AMERICAN CRIMINAL PROCEDURE

CASES AND COMMENTARY

Seventh Edition

By

Stephen A. Saltzburg
Wallace and Beverley Woodbury University Professor,
George Washington University Law School

Daniel J. Capra
Philip Reed Professor of Law
Fordham University School of Law

AMERICAN CASEBOOK SERIES®

THOMSON
™
WEST

Mat # 40127489

American Casebook Series and West Group are trademarks registered in the U.S. Patent and Trademark Office.

COPYRIGHT © 1980, 1984, 1988, 1992, 1996 WEST PUBLISHING CO.
COPYRIGHT © 2000 By WEST GROUP
© 2004 West, a Thomson business
      610 Opperman Drive
      P.O. Box 64526
      St. Paul, MN 55164–0526
      1–800–328–9352

ISBN 0–314–14534–6

TEXT IS PRINTED ON 10% POST CONSUMER RECYCLED PAPER

To the women we love,
Susan Lee and Anne Capra

*

Preface

This Seventh Edition plays to what we feel were the strengths of the first six editions. While the predominant focus is on Supreme Court jurisprudence, we have tried wherever possible to give the reader a sense of what the lower courts are doing with the interesting and exciting issues that abound in criminal procedure. The lower courts are where the day-to-day law is made, and where many of the most interesting fact situations arise. Since our topic is "American" Criminal Procedure, we have made an effort to include cases from all the circuits and state courts throughout the book. As with prior editions, extensive commentary and interesting fact situations are included to assist in doctrinal development. We have also added extensive academic commentary on some of the cutting issues in criminal procedure. Finally, the book covers all problems of criminal investigation and adjudication. It is not limited to constitutional issues. Yet despite the breadth of the book, we have made a special effort to keep it to a manageable and readable length.

The format of the book is the same as the prior editions, although much of the material has been reorganized and updated. Citations to Supreme Court opinions are limited to United States Reports, unless the case is so recent that the U.S. cite is not available. Certiorari denied citations are omitted on the ground that they unnecessarily clutter a book that is primarily for classroom use. Citations included in cases are often omitted without so specifying. Lettered footnotes are from the original materials. Numbered footnotes are ours. Omissions from the text of original material are indicated by asterisks and brackets. We have added more than 1000 headnotes in an effort to make the book as user friendly as possible.

This Edition gives special treatment to some of the more active areas of criminal procedure in the past four years, including important developments after the terrorist attack on 911. Racially-based stops and encounters are discussed in Chapter Two. Detention of suspected terrorists as "material witnesses" and "enemy combatants" is discussed throughout the Book. Important questions concerning the right to retained counsel and to counsel's role are also explored in Chapter Ten. The fundamental changes wrought by the Sentencing Guidelines, which take up much of the lower courts' time and effort and which have resulted in a shift of power from courts to prosecutors, are explored in Chapters Nine and Eleven.

Because every criminal procedure teacher likes to cover different material, we have tried to divide the book into numerous subdivisions to enable teachers to pick and choose the subjects they most want to cover. We think that an advanced criminal procedure course is a useful and popular addition to the curriculum. If an advanced course is contemplated, Chapters Nine through Thirteen could be reserved for that course. An alternative approach is to include Chapter Nine in the basic course and move Chapters Eight and Five into the advanced course. A third approach is to cover parts of all, or almost all, chapters in the basic course, and to finish them in the advanced course. We believe and hope that the material lends itself to several different divisions that all work well in class and make either a single course or a tandem interesting for all students.

STEPHEN A. SALTZBURG,
Washington, D.C.

DANIEL J. CAPRA
New York, N.Y.

March 2004

Introduction

Criminal procedure is one of the courses in law school that generates class-room excitement that continues from the first to the last day of class. Whether it is the opportunity to compare the Warren and the Burger Courts and to predict the likely course of the Rehnquist Court, the fact that criminal procedure as a subject of study has developed only relatively recently so that one is almost always on the cutting edge of the law, a fascination with the battle between government and individual and the true adversary clash that often results, the fact that the Bill of Rights holds an important place in the hearts and minds of future lawyers, or all of these things to some extent, people like to talk and argue about criminal procedure, and they mind studying it less than they mind studying many other things.

As excited as students of criminal procedure are, too often they leave their courses feeling somewhat frustrated. They have learned a lot of recent law and they know what the latest decisions of the Supreme Court are, but they do not feel comfortable in their understanding of the criminal justice system (to the extent that it is accurate to call the way criminal cases are handled a system) as a whole, or in their knowledge of the doctrinal roots of the numerous concepts that they have examined. This book is an effort to remove some of that frustration, to clarify the way in which the parts of the criminal justice system relate to one another, and to explain how we arrived where we now find ourselves.

To accomplish this task, the book utilizes far more original text and scholarly commentary than is typically found in casebooks on the subject. The text attempts to develop the history of the rules discussed, to point out how judicial treatment of various concepts has changed over time, and to indicate the vices and the virtues of various approaches, past and present. An effort is made to provide students with citations to law journals, books and cases not presented in this book so that those who are interested can examine topics more fully on their own with easy access to the relevant literature.

When a subject is examined, an effort is made to point out inadequacies in judicial opinions or legislative reactions to judicial opinions. Sometimes our own views are stated, either explicitly or implicitly, in an effort to stimulate thinking about new approaches to familiar problems. Where appropriate, students are asked to think about the concepts they have learned in connection with problems that encourage them to develop their own ideas about how best to handle hard cases and close questions.

An effort has been made to reproduce only those Supreme Court cases that are most important. Less important cases are discussed in the textual material. Some of the cases that are offered are not yesterday's Supreme Court decisions, but those of a more distant Court, because the important opinions may be those that were seminal.

The emphasis on the development of concepts over time indicates a bias that should be confessed here: We believe that the judiciary, especially the Supreme Court, and legislatures, to the extent that they become involved in establishing procedures for criminal cases, attempt to articulate and apply doctrines that will hold their own over time. In other words, we believe that they struggle "to get it right" eventually, if not always at the first crack.

This is not to suggest that right answers are clear or easy to ascertain. In many instances, reasonable minds will differ on the proper solution to questions, and often reasonable minds will find proper solutions to be elusive. We suggest only that approaches that are plainly defective are almost always abandoned or changed, and that it seems that courts and legislatures do attempt to refine the procedures that govern criminal investigations and prosecutions as a result of experience.

Like most criminal procedure books, this one places much emphasis on constitutional rules. This hardly can be avoided, since the Constitution as now interpreted does set minimum standards for many parts of the criminal justice system. But, an attempt is made to indicate when nonconstitutional rules may be more important or more useful than constitutional ones.

To sum up, this book combines elements of traditional casebooks with textual material that might more typically be found in a treatise or hornbook, and it intersperses problems in many chapters. Overall, the idea is to identify clearly the problems of criminal procedure, to offer various ideas about how to handle the problems, and to describe the work that still needs to be done if criminal cases are to be processed fairly.

Some comments on the particular chapters of the book may help to explain how we have approached various topics.

Chapter One begins with a development of the criminal justice system. The importance of constitutional rules is discussed, and the incorporation and retroactivity doctrines are examined, since they arise again and again in the cases that are discussed in the following chapters.

Chapter Two examines all aspects of Fourth Amendment law. It begins with a careful examination of the Amendment's language and an exploration of the relationship between the warrant clause and the reasonableness clause. The concepts of probable cause, valid warrants, arrest, stop and frisk, and scrutiny by a detached magistrate are all covered at length. Eavesdropping and wiretapping are looked at afterwards. The chapter reserves an examination of the exclusionary rule until the end and attempts thereby to promote an understanding of what the rule is and what its true costs are. This is the longest chapter of the book, covering the many facets of search and seizure law.

Chapter Three covers self-incrimination and confessions. More than usual attention is paid to traditional Fifth Amendment law and how it relates to the law of confessions. Much space is devoted to laying the historical foundation for present law. Only then are *Miranda, Massiah, Brewer, Henry* and other major cases discussed.

Identification evidence is scrutinized in Chapter Four. The major Supreme Court cases take up most of the chapter, but an attempt is made to point out the shortcomings in the Court's work and to suggest how identification procedures might be improved and how fairer trials might result.

Chapter Five is about the right to counsel. Since the right to counsel may be important in connection with confessions and identifications, as well as later in the process, it might seem strange for this chapter to follow the two previous ones. But we believe that the order works and that it is helpful to treat the counsel cases in one place—at the point at which counsel is likely to be involved for the remainder of the process. The doctrines of ineffective assistance and self-representation are not treated here, but are reserved for Chapter Ten.

Chapter Six looks at the decision whether or not to charge a suspect. The roles of the police, the prosecutor and the grand jury are examined, and an effort is made to show how interdependent they are. The current controversy over the utility of the grand jury as a screening device and the dangers of the grand jury serving as an arm of the executive are described and discussed. Preliminary hearings and their relationship to grand juries and charging decisions generally are considered in some detail.

Chapter Seven covers bail and pretrial release. Both constitutional and nonconstitutional rules, especially the 1984 Federal Bail Reform Act, are analyzed. The purposes of bail and the controversy over preventive detention are discussed. Some emphasis is placed on the traditional role of the bondsman and the need for bail reform.

Chapter Eight presents criminal discovery. After a general overview, attention is paid to what the defendant can get from the prosecutor and what the prosecutor can get from the defendant without violating the Constitution. Proposals for liberalizing discovery are considered.

Chapter Nine is devoted to guilty pleas and plea bargaining. An extensive excerpt from a comprehensive study of plea bargaining in the United States begins the chapter. It is followed by a scholarly debate about the merits of plea bargaining, and then by a discussion of the requirements of a valid plea and an analysis of the finality of a plea.

Trial and trial-related rights are treated in Chapter Ten. Among the topics covered are speedy trial, joinder of defendants and charges, burdens of persuasion, jury trial, fair-trial—free press conflicts, and effective representation and self-representation. This is the second longest chapter in the book. It addresses in the context of criminal trials many issues that are considered in the context of civil trials in the typical course in Civil Procedure.

Sentencing is the exclusive concern of Chapter Eleven. Basic options in sentencing are described, as are the roles of judge and jury. The determinate versus indeterminate sentencing controversy is explored, and the Federal Sentencing Guidelines are carefully examined. Also, the procedures that are generally employed in sentencing, and the applicable constitutional rules are set forth.

Chapter Twelve covers all aspects of double jeopardy. Most attention is paid to recent decisions of the Supreme Court that clarify (or further confuse, depending on how the decisions are read) a subject that has been puzzling criminal procedure students for years. Collateral estoppel and vindictive prosecutorial conduct also are discussed.

Finally, Chapter Thirteen focuses on post-trial motions, appeals, and collateral attacks on convictions. An effort is made to examine all important post-sentencing challenges that can be made to a conviction. The section on collateral attack endeavors to explain the development of habeas corpus by the Supreme Court and Congress and the high points of the debate over how much post-conviction attack is desirable in a criminal justice system.

It should be obvious that we have tried to cover all of the significant parts of the criminal justice system and to do so in a reasonable number of pages. To accomplish this, we have worked hard to make the textual portions of the book as informative as possible. This Edition cannot yet be called a short book, but criminal procedure is not a subject that is easily confined to a few pages. To make the length somewhat more tolerable, we have endeavored to use headnotes as well as several different typesizes, not only for purposes of emphasis, but also to break the monotony of the printed page. To make the book easier to read, we also delete most internal citations in material that we quote from other sources. Thus, most internal cites in the Supreme Court opinions found throughout the book are missing. Footnotes in quoted material generally are deleted also. When we leave internal citations and original footnotes in the quoted material, we do so in the belief that they make a contribution to the overall coverage of the materials. Footnotes that are taken from the original source all have small letters to identify them—i.e., a, b, c, etc. Our own footnotes are identified by number—i.e., 1, 2, 3, etc. We hope that these choices enhance the "readability" of the book, and that by choosing to delete unnecessary baggage in quoted material, we have been able to pay more attention to the important and interesting questions that make criminal procedure a joy to study.

STEPHEN A. SALTZBURG
Washington, D.C.

DANIEL J. CAPRA
New York, N.Y.

March, 2004

Summary of Contents

*

Table of Contents

*

Table of Cases

The principal cases are in bold type. Cases cited or discussed in the text are roman type. References are to pages. Cases cited in principal cases and within other quoted materials are not included.

li

Table of Authorities

*

AMERICAN CRIMINAL PROCEDURE

CASES AND COMMENTARY

Seventh Edition

*

Chapter One

BASIC PRINCIPLES

I. A CRIMINAL CASE

A course in criminal procedure obviously is intended to cover the procedures that are employed as a criminal case is processed. It could be said that the course covers the processing of those cases that are studied in criminal law. Although such a statement would be fairly accurate, it would fail to address the question of when a case is sufficiently "criminal" to require the procedures that are the focus of this book.

An important threshold question is whether a sanction that has been chosen is properly classified as "criminal" for purposes of assigning procedural rights to parties. An answer that is frequently given is that criminal cases require proof beyond a reasonable doubt, whereas civil and administrative cases generally do not. But this answer is too circular to be helpful. Proof beyond a reasonable doubt is required once a case is identified as criminal. Similarly, rights to counsel, to invoke the privilege against self-incrimination, to suppress illegally seized evidence, and others as well, may be triggered when a case is identified as criminal. But these rights arise after the identification is made.

Another answer is that the label "criminal" implies jail and prison. But jail and prison are not the usual penalties for many lesser criminal offenses. It is at least generally true that if jail and prison are prescribed penalties for a violation of the law, the law is criminal. But, fines, restitution and other sanctions might be employed as criminal sanctions. If the existence or absence of jail and prison penalties does not determine whether or not a case is criminal, could the determinative factor be whether a penalty is a punishment or not? This would appear to be somewhat closer to the mark. Yet, deciding whether a sanction is a punishment itself may present difficulties. Moreover, punitive damages and civil fines are hardly unknown to American law. Thus, the penalty aspect alone cannot identify a criminal case.

Another answer might be that the party seeking to impose the penalty is the state. One characteristic of criminal cases is that they are brought in the name of the government on behalf of the community. But while the presence of the state as a party is a feature of criminal cases, it is also a feature of many civil cases and of administrative proceedings brought by government agencies, which are generally thought to be civil.

Moreover, recent attempts by the government to prosecute alleged terrorists after the September 11 tragedy further complicate the determination of whether

1

an action is "criminal." The government has argued that "enemy combatants" are not entitled to the ordinary protections afforded a criminal defendant. And yet those combatants are punished in the same way as criminal defendants found guilty beyond a reasonable doubt.

Legislative Designation

Thus, something more is needed to identify criminal cases. That something is so obvious that it may appear unsatisfactory at first; it is the label that the legislature chooses to give a sanction. If the legislature calls something criminal, presumably it wants the public to treat an offense as criminal. When this happens, the special procedures of criminal cases will be invoked. See generally Cheh, Constitutional Limits on Using Civil Remedies To Achieve Criminal Law Objectives: Understanding and Transcending the Criminal–Civil Law Distinction, 42 Hastings L.J. 1325 (1991)(proceeding is criminal where labeled as such by the legislature). The question remains, however, whether the legislature's designation of a sanction as other than criminal should always be dispositive.

Civil Penalty: United States v. L.O. Ward

Usually it is a defendant who argues that his alleged violation is criminal; as such he is seeking to take advantage of certain constitutional rights that are only available in criminal prosecutions. A decision that the defendant faces a civil sanction means that the claim of right will be denied. In United States v. L. O. Ward, 448 U.S. 242 (1980), for example, the Supreme Court held that a penalty imposed upon persons discharging hazardous substances into navigable waters was a civil penalty and, therefore, that a reporting requirement for violators did not violate the Fifth Amendment's privilege against compelled self-incrimination. The Court said that the question whether a penalty is criminal or civil is a matter of statutory construction.

> Our inquiry in this regard has traditionally proceeded on two levels. First, we have set out to determine whether Congress, in establishing the penalizing mechanism, indicated either expressly or impliedly a preference for one label or the other. Second, where Congress has indicated an intention to establish a civil penalty, we have inquired further whether the statutory scheme was so punitive either in purpose or effect as to negate that intention. In regard to this latter inquiry, we have noted that "only the clearest proof could suffice to establish the unconstitutionality of a statute on such a ground."

The Court accepted the congressional label of "civil," although Justice Stevens dissented.

Commitment of Sex Offenders: Allen v. Illinois and Kansas v. Hendricks

In Allen v. Illinois, 478 U.S. 364 (1986), the Court held that commitment proceedings under the Illinois Sexually Dangerous Persons Act were not criminal, and therefore that the Fifth Amendment self-incrimination clause was not applicable. In *Allen,* the Court found that the legislature's characterization of the statute as civil and treatment-oriented was crucial, even though persons committed under the Act were kept in a maximum security institution that also housed prisoners in need of psychiatric care.

The Court relied heavily on *Allen* in Kansas v. Hendricks, 521 U.S. 346 (1997). Hendricks challenged a Kansas statute imposing involuntary civil commitment on sexual predators. Hendricks was committed under the Act just before he was to be released from prison, where he had been incarcerated after a series of sex crime convictions. Hendricks argued that the civil commitment violated his constitutional right against double jeopardy, and also that it operated as an ex post facto law (because the civil commitment statute was passed well after the sexually abusive acts had been committed). Both of these constitutional claims are triggered only when the state imposes criminal "punishment" on the citizen. The case therefore boiled down to whether the involuntary commitment statute was civil or criminal in nature.

Justice Thomas, writing for five members of the Court, held that the statute was civil rather than criminal in nature. He wrote as follows:

> The categorization of a particular proceeding as civil or criminal "is first of all a question of statutory construction." *Allen*, 478 U.S., at 368. We must initially ascertain whether the legislature meant the statute to establish "civil" proceedings. If so, we ordinarily defer to the legislature's stated intent. Here, Kansas' objective to create a civil proceeding is evidenced by its placement of the Sexually Violent Predator Act within the Kansas probate code, instead of the criminal code, as well as its description of the Act as creating a "civil commitment procedure." Nothing on the face of the statute suggests that the legislature sought to create anything other than a civil commitment scheme designed to protect the public from harm.

> Although we recognize that a civil label is not always dispositive, we will reject the legislature's manifest intent only where a party challenging the statute provides "the clearest proof" that "the statutory scheme [is] so punitive either in purpose or effect as to negate [the State's] intention" to deem it "civil." United States v. Ward. * * * Hendricks, however, has failed to satisfy this heavy burden.

> As a threshold matter, commitment under the Act does not implicate either of the two primary objectives of criminal punishment: retribution or deterrence. The Act's purpose is not retributive because it does not affix culpability for prior criminal conduct. Instead, such conduct is used solely for evidentiary purposes, either to demonstrate that a "mental abnormality" exists or to support a finding of future dangerousness. * * * In addition, the Kansas Act does not make a criminal conviction a prerequisite for commitment—persons absolved of criminal responsibility may nonetheless be subject to confinement under the Act. An absence of the necessary criminal responsibility suggests that the State is not seeking retribution for a past misdeed. * * *

> Moreover, unlike a criminal statute, no finding of scienter is required to commit an individual who is found to be a sexually violent predator; instead, the commitment determination is made based on a "mental abnormality" or "personality disorder" rather than on one's criminal intent. The existence of a scienter requirement is customarily an important element in distinguishing criminal from civil statutes. The absence of such a requirement

here is evidence that confinement under the statute is not intended to be retributive.

Nor can it be said that the legislature intended the Act to function as a deterrent. Those persons committed under the Act are, by definition, suffering from a "mental abnormality" or a "personality disorder" that prevents them from exercising adequate control over their behavior. Such persons are therefore unlikely to be deterred by the threat of confinement. And the conditions surrounding that confinement do not suggest a punitive purpose on the State's part. The State has represented that an individual confined under the Act is not subject to the more restrictive conditions placed on state prisoners, but instead experiences essentially the same conditions as any involuntarily committed patient in the state mental institution. Because none of the parties argues that people institutionalized under the Kansas general civil commitment statute are subject to punitive conditions, even though they may be involuntarily confined, it is difficult to conclude that persons confined under this Act are being "punished."

Justice Thomas emphasized that involuntary confinement could be "civil", even if it might be permanent:

Hendricks focuses on his confinement's potentially indefinite duration as evidence of the State's punitive intent. That focus, however, is misplaced. Far from any punitive objective, the confinement's duration is instead linked to the stated purposes of the commitment, namely, to hold the person until his mental abnormality no longer causes him to be a threat to others. If, at any time, the confined person is adjudged "safe to be at large," he is statutorily entitled to immediate release.

Hendricks' final argument was that the commitment procedure could not be deemed civil in nature because he never received any treatment for his mental abnormality. Justice Thomas noted the findings of the lower courts that Hendricks' condition was not treatable. It therefore rejected his argument that the failure to provide treatment rendered the scheme punitive in nature.

While we have upheld state civil commitment statutes that aim both to incapacitate and to treat, see *Allen*, supra, we have never held that the Constitution prevents a State from civilly detaining those for whom no treatment is available, but who nevertheless pose a danger to others. A State could hardly be seen as furthering a "punitive" purpose by involuntarily confining persons afflicted with an untreatable, highly contagious disease. Similarly, it would be of little value to require treatment as a precondition for civil confinement of the dangerously insane when no acceptable treatment existed. To conclude otherwise would obligate a State to release certain confined individuals who were both mentally ill and dangerous simply because they could not be successfully treated for their afflictions.

Justice Thomas summed up as follows:

Where the State has "disavowed any punitive intent"; limited confinement to a small segment of particularly dangerous individuals; provided strict procedural safeguards; directed that confined persons be segregated from the general prison population and afforded the same status as others who have been civilly committed; recommended treatment if such is possible; and permitted immediate release upon a showing that the individual is no longer dangerous or mentally impaired, we cannot say that it acted with punitive intent. We therefore hold that the Act does not establish criminal proceedings and that involuntary confinement pursuant to the Act is not punitive. Our conclusion that the Act is nonpunitive thus removes an essential prerequisite for both Hendricks' double jeopardy and ex post facto claims.

Justice Breyer, joined by Justices Stevens, Souter and Ginsburg, dissented in *Hendricks*. Justice Breyer contended that the Kansas procedure was punitive and therefore violated the constitutional prohibition against ex post facto laws. He based his conclusion on the fact that Hendricks received no treatment for his illness.

Registration of Sex Offenders—Civil Regulation or Criminal Punishment?: Smith v. Doe

In Smith v. Doe, 538 U.S. 84 (2003), the Court upheld Alaska's version of a "Megan's Law" against a challenge that it violated the Ex Post Facto Clause (a clause that applies only to criminal punishment). Megan's Laws, adopted by legislatures throughout the country, require those convicted as sex offenders to register with their state of residence. Information about the offenders is then published over the internet. Alaska's version required sex offenders to register even if they were convicted before the date of the legislation. The Court, in an opinion by Justice Kennedy for five Justices, held that the statutory scheme was civil rather than punitive, and therefore the Ex Post Facto Clause did not apply. The Court noted that the purpose of the law, as expressed in the statutory text, was to protect the public from sex offenders. Justice Kennedy cited *Hendricks* and declared that "an imposition of restrictive measures on sex offenders adjudged to be dangerous is a legitimate nonpunitive governmental objective" and that "nothing on the face of the statute suggests that the legislature sought to create anything other than a civil scheme designed to protect the public from harm." The Court also noted that the Alaska law simply requires registration; it "imposes no physical restraint, and so does not resemble the punishment of imprisonment, which is the paradigmatic affirmative disability or restraint."

Justice Kennedy rejected the argument that the registration system was punitive because it was tantamount to probation or supervised release, which clearly are aspects of the criminal justice system. He distinguished registration from probation or supervised release as follows:

Probation and supervised release entail a series of mandatory conditions and allow the supervising officer to seek the revocation of probation or release in case of infraction. By contrast, offenders subject to the Alaska statute are free to move where they wish and to live and work as other citizens, with no supervision. Although registrants must inform the authorities after they change their facial features (such as growing a beard), borrow a car, or seek psychiatric treatment, they are not required to seek permission to do so. A sex offender who fails to comply with the reporting requirement may be subjected to a criminal prosecution for that failure, but any prosecution is a proceeding separate from the individual's original offense. Whether other constitutional objections can be raised to a mandatory reporting require-ment, and how those questions might be resolved, are concerns beyond the scope of this opinion. It suffices to say the registration requirements make a valid regulatory program effective and do not impose punitive restraints in violation of the *Ex Post Facto* Clause.

Justice Thomas wrote a short concurring opinion.

Justice Souter concurred in the judgment. He noted that the Alaska scheme did present some indications of punishment. For example, some of the provisions were located in the criminal code; the touchstone for regulation was the commission of a past crime rather than current dangerousness; and the statute made written notification of the registration requirement a condition of a guilty plea to any sex offense. He also noted that the publication of sex offender status on the internet might be seen to bear "some resemblance to shaming punishments that were used earlier in our history to disable offenders from living normally in the community." Justice Souter, however, concluded as follows:

> To me, the indications of punitive character stated above and the civil indications weighed heavily by the Court are in rough equipoise. * * * What tips the scale for me is the presumption of constitutionality normally accorded a State's law. That presumption gives the State the benefit of the doubt in close cases like this one, and on that basis alone I concur in the Court's judgment.

Justice Stevens dissented in *Smith*. He declared as follows:

> No matter how often the Court may repeat and manipulate multifactor tests that have been applied in wholly dissimilar cases involving only one or two of these three aspects of these statutory sanctions, it will never persuade me that the registration and reporting obligations that are imposed on convicted sex offenders *and on no one else* as a result of their convictions are not part of their punishment. In my opinion, a sanction that (1) is imposed on everyone who commits a criminal offense, (2) is not imposed on anyone else, and (3) severely impairs a person's liberty is punishment.

Justice Ginsburg, joined by Justice Breyer, wrote a separate dissent. She argued that the registration and reporting requirements are comparable to conditions of supervised release or parole, and that the public notification regimen called to mind the shaming punishments of the past. She concluded as follows:

> What ultimately tips the balance for me is the Act's excessiveness in relation to its nonpunitive purpose. * * * [T]he Act has a legitimate civil purpose: to promote public safety by alerting the public to potentially recidivist sex offenders in the community. But its scope notably exceeds this purpose. The Act applies to all convicted sex offenders, without regard to their future dangerousness. And the duration of the reporting requirement is keyed not to any determination of a particular offender's risk of reoffending, but to whether the offense of conviction qualified as aggravated. The reporting requirements themselves are exorbitant: The Act requires aggravated offenders to engage in perpetual quarterly reporting, even if their personal information has not changed. And meriting heaviest weight in my judgment, the Act makes no provision whatever for the possibility of rehabilitation: Offenders cannot shorten their registration or notification

period, even on the clearest demonstration of rehabilitation or conclusive proof of physical incapacitation.

Distinguishing Civil and Criminal Contempt Proceedings: UMWA v. Bagwell

Sanctions for contempt of court present difficult problems of delineation between civil and criminal proceedings. Some contempt proceedings are designated as "criminal" and therefore the alleged offending party is entitled to the procedural protections accorded other criminal defendants. Other contempt citations are styled as "civil" with accordingly less protections extended the alleged offender. The Court discussed the problematic distinction between civil and criminal contempt in International Union, United Mine Workers of America v. Bagwell, 512 U.S. 821 (1994). A state court issued a complex injunction prohibiting the union from conducting unlawful strike activities against certain mining companies. The union allegedly violated the terms of the injunction. A month after issuing the injunction, the trial court held a contempt hearing and announced that the union would be fined for any future breach of the injunction. In subsequent contempt hearings, the court levied over $64,000,000 in what it termed coercive, civil fines, ordering most of the money ($52,000,000) to be paid to the Commonwealth and the counties affected by the unlawful activities. In the Supreme Court, the question was whether the contempt fines were civil or criminal; the parties and all Justices agreed that if the fines were criminal, the union was entitled to a criminal jury trial before the fines could be imposed.

The Court, in an opinion by Justice Blackmun, held that the fines constituted criminal punishment. Justice Blackmun ultimately relied upon several considerations to determine that the fines were criminal sanctions:

> The union's sanctionable conduct did not occur in the court's presence or otherwise implicate the court's ability to maintain order and adjudicate the proceedings before it. Nor did the union's contumacy involve simple, affirmative acts * * *. Instead, the Virginia trial court levied contempt fines for widespread, ongoing, out-of-court violations of a complex injunction. In so doing, the court effectively policed petitioners' compliance with an entire code of conduct that the court itself had imposed. The union's contumacy lasted many months and spanned a substantial portion of the State. The fines assessed were serious, totalling over $52,000,000. Under such circumstances, disinterested factfinding and even-handed adjudication were essential, and petitioners were entitled to a criminal jury trial.

Justice Ginsburg, joined by Chief Justice Rehnquist, wrote an opinion concurring in part and concurring in the judgment. She was persuaded that "the Virginia courts' refusal to vacate the fines, despite the parties' settlement * * * is characteristic of criminal, not civil proceedings."

Criminal Procedure Issues in a Civil Context

Occasionally, constitutional guarantees covered in the criminal procedure course will arise in a civil context. The most prevalent situation is an action for damages brought against a police officer under 42 U.S.C. § 1983 for violation of the plaintiff's constitutional rights. For example, if the plaintiff claims that he was wrongly arrested or illegally searched, the court applies Fourth Amendment principles in the same way as if a criminal defendant moves to suppress evidence allegedly obtained in violation of the Fourth Amendment. Many such cases will be discussed in this book.

II. THE NATURE OF THE PROCEDURAL SYSTEM AND THE SOURCES OF PROCEDURAL RULES

Many of the procedural rules that will be discussed in this book have their roots in the United States Constitution. The Bill of Rights contains several provisions that have exclusive applicability to criminal cases, and others that have had their principal impact on the criminal justice system. Many of these same rights are found in the constitutions of the fifty states, and as the next section of this Chapter will explain, most provisions of the Bill of Rights are now binding on the states.

It must be recognized that constitutional rules represent only the minimum protections that must be afforded criminal defendants. Statutes and court rules can and do build upon or add to constitutional minima and fill out the interstices of the criminal justice process.

As you examine American criminal justice, you will not be surprised to see that law enforcement officials find that constitutional, statutory and judge-made rules may make it difficult for them to carry out the duties assigned to them. The course in criminal procedure presents a tension between goals having to do with protecting individual defendants and promoting individual freedom, and goals having to do with ferreting out, prosecuting, and, ultimately, stopping crime. See generally Hall, Objectives of Federal Criminal Procedural Revision, 51 Yale L.J. 723 (1942). Professor Packer described the conflict by positing two possible, competing models of the criminal justice system: the crime control model and the due process model. See generally, The Limits of the Criminal Sanction (1968).

Pay attention to the kind of system that develops in the pages that follow. Like so many systems, it attempts to reconcile competing values, resulting in compromises that are often unsatisfactory. As you wonder about the worth of the end product, remember that many of the rules that have been developed, constitutional and non-constitutional alike, attempt to separate power in the processing of criminal cases. Others are designed to assure that the defendant can participate in and take control of her own case. In each section, and with each new rule, it will be helpful to ask what kind of system would be created if the rules were changed.

III. TWO SPECIAL ASPECTS OF CONSTITUTIONAL LAW: THE INCORPORATION DOCTRINE AND RETROACTIVE APPLICATION OF CONSTITUTIONAL DECISIONS

Most of the cases you will read in this course are decisions of the United States Supreme Court. Before discussing the constitutional law developed by the Supreme Court in these decisions, we believe it is useful to analyze the practical *impact* of a constitutionally-based decision by the Supreme Court. The impact of a Supreme Court decision is governed by two general principles—incorporation and retroactivity. Under the doctrine of incorporation, a constitutionally-based decision ordinarily will bind both the states and the Federal government. Retroactivity principles, on the other hand, determine whether the Court's decision will have any effect on official activity occurring before the date of the decision.

A. INCORPORATION

Few individual rights were guaranteed by the original Constitution prior to the adoption of the Bill of Rights. But the ratification of the first ten Amendments in 1791 provided procedural protections that comprise much of what will be examined in this book.

In Barron v. Baltimore, 32 U.S. (7 Pet.) 243 (1833), Chief Justice Marshall, writing for the Court, concluded that the Bill of Rights applied only against the Federal government and not against the states. Although the clarity of the Marshall view leaves little doubt as to his reluctance to apply any of the original Amendments against the states, there have been suggestions that some Amendments might have been intended to be applicable to both the states and the Federal government. See 2 Crosskey, Politics and the Constitution in the History of the United States 1050 (1953).

After the Civil War and the adoption of the Thirteenth, Fourteenth and Fifteenth Amendments, a new question arose: whether these Amendments, particularly the Fourteenth, incorporated the Bill of Rights protections, thus making them applicable against the states. Early cases, like the *Slaughter-House Cases*, 83 U.S. (16 Wall.) 36 (1872), took a narrow view of the Amendments. But four dissenters would have read the Fourteenth Amendment more broadly, as altering the fundamental relationship of the Federal government and the states, and imposing obligations on the states to protect individual rights.[1]

For approximately three quarters of a century the Court struggled to interpret the open-ended language of the Fourteenth Amendment. In 1884, in Hurtado v. California, 110 U.S. 516, the Court held that California could permit criminal proceedings to be instituted by information, rather than by grand jury indictment. And in 1908, the Court, in Twining v. New Jersey, 211 U.S. 78, held that the privilege against self-incrimination was not binding on the states. But in 1932, in Powell v. Alabama, 287 U.S. 45, the Court held that denial of counsel in a capital case effectively denied the denied the defendant their Fourteenth Amendment right to due process.

Five years later, in Palko v. Connecticut, 302 U.S. 319 (1937), Justice Cardozo wrote for the Court to uphold a state procedure that permitted the state to appeal in a criminal case and obtain a new trial. He assumed that the Double Jeopardy Clause of the Fifth Amendment would have invalidated such an appeal and retrial by the Federal government, but found that the states could take a different approach. Discussing the question whether the Bill of Rights was "absorbed" into the Fourteenth Amendment, Justice Cardozo wrote that the "specific pledges of particular amendments have been found to be implicit in the concept of ordered liberty, and thus, through the Fourteenth Amendment, become valid as against the states." But according to Justice Cardozo, the

---

1. Professor Ely has observed that the opinions in the case can be read to support a claim that all nine justices would have incorpo- rated the Bill of Rights into the Fourteenth Amendment. J. Ely, Democracy and Distrust 196 n. 59 (1980).

Double Jeopardy Clause was not one of those guarantees "implicit in the concept of ordered liberty."

A decade after *Palko*, a majority of the Court reaffirmed *Twining* in Adamson v. California, 332 U.S. 46 (1947). Justice Black, joined by Justice Douglas, dissented. Justice Black argued that the language of the first section of the Fourteenth Amendment was intended to assure that no state could deprive its citizens of the privileges and protections of the Bill of Rights. Also, Justice Black rejected what he called the "natural law" formula of *Palko,* which invited the Court to recognize rights "implicit in the concept of ordered liberty" and yet not found in the Bill of Rights.[2] Responding to the opinion by Justice Black and its appendix of constitutional history, Justice Frankfurter took vigorous exception to Black's argument.[3]

Justices Black and Frankfurter continued to disagree for years over the relationship of the Bill of Rights and the Fourteenth Amendment, with Justice Frankfurter generally prevailing on the theory that the Amendment did not make the Bill of Rights applicable to the States, but that it did incorporate such protections as were "implicit in the concept of ordered liberty." See, e.g., Wolf v. Colorado, 338 U.S. 25 (1949); Rochin v. California, 342 U.S. 165 (1952); Irvine v. California, 347 U.S. 128 (1954); Breithaupt v. Abram, 352 U.S. 432 (1957).

In the 1960's a shift took place, subtle at first, but less so over time. The Warren Court—without ever formally abandoning the fundamental fairness standard—began to incorporate more and more Bill of Rights guarantees into the Fourteenth Amendment, pursuant to an approach referred to by Justice Black as "selective incorporation." The Court paid little attention to the facts of the case presenting the incorporation issue, and proceeded instead to determine whether the right asserted was fundamental to the American system of justice. Moreover, the Court insisted that, once incorporated, the scope of the Constitutional guarantee would be the same in state as in Federal cases: every detail of the incorporated provision was applicable "jot-for-jot" to the states.

The current approach of the Court, and the competing theories also, are well illustrated by Duncan v. Louisiana. *Duncan* held that the right to jury trial, guaranteed by the Sixth Amendment, is binding on the states. That particular holding is not the subject of attention here [see Chapter Ten for that part of the case]; rather, the focus is on how the Court reached its result. The change in the Court's analysis over time is well-rendered by the long footnote in the majority opinion.

---

2. Justice Murphy, joined by Justice Rutledge, also dissented. Justice Murphy would have reserved the right to recognize procedural protections not explicitly recognized in the Bill of Rights. Later, Justice Douglas also would move to this position.

3. Justice Frankfurter relied heavily on the historical analysis in Fairman, Does the Fourteenth Amendment Incorporate the Bill of Rights? The Original Understanding, 2 Stan. L.Rev. 5 (1949). Both Justice Black and Professor Fairman are criticized in Kelly, Clio and the Court: An Illicit Love Affair, 1965 Sup.Ct. Rev. 119. Professor Amar has written an important article that criticizes the Fairman view and concludes that the Fourteenth Amendment was designed to apply the Bill of Rights protections to the States. See Amar, The Bill of Rights and the Fourteenth Amendment, 101 Yale L.J. 1193 (1991).

DUNCAN v. LOUISIANA

Supreme Court of the United States, 1968.
391 U.S. 145.

Mr. Justice White **delivered the opinion of the Court.**

* * *

I

The Fourteenth Amendment denies the States the power to "deprive any person of life, liberty, or property, without due process of law." In resolving conflicting claims concerning the meaning of this spacious language, the Court has looked increasingly to the Bill of Rights for guidance; many of the rights guaranteed by the first eight Amendments to the Constitution have been held to be protected against state action by the Due Process Clause of the Fourteenth Amendment. That clause now protects the right to compensation for property taken by the State;[a] the rights of speech, press, and religion covered by the First Amendment;[b] the Fourth Amendment rights to be free from unreasonable searches and seizures and to have excluded from criminal trials any evidence illegally seized;[c] the right guaranteed by the Fifth Amendment to be free of compelled self-incrimination;[d] and the Sixth Amendment rights to counsel,[e] to a speedy[f] and public[g] trial, to confrontation of opposing witnesses,[h] and to compulsory process for obtaining witnesses.[i]

a. Chicago, B. & Q. R. Co. v. Chicago, 166 U.S. 226 (1897).

b. See, e.g., Fiske v. Kansas, 274 U.S. 380 (1927).

c. See Mapp v. Ohio, 367 U.S. 643 (1961).

d. Malloy v. Hogan, 378 U.S. 1 (1964).

e. Gideon v. Wainwright, 372 U.S. 335 (1963).

f. Klopfer v. North Carolina, 386 U.S. 213 (1967).

g. In re Oliver, 333 U.S. 257 (1948).

h. Pointer v. Texas, 380 U.S. 400 (1965).

i. Washington v. Texas, 388 U.S. 14 (1967).

j. In one sense recent cases applying provisions of the first eight Amendments to the

The test for determining whether a right extended by the Fifth and Sixth Amendments with respect to federal criminal proceedings is also protected against state action by the Fourteenth Amendment has been phrased in a variety of ways in the opinions of this Court. The question has been asked whether a right is among those " 'fundamental principles of liberty and justice which lie at the base of all our civil and political institutions,' "Powell v. Alabama, 287 U.S. 45, 67 (1932); whether it is "basic in our system of jurisprudence," In re Oliver, 333 U.S. 257, 273 (1948); and whether it is "a fundamental right, essential to a fair trial," Gideon v. Wainwright, 372 U.S. 335, 343–344 (1963). The claim before us is that the right to trial by jury guaranteed by the Sixth Amendment meets these tests. The position of Louisiana, on the other hand, is that the Constitution imposes upon the States no duty to give a jury trial in any criminal case, regardless of the seriousness of the crime or the size of the punishment which may be imposed. Because we believe that trial by jury in criminal cases is fundamental to the American scheme of justice, we hold that the Fourteenth Amendment guarantees a right of jury trial in all criminal cases which—were they to be tried in a federal court—would come within the Sixth Amendment's guarantee.[j]

States represent a new approach to the "incorporation" debate. Earlier the Court can be seen as having asked, when inquiring into whether some particular procedural safeguard was required of a State, if a civilized system could be imagined that would not accord the particular protection. For example, Palko v. Connecticut, 302 U.S. 319, 325 (1937) stated: "The right to trial by jury and the immunity from prosecution except as the result of an indictment may have value and importance. Even so, they are not of the very essence of a scheme of ordered liberty * * *. Few would be so narrow or provincial as to maintain that a fair and enlightened system of justice would be impossible without them." The recent cases, on the other hand, have proceeded upon the valid assumption that state criminal processes

Since we consider the appeal before us to be such a case, we hold that the Constitution was violated when appellant's demand for jury trial was refused.

* * *

MR. JUSTICE BLACK, with whom MR. JUSTICE DOUGLAS joins, concurring.

* * *

All of these holdings making Bill of Rights' provisions applicable as such to the States mark, of course, a departure from the *Twining* doctrine holding that none of those provisions were enforceable as such against the States. The dissent in this case, however, makes a spirited and forceful defense of that now discredited doctrine. I do not believe that it is necessary for me to repeat the historical and logical reasons for my challenge to the *Twining* holding contained in my *Adamson* dissent and Appendix to it. What I wrote there in 1947 was the product of years of study and research. My appraisal of the legislative history followed 10 years of legislative experience as a Senator of the United States, not a bad

way, I suspect, to learn the value of what is said in legislative debates, committee discussions, committee reports, and various other steps taken in the course of passage of bills, resolutions, and proposed constitutional amendments. My Brother Harlan's objections to my *Adamson* dissent history, like that of most of the objectors, relies most heavily on a criticism written by Professor Charles Fairman and published in the Stanford Law Review. 2 Stan.L.Rev. 5 (1949). I have read and studied this article extensively, including the historical references, but am compelled to add that in my view it has completely failed to refute the inferences and arguments that I suggested in my *Adamson* dissent. Professor Fairman's "history" relies very heavily on what was *not* said in the state legislatures that passed on the Fourteenth Amendment. Instead of relying on this kind of negative pregnant, my legislative experience has convinced me that it is far wiser to rely on what *was* said, and most importantly, said by the men who actually sponsored the Amendment in the Congress.
* * *

are not imaginary and theoretical schemes but actual systems bearing virtually every characteristic of the common-law system that has been developing contemporaneously in England and in this country. The question thus is whether given this kind of system a particular procedure is fundamental—whether, that is, a procedure is necessary to an Anglo–American regime of ordered liberty. It is this sort of inquiry that can justify the conclusions that state courts must exclude evidence seized in violation of the Fourth Amendment, Mapp v. Ohio, 367 U.S. 643 (1961); that state prosecutors may not comment on a defendant's failure to testify, Griffin v. California, 380 U.S. 609 (1965); and that criminal punishment may not be imposed for the status of narcotics addiction, Robinson v. California, 370 U.S. 660 (1962). Of immediate relevance for this case are the Court's holdings that the States must comply with certain provisions of the Sixth Amendment, specifically that the States may not refuse a speedy trial, confrontation of witnesses, and the assistance, at state expense if necessary, of counsel. See cases cited supra. Of each of these determinations that a constitu-

tional provision originally written to bind the Federal Government should bind the States as well it might be said that the limitation in question is not necessarily fundamental to fairness in every criminal system that might be imagined but is fundamental in the context of the criminal processes maintained by the American States.

* * * A criminal process, which was fair and equitable but used no juries is easy to imagine. It would make use of alternative guarantees and protections which would serve the purposes that the jury serves in the English and American systems. Yet no American State has undertaken to construct such a system. Instead, every American State, including Louisiana, uses the jury extensively, and imposes very serious punishments only after a trial at which the defendant has a right to a jury's verdict. In every State, including Louisiana, the structure and style of the criminal process—the supporting framework and the subsidiary procedures—are of the sort that naturally complement jury trial, and have developed in connection with and in reliance upon jury trial.

In addition to the adoption of Professor Fairman's "history," the dissent states that "the great words of the four clauses of the first section of the Fourteenth Amendment would have been an exceedingly peculiar way to say that 'The rights heretofore guaranteed against federal intrusion by the first eight Amendments are henceforth guaranteed against state intrusion as well.'" In response to this I can say only that the words "No State shall make or enforce any law which shall abridge the privileges or immunities of citizens of the United States" seem to me an eminently reasonable way of expressing the idea that henceforth the Bill of Rights shall apply to the States. What more precious "privilege" of American citizenship could there be than that privilege to claim the protections of our great Bill of Rights? I suggest that any reading of "privileges or immunities of citizens of the United States" which excludes the Bill of Rights' safeguards renders the words of this section of the Fourteenth Amendment meaningless. * * *

While I do not wish at this time to discuss at length my disagreement with Brother Harlan's forthright and frank restatement of the now discredited *Twining* doctrine, I do want to point out what appears to me to be the basic difference between us. His view, as was indeed the view of *Twining,* is that "due process is an evolving concept" and therefore that it entails a "gradual process of judicial inclusion and exclusion" to ascertain those "immutable principles * * * of free government which no member of the Union may disregard." Thus the Due Process Clause is treated as prescribing no specific and clearly ascertainable constitutional command that judges must obey in interpreting the Constitution, but rather as leaving judges free to decide at any particular time whether a particular rule or judicial formulation embodies an "immutable principl[e] of free government" or is "implicit in the concept of ordered liberty," or whether certain conduct "shocks the judge's conscience" or runs counter to some other similar, undefined and undefinable standard. Thus due process, according to my Brother Harlan, is to be a phrase with no permanent meaning, but one which is found to shift from time to time in accordance with judges' predilections and understandings of what is best for the country. If due process means this, the Fourteenth Amendment, in my opinion, might as well have been written that "no person shall be deprived of life, liberty or property except by laws that the judges of the United States Supreme Court shall find to be consistent with the immutable principles of free government." It is impossible for me to believe that such unconfined power is given to judges in our Constitution that is a written one in order to limit governmental power.

Another tenet of the *Twining* doctrine as restated by my Brother Harlan is that "due process of law requires only fundamental fairness." But the "fundamental fairness" test is one on a par with that of shocking the conscience of the Court. Each of such tests depends entirely on the particular judge's idea of ethics and morals instead of requiring him to depend on the boundaries fixed by the written words of the Constitution. Nothing in the history of the phrase "due process of law" suggests that constitutional controls are to depend on any particular judge's sense of values. * * *

Finally I want to add that I am not bothered by the argument that applying the Bill of Rights to the States, "according to the same standards that protect those personal rights against federal encroachment," interferes with our concept of federalism in that it may prevent States from trying novel social and economic experiments. I have never believed that under the guise of federalism the States should be able to experiment with the protections afforded our citizens through the Bill of Rights. It seems to me totally inconsistent to advocate, on the one hand, the power of this Court to strike down any state law or practice which it finds "unreasonable" or "unfair" and, on the other hand, urge that the States be given maximum power to develop their own laws and procedures. * * *

In closing I want to emphasize that I believe as strongly as ever that the Fourteenth Amendment was intended to make the Bill of Rights applicable to the States. I have been willing to support the selective incorporation doctrine, however, as an alternative, although perhaps less historically supportable than complete incorporation. The selective incorporation process, if used properly, does limit the Supreme Court in the Fourteenth Amendment field to specific Bill of Rights' protections only and keeps judges from roaming at will in their own notions of what policies outside the Bill of Rights are desirable and what are not. And, most importantly for me, the selective incorporation process has the virtue of having already worked to make most of the Bill of Rights' protections applicable to the States.

MR. JUSTICE HARLAN, **whom** MR. JUSTICE STEWART **joins, dissenting.**

* * *

The Court's approach to this case is an uneasy and illogical compromise among the views of various Justices on how the Due Process Clause should be interpreted. The Court does not say that those who framed the Fourteenth Amendment intended to make the Sixth Amendment applicable to the

States. And the Court concedes that it finds nothing unfair about the procedure by which the present appellant was tried. Nevertheless, the Court reverses his conviction: it holds, for some reason not apparent to me that the Due Process Clause incorporates the particular clause of the Sixth Amendment that requires trial by jury in federal criminal cases—including, as I read its opinion, the sometimes trivial accompanying baggage of judicial interpretation in federal contexts. I have raised my voice many times before against the Court's continuing undiscriminating insistence upon fastening on the States federal notions of criminal justice and I must do so again in this instance. With all respect, the Court's approach and its reading of history are altogether topsy-turvy.

I

I believe I am correct in saying that every member of the Court for at least the last 135 years has agreed that our Founders did not consider the requirements of the Bill of Rights so fundamental that they should operate directly against the States. They were wont to believe rather that the security of liberty in America rested primarily upon the dispersion of governmental power across a federal system. The Bill of Rights was considered unnecessary by some but insisted upon by others in order to curb the possibility of abuse of power by the strong central government they were creating.

The Civil War Amendments dramatically altered the relation of the Federal Government to the States. The first section of the Fourteenth Amendment imposes highly significant restrictions on state action. But the restrictions are couched in very broad and general terms: citizenship; privileges and immunities; due process of law; equal protection of the laws. * * * Where does the Court properly look to find the specific rules that define and give content to such terms as "life, liberty, or property" and "due process of law"?

A few members of the Court have taken the position that the intention of those who drafted the first section of the Fourteenth Amendment was simply, and exclusively, to make the provisions of the first eight Amendments applicable to state action. This view has never been accepted by this Court. In my view, often expressed elsewhere, the first section of the Fourteenth Amendment was meant neither to incorporate, nor to be limited to, the specific guarantees of the first eight Amendments. The overwhelming historical evidence marshalled by Professor Fairman demonstrates, to me conclusively, that the Congressmen and state legislators who wrote, debated, and ratified the Fourteenth Amendment did not think they were "incorporating" the Bill of Rights[k] and the very breadth and generality of the Amendment's provisions suggest that its authors did not suppose that the Nation would always be limited to mid–19th century conceptions of "liberty" and "due process of law" * * *.

In short, neither history, nor sense, supports using the Fourteenth Amendment to put the States in a constitutional straitjacket with respect to their own development in the administration of criminal or civil law.

Although I therefore fundamentally disagree with the total incorporation view of the Fourteenth Amendment, it seems to me that such a position does at least have the virtue, lacking in the Court's selective incorporation approach, of internal consistency: we look to the Bill of Rights, word for word, clause for clause, precedent for precedent because, it is said, the men who wrote the Amendment wanted it that way. * * *.

Apart from the approach taken by the absolute incorporationists, I can see only one method of analysis that has any internal logic. That is to start with the words "liberty" and "due process of law" and attempt to define them in a way that accords with American traditions and our system of government. This approach * * * entails a "gradual process of judicial inclusion and exclusion," seeking, with due rec-

k. Fairman, Does the Fourteenth Amendment Incorporate the Bill of Rights? The Original Understanding, 2 Stan.L.Rev. 5 (1949). Professor Fairman was not content to rest upon the overwhelming fact that the great words of the four clauses of the first section of the Fourteenth Amendment would have been an exceedingly peculiar way to say that "The rights heretofore guaranteed against federal intrusion by the first eight Amendments are henceforth guaranteed against state intrusion as well." He therefore sifted the mountain of material comprising the debates and committee reports relating to the Amendment in both Houses of Congress and in the state legislatures that passed upon it. He found that in the immense corpus of comments on the purpose and effects of the proposed amendment, and on its virtues and defects, there is almost no evidence whatever for "incorporation." The first eight Amendments are so much as mentioned by only two members of Congress, one of whom effectively demonstrated (a) that he did not understand Barron v. Baltimore, 7 Pet. 243, and therefore did not understand the

question of incorporation, and (b) that he was not himself understood by his colleagues. One state legislative committee report, rejected by the legislature as a whole, found § 1 of the Fourteenth Amendment superfluous because it duplicated the Bill of Rights: the committee obviously did not understand Barron v. Baltimore either. That is all Professor Fairman could find, in hundreds of pages of legislative discussion prior to passage of the Amendment, that even suggests incorporation.

To this negative evidence the judicial history of the Amendment could be added. For example, it proved possible for a Court whose members had lived through Reconstruction to reiterate the doctrine of Barron v. Baltimore, that the Bill of Rights did not apply to the States, without so much as questioning whether the Fourteenth Amendment had any effect on the continued validity of that principle. E.g., Walker v. Sauvinet, 92 U.S. 90; see generally Morrison, Does the Fourteenth Amendment Incorporate the Bill of Rights? The Judicial Interpretation, 2 Stan.L.Rev. 140 (1949).

ognition of constitutional tolerance for state experimentation and disparity, to ascertain those "immutable principles * * * of free government which no member of the Union may disregard." * * *

* * *

Today's Court still remains unwilling to accept the total incorporationists' view of the history of the Fourteenth Amendment. This, if accepted, would afford a cogent reason for applying the Sixth Amendment to the States. The Court is also, apparently, unwilling to face the task of determin-

ing whether denial of trial by jury in the situation before us, or in other situations, is fundamentally unfair. Consequently, the Court has compromised on the ease of the incorporationist position, without its internal logic. It has simply assumed that the question before us is whether the Jury Trial Clause of the Sixth Amendment should be incorporated into the Fourteenth, jot-for-jot and case-for-case, or ignored. Then the Court merely declares that the clause in question is "in" rather than "out."

The Court has justified neither its starting place nor its conclusion. * * *

Note on Incorporation

The Court has never accepted Justice Black's view that the Fourteenth Amendment incorporates the entirety of the Bill of Rights. So for example, the right to indictment by grand jury is not binding on the states. The Seventh Amendment jury trial right is not binding upon the states in civil cases. And the bail clause of the Eighth Amendment has not yet been incorporated into the Fourteenth Amendment by the Supreme Court. But, the "fundamental fairness" approach of *Palko* and *Adamson* has given way to a selective incorporation view that, as Justice Black correctly notes in *Duncan,* has moved the Court a long way toward the total incorporation result that he advocated.

If Justice Black was wrong about the intent of the drafters of the Fourteenth Amendment and they did not intend incorporation, is there any rhyme or reason to the selective incorporation idea? If there is, it has to be that the Court has been willing to assume that the drafters of the Fourteenth Amendment wanted to enforce against the states only those portions of the Bill of Rights whose fundamentality remained evident many years after the first ten Amendments were adopted. Justice Black argued that incorporation of the Bill of Rights is preferable to a case-by-case, fundamental fairness approach, because the latter gives rise to judicial subjectivity in applying the vague term "due process." Are the Bill of Rights protections less susceptible to judicial subjectivity? For instance, does the term "unreasonable searches and seizures" in the Fourth Amendment provide more limitation on judicial subjectivity than the term "due process"?

Note on Relationship Between Due Process and Incorporated Rights

Does the Fourteenth Amendment provide supplemental protection *beyond* that granted by the Bill of Rights? For example, assume that police arrest a suspect after obtaining a warrant based upon probable cause. Are there some circumstances in which the police activity, though legal under the Fourth Amendment, can nonetheless violate due process? Another question is: if the police activity is illegal under the Fourth Amendment, can it also be found illegal as an independent deprivation of liberty without due process? The Supreme Court has discussed the relationship between the Fourteenth Amendment due process protection and the enumerated Bill of Rights protections in several cases, and the answers are not entirely consistent.

In Graham v. Connor, 490 U.S. 386 (1989), the Court held that constitutional claims against police officers for excessive force in making an arrest could not be analyzed under the doctrine of "substantive" due process. The Court stated that "the Fourth Amendment provides an explicit textual source of constitutional protection" for citizens faced with arrest. Therefore, "that Amendment, not the more generalized notion of substantive due process, must be the guide for analyzing these claims." Likewise, in Gerstein v. Pugh, 420 U.S. 103 (1975), the Court applied Fourth Amendment standards, rather than notions of procedural due process, to determine when and whether an arrestee is entitled to a judicial determination of probable cause. The Court explained that exclusive reliance on the Fourth Amendment was appropriate in the arrest context because that Amendment was "tailored explicitly for the criminal justice system," and its "balance between individual and public interest always has been thought to define the 'process that is due' for seizures of persons or property in criminal cases."

In contrast, the Court in United States v. James Daniel Good Real Property, 510 U.S. 43 (1993), held that compliance with the Fourth Amendment is not sufficient when the government seizes property for purposes of civil forfeiture. Police found a large quantity of drugs in Good's home, and Good pled guilty to state drug offenses. Over four years later, the United States filed an *in rem* action against Good's house and land, on the ground that the property had been used to commit or facilitate a drug transaction. Following an *ex parte* proceeding, a Magistrate Judge issued a warrant authorizing the seizure of the property, and the government executed the warrant without prior notice to Good or an adversary hearing. Good challenged the seizure of property under the Due Process Clause. The government argued that it need only comply with the Fourth Amendment when seizing forfeitable property; this it had done by obtaining a warrant based upon probable cause.

In a 5–4 decision written by Justice Kennedy, the Court distinguished *Gerstein* and held that the Due Process Clause was applicable to civil forfeiture proceedings. Justice Kennedy explained that *Gerstein* "concerned not the seizure of property but the arrest or detention of criminal suspects, subjects we have considered to be governed by the provisions of the Fourth Amendment without reference to other constitutional guarantees." He also noted that "unlike the seizure presented by this case, the arrest or detention of a suspect occurs as part of the regular criminal process, where other safeguards ordinarily ensure compliance with due process." The Court found that under the Due Process Clause, a property owner is entitled to notice and an opportunity to be heard before the Government seizes real property allegedly subject to civil forfeiture.

Chief Justice Rehnquist dissented in *Good* in an opinion joined by Justices O'Connor and Scalia. He argued that *Gerstein* could not be distinguished and that the Fourth Amendment provided an "explicit textual source" of protection that did not permit supplementation under the more general Due Process Clause. He stated that "[i]t is paradoxical indeed to hold that a criminal defendant can be temporarily deprived of liberty on the basis of an *ex parte* probable cause determination, yet respondent Good cannot be temporarily deprived of property on the same basis." Justices O'Connor and Thomas also wrote separate dissents.

Shortly after *Good*, the Court again discussed the interrelationship between the Due Process Clause and incorporated Bill of Rights protections in Albright v. Oliver, 510 U.S. 266 (1994). Albright brought an action for violation of his constitutional rights when he was arrested and prosecuted without probable cause. The charges were ultimately dropped. Albright relied specifically on his alleged "substantive" due process right to be free from an arbitrary deprivation of liberty. He did not bring a constitutional claim under the Fourth Amendment, apparently because he thought: 1) that it would not cover the damages he suffered from being charged as opposed to being arrested; and 2) that a Fourth Amendment claim would have been untimely, in that the statutory period would begin to run upon arrest rather than upon prosecution.

In a plurality opinion written for four members of the Court, Chief Justice Rehnquist declared that there is no "substantive right under the Due Process Clause to be free from criminal prosecution except upon probable cause." The Chief Justice relied on *Graham* and did not cite *Good*. He reasoned as follows:

> *Hurtado* held that the Due Process Clause did not make applicable to the States the Fifth Amendment's requirement that all prosecutions for an infamous crime be instituted by the indictment of a grand jury. In the more than 100 years since *Hurtado* was decided, the Court has concluded that a number of the procedural protections contained in the Bill of Rights were made applicable to the States by the Fourteenth Amendment.

> This course of decision has substituted, in these areas of criminal procedure, the specific guarantees of the various provisions of the Bill of Rights * * * for the more generalized language contained in the earlier cases construing the Fourteenth Amendment. * * * Where a particular amendment provides an explicit textual source of constitutional protection against a particular sort of government behavior, that amendment, not the more generalized notion of "substantive due process," must be the guide for analyzing these claims.

In a concurring opinion, Justice Scalia stated that he accepted the doctrine of incorporation, "because it is both long established and narrowly limited." He recognized that the doctrine of substantive due process had been applied in some civil contexts, but concluded that the doctrine could not be used "to impose additional requirements upon such of the states' criminal processes as are already addressed (and left without such requirements) by the Bill of Rights."

Justice Kennedy, joined by Justice Thomas, concurred in the judgment. He asserted that the Due Process Clause could not be relied upon where it would provide exactly the same protection as a specific guarantee contained in the Bill of Rights. Justice Ginsburg took a similar position in a separate concurring opinion.

Justice Souter wrote a separate opinion concurring in the judgment. Relying on *Good*, he rejected the proposition "that the Constitution's application to a general subject (like prosecution) is necessarily exhausted by protection under particular textual guarantees addressing specific events within that subject (like search and seizure), on a theory that one specific constitutional provision can pre-empt a broad field as against another more general one." However, Justice Souter nonetheless rejected Albright's substantive due process argument because it merely "duplicated protection that a more specific provision [the Fourth Amendment] already bestowed."

Justice Stevens, joined by Justice Blackmun, dissented. He contended that Albright was seeking damages for illegal prosecution. Because the right to a grand jury determination of probable cause has *not* been incorporated under the Fourteenth Amendment, Justice Stevens concluded that the Due Process Clause could be construed to provide an independent right to be free from prosecution-without-cause. Justice Stevens attacked the "cramped" view of the plurality that the Bill of Rights marks the outer limits of the protection provided by the Fourteenth Amendment.

Recap on Residual Protection Provided
By the Due Process Clause

The following principles can be gleaned from the morass of opinions set forth above:

    1.   A citizen cannot rely on a right to "due process" if a specific Bill of Rights guarantee would provide the same constitutional protection.

    2.   Where a specific Bill of Rights protection has traditionally regulated an area of criminal investigation or prosecution, and yet provides no protection in a particular case, it is very unlikely that a citizen can rely upon a more general due process guarantee.

    3.   Independent protection under the Due Process Clause remains viable where governmental activity, as in *Good*, has some purpose other than enforcement of the criminal law.

    4.   Independent protection under the Due Process Clause remains viable even in criminal cases where no specific Bill of Rights guarantee has traditionally applied. See e.g., Godinez v. Moran, 509 U.S. 389 (1993) (defendant has a right under the Due Process Clause to be tried only if competent).

Note on State Constitutional Protections

The Supreme Court has the final say in interpreting federal constitutional protections concerning criminal procedure. But state courts have sometimes provided enhanced protection of constitutional rights through reliance on state constitutions. Advocates of expansive readings of constitutional protections, who once asserted that state courts could not be trusted to protect fundamental liberties, are now turning to those courts and asking them to use their state constitutions to go beyond the decisions of the United States Supreme Court. The result is that states may not experiment in ways that provide less protection than is guaranteed by the Bill of Rights, but they may provide more.

While some states have been more active than others, virtually every state has rejected at least one Supreme Court decision as insufficiently protective of the rights of citizens. Many of these decisions will be discussed in the context of particular Supreme Court rulings, *infra*. It must be remembered that if the state court explicitly relies on state constitutional law to provide more protection to citizens than the Federal Constitution, the state court's decision on this matter cannot be reviewed by the Supreme Court. This is because there is no Federal question which would control the case. See generally Michigan v. Long, 463 U.S. 1032 (1983)(state court must place explicit reliance on state law in order to avoid Supreme Court review; otherwise it will be presumed that the state court was construing Federal constitutional law). For extensive discussions about what has come to be called "state court activism," see Brennan, J., State Constitutions and the Protection of Individual Rights, 90 Harv.L.Rev. 489 (1977); Symposium on Emerging Issues in State Constitutional Law, 65 Temple L.Rev. 1119 (1992); Hancock, State Court Activism and Searches Incident to Arrest, 68 Va.L.Rev. 1085, 1110 (1982). For a critical view, see Gardner, The Failed Discourse of State Constitutionalism, 90 Mich.L.Rev. 685 (1992).

B. RETROACTIVITY

1. *The Impact of New Decisions*

When the Supreme Court reviews the conduct of government officials in a criminal case, the legal rule it promulgates will obviously apply to all similar government conduct arising after the date of the decision. But an important question is whether the legal rule should also be applied to government conduct occurring *before* the date of the decision. The question of retroactive application is one of competing policies and interests.

For example, when the Supreme Court overrules a prior decision that had permitted certain police behavior, the Court might be concerned that law enforcement officers, who relied on the case law existing at the time of their conduct, in fact acted as competent officers should. The Court might, therefore, be reluctant to see the government disadvantaged as a result of justifiable reliance by government agents. The Court also might be concerned that trial courts that relied on the old rule may be burdened with numerous retrials once the new decision is announced.

On the other hand, if a decision is important enough to be called a "constitutional decision," it is arguable that it ought to benefit all those who suffered the conduct now found to be wrongful.

For many years, the Supreme Court's position on retroactive application was complicated and often inconsistent. But one rule that the Court always has followed is to give the benefit of the new rule to the litigant who establishes it, even though that constitutes retroactive application. The Court has done so for two reasons: 1) to provide litigants with incentives to improve past decisions of the Court, because few litigants would ask the Court to establish a new rule that they could not use; and 2) to assure that there is a concrete case or controversy before the Court.

2. *Prior Supreme Court Law on Retroactivity, and the Harlan Approach*

In Stovall v. Denno, 388 U.S. 293 (1967) and Desist v. United States, 394 U.S. 244 (1969), the Court refused to apply its decisions requiring counsel at certain lineups and its holding in an earlier Fourth Amendment case, Katz v. United States, 389 U.S. 347 (1967), to other cases still pending on direct review. Rather, the Court applied its earlier decisions to reach only the police activity that followed the announcement of the new rules. Essentially, the rulings were given only prospective effect, other than for the litigants in the cases in which the new rule was established.

Justice Harlan dissented in *Desist* and concluded that new constitutional rules must be applied, at a minimum, to all cases pending on direct review when the rules are handed down. (A case is on "direct review" when it is still on appeal from a judgment of conviction. This includes all appellate activity up to and including the Supreme Court's denial of a writ of certiorari). Justice Harlan charged that a decision to apply a ruling on direct review of one case (i.e., the case before the Court), but not another, is an assertion of legislative, not adjudicatory, power. Justice Harlan argued further that, as a general matter, a new rule should *not* be applied in collateral attack (i.e., habeas corpus) proceedings. (Habeas corpus proceedings usually involve federal court review of a state judgment of conviction, and are brought after a defendant's direct appeals through the state appellate courts and the United States Supreme Court have been rejected or foregone; see the discussion in Chapter 13). Justice Harlan identified two situations in which the presumption of nonretroactivity of new rules for habeas corpus cases could be overcome; these were exceptions to the general principle of nonretroactivity in habeas cases. The first exception encompassed habeas corpus petitioners who sought the benefit of a new rule that is so fundamental that it is "implicit in the concept of ordered liberty" (quoting Justice Cardozo's opinion in *Palko*). The second exception covered a petitioner who relied upon a new rule to demonstrate that the conduct for which he was tried was constitutionally protected, so that a trial should never have occurred in the first place. Justice Harlan's view is fully discussed and analyzed by the Court in Teague v. Lane, below.

3. *Current Supreme Court Approach to Retroactivity*

In a series of cases, the Court finally adopted the Harlan approach to retroactivity, with one slight modification as to the "fundamental fairness" exception to non-retroactivity on habeas. In Griffith v. Kentucky, 479 U.S. 314 (1987), the Court held that its decision the previous term in Batson v. Kentucky, 476 U.S. 79 (1986)(defendant could establish a prima facie case of racial discrimination based on the prosecution's use of peremptory challenges in a single case), would be applied retroactively to all cases still pending on direct review when the decision was announced. Although *Batson* overruled a decision that had withstood attack for more than twenty years, the Court declined to follow *Stovall* and other cases that had barred some or all defendants from benefitting from recently announced decisions even while pursuing direct appeal or review in the Supreme Court. Instead the Court adopted Justice Harlan's analysis of direct review: a new rule is applicable to all cases that are still under court review, up to the time that a petition for certiorari in the United States Supreme Court has been denied or the time to file such a petition has run out. Justice Blackmun wrote in *Griffith* for six Justices. The Court's analysis in *Griffith* is discussed in Teague v. Lane, immediately below, where the Court adopted the Harlan view that new rules are generally inapplicable to habeas cases.

The applicability of *Teague* has been limited somewhat by subsequent Congressional legislation restricting habeas corpus relief. Yet *Teague* is still important because that legislation was promulgated in the spirit of *Teague* (which is generally to limit the retroactive effect of new rules in habeas corpus cases), and there are some situations in which the legislation is inapplicable, thus rendering *Teague* the governing principle. The effect of the legislation is discussed in a Note following *Teague*.

TEAGUE v. LANE

Supreme Court of the United States, 1989.
489 U.S. 288.

Justice O'Connor **announced the judgment of the Court and delivered the opinion of the Court with** respect to Parts I, II, and III, and an **opinion with respect to Parts IV and V, in which** Chief Justice Rehnquist,

JUSTICE SCALIA, and JUSTICE KENNEDY join.

In Taylor v. Louisiana, 419 U.S. 522 (1975), this Court held that the Sixth Amendment required that the jury venire be drawn from a fair cross section of the community. * * * The principal question presented in this case is whether the Sixth Amendment's fair cross section requirement should now be extended to the petit jury. Because we adopt Justice Harlan's approach to retroactivity for cases on collateral review, we leave the resolution of that question for another day.

I

Petitioner, a black man, was convicted by an all-white Illinois jury of three counts of attempted murder, two counts of armed robbery, and one count of aggravated battery. During jury selection for petitioner's trial, the prosecutor used all 10 of his peremptory challenges to exclude blacks. * * *

On appeal, petitioner argued that the prosecutor's use of peremptory challenges denied him the right to be tried by a jury that was representative of the community. The Illinois Appellate Court rejected petitioner's fair cross section claim. The Illinois Supreme Court denied leave to appeal, and we denied certiorari.

Petitioner then filed a petition for a writ of habeas corpus in the United States District Court for the Northern District of Illinois. Petitioner repeated his fair cross section claim * * *. [Both the District Court and the Court of Appeals en banc denied Teague's claim for habeas relief. The Court of Appeals held that the Constitution's fair cross-section requirement was limited to the jury venire—the pool from which the jury that sits in the case (the petit jury) is drawn].

II

* * *

III

* * *

IV

Petitioner's * * * contention is that the Sixth Amendment's fair cross section requirement applies to the petit jury. * * * Petitioner * * * contends that the *ratio decidendi* of *Taylor* cannot be limited to the jury venire, and he urges adoption of a new rule. Because we hold that the rule urged by petitioner should not be applied retroactively to cases on collateral review, we decline to address petitioner's contention.

A

In the past, the Court has, without discussion, often applied a new constitutional rule of criminal procedure to the defendant in the case announcing the new rule, and has confronted the question of retroactivity later when a different defendant sought the benefit of that rule. In several cases, however, the Court has addressed the retroactivity question in the very case announcing the new rule. These two lines of cases do not have a unifying theme, and we think it is time to clarify how the question of retroactivity should be resolved for cases on collateral review.

* * *

In our view, the question "whether a decision [announcing a new rule should] be given prospective or retroactive effect should be faced at the time of [that] decision." Mishkin, Foreword: the High Court, the Great Writ, and the Due Process of Time and Law, 79 Harv. L. Rev. 56, 64 (1965). Retroactivity is properly treated as a threshold question, for, once a new rule is applied to the defendant in the case announcing the rule, evenhanded justice requires that it be applied retroactively to all who are similarly situated. Thus, before deciding whether the fair cross section requirement should be extended to the petit jury, we should ask whether such a rule would be applied retroactively to the case at issue. * * *

It is admittedly often difficult to determine when a case announces a new rule, and we do not attempt to define the spectrum of what may or may not constitute a new rule for retroactivity purposes. In general, however, a case announces a new rule when it breaks new ground or imposes a new obligation on the States or the Federal Government. To put it differently, a case announces a new rule if the result was not dictated by precedent existing at the time the defendant's conviction became final. Given the strong language in *Taylor* and our statement in Akins v. Texas, 325 U.S. 398, 403 (1945), that "[f]airness in [jury] selection has never been held to require proportional representation of races upon a jury," application of the fair cross section requirement to the petit jury would be a new rule.

Not all new rules have been uniformly treated for retroactivity purposes. Nearly a quarter of a century ago, in Linkletter v. Walker, 381 U.S. 618 (1965), the Court attempted to set some standards by which to determine the retroactivity of new rules. The question in *Linkletter* was whether Mapp v. Ohio, which made the exclusionary rule applicable to the States, should be applied retroactively to cases on collateral review. The Court determined that the retroactivity of *Mapp* should be determined by examining the purpose of the exclusionary rule, the reliance of the States on prior law, and the effect on the administration of justice of a retroactive application of the exclusionary rule. Using

that standard, the Court held that *Mapp* would only apply to trials commencing after that case was decided.

The *Linkletter* retroactivity standard has not led to consistent results. Instead, it has been used to limit application of certain new rules to cases on direct review, other new rules only to the defendants in the cases announcing such rules, and still other new rules to cases in which trials have not yet commenced. * * *

Application of the *Linkletter* standard led to the disparate treatment of similarly situated defendants on direct review. For example, in * * * Johnson v. New Jersey, 384 U.S. 719, 733–735 (1966), the Court held, under the *Linkletter* standard, that *Miranda* would only be applied to trials commencing after that decision had been announced. Because the defendant in *Johnson*, like the defendants in *Miranda*, was on direct review of his conviction, the Court's refusal to give *Miranda* retroactive effect resulted in unequal treatment of those who were similarly situated. * * *

In Griffith v. Kentucky, 479 U.S. 314 (1987), we rejected as unprincipled and inequitable the *Linkletter* standard for cases pending on direct review at the time a new rule is announced, and adopted the first part of the retroactivity approach advocated by Justice Harlan. We agreed with Justice Harlan that "failure to apply a newly declared constitutional rule to criminal cases pending on direct review violates basic norms of constitutional adjudication." We gave two reasons for our decision. First, because we can only promulgate new rules in specific cases and cannot possibly decide all cases in which review is sought, "the integrity of judicial review" requires the application of the new rule to "all similar cases pending on direct review." * * * Second, because "selective application of new rules violates the principle of treating similarly situated defendants the same," we refused to continue to tolerate the inequity that resulted from not applying new rules retroactively to defendants whose cases had not yet become final. Although new rules that constituted clear breaks with the past generally were not given retroactive effect under the *Linkletter* standard, we held that "a new rule for the conduct of criminal prosecutions is to be applied retroactively to all cases, state or federal, pending on direct review or not yet final, with no exception for cases in which the new rule constitutes a 'clear break' with the past."

The *Linkletter* standard also led to unfortunate disparity in the treatment of similarly situated defendants on collateral review. An example will best illustrate the point. In Edwards v. Arizona, 451 U.S. 477, 484–487 (1981), the Court held that once a person invokes his right to have counsel present during custodial interrogation, a valid waiver of that right cannot be inferred from the fact that the person responded to police-initiated questioning. It was not until Solem v. Stumes, 465 U.S. 638 (1984), that the Court held, under the *Linkletter* standard, that *Edwards* was not to be applied retroactively to cases on collateral review. In the interim, several lower federal courts had come to the opposite conclusion and had applied *Edwards* to cases that had become final before that decision was announced. Thus, some defendants on collateral review whose *Edwards* claims were adjudicated prior to *Stumes* received the benefit of *Edwards*, while those whose *Edwards* claims had not been addressed prior to *Stumes* did not. This disparity in treatment was a product of two factors: our failure to treat retroactivity as a threshold question and the *Linkletter* standard's inability to account

for the nature and function of collateral review. Having decided to rectify the first of those inadequacies, we now turn to the second.

B

Justice Harlan believed that new rules generally should not be applied retroactively to cases on collateral review. * * * Given the "broad scope of constitutional issues cognizable on habeas," Justice Harlan argued that it is "sounder, in adjudicating habeas petitions, generally to apply the law prevailing at the time a conviction became final than it is to seek to dispose of [habeas] cases on the basis of intervening changes in constitutional interpretation." As he had explained in *Desist*, "the threat of habeas serves as a necessary additional incentive for trial and appellate courts throughout the land to conduct their proceedings in a manner consistent with established constitutional standards. In order to perform this deterrence function, * * * the habeas court need only apply the constitutional standards that prevailed at the time the original proceedings took place."

Justice Harlan identified only two exceptions to his general rule of nonretroactivity for cases on collateral review. First, a new rule should be applied retroactively if it places "certain kinds of primary, private individual conduct beyond the power of the criminal law-making authority to proscribe." Second, a new rule should be applied retroactively if it requires the observance of "those procedures that ... are 'implicit in the concept of ordered liberty.'"

* * *

We agree with Justice Harlan's description of the function of habeas corpus. "[T]he Court never has defined the scope of the writ simply by reference to a perceived need to assure that an individual accused of crime is afforded a trial free of constitutional error." Rather, we have recognized that interests of comity and finality must also be considered in determining the proper scope of habeas review. * * *

* * * Application of constitutional rules not in existence at the time a conviction became final seriously undermines the principle of finality which is essential to the operation of our criminal justice system. Without finality, the criminal law is deprived of much of its deterrent effect. The fact that life and liberty are at stake in criminal prosecutions "shows only that 'conventional notions of finality' should not have as much place in criminal as in civil litigation, not that they should have none." Friendly, Is Innocence Irrelevant? Collateral Attacks on Criminal Judgments, 38 U. Chi. L. Rev. 142, 150 (1970). See also Mackey v. United States, 401 U.S., at 691 (Harlan, J.)("No one, not criminal defendants, not the judicial system, not society as a whole is benefitted by a judgment providing a man shall tentatively go to jail today, but tomorrow and every day thereafter his continued incarceration shall be subject to fresh litigation").

* * *

The "costs imposed upon the State[s] by retroactive application of new rules of constitutional law on habeas corpus * * * generally far outweigh the benefits of this application." In many ways the application of new rules to cases on collateral review may be more intrusive than the enjoining of criminal prosecutions, for it continually forces the States to marshal resources in order to keep in prison defendants whose trials and appeals conformed to then-existing constitutional standards. Furthermore, * * * "[s]tate courts are understandably

frustrated when they faithfully apply existing constitutional law only to have a federal court discover, during a [habeas] proceeding, new constitutional commands."

We find these criticisms to be persuasive, and we now adopt Justice Harlan's view of retroactivity for cases on collateral review. Unless they fall within an exception to the general rule, new constitutional rules of criminal procedure will not be applicable to those cases which have become final before the new rules are announced.

V

Petitioner's conviction became final in 1983. As a result, the rule petitioner urges would not be applicable to this case, which is on collateral review, unless it would fall within an exception.

The first exception suggested by Justice Harlan—that a new rule should be applied retroactively if it places "certain kinds of primary, private individual conduct beyond the power of the criminal law-making authority to proscribe"—is not relevant here. Application of the fair cross section requirement to the petit jury would not accord constitutional protection to any primary activity whatsoever.

The second exception suggested by Justice Harlan—that a new rule should be applied retroactively if it requires the observance of "those procedures that * * * are 'implicit in the concept of ordered liberty,'"(quoting Palko v Connecticut)—we apply with a modification. * * *

* * * Were we to employ the *Palko* test without more, we would be doing little more than importing into a very different context the terms of the debate over incorporation. Reviving the *Palko* test now, in this area of law, would be unnecessarily anachronistic. * * * [W]e believe that Justice Harlan's concerns about the difficulty in

identifying both the existence and the value of accuracy-enhancing procedural rules can be addressed by limiting the scope of the second exception to those new procedures without which the likelihood of an accurate conviction is seriously diminished.

Because we operate from the premise that such procedures would be so central to an accurate determination of innocence or guilt, we believe it unlikely that many such components of basic due process have yet to emerge. * * *

* * * Because the absence of a fair cross section on the jury venire does not undermine the fundamental fairness that must underlie a conviction or seriously diminish the likelihood of obtaining an accurate conviction, we conclude that a rule requiring that petit juries be composed of a fair cross section of the community would not be a "bedrock procedural element" that would be retroactively applied under the second exception we have articulated.

Were we to recognize the new rule urged by petitioner in this case, we would have to give petitioner the benefit of that new rule even though it would not be applied retroactively to others similarly situated. * * *

If there were no other way to avoid rendering advisory opinions, we might well agree that the inequitable treatment described above is "an insignificant cost for adherence to sound principles of decision-making." But there is a more principled way of dealing with the problem. We can simply refuse to announce a new rule in a given case unless the rule would be applied retroactively to the defendant in the case and to all others similarly situated. We think this approach is a sound one. Not only does it eliminate any problems of rendering advisory opinions, it also avoids the inequity resulting from the uneven application of new rules to similarly situated defendants. We therefore hold that, implicit in the retroactivity approach we adopt today, is the principle that habeas corpus cannot be used as a vehicle to create new constitutional rules of criminal procedure unless those rules would be applied retroactively to all defendants on collateral review through one of the two exceptions we have articulated. * * *

[The opinion of JUSTICE WHITE, concurring in part and concurring in the judgment, is omitted.]

JUSTICE STEVENS, with whom JUSTICE BLACKMUN joins as to Part I, concurring in part and concurring in the judgment.

* * *

In general, I share Justice Harlan's views about retroactivity. * * * I am persuaded that the Court should adopt Justice Harlan's analysis of retroactivity for habeas corpus cases as well for cases still on direct review.

I do not agree, however, with the plurality's dicta proposing a "modification" of Justice Harlan's fundamental fairness exception. * * *

* * * I cannot agree that it is "unnecessarily anachronistic" to issue a writ of habeas corpus to a petitioner convicted in a manner that violates fundamental principles of liberty. Furthermore, a touchstone of factual innocence would provide little guidance in certain important types of cases, such as those challenging the constitutionality of capital sentencing hearings. Even when assessing errors at the guilt phase of a trial, factual innocence is too capricious a factor by which to determine if a procedural change is sufficiently "bedrock" or "watershed" to justify application of the fundamental fairness exception. * * *

* * *

JUSTICE BRENNAN, **with whom** JUSTICE MARSHALL **joins, dissenting.**

* * * Out of an exaggerated concern for treating similarly situated habeas petitioners the same, the plurality would for the first time preclude the federal courts from considering on collateral review a vast range of important constitutional challenges; where those challenges have merit, it would bar the vindication of personal constitutional rights and deny society a check against further violations until the same claim is presented on direct review. * * *

* * *

[F]rom the plurality's exposition of its new rule, one might infer that its novel fabrication will work no great change in the availability of federal collateral review of state convictions. Nothing could be further from the truth. * * * Few decisions on appeal or collateral review are "dictated" by what came before. Most such cases involve a question of law that is at least debatable, permitting a rational judge to resolve the case in more than one way. Virtually no case that prompts a dissent on the relevant legal point, for example, could be said to be "dictated" by prior decisions. * * * The plurality's approach today can thus be expected to contract substantially the Great Writ's sweep.

* * *

Commentary on the Teague Rule

While Justice O'Connor's modified Harlan view was joined only by a plurality in *Teague*, it has subsequently been adopted by a majority of the Court in a series of cases. See, e.g., Penry v. Lynaugh, 492 U.S. 302 (1989)(applying *Teague* to preclude some claims brought in a collateral attack of a death sentence).

In Collins v. Youngblood, 497 U.S. 37 (1990), the Court held that the rule in *Teague*, prohibiting retroactive application or promulgation of new rules to habeas corpus cases, was not jurisdictional and therefore would not be raised by the Court *sua sponte*.

Under the Harlan-*Teague* view, defendants are subject to different treatment depending on the efficiency of the appellate courts in the state in which they are convicted. The slower the appellate system, the more likely that the defendant would benefit from new rules, because it is more likely that the case will still be on direct review when the new rule is promulgated.

A different criticism of the Harlan approach, as applied to cases on direct review, is that if new rules are generally applicable to cases not finalized, the cost of a new rule will often be significant. That may deter the Court from promulgating new rules in the first place. See Jenkins v. Delaware, 395 U.S. 213 (1969)(non-retroactivity provides an impetus for the "implementation of long overdue reforms which otherwise could not be practicably effected."); People v. Mitchell, 80 N.Y.2d 519, 591 N.Y.S.2d 990, 606 N.E.2d 1381 (1992)(rejecting Harlan view and holding that under state law, a new rule was not applicable to cases on direct review: denying retroactive effect to new rules "permits this Court to expand the protection accorded defendants when we might otherwise hesitate to do so because retroactive application threatens to wreak more havoc in society that society's interest in stability will tolerate.").

The academic commentary on *Teague* has been almost uniformly negative. Some examples are: Liebman, More Than "Slightly Retro": The Rehnquist Court's Rout of Habeas Corpus Jurisdiction in Teague v. Lane, 18 N.Y.U. Rev. of Law & Social Change 537 (1991); Dubber, Prudence and Substance: How the Supreme Court's New Habeas Retroactivity Doctrine Mirrors and Affects Substantive Constitutional Law, 30 Am.Crim.L.Rev. 1 (1992); Meyer, "Nothing We Say Matters": *Teague* and New Rules, 61 Univ.Chi.L.Rev. 423 (1994).

It is difficult to appreciate the lines the Court has drawn between prospective and retrospective decisions without focusing on specific holdings. The subject is raised at the outset of the book to put you on notice that it is an important part of the Court's work. See whether you would have cushioned the force of some decisions even more than the Court did by limiting retroactive application, or whether you would adopt a rule giving all defendants the benefit of constitutional decisions no matter when a precedent is established. In the final chapter you will have a chance to examine habeas corpus and the subject of collateral remedies generally.

What Is a "New Rule"?

After *Teague,* new rules are generally inapplicable to those whose convictions have been finalized—including the petitioner who initially brings the claim for a new rule on collateral review. Finalization is defined as the date on which the United States Supreme Court has denied certiorari of the defendant's direct appeal, or when the time to petition for certiorari has run out. However, Justice Harlan, whose views were generally adopted in *Teague,* emphasized that some "new" holdings are not "new" at all, but are merely applications of well-settled principles to different fact situations.

The Court, following Justice Harlan's approach, has mandated that when a decision merely applies settled precedent it is not a "new" rule at all, and is thus completely retroactive. See Yates v. Aiken, 484 U.S. 211 (1988). The rationale is that if a constitutional rule is not "new", the state court should have applied it correctly, and therefore the failure to apply it is proper grounds for habeas relief. The difficulty is in determining if a rule is "new" or merely an old rule applied to a different fact situation. In *Teague,* the Court stated that a case announces a new rule when it was "not dictated by existing precedent."

In Butler v. McKellar, 494 U.S. 407 (1990), the Court expounded further on the *Teague* definition of a "new" rule. The issue was whether Arizona v. Roberson was a new rule or merely an application of Edwards v. Arizona[4] to a somewhat different fact situation. When Butler was tried in state court, *Edwards* had been decided, but *Roberson* was not decided until Butler's conviction had been finalized. *Edwards* held that once a person in custody has requested counsel, the police may not conduct further interrogation unless counsel is provided or the suspect initiates communications. *Roberson* held that the *Edwards* rule applied even when the officer wants to question the suspect about a crime unrelated to that for which he has been arrested. Butler, who confessed to a crime unrelated to that for which he was arrested, argued that the rule in *Roberson* should be retroactively applied to him, on the ground that the

4. Both of these cases are discussed in the material on confessions in Chapter Three.

Roberson Court itself had stated that the rule was not new but merely an application of *Edwards*.

Chief Justice Rehnquist, writing for the majority, stated that a rule is "new" if reasonable minds could have differed about the result of the decision before it was rendered. The majority held that *Roberson* was a new rule, because reasonable-minded lower courts before *Roberson* had differed about whether *Edwards* would apply to questioning about unrelated investigations. The fact that the majority in *Roberson* characterized its decision as indistinguishable from *Edwards* and as a refusal to create an "exception" was not dispositive. According to the Chief Justice, "courts frequently view their decisions as being 'controlled' or 'governed' by prior opinions even when aware of reasonable contrary conclusions reached by lower courts." He stated that "[t]he 'new rule' principle * * * validates reasonable, good-faith interpretations of existing precedents made by state courts even though they are shown to be contrary to later decisions."

Justice Brennan, joined by Justices Marshall, Blackmun and Stevens, dissented in *Butler*. Justice Brennan complained that *Butler,* when combined with *Teague,* drastically limits the scope of habeas corpus relief by a "virtually all-encompassing definition of 'new rule'." The Federal court reviewing a state court decision cannot grant the petition if reasonable minds could differ about the state court result: granting a petition in such circumstances would be tantamount to applying a new rule on habeas, which is prohibited by *Teague.* Consequently, the petition will only be granted if the state court was so incorrect about the meaning of federal law as to be completely unreasonable. According to Justice Brennan, such a permissive standard is contrary to the "deterrence function" of habeas review.

Refusal to Promulgate a New Rule as a Decision on the Merits

When the Court refuses to decide a question in a habeas case because to do so would result in the promulgation of a "new rule," has the Court given an opinion on the merits of the proposed rule itself? For example, in *Teague*, did the Court, by refusing to decide the issue of whether the fair cross section requirement applied to the petit jury, effectively signal to the lower courts its view about the merits of such a claim? If you were a lower court judge, would you be inclined to adopt a "new rule" in a direct review case after the Supreme Court had declined to adopt the rule in a habeas case?

The Supreme Court has given some indication that a refusal to render what would be a "new rule" on habeas is similar to a rejection of the proposed rule on the merits. In Johnson v. Texas, 509 U.S. 350 (1993), the Court considered a question of the constitutionality of a capital sentencing statute on direct review. This question was identical to that which the Court had, earlier in the same term, refused to consider on habeas review on the ground that granting relief would require promulgation of a "new rule." Acting on direct review "without the constraints of *Teague*," the Court rejected the constitutional claim on the merits, relying on "much of the reasoning" in the previous habeas case. Justice O'Connor, the author of *Teague*, wrote a dissent in *Johnson* for four Justices. She argued that "cases that reject a claim as requiring a new rule cannot constitute stare decisis on direct review," since a rejection on habeas means only that the issue is "susceptible to debate among reasonable minds."

Is it possible to separate the question of whether a proposed rule is "new" from the question whether a proposed rule is meritorious? See Arkin, The Prisoner's Dilemma: Life in the Lower Federal Courts After Teague v. Lane, 69 No.Car.L.Rev. 371 (1991)(whether a rule is new requires a view into the merits of the rule).

The Teague Rule and Statutory Limitations on Habeas Corpus Relief

The result mandated by *Teague* and *Butler* essentially has been incorporated as part of the substantive limitations imposed on habeas corpus relief by the 1996 Antiterrorism and Effective Death Penalty Act (AEDPA). AEDPA severely limits Federal habeas review over state court determinations of constitutional law, but the rule is now phrased as merit-based rather than retroactivity-based. The Act provides, in pertinent part:

> *(d) An application for a writ of habeas corpus on behalf of a person in custody pursuant to the judgment of a State court shall not be granted with respect to any claim that was adjudicated on the merits in State court proceedings unless the adjudication of the claim—*

> *(1) resulted in a decision that was contrary to, or involved an unreasonable application of, clearly established Federal law, as determined by the Supreme Court of the United States; or*

> *(2) resulted in a decision that was based on an unreasonable determination of the facts in light of the evidence presented in the State court proceeding.*

In Williams v. Taylor, 529 U.S. 362 (2000), the Court, in an opinion by Justice O'Connor, declared that the AEDPA essentially codified a standard of review of state court decisions that is equivalent to the "new rule" jurisprudence of *Teague*. Under AEDPA, a federal court cannot grant relief unless the state court decision is "contrary to, or involved an unreasonable application of, clearly established Federal law, as determined by the Supreme Court of the United States." In *Williams*, Justice O'Connor declared that "whatever would qualify as an old rule under our *Teague* jurisprudence will constitute 'clearly established Federal law, as determined by the Supreme Court of the United States' under § 2254(d)(1). The one caveat, as the statutory language makes clear, is that § 2254(d)(1) restricts the source of clearly established law to this Court's jurisprudence." Consequently, if a habeas petitioner is claiming that a state court misapplied constitutional law that was not clearly established by the United States Supreme Court at the time, the habeas petition must be denied— because the state court decision is not "contrary to" clearly established law as defined by the Supreme Court. It follows that the *Teague* "new rule" jurisprudence has been codified, for all practical purposes, by AEDPA.

Note that in AEDPA there are no exceptions provided comparable to the two limited exceptions permitting retroactive application in *Teague*, i.e., "watershed" rules of constitutional law, or rules that hold certain conduct beyond criminal proscription. The rationale for rejecting these exceptions, according to an official at the Justice Department who was instrumental in drafting the provision, is that the *Teague* exceptions are so narrow that they can never be invoked as a practical matter. The result under AEDPA is that a habeas petitioner cannot seek to invoke a rule of law unless it was already clearly established at the time of the trial—and it makes no difference whether the rule of law proposed by the habeas claimant is a "watershed" rule or a rule that holds certain conduct beyond criminal proscription.

Finally, note that *Teague* itself remains directly applicable in cases where AEDPA does not apply. For example, where a state court never considered a defendant's claim on the merits, the standard of review set forth in AEDPA is by its terms inapplicable. However, for habeas corpus relief to be granted in such a situation, the petitioner's claim must still be based on constitutional law as it existed at the time of his conviction. Any attempt to extend that then-existing law will run into the "new rule" jurisprudence of *Teague* and its progeny. Thus, in Weeks v. Angelone, 176 F.3d 249 (4th Cir. 1999) the habeas petitioner claimed that his due process rights were denied by the state court's failure to provide him an expert in ballistics to assist in his defense. This claim was not covered by AEDPA because the state court had never considered it on the merits, even though asked to do so. But the constitutional claim was still barred by *Teague*, because the law existing at the time of the petitioner's conviction provided only that a defendant was entitled, upon a sufficient showing of need, to a state-appointed *psychiatrist* to assist in the defense. This precedent did not mandate appointment of non-psychiatric experts. Extending Supreme Court precedent to provide a guarantee of a non-psychiatric expert would constitute a "new rule", barred by *Teague.*

Retroactive Application Against the Defendant?

The cases and statute discussed above all deal with whether a defendant can, through retroactive application, receive a benefit from a change in law. But what about changes in law that are detrimental to a defendant? Do the same principles apply? For example, what if a habeas petitioner's conviction was obtained in violation of then-existing case law, but that law was subsequently overruled? Is the conviction assessed in light of the law at the time (resulting in relief), or is the state permitted to take advantage of a change in the law to the defendant's detriment? In Lockhart v. Fretwell, 506 U.S. 364 (1993), the Supreme Court, in an opinion by Chief Justice Rehnquist, held that detrimental changes in the law must be applied retroactively against petitioners on habeas review. The Chief Justice distinguished *Teague* and reasoned as follows:

> *Teague* stands for the proposition that new constitutional rules of criminal procedure will not be announced or applied on collateral review. * * * [T]his retroactivity rule was motivated by a respect for the States' strong interest in the finality of criminal convictions, and the recognition that a State should not be penalized for relying on the constitutional standards that prevailed at the time the original proceedings took place. The "new rule" principle therefore validates reasonable, good-faith interpretations of existing precedents made by state courts even though they are shown to be contrary to later decisions.

> A federal habeas petitioner has no interest in the finality of the state court judgment under which he is incarcerated: indeed, the very purpose of his habeas petition is to overturn that judgment. Nor does such a petitioner ordinarily have any claim of reliance on past judicial precedent as a basis for his actions * * *. The result of these differences is that the State will

benefit from our *Teague* decision in some federal habeas cases, while the habeas petitioner will not.

Justice Stevens, joined by Justice Blackmun, dissented and argued that an "even-handed approach to retroactivity would seem to require that we continue to evaluate defendants' claims under the law as it stood at the time of trial." He reasoned that since, under *Teague*, a defendant may not take advantage of subsequent changes in the law when they are favorable to him, "there is no self-evident reason why a State should be able to take advantage of subsequent changes in the law when they are adverse to his interests." The dissenters concluded that a "rule that generally precludes defendants from taking advantage of post-conviction changes in the law, but allows the State to do so, cannot be reconciled with this Court's duty to administer justice impartially."

Chapter Two

SEARCHES AND SEIZURES OF PERSONS AND THINGS

I. AN INTRODUCTION TO THE FOURTH AMENDMENT

A. THE PROBLEM OF GATHERING EVIDENCE

When government focuses its attention on crime detection and crime prevention, frequently it encounters uncooperative individuals. But the police are not compelled to forego investigative and preventive measures for lack of voluntary cooperation. They can exert themselves in order to gather information, evidence and suspects. When they do, they must consider the limitations imposed by the Fourth Amendment, which reads as follows:

> The right of the people to be secure in their persons, houses, papers and effects, against unreasonable searches and seizures shall not be violated, and no Warrants shall issue, but upon probable cause, supported by Oath or affirmation, and particularly describing the place to be searched, and the persons or things to be seized.

B. THE BASICS OF THE FOURTH AMENDMENT

A number of points will seem obvious from a reading of the language of the Amendment, even without knowledge of its history and interpretation.

First, the language ascribes the right to the people, not to one person as under the Fifth Amendment, or to an accused as under the Sixth Amendment. Hence, the wording resembles that found in the Ninth and Tenth Amendments. Professor Amsterdam has suggested that the choice of language might well be important in properly interpreting the Amendment; in his view the courts might be well advised to focus on problems of how to regulate or control the conduct of the government so that Fourth Amendment violations do not occur, rather than on fashioning remedies for only those individuals who have suffered a personal Fourth Amendment wrong. See Perspectives on the Fourth Amendment, 58 Minn.L.Rev. 335, 367 (1974). But the Supreme Court has instead invoked the term "the people" to narrow the class of those protected by the Fourth Amendment.

"The People" as a Limiting Term: United
States v. Verdugo–Urquidez

In United States v. Verdugo—Urquidez, 494 U.S. 259 (1990), a Mexican citizen and resident was apprehended by Mexican police and transported to the United States for trial on drug charges. After his arrest, United States law enforcement officials, working with Mexican officials, conducted warrantless searches of the defendant's residences in Mexico. The lower courts held that the searches violated the Fourth Amendment.

The Supreme Court held that the Fourth Amendment does not apply to a search of property that is owned by a non-resident alien and located in a foreign country. Chief Justice Rehnquist for the Court reasoned that the Fourth Amendment's reference to "the people," as opposed to a particular person, was a "term of art." He asserted that the term was intended to refer only to a class of persons "who are part of a national community or who have otherwise developed sufficient connection with this country to be considered a part of that community."

The Court held that the defendant, who had been transported against his will to the United States three days before the foreign search was conducted, lacked sufficient connection with the United States to be one of "the people" protected by the Fourth Amendment. The Chief Justice looked to the history of the Amendment and concluded that its purpose was to protect the people of the United States from abuses by their own government; he contended that this history could not fairly be read to limit government action against aliens, outside the United States.

Justice Brennan, joined by Justice Marshall, dissented. Justice Brennan noted that the defendant was convicted for violating a Federal law, even though his conduct had been completely outside the United States. Thus, the defendant had been subject to an extraterritorial application of American criminal law. Justice Brennan argued that it was unfair for the Federal Government to require aliens outside the country to obey Federal laws, and yet refuse to obey its own laws in the course of investigating the very extraterritorial activity that the government has criminalized. According to Justice Brennan, the Fourth Amendment is an "unavoidable correlative" of the government's power to enforce the criminal law. Justice Blackmun wrote a separate dissenting opinion.

Searches Against Illegal Aliens in the United States?

In *Verdugo–Urquidez,* the Court specifically refused to decide whether an illegal alien who lived in the United States would be one of "the people" protected by the Fourth Amendment. Five Justices, however, (Stevens, Kennedy, Brennan, Marshall and Blackmun), in various opinions in *Verdugo–Urquidez,* indicated that they would hold the Fourth Amendment applicable to searches of illegal aliens conducted within the United States. The reasoning was that an illegal alien living in the United States would have the "connection" with this country required to be one of "the people" protected by the Fourth Amendment.

But *Verdugo-Urquidez* was decided before the terrorist attack of September 11, 2001. Since that time, various government officials have argued that illegal aliens living in the United States do not have the right to invoke Fourth

Amendment protections as they do not have a legitimate connection to the United States. Do you agree?

The Reasonableness Clause and the Warrant Clause

As a second introductory point, the Fourth Amendment is set forth in two parts, the first dealing with unreasonable searches and the second dealing with warrants. Because the term "unreasonable" is used first, it might be thought to predominate so that all searches and seizures must satisfy its command, whereas the warrant clause would come into play only when a warrant is sought to justify government action. But the Supreme Court has purported not to read the language in this way. One observer has suggested that the Court has "stood the amendment on its head" by reading the warrant clause as the controlling clause of the Amendment. T. Taylor, Two Studies in Constitutional Interpretation 23–24 (1969). The Court has stated that searches and seizures are *presumed* to be unreasonable unless carried out pursuant to a warrant. But important exceptions to the presumptive warrant requirement have been created. When an exception to the warrant requirement is applicable, only the reasonableness requirement must be satisfied. It must also be noted that in recent years, the Court has in some cases explicitly invoked the reasonableness clause as the predominant clause of the Fourth Amendment, most notably when the government's search or seizure serves "special needs" beyond criminal law enforcement.

"Probable Cause"

Third, the term "probable cause" is used to define the minimum showing necessary to support a warrant application; it is not used to demarcate reasonableness generally in search and seizure situations. Despite the placement of the words, the decisions make probable cause a limitation on many searches and seizures even though no warrant is deemed necessary under the circumstances. Also, note that the definition of probable cause is not altogether clear; the Amendment itself contains not a hint as to its meaning. The courts have been left to give meaning to the term, and their efforts will be analyzed later in this Chapter.

State Action Requirement

Fourth, the Amendment plainly recognizes a right, but does not indicate against whom it applies. Arguably, the people have a right to be free from all searches and seizures that are not reasonable, even if conducted by private persons. But, unlike the Thirteenth Amendment, the Fourth is interpreted as providing protection only against the government and those acting in conjunction with it. On the other hand, nothing in the language of the Amendment limits the applicability to criminal investigations or to the police. The protection is against all unreasonable searches and seizures conducted by government officials regardless of the purpose of the investigation or the identity of the investigator. Courts have accepted this reading, but do take the nature of the investigation into account in assessing the reasonableness of particular searches and in defining the requirements of a proper warrant.

The Question of Remedies

Fifth, the Amendment establishes a right, but does not mention the consequences of a violation of that right; as with other provisions of the Bill of Rights, remedies are not specified. Whether the Constitution mandates certain remedies for a violation of the Fourth Amendment is a question considered in connection with the exclusionary rule.

C. THE PURPOSE OF THE AMENDMENT

The Fourth Amendment, like most provisions of the Constitution, is hardly a black letter expression of an easily grasped rule of law. It is more an expression of a philosophy that grew out of offensive British procedures prior to the Revolution and was written into the fundamental law of the land by framers who hoped to assure that government must always respect the sanctity of the people and the effects they hold dear.

The cases, especially those decided after 1960, will suggest that the Amendment protects privacy. To some extent this must be true. Insofar as the Amendment restricts the availability of warrants and bars all unreasonable searches, the capacity of people to keep things secret (or private) from the government is enhanced. But on the face of the Amendment it is apparent that privacy is not absolutely protected. In fact, the Amendment implicitly recognizes the legitimacy of reasonable searches, the propriety of warrants directing the seizure of persons and things, and perhaps most importantly, that the probable cause standard for a warrant (and for warrantless searches and seizures) requires significantly less of the government than the proof beyond a reasonable doubt required in a criminal case, or even the preponderant proof necessary in a civil case. Privacy is thus protected by language implying the government's authority to search and seize. The tension between the protection afforded the people and the power of their government is what this Chapter is about.

D. THE AMENDMENT AND THE EXCLUSIONARY RULE

Before turning to specifics, one suggestion is in order: It is useful to distinguish two questions in thinking about Fourth Amendment problems. First, there is the question whether the Amendment prohibits the kind of conduct described in the cases. If so, the second question is whether evidence obtained by means of a Fourth Amendment violation should be available as proof in criminal trials and other proceedings. The debate over the wisdom of an exclusionary rule is a debate over the second question. Yet, too often analysis of the first question is confused in the process of debating the second. Consider, for example, the following personal editorial by Judge Wilkey of the United States Court of Appeals for the District of Columbia Circuit:

> Among nations of the civilized world we are unique in two respects: (1) We suffer the most extraordinary crime rate with firearms. (2) In criminal prosecutions, by a rule of evidence which exists in no other country, we exclude the most trustworthy and convincing evidence.

> These two aberrations are not unconnected. In fact, the "exclusionary rule" has made unenforceable the gun control laws we have and will make ineffective any stricter controls which may be devised. Its fetters particular-

ly paralyze police efforts to prevent, detect and punish street crimes involving not only weapons but narcotics.

* * *

The exclusionary rule has been devastating to gun control laws. Unless a police officer has "probable cause" to make a reasonable search, nothing found during the search—no sawed-off shotgun, automatic pistol or submachine gun—can be introduced as evidence. Therefore, since it is virtually impossible to be convicted in the U.S. of carrying a weapon illegally, American criminals do carry guns and use them. Since police know they carry and use them, they engage in far more searches and seizures than in the countries mentioned above, and some of those searches and seizures are blatantly illegal.

* * *

Why Suppress Valid Evidence, Wall Street Journal, Oct. 7, 1977, at 1, col. 1.

This is an argument by a distinguished jurist who pondered search and seizure problems for years. Yet, it is fundamentally flawed. Can you see the logical error on the basis of your brief exposure to the language of the Fourth Amendment? "Probable cause" is a term found in the language chosen by the framers. If the Court correctly interprets the Fourth Amendment as requiring probable cause for particular police action, then it is the Amendment itself, not the remedy for a violation, that truly concerns Judge Wilkey. Immediate abolition of the exclusionary rule does not signify that police officers may engage in searches and seizures without probable cause. They remain bound by the Constitution.[1] Hence, even with the demise of the exclusionary rule, gun control laws, as well as other criminal laws, still will be hard to enforce. If more vigorous enforcement is desired, the Constitution can be amended or the prevailing interpretation challenged. But changing the reach, as it is now understood, of the Amendment raises issues different from those raised by the exclusionary rule debate.

The cases that comprise the bulk of this Chapter assume that the remedy for an unconstitutional search and seizure is exclusion, though the resolution of the Fourth Amendment questions in these cases is not dependent on exclusion. The costs and benefits of the exclusionary rule are not discussed until late in the Chapter. Delay should provide an adequate opportunity for an understanding of the different circumstances in which a Fourth Amendment violation occurs. But delay in no way is intended to imply that the exclusionary rule is plainly desirable and that the debate over it is not important. The debate is important for practical and symbolic reasons, and delay in reaching it is tantamount to deference to its significance. But, it is true that even without the exclusionary rule, the basic problems of deciding what the Amendment means, which form the heart of most of the cases considered herein, would remain. As you read the cases, keep in mind that despite the fact that the issues usually are cast in terms of whether evidence should have been excluded at trial, the same issues could arise in some form or other—perhaps in civil suits rather than

---

1. This point is made by another experienced jurist, Justice Stewart, in The Road to *Mapp v. Ohio* and Beyond: The Origins, Development, and Future of the Exclusionary Rule in Search-and-Seizure Cases, 83 Colum.L.Rev. 1365 (1989).

criminal cases—even without an exclusionary rule. Hence, you cannot avoid grappling with the meaning and proper interpretation of the Fourth Amendment simply by doing away with the exclusionary rule.

II. THRESHOLD REQUIREMENTS FOR FOURTH AMENDMENT PROTECTIONS: WHAT IS A "SEARCH?" WHAT IS A "SEIZURE?"

The Fourth Amendment prohibits unreasonable searches and seizures. If the government activity is neither a "search" nor a "seizure" it is not regulated by the Fourth Amendment, and therefore it does not have to be reasonable.

It has been argued that in deciding the threshold question of whether a government intrusion is a search or seizure, one should err on the side of the citizen. The consequence of finding a search or seizure is merely that the government is required to act reasonably, whereas the consequence of not finding a search or seizure is that government officials can act unreasonably and arbitrarily. See Amsterdam, Perspectives on the Fourth Amendment, 58 Minn. L.Rev. 349 (1974). In fact, however, the Court in recent years has sometimes held that certain police investigative activity is neither a search nor a seizure, and is thus free from the strictures of the Fourth Amendment.

A. THE REASONABLE EXPECTATION TEST

In the following landmark case, the Court established a general test for determining whether government investigative activity rises to the level of a search.

KATZ v. UNITED STATES

Supreme Court of the United States, 1967.
389 U.S. 347.

MR. JUSTICE STEWART **delivered the opinion of the Court.**

The petitioner was convicted in the District Court for the Southern District of California under an eight-count indictment charging him with transmitting wagering information by telephone from Los Angeles to Miami and Boston, in violation of a Federal statute. At trial the Government was permitted, over the petitioner's objection, to introduce evidence of the petitioner's end of telephone conversations, overheard by FBI agents who had attached an electronic listening and recording device to the outside of the public telephone booth from which he had placed his calls. In affirming his conviction, the Court of Appeals rejected the contention that the recordings had been obtained in violation of the Fourth Amendment, because "[t]here was no physical entrance into the area occupied by [the petitioner]." We granted certiorari in order to consider the constitutional questions thus presented.

The petitioner has phrased those questions as follows:

"A. Whether a public telephone booth is a constitutionally protected area so that evidence obtained by attaching an electronic listening recording device to the top of such a booth is obtained in violation of the right to privacy of the user of the booth.

"B. Whether physical penetration of a constitutionally protected area is necessary before a search and seizure can be said to be violative of the Fourth Amendment to the United States Constitution."

We decline to adopt this formulation of the issues. In the first place, the correct solution of Fourth Amendment problems is not necessarily promoted by incantation of the phrase "constitutionally protected area." Secondly, the Fourth Amendment cannot be translated into a general constitutional "right to privacy." That Amendment protects individual privacy against certain kinds of governmental intrusion, but its protections go further, and often have nothing to do with privacy at all. Other provisions of the Constitution protect personal privacy from other forms of governmental invasion. But the protection of a person's *general* right to privacy—his right to be let alone by other people—is like the protection of his property and of his very life, left largely to the law of the individual States.

Because of the misleading way the issues have been formulated, the parties have attached great significance to the characterization of the telephone booth from which the petitioner placed his calls. The petitioner has strenuously argued that the booth was a "constitutionally protected area." The Government has maintained with equal vigor that it was not. But this effort to decide whether or not a given "area," viewed in the abstract, is "constitutionally protected" deflects attention from the problem presented by this case. For the Fourth Amendment protects people, not places. What a person knowingly exposes to the public, even in his own home or office, is not a subject of Fourth Amendment protection. But what he seeks to preserve as private, even in an area accessible to the public, may be constitutionally protected.

The Government stresses the fact that the telephone booth from which the petitioner made his calls was constructed partly of glass, so that he was as visible after he entered it as he would have been if he had remained outside. But what he sought to exclude when he entered the booth was not the intruding eye—it was the uninvited ear. He did not shed his right to do so simply because he made his calls from a place where he might be seen. No less than an individual in a business office, in a friend's apartment, or in a taxicab, a person in a telephone booth may rely upon the protection of the Fourth Amendment. One who occupies it, shuts the door behind him, and pays the toll that permits him to place a call is surely entitled to assume that the words he utters into the mouthpiece will not be broadcast to the world. To read the Constitution more narrowly is to ignore the vital role that the public telephone has come to play in private communication.

The Government contends, however, that the activities of its agents in this case should not be tested by Fourth Amendment requirements, for the surveillance technique they employed involved no physical penetration of the telephone booth from which the petitioner placed his calls. It is true that the absence of such penetration was at one time thought to foreclose further Fourth Amendment inquiry, Olmstead v. United States, 277 U.S. 438, 457, 464, 466; Goldman v. United States, 316 U.S. 129, 134–136, for that Amendment was thought to limit only searches and seizures of tangible property. But "[t]he premise that property interests control the right of the Government to search and seize has been discredited." Warden v. Hayden, 387 U.S. 294, 304. Thus, although a closely divided Court supposed in *Olmstead* that surveillance without any trespass and without the seizure of any material object fell outside the ambit of the Constitution, we have since departed from the narrow view on which that decision rested. Indeed, we have expressly held that the Fourth Amendment governs not only the seizure of tangible items, but extends as well to the recording of oral statements, overheard without any "technical trespass under * * * local property law." Silverman v. United States, 365 U.S. 505, 511. Once this much is acknowledged, and once it is recognized that the Fourth Amendment protects people—and not simply "areas"—against unreasonable searches and seizures, it becomes clear that the reach of that Amendment cannot turn upon the presence or absence of a physical intrusion into any given enclosure.

We conclude that the underpinnings of *Olmstead* and *Goldman* have been so eroded by our subsequent decisions that the "trespass" doctrine there enunciated can no longer be regarded as controlling. The Government's activities in electronically listening to and recording the petitioner's words violated the privacy upon which he justifiably relied while using the telephone booth and thus constituted a "search and seizure" within the meaning of the Fourth Amendment. The fact that the electronic device employed to achieve that end did not happen to penetrate the wall of the booth can have no constitutional significance.

The question remaining for decision, then, is whether the search and seizure conducted in this case complied with constitutional standards. In that regard, the Government's position is that its agents acted in an entirely defensible manner: They did not begin their electronic surveillance until investigation of the petitioner's activities had established a strong probability that he was using the telephone in question to transmit gambling information to persons in other States, in violation of Federal law. Moreover, the surveillance was limited, both in scope and in duration, to the specific purpose of establishing the contents of the petitioner's unlawful telephonic communications. The agents confined their surveillance to the brief periods during which he used the telephone booth, and they took great care to overhear only the conversations of the petitioner himself.

Accepting this account of the Government's actions as accurate, it is clear that this surveillance was so narrowly circumscribed that a duly authorized magistrate, properly notified of the need for such investigation, specifically informed of the basis on which it was to proceed, and clearly apprised of the precise intrusion it would entail, could constitutionally have authorized, with appropriate safeguards, the very limited search and seizure that the Government asserts in fact took place. * * *

* * * Yet the inescapable fact is that this restraint was imposed by the agents themselves, not by a judicial officer. They were not required, before commencing the search, to present their estimate of probable cause for detached scrutiny by a neutral magistrate. They were not compelled, during the conduct of the search itself, to observe precise limits established in advance by a specific court order. Nor were they directed, after the search had been completed, to notify the authorizing magistrate in detail of all that had been seized. In the absence of such safeguards, this Court has never sustained a search upon the sole ground that officers reasonably expected to find evidence of a particular

crime and voluntarily confined their activities to the least intrusive means to that end * * *.

* * *

The Government does not question these basic principles. Rather, it urges the creation of a new exception to cover this case. It argues that surveillance of a telephone booth should be exempted from the usual requirement of advance authorization by a magistrate upon a showing of probable cause. We cannot agree. Omission of such authorization

"bypasses the safeguards provided by an objective predetermination of probable cause, and substitutes instead the far less reliable procedure of an after-the-event justification for the * * * search, too likely to be subtly influenced by the familiar shortcomings of hindsight judgment." Beck v. Ohio, 379 U.S. 89, 96.

And bypassing a neutral predetermination of the *scope* of a search leaves individuals secure from Fourth Amendment violations "only in the discretion of the police."

These considerations do not vanish when the search in question is transferred from the setting of a home, an office, or a hotel room to that of a telephone booth. Wherever a man may be, he is entitled to know that he will remain free from unreasonable searches and seizures. The government agents here ignored "the procedure of antecedent justification * * * that is central to the Fourth Amendment," a procedure that we hold to be a constitutional precondition of the kind of electronic surveillance involved in this case. Because the surveillance here failed to meet that condition, and because it led to

the petitioner's conviction, the judgment must be reversed.

* * *

MR. JUSTICE HARLAN, concurring.

I join the opinion of the Court, which I read to hold only (a) that an enclosed telephone booth is an area where, like a home, and unlike a field, a person has a constitutionally protected reasonable expectation of privacy; (b) that electronic as well as physical intrusion into a place that is in this sense private may constitute a violation of the Fourth Amendment; and (c) that the invasion of a constitutionally protected area by Federal authorities is, as the Court has long held, presumptively unreasonable in the absence of a search warrant.

As the Court's opinion states, "the Fourth Amendment protects people, not places." The question, however, is what protection it affords to those people. Generally, as here, the answer to that question requires reference to a "place." My understanding of the rule that has emerged from prior decisions is that there is a twofold requirement, first that a person have exhibited an actual (subjective) expectation of privacy and, second, that the expectation be one that society is prepared to recognize as "reasonable." Thus a man's home is, for most purposes, a place where he expects privacy, but objects, activities, or statements that he exposes to the "plain view" of outsiders are not "protected" because no intention to keep them to himself has been exhibited. On the other hand, conversations in the open would not be protected against being overheard, for the expectation of privacy under the circumstances would be unreasonable.

The critical fact in this case is that "[o]ne who occupies it, [a telephone booth] shuts the door behind him, and pays the toll that permits him to place a call is surely entitled to assume" that his conversation is not being intercepted. The point is not that the booth is "accessible to the public" at other times, but that it is a temporarily private place whose momentary occupants' expectations of freedom from intrusion are recognized as reasonable.

* * *

MR. JUSTICE BLACK, **dissenting.**

* * *

My basic objection is twofold: (1) I do not believe that the words of the Amendment will bear the meaning given them by today's decision, and (2) I do not believe that it is the proper role of this Court to rewrite the Amendment in order "to bring it into harmony with the times" and thus reach a result that many people believe to be desirable.

While I realize that an argument based on the meaning of words lacks the scope, and no doubt the appeal, of broad policy discussions and philosophical discourses on such nebulous subjects as privacy, for me the language of the Amendment is the crucial place to look in construing a written document such as our Constitution. * * *

The first clause protects "persons, houses, papers, and effects, against unreasonable searches and seizures

* * *." These words connote the idea of tangible things with size, form, and weight, things capable of being searched, seized, or both. The second clause of the Amendment still further establishes its Framers' purpose to limit its protection to tangible things by providing that no warrants shall issue but those "particularly describing the place to be searched, and the persons or things to be seized." A conversation overheard by eavesdropping, whether by plain snooping or wiretapping, is not tangible and, under the normally accepted meanings of the words, can neither be searched nor seized. * * *

Tapping telephone wires, of course, was an unknown possibility at the time the Fourth Amendment was adopted. But eavesdropping (and wiretapping is nothing more than eavesdropping by telephone) was * * * an ancient practice which at common law was condemned as a nuisance. * * * There can be no doubt that the Framers were aware of this practice, and if they had desired to outlaw or restrict the use of evidence obtained by eavesdropping, I believe that they would have used the appropriate language to do so in the Fourth Amendment. They certainly would not have left such a task to the ingenuity of language-stretching judges.

* * *

[Justice Marshall took no part in the consideration or decision of this case. Concurring opinions by Douglas, J., joined by Brennan, J., and by White, J. are omitted.]

Katz as a Two–Pronged Test

Katz has been read to set forth a two-pronged test for determining whether government conduct constitutes a search. First, the government conduct must offend the citizen's subjective manifestation of a privacy interest. Second, the privacy interest invaded must be one that society is prepared to accept as legitimate. This two-pronged test comes not from Justice Stewart's majority opinion but rather from Justice Harlan's concurring opinion. It is notable that in the later case of United States v. White, 401 U.S. 745 (1971) (holding that no search occurred where police electronically eavesdropped on a two-party conversation with the consent of one of the parties), Justice Harlan dissented and expressed misgivings about the test that he had promulgated in *Katz:*

> While these formulations represent an advance over the unsophisticated trespass analysis of the common law, they too have their limitations and can, ultimately, lead to the substitution of words for analysis. The analysis must, in my view, transcend the search for subjective expectations or legal attribution of assumptions of risk. Our expectations, and the risks we assume, are in large part reflections of laws that translate into rules the customs and values of the past and present.

Thus, Justice Harlan's concern was that the reasonableness of an expectation of privacy would be determined by existing laws and practices, and that this could result in the diminution of protected privacy interests. As Professor Amsterdam has put it, under the *Katz* expectation test, the government could control the extent of privacy interests by simply announcing "that we were all forthwith being placed under comprehensive electronic surveillance." Amsterdam, Perspectives on the Fourth Amendment, 58 Minn.L.Rev. 349, 384 (1974).

Should the Fourth Amendment threshold be dependent on what we should *expect* from government, or rather on what we can *demand* from government? Consider Professor Clancy's critique of *Katz:*

> The ability to exclude must extend to all invasions, tangible and intangible, and must protect both tangible and intangible aspects of the amendment's protected objects. That was the essential lesson of *Katz. Katz* and the privacy theory, however, failed to grasp the essence of the interest protected. Although it may have been Katz's *expectation* that his conversation was not being heard, it was his *right* to exclude others from hearing. It is not privacy which may motivate a person to assert his or her right. It is the right to prevent intrusions—to exclude—which affords personal security.

Clancy, What Does the Fourth Amendment Protect: Property, Privacy, or Security?, 33 Wake Forest L. Rev. 307, 367–8 (1998).

B. INTERESTS PROTECTED BY THE FOURTH AMENDMENT AFTER KATZ

The Court has held on several occasions after *Katz* that there is no legitimate privacy interest in illegal activity. See United States v. Place, infra (no privacy interest in possession of contraband). If that is the case, it may be wondered why Katz was entitled to protection in the phone booth. Katz was not expressing private, personal thoughts; he was engaging in illegal betting transactions.

One possible answer is that Katz received the protection of the Fourth Amendment because the government was not certain that his activity was illegal until officials listened to the conversations. Where guilt is not certain before the intrusion, the police may be invading the legitimate privacy and possessory interests of those who are actually innocent. See Loewy, The Fourth Amendment as a Device for Protecting the Innocent, 81 Mich.L.Rev. 907 (1983) (Fourth Amendment can be invoked by the guilty "when necessary to protect the innocent"); Colb, Innocence, Privacy, and Targeting in Fourth Amendment

Jurisprudence, 96 Colum.L.Rev. 1456 (1996) (discussing the "Innocence Model" of the Fourth Amendment).

But even if Katz is "presumed innocent" before the phone is tapped, couldn't the government in *Katz* have argued that if Katz were placing an innocent call, he should have no complaint about government surveillance? If the private activity is not criminal, what does the citizen have to hide?

Courts after *Katz* have found three legitimate interests, held by all citizens, that can be impaired by a government intrusion. First, there is an interest in being free from physical disruption and inconvenience. Thus, an innocent person who is subject to a bodily seizure suffers a Fourth Amendment intrusion; the fact that he or she had nothing to hide is irrelevant. Second, certain information, even though not indicative of criminal activity, may be personal or embarrassing; innocent citizens have a legitimate interest in keeping such information private. Third, the Fourth Amendment prohibits unreasonable seizures of property as well as searches. The citizen has a legitimate interest in control over and use of his or her property, and that interest is obviously implicated when the government exercises dominion and control over such property.

Seizures and Searches Implicate Different Interests

Note that a seizure may occur without a search, and a search may occur without a seizure. As Justice Stevens explained in his concurring opinion in Texas v. Brown, 460 U.S. 730, 747–48 (1983):

> Although our Fourth Amendment cases sometimes refer indiscriminately to searches and seizures, there are important differences between the two * * *. The Amendment protects two different interests of the citizen—the interest in retaining possession of property and the interest in maintaining personal privacy. A seizure threatens the former, a search the latter. As a matter of timing, a seizure is usually preceded by a search, but when a container is involved the converse is often true. Significantly, the two protected interests are not always present to the same extent; for example, the seizure of a locked suitcase does not necessarily compromise the secrecy of its contents, and the search of a stopped vehicle does not necessarily deprive its owner of possession.

Justice Stevens' point is that searches and seizures are different, and that the Fourth Amendment regulates searches and seizures independently. This point was made again by the Court in Soldal v. Cook County, 506 U.S. 56 (1992). The Soldal family resided in a trailer on a rented lot. The owner of the lot removed and towed the trailer prior to an eviction hearing while deputy sheriffs at the scene declined to intervene. The Soldals brought an action under 42 U.S.C. § 1983, claiming that their Fourth Amendment rights had been violated when their trailer was taken away.

The lower court had dismissed the action, reasoning that the Fourth Amendment was not implicated because the removal and towing did not occur in the course of an investigation for evidence, and did not involve invasion of the privacy interests of those living in the trailer. Justice White, writing for the Court, rejected this position and stated that for Fourth Amendment purposes a "seizure" of property occurs whenever "there is some meaningful interference with an individual's possessory interests in that property." He concluded: "[w]e fail to see how being unceremoniously dispossessed of one's home in the manner alleged to have occurred here can be viewed as anything but a seizure invoking the protection of the Fourth Amendment."

Justice White cited *Katz* for the proposition that privacy rights are not the sole measure of Fourth Amendment violations, and noted that "seizures of property are subject to Fourth Amendment scrutiny even though no search within the meaning of the Amendment has taken place." He rejected the lower court's notion that the Fourth Amendment only applies to efforts to collect evidence:

> In our view, the reason why an officer might enter a house or effectuate a seizure is wholly irrelevant to the threshold question of whether the Amendment applies. What matters is the intrusion on the people's security from governmental interference. Therefore, the right against unreasonable seizures would be no less transgressed if the seizure of the house was undertaken to collect evidence, verify compliance with a housing regulation, effect an eviction by the police, or on a whim, for no reason at all.

After *Soldal*, the question of whether a seizure of property has or has not occurred is usually obvious and is rarely contested. More difficult questions have arisen concerning whether police efforts to detain an individual constitute a seizure of the *person* triggering Fourth Amendment protection. These questions are considered in the discussion of stop and frisk, later in this Chapter.

C. APPLICATIONS OF THE KATZ PRINCIPLE:

The Court has on many occasions applied the *Katz* principle, usually by referring to the concurring opinion of Justice Harlan, which set forth a two-pronged test for whether a government intrusion triggers the Fourth Amendment. First, has the individual manifested a subjective expectation of privacy? Second, is the expectation one that society is prepared to accept as legitimate?

The cases discussed below illustrate the difficulty that courts have had in applying the Fourth Amendment and the *Katz* test to modern investigative techniques. As you go through this material, keep in mind that if the court finds that the police conduct is a search or seizure, it means only that the Fourth Amendment is applicable—the police activity will still be permissible if it satisfies the requirements of the Fourth Amendment. On the other hand, if the court finds that the police conduct is not a search or seizure, it means that the Fourth Amendment is completely inapplicable; consequently, as far as that Amendment is concerned, the police do not have to have a reason for doing what they are doing.

The cases discussed below address a number of now-common investigative techniques, and provide an opportunity for you to assess how well the *Katz* test has worked in practice.

1. *Subjective Manifestation*

Individuals must take affirmative steps to protect their privacy interests; otherwise, a police inspection will not constitute a search, due to failure to satisfy the "subjective manifestation" prong of *Katz*. See, e.g., United States v. Bellina, 665 F.2d 1335 (4th Cir.1981) (no search where officer used a step ladder to peer into the interior of a plane; the defendant made no attempt to cover the windows, and therefore did not sufficiently manifest a subjective interest in privacy).

Many cases hold, for example, that abandonment of property is inconsistent with the retention of any subjective privacy or possessory interests, so police detention and investigation of abandoned property does not trigger Fourth Amendment protection. Moreover, abandonment need not be explicit. "Whether abandonment has occurred is a question of intent that may be inferred from acts, words, and other objective facts." United States v. Cofield, 272 F.3d 1303 (11th Cir. 2001). Thus, in United States v. Hoey, 983 F.2d 890 (8th Cir.1993), police entered into an apartment where Hoey had lived, and discovered evidence that was used against her at trial. The Court held that the government activity did not constitute a search because the defendant had abandoned the apartment. At the time of the police entry, the defendant was six weeks behind on her rent; she had held a moving sale; and she was seen leaving the apartment two days before the police entry and had not returned. In contrast, in Smith v. Ohio, 494 U.S. 541 (1990), a defendant carrying a brown paper bag was approached by two plainclothes officers. When the officers identified themselves, the defendant threw the bag on the hood of his car. The officers asked what was in the bag and the defendant tried to grab it. One officer pushed the defendant's hand away and opened the bag. The Court declared that "a citizen who attempts to protect his private property from inspection after throwing it on a car to respond to a police officer's inquiry clearly has not abandoned that property."

Abandonment is often found when a person denies ownership of a container in the face of police inquiries. See, e.g., United States v. McDonald, 100 F.3d 1320 (7th Cir.1996) (police officers discovered contraband in a bag placed in the overhead bin of the passenger compartment of a bus; when the police asked the owner of the bag to claim it, McDonald did not come forward; this constituted an abandonment of McDonald's privacy interest in the bag); United States v. Sanders, 196 F.3d 910 (8th Cir. 1999) ("statements to the officers that he did not own the bag were sufficient to constitute abandonment").

Often the issue of abandonment is considered as a question of whether the defendant has "standing" to assert a Fourth Amendment issue. See, e.g., United States v. Garzon, 119 F.3d 1446 (10th Cir.1997) ("Abandonment is akin to the issue of standing because a defendant lacks standing to complain of an illegal search or seizure of property which has been abandoned.") The concept of "standing" is discussed in the materials on the exclusionary rule, *infra*.

2. *Open Fields*

Prior to *Katz*, the Court had established an "open fields" rule. In Hester v. United States, 265 U.S. 57 (1924), the Court distinguished open fields from constitutionally protected areas like houses, and held that a police entry into open fields was not regulated by the Fourth Amendment. The Court in Oliver v. United States, 466 U.S. 170 (1984) held that the "open fields" doctrine was consistent with *Katz*, because a person does not have a legitimate expectation of privacy in an open field. An important thing to note about *Oliver* is that the term "open fields" was a misnomer as applied to the area searched in that case.[2]

---

2. See United States v. Van Damme, 48 F.3d 461 (9th Cir.1995) ("The unfortunate use of the term 'open fields' in this body of law causes misunderstanding and confusion, and should be replaced by a term which means what it says, such as 'unprotected area.' ").

Oliver complained that two state police officers trespassed on his farm to investigate reports that he was growing marijuana. They drove past his house to a locked gate with a "No Trespassing" sign on it. A footpath led around one side of the gate. The officers took it, walked around the gate and along the road for several hundred yards. They found a field of marijuana on the property, about a mile from Oliver's house. The question for the Court was whether this police investigation amounted to a search.

Justice Powell wrote the Court's opinion and was fully supported by four other Justices. Justice White joined the majority on the proposition that the Fourth Amendment "indicates with some precision the places and things encompassed by its protections" and that open fields are not "effects" within the coverage of the Amendment. Justice White did not join the longer parts of the majority opinion concluding that a citizen has no legitimate expectation of privacy in an open field. The lengthy opinion contained the following statements:

1. "An individual may not legitimately demand privacy for activities conducted out of doors in fields, except in the area immediately surrounding the home."

2. "Open fields do not provide the setting for those intimate activities that the Amendment is intended to shelter from government interference or surveillance. There is no societal interest in protecting the privacy of those activities, such as the cultivation of crops, that occur in open fields."

3. "It is not generally true that fences or no trespassing signs effectively bar the public from viewing open fields in rural areas."

4. "[O]nly the curtilage, not the neighboring open fields, warrants the Fourth Amendment protections that attach to the home."

5. "[C]ourts * * * have extended Fourth Amendment protection to the curtilage; and they have defined the curtilage, as did the common law, by reference to the factors that determine whether an individual may expect that an area immediately adjacent to the home will remain private."

6. "An open field need be neither 'open' nor a 'field.'"

The majority in *Oliver* rejected "the suggestion that steps taken to protect privacy establish that expectations of privacy in an open field are legitimate." Although it recognized that Oliver "planted the marijuana upon secluded land and erected fences and no trespassing signs around the property," the Court found that these efforts did not establish that any expectation of privacy was legitimate. In other words, Oliver might have had a *subjective* expectation of privacy in light of his efforts to cordon off his property; but it was not an expectation that society was prepared to accept as legitimate, because there is no legitimate expectation of privacy in an open field.

The *Oliver* majority concluded that even if the officers committed a trespass under state law, the Fourth Amendment was not violated: "in the case of open fields, the general rights of property protected by the common law of trespass have little or no relevancy to the applicability of the Fourth Amendment."

Finally, the Court rejected the suggestion that a case-by-case approach should be used to determine whether a person had sufficiently closed off the property beyond the curtilage to public access, so as to justify Fourth Amendment protection. Justice Powell stated that such an approach would not provide "a workable accommodation between the needs of law enforcement and the interests protected by the Fourth Amendment." Apparently, the best "accommodation" between the needs of law enforcement and Fourth Amendment interests was to provide no protection at all for open fields.

Justice Marshall, joined by Justices Brennan and Stevens, dissented. He challenged the majority's reasoning that open fields are not protected by the language of the Fourth Amendment, observing that telephone booths and commercial establishments do not fit the language of the Amendment any more than open fields do, yet Supreme Court decisions have found them to be protected by the Fourth Amendment. He also noted that many private activities occur on property outside the curtilage of a home—including romantic activities, nature walks, and secret meetings.

Questions About Oliver and the Open Fields Doctrine

Is it now the case that no one—scientist, naturalist, lover, or simply a private person who prefers outdoors to indoors—can rely on the Fourth Amendment to protect against police surveillance of land areas not immediately adjacent to a house? May the police engage in as much surveillance as they care to as often as they want on the theory that there is no violation of any reasonable expectation of privacy? See United States v. Van Damme, 48 F.3d 461 (9th Cir.1995) (no search where police officer trespassed on the defendant's land in the middle of the night, walked through the defendant's forest, and climbed over his wire fence to conduct surveillance).

The Court in *Oliver* takes a literal approach to the words of the Fourth Amendment, and finds that a field is neither a person, house, paper, nor effect. Recall Justice Black's dissent in *Katz*. Does Katz's telephone conversation fit within the literal terms of the Fourth Amendment? If not, why is it protected?

Suppose police officers jump over a property owner's fence and are traipsing through the owner's field when they come upon a barrel with a lid. If they pry open the lid and look into the barrel, is that a search? May officers in an "open field" lift up a tarpaulin to see what is beneath it? Does it make a difference if the tarpaulin is tied to the ground with stakes? If you would not be willing to let officers open barrels or lift up covers on objects, are you more willing to permit them to roam about and look at uncovered objects? Might the reason that objects are uncovered be that landowners rely on their fence to keep out intruders?

In Husband v. Bryan, 946 F.2d 27 (5th Cir.1991), officers looking for a body used bulldozers to dig up three acres of a pasture owned by Husband. They had no warrant or probable cause, and a body was never found. Husband sued the officers, alleging a violation of her Fourth Amendment rights. The officers contended that under the open fields doctrine, Husband had no right to be free from unreasonable searches of her pasture. The court held that the open fields doctrine could not be extended to anything beyond "observation searches" and accordingly that Husband's Fourth Amendment rights had been violated. Do you agree? Would the Supreme Court agree?[3]

Note on Curtilage

The Fourth Amendment does not protect open fields, but, as *Oliver* notes, the Amendment does protect "curtilage." How far the curtilage extends is now an issue

3. The Supreme Court's open field cases are criticized in Saltzburg, Another Victim of Illegal Narcotics: The Fourth Amendment (As Illustrated By the Open Fields Doctrine) 48 U.Pitt.L.Rev. 1 (1986). See also Wilkins, Defining the "Reasonable Expectation of Privacy": An Emerging Tripartite Analysis, 40 Vand. L.Rev. 1077 (1987).

that every police officer must confront. In United States v. Dunn, 480 U.S. 294 (1987), the Supreme Court held that a barn located approximately fifty yards from the fence surrounding a residence on almost two hundred acres of property was outside the curtilage—therefore police intrusion into that area did not constitute a search. Although Dunn's entire ranch was encircled by a fence and interior fences constructed of posts and barbed wires also were present, Federal and state officers ignored the fences and trespassed without a warrant upon Dunn's land. They crossed over the outer fence and one interior fence before smelling the odor of an acid used in the manufacture of certain drugs. The officers then crossed an interior barbed wire fence surrounding one smaller barn, and another barbed wire interior fence surrounding a larger barn. The larger barn had an open overhang, a wooden fence around it, locked, waist-high gates barring entry into the barn, and netting above the gates. From a distance the officers could not see through the netting. They approached the gates, shined a light through the netting and saw what appeared to a drug laboratory. They left the property without entering the barn, but twice reentered the property without a warrant before obtaining a warrant to search the barn from a Federal magistrate.

Justice White's opinion for the Court reasoned "that curtilage questions should be resolved with particular reference to four factors: the proximity of the area claimed to be curtilage to the home; whether the area is included within an enclosure surrounding the home; the nature of the uses to which the area is put; and the steps taken by the resident to protect the area from observation by people passing by." He rejected the government's "invitation to adopt a 'bright-line' rule that 'the curtilage should extend no farther than the nearest fence surrounding a fenced house.' " Justice White applied the factors and found that the barn was 60 yards from the house itself, not within the area enclosed by the house fence, there was no objective indication that the barn was used for intimate activities associated with the home, and there was no protection from observation by those standing in open fields. The Court accepted arguendo, but did not decide, Dunn's contention that an entry into the barn would have been impermissible even though the barn itself was in an open field.

Justice Scalia concurred in the opinion, except for the portion that focused on whether law enforcement officials possessed objective data indicating that the barn was not being used for intimate activities of the home. He indicated that the significant point was that the barn was not being so used, not whether the law enforcement officers knew that. Justice Brennan, joined by Justice Marshall, dissented.[4]

Even if property is within the curtilage, a visual inspection of that property from *outside* the curtilage does not constitute a search. See United States v. Hatfield, 333 F.3d 1189 (10th Cir. 2003) ("[W]e hold that police observation of a defendant's curtilage from a vantage point in the defendant's open field is not a search under the Fourth Amendment. Even though we can conclude that Hatfield had a subjective expectation of privacy in the space immediately behind

4. For lower court cases applying the *Dunn* factors, see Daughenbaugh v. City of Tiffin, 150 F.3d 594 (6th Cir.1998) (unattached garage was within curtilage of the house, where it was 50 yards away from the house, within natural boundaries of a river and trees that circled the property, set far back from the road, and the officers had no indication that the defendant was using the garage for any illegal activity); United States v. Traynor, 990 F.2d 1153 (9th Cir.1993) (workshop not within curtilage, where it was 70 feet from the house, and shop and house were not enclosed within a single fenced-in area); United States v. McKeever, 5 F.3d 863 (5th Cir.1993) (area not curtilage where it was 50 feet from home and not within an immediate fenced-in area); United States v. Swepston, 987 F.2d 1510 (10th Cir.1993) (chicken shed within the curtilage but barn was not).

his house, this is not an expectation of privacy that society regards as reasonable, at least with respect to visual observations made from an adjoining open field.").

3. Access by Members of the Public

Even if a citizen tries to keep information private, it is sometimes the case in society that the citizen will not get his or her wish. One cannot walk along a public street and have a reasonable expectation that one's movement will be free from public viewing. A homeowner cannot demand that planes not fly overhead. Society is not prepared to accept such demands as legitimate. After *Katz,* the Supreme Court has held in a series of cases that if an aspect of a person's life is subject to scrutiny by society, then that person has no legitimate expectation in denying equivalent access to police. There is thus no search if the police obtain information that members of the public could obtain.

a. Consensual Electronic Surveillance

In United States v. White, 401 U.S. 745 (1971), a government informer carrying a radio transmitter engaged the defendant in conversations that were overheard by an agent using a radio receiver. Justice White's opinion for himself, Chief Justice Burger, Justice Stewart and Justice Blackmun concluded that the defendant had no reasonable expectation of privacy in the conversations. The plurality stated that "the law permits the frustration of actual expectations of privacy by permitting authorities to use the testimony of those associates who for one reason or another have determined to turn to the police" and that "one contemplating illegal activities must realize and risk that his companions may be reporting to the police." Justice Black concurred in the judgment for the reasons he stated in *Katz.* Justice Douglas dissented, questioning whether a citizen must "live in fear that every word he speaks may be transmitted or recorded and later repeated to the entire world." Justice Harlan in dissent argued that the assumption of risk approach was not an adequate guide to controlling new threats to privacy. As he put the question, it was not whether the defendant knew there was a risk of third party bugging but whether "we should impose on our citizens the risks of the electronic listener or observer without at least the protection of a warrant requirement." He concluded that "[t]he impact of third-party bugging must * * * be considered to undermine that confidence and sense of security in dealing with another that is characteristic of individual relationships between citizens in a free society." Justice Marshall also dissented.[5] Justice Brennan concurred in the result on a different ground. Where do you come out on the question?[6]

---

5. Some state courts have sided with the dissenters. See, e.g., People v. Beavers, 393 Mich. 554, 227 N.W.2d 511 (1975); State v. Glass, 583 P.2d 872 (Alaska 1978).

The "assumption of risk" analysis applied in *White* is assailed by Professor Maclin in Informants and the Fourth Amendment: a Reconsideration, 74 Wash.Univ.L.Q. 573 (1996) ("A home or private conversation should not lose its constitutional protection against promiscuous police intrusion merely because an individual has allowed a third party's presence. When it comes to Fourth Amendment rights, the

difference between the police and everyone else matters.").

6. Justice O'Connor wrote for seven Justices in Maryland v. Macon, 472 U.S. 463 (1985), as the Court held that undercover officers did not engage in a "search" or "seizure" within the ambit of the Fourth Amendment when they purchased magazines from a bookstore salesclerk with a marked bill prior to making a warrantless arrest of the clerk for distributing obscene materials. The Court reasoned that "[a]n undercover officer does not violate the Fourth Amendment by accepting an

Courts have applied the *White* analysis to video surveillance as well. In United States v. Gonzalez, 328 F.3d 543 (9th Cir. 2003), Gonzalez and an associate arranged to receive a shipment of drugs in a package addressed to a hospital, where one of them worked in the mailroom. Officers were tipped off to the shipment, and obtained the consent of the hospital to install a hidden video camera in the mailroom. The video showed that when the package arrived, Gonzalez clapped his hands and acted "in a manner usually reserved for post-touchdown endzone celebrations." Gonzalez argued that the suspicious conduct on the video could not be used at trial because the video surveillance was an illegal search. But the court noted that the mailroom was a large, "quasi-public" space at a public hospital, with large windows through which the room was visible, and that it was accessed frequently by hospital employees. The Court concluded as follows:

> Gonzalez would have us adopt a theory of the Fourth Amendment akin to J.K. Rowling's Invisibility Cloak, to create at will a shield impenetrable to law enforcement view even in the most public places. However, the fabric of the Fourth Amendment does not stretch that far. He did not have an expectation of privacy in the public mailroom that society would accept as reasonable.

If Gonzalez did not have a legitimate expectation to be free from video surveillance, why did Katz have a legitimate expectation of privacy in the public telephone booth?

b. *Financial Records*

California Bankers Ass'n v. Shultz, 416 U.S. 21 (1974), analyzed whether the recordkeeping and reporting requirements imposed upon banks and individuals by the Bank Secrecy Act of 1970 violated the Fourth Amendment. Banks were required by Title I of the Act to maintain records of their client's identities and to microfilm certain checks and to keep records of other items. Part of Title II authorized the Secretary of the Treasury to require financial institutions to file reports of certain payments, receipts, or transfers of currency or other monetary instruments. Implementing regulations required banks to report each deposit, withdrawal, exchange of currency, or other payment or transfer involving more than $10,000. The information could be made available to other agencies of the government. The ACLU and others challenging the recordkeeping provisions argued that the Act made banks agents of the government and, thus, the recordkeeping provisions amounted to a search and seizure of customers' records. The Court rejected the argument on the ground that banks were parties to any transactions of the depositors. The depositors of necessity granted access to the banks, so this precluded any legitimate expectation that the government would not have the same access. A similar analysis was used to uphold the currency reporting requirement. Justice Douglas dissented, arguing that "[o]ne's bank accounts are within the 'expectations of privacy' category. For they mirror not only one's finances but his interests, his debts, his way of life, his family, and his civil commitments." Justice Marshall agreed in his

offer to do business that is freely made to the public." Justice Brennan, joined by Justice Marshall, dissented and argued that seizure of a person for distributing obscene materials should be preceded by a prior judicial determi-

nation of probable obscenity. While *Macon* did not involve electronic surveillance, the case is really the same as *White* from a Fourth Amendment standpoint.

dissent, as he relied heavily on *Katz*. He stated that "[t]he fact that one has disclosed private papers to the bank, for a limited purpose, within the context of a confidential customer-bank relationship, does not mean that one has waived all right to the privacy of the papers."

In United States v. Miller, 425 U.S. 435 (1976), Justice Powell's opinion for the Court held that the Fourth Amendment was not implicated by a subpoena issued to a bank to obtain a depositor's records compiled by the bank. Over dissents by Justices Brennan and Marshall, the Court found that because the depositor made the records accessible to the bank, there was no reasonable expectation that they would be free from government surveillance.

Under Section 215 of the "Uniting And Strengthening America By Providing Appropriate Tools Required To Intercept And Obstruct Terrorism (USA Patriot Act) Act of 2001," the FBI's authority under the Foreign Intelligence Surveillance Act (FISA) is expanded. The FBI may apply for a court order requesting the production of "any tangible thing (including books, records, papers, documents and other items)." The statute covers, but is not limited to, financial records. The judge is required to enter the order so long as the FBI officer provides a written statement declaring that the items are being sought for an ongoing investigation related to international terrorism or clandestine intelligence activities. Before the Patriot Act, FISA orders could only be used to obtain records relating to foreign powers or their agents. The Patriot Act expands the authority to reach records of "United States persons," a category which includes both U.S. citizens and lawful U.S. residents. Section 215 bars investigations of U.S. persons based solely on the exercise of First Amendment rights, but it permits other investigations even though there is only a weak connection to a terrorism or clandestine intelligence activities.

c. Pen Registers

In Smith v. Maryland, 442 U.S. 735 (1979), police installed a pen register device in the phone company offices. This device recorded the numbers called by the defendant from his home telephone. Justice Blackmun, writing for six members of the Court, found that the use of the pen register did not constitute a search, and hence no warrant or probable cause was required. The majority stated that "a person has no legitimate expectation of privacy in information he voluntarily turns over to third parties" and that "when he used his phone, petitioner voluntarily conveyed numerical information to the telephone company." The Court held that Smith "assumed the risk that the company would reveal to the police the numbers he dialed." Justice Stewart, joined by Justice Brennan, dissented, arguing that since private telephone conversations were protected by *Katz,* the numbers dialed from a private telephone were equally protected. Justice Marshall's dissent asserted that "privacy is not a discrete commodity, possessed absolutely or not at all" and that those who disclose information for "a limited business purpose need not assume that this information will be released to other persons for other purposes." Is the majority correct in its assessment of societal expectations? Is the dissent?

Despite the fact that the use of a pen register is not a search under the Fourth Amendment, Congress has imposed statutory limitations on the use of pen registers. The most important statutory enactment is the "pen register" provisions of the Electronic Communications Privacy Act of 1986, 18 U.S.C.

§ 3121 et seq. The statute prohibits the use of pen registers unless 1) the "provider" gives consent, or 2) a court order is obtained. The court is authorized to issue an order to install a pen register upon a certified statement of a government official that the pen register is likely to uncover information relevant to a criminal investigation. Note that the government does not need to show probable cause, as it would have to do were the use of a pen register a search.

Carnivore and Computers

The FBI has developed a computer surveillance program called "Carnivore." The program can monitor activity over the internet. Carnivore is an electronic surveillance system that monitors a targeted user's e-mail, web browsing, and file transfer activity. The system is capable of gathering information associated with internet activities at two levels. First, in "full collection" mode, Carnivore intercepts the addressing information and content of a targeted user's electronic communication. The FBI readily admits that in "full collection" mode, the use of Carnivore constitutes a search that is regulated by the Fourth Amendment. Second, in "pen collection" mode, Carnivore primarily gathers only the addressing information associated with e-mail, web browsing, and file transfer activity. The FBI argues that this information is equivalent to the numbers dialed on a telephone, and therefore the "pen collection" mode is not a search and is regulated only by the statutory provisions of the Electronic Communications Privacy Act, discussed above. The argument is that a computer user has no legitimate expectation of privacy in the web addresses that he visits or the e-mail addresses to which he sends e-mail, as this information is accessible to his internet service provider. Do you agree? For more discussion of the use of Carnivore, see Schultz, Unrestricted Federal Agent: "Carnivore" and the Need to Revise the Pen Register Statute, 76 Notre Dame L. Rev. 1215 (2001). See also Guest v. Leis, 255 F.3d 325 (6th Cir. 2001) ("computer users do not have a legitimate expectation of privacy in their subscriber information because they have conveyed it to another person—the system operator).

The USA Patriot Act, passed quickly to combat terrorism after September 11, 2001, amends the relevant electronic surveillance statutes to permit the pen collection mode of Carnivore. See sections 214 and 216 of the Patriot Act, set forth in the statutory supplement.

d. Electronic Pagers

The pen register cases hold that there is no reasonable expectation of privacy in the numbers dialed on a telephone. Does the pen register principle apply to numbers stored in an electronic pager? In United States v. Meriwether, 917 F.2d 955 (6th Cir.1990), a government agent seized a pager from a suspected drug dealer. The pager was seized in the "on" position, and the agent recorded the next forty telephone numbers received by the pager. The agents traced one of the numbers to the defendant, and subsequent investigation implicated the defendant in a drug deal. The defendant argued that the officers had conducted an illegal search of his private information, i.e., the fact that he had called the person who owned the pager. But the Court rejected the defendant's argument that he had a reasonable expectation of privacy when he transmitted his number to the pager. It reasoned that the defendant had, in making the call, disclosed information to another member of the public, and therefore assumed the risk that his message would be received by whomever happened to be in possession of the pager at the time.

In contrast, the court in United States v. Chan, 830 F.Supp. 531 (N.D.Cal. 1993), held that the person *in possession* of a pager has a legitimate privacy interest in the numbers stored in the pager's memory. Chan was legally arrested and his pager was seized. The arresting officer activated the pager's memory and retrieved two telephone numbers that connected Chan to a drug transaction. The court distinguished *Meriwether* and held that the officer's activation of the pager was a search. The court noted that "[i]n contrast to the transmitter of a message to a pager, the possessor of the pager has control over the electronically stored information." It concluded that the "expectation of privacy in an electronic repository for personal data is therefore analogous to that in a personal address book or other repository for such information." Nonetheless, the *Chan* court did not suppress the evidence. While the officer's conduct constitutes a search, this does not mean that the conduct is prohibited. It only means that the conduct must be reasonable. Here, the officer's conduct was found reasonable because he seized the pager and activated its memory while conducting a valid arrest.[7]

e. Trash

In California v. Greenwood, 486 U.S. 35 (1988), police officers asked a neighborhood trash collector to pick up plastic garbage bags that Greenwood left on the curb in front of his house and to turn the bags over to the police. The police rummaged through the bags and found items indicating narcotics use. This information was used to obtain warrants to search Greenwood's house. Greenwood challenged the warrants as the fruit of an illegal search of his trash. Justice White, writing for seven members of the Court, concluded that the officer's inspection of the trash was not a search and therefore was permissible without a warrant or probable cause. Justice White relied on *Smith* (the pen register case) and asserted that "respondents exposed their garbage to the public sufficiently to defeat their claim to Fourth Amendment protection. It is common knowledge that plastic garbage bags left on or at the side of a public street are readily accessible to animals, children, scavengers, snoops, and other members of the public." Because the public had access to the trash, Justice White reasoned that "the police cannot be reasonably expected to avert their eyes from evidence of criminal activity that could have been observed by any member of the public." Justice White therefore found it irrelevant that Greenwood was prohibited by city ordinance from disposing of his trash in any way other than leaving it for the trash service. The ruling was not based on Greenwood's "abandonment" of property, as that would require some showing of a voluntary relinquishment. Rather, the ruling was based squarely on the premise that Greenwood had no expectation of privacy in property to which members of the public had access.

Justice Brennan, joined by Justice Marshall, dissented. He argued that "scrutiny of another's trash is contrary to commonly accepted notions of civilized behavior" and that "society will be shocked to learn that the Court, the ultimate guarantor of liberty, deems unreasonable our expectation that the

---

7. See the discussion of the arrest power rule later in this Chapter.

aspects of our private lives that are concealed safely in a trash bag will not become public." Justice Brennan concluded as follows:

> The mere *possibility* that unwelcome meddlers *might* open and rummage through the containers does not negate the expectation of privacy in its contents any more than the possibility of a burglary negates an expectation of privacy in the home; or the possibility of a private intrusion negates an expectation of privacy in an unopened package; or the possibility that an operator will listen in on a telephone conversation negates an expectation of privacy in the words spoken on the telephone.

Who more accurately captures societal expectations of the American people, Justice White or Justice Brennan?[8]

Questions About Greenwood

What if Greenwood had placed his garbage bags in a trash can just inside his fenced-in backyard? See United States v. Hedrick, 922 F.2d 396 (7th Cir.1991) (not a search even though trash was located near garage, well inside property, because member of the public could still have reached into the trash can). See also United States v. Redmon, 138 F.3d 1109 (7th Cir.1998) (en banc) (no search where officers walked up the defendant's driveway, took trash out of a trashcan located next to the garage, and rummaged through the trash; the court reasons that members of the public, as well as raccoons, could have obtained access to the trash, so police officers could not be excluded).

Would it make any difference if Greenwood had shredded documents and papers into tiny pieces before depositing them in the trash? The Court in United States v. Scott, 975 F.2d 927 (1st Cir.1992), held that an officer's investigation of shredded trash did not constitute a search:

> What we have here is a failed attempt at secrecy by reason of underestimation of police resourcefulness, not invasion of constitutionally protected privacy. There is no constitutional protection from police scrutiny as to information received from a failed attempt at secrecy. * * * The Fourth Amendment * * * does not protect appellee when a third party expends the effort and expense to solve the jigsaw puzzle created by shredding.

f. Public Areas

The "public access" prong of the *Katz* test means that most acts conducted in public are not protected by the Fourth Amendment. But sometimes the question arises as to whether an area is truly "public." For example, can police officers look through the effects of a homeless person (such as a closed cardboard box) without a warrant? Is *Greenwood* good authority for holding that such an inspection is not a search? In Connecticut v. Mooney, 218 Conn. 85, 588 A.2d 145 (1991), the court held that a homeless person had a reasonable expectation of privacy in the contents of a duffel bag and cardboard box kept on public property. The court distinguished *Greenwood* as a case in which defendants placed trash at the curb for the purpose of conveying it to a third party. Is this distinction persuasive? Compare D'Aguanno v. Gallagher, 50 F.3d 877 (11th

8. Professors Slobogin and Schumacher have argued, on the basis of some empirical research, that the Court's conclusions about societal expectations are often at odds with the actual views of most members of society. See Slobogin and Schumacher, Reasonable Expectations of Privacy and Autonomy in Fourth Amendment Cases: An Empirical Look at "Understandings Recognized and Permitted by Society," 42 Duke L.J.727 (1993).

Cir.1995) (homeless persons did not have reasonable expectation of privacy in belongings stored on private property without landowner's permission).

Is it a search if a police officer peers into a closed public bathroom stall? In United States v. White, 890 F.2d 1012 (8th Cir.1989), an officer surreptitiously observed the defendant in a bathroom stall by looking through the gap between the bathroom stall door and the wall of the stall. In this manner the officer saw the defendant engaged in criminal activity. The court held that the officer's activity did not constitute a search. It stated that while the defendant "could reasonably expect a significant amount of privacy in the bathroom stall," that expectation was not violated "because the design of the stall allowed the officer to make her observations without placing herself in any position that would be unexpected by an occupant of the stall." See also United States v. Delaney, 52 F.3d 182 (8th Cir.1995) (no search where officer peers into closed bathroom stall in airport and sees the defendant trying to flush drugs down the toilet).

g. Aerial Surveillance

The Court has applied the public-access-therefore-police-access rationale of *Smith* and *Greenwood* to aerial surveillance of private property. In California v. Ciraolo, 476 U.S. 207 (1986), Chief Justice Burger wrote for the Court as it held, 5–4, that the Fourth Amendment was not violated by aerial observation of a fenced-in backyard, from an altitude of 1,000 feet, even though the officers were operating without a warrant or probable cause. Ciraolo had erected two fences, a six foot outer and a ten foot inner fence, to protect his backyard from observation on the ground. But the aerial overflight revealed the fact that Ciraolo was growing marijuana. The majority reasoned that "the mere fact that an individual has taken measures to restrict some views of his activities [does not] preclude an officer's observations from a public vantage point where he has a right to be and which renders the activities clearly visible." Because any member of the public flying in the public airspace could have peered into the yard, the majority concluded that Ciraolo had no reasonable expectation of privacy against aerial surveillance by the police. The defendant argued that a flyover by members of the public would be different in character and purpose from a flyover by law enforcement officers. But the majority rejected any such distinction, and had "difficulty understanding exactly how respondent's expectations of privacy from aerial observation might differ when two airplanes pass overhead at identical altitudes, simply for different purposes."

Justice Powell, joined by Justices Brennan, Marshall and Blackmun, dissented. He relied upon *Katz* and argued that the Court erred in relying solely on the manner of surveillance rather than "focusing on the interests of the individual and of a free society" and suggested that "[a]erial surveillance is nearly as intrusive on family privacy as physical trespass into the curtilage."

Dow Chemical Co. v. United States, 476 U.S. 227 (1986), was decided the same day by the same vote as *Ciraolo*. The Environmental Protection Agency engaged in aerial photographing of Dow Chemical Co.'s manufacturing plant in Michigan. Dow had maintained elaborate ground security that barred public views of its plant from the ground and had investigated low flights over the plant. It sued for injunctive relief against the EPA, arguing that its Fourth Amendment rights were violated by the aerial overflights. Chief Justice Burger's majority opinion concluded that "the taking of aerial photographs of an industrial plant complex from navigable airspace is not a search prohibited by the Fourth Amendment."

Again Justice Powell wrote for the four dissenters. He relied upon *Katz* to argue that trade secrets laws demonstrate societal recognition of legitimate interests in business privacy, and distinguished *Ciraolo* on the ground that the EPA needed to use a sophisticated camera to discover the details revealed in its photographs.

Ordinary Overflights: Florida v. Riley

The Court applied *Ciraolo* in Florida v. Riley, 488 U.S. 445 (1989), and held that surveillance of a backyard from a helicopter hovering at 400 feet was not a search. Justice White, writing for a plurality, relied on prior cases for the proposition that if information is made available to the public, then an officer can act as any member of the public could and obtain the information free from Fourth Amendment restrictions. The crucial question in *Riley* was whether the public could gain access to the information in Riley's backyard by way of aerial surveillance; the information was partially obscured by a greenhouse, precluding observation by airplane. The officers found it necessary to hover over the property in a helicopter at a height of 400 feet. Justice White noted that no law prohibited the public from hovering over Riley's property in a helicopter at a low level; therefore the police could do so as well. Justice White relied on FAA regulations that allow helicopters to be operated at virtually any altitude so long as they do not pose a safety hazard. He added that there was no injury to the property or any dust or threat from the visual inspection, and that no intimate activities in the house or curtilage had been observed.

Justice O'Connor concurred in the judgment. She disagreed with the plurality's analysis and contended that the proper test for determining the reasonableness of an expectation of privacy was whether the public *ordinarily* had access to the information sought by the police, not whether it was legally possible for a member of the public to obtain it. Thus, for Justice O'Connor, the question was whether members of the public *ordinarily* hovered over Riley's property at 400 feet in helicopters—if not, the police conduct would be a search. Justice O'Connor nonetheless concurred in the result, asserting that the burden was on Riley, the moving party, to show that members of the public did not regularly hover over his property in helicopters. Because Riley had offered no proof on this point in the lower court, she agreed that a search was not shown on the facts in *Riley*.

Justice Brennan wrote a dissenting opinion joined by Justices Marshall and Stevens. He agreed with Justice O'Connor that the reasonableness of a privacy expectation should be determined by whether the public ordinarily has access to the information, not by whether it is legally possible to obtain access. Justice Brennan urged that judicial notice could be taken of the infrequent nature of lowflying helicopters, and that the burden should be placed upon the government to show that this type of aerial surveillance is so frequent as to render unreasonable a privacy expectation. Justice Blackmun also dissented. He agreed with Justices Brennan and O'Connor that the appropriate test is one of whether public access to the property is potentially frequent as opposed to merely possible. Justice Blackmun agreed with Justice Brennan that the burden should be placed upon the government to show frequency of public access. He argued that a remand would give the government the opportunity to satisfy the burden.

In *Riley* five members of the Court agreed that the mere *possibility* of public access is not enough to render a privacy expectation unreasonable. Isn't that the same point that Justice Brennan made in dissent in *Greenwood*? How can *Riley* and *Greenwood* be reconciled?

Views From Above

In light of the aerial overflight cases, how would you rule if police officers shimmy up a telephone pole, or use a ladder, to peer over a homeowner's seven foot high fence? Would this conduct be a search? What if an officer is given a propulsion package that enables him to fly from one border of the property over the property to the other side? Would this be a search? See e.g., Sarantopoulos v. State, 629 So.2d 121 (Fla.1993) (no search where very tall officer stands on tiptoes to peer over a seven-foot fence into a yard; nor would it have been a search if the officer had used a ladder).

h. *Manipulation of Bags in Public Transit*

In recent years, officers have used many techniques to halt the flow of drug traffic on interstate buses and trains. One recent innovation is for officers to enter a bus or train and examine, by touch, the outside of bags that have been placed in the overhead baggage rack. Soft bags are manipulated to determine whether they contain hard objects that could be guns or drugs. In the following case, the Supreme Court determined whether the Fourth Amendment regulated this practice.

BOND v. UNITED STATES

Supreme Court of the United States, 2000.
529 U.S. 334.

CHIEF JUSTICE REHNQUIST **delivered the opinion of the Court.**

This case presents the question whether a law enforcement officer's physical manipulation of a bus passenger's carry-on luggage violated the Fourth Amendment's proscription against unreasonable searches. We hold that it did.

Petitioner Steven Dewayne Bond was a passenger on a Greyhound bus that left California bound for Little Rock, Arkansas. The bus stopped, as it was required to do, at the permanent Border Patrol checkpoint in Sierra Blanca, Texas. Border Patrol Agent Cesar Cantu boarded the bus to check the immigration status of its passengers. After reaching the back of the bus, having satisfied himself that the passengers were lawfully in the United

States, Agent Cantu began walking toward the front. Along the way, he squeezed the soft luggage which passengers had placed in the overhead storage space above the seats.

Petitioner was seated four or five rows from the back of the bus. As Agent Cantu inspected the luggage in the compartment above petitioner's seat, he squeezed a green canvas bag and noticed that it contained a "brick-like" object. Petitioner admitted that the bag was his and agreed to allow Agent Cantu to open it. [The Government has not argued here that petitioner's consent to Agent Cantu's opening the bag is a basis for admitting the evidence.] Upon opening the bag, Agent Cantu discovered a "brick" of methamphetamine. The brick had been wrapped in duct tape until it was oval-shaped and then rolled in a pair of pants.

Petitioner was indicted for conspiracy to possess, and possession with intent to distribute, methamphetamine in violation of 21 U.S.C. § 841(a)(1). He moved to suppress the drugs, arguing that Agent Cantu conducted an illegal search of his bag. Petitioner's motion was denied, and the District Court found him guilty on both counts and sentenced him to 57 months in prison. On appeal, he conceded that other passengers had access to his bag, but contended that Agent Cantu manipulated the bag in a way that other passengers would not. The Court of Appeals rejected this argument, stating that the fact that Agent Cantu's manipulation of petitioner's bag was calculated to detect contraband is irrelevant for Fourth Amendment purposes. Thus, the Court of Appeals affirmed the denial of the motion to suppress, holding that Agent Cantu's manipulation of the bag was not a search within the meaning of the Fourth Amendment. We granted certiorari, and now reverse.

The Fourth Amendment provides that "[t]he right of the people to be secure in their persons, houses, papers, and effects, against unreasonable searches and seizures, shall not be violated. . . ." A traveler's personal luggage is clearly an "effect" protected by the Amendment. See United States v. Place, 462 U.S. 696 (1983). Indeed, it is undisputed here that petitioner possessed a privacy interest in his bag.

But the Government asserts that by exposing his bag to the public, petitioner lost a reasonable expectation that his bag would not be physically manipulated. * * *

Here, petitioner concedes that, by placing his bag in the overhead compartment, he could expect that it would be exposed to certain kinds of touching and handling. But petitioner argues that Agent Cantu's physical manipulation of his luggage "far exceeded the casual contact [petitioner] could have expected from other passengers." The Government counters that it did not.

Our Fourth Amendment analysis embraces two questions. First, we ask whether the individual, by his conduct, has exhibited an actual expectation of privacy; that is, whether he has shown that "he [sought] to preserve [something] as private." Smith v. Maryland, 442 U.S. 735 (1979) Here, petitioner sought to preserve privacy by using an opaque bag and placing that bag directly above his seat. Second, we inquire whether the individual's expectation of privacy is "one that society is prepared to recognize as reasonable." When a bus passenger places a bag in an overhead bin, he expects that other passengers or bus employees may move it for one reason or another. Thus, a bus passenger clearly expects that his bag may be handled. He does not expect that other passengers or bus employees will, as a matter of course, feel the bag in an exploratory manner. But this is exactly what the agent did here. We therefore hold that the agent's physical manipulation of petitioner's bag violated the Fourth Amendment.

The judgment of the Court of Appeals is

Reversed.

JUSTICE BREYER, with whom JUSTICE SCALIA joins, dissenting.

Does a traveler who places a soft-sided bag in the shared overhead storage compartment of a bus have a "reasonable expectation" that strangers will not push, pull, prod, squeeze, or otherwise manipulate his luggage? Unlike the majority, I believe that he does not.

Petitioner argues—and the majority points out—that, even if bags in overhead bins are subject to general "touching" and "handling," this case is special because "Agent Cantu's physical manipulation of [petitioner's] luggage far exceeded the casual contact [he] could have expected from other passengers." But the record shows the contrary. * * * On the occasion at issue here, Agent Cantu "felt a green bag" which had "a brick-like object in it." He explained that he felt "the edges of the brick in the bag," and that it was a "[b]rick-like object ... that, when squeezed, you could feel an outline of something of a different mass inside of it." Although the agent acknowledged that his practice was to "squeeze [bags] very hard," he testified that his touch ordinarily was not "[h]ard enough to break something inside that might be fragile." Petitioner also testified that Agent Cantu "reached for my bag, and he shook it a little, and squeezed it."

How does the "squeezing" just described differ from the treatment that overhead luggage is likely to receive from strangers in a world of travel that is somewhat less gentle than it used to be? I think not at all. See United States v. McDonald, 100 F.3d 1320, 1327 (C.A.7 1996) (" '[A]ny person who has travelled on a common carrier knows that luggage placed in an overhead compartment is always at the mercy of all people who want to rearrange or move previously placed luggage' "); Eagan, Familiar Anger Takes Flight with Airline Tussles, Boston Herald, Aug. 15, 1999, p. 8 ("It's dog-eat-dog trying to cram half your home into overhead compartments"); Massingill, Airlines Ride on the Wings of High–Flying Economy and Travelers Pay Price in Long Lines, Cramped Airplanes, Kansas City Star, May 9, 1999, p. F4 ("[H]undreds of passengers fill overhead compartments with bulky carry-on bags that they have to cram, recram, and then remove"); Flynn, Confessions of a Once–Only Carry–On Guy, San Francisco Examiner, Sept. 6, 1998, p. T2 (flight attendant "rearranged the contents of three different overhead compartments to free up some room" and then "shoved and pounded until [the] bag squeezed in"). The trial court, which heard the evidence, saw nothing unusual, unforeseeable, or special about this agent's squeeze. It found that Agent Cantu simply "felt the outside of Bond's softside green cloth bag," and it viewed the agent's activity as "minimally intrusive touching."

* * * Privacy itself implies the exclusion of uninvited strangers, not just strangers who work for the Government. Hence, an individual cannot reasonably expect privacy in respect to objects or activities that he knowingly exposes to the public.

* * *

* * * At best, this decision will lead to a constitutional jurisprudence of "squeezes," thereby complicating further already complex Fourth Amendment law, increasing the difficulty of deciding ordinary criminal matters, and hindering the administrative guidance (with its potential for control of unreasonable police practices) that a less complicated jurisprudence might provide. At worst, this case will deter law enforcement officers searching for drugs near borders from using even the most non-intrusive touch to help investigate publicly exposed bags. At the same time, the ubiquity of non-governmental pushes, prods, and squeezes (delivered by driver, attendant, passenger, or some other stranger) means that this decision cannot do much to protect true privacy. Rather, the traveler who wants to place a bag in a shared overhead bin and yet safe-

guard its contents from public touch should plan to pack those contents in a suitcase with hard sides, irrespective of the Court's decision today.

For these reasons, I dissent.

Question About Bond

Bond was decided before September 11, 2001. Do you think it would be decided the same way today? If so, then how is it permissible to conduct the intrusive searches of the luggage and even the persons of air travelers that have become common practice after 9/11?

4.   *Investigation That Can Only Reveal Illegal Activity*

Investigation that threatens to uncover innocent, private activity can constitute a search, because it invades a legitimate Fourth Amendment secrecy interest. In contrast, the Supreme Court has held that there is no legitimate expectation of privacy in illegal activity. Therefore, an investigative activity is not a search if it can *only* reveal illegal activity.

a.   *Canine Sniffs*

In United States v. Place, 462 U.S. 696 (1983), the Supreme Court held that a canine sniff of closed luggage for drugs was not a search.

The Court, in an opinion by Justice O'Connor, said this about "canine sniffs":

> A "canine sniff" by a well-trained narcotics detection dog * * * does not require opening the luggage. It does not expose noncontraband items that otherwise would remain hidden from public view, as does, for example, an officer's rummaging through the contents of the luggage. Thus, the manner in which information is obtained through this investigative technique is much less intrusive than a typical search. Moreover, the sniff discloses only the presence or absence of narcotics, a contraband item. Thus, despite the fact that the sniff tells the authorities something about the contents of the luggage, the information obtained is limited. This limited disclosure also ensures that the owner of the property is not subjected to the embarrassment and inconvenience entailed in less discriminate and more intrusive investigative methods.

> In these respects, the canine sniff is *sui generis*. We are aware of no other investigative procedure that is so limited both in the manner in which the information is obtained and in the content of the information revealed by the procedure. Therefore, we conclude that the particular course of investigation that the agents intended to pursue here—exposure of respondent's luggage, which was located in a public place, to a trained canine—did not constitute a "search" within the meaning of the Fourth Amendment.

While the dog sniff in *Place* was not a search, the Court nonetheless held that the cocaine found in Place's luggage was illegally obtained. This was because police did not have the dog ready when Place's luggage arrived at an airport; it took 90 minutes to bring the dog to the scene, and Place's luggage was detained for that time. This detention was an exercise of dominion and control over the luggage, which implicated the Fourth Amendment's prohibition against unreasonable seizures; and the Court found the 90 minute seizure unreasonable under the circumstances, because the officers were not diligent in their investigation and had no probable cause to detain the luggage.

Dog Problems

If a dog trained to alert to drugs positively alerts to luggage, can the officers open the luggage immediately? The answer is no. While the dog sniff itself is not a search, the *opening* of the luggage would be a search because it could uncover legitimate private activity. This is because a dog's positive alert to a piece of luggage does not always mean that drugs are located there. Dogs are fallible; some are trained better than others. Moreover, even if the dog is reliable, it will often make a positive alert to trace amounts of narcotics. The problem with trained canine hypersensitivity is that there are trace amounts of cocaine on almost all of the money supply in America. See Curriden, Courts Reject Drug–Tainted Evidence, ABA Journal, August, 1993, p.22 (noting that 11 prominent citizens in Miami supplied a $20 bill in their possession for drug-testing; ten of the eleven bills tested positive for trace amounts of cocaine, including the bills provided by the Archbishop of Miami and former Attorney General Janet Reno); Crime and Chemical Analysis, 243 Science 1554 (1989) (study indicating that 97% of all bills in circulation in the country are contaminated by cocaine, with an average of 7.3 micrograms per bill).

If a dog positively alerts, this constitutes legally obtained information that can be brought to a Magistrate in an attempt to obtain a warrant. It is up to the Magistrate, and the reviewing court, to assess whether a positive alert, either by itself or with other evidence, constitutes probable cause. See, e.g., United States v. $49,576.00 in Currency, 116 F.3d 425 (9th Cir.1997) (noting that positive dog alert was entitled to "little weight" in the probable cause determination, "because of the widespread contamination of money with drug residue in the Los Angeles area"); United States v. Ludwig, 10 F.3d 1523 (10th Cir.1993) (positive alert suffices for probable cause where dog has a reliable track record); United States v. $5000.00 in Currency, 40 F.3d 846 (6th Cir.1994) (given widespread currency contamination, "we conclude that Maggie's reaction is insufficiently indicative of probable cause"); United States v. Trayer, 898 F.2d 805 (D.C.Cir.1990) (noting that "less than scrupulously neutral procedures, which create at least the possibility of unconscious 'cuing,' may well jeopardize the reliability of dog sniffs"; finding probable cause in the instant case where dog was reliable and cuing had not occurred); United States v. United States Currency, $30,060.00, 39 F.3d 1039 (9th Cir.1994) (a positive dog alert is probative but, because of currency contamination, it must be combined with other suspicious facts in order to constitute probable cause).[9]

Another problem that can arise with the use of dogs is that some dogs get so excited that they go beyond simply sniffing the suspect container. For example, in United States v. Lyons, 957 F.2d 615 (8th Cir.1992), an officer used Grady, a drug-detecting dog, to conduct a sniff of a mailed package in accordance with *Place.* When Grady alerted, however, he became agitated and tore the package in two, spewing the contents on the floor. The contents turned out to be cocaine; Grady had to be treated with drugs to counteract the cocaine he had eaten.

---

9. For a thorough discussion of all the problems presented by canine sniffs, see Tasz-litz, Does the Cold Nose Know? The Unscien-tific Myth of the Dog Scent Lineup, 42 Hast. L.J.15 (1990).

Lyons argued that Grady's conduct constituted an illegal search, because it was much more than the simple canine sniff upheld in *Place*. But the court held that the dog's tearing open the package did not constitute a search. The court likened Grady's act to a natural occurrence, and held that his conduct could not be attributed to the police unless there was some police misconduct involved. The court declared that "in this case the entire event happened in seconds, so quickly that police had no chance to stop Grady from tearing the package." Accordingly, "the dog's instinctive actions did not violate the fourth amendment."

Dog Sniffs of People and Places

Do the police implicate the Fourth Amendment if they conduct a dog sniff of a person? See United States v. Garcia–Garcia, 319 F.3d 726 (5th Cir. 2003) (dog sniff of a person is equivalent to a *Terry* frisk if the dog makes contact with the person). What if they send the dog down the block in a neighborhood, and the dog alerts to a certain house? What if they send the dog down the aisle of a passenger train, and the dog alerts to a sleeper compartment? In United States v. Thomas, 757 F.2d 1359 (2d Cir.1985), the court held that the use of a marijuana-sniffing dog outside an apartment was a search. The court reasoned that because of the greater expectation of privacy in the home, the dog sniff of Thomas' apartment was a greater intrusion than the dog sniff of Place's luggage. Was it? In contrast, in United States v. Colyer, 878 F.2d 469 (D.C.Cir.1989), the court held that a dog sniff outside an Amtrak sleeping compartment was not a search. The court stated that *Place* stood for the proposition that "governmental conduct that can reveal nothing about noncontraband items * * * interferes with no legitimate privacy expectation." The court was also concerned about the specter of police officer liability if canine sniffs were searches:

> [I]f we were to hold that the corridor sniff were a search, those whose sleeper cars were sniffed in order to ensure that Max 25 was not falsely alerting—and of whom the agents had no reason to suspect possession of illicit drugs—could maintain a civil action, although no information pertaining to their private affairs was obtained, and neither they nor their belongings were seized.

See also United States v. Reed, 141 F.3d 644 (6th Cir.1998) (declaring that the holding in *Thomas* "ignores the Supreme Court's determination in *Place* that a person has no legitimate privacy interest in the possession of contraband, thus rendering the location of the contraband irrelevant to the Court's holding that a canine sniff does not constitute a search.").

Would you hold a canine sniff to be a search under some circumstances? Would you distinguish the sniffing of a person from the sniffing of property? See United States v. Roby, 122 F.3d 1120 (8th Cir.1997) (canine sniff of an apartment from an outside hallway does not constitute a search); United States v. Ludwig, 10 F.3d 1523 (10th Cir.1993) (random dog-sniffing of vehicles are not searches subject to the Fourth Amendment); United States v. Lingenfelter, 997 F.2d 632 (9th Cir.1993) ("Whether the canine sniff is of luggage or the exterior of a warehouse, it discloses only the presence of absence of a contraband item"; leaving open, however, whether a dog sniff of a person constitutes a search).

b. *Chemical Testing for Drugs*

The Court applied the reasoning in *Place* when it upheld the warrantless chemical field-testing of a powder that a Federal agent obtained from a package opened by Federal Express employees in United States v. Jacobsen, 466 U.S. 109 (1984).[10] Justice Stevens' opinion for the Court stated that "[a] chemical test that merely discloses whether or not a particular substance is cocaine does not compromise any legitimate interest in privacy." Even if the results of the test are negative, the results reveal "nothing of special interest." Thus, "[h]ere, as in *Place*, the likelihood that official conduct * * * will actually compromise any legitimate interest in privacy seems much too remote to characterize the testing as a search subject to the Fourth Amendment."

While the field test in *Jacobsen* was not a search, it did constitute a seizure, because the powder sample that is tested is destroyed in the process. Thus, the test affected "possessory interests protected by the Amendment, since by destroying a quantity of the powder it converted what had been only a temporary deprivation of possessory interests into a permanent one." However, Justice Stevens found that the seizure involved in a field test was reasonable under the Fourth Amendment because only a minimal amount of the powder was destroyed, and the officer had a clear indication that the powder was some kind of contraband before he tested it.

Justice Brennan, joined by Justice Marshall, wrote a dissenting opinion in *Jacobsen*. The dissent found it "most startling" that in this case and in *Place* the Court put "its exclusive focus on the nature of the information or item sought and revealed through the use of a surveillance technique, rather than on the context in which the information or item is concealed." Rather than hold that a technique either always or never violates reasonable expectations of privacy, Justice Brennan urged the Court to examine the private nature of the area or item subjected to intrusion.

Other Drug Testing

Does *Jacobsen* mean that drug tests on urine samples are not searches? In Skinner v. Railway Labor Executives' Ass'n, 489 U.S. 602 (1989), the Court unanimously held that drug testing of urine was a search. The Court noted that unlike the field testing in *Jacobsen,* drug testing of urine samples could uncover such innocent secret information as epilepsy, pregnancy, or the use of prescription drugs. Moreover, the process of collecting urine samples (including aural observation) was intrusive and embarrassing. The Court concluded that "the collection and testing of urine intrudes upon expectations of privacy that society has long recognized as reasonable."

5.   Use of Technology to Enhance Inspection

Under *Katz*, visual inspection is not always a "search", as seen in the aerial overflight cases. But what if visual inspection is aided by sophisticated technological devices?

a.   Thermal Detection Devices

One recent technological advance in law enforcement has been the development of an infrared thermal detection device. The use of such a device in

---

10. The portion of the Court's opinion upholding the visual examination and seizure of the plastic bags containing the powder is dis-   cussed in the section on mixed public and private searches, *infra.*

detecting a drug-growing operation was reviewed by the Supreme Court in the following case.

KYLLO v. UNITED STATES

United States Supreme Court, 2001.
533 U.S. 27.

JUSTICE SCALIA **delivered the opinion of the Court.**

This case presents the question whether the use of a thermal-imaging device aimed at a private home from a public street to detect relative amounts of heat within the home constitutes a "search" within the meaning of the Fourth Amendment.

I

In 1991 Agent William Elliott of the United States Department of the Interior came to suspect that marijuana was being grown in the home belonging to petitioner Danny Kyllo, part of a triplex on Rhododendron Drive in Florence, Oregon. Indoor marijuana growth typically requires high-intensity lamps. In order to determine whether an amount of heat was emanating from petitioner's home consistent with the use of such lamps, at 3:20 a.m. on January 16, 1992, Agent Elliott and Dan Haas used an Agema Thermovision 210 thermal imager to scan the triplex. Thermal imagers detect infrared radiation, which virtually all objects emit but which is not visible to the naked eye. The imager converts radiation into images based on relative warmth—black is cool, white is hot, shades of gray connote relative differences; in that respect, it operates somewhat like a video camera showing heat images. The scan of Kyllo's home took only a few minutes and was performed from the passenger seat of Agent Elliott's vehicle across the street from the front of the house and also from the street in back of the house. The scan showed that the roof over the garage and a side wall of petition-

er's home were relatively hot compared to the rest of the home and substantially warmer than neighboring homes in the triplex. Agent Elliott concluded that petitioner was using halide lights to grow marijuana in his house, which indeed he was. Based on tips from informants, utility bills, and the thermal imaging, a Federal Magistrate Judge issued a warrant authorizing a search of petitioner's home, and the agents found an indoor growing operation involving more than 100 plants. Petitioner was indicted on one count of manufacturing marijuana, in violation of 21 U.S.C. § 841(a)(1). He unsuccessfully moved to suppress the evidence seized from his home and then entered a conditional guilty plea.

The Court of Appeals for the Ninth Circuit remanded the case for an evidentiary hearing regarding the intrusiveness of thermal imaging. On remand the District Court found that the Agema 210 "is a non-intrusive device which emits no rays or beams and shows a crude visual image of the heat being radiated from the outside of the house"; it "did not show any people or activity within the walls of the structure"; "[t]he device used cannot penetrate walls or windows to reveal conversations or human activities"; and "[n]o intimate details of the home were observed." Based on these findings, the District Court upheld the validity of the warrant that relied in part upon the thermal imaging, and reaffirmed its denial of the motion to suppress. A divided Court of Appeals initially reversed, but that opinion was withdrawn and the panel (after a change in composition) affirmed, with

Judge Noonan dissenting. The court held that petitioner had shown no subjective expectation of privacy because he had made no attempt to conceal the heat escaping from his home, and even if he had, there was no objectively reasonable expectation of privacy because the imager "did not expose any intimate details of Kyllo's life," only "amorphous 'hot spots' on the roof and exterior wall." We granted certiorari.

II

The Fourth Amendment provides that "[t]he right of the people to be secure in their persons, houses, papers, and effects, against unreasonable searches and seizures, shall not be violated." "At the very core" of the Fourth Amendment "stands the right of a man to retreat into his own home and there be free from unreasonable governmental intrusion." Silverman v. United States, 365 U.S. 505, 511 (1961). With few exceptions, the question whether a warrantless search of a home is reasonable and hence constitutional must be answered no.

On the other hand, the antecedent question of whether or not a Fourth Amendment "search" has occurred is not so simple under our precedent. The permissibility of ordinary visual surveillance of a home used to be clear because, well into the 20th century, our Fourth Amendment jurisprudence was tied to common-law trespass. Visual surveillance was unquestionably lawful because "the eye cannot by the laws of England be guilty of a trespass." Boyd v. United States, 116 U.S. 616, 628 (1886). We have since decoupled violation of a person's Fourth Amendment rights from trespassory violation of his property, see Rakas v. Illinois, 439 U.S. 128 (1978), but the lawfulness of warrantless visual surveillance of a home has still been preserved. As we

observed in California v. Ciraolo, 476 U.S. 207, 213 (1986), "[t]he Fourth Amendment protection of the home has never been extended to require law enforcement officers to shield their eyes when passing by a home on public thoroughfares."

One might think that the new validating rationale would be that examining the portion of a house that is in plain public view, while it is a "search" despite the absence of trespass, is not an "unreasonable" one under the Fourth Amendment. But in fact we have held that visual observation is no "search" at all—perhaps in order to preserve somewhat more intact our doctrine that warrantless searches are presumptively unconstitutional. See Dow Chemical Co. v. United States, 476 U.S. 227, 234–235, 239 (1986). In assessing when a search is not a search, we have applied somewhat in reverse the principle first enunciated in Katz v. United States, 389 U.S. 347 (1967). *Katz* involved eavesdropping by means of an electronic listening device placed on the outside of a telephone booth—a location not within the catalog ("persons, houses, papers, and effects") that the Fourth Amendment protects against unreasonable searches. We held that the Fourth Amendment nonetheless protected Katz from the warrantless eavesdropping because he "justifiably relied" upon the privacy of the telephone booth. As Justice Harlan's oft-quoted concurrence described it, a Fourth Amendment search occurs when the government violates a subjective expectation of privacy that society recognizes as reasonable. We have subsequently applied this principle to hold that a Fourth Amendment search does not occur—even when the explicitly protected location of a house is concerned—unless "the individual manifested a subjective expectation of privacy in the object of the challenged search," and "society [is] willing to recognize that expectation as reasonable." We have applied this test in holding that it is not a search for the police to use a pen register at the phone company to determine what numbers were dialed in a private home, and we have applied the test on two different occasions in holding that aerial surveillance of private homes and surrounding areas does not constitute a search.

The present case involves officers on a public street engaged in more than naked-eye surveillance of a home. We have previously reserved judgment as to how much technological enhancement of ordinary perception from such a vantage point, if any, is too much. While we upheld enhanced aerial photography of an industrial complex in *Dow Chemical*, we noted that we found "it important that this is not an area immediately adjacent to a private home, where privacy expectations are most heightened."

III

It would be foolish to contend that the degree of privacy secured to citizens by the Fourth Amendment has been entirely unaffected by the advance of technology. For example, as the cases discussed above make clear, the technology enabling human flight has exposed to public view (and hence, we have said, to official observation) uncovered portions of the house and its curtilage that once were private. The question we confront today is what limits there are upon this power of technology to shrink the realm of guaranteed privacy.

The *Katz* test—whether the individual has an expectation of privacy that society is prepared to recognize as reasonable—has often been criticized as circular, and hence subjective and unpredictable. See Posner, The Uncertain Protection of Privacy by the Supreme Court, 1979 S. Ct. Rev. 173, 188; Minnesota v. Carter, 525 U.S. 83, 97 (SCALIA, J., concurring). While it may be difficult to refine *Katz* when the search of areas such as telephone booths, automobiles, or even the curtilage and uncovered portions of residences are at issue, in the case of the search of the interior of homes—the prototypical and hence most commonly litigated area of protected privacy—there is a ready criterion, with roots deep in the common law, of the minimal expectation of privacy that exists, and that is acknowledged to be reasonable. To withdraw protection of this minimum expectation would be to permit police technology to erode the privacy guaranteed by the Fourth Amendment. We think that obtaining by sense-enhancing technology any information regarding the interior of the home that could not otherwise have been obtained without physical "intrusion into a constitutionally protected area," constitutes a search—at least where (as here) the technology in question is not in general public use. This assures preservation of that degree of privacy against government that existed when the Fourth Amendment was adopted. On the basis of this criterion, the information obtained by the thermal imager in this case was the product of a search.[a]

a. The dissent's repeated assertion that the thermal imaging did not obtain information regarding the interior of the home is simply inaccurate. A thermal imager reveals the relative heat of various rooms in the home. The dissent may not find that information particularly private or important, but there is no basis for saying it is not information regarding the interior of the home. The dissent's comparison of the thermal imaging to various circumstances in which outside observers might be able to perceive, without technology, the heat of the home—for example, by observing snow-melt on the roof—is quite irrelevant. The fact that equivalent information could sometimes be obtained by other means does not make lawful the use of means that violate the Fourth Amendment. The police might, for example,

The Government maintains, however, that the thermal imaging must be upheld because it detected "only heat radiating from the external surface of the house." The dissent makes this its leading point, contending that there is a fundamental difference between what it calls "off-the-wall" observations and "through-the-wall surveillance." But just as a thermal imager captures only heat emanating from a house, so also a powerful directional microphone picks up only sound emanating from a house-and a satellite capable of scanning from many miles away would pick up only visible light emanating from a house. We rejected such a mechanical interpretation of the Fourth Amendment in *Katz*, where the eavesdropping device picked up only sound waves that reached the exterior of the phone booth. Reversing that approach would leave the homeowner at the mercy of advancing technology—including imaging technology that could discern all human activity in the home. While the technology used in the present case was relatively crude, the rule we adopt must take account of more sophisticated systems that are already in use or in development. * * * As for the dissent's extraordinary assertion that anything learned through "an inference" cannot be a search, that would validate even the "through-the-wall" technologies that the dissent purports to disapprove. Surely the dissent does not believe that the through-the-wall radar or ultrasound technology produces an 8–by–10 Kodak glossy that needs no analysis (i.e., the making of inferences). * * *

The Government also contends that the thermal imaging was constitutional because it did not "detect private ac-

tivities occurring in private areas." It points out that in *Dow Chemical* we observed that the enhanced aerial photography did not reveal any "intimate details." *Dow Chemical*, however, involved enhanced aerial photography of an industrial complex, which does not share the Fourth Amendment sanctity of the home. The Fourth Amendment's protection of the home has never been tied to measurement of the quality or quantity of information obtained. In *Silverman*, for example, we made clear that any physical invasion of the structure of the home, "by even a fraction of an inch," was too much, 365 U.S., at 512, and there is certainly no exception to the warrant requirement for the officer who barely cracks open the front door and sees nothing but the nonintimate rug on the vestibule floor. In the home, our cases show, all details are intimate details, because the entire area is held safe from prying government eyes. Thus, in [United States v.] *Karo*, [discussed in the section on beepers, below] the only thing detected was a can of ether in the home; and in Arizona v. Hicks, 480 U.S. 321 (1987), the only thing detected by a physical search that went beyond what officers lawfully present could observe in "plain view" was the registration number of a phonograph turntable. These were intimate details because they were details of the home, just as was the detail of how warm—or even how relatively warm—Kyllo was heating his residence.

Limiting the prohibition of thermal imaging to "intimate details" would not only be wrong in principle; it would be impractical in application * * *. To begin with, there is no necessary connection between the sophistication of the surveillance equip-

---

learn how many people are in a particular house by setting up year-round surveillance; but that does not make breaking and entering to find out the same information lawful. In any

event, on the night of January 16, 1992, no outside observer could have discerned the relative heat of Kyllo's home without thermal imaging.

ment and the "intimacy" of the details that it observes—which means that one cannot say (and the police cannot be assured) that use of the relatively crude equipment at issue here will always be lawful. The Agema Thermovision 210 might disclose, for example, at what hour each night the lady of the house takes her daily sauna and bath—a detail that many would consider "intimate"; and a much more sophisticated system might detect nothing more intimate than the fact that someone left a closet light on. We could not, in other words, develop a rule approving only that through-the-wall surveillance which identifies objects no smaller than 36 by 36 inches, but would have to develop a jurisprudence specifying which home activities are "intimate" and which are not. And even when (if ever) that jurisprudence were fully developed, no police officer would be able to know in advance whether his through-the-wall surveillance picks up "intimate" details—and thus would be unable to know in advance whether it is constitutional.

The dissent's proposed standard—whether the technology offers the "functional equivalent of actual presence in the area being searched"—would seem quite similar to our own at first blush. The dissent concludes that *Katz* was such a case, but then inexplicably asserts that if the same listening device only revealed the volume of the conversation, the surveillance would be permissible. Yet if, without technology, the police could not discern volume without being actually present in the phone booth, JUSTICE STEVENS should conclude a

search has occurred. The same should hold for the interior heat of the home if only a person present in the home could discern the heat. Thus the driving force of the dissent, despite its recitation of the above standard, appears to be a distinction among different types of information—whether the "homeowner would even care if anybody noticed." The dissent offers no practical guidance for the application of this standard, and for reasons already discussed, we believe there can be none. The people in their houses, as well as the police, deserve more precision.[b]

We have said that the Fourth Amendment draws "a firm line at the entrance to the house." That line, we think, must be not only firm but also bright—which requires clear specification of those methods of surveillance that require a warrant. While it is certainly possible to conclude from the videotape of the thermal imaging that occurred in this case that no "significant" compromise of the homeowner's privacy has occurred, we must take the long view, from the original meaning of the Fourth Amendment forward.

Where, as here, the Government uses a device that is not in general public use, to explore details of the home that would previously have been unknowable without physical intrusion, the surveillance is a "search" and is presumptively unreasonable without a warrant.

Since we hold the Thermovision imaging to have been an unlawful search, it will remain for the District Court to determine whether, without the evi-

---

b. The dissent argues that we have injected potential uncertainty into the constitutional analysis by noting that whether or not the technology is in general public use may be a factor. That quarrel, however, is not with us but with this Court's precedent. See *Ciraolo*, supra, at 215 ("In an age where private and commercial flight in the public airways is rou-

tine, it is unreasonable for respondent to expect that his marijuana plants were constitutionally protected from being observed with the naked eye from an altitude of 1,000 feet"). Given that we can quite confidently say that thermal imaging is not "routine," we decline in this case to reexamine that factor.

dence it provided, the search warrant issued in this case was supported by probable cause—and if not, whether there is any other basis for supporting admission of the evidence that the search pursuant to the warrant produced.

* * *

The judgment of the Court of Appeals is reversed; the case is remanded for further proceedings consistent with this opinion.

JUSTICE STEVENS, **with whom** THE CHIEF JUSTICE, JUSTICE O'CONNOR, **and** JUSTICE KENNEDY **join, dissenting.**

There is, in my judgment, a distinction of constitutional magnitude between "through-the-wall surveillance" that gives the observer or listener direct access to information in a private area, on the one hand, and the thought processes used to draw inferences from information in the public domain, on the other hand. The Court has crafted a rule that purports to deal with direct observations of the inside of the home, but the case before us merely involves indirect deductions from "off-the-wall" surveillance, that is, observations of the exterior of the home. Those observations were made with a fairly primitive thermal imager that gathered data exposed on the outside of petitioner's home but did not invade any constitutionally protected interest in privacy. Moreover, I believe that the supposedly "bright-line" rule the Court has created in response to its concerns about future technological developments is unnecessary, unwise, and inconsistent with the Fourth Amendment.

I

* * *

While the Court "take[s] the long view" and decides this case based largely on the potential of yet-to-be-developed technology that might allow "through-the-wall surveillance," this case involves nothing more than off-the-wall surveillance by law enforcement officers to gather information exposed to the general public from the outside of petitioner's home. All that the infrared camera did in this case was passively measure heat emitted from the exterior surfaces of petitioner's home; all that those measurements showed were relative differences in emission levels, vaguely indicating that some areas of the roof and outside walls were warmer than others. As still images from the infrared scans show, no details regarding the interior of petitioner's home were revealed. Unlike an x-ray scan, or other possible "through-the-wall" techniques, the detection of infrared radiation emanating from the home did not accomplish "an unauthorized physical penetration into the premises." * * *

Indeed, the ordinary use of the senses might enable a neighbor or passerby to notice the heat emanating from a building, particularly if it is vented, as was the case here. Additionally, any member of the public might notice that one part of a house is warmer than another part or a nearby building if, for example, rainwater evaporates or snow melts at different rates across its surfaces. Such use of the senses would not convert into an unreasonable search if, instead, an adjoining neighbor allowed an officer onto her property to verify her perceptions with a sensitive thermometer. Nor, in my view, does such observation become an unreasonable search if made from a distance with the aid of a device that merely discloses that the exterior of one house, or one area of the house, is much warmer than another. Nothing more occurred in this case.

Thus, the notion that heat emissions from the outside of a dwelling is a private matter implicating the protections of the Fourth Amendment (the text of which guarantees the right of people "to be secure in their ... houses" against unreasonable searches and seizures (emphasis added)) is not only unprecedented but also quite difficult to take seriously. Heat waves, like aromas that are generated in a kitchen, or in a laboratory or opium den, enter the public domain if and when they leave a building. A subjective expectation that they would remain private is not only implausible but also surely not "one that society is prepared to recognize as reasonable."

* * *

Notwithstanding the implications of today's decision, there is a strong public interest in avoiding constitutional litigation over the monitoring of emissions from homes, and over the inferences drawn from such monitoring. Just as "the police cannot reasonably be expected to avert their eyes from evidence of criminal activity that could have been observed by any member of the public," *Greenwood*, 486 U.S., at 41, so too public officials should not have to avert their senses or their equipment from detecting emissions in the public domain such as excessive heat, traces of smoke, suspicious odors, odorless gases, airborne particulates, or radioactive emissions, any of which could identify hazards to the community. In my judgment, monitoring such emissions with "sense-enhancing technology," and drawing useful conclusions from such monitoring, is an entirely reasonable public service.

* * *

II

* * *

Despite the Court's attempt to draw a line that is "not only firm but also bright," the contours of its new rule are uncertain because its protection apparently dissipates as soon as the relevant technology is "in general public use." Yet how much use is general public use is not even hinted at by the Court's opinion, which makes the somewhat doubtful assumption that the thermal imager used in this case does not satisfy that criterion. In any event, putting aside its lack of clarity, this criterion is somewhat perverse because it seems likely that the threat to privacy will grow, rather than recede, as the use of intrusive equipment becomes more readily available.

* * *

III

Although the Court is properly and commendably concerned about the threats to privacy that may flow from advances in the technology available to the law enforcement profession, it has unfortunately failed to heed the tried and true counsel of judicial restraint. Instead of concentrating on the rather mundane issue that is actually presented by the case before it, the Court has endeavored to craft an all-encompassing rule for the future. It would be far wiser to give legislators an unimpeded opportunity to grapple with these emerging issues rather than to shackle them with prematurely devised constitutional constraints.

I respectfully dissent.

Questions About Kyllo

What happens if police use a thermal imaging device on a warehouse rather than a home? Is *Kyllo's* emphasis on the sanctity of the home determinative? Professor Maclin, in *Katz, Kyllo,* and Technology: Virtual Fourth Amendment Protection in the

Twenty–First Century, 72 Miss. L.J. 51 (2002), comments that it may be possible in future cases to distinguish the thermal imaging directed at a home from thermal imaging directed at an office or other business facility. Why? Doesn't the citizen have the same right to preserve information as private in her warehouse as she does in her home? See United States v. Elkins, 300 F.3d 638 (6th Cir. 2002), where the trial court held that the use of a thermal imaging device on a warehouse constituted a search after *Kyllo,* but the Court of Appeals found it unnecessary to decide the question because the officers had enough information without the results of the thermal imaging to justify a search of the warehouse. The Court of Appeals did note, however, the following:

> While *Kyllo* broadly protects homes against warrantless thermal imaging, the case before us involves the use of a thermal imager to scan the Elkinses' commercial buildings. There is a reasonable expectation of privacy in business premises, yet it is less than the reasonable expectation of privacy enjoyed by the home.

What happens if the use of thermal imaging devices becomes commonplace among members of the public? Doesn't the majority in *Kyllo* admit that the use of the devices by police officers at that point will not be a search? If that is so, then how much has the Court done to protect citizens from technological advances in official investigations?

Note that at least at this point, the Court's holding in *Kyllo* puts an end to the law enforcement use of thermal imaging devices to scan homes. Such a scan would be a search, and searches require probable cause. If an officer has the probable cause necessary to conduct a thermal imaging scan, then he has no need for the thermal imaging scan. He can just get a warrant to search the home. Before *Kyllo,* thermal imagers were used to *obtain* the probable cause necessary to get a warrant. Moreover, thermal imagers rely on a relative comparison of heat emanation. So typically,(and as in *Kyllo*), an officer would have to scan other houses in the neighborhood to determine whether the suspect's house emanated heat more than those other houses. Under *Kyllo,* the scan of each of the houses in the neighborhood is an illegal search.

How does the analysis in *Kyllo* relate to the use of other new technological toys being used by law enforcement? One example is the use of "face-recognition" technology. This technology scans faces in public places and reviews the results against a database of wanted criminals and suspects. It was used at the Super Bowl in Tampa. Officials scanned the entire crowd and found many in attendance who were criminals at large. Does *Kyllo* mean that the use of face technology is a search? Another new device is known as "Sentor". It looks like a large flashlight. It is pointed at a person and, when the officer turns a switch, the Sentor acts like a vacuum cleaner. It sucks in large quantities of air and other particles surrounding the citizen. The Sentor is then placed into another machine, which heats the collected samples and uses high-speed chromatography to separate out the chemical compounds contained in the particles. In this way it detects whether the chemical compounds used in narcotics or bombs are surrounding the citizen. Does the use of Sentor constitute a search under *Kyllo*?

b. Electronic Beepers

Tracking Public Movements: United States v. Knotts

The Court discussed the use of electronic beepers to track a person's public movements in United States v. Knotts, 460 U.S. 276 (1983). State officers, suspicious that a purchaser of chemicals, Armstrong, might be using them to manufacture drugs, obtained the consent of the company selling the chemicals to install a beeper inside a 5 gallon container of chloroform before Armstrong picked it up. Armstrong placed the container in his car. The officers monitored the beeper signal from the container and followed Armstrong to Petschen's house where the container was transferred to his car. Ultimately the signal became stationary at a location identified as a cabin belonging to Knotts. Because Knotts did not (and could not, for lack of standing) challenge the warrantless installation of the beeper in the container, the Court had no occasion to address the permissibility of that intrusion. Justice Rehnquist's opinion for six Justices quoted from *Katz* and *Smith* (the pen register case) and framed the question presented as whether the officers had invaded any legitimate expectation of privacy held by Knotts when they tracked the container's movement by use of the beeper. The opinion reasoned as follows:

> Visual surveillance from public places along Petschen's route or adjoining Knotts' premises would have sufficed to reveal all of these facts to the police. The fact that the officers in this case relied not only on visual surveillance, but on the use of the beeper to signal the presence of Petschen's automobile to the police receiver, does not alter the situation. Nothing in the Fourth Amendment prohibited the police from augmenting the sensory faculties bestowed upon them at birth with such enhancement as science and technology afforded them in this case.

Knotts argued that if the tracking by beeper was not even a search, it would mean that unlimited surveillance of any citizen would be possible without judicial supervision. But the Court responded that "if such dragnet type law enforcement practices * * * should eventually occur, there will be time enough then to determine whether different constitutional principles may be applicable." It noted too that nothing in the record indicated that the beeper signal was used to monitor any activity in the cabin.

Does *Knotts,* then, provide authority for the use of face-recognition technology in public places, as discussed above? If so, is there a conflict between *Knotts* and *Kyllo*?

Complex Beeper Issues: United States v. Karo

United States v. Karo, 468 U.S. 705 (1984), answered some of the difficult questions left open in *Knotts*. A DEA agent learned that Karo, Horton and Harley had ordered 50 gallons of ether from a government informant, who told the agent that the ether was to be used to extract cocaine from clothing that had been imported into the United States. The government obtained a court order authorizing the installation and monitoring of a beeper in one of the cans of ether—but this order was later found to be invalid. Agents saw Karo pick up the ether from the informant and followed him to his house. They used the beeper to determine that the ether was still in the house, and they subsequently used it to detect that the ether had been moved to Horton's house. From this house, agents could smell the ether while standing on the sidewalk. A third use of the beeper helped agents discover that the ether had been moved to Horton's father's house, and a fourth use revealed it had been taken to a commercial storage facility. Agents could smell the ether in a row of lockers and used the beeper a fifth time to discover the exact location of the ether. The sixth use led agents to another storage facility where they detected the smell of ether from a locker. They obtained consent to install a closed-circuit camera in the facility and observed a man and woman load the ether into Horton's pick-up truck. While undertaking to follow the truck to another house, the agents used the beeper a seventh time. The eighth use assured the agents that the ether remained in the house when the truck left. Finally, agents obtained a search warrant for the house. They found cocaine and laboratory equipment and made arrests.

Justice White wrote for the Court. He concluded first that no authorization was necessary to place a beeper in the can of ether. Therefore it did not matter that the court order authorizing the installation was invalid.

> It is clear that the actual placement of the beeper into the can violated no one's Fourth Amendment rights. The can into which the beeper was placed belonged at the time to the DEA, and by no stretch of the imagination could it be said that respondents then had any legitimate expectation of privacy in it.

Justice White next concluded that the Fourth Amendment was not implicated by the fact that Karo received a can that contained an electronic tracking device.

> The mere transfer to Karo of a can containing an unmonitored beeper infringed no privacy interest. It conveyed no information that Karo wished to keep private, for it conveyed no information at all. To be sure, it created a *potential* for an invasion of privacy, but we have never held that potential, as opposed to actual, invasions of privacy constitute searches for purposes of the Fourth Amendment. A holding to that effect would mean that a policeman walking down the street carrying a parabolic microphone capable of picking up conversations in nearby homes would be engaging in a search even if the microphone were not turned on. It is the exploitation of technological advances that implicates the Fourth Amendment, not their mere existence.

> We likewise do not believe that the transfer of the container constituted a seizure. A "seizure" of property occurs when "there is some meaningful interference with an individual's possessory interests in that property." Although the can may have contained an unknown and unwanted foreign object, it cannot be said that anyone's possessory interest was interfered with in a meaningful way. * * * Of course, if the presence of a beeper in the can constituted a seizure merely because of its occupation of space, it would follow that the presence of any object, regardless of its nature, would violate the Fourth Amendment.

> We conclude that no Fourth Amendment interest of Karo or of any other respondent was infringed by the installation of the beeper. Rather, any impairment of their privacy interests that may have occurred was occasioned by the monitoring of the beeper.

Beepers in the House

Justice White reached a different conclusion in *Karo* as to the monitoring of the beeper "in a private residence, a location not open to visual surveillance".

The monitoring of an electronic device such as a beeper is, of course, less intrusive than a full-scale search, but it does reveal a critical fact about the interior of the premises that the Government is extremely interested in knowing and that it could not have otherwise obtained without a warrant. The case is thus not like *Knotts*, for there the beeper told the authorities nothing about the interior of *Knotts'* cabin. The information obtained in *Knotts* was "voluntarily conveyed to anyone who wanted to look. * * * *"; here, as we have said, the monitoring indicated that the beeper was inside the house, a fact that could not have been visually verified.

We cannot accept the Government's contention that it should be completely free from the constraints of the Fourth Amendment to determine by means of an electronic device, without a warrant and without probable cause or reasonable suspicion, whether a particular article—or a person, for that matter—is in an individual's home at a particular time. Indiscriminate monitoring of property that has been withdrawn from public view would present far too serious a threat to privacy interests in the home to escape entirely some sort of Fourth Amendment oversight.

Although the Court condemned warrantless monitoring of a beeper inside a private house, it sustained the search warrant that agents obtained at the end of their surveillance. The knowledge that the agents obtained without using the beeper, together with their proper use of the beeper in monitoring travel outside the house, provided sufficient independent information to justify the issuance of a search warrant. Thus, the illegally obtained information (i.e., that the can was inside a house for some period of time) had no effect on the Magistrate's issuance of the warrant.

Justice Stevens, joined by Justices Brennan and Marshall, dissented in part. Justice Stevens observed that "the character of the property is profoundly different when infected with an electronic bug than when it is entirely germ free." He concluded that agents asserted dominion and control over the property when they inserted the beeper and that this amounted to a seizure covered by the Fourth Amendment. He contended that "the private citizen is entitled to assume, and in fact does assume, that his possessions are not infected with concealed electronic devices." He found "little comfort in the Court's notion that no invasion of privacy occurs until a listener obtains some significant information by use of the device."

But if Justice Stevens felt this way with respect to the use of the beeper in *Karo*, how could he then accept the use of the thermal imaging device in his dissent in *Kyllo*? The apparent distinction is that the thermal imager operates "on-the-wall" while the beeper operates "through the wall." But why should that make any difference?

Informants, Beepers, and Stolen Property

Justice O'Connor, joined by Justice Rehnquist, wrote a separate opinion in *Karo* concurring in most of the Court's opinion and in its judgment. She wrote separately to state her view that a home owner might not be able to claim that his privacy rights are violated if he permits a third person to enter the home with property that contains a beeper. If, for example, a government undercover agent posing as a drug buyer entered a suspect's home and carried a beeper, the home owner might not have a valid complaint. Justice White responded in a footnote by saying that he did not necessarily disagree with this analysis. Justice White found it inapplicable to the instant case, where the defendant himself had purchased the beepered can and brought it into the house.

The point that Justice O'Connor raised might well be crucial if an informant agrees to have a beeper placed in property that he acquires and brings to the homes of other suspects. It might also mean that it is permissible to place a beeper on property that is later stolen, and then track the movement of the property, even into private areas. Thus, in United States v. Jones, 31 F.3d 1304 (4th Cir.1994), officials suspected that a postal worker was stealing mail. They placed a beeper in a particularly attractive mail pouch. The beeper was activated when the pouch was opened, and the officers tracked the beeper into the defendant's van. The court relied on Justice O'Connor's opinion in *Karo*, and held that the use of the beeper was not a search. The court distinguished the facts of *Karo* in the following analysis:

> *Karo* * * * raises the disturbing specter of government agents hiding electronic devices in all sorts of personal property and then following private citizens who own such property as they go about their business. This case presents no such danger. Here, the government has placed the electronic device in its own property. Only purloiners of such property need fear adverse consequences.

c. *Other Sensory Enhancement Devices*

United States v. Taborda, 635 F.2d 131 (2d Cir.1980), holds that agents invaded a person's reasonable expectation of privacy when they used a telescope to see activities not visible with the naked eye from across the street from a suspect's apartment. The same court opined that observations made with binoculars or other visual aids were not proscribed in places where a suspect otherwise had exposed himself to public view, United States v. Lace, 669 F.2d 46 (2d Cir.1982). Would you agree that use of a telescope may violate *Katz?*

The court found no constitutional violation in United States v. Mankani, 738 F.2d 538 (2d Cir.1984), where a Federal agent managed to overhear conversations in an adjoining hotel room through a pre-existing hole in the wall. The court reasoned that the agent had a legal right to be in the adjoining room and that the transitory nature of a hotel diminished the expectation of privacy that a person may rely upon while there. Would this reasoning have authorized the agent to drill a hole?

If the police officer shines a flashlight into a darkened car, is that a search? Can it be argued that the flashlight does not prejudice the citizen, since it merely provides the officer with information that could be obtained from sensory perception? See Texas v. Brown, 460 U.S. 730 (1983) ("the use of artificial means to illuminate a darkened area simply does not constitute a search, and thus triggers no Fourth Amendment protection").

In Dow Chemical Co. v. United States, 476 U.S. 227 (1986), Government officials flew over Dow's commercial property, and used a $22,000 camera to take pictures of the areas between Dow's buildings. The photographs could be magnified so that objects one-half inch in diameter could be seen. Chief Justice Burger, writing for the Court, relied on *Knotts* and *Oliver* and held that Dow had no privacy interest in the area between its buildings, at least not from aerial surveillance, and therefore the use of the camera was not a search. The majority noted that "surveillance of private property by using highly sophisticated surveillance equipment not generally available to the public, such as satellite technology, might be constitutionally proscribed absent a warrant." However, the Court found that the photographs at issue did not rise to that level. The Chief Justice stated that "the mere fact that human vision is enhanced somewhat, at least to the degree here, does not give rise to constitutional problems," and that "Fourth Amendment cases must be decided on the facts of each case, not by extravagant generalizations."

Justice Powell, joined by Justices Brennan, Marshall, and Blackmun, dissented. Justice Powell argued that the Government activity constituted a search, because the magnification gave information that could not have been obtained through the senses. Is *Dow* based on the fact that the photographic magnification would never be problematic, or on the fact that Dow had no expectation of privacy in the first place in the area that was observed? If the citizen has no expectation of privacy that would be implicated by a government investigation, why would it matter if the government used high-tech surveillance techniques? Can *Dow Chemical* be squared with *Kyllo*?

6. *Investigative Activity Conducted by Private Citizens*

a. *Private Activity*

The Fourth Amendment, along with other protections in the Bill of Rights, is intended to regulate state actors. Consequently, a search or seizure conducted by a private citizen is not a "search or seizure" within the meaning of the Fourth Amendment. In Burdeau v. McDowell, 256 U.S. 465 (1921), the Supreme Court held that private papers stolen from office safes that were blown open, and a desk that was forced open, could be presented to a grand jury by a government prosecutor, because the search was conducted by private parties and so it was not a violation of the Fourth Amendment. The Court noted that the victim of the thefts had a private right of action against the thieves, but refused to bar the government from using the evidence. Justice Brandeis, joined by Justice Holmes, dissented. See also United States v. Young, 153 F.3d 1079 (9th Cir.1998) (Fourth Amendment not implicated where Federal Express employee opened a suspicious package, discovered contraband, and turned it over to law enforcement officers).

Mixed Public and Private Action

Courts have found the Fourth Amendment to apply if a private individual is acting, under the circumstances, as an agent for the government. Government officials may not avoid Fourth Amendment requirements by enlisting private individuals to do what government officials cannot. See United States v. Walther, 652 F.2d 788 (9th Cir.1981) (airline employee acted as government agent when he expected a DEA reward for his actions and the agency had encouraged him). Yet it is often difficult to determine when such an agency, or joint venture, has been established.

Relevant Factors for Determining Agency

Whenever a claim is made that a private person is acting as a police agent, the question is whether the private person believed at the time of a search or seizure that her action had been explicitly or implicitly requested or required by police or other government agents, who had reason to know that their actions might well give rise to such belief or that such a belief existed. If the belief existed and the government had reason to know that it might or actually did exist, the search by the private person will come within the reach of the Fourth Amendment.

For example, in Skinner v. Railway Labor Executives' Ass'n, 489 U.S. 602 (1989), the Court held that drug-testing procedures promulgated by private railroad companies, pursuant to Federal regulations granting authority to the railroads, implicated the Fourth Amendment. The government had mandated that the railroads not bargain away the drug-testing authority granted by the Federal regulations. Also, the Federal regulations made plain a strong preference for testing as well as the government's desire to have access to the results. The Court held that the Fourth Amendment could be applicable even if the government does not actually compel a search by a private party. The Court found "clear indices of the Government's encouragement, endorsement, and participation" sufficient to make the drug testing a government search regulated by the Fourth Amendment. See also United States v. Pierce, 893 F.2d 669 (5th Cir.1990) (for a search by a private person to trigger Fourth Amendment protection, the government must have known about the search in advance, and the private party must be acting for law enforcement purposes).

b. Government Investigative Activity Subsequent to Private and Other Legal Searches

Limits Imposed by the Initial Search: Walter v. United States

Difficult questions can arise when government agents follow up on a private search. Walter v. United States, 447 U.S. 649 (1980), divided the Court on the question whether FBI agents, who received a package of films from a recipient to whom it was misdelivered by a private carrier, could view the films without a warrant. The recipient had opened the package but had not viewed the films. Justice Stevens' opinion, joined by Justice Stewart, concluded that "the unauthorized exhibition of the films constituted an unreasonable invasion of their owner's constitutionally protected interest in privacy," and that "an officer's authority to possess a package is distinct from his authority to examine its contents." Hence, although the agents could receive the films, they could not view them without a warrant, even though a private person not covered by the Fourth Amendment had opened the package. These Justices reasoned that "[a] partial invasion of privacy cannot automatically justify a total invasion." Justice White, joined by Justice Brennan, concurred in part and disagreed with a footnote of Justice Stevens that left open the question "whether the Government projection of the films would have infringed any Fourth Amendment interest if private parties had projected the films before turning them over to the Government." Justice White agreed that a search by private persons could provide probable cause for a warrant, but said it could not excuse the government from the warrant requirement for its own search. Apparently, both opinions agreed that what the FBI observed in plain view was properly observed. Justice Marshall concurred in the judgment without opinion. Justice Blackmun's dissent, joined by Chief Justice Burger and Justices Powell and Rehnquist, argued "that, by the time the FBI received the films, these petitioners had no remaining expectation of privacy in their contents."

Reopening Permitted: United States v. Jacobsen

The extent to which government agents may search or seize evidence following searches by private individuals again divided the Court in United States v. Jacobsen, 466 U.S. 109 (1984). A Federal Express supervisor asked an office manager to examine a package that had been torn by a fork lift. Inside a cardboard outer container, the supervisor and manager found, cushioned by five or six pieces of crumpled newspaper, a ten-inch long tube wrapped with the kind of silver tape used on basement ducts. They cut open the tube and found a series of zip-lock bags that contained white powder; they then put the bags back into the tube and closed but did not reseal the tube. They notified the Drug Enforcement Administration of their finding, and an agent arrived at the office, reopened the tube, opened the zip-lock bags, removed a trace of the powder from each, did a "field test," and discovered that the powder was cocaine.

The Court sustained the agent's actions. Justice Stevens' opinion commanded six votes. He reasoned that the Federal Express employees' actions were not covered by the Fourth Amendment and that *Walter* required an analysis of the extent to which the government exceeded the bounds of the private search.

Justice Stevens observed that there was no Fourth Amendment violation in the employees' describing what they saw and reasoned as follows: when the officer first saw the package he knew that it contained "nothing of significance except a tube containing plastic bags and, ultimately, white powder"; "a manual inspection of the tube and its contents would not tell [the officer] anything more than he already had been told"; the only reason for the inspection was to avoid "the risk of a flaw in the employees' recollection," which did not involve an infringing of privacy rights; the removal of the plastic bags from the tube and the officer's visual inspection "enabled the agent to learn nothing that had not previously been learned during the private search"; the officer's seizure was reasonable since the package already had been opened, it remained unsealed, and the employees invited the agent to inspect its contents; and the warrantless seizure of the bags was reasonable on the ground that they probably contained contraband.

Finally, Justice Stevens reasoned that the field test—to determine only one thing, whether the powder was cocaine—compromised "no legitimate privacy interest." This portion of his opinion, discussed earlier in this Chapter, reasoned that a citizen has no legitimate expectation of privacy in contraband, and therefore an investigation cannot constitute a search if it can only determine whether a substance is contraband or not.

Justice White concurred in part and in the judgment. He argued that the effect of the Court's decision was to permit police to break into a locked car, suitcase, or even a house, if a private person previously did so and reported what he found to the police. Justice White concluded that a warrant should be required in these cases. Justice Brennan, joined by Justice Marshall, dissented and agreed with Justice White's criticism of the majority opinion.

In thinking about the majority's approach in *Jacobsen*, consider whether it really is important that the employees told the agent that the package contained only the bags with the powder. Justice Stevens states that there was nothing of significance in the package other than the bags. On these facts, he probably is correct. What, however, if the newspapers had not been crumpled, or if something else was in the package besides the bags? Does the agent decide what is significant? Or should a magistrate decide?

Police Entry Into a Residence After Private Entry

Justice White, dissenting in *Jacobsen*, assailed the majority opinion on the ground that it would permit police officers to enter a home without a warrant or probable cause, simply because some private citizen (even a trespasser or robber) had done so. Lower courts after *Jacobsen* have encountered fact situations similar to Justice White's hypothetical, and have sought to impose some limits on the *Jacobsen* principle in the context of a search of a residence. In United States v. Paige, 136 F.3d 1012 (5th Cir.1998), roofers working on Paige's house inadvertently damaged a section of siding on the house. They went into Paige's garage to look for additional siding to replace it. Paige had told them to go to the garage if they needed anything. A worker looking for siding crawled up into the attic space of the garage, and discovered marijuana. A narcotics detective was eventually summoned, and he did the same investigation as had the worker. The detective's discovery of the marijuana was challenged as an illegal search.

The government in *Paige* relied on *Jacobsen* for the broad proposition "that a police officer's search is constitutionally permissible so long as his search does not exceed the scope of a prior private-party search." But the Court refused to treat *Jacobsen* as an "inflexible rule" when applied to an officer's search of a residence. The Court explained as follows:

Unlike the package at issue in *Jacobsen*, which contained "nothing but contraband," people's homes contain countless personal, non-contraband possessions. Certainly, a homeowner's legitimate and significant privacy expectation in these possessions cannot be entirely frustrated simply because, ipso facto, a private party (e.g., an exterminator, a carpet cleaner, or a roofer) views some of those possessions. Because *Jacobsen* was concerned primarily with measuring "the scope of a private search of a mail package, the entire contents of which were obvious," *Jacobsen's* holding [should not be extended] to cases involving private searches of residences. A decision any other way would make the government the undeserving recipient of considerable private information of a home's contents strictly through application of an inflexible rule. We refuse to reward the government with such a windfall * * *.

The *Paige* court decided that the concept of *foreseeability* would provide an appropriate limit on law enforcement investigative activity occurring after a private search.

[W]e find that the proper Fourth Amendment inquiry, when confronted with a police search of a home that extends no further than a previously-conducted private party search, is to determine whether the homeowner or occupant continues to possess a reasonable expectation of privacy after the private search occurs. In making this determination, consideration must be given to whether the activities of the home's occupants or the circumstances within the home at the time of the private search created a risk of intrusion by the private party that was reasonably foreseeable. If indeed the private party's intrusion was reasonably foreseeable (based on such activities or circumstances), the occupant will no longer possess a reasonable expectation of privacy in the area or thing searched, and the subsequent police search will not trigger the Fourth Amendment. If, however, the private party's initial intrusion was not reasonably foreseeable, the occupant's reasonable expectation of privacy will survive, and the subsequent police search will indeed activate the Fourth Amendment.

Applying this foreseeability concept to the facts, the *Paige* Court found that the workers' intrusion into the attic of Paige's garage was reasonably foreseeable, and therefore the officer's later inspection of the same space did not constitute a search.

In the instant case, both Paige's conduct and the circumstances of the situation created a risk of intrusion into his garage's attic that was reasonably foreseeable. Paige himself had hired W.R. Cox Enterprises to repair his roof, and the roofing employees' search for siding began only after they inadvertently damaged the side of his home. Accidents of this type, related to the task at hand and arising contemporaneously therewith, are reasonably expected to occur. * * * Paige had advised the workers that they could go into the garage if they needed "anything;" moreover, Paige had specifically directed the workers to the garage and pointed out various tools and supplies they could access. * * * Given that [the worker's] entry into the garage was thus sufficiently justified, we do not find unreasonable [the worker's] decision to explore the attic, as it was rational to believe that siding could be stored there. * * * Both the conduct of Paige, and the circumstances of the situation, made these intrusions reasonably foreseeable. Consequently, we find that Detective Croft's subsequent examination of the attic did not qualify as a "search" for Fourth Amendment purposes.

When would a private entry not be "foreseeable", so as to limit a subsequent entry by police officers?

Controlled Deliveries: Illinois v. Andreas

Jacobsen establishes that if an initial intrusion (at least into a container) is not covered by the Fourth Amendment, a later intrusion by police officers to the same extent is also free from Fourth Amendment constraints. While *Jacobsen* dealt with an initial search to which the Fourth Amendment did not apply, its principle has been held equally applicable when initial searches of containers are valid under the Fourth Amendment. For example, in Illinois v. Andreas, 463 U.S. 765 (1983), government agents conducted a legal customs search of a wooden crate that was being shipped to an address in the United States, and found drugs hidden in a table therein. They then resealed the crate, and followed it to its destination using a surveillance process called a "controlled delivery." Surveilling police ultimately saw Andreas drag the container into his apartment; when he re-emerged with it 30 to 45 minutes later, the agents searched the container without a warrant. Chief Justice Burger, writing for the Court, reasoned that "the simple act of resealing the container to enable the police to make a controlled delivery does not operate to revive or restore the lawfully invaded privacy rights." Thus, the reopening of the container was not a search, because no legitimate expectation of privacy existed in the container at that time.

What if Andreas came out with the crate two days later? If a customs official legally searches a suitcase, can government agents search the same suitcase without a warrant a year later? In *Andreas,* Chief Justice Burger recognized that there may be a gap in surveillance, during which "it is possible that the container will be put to other uses—for example, the contraband may be removed or other items may be placed inside." He concluded, however, that the Fourth Amendment would be applicable to a subsequent reopening only if there is "a substantial likelihood that the contents of the container have been changed during the gap in surveillance." Otherwise, "there is no legitimate expectation of privacy in the contents of a container previously opened under lawful authority." On the facts, the Court found that the re-opening did not implicate a revived privacy interest, due to the unusual size of the container, its specialized purpose, and the relatively short time that Andreas had the container in his apartment.

7. *Foreign Officials*

Courts have uniformly held that "[e]vidence obtained by foreign police officials from searches conducted in their country is generally admissible * * * regardless of whether the search complied with the Fourth Amendment." United States v. Behety, 32 F.3d 503 (11th Cir.1994). This is because searches by foreign officials do not constitute the kind of "state action" that is circumscribed by the Bill of Rights. There are, however, two very limited exceptions to this general rule. These exceptions are set forth by the court in United States v. Barona, 56 F.3d 1087 (9th Cir.1995):

> One exception * * * occurs if the circumstances of the foreign search and seizure are so extreme that they shock the judicial conscience, so that a federal appellate court in the exercise of its supervisory powers can require exclusion of the evidence. This type of exclusion is not based on our Fourth Amendment jurisprudence, but rather on the recognition that we may employ our supervisory powers when absolutely necessary to preserve the integrity of the criminal justice system. * * *

> The second exception * * * applies when United States agents' participation in the investigation is so substantial that the action is a joint venture between United States and foreign officials.

A suggested approach for identifying foreign searches subject to American constitutional restraints is offered in Saltzburg, The Reach of the Bill of Rights Beyond the Terra Firma of the United States, 20 Va.J.Int'l L. 741 (1980).

Even if the foreign search is conducted by or at the behest of American officials, it will not implicate the Fourth Amendment if the victim of the search is a non-resident alien. In United States v. Verdugo–Urquidez, 494 U.S. 259 (1990), discussed earlier in the Chapter, the Court held that non-resident aliens lack sufficient connection with this Country to be considered as part of "the people" covered by the Fourth Amendment.

8. *Jails, Prison Cells, and Convicts*

Chief Justice Burger wrote for the Court in Hudson v. Palmer, 468 U.S. 517 (1984), as it held that a prisoner has no constitutionally protected expectation of privacy in his prison cell or in papers or property in his cell. Therefore, the Fourth Amendment was not implicated when prison officials rummaged through Hudson's cell and personal effects and destroyed some of his property in the course of their conduct. The Court concluded that "[t]he uncertainty that attends random searches of cells renders these searches perhaps the most effective weapon of the prison administrator in the constant fight against the proliferation of knives and guns, illicit drugs, and other contraband." It added that prison officials must be free to seize any articles from cells when necessary to serve legitimate institutional interests.

Justice Stevens, joined by Justices Brennan, Marshall and Blackmun, dissented. He did not disagree that prison officials should be able to conduct random searches to protect prison security, but he took exception to the holding that "no matter how malicious, destructive or arbitrary a cell search and seizure may be, it cannot constitute an unreasonable invasion of any privacy or possessory interest that society is prepared to recognize as reasonable." In his opinion, "[t]o hold that a prisoner's possession of a letter from his wife, or a picture of his baby, has no protection against arbitrary or malicious perusal, seizure or destruction would not * * * comport with any civilized standard of decency."

Justice Stevens noted that the majority's holding was limited to a prisoner's papers and effects located in his cell, and that the Court apparently "believes that at least a prisoner's person is secure from unreasonable search and seizure." In Bell v. Wolfish, 441 U.S. 520 (1979), the Court stated that at best prisoners have a reasonable expectation of privacy "of diminished scope" and that strip searches and body cavity searches of pretrial detainees after contact visits were governed by the Fourth Amendment but were reasonable under the circumstances.

9. *Public Schools and Public Employees*

In New Jersey v. T.L.O., 469 U.S. 325 (1985), the Court rejected a state's arguments that students have no legitimate expectation of privacy when they attend public schools. Although the Court recognized the need for schools to maintain discipline, it declined to apply its decision in the prisoner case, Hudson v. Palmer, *supra*, to the school context. Justice White wrote for the Court and stated that "[w]e are not yet ready to hold that the schools and the prisons need be equated for purposes of the Fourth Amendment." His opinion also rejected the state's suggestion that a student is free to maintain any privacy interest in personal property simply by leaving the property at home. The opinion concluded that "schoolchildren may find it necessary to carry with them a variety of legitimate, noncontraband items, and there is no reason to conclude that they have necessarily waived all rights to privacy in such items merely by bringing them onto school grounds."

It is important to remember however, that a finding of a legitimate expectation of privacy is simply the first step in the Fourth Amendment inquiry. If the citizen has a legitimate expectation of privacy, then the official intrusion is reviewed for its reasonableness. In *T.L.O.*, the Court held that the school official's inspection of a student's handbag was a search, but concluded that the search was reasonable because the official could reasonably suspect that the student had cigarettes in her bag.

The Supreme Court in O'Connor v. Ortega, 480 U.S. 709 (1987), unanimously rejected an argument that governmental employees "can never have a reasonable expectation of privacy in their place of work," although the Justices could not agree on an opinion for the Court. State hospital officials, investigating various charges made against a psychiatrist, entered the psychiatrist's office and seized various items from his desk and file cabinets. The psychiatrist brought a civil rights action against the officials, claiming that they had violated his Fourth Amendment rights.

Justice O'Connor's plurality opinion, joined by Chief Justice Rehnquist and Justices White and Powell, declined to decide whether the psychiatrist had a reasonable expectation of privacy in his office, but found that he definitely had one in his desk and file cabinets. The plurality concluded "that public employers' intrusions upon the constitutionally protected privacy interests of government employees for noninvestigatory, work-related purposes, as well as for investigations of work-related misconduct should be judged by the standard of reasonableness under all the circumstances." Applying those reasonableness standards, Justice O'Connor found that the search of the public employee's office was permissible because investigating officials had reasonable suspicion to believe that the employee had stolen government property.

Justice Scalia concurred in the judgment. He objected to the vagueness of the plurality opinion and "would hold * * * that the offices of government employees, and *a fortiori* the drawers and files within those offices, are covered by the Fourth Amendment protections as a general matter. (The qualification is necessary to cover such unusual situations as that in which the office is subject to unrestricted public access * * *.)" But, Justice Scalia also "would hold that government searches to retrieve work-related materials or to investigate violations of workplace rules—searches of the sort that are regarded as reasonable and normal in the private-employer context—do not violate the Fourth Amendment." He agreed with Justice O'Connor that the search in the instant case was reasonable because officials had reasonable suspicion to believe that the employee had stolen property.

Justice Blackmun, joined by Justices Brennan, Marshall, and Stevens, dissented in *Ortega.* The dissenters agreed with Justice Scalia's view that government employees had a reasonable expectation of privacy in their offices. But they argued that the reasonableness of the search should be judged by standards of probable cause rather than the lesser standards of reasonable suspicion.

10. Re-cap on Limitations Wrought by Katz

At the time of *Katz,* there was general agreement that traditional entries and inspections by law enforcement officers were regulated by the Fourth Amendment, and that the *Katz* test was designed to limit government activity at the margins, such as in the use of electronic surveillance. Since *Katz,* however, the courts have often used the expectation of privacy test to limit Fourth Amendment protection, so that much law enforcement activity that *looks like* a search (as that word would be commonly understood) is not in fact a search for Fourth Amendment purposes. Recall *Greenwood* and *Hudson,* where the police rummaged through property, and yet the activity in each case was found not to be a search.

The contraction of Fourth Amendment protection after *Katz* is brought into sharp relief by Professor Sundby in "Everyman's" Fourth Amendment: Privacy or Mutual Trust Between Government and Citizen?, 94 Colum.L.Rev.1751, 1789 (1994):

> To see just how far afield the Court has strayed, it is instructive to imagine compiling the Court's holdings concerning when the Fourth Amendment applies or, more accurately, does not apply into an *"Accidental Tourist's Guide to Maintaining Privacy Against Government Surveillance."* The advice would be rather astonishing:

>> To maintain privacy, one must not write any checks nor make any phone calls. It would be unwise to engage in conversation with any other person, or to walk, even on private property, outside one's house. If one is to barbecue or read in the backyard, do so only if surrounded by a fence higher than a double-decker bus and while sitting beneath an opaque awning. The wise individual might also consider purchasing anti-aerial spying devices if available (be sure to check the latest Sharper Image catalogue). Upon retiring inside, be sure to pull the shades together tightly so that no crack exists and to converse only in quiet tones. When discarding letters or other delicate materials * * * take the trash personally to the disposal site and bury it deep within. Finally, when buying items, carefully inspect them for any electronic tracking devices that may be attached.

Professor Sundby argues that in severely restricting the scope of the Fourth Amendment as it has, the Court might have been influenced "by the fact that the privacy interests they are examining in these cases are not those of Farmer McGregor raising corn in the back forty or tending sheep in the barn, but involve activities like the cultivation of marijuana and the running of an amphetamine laboratory." Similarly, Professor Maclin has argued that the Court, "if pushed" would acknowledge that people have a legitimate expectation of privacy in many kinds of activities; however, the Court has used *Katz* to limit Fourth Amendment protection because it "assumes that these intrusions will only happen" to people engaged in criminal activity, and trusts the police to target the right people. See Maclin, Justice Thurgood Marshall, Taking the Fourth Amendment Seriously, 77 Cornell L.Rev. 723, 745 (1992). Others have hypothesized that the Court has defined the "reasonableness" of an expectation of privacy to include the need for effective law enforcement. See Bookspan, Reworking the Warrant Requirement: Resuscitating the Fourth Amendment, 44 Vand.L.Rev.473, 495 (1991) (attributing the Court's "definitional limitations" on what constitutes a search in part to "a desire to allow more aggressive police investigative methods" to combat crime).

What is your view of the *Katz* line of cases? Do you think that the Court has got it about right, given the general lack of privacy in modern society? Would these cases have been decided differently if they were all civil cases brought by innocent victims of intrusive government surveillance? If so, does this tell you anything about the merits of the exclusionary rule, as compared to a civil remedy for an officer's violation of a citizen's Fourth Amendment rights?

III. THE TENSION BETWEEN THE REASONABLENESS AND THE WARRANT CLAUSES

A. THE IMPORTANCE OF THE WARRANT CLAUSE GENERALLY

Today it is well established that searches and seizures conducted without a warrant are presumed to be unreasonable. The language of the Court is that "searches conducted outside the judicial process, without prior approval by judge or magistrate are *per se* unreasonable under the Fourth Amendment—subject only to a few specifically established and well-delineated exceptions." Katz v. United States, 389 U.S. 347, 357 (1967). The Court has deemed this "a cardinal principle" of Fourth Amendment law. Mincey v. Arizona, 437 U.S. 385 (1978).

But the vision of a tough, sweeping per se warrant rule yielding only to the most demanding claims for exceptions is at odds with reality. Despite the Court's ringing language, the so-called per se rule can be restated as follows:

> A search and seizure in some circumstances is presumed to be unconstitutional if no prior warrant is obtained, but in other circumstances the prior warrant is unnecessary to justify a search and seizure.

The line of demarcation is most difficult to draw. Undoubtedly, there is a per se rule that applies in *some* situations, but it would be gross exaggeration for anyone to suggest even that most searches and seizures require a warrant. As Justice Scalia stated in his concurring opinion in California v. Acevedo, 500 U.S. 565 (1991), the Court's jurisprudence with respect to the warrant requirement has "lurched back and forth between imposing a categorical warrant requirement and looking to reasonableness alone." According to Justice Scalia, the result is that the warrant requirement has become "so riddled with exceptions that it [is] basically unrecognizable."

B. THE REASON FOR THE WARRANT REQUIREMENT

The following case is probably the Supreme Court's most thorough explication and justification of the warrant requirement. It lays the foundation of the current "per se" rule that warrants are required for searches and seizures, subject to "a few carefully delineated" exceptions.

JOHNSON v. UNITED STATES

Supreme Court of the United States, 1948.
333 U.S. 10.

Mr. Justice Jackson **delivered the opinion of the Court.**

Petitioner was convicted of four counts charging violation of federal narcotic laws. The only question which brings the case here is whether it was lawful, without a warrant of any kind, to arrest petitioner and to search her living quarters.

Taking the Government's version of disputed events, decision would rest on these facts:

At about 7:30 p.m. Detective Lieutenant Belland, an officer of the Seattle police force narcotic detail, received information from a confidential informer, who was also a known narcotic user, that unknown persons were smoking opium in the Europe Hotel.

The informer was taken back to the hotel to interview the manager, but he returned at once saying he could smell burning opium in the hallway. Belland communicated with federal narcotic agents and between 8:30 and 9 o'clock went back to the hotel with four such agents. All were experienced in narcotic work and recognized at once a strong odor of burning opium which to them was distinctive and unmistakable. The odor led to Room 1. The officers did not know who was occupying that room. They knocked and a voice inside asked who was there. "Lieutenant Belland," was the reply. There was a slight delay, some "shuffling or noise" in the room and then the defendant opened the door. The officer said, "I want to talk to you a little bit." She then, as he describes it, "stepped back acquiescently and admitted us." He said, "I want to talk to you about this opium smell in the room here." She denied that there was such a smell. Then he said, "I want you to consider yourself under arrest because we are going to search the room." The search turned up incriminating opium and smoking apparatus, the latter being warm, apparently from recent use. This evidence the District Court refused to suppress before trial and admitted over defendant's objection at the trial. Conviction resulted and the Circuit Court of Appeals affirmed.

The defendant challenged the search of her home as a violation of the rights secured to her, in common with others, by the Fourth Amendment to the Constitution.

I

* * *

Entry to defendant's living quarters, which was the beginning of the search, was demanded under color of office. It was granted in submission to authority rather than as an understanding and intentional waiver of a constitutional right.

At the time entry was demanded the officers were possessed of evidence which a magistrate might have found to be probable cause for issuing a search warrant. * * * If the presence of odors is testified to before a magistrate and he finds the affiant qualified to know the odor, and it is one sufficiently distinctive to identify a forbidden substance, * * * it might very well be found to be evidence of most persuasive character.

The point of the Fourth Amendment, which often is not grasped by zealous officers, is not that it denies law enforcement the support of the usual inferences which reasonable men draw from evidence. Its protection consists in requiring that those inferences be drawn by a neutral and detached magistrate instead of being judged by the officer engaged in the often competitive enterprise of ferreting out crime. Any assumption that evidence sufficient to support a magistrate's disinterested determination to issue a search warrant will justify the officers in making a search without a warrant would reduce the Amendment to a nullity and leave the people's homes secure only in the discretion of police officers. Crime, even in the privacy of one's own quarters, is, of course, of grave concern to society, and the law allows such crime to be reached on proper showing. The right of officers to thrust themselves into a home is also a grave concern, not only to the individual but to a society which chooses to dwell in reasonable security and freedom from surveillance. When the right of privacy must reasonably yield to the right of search is, as a rule, to be decided by a judicial officer, not by a policeman or government enforcement agent.

There are exceptional circumstances in which, on balancing the need for effective law enforcement against the right of privacy, it may be contended that a magistrate's warrant for search may be dispensed with. But this is not such a case. No reason is offered for not obtaining a search warrant except the inconvenience to the officers and some slight delay necessary to prepare papers and present the evidence to a magistrate. These are never very convincing reasons and, in these circumstances, certainly are not enough to by-pass the constitutional requirement. No suspect was fleeing or likely to take flight. The search was of permanent premises, not of a movable vehicle. No evidence or contraband was threatened with removal or destruction, except perhaps the fumes which we suppose in time would disappear. But they were not capable at any time of being reduced to possession for presentation to court. The evidence of their existence before the search was adequate and the testimony of the officers to that effect would not perish from the delay of getting a warrant.

If the officers in this case were excused from the constitutional duty of presenting their evidence to a magistrate, it is difficult to think of a case in which it should be required.

II

[The Court held that the officers had no probable cause to arrest the defendant until they entered the defendant's quarters, and reasoned that the search (entry and visual inspection) preceded the arrest. It was not possible, therefore, to justify the officers' conduct on a search incident to a valid arrest theory. Justices Black, Reed, and Burton, together with Chief Justice Vinson, dissented without opinion.]

Note on Johnson

Johnson represents a victory for those who would have the police secure warrants. As the majority intimates, there almost certainly was enough evidence known to the police to justify a magistrate's issuance of a warrant. Yet, because no warrant was sought, the search is deemed constitutionally "unreasonable" or invalid. Why is this the correct result? If you would answer that the framers assumed that warrants generally would be required, you must recognize that those same framers were familiar with warrantless searches incident to arrest and therefore presumably had in mind that some searches would not require warrants. Could *Johnson* have been viewed as a case in which no warrant was necessary?

C. THE FUNCTION OF THE WARRANT REQUIREMENT

Professor Amsterdam has made the following suggestion:

Indiscriminate searches or seizures might be thought to be bad for either or both of two reasons. The first is that they expose people and their possessions to interferences by government when there is no good reason to do so. The concern here is against *unjustified* searches and seizures: it rests upon the principle that every citizen is entitled to security of his person and property unless and until an adequate justification for disturbing that security is shown. The second is that indiscriminate searches and seizures are conducted at the discretion of executive officials, who may act despotically and capriciously in the exercise of the power to search and seize. This latter concern runs against arbitrary searches and seizures: it condemns the petty tyranny of unregulated rummagers.

Perspectives on the Fourth Amendment, 58 Minn.L.Rev. 349, 411 (1974).

With searches and seizures that are subject to the warrant requirement, probable cause represents the threshold of proof that must be satisfied before the power to search and seize is legitimated. The existence of such a proof requirement strongly suggests that the government must be able to demonstrate a factually-based interest in people, places or things *before* using its power to disturb them. The proof requirement protects against *unjustified* searches and seizures.

Related to the proof requirement are the "Oath or affirmation" and particularity provisions of the Amendment. Probable cause is to be shown by persons willing to swear to or affirm the truth of their statements and thus to be held accountable for their representations. In addition, the applicant for the warrant is committing to a public record the information that is known *before* the search so that, after the search takes place, there is no confusion between the ex-post and ex-ante positions of the applicant. Without an antecedent warrant requirement, an officer questioned about probable cause can work backwards from the search, and fill in the facts as if they were known beforehand.

The specificity requirement implies that the government can only interfere with those persons, places or things that it has shown a valid interest in. Here, too, the written record made in advance of the search may decrease the danger that after a search is completed, the police will claim that whatever is found is exactly what was sought. Also, the specification of objects sought to be seized may inform the magistrate's decision on whether the proposed search is reasonable or excessive. A showing of probable cause, then, does not mean any search and seizure authorized by a warrant is valid; it means that any search and seizure directed by warrant at the people, places, or things to which the probable cause specifically relates satisfies the warrant clause of the Fourth Amendment. These limitations guard against what Amsterdam called *arbitrary* searches and seizures.

By placing a magistrate between the citizen and the police, the Amendment, in the words of the *Johnson* majority, establishes that a neutral observer is to decide whether the probable cause and specificity requirements have been satisfied. This is one way in which the Amendment operates to prevent unjustified searches and seizures; the presumption is that a magistrate will make fewer errors than "the officer engaged in the often competitive enterprise of ferreting out crime." *Johnson*, 333 U.S., at 14.

By interposing the magistrate between the "competitors"—the police and the suspect—the Amendment may also serve another function. It may afford the neutral magistrate an opportunity to refuse a warrant, even if the application is supported by oath, probable cause and specifics, on the ground that a search and seizure is unreasonable under the circumstances. For example, if the police have probable cause to believe that A has marijuana cigarettes in his home, and if possession of small quantities of marijuana is punishable by fine only, a magistrate might be inclined to disapprove a warrant to search A's entire house on the ground that the scope of the search would be beyond what reasonable persons would accept in light of the government's minimal interests at stake. The same magistrate might be persuaded to permit a search of A's briefcase. Similarly, if the police obtain a warrant to search A's house on Monday and execute the warrant that same day, but find nothing, a magistrate might hesitate to issue another warrant to search on Tuesday, and perhaps another to look again on Wednesday, even if the police still have probable cause. Or, in an income tax evasion case, if the police asked for authority to search for and seize everything found in a home as evidence of an income greater than that recorded on a tax return, a magistrate might balk at issuing such a warrant. However, the same magistrate might authorize an entry into the house to take photographs. By imposing limitations on searches, a magistrate may prevent *excessive* governmental intrusions.

Another important function of the warrant requirement was identified by the Court in Illinois v. Gates, discussed later in this Chapter. The Court stated that "the possession of a warrant by officers conducting an arrest or search greatly reduces the perception of unlawful or intrusive police conduct, by assuring the individual whose property is searched or seized of the lawful authority of the executing officer, his need to search, and the limits of his power to search."

As you go through the remainder of the Chapter, see if you can identify other goals of the warrant requirement. Might one be to remind police of their obligation to comply with the legal constraints placed upon them? Could it also be argued that without the specific limitation of the warrant requirement, the Fourth Amendment's general command that a search be "reasonable" would be inherently ambiguous and subject to the case-by-case balancing of shifting majorities in the courts? Is it possible for the Supreme Court to give specific and principled guidance under the reasonableness clause?

The Warrant Requirement in Reality

The above discussion articulated a number of theoretically sound reasons for the warrant requirement. But does the warrant process, in practice, serve these purposes? For example, the Administrative Office of the United States Courts compiled statistics on warrants issued for electronic surveillance. The New York Times reported on these statistics as follows:

> The figures show that Federal and state judges are largely rubber stamps for law enforcement when it comes to electronic surveillance, despite all the talk of the need for an independent review by the courts of bugs and wiretaps. The last time a court denied a wiretap application was in 1988; all told, only 7 applications out of 8,950 since 1983 have been turned down.

Labaton, Before the Explosion, Officials Saw Little Risk for Building in Oklahoma City, New York Times, May 2, 1995, p. A19. What is the point of requiring a warrant if the warrant process is simply a formality as a practical matter? Could this be a reason for the Court's expansion of the exceptions to the warrant requirement? Is the Court attempting to focus the warrant requirement on those few areas in which a magistrate's determination might make a difference?

The exceptions to the warrant requirement will be considered shortly. Before reaching them, it is useful to understand what practical protections the warrant application procedure affords, so that you know what it really means to say that the warrant clause, with its dependence on the neutral magistrate, is a fundamental part of American freedom.

IV. OBTAINING A SEARCH WARRANT: CONSTITUTIONAL PREREQUISITES

A. DEMONSTRATING PROBABLE CAUSE

1. *Source Of Information On Which Probable Cause Is Based*

The Fourth Amendment mandates a showing of probable cause as justification for a search warrant. As noted above, this is the threshold proof requirement. The higher it is set, the greater the theoretical role of the magistrate in the warrant process and the protection against police searches and seizures. Scant attention was paid to the term probable cause until the 1960's, when two major cases were decided, Aguilar v. Texas, 378 U.S. 108 (1964) and Spinelli v. United States, 393 U.S. 410 (1969). *Spinelli* is set forth below; the earlier *Aguilar* decision is discussed in the majority opinion. Both of these cases deal with regulation of the source of information on which probable cause is based.

SPINELLI v. UNITED STATES

Supreme Court of the United States, 1969.
393 U.S. 410.

MR. JUSTICE HARLAN **delivered the opinion of the Court.**

William Spinelli was convicted * * * of traveling to St. Louis, Missouri, from a nearby Illinois suburb with the intention of conducting gambling activities proscribed by Missouri law. At every appropriate stage in the proceedings in the lower courts, the petitioner challenged the constitutionality of the warrant which authorized the FBI search that uncovered the evidence necessary for his conviction. * * *

In *Aguilar*, a search warrant had issued upon an affidavit of police officers who swore only that they had "received reliable information from a credible person and do believe" that narcotics were being illegally stored on the described premises. While recognizing that the constitutional requirement of probable cause can be satisfied by hearsay information, this Court held the affidavit inadequate for two reasons. First, the application failed to set forth any of the "underlying circumstances" necessary to enable the magistrate independently to judge of the validity of the informant's conclusion that the narcotics were where he said they were. Second, the affiant-officers did not attempt to support their claim that their informant was " 'credible' or his information 'reliable.' " The Government is, however, quite right in saying that the FBI affidavit in the present case is more ample than that in *Aguilar*. Not only does it contain a report from an anonymous informant, but it also contains a report of an independent FBI investigation which is said to corroborate the informant's tip. We are, then, required to delineate the manner in which *Aguilar's* two-pronged test should be applied in these circumstances.

In essence, the affidavit * * * contained the following allegations:[a]

1. The FBI had kept track of Spinelli's movements on five days during the month of August 1965. On four of

---

a. It is, of course, of no consequence that the agents might have had additional information which could have been given to the Commissioner. "It is elementary that in passing on the validity of a warrant, the reviewing court may consider *only* information brought to the magistrate's attention." Aguilar v. Texas, 378 U.S. 108, 109, n. 1 (emphasis in original). * * *

these occasions, Spinelli was seen crossing one of two bridges leading from Illinois into St. Louis, Missouri, between 11 a.m. and 12:15 p.m. On four of the five days, Spinelli was also seen parking his car in a lot used by residents of an apartment house at 1108 Indian Circle Drive in St. Louis, between 3:30 p.m. and 4:45 p.m. On one day, Spinelli was followed further and seen to enter a particular apartment in the building.

2. An FBI check with the telephone company revealed that this apartment contained two telephones listed under the name of Grace P. Hagen, and carrying the numbers WYdown 4–0029 and WYdown 4–0136.

3. The application stated that "William Spinelli is known to this affiant and to federal law enforcement agents and local law enforcement agents as a bookmaker, an associate of bookmakers, a gambler, and an associate of gamblers."

4. Finally, it was stated that the FBI "has been informed by a confidential reliable informant that William Spinelli is operating a handbook and accepting wagers and disseminating wagering information by means of the telephones which have been assigned the numbers WYdown 4–0029 and WYdown 4–0136."

There can be no question that the last item mentioned, detailing the informant's tip, has a fundamental place in this warrant application. Without it, probable cause could not be established. The first two items reflect only innocent-seeming activity and data. Spinelli's travels to and from the apartment building and his entry into a particular apartment on one occasion could hardly be taken as bespeaking gambling activity; and there is surely nothing unusual about an apartment containing two separate telephones. Many a householder indulges himself in this petty luxury. Finally, the allegation that Spinelli was "known" to the affiant and to other federal and local law enforcement officers as a gambler and an associate of gamblers is but a bald and unilluminating assertion of suspicion that is entitled to no weight in appraising the magistrate's decision.

So much indeed the Government does not deny. Rather, * * * the Government claims that the informant's tip gives a suspicious color to the FBI's reports detailing Spinelli's innocent-seeming conduct and that, conversely, the FBI's surveillance corroborates the informant's tip, thereby entitling it to more weight. It is true, of course that the magistrate is obligated to render a judgment based upon a common-sense reading of the entire affidavit. We believe, however, that the "totality of circumstances" approach taken by the Court of Appeals paints with too broad a brush. Where, as here, the informer's tip is a necessary element in a finding of probable cause, its proper weight must be determined by a more precise analysis.

The informer's report must first be measured against *Aguilar's* standards so that its probative value can be assessed. If the tip is found inadequate under *Aguilar*, the other allegations which corroborate the information contained in the hearsay report should then be considered. At this stage as well, however, the standards enunciated in *Aguilar* must inform the magistrate's decision. He must ask: Can it fairly be said that the tip, even when certain parts of it have been corroborated by independent sources, is as trustworthy as a tip which would pass *Aguilar's* tests without independent corroboration? *Aguilar* is relevant at this stage of the inquiry as well because the tests it establishes were designed to implement the long-standing principle that probable cause must be determined by a "neutral and detached magistrate," and not by "the officer engaged in the often competitive enterprise of ferreting out crime." Johnson v. United States, 333 U.S. 10 (1948). A magistrate cannot be said to have properly discharged his constitutional duty if he relies on an informer's tip which—even when partially corroborated—is not as reliable as one which passes *Aguilar's* requirements when standing alone.

Applying these principles to the present case, we first consider the weight to be given the informer's tip when it is considered apart from the rest of the affidavit. It is clear that a Commissioner could not credit it without abdicating his constitutional function. Though the affiant swore that his confidant was "reliable," he offered the magistrate no reason in support of this conclusion. Perhaps even more important is the fact that *Aguilar's* other test has not been satisfied. The tip does not contain a sufficient statement of the underlying circumstances from which the informer concluded that Spinelli was running a bookmaking operation. We are not told how the FBI's source received his information—it is not alleged that the informant personally observed Spinelli at work or that he had ever placed a bet with him. Moreover, if the informant came by the information indirectly, he did not explain why his sources were reliable. In the absence of a statement detailing the manner in which the information was gathered, it is especially important that the tip describe the accused's criminal activity in sufficient detail that the magistrate may know that he is relying on something more substantial than a casual rumor circulating in the underworld or an accusa-

tion based merely on an individual's general reputation.

The detail provided by the informant in Draper v. United States, 358 U.S. 307 (1959), provides a suitable benchmark. While Hereford, the Government's informer in that case, did not state the way in which he had obtained his information, he reported that Draper had gone to Chicago the day before by train and that he would return to Denver by train with three ounces of heroin on one of two specified mornings. Moreover, Hereford, went on to describe, with minute particularity, the clothes that Draper would be wearing upon his arrival at the Denver station. A magistrate, when confronted with such detail, could reasonably infer that the informant had gained his information in a reliable way.[b] Such an inference cannot be made in the present case. Here, the only facts supplied were that Spinelli was using two specified telephones and that these phones were being used in gambling operations. This meager report could easily have been obtained from an offhand remark heard at a neighborhood bar.

Nor do we believe that the patent doubts *Aguilar* raises as to the report's reliability are adequately resolved by a consideration of the allegations detailing the FBI's independent investigative efforts. At most, these allegations indicated that Spinelli could have used the telephones specified by the informant for some purpose. This cannot by itself be said to support both the inference that the informer was generally trustworthy and that he had made his charge against Spinelli on the basis of information obtained in a reliable way. Once

---

b. While *Draper* involved the question whether the police had probable cause for an arrest without a warrant, the analysis required for an answer to this question is basically similar to that demanded of a magistrate when he considers whether a search warrant should issue.

again, *Draper* provides a relevant comparison. Independent police work in that case corroborated much more than one small detail that had been provided by the informant. There, the police, upon meeting the inbound Denver train on the second morning specified by informer Hereford, saw a man whose dress corresponded precisely to Hereford's detailed description. It was then apparent that the informant had not been fabricating his report out of whole cloth; since the report was of the sort which in common experience may be recognized as having been obtained in a reliable way, it was perfectly clear that probable cause had been established.

We conclude, then, that in the present case the informant's tip—even when corroborated to the extent indicated—was not sufficient to provide the basis for a finding of probable cause. This is not to say that the tip was so insubstantial that it could not properly have counted in the magistrate's determination. Rather, it needed some further support. When we look to the other parts of the application, however, we find nothing alleged which would permit the suspicions engendered by the informant's report to ripen into a judgment that a crime was probably being committed. As we have already seen, the allegations detailing the FBI's surveillance of Spinelli and its investigation of the telephone company records contain no suggestion of criminal conduct when taken by themselves—and they are not endowed with an aura of suspicion by virtue of the informer's tip. Nor do we find that the FBI's reports take on a sinister color when read in light of common knowledge that bookmaking is often

carried on over the telephone and from premises ostensibly used by others for perfectly normal purposes. Such an argument would carry weight in a situation in which the premises contain an unusual number of telephones or abnormal activity is observed, but it does not fit this case where neither of these factors is present.[c] All that remains to be considered is the flat statement that Spinelli was "known" to the FBI and others as a gambler. But just as a simple assertion of police suspicion is not itself a sufficient basis for a magistrate's finding of probable cause, we do not believe it may be used to give additional weight to allegations that would otherwise be insufficient.

The affidavit, then, falls short of the standards set forth in *Aguilar, Draper,* and our other decisions that give content to the notion of probable cause. In holding as we have done, we do not retreat from the established propositions that only the probability, and not a prima facie showing, of criminal activity is the standard of probable cause; that affidavits of probable cause are tested by much less rigorous standards than those governing the admissibility of evidence at trial; that in judging probable cause issuing magistrates are not to be confined by niggardly limitations or by restrictions on the use of their common sense; and that their determination of probable cause should be paid great deference by reviewing courts. But we cannot sustain this warrant without diluting important safeguards that assure that the judgment of a disinterested judicial officer will interpose itself between the police and the citizenry.

* * *

c. A box containing three uninstalled telephones was found in the apartment, but only

after execution of the search warrant.

MR. JUSTICE MARSHALL took no part in the consideration or decision of this case.

MR. JUSTICE WHITE, concurring.

* * * An investigator's affidavit that he has seen gambling equipment being moved into a house at a specified address will support the issuance of a search warrant. The oath affirms the honesty of the statement and negatives the lie or imagination. Personal observation attests to the facts asserted— that there is gambling equipment on the premises at the named address.

But if the officer simply avers, without more, that there is gambling paraphernalia on certain premises, the warrant should not issue, even though the belief of the officer is an honest one, as evidenced by his oath, and even though the magistrate knows him to be an experienced, intelligent officer who has been reliable in the past. This much was settled in Nathanson v. United States, 290 U.S. 41 (1933), where the Court held insufficient an officer's affidavit swearing he had cause to believe that there was illegal liquor on the premises for which the warrant was sought. The unsupported assertion or belief of the officer does not satisfy the requirement of probable cause.

What is missing in *Nathanson* and like cases is a statement of the basis for the affiant's believing the facts contained in the affidavit—the good "cause" which the officer in *Nathanson* said he had. If an officer swears that there is gambling equipment at a certain address, the possibilities are (1) that he has seen the equipment; (2) that he has observed or perceived facts from which the presence of the equipment may reasonably be inferred; and (3) that he has obtained the information from someone else. If (1) is true, the affidavit is good. But in (2), the affidavit is insufficient unless the perceived facts are given, for it is the magistrate, not the officer, who is to judge the existence of probable cause. With respect to (3), where the officer's information is hearsay, no warrant should issue absent good cause for crediting that hearsay. Because an affidavit asserting, without more, the location of gambling equipment at a particular address does not claim personal observation of any of the facts by the officer, and because of the likelihood that the information came from an unidentified third party, affidavits of this type are unacceptable. * * *

If the affidavit rests on hearsay—an informant's report—what is necessary under *Aguilar* is one of two things: the informant must declare either (1) that he has himself seen or perceived the fact or facts asserted; or (2) that his information is hearsay, but there is good reason for believing it—perhaps one of the usual grounds for crediting hearsay information. The first presents few problems: since the report, although hearsay, purports to be first-hand observation, remaining doubt centers on the honesty of the informant, and that worry is dissipated by the officer's previous experience with the informant. The other basis for accepting the informant's report is more complicated. But if, for example, the informer's hearsay comes from one of the actors in the crime in the nature of admission against interest, the affidavit giving this information should be held sufficient.

I am inclined to agree with the majority that there are limited special circumstances in which an "honest" informant's report, if sufficiently detailed, will in effect verify itself—that is, the magistrate when confronted with such detail could reasonably infer that the informant had gained his information in a reliable way. * * *

So too in the special circumstances of Draper v. United States, 358 U.S. 307 (1959), the kind of information related by the informant is not generally sent ahead of a person's arrival in a city except to those who are intimately connected with making careful arrangements for meeting him. The informant, posited as honest, somehow had the reported facts, very likely from one of the actors in the plan, or as one of them himself. The majority's suggestion is that a warrant could have been obtained based only on the informer's report. I am inclined to agree, although it seems quite plain that if it may be so easily inferred from the affidavit that the informant has himself observed the facts or has them from an actor in the event, no possible harm could come from requiring a statement to that effect, thereby removing the difficult and recurring questions which arise in such situations.

Of course, *Draper* itself did not proceed on this basis. Instead, the Court pointed out that when the officer saw a person getting off the train at the specified time, dressed and conducting himself precisely as the informant had predicted, all but the critical fact with respect to possessing narcotics had then been verified and for that reason the officer had "reasonable grounds" to believe also that Draper was carrying narcotics. Unquestionably, verification of arrival time, dress, and gait reinforced the honesty of the informant—he had not reported a made-up story. But if what *Draper* stands for is that the existence of the tenth and critical fact is made sufficiently probable to justify the issuance of a warrant by verifying nine other facts coming from the same source, I have my doubts about that case.

In the first place, the proposition is not that the tenth fact may be logically inferred from the other nine or that the tenth fact is usually found in conjunction with the other nine. No one would suggest that just anyone getting off the 10:30 train dressed as Draper was, with a brisk walk and carrying a zipper bag, should be arrested for carrying narcotics. The thrust of *Draper* is not that the verified facts have independent significance with respect to proof of the tenth. The argument instead relates to the reliability of the source: because an informant is right about some things, he is more probably right about other facts, usually the critical, unverified facts.

But the Court's cases have already rejected for Fourth Amendment purposes the notion that the past reliability of an officer is sufficient reason for believing his current assertions. Nor would it suffice, I suppose, if a reliable informant states there is gambling equipment in Apartment 607 and then proceeds to describe in detail Apartment 201, a description which is verified before applying for the warrant. He was right about 201, but that hardly makes him more believable about the equipment in 607. But what if he states that there are narcotics locked in a safe in Apartment 300, which is described in detail, and the apartment manager verifies everything but the contents of the safe? I doubt that the report about the narcotics is made appreciably more believable by the verification. The informant could still have gotten his information concerning the safe from others about whom nothing is known or could have inferred the presence of narcotics from circumstances which a magistrate would find unacceptable.

The tension between *Draper* and the *Nathanson-Aguilar* line of cases is evident from the course followed by the majority opinion. First, it is held that the report from a reliable informant that Spinelli is using two telephones with specified numbers to conduct a gambling business plus Spinelli's reputation in police circles as a gambler does not add up to probable cause. This is wholly consistent with *Aguilar* and *Nathanson:* the informant did not reveal whether he had personally observed the facts or heard them from another and, if the latter, no basis for crediting the hearsay was presented. Nor were the facts, as Mr. Justice Harlan says, of such a nature that they normally would be obtainable only by the personal observation of the informant himself. The police, however, did not stop with the informant's report. Independently, they established the existence of two phones having the given numbers and located them in an apartment house which Spinelli was regularly frequenting away from his home. * * * The *Draper* approach would reasonably justify the issuance of a warrant in this case, particularly since the police had some awareness of Spinelli's past activities. The majority, however, while seemingly embracing *Draper,* confines that case to its own facts. Pending full-scale reconsideration of that case, on the one hand, or of the *Nathanson-Aguilar* cases on the other, I join the opinion of the Court and the judgment of reversal, especially since a vote to affirm would produce an equally divided Court.

MR. JUSTICE BLACK, **dissenting.**

In my view, this Court's decision in Aguilar v. Texas, 378 U.S. 108 (1964), was bad enough. That decision went very far toward elevating the magistrate's hearing for issuance of a search warrant to a full-fledged trial, where witnesses must be brought forward to attest personally to all the facts alleged. But not content with this, the Court today expands *Aguilar* to almost unbelievable proportions. * * * Nothing in our Constitution * * * requires that the facts be established with that degree of certainty and with such elaborate specificity before a policeman can be authorized by a disinterested magistrate to conduct a carefully limited search.

* * *

MR. JUSTICE FORTAS, **dissenting.**

* * *

A policeman's affidavit should not be judged as an entry in an essay contest. It is not "abracadabra." As the majority recognizes, a policeman's affidavit is entitled to common-sense evaluation. * * *

MR. JUSTICE STEWART, **dissenting.**

For substantially the reasons stated by my Brothers Black and Fortas, I believe the warrant in this case was supported by a sufficient showing of probable cause. * * *

Applying Spinelli

The majority in *Spinelli* appears to accept the following propositions:

a.   A police officer is presumed to be honest when making an affidavit. Thus, credibility of the officer is never to be questioned.

b.   What may be questioned, however, is the source of the officer's information.

c.   If the officer avers that she has first-hand knowledge of the facts used to demonstrate probable cause, the only question is whether the sworn facts are sufficient to meet the threshold. The magistrate is informed of what the officer knows and makes an independent determination of sufficiency.

d. If the officer is relying on someone else for part or all of the information, then it is necessary to make three additional determinations:

(i.) Who is the source of the information, and is the source reliable? Reliability is the first prong of the *Spinelli* test.

(ii.) What are the bases and details of the source's knowledge? Credible information is the second prong of the test.

(iii.) Assuming reliability of the source, are the facts, either standing alone or taken together with other facts provided by the affiant, sufficient to satisfy the proof threshold, probable cause?

e. If the source is not known to the police to be reliable under d, i, above, the police may be able to demonstrate reliability by corroborating the details provided by the informant. The Court in *Spinelli* required a substantial amount of corroboration in such circumstances. Corroborating the fact that Spinelli had two telephone lines in his apartment was not enough to eliminate the concerns about the informant's reliability.

f. If the informant's basis of information is unclear, it may be sufficient that the information is so detailed that it could only have come from the informant's personal observation and so it may satisfy d, ii, above.

g. If the information provided by the informant falls short of demonstrating probable cause, the police can gather other information to be included in the application for a warrant.

h. When the magistrate looks at all the information provided to assess whether probable cause is shown, she is to take a common sense approach to the application and ask whether the government has shown "the probability" of criminal activity.

Spinelli does not purport to deal with circumstances in which a crime victim or eyewitness reports an alleged crime immediately after he or she says it took place. It addresses warrant applications in which the police rely on tipsters who generally are not themselves personally involved as participants or witnesses in the very criminal activity they report, but who have an ongoing relationship with police. It is these informants whose reliability is most questionable.

The *Spinelli* majority shows a mistrust of informants. Is that justified? Consider an anecdote from Dallas, where informants were paid millions of dollars based on tips that certain people were carrying drugs. The informants would pick up migrant laborers, give them a backpack, and tell them to wait to be picked up at a certain corner, where they would be taken to a factory for employment for the day. The bag would contain a powdery substance with trace amounts of cocaine. Then the informants would "tip" the police that a person was standing at a street corner holding a backpack containing narcotics. The "tip" would include a detailed description of the person holding the bag. The scam was not uncovered until years later when the substances were retested and found to be largely ground up masonry, with only trace amounts of cocaine.

Whatever your own opinion is, you should know that *Spinelli* was not well received by law enforcement officials. This reaction was predictable, especially in view of the dissenters' warning that law enforcement efforts would suffer greatly from the majority's position. Also, the decision may have appeared to be more complicated and even more hostile to police than it was intended to be.

2. *Rejection of a Rigid Two–Pronged Test*

In the following case, the Court held that the two-pronged test of *Aguilar* and *Spinelli* would no longer control the determination of probable cause. Yet the Court took some pains to emphasize that the *Aguilar-Spinelli* structure still has continuing relevance when police rely in whole or in part on an informant's tip.

ILLINOIS v. GATES

Supreme Court of the United States, 1983.
462 U.S. 213.

JUSTICE REHNQUIST **delivered the opinion of the Court.**

Respondents Lance and Susan Gates were indicted for violation of state drug laws after police officers, executing a search warrant, discovered marijuana and other contraband in their automobile and home. Prior to trial the Gates' moved to suppress evidence seized during this search. The Illinois Supreme Court affirmed the decisions of lower state courts granting the motion. * * *

We granted certiorari to consider the application of the Fourth Amendment to a magistrate's issuance of a search warrant on the basis of a partially corroborated anonymous informant's tip. * * *

* * *

II

* * * Bloomingdale, Ill., is a suburb of Chicago located in DuPage County. On May 3, 1978, the Bloomingdale Police Department received by mail an anonymous handwritten letter which read as follows:

"This letter is to inform you that you have a couple in your town who strictly make their living on selling drugs. They are Sue and Lance Gates, they live on Greenway, off Bloomingdale Rd. in the condominiums. Most of their buys are done in Florida. Sue his wife drives their car to Florida, where she leaves it to be loaded up with drugs, then Lance flys down and drives it back. Sue flys back after she drops the car off in Florida. May 3 she is driving down there again and Lance will be flying down in a few days to drive it back. At the time Lance drives the car back he has the trunk loaded with over $100,000.00 in drugs. Presently they have over $100,000.00 worth of drugs in their basement.

They brag about the fact they never have to work, and make their entire living on pushers.

I guarantee if you watch them carefully you will make a big catch. They are friends with some big drugs dealers, who visit their house often.

Lance & Susan
Gates

Greenway

in Condominiums"

The letter was referred by the Chief of Police of the Bloomingdale Police Department to Detective Mader, who decided to pursue the tip. Mader learned, from the office of the Illinois Secretary of State, that an Illinois driver's license had been issued to one Lance Gates, residing at a stated address in Bloomingdale. He contacted a confidential informant, whose examination of certain financial records revealed a more recent address for the Gates, and he also learned from a police officer assigned to O'Hare Airport that "L. Gates" had made a reservation on Eastern Airlines flight 245 to West Palm Beach, Fla., scheduled to depart from Chicago on May 5 at 4:15 p.m.

Mader then made arrangements with an agent of the Drug Enforcement Administration for surveillance of the May 5 Eastern Airlines flight. The agent later reported to Mader that Gates had boarded the flight, and that federal agents in Florida had observed him arrive in West Palm Beach and take a taxi to the nearby Holiday Inn. They also reported that Gates went to a room registered to one Susan Gates and that, at 7:00 a.m. the next morning, Gates and an unidentified woman left the motel in a Mercury bearing Illinois license plates and drove northbound on an interstate frequently used by travelers to the Chicago area. In addition, the DEA agent informed Mader that the license plate number on the Mercury registered to a Hornet station wagon owned by Gates. The agent also advised Mader that the driving time between West Palm Beach and Bloomingdale was approximately 22 to 24 hours.

Mader signed an affidavit setting forth the foregoing facts, and submitted it to a judge of the Circuit Court of DuPage County, together with a copy of the anonymous letter. The judge of that court thereupon issued a search warrant for the Gates' residence and for their automobile. The judge, in deciding to issue the warrant, could have determined that the *modus operandi* of the Gates had been substantially corroborated. As the anonymous letter predicted, Lance Gates had flown from Chicago to West Palm Beach late in the afternoon of May 5th, had checked into a hotel room registered in the name of his wife, and, at 7:00 a.m. the following morning, had headed north, accompanied by an unidentified woman, out of West Palm

Beach on an interstate highway used by travelers from South Florida to Chicago in an automobile bearing a license plate issued to him.

At 5:15 a.m. on March 7th, only 36 hours after he had flown out of Chicago, Lance Gates, and his wife, returned to their home in Bloomingdale, driving the car in which they had left West Palm Beach some 22 hours earlier. The Bloomingdale police were awaiting them, searched the trunk of the Mercury, and uncovered approximately 350 pounds of marijuana. A search of the Gates' home revealed marijuana, weapons, and other contraband. The Illinois Circuit Court ordered suppression of all these items, on the ground that the affidavit submitted to the Circuit Judge failed to support the necessary determination of probable cause to believe that the Gates' automobile and home contained the contraband in question. This decision was affirmed in turn by the Illinois Appellate Court and by a divided vote of the Supreme Court of Illinois.

The Illinois Supreme Court concluded—and we are inclined to agree—that, standing alone, the anonymous letter sent to the Bloomingdale Police Department would not provide the basis for a magistrate's determination that there was probable cause to believe contraband would be found in the Gates' car and home. The letter provides virtually nothing from which one might conclude that its author is either honest or his information reliable; likewise, the letter gives absolutely no indication of the basis for the writer's predictions regarding the Gates' criminal activities. Something more was required, then, before a magistrate could conclude that there was probable cause to believe that contraband would be found in the Gates' home and car.

The Illinois Supreme Court also properly recognized that Detective Mader's affidavit might be capable of supplementing the anonymous letter with information sufficient to permit a determination of probable cause. In holding that the affidavit in fact did not contain sufficient additional information to sustain a determination of probable cause, the Illinois court applied a "two-pronged test," derived from our decision in Spinelli v. United States. The Illinois Supreme Court, like some others, apparently understood *Spinelli* as requiring that the anonymous letter satisfy each of two independent requirements before it could be relied on. According to this view, the letter, as supplemented by Mader's affidavit, first had to adequately reveal the "basis of knowledge" of the letter writer—the particular means by which he came by the information given in his report. Second, it had to provide facts sufficiently establishing either the "veracity" of the affiant's informant, or, alternatively, the "reliability" of the informant's report in this particular case.

The Illinois court, alluding to an elaborate set of legal rules that have developed among various lower courts to enforce the "two-pronged test," found that the test had not been satisfied. First, the "veracity" prong was not satisfied because, "there was simply no basis [for] * * * conclud[ing] that the anonymous person [who wrote the letter to the Bloomingdale Police Department] was credible." The court indicated that corroboration by police of details contained in the letter might never satisfy the "veracity" prong, and in any event, could not do so if, as in the present case, only "innocent" details are corroborated. In addition, the letter gave no indication of the basis of its writer's knowledge of the Gates' activities. The Illinois court understood *Spinelli* as permit-

ting the detail contained in a tip to be used to infer that the informant had a reliable basis for his statements, but it thought that the anonymous letter failed to provide sufficient detail to permit such an inference. Thus, it concluded that no showing of probable cause had been made.

We agree with the Illinois Supreme Court that an informant's "veracity," "reliability" and "basis of knowledge" are all highly relevant in determining the value of his report. We do not agree, however, that these elements should be understood as entirely separate and independent requirements to be rigidly exacted in every case, which the opinion of the Supreme Court of Illinois would imply. Rather, as detailed below, they should be understood simply as closely intertwined issues that may usefully illuminate the commonsense, practical question whether there is "probable cause" to believe that contraband or evidence is located in a particular place.

III

This totality of the circumstances approach is far more consistent with our prior treatment of probable cause than is any rigid demand that specific "tests" be satisfied by every informant's tip. Perhaps the central teaching of our decisions bearing on the probable cause standard is that it is a "practical, nontechnical conception." * * *

[P]robable cause is a fluid concept—turning on the assessment of probabilities in particular factual contexts—not readily, or even usefully, reduced to a neat set of legal rules. Informants' tips doubtless come in many shapes and sizes from many different types of persons. * * *

[T]he "two-pronged test" directs analysis into two largely independent channels—the informant's "veracity" or "reliability" and his "basis of knowledge." There are persuasive arguments against according these two elements such independent status. Instead, they are better understood as relevant considerations in the totality of circumstances analysis that traditionally has guided probable cause determinations: a deficiency in one may be compensated for, in determining the overall reliability of a tip, by a strong showing as to the other, or by some other indicia of reliability.

* * * Unlike a totality of circumstances analysis, which permits a balanced assessment of the relative weights of all the various indicia of reliability (and unreliability) attending an informant's tip, the "two-pronged test" has encouraged an excessively technical dissection of informants' tips,[a] with undue attention being focused on isolated issues that cannot sensibly be divorced from the other facts presented to the magistrate.

* * * Finely-tuned standards such as proof beyond a reasonable doubt or by a preponderance of the evidence, useful in formal trials, have no place in the magistrate's decision. While an effort to fix some general, numerically precise degree of certainty corresponding to "probable cause" may not be helpful, it is clear that "only the probability, and not a prima facie

showing, of criminal activity is the standard of probable cause." *Spinelli,* supra.

We have also recognized that affidavits are normally drafted by nonlawyers in the midst and haste of a criminal investigation. * * * The rigorous inquiry into the *Spinelli* prongs and the complex superstructure of evidentiary and analytical rules that some have seen implicit in our *Spinelli* decision, cannot be reconciled with the fact that many warrants are—quite properly—issued on the basis of nontechnical, common-sense judgments of laymen applying a standard less demanding than those used in formal legal proceedings.

* * *

If the affidavits submitted by police officers are subjected to the type of scrutiny some courts have deemed appropriate, police might well resort to warrantless searches, with the hope of relying on consent or some other exception to the warrant clause that might develop at the time of the search. In addition, the possession of a warrant by officers conducting an arrest or search greatly reduces the perception of unlawful or intrusive police conduct, by assuring "the individual whose property is searched or seized of the lawful authority of the executing officer, his need to search, and the

---

a. Some lower court decisions, brought to our attention by the State, reflect a rigid application of such rules. In Bridger v. State, 503 S.W.2d 801 (Tex.Cr.App.1974), the affiant had received a confession of armed robbery from one of two suspects in the robbery; in addition, the suspect had given the officer $800 in cash stolen during the robbery. The suspect also told the officer that the gun used in the robbery was hidden in the other suspect's apartment. A warrant issued on the basis of this was invalidated on the ground that the affidavit did not satisfactorily describe how the accomplice had obtained his information regarding the gun.

Likewise, in People v. Palanza, 371 N.E.2d 687 (Ill.App.1978), the affidavit submitted in support of an application for a search warrant

stated that an informant of proven and uncontested reliability had seen, in specifically described premises, "a quantity of a white crystalline substance which was represented to the informant by a white male occupant of the premises to be cocaine. Informant has observed cocaine on numerous occasions in the past and is thoroughly familiar with its appearance. The informant states that the white crystalline powder he observed in the above described premises appeared to him to be cocaine." The warrant issued on the basis of the affidavit was invalidated because "There is no indication as to how the informant or for that matter any other person could tell whether a white substance was cocaine and not some other substance such as sugar or salt."

* * *

limits of his power to search." Reflecting this preference for the warrant process, the traditional standard for review of an issuing magistrate's probable cause determination has been that so long as the magistrate had a "substantial basis for * * * conclud[ing]" that a search would uncover evidence of wrongdoing, the Fourth Amendment requires no more. * * *

Finally, the direction taken by decisions following *Spinelli* poorly serves "the most basic function of any government": "to provide for the security of the individual and of his property." The strictures that inevitably accompany the "two-pronged test" cannot avoid seriously impeding the task of law enforcement. If, as the Illinois Supreme Court apparently thought, that test must be rigorously applied in every case, anonymous tips would be of greatly diminished value in police work. Ordinary citizens * * * generally do not provide extensive recitations of the basis of their everyday observations. Likewise, as the Illinois Supreme Court recognized in this case, the veracity of persons supplying anonymous tips is by hypothesis largely unknown, and unknowable. As a result, anonymous tips seldom could survive a rigorous application of either of the *Spinelli* prongs. Yet, such tips, particularly when supplemented by independent police investigation, frequently contribute to the solution of otherwise "perfect crimes." While a conscientious assessment of the basis for crediting such tips is required by the Fourth Amendment, a standard that leaves virtually no place for anonymous citizen informants is not.

For all these reasons, we conclude that it is wiser to abandon the "two-pronged test" established by our decisions in *Aguilar* and *Spinelli*.[b] In its place we reaffirm the totality of the circumstances analysis that traditionally has informed probable cause determinations. The task of the issuing magistrate is simply to make a practical, common-sense decision whether, given all the circumstances set forth in the affidavit before him, including the "veracity" and "basis of knowledge" of persons supplying hearsay information, there is a fair probability that contraband or evidence of a crime will be found in a particular place. And the duty of a reviewing court is simply to ensure that the magistrate had a "substantial basis for * * * conclud[ing]" that probable cause existed. * * *

Our earlier cases illustrate the limits beyond which a magistrate may not venture in issuing a warrant. A sworn statement of an affiant that "he has cause to suspect and does believe that" liquor illegally brought into the United States is located on certain premises will not do. Nathanson v. United States, 290 U.S. 41 (1933). An affidavit must provide the magistrate with a substantial basis for determining the existence of probable cause, and the wholly conclusory statement at issue in *Nathanson* failed to meet this requirement. An officer's statement that "affiants have received reliable information from a credible person and believe" that heroin is stored in a home, is likewise inadequate. Aguilar v. Texas. As in *Nathanson,* this is a mere conclusory statement that gives the magistrate virtually no basis

b. * * *

Whether the allegations submitted to the magistrate in *Spinelli* would, under the view we now take, have supported a finding of probable cause, we think it would not be profitable to decide. There are so many variables in the probable cause equation that one determination will seldom be a useful "precedent" for

another. Suffice it to say that while we in no way abandon *Spinelli*'s concern for the trustworthiness of informers and for the principle that it is the magistrate who must ultimately make a finding of probable cause, we reject the rigid categorization suggested by some of its language.

at all for making a judgment regarding probable cause. Sufficient information must be presented to the magistrate to allow that official to determine probable cause; his action cannot be a mere ratification of the bare conclusions of others. In order to ensure that such an abdication of the magistrate's duty does not occur, courts, must continue to conscientiously review the sufficiency of affidavits on which warrants are issued. But when we move beyond the "bare bones" affidavits present in cases such as *Nathanson* and *Aguilar,* this area simply does not lend itself to a prescribed set of rules, like that which had developed from *Spinelli.* Instead, the flexible, common-sense standard * * * better serves the purposes of the Fourth Amendment's probable cause requirement.

Justice Brennan's dissent suggests in several places that the approach we take today somehow downgrades the role of the neutral magistrate, because *Aguilar* and *Spinelli* "preserve the role of magistrates as independent arbiters of probable cause. * * * "Quite the contrary, we believe, is the case. * * * Nothing in our opinion in any way lessens the authority of the magistrate to draw such reasonable inferences as he will from the material supplied to him by applicants for a warrant; indeed, he is freer than under the regime of *Aguilar* and *Spinelli* to draw

such inferences, or to refuse to draw them if he is so minded.

* * *

IV

[The Court describes Draper v. United States, a case discussed in *Spinelli.*]

The showing of probable cause in the present case was fully as compelling as that in *Draper.* Even standing alone, the facts obtained through the independent investigation of Mader and the DEA at least suggested that the Gateses were involved in drug trafficking. In addition to being a popular vacation site, Florida is well-known as a source of narcotics and other illegal drugs. Lance Gates' flight to Palm Beach, his brief, overnight stay in a motel, and apparent immediate return north to Chicago in the family car, conveniently awaiting him in West Palm Beach, is as suggestive of a prearranged drug run, as it is of an ordinary vacation trip.

In addition, the magistrate could rely on the anonymous letter which had been corroborated in major part by Mader's efforts—just as had occurred in *Draper.*[c] The Supreme Court of Illinois reasoned that *Draper* involved an informant who had given reliable information on previous occasions, while the honesty and reliability of the anonymous informant in this case were unknown to the

---

c. The Illinois Supreme Court thought that the verification of details contained in the anonymous letter in this case amounted only to "the corroboration of innocent activity," and that this was insufficient to support a finding of probable cause. We are inclined to agree, however with the observation of Justice Moran in his dissenting opinion that "In this case, just as in *Draper,* seemingly innocent activity became suspicious in the light of the initial tip." And it bears noting that *all* of the corroborating detail established in *Draper, supra,* was of entirely innocent activity * * *.

This is perfectly reasonable. As discussed previously, probable cause requires only a probability or substantial chance of criminal

activity, not an actual showing of such activity. By hypothesis, therefore, innocent behavior frequently will provide the basis for a showing of probable cause; to require otherwise would be to *sub silentio* impose a drastically more rigorous definition of probable cause than the security of our citizens demands. We think the Illinois court attempted a too rigid classification of the types of conduct that may be relied upon in seeking to demonstrate probable cause. In making a determination of probable cause the relevant inquiry is not whether particular conduct is "innocent" or "guilty," but the degree of suspicion that attaches to particular types of non-criminal acts.

Bloomingdale police. While this distinction might be an apt one at the time the police department received the anonymous letter, it became far less significant after Mader's independent investigative work occurred. The corroboration of the letter's predictions that the Gateses' car would be in Florida, that Lance Gates would fly to Florida in the next day or so, and that he would drive the car north toward Bloomingdale all indicated, albeit not with certainty, that the informant's other assertions also were true. "Because an informant is right about some things, he is more probably right about other facts"—including the claim regarding the Gateses' illegal activity. This may well not be the type of "reliability" or "veracity" necessary to satisfy some views of the "veracity prong" of *Spinelli*, but we think it suffices for the practical, common-sense judgment called for in making a probable cause determination. It is enough, for purposes of assessing probable cause, that "corroboration through other sources of information reduced the chances of a reckless or prevaricating tale," thus providing "a substantial basis for crediting the hearsay."

Finally, the anonymous letter contained a range of details relating not just to easily obtained facts and conditions existing at the time of the tip, but to future actions of third parties ordinarily not easily predicted. The letter writer's accurate information as to the travel plans of each of the Gateses' was of a character likely obtained only from the Gateses' themselves, or from someone familiar with their not entirely ordinary travel plans. If the informant had access to accurate information of this type a magistrate could properly conclude that it was not unlikely that he also had access to reliable information of the Gateses' alleged illegal activities.[d] Of course, the Gateses' travel plans might have been learned from a talkative neighbor or travel agent; under the "two-pronged test" developed from *Spinelli*, the character of the details in the anonymous letter might well not permit a sufficiently clear inference regarding the letter writer's "basis of knowledge." But, as discussed previously, probable cause does not demand the certainty we associate with formal trials. It is enough that there was a fair

---

d. Justice Stevens' dissent seizes on one inaccuracy in the anonymous informant's letter—its statement the Sue Gates would fly from Florida to Illinois, when in fact she drove—and argues that the probative value of the entire tip was undermined by this allegedly "material mistake." We have never required that informants used by the police be infallible, and can see no reason to impose such a requirement in this case. Probable cause, particularly when police have obtained a warrant, simply does not require the perfection the dissent finds necessary.

Likewise, there is no force to the dissent's argument that the Gateses' action in leaving their home unguarded undercut the informant's claim that drugs were hidden there. Indeed, the line-by-line scrutiny that the dissent applies to the anonymous letter is akin to that we find inappropriate in reviewing magistrate's decisions. The dissent apparently attributes to the magistrate who issued the warrant in this case the rather implausible notion that persons dealing in drugs always stay at home,

apparently out of fear that to leave might risk intrusion by criminals. If accurate, one could not help sympathizing with the self-imposed isolation of people so situated. In reality, however, it is scarcely likely that the magistrate ever thought that the anonymous tip "kept one spouse" at home, much less that he relied on the theory advanced by the dissent. The letter simply says that Sue would fly from Florida to Illinois, without indicating whether the Gateses' made the bitter choice of leaving the drugs in their house, or those in their car, unguarded. The magistrate's determination that there might be drugs or evidence of criminal activity in the Gateses' home was well-supported by the less speculative theory, noted in text, that if the informant could predict with considerable accuracy the somewhat unusual travel plans of the Gateses, he probably also had a reliable basis for his statements that the Gateses kept a large quantity of drugs in their home and frequently were visited by other drug traffickers there.

probability that the writer of the anonymous letter had obtained his entire story either from the Gateses or someone they trusted. And corroboration of major portions of the letter's predictions provides just this probability. It is apparent, therefore, that the judge issuing the warrant had a "substantial basis for * * * conclud[ing]" that probable cause to search the Gateses' home and car existed. The judgment of the Supreme Court of Illinois therefore must be

Reversed.

JUSTICE WHITE, concurring in the judgment.

* * * [I]t is not at all necessary to overrule *Aguilar-Spinelli* in order to reverse the judgment below. Therefore, because I am inclined to believe that, when applied properly, the *Aguilar-Spinelli* rules play an appropriate role in probable cause determinations, and because the Court's holding may foretell an evisceration of the probable cause standard, I do not join the Court's holding.

The Court reasons that the "veracity" and "basis of knowledge" tests are not independent, and that a deficiency as to one can be compensated for by a strong showing as to the other. Thus, a finding of probable cause may be based on a tip from an informant "known for the unusual reliability of his predictions" or from "an unquestionably honest citizen," even if the report fails thoroughly to set forth the basis upon which the information was obtained. If this is so, then it must follow *a fortiori* that "the affidavit of an officer, known by the magistrate to be honest and experienced, stating that [contraband] is located in a certain building" must be acceptable. It would be "quixotic" if a similar statement from an honest informant, but not one from an honest officer, could furnish probable cause. But we have

repeatedly held that the unsupported assertion or belief of an officer does not satisfy the probable cause requirement. Thus, this portion of today's holding can be read as implicitly rejecting the teachings of these prior holdings.

The Court may not intend so drastic a result. Indeed, the Court expressly reaffirms the validity of cases such as *Nathanson* that have held that, no matter how reliable the affiant-officer may be, a warrant should not be issued unless the affidavit discloses supporting facts and circumstances. The Court limits these cases to situations involving affidavits containing only "bare conclusions" and holds that, if an affidavit contains anything more, it should be left to the issuing magistrate to decide, based solely on "practical[ity]" and "common-sense," whether there is a fair probability that contraband will be found in a particular place.

Thus, as I read the majority opinion, it appears that the question whether the probable cause standard is to be diluted is left to the common-sense judgments of issuing magistrates. I am reluctant to approve any standard that does not expressly require, as a prerequisite to issuance of a warrant, some showing of facts from which an inference may be drawn that the informant is credible and that his information was obtained in a reliable way. * * *

JUSTICE BRENNAN, with whom JUSTICE MARSHALL joins, dissenting.

* * *

Although the rules drawn from [*Aguilar-Spinelli*] are cast in procedural terms, they advance an important underlying substantive value: Findings of probable cause, and attendant intrusions, should not be authorized unless there is some assurance that the information on which they are based has been obtained in a reliable way by an honest or credible person. * * *

* * *

[O]ne can concede that probable cause is a "practical, nontechnical" concept without betraying the values that *Aguilar* and *Spinelli* reflect. *Aguilar* and *Spinelli* require the police to provide magistrates with certain crucial information. They also provide structure for magistrates' probable cause inquiries. In so doing, *Aguilar* and *Spinelli* preserve the role of magistrates as independent arbiters of probable cause, insure greater accuracy in probable cause determinations, and advance the substantive value of precluding findings of probable cause, and attendant intrusions, based on anything less than information from an honest or credible person who has acquired his information in a reliable way. Neither the standards nor their effects are inconsistent with a "practical, nontechnical" conception of probable cause. Once a magistrate has determined that he has information before him that he can reasonably say has been obtained in a reliable way by a credible person, he has ample room to use his common sense and to apply a practical, nontechnical conception of probable cause.

* * *

JUSTICE STEVENS, **with whom** JUSTICE BRENNAN **joins, dissenting.**

The fact that Lance and Sue Gates made a 22–hour nonstop drive from West Palm Beach, Florida, to Bloomingdale, Illinois, only a few hours after Lance had flown to Florida provided persuasive evidence that they were engaged in illicit activity. That fact, however, was not known to the magistrate when he issued the warrant to search their home.

What the magistrate did know at that time was that the anonymous informant had not been completely accurate in his or her predictions. The informant had indicated that "Sue drives their car to Florida *where she leaves it to be loaded up with drugs* * * *. Sue flies back after she drops the car off in Florida.*" Yet Detective Mader's affidavit reported that she "left the West Palm Beach area driving the Mercury northbound."

The discrepancy between the informant's predictions and the facts known to Detective Mader is significant for three reasons. First, it cast doubt on the informant's hypothesis that the Gateses already had "over $100,000 worth of drugs in their basement." The informant had predicted an itinerary that always kept one spouse in Bloomingdale, suggesting that the Gateses did not want to leave their home unguarded because something valuable was hidden within. That inference obviously could not be drawn when it was known that the pair was actually together over a thousand miles from home.

Second, the discrepancy made the Gateses' conduct seem substantially less unusual than the informant had predicted it would be. It would have been odd if, as predicted, Sue had driven down to Florida on Wednesday, left the car, and flown right back to Illinois. But the mere facts that Sue was in West Palm Beach with the car, that she was joined by her husband at the Holiday Inn on Friday, and that the couple drove north together the next morning are neither unusual nor probative of criminal activity.

Third, the fact that the anonymous letter contained a material mistake undermines the reasonableness of relying on it as a basis for making a forcible entry into a private home.

* * * No one knows who the informant in this case was, or what motivated him or her to write the note. Given that the note's predictions were faulty in one significant respect, and were corroborated by nothing except ordinary innocent activity, I must surmise that the Court's evaluation of the warrant's validity has been colored by subsequent events.

* * *

Note on Gates

The Court moves to a totality of the circumstances test and abandons, as too rigid, the two-pronged test that it had previously established. Is there any way for a magistrate to independently screen applications for warrants without looking at who provides the underlying information that appears in the applications and how these people obtained their information? Does the substitution of a totality of the circumstances test for the two-pronged test mean that the two-pronged test is no longer relevant? Or does Illinois v. Gates in large measure reaffirm the logical importance of both prongs of the *Aguilar* and *Spinelli* test while establishing that one prong may be strong enough to overcome weaknesses in the other? See, e.g., United States v. Morales, 171 F.3d 978 (5th Cir.1999) (noting that the *Gates* totality of the circumstances test "includes four factors: (1) the nature of the information; (2) whether there has been an opportunity for the police to see or hear the matter reported; (3) the veracity and the basis of knowledge of the informant; (4) whether there has been any independent verification of the matters reported through police investigation.").

If you were teaching magistrates, which test, the two-pronged *Spinelli* test or the *Gates* totality of the circumstances test, would be more helpful to you in explaining how magistrates are to evaluate warrant applications?

Gates finds scholarly support in Grano, Probable Cause and Common Sense: A Reply to the Critics of Illinois v. Gates, 17 Mich.J.L.Reform 465 (1984). But the two-pronged test remains the choice of some state courts.

The New York Court of Appeals rejected *Gates* in the context of warrantless police activity in People v. Johnson, 66 N.Y.2d 398, 497 N.Y.S.2d 618, 488 N.E.2d 439 (1985). In so holding, the court followed the lead of the Washington Supreme Court in State v. Jackson, 102 Wash.2d 432, 688 P.2d 136 (1984). See also State v. Jacumin, 778 S.W.2d 430 (Tenn.1989) and State v. Jones, 706 P.2d 317 (Alaska 1985), both rejecting *Gates* in favor of the *Spinelli* two-pronged test. All of these decisions are based on a construction of the respective court's State constitution.

Strong Prong/Weak Prong

Does it make sense that a strong showing on one of the *Spinelli* prongs can make up for a weak showing on the other? For cases in which courts used this reasoning from *Gates* to uphold a finding of probable cause, see Carter v. United States, 729 F.2d 935 (8th Cir.1984) (no specific statement as to informant's basis of knowledge for stating that marijuana was growing on certain property; however, some detail concerning the location of the property was given, and any deficiency in basis of knowledge is compensated for by informant's prior track record of reliable tips); United States v. Phillips, 727 F.2d 392 (5th Cir.1984) (questionable veracity of citizen-informant who hated defendant was overcome by wealth of detail in the tip).

The Function of Corroboration after Gates

The biggest effect of *Gates* is its more permissive view of the nature and extent of corroboration necessary to shore up a defective tip. For a post-*Gates* example of the use of corroboration, consider United States v. Warner, 894 F.2d 957 (8th Cir.1990). A "confidential and reliable source" informed the Sheriff's office that he had seen Warner fire a machinegun at Warner's residence. The next day, an anonymous caller reported that Warner had shot a machinegun the previous day at Warner's residence. The officer checked firearms registrations and found that Warner had no registered firearms. On the basis of this information, a warrant was issued to search Warner's house for an unregistered firearm. The court of appeals upheld the magistrate's determination of probable cause, reasoning that the two tips were "mutually corroborative," and that the officer's check of firearms records provided further crucial corroboration. Would this corroboration have been sufficient under *Spinelli*? Did the officer's corroboration mean that Warner had an unlicensed gun, or that he had no gun? How did the court know that the "mutually corroborative" tips came from two different people?

The effect of *Gates* is apparent in cases like United States v. Peyko, 717 F.2d 741 (2d Cir.1983). An officer received an anonymous tip that Peyko was receiving weekly deliveries of drugs by Federal Express. The officer investigated and found that Peyko had been using Federal Express to send and receive packages regularly. The court found that the tip, together with the corroboration, provided probable cause to seize a Federal Express package addressed to Peyko. While the corroboration was of completely innocent activity (regularly sending and receiving packages), it lent color to the tip, which lent color to the corroboration, which led to probable cause under the *Gates* totality of circumstances approach. In light of *Peyko*, is there any risk that an innocent person with enemies will be subject to a search of his house or possessions?

Insufficient Corroboration

There are a few reported cases finding that police corroboration was insufficient to shore up a defective tip, even under the *Gates* totality of the circumstances approach. One such case is United States v. Leake, 998 F.2d 1359 (6th Cir.1993). An anonymous informant phoned the police narcotics office and stated that he was a tradesman hired to do some work at 4825 Westport Road. While working, he smelled and saw marijuana in the basement. When questioned as to how he knew it was marijuana, he stated that in his "younger days" he had been a marijuana user, but that now he was older, with children, and was very "anti-drug." Surveillance was initiated at 4825 Westport Road. No undue amount of traffic was observed. It was confirmed that the house had a basement. Two vehicles were registered to the address, one owned by Leake. On the basis of the tip and the investigation, the magistrate issued a warrant to search the premises at 4825 Westport Road, and officers recovered over 300 pounds of marijuana in the basement.

The court in *Leake* held that the warrant lacked probable cause. The court first observed that unlike *Gates*, the anonymous caller in *Leake* had not provided much detail. No names of particular individuals were ever mentioned, no dates were provided, and "no planned future activity was described as in *Gates*." Nor was the corroboration sufficient to overcome the defective tip. The court reasoned as follows:

> Detective Murphy's corroboration of the information provided by the caller was simply insufficient. * * * Murphy admitted noticing nothing out of the ordinary at the Westport Road residence. Although he noted the license plates on the cars and ultimately traced their registration, he had no information provided by the caller establishing the significance of the ownership and registration of the cars. He did verify that the residence had a basement but, standing alone, this was relatively unimportant. His investigation fell far short of the corroborations provided in *Gates* * * *. In *Gates*, nearly every detail in the tipster's letter was confirmed.

The *Leake* court found a moral in this story:

> Ultimately, this case demonstrates the importance of taking sufficient time to verify an anonymous tip before a warrant is requested. Detective Murphy's investigation of the caller's information was inadequate. More police work was needed. The supporting affidavit was too vague and Detective Murphy's limited two-night surveillance was insufficient to verify important elements of the anonymous caller's information.

See also United States v. Wilhelm, 80 F.3d 116 (4th Cir.1996), where the officer received information from a "reliable source" who observed marijuana in the defendant's home and provided directions to that home. The court found, understandably, that this barebones information was not sufficient to establish probable cause, but the government argued that the tip had been corroborated by the facts that: 1) the informant had given accurate directions to the defendant's home and 2) the informant, in describing the defendant's activity, had accurately described what marijuana looks like and how it is packaged and sold. The court found that this corroboration was not enough to cure the defect in the tip under *Gates,* because "[a]lmost anyone can give directions to a particular house without knowing anything of substance about what goes on inside that house, and anyone who occasionally watches the evening news can make generalizations about what marijuana looks like and how it is packaged and sold."

The Gates Test Applied: Massachusetts v. Upton

The Court reiterated its "totality of the circumstances" test in Massachusetts v. Upton, 466 U.S. 727 (1984), a per curiam disposition reversing the state supreme court. The Court described the facts as follows:

> At noon on September 11, 1980, Lt. Beland of the Yarmouth Police Department assisted in the execution of a search warrant for a motel room reserved by one Richard Kelleher at the Snug Harbor Motel in West Yarmouth. The search produced several items of identification, including credit cards, belonging to two persons whose homes had recently been burglarized. Other items taken in the burglaries, such as jewelry, silver and gold, were not found at the motel.

> At 3:20 p.m. on the same day, Lt. Beland received a call from an unidentified female who told him that there was "a motor home full of stolen stuff" parked behind #5 Jefferson Ave., the home of respondent

George Upton and his mother. She stated that the stolen items included jewelry, silver and gold. As set out in Lt. Beland's affidavit in support of a search warrant:

> She further stated that George Upton was going to move the motor home any time now because of the fact that Ricky Kelleher's motel room was raided and that George Upton had purchased these stolen items from Ricky Kelleher. This unidentified female stated that she had seen the stolen items but refused to identify herself because "he'll kill me," referring to George Upton. I then told this unidentified female that I knew who she was, giving her the name of Lynn Alberico, who I had met on May 16, 1980, at George Upton's repair shop off Summer St., in Yarmouthport. She was identified to me by George Upton as being his girlfriend, Lynn Alberico. The unidentified female admitted that she was the girl that I had named, stating that she was surprised that I knew who she was. She then told me that she'd broken up with George Upton and wanted to burn him. She also told me that she wouldn't give me her address or phone number but that she would contact me in the future, if need be.

Following the phone call, Lt. Beland went to Upton's house to verify that a motor home was parked on the property. Then, while other officers watched the premises, Lt. Beland prepared the application for a search warrant, setting out all the information noted above in an accompanying affidavit. He also attached the police reports on the two prior burglaries, along with lists of the stolen property. A magistrate issued the warrant, and a subsequent search of the motor home produced the items described by the caller and other incriminating evidence. The discovered evidence led to Upton's conviction on multiple counts of burglary, receiving stolen property, and related crimes.

The Court explained why the state supreme court's invalidation of the warrant was inconsistent with *Gates*:

> [T]he Massachusetts court reasoned, first, that the basis of the informant's knowledge was not "forcefully apparent" in the affidavit. Although the caller stated that she had seen the stolen items and that they were in the motor home, she did not specifically state that she saw them in the motor home. Second, the court concluded that "[n]one of the common bases for determining the credibility of an informant or the reliability of her information is present here." The caller was not a "tried and true" informant, her statement was not against penal interest, and she was not an "ordinary citizen" providing information as a witness to a crime. "She was an anonymous informant, and her unverified assent to the suggestion that she was Lynn Alberico does not take her out of that category."

Finally, the court felt that there was insufficient corroboration of the informant's tip to make up for its failure to satisfy the two-pronged test. The facts that tended to corroborate the informant's story were that the motor home was where it was supposed to be, that the caller knew of the motel raid which took place only three hours earlier, and that the caller knew the name of Upton and his girlfriend. But, much as the Supreme Court of Illinois did in the opinion we reviewed in *Gates*, the Massachusetts court reasoned that each item of corroborative evidence either related to innocent, nonsuspicious conduct or related to an event that took place in public. * * *

The Supreme Court took the Massachusetts Court to task in the following analysis:

We think that the Supreme Judicial Court of Massachusetts misunderstood our decision in *Gates*. We did not merely refine or qualify the "two-pronged test." We rejected it as hypertechnical and divorced from "the factual and practical considerations of everyday life on which reasonable and prudent men, not legal technicians, act." * * *

* * * The court did not consider Lt. Beland's affidavit in its entirety, giving significance to each relevant piece of information and balancing the relative weights of all the various indicia of reliability (and unreliability) attending the tip. Instead, the court insisted on judging bits and pieces of information in isolation against the artificial standards provided by the two-pronged test.

The Supreme Judicial Court also erred in failing to grant any deference to the decision of the magistrate to issue a warrant. Instead of merely deciding whether the evidence viewed as a whole provided a "substantial basis" for the magistrate's finding of probable cause, the court conducted a de novo probable cause determination. We rejected just such after-the-fact, de novo scrutiny in *Gates*. * * *

Examined in light of *Gates*, Lt. Beland's affidavit provides a substantial basis for the issuance of the warrant. No single piece of evidence in it is conclusive. But the pieces fit neatly together and, so viewed, support the magistrate's determination that there was "a fair probability that contraband or evidence of crime" would be found in Upton's motor home. The informant claimed to have seen the stolen goods and gave a description of them which tallied with the items taken in recent burglaries. She knew of the raid on the motel room—which produced evidence connected to those burglaries—and that the room had been reserved by Kelleher. She explained the connection between Kelleher's motel room and the stolen goods in Upton's motor home. And she provided a motive both for her attempt at anonymity—fear of Upton's retaliation—and for furnishing the information—her recent breakup with Upton and her desire "to burn him."

The Massachusetts court dismissed Lt. Beland's identification of the caller as a mere "unconfirmed guess." But "probable cause does not demand the certainty we associate with formal trials." Lt. Beland noted that the caller "admitted that she was the girl I had named, stating that she was surprised that I knew who she was." It is of course possible that the caller merely adopted Lt. Beland's suggestion as "a convenient cover for her true identity." But given the caller's admission, her obvious knowledge of who Alberico was and how she was connected with Upton, and her explanation of her motive in calling, Lt. Beland's inference appears stronger than a mere uninformed and unconfirmed guess. It is enough that the inference was a reasonable one and conformed with the other pieces of evidence making up the total showing of probable cause.[11]

---

11. Justice Stevens concurred in the judgment, expressing the opinion that the state supreme court should have indicated whether the warrant was valid under state law. Justices

3. The Citizen Informant

Under both *Spinelli* and *Gates*, the courts have distinguished police informants and anonymous informants from an ordinary citizen who identifies himself and reports a crime. The reason for this distinction is that paid informants are presumptively unreliable given their dubious character and financial (or other) arrangements, and anonymous informants must be presumed unreliable because they may be using their anonymity for suspect reasons (e.g., to frame or harass an enemy). In contrast, identified citizen informants are presumed reliable because the motivations, which are "concern for society or for his own safety," suggest that there is little chance of fabrication. State v. Paszek, 50 Wis.2d 619, 184 N.W.2d 836 (1971). See also United States v. Decoteau, 932 F.2d 1205 (7th Cir.1991) (where citizen-informant known to the officer told him that she had seen the defendant with a sawed-off shotgun, the informant's statement itself provides probable cause and corroboration is unnecessary); United States v. Blount, 123 F.3d 831 (5th Cir.1997) (en banc) (information coming from an identified neighbor of the defendant constituted probable cause, because the officers "had no reason to disbelieve Ms. Cooksey, or to question her motives or credibility").

Are you persuaded that citizen informants should be presumed reliable? If you are, would you require that an officer applying for a warrant demonstrate that the informant is an ordinary citizen and not a routine informant? For such a requirement, see People v. Smith, 17 Cal.3d 845, 132 Cal.Rptr. 397, 553 P.2d 557 (1976). Would you be willing to presume reliability as readily in some cases as others? Or would you carefully scrutinize the circumstances that result in an informant's emerging to cooperate with the police?

Who qualifies as a citizen informant? In Rutledge v. United States, 392 A.2d 1062 (D.C.App.1978), the court concluded that a first-time volunteer, paid informant was closer to a typical or ordinary informant than to the usual unrewarded citizen who comes forward. Do you agree?

4. Accomplices

In United States v. Patterson, 150 F.3d 382 (4th Cir.1998), the police arrested Greene after two masked men robbed a bank. Greene confessed and identified Patterson as his accomplice. On the basis of this statement, the officers searched Patterson's car and found incriminating evidence. Patterson challenged the search as lacking probable cause. But the court held that the confession of a co-participant is itself sufficient to establish probable cause—no corroboration is required. The court noted that a defendant can be convicted solely on the basis of the uncorroborated testimony of an accomplice, and reasoned that "it would be contradictory to allow a defendant to be convicted based on the uncorroborated testimony of his co-perpetrator while refusing to find that the same statement would be sufficient to support probable cause."

Brennan and Marshall dissented from the summary reversal of the state court.

On remand in *Upton*, the Massachusetts Supreme Judicial Court declined to follow *Gates* and reaffirmed its commitment to the two-pronged test under the state constitution. Commonwealth v. Upton, 394 Mass. 363, 476 N.E.2d 548 (1985). It reasoned that the two-pronged test "aids lay people, such as the police and certain lay magistrates, in a way that the 'totality of the circumstances' test never could." Do you believe that the state supreme court correctly applied the *Spinelli* test to the *Upton* facts?

But is the accomplice's testimony under oath at trial really the "same statement" as the accomplice's stationhouse confession implicating another in the crime?

5. Quantity of Information Required for Probable Cause

Gates dealt with the quality of information that could be considered in the probable cause determination, i.e., whether the informant's tip is reliable enough to be considered as proof of probable cause. Assuming that all the information is reliable, another question arises: has the information submitted established a "fair probability" of criminal activity? This question arises not only with respect to affidavits submitted to magistrates, but also with warrantless searches and seizures; even if the search or seizure is conducted pursuant to an exception to the warrant requirement, the officer is ordinarily required to have probable cause.

Equivocal Activity

One circumstance in which a "fair probability" question is presented is where it is unknown whether a crime has been or is being committed. For example, what if the officer sees a person at 2:00 a.m. carrying a television and a stereo down the street in a shopping cart? There are many innocent explanations for this activity. Does that mean that there is no fair probability of criminal activity?

Consider United States v. Prandy–Binett, 995 F.2d 1069 (D.C.Cir.1993). Judge Randolph introduced the facts as follows:

> Some opaque containers induce assumptions about their contents. Refrigerators contain food. Under the hoods of automobiles are engines. These are predictions, based on experience. Narcotics officers have their own specialized experience and training. Detective John Centrella saw a small rectangular block wrapped in silver duct tape. To the uninitiated, the object's outward appearance said nothing about its contents. To Detective Centrella, the size, shape and wrapping of the object signified one kilogram of illegal narcotics. * * *

> Detective Centrella and another narcotics detective were on duty at Union Station, meeting trains arriving from New York City, a "source city" for drugs. As they watched departing passengers, their attention was drawn to an individual walking through the station faster than the others and trying to get around them. When the individual—Prandy–Binett—made eye contact with the detectives, who were in plain clothes, he moved even more quickly toward the exit. The detectives approached him and identified themselves. After telling the officers he had come from New Jersey, Prandy–Binett produced a one-way train ticket, purchased with cash, showing that his trip originated at Penn Station, New York City. After saying he lived in Washington, D.C., he handed the officers a driver's license showing Hyattsville, Maryland, as his residence. Detective Centrella's suspicions, aroused by these possible inconsistencies, were heightened by the cloth "tote" or "gym" bag Prandy–Binett carried on his shoulder. Prandy–Binett reported having spent a week working in New Jersey. Yet his only luggage was the small bag, which did not appear full. Asked whether the bag contained drugs

or guns, Prandy–Binett said no. Detective Centrella then requested permission to search the bag. Prandy–Binett replied that he did not have to consent and that the bag contained only clothing. He took the bag from his shoulder, placed it on the ground, knelt down (as did the detective next to him), unzipped the bag and began pulling out a pair of blue jeans. This action uncovered a miniature shopping bag lying on its side, deep purple in color, a "perfume or a cologne bag" from Elizabeth Taylor Perfume. Unprompted, Prandy–Binett said, in evident reference to the perfume bag, "this is a gift." As Prandy–Binett continued to manipulate the blue jeans, a portion of a rectangular block, wrapped in silver duct tape, slid out of the perfume bag. Believing the block to contain illegal drugs, Detective Centrella handcuffed Prandy–Binett, examined the wrapped object further, and seized it and the gym bag. A later field test on the contents of the wrapped block revealed cocaine.

Judge Randolph concluded that, based on the totality of circumstances, there was a fair probability that the rectangular block contained drugs, and upheld the narcotics conviction on which the search and seizure were based. He analyzed the fair probability question as follows:

Somewhere between "less than evidence which would justify conviction" and "more than bare suspicion," probable cause is satisfied. The precise point is indeterminate. We are concerned not simply with probabilities, but with conditional probabilities: if one event occurs, how likely is it that another event will occur? This is why the detectives' observations up to the time the block slipped out of the perfume bag cannot be disregarded. It is why in similar cases we ask, although sometimes tacitly, what is the probability that a train passenger arriving at Union Station from New York City will be carrying cocaine? Quite low, we trust, despite New York's status as a source city for narcotics. Is the probability increased if the passenger moves quickly through the station after leaving the train? Greater if the passenger also gives apparently deceptive answers when the police question him? Greater still if the passenger opens his bag and refers to a package wrapped in duct tape inside a fancy perfume bag as a "gift?" Neither courts nor law enforcement officers, nor anyone else for that matter, can quantify any of this. A mathematician could not perform the calculations because there is no way of assigning probabilities to the individual events. The information is simply unavailable, as will doubtless be true in every Fourth Amendment case. Still, we are convinced that, up to the sighting of the duct tape package, the conditional probability was low, much too low to have satisfied the Fourth Amendment in light of the interests it protects.

The case thus comes down to the detectives' inference of narcotics from the appearance of the wrapped block, and on the extent to which that inference enhanced the probability of Prandy–Binett's possessing drugs. We put the question in these terms because "probable cause" is evaluated not only from the perspective of a "prudent man," but also from the particular viewpoint of the officer involved in the search or seizure. * * *

Judge Randolph concluded that the sighting of the rectangular block wrapped in duct tape added enough to the other facts to constitute a fair probability of criminal activity. He noted three factors bearing on this probability assessment:

There was first the block's bulk. * * * Detective Centrella was quite familiar with the bulk of packages containing one kilogram of cocaine. During his 20 years of service, he personally had seized 100 such kilos and had seen many more. Both Detective Centrella, and his partner, an experienced narcotics detective who had undergone training at the Drug Enforcement Administration, thus had good reason for believing that the wrapped block in Prandy–Binett's gym bag was about the size of a package containing one kilogram of cocaine or heroin.

The second consideration was the rectangular shape of the object. The portion protruding from the perfume bag was consistent with what the detectives knew to be the standard configuration, the typical "kilo brick." The bag itself, roughly four inches wide and between six and ten inches deep, was the right size for holding a kilo of narcotics so packaged. The brick-like shape of the object thus further alerted the detectives, in light of their training and experience, to the possible presence of narcotics.

The third factor was wrapping—silver duct tape (over plastic). Duct tape is attractive to traffickers because fingerprints are difficult to lift from its surface and because some criminals believe—erroneously—that it masks the odor of the drugs from police dogs. Detective Centrella testified that he had seen "several hundred" packages wrapped in silver duct tape similar in appearance to the one in Prandy–Binett's bag. Every one contained contraband. He also reported that approximately 95 percent of the kilogram-sized quantities of cocaine he had seized in his career were so packaged. * * *

To Detective Centrella the wrapped block thus conveyed the message "one kilo of narcotics" just as surely as if the words were written on the tape. The circumstances leading up to the arrest and the incongruity of the crudely wrapped block inside the fancy perfume bag, together with Prandy–Binett's unsolicited disclaimer "This is a gift," must have confirmed what the detective saw in his mind's eye. * * * We cannot say exactly how probable it was that the block contained drugs, but we are convinced that it amounted, at the least, to a " 'fair probability' "Prandy–Binett was committing an offense.

Judge Randolph rejected the argument that probable cause was lacking because the officers could not be sure that Prandy–Binett was carrying cocaine rather than some other contraband such as heroin. He stated: "It is simply not the law that officers must be aware of the specific crime an individual is likely committing. It is enough that they have probable cause to believe the defendant has committed one or the other of several offenses, even though they cannot be sure which one."

Judge Edwards wrote a vigorous dissent in *Prandy-Binett*. He complained that the majority, "relying on a bizarre theory of 'conditional probabilities,' holds that probable cause can be based on the appearance of duct tape." He argued that the officers were motivated more by racial classification than by any assessment of probability:

The circumstances that actually arouse police "suspicion" are obvious to anyone who bothers to look—individuals traveling through Union Station who are evidently poor, or people of color, are the individuals who are approached, questioned, stopped and searched. See Sheri Lynn Johnson, Race and the Decision to Detain a Suspect, 93 Yale L.J. 214, 225–37 (1983) (describing the varied uses of race as a motivation for police detention, and as an element in probable cause and reasonable suspicion analyses); Developments in the Law: Race and the Criminal Process, 101 Harv. L. Rev. 1472, 1496 (1988) (noting studies that reveal that "police use race as an independently significant, if not determinative, factor in deciding whom to follow, detain, search, or arrest").

Judge Edwards dismissed as irrelevant any factors other than the duct tape. According to Judge Edwards, Prandy–Binett's answers about his itinerary were not suspicious at all:

> Given the metropolitan nature of the Washington and New York areas, it is hardly inconsistent or even unusual for someone to say that he lives in Washington, but to have a Maryland address and driver's license; or to say that he was travelling from New Jersey, but to have boarded the train in New York. Nor is there anything unusual about living in one town and working in another, or in carrying a small bag when one has been out of town for a week—especially if one is poor.

Likewise, the supposed incongruity of carrying a package wrapped in duct tape as a gift in an expensive bag was dismissed by Judge Edwards:

> The majority also finds suspicious the "incongruity" of the sight of a "crudely wrapped block inside the fancy perfume bag." Such comment reveals a distinct lack of empathy for some members of our society—those without much disposable income, for example—who readily find use for a discarded shopping bag and who might very well wrap a gift with whatever packaging material is on hand, including duct tape.

Judge Edwards concluded that the placement of a rectangular object wrapped in duct tape inside one's luggage was simply not enough to rise to a fair probability of criminal activity. He argued that the "brick-like shape of a package might provide the observer with a general hint about the size of its contents, but the shape of such a package is too generic to make reasonable the inference that the contents of the package are also brick-shaped."

Who has the better argument in *Prandy-Binett*? Of course it is true that Prandy–Binett might have wrapped some figurines into a rectangular mass of duct tape. But does that mean there wasn't a fair probability that the package contained contraband?

Probable Cause to Arrest

The probable cause requirement applies to arrests as well as to searches. Probable cause to search is determined by whether there is a fair probability that the area or object searched contains evidence of a crime. Probable cause to arrest is determined by whether there is a fair probability to believe that the person arrested has committed a crime. Often these two fair probability assessments are actually one. For example, if there was probable cause to believe that the rectangular object in Prandy–Binett's luggage contained contraband, then there was also probable cause to arrest Prandy–Binett on a narcotics offense. In some situations, however, there may be probable cause to arrest, but not probable cause to search. For example, there may be a fair probability that a person robbed a bank five years ago; but that does not mean there is a fair probability to believe that the defendant's briefcase contains any evidence of the five year-old bank robbery. In other cases, there may be probable cause to search but not probable cause to arrest, such as where a criminal leaves a suitcase full of drugs in the home of an unsuspecting friend.

In the arrest context, the question of fair probability sometimes arises where police know that a crime has been committed, but they are not certain that a suspect is the perpetrator. Consider United States v. Valez, 796 F.2d 24 (2d Cir.1986) where the court set forth the following facts and analysis:

> At 4:30 p.m. on October 16, 1984, New York City Police Sergeant Albert Zarr and Officer James Allen were parked in a surveillance vehicle on West 48th Street between Eighth and Ninth Avenues in Manhattan. Zarr sat near the rear window watching the street with binoculars; Allen remained in the front seat. After observing what appeared to be a narcotics sale on the southeast corner of 48th and Ninth, Zarr sent one of his undercover police officers to make a drug buy.

> Zarr saw the undercover officer hand money to two men at the corner and in return receive two packets that later proved to contain cocaine. Zarr observed that one of the sellers was an Hispanic male in his twenties, wearing a black leather jacket, grey pants with a comb in the back pocket, and a white or off-white V-neck shirt with dark trim on the collar.

> Zarr described the sellers to Allen and radioed the description to the field team. At that point, the seller with the black jacket walked around the corner and disappeared from view. Zarr instructed Allen to follow the subject and make an arrest.

> Allen left the van immediately and proceeded west on 48th Street and then south on Ninth Avenue in search of the seller. Allen walked to the next corner, but did not see his subject. He decided to turn back on the hunch that the seller had ducked into one of the stores. When Allen returned to the corner of 48th and Ninth, he saw a man coming out of a Blimpie's fast food restaurant who matched the description that Zarr had given him. At 4:40 p.m., five to ten minutes after Allen left the surveillance van, he arrested the man. The person whom Allen had arrested was Valez. [Valez was brought to the station, and a search of his person uncovered packets of cocaine.]

> When Sergeant Zarr and the undercover officer who made the "buy" returned to the stationhouse, they realized that Allen had arrested the wrong man. [Valez moved to suppress the cocaine on the ground that the arrest was illegal for lack of probable cause.] Valez relied primarily on the fact that Zarr's description did not include any mention of facial hair, whereas Valez had a small goatee and a thick moustache. Valez also argued that Zarr's description of the seller was overly general and that the mistaken arrest resulted from the negligent and unorganized conduct of the surveillance team.

The *Valez* Court held that the description of the perpetrator was not overly general, and that the officers had acted properly in arresting Valez:

> Given Zarr's detailed description of the seller's clothing, his failure to mention that the seller was clean-shaven does not constitute an unreasonable oversight. * * * [T]he police may justifiably place little reliance on the

presence or absence of facial hair on a suspect who otherwise matches a description because facial hair may be worn or taken off as a disguise. * * *

We also believe that Zarr's description was sufficiently detailed to provide Allen with probable cause to believe that Valez was the seller, particularly because Allen encountered Valez, who matched every detail of the description, within the immediate vicinity of the drug sale and not more than 10 minutes after Zarr gave Allen the description. * * *

We find that there was probable cause to arrest Valez. Thus, although Valez may be the victim of a mistake, no purpose would be served by suppressing clear evidence of Valez's guilt, which evidence came to the attention of the police as a result of their well-intentioned but misguided actions.

Dissenting Judge Oakes argued that Officer Zarr's description was too general to support the conclusion that there was probable cause to arrest:

By sending an officer into the area with a description only of race, approximate age, and clothing and, oh yes, of a comb in the hip pocket—but not mentioning facial hair or its absence, or the length of the suspect's haircut—Zarr was insufficiently distinguishing the person who made the sale from other Latin males of not uncommon appearance in the immediate area. It was the equivalent of "identifying" a suspect in the Wall Street area by describing him as a white, thirty-ish man with a button-down shirt and dark pinstripe suit, carrying a leather attache case.

Who has the better of the argument on probable cause, the majority or the dissent? Would it have mattered if Zarr had arrested the real seller before Allen had arrested Valez?

Compare the result in *Valez* with that of United States v. Kithcart, 134 F.3d 529 (3d Cir. 1998). Officers received three radio transmissions reporting separate armed robberies. Two robberies were reported in Bensalem Township and one in the adjacent Bristol Township. The time and the exact location of the robbery in Bristol Township was not specified. The perpetrators were described as "two black males in a black sports car." One of the perpetrators might have been wearing white clothes, and the vehicle was described as a "possible Z–28, possible Camaro." Ten minutes after the last radio transmission, concerning the robbery in Bristol Township, Officer Nelson spotted a black Nissan 300ZX, about a mile from Bristol Township. The vehicle was being driven by an African–American male, who appeared to be the only person in the car. Officer Nelson testified that since she had received the last radio transmission, this was the first time she had come upon either a black car or an African–American driver. She signalled the car to pull over, and "saw two sets of arms raised toward the roof of the car, and she realized that there were two people in the car." Eventually the officer searched the car, and found firearms. Kithcart, the driver, was charged with being a felon in possession of a firearm. The trial court denied Kithcart's suppression motion, holding that Officer Nelson had probable cause to arrest Kithcart when she pulled him over, and therefore that the search of the car was a proper search incident to a valid arrest.

The court of appeals, however, held that Officer Nelson did not have probable cause to arrest Kithcart when she pulled him over. The court analyzed the probable cause standard, in light of the facts, as follows:

The district court erred in concluding that there was probable cause to arrest and search Kithcart prior to the discovery of the guns. The mere fact that Kithcart is black and the perpetrators had been described as two black males is plainly insufficient. As we have previously noted, a description of " 'two negro males' and two 'black males' ... without more ... would not have been sufficient to provide probable cause to arrest [the suspect]." Edwards v. City of Philadelphia, 860 F.2d 568, 571 n. 2 (3d Cir.1988). Moreover, the match between the description of the perpetrators' car (a black sports car, "possible Z–28, possible Camaro)" and the vehicle in which Kithcart was spotted (a black Nissan 300ZX) was far from precise. Although the Camaro Z–28 and the Nissan 300ZX could be considered "sports cars," there was no evidence offered at the suppression hearing that the shapes of the two cars were sufficiently similar so as to warrant an inference that a 300ZX could be mistaken for a Z–28.

Nor is probable cause established by either the location or time of the stop. There was no evidence presented as to where in Bristol Township the final robbery occurred; nor was there evidence presented that the Bristol robbery occurred shortly before Officer Nelson stopped the car carrying Kithcart. Although the radio transmission regarding the Bristol robbery came approximately 10 minutes before the vehicle was stopped, Officer Nelson testified that she did not recall that the radio transmission revealed when the Bristol robbery occurred, other than that it occurred that same evening. Compare *Edwards*, 860 F.2d at 571 n. 2 (although the description "two negro males" was insufficient by itself to provide probable cause to arrest suspect, other evidence closely linking suspect to scene of reported crime was sufficient). In sum, we think that it is clear that the facts and circumstances within Officer Nelson's knowledge at the time she stopped the Nissan were insufficient to allow a prudent person to believe that the car and its occupants had committed or were committing an offense. In other words, armed with information that two black males driving a black sports car were believed to have committed three robberies in the area some relatively short time earlier, Officer Nelson could not justifiably arrest any African–American man who happened to drive by in any type of black sports car.

What accounts for the different results in *Valez* and *Kithcart*? What more could the officer in *Kithcart* have found to make the case for probable cause?

For another interesting case on probable cause, see Valente v. Wallace, 332 F.3d 30 (1st Cir. 2003), where the Court found probable cause to arrest an employee for writing notes to the employer containing bomb threats. The arrest was based mostly on the conclusion of a handwriting analyst. The Court recognized that handwriting analysis was an "inexact science" but found the expert's conclusion to be a "powerful start" toward probable cause. Added to this was the fact that the letters began shortly after the employee started working for the company; that they were found in the building where she worked; and that she acted nervously when questioned about the notes.

Mistaken Arrests

As is indicated by *Valez*, probable cause to arrest (or to search) can exist even though the police are mistaken in believing that the person arrested committed a crime. The question for probable cause is not accuracy but rather fair probability. See Hill v. California, 401 U.S. 797 (1971) (if police have probable cause to arrest Hill and have probable cause to believe that Miller is Hill, they act properly if they arrest Miller); Hirsch v. Burke, 40 F.3d 900 (7th Cir.1994) (police had probable cause to arrest a person for public drunkenness, even though in fact the person was a diabetic in a state of insulin shock).

Probabilities With Multiple Suspects

If a police officer finds drugs in a car, does he have probable cause to arrest everyone in the car? That is the question in the following case.

MARYLAND v. PRINGLE

Supreme Court of the United States, 2003
124 S.Ct. 795.

CHIEF JUSTICE REHNQUIST **delivered the opinion of the Court.**

* * *

At 3:16 a.m. on August 7, 1999, a Baltimore County Police officer stopped a Nissan Maxima for speeding. There were three occupants in the car: Donte Partlow, the driver and owner, respondent Pringle, the front-seat passenger, and Otis Smith, the back-seat passenger. The officer asked Partlow for his license and registration. When Partlow opened the glove compartment to retrieve the vehicle registration, the officer observed a large amount of rolled-up money in the glove compartment. The officer returned to his patrol car with Partlow's license and registration to check the computer system for outstanding violations. The computer check did not reveal any violations. The officer returned to the stopped car, had Partlow get out, and issued him an oral warning.

After a second patrol car arrived, the officer asked Partlow if he had any weapons or narcotics in the vehicle. Partlow indicated that he did not. Partlow then consented to a search of the vehicle. The search yielded $763 from the glove compartment and five plastic glassine baggies containing cocaine

from behind the back-seat armrest. When the officer began the search the armrest was in the upright position flat against the rear seat. The officer pulled down the armrest and found the drugs, which had been placed between the armrest and the back seat of the car.

The officer questioned all three men about the ownership of the drugs and money, and told them that if no one admitted to ownership of the drugs he was going to arrest them all. The men offered no information regarding the ownership of the drugs or money. All three were placed under arrest and transported to the police station.

Later that morning, Pringle waived his rights under Miranda v. Arizona, and gave an oral and written confession in which he acknowledged that the cocaine belonged to him, that he and his friends were going to a party, and that he intended to sell the cocaine or "use it for sex." Pringle maintained that the other occupants of the car did not know about the drugs, and they were released.

The trial court denied Pringle's motion to suppress his confession as the fruit of an illegal arrest, holding that the officer had probable cause to arrest Pringle. A jury convicted Pringle of possession with intent to distribute cocaine and possession of cocaine. * * * The Court of Appeals of Maryland, by divided vote, reversed, holding that, absent specific facts tending to show Pringle's knowledge and dominion or control over the drugs, "the mere finding of cocaine in the back armrest when [Pringle] was a front seat passenger in a car being driven by its owner is insufficient to establish probable cause for an arrest for possession." We granted certiorari, and now reverse.

* * * Maryland law authorizes police officers to execute warrantless arrests, *inter alia*, for felonies committed in an officer's presence or where an officer has probable cause to believe that a felony has been committed or is being committed in the officer's presence. A warrantless arrest of an individual in a public place for a felony, or a misdemeanor committed in the officer's presence, is consistent with the Fourth Amendment if the arrest is supported by probable cause.

It is uncontested in the present case that the officer, upon recovering the five plastic glassine baggies containing suspected cocaine, had probable cause to believe a felony had been committed. The sole question is whether the officer had probable cause to believe that Pringle committed that crime. Maryland law defines "possession" as "the exercise of actual or constructive dominion or control over a thing by one or more persons."

The long-prevailing standard of probable cause protects "citizens from rash and unreasonable interferences with privacy and from unfounded charges of crime," while giving "fair leeway for enforcing the law in the community's protection." Brinegar v.United States, 338 U.S. 160 (1949). On many occasions, we have reiterated that the probable-cause standard is a "practical, nontechnical conception"

that deals with "'the factual and practical considerations of everyday life on which reasonable and prudent men, not legal technicians, act.'" Illinois v. Gates. Probable cause is a fluid concept—turning on the assessment of probabilities in particular factual contexts—not readily, or even usefully, reduced to a neat set of legal rules.

The probable-cause standard is incapable of precise definition or quantification into percentages because it deals with probabilities and depends on the totality of the circumstances. * * * To determine whether an officer had probable cause to arrest an individual, we examine the events leading up to the arrest, and then decide whether these historical facts, viewed from the standpoint of an objectively reasonable police officer, amount to probable cause.

In this case, Pringle was one of three men riding in a Nissan Maxima at 3:16 a.m. There was $763 of rolled-up cash in the glove compartment directly in front of Pringle. Five plastic glassine baggies of cocaine were behind the back-seat armrest and accessible to all three men. Upon questioning, the three men failed to offer any information with respect to the ownership of the cocaine or the money.

We think it an entirely reasonable inference from these facts that any or all three of the occupants had knowledge of, and exercised dominion and control over, the cocaine. Thus a reasonable officer could conclude that there was probable cause to believe Pringle committed the crime of possession of cocaine, either solely or jointly.

Pringle's attempt to characterize this case as a guilt-by-association case is unavailing. His reliance on Ybarra v. Illinois [discussed in the section on stop and frisk, infra], and United States v. Di Re, 332 U.S. 581 (1948), is misplaced. In *Ybarra*, police officers obtained a warrant to search a tavern and its bartender for evidence of possession of a controlled substance. Upon entering the tavern, the officers conducted patdown searches of the customers present in the tavern, including Ybarra. Inside a cigarette pack retrieved from Ybarra's pocket, an officer found six tinfoil packets containing heroin. We stated:

> "[A] person's mere propinquity to others independently suspected of criminal activity does not, without more, give rise to probable cause to search that person. Where the standard is probable cause, a search or seizure of a person must be supported by probable cause particularized with respect to that person. This requirement cannot be undercut or avoided by simply pointing to the fact that coincidentally there exists probable cause to search or seize another or to search the premises where the person may happen to be."

We held that the search warrant did not permit body searches of all of the tavern's patrons and that the police could not pat down the patrons for weapons, absent individualized suspicion.

This case is quite different from *Ybarra*. Pringle and his two companions were in a relatively small automobile, not a public tavern. In Wyoming v. Houghton, 526 U.S. 295 (1999) [discussed in the section on automobile searches, infra], we noted that "a car passenger—unlike the unwitting tavern patron in *Ybarra*—will often be engaged in a common enterprise with the driver, and have the same interest in concealing the fruits or the evidence of their wrongdoing." Here we think it was reasonable for the officer to infer a common enterprise among the three men. The quantity of drugs and cash in the car indicated the likeli-

hood of drug dealing, an enterprise to which a dealer would be unlikely to admit an innocent person with the potential to furnish evidence against him.

In *Di Re*, a federal investigator had been told by an informant, Reed, that he was to receive counterfeit gasoline ration coupons from a certain Buttitta at a particular place. The investigator went to the appointed place and saw Reed, the sole occupant of the rear seat of the car, holding gasoline ration coupons. There were two other occupants in the car: Buttitta in the driver's seat and Di Re in the front passenger's seat. Reed informed the investigator that Buttitta had given him counterfeit coupons. Thereupon, all three men were arrested and searched. After noting that the officers had no information implicating Di Re and no information pointing to Di Re's possession of coupons, unless presence in the car warranted that inference, we concluded that the officer lacked probable cause to believe that Di Re was involved in the crime. We said "any inference that everyone on the scene of a crime is a party to it must disappear if the Government informer singles out the guilty person." No such singling out occurred in this case; none of the three men provided information with respect to the ownership of the cocaine or money.

We hold that the officer had probable cause to believe that Pringle had committed the crime of possession of a controlled substance. Pringle's arrest therefore did not contravene the Fourth and Fourteenth Amendments. Accordingly, the judgment of the Court of Appeals of Maryland is reversed, and the case is remanded for further proceedings not inconsistent with this opinion.

It is so ordered.

Questions on Pringle

Would the officers have had probable cause to arrest Pringle's 15 year-old son if he were a fourth occupant in the car? What about Pringle's 87 year-old great grandfather? Would the result in Pringle have been the same if the officer found no drugs in the car but obtained consent to search the trunk and found the drugs there?

6. Collective Knowledge

In Whiteley v. Warden, 401 U.S. 560 (1971), the Supreme Court said that "[c]ertainly police officers called upon to aid other officers in executing arrest warrants are entitled to assume that the officers requesting aid offered the magistrate the information requisite to support an independent judicial assessment of probable cause." This sensible approach means that once Officer A demonstrates to a magistrate probable cause to arrest a suspect, any other officer can make the arrest on the assumption that the warrant is valid. The arresting officer need not have independent knowledge of the arrestee's criminal activity. The same rule applies in warrantless arrest cases. If Officer B makes an arrest pursuant to orders from Officer A, and the latter had probable cause for the order, the arrest is valid. Why? Likewise with searches—the officer who actually conducts the search need not have personal knowledge of the facts supporting probable cause. All that is required is collective knowledge that rises to the level of probable cause. Why?

7. Staleness of Information

One problem that sometimes arises in assessing probable cause is that the officer's information is dated. For example, an officer may receive information from a reliable informant that the defendant had an ounce of marijuana in his home on January 1. Assuming that the informant's tip satisfies *Gates*, there is still a problem if the search of the defendant's home is conducted on July 1. Certainly, there is no fair probability that the same ounce of marijuana is still in the defendant's house six months later.

An example of a staleness problem arose in United States v. Harris, 20 F.3d 445 (11th Cir.1994). There was probable cause to believe that Ford was involved in a narcotics conspiracy in 1988. However, the warrant to search Ford's house was not issued until 1990. 1989 had apparently been a bad year for the conspiracy: several drug couriers had been arrested and large amounts of drugs had been seized. Two of Ford's top coconspirators had become embroiled in an altercation, and each had reported the other to the authorities. Ford argued that, under these circumstances, the information that he was involved in a narcotics conspiracy had become stale. The *Harris* Court had this to say about the staleness inquiry:

> When reviewing staleness challenges we do not apply some talismanic rule which establishes arbitrary time limitations * * *. In this case-by-case determination we may consider the maturity of the information, nature of the suspected crime (discrete crimes or ongoing conspiracy), habits of the accused, character of the items sought, and nature and function of the premises to be searched.

Applying these factors, the *Harris* Court found that the information provided to the magistrate established a fair probability that Ford was still involved in a narcotics conspiracy in 1990. The court noted that the conspiracy was "long-standing and protracted" and that the affidavit showed that Ford "had no visible source of income, yet owned a large house" and was still associated with some of his coconspirators. See also United States v. Spikes, 158 F.3d 913 (6th Cir.1998) (four-year-old information concerning drug activity was not stale where it was corroborated by more recent information, to lead to a fair conclusion that the defendant was engaged in continuous large-scale drug activity); United States v. Harvey, 2 F.3d 1318 (3d Cir.1993) (delivery of child pornography to defendant's home two to fifteen months before the search; information was not stale where police submitted with their warrant application an expert's affidavit indicating that "pedophiles rarely, if ever, dispose of sexually explicit material"); United States v. Diecidue, 603 F.2d 535 (5th Cir. 1979) (four-month-old report of projectiles in the walls and floors of a dwelling as a result of the test-firing of a murder weapon were not stale because the "floors and walls of a house are relatively permanent fixtures and would not likely be subject to removal over the period of four months").

8. *First Amendment Concerns*

In New York v. P.J. Video, 475 U.S. 868 (1986), Justice Rehnquist wrote for the Court as it held that warrants authorizing the seizure of "adult" tapes from a video store were supported by probable cause to believe that the tapes were pornographic. Justice Rehnquist first noted that "an application for a warrant authorizing the seizure of materials presumptively protected by the First Amendment should be evaluated under the same standard of probable cause used to review warrants generally."[12] The Court found that the affidavits in the instant case contained more than enough information to conclude that there was a "fair probability" that the movies satisfied the statutory definition of obscenity (i.e., predominant appeal to prurient interest in sex, specific sexual conduct presented in patently offensive manner, and no serious redeeming social value). Justice Marshall, joined by Justices Brennan and Stevens, dissented. He argued that the affidavits described only some excerpted scenes, and not the entirety of each film. So in his view the magistrate could not have determined that the sex acts pervaded the films or that the films as a whole lacked artistic value; while the *affidavits* were pervaded with sex acts, it did not necessarily follow that the *films* were obscene. The majority's response to Justice Marshall's argument was that one of the affidavits, for example, described five hardcore sex scenes, taking place in a 93 minute film; therefore the sheer volume of sex acts depicted in the such an affidavit established at least a fair probability that there was no time left for the film to include any matters of redeeming social value.

---

12. The Court observed that First Amendment decisions in Roaden v. Kentucky, 413 U.S. 496 (1973), A Quantity of Copies of Books v. Kansas, 378 U.S. 205 (1964), Marcus v. Search Warrants, 367 U.S. 717 (1961), Heller v. New York, 413 U.S. 483 (1973), and Lee Art Theatre, Inc. v. Virginia, 392 U.S. 636 (1968), provided various protections against seizure of films and books on the basis of their content. *Roaden* barred reliance on "exigent circumstances" to seize allegedly obscene materials if the seizure would amount to a prior restraint. *A Quantity of Books* and *Marcus* prohibited large-scale seizures constituting a prior restraint without an adversary hearing first. *Heller* restricted seizure of allegedly obscene materials, even where there is no prior restraint, to searches pursuant to a warrant with a prompt post-seizure hearing provided. *Lee Art Theatres* barred the issuance of a warrant based upon the conclusory statements of a police officer that materials are obscene. After *P.J. Video*, the Court held in Fort Wayne Books, Inc. v. Indiana, 489 U.S. 46 (1989) that the First Amendment prohibits the seizure of more than one copy of a book or film until there has been a determination of obscenity following an adversary hearing.

When *P.J. Video* returned to the state courts, the New York Court of Appeals held in New York v. P.J. Video, Inc., 68 N.Y.2d 296, 508 N.Y.S.2d 907, 501 N.E.2d 556 (1986), that the state constitution barred reliance on the totality of circumstances approach for warrants directed at allegedly obscene materials. It reasoned that all aspects of the statutory definition of obscenity are significant and that the Supreme Court's approach effectively ignored some of the statutory elements.

B. PROBABLE CAUSE, SPECIFICITY AND REASONABLENESS

1. *The Things That Can Be Seized*

Up until 1967, the Court had consistently held that the Fourth Amendment prohibited the government from searching for or seizing anything other that the "fruits and instrumentalities" of a crime. "Mere evidence" of a crime was considered beyond the scope of a permissible Fourth Amendment search. So for example, if officers had probable cause to believe that the defendant was a narcotics dealer, they could search for and seize narcotics and related paraphernalia, but they would not be permitted to look for phone records or storage locker rental agreements, because these things were "mere evidence" of the crime. Obviously, the mere evidence rule severely constricted the scope of a search that a magistrate could authorize.

In the following case, the Warren Court dramatically expanded the possibilities for law enforcement, both when searching pursuant to a warrant and when searching pursuant to an exception to the warrant requirement.

WARDEN v. HAYDEN

Supreme Court of the United States, 1967.
387 U.S. 294.

JUSTICE BRENNAN **delivered the opinion of the Court.**

We review in this case the validity of the proposition that there is under the Fourth Amendment a "distinction between merely evidentiary materials, on the one hand, which may not be seized either under the authority of a search warrant or during the course of a search incident to arrest, and on the other hand, those objects which may validly be seized including the instrumentalities and means by which a crime is committed, the fruits of crime such as stolen property, weapons by which escape of the person arrested might be effected, and property the possession of which is a crime."

A Maryland court sitting without a jury convicted respondent of armed robbery. Items of his clothing, a cap,

jacket, and trousers, among other things, were seized during a search of his home, and were admitted in evidence without objection. After unsuccessful state court proceedings, he sought and was denied federal habeas corpus relief in the District Court for Maryland. A divided panel of the Court of Appeals for the Fourth Circuit reversed. The Court of Appeals believed that * * * respondent was correct in his contention that the clothing seized was improperly admitted in evidence because the items had "evidential value only" and therefore were not lawfully subject to seizure. * * * We reverse.

I.

* * *

II.

[The Court held that the search of Hayden's house, while without a warrant, was justified by exigent circumstances].

III.

We come, then, to the question whether, even though the search was lawful, the Court of Appeals was correct in holding that the seizure and introduction of the items of clothing violated the Fourth Amendment because they are "mere evidence." The distinction made by some of our cases between seizure of items of evidential value only and seizure of instrumentalities, fruits, or contraband has been criticized by courts and commentators. * * * We today reject the distinction as based on premises no longer accepted as rules governing the application of the Fourth Amendment.

* * *

Nothing in the language of the Fourth Amendment supports the distinction between "mere evidence" and instrumentalities, fruits of crime, or contraband. On its face, the provision assures the "right of the people to be secure in their persons, houses, papers, and effects . . . ," without regard to the use to which any of these things are applied. This "right of the people" is certainly unrelated to the "mere evidence" limitation. Privacy is disturbed no more by a search directed to a purely evidentiary object than it is by a search directed to an instrumentality, fruit, or contraband. A magistrate can intervene in both situations, and the requirements of probable cause and specificity can be preserved intact. Moreover, nothing in the nature of property seized as evidence renders it more private than property seized, for example, as an instrumentality; quite the opposite may be true. Indeed, the distinction is wholly irrational, since,

depending on the circumstances, the same "papers and effects" may be "mere evidence" in one case and "instrumentality" in another.

* * *

The requirement that the Government assert in addition some property interest in material it seizes has long been a fiction, obscuring the reality that government has an interest in solving crime. * * * The requirements of the Fourth Amendment can secure the same protection of privacy whether the search is for "mere evidence" or for fruits, instrumentalities or contraband. There must, of course, be a nexus—automatically provided in the case of fruits, instrumentalities or contraband—between the item to be seized and criminal behavior. Thus in the case of "mere evidence," probable cause must be examined in terms of cause to believe that the evidence sought will aid in a particular apprehension or conviction. In so doing, consideration of police purposes will be required. But no such problem is presented in this case. The clothes found * * * matched the description of those worn by the robber and the police therefore could reasonably believe that the items would aid in the identification of the culprit.

* * *

The rationale most frequently suggested for the rule preventing the seizure of evidence is that "limitations upon the fruit to be gathered tend to limit the quest itself." But privacy "would be just as well served by a restriction on search to the even-numbered days of the month. * * * And it would have the extra advantage of avoiding hair-splitting questions * * *." The "mere evidence" limitation has spawned exceptions so numerous and confusion so great, in fact, that it is questionable whether it affords meaningful protection. But if its rejection does enlarge the area of permissible searches, the intrusions are nevertheless made after fulfilling the probable cause and particularity requirements of the Fourth Amendment and after the intervention of "a neutral and detached magistrate." The Fourth Amendment allows intrusions upon privacy under these circumstances, and there is no viable reason to distinguish intrusions to secure "mere evidence" from intrusions to secure fruits, instrumentalities, or contraband.

The judgment of the Court of Appeals is reversed.

JUSTICE BLACK concurs in the result.

[The concurring opinion by Justice Fortas, joined by Chief Justice Warren, is omitted].

JUSTICE DOUGLAS, **dissenting.**

* * *

* * * The personal effects and possessions of the individual (all contraband and the like excepted) are sacrosanct from prying eyes, from the long arm of the law, from any rummaging by police. Privacy involves the choice of the individual to disclose or to reveal what he believes, what he thinks, what he possesses. * * * The Framers, who were as knowledgeable as we, knew what police surveillance meant and how the practice of rummaging through one's personal effects could destroy freedom.

* * *

* * * I would * * * leave with the individual the choice of opening his private effects (apart from contraband and the like) to the police or keeping their contents a secret and their integrity inviolate. The existence of that choice is the very essence of the right of privacy. Without it the Fourth Amendment and the Fifth are ready instruments for the police state that the Framers sought to avoid.

Note on the Mere Evidence Rule

Is Justice Brennan correct that a "mere evidence" distinction makes no sense? Could the mere evidence distinction be justified by the practical problems that the lack of such a distinction can create? For example, if mere evidence can be the target of a search, then it is certainly a challenge to administer the particularity requirement of the warrant clause. How can you describe mere evidence with any particularity? "Evidence of a large scale drug operation" could cover everything in the premises, from electric bills to dollar bills, from trace elements on a table to the food in the refrigerator that could be used to entertain buyers.

Societal privacy interests are also undoubtedly threatened by the abrogation of the mere evidence rule. Without a mere evidence limitation, an innocent third party's home or office may be the legitimate object of a search; evidence that might be relevant to a crime can be spread far and wide, while the fruits and instrumentalities of a crime are more often kept with the perpetrators. As you proceed through this Chapter, try to determine how the cases discussed would have been resolved under a mere evidence limitation. You will undoubtedly conclude that Warden v. Hayden had a fundamental, pro-prosecution effect on Fourth Amendment law.

Does the result in Warden v. Hayden comport with your impression of the Warren Court's criminal procedure jurisprudence? See Saltzburg, Criminal Procedure in the 1960s: A Reality Check, 42 Drake L.J.179 (1993) (noting that the Warren Court's pro-defendant reputation is belied by cases like Warden v. Hayden).

2. *Probable Cause as to Location of Evidence*

It is sometimes the case that police have probable cause to believe that a suspect has committed a crime and is in control of certain evidence, but are less sure where the evidence is located. Can they obtain a search warrant for the premises where the suspect lives on the theory that it is the most likely place to search for evidence? The premises where the suspect works? The places that the suspect frequents? In Zurcher v. Stanford Daily, 436 U.S. 547, 556 (1978), the majority stated that "[t]he critical element * * * is reasonable cause to believe that the specific 'things' to be searched for and seized are located on the property to which entry is sought." This will depend on "the type of crime, the nature of the items sought, the suspect's opportunity for concealment and normal inferences about where a criminal might hide" evidence of a crime. See United States v. Jones, 994 F.2d 1051 (3d Cir.1993) (sufficient nexus between robbery and defendants' homes, because items sought, such as cash, were the kinds of things "that criminals like to keep in secure places like their homes").

It follows that probable cause does not automatically exist to search a person's home simply because that person has been involved in a crime. For example, in United States v. Lalor, 996 F.2d 1578 (4th Cir.1993), the court held that a warrant to search Lalor's residence was invalid. Investigation showed only that Lalor and others sold drugs on the street. The court reasoned that this was insufficient to establish probable cause that Lalor kept evidence of drug activity at his house. No attempt was made to link the street sales with any activity at Lalor's house. The court, citing cases, declared that "residential searches have been upheld only where some information links the criminal activity to the defendant's residence." Compare United States v. Pitts, 6 F.3d 1366 (9th Cir.1993) (finding a sufficient nexus between defendant's narcotics activity and his home: "in the case of drug dealers, evidence is likely to be found where the dealers live"). Considering the purposes of the warrant requirement, what do you think the correct standard is?

3. *Searches of Non–Suspects' Premises*

In some investigations, police may have probable cause to search one person's premises for evidence that could be used against another. That and several other problems arose in Zurcher v. Stanford Daily, 436 U.S. 547 (1978). Officers had probable cause to believe that a Stanford Daily photographer had taken pictures of demonstrators who attacked a group of police officers. A warrant was obtained to search the Daily's offices for negatives, film, and pictures taken at the demonstration. The warrant affidavit contained no allegation that members of the Daily staff were in any way involved in unlawful acts. The search pursuant to the warrant was conducted by four police officers in the presence of some members of the Daily staff. The Daily's photographic laboratories, filing cabinets, desks, and wastepaper baskets were searched. Locked drawers and rooms were not opened. No evidence pertinent to the assault on the officers was uncovered. Thereafter, the Daily and some members of its staff brought a civil action seeking declaratory and injunctive relief, alleging that the entry, even though with a warrant, was in violation of the Fourth Amendment.

The lower court in *Zurcher* held that the Fourth Amendment did not permit a warrant to search for materials in possession of one not suspected of a crime, unless it was apparent that a subpoena and a court order would be futile. But the Supreme Court reversed and found the warrant valid, in an opinion by Justice White.

Justice White defined the question presented:

> The issue here is how the Fourth Amendment is to be construed and applied to the "third party" search, the recurring situation where state authorities have probable cause to believe that fruits, instrumentalities, or other evidence of crime is located on identified property but do not then have probable cause to believe that the owner or possessor of the property is himself implicated in the crime that has occurred or is occurring.

Justice White declared that there was nothing special about the search of a third party's premises. The question in any case is whether there is probable cause to believe that evidence of a crime will be found in the place to be searched:

> Under existing law, valid warrants may be issued to search *any* property, whether or not occupied by a third party, at which there is probable cause to believe that fruits, instrumentalities, or evidence of a crime will be found. Nothing on the face of the Amendment suggests that a third-party search warrant should not normally issue. The Warrant Clause speaks of search warrants issued on "probable cause" and "particularly describing the place to be searched, and the persons or things to be seized." * * *.

* * *

> The critical element in a reasonable search is not that the owner of the property is suspected of crime but that there is reasonable cause to believe that the specific "things" to be searched for and seized are located on the property to which entry is sought. * * *

Justice White emphasized the practical problems that would arise for law enforcement if search warrants could not be issued for third party premises:

> [S]earch warrants are often employed early in an investigation, perhaps before the identity of any likely criminal and certainly before all the perpetrators are or could be known. The seemingly blameless third party in possession of the fruits or evidence may not be innocent at all; and if he is, he may nevertheless be so related to or so sympathetic with the culpable party that he cannot be relied upon to retain and preserve the articles that may implicate his friends, or at least not to notify those who would be damaged by the evidence that the authorities are aware of its location. In any event, it is likely that the real culprits will have access to the property, and the delay involved in employing the subpoena *duces tecum,* offering as it does the opportunity to litigate its validity, could easily result in the disappearance of the evidence, whatever the good faith of the third party.

Justice White intimated that the reasonableness clause of the Fourth Amendment might impose some limitations on the execution of a search, even if the search was supported by a warrant issued upon probable cause. However, "the courts may not, in the name of Fourth Amendment reasonableness, forbid the States from issuing warrants to search for evidence simply because the owner or possessor of the place to be searched is not then reasonably suspected of criminal involvement."

Finally, Justice White rejected the argument that First Amendment concerns required a limitation on the use of warrants to search the office of a newspaper:

> There is no reason to believe * * * that magistrates cannot guard against searches of the type, scope, and intrusiveness that would actually interfere with the timely publication of a newspaper. Nor, if the requirements of specificity and reasonableness are properly applied, policed, and observed, will there be any occasion or opportunity for officers to rummage at large in newspaper files or to intrude into or to deter normal editorial and publication decisions. * * * Nor are we convinced * * * that confidential sources will disappear and that the press will suppress news because of fears of warranted searches.

Justice Stewart, joined by Justice Marshall, dissented in *Zurcher* and argued that the use of a warrant to search a newspaper constituted an infringement on First Amendment rights.

Justice Stevens wrote a separate dissent, in which he noted that the problem of third party searches had been created by "the profound change in Fourth Amendment law that occurred in 1967, when Warden v. Hayden was decided." He elaborated as follows:

> In the pre-*Hayden* era warrants were used to search for contraband, weapons, and plunder, but not for "mere evidence." The practical effect of the rule prohibiting the issuance of warrants to search for mere evidence was to narrowly limit not only the category of objects, but also the category of persons and the character of the privacy interests that might be affected by an unannounced police search.

> Just as the witnesses who participate in an investigation or a trial far outnumber the defendants, the persons who possess evidence that may help to identify an offender, or explain an aspect of a criminal transaction, far outnumber those who have custody of weapons or plunder. Countless law-abiding citizens—doctors, lawyers, merchants, customers, bystanders—may have documents in their possession that relate to an ongoing criminal investigation. The consequences of subjecting this large category of persons to unannounced police searches are extremely serious. The *ex parte* warrant procedure enables the prosecutor to obtain access to privileged documents that could not be examined if advance notice gave the custodian an opportunity to object. The search for the documents described in a warrant may involve the inspection of files containing other private matter. The dramatic character of a sudden search may cause an entirely unjustified injury to the reputation of the persons searched.

Justice Stevens argued that a "showing of probable cause that was adequate to justify the issuance of a warrant to search for stolen goods in the 18th century does not automatically satisfy the new dimensions of the Fourth Amendment in the post-*Hayden* era." He concluded that "[t]he only conceivable justification for an unannounced search of an innocent citizen is the fear that, if notice were given, he would conceal or destroy the object of the search." Since there was nothing in the warrant application to indicate that the Daily would destroy evidence, Justice Stevens contended that the search, even though pursuant to a warrant, was unreasonable.

Law Office Searches

While searches of third-party premises are governed by the Fourth Amendment standards applicable to searches generally, special problems of confidentiality arise if the officer has probable cause to search a lawyer's office for evidence against the client. After *Zurcher,* the Minnesota Supreme Court held that under the state constitution and the Fourth Amendment, it is unreasonable for police to secure a warrant to search an attorney's office for records belonging to a client, unless the attorney also is suspected of wrongdoing or there is a threat of destruction of the records. O'Connor v. Johnson, 287 N.W.2d 400 (Minn.1979). Wisconsin has accomplished the same thing as Minnesota, but through legislation. Wis.Stat.Ann. § 968.13 (1979).

Whatever extra protections might otherwise exist with respect to law office searches, they do not apply if there is probable cause to believe that the lawyer is engaged in criminal activity unrelated to representing clients. See United States v. Czuprynski, 46 F.3d 560 (6th Cir.1995) (en banc) (warrant authorizing law office search for marijuana on the basis of report by a dismissed associate; lawyer sentenced to 14 months' imprisonment for possession of 1.6 grams of marijuana; conviction affirmed).

National City Trading Corp. v. United States, 635 F.2d 1020 (2d Cir.1980), illustrates how broad the search of a law office can be: the court approved the search of a suite of rooms which were used for business purposes and as a lawyer's office. The court stated:

Although a law office search should be executed with special care to avoid unnecessary intrusion on attorney-client communications, it is nevertheless proper if there is reasonable cause to believe that the specific items are located on the property to be searched. * * * A criminal enterprise does not exempt itself from a search warrant by conducting its business and keeping its records in its lawyer's office.

4. Describing the Place to Be Searched

The warrant clause requires a particularized description of the place to be searched. The Colonial experience with general warrants was the major reason for including the Fourth Amendment in the Bill of Rights; the particularity requirement is designed to protect against the use of a warrant as a general warrant.

Function of the Particularity Requirement

The requirement of a particular description of the place to be searched provides at least three protections:

First, if the executing officer has no knowledge of the underlying facts, the particular description of the premises in the warrant operates as a necessary control on his discretion. Without a particular description, the unknowing officer may conduct a search in every place that fits a general description. We would not want an officer, armed with a single search warrant, to search every "house on Second Avenue," for example. See, e.g., United States v. Nafzger, 965 F.2d 213 (7th Cir.1992) ("By accepting 'the Western District of Wisconsin' as a particular description of the place the truck was to be found we would be giving the government carte blanche to search anywhere in that district that the truck might conceivably be found, condoning the use of the pernicious general warrant, and redacting the particularity requirement from the fourth amendment."). See also United States v. Stefonek, 179 F.3d 1030 (7th Cir.1999) (particularity requirement is necessary to "make sure that the law enforcement officer who executes the warrant stays within the bounds set by the issuer").

Second, even if the executing officer knows the place she wants to search, the particular description in the warrant establishes a specific record of probable cause as to location prior to the search. The officer is not permitted, after the fact, to construct the case that would have supported probable cause to search the place she eventually chose.

Finally, the particularity requirement prevents the officer from using the warrant as a blank check to expand a search by relying on an overly general description of the place to be searched. See, e.g., United States v. Cannon, 264 F.3d 875 (9th Cir. 2001) (warrant to search a house did not permit officers to search a building that was unconnected to the house).

Reasonable Particularity

The Fourth Amendment requires that the warrant must set forth the location of the place to be searched with reasonable particularity. Technical precision is not required in all cases. The degree of particularity that is reasonable depends on the nature of the place to be searched and on the information that an officer could reasonably obtain about the location before a warrant is issued. Consider the following cases.

It is well accepted that "two or more apartments in the same building stand on the same footing as two or more houses. A single warrant cannot describe an entire building when cause is shown for searching only one apartment." Moore v. United States, 461 F.2d 1236, 1238 (D.C.Cir.1972). But in Maryland v. Garrison, 480 U.S. 79 (1987), the Court upheld a warrant authorizing the search of a "third floor apartment" even though there were actually two apartments on the third floor. Baltimore police officers had probable cause to believe that illegal activity was being conducted in an apartment on the third floor of a four-story building, and they conducted an investigation to determine whether there was more than one apartment on the floor. An officer obtained information from the utility company and telephone company which appeared to indicate that the entire third floor consisted of one apartment. The officer checked out the door buzzers outside the apartment building, but this did not indicate how many apartments were on any particular floor. There were seven apartments listed in the four-story building. The officer then obtained a warrant that authorized the search of the "third floor apartment." After entering the apartment building, the officers eventually found that there were two apartments on the third floor, with one door to both apartments, and a shared entryway. McWebb, the suspect, occupied one of the apartments, and Garrison occupied the other. Before the officers realized that they were mistakenly in Garrison's apartment, they discovered contraband leading to Garrison's arrest and conviction.

The Court in *Garrison*, in an opinion written by Justice Stevens for six Justices, held that the description in the warrant of the place to be searched was sufficiently particular. Justice Stevens reasoned as follows:

Plainly, if the officers had known, or even if they should have known, that there were two separate dwelling units on the third floor of 2036 Park Avenue, they would have been obligated to exclude [Garrison's] apartment from the scope of the requested warrant. But we must judge the constitutionality of their conduct in light of the information available to them at the time they acted. Those items of evidence that emerge after the warrant is issued have no bearing on whether or not a warrant was validly issued. * * * The validity of the warrant must be assessed on the basis of the information that the officers disclosed, or had a duty to discover and to disclose, to the issuing Magistrate. On the basis of that information, we agree with the conclusion of all three Maryland courts that the warrant, insofar as it authorized a search that turned out to be ambiguous in scope, was valid when it issued.[13]

Compare United States v. Johnson, 26 F.3d 669 (7th Cir.1994), where the warrant authorized the search of an entire duplex occupied by several members of a narcotics conspiracy. Even though the officer was aware that it was a multiple dwelling, the court upheld the warrant as sufficiently particular:

The defendant argues that in "multiple dwelling" cases we must suppress all the evidence seized pursuant to the overbroad warrant. While that may be true when the warrant authorizes the search of an entire structure and the officers do not know which unit contains the evidence of illegal conduct, that analysis does not apply when (1) the officer knows that there are multiple units and believes there is probable cause to search each unit, or (2) the targets of the investigation have access to the entire structure.

Single family dwellings usually present less of a problem of particular description than the multi-family dwellings discussed above. In urban areas, a street address is considered sufficiently particular. In rural areas, less particularized descriptions may be reasonable due to the absence of street addresses. See United States v. Dorrough, 927 F.2d 498 (10th Cir.1991) (warrant sufficiently particular where it describes a well-marked turnoff leading to the house, a quarter mile up a mountain, and the defendant's house is the only one up the mountain). The ultimate question is "whether the place to be searched is described with sufficient particularity to enable the executing officer to locate and identify the premises with reasonable effort, and whether there is any reasonable probability that another premise might be mistakenly searched." United States v. Pelayo–Landero, 285 F.3d 491 (6th Cir. 2002) (trailer home sufficiently described where directions are given to the trailer park and the warrant describes the particular trailer by color, by a certain exterior trim and by a wooden deck).

The Wrong Address

In some cases, warrants have misdescribed an address. These mistakes arise most often where a building is on a corner or is set back from a street. For

13. Of course, a validly issued warrant may be improperly executed. In *Garrison*, however, the Court found that the officers acted reasonably, though mistakenly, by searching Garrison's apartment, because the layout of the two apartments made it appear as if it was actually one apartment on the third floor. By the time the officers discovered that there were two separate apartments (presumably when they found two kitchens) they had already discovered the evidence that was used against Garrison.

example, in Lyons v. Robinson, 783 F.2d 737 (8th Cir.1985), the warrant listed the place to be searched as 325 Adkinson Street; Lyons' residence was actually 325 Short Street, on the corner of Short and Adkinson. The *Lyons* Court stated that the description, though inaccurate, was sufficiently particular because it made it unlikely under the circumstances that another premises might be mistakenly searched.

In light of the result in *Lyons*, consider United States v. Ellis, 971 F.2d 701 (11th Cir.1992). The court described the facts surrounding the search as follows:

On May 6, 1988, Deputy Nick LaManna prepared an affidavit for a search warrant. Based on his observations, LaManna requested a warrant to search "the third mobile home on the north side of Christian Acres Road" in Grand Bay, Alabama. The warrant and accompanying affidavit did not give any other information to narrow the search, and LaManna (at that time) did not know who inhabited the home. The documents did not indicate that the mobile home was owned or inhabited by Billy Ellis, but in fact indicated that the "occupant [was] unknown to affiant." Moreover, the documents did not describe the physical appearance of Ellis' mobile home in any way. In fact, the affidavit added nothing to the warrant.

Officers other than LaManna executed the search. Although by this time the officers knew that they were looking for Billy Ellis' mobile home, they had no knowledge of what the mobile home looked like or where it was, apart from the information in the warrant and affidavit. As a result, the officers relied on the warrant and went to the third mobile home. Its inhabitant informed them that Billy Ellis actually lived at the fifth mobile home on the north side of the road. At this point, the officers did not call the station to corroborate this information, nor did they bother to procure a corrected warrant. Furthermore, the officers did not contact LaManna; although he was apparently nearby, he did not arrive at the fifth mobile home until after the officers had already begun the search. Rather, the officers accepted the neighbor's word at face value and went directly to the fifth mobile home. After the officers had begun to search it, Deputy LaManna arrived and confirmed that this was the home he had observed, i.e., Billy Ellis' residence.

The *Ellis* Court held that the mistaken address rendered the warrant defective, and that the information given by the neighbor did not correct the defect:

The warrant did not describe the mobile home physically, unlike numerous warrants that have previously been upheld despite a mistaken address. Similarly, the name "Billy Ellis" did not appear anywhere on the warrant or the affidavit. * * * Considering that the only information in the warrant was erroneous, we believe that the warrant did not describe the place to be searched with sufficient particularity.

* * *

* * * The procedure employed in this case risked a general search. Had the neighbor given the officers the wrong address, they might have gone from home to home and attempted to search numerous mistaken residences. * * * [A]n erroneous search was averted in this case by pure serendipity: the inhabitant of the third mobile home just happened to be home to stop

the officers from searching that residence, and that inhabitant just happened to direct the officers to the correct mobile home. This is not a case where the officers took every step that could reasonably be expected of them. Once the officers recognized that the warrant specified the wrong address, they could have attempted to contact Detective LaManna, who could have insured that the officers' next stab was a correct one. Alternatively, the officers could have used the information from the inhabitant of the third mobile home to obtain a new, corrected warrant.

Do you agree with the court's analysis? How likely is it that the neighbor would have been wrong about the location of Ellis' mobile home?

The Breadth of the Place to Be Searched

The cases discussed above deal with whether the warrant sufficiently describes the location of the premises to be searched. A different particularity question that sometimes arises is whether the warrant sufficiently describes particular places in the general area to be searched. For example, if the warrant authorizes the search of the "premises" at 1825 Elm Street, do the police have the authority to search a freestanding garage behind the house at that address?

In United States v. Earls, 42 F.3d 1321 (10th Cir.1994), the court held that a warrant to search "the premises" at a particular location covered a detached garage, a shed, and an office, each of which was located within the curtilage of the house described in the warrant. Similarly, courts have generally held that "a search warrant authorizing a search of a certain premises generally includes any vehicles located within its curtilage if the objects of the search might be located" in those vehicles. See United States v. Gorman, 104 F.3d 272 (9th Cir.1996) (container found in the curtilage was within the scope of a warrant authorizing the search of a bus used as a home). See also United States v. Kyles, 40 F.3d 519 (2d Cir.1994) (warrant to search an apartment authorized the agent to search the defendant's locked bedroom, even though the defendant was not named as a suspect; the room was not a separate residence outside the scope of the warrant); United States v. Ferreras, 192 F.3d 5 (1st Cir. 1999) (warrant to search a second floor apartment authorizes the search of an attic on the third floor where the attic was open to the second floor, but not to the street or the first floor apartment, and the attic was not equipped for independent living).

One of the most difficult problems for the courts has been the scope of the search of the property of persons who happen to be on the premises that are being searched pursuant to a warrant. Most courts have held that any person's property is subject to search so long as the property could contain the items described in the warrant. United States v. Gonzalez, 940 F.2d 1413 (11th Cir.1991) (court upholds search of a visitor's briefcase capable of concealing evidence sought in the warrant).

All of these scope rulings are simply an application of the principle that a warrant permitting a search of a house or a building authorizes the police to search anywhere within the building (or curtilage) that is large enough to contain the evidence the police are looking for. The scope of the authority to search a described area is set forth in colorful language by Judge Posner in United States v. Evans, 92 F.3d 540 (7th Cir.1996):

If they are looking for a canary's corpse, they can search a cupboard, but not a locket. If they are looking for an adolescent hippopotamus, they can search the living room or garage but not the microwave oven. If they are searching for cocaine, they can search a container large enough to hold a gram, or perhaps less.

In *Evans,* the defendant objected to the search of the trunk of his car, which was parked in the detached garage of a house. The warrant authorized a search for drugs in both the house and detached garage. Evans complained, among other things, that he resided at the house (and parked his car there) only intermittently. But Judge Posner found no problem with the search:

> It seems to us that a car parked in a garage is just another interior container, like a closet or a desk. If, as in this case, the trunk or glove compartment is not too small to hold what the search warrant authorizes the police to look for, they can search the trunk and the glove compartment. * * * It does not matter whose [car] it is unless it obviously belonged to someone wholly uninvolved in the criminal activities going on in the house. If an innocent guest leaves a trunk in the host's house and the police obtain a search warrant to search the house for something small enough to fit in the trunk, then, unless it is apparent that the trunk does not belong to anyone connected with the illegal activity—a condition that will rarely be satisfied—the police can search the trunk and if it happens to contain evidence that the guest is a criminal after all, albeit innocent of any involvement in the criminal activities of his host, he is out of luck.

5. *Particularity for Arrest Warrants*

An arrest warrant must describe the person to be seized with sufficient particularity. Does the fact that the officers have probable cause to arrest a person mean that the person can be specifically described? Is a warrant authorizing the arrest of "John Doe a/k/a Ed" sufficiently particular? The court in United States v. Doe, 703 F.2d 745 (3d Cir.1983), held that such a warrant was overbroad, and held further that the insufficient description was not cured by the fact that the officer who executed the warrant had independent personal knowledge that the arrestee was the person for whom the warrant was intended. Why doesn't the officer's personal knowledge solve the problem? Would the warrant have been sufficiently particular if it described "John Doe, a/k/a Ed, a white male six feet tall and 200 pounds"?

6. *Describing the Things to Be Seized*

The breadth of possible searches makes the probable cause and specificity requirements of the warrant clause critical, if the magistrate is to limit "unreasonable" searches and seizures. The following case is the Supreme Court's major pronouncement on the permissible breadth of an authorized seizure.

ANDRESEN v. MARYLAND

Supreme Court of the United States, 1976.
427 U.S. 463.

Mr. Justice Blackmun delivered the opinion of the Court.

* * *

I

In early 1972, a Bi–County Fraud Unit, acting under the joint auspices of the State's Attorneys' Offices of Montgomery and Prince George's Counties, Md., began an investigation of real estate settlement activities in the Washington, D.C., area. At the time, petitioner Andresen was an attorney who, as a sole practitioner, specialized in real estate settlements in Montgomery County. During the Fraud Unit's investigation, his activities came under scrutiny, particularly in connection with a transaction involving Lot 13T in the Potomac Woods subdivision of Montgomery County. The investigation, which included interviews with the purchaser, the mortgage holder, and other lienholders of Lot 13T, as well as an examination of county land records, disclosed that petitioner, acting as settlement attorney, had defrauded Standard–Young Associates, the purchaser of Lot 13T. Petitioner had represented that the property was free of liens and that, accordingly, no title insurance was necessary, when in fact, he knew that there were two outstanding liens on the property. In addition, investigators learned that the lienholders, by threatening to foreclose their liens, had forced a halt to the purchaser's construction on the property. When Standard–Young had confronted petitioner with this information, he responded by issuing, as an agent of a title insurance company, a title policy guaranteeing clear title to the property. By this action, petitioner also defrauded that insurance company by requiring it to pay the outstanding liens.

The investigators * * * applied for warrants to search petitioner's law office and the separate office of Mount Vernon Development Corporation, of which petitioner was incorporator, sole shareholder, resident agent, and director. The application sought permission to search for specified documents pertaining to the sale and conveyance of Lot 13T. A judge of the Sixth Judicial Circuit of Montgomery County concluded that there was probable cause and issued the warrants.

The searches of the two offices were conducted simultaneously during daylight hours on October 31, 1972.[a] Petitioner was present during the search of his law office and was free to move about. Counsel for him was present during the latter half of the search. Between 2% and 3% of the files in the office were seized. A single investigator, in the presence of a police officer, conducted the search of Mount Vernon Development Corporation. This search, taking about four hours, resulted in the seizure of less than 5% of the corporation's files.

* * *

III

[Petitioner contends] that rights guaranteed him by the Fourth Amend-

---

a. Before these search warrants were executed, the Bi–County Fraud Unit had also received complaints concerning other Potomac Woods real estate transactions conducted by petitioner. The gist of the complaints was that petitioner, as settlement attorney, took money from three sets of home purchasers upon assurances that he would use it to procure titles to their properties free and clear of all encumbrances. It was charged that he had misappropriated the money so that they had not received clear title to the properties as promised.

ment were violated because the descriptive terms of the search warrants were so broad as to make them impermissible "general" warrants * * *.

The specificity of the search warrants. Although petitioner concedes that the warrants for the most part were models of particularity, he contends that they were rendered fatally "general" by the addition, in each warrant, to the exhaustive list of particularly described documents, of the phrase "together with other fruits, instrumentalities and evidence of crime at this [time] unknown." The quoted language, it is argued, must be read in isolation and without reference to the rest of the long sentence at the end of which it appears. When read "properly," petitioner contends, it permits the search for and seizure of any evidence of any crime.

* * *

In this case we agree with the determination of the Court of Special Appeals of Maryland that the challenged phrase must be read as authorizing only the search for and seizure of evidence relating to "the crime of false pretenses with respect to Lot 13T." The challenged phrase is not a separate sentence. Instead, it appears in each warrant at the end of a sentence containing a lengthy list of specified and particular items to be seized, all pertaining to Lot 13T.[b] We think it clear from the context that the term "crime" in the warrants refers only to the crime of false pretenses with respect to the sale of Lot 13T. The "other fruits" clause is one of a series that follows the colon after the word "Maryland." All clauses in the series are limited by what precedes that colon, namely, "items pertaining to * * * lot 13, block T." The warrants, accordingly, did not authorize the executing officers to conduct a search for evidence of other crimes but only to search for and seize evidence relevant to the crime of false pretenses and Lot 13T.[c]

* * *

b. "[T]he following items pertaining to sale, purchase, settlement and conveyance of lot 13, block T, Potomac Woods subdivision, Montgomery County, Maryland:

"title notes, title abstracts, title rundowns; contracts of sale and/or assignments from Raffaele Antonelli and Rocco Caniglia to Mount Vernon Development Corporation and/or others; lien payoff correspondence and lien payoff memoranda to and from lienholders and noteholders; correspondence and memoranda to and from trustees of deeds of trust; lenders instructions for a construction loan or construction and permanent loan; disbursement sheets and disbursement memoranda; checks, check stubs and ledger sheets indicating disbursement upon settlement; correspondence and memoranda concerning disbursements upon settlement; settlement statements and settlement memoranda; fully or partially prepared deed of trust releases, whether or not executed and whether or not recorded; books, records, documents, papers, memoranda and correspondence, showing or tending to show a fraudulent intent, and/or knowledge as elements of the crime of false pretenses, in violation of Article 27, Section 140, of the Annotated Code of Maryland, 1957 Edition, as amended and revised, together with other

fruits, instrumentalities and evidence of crime at this [time] unknown."

Petitioner also suggests that the specific list of the documents to be seized constitutes a "general" warrant. We disagree. Under investigation was a complex real estate scheme whose existence could be proved only by piecing together many bits of evidence. Like a jigsaw puzzle, the whole "picture" of petitioner's false-pretense scheme with respect to Lot 13T could be shown only by placing in the proper place the many pieces of evidence that, taken singly, would show comparatively little. The complexity of an illegal scheme may not be used as a shield to avoid detection when the State has demonstrated probable cause to believe that a crime has been committed and probable cause to believe that evidence of this crime is in the suspect's possession.

c. The record discloses that the officials executing the warrants seized numerous papers that were not introduced into evidence. Although we are not informed of their content, we observe that to the extent such papers were not within the scope of the warrants or were otherwise improperly seized, the State was correct in returning them voluntarily and the trial judge was correct in suppressing others.

We recognize that there are grave dangers inherent in executing a warrant authorizing a

Mr. Justice Brennan, **dissenting.**

* * *

* * * After a lengthy and admittedly detailed listing of items to be seized, the warrants in this case further authorized the seizure of "other fruits, instrumentalities and evidence of crime at this [time] unknown." The Court construes this sweeping authorization to be limited to evidence pertaining to the crime of false pretenses with respect to the sale of Lot 13T. * * * The question is not how those warrants are to be viewed in hindsight, but how they were in fact viewed by those executing them. The overwhelming quantity of seized material that was either suppressed or returned to petitioner is irrefutable testimony to the unlawful generality of the warrants. The Court's attempt to cure this defect by *post hoc* judicial construction evades principles settled in this Court's Fourth Amendment decisions. * * *

[Justice Marshall also dissented, agreeing with Justice Brennan's Fourth Amendment analysis.]

Note On Andresen and Particularity

Justice Blackmun reads the last portion of the *Andresen* warrant as authorizing the police "only to search for and seize evidence relevant to the crime of false pretenses and Lot 13T." Justice Brennan complains that the police reasonably believed the warrant was broader and authorized a search for evidence of other crimes. If a warrant is drafted in such a way that it is subject to two readings, one which would render it valid and another which would invalidate it, should a reviewing court adopt the reading that the police give the warrant, or the reading that the reviewing court believes that the magistrate, presumed to be acting constitutionally, intended? Which approach is more in line with the goals of the Fourth Amendment?

Searches of Computers

The Court in *Andresen* notes that in a search for documents, it is all but inevitable that the police will be required to peruse innocuous private documents. The same problem arises when the police search for information stored in a computer. Even a requirement of reasonable particularity will not shield most information stored in a computer from inspection, where police have probable cause to believe that incriminating evidence is somewhere on the hard drive. Assume, for example, that an officer has a warrant to search for child pornography stored on a computer. In his search, he comes across a folder labelled "grocery lists." Can he open the folder? It would seem that he could, because otherwise a criminal could shield incriminating information from view by simply labelling the folder in a certain way. But this means that the search of the computer will by necessity be extensive and thorough, covering all files, including "cookies", history, deleted files, etc. See Guest v. Leis, 255 F.3d 325 (6th Cir. 2001) (officers with a warrant to search information located on a computer are

search and seizure of a person's papers that are not necessarily present in executing a warrant to search for physical objects whose relevance is more easily ascertainable. In searches for papers, it is certain that some innocuous documents will be examined, at least cursorily, in order to determine whether they are, in fact, among those papers authorized to be seized.

Similar dangers, of course, are present in executing a warrant for the "seizure" of telephone conversations. In both kinds of searches, responsible officials, including judicial officials, must take care to assure that they are conducted in a manner that minimizes unwarranted intrusions upon privacy.

permitted to seize the computer and conduct a thorough search of all files on the computer, as they are allowed to separate relevant files from unrelated files).

Reasonable Particularity

Regarding the particularity requirement as to things to be seized, one commentator has suggested that "[t]he nature of the property will often give some indication as to how detailed a description is necessary." LaFave, Search and Seizure, The Course of True Law * * * Has Not * * * Run Smooth, 1966 U.Ill.L.For. 255, 268. Some property may not be susceptible to anything more than a general description (e.g., "United States currency"). Another factor relevant to particularity is how much an officer would be expected to know about the property in the course of obtaining probable cause to seize it. See United States v. Fuccillo, 808 F.2d 173 (1st Cir.1987) (warrant to seize "stolen clothing" held insufficiently particular where officers were given a detailed list of the articles stolen before applying for the warrant). Compare United States v. Upham, 168 F.3d 532 (1st Cir.1999) (in a child pornography case, a description of the property to be seized as "any and all visual depictions, in any format or media, or minors engaged in sexually explicit conduct" was sufficiently particular because the officers could not be expected to describe the materials with any more specificity).

In United States v. Strand, 761 F.2d 449 (8th Cir.1985), postal inspectors suspected that Strand, a mail carrier, was stealing items from the mail. They obtained a warrant authorizing the seizure of "stolen mail" from Strand's house. The court held that some items seized from Strand's home were legally obtained, others illegally obtained. The court explained as follows:

> We believe that the term "stolen mail" is sufficiently definite to enable a postal inspector to identify and seize items which clearly fit within such a generic class, such as letters and parcels, neither addressed to nor sent by the person whose property is being searched, bearing postage stamps or marks. A search for "stolen mail" does not, however, permit the seizure of items which do not fit into the generic category. Many of the items seized in the present case under the rubric of stolen mail were not found in parcels of mail, and included items such as socks, a sweatshirt, cosmetics, a sweater, a thermometer, a china plate, and gloves; * * *

Has the court in *Strand* given the searching officers too much or too little discretion to determine whether an item constitutes "stolen mail"?

Severability

Even if a clause in the warrant is overbroad, the defect will not ordinarily taint the entire search. Thus, in LeBron v. Vitek, 751 F.2d 311 (8th Cir.1985) the court "affirmed the concept of severability" and held that an item seized pursuant to a particularized clause in a warrant was properly admitted at trial, even though other items were improperly seized pursuant to a clause allowing seizure of "records and other stolen property." Similarly, in United States v. Brown, 984 F.2d 1074 (10th Cir.1993), a warrant to search a vehicle dismantling business described with particularity over forty items, including "bumpers, grills, fenders, hoods * * * blank registration forms", etc. But a catch-all clause was included to permit seizure of "[a]ny other item which the Officers determine or have reasonable belief is stolen while executing this search warrant." The Court held that the catch-all provision was overbroad. But this did not taint the evidence seized pursuant to the particular descriptions in the warrant. The Court stated:

> At least eight circuits have held that where a warrant contains both specific as well as unconstitutionally broad language, the broad portion may be redacted and the balance of the warrant considered valid. In such cases only those items confiscated under the overbroad portion of the warrant are suppressed.

7. Reasonableness and Warrants

In *Zurcher,* Justice White left open the possibility that reasonableness is an upper limitation on searches even when officers have probable cause and a warrant. That is, a search may be so intrusive and extreme that it is unreasonable even though pursuant to a warrant based on probable cause. But he stated that the Constitution should not be read to prohibit absolutely searches of third parties absent a showing that a subpoena would be inadequate to gather evidence. Is the magistrate in an *ex parte* proceeding obliged to consider the likely impact of the police search on the person or organization at whom the warrant is directed? If not, the impact of Warden v. Hayden becomes even more profound.

Certain rules, like Fed.R.Crim.P. 41(d) provide that "a magistrate judge or judge of a state court of record must issue the warrant if there is probable cause to search for and seize a person or property. . . ." Although the language appears to be mandatory, a magistrate cannot issue a warrant that violates the reasonableness portion of the Fourth Amendment.

There are a few cases in which searches have been found unreasonable even though conducted with a warrant and probable cause. Most of these cases involve medical procedures. In Winston v. Lee, 470 U.S. 753 (1985), the defendant had been wounded in the course of committing a robbery. The state obtained a court order forcing the defendant to undergo surgery under a general anesthetic to remove a bullet lodged at least 2.5 to 3 centimeters beneath the surface of his skin; the state clearly had probable cause that the search would uncover evidence, and had obtained a court order authorizing the procedure (tantamount to a warrant), but the defendant argued that the procedure was still unreasonable under the Fourth Amendment. Justice Brennan, writing for the Court, agreed with the defendant. He noted that the medical risks of the operation were disputed, and reasoned that the uncertainty militated against a finding that the operation was a reasonable search. Moreover, the Commonwealth failed to show a compelling need for the bullet, since it had substantial other evidence tying the defendant to the robbery and could offer evidence of the location of the bullet in the defendant's body.

It is possible, in light of Supreme Court cases like *Lee,* Griswold v. Connecticut, 381 U.S. 479 (1965) (asking "[w]ould we allow the police to search the sacred precincts of marital bedrooms for telltale signs of the use of contraceptives?"), and Stanley v. Georgia, 394 U.S. 557 (1969) (private possession of obscene material in home constitutionally protected), that some magistrates might decline to issue warrants that would invade areas that traditionally have been regarded as off limits to the government. Similarly, some magistrates might decide that the scope of a warrant is too broad, even though there is probable cause to search and a particularized description of the things to be seized (e.g., a requested authorization to seize all books and records).

8. *Details of the Warrant*

Section 220.2(2) of the ALI Model Code of Pre–Arraignment Procedure sets forth the information that should be included in the warrant.

Section 220.2. Contents of Search Warrant

(1) **Date and Address.** A search warrant issued pursuant to [this Code] shall be dated, and shall be addressed to and authorize its execution by an officer authorized by law to execute search warrants issued by the issuing authority.

(2) **Scope of Contents.** The warrant shall state, or describe with particularity:

(a) the identity of the issuing authority, and the date when and place where application for the warrant was made;

(b) the identity of the applicant and all persons whose affidavits were submitted in support of the application;

(c) the issuing authority's finding of sufficiency of the application and of reasonable cause for issuance of the warrant;

(d) the identity of the individual to be searched, and the location and designation of the places to be searched;

(e) the individuals or things constituting the object of the search and authorized to be seized;

(f) the times of day or night and the period of time during which execution of the warrant is authorized; and

(g) the period of time, not to exceed five days, after execution of the warrant, within which the warrant is to be returned to the issuing authority.

The requirement that affiants be disclosed does not mean that the names of informants must be revealed. It is included so that the person served can decide whether to challenge the warrant and is, therefore, not really a limitation on searches and seizures. The warrant must indicate that the magistrate has found the supporting application to be sufficient. Can you see why this is required? Individuals and things to be searched and seized, the times when service is authorized and the time for the return are all to be specified. Time limits on execution are often found in statutes or court rules.

Fed.R.Crim.P. 41(e)(2) places the following restrictions on a search warrant.

The warrant must identify the person or property to be searched, identify any person or property to be seized, and designate the magistrate judge to whom it must be returned. The warrant must command the officer to:

(A) execute the warrant within a specified time no longer than 10 days;

(B) execute the warrant during the daytime, unless the judge for good cause expressly authorizes the execution at another time; and

(C) return the warrant to the magistrate judge designated in the warrant.

Daytime means the hours from 6:00 a.m. to 10:00 p.m. according to local time. Fed.R.Crim.P. 41(a)(2)(B). Searches for narcotics, however, are covered by a specific statute that "requires no special showing for a nighttime search, other than a showing that the contraband is likely to be on the property or person to be searched at the time." Gooding v. United States, 416 U.S. 430 (1974) (citing 21 U.S.C. § 879). In United States v. Tucker, 313 F.3d 1259 (10th Cir. 2002), the Court found a nighttime search to be reasonable under the Fourth Amendment, at least where there is some showing of necessity for nighttime execution. In *Tucker*, necessity was found due to the volatile nature of the chemicals on the premises to be searched.

9. *Anticipatory Warrants*

Can government agents obtain an "anticipatory" search warrant conditioned upon future events that, if fulfilled, would create probable cause? The court in United States v. Garcia, 882 F.2d 699 (2d Cir.1989), found such a warrant valid. The warrant in *Garcia* was issued before cocaine was delivered to the house to be searched. Execution of the warrant was contingent upon the delivery of cocaine by two designated messengers. The court found itself presented with the following choice:

> whether the objective of the Fourth Amendment is better served by allowing an agent to obtain a warrant in advance of the delivery, or whether it is better served by forcing him to go to the scene without a warrant, and, if necessary, proceed under the constraints of the exigent circumstances exception, subject always to the risk of being second-guessed by judicial authorities at a later date as to whether the known facts legally justified the search.

In essence the court found that the anticipatory warrant was better than no warrant at all. The court stated, however, that to be valid, the warrant must set forth explicit conditions to limit the discretion of the officers in determining whether the triggering event has occurred. Many other lower courts have upheld anticipatory warrants. See, e.g., United States v. Hugoboom, 112 F.3d 1081 (10th Cir.1997) (noting that anticipatory warrants may offer "greater, not lesser protection against unreasonable invasion of a citizen's privacy" because it is more likely, given the triggering event, "that probable cause will exist at the time of the search than the typical warrant based solely upon the known prior location of the items to be searched at the place to be searched"); United States v. Bieri, 21 F.3d 811 (8th Cir.1994) ("An anticipatory warrant should be upheld if independent evidence shows the delivery of contraband will or is likely to occur and the warrant is conditioned on that delivery."). Of course, for an anticipatory warrant to be valid, the triggering event must be set forth with specificity, either in the warrant itself or in an attached affidavit. See United States v. Hotal, 143 F.3d 1223 (9th Cir.1998) (where probable cause to search a premises was conditioned on a future delivery of child pornography, a warrant to search the premises "forthwith" was invalid; the fact that the condition of future delivery was expressed in the officer's affidavit was insufficient, because the affidavit was not attached to the warrant). See the thorough discussion in Adams, Anticipatory Search Warrants: Constitutionality, Requirements, and Scope, 79 Ky.L.J. 681 (1991).

C. EXECUTING THE WARRANT

1. *The Knock and Announce Requirement*

Statutes throughout the country require that officers executing a warrant knock and announce their presence before attempting to enter a dwelling. Typical of these statutes is 18 U.S.C.A. § 3109.

> The officer may break open any outer or inner door or window of a house, or any part of a house, or anything therein, to execute a search warrant, if, after notice of his authority and purpose, he is refused admittance or when necessary to liberate himself or a person aiding him in the execution of the warrant.

The purposes of the knock and announce requirement are set forth by the court in United States v. Contreras–Ceballos, 999 F.2d 432 (9th Cir.1993):

> The requirement that law enforcement officers give notice of their authority and purpose prior to forcing entry to execute a warrant serves three purposes: it protects citizens and law enforcement officials from violence; it protects individual privacy rights; and it protects against needless destruction of private property.

"Refused Admittance"

The statute provides that an officer can break open premises if he has announced his authority and purpose and is refused admittance. Clearly, if the homeowner says "you can't come in", this will justify a forced entry. But refusal of admittance may also be implied from the circumstances. Thus, in United States v. Knapp, 1 F.3d 1026 (10th Cir.1993), officers smashed down the defendant's door with a battering ram after announcing their presence and waiting in vain for twelve seconds for a response from the defendant, whom they knew was inside. The court found that the failure to respond within twelve seconds constituted a refusal of entry. The court noted that "the phrase 'refused admittance' is not restricted to an affirmative refusal, but encompasses circumstances that constitute constructive or reasonably inferred refusal." On the other hand, in United States v. Moore, 91 F.3d 96 (10th Cir.1996), the officers announced their presence, waited three seconds, and when they got no response, they entered the premises by force. The court found that the forced entry was "virtually instantaneous" with the announcement and that this "precluded any claim that the officers were constructively refused admittance."

Whether refusal to admit can be deemed from a refusal to answer the door within a certain period of time is dependent on the circumstances. For example, it has been held that citizens should be allowed more time to answer the door when the warrant is executed in the nighttime hours, and accordingly less time can be granted during the day. See United States v. Jenkins, 175 F.3d 1208 (10th Cir.1999) (where officers waited for 14 seconds after twice announcing their presence, a forced entry was reasonable; the required waiting period "was somewhat reduced because the officers executed the warrant at 10:00 a.m., when most people are awake and engaged in everyday activities."). Another factor is whether the residence is small or large. See United States v. Sargent, 319 F.3d 4 (1st Cir. 2003) (lack of response for five seconds was especially significant given the small size of the defendant's apartment).

Constitutional Basis of the Knock and Announce Requirement

In Wilson v. Arkansas, 514 U.S. 927 (1995), the Court considered whether the Fourth Amendment requires the police to announce their presence before entering a premises. Justice Thomas, writing for a unanimous Court, surveyed the common-law precedents, and concluded as follows:

> Given the longstanding common-law endorsement of the practice of announcement, we have little doubt that the Framers of the Fourth Amendment thought that the method of an officer's entry into a dwelling was among the factors to be considered in assessing the reasonableness of a search or seizure. * * * [W]e hold that in some circumstances an officer's unannounced entry into a home might be unreasonable under the Fourth Amendment.

Justice Thomas stressed, however, that the announcement rule was not a rigid constitutional requirement, but rather a component of the Fourth Amendment reasonableness inquiry. He stated that the "Fourth Amendment's flexible requirement of reasonableness should not be read to mandate a rigid rule of announcement that ignores countervailing law enforcement interests." Among the countervailing circumstances that might permit an unannounced entry, the Court mentioned hot pursuit of a suspect, the risk of destruction of evidence, and the safety of officers. Justice Thomas concluded as follows:

> We need not attempt a comprehensive catalog of the relevant countervailing factors here. For now, we leave to the lower courts the task of determining the circumstances under which an unannounced entry is reasonable under the Fourth Amendment. We simply hold that although a search or seizure of a dwelling might be constitutionally defective if police officers enter without prior announcement, law enforcement interests may also establish the reasonableness of an unannounced entry.

The Court remanded to allow the state courts to determine whether circumstances existed sufficient to excuse the fact that officers entered Wilson's home without announcing their presence.

Proving a Knock and Announce Violation

In United States v. Mueller, 902 F.2d 336 (5th Cir.1990), the court stated that the defendant must establish a prima facie case that entry was unannounced. In *Mueller,* the defendant averred that at the time of the police entry, he was sleeping on the other side of the house and that he would have heard the officers knock if they had done so. The court found that this assertion was not enough to establish a prima facie case; even though the state offered no affirmative evidence of knocking, the defendant had not met his burden of going forward. How much more evidence should Mueller have had to provide that the officers failed to knock?

2. *Exceptions to the Notice Rule*

No "Breaking"

If the door to a residence is already open, are police required to announce their presence before entering? In United States v. Remigio, 767 F.2d 730 (10th Cir.1985), the court held that such an entry was not a "breaking," so that the knock and announce statute was inapplicable. The court noted that this was the majority view. See also United States v. Contreras–Ceballos, 999 F.2d 432 (9th Cir.1993) (officer who said he was a Federal Express agent did not violate the knock and announce statute when occupant opened door in response to the ploy and officer placed his foot in the entryway so that the door could not be closed again; this was not a breaking); United States v. Mendoza, 281 F.3d 712 (8th Cir. 2002) (police officers are not required to knock on the front door of a duplex, as the door opened to a common hallway as to which the defendant had no legitimate expectation of privacy; and they were not required to knock before entering the defendant's own apartment, as that apartment did not have a door on it).

Emergency Circumstances: Richards v. Wisconsin

As the Supreme Court stated in *Wilson*, supra, officers will be permitted to make an unannounced entry if announcement would create a risk of destruction of evidence or a risk of harm to the officers or others.[14] In Richards v. Wisconsin, 520 U.S. 385 (1997), the Court considered the exigent circumstances exception to the knock and announce requirement in the context of a search for drugs. Justice Stevens, writing for the Court, set forth the facts of the case:

> On December 31, 1991, police officers in Madison, Wisconsin obtained a warrant to search Steiney Richards' hotel room for drugs and related paraphernalia. The search warrant was the culmination of an investigation that had uncovered substantial evidence that Richards was one of several individuals dealing drugs out of hotel rooms in Madison. The police requested a warrant that would have given advance authorization for a "no-knock" entry into the hotel room, but the magistrate explicitly deleted those portions of the warrant.

> The officers arrived at the hotel room at 3:40 a.m. Officer Pharo, dressed as a maintenance man, led the team. With him were several plainclothes officers and at least one man in uniform. Officer Pharo knocked on Richards' door and, responding to the query from inside the room, stated that he was a maintenance man. With the chain still on the door, Richards cracked it open. Although there is some dispute as to what occurred next, Richards acknowledges that when he opened the door he saw the man in

---

14. Remember that while exigent circumstances permits a completely unannounced entry, officers who announce their presence need not always have exigent circumstances to enter the premises to be searched. If there is no response to their announcement, officers can deem the lack of response a refusal under the statute and enter by breaking. See United States v. Knapp, 1 F.3d 1026 (10th Cir.1993)

(exigent circumstances did not exist to dispense with announcement, where the occupant was an amputee who could not easily destroy the evidence; however, the occupant's failure to respond to the announcement constituted a refusal to permit entry, justifying the officers' use of a battering ram to knock the door down).

uniform standing behind Officer Pharo. He quickly slammed the door closed and, after waiting two or three seconds, the officers began kicking and ramming the door to gain entry to the locked room. At trial, the officers testified that they identified themselves as police while they were kicking the door in. When they finally did break into the room, the officers caught Richards trying to escape through the window. They also found cash and cocaine hidden in plastic bags above the bathroom ceiling tiles.

The Wisconsin Supreme Court had held that the knock and announce requirement was automatically excused in any case in which the police were authorized to search for evidence of a felony drug crime. That court in establishing a bright-line rule reasoned that exigent circumstances justifying a no-knock entry are virtually always present in felony drug cases, due to the high risk of destruction of evidence and the likelihood that drug dealers will be armed and dangerous. But the Supreme Court rejected this per se exigent circumstances rule. Justice Stevens reasoned as follows:

> The Wisconsin court explained its blanket exception as necessitated by the special circumstances of today's drug culture, and the State asserted at oral argument that the blanket exception was reasonable in "felony drug cases because of the convergence in a violent and dangerous form of commerce of weapons and the destruction of drugs." But creating exceptions to the knock-and-announce rule based on the "culture" surrounding a general category of criminal behavior presents at least two serious concerns.

> First, the exception contains considerable overgeneralization. For example, while drug investigation frequently does pose special risks to officer safety and the preservation of evidence, not every drug investigation will pose these risks to a substantial degree. For example, a search could be conducted at a time when the only individuals present in a residence have no connection with the drug activity and thus will be unlikely to threaten officers or destroy evidence. Or the police could know that the drugs being searched for were of a type or in a location that made them impossible to destroy quickly. In those situations, the asserted governmental interests in preserving evidence and maintaining safety may not outweigh the individual privacy interests intruded upon by a no-knock entry. Wisconsin's blanket rule impermissibly insulates these cases from judicial review.

> A second difficulty with permitting a criminal-category exception to the knock-and-announce requirement is that the reasons for creating an exception in one category can, relatively easily, be applied to others. Armed bank robbers, for example, are, by definition, likely to have weapons, and the fruits of their crime may be destroyed without too much difficulty. If a per se exception were allowed for each category of criminal investigation that included a considerable—albeit hypothetical—risk of danger to officers or destruction of evidence, the knock-and-announce element of the Fourth Amendment's reasonableness requirement would be meaningless.

> Thus, the fact that felony drug investigations may frequently present circumstances warranting a no-knock entry cannot remove from the neutral scrutiny of a reviewing court the reasonableness of the police decision not to knock and announce in a particular case. Instead, in each case, it is the duty of a court confronted with the question to determine whether the facts and

circumstances of the particular entry justified dispensing with the knock-and-announce requirement.

The Court's rejection of a per se exigent circumstances rule did not mean that the no-knock entry in *Richards* was unreasonable. Balancing the interests of the state and the individual, the Court set the standard of exigency that would be sufficient justify a no-knock entry:

> In order to justify a "no-knock" entry, the police must have a reasonable suspicion that knocking and announcing their presence, under the particular circumstances, would be dangerous or futile, or that it would inhibit the effective investigation of the crime by, for example, allowing the destruction of evidence. This standard—as opposed to a probable cause requirement—strikes the appropriate balance between the legitimate law enforcement concerns at issue in the execution of search warrants and the individual privacy interests affected by no-knock entries. Cf. Terry v. Ohio, (requiring a reasonable and articulable suspicion of danger to justify a pat-down search). This showing is not high, but the police should be required to make it whenever the reasonableness of a no-knock entry is challenged.

Thus, the officers do not need probable cause to believe that evidence will be destroyed if they announce their presence. The lesser standard of reasonable suspicion is all that is required. Applying this standard to the facts of the case, the Court had little difficulty in determining that the no-knock entry in *Richards* was justified:

> Although we reject the Wisconsin court's blanket exception to the knock-and-announce requirement, we conclude that the officers' no-knock entry into Richards' hotel room did not violate the Fourth Amendment.* * * [T]he circumstances in this case show that the officers had a reasonable suspicion that Richards might destroy evidence if given further opportunity to do so. The judge who heard testimony at Richards' suppression hearing concluded that it was reasonable for the officers executing the warrant to believe that Richards knew, after opening the door to his hotel room the first time, that the men seeking entry to his room were the police. Once the officers reasonably believed that Richards knew who they were, the court concluded, it was reasonable for them to force entry immediately given the disposable nature of the drugs.

For other cases finding reasonable suspicion of exigent circumstances justifying a no-knock entry, see United States v. Sutton, 336 F.3d 550 (7th Cir. 2003) (information that pit bulls had been seen on the property and that individuals with drug or weapons convictions had been seen entering the home, when added to the lack of cover for officers approaching the home, gave officers reasonable suspicion that compliance with the knock and announce requirement might place them in danger); United States v. Cooper, 168 F.3d 336 (8th Cir.1999) (SWAT team's no-knock entry was justified where the defendant was dealing drugs from his house, weapons were inside, the house was barricaded, and the defendant had a violent criminal history); United States v. Weeks, 160 F.3d 1210 (8th Cir.1998) (no-knock entry of drug stash house was justified where officers were informed that the residents answered the door with guns in their hands, one of the residents had been convicted of a firearms offense, and the front door was braced). Compare United States v. Brown, 251 F.3d 286 (1st Cir. 2001) (no-knock entry unjustified simply because drugs and weapons were present; government made no showing that weapons were likely to be used, and the quantity of drugs on the premises was so large that it could not easily be destroyed).

Does the Violation of the Knock and Announce Requirement Justify Exclusion of Evidence?

In Wilson v. Arkansas, *supra*, the Court reserved decision on whether the violation of the knock and announce requirement would require exclusion of any evidence found in the subsequent search. In United States v. Langford, 314 F.3d 892 (7th Cir. 2002), the Court held that evidence obtained after an improper no-knock entry could not be excluded. It reasoned that "it is hard to understand how the discovery of evidence inside a house could be anything but inevitable once the police arrive with a warrant.... Armed with a valid search warrant, the police in our case would have discovered the defendant's gun even if they had given him enough time to answer their knock before they broke the front door down." The Court noted that in some cases the delay required for properly entering the premises would have permitted the defendant to destroy or hide evidence; but "in such cases the rule is waived."

Most courts have agreed with *Langford*, as the cases cited in that case indicate. However, other courts have reasoned that exclusion is required because the violation of the knock and announce requirement makes the search unreasonable under the Fourth Amendment, and exclusion is required to deter police misconduct. See United States v. Banks, 282 F.3d 699 (9th Cir. 2002).

No-Knock Warrants

In *Richards*, the officers determined at the scene that the circumstances justified a no-knock entry, and this decision was upheld by the Supreme Court. Is it ever reasonable for this decision to be made in advance by the magistrate? In a footnote in *Richards*, the Court observed that "[a] number of States give magistrate judges the authority to issue 'no-knock' warrants if the officers demonstrate ahead of time a reasonable suspicion that entry without prior announcement will be appropriate in a particular context." The *Richards* Court stated that the practice of allowing magistrates to issue no-knock warrants "seems entirely reasonable when sufficient cause to do so can be demonstrated ahead of time." See also United States v. Banks, infra (upholding the use of no-knock warrants where it is shown that announcement would be futile or that exigency would arise upon knocking).

No-Knock Entries and Destruction of Property: United States v. Ramirez

In United States v. Ramirez, 523 U.S. 65 (1998), officers had a no-knock warrant to search a house for a dangerous escaped prisoner. Approaching the house in the early morning hours, they announced over a loud speaker system that they had a search warrant. Simultaneously, they broke a single window in the garage and pointed a gun through the opening, hoping to prevent the occupants of the house from rushing to the weapons stash that an informant had told them was in the garage. Awakened by the noise and fearful that his house was being burglarized, the owner of the house, Ramirez, grabbed a pistol and fired it into the garage ceiling. When the officers shouted "police," Ramirez surrendered and was taken into custody. Ramirez was indicted on federal charges of being a felon in possession of a firearm. As it turned out, the escaped prisoner was not on the premises. However, Ramirez did not argue that the police lacked probable cause to search for the escaped prisoner. Rather, he argued that a heightened degree of exigent circumstances is required if the police are going to destroy property during a no-knock warrant entry.

Chief Justice Rehnquist, writing for a unanimous Court, held that officers are not held to a higher standard when a no-knock entry results in the destruction of property. He declared: "Under *Richards*, a no-knock entry is justified if police have a 'reasonable suspicion' that knocking and announcing would be dangerous, futile, or destructive to the purposes of the investigation. Whether such a 'reasonable suspicion' exists depends in no way on whether police must destroy property in order to enter." The Chief Justice recognized that the general Fourth Amendment reasonableness requirement imposes some limitation on the destructiveness of a search. However, in this case, the very limited destruction of property was reasonable, given the fact that the officers were acting to prevent possible violent activity.

The Court also rejected the argument that the knock-and-announce statute, 18 U.S.C. § 3109, prohibited the destruction of property during the execution of a no-knock entry. The Chief Justice declared that the knock-and-announce statute "codifies the exceptions to the common-law announcement requirement" and that "the common law in turn informs the Fourth Amendment." Therefore, the Court's recent decisions in *Wilson* and *Richards* "serve as guideposts in construing the statute." The Chief Justice analyzed *Wilson* and *Richards* in the following passage:

> In Wilson v. Arkansas, 514 U.S. 927 (1995), we concluded that the common-law principle of announcement is "an element of the reasonableness inquiry under the Fourth Amendment," but noted that the principle "was never stated as an inflexible rule requiring announcement under all circumstances." In Richards v. Wisconsin, 520 U.S. 385 (1997), we articulated the test used to determine whether exigent circumstances justify a particular no-knock entry. We therefore hold that § 3109 includes an exigent circumstances exception and that the exception's applicability in a given instance is measured by the same standard we articulated in *Richards*. The police met that standard here and § 3109 was therefore not violated.

Compare Mena v. City of Simi Valley, 226 F.3d 1031 (9th Cir. 2000) (Fourth Amendment violated where officers unnecessarily broke down doors that were unlocked and open, with one officer stating "I like to destroy these kind of materials, it's cool").

3. Exigent Circumstances After Knocking

In the following case, the Court discusses how and whether exigent circumstances can allow police to break a door down *after* knocking.

UNITED STATES v. BANKS

Supreme Court of the United States, 2003.
124 S.Ct. 521.

JUSTICE SOUTER **delivered the opinion of the Court**.

Officers executing a warrant to search for cocaine in respondent Banks's apartment knocked and announced their authority. The question is whether their 15–to–20–second wait before a forcible entry satisfied the Fourth Amendment and 18 U.S.C. § 3109. We hold that it did.

I

With information that Banks was selling cocaine at home, North Las Vegas Police Department officers and Federal Bureau of Investigation agents got a warrant to search his two-bedroom apartment. As soon as they arrived there, about 2 o'clock on a Wednesday afternoon, officers posted in front called out "police search warrant" and rapped hard enough on the door to be heard by officers at the back door. There was no indication whether anyone was home, and after waiting for 15 to 20 seconds with no answer, the officers broke open the front door with a battering ram. Banks was in the shower and testified that he heard nothing until the crash of the door, which brought him out dripping to confront the police. The search produced weapons, crack cocaine, and other evidence of drug dealing.

In response to drug and firearms charges, Banks moved to suppress evidence, arguing that the officers executing the search warrant waited an unreasonably short time before forcing entry, and so violated both the Fourth Amendment and 18 U.S.C. § 3109. The District Court denied the motion, and Banks pleaded guilty, reserving his right to challenge the search on appeal.

A divided panel of the Ninth Circuit reversed and ordered suppression of the evidence found.

We granted certiorari to consider how to go about applying the standard of reasonableness to the length of time police with a warrant must wait before entering without permission after knocking and announcing their intent in a felony case. We now reverse.

II

There has never been a dispute that these officers were obliged to knock and announce their intentions when executing the search warrant, an obligation they concededly honored. Despite this agreement, we start with a word about standards for requiring or dispensing with a knock and announcement, since the same criteria bear on when the officers could legitimately enter after knocking.

The Fourth Amendment says nothing specific about formalities in exercising a warrant's authorization, speaking to the manner of searching as well as to the legitimacy of searching at all simply in terms of the right to be "secure . . . against unreasonable searches and seizures." Although the notion of reasonable execution must therefore be fleshed out, we have done that case by case, largely avoiding categories and protocols for searches. Instead, we have treated reasonableness as a function of the facts of cases so various that no template is likely to produce sounder results than examining the totality of circumstances in a given case; * * *. We have, however, pointed out factual considerations of unusual, albeit not dispositive, significance.

[Justice Souter discusses *Wilson* and *Richards*.] When a warrant applicant gives reasonable grounds to expect futility or to suspect that one or another such exigency already exists or will arise instantly upon knocking, a magistrate judge is acting within the Constitution to authorize a "no-knock" entry. And even when executing a warrant silent about that, if circumstances support a reasonable suspicion of exigency when the officers arrive at the door, they may go straight in.

Since most people keep their doors locked, entering without knocking will normally do some damage, a circumstance too common to require a heightened justification when a reasonable suspicion of exigency already justifies an unwarned entry. We have accordingly held that police in exigent circumstances may damage premises so far as necessary for a no-knock entrance without demonstrating the suspected risk in any more detail than the law demands for an unannounced intrusion simply by lifting the latch. United States v. Ramirez, 523 U.S. 65, 70–71 (1998). Either way, it is enough that the officers had a reasonable suspicion of exigent circumstances.

III

* * * Although the police concededly arrived at Banks's door without reasonable suspicion of facts justifying a no-knock entry, they argue that announcing their presence started the clock running toward the moment of apprehension that Banks would flush away the easily disposable cocaine, prompted by knowing the police would soon be coming in. * * *

Banks does not, of course, deny that exigency may develop in the period beginning when officers with a warrant knock to be admitted, and the issue comes down to whether it was reasonable to suspect imminent loss of evidence after the 15 to 20 seconds the officers waited prior to forcing their way. Though we agree * * * that this call is a close one, we think that after 15 or 20 seconds without a response, police could fairly suspect that cocaine would be gone if they were reticent any longer. Courts of Appeals have, indeed, routinely held similar wait times to be reasonable in drug cases with similar facts including easily disposable evidence (and some courts have found even shorter ones to be reasonable enough).

A look at Banks's counterarguments shows why these courts reached sensible results, for each of his reasons for saying that 15 to 20 seconds was too brief rests on a mistake about the relevant enquiry: the fact that he was actually in the shower and did not hear the officers is not to the point, and the same is true of the claim that it might have taken him longer than 20 seconds if he had heard the knock and headed straight for the door. As for the shower, it is enough to say that the facts known to the police are what count in judging reasonable waiting time, and there is no indication that the police knew that Banks was in the shower and thus unaware of an impending search that he would otherwise have tried to frustrate.

And the argument that 15 to 20 seconds was too short for Banks to have come to the door ignores the very risk that justified prompt entry. True, if the officers were to justify their timing here by claiming that Banks's failure to admit them fairly suggested a refusal to let them in, Banks could at least argue that no such suspicion can arise until an occupant has had time to get to the door, a time that will vary with the size of the establishment, perhaps five seconds to open a motel room door, or several minutes to move through a townhouse. In this case, however, the police claim exigent need to enter, and the crucial fact in examining their actions is not time to reach the door but the particular exigency claimed. On the record here, what matters is the opportunity to get rid of cocaine, which a prudent dealer will keep near a commode or kitchen sink. The significant circumstances include the arrival of the police during the day, when anyone inside would probably have been up and around, and the sufficiency of 15 to 20 seconds for getting to the bathroom or the kitchen to start flushing cocaine down the drain. That is, when circumstances are exigent because a pusher may be near the point of putting his drugs beyond reach, it is imminent disposal, not travel time to the entrance, that governs when the police may reasonably enter; since the bathroom and kitchen are usually in the interior of a dwelling, not the front hall, there is no reason generally to peg the travel time to the location of the door, and no reliable basis for giving the proprietor of a mansion a longer wait than the resident of a bungalow, or an apartment like Banks's. And 15 to 20 seconds does not seem an unrealistic guess about the time someone would need to get in a position to rid his quarters of cocaine.

Once the exigency had matured, of course, the officers were not bound to learn anything more or wait any longer before going in, even though their entry entailed some harm to the build-

ing. *Ramirez* held that the exigent need of law enforcement trumps a resident's interest in avoiding all property damage, and there is no reason to treat a post-knock exigency differently from the no-knock counterpart in *Ramirez* itself.

IV

* * * One point in making an officer knock and announce * * * is to give a person inside the chance to save his door. That is why, in the case with no reason to suspect an immediate risk of frustration or futility in waiting at all, the reasonable wait time may well be longer when police make a forced entry, since they ought to be more certain the occupant has had time to answer the door. It is hard to be more definite than that * * *. Suffice it to say that the need to damage property in the course of getting in is a good reason to require more patience than it would be reasonable to expect if the door were open. Police seeking a stolen piano may be able to spend more time to make sure they really need the battering ram.

* * *

V

[The Court finds the same exigent circumstances exception in the knock-and-announce statute].

The judgment of the Court of Appeals is reversed.

4. *Timing and Scope of Execution*

It is frequently the case that statutes or rules of court define a time period in which a warrant must be served. See Fed.R.Crim.P. 41(e)(2) (warrant must be served within ten days of issuance). Some courts hold that the exact time of execution within that period should be left to the officer's discretion. See, e.g., State v. Morgan, 222 Kan. 149, 563 P.2d 1056 (1977). However, delay may leave officers unable to execute their warrant if intervening circumstances negate the previous showing of probable cause. See the discussion of staleness of information in the section on probable cause, supra.

In view of the number of search and seizure cases that have been decided, it is surprising that few have discussed the permissible latitude that officers have in executing a warrant. Clearly they can only look in places where the objects specified might be found. As the Court stated in United States v. Ross, 456 U.S. 798 (1982): "A lawful search of fixed premises generally extends to the entire area in which the object of the search may be found and is not limited by the possibility that separate acts of entry or entry or opening may be required to complete the search."

Destruction and Excessiveness

Does the authorization to search wherever evidence may be found mean that officers can break open walls, tear up floors and ceilings, and inflict other permanent damage? The case law, most of it old, offers little guidance. One case with a helpful discussion is Buckley v. Beaulieu, 104 Me. 56, 71 A. 70 (1908), where the court held that officers acted excessively and unreasonably when they searched unsuccessfully for liquor by tearing out the interior walls of a house. The court noted that the officers could have searched for any liquor concealed within the walls by using "some slender probe with comparatively little injury."

In contrast, the court in United States v. Weinbender, 109 F.3d 1327 (8th Cir.1997), found it reasonable for officers to remove a piece of drywall to search for clothes that would have tied the defendant to a crime. The officers found guns in the space behind the drywall. The court observed that the drywall was unfinished; it was a small square apparently covering a storage space; it was removed in a few seconds without tools; and the officers had been informed that Weinbender used hiding places in his home. The court observed that "the manner in which a warrant is executed is always subject to judicial review to ensure that it does not traverse the general Fourth Amendment proscription against reasonableness." But in this case, the information possessed by the officers and the ease with which the drywall was removed led the court to conclude that the officers' actions were reasonable.

Use of Distraction and Intimidation Devices

Is it ever reasonable for officers to employ distraction and intimidation devices in the course of a warranted search? Is it always reasonable? The use of such a device was considered by the court in United States v. Myers, 106 F.3d 936 (10th Cir.1997). The Kansas Bureau of Investigation (KBI) had probable cause to believe that Myers was growing marijuana inside his home. KBI agents also discovered that Mr. Myers had prior convictions for burglary and theft, and cocaine trafficking. They also found out that, as a juvenile, Myers had been involved in the fire bombing of a jail or police vehicle and had been convicted of possession of an unregistered firearm and possession of a fire bomb.

The KBI obtained a warrant to search Myers's residence; the warrant authorized a night-time search. The search was conducted in the following manner, as described by the court:

> On March 9, 1994, at approximately 6:09 a.m., agents of the KBI, dressed completely in black and wielding automatic machine guns, knocked on Mr. Myers's front door and announced that they had a search warrant. The agents waited ten seconds, then battered down the door and rolled a Deftec Model 25 Distraction Device, also known as a "flash-bang," into the living room. The device exploded, and the agents then stormed the house,

finding Mr. Myers, his wife, nineteen-year-old stepson, nine-year-old step-daughter, and seventeen-month-old daughter.

After subduing Mr. Myers and his wife and children, the KBI conducted a search of the house, which revealed a substantial marijuana growing operation in the attic.

The court noted that the purpose of the flash-bang device is "to distract and disorient any occupants in the vicinity of the entry" and that the device explodes with a "brilliant flash of light and a loud bang." Myers argued that the use of the flash-bang device amounted to a "military-style assault" and was unreasonable. The court was not unsympathetic to the argument, but ultimately rejected it.

The use of a "flashbang" device in a house where innocent and unsuspecting children sleep gives us great pause. Certainly, we could not countenance the use of such a device as a routine matter. However, we also recognize that we must review the agents' actions from the perspective of reasonable agents on the scene, who are legitimately concerned with not only doing their job but with their own safety. Although it might seem that the KBI's actions in this case come dangerously close to a Fourth Amendment violation, we cannot say that their actions were objectively unreasonable given the district court's factual findings. * * * The district court obviously credited police testimony that Mr. Myers's lengthy pattern of criminal activity—beginning with the fire bombing in 1971 and continuing until the cocaine conviction in 1988—made them apprehensive. The district court also found that the agents knew that there was a fair probability that Mr. Myers's residence contained an illegal marijuana growing operation.

Given the likelihood that a person involved in drugs may also have access to weapons, and may also have committed other crimes, will there ever be a situation during drug searches in which the use of a flash-bang device will be unreasonable? Will flash-bang devices always be reasonable in searches of the premises of prospective terrorists?

If the use of a flash-bang device is unreasonable under the circumstances, should the evidence found in the search be excluded? In United States v. Jones, 214 F.3d 836 (7th Cir. 2000), the court questioned whether the use of a flash-bang device was reasonable where officers invaded the house of a suspected drug dealer, knowing that his girlfriend and her six-year-old child was present. The court noted that "police cannot automatically throw bombs into drug dealers' houses, even if the bomb goes by the euphemism 'flash-bang device.'" But on the question of exclusion, the court reasoned as follows:

If this were a damages action * * * the claim would be a serious one. But * * * Jones wants us to hold that the fourth amendment precludes the use of the evidence that the officers found in his apartment. That argument must be rejected for a reason unrelated to the strength of the contention that the officers behaved inappropriately: the exclusionary rule depends on causation. * * * A battering ram, flash-bang device, or blow to the neck could affect the seizure [of evidence] only by surprising or stunning the occupants so that they could not destroy evidence. * * * An argument that the occupants could have destroyed the drugs, if only they had more time and full possession of their faculties, is not a good reason to suppress probative evidence of crime.

Unnecessarily Intrusive Searches

An example of an unreasonably intense search arose in Hummel–Jones v. Strope, 25 F.3d 647 (8th Cir.1994), which was a civil rights action brought by a husband (Jones) and wife (Hummel–Jones) after a 2:00 a.m. raid of the small birthing clinic at which they were staying. The court set forth the facts surrounding the search as follows:

This dispute arises out of an investigation of the Country Cradle, a well-established and openly-operated alternative birthing clinic located in rural Missouri. A registered nurse operated the clinic. Evidently, the defendants' concern that the nurse might be practicing medicine without a license prompted the search at issue.

On the afternoon of January 23, 1991, Board of Healing Arts Inspector Kistler became convinced that the nurse was delivering a baby at the clinic, and thereby practicing medicine without a license. Kistler contacted Deputy Sheriff Popplewell about the possibility of an investigation or a search. As a result, a reserve deputy was sent to the clinic that evening at 10 P.M. The couple, their toddler, and their four-hour old newborn were the only occupants at the time the deputy knocked on the door. The deputy told the family that he was a soldier on his way to the Gulf War. He claimed to be having car trouble, so the family admitted him to telephone for help. In reality, he was telephoning waiting officers to inform them that the Country Cradle was occupied by a family with a newborn infant.

At approximately 11:00 P.M., Investigator Kistler and Deputy Sheriff Popplewell went to the home of Miller County Assistant Prosecuting Attorney Marmion to discuss the advisability of procuring a search warrant. Marmion prepared the application for a warrant and the accompanying affidavit. * * * The magistrate issued the warrant at approximately 1:00 A.M., and authorized a search for "video tapes, medical records, medical supplies, financial records, video equipment, medications or narcotics, sheets, [and] medical textbooks" being kept at the Country Cradle.

At 2:00 A.M. four uniformed and armed officers, two prosecuting attorneys, and the inspector raided the Country Cradle. The officers entered after knocking and awakening Jones. They refused his request to return later in the morning. Jones was ordered to sit on the waiting room couch and was questioned. Several others of the search party went into the separate bedroom where the pajama clad Hummel–Jones was attempting to nurse her newborn son, and began to question her. The couple declined to identify themselves. The searchers seized the couple and restricted them to the waiting room couch while the search was conducted. Whenever Hummel–Jones left the couch, an officer accompanied her. Inspector Kistler photographed the family as "evidence." Kistler also photographed Hummel–Jones's lingerie soaking in the bathroom sink. Popplewell searched Hummel–Jones's overnight bag against her wishes. The searchers seized one of the family's banking slips to establish their identity. The searchers also seized the couple's personal video-tape of Hummel–Jones's afterbirth experience, despite the couple's objections. The search lasted for three and a half hours, or, essentially, throughout the night.

The court of appeals reversed the lower court's grant of summary judgment in favor of the investigating officers. The court held that the search was so excessive, even though conducted pursuant to a warrant and probable cause, as to be unreasonable, and that the officers were not entitled to qualified immunity because they had violated clearly established law regulating the scope of a warranted search. The court analyzed these questions as follows:

> Although how best to proceed in performing a search is generally left to the discretion of officers executing a warrant, possession of a search warrant does not give the executing officers a license to proceed in whatever manner suits their fancy. The manner in which a warrant is executed is always subject to judicial review to ensure that it does not traverse the general Fourth Amendment proscription against unreasonableness. The "when" and "how" of otherwise legitimate law enforcement actions may always render such actions unreasonable. * * * [W]e have no doubt that this search exceeded all bounds of reasonableness.

> * * *

> The primary justification the appellees put forth for performing this search of a well-established and openly-operating birthing clinic at 2:00 A.M. was to ensure that the mother and newborn would be present. Otherwise, we are told, items of evidence, to wit, the mother, newborn, and bloody sheets, might have been lost. Mothers and newborns at a birthing clinic are not "items of evidence." And, neither the warrant nor the warrant application mention either a mother or a newborn when particularly describing the "items" to be searched for and seized. In any case, the mother and newborn were not going to disappear. At worst, they were going to go home. Photographing the mother and her newborn on the clinic premises could not help establish whether or not there was unlicensed practice of medicine occurring at the clinic because it is not illegal to give birth wherever one happens to be when the moment arrives. Nor were the bloody sheets and lingerie attendant to a birth evidence of any illegality.

What should the officers have done in *Hummel-Jones* to make the search reasonable? Is the court simply saying that the crime that the officers suspected was not worth all the havoc they caused? Would the result have been the same if Hummel–Jones had been nursing her newborn in a house full of suspected terrorists?

When Is the Search Completed?

It is obvious that officers must terminate a search when all of the materials described in the warrant have been found. This standard works pretty well if officers are looking for a discrete object, like a particular stolen television. But sometimes it is difficult to determine whether all the evidence described in the warrant has been found. For example, if officers have a warrant to search for narcotics and paraphernalia, the search need not be terminated as soon as the officers find some narcotics. There may well be more on the premises. But does it follow that there is really no limitation on the scope and duration of a search for narcotics?

The courts do not seem very interested in imposing temporal or spatial limitations on searches for narcotics and related evidence. For example, in

United States v. Stiver, 9 F.3d 298 (3d Cir.1993), officers armed with a search warrant for narcotics, paraphernalia, and proof of residency, entered Stiver's apartment. During the course of the search, which lasted about 80 minutes, the telephone rang many times. An officer answered the phone and pretended to be one of Stiver's associates; he took 12 orders for drugs from the callers. Stiver argued that the officers exceeded their authority by answering the phone and taking orders from his customers. But the court held that this activity was within the scope of the search authorized by the warrant. The court noted that officers are not required to interpret narrowly the terms of the warrant, and reasoned as follows:

> [T]he warrant authorized the officers to search for and seize, among other things, "all drug paraphernalia." In ordinary usage, the term "paraphernalia" is defined to mean "equipment and apparatus used in or necessary for a particular activity." [quoting the Random House Dictionary]. In light of the fact that the officers had ample cause to believe that the defendant had been using the apartment for heroin sales, * * * the officers had an entirely reasonable basis for concluding that the defendant's telephone was a piece of "equipment" or "apparatus" that was used in [drug activity]. The officers therefore acted properly in "searching" the telephone, i.e., answering it.
>
> We also believe that the officers' conduct was authorized by the portion of the warrant permitting them to search for "any items to prove residency." Telephone calls for the defendant at the premises would provide evidence that he resided there.

Does the court's reasoning mean that the officers could occupy Stiver's apartment for a week in order to take more calls from his customers? Could they occupy the apartment for a year?

Presence of the Occupant

Should officers be required to conduct searches in the presence of the owner or possessor of property, unless it would be unduly burdensome for them to do so? Most courts recognize the advisability of such a procedure. See, e.g., Commonwealth v. Prokopchak, 279 Pa.Super. 284, 420 A.2d 1335 (1980) (noting that officers both notified a number of people to admit them into the house, and waited 15 minutes past the time the occupants should have returned to the house before forcibly entering the premises under the reasonable assumption that no one was planning to arrive and voluntarily let the officers inside). But most courts hold that the Fourth Amendment does not *require* the officers to try to conduct the search in the presence of the occupant. See, e.g., United States v. Gervato, 474 F.2d 40 (3d Cir.1973).

Sneak and Peak Warrants

Section 213 of Public Law 107–56, 115 Stat. 272, the "Uniting And Strengthening America By Providing Appropriate Tools Required To Intercept And Obstruct Terrorism (USA Patriot Act) Act of 2001," authorizes so-called "sneak and peek" warrants. These warrants permit federal agents to enter a person's home or office covertly. The government can delay notice of a search if it can show "reasonable cause to believe that providing immediate notification of the execution of the warrant may have an adverse result." The government can also seize items without prior notice if it can show a "reasonable necessity" for the seizure. Section 213 amends 18 U. S. C. § 3103a, relating to warrants for the search and seizure of evidence of federal crimes. The statute adds the following language: "With respect to the issuance of any warrant or court order under this section, or any other rule of law, to search for and seize any property or material that constitutes evidence of a criminal offense in violation of the laws of the United States, any notice required, or that may be required, to be given may be delayed if ... (1) the court finds reasonable cause to believe that providing immediate notification of the execution of the warrant may have an adverse result (as defined in section 2705); (2) the warrant prohibits the seizure of any tangible property ... except where the court finds reasonable necessity for the seizure; and (3) the warrant provides for the giving of such notice within a reasonable period of its execution, which period may thereafter be extended by the court for good cause shown." 18 U. S. C. § 2705(a)(2) defines "adverse result" to be (1) endangering the life or physical safety of an individual, (2) flight from prosecution, (3) destruction of or tampering with evidence, (4) intimidation of potential witnesses, or (5) otherwise seriously jeopardizing an investigation or unduly delaying a trial.

Under what circumstances would it be necessary to employ a sneak and peek warrant?

5. *Presence of the Warrant*

Must the officer who executes a search warrant actually have the warrant in hand at the time of the search? Courts have held that while Fed.R.Crim.P. 41(f) requires the officer to serve upon the person searched a copy of the warrant, it does not require that this be done before the search takes place. See, e.g., United States v. Hepperle, 810 F.2d 836, 839 (8th Cir.1987) ("[w]hile it may be foolhardy to proceed in the absence of the physical presence of the warrant, it is not unconstitutional"). Considering that one reason for the warrant is to provide the executing officer with a lawful show of authority, does this result make sense?

6. *Enlisting Private Citizens to Help Search*

Unwilling Assistance

In United States v. New York Tel. Co., 434 U.S. 159 (1977), the Court, per Justice White, held that, upon a showing of probable cause, a district judge had power to order an unwilling telephone company to assist the government in installing pen registers. The All Writs Act, 28 U.S.C.A. § 1651(a) states: "The Supreme Court and all courts established by Act of Congress may issue all writs necessary or appropriate in aid of their respective jurisdictions and agreeable to the usages and principles of law." The Act was thought to be sufficient authority for a court to compel a private person to act. Justice Stevens wrote for himself and Justices Brennan and Marshall in dissent. Their position was that Congress did not empower Federal courts to compel private parties to carry out this kind of surveillance. Justice Stewart, also in dissent, agreed with this point. Justice Stevens argued that the majority's decision provides a sweeping grant of authority without precedent in our Nation's history. Of course, there is precedent for such authority in the common law—the writ of assistance.

If a warrant is otherwise valid, why shouldn't a person be subject to an order to help the police enforce it? Sometimes such an order might minimize the intrusion the police otherwise would have to make. Would people like Andresen be worse off if secretaries and employees could be compelled to participate in searches in order to minimize intrusions? In the *New York Telephone* case, the majority said that without assistance from the company, the government could not have conducted the surveillance. Should this make a difference in Fourth Amendment analysis?

Willing Assistance

New York Telephone involved individuals who were unwilling to assist the government. Is the Fourth Amendment question different if an individual *wants* to assist the government in conducting a search of another person's property? In United States v. Clouston, 623 F.2d 485 (6th Cir.1980), the court upheld a search conducted with the willing assistance of two telephone company employees where the warrant authorized seizure of certain electronic devices used in surreptitious interception of wire communications. The court found no problem with officers seeking the voluntary assistance of private citizens, in order to make the search proceed more efficiently. In contrast, in Bills v. Aseltine, 958 F.2d 697 (6th Cir.1992), officers had a warrant to search for a stolen generator in the Bills' residence. They also suspected that the Bills had other stolen property on the premises, though the warrant listed only the generator. The officers asked a General Motors official if he wanted to come along on the search for the generator to see if he could identify any property which might have been stolen from General Motors. During the search, the GM official took 231 photographs of various parts and equipment. The court distinguished *Clouston* and declared:

> [The GM official] was present, not in aid of the officers or their mission, but for his own purposes, involving the recovery of stolen General Motors property not mentioned in any warrant. * * *

> * * * Officers * * * may * * * exceed the scope of the authority implicitly granted them by their warrant when they permit unauthorized invasions of privacy by third parties who have no connection to the search warrant or the officers' purposes for being on the premises.

Compare United States v. Robertson, 21 F.3d 1030 (10th Cir.1994) (holding that Federal law allows officers executing a valid warrant to bring along the victim of a theft, in order to assist the officers in identifying the items covered by the warrant); United States v. Bach, 310 F.3d 1063 (8th Cir. 2002) (no error for officers to allow Yahoo! technicians to retrieve all of the information from the defendant's Yahoo! account in an investigation of child pornography; the court noted that "the technical expertise of Yahoo!s technicians far outweighs that of the officers").

7. Media Ride Alongs

Are Fourth Amendment problems raised when officers invite the media along when they execute a search? This question was presented in Wilson v.

Layne, 526 U.S. 603 (1999). Officers executing an arrest warrant for Dominic Wilson entered the home of his parents late at night. They brought a photographer and a reporter from the Washington Post along with them. Dominic's father became upset, and was subdued on the floor. Dominic's mother came out of the bedroom and witnessed the conflagration in her nightgown. Numerous photographs were taken, but none were ever published.

The Wilsons brought a civil rights action against the officers, contending that the "media ride along" violated their Fourth Amendment rights. The Supreme Court, in an opinion by Chief Justice Rehnquist, unanimously agreed that the media observation of the execution of the arrest warrant in the Wilson's home constituted a Fourth Amendment violation.

The Chief Justice noted that police actions undertaken in execution of a warrant need not always be explicitly authorized by the text of the warrant. However, "the Fourth Amendment does require that police actions in execution of a warrant be related to the objectives of the authorized intrusion." In this case, "the presence of reporters inside the home was not related to the objectives of the authorized intrusion." The Chief Justice emphasized that this was not a case "in which the presence of the third parties directly aided in the execution of the warrant. Where the police enter a home under the authority of a warrant to search for stolen property, the presence of third parties for the purpose of identifying the stolen property has long been approved by this Court and our common-law tradition."

The officers cited a number of law enforcement objectives that might be met by a media ride along. But the Court rejected these interests as insufficient. The Chief Justice elaborated in the following passage:

> Respondents argue that the presence of the Washington Post reporters in the Wilsons' home nonetheless served a number of legitimate law enforcement purposes. They first assert that officers should be able to exercise reasonable discretion about when it would "further their law enforcement mission to permit members of the news media to accompany them in executing a warrant." But this claim ignores the importance of the right of residential privacy at the core of the Fourth Amendment. It may well be that media ride-alongs further the law enforcement objectives of the police in a general sense, but that is not the same as furthering the purposes of the search. Were such generalized "law enforcement objectives" themselves sufficient to trump the Fourth Amendment, the protections guaranteed by that Amendment's text would be significantly watered down.

> Respondents next argue that the presence of third parties could serve the law enforcement purpose of publicizing the government's efforts to combat crime, and facilitate accurate reporting on law enforcement activities. * * * Surely the possibility of good public relations for the police is simply not enough, standing alone, to justify the ride-along intrusion into a private home. And even the need for accurate reporting on police issues in general bears no direct relation to the constitutional justification for the police intrusion into a home in order to execute a felony arrest warrant.

> Finally, respondents argue that the presence of third parties could serve in some situations to minimize police abuses and protect suspects, and also to protect the safety of the officers. While it might be reasonable for police officers to themselves videotape home entries as part of a "quality control"

effort to ensure that the rights of homeowners are being respected, or even to preserve evidence, such a situation is significantly different from the media presence in this case. The Washington Post reporters in the Wilsons' home were working on a story for their own purposes. They were not present for the purpose of protecting the officers, much less the Wilsons. A private photographer was acting for private purposes, as evidenced in part by the fact that the newspaper and not the police retained the photographs. Thus, although the presence of third parties during the execution of a warrant may in some circumstances be constitutionally permissible, the presence of these third parties was not.

But even though the media ride along violated the Wilsons' Fourth Amendment Rights, the Court held that the Wilsons were not entitled to a monetary recovery. This was because the officers were entitled to qualified immunity—meaning that even if they violated the Constitution, they would be liable for damages only if they transgressed constitutional law that was "clearly established" at the time of their actions. The Chief Justice declared that the unconstitutionality of the media ride along was not clearly established at the time of the entry into the Wilson household. Justice Stevens dissented from this aspect of the decision.

Wilson was a civil action for damages, so the exclusionary rule was not operative. In a footnote, however, the Chief Justice took pains to note that with respect to media ride alongs, "if the police are lawfully present, the violation of the Fourth Amendment is the presence of the media and not the presence of the police in the home." The Court had "no occasion here to decide whether the exclusionary rule would apply to any evidence discovered or developed by the media representatives." For a lower court answer to that question, see United States v. Hendrixson, 234 F.3d 494 (11th Cir. 2000):

> Although the media were present for the search of Stephens' residence, media presence did not expand the scope of the search (the search actually carried out by the police themselves) beyond that allowed by the terms of the warrant. There is no allegation that the reporter aided the search; he did not touch, move, or handle anything in the residence. The police thus conducted a search within the perameters of the warrant, and the evidence obtained during the search is not subject to the exclusionary rule.

D. THE SCREENING MAGISTRATE

1. *Neutral and Detached*

Because of the important position the magistrate holds under the Supreme Court's view of the warrant requirement, it would be natural to expect that the magistrate must be a person of some learning, good legal sense, and sensitivity to constitutional doctrines. In many jurisdictions, the sad truth is that there are few, if any, magistrates who possess these qualifications. See generally Nock, The Point of the Fourth Amendment and the Myth of Magisterial Discretion, 23 Conn. L.Rev. 1 (1990) (arguing that the fact that most state magistrates are elected impairs their neutral and detached function).

In Coolidge v. New Hampshire, 403 U.S. 443, 449–453 (1971), the Court invalidated a warrant issued by the state's Attorney General, who was authorized by state law to act as a justice of the peace. The Court concluded that an executive officer, the head of law enforcement in the State, could not be the neutral and detached magistrate required by the Constitution. Justice Black, joined by Chief Justice Burger and Justice Blackmun, dissented. That three justices were willing to hold that a law enforcement officer could be the screener in the warrant process suggests something about the teeth they wanted to see that process have. However, in Connally v. Georgia, 429 U.S. 245 (1977), the Court was unanimous in holding that a magistrate who was paid a fee if he issued a warrant, and nothing if he denied an application, was not neutral and detached.

In United States v. McKeever, 906 F.2d 129 (5th Cir.1990), the defendant complained of the magistrate's neutrality on the following grounds: she was formerly involved in law enforcement and retained reserve officer status; her husband was a deputy; and she visited the site of the search while it was being conducted. The court found these factors "troubling" but not enough to show a lack of neutrality. The court stated that a magistrate may retain certain law enforcement duties without losing neutrality; that no showing was made that the magistrate's husband participated in the issuance of the warrant or the search; and that the magistrate went to the site solely out of "curiosity" and did not assist in the search. Compare Lo–Ji Sales, Inc. v. New York, 442 U.S. 319 (1979) (magistrate loses neutral and detached status when he assists in the search).

Rubber Stamp

Of course, if the magistrate issues the warrant without even reading the application, he has become a rubber stamp and cannot be found neutral and detached. See United States v. Decker, 956 F.2d 773 (8th Cir.1992) (magistrate loses neutral and detached status when he fails to read a warrant because he was "intrigued" by the manner in which the officer became suspicious of the defendant). But it is difficult for the defendant to prove that the magistrate actually acted as a rubber stamp. For example, in United States v. Brown, 832 F.2d 991 (7th Cir.1987), the defendant sought to prove that the municipal judge who issued the warrant against him had acted as a rubber stamp. Brown submitted into evidence hundreds of search warrants issued by the municipal judge. Most of the affidavits approved by the judge were form affidavits. The court stated that the volume of warrants issued, especially in comparison to lesser amounts issued by other judges, proved not that the judge was a rubber stamp, but rather that the judge had "extraordinary experience in reviewing warrant applications." The court noted, with considerable understatement, that "it might be difficult for a litigant to establish" that a judge has abandoned her neutral and detached role.

2. Legal Training

In Shadwick v. City of Tampa, 407 U.S. 345 (1972), the Court considered whether the Fourth Amendment required a magistrate to have legal training. In Tampa, municipal clerks, who were not lawyers, were authorized to issue arrest warrants for minor offenses. Justice Powell, writing for a unanimous Court, held that the clerks qualified as neutral and detached magistrates despite their lack of legal training. Justice Powell declared as follows:

The substance of the Constitution's warrant requirement does not turn on the labeling of the issuing party. The warrant traditionally has represented an independent assurance that a search and arrest will not proceed without probable cause to believe that a crime has been committed and that the person or place named in the warrant is involved in the crime. Thus, an issuing magistrate must meet two tests. He must be neutral and detached, and he must be capable of determining whether probable cause exists for the requested arrest or search.

Justice Powell found that the two standards, of neutrality and competence, were met by the Tampa municipal clerks:

> The clerk's neutrality has not been impeached: he is removed from prosecutor or police and works within the judicial branch subject to the supervision of the municipal court judge.

> Appellant likewise has failed to demonstrate that these clerks lack capacity to determine probable cause. The clerk's authority extends only to the issuance of arrest warrants for breach of municipal ordinances. We presume from the nature of the clerk's position that he would be able to deduce from the facts on an affidavit before him whether there was probable cause to believe a citizen guilty of impaired driving, breach of peace, drunkenness, trespass, or the multiple other common offenses covered by a municipal code. There has been no showing that this is too difficult a task for a clerk to accomplish. Our legal system has long entrusted nonlawyers to evaluate more complex and significant factual data than that in the case at hand. Grand juries daily determine probable cause prior to rendering indictments, and trial juries assess whether guilt is proved beyond a reasonable doubt. The significance and responsibility of these lay judgments betray any belief that the Tampa clerks could not determine probable cause for arrest.

Justice Powell emphasized that the Court was not making a categorical rule that the issuance of warrants by non-lawyers would always satisfy the Fourth Amendment requirements of neutrality and detachment. Rather, the Court simply rejected the categorical rule that non-lawyers could never act as neutral and detached magistrates. Justice Powell concluded: "States are entitled to some flexibility and leeway in their designation of magistrates, so long as all are neutral and detached and capable of the probable-cause determination required of them."

Note on Shadwick

Shadwick dealt with arrest warrants, not search warrants. But, the Court's disclaimers notwithstanding, it is clear that the Court was defining the term "magistrate" for Fourth Amendment purposes. The *Shadwick* Court cited arrest and search cases interchangeably. In Illinois v. Gates, 462 U.S. 213 (1983), considered supra, the Court assumed that non-lawyers may issue search warrants. Do you believe that the warrant clause is meaningful when the magistrate is not a lawyer? What message, if any, does *Shadwick* send to magistrates about the importance of their screening function?

Notice that in Fed.R.Crim.P. 41, Congress limited the class of persons who could issue warrants. Rule 41(a) provides that a search warrant may be issued only by "a federal magistrate judge or a judge of a state court of record."

3. *Magistrate Decisions*

There is no requirement that a magistrate give reasons for finding probable cause or for rejecting a warrant application. Is there an argument that magistrates should have to signify in writing their reasons for finding probable cause before issuing a warrant? Would you be persuaded by a counter-argument that it does not matter whether the magistrate reasoned properly as long as the Fourth Amendment probable cause standard actually is satisfied by the warrant application? Can the Fourth Amendment be satisfied if the magistrate is not reasoning properly? Could it be satisfied, for example, if the issuing magistrate approves the warrant in reliance on the professionalism of the police? See People v. Potwora, 48 N.Y.2d 91, 421 N.Y.S.2d 850, 397 N.E.2d 361 (1979) (holding that a magistrate cannot delegate his screening function, even by relying on other magistrates' conclusions that magazines were obscene).

V. TO APPLY OR NOT APPLY THE WARRANT CLAUSE

As stated previously, the Court has held that a search or seizure is presumptively unreasonable in the absence of a warrant based upon probable cause. However, the Court has found that the presumption of unreasonableness can be overcome in a variety of circumstances. Some of the circumstances excuse the officer from obtaining a warrant, but still require the officer to have probable cause. Other circumstances permit a search or seizure even though the officer has neither a warrant nor probable cause. As you read through the "exceptions" to the warrant clause discussed below, be sure to keep straight exactly what requirements the Court retains for each exception. In order to do this, it is helpful to begin with the justification for each exception.

A. ARRESTS IN PUBLIC AND IN THE HOME

1. *Standards for Warrantless Arrests*

Once the point is made that warrants are necessary to search for property and seize it, it might seem that to search for and seize a person would *a fortiori* require a warrant. But this is not the law.

Section 120.1 of the ALI Model Code of Pre–Arraignment Procedure illustrates the powers that police may be given to proceed without a warrant.

Section 120.1. Arrest Without a Warrant

(1) **Authority to Arrest Without a Warrant.** A law enforcement officer may arrest a person without a warrant if the officer has reasonable cause to believe that such person has committed

    (a) a felony;

    (b) a misdemeanor, and the officer has reasonable cause to believe that such person

        (i) will not be apprehended unless immediately arrested; or

        (ii) may cause injury to himself or others or damage to property unless immediately arrested; or

(c) a misdemeanor or petty misdemeanor in the officer's presence.

* * *

Note that even though an arrest is permitted in certain circumstances without a warrant, the officer must always have probable cause to arrest a suspect. See the discussion of probable cause to arrest, earlier in this Chapter.

2. *Arrest Versus Summons*

Why is it reasonable under the Fourth Amendment to begin the criminal process by arresting a suspect, rather than by simply notifying him to appear in court? In 1791, when the Fourth Amendment was adopted, the prevalence of the death penalty and the incentive it provided offenders to escape might have provided a reason for seizing a person at the time he was charged with any felony. Then, and now, arresting someone who is committing an offense in the officer's presence, especially one who is disturbing the public peace, could be defended on the ground that officers should stop criminal activities before they are completed, if reasonably possible. See, e.g., Diaz v. City of Fitchburg, 176 F.3d 560 (1st Cir.1999) (not unreasonable to effect custodial arrest on persons who violated an ordinance that prohibits the obstruction of public passages: "If the officer always were obligated to allow the criminal obstruction to continue, he or she would be unable to satisfy the Ordinance's apparent purpose of assuring public convenience and safety."). But, why should other cases begin with forcible detention? Is it clear that persons charged with criminal offenses are much more likely to flee than persons named as defendants in civil actions? Undoubtedly, civil defendants cannot be arrested today without a special showing of need. What justifies different treatment for criminal defendants?

In Gustafson v. Florida, 414 U.S. 260, 267 (1973), Justice Stewart suggested that "a persuasive claim might have been made * * * that the custodial arrest of the petitioner for a minor traffic offense violated his rights under the Fourth and Fourteenth Amendments."

In Atwater v. City of Lago Vista, 532 U.S. 318 (2001), the Court opted for a bright-line rule that a custodial arrest is *always* reasonable if the officer has probable cause of a criminal violation. Atwater was arrested for a minor traffic offense (a seat belt violation) that was punishable only by a fine. Yet instead of getting a ticket that would operate as a notice to appear, Atwater was detained, brought to the police station and booked. She argued that these custodial actions were unreasonable for such a minor offense. But the Court reasoned, among other things, that it would be too difficult to distinguish among offenses that could justify custodial arrest and those that could not. *Atwater* is set forth in full in the section on arrest powers, *infra*. It is clear after *Atwater* that the decision to proceed by arrest or summons is totally within the police officer's discretion.

Atwater holds that an officer does not need to proceed by summons, even for minor offenses. Is it possible to argue, on the other hand, that there are certain offenses that *must not* proceed by summons? Should the officer be *required* to arrest a suspect for certain types of offenses?

Two well-publicized cases have focused attention on whether the police need to arrest suspects as opposed to have them appear on their own. In one, Congressman Dan Rostenkowski was indicted on seventeen federal felony counts for abusing his official position. Yet he was permitted simply to appear for booking without arrest. In the other, O.J. Simpson, the Hall-of-Fame football star turned actor, was allowed time to surrender himself on charges that he committed the double murder of his former wife and a friend who had stopped by her house. When Simpson failed to surrender, police combed the Los Angeles area until they located Simpson in the car of a friend. With spectators lining the freeways, police trailed the car for miles after Simpson's friend said that Simpson had a gun to his head and wanted to see his mother. Ultimately, Simpson surrendered, and many critics argued that he should have been arrested initially rather than permitted to remain free upon his promise to appear.

Were officers wrong in one or both of these cases not to forcibly arrest upon a determination that probable cause existed? Are there some categories of cases in which public safety requires an arrest, and other categories in which a summons to appear combined with a planned booking satisfy public safety concerns? Does equal justice require that all suspects be arrested? Or is equal justice compatible with reasonable classification of suspects?

Note that O.J. Simpson previously had been charged with beating his wife. At that time, he was allowed to appear and plead nolo contendere to a reduced charge. In response to the Simpson case, state legislatures have considered bills to *require* police officers to arrest anyone suspected of seriously beating a spouse; some such laws have been passed. See "Albany Set to Require Arrest In Domestic Violence Cases," New York Times, June 22, 1994, p.A1, col. 5 (noting the view of the sponsors of such a bill that it "would sharply reduce police discretion in such cases and remedy spotty enforcement of domestic violence laws", and also noting that currently, at least 15 states have policies which require arrests in cases of serious domestic violence). These bills have been criticized by some law enforcement officials on the grounds that they "hamstring police officers" and "force the police to make unwarranted arrests." Id. Does a law *requiring* arrests for serious crimes make as much sense as a law *prohibiting* arrests for minor crimes? Is it better to leave the entire question of "arrest versus summons" to the discretion of police officers?

3. The Constitutional Rule: Arrests in Public

The following case sets forth the constitutional basis for permitting a public arrest in the absence of a warrant.

UNITED STATES v. WATSON

Supreme Court of the United States, 1976.
423 U.S. 411.

MR. JUSTICE WHITE **delivered the opinion of the Court.**

This case presents questions under the Fourth Amendment as to the legality of a warrantless arrest * * *.

I

The relevant events began on August 17, 1972, when an informant, one

Khoury, telephoned a postal inspector informing him that respondent Watson was in possession of a stolen credit card and had asked Khoury to cooperate in using the card to their mutual advantage. On five to 10 previous occasions Khoury had provided the inspector with reliable information on postal inspection matters, some involving Watson. Later that day Khoury delivered the card to the inspector. On learning that Watson had agreed to furnish additional cards, the inspector asked Khoury to arrange to meet with Watson. * * * Khoury met with Watson at a restaurant designated by the latter. Khoury had been instructed that if Watson had additional stolen credit cards, Khoury was to give a designated signal. The signal was given, the officers closed in, and Watson was forthwith arrested. * * * A search having revealed that Watson had no credit cards on his person, the inspector asked if he could look inside Watson's car, which was standing within view. Watson said, "Go ahead," and repeated these words when the inspector cautioned that "[i]f I find anything, it is going to go against you." Using keys furnished by Watson, the inspector entered the car and found under the floor mat an envelope containing two credit cards in the names of other persons. * * *

Prior to trial, Watson moved to suppress the cards, claiming that his arrest was illegal for want of * * * an arrest warrant * * *. The motion was denied, and Watson was convicted of illegally possessing the two cards seized from his car.

[The court of appeals held that Watson's arrest was illegal because the officers had not obtained an arrest warrant, and there were no exigent circumstances to justify the absence of a warrant. The court of appeals further held that the credit cards should have been suppressed as the fruits of the illegal arrest.]

II

* * *

Contrary to the Court of Appeals' view, Watson's arrest was not invalid because executed without a warrant. [The Court noted that Watson's war-

rantless arrest was authorized by statute, 18 U.S.C. § 3061.]

* * *

[T]here is nothing in the Court's prior cases indicating that under the Fourth Amendment a warrant is required to make a valid arrest for a felony. Indeed, the relevant prior decisions are uniformly to the contrary.

"The usual rule is that a police officer may arrest without warrant one believed by the officer upon reasonable cause to have been guilty of a felony * * *." Carroll v. United States, 267 U.S. 132, 156 (1925). * * *

The cases construing the Fourth Amendment thus reflect the ancient common-law rule that a peace officer was permitted to arrest without a warrant for a misdemeanor or felony committed in his presence as well as for a felony not committed in his presence if there was reasonable ground for making the arrest. This has also been the prevailing rule under state constitutions and statutes. * * *.

* * *

The balance struck by the common law in generally authorizing felony arrests on probable cause, but without a warrant, has survived substantially intact. It appears in almost all of the States in the form of express statutory authorization. * * *

This is the rule Congress has long directed its principal law enforcement officers to follow. Congress has plainly decided against conditioning warrantless arrest power on proof of exigent circumstances. Law enforcement officers may find it wise to seek arrest warrants where practicable to do so, and their judgments about probable cause may be more readily accepted where backed by a warrant issued by a magistrate. But we decline to transform this judicial preference into a constitutional rule when the judgment of the Nation and Congress has for so long been to authorize warrantless public arrests on probable cause rather than to encumber criminal prosecutions with endless litigation with respect to the existence of exigent circumstances, whether it was practicable to get a warrant, whether the suspect was about to flee, and the like.

Watson's arrest did not violate the Fourth Amendment, and the Court of Appeals erred in holding to the contrary.

* * *

MR. JUSTICE STEVENS took no part in the consideration or decision of this case.

[Justice Stewart's one paragraph opinion concurring in the judgment is omitted.]

MR. JUSTICE POWELL, concurring.

* * *

On its face, our decision today creates a certain anomaly. There is no more basic constitutional rule in the Fourth Amendment area than that which makes a warrantless search unreasonable except in a few "jealously and carefully drawn" exceptional circumstances. * * *

* * *

Since the Fourth Amendment speaks equally to both searches and seizures, and since an arrest, the taking hold of one's person, is quintessentially a seizure, it would seem that the constitutional provision should impose the same limitations upon arrests that it does upon searches. Indeed, as an abstract matter an argument can be made that the restrictions upon arrest perhaps should be greater. A search may cause only annoyance and temporary inconvenience to the law-abiding citizen, assuming more serious dimen-

sion only when it turns up evidence of criminality. An arrest, however, is a serious personal intrusion regardless of whether the person seized is guilty or innocent. * * *.

But logic sometimes must defer to history and experience. The Court's opinion emphasizes the historical sanction accorded warrantless felony arrests. * * *

[A] constitutional rule permitting felony arrests only with a warrant or in exigent circumstances could severely hamper effective law enforcement. Good police practice often requires postponing an arrest, even after probable cause has been established, in order to place the suspect under surveillance or otherwise develop further evidence necessary to prove guilt to a jury. Under the holding of the Court of Appeals such additional investigative work could imperil the entire prosecution. Should the officers fail to obtain a warrant initially, and later be required by unforeseen circumstances to arrest immediately with no chance to procure a last-minute warrant, they would risk a court decision that the subsequent exigency did not excuse their failure to get a warrant in the interim since they first developed probable cause. If the officers attempted to meet such a contingency by procuring a warrant as soon as they had probable cause and then merely held it during their subsequent investigation, they would risk a court decision that the warrant had grown stale by the time it was used. Law enforcement personnel caught in this squeeze could ensure validity of their arrests only by obtaining a warrant and arresting as soon as probable cause existed, thereby foreclosing the possibility of gathering vital additional evidence from the suspect's continued actions.

In sum, the historical and policy reasons sketched above fully justify the Court's sustaining of a warrantless arrest upon probable cause, despite the resulting divergence between the constitutional rule governing searches and that now held applicable to seizures of the person.

* * *

MR. JUSTICE MARSHALL, **with whom** MR. JUSTICE BRENNAN **joins, dissenting.**

By granting police broad powers to make warrantless arrests, the Court today sharply reverses the course of our modern decisions construing the Warrant Clause of the Fourth Amendment. * * *

* * *

A warrant requirement for arrests would, of course, minimize the possibility that * * * an intrusion into the individual's sacred sphere of personal privacy would occur on less than probable cause. Primarily for this reason, a warrant is required for searches. Surely there is no reason to place greater trust in the partisan assessment of a police officer that there is probable cause for an arrest than in his determination that probable cause exists for a search. * * *

The Government's assertion that a warrant requirement would impose an intolerable burden stems, in large part, from the specious supposition that procurement of an arrest warrant would be necessary as soon as probable cause ripens. There is no requirement that a search warrant be obtained the moment police have probable cause to search. The rule is only that present probable cause be shown and a warrant obtained before a search is undertaken. The same rule should obtain for arrest warrants, where it may even make more sense. Certainly, there is less need for prompt procurement of a warrant in the arrest situation. Unlike probable cause to search, probable cause to arrest, once formed, will continue to exist for the indefinite future, at least if no intervening exculpatory facts come to light.

* * *

It is suggested, however, that even if application of this rule does not require police to secure a warrant as soon as they obtain probable cause, the confused officer would nonetheless be prone to do so. If so, police "would risk a court decision that the warrant had grown stale by the time it was used." This fear is groundless. * * * Just as it is virtually impossible for probable cause for an arrest to grow stale between the time of formation and the time a warrant is procured, it is virtually impossible for probable cause to become stale between procurement and arrest. Delay by law enforcement officers in executing an arrest warrant does not ordinarily affect the legality of the arrest. In short, staleness should be the least of an arresting officer's worries.[a]

* * *

Note on the Use of Excessive Force in Making an Arrest

Based on your knowledge of the background and purposes of the Fourth Amendment, are you satisfied with the balance struck by the *Watson* court? In

---

a. It is suggested that staleness would be most serious in situations where the original probable cause justifying a warrant is undercut by exculpatory evidence, only to be reaffirmed by further inculpatory evidence. Why this should be a problem baffles me. It should be obvious that when the probable cause support-

ing a warrant no longer exists, the warrant is void and the suspect cannot be arrested. That probable cause is thereafter again found only tells us that, absent exigency, a subsequent warrant should be obtained, not that the void warrant should somehow be resurrected.

evaluating the need for pre-arrest screening, you might want to consider that police can use reasonable force to effect an arrest.

The Supreme Court limited the use of deadly force to apprehend a suspect in Tennessee v. Garner, 471 U.S. 1 (1985). The Court held that under the Fourth Amendment, deadly force may not be used to prevent the escape of a felon unless it is necessary to prevent the escape *and* the officer has probable cause to believe that the suspect poses a significant threat of death or serious physical injury to the officer or others. The felon who was running from the police in *Garner* had committed a non-violent felony and was not known to be violent. The Court concluded that the felon's Fourth Amendment rights were violated when he was shot and killed by an officer who chased and could not catch him. Justice White wrote for six Justices that "[i]t is not better that all felony suspects die than that they escape." The majority declined to interpret the Fourth Amendment in light of the common-law rule that permitted the use of deadly force to prevent the escape of fleeing felons. It observed that "[b]ecause of sweeping change in the legal and technological context, reliance on the common-law rule in this case would be a mistaken literalism that ignores the purposes of a historical inquiry." The Court noted that the common law made most felonies punishable by death and recognized most felons as especially dangerous, while few felonies are punishable by death today and numerous modern misdemeanors involve conduct more dangerous than felonies. Moreover, the common-law rule developed when weapons were rudimentary and deadly force was inflicted by hand-to-hand combat in many instances, whereas today the use of firearms makes the implementation of deadly force very different.

Justice O'Connor, joined by Chief Justice Burger and Justice Rehnquist, dissented in *Garner*. She argued that "the Court effectively creates a Fourth Amendment right allowing a burglary suspect to flee unimpeded from a police officer who has probable cause to arrest, who has ordered the suspect to halt, and who has no means short of firing his weapon to prevent escape."

After *Garner*, the Supreme Court held in Graham v. Connor, 490 U.S. 386 (1989), that all claims of excessive force in the making of an arrest (whether deadly or not) are to be governed by Fourth Amendment standards of reasonableness. Chief Justice Rehnquist, writing for the Court, indicated that some of the relevant factors in the Fourth Amendment reasonableness inquiry "include the severity of the crime at issue, whether the suspect poses an immediate threat to the safety of the officers or others, and whether he is actively resisting arrest or attempting to evade arrest by flight." Consequently, while an officer may use non-deadly force in apprehending a fleeing felon, the manner in which the force is asserted might be unreasonable. For example, if the officer uses a police dog that is improperly trained, or fails to give a proper warning or instruction before letting the dog loose, this might be found to be an unreasonable use of force. See, e.g., Vathekan v. Prince George's County, 154 F.3d 173 (4th Cir.1998) (officer who releases an attack dog during a burglary investigation, without giving verbal warning to the suspect, would act unreasonably under the Fourth Amendment).

Excessive Force and Public Protest

Given the factors set forth in *Graham*, how would you decide a case based on the following facts:

>   In March 1989, San Diego police became aware that Operation Rescue planned to stage several anti-abortion demonstrations in the city. Cognizant of the protest tactics used by Operation Rescue members in other demon-

strations, San Diego Police Chief Burgreen met with his staff to formulate a plan of action. After considering several options, Burgreen adopted a policy for dispersing and arresting demonstrators who trespassed on and blocked entrances to private medical clinics.

The policy provided for the police first to give the protesters an opportunity to avoid arrest by leaving the premises after a verbal warning. The police were then to arrest those who refused to leave and give them another opportunity to move voluntarily. Finally, the police were to remove the remaining demonstrators with "pain compliance techniques" involving the application of pain as necessary to coerce movement. The "pain compliance" policy provided for the police to use either "Orcutt Police Nonchakus" (OPNs) (two sticks of wood connected at one end by a cord, used to grip a demonstrator's wrist) or direct physical contact (firm grip, wrist-and arm-twisting, and pressure point holds).

Although San Diego police officers generally have discretion either to use pain compliance or to drag and carry arrestees, Burgreen's policy absolutely prohibited officers from using the drag and carry method. Burgreen changed the existing rule in anticipation of the Operation Rescue protests for two reasons. First, he wanted to prevent the back injuries that multiple dragging and carrying causes to police and arrestees. And, second, he wanted to maximize police control over the large crowds he anticipated.

In each of the three demonstrations at issue, protesters converged upon a medical building, blocking entrances, filling stairwells and corridors, and preventing employees and patients from entering. When police or property owners attempted to remove them, the demonstrators "passively" resisted by remaining seated, refusing to move, and refusing to bear weight. * * * [T]he officers implemented Burgreen's policy and used only pain compliance techniques.

For each arrest, the officers warned the demonstrators that they would be subject to pain compliance measures if they did not move, that such measures would hurt, and that they could reduce the pain by standing up, eliminating the tension on their wrists and arms. The officers then forcibly moved the arrestees by tightening OPNs around their wrists until they stood up and walked. All arrestees complained of varying degrees of injury to their hands and arms, including bruises, a pinched nerve, and one broken wrist.

Several subsequently filed suit, claiming that the police violated the Fourth Amendment by using excessive force in executing the arrests * * *. After viewing a videotape of the arrests, the jury concluded that none involved excessive force and returned a verdict for the city.

On appeal, the court in Forrester v. City of San Diego, 25 F.3d 804 (9th Cir.1994), upheld the jury verdict and concluded that the use of the nonchakus did not constitute excessive force. Judge Hall analyzed the excessive force question as follows:

The evidence satisfies the *Graham* inquiry of reasonableness. First, the nature and quality of the intrusion upon the arrestees' personal security was less significant than most claims of force. The police did not threaten or use deadly force and did not deliver physical blows or cuts. Rather, the force consisted only of physical pressure administered on the demonstrators' limbs in increasing degrees, resulting in pain.

Second, the city clearly had a legitimate interest in quickly dispersing and removing lawbreakers with the least risk of injury to police and others. The arrestees were part of a group of more than 100 protesters operating in an organized and concerted effort to invade private property, obstruct business, and hinder law enforcement. Although many of these crimes were misdemeanors, the city's interest in preventing their widespread occurrence was significant. The city had a substantial interest in preventing the organized lawlessness conducted by the plaintiffs in this case, and the police were also justifiably concerned about the risk of injury to the medical staff, patients of the clinic, and other protesters.

Judge Hall rejected the plaintiffs' claims that the officers were constitutionally required to use less painful techniques, such as the "drag and carry" method, to arrest them:

Police officers * * * are not required to use the least intrusive degree of force possible. Rather * * * the inquiry is whether the force that was used to effect a particular seizure was reasonable, viewing the facts from the perspective of a reasonable officer on the scene. Whether officers hypothetically could have used less painful, less injurious, or more effective force in executing an arrest is simply not the issue.

Judge Kleinfeld dissented in *Forrester*. He emphasized the peacefulness of the demonstrators, the petty nature of the crime of trespassing, and the pain inflicted by the police. He concluded as follows:

To be reasonable, force has to be designed to accomplish a legitimate objective efficiently. The objective was to make the demonstrators move from where they were seated to the vans. But the force was not used to move the demonstrators into the vans. It was used to punish them for refusing to get up and walk to the vans. It worked as punishment does, by hurting people enough so that they do something to avoid it. * * *

In this case, a more efficient pain compliance technique would have been for the officers to warn demonstrators that if they did not move voluntarily they would be burned with lighted cigarettes, and then hold the cigarettes against their skin until they complied. The pain would have been comparable, the risk of long term disability less than from tendon injury or fractures in the wrist, and the officers would have been able to keep one hand free. Probably one officer instead of two could have accomplished each arrest. I am quite sure we would not accept the use of lighted cigarettes against the skin as reasonable force in this case. Yet the nonchakus were worse. They inflicted more serious injuries, with longer lasting consequences, without working any better to arrest people rapidly with minimum police effort. * * *

Watching the videotape, and seeing small, middle aged women scream in agony as the nonchakus were twisted around their wrists made me physically ill. * * * The crimes being committed looked about the same as those committed by Freedom Riders in the 1960's: trespass and failure to disperse. * * *

While we value law and order, we value individual liberty and compassion so profoundly that we tolerate a good deal of disorder, and are lenient, compared to many regimes, about lesser violations of law. The intentional infliction of severe pain during an arrest of a passively resisting demonstrator, when it is not incidental to an efficient means of making the arrest, is inconsistent with those values. Passive resistance tests our level of civilization.

Forrester was distinguished in Headwaters Forest Defense v. County of Humboldt, 211 F.3d 1121 (9th Cir. 2000). In that case, environmentalists locked themselves together in a lumber company lobby as a form of peaceful protest. Others locked themselves to bulldozers. Officers used pepper spray on all of these protesters to force them to unlock themselves. The court found that the use of the pepper spray was unreasonable. The court noted that pepper spray continues to hurt even after it is employed—unlike the nunchakus in *Forrester*. Moreover, the protesters posed no safety threat to anyone.

For a perceptive critique of the law concerning excessive force, see Urbonya, Dangerous Misperceptions: Protecting Police Officers, Society, and the Fourth Amendment Right to Personal Security, 22 Hast.Con.L.Q. 623 (1995).

4. *Protections Against Erroneous Warrantless Arrests*

Watson holds that if an officer has probable cause to believe that a person has committed a felony, he can arrest the suspect in a public place without a warrant. As discussed earlier in this Chapter, the risk of a warrantless search or seizure is that an officer, in the competitive enterprise of ferreting out crime, may be mistaken in his assessment of probable cause. The Supreme Court has held that while a warrant is not required for a public arrest, certain post-arrest protections are necessary to minimize the harm to a person who is arrested without probable cause. In Gerstein v. Pugh, 420 U.S. 103 (1975), the Court declared that if a person is arrested without a warrant, he is entitled to a "prompt" post-arrest assessment of probable cause by a magistrate. The *Gerstein* Court also held, however, that the state need not provide the adversary safeguards associated with a trial. The Court reasoned that the probable cause standard traditionally has been decided by a magistrate in a nonadversary hearing on the basis of hearsay and written testimony. In the following case the Court considered how prompt the probable cause hearing must be.

COUNTY OF RIVERSIDE v. McLAUGHLIN

Supreme Court of the United States, 1991.
500 U.S. 44.

JUSTICE O'CONNOR **delivered the opinion of the Court.**

In Gerstein v. Pugh, this Court held that the Fourth Amendment requires a prompt judicial determination of probable cause as a prerequisite to an extended pretrial detention following a warrantless arrest. This case requires us to define what is "prompt" under *Gerstein*.

I

This is a class action brought under 42 U.S.C. § 1983 challenging the manner in which the County of Riverside, California (County), provides probable cause determinations to persons arrested without a warrant. At issue is the County's policy of combining probable cause determinations with its arraignment procedures. Under County policy, * * * arraignments must be conducted without unnecessary delay and, in any event, within two days of arrest. This two-day requirement excludes from computation weekends and holidays. Thus, an individual arrested without a warrant late in the week may in some cases be held for as long as five days before receiving a probable cause determination. Over the Thanksgiving holiday, a 7–day delay is possible.

* * *

Plaintiffs asked the District Court to issue a preliminary injunction requiring the County to provide all persons arrested without a warrant a judicial determination of probable cause within 36 hours of arrest. The District Court issued the injunction, holding that the County's existing practice violated this Court's decision in *Gerstein.* Without discussion, the District Court adopted a rule that the County provide probable cause determinations within 36 hours of arrest, except in exigent circumstances. * * *

The Court of Appeals * * * determined that the County's policy of providing probable cause determinations at arraignment within 48 hours was "not in accord with *Gerstein*'s requirement of a determination 'promptly after arrest'" because no more than 36 hours were needed "to complete the administrative steps incident to arrest."

* * *

III

A

In *Gerstein,* this Court held unconstitutional Florida procedures under which persons arrested without a war-

rant could remain in police custody for 30 days or more without a judicial determination of probable cause. In reaching this conclusion we attempted to reconcile important competing interests. On the one hand, States have a strong interest in protecting public safety by taking into custody those persons who are reasonably suspected of having engaged in criminal activity, even where there has been no opportunity for a prior judicial determination of probable cause. On the other hand, prolonged detention based on incorrect or unfounded suspicion may unjustly "imperil [a] suspect's job, interrupt his source of income, and impair his family relationships." We sought to balance these competing concerns by holding that States "must provide a fair and reliable determination of probable cause as a condition for any significant pretrial restraint of liberty, and this determination must be made by a judicial officer either before *or promptly after* arrest."

The Court thus established a "practical compromise" between the rights of individuals and the realities of law enforcement. * * * Significantly, the Court stopped short of holding that jurisdictions were constitutionally compelled to provide a probable cause hearing immediately upon taking a suspect into custody and completing booking procedures. We acknowledged the burden that proliferation of pretrial proceedings places on the criminal justice system and recognized that the interests of everyone involved, including those persons who are arrested, might be disserved by introducing further procedural complexity into an already intricate system. Accordingly, we left it to the individual States to integrate prompt probable cause determinations into their differing systems of pretrial procedures.

In so doing, we gave proper deference to the demands of federalism.

* * * Our purpose in *Gerstein* was to make clear that the Fourth Amendment requires every State to provide prompt determinations of probable cause, but that the Constitution does not impose on the States a rigid procedural framework. Rather, individual States may choose to comply in different ways.

Inherent in *Gerstein*'s invitation to the States to experiment and adapt was the recognition that the Fourth Amendment does not compel an immediate determination of probable cause upon completing the administrative steps incident to arrest. Plainly, if a probable cause hearing is constitutionally compelled the moment a suspect is finished being "booked," there is no room whatsoever for "flexibility and experimentation by the States." * * * Waiting even a few hours so that a bail hearing or arraignment could take place at the same time as the probable cause determination would amount to a constitutional violation. Clearly, *Gerstein* is not that inflexible.

Notwithstanding *Gerstein*'s discussion of flexibility, the [lower court] construed *Gerstein* as "requir[ing] a probable cause determination to be made *as soon as the administrative steps incident to arrest were completed,* and that such steps should require only a brief period." * * * The foregoing discussion readily demonstrates the error of this approach. *Gerstein* held that probable cause determinations must be prompt—not immediate. * * *

* * *

B

Given that *Gerstein* permits jurisdictions to incorporate probable cause determinations into other pretrial procedures, some delays are inevitable. For example, where, as in Riverside County, the probable cause determination is combined with arraignment, there will be delays caused by paperwork and logistical problems. * * * On weekends, when the number of arrests is often higher and available resources tend to be limited, arraignments may get pushed back even further. In our view, the Fourth Amendment permits a reasonable postponement of a probable cause determination while the police cope with the everyday problems of processing suspects through an overly burdened criminal justice system.

But flexibility has its limits; *Gerstein* is not a blank check. A State has no legitimate interest in detaining for extended periods individuals who have been arrested without probable cause. * * *

Unfortunately, as lower court decisions applying *Gerstein* have demonstrated, it is not enough to say that probable cause determinations must be "prompt." This vague standard simply has not provided sufficient guidance. * * *

Our task in this case is to articulate more clearly the boundaries of what is permissible under the Fourth Amendment. Although we hesitate to announce that the Constitution compels a specific time limit, it is important to provide some degree of certainty so that States and counties may establish procedures with confidence that they fall within constitutional bounds. Taking into account the competing interests articulated in *Gerstein,* we believe that a jurisdiction that provides judicial determinations of probable cause within 48 hours of arrest will, as a general matter, comply with the promptness requirement of *Gerstein.* For this reason, such jurisdictions will be immune from systemic challenges.

This is not to say that the probable cause determination in a particular case passes constitutional muster simply because it is provided within 48 hours. Such a hearing may nonetheless violate *Gerstein* if the arrested individual can prove that his or her probable cause determination was delayed unreasonably. Examples of unreasonable delay are delays for the purpose of gathering additional evidence to justify the arrest, a delay motivated by ill will against the arrested individual, or delay for delay's sake. In evaluating whether the delay in a particular case is unreasonable, however, courts must allow a substantial degree of flexibility. Courts cannot ignore the often unavoidable delays in transporting arrested persons from one facility to another, handling late-night bookings where no magistrate is readily available, obtaining the presence of an arresting officer who may be busy processing other suspects or securing the premises of an arrest, and other practical realities.

Where an arrested individual does not receive a probable cause determination within 48 hours, the calculus changes. In such a case, the arrested individual does not bear the burden of proving an unreasonable delay. Rather, the burden shifts to the government to demonstrate the existence of a bona fide emergency or other extraordinary circumstance. The fact that in a particular case it may take longer than 48 hours to consolidate pretrial proceedings does not qualify as an extraordinary circumstance. Nor, for that matter, do intervening weekends. A jurisdiction that chooses to offer combined proceedings must do so as soon as is reasonably feasible, but in no event later than 48 hours after arrest.

* * * In advocating a 24–hour rule, the dissent would compel Riverside County—and countless others across the Nation—to speed up its criminal justice mechanisms substantially, presumably by allotting local tax dollars to hire additional police officers and

magistrates. There may be times when the Constitution compels such direct interference with local control, but this is not one. As we have explained, *Gerstein* clearly contemplated a reasonable accommodation between legitimate competing concerns. We do no more than recognize that such accommodation can take place without running afoul of the Fourth Amendment.

* * * Under *Gerstein*, jurisdictions may choose to combine probable cause determinations with other pretrial proceedings, so long as they do so promptly. This necessarily means that only certain proceedings are candidates for combination. Only those proceedings that arise very early in the pretrial process—such as bail hearings and arraignments—may be chosen. Even then, every effort must be made to expedite the combined proceedings.

* * *

JUSTICE MARSHALL, **with whom** JUSTICE BLACKMUN **and** JUSTICE STEVENS **join, dissenting.**

In Gerstein v. Pugh, this Court held that an individual detained following a warrantless arrest is entitled to a "prompt" judicial determination of probable cause as a prerequisite to any further restraint on his liberty. I agree with Justice Scalia that a probable-cause hearing is sufficiently "prompt" under *Gerstein* only when provided immediately upon completion of the "administrative steps incident to arrest."

JUSTICE SCALIA, **dissenting.**

* * *

The Court views the task before it as one of "balanc[ing] [the] competing concerns" of "protecting public safety," on the one hand, and avoiding "prolonged detention based on incorrect or unfounded suspicion," on the other hand.* * * There is assuredly room for such an approach in resolving novel questions of search and seizure under the "reasonableness" standard that the Fourth Amendment sets forth. But not, I think, in resolving those questions on which a clear answer already existed in 1791 and has been generally adhered to by the traditions of our society ever since. As to those matters, the "balance" has already been struck, the "practical compromise" reached—and it is the function of the Bill of Rights to *preserve* that judgment, not only against the changing views of Presidents and Members of Congress, but also against the changing views of Justices whom Presidents appoint and Members of Congress confirm to this Court.

The issue before us today is of precisely that sort. As we have recently had occasion to explain, the Fourth Amendment's prohibition of "unreasonable seizures," insofar as it applies to seizure of the person, preserves for our citizens the traditional protections against unlawful arrest afforded by the common law. See California v. Hodari D. [discussed in the section on stop and frisk, infra]. One of those—one of the most important of those—was that a person arresting a suspect without a warrant must deliver the arrestee to a magistrate "as soon as he reasonably can." 2 M. Hale, Pleas of the Crown 95, n. 13 (1st Am. ed. 1847). * * * The practice in the United States was the same. See e.g., Perkins, The Law of Arrest, 25 Iowa L.Rev. 201, 254 (1940). It was clear, moreover, that the only element bearing upon the reasonableness of delay was, not such circumstances as the pressing need to conduct further investigation, but the arresting officer's ability, once the prisoner had been secured, to reach a magistrate who could issue the needed warrant for further detention. Any detention beyond the period within

which a warrant could have been obtained rendered the officer liable for false imprisonment.

* * *

* * * Mr. McLaughlin was entitled to have a *prompt* impartial determination that there was reason to deprive him of his liberty—not according to a schedule that suits the State's convenience in piggybacking various proceedings, but as soon as his arrest was completed and the magistrate could be procured.

* * *

I do not know how the Court calculated its outer limit of 48 hours. I must confess, however, that I do not know how I would do so either, if I thought that one justification for delay could be the State's "desire to combine." * * * So as far as I can discern (though I cannot pretend to be able to do better), the Court simply decided that, given the administrative convenience of "combining," it is not so bad for an utterly innocent person to wait 48 hours in jail before being released.

If one eliminates (as one should) that novel justification for delay, determining the outer boundary of reasonableness is a more objective and more manageable task. * * *

With one exception, no federal court considering the question has regarded 24 hours as an inadequate amount of time to complete arrest procedures, and with the same exception every court actually setting a limit for probable-cause determination based on those procedures has selected 24 hours. (The exception would not count Sunday within the 24–hour limit.) See Brandes, Post–Arrest Detention and the Fourth Amendment: Refining the Standard of *Gerstein v. Pugh*, 22 Colum.J.L. & Soc.Prob. 445, 474–475 (1989). Federal courts have reached a similar conclusion in applying Federal Rules of Criminal Procedure 5(a), which requires presentment before a federal magistrate "without unnecessary delay." And state courts have similarly applied a 24–hour limit under state statutes requiring presentment without "unreasonable delay." New York, for example, has concluded that no more than 24 hours is necessary from arrest to *arraignment.* Twenty-nine States have statutes similar to New York's, which require either presentment or arraignment "without unnecessary delay" or "forthwith"; eight States explicitly require presentment or arraignment within 24 hours; and only seven States have statutes explicitly permitting a period longer than 24 hours. Since the States requiring a probable-cause hearing within 24 hours include both New York and Alaska, it is unlikely that circumstances of population or geography demand a longer period. Twenty-four hours is consistent with the American Law Institute's Model Code. ALI, Model Code of Pre–Arraignment Procedure § 310.1 (1975). * * *

In my view, absent extraordinary circumstances, it is an "unreasonable seizure" within the meaning of the Fourth Amendment for the police, having arrested a suspect without a warrant, to delay a determination of probable cause for the arrest either (1) for reasons unrelated to arrangement of the probable-cause determination or completion of the steps incident to

arrest, or (2) beyond 24 hours after the arrest. Like the Court, I would treat the time limit as a presumption; when the 24 hours are exceeded the burden shifts to the police to adduce unforeseeable circumstances justifying the additional delay.

* * *

* * * One hears the complaint, nowadays, that the Fourth Amendment has become constitutional law for the guilty; that it benefits the career criminal (through the exclusionary rule) often and directly, but the ordinary citizen remotely if at all. By failing to protect the innocent arrestee, today's opinion reinforces that view. * * * While in recent years we have invented novel applications of the Fourth Amendment to release the unquestionably guilty, we today repudiate one of its core applications so that the presumptively innocent may be left in jail. Hereafter a law-abiding citizen wrongfully arrested may be compelled to await the grace of a Dickensian bureaucratic machine, as it churns its cycle for up to two days—never once given the opportunity to show a judge that there is absolutely no reason to hold him, that a mistake has been made. In my view, this is the image of a system of justice that has lost its ancient sense of priority, a system that few Americans would recognize as our own.

Detentions for Less Than 48 Hours

The Court in *McLaughlin* noted that no systemic relief can be granted for warrantless detentions less than 48 hours duration. However, it also noted that an individual detention might be unreasonable even if it is less than 48 hours. The court in *United States v. Davis,* 174 F.3d 941 (8th Cir.1999), found a warrantless detention unreasonable even though it lasted only two hours. Officers arrested Davis for falsely reporting a theft. She was placed in a holding cell for two hours, and was then questioned about her boyfriend, who was suspected of illegally trafficking in firearms. She was released after agreeing to obtain evidence against her boyfriend. Booking procedures on the false report charge were never initiated, and she was never taken before a magistrate to determine whether there was probable cause to arrest her on that charge. Under these circumstances, the court found that Davis had been detained illegally. The court read *McLaughlin* and subsequent lower court cases as having made clear "that a delay may be unreasonable if it is motivated by a desire to uncover additional evidence to support the arrest or to use the suspect's presence solely to investigate the suspect's involvement in other crimes." The court concluded that *McLaughlin* "does not establish a per se rule that an individual may be detained for 48 hours by local authorities for any purpose whatsoever. Nor does it stand for the proposition that authorities may violate the Constitution as long as they do so for only a brief period of time."

Is the court saying that Davis' detention was illegal because the officer had an improper motive in detaining her? Isn't a focus on an officer's motive inconsistent with the Fourth Amendment's standard of objective reasonableness?

Remedy for a McLaughlin Violation

What is the remedy for an unreasonable delay in presentment to a magistrate? In Powell v. Nevada, 511 U.S. 79 (1994), Powell was arrested for child abuse, and his *Gerstein* hearing was not held until at least 72 hours after his arrest. In the time between 48 and 72 hours after his arrest, the defendant made an inculpatory statement, but the magistrate determined that probable cause to arrest him existed solely on the basis of information obtained before Powell's arrest. Powell's inculpatory statement was introduced against him at trial, and he was found guilty. Powell challenged his conviction, arguing that his inculpatory statement was illegally obtained and should have been excluded. The lower court rejected this argument by reasoning, among other things, that Powell was convicted before the date that *McLaughlin* was decided.

Justice Ginsburg, in an opinion for seven members of the Court, held that *McLaughlin* was retroactive to all defendants whose convictions were not final on the date of that decision; thus Powell was entitled to the benefit of that decision. She noted, however, that it did not necessarily follow that Powell's inculpatory statement had to be excluded from his trial. She stated that the Court in *McLaughlin* had not resolved "the appropriate remedy for a delay in determining probable cause." The Court remanded the case for a determination of this question.[15]

Justice Thomas, joined by Chief Justice Rehnquist, dissented. Justice Thomas agreed that *McLaughlin* applied retroactively to Powell's conviction, but he disagreed that a remand was necessary to determine the appropriate remedy. In Justice Thomas' view, "the violation of *McLaughlin* (as opposed to his *arrest* and *custody*) bore no causal relationship whatsoever" to Powell's subsequent inculpatory statement. Justice Thomas reasoned as follows:

> The timing of the probable cause determination would have affected petitioner's statement only if a proper hearing at or before the 48–hour mark would have resulted in a finding of no probable cause. Yet, as the magistrate found, the police had probable cause to suspect petitioner of child

---

15. On remand, the Nevada Supreme Court avoided the question. It held that error, if any, in admitting Powell's jailhouse statement was harmless, because he had made a similar statement when he was arrested. 113 Nev. 41, 930 P.2d 1123 (1997).

abuse, and there is no suggestion that the delay in securing a determination of probable cause permitted the police to gather additional evidence to be presented to the magistrate. On the contrary, the magistrate based his determination on the facts included in the declaration of arrest that was completed within an hour of petitioner's arrest. Thus, if the probable cause determination had been made within 48 hours as required by *McLaughlin*, the same information would have been presented, the same result would have been obtained, and none of the circumstances of petitioner's custody would have been altered.

See also State v. Tucker, 137 N.J. 259, 645 A.2d 111 (1994) (confession made after 48 hour period was admissible, where evidence against the defendant was so strong that he would not have been released had a hearing been held earlier); United States v. Fullerton, 187 F.3d 587 (6th Cir. 1999) (even though the defendant was detained for 72 hours without a hearing, this did not result in exclusion of evidence obtained from him at the time of the arrest, as there was no causal connection between the *McLaughlin* violation and the seizure of the evidence).

5.   *Arrests in the Home*

The Payton Rule

Watson and *Gerstein* left open the question whether a warrant is necessary to enter a home to make an arrest. The Court answered the question concerning arrests in the home in Payton v. New York, 445 U.S. 573 (1980). The Court described the facts as follows:

> On January 14, 1970, after two days of intensive investigation, New York detectives had assembled evidence sufficient to establish probable cause to believe that Theodore Payton had murdered the manager of a gas station two days earlier. At about 7:30 a.m. on January 15, six officers went to Payton's apartment in the Bronx, intending to arrest him. They had not obtained a warrant. Although light and music emanated from the apartment, there was no response to their knock on the metal door. They summoned emergency assistance and, about 30 minutes later, used crowbars to break open the door and enter the apartment. No one was there. In plain view, however, was a .30–caliber shell casing that was seized and later admitted into evidence at Payton's murder trial.

> In due course Payton surrendered to the police, was indicted for murder, and moved to suppress the evidence taken from his apartment.

The New York Court of Appeals held that no warrant was required to enter a home to make an arrest of a person living there. The Supreme Court disagreed.

Justice Stevens' majority opinion emphasized that the home has always been viewed as an especially private place; set forth a history that indicated there were doubts at common law concerning authority to invade a home to make an arrest; conceded that a majority of state courts addressing the question had permitted warrantless arrests in the home, but observed a trend in the opposite direction in the previous decade; and finally decided that the home deserved special protection. Justice Stevens concluded that "the Fourth Amendment has drawn a firm line at the entrance to the house" and that "absent exigent circumstances, that threshold may not reasonably be crossed without a warrant."[16]

In its penultimate paragraph, the opinion addressed the kind of warrant it required:

> Finally, we note the State's suggestion that only a search warrant based upon probable cause to believe the suspect is at home at a given time can adequately protect the privacy interests at stake, and since such a warrant requirement is manifestly impractical, there need be no warrant of any kind. We find this ingenious argument unpersuasive. It is true that an arrest warrant requirement may afford less protection than a search warrant requirement, but it will suffice to interpose the magistrate's determination of probable cause between the zealous officer and the citizen. If there is sufficient evidence of a citizen's participation in a felony to persuade a judicial officer that his arrest is justified, it is constitutionally reasonable to require him to open his doors to the officers of the law. Thus, for Fourth Amendment purposes, an arrest warrant founded on probable cause implicitly carries with it the limited authority to enter a dwelling in which the suspect lives when there is reason to believe the suspect is within.[17]

The *Payton* rule was reaffirmed in the Court's unanimous per curiam opinion in Kirk v. Louisiana, 536 U.S. 635 (2002). The Court summarily reversed a conviction based on evidence found on the defendant when he was arrested in his home without a warrant and without a showing of exigent circumstances.

Reason to Believe the Suspect Is at Home

Payton leaves it to the officer executing the arrest warrant to determine whether there is "reason to believe the suspect is within" the home. Is this consistent with the theory of the warrant clause? Is the officer who executes a search warrant free to determine whether enough information exists to believe that evidence described in the warrant is located in a certain place?

Does the Court in *Payton* mean that an arresting officer must have probable cause to believe the suspect is at home? Or does "reason to believe" mean something less than probable cause? The court in United States v. Magluta, 44 F.3d 1530 (11th Cir.1995), confronted this problem. The defendant argued that there was no probable cause to believe that he was at home when the officers entered with an arrest warrant, and the government argued that officers only needed "reason to believe" that he was at home, not probable cause. The court, noting that *Payton* was vague at best on this point, declared as follows:

> We think it sufficient to hold that in order for law enforcement officials to enter a residence to execute an arrest warrant for a resident of the premises, the facts and circumstances within the knowledge of the law

16. If negative consequences could occur in the time it takes to obtain a warrant, the officers are excused from obtaining one under the doctrine of "exigent circumstances." This doctrine applies both to arrest warrants otherwise required by *Payton*, and to search warrants. See the discussion of exigent circumstances later in this Chapter.

17. Justice Blackmun wrote a one paragraph concurring opinion. Justice White dissented and was joined by the Chief Justice and Justice Rehnquist. Justice Rehnquist also added a short dissent.

enforcement agents, when viewed in the totality, must warrant a reasonable belief that the location to be searched is the suspect's dwelling, and that the suspect is within the residence at the time of entry. * * * In evaluating this on the spot determination * * * courts must be sensitive to common sense factors indicating a resident's presence. For example, officers may take into consideration the possibility that the resident may be aware that police are attempting to ascertain whether or not the resident is at home, and officers may presume that a person is at home at certain times of the day—a presumption which can be rebutted by contrary evidence regarding the suspect's known schedule.

The *Magluta* court found that the officers had reason to believe Magluta was at home, because a visitor was on the premises, Magluta's car was in the driveway, and a porch light was on. The fact that the officers had not seen Magluta about the premises that day was not dispositive, because "the officers were entitled to consider that Magluta was a fugitive from justice, wanted on a 24 count drug trafficking indictment, who might have been concealing his presence." See also United States v. Edmonds, 52 F.3d 1236 (3d Cir.1995) (reason to believe that suspect was at home at 6:45 a.m., when his car was parked outside the premises, "and this expectation was not dispelled by the fact that someone probably involved in a drug operation did not appear when the agents announced themselves at his door"). What is the difference between "reason to believe" and "probable cause to believe" that a suspect is at home? See United States v. Gorman, 314 F.3d 1105 (9th Cir. 2002) (noting that the "reason to believe" standard was undefined in *Payton*: "We now conclude that the 'reason to believe' standard of *Payton* * * * embodies the same standard of reasonableness inherent in probable cause.").

Is the Arrest at Home or in Public?

In light of *Payton* and *Watson*, it becomes important to determine whether an arrest occurs in the home, where a warrant is generally required, or in public, where it is not. In United States v. Holland, 755 F.2d 253 (2d Cir.1985), the defendant was in his second-floor apartment in a two-family house when he heard someone ring the doorbell to his apartment. To answer the bell, he had to walk down a flight of stairs through a common hallway and open the door in the front of the building. There he was arrested without a warrant. The court found no intent in *Payton* to broaden the definition of "home" so as to include the entranceway to a common hallway. Judge Newman in dissent noted that if Holland had been living in a modern building with a buzzer mechanism, the officer would have had to arrest him at the door to his apartment. He concluded that *Payton* should apply as well to the "humble surroundings" in which the defendant lived.

What if the officers announce their presence and order the citizen to open the door, and the citizen opens the door to his home and is placed under arrest right there? Is that arrest made in the home or in public? Lower courts have split on this question. Some courts have stated that if the defendant is ordered to open the door under a lawful claim of authority, and is arrested upon opening the door, then the arrest occurs in the home and a warrant is required. See United States v. Flowers, 336 F.3d 1222 (10th Cir. 2003). Compare United States v. Vaneaton, 49 F.3d 1423 (9th Cir.1995) (no arrest warrant required where the defendant voluntarily opened the door, and thus "his actions were not taken in response to a claim of lawful authority"). Other courts hold that if the officers remain outside the doorway and inform the defendant that he is under arrest, then the arrest is made in public because the officers never physically entered the home. This latter view leads to difficult fact questions when the officer subsequently enters the home, for example to secure the premises or to follow the defendant while he gets his coat. Under this latter "officer was outside" view, if the arrest was made before the physical entry, then the entry can be justified as incident to the arrest and information discovered during the incident search will be considered legally obtained. However, if the arrest is made after the entry and without a warrant, then there has been a *Payton* violation, and the information discovered during the entry is illegally obtained. See United States v. Berkowitz, 927 F.2d 1376 (7th Cir.1991) (remanding to determine whether the officers informed the defendant that he was under arrest before or after entering his home). Courts holding that a doorway arrest constitutes an arrest in the home do not have to deal with such fine-line distinctions.

If the defendant is in his home, can the officer wait for ten hours for the defendant to come outside and then arrest him without a warrant? See United States v. Bustamante–Saenz, 894 F.2d 114 (5th Cir.1990) (yes). The holding in *Bustamante–Saenz* receives support from the Supreme Court decision in New York v. Harris, 495 U.S. 14 (1990), in which the Court held that a violation of *Payton* constitutes an illegal *search* of the home, but that the warrantless in-home *arrest* is not itself illegal so long as the officer has probable cause to arrest. *Harris* concerned the fruits of an alleged *Payton* violation, and is discussed in the material on the exclusionary rule later in this Chapter.

Homeless Persons

Is a warrant ever required to arrest a homeless person? Some courts have held that the arrest of a homeless person cannot violate *Payton*, even if the arrest occurs in a place that the person calls "home." See United States v. Ruckman, 806 F.2d 1471 (10th Cir.1986) (warrantless arrest of the defendant in a cave on government-owned property did not violate *Payton*). Increasingly, however, courts have been sympathetic to the privacy interests of homeless persons, and have held that the term "home" must be applied flexibly to include a public area in which a homeless person has established a living space—at least if the person is not trespassing. See, e.g., Community for Creative Non–Violence v. U.S. Marshals Service, 797 F.Supp. 7 (D.C.D.C.1992) (*Payton* applies to arrests conducted in a homeless shelter).

Hotels and Motels

The protections against warrantless intrusions into the home announced in *Payton* apply with equal force to a properly rented hotel or motel room during the rental period. See, e.g., United States v. Morales, 737 F.2d 761 (8th Cir.1984). However, this is only the case as long as the arrestee has rightful possession of the room. If the rental period has terminated, or if the person has been ejected from the premises, then the premises can no longer be considered a "home," and an arrest warrant is not required. See, e.g., United States v. Larson, 760 F.2d 852 (8th Cir.1985). See also United States v. Gooch, 6 F.3d 673

(9th Cir.1993) (arrest warrant required for an arrest inside a tent pitched in a public campground: "A guest in Yellowstone Lodge, a hotel on government park land, would have no less an expectation of privacy in his hotel room than a guest in a private hotel, and the same logic would extend to a campsite where the opportunity is extended to spend the night.").

Arrests in the Home of a Third Party

After *Payton*, the Court addressed the standard to be used when an arrest of one suspect is made in the home of a third person in Steagald v. United States, 451 U.S. 204 (1981). Officers obtained an arrest warrant for Ricky Lyons, a federal fugitive wanted on drug charges. They received information that Lyons was staying at a certain house for the next 24 hours. Armed with the arrest warrant, they searched the house. They did not find Lyons, but they did find drugs in the house. These drugs were offered against Steagald, the owner of the house. Steagald moved to suppress the drugs on the ground that the officers failed to secure a search warrant before entering the house to look for Lyons.

Justice Marshall's majority opinion in *Steagald* concluded that a search warrant must be obtained to look for a suspect in the home of a third party, absent exigent circumstances or consent. [The difference between an arrest warrant and a search warrant in this context is that the arrest warrant only requires the magistrate's determination that there is probable cause to arrest a person; it is not specific as to location. A search warrant would require a magistrate to determine that there is probable cause to believe that the suspect is located in the home of the third party.] The majority held that an arrest warrant did not sufficiently protect the privacy interests of the third party homeowner. Justice Marshall noted that Steagald's only protection from an illegal search "was the agent's personal determination of probable cause" to believe that Lyons was in Steagald's house. The majority was concerned with the possibility of abuse that could arise if a search warrant were not required in the absence of exigent circumstances: "Armed solely with an arrest warrant for a single person, the police could search all the homes of that individual's friends and acquaintances." Justice Rehnquist's dissent was joined by Justice White. They focused on the mobility of fugitives and the likelihood of escape. They also observed that when a suspect lives in another's place for a significant period, this may convert the place into the suspect's home and thus justify a search for that suspect under an arrest warrant.

The majority in *Steagald* showed concern that a third party may be the victim of a search where there is no probable cause to believe that the arrestee is on the premises. But what about those third parties who live with the arrestee? See United States v. Litteral, 910 F.2d 547 (9th Cir.1990) ("if the suspect is a co-resident of the third party, then *Steagald* does not apply, and *Payton* allows both arrest of the subject of the arrest warrant and use of evidence found against the third party"). As an arrest warrant is sufficient to arrest a person in his home, aren't those who live with him subject to the same risk that concerned the Court in *Steagald?* Is the real difference between *Payton* and *Steagald* that the officer's error as to probable cause can result in a greater number of mistaken searches in the latter case than in the former? Or does the difference lie in the risk that a person assumes in living with somebody, as opposed to having somebody visit their home temporarily? See United States v. Lovelock, 170 F.3d

339 (2d Cir. 1999) ("A person who occupies premises jointly with another has a reduced expectation of privacy since he assumes the risk that his housemate may engage in conduct that authorized entry into the premises.").

After *Steagald,* it is important for the officer to determine whether the suspect lives in the premises (in which case an arrest warrant is sufficient) or is merely a visitor (in which case a search warrant is required). What considerations should an officer take into account? See United States v. Pallais, 921 F.2d 684 (7th Cir.1990) (suspect who was staying in garage overseeing the renovation of his children's home was a resident, so that arrest warrant was sufficient). What if the officer wants to arrest a person in a third party's home, and knows that the suspect has a residence somewhere else? Does this prohibit the officer from reasonably believing that the suspect might reside in the third party's home as well? See United States v. Risse, 83 F.3d 212 (8th Cir.1996) (officer could enter defendant's home with an arrest warrant to arrest the defendant's girlfriend, even though the officer knew that the girlfriend had her own apartment: "We have found no authority to support Risse's implicit assumption that a person can have only one residence for Fourth Amendment purposes.").

Questions of Standing

In *Steagald*, the officers entered Steagald's home to arrest the suspect *Lyons*. While trying to find Lyons, the officers discovered evidence that was used against Steagald at trial. The Court held that the evidence should have been suppressed because Steagald's Fourth Amendment rights were violated in the absence of a search warrant. Does that mean that Lyons, the suspect, could have objected to the lack of a search warrant if the officers had found him in the home? The courts have answered in the negative, reasoning that *Steagald* was concerned with the privacy rights of the third-party homeowner, not with the visiting arrestee. See United States v. Underwood, 717 F.2d 482 (9th Cir.1983) (*Steagald* addressed only the right of a third party not named in the arrest warrant to the privacy of his or her home; this right is personal and cannot be asserted vicariously by the person named in the arrest warrant). A contrary rule would be anomalous: the suspect would be entitled to demand a search warrant when arrested in the home of another, while under *Payton* he could demand only an arrest warrant when arrested in his own home. See United States v. Kaylor, 877 F.2d 658 (8th Cir.1989) ("Kaylor cannot claim any greater Fourth Amendment protection in the Lindgren home than he possessed in his own home").

The Rights of an Overnight Guest: Minnesota v. Olson

The Court concluded in Minnesota v. Olson, 495 U.S. 91 (1990), that an arrest warrant was required under *Payton* to arrest an overnight guest in the home of a third person. Justice White wrote the majority opinion. Chief Justice Rehnquist and Justice Blackmun dissented without opinion. Justice White stressed that a person's "status as an overnight guest is alone enough to show that he had an expectation of privacy in the home that society is prepared to accept as reasonable." The Court specifically rejected the State's argument that a place must be one's own home in order to have a legitimate expectation of privacy there.

Temporary Visitors

The Court in *Olson* held that an overnight guest had a sufficient expectation of privacy in the premises to be entitled to the protections of the warrant requirement. What if the guest's connection with the premises is less substantial than that of an overnight guest? In Minnesota v. Carter, 525 U.S. 83 (1998), Carter and Johns objected to a warrantless search of an apartment. Their connection with the apartment was that they were there for a couple of hours cutting up cocaine. Chief Justice Rehnquist, writing for the Court, held that the defendants had no expectation of privacy sufficient to trigger their Fourth Amendment rights. The Chief Justice explained as follows:

> If we regard the overnight guest in Minnesota v. Olson as typifying those who may claim the protection of the Fourth Amendment in the home of another, and one merely "legitimately on the premises" as typifying those who may not do so, the present case is obviously somewhere in between. But the purely commercial nature of the transaction engaged in here, the relatively short period of time on the premises, and the lack of any previous connection between respondents and the householder, all lead us to conclude that respondents' situation is closer to that of one simply permitted on the premises. We therefore hold that any search which may have occurred did not violate their Fourth Amendment rights.

Justice Scalia, joined by Justice Thomas, wrote a concurring opinion. He noted that the text of the Fourth Amendment provides protection to people in "their" houses—and Carter and Johns were not in "their" house when the search occurred. He reasoned as follows:

> [I]n deciding the question presented today we write upon a slate that is far from clean. The text of the Fourth Amendment, the common-law background against which it was adopted, and the understandings consistently displayed after its adoption make the answer clear. * * * We went to the absolute limit of what text and tradition permit in Minnesota v. Olson, when we protected a mere overnight guest against an unreasonable search of his hosts' apartment. But whereas it is plausible to regard a person's overnight lodging as at least his "temporary" residence, it is entirely impossible to give that characterization to an apartment that he uses to package cocaine. Respondents here were not searched in "their ... hous[e]" under any interpretation of the phrase that bears the remotest relationship to the well understood meaning of the Fourth Amendment.

Justice Kennedy wrote a concurring opinion in which he distinguished between business guests and social guests. He joined the Court's opinion "for its reasoning is consistent with my view that almost all social guests have a legitimate expectation of privacy, and hence protection against unreasonable searches, in their host's home."

Justice Ginsburg, joined by Justices Stevens and Souter, dissented in *Carter*. In her view, "when a homeowner or lessor personally invites a guest into her home to share in a common endeavor, whether it be for conversation, to engage in leisure activities, or for business purposes licit or illicit, that guest should share his host's shelter against unreasonable searches and seizures."

Justice Breyer concurred in the judgment in *Carter*. He agreed with Justice Ginsburg that the Fourth Amendment protects any invitee to a home, whatever the purpose for their presence. He concluded, however, that the officer in *Carter* had not even engaged in a search—he had simply peered through the blinds into a basement apartment, and saw Carter and Johns cutting up the cocaine.

6. *Material Witness*

The power to arrest is usually applied to persons suspected of criminal activity. However, the police also have the power to arrest and detain a material witness to a crime "if it is shown that it may become impracticable to secure his presence by subpoena." 18 U.S.C.A. § 3144. In addition to the Federal statute, every state provides for detention of material witnesses. The Supreme Court has cited the practice with approval in Stein v. New York, 346 U.S. 156, 184 (1953) and Barry v. United States ex rel. Cunningham, 279 U.S. 597, 617 (1929). The expansiveness of the power to arrest a material witness was shown when James Nichols was arrested after the bombing of the Oklahoma City Federal Building. The officers did not have probable cause to believe that James Nichols was involved in the bombing; but they did have probable cause to believe that he had pertinent information about the crime. Nichols was detained for several days as a material witness. His brother Terry Nichols was arrested as a material witness on April 19, 1995, and not charged with direct involvement in the crime until May 9. (See Bombing Prosecutors Invoke Seldom–Used Statute, National Law Journal, June 26, 1995, p. A11).

What are the constitutional limitations on this power? In Bacon v. United States, 449 F.2d 933 (9th Cir.1971), it was held that a warrant to arrest a material witness must be based on probable cause to believe, first, that the testimony of the witness will be material, and second, that it may become impracticable to secure his presence by a subpoena. Should arrests without warrant ever be permitted? Only in exigent circumstances?

18 U.S.C.A. § 3144 provides for release if the witness' testimony can be adequately secured by deposition. But in most states, there is no statutory limit on the permissible length of detention of a witness who cannot pay the required bond. See, e.g., Quince v. State, 94 R.I. 200, 179 A.2d 485 (1962) (witness confined with convicted offenders for 158 days). States differ widely in the procedural protections they afford to a detained witness, e.g., preliminary hearing, assistance of counsel, appeal, and compensation. See Application of Cochran, 434 F.Supp. 1207 (D.C.Neb.1977) (outlining minimum due process requirements).

There is no constitutional right to monetary compensation for time spent in confinement as a material witness. In Hurtado v. United States, 410 U.S. 578 (1973), the Court held that payment of one dollar per day as compensation did not constitute a "taking" without just compensation or a denial of equal protection.

The material witness statute has been used with some frequency after the 9/11 attacks, to detain Muslims with suspected ties to terrorists. The following case is an example of the use of the statute after 9/11.

UNITED STATES v. AWADALLAH

United States Court of Appeals for the Second Circuit, 2003.
349 F.3d 42 (2d Cir. 2003).

JACOBS, **Circuit Judge:**

This appeal, which arises from the government's investigation of the September 11, 2001 terrorist attacks, presents questions about the scope of the federal material witness statute and the government's powers of arrest and detention thereunder. See 18 U.S.C. § 3144. The district court (Scheindlin, J.) ruled that the statute cannot be applied constitutionally to a grand jury witness such as the defendant-appellee, Osama Awadallah, and dismissed the perjury indictment against him as fruit of an illegal detention. The court also suppressed his grand jury testimony as fruit of an illegal detention on the alternative ground that the affidavit in support of the arrest warrant included material misrepresentations.

We conclude that these rulings must be reversed and the indictment reinstated. We also reverse the district court's independent ruling that the FBI's unreasonable searches and seizures on September 20 and 21, 2001, before Awadallah was arrested as a material witness, require suppression at trial of certain statements and physical evidence.

BACKGROUND

In the days immediately following September 11, 2001, the United States Attorney for the Southern District of New York initiated a grand jury investigation into the terrorist attacks. Investigators quickly identified Nawaf Al–Hazmi and Khalid Al–Mihdhar as two of the hijackers on American Airlines Flight 77, which crashed into the Pentagon. The Justice Department released the identities of all nineteen hijackers on Friday, September 14, 2001, and news media around the country publicized their names and photographs the following day.

A search of the car Al–Hazmi abandoned at Dulles Airport in Virginia produced a piece of paper with the notation, "Osama 589–5316." Federal agents tracked this number to a San Diego address at which the defendant, Osama Awadallah, had lived approximately eighteen months earlier. Al–Hazmi and Al–Mihdhar also had lived in the San Diego vicinity around that time.

* * *

On the morning of September 20, 2001, federal agents went to Awadallah's current residence in San Diego. When the agents arrived at the apartment, Awadallah was attending a course in English as a second language at nearby Grossmont College, where he was enrolled. The agents interviewed Awadallah's roommate in their apartment for several hours.

When Awadallah came home at around 2:00 p.m. that afternoon, several agents approached him as he entered the parking lot and got out of his car (a gray Honda). They questioned him in the parking lot for a few minutes and then told him that he had to accompany them to the FBI office for questioning. Awadallah insisted on returning to his apartment first to observe the afternoon Muslim prayer, which he did as the agents watched. When Awadallah went into the bathroom, the agents insisted that the bathroom door be left open.

Before leaving for the FBI office, an agent asked Awadallah to sign a consent form allowing them to search his apartment and car. Otherwise, the agent told him, they would get a warrant and "tear up" his home. Believing he had no choice, Awadallah signed the form without reading it. The agents then put him in their car and drove him to the FBI office. Awadallah told them that he had to return in time for a 6:00 p.m. computer class; they told him that would be no problem.

At the FBI office, agents offered Awadallah a drink, but he declined because he was fasting. They asked him to sign another consent form for the search of his second car, an inoperative white Honda in the parking lot of his apartment building. This time, Awadallah read the form and learned that he had a right to refuse consent; and though he signed the consent form for his second car, he explicitly revoked his consent for the search of the first car. An agent tried to reach the agents at the apartment building by cell phone, but did not reach them until fifteen minutes later, after the search of the first car had been completed. The agents at the scene then searched the apartment and the second car. The search of Awadallah's home produced several computer-generated photographs of Osama bin Laden; the searches of his cars produced two videotapes on Bosnia and one on Islam and a retractable razor which could be described as a box-cutter or a carpet knife.

Awadallah was alone in a locked interview room for a while, until agents arrived to question him. They did not advise him of his rights or tell him that he could leave. They asked him about the September 11 hijackers and about his life and acquaintances. He told the agents that he knew Al–Hazmi, and that he had frequently seen another man with him, whose name he did not know.

* * *

When 6:00 p.m. approached, the agents told Awadallah that they had called his school and that it was alright for him to miss class. They told him he would "have to stay" with them until they were finished. The entire interview lasted approximately six hours, ending at nearly 11:00 p.m. Before allowing Awadallah to leave, the agents scheduled a polygraph examination for the next morning. * * * At 6:30 a.m. the following day, September 21, 2001, Awadallah called the FBI and refused to come in for the polygraph test until he had a lawyer. The agent told him they would get an arrest warrant. Believing he had no choice, Awadallah went with two agents who picked him up at his apartment at 7:00 a.m.

At the FBI office, agents advised Awadallah of his rights and he signed an advice-of-rights acknowledgment form. The polygraph exam lasted one-and-a-half to two hours. Afterward, the agents told Awadallah that the polygraph registered lies in response to two questions: whether he had advance knowledge of the September 11 attacks and whether he had participated in them in any way. It is unclear whether these were in fact the results. The conversation became heated as the agents accused Awadallah of being a terrorist. They refused Awadallah's requests to call a lawyer and his brother, and did not release him in time for Friday prayer.

Throughout the questioning that day, the FBI agents in San Diego had been in contact with an Assistant United States Attorney ("AUSA") in New York. At approximately 2:00 p.m. Eastern time, the AUSA instructed the agents to arrest Awadallah as a material witness. The agents handcuffed Awadallah and took him to the San Diego correctional center for booking.

Meanwhile, prosecutors and agents in New York prepared an application for a material witness warrant. In the supporting affidavit, FBI Special Agent Ryan Plunkett recounted how the FBI found the phone number in Al–Hazmi's car, Awadallah's admission that he knew Al–Hazmi, and the results of the agents' searches, including the "box-cutter" and the photographs of bin Laden. Agent Plunkett stated that it might become difficult to secure Awadallah's grand jury testimony because he had extensive family ties in Jordan and might be a flight risk. The affidavit did not say when Awadallah said he had last seen Al–Hazmi (over a year earlier); that Awadallah had moved eighteen months earlier from the address associated with the phone number; that Awadallah had used the "box-cutter" recently to install a new carpet in his apartment; that Awadallah had been (ostensibly) cooperative with the FBI agents in San Diego; or that Awadallah had three brothers who lived in San Diego, one of whom was an American citizen. Also, the affidavit stated that the "box-cutter" had been found in Awadallah's apartment when, in fact, it had been found in his inoperative second car.

Shortly before 6:00 p.m. Eastern time, Agent Plunkett and an AUSA presented the material witness warrant application to Chief Judge Mukasey of the United States District Court for the Southern District of New York. Based solely on the contents of Agent Plunkett's affidavit, Chief Judge Mukasey issued a warrant to arrest Awadallah as a material witness pursuant to 18 U.S.C. § 3144. The court was unaware that Awadallah had already been arrested as a material witness three hours earlier.

On September 25, 2001, Awadallah appeared before a Magistrate Judge Ruben B. Brooks in the Southern District of California, who declined to re-

lease him on bail and ordered that he be removed to New York. On October 2, 2001, the day after he arrived in New York, Awadallah appeared before Chief Judge Mukasey for a second bail hearing. Chief Judge Mukasey also declined to release Awadallah on bail, finding his continued detention to be "reasonable under the circumstances."

During the period of his detention, Awadallah spent time in four prisons as he was transferred to the New York correctional center by way of Oklahoma City. He alleges that he received harsh and improper treatment during this period. Because these allegations of abuse and mistreatment were immaterial to the issues before the district court, Judge Scheindlin expressly declined to make "findings of fact on disputed issues regarding the conditions of confinement." Nonetheless, Judge Scheindlin noted that Awadallah spent most of his time in solitary confinement; at times lacked access to his family, his lawyer, or a phone; and was repeatedly strip-searched. The government did not dispute that, by October 4, 2001, "Awadallah had bruises on his upper arms," and an agent's report indicated several other injuries on his shoulder, ankles, hand, and face. Awadallah sometimes refrained from eating because the meals provided did not comply with his religious dietary restrictions.

On October 10, 2001, twenty days after his arrest as a material witness, Awadallah testified before the grand jury in the Southern District of New York. The prosecutor questioned him for most of the day. In the course of his testimony, Awadallah denied knowing anyone named Khalid Al–Mihdhar or Khalid. The government then showed him an examination booklet he had written in September, which the government obtained from his English teacher in San Diego. The booklet contained the following handwritten sentence: "One of the quietest people I have met is Nawaf. Another one his name Khalid. They have stayed in S.D. [San Diego] for 6 months." Awadallah acknowledged that it was his examination booklet, and that most of the writing in it was his own, but he denied that the name Khalid and a few other words on the page were written in his handwriting. On October 15, 2001, when Awadallah again appeared before the grand jury, he stated that his recollection of Khalid's name had been refreshed by his October 10 testimony and that the disputed writing in the exam booklet was in fact his own. However, he did not admit to making false statements in his first grand jury appearance.

The United States Attorney for the Southern District of New York filed charges against Awadallah on two counts of making false statements to the grand jury in violation of 18 U.S.C. § 1623: falsely denying that he knew Khalid Al–Mihdhar (Count One); and falsely denying that the handwriting in the exam booklet was his own (Count Two).

On November 27, 2001, the district court (Scheindlin, J.) granted Awadallah's bail application. He satisfied the bail conditions and was released approximately two weeks later.

In December 2001, Awadallah moved to dismiss the indictment * * *. [The district court granted the motion on the ground that] the federal material witness statute, 18 U.S.C. § 3144, did not apply to grand jury witnesses.* * * The court held that Awadallah's arrest and detention were therefore unlawful. * * * Judge Scheindlin ruled that Awadallah's perjured grand jury testimony had to be suppressed as fruit of this illegal arrest and detention.

* * *

DISCUSSION

* * *

I. Applicability of 18 U.S.C. § 3144

The first issue presented is whether the federal material witness statute, 18 U.S.C. § 3144, allows the arrest and detention of grand jury witnesses. * * * Section 3144, titled "release or detention of a material witness," provides in its entirety:

> If it appears from an affidavit filed by a party that the testimony of a person is material in a criminal proceeding, and if it is shown that it may become impracticable to secure the presence of the person by subpoena, a judicial officer may order the arrest of the person and treat the person in accordance with the provisions of section 3142 of this title. No material witness may be detained because of inability to comply with any condition of release if the testimony of such witness can adequately be secured by deposition, and if further detention is not necessary to prevent a failure of justice. Release of a material witness may be delayed for a reasonable period of time until the deposition of the witness can be taken pursuant to the Federal Rules of Criminal Procedure.

18 U.S.C. § 3144. The statute is cast in terms of a material witness in "a criminal proceeding." The decisive question here is whether that term encompasses proceedings before a grand jury.

Based on its study of the statutory wording, context, legislative history, and case law, the district court held that "Section 3144 only allows the detention of material witnesses in the pretrial (as opposed to the grand jury) context." We have found no other decision that has arrived at this conclusion.

The only prior case that squarely considered the issue held that 18 U.S.C. § 3149, the precursor to today's material witness statute, allowed detention of grand jury witnesses. See Bacon v. United States, 449 F.2d 933, 936–41 (9th Cir. 1971). * * * Other courts, including this one, have assumed that the material witness statute authorizes detention of grand jury witnesses. * * *

In In re Material Witness Warrant, 213 F.Supp.2d 287 (S.D.N.Y. 2002), Chief Judge Mukasey "decline[d] to follow the reasoning and holding in *Awadallah*," holding instead:

> Given the broad language of the statute, its legislative history ..., the substantial body of case law indicating that there is no constitutional impediment to detention of grand jury witnesses, and the unquestioned application of the statute to grand jury witnesses over a period of decades before Awadallah, to perceive a Congressional intention that grand jury witnesses be excluded from the reach of section 3144 is to perceive something that is not there.

Having the benefit of thorough opinions on both sides of the question, we conclude that the district court's ruling in this case must be reversed.

* * *

B. Language of the Statute

As noted above, § 3144 applies to witnesses whose testimony is material in "a criminal proceeding." 18 U.S.C. § 3144. "Criminal proceeding" is a broad and capacious term, and there is good reason to conclude that it includes a grand jury proceeding. First, it has long been recognized that "the word 'proceeding' is not a technical one, and is aptly used by courts to designate an inquiry before a grand jury."

* * *

Notwithstanding this support for the general view that "criminal proceedings" encompass grand jury proceedings, however, we cannot say that the statutory wording alone compels that conclusion. Black's Law Dictionary defines a "criminal proceeding" as "[a] proceeding instituted to determine a person's guilt or innocence or to set a convicted person's punishment; a criminal hearing or trial." Black's Law Dictionary 1221 (7th ed. 1999). It defines a "grand jury" as "[a] body of ... people ... who, in ex parte proceedings, decide whether to issue indictments. If the grand jury decides that evidence is strong enough to hold a suspect for trial, it returns a bill of indictment ... charging the suspect with a specific crime." Defined this way, a grand jury proceeding is not a "proceeding instituted to determine a person's guilt or innocence or to set a convicted person's punishment," but rather a proceeding to "decide whether to issue indictments." A grand jury proceeding is certainly a stage of criminal justice; and it is certainly a proceeding. As a proceeding, it is certainly not civil, administrative, arbitral, commercial, social, or any type of proceeding other than (or as much as) criminal. Even so, the dictionary entries could suggest that grand jury proceedings lie outside the scope of § 3144.

* * *

C. Legislative History

The legislative history of § 3144 makes clear Congress's intent to include grand jury proceedings within the definition of "criminal proceeding." Congress enacted § 3144 in its current form as part of the Bail Reform Act of 1984. Its language is nearly identical to the text of its predecessor statute, 18 U.S.C. § 1349 (1966) * * *.

The most telling piece of legislative history appears in the Senate Judiciary Committee Report that accompanied the 1984 enactment of § 3144. The Report stated that, "if a person's testimony is material in any criminal proceeding, and if it is shown that it may become impracticable to secure his presence by subpoena, the government is authorized to take such person into custody." A footnote to this statement advised categorically that "[a] grand jury investigation is a 'criminal proceeding' within the meaning of this section.* * *

D. Constitutional Considerations

In concluding that § 3144 does not apply to grand jury witnesses, the district court invoked the canon of constitutional avoidance, under which a court should construe an ambiguous statute to avoid constitutional problems if a viable alternative interpretation exists. This rule, which facilitates a choice between alternative interpretations of an ambiguous statute, has no bearing if the meaning of the statute is known.

Assuming arguendo that there are two viable interpretations of § 3144, "the canon ... applies only when there are serious concerns about the statute's constitutionality." The district court determined that "imprisoning a material witness for a grand jury investigation raises a serious constitutional question" under the Fourth Amendment's prohibition against unreasonable search and seizure. We respectfully disagree.

As a threshold matter, the detention of material witnesses for the purpose of securing grand jury testimony has withstood constitutional challenge. In New York v. O'Neill, 359 U.S. 1 (1959), the Supreme Court considered "the constitutionality of a Florida statute entitled 'Uniform Law to Secure the Attendance of Witnesses from Within or Without a State in Criminal Proceedings.'" This statute * * * enabled a judge of one state to certify "the necessity of the appearance of [a] witness in a criminal prosecution or grand jury investigation," and concomitantly enabled the state where that witness could be found to "take the witness into immediate custody" and "deliver the witness to an officer of the requesting State." The Court held that this statute did not violate the Privileges and Immunities Clause of the Fourteenth Amendment. In doing so, it observed that "Florida undoubtedly could have held respondent within Florida if he had been a material witness in a criminal proceeding within that State." The Court observed that "[a] citizen cannot shirk his duty, no matter how inconvenienced thereby, to testify in criminal proceedings and grand jury investigations in a State where he is found. There is no constitutional provision granting him relief from this obligation to testify even though he must travel to another State to do so."

* * *

Similarly, the Court has observed that the Senate has "the power in some cases to issue a warrant of arrest to compel" the "attendance of witnesses," and that this power was "a necessary incident of the power to adjudge, in no wise inferior under like circumstances to that exercised by a court of justice." Barry v. United States ex rel. Cunningham, 279 U.S. 597, 616 (1929). * * *

The district court failed to account for these cases in detecting a constitutional problem in the detention of a material witness, and focused instead on developing its own Fourth Amendment analysis. Even meeting the district court decision on those terms, we see no serious constitutional problem that would warrant the exclusion of grand jury proceedings from the scope of § 3144.

* * * Determining the reasonableness of a seizure involves a balancing of competing interests:

> The essential purpose of the proscriptions in the Fourth Amendment is to impose a standard of "reasonableness" upon the exercise of discretion by government officials, including law enforcement agents, in order "to safeguard the privacy and security of individuals against arbitrary invasions...." Thus, the permissibility of a particular law enforcement practice is judged by balancing its intrusion on the individual's Fourth Amendment interests against its promotion of legitimate governmental interests.

Delaware v. Prouse, 440 U.S. 648 (1979). Thus we must consider both "the nature and quality of the intrusion on the individual's Fourth Amendment interests" and "the importance of the governmental interests alleged to justify the intrusion." Tennessee v. Garner, 471 U.S. 1, 8 (1985).

In its balancing analysis, the district court found that "the only legitimate reason to detain a grand jury witness is to aid in an ex parte investigation to determine whether a crime has been committed and whether criminal proceedings should be instituted against any person." This is no small interest. In United States v. Mandujano, 425 U.S. 564 (1976), the Supreme Court explained:

> The grand jury is an integral part of our constitutional heritage which was brought to this country with the common law.... Indispensable to the exercise of its power is the authority to compel the attendance and the testimony of witnesses....

When called by the grand jury, witnesses are thus legally bound to give testimony. This principle has long been recognized.

* * *

The district court noted (and we agree) that it would be improper for the government to use § 3144 for other ends, such as the detention of persons suspected of criminal activity for which probable cause has not yet been established. However, the district court made no finding (and we see no evidence to suggest) that the government arrested Awadallah for any purpose other than to secure information material to a grand jury investigation. Moreover, that grand jury was investigating the September 11 terrorist attacks. The particular governmental interests at stake therefore were the indictment and successful prosecution of terrorists whose attack, if committed by a sovereign, would have been tantamount to war, and the discovery of the conspirators' means, contacts, and operations in order to forestall future attacks.

On the other side of the balance, the district court found in essence that § 3144 was not calibrated to minimize the intrusion on the liberty of a grand jury witness. According to the district court, several procedural safeguards available to trial witnesses are not afforded in the grand jury context. We agree with the district court, of course, that arrest and detention are significant infringements on liberty, but we conclude that § 3144 sufficiently limits that infringement and reasonably balances it against the government's countervailing interests.

The first procedural safeguard to be considered is § 3144's provision that "no material witness may be detained because of inability to comply with any condition of release if the testimony of such witness can adequately be secured by deposition, and if further detention is not necessary to prevent a failure of justice." The district court agreed with the government that this deposition provision does not apply to grand jury witnesses. The government's altered position on appeal is that "Congress intended depositions to be available as a less restrictive alternative to detaining a grand jury witness." Such a pivot by the government on appeal is awkward, but we accept the government's explanation that it was persuaded by Chief Judge Mukasey's view in In re Material Witness Warrant, 213 F. Supp. 2d at 296.

We conclude that the deposition mechanism is available for grand jury witnesses detained under § 3144. [Under Fed.R.Crim.P. 15 a district court is] authorized to order a deposition and to release the witness once it has been taken. * * *

The district court found the deposition provision inapplicable in the grand jury context in part because a conventional deposition is inconsistent with the procedural and evidentiary rules of a grand jury hearing. However, the district court may set additional conditions for the conduct of a deposition. The court thus can limit the deposition according to grand jury protocol, for example by limiting the witness's right to have counsel present during the deposition or by permitting the use of hearsay.

* * *

The second procedural safeguard at issue is § 3144's express invocation of the bail and release provisions set forth in 18 U.S.C. § 3142. Section 3144 directs that "a judicial officer may ... treat the [detained] person in accordance with the provisions of section 3142 of this title." 18 U.S.C. § 3144. As noted above, § 3142 sets conditions for the "release or deten-

tion of a defendant pending trial," as follows:

> Upon the appearance before a judicial officer of a person charged with an offense, the judicial officer shall issue an order that, pending trial, the person be—(1) released on personal recognizance or upon execution of an unsecured appearance bond ...; (2) released on a condition or combination of conditions ...; (3) temporarily detained to permit revocation of conditional release, deportation, or exclusion ...; or (4) detained....

18 U.S.C. § 3142(a).

As the district court observed, some of the terms used in § 3142—namely, "a person charged with an offense" and "pending trial"—do not comport with the structure of grand jury proceedings. However, we do not deduce (as the district court did) that "it is plain that section 3142 cannot apply to grand jury proceedings." We agree with Chief Judge Mukasey that the provisions of § 3142 govern insofar as they are applicable in the grand jury setting * * *. Thus, a person detained as a material witness in a grand jury investigation may obtain a hearing on the propriety of his continued detention and the conditions, if any, which will allow his release.

* * *

Finally, Awadallah and the NYCDL argue that § 3144 provides no limit on how long a grand jury witness may be detained, whereas the detention of a trial witness is implicitly limited (or speeded) by the time limits on prosecution contained in the Speedy Trial Act, 18 U.S.C. § 3161 et seq. However, the Speedy Trial Act permits delay for various reasons, see 18 U.S.C. § 3161(h), which may have the collateral effect of extending the detention of a material witness; and nothing in the Speedy Trial Act requires a court to consider the effect of a continuance or delay on a detained witness. The Act therefore provides cold comfort to a detained trial witness.

While § 3144 contains no express time limit, the statute and related rules require close institutional attention to the propriety and duration of detentions: "no material witness may be detained because of inability to comply with any condition of release if the testimony of such witness can adequately be secured by deposition, and if further detention is not necessary to prevent a failure of justice." 18 U.S.C. § 3144. The court must "treat the person in accordance with the provisions of section 3142," which provides a mechanism for release. And release may be delayed only "for a reasonable period of time until the deposition of the witness can be taken pursuant to the Federal Rules of Criminal Procedure." Perhaps most important, [Fed. R.Crim.P.] 46 requires the government to make a "biweekly report" to the court listing each material witness held in custody for more than ten days and justifying the continued detention of each witness. These measures tend to ensure that material witnesses are detained no longer than necessary.

In light of the foregoing analysis, we must ask whether Awadallah was properly detained when he was held for several weeks without being allowed to give his deposition and obtain release. Such a detention constitutes a significant intrusion on liberty, since a material witness can be arrested with little or no notice, transported across the country, and detained for several days or weeks. Under the circumstances of this case, however, we are satisfied that Awadallah's detention was not unreasonably prolonged.

As indicated above, the deposition mechanism invoked in § 3144 is avail-

able to grand jury witnesses, but it is not required in every instance. Section 3144 requires release after deposition only if "the testimony of such witness can adequately be secured by deposition" and "further detention is not necessary to prevent a failure of justice." Similarly, § 3142 provides that a person may be detained if, "after a hearing ..., the judicial officer finds that no condition or combination of conditions will reasonably assure the appearance of the person as required and the safety of any other person and the community." 18 U.S.C. § 3142(e).

The procedural history demonstrates that Awadallah received adequate process to ensure that the duration of his detention was reasonable. * * * All told, Awadallah spent 20 days in detention as a material witness before testifying before the grand jury and uttering the allegedly perjurious statements. The undisputed facts establish that he received two bail hearings pursuant to § 3142 within days of his arrest, and that the judges in both hearings found his continued detention to be both reasonable and necessary. Under these circumstances, Awadallah's detention as a material witness was a scrupulous and constitutional use of the federal material witness statute.

[The Court goes on to reverse the district court's finding that the material witness warrant was invalid as based on material misrepresentations by the FBI. It also reverses the district judge's ruling that the government illegally arrested Awadallah and that his statements to the grand jury had to be suppressed as fruits of the illegal arrest. The Court noted that even if Awadallah had been seized illegally, the exclusionary rule does not apply when the perjury alleged in the indictment was committed after the constitutional violation. The Court declared that "statements obtained as fruit of an illegal arrest may be introduced in a perjury trial, if the alleged perjury occurred after the illegal arrest and there is no actual evidence of collusion between the proponents of the evidence and the arresting officers." The Court reasoned that the officers were sufficiently deterred by the prospect that Awadallah was a suspect in the 9/11 conspiracy and therefore would not have wanted the evidence to be suppressed in a substantive prosecution.]

Conclusion

For the foregoing reasons, we reverse the decisions of the district court and remand for reinstatement of the indictment and further proceedings consistent with this opinion.

[The concurring opinion of Judge Straub is omitted.]

Questions on the Use of the Material Witness Statute After 9/11

Was the Court in *Awadallah* influenced by the fact that Awadallah appeared to have at least some information about 9/11, as opposed to, say, a drug crime?

The Court states that the material witness statute cannot be used as a pretext for an extended detention of someone as to whom there is no probable cause to arrest for a crime. But how is such pretext to be determined? The dangers of material witness detention are emphasized by Stacey Studnicki and John Apol, Witness Detention and Intimidation: The History and Future of Material Witness Law, 76 St. John's L.Rev. 483 (2002):

> Material witness law is unique because of the potential *carte blanche* it provides to the government and law enforcement officials who may abuse it. In the aftermath of the September 11, 2001 terrorist attacks, the FBI has been accused of misusing the material witness law to detain people while investigating their backgrounds and activities. Indeed, the United States Attorney General announced that the "aggressive detention" of material witnesses in the wake of September 11th would be the norm. The secrecy surrounding the detention of material witnesses adds to the potential of misuse of this authority as an investigatory tool, rather than a legitimate means of obtaining testimony or protecting a witness. Further, it is easier to arrest an individual as a material witness than as a criminal defendant since there is no required showing of probable cause that the witness has committed a crime.

7. Enemy Combatants

After 9/11, many suspected terrorists have been detained as "enemy combatants". The government detains "enemy combatants" without making a showing to a civilian court that there is probable cause for the detention. The theory is that "enemy combatants" are essentially prisoners of war and therefore are outside the jurisdiction of civilian courts—at best there is only a limited, deferential review at some point on whether the "enemy combatant" status is justified. "Enemy combatant" status is treated extensively in Chapter 10, *infra*, as its consequences are not only detention, but also determination of guilt by a military tribunal rather than a civilian jury trial.

B. STOP AND FRISK

There are numerous situations in which the police recognize that they do not have probable cause to act, but want "to stop suspicious persons for questioning and, occasionally, to search these persons for dangerous weapons." LaFave, "Street Encounters" and the Constitution: Terry, Sibron, Peters and

Beyond, 67 Mich.L.Rev. 40, 42 (1968). From the police perspective, if officers have to wait for probable cause to develop before conducting these preliminary investigations, they would be severely hampered in their efforts to prevent crime. In their view, a standard of proof less demanding than probable cause is needed to nip a crime problem in the bud. Following the adoption in 1964 of a New York statute that became known as the "stop and frisk" law and the conclusion of several important studies of what police do in the real world, the United States Supreme Court placed its first imprimatur on searches and seizures of persons and things without probable cause.

1. Stop and Frisk Established

TERRY v. OHIO

Supreme Court of the United States, 1968.
392 U.S. 1.

MR. CHIEF JUSTICE WARREN delivered the opinion of the Court.

This case presents serious questions concerning the role of the Fourth Amendment in the confrontation on the street between the citizen and the policeman investigating suspicious circumstances.

Petitioner Terry was convicted of carrying a concealed weapon and sentenced to the statutorily prescribed term of one to three years in the penitentiary. Following the denial of a pretrial motion to suppress, the prosecution introduced in evidence two revolvers and a number of bullets seized from Terry and a codefendant, Richard Chilton, by Cleveland Police Detective Martin McFadden. At the hearing on the motion to suppress this evidence, Officer McFadden testified that while he was patrolling in plain clothes in downtown Cleveland at approximately 2:30 in the afternoon of October 31, 1963, his attention was attracted by two men, Chilton and Terry, standing on the corner of Huron Road and Euclid Avenue. He had never seen the two men before, and he was unable to say precisely what first drew his eye to them. However, he testified that he had been a policeman for 39 years and a detective for 35 and that he had been as-

signed to patrol this vicinity of downtown Cleveland for shoplifters and pickpockets for 30 years. He explained that he had developed routine habits of observation over the years and that he would "stand and watch people or walk and watch people at many intervals of the day." He added: "Now, in this case when I looked over they didn't look right to me at the time."

His interest aroused, Officer McFadden took up a post of observation in the entrance to a store 300 to 400 feet away from the two men. * * * He saw one of the men leave the other one and walk southwest on Huron Road, past some stores. The man paused for a moment and looked in a store window, then walked on a short distance, turned around and walked back toward the corner, pausing once again to look in the same store window. He rejoined his companion at the corner, and the two conferred briefly. Then the second man went through the same series of motions, strolling down Huron Road, looking in the same window, walking on a short distance, turning back, peering in the store window again, and returning to confer with the first man at the corner. The two men repeated this ritual alternately between five and six times apiece—

in all, roughly a dozen trips. At one point, while the two were standing together on the corner, a third man approached them and engaged them briefly in conversation. This man then left the two others and walked west on Euclid Avenue. Chilton and Terry resumed their measured pacing, peering, and conferring. After this had gone on for 10 to 12 minutes, the two men walked off together, heading west on Euclid Avenue, following the path taken earlier by the third man.

By this time Officer McFadden had become thoroughly suspicious. He testified that after observing their elaborately casual and oft-repeated reconnaissance of the store window on Huron Road, he suspected the two men of "casing a job, a stick-up," and that he considered it his duty as a police officer to investigate further. He added that he feared "they may have a gun." Thus, Officer McFadden followed Chilton and Terry and saw them stop in front of Zucker's store to talk to the same man who had conferred with them earlier on the street corner. Deciding that the situation was ripe for direct action, Officer McFadden approached the three men, identified himself as a police officer and asked for their names. * * * When the men "mumbled something" in response to his inquiries, Officer McFadden grabbed petitioner Terry, spun him around so that they were facing the other two, with Terry between McFadden and the others, and patted down the outside of his clothing. In the left breast pocket of Terry's overcoat Officer McFadden felt a pistol. He reached inside the overcoat pocket, but was unable to remove the gun. At this point, keeping Terry between himself and the others, the officer ordered all three men to enter Zucker's store. As they went in, he removed Terry's overcoat completely, removed a .38–caliber revolver from

the pocket and ordered all three men to face the wall with their hands raised. Officer McFadden proceeded to pat down the outer clothing of Chilton and the third man, Katz. He discovered another revolver in the outer pocket of Chilton's overcoat, but no weapons were found on Katz. The officer testified that he only patted the men down to see whether they had weapons, and that he did not put his hands beneath the outer garments of either Terry or Chilton until he felt their guns. So far as appears from the record, he never placed his hands beneath Katz' outer garments. Officer McFadden seized Chilton's gun, asked the proprietor of the store to call a police wagon, and took all three men to the station, where Chilton and Terry were formally charged with carrying concealed weapons.

On the motion to suppress the guns the prosecution took the position that they had been seized following a search incident to a lawful arrest. The trial court rejected this theory, stating that it "would be stretching the facts beyond reasonable comprehension" to find that Officer McFadden had had probable cause to arrest the men before he patted them down for weapons. However, the court denied the defendants' motion on the ground that Officer McFadden, on the basis of his experience, "had reasonable cause to believe * * * that the defendants were conducting themselves suspiciously, and some interrogation should be made of their action." Purely for his own protection, the court held, the officer had the right to pat down the outer clothing of these men, who he had reasonable cause to believe might be armed. The court distinguished between an investigatory "stop" and an arrest, and between a "frisk" of the outer clothing for weapons and a full-blown search for evidence of crime. The frisk, it held, was essential to the proper performance of the officer's investigatory duties, for without it "the answer to the police officer may be a bullet, and a loaded pistol discovered during the frisk is admissible."

* * *

I

The Fourth Amendment provides that "the right of the people to be secure in their persons, houses, papers, and effects, against unreasonable searches and seizures shall not be violated * * *." This inestimable right of personal security belongs as much to the citizen on the streets of our cities as to the homeowner closeted in his study to dispose of his secret affairs. * * *

We would be less than candid if we did not acknowledge that this question thrusts to the fore difficult and troublesome issues regarding a sensitive area of police activity—issues which have never before been squarely presented to this Court. Reflective of the tensions involved are the practical and constitutional arguments pressed with great vigor on both sides of the public debate over the power of the police to "stop and frisk"—as it is sometimes euphemistically termed—suspicious persons.

* * *

In this context we approach the issues in this case mindful of the limitations of the judicial function in controlling the myriad daily situations in which policemen and citizens confront each other on the street. The State has characterized the issue here as "the right of a police officer * * * to make an on-the-street stop, interrogate and pat down for weapons (known in street vernacular as 'stop and frisk')." But this is only partly accurate. For the issue is not the abstract propriety of the police conduct, but the admissibility against petitioner of the evidence uncovered by the search and seizure. [The Court suggests that the exclusionary rule may not deter all Fourth Amendment violations. For example, where an officer is bent on harassment, and doesn't care about whether he finds evidence, the exclusionary rule cannot deter the officer because the exclusionary rule is dependent on litigation-oriented disincentives.]

* * *

Proper adjudication of cases in which the exclusionary rule is invoked demands a constant awareness of these limitations. The wholesale harassment by certain elements of the police community, of which minority groups, particularly Negroes, frequently complain,[a] will not be stopped by

a. The President's Commission on Law Enforcement and Administration of Justice found that "[i]n many communities, field interrogations are a major source of friction between the police and minority groups." President's Commission on Law Enforcement and Administration of Justice, Task Force Report: The Police 183 (1967). It was reported that the friction caused by "[m]isuse of field interrogations" increases "as more police departments adopt 'aggressive patrol' in which officers are encouraged routinely to stop and question persons on the street who are unknown to them, who are suspicious, or whose purpose for being abroad is not readily evident." While the frequency with which "frisking" forms a part of field interrogation practice varies tremendously

with the locale, the objective of the interrogation, and the particular officer, it cannot help but be a severely exacerbating factor in police-community tensions. This is particularly true in situations where the "stop and frisk" of youths or minority group members is "motivated by the officers' perceived need to maintain the power image of the beat officer, an aim sometimes accomplished by humiliating anyone who attempts to undermine police control of the streets."

[Editors' note: For a general discussion of problems of police stopping suspects for reasons other than arrest, see Dix, Nonarrest Investigatory Detentions in Search and Seizure Law, 1985 Duke L.J. 849. For a discussion of how race plays a role in the use of the stop and

the exclusion of any evidence from any criminal trial. Yet a rigid and unthinking application of the exclusionary rule, in futile protest against practices which it can never be used effectively to control, may exact a high toll in human injury and frustration of efforts to prevent crime. * * *

* * *

II

Our first task is to establish at what point in this encounter the Fourth Amendment becomes relevant. That is, we must decide whether and when Officer McFadden "seized" Terry and whether and when he conducted a "search." There is some suggestion in the use of such terms as "stop" and "frisk" that such police conduct is outside the purview of the Fourth Amendment because neither action rises to the level of a "search" or "seizure" within the meaning of the Constitution. We emphatically reject this notion. It is quite plain that the Fourth Amendment governs "seizures" of the person which do not eventuate in a trip to the station house and prosecution for crime—"arrests" in traditional terminology. It must be recognized that whenever a police officer accosts an individual and restrains his freedom to walk away, he has "seized" that person. And it is nothing less than sheer torture of the English language to suggest that a careful exploration of the outer surfaces of a person's clothing all over his or her body in an attempt to find weapons is not a "search." Moreover, it is simply fantastic to urge that such a procedure performed in public by a policeman while the citizen stands helpless, perhaps facing a wall with his hands raised, is a "petty indignity." It is a serious intrusion upon the sanctity of the person,

which may inflict great indignity and arouse strong resentment, and it is not to be undertaken lightly.

The danger in the logic which proceeds upon distinctions between a "stop" and an "arrest," or "seizure" of the person, and between a "frisk" and a "search" is twofold. It seeks to isolate from constitutional scrutiny the initial stages of the contact between the policeman and the citizen. And by suggesting a rigid all-or-nothing model of justification and regulation under the Amendment, it obscures the utility of limitations upon the scope, as well as the initiation, of police action as a means of constitutional regulation. * * *

The distinctions of classical "stop-and-frisk" theory thus serve to divert attention from the central inquiry under the Fourth Amendment—the reasonableness in all the circumstances of the particular governmental invasion of a citizen's personal security. "Search" and "seizure" are not talismans. We therefore reject the notions that the Fourth Amendment does not come into play at all as a limitation upon police conduct if the officers stop short of something called a "technical arrest" or a "full-blown search."

In this case there can be no question, then, that Officer McFadden "seized" petitioner and subjected him to a "search" when he took hold of him and patted down the outer surfaces of his clothing. We must decide whether at that point it was reasonable for Officer McFadden to have interfered with petitioner's personal security as he did. And in determining whether the seizure and search were "unreasonable" our inquiry is a dual one—whether the officer's action was justified at its inception, and whether

frisk power, see Maclin, The Decline of the Right of Locomotion: The Fourth Amendment

on the Streets, 75 Cornell L.Rev.128 (1990).]

it was reasonably related in scope to the circumstances which justified the interference in the first place.

III

If this case involved police conduct subject to the Warrant Clause of the Fourth Amendment, we would have to ascertain whether "probable cause" existed to justify the search and seizure which took place. However, that is not the case. We do not retreat from our holdings that the police must, whenever practicable, obtain advance judicial approval of searches and seizures through the warrant procedure or that in most instances failure to comply with the warrant requirement can only be excused by exigent circumstances. But we deal here with an entire rubric of police conduct—necessarily swift action predicated upon the on-the-spot observations of the officer on the beat—which historically has not been, and as a practical matter could not be, subjected to the warrant procedure. Instead the conduct involved in this case must be tested by the Fourth Amendment's general proscription against unreasonable searches and seizures.

Nonetheless, the notions which underlie both the warrant procedure and the requirement of probable cause remain fully relevant in this context. In order to assess the reasonableness of Officer McFadden's conduct as a general proposition, it is necessary "first to focus upon the governmental interest which allegedly justifies official intrusion upon the constitutionally protected interests of the private citizen," for there is "no ready test for determining reasonableness other than by balancing the need to search [or seize] against the invasion which the search [or seizure] entails." Camara v. Municipal Court, 387 U.S. 523, 534–535, 536–537 (1967). And in justifying the particular intrusion the police officer must be able to point to specific and articulable facts which, taken together with rational inferences from those facts, reasonably warrant that intrusion. * * * And in making that assessment it is imperative that the facts be judged against an objective standard: would the facts available to the officer at the moment of the seizure or the search "warrant a man of reasonable caution in the belief" that the action taken was appropriate? Anything less would invite intrusions upon constitutionally guaranteed rights based on nothing more substantial than inarticulate hunches, a result this Court has consistently refused to sanction. And simple " 'good faith on the part of the arresting officer is not enough.' * * * If subjective good faith alone were the test, the protections of the Fourth Amendment would evaporate, and the people would be 'secure in their persons, houses, papers, and effects,' only in the discretion of the police."

Applying these principles to this case, we consider first the nature and extent of the governmental interests involved. One general interest is of course that of effective crime prevention and detection; it is this interest which underlies the recognition that a police officer may in appropriate circumstances and in an appropriate manner approach a person for purposes of investigating possibly criminal behavior even though there is no probable cause to make an arrest. It was this legitimate investigative function Officer McFadden was discharging when he decided to approach petitioner and his companions. He had observed Terry, Chilton, and Katz go through a series of acts, each of them perhaps innocent in itself, but which taken together warranted further investigation. There is nothing unusual in two men standing together on a street corner, perhaps waiting for someone. Nor is there anything suspicious about people in such circumstances strolling up and down the street, singly or in pairs. Store windows, moreover, are made to be looked in. But the story is quite different where, as here, two men hover about a street corner for an extended period of time, at the end of which it becomes apparent that they are not waiting for anyone or anything; where these men pace alternately along an identical route, pausing to stare in the same store window roughly 24 times; where each completion of this route is followed immediately by a conference between the two men on the corner; where they are joined in one of these conferences by a third man who leaves swiftly; and where the two men finally follow the third and rejoin him a couple of blocks away. It would have been poor police work indeed for an officer of 30 years' experience in the detection of thievery from stores in this same neighborhood to have failed to investigate this behavior further.

The crux of this case, however, is not the propriety of Officer McFadden's taking steps to investigate petitioner's suspicious behavior, but rather, whether there was justification for McFadden's invasion of Terry's personal security by searching him for weapons in the course of that investigation. We are now concerned with more than the governmental interest in investigating crime; in addition, there is the more immediate interest of the police officer in taking steps to assure himself that the person with whom he is dealing is not armed with a weapon that could unexpectedly and fatally be used against him. Certainly it would be unreasonable to require that police officers take unnecessary risks in the performance of their duties. American criminals have a long tradition of armed violence, and every year in this country many law enforcement officers are killed in the line of duty, and thousands more are wounded. Virtually all of these deaths and a substantial portion of the injuries are inflicted with guns and knives.

In view of these facts, we cannot blind ourselves to the need for law enforcement officers to protect themselves and other prospective victims of violence in situations where they may lack probable cause for an arrest. When an officer is justified in believing that the individual whose suspicious behavior he is investigating at close range is armed and presently dangerous to the officer or to others, it would appear to be clearly unreasonable to deny the officer the power to take necessary measures to determine whether the person is in fact carrying a weapon and to neutralize the threat of physical harm.

* * *

Our evaluation of the proper balance that has to be struck in this type of case leads us to conclude that there must be a narrowly drawn authority to permit a reasonable search for weapons for the protection of the police officer, where he has reason to believe that he is dealing with an armed and dangerous individual, regardless of whether he has probable cause to arrest the individual for a crime. The officer need not be absolutely certain that the individual is armed; the issue is whether a reasonably prudent man in the circumstances would be warranted in the belief that his safety or that of others was in danger. And in determining whether the officer acted reasonably in such circumstances, due weight must be given, not to his inchoate and unparticularized suspicion or "hunch," but to the specific reasonable inferences which he is entitled to draw from the facts in light of his experience.

IV

* * *

We need not develop at length in this case * * * the limitations which the Fourth Amendment places upon a protective seizure and search for weapons. These limitations will have to be developed in the concrete factual circumstances of individual cases. Suffice it to note that such a search, unlike a search without a warrant incident to arrest, is not justified by any need to prevent the disappearance or destruction of evidence of crime. The sole justification of the search in the present situation is the protection of the police officer and others nearby, and it must therefore be confined in scope to an intrusion reasonably designed to discover guns, knives, clubs, or other hidden instruments for the assault of the police officer.

The scope of the search in this case presents no serious problem in light of these standards. * * *

V

We conclude that the revolver seized from Terry was properly admitted in evidence against him. At the time he seized petitioner and searched him for weapons, Officer McFadden had reasonable grounds to believe that petitioner was armed and dangerous, and it was necessary for the protection of himself and others to take swift measures to discover the true facts and neutralize the threat of harm if it materialized. The policeman carefully restricted his search to what was appropriate to the discovery of the particular items which he sought. Each case of this sort will, of course, have to be decided on its own facts. We merely hold today that where a police officer observes unusual conduct which leads him reasonably to conclude in light of his experience that criminal activity may be afoot and that the persons with whom he is dealing may be armed and presently dangerous, where in the course of investigating this behavior he identifies himself as a policeman and makes reasonable inquiries, and where nothing in the initial stages of the encounter serves to dispel his reasonable fear for his own or others' safety, he is entitled for the protection of himself and others in the area to conduct a carefully limited search of the outer clothing of such persons in an attempt to discover weapons which might be used to assault him. Such a search is a reasonable search under the Fourth Amendment, and any weapons seized may properly be introduced in evidence against the person from whom they were taken.

MR. JUSTICE BLACK concurs in the judgment and the opinion except where the opinion quotes from and relies upon this Court's opinion in Katz v. United States and the concurring opinion in Warden v. Hayden.

MR. JUSTICE HARLAN, concurring.

While I unreservedly agree with the Court's ultimate holding in this case, I am constrained to fill in a few gaps, as I see them, in its opinion. I do this because what is said by this Court today will serve as initial guidelines for law enforcement authorities and courts throughout the land as this important new field of law develops.

A police officer's right to make an on-the-street "stop" and an accompanying "frisk" for weapons is of course bounded by the protections afforded by the Fourth and Fourteenth Amendments. The Court holds, and I agree, that while the right does not depend upon possession by the officer of a valid warrant, nor upon the existence of probable cause, such activities must be reasonable under the circumstances as the officer credibly relates them in court. * * *

* * * The holding has, however, two logical corollaries that I do not think the Court has fully expressed.

In the first place, if the frisk is justified in order to protect the officer during an encounter with a citizen, the officer must first have constitutional grounds to insist on an encounter, to make a *forcible* stop. Any person, including a policeman, is at liberty to avoid a person he considers dangerous. If and when a policeman has a right instead to disarm such a person for his own protection, he must first have a right not to avoid him but to be in his presence. That right must be more than the liberty (again, possessed by every citizen) to address questions to other persons, for ordinarily the person addressed has an equal right to ignore his interrogator and walk away; he certainly need not submit to a frisk for the questioner's protection. I would make it perfectly clear that the right to frisk in this case depends upon the reasonableness of a forcible stop to investigate a suspected crime.

Where such a stop is reasonable, however, the right to frisk must be immediate and automatic if the reason for the stop is, as here, an articulable suspicion of a crime of violence. Just as a full search incident to a lawful arrest requires no additional justification, a limited frisk incident to a lawful stop must often be rapid and routine. There is no reason why an officer, rightfully but forcibly confronting a person suspected of a serious crime, should have to ask one question and take the risk that the answer might be a bullet.

* * *

Mr. Justice White, concurring.

* * * I think an additional word is in order concerning the matter of interrogation during an investigative stop. There is nothing in the Constitution which prevents a policeman from addressing questions to anyone on the street. Absent special circumstances, the person approached may not be detained or frisked but may refuse to cooperate and go on his way. However, given the proper circumstances, such as those in this case, it seems to me the person may be briefly detained against his will while pertinent questions are directed to him. Of course, the person stopped is not obliged to answer, answers may not be compelled, and refusal to answer furnishes no basis for an arrest, although it may alert the officer to the need for continued observation. * * *

Mr. Justice Douglas, dissenting.

I agree that petitioner was "seized" within the meaning of the Fourth Amendment. I also agree that frisking petitioner and his companions for guns was a "search." But it is a mystery how that "search" and that "seizure" can be constitutional by Fourth Amendment standards, unless there was "probable cause" to believe that (1) a crime had been committed or (2) a crime was in the process of being committed or (3) a crime was about to be committed.

* * *

The infringement on personal liberty of any "seizure" of a person can only be "reasonable" under the Fourth Amendment if we require the police to possess "probable cause" before they seize him. Only that line draws a meaningful distinction between an officer's mere inkling and the presence of facts within the officer's personal knowledge which would convince a reasonable man that the person seized has committed, is committing, or is about to commit a particular crime. * * *

To give the police greater power than a magistrate is to take a long step down the totalitarian path. Perhaps such a step is desirable to cope with modern forms of lawlessness. But if it is taken, it should be the deliberate choice of the people through a constitutional amendment. * * *.

Note on the Impact of Terry

It would be hard to overestimate the effect of *Terry* on Fourth Amendment jurisprudence. The Court not only permitted stops and frisks on less than probable cause; it also explicitly invoked the reasonableness clause over the warrant clause as the governing standard. Perhaps the Court intended to limit use of the reasonableness clause and its balancing approach to the area of stop and frisk; but once that balancing process was undertaken in one area, it became difficult to prevent its application to other searches and seizures. See Sundby, A Return to Fourth Amendment Basics: Undoing the Mischief of *Camara* and *Terry,* 72 Minn.L.Rev. 383 (1988) (noting that *Terry* has led, in time, to a general diminution of Fourth Amendment protection).

Critique of Terry

Professor Maclin provides a critique on *Terry*, and assesses the impact of that decision on minorities, in Terry v. Ohio's Fourth Amendment Legacy: Black Men and Police Discretion, 72 St.John's L.Rev. 1271, 1278 (1998):

> Without saying so, *Terry* fundamentally changed Fourth Amendment law. Garden-variety search and seizure cases, the types that patrol officers are most likely to undertake, would no longer be judged by whether government officials had obtained judicial warrants or possessed probable cause before invading the privacy and personal security of individuals. After *Terry*, police intrusions would be controlled by a malleable "reasonableness" standard that gave enormous discretion to the police. When this reasonableness norm was applied to street encounters between the police and urban residents, the result was predictable—expanded police powers and diminished individual freedom. One of the flaws of *Terry* was that this shift in constitutional doctrine was implemented without a full examination of the consequences for blacks and other disfavored persons most affected by police investigatory methods. Moreover, the result in *Terry* provided a springboard for modern police methods that target black men and others for arbitrary and discretionary intrusions. Unsurprisingly, the Burger and Rehnquist Courts have sanctioned several forms of investigatory police conduct by invoking the reasonableness rationale announced in *Terry*. For this reason alone, the result in *Terry* deserves censure.

> * * *

> For some, the *Terry* Court made the right choice. The need for police safety justified the loss of Fourth Amendment freedom. But those that have been the most vocal defenders of *Terry* tend to come from socioeconomic and racial backgrounds that are predominantly free from police harassment. For many blacks and other disfavored groups, however, the *Terry* Court wrongly subordinated their Fourth Amendment rights to police safety. The Court's failure to treat as dispositive the clear correlation between stop and frisk and the violation of their Fourth Amendment rights only served to remind blacks and other minorities of their second-class status in America.

Professor Richman, in The Process of *Terry* Lawmaking, 72 St. John's L.Rev. 1043 (1998), takes issue with Professor Maclin's critique on *Terry*, arguing that the *Terry* Court was pragmatic in validating, but imposing limits on, a necessary and inevitable police practice:

> Without *Terry*, courts would have to choose between ignoring the constitutional implications of street stops, or applying a probable-cause standard to them, and possibly watering down that standard in the process. Some may find *Terry* and its progeny too deferential toward the judgment calls of police officers in such encounters, but without *Terry*, such judgments might have gone completely unregulated. Moreover, by looking only to "reasonableness," these cases ensure that probable cause remains a meaningful standard, reserved for full-fledged searches and seizures. At the heart of the Supreme Court's *Terry* decision is thus an appreciation of a police officer's job and knowledge, and a desire to give him some degree of protection when he's doing that job. The idea * * * is to have judges approach cases from the perspective of law enforcement officers. Just as we recognize a special province for jurors, in which they draw on their "common sense conclusions about human behavior," so should we give some deference to the competence of police officers. Let cops do what they do best, with courts ensuring only that they don't act arbitrarily, or worse.

What do you think would have happened to police practices, and court rulings, if the Court in *Terry* had required probable cause for all temporary detentions?

An Early Application of Terry—Adams v. Williams

The *Terry* decision with its companion cases—Sibron v. New York, and Peters v. New York, 392 U.S. 40 (1968)—was only the first step in the articulation of what the Fourth Amendment permits the police to do without probable cause. The Supreme Court's first post-*Terry* effort was Adams v. Williams, 407 U.S. 143 (1972). Williams was convicted of illegal possession of a handgun and possession of heroin, after unsuccessfully challenging a stop and frisk. Justice Rehnquist, writing for the Court, set forth the facts surrounding the stop and frisk as follows:

> Police Sgt. John Connolly was alone early in the morning on car patrol duty in a high-crime area of Bridgeport, Connecticut. At approximately 2:15 a.m. a person known to Sgt. Connolly approached his cruiser and informed him that an individual seated in a nearby vehicle was carrying narcotics and had a gun at his waist.

> After calling for assistance on his car radio, Sgt. Connolly approached the vehicle to investigate the informant's report. Connolly tapped on the car window and asked the occupant, Robert Williams, to open the door. When Williams rolled down the window instead, the sergeant reached into the car and removed a fully loaded revolver from Williams' waistband. The gun had not been visible to Connolly from outside the car, but it was in precisely the place indicated by the informant. Williams was then arrested by Connolly for unlawful possession of the pistol. A search incident to that arrest was conducted after other officers arrived. They found substantial quantities of heroin on Williams' person and in the car, and they found a machete and a second revolver hidden in the automobile.

Williams argued that the informant's tip was not a reliable basis on which to conduct the initial stop. But Justice Rehnquist disagreed:

[W]e believe that Sgt. Connolly acted justifiably in responding to his informant's tip. The informant was known to him personally and had provided him with information in the past. This is a stronger case than obtains in the case of an anonymous telephone tip. The informant here came forward personally to give information that was immediately verifiable at the scene. Indeed, under Connecticut law, the informant might have been subject to immediate arrest for making a false complaint had Sgt. Connolly's investigation proved the tip incorrect. Thus, while the Court's decisions indicate that this informant's unverified tip may have been insufficient for a narcotics arrest or search warrant, the information carried enough indicia of reliability to justify the officer's forcible stop of Williams.

In reaching this conclusion, we reject respondent's argument that reasonable cause for a stop and frisk can only be based on the officer's personal observation rather than on information supplied by another person. Informants' tips, like all other clues and evidence coming to a policeman on the scene, may vary greatly in their value and reliability.

Justice Rehnquist also held that the frisk was permissible in light of the circumstances under which Williams was detained:

While properly investigating the activity of a person who was reported to be carrying narcotics and a concealed weapon and who was sitting alone in a car in a high-crime area at 2:15 in the morning, Sgt. Connolly had ample reason to fear of his safety. When Williams rolled down his window, rather than complying with the policeman's request to step out of the car so that his movements could more easily be seen, the revolver allegedly at Williams' waist became an even greater threat. Under these circumstances the policeman's action in reaching to the spot where the gun was thought to be hidden constituted a limited intrusion designed to insure his safety, and we conclude that it was reasonable.

Finally, Justice Rehnquist concluded that the search of the passenger compartment of the car, which led to discovery of the heroin, was permissible in light of everything that had gone before:

Once Sgt. Connolly had found the gun precisely where the informant had predicted, probable cause existed to arrest Williams for unlawful possession of the weapon. * * * In the present case the policeman found Williams in possession of a gun in precisely the place predicted by the informant. This tended to corroborate the reliability of the informant's further report of narcotics and, together with the surrounding circumstances, certainly suggested no lawful explanation for possession of the gun. * * * Under the circumstances surrounding Williams' possession of the gun seized by Sgt. Connolly, the arrest on the weapons charge was supported by probable cause, and the search of his person and of the car incident to that arrest was lawful. The fruits of the search were therefore properly admitted at Williams' trial * * *.

Justice Douglas, joined by Justice Marshall, dissented in *Williams*. He argued that Williams was illegally arrested, because there was no indication at the time of arrest that Williams possessed the gun illegally.

Justice Brennan wrote a separate dissent in *Williams*, arguing that *Terry* should not be applicable to crimes like narcotics possession, because "[t]here is too much danger that, instead of the stop being the object and the protective frisk an incident thereto, the reverse will be true."

Justice Marshall, joined by Justice Douglas, also wrote a separate dissent in *Williams*. He observed that the informant, on whom the officer relied to stop Williams, had no track record of giving reliable information. He concluded as follows:

> If the Court does not ignore the care with which we examined the knowledge possessed by the officer in *Terry* when he acted, then I cannot see how the actions of the officer in this case can be upheld. The Court explains what the officer knew about respondent before accosting him. But what is more significant is what he did not know. With respect to the scene generally, the officer had no idea how long respondent had been in the car, how long the car had been parked, or to whom the car belonged. With respect to the gun, the officer did not know if or when the informant had ever seen the gun, or whether the gun was carried legally, as Connecticut law permitted, or illegally. And with respect to the narcotics, the officer did not know what kind of narcotics respondent allegedly had, whether they were legally or illegally possessed, what the basis of the informant's knowledge was, or even whether the informant was capable of distinguishing narcotics from other substances.

> Unable to answer any of these questions, the officer nevertheless determined that it was necessary to intrude on respondent's liberty. I believe that his determination was totally unreasonable. As I read *Terry*, an officer may act on the basis of *reliable* information short of probable cause to make a stop, and ultimately a frisk, if necessary; but the officer may not use unreliable, unsubstantiated, conclusory hearsay to justify an invasion of liberty. *Terry* never meant to approve the kind of knee-jerk police reaction that we have before us in this case.

Questions about Adams v. Williams

What guidance do the police have from the Supreme Court after Adams v. Williams? Do they know what kinds of information can be used to satisfy *Terry*? Does the Court identify the points when a stop under *Terry* occurs and when a touching of a person amounts to a frisk? Do you see anything in the language or tone of *Terry* which indicates that the Court never meant to approve the kind of police conduct at issue in *Williams*? Or is Justice Marshall simply regretful that he didn't join Justice Douglas in dissent in *Terry*?

Bright Line Rules Under Terry—Pennsylvania v. Mimms

Another case in the Court's early development of the *Terry* doctrine was the per curiam decision in Pennsylvania v. Mimms, 434 U.S. 106 (1977). While on routine patrol, two Philadelphia police officers observed Mimms driving a car with an expired license plate. The officers stopped the car to issue a traffic summons. One of the officers approached the car and told Mimms to step out of the car and produce his owner's card and operator's license. When Mimms got out of the car, the officer noticed a large bulge under his sports jacket. Thinking that Mimms might be carrying a weapon, the officer frisked Mimms and found that the bulge was a loaded revolver. Mimms unsuccessfully moved to suppress the gun, and was convicted for firearms violations.

The Court held that the officer had acted properly under the *Terry* doctrine, and therefore that the revolver was properly admitted at Mimms' trial. The Court noted that the parties agreed (1) that the officer was justified in stopping Mimms for the traffic violation, and (2) that the officer had sufficient cause to frisk Mimms for a weapon once he observed the bulge. The question in dispute was whether the officer was justified in ordering Mimms to get out of the car. If this seizure was unlawful under *Terry*, then the subsequent frisk would be unlawful as well. But the Court held that officers in the course of a legal stop of an automobile have an *automatic* right under *Terry* to order the driver out of the vehicle. The Court came to its bright line rule in the following analysis:

> [W]e look first to that side of the balance which bears the officer's interest in taking the action that he did. The State freely concedes the officer had no reason to suspect foul play from the particular driver at the time of the stop, there having been nothing unusual or suspicious about his behavior. It was apparently his practice to order all drivers out of their vehicles as a matter of course whenever they had been stopped for a traffic violation. The State argues that this practice was adopted as a precautionary measure to afford a degree of protection to the officer and that it may be justified on that ground. Establishing a face-to-face confrontation diminishes the possibility, otherwise substantial, that the driver can make unobserved movements; this, in turn, reduces the likelihood that the officer will be the victim of an assault.
>
> We think it too plain for argument that the State's proffered justification—the safety of the officer—is both legitimate and weighty. * * * According to one study, approximately 30% of police shootings occurred when a police officer approached a suspect seated in an automobile. Bristow, Police Officer Shootings—A Tactical Evaluation, 54 J.Crim.L.C. & P.S. 93 (1963). We are aware that not all these assaults occur when issuing traffic summons, but we have before expressly declined to accept the argument that traffic violations necessarily involve less danger to officers than other types of confrontations. * * *
>
> The hazard of accidental injury from passing traffic to an officer standing on the driver's side of the vehicle may also be appreciable in some situations. Rather than conversing while standing exposed to moving traffic, the officer prudently may prefer to ask the driver of the vehicle to step out of the car and off onto the shoulder of the road where the inquiry may be pursued with greater safety to both.
>
> Against this important interest we are asked to weigh the intrusion into the driver's personal liberty occasioned not by the initial stop of the vehicle, which was admittedly justified, but by the order to get out of the car. We think this additional intrusion can only be described as *de minimis*. The driver is being asked to expose to view very little more of his person than is already exposed. * * * What is at most a mere inconvenience cannot prevail when balanced against legitimate concerns for the officer's safety.

Justice Marshall dissented in *Mimms*. He argued that *Terry* requires a nexus between the reason for the stop and the need for self-protection that justifies a further intrusion. He found no nexus between the traffic violation and a subsequent order to get out of the car.

Justice Stevens, joined by Justices Brennan and Marshall, wrote a separate dissent in *Mimms*. He argued that the rule chosen by the Court could not be supported by safety concerns:

> [Ordering the suspect out of the car] could actually aggravate the officer's danger because the fear of a search might cause a serious offender to take desperate action that would be unnecessary if he remained in the vehicle while being ticketed. Whatever the reason, it is significant that some experts in this area of human behavior strongly recommend that the police officer "never allow the violator to get out of the car * * *."[18] Obviously it is not my purpose to express an opinion on the safest procedure to be followed in making traffic arrests or to imply that the arresting officer faces no significant hazard, even in the apparently routine situation. I do submit, however, that no matter how hard we try we cannot totally eliminate the danger associated with law enforcement, and that, before adopting a nation-wide rule, we should give further consideration to the infinite variety of situations in which today's holding may be applied.

Justice Stevens strenuously objected to the Court's adoption of a bright line rule to cover all vehicle stops, regardless of the circumstances:

> Until today the law applicable to seizures of a person has required individualized inquiry into the reason for each intrusion, or some comparable guarantee against arbitrary harassment. * * * [T]o eliminate any requirement that an officer be able to explain the reasons for his actions signals an abandonment of effective judicial supervision of this kind of seizure and leaves police discretion utterly without limits. Some citizens will be subjected to this minor indignity while others—perhaps those with more expensive cars, or different bumper stickers, or different-colored skin—may escape it entirely.

Questions About Mimms

Two arguments are accepted by the majority in *Mimms*—one is that officers, to avoid assaults, should be able to order out of their cars those drivers stopped for violations; and the other is that such an order is a valid attempt to avoid traffic injuries. Are you persuaded by these arguments? Does the merit of these arguments depend on the facts of a particular case? Or are these safety concerns likely to arise so often that the Court is justified in adopting a bright line rule? The dissenters consider the safety concerns overstated; but they do not argue that the Court's assessment of the individual right at stake is understated. Given the minimal nature of the intrusion at issue in *Mimms*, why are the dissenters so upset?

---

18. "2. *Never allow the violator to get out of the car* and stand to its left. If he does get out, which should be avoided, walk him to the rear and right side of the car. Quite obviously this is a much safer area to conduct a conversation." V. Folley, Police Patrol Techniques and Tactics 95 (1973)(emphasis in original).

Another authority is even more explicit:

"The officer should stand slightly to the rear of the front door and doorpost. This will prevent the violator from suddenly opening the door and striking the officer. In order to thoroughly protect himself as much as possible, the officer should reach with his weak hand and push the lock button down if the window is open. This will give an indication to the driver that he is to remain inside the vehicle." A. Yount, Vehicle Stops Manual, Misdemeanor and Felony 2–3 (1976).

What if the driver of the car wants to get out, and the officer (perhaps thinking it the safest procedure) wants the driver to stay in the car? Is this an additional seizure for Fourth Amendment purposes? Is the dissent's position that the driver can do whatever she wants? What if the officer permits the driver to remain in the car, but says "keep your hands where I can see them"? Is this an invalid seizure if unaccompanied by articulable suspicion?

Do real possibilities of harassment and racially discriminatory law enforcement exist under the majority's bright line rule? Identify them. Does the case-by-case approach of *Terry* provide protection against harassment and discrimination in contexts like *Mimms?*

Mimms and Passengers

In Maryland v. Wilson, 519 U.S. 408 (1997), the Court considered whether the automatic rule established in *Mimms* applied to passengers as well as drivers. An officer stopped a car traveling on Interstate 95. The car was going 64 miles per hour in a 55 mile per hour zone. The officer ordered the driver and Wilson, a passenger, to get out of the car. The officer did not have reasonable suspicion to believe that Wilson was up to anything special. When Wilson stepped out of the car, a quantity of cocaine allegedly fell to the ground. The state court had held that the *Mimms* rule did not apply to passengers, and therefore that Wilson could not be ordered out of the car in the absence of reasonable suspicion to believe he was involved in a crime. But the Supreme Court, in an opinion by Chief Justice Rehnquist for seven members of the Court, disagreed and held that the bright-line rule of *Mimms* applied to passengers. The Chief Justice balanced the factors discussed in *Mimms*:

> On the public interest side of the balance, the same weighty interest in officer safety is present regardless of whether the occupant of the stopped car is a driver or passenger. Regrettably, traffic stops may be dangerous encounters. In 1994 alone, there were 5,762 officer assaults and 11 officers killed during traffic pursuits and stops. In the case of passengers, the danger of the officer's standing in the path of oncoming traffic would not be present except in the case of a passenger in the left rear seat, but the fact that there is more than one occupant of the vehicle increases the possible sources of harm to the officer.

> On the personal liberty side of the balance, the case for the passengers is in one sense stronger than that for the driver. There is probable cause to believe that the driver has committed a minor vehicular offense, but there is no such reason to stop or detain the passengers. But as a practical matter, the passengers are already stopped by virtue of the stop of the vehicle. The only change in their circumstances which will result from ordering them out of the car is that they will be outside of, rather than inside of, the stopped car. Outside the car, the passengers will be denied access to any possible weapon that might be concealed in the interior of the passenger compartment. It would seem that the possibility of a violent encounter stems not from the ordinary reaction of a motorist stopped for a speeding violation, but from the fact that evidence of a more serious crime might be uncovered during the stop. And the motivation of a passenger to employ violence to

prevent apprehension of such a crime is every bit as great as that of the driver.

* * *

In summary, danger to an officer from a traffic stop is likely to be greater when there are passengers in addition to the driver in the stopped car. While there is not the same basis for ordering the passengers out of the car as there is for ordering the driver out, the additional intrusion on the passenger is minimal. We therefore hold that an officer making a traffic stop may order passengers to get out of the car pending completion of the stop.

Justice Stevens, joined by Justice Kennedy, dissented in *Wilson.* He argued that police officers are rarely at risk from passengers during routine automobile stops, and that any "limited additional risk to police officers must be weighed against the unnecessary invasion that will be imposed on innocent citizens under the majority's rule in the tremendous number of routine stops that occur each day." He asserted that "the aggregation of thousands upon thousands of petty indignities has an impact on freedom that I would characterize as substantial, and which in my view clearly outweighs the evanescent safety concerns pressed by the majority." Justice Stevens concluded as follows:

> In my view, wholly innocent passengers in a taxi, bus, or private car have a constitutionally protected right to decide whether to remain comfortably seated within the vehicle rather than exposing themselves to the elements and the observation of curious bystanders. The Constitution should not be read to permit law enforcement officers to order innocent passengers about simply because they have the misfortune to be seated in a car whose driver has committed a minor traffic offense.

Justice Kennedy wrote a separate dissent in which he stated that officers should be able to order a passenger out of a car only if necessary under the circumstances to investigate a crime or to protect the officer.

Scope of the Mimms Bright Line Approach

Can the *Mimms* bright-line analysis be applied to justify other automatic rights of police in the context of a vehicle stop? What if an officer stops the car and cannot see into the interior? Should there be an automatic right to open the door to check for any danger to the officer? The court in United States v. Stanfield, 109 F.3d 976 (4th Cir.1997), noted that the "advent of tinted automobile windows has threatened to bring to naught" the protections accorded police officers in *Terry.* Relying on *Mimms,* the court balanced the police interest against the interest of the citizen, and declared as follows:

> [W]e believe that the Court's decisions in *Mimms* and *Wilson* in particular would support a holding that whenever, during a lawful traffic stop, officers are required to approach a vehicle with windows so heavily tinted that they are unable to view the interior of the stopped vehicle, they may, when it appears in their experienced judgment prudent to do so, open at least one of the vehicle's doors and, without crossing the plane of the vehicle, visually inspect its interior in order to ascertain whether the driver is armed, whether he has access to weapons, or whether there are other occupants of the vehicle who might pose a danger to the officers.

How far can this analysis go? Should an officer have the automatic right to pop the trunk after stopping a car, just in case somebody might be hiding in there? How about the automatic right to search the glove compartment for weapons? If your answer is that such searches should depend on actual facts supporting the belief that the police officer is in danger, then how do you justify or distinguish *Mimms* and *Wilson*?

Mimms Applied: New York v. Class

The Court authorized a limited investigative entry into a car during the course of a stop in New York v. Class, 475 U.S. 106 (1986). Class was stopped for a traffic violation. Officers peered through the windshield of Class's car to obtain the vehicle identification, but the number was covered by papers on the dashboard. One officer entered the car to move the papers away, and at that point discovered a gun, which was admitted against Class at his trial for firearms violations. The Court, in a 6–3 opinion by Justice O'Connor, relied on *Mimms* and held that the officer acted reasonably. The Court held that "in order to observe a Vehicle Identification Number (VIN) generally visible from outside an automobile, a police officer may reach into the passenger compartment of a vehicle to move papers obscuring the VIN after its driver has been stopped for a traffic violation and has exited the car." Justice O'Connor reasoned that "[t]he VIN is a significant thread in the web of regulation of the automobile" and that "[a] motorist must surely expect that such regulation will on occasion require the State to determine the VIN of his or her vehicle, and the individual's reasonable expectation of privacy in the VIN is thereby diminished," especially for a driver who has committed a traffic violation.

Class argued that he should have been permitted to re-enter the car to move his papers away. But Justice O'Connor relied upon *Mimms* to reason that officers may detain an individual outside a car to protect themselves from danger; therefore, the officers were not required to ask Class to re-enter the car to remove his papers. Justice O'Connor noted that the Court's holding "does not authorize a police officer to enter a vehicle to obtain a dashboard-mounted VIN when the VIN is visible from outside the automobile," since "[i]f the VIN is in the plain view of someone outside the vehicle, there is no justification for governmental intrusion into the passenger compartment to see it."

Justice Powell, joined by Chief Justice Burger, concurred in *Class*, emphasizing the important governmental interest in the VIN, and concluding that "the Fourth Amendment question may be stated simply as whether the officer's efforts to inspect the VIN were reasonable." Justice Brennan, joined by Justices Marshall and Stevens, dissented. He argued that "the mere fact that the state utilizes the VIN in conjunction with regulations designed to promote highway safety does not give the police a reason to *search* for such information every time a motorist violates a traffic law." Justice White, joined by Justice Stevens, also dissented, stating that he was unprepared to accept the Court's reasoning that "the governmental interest in obtaining the VIN by entering a protected area is sufficient to outweigh the owner's privacy interest in the interior of the car."

Class is assailed in Maclin, New York v. Class: A Little–Noticed Case with Disturbing Implications, 78 J. Crim.L. & Crim. 1 (1987). Professor Maclin asks whether the police could search a glove compartment for a registration certificate? Whether they could enter a vehicle to search for a driver's license inadvertently left behind in a purse, suitcase, or other container? Whether they could enter a car to inspect the VIN after stopping a motorist at a roadblock to check for license and registrations? Are these situations distinguishable from the facts of *Class*?

Detention of Occupants of a Residence: Note on Michigan v. Summers

In Michigan v. Summers, 452 U.S. 692 (1981), the Court held, 6–3, that police officers with a search warrant for a home can require occupants of the premises, even if leaving when the police arrive, to remain while the search warrant is executed. The Court held that such a seizure would always be reasonable, given the state's interest in preventing flight, and the risk that persons leaving the premises would attempt to destroy evidence. The Court noted that the detention in *Summers* was less serious than the street stops sanctioned in *Terry*, because the occupant was being detained inside his home. The Court also observed that the search warrant provided protection against overreaching by the police officers. Does *Mimms* lend support to the result in *Summers*? See also United States v. Fountain, 2 F.3d 656 (6th Cir.1993)(under *Summers*, police may detain non-residents of the premises while conducting a warranted search).

2. When Does a Seizure Occur? The Line Between "Stop" and "Encounter"

In *Terry,* it was not difficult to determine the precise point at which the stop occurred: the officer physically grabbed Terry and spun him around. However, the Court has had more difficulty determining whether a stop has occurred when the police conduct is not as affirmatively coercive or as physically intrusive as in *Terry.*

The Mendenhall "Free to Leave" Test

In United States v. Mendenhall, 446 U.S. 544 (1980), Mendenhall was observed by Drug Enforcement Administration agents at the Detroit Airport as she arrived on a flight from Los Angeles. They suspected her of being a drug courier. The agents approached her as she was walking through the concourse, identified themselves as DEA agents, and one agent asked to see her identification and airline ticket. The driver's license she produced was in her name, but her ticket was not. She became extremely nervous. The agent gave her back her license and ticket and asked Mendenhall to accompany him to the airport DEA office for further questions. Without saying anything, she did so. In the office the agent asked Mendenhall if she would allow a search of her person and handbag. She said yes. In a strip search of her person drugs were found. Mendenhall was arrested, prosecuted, and convicted.

Justice Stewart, joined only by Justice Rehnquist, addressed an argument that the government had not made in the lower courts and concluded that when Mendenhall was approached in the airport, no "seizure" had occurred, and therefore this initial police-citizen contact was outside the scope of the Fourth Amendment. Just Stewart explained:

The events took place in the public concourse. The agents wore no uniforms and displayed no weapons. They did not summon the respondent to their presence, but instead approached her and identified themselves as federal agents. They requested, but did not demand to see the respondent's identification and ticket. Such conduct, without more, did not amount to an intrusion upon any constitutionally protected interest. * * *

This conclusion resulted from application of the following rule:

A person has been "seized" within the meaning of the Fourth Amendment only if, in view of all the circumstances surrounding the incident, a reasonable person would have believed that he was not free to leave. Examples of circumstances that might indicate a seizure, even where the person did not attempt to leave, would be the threatening presence of several officers, the display of a weapon by an officer, some physical touching of the person of the citizen, or the use of language or tone of voice indicating that compliance with the officer's request might be compelled.

Justice Stewart's "free to leave" test did not command a majority of the Court in *Mendenhall;* seven Justices found that the question of whether a seizure had occurred was not properly raised in the lower court. But subsequent cases have established the "free to leave" test as the initial benchmark for determining whether a person has been stopped within the meaning of *Terry*.[19]

Applying the "Free to Leave" Test: Florida v. Royer

A plurality of the Court applied the Stewart "free to leave" test in Florida v. Royer, 460 U.S. 491 (1983). Justice White, writing for himself and Justices Marshall, Powell, and Stevens, stated the facts:

On January 3, 1978, Royer was observed at Miami International Airport by two plain-clothes detectives of the Dade County, Florida, Public Safety Department assigned to the County's Organized Crime Bureau, Narcotics Investigation Section. Detectives Johnson and Magdalena believed that Royer's appearance, mannerisms, luggage, and actions fit the so-called "drug courier profile." Royer, apparently unaware of the attention he had attracted, purchased a one-way ticket to New York City and checked his two suitcases, placing on each suitcase an identification tag bearing the name "Holt" and the destination, "LaGuardia". As Royer made his way to the concourse which led to the airline boarding area, the two detectives approached him, identified themselves as policemen working out of the sheriff's office, and asked if Royer had a "moment" to speak with them; Royer said "Yes."

Upon request, but without oral consent, Royer produced for the detectives his airline ticket and his driver's license. The airline ticket, like the baggage identification tags, bore the name "Holt," while the driver's license carried respondent's correct name, "Royer." When the detectives asked about the discrepancy, Royer explained that a friend had made the reservation in the name of "Holt." Royer became noticeably more nervous during

---

19. As will be seen later in this section, the Stewart test has been modified by more recent cases, such as *Bostick* and *Hodari*, to accommodate some specific fact situations arising in police-citizen encounters. But it still remains the basic test for determining whether a person has been stopped under *Terry*.

this conversation, whereupon the detectives informed Royer that they were in fact narcotics investigators and that they had reason to suspect him of transporting narcotics.

The detectives did not return his airline ticket and identification but asked Royer to accompany them to a room, approximately forty feet away, adjacent to the concourse. Royer said nothing in response but went with the officers as he had been asked to do. The room was later described by Detective Johnson as a "large storage closet," located in the stewardesses' lounge and containing a small desk and two chairs. Without Royer's consent or agreement, Detective Johnson, using Royer's baggage check stubs, retrieved the "Holt" luggage from the airline and brought it to the room where respondent and Detective Magdalena were waiting. Royer was asked if he would consent to a search of the suitcases. Without orally responding to this request, Royer produced a key and unlocked one of the suitcases, which the detective then opened without seeking further assent from Royer. Drugs were found in that suitcase. According to Detective Johnson, Royer stated that he did not know the combination to the lock on the second suitcase. When asked if he objected to the detective opening the second suitcase, Royer said "no, go ahead," and did not object when the detective explained that the suitcase might have to be broken open. The suitcase was pried open by the officers and more marihuana was found. Royer was then told that he was under arrest. Approximately fifteen minutes had elapsed from the time the detectives initially approached respondent until his arrest upon the discovery of the contraband.

Justice White observed that Royer had testified that he believed he was not free to leave the officers' presence and that Detective Johnson stated that he did not believe he had probable cause to arrest until after he opened the suitcases. Justice White summarized some of the law regarding "stops."

Some preliminary observations are in order. First, it is unquestioned that without a warrant to search Royer's luggage and in the absence of probable cause and exigent circumstances, the validity of the search depended on Royer's purported consent. Neither is it disputed that where the validity of a search rests on consent, the State has the burden of proving that the necessary consent was obtained and that it was freely and voluntarily given, a burden that is not satisfied by showing a mere submission to a claim of lawful authority.

Second, law enforcement officers do not violate the Fourth Amendment by merely approaching an individual on the street or in another public place, by asking him if he is willing to answer some questions, by putting questions to him if the person is willing to listen, or by offering in evidence in a criminal prosecution his voluntary answers to such questions. Nor would the fact that the officer identifies himself as a police officer, without more, convert the encounter into a seizure requiring some level of objective justification. The person approached, however, need not answer any question put to him; indeed, he may decline to listen to the questions at all and may go on his way. He may not be detained even momentarily without reasonable, objective grounds for doing so; and his refusal to listen or answer does not, without more, furnish those grounds. If there is no detention—no seizure within the meaning of the Fourth Amendment—then no constitutional rights have been infringed.

The plurality rejected the State's argument that the police activity could be justified as a consensual encounter.

> Asking for and examining Royer's ticket and his driver's license were no doubt permissible in themselves, but when the officers identified themselves as narcotics agents, told Royer that he was suspected of transporting narcotics, and asked him to accompany them to the police room, while retaining his ticket and driver's license and without indicating in any way that he was free to depart, Royer was effectively seized for the purposes of the Fourth Amendment. These circumstances surely amount to a show of official authority such that "a reasonable person would have believed he was not free to leave." * * *

> * * * Here, Royer's ticket and identification remained in the possession of the officers throughout the encounter; the officers also seized and had possession of his luggage. As a practical matter, Royer could not leave the airport without them. In *Mendenhall,* no luggage was involved, the ticket and identification were immediately returned, and the officers were careful to advise that the suspect could decline to be searched. Here, the officers had seized Royer's luggage and made no effort to advise him that he need not consent to the search.

Justice Brennan concurred in the result. Four Justices dissented in *Royer* on the ground that, while Royer may have been seized, the seizure was supported by reasonable suspicion and the police lawfully obtained Royer's consent. Thus, none of the Justices disagreed with the proposition that Royer was seized within the meaning of the Fourth Amendment when the officers retained Royer's ticket and identification.

Does the *Royer* Court give sufficient guidance to the police to determine what type of conduct triggers a Fourth Amendment seizure? Lower courts have tried to impart some guidance. See Johnson v. Campbell, 332 F.3d 199 (3rd Cir. 2003) (motorist was stopped when officer persisted in telling him to roll his window down even after motorist refused: "At that time, Campbell made it clear that Johnson was not free to ignore him and would not be left alone until he complied."); United States v. Jefferson, 906 F.2d 346 (8th Cir.1990)(implying that failing to return necessary documentation such as a driver's license always constitutes a stop); United States v. High, 921 F.2d 112 (7th Cir. 1990)(suggesting that officers "preface their questions with a statement that the encounter is consensual and that the citizen is free to go").

Airport Confrontations After Royer

Despite the Court's decision in *Royer*, lower courts have often had difficulty in determining when and whether a seizure occurs during an airport confrontation. A court must look at the totality of the circumstances, and results may differ depending on minor variations in the facts, as well as the perspective of the particular court. In Wilson v. Superior Court, 34 Cal.3d 777, 195 Cal.Rptr. 671, 670 P.2d 325 (1983), the court found that a seizure had taken place when a police officer approached a passenger who had picked up his luggage and put it into a car, told him that the police had received information that the passenger would be carrying a lot of drugs, and asked the passenger for permission to search the luggage. Compare United States v. Berke, 930 F.2d 1219 (7th Cir.1991)(police contact was an encounter, not a seizure, where officers sat on either side of the defendant in a terminal, notified him that they were officers looking for narcotics, asked for consent to search, and informed the defendant that he had the right to leave and to refuse consent).

In one of the most notorious airport confrontations ever, Los Angeles Police Officer Searle approached Joe Morgan, the Hall of Fame baseball player, while Morgan was making a telephone call during a layover at LAX. The officer suspected that Morgan was a drug courier, traveling with another African American who was acting as a lookout. The officer tapped Morgan on the shoulder, and asked him to accompany him to determine whether he was traveling with another person. Morgan told the officer to go away. The officer persisted, and Morgan continued to refuse to cooperate. A bystander came up to identify Morgan as a famous baseball player, but the officer flashed his badge and told him to back off. Morgan became increasingly upset. Eventually the situation escalated to such a point that Morgan was thrown to the ground, handcuffed, and brought into a detention room with the officer's hand over Morgan's face and mouth. Morgan was released shortly thereafter; no charges were filed. Morgan brought an action against the officer for a violation of his Fourth Amendment rights. The court of appeals affirmed a judgment in favor of Morgan (though vacating and remanding an award of punitive damages). The officer argued that Morgan was not seized until *after* he became so unruly that he had to be handcuffed; thus, in the officer's view, his seizure of Morgan was reasonable because it was justified by Morgan's response to what had been an encounter rather than a stop. But the court rejected this argument:

> By definition, a "consensual" exchange between police and citizens cannot take place in the absence of consent. When a citizen expresses his or her desire *not* to cooperate, continued questioning cannot be deemed consensual. * * * Searle testified that after he approached Morgan, Morgan indicated in no uncertain terms that he did not want to be bothered. * * * We find that Morgan's unequivocal expression of his desire to be left alone demonstrates that the exchange between Morgan and Searle was not consensual. Because the exchange was nonconsensual, we do not hesitate to find that Morgan was indeed seized well before he allegedly became violent.

Do you think that Joe Montana, the Hall of Fame quarterback runs the same risk of police confrontation in an airport as does Joe Morgan? If Joe Montana had refused to cooperate with an inquiry, would the officer have allowed him to walk away?

Factory Sweeps: INS v. Delgado

A majority of the Court finally adopted and applied the *Mendenhall* test in Immigration and Naturalization Service v. Delgado, 466 U.S. 210 (1984), which held that INS officers did not seize workers when they conducted factory surveys in search of illegal aliens. Justice Rehnquist described the surveys as follows:

> At the beginning of the surveys several agents positioned themselves near the buildings' exits, while other agents dispersed throughout the factory to question most, but not all, employees at their work stations. The

agents displayed badges, carried walkie-talkies, and were armed, although at
no point during any of the surveys was a weapon ever drawn. Moving
systematically through the factory, the agents approached employees and,
after identifying themselves, asked them from one to three questions relating to their citizenship. If the employee gave a credible reply that he was a
United States citizen, the questioning ended, and the agent moved on to
another employee. If the employee gave an unsatisfactory response or
admitted that he was an alien, the employee was asked to produce his
immigration papers. During the survey, employees continued with their
work and were free to walk around within the factory.

Four employees questioned in one of the surveys filed suit, claiming
that the factory sweeps violated the Fourth Amendment and seeking declaratory and injunctive relief. The employees lost in the district court, prevailed in the court of appeals, and lost again in the Supreme Court.

Justice Rehnquist noted that "police questioning, by itself, is unlikely to
result in a Fourth Amendment violation. While most citizens will respond to a
police request, the fact that people do so, and do so without being told they are
free not to respond, hardly eliminates the consensual nature of the response."
He rejected the argument that the employees were seized during the entire
survey, finding that even though there were agents at the exits, they were placed
there to insure that questions were put to all employees. Because the employees
were at work and thus were not going to leave the factory in any event, Justice
Rehnquist concluded that the guards at the exit could not have had a coercive or
custodial effect. The majority reasoned that "[t]his conduct should have given
[the employees] no reason to believe that they would be detained if they gave
truthful answers to the questions put to them or if they simply refused to
answer." And the majority also rejected an argument that individual employees
were seized when they were questioned.

Justice Powell concurred in the result with an opinion stating that the
majority opinion was "persuasive," but that the question of whether a seizure
took place was a close one. He found it unnecessary to resolve the question, since
he concluded that any seizure was reasonable given the importance of the
government's interest in finding illegal aliens.

Justice Brennan, joined by Justice Marshall, dissented from the holding that
the individual interrogations were not seizures and argued that the testimony in
the case "paints a frightening picture of people subjected to wholesale interrogation under conditions designed not to respect personal security and privacy, but
rather to elicit prompt answers from completely intimidated workers."

Put yourself in the workers' place. Would you feel free to leave? Would you
assume the armed guards at the exits were placed there to keep you inside the
factory? Suppose the building was a law school rather than a factory and you
were present as a student who had read *Delgado*. Would you attempt to leave a
building secured in the way the *Delgado* factory was?

Street Encounters

Officers in police cars, marked and unmarked, often seek to question people
on the street. When officers pull up to question a person on the street in the
absence of any articulable reasonable suspicion, have they violated the person's

Fourth Amendment rights? This will depend on whether the officer's conduct amounts to a seizure, or is rather simply an encounter. United States v. Cardoza, 129 F.3d 6 (1st Cir.1997), represents a fairly typical case. The court described the facts as follows:

> In July of 1995, a sixteen-year-old acquaintance of Cardoza, Myron Ragsdale, asked Cardoza to secure a handgun for him to purchase. Cardoza found a dealer willing to sell a nine-millimeter semiautomatic handgun to Ragsdale for $200.00. On the night of July 14, 1995, Cardoza and Ragsdale went to Walnut Park in Roxbury, Massachusetts, to make the gun purchase. Ragsdale paid $200.00 for the handgun and nine rounds of ammunition. Ragsdale loaded the gun with eight rounds of ammunition, and Cardoza took possession of the ninth round. Sometime after the transaction was completed, Cardoza and Ragsdale began walking along Humboldt Avenue. As they walked, Ragsdale had the handgun in his waistband and Cardoza carried the single round of ammunition in his hand. By this time it was approximately 2:00 a.m. on the morning of July 15. They were spotted walking along Humboldt Avenue by four officers of the Boston Police's Youth Violence Strike Force who were patrolling the area in an unmarked police car. One of the officers in the car, Gregory Brown, noticed that Cardoza and Ragsdale were acting indecisively about whether to continue walking up Humboldt, or instead cross the street in front of the police car. Moving slowly, the police car approached Cardoza and Ragsdale from behind. As the patrol car approached, Cardoza and Ragsdale crossed Humboldt Avenue in order to walk up the sidewalk of Ruthven Street, a one-way thoroughfare that emptied onto Humboldt Avenue. As they crossed in front of the car, Officer Brown, who was sitting in the back seat on the driver's side, recognized Cardoza and directed the driver to make a left turn off Humboldt, and proceed the wrong way up Ruthven for a short distance. Officer Brown testified that he wanted to ask Cardoza some questions concerning a shooting incident that had occurred some days earlier. The driver took the left turn, and pulled over to the curb just off Humboldt, facing the wrong way on Ruthven Street.

> Officer Brown, whose window was rolled down, called out to Cardoza, asking "What's up Freddie? What are you doing out this time of night?" Cardoza stopped, turned, and approached the patrol car. Ragsdale continued walking a short distance. Officer Brown remained in the car conversing with Cardoza through the open car window. As he talked with Officer Brown, Cardoza began to gesture with his hand, exposing the round of ammunition. Seeing the round of ammunition, Brown exited the patrol car, and began to pat-frisk Cardoza. At the same time, two other officers exited the car and approached and pat-frisked Ragsdale, discovering the handgun loaded with eight rounds of ammunition.

Cardoza was convicted of possession of being a felon in possession of a firearm and ammunition. He argued that the evidence should be suppressed because, by the time the officer saw the ammunition, he had been stopped by the officer without reasonable suspicion. But the court disagreed, and found that Cardoza had not been seized within the meaning of the Fourth Amendment. It explained as follows:

Our inquiry is not directed at whether the police conduct objectively communicated police desire to speak to Cardoza, or ask him a question. Rather, we must determine whether their conduct indicated that they were interfering with his liberty to such an extent that he was not free to leave. We think the distinction important, and are left, therefore, with the conclusion that the police officers' conduct on the night in question would not have communicated to a reasonable person that the police were attempting to intrude upon Cardoza's freedom of movement.

To begin with, no sirens or flashing lights were used by the officers to indicate to Cardoza that he should stop in his tracks. Similarly, the police cruiser pulled over and stopped at the curb before Officer Brown called out to Cardoza. And Officer Brown remained in the car when he called out to Cardoza. * * * Officer Brown did not ask Cardoza to stop, or even to approach the car. He simply called out through an open car window with the question "what are you doing out at this time of night?" Those words do not objectively communicate an attempt to restrain Cardoza's liberty. We are therefore unpersuaded that the police officers' actions transformed mere police questioning into a seizure.

If a police car pulled up against traffic on a one-way street to speak to you, would you feel free to leave? Would any person in their right mind (much less reasonable mind) feel free to leave? Obviously not. But the *Cardoza* court had a response to this argument:

We recognize, of course, the import of Cardoza's observation that few people, including himself, would ever feel free to walk away from any police question. Under this reasoning, however, * * * every police-citizen encounter [is transformed] into a seizure. The "free to walk away" test, however, must be read in conjunction with the Court's frequent admonitions that "a seizure does not occur simply because a police officer approaches an individual and asks a few questions." What emerges between the two imperatives, therefore, is the directive that police conduct, viewed from the totality of the circumstances, must objectively communicate that the officer is exercising his or her official authority to restrain the individual's liberty of movement before we can find that a seizure occurred. Because there was no such objective communication in the instant case, we affirm the district court's denial of Cardoza's motion to suppress.

So the court held that the question is not whether a reasonable person would feel free to leave, but rather whether the police officer was acting coercively. But even under that test, isn't an officer acting coercively when he drives the wrong way down a one-way street at 2 a.m., pulls over, and asks the citizen what he is up to?

Problem With the "Freedom to Walk Away" Test

Daniel Steinbeck takes the Court's "freedom to walk away" test to task in The Wrong Line Between Freedom and Restraint: The Unreality, Obscurity, and Incivility of the Fourth Amendment Consensual Encounter Doctrine, 38 San Diego L.Rev. 507 (2001):

There are legal fictions and there are legal fictions. One means of differentiating good from bad legal fictions is their relationship to reality

* * *. By that measure, in light of the available evidence, the consensual encounter doctrine paints a false picture of reality as applied to encounters involving investigation of the individual being questioned. In so doing, it mislocates the dividing line between freedom and restraint, including on the "freedom" side of this line many people who are effectively restrained or—to put it another way—are restrained in all but the eyes of the law.

* * * The obscurity of the line between freedom and detention bespeaks an uncivil distrust of the persons whose liberty is at stake. It plays on their ignorance and understandable sense of powerlessness in relation to law enforcement officers. Moreover, attempts by citizens to clarify their status, or assert the rights they believe they have, produce additional incivility and friction on both sides. The consensual encounter doctrine virtually invites citizens, as an initial response, to question or rebuff police approaches. * * * Rudeness and confrontation by citizens, which are virtually required in order for citizens to determine whether they are free to go, stimulates rudeness and confrontation in response. This, in turn, poisons the relationship between citizens and their government, creating social friction and disunity.

But what is the alternative? Should it be considered a stop whenever a police officer approaches a citizen to ask questions?

Bus Sweeps: Florida v. Bostick and United States v. Drayton

In the following case, the Court considers the permissibility of a "bus sweep" in the absence of reasonable suspicion. The case discusses and applies the Court's first analysis of this subject in Florida v. Bostick.

UNITED STATES v. DRAYTON

Supreme Court of the United States, 2002.
536 U.S. 194.

JUSTICE KENNEDY **delivered the opinion of the Court.**

The Fourth Amendment permits police officers to approach bus passengers at random to ask questions and to request their consent to searches, provided a reasonable person would understand that he or she is free to refuse. Florida v. Bostick, 501 U.S. 429 (1991). This case requires us to determine whether officers must advise bus passengers during these encounters of their right not to cooperate.

I

On February 4, 1999, respondents Christopher Drayton and Clifton Brown, Jr., were traveling on a Greyhound bus en route from Ft. Lauderdale, Florida, to Detroit, Michigan. The bus made a scheduled stop in Tallahassee, Florida. The passengers were required to disembark so the bus could be refueled and cleaned. As the passengers reboarded, the driver checked their tickets and then left to complete paperwork inside the terminal. As he left, the driver allowed three members of the Tallahassee Police Department to board the bus as part of a routine drug and weapons interdiction effort. The officers were dressed in plain clothes and carried concealed weapons and visible badges.

Once onboard Officer Hoover knelt on the driver's seat and faced the rear of the bus. He could observe the passengers and ensure the safety of the two other officers without blocking the aisle or otherwise obstructing the bus exit. Officers Lang and Blackburn went to the rear of the bus. Blackburn remained stationed there, facing forward. Lang worked his way toward the front of the bus, speaking with individual passengers as he went. He asked the passengers about their travel plans and sought to match passengers with luggage in the overhead racks. To avoid blocking the aisle, Lang stood next to or just behind each passenger with whom he spoke.

According to Lang's testimony, passengers who declined to cooperate with him or who chose to exit the bus at any time would have been allowed to do so without argument. In Lang's experience, however, most people are willing to cooperate. Some passengers go so far as to commend the police for their efforts to ensure the safety of their travel. Lang could recall five to six instances in the previous year in which passengers had declined to have their luggage searched. It also was common for passengers to leave the bus for a cigarette or a snack while the officers were on board. Lang sometimes informed passengers of their right to refuse to cooperate. On the day in question, however, he did not.

Respondents were seated next to each other on the bus. Drayton was in the aisle seat, Brown in the seat next to the window. Lang approached respondents from the rear and leaned over Drayton's shoulder. He held up his badge long enough for respondents to identify him as a police officer. With his face 12–to–18 inches away from Drayton's, Lang spoke in a voice just loud enough for respondents to hear:

I'm Investigator Lang with the Tallahassee Police Department. We're conducting bus interdiction [sic], attempting to deter drugs and illegal

weapons being transported on the bus. Do you have any bags on the bus?

Both respondents pointed to a single green bag in the overhead luggage rack. Lang asked, "Do you mind if I check it?," and Brown responded, "Go ahead." Lang handed the bag to Officer Blackburn to check. The bag contained no contraband.

Officer Lang noticed that both respondents were wearing heavy jackets and baggy pants despite the warm weather. In Lang's experience drug traffickers often use baggy clothing to conceal weapons or narcotics. The officer thus asked Brown if he had any weapons or drugs in his possession. And he asked Brown: "Do you mind if I check your person?" Brown answered, "Sure," and cooperated by leaning up in his seat, pulling a cell phone out of his pocket, and opening up his jacket. Lang reached across Drayton and patted down Brown's jacket and pockets, including his waist area, sides, and upper thighs. In both thigh areas, Lang detected hard objects similar to drug packages detected on other occasions. Lang arrested and handcuffed Brown. Officer Hoover escorted Brown from the bus.

Lang then asked Drayton, "Mind if I check you?" Drayton responded by lifting his hands about eight inches from his legs. Lang conducted a pat-down of Drayton's thighs and detected hard objects similar to those found on Brown. He arrested Drayton and escorted him from the bus. A further search revealed that respondents had duct-taped plastic bundles of powder cocaine between several pairs of their boxer shorts. Brown possessed three bundles containing 483 grams of cocaine. Drayton possessed two bundles containing 295 grams of cocaine.

[The defendants were charged with drug crimes. The trial court denied motions to suppress the drugs on the ground that the entire procedure was a consensual encounter.]

The Court of Appeals for the Eleventh Circuit reversed and remanded with instructions to grant respondents' motions to suppress. The court held that this disposition was compelled by its previous decisions in United States v. Washington, 151 F. 3d 1354 (1998), and United States v. Guapi, 144 F. 3d 1393 (1998). Those cases had held that bus passengers do not feel free to disregard police officers' requests to search absent "some positive indication that consent could have been refused."

We granted certiorari. The respondents, we conclude, were not seized and their consent to the search was voluntary; and we reverse.

II

Law enforcement officers do not violate the Fourth Amendment's prohibition of unreasonable seizures merely by approaching individuals on the street or in other public places and putting questions to them if they are willing to listen. Even when law enforcement officers have no basis for suspecting a particular individual, they may pose questions, ask for identification, and request consent to search luggage—provided they do not induce cooperation by coercive means. See *Florida v. Bostick,* 501 U.S., at 434–435. If a reasonable person would feel free to terminate the encounter, then he or she has not been seized.

The Court has addressed on a previous occasion the specific question of drug interdiction efforts on buses. In *Bostick,* two police officers requested a bus passenger's consent to a search of his luggage. The passenger agreed, and the resulting search revealed cocaine in his suitcase. The Florida Supreme Court suppressed the cocaine. In doing so it adopted a *per se* rule that due to the cramped confines onboard a bus the act of questioning would deprive a person of his or her freedom of movement and so constitute a seizure under the Fourth Amendment.

This Court reversed. *Bostick* first made it clear that for the most part *per se* rules are inappropriate in the Fourth Amendment context. The proper inquiry necessitates a consideration of "all the circumstances surrounding the encounter." The Court noted next that the traditional rule, which states that a seizure does not occur so long as a reasonable person would feel free "to disregard the police and go about his business," is not an accurate measure of the coercive effect of a bus encounter. A passenger may not want to get off a bus if there is a risk it will depart before the opportunity to reboard. A bus rider's movements are confined in this sense, but this is the natural result of choosing to take the bus; it says nothing about whether the police conduct is coercive. The proper inquiry "is whether a reasonable person would feel free to decline the officers' requests or otherwise terminate the encounter." Finally, the Court rejected Bostick's argument that he must have been seized because no reasonable person would consent to a search of luggage containing drugs. The reasonable person test, the Court explained, is objective and "presupposes an *innocent* person."

In light of the limited record, *Bostick* refrained from deciding whether a seizure occurred. The Court, however, identified two factors "particularly worth noting" on remand. First, although it was obvious that an officer was armed, he did not remove the gun from its pouch or use it in a threatening way. Second, the officer advised the passenger that he could refuse consent to the search.

Relying upon this latter factor, the Eleventh Circuit has adopted what is in effect a *per se* rule that evidence obtained during suspicionless drug interdiction efforts aboard buses must be suppressed unless the officers have advised passengers of their right not to cooperate and to refuse consent to a search. * * *

The Court of Appeals erred in adopting this approach.

Applying the *Bostick* framework to the facts of this particular case, we conclude that the police did not seize respondents when they boarded the bus and began questioning passengers. The officers gave the passengers no reason to believe that they were required to answer the officers' questions. When Officer Lang approached respondents, he did not brandish a weapon or make any intimidating movements. He left the aisle free so that respondents could exit. He spoke to passengers one by one and in a polite, quiet voice. Nothing he said would suggest to a reasonable person that he or she was barred from leaving the bus or otherwise terminating the encounter.

* * * There was no application of force, no intimidating movement, no overwhelming show of force, no brandishing of weapons, no blocking of exits, no threat, no command, not even an authoritative tone of voice. It is beyond question that had this encounter occurred on the street, it would be constitutional. The fact that an encounter takes place on a bus does not on its own transform standard police questioning of citizens into an illegal seizure. Indeed, because many fellow passengers are present to witness officers' conduct, a reasonable person may feel even more secure in his or her decision not to cooperate with police on a bus than in other circumstances.

Respondents make much of the fact that Officer Lang displayed his badge. In Florida v. Rodriguez, 469 U.S., at 5–6, however, the Court rejected the claim that the defendant was seized when an officer approached him in an airport, showed him his badge, and asked him to answer some questions. Likewise, in INS v. Delgado, 466 U.S. 210, 212–213 (1984), the Court held that INS agents' wearing badges and questioning workers in a factory did not constitute a seizure. And while neither Lang nor his colleagues were in uniform or visibly armed, those factors should have little weight in the analysis. Officers are often required to wear uniforms and in many circumstances this is cause for assurance, not discomfort. Much the same can be said for wearing sidearms. That most law enforcement officers are armed is a fact well known to the public. The presence of a holstered firearm thus is unlikely to contribute to the coerciveness of the encounter absent active brandishing of the weapon.

Officer Hoover's position at the front of the bus also does not tip the scale in respondents' favor. Hoover did nothing to intimidate passengers, and he said nothing to suggest that people could not exit and indeed he left the aisle clear. In *Delgado*, the Court determined there was no seizure even though several uniformed INS officers were stationed near the exits of the factory. The Court noted: "The presence of agents by the exits posed no reasonable threat of detention to these workers, ... the mere possibility that they would be questioned if they sought to leave the buildings should not have resulted in any reasonable apprehension by any of them that they would be seized or detained in any meaningful way."

Finally, the fact that in Officer Lang's experience only a few passengers have refused to cooperate does not suggest that a reasonable person would not feel free to terminate the bus encounter. In Lang's experience it was common for passengers to leave the bus for a cigarette or a snack while the officers were questioning passengers. And of more importance, bus passengers answer officers' questions and otherwise cooperate not because of coercion but because the passengers know that their participation enhances their own safety and the safety of those around them. * * *

Drayton contends that even if Brown's cooperation with the officers was consensual, Drayton was seized because no reasonable person would feel free to terminate the encounter with the officers after Brown had been arrested. * * * The arrest of one person does not mean that everyone around him has been seized by police. If anything, Brown's arrest should have put Drayton on notice of the consequences of continuing the encounter by answering the officers' questions. Even after arresting Brown, Lang addressed Drayton in a polite manner and provided him with no indication that he was required to answer Lang's questions.

We turn now from the question whether respondents were seized to whether they were subjected to an unreasonable search, *i.e.,* whether their consent to the suspicionless search was involuntary. In circumstances such as these, where the question of voluntariness pervades both the search and seizure inquiries, the respective analyses turn on very similar facts. And, as the facts above suggest, respondents' consent to the search of their luggage and their persons was voluntary. Nothing Officer Lang said indicated a command to consent to the search. Rather, when

respondents informed Lang that they had a bag on the bus, he asked for their permission to check it. And when Lang requested to search Brown and Drayton's persons, he asked first if they objected, thus indicating to a reasonable person that he or she was free to refuse. Even after arresting Brown, Lang provided Drayton with no indication that he was required to consent to a search. To the contrary, Lang asked for Drayton's permission to search him ("Mind if I check you?"), and Drayton agreed.

* * * Although Officer Lang did not inform respondents of their right to refuse the search, he did request permission to search, and the totality of the circumstances indicates that their consent was voluntary, so the searches were reasonable.

In a society based on law, the concept of agreement and consent should be given a weight and dignity of its own. Police officers act in full accord with the law when they ask citizens for consent. It reinforces the rule of law for the citizen to advise the police of his or her wishes and for the police to act in reliance on that understanding. When this exchange takes place, it dispels inferences of coercion.

We need not ask the alternative question whether, after the arrest of Brown, there were grounds for a *Terry* stop and frisk of Drayton, though this may have been the case. It was evident that Drayton and Brown were traveling together—Officer Lang observed the pair reboarding the bus together; they were each dressed in heavy, baggy clothes that were ill-suited for the day's warm temperatures; they were seated together on the bus; and they each claimed responsibility for the single piece of green carry-on luggage. Once Lang had identified Brown as carrying what he believed to be narcotics, he may have had reasonable suspicion to conduct a *Terry* stop and frisk on Drayton as well. That question, however, has not been presented to us. The fact the officers may have had reasonable suspicion does not prevent them from relying on a citizen's consent to the search. It would be a paradox, and one most puzzling to law enforcement officials and courts alike, were we to say, after holding that Brown's consent was voluntary, that Drayton's consent was ineffectual simply because the police at that point had more compelling grounds to detain him. After taking Brown into custody, the officers were entitled to continue to proceed on the basis of consent and to ask for Drayton's cooperation.

The judgment of the Court of Appeals is reversed, and the case is remanded for further proceedings consistent with this opinion.

JUSTICE SOUTER, with whom JUSTICE STEVENS and JUSTICE GINSBURG join, dissenting.

Anyone who travels by air today submits to searches of the person and luggage as a condition of boarding the aircraft. It is universally accepted that such intrusions are necessary to hedge against risks that, nowadays, even small children understand. The commonplace precautions of air travel have not, thus far, been justified for ground transportation, however, and no such conditions have been placed on passengers getting on trains or buses. There is therefore an air of unreality about the Court's explanation that bus passengers consent to searches of their luggage to "enhanc[e] their own safety and the safety of those around them." * * *

* * * [F]or reasons unexplained, the driver with the tickets entitling the passengers to travel had yielded his custody of the bus and its seated travelers to three police officers, whose authority apparently superseded the driver's own. The officers took control of the entire passenger compartment, one stationed at the door keeping surveillance of all the occupants, the others working forward from the back. With one officer right behind him and the other one forward, a third officer accosted each passenger at quarters extremely close and so cramped that as many as half the passengers could not even have stood to face the speaker. None was asked whether he was willing to converse with the police or to take part in the enquiry. Instead the officer said the police were "conducting bus interdiction," in the course of which they "would like . . . cooperation." The reasonable inference was that the "interdiction" was not a consensual exercise, but one the police would carry out whatever the circumstances; that they would prefer "cooperation" but would not let the lack of it stand in their way. There was no contrary indication that day, since no passenger had refused the cooperation requested, and there was no reason for any passenger to believe that the driver would return and the trip resume until the police were satisfied. The scene was set and an atmosphere of obligatory participation was established by this introduction. Later requests to search prefaced with "Do you mind . . ." would naturally have been understood in the terms with which the encounter began.

It is very hard to imagine that either Brown or Drayton would have believed that he stood to lose nothing if he refused to cooperate with the police, or that he had any free choice to ignore the police altogether. No reasonable passenger could have believed that, only an uncomprehending one. * * * While I am not prepared to say that no bus interrogation and search can pass the *Bostick* test without a warning that passengers are free to say no, the facts here surely required more from the officers than a quiet tone of voice. A police officer who is certain to get his way has no need to shout.

Note on Bus Sweeps

Janice Nadler, in No Need to Shout: Bus Sweeps and the Psychology of Coercion, 2002 Sup.Ct. Rev. 153, argues that the Court's bus sweep cases, while understandable after 9/11, are out of line with social science evidence concerning coercion and consent. She concludes as follows:

> It may be the case that, on balance, it is desirable to permit police to board intercity buses and pose questions to passengers and, in some circumstances, conduct searches of baggage and persons, especially with the current need to be vigilant about potential risks of terrorism. In this way, it is understandable that the *Drayton* Court scrupulously avoided announcing rules in drug cases that would restrict the ability of police to investigate terrorism and other serious threats to public security.
>
> On the other hand, in its effort to be sensitive to the order-maintenance needs of the government, the Court has promulgated a standard to determining the bounds of consensual police-citizen encounters and voluntary searches that struggles against a wealth of social science evidence, that subjects many innocent people to suspicionless searches and seizures against their will, and that produces disagreement and confusion in the lower courts. It may be that large-scale, suspicionless searches of passengers on common carriers is a price that we ought to be willing to pay to stem the flow of illegal narcotics transported on intercity buses and trains. If this is the determination that underlies the decision in *Drayton*, then the Court should have explicitly stated it and justified it—rather than relying on the implausible assertion that bus passengers, when they are individually confronted by armed police officers who want to search them, feel free to ignore the police or outright refuse their requests.

State of Mind Required for a Stop: Brower v. County of Inyo

Must an officer have a certain state of mind in order to seize a person? Justice Scalia wrote for the Court in Brower v. County of Inyo, 489 U.S. 593 (1989), where officers set up a "blind" roadblock in an attempt to apprehend a fleeing suspect. The suspect, approaching the roadblock from around a curve, was not able to stop before crashing into it. The suspect died in the crash and a wrongful death action was brought alleging that the suspect had been illegally "seized" by the roadblock. Justice Scalia agreed with the plaintiff that a seizure had occurred. He declared that "a Fourth Amendment seizure does not occur whenever there is a governmentally caused termination of an individual's freedom of movement * * *, nor even whenever there is a governmentally *desired* termination of an individual's freedom of movement * * *, but only when there is a governmental termination of freedom of movement *through means intentionally applied*." In this case, the officers placed the roadblock with the intent to stop the suspect; and in fact the suspect was stopped by means of the roadblock. Therefore, the suspect was seized, even though he was not stopped in precisely the way that the officers intended for him to stop. The means used to stop him were intentionally applied.[20]

---

20. The Court in *Brower* remanded for a determination of whether the seizure was unreasonable under the circumstances.

To further elaborate on this intent-based test, Justice Scalia posed the following hypothetical: police officers park and leave their squad car on a hill, the parking brake accidentally disengages, the car rolls down the hill and just happens to pin a suspected criminal against a wall. Has the criminal been seized? Justice Scalia's answer was "no", because the officers never intentionally applied any means to stop the suspect's freedom of movement. They just got lucky.

Justice Stevens, joined by Justices Brennan, Marshall, and Blackmun, concurred in the judgment. He objected to Justice Scalia's emphasis on an intentional acquisition of physical control as marking the onset of a seizure, and suggested that, since it was clear in the instant case that the roadblock was intended to stop the deceased, "[d]ecision in the case before us is thus not advanced by pursuing a hypothetical inquiry concerning whether an unintentional act might also violate the Fourth Amendment."

How would the *Brower* test apply in the following circumstance? A gunman commandeers a school bus and takes a student as a hostage. A police standoff ensues, and a police officer fires into the bus in an attempt to kill the gunman. The bullet, however, hits the student instead. Has the student been unreasonably seized? The court in Medeiros v. O'Connell, 150 F.3d 164 (2d Cir.1998), held that the police conduct did not constitute a seizure of the student, and therefore that summary judgment was properly granted to the officer in a section 1983 case. The court declared that a police officer's deliberate decision to shoot for the purpose of stopping the *gunman* "does not result in the sort of willful detention of the hostage that the Fourth Amendment was designed to govern." The court noted that the officer's intent was not to restrain the hostage's movement—far from it. The court also observed that the instant case was distinguishable "from those in which the police shoot an innocent victim mistakenly believing that he is the suspect whom they are pursuing." In such cases, a seizure occurs because "the victim was indeed the object of an intentional act of seizure, even if the police were mistaken as to the victim's identity." But where a hostage is hit by a bullet intended for the hostage-taker, there is no intentional seizure of the hostage within the meaning of *Brower*.

The Suspect Who Does Not Submit: California v. Hodari D.

In *Mendenhall*, *Bostick*, and *Drayton*, the suspects each agreed to cooperate with the police, and the question was whether a reasonable innocent person would have felt free to refuse to cooperate. But what if the suspect actually *does* refuse to cooperate? Justice Scalia, writing for the Court in California v. Hodari D., 499 U.S. 621 (1991), considered the applicability of the *Mendenhall* test to situations in which the suspect refuses to submit to a show of authority. The case arose when officers encountered a group of youths who were huddled around a car and who fled when they saw the officers. Hodari, one of the group who ran, threw away a small rock as a pursuing officer was about to catch him. One officer tackled Hodari, handcuffed him and radioed for assistance. Subsequently, the officer discovered that the discarded rock was crack cocaine. Hodari claimed that the pursuit was a seizure, and because there was no legal cause for the pursuit there was a Fourth Amendment violation, requiring suppression of the fruits including the cocaine.

Justice Scalia "consulted the common law" and cited law dictionaries to support the notion that the word "seizure" has meant a "taking possession." Justice Scalia separated seizures into two types: those in which the officer has physically touched the citizen, and those in which the officer has used a non-physical show of authority. As to the former category, Justice Scalia noted that "[t]o constitute an arrest, * * *—the quintessential 'seizure of the person' under our Fourth Amendment jurisprudence—the mere grasping or application of physical force with lawful authority, whether or not it succeeded in subduing the arrestee, was sufficient." However, although "an arrest is effected by the slightest application of physical force," Justice Scalia rejected the idea that "there is a *continuing* arrest during the period of fugitivity."

As to the latter category of non-physical displays of authority such as pursuit, at issue under the facts of *Hodari,* Justice Scalia framed the question before the Court as "whether, with respect to a show of authority as with respect to application of physical force, a seizure occurs even though the subject does not yield." The answer was "that it does not."

Justice Scalia recognized that *Mendenhall* dealt with non-physical displays of authority, and focused only on whether a reasonable person would feel that he or she was free to leave, rather than on actual submission. Justice Scalia concluded, however, that the "free to leave" test was a necessary, but not sufficient, test for determining whether a seizure occurs. He stated that the *Mendenhall* test when "read carefully" says that a person has been seized "only if", not "whenever" the officer uses a show of authority. Thus, where the officer engages in a non-physical show of authority, it must be such that a reasonable person would not feel free to leave, *and* the citizen must actually submit. This is in contrast to physical touching or grasping, which if intentional is a seizure in any case.

As a matter of policy, Justice Scalia reasoned that the public should be encouraged to comply with police orders, therefore it would not do to reward suspects like Hodari for noncompliance by finding a seizure. Justice Scalia rejected the argument that police officers would abuse a rule that they may automatically chase non-complying suspects. The perceived risk of abuse was that officers, having no reasonable suspicion to support a stop, would routinely use non-physical displays of authority in the hope that suspects would disobey them and evidence would be found. Justice Scalia found this risk overrated. He reasoned that police do not issue orders expecting them to be ignored. Thus, officers would not take the risk that suspects would comply with their orders and render the seizure illegal in the absence of reasonable suspicion.

Justice Stevens, joined by Justice Marshall, dissented. He criticized the majority's "narrow construction" of the term "seizure" as meaning "that a police officer may now fire his weapon at an innocent citizen and not implicate the Fourth Amendment—as long as he misses his target." The dissenters argued that the common law distinction between touching and a show of force was not determinative for Fourth Amendment purposes. Justice Stevens suggested that the common law ought not to govern analyses of current law enforcement practices.

Justice Stevens concluded that the majority erred in focusing on the citizen's reaction to an officer's conduct rather than on the officer's conduct itself. He noted that under the majority's test, police officers could take advantage of citizens by using all their conduct against them in the seconds before they actually submit to authority. For example, an officer could flash his lights to stop a car without adequate cause, and then use any observations made before the car comes to a complete stop. Similarly, a drug enforcement agent could approach a group of passengers in an airport with a drawn gun, announce a baggage search, and then rely on the passengers' reaction to justify a subsequent investigative stop.

Justice Stevens concluded that it was "anomalous, at best" to establish different rules for seizures effected by touching and those effected by a show of force. He argued that it was important for an officer to know in advance whether certain conduct would constitute a seizure, and that the majority's test makes this impossible when the officer is using a non-physical show of force.

Questions After Hodari

Suppose an officer pulls a gun, tells a suspect to stop, the suspect turns toward the officer, and has a heart attack and dies. Has the suspect been seized? What if an officer fires a warning shot in the air and a fleeing suspect stops suddenly and a package falls from his pocket as a result of this sudden stop? Is the package the fruit of a seizure?

It should be noted that Hodari was a young, African American, urban male. How suspicious is it for such a person to run when a number of uniformed police come around the corner? See generally Maclin, "Black and Blue Encounters"—Some Preliminary Thoughts About Fourth Amendment Seizures: Should Race Matter?, 26 Val.U.L.Rev. 243 (1991)(arguing that the Court should take account of the race of the citizen in assessing the legality of a police-citizen confrontation under *Terry*).

When Does Submission Occur?

One of the problems left for police officers and the courts after *Hodari* is to determine when, precisely, a suspect has submitted to a non-physical show of authority. Exemplary is United States v. Hernandez, 27 F.3d 1403 (9th Cir. 1994). Officers were taking a person into custody outside an apartment building when they saw Hernandez jump over a fence into an alley and run to the apartment building's gate. Suspecting illegal activity, Officer Sadar approached Hernandez, and stated that he was a police officer and needed to talk to him. As Sadar walked towards him, Hernandez stopped momentarily, looked at Sadar, and then turned and attempted to climb over the gate. Sadar grabbed Hernandez, they struggled, the gate came down, Hernandez broke free and began running, and then threw a gun away which was recovered by the police. Hernandez was charged with felon firearm possession.

Hernandez moved to suppress the gun, arguing that he was seized when he briefly submitted (i.e., hesitated briefly) to the officer's show of authority before fleeing, and that at that point the officer had no reasonable suspicion to stop him. From this premise he concluded that the discarded gun was a fruit of the illegal seizure. But the Court disagreed with the premise, and held that Hernandez was never actually seized by Officer Sadar:

> We decline to adopt a rule whereby momentary hesitation and direct eye contact prior to flight constitute submission to a show of authority. Such a rule would encourage suspects to flee after the slightest contact with an

officer in order to discard evidence, and yet still maintain Fourth Amendment protections.

The court found that Hernandez was never seized "because he never submitted to authority, nor was he physically subdued." Therefore, the gun discovered as a result of Sadar's "encounter" with Hernandez was legally obtained, even if there was no reasonable suspicion to detain Hernandez. Do you agree with the *Hernandez* Court that criminals could be so savvy as to take advantage of a rule by which a momentary hesitation would constitute submission to authority? Are criminals that up on their Fourth Amendment law? See also United States v. Lender, 985 F.2d 151 (4th Cir.1993)(defendant's momentary halt on the sidewalk with his back to the officers, while fumbling for something on his person, did not constitute submission to authority; consequently, the gun that he dropped thereafter was obtained legally).

Controlling Gang Activity Through Anti–Loitering Ordinances: City of Chicago v. Morales

Hodari shows one means by which police officers attempt to control gang-related activity—they simply present themselves and hope to see something suspicious; failing that, they hope that their presence will cause a suspicious reaction. But what if the presence of the police actually stops the suspected gang members from conducting suspicious activity—only to have the activity begin again when the police leave the scene? This possible gap in enforcement has led to the use of anti-loitering laws in many municipalities. In *City of Chicago v. Morales*, 527 U.S. 41 (1999), the Supreme Court invalidated one such law on due process grounds. The law established a criminal offense on the basis of four predicates: First, the police officer must reasonably believe that at least one of the two or more persons present in a "public place" is a "criminal street gang membe[r]." Second, the persons must be "loitering," which the ordinance defined as "remain[ing] in any one place with no apparent purpose." Third, the officer must then order "all" of the persons to disperse and remove themselves "from the area." Fourth, a person to be guilty must wilfully disobey the officer's order. If any person, whether a gang member or not, wilfully disobeyed the officer's order, that person would be guilty of violating the ordinance.

A majority of the Court, in a number of separate opinions, found that the ordinance was unconstitutionally vague because, in the words of Justice Stevens' plurality opinion, it violated "the requirement that a legislature establish minimal guidelines to govern law enforcement." That is, the ordinance provided essentially unlimited discretion for an officer to determine who was loitering and who was not.

The Justices in the majority in their various opinions took pains to note that the Court was not invalidating all anti-loitering legislation. Justice O'Connor's tempering language in her separate opinion is typical:

> It is important to courts and legislatures alike that we characterize more clearly the narrow scope of today's holding. As the ordinance comes to this Court, it is unconstitutionally vague. Nevertheless, there remain open to Chicago reasonable alternatives to combat the very real threat posed by gang intimidation and violence. For example, the Court properly and expressly distinguishes the ordinance from laws that require loiterers to have

a "harmful purpose," from laws that target only gang members, and from laws that incorporate limits on the area and manner in which the laws may be enforced. In addition, the ordinance here is unlike a law that directly prohibits the presence of a large collection of obviously brazen, insistent, and lawless gang members and hangers-on on the public ways that intimidates residents. Indeed, as the plurality notes, the city of Chicago has several laws that do exactly this. Chicago has even enacted a provision that "enables police officers to fulfill . . . their traditional functions," including "preserving the public peace." Specifically, Chicago's general disorderly conduct provision allows the police to arrest those who knowingly "provoke, make or aid in making a breach of peace."

Justice Scalia wrote a dissenting opinion. Justice Thomas wrote a separate dissent that was joined by the Chief Justice and Justice Scalia. The dissenters argued that the Court had impermissibly established a constitutional right to loiter; that the ordinance was not vague because police officers could not order dispersal unless a gang member was present and those who were loitering had no apparent purpose; and that the alternative forms of legislation suggested by the majority would be insufficient to protect against gang intimidation, because gang members often cease intimidating activity when police are present, only to begin again when police leave the scene.

Note on Hodari's Impact on Civil Rights Actions

The Court's decision in *Hodari* has had an effect on certain civil rights actions brought by those who are injured by police officers attempting to make an arrest. Where the claim for injury is based on the Fourth Amendment, the plaintiff must prove an unreasonable seizure. The Court in *Hodari* made clear that police activity preceding a seizure is not governed by the Fourth Amendment, and that a person who fails to submit to a non-physical show of authority is not protected by the Fourth Amendment.

The case of Carter v. Buscher, 973 F.2d 1328 (7th Cir.1992), illustrates the impact of *Hodari*. Lisa Ruhl Carter brought an action under 42 U.S.C. § 1983, for a violation of her husband Raymond Ruhl's Fourth Amendment rights, after Ruhl was killed during an attempted arrest. The court of appeals sets forth the facts as follows:

> If fact is stranger than fiction, this case is a prime example. Initially, the facts read like the script from Keystone Cops. But what began as a dubious scheme ended in tragic bloodshed.

> In January 1988, the Illinois State Police were investigating Ruhl for solicitation to murder his wife, Lisa Ruhl Carter. With the assistance of Ruhl's co-conspirator, the state police obtained sufficient evidence to authorize Ruhl's arrest. Arresting Ruhl, however, proved nettlesome. Based on reliable information, the state police knew that Ruhl ran a gun shop out of his home and bragged that he was always armed—even while working inside a prison as a correctional officer for the Illinois Department of Corrections ("DOC"), in violation of DOC regulations. To minimize Ruhl's access to weapons and thereby reduce the risk of injury to state police officers and bystanders, the state police officers concocted a scheme to arrest Ruhl on U.S. 51, just south of the Oconee, Illinois intersection.

> On January 15, 1988, state police officers Tamara Ann Byers, David P. McLearin and the late Virgil Lee Bensyl together with DOC officers Michael Heltsley and Michael McKinney carried out their ill-fated scheme. To set the

plan in motion, McKinney telephoned defendant Alfred E. Buscher, an assistant warden with the DOC. Buscher then telephoned Ruhl and asked Ruhl to assist his niece who was supposedly having car trouble on U.S. 51. According to the script, Byers would portray the stranded niece and Bensyl and McLearin would portray two friends who had been riding with her. All three wore street clothes in keeping with their roles. Heltsley and McKinney planned to stay in their car a short distance from the scene and wait for a signal from the officers on the scene indicating that Ruhl had been arrested. When Ruhl arrived, Byers would ask him to look at her car, and when Ruhl came to inspect the engine, Bensyl would shine a flashlight in Ruhl's eyes, announce that the three stranded motorists were state police and place Ruhl under arrest. Unfortunately, Ruhl followed a different script.

When Ruhl arrived at the scene, it was dark. Ruhl remained in his car with the motor on and the car in gear 20 to 25 feet behind the "stranded" car. While Bensyl and McLearin waited by the hood of Byers' car, Byers walked back to Ruhl's car alone, leaned down to talk with him through the driver's window and tried to persuade him to take a look at her engine. According to Byers, Ruhl appeared nervous. Apparently impatient with Byers' progress, Bensyl came back to Ruhl's car and stood behind Byers. Drawing his police flashlight, Bensyl shone it into Ruhl's eyes and announced, "state police."

Ruhl responded by drawing an automatic weapon and shooting over Byers' shoulder striking Bensyl in the chest. As Bensyl fell to the ground, Byers drew her weapon and began to fire at Ruhl through the rear side window and then through the rear window of the car. As the gunfire erupted, McLearin rushed toward Ruhl's car, but Ruhl shot at him three times through the windshield, and McLearin hit the ground wounded. Ruhl then turned his weapon on Byers who was still firing at him through his rear window. Kicking his car door open, Ruhl spun out of the car and fired another round at Byers, and Byers fired her last round in return. As Ruhl stepped toward Byers and raised his gun again, McLearin surfaced from a ditch behind Ruhl's car. Startled, Ruhl shot at McLearin. Meanwhile, Heltsley and McKinney arrived on the scene. Heltsley fired his shotgun, striking Ruhl in the chest. Ruhl collapsed, but when he reached for the handgun he had dropped, Byers grabbed it and fired once more at Ruhl. At the end of the shootout, which had lasted approximately a minute, Ruhl and Bensyl lay dead and McLearin lay bleeding on the side of the highway.

Nearly two years later, * * * Carter, ironically the intended victim of Ruhl's murder plot, filed this section 1983 action as administrator of Ruhl's estate alleging "that by reason of their ill conceived plan in the attempt to arrest [Ruhl] along a darkened highway instead of inside the correctional institution where he worked, the Defendants ... provoked a situation whereby unreasonable deadly force was used in the attempt to seize his person in violation of the Fourth Amendment...."

The court of appeals found that the Fourth Amendment did not protect against an ill-conceived and dangerous plan to effectuate an arrest. Rather, the question was whether Ruhl was unreasonably seized. The seizure did not occur until he submitted to authority—i.e., when he was shot dead. At that point, the seizure was eminently reasonable, because Ruhl had been firing at the officers. The court elaborated as follows:

> The Fourth Amendment prohibits unreasonable seizures not unreasonable, unjustified or outrageous conduct in general. Therefore, pre-seizure conduct is not subject to Fourth Amendment scrutiny. * * * Illinois DOC officer Heltsley

unquestionably seized Ruhl by shooting him in the chest. Prior to that, however, no "seizure" occurred, not even when officer Bensyl flashed his light and announced "state police." * * * [A] seizure requires not only that the reasonable person feel that he is not free to leave, but also that the subject actually yield to a show of authority from the police or be physically touched by the police. California v. Hodari. Carter has not argued (and there is no indication in the record) that prior to shooting Ruhl, the state police officers physically restrained Ruhl or that Ruhl yielded to any show of authority. Quite to the contrary, when Bensyl announced "state police," Ruhl did not submit to Bensyl; he shot him. Shooting Ruhl, then, constitutes the only "seizure" we must scrutinize under the Fourth Amendment.

Was shooting Ruhl "reasonable" under the Fourth Amendment? We need not linger long on this question. Ruhl's shooting rampage threatened the lives of all the officers at the scene. * * *

See also Mettler v. Whitledge, 165 F.3d 1197 (8th Cir.1999) (sending in an attack dog did not constitute an unreasonable seizure, where the citizen shot the dog before the dog got to him).

Summary of Seizure Cases

Professor Sundby has set forth the following "Accidental Tourist's guide-book" on the state of the law concerning seizures of persons under *Terry*:

> Travel is a considerable problem. One should be aware that law enforcement officers may stop someone and ask permission to look in his luggage even if the traveler has not acted in a fashion that would provoke articulable suspicion of wrongdoing. This is true whether traveling by land, air, or sea. If approached, the innocent traveler should not be alarmed but should state to the officer that he or she has no desire to converse and has other, more important appointments to keep. Although this might strike the traveler at first as rude and abrupt, and perhaps a bit frightening if the questioner is armed, the Supreme Court has made clear that the Fourth Amendment is not for the timid. Consequently, the wise traveler should carry a copy of the Fourth Amendment and display it to the questioner and thus avoid any unnecessary discourse. It is this writer's fervent hope that travel agents soon shall issue copies of the Fourth Amendment as standard procedure when writing airplane, bus, or train tickets.

Sundby, "Everyman's" Fourth Amendment: Privacy or Mutual Trust Between Government and Citizen?, 94 Colum.L.Rev.1751, 1793 (1994). Is Professor Sundby's assessment overly critical, or just about right?

3.   *Grounds for a Stop: Reasonable Suspicion*

The degree of suspicion required to make a stop is referred to as "reasonable suspicion" by the courts. See United States v. Brignoni–Ponce, 422 U.S. 873 (1975). As with the higher standard of probable cause, two separate questions arise in determining whether reasonable suspicion exists. The court must investigate the *source* of information upon which reasonable suspicion is based; and the court must evaluate whether that information is *sufficiently suspicious* to justify a stop.

a. Source of Information

In Adams v. Williams, supra, the Court considered whether an informant's tip could be credited toward reasonable suspicion. *Adams* did not consider, however, whether reasonable suspicion could be based on a tip from an anonymous informant.

Anonymous Tips: Alabama v. White

The Court relied heavily on *Adams* and Illinois v. Gates (discussed in the material on probable cause) in Alabama v. White, 496 U.S. 325 (1990), and held that an anonymous informant's tip that was "significantly corroborated" by a police officer's investigation provided reasonable suspicion for a stop. The police received an anonymous tip that White would be leaving a particular apartment in a brown Plymouth station wagon with the right taillight lens broken, and would be driving to Dobey's Motel with a brown attache case containing cocaine. The officers went to the apartment, and saw White enter a brown Plymouth station wagon with a broken right taillight. She was not carrying an attache case. They followed the station wagon as it took the most direct route toward Dobey's Motel. White was stopped just short of Dobey's Motel, and consented to the search of a brown attache case that was in the car. The officers found marijuana in the attache case, and three milligrams of cocaine in White's purse, which was searched during processing at the station. White argued that the stop was illegal because the officers did not have reasonable suspicion, and the evidence should therefore have been excluded as a product of the illegal stop.

Justice White, writing for a six-person majority, held that the stop was supported by reasonable suspicion. He noted that under the *Gates* "totality of the circumstances" approach to probable cause, an informant's veracity and basis of knowledge remain "highly relevant" in determining the value of the report of an informant. Justice White stated: "These factors are also relevant in the reasonable suspicion context, although allowance must be made in applying them for the lesser showing required to meet that standard."

Even given the lesser showing required, Justice White acknowledged that the anonymous tip did not itself provide reasonable suspicion, since it failed to show that the informant was reliable, and it gave no indication of the informant's basis for predicting White's activities. But the majority stated: "As there was in *Gates,* however, in this case there is more than the tip itself."

Justice White determined that the corroboration in *White* was not as substantial as that in *Gates.* Yet this was not fatal, since reasonable suspicion is a less stringent standard than probable cause. Justice White explained as follows:

> Reasonable suspicion is a less demanding standard than probable cause not only in the sense that reasonable suspicion can be established with information that is different in quantity or content than that required to establish probable cause, but also in the sense that reasonable suspicion can arise from information that is less reliable than that required to show probable cause.

The Court found that reasonable suspicion existed even though the corroboration of the tip was not complete, and even though the tip was not correct in some details. Justice White acknowledged that the officer's corroboration of the existence of the car was insignificant, since "anyone could have predicted that fact because it was a condition presumably existing at the time of the call." However, the caller's ability to predict White's future behavior (i.e., getting in the car and driving toward Dobey's motel) was "important" because:

> [I]t demonstrated inside information—a special familiarity with respondent's affairs. The general public would have had no way of knowing that respondent would shortly leave the building, get in the described car, and drive the most direct route to Dobey's Motel. Because only a small number of people are generally privy to an individual's itinerary, it is reasonable for police to believe that a person with access to such information is likely to also have access to reliable information about that individual's illegal activities. * * * When significant aspects of the caller's predictions were verified, there was reason to believe not only that the caller was honest but also that he was well informed, at least well enough to justify the stop.

Justice Stevens wrote a short dissenting opinion, joined by Justices Brennan and Marshall. The dissenters argued that the activity predicted by the informant and corroborated by the police (leaving an apartment and driving toward a motel) was completely innocent. Justice Stevens concluded as follows:

> Millions of people leave their apartments at about the same time every day carrying an attache case and heading for a destination known to their neighbors. Usually, however, the neighbors do not know what the briefcase contains. An anonymous neighbor's prediction about somebody's time of departure and probable destination is anything but a reliable basis for assuming that the commuter is in possession of an illegal substance— particularly when the person is not even carrying the attache case described by the tipster.

Questions After White

Does it make sense that the reasonable suspicion standard is less demanding as to both quantity and *quality* of information? Does the Court mean that certain information may be too unreliable to credit toward probable cause, but reliable enough to credit toward reasonable suspicion? Do you agree with the Court's premise that an informant's accurate prediction of future innocent activity makes it more likely that the informant is correct in his conclusion about the suspect's criminal activity? Reconsider Justice White's concurring opinion in *Spinelli* (discussed in the material on probable cause). Is it consistent with his majority opinion in *White?* See generally Rudstein, White on *White:* Anonymous Tips, Reasonable Suspicion, and the Constitution, 79 Ky.L.J. 661 (1991).

Anonymous Tips Concerning Gun Possession

In the following case, the Court considered whether an anonymous tip concerning possession of a gun constitutes reasonable suspicion when it is not corroborate by any predicted activity.

FLORIDA v. J.L.

Supreme Court of the United States, 2000.
529 U.S. 266.

Justice Ginsburg **delivered the opinion of the Court.**

The question presented in this case is whether an anonymous tip that a person is carrying a gun is, without more, sufficient to justify a police officer's stop and frisk of that person. We hold that it is not.

I

On October 13, 1995, an anonymous caller reported to the Miami–Dade Police that a young black male standing at a particular bus stop and wearing a plaid shirt was carrying a gun. So far as the record reveals, there is no audio recording of the tip, and nothing is known about the informant. Sometime after the police received the tip—the record does not say how long—two officers were instructed to respond. They arrived at the bus stop about six minutes later and saw three black males "just hanging out [there]." One of the three, respondent J.L., was wearing a plaid shirt. Apart from the tip, the officers had no reason to suspect any of the three of illegal conduct. The officers did not see a firearm, and J.L. made no threatening or otherwise unusual movements. One of the officers approached J.L., told him to put his hands up on the bus stop, frisked him, and seized a gun from J.L.'s pocket. The second officer frisked the other two individuals, against whom no allegations had been made, and found nothing. J.L., who was at the time of the frisk 10 days shy of his 16th birthday, was charged under state law with carrying a concealed firearm without a license and possessing a firearm while under the age of 18. He moved to suppress the gun as the fruit of an unlawful search, and the trial court granted his

motion. The intermediate appellate court reversed, but the Supreme Court of Florida quashed that decision and held the search invalid under the Fourth Amendment.

Anonymous tips, the Florida Supreme Court stated, are generally less reliable than tips from known informants and can form the basis for reasonable suspicion only if accompanied by specific indicia of reliability, for example, the correct forecast of a subject's "not easily predicted" movements. The tip leading to the frisk of J.L., the court observed, provided no such predictions, nor did it contain any other qualifying indicia of reliability. Two justices dissented. The safety of the police and the public, they maintained, justifies a "firearm exception" to the general rule barring investigatory stops and frisks on the basis of bare-boned anonymous tips.

* * * We granted certiorari, and now affirm the judgment of the Florida Supreme Court.

II

* * *

In the instant case, the officers' suspicion that J.L. was carrying a weapon arose not from any observations of their own but solely from a call made from an unknown location by an unknown caller. Unlike a tip from a known informant whose reputation can be assessed and who can be held responsible if her allegations turn out to be fabricated, see Adams v. Williams, 407 U.S. 143 (1972), "an anonymous tip alone seldom demonstrates the informant's basis of knowledge or veracity," Alabama v. White,

496 U.S., at 329. As we have recognized, however, there are situations in which an anonymous tip, suitably corroborated, exhibits "sufficient indicia of reliability to provide reasonable suspicion to make the investigatory stop." The question we here confront is whether the tip pointing to J.L. had those indicia of reliability.

In *White*, the police received an anonymous tip asserting that a woman was carrying cocaine and predicting that she would leave an apartment building at a specified time, get into a car matching a particular description, and drive to a named motel. Standing alone, the tip would not have justified a *Terry* stop. Only after police observation showed that the informant had accurately predicted the woman's movements, we explained, did it become reasonable to think the tipster had inside knowledge about the suspect and therefore to credit his assertion about the cocaine. Although the Court held that the suspicion in *White* became reasonable after police surveillance, we regarded the case as borderline. Knowledge about a person's future movements indicates some familiarity with that person's affairs, but having such knowledge does not necessarily imply that the informant knows, in particular, whether that person is carrying hidden contraband. We accordingly classified *White* as a "close case."

The tip in the instant case lacked the moderate indicia of reliability present in *White* and essential to the Court's decision in that case. The anonymous call concerning J.L. provided no predictive information and therefore left the police without means to test the informant's knowledge or credibility. That the allegation about the gun turned out to be correct does not suggest that the officers, prior to the frisks, had a reasonable basis for suspecting J.L. of engaging in unlawful conduct: The reasonableness of official suspicion must be measured by what the officers knew before they conducted their search. All the police had to go on in this case was the bare report of an unknown, unaccountable informant who neither explained how he knew about the gun nor supplied any basis for believing he had inside information about J.L. If *White* was a close case on the reliability of anonymous tips, this one surely falls on the other side of the line.

Florida contends that the tip was reliable because its description of the suspect's visible attributes proved accurate: There really was a young black male wearing a plaid shirt at the bus stop. * * * These contentions misapprehend the reliability needed for a tip to justify a *Terry* stop.

An accurate description of a subject's readily observable location and appearance is of course reliable in this limited sense: It will help the police correctly identify the person whom the tipster means to accuse. Such a tip, however, does not show that the tipster has knowledge of concealed criminal activity. The reasonable suspicion here at issue requires that a tip be reliable in its assertion of illegality, not just in its tendency to identify a determinate person.

A second major argument advanced by Florida and the United States as amicus is, in essence, that the standard *Terry* analysis should be modified to license a "firearm exception." Under such an exception, a tip alleging an illegal gun would justify a stop and frisk even if the accusation would fail standard pre-search reliability testing. We decline to adopt this position.

Firearms are dangerous, and extraordinary dangers sometimes justify unusual precautions. Our decisions recognize the serious threat that armed criminals pose to public safety;

Terry's rule, which permits protective police searches on the basis of reasonable suspicion rather than demanding that officers meet the higher standard of probable cause, responds to this very concern. But an automatic firearm exception to our established reliability analysis would rove too far. Such an exception would enable any person seeking to harass another to set in motion an intrusive, embarrassing police search of the targeted person simply by placing an anonymous call falsely reporting the target's unlawful carriage of a gun. Nor could one securely confine such an exception to allegations involving firearms. Several Courts of Appeals have held it per se foreseeable for people carrying significant amounts of illegal drugs to be carrying guns as well. If police officers may properly conduct *Terry* frisks on the basis of bare-boned tips about guns, it would be reasonable to maintain under the above-cited decisions that the police should similarly have discretion to frisk based on bareboned tips about narcotics. As we clarified when we made indicia of reliability critical in *Adams* and *White*, the Fourth Amendment is not so easily satisfied. Cf. Richards v. Wisconsin, 520 U.S. 385 (1997) (rejecting a per se exception to the "knock and announce" rule for narcotics cases partly because "the reasons for creating an exception in one category [of Fourth Amendment cases] can, relatively easily, be applied to others," thus allowing the exception to swallow the rule).

The facts of this case do not require us to speculate about the circumstances under which the danger alleged in an anonymous tip might be so great as to justify a search even without a showing of reliability. We do not say, for example, that a report of a person carrying a bomb need bear the indicia of reliability we demand for a report of a person carrying a firearm

before the police can constitutionally conduct a frisk. Nor do we hold that public safety officials in quarters where the reasonable expectation of Fourth Amendment privacy is diminished, such as airports, see Florida v. Rodriguez, 469 U.S. 1 (1984) (per curiam), and schools, see New Jersey v. T.L.O., 469 U.S. 325 (1985), cannot conduct protective searches on the basis of information insufficient to justify searches elsewhere.

Finally, the requirement that an anonymous tip bear standard indicia of reliability in order to justify a stop in no way diminishes a police officer's prerogative, in accord with *Terry*, to conduct a protective search of a person who has already been legitimately stopped. We speak in today's decision only of cases in which the officer's authority to make the initial stop is at issue. In that context, we hold that an anonymous tip lacking indicia of reliability of the kind contemplated in *Adams* and *White* does not justify a stop and frisk whenever and however it alleges the illegal possession of a firearm.

The judgment of the Florida Supreme Court is affirmed.

JUSTICE KENNEDY, with whom THE CHIEF JUSTICE joins, concurring.

On the record created at the suppression hearing, the Court's decision is correct. The Court says all that is necessary to resolve this case, and I join the opinion in all respects. It might be noted, however, that there are many indicia of reliability respecting anonymous tips that we have yet to explore in our cases.

When a police officer testifies that a suspect aroused the officer's suspicion, and so justifies a stop and frisk, the courts can weigh the officer's credibility and admit evidence seized pursuant to the frisk even if no one, aside from the officer and defendant themselves, was present or observed the seizure. An anonymous telephone tip without more is different, however; for even if the officer's testimony about receipt of the tip is found credible, there is a second layer of inquiry respecting the reliability of the informant that cannot be pursued. If the telephone call is truly anonymous, the informant has not placed his credibility at risk and can lie with impunity. The reviewing court cannot judge the credibility of the informant and the risk of fabrication becomes unacceptable.

On this record, then, the Court is correct in holding that the telephone tip did not justify the arresting officer's immediate stop and frisk of respondent. There was testimony that an anonymous tip came in by a telephone call and nothing more. The record does not show whether some notation or other documentation of the call was made either by a voice recording or tracing the call to a telephone number. * * *

It seems appropriate to observe that a tip might be anonymous in some sense yet have certain other features, either supporting reliability or narrowing the likely class of informants, so that the tip does provide the lawful basis for some police action. One such feature, as the Court recognizes, is that the tip predicts future conduct of the alleged criminal. There may be others. For example, if an unnamed caller with a voice which sounds the same each time tells police on two successive nights about criminal activity

which in fact occurs each night, a similar call on the third night ought not be treated automatically like the tip in the case now before us. In the instance supposed, there would be a plausible argument that experience cures some of the uncertainty surrounding the anonymity, justifying a proportionate police response. * * *

If an informant places his anonymity at risk, a court can consider this factor in weighing the reliability of the tip. An instance where a tip might be considered anonymous but nevertheless sufficiently reliable to justify a proportionate police response may be when an unnamed person driving a car the police officer later describes stops for a moment and, face to face, informs the police that criminal activity is occurring. * * *

Instant caller identification is widely available to police, and, if anonymous tips are proving unreliable and distracting to police, squad cars can be sent within seconds to the location of the telephone used by the informant. Voice recording of telephone tips might, in appropriate cases, be used by police to locate the caller. It is unlawful to make false reports to the police, and the ability of the police to trace the identity of anonymous telephone informants may be a factor which lends reliability to what, years earlier, might have been considered unreliable anonymous tips.

These matters, of course, must await discussion in other cases, where the issues are presented by the record.

J.L. and a Tip About Reckless Driving

How does the Court's analysis in *J.L.* apply if police receive an anonymous tip that a car is engaged in reckless driving and, when police officers observe the car on the road, where the informant said it would be, the driver is not at that point driving recklessly? Can the officers stop the car despite the lack of corroboration as to predictive activity? The court in United States v. Wheat, 278 F.3d 722 (8th Cir. 2001) considered this question and upheld the stop of the identified car. It relied on the language in *J.L.*, implying that the decision would be different if public safety were in imminent risk:

An erratic and possibly drunk driver poses an imminent threat to public safety. Of course, arguably so too does a citizen armed with a gun, yet the Supreme Court firmly declined to adopt an automatic firearm exception to the reliability requirement on that basis. However, there is a critical distinction between gun possession cases and potential drunk driving cases. In the possessory offense cases, law enforcement officers have two less invasive options not available to officers responding to a tip about a drunk driver. First, they may initiate a simple consensual encounter, for which no articulable suspicion is required. Needless to say, that is not possible when the suspect is driving a moving vehicle.

Alternatively, officers responding to a tip about a possessory violation may quietly observe the suspect for a considerable length of time, watching for other indications of incipient criminality that would give them reasonable suspicion to make an investigatory stop—as, for example, in *Terry*, where an experienced officer witnessed several men casing a joint. By contrast, where an anonymous tip alleges erratic and possibly drunk driving, a responding officer faces a stark choice. * * * [H]e can intercept the vehicle immediately and ascertain whether its driver is operating under the influence of drugs or alcohol. Or he can follow and observe, with three possible outcomes: the suspect drives without incident for several miles; the suspect drifts harmlessly onto the shoulder, providing corroboration of the tip and probable cause for an arrest; or the suspect veers into oncoming traffic, or fails to stop at a light, or otherwise causes a sudden and potentially devastating accident. In contradistinction to *J.L.*, where the suspect was merely standing at the bus stop, in this context the suspect is extremely mobile, and potentially highly dangerous. A drunk driver is not at all unlike a "bomb," and a mobile one at that. Thus, we think that there is a substantial government interest in effecting a stop as quickly as possible.

b. Quantum of Suspicion

The Supreme Court in United States v. Cortez, 449 U.S. 411 (1981), set forth the following oft-cited test for determining whether reasonable suspicion exists in a given set of circumstances:

[T]he totality of the circumstances—the whole picture—must be taken into account. Based upon that whole picture the detaining officers must have a particularized and objective basis for suspecting the particular person stopped of criminal activity. * * * [P]articularized suspicion contains two elements, each of which must be present before a stop is permissible. First, the assessment must be based upon all the circumstances. The analysis proceeds with various objective observations, information from police reports, if such are available, and considerations of the modes or patterns of operation of certain kinds of lawbreakers. From these data, a trained officer draws inferences and makes deductions—inferences and deductions that might well elude an untrained person.

The process does not deal with hard certainties, but with probabilities. Long before the law of probabilities was articulated as such, practical people formulated certain common sense conclusions about human behavior; * * *.

The second element contained in the idea that an assessment of the whole picture must yield a particularized suspicion is the concept that the process just described must raise a suspicion that the particular individual being stopped is engaged in wrongdoing.

Comparison to Probable Cause

The Court in *Terry* reasoned that, because a stop was less intrusive than an arrest, it could be justified upon a lesser showing of proof than the probable cause required for an arrest. Courts have struggled with the meaning of reasonable suspicion and with how the reasonable suspicion standard differs from that of probable cause. It is clear, however, that the standards are materially different. There are many cases in which the courts have held that reasonable suspicion existed but probable cause did not. See Florida v. Royer, 460 U.S. 491 (1983) (consent tainted where it was obtained while Royer was under arrest and officers had only reasonable suspicion and not probable cause to believe that Royer was involved in drug activity); United States v. Anderson, 981 F.2d 1560 (10th Cir.1992)(reasonable suspicion, but not probable cause existed, where the defendant was twice seen leaving a house in which narcotics were sold, and parked his car a few blocks from the house, near a truck where narcotics were stored; since the defendant was arrested rather than stopped, the evidence obtained as a result of the detention should have been suppressed).

The analytical framework used by the courts in assessing reasonable suspicion is similar to that employed in assessing probable cause. Thus, a court will undertake a common sense analysis of the facts presented; it will give deference to the expertise of law enforcement officers, who may know through experience that certain facts are indicative of criminal activity (e.g., that drug dealers often carry beepers or cellular phones); it will consider the totality of the circumstances because, while each fact may seem innocent if considered individually, the factors considered in their totality may not be so easily explained away; and it will not expect the officers to be infallible.

The most important difference between reasonable suspicion and probable cause is that reasonable suspicion is a less demanding standard of proof—a stop is permissible upon something less than the fair probability standard that defines probable cause. Some courts have defined reasonable suspicion as a fair *possibility* (as opposed to probability) of criminal activity. It is appropriate to think of reasonable suspicion as "possible cause."

A probability-based example of the difference between reasonable suspicion and probable cause is presented by the facts of United States v. Winsor, 846 F.2d 1569 (9th Cir.1988). Officers chased suspected bank robbers fleeing from the bank into a hotel. The hotel had approximately 40 guest rooms, and the officers had no idea where in the hotel the robbers were hiding. The question was whether there was probable cause to search each of the hotel rooms for the suspects. The court found that a one-in-forty probability was too small to support probable cause, but that the low probability did amount to reasonable suspicion: "The odds on discovering the suspect in the first room upon whose door the police knocked were high enough to support a founded suspicion. The odds favoring discovery increase as rooms are searched. At some point, perhaps at the last two or three unsearched rooms, probable cause may be said to exist." Conversely, at some point of improbability, reasonable suspicion would not have existed—for example, if the hotel had 600 rooms, there would not have been reasonable suspicion to believe that the suspects were in any particular room. Because there was only reasonable suspicion and not probable cause in *Winsor*, the court held that the search of the hotel room in which the suspects were actually found was illegal. A search for law enforcement purposes requires probable cause and cannot be justified under *Terry*.

Assessment of Probabilities

The Court applied the *Cortez* totality of circumstances test in the following case.

UNITED STATES v. ARVIZU

Supreme Court of the United States, 2002.
534 U.S. 266.

CHIEF JUSTICE REHNQUIST **delivered the opinion of the Court**.

Respondent Ralph Arvizu was stopped by a border patrol agent while driving on an unpaved road in a remote area of southeastern Arizona. A search of his vehicle turned up more than 100 pounds of marijuana. The District Court for the District of Arizona denied respondent's motion to suppress, but the Court of Appeals for the Ninth Circuit reversed. In the course of its opinion, it categorized certain factors relied upon by the District Court as simply out of bounds in deciding whether there was "reasonable suspicion" for the stop. We hold that the Court of Appeals' methodology was contrary to our prior decisions and that it reached the wrong result in this case.

On an afternoon in January 1998, Agent Clinton Stoddard was working at a border patrol checkpoint along U.S. Highway 191 approximately 30 miles north of Douglas, Arizona. Douglas has a population of about 13,000 and is situated on the United States–Mexico border in the southeastern part of the State. Only two highways lead north from Douglas. See App. 157. Highway 191 leads north to Interstate 10, which passes through Tucson and Phoenix. State Highway 80 heads

northeast through less populated areas toward New Mexico, skirting south and east of the portion of the Coronado National Forest that lies approximately 20 miles northeast of Douglas.

The checkpoint is located at the intersection of 191 and Rucker Canyon Road, an unpaved east-west road that connects 191 and the Coronado National Forest. When the checkpoint is operational, border patrol agents stop the traffic on 191 as part of a coordinated effort to stem the flow of illegal immigration and smuggling across the international border. Agents use roving patrols to apprehend smugglers trying to circumvent the checkpoint by taking the backroads, including those roads through the sparsely populated area between Douglas and the national forest. Magnetic sensors, or "intrusion devices," facilitate agents' efforts in patrolling these areas. Directionally sensitive, the sensors signal the passage of traffic that would be consistent with smuggling activities.

Sensors are located along the only other northbound road from Douglas besides Highways 191 and 80: Leslie Canyon Road. Leslie Canyon Road runs roughly parallel to 191, about halfway between 191 and the border of the Coronado National Forest, and ends when it intersects Rucker Canyon Road. It is unpaved beyond the 10–mile stretch leading out of Douglas and is very rarely traveled except for use by local ranchers and forest service personnel. Smugglers commonly try to avoid the 191 checkpoint by heading west on Rucker Canyon Road from Leslie Canyon Road and thence to Kuykendall Cutoff Road, a primitive dirt road that leads north approximately 12 miles east of 191. From there, they can gain access to Tucson and Phoenix.

Around 2:15 p.m., Stoddard received a report via Douglas radio that a Leslie Canyon Road sensor had triggered. This was significant to Stoddard for two reasons. First, it suggested to him that a vehicle might be trying to circumvent the checkpoint. Second, the timing coincided with the point when agents begin heading back to the checkpoint for a shift change, which leaves the area unpatrolled. Stoddard knew that alien smugglers did extensive scouting and seemed to be most active when agents were en route back to the checkpoint. Another border patrol agent told Stoddard that the same sensor had gone off several weeks before and that he had apprehended a minivan using the same route and witnessed the occupants throwing bundles of marijuana out the door.

Stoddard drove eastbound on Rucker Canyon Road to investigate. As he did so, he received another radio report of sensor activity. It indicated that the vehicle that had triggered the first sensor was heading westbound on Rucker Canyon Road. He continued east, passing Kuykendall Cutoff Road. He saw the dust trail of an approaching vehicle about a half mile away. Stoddard had not seen any other vehicles and, based on the timing, believed that this was the one that had tripped the sensors. He pulled off to the side

of the road at a slight slant so he could get a good look at the oncoming vehicle as it passed by.

It was a minivan, a type of automobile that Stoddard knew smugglers used. As it approached, it slowed dramatically, from about 50–55 to 25–30 miles per hour. He saw five occupants inside. An adult man was driving, an adult woman sat in the front passenger seat, and three children were in the back. The driver appeared stiff and his posture very rigid. He did not look at Stoddard and seemed to be trying to pretend that Stoddard was not there. Stoddard thought this suspicious because in his experience on patrol most persons look over and see what is going on, and in that area most drivers give border patrol agents a friendly wave. Stoddard noticed that the knees of the two children sitting in the very back seat were unusually high, as if their feet were propped up on some cargo on the floor.

At that point, Stoddard decided to get a closer look, so he began to follow the vehicle as it continued westbound on Rucker Canyon Road toward Kuykendall Cutoff Road. Shortly thereafter, all of the children, though still facing forward, put their hands up at the same time and began to wave at Stoddard in an abnormal pattern. It looked to Stoddard as if the children were being instructed. Their odd waving continued on and off for about four to five minutes.

Several hundred feet before the Kuykendall Cutoff Road intersection, the driver signaled that he would turn. At one point, the driver turned the signal off, but just as he approached the intersection he put it back on and abruptly turned north onto Kuykendall. The turn was significant to Stoddard because it was made at the last place that would have allowed the minivan to avoid the checkpoint. Also,

Kuykendall, though passable by a sedan or van, is rougher than either Rucker Canyon or Leslie Canyon roads, and the normal traffic is four-wheel-drive vehicles. Stoddard did not recognize the minivan as part of the local traffic agents encounter on patrol and he did not think it likely that the minivan was going to or coming from a picnic outing. He was not aware of any picnic grounds on Turkey Creek, which could be reached by following Kuykendall Cutoff all the way up. * * * And he had never seen anyone picnicking or sightseeing near where the first sensor went off.

Stoddard radioed for a registration check and learned that the minivan was registered to an address in Douglas that was four blocks north of the border in an area notorious for alien and narcotics smuggling. After receiving the information, Stoddard decided to make a vehicle stop. He approached the driver and learned that his name was Ralph Arvizu. Stoddard asked if respondent would mind if he looked inside and searched the vehicle. Respondent agreed, and Stoddard discovered marijuana in a black duffel bag under the feet of the two children in the back seat. Another bag containing marijuana was behind the rear seat. In all, the van contained 128.85 pounds of marijuana, worth an estimated $99,080.

Respondent was charged with possession with intent to distribute marijuana in violation of 21 U.S.C. § 841(a)(1) (1994 ed.). He moved to suppress the marijuana, arguing among other things that Stoddard did not have reasonable suspicion to stop the vehicle as required by the Fourth Amendment. After holding a hearing where Stoddard and respondent testified, the District Court for the District of Arizona ruled otherwise. It pointed to a number of the facts described above and noted particularly that any

recreational areas north of Rucker Canyon would have been accessible from Douglas via 191 and another paved road, making it unnecessary to take a 40–to–50–mile trip on dirt roads.

The Court of Appeals for the Ninth Circuit reversed. In its view, fact-specific weighing of circumstances or other multifactor tests introduced "a troubling degree of uncertainty and unpredictability" into the Fourth Amendment analysis. It therefore "attempt[ed] . . . to describe and clearly delimit the extent to which certain factors may be considered by law enforcement officers in making stops such as the stop involv[ing]" respondent. After characterizing the District Court's analysis as relying on a list of 10 factors, the Court of Appeals proceeded to examine each in turn. It held that 7 of the factors, including respondent's slowing down, his failure to acknowledge Stoddard, the raised position of the children's knees, and their odd waving carried little or no weight in the reasonable-suspicion calculus. The remaining factors—the road's use by smugglers, the temporal proximity between respondent's trip and the agents' shift change, and the use of minivans by smugglers—were not enough to render the stop permissible. We granted certiorari to review the decision of the Court of Appeals because of its importance to the enforcement of federal drug and immigration laws.

* * *

When discussing how reviewing courts should make reasonable-suspicion determinations, we have said repeatedly that they must look at the "totality of the circumstances" of each case to see whether the detaining officer has a "particularized and objective basis" for suspecting legal wrongdoing. This process allows officers to draw on their own experience and specialized training to make inferences from and deductions about the cumulative information available to them that "might well elude an untrained person." Although an officer's reliance on a mere "hunch" is insufficient to justify a stop, the likelihood of criminal activity need not rise to the level required for probable cause, and it falls considerably short of satisfying a preponderance of the evidence standard.

Our cases have recognized that the concept of reasonable suspicion is somewhat abstract. But we have deliberately avoided reducing it to a neat set of legal rules. * * *

We think that the approach taken by the Court of Appeals here departs sharply from the teachings of these cases. The court's evaluation and rejection of seven of the listed factors in isolation from each other does not take into account the "totality of the circumstances," as our cases have understood that phrase. The court appeared to believe that each observation by Stoddard that was by itself readily susceptible to an innocent explanation was entitled to "no weight." *Terry*, however, precludes this sort of divide-and-conquer analysis. The officer in *Terry* observed the petitioner and his companions repeatedly walk back and forth, look into a store window, and confer with one another. Although each of the series of acts was "perhaps innocent in itself," we held that, taken together, they "warranted further investigation."

The Court of Appeals' view that it was necessary to "clearly delimit" an officer's consideration of certain factors to reduce "troubling ... uncertainty," also runs counter to our cases and underestimates the usefulness of the reasonable-suspicion standard in guiding officers in the field.

* * * Take, for example, the court's positions that respondent's deceleration could not be considered because "slowing down after spotting a law enforcement vehicle is an entirely normal response that is in no way indicative of criminal activity" and that his failure to acknowledge Stoddard's presence provided no support because there were "no 'special circumstances' rendering 'innocent avoidance ... improbable.' "We think it quite reasonable that a driver's slowing down, stiffening of posture, and failure to acknowledge a sighted law enforcement officer might well be unremarkable in one instance (such as a busy San Francisco highway) while quite unusual in another (such as a remote portion of rural southeastern Arizona). Stoddard was entitled to make an assessment of the situation in light of his specialized training and familiarity with the customs of the area's inhabitants. To the extent that a totality of the circumstances approach may render appellate review less circumscribed by precedent than otherwise, it is the nature of the totality rule.

* * *

Having considered the totality of the circumstances and given due weight to the factual inferences drawn by the law enforcement officer and District Court Judge, we hold that Stoddard had reasonable suspicion to believe that respondent was engaged in illegal activity. It was reasonable for Stoddard to infer from his observations, his registration check, and his experience as a border patrol agent that respondent had set out from Douglas along a little-traveled route used by smugglers to avoid the 191 checkpoint. Stoddard's knowledge further supported a commonsense inference that respondent intended to pass through the area at a time when officers would be leaving their backroads patrols to change shifts. The likelihood that respondent and his family were on a picnic outing was diminished by the fact that the minivan had turned away from the known recreational areas accessible to the east on Rucker Canyon Road. Corroborating this inference was the fact that recreational areas farther to the north would have been easier to reach by taking 191, as opposed to the 40–to–50–mile trip on unpaved and primitive roads. The children's elevated knees suggested the existence of concealed cargo in the passenger compartment. Finally * * * Stoddard's assessment of respondent's reactions upon seeing him and the children's mechanical-like waving, which continued for a full four to five minutes, were entitled to some weight.

Respondent argues that we must rule in his favor because the facts suggested a family in a minivan on a holiday outing. A determination that reasonable suspicion exists, however, need not rule out the possibility of innocent conduct. Undoubtedly, each of these factors alone is susceptible to innocent explanation, and some factors are more probative than others. Taken together, we believe they sufficed to form a particularized and objective basis for Stoddard's stopping the vehicle, making the stop reasonable within the meaning of the Fourth Amendment.

The judgment of the Court of Appeals is therefore reversed, and the case is remanded for further proceedings consistent with this opinion.

It is so ordered.

[The concurring opinion of Justice Scalia is omitted.]

Examples of Reasonable Suspicion

As stated in *Arvizu*, a determination of whether reasonable suspicion exists requires a review of the totality of the circumstances. No two cases are exactly alike. The best way to get a handle on the quantum of evidence required for reasonable suspicion is to review some of the cases. The following are the facts of a case in which reasonable suspicion was found:

On Wednesday, August 30, 1995, Felix Barron–Cabrera was driving north on New Mexico Highway 180, in a rented Ryder truck. The City of Deming, New Mexico (pop.15,000) was behind him, and Silver City was ahead. Except during morning and afternoon rush hours, when some workers commute between Deming and Silver City, Highway 180 is lightly traveled. There are no established Border Patrol checkpoints on Highway 180, which bypasses other north-south routes with established checkpoints. However, in April 1995, the Northern County Unit of the Deming Border Patrol station began daily patrols of Highway 180 north of Deming. Between April 1995 and October 1995, that Unit apprehended 30 "smuggling loads" carrying a total of 140 illegal aliens on Highway 180 north of Deming.

At about 2:45 p.m., Barron–Cabrera drove a Ryder truck past a marked Border Patrol vehicle (a white Chevy Suburban) which was being driven southbound by Officer Robert Glenn Garcia. Officer Carlos Roches was a passenger in the Border Patrol vehicle. At that time, Barron–Cabrera was driving north at about 55 mph, and Officer Garcia was driving south at 45 mph. Officer Garcia testified that he was suspicious of Ryder trucks because he knew that a Border Patrol unit operating out of Lordsburg, New Mexico had recently apprehended a rental truck filled with either illegal aliens or narcotics. He was especially suspicious of Ryder trucks, such as Barron–Cabrera's, which were neither towing nor driving in tandem with another vehicle. This was because, in Officer Garcia's life experience, "[n]ormally you would see a Ryder truck with the personally owned vehicle of the driver, say, in tow behind it, or there may be a husband and wife, a spouse, driving their personally owned vehicle behind it as they were moving to wherever they were going."

Officer Garcia testified that he was first able to observe Barron–Cabrera when the two vehicles were about 120 feet apart from each other. Garcia claimed that he and his partner Officer Roches then made the following observations as the cars drew closer: (1) Barron–Cabrera had a passenger in the cab of the truck; (2) Barron–Cabrera, the driver, looked at Garcia with a surprised look as the two vehicles passed; (3) Barron–Cabrera's eyes got wider after looking at the Border Patrol vehicle; (4) Barron–Cabrera then looked straight forward at the road, with both hands on the steering wheel in the 10:00 and 2:00 position; and (5) Barron–Cabrera's passenger also looked at the Border Patrol vehicle once, looked a second time, and then stared straight forward. At the speeds the two vehicles were moving, Officer Garcia would have had nine-elevenths of one second to make these observations, before the two vehicles passed each other.

Officer Garcia then pulled onto the southbound shoulder of the road, to maintain surveillance of the northbound Ryder truck in his side-view mirror. As soon as Officer Garcia pulled over, however, he saw the Ryder truck hit its brake lights. He then immediately turned his Border Patrol vehicle around, and began to "tail" Barron–Cabrera's Ryder truck as it proceeded north on Highway 180. Garcia testified that as he approached the Ryder truck from behind, he and Officer Roches could see in the Ryder truck's outside mirrors that Barron–Cabrera and his passenger were "keeping an eye" on the Border Patrol vehicle by moving their heads in jerky fashions to see into the outside mirrors.

While the Border Patrol vehicle "tailed" the Ryder truck at close distance for about two miles, the Ryder truck slowed down from about 58 mph to about 45 mph (the speed limit was 55 mph). Officer Garcia also testified that, while tailing the Ryder Truck, he observed it touch both the shoulder of the road and the center line. However, he explicitly stated that he stopped the truck not for any traffic violation, but exclusively "[t]o ascertain whether or not they were illegal aliens."

After following the Ryder truck north on Highway 180 for about two miles, Officer Garcia pulled it over. [A subsequent search of the truck found 21 illegal aliens.]

Barron–Cabrera proffered two arguments in support of his motion to suppress. First, he contended that the officer's testimony concerning the driver's and passenger's reaction was not credible and therefore could not count toward a finding of reasonable suspicion. Second, he contended that even if the officer's account was credible, the facts were insufficient to constitute reasonable suspicion.

On the question of credibility, the court noted that the trial judge found the officer to be credible, and that this determination was entitled to substantial deference:

In the present case, the district court credited Officer Garcia's testimony, and thereby found that the factual events at issue occurred as Officer Garcia described them. The court's finding in this regard is a "finding of historical fact" which we review only for "clear error" * * * for only the trial judge can be aware of the variations in demeanor and tone of voice that bear so heavily on the listener's understanding of and belief in what is said. This is not to suggest that the trial judge may insulate his findings from review by denominating them credibility determinations, for factors other than demeanor and inflection go into the decisions whether or not to believe a witness. Documents or objective evidence may contradict the witness' story; or the story itself may be so internally inconsistent or implausible on its face that a reasonable factfinder would not credit it. Where such factors are present, the court of appeals may well find clear error even in a finding purportedly based on a credibility determination. But when a trial judge's finding is based on his decision to credit the testimony of one of two or more witnesses, each of whom has told a coherent and facially plausible story that is not contradicted by extrinsic evidence, that finding, if not internally inconsistent, can virtually never be clear error.

Barron–Cabrera argued that the trial court did clearly err, because the officer had only nine-elevenths of one second to observe Barron–Cabrera and his passenger exhibit "surprised or scared" facial expressions, widen their eyes, look back to watch the Border Patrol vehicle go by, return to looking straight forward with both hands gripping the steering wheel, look a second time, and then stare straight forward again. This was because Officer Garcia testified that he was traveling southbound at 45 mph, that Barron–Cabrera was traveling northbound at 55 mph, and that Garcia was first able to observe Barron–Cabrera and his companion from a distance of 120 feet. But even given that limited time period, the court found no clear error in the trial court's crediting of the officer's testimony:

> While nine-elevenths of a second is in many respects a short duration of time, we note that it is nearly twice the interval in which a major-league baseball batter must observe the trajectory of an approaching pitch, determine what kind of pitch it is, decide whether or not to swing at it, and then, if indicated, swing his bat into a proper position to hit the ball. We recognize, of course, that Officer Garcia is not a major-league baseball player. However, nine-elevenths of a second is roughly the interval in which a high-school baseball player must complete the same calculations. Further, Officer Garcia could draw upon three-and-a-half years of experience at observing the reactions of motorists in helping him decipher what he was quickly observing.

> In addition, we reiterate that the district court expressly found that Officer Garcia was "a credible witness" generally, and also that "the agent's testimony was credible" with respect to the particular stop at issue. Here, we cannot say that Officer Garcia's testimony was so implausible on its face that no reasonable trier of fact would have credited it. We therefore hold that the district court did not commit clear error when it credited Officer Garcia's factual account of the events leading up to the traffic stop.

On the question of whether there was reasonable suspicion, the court agreed with the trial court that the totality of circumstances made it reasonably possible that illegal aliens were being transported in the Ryder truck. The court summarized as follows:

> In sum, the "totality of the circumstances" in the present case amount to this: Barron–Cabrera and a companion were driving: (1) a Ryder truck unaccompanied by another vehicle towed or driving in tandem; (2) on Highway 180, a lightly traveled road rarely used for household moves; (3) which was reasonably near the Mexican border; (4) which was a known smuggling corridor which bypassed every permanent border checkpoint in the vicinity; and (5) upon which four vehicles carrying 32 aliens had already been apprehended within the same month. When Barron–Cabrera spotted a Border Patrol vehicle, (6) he became noticeably agitated; (7) he tapped on his brakes and slowed to nearly ten miles per hour below the speed limit; (8) he drove over the center line and the shoulder line; and (9) he drove in a stiff manner which Officer Garcia had observed other smugglers assume when tailed by a law enforcement vehicle. In our opinion, these factors, considered as a whole, establish sufficient reasonable suspicion to support Officer Garcia's traffic stop.

Is it really suspicious that a Ryder truck is traveling unaccompanied by another vehicle? What difference does it make that other illegal aliens had been transported along the same route, if there is no indication that Barron–Cabrera was involved in these previous acts? Would you be nervous if a Border Patrol vehicle passed you, pulled over, turned around, and began to tail you, all on a remote highway, and with you in a Ryder truck? Would that make you drive in a "stiff" manner? If all of the listed factors can be explained innocently, is there something about all the factors put together that makes Barron–Cabrera's activity suspicious? If so, what factors could you take out to make the totality *not* sufficiently suspicious to support a stop?

Here are the facts of another case in which reasonable suspicion was found:

> At 1:00 p.m. two Boston police detectives in an unmarked car were patrolling that portion of Boston known as the "Combat Zone." The Combat Zone is a high crime area known for prostitution and drug-dealing. As the officers were stopped at a light, they noticed a grey Thunderbird automobile stopped on the curb of Washington Street with a man at the wheel. As the officers watched, a second man approached the Thunderbird from the sidewalk and engaged the driver in a twenty second conversation through the open passenger-side window. The second man got into the car and had an additional five or ten second conversation with the driver. The car then pulled out and proceeded for two blocks until it made a right turn onto Hayward Place, a short street which connects Washington Street and Harrison Avenue. The officers followed in their unmarked car. Hayward Place was deserted. The Thunderbird parked on Hayward Place, and the officers parked well behind it with an unobstructed view. The officers observed the driver and passenger engaged in a thirty second discussion with their heads inclined toward each other. The passenger then got out of the car and walked back toward Washington Street. One officer approached the car, ordered the driver out, noticed a bulge, and pursuant to a pat-down frisk uncovered a spring-activated knife. The officer arrested the driver for carrying an illegal weapon, and in a search incident to arrest eleven grams of cocaine were uncovered.

The court confronted with these facts in United States v. Trullo, 809 F.2d 108 (1st Cir.1987), stated that the officer's seizure of the driver went to the "outermost reaches of a permissible *Terry* stop," and that "today's satisfactory explanation may very well be tomorrow's lame excuse." But the court did uphold the police conduct, relying on the high crime area, the officers' expertise in determining whether drug activity was afoot, the short nature of the conversation between the driver and passenger, and the fact that the passenger walked back toward the place where he had met the car. This latter factor meant that it was "unlikely that the man was seeking transportation." The court concluded that while it would be possible to "hypothesize some innocent explanation" for the conduct, the test for a stop is whether there is reasonable suspicion of criminal activity, and not whether the facts can be construed as innocent. Judge Bownes, in dissent, asked the following question: "If a citizen lets another person into his car on Washington Street, where must he let him off to avoid an armed stop by the police?" Judge Bownes claimed that the majority "seems to allow armed stops of individuals who meet in the Combat Zone on the basis of unlimited deference to police discretion." Who has the better of the argument? Who has more accurately applied the *Cortez* test?

Example of Reasonable Suspicion Lacking

While most of the reported cases assessing reasonable suspicion have found that the officers in question had sufficient proof to justify a stop, there are a few cases in which the facts are so innocent that the reviewing court finds the stop invalid. An example is United States v. Rodriguez, 976 F.2d 592 (9th Cir.1992). Officers sitting in a marked car alongside Interstate 8 in California saw Rodriguez drive toward them in a 1976 Ford Ranchero. They noticed that he looked Hispanic, sat up straight, kept both hands on the wheel, and looked straight ahead. He did not "acknowledge" the agents' presence, which they thought suspicious because all the other traffic passing by had acknowledged the presence of the officers. The agents testified that Interstate 8 is a "notorious route for alien smugglers" and that Ford Rancheros have a space behind the seat where illegal aliens can be concealed. The agents followed Rodriguez. They testified that his car responded sluggishly when it went over a bump, as if heavily loaded, rather than with a "crisp, light movement" that was typical of a Ford Ranchero. They also noted that, while being followed, Rodriguez looked often into his rear view mirror and swerved slightly within his lane. On the basis of this information, the officers stopped Rodriguez's vehicle. A subsequent search pursuant to consent yielded 168 pounds of marijuana. Rodriguez argued that the consent was tainted as a product of an unlawful stop.

The court held that reasonable suspicion did not exist to stop Rodriguez, and therefore the evidence was illegally obtained. It first noted that the testimony of the officers at the suppression hearing was eerily similar to that provided in other cases, so similar that "an inquiring mind may wonder about the recurrence of such fortunate parallelism in the experiences of the arresting agents." The court stated that it could not accept "what has come to appear to be a prefabricated or recycled profile of suspicious behavior very likely to sweep many ordinary citizens into a generality of suspicious appearance merely on hunch." According to the court, the factors cited by the agents "describe too many individuals to create a reasonable suspicion that this particular defendant was engaged in criminal activity." The court concluded as follows:

> In short, the agents in this case saw a Hispanic man cautiously and attentively driving a 16 year-old Ford with a worn suspension, who glanced in his rear view mirror while being followed by agents in a marked Border Patrol car. This profile could certainly fit hundreds or thousands of law abiding daily users of the highways of Southern California.

Is the court's finding of no reasonable suspicion sustainable after *Arvizu*? Are the facts of *Arvizu*, in their totality, more suspicious? See also United States v. Peters, 10 F.3d 1517 (10th Cir.1993)(where two Nigerians in a Ryder truck were pulled over for a traffic violation, and consented to a search that uncovered no evidence, they could not be stopped later down the road on the basis that they appeared nervous when being followed by another marked police car); United States v. Davis, 94 F.3d 1465 (10th Cir.1996) (no reasonable suspicion to stop a person with a criminal record who parked outside a store that sold liquor without a license, made and broke eye contact with police officers, and walked away with his hands in his pockets).

Reasonable Suspicion of a Completed Crime: United States v. Hensley

Most of the cases discussed above evaluated whether the officer had reasonable suspicion that the suspect was either committing a crime or about to commit a crime. Can a *Terry* stop be made on the basis of reasonable suspicion to believe that the suspect has *already* committed a crime? The Court in United States v. Hensley, 469 U.S. 221 (1985), confronted these facts:

> Several days after a tavern robbery in St. Bernard, Ohio (a Cincinnati suburb), a St. Bernard police officer interviewed an informant who stated that Hensley drove the getaway car. The officer obtained a written statement from the informant and immediately issued a "wanted flyer" to other police departments in the metropolitan area. The flyer stated that Hensley was wanted for investigation of an aggravated robbery, described Hensley and the date and location of the robbery, warned that Hensley should be considered armed and dangerous, and asked other departments to pick up and hold Hensley for the St. Bernard police.

> In a Kentucky suburb of Cincinnati, an officer who had heard the flyer read aloud several times stopped a car driven by Hensley. Although the officer let Hensley drive away, he inquired whether there was an outstanding warrant for his arrest. Two other officers in separate patrol cars interrupted to say that there might be an Ohio warrant on Hensley. The three officers then looked for Hensley while the dispatcher looked for the flyer and mistakenly telephoned Cincinnati to inquire about the flyer. One of the officers spotted Hensley's car and, after being advised by the dispatcher that Cincinnati was hunting for a warrant, he pulled the car over and approached with a drawn service revolver. A second officer arrived at the scene, saw a gun under the seat of a passenger known to be a convicted felon, arrested the passenger, and searched the car. When another gun was found, Hensley was arrested for illegal handgun possession.

Justice O'Connor, writing for a unanimous Court, held that *Terry* was not confined to prospective crimes; the power granted by *Terry* may also be exercised to investigate completed crimes. Her opinion approved stops where "police have a reasonable suspicion, grounded in specific and articulable facts, that a person they encounter was involved in or is wanted in connection with a completed felony." Relying on the "collective knowledge" doctrine established in Whiteley v. Warden, [discussed in the materials on probable cause], Justice O'Connor concluded that one department or officer could act to make a stop if another officer or department had sufficient cause to make the stop and asked for assistance. She applied her analysis to the facts and concluded that the St. Bernard police had a reasonable suspicion that Hensley committed a crime, that the Kentucky officers properly relied on the flyer, and that the stop was carried out in compliance with *Terry*.

Relevance of the Race of the Suspect

The court in *Rodriguez, supra,* expressed concern that an overly broad test of reasonable suspicion could result in a dragnet for Hispanics. Can the suspect's race ever be taken into account explicitly in determining whether reasonable suspicion exists? When the question is whether the suspect sufficiently matches the description of a perpetrator of a completed crime, the suspect's race must obviously be considered relevant. For example, if a bank teller describes a robber as an Asian male in his 40's, an officer assessing reasonable suspicion must necessarily consider a person's race in determining whether to stop him. More difficult questions arise, however, when an officer considers a person suspicious simply because he is found in an area ordinarily not frequented by members of the suspect's racial group. Is it appropriate to consider it suspicious that an African–American male is walking down the street of an affluent suburb at 11 p.m., where the same conduct from a white male would not be suspicious in the least? Similarly, difficult questions exist when officers argue that certain crimes are more commonly committed by certain races (such as men of Arab descent and crimes of terrorism). In these cases, police officers essentially argue that activity of a member of a certain race is suspicious while the same activity by a member of a different race would not be suspicious.

How would the test articulated in *Cortez* apply to the following facts?

A St. Paul police officer observed Uber's vehicle at about 2:15 a.m. The officer saw the vehicle again about 30 minutes later in the same area. At that time the officer ran a check on the license number and determined that the vehicle was registered to a person in Moundsview, Minnesota, a suburb about 20 miles from St. Paul. Upon learning this information, the officer decided to stop the vehicle, because he thought the driver was seeking to solicit a prostitute. The Summit–University area, in which Uber's car was spotted, is well known as one where prostitution flourishes. The officer did not at that time see prostitutes in the area, nor had Uber slowed down or talked to anyone.

The court in City of St. Paul v. Uber, 450 N.W.2d 623 (Minn.App.1990), held that this information did not create reasonable suspicion to support a stop. The court stated as follows:

We know of no authority that requires a resident of the State of Minnesota to have any reason to be on the public streets of another town * * *. No one from any suburb needs to justify his or her lawful presence on a public street in Minneapolis or St. Paul. * * * The officer's assumption that [Uber] was seeking prostitution was an inadvertent, but nevertheless invidious, form of discrimination. We would not tolerate the blatant discriminatory proposition that any member of a minority group found on a public street in Edina [an affluent suburb] had better live there, or be required to stop and justify his or her presence to the authorities. * * * Once we clear away the smoke from this case, it is clear that the stop of [Uber] is premised on the belief that after midnight, Caucasian males from the suburbs are only in the Summit–University area for no good, and that after midnight, no good is all the Summit–University area has to offer. Neither the residents of Summit–University nor the residents of Moundsview deserve the implications of this case. * * * Simply being on a public street in an area where one "might" find a prostitute or a drug dealer does not, without more, meet any constitutional standard for a stop by the authorities. See e.g. Brown v. Texas, 443 U.S. 47 (1979) (defendant's mere presence in a neighborhood frequented by drug users held insufficient to justify a stop).

While a person's race, or the existence of a high crime area, may not "without more" constitute reasonable suspicion, how much more is required? What if Uber had been driving ten miles below the speed limit and looking out along the street? Would such conduct be sufficiently suspicious, given the neighborhood, regardless of the suspect's race?[21] For a case consistent with *Uber*, see State v. Barber, 118 Wn.2d 335, 823 P.2d 1068 (1992)("racial incongruity, i.e., a person of any race being allegedly out of place in a particular geographic area," could not be considered in the reasonable suspicion inquiry).

Some courts, in contrast to *Uber*, have found it permissible for an officer to consider the race of a person in determining whether the person's conduct is suspicious. These courts hold that while the suspect's race cannot be the only factor supporting a stop, it can be considered together with other suspicious factors. In other words, these courts appear to permit a form of racial profiling, so long as race is not the only basis for the stop. As the court put it in United States v. Weaver, 966 F.2d 391 (8th Cir.1992), a case in which the defendant, the only African–American male on a flight from Los Angeles to Kansas City, was stopped on suspicion of drug trafficking:

> Had [Officer] Hicks relied solely on Weaver's race as a basis for his suspicions, we would have a different case before us. As it is, however, facts are not to be ignored simply because they may be unpleasant—and the unpleasant fact in this case is that Hicks had knowledge * * * that young black Los Angeles gangs were flooding the Kansas City area with cocaine. To that extent, then, race, when coupled with the other factors Hicks relied upon, [i.e., that Weaver came from a source city for drugs, had no identifica-

---

21. Professor Harris, in Factors for Reasonable Suspicion: When Black and Poor Means Stopped and Frisked, 69 Ind.L.J.659 (1994), argues that *Terry* stops have a disproportionate effect on minorities, even if race is not explicitly taken into account in determining reasonable suspicion. This is because in many courts "an individual's presence in a high crime location plus evasion of the police equals suspicion reasonable enough to allow a stop under *Terry*." Professor Harris argues that minorities, because of where they usually live and how they understandably react toward police, are more likely to trigger these two "suspicious" factors.

tion, and appeared unusually nervous when encountered by police officers] was a factor in the decision to approach and ultimately detain Weaver. We wish it were otherwise, but we take the facts as they are presented to us, and not as we would like them to be.

Should the court in *Weaver* have taken the facts as they would have liked them to be, instead of how they were presented? Would it be worth it to hold a person's race as non-suspicious as a matter of law, regardless of "reality"? Would that encourage the police to be more "race-blind" in their use of the *Terry* power?

For more on the problem of racial profiling after 9/11, see Deborah Ramirez, Defining Racial Profiling in a Post–September 11th World, 40 Am.Crim.L.Rev. 1195 (2003).

The Use of Race in Encounters, in the Absence of Reasonable Suspicion

Assume, as some courts have held, that a person's behavior cannot be considered suspicious simply because the person is a member of a certain racial group. Aren't police officers easily able to avoid this principle simply by encountering, as opposed to stopping, a person because of their race? Remember, if an officer's conduct is not a "seizure", it is completely outside the coverage of the Fourth Amendment. Thus, the Fourth Amendment does not prohibit an officer from encountering a person, asking him questions, etc., solely on account of the person's race. As far as the Fourth Amendment is concerned, an officer can do anything short of a seizure, for any reason or no reason.

This does not mean that the Constitution has nothing to say about racially-based encounters. The court in United States v. Avery, 137 F.3d 343 (6th Cir.1997), explained as follows:

> Although Fourth Amendment principles regarding unreasonable seizures do not apply to consensual encounters, an officer does not have unfettered discretion to conduct an investigatory interview with a citizen. The Equal Protection Clause of the Fourteenth Amendment provides citizens a degree of protection independent of the Fourth Amendment protection against unreasonable searches and seizures. This protection becomes relevant even before a seizure occurs.

The court in *Avery* held that the Equal Protection Clause imposes limits on an officer's decision as to who to encounter, and also imposes similar limits on an officer's decision to track somebody *before* an encounter (i.e., the pre-contact stage). At both the contact and pre-contact stage, an officer cannot discriminate on the basis of race. The court concluded that "citizens are entitled to equal protection of the laws at all times. If law enforcement adopts a policy, employs a practice, or in a given situation takes steps to initiate an investigation of a citizen based solely upon that citizen's race, without more, then a violation of the Equal Protection Clause has occurred."

Proving an equal protection violation at the contact or pre-contact stage is not an easy matter, however. In *Avery*, an African–American male was encountered by police officers while moving through an airport. He "failed" his encounter by giving implausible answers, and eventually his bag was searched and drugs were discovered. Avery relied on statistics indicating that a disproportionate number of African–American travelers are investigated and encountered in airports. But the court found that the statistics were not compiled in a systematic manner, and were sketchy and ultimately "unpersuasive." Moreover, even if the statistics established a prima facie case of discrimination at the contact and pre-contact stage, this not prove a case of intent to discriminate. Rather, it would simply shift the burden to the government to articulate a non-discriminatory reason for the investigation and encounter. In this case, the officers had a plausible, non-racially-based reason for investigation and encounter. The *Avery* court summarized as follows:

> When the officers began to follow Avery they knew: (1) he was in a hurry; (2) he appeared focused and looked straight ahead; (3) he was attired in a sweat suit with short sleeves in December; and (4) he carried a gym-type, carry-on bag. These factors, when combined with the observation at the gate of Avery sitting in an empty row of seats closest to the podium, provided the officers with sufficient reason to begin an investigation of Avery. An officer is not held to a "suspicion of criminal activity standard" when he embarks to investigate someone. The officer merely is prohibited from his pursuit if he acts based solely on race. Consequently, there was no equal protection violation in this case.

See also United States v. Chavez, 281 F.3d 479 (5th Cir. 2002) (defendant failed to show that officers' targeting of certain bars frequented by Hispanics was racially motivated; proof of discriminatory purpose is "a necessary predicate of an equal protection violation").

Use of Profiles

In several of the cases above it is apparent that the officers were comparing the activity of the suspect to a profile of a person engaged in certain criminal activity. Officers often use profiles to determine whether the conduct of citizens is sufficiently suspicious to justify a stop. A profile is a list of characteristics compiled by a law enforcement agency, which have been found through experience to be common characteristics of those engaged in a certain type of criminal activity. The most common example is a drug courier profile, but officers also employ other profiles for specific criminal activity. See United States v. Malone, 886 F.2d 1162 (9th Cir.1989)(officer stops the defendant on the basis of a gang member profile). The use of drug courier profiles was discussed extensively in United States v. Berry, 670 F.2d 583 (5th Cir.1982)(en banc):

> The precise characteristics in the profile appear to vary, but those most commonly mentioned in cases in this Circuit as constituting the profile are described in United States v. Elmore, 595 F.2d 1036, 1039 n. 3 (5th Cir.1979), cert. denied, 447 U.S. 910 (1980):
>
> > The seven primary characteristics are: (1) arrival from or departure to an identified source city; (2) carrying little or no luggage, or large quantities of empty suitcases; (3) unusual itinerary, such as rapid turnaround time for a very lengthy airplane trip; (4) use of an alias; (5) carrying unusually large amounts of currency in the many thousands of dollars, usually on their person, in briefcases or bags; (6) purchasing airline tickets with a large amount of small denomination currency; and (7) unusual nervousness beyond that ordinarily exhibited by passengers.

The secondary characteristics are (1) the almost exclusive use of public transportation, particularly taxicabs, in departing from the airport; (2) immediately making a telephone call after deplaning; (3) leaving a false or fictitious call-back telephone number with the airline being utilized; and (4) excessively frequent travel to source or distribution cities.

* * * We conclude that the profile is nothing more than an administrative tool of the police. The presence or absence of a particular characteristic on any particular profile is of *no* legal significance in the determination of reasonable suspicion.

Two consequences stem from this holding. First, a match between certain characteristics listed on the profile and characteristics exhibited by a defendant does not automatically establish reasonable suspicion. * * * Any checklist of suspicious characteristics cannot be mechanically applied by a court to determine whether a particular search or seizure meets the Supreme Court's standards. A profile does not focus on the particular circumstances at issue. Nor does such a profile indicate in every case that a specific individual who happens to match some of the profile's vague characteristics is involved in actions sufficiently suspicious as to justify a stop.

The second consequence of our holding flows from the first. Although a match between a defendant's characteristics and some of the characteristics on a drug courier profile does not automatically support a finding of reasonable suspicion, the fact that a characteristic of a defendant also happens to appear on the profile does not preclude its use as a justification providing reasonable suspicion for a stop. If an officer can demonstrate why some factor, interpreted with due regard for the officer's experience and not merely in light of its presence on the profile, was, in the particular circumstances of the facts at issue, of such import as to support a reasonable suspicion that an individual was involved in drug smuggling, we do not believe that a court should downgrade the importance of that factor merely because it happens to be part of the profile. Our holding is only that we will assign no characteristic greater or lesser weight merely because the characteristic happens to be present on, or absent from, the profile.

The Supreme Court essentially adopted the *Berry* approach toward profiles in United States v. Sokolow, 490 U.S. 1 (1989). DEA agents stopped Sokolow after they learned that he paid $2100 for two airplane tickets from a roll of $20 bills, he traveled under a name that did not match the name under which his telephone was listed, he traveled to Honolulu from Miami and stayed only 48 hours even though a round-trip flight takes 20 hours, he appeared nervous during the trip, and he checked no luggage. Chief Justice Rehnquist wrote for the majority, which found that the above facts, taken together, amounted to reasonable suspicion. The Chief Justice reviewed the facts known to the officers concerning Sokolow, and recognized that "any one of these factors is not by itself proof of any illegal conduct and is quite consistent with innocent travel." But he stated that the relevant inquiry "is not whether particular conduct is innocent or guilty, but the degree of suspicion that attaches to particular types of noncriminal acts."

The Chief Justice rejected Sokolow's argument that the officer's use of a drug courier profile tainted the stop:

A court sitting to determine the existence of reasonable suspicion must require the agent to articulate the factors leading to that conclusion, but the fact that these factors may be set forth in a "profile" does not somehow detract from their evidentiary significance as seen by a trained agent.

The Chief Justice also rejected Sokolow's argument that agents were obligated to use the least intrusive means available to verify or dispel their suspicions—in this case by engaging in an encounter rather than a stop. The majority reasoned that any rule requiring a least intrusive alternative approach would hamper the police in making on-the-spot decisions.

Justice Marshall, joined by Justice Brennan, dissented and complained about the officers' use of the drug courier profile.

It is highly significant that the DEA agents stopped Sokolow because he matched one of the DEA's "profiles" of a paradigmatic drug courier. * * * Reflexive reliance on a profile of drug courier characteristics runs a far greater risk than does ordinary, case-by-case police work, of subjecting innocent individuals to unwarranted police harassment and detention. This risk is enhanced by the profile's chameleon-like way of adapting to any particular set of observations. Compare, e.g., United States v. Moore, 675 F.2d 802, 803 (C.A.6 1982)(suspect was first to deplane), with United States v. Mendenhall, 446 U.S. 544, 564 (1980)(last to deplane), with United States v. Buenaventura–Ariza, 615 F.2d 29, 31 (C.A.2 1980)(deplaned from middle); United States v. Sullivan, 625 F.2d 9, 12 (C.A.4 1980)(one-way tickets), with United States v. Craemer, 555 F.2d 594, 595 (C.A.6 1977)(round-trip tickets), with United States v. McCaleb, 552 F.2d 717, 720 (C.A.6 1977) (non-stop flight), with United States v. Sokolow, 808 F.2d 1366, 1370 (C.A.9 1987), vacated, 831 F.2d 1413 (C.A.9 1987)(changed planes); *Craemer,* supra, at 595 (no luggage), with United States v. Sanford, 658 F.2d 342, 343 (C.A.5 1981)(gym bag), with *Sullivan,* supra, at 12 (new suitcases); United States v. Smith, 574 F.2d 882, 883 (C.A.6 1978)(traveling alone), with United States v. Fry, 622 F.2d 1218, 1219 (C.A.5 1980)(traveling with companion); United States v. Andrews, 600 F.2d 563, 566 (C.A.6 1979)(acted nervously), with United States v. Himmelwright, 551 F.2d 991, 992 (CA5 1977)(acted too calmly).

Overbroad Profile Factors

It is clear that some profile factors relied on by police are far too broad to support reasonable suspicion in the courts. For example, in United States v. Beck, 140 F.3d 1129 (8th Cir.1998), an officer sought to justify the stop of a motorist in part because he was driving through Arkansas in a car from California, and California was a "source state" for drugs. The criteria for considering the entire state of California to be a profile factor was unexplained. Indeed, the officer testified that he considered not only California to be a drug source state, but also Arizona, Texas, New Mexico, Florida, and Louisiana. The court held that the profile factor was far too broad to be useful in a consideration of reasonable suspicion.

While we do not suggest that geography is an entirely irrelevant factor, we do not think that the entire state of California, the most populous state in the union, can properly be deemed a source of illegal narcotics such that mere residency in that state constitutes a factor supporting reasonable suspicion. Because millions of law-abiding Americans reside in California and travel, mere residency in and travel from the State of California means the officer's "source state" factor must be considered in this context. Innumerable other Americans travel to that state or through there for pleasure or lawful business. Clearly, the vast number of individuals coming from that state must relegate this factor to a relatively insignificant role. Indeed, Officer Taylor conceded at the suppression hearing that interstate motorists have a better than equal chance of traveling from a source state to a demand state. We conclude, in the circumstances of this case, that no specific, articulable basis warranting a reasonable belief that Beck's Buick contained contraband can be gleaned from the mere fact that Beck's Buick was registered and licensed in California.

Note that the *Beck* court does not prevent the officer from using the California profile factor in *deciding* whether to stop a motorist. He simply cannot justify the stop by this factor. If the officer had reasonable suspicion to stop the car on other grounds, the use of the California profile factor would not raise a Fourth Amendment issue.

Reasonable Suspicion and Flight From the Police

If a person runs upon seeing the police, is this enough to justify a stop of that person? This was a question presented in Illinois v. Wardlow, 528 U.S. 119 (2000). Wardlow fled upon seeing a caravan of police vehicles converge on an area of Chicago known for heavy narcotics trafficking. When Officers Nolan and Harvey caught up with him on the street, Nolan stopped him and conducted a protective pat-down search for weapons because in his experience there were usually weapons in the vicinity of narcotics transactions. Discovering a handgun, the officers arrested Wardlow. The Illinois appellate courts reversed Wardlow's conviction for a firearm violation, reasoning that his flight from the police in a high crime area did not constitute reasonable suspicion. The Supreme Court, in an opinion by Chief Justice Rehnquist for five Justices, found that the officers did have reasonable suspicion under the circumstances, and reinstated Wardlow's conviction.

The Chief Justice analyzed the relevance of Wardlow's flight in a high crime area in the following passage:

> An individual's presence in an area of expected criminal activity, standing alone, is not enough to support a reasonable, particularized suspicion that the person is committing a crime. Brown v. Texas, 443 U. S. 47 (1979). But officers are not required to ignore the relevant characteristics of a location in determining whether the circumstances are sufficiently suspicious to warrant further investigation. Accordingly, we have previously noted the fact that the stop occurred in a high crime area among the relevant contextual considerations in a Terry analysis. Adams v. Williams.
>
> In this case, moreover, it was not merely respondent's presence in an area of heavy narcotics trafficking that aroused the officers' suspicion but his unprovoked flight upon noticing the police. * * * Headlong flight— wherever it occurs—is the consummate act of evasion: it is not necessarily indicative of wrongdoing, but it is certainly suggestive of such. In reviewing

the propriety of an officer's conduct, courts do not have available empirical studies dealing with inferences drawn from suspicious behavior, and we cannot reasonably demand scientific certainty from judges or law enforcement officers where none exists. Thus, the determination of reasonable suspicion must be based on commonsense judgments and inferences about human behavior. See United States v. Cortez. We conclude Officer Nolan was justified in suspecting that Wardlow was involved in criminal activity, and, therefore, in investigating further.

Such a holding is entirely consistent with our decision in Florida v. Royer, where we held that when an officer, without reasonable suspicion or probable cause, approaches an individual, the individual has a right to ignore the police and go about his business. And any refusal to cooperate, without more, does not furnish the minimal level of objective justification needed for a detention or seizure. But unprovoked flight is simply not a mere refusal to cooperate. Flight, by its very nature, is not going about one's business; in fact, it is just the opposite. Allowing officers confronted with such flight to stop the fugitive and investigate further is quite consistent with the individual's right to go about his business or to stay put and remain silent in the face of police questioning.

Respondent and amici also argue that there are innocent reasons for flight from police and that, therefore, flight is not necessarily indicative of ongoing criminal activity. This fact is undoubtedly true, but does not establish a violation of the Fourth Amendment. Even in *Terry*, the conduct justifying the stop was ambiguous and susceptible of an innocent explanation. * * * *Terry* accepts the risk that officers may stop innocent people. Indeed, the Fourth Amendment accepts that risk in connection with more drastic police action; persons arrested and detained on probable cause to believe they have committed a crime may turn out to be innocent. The *Terry* stop is a far more minimal intrusion, simply allowing the officer to briefly investigate further. If the officer does not learn facts rising to the level of probable cause, the individual must be allowed to go on his way. But in this case the officers found respondent in possession of a handgun, and arrested him for violation of an Illinois firearms statute.

Justice Stevens concurred in part and dissented in part in an opinion joined by Justices Souter, Ginsburg and Breyer. Justice Stevens stated that the defendant was pressing for a rule that flight from police officers would *never* equal reasonable suspicion, while the State was pressing for a rule that flight from police officers would *always* equal reasonable suspicion. He agreed with the majority that neither per se rule was appropriate, and that the relevance of flight in the reasonable suspicion inquiry depends on the circumstances. He dissented, however, from the Court's ruling that Wardlow's flight in a high crime area was sufficiently suspicious to justify a *Terry* stop under the circumstances. Justice Stevens stated that "even in a high crime neighborhood unprovoked flight does not invariably lead to reasonable suspicion. On the contrary, because many factors providing innocent motivations for unprovoked flight are concentrated in high crime areas, the character of the neighborhood arguably makes an inference of guilt less appropriate, rather than more so. Like unprovoked flight itself, presence in a high crime neighborhood is a fact too generic and susceptible to innocent explanation to satisfy the reasonable suspicion inquiry."

Justice Stevens emphasized why flight from the police might not be suspicious, particularly in minority communities and high crime neighborhoods:

> Among some citizens, particularly minorities and those residing in high crime areas, there is * * * the possibility that the fleeing person is entirely innocent, but, with or without justification, believes that contact with the police can itself be dangerous, apart from any criminal activity associated with the officer's sudden presence. For such a person, unprovoked flight is neither "aberrant" nor "abnormal." * * *

4. Limited Searches for Police Protection Under the Terry Doctrine

Terry and *Adams* indicate that an officer can frisk a suspect, and pull out objects found on the suspect, if there is reasonable suspicion to believe that this is necessary to protect the officer from bodily harm. Are you concerned that an officer may testify in support of the frisk that she felt a fear of bodily harm, when in fact she was looking for evidence without having probable cause? Is there an easy way to distinguish *Terry* frisks from impermissible searches for evidence?

Frisk Cannot Be Used to Search for Evidence: Minnesota v. Dickerson

In Minnesota v. Dickerson, 508 U.S. 366 (1993), the Court reaffirmed the principle that *Terry* frisks are justified only for protective purposes and that a search for evidence is not permitted under *Terry*. The officer in *Dickerson* conducted a lawful stop and patdown, and felt a small, hard object in Dickerson's pocket. The officer determined that it was not a weapon, but nonetheless continued to squeeze and prod the object. This additional investigation led him to the conclusion that the object was crack cocaine. The officer then pulled the object out from Dickerson's pocket, and found that his conclusion was correct. Justice White, writing for the Court, declared that "the police officer in this case overstepped the bounds of the strictly circumscribed search for weapons allowed under *Terry*." He concluded as follows:

> Here, the officer's continued exploration of respondent's pocket after having concluded that it contained no weapon was unrelated to the sole justification of the search under *Terry*: the protection of the police officer and others nearby. It therefore amounted to the sort of evidentiary search that *Terry* expressly refused to authorize, and that we have condemned in subsequent cases.

See also United States v. Miles, 247 F.3d 1009 (9th Cir. 2001) (officer exceeded scope of *Terry* frisk by shaking a small box found in the outer pocket of the suspect's clothing, where the box clearly could not have contained a weapon); United States v. Schiavo, 29 F.3d 6 (1st Cir.1994)(officer went beyond the bounds of a permissible *Terry* frisk by continuing to probe a paper bag inside the defendant's jacket after having concluded that it contained no weapon; drugs found in the bag were therefore properly excluded).

Suspicion Required to Support the Right to Frisk

Evaluate the following facts in light of *Terry* and *Adams*.

The officer received a radio report of an anonymous 911 call in which the informant stated that he had seen a woman in a blue car with a white top parked in front of 123 West 112th Street, a high crime area in New York City. The woman had passed a handgun to a man seated in the car with her. Finding defendant in a car meeting the description at the specific location indicated by the informant, the officer ordered the defendant out of the car, frisked her, and took a pistol from the area of her waistband.

The New York Court of Appeals held that while the stop was permissible, the frisk was not. The court reasoned as follows:

A frisk requires reliable knowledge of facts providing reasonable basis for suspecting that the individual to be subjected to that intrusion is armed and may be dangerous. Here, there was no such predicate either in the information received, which indicated that defendant had given a gun to the man but provided no basis for inferring that she had another or that it had been returned to her, or in what occurred during the officer's encounter with defendant. No inquiry was made of defendant so she neither refused to answer nor answered evasively; no suspicious bulge was perceived in her clothing; no furtive movements were made by her; her appearance and movements were not concealed by darkness.

People v. Russ, 61 N.Y.2d 693, 472 N.Y.S.2d 601, 460 N.E.2d 1086 (1984). If you were a police officer, would you have found it necessary to frisk Russ for a gun, after she had already passed a gun in a high crime area?

Most courts have given considerably more deference to police concerns about the risk of harm involved in making a stop. Consider United States v. Rideau, 969 F.2d 1572 (5th Cir.1992)(en banc). Two officers were on patrol in a high crime area of Beaumont, Texas, "where people often carried weapons and transacted drug deals on the street, and where public drunkenness was a recurrent problem." The officers saw a man standing in the road. They flashed a bright light at him. The man turned to step up to the curb, and he stumbled. Officer Ellison, suspecting that the man was drunk, got out of his car and approached. Ellison asked the man his name. The man appeared nervous, did not answer, and began to back away. Ellison "immediately closed the gap and reached out to pat the man's outer clothing." The first place he touched was the man's right front pants pocket, where he felt a gun. The officer put the man up against the patrol car, removed the gun, and arrested him. The man, subsequently identified as Rideau, was convicted for felon firearm possession.

Judge Higginbotham, writing for the majority of the en banc court of appeals, held that the frisk was justified because Officer Ellison had reasonable cause to believe that Rideau posed a threat of harm:

A reasonably prudent man in Ellison's situation could have believed that his safety and that of his partner was in danger. Ellison already had some reason to believe that Rideau might be intoxicated or perhaps injured. When approached and asked his name, Rideau did not respond but appeared nervous and, critically, backed away. It was not unreasonable under the circumstances for Ellison to have feared that Rideau was moving back to give himself time and space to draw a weapon. It was not then unreasonable for Ellison simply to touch Rideau's front pants pocket to determine whether he had a gun.

Judge Higginbotham emphasized that the officer's safety was especially at risk given the time and location of the stop:

> Rideau's specific moves took place after a detention, at night, in a high crime area where the carrying of weapons is common. * * * Stripped from their context, the backward steps offer no threat, but to a police officer in Ellison's situation, they become very significant in the matrix of the general facts. * * * Of course, that an individual is in a high crime neighborhood at night is not in and of itself enough to support an officer's decision to stop and frisk him. But when someone engages in suspicious activity in a high crime area, where weapons and violence abound, police officers must be particularly cautious in approaching and questioning him.

Judge Smith, together with four other judges of the en banc panel, dissented in *Rideau*. He argued that under the majority's permissive approach, Rideau could have been frisked no matter what he did when Officer Ellison approached: if he had moved forward, this would have been deemed threatening as well; if he had moved to the side, this would have been deemed nervousness or flight; if he had remained motionless, it would have been viewed as "abnormal behavior caused by drugs or alcohol." Judge Smith concluded as follows:

> Perhaps if Rideau had graduated from charm school and had been taught how to look "cool and collected" in the face of approaching uniformed officers, he could have managed to avoid the patdown. Otherwise, he was doomed to the intrusion that in fact occurred. * * *
>
> * * * [O]ne can surmise that many totally innocent persons, upon seeing the approach of two uniformed officers, would take a couple of steps backward and would be surprised to learn that that normal reaction could subject them to a search of their person * * *. Rideau was searched not because of anything he did but because of his *status*—a person in a "bad part of town" where, presumably, people do not belong late at night, on the street, unless they are "up to no good." By that measure, almost any person in the vicinity of Martin Luther King Boulevard and Bonham Street that night could have been stopped and frisked.

Arguably, the New York court in *Russ* gave too little credence to an officer's concern for his safety in making a stop explicitly on a weapons charge. Did the majority in *Rideau* give too much credence to an officer's concern for his safety where the stop had nothing to do with weapons and was at least purportedly an attempt to help Rideau, who appeared drunk?

Note that reasonable suspicion to conduct a frisk will depend in part on the nature of the crime for which the citizen is suspected. Thus, if there is reasonable suspicion to believe that a person is going to commit a crime of violence with a weapon, there will automatically be reasonable suspicion to frisk that person. On the other hand, if the citizen is suspected of a financial crime, it is less likely that reasonable suspicion to frisk will be found. See Leveto v. Lapina, 258 F.3d 156 (3rd Cir. 2001) (frisk of person suspected of tax offense was illegal, as there was no reason to think that the person was armed and dangerous).

Professor Harris has surveyed the lower court decisions on *Terry* frisks and has concluded that the courts have generally moved "toward one goal: allowing police to make more frisks by assuming that more and more crimes, persons and situations *could* present danger to officers, when in fact they *may not*. The result has been a steady progression toward a point at which anyone, anytime, may be searched if they are stopped, with no limits on police discretion." Harris, Frisking Every Suspect: The Withering of *Terry*, 28 U.C.D.L.Rev.1 (1994).

Terry Frisks and Rising Violence

Could this steady expansion of the power to frisk be explained as the courts' reaction to the rising violence in our society? Consider United States v. Michelletti, 13 F.3d 838 (5th Cir.1994)(en banc), where the court upheld a frisk by an officer who approached a man with an open can of beer and his hand in his right pocket, at night, in a high crime area. The court implied that the power of an officer to frisk a suspect had to be expanded with the changing times:

> Officer Perry's concern for his safety, dramatized by the recent loss of his friend [a fellow officer killed in the line of duty], is hardly groundless in this day and age. The number of police officers killed annually in the line of duty has tripled since *Terry* was decided; the number of those assaulted and wounded has risen by a factor of twenty. Surely the constitutional legitimacy of a brief patdown * * * may and should reflect the horrendously more violent society in which we live, twenty-five years after *Terry*.

Does *Terry* need to be applied more liberally in light of the changing times? Or was it too permissive to begin with?

Protective Searches Beyond the Suspect's Person: Michigan v. Long

The Court held in Michigan v. Long, 463 U.S. 1032 (1983), that the power to search under *Terry* can extend to protective examinations of areas beyond the person of the suspect. Long was stopped by officers who saw him driving erratically before he swerved into a ditch. When the officers stopped, Long was out of his car and he appeared to be under the influence of something. Long failed to respond to initial requests that he produce a license and registration and then began to walk toward the passenger compartment of his car. An officer flashed a light into the car and saw a hunting knife. A protective search for weapons was conducted in the passenger compartment and marijuana was found and seized. Justice O'Connor's opinion for the Court reasoned that *Terry* permits a limited examination of an area from which a person, who police reasonably believe is dangerous, might gain immediate control of a weapon. The Court upheld the examination of the passenger compartment.[22]

Considering that Long was outside the car at the time that it was searched, how could the officers have had a reasonable fear that harm could come from something inside the car? Justice O'Connor explained that because a stop is only a temporary intrusion, the suspect "will be permitted to reenter his automobile, and he will then have access to any weapons inside." The New York Court of Appeals, in People v. Torres, 74 N.Y.2d 224, 544 N.Y.S.2d 796, 543 N.E.2d 61 (1989), rejected this reasoning in *Long* as a matter of state constitutional law. The *Torres* court declared:

---

22. Justice Blackmun concurred in part and in the judgment. Justice Brennan, joined by Justice Marshall, and Justice Stevens filed dissenting opinions.

[I]t is unrealistic to assume, as the Supreme Court did in Michigan v. Long, that having been stopped and questioned without incident, a suspect who is about to be released and permitted to proceed on his way would, upon reentry into his vehicle, reach for a concealed weapon and threaten the departing police officer's safety. Certainly, such a far-fetched scenario is an insufficient basis upon which to predicate the substantial intrusion that occurred here.

Is it "far-fetched" to believe that a suspect could present a risk of harm to the officer in a post-stop situation? Would you think it far-fetched if you were a police officer?

Applying Michigan v. Long

Is it reasonable to assume that those suspected of drug dealing always present a risk of harm to the officer when stopped? In United States v. Brown, 913 F.2d 570 (8th Cir.1990), the court relied on *Long* to uphold a search of a locked glove compartment, when the officers had reasonable suspicion of drug activity. The court concluded that "since weapons and violence are frequently associated with drug transactions, the officers reasonably believed that the individuals with whom they were dealing were armed and dangerous." Is there now a per se rule that a full-fledged search of a passenger compartment can be conducted upon reasonable suspicion to believe the driver is a drug dealer? See Harris, Frisking Every Suspect, supra (noting that courts originally permitted an automatic protective search of those suspected of being major drug traffickers, but that the automatic rule has now been extended to virtually anyone suspected of a narcotics violation). See also United States v. Sakyi, 160 F.3d 164 (4th Cir.1998) (finding it permissible to frisk all occupants of a car after a cigar box of marijuana was found in the car; court reasons that "guns often accompany drugs").

The *Long* rationale is not limited to protective searches of cars. Thus, in United States v. Johnson, 932 F.2d 1068 (5th Cir.1991), the court upheld a cursory inspection of a pair of overalls located a few feet away from a suspect who appeared to be attempting to burglarize a house. The court found that merely separating the suspect from his effects during the stop would not provide sufficient protection to the officers, since if the stop was terminated, the officers would have to return the property to the suspect.

Protective Searches of Persons Other Than the Suspect

In the course of detaining suspects either by a stop or an arrest, officers are often confronted with whether they can frisk persons other than the suspect. In United States v. Berryhill, 445 F.2d 1189 (9th Cir.1971), the court adopted an "automatic companion" rule, whereby the companion of an arrestee could automatically be subject to a frisk—even if the companion presents no risk of harm to the officer on the facts. Other courts have rejected this rule on the ground that it is inconsistent with the case-by-case approach to protective searches mandated by *Terry*. See United States v. Bell, 762 F.2d 495 (6th Cir.1985). See also United States v. Menard, 95 F.3d 9 (8th Cir.1996) (rejecting the automatic companion rule but finding that the officer had reasonable suspicion on the facts to conduct a frisk of the companion of an arrestee, where the car was stopped on a remote highway in the middle of the night).

In Ybarra v. Illinois, 444 U.S. 85 (1979), the Court refused to uphold the frisk of a patron of a bar who happened to be present when the police arrived to conduct a search of the bar pursuant to a valid search warrant. The Court noted that the patron's mere presence in the bar was not enough to provide a reasonable belief that he posed a risk of harm to the officers, and that no specific facts were shown to indicate that Ybarra was armed and dangerous. Does *Ybarra* support the courts which have adopted the automatic companion rule, or the courts which have rejected it? How much information does an officer need, other than mere presence, to support a frisk of a person in the vicinity of an arrest? See United States v. Reid, 997 F.2d 1576 (D.C.Cir.1993)(defendant could be frisked after officers saw him exit from a suspected crack house that they were about to search: "Common sense suggests that there is a much greater likelihood that a person found in a small private residence containing drugs will be involved in the drug activity occurring there than an individual who happens to be in a public tavern where the bartender is suspected of possessing drugs.").

Inspecting Objects During the Course of a Protective Frisk

Assume that an officer has properly stopped a person and has reasonable suspicion to believe that the person presents a safety risk. The officer then conducts a pat-down and feels an object inside the suspect's coat. Can the officer pull the object out and inspect it? Under *Dickerson*, the answer is that the officer can inspect the object only if it is reasonably likely to be a weapon—*Terry* does not justify a search for evidence. But sometimes there is a vigorous dispute about whether an object could reasonably be a weapon.

A case in point is United States v. Swann, 149 F.3d 271 (4th Cir.1998). Officers responded to a report of a theft of a wallet in an office building. Witness reports indicated that the thief had been detained by employees, but broke free and tossed the wallet in the direction of three black males standing near the elevator. One of the men retrieved the wallet and all three men fled the scene. An officer spotted two black males in the basement parking garage. According to the officer, they appeared "really nervous and uneasy and kind of edgy; didn't want to hang around." When the officer told them that he needed to speak with them, one of them tried to circle around him to get behind his back. The officer felt threatened by this action and called for back-up. When another officer arrived, the men were patted down. The officer patting down Swann found a hard object in Swann's left sock. The officer pulled it out and it turned out to be five credit cards belonging to the victim of the theft.

Swann moved to suppress the credit cards on the ground that *Terry* did not permit the officer to inspect the object found in his sock. But the court disagreed, concluding that a reasonable officer "could justifiably have believed that the item was a weapon." The court elaborated:

[T]he object in Swann's sock was approximately the same size and shape as a box cutter with a sharp blade, which is often used as a weapon.

The location of the object in the sock, as well as its hard character and its shape, made it suspicious. A similarly shaped hard object in Swann's pocket surely would have raised no alarms, as there could be inummerable innocent explanations for it. And a hard rectangular object in one's sock might not be suspicious on a jogger or someone similarly dressed. But these men were both fully dressed, and Swann's pants had pockets that could have contained an item of that size and shape.

Given all the circumstances, it was objectively reasonable for the officer to believe that this particular hard object could likely be a weapon and to seize the item to satisfy himself that it was not something that could be used to inflict harm. Officers making *Terry* stops must make quick decisions as to how to protect themselves and others from possible danger. Were we to disapprove of Officer Martin's actions, we would require an officer to allow a suspicious object to remain within easy reach of demonstrably nervous and potentially aggressive subjects. Our respect for the privacy rights of citizens does not require such an increase in the danger that police officers must face.

Why is it relevant that Swann had pockets and yet decided to use his sock as a storage space? Does that fact indicate that he was trying to hide a weapon? Or rather that he was trying to hide evidence of a crime? Would the result in *Swann* change if the object in Swann's sock was soft to the touch?

Protective Sweeps: Maryland v. Buie

In Maryland v. Buie, 494 U.S. 325 (1990), the Court considered the legality of a "protective sweep," which it defined as a "quick and limited search of a premises, incident to an arrest and conducted to protect the safety of police officers or others." Officers had probable cause to believe that Buie and an associate committed an armed robbery. They arrested Buie at his home, and conducted a protective sweep of the premises. During the sweep, the officers discovered clothing that tied Buie to the robbery. At the time of the sweep, the officers had reasonable suspicion, but not probable cause, to believe that a dangerous person such as Buie's associate might be hiding in the premises. Buie argued that a protective sweep could not be conducted in the absence of probable cause to believe that there were individuals on the premises who would harm the officers or others. The Court, by a 7–2 vote, rejected Buie's argument. Justice White, writing for the majority, relied heavily on *Terry* and *Long* to find that a protective sweep could be justified by an officer's reasonable suspicion "that the area swept harbored an individual posing danger to the officer or others." According to Justice White, the reasonable suspicion standard was an appropriate balance between the arrestee's remaining privacy interest in the home and the officer's interest in safety. Justice White emphasized that a protective sweep is a relatively limited intrusion because it "may extend only to a cursory inspection of those spaces where a person may be found," and the sweep can last "no longer than is necessary to dispel the reasonable suspicion of danger." Justice Stevens concurred to emphasize that a protective sweep could only be conducted for safety purposes, not to prevent destruction of evidence.[23] Justice Brennan, joined by Justice Marshall, dissented and noted his continuing criticism "of the emerging tendency on the part of the Court to convert the *Terry* decision from a narrow exception into one that swallows the general rule that searches are 'reasonable' only if based upon probable cause."

23. See United States v. Hogan, 38 F.3d 1148 (10th Cir.1994)("[I]t appears that once inside Hogan's property, officers went on a fishing expedition for evidence linking Hogan to the murder. This greatly exceeded the permissible scope of a protective sweep.").

Note that a protective sweep is not permissible simply because the arrestee is dangerous. The question is whether there is reasonable suspicion to believe that there is someone other than the arrestee who, under the circumstances, could present a risk of harm to officers or others. See United States v. Colbert, 76 F.3d 773 (6th Cir.1996) (protective sweep not permitted where there is no indication that anyone other than the arrestee is on the premises: "The facts upon which officers may justify a *Buie* protective sweep are those facts giving rise to a suspicion of danger from attack by a third party during the arrest, not the dangerousness of the arrested individual.").

Protective Sweep Where Arrest Is Made Outside the Premises

In *Buie*, the officers entered a residence to arrest a person for armed robbery, and their protective sweep of the premises was upheld by the Supreme Court. Would the *Buie* premise ever permit officers to conduct a protective sweep of a residence if the officers arrested the suspect *outside*? The court in United States v. Henry, 48 F.3d 1282 (D.C.Cir.1995), had this to say:

> Although *Buie* concerned an arrest made in the home, the principles enunciated by the Supreme Court are fully applicable where, as here, the arrest takes place just outside the residence. That the police arrested the defendant outside rather than inside his dwelling is relevant to the question of whether they could reasonably fear an attack by someone within it. The officers' exact location, however, does not change the nature of the appropriate inquiry: Did articulable facts exist that would lead a reasonably prudent officer to believe a sweep was required to protect the safety of those on the arrest scene?

The *Henry* court found sufficient cause for a protective sweep, even though Henry was arrested outside his house, where Henry had been convicted previously of a weapons violation, and the officers were reliably informed that Henry's criminal associates were inside the house.

5. Brief and Limited Detentions: The Line Between "Stop" and "Arrest"

Terry allows a stop upon a standard of proof less than probable cause, in part because a stop is less intrusive than an arrest. But it is often difficult to determine when an intrusion crosses over from a stop to an arrest requiring probable cause. What is there about an arrest that makes it different from a stop? Is it that the officers force the suspect to move to a detention area? Is it that the officers draw their guns or use handcuffs? Is it the length of the detention? What guidelines would you set to determine whether the officer has crossed the line and effectuated an arrest? This section considers the factors found relevant by the courts.

a. Forced Movement of the Suspect to a Custodial Area

In Florida v. Royer, supra, Royer was taken from the public area of an airport into a small room, where the officers sought and obtained Royer's consent to a search of his luggage. The plurality in *Royer* held that the consent was invalid because it was obtained as the result of an arrest without probable cause. Justice White, writing for the plurality, first set forth general principles governing stops and arrests:

The predicate permitting seizures on suspicion short of probable cause is that law enforcement interests warrant a limited intrusion on the personal security of the suspect. The scope of the intrusion permitted will vary to some extent with the particular facts and circumstances of each case. This much, however, is clear: an investigative detention must be temporary and last no longer than is necessary to effectuate the purpose of the stop. Similarly, the investigative methods employed should be the least intrusive means reasonably available to verify or dispel the officer's suspicion in a short period of time. It is the State's burden to demonstrate that the seizure it seeks to justify on the basis of a reasonable suspicion was sufficiently limited in scope and duration to satisfy the conditions of an investigative seizure.

The plurality found that Royer had been illegally detained.

[A]t the time Royer produced the key to his suitcase, the detention to which he was then subjected was a more serious intrusion on his personal liberty than is allowable on mere suspicion of criminal activity.

By the time Royer was informed that the officers wished to examine his luggage, he had identified himself when approached by the officers and had attempted to explain the discrepancy between the name shown on his identification and the name under which he had purchased his ticket and identified his luggage. The officers were not satisfied, for they informed him they were narcotics agents and had reason to believe that he was carrying illegal drugs. They requested him to accompany them to the police room. Royer went with them. He found himself in a small room—a large closet—equipped with a desk and two chairs. He was alone with two police officers who again told him that they thought he was carrying narcotics. He also found that the officers, without his consent, had retrieved his checked luggage from the airlines. What had begun as a consensual inquiry in a public place had escalated into an investigatory procedure in a police interrogation room, where the police, unsatisfied with previous explanations, sought to confirm their suspicions. The officers had Royer's ticket, they had his identification, and they had seized his luggage. Royer was never informed that he was free to board his plane if he so chose, and he reasonably believed that he was being detained. * * * As a practical matter, Royer was under arrest. * * *

Justice White noted that some forced movements of a suspect might be justifiable during a *Terry* stop; he emphasized, however, that probable cause is required if the officer forces the suspect to move in order to further the investigation or to place more pressure on the suspect:

[T]here are undoubtedly reasons of safety and security that would justify moving a suspect from one location to another during an investigatory detention, such as from an airport concourse to a more private area. There is no indication in this case that such reasons prompted the officers to transfer the site of the encounter from the concourse to the interrogation room. It appears, rather, that the primary interest of the officers was not in having an extended conversation with Royer but in the contents of his luggage, a matter which the officers did not pursue orally with Royer until after the encounter was relocated to the police room. The record does not reflect any facts which would support a finding that the legitimate law enforcement purposes which justified the detention in the first instance were furthered by removing Royer to the police room prior to the officer's attempt to gain his consent to a search of his luggage.

Justice Blackmun dissented in *Royer* and argued that Royer was only detained for 15 minutes, the officers were polite, and the intrusion was minimal. He concluded that Royer was only stopped, not arrested, when he gave consent to the luggage search.

Justice Rehnquist, joined by Chief Justice Burger and Justice O'Connor, also dissented, arguing as follows:

> Would it have been more "reasonable" to interrogate Royer about the contents of his suitcases, and to seek his permission to open the suitcases when they were retrieved, in the busy main concourse of the Miami Airport, rather than to find a room off the concourse where the confrontation would surely be less embarrassing to Royer? If the room had been large and spacious, rather than small, if it had possessed three chairs rather than two, would the officers' conduct have been made reasonable by these facts?

See also United States v. Ricardo D., 912 F.2d 337 (9th Cir.1990)(taking person by the arm and placing him in squad car for questioning held impermissible under *Terry*, where there was no showing that the police procedure was "necessary for safety or security reasons").

b. Forced Movement for Identification Purposes

In *Royer,* the Court held that an arrest occurred when Royer was forcibly moved to a custodial atmosphere, for purposes of extracting consent to search. The Court noted, however, that an officer can, within the confines of a *Terry* stop, force the suspect to move for purposes of safety and security. Are there any other legitimate reasons to force a suspect to move without probable cause to arrest? Many courts have found that if reasonable suspicion exists, it is permissible to transport the suspect a short distance for purposes of identification by witnesses. In People v. Hicks, 68 N.Y.2d 234, 508 N.Y.S.2d 163, 500 N.E.2d 861 (1986), the New York Court of Appeals found that coercive movement to the crime scene for purposes of identification was within the confines of a permissible *Terry* stop. It explained as follows:

> There were witnesses within a quarter mile of the place of inquiry— approximately one minute away by car—who had just seen the perpetrators and would either identify defendant (in which event he would be arrested) or not identify him (in which event he would be released). A speedy on-the-scene viewing thus was of value both to law enforcement authorities and to defendant, and was appropriate here. The transportation did not unduly prolong the detention. Defendant might, alternatively, have been momentarily detained where he had been stopped and the witnesses brought there, but such a procedure would have entailed first securing defendant and his companion and then arranging transportation for the witnesses, possibly even a more time-consuming process than that chosen. At all events, given the time and distance involved this is a difference without constitutional significance.

c. Investigative Techniques That are Permissible Within the Confines of a Terry Stop

The purpose of a *Terry* stop is to permit an officer to investigate the facts on which reasonable suspicion is based, in order to determine whether the suspect is involved in criminal activity. It therefore follows that some preliminary investigation, designed to clear up or develop reasonable suspicion, is permissible within the confines of a stop. However, probable cause will be required for more intrusive or long-term custodial investigative techniques. The difficulty, again, is in drawing the line between these two principles.

The most common investigative techniques permitted pursuant to a *Terry* stop are preliminary investigation of the suspect's identity, and questioning concerning the suspicious circumstances giving rise to the stop. See United States v. Holzman, 871 F.2d 1496 (9th Cir.1989)(request for identification was a legitimate investigative technique in the course of a *Terry* stop); United States v. Guzman, 864 F.2d 1512 (10th Cir.1988)("An officer conducting a routine traffic stop may request a driver's license and vehicle identification."). The officer may also verify the information obtained from the suspect by communicating with others, or by conducting preliminary investigations such as a vehicle registration check, license check, or a computer search for outstanding warrants. See United States v. Glover, 957 F.2d 1004 (2d Cir.1992)(permissible within the confines of a *Terry* stop to conduct a computer check to verify the accuracy of the suspect's "rather dubious" proof of identification); United States v. Lego, 855 F.2d 542 (8th Cir.1988)(proper within the confines of a *Terry* stop to check for outstanding warrants); United States v. Mendez, 118 F.3d 1426 (10th Cir.1997) ("An officer conducting a routine traffic stop may run computer checks on the driver's license, the vehicle registration papers, and on whether the driver has any outstanding warrants or the vehicle has been reported stolen"). Courts have also permitted officers to detain suspects on reasonable suspicion in order to conduct a canine sniff or to conduct a preliminary investigation of other suspicious circumstances. See United States v. Bloomfield, 40 F.3d 910 (8th Cir. 1994)(where officers had reasonable suspicion that drugs were in a car, it was proper to detain the suspects while a dog was brought to the scene to sniff the vehicle, because the investigation was "reasonably related in scope to the circumstances that justified the interference in the first place").

d. Overly Intrusive Investigation Techniques

On the other hand, some investigative techniques are themselves so intrusive or extensive as to require probable cause. The most obvious example is a search for evidence, which, as stated above, goes beyond the scope of a *Terry* stop. Also, some courts have held that probable cause is required before a suspect can be subjected to a series of demanding physical tests to determine whether he is intoxicated. See People v. Carlson, 677 P.2d 310 (Colo. 1984)(holding that the full battery of tests employed was so intrusive as to constitute an arrest). Roadside sobriety tests that are less demanding may be permissible under *Terry*, however. See State v. Wyatt, 67 Haw. 293, 687 P.2d 544 (1984)(limited field sobriety test permissible on reasonable suspicion).

e. Investigation of Matters Other than the Reasonable Suspicion That Supported the Stop: Stop After a Stop

Many courts have held that *Terry* does not permit questioning or other investigation that goes beyond the scope of the reasonable suspicion for which the suspect was stopped. For example, an officer who stops someone for a traffic violation cannot continue the stop in order to investigate for drug or gun crimes, in the absence of reasonable suspicion to support such an independent inquiry. See United States v. Salzano, 158 F.3d 1107 (10th Cir.1998) (traffic stop could not be prolonged to investigate possible drug activity, where officer did not have reasonable suspicion that the defendant was involved in drug activity). The reasoning is that if the initial reasonable suspicion that supported the stop has either been cleared up or not quickly resolved, the suspect must be released: a *Terry* stop cannot be used as an excuse for a fishing expedition. United States v. Santiago, 310 F.3d 336 (5th Cir. 2002) (detention after a valid traffic stop was impermissible: "Once a computer check is completed and the officer either issues a citation or determines that no citation should be issued, the detention should end and the driver should be free to leave. In order to continue a detention after such a point, the officer must have a reasonable suspicion supported by articulable facts that a crime has been or is being committed.").

For example, in United States v. Millan–Diaz, 975 F.2d 720 (10th Cir.1992), officers stopped the defendant's vehicle on reasonable suspicion that he was transporting illegal aliens. When no aliens were found, one officer tapped the car door panels and heard a dull thud. The panel was opened and marijuana was found, but the court found that it had to be suppressed, because the purpose of the stop "was satisfied" as soon as the agents determined that there were no illegal aliens hiding in the car, and "the reasonable suspicion necessary to continue the encounter with Defendant had disappeared."

Reasonable Suspicion as to Another Crime

Note that the rulings in the above cases are based on the fact that the officers had no reasonable suspicion to investigate any matter other than the one for which the suspect was stopped. If, however, in the course of a stop to investigate crime "A", the officer obtains reasonable suspicion to investigate crime "B", then the detention can be extended to investigate crime "B" even though the initial justification for the stop no longer exists. There will then be a permissible stop after a stop. Thus, in United States v. Erwin, 155 F.3d 818 (6th Cir.1998) (en banc), officers pulled Ervin over because they had reasonable suspicion to believe that he was driving while intoxicated. While going through the drill of the traffic stop, it became apparent that Ervin was not intoxicated. But this investigation also uncovered evidence indicating that Ervin was a drug dealer. The court analyzed the situation as follows:

> After the deputies satisfied themselves that Erwin was not drunk or otherwise impaired, they were justified in continuing to detain Erwin if, by then, they had reasonable and articulable suspicion that Erwin was engaged in other criminal activity. We think, as the district court did, that the deputies were reasonably entitled to conclude that Erwin may have been a drug dealer, based on the facts that he (1) was nervous, (2) seemed to try to avoid being questioned by attempting to leave, (3) seemed to have used or was preparing to use a pay telephone to make a call when a cellular telephone was available, (4) seemed to have drug paraphernalia in his vehicle, (5) had a large amount of cash, (6) had no registration or proof of insurance, (7) had a criminal record of drug violations, and (8) had an out-of-place backseat cushion. Although many of these facts are consistent with

innocence, all that is required is that the deputies' suspicion be "reasonable" and "articulable," as determined by the totality of the circumstances. We find this standard was met.

See also United States v. Rivera, 906 F.2d 319 (7th Cir.1990)(where a car was stopped for traffic offenses, questions outside the scope of traffic offenses were permissible where they were prompted by inconsistent answers given by the driver and passengers and where the questions were "not egregious enough to make the scope of the trooper's investigation unconstitutional").

Consensual Encounters After a Stop Has Ended

As discussed above, a suspect cannot be detained for investigation of matters different from those which support a stop, in the absence of founded suspicion as to those other matters. But what if the suspect is simply *asked* about another crime while the initial stop is ending? Can there be a permissible *encounter* after a stop? The Supreme Court addressed this question in Ohio v. Robinette, 519 U.S. 33 (1996). Robinette was legally stopped for speeding and given a verbal warning. When the officer returned Robinette's license, he said: "One question before you get gone: Are you carrying any illegal contraband in your car? Any weapons of any kind, drugs, anything like that?" Robinette answered "no" to these questions, after which the officer asked if he could search the car. Robinette consented. The officer found drugs and arrested Robinette.

Robinette argued that before valid consent could be obtained, the officer had to tell him that he was free to leave. Otherwise, the detention would still be continuing, and would amount to an illegal arrest as it was proceeding on a matter other than that which gave rise to the initial stop. But Chief Justice Rehnquist, in an opinion for seven members of the Court, disagreed. The Court held that Robinette voluntarily consented to the search, and rejected any bright-line requirement that the suspect be told that the stop is over and he is free to go. Justice Ginsburg concurred in the judgment. Justice Stevens dissented.

f. Interrogations and Fingerprinting

Interrogation Beyond the Confines of Terry

In Dunaway v. New York, 442 U.S. 200 (1979), the Court distinguished *Terry* stops from cases in which the police detain a suspect for sustained interrogation. The Court emphasized that *Terry* was a narrow decision and concluded that police cannot detain a suspect and transport him to the stationhouse for questioning without probable cause, even if the detention is not deemed to be an arrest under state law (and there would be no arrest record or formal booking procedure). Justice Brennan, writing for the Court, concluded that "detention for custodial interrogation—regardless of its label—intrudes so severely on interests protected by the Fourth Amendment as necessarily to trigger the traditional safeguards against illegal arrest." He noted that "any 'exception' that could cover a seizure as intrusive as that in this case would threaten to swallow the general rule that Fourth Amendment seizures are reasonable only if based upon probable cause."[24]

---

24. Justice White wrote a short opinion concurring in the judgment. Justice Stevens also wrote a brief concurring opinion. Justice Rehnquist, joined by Chief Justice Burger, dissented.

The Court in Kaupp v. Texas, 123 S.Ct. 1843 (2003) (per curiam) confirmed that a forced transportation and interrogation of a suspect constitutes an arrest for which probable cause is required. Police officers suspected Kaupp, an adolescent, of involvement in a murder, but did not have probable cause to arrest him. The officers entered Kaupp's house at 3 a.m., went to his bedroom, woke him up, placed him in handcuffs, and transported him in a patrol car while he was still in his underwear. The patrol car stopped for 5 to 10 minutes at the site where the victim's body had been found, and then went on to the sheriff's headquarters, where police removed Kaupp's handcuffs, gave him *Miranda* warnings, and told him that the victim's brother had confessed to the crime and implicated him as an accomplice. Kaupp then admitted to some part in the crime.

The state courts held that Kaupp had not been arrested, because he answered "okay" when he was told in his bedroom that he needed to go with the officers. The state courts brushed off the officers' use of handcuffs as "routine" practice of the police department. The Court reversed, finding it clear that Kaupp had been arrested without probable cause. The Court reasoned as follows:

> Although certain seizures may be justified on something less than probable cause, we have never sustained against Fourth Amendment challenge the involuntary removal of a suspect from his home to a police station and his detention there for investigative purposes absent probable cause or judicial authorization. Such involuntary transport to a police station for questioning is sufficiently like arrest to invoke the traditional rule that arrests may constitutionally be made only on probable cause.

> The state does not claim to have had probable cause here, and a straightforward application of the test just mentioned shows beyond cavil that Kaupp was arrested within the meaning of the Fourth Amendment * * *. A 17-year-old boy was awakened in his bedroom at three in the morning by at least three police officers, one of whom stated "we need to go and talk." He was taken out in handcuffs, without shoes, dressed only in his underwear in January, placed in a patrol car, driven to the scene of a crime and then to the sheriff's offices, where he was taken into an interrogation room and questioned. This evidence points to arrest even more starkly than the facts in Dunaway v. New York, 442 U.S. 200, 212 (1979), where the petitioner "was taken from a neighbor's home to a police car, transported to a police station, and placed in an interrogation room." There we held it clear that the detention was "in important respects indistinguishable from a traditional arrest" and therefore required probable cause or judicial authorization to be legal. The same is, if anything, even clearer here.

> Contrary reasons mentioned by the state courts are no answer to the facts. Kaupp's " 'Okay' " in response to Pinkins's statement [telling Kaupp to come with them to "have a talk"] is no showing of consent under the circumstances. Pinkins offered Kaupp no choice, and a group of police officers rousing an adolescent out of bed in the middle of the night with the words "we need to go and talk" presents no option but "to go." * * * If reasonable doubt were possible on this point, the ensuing events would

resolve it: removal from one's house in handcuffs on a January night with nothing on but underwear for a trip to a crime scene on the way to an interview room at law enforcement headquarters. Even "an initially consensual encounter . . . can be transformed into a seizure or detention within the meaning of the Fourth Amendment." INS v. Delgado, 466 U.S. 210, 215 (1984). It cannot seriously be suggested that when the detectives began to question Kaupp, a reasonable person in his situation would have thought he was sitting in the interview room as a matter of choice, free to change his mind and go home to bed.

Nor is it significant, as the state court thought, that the sheriff's department "routinely" transported individuals, including Kaupp on one prior occasion, while handcuffed for safety of the officers, or that Kaupp "did not resist the use of handcuffs or act in a manner consistent with anything other than full cooperation." The test is an objective one, and stressing the officers' motivation of self-protection does not speak to how their actions would reasonably be understood. As for the lack of resistance, failure to struggle with a cohort of deputy sheriffs is not a waiver of Fourth Amendment protection, which does not require the perversity of resisting arrest or assaulting a police officer.

Fingerprinting

In Davis v. Mississippi, 394 U.S. 721 (1969), cited in *Dunaway,* the Court held that a round-up of twenty-five African–American youths for questioning and fingerprinting, in an effort to match prints found around a window entered by a rape suspect, violated the Fourth Amendment. Justice Brennan wrote for the Court that "[i]t is arguable * * * that because of the unique nature of the fingerprinting process, such detentions might, under narrowly defined circumstances, be found to comply with the Fourth Amendment even though there is no probable cause in the traditional sense." He explained that fingerprinting is less serious an intrusion on liberty than other searches, that repeated fingerprinting is not a real danger because it would not be necessary, that fingerprinting is extremely reliable, and that it can be done at a convenient time and does not offer opportunities for harassment. In this case, however, the fingerprinting did not comply with the Fourth Amendment because, among other things, "petitioner was unnecessarily required to undergo two fingerprinting sessions; and petitioner was not merely fingerprinted * * * but also subjected to interrogation."

Isn't fingerprinting simply a means of identification, and isn't investigation of the suspect's identity permitted in a *Terry* stop? If there is reasonable suspicion but not probable cause, and the officer who makes a stop knows that there were fingerprints found at the scene of a crime, is it permissible for the officer to take fingerprints and delay the suspect long enough to obtain a match?

Justice White addressed some of these questions as he wrote for the Court in Hayes v. Florida, 470 U.S. 811 (1985). Police officers who were investigating a series of rapes had reasonable suspicion but not probable cause to believe that Hayes was the perpetrator. The officers took Hayes to the stationhouse, without his consent, to be fingerprinted. Justice White concluded that this procedure amounted to an arrest. He indicated that the Court adhered to the view that when police forcibly remove a person to the stationhouse, they are making a seizure that must be considered an arrest, requiring probable cause. Justice White added, however, that the Court's reasoning did not imply "that a brief detention in the field for the purpose of fingerprinting, where there is only reasonable suspicion not amounting to probable cause, is necessarily impermissible under the Fourth Amendment." He relied on *Davis* and noted that fingerprinting in itself is a relatively minimal intrusion and a means of identification not unlike other methods of identification permitted under *Terry*.[25]

Would you permit fingerprinting as part of a *Terry* stop? Would you permit the police to photograph persons who are stopped? What about taking DNA samples of persons who are stopped?

g.   *Time Limits on Terry Stops*

The Supreme Court rejected an absolute time limit for *Terry* stops in United States v. Sharpe, 470 U.S. 675 (1985). The facts are described in the next two paragraphs.

A Drug Enforcement agent was on patrol in an unmarked car on a coastal road in North Carolina at approximately 6:30 a.m. when he saw a blue pickup truck with an attached camper "traveling in tandem with a blue Pontiac Bonneville." The agent saw that the truck was riding low, the camper did not bounce or sway appreciably around turns, and that a quilted material covered the rear and side windows of the camper. The agent followed the vehicles for 20 miles into South Carolina where he decided to make an "investigative stop." He radioed the highway patrol for help and a trooper in a marked patrol car responded to the call. Almost immediately after the trooper caught up with the vehicles, the Pontiac and the pickup turned off the highway onto a campground road. The agent and trooper followed the two vehicles as they sped along the road at double the legal speed until they returned to the main road. The trooper pulled alongside the Pontiac, which was in the lead, turned on his flashing light and motioned for the driver to pull over. As the Pontiac moved to the side, the pickup truck cut between it and the trooper's car, nearly hitting the latter. The trooper pursued the truck while the agent approached the Pontiac and requested identification.

The agent examined the driver's license. After unsuccessfully attempting to radio the trooper, he radioed the local police for assistance. Two local officers arrived and the agent asked them to "maintain the situation" while he went to find the trooper. The trooper had stopped the pickup, removed the driver from the truck, examined his license and a bill of sale for the truck, and patted him down. When the trooper told the driver that he would be held until a DEA agent arrived, the driver became nervous, stated that he wanted to leave, and asked for the return of the driver's license. Approximately 15 minutes after the truck was stopped, the DEA agent arrived and learned that the name on the registration was the same as the name on the driver's license of the Pontiac's driver. The driver of the pickup denied two requests for permission to search the truck before the agent examined the truck and stated that he could smell marijuana. Without asking again for permission, he removed the keys from the ignition, opened the rear of the camper, and observed a large number of burlap-wrapped

---

25. Justice Brennan, joined by Justice Marshall, concurred in the judgment. He objected to "the Court's strained effort to reach the question" of "[t]he validity of on-site finger- printing." Justice Blackmun concurred in the judgment without opinion. Justice Powell did not participate in the case.

bales resembling marijuana. The agent arrested the driver and returned to the Pontiac to arrest its occupants. The total time between his initial stop of the Pontiac and the arrests of its occupants was between 30 and 40 minutes. The defendants argued that the evidence was illegally obtained as a result of an arrest in the absence of probable cause. The government argued that there was reasonable suspicion to detain the pickup, that the length of the detention by the trooper did not exceed that permitted by *Terry*, and that the DEA agent had probable cause to search the pickup after he smelled marijuana. The case boiled down to whether the pickup and its occupants had been detained beyond the time limits permitted by *Terry*.

Chief Justice Burger wrote for the Court and held that the detention did not exceed the time limits of a permissible *Terry* stop. The Chief Justice noted the "difficult linedrawing problems in distinguishing an investigative stop from a de facto arrest". He recognized that "if an investigative stop continues indefinitely, at some point it can no longer be justified as an investigative stop." Defendants suggested a bright-line time limit on *Terry* stops of 20 minutes. But the Court rejected a "hard-and-fast time limit" and concluded that it was "appropriate to examine whether the police diligently pursued a means of investigation that was likely to confirm or dispel their suspicions quickly, during which time it was necessary to detain the defendant." The officers satisfied that test, since the case did "not involve any delay unnecessary to the legitimate investigation of the law enforcement officers"; in part this was because the suspects contributed to the delay through their own actions, by refusing to pull over.

Justice Marshall concurred in the judgment because the evasive actions of the suspects turned a brief encounter with the officers into an extended one. He emphasized, however, that *Terry* stops must be brief "no matter what the needs of law enforcement in the particular case."

Justice Brennan dissented. He objected to treating the brevity limitation upon a stop as an "accordion-like concept that may be expanded outward depending on the law enforcement purposes to be served by the stop." He criticized the officers' handling of the investigation and found that the stop was unduly and unnecessarily lengthy. Justice Stevens dissented without reaching the merits.

Questions After Sharpe

After *Sharpe* what kind of conduct, if any, will be considered impermissible delay, as opposed to diligent investigation? See United States v. Davies, 768 F.2d 893 (7th Cir.1985)(reasonable to detain suspects for an additional thirty minutes to await advice from superiors, where detaining officers were inexperienced); United States v. Bloomfield, 40 F.3d 910 (8th Cir.1994)(en banc)("The one-hour period between the time Roberts pulled Bloomfield over and the time Roberts arrested Bloomfield was not an unreasonable period to wait for a drug dog to verify Roberts' suspicion."); United States v. Simmons, 172 F.3d 775 (11th Cir.1999) (officer did not exceed the limits of a *Terry* stop when he pulled a person over for a traffic violation, ran a warrant check, and waited for further information when it appeared that the defendant generally matched a description in an arrest warrant; 40 minute detention was not excessive).

Is it consistent for the Court to say that at some point a stop can continue for so long as to constitute an arrest, and yet that there is no hard and fast rule on how long a *Terry* stop can be?

h. Show of Force During a Terry Stop

A traditional arrest is sometimes accompanied by the officer's use of handcuffs and drawn gun. Can the officer use such coercive tactics within the confines of a *Terry* stop? Courts have routinely relied on *Terry* and *Adams* to uphold the use of handcuffs and guns where there is reasonable suspicion to believe that they are necessary to protect the officer from harm. See People v. Allen, 73 N.Y.2d 378, 540 N.Y.S.2d 971, 538 N.E.2d 323 (1989)(officers handcuffed suspect who matched the description of an armed bank robber, after chasing him down a dark alley in a high crime area); United States v. Merkley, 988 F.2d 1062 (10th Cir.1993)("because safety may require the police to freeze temporarily a potentially dangerous situation, both the display of firearms and the use of handcuffs may be part of a reasonable *Terry* stop"; use of such tactics was found permissible in this case where the defendant was suspected of threatening to kill someone).

In United States v. Alexander, 907 F.2d 269 (2d Cir.1990), the court held that officers acted properly when they unholstered their guns to detain two men suspected of purchasing drugs. The two men were in a Jaguar at 6:00 p.m., parked in an area known for drug activity. The court emphasized the "dangerous nature of the drug trade and the genuine need of law enforcement agents to protect themselves from the deadly threat it may pose." Has the court established a per se rule for those who are reasonably suspected of drug activity? Compare United States v. Novak, 870 F.2d 1345 (7th Cir.1989), where nine law enforcement officers working in an airport stopped two suspected drug couriers. One officer drew her gun and pointed it directly at one suspect's head at close range. The court found that an arrest had occurred. Do you agree?

The use of tactics such as handcuffing and drawn guns has sometimes resulted in a civil rights action being brought against the officers. Consider the facts behind the claim in Oliveira v. Mayer, 23 F.3d 642 (2d Cir.1994):

> On January 4, 1991, a private motorist spotted the plaintiffs, three dark-skinned males, handling an expensive video camera while driving in a dilapidated station wagon through an affluent area of North Stamford, Connecticut. Suspicious merely because the camera appeared quite valuable and because the vehicle had New York license plates and had emerged from a dead-end street, the motorist called the police from his car phone and reported that there may have been a burglary.

> The Stamford Police Department dispatched many officers in response to the motorist's report. They quickly located what they correctly believed was the station wagon the motorist had reported, and six police cruisers formed a wedge around the plaintiffs' vehicle * * *. The police officers then followed "high risk" or "felony" stop procedures. By loud-speaker, the plaintiffs were ordered to stop their vehicle, toss out the keys, and keep their hands outside the windows. With guns drawn, the police ordered the driver, Luis Oliveira, to leave the car, keep his hands above his head, and walk backwards towards them. Luis was then ordered to kneel, was handcuffed, was searched while spread over the hood of a car, and was placed into the rear of one of the police cruisers. The other two plaintiffs were similarly removed from the station wagon, handcuffed, searched, and segregated. Though the plaintiffs were at times slow to respond to the officers'

commands due to their limited mastery of English, they followed the officers' orders without resistance.

After thoroughly searching the defendants, the police also searched the entire interior of the station wagon and the contents of the shoulder bag found in the vehicle. Each plaintiff was separately questioned and at least one was read *Miranda* rights. While questioned, the plaintiffs stated they had been working as masons in North Stamford, but they could not provide an exact location or identify their employer. Luis Oliveira provided the police with a phone number, which was called, but the person that answered did not speak English. About 30 minutes after the plaintiffs were stopped, other officers completed a canvass of the neighborhood where the plaintiffs had initially been spotted and found no signs of a burglary, at which point the plaintiffs were released.

The officers argued that they had reasonable suspicion to believe the plaintiffs were involved in a crime, and that their use of coercive procedures was within the confines of a *Terry* stop. But the *Oliveira* court, assessing the above facts, concluded as follows:

When we consider (1) the numerous oppressive elements of the encounter between the police and the plaintiffs, (2) the limited evidence that there was a crime, and (3) the absence of any indication the plaintiffs were armed or dangerous, we must conclude, as a matter of law, that the plaintiffs were subject to a degree of restraint that was too intrusive to be classified as an investigative detention.

Do you agree, or can reasonable minds differ on this point? The *Oliveira* court also held that, as a matter of law, the officers did not have probable cause to arrest the plaintiffs. Do you agree, or can reasonable minds differ on this point?

Aggressive Tactics Employed Against Minorities

Do you think it made a difference to the *Oliveira* court that the persons subject to the use of force were members of a minority group, found in an affluent neighborhood? In Washington v. Lambert, 98 F.3d 1181 (9th Cir.1996), another civil rights action brought against police officers using force during an alleged *Terry* stop, the court explicitly noted its concerns that these police tactics were used disproportionately against minorities. In *Washington,* the plaintiffs were stopped because they fit a general description of two African–Americans wanted in a string of burglaries. Seven officers used spotlights on the plaintiffs, ordered them by bullhorn to get out of their car, handcuffed them, and placed them in separate squad cars. One officer had a police dog in tow. The plaintiffs were eventually released. The court evaluated the use of force on minorities in the context of a *Terry* stop:

In balancing the interests in freedom from arbitrary government intrusion and the legitimate needs of law enforcement officers, we cannot help but be aware that the burden of aggressive and intrusive police action falls disproportionately on African–American, and sometimes Latino, males. * * * Cases, newspaper reports, books, and scholarly writings all make clear that the experience of being stopped by the police is a much more common one for black men than it is for white men. See, e.g., Kolender v. Lawson, 461 U.S. 352, 354 (1983) (Lawson, a law abiding African–American man, was stopped or arrested fifteen times in primarily white neighborhoods in a 22–month period); Jeff Brazil and Steve Berry, Color of Driver is Key to Stops in I–95 Videos, Orl. Sent., Aug. 23, 1992, at A1 and Henry Curtis, Statistics Show Pattern of Discrimination, Orl. Sent. Aug. 23, 1992 at A11 (videotapes show that 70% of stops made by drug interdiction unit on portion of I–95 in Florida are of African–Americans or Hispanics, although they made up only 5% of the drivers on that stretch of the interstate. Only about 5% of these stops lead to arrests); Michael Schneider, State Police I–95 Drug Unit Found to Search Black Motorists 4 Times More Often Than White, Balt. Sun, May 23, 1996, at B2 (reporting similar statistics in Maryland four years later); David A. Harris, Factors for Reasonable Suspicion: When Black and Poor Means Stopped and Frisked, 69 Ind. L.J. 659, 679–80 (1994); Elizabeth A. Gaynes, The Urban Criminal Justice System: Where Young + Black + Male = Probable Cause, 20 Ford. Urb. L.J. 621, 623–25 (1993); Tracey Maclin, Black and Blue Encounters—Some Preliminary Thoughts About Fourth Amendment Seizures: Should Race Matter?, 26 Val. U.L.Rev. 243, 250–57 (documenting incidents); Developments in the Law—Race and the Criminal Process, 101 Harv. L.Rev. 1472, 1505 (1988) ("[P]olice often lower their standards of investigation when a suspect has been described as a minority, thus intruding upon a greater number of individuals who meet the racial description than if the suspect had been described as white.").

Although much of the evidence concerns the disproportionate burden police action imposes on African–American males who are young and poor, there is substantial evidence that the experience of being stopped by police is also common both for older African–Americans and for those who are professionals—lawyers, doctors, businessmen, and academics. E.g., Schneider, I–95 Drug Unit, at B2 (reporting complaints of an African–American couple in their mid-sixties whose minivan was pulled over and searched for drugs on their 40th wedding anniversary); Gaynes, Probable Cause, 20 Ford. Urb. L.J. at 625 ("Most black professionals can recount at least one incident of being stopped, roughed up, questioned, or degraded by white police officers."). For example, Deval Patrick, formerly a partner in a prestigious Boston law firm and an Assistant Attorney General of the United States and head of the Civil Rights Division at the Department of Justice, recently reported that "I still get stopped if I'm driving a nice car in the 'wrong' neighborhood." Deval Patrick, Have Americans Forgotten Who They Are?, L.A. Times, Sept. 2, 1996, at B5. Christopher Darden, a suddenly well-known prosecutor, recently wrote that he is stopped by police five times a year because "I always seem to get pulled over by some cop who is suspicious of a black man driving a Mercedes." Christopher Darden, In Contempt 110 (1996). Henry L. Gates, Jr. has written, poignantly, "[n]or does [University of Chicago Professor] William Julius Wilson ... wonder why he was stopped near a small New England town by a policeman who wanted to know what he was doing in those parts. There's a moving violation that many African–Americans know as D.W.B.: Driving While Black." Thirteen Ways of Looking at a Black Man, New Yorker, Oct. 23, 1995 at 59; see also Michael A. Fletcher, Driven to Extremes; Black Men Take Steps to Avoid Police Stops, Wash. Post, March 29, 1996, at A1 (reporting frequent stops by police of black professionals). These encounters are humiliating, damaging to the detainees' self-esteem, and reinforce the reality that racism and intolerance are for many African–Americans a regular part of their daily lives. See, e.g., Charles N. Jamison, Jr., Racism: The Hurt That Men Won't Name, Essence, Nov. 1992 at 64; Patrick, Have Americans Forgotten?

The *Washington* court held that the officers' use of handcuffs and drawn guns resulted in an arrest in the absence of probable cause, given the fact that the plaintiffs were cooperative, and that such tactics were unnecessary given the presence of a large number of police officers and a dog. In fact, the violation of the plaintiffs' constitutional rights was found to be so clear under the circumstances that the officers were not entitled to qualified immunity. But what, exactly, does the court's discussion of *stops* of minorities by police officers have to do with the *tactics* used by police officers during this stop?

6. Detention of Property Under Terry

Terry concerned seizures of the person, but its principles have been applied to seizures of property as well. The Court in United States v. Van Leeuwen, 397 U.S. 249 (1970), held that some detentions of property could occur upon reasonable suspicion. Officers, acting upon reasonable suspicion, detained a mailed package for more than a day, while an investigation was made for purposes of developing probable cause and obtaining a warrant. A unanimous Court recognized that detention of mail could at some point become an unreasonable seizure, but found that in the instant case the investigation was conducted promptly and diligently. The Court concluded that "[d]etention for this limited time was, indeed, the prudent act rather than letting the packages enter the mails and then, in case the initial suspicions were confirmed, trying to locate them en route." The Court emphasized that the privacy interest in the packages was "not disturbed or invaded until the approval of the magistrate was obtained." Compare United States v. Dass, 849 F.2d 414 (9th Cir. 1988)(reasonable suspicion does not justify detention of mail for 7–23 days, where the delay could have been reduced to 32 hours if officers had acted diligently); United States v. Aldaz, 921 F.2d 227 (9th Cir.1990)(three day detention of mail permissible upon reasonable suspicion, where drug-sniffing dogs were 700 air miles away, and other delays were caused by remoteness of post office).

The Court in *Van Leeuwen* upheld a one-day detention without probable cause, while an investigation was conducted. Recall the facts of *Sharpe*. Do you think the Court would have allowed the suspects to be detained without probable cause for more than a day, while a diligent investigation was being conducted?[26] If not, what is the difference between the seizure in *Sharpe* and that in *Van Leeuwen?* Could it be argued that the detention in *Van Leeuwen* was no seizure at all, since a person to whom mail is sent has no legitimate expectation of receiving it on a particular day? See United States v. Johnson, 990 F.2d 1129 (9th Cir.1993)(no seizure where the defendant had a two-hour layover at an airport, and the entire process of removing the defendant's luggage from a baggage cart, taking it into an office, and having a dog sniff it, was completed

---

26. See United States v. $191,910.00 in Currency, 16 F.3d 1051, 1060 n. 16 (9th Cir. 1994)("[I]f a police officer had sufficient reasonable suspicion to detain a person, he could not hold that person for 24 hours before obtaining probable cause, even if the government was working as quickly as it could to gather evidence establishing probable cause.").

prior to the time that the luggage would have been placed on the airplane); United States v. Terriques, 319 F.3d 1051 (8th Cir. 2003)(handling and observation of package by mail clerk was not a seizure as it did not delay the time of delivery).

Unreasonable Detention: United States v. Place

The Court in United States v. Place, 462 U.S. 696 (1983), noted that it is often necessary to seize property upon reasonable suspicion, while an investigation of criminal activity continues. The Court recognized, however, that if a person is traveling with his property, then a seizure of that property "intrudes on both the suspect's possessory interest in his luggage as well as his liberty interest in proceeding with his itinerary." It concluded that "the limitations applicable to investigative detentions of the person should define the permissible scope of the person's luggage on less than probable cause."

On the facts, the Court held that the officers detained Place's luggage for such a long period that probable cause was required to support the detention; because the officers had only reasonable suspicion, the detention was illegal. Police officers seized Place's luggage as he arrived at LaGuardia Airport on a flight from Miami. 90 minutes later, they subjected the luggage to a canine sniff. Justice O'Connor, writing for the Court, stated that the 90 minute detention was unreasonable in the absence of probable cause, because the delay was caused by the failure to transport the drug detecting dog from one New York metropolitan airport to another. She reasoned that the dog could have been transported while Place was in the air en route to New York, since the officers had reasonable suspicion during that time. She concluded that the officers had not diligently pursued the investigation, and that "we have never approved a seizure of the person for the prolonged 90–minute period involved here." Finally, the Court noted that the Fourth Amendment violation was "exacerbated by the failure of the agents to inform the respondent of the place to which they were transporting his luggage, of the length of time he might be dispossessed, and of what arrangements would be made for return of the luggage if the investigation dispelled the suspicion." Under these circumstances, the detention of Place's luggage was tantamount to a detention of Place himself. Justice Brennan, joined by Justice Marshall, concurred in the result. He argued that the *Terry* balancing approach "should not be conducted except in the most limited circumstances." Justice Blackmun also concurred in the result, similarly expressing concern "with what appears to me to be an emerging tendency on the part of the Court to convert the *Terry* decision into a general statement that the Fourth Amendment requires only that any seizure be reasonable."

Questions After Place

Does *Place* mean that a 90–minute detention of luggage is always unreasonable in the absence of probable cause? The Court in United States v. $191,910.00 in Currency, 16 F.3d 1051 (9th Cir.1994) held that a two-hour detention of a traveler's luggage, pending a dog sniff, violated the Fourth Amendment solely because of its length. Even if "an unforeseeable canine virus" had suddenly afflicted all the available drug-sniffing dogs, that court would have invalidated the two-hour seizure of the person's luggage. Do you agree, or should the officer's diligence in pursuing the investigation be the only factor for determining the reasonableness of the length of the seizure?

Does *Place* mean that officers must have the drug sniffing dog on the premises at the time the luggage is seized? See United States v. Alpert, 816 F.2d 958 (4th Cir.1987)(50–minute detention of luggage reasonable, and *Place* does not establish a per se requirement that narcotics dogs must be kept at each airport); United States v. Frost, 999 F.2d 737 (3d Cir.1993)(80–minute detention of luggage pending dog sniff was reasonable: "It does not demonstrate a lack of diligence on the part of the detectives that a drug-sniffing unit was not on duty that day, so that he had to be summoned to the airport"; *Place* distinguished because officers in that case had substantial time to bring the dog to the airport before the luggage arrived).

Seizure of Property With No Deprivation of a Liberty Interest

In United States v. LaFrance, 879 F.2d 1 (1st Cir.1989), police had reasonable suspicion to believe that a Federal Express package, addressed to LaFrance, contained drugs. The package was guaranteed for delivery that day by noon. The officers arranged for a dog sniff, but the dog was several miles away. The sniff began at 1:15 p.m., and was completed by 2:15; the test was positive. Then a warrant was obtained to search the package. LaFrance challenged the reasonableness of the detention of the package. He testified at the suppression hearing that on the basis of prior experience, he expected to receive the package by 11:00 a.m. The court held that "LaFrance's anticipation that he would receive the goods soon after 11 a.m., though based on earlier experiences, is irrelevant. It is hornbook contract law that where a delivery time is agreed upon, a court should not intrude to imply a different reasonable time for delivery." The court recognized that "once noon arrived, the constitutional chemistry was altered" but that the detention from that point was for a limited time, and that the police were diligent in their investigation during that time.

In *LaFrance*, the detention of the package on reasonable suspicion was longer than that held impermissible in *Place*; however, the court reasoned that unlike the traveler in *Place*, LaFrance's liberty interest was not impaired by the detention of the Federal Express package. Place could not really go anywhere without his luggage, whereas LaFrance was at home and free to go wherever he wanted. Since the intrusion was not as severe as that in *Place*, the court reasoned that the somewhat longer detention of the package was permissible so long as the police were acting diligently. Do you agree with the court that LaFrance's liberty interest was not impaired by the detention of the package? Wasn't LaFrance essentially confined to his home by his need to wait for the package?

7. Limited Searches for Evidence by Law Enforcement Officers Under Terry

Terry allows limited investigative seizures of the person or property on the basis of reasonable suspicion. *Terry* also allows limited searches for self-protection on the basis of reasonable suspicion. Does *Terry* permit limited, cursory inspections by law enforcement officers searching for *evidence* on the basis of reasonable suspicion rather than probable cause? This was one question encountered by the Court in Arizona v. Hicks, 480 U.S. 321 (1987). Police lawfully entered premises from which a weapon had been fired, and noticed two sets of expensive stereo components in an otherwise squalid apartment. Suspecting that the components were stolen, one officer moved a turntable in order to read the serial number that was on the underside of the unit. The serial number matched that of a turntable that had been reported stolen. The State did not argue that probable cause existed to move the turntable, but rather that the movement and inspection was a "cursory" search that was justified by reasonable suspicion.

Justice Scalia, writing for the Court, rejected this argument and held that probable cause was required for the search, even though it was cursory. He declared that "a search is a search, even if it happens to disclose nothing but the bottom of a turntable." He concluded that "we are unwilling to send police and judges into a new thicket of Fourth Amendment law, to seek a creature of uncertain description that is neither a plain-view inspection nor yet a full-blown search. Nothing in the prior opinions of this Court supports such a distinction." Why doesn't the prior opinion of the Court in *Terry* support the distinction that Justice Scalia rejected?

Justice O'Connor, joined by Chief Justice Rehnquist and Justice Powell, dissented. She argued that police officers who have reasonable, articulable suspicion that an object they come across in a lawful search is evidence of crime may make a cursory inspection of the object to verify their suspicion. Justice Powell added a dissenting opinion, joined by the Chief Justice and Justice O'Connor, that suggested that the majority's distinction between observing a serial number while searching (permissible) and moving an object to read a serial number (impermissible) trivialized the Fourth Amendment and would cause uncertainty. See also Minnesota v. Dickerson, 508 U.S. 366 (1993)(*Terry* protective search can be conducted if the officer has reasonable suspicion that the suspect poses a risk of harm to the officer or others; however, a search for contraband by law enforcement officers is outside the *Terry* doctrine and requires probable cause).

Questions After Hicks

The State in *Hicks* did not argue that the presence of two new stereos in a squalid apartment constituted probable cause to believe they were stolen. Should this argument have been made?

The holding in *Hicks* has not deterred the government from arguing that cursory inspections can be conducted on reasonable suspicion. In United States v. Winsor, 846 F.2d 1569 (9th Cir.1988) (en banc), officers chased suspected bank robbers fleeing from the crime into a hotel. Given the large number of rooms in the hotel, the court found that there was reasonable suspicion, but not probable cause, to believe that the robbers were in any particular room. At each room, the officers knocked on the door and announced "Police, open the door." After checking a few rooms, they knocked on a door answered by Dennis Winsor. They recognized him as the robber. At this point, the police had probable cause to enter, whereupon they found Peter Winsor, the other robber, as well as incriminating evidence. The Winsors argued that under *Hicks,* the police conducted a search of their room when they knocked on the door, commanded that it be opened, and looked inside. The government argued that the officers had not conducted a full-blown search for evidence, but rather a cursory inspection requiring only reasonable suspicion. The court of appeals held that the evidence the officers discovered when the door opened (and all evidence found in the room thereafter) was illegally obtained:

We refuse the government's invitation to decide this case by balancing the competing interests at stake. Instead, we adhere to the bright-line rule that *Hicks* appears to have announced: The Fourth Amendment prohibits searches of dwellings without probable cause.

Would *Winsor* have come out differently if the officers had searched all but 30 rooms before finding the Winsors? All but 20? All but 10?

In United States v. Colyer, 878 F.2d 469 (D.C.Cir.1989), the court found it difficult to reconcile the *Terry* doctrine with the Court's rejection of Justice O'Connor's balancing approach for searches in *Hicks*.

To be sure, the Supreme Court has upheld on reasonable suspicion a variety of minimally intrusive *seizures* * * *. Although there may be no compelling reason to differentiate between seizures on the basis of their intrusiveness and failing to likewise differentiate between types of searches, the fact remains that we are unable to point to a single Supreme Court case that has upheld a search on reasonable suspicion merely because it was minimally intrusive.

Other courts have taken the contrary view and held that a minimally intrusive search for evidence is permissible if supported by reasonable suspicion. For example, in United States v. Concepcion, 942 F.2d 1170 (7th Cir.1991), officers took a key found on the defendant, and inserted it into a lock on a door to an apartment in which drugs had been found. The court held that this was a search, since the use of the key in the lock gave the officers information they did not otherwise have, i.e., that the defendant had a key to the apartment. But the search was upheld even though, at the time they used the key, the officers had only reasonable suspicion and not probable cause to connect the defendant with the apartment. The court reasoned that the search was minimally intrusive. It distinguished *Hicks* on the ground that the information uncovered in *Hicks* was more private: the officers in *Concepcion* could have connected the defendant with the apartment in a variety of ways. Is this a meaningful distinction?

Is there any persuasive distinction between searches and seizures that supports the difference in result between *Terry* and *Hicks*?

8. *Application of the Terry Reasonableness Analysis Outside the Stop and Frisk Context*

The *Terry* analysis balances the nature of the individual interest at stake in a search and seizure against the interest of the government in investigating and preventing crime. *Terry* applied this reasonableness analysis in the context of the limited intrusion known as stop and frisk. But it is apparent that the balancing analysis could be applied in a wide variety of contexts to allow intrusions on reasonable suspicion rather than probable cause, and without a warrant. In the following case, the Court applied the *Terry* analysis to a full-blown search of the residence of a probationer.

UNITED STATES v. KNIGHTS

Supreme Court of the United States, 2001.
534 U.S. 112.

Chief Justice Rehnquist **delivered the opinion of the Court.**

A California court sentenced respondent Mark James Knights to summary probation for a drug offense. The probation order included the following condition: that Knights would "[s]ubmit his ... person, property, place of residence, vehicle, personal effects, to search at anytime, with or without a search warrant, warrant of arrest or reasonable cause by any probation officer or law enforcement officer." Knights signed the probation order, which stated immediately above his signature that "I HAVE RECEIVED A COPY, READ AND UNDERSTAND THE ABOVE TERMS AND CONDITIONS OF PROBATION AND AGREE TO ABIDE BY SAME." In this case, we decide whether a search pursuant to this probation condition, and supported by reasonable suspicion, satisfied the Fourth Amendment.

Three days after Knights was placed on probation, a Pacific Gas & Electric (PG & E) power transformer and adjacent Pacific Bell telecommunications vault near the Napa County Airport were pried open and set on fire, causing an estimated $1.5 million in damage. Brass padlocks had been removed and a gasoline accelerant had been used to ignite the fire. This incident was the latest in more than 30 recent acts of vandalism against PG & E facilities in Napa County. Suspicion for these acts had long focused on Knights and his friend, Steven Simoneau. The incidents began after PG & E had filed a theft-of-services complaint against Knights and discontinued his electrical service for failure to pay his bill. Detective Todd Hancock of the Napa County Sheriff's Department had noticed that the acts of vandalism coincided with Knights's court appearance dates concerning the theft of PG & E services. And just a week before the arson, a sheriff's deputy had stopped Knights and Simoneau near a PG & E gas line and observed pipes and gasoline in Simoneau's pickup truck.

After the PG & E arson, a sheriff's deputy drove by Knights's residence, where he saw Simoneau's truck parked in front. The deputy felt the hood of the truck. It was warm. Detective Hancock decided to set up surveillance of Knights's apartment. At about 3:10 the next morning, Simoneau exited the apartment carrying three cylindrical items. Detective Hancock believed the items were pipe bombs. Simoneau walked across the street to the bank of the Napa River, and Hancock heard three splashes. Simoneau returned without the cylinders and drove away in his truck. Simoneau then stopped in a driveway, parked, and left the area. Detective Hancock entered the driveway and observed a number of suspicious objects in the truck: a Molotov cocktail and explosive materials, a gasoline can, and two brass padlocks that fit the description of those removed from the PG & E transformer vault.

After viewing the objects in Simoneau's truck, Detective Hancock decided to conduct a search of Knights's apartment. Detective Hancock was aware of the search condition in Knights's probation order and thus believed that a warrant was not necessary. The search revealed a detonation cord, ammunition, liquid chemicals, instruction manuals on chemistry and electrical circuitry, bolt cutters, telephone pole-climbing spurs, drug paraphernalia, and a brass padlock stamped "PG & E."

Knights was arrested, and a federal grand jury subsequently indicted him for conspiracy to commit arson, for possession of an unregistered destructive device, and being a felon in possession of ammunition. Knights moved to suppress the evidence obtained during the search of his apartment. The District Court held that Detective Hancock had "reasonable suspicion" to believe that Knights was involved with incendiary materials. The District Court nonetheless granted the motion to suppress on the ground that the search was for "investigatory" rather than "probationary" purposes. The Court of Appeals for the Ninth Circuit affirmed. The Court of Appeals relied on its earlier decisions holding that the search condition in Knights's probation order "must be seen as limited to probation searches, and must stop short of investigation searches."

The Supreme Court of California has rejected this distinction and upheld searches pursuant to the California probation condition "whether the purpose of the search is to monitor the probationer or to serve some other law enforcement purpose." People v. Woods, 21 Cal.4th 668, 681, 88 Cal. Rptr.2d 88, 981 P.2d 1019, 1027 (1999). We granted certiorari, to assess the constitutionality of searches made pursuant to this common California probation condition.

Certainly nothing in the condition of probation suggests that it was confined to searches bearing upon probationary status and nothing more. The search condition provides that Knights will submit to a search "by any probation officer or law enforcement officer" and does not mention anything about purpose. The question then is whether the Fourth Amendment limits searches pursuant to this probation condition to those with a "probationary" purpose.

Knights argues that this limitation follows from our decision in Griffin v. Wisconsin, 483 U.S. 868 (1987) [see the discussion of *Griffin* in the section on "special needs" searches, later in this chapter]. In *Griffin*, we upheld a search of a probationer conducted pursuant to a Wisconsin regulation permitting "any probation officer to search a probationer's home without a warrant as long as his supervisor approves and as long as there are 'reasonable grounds' to believe the presence of contraband," The Wisconsin regulation that authorized the search was not an express condition of Griffin's probation; in fact, the regulation was not even promulgated at the time of Griffin's sentence. The regulation applied to all Wisconsin probationers, with no need for a judge to make an individualized determination that the probationer's conviction justified the need for warrantless searches. We held that a State's operation of its probation system presented a "special need" for the "exercise of supervision to assure that [probation] restrictions are in fact observed." That special need for supervision justified the Wisconsin regulation and the search pursuant to the regulation was thus reasonable.

In Knights's view, apparently shared by the Court of Appeals, a warrantless search of a probationer satisfies the Fourth Amendment only if it is just like the search at issue in *Griffin*—i.e., a "special needs" search conducted by a probation officer monitoring whether the probationer is complying with probation restrictions. This dubious logic—that an opinion upholding the constitutionality of a particular search implicitly holds unconstitutional any search that is not like it—runs contrary to *Griffin's* express statement that its "special needs" holding made it "unnecessary to consider whether" warrantless searches of probationers were otherwise reasonable within the meaning of the Fourth Amendment.

* * *

We need not decide whether Knights's acceptance of the search condition constituted consent in the

* * * sense of a complete waiver of his Fourth Amendment rights * * * because we conclude that the search of Knights was reasonable under our general Fourth Amendment approach of "examining the totality of the circumstances," Ohio v. Robinette, 519 U.S. 33, 39 (1996), with the probation search condition being a salient circumstance.

The touchstone of the Fourth Amendment is reasonableness, and the reasonableness of a search is determined by assessing, on the one hand, the degree to which it intrudes upon an individual's privacy and, on the other, the degree to which it is needed for the promotion of legitimate governmental interests. Knights's status as a probationer subject to a search condition informs both sides of that balance. "Probation, like incarceration, is a form of criminal sanction imposed by a court upon an offender after verdict, finding, or plea of guilty." *Griffin, supra,* at 874. * * * Inherent in the very nature of probation is that probationers do not enjoy the absolute liberty to which every citizen is entitled. Just as other punishments for criminal convictions curtail an offender's freedoms, a court granting probation may impose reasonable conditions that deprive the offender of some freedoms enjoyed by law-abiding citizens.

The judge who sentenced Knights to probation determined that it was necessary to condition the probation on Knights's acceptance of the search provision. It was reasonable to conclude that the search condition would further the two primary goals of proba-

tion—rehabilitation and protecting society from future criminal violations. The probation order clearly expressed the search condition and Knights was unambiguously informed of it. The probation condition thus significantly diminished Knights's reasonable expectation of privacy.[a]

In assessing the governmental interest side of the balance, it must be remembered that the very assumption of the institution of probation is that the probationer is more likely than the ordinary citizen to violate the law. The recidivism rate of probationers is significantly higher than the general crime rate. See U.S. Dept. of Justice, Office of Justice Programs, Bureau of Justice Statistics, Recidivism of Felons on Probation, 1986–89, pp. 1, 6 (Feb. 1992) (reporting that 43% of 79,000 felons placed on probation in 17 States were rearrested for a felony within three years while still on probation). And probationers have even more of an incentive to conceal their criminal activities and quickly dispose of incriminating evidence than the ordinary criminal because probationers are aware that they may be subject to supervision and face revocation of probation, and possible incarceration, in proceedings in which the trial rights of a jury and proof beyond a reasonable doubt, among other things, do not apply.

The State has a dual concern with a probationer. On the one hand is the hope that he will successfully complete probation and be integrated back into the community. On the other is the concern, quite justified, that he will be more likely to engage in crimi-

a. We do not decide whether the probation condition so diminished, or completely eliminated, Knights's reasonable expectation of privacy (or constituted consent, see supra, at 6) that a search by a law enforcement officer without any individualized suspicion would have satisfied the reasonableness requirement of the Fourth Amendment. The terms of the probation condition permit such a search, but we need not address the constitutionality of a suspicionless search because the search in this case was supported by reasonable suspicion.

nal conduct than an ordinary member of the community. The view of the Court of Appeals in this case would require the State to shut its eyes to the latter concern and concentrate only on the former. But we hold that the Fourth Amendment does not put the State to such a choice. Its interest in apprehending violators of the criminal law, thereby protecting potential victims of criminal enterprise, may therefore justifiably focus on probationers in a way that it does not on the ordinary citizen.

We hold that the balance of these considerations requires no more than reasonable suspicion to conduct a search of this probationer's house. The degree of individualized suspicion required of a search is a determination of when there is a sufficiently high probability that criminal conduct is occurring to make the intrusion on the individual's privacy interest reasonable. See United States v. Cortez, 449 U.S. 411, 418 (1981) (individualized suspicion deals "with probabilities"). Although the Fourth Amendment ordinarily requires the degree of probability embodied in the term "probable cause," a lesser degree satisfies the Constitution when the balance of governmental and private interests makes such a standard reasonable. See, e.g., Terry v. Ohio, 392 U.S. 1 (1968). Those interests warrant a lesser than probable-cause standard here. When

an officer has reasonable suspicion that a probationer subject to a search condition is engaged in criminal activity, there is enough likelihood that criminal conduct is occurring that an intrusion on the probationer's significantly diminished privacy interests is reasonable.

The same circumstances that lead us to conclude that reasonable suspicion is constitutionally sufficient also render a warrant requirement unnecessary. See Illinois v. McArthur, 531 U.S. 326, 330 (2001) (noting that general or individual circumstances, including "diminished expectations of privacy," may justify an exception to the warrant requirement).

* * *

The District Court found, and Knights concedes, that the search in this case was supported by reasonable suspicion. We therefore hold that the warrantless search of Knights, supported by reasonable suspicion and authorized by a condition of probation, was reasonable within the meaning of the Fourth Amendment. The judgment of the Court of Appeals is reversed, and the cause is remanded for further proceedings not inconsistent with this opinion.

It is so ordered.

[The concurring opinion of Justice Souter is omitted.]

C. SEARCH INCIDENT TO ARREST: THE ARREST POWER RULE

A warrantless search incident to a valid arrest was an accepted practice at the time the Bill of Rights was adopted. While the principle was and is well-accepted, its application to various fact situations, and even the rationale underlying the exception, have been subject to dispute and inconsistent application in the Supreme Court. In the following case, the Court sought to explain the rationale of the search incident to arrest exception, and to limit the scope of an incident search to the rationale supporting the exception.

1. Spatial Limitations

CHIMEL v. CALIFORNIA

Supreme Court of the United States, 1969.
395 U.S. 752.

MR. JUSTICE STEWART **delivered the opinion of the Court.**

This case raises basic questions concerning the permissible scope under the Fourth Amendment of a search incident to a lawful arrest.

The relevant facts are essentially undisputed. Late in the afternoon of September 13, 1965, three police officers arrived at the Santa Ana, California, home of the petitioner with a warrant authorizing his arrest for the burglary of a coin shop. The officers knocked on the door, identified themselves to the petitioner's wife, and asked if they might come inside. She ushered them into the house, where they waited 10 or 15 minutes until the petitioner returned home from work. When the petitioner entered the house, one of the officers handed him the arrest warrant and asked for permission to "look around." The petitioner objected, but was advised that "on the basis of the lawful arrest," the officers would nonetheless conduct a search. No search warrant had been issued.

Accompanied by the petitioner's wife, the officers then looked through the entire three-bedroom house, including the attic, the garage, and a small workshop. In some rooms the search was relatively cursory. In the master bedroom and sewing room, however, the officers directed the petitioner's wife to open drawers and "to physically move contents of the drawers from side to side so that [they] might view any items that would have come from [the] burglary." After completing the search, they seized numerous items—primarily coins, but also several medals, tokens, and a few oth-

er objects. The entire search took between 45 minutes and an hour.

At the petitioner's subsequent state trial on two charges of burglary, the items taken from his house were admitted into evidence against him, over his objection that they had been unconstitutionally seized. * * *

Without deciding the question, we proceed on the hypothesis that the California courts were correct in holding that the arrest of the petitioner was valid under the Constitution. This brings us directly to the question whether the warrantless search of the petitioner's entire house can be constitutionally justified as incident to that arrest. The decisions of this Court bearing upon that question have been far from consistent, as even the most cursory review makes evident.

* * *

[The Court describes its erratic decisions beginning with dictum in Weeks v. United States, 232 U.S. 383 (1914), and continuing through Harris v. United States, 331 U.S. 145 (1947), Trupiano v. United States, 334 U.S. 699 (1948), and United States v. Rabinowitz, 339 U.S. 56 (1950).]

Rabinowitz has come to stand for the proposition, *inter alia,* that a warrantless search "incident to a lawful arrest" may generally extend to the area that is considered to be in the "possession" or under the "control" of the person arrested. And it was on the basis of that proposition that the California courts upheld the search of the petitioner's entire house in this case. That doctrine, however, at least in the broad sense in which it was applied by the California courts in this case, can withstand neither historical nor rational analysis.

* * *

* * * When an arrest is made, it is reasonable for the arresting officer to search the person arrested in order to remove any weapons that the latter might seek to use in order to resist arrest or effect his escape. Otherwise, the officer's safety might well be endangered, and the arrest itself frustrated. In addition, it is entirely reasonable for the arresting officer to search for and seize any evidence on the arrestee's person in order to prevent its concealment or destruction. And the area into which an arrestee might reach in order to grab a weapon or evidentiary items must, of course, be governed by a like rule. A gun on a table or in a drawer in front of one who is arrested can be as dangerous to the arresting officer as one concealed in the clothing of the person arrested. There is ample justification, therefore, for a search of the arrestee's person and the area "within his immediate control"—construing that phrase to mean the area from within which he might gain possession of a weapon or destructible evidence.

There is no comparable justification, however, for routinely searching any room other than that in which an arrest occurs—or, for that matter, for searching through all the desk drawers or other closed or concealed areas in that room itself. Such searches, in the absence of well-recognized exceptions, may be made only under the authority of a search warrant. The "adherence to judicial processes" mandated by the Fourth Amendment requires no less.

* * *

It is argued in the present case that it is "reasonable" to search a man's house when he is arrested in it. But that argument is founded on little more than a subjective view regarding the acceptability of certain sorts of police conduct, and not on considerations relevant to Fourth Amendment interests. Under such an unconfined analysis, Fourth Amendment protection in this area would approach the evaporation point. It is not easy to explain why, for instance, it is less subjectively "reasonable" to search a man's house when he is arrested on his front lawn—or just down the street—than it is when he happens to be in the house at the time of arrest. * * * Thus, although "[t]he recurring questions of the reasonableness of searches" depend upon "the facts and circumstances—the total atmosphere of the case," those facts and circumstances must be viewed in the light of established Fourth Amendment principles.

It would be possible, of course, to draw a line between *Rabinowitz* and *Harris* on the one hand, and this case on the other. For *Rabinowitz* involved a single room, and *Harris* a four-room apartment, while in the case before us an entire house was searched. But such a distinction would be highly artificial. The rationale that allowed the searches and seizures in *Rabinowitz* and *Harris* would allow the searches and seizures in this case. No consideration relevant to the Fourth Amendment suggests any point of rational limitation, once the search is allowed to go beyond the area from which the person arrested might obtain weapons or evidentiary items. The only reasoned distinction is one between a search of the person arrested and the area within his reach on the one hand, and more extensive searches on the other.

The petitioner correctly points out that one result of decisions such as *Rabinowitz* and *Harris* is to give law enforcement officials the opportunity to engage in searches not justified by probable cause, by the simple expedient of arranging to arrest suspects at home rather than elsewhere. We do not suggest that the petitioner is necessarily correct in his assertion that such a strategy was utilized here, but the fact remains that had he been arrested earlier in the day, at his place of employment rather than at home, no search of his house could have been made without a search warrant. * * *

[The concurring opinion of Justice Harlan is omitted.]

Mr. Justice White, **with whom Mr. Justice Black joins, dissenting.**

* * *

* * * Search of an arrested man and of the items within his immediate reach must in almost every case be reasonable. There is always a danger that the suspect will try to escape, seizing concealed weapons with which to overpower and injure the arresting officers, and there is a danger that he may destroy evidence vital to the prosecution. Circumstances in which these justifications would not apply are sufficiently rare that inquiry is not made into searches of this scope, which have been considered reasonable throughout.

The justifications which make such a search reasonable obviously do not apply to the search of areas to which the accused does not have ready physical access. This is not enough, however, to prove such searches unconstitutional. The Court has always held, and does not today deny, that when there is probable cause to search and it is "impracticable" for one reason or another to get a search warrant, then a warrantless search may be reasonable. This is the case whether an arrest was made at the time of the search or not.

This is not to say that a search can be reasonable without regard to the probable cause to believe that seizable items are on the premises. But when there are exigent circumstances, and probable cause, then the search may be made without a warrant, reasonably. An arrest itself may often create an emergency situation making it impracticable to obtain a warrant before embarking on a related search. Again assuming that there is probable cause to search premises at the spot where a suspect is arrested, it seems to me unreasonable to require the police to leave the scene in order to obtain a search warrant when they are already legally there to make a valid arrest, and when there must almost always be a strong possibility that confederates of the arrested man will in the meanwhile remove the items for which the police have probable cause to search. This must so often be the case that it seems to me as unreasonable to require a warrant for a search of the premises as to require a warrant for search of the person and his very immediate surroundings.

* * *

Application of Chimel's Case–By–Case Approach

What are the precise spatial limitations on the arrest power rule after *Chimel*? Is the permissible scope of the search determined by where the suspect was arrested, or by where the search occurred? Does it make a difference that the suspect is handcuffed? Infirm? Consider United States v. Lucas, 898 F.2d 606 (8th Cir.1990), where the defendant was convicted of bank robbery based in part upon evidence found in the following search incident to arrest:

The magistrate found that Lucas was seated at a kitchen table with two other men as the officers stood in the front doorway of the apartment in which he was arrested. As Lucas began to get up from the table, the officers entered the apartment and ran into the kitchen. Two officers attempted to apprehend Lucas, and one officer monitored the other two men seated at the table. By the time the officers reached Lucas, his hand was within inches of the handle on a cabinet door. During the ensuing struggle, which lasted for approximately forty seconds, Lucas and the two officers slid around on the slick floor. At one point, Lucas fell to the floor, and the skirmish continued until Lucas was handcuffed. As an officer pulled Lucas from the floor and moved him toward the living room, another officer immediately stood up, opened the cabinet door that Lucas had been attempting to reach, and found a chrome automatic pistol inside the cabinet. The two men seated at the kitchen table were not handcuffed until after the gun was discovered.

The court upheld the search under *Chimel:*

> Lucas argues that *Chimel* does not justify the search here because he was being escorted, handcuffed, from the kitchen when the search occurred. While relevant under *Chimel*, this is not a determinative factor. * * * [A] warrantless search incident to an arrest may be valid even though a court, operating with the benefit of hindsight in an environment well removed from the scene of the arrest, doubts that the defendant could have reached the items seized during the search. The officers in this case searched a cabinet in a small kitchen immediately after handcuffing Lucas and while removing him from the kitchen. Moreover, two of Lucas' friends who had not been handcuffed were still at the kitchen table when the search took place. On these facts, we conclude that this was a valid warrantless search incident to Lucas' arrest. This conclusion is consistent not only with [this Circuit's opinions] but also with opinions from other circuits. See United States v. Queen, 847 F.2d at 352–54 (holding search valid even though it occurred when arrestee was handcuffed and guarded by two police officers several feet from the searched area); United States v. Silva, 745 F.2d 840, 847 (4th Cir.1984)(upholding search begun after arrestees were handcuffed, placed on beds, and monitored by federal agents); United States v. Fleming, 677 F.2d 602, 606–08 (7th Cir.1982)(approving the search, after arrestees were handcuffed, of a paper bag that was in police custody).

Does the court in *Lucas* show too much or just enough concern for the safety of the officers? Compare United States v. Blue, 78 F.3d 56 (2d Cir.1996) (search of an area between a mattress and a box spring could not be justified under the arrest power rule; the suspects were on the floor, handcuffed with their hands behind their backs, and many officers were controlling them).

Timing of Grab Area Determination

Should the grab area be determined by where the arrestee is at the time of the *search*, or rather by where the arrestee *was* at the time of *arrest*? In Davis v. Robbs, 794 F.2d 1129 (6th Cir.1986), the court upheld the seizure of a rifle that had been in close proximity to the arrestee at the time of the arrest. Judge Wellford dissented on this point, noting that the search and seizure occurred after the arrestee was put in the squad car:

> The rationale justifying the search incident to arrest exception is that some exigency exists at the time of the search or seizure, not arrest.

Otherwise, no actual exigency, such as danger to the safety of the police or others, would exist. The actual exigency at the time of arrest would become fictional through transplantation to the time of the search and seizure. At the time the police seized the rifle in the present case, [the arrestee] was handcuffed and in the squad car. He no longer had access to the gun nor posed any danger to the police. * * * Thus, the rationale justifying the exception does not support the seizure of the rifle. The danger had passed.

The court in United States v. Abdul–Saboor, 85 F.3d 664 (D.C.Cir.1996) agreed with the majority in *Davis* that the grab area should be determined as of the time of the arrest, not at the time of the search. Thus, an officer's search of an area after the arrestee had been taken out of the room was permissible. The court reasoned that "if the courts were to focus exclusively upon the moment of the search, we might create a perverse incentive for an arresting officer to prolong the period during which the arrestee is kept in an area where he could pose a danger to the officer." Do you think this is a realistic possibility? Compare United States v. Myers, 308 F.3d 251 (3rd Cir. 2002)(arrest power grab area must be determined as of the time of the search; therefore search of bag was illegal when it occurred after the defendant was restrained, physically incapacitated, and under the control of two armed officers).

For arguments that the search incident to arrest doctrine has been interpreted too broadly by the courts, see Wayne Logan, An Exception Swallows a Rule: Police Authority to Search Incident to Arrest, 19 Yale L. & Pol. Rev. 381 (2001); Myron Moskowitz, A Rule in Search of a Reason: An Empirical Reexamination of *Chimel* and *Belton*, 2002 Wis. L. Rev. 657.

Creating Grab Areas

The arrest power rule, after *Chimel*, is based on the need to prevent the arrestee from reaching evidence or a weapon. In United States v. Perea, 986 F.2d 633 (2d Cir.1993), officers stopped a cab in which Perea was a passenger, and arrested him on a narcotics charge. They found a duffel bag in the trunk of the cab. One officer took Perea out of the cab and brought him next to the duffel bag, and asked him to identify it as his. Perea implied that he was transporting the bag for another person. The officers thereupon searched the bag and found narcotics. The court held that this search could not be justified under the arrest power rule, because "arresting agents are not allowed to simulate circumstances warranting application of the incident-to-arrest exception merely by bringing the item they wish to search into the area near the person arrested, or vice versa." But didn't the officer have a permissible motive for bringing Perea next to the bag? Is there any other way that Perea could have been asked to identify the bag?

Post-Arrest Movements: Washington v. Chrisman

Does the rationale of *Chimel*, allowing search incident to arrest to protect the officer and preserve the evidence, apply to every arrest? Does it apply even if the arrestee is allowed to move about? In Washington v. Chrisman, 455 U.S. 1 (1982), Chief Justice Burger, writing for the Court, declared that "the absence of an affirmative indication that an arrested person might have a weapon available or might attempt to escape does not diminish the arresting officer's authority to maintain custody over the arrested person." The Court stated that "every arrest must be presumed to present a risk of danger to the arresting officer," because "there is no way for an officer to predict reliably how a particular subject will react to arrest of the degree of potential danger." The Court upheld a search and seizure incident to arrest under the following circumstances: A police officer saw a person who appeared to be underage carrying liquor. He asked for identification and the suspect said it was in his dormitory room. The suspect agreed that the officer could accompany him while he retrieved it. As the suspect entered the room the officer remained in the open doorway from where he saw the suspect's roommate become nervous. The officer entered the room and noticed seeds and a small pipe that he concluded were used in marijuana smoking. After warning both roommates of their rights, the officer asked about other drugs and was given additional marijuana. The officer subsequently obtained consent to search the room and found LSD.

Chief Justice Burger reasoned that once the officer placed his suspect under arrest before returning to the suspect's room "[t]he officer had a right to remain literally at the suspect's elbow at all times." The opinion referred to the initial actions of the officer in waiting in the doorway as exhibiting restraint and concluded that since he had a valid right to enter the room at any time to monitor the movements of the arrested person, he had a right to be where he was when he first saw the seeds and the pipe.

Justice White, joined by Justices Brennan and Marshall, dissented. The thrust of the dissent was that an officer "should not be permitted to invade living quarters any more than is necessary to maintain control and protect himself," which were not the reasons for the invasion in this case.[27]

Post-Arrest Movements Ordered by the Officer

In *Chrisman*, the defendant voluntarily went to his room to get identification. What if the arrestee does not want to retrieve something from his house—like his clothes? Can the officer require the arrestee to retrieve an item, and then invoke *Chrisman* and follow the arrestee through the house? A court confronted this question in United States v. Butler, 980 F.2d 619 (10th Cir. 1992). Officers went to Butler's trailer armed with an arrest warrant. The grounds were strewn with litter, broken glass, and several hundred beer cans. The officers called for Butler to come outside, where he was placed under arrest. They noticed that Butler was not wearing shoes, and that there was broken glass near his feet. The officers directed Butler to go in and get some shoes on; they followed him as he did so, and they saw and seized illegal weapons in the trailer. The court relied on *Chrisman* and held that the officers' actions were proper. It found that the officers acted out of a concern for Butler's welfare, and noted several decisions holding that "police may conduct a limited entry into an area for the purpose of protecting the health or safety of an arrestee." See, e.g.,

---

27. Although the Supreme Court reversed the Washington Supreme Court in *Chrisman*, it was the state supreme court that was to have the last word. On remand, it held that the officer violated the state constitution, which it interpreted to prohibit warrantless entry into a private dwelling by an officer unless he has specific articulable facts justifying the entry. The court found that the officer had no reason to perceive a threat to his safety or to fear destruction of evidence or escape, and that his entry was therefore invalid. State v. Chrisman, 100 Wash.2d 814, 676 P.2d 419 (1984).

United States v. Titus, 445 F.2d 577 (2d Cir.1971)(where defendant was naked when arrested, the officers "were bound to find some clothing for Titus rather than take him nude to FBI headquarters on a December night"). Compare United States v. Anthon, 648 F.2d 669 (10th Cir.1981)(officers could not force arrestee to "complete his wardrobe" where he was arrested in swimming trunks).

Arrest Leading to Exigent Circumstances

Justice White, dissenting in *Chimel,* argues that when a person is arrested, the fact of the arrest itself will in almost all cases give rise to exigent circumstances to search beyond the grab area of the arrestee. He reasoned that friends, family or business associates of the arrestee will almost always become aware of an arrest and will almost always try to destroy evidence when they learn about the arrest. Justice White does not contend that exigent circumstances will arise after *every* arrest, nor could he: if Chimel had been arrested while his wife was at work, there could be no threat that the wife would immediately destroy evidence. Rather, Justice White argues that exigent circumstances will arise so often upon an arrest that it makes sense to establish a bright line rule permitting a search, so as to avoid the negative effects of ad hoc judgments and a case-by-case approach. Why did this argument not persuade the majority? If, as *Chrisman* states, we presume that the arrestee will destroy evidence or harm the officer even if that is not so in a particular case, why do we not presume that the arrestee's associates will learn about the arrest and destroy evidence or harm the officer?

The exigent circumstances exception will be discussed later in this Chapter, but for now it is important to note that the Court requires a showing of exigency on the particular facts of the case, and that the arrest of a person, while certainly relevant, is not dispositive of whether there is a risk of destruction of evidence or harm to the officers or public that would excuse the warrant requirement. Illustrative is Vale v. Louisiana, 399 U.S. 30 (1970). Officers observing Vale had probable cause to believe that he had engaged in a drug transaction outside his house. When they approached, Vale walked quickly toward the house. He was arrested on his front steps. The officers then searched the house, and found narcotics in the back bedroom. Three minutes after the officers entered the house, Vale's mother and brother came home carrying groceries. Justice Stewart wrote for the Court as it held that the officers' warrantless search of the bedroom violated the Fourth Amendment. The Court found that the State had not met its burden of showing that exigent circumstances existed. Justice Stewart stated that "the goods ultimately seized were not in the process of destruction," and rejected the argument that "an arrest on the street can provide its own exigent circumstance so as to justify a warrantless search of the arrestee's house." Justice Blackmun did not take part. Justice Black, joined by Chief Justice Burger, dissented. He concluded that the State's burden of showing exigent circumstances was met.

Notwithstanding *Vale,* in many cases an arrest will create exigent circumstances due to the risk that the arrestee's friends, family, or associates will destroy evidence. See United States v. Chavez, 812 F.2d 1295 (10th Cir. 1987)(exigent circumstances allowed warrantless entry into garage, where lights therein were turned off shortly after drug seller was arrested in front of the garage). In United States v. Socey, 846 F.2d 1439 (D.C.Cir.1988), the court set forth the following standard for determining whether exigent circumstances arise after an arrest:

> Consistent with *Vale,* we believe that a police officer can show an objectively reasonable belief that contraband is being, or will be, destroyed within a home if he can show 1) a reasonable belief that third persons were inside a private dwelling and 2) a reasonable belief that these third persons are aware of an * * * arrest of a confederate outside the premises so that they might see a need to destroy evidence.

The court in *Socey* found that exigent circumstances existed where an arrest was made outside a house in which a large-scale drug operation was being conducted. The court stated that it was not unreasonable for the officers to believe "that such an operation would have some type of look-out system." The court also emphasized the fact that drugs are easily destroyed. Has the court in *Socey* applied a per se rule of exigent circumstances for arrests outside suspected drug operations? Is that consistent with *Chimel* and *Vale?*

Protective Sweep After an Arrest

Even in the absence of exigent circumstances, police may, pursuant to the *Terry* doctrine, search beyond the *Chimel* spatial limitations if it is necessary to conduct a "protective sweep" of the place where the arrest is made. In Maryland v. Buie, 494 U.S. 325 (1990), the Court defined a "protective sweep" as a "quick and limited search of a premises, incident to an arrest and conducted to protect the safety of police officers or others." The Court held that a protective sweep could be justified by reasonable suspicion "that the area swept harbored an individual posing a danger to the officer or others." Probable cause was not necessary for such a sweep. Justice White, writing for the Court, concluded that the spatial limitations of *Chimel* were not undermined by allowing a protective sweep on reasonable suspicion. Unlike a search incident to arrest, the protective sweep is limited to areas where persons may be hidden. Nor does the officer have an automatic right to conduct a protective sweep (unlike the automatic right to conduct a search incident to arrest). Justice Stevens concurred to emphasize that a protective sweep could not be conducted to root out those who might destroy evidence but who would not present a safety risk to the officers or others. That is, the protective sweep is a safety-based and not an evidence-based doctrine. Justice Brennan, joined by Justice Marshall dissented.

2.   Temporal Limitations

Sequence of Search and Arrest

Generally, a search incident to arrest takes place immediately after the arrest itself. But courts will not concern themselves with the technicality of which came first—the arrest or the search—when both are nearly simultaneous and probable cause to arrest existed before the search was conducted. As the Court stated in Rawlings v. Kentucky, 448 U.S. 98 (1980): "Where the formal arrest followed quickly on the heels of the challenged search of petitioner's person, we do not believe it particularly important that the search preceded the arrest rather than vice versa." See also United States v. Cutchin, 956 F.2d 1216

(D.C.Cir.1992)("The sequence makes no difference since police did not need the fruits of the search to establish probable cause.").

While a search can precede the arrest, a search cannot be used to provide the probable cause necessary to make the arrest. As the Court stated in the per curiam opinion in Smith v. Ohio, 494 U.S. 541 (1990): "That reasoning, * * * justifying the arrest by the search and at the same time * * * the search by the arrest, just will not do."

Removal From the Arrest Scene

The term "incident to" implies that if the search is too removed from the arrest, it will not qualify for the exception. But how removed is too removed? In Chambers v. Maroney, 399 U.S. 42 (1970), officers searched an automobile that had been impounded and brought to the police station after the arrest of its occupants. The Court held that this search could not be justified as incident to the arrests, stating that "once an accused is under arrest and in custody, then a search made at another place, without a warrant, is simply not incident to the arrest." The Court concluded that the reasons for a search incident to arrest "no longer obtain when the accused is safely in custody at the station house." The Court applied the same principle in United States v. Chadwick, 433 U.S. 1 (1977), where a footlocker was searched at the police station, 90 minutes after the arrest of its owner. The Court stated that the search "cannot be viewed as incidental to the arrest or as justified by any other exigency."

In United States v. Edwards, 415 U.S. 800 (1974), the Court held that a suspect, who was arrested for attempting to break into a post office and jailed close to midnight, could be searched incident to arrest the next morning. After the arrest, the police discovered that entry into the post office apparently involved prying open a window with an iron bar that caused paint to chip. They seized Edwards' shirt and trousers in the morning and subjected them to analysis that revealed paint chips. Justice White's majority opinion said "that searches and seizures that could be made on the spot at the time of arrest may legally be conducted later when the accused arrives at the place of detention." He went on to conclude "that the normal processes incident to arrest and custody had not yet been completed when Edwards was placed in his cell." Justice White left open the possibility that a warrant might be required for some post-seizure searches of arrestees, but strongly implied that most searches and seizures of the arrestee's person and things in his possession at the time of the arrest could be examined automatically. Justice Stewart, joined by Justices Douglas, Brennan and Marshall dissented, taking the view that "the considerations that typically justify a warrantless search incident to a lawful arrest were wholly absent here."

Edwards was cited by Justice Blackmun in dissent in *Chadwick*. Is there any way to reconcile the two cases? Do they take a different view of what is incident to arrest, or do they merely deal with different types of searches? The next case may have some bearing on this question.

3. *Searches of the Person Incident to Arrest*

UNITED STATES v. ROBINSON

Supreme Court of the United States, 1973.
414 U.S. 218.

Mr. Justice Rehnquist **delivered the opinion of the Court.**

Respondent Robinson was convicted in United States District Court for the District of Columbia of the possession and facilitation of concealment of heroin * * *. [T]he Court of Appeals en banc reversed the judgment of conviction, holding that the heroin introduced in evidence against respondent had been obtained as a result of a search which violated the Fourth Amendment to the United States Constitution. * * *

On April 23, 1968, at approximately 11 p.m., Officer Richard Jenks, a 15–year veteran of the District of Columbia Metropolitan Police Department, observed the respondent driving a 1965 Cadillac near the intersection of 8th and C Streets, N.E., in the District of Columbia. Jenks, as a result of previous investigation following a check of respondent's operator's permit four days earlier, determined there was reason to believe that respondent was operating a motor vehicle after the revocation of his operator's permit. This is an offense defined by statute in the District of Columbia which carries a mandatory minimum jail term, a mandatory minimum fine, or both.

Jenks signaled respondent to stop the automobile, which respondent did, and all three of the occupants emerged from the car. At that point Jenks informed respondent that he was under arrest for "operating after revocation and obtaining a permit by misrepresentation." It was assumed by the Court of Appeals, and is conceded by the respondent here, that Jenks had probable cause to arrest respondent, and that he effected a full-custody arrest.

In accordance with procedures prescribed in police department instructions, Jenks then began to search respondent. He explained at a subsequent hearing that he was "face-to-face" with the respondent, and "placed [his] hands on [the respondent], my right-hand to his left breast like this (demonstrating) and proceeded to pat him down thus [with the right hand]." During this patdown, Jenks felt an object in the left breast pocket of the heavy coat respondent was wearing, but testified that he "couldn't tell what it was" and also that he "couldn't actually tell the size of it." Jenks then reached into the pocket and pulled out the object, which turned out to be a "crumpled up cigarette package." Jenks testified that at this point he still did not know what was in the package. * * *

The officer then opened the cigarette pack and found 14 gelatin capsules of white powder which he thought to be, and which later analysis proved to be, heroin. Jenks then continued his search of respondent to completion, feeling around his waist and trouser legs, and examining the remaining pockets. The heroin seized from the respondent was admitted into evidence at the trial which resulted in his conviction in the District Court.

* * * We conclude that the search conducted by Jenks in this case did not offend the limits imposed by the Fourth Amendment, and we therefore reverse the judgment of the Court of Appeals.

I

It is well settled that a search incident to a lawful arrest is a traditional exception to the warrant requirement of the Fourth Amendment. This general exception has historically been formulated into two distinct propositions. The first is that a search may be made of the *person* of the arrestee by virtue of the lawful arrest. The second is that a search may be made of the area within the control of the arrestee.

Examination of this Court's decisions shows that these two propositions have been treated quite differently. The validity of the search of a person incident to a lawful arrest has been regarded as settled from its first enunciation, and has remained virtually unchallenged until the present case. The validity of the second proposition, while likewise conceded in principle, has been subject to differing interpretations as to the extent of the area which may be searched. * * *

* * *

Throughout the series of cases in which the Court has addressed the second proposition relating to a search incident to a lawful arrest—the permissible area beyond the person of the arrestee which such a search may cover—no doubt has been expressed as to the unqualified authority of the arresting authority to search the person of the arrestee.

* * * Since the statements in the cases speak not simply in terms of an exception to the warrant requirement, but in terms of an affirmative authority to search, they clearly imply that such searches also meet the Fourth Amendment's requirement of reasonableness.

II

In its decision of this case, the Court of Appeals decided that even after a police officer lawfully places a suspect under arrest for the purpose of taking him into custody, he may not ordinarily proceed to fully search the prisoner. He must, instead, conduct a limited frisk of the outer clothing and remove such weapons that he may, as a result of that limited frisk, reasonably believe and ascertain that the suspect has in his possession. While recognizing that Terry v. Ohio dealt with a permissible "frisk" incident to an investigative stop based on less than probable cause to arrest, the Court of Appeals felt that the principles of that case should be carried over to this probable-cause arrest for driving while one's license is revoked. Since there would be no further evidence of such a crime to be obtained in a search of the arrestee, the court held that only a search for weapons could be justified.

* * *

III

* * *

The Court of Appeals in effect determined that the *only* reason supporting the authority for a *full* search incident to lawful arrest was the possibility of discovery of evidence or fruits. Concluding that there could be no evidence or fruits in the case of an offense such as that with which respondent was charged, it held that any protective search would have to be limited by the conditions laid down in *Terry* for a search upon less than probable cause to arrest. Quite apart from the fact that *Terry* clearly recognized the distinction between the two types of searches, and that a different rule governed one than governed the other, we find additional reason to disagree with the Court of Appeals.

The justification or reason for the authority to search incident to a lawful arrest rests quite as much on the need to disarm the suspect in order to take him into custody as it does on the need to preserve evidence on his person for later use at trial. The standards traditionally governing a search incident to lawful arrest are not, therefore, commuted to the stricter *Terry* standards by the absence of probable fruits or further evidence of the particular crime for which the arrest is made.

Nor are we inclined, on the basis of what seems to us to be a rather speculative judgment, to qualify the breadth of the general authority to search incident to a lawful custodial arrest on an assumption that persons arrested for the offense of driving while their licenses have been revoked are less likely to possess dangerous weapons than are those arrested for other crimes. It is scarcely open to doubt that the danger to an officer is far greater in the case of the extended exposure which follows the taking of a suspect into custody and transporting him to the police station than in the case of the relatively fleeting contact resulting from the typical *Terry*-type stop. This is an adequate basis for treating all custodial arrests alike for purposes of search justification.

But quite apart from these distinctions, our more fundamental disagreement with the Court of Appeals arises from its suggestion that there must be litigated in each case the issue of whether or not there was present one of the reasons supporting the authority for a search of the person incident to a lawful arrest. * * * A police officer's determination as to how and where to search the person of a suspect whom he has arrested is necessarily a quick *ad hoc* judgment which the Fourth Amendment does not require to be broken down in each instance into an analysis of each step in the search. The authority to search the person incident to a lawful custodial arrest, while based upon the need to

disarm and to discover evidence, does not depend on what a court may later decide was the probability in a particular arrest situation that weapons or evidence would in fact be found upon the person of the suspect. A custodial arrest of a suspect based on probable cause is a reasonable intrusion under the Fourth Amendment; that intrusion being lawful, a search incident to the arrest requires no additional justification. It is the fact of the lawful arrest which establishes the authority to search, and we hold that in the case of a lawful custodial arrest a full search of the person is not only an exception to the warrant requirement of the Fourth Amendment, but is also a "reasonable" search under that Amendment.

* * *

MR. JUSTICE POWELL, **concurring.**

* * *

* * * I believe that an individual lawfully subjected to a custodial arrest retains no significant Fourth Amendment interest in the privacy of his person. Under this view the custodial arrest is the significant intrusion of state power into the privacy of one's person. If the arrest is lawful, the privacy interest guarded by the Fourth Amendment is subordinated to a legitimate and overriding governmental concern. No reason then exists to frustrate law enforcement by requiring some independent justification for a search incident to a lawful custodial arrest. This seems to me the reason that a valid arrest justifies a full search of the person, even if that search is not narrowly limited by the twin rationales of seizing evidence and disarming the arrestee. The search incident to arrest is reasonable under the Fourth Amendment because the privacy interest protected by that constitutional guarantee is legitimately abated by the fact of arrest.

MR. JUSTICE MARSHALL, **with whom MR. JUSTICE DOUGLAS and MR. JUSTICE BRENNAN join, dissenting.**

* * *

* * * As the majority itself is well aware, the powers granted the police in this case are strong ones, subject to potential abuse. Although, in this particular case, Officer Jenks was required by police department regulations to make an in-custody arrest rather than to issue a citation, in most jurisdictions and for most traffic offenses the determination of whether to issue a citation or effect a full arrest is discretionary with the officer. There is always the possibility that a police officer, lacking probable cause to obtain a search warrant, will use a traffic arrest as a pretext to conduct a search. * * *

The majority opinion fails to recognize that the search conducted by Officer Jenks did not merely involve a search of respondent's person. It also included a separate search of effects found on his person. And even were we to assume, *arguendo,* that it was reasonable for Jenks to remove the object he felt in respondent's pocket, clearly there was no justification consistent with the Fourth Amendment which would authorize his opening the package and looking inside.

To begin with, after Jenks had the cigarette package in his hands, there is no indication that he had reason to believe or did in fact believe that the package contained a weapon. More importantly, even if the crumpled-up cigarette package had in fact contained some sort of small weapon, it would have been impossible for respondent to have used it once the package was in the officer's hands. Opening the package, therefore, did not further the

protective purpose of the search. * * *

It is suggested, however, that since the custodial arrest itself represents a significant intrusion into the privacy of the person, any additional intrusion by way of opening or examining effects found on the person is not worthy of constitutional protection. But such an approach was expressly rejected by the Court in *Chimel.* * * *

* * *

The Government argues that it is difficult to see what constitutionally protected ''expectation of privacy'' a prisoner has in the interior of a cigarette pack. One wonders if the result in this case would have been the same were respondent a businessman who was lawfully taken into custody for driving without a license and whose wallet was taken from him by the police. Would it be reasonable for the police officer, because of the possibility that a razor blade was hidden somewhere in the wallet, to open it, remove all the contents, and examine each item carefully? Or suppose a lawyer lawfully arrested for a traffic offense is found to have a sealed envelope on his person. Would it be permissible for the arresting officer to tear open the envelope in order to make sure that it did not contain a clandestine weapon—perhaps a pin or a razor blade? Would it not be more consonant with the purpose of the Fourth Amendment and the legitimate needs of the police to require the officer, if he has any question whatsoever about what the wallet or letter contains, to hold on to it until the arrestee is brought to the precinct station?[a]

* * *

a. Nor would it necessarily have been reasonable for the police to have opened the cigarette package at the police station. The

Government argued below, as an alternative theory to justify the search in this case, that when a suspect is booked and is about to be

Discretion to Arrest: Note on Gustafson v. Florida

Decided together with *Robinson* was Gustafson v. Florida, 414 U.S. 260 (1973). In that case, both the decision whether to arrest for a traffic offense (or issue a citation) and whether to conduct a full scale search were left to the officer on the scene. The majority said that "we do not find these differences determinative of the constitutional issue." The lineup of the Justices was the same as in *Robinson,* except that Mr. Justice Stewart noted in a one paragraph concurrence "that a persuasive claim might have been made in this case that the custodial arrest * * * for a minor traffic offense violated * * * rights under the Fourth and Fourteenth Amendments." 414 U.S. at 266–67. Professor Amsterdam argued that had the Court condemned the amount of discretion left to the officer in *Gustafson* and distinguished *Robinson's* rule-oriented, discretionless system, "it would * * * have made by far the greatest contribution to the jurisprudence of the fourth amendment since James Otis argued against the writs of assistance in 1761." Perspectives on the Fourth Amendment, 58 Minn.L.Rev. 349, 416 (1974).

Can it be argued that Professor Amsterdam overestimates the effect of a contrary result in *Gustafson*? That case allowed the officer discretion to determine whether to make a custodial or non-custodial arrest. But didn't the officer in *Robinson* have discretion as to whether even to place the suspect under arrest? Can an officer be required to arrest a person when the officer determines that probable cause exists? Would that be a beneficial rule?

Custodial Arrests for Minor Offenses

Why is it reasonable under the Fourth Amendment to permit an officer to conduct a full-scale custodial arrest for a traffic violation? One possible limitation on the broad search rights given to police under *Robinson* would be to hold that certain violations are so minimal as to not justify a custodial arrest. But this option was rejected by the Supreme Court in the following case.

placed in station house detention, it is reasonable to search his person to prevent the introduction of weapons or contraband into the jail facility and to inventory the personal effects found on the suspect. Since respondent's cigarette package would have been removed and opened at the station house anyway, the argument goes, the search might just as well take place in the field at the time of the arrest. This argument fails * * *. [A]s the Court of Appeals had indicated in its opinion in United States v. Mills, 472 F.2d 1231 (1972)(en banc), the justification for station-house searches is not the booking process itself, but rather the fact that the suspect will be placed in jail. In the District of Columbia, petty offenses of the sort involved in the present case are bailable, and, as the Government stipulated in *Mills,* the normal procedure is for offenders to be advised of the opportunity to post collateral at the station house and to avoid an inventory search unless they are unable or refuse to do so. One cannot justify a full search in the field on a subsequent event that quite possibly may never take place.

The Government also suggested in oral argument before this Court that it would be administratively inconvenient to require a police officer, after removing an object from an arrestee, to hold on to the object rather than to look inside and determine what it contained. Mere administrative inconvenience, however, cannot justify invasion of Fourth Amendment rights. One can no doubt imagine cases where the inconvenience might be so substantial as to interfere with the task of transporting the suspect into custody. While these situations might necessitate a different rule, certainly in this case there would have been no inconvenience whatsoever. Officer Jenks could easily have placed the cigarette package in his own pocket or handed it to his partner to hold onto until they reached the precinct station.

ATWATER v. CITY OF LAGO VISTA

United States Supreme Court, 2001.
532 U.S. 318.

JUSTICE SOUTER delivered the opinion of the Court.

The question is whether the Fourth Amendment forbids a warrantless arrest for a minor criminal offense, such as a misdemeanor seatbelt violation punishable only by a fine. We hold that it does not.

I

A

In Texas, if a car is equipped with safety belts, a front-seat passenger must wear one, Tex. Tran. Code Ann. § 545.413(a) (1999), and the driver must secure any small child riding in front, § 545.413(b). Violation of either provision is "a misdemeanor punishable by a fine not less than $25 or more than $50." § 545.413(d). Texas law expressly authorizes "[a]ny peace officer [to] arrest without warrant a person found committing a violation" of these seatbelt laws, § 543.001, although it permits police to issue citations in lieu of arrest, §§ 543.003–543.005.

In March 1997, Petitioner Gail Atwater was driving her pickup truck in Lago Vista, Texas, with her 3-year-old son and 5-year-old daughter in the front seat. None of them was wearing a seatbelt. Respondent Bart Turek, a Lago Vista police officer at the time, observed the seatbelt violations and pulled Atwater over. According to Atwater's complaint (the allegations of which we assume to be true for present purposes), Turek approached the truck and "yell [ed]" something to the effect of "[w]e've met before" and "[y]ou're going to jail." [Turek had previously stopped Atwater for what he had thought was a seatbelt violation, but then had realized that Atwater's son, although seated on the vehicle's armrest, was in fact belted in.

Atwater acknowledged that her son's seating position was unsafe, and Turek had issued a verbal warning.] He then called for backup and asked to see Atwater's driver's license and insurance documentation, which state law required her to carry. When Atwater told Turek that she did not have the papers because her purse had been stolen the day before, Turek said that he had "heard that story two-hundred times." Atwater asked to take her "frightened, upset, and crying" children to a friend's house nearby, but Turek told her, "[y]ou're not going anywhere." As it turned out, Atwater's friend learned what was going on and soon arrived to take charge of the children. Turek then handcuffed Atwater, placed her in his squad car, and drove her to the local police station, where booking officers had her remove her shoes, jewelry, and eyeglasses, and empty her pockets. Officers took Atwater's "mug shot" and placed her, alone, in a jail cell for about one hour, after which she was taken before a magistrate and released on $310 bond. Atwater was charged with driving without her seatbelt fastened, failing to secure her children in seatbelts, driving without a license, and failing to provide proof of insurance. She ultimately pleaded no contest to the misdemeanor seatbelt offenses and paid a $50 fine; the other charges were dismissed.

B

Atwater and her husband * * * filed suit * * * under 42 U.S.C. § 1983 against Turek and respondents City of Lago Vista and Chief of Police Frank Miller. So far as concerns us, petitioners (whom we will simply call Atwater) alleged that respondents (for simplicity, the City) had violated Atwater's Fourth Amendment "right to be free from unreasonable seizure," and sought compensatory and punitive damages. * * * Given Atwater's admission that she had "violated the law" * * * the District Court ruled the Fourth Amendment claim "meritless" and granted the City's summary judgment motion. A panel of the United States Court of Appeals for the Fifth Circuit reversed. It concluded that "an arrest for a first-time seat belt offense" was an unreasonable seizure within the meaning of the Fourth Amendment * * *. Sitting en banc, the Court of Appeals vacated the panel's decision and affirmed the District Court's summary judgment for the City. Relying on Whren v. United States, 517 U.S. 806 (1996), the en banc court observed that, although the Fourth Amendment generally requires a balancing of individual and governmental interests, where "an arrest is based on probable cause then with rare exceptions * * * the result of that balancing is not in doubt." Because "[n]either party dispute[d] that Officer Turek had probable cause to arrest Atwater," and because "there [was] no evidence in the record that Officer Turek conducted the arrest in an extraordinary manner, unusually harmful to Atwater's privacy interests," the en banc court held that the arrest was not unreasonable for Fourth Amendment purposes. * * *

We granted certiorari to consider whether the Fourth Amendment, either by incorporating common-law restrictions on misdemeanor arrests or otherwise, limits police officers' authority to arrest without warrant for minor criminal offenses. We now affirm.

II

* * * Atwater's specific contention is that "founding-era common-law rules" forbade peace officers to make warrantless misdemeanor arrests except in cases of "breach of the peace," a category she claims was then understood narrowly as covering only those nonfelony offenses "involving or tending toward violence." Although her historical argument is by no means insubstantial, it ultimately fails.

A

[Justice Souter engaged in an extensive and detailed analysis of pre-founding English common law and concluded that, "the common-law commentators (as well as the sparsely reported cases) reached divergent conclusions with respect to officers' warrantless misdemeanor arrest power. Moreover, in the years leading up to American independence, Parliament repeatedly extended express warrantless arrest authority to cover misdemeanor-level offenses not amounting to or involving any violent breach of the peace."]

B

An examination of specifically American evidence is to the same effect. Neither the history of the framing era nor subsequent legal development indicates that the Fourth Amendment was originally understood, or has traditionally been read, to embrace Atwater's position.

1

[Justice Souter engages in another extensive and detailed analysis of American practice with respect to arrests, both pre- and post-founding. He concludes that there was a basic assumption that a custodial arrest was reasonable for nonviolent misdemeanors.]

* * * Small wonder, then, that today statutes in all 50 States and the District of Columbia permit warrantless misdemeanor arrests by at least some (if not all) peace officers without requiring any breach of the peace, as

do a host of congressional enactments. * * * This, therefore, simply is not a case in which the claimant can point to "a clear answer [that] existed in 1791 and has been generally adhered to by the traditions of our society ever since." County of Riverside v. McLaughlin, 500 U.S. 44, 60 (1991) (SCALIA, J., dissenting).

III

* * * Atwater does not wager all on history. Instead, she asks us to mint a new rule of constitutional law on the understanding that when historical practice fails to speak conclusively to a claim grounded on the Fourth Amendment, courts are left to strike a current balance between individual and societal interests by subjecting particular contemporary circumstances to traditional standards of reasonableness. Atwater accordingly argues for a modern arrest rule, one not necessarily requiring violent breach of the peace, but nonetheless forbidding custodial arrest, even upon probable cause, when conviction could not ultimately carry any jail time and when the government shows no compelling need for immediate detention.

If we were to derive a rule exclusively to address the uncontested facts of this case, Atwater might well prevail. She was a known and established resident of Lago Vista with no place to hide and no incentive to flee, and common sense says she would almost certainly have buckled up as a condition of driving off with a citation. In her case, the physical incidents of arrest were merely gratuitous humiliations imposed by a police officer who was (at best) exercising extremely poor judgment. Atwater's claim to live free of pointless indignity and confinement clearly outweighs anything the City can raise against it specific to her case.

But we have traditionally recognized that a responsible Fourth Amendment balance is not well served by standards requiring sensitive, case-by-case determinations of government need, lest every discretionary judgment in the field be converted into an occasion for constitutional review. See, e.g., United States v. Robinson, 414 U.S. 218, 234–235 (1973). Often enough, the Fourth Amendment has to be applied on the spur (and in the heat) of the moment, and the object in implementing its command of reasonableness is to draw standards sufficiently clear and simple to be applied with a fair prospect of surviving judicial second-guessing months and years after an arrest or search is made. Courts attempting to strike a reasonable Fourth Amendment balance thus credit the government's side with an essential interest in readily administrable rules.

At first glance, Atwater's argument may seem to respect the values of clarity and simplicity, so far as she claims that the Fourth Amendment generally forbids warrantless arrests for minor crimes not accompanied by violence or some demonstrable threat of it (whether "minor crime" be defined as a fine-only traffic offense, a fine-only offense more generally, or a misdemeanor). But the claim is not ultimately so simple, nor could it be, for complications arise the moment we begin to think about the possible applications of the several criteria Atwater proposes for drawing a line between minor crimes with limited arrest authority and others not so restricted.

One line, she suggests, might be between "jailable" and "fine-only" offenses, between those for which conviction could result in commitment and those for which it could not. The trouble with this distinction, of course, is that an officer on the street might not be able to tell. It is not merely that we cannot expect every police officer to know the details of frequently complex penalty schemes, but that penalties for ostensibly identical conduct can vary on account of facts difficult (if not impossible) to know at the scene of an arrest. Is this the first offense or is the suspect a repeat offender? Is the weight of the marijuana a gram above or a gram below the fine-only line? Where conduct could implicate more than one criminal prohibition, which one will the district attorney ultimately decide to charge? And so on. But Atwater's refinements would not end there. She represents that if the line were drawn at nonjailable traffic offenses, her proposed limitation should be qualified by a proviso authorizing warrantless arrests where "necessary for enforcement of the traffic laws or when [an] offense would otherwise continue and pose a danger to others on the road." * * * The proviso only compounds the difficulties. Would, for instance, either exception apply to speeding? At oral argument, Atwater's counsel said that "it would not be reasonable to arrest a driver for speeding unless the speeding rose to the level of reckless driving." But is it not fair to expect that the chronic speeder will speed again despite a citation in his pocket, and should that not qualify as showing that the "offense would * * * continue" under Atwater's rule? And why, as a constitutional matter, should we assume that only reckless driving will "pose a danger to others on the road" while speeding will not?

There is no need for more examples to show that Atwater's general rule and limiting proviso promise very little in the way of administrability. * * * Atwater's rule therefore would not only place police in an almost impossible spot but would guarantee increased litigation over many of the arrests that would occur. For all these reasons, Atwater's various distinctions between permissible and impermissible arrests for minor crimes strike us as very unsatisfactory lines to require police officers to draw on a moment's notice. One may ask, of course, why these difficulties may not be answered by a simple tie breaker for the police to follow in the field: if in doubt, do not arrest. The first answer is that in practice the tie breaker would boil down to something akin to a least-restrictive-alternative limitation, which is itself one of those "ifs, ands, and buts" rules * * *. Beyond that, whatever help the tie breaker might give would come at the price of a systematic disincentive to arrest in situations where even Atwater concedes that arresting would serve an important societal interest. An officer not quite sure that the drugs weighed enough to warrant jail time or not quite certain about a suspect's risk of flight would not arrest, even though it could perfectly well turn out that, in fact, the offense called for incarceration and the defendant was long gone on the day of trial. Multiplied many times over, the costs to society of such underenforcement could easily outweigh the costs to defendants of being needlessly arrested and booked * * *.

Just how easily the costs could outweigh the benefits may be shown by asking, as one Member of this Court did at oral argument, "how bad the problem is out there." The very fact that the law has never jelled the way Atwater would have it leads one to wonder whether warrantless misdemeanor arrests need constitutional attention, and there is cause to think the answer is no. So far as such arrests might be thought to pose a threat to the probable-cause requirement, anyone arrested for a crime without formal process, whether for felony or misdemeanor, is entitled to a magistrate's review of probable cause within 48 hours, County of Riverside v. McLaughlin, 500 U.S., at 55–58, and there is no reason to think the procedure in this case atypical in giving the suspect a prompt opportunity to request release. Many jurisdictions, moreover, have chosen to impose more restrictive safeguards through statutes limiting warrantless arrests for minor offenses. It is of course easier to devise a minor-offense limitation by statute than to derive one through the Constitution, simply because the statute can let the arrest power turn on any sort of practical consideration without having to subsume it under a broader principle. It is, in fact, only natural that States should resort to this sort of legislative regulation, for, as Atwater's own amici emphasize, it is in the interest of the police to limit petty-offense arrests, which carry costs that are simply too great to incur without good reason. Finally, and significantly, under current doctrine the preference for categorical treatment of Fourth Amendment claims gives way to individualized review when a defendant makes a colorable argument that an arrest, with or without a warrant, was "conducted in an extraordinary manner, unusually harmful to [his] privacy or even physical interests." Whren v. United States, 517 U.S., at 818; see also Graham v. Connor, 490 U.S. 386, 395–396 (1989) (excessive force actionable under § 1983). The upshot of all these influences, combined with the good sense (and, failing that, the political accountability) of most local lawmakers and law-enforcement officials, is a dearth of horribles demanding redress. Indeed, when Atwater's counsel was asked at oral argument for any indications of comparably foolish, warrantless misdemeanor arrests, he could offer only one. We are sure that there are others, but just as surely the country is not confronting anything like an epidemic of unnecessary minor-offense arrests. That fact caps the reasons for rejecting Atwater's request for the development of a new and distinct body of constitutional law.

Accordingly, we confirm today what our prior cases have intimated: the standard of probable cause "applies to all arrests, without the need to balance the interests and circumstances involved in particular situations." Dunaway v. New York, 442 U.S. 200, 208 (1979). If an officer has probable cause to believe that an individual has committed even a very minor criminal offense in his presence, he may, without violating the Fourth Amendment, arrest the offender.

IV

Atwater's arrest satisfied constitutional requirements. There is no dispute that Officer Turek had probable cause to believe that Atwater had committed a crime in his presence. * * * Turek was accordingly authorized (not required, but authorized) to make a custodial arrest without balancing costs and benefits or determining whether or not Atwater's arrest was in some sense necessary.

Nor was the arrest made in an "extraordinary manner, unusually harmful to [her] privacy or * * * physical interests." * * * Atwater's arrest was surely "humiliating," as she says in her brief, but it was no more "harmful to privacy or physical interests" than the normal custodial arrest. She was handcuffed, placed in a squad car, and taken to the local police station, where officers asked her to remove her shoes, jewelry, and glasses, and to empty her pockets. They then took her photograph and placed her in a cell, alone, for about an hour, after which she was taken before a magistrate, and released on $310 bond. The arrest and booking were inconvenient and embarrassing to Atwater, but not so extraordinary as to violate the Fourth Amendment.

The Court of Appeals's en banc judgment is affirmed.

JUSTICE O'CONNOR, **with whom** JUSTICE STEVENS, JUSTICE GINSBURG, **and** JUSTICE BREYER **join, dissenting**.

* * *

I

* * * While probable cause is surely a necessary condition for warrantless arrests for fine-only offenses, any realistic assessment of the interests implicated by such arrests demonstrates that probable cause alone is not a sufficient condition.

* * *

A custodial arrest exacts an obvious toll on an individual's liberty and privacy, even when the period of custody is relatively brief. The arrestee is subject to a full search of her person and confiscation of her possessions. If the arrestee is the occupant of a car, the entire passenger compartment of the car, including packages therein, is subject to search as well. The arrestee may be detained for up to 48 hours without having a magistrate determine whether there in fact was probable cause for the arrest. Because people arrested for all types of violent and nonviolent offenses may be housed together awaiting such review, this detention period is potentially dangerous. And once the period of custody is over, the fact of the arrest is a permanent part of the public record. * * * If the State has decided that a fine, and not imprisonment, is the appropriate punishment for an offense, the State's interest in taking a person suspected of committing that offense into custody is surely limited, at best. This is not to say that the State will never have such an interest. A full custodial arrest may on occasion vindicate legitimate state interests, even if the crime is punishable only by fine. Arrest is the

surest way to abate criminal conduct. It may also allow the police to verify the offender's identity and, if the offender poses a flight risk, to ensure her appearance at trial. But when such considerations are not present, a citation or summons may serve the State's remaining law enforcement interests every bit as effectively as an arrest.

* * * In light of the availability of citations to promote a State's interests when a fine-only offense has been committed, I cannot concur in a rule which deems a full custodial arrest to be reasonable in every circumstance. * * * Instead, I would require that when there is probable cause to believe that a fine-only offense has been committed, the police officer should issue a citation unless the officer is "able to point to specific and articulable facts which, taken together with rational inferences from those facts, reasonably warrant [the additional] intrusion" of a full custodial arrest. Terry v. Ohio, 392 U.S., at 21.

* * * The rule I propose—which merely requires a legitimate reason for the decision to escalate the seizure into a full custodial arrest—thus does not undermine an otherwise "clear and simple" rule. While clarity is certainly a value worthy of consideration in our Fourth Amendment jurisprudence, it by no means trumps the values of liberty and privacy at the heart of the Amendment's protections. What the *Terry* rule lacks in precision it makes up for in fidelity to the Fourth Amendment's command of reasonableness and sensitivity to the competing values protected by that Amendment. Over the past 30 years, it appears that the *Terry* rule has been workable and easily applied by officers on the street.

* * *

II

* * *

III

* * * The per se rule that the Court creates has potentially serious consequences for the everyday lives of Americans. A broad range of conduct falls into the category of fine-only misdemeanors. In Texas alone, for example, disobeying any sort of traffic warning sign is a misdemeanor punishable only by fine, as is failing to pay a highway toll, and driving with expired license plates. Nor are fine-only crimes limited to the traffic context. In several States, for example, littering is a criminal offense punishable only by fine. * * * My concern lies not with the decision to enact or enforce these laws, but rather with the manner in which they may be enforced. Under today's holding, when a police officer has probable cause to believe that a fine-only misdemeanor offense has occurred, that officer may stop the suspect, issue a citation, and let the person continue on her way. Or, if a traffic violation, the officer may stop the car, arrest the driver, search the driver, see United States v. Robinson, 414 U.S., at 235, search the entire passenger compartment of the car including any purse or package inside, see New York v. Belton, 453 U.S., at 460, and impound the car and inventory all of its contents, see Colorado v. Bertine, 479 U.S. 367, 374 (1987). Although the Fourth Amendment expressly requires that the latter course be a reasonable and proportional response to the circumstances of the offense, the majority gives officers unfettered discretion to choose that course without articulating a single reason why such action is appropriate.

Such unbounded discretion carries with it grave potential for abuse. The majority takes comfort in the lack of evidence of "an epidemic of unnecessary minor-offense arrests." But the relatively small number of published cases dealing with such arrests proves little and should provide little solace. Indeed, as the recent debate over racial profiling demonstrates all too clearly, a relatively minor traffic infraction may often serve as an excuse for stopping and harassing an individual. After today, the arsenal available to any officer extends to a full arrest and the searches permissible concomitant to that arrest. An officer's subjective motivations for making a traffic stop are not relevant considerations in determining the reasonableness of the stop. But it is precisely because these motivations are beyond our purview that we must vigilantly ensure that officers' poststop actions—which are properly within our reach—comport with the Fourth Amendment's guarantee of reasonableness.

* * *

Robinson and Containers in the Arrestee's Grab Area

The Court in *Robinson* established an automatic right to search everything found on a person who has been subjected to a custodial arrest. Does that automatic search power extend to containers found in the arrestee's grab area? In United States v. Chadwick, supra, the Court held that a search of a footlocker at the police station could not be justified as a search incident to arrest because it occurred long after Chadwick was in custody. In a footnote, the Court referred to *Robinson* and stated as follows:

> Unlike searches of the person, searches of possessions within an arrestee's immediate control cannot be justified by any reduced expectations of privacy caused by the arrest. Respondents' privacy interest in the contents of the footlocker was not eliminated simply because they were under arrest.

Does this passage mean that the officer has no automatic right to search containers incident to arrest when they are within the control area but not on the person? This would mean that briefcases, pocketbooks and bookbags could be seized, but not searched without a warrant or exigent circumstances (such as a ticking briefcase); whereas wallets and cigarette packs found on the person could be thoroughly and automatically searched under *Robinson*. Does this distinction based on privacy interests make sense? Wouldn't the things one carries on one's person be more and not less private? Most lower courts have applied the automatic arrest power rule of *Robinson* to searches of briefcases and the like in the arrestee's grab area. See, e.g., United States v. Morales, 923 F.2d 621 (8th Cir.1991) (distinguishing *Chadwick* as a case involving a search that occurred too long after the arrest was completed and upholding search of a container under the arrest power rule); United States v. Herrera, 810 F.2d 989 (10th Cir.1987)(same). But see United States v. Gorski, 852 F.2d 692 (2d Cir. 1988)(search of bag during arrest must be justified by exigent circumstances, otherwise seizure is all that is permitted). The following case, though ostensibly dealing with automobiles, may have some bearing on whether any container in the control area may be searched incident to a lawful arrest.

4.   *The Arrest Power Rule Applied to Automobiles*

NEW YORK v. BELTON

Supreme Court of the United States, 1981.
453 U.S. 454.

JUSTICE STEWART **delivered the opinion of the Court.**

When the occupant of an automobile is subjected to a lawful custodial arrest, does the constitutionally permissible scope of a search incident to his arrest include the passenger compartment of the automobile in which he was riding? That is the question at issue in the present case.

I

On April 9, 1978, Trooper Douglas Nicot, a New York State policeman driving an unmarked car on the New York Thruway, was passed by another automobile travelling at an excessive rate of speed. Nicot gave chase, overtook the speeding vehicle, and ordered its driver to pull it over to the side of the road and stop. There were four men in the car, one of whom was Roger Belton, the respondent in this case. The policeman asked to see the driver's license and automobile regis-

tration, and discovered that none of the men owned the vehicle or was related to its owner. Meanwhile, the policeman had smelled burnt marihuana and had seen on the floor of the car an envelope marked "Supergold" that he associated with marihuana. He therefore directed the men to get out of the car, and placed them under arrest for the unlawful possession of marihuana. He patted down each of the men and "split them up into four separate areas of the Thruway at this time so they would not be in physical touching area of each other." He then picked up the envelope marked "Supergold" and found that it contained marihuana. After giving the arrestees the warnings required by Miranda v. Arizona, the state policeman searched each one of them. He then searched the passenger compartment of the car. On the back seat he found a black leather jacket belonging to Belton. He unzipped one of the pockets of the jacket and discovered cocaine. Placing the jacket in his automobile, he drove the four arrestees to a nearby police station.

Belton was subsequently indicted for criminal possession of a controlled substance. In the trial court he moved that the cocaine the trooper had seized from the jacket pocket be suppressed. The court denied the motion. * * *

The New York Court of Appeals reversed, holding that "[a] warrantless search of the zippered pockets of an unaccessible jacket may not be upheld as a search incident to a lawful arrest where there is no longer any danger that the arrestee or a confederate might gain access to the article." Two judges dissented. * * *

II

* * *

Although the principle that limits a search incident to a lawful custodial arrest may be stated clearly enough, courts have discovered the principle difficult to apply in specific cases. Yet, as one commentator has pointed out, the protection of the Fourth and Fourteenth Amendments "can only be realized if the police are acting under a set of rules which, in most instances, makes it possible to reach a correct determination beforehand as to whether an invasion of privacy is justified in the interest of law enforcement." LaFave, "Case-by-Case Adjudication" versus "Standardized Procedures": The Robinson Dilemma, 1974 Sup.Ct.Rev. 127, 142. * * * In short, "A single, familiar standard is essential to guide police officers, who have only limited time and expertise to reflect on and balance the social and individual interests involved in

the specific circumstances they confront."

So it was that, in United States v. Robinson, the Court hewed to a straightforward rule, easily applied, and predictably enforced. * * *

But no straightforward rule has emerged from the litigated cases respecting the question involved here— the question of the proper scope of a search of the interior of an automobile incident to a lawful custodial arrest of its occupants. * * *

When a person cannot know how a court will apply a settled principle to a recurring factual situation, that person cannot know the scope of his constitutional protection, nor can a policeman know the scope of his authority. While the *Chimel* case established that a search incident to an arrest may not stray beyond the area within the immediate control of the arrestee, courts have found no workable definition of "the area within the immediate control of the arrestee" when that area arguably includes the interior of an automobile and the arrestee is its recent occupant. Our reading of the cases suggests the generalization that articles inside the relatively narrow compass of the passenger compartment of an automobile are in fact generally, even if not inevitably, within "the area into which an arrestee might reach in order to grab a weapon or evidentiary item." In order to establish the workable rule this category of cases requires, we read *Chimel's* definition of the limits of the area that may be searched in light of that generalization. Accordingly, we hold that when a policeman has made a lawful custodial arrest of the occupant of an automobile, he may, as a contemporaneous incident of that arrest, search the passenger compartment of that automobile.[a]

a. Our holding today does no more than determine the meaning of *Chimel's* principles

in this particular and problematic context. It in no way alters the fundamental principles es-

It follows from this conclusion that the police may also examine the contents of any containers found within the passenger compartment, for if the passenger compartment is within reach of the arrestee, so also will containers in it be within his reach.[b] Such a container may, of course, be searched whether it is open or closed, since the justification for the search is not that the arrestee has no privacy interest in the container, but that the lawful custodial arrest justifies the infringement of any privacy interest the arrestee may have. * * *

It is true, of course, that these containers will sometimes be such that they could hold neither a weapon nor evidence of the criminal conduct for which the suspect was arrested. However, in United States v. Robinson, supra, the Court rejected the argument that such a container—there a "crumpled up cigarette package"—located during a search of Robinson incident to his arrest could not be searched * * *.[c]

[The Court distinguishes automobile search cases and upholds the search and seizure.]

JUSTICE BRENNAN, **with whom** JUSTICE MARSHALL, **joins, dissenting.**

* * *

* * * While the "interior/trunk" distinction may provide a workable guide in certain routine cases—for example, where the officer arrests the driver of a car and then immediately searches the seats and floor—in the long run, I suspect it will create far more problems than it solves. The Court's new approach leaves open too many questions and, more important, it provides the police and the courts with too few tools with which to find the answers.

Thus, although the Court concludes that a warrantless search of a car may take place even though the suspect was arrested outside the car, it does not indicate how long after the suspect's arrest that search may validly be conducted. Would a warrantless search incident to arrest be valid if conducted five minutes after the suspect left his car? Thirty minutes? Three hours? Does it matter whether the suspect is standing in close proximity to the car when the search is conducted? Does it matter whether the police formed probable cause to arrest before or after the suspect left his car? And *why* is the rule announced today necessarily limited to searches of cars? What if a suspect is seen walking out of a house where the police, peering in from outside, had formed probable cause to believe a crime was being committed? Could the police then arrest that suspect and enter the house to conduct a search incident to arrest? Even assuming today's rule is limited to searches of the "interior" of cars— an assumption not demanded by logic—what is meant by "interior"? Does it include locked glove compartments, the interior of door panels, or the area under the floorboards? Are special

---

tablished in the *Chimel* case regarding the basic scope of searches incident to lawful custodial arrests.

b. "Container" here denotes any object capable of holding another object. It thus includes closed or open glove compartments, consoles, or other receptacles located anywhere within the passenger compartment, as well as luggage, boxes, bags, clothing, and the like. Our holding encompasses only the interior of the passenger compartment of an automobile and does not encompass the trunk.

c. It seems to have been the theory of the Court of Appeals that the search and seizure in the present case could not have been incident to the respondent's arrest, because Trooper Nicot, by the very act of searching the respondent's jacket and seizing the contents of its pocket, had gained "exclusive control" of them. But under this fallacious theory no search or seizure incident to a lawful arrest could ever be valid; by seizing an article even on the arrestee's person, an officer may be said to have reduced that article to his "exclusive control."

rules necessary for station wagons and hatchbacks, where the luggage compartment may be reached through the interior, or taxicabs, where a glass panel might separate the driver's compartment from the rest of the car? Are the only containers that may be searched those that are large enough to be "capable of holding another object"? Or does the new rule apply to any container, even if it "could hold neither a weapon nor evidence of the criminal conduct for which the suspect was arrested"?

The Court does not give the police any "bright line" answers to these questions. More important, because the Court's new rule abandons the justifications underlying *Chimel*, it offers no guidance to the police officer seeking to work out these answers for himself. As we warned in *Chimel*, "no consideration relevant to the Fourth Amendment suggests any point of rational limitation, once the search is allowed to go beyond the area from which the person arrested might obtain weapons or evidentiary items." * * *

* * * I continue to believe that *Chimel* provides a sound, workable rule for determining the constitutionality of a warrantless search incident to arrest. * * * While it may be difficult in some cases to measure the exact scope of the arrestee's immediate control, relevant factors would surely include the relative number of police officers and arrestees, the manner of restraint placed on the arrestee, and the ability of the arrestee to gain access to a particular area or container. Certainly there will be some close cases, but when in doubt the police can always turn to the rationale underlying *Chimel*—the need to prevent the arrestee from reaching weapons or contraband—before exercising their judgment.* * *

[The one paragraph concurring opinion of Justice Rehnquist, the one paragraph opinion concurring in the judgment by Justice Stevens, and the one paragraph dissent by Justice White (joined by Justice Marshall) are omitted.]

Note on Bright Line Rules

The result in *Belton* is hardly shocking after *Robinson*. Both are "bright line" rule cases as is the later decision in *Atwater*. In fact, the entire search incident to arrest doctrine assumes a necessity for a single rule by positing danger of physical harm and destruction of evidence in all custodial arrest situations. The justification for a bright line rule is that it is needed for predictability and easy application. Of course, this rationale does not determine *which* bright line rule a court should choose. For example, the *Belton* Court could have adopted a bright line rule that the passenger compartment is never, rather than always, within the occupant's immediate control. Or the Court could have decided that the passenger compartments of all American-built cars are within the occupant's immediate control. Why choose one bright line rule over another?

The reason given by the *Belton* Court for choosing its bright line rule is that it will almost always be correct on the facts; while it is not always true that the passenger compartment is within the control of the occupant during an arrest, it will be true so often that the cost of overinclusiveness in a few cases is outweighed by the virtues of bright line adjudication. Is the Court in *Belton* justified in establishing a bright line rule that the passenger compartment is always in the control area of the arrestee? Is that almost always true as an empirical matter? Isn't it more likely that at the time of the search of a vehicle, the arrestees have been placed so far from the car that there is no way for them to get access to the passenger compartment? For a criticism of the Court's bright-line adjudication in *Belton,* see Alschuler, Bright Line Fever and the Fourth Amendment, 45 U.Pitt.L.Rev. 227 (1981).

United States v. Cotton, 751 F.2d 1146 (10th Cir.1985), indicates the extent of the *Belton* bright line rule by holding that "where an officer has made a lawful arrest of a suspect in an automobile, he may seize articles found within the interior of the automobile as part of a search incident to a lawful arrest, even where the arrestee is outside of the vehicle and handcuffed." What justifies this result?

Problems After Belton: The Arrestee's Relationship to the Car

Justice Brennan in *Belton* asserted that the majority's bright line rule was not as bright as it appeared. There seems to be some merit to his point, because the lower courts have struggled with various questions about *Belton's* application.

One such question is whether *Belton* is applicable when a person is arrested away from his car. For example, in United States v. Strahan, 984 F.2d 155 (6th Cir.1993), police officers arrested the defendant after he had parked his car and was walking towards a bar. The officers then searched the defendant's car and found a gun. Although the court noted that *Belton* allows the search of a passenger compartment after an arrestee is removed from the car, the court found that *Belton* "clearly limits its application to only those settings where an officer makes a custodial arrest of the *occupant* of an automobile." Because the police did not make an arrest of an occupant of a vehicle, the court held that the *Chimel* test for determining the grab area, rather than *Belton's* bright line rule, was applicable. Since Strahan was arrested 30 feet from his vehicle, the court held that the "passenger compartment of the vehicle was not within Strahan's immediate control at the time of the arrest" and therefore that the arrest power rule was not applicable. Compare United States v. Franco, 981 F.2d 470 (10th Cir.1992) (*Belton* applies where the defendant drove his car to a drug transaction, got into the car of an undercover officer to complete the transaction, and was arrested while in the officer's car: "Mr. Franco exercised control over his vehicle and its contents at the time of the arrest and during the commission of the offense, and was its immediate occupant.").

The Supreme Court granted certiorari in United States v. Thornton, 325 F.3d 189 (4th Cir. 2003), to decide whether the bright-line *Belton* rule is "confined to situations in which police initiate contact with the occupant of a vehicle while that person is in the vehicle." In *Thornton,* the Court of Appeals rejected the "arrestee in the vehicle" limitation, reasoning that it would require officers to alert a suspect to their presence while the suspect was still in the car, thus forcing officers to choose "between forfeiting the opportunity to preserve evidence for later use at trial and increasing the risk to their own lives and the lives of others." The Court also noted that this limitation would "encourage individuals to avoid lawful searches of their vehicles by rapidly exiting or moving away from the vehicle as officers approached." [This point presumes that people about to be arrested in their cars are current on their Fourth Amendment law.] The *Thornton* Court upheld the search of the defendant's car because he was in "close proximity" with the vehicle when he was arrested. The Supreme Court's decision in *Thornton* will be included in the Supplement to this Casebook.

Problems After Belton: What Is The Passenger Compartment?

The Court in *Belton* distinguished passenger compartments, which can be automatically searched, from trunks, which cannot. This has created the "hatchback" problem. Is a hatchback a trunk, or part of the passenger compartment? The courts have generally held that the passenger compartment includes any area "generally reachable without exiting the vehicle, without regard to the likelihood in a particular case that such a reaching was possible": which would mean that a hatchback area is part of the passenger compartment. United States v. Doward, 41 F.3d 789 (1st Cir.1994). See also United States v. Olguin–Rivera, 168 F.3d 1203 (10th Cir. 1999) (search of luggage area in a sport utility vehicle is permissible under *Belton*, even though the area was covered by a retractable vinyl cover). Does it make any sense to define the passenger compartment in this manner, when the arrestee is ordinarily *outside* the vehicle at the time of the search?

Problems After Belton: What Is A Container?

Another question left after *Belton* is, what is a container? The Court in *Belton* specifically held that the police can automatically open all loose containers in the passenger compartment. Are the door panels considered containers because they have an empty space in which something can be stored? Lower courts have generally limited searches under *Belton* to areas in the passenger compartment that can be investigated without causing serious damage to the vehicle. See, e.g., United States v. Diaz–Lizaraza, 981 F.2d 1216 (11th Cir.1993)(holding search of defendant's truck as within the scope allowed by *Belton* where police officer "looked under the seats on floor of the truck, but did not rip the upholstery, look under the hood, or damage the trunk in any way."). See also United States v. Holifield, 956 F.2d 665 (7th Cir. 1992)(search of locked glove compartment permissible under *Belton*, where it can be opened without damage to the vehicle). Does this limitation on *Belton* make any sense?

Applicability of Belton to Searches of Places Other Than Vehicles

Despite the footnote in *Belton* limiting its application to automobiles, lower courts have often looked at *Belton* more expansively. There are two bright line rules in *Belton*, and each has potential application outside the context of a vehicle search. The first bright line rule is that a passenger compartment is always within the arrestee's grab area. This principle could be extended to other enclosed spaces, though to do so would be in obvious conflict with *Chimel's* case-by-case approach to an arrestee's grab area. The court in United States v. Palumbo, 735 F.2d 1095 (8th Cir.1984), opted for *Belton* over *Chimel*, and held that a search of a dresser drawer in a motel room was within the arrestee's control area, even though the defendant was handcuffed and surrounded by several officers. The court relied on *Belton* for the proposition that the arrest power rule "is not constrained because the arrestee is unlikely at the time of the arrest to actually reach into an area." Is this a fair reading of *Belton*? Is there a problem in applying *Belton* to searches of rooms, houses, offices, parks, etc.?

The second bright line rule of *Belton* is that containers in the arrestee's grab area can be opened automatically. Any extension of this rule is potentially in conflict with the Court's decision in United States v. Chadwick, supra, where the Court held that a search of the arrestee's footlocker could not be justified under the arrest power rule because, among other things, the footlocker had been brought to the police station and so there was no risk of destruction of evidence or peril to the officers at the time of the search. The court in United States v. Johnson, 846 F.2d 279 (5th Cir.1988), opted for *Belton* over *Chadwick* and held that containers within the arrestee's "grab" area could be immediately searched, even though the arrest did not occur in or near a car. The court reasoned as follows:

> Although the Court in *Chadwick* seemed to have drawn a distinction between searches of persons and searches of possessions in the arrestee's immediate control, the Court discarded that distinction in *Belton*. * * * We conclude that *Belton* eradicates any differences between searches of the person and searches within the arrestee's immediate control. Law enforcement officers may, pursuant to a valid arrest, search any container on the person or within his reach. Of course, the search must be contemporaneous with the arrest. Cf. *Chadwick*.

Judge Williams, concurring, went even further and stated that

> *Belton* constituted a virtual overruling of the rationale of *Chimel*. *Belton* overruled this rationale in spite of the fact that the opinion * * * stated its limitation upon *Chimel* solely in terms of the search of the passenger compartment of an automobile * * *. The only limitation upon this conclusion was contained in a footnote * * *. I am now convinced that the Supreme Court * * * would push *Belton* beyond its facts and treat the *Chimel* rationale as no longer accurately reflecting the law.

Do you agree with Judge Williams' prediction? What could be the rationale, and corresponding limitation, of the search incident to arrest exception if *Chimel* is overruled?

In United States v. $639,558.00 in United States Currency, 955 F.2d 712 (D.C.Cir.1992), the court relied on *Chimel* and *Chadwick*, rather than *Belton*, and invalidated a search of luggage conducted after the holder of the forfeited currency had been arrested and handcuffed to a chair. The court held that the search could not be justified as incident to arrest because there was no possibility that the arrestee could destroy any evidence, and "any need for swift action had by that time disappeared." The court stated that "[i]n the language of *Chadwick,* no exigency existed at the time of this search, by which *Chadwick* meant 'no danger that the arrestee might gain access to the property to seize a weapon or destroy evidence.'" The government argued that *Chadwick* was not controlling because it had been effectively overruled by *Belton*—as the Fifth Circuit implied in *Palumbo*. But the court held that *Belton* was limited to vehicle searches, and rejected the government's argument in the following language:

> Whatever merit there is to the government's point that *Chadwick* is wobbly, an inferior court cannot disregard it. * * * *Chadwick* rejected the argument that because an immediate search without a warrant could have been justified as incident to arrest, that exception would justify a warrantless search of a closed container conducted later, after the exigency had ended. Since our duty is to apply *Chadwick,* we hold that the search of [the arrestee's] luggage cannot be sustained as incident to his arrest.

Most courts, however, have applied the automatic-opening rule of *Belton* to searches of items in the grab area, such as briefcases, even where a car is not involved. See, e.g., United States v. Morales, 923 F.2d 621 (8th Cir.1991) (distinguishing *Chadwick* as a case involving a search that occurred too long after the arrest was completed). Which view do you prefer?

5. *The Arrest Power Rule Where No Arrest Takes Place*

In *Robinson,* the Court established a bright-line rule permitting full-blown searches when a person has been subjected to a custodial arrest; *Belton* extended these bright line principles to cases in which an occupant of a car is subjected to custodial arrest. Each case involved a traffic stop, and in each case a custodial arrest was authorized, but it was not mandatory. What if the officers in *Belton* and *Robinson* had simply issued a ticket? Would the arrest-power rule apply? That question was considered by the Supreme Court in the following case.

KNOWLES v. IOWA

Supreme Court of the United States, 1998.
525 U.S. 113.

CHIEF JUSTICE REHNQUIST **delivered the opinion of the Court.**

An Iowa police officer stopped petitioner Knowles for speeding, but issued him a citation rather than arresting him. The question presented is whether such a procedure authorizes the officer, consistently with the Fourth Amendment, to conduct a full search of the car. We answer this question "no."

Knowles was stopped in Newton, Iowa, after having been clocked driving 43 miles per hour on a road where the speed limit was 25 miles per hour. The police officer issued a citation to Knowles, although under Iowa law he might have arrested him. The officer then conducted a full search of the car, and under the driver's seat he found a bag of marijuana and a "pot pipe." Knowles was then arrested and charged with violation of state laws dealing with controlled substances.

Before trial, Knowles moved to suppress the evidence so obtained. He argued that the search could not be sustained under the "search incident to arrest" exception recognized in United States v. Robinson, because he had not been placed under arrest. At the hearing on the motion to suppress, the police officer conceded that he had neither Knowles' consent nor probable cause to conduct the search.

He relied on Iowa law dealing with such searches.

Iowa Code Ann. § 321.485(1)(a) (West 1997) provides that Iowa peace officers having cause to believe that a person has violated any traffic or motor vehicle equipment law may arrest the person and immediately take the person before a magistrate. Iowa law also authorizes the far more usual practice of issuing a citation in lieu of arrest or in lieu of continued custody after an initial arrest. See Iowa Code Ann. § 805.1(1) (West Supp.1997). Section 805.1(4) provides that the issuance of a citation in lieu of an arrest "does not affect the officer's authority to conduct an otherwise lawful search." The Iowa Supreme Court has interpreted this provision as providing authority to officers to conduct a full-blown search of an automobile and driver in those cases where police elect not to make a custodial arrest and instead issue a citation—that is, a search incident to citation.

Based on this authority, the trial court denied the motion to suppress and found Knowles guilty. The Supreme Court of Iowa * * * affirmed by a divided vote. * * * [T]he Iowa Supreme Court upheld the constitutionality of the search under a bright-line "search incident to citation" exception to the Fourth Amendment's warrant requirement, reasoning that so long as the arresting officer had probable cause to make a custodial arrest, there need not in fact have been a custodial arrest. We granted certiorari, and we now reverse.

* * *

In *Robinson*, supra, we noted the two historical rationales for the "search incident to arrest" exception: (1) the need to disarm the suspect in order to take him into custody, and (2) the need to preserve evidence for later use at trial. But neither of these underlying rationales for the search incident to arrest exception is sufficient to justify the search in the present case.

We have recognized that the first rationale—officer safety—is " 'both legitimate and weighty,' " Maryland v. Wilson, 519 U.S. 408 (1997). The threat to officer safety from issuing a traffic citation, however, is a good deal less than in the case of a custodial arrest. In *Robinson*, we stated that a custodial arrest involves "danger to an officer" because of "the extended exposure which follows the taking of a suspect into custody and transporting him to the police station." We recognized that "[t]he danger to the police officer flows from the fact of the arrest, and its attendant proximity, stress, and uncertainty, and not from the grounds for arrest." A routine traffic stop, on the other hand, is a relatively brief encounter and "is more analogous to a so-called '*Terry* stop' . . . than to a formal arrest."

This is not to say that the concern for officer safety is absent in the case of a routine traffic stop. It plainly is not. But while the concern for officer safety in this context may justify the "minimal" additional intrusion of ordering a driver and passengers out of the car, it does not by itself justify the often considerably greater intrusion attending a full field-type search. Even without the search authority Iowa

urges, officers have other, independent bases to search for weapons and protect themselves from danger. For example, they may order out of a vehicle both the driver, and any passengers; perform a "patdown" of a driver and any passengers upon reasonable suspicion that they may be armed and dangerous; conduct a "*Terry* patdown" of the passenger compartment of a vehicle upon reasonable suspicion that an occupant is dangerous and may gain immediate control of a weapon, Michigan v. Long, 463 U.S. 1032 (1983); and even conduct a full search of the passenger compartment, including any containers therein, pursuant to a custodial arrest, New York v. Belton, 453 U.S. 454, 460 (1981).

Nor has Iowa shown the second justification for the authority to search incident to arrest—the need to discover and preserve evidence. Once Knowles was stopped for speeding and issued a citation, all the evidence necessary to prosecute that offense had been obtained. No further evidence of excessive speed was going to be found either on the person of the offender or in the passenger compartment of the car.

Iowa nevertheless argues that a "search incident to citation" is justified because a suspect who is subject to a routine traffic stop may attempt to hide or destroy evidence related to his identity (e.g., a driver's license or vehicle registration), or destroy evidence of another, as yet undetected crime. As for the destruction of evidence relating to identity, if a police officer is not satisfied with the identification furnished by the driver, this may be a basis for arresting him rather than merely issuing a citation. As for destroying evidence of other crimes, the possibility that an officer would stumble onto evidence wholly unrelated to the speeding offense seems remote.

In *Robinson*, we held that the authority to conduct a full field search as incident to an arrest was a "bright-line rule," which was based on the concern for officer safety and destruction or loss of evidence, but which did not depend in every case upon the existence of either concern. Here we are asked to extend that "bright-line rule" to a situation where the concern for officer safety is not present to the same extent and the concern for destruction or loss of evidence is not present at all. We decline to do so. The judgment of the Supreme Court of Iowa is reversed, and the cause remanded for further proceedings not inconsistent with this opinion.

Question on Knowles

Is the court saying that the search of Knowles' car would have been permissible if the officer had decided to bring Knowles into custody rather than giving him a ticket? If so, isn't the Court providing police officers with an incentive to use a custodial arrest rather than a ticket for a minor traffic offense? How does encouraging police officers to act more intrusively further Fourth Amendment values?

D. PRETEXTUAL STOPS AND ARRESTS

Belton, Robinson, and the *Terry* doctrine give police officers the right to conduct certain searches on the basis of a stop or arrest for a minor offense, such as a traffic offense. Is it possible that these investigatory powers as to minor crimes can be used to search for evidence of a more serious crime for which probable cause or reasonable suspicion does not exist? Are you concerned with that possibility? Is it possible that the right to stop/arrest/search for a minor traffic offense could be used by police as a tool for harassing citizens, particularly minorities? Does the Fourth Amendment protect a citizen from pretextual stops, arrests and searches if the citizen has in fact committed a minor offense? The Supreme Court considered these questions in the following case.

WHREN v. UNITED STATES

Supreme Court of the United States, 1996.
517 U.S. 806.

JUSTICE SCALIA **delivered the opinion of the Court.**

In this case we decide whether the temporary detention of a motorist who the police have probable cause to believe has committed a civil traffic violation is inconsistent with the Fourth Amendment's prohibition against unreasonable seizures unless a reasonable officer would have been motivated to stop the car by a desire to enforce the traffic laws.

I

On the evening of June 10, 1993, plainclothes vice-squad officers of the District of Columbia Metropolitan Po-

lice Department were patrolling a "high drug area" of the city in an unmarked car. Their suspicions were aroused when they passed a dark Pathfinder truck with temporary license plates and youthful occupants waiting at a stop sign, the driver looking down into the lap of the passenger at his right. The truck remained stopped at the intersection for what seemed an unusually long time—more than 20 seconds. When the police car executed a U-turn in order to head back toward the truck, the Pathfinder turned suddenly to its right, without signalling, and sped off at an "unreasonable" speed. The policemen followed, and in a short while overtook the Pathfinder when it stopped behind other traffic at a red light. They pulled up alongside, and Officer Ephraim Soto stepped out and approached the driver's door, identifying himself as a police officer and directing the driver, petitioner Brown, to put the vehicle in park. When Soto drew up to the driver's window, he immediately observed two large plastic bags of what appeared to be crack cocaine in petitioner Whren's hands. Petitioners were arrested, and quantities of several types of illegal drugs were retrieved from the vehicle.

Petitioners were charged in a four-count indictment with violating various federal drug laws, * * *. At a pretrial suppression hearing, they challenged the legality of the stop and the resulting seizure of the drugs. They argued that the stop had not been justified by probable cause to believe, or even reasonable suspicion, that petitioners were engaged in illegal drug-dealing activity; and that Officer Soto's asserted ground for approaching the vehicle—to give the driver a warning concerning traffic violations—was pretextual. The District Court denied the suppression motion, concluding that "the facts of the stop were not controverted," and "there was nothing to really demonstrate that the actions of the officers were contrary to a normal traffic stop."

Petitioners were convicted of the counts at issue here. The Court of Appeals affirmed the convictions, holding with respect to the suppression issue that, "regardless of whether a police officer subjectively believes that the occupants of an automobile may be engaging in some other illegal behavior, a traffic stop is permissible as long as a reasonable officer in the same circumstances could have stopped the car for the suspected traffic violation." We granted certiorari.

II

* * *

Petitioners accept that Officer Soto had probable cause to believe that various provisions of the District of Columbia traffic code had been violated. See 18 D. C. Mun. Regs. §§ 2213.4 (1995)("An operator shall . . . give full time and attention to the operation of the vehicle"); 2204.3 ("No person shall turn any vehicle . . . without giving an appropriate signal"); 2200.3 ("No person shall drive a vehicle . . . at a speed greater than is reasonable and prudent under the conditions"). They argue, however, that "in the unique context of civil traffic regulations" probable cause is not enough. Since, they contend, the use of automobiles is so heavily and minutely regulated that total compliance with traffic and safety rules is nearly impossible, a police officer will almost invariably be able to catch any given motorist in a technical violation. This creates the temptation to use traffic stops as a means of investigating other law violations, as to which no probable cause or even articulable suspicion exists. Petitioners, who are both black, further contend that police officers might decide which motorists to stop based on decidedly impermissible factors, such as the race of the car's occupants. To avoid this danger, they say, the Fourth Amendment test for traffic stops should be, not the normal one (applied by the Court of Appeals) of whether probable cause existed to justify the stop; but rather, whether a police officer, acting reasonably, would have made the stop for the reason given.

A

Petitioners contend that the standard they propose is consistent with our past cases' disapproval of police attempts to use valid bases of action against citizens as pretexts for pursuing other investigatory agendas. We are reminded that in Florida v. Wells, 495 U.S. 1 (1990), we stated that "an inventory search must not be used as a ruse for a general rummaging in order to discover incriminating evidence"; that in Colorado v. Bertine, 479 U.S. 367 (1987), in approving an inventory search, we apparently thought it significant that there had been "no showing that the police, who were following standard procedures, acted in bad faith or for the sole purpose of investigation"; and that in New York v. Burger, 482 U.S. 691 (1987), we observed, in upholding the constitutionality of a warrantless administrative inspection, that the search did not appear to be "a 'pretext' for obtaining evidence of . . . violation of . . . penal laws." But only an undiscerning reader would regard these cases as endorsing the principle that ulterior motives can invalidate police conduct that is justifiable on the basis of probable cause to believe that a violation of law has occurred. In each case we were addressing the validity of a search conducted in the absence of probable cause. Our quoted statements simply explain that the exemption from the need for probable cause (and warrant), which is accorded to searches made for the purpose of inventory or administrative regulation, is not accorded to searches that are not made for those purposes.

* * *

* * * Not only have we never held, outside the context of inventory search or administrative inspection (discussed above), that an officer's motive invalidates objectively justifiable behavior under the Fourth Amendment; but we have repeatedly held and asserted the contrary. * * * In United States v. Robinson, 414 U.S. 218 (1973), we held that a traffic-violation arrest (of the sort here) would not be rendered

invalid by the fact that it was "a mere pretext for a narcotics search," and that a lawful postarrest search of the person would not be rendered invalid by the fact that it was not motivated by the officer-safety concern that justifies such searches. And in Scott v. United States, 436 U.S. 128 (1978), in rejecting the contention that wiretap evidence was subject to exclusion because the agents conducting the tap had failed to make any effort to comply with the statutory requirement that unauthorized acquisitions be minimized, we said that "subjective intent alone . . . does not make otherwise lawful conduct illegal or unconstitutional." We described *Robinson* as having established that "the fact that the officer does not have the state of mind which is hypothecated by the reasons which provide the legal justification for the officer's action does not invalidate the action taken as long as the circumstances, viewed objectively, justify that action."

We think these cases foreclose any argument that the constitutional reasonableness of traffic stops depends on the actual motivations of the individual officers involved. We of course agree with petitioners that the Constitution prohibits selective enforcement of the law based on considerations such as race. But the constitutional basis for objecting to intentionally discriminatory application of laws is the Equal Protection Clause, not the Fourth Amendment. Subjective intentions play no role in ordinary, probable-cause Fourth Amendment analysis.

B

Recognizing that we have been unwilling to entertain Fourth Amendment challenges based on the actual motivations of individual officers, petitioners disavow any intention to make the individual officer's subjective good faith the touchstone of "reasonableness." They insist that the standard they have put forward—whether the officer's conduct deviated materially from usual police practices, so that a reasonable officer in the same circumstances would not have made the stop for the reasons given—is an "objective" one.

But although framed in empirical terms, this approach is plainly and indisputably driven by subjective considerations. Its whole purpose is to prevent the police from doing under the guise of enforcing the traffic code what they would like to do for different reasons. Petitioners' proposed standard may not use the word "pretext," but it is designed to combat nothing other than the perceived "danger" of the pretextual stop, albeit only indirectly and over the run of cases. Instead of asking whether the individual officer had the proper state of mind, the petitioners would have us ask, in effect, whether (based on general police practices) it is plausible to believe that the officer had the proper state of mind.

Why one would frame a test designed to combat pretext in such fashion that the court cannot take into account actual and admitted pretext is a curiosity that can only be explained by the fact that our cases have foreclosed the more sensible option. If those cases were based only upon the evidentiary difficulty of establishing subjective intent, petitioners' attempt to root out subjective vices through objective means might make sense. But they were not based only upon that, or indeed even principally upon that. Their principal basis—which applies equally to attempts to reach subjective intent through ostensibly objective means—is simply that the Fourth Amendment's concern with "reasonableness" allows certain actions to be taken in certain circumstances, what-

ever the subjective intent. But even if our concern had been only an evidentiary one, petitioners' proposal would by no means assuage it. Indeed, it seems to us somewhat easier to figure out the intent of an individual officer than to plumb the collective consciousness of law enforcement in order to determine whether a "reasonable officer" would have been moved to act upon the traffic violation. While police manuals and standard procedures may sometimes provide objective assistance, ordinarily one would be reduced to speculating about the hypothetical reaction of a hypothetical constable—an exercise that might be called virtual subjectivity.

Moreover, police enforcement practices, even if they could be practicably assessed by a judge, vary from place to place and from time to time. We cannot accept that the search and seizure protections of the Fourth Amendment are so variable, and can be made to turn upon such trivialities. The difficulty is illustrated by petitioners' arguments in this case. Their claim that a reasonable officer would not have made this stop is based largely on District of Columbia police regulations which permit plainclothes officers in unmarked vehicles to enforce traffic laws "only in the case of a violation that is so grave as to pose an immediate threat to the safety of others." This basis of invalidation would not apply in jurisdictions that had a different practice. And it would not have applied even in the District of Columbia, if Officer Soto had been wearing a uniform or patrolling in a marked police cruiser.

* * *

III

In what would appear to be an elaboration on the "reasonable officer" test, petitioners argue that the balancing inherent in any Fourth Amendment inquiry requires us to weigh the governmental and individual interests implicated in a traffic stop such as we have here. That balancing, petitioners claim, does not support investigation of minor traffic infractions by plainclothes police in unmarked vehicles; such investigation only minimally advances the government's interest in traffic safety, and may indeed retard it by producing motorist confusion and alarm—a view said to be supported by the Metropolitan Police Department's own regulations generally prohibiting this practice. And as for the Fourth Amendment interests of the individuals concerned, petitioners point out that our cases acknowledge that even ordinary traffic stops entail "a possibly unsettling show of authority"; that they at best "interfere with freedom of movement, are inconvenient, and consume time" and at worst "may create substantial anxiety". That anxiety is likely to be even more pronounced when the stop is conducted by plainclothes officers in unmarked cars.

It is of course true that in principle every Fourth Amendment case, since it turns upon a "reasonableness" determination, involves a balancing of all relevant factors. With rare exceptions not applicable here, however, the result of that balancing is not in doubt where the search or seizure is based upon probable cause. * * *

Where probable cause has existed, the only cases in which we have found it necessary actually to perform the "balancing" analysis involved searches or seizures conducted in an extraordinary manner, unusually harmful to an individual's privacy or even physical interests—such as, for example, seizure by means of deadly force, see Tennessee v. Garner, unannounced entry into a home, see Wilson v. Arkansas, entry into a home without a warrant, see Welsh v. Wisconsin, or physical penetration of the body, see Winston v. Lee. The making of a traffic stop out-of-uniform does not remotely qualify as such an extreme practice, and so is governed by the usual rule that probable cause to believe the law has been broken "outbalances" private interest in avoiding police contact.

Petitioners urge as an extraordinary factor in this case that the "multitude of applicable traffic and equipment regulations" is so large and so difficult to obey perfectly that virtually everyone is guilty of violation, permitting the police to single out almost whomever they wish for a stop. But we are aware of no principle that would allow us to decide at what point a code of law becomes so expansive and so commonly violated that infraction itself can no longer be the ordinary measure of the lawfulness of enforcement. And even if we could identify such exorbitant codes, we do not know by what standard (or what right) we would decide, as petitioners would have us do, which particular provisions are sufficiently important to merit enforcement.

For the run-of-the-mine case, which this surely is, we think there is no realistic alternative to the traditional common-law rule that probable cause justifies a search and seizure.

Here the District Court found that the officers had probable cause to believe that petitioners had violated the traffic code. That rendered the stop reasonable under the Fourth Amendment, the evidence thereby discovered admissible, and the upholding of the convictions by the Court of Appeals for the District of Columbia Circuit correct.

Judgment affirmed.

Questions About Whren

Professor Maclin, in Race and the Fourth Amendment, 51 Vand. L.Rev. 333 (1998), cites some statistics that might give some perspective to the impact of *Whren* on Fourth Amendment protections. These statistics were compiled in two separate actions in Maryland and New Jersey, alleging that State Troopers were engaged in racial profiling of Black motorists. The New Jersey Turnpike data revealed the following:

A count of the traffic indicated that 13.5% of the automobiles carried a black occupant. A count of the traffic surveyed for speeding indicated that 98.1% of the vehicles on the road exceeded the speed limit. Fifteen percent of the speeding vehicles had a black occupant. Fifteen percent of the automobiles that both violated the speed limit and committed some other moving violation also had a black occupant.* * * [W]hile automobiles with black occupants represented only 15% of the motorists who violated the speeding laws, * * * 35.6% of the race identified stops * * * involved vehicles with black occupants.

In the Maryland case, Wilkins v. Maryland State Police, a state trooper stopped an automobile with four black occupants for speeding in April 1992 in Allegheny County. One of the occupants was Robert Wilkins, a Washington, D.C., criminal defense lawyer, who with his family, was returning to Washington after attending a funeral in Chicago. He was detained for more than 30 minutes, and the officer had a drug-sniffing dog brought to the scene. The canine sniff revealed no narcotics; the officer then permitted Wilson and his family to leave after writing out a speeding ticket.

Wilkins subsequently filed a class action lawsuit alleging Maryland troopers were illegally stopping black motorists because of their race. In addition to the police data, the plaintiffs' expert designed a statistical plan to determine whether Maryland troopers stop and search black motorists at a rate disproportionate to their numbers on the roads. This survey indicated that

93.3% of the drivers on Interstate 95 "were violating traffic laws and thus were eligible to be stopped by State Police. Of the violators, 17.5% were black, and 74.7% were white." Data from the Maryland State Police measured the number of motorists stopped and searched by troopers on Interstate 95, north of Baltimore between January 1995 and September 1996. The police data indicated the following: 72.9% of the motorists stopped and searched were black; 80.3% of the motorists searched were black, Hispanic or some other racial minority group; 19.7% of those searched were white.

The police data also measured the number of searches conducted by individual troopers on Interstate 95 north of Baltimore. This data indicated that thirteen troopers conducted 85.4% of the searches. With the exception of one trooper, all of these troopers searched black and other minority motorists at much higher rates than these motorists travel on the highway. The trooper (omitting the trooper who searched black motorists at a rate close to their presence on the roads) with the lowest percentage of black motorist searches still searched black motorists at nearly twice the rate they were found to travel on the highway. The trooper with the highest percentage of black motorist searches searched only black motorists. Ten of the thirteen troopers searched minority motorists at least 80% of the time.

The police data also included information on motorists searched by the police who traveled on roads outside of the northern portion of Interstate 95. This data contrasted significantly with the searches conducted on Interstate 95. For example, while troopers searched white motorists 19.7% of the time on Interstate 95, troopers patrolling outside of Interstate 95 searched white motorists 63.7% of the time. Troopers searched 72.9% of the black motorists on Interstate 95, but only 32% on other state roads. * * *

Finally, the police data included information on the number of searches that revealed contraband. Troopers found contraband in 28.1% of the cars they searched. The success rate of troopers on Interstate 95 was approximately the same as for searches on other state roads: Troopers found contraband in 29.9% of the cars on Interstate 95 and in 27.1% of the cars on roads outside of Interstate 95. According to the plaintiffs' expert, the police data reported no statewide differences in the success rate of troopers when searching black and white motorists: Troopers recovered contraband from 28.4% of the black motorists searched and from 28.8% of the white motorists searched. Thus, seventy percent of the searches uncovered no contraband.

The plaintiff's expert in *Wilkins* concluded that "the probability that black Interstate 95 drivers are subjected to searches at so high a rate by chance is less than one in one quintillion. It is wildly significant by statistical measures."

In light of these statistics, did the Court reach the right result in *Whren* when it held that probable cause of a traffic violation ends the Fourth Amendment inquiry? If that is the wrong result, what should the Court have done? Should it have held that officers cannot make stops or arrests for traffic violations? Should it have held that officers can make stops for traffic violations, but that any evidence they find of some other violation cannot be admitted at trial? Would excluding the evidence, even though "legally" found, be justified? Would it deter police officers from stopping for traffic violations simply to harrass minority drivers?

For a critique of *Whren*, see O'Neill, Beyond Privacy, Beyond Probable Cause, Beyond the Fourth Amendment: New Strategies for Fighting Pretext Arrests, 69 Colo.L.Rev. 693 (1998). Professor O'Neill argues that instead of focusing on privacy, the Court in *Whren* should have focused on whether the police officer's conduct in *Whren* was abusive and arbitrary.

The police officer in *Whren* testified that when he stopped the suspects' vehicle and approached the car, he observed two large plastic bags of crack cocaine in Whren's hands. Was Whren stupid or something? When he saw the officer approach the car, why didn't he try to hide the drugs? Professor Maclin, in Race and the Fourth Amendment, supra, has this to say about this aspect of *Whren:*

> After reviewing so many cases where police officers testify that they discovered illegal drugs in plain view or after a consent search, judges may begin to wonder why drug dealers are so stupid. * * * Of course, there is an alternative explanation other than drug dealers' desire to cooperate with the police for the type of police testimony seen in *Whren* and other cases where drugs are claimed to be found in plain view or after a consent search: police perjury. As Joseph D. McNamara, the former Police Chief of Kansas City and San Jose, has explained:
>
> > (H)undreds of thousands of police officers swear under oath that the drugs were in plain view or that the defendant gave consent to a search. This may happen occasionally but it defies belief that so many drug users are careless enough to leave illegal drugs where the police can see them or so dumb as to give cops consent to search them when they possess drugs.

* * * We can suppose that criminals are not rocket scientists and that Freud's insights apply to criminals no less than to anyone else. But even if a self-destructive error of the sort posited by the police is possible, it is not probable.

Equal Protection Issues

Are there limitations other than those of the Fourth Amendment that might constrain officers who use traffic stops as a pretext to search or harass? In United States v. Scopo, 19 F.3d 777 (2d Cir.1994), the court upheld a firearms conviction based on evidence discovered during a stop for a traffic offense. Judge Newman, concurring, declared as follows:

> In upholding Scopo's arrest, we should not be understood to be giving police officers carte blanche to skew their law enforcement activity against any group that displeases them. Though the Fourth Amendment permits a pretext arrest, if otherwise supported by probable cause, the Equal Protection Clause still imposes restraint on impermissibly class-based discriminations.

The Court in *Whren* also cited the Equal Protection Clause as a constraint on police officers in cases where the stop or arrest is reasonable under the Fourth Amendment. As discussed in the section on *Terry*, *supra* however, it is extremely difficult to prove an equal protection violation when it comes to police officer conduct in the streets. Professor Maclin, in Race and the Fourth Amendment, supra, elaborates:

> Before a black motorist can obtain access to or challenge an officer's past practices regarding traffic stops under an equal protection challenge, the defense may have to overcome a heavy evidentiary burden. In United States v. Armstrong, [discussed in Chapter Six, infra] decided three weeks before *Whren*, the Court held that the essential elements of a selective prosecution claim must be shown before the prosecution is required to provide access to its files for discovery purposes. Thus, the defense must show both a discriminatory effect and purpose by governmental actors. Under *Armstrong*, "(t)o establish a discriminatory effect in a race case, the claimant must show that similarly situated individuals of a different race were not prosecuted." * * *

> Of course, a black motorist might argue that the reasoning of *Armstrong* follows from the Court's reluctance to examine executive branch decisions on whom to prosecute, and is thus inapplicable where the enforcement policies of the police are challenged, because police are not entitled to the same degree of deference accorded prosecutors. But lower court decisions subsequent to *Armstrong* and *Whren* have not read *Armstrong* narrowly, and have applied its strict evidentiary burden to claims of selective enforcement by the police. See United States v. Bullock, 94 F.3d 896, 899 (4th Cir.1996) (applying *Armstrong* to affirm district court's ruling refusing defendant's attempt to present evidence and to cross-examine the arresting officer about his past practice of using traffic stops of young black males as a pretext for drug searches because the defendant "failed to lay any foundation for an equal protection challenge based on racially selective enforcement procedures"); United States v. Bell, 86 F.3d 820, 823 (8th Cir.1996) (holding that a black defendant raising discriminatory enforcement claim

against the police must show "people of another race violated the law and the law was not enforced against them" and while Bell showed that only blacks were arrested for violating bicycle headlamp law during a certain month, he "failed to show white bicyclists also violated the statute and police chose not to arrest them"). * * *

Even if a defendant is able to overcome the obstacles to discovery erected by *Armstrong*, to prevail on the merits of an equal protection claim, he will have to show that he was singled out because of his race or ethnicity, and that similarly situated white motorists were not stopped. In the typical case, this means that a black defendant must show a specific intent or purpose by either the officer or his department to target blacks for traffic stops. * * * Unless an officer were to testify that the motorist was stopped because he was black or Hispanic, the specific intent standard will doom the typical pretextual traffic stop case involving a black motorist. In the atypical case involving a defense able to conduct a systematic study of the enforcement practices of a particular police department, there is a better chance of success if statistics suggest that officers are targeting black motorists. But even where statistics show a strong correlation between race and a particular outcome, the Court has still required the individual criminal defendant to prove that the government officials in his case were motivated by a discriminatory intent.

Finally, even if a black defendant challenging a pretextual traffic stop is able to obtain discovery and prevail on the merits of an equal protection claim, there is the question of remedy. The Court has shown no sign that it interprets the Equal Protection Clause to embody an exclusionary rule remedy, or that the Clause even requires the dismissal of criminal charges in a case involving a race-based prosecution. * * *

For these reasons, successful equal protection challenges to pretextual traffic stops by minority motorists will be rare. Thus, the *Whren* Court's apparent accord with the constitutional challenge in that case, ("We of course agree with petitioners that the Constitution prohibits selective enforcement of the law based on considerations such as race."), seems hollow.

For cases rejecting equal protection challenges to police searches and seizures after *Whren*, see, e.g., Johnson v. Crooks, 326 F.3d 995 (8th Cir. 2003) (even though officer followed a black motorist 11 miles before making a traffic stop, there was no showing of an equal protection violation, as the plaintiff "offered no evidence that Crooks does not stop non-African Americans under similar circumstances."); Bingham v. City of Manhattan Beach, 329 F.3d 723 (9th Cir. 2003) ("Essentially, Bingham argues that because he is African–American, the officer is white, and they disagree about the reasonableness of the traffic stop, these circumstances are sufficient to raise an inference of discrimination. We disagree that this is sufficient to state an equal protection claim."); Bradley v. United States, 299 F.3d 197 (3rd Cir. 2002) (the fact that the plaintiff, an African–American, was thoroughly searched at a Customs checkpoint while several white males were allowed to pass is not enough to show discriminatory intent).

Is it possible that the solution to pretextual stops after *Whren* has been shifted from constitutional regulation to regulation by public outrage and possible legislation? Public outrage over racial profiling in the use of traffic stops led to personnel changes in New Jersey, as well as new rules requiring Troopers to file reports concerning the race of motorists whom they stop. See "Whitman Admits Police Used Race in Turnpike Stops," New York Times, April 21, 1999, at B1. Legislation has been introduced in 18 states requiring studies of how often racial profiling occurs and requiring police to record the race of each person stopped for a traffic violation. Samborn, "Profiled and Pulled Over," ABA Journal, October, 1999, at 18. The President has issued an Executive Order prohibiting racial profiling by federal officers. Can you think of any other legislation that might be useful in regulating the pretextual use of traffic stops?

Probable Cause of a Traffic Violation

A traffic stop can only be used as a pretext under *Whren* if the officer has reasonable cause to believe that the motorist has actually violated a traffic law. Consider the facts set out by the court in United States v. Miller, 146 F.3d 274 (5th Cir.1998):

> Shortly before 1:00 p.m. on September 27, 1996, Randell County Deputy Sheriff John Sheets spotted Richard Eugene Miller driving a motor home east on Interstate 40, near Amarillo, Texas. Sheets was working as a member of the Criminal Interdiction Unit of the Panhandle Regional Narcotics Trafficking Task Force, which, according to Sheets, sought to interdict illegal drugs by stopping motorists under the pretext of enforcing traffic laws in order to obtain voluntary consent to search their vehicles. Sheets, observing that Miller's motor home had no front license plate, turned around to follow it to see if it had the required license registration in the rear. As Sheets was following, Miller exited Interstate 40, turning south onto Soncy Road. Sheets then saw that the motor home had a temporary Colorado registration tag, but also noticed that it had its left turn signal on for a period of time during which it proceeded through an intersection but did not turn left nor change lanes to the left. Sheets pulled Miller over, and they were joined shortly thereafter by Brent Clay, an Amarillo police officer who was also a member of the Regional Narcotics Task Force.

> After pulling him over, Sheets informed Miller that he was going to issue him a warning citation for improper use of his left turn signal. He then told Miller that he and Clay were looking for illegal contraband and asked if Miller would mind if he and Clay searched the motor home. Miller indicated that he did not object to a search. The officers undertook a search and found approximately eighty kilograms of marijuana in a compartment under a bed in the motor home and they arrested Miller.

The court conducted an extensive review of Texas traffic laws. It found that nothing in the Texas traffic laws prohibited motorists from having a turn signal on without turning or changing lanes. Therefore, the traffic stop was illegal, and the drugs were suppressed as the fruit of an unlawful stop. The court concluded as follows:

> The rule articulated by the Supreme Court in *Whren* provides law enforcement officers broad leeway to conduct searches and seizures regardless of whether their subjective intent corresponds to the legal justifications for their actions. But the flip side of that leeway is that the legal justification must be objectively grounded. Here, given that having a turn signal on

is not a violation of Texas law, no objective basis for probable cause justified the stop of Miller.

See also United States v. Mariscal, 285 F.3d 1127 (9th Cir. 2002) (*Whren* not applicable because the officer stopped the defendant for something that was not a traffic violation: the defendant turned right without signalling, but the local traffic law prohibited such turns only if "other traffic" would be affected by the turn; in this case, there was no "other traffic" on the road; the fact that the police officer's car was affected by the defendant's turn was irrelevant, because it was affected only "to the extent that the turn energized the officers to swoop down upon their prey.").

E. PLAIN VIEW AND PLAIN TOUCH SEIZURES

The concept of plain view underlies much of the law and practice under the *Terry* doctrine and the arrest power rule, and it applies as well during searches conducted pursuant to a warrant or another exception to the warrant requirement. For example, the officers in *Robinson* and *Belton* seized narcotics in plain view during the course of a search incident to arrest; the officers in *Long* seized weapons in plain view in Long's car during the course of a search for self-protection under *Terry;* the officer in *Whren* seized evidence that he saw in Whren's hands after making a lawful traffic stop; and an officer searching pursuant to a warrant can seize contraband that comes into view during the lawful course of that search.

In Coolidge v. New Hampshire, 403 U.S. 443 (1971), Justice Stewart's plurality opinion stated that if officers have a right to be in a particular place and come upon evidence that they have probable cause to believe is subject to seizure, they may seize it. In the following case, the Court explains the plain view doctrine in detail, and revisits some of the problems of applying that doctrine that divided the Court in *Coolidge*.

HORTON v. CALIFORNIA

Supreme Court of the United States, 1990.
496 U.S. 128.

JUSTICE STEVENS **delivered the opinion of the Court.**

In this case we revisit an issue that was considered, but not conclusively resolved, in Coolidge v. New Hampshire: Whether the warrantless seizure of evidence of crime in plain view is prohibited by the Fourth Amendment if the discovery of the evidence was not inadvertent. We conclude that even though inadvertence is a characteristic of most legitimate "plain view" seizures, it is not a necessary condition.

I

Petitioner was convicted of the armed robbery of Erwin Wallaker, the treasurer of the San Jose Coin Club. * * *

Sergeant LaRault, an experienced police officer, investigated the crime and determined that there was probable cause to search petitioner's home for the proceeds of the robbery and for the weapons used by the robbers. His affidavit for a search warrant referred to police reports that described the weapons as well as the proceeds, but the warrant issued by the Magistrate only authorized a search for the proceeds, including three specifically described rings.

Pursuant to the warrant, LaRault searched petitioner's residence, but he did not find the stolen property. During the course of the search, however, he discovered the weapons in plain view and seized them. * * * LaRault testified that while he was searching for the rings, he also was interested in finding other evidence connecting petitioner to the robbery. Thus, the seized evidence was not discovered "inadvertently."

* * *

II

* * *

The right to security in person and property protected by the Fourth Amendment may be invaded in quite different ways by searches and seizures. A search compromises the individual interest in privacy; a seizure deprives the individual of dominion over his or her person or property. The "plain view" doctrine is often considered an exception to the general rule that warrantless searches are presumptively unreasonable, but this characterization overlooks the important difference between searches and seizures. If an article is already in plain view, neither its observation nor its seizure would involve any invasion of privacy. A seizure of the article, however, would obviously invade the owner's possessory interest. If "plain view" justifies an exception from an otherwise applicable warrant requirement, therefore, it must be an exception that is addressed to the concerns that are implicated by seizures rather than by searches.

The criteria that generally guide "plain view" seizures were set forth in Coolidge v. New Hampshire. The Court held that the seizure of two automobiles parked in plain view on the defendant's driveway in the course of arresting the defendant violated the Fourth Amendment. Accordingly, particles of gun powder that had been subsequently found in vacuum sweepings from one of the cars could not be introduced in evidence against the defendant. The State endeavored to justify the seizure of the automobiles, and their subsequent search at the police station, on four different grounds, including the "plain view" doctrine. The scope of that doctrine as it had developed in earlier cases was fairly summarized in * * * Justice Stewart's opinion:

* * *

"An example of the applicability of the 'plain view' doctrine is the situation in which the police have a warrant to search a given area for specified objects, and in the course of the search come across some other article of incriminating character. Where the initial intrusion that brings the police within plain view of such an article is supported, not by a warrant, but by one of the recognized exceptions to the warrant requirement, the seizure is also legitimate. Thus * * * an object that comes into view during a search incident to arrest that is appropriately limited in scope under existing law may be seized without a warrant. Chimel v. California. * * *

"What the 'plain view' cases have in common is that the police officer in each of them had a prior justification for an intrusion in the course of which he came inadvertently across a piece of evidence incriminating the accused. The doctrine serves to supplement the prior justification— whether it be a warrant for another object, hot pursuit, search incident to lawful arrest, or some other legitimate reason for being present unconnected with a search directed against the accused—and permits the warrantless seizure. Of course, the extension of the original justification is legitimate only where it is immediately apparent to the police that they have evidence before them; the 'plain view' doctrine may not be used to extend a general exploratory search from one object to another until something incriminating at last emerges."

Justice Stewart then described the two limitations on the doctrine that he found implicit in its rationale: First, "that plain view *alone* is never enough to justify the warrantless seizure of evidence"; and second, "that the discovery of evidence in plain view must be inadvertent."

* * *

III

Justice Stewart concluded that the inadvertence requirement was necessary to avoid a violation of the express constitutional requirement that a valid warrant must particularly describe the things to be seized. He explained:

"The rationale of the exception to the warrant requirement, as just stated, is that a plain-view seizure will not turn an initially valid (and therefore limited) search into a 'general' one, while the inconvenience of procuring a warrant to cover an inadvertent discovery is great. But where the discovery is anticipated, where the police know in advance the location of the evidence and intend to seize it, the situation is altogether different. The requirement of a warrant to seize imposes no inconvenience whatever, or at least none which is constitutionally cognizable in a legal system that regards warrantless searches as '*per se* unrea-

sonable' in the absence of 'exigent circumstances.' "

* * *

We find two flaws in this reasoning. First, evenhanded law enforcement is best achieved by the application of objective standards of conduct, rather than standards that depend upon the subjective state of mind of the officer. The fact that an officer is interested in an item of evidence and fully expects to find it in the course of a search should not invalidate its seizure if the search is confined in area and duration by the terms of a warrant or a valid exception to the warrant requirement. If the officer has knowledge approaching certainty that the item will be found, we see no reason why he or she would deliberately omit a particular description of the item to be seized from the application for a search warrant. Specification of the additional item could only permit the officer to expand the scope of the search. On the other hand, if he or she has a valid warrant to search for one item and merely a suspicion concerning the second, whether or not it amounts to probable cause, we fail to see why that suspicion should immunize the second item from seizure if it is found during a lawful search for the first.

* * *

Second, the suggestion that the inadvertence requirement is necessary to prevent the police from conducting general searches, or from converting specific warrants into general warrants, is not persuasive because that interest is already served by the requirements that no warrant issue unless it "particularly describ[es] the place to be searched and the persons or things to be seized," and that a warrantless search be circumscribed by the exigencies which justify its initiation. Scrupulous adherence to these requirements serves the interests in limiting the area and duration of the search that the inadvertence requirement inadequately protects. Once those commands have been satisfied and the officer has a lawful right of access, however, no additional Fourth Amendment interest is furthered by requiring that the discovery of evidence be inadvertent. If the scope of the search exceeds that permitted by the terms of a validly issued warrant or the character of the relevant exception from the warrant requirement, the subsequent seizure is unconstitutional without more.

* * *

In this case, the scope of the search was not enlarged in the slightest by the omission of any reference to the weapons in the warrant. Indeed, if the three rings and other items named in the warrant had been found at the outset—or if petitioner had them in his possession and had responded to the warrant by producing them immediately—no search for weapons could have taken place. * * *

* * * The prohibition against general searches and general warrants serves primarily as a protection against unjustified intrusions on privacy. But reliance on privacy concerns that support that prohibition is misplaced when the inquiry concerns the scope of an exception that merely authorizes an officer with a lawful right of access to an item to seize it without a warrant.

* * *

[Based on the above reasoning, the Court rejects the implication in *Coolidge* that a plain view seizure must be inadvertent.]

JUSTICE BRENNAN, **with whom** JUSTICE MARSHALL **joins, dissenting.**

* * *

[T]here are a number of instances in which a law enforcement officer might deliberately choose to omit certain items from a warrant application even though he has probable cause to seize them, knows they are on the premises, and intends to seize them when they are discovered in plain view. For example, the warrant application process can often be time-consuming, especially when the police attempt to seize a large number of items. An officer interested in conducting a search as soon as possible might decide to save time by listing only one or two hard-to-find items, such as the stolen rings in this case, confident that he will find in plain view all of the other evidence he is looking for before he discovers the listed items. Because rings could be located almost anywhere inside or outside a house, it is unlikely that a warrant to search for and seize the rings would restrict the scope of the search. An officer might rationally find the risk of immediately discovering the items listed in the warrant—thereby forcing him to conclude the search immediately—outweighed by the time saved in the application process.

* * * It is true that the inadvertent discovery requirement furthers no privacy interests. * * * But it does protect possessory interests. * * * The Court today eliminates a rule designed to further possessory interests on the ground that it fails to further privacy interests. I cannot countenance such constitutional legerdemain.

* * *

Note on Horton

What dangers, if any, exist when an officer omits items from a warrant request? Does omission impair the magistrate's ability to make the probable cause determination before a search is conducted? Can the decision in *Horton* be used to evade the particularity requirement of the warrant clause? See United States v. Soussi, 29 F.3d 565 (10th Cir.1994)("[I]tems named in an impermissibly broad portion of a warrant may nevertheless be seized pursuant to the plain view doctrine so long as the government's plain view seizure scrupulously adheres to the three-prong *Horton* test.").

Probable Cause to Seize an Item in Plain View: Arizona v. Hicks

One of the difficult plain view issues is how closely the police may examine an object to decide whether it is subject to seizure. In the 6–3 decision in Arizona v. Hicks, 480 U.S. 321 (1987), Justice Scalia wrote for the Court as it held that probable cause is necessary to justify a search that precedes a plain view seizure. Arizona police entered Hicks' apartment after a bullet was fired through its floor into the apartment below, injuring a man. The officers looked for the shooter, other victims and weapons. One officer noticed two sets of expensive stereo components that seemed out of place in an "ill-appointed four-room apartment." The officer moved some of the components in order to find serial numbers, telephoned in the numbers, and learned that one turntable he had moved was stolen. He seized the turntable immediately. Later it was learned that other equipment was stolen, and a warrant was obtained.

Justice Scalia rejected the state's argument that the officer's inspection of the underside of the turntable did not amount to a search: "A search is a search, even if it happens to disclose nothing but the bottom of a turntable." He also rejected the argument that the officer had sufficient cause to justify his actions. The state conceded that the officer lacked probable cause for a search, but sought to justify his actions on the basis of reasonable suspicion. Justice Scalia described the plain view doctrine as resting on the "desirability of sparing police, whose viewing of the object in the course of a lawful search is as legitimate as it would have been in a public place, the inconvenience and the risk—to themselves or to preservation of the evidence—of going to get a warrant." He further observed that "[n]o reason is apparent why an object should routinely be seizable on lesser grounds, during an unrelated search and seizure, than would have been needed to obtain a warrant for that same object if it had been known to be on the premises." Justice O'Connor, joined by Chief Justice Rehnquist and Justice Powell, dissented.

After *Hicks*, an officer must have probable cause to seize an item in plain view during the course of legal activity. And that probable cause must be readily apparent, meaning that probable cause must exist without the necessity of a further search. For cases discussing the probable cause requirement for plain view seizures after *Hicks*, see United States v. Benish, 5 F.3d 20 (3d Cir. 1993)(probable cause to seize a marijuana plant was immediately apparent, as the officer had taken classes on identifying marijuana); United States v. Cooper, 19 F.3d 1154 (7th Cir.1994)(probable cause to seize an empty ammunition box was immediately apparent, where it was found together with drugs and weapons: "The ammunition box, unlike a cigar box, is probative of weapons possession and drug dealing."); United States v. Pindell, 336 F.3d 1049 (D.C.Cir. 2003) (probable cause to seize a notebook was immediately apparent, as the victim of a robbery had told the officer that the perpetrator had been disguised as a police officer and had recorded information in a notebook during the robbery; the officer found the notebook lying next to a police uniform in the defendant's car).

The Plain Touch Doctrine

If an officer, acting in the course of lawful activity, can determine by touch that an object is evidence or contraband, can he seize the object? This was the question in Minnesota v. Dickerson, 508 U.S. 366 (1993), where an officer, in the course of a stop and frisk permitted by the *Terry* doctrine, patted-down the suspect and felt a small, hard, pea-shaped object in the suspect's shirt pocket. At the suppression hearing, the officer testified that he examined the object with his fingers "and it slid and it felt to be a lump of crack cocaine in cellophane." Because the suspect had left a house known to be a place for drug activity, the officer concluded that there was probable cause to believe that the pea-shaped object was contraband, and he pulled the object from the suspect's pocket; the object turned out to be a small plastic bag containing crack cocaine.

The state in *Dickerson* argued that the seizure was permissible because the officer obtained probable cause by "plain touch" during a lawful frisk, which was analogous to obtaining probable cause by plain view during a lawful search. The Minnesota Supreme Court rejected the argument that the Fourth Amendment contained a plain touch exception to the warrant requirement. It further held that even if there is a plain touch exception, it would not apply to the facts of the case, because the officer had squeezed and prodded the package in Dickerson's pocket in order to determine what it was. Thus, the fact that it was contraband was not immediately apparent to the officer. The Supreme Court, in an opinion by Justice White, rejected the lower court's reasoning as to the existence of a plain touch exception, and found that such an exception to the warrant requirement does exist; but the Court nonetheless affirmed the lower court on the ground that the officer's activity went beyond the scope of the plain touch exception.

Justice White stated that the plain view doctrine "has an obvious application by analogy to cases in which an officer discovers contraband through the sense of touch during an otherwise lawful search." He elaborated as follows:

> The rationale of the plain view doctrine is that if contraband is left in open view and is observed by a police officer from a lawful vantage point, there has been no invasion of a legitimate expectation of privacy and thus no "search" within the meaning of the Fourth Amendment—or at least no search independent of the initial intrusion that gave the officers their vantage point. The warrantless seizure of contraband that presents itself in this manner is deemed justified by the realization that resort to a neutral magistrate under such circumstances would often be impracticable and would do little to promote the objectives of the Fourth Amendment. The same can be said of tactile discoveries of contraband. If a police officer lawfully pats down a suspect's outer clothing and feels an object whose contour or mass makes its identity immediately apparent, there has been no invasion of the suspect's privacy beyond that already authorized by the officer's search for weapons; if the object is contraband, its warrantless seizure would be justified by the same practical considerations that inhere in the plain view context.

While the Court found that the Fourth Amendment permits the seizure of evidence discovered through the sense of touch in the course of a lawful search, it also found that the plain touch exception was not applicable to the facts of *Dickerson*. This was because the officer did more than merely touch the object in the course of a lawful *Terry* frisk. Rather, he went beyond the scope of a *Terry* protective frisk, by pushing and prodding the object, after concluding that it was not a weapon, in order to determine whether it was contraband. The Court noted that the facts in *Dickerson* were "very similar" to those presented in Arizona v. Hicks. Justice White evaluated the facts of *Dickerson* as follows:

> Although the officer was lawfully in a position to feel the lump in respondent's pocket, because *Terry* entitled him to place his hands upon respondent's jacket, the court below determined that the incriminating character of the object was not immediately apparent. Rather, the officer determined that the item was contraband only after conducting a further search, one not authorized by *Terry* or any other exception to the warrant requirement. Because the further search of respondent's jacket was constitutionally invalid, the seizure of the cocaine that followed is likewise unconstitutional.

Justice Scalia wrote a short concurring opinion. Chief Justice Rehnquist wrote a short dissenting opinion joined by Justices Blackmun and Thomas. He agreed with the majority's position on the plain touch exception, but argued that a remand was necessary to allow the Minnesota court to apply the exception to the facts of the case. How much more information would have been required for the officer to find probable cause to believe that a hard, pea-shaped object in Dickerson's pocket was crack cocaine? See United States v. Williams, 139 F.3d 628 (8th Cir.1998)(officer who conducted *Terry* frisk and felt a package, had probable cause to seize it because the suspect had just been observed taking part in a drug transaction).

F. AUTOMOBILES AND OTHER MOVABLE OBJECTS

One of the well-recognized exceptions to the warrant requirement is that which is commonly referred to as the "automobile exception." Broadly stated, the doctrine holds that the police may search an automobile without a warrant, so long as they have probable cause to believe it contains evidence of criminal activity. The Court first created the exception in Carroll v. United States, 267 U.S. 132 (1925), and it is sometimes called "the *Carroll* Doctrine." As you study the following material, consider three questions: whether the rationale for the exception can withstand analysis, how consistently the Court has applied the articulated rationale to new sets of facts, and whether acceptance of the rationale might logically require its extension to objects other than cars.

1. The Carroll Doctrine

Carroll v. United States involved a violation of the National Prohibition Act, as did many early search and seizure cases. In December 1921, the two defendants were driving westward on a highway between Detroit and Grand Rapids when they were stopped by federal prohibition agents who were patrolling the road. Bootlegging traffic was known to be heavy in the area, due to its proximity to Canada. The defendant's car was searched without a warrant, and 68 quarts of whiskey and gin were found behind the upholstering of the seats. The officers had not anticipated that the defendants would be traveling the highway at that particular time, but their past experiences with these men led them to believe that the defendants were presently engaged in transporting liquor. The defendants were convicted of illegal transportation of intoxicating liquor, a misdemeanor.

The Court, in a 7–2 decision written by Chief Justice Taft, found the search to be constitutional. The major contention was not probable cause, but whether a warrant was required for the search. Justice Taft declared that a warrant could not reasonably have been demanded in light of the mobility of the vehicle:

> [T]he guaranty of freedom from unreasonable searches and seizures by the Fourth Amendment has been construed, practically since the beginning of the Government, as recognizing a necessary difference between a search of a store, dwelling house or other structure in respect of which a proper official warrant readily may be obtained, and a search of a ship, motor boat, wagon or automobile, for contraband goods, where it is not practicable to secure a warrant because the vehicle can be quickly moved out of the locality or jurisdiction in which the warrant must be sought.

Taft further noted that the right to search and the validity of the seizure were not dependent on the right to arrest, thus clearly distinguishing this search from that of an automobile incident to the arrest of the driver.

2. *Distinguishing Carroll From Search Incident to Arrest*

Under the automobile exception, the officer must still have probable cause to believe that evidence will be found in the area of the car that she searches. In contrast, all that is needed for a search incident to arrest is probable cause to arrest—and as shown in *Belton*, that probable cause could be for a minor crime such as a traffic offense. Recall the discussion on pretextual stops and arrests. Will the arrest power rule be more or less likely than the car exception to be invoked to justify a pretextual search? Justice Stevens concurred in the judgment in *Belton* on the ground that it could and should have been decided under the automobile exception. He argued that under the majority opinion in *Belton*, the officer may find reason to make a custodial arrest on a minor offense "whenever he sees an interesting looking briefcase or package in a vehicle that has been stopped for a traffic violation." He contended that by taking "the giant step of permitting searches in the absence of probable cause, the Court misses the shorter step of relying on the automobile exception." Is the automobile exception a shorter step than the search incident to arrest exception? When would the government seek to justify a search under one exception but not the other?

3. *The Progeny of Carroll*

In the following case, the Court considered whether the *Carroll* doctrine, and its reliance on a car's mobility, could be invoked when a warrantless search of a car occurred after the car had been removed to the police station. A car impounded by the police is hardly mobile within the meaning of *Carroll*. So what can justify a warrantless search of an immobile car?

CHAMBERS v. MARONEY

Supreme Court of the United States, 1970.
399 U.S. 42.

MR. JUSTICE WHITE **delivered the opinion of the Court.**

The principal question in this case concerns the admissibility of evidence seized from an automobile, in which petitioner was riding at the time of his arrest, after the automobile was taken to a police station and was there thoroughly searched without a warrant. The Court of Appeals for the Third Circuit found no violation of petitioner's Fourth Amendment rights. We affirm.

I

During the night of May 20, 1963, a Gulf service station in North Braddock, Pennsylvania, was robbed by two men, each of whom carried and displayed a gun. The robbers took the currency from the cash register; the service station attendant, one Stephen Kovacich, was directed to place the coins in his right-hand glove, which was then taken by the robbers. Two teen-agers, who had earlier noticed a blue compact station wagon circling the block in the vicinity of the Gulf station, then saw the station wagon speed away from a parking lot close to the Gulf station. About the same time, they learned that the Gulf station had been robbed. They reported to police, who arrived immediately, that four men were in the station wagon and one was wearing a green sweater. Kovacich told the police that one of the men who robbed him was wearing a green sweater and the other was wearing a trench coat. A description of the car and the two robbers was broadcast over the police radio. Within an hour, a light blue compact station wagon answering the description and carrying four men was stopped by the police about two miles from the Gulf station.

Petitioner was one of the men in the station wagon. He was wearing a green sweater and there was a trench coat in the car. The occupants were arrested and the car was driven to the police station. In the course of a thorough search of the car at the station, the police found concealed in a compartment under the dashboard two .38–caliber revolvers (one loaded with dumdum bullets), a right-hand glove containing small change, and certain cards bearing the name of Raymond Havicon, the attendant at a Boron service station in McKeesport, Pennsylvania, who had been robbed at gunpoint on May 13, 1963. * * *

II

[The Court holds that the police had probable cause to make an arrest, but that the search of the car at the police station was too removed from the arrest to be justified as a search incident to arrest.]

In terms of the circumstances justifying a warrantless search, the Court has long distinguished between an automobile and a home or office. * * * [The Court quotes from *Carroll* and cites its other early cases.]

* * *

Neither *Carroll,* supra, nor other cases in this Court require or suggest that in every conceivable circumstance the search of an auto even with probable cause may be made without the extra protection for privacy that a warrant affords. But the circumstances that furnish probable cause to search a particular auto for particular articles are most often unforeseeable; moreover, the opportunity to search is fleeting since a car is readily movable. Where this is true, as in *Carroll* and the case before us now, if an effective search is to be made at any time, either the search must be made immediately without a warrant or the car itself must be seized and held without a warrant for whatever period is necessary to obtain a warrant for the search.[a]

* * * *Carroll,* supra, holds a search warrant unnecessary where there is probable cause to search an automobile stopped on the highway; the car is movable, the occupants are alerted, and the car's contents may never be found again if a warrant must be obtained. Hence an immediate search is constitutionally permissible.

Arguably, because of the preference for a magistrate's judgment only the immobilization of the car should be permitted until a search warrant is obtained; arguably, only the "lesser" intrusion is permissible until the magistrate authorizes the "greater." But which is the "greater" and which the "lesser" intrusion is itself a debatable question and the answer may depend on a variety of circumstances. For constitutional purposes, we see no difference between on the one hand seizing and holding a car before presenting the probable cause issue to a magistrate and on the other hand carrying out an immediate search without a warrant. Given probable cause to search, either course is reasonable under the Fourth Amendment.

On the facts before us, the blue station wagon could have been searched on the spot when it was stopped since there was probable cause to search and it was a fleeting target for a search. The probable-cause factor still obtained at the station house and so did the mobility of the car unless the Fourth Amendment permits a warrantless seizure of the car and the denial of its use to anyone until a warrant is secured. In that event there is little to choose in terms of practical consequences between an immediate search without a warrant and the car's immobilization until a warrant is obtained.[b] The same consequences may not follow where there is unforeseeable cause to search a house. Compare Vale v. Louisiana [discussed in the section on exigent circumstances]. But as *Carroll,* supra, held, for the purposes of the Fourth Amendment there is a constitutional difference between houses and cars.

* * *

MR. JUSTICE BLACKMUN took no part in the consideration or decision of this case.

MR. JUSTICE HARLAN, concurring in part and dissenting in part.

* * *

The Court concedes that the police could prevent removal of the evidence by temporarily seizing the car for the time necessary to obtain a warrant. It does not dispute that such a course would fully protect the interests of effective law enforcement; rather it states that whether temporary seizure is a "lesser" intrusion than warrantless search "is itself a debatable question and the answer may depend on a vari-

---

a. Following the car until a warrant can be obtained seems an impractical alternative since, among other things, the car may be taken out of the jurisdiction. Tracing the car and searching it hours or days later would of course permit instruments or fruits of crime to be removed from the car before the search.

b. It was not unreasonable in this case to take the car to the station house. All occupants

in the car were arrested in a dark parking lot in the middle of the night. A careful search at that point was impractical and perhaps not safe for the officers, and it would serve the owner's convenience and the safety of his car to have the vehicle and the keys together at the station house.

ety of circumstances.''[c] I believe it clear that a warrantless search involves the greater sacrifice of Fourth Amendment values.

* * * [I]n the circumstances in which this problem is likely to occur, the lesser intrusion will almost always be the simple seizure of the car for the period—perhaps a day—necessary to enable the officers to obtain a search warrant. In the first place, as this case shows, the very facts establishing probable cause to search will often also justify arrest of the occupants of the vehicle. Since the occupants themselves are to be taken into custody, they will suffer minimal further inconvenience from the temporary immobilization of their vehicle. Even where no arrests are made, persons who wish to avoid a search—either to protect their privacy or to conceal incriminating evidence—will almost certainly prefer a brief loss of the use of the vehicle in exchange for the opportunity to have a magistrate pass upon the justification for the search. To be sure, one can conceive of instances in which the occupant, having nothing to hide and lacking concern for the privacy of the automobile, would be more deeply offended by a temporary immobilization of his vehicle than by a prompt search of it. However, such a person always remains free to consent to an immediate search, thus avoiding any delay. Where consent is not forthcoming, the occupants of the car have an interest in privacy that is protected by the Fourth Amendment even where the circumstances justify a temporary seizure. The Court's endorsement of a warrantless invasion of that privacy where another course would suffice is simply inconsistent with our repeated stress on the Fourth Amendment's mandate of " 'adherence to judicial processes.' "[d]

* * *

Questions After Chambers

What implications does *Chambers* have for searches of parked cars, where the police do not make an initial stop? Does it matter where the car is parked, or whether the initial police-vehicle encounter is deliberate or by chance? Not surprisingly, a discussion of these issues had to arise. It did in Coolidge v. New Hampshire, 403 U.S. 443 (1971). In *Coolidge,* the police obtained warrants to arrest the defendant and to search his car. The automobile was seized from his driveway shortly after the defendant's arrest, and was searched two days later at the police station, and twice more in the following months. The warrants were held to be defective, because they had not been issued by a neutral magistrate. Thus, the Court considered whether the search could be justified under any other theories, including the *Carroll* doctrine. A plurality held *Carroll* to be inapplicable here, because of the

c. The Court, unable to decide whether search or temporary seizure is the "lesser" intrusion, in this case authorizes both. The Court concludes that it was reasonable for the police to take the car to the station, where they searched it once to no avail. The searching officers then entered the station, interrogated petitioner and the car's owner, and returned later for another search of the car—this one successful. At all times the car and its contents were secure against removal or destruction. Nevertheless, the Court approves the searches without even an inquiry into the officers' ability promptly to take their case before a magistrate.

d. Circumstances might arise in which it would be impracticable to immobilize the car for the time required to obtain a warrant—for example, where a single police officer must take arrested suspects to the station, and has no way of protecting the suspects' car during his absence. In such situations it might be wholly reasonable to perform an on-the-spot search based on probable cause. However, where nothing in the situation makes impracticable the obtaining of a warrant, I cannot join the Court in shunting aside that vital Fourth Amendment safeguard.

absence of exigency. This is the first and last Supreme Court case where a warrantless automobile search was held to be unconstitutional for that reason. Obviously, it could not be seriously argued that it was impracticable to obtain a warrant when a warrant had in fact been obtained, albeit a defective one. The Court nevertheless considered whether an exigency existed justifying the warrantless seizure of the car because of its potential mobility (and therefore justifying a warrantless search of the car under *Chambers*). Justice Stewart, writing for the plurality, found no exigency since Coolidge had been arrested, his wife had been removed from the premises, and the police had control of the car as it was parked outside Coolidge's house. Justice Stewart declared as follows:

> The word "automobile" is not a talisman in whose presence the Fourth Amendment fades away and disappears. And surely there is nothing in this case to invoke the meaning and purpose of the rule of Carroll v. United States—no alerted criminal bent on flight, no fleeting opportunity on an open highway after a hazardous chase, no contraband or stolen goods or weapons, no confederates waiting to move the evidence, not even the inconvenience of a special police detail to guard the immobilized automobile. In short, by no possible stretch of the legal imagination can this be made into a case where "it is not practicable to secure a warrant," and the "automobile exception," despite its label, is simply irrelevant.

Justice Stewart distinguished *Chambers* on the ground that, in the present case, the *initial* intrusion by the police was unjustified. That is, the officers did not obtain a proper warrant even though they knew precisely where Coolidge's car was parked at all times, and had been investigating him for weeks. This was unlike the situation in *Chambers*, where the officers were on patrol and happened to *come upon* a car that fit the description of one seen at a gas station robbery; there was no way in which the officers in *Chambers* could have been expected to obtain a warrant *before* they even seized the car. And because they could seize it without a warrant, under the rationale of *Chambers*, they could also search it without a warrant.

A few state courts have imposed an "exigency" requirement on warrantless automobile searches.[28] But the Supreme Court has narrowed *Coolidge* to its facts and has abjured fact-specific analysis.

In one post-*Coolidge* case, Cardwell v. Lewis, 417 U.S. 583 (1974), a plurality of the Court explicitly rejected the contention that mobility of the car before it is seized makes a difference: "The fact that the car in *Chambers* was seized after being stopped on a highway, whereas Lewis' car was seized from a public parking lot, has little, if any, legal significance." Similarly, in Texas v. White, 423 U.S. 67 (1975), the Court upheld the warrantless search of an automobile that had been towed to the police department's impound lot. The Court rejected the argument of the dissenters that the police should have been required to provide a justification for removing the car to the stationhouse rather than searching it on the scene. See also Michigan v. Thomas, 458 U.S. 259 (1982)(holding "that the justification to conduct such a warrantless search does not vanish once the car has been immobilized"). An impatient Supreme Court summarily reversed a Florida intermediate appellate court in Florida v. Meyers, 466 U.S. 380 (1984)(per curiam), and, as in Michigan v. Thomas, reiterated the *Chambers* holding that a warrantless search of an auto may

---

28. See Clark v. State, 574 P.2d 1261 (Alaska 1978)(factual circumstances must be considered rather than abstract potentiality for mobility or destruction; search of car parked in public place was reasonable when known ac-complice was at large); State v. Parker, 355 So.2d 900 (La.1978) (no exigent circumstances existed when van was parked and unattended and guard could have been posted until a warrant was obtained).

be conducted after the auto has been immobilized, as long as there is probable cause to believe that the auto contains evidence of criminal activity.

In light of *White* and *Thomas,* lower courts have interpreted *Coolidge* to mean that a warrant is required only if the officers had a clear opportunity to obtain a warrant before *seizing* the car. Under this view, *Chambers* is based on the rationale that due to its mobility, a car can be seized pending the obtaining of a warrant; and a search without a warrant is permitted because the search of a car is no more intrusive than would be the seizure of the car pending a warrant. But if the original seizure itself could have been preceded by a warrant, then the premise of *Chambers* is missing and the car exception ought not to apply. This explanation is consistent with the facts of *Chambers,* where the officers clearly could not have obtained a warrant before seizing the car, and with the facts of *Coolidge,* where the officers could have obtained a warrant (in fact they did so, but it was invalid because issued by a law enforcement officer) before seizing the car. See, e.g., United States v. Moscatiello, 771 F.2d 589 (1st Cir.1985) (*Coolidge* distinguished where officers seized car after pursuing it in a rapidly developing situation); United States v. Reed, 26 F.3d 523 (5th Cir.1994)(warrantless search of car permitted; *Coolidge* distinguished because the officers "did not know where the car was, nor that it contained the money, until they completed their tracking upon arrival at the house").

The Diminished Expectation of Privacy Rationale: California v. Carney

It is apparent that exigency is not a sufficient basis for the automobile exception after cases like *Chambers, White* and *Thomas.* Exigency derives from mobility; but the Court has explicitly held that the car exception permits a warrantless search even if the vehicle is immobile. In California v. Carney, 471 U.S. 386 (1985), the Court re-evaluated the automobile exception to the warrant requirement and concluded that "the reasons for the vehicle exception are twofold." Chief Justice Burger, writing for the Court, explained as follows:

> The capacity to be quickly moved was clearly the basis of the holding in *Carroll,* and our cases have consistently recognized ready mobility as one of the principal bases of the automobile exception. * * *

> However, although ready mobility alone was perhaps the original justification for the vehicle exception, our later cases have made clear that ready mobility is not the only basis for the exception. * * * Besides the element of mobility, less rigorous warrant requirements govern because the expectation of privacy with respect to one's automobile is significantly less than that relating to one's home or office.

> Even in cases where an automobile was not immediately mobile, the lesser expectation of privacy resulting from its use as a readily mobile vehicle justified application of the vehicular exception.

See also United States v. Matthews, 32 F.3d 294 (7th Cir.1994)("[T]he mobility of the vehicle is not essential to the application of the automobile exception" because "the diminished expectation of privacy alone is sufficient to conduct a search on probable cause.").

Why do citizens have a diminished expectation of privacy with respect to their automobiles? The Chief Justice in *Carney* explained that these reduced expectations "derive not from the fact that the area to be searched is in plain view, but from the pervasive regulation of vehicles capable of traveling on the public highways." He stressed that automobiles are "subjected to pervasive and continuing governmental regulation and controls." Has the Court correctly assessed societal expectations with regard to automobiles?

In Pennsylvania v. Labron, 518 U.S. 938 (1996), the Court, in a per curiam decision, reaffirmed the principle that exigent circumstances are not required to justify the warrantless search of an automobile. Relying explicitly on the diminished expectation of privacy rationale articulated in *Carney,* the Court declared that if a car "is readily mobile and probable cause exists to believe it contains contraband, the Fourth Amendment thus permits police to search the vehicle without more." The Court upheld warrantless searches of two cars where the police had probable cause to believe that each contained drugs. It did not matter that there was no risk of destruction of evidence at the time the searches were conducted. Thereafter, in Maryland v. Dyson, 527 U.S. 465 (1999) (per curiam), the Court once again reaffirmed the *Carroll* doctrine, relying on *Labron* to overturn a state court's suppression of evidence. Officers had probable cause to believe that Dyson's car contained drugs, and they conducted a warrantless search. The Maryland court suppressed the evidence because there was no indication of any exigency that would have precluded the police from obtaining a warrant before the search. The Court stated categorically that "the automobile exception has no separate exigency requirement" and that the probable cause finding "alone satisfies the automobile exception to the Fourth Amendment's warrant requirement." Justices Breyer and Stevens dissented on procedural grounds, but they agreed with the Court's statement concerning the scope of the automobile exception.

Motor Homes

The Court in *Carney* considered whether the dual justification for the automobile exception (mobility and diminished expectation of privacy) applied to the warrantless search of a motor home. A six-person majority held that police officers validly searched a "Dodge Mini Motor Home" with probable cause but no warrant when the motor home was parked in a lot in a downtown area. Officers had received uncorroborated information that the motor home was used by a person who exchanged marijuana for sex. They watched a youth enter the motor home and remain there for more than an hour. When he left, the officers stopped him and learned that he had received marijuana in exchange for sexual contacts. The officers knocked on the door and the suspect stepped out. They identified themselves as officers and entered the motor home where they saw marijuana and related paraphernalia.

Chief Justice Burger rejected the argument that the motor home was different from other vehicles because it was capable of functioning as a home as well as a vehicle, reasoning that "[t]o distinguish between respondent's motor home and an ordinary sedan for purposes of the vehicle exception would require that we apply the exception depending upon the size of the vehicle and the quality of its appointments" and "to fail to apply the exception to vehicles such as a motor home ignores the fact that a motor home lends itself easily to use as an instrument of illicit drug traffic and other illegal activity." Thus, the Court declined "to distinguish between 'worthy' and 'unworthy' vehicles which are either on the public roads and highways, or situated such that it is reasonable to conclude that the vehicle is not being used as a residence." In a footnote, the Court noted that it did not "pass on the application of the vehicle to a motor home that is situated in a way or place that objectively indicates that it is being used as a residence." It suggested, however, some factors that might be relevant in determining whether a warrant should be required: "its location, whether the vehicle is licensed, whether it is connected to utilities, and whether it has convenient access to a public road."

Justice Stevens, joined by Justices Brennan and Marshall, dissented. He argued that the Court "accorded priority to an exception rather than to the general rule." He concluded that because motor homes were a combination of homes and autos, the general preference for a warrant should govern a close case.

Questions after Carney

Suppose that a motor home is parked in the garage of a private home, and that officers learn that marijuana has been traded for sexual contact inside the motor home while it was in the garage. Does the warrant clause apply since officers have to enter the garage to search the motor home? Would it make a difference if the motor home were parked in the driveway outside the garage rather than inside it? What if the motor home is parked in front of the house on the street? What if officers learn that a suspect has marijuana in his house and a motor home parked in front of the house. May they enter the house without a warrant on the theory that the suspect has a vehicle that could be used to move the marijuana?

The automobile exception extends to airplanes, according to United States v. Nigro, 727 F.2d 100 (6th Cir.1984)(en banc). Three dissenters argued that once officers had immobilized a plane, they should have obtained a warrant before searching it. But the majority cited the Supreme Court's auto search cases and concluded that mobility of the vehicle is not a prerequisite to the exception. Do you believe the automobile cases should apply to commercial carriers? May police search a cruise liner without a warrant?

Carroll and Forfeiture of Automobiles

In Florida v. White, 526 U.S. 559 (1999), the Court considered whether the *Carroll* doctrine permits the warrantless *seizure* of a car when the officer has probable cause to believe that the car is subject to forfeiture. Officers observed White using his car to deliver cocaine. Two months later, he was arrested at his workplace on unrelated charges. At that time, the arresting officers seized his car without securing a warrant because they believed that it was subject to forfeiture under the Florida Contraband Forfeiture Act (Act). The Florida Act authorizes the seizure of "contraband", which includes any "vehicle of any kind, * * * which was used * * * as an instrumentality in the commission of, or in aiding or abetting in the commission of, any felony." During a subsequent inventory search, the police discovered cocaine in the car. White was then charged with a state drug violation. At his trial on the drug charge, he moved to suppress the evidence discovered during the search, arguing that the car's warrantless seizure violated the Fourth Amendment, thereby making the cocaine the "fruit of the poisonous tree."

The Court, in an opinion by Justice Thomas for seven Justices, held that the officers were not required to obtain a warrant to seize the car pursuant to the state forfeiture law. Justice Thomas discussed the relevance of the *Carroll* doctrine in the following passage:

> The principles underlying the rule in *Carroll* and the founding-era statutes upon which they are based fully support the conclusion that the warrantless seizure of respondent's car did not violate the Fourth Amendment. Although * * * the police lacked probable cause to believe that respondent's car contained contraband they certainly had probable cause to believe that the vehicle itself was contraband under Florida law. Recognition of the need to seize readily movable contraband before it is spirited away undoubtedly underlies the early federal laws relied upon in *Carroll*. This need is equally weighty when the automobile, as opposed to its contents, is the contraband that the police seek to secure.

Justice Thomas also noted that the vehicle was seized in a public place, and therefore did not implicate any privacy interest.

Justice Stevens, joined by Justice Ginsburg, dissented in *White*. He saw no reason for dispensing with the preference for a warrant, and noted that

> the particularly troubling aspect of this case is not that the State provides a weak excuse for failing to obtain a warrant either before or after White's arrest, but that it offers us no reason at all. * * * On this record, one must assume that the officers who seized White's car simply preferred to avoid the hassle of seeking approval from a judicial officer. I would not permit bare convenience to overcome our established preference for the warrant process as a check against arbitrary intrusions by law enforcement agencies "engaged in the often competitive"—and, here, potentially lucrative—"enterprise of ferreting out crime."

4. *Movable Property—In and Out of Cars*

If the automobile exception were based totally on exigency due to mobility of the car, then it should also permit warrantless searches of other mobile containers such as briefcases, suitcases, and footlockers. However, as seen in *Carney*, the exception is also (and probably primarily) based on the reduced expectation of privacy accorded an automobile. Is there any way to distinguish mobile containers from automobiles on privacy grounds? The Supreme Court did just that in United States v. Chadwick, 433 U.S. 1 (1977), where it held that the mobility of a footlocker justified its *seizure* upon probable cause, but that a warrant was required to *search* the footlocker, unless emergency circumstances rendered a seizure insufficient to protect the state interest (e.g., if the footlocker was ticking). Chief Justice Burger, writing for the Court, distinguished mobile containers from cars on the following grounds:

> The factors which diminish the privacy aspects of an automobile do not apply to respondents' footlocker. Luggage contents are not open to public view, except as a condition to a border entry or common carrier travel; nor is luggage subject to regular inspections and official scrutiny on a continuing basis. Unlike an automobile, whose primary function is transportation, luggage is intended as a repository of personal effects. In sum, a person's expectations of privacy in personal luggage are substantially greater than in an automobile.

Because of the higher expectation of privacy in the footlocker, it could not be said, as it could in *Chambers,* that an immediate search would be no more intrusive than a seizure pending a warrant. As the Chief Justice explained in a footnote:

> A search of the interior [of the footlocker] was therefore a far greater intrusion into Fourth Amendment values than the impoundment of the footlocker. Though surely a substantial infringement of respondents' use and possession, the seizure did not diminish respondents' legitimate expectation that the footlocker's contents would remain private.

It was the greatly reduced expectation of privacy in the automobile, coupled with the transportation function of the vehicle, that made the Court in *Chambers* unwilling to decide whether an immediate search of an automobile, or its seizure and indefinite mobilization, constituted a greater interference with the rights of the owner. This is clearly not the case with locked luggage.

Questions after Chadwick

The crux of the majority's argument in *Chadwick* lies in the contention that one has a lesser expectation of privacy in one's car than in movable chattel such as luggage. Is this argument convincing? Is the lesser expectation of privacy surrounding autos simply the result of the Supreme Court having said so?

Does the fact that vehicles are used essentially for transportation demand, or even allow, the conclusion that they are seldom used as repositories for personal effects? Would that assertion hold true in the case of a traveling salesman who lives out of his car for several days each week? Do the particular facts of any case make a difference in light of the Court's categorical "diminished expectation" analysis?

The Fourth Amendment extends beyond homes to all effects, including cars and suitcases. If the least intrusive alternative to searches must be taken when a suitcase or a house is involved, why not when a car is involved? Is the difference between the intrusiveness of a search, and that of a seizure, negligible if the object searched is a car, but of constitutional dimensions when a footlocker is concerned?

Mobile Containers in the Car

With a warrant required for the search of a mobile container, but not required for the search of an automobile, it was only a matter of time before the Court was presented with cases in which the two rules would collide. Which rule applies when an officer finds a mobile container while searching a car without a warrant? In Arkansas v. Sanders, 442 U.S. 753 (1979), the Court held that a warrant was required to search a suitcase that had been placed in the trunk of a taxi. In *Sanders,* officers had probable cause to search the passenger's suitcase, but no probable cause to search anywhere else in the taxi. Thereafter, in United States v. Ross, 456 U.S. 798 (1982), the Court upheld the warrantless search of a paper bag and pouch found during the search of a car. Justice Stevens, writing for a six-person majority, noted that "in neither *Chadwick* nor *Sanders* did the police have probable cause to search the vehicle or anything within it except the footlocker in the former case and the green suitcase in the latter." In contrast, in *Ross* the officers had probable cause to search the entire car for drugs. Justice Stevens noted that the *Carroll* doctrine would largely be nullified if it did not extend to containers such as those in *Ross,* because "contraband goods rarely are strewn across the trunk or floor of a car."

Justice Marshall, joined by Justice Brennan in dissent in *Ross,* emphasized the anomalous results that could occur due to the fine lines drawn between *Ross* and *Sanders.* For example, if officers are informed that a person has drugs in a bag in the trunk, it would appear that probable cause is localized in the bag, and hence *Sanders* would apply. But if they are more generally informed that there are drugs in the trunk, *Ross* would apply. Yet it is notable that the *Ross* dissenters did not challenge the primacy of the *Carroll* doctrine, and accepted the majority's premise that there is a diminished expectation of privacy in an automobile. *Sanders, Ross,* and *Chadwick* are extensively discussed in the next case, in which the Court again tries to resolve the question of whether a warrant is required to search a container placed in a car.

CALIFORNIA v. ACEVEDO

Supreme Court of the United States, 1991.
500 U.S. 565.

JUSTICE BLACKMUN **delivered the opinion of the Court.**

This case requires us once again to consider the so-called "automobile exception" to the warrant requirement of the Fourth Amendment and its application to the search of a closed container in the trunk of a car.

I

On October 28, 1987, Officer Coleman of the Santa Ana, Cal., Police Department received a telephone call from a federal drug enforcement agent in Hawaii. The agent informed Coleman that he had seized a package containing marijuana which was to have been delivered to the Federal Express office in Santa Ana and which was addressed to J.R. Daza at 805 West Stevens Avenue in that city. The agent arranged to send the package to Coleman instead. Coleman then was to take the package to the Federal Express office and arrest the person who arrived to claim it.

* * * At about 10:30 a.m. on October 30, a man, who identified himself as Jamie Daza, arrived to claim the package. He accepted it and drove to his apartment on West Stevens. He carried the package into the apartment.

* * *

At 12:30 p.m., respondent Charles Steven Acevedo arrived. He entered Daza's apartment, stayed for about 10 minutes, and reappeared carrying a brown paper bag that looked full. The officers noticed that the bag was the size of one of the wrapped marijuana packages sent from Hawaii. Acevedo walked to a silver Honda in the parking lot. He placed the bag in the trunk of the car and started to drive away. Fearing the loss of evidence, officers in a marked police car stopped him. They opened the trunk and the bag, and found marijuana.

* * *

The California Court * * * concluded that the marijuana found in the paper bag in the car's trunk should have been suppressed. The court concluded that the officers had probable cause to believe that the paper bag contained drugs but lacked probable cause to suspect that Acevedo's car, itself, otherwise contained contraband. Because the officers' probable cause was directed specifically at the bag, the court held that the case was controlled by United States v. Chadwick rather than by United States v. Ross. Although the court agreed that the officers could seize the paper bag, it held that, under *Chadwick,* they could not open the bag without first obtaining a warrant for that purpose. The court then recognized "the anomalous nature" of the dichotomy between the rule in *Chadwick* and the rule in *Ross.* That dichotomy dictates that if there is probable cause to search a car, then the entire car—including any closed container found therein—may be searched without a warrant, but if there is probable cause only as to a container in the car, the container may be held but not searched until a warrant is obtained.

* * *

II

* * *

In United States v. Ross, we held that a warrantless search of an automobile under the *Carroll* doctrine could include a search of a container or package found inside the car when such a search was supported by probable cause. * * * Thus, "[i]f probable cause justifies the search of a lawfully stopped vehicle, it justifies the search of every part of the vehicle and its contents that may conceal the object of the search." In *Ross,* therefore, we clarified the scope of the *Carroll* doctrine as properly including a "probing search" of compartments and containers within the automobile so long as the search is supported by probable cause.

In addition to this clarification, *Ross* distinguished the *Carroll* doctrine from the separate rule that governed the search of closed containers. The Court had announced this separate rule, unique to luggage and other closed packages, bags, and containers, in United States v. Chadwick. In *Chadwick,* federal narcotics agents had probable cause to believe that a 200–pound double-locked footlocker contained marijuana. The agents tracked

the locker as the defendants removed it from a train and carried it through the station to a waiting car. As soon as the defendants lifted the locker into the trunk of the car, the agents arrested them, seized the locker, and searched it. In this Court, the United States did not contend that the locker's brief contact with the automobile's trunk sufficed to make the *Carroll* doctrine applicable. Rather, the United States urged that the search of movable luggage could be considered analogous to the search of an automobile.

The Court rejected this argument because, it reasoned, a person expects more privacy in his luggage and personal effects than he does in his automobile. * * *

In Arkansas v. Sanders, the Court extended *Chadwick's* rule to apply to a suitcase actually being transported in the trunk of a car. In *Sanders,* the police had probable cause to believe a suitcase contained marijuana. They watched as the defendant placed the suitcase in the trunk of a taxi and was driven away. The police pursued the taxi for several blocks, stopped it, found the suitcase in the trunk, and searched it. Although the Court had applied the *Carroll* doctrine to searches of integral parts of the automobile itself, (indeed, in *Carroll,* contraband whiskey was in the upholstery of the seats) it did not extend the doctrine to the warrantless search of personal luggage "merely because it was located in an automobile lawfully stopped by the police." * * *

In *Ross,* the Court endeavored to distinguish between *Carroll,* which governed the *Ross* automobile search, and *Chadwick,* which governed the *Sanders* automobile search. It held that the *Carroll* doctrine covered searches of automobiles when the police had probable cause to search an entire vehicle but that the *Chadwick* doctrine governed searches of luggage when the officers had probable cause to search only a container within the vehicle. Thus, in a *Ross* situation, the police could conduct a reasonable search under the Fourth Amendment without obtaining a warrant, whereas in a *Sanders* situation, the police had to obtain a warrant before they searched.

* * * *Ross* held that closed containers encountered by the police during a warrantless search of a car pursuant to the automobile exception could also be searched. Thus, this Court in *Ross* took the critical step of saying that closed containers in cars could be searched without a warrant because of their presence within the automobile. Despite the protection that *Sanders* purported to extend to closed containers, the privacy interest in those closed containers yielded to the broad scope of an automobile search.

III

* * *

This Court in *Ross* rejected *Chadwick's* distinction between containers and cars. It concluded that the expectation of privacy in one's vehicle is equal to one's expectation of privacy in the container, and noted that "the privacy interests in a car's trunk or glove compartment may be no less than those in a movable container." * * * It concluded that the time and expense of the warrant process would be misdirected if the police could search every cubic inch of an automobile until they discovered a paper sack, at which point the Fourth Amendment required them to take the sack to a magistrate for permission to look inside. We now must decide the question deferred in *Ross:* whether the Fourth Amendment requires the police to obtain a warrant to open the sack in

a movable vehicle simply because they lack probable cause to search the entire car. We conclude that it does not.

IV

Dissenters in *Ross* asked why the suitcase in *Sanders* was "more private, less difficult for police to seize and store, or in any other relevant respect more properly subject to the warrant requirement, than a container that police discover in a probable-cause search of an entire automobile?" We now agree that a container found after a general search of the automobile and a container found in a car after a limited search for the container are equally easy for the police to store and for the suspect to hide or destroy. In fact, we see no principled distinction in terms of either the privacy expectation or the exigent circumstances between the paper bag found by the police in *Ross* and the paper bag found by the police here. Furthermore, by attempting to distinguish between a container for which the police are specifically searching and a container which they come across in a car, we have provided only minimal protection for privacy and have impeded effective law enforcement.

The line between probable cause to search a vehicle and probable cause to search a package in that vehicle is not always clear, and separate rules that govern the two objects to be searched may enable the police to broaden their power to make warrantless searches and disserve privacy interests. * * * At the moment when officers stop an automobile, it may be less than clear whether they suspect with a high degree of certainty that the vehicle contains drugs in a bag or simply contains drugs. If the police know that they may open a bag only if they are actually searching the entire car, they may search more extensively than they otherwise would in order to establish the general probable cause required by *Ross.*

* * * We cannot see the benefit of a rule that requires law enforcement officers to conduct a more intrusive search in order to justify a less intrusive one.

To the extent that the *Chadwick–Sanders* rule protects privacy, its protection is minimal. Law enforcement officers may seize a container and hold it until they obtain a search warrant. *Chadwick.* Since the police, by hypothesis, have probable cause to seize the property, we can assume that a warrant will be routinely forthcoming in the overwhelming majority of cases. And the police often will be able to search containers without a warrant, despite the *Chadwick–Sanders* rule, as a search incident to a lawful arrest. New York v. Belton.

* * *

Finally, the search of a paper bag intrudes far less on individual privacy than does the incursion sanctioned long ago in *Carroll.* In that case, prohibition agents slashed the upholstery of the automobile. This Court nonetheless found their search to be reasonable under the Fourth Amendment. If destroying the interior of an automobile is not unreasonable, we cannot conclude that looking inside a closed container is. In light of the minimal protection to privacy afforded by the *Chadwick–Sanders* rule, and our serious doubt whether that rule substantially serves privacy interests, we now hold that the Fourth Amendment does not compel separate treatment for an automobile search that extends only to a container within the vehicle.

V

The *Chadwick–Sanders* rule not only has failed to protect privacy but it has also confused courts and police

officers and impeded effective law enforcement. * * *

The discrepancy between the two rules has led to confusion for law enforcement officers. For example, when an officer, who has developed probable cause to believe that a vehicle contains drugs, begins to search the vehicle and immediately discovers a closed container, which rule applies? The defendant will argue that the fact that the officer first chose to search the container indicates that his probable cause extended only to the container and that *Chadwick* and *Sanders* therefore require a warrant. On the other hand, the fact that the officer first chose to search in the most obvious location should not restrict the propriety of the search. The *Chadwick* rule, as applied in *Sanders,* has devolved into an anomaly such that the more likely the police are to discover drugs in a container, the less authority they have to search it. We have noted the virtue of providing "clear and unequivocal guidelines to the law enforcement profession." The *Chadwick–Sanders* rule is the antithesis of a "clear and unequivocal guideline."

* * *

Although we have recognized firmly that the doctrine of stare decisis serves profoundly important purposes in our legal system, this Court has overruled a prior case on the comparatively rare occasion when it has bred confusion or been a derelict or led to anomalous results. * * * [T]he existence of the dual regimes for automobile searches that uncover containers has proved as confusing as the *Chadwick* and *Sanders* dissenters predicted. We conclude that it is better to adopt one clear-cut rule to govern automobile searches and eliminate the warrant requirement for closed containers set forth in *Sanders.*

VI

* * *

Until today, this Court has drawn a curious line between the search of an automobile that coincidentally turns up a container and the search of a container that coincidentally turns up in an automobile. The protections of the Fourth Amendment must not turn on such coincidences. We therefore interpret *Carroll* as providing one rule to govern all automobile searches. The police may search an automobile and the containers within it where they have probable cause to believe contraband or evidence is contained.

* * *

JUSTICE SCALIA, **concurring in the judgment.**

I agree with the dissent that it is anomalous for a briefcase to be protected by the "general requirement" of a prior warrant when it is being carried along the street, but for that same briefcase to become unprotected as soon as it is carried into an automobile. On the other hand, I agree with the Court that it would be anomalous for a locked compartment in an automobile to be unprotected by the "general requirement" of a prior warrant, but for an unlocked briefcase within the automobile to be protected. I join in the judgment of the Court because I think its holding is more faithful to the text and tradition of the Fourth Amendment, and if these anomalies in our jurisprudence are ever to be eliminated that is the direction in which we should travel.

* * *

Although the Fourth Amendment does not explicitly impose the requirement of a warrant, it is of course textually possible to consider that implicit within the requirement of reasonableness. For some years after the (still continuing) explosion in Fourth Amendment litigation that followed our announcement of the exclusionary rule in Weeks v United States, our jurisprudence lurched back and forth between imposing a categorical warrant requirement and looking to reasonableness alone. (The opinions preferring a warrant involved searches of structures.) See generally Chimel v. California. By the late 1960's, the preference for a warrant had won out, at least rhetorically. See *Chimel;* Coolidge v. New Hampshire.

The victory was illusory. Even before today's decision, the "warrant requirement" had become so riddled with exceptions that it was basically unrecognizable. In 1985, one commentator cataloged nearly 20 such exceptions, including "searches incident to arrest ... automobile searches ... border searches ... administrative searches of regulated businesses ... exigent circumstances ... search[es] incident to nonarrest when there is probable cause to arrest ... boat boarding for document checks ... welfare searches ... inventory searches ... airport searches ... school search[es]...." Bradley, Two Models of the Fourth Amendment, 83 Mich.L.Rev. 1468, 1473–1474 (1985)(footnotes omitted). * * * Our intricate body of law regarding "reasonable expectation of privacy" has been developed largely as a means of creating these exceptions, enabling a search to be denominated not a Fourth Amendment "search" and therefore not subject to the general warrant requirement.

Unlike the dissent, therefore, I do not regard today's holding as some momentous departure, but rather as merely the continuation of an inconsistent jurisprudence that has been with us for years. Cases like United States v. Chadwick and Arkansas v. Sanders have taken the "preference for a warrant" seriously, while cases like United States v. Ross and Carroll v. United States have not. There can be no clarity in this area unless we make up our minds, and unless the principles we express comport with the actions we take.

In my view, the path out of this confusion should be sought by returning to the first principle that the "reasonableness" requirement of the Fourth Amendment affords the protection that the common law afforded. I have no difficulty with the proposition that that includes the requirement of a warrant, where the common law required a warrant; and it may even be that changes in the surrounding legal rules * * * may make a warrant indispensable to reasonableness where it once was not. But the supposed "general rule" that a warrant is always required does not appear to have any basis in the common law and confuses rather than facilitates any attempt to develop rules of reasonableness in light of changed legal circumstances, as the anomaly eliminated and the anomaly created by today's holding both demonstrate.

And there are more anomalies still. Under our precedents (as at common law), a person may be arrested outside the home on the basis of probable cause, without an arrest warrant. United States v. Watson. Upon arrest, the person, as well as the area within his grasp, may be searched for evidence related to the crime. Chimel v. California. Under these principles, if a known drug dealer is carrying a briefcase reasonably believed to contain marijuana (the unauthorized possession of which is a crime), the police may arrest him and search his person on the basis of probable cause alone. And, under our precedents, upon arrival at the station house, the police may inventory his possessions, including the briefcase, even if there is no reason to suspect that they contain contraband. Illinois

v. Lafayette [discussed in the section on inventory searches in this Chapter]. According to our current law, however, the police may not, on the basis of the same probable cause, take the less intrusive step of stopping the individual on the street and demanding to see the contents of his briefcase. That makes no sense a priori, and in the absence of any common law tradition supporting such a distinction, I see no reason to continue it.

* * *

JUSTICE WHITE, **dissenting.**

Agreeing as I do with most of Justice Stevens' opinion and with the result he reaches, I dissent and would affirm the judgment below.

JUSTICE STEVENS, **with whom** JUSTICE MARSHALL **joins, dissenting.**

* * *

To the extent there was any "anomaly" in our prior jurisprudence, the Court has "cured" it at the expense of creating a more serious paradox. For, surely it is anomalous to prohibit a search of a briefcase while the owner is carrying it exposed on a public street yet to permit a search once the owner has placed the briefcase in the locked trunk of his car. One's privacy interest in one's luggage can certainly not be diminished by one's removing it from a public thoroughfare and placing it—out of sight—in a privately owned vehicle. Nor is the danger that evidence will escape increased if the luggage is in a car rather than on the street. In either location, if the police have probable cause, they are authorized to seize the luggage and to detain it until they obtain judicial approval for a search. Any line demarking an exception to the warrant requirement will appear blurred at the edges, but the Court has certainly erred if it believes that, by erasing one line and drawing another, it has drawn a clearer boundary.

* * *

To support its argument that today's holding works only a minimal intrusion on privacy, the Court suggests that "[i]f the police know that they may open a bag only if they are actually searching the entire car, they may search more extensively than they otherwise would in order to establish the general probable cause required by *Ross*." * * * [T]his fear is unexplained and inexplicable. Neither evidence uncovered in the course of a search nor the scope of the search conducted can be used to provide post hoc justification for a search unsupported by probable cause at its inception.

The Court also justifies its claim that its holding inflicts only minor damage by suggesting that, under New York v. Belton, the police could have arrested respondent and searched his bag if respondent had placed the bag in the passenger compartment of the automobile instead of the trunk. * * * Even accepting *Belton*'s application to a case like this one, however, the Court's logic extends its holding to a container placed in the *trunk* of a vehicle, rather than in the passenger compartment. And the Court makes this extension without any justification whatsoever other than convenience to law enforcement.

* * *

* * * No impartial observer could criticize this Court for hindering the progress of the war on drugs. On the contrary, decisions like the one the Court makes today will support the conclusion that this Court has become a loyal foot soldier in the Executive's fight against crime.

* * *

Probable Cause Issues After Acevedo

Professor Green has pointed out that the rule in *Acevedo* does not eliminate all the uncertainty of the previous law. The difficult question of whether probable cause exists to search a certain part of the car still exists. See Green, "Power, Not Reason": Justice Marshall's Valedictory and the Fourth Amendment in the Supreme Court's 1990–91 Term, 70 No.Car.L.Rev. 373 (1992). Not surprisingly, the lower courts have reached divergent results on the probable cause/location question after *Acevedo*. Compare United States v. McSween, 53 F.3d 684 (5th Cir.1995)(when officer smelled burnt marijuana, he had probable cause to search under the hood of the defendant's car, even though a search of the passenger compartment had turned up nothing), with United States v. Nielsen, 9 F.3d 1487 (10th Cir.1993)(when officer smelled burnt marijuana and a search of the passenger compartment turned up nothing, his search of the trunk was illegal: "We do not believe under the circumstances that there was a fair probability that the *trunk* contained marijuana, or that a disinterested magistrate would so hold if asked to issue a search warrant.").

Delayed Search of Containers

In United States v. Johns, 469 U.S. 478 (1985), the Court considered whether there are any temporal limitations on the power to search containers in cars without a warrant. Customs agents removed packages from a trunk, placed them in a Drug Enforcement Agency warehouse, and searched the packages three days thereafter. The officers had probable cause, but no warrant. Writing for the Court, Justice O'Connor reasoned that *Ross* would have authorized a warrantless search of the packages when they were removed from the trunk, that previous cases—e.g., Chambers v. Maroney, Texas v. White—authorized a delayed search of the trunk, and that "searches of containers discovered in the course of a vehicle search are [not] subject to temporal restrictions not applicable to the vehicle search itself." The Court indicated that it did not intend to authorize indefinite retention of vehicles or "to foreclose the possibility that the owner of a vehicle or its contents might attempt to prove that delay in the completion of a vehicle search was unreasonable because it adversely affected a privacy or possessory interest." The Court also rejected the defendant's argument that the automobile exception was inapplicable because the agents had taken the packages from the trunk before searching them. Justice O'Connor saw no reason to require officers to keep a container in a car while the search of that container is conducted. Justice Brennan, joined by Justice Marshall, dissented and argued that no exigency precluded reasonable efforts to obtain a warrant.

Search of Passenger's Property: Wyoming v. Houghton

In *Ross* and *Acevedo*, the Court upheld warrantless searches of containers that were clearly owned by the driver of the car. Should the situation change if the officer conducts a warrantless search of a passenger's property? The Supreme Court considered this question in Wyoming v. Houghton, 526 U.S. 295, (1999). Justice Scalia, writing for the Court, set forth the facts:

> In the early morning hours of July 23, 1995, a Wyoming Highway Patrol officer stopped an automobile for speeding and driving with a faulty brake light. There were three passengers in the front seat of the car: David Young (the driver), his girlfriend, and respondent. While questioning Young, the officer noticed a hypodermic syringe in Young's shirt pocket. He left the occupants under the supervision of two backup officers as he went to get gloves from his patrol car. Upon his return, he instructed Young to step out of the car and place the syringe on the hood. The officer then asked Young why he had a syringe; with refreshing candor, Young replied that he used it to take drugs.

> At this point, the backup officers ordered the two female passengers out of the car and asked them for identification. Respondent falsely identified herself as "Sandra James" and stated that she did not have any identification. Meanwhile, in light of Young's admission, the officer searched the passenger compartment of the car for contraband. On the back seat, he found a purse, which respondent claimed as hers. He removed from the purse a wallet containing respondent's driver's license, identifying her properly as Sandra K. Houghton. When the officer asked her why she had lied about her name, she replied: "In case things went bad."

> Continuing his search of the purse, the officer found a brown pouch and a black wallet-type container. Respondent denied that the former was hers, and claimed ignorance of how it came to be there; it was found to contain drug paraphernalia and a syringe with 60 ccs of methamphetamine. Respondent admitted ownership of the black container, which was also found to contain drug paraphernalia, and a syringe (which respondent acknowledged was hers) with 10 ccs of methamphetamine—an amount insufficient to

support the felony conviction at issue in this case. The officer also found fresh needle-track marks on respondent's arms. He placed her under arrest.

The Wyoming Supreme Court found that the search of Houghton's purse violated the Fourth Amendment, because the officer "knew or should have known that the purse did not belong to the driver, but to one of the passengers," and because "there was no probable cause to search the passengers' personal effects and no reason to believe that contraband had been placed within the purse."

Justice Scalia disagreed with the Wyoming Court's assumption that a passenger's property is subject to greater protection than that of the driver. He relied heavily on *Ross* to conclude that a warrant was not required to search Houghton's purse, because there was probable cause to believe that drugs were in the car in which the purse was located. Under *Ross*, "[i]f probable cause justifies the search of a lawfully stopped vehicle, it justifies the search of every part of the vehicle and its contents that may conceal the object of the search." While there was no passenger in *Ross*, Justice Scalia reasoned that "if the rule of law that *Ross* announced were limited to contents belonging to the driver, or contents other than those belonging to passengers, one would have expected that substantial limitation to be expressed." * * * Justice Scalia also relied on the holding in Zurcher v. Stanford Daily (discussed in the section on warrants, *supra*) for the proposition that "the critical element in a reasonable search is not that the owner of the property is suspected of crime but that there is reasonable cause to believe that the specific things to be searched for and seized are located on the property to which entry is sought." Justice Scalia concluded as follows:

> When there is probable cause to search for contraband in a car, it is reasonable for police officers—like customs officials in the Founding era—to examine packages and containers without a showing of individualized probable cause for each one. A passenger's personal belongings, just like the driver's belongings or containers attached to the car like a glove compartment, are "in" the car, and the officer has probable cause to search for contraband in the car.

> * * * Passengers, no less than drivers, possess a reduced expectation of privacy with regard to the property that they transport in cars, which travel public thoroughfares, seldom serve as the repository of personal effects, are subjected to police stop and examination to enforce pervasive governmental controls as an everyday occurrence, and, finally, are exposed to traffic accidents that may render all their contents open to public scrutiny.

Houghton relied on the case of United States v. Di Re, 332 U.S. 581 (1948), where the Court had held that probable cause to search a car did not justify a body search of a passenger. But Justice Scalia distinguished *DiRe* on the basis of "the unique, significantly heightened protection afforded against searches of one's person." Quoting *Terry*, he observed that the search of one's person "must surely be an annoying, frightening, and perhaps humiliating experience" and concluded that "[s]uch traumatic consequences are not to be expected when the police examine an item of personal property found in a car."

In contrast to a passenger's minimal privacy expectations in property placed in a car, Justice Scalia found the governmental interests at stake to be "substantial." This was because "[e]ffective law enforcement would be appreciably impaired without the ability to search a passenger's personal belongings when there is reason to believe contraband or evidence of criminal wrongdoing is hidden in the car." Justice Scalia explained that a passenger "will often be engaged in a common enterprise with the driver, and have the same interest in concealing the fruits or the evidence of their wrongdoing. A criminal might be able to hide contraband in a passenger's belongings as readily as in other containers in the car—perhaps even surreptitiously, without the passenger's knowledge or permission." Justice Scalia elaborated:

> To be sure, these factors favoring a search will not always be present, but the balancing of interests must be conducted with an eye to the generality of cases. To require that the investigating officer have positive reason to believe that the passenger and driver were engaged in a common enterprise, or positive reason to believe that the driver had time and occasion to conceal the item in the passenger's belongings, surreptitiously or with friendly permission, is to impose requirements so seldom met that a "passenger's property" rule would dramatically reduce the ability to find and seize contraband and evidence of crime. * * * [O]nce a "passenger's property" exception to car searches became widely known, one would expect passenger-confederates to claim everything as their own. And one would anticipate a bog of litigation—in the form of both civil lawsuits and motions to suppress in criminal trials—involving such questions as whether the officer should have believed a passenger's claim of ownership, whether he should have inferred ownership from various objective factors, whether he had probable cause to believe that the passenger was a confederate, or to believe that the driver might have introduced the contraband into the package with or without the passenger's knowledge. When balancing the competing interests, our determinations of "reasonableness" under the Fourth Amendment must take account of these practical realities. We think they militate in favor of the needs of law enforcement, and against a personal-privacy interest that is ordinarily weak.

                                * * *

We hold that police officers with probable cause to search a car may inspect passengers' belongings found in the car that are capable of concealing the object of the search.

Justice Breyer wrote a short concurring opinion in *Houghton,* reasoning that "[i]f the police must establish a container's ownership prior to the search of that container (whenever, for example, a passenger says 'that's mine'), the resulting uncertainty will destroy the workability of the bright-line rule set forth in United States v. Ross. At the same time, police officers with probable cause to search a car for drugs would often have probable cause to search containers regardless. Hence a bright-line rule will authorize only a limited number of searches that the law would not otherwise justify."

Justice Stevens, joined by Justices Souter and Ginsburg, dissented in *Houghton*. He argued that the Court had gone farther than it had in *Ross* because it upheld the search of Houghton's purse *even though the officer did not have probable cause to believe that there was contraband in the purse*:

> * * * Ironically, while we concluded in *Ross* that "[p]robable cause to believe that a container placed in the trunk of a taxi contains contraband or evidence does not justify a search of the entire cab," the rule the Court

fashions would apparently permit a warrantless search of a passenger's briefcase if there is probable cause to believe the taxidriver had a syringe somewhere in his vehicle.

Nor am I persuaded that the mere spatial association between a passenger and a driver provides an acceptable basis for presuming that they are partners in crime or for ignoring privacy interests in a purse. Whether or not the Fourth Amendment required a warrant to search Houghton's purse, at the very least the trooper in this case had to have probable cause to believe that her purse contained contraband. The Wyoming Supreme Court concluded that he did not.

Finally, in my view, the State's legitimate interest in effective law enforcement does not outweigh the privacy concerns at issue. I am as confident in a police officer's ability to apply a rule requiring a warrant or individualized probable cause to search belongings that are—as in this case—obviously owned by and in the custody of a passenger as is the Court in a "passenger-confederate[']s" ability to circumvent the rule. Certainly the ostensible clarity of the Court's rule is attractive. But that virtue is insufficient justification for its adoption. Moreover, a rule requiring a warrant or individualized probable cause to search passenger belongings is every bit as simple as the Court's rule; it simply protects more privacy.

Questions After Houghton

Assume the following facts: the officer properly stops the car driven by Young. Young admits that he is a drug user and that syringes and drugs are in the car. He also says that Houghton, his passenger, is accompanying him to a drug counseling center. Houghton explains that she is a drug counselor fiercely opposed to drug use. Houghton produces identification and a business card that supports her statement. The officer searches under the driver's seat and finds drugs. Can he now search Houghton's purse? The answer appears to be yes under the Court's bright-line rule, because the officer has probable cause to search the car and therefore "may inspect passengers' belongings found in the car that are capable of concealing the object of the search." Does this result make sense under these facts? Are these facts so unlikely that it makes sense to have a bright line rule?

G. EXIGENT CIRCUMSTANCES

1. Exigent Circumstances Generally

It takes time to obtain a warrant. In some cases where police have probable cause to search or arrest, they have to work quickly, because delay could give a suspect the opportunity to escape; or delay could give the suspect, or others, an opportunity to take up and use weapons; or delay could give the suspect or others the opportunity to destroy evidence. The exigent circumstance cases concern fact-specific situations in which the state must show that immediate action was reasonably necessary to prevent flight, or to safeguard the police or public, or to protect against the loss of evidence.

In exigent circumstance cases, courts address situations in which an officer had probable cause to search, but had insufficient time to seek a warrant. The exigent circumstances exception merely excuses the officer from having to obtain a magistrate's determination that probable cause exists; it does not permit a search in the absence of probable cause. Besides needing probable cause to search, the officer must have probable cause to believe that the persons or items to be searched or seized might be gone, or that some other danger would arise, before a warrant could be obtained.

The exigent circumstances exception applies equally to arrests and to searches. Recall that under Payton v. New York, supra, a warrant is required to arrest a person in his home. However, if exigent circumstances are present, a warrant for an in-home arrest is excused. Likewise, officers may search a container, premises, etc. without a warrant if they have probable cause and if exigent circumstances are present. The materials below discuss arrest cases and search cases interchangeably.

The argument for warrantless, exigent circumstance searches is attractive. Because probable cause exists, a magistrate could issue a warrant to make the search; where there is no time to consult the magistrate, the warrant clause should not stand in the way of gathering the same evidence that could be gathered pursuant to a warrant when there is time to obtain one. But, the problems with the argument are almost self-evident by now. It assumes that probable cause exists, whereas the warrant clause cases assume that the zealous officer may overreact to observed facts, and misjudge whether probable cause is present. Moreover, the argument is inattentive to the reasonable concern that the very exigencies that justify immediate action may affect an officer's perceptions and distort his usual judgment on the probable cause question. It assumes that a magistrate who could issue a warrant would issue one, when, in theory at least, the magistrate might refuse in an effort to prevent an unreasonable search. Also, the argument blinks the fact that the officer who makes an exigent circumstance search is personally deciding the scope and particulars of the intrusion.

2. Hot Pursuit

If officers are in hot pursuit of a suspect, this will excuse an arrest warrant where one would otherwise be required, and it will also excuse a search warrant where a search of an area must be conducted in order to find and apprehend the suspect. The rationale is that it is unrealistic to expect police officers to stop in the middle of a chase and resort to the warrant process. To do so could allow the suspect to get away and thus render the warrant meaningless. The delay of obtaining a warrant could also allow the suspect to destroy evidence or to create a dangerous situation for police officers or members of the public. In these latter respects, the hot pursuit doctrine is really just a variant of the "public safety" and "destruction of evidence" aspects of the exigent circumstances doctrine, to be discussed below.

The leading hot pursuit case in the Supreme Court is Warden v. Hayden, 387 U.S. 294 (1967). Officers pursued a robbery suspect into what was subsequently determined to be the suspect's house. The suspect's wife answered the door, and the police entered the house to search for the suspect. In the course of looking for him, they also looked for weapons which he might have concealed during the pursuit. The officers found incriminating clothing in a washing machine. The Court held that the warrantless search was justified by the "hot pursuit" exception. The fact that the officers found clothing as opposed to weapons in the washing machine was not problematic, since the officers had the right, in these emergency circumstances, to search the washing machine to look for weapons, and thus the seizure of the clothing was permissible under the plain view doctrine.

The "hot pursuit" doctrine is based on the premise that the suspect, knowing that he is being pursued, may seek to escape, or to destroy evidence or create a threat to public safety. It follows that the "hot pursuit" doctrine cannot apply where the suspect is unaware that he is being pursued by police officers. Thus, in Welsh v. Wisconsin, 466 U.S. 740 (1984), officers were notified that a car had been driven into a ditch. Eyewitnesses told the officers that the driver had been driving erratically, and had walked away from the scene. The officers quickly went to the address listed on the vehicle registration, and arrested Welsh in his home for driving while intoxicated. The Court held that the "hot pursuit" doctrine could not apply in these circumstances, since Welsh was never aware until he was arrested that he was being pursued by police officers. If the "hot pursuit" doctrine were controlled by how expeditiously the police were pursuing the suspect, then it would exist in virtually every case.

On the other hand, the "hot pursuit" doctrine can cover situations significantly short of high speed car chases. For example, in United States v. Santana, 427 U.S. 38 (1976), officers approached Santana while she was standing in the doorway of her home. They had probable cause to arrest her. When Santana saw the officers, she quickly retreated into her house. The officers told her she was under arrest and then followed her into the house to catch her and place her in custody. The Court, in an opinion by Justice Rehnquist, held that the police officers were permitted to follow Santana into her house under the doctrine of "hot pursuit." Justice Rehnquist noted that the hot pursuit doctrine serves to ensure that "a suspect may not defeat an arrest which has been set in motion in a public place * * * by the expedient of escaping into a private place." He concluded: "the fact that the pursuit here ended almost as soon as it began did not render it any the less a 'hot pursuit' sufficient to justify the warrantless entry."

3. Police and Public Safety

A warrant is excused if the delay in obtaining a warrant would result in a significant risk of harm to the police or to members of the public. A notable example of the loosely-termed "public safety" doctrine arose in the O.J. Simpson case. After finding the bodies of Nicole Simpson and her friend, officers went to Simpson's residence, scaled the fence, entered the yard, and found evidence that incriminated Simpson. The state argued that the officers had a legitimate concern that, in light of the recent murders and Simpson's celebrity status, either Simpson or his family might be in danger. The trial court found that the imminent risk to the safety of persons at the Simpson residence excused the officers from obtaining a warrant. Of course, as it turned out, there was no danger to anyone on the premises, but exigency is determined as of the time of the police action, and not in hindsight. See, e.g., United States v. Salava, 978 F.2d 320 (7th Cir.1992)(risk to public safety excuses warrant where the defendant was found outside his home with blood on his clothes, and stated that he shot someone inside the home; while it was subsequently discovered that the defendant had wounded himself in a fight with an imaginary opponent, the court must evaluate the risk to public safety from the point of view of the officer at the time of the search). See also Tierney v. Davidson, 133 F.3d 189 (2d Cir.1998) (it was proper for police to enter a home without a warrant, after they had received reports of a serious domestic disturbance, and the house was quiet when they arrived; even though nobody had actually been injured, it was reasonable for the officer "to believe that someone inside had been injured or was in danger, that both antagonists remained in the house, and that this situation satisfied the exigent circumstances exception.").

4. *The Risk of Destruction of Evidence*

If evidence will be destroyed in the time it takes to obtain a warrant, then the warrant requirement is excused. The question usually disputed in the cases is whether there was really an imminent risk of destruction of evidence under the facts presented.

Not surprisingly, destruction of evidence issues often arise in drug cases. One such case is the en banc decision of United States v. MacDonald, 916 F.2d 766 (2d Cir.1990). The court recited the facts surrounding the search as follows:

In May 1988, an informant alerted the New York Drug Enforcement Task Force ("Task Force") of a possible narcotics operation utilizing two apartments in a Manhattan apartment building located at 321 Edgecombe Avenue. On the evening of September 8, 1988, agents of the Task Force established surveillance outside the apartment building. The agents observed numerous indications that a retail narcotics exchange was being operated out of Apartment 1–O, a one-room efficiency on the first floor.

Shortly before ten o'clock that evening, one of the agents of the Task Force, James Agee, went to Apartment 1–O in an attempt to transact an undercover purchase of narcotics. After knocking and being admitted by an unidentified man, Agent Agee encountered Paul Thomas, who was sitting in a chair next to the door and pointing a cocked 9 mm. semi-automatic weapon at the floor, but in Agee's direction. Defendant Errol MacDonald, who was sitting on a couch counting a stack of money, was within easy reach of a .357 magnum revolver. There were four other men, including the man who admitted Agee, in the apartment which contained large quantities of what appeared to Agee to be marijuana and cocaine. Agee detected the distinct odor of marijuana smoke. He handed the unidentified doorman a prerecorded five dollar bill in return for a package of marijuana. Agee then immediately left the building and reported his observations to the other Task Force members waiting outside.

Approximately ten minutes after the controlled purchase, Agee returned to the apartment with reinforcements. After knocking on the door and identifying themselves, the agents heard the sounds of shuffling feet. They also simultaneously received a radio communication from agents remaining outside the building informing them that the occupants of the first floor apartment were attempting to escape through a bathroom window. The agents at the apartment door then used a battering ram to force entry.

The agents arrested five men in the apartment, four in the bathroom and one hiding in a closet. As they performed a security sweep of the apartment, they discovered in plain view the two loaded weapons, large quantities of cocaine and marijuana, narcotics paraphernalia, packaging materials and several thousand dollars in cash. Additional cash was recovered from the persons of the suspects.

The majority of the en banc court found that exigent circumstances existed even before the officers knocked on the door and heard people scurrying around. The court stated as follows:

> The essential question in determining whether exigent circumstances justified a warrantless entry is whether law enforcement agents were confronted by an "urgent need" to render aid or take action. Dorman v. United States, 435 F.2d 385, 391 (D.C.Cir.1970)(in banc). We have adopted the factors set out in *Dorman* as guideposts intended to facilitate the district court's determination. The *Dorman* factors have been summarized as follows:
>
> > (1) the gravity or violent nature of the offense with which the suspect is to be charged; (2) whether the suspect "is reasonably believed to be armed"; (3) "a clear showing of probable cause ... to believe that the suspect committed the crime"; (4) "strong reason to believe that the suspect is in the premises being entered"; (5) "a likelihood that the suspect will escape if not swiftly apprehended"; and (6) the peaceful circumstances of the entry.

* * *

Applying the *Dorman* factors to the case at hand, the district court's determination [that exigent circumstances existed] was far from clearly erroneous. First, the ongoing sale and distribution of narcotics constituted a grave offense. Second, the defendant and at least one of his associates were armed with loaded, semi-automatic weapons. Third, the law enforcement agents had not only probable cause to suspect that a crime had been perpetrated but firsthand knowledge that ongoing crimes were transpiring. Fourth, the agents further knew that the defendant and his associates were in the apartment. Fifth, the likelihood that a suspect might escape if not swiftly apprehended was confirmed by the fact that the man who actually made the sale to Agent Agee had apparently escaped during the ten-minute interval that elapsed after the controlled purchase and before the agents entered the apartment. Sixth, the agents acted in accordance with the law, and first attempted to effect a peaceful entry by knocking and announcing themselves.

* * * In addition, the district court's finding that the agents were confronted by an urgent need to prevent the possible loss of evidence cannot be said to be clearly erroneous in light of the information that the suspects were using an unidentified apartment in the building to store narcotics, the ease with which the suspects could have disposed of the cocaine by flushing it down the toilet, and the possibility that the prerecorded five dollar bill used by Agent Agee in the undercover buy would be lost if the ongoing drug transactions were permitted to continue while the agents sought a warrant. Finally, the dangers of harm to law enforcement agents and the public, of the loss of evidence and of the escape of the suspects were aggravated by the additional time required for, and the impracticability of, obtaining a warrant at the late hour of day, while the apartment continued to be used as a retail drug outlet.

The *MacDonald* majority was unsympathetic to the defendant's claim that it had created a per se exigent circumstances exception in large-scale narcotics cases.

> The defendant also argues that narcotics-related crimes so frequently involve exigent circumstances that the exception threatens to eviscerate the rule. * * * If it is true that ongoing retail narcotics operations often confront law enforcement agents with exigent circumstances, we fail to see how such a sad reality constitutes a ground for declaring that the exigencies do not, in fact, exist. To disallow the exigent circumstances exception in these cases would be to tie the hands of law enforcement agents who are entrusted with the responsibility of combatting grave, ongoing crimes * * *.

Judge Kearse dissented from the majority's decision in *MacDonald*. In her view, the government had not made a factual showing that a risk of destruction of evidence existed at the time that the officers decided to knock on the door.

> There has never been an exigent circumstances exception permitting a warrantless entry simply because the offense involves narcotics. Nor was an exigency created in the present case by the fact that there were firearms in the apartment. We often have taken judicial notice that, to substantial dealers in narcotics, firearms are as much tools of the trade as are the commonly recognized articles of narcotics paraphernalia. Thus, emphasis on the presence of firearms for the view that the circumstances were exigent suggests that whenever there is probable cause to believe that narcotics offenses are being committed, the agents should be allowed to ignore the warrant requirement.

* * *

> The total lack of awareness by the suspects in the present case, prior to the agents' return to the apartment, is virtually ignored by the majority. Thus, in concluding that there was a likelihood that the suspects would escape and evidence would be destroyed, the majority apparently sees no significance in the fact that this operation had been ongoing in Apartment 1–O since May, i.e., some four months before the agents' surveillance, and that there was no reason to believe it would be moved. * * * There was no basis for believing that the occupants of the apartment had been alerted to the September 8 surveillance prior to the agents' announcement of their official presence. The agents had received no information and had seen no indication that the suspects had any kind of security devices in the apartment or had posted any lookouts in the area. The surveillance was conducted by a team of agents whose ethnic makeup matched that of the civilians coming and going in the neighborhood. The surveillance was inconspicuous; the building was large, and there was a good deal of traffic in and out with respect to apartments other than 1–O; the agents' vehicles were placed so circumspectly that even Agee did not know where those other than his own were parked. * * * Nor did anything that occurred during Agee's subsequent purchase appear to alert the suspects. * * * There was simply nothing in the record to suggest that the suspects would suddenly, after at least four months of operation, start to destroy their business assets * * *.

* * *

The majority's ruling today gives law enforcement officers broad license to enter premises without a warrant. * * * Indeed, it appears that the majority would allow the agents to enter simply on the basis that one agent had recently been on the premises by consent and witnessed the trafficking. After this decision there appears to be little left of the warrant requirement in narcotics cases.

Judge Kearse's dissent was joined by Judge Oakes who had also dissented in United States v. Cattouse, 846 F.2d 144 (2d Cir.1988), a similar narcotics case in which the court found exigent circumstances due to the risk of destruction of evidence. In *Cattouse,* Judge Oakes stated that "we should be more forthright and say that the Fourth Amendment's warrant requirement is simply inapplicable in drug buy cases." See also United States v. Howard, 106 F.3d 70 (5th Cir.1997) (exigent circumstances existed to search for drugs, given their easy destructibility and the inevitable presence of guns).

Is the en banc decision in *MacDonald* consistent with the Supreme Court's decision in Vale v. Louisiana, 399 U.S. 30 (1970)? In *Vale,* the Court emphasized the fact-based nature of the exigent circumstances inquiry, and held that exigent circumstances did not exist to search Vale's home, when Vale was arrested outside his home for engaging in a drug transaction and there was no indication that anyone was inside destroying evidence. The Court noted that at the time of the officers' entry into the home, the narcotics were not "in the process of destruction." Does the Court in *Vale* mean that the destruction must have already begun before a warrant is excused? Is the issue whether destruction is "imminent?" Was there an imminent risk of destruction of narcotics in *MacDonald?*

Any suggestion in *MacDonald* that exigent circumstances *always* exist in the search of large scale drug operations must also be evaluated in light of the Supreme Court's subsequent decision in Richards v. Wisconsin, 520 U.S. 385 (1997). The question in *Richards* was whether officers would be excused from complying with the constitutional requirement that they knock and announce their presence before engaging in a warranted search of a premises. The knock-and-announce requirement is excused if there is an imminent risk of destruction of evidence, and thus the exigent circumstances exception applies both to the warrant requirement itself and to the knock-and-announce requirement. See the discussion of the knock-and-announce requirement earlier in this Chapter.

The government in *Richards* argued that exigent circumstances excusing the knock-and-announce requirement *automatically* arise in the search of a large-scale drug operation. But the Supreme Court unanimously rejected this bright-line rule in favor of a case-by-case approach. Justice Stevens, writing for the Court, argued that there could be situations in which the risk of destruction of evidence might not be imminent:

> [A] search could be conducted at a time when the only individuals present in a residence have no connection with the drug activity and thus will be unlikely to threaten officers or destroy evidence. Or the police could know that the drugs being searched for were of a type or in a location that made them impossible to destroy quickly. * * * Wisconsin's blanket rule impermissibly insulates these cases from judicial review.

While the *Richards* Court rejected the government's *per se* exigent circumstances argument, it found that the officer's failure to knock and announce was justified under the circumstances. The defendant was aware of the presence of police officers, and the evidence was in fact in imminent risk of destruction. Similarly, in *MacDonald,* even without a bright line rule of exigency, the court could rely on the fact that the drugs could be destroyed easily, the crime was grave, and the marked money could have been lost in the time it would take to get a warrant. Which is to say there will almost always be exigent circumstances for a warrantless search of a large scale drug operation, even taking a case-by-case approach.

The Seriousness of the Offense

In assessing whether there is a risk of destruction of evidence sufficient to excuse a warrant, the courts take into account not only the destructibility of the evidence but also the seriousness of the offense. For example, the serious nature of a narcotics offense was central to the *MacDonald* Court's finding of exigent circumstances.

The "seriousness" factor raises two questions: 1) Could an offense be so serious that exigency should be deemed automatic, without regard to the actual risk of destruction of evidence? and 2) Could an offense be so minor that a warrant should be required regardless of the actual risk of destruction of evidence? The Supreme Court has had something to say about both of these questions.

Murder Scene

As to the first question, the Court in Mincey v. Arizona, 437 U.S. 385 (1978), considered the government's argument that there should be a "murder scene" exception to the warrant requirement. Mincey shot and killed an officer during a drug bust. Mincey himself was seriously wounded. A protective sweep of the premises resulted in the detention of Mincey's associates. Ten minutes later, homicide detectives entered the premises without a warrant and began a search for evidence that lasted four days. Every item in the apartment was closely examined and inventoried, and two to three hundred objects were seized.

Justice Stewart wrote for a unanimous Court. He rejected a "scene of the homicide" exception to the warrant requirement and stated that the government must make a factual showing of exigent circumstances. Justice Stewart wrote as follows:

> * * * We do not question the right of the police to respond to emergency situations. Numerous state and federal cases have recognized that the Fourth Amendment does not bar police officers from making warrantless entries and searches when they reasonably believe that a person within is in need of immediate aid. Similarly, when the police come upon the scene of a homicide they may make a prompt warrantless search of the area to see if there are other victims or if a killer is still on the premises. * * *

> But a warrantless search must be "strictly circumscribed by the exigencies which justify its initiation," and it simply cannot be contended that this search was justified by any emergency threatening life or limb. All the persons in Mincey's apartment had been located before the investigating homicide officers arrived there and began their search. And a four-day

search that included opening dresser drawers and ripping up carpets can hardly be rationalized in terms of the legitimate concerns that justify an emergency search.

    * * * [T]he State points to the vital public interest in the prompt investigation of the extremely serious crime of murder. No one can doubt the importance of this goal. But the public interest in the investigation of other serious crimes is comparable. If the warrantless search of a homicide scene is reasonable, why not the warrantless search of the scene of a rape, a robbery, or a burglary? No consideration relevant to the Fourth Amendment suggests any point of rational limitation of such a doctrine.

What would be wrong with a rule that allowed automatic searches at the scene of a homicide, rape, or robbery, even the day after the crime has occurred? Won't a search warrant be issued automatically for these kinds of crimes? If the warrant application is perfunctory, what is gained by having the police, who are already at the scene of the crime, seek a warrant? Would a warrant requirement have prevented the intensive nature of the search and seizure that most bothered the Court in *Mincey?*[29]

Minor Offenses

As to the second question, the Court in Welsh v. Wisconsin, 466 U.S. 740 (1984), considered whether an offense could be so minor as not to justify an exception to the warrant requirement even given an imminent risk of destruction of evidence. Officers arrested Welsh in his home shortly after receiving a report from an observer that Welsh had been driving his car while being intoxicated or very sick. After seeing Welsh driving erratically and ultimately swerving off the road into a ditch, the observer blocked Welsh's car with his own car and saw Welsh walk away from the ditch after being refused a ride. Police came to the scene and discovered a motor vehicle registration in Welsh's abandoned car. The police went to the address listed on the registration and arrested Welsh in his home for driving while under the influence of an intoxicant. Welsh subsequently refused to submit to a breathalyzer test. The state revoked his license due to his failure to submit to a breathalyzer test, and Welsh challenged this action, arguing that his refusal came about as a result of an illegal warrantless in-home arrest. The state argued that the warrantless arrest was legal because, among other things, the delay in obtaining a warrant would

---

29. In a unanimous per curiam opinion in Thompson v. Louisiana, 469 U.S. 17 (1984), the Court found that *Mincey* required reversal of a state court decision upholding the warrantless "murder scene" search of the defendant's home. Sheriff's deputies came to the defendant's home in response to a call from her daughter reporting a homicide. The deputies entered the home, made a cursory search and found the defendant's husband dead of a gunshot wound in a bedroom and the defendant unconscious in another bedroom due to an apparent drug overdose. The daughter apparently told the deputies that the defendant had shot the victim, took a large quantity of pills in a suicide attempt, changed her mind, and called the daughter and asked for help.

The deputies transported the defendant to the hospital and secured the scene after searching for other victims or suspects. Thirty-five minutes later, officers from the homicide unit arrived and conducted a two hour follow-up investigation in which they examined each room of the house. The defendant moved to suppress a pistol taken from a chest of drawers in the room where the deceased's body was found, a torn up note found in a wastepaper basket in an adjoining bathroom, and a letter (alleged to be a suicide note) found inside an envelope containing a Christmas card on the top of a chest of drawers. The Court found that *Mincey* was squarely in point. Do you agree? If so, are you more or less convinced that *Mincey* was correctly decided?

have resulted in the loss of evidence—specifically the loss of proof of Welsh's intoxication.

Justice Brennan's opinion for six members of the Court rejected the destruction of evidence argument and found the arrest illegal. Justice Brennan stated that the concept of exigent circumstances must be narrowly construed when the home is the target of police conduct, "especially when the underlying offense for which there is probable cause to arrest is relatively minor."

Justice Brennan declared that "it is difficult to conceive of a warrantless home arrest that would not be unreasonable under the Fourth Amendment when the underlying offense is extremely minor." He held that "an important factor to be considered when determining whether any exigency exists is the gravity of the underlying offense for which the arrest is being made" and declared that "application of the exigent-circumstances exception in the context of a home entry should rarely be sanctioned when there is probable cause to believe that only a minor offense, such as the kind at issue in this case, has been committed."

Applying these principles to the facts of the case, Justice Brennan noted that "[t]he State of Wisconsin has chosen to classify the first offense for driving while intoxicated as a noncriminal, civil forfeiture offense for which no imprisonment is possible," and that "[g]iven this expression of the state's interest, a warrantless home arrest cannot be upheld simply because evidence of the petitioner's blood-alcohol level might have dissipated while the police obtained a warrant."

Justice White, joined by Justice Rehnquist, dissented. He reasoned that a warrantless home entry is no more intrusive for a minor offense than a major one and that the majority's approach will force officers who must make quick decisions to assess whether a violation is major or minor for purposes of making an exigency determination. Justice White noted that a misdemeanor-felony distinction could have been adopted, but opined that the majority wisely did not adopt it, since "the category of misdemeanors today includes enough serious offenses to call into question the desirability of such line drawing."

5. *Impermissibly Created Exigency*

In some cases suspects are alerted to the presence of police activity, and then there is little dispute about the risk of destruction of evidence or other danger when the officers make an entry. Instead, defendants argue that the police acted impermissibly in revealing their presence, and thus manufactured the exigent circumstances. It is well-recognized that officers should not be allowed to evade the warrant requirement by impermissibly creating exigent circumstances. But there is dispute about whether officers act impermissibly by revealing their presence.

The issue of manufactured exigency arose in *MacDonald,* discussed above. Recall that the officers went to the door of the drug operation and knocked on it, announcing their presence (called in the trade a "knock and talk"). At that point, they heard people scurrying around. The officers used a battering ram, which they happened to have with them, to knock down the door. An officer who testified at the suppression hearing stated that they knocked on the door to obtain consent. The court of appeals, as discussed above, held that exigent circumstances existed even before the officers knocked on the door. But even assuming that was not the case, the court found in the alternative that exigent circumstances existed after the knocking and that the officers did not impermissibly create that exigency. The majority analyzed the "creation of exigency" issue as follows:

> [T]he agents' conduct was perfectly proper. By knocking and announcing themselves, they acted in accordance with the law, attempting the "peaceful entry" contemplated in *Dorman,* 435 F.2d at 393. Exigent circumstances are not to be disregarded simply because the suspects chose to respond to the agents' lawful conduct by attempting to escape, destroy evidence, or engage in any other unlawful activity. The fact that the suspects may reasonably be expected to behave illegally does not prevent law enforcement agents from acting lawfully to afford the suspects the opportunity to do so. Thus, assuming *arguendo* that there were no exigent circumstances before the knock, the agents' conduct did not impermissibly create the circumstances occurring thereafter.

The argument that law enforcement agents created exigent circumstances in bad faith has been rejected in numerous other contexts. We have previously reasoned that agents did not intentionally design exigent circumstances by using: (1) an all white surveillance team in a predominantly black neighborhood, and thus exposing the agents to a great risk of detection, [United States v.] Cattouse, 846 F.2d at 147, 148; (2) marked buy money in a controlled drug deal, and thus compelling the agents to act immediately lest the money be dissipated, id.; and (3) counterfeit tickets marked void, and thus endangering the lives of agents and occasioning the possibility of destruction of evidence when the suspect unwrapped the package and discovered the markings, [United States] v. Zabare, 871 F.2d at 290. The United States Court of Appeals for the First Circuit has held that a deceptive telephone call by agents advising the occupants of a motel room to vacate since their associates in a narcotics deal had been arrested was "a creative investigative effort and simply an example of good police work" rather than an impermissible effort to circumvent the arrest warrant requirement. United States v. Rengifo, 858 F.2d 800, 803 (1st Cir.1988).

* * *

* * * [W]e have repeatedly held that the determination of exigent circumstances is an objective one based on the totality of the circumstances confronting law enforcement agents. The Supreme Court's recent decision in Horton v. California [discussed in the material on plain view, supra] confirms our approach.

* * * We simply shall not engage in futile speculation as to whether the agents actually expected the suspects to respond lawfully to their knock at the door. The fact that the agents brought along a battering ram changes nothing. The exigent circumstances known to the agents before they knocked sufficiently alerted them to the possibility that a forced entry would be necessary.

* * * Therefore, we hold that when law enforcement agents act in an entirely lawful manner, they do not impermissibly create exigent circumstances. Law enforcement agents are required to be innocent but not naive.

Judge Kearse in dissent argued that the officers had impermissibly created exigent circumstances.

> I find it difficult to conceive of the officers' return to the apartment as anything other than pretext, in an effort to precipitate a crisis that did not then exist. Though Agee stated that he returned in the hope that the occupants would give him consent to search the apartment, that explanation should, in the circumstances, be found not credible as a matter of law. Agee testified that when he made his undercover purchase, he saw two firearms in the apartment, and one of them was held cocked and pointed in his direction while he was in the apartment. It was not objectively reasonable for the officers to hold any belief that suspects who took such precautions during an apparently innocuous buy would voluntarily consent to a search by law enforcement officers. Since the agents' suggestion that they returned because they thought they could gain entrance to search by consent defies credulity, and since the agents plainly anticipated that the announcement of their identity would precipitate an exigency, for they came armed with a battering ram, I think the agents must be regarded as having deliberately created the exigency precisely to justify their warrantless entry. We should not endorse such contrivances by law enforcement officials in their efforts to circumvent the Fourth Amendment's warrant requirement.

The *MacDonald* Court refused to find impermissible creation of exigent circumstances because the officers' activity that created the exigency was objectively lawful—even though it was apparent that the officers acted with the intent to create a situation in which the suspects would attempt to destroy evidence, they did nothing illegal. Under this view there is no impermissible creation of exigency unless the creation itself is an illegal search or seizure. Recall the discussion of pretext stops and arrests, and the Supreme Court's holding in *Whren*, adopting an objective standard for assessing an officer's conduct under the Fourth Amendment. Is *Whren* determinative of the result in a case like *MacDonald?* Could it be argued that *Whren* found pretext arguments concerning arrests to be answered by probable cause, whereas probable cause is not the issue when exigent circumstances are created by the police?

Other courts have held more broadly that police activity that is not illegal itself can nonetheless constitute impermissible creation of exigent circumstances. For example, the court in United States v. Timberlake, 896 F.2d 592 (D.C.Cir.1990), confronted facts similar to those in *MacDonald*—officers without a warrant knocked on the door of a suspected drug den, announced their presence, and entered after hearing people scurrying around. The *Timberlake* Court stated that "police officers cannot deliberately create exigent circumstances," and held the entry invalid because there was "no evidence that the police, when they knocked on the door, intended anything other than a warrantless search of the apartment."

The courts, such as *Timberlake*, that follow a broader view, nonetheless recognize that not all police-created exigencies are impermissible. That is, police are not required to go out of their way to avoid creating exigencies. For example, in United States v. Rico, 51 F.3d 495 (5th Cir.1995), exigent circumstances were created when a drug conspirator was arrested outside a drug den after stashing what appeared to be narcotics in a car. The defendant argued that the exigent circumstances exception was inapplicable because the risk of destruction of evidence arose from the fact that the officer arrested the conspirator right in front of the premises, thus inevitably alerting his cohorts to the police presence. But the court held that the exigent circumstances were not impermissibly created:

> Perhaps Agent Bingham could have pursued a different course; he might have waited until Cuero drove away from the house and then have him apprehended by the other agents well out of sight and earshot of the other suspects. But we will not second-guess law enforcement tactics as long as those tactics are neither unreasonable nor employed with specific intent to create an emergency simply to circumvent the warrant requirement.

How does one determine whether the officers acted "deliberately" in creating exigent circumstances? Why should that matter?

6. *Prior Opportunity to Obtain a Warrant*

If the police can foresee that an exigency would arise at a certain time in the future, and have a strong case of probable cause and ample time to obtain a warrant before that exigency occurs, then that opportunity to obtain the warrant precludes the later invocation of the exigent circumstances exception. For example, assume that an officer knows that a terrorist suspect vacuums his carpet every Wednesday morning, and that this would destroy relevant forensic evidence. On Wednesday morning, there are exigent circumstances due to the risk of destruction of evidence. But if the officer learned this information on Monday, and had probable cause to search at that time, then he should not be able to invoke the exigent circumstances exception two days later.

The decided cases do not usually present such clean facts, however. In the typical case, the state argues that the officer did not have probable cause until the exigency arose, and therefore had no prior opportunity to obtain a warrant. The defendant then makes the anomalous argument that the officer had probable cause well before that. The state also argues that the officer should not be required to go to the magistrate at the very first moment that probable cause exists, and that a contrary rule would jeopardize undercover activity and ongoing investigations.[30]

How the court resolves these contentions will depend on the facts. In United States v. Miles, 889 F.2d 382 (2d Cir.1989), the court was confronted with the following facts: Joy, a reliable informant for the DEA, had arranged a cocaine buy in Miles' apartment. He gave DEA agents Miles' name and address, and the agents monitored a phone call between Joy and Miles indicating Miles' willingness to make the narcotics deal. Several hours later, the transaction took place in the apartment. The seller was one Rodriguez, with Miles acting as a broker. Joy was present when Rodriguez delivered a kilogram of cocaine to Miles' apartment. Joy so notified DEA agents outside the building by beeper. Then Joy left the apartment telling Rodriguez and Miles that he was going to get the money for the buy. At that point, the DEA agents entered the apartment, without a warrant. The court found that the entry was supported by exigent

---

30. See United States v. Foxworth, 8 F.3d 540 (7th Cir.1993) (warrantless arrest in a motel room was supported by exigent circumstances: "[A]lthough the police had the motel under surveillance for two hours, the focus of their concern was Foxworth, who did not arrive until sometime after the police had begun their observations. Only after the police had observed the events at the motel did they gather the necessary probable cause to arrest Foxworth. By then, people and drugs were moving quickly.").

circumstances, stating that "Joy's absence for an extended period of time while the agents sought a warrant would create a substantial risk of alerting Miles and Rodriguez to the imminence of an arrest" and that, if alerted, they might destroy the cocaine. The court rejected Miles' argument that the officer had a prior opportunity to obtain a warrant, which existed at least from the time they monitored Joy's phone conversation with Miles earlier in the day. The court stated that "law enforcement officers may delay obtaining a warrant until events have proceeded to a point where the agents could be reasonably certain that the evidence would ultimately support a conviction;" and it was not until the transaction actually took place that this reasonable certainty existed. In other words, officers are not required to obtain a warrant at the very first moment that probable cause could be said to arise—they have the right to continue their investigation and strengthen the showing of probable cause. The court further concluded that "even if the agents might have been able to obtain a warrant earlier in the day, their failure to do so at the first opportunity does not bar them from acting on an exigency that arises later." Does the court in *Miles* mean that officers must have proof greater than probable cause before they are required to go to a magistrate?

7. *Electronic Warrants*

Fed.R.Crim.P. 41(d)(3)(A) provides that warrants may be obtained by telephone "or other appropriate means, including facsimile transmission." Presumably the language "other appropriate means" permits email warrants as well. Telephonic and fax warrants are available in most states. This does not mean that warrants can be obtained immediately, however. Basically, the electronic warrant merely saves travel time. Under Rule 41, a duplicate original warrant must be prepared by the officer, and must be read or sent in written form verbatim to the magistrate, who must transcribe it and prepare an original warrant for the record. These recording requirements are considered necessary to prevent post hoc reconstructions of probable cause and particularity. It must also be remembered that at certain times (e.g., late at night or on the weekend), it may be difficult to reach a magistrate, telephonically or otherwise.

While not instantaneous, the time involved in obtaining an electronic warrant can be significantly less than it would take to obtain a warrant in person. In United States v. Cuaron, 700 F.2d 582 (10th Cir.1983), the court held that exigent circumstances must be determined by whether the officer could have obtained a telephone warrant before the entry:

> The time necessary to obtain a warrant is relevant to a determination whether circumstances are exigent. Therefore, courts should consider the amount of time required to obtain a telephone warrant in assessing the urgency of the situation. Although warrants obtained by telephone generally take less time to procure than traditional warrants, the time required for a telephone warrant varies from case to case. * * * [T]rial courts must consider the availability of a telephone warrant in determining whether exigent circumstances existed, unless the critical nature of the circumstances clearly prevented the effective use of *any* warrant procedure.

See also United States v. Berick, 710 F.2d 1035 (5th Cir.1983)(risk of destruction of evidence resulting from arrest of drug seller was so imminent that recourse to even a telephone warrant was unavailable); United States v. Patino, 830 F.2d

1413 (7th Cir.1987)(agent who observed fugitive in defendant's yard had adequate opportunity to obtain a telephone warrant during 30–minute wait for back-up assistance). Presumably, the possibility of email will shorten the time period for obtaining a warrant, and therefore narrow the window of time in which an officer can claim exigent circumstances.

8.   *Seizing Premises in the Absence of Exigent Circumstances*

If exigent circumstances do not exist to search a house or other premises, the officers must obtain a search warrant. But can the officers take any protective action to preserve the status quo while a warrant is being obtained? In Segura v. United States, 468 U.S. 796 (1984), officers had probable cause to believe that two individuals, Segura and Luz Colon, were trafficking in cocaine from their New York apartment. They established surveillance, and arrested Segura as he entered the lobby of his apartment building. The agents took Segura to his apartment, and knocked on the door. Luz Colon answered the door. The agents entered without receiving permission, placed Luz Colon under arrest, and conducted a limited security sweep. In the process of the sweep, they saw evidence of drug activity. Luz Colon and Segura were incarcerated, and two officers waited in Segura's apartment while a search warrant was being obtained. Due to "administrative delay" it was 19 hours before the search of the apartment was eventually conducted.

A majority of the Court found it unnecessary to reach the question of whether the officers acted illegally. The majority reasoned that, even if the warrantless entry of the premises was illegal, the later search conducted pursuant to a warrant was based on an independent legal source, i.e., the information the officers already had before they seized the premises. This aspect of the opinion will be discussed later in this Chapter in the materials on the exclusionary rule. Chief Justice Burger, joined by Justice O'Connor, went further, however, and declared that the seizure of the premises pending a warrant was reasonable, even in the absence of exigent circumstances.

Chief Justice Burger's opinion in *Segura* was adopted by a majority of the Court in Murray v. United States, 487 U.S. 533 (1988). See also United States v. Veillette, 778 F.2d 899 (1st Cir.1985)(48 hour seizure of premises, pending a warrant, held reasonable under *Segura*).

Prohibiting Entry While a Warrant Is Being Obtained: Illinois v. McArthur

In the following case, the Court expanded upon the analysis in *Segura* and firmly established the authority of police officers to maintain the status quo while a warrant is being obtained.

ILLINOIS v. McARTHUR

Supreme Court of the United States, 2001.
531 U.S. 326.

Justice Breyer **delivered the opinion of the Court.**

Police officers, with probable cause to believe that a man had hidden marijuana in his home, prevented that man from entering the home for about two hours while they obtained a search warrant. We must decide whether those officers violated the Fourth Amendment. We conclude that the officers acted reasonably. They did not violate the Amendment's requirements. And we reverse an Illinois court's holding to the contrary.

I

A

On April 2, 1997, Tera McArthur asked two police officers to accompany her to the trailer where she lived with her husband, Charles, so that they could keep the peace while she removed her belongings. The two officers, Assistant Chief John Love and Officer Richard Skidis, arrived with Tera at the trailer at about 3:15 p.m. Tera went inside, where Charles was present. The officers remained outside.

When Tera emerged after collecting her possessions, she spoke to Chief Love, who was then on the porch. She suggested he check the trailer because "Chuck had dope in there." She added (in Love's words) that she had seen Chuck "slid[e] some dope underneath the couch."

Love knocked on the trailer door, told Charles what Tera had said, and asked for permission to search the trailer, which Charles denied. Love then sent Officer Skidis with Tera to get a search warrant.

Love told Charles, who by this time was also on the porch, that he could not reenter the trailer unless a police officer accompanied him. Charles subsequently reentered the trailer two or three times (to get cigarettes and to make phone calls), and each time Love stood just inside the door to observe what Charles did.

Officer Skidis obtained the warrant by about 5 p.m. He returned to the trailer and, along with other officers, searched it. The officers found under the sofa a marijuana pipe, a box for marijuana (called a "one-hitter" box), and a small amount of marijuana. They then arrested Charles.

B

Illinois subsequently charged Charles McArthur with unlawfully possessing drug paraphernalia and marijuana (less than 2.5 grams), both misdemeanors. McArthur moved to suppress the pipe, box, and marijuana on the ground that they were the "fruit" of an unlawful police seizure, namely, the refusal to let him reenter the trailer unaccompanied, which would have permitted him, he said, to "have destroyed the marijuana."

The trial court granted McArthur's suppression motion. The Appellate Court of Illinois affirmed, and the Illinois Supreme Court denied the State's petition for leave to appeal. We granted certiorari to determine whether the Fourth Amendment prohibits the kind of temporary seizure at issue here.

II

A

* * *

In the circumstances of the case before us, we cannot say that the warrantless seizure was *per se* unreasonable. It involves a plausible claim of specially pressing or urgent law enforcement need, *i.e.,* "exigent circumstances." Moreover, the restraint at issue was tailored to that need, being limited in time and scope, and avoiding significant intrusion into the home itself. Consequently, rather than employing a *per se* rule of unreasonableness, we balance the privacy-related and law enforcement-related concerns to determine if the intrusion was reasonable.

We conclude that the restriction at issue was reasonable, and hence lawful, in light of the following circumstances, which we consider in combination. First, the police had probable cause to believe that McArthur's trailer home contained evidence of a crime and contraband, namely, unlawful drugs. The police had had an opportunity to speak with Tera McArthur and make at least a very rough assessment of her reliability. They knew she had had a firsthand opportunity to observe her husband's behavior, in particular with respect to the drugs at issue. And they thought, with good reason, that her report to them reflected that opportunity. Cf. Massachusetts v. Upton, 466 U.S. 727, 732–734 (1984) *(per curiam)* (upholding search warrant issued in similar circumstances).

Second, the police had good reason to fear that, unless restrained, McArthur would destroy the drugs before they could return with a warrant. They reasonably might have thought that McArthur realized that his wife knew about his marijuana stash; observed that she was angry or frightened enough to ask the police to accompany her; saw that after leaving the trailer she had spoken with the police; and noticed that she had walked off with one policeman while leaving the other outside to observe the trailer. They reasonably could have concluded that McArthur, consequently suspecting an imminent search, would, if given the chance, get rid of the drugs fast.

Third, the police made reasonable efforts to reconcile their law enforcement needs with the demands of personal privacy. They neither searched the trailer nor arrested McArthur before obtaining a warrant. Rather, they imposed a significantly less restrictive restraint, preventing McArthur only from entering the trailer unaccompanied. They left his home and his belongings intact—until a neutral Magistrate, finding probable cause, issued a warrant.

Fourth, the police imposed the restraint for a limited period of time, namely, two hours. Cf. Terry v. Ohio (manner in which police act is a vital part of the inquiry). As far as the record reveals, this time period was no longer than reasonably necessary for the police, acting with diligence, to obtain the warrant. Compare United States v. Place, *supra,* at 709–710, (holding 90–minute detention of luggage unreasonable based on nature of interference with person's travels and lack of diligence of police), with United States v. Van Leeuwen, 397 U.S. 249, 253 (1970) (holding 29–hour detention of mailed package reasonable given unavoidable delay in obtaining warrant and minimal nature of intrusion). Given the nature of the intrusion and the law enforcement interest at stake, this brief seizure of the premises was permissible.

B

Our conclusion that the restriction was lawful finds significant support in this Court's case law. In Segura v. United States, 468 U.S. 796 (1984), the Court considered the admissibility of drugs which the police had found in a lawful, warrant-based search of an apartment, but only after unlawfully entering the apartment and occupying it for 19 hours. The majority held that the drugs were admissible because, had the police acted lawfully throughout, they could have discovered and seized the drugs pursuant to the validly issued warrant. The minority disagreed. However, when describing alternative lawful search and seizure methods, both majority and minority assumed, at least for argument's sake, that the police, armed with reliable information that the apartment contained drugs, might lawfully have sealed the apartment from the outside, restricting entry into the apartment while waiting for the warrant.

In various other circumstances, this Court has upheld temporary restraints where needed to preserve evidence until police could obtain a warrant. See, *e.g.,* United States v. Place (reasonable suspicion justifies brief detention of luggage pending further investigation); Carroll v. United States (warrantless search of automobile constitutionally permissible).

We have found no case in which this Court has held unlawful a temporary seizure that was supported by probable cause and was designed to prevent the loss of evidence while the police diligently obtained a warrant in a reasonable period of time. But cf. Welsh v. Wisconsin (holding warrantless entry into and arrest in home unreasonable despite possibility that evidence of noncriminal offense would be lost while warrant was being obtained).

C

Nor are we persuaded by the countervailing considerations that the parties or lower courts have raised. * * * The Appellate Court of Illinois concluded that the police could not order McArthur to stay outside his home because McArthur's porch, where he stood at the time, was part of his home; hence the order "amounted to a constructive eviction" of McArthur from his residence. This Court has held, however, that a person standing in the doorway of a house is "in a 'public' place," and hence subject to arrest without a warrant permitting entry of the home. United States v. Santana, 427 U.S. 38 (1976). Regardless, we do not believe the difference to which the Appellate Court points—porch versus, *e.g.,* front walk—could make a significant difference here as to the reasonableness of the police restraint; and that, from the Fourth Amendment's perspective, is what matters.

The Appellate Court also found negatively significant the fact that Chief Love, with McArthur's consent, stepped inside the trailer's doorway to observe McArthur when McArthur reentered the trailer on two or three occasions. McArthur, however, reentered simply for his own convenience, to make phone calls and to obtain cigarettes. Under these circumstances, the reasonableness of the greater restriction (preventing reentry) implies the reasonableness of the lesser (permitting reentry conditioned on observation).

Finally, McArthur points to a case (and we believe it is the only case) that he believes offers direct support, namely, Welsh v. Wisconsin, *supra*. *In Welsh, this Court held that police could not enter a home without a warrant in order to prevent the loss of evidence (namely, the defendant's blood alcohol level) of the "nonjailable traffic offense" of driving while intoxicated. McArthur notes that his two convictions are for misdemeanors, which, he says, are as minor, and he adds that the restraint, keeping him out of his home, was nearly as serious.*

We nonetheless find significant distinctions. The evidence at issue here was of crimes that were "jailable," not "nonjailable." In *Welsh,* we noted that, "[g]iven that the classification of state crimes differs widely among the States, the penalty that may attach to any particular offense seems to provide the clearest and most consistent indication of the State's interest in arresting individuals suspected of committing that offense." The same reasoning applies here, where class C misdemeanors include such widely diverse offenses as drag racing, drinking alcohol in a railroad car or on a railroad platform, bribery by a candidate for public office, and assault.

And the restriction at issue here is less serious. Temporarily keeping a person from entering his home, a consequence whenever police stop a person on the street, is considerably less intrusive than police entry into the home itself in order to make a warrantless arrest or conduct a search.

We have explained above why we believe that the need to preserve evidence of a "jailable" offense was sufficiently urgent or pressing to justify the restriction upon entry that the police imposed. We need not decide whether the circumstances before us would have justified a greater restriction for this type of offense or the same restriction were only a "nonjailable" offense at issue.

III

In sum, the police officers in this case had probable cause to believe that a home contained contraband, which was evidence of a crime. They reasonably believed that the home's resident, if left free of any restraint, would destroy that evidence. And they imposed a restraint that was both limited and tailored reasonably to secure law enforcement needs while protecting privacy interests. In our view, the restraint met the Fourth Amendment's demands.

The judgment of the Illinois Appellate Court is reversed, and the case is remanded for further proceedings not inconsistent with this opinion.

[Justice Souter, concurring, noted that the law "can hardly raise incentives to obtain a warrant without giving the police a fair chance to take their probable cause to a magistrate and get one."]

JUSTICE STEVENS, **dissenting.**

* * * As the majority explains, the essential inquiry in this case involves a balancing of the "privacy-related and law enforcement-related concerns to determine if the intrusion was reasonable." Under the specific facts of this case, I believe the majority gets the balance wrong. Each of the Illinois jurists who participated in the decision of this case placed a higher value on the sanctity of the ordinary citizen's home than on the prosecution of this petty offense. They correctly viewed that interest—whether the home be a humble cottage, a secondhand trailer, or a stately mansion—as one meriting the most serious constitutional protection. Following their analysis and the reasoning in our decision in Welsh v. Wisconsin (holding that some offenses may be so minor as to make it unreasonable for police to undertake searches that would be constitutionally permissible if graver offenses were suspected), I would affirm.

H. ADMINISTRATIVE SEARCHES AND OTHER SEARCHES AND SEIZURES BASED ON "SPECIAL NEEDS"

While the warrant clause is still, at least rhetorically, the predominant clause of the Fourth Amendment, the Supreme Court has applied the reasonableness clause to searches conducted for purposes other than traditional criminal law enforcement. The Court has reasoned that the traditional requirement of a warrant based on probable cause is not well-suited to searches for purposes as varied as enforcing school discipline, public safety, and administrative efficiency. If the government search or seizure is designed to effectuate special needs beyond criminal law enforcement, then the Court engages in a balancing of interests under the reasonableness clause to determine what safeguards must apply. Reasonableness analysis balances the need for a particular search or seizure against the degree of invasion upon personal rights that the search or seizure entails. And if the probable cause standard and/or the warrant requirement takes insufficient account of the state interest in light of the degree of the intrusion, then the Court finds it reasonable to dispense with such requirements in favor of lesser standards such as reasonable suspicion, area warrants, or other controls on official discretion.

On the other hand, if the purpose of the search is simply to obtain evidence for purposes of criminal law enforcement, then probable cause and a warrant are presumptively required. See Arizona v. Hicks, 480 U.S. 321 (1987)(holding that, absent "special operational necessities," probable cause is required for a search for evidence); Romo v. Champion, 46 F.3d 1013 (10th Cir.1995)(probable cause not required to search a person driving into a prison parking lot, where the search is conducted for safety purposes; however, if the officers "had executed the search for traditional law enforcement purposes, they presumptively would have needed probable cause.").

As you go through the following cases, it may be helpful to keep the following questions in mind. Has the state established a special need beyond criminal law enforcement for conducting the search or seizure? Why is a need to search for purposes other than criminal law enforcement more important than the need to search to enforce the criminal law? And most importantly, does it make any difference to the citizen that the state intrusion is for a purpose other than traditional criminal law enforcement?

1. *Safety Inspections of Homes*

In Camara v. Municipal Court, 387 U.S. 523 (1967), a homeowner claimed the right to refuse a warrantless entry by a health inspector who desired to inspect the house as provided for in the San Francisco housing code. The Court held that the Fourth Amendment covered these administrative searches. But Justice White's majority opinion said that government safety inspectors were not required to have probable cause to believe that a particular dwelling was in violation of the code being enforced. Rather, area-wide safety inspections are permissible and "it is obvious that 'probable cause' to issue a warrant to inspect must exist if reasonable legislative or administrative standards for conducting an area inspection are satisfied with respect to a particular dwelling." Thus, while a warrant is required for an administrative safety inspection of a home, the warrant need not be based upon a finding of probable cause that a particular home is in violation of a safety code. Instead, the warrant can be issued upon a finding that a search is in compliance with a reasonable administrative scheme. Finally, the opinion noted that "nothing we say today is intended to foreclose prompt inspections, even without a warrant, that the law had traditionally upheld in emergency situations."

In a companion case, See v. City of Seattle, 387 U.S. 541 (1967), the Court, per Justice White, applied the *Camara* requirements—i.e., a warrant based on either probable cause or demonstrated compliance with some reasonable administrative inspection scheme—to inspections of non-residential commercial structures. But, the Court did "not in any way imply that business premises may not reasonably be inspected in many more situations than private homes."

Justice Clark, joined by Justices Harlan and Stewart, dissented in both *Camara* and *See.* They argued that the area warrant concept and the "boxcar" warrant would degrade the Fourth Amendment, and asked: "Why the ceremony, the delay, the expense, the abuse of the search warrant?"

The Assessment of Cause for a Safety Inspection

An official who issues a warrant for a home safety inspection under *Camara* necessarily performs a different function than the magistrate assessing a search warrant application in a criminal investigation. This is because the standard of proof required for a home safety inspection is different from the traditional probable cause standard. A home inspection can be conducted on the basis of such generalized facts as passage of time and the nature of the building, and as part of an area-wide inspection. The Court in *Camara* stressed that review of the reasons for a safety inspection should occur "without any reassessment of the basic agency decision to canvass an area." Thus, the officer issuing a safety inspection warrant is not charged with evaluating the legislative and administrative policy decisions as to frequency of inspection, resource expenditures, and the like. The officer need only decide whether an established inspection policy exists and whether the inspection for which a warrant is sought fits within that program.

What danger does an area-wide warrant, which is not based upon probable cause as to any specific home, guard against? What would be wrong with a rule that safety inspectors could not enter a house without probable cause to believe that there was a safety violation? How would a safety inspector obtain enough information to constitute probable cause? Is a safety inspection of a home less intrusive than a search of a home by law enforcement officers investigating a crime?

Warrants Without Probable Cause?

The *Camara* Court imposed a unique requirement—that a warrant would be required, but that the warrant would be issued upon some objective standard other than probable cause. Subsequently, in Griffin v. Wisconsin, 483 U.S. 868 (1987), the Court again addressed the question whether the Fourth Amendment envisions a warrant that is not based upon particularized probable cause. Griffin, a probationer, challenged the search of his home by his probation officer. One argument in the case was that, even if probable cause was not required for the search of a probationer's home (due to a probationer's diminished expectation of privacy and the state's administrative interest in regulating a probationer), the Court should nonetheless require a warrant to be obtained. Justice Scalia, writing for the Court, contended that the Fourth Amendment could not be read to provide for such a warrant. He reasoned that a warrant based on something other than probable cause would violate the specific language in the Fourth Amendment that "no warrant shall issue, but upon probable cause." He distinguished *Camara* as a case where the Court "arguably came to permit an exception to that prescription for administrative search warrants, which may but do not necessarily have to be issued by courts." Justice Scalia emphasized that the general rule for judicial search warrants is that they can only be issued upon particularized probable cause. Thus, the Court refused to accept the solution of a warrant based on less than probable cause as a means of balancing state and individual interests. It held that a probation officer can conduct a warrantless search of a probationer's house, upon reasonable suspicion of a probation violation.

2. *Administrative Searches of Businesses*

The Court applied the *Camara* protections to businesses in *See*, but it is apparent that administrative searches of businesses involve different issues from searches of residences. For one thing, some entries into business premises may not be searches at all, i.e., if the area inspected is open to the general public. Thus, if the inspector walks through a hotel lobby and looks for fire exits, no reasonable expectation of privacy is implicated. See Donovan v. Lone Steer, Inc., 464 U.S. 408 (1984). Also, an administrative search of a business implicates more complex regulatory concerns: the state has an administrative interest not only in whether the business structure is safe, but also in whether the business is being safely and properly conducted. Moreover, the businessperson may have a diminished expectation of privacy given the nature of the business conducted. But on the other hand, the risk of an arbitrary use of official power to conduct a regulatory search of a business must be a cause for special concern. It is no secret that businesspersons have occasionally been subject to harassment and extortion by unscrupulous investigators. All of these considerations, and the special rules applicable to "closely regulated" businesses, are discussed in the following case.

NEW YORK v. BURGER

Supreme Court of the United States, 1987.
482 U.S. 691.

JUSTICE BLACKMUN **delivered the opinion of the Court.**

This case presents the question whether the warrantless search of an automobile junkyard, conducted pursuant to a statute authorizing such a search, falls within the exception to the warrant requirement for administrative inspections of pervasively regulated industries. The case also presents the question whether an otherwise proper administrative inspection is unconstitutional because the ultimate purpose of the regulatory statute pursuant to which the search is done—the deterrence of criminal behavior—is the same as that of penal laws, with the result that the inspection may dis-

close violations not only of the regulatory statute but also of the penal statutes.

I

Respondent Joseph Burger is the owner of a junkyard in Brooklyn, N.Y. His business consists, in part, of the dismantling of automobiles and the selling of their parts. * * * At approximately noon on November 17, 1982, Officer Joseph Vega and four other plainclothes officers, all members of the Auto Crimes Division of the New York City Police Department, entered respondent's junkyard to conduct an inspection pursuant to N.Y.Veh. & Traf.Law § 415–a5 (McKinney 1986).[a]

a. This statute reads in pertinent part: "Records and identification. (a) * * * Every person required to be registered pursuant to this section shall maintain a record of all motor vehicles, trailers, and major component parts thereof, coming into his possession to-

gether with a record of the disposition of any such motor vehicle, trailer or part thereof and shall maintain proof of ownership for any motor vehicle, trailer or major component part thereof while in his possession. * * * Upon request of an agent of the commissioner or of

On any given day, the Division conducts from 5 to 10 inspections of vehicle dismantlers, automobile junkyards, and related businesses.

Upon entering the junkyard, the officers asked to see Burger's license and his "police book"—the record of the automobiles and vehicle parts in his possession. Burger replied that he had neither a license nor a police book. The officers then announced their intention to conduct a § 415–a5 inspection. * * * In accordance with their practice, the officers copied down the Vehicle Identification Numbers (VINs) of several vehicles and parts of vehicles that were in the junkyard. After checking these numbers against a police computer, the officers determined that respondent was in possession of stolen vehicles and parts. Accordingly, Burger was arrested and charged with five counts of possession of stolen property and one count of unregistered operation as a vehicle dismantler, in violation of § 415–a1.

[The trial court denied a motion to suppress, but the New York Court of Appeals reversed, finding that the statute authorizing the warrantless inspection was unconstitutional.]

II

A

The Court long has recognized that the Fourth Amendment's prohibition on unreasonable searches and seizures is applicable to commercial premises, as well as to private homes. See v. City of Seattle. An owner or operator of a business thus has an expectation of privacy in commercial property, which society is prepared to consider to be reasonable, see Katz v. United States (Harlan, J., concurring). This expectation exists not only with respect to traditional police searches conducted for the gathering of criminal evidence but also with respect to administrative inspections designed to enforce regulatory statutes. See Marshall v. Barlow's, Inc., 436 U.S. 307, 312–313 (1978). An expectation of privacy in commercial premises, however, is different from, and indeed less than, a similar expectation in an individual's home. This expectation is particularly attenuated in commercial property employed in "closely regulated" industries. * * *

The Court first examined the "unique" problem of inspections of "closely regulated" businesses in two enterprises that had "a long tradition of close government supervision." In Colonnade Corp. v. United States, 397 U.S. 72 (1970), it considered a warrantless search of a catering business pursuant to several federal revenue statutes authorizing the inspection of the premises of liquor dealers. Although the Court disapproved the search because the statute provided that a sanction be imposed when entry was refused, and because it did not authorize entry without a warrant as an alternative in this situation, it recognized that "the liquor industry [was] long subject to close supervision and inspection." We returned to this issue in United States v. Biswell, 406 U.S. 311 (1972), which [upheld] a warrantless inspection of the premises of a pawnshop operator, who was federally licensed to sell sporting weapons pursuant to the Gun Control Act of 1968. * * * We observed: "When a dealer chooses to engage in this perva-

---

any police officer and during his regular and usual business hours, a vehicle dismantler shall produce such records and permit said agent or police officer to examine them and any vehicles or parts of vehicles which are subject to the record keeping requirements of this section and which are on the premises.... The failure to produce such records or to permit such inspection on the part of any person required to be registered pursuant to this section as required by this paragraph shall be a class A misdemeanor."

sively regulated business and to accept a federal license, he does so with the knowledge that his business records, firearms, and ammunition will be subject to effective inspection."

The *"Colonnade–Biswell"* doctrine, stating the reduced expectation of privacy by an owner of commercial premises in a "closely regulated" industry, has received renewed emphasis in more recent decisions. In Marshall v. Barlow's, Inc., we noted its continued vitality but declined to find that warrantless inspections, made pursuant to the Occupational Safety and Health Act of 1970, of *all* businesses engaged in interstate commerce fell within the narrow focus of this doctrine. However, we found warrantless inspections made pursuant to the Federal Mine Safety and Health Act of 1977, proper because they were of a "closely regulated" industry. Donovan v. Dewey, 452 U.S. 594 (1981).

Indeed, in Donovan v. Dewey, we declined to limit our consideration to the length of time during which the business in question—stone quarries—had been subject to federal regulation. We pointed out that the doctrine is essentially defined by "the pervasiveness and regularity of the federal regulation" and the effect of such regulation upon an owner's expectation of privacy. We observed, however, that "the duration of a particular regulatory scheme" would remain an "important factor" in deciding whether a warrantless inspection pursuant to the scheme is permissible.[b]

B

Because the owner or operator of commercial premises in a "closely reg-

ulated" industry has a reduced expectation of privacy, the warrant and probable-cause requirements, which fulfill the traditional Fourth Amendment standard of reasonableness for a government search, have lessened application in this context. Rather, we conclude that, as in other situations of "special need" where the privacy interests of the owner are weakened and the government interests in regulating particular businesses are concomitantly heightened, a warrantless inspection of commercial premises may well be reasonable within the meaning of the Fourth Amendment.

This warrantless inspection, however, even in the context of a pervasively regulated business, will be deemed to be reasonable only so long as three criteria are met. First, there must be a "substantial" government interest that informs the regulatory scheme pursuant to which the inspection is made. See Donovan v. Dewey ("substantial federal interest in improving the health and safety conditions in the Nation's underground and surface mines").

Second, the warrantless inspections must be "necessary to further [the] regulatory scheme." For example, in *Dewey* we recognized that forcing mine inspectors to obtain a warrant before every inspection might alert mine owners or operators to the impending inspection, thereby frustrating the purposes of the Mine Safety and Health Act—to detect and thus to deter safety and health violations.

Finally, "the statute's inspection program, in terms of the certainty and regularity of its application, [must] provid[e] a constitutionally adequate substitute for a warrant." In other

b. We explained in Donovan v. Dewey: "If the length of regulation were the only criterion, absurd results would occur. Under appellees' view, new or emerging industries, including ones such as the nuclear power industry that pose enormous potential safety and health problems, could never be subject to warrantless searches even under the most carefully structured inspection program simply because of the recent vintage of regulation."

words, the regulatory statute must perform the two basic functions of a warrant: it must advise the owner of the commercial premises that the search is being made pursuant to the law and has a properly defined scope, and it must limit the discretion of the inspecting officers. To perform this first function, the statute must be "sufficiently comprehensive and defined that the owner of commercial property cannot help but be aware that his property will be subject to periodic inspections undertaken for specific purposes." Donovan v. Dewey. In addition, in defining how a statute limits the discretion of the inspectors, we have observed that it must be "carefully limited in time, place, and scope." United States v. Biswell.

III

A

Searches made pursuant to § 415–a5, in our view, clearly fall within this established exception to the warrant requirement for administrative inspections in "closely regulated" businesses. First, the nature of the regulatory statute reveals that the operation of a junkyard, part of which is devoted to vehicle dismantling, is a "closely regulated" business in the State of New York. The provisions regulating the activity of vehicle dismantling are extensive. An operator cannot engage in this industry without first obtaining a license, which means that he must meet the registration requirements and must pay a fee. Under § 415–a5(a), the operator must maintain a police book recording the acquisition and disposition of motor vehicles and vehicle parts, and make such records and inventory available for inspection by the police or any agent of the Department of Motor Vehicles. The operator also must display his registration number prominently at his place of business, on business documentation,

and on vehicles and parts that pass through his business. Moreover, the person engaged in this activity is subject to criminal penalties, as well as to loss of license or civil fines, for failure to comply with these provisions. That other States besides New York have imposed similarly extensive regulations on automobile junkyards further supports the "closely regulated" status of this industry.

In determining whether vehicle dismantlers constitute a "closely regulated" industry, the "duration of [this] particular regulatory scheme" has some relevancy. Section 415–a could be said to be of fairly recent vintage, and the inspection provision of § 415–a5 was added only in 1979. But because the automobile is a relatively new phenomenon in our society and because its widespread use is even newer, automobile junkyards and vehicle dismantlers have not been in existence very long and thus do not have an ancient history of government oversight. * * *

The automobile-junkyard business, however, is simply a new branch of an industry that has existed, and has been closely regulated, for many years. The automobile junkyard is closely akin to the secondhand shop or the general junkyard. * * * As such, vehicle dismantlers represent a modern, specialized version of a traditional activity. In New York, general junkyards and secondhand shops long have been subject to regulation. * * * The history of government regulation of junk-related activities argues strongly in favor of the "closely regulated" status of the automobile junkyard.

Accordingly, in light of the regulatory framework governing his business and the history of regulation of related industries, an operator of a junkyard engaging in vehicle dismantling has a reduced expectation of privacy in this "closely regulated" business.

B

The New York regulatory scheme satisfies the three criteria necessary to make reasonable warrantless inspections pursuant to § 415–a5. First, the State has a substantial interest in regulating the vehicle-dismantling and automobile-junkyard industry because motor vehicle theft has increased in the State and because the problem of theft is associated with this industry. In this day, automobile theft has become a significant social problem, placing enormous economic and personal burdens upon the citizens of different States. * * *

Second, regulation of the vehicle-dismantling industry reasonably serves the State's substantial interest in eradicating automobile theft. It is well established that the theft problem can be addressed effectively by controlling the receiver of, or market in, stolen property. Automobile junkyards and vehicle dismantlers provide the major market for stolen vehicles and vehicle parts. Thus, the State rationally may believe that it will reduce car theft by regulations that prevent automobile junkyards from becoming markets for stolen vehicles and that help trace the origin and destination of vehicle parts.

Moreover, the warrantless administrative inspections pursuant to § 415–a5 "are necessary to further [the] regulatory scheme." Donovan v. Dewey. * * * We explained in *Biswell:*

"[I]f inspection is to be effective and serve as a credible deterrent, unannounced, even frequent, inspections are essential. In this context, the prerequisite of a warrant

could easily frustrate inspection; and if the necessary flexibility as to time, scope, and frequency is to be preserved, the protections afforded by a warrant would be negligible."

* * * Because stolen cars and parts often pass quickly through an automobile junkyard, "frequent" and "unannounced" inspections are necessary in order to detect them. In sum, surprise is crucial if the regulatory scheme aimed at remedying this major social problem is to function at all.

Third, § 415–a5 provides a "constitutionally adequate substitute for a warrant." The statute informs the operator of a vehicle dismantling business that inspections will be made on a regular basis. Thus, the vehicle dismantler knows that the inspections to which he is subject do not constitute discretionary acts by a government official but are conducted pursuant to statute. Section 415–a5 also sets forth the scope of the inspection and, accordingly, places the operator on notice as to how to comply with the statute. In addition, it notifies the operator as to who is authorized to conduct an inspection.

Finally, the "time, place, and scope" of the inspection is limited to place appropriate restraints upon the discretion of the inspecting officers. The officers are allowed to conduct an inspection only "during [the] regular and usual business hours."ᶜ The inspections can be made only of vehicle-dismantling and related industries. And the permissible scope of these searches is narrowly defined: the inspectors may examine the records, as well as "any vehicles or parts of vehicles which are subject to the record

---

c. Respondent contends that § 415–a5 is unconstitutional because it fails to limit the number of searches that may be conducted of a particular business during any given period. While such limitations, or the absence thereof,

are a factor in an analysis of the adequacy of a particular statute, they are not determinative of the result so long as the statute, as a whole, places adequate limits upon the discretion of the inspecting officers. * * *

keeping requirements of this section and which are on the premises."

IV

* * * The Court of Appeals, nevertheless, struck down the statute as violative of the Fourth Amendment because, in its view, the statute had no truly administrative purpose but was "designed simply to give the police an expedient means of enforcing penal sanctions for possession of stolen property." The court rested its conclusion that the administrative goal of the statute was pretextual and that § 415–a5 really "authorize[d] searches undertaken solely to uncover evidence of criminality" particularly on the fact that, even if an operator failed to produce his police book, the inspecting officers could continue their inspection for stolen vehicles and parts. The court also suggested that the identity of the inspectors—police officers—was significant in revealing the true nature of the statutory scheme.

In arriving at this conclusion, the Court of Appeals failed to recognize that a State can address a major social problem *both* by way of an administrative scheme *and* through penal sanctions. Administrative statutes and penal laws may have the same *ultimate* purpose of remedying the social problem, but they have different subsidiary purposes and prescribe different methods of addressing the problem. An administrative statute establishes how a particular business in a "closely regulated" industry should be operated, setting forth rules to guide an operator's conduct of the business and allowing government officials to ensure that those rules are followed. Such a regulatory approach contrasts with that of the penal laws, a major emphasis of which is the punishment of individuals for specific acts of behavior.

* * * The New York penal laws address automobile theft by punishing it

or the possession of stolen property, including possession by individuals in the business of buying and selling property. In accordance with its interest in regulating the automobile-junkyard industry, the State also has devised a regulatory manner of dealing with this problem. Section 415–a, as a whole, serves the regulatory goals of seeking to ensure that vehicle dismantlers are legitimate businesspersons and that stolen vehicles and vehicle parts passing through automobile junkyards can be identified. * * *

If the administrative goals of § 415–a5 are recognized, the difficulty the Court of Appeals perceives in allowing inspecting officers to examine vehicles and vehicle parts even in the absence of records evaporates. The regulatory purposes of § 415–a5 certainly are served by having the inspecting officers compare the records of a particular vehicle dismantler with vehicles and vehicle parts in the junkyard. The purposes of maintaining junkyards in the hands of legitimate businesspersons and of tracing vehicles that pass through these businesses, however, *also* are served by having the officers examine the operator's inventory even when the operator, for whatever reason, fails to produce the police book. Forbidding inspecting officers to examine the inventory in this situation would permit an illegitimate vehicle dismantler to thwart the purposes of the administrative scheme and would have the absurd result of subjecting his counterpart who maintained records to a more extensive search.

Nor do we think that this administrative scheme is unconstitutional simply because, in the course of enforcing it, an inspecting officer may discover evidence of crimes, besides violations of the scheme itself. * * * The discovery of evidence of crimes in the course of an otherwise proper administrative inspection does not render that search illegal or the administrative scheme suspect.

Finally, we fail to see any constitutional significance in the fact that police officers, rather than "administrative" agents, are permitted to conduct the § 415–a5 inspection. The significance respondent alleges lies in the role of police officers as enforcers of the penal laws and in the officers' power to arrest for offenses other than violations of the administrative scheme. It is, however, important to note that state police officers, like those in New York, have numerous duties in addition to those associated with traditional police work. As a practical matter, many States do not have the resources to assign the enforcement of a particular administrative scheme to a specialized agency. So long as a regulatory scheme is properly administrative, it is not rendered illegal by the fact that the inspecting officer has the power to arrest individuals for violations other than those created by the scheme itself. In sum, we decline to impose upon the States the burden of requiring the enforcement of their regulatory statutes to be carried out by specialized agents.

* * *

JUSTICE BRENNAN, with whom JUSTICE MARSHALL joins, and with whom JUSTICE O'CONNOR joins as to all but Part III, dissenting.

* * *

I

* * *

The provisions governing vehicle dismantling in New York simply are not extensive. A vehicle dismantler must register and pay a fee, display the registration in various circumstances, maintain a police book, and allow inspections. Of course, the inspections themselves cannot be cited as proof of pervasive regulation justifying elimination of the warrant requirement; that would be obvious bootstrapping. Nor can registration and recordkeeping requirements be characterized as close regulation. New York City, like many States and municipalities, imposes similar, and often more stringent licensing, recordkeeping, and other regulatory requirements on a myriad of trades and businesses. Few substantive qualifications are required of an aspiring vehicle dismantler; no regulation governs the condition of the premises, the method of operation, the hours of operation, the equipment utilized, etc. This scheme stands in marked contrast to, e.g., the mine safety regulations relevant in Donovan v. Dewey.

In sum, if New York City's administrative scheme renders the vehicle-dismantling business closely regulated, few businesses will escape such a finding. * * *

II

Even if vehicle dismantling were a closely regulated industry, I would nonetheless conclude that this search violated the Fourth Amendment. * * *

* * * There is neither an upper nor a lower limit on the number of searches that may be conducted at any given operator's establishment in any given time period. Neither the statute, nor any regulations, nor any regulatory body, provides limits or guidance on the selection of vehicle dismantlers for inspection. * * *

The Court also maintains that this statute effectively limits the scope of the search. * * * Plainly, a statute authorizing a search which can uncover *no* administrative violations is not sufficiently limited in scope to avoid the warrant requirement. This statute fails to tailor the scope of administrative inspection to the particular concerns posed by the regulated business. * * * The conduct of the police in this case underscores this point. The police removed identification numbers from a walker and a wheelchair, neither of which fell within the statutory scope of a permissible administrative search.

* * * The *sole* limitation I see on a police search of the premises of a vehicle dismantler is that it must occur during business hours; otherwise it is open season. The unguided discretion afforded police in this scheme precludes its substitution for a warrant.

III

The fundamental defect in § 415–a5 is that it authorizes searches intended solely to uncover evidence of criminal acts. * * *

Here the State has * * * circumvented the requirements of the Fourth Amendment by altering the label placed on the search. This crucial point is most clearly illustrated by the fact that the police copied the serial numbers from a wheelchair and a handicapped person's walker that were found on the premises, and determined that these items had been stolen. * * * The scope of the search alone reveals that it was undertaken solely to uncover evidence of criminal wrongdoing.

Moreover, it is factually impossible that the search was intended to discov-

er wrongdoing subject to administrative sanction. Burger stated that he was not registered to dismantle vehicles as required by § 415–a1, and that he did not have a police book, as required by § 415–a5(a). At that point he had violated every requirement of the administrative scheme. There is no administrative provision forbidding possession of stolen automobiles or automobile parts. The inspection became a search for evidence of criminal acts when all possible administrative violations had been uncovered.

* * *

The Court thus implicitly holds that if an administrative scheme has certain goals and if the search serves those goals, it may be upheld even if no concrete administrative consequences could follow from a particular search. This is a dangerous suggestion, for the goals of administrative schemes often overlap with the goals of the criminal law. * * * If the Fourth Amendment is to retain meaning in the commercial context, it must be applied to searches for evidence of criminal acts even if those searches would also serve an administrative purpose, unless that administrative purpose takes the concrete form of seeking an administrative violation.

* * *

Administrative Searches of Businesses After Burger

What precisely are the limitations on administrative inspections of businesses after *Burger*? Has the Court imposed sufficient controls on official discretion? Did Justice Brennan overreact? Analysis in some lower court cases after *Burger* would suggest that he did not. In United States v. Hernandez, 901 F.2d 1217 (5th Cir.1990), an FBI agent who suspected that a commercial truck was carrying drugs followed the truck for twenty-four hours and 600 miles. He then notified the Texas Department of Public Safety that a truck believed to be carrying drugs was traveling on the interstate with no license plates. The DPS officer stopped the truck and demanded a driver's license and a bill of lading describing the cargo. The driver failed to produce evidence of Texas Interstate Commerce Commission Motor Carrier authorization. The officer then walked to the back of the truck and opened an inspection port, a small door used to check the temperature of the cargo. He smelled marijuana, obtained the keys to the cargo door, and a search of the truck uncovered 98 bales of marijuana. The court of appeals found that, while there was probable cause to arrest for the license plate violation, this did not provide probable cause to search the truck; nor was the search permissible as a search incident to arrest, because it went beyond the passenger compartment; nor was it permissible as a protective search under *Terry,* because the officer had no reasonable suspicion of bodily harm that necessitated looking into the cargo area. But the search was permissible as an administrative search under *Burger.* The court concluded that a Texas civil statute regulating motor carriers authorized any Department of Public Safety Officer to inspect any load of commodities being transported for hire over the highways of the state. Could the DPS officer have searched a car to determine whether it was carrying commercial goods without a commercial license? If so, wouldn't that mean that the DPS officer could search any car on the highway without suspicion?

The Element of Surprise

The Court justified the warrantless search in *Burger* partly because surprise was necessary. The concern was that the officer would go to Burger's business without a warrant, and would be refused admission; then, when the officer went to get a warrant, Burger would destroy or dispose of evidence of an administrative violation. The Court therefore held that Burger had no right to refuse a warrantless inspection; to permit such refusal would deprive the inspector of the element of surprise that is often necessary to further regulatory interests.

Of course, the concern about loss of the surprise factor does not really answer why an officer couldn't be required to get a warrant *before* approaching Burger's business the first time around. Then the officer could conduct a surprise inspection *with a warrant.* The court in Lesser v. Espy, 34 F.3d 1301 (7th Cir.1994), confronted the question about the element of surprise discussed in *Burger*, and proffered an explanation. *Lesser* involved the constitutionality of a warrantless inspection of a farm that raised rabbits to be used as laboratory animals. The court discussed the surprise element as follows:

> In rabbit farming many of the potential deficiencies that would violate the [Animal Welfare] Act can be quickly concealed. See, e.g., 9 C.F.R. §§ 3.50(c) (improper storage of food); 3.50(d) (improper waste disposal); 3.50(e) (unclean washrooms); 3.56(a) (unsanitary primary enclosures). Thus the Department correctly observes that preserving the element of surprise and the possibility of frequent inspections is necessary in order to detect violators. In response the Lessers rightly point out that the element of surprise may be easily maintained even with a warrant requirement—a warrant may be issued ex parte and executed without prior notice. Nevertheless, we believe a warrant requirement for the most routine inspection would interfere with the Department's ability to function and unnecessarily increase the cost of the Secretary's operations without a significant increase in privacy, especially since all licensed suppliers of research animals have a reasonable expectation of at least a couple of regular inspections * * * each year.

Thus, the need for surprise is really a false issue—the question is whether officials who undoubtedly need to make surprise inspections should be burdened with a warrant requirement. The *Lesser* Court, following *Burger*, determines that the minimal privacy interest protected by a warrant requirement is outweighed by the inconvenience of having to obtain a warrant before every single administrative inspection. Would you balance the interests in the same way? Is the *Lesser* reasoning based on the fact that most businesspersons would find it in their interest to submit to an administrative inspection in the first instance, which would mean that administrative inspectors would be obtaining warrants that they would by and large never have to use? Is that a legitimate reason for dispensing with the warrant requirement?

By the way, what would be wrong with having the rabbit farmer "cover up" his violations during the period after his refusal when the administrative inspector would have to go and get a warrant (assuming the inspector did not get one in the first instance)? Doesn't "cover up" mean "fix" in this circumstance? Isn't the goal of the administrative inspection to get the owner to repair the premises?

Administrative Inspections by Law Enforcement Officers

The Court in *Burger* held that the administrative nature of an inspection was not negated simply because the inspector was a law enforcement officer. Nonetheless, courts after *Burger* have applied a stricter scrutiny to so-called "administrative" searches when they are conducted by law enforcement officers. For example, in United States v. Johnson, 994 F.2d 740 (10th Cir.1993), an FBI agent received information (not amounting to probable cause) that Johnson, a taxidermist, was involved in the illegal smuggling of protected animals. He called a state agent, who agreed to accompany the federal agent, ostensibly to conduct an administrative taxidermy inspection. The applicable statute authorized warrantless administrative inspections of taxidermists, but only when performed by state agents. The federal agent drove 300 miles to Johnson's taxidermy shop in order to be present for the inspection; he also participated actively in the search of the business. The investigators discovered several specimens of illegally imported animals. The court held that "the administrative search was employed solely as an instrument of criminal law enforcement." Consequently, all of the evidence was illegally obtained. The court reasoned as follows:

> The presence and active participation of the federal agent during the search of Mr. Johnson's shop, and the federal agent's insistence that the state agent accompany him establish as a matter of law that the federal agent used the state regulatory inspection as a pretext for an investigatory search. Federal agents may not cloak themselves with the authority granted by state inspection statutes in order to seek evidence of criminal activity and avoid the Fourth Amendment's warrant requirement.

Recall the discussion of pretext earlier in this Chapter. Was the inspection in *Johnson* really pretextual, given the fact that the state agent had the right to conduct a warrantless administrative inspection? Or, can it be argued that *Whren* permits otherwise pretextual searches and arrests only when there is probable cause? If that is so, then courts can still regulate for pretext when police officers seek to conduct a suspicionless "administrative" search that is really for purposes of criminal law enforcement. See also United States v. Knight, 306 F.3d 534 (8th Cir. 2002) (police officer's search of truck, purportedly pursuant to a state safety inspection program, was illegal when officer searched the trucker's briefcase: "We believe that, as a general matter, rummaging through a persons' belongings is more likely to serve the purpose of 'crime control' than the enforcement of a regulatory scheme.").

3. Searches and Seizures of Individuals Pursuant to "Special Needs"

The Court has used its special needs balancing analysis in a series of cases to uphold civil-based searches of individuals in the absence of a warrant and probable cause. The first cases upheld suspicion-based searches, where the government had reasonable suspicion, but not probable cause, to justify a civil-based search. Then the Court decided a series of cases raising the question whether civil-based searches could be conducted in the absence of any suspicion at all.

a. Searches and Seizures on the Basis of Reasonable Suspicion Rather Than Probable Cause

In New Jersey v. T.L.O., 469 U.S. 325 (1985), a school official searched the handbag of a student. The official had reasonable suspicion, but not probable cause to believe that cigarettes were in the student's purse. In the absence of probable cause, the search could not be justified as a criminal-based search for evidence. Nor could the search be justified under the *Terry* doctrine, since the administrator had no basis for believing that the student posed a risk of bodily harm. Nonetheless, the Court upheld the search. The Court reasoned that the search effectuated "special needs" beyond ordinary criminal law enforcement— specifically the state's need to assure a safe and healthy learning environment. This finding of special needs permitted the Court to balance the state interest at stake in the search against the student's interest in privacy.

The *T.L.O.* Court found that the reasonable suspicion standard was sufficient to protect the student's diminished expectation of privacy in the school environment, while permitting the government the proper degree of leeway in maintaining standards of school discipline. If probable cause was required, school officials would be unable to regulate disciplinary problems at an early stage. Finally, the Court held that a warrant would not be required for searches conducted by school officials; school officials could not be expected to obtain a judicial warrant before seeking to enforce school disciplinary standards.

The *T.L.O.* analysis was used by the Court to uphold warrantless searches of the office of a government official, and of the house of a probationer. O'Connor v. Ortega, 480 U.S. 709 (1987); Griffin v. Wisconsin, supra. In both *O'Connor* and *Griffin*, as in *T.L.O.*, the Court found that conditioning searches on probable cause would be deleterious to the state interest, and that the reasonable suspicion standard was an appropriate balance between state and individual interests.

Note on More Intrusive Searches

In *T.L.O.*, the Court required individualized suspicion for a search of a student's handbag. This raises the question whether a "special needs" search could be so intrusive as to require the more stringent standard of probable cause. Consider the facts of Cornfield by Lewis v. School Dist. No. 230, 991 F.2d 1316 (7th Cir.1993):

Brian Cornfield was enrolled in a behavioral disorder program at Carl Sandburg High School. Kathy Stacy, a teacher's aide in that program, found him outside the school building in violation of school rules * * *. When she reported the infraction to Richard Spencer, Cornfield's teacher, and Dean Richard Frye, Stacy also alerted them to her suspicion that Cornfield appeared "too well-endowed." [Other teachers] corroborated Stacy's observation of an unusual bulge in Cornfield's crotch area. * * * Believing the sixteen-year Cornfield was "crotching" drugs, Spencer and Frye asked him to accompany them * * *.

* * * Believing a pat down to be excessively intrusive and ineffective at detecting drugs, Spencer and Frye escorted Cornfield to the boys' locker room to conduct a strip search. After making certain that no one else was present in the locker room, they locked the door. Spencer then stood about fifteen feet from Cornfield, and Frye was standing on the opposite side, approximately ten to twelve feet away, while they had him remove his street clothes and put on a gym uniform. Spencer and Frye visually inspected his naked body and physically inspected his clothes. Neither man performed a body cavity search. They found no evidence of drugs or any other contraband.

Cornfield brought a civil rights action for a violation of his Fourth Amendment rights. The court noted that "as the intrusiveness of the search of a student intensifies, so too does the Fourth Amendment standard of reasonableness," and that probable cause might well be required for an extremely intrusive search. Cornfield argued that the search in the locker room was so intrusive as to be unreasonable in the absence of probable cause. But the court found the search to be reasonable, downplaying the seriousness of the intrusion:

> On the one hand, the sixteen-year-old Cornfield was of an age at which children are extremely self-conscious about their bodies; thus, the potential impact of a strip search was substantial. However, given Spencer and Frye's suspicion that Cornfield was crotching drugs, their conclusion that a strip search was the least intrusive way to confirm or deny their suspicions was not unreasonable. As administered, two male school personnel performed the search and did so in the privacy of the boys' locker room. * * * Spencer and Frye did not physically touch him or subject him to a body cavity search, nor did they have him suffer the indignity of standing naked before them but allowed him to put on a gym uniform while they searched his street clothes.

What would the school officials have had to do before probable cause would be required to support their actions? Could they have inspected Cornfield's body cavities on reasonable suspicion that he was hiding drugs?

See also Jenkins by Hall v. Talladega City Board of Education, 115 F.3d 821 (11th Cir.1997), a civil rights action brought on behalf of two second-grade students. A school official strip-searched them, having only reasonable suspicion and not probable cause to believe that they had stolen $7.00 from a classmate's purse. The court did not find it necessary to determine whether the students' Fourth Amendment rights had been violated. This was because government officials are entitled to qualified immunity in civil rights actions brought under 42 U.S.C. § 1983; this means that officials are not liable unless they have violated "clearly established" constitutional law. The court concluded that the general balancing of interests test set forth by the Supreme Court in *T.L.O.* was insufficiently specific to provide any clearly established law on the subject of school searches. Judge Kravitch dissented, declaring that the theft of $7.00, "although morally reprehensible, poses no threat of physical danger to other students and cannot, therefore, serve as the basis for a search of this magnitude." Could it be argued that a strip search of second-graders would be unreasonable even if the school official had probable cause to believe that the students had stolen $7.00?

    b.   Suspicionless Searches of Persons on the Basis of "Special Needs"

Drug-Testing of Employees

    T.L.O, O'Connor, and *Griffin* each permitted "special needs" searches on the basis of reasonable suspicion rather than probable cause. None of those cases considered whether a "special needs" search could be conducted without any suspicion that the person searched has violated any law or regulation. Subsequently the Court, in companion cases, considered the constitutionality of suspicionless drug-testing of public employees. In Skinner v. Railway Labor Executives' Ass'n, 489 U.S. 602 (1989), the Court upheld a program mandating drug tests for all railroad personnel involved in certain train accidents. Thus, the plan called for suspicionless testing of all personnel involved in the accident. Failing the test would result in loss of employment. Justice Kennedy, writing for the Court, made the following points:

    1.   The program was subject to Fourth Amendment scrutiny, because the drug-testing was essentially required by federal regulation. Therefore, even though it was administered by a private employer, it was not a private party search beyond the purview of the Fourth Amendment.

    2.   Drug testing of urine is a search within the meaning of the Fourth Amendment, because it can reveal private information (such as pregnancy or epilepsy), and because the process of monitoring the employee's act of urination implicates privacy interests.

    3.   The government's interest in regulating the conduct of railroad employees to ensure safety "presents 'special needs' beyond normal law enforcement that may justify departures from the usual warrant and probable-cause requirements."

    4.   A warrant was not required to subject the railroad employees to drug-testing, because, "in light of the standardized nature of the tests and the minimal discretion vested in those charged with administering the program, there are virtually no facts for a neutral magistrate to evaluate." Moreover, the railroad supervisors responsible for administering the testing program "are not in the business of investigating violations of the criminal laws or enforcing administrative codes, and otherwise have little occasion to become familiar with the intricacies of this Court's Fourth Amendment jurisprudence."

    5.   The drug-testing program was reasonable even though it provided for testing in the absence of any individualized suspicion of drug use. Justice Kennedy declared: "where the privacy interests implicated by the search are minimal, and where an important governmental interest furthered by the intrusion would be placed in jeopardy by a requirement of individualized suspicion, a search may be reasonable despite the absence of such suspicion." The urine testing was not very intrusive, because "[t]he regulations do not require that samples be furnished under the direct observation of a monitor, despite the desirability of such a procedure to ensure the integrity of the sample. The sample is also collected in a medical environment, by

personnel unrelated to the railroad employer, and is thus not unlike similar procedures encountered often in the context of a regular physical examination." Furthermore, the expectations of privacy of covered employees was "diminished by reason of their participation in an industry that is regulated pervasively to ensure safety, a goal dependent, in substantial part, on the health and fitness of covered employees." Finally, the state interests at stake were "compelling," and could not be accommodated by a requirement of individualized suspicion. Employees subject to the tests "discharge duties fraught with such risks of injury to others that even a momentary lapse of attention can have disastrous consequences." Drug-testing provides an effective means of deterring drug use, because employees in safety-sensitive positions "know they will be tested upon the occurrence of a triggering event, the timing of which no employee can predict with certainty." Also, drug-testing will "help railroads obtain invaluable information about the causes of major accidents, and to take appropriate measures to safeguard the general public."

6. A requirement of particularized suspicion of drug use would "seriously impede an employer's ability to obtain this information, despite its obvious importance." This is because "[o]btaining evidence that might give rise to the suspicion that a particular employee is impaired, a difficult endeavor in the best of circumstances, is most impracticable in the aftermath of a serious accident."

Justice Stevens concurred in part and in the judgment in *Skinner*. He was dubious, however, about the deterrent effect of drug-testing in the railroad context, reasoning that workers would "not go to work with the expectation that they may be involved in a major accident," and that "if the risk of serious personal injury does not deter their use of these substances, it seems highly unlikely that the additional threat of loss of employment would have any effect on their behavior."

Justice Marshall, joined by Justice Brennan, dissented in *Skinner*. He argued that the Court's reliance on the reasonableness clause was fundamentally flawed. He criticized the Court for rejecting the probable cause requirement for "a manipulable balancing inquiry under which, upon the mere assertion of a 'special need,' even the deepest dignitary and privacy interests become vulnerable to governmental incursion."

In National Treasury Employees Union v. Von Raab, 489 U.S. 656 (1989), a case decided the same day as *Skinner,* the Court upheld compelled urinalysis of certain Customs Service employees. Drug tests were made a condition of obtaining employment for three types of positions in the Customs Service: those involving drug interdiction, those requiring the employee to carry a firearm, and those in which the employee would handle "classified documents." The employee was allowed to produce the sample privately, but to protect against adulteration, "a monitor of the same sex as the employee remains close at hand to listen for the normal sounds of urination." Customs employees who tested positive for drugs and who could offer no satisfactory explanation were subject to dismissal from the Service; but the testing results could not be turned over to a criminal prosecutor without the employee's consent.

Justice Kennedy again wrote the opinion for the Court. He found that the drug-testing served special needs beyond criminal law enforcement, specifically the need for safety and to ensure that customs employees responsible for controlling the flow of drugs into the country are not on drugs themselves. Balancing the state and individual interests, Justice Kennedy concluded that a warrant was not required for the testing, since the event which triggered the testing—the employee's decision to apply for a covered position—could admit of no discretion. The Court found that suspicionless testing was reasonable as applied to two of the three covered types of employees—those involved in drug interdiction and those carrying handguns. Justice Kennedy noted that "the Government has a compelling interest in ensuring that front-line personnel are physically fit, and have unimpeachable integrity and judgment," and that the public interest "likewise demands effective measures to prevent the promotion of drug users to positions that require the incumbent to carry a firearm." The majority asserted that these two classes of employees had a diminished expectation of privacy, because the positions depended uniquely on the employees' "judgment and dexterity." Justice Kennedy also emphasized that the testing procedures were designed to minimize the intrusion involved, to the extent possible without sacrificing the reliability of the test.

The Court in *Von Raab* found itself unable to assess the reasonableness of suspicionless testing as applied to the third category of employees, those handling classified documents. The Court remanded this aspect of the case, and explained as follows:

> It is not clear * * * whether the category defined by the Service's testing directive encompasses only those Customs employees likely to gain access to sensitive information. Employees who are tested under the Service's scheme include those holding such diverse positions as "Accountant," "Accounting Technician," "Animal Caretaker," "Attorney (All)," "Baggage Clerk," "Co-op Student (All)," "Electric Equipment Repairer," "Mail Clerk/Assistant," and "Messenger." * * * [I]t is not evident that those occupying these positions are likely to gain access to sensitive information, and this apparent discrepancy raises in our minds the question whether the Service has defined this category of employees more broadly than is necessary to meet the purposes of the Commissioner's directive.

What If There Is No Record of Drug Abuse?

The most difficult issue for the majority in *Von Raab* was that the Customs Service had implemented the drug-testing program even though there was no documented drug problem among Customs employees. This was unlike the situation in *Skinner,* where the drug problem among railroad employees, and the risk therefrom, was well-documented. Those who challenged the plan in *Von Raab* argued that suspicionless drug-testing was unreasonable unless it could be justified as responsive to and effective against a documented drug problem. Justice Kennedy rejected this argument in the following analysis:

> Detecting drug impairment on the part of employees can be a difficult task, especially where, as here, it is not feasible to subject employees and their work product to the kind of day-to-day scrutiny that is the norm in more traditional office environments. Indeed, the almost unique mission of the Service gives the Government a compelling interest in ensuring that many of these covered employees do not use drugs even off duty, for such use

creates risks of bribery and blackmail against which the Government is entitled to guard. In light of the extraordinary safety and national security hazards that would attend the promotion of drug users to positions that require the carrying of firearms or the interdiction of controlled substances, the Service's policy of deterring drug users from seeking such promotions cannot be deemed unreasonable.

The mere circumstance that all but a few of the employees tested are entirely innocent of wrongdoing does not impugn the program's validity. * * * The Service's program is designed to prevent the promotion of drug users to sensitive positions as much as it is designed to detect those employees who use drugs. Where, as here, the possible harm against which the Government seeks to guard is substantial, the need to prevent its occurrence furnishes an ample justification for reasonable searches calculated to advance the Government's goal.

In a footnote, Justice Kennedy compared suspicionless drug-testing to suspicionless searches at airports.

As Judge Friendly explained in a leading case upholding such searches:

"When the risk is the jeopardy to hundreds of human lives and millions of dollars of property inherent in the pirating or blowing up of a large airplane, that danger *alone* meets the test of reasonableness, so long as the search is conducted in good faith for the purpose of preventing hijacking or like damage and with reasonable scope and the passenger has been given advance notice of his liability to such a search so that he can avoid it by choosing not to travel by air." United States v. Edwards, 498 F.2d 496, 500 (C.A.2 1974) (emphasis in original).

* * * [W]e would not suppose that, if the validity of these searches be conceded, the Government would be precluded from conducting them absent a demonstration of danger as to any particular airport or airline. It is sufficient that the Government have a compelling interest in preventing an otherwise pervasive societal problem from spreading to the particular context.

Nor would we think, in view of the obvious deterrent purpose of these searches, that the validity of the Government's airport screening program necessarily turns on whether significant numbers of putative air pirates are actually discovered by the searches conducted under the program. * * * When the Government's interest lies in deterring highly hazardous conduct, a low incidence of such conduct, far from impugning the validity of the scheme for implementing this interest, is more logically viewed as a hallmark of success.

Justice Marshall, joined by Justice Brennan, dissented in *Von Raab* for the reasons stated in *Skinner*. Justice Scalia, joined by Justice Stevens, both of whom found suspicionless drug-testing to be reasonable in *Skinner,* dissented in *Von Raab*. Justice Scalia explained his differing votes in the two cases as follows:

I joined the Court's opinion [in *Skinner*] because the demonstrated frequency of drug and alcohol use by the targeted class of employees, and the demonstrated connection between such use and grave harm, rendered the search a reasonable means of protecting society. I decline to join the Court's opinion in the present case because neither frequency of use nor connection to harm is demonstrated or even likely. In my view the Customs Service rules are a kind of immolation of privacy and human dignity in symbolic opposition to drug use.

Justice Scalia rejected the majority's generalization that no American workplace is free from the drug problem. He responded that such a generalization could perhaps suffice "if the workplace at issue could produce such catastrophic social harm that no risk whatever is tolerable—the secured areas of a nuclear power plant for example." Justice Scalia noted that suspicionless testing for nuclear power plant employees in sensitive jobs had been upheld even without a showing of a drug problem. See Rushton v. Nebraska Public Power District, 844 F.2d 562 (8th Cir.1988). See also Thomson v. Marsh, 884 F.2d 113 (4th Cir.1989) (suspicionless testing of personnel in chemical weapons plant upheld). He responded, however, that if the majority considered that the threat posed by drug-addicted Customs officials was comparable to that found in *Rushton*, "then the Fourth Amendment has become frail protection indeed." He noted that this reasoning would extend approval of suspicionless drug testing to vast numbers of public employees, including "automobile drivers, operators of other potentially dangerous equipment, construction workers, school crossing guards."

Drug–Testing of Schoolchildren

In *T.L.O.*, the Court upheld a search of a student's handbag where the school official had reasonable suspicion that the bag contained cigarettes. The Court did not foreclose the possibility that suspicionless searches of schoolchildren might be reasonable in certain circumstances. The Supreme Court has taken up that question in two cases: *Vernonia School District 47J v. Acton,* and the following case, which discusses *Vernonia* in detail.

BOARD OF EDUCATION OF INDEPENDENT SCHOOL DISTRICT NO. 92 OF POTTAWATOMIE COUNTY v. EARLS

Supreme Court of the United States, 2002.
536 U.S. 822.

JUSTICE THOMAS **delivered the opinion of the Court.**

The Student Activities Drug Testing Policy implemented by the Board of Education of Independent School District No. 92 of Pottawatomie County (School District) requires all students who participate in competitive extracurricular activities to submit to drug testing. Because this Policy reasonably serves the School District's important interest in detecting and preventing drug use among its students, we hold that it is constitutional.

I

The city of Tecumseh, Oklahoma, is a rural community located approximately 40 miles southeast of Oklahoma City. The School District administers all Tecumseh public schools. In the fall of 1998, the School District adopted the Student Activities Drug Testing Policy (Policy), which requires all middle and high school students to consent to drug testing in order to participate in any extracurricular activity. In practice, the Policy has been applied only to competitive extracurricular activities sanctioned by the Oklahoma Secondary Schools Activities

Association, such as the Academic Team, Future Farmers of America, Future Homemakers of America, band, choir, pom pon, cheerleading, and athletics. Under the Policy, students are required to take a drug test before participating in an extracurricular activity, must submit to random drug testing while participating in that activity, and must agree to be tested at any time upon reasonable suspicion. The urinalysis tests are designed to detect only the use of illegal drugs, including amphetamines, marijuana, cocaine, opiates, and barbituates, not medical conditions or the presence of authorized prescription medications.

At the time of their suit, both respondents attended Tecumseh High School. Respondent Lindsay Earls was a member of the show choir, the marching band, the Academic Team, and the National Honor Society. Respondent Daniel James sought to participate in the Academic Team. Together with their parents, Earls and James brought a 42 U.S.C. § 1983 action against the School District, challenging the Policy both on its face and as applied to their participation in extracurricular activities. They alleged that the Policy violates the Fourth Amendment as incorporated by the Fourteenth Amendment and requested injunctive and declarative relief. They also argued that the School District failed to identify a special need for testing students who participate in extracurricular activities, and that the "Drug Testing Policy neither addresses a proven problem nor promises to bring any benefit to students or the school."

Applying the principles articulated in Vernonia School Dist. 47J v. Acton, 515 U.S. 646 (1995), in which we upheld the suspicionless drug testing of school athletes, the United States District Court for the Western District of Oklahoma rejected respondents' claim

that the Policy was unconstitutional and granted summary judgment to the School District. The court noted that "special needs" exist in the public school context and that, although the School District did "not show a drug problem of epidemic proportions," there was a history of drug abuse starting in 1970 that presented "legitimate cause for concern." The District Court also held that the Policy was effective because "[i]t can scarcely be disputed that the drug problem among the student body is effectively addressed by making sure that the large number of students participating in competitive, extracurricular activities do not use drugs."

The United States Court of Appeals for the Tenth Circuit reversed, holding that the Policy violated the Fourth Amendment. The Court of Appeals agreed with the District Court that the Policy must be evaluated in the "unique environment of the school setting," but reached a different conclusion as to the Policy's constitutionality. Before imposing a suspicionless drug testing program, the Court of Appeals concluded that a school "must demonstrate that there is some identifiable drug abuse problem among a sufficient number of those subject to the testing, such that testing that group of students will actually redress its drug problem." * * *. We granted certiorari, and now reverse.

II

* * * Searches by public school officials, such as the collection of urine samples, implicate Fourth Amendment interests. We must therefore review the School District's Policy for "reasonableness," which is the touchstone of the constitutionality of a governmental search.

In the criminal context, reasonableness usually requires a showing of probable cause. The probable-cause standard, however, "is peculiarly related to criminal investigations" and may be unsuited to determining the reasonableness of administrative searches where the "Government seeks to *prevent* the development of hazardous conditions." Treasury Employees v. Von Raab. The Court has also held that a warrant and finding of probable cause are unnecessary in the public school context because such requirements "would unduly interfere with the maintenance of the swift and informal disciplinary procedures that are needed." *Vernonia, supra,* at 653.

Given that the School District's Policy is not in any way related to the conduct of criminal investigations, see Part II–B, *infra,* respondents do not contend that the School District requires probable cause before testing students for drug use. Respondents instead argue that drug testing must be based at least on some level of individualized suspicion. It is true that we generally determine the reasonableness of a search by balancing the nature of the intrusion on the individual's privacy against the promotion of legitimate governmental interests. But we have long held that "the Fourth Amendment imposes no irreducible requirement of [individualized] suspicion." United States v. Martinez—Fuerte, 428 U.S. 543, 561 (1976). "[I]n certain limited circumstances, the Government's need to discover such latent or hidden conditions, or to prevent their development, is sufficiently compelling to justify the intrusion on privacy entailed by conducting such searches without any measure of individualized suspicion." *Von Raab, supra,* at 668. Therefore, in the context of safety and administrative regulations, a search unsupported by probable cause may be reasonable "when 'special needs, beyond the normal need for law enforcement, make the

warrant and probable-cause requirement impracticable.' "Griffin v. Wisconsin, 483 U.S. 868, 873 (1987).

Significantly, this Court has previously held that "special needs" inhere in the public school context. See *Vernonia, supra,* at 653. While schoolchildren do not shed their constitutional rights when they enter the schoolhouse, "Fourth Amendment rights . . . are different in public schools than elsewhere; the 'reasonableness' inquiry cannot disregard the schools' custodial and tutelary responsibility for children." *Vernonia, supra,* at 656. In particular, a finding of individualized suspicion may not be necessary when a school conducts drug testing.

In *Vernonia,* this Court held that the suspicionless drug testing of athletes was constitutional. The Court, however, did not simply authorize all school drug testing, but rather conducted a fact-specific balancing of the intrusion on the children's Fourth Amendment rights against the promotion of legitimate governmental interests. Applying the principles of *Vernonia* to the somewhat different facts of this case, we conclude that Tecumseh's Policy is also constitutional.

A

We first consider the nature of the privacy interest allegedly compromised by the drug testing. As in *Vernonia,* the context of the public school environment serves as the backdrop for the analysis of the privacy interest at stake and the reasonableness of the drug testing policy in general.

A student's privacy interest is limited in a public school environment where the State is responsible for maintaining discipline, health, and safety. Schoolchildren are routinely required to submit to physical examinations and vaccinations against disease. Securing order in the school environment sometimes requires that students be subjected to greater controls than those appropriate for adults.

Respondents argue that because children participating in nonathletic extracurricular activities are not subject to regular physicals and communal undress, they have a stronger expectation of privacy than the athletes tested in *Vernonia.* This distinction, however, was not essential to our decision in *Vernonia,* which depended primarily upon the school's custodial responsibility and authority.

In any event, students who participate in competitive extracurricular activities voluntarily subject themselves to many of the same intrusions on their privacy as do athletes. Some of these clubs and activities require occasional off-campus travel and communal undress. All of them have their own rules and requirements for participating students that do not apply to the student body as a whole. * * * This regulation of extracurricular activities further diminishes the expectation of privacy among schoolchildren. We therefore conclude that the students affected by this Policy have a limited expectation of privacy.

B

Next, we consider the character of the intrusion imposed by the Policy. Urination is an excretory function traditionally shielded by great privacy. But the "degree of intrusion" on one's privacy caused by collecting a urine sample "depends upon the manner in which production of the urine sample is monitored." *Vernonia, supra,* at 658.

Under the Policy, a faculty monitor waits outside the closed restroom stall for the student to produce a sample and must "listen for the normal sounds of urination in order to guard against tampered specimens and to in-

sure an accurate chain of custody." The monitor then pours the sample into two bottles that are sealed and placed into a mailing pouch along with a consent form signed by the student. This procedure is virtually identical to that reviewed in *Vernonia,* except that it additionally protects privacy by allowing male students to produce their samples behind a closed stall. Given that we considered the method of collection in *Vernonia* a "negligible" intrusion, the method here is even less problematic.

In addition, the Policy clearly requires that the test results be kept in confidential files separate from a student's other educational records and released to school personnel only on a "need to know" basis. Respondents nonetheless contend that the intrusion on students' privacy is significant because the Policy fails to protect effectively against the disclosure of confidential information and, specifically, that the school "has been careless in protecting that information: for example, the Choir teacher looked at students' prescription drug lists and left them where other students could see them." But the choir teacher is someone with a "need to know," because during off-campus trips she needs to know what medications are taken by her students. * * * In any event, there is no allegation that any other student did see such information. This one example of alleged carelessness hardly increases the character of the intrusion.

Moreover, the test results are not turned over to any law enforcement authority. Nor do the test results here lead to the imposition of discipline or have any academic consequences. Rather, the only consequence of a failed drug test is to limit the student's privilege of participating in extracurricular activities. Indeed, a student may test positive for drugs twice and still be allowed to participate in extracurricular activities. After the first positive test, the school contacts the student's parent or guardian for a meeting. The student may continue to participate in the activity if within five days of the meeting the student shows proof of receiving drug counseling and submits to a second drug test in two weeks. For the second positive test, the student is suspended from participation in all extracurricular activities for 14 days, must complete four hours of substance abuse counseling, and must submit to monthly drug tests. Only after a third positive test will the student be suspended from participating in any extracurricular activity for the remainder of the school year, or 88 school days, whichever is longer.

Given the minimally intrusive nature of the sample collection and the limited uses to which the test results are put, we conclude that the invasion of students' privacy is not significant.

C

Finally, this Court must consider the nature and immediacy of the government's concerns and the efficacy of the Policy in meeting them. See *Vernonia,* 515 U.S., at 660. This Court has already articulated in detail the importance of the governmental concern in preventing drug use by schoolchildren. The drug abuse problem among our Nation's youth has hardly abated since *Vernonia* was decided in 1995. * * * As in *Vernonia,* "the necessity for the State to act is magnified by the fact that this evil is being visited not just upon individuals at large, but upon children for whom it has undertaken a special responsibility of care and direction." The health and safety risks identified in *Vernonia* apply with equal force to Tecumseh's children. Indeed, the nationwide drug epidemic makes the war against drugs a pressing concern in every school.

Additionally, the School District in this case has presented specific evidence of drug use at Tecumseh schools. Teachers testified that they had seen students who appeared to be under the influence of drugs and that they had heard students speaking openly about using drugs. A drug dog found marijuana cigarettes near the school parking lot. Police officers once found drugs or drug paraphernalia in a car driven by a Future Farmers of America member. And the school board president reported that people in the community were calling the board to discuss the "drug situation." We decline to second-guess the finding of the District Court that "[v]iewing the evidence as a whole, it cannot be reasonably disputed that the [School District] was faced with a 'drug problem' when it adopted the Policy."

Respondents consider the proffered evidence insufficient and argue that there is no "real and immediate interest" to justify a policy of drug testing nonathletes. We have recognized, however, that "[a] demonstrated problem of drug abuse ... [is] not in all cases necessary to the validity of a testing regime," but that some showing does "shore up an assertion of special need for a suspicionless general search program." Chandler v. Miller, 520 U.S. 305, 319 (1997). The School District has provided sufficient evidence to shore up the need for its drug testing program.

Furthermore, this Court has not required a particularized or pervasive drug problem before allowing the government to conduct suspicionless drug testing. For instance, in *Von Raab* the Court upheld the drug testing of customs officials on a purely preventive basis, without any documented history of drug use by such officials. In response to the lack of evidence relating to drug use, the Court noted generally that "drug abuse is one of the most serious problems confronting our society today," and that programs to prevent and detect drug use among customs officials could not be deemed unreasonable. Likewise, the need to prevent and deter the substantial harm of childhood drug use provides the necessary immediacy for a school testing policy. Indeed, it would make little sense to require a school district to wait for a substantial portion of its students to begin using drugs before it was allowed to institute a drug testing program designed to deter drug use.

Given the nationwide epidemic of drug use, and the evidence of increased drug use in Tecumseh schools, it was entirely reasonable for the School District to enact this particular drug testing policy. * * * As we cannot articulate a threshold level of drug use that would suffice to justify a drug testing program for schoolchildren, we refuse to fashion what would in effect be a constitutional quantum of drug use necessary to show a "drug problem."

Respondents also argue that the testing of nonathletes does not implicate any safety concerns, and that safety is a "crucial factor" in applying the special needs framework. * * *. Respondents are correct that safety factors into the special needs analysis, but the safety interest furthered by drug testing is undoubtedly substantial for all children, athletes and nonathletes alike. We know all too well that drug use carries a variety of health risks for children, including death from overdose.

We also reject respondents' argument that drug testing must presumptively be based upon an individualized reasonable suspicion of wrongdoing because such a testing regime would be less intrusive. In this context, the Fourth Amendment does not require a finding of individualized suspicion, and we decline to impose such a requirement on schools attempting to prevent and detect drug use by students. Moreover, we question whether testing based on individualized suspicion in fact would be less intrusive. Such a regime would place an additional burden on public school teachers who are already tasked with the difficult job of maintaining order and discipline. A program of individualized suspicion might unfairly target members of unpopular groups. The fear of lawsuits resulting from such targeted searches may chill enforcement of the program, rendering it ineffective in combating drug use. See *Vernonia*, 515 U.S., at 663–664 (offering similar reasons for why "testing based on 'suspicion' of drug use would not be better, but worse"). In any case, this Court has repeatedly stated that reasonableness under the Fourth Amendment does not require employing the least intrusive means, because "[t]he logic of such elaborate less-restrictive-alternative arguments could raise insuperable barriers to the exercise of virtually all search-and-seizure powers." *Martinez–Fuerte*, 428 U.S., at 556–557, n. 12.

Finally, we find that testing students who participate in extracurricular activities is a reasonably effective means of addressing the School District's legitimate concerns in preventing, deterring, and detecting drug use. While in *Vernonia* there might have been a closer fit between the testing of athletes and the trial court's finding that the drug problem was "fueled by the 'role model' effect of athletes' drug use," such a finding was not essential to the holding. *Vernonia* did not require the school to test the group of students most likely to use drugs, but rather considered the constitutionality of the program in the context of the public school's custodial responsibilities. Evaluating the Policy in this context, we conclude that the drug testing of Tecumseh students who participate in extracurricular activities effectively serves the School District's interest in protecting the safety and health of its students.

III

Within the limits of the Fourth Amendment, local school boards must assess the desirability of drug testing schoolchildren. In upholding the constitutionality of the Policy, we express no opinion as to its wisdom. Rather, we hold only that Tecumseh's Policy is a reasonable means of furthering the School District's important interest in preventing and deterring drug use among its schoolchildren. Accordingly, we reverse the judgment of the Court of Appeals.

It is so ordered.

Justice Breyer, concurring.

* * * The school's drug testing program addresses a serious national problem by focusing upon demand, avoiding the use of criminal or disciplinary sanctions, and relying upon professional counseling and treatment. In my view, this program does not violate the Fourth Amendment's prohibition of "unreasonable searches and seizures." I reach this conclusion primarily for the reasons given by the Court, but I would emphasize several underlying considerations, which I understand to be consistent with the Court's opinion.

I

* * *

II

In respect to the privacy-related burden that the drug testing program imposes upon students, I would emphasize the following: First, not everyone would agree with this Court's characterization of the privacy-related significance of urine sampling as "negligible." Some find the procedure no more intrusive than a routine medical examination, but others are seriously embarrassed by the need to provide a urine sample with someone listening "outside the closed restroom stall." When trying to resolve this kind of close question involving the interpretation of constitutional values, I believe it important that the school board provided an opportunity for the airing of these differences at public meetings designed to give the entire community "the opportunity to be able to participate" in developing the drug policy. The board used this democratic, participatory process to uncover and to resolve differences, giving weight to the fact that the process, in this instance, revealed little, if any, objection to the proposed testing program.

Second, the testing program avoids subjecting the entire school to testing. And it preserves an option for a conscientious objector. He can refuse testing while paying a price (nonparticipation) that is serious, but less severe than expulsion from the school.

Third, a contrary reading of the Constitution, as requiring "individualized suspicion" in this public school context, could well lead schools to push the boundaries of "individualized suspicion" to its outer limits, using subjective criteria that may "unfairly target members of unpopular groups," or leave those whose behavior is slightly abnormal stigmatized in the minds of others. See Belsky, Random vs. Suspicion–Based Drug Testing in the Public Schools—A Surprising Civil Liberties Dilemma, 27 Okla. City U.L.Rev. 1, 20–21 (forthcoming 2002) (listing court-approved factors justifying suspicion-based drug testing, including tiredness, overactivity, quietness, boisterousness, sloppiness, excessive meticulousness, and tardiness).

* * *

JUSTICE GINSBURG, **with whom** JUSTICE STEVENS, JUSTICE O'CONNOR, **and** JUSTICE SOUTER **join, dissenting.**

Seven years ago, in Vernonia School Dist. 47J v. Acton, 515 U.S. 646 (1995), this Court determined that a school district's policy of randomly testing the urine of its student athletes for illicit drugs did not violate the Fourth Amendment. In so ruling, the Court emphasized that drug use "increase[d] the risk of sports—related injury" and that Vernonia's athletes were the "leaders" of an aggressive local "drug culture" that had reached " 'epidemic proportions.' "*Id.*, at 649. Today, the Court relies upon *Vernonia* to permit a school district with a drug problem its superintendent repeatedly described as "not . . . major," to test the urine of an academic team member solely by reason of her participation in a nonathletic, competitive extracurricular activity—participation associated with neither special dangers from, nor particular predilections for, drug use.

* * *

I

A

* * *

This case presents circumstances dispositively different from those of *Vernonia*. True, as the Court stresses, Tecumseh students participating in competitive extracurricular activities other than athletics share two relevant characteristics with the athletes of *Vernonia*. First, both groups attend public schools. * * * Concern for student health and safety is basic to the school's caretaking, and it is undeniable that "drug use carries a variety of health risks for children, including death from overdose."

Those risks, however, are present for *all* schoolchildren. *Vernonia* cannot be read to endorse invasive and suspicionless drug testing of all students upon any evidence of drug use, solely because drugs jeopardize the life and health of those who use them. Many children, like many adults, engage in dangerous activities on their own time; that the children are enrolled in school scarcely allows government to monitor all such activities. * * * Had the *Vernonia* Court agreed that public school attendance, in and of itself, permitted the State to test each student's blood or urine for drugs, the opinion in *Vernonia* could have saved many words. See, *e.g.,* 515 U.S., at 662 ("[I]t must not be lost sight of that [the Vernonia School District] program is directed . . . to drug use by school athletes, where the risk of immediate physical harm to the drug user or those with whom he is playing his sport is particularly high.").

The second commonality to which the Court points is the voluntary character of both interscholastic athletics and other competitive extracurricular activities. * * *

While extracurricular activities are "voluntary" in the sense that they are not required for graduation, they are part of the school's educational program; for that reason, the petitioner (hereinafter School District) is justified in expending public resources to make them available. Participation in such activities is a key component of school life, essential in reality for students applying to college, and, for all participants, a significant contributor to the breadth and quality of the educational experience. Students "volunteer" for extracurricular pursuits in the same way they might volunteer for honors classes: They subject themselves to additional requirements, but they do so in order to take full advantage of the education offered them.

Voluntary participation in athletics has a distinctly different dimension: Schools regulate student athletes discretely because competitive school sports by their nature require communal undress and, more important, expose students to physical risks that schools have a duty to mitigate. For the very reason that schools cannot offer a program of competitive athletics without intimately affecting the privacy of students, *Vernonia* reasonably analogized school athletes to "adults who choose to participate in a closely regulated industry." * * * Interscholastic athletics similarly require close safety and health regulation; a school's choir, band, and academic team do not.

In short, *Vernonia* applied, it did not repudiate, the principle that "the legality of a search of a student should depend simply on the reasonableness, *under all the circumstances*, of the search." Enrollment in a public school, and election to participate in school activities beyond the bare minimum that the curriculum requires, are indeed factors relevant to reasonableness, but they do not on their own justify intrusive, suspicionless searches. * * *

B

* * *

[T]he "nature and immediacy of the governmental concern," *Vernonia*, 515 U.S., at 660, faced by the Vernonia School District dwarfed that confronting Tecumseh administrators. Vernonia initiated its drug testing policy in response to an alarming situation: "[A] large segment of the student body, particularly those involved in interscholastic athletics, was in a state of

rebellion ... fueled by alcohol and drug abuse as well as the student[s'] misperceptions about the drug culture." *Id.*, at 649. Tecumseh, by contrast, repeatedly reported to the Federal Government during the period leading up to the adoption of the policy that "types of drugs [other than alcohol and tobacco] including controlled dangerous substances, are present [in the schools] but have not identified themselves as major problems at this time." * * *

The School District cites Treasury Employees v. Von Raab, in which this Court permitted random drug testing of customs agents absent "any perceived drug problem among Customs employees," given that "drug abuse is one of the most serious problems confronting our society today." See also Skinner v. Railway Labor Executives' Assn. (upholding random drug and alcohol testing of railway employees based upon industry-wide, rather than railway-specific, evidence of drug and alcohol problems). The tests in *Von Raab* and *Railway Labor Executives*, however, were installed to avoid enormous risks to the lives and limbs of others, not dominantly in response to the health risks to users invariably present in any case of drug use.

Not only did the Vernonia and Tecumseh districts confront drug problems of distinctly different magnitudes, they also chose different solutions: Vernonia limited its policy to athletes; Tecumseh indiscriminately subjected to testing all participants in competitive extracurricular activities. * * *

At the margins, of course, no policy of *random* drug testing is perfectly tailored to the harms it seeks to address. The School District cites the dangers faced by members of the band, who must "perform extremely precise routines with heavy equipment and instruments in close proximity to other students," and by Future Farmers of America, who "are required to individually control and restrain animals as large as 1500 pounds." For its part, the United States acknowledges that "the linebacker faces a greater risk of serious injury if he takes the field under the influence of drugs than the drummer in the halftime band," but parries that "the risk of injury to a student who is under the influence of drugs while playing golf, cross country, or volleyball (sports covered by the policy in *Vernonia*) is scarcely any greater than the risk of injury to a student ... handling a 1500–pound steer (as [Future Farmers of America] members do) or working with cutlery or other sharp instruments (as [Future Homemakers of America] members do)." * * * Notwithstanding nightmarish images of out-of-control flatware, livestock run amok, and colliding tubas disturbing the peace and quiet of Tecumseh, the great majority of students the School District seeks to test in truth are engaged in activities that are not safety sensitive to an unusual degree. There is a difference between imperfect tailoring and no tailoring at all.

The Vernonia district, in sum, had two good reasons for testing athletes: Sports team members faced special health risks and they "were the leaders of the drug culture." *Vernonia*, 515 U.S., at 649. No similar reason, and no other tenable justification, explains Tecumseh's decision to target for testing all participants in every competitive extracurricular activity.

Nationwide, students who participate in extracurricular activities are significantly less likely to develop substance abuse problems than are their less-involved peers. * * * Tecumseh's policy thus falls short doubly if deterrence is its aim: It invades the privacy of students who need deterrence least, and risks steering students at greatest risk for substance abuse away from extracurricular involvement that potentially may palliate drug problems.

To summarize, this case resembles *Vernonia* only in that the School Districts in both cases conditioned engagement in activities outside the obligatory curriculum on random subjection to urinalysis. The defining characteristics of the two programs, however, are entirely dissimilar. The Vernonia district sought to test a subpopulation of students distinguished by their reduced expectation of privacy, their special susceptibility to drug-related injury, and their heavy involvement with drug use. The Tecumseh district seeks to test a much larger population associated with none of these factors. It does so, moreover, without carefully safeguarding student confidentiality and without regard to the program's untoward effects. A program so sweeping is not sheltered by *Vernonia;* its unreasonable reach renders it impermissible under the Fourth Amendment.

II

* * *

For the reasons stated, I would affirm the judgment of the Tenth Circuit declaring the testing policy at issue unconstitutional.

Question After Earls

Can a school district now mandate random drug-testing of *all* public school students, whether or not they wish to participate in extracurricular activities? If not, why not?

Drug-Testing of Politicians

In the following case, the Court appeared to draw back somewhat from its previous cases supporting suspicionless drug-testing on the basis of "special needs." Note, however, that *Earls* was decided *after* this case–so it might be concluded that whatever protections exist under the following opinion are not available to public school students.

CHANDLER v. MILLER

Supreme Court of the United States, 1997.
520 U.S. 305.

JUSTICE GINSBURG **delivered the opinion of the Court.**

* * *

Georgia requires candidates for designated state offices to certify that they have taken a drug test and that the test result was negative. We confront in this case the question whether that requirement ranks among the limited circumstances in which suspicionless searches are warranted. Relying on this Court's precedents sustaining drug-testing programs for student athletes, customs employees, and railway employees, see Vernonia School Dist. 47J v. Acton (random drug testing of students who participate in interscholastic sports); Treasury Dept. v. Von Raab (drug tests for United States Customs Service employees who seek transfer or promotion to certain positions); Skinner v. Railway Labor Executives' Assn. (drug and alcohol tests for railway employees involved in train accidents and for those who violate particular safety rules), the United States Court of Appeals for the Eleventh Circuit judged Georgia's law constitutional. We reverse that judgment. Georgia's requirement that candidates for state office pass a drug test, we hold, does not fit within the closely guarded category of constitutionally permissible suspicionless searches.

* * *

I

The prescription at issue, approved by the Georgia Legislature in 1990, orders that "each candidate seeking to qualify for nomination or election to a state office shall as a condition of such qualification be required to certify that such candidate has tested negative for illegal drugs." Georgia was the first, and apparently remains the only, State to condition candidacy for state office on a drug test.

Under the Georgia statute, to qualify for a place on the ballot, a candidate must present a certificate from a state-approved laboratory, in a form approved by the Secretary of State, reporting that the candidate submitted to a urinalysis drug test within 30 days prior to qualifying for nomination or election and that the results were negative. The statute lists as "illegal drugs": marijuana, cocaine, opiates, amphetamines, and phencyclidines. The designated state offices are: "the Governor, Lieutenant Governor, Secretary of State, Attorney General, State School Superintendent, Commissioner of Insurance, Commissioner of Agriculture, Commissioner of Labor, Justices of the Supreme Court, Judges of the Court of Appeals, judges of the superior courts, district attorneys, members of the General Assembly, and members of the Public Service Commission."

Candidate drug tests are to be administered in a manner consistent with the United States Department of Health and Human Services Guidelines, or other professionally valid procedures approved by Georgia's Commissioner of Human Resources. A candidate may provide the test specimen at a laboratory approved by the State, or at the office of the candidate's personal physician. Once a urine sample is obtained, an approved laboratory determines whether any of the five specified illegal drugs are present, and prepares a certificate reporting the test results to the candidate.

Petitioners were Libertarian Party nominees in 1994 for state offices subject to the requirements of [the statute]. * * ** * * Naming as defendants Governor Zell D. Miller and two other state officials involved in the administration of § 21–2–140, petitioners requested declaratory and injunctive relief barring enforcement of the statute. * * * In January 1995, the District Court entered final judgment for respondents.

[The Eleventh Circuit upheld the statute, despite any showing of a drug problem among candidates for office. The Court of Appeals relied heavily on *Von Raab*. It stated that "those vested with the highest executive authority to make public policy in general and frequently to supervise Georgia's drug interdiction efforts in particular must be persons appreciative of the perils of drug use." It also found that candidates have a diminished expectation of privacy, because "candidates for high office must expect the voters to demand some disclosures about their physical, emotional, and mental fitness for the position."]

* * *

II

* * *

To be reasonable under the Fourth Amendment, a search ordinarily must be based on individualized suspicion of wrongdoing. See *Vernonia*. But particularized exceptions to the main rule are sometimes warranted based on "special needs, beyond the normal need for law enforcement." When such "special needs"—concerns other than crime detection—are alleged in justification of a Fourth Amendment intrusion, courts must undertake a context-specific inquiry, examining closely the competing private and public interests advanced by the parties. * * *

A

[The Court reviews *Skinner, Von Raab, and Vernonia*, noting as to *Vernonia* that the drug-testing program's "context was critical, for local governments bear large responsibilities, under a public school system, as guardian and tutor of children entrusted to its care", and noting further that the District Court's findings in *Vernonia* established that student athletes were "leaders of the drug culture."]

B

* * * Because the State has effectively limited the invasiveness of the testing procedure, we concentrate on the core issue: Is the certification requirement warranted by a special need?

Our precedents establish that the proffered special need for drug testing must be substantial—important enough to override the individual's acknowledged privacy interest, sufficiently vital to suppress the Fourth Amendment's normal requirement of individualized suspicion. Georgia has failed to show * * * a special need of that kind.

Respondents' defense of the statute rests primarily on the incompatibility of unlawful drug use with holding high state office. The statute is justified, respondents contend, because the use of illegal drugs draws into question an official's judgment and integrity; jeopardizes the discharge of public functions, including antidrug law enforcement efforts; and undermines public confidence and trust in elected officials. The statute, according to respondents, serves to deter unlawful drug users from becoming candidates and thus stops them from attaining high state office. Notably lacking in respondents' presentation is any indication of a concrete danger demanding departure from the Fourth Amendment's main rule.

Nothing in the record hints that the hazards respondents broadly describe are real and not simply hypothetical for Georgia's polity. The statute was not enacted, as counsel for respondents readily acknowledged at oral argument, in response to any fear or suspicion of drug use by state officials * * *. A demonstrated problem of drug abuse, while not in all cases necessary to the validity of a testing regime, see *Von Raab*, would shore up an assertion of special need for a suspicionless general search program. Proof of unlawful drug use may help to clarify—and to substantiate—the precise hazards posed by such use. Thus, the evidence of drug and alcohol use by railway employees engaged in safety-sensitive tasks in *Skinner*, and the immediate crisis prompted by a sharp rise in students' use of unlawful drugs in *Vernonia*, bolstered the government's and school officials' arguments that drug-testing programs were warranted and appropriate.

In contrast to the effective testing regimes upheld in *Skinner, Von Raab*, and *Vernonia*, Georgia's certification requirement is not well designed to identify candidates who violate antidrug laws. Nor is the scheme a credible means to deter illicit drug users

from seeking election to state office. The test date—to be scheduled by the candidate anytime within 30 days prior to qualifying for a place on the ballot—is no secret. As counsel for respondents acknowledged at oral argument, users of illegal drugs, save for those prohibitively addicted, could abstain for a pretest period sufficient to avoid detection.* * * Moreover, respondents have offered no reason why ordinary law enforcement methods would not suffice to apprehend such addicted individuals, should they appear in the limelight of a public stage. * * *

Respondents and the United States as amicus curiae rely most heavily on our decision in *Von Raab*, which sustained a drug-testing program for Customs Service officers prior to promotion or transfer to certain high-risk positions, despite the absence of any documented drug abuse problem among Service employees. * * *

Hardly a decision opening broad vistas for suspicionless searches, *Von Raab* must be read in its unique context. As the Customs Service reported in announcing the testing program, "[Customs employees], more than any other Federal workers, are routinely exposed to the vast network of organized crime that is inextricably tied to illegal drug use." We stressed that "drug interdiction had become the agency's primary enforcement mission," and that the employees in question would have "access to vast sources of valuable contraband." Furthermore, Customs officers "had been the targets of bribery by drug smugglers on numerous occasions," and several had succumbed to the temptation.

Respondents overlook a telling difference between *Von Raab* and Georgia's candidate drug-testing program. In *Von Raab* it was "not feasible to subject employees [required to carry firearms or concerned with interdiction of controlled substances] and their work product to the kind of day-to-day scrutiny that is the norm in more traditional office environments." Candidates for public office, in contrast, are subject to relentless scrutiny—by their peers, the public, and the press. Their day-to-day conduct attracts attention notably beyond the norm in ordinary work environments.

What is left, after close review of Georgia's scheme, is the image the State seeks to project. By requiring candidates for public office to submit to drug testing, Georgia displays its commitment to the struggle against drug abuse. The suspicionless tests, according to respondents, signify that candidates, if elected, will be fit to serve their constituents free from the influence of illegal drugs. But Georgia asserts no evidence of a drug problem among the State's elected officials, those officials typically do not perform high-risk, safety-sensitive tasks, and the required certification immediately aids no interdiction effort. The need revealed, in short, is symbolic, not "special," as that term draws meaning from our case law.

* * *

* * * However well-meant, the candidate drug test Georgia has devised diminishes personal privacy for a symbol's sake. The Fourth Amendment shields society against that state action.

III

* * *

We reiterate * * * that where the risk to public safety is substantial and real, blanket suspicionless searches calibrated to the risk may rank as "rea-

sonable"—for example, searches now routine at airports and at entrances to courts and other official buildings. But where, as in this case, public safety is not genuinely in jeopardy, the Fourth Amendment precludes the suspicionless search, no matter how conveniently arranged.

* * *

Reversed.

CHIEF JUSTICE REHNQUIST, **dissenting.**

* * * It would take a bolder person than I to say that * * * widespread drug usage could never extend to candidates for public office such as Governor of Georgia. The Court says that "nothing in the record hints that the hazards respondents broadly describe are real and not simply hypothetical for Georgia's polity." But surely the State need not wait for a drug addict, or one inclined to use drugs illegally, to run for or actually become Governor before it installs a prophylactic mechanism.

* * *

Under normal Fourth Amendment analysis, the individual's expectation of privacy is an important factor in the equation. But here, the Court perversely relies on the fact that a candidate for office gives up so much privacy * * * as a reason for sustaining a Fourth Amendment claim. The Court says, in effect, that the kind of drug test for candidates required by the Georgia law is unnecessary, because the scrutiny to which they are already subjected by reason of their candidacy will enable people to detect any drug use on their part.

* * *

Note on Vernonia, Earls and Chandler

Does it make sense to you that a 13-year-old who wants to join the school chess team can be forced to take a drug test, while a candidate for Governor of a State cannot be so forced? In light of the privacy interests that each of these people could be thought to have, shouldn't it be the other way around? Can it simply be explained by the fact that the Court considers the school environment, and the state's relationship to schoolchildren, unique? For a critique of the school drug-testing cases and *Chandler*, see Dery, Are Politicians More Deserving of Privacy than Schoolchildren? How Chandler v. Miller Exposed the Absurdities of Fourth Amendment "Special Needs" Balancing, 40 Ariz.L.Rev. 73 (1998).

Drug-Testing Cases After Chandler

It should come as no surprise that drug-testing cases are all over the map after *Chandler*. In *Chandler,* the Court second-guessed whether a drug-testing plan would be effective in controlling drug abuse—such second-guessing was missing in the Court's previous cases, and in the subsequent case of *Earls.* In *Chandler*, the Court held that people with minimal privacy interests could not be subject to drug-testing that was relatively non-intrusive. The emphasis in the previous cases, and in *Earls*, was to the contrary.

For a taste of the differing results after *Chandler,* see, e.g., 19 Solid Waste Dept. Mech. v. City of Albuquerque, 156 F.3d 1068 (10th Cir.1998) (invalidating suspicionless searches of trash truck mechanics as not justified by a "special need"; stating that after *Chandler,* "even if the privacy interest is virtually non-existent, the special need requirement prevents suspicionless searches where the government has failed to show either that it has a real interest in testing or that its test will further its proffered interest."); Knox County Educ. Assoc. v. Knox County Board of Education, 158 F.3d 361 (6th Cir.1998) (random testing of all teachers permitted, even though no showing of a drug problem was made; *Chandler* is distinguished on the grounds that teachers are more important than politicians, and teachers "are not subject to the same day-to-day scrutiny as are candidates for public office"); United Teachers v. School Bd. Through Holmes, 142 F.3d 853 (5th Cir.1998) (suspicionless testing of all teachers injured in the course of employment violates the Fourth Amendment; the court concluded that "there is an insufficient nexus between suffering an injury at work and drug impairment").

In *19 Solid Waste Dept.,* supra, the Court found it necessary after *Chandler* to inquire into the effectiveness of the drug-testing plan. It held the plan ineffective (thus not furthering a "special need") in part because the employees were tested only once every four years. It therefore concluded that "this program is not at all well-designed to detect drug use among its employees and lacks deterrent effect." Would the court have been happier with a plan that required employees to be tested every day? Does the court mean that the more pervasive (and intrusive) the testing plan, the more it is likely to fulfil a special need and thus be reasonable? Can't the same perverse argument be found in *Chandler*, where the Court says that the plan is unreasonable because candidates receive 30 days advance notice? Is the court saying that surprise inspections, though obviously more upsetting to the citizen, are more reasonable?

HIV Testing

Can suspicionless, mandatory testing for HIV ever be considered reasonable? Does HIV testing raise different privacy concerns than drug-testing? In

People v. Adams, 149 Ill.2d 331, 173 Ill.Dec. 600, 597 N.E.2d 574 (1992), the court rejected a Fourth Amendment challenge to an Illinois statute that required mandatory HIV testing for defendants convicted of prostitution-related crimes and other sexual misconduct. The court found that the government has a "special need" in stopping the spread of AIDS and in informing and treating those who may have had sexual contact with a person who is HIV-positive. This need was effectuated by targeting defendants convicted of sex-related crimes. The court recognized that those tested had a substantial privacy interest in the results (including an interest in not knowing that they are HIV positive). But the court held that the statute was written to minimize any intrusion on privacy interests; the statute provides that the results of the test are to be sealed and delivered to the trial judge for a determination of whether and to whom the results may be revealed. The court reasoned that a requirement of individualized suspicion would be unworkable, because outward manifestations of AIDS do not occur until long after a person becomes infected with the virus.

Do you agree with the result in *Adams*? If the purpose of the statute is to control the spread of AIDS and to inform persons who have come into contact with them, how can this interest be effectuated if the results of the test remain confidential? Other cases upholding suspicionless HIV testing include Dunn v. White, 880 F.2d 1188 (10th Cir.1989) (random HIV testing of prisoners upheld, even though no showing was made that there was an AIDS problem in the prison); Love v. Superior Court, 226 Cal.App.3d 736, 276 Cal.Rptr. 660 (1990) (upholding suspicionless HIV testing of persons convicted of soliciting an act of prostitution); In re Juveniles, 121 Wn.2d 80, 847 P.2d 455 (1993) (upholding statute requiring mandatory testing of all convicted sex offenders; noting that traditional standards that require individualized suspicion are impractical because HIV-infected sexual offenders have no outward manifestation of infection); United States v. Ward, 131 F.3d 335 (3d Cir. 1997) (HIV testing of defendant charged with sexual assault held reasonable: "Early HIV testing of an admitted rapist, or even an accused rapist, provides necessary information for the prompt and vital treatment and mental well-being of the victim.").

Drug-Testing of Pregnant Mothers

In the following case the Court continued along the difficult path of distinguishing those searches that serve special needs beyond ordinary criminal law enforcement and those that do not. Note that this case was decided after *Chandler* but before *Earls*.

FERGUSON v. CITY OF CHARLESTON

Supreme Court of the United States, 2001.
532 U.S. 67.

JUSTICE STEVENS delivered the opinion of the Court.

In this case, we must decide whether a state hospital's performance of a diagnostic test to obtain evidence of a patient's criminal conduct for law enforcement purposes is an unreasonable search if the patient has not consented to the procedure. * * *

I

In the fall of 1988, staff members at the public hospital operated in the city of Charleston by the Medical University of South Carolina (MUSC) became concerned about an apparent increase in the use of cocaine by patients who were receiving prenatal treatment. In response to this perceived increase, as of April 1989, MUSC began to order drug screens to be performed on urine samples from maternity patients who were suspected of using cocaine. If a patient tested positive, she was then referred by MUSC staff to the county substance abuse commission for counseling and treatment. However, despite the referrals, the incidence of cocaine use among the patients at MUSC did not appear to change.

Some four months later, Nurse Shirley Brown, the case manager for the MUSC obstetrics department, heard a news broadcast reporting that the police in Greenville, South Carolina, were arresting pregnant users of cocaine on the theory that such use harmed the fetus and was therefore child abuse. Nurse Brown discussed the story with MUSC's general counsel, Joseph C. Good, Jr., who then contacted Charleston Solicitor Charles Condon in order to offer MUSC's cooperation in prosecuting mothers whose children tested positive for drugs at birth.

After receiving Good's letter, Solicitor Condon took the first steps in developing the policy at issue in this case. He organized the initial meetings, decided who would participate, and issued the invitations, in which he described his plan to prosecute women who tested positive for cocaine while pregnant. The task force that Condon formed included representatives of MUSC, the police, the County

Substance Abuse Commission and the Department of Social Services. Their deliberations led to MUSC's adoption of a 12–page document entitled "POLICY M–7," dealing with the subject of "Management of Drug Abuse During Pregnancy." The first three pages of Policy M–7 set forth the procedure to be followed by the hospital staff to "identify/assist pregnant patients suspected of drug abuse." The first section, entitled the "Identification of Drug Abusers," provided that a patient should be tested for cocaine through a urine drug screen if she met one or more of nine criteria.[a] It also stated that a chain of custody should be followed when obtaining and testing urine samples, presumably to make sure that the results could be used in subsequent criminal proceedings. The policy also provided for education and referral to a substance abuse clinic for patients who tested positive. Most important, it added the threat of law enforcement intervention that "provided the necessary leverage to make the [p]olicy effective." That threat was, as respondents candidly acknowledge, essential to the program's success in getting women into treatment and keeping them there.

The threat of law enforcement involvement was set forth in two protocols, the first dealing with the identification of drug use during pregnancy, and the second with identification of drug use after labor. * * * [A]fter the initial positive drug test, the police were to be notified (and the patient arrested) only if the patient tested positive for cocaine a second time or if

---

a.   Those criteria were as follows:

1.   No prenatal care

2.   Late prenatal care after 24 weeks gestation

3.   Incomplete prenatal care

4.   Abruptio placentae

5.   Intrauterine fetal death

6.   Preterm labor of no obvious cause

7.   IUGR [intrauterine growth retardation] of no obvious cause

8.   Previously known drug or alcohol abuse

9.   Unexplained congenital anomalies.

she missed an appointment with a substance abuse counselor. * * *

The last six pages of the policy contained forms for the patients to sign, as well as procedures for the police to follow when a patient was arrested. The policy also prescribed in detail the precise offenses with which a woman could be charged, depending on the stage of her pregnancy. If the pregnancy was 27 weeks or less, the patient was to be charged with simple possession. If it was 28 weeks or more, she was to be charged with possession and distribution to a person under the age of 18—in this case, the fetus. If she delivered "while testing positive for illegal drugs," she was also to be charged with unlawful neglect of a child. Under the policy, the police were instructed to interrogate the arrestee in order "to ascertain the identity of the subject who provided illegal drugs to the suspect." Other than the provisions describing the substance abuse treatment to be offered to women who tested positive, the policy made no mention of any change in the prenatal care of such patients, nor did it prescribe any special treatment for the newborns.

II

Petitioners are 10 women who received obstetrical care at MUSC and who were arrested after testing positive for cocaine. * * * Respondents include the city of Charleston, law enforcement officials who helped develop and enforce the policy, and representatives of MUSC.

Petitioners' complaint challenged the validity of the policy under various theories, including the claim that warrantless and nonconsensual drug tests conducted for criminal investigatory purposes were unconstitutional searches. Respondents advanced two principal defenses to the constitutional claim: (1) that, as a matter of fact, petitioners had consented to the searches; and (2) that, as a matter of law, the searches were reasonable, even absent consent, because they were justified by special non-law-enforcement purposes. The District Court rejected the second defense because the searches in question "were not done by the medical university for independent purposes. [Instead,] the police came in and there was an agreement reached that the positive screens would be shared with the police." Accordingly, the District Court submitted the factual defense to the jury with instructions that required a verdict in favor of petitioners unless the jury found consent. The jury found for respondents.

Petitioners appealed, arguing that the evidence was not sufficient to support the jury's consent finding. The Court of Appeals for the Fourth Circuit affirmed, but without reaching the question of consent. Disagreeing with the District Court, the majority of the appellate panel held that the searches were reasonable as a matter of law under our line of cases recognizing that "special needs" may, in certain exceptional circumstances, justify a search policy designed to serve non-law—enforcement ends. * * *

We granted certiorari to review the appellate court's holding on the "special needs" issue. Because we do not reach the question of the sufficiency of the evidence with respect to consent, we necessarily assume for purposes of our decision—as did the Court of Appeals—that the searches were conducted without the informed consent of the patients. We conclude that the judgment should be reversed and the case remanded for a decision on the consent issue.

III

* * *

Because the hospital seeks to justify its authority to conduct drug tests and to turn the results over to law enforcement agents without the knowledge or consent of the patients, this case differs from the four previous cases in which we have considered whether comparable drug tests "fit within the closely guarded category of constitutionally permissible suspicionless searches." [The Court discusses the previous case law.]

The critical difference between those four drug-testing cases and this one, however, lies in the nature of the "special need" asserted as justification for the warrantless searches. In each of those earlier cases, the "special need" that was advanced as a justification for the absence of a warrant or individualized suspicion was one divorced from the State's general interest in law enforcement. * * * In this case, however, the central and indispensable feature of the policy from its inception was the use of law enforcement to coerce the patients into substance abuse treatment. This fact distinguishes this case from circumstances in which physicians or psychologists, in the course of ordinary medical procedures aimed at helping the patient herself, come across information that under rules of law or ethics is subject to reporting requirements, which no one has challenged here. *See, e.g.,* Ark. Code Ann. § 12–12–602 (1999) (requiring reporting of intentionally inflicted knife or gunshot wounds); Ariz. Rev.Stat. Ann. § 13–3620 (Supp.2000) (requiring "any ... person having responsibility for the care or treatment of children" to report suspected abuse or neglect to a peace officer or child protection agency).

Respondents argue in essence that their ultimate purpose—namely, protecting the health of both mother and child—is a beneficent one. In *Chandler*, however, we did not simply accept the State's invocation of a "special need." Instead, we carried out a "close review" of the scheme at issue before concluding that the need in question was not "special," as that term has been defined in our cases. In this case, a review of the M–7 policy plainly reveals that the purpose actually served by the MUSC searches "is ultimately indistinguishable from the general interest in crime control." Indianapolis v. Edmond, [*Edmond* follows immediately, in the section on roadblocks and checkpoints].

In looking to the programmatic purpose, we consider all the available evidence in order to determine the relevant primary purpose. In this case it is clear from the record that an initial and continuing focus of the policy was on the arrest and prosecution of drug-abusing mothers. Tellingly, the document codifying the policy incorporates the police's operational guidelines. It devotes its attention to the chain of custody, the range of possible criminal charges, and the logistics of police notification and arrests. Nowhere, however, does the document discuss different courses of medical treatment for either mother or infant, aside from treatment for the mother's addiction.

Moreover, throughout the development and application of the policy, the Charleston prosecutors and police were extensively involved in the day-to-day administration of the policy. Police and prosecutors decided who would receive the reports of positive drug screens and what information would be included with those reports. Law enforcement officials also helped determine the procedures to be followed when performing the screens. * * * Police took pains to coordinate the timing and circumstances of the arrests with MUSC staff, and, in particular, Nurse Brown.

While the ultimate goal of the program may well have been to get the women in question into substance abuse treatment and off of drugs, the immediate objective of the searches was to *generate evidence for law enforcement purposes* in order to reach that goal.[b] The threat of law enforcement may ultimately have been intended as a means to an end, but the direct and primary purpose of MUSC's policy was to ensure the use of those means. In our opinion, this distinction is critical. Because law enforcement involvement always serves some broader social purpose or objective, under respondents' view, virtually any nonconsensual suspicionless search could be immunized under the special needs doctrine by defining the search solely in terms of its ultimate, rather than immediate, purpose. Such an approach is inconsistent with the Fourth Amendment. Given the primary purpose of the Charleston program, which was to use the threat of arrest and prosecution in order to force women into treatment, and given the extensive involvement of law enforcement officials at every stage of the policy, this case simply does not fit within the closely guarded category of "special needs."

* * *

As respondents have repeatedly insisted, their motive was benign rather than punitive. Such a motive, however, cannot justify a departure from Fourth Amendment protections, given the pervasive involvement of law enforcement with the development and application of the MUSC policy. The stark and unique fact that characterizes this case is that Policy M–7 was designed to obtain evidence of criminal conduct by the tested patients that would be turned over to the police and that could be admissible in subsequent criminal prosecutions. While respondents are correct that drug abuse both was and is a serious problem, the gravity of the threat alone cannot be dispositive of questions concerning what means law enforcement officers may employ to pursue a given purpose.

* * *

Accordingly, the judgment of the Court of Appeals is reversed, and the case is remanded for further proceedings consistent with this opinion.

JUSTICE KENNEDY, concurring in the judgment.

* * * None of our special needs precedents has sanctioned the routine inclusion of law enforcement, both in the design of the policy and in using arrests, either threatened or real, to

---

b. Accordingly, this case differs from New York v. Burger, 482 U.S. 691 (1987), in which the Court upheld a scheme in which police officers were used to carry out administrative inspections of vehicle dismantling businesses. That case involved an industry in which the expectation of privacy in commercial premises was "particularly attenuated" given the extent to which the industry in question was closely regulated. More important for our purposes, the Court relied on the "plain administrative purposes" of the scheme to reject the contention that the statute was in fact "designed to gather evidence to enable convictions under the penal laws." The discovery of evidence of other violations would have been merely incidental to the purposes of the administrative search. In contrast, in this case, the policy was specifically designed to gather evidence of violations of penal laws.

This case also differs from the handful of seizure cases in which we have applied a balancing test to determine Fourth Amendment reasonableness. *See, e.g.,* Michigan Dept. of State Police v. Sitz, 496 U.S. 444, 455 (1990); United States v. Martinez–Fuerte, 428 U.S. 543 (1976). First, those cases involved roadblock seizures, rather than "the intrusive search of the body or the home." See Indianapolis v. Edmond (REHNQUIST, C. J., dissenting); *Martinez-Fuerte*, 428 U.S., at 561 ("[W]e deal neither with searches nor with the sanctity of private dwellings, ordinarily afforded the most stringent Fourth Amendment protection"). Second, the Court explicitly distinguished the cases dealing with checkpoints from those dealing with "special needs." *Sitz*, 496 U.S., at 450.

implement the system designed for the special needs objectives. The special needs cases we have decided do not sustain the active use of law enforcement, including arrest and prosecutions, as an integral part of a program which seeks to achieve legitimate, civil objectives. The traditional warrant and probable-cause requirements are waived in our previous cases on the explicit assumption that the evidence obtained in the search is not intended to be used for law enforcement purposes. Most of those tested for drug use under the policy at issue here were not brought into direct contact with law enforcement. This does not change the fact, however, that, as a systemic matter, law enforcement was a part of the implementation of the search policy in each of its applications. Every individual who tested positive was given a letter explaining the policy not from the hospital but from the solicitor's office. Everyone who tested positive was told a second positive test or failure to undergo substance abuse treatment would result in arrest and prosecution. As the Court holds, the hospital acted, in some respects, as an institutional arm of law enforcement for purposes of the policy. Under these circumstances, while the policy may well have served legitimate needs unrelated to law enforcement, it had as well a penal character with a far greater connection to law enforcement than other searches sustained under our special needs rationale.

* * *

The holding of the Court, * * * does not call into question the validity of mandatory reporting laws such as child abuse laws which require teachers to report evidence of child abuse to the proper authorities, even if arrest and prosecution is the likely result. That in turn highlights the real difficulty. As this case comes to us * * * we

must accept the premise that the medical profession can adopt acceptable criteria for testing expectant mothers for cocaine use in order to provide prompt and effective counseling to the mother and to take proper medical steps to protect the child. If prosecuting authorities then adopt legitimate procedures to discover this information and prosecution follows, that ought not to invalidate the testing. One of the ironies of the case, then, may be that the program now under review, which gives the cocaine user a second and third chance, might be replaced by some more rigorous system. We must, however, take the case as it comes to us; and the use of handcuffs, arrests, prosecutions, and police assistance in designing and implementing the testing and rehabilitation policy cannot be sustained under our previous cases concerning mandatory testing.

* * *

JUSTICE SCALIA, with whom THE CHIEF JUSTICE and JUSTICE THOMAS join as to Part II, dissenting.

* * *

I

The first step in Fourth Amendment analysis is to identify the search or seizure at issue. What petitioners, the Court, and to a lesser extent the concurrence really object to is not the urine testing, but the hospital's reporting of positive drug-test results to police. But the latter is obviously not a search. * * * There is only one act that could conceivably be regarded as a search of petitioners in the present case: the taking of the urine sample. I suppose the testing of that urine for traces of unlawful drugs could be considered a search of sorts, but the Fourth Amendment protects only against searches of citizens' "persons, houses, papers, and effects"; and it is entirely unrealistic to regard urine as one of the "effects" (i.e., part of the property) of the person who has passed and abandoned it. Some would argue, I suppose, that testing of the urine is prohibited by some generalized privacy right "emanating" from the "penumbras" of the Constitution (a question that is not before us); but it is not even arguable that the testing of urine that has been lawfully obtained is a Fourth Amendment search. * * *

It is rudimentary Fourth Amendment law that a search which has been consented to is not unreasonable. There is no contention in the present case that the urine samples were extracted forcibly.* * *

Until today, we have never held—or even suggested—that material which a person voluntarily entrusts to someone else cannot be given by that person to the police, and used for whatever evidence it may contain. Without so much as discussing the point, the Court today opens a hole in our Fourth Amendment jurisprudence, the size and shape of which is entirely indeterminate. * * * Since the Court declines even to discuss the issue, it leaves law enforcement officials entirely in the dark as to when they can use incriminating evidence obtained from "trusted" sources. * * *

II

I think it clear, therefore, that there is no basis for saying that obtaining of the urine sample was unconstitutional. The special-needs doctrine is thus quite irrelevant, since it operates only to validate searches and seizures that are otherwise unlawful. In the ensuing discussion, however, I shall assume (contrary to legal precedent) that the taking of the urine sample was (either because of the patients' necessitous circumstances, or because of failure to disclose that the urine would be tested for drugs, or because of failure to disclose that the results of the test would be given to the police) coerced. Indeed, I shall even assume (contrary to common sense) that the testing of the urine constituted an unconsented search of the patients' effects. On those assumptions, the special-needs doctrine would become relevant; and, properly applied, would validate what was done here.

* * *

The initial goal of the doctors and nurses who conducted cocaine-testing in this case was to refer pregnant drug addicts to treatment centers, and to prepare for necessary treatment of their possibly affected children. When the doctors and nurses agreed to the program providing test results to the police, they did so because (in addition to the fact that child abuse was required by law to be reported) they wanted to use the sanction of arrest as a strong incentive for their addicted patients to undertake drug-addiction treatment. And the police themselves used it for that benign purpose, as is shown by the fact that only 30 of 253 women testing positive for cocaine were ever arrested, and only 2 of those prosecuted. It would not be unreasonable to conclude that today's judgment, authorizing the assessment of damages against the county solicitor and individual doctors and nurses who participated in the program, proves once again that no good deed goes unpunished.

Note on Ferguson

Is the majority's footnote distinguishing *Burger* persuasive? *Burger* seems to hold that criminal law objectives can be pursued through civil-based means under the "special needs" doctrine. *Ferguson* seems to hold that civil law objectives cannot be pursued through criminal-based means under the "special needs" doctrine. Does that make sense? Recall that the Court in *Burger* upheld suspicionless searches by police officers rather than administrative officials, and the evidence found was turned over to prosecutors.

On remand, the Fourth Circuit held that the mothers did not consent to use of the urine tests in a criminal prosecution. Ferguson v. City of Charleston, 308 F.3d 380 (4th Cir. 2002). The Court remanded for a determination of damages.

4. Roadblocks, Checkpoints and Suspicionless Seizures

Individual Stops Without Suspicion

In Delaware v. Prouse, 440 U.S. 648 (1979), the Court held that an officer could not, in the absence of reasonable suspicion, stop an automobile and detain the driver in order to check his license and registration. The officer in *Prouse* made an ad hoc, suspicionless stop, and the Court expressed its concern with "the unconstrained exercise of discretion." The Court noted that such an ad hoc stop was not "a sufficiently productive mechanism to justify the intrusion" and that there were other, better ways to effectuate the state interest in vehicle registration and safety, such as yearly inspections. The majority emphasized that it was not foreclosing as one possible alternative the "questioning of all oncoming traffic at roadblock-type stops." In response to the majority's roadblock alternative, Justice Rehnquist argued in dissent that the majority had "elevated the adage 'misery loves company' to a novel role in Fourth Amendment jurisprudence." Why is it better to stop everybody rather than anybody?

Permanent Checkpoints

The dictum in *Prouse* concerning roadblock-type stops was supported by the Court's earlier decision in United States v. Martinez—Fuerte, 428 U.S. 543 (1976). In that case, the Court, invoking *Terry* principles, approved suspicionless stops at permanent checkpoints removed from the border. The Court emphasized that suspicionless stops were necessary to implement the state interest in regulating the flow of illegal aliens, and noted that the fixed checkpoint was minimally intrusive. Justice Powell, writing for the Court, argued that motorists are not surprised by a fixed checkpoint; that such checkpoints limit the discretion of the officer; and that "the location of a fixed checkpoint is not chosen by officers in the field, but by officials responsible for making overall decisions as to the most effective allocation of limited enforcement resources." Justice Powell stressed that it was permissible to dispense with particularized suspicion because "we deal neither with searches nor with the sanctuary of private dwellings."

Temporary Checkpoints to Check for DUI

The Court upheld suspicionless stops at temporary sobriety checkpoints in Michigan Department of State Police v. Sitz, 496 U.S. 444 (1990). The Michigan program allowed checkpoints to be set up by officers in the field according to a list of considerations including "safety of the location," "minimum inconvenience for the driver," and available space "to pull the vehicle off the traveled portion of the roadway for further inquiry if necessary." Under the program, all motorists passing through the checkpoint would be stopped and briefly examined for signs of intoxication. If the driver appeared intoxicated, he or she would be directed to another area where license and registration would be checked, and further sobriety tests would be conducted if warranted. The only checkpoint operated under the program resulted in a stop of 126 vehicles, and one arrest for drunk driving. The challenge in the Supreme Court focused solely on the initial detention and associated preliminary investigation of motorists for signs of intoxication.

Chief Justice Rehnquist's opinion for five members of the Court relied heavily on *Martinez—Fuerte,* and applied the "misery loves company" rationale that then-Justice Rehnquist had criticized in *Prouse.*

Respondents in *Sitz* argued that a reasonableness balancing approach could not be employed to evaluate sobriety checkpoints, because there was no special need beyond criminal law enforcement at stake. They argued that sobriety checkpoints are used to enforce criminal laws prohibiting drunk driving.

The majority responded that a special need beyond criminal law enforcement was not required to support reasonableness balancing for stops at fixed checkpoints. The Chief Justice stated that the special needs analysis of *Skinner* et al. "was in no way designed to repudiate our prior cases dealing with police stops." Thus, the Court relied on the *Terry* line of cases rather than on the "special needs" line of cases.

Balancing the interests of the state and the individual, as permitted for law enforcement seizures by *Terry,* the Chief Justice quoted from *Martinez—Fuerte,* and concluded that the intrusiveness of a sobriety checkpoint was extremely limited:

> At traffic checkpoints the motorist can see that other vehicles are being stopped, he can see visible signs of the officers' authority, and he is much less likely to be frightened or annoyed by the intrusion. * * * Here, checkpoints are selected pursuant to the guidelines, and uniformed police officers stop every approaching vehicle. The intrusion resulting from the brief stop at the sobriety checkpoint is for constitutional purposes indistinguishable from the checkpoint stops we upheld in *Martinez—Fuerte.*

Against this limited intrusion, the Court balanced the State's heavy interest in eradicating drunken driving. Chief Justice Rehnquist rejected the argument that sobriety checkpoints did not effectively advance this undeniable state interest. He stated that references to effectiveness of searches and seizures in previous cases, such as *Prouse,* were not intended "to transfer from politically accountable officials to the courts the decision as to which among reasonable alternative law enforcement techniques should be employed to deal with a serious public danger." The Court concluded that "the choice among such reasonable alternatives remains with the government officials who have a unique understanding of, and a responsibility for, limited public resources." The majority faulted the lower court for its "searching examination" of the effectiveness of sobriety checkpoints.

Justice Stevens wrote a dissenting opinion joined in large part by Justices Brennan and Marshall. He argued that unlike the permanent, fixed checkpoint, the police operating a sobriety checkpoint "have extremely broad discretion in determining the exact timing and placement of the roadblock." Moreover, a temporary checkpoint is more intrusive because of the element of surprise that it presents:

> A driver who discovers an unexpected checkpoint on a familiar local road will be startled and distressed. She may infer, correctly, that the checkpoint is not simply "business as usual," and may likewise infer, again correctly, that the police have made a discretionary decision to focus their law enforcement efforts upon her and others who pass the chosen point.

Questions After Sitz

The Court in *Sitz* chided the lower court for second-guessing the legislature's determination that roadblocks would be an effective means of investigating and deterring drunk driving. Yet in *Chandler*, supra, the Court second-guessed the legislature's determination that its drug-testing plan would be an effective means of detecting and deterring drug use in candidates for public office. How do you square the two cases?

If *Martinez—Fuerte* is the correct analogy, can *Sitz* stand for the proposition that daily stops are permissible at various locations? Can *Martinez—Fuerte* justify roving or moveable checkpoints? If so, who decides where these checkpoints should be placed? Does it make a difference that the location of the checkpoint in *Martinez—Fuerte* was chosen by high level officials rather than by officers in the field? Do the considerations set forth in the Michigan program restrict police discretion or promote it?

Drug Checkpoints

In the following case, the Court essentially revised its analysis in *Sitz* and distinguished sobriety roadblocks from checkpoints designed to check for drugs. The Court invalidates a roadblock program because its primary purpose was to enforce the criminal law. How is a court supposed to determine whether the state has an improper purpose after this case?

CITY OF INDIANAPOLIS v. EDMOND

Supreme Court of the United States, 2000.
531 U.S. 32.

JUSTICE O'CONNOR **delivered the opinion of the Court.**

In Michigan Dept. of State Police v. Sitz and United States v. Martinez—Fuerte we held that brief, suspicionless seizures at highway checkpoints for the purposes of combating drunk driving and intercepting illegal immigrants were constitutional. We now consider the constitutionality of a highway checkpoint program whose primary purpose is the discovery and interdiction of illegal narcotics.

I

In August 1998, the city of Indianapolis began to operate vehicle checkpoints on Indianapolis roads in an effort to interdict unlawful drugs. The city conducted six such roadblocks between August and November that year, stopping 1,161 vehicles and arresting 104 motorists. Fifty-five arrests were for drug-related crimes, while 49 were for offenses unrelated to drugs. The overall "hit rate" of the program was thus approximately nine percent.

The parties stipulated to the facts concerning the operation of the checkpoints by the Indianapolis Police Department (IPD) for purposes of the preliminary injunction proceedings instituted below. At each checkpoint location, the police stop a predetermined number of vehicles. Approximately 30 officers are stationed at the checkpoint. Pursuant to written directives issued by the chief of police, at least one officer approaches the vehicle, advises the driver that he or she is being stopped briefly at a drug checkpoint, and asks the driver to produce a license and registration. The officer also looks for signs of impairment and conducts an open-view examination of the vehicle from the outside. A narcotics-detection dog walks around the outside of each stopped vehicle.

The directives instruct the officers that they may conduct a search only by consent or based on the appropriate quantum of particularized suspicion. The officers must conduct each stop in the same manner until particularized suspicion develops, and the officers have no discretion to stop any vehicle out of sequence. The city agreed in the stipulation to operate the checkpoints in such a way as to ensure that the total duration of each stop, absent reasonable suspicion or probable cause, would be five minutes or less.

* * * [C]heckpoint locations are selected weeks in advance based on such considerations as area crime statistics and traffic flow. The checkpoints are generally operated during daylight hours and are identified with lighted signs reading, "NARCOTICS CHECKPOINT ___ MILE AHEAD, NARCOTICS K–9 IN USE, BE PREPARED TO STOP." Once a group of cars has been stopped, other traffic proceeds without interruption until all the stopped cars have been processed or diverted for further processing. * * * [T]he average stop for a vehicle not subject to further processing lasts two to three minutes or less.

Respondents James Edmond and Joell Palmer were each stopped at a narcotics checkpoint in late September 1998. Respondents then filed a lawsuit on behalf of themselves and the class of all motorists who had been stopped or were subject to being stopped in the future at the Indianapolis drug checkpoints. Respondents claimed that the roadblocks violated the Fourth Amendment of the United States Constitution and the search and seizure provision of the Indiana Constitution. Respondents requested declaratory and injunctive relief for the class, as well as damages and attorney's fees for themselves.

Respondents then moved for a preliminary injunction. * * * The United States District Court for the Southern District of Indiana agreed to class certification and denied the motion for a preliminary injunction, holding that the checkpoint program did not violate the Fourth Amendment. A divided panel of the United States Court of Appeals for the Seventh Circuit reversed, holding that the checkpoints contravened the Fourth Amendment. We granted certiorari, and now affirm.

II

The Fourth Amendment requires that searches and seizures be reasonable. A search or seizure is ordinarily unreasonable in the absence of individualized suspicion of wrongdoing. Chandler v. Miller. While such suspicion is not an "irreducible" component of reasonableness, *Martinez–Fuerte*, we have recognized only limited circumstances in which the usual rule does not apply. For example, we have upheld certain regimes of suspicionless searches where the program was designed to serve "special needs, beyond the normal need for law enforcement." [The Court describes its drug-testing cases.] We have also allowed searches for certain administrative purposes without particularized suspicion of misconduct, provided that those searches are appropriately limited. See, *e.g.,* New York v. Burger (warrantless administrative inspection of premises of "closely regulated" business); Camara v. Municipal Court of City and County of San Francisco (administrative inspection to ensure compliance with city housing code).

We have also upheld brief, suspicionless seizures of motorists at a fixed Border Patrol checkpoint designed to intercept illegal aliens, *Martinez-Fuerte,* supra, and at a sobriety checkpoint aimed at removing drunk drivers from the road, Michigan Dept. of State Police v. Sitz. In addition, in Delaware v. Prouse, we suggested that a similar type of roadblock with the purpose of verifying drivers' licenses and vehicle registrations would be permissible. In none of these cases, however, did we indicate approval of a checkpoint program whose primary purpose was to detect evidence of ordinary criminal wrongdoing.

* * *

In *Sitz,* we evaluated the constitutionality of a Michigan highway sobriety checkpoint program. The *Sitz* checkpoint involved brief suspicionless stops of motorists so that police officers could detect signs of intoxication and remove impaired drivers from the road. * * * This checkpoint program was clearly aimed at reducing the immediate hazard posed by the presence of drunk drivers on the highways, and there was an obvious connection between the imperative of highway safety and the law enforcement practice at issue. The gravity of the drunk driving problem and the magnitude of the State's interest in getting drunk drivers off the road weighed heavily in our determination that the program was constitutional.

In *Prouse,* we invalidated a discretionary, suspicionless stop for a spot check of a motorist's driver's license and vehicle registration. The officer's conduct in that case was unconstitutional primarily on account of his exercise of "standardless and unconstrained discretion." We nonetheless acknowledged the States' "vital interest in ensuring that only those qualified to do so are permitted to operate motor vehicles, that these vehicles are fit for safe operation, and hence that licensing, registration, and vehicle inspection requirements are being observed." Accordingly, we suggested that "[q]uestioning of all oncoming traffic at roadblock-type stops" would be a lawful means of serving this interest in highway safety.

We further indicated in *Prouse* that we considered the purposes of such a hypothetical roadblock to be distinct from a general purpose of investigating crime. The State proffered the additional interests of "the apprehension of stolen motor vehicles and of drivers under the influence of alcohol or narcotics" in its effort to justify the discretionary spot check. We attributed the entirety of the latter interest to the State's interest in roadway safety. We also noted that the interest in apprehending stolen vehicles may be partly subsumed by the interest in roadway safety. We observed, however, that "[t]he remaining governmental interest in controlling automobile thefts is not distinguishable from the general interest in crime control." Not only does the common thread of highway safety thus run through *Sitz* and *Prouse,* but *Prouse* itself reveals a difference in the Fourth Amendment significance of highway safety interests and the general interest in crime control.

III

It is well established that a vehicle stop at a highway checkpoint effectuates a seizure within the meaning of the Fourth Amendment. The fact that officers walk a narcotics-detection dog around the exterior of each car at the Indianapolis checkpoints does not transform the seizure into a search. See United States v. Place, 462 U.S. 696, 707 (1983). Just as in *Place*, an exterior sniff of an automobile does not require entry into the car and is not designed to disclose any information other than the presence or absence of narcotics. * * * Rather, what principally distinguishes these checkpoints from those we have previously approved is their primary purpose.

As petitioners concede, the Indianapolis checkpoint program unquestionably has the primary purpose of interdicting illegal narcotics. In their stipulation of facts, the parties repeatedly refer to the checkpoints as "drug checkpoints" and describe them as "being operated by the City of Indianapolis in an effort to interdict unlawful drugs in Indianapolis." In addition, the first document attached to the parties' stipulation is entitled "DRUG CHECKPOINT CONTACT OFFICER DIRECTIVES BY ORDER OF THE CHIEF OF POLICE.". These directives instruct officers to "[a]dvise the citizen that they are being stopped briefly at a drug checkpoint." * * * Further, * * * the checkpoints are identified with lighted signs reading, "NARCOTICS CHECKPOINT ___ MILE AHEAD, NARCOTICS K–9 IN USE, BE PREPARED TO STOP." Finally, both the District Court and the Court of Appeals recognized that the primary purpose of the roadblocks is the interdiction of narcotics.

We have never approved a checkpoint program whose primary purpose was to detect evidence of ordinary criminal wrongdoing. Rather, our checkpoint cases have recognized only limited exceptions to the general rule that a seizure must be accompanied by some measure of individualized suspicion. * * * [E]ach of the checkpoint programs that we have approved was designed primarily to serve purposes closely related to the problems of policing the border or the necessity of ensuring roadway safety. Because the primary purpose of the Indianapolis narcotics checkpoint program is to uncover evidence of ordinary criminal wrongdoing, the program contravenes the Fourth Amendment.

Petitioners propose several ways in which the narcotics-detection purpose of the instant checkpoint program may instead resemble the primary purposes of the checkpoints in *Sitz* and *Martinez-Fuerte*. Petitioners state that the checkpoints in those cases had the same ultimate purpose of arresting those suspected of committing crimes. Securing the border and apprehending drunk drivers are, of course, law enforcement activities, and law enforcement officers employ arrests and criminal prosecutions in pursuit of these goals. If we were to rest the case at this high level of generality, there would be little check on the ability of the authorities to construct roadblocks for almost any conceivable law enforcement purpose. Without drawing the line at roadblocks designed primarily to serve the general interest in crime control, the Fourth Amendment would do little to prevent such intrusions from becoming a routine part of American life.

Petitioners also emphasize the severe and intractable nature of the drug problem as justification for the checkpoint program. There is no doubt that traffic in illegal narcotics creates social harms of the first magnitude. * * * But the gravity of the threat alone cannot be dispositive of questions concerning what means law enforcement officers may employ to pursue a given purpose. Rather, in determining whether individualized suspicion is required, we must consider the nature of the interests threatened and their connection to the particular law enforcement practices at issue. We are particularly reluctant to recognize exceptions to the general rule of individualized suspicion where governmental authorities primarily pursue their general crime control ends.

Nor can the narcotics-interdiction purpose of the checkpoints be rationalized in terms of a highway safety concern similar to that present in *Sitz*. The detection and punishment of almost any criminal offense serves broadly the safety of the community, and our streets would no doubt be safer but for the scourge of illegal drugs. Only with respect to a smaller class of offenses, however, is society confronted with the type of immediate, vehicle-bound threat to life and limb that the sobriety checkpoint in *Sitz* was designed to eliminate.

Petitioners also liken the anticontraband agenda of the Indianapolis checkpoints to the antismuggling purpose of the checkpoints in *Martinez-Fuerte*. Petitioners cite this Court's conclusion in *Martinez-Fuerte* that the flow of traffic was too heavy to permit "particularized study of a given car that would enable it to be identified as a possible carrier of illegal aliens," and claim that this logic has even more force here. The problem with this argument is that the same logic prevails any time a vehicle is employed to conceal contraband or other evidence of a crime. This type of connection to the roadway is very different from the close connection to roadway safety that was present in *Sitz* and *Prouse*. Further, the Indianapolis checkpoints are far removed from the border context that was crucial in *Martinez-*

Fuerte. While the difficulty of examining each passing car was an important factor in validating the law enforcement technique employed in *Martinez-Fuerte*, this factor alone cannot justify a regime of suspicionless searches or seizures. Rather, we must look more closely at the nature of the public interests that such a regime is designed principally to serve.

* * * We decline to suspend the usual requirement of individualized suspicion where the police seek to employ a checkpoint primarily for the ordinary enterprise of investigating crimes. We cannot sanction stops justified only by the generalized and ever-present possibility that interrogation and inspection may reveal that any given motorist has committed some crime.

Of course, there are circumstances that may justify a law enforcement checkpoint where the primary purpose would otherwise, but for some emergency, relate to ordinary crime control. For example * * * the Fourth Amendment would almost certainly permit an appropriately tailored roadblock set up to thwart an imminent terrorist attack or to catch a dangerous criminal who is likely to flee by way of a particular route. The exigencies created by these scenarios are far removed from the circumstances under which authorities might simply stop cars as a matter of course to see if there just happens to be a felon leaving the jurisdiction. While we do not limit the purposes that may justify a checkpoint program to any rigid set of categories, we decline to approve a program whose primary purpose is ultimately indistinguishable from the general interest in crime control.

Petitioners argue that our prior cases preclude an inquiry into the purposes of the checkpoint program. For example, they cite Whren v. United

States, 517 U.S. 806 (1996), and Bond v. United States, 529 U.S. 334 (2000), to support the proposition that "where the government articulates and pursues a legitimate interest for a suspicionless stop, courts should not look behind that interest to determine whether the government's 'primary purpose' is valid." These cases, however, do not control the instant situation.

In *Whren*, we held that an individual officer's subjective intentions are irrelevant to the Fourth Amendment validity of a traffic stop that is justified objectively by probable cause to believe that a traffic violation has occurred. We observed that our prior cases "foreclose any argument that the constitutional reasonableness of traffic stops depends on the actual motivations of the individual officers involved." In so holding, we expressly distinguished cases where we had addressed the validity of searches conducted in the absence of probable cause. See *Whren* (distinguishing Florida v. Wells, 495 U.S. 1, 4 (1990) (stating that "an inventory search must not be a ruse for a general rummaging in order to discover incriminating evidence"), Colorado v. Bertine, 479 U.S. 367, 372 (1987) (suggesting that the absence of bad faith and the lack of a purely investigative purpose were relevant to the validity of an inventory search), and *Burger*, 482 U.S., at 716–717, n. 27 (observing that a valid administrative inspection conducted with neither a warrant nor probable cause did not appear to be a pretext for gathering evidence of violations of the penal laws)).

Whren therefore reinforces the principle that, while "[s]ubjective intentions play no role in ordinary, probable-cause Fourth Amendment analysis," programmatic purposes may be relevant to the validity of Fourth Amendment intrusions under-

taken pursuant to a general scheme without individualized suspicion. Accordingly, *Whren* does not preclude an inquiry into programmatic purpose in such contexts. It likewise does not preclude an inquiry into programmatic purpose here.

Last Term in *Bond*, we addressed the question whether a law enforcement officer violated a reasonable expectation of privacy in conducting a tactile examination of carry-on luggage in the overhead compartment of a bus. In doing so, we simply noted that the principle of *Whren* rendered the subjective intent of an officer irrelevant to this analysis. While, as petitioners correctly observe, the analytical rubric of *Bond* was not "ordinary, probable-cause Fourth Amendment analysis," nothing in *Bond* suggests that we would extend the principle of *Whren* to all situations where individualized suspicion was lacking. Rather, subjective intent was irrelevant in *Bond* because the inquiry that our precedents required focused on the objective effects of the actions of an individual officer. By contrast, our cases dealing with intrusions that occur pursuant to a general scheme absent individualized suspicion have often required an inquiry into purpose at the programmatic level.

Petitioners argue that the Indianapolis checkpoint program is justified by its lawful secondary purposes of keeping impaired motorists off the road and verifying licenses and registrations. If this were the case, however, law enforcement authorities would be able to establish checkpoints for virtually any purpose so long as they also included a license or sobriety check. For this reason, we examine the available evidence to determine the primary purpose of the checkpoint program. While we recognize the challenges inherent in a purpose inquiry, courts routinely engage in this enterprise in many areas of constitutional jurisprudence as a means of sifting abusive governmental conduct from that which is lawful. As a result, a program driven by an impermissible purpose may be proscribed while a program impelled by licit purposes is permitted, even though the challenged conduct may be outwardly similar. While reasonableness under the Fourth Amendment is predominantly an objective inquiry, our special needs and administrative search cases demonstrate that purpose is often relevant when suspicionless intrusions pursuant to a general scheme are at issue.[a]

It goes without saying that our holding today does nothing to alter the constitutional status of the sobriety and border checkpoints that we approved in *Sitz* and *Martinez-Fuerte*, or of the type of traffic checkpoint that we suggested would be lawful in *Prouse*. The constitutionality of such checkpoint programs still depends on a balancing of the competing interests at stake and the effectiveness of the program. When law enforcement authorities pursue primarily general crime control purposes at checkpoints such as here, however, stops can only be justified by some quantum of individualized suspicion.

Our holding also does not affect the validity of border searches or searches at places like airports and government buildings, where the need for such measures to ensure public safety can be particularly acute. Nor does our opinion speak to other intrusions aimed primarily at purposes beyond the general interest in crime control. Our holding also does not impair the

ability of police officers to act appropriately upon information that they properly learn during a checkpoint stop justified by a lawful primary purpose, even where such action may result in the arrest of a motorist for an offense unrelated to that purpose. Finally, we caution that the purpose inquiry in this context is to be conducted only at the programmatic level and is not an invitation to probe the minds of individual officers acting at the scene.

Because the primary purpose of the Indianapolis checkpoint program is ultimately indistinguishable from the general interest in crime control, the checkpoints violate the Fourth Amendment. The judgment of the Court of Appeals is accordingly affirmed.

CHIEF JUSTICE REHNQUIST, **with whom** JUSTICE THOMAS **joins, and with whom** JUSTICE SCALIA **joins as to Part I, dissenting**.

* * *

I

* * *

This case follows naturally from *Martinez-Fuerte* and *Sitz*. Petitioners acknowledge that the "primary purpose" of these roadblocks is to interdict illegal drugs, but this fact should not be controlling. Even accepting the Court's conclusion that the checkpoints at issue in *Martinez-Fuerte* and *Sitz* were not primarily related to criminal law enforcement, the question whether a law enforcement purpose could support a roadblock seizure is not presented in this case. The District Court found that another "purpose of

---

a. Because petitioners concede that the primary purpose of the Indianapolis checkpoints is narcotics detection, we need not decide whether the State may establish a checkpoint program with the primary purpose of checking licenses or driver sobriety and a secondary

purpose of interdicting narcotics. Specifically, we express no view on the question whether police may expand the scope of a license or sobriety checkpoint seizure in order to detect the presence of drugs in a stopped car.

the checkpoints is to check driver's licenses and vehicle registrations," and the written directives state that the police officers are to "[l]ook for signs of impairment." The use of roadblocks to look for signs of impairment was validated by *Sitz*, and the use of roadblocks to check for driver's licenses and vehicle registrations was expressly recognized in Delaware v. Prouse. * * *

Because of the valid reasons for conducting these roadblock seizures, it is constitutionally irrelevant that petitioners also hoped to interdict drugs. In Whren v. United States, we held that an officer's subjective intent would not invalidate an otherwise objectively justifiable stop of an automobile. The reasonableness of an officer's discretionary decision to stop an automobile, at issue in *Whren*, turns on whether there is probable cause to believe that a traffic violation has occurred. The reasonableness of highway checkpoints, at issue here, turns on whether they effectively serve a significant state interest with minimal intrusion on motorists. The stop in *Whren* was objectively reasonable because the police officers had witnessed traffic violations; so too the roadblocks here are objectively reasonable because they serve the substantial interests of preventing drunken driving and checking for driver's licenses and vehicle registrations with minimal intrusion on motorists.

Once the constitutional requirements for a particular seizure are satisfied, the subjective expectations of those responsible for it, be it police officers or members of a city council, are irrelevant. Cf. Scott v. United States, 436 U.S. 128 (1978) ("Subjective intent alone ... does not make otherwise lawful conduct illegal or unconstitutional"). It is the objective effect of the State's actions on the privacy of the individual that animates the Fourth Amendment. * * *

* * * The only difference between this case and *Sitz* is the presence of the dog. We have already held, however, that a "sniff test" by a trained narcotics dog is not a "search" within the meaning of the Fourth Amendment because it does not require physical intrusion of the object being sniffed and it does not expose anything other than the contraband items. And there is nothing in the record to indicate that the dog sniff lengthens the stop. Finally, the checkpoints' success rate—49 arrests for offenses unrelated to drugs—only confirms the State's legitimate interests in preventing drunken driving and ensuring the proper licensing of drivers and registration of their vehicles. These stops effectively serve the State's legitimate interests; they are executed in a regularized and neutral manner; and they only minimally intrude upon the privacy of the motorists. They should therefore be constitutional.

II

The Court, unwilling to adopt the straightforward analysis that these precedents dictate, adds a new non-law-enforcement primary purpose test lifted from a distinct area of Fourth Amendment jurisprudence relating to the *searches* of homes and businesses. * * * [W]hatever sense a non-law-enforcement primary purpose test may make in the search setting, it is ill suited to brief roadblock seizures, where we have consistently looked at "the scope of the stop" in assessing a program's constitutionality.

* * *

[T]he Court's newfound non-law-enforcement primary purpose test is both unnecessary to secure Fourth Amendment rights and bound to produce wide-ranging litigation over the "purpose" of any given seizure. Police designing highway roadblocks can never be sure of their validity, since a jury might later determine that a forbidden purpose exists.

* * * [I]f the Indianapolis police had assigned a different purpose to their activity here, but in no way changed what was done on the ground to individual motorists, it might well be valid. [The Chief Justice cites the majority's footnote concerning the possible permissibility of a checkpoint whose secondary purpose is drug interdiction.] The Court's non-law-enforcement primary purpose test simply does not serve as a proxy for anything that the Fourth Amendment is, or should be, concerned about in the automobile seizure context.

* * *

JUSTICE THOMAS, **dissenting**.

Taken together, our decisions in Michigan Dept. of State Police v. Sitz and United States v. Martinez–Fuerte stand for the proposition that suspicionless roadblock seizures are constitutionally permissible if conducted according to a plan that limits the discretion of the officers conducting the stops. I am not convinced that *Sitz* and *Martinez-Fuerte* were correctly decided. Indeed, I rather doubt that the Framers of the Fourth Amendment would have considered "reasonable" a program of indiscriminate stops of individuals not suspected of wrongdoing.

Respondents did not, however, advocate the overruling of *Sitz* and *Martinez-Fuerte*, and I am reluctant to consider such a step without the benefit of briefing and argument. For the reasons given by THE CHIEF JUSTICE, I believe that those cases compel upholding the program at issue here. I, therefore, join his opinion.

Note on Edmond and Checkpoints After 9/11

The majority was concerned that checkpoints would become "a routine part of American life." After 9/11, checkpoints have indeed become a routine part of American life. Many of the checkpoints are not simply seizures, but intrusive searches as well (e.g., airport checkpoints). But the checkpoints seem to fall within the majority's perhaps prophetic paragraph that permits terrorism-related checkpoints without any showing of suspicion. And if these are "special needs" checkpoints, then a search can usually be justified by balancing the government's interest in rooting out terrorism against the individual's diminished interest in privacy.

Terrorism-related checkpoints after 9/11 have been upheld. An example is United States v. Green, 293 F.3d 855 (5th Cir. 2002), upholding a suspicionless roadblock check on an open military installation. The court declared as follows:

> We believe that this case differs substantially from *Edmond* in two respects. First, the protection of the nation's military installations from acts of domestic or international terrorism is a unique endeavour, akin to the policing of our borders, and one in which a greater degree of intrusiveness may be allowed. Second, those cases focusing not on unique, national challenges, but instead on road safety, are concerned with dangers specifically associated with vehicles and therefore justify suspicionless checkpoint seizures. Since we know from painful experience that vehicles are often used to transport and deliver explosives in the form of "car bombs," and that military installations have historically faced greater risk than civilian communities of such a bombing, vehicles pose a special risk.

The majority in *Edmond* also seemed to approve of emergency roadblocks to catch a dangerous criminal, such as were used during the Washington, D.C. area sniper attacks. Where is the line, then, between crime enforcement and special needs?

Drug Interdiction as a Secondary Purpose

The majority in *Edmond* dropped a footnote that is was not deciding whether otherwise valid checkpoints become invalid if a *secondary* purpose is drug interdiction. Throughout the opinion, the Court emphasizes that the *primary* purpose of the Indianapolis checkpoint was drug interdiction, as opposed to a vehicle-related threat to public safety. After *Edmund,* courts have upheld checkpoints where the primary purpose effectuates special needs beyond law enforcement, even though there is also a secondary purpose of drug interdiction. See, e.g., United States v. Davis, 270 F.3d 977 (D.C.Cir. 2001) (checkpoint not invalidated by secondary purpose of drug interdiction, noting that the footnote in *Edmond* "seems divorced from the rest of the opinion" and that the opinion as a whole "more than suggests that if the 'primary purpose' had been for a purpose the Court endorsed–such as detecting drunk drivers, or checking licenses–the roadblock would be constitutional."); United States v. Moreno–Vargas, 315 F.3d 489 (5th Cir. 2002) (use of drug-detecting dogs at a permanent fixed immigration checkpoint does not invalidate the checkpoint stops; drug interdiction was a permissible secondary purpose of the checkpoint).

Assuming there is a constitutional distinction between primary and secondary purposes, how hard is it for the government to evade the Court's holding in *Edmond*? What stops the government from calling its checkpoint a "sobriety" or "registration" checkpoint, and keeping a drug detecting dog at the checkpoint as part of a specified "secondary" purpose?

Drug-Detection as a Vehicle–Related Safety Interest

The *Edmund* Court distinguished sobriety checkpoints from the Indianapolis drug interdiction checkpoint on the ground that drunk drivers present an immediate, vehicle-related safety throughout while drug dealers do not raise a specific safety issue merely by driving. Does this mean that suspicionless drug checkpoints would be permitted if they are styled as an attempt to detect those who are driving *under the influence* of drugs?

What if the state can make a reasonable argument that drug dealers do indeed create a vehicle-related threat to safety? After all, drug dealers are likely to double park, commit illegal u-turns, and generally act without concern of the traffic laws. In United States v. Davis, 270 F.3d 977 (D.C.Cir. 2001), the court upheld a checkpoint that was in response to community complaints that drug dealers and buyers in cars were speeding, committing illegal u-turns, and causing traffic congestion. The Court noted that the primary purpose of the roadblock was to remedy the traffic problems caused by drug-dealing and "[w]hatever advantage was gained in drug enforcement was coincidental to the principal purpose of the traffic roadblocks." If this is correct, how much is left of the majority opinion in *Edmond*?

Suspicionless Checkpoints to Obtain
Information About a Crime

In the following case the Court distinguished *Edmond* and upheld a suspicionless checkpoint. What is the basis for the distinction?

ILLINOIS v. LIDSTER

Supreme Court of the United States, 2004.
124 S.Ct. 885.

JUSTICE BREYER delivered the opinion of the Court.

This Fourth Amendment case focuses upon a highway checkpoint where police stopped motorists to ask them for information about a recent hit-and-run accident. We hold that the police stops were reasonable, hence, constitutional.

I

The relevant background is as follows: On Saturday, August 23, 1997, just after midnight, an unknown motorist traveling eastbound on a highway in Lombard, Illinois, struck and killed a 70–year-old bicyclist. The motorist drove off without identifying himself. About one week later at about the same time of night and at about the same place, local police set up a highway checkpoint designed to obtain more information about the accident from the motoring public.

Police cars with flashing lights partially blocked the eastbound lanes of the highway. The blockage forced traffic to slow down, leading to lines of up to 15 cars in each lane. As each vehicle drew up to the checkpoint, an officer would stop it for 10 to 15 seconds, ask the occupants whether they had seen anything happen there the previous weekend, and hand each driver a flyer. The flyer said "ALERT ... FATAL HIT & RUN ACCIDENT" and requested "assistance in identifying the vehicle and driver in this accident which killed a 70 year old bicyclist."

Robert Lidster, the respondent, drove a minivan toward the checkpoint. As he approached the checkpoint, his van swerved, nearly hitting one of the officers. The officer smelled alcohol on Lidster's breath. He directed Lidster to a side street where another officer administered a sobriety test and then arrested Lidster. Lidster was tried and convicted in Illinois state court of driving under the influence of alcohol.

Lidster challenged the lawfulness of his arrest and conviction on the ground that the government had obtained much of the relevant evidence through use of a checkpoint stop that violated the Fourth Amendment. The trial court rejected that challenge. But an Illinois appellate court reached the opposite conclusion. The Illinois Supreme Court agreed with the appellate court. It held * * * that our decision in Indianapolis v. Edmond required it to find the stop unconstitutional. * * * We now reverse the Illinois Supreme Court's determination.

II

The Illinois Supreme Court basically held that our decision in *Edmond* governs the outcome of this case. We do not agree. *Edmond* involved a checkpoint at which police stopped vehicles to look for evidence of drug crimes committed by occupants of those vehicles. After stopping a vehicle at the checkpoint, police would examine (from outside the vehicle) the vehicle's interior; they would walk a drug-sniffing dog around the exterior; and, if they found sufficient evidence of drug (or other) crimes, they would arrest the vehicle's occupants. We found that police had set up this checkpoint primarily for general "crime control" purposes, *i.e.*, "to detect evidence of ordinary criminal wrongdoing." We noted that the stop was made without individualized suspicion. And we held that the Fourth Amendment forbids such a stop, in the absence of special circumstances.

The checkpoint stop here differs significantly from that in *Edmond*. The stop's primary law enforcement purpose was *not* to determine whether a vehicle's occupants were committing a crime, but to ask vehicle occupants, as members of the public, for their help in providing information about a crime in all likelihood committed by others. The police expected the information elicited to help them apprehend, not the vehicle's occupants, but other individuals.

Edmond's language, as well as its context, makes clear that the constitutionality of this latter, information-seeking kind of stop was not then before the Court. *Edmond* refers to the subject matter of its holding as "stops justified only by the generalized and ever-present possibility that interrogation and inspection may reveal that *any given motorist has committed some crime.*" We concede that *Edmond* describes the law enforcement objective there in question as a "general interest in crime control," but it specifies that the phrase "general interest in crime control" does not refer to every "law enforcement" objective. We must read this and related general language in *Edmond* as we often read general language in judicial opinions—as referring in context to circumstances similar to the circumstances then before the Court and not referring to quite different circumstances that the Court was not then considering.

Neither do we believe, *Edmond* aside, that the Fourth Amendment would have us apply an *Edmond*-type rule of automatic unconstitutionality to brief, information-seeking highway stops of the kind now before us. For one thing, the fact that such stops normally lack individualized suspicion cannot by itself determine the constitutional outcome. As in *Edmond*, the stop here at issue involves a motorist. The Fourth Amendment does not treat a motorist's car as his castle. And special law enforcement concerns will sometimes justify highway stops without individualized suspicion. See Michigan Dept. of State Police v. Sitz (sobriety checkpoint); United States v. Martinez–Fuerte (Border Patrol checkpoint). Moreover, unlike *Edmond*, the context here (seeking information from the public) is one in which, by definition, the concept of individualized suspicion has little role to play. Like certain other forms of police activity, say, crowd control or public safety, an information-seeking stop is not the kind of event that involves suspicion, or lack of suspicion, of the relevant individual.

For another thing, information-seeking highway stops are less likely to provoke anxiety or to prove intrusive. The stops are likely brief. The police are not likely to ask questions designed to elicit self-incriminating information. And citizens will often react positively when police simply ask for their help as responsible citizens to give whatever information they may have to aid in law enforcement.

Further, the law ordinarily permits police to seek the voluntary cooperation of members of the public in the investigation of a crime. "Law enforcement officers do not violate the Fourth

Amendment by merely approaching an individual on the street or in another public place, by asking him if he is willing to answer some questions, [or] by putting questions to him if the person is willing to listen." Florida v. Royer [discussed *supra* in the section on *Terry* stops.]. * * *

The importance of soliciting the public's assistance is offset to some degree by the need to stop a motorist to obtain that help—a need less likely present where a pedestrian, not a motorist, is involved. The difference is significant in light of our determinations that such an involuntary stop amounts to a "seizure" in Fourth Amendment terms. That difference, however, is not important enough to justify an *Edmond*-type rule here. After all, as we have said, the motorist stop will likely be brief. Any accompanying traffic delay should prove no more onerous than many that typically accompany normal traffic congestion. And the resulting voluntary questioning of a motorist is as likely to prove important for police investigation as is the questioning of a pedestrian. Given these considerations, it would seem anomalous were the law (1) ordinarily to allow police freely to seek the voluntary cooperation of pedestrians but (2) ordinarily to forbid police to seek similar voluntary cooperation from motorists.

Finally, we do not believe that an *Edmond*-type rule is needed to prevent an unreasonable proliferation of police checkpoints. Practical considerations—namely, limited police resources and community hostility to related traffic tie-ups—seem likely to inhibit any such proliferation. And, of course, the Fourth Amendment's normal insistence that the stop be reasonable in context will still provide an important legal limitation on police use of this kind of information-seeking checkpoint.

These considerations, taken together, convince us that an *Edmond*-type presumptive rule of unconstitutionality does not apply here. That does not mean the stop is automatically, or even presumptively, constitutional. It simply means that we must judge its reasonableness, hence, its constitutionality, on the basis of the individual circumstances. And as this Court said in Brown v. Texas, 443 U.S. 47, 51 (1979), in judging reasonableness, we look to "the gravity of the public concerns served by the seizure, the degree to which the seizure advances the public interest, and the severity of the interference with individual liberty."

III

We now consider the reasonableness of the checkpoint stop before us in light of the factors just mentioned * * * . We hold that the stop was constitutional.

The relevant public concern was grave. Police were investigating a crime that had resulted in a human death. No one denies the police's need to obtain more information at that time. And the stop's objective was to help find the perpetrator of a specific and known crime, not of unknown crimes of a general sort.

The stop advanced this grave public concern to a significant degree. The police appropriately tailored their checkpoint stops to fit important criminal investigatory needs. The stops took place about one week after the hit-and-run accident, on the same highway near the location of the accident, and at about the same time of night. And police used the stops to obtain information from drivers, some of whom might well have been in the vicinity of the crime at the time it occurred.

Most importantly, the stops interfered only minimally with liberty of the sort the Fourth Amendment seeks to protect. Viewed objectively, each stop required only a brief wait in line—a very few minutes at most. Contact with the police lasted only a few seconds. Police contact consisted simply of a request for information and the distribution of a flyer. Viewed subjectively, the contact provided little reason for anxiety or alarm. The police stopped all vehicles systematically. And there is no allegation here that the police acted in a discriminatory or otherwise unlawful manner while questioning motorists during stops.

For these reasons we conclude that the checkpoint stop was constitutional.

The judgment of the Illinois Supreme Court is

Reversed.

JUSTICE STEVENS, **with whom** JUSTICE SOUTER **and** JUSTICE GINSBURG **join, concurring in part and dissenting in part.**

There is a valid and important distinction between seizing a person to determine whether she has committed a crime and seizing a person to ask whether she has any information about an unknown person who committed a crime a week earlier. I therefore join Parts I and II of the Court's opinion explaining why our decision in Indianapolis v. Edmond is not controlling in this case. However, I find the issue discussed in Part III of the opinion closer than the Court does and believe it would be wise to remand the case to the Illinois state courts to address that issue in the first instance.

In contrast to pedestrians, who are free to keep walking when they encounter police officers handing out flyers or seeking information, motorists who confront a roadblock are required to stop, and to remain stopped for as long as the officers choose to

detain them. Such a seizure may seem relatively innocuous to some, but annoying to others who are forced to wait for several minutes when the line of cars is lengthened—for example, by a surge of vehicles leaving a factory at the end of a shift. Still other drivers may find an unpublicized roadblock at midnight on a Saturday somewhat alarming.

On the other side of the equation, the likelihood that questioning a random sample of drivers will yield useful information about a hit-and-run accident that occurred a week earlier is speculative at best. To be sure, the sample in this case was not entirely random: The record reveals that the police knew that the victim had finished work at the Post Office shortly before the fatal accident, and hoped that other employees of the Post Office or the nearby industrial park might work on similar schedules and, thus, have been driving the same route at the same time the previous week. That is a plausible theory, but there is no evidence in the record that the police did anything to confirm that the nearby businesses in fact had shift changes at or near midnight on Saturdays, or that they had reason to believe that a roadblock would be more effective than, say, placing flyers on the employees' cars.

In short, the outcome of the multifactor test prescribed in Brown v. Texas is by no means clear on the facts of this case. Because the Illinois Appellate Court and the State Supreme Court held that the Lombard roadblock was *per se* unconstitutional under Indianapolis v. Edmond, neither court attempted to apply the *Brown* test. * * * We should be especially reluctant to abandon our role as a court of review in a case in which the constitutional inquiry requires analysis of local conditions and practices more familiar to judges closer to the scene. I would therefore remand the case to the Illinois courts to undertake the initial analysis of the issue that the Court resolves in Part III of its opinion. To that extent, I respectfully dissent.

5. Inventory Searches

By now it should be apparent that the line between regulatory searches and law enforcement searches is often blurred. Another example of this overlap occurs with inventory searches. In most jurisdictions it is standard procedure for the police to inventory the contents of automobiles and other containers being held in their custody. An inventory search has nothing to do with probable cause, and *ostensibly,* is unrelated to criminal investigation of any kind. As one court has put it, the police are allowed to conduct inventory searches in order "to protect the owner's property while it is in police custody, to protect the police against claims of lost or stolen property, and to protect the police and the public from potential danger." The traditional requirements of warrant and probable cause are excused because inventory searches serve a "caretaking" function and "are not designed to uncover evidence of criminal activity." United States v. Andrews, 22 F.3d 1328 (5th Cir.1994).

Community Caretaking Function

The Supreme Court has discussed these warrantless searches in several instances. In Cady v. Dombrowski, 413 U.S. 433 (1973), the Court approved the search of a car towed to a private garage after an accident that resulted in the hospitalization of the driver. The driver was a Chicago policeman, and the officer who conducted the search testified that he was looking for the driver's service revolver, which he believed Chicago policemen were required to carry at all times. In the course of the search, blood-stained garments were discovered in the trunk, which were later used to convict the defendant of murder. In a 5–4 decision, Justice Rehnquist found that the initial intrusion to search for the gun was reasonable as a "community caretaking function," to protect the public from the possibility that it would fall into the hands of vandals. Therefore, the seizure of evidence found in plain view was also justified.[31]

Warrantless, Suspicionless Searches: South Dakota v. Opperman

Two years after *Cady,* the Court upheld the warrantless inventory search of a car impounded for a parking violation. Chief Justice Burger, writing for the Court in South Dakota v. Opperman, 428 U.S. 364 (1976), emphasized that the search was conducted pursuant to standard police procedures, which helped to guarantee that the intrusion "would be limited to the scope necessary to carry out the caretaking function." The majority found the search of Opperman's impounded car to be a reasonable means of protecting valuables, which could be seen in plain view on the dashboard. Opperman argued that it was unreasonable

---

31. Note that the search in *Cady* could not have been justified under the automobile exception, even though there was reasonable cause to believe that the car contained a re- volver. The defendant was under arrest for drunk driving, and he was permitted to carry a gun, so the search could not be explained as a search for evidence of crime or contraband.

for the officers to break open the lock of his car and search the glove compartment, where they found marijuana that was used against him at trial. But the Court held that these actions were reasonable because they were authorized, and indeed mandated, by local police regulations. As with other special needs cases, the Court balanced the state interest against the nature of the intrusion to determine whether inventory searches were reasonable. The Court found that three legitimate state interests supported an inventory search: 1) protection of the police department from false property claims; 2) protection of the property interests of the owner; and 3) protection of the police and public from dangerous items. These interests outweighed the owner's privacy interests, especially given the diminished expectation of privacy in automobiles.

Justice Powell, in a concurring opinion, explained why the warrant requirement is inapposite where inventory searches conducted pursuant to departmental regulations are involved. First, there are no special facts for a neutral magistrate to evaluate so as to determine whether probable cause exists, since inventory searches are non-criminal in nature. Second, there is no danger of discretionary searches or hindsight justifications when searches are conducted in accordance with standard procedures. Third, the danger of arbitrariness is not present where routine searches of all impounded cars are conducted.

Justice Marshall—in a dissent joined by Justices Brennan and Stewart, and in part by Justice White—argued that warrantless, suspicionless inventory searches could not be justified by any "special need." He found the safety rationale—i.e., that inventory searches protected the police and public from dangerous items—to be overbroad. Every automobile and container poses at least some hypothetical threat to safety. Justice Marshall concluded that an "undifferentiated possibility of harm" cannot serve as a basis for an inventory, and that the safety rationale was only implicated where specific circumstances indicate the possibility of a particular danger—such as in *Cady*, where the officers reasonably believed that the defendant had a gun in his car.

Next, Justice Marshall considered the assertion that inventories are necessary to protect the police against lost property claims. In this case, the concern was irrelevant because South Dakota law absolved police of responsibility as "gratuitous depositors" beyond inventorying objects in plain view and locking the car. Furthermore, an inventory does not discourage false claims that an item was stolen prior to the search, or was intentionally omitted from police records. Nor does it ensure that such police misconduct did not in fact occur.

Finally, Justice Marshall derided the assertion that impoundment and search of property is a reasonable means of protecting the owner's property interests. In his view, the property owner's interests are best known by the property owner himself; if the owner feels that impoundment and search are needed to protect his property, then he can simply consent to these intrusions.

Property Carried by an Arrestee: Illinois v. Lafayette

The Supreme Court relied on South Dakota v. Opperman in Illinois v. Lafayette, 462 U.S. 640 (1983), as it upheld the inventory search at the police station of a shoulder bag belonging to a man arrested for disturbing the peace. The search uncovered drugs. Chief Justice Burger reasoned that the government's interests in an inventory search at the stationhouse "may in some circumstances be even greater that those supporting a search incident to arrest'' and that police conduct that might be embarrassingly intrusive on the street could be handled privately at the stationhouse. The Chief Justice asserted that the three interests supporting an inventory search were fully applicable to a stationhouse search of an arrestee's possessions: police need to protect the property of arrested persons, to protect themselves from claims of theft or damage to property, and to remove dangerous instrumentalities from arrestees.

The lower court in *Lafayette* had found the inventory search unreasonable on the ground that preservation of the property could have been achieved in a less intrusive manner, such as by storing the bag rather than investigating its contents. Chief Justice Burger rejected this reasoning, stating as follows:

> The reasonableness of any particular governmental activity does not necessarily or invariably turn on the existence of alternative less intrusive means. * * * Even if less intrusive means existed of protecting some particular types of property, it would be unreasonable to expect police officers in the everyday course of business to make fine and subtle distinctions in deciding which containers or items may be searched and which must be sealed as a unit. [citing New York v. Belton]

In a footnote, the Court stated that the inventory search of Lafayette's bag may have been invalid if he was not going to be incarcerated after being booked for disturbing the peace.[32] If the arrestee is going to be released immediately, then the interests supporting an inventory search would not appear to be implicated. Justice Marshall, joined by Justice Brennan, concurred in the judgment.

Limits on Police Discretion: Colorado v. Bertine

Opperman and *Lafayette* supported the Supreme Court's decision in Colorado v. Bertine, 479 U.S. 367 (1987), holding that police officers could inventory the contents of a van, including a closed backpack and a nylon bag and other containers within it. Chief Justice Rehnquist's opinion for the Court rejected an argument that the impoundment of the car was unjustified because the driver could have been offered the opportunity to make arrangements for the safekeeping of his property. The Court concluded that "reasonable police regulations relating to inventory procedures administered in good faith satisfy the Fourth Amendment, even though courts might as a matter of hindsight be able to devise equally reasonable rules requiring a different procedure."

The *Bertine* Court also rejected the defendant's claim that the inventory was impermissible because departmental regulations gave police officers discretion to decide whether to impound the van or to park and lock it in a public parking lot. The Chief Justice noted that the regulations established several factors by which the officer was to determine whether to impound the vehicle or instead exercise a park and lock alternative. The regulations permitted impoundment only in two conditions: if leaving the car would present a real risk of damage or vandalism to the car; or if approval to leave the car could not be obtained from the owner. The majority held that these conditions were sufficiently concrete and understanda-

---

32. A number of courts have held that a preincarceration inventory search is improper if the arrestee, upon posting collateral, has a right to release without any incarceration. See, e.g., United States v. Mills, 472 F.2d 1231 (D.C.Cir.1972); People v. Dixon, 392 Mich. 691, 222 N.W.2d 749 (1974).

ble to reasonably limit the discretion of the officer. The Court concluded that "nothing in *Opperman* or *Lafayette* prohibits the exercise of police discretion so long as that discretion is exercised according to standard criteria and on the basis of something other than suspicion of criminal activity."

Bertine also challenged the opening of the containers found in his car, on the ground that the inventorying officer did not properly weigh the privacy interest in the container against the risk that it might serve as a repository for dangerous or valuable items. The majority again rejected a less intrusive means analysis for opening containers in an inventory search. In a footnote, the Court emphasized that "the police department procedures mandated the opening of closed containers and the listing of their contents." Thus, the officer's discretion as to what to open was limited by the inventory rules that were in place.

Justice Blackmun, joined by Justices Powell and O'Connor, concurred and wrote separately "to underscore the importance of having such inventories conducted only pursuant to standardized police procedures." Justice Marshall, joined by Justice Brennan, dissented. He urged that the officers did not act according to standards that sufficiently controlled their discretion and he repeated the arguments he made in *Opperman* that the government's interests in conducting an inventory did not outweigh the property owner's privacy interests.

Limits on Police Discretion: Florida v. Wells

The Court revisited the subject of police discretion in conducting inventory searches in Florida v. Wells, 495 U.S. 1 (1990). The Court unanimously found that the opening of a locked suitcase could not be justified as an inventory search where the Florida Highway Patrol had no policy whatever concerning the opening of closed containers. Chief Justice Rehnquist, writing for the Court, found the search to be insufficiently regulated by standardized police procedures. However, the Chief Justice took issue with a statement by the Florida Supreme Court that "the police under *Bertine* must mandate either that all containers will be opened during an inventory search, or that no containers will be opened. There can be no room for discretion." According to the Court in *Wells*, the Fourth Amendment does allow the officer some latitude to decide whether a container may be opened in an inventory search. This discretion can be exercised, pursuant to departmental regulations, "in light of the nature of the search and the characteristics of the container itself." The Chief Justice concluded:

> While policies of opening all containers or of opening no containers are unquestionably permissible, it would be equally permissible, for example, to allow the opening of closed containers whose contents officers determine they are unable to ascertain from examining the contents' exteriors. The allowance of the exercise of judgment based on concerns related to the purpose of an inventory search does not violate the Fourth Amendment.

This dictum prompted sharp responses in opinions by Justice Brennan (joined by Justice Marshall), Justice Blackmun, and Justice Stevens, all of whom concurred in the judgment. These Justices generally argued that to allow the individual officer any discretion to determine whether a container should be opened would create an unacceptable risk of abuse. Justice Brennan noted that the *Bertine* Court had allowed the officer some discretion as to whether to impound a car, but no discretion as to whether to open a container therein. He concluded that "attempting to cast doubt on the vitality of the holding in *Bertine* in this otherwise easy case is not justified." In response to Justice Brennan's characterization of the *Bertine* "holding", the Chief Justice stated that while the departmental rules at issue in *Bertine* called for an opening of all containers, the Court did not actually hold that such an all-or-nothing rule was required by the Fourth Amendment.

After *Wells,* would a policy allowing police officers to open containers "if they reasonably appear to contain valuables" be upheld? See United States v. Andrews, 22 F.3d 1328 (5th Cir.1994) (upholding a search of a notebook pursuant to departmental regulations that authorized officers to search property insofar as necessary "to protect the city from claims of lost property"). Why does Justice Brennan prefer that all containers be opened rather than some? Is it better that everybody suffer an invasion of privacy rather than a few?

In the end, there may be no way to eliminate the exercise of discretion in an inventory seizure and search. Certainly an all-or-nothing rule of impoundment would not be practicable, given the various fact situations in which officers come upon cars subject to impoundment. While an all-or-nothing rule could be applied to opening containers, discretion would still have to be exercised to determine whether a certain item is or is not a container. See generally United States v. Judge, 864 F.2d 1144 (5th Cir.1989). For example, if the inventorying officer finds a fountain pen in a car, can he open up the pen under a policy requiring the opening of all containers? What if he finds a teddy bear?

The Problem of Pretext

One issue that arises from a consideration of the justifications for an inventory is whether the procedure is a pretext for conducting a warrantless search for evidence of crime. The emphasis in *Opperman* and *Bertine* on standardized inventory procedures reflects concern that, absent such guidelines, investigatory searches may be conducted under the guise of inventories. As we have seen in other areas, however (most notably with roadblocks and searches incident to arrest), the fact that the officer is guided by bright line, all-or-nothing rules does not eliminate the possibility of pretextual searches. And as in other areas, the fact that the officer may have a pretextual motive is usually held irrelevant if the search itself is objectively reasonable. See, e.g., United States v. Lewis, 3 F.3d 252 (8th Cir.1993) (inventory search finds drugs in the engine compartment of the car; search held reasonable because conducted pursuant to standard inventory procedures); United States v. Hawkins, 279 F.3d 83 (1st Cir. 2002) ("Appellant also challenges the search saying that the inventory was clearly a 'ruse' used to search for drugs. Regardless of what appellant suggests, the law is clear. The subjective intent of the officers is not relevant so long as they conduct a search according to a standardized inventory policy.")' United States v. Garner, 181 F.3d 988 (8th Cir.1999) ("The presence of an investigative motive does not invalidate an otherwise valid inventory search.").

On the other hand, if the officer is acting without guidelines, as in *Wells,* or if the officer disregards guidelines to obtain evidence, then the search cannot be justified as an inventory search. An example of the latter is where the officer opens only a few containers in an impounded automobile, or fails to file an inventory list where such a filing is required. See United States v. Parr, 716 F.2d 796 (11th Cir.1983) (search cannot be justified as an inventory search where items were selectively investigated). As the court put it in United States v. Rowland, 341 F.3d 774 (8th Cir. 2003), a case where officers inventoried the evidence of crime but not other items of value in the car:

> In sum, law enforcement had standardized procedures in place but failed to follow them here. Such failure, coupled with the fact the officers disregarded items without evidentiary value * * * suggests they did not search the vehicle in order to safeguard the vehicle's contents from loss, or to protect law enforcement personnel from harm, or even to guard the department and county against a possible lawsuit. Rather, it appears law enforcement sifted through the vehicle's contents searching only for and recording only incriminating evidence; something law enforcement may not do.

Less Onerous Alternatives

The problem of pretext inventory searches could be regulated by requiring police officers to use the least onerous alternative in effectuating the state interests involved. For example, impoundment of a car could be prohibited if the owner was on the scene and could simply drive it away—the "drive away" alternative would protect the police from false claims, protect the owner's interest, and protect against safety risks, without necessitating an intrusive seizure. Similarly, a search of the car and containers in the car could be prohibited if the officer could simply seal the car to prevent entry. It would seem that in some circumstances, a container can be sealed or locked, thus protecting the owner's valuables and protecting the police from false claims, without the intrusion of a search. However, these arguments are based on a less intrusive means analysis, which the Supreme Court has rejected in *Lafayette* and *Bertine*. According to those cases, the issue is not whether a less intrusive alternative exists that would equally effectuate state interests. Rather, the issue is whether the alternative chosen is a reasonable means of accommodating the (high) interests of the state and the (low) privacy interests of citizens.

Why did the Supreme Court reject the less intrusive alternative arguments in the inventory cases? Professor Maclin points out that the Court has required the State to employ less intrusive means when other constitutional rights, such as First Amendment rights, are involved. He proffers the following explanation for this apparent disparity in constitutional standards.

> The Court is uninterested in placing the Fourth Amendment in the category of preferred constitutional rights, including the rights of free speech, freedom of religion, and freedom from racial discrimination, despite its specific placement in the Bill of Rights.

> * * *

> Why is the Fourth Amendment considered a second-class right? My guess is that the Court sees the typical Fourth Amendment claimant as a second-class citizen, and sees the typical police officer as being overwhelmed with the responsibilities and duties of maintaining law and order in our crime-prone society. This dual perception may explain the Court's reluctance to subject police conduct to vigorous judicial oversight.

Maclin, The Central Meaning of the Fourth Amendment, 35 Wm & Mary L.Rev.197, 237 (1993). Can you see any reason to distinguish between, for example, First and Fourth Amendment protections? Is the difference that the Fourth Amendment emphasizes reasonableness, while the First Amendment is written in more absolute terms?

Searches and Seizures That Serve No Inventory Interest

An impoundment or search that effectuates the state interests supporting an inventory search, even though those interests could be met less intrusively, must be distinguished from an impoundment or search that effectuates none of those state interests. It is reasonable, under *Bertine,* to impound a vehicle even where alternative arrangements could be made to protect the car. It is also reasonable, under *Bertine* and *Lafayette,* to open a container even though it could otherwise be secured. It is not, however, reasonable to impound a vehicle that is parked in a locked garage attached to the arrestee's home; such a seizure is not necessary to effectuate the interests that support an impoundment in the first place. Likewise, it is not reasonable to vacuum a car's interior to "inventory" carpet fibers: there is no safety risk, no chance of a claim for lost property, and no need to protect the owner from the chance that his carpet fibers will be stolen. See United States v. Showalter, 858 F.2d 149 (3d Cir.1988), where the government sought to justify the search of an entire *residence* under the inventory exception. The court stated that "none of the factors which have been used to justify the warrantless inventory search of an automobile are present * * * when generally applied to the home." See also United States v. Best, 135 F.3d 1223 (8th Cir.1998), where the officer, in the course of an "inventory" search, pried open the door panel of a car and discovered drugs. The court held the search invalid, because it "did not serve the purpose of protecting the car and its contents." The court noted that "Best would not have a legitimate claim for protection of property hidden in the door panel" of his car, and therefore the officer "did not have a legitimate interest in seeking such property."

6. *Border Searches*

Courts are not always persuasive in their inventory search opinions, but they try to state a rationale for not requiring a warrant. This is in sharp contrast with the cases establishing the border search exception to the warrant and probable cause requirements. These cases make little effort to justify the exception on policy grounds. The most persuasive rationale is similar to that used in *Skinner* and *Von Raab*: border searches serve a special need beyond traditional criminal law enforcement. The special need is the interest in protecting American borders, "in order to regulate the collection of duties and to prevent the introduction of contraband into this country." United States v. Johnson, 991 F.2d 1287 (7th Cir.1993). As the Court stated in United States v. Montoya de Hernandez, 473 U.S. 531 (1985):

> At the border, customs officials have more than merely an investigative law enforcement role. They are also charged, along with immigration officials, with protecting this Nation from entrants who may bring anything harmful into this country, whether that be communicable diseases, narcotics, or explosives.

Because the border search serves special needs, it is evaluated under the reasonableness clause of the Fourth Amendment. And given the heavy state interest just stated, as well as the diminished expectation of privacy attendant to a border crossing, border searches are ordinarily reasonable even without a warrant or probable cause, and often without any suspicion at all. See United States v. Robles, 45 F.3d 1 (1st Cir.1995) ("routine border searches, conducted for the purposes of collecting duties and intercepting contraband destined for the interior of the United States, do not require reasonable suspicion, probable cause, or a warrant").

Routine border searches have been authorized by statute to prevent entrance into the country of illegal aliens or goods, and to enforce customs regulations. The constitutionality of routine border searches, conducted without warrant or probable cause, has been assumed since the beginning of the nation. In 1976, the Supreme Court repeated the assumption in a case in which the Court was asked by the government to uphold the warrantless search of first class international mail by customs officials.[33]

UNITED STATES v. RAMSEY

Supreme Court of the United States, 1977.
431 U.S. 606.

MR. JUSTICE REHNQUIST **delivered the opinion of the Court.**

[The case involved an investigation of a heroin-by-mail enterprise in the Washington, D.C. area. Customs officials developed a reasonable suspicion that eight envelopes from Thailand might contain heroin. The envelopes were opened without a warrant and each did, in fact, contain heroin.]

* * *

III

A

That searches made at the border, pursuant to the longstanding right of the sovereign to protect itself by stopping and examining persons and property crossing into this country, are reasonable simply by virtue of the fact that they occur at the border should, by now, require no extended demonstration. The Congress which proposed the Bill of Rights, including the Fourth Amendment, to the state legislatures on September 25, 1789, 1 Stat. 97, had, some two months prior to that proposal, enacted the first customs statute, Act of July 31, 1789, c. 5, 1 Stat. 29. Section 24 of this statute granted customs officials "full power and authority" to enter and search "any ship or vessel, in which they shall have reason to suspect any goods, wares or merchandise subject to duty shall be concealed * * *." This acknowledgment of plenary customs power was differentiated from the more limited power to enter and search "any particular dwelling-house, store, building, or other place * * * "

---

33. The Court upheld the suspicionless stop of a ship in United States v. Villamonte–Marquez, 462 U.S. 579 (1983). It traced 19 U.S.C. § 1581(a), which authorizes a customs officer to board any vessel to examine the manifest and other documents and papers, to a similar 1790 statute and concluded that the framers of the Fourth Amendment considered it reasonable for officials to board vessels in waters providing ready access to the open sea, even without any suspicion of wrongdoing.

If a vessel on the high seas is owned by a non-resident alien, the search need not be justified under the border exception, because the Fourth Amendment is not applicable to searches of a non-resident alien's property that is located outside the United States. Such an alien is not one of "the people" entitled to Fourth Amendment protection. See United States v. Verdugo–Urquidez (discussed in the introduction to this Chapter); United States v. Davis, 905 F.2d 245 (9th Cir.1990) (applying *Verdugo–Urquidez* to a search on the high seas).

where a warrant upon "cause to suspect" was required. The historical importance of the enactment of this customs statute by the same Congress which proposed the Fourth Amendment is, we think, manifest. * * *

* * *

Border searches, then, from before the adoption of the Fourth Amendment, have been considered to be "reasonable" by the single fact that the person or item in question had entered into our country from outside. There has never been any additional requirement that the reasonableness of a border search depended on the existence of probable cause. This longstanding recognition that searches at our borders without probable cause and without a warrant are nonetheless "reasonable" has a history as old as the Fourth Amendment itself. We reaffirm it now.

B

Respondents urge upon us, however, the position that mailed letters are somehow different, and, whatever may be the normal rule with respect to border searches, different considerations, requiring the full panoply of Fourth Amendment protections, apply to international mail. * * *

The border-search exception is grounded in the recognized right of the sovereign to control, subject to substantive limitations imposed by the Constitution, who and what may enter the country. It is clear that there is nothing in the rationale behind the border-search exception which suggests that the mode of entry will be critical. It was conceded at oral argument that customs officials could search, without probable cause and

without a warrant, envelopes carried by an entering traveler, whether in his luggage or on his person. Surely no different constitutional standard should apply simply because the envelopes were mailed, not carried. The critical fact is that the envelopes cross the border and enter this country, not that they are brought in by one mode of transportation rather than another. It is their entry into this country from without it that makes a resulting search "reasonable."

* * *

* * * The historically recognized scope of the border-search doctrine, suggests no distinction in constitutional doctrine stemming from the mode of transportation across our borders. The contrary view of the Court of Appeals and respondents stems, we think, [on the lower court's reasoning] that "the rationale of the border search exception * * * is based upon * * * the difficulty of obtaining a warrant when the subject of the search is mobile, as a car or person * * *."

The fundamental difficulty with this position is that the "border search" exception is not based on the doctrine of "exigent circumstances" at all. It is a longstanding, historically recognized exception to the Fourth Amendment's general principle that a warrant be obtained * * *.

* * *

In view of the wealth of authority establishing the border search as "reasonable" within the Fourth Amendment even though there be neither probable cause nor a warrant, we reject the distinctions made by the Court of Appeals in its opinion.[a]

a. Justice Stevens, joined by Justices Brennan and Marshall, dissented, arguing that Congress did not confer authority to open letters without probable cause. Justice Powell wrote a concurring opinion.

Note on Routine Border Searches

The court in United States v. Charleus, 871 F.2d 265 (2d Cir.1989), states the well-accepted proposition that "routine border searches of the personal belongings and effects of entrants may be conducted without regard to probable cause or reasonable suspicion." Such searches are deemed reasonable because of the important state interest involved in regulating the border, the diminished expectation of privacy attendant to crossing the border, and the limited intrusiveness of a routine border search. Does the lesser expectation of privacy in luggage carried into the country justify warrantless border searches, or does the existence of such searches reduce one's expectation of privacy?

Routine vs. Non-routine Border Searches

While suspicionless routine border searches have been well-accepted, "the rule as to nonroutine border searches is, however, different." United States v. Robles, 45 F.3d 1 (1st Cir.1995). Because they are more intrusive, non-routine border searches must be supported by some level of individualized suspicion.

But where do you draw the line between routine and non-routine border searches? In United States v. Sandoval Vargas, 854 F.2d 1132 (9th Cir.1988), Customs Inspectors referred the defendant's car to a secondary inspection area, and conducted a thorough search of the passenger compartment and the trunk. The court found this a routine search, noting that it was "typical of those conducted at the border." In contrast, in United States v. Puig, 810 F.2d 1085 (11th Cir.1987), the court held that individualized suspicion was required for a customs official to drill a hole into the hull of a boat. Do you see any material difference between these two intrusions? See also United States v. Molina–Tarazon, 279 F.3d 709 (9th Cir. 2002) (dismantling and search of an automobile gas tank was not a routine border search: "Three aspects of the search here render it non-routine: Force was used to remove and disassemble the fuel tank; the procedure involved some risk of harm; and someone whose vehicle was subjected to such a search is likely to feel a diminished sense of security.").

Searches of persons can fall on either side of the line between routine and non-routine border searches. For example, in United States v. Sanders, 663 F.2d 1 (2d Cir.1981), customs officials forced the defendant to take off his artificial leg and inspected it, finding drugs. The court likened the police activity to a body cavity search, well-recognized as more intrusive than the routine border search. In contrast, in United States v. Charleus, 871 F.2d 265 (2d Cir.1989), a customs inspector patted down the defendant, felt a hard lump under his clothing, and lifted the back of his shirt, whereupon he found packages of narcotics taped to the defendant's body. The court analyzed the intrusion as follows:

> The [intrusion] arguably straddles the line between the two categories of border searches—searching more than personal belongings or effects such as a purse, wallet, or even outer jacket was involved; but the search was not nearly as intrusive as a body cavity or full strip search. Since the potential indignity resulting from a pat on the back followed by a lifting of one's shirt simply fails to compare with the much greater level of intrusion associated with a body cavity or full strip search, we decline to hold that reasonable suspicion was here required.

See also United States v. Kelly, 302 F.3d 291 (5th Cir. 2002) (canine sniff of a person, including contact with the dog's nose, was a routine border search: "Certainly, a canine sniff, even one involving some bodily contact, is no more intrusive than a frisk or a pat-down, both of which clearly qualify as routine border searches.'').

The court in United States v. Braks, 842 F.2d 509 (1st Cir.1988), listed factors it considered relevant in assessing whether a border search is non-routine:

(i) whether the search results in the exposure of intimate body parts or requires the suspect to disrobe;

(ii) whether physical contact between Customs officials and the suspect occurs during the search;

(iii) whether force is used to effect the search;

(iv) whether the type of search exposes the suspect to pain or danger;

(v) the overall manner in which the search is conducted; and

(vi) whether the suspect's reasonable expectations of privacy, if any, are abrogated by the search.

The *Braks* court applied these principles to a case in which a female traveler was taken to a private room by female officers and forced to lift her skirt and expose her undergarments, at which point the officers discovered a bulge in Braks' girdle that turned out to be cocaine. The court held that this was a routine border search, and therefore no suspicion was required. Do you agree? Would the result have been the same if Braks had been forced to lift her skirt in public? If the officers had been male?

The Degree of Suspicion Required for a Non–Routine Border Intrusion

Assume that a border intrusion is so severe as to be considered "non-routine." What standard of proof is required for such an intrusion? The Court addressed this question in United States v. Montoya de Hernandez, 473 U.S. 531 (1985). Justice Rehnquist, writing for a six-person majority, stated that "the detention of a traveler at the border, beyond the scope of a routine customs search and inspection, is justified at its inception if customs agents, considering all the facts surrounding the traveler and her trip, reasonably suspect that the traveler is smuggling contraband in her alimentary canal."

Montoya de Hernandez went though customs in Los Angeles after arriving on a plane from Colombia. Her eight recent trips to either Miami or Los Angeles caused agents to question her about the purpose for her trip. She carried $5,000 cash, mostly $50 bills, with no billfold and stated that she came to purchase goods for her husband's store in Colombia. Although she had no appointments with sellers and no hotel reservation, she stated that she planned to ride around the city visiting retail stores and that she planned to stay at a Holiday Inn. She could not recall how her airline ticket was purchased. In her valise inspectors found four changes of "cold weather" clothing.

These facts, the Court held, were sufficient to warrant seasoned inspectors in arriving at a reasonable suspicion that Montoya de Hernandez was a "balloon swallower" attempting to smuggle drugs into the country. A strip search by a female inspector revealed a fullness in the suspect's abdomen. The inspector noticed that the suspect was wearing two pair of elastic underpants with a paper towel lining the crotch area. Upon receiving this information, the inspector in charge informed the suspect of his suspicion. The inspector gave her the option of returning to Colombia on the next available flight, agreeing to an x-ray or remaining in detention until she produced a monitored bowel movement. She chose the first option, but inspectors were unable to arrange a flight. Sixteen hours later, the suspect had not defecated or urinated and had refused food or drink. It appeared that she was struggling to avoid use of the toilet. Inspectors sought and obtained a warrant authorizing a rectal examination and x-ray, provided that the physician consider the suspect's claim of pregnancy. A pregnancy test was negative, and a rectal examination produced a balloon containing a foreign substance. Investigators arrested the suspect. She later passed 88 balloons through her system containing 80% pure cocaine hydrochloride.

The Supreme Court upheld both the initial inspection and the detention, finding that the delay was attributable to the suspect's "heroic" efforts "to resist the call of nature" and that the detention was not unreasonably long even though it "undoubtedly exceed[ed] any other detention we have approved under reasonable suspicion." Justice Rehnquist emphasized not only the suspect-created delay, but also the heavy state interest and diminished expectation of privacy attendant to a border crossing. He noted that "alimentary canal smuggling cannot be detected in the amount of time in which other illegal activity may be investigated through brief *Terry*-type stops." Justice Stevens concurred in the judgment on the ground that the prolonged detention was attributable to the suspect's choice not to consent to an x-ray. Justice Brennan, joined by Justice Marshall, described the facts as a "disgusting and saddening episode" involving a detention based upon a profile that justified at most reasonable suspicion, and he dissented. He argued that "[i]ndefinite involuntary *incommunicado* detentions 'for investigation' are the hallmark of a police state, not a free society."

Standard of Proof Between Probable Cause and Reasonable Suspicion?

The lower court in *Montoya* had found that the intrusion was so severe that it had to be justified by a "clear indication" of criminal activity. This was a standard of proof somewhere between reasonable suspicion and probable cause. In *Montoya,* the majority emphatically rejected this approach, and stated that as in *Terry,* there is no relevant standard of proof between reasonable suspicion and probable cause. Justice Rehnquist concluded as follows:

> We do not think that the Fourth Amendment's emphasis upon reasonableness is consistent with the creation of a third verbal standard in addition to reasonable suspicion and probable cause; * * * subtle verbal gradations may obscure rather than elucidate the meaning of the provision in question.

> The reasonable suspicion standard has been applied in a number of contexts and effects a needed balance between private and public interests when law enforcement officials must make a limited intrusion on less than probable cause.

After *Montoya,* there are apparently only two types of intrusions at the border— a routine border intrusion that can be done without suspicion, and a non-routine border intrusion that requires reasonable suspicion. It could be argued that some intrusions at the border could be so severe as to require probable cause, but given the facts of *Montoya* and the state interest supporting border searches, can you envision such an intrusion? Perhaps compelled surgery?

Note that lower courts have read *Montoya de Hernandez* as holding that officers do not need probable cause for a border detention of an internal carrier, no matter how long a detention is required; thus, the lesser standard of reasonable suspicion sets the benchmark for these detentions. See United States v. Adekunle, 2 F.3d 559 (5th Cir.1993) (reasonable suspicion sufficient for 100 hour incommunicado detention, forced use of laxatives, and monitored bowel movement); United States v. Odofin, 929 F.2d 56 (2d Cir.1991) (24 day detention before bowel movement; reasonable suspicion sufficient).

Is a Warrant Ever Required?

The Court in *Montoya de Hernandez* held that the Customs officials did not need a warrant to detain the defendant for over 16 hours while waiting for nature to take its course. This has led some lower courts to conclude that no judicial intervention is ever required for a border detention—regardless of how long that detention may be—until the defendant is actually arrested and then entitled to a post-arrest determination of probable cause. See United States v. Esieke, 940 F.2d 29 (2d Cir.1991) (36–hour detention until bowel movement: "an extended border detention of a suspected alimentary canal smuggler does not implicate the Fourth Amendment's warrant clause and, accordingly, does not require judicial approval. * * * The length of an extended border detention is governed by the detainee's bodily processes, not by a clock."). Other courts have imposed procedural safeguards requiring judicial supervision of extended detentions, without specifically stating that such safeguards are required by the Fourth Amendment. See United States v. Adekunle, 2 F.3d 559 (5th Cir.1993) (concerned with the "incommunicado" nature of a long-term detention, the court stated: "Failure to obtain a judicial determination within 48 hours shifts the burden to the government to demonstrate a bona fide emergency or extraordinary circumstance" for the border detention).

Searches Away From the Border

While the constitutionality of border searches has never been questioned, considerable controversy has arisen over the question, "what is a border?" The right to search at the border has generally been recognized as extending to its functional equivalent as well. For example, if a plane flies from Mexico City nonstop to Denver, a search by customs officials at the Denver airport is considered a border search. Before aircraft may be searched at an internal checkpoint, however, there must be a high degree of probability that a border crossing took place, or that the object of search has just entered the country. United States v. Ivey, 546 F.2d 139 (5th Cir.1977). The same standard applies to searches of ships. United States v. Tilton, 534 F.2d 1363 (9th Cir.1976). In Torres v. Puerto Rico, 442 U.S. 465 (1979), the Court unanimously agreed that a trip from the mainland to Puerto Rico did not result in the crossing of an *international* border and that the border search exception to the warrant requirement did not apply.

A more troubling problem has arisen in connection with searches of vehicles inside the border, pursuant to § 287(a) of the Immigration and Nationality Act

[8 U.S.C.A. § 1357(a)], which allows searches for aliens "within a reasonable distance from any external boundary of the United States." A reasonable distance has been defined as 100 air miles from any external border, 8 CFR § 287.1. The reasons for this legislative extension of border search powers, and the regulatory response, is explained in the following excerpt from United States v. Martinez–Fuerte, 428 U.S. 543, 552–53 (1976):

> Interdicting the flow of illegal entrants from Mexico poses formidable law enforcement problems. The principal problem arises from surreptitious entries. The United States shares a border with Mexico that is almost 2,000 miles long, and much of the border area is uninhabited desert or thinly populated arid land. Although the Border Patrol maintains personnel, electronic equipment, and fences along portions of the border, it remains relatively easy for individuals to enter the United States without detection. It also is possible for an alien to enter unlawfully at a port of entry by the use of falsified papers or to enter lawfully but violate restrictions of entry in an effort to remain in the country unlawfully. Once within the country, the aliens seek to travel inland to areas where employment is believed to be available, frequently meeting by prearrangement with friends or professional smugglers who transport them in private vehicles.

> The Border Patrol conducts three kinds of inland traffic-checking operations in an effort to minimize illegal immigration. Permanent checkpoints, such as those at San Clemente and Sarita, are maintained at or near intersections of important roads leading away from the border. They operate on a coordinated basis designed to avoid circumvention by smugglers and others who transport the illegal aliens. Temporary checkpoints, which operate like permanent ones, occasionally are established in other strategic locations. Finally, roving patrols are maintained to supplement the checkpoint system.

*

> [P]ermanent checkpoints are chosen on the basis of a number of factors. The Border Patrol believes that to assure effectiveness, a checkpoint must be (i) distant enough from the border to avoid interference with traffic in populated areas near the border, (ii) close to the confluence of two or more significant roads leading away from the border, (iii) situated in terrain that restricts vehicle passage around the checkpoint, (iv) on a stretch of highway compatible with safe operation, and (v) beyond the 25–mile zone in which "border passes" are valid.

The operation of the checkpoints is outlined in United States v. Ortiz, 422 U.S. 899, 910–911, 914 (1975) (Appendix to Burger, C.J., concurring).

> When the checkpoints, whether permanent or temporary, are in operation, an officer standing at the "point" in full dress uniform on the highway will view the decelerating oncoming vehicles and their passengers, and will visually determine whether he has reason to believe the occupants of the vehicle are aliens (i.e., "breaks the pattern" of usual traffic). If so, the vehicle will be stopped (if the traffic at the checkpoint is heavy, as at the San Clemente checkpoint, the vehicle will be actually directed off the highway) for inquiries to be made by the agent. If the agent does not have reason to believe that the vehicle approaching the checkpoint is carrying

aliens, he may exchange salutations, or merely wave the vehicle through the checkpoint.

If, after questioning the occupants, the agent then believes that illegal aliens may be secreted in the vehicle (because of a break in the "pattern" indicating the possibility of smuggling) he will inspect the vehicle by giving a cursory visual inspection of those areas of the vehicle not visible from the outside (i.e. trunk, interior portion of camper, etc.).

Beginning with Almeida–Sanchez v. United States, 413 U.S. 266 (1973), the Supreme Court decided a series of cases dealing with the constitutionality of these law enforcement efforts in border areas. In *Almeida-Sanchez* the defendant was stopped by a roving Border Patrol on an east-west road in California about 25 air miles north of the Mexican border. The officers had no warrant and no probable cause to stop or search. They nevertheless searched the defendant's vehicle for illegal aliens, discovering instead a large quantity of marijuana. The Court held the search unconstitutional because the search was not conducted at the border nor at a functional equivalent thereof. In a 5–4 decision, Justice Stewart wrote for the majority that a roving border patrol could not conduct a vehicle search without probable cause. Justice White's dissent found the search to be a reasonable response to the unique problems of enforcing immigration laws in border areas.

Two years later, the Court held that stops by roving border patrols, absent reasonable cause to suspect that aliens were being illegally transported, were unconstitutional. However, in light of significant enforcement needs and the limited intrusion entailed in a stop for questioning, reasonable suspicion rather than probable cause would justify the stop. Any additional detention, however, would require probable cause. United States v. Brignoni–Ponce, 422 U.S. 873 (1975). Thus, roving border patrols are subject to the same standards as other law enforcement stops under *Terry*.

The use of traffic checkpoints removed from the border also came under scrutiny. In United States v. Ortiz, supra, warrantless searches at internal checkpoints were held unconstitutional unless based on probable cause. The Court found that, at least insofar as searches were concerned, the risk of official abuse of discretion was just as great at a checkpoint as it was at a roving patrol; officers at checkpoints decided which cars to search, and only 3% of the vehicles that were stopped were also searched.

The following year, the Court approved warrantless *stops* of vehicles at permanent checkpoints for limited questioning of the occupants. United States v. Martinez–Fuerte, 428 U.S. 543 (1976). No probable cause or reasonable suspicion was required to justify the stops. The Court reasoned that suspicionless checkpoint stops are necessary tools of law enforcement, and that the public interest in making these stops outweighed the constitutionally protected interests of private citizens. In addition, Justice Powell, writing for the Court, stated that motorists could be selectively referred to secondary inspection areas for further questioning, again without any articulable suspicion. He argued that the additional intrusion—although admittedly a seizure—was limited and inoffensive and that use of the questioning techniques tended to minimize the intrusion on the general motoring public, thus protecting other Fourth Amendment interests. However, if the secondary inspection was unduly offensive or intrusive, then individualized suspicion would be required. See also United States v.

Machuca–Barrera, 261 F.3d 425 (5th Cir. 2001) (stop at immigration checkpoint can last no longer than necessary to fulfil its immigration-related purpose).

A final issue dealt with in *Martinez-Fuerte* was whether a judicial warrant is required to authorize a particular checkpoint location and the practice of routine stops. Justice Powell contrasted the border checkpoint situation with those circumstances that justified the administrative warrant requirement in *Camara*. He argued that *Martinez-Fuerte* involved a lesser intrusion, that the motorist at a checkpoint knows that the officers present have authority to act, and that high ranking executive officials make decisions on the location of checkpoints, thereby minimizing the field officer's discretion.

Justice Brennan, in a dissent joined by Justice Marshall, ignored the warrant issue. Instead, he attacked the majority's distinction between roving patrol and checkpoint stops, finding both to be unreasonable under the Fourth Amendment. Justice Brennan dismissed the contentions that checkpoint stops were subjectively less intrusive, and that selective referral to secondary detention areas was any less discretionary or stigmatizing than roving patrol stops. He suggested that reasonable suspicion should be required for checkpoint stops, or, at the very least, for the additional detention.

The Reverse Border Exception

Should border officials have the same broad powers to search outgoing persons and vehicles as they have to search those entering the country? Do any of the considerations that justify regular border searches apply to searches of persons and things leaving the country? See United States v. Duncan, 693 F.2d 971 (9th Cir.1982) (holding, 2–1, that search of departing passenger was a border search, requiring no suspicion). In United States v. Berisha, 925 F.2d 791 (5th Cir.1991), the court stated that "both incoming and outgoing border searches have several features in common; for example, the government is interested in protecting some interest of United States citizens, there is a likelihood of smuggling attempts at the border, and the individual is on notice that his privacy may be invaded when he crosses the border." The court therefore upheld a warrantless, suspicionless patdown search of a departing traveler, which uncovered $17,000 of domestic currency.

Do you agree that the principles supporting the border exception apply equally to the "reverse" border exception? Consider the arguments of Judge Kozinski, dissenting in United States v. Nates, 831 F.2d 860 (9th Cir.1987), a case in which the court upheld the suspicionless search of outgoing luggage under the reverse border exception, after the defendant had checked it with the airline:

> We * * * don't know precisely how many suitcases are opened and searched every day without the knowledge or consent of their owners, but the number appears to be very substantial. In a case recently decided by the Eleventh Circuit, the record disclosed that in a seven-month period during 1985, *a single customs agent* surreptitiously "opened about 50,000 suitcases." United States v. Hernandez–Salazar, 813 F.2d 1126, 1130 n. 16 (11th Cir.1987). If this rate is typical, it would amount to about 100,000 bags opened per agent per year. Assuming that the customs service assigns even a modest number of agents to this task, the number of surreptitious

intrusions into the property and privacy of travelers is potentially staggering. It is a matter that should give us serious pause lest we overlook, and implicitly approve, what may amount to wholesale violations of the fourth amendment rights of the traveling public.

* * * [W]hen the search is conducted outside the passengers' presence, they are unable to protect the physical security or integrity of their possessions. Thus, bags might be damaged when they are forced open, or their contents might be broken, lost or stolen. When passengers are present during the search, they can minimize the risk by opening suitcases themselves and alerting the agents about any items that may be subject to damage. Also, they can witness any mishap and hold the agent responsible. Agents, for their part, may be more careful if passengers are watching. * * * The fact of the matter is, when agents secretly break into people's suitcases and search through them by the hundreds of thousands, occasionally something will go wrong—someone will be tempted, or careless, or even do something that seems perfectly reasonable yet causes damage, such as opening a canister of undeveloped film.

Finally, there is a separate intrusion because passengers whose luggage is searched are generally never told about it. This means that when something is lost, stolen, mislaid or broken, the passenger will be completely mystified as to what happened. He will have no idea where to inquire as to its whereabouts or demand compensation. He may spend countless hours looking for the item in places he might have left it, harassing people who might have taken it, never suspecting that a government agent used a passkey to go through his luggage. Being subject to a secret search and then never being told about it is something I think most people would find especially offensive, and this then bears on the reasonableness of the procedure employed by the government.

All of this might be beside the point if there were no reasonably available alternatives. But there clearly are. * * *

One simple way of handling the matter would be for passengers to exit the country through customs—with occasional spot checks—much as they do when entering.

Are reverse border searches tolerated because of the concern that if a search is not conducted, the property in question will get away forever? Does the government have a legitimate concern about property that will no longer be within the United States?

I. CONSENT SEARCHES

1. *Voluntary Consent*

Voluntariness Distinguished From Waiver: Schneckloth v. Bustamonte

A search based upon voluntary consent is reasonable even in the absence of a warrant or any articulable suspicion. The Supreme Court addressed the requirements for valid consent in Schneckloth v. Bustamonte, 412 U.S. 218 (1973). A California police officer at 2:40 a.m. stopped an automobile with a headlight and a license plate light burned out. Six men were in the car. The driver had no license, only one passenger produced his license, and he explained that the car was his brother's. The officer asked the men to step out of the car, they complied, and after two additional officers arrived, the officer asked the person who produced the license if he could search the car. The man replied, "Sure, go ahead," and opened the trunk for the officer. The search produced three stolen checks. The court of appeals held that consent was not valid because the consenting party was never told that he could refuse to give consent. The Supreme Court disagreed.

Justice Stewart's majority opinion cited voluntariness concepts developed in confession cases and concluded that

> the question whether a consent to a search was in fact voluntary or was the product of duress or coercion, express or implied, is a question of fact to be determined from the totality of the circumstances. While knowledge of the right to refuse consent is one factor to be taken into account, the government need not establish such knowledge as the sine qua non of an effective consent.

The defendant argued that warnings—like the *Miranda* warnings, which we shall examine in connection with police interrogation—should be required before consent can be sought. The majority responded that it would be impractical to give such warnings under the "informal and unstructured conditions" in which consent requests are usually made.

Justice Stewart distinguished the traditional concept of waiver of "the safeguards of a fair criminal trial" from consent to search. He concluded that a defendant was to be given "the greatest possible opportunity to utilize every facet of the constitutional model of a fair criminal trial," and that "[a]ny trial conducted in derogation of that model leaves open the possibility that the trial reached an unfair result." But, he found, that "[t]he protections of the Fourth Amendment are of a wholly different order." Justice Stewart concluded that the proper test in consent search cases is not whether there was a waiver of the defendant's Fourth Amendment rights, but whether the consent to search was voluntary under the totality of circumstances. He argued that there was nothing unfair or suspect about consent to a search, and that the Fourth and Fourteenth Amendments did not require that citizens be discouraged from cooperating with the police. The Court held that whether a consent was voluntary must be determined by the totality of the circumstances. The suspect's knowledge of his right to refuse consent is therefore relevant in determining the voluntariness of the consent. But absence of a consent warning is not dispositive.

As applied to the facts of the case, Justice Stewart had no trouble in concluding that the suspect's consent was voluntary—the suspect was not under arrest; the officer used no force and made no threats; and the suspect expressed no unwillingness to consent.

Justice Brennan dissented, arguing that "[i]t wholly escapes me how our citizens can meaningfully be said to have waived something as precious as a constitutional guarantee without ever being aware of its existence." Justice Marshall also dissented. He argued that consent searches are permissible because we permit our citizens to choose not to exercise their constitutional rights, and that "consent cannot be considered a meaningful choice unless he knew that he could in fact exclude the police." His solution was to have the government bear the burden of showing knowledge, which burden could be satisfied by a warning before asking for consent.

Reaffirming Schneckloth: United States v. Drayton

The Court reaffirmed its totality of the circumstances analysis in United States v. Drayton, 536 U.S. 194 (2002), in which the Court upheld searches of bags and persons made during a bus sweep. The Court found that while the officer did not inform the suspects of their right to refuse consent, "he did request permission to search, and the totality of the circumstances indicates that their consent was voluntary, so the searches were reasonable. The *Drayton* Court concluded as follows:

> In a society based on law, the concept of agreement and consent should be given a weight and dignity of its own. Police officers act in full accord with the law when they ask citizens for consent. It reinforces the rule of law for the citizen to advise the police of his or her wishes and for the police to act in reliance on that understanding. When this exchange takes place, it dispels inferences of coercion.

The Court's opinion in *Drayton* is fully set forth in the section on stops and frisks, supra.

The Consequences of Refusing Consent

Is refusal to consent suspicious? Can an officer conclude that a person who refuses to permit a search has something to hide? In United States v. Prescott, 581 F.2d 1343 (9th Cir.1978), the court held that a person cannot be penalized for exercising the right to refuse to permit a search, and that "passive refusal to consent to a warrantless search is privileged conduct which cannot be considered as evidence of criminal wrongdoing." The majority said that its reasoning was necessary "to protect the exercise of a constitutional right." Surprisingly, there was a dissenting opinion that argued that no harm would come if a citizen's decision to invoke Fourth Amendment rights were admissible in evidence against the citizen. See also United States v. Torres, 65 F.3d 1241 (4th Cir.1995) ("Officers cannot use a traveler's refusal to consent to the search of his bags as support for the requisite reasonable, articulable suspicion.").

Thus, an officer is not permitted to consider a refusal to permit consent as evidence of guilt. But what if the citizen permits a search because he thinks, incorrectly, that if he refuses, this will count against him? Can such consent be voluntary? Must the citizen be informed that refusal to consent cannot be used against him? How would the Court's reasoning in *Schneckloth* resolve these questions?

The Impact of Custody

In *Schneckloth,* consent was obtained from a person not in the custody of the police, a fact emphasized by the Court in its conclusion that its decision was "a narrow one." But in United States v. Watson, 423 U.S. 411 (1976), the Court found that the absence of consent warnings or of proof that Watson knew he could withhold consent was not controlling where the defendant "had been arrested and was in custody, but his consent was given while on a public street, not in the confines of the police station." The majority added that "to hold that illegal coercion is made out from the fact of arrest and the failure to inform the arrestee that he could withhold consent would not be consistent with *Schneckloth.*" *Watson* made clear that *Schneckloth* was not quite as narrow as Justice Stewart had proclaimed. Justice Marshall, joined by Justice Brennan, adhered to his opinion in *Schneckloth,* but added that "even short of this position there are valid reasons for application of such a rule to consents procured from suspects held in custody."

Not surprisingly, *Watson* has been extended to uphold consent extracted in all types of custodial situations; while the person's custodial status is relevant to whether the consent was voluntary, it is not dispositive. See, e.g., United States v. Hidalgo, 7 F.3d 1566 (11th Cir.1993) (consent voluntary even though the defendant "was arrested by SWAT team members who broke into his home in the early morning, woke him, and forced him to the ground at gun point"); United States v. Duran, 957 F.2d 499 (7th Cir.1992) (consent voluntary even though the suspect was under arrest and in the police station).

Totality of the Circumstances

After *Schneckloth* the totality of the circumstances must be examined to determine whether a person has voluntarily consented to a search. In Bumper v. North Carolina, 391 U.S. 543 (1968), the Court placed the burden of proving that consent "was, in fact, freely and voluntarily given" on the government, and "[t]his burden cannot be discharged by showing no more than acquiescence to a claim of lawful authority." See also United States v. Lindsay, 506 F.2d 166 (D.C.Cir.1974) (silence not consent).

The Supreme Court applied *Schneckloth* and found a valid consent in United States v. Mendenhall, 446 U.S. 544 (1980). Officers encountered Mendenhall in an airport, suspected she was a drug courier, and asked her to accompany them to a private room. She agreed. After a series of polite questions, Mendenhall ultimately agreed to a strip search and a search of her purse. Narcotics were found in the purse and on her person. Although a majority of the Court did not agree on whether to treat Mendenhall as "seized" when federal agents first approached her, a majority did agree that she voluntarily consented to accompany the agents to their airport office and to have her purse and person searched. In deciding that Mendenhall voluntarily accompanied the agents to their office, the Court observed that she was simply asked to go and was not threatened or physically forced. In deciding that the searches in the office were consensual, the Court emphasized that Mendenhall was twice told that she was free to decline consent. Justice White's dissent for four members of the Court argued that the government failed to meet its burden of proving that Mendenhall consented to accompany the officers to their office. "[T]he Court's conclusion can only be based on the notion that consent can be assumed from the absence of proof that a suspect resisted police authority. This is a notion that we have squarely rejected."

In United States v. Gonzalez–Basulto, 898 F.2d 1011 (5th Cir.1990), the court set forth a non-exclusive list of six factors relevant to whether consent is voluntarily obtained.

(1) the voluntariness of the defendant's custodial status; (2) the presence of coercive police procedures; (3) the extent and level of the defendant's cooperation with the police; (4) the defendant's awareness of his right to refuse consent; (5) the defendant's education and intelligence; and (6) the defendant's belief that no evidence will be found.

Obviously, none of these factors are dispositive. For example, *Watson* found a consent voluntary even though the defendant was under arrest, and *Schneckloth* found voluntary consent even though the defendant was unaware of his right to refuse. However, a weak showing by the government on several of the factors substantially increases the likelihood that consent will be found involuntary.

The facts and resolution of *Gonzalez–Basulto,* supra, are typical of consent cases after *Schneckloth.* Border patrol agents at a permanent checkpoint suspected that Gonzalez–Basulto was carrying drugs in a refrigerated tractor-trailer rig. He was referred to a secondary inspection area to verify his claim that he was an American citizen. Gonzalez produced immigration documentation, and looked nervously about at the drug sniffing dogs present at the checkpoint. The agent asked whether Gonzalez would mind opening the trailer for an inspection. Gonzalez replied "no problem" and unlocked and opened the trailer, which contained boxes of oranges and lemons. A drug-sniffing dog was hoisted into the trailer, and gave a positive alert. The agents opened many boxes, and finally found cocaine in boxes near the front of the trailer. The court found that Gonzalez voluntarily consented to the search.

> The agents did not brandish weapons or threaten Gonzalez in any way. Gonzalez was not placed under arrest until the search uncovered the cocaine. Gonzalez cooperated with the agent who requested permission to search by responding "no problem" to the request and by unlocking and opening the trailer doors. While the agent admitted that he did not inform Gonzalez of his right to refuse to consent, the agent emphasized that he did not put any kind of pressure on Gonzalez to get his consent. He merely asked for permission. Gonzalez was not well-educated but he exhibited a sufficient degree of understanding to indicate his "no problem" response was intelligent. Gonzalez may well have believed that no drugs would be found because the cocaine was hidden in boxes toward the front of the trailer and there was little crawl space in the trailer.

Consider the sixth factor discussed in *Gonzalez–Basulto,* i.e. the defendant's belief that no evidence would be found. In United States v. Mendenhall, supra, the Court categorically rejected the argument that Mendenhall could not have voluntarily consented to a strip search because it would disclose the drugs that she carried. The Court stated that, while the suspect may later regret having given consent, "the question is not whether she acted in her ultimate self-interest, but whether she acted voluntarily." Wouldn't the contrary view—that a person could not give voluntary consent if the search would be likely to uncover incriminating evidence—all but do away with consent searches? Is there any plausible reason for a suspect to voluntarily consent to a search that will uncover evidence?

Threats of Action if Consent Is Refused

Suppose an officer says, "I would like you to consent, but if you don't, I'll just come back a little later with a warrant." Does this threat render a subsequent consent involuntary? The court considered this question in United States v. Duran, 957 F.2d 499 (7th Cir.1992), in which Karen Duran consented to the search of an outbuilding after officers told her that they would obtain a warrant if she didn't consent. The court stated:

> This may have induced Karen to grant her consent, but it was not coercive under the fourth amendment. Although empty threats to obtain a warrant may at times render a subsequent consent involuntary, see United States v. Talkington, 843 F.2d 1041 (7th Cir.1988) (consent invalid when police lied in telling suspect that they were in the process of getting a search warrant); Dotson v. Somers, 175 Conn. 614, 402 A.2d 790 (1978) (consent invalid where police had insufficient grounds upon which to base a warrant application), the threat in this case was firmly grounded. Karen's admission that [her husband, the defendant] dealt marijuana would have provided the police probable cause had they sought a search warrant, so their threat to do so in the event she refused consent was entirely proper.

What if an officer thinks he has probable cause, and threatens to obtain a warrant, but the reviewing court finds that he was mistaken and that probable cause did not exist? Was the officer's threat to obtain a warrant an "empty" one rendering a subsequent consent involuntary?

In United States v. Ivy, 165 F.3d 397 (6th Cir.1998), officers looking for drugs placed Ivy in custody in his house, together with his girlfriend Jones, and their infant child. Officers had found drugs on the premises in a legal search, and wanted to obtain consent to conduct a more detailed search. Jones was cuffed to a table by her leg. For a period of 90 minutes, police officers sought consent first from Ivy and then from Jones. When asked what would happen if he did not consent, Ivy was informed that a search warrant would be sought; that he and his girlfriend would be arrested; and that the child would be placed in foster care. Ivy then signed the consent form. The court found the consent to be involuntary. It explained as follows:

> The Government argues that Setliff's statements were lawful references to the fact that the officers could obtain a search warrant. It is true that an agent's statements to the effect that he would obtain a warrant if the suspect did not consent to the search does not taint the suspect's consent to a search. Setliff's remarks, however, went far beyond a mere reference to the fact that he could obtain a warrant. Rather, he explicitly stated that if Ivy did not sign the form, he would arrest Ivy's girlfriend and take away their small child.

* * *

In this case, Sergeant Setliff was uncertain as to Jones' level of involvement, if any, in the drugs found on the premises when he stated he would arrest her. Under the circumstances, it appears the statements made by Setliff were not merely informative, but were specifically calculated to induce fear and apply pressure. The intimidating nature of Setliff's statement is particularly striking when one considers that Setliff not only threatened to arrest Jones, but also to take Ivy and Jones' child from their custody. Even if Setliff was correct in that both parents were about to be arrested and taken to jail, there were supervision alternatives to state custody, such as having the child stay with a friend or relative. That Setliff stated, unequivocally, that the child would go into government custody if Ivy and Jones did not consent to a search indicates that Setliff was not merely trying to provide Ivy with data upon which to base his decision to consent, but rather was attempting to overcome Ivy's resolution not to consent. * * *

Even more disturbing than Sergeant Setliff's foreboding statements are the actions the police took with regard to Jones and her child while awaiting either consent or a warrant to search Ivy's house. The police handcuffed Jones, by her legs, to the kitchen table. At points during the hour and a half while police attempted to induce either Jones or Ivy to sign a consent, the police took Jones' child from her. Jones was finally allowed to keep her child after Ivy signed the consent form. Courts have found that antagonistic actions by the police against a suspect's family taint the voluntariness of any subsequent consent. See, e.g., United States v. Hurston, 12 F.Supp.2d 630, 637 (E.D.Mich.1998) (suspect's consent to search home was not given voluntarily, in light of "hectic" police entry, in which police "rounded up" suspect's children and fiancee); United States v. Eggers, 21 F.Supp.2d 261, 270–71 (S.D.N.Y.1998) (police statement that suspect's children would be locked out of house until search was executed constituted duress and coercion, annulling resultant consent). This Court now finds that such hostile police action against a suspect's family is a factor which significantly undermines the voluntariness of any subsequent consent given by the suspect.

After an hour and a half of this situation * * * Ivy finally acquiesced and signed the consent to search form. Perhaps this was a form of coerced chivalry on Ivy's behalf. Perhaps his will was overcome by the time, the threats, the police handling his child, and the sight of his girlfriend chained to a table. One thing is certain: Ivy's consent was not voluntarily imparted; his will was indeed overcome.

Must a Person Who Is Stopped Be Told That He Is Free to Leave?

In Ohio v. Robinette, 519 U.S. 33 (1996), Robinette was lawfully stopped for speeding and given a warning. After the officer returned his license, he asked Robinette: "One question before you get gone: Are you carrying any illegal contraband in your car? Any weapons of any kind, drugs, anything like that?" Robinette answered in the negative, and when the officer asked to search the car, Robinette consented. The officer found drugs in the car.

The state court held that Robinette's consent could not be voluntary because the officer never informed him that the stop had ended and he was free to go. The Supreme Court considered whether the Fourth Amendment requires an officer to inform a suspect after a stop has concluded that he is free to go before consent can be found voluntary. The Court, in an opinion by Chief Justice

Rehnquist for seven Justices, found no such bright-line requirement in the Fourth Amendment. The Chief Justice reasoned as follows:

> We have previously rejected a per se rule very similar to that adopted by the Supreme Court of Ohio in determining the validity of a consent to search. In Schneckloth v. Bustamonte, it was argued that such a consent could not be valid unless the defendant knew that he had a right to refuse the request. We rejected this argument: "While knowledge of the right to refuse consent is one factor to be taken into account, the government need not establish such knowledge as the sine qua non of an effective consent." And just as it "would be thoroughly impractical to impose on the normal consent search the detailed requirements of an effective warning," so too would it be unrealistic to require police officers to always inform detainees that they are free to go before a consent to search may be deemed voluntary.

> The Fourth Amendment test for a valid consent to search is that the consent be voluntary, and "voluntariness is a question of fact to be determined from all the circumstances." The Supreme Court of Ohio having held otherwise, its judgment is reversed, and the case is remanded for further proceedings not inconsistent with this opinion.

Justice Ginsburg concurred in the judgment in *Robinette*, emphasizing that while a "tell-then-ask" rule made good sense, imposing it as a constitutional requirement was inconsistent with the totality of circumstances approach mandated by *Schneckloth*.

Justice Stevens dissented. He argued that, by asking whether Robinette had contraband, the officer was continuing the detention, even though the initial reason for the detention had ended. Justice Stevens concluded from this that the continued interrogation, in the absence of reasonable suspicion, constituted an illegal seizure, which tainted Robinette's consent.

Subjective Attitudes Toward Authority

In United States v. Zapata, 997 F.2d 751 (10th Cir.1993), the defendant, a Mexican National, was traveling on a train. He was approached by DEA Agent Kevin Small. After a few questions from Agent Small concerning his itinerary and possible drug activity, Zapata consented to a search of his luggage, which contained narcotics. At his suppression hearing, Zapata testified as follows:

Q. Why did you allow Mr. Small to search your luggage?

A. Because I saw that he was a police officer.

Q. And of what significance was the fact he was a police officer?

A. I didn't know because I thought that when a policeman asks you something one has to answer.

Q. Did you think that when he was asking you, that he was really telling you what to do?

A. Yes, sir.

Q. Did you believe that you had any choice in not doing what he said?

A. At the moment I thought that if I didn't do it he would get angry or he would do something else.

When questioned by the court, Zapata indicated that he had heard that Mexican police "strike you, they hit you" when a citizen encounters a policeman. The district court held that Zapata's consent was involuntary, relying in large part on the fact that because of his upbringing in Mexico, "Defendant believed that he must acquiesce to all police requests because failure to do so could result in dire consequences, including physical harm." But the Court of Appeals reversed, reasoning as follows:

> [E]ven assuming some subjective characteristics are relevant to the validity of Mr. Zapata's consent, we reject the notion that his attitude toward police, from whatever source, can constitute such a relevant subjective characteristic. While such attributes as the age, gender, education, and intelligence of the accused have been recognized as relevant, an intangible characteristic such as attitude toward authority is inherently unverifiable and unquantifiable. Generalities about attitudes are even more vaporous. The district court's finding that Mr. Zapata's consent was not freely and voluntarily given is clearly erroneous.

Does a case like *Zapata* give the police too much leeway to take advantage of people from other cultures? Can we expect police to take part in an acculturation process when they are trying to obtain consent?

Did the Person Consent?

In some cases, the question is not whether the defendant consented voluntarily, but whether he consented at all. For example, in United States v. Price, 54 F.3d 342 (7th Cir.1995), Officer Brown stopped Pierce's car, became suspicious, and asked whether there were any drugs in the car. Pierce replied in the negative. Officer Brown then asked Pierce, "Do you mind if I take a look?" and Pierce quickly replied "Sure." Brown searched the car, and Pierce looked on without objection. Narcotics were discovered. At the suppression hearing, Pierce testified that when he said "Sure" what he meant was "Sure, I *mind*." The court of appeals responded to this argument as follows:

> Perhaps in the abstract one could say that given the phrasing of Brown's question, Pierce's response to it is ambiguous and thus capable of being interpreted as either "Go ahead" or "No way." But * * * [t]he only conclusion to be drawn from the totality of the evidence is that Pierce's immediate response "Sure" meant, "Sure, go ahead." The crucial fact is Pierce's failure to protest upon learning that Brown understood his response as a consent to the search. Had Pierce not agreed to the search, now was the time to make that clear. Yet when confronted with Brown's understanding of his response, Pierce offered no objection at all; instead, he submitted to a pat-down search and took a seat in Brown's patrol car in order to get out of the rain. Given these circumstances it was not clear error for the district court to find that Pierce's response "Sure" meant that he agreed to the search.

Assume that you are in Pierce's situation and that you really mean "Sure, I mind," not "Sure, go ahead." What would your reaction be if Officer Brown ignores you and goes ahead with the search anyway? Would telling him to stop have a positive effect, do you think? See also United States v. Worley, 193 F.3d 380 (6th Cir. 1999) ("the district court did not commit clear error in granting

Worley's motion to suppress after determining that his statement 'You've got the badge, I guess you can,' did not indicate consent to the search.'').

"Reluctant" Consent

In United States v. Rivas, 99 F.3d 170 (5th Cir.1996), Rivas was asked to sign a consent form for the search of his house. He signed the form, but added the word "reluctantly" at the signature line. Rivas argued that this stated reluctance indicated that the consent was involuntary. But the court disagreed. It reasoned that the fact that Rivas added the word "reluctantly" to the form, and then told the police that they could go ahead and search the house, "evidenced his awareness that he had the right to refuse to consent to the search." Thus, Rivas' addition to the form cut in favor of a finding of voluntariness, not against it. Do you agree?

2. Third Party Consent

Can a third party consent to the search of an area in which a suspect has an expectation of privacy? Frazier v. Cupp, 394 U.S. 731 (1969), upheld the search of a defendant's duffle bag when his cousin, a joint user of the bag, voluntarily consented. The Court rejected the argument that because the cousin had authority to use only one compartment of the bag, he could not consent to a search of the remainder, stating that it would not "engage in such metaphysical subtleties," and that the defendant, who allowed his cousin to use the bag, must "have assumed the risk" he would consent to let others see inside.

Actual Authority: United States v. Matlock

The leading third-party consent case is United States v. Matlock, 415 U.S. 164 (1974). Matlock was arrested in the front yard of a house. Mrs. Graff admitted the police to the house and told them she shared the house with Matlock. She consented to a search. The lower courts held that the third party consent doctrine depended upon not only the reasonable appearance of authority to consent but also upon actual authority to consent, and they found insufficient evidence to show actual authority. The Supreme Court reversed, finding actual authority. It did not reach the question whether apparent authority is sufficient. The Court stated the rationale for permitting third-party consent searches in the following analysis:

> The authority which justifies the third-party consent does not rest upon the law of property, with its attendant historical and legal refinements, but rests rather on mutual use of the property by persons generally having joint access or control for most purposes, so that it is reasonable to recognize that any of the co-inhabitants has the right to permit the inspection in his own right and that the others have assumed the risk that one of their number might permit the common area to be searched.

Apparent Authority: Illinois v. Rodriguez

The Court in Illinois v. Rodriguez, 497 U.S. 177 (1990), considered the issue it left open in *Matlock:* whether a search is valid when based on the consent of a third party who has apparent but not actual authority. The third party in

Rodriguez was Rodriguez's woman friend, who had, unknown to the officers, moved out of his apartment a month before the search and retained a key without permission. When speaking to the officers, she referred to the premises as "our apartment."

Justice Scalia, writing for a six-person majority, agreed with the lower courts that the friend did not have actual authority to consent to a search of the apartment, in that she had no joint access or control of the premises after moving out. According to the majority, however, the officers' reasonable belief that the friend had authority to consent would validate the entry. The Court rejected the defendant's argument that permitting a search on the basis of apparent but not actual authority would amount to an unauthorized waiver of the defendant's Fourth Amendment rights. Justice Scalia relied on *Schneckloth* and distinguished between a waiver of constitutional rights and the voluntary consent to search. He explained that while a waiver of a constitutional right must be personal, the validity of a consent search is determined by whether the search is reasonable:

> We would assuredly not permit * * * evidence seized in violation of the Fourth Amendment to be introduced on the basis of a trial court's mere 'reasonable belief'—derived from statements by unauthorized persons—that the defendant has waived his objection. But one must make a distinction between, on the one hand, trial rights that derive from the violation of constitutional guarantees and, on the other hand, the nature of those constitutional guarantees themselves. * * *
>
> What Rodriguez is assured by the trial right of the exclusionary rule, where it applies, is that no evidence seized in violation of the Fourth Amendment will be introduced at his trial unless he consents. What he is assured by the Fourth Amendment itself, however, is not that no government search of his house will occur unless he consents; but that no search will occur that is "unreasonable." * * * There are various elements, of course, that can make a search of a person's house reasonable—one of which is the consent of the person or his cotenant. The essence of respondent's argument is that we should impose upon this element a requirement that we have not imposed upon other elements that regularly compel government officers to exercise judgment regarding the facts: namely, the requirement that their judgment be not only responsible but correct.

Justice Scalia concluded that the question of authority to consent should be governed by the same standard of reasonableness—and allowance for reasonable mistakes—as had been applied in other areas of Fourth Amendment jurisprudence, such as probable cause, the execution of a warrant, and the existence of exigent circumstances. The Court remanded for a determination of whether the officers could have reasonably believed that Rodriguez's friend had actual authority to consent to a search of his apartment.

Justice Marshall, joined by Justices Brennan and Stevens, dissented. Justice Marshall contended that third party consent searches are permissible not because they are reasonable, but because a person "may voluntarily limit his expectation of privacy by allowing others to exercise authority over his possessions" and thus they are not searches at all. Justice Marshall concluded that if an individual did not actually voluntarily assume the risk of third party consent, there would then be a "search," and the consent of a third party does not make a search reasonable.

Mistakes of Law

In Stoner v. California, 376 U.S. 483 (1964), the government argued that the officers relied on the apparent authority of the hotel desk clerk to consent to a search of Stoner's room. The Court rejected that argument, stating that "the rights protected by the Fourth Amendment are not to be eroded by unrealistic doctrines of apparent authority." Is the result and language in *Stoner* inconsistent with *Rodriguez?* Or can it be explained by the reasonableness standards that are applicable to third party consent searches? Is *Stoner* really an apparent authority case? See, e.g., United States v. Brown, 961 F.2d 1039 (2d Cir.1992) (stating that *Rodriguez* does not validate "a search premised upon an erroneous view of the law" and that "an investigator's erroneous belief that landladies are generally authorized to consent to a search of a tenant's premises could not provide the authorization necessary for a warrantless search").

The Duty to Investigate

Does *Rodriguez* mean that the police can presume third party consent upon the assertion of the third party that he has common authority? If a babysitter answers the door, and asserts that she has common authority over the entire premises, can police search the entire house upon the babysitter's consent? What if the consent is obtained from a live-in babysitter? In United States v. Dearing, 9 F.3d 1428 (9th Cir.1993), the court held that a live-in babysitter lacked apparent authority to consent to a search of his employer's bedroom. The court declared that "the police are not allowed to proceed on the theory that ignorance is bliss," and concluded that the officer should have inquired into the extent of the babysitter's authorized access into his employer's bedroom. If the officer had made such an inquiry, and the babysitter lied and said that he had uninhibited access to the bedroom, would the search of the bedroom have been reasonable? Does *Dearing* require a cross-examination of every person who claims to have authority to consent? See also United States v. Whitfield, 939 F.2d 1071 (D.C.Cir.1991) (government's burden of proving valid consent "cannot be met if agents, faced with an ambiguous situation, nevertheless proceed without making further inquiry").

Actual But Not Apparent Authority

What if the babysitter in the above example really had actual authority, but could not reasonably be believed to have apparent authority? What if the officer did not believe that the babysitter had either apparent or actual authority, but in fact she had actual authority? In light of the pretext cases discussed throughout this Chapter, would the courts find that a search pursuant to the babysitter's consent was reasonable? See, e.g., United States v. Chaidez, 919 F.2d 1193, 1201–02 (7th Cir.1990) (it was unreasonable to infer authority when person consenting to search said that she did not live in the house and was there only to do laundry, and that she rented the property for her father; however, the fact that she had actual authority justified the search).

Three Kinds of Apparent Authority Questions

The court in United States v. Jenkins, 92 F.3d 430 (6th Cir.1996), set forth a helpful structure for determining whether third-party consent can be found on grounds of apparent authority. In *Jenkins,* the driver of a rig gave written consent to search the rig's trailer. When he signed the consent form, he said, "It's not up to me; I don't own the stuff." The officers knew that Jenkins, and not the driver, owned the rig. There was no lock on the trailer door. Drugs were found in his trailer, and Jenkins moved to suppress them on the ground that the driver had no actual or apparent authority to consent to a search of his trailer. The court analyzed the third-party consent problem in the following passage:

> In order to clarify the type of statements to an officer that would be necessary to put the officer on notice of an apparent consenter's lack of authority over a space, it is useful to identify three categories of situations. In the first class of situations, an officer would never be justified in believing that the consenter has authority, regardless of what the consenter says. An obvious example is where the officer is aware that the consenter has no rights to the property and no authority to consent, for example, asking the mailman, whom the officer sees delivering a letter, for consent to search a house. Another is where the consenter is obviously only a custodian with limited authority over a particular space, for example, a hotel clerk.

> In the second set of situations, a reasonable officer would usually think that the consenter does not have authority, but the officer could be justified in thinking otherwise if the consenter provides additional information indicating common authority. For example, an officer usually cannot assume that a landlord has authority to consent to search of property used by a tenant, but if the landlord asserts that he stores property or occasionally lives with the tenant, then a reasonable officer may be justified in assuming that the consenter has common authority. United States v. Yarbrough, 852 F.2d 1522, 1533–34 (9th Cir.1988) (landlord stored furniture on property, sometimes slept there, had a spare key); United States v. Hall, 979 F.2d 77, 79 (6th Cir.1992) (owner of room rented to defendant kept personal property in the room, the room was never locked, and "there was never an agreement or understanding between him and [the defendant] that he was not to go into the room"). In such cases, a simple "yes" to a request to search means "no"; but an elaborate "yes" describing a basis for common authority means "yes." (We do not mean to imply that the consenter's words are the only basis for the additional information that makes "yes" convincing—an officer is justified in relying on his own observations, or believable statements by others, concerning the scope of the consenter's authority over a space.)

> In the third category of situations, a reasonable officer would usually assume that a person in the position of the consenter does have authority over the space. This is the general rule for people in possession of movable containers, or someone who comes to the door of a house after the police knock. Of course, if the consenter provides additional information, the context may change in such a manner that no reasonable officer would maintain the default assumption. See United States v. Salinas–Cano, 959 F.2d 861, 864–65 (10th Cir.1992) (girlfriend cannot consent to search of

boyfriend's bag); United States v. Most, 876 F.2d 191, 199–200 (D.C.Cir. 1989) (store employee cannot consent to search of bag left in his custody by defendant).

The *Jenkins* court found that the consent of a driver of a rig falls into the third category, i.e., apparent authority reasonably can be assumed in the absence of contrary indicators.

The generic relationship between the owner of a rig and its driver is characterized by a considerable grant of authority to the driver. The driver has complete control of the tractor part of the rig, and almost always has keys to the trailer. The driver is typically allowed to enter the trailer on the occurrence of any of a certain number of conditions: loading, unloading, an inspection after an ominous noise, or an emergency. Moreover, the driver may actually be the owner of the rig, or someone with a position in the trucking company that is the practical equivalent of an owner. Therefore, when a driver consents—an act that suggests some authority to consent—a police officer is not required to run down a check list of questions about the details of the driver's relationship to his rig.

* * *

For these reasons, we hold that a request to the driver of a rig to search the rig's trailer is firmly within the third of the three categories outlined above. That means that an officer is justified in thinking that the driver has authority to consent unless the officer knows (or is told) other information indicating that the usual assumption is incorrect. On the facts of this case, we do not believe that Holt's quick statement, "It's not up to me; I don't own the stuff"—said while he was signing the consent form—was sufficient to put Trooper Lopez on notice that Holt did not have authority to consent. This is not a case where the driver said: "Sorry, there is a company policy that forbids me from allowing you to search the trailer. Call my boss at 1–800–GOSEARCH." We also note that the absence of a lock-seal on the trailer door further supports the officer's assumption. Because a reasonable officer in Trooper Lopez's position could have thought Holt had authority to consent to a search of the trailer, the consent validates the otherwise unreasonable search.

See also United States v. Fultz, 146 F.3d 1102 (9th Cir.1998) (where homeowner allowed the defendant to store a box in the garage, and homeowner told the police that she had no right to open the box, the homeowner's consent did not give the officers authority to search the box); United States v. Basinski, 226 F.3d 829 (7th Cir. 2000) (defendant gave a locked briefcase for safekeeping to a friend with instructions not to open it, and did not give the friend the combination to the lock; under these circumstances, the friend had no actual or apparent authority to consent to the search of the briefcase).

Consent Among Family Members

Courts generally allow parents with control over entire premises to consent to the search of the entire house, even a minor's bedroom, see, e.g., United States v. Peterson, 524 F.2d 167 (4th Cir.1975). However, consent will not be valid if it is clear that part of the premises is exclusively reserved for a child, see, e.g., In re Scott K, 24 Cal.3d 395, 155 Cal.Rptr. 671, 595 P.2d 105 (1979); People

v. Nunn, 55 Ill.2d 344, 304 N.E.2d 81 (1973). Courts have also held that minors have authority to permit the search of a residence, except again as to exclusive zones where they have no right of access. See, e.g., United States v. Gutierrez–Hermosillo, 142 F.3d 1225 (10th Cir.1998) (noting that "the compromise of the expectation of privacy is no less the case for a minor co-occupant than for an adult"). Siblings frequently have been permitted to consent to searches of jointly occupied premises. See, e.g., United States v. Boston, 508 F.2d 1171 (2d Cir. 1974).

Spouses are generally presumed to have authority to consent to the search of a premises jointly occupied by both spouses. However, the court in United States v. Duran, 957 F.2d 499 (7th Cir.1992), rejected the government's argument for a per se rule that spouses always have the authority to consent to the search of every part of jointly owned property. The court declared that a per se rule "is defective because it presumes that spouses, in forging a marital bond, remove any and all boundaries between them." While the *Duran* court left open the possibility that spouses might have exclusive zones of privacy, it found on the facts of the case that the defendant's wife had authority to consent to the search of a farmhouse on jointly held property. The court held that a nonconsenting spouse must overcome a presumption of joint control by showing that "the consenting spouse was denied access to the particular area searched." While Mrs. Duran testified that she had never gone into the farmhouse, she admitted that she was never specifically excluded. Consequently, she had actual authority to consent to a search.

3. Scope of Consent

Even if a person voluntarily gives consent, there may be a question about whether the consent extended to the areas actually searched by the officer. A search beyond the scope of consent cannot be justified as a consent search. The question is whether a given search is beyond the scope of a given consent. In United States v. Blake, 888 F.2d 795 (11th Cir.1989), officers approached Blake while he was walking to his plane at an airport. After receiving identification and examining his tickets, the officers asked Blake if he would consent to a search of his "person." They informed him of his right to refuse. Within seconds of receiving consent, one officer reached into Blake's groin region where he did a "frontal touching" of Blake's genitals. The officer felt an object and heard a crinkling sound, and a subsequent search incident to arrest revealed crack cocaine. The court held that the frontal touching was a search beyond the scope of Blake's consent. It stated that, given the public location of the police-citizen encounter, "it cannot be said that a reasonable individual would understand that a search of one's person would entail an officer touching his or her genitals." Do you agree? What if, before asking Blake for permission to search his person, the officers had conducted frontal touchings of five other people in the airport in full view of Blake? See also United States v. Towns, 913 F.2d 434 (7th Cir.1990) (consent for entry into an apartment to look at defendant's identification did not permit thorough seven hour search of the apartment).

Scope Defined by the Object of the Search: Florida v. Jimeno

In Florida v. Jimeno, 500 U.S. 248 (1991), Chief Justice Rehnquist, writing for a majority of seven justices, relied on *Rodriguez* and *Schneckloth* to conclude that the scope of a consent is determined by a standard of objective reasonableness. The Court held that an officer could reasonably conclude that when a suspect gave general consent to a search of his car, he also consented to a search of a paper bag lying on the floor of the car. The officer had informed Jimeno that he was looking for narcotics in the car and obtained consent to search. Jimeno did not place any explicit limitation on the scope of the search. The Chief Justice reasoned that the general consent to search the car included consent to search containers in the car that might contain drugs. He stated that "the scope of a search is generally defined by its expressed object" and that "a reasonable person might be expected to know that narcotics are carried in some form of container." The Chief Justice distinguished the instant case from one in which an officer, given consent to search the trunk of a car, pried open a locked briefcase found inside the trunk. He explained that "it is very likely unreasonable to think that a suspect, by consenting to the search of his trunk, has agreed to the breaking open of a locked briefcase within the trunk, but it is otherwise with a paper bag."

The *Jimeno* majority rejected the defendant's argument that police officers should be required to request separate permission to search each container found in a car. The Chief Justice saw "no basis for adding this sort of superstructure to the Fourth Amendment's basic tenet of reasonableness." He noted that a container-by-container requirement would result in fewer consents, which would be contrary to the community's interest in encouraging citizens to cooperate with the authorities.

Justice Marshall, joined by Justice Stevens, dissented. Justice Marshall noted that, at best, general consent is ambiguous, and police can avoid ambiguity by asking at the outset for permission to search a car and its contents or by asking for additional permission to search a container when it is found within a car. Justice Marshall concluded by attacking the majority's expressed interest in encouraging consent searches:

> The majority's real concern is that if the police were required to ask for additional consent to search a closed container * * *, an individual who did not mean to authorize such additional searching would have an opportunity to say no. In essence, then, the majority is claiming that 'the community has a real interest' not in encouraging citizens to *consent* to investigatory efforts of their law enforcement agents, but rather in encouraging individuals to be *duped* by them. That is not the community that the Fourth Amendment contemplates.

In terms of providing guidance to the police, is the dissent's approach more or less helpful than the majority's? Which approach provides a suspect with the clearest choice? Which approach is more likely to communicate to a suspect that consent may be limited or general? Which approach is most likely to generate consent?

Ambiguity Construed Against the Citizen

After *Jimeno,* it is up to the citizen rather than the officer to clarify any ambiguity concerning the scope of consent. See United States v. Berke, 930 F.2d 1219 (7th Cir.1991) (consent to officer's "looking" into bag allows a thorough search of the bag; defendant did not ask for clarification of what the officers meant when they said they wanted to "look"); United States v. Zapata, 180 F.3d 1237 (11th Cir.1999) (consent to search a car permits the officer to unscrew and open a secret compartment). But see United States v. Strickland, 902 F.2d 937 (11th Cir.1990) (consent to search a car does not extend to officer's slashing open a spare tire). Recall the facts of *Blake, supra,* in which the court held that Blake's consent to search his "person" did not extend to a pat-down of his genitalia. Is this result correct after *Jimeno*? See United States v. Rodney, 956 F.2d 295 (D.C.Cir.1992) (Thomas, J.) (consent to a body search permits the search of defendant's crotch area).

Imagine that you are in Blake's position and the officer asks if he can search your person. Assume further that you want to limit the scope of this search. Since it is up to you to clarify any ambiguity, how would you go about doing so? Would you be concerned that by limiting the scope of the search, you will direct the officer's attention to the very area that you want to exclude from the search?

While ambiguity is construed against the citizen, there are certainly situations in which the officers' search will be beyond what could be reasonably contemplated by the consent. For example, in United States v. Turner, 169 F.3d 84 (1st Cir.1999), Turner's next door neighbor was attacked with a knife, and blood was found around Turner's window. Officers thought the assailant might be hiding in Turner's house and asked for consent to search. They also had thoughts that Turner might be the assailant. They asked to search for any signs that the suspect might have been inside Turner's apartment, or might have left evidence of his presence there. Turner consented. An officer saw a picture on Turner's computer screen that resembled the victim. This got him curious, and so he sat down and started searching through the computer's hard drive. He discovered files containing child pornography, and Turner was prosecuted for that offense. But the court held that the search exceeded the scope of consent, and therefore that the files were illegally obtained:

> We think that an objectively reasonable person assessing in context the exchange between Turner and these detectives would have understood that the police intended to search only in places where an intruder hastily might have disposed of any physical evidence of the Thomas assault immediately after it occurred; for example, in places where a fleeing suspect might have tossed a knife or bloody clothing. Whereas, in sharp contrast, it obviously would have been impossible to abandon physical evidence of this sort in a personal computer hard drive, and bizarre to suppose—nor has the government suggested—that the suspected intruder stopped to enter incriminating evidence into the Turner computer.

See also United States v. Osage, 235 F.3d 518 (10th Cir. 2000) (consent to search a bag does not permit the opening of a sealed can labeled "Tamales in Gravy" found in the bag: "before an officer may actually destroy or render completely useless a container which would otherwise be within the scope of a permissive search, the officer must obtain explicit authorization, or have some other, lawful, basis upon which to proceed.").

4. *Withdrawing Consent*

Because there is a right to refuse consent initially, and a right to control the scope of consent, it follows that there is also a right to revoke a consent once given. Of course, consent cannot be revoked retroactively after the officer has found incriminating information. United States v. Dyer, 784 F.2d 812 (7th Cir.1986) (revocation must be made before the search is completed). Also, the revocation of consent must be clear and explicit. See State v. Luther, 63 Or.App. 86, 663 P.2d 1261 (1983) (consent not withdrawn where defendant closes and locks a door in his apartment, but later acquiesces in efforts to open the door for the police); United States v. Lattimore, 87 F.3d 647 (4th Cir.1996) (refusal to sign a written consent form does not constitute withdrawal of oral consent). But it is clear that the officer's right to continue with a consent search can be terminated by the defendant—or by a third party if the officer is relying on third party consent. See United States v. Springs, 936 F.2d 1330 (D.C.Cir.1991) ("even after consent to search is initially given, a person may subsequently limit or withdraw that consent").

Suppose that an officer obtains voluntary consent to search a home and then, when he is about to enter a closet, the defendant revokes consent and forbids entry to the closet. Can the officer consider the defendant's actions as proof that there is something incriminating in the closet? As one court put it: "The constitutional right to withdraw one's consent would be of little value if the very fact of choosing to exercise that right could serve as any part of the basis for finding the reasonable suspicion that makes consent unnecessary." United States v. Carter, 985 F.2d 1095 (D.C.Cir.1993).

This principle is fact-sensitive, however. For example, in *Carter,* where the court set forth the principle that revocation of consent cannot be considered suspicious, the court actually upheld a search that was made after consent was revoked. The court found the principle it stated "immaterial" where the following sequence of events occurred: 1) Officers suspected Carter of drug trafficking based on various profile factors and suspicious answers to questions during the encounter; 2) Carter permitted the officer to look through his tote bag; 3) the officer pulled out a paper bag from the tote bag; 4) Carter snatched the paper bag from the officer and volunteered to show the officer the food that he claimed was in the paper bag; 5) Carter put his hand inside the paper bag, felt around, and finally withdrew his hand—which was empty; and 6) Carter then rolled up the paper bag and stood looking at the officer.

The court held that the officer could reasonably take Carter's conduct with respect to the paper bag into account, "as part of the totality of the circumstances, regardless whether it occurred before or, as here, after Carter had given and then withdrawn his consent to a search." This was because Carter's "peculiar" way of retracting consent could legitimately be considered suspicious, independent of the withdrawal of consent itself.

Judge Wald, in dissent, complained that while Carter "was entitled to just say no to any further search of the bag, he had to do so in a way that would not raise the detective's suspicion that he had something to hide; not an easy feat under the circumstances." She stated that the majority's approach "effectively eviscerates the right to withdraw consent (certainly midway through a previously consented-to search) to nothing more than a pious throwaway sentence in judicial opinions approving searches." She concluded as follows:

> The reality is that so-called consensual encounters with the police are bound to be unnerving, and that most citizens—innocent or guilty—will feel the need to explain or excuse themselves when refusing to comply with a police request to search their luggage or anything contained therein, and, in so

doing, create the very suspicion that will be used to justify the previously unauthorized detention. * * * Permitting the police to rely on the atmospherics of the refusal or withdrawal of consent to supply the reasonable suspicion necessary to objectively justify an otherwise unlawful search strips the legal right of withdrawal of all practical value. * * * If the right to withdraw consent for a "consensual" encounter is to have any meaning on the streets, as well as in the jurisprudence, it must encompass the manner as well as the fact of its exercise.

For a different perspective on "suspicious" withdrawal of consent, see United States v. Wilson, 953 F.2d 116 (4th Cir.1991) (angry refusal to allow search of coat, after consenting to search of luggage and person, should not have counted as a factor in the analysis of reasonable suspicion; except in extraordinary circumstances, officers must have evidence independent of the withdrawal of consent and the manner in which it is executed).

5. Credibility Determinations

Consent cases often come down to a credibility determination between the officer's account of what happened and the defendant's account of what happened. Typically, the officers testify that they acted politely, asked the defendant to consent, informed him of his right to refuse, and the defendant readily consented. In contrast, defendants testify that the officers either never even sought consent, or obtained consent by way of threatening and coercive tactics. In the typical consent case, there is little evidence other than the testimony of the opposing sides that is or can be produced on the consent question. It is fair to state, at least by viewing the reported opinions, that courts routinely find officers to be more credible than defendants. Is this the way it should be?

A typical example of a credibility dispute arose in United States v. Heath, 58 F.3d 1271 (8th Cir.1995). Officers received a tip about drug trafficking out of a motel room. They knocked on the door, which was then opened a crack. The officers testified at the suppression hearing that they informed the defendant, who answered the door, that they were aware of possible drug activity in the room. They asked if they could come in, and the defendant opened the door and said "yes." The officers informed him that he did not have to speak with them, and did not have to consent to any searches, and the defendant nodded affirmatively. The officers noticed that the defendant was trying to slide a shoebox under the bed. They asked him if they could look inside it, and he said "yes." Inside the shoebox was crack cocaine and other incriminating evidence.

Heath's version of the events was "much different." He testified that the officers knocked on the door, stated that they had probable cause to search the room for narcotics, and that they needed to check the room. One officer's voice turned harsh and he stated that "if you don't let me in I am going to get a f* * * * * * search warrant and tear apart your room." Heath let go of the door and the officers pushed their way in. Once in the room, the officers did not tell him that he had a right to refuse consent. One officer grabbed the shoebox and opened it.

The officers then testified in rebuttal; they stuck to their story and categorically denied Heath's version. The district court believed the officers and denied Heath's motion to suppress. On appeal, the court stated that "a district court's decision to credit a witness's testimony over that of another can almost never be clear error unless there is extrinsic evidence that contradicts the witness's story or the story is so internally inconsistent or implausible on its face that a reasonable fact-finder would not credit it." The court refused to grant relief, noting that "[t]here was no extrinsic evidence to contradict the deputies' story other than Heath's own testimony." Moreover, the testimony was not so implausible as to be unworthy of belief.

Judge McMillian concurred in *Heath*, but only because "it is not the province of the appeals court to make credibility assessments." He was dubious about the truthfulness of the officers' version of the events:

> The police officers' saccharine account of the events * * * ironically leaves a bitter aftertaste. Rarely, if ever, have I encountered a case in which the police conduct was so mild-mannered and the suspect so acquiescent. The "fact" that Heath would so willingly consent to the search of his motel room and, more specifically, the shoe box, which he knew contained drugs and drug paraphernalia, is surprising, to say the least.

What can be done about the problem of retroactively manufacturing consent through suppression hearing testimony? What extrinsic evidence could Heath hope to produce that would contradict the officers' account? Compare United States v. Forbes, 181 F.3d 1 (1st Cir.1999) (court remands for further factfinding where officer's account of a consent search was rendered implausible by the fact that it was inconsistent with the physical evidence, trial court said it did not believe some of the details testified to by the officer, and the officer gave no explanation for why he sought consent when he also maintained that he had probable cause to search the defendant's car).

In New York City, the Mollen Commission reviewed the activities of the New York City Police Department and concluded that police officers often commit perjury on the witness stand. The Commission found that perjury is "prevalent enough in the department that it has its own nickname: 'testilying.'" Sexton, New York Police Often Lie Under Oath, Report Says, New York Times, April 22, 1994, p.1, col. 1. See also Slobogin, Testilying and What To Do About It, 67 Colo. L.Rev. 1037 (1996) (citing surveys of defense attorneys, prosecutors and judges, who estimated that police perjury at Fourth Amendment suppression hearings occurs in twenty to fifty percent of the cases). On the other hand, the defendant has a strong incentive to lie at the suppression hearing as well, doesn't he?

Are there any solutions? Professor Slobogin, in Testilying and What To Do About It, 67 Colo. L.Rev. 1037 (1996), argues that if the exclusionary rule were replaced with an effective civil remedy, testilying would be reduced. He asserts that under the current system, prosecutors either encourage or do not discourage testilying, because they have a desire to prosecute obvious criminals. This incentive to put on perjured testimony would be eliminated if illegally obtained evidence could be admitted at a criminal trial. Moreover, prosecutors would be more likely to prosecute officers for perjury where no loss of evidence is at stake.

Professor Lassiter, in Eliminating Consent from the Lexicon of Traffic Stop Interrogations, 27 Cap. L.Rev. 79 (1998), proffers a different solution. He argues first that testilying goes hand in hand with racial profiling. That is, officers single out minorities for traffic and other stops, and then lie at the suppression hearing about things like consent. He considers whether a rule should be promulgated that a suspect cannot consent to a search without a lawyer present, but dismisses that solution as "impractical" when applied to consents obtained on the street. He states that in light of the twin problems of racial profiling and testilying, the possibility that citizens truly and voluntarily consent to a search that uncovers evidence is so remote that the *entire concept of voluntary consent should be rejected*. He concludes that "voluntary uncounseled consent to search and seizure which would lead to the discovery of self-incriminating evidence strains faith in the law. Logic compels the elimination of uncounseled consent from permissible invasions of privacy and property rights. If a repentant criminal suspect truly consents to the discovery of evidence that would seal his demise he has many opportunities to do so upon his own initiative, after he has obtained counsel." Would Professor Lassiter's solution permit third parties to consent to a search without advice of counsel?

Can you think of any other solutions to the problem of testilying? What about subjecting officers to polygraph tests before they testify that the defendant voluntarily consented to a search that uncovered incriminating evidence? See also McClurg, Good Cop, Bad Cop: Using Cognitive Dissonance Theory to Reduce Police Lying, 32 U.C. Davis L.Rev. 389 (1999) (suggesting changes in police training and mentoring to reduce testilying).

VI. WIRETAPPING, UNDERCOVER ACTIVITY, AND THE OUTER REACHES OF THE FOURTH AMENDMENT

The Supreme Court has struggled in its attempts to consider the Fourth Amendment's applicability to various types of undercover investigative activity.

A. CONSTITUTIONAL LIMITATIONS ON ELECTRONIC SURVEILLANCE

Physical Trespass Required: Olmstead v. United States

In 1928, Chief Justice Taft's majority opinion in Olmstead v. United States, 277 U.S. 438, declared that the interception of voice communications over telephone lines without entry into Olmstead's premises was not within the coverage of the Amendment. "The evidence was secured by the use of the sense of hearing and that only. There was no entry of the house or offices of the defendants." Justices Brandeis and Holmes wrote separate dissenting opinions. Justice Brandeis observed that "[t]he makers of our Constitution * * * conferred, as against the government, the right to be let alone—the most comprehensive of rights and the right most valued by civilized men." He argued that "every unjustifiable intrusion upon the privacy of the individual, by whatever means employed, must be deemed a violation of the Fourth Amendment." And he warned, in now familiar words, that "[o]ur government is the potent, the omnipresent teacher. For good or ill, it teaches the whole people by its example. Crime is contagious. If the government becomes a lawbreaker, it breeds contempt for law; it invites every man to become a law unto himself; it invites anarchy."

Continuing the Trespass Analysis: Goldman v. United States and on Lee v. United States

In Goldman v. United States, 316 U.S. 129 (1942), the Court found that the use of a detectaphone placed against an office wall to hear conversations next door did not violate the Fourth Amendment because there was no trespass. A decade later the Court held by a 5–4 majority in On Lee v. United States, 343 U.S. 747 (1952), that the Fourth Amendment was not implicated when the government wired an undercover agent for sound by means of a microphone that transmitted sounds to another officer outside the laundry in which the undercover agent was conversing with On Lee. There was no trespass. In a separate opinion, Justice Frankfurter said that the dissenting view in *Goldman* was correct: *Olmstead* and its trespass analysis should be overruled. Justice Douglas' dissent expressed dissatisfaction that he had voted with the majority in *Goldman*.

Rejecting the Trespass Rationale: Silverman v. United States and Katz v. United States

Nine years later came the first Supreme Court condemnation of eavesdropping under the Fourth Amendment. Justice Stewart's unanimous opinion in Silverman v. United States, 365 U.S. 505 (1961), found a constitutional violation in the placement of a spike, a foot long with a microphone attached, under a baseboard into a party wall, so that it made contact with the heating duct that ran through the entire house and served as a sounding board. The Court said that its decision did "not turn upon the technicality of a trespass upon a party wall as a matter of local law. It is based upon the reality of an intrusion into a constitutionally protected area." Finally, in Katz v. United States, 389 U.S. 347 (1967), the Court overruled *Olmstead* and *Goldman*, and scrapped the trespass rationale. The Court stated that the Fourth Amendment would apply to electronic surveillance whenever it violated a person's justifiable expectation of privacy. *Katz* is set forth, and discussed in detail, in the section on the threshold requirements for Fourth Amendment protection, *supra*.

B. UNDERCOVER AGENTS

Surreptitious Recording: Lopez v. United States

Lopez v. United States, 373 U.S. 427 (1963), involved an IRS agent who, having received an unsolicited bribe and having reported it to his superiors, concealed a wire recorder on his person, as directed by his superiors, when he met Lopez. Justice Harlan's majority opinion found no Fourth Amendment violation. "[T]he device was used only to obtain the most reliable evidence possible of a conversation in which the Government's own agent was a participant and which that agent was fully entitled to disclose." The opinion concluded that "the risk that petitioner took in offering a bribe * * * fairly included the risk that the offer would be accurately reproduced in court, whether by faultless memory or mechanical recording."

Undercover Agents in the Home: Lewis v. United States

Chief Justice Warren wrote for the Court in Lewis v. United States, 385 U.S. 206 (1966), and shed additional light on the Fourth Amendment's application to undercover government investigative activities. An undercover narcotics agent had telephoned Lewis' home asking about the possibility of purchasing marijuana. Arrangements were made and a sale was consummated. Subsequently, another sale took place in Lewis' home. Only Justice Douglas dissented from the Warren view that, because Lewis invited the agent into his home "for the specific purpose of executing a felonious sale of narcotics," the fact that Lewis believed he was dealing with a fellow lawbreaker did not require constitutional protection for the belief. The Chief Justice rejected the defendant's argument that the privacy interests in a home required heightened protection:

> [W]hen, as here, the home is converted into a commercial center to which outsiders are invited for purposes of transacting unlawful business, that business is entitled to no greater sanctity than if it were carried on in a store, a garage, a car, or on the street. A government agent, in the same manner as a private person, may accept an invitation to do business and may enter upon the premises for the very purposes contemplated by the occupant.

Limits on the Scope of Undercover Activity: Gouled v. United States

In upholding the undercover activity in *Lewis*, the Court took pains to distinguish Gouled v. United States, 255 U.S. 298 (1921). In *Gouled,* a business associate of the defendant, acting under orders from federal officers, obtained entry into the defendant's office by pretending that he was paying a social visit, when in fact he rummaged through papers in the office while Gouled was temporarily absent. The Court in *Gouled* invalidated the search. The *Lewis* Court explained that the search in *Gouled* was invalidated because the undercover informant's search went well beyond the scope of Gouled's invitation into the home. Does this mean that if an officer masquerades as a television repairman, is his undercover investigative activity permissible if he investigates no further than an ordinary television repairman would do?

Misplaced Confidence: Hoffa v. United States

A similar result to that in *Lewis* was reached in Hoffa v. United States, 385 U.S. 293 (1966). Union leader James Hoffa was convicted for attempting to bribe jurors in a previous trial. Much of the government's case depended on the testimony of a local union official who, after being released from jail with federal and state charges pending against him, spent a great deal of time in the Hoffa camp at the time of the bribe attempts. Justice Stewart's majority opinion assumed that the witness had been an undercover agent from the first visit to Hoffa, but found that "no interest legitimately protected by the Fourth Amendment" was involved in the case. Justice Stewart wrote that "[w]hat the Fourth Amendment protects is the security a man relies upon when he places himself or his property within a constitutionally protected area * * *." He concluded that the undercover agent invaded no protected area because he was invited into

Hoffa's hotel room. Under these circumstances, Hoffa was not relying on the security of the hotel room, but upon his "misplaced confidence" that the union official would not reveal his statements. Such a risk, according to Justice Stewart, is "the kind of risk we necessarily assume whenever we speak."[34]

Analysis of Eavesdropping and Undercover Informant Cases

The Court struggled in the early wiretapping and eavesdropping cases just to identify the right issues. Faced with new techniques of evidence gathering, the Court first found no Fourth Amendment violation unless a trespass occurred. Then, it suggested that any trespass was enough to require a finding that the Fourth Amendment was violated. *Katz* ultimately rejected a trespass test and substituted a reasonable expectation of privacy test. But the *Katz* test does not change the results in *Lewis, Hoffa,* or *Osborn,* because the Court in those cases held that the defendants had no reasonable expectation of privacy from undercover activity, having assumed the risk that their friends or associates would disclose their guilty secrets. See also United States v. Davis, 326 F.3d 361 (2d Cir. 2003) (no Fourth Amendment violation where defendant invited an undercover informant into his home for a drug transaction, and the informant secretly videotaped the proceedings; the court noted that it was not deciding "the constitutionality of video surveillance conducted by an invited visitor equipped with a hidden camera with the power to depict items and details unobservable by the human eye").

Is the assumption of risk analysis a better way to handle these problems than the old trespass analysis? How do we know what risks we assume until the Court tells us? Why does a person assume the risk that a friend will record an incriminating conversation, but not the risk that the government will use a wiretap and record an incriminating conversation?

C. WIRETAPPING AND EAVESDROPPING STATUTES

Procedural Protections Required: Berger v. New York

Berger v. New York, 388 U.S. 41 (1967), seemed to evince a different judicial attitude toward electronic eavesdropping. The case arose out of a state investigation of alleged bribery of officials responsible for liquor licenses. An eavesdropping order was obtained pursuant to a New York statute, which read as follows:

> An ex parte order for eavesdropping * * * may be issued by any justice of the supreme court or judge of a county court or of the court of general sessions of the county of New York upon oath or affirmation * * * that

---

34. The Court relied on *Lopez* and *Hoffa* in Osborn v. United States, 385 U.S. 323 (1966), which arose out of the attempt to bribe the Hoffa jurors. A man (Vick) hired by Hoffa's lawyer to investigate prospective jurors was cooperating with the government. He related a conversation during which a juror bribe was discussed. Responding to a government request for court authorization, two district judges approved the utilization of a tape recorder on Vick's person during his next scheduled meeting with the lawyer. The recording was used as evidence leading to the lawyer's conviction. Justice Stewart's majority opinion found *Lopez* and *Hoffa* good authority for sustaining the use of the evidence, and added that the judicial approval for a "narrow and particularized purpose" also validated the procedure. Justice Douglas dissented.

there is reasonable ground to believe that evidence of crime may be thus obtained, and particularly describing the person or persons whose communications, conversations or discussions are to be overheard or recorded and the purpose thereof, and, in the case of a telegraphic or telephonic communication, identifying the particular telephone number or telegraph line involved. In connection with the issuance of such an order the justice or judge may examine on oath the applicant and any other witness he may produce and shall satisfy himself of the existence of reasonable grounds for the granting of such application. Any such order shall be effective for the time specified therein but not for a period of more than two months unless extended or renewed by the justice or judge who signed and issued the original order upon satisfying himself that such extension or renewal is in the public interest. Any such order together with the papers upon which the application was based, shall be delivered to and retained by the applicant as authority for the eavesdropping authorized therein.

The orders at issue in *Berger* permitted the installation of recording devices in an attorney's office and another person's office for 60 days. After two weeks, a conspiracy was uncovered and Berger was indicted as part of it. Relevant portions of the recordings were admitted into evidence. Justice Clark's majority opinion found serious fault with the New York statute. Justice Clark viewed the statute as a "blanket grant" of permission to eavesdrop, "without adequate supervision or protective procedures." Among the procedural flaws, Justice Clark noted that: 1) there was a conspicuous absence of any requirement that a particular crime be named; 2) there was no requirement of a particular description of the conversations sought; 3) the length of time eavesdropping was permitted was too extensive; 4) extensions of the time period were granted on an insufficient showing that such extensions were "in the public interest"; 5) there was no provision for terminating the conversation once the evidence sought was found; and 6) the statute lacked notice and return procedures. The opinion concluded as follows: "Our concern with the statute here is whether its language permits a trespassory invasion of the home, by general warrant, contrary to the command of the Fourth Amendment. As it is written, we believe that it does."

The Federal Statutory Response: Title III and Its Amendments

One year after *Berger*, Congress enacted a new scheme of regulating wiretapping and electronic eavesdropping as part of the 1968 Omnibus Crime Control and Safe Streets Act. This legislation, which does not regulate eavesdropping conducted with the consent of one of the parties, is commonly known as "Title III." Title III was subsequently modified by Title I of the 1986 Electronic Communications Privacy Act, to account for technological advances and to correct perceived gaps in the statute. Subsequent amendments were made by the Storage Communications Act. Title III was most recently amended by the USA PATRIOT ACT, passed almost immediately after the 9/11 terrorist attacks, and then again by the Homeland Security Act of 2002 (which makes it easier for agencies to share information obtained through interceptions permitted by Title III). Portions of Title III, as modified by these later amendments, are set forth below. Compare these provisions with the New York statute invalidated in *Berger*.

Title III of the Omnibus Crime Control and Safe Streets Act of 1968, as amended, 18 U.S.C.A. §§ 2510–2520.

CHAPTER 119—WIRE INTERCEPTION AND INTERCEPTION OF ORAL COMMUNICATIONS

§ 2510. Definitions

As used in this chapter—

(1) "wire communication" means any aural transfer made in whole or in part through the use of facilities for the transmission of communications by the aid of wire, cable, or other like connection between the point of origin and the point of reception (including the use of such connection in a switching station) furnished or operated by any person engaged in providing or operating such facilities for the transmission of interstate or foreign communications or communications affecting interstate or foreign commerce;

(2) "oral communication" means any oral communication uttered by a person exhibiting an expectation that such communication is not subject to interception under circumstances justifying such expectation, but such term does not include any electronic communication;

* * *

(4) "intercept" means the aural acquisition or other acquisition of the contents of any wire, electronic, or oral communication through the use of any electronic, mechanical, or other device;[35]

(5) "electronic, mechanical, or other device" means any device or apparatus which can be used to intercept a wire, oral, or electronic communication other than—

(a) any telephone or telegraph instrument, equipment or facility, or any component thereof,

(i) furnished to the subscriber or user by a provider of wire or electronic communication service in the ordinary course of its business and being used by the subscriber or user in the ordinary course of its business or furnished by such subscriber or user for connection to the facilities of such service and used in the ordinary course of its business; or

---

35. In United States v. New York Tel. Co., 434 U.S. 159 (1977), the Court held that pen registers were not interceptions within the meaning of the statute, because they do not hear sound and thus do not involve the "aural acquisition" of anything.

The result in *New York Tel. Co.* is now codified in 18 U.S.C. § 2511(2)(h). However, in the 1986 Electronic Communications Privacy Act, 18 U.S.C. § 3121, Congress provided that pen register surveillance must be court-approved; however, it is not subject to all the procedural safeguards governing court-ordered electronic surveillance.

In United States v. Koyomejian, 970 F.2d 536 (9th Cir.1992) (en banc), the court held consistently with other lower courts that domestic silent *video* surveillance is not covered by Title I or Title III. However, the court looked to these statutes "for guidance in implementing the Fourth Amendment" as applied to video surveillance. The court concluded that domestic video surveillance is constitutional only if four requirements, in addition to a finding of probable cause, are met: (1) the judge issuing the warrant must find that video surveillance is the least intrusive alternative; (2) the warrant must particularly describe the activity to be videotaped; (3) the warrant must limit the period of surveillance to no longer than necessary and in any event no longer than 30 days; and (4) the warrant must require that the surveillance be conducted in such a way as to minimize the videotaping of conduct not subject to surveillance. See also United States v. Williams, 124 F.3d 411 (3d Cir. 1997) (holding that video surveillance can be ordered for any crime that could be the subject of a wiretap order under Title III).

(ii) being used by a provider of wire or electronic communication service in the ordinary course of its business, or by an investigative or law enforcement officer in the ordinary course of his duties;

(b) a hearing aid or similar device being used to correct subnormal hearing to not better than normal;

* * *

(9) ["Judges" mean federal district and appeals judges and state court of general jurisdiction judges authorized by state statute to authorize interceptions.]

* * *

(11) "aggrieved person" means a person who was a party to any intercepted wire, oral, or electronic communication or a person against whom the interception was directed.

* * *

(12) "electronic communication" means any transfer of signs, signals, writing, images, sounds, data, or intelligence of any nature transmitted in whole or in part by a wire, radio, electromagnetic, photoelectronic or photooptical system that affects interstate or foreign commerce, but does not include—

(A) any wire or oral communication;

(B) any communication made through a tone-only paging device;

(C) any communication from a tracking device (as defined in section 3117 of this title); or

(D) electronic funds transfer information stored by a financial institution in a communications system used for the electronic storage and transfer of funds;

(13) "user" means any person or entity who—

(A) uses an electronic communication service; and

(B) is duly authorized by the provider of such service to engage in such use;

(14) "electronic communications system" means any wire, radio, electromagnetic, photooptical or photoelectronic facilities for the transmission of wire or electronic communications, and any computer facilities or related electronic equipment for the electronic storage of such communications;

(15) "electronic communication service" means any service which provides to users thereof the ability to send or receive wire or electronic communications;

(16) "readily accessible to the general public" means, with respect to a radio communication, that such communication is not—

(A) scrambled or encrypted;

(B) transmitted using modulation techniques whose essential parameters have been withheld from the public with the intention of preserving the privacy of such communication;

(C) carried on a subcarrier or other signal subsidiary to a radio transmission;

(D) transmitted over a communication system provided by a common carrier, unless the communication is a tone only paging system communication; or

(E) transmitted on frequencies allocated under part 25, subpart D, E, or F of part 74, or part 94 of the Rules of the Federal Communications Commission, unless, in the case of a communication transmitted on a frequency allocated under part 74 that is not exclusively allocated to broadcast auxiliary services, the communication is a two-way voice communication by radio;

(17) "electronic storage" means—

(A) any temporary, intermediate storage of a wire or electronic communication incidental to the electronic transmission thereof; and

(B) any storage of such communication by an electronic communication service for purposes of backup protection of such communication;

(18) "aural transfer" means a transfer containing the human voice at any point between and including the point of origin and the point of reception;

(19) "foreign intelligence information" * * * means—

(A) information, whether or not concerning a United States person, that relates to the ability of the United States to protect against—

(i) actual or potential attack or other grave hostile acts of a foreign power or an agent of a foreign power;

(ii) sabotage or international terrorism by a foreign power or an agent of a foreign power; or

(iii) clandestine intelligence activities by an intelligence service or network of a foreign power or by an agent of a foreign power; or

(B) information, whether or not concerning a United States person, with respect to a foreign power or foreign territory that relates to—

(i) the national defense or the security of the United States; or

(ii) the conduct of the foreign affairs of the United States;

* * *

(21) "computer trespasser"—

(A) means a person who accesses a protected computer without authorization and thus has no reasonable expectation of privacy in any communication transmitted to, through, or from the protected computer; and

(B) does not include a person known by the owner or operator of the protected computer to have an existing contractual relationship with the owner or operator of the protected computer for access to all or part of the protected computer.

§ 2511. Interception and disclosure of wire or oral communications prohibited

[This section bars the wilful interception, use, or disclosure of wire, oral, or electronic communications covered by the Act; but it does not apply to interception conducted with the consent of one of the parties.][36]

* * *

(2)(f) Nothing contained [herein], shall be deemed to affect the acquisition by the United States Government of foreign intelligence information from international or foreign communications, or foreign intelligence activities conducted in accordance with otherwise applicable Federal law involving a foreign electronic communications system, utilizing a means other than electronic surveillance as defined in section 101 of the Foreign Intelligence Surveillance Act of 1978, and procedures in this chapter and the Foreign Intelligence Surveillance Act of 1978 shall be the exclusive means by which electronic surveillance, as defined in section 101 of such Act, and the interception of domestic wire, oral and electronic communications may be conducted.[37]

   (i) It shall not be unlawful under this chapter for a person acting under color of law to intercept the wire or electronic communications of a computer trespasser transmitted to, through, or from the protected computer, if—

      (I) the owner or operator of the protected computer authorizes the interception of the computer trespasser's communications on the protected computer;

36. Inadvertent interceptions do not violate the Act. See Adams v. Sumner, 39 F.3d 933 (9th Cir.1994) (switchboard operator at hotel inadvertently hears an incriminating conversation; no error to admit at trial). See also United States v. Wuliger, 981 F.2d 1497 (6th Cir. 1992) (attorney who uses intercepted conversations to cross-examine a witness cannot be convicted under the Act unless he knows or has reason to know that the communications were intercepted in violation of the Act).

37. In United States v. United States District Court, 407 U.S. 297 (1972), the Court, without a dissent, held that the President had no power to conduct warrantless searches in domestic security investigations. But the Court left open the question whether there could be warrantless taps in foreign security investigations.

United States v. Truong Dinh Hung, 629 F.2d 908 (4th Cir.1980), discusses the Congressional response to the Supreme Court's national security wiretap case, the Foreign Intelligence Surveillance Act of 1978, 50 U.S.C.A. § 1801 et seq., (referred to in the statute quoted above) which requires judicial approval for some foreign intelligence surveillance and authorizes approval upon a less demanding showing than is required for ordinary warrants. The court upheld warrantless electronic surveillance in the instant case, concluding that the government did not need a warrant "when the object of the search or the surveillance is a foreign power, its agent or collaborators," and the surveillance is conducted "primarily" for foreign intelligence reasons. Even when a warrant is not required, the court said that the search must satisfy the reasonableness requirement of the Fourth Amendment. Note that FISA regulates video surveillance whereas Title III does not. United States v. Koyomejian, 970 F.2d 536 (9th Cir.1992) (en banc). FISA is discussed in Note, The Foreign Intelligence Surveillance Act: Legislating a Judicial Role in National Security Surveillance, 78 Mich.L.Rev. 1116 (1980).

Congress enacted Public Law 107–56, 115 Stat. 272, on October 26, 2001. The formal title is the "Uniting And Strengthening America By Providing Appropriate Tools Required To Intercept And Obstruct Terrorism (USA Patriot Act) Act of 2001." The statute included 10 titles that amended 15 criminal statutes. It created many new laws against terrorism and expanded the authority of the government to conduct both electronic surveillance and physical searches. Among its provisions, the Act expanded power to seek roving wiretaps (Section 206), engage in electronic and computer surveillance (Sections 209–212), and use "sneak and peak" searches (Section 213) and pen registers and "trap and trace" surveillance (Section 216). The Act also provides for nationwide search warrants (Sections 219 and 220). It permits intelligence agencies and law enforcement agencies to share information with each other, and provides that FISA orders may be obtained when a "significant" purpose is to gather intelligence. (Section 218). The predominant purpose need not be, as most courts had previously held when they interpreted the previous language ("the purpose"), to gather intelligence. Section 224 provides for the "sunset" of some, but not all and not necessarily the most controversial, of the new provisions on December 31, 2005, unless Congress affirmatively extends them.

(II) the person acting under color of law is lawfully engaged in an investigation;

(III) the person acting under color of law has reasonable grounds to believe that the contents of the computer trespasser's communications will be relevant to the investigation; and

(IV) such interception does not acquire communications other than those transmitted to or from the computer trespasser.

§ 2515. Prohibition of use as evidence of intercepted wire or oral communications

Whenever any wire or oral communication has been intercepted, no part of the contents of such communication and no evidence derived therefrom may be received in evidence in any trial, hearing, or other proceeding in or before any court, grand jury, department, officer, agency, regulatory body, legislative committee, or other authority of the United States, a State, or a political subdivision thereof if the disclosure of that information would be in violation of this chapter.

§ 2516. Authorization for interception of wire, oral, or electronic communications

(1) The Attorney General, Deputy Attorney General, Associate Attorney General, or any Assistant Attorney General, any acting Assistant Attorney General, or any Deputy Assistant Attorney General or Acting Deputy Assistant Attorney General in the Criminal Division specially designated by the Attorney General, may authorize an application to a Federal judge of competent jurisdiction for * * * an order authorizing or approving the interception of wire or oral communications * * * when such interception may provide or has provided evidence of—

[The statute provides a long list of crimes that can be investigated, and it was amended by the USA PATRIOT ACT to include crimes related to computer fraud and abuse, use of chemical weapons, and terrorism]

(2) The principal prosecuting attorney of any State, or the principal prosecuting attorney of any political subdivision thereof, if such attorney is authorized by a statute of that State to make application to a State court judge of competent jurisdiction for an order authorizing or approving the interception of wire or oral communications, may apply to such judge for * * * an order * * * when such interception may provide or has provided evidence of the commission of the offense of murder, kidnapping, gambling, robbery, bribery, extortion, or dealing in narcotic drugs, marihuana or other dangerous drugs, or other crime dangerous to life, limb, or property, and punishable by imprisonment for more than one year, designated in any applicable State statute authorizing such interception, or any conspiracy to commit any of the foregoing offenses.

§ 2517. Authorization for disclosure and use of intercepted wire, oral, or electronic communications

(1) Any investigative or law enforcement officer who, by any means authorized by this chapter, has obtained knowledge of the contents of any wire, oral, or electronic communication, or evidence derived therefrom, may disclose such contents to another investigative or law enforcement officer to the extent that such disclosure is appropriate to the proper performance of the official duties of the officer making or receiving the disclosure.

(2) Any investigative or law enforcement officer who, by any means authorized by this chapter, has obtained knowledge of the contents of any wire, oral, or electronic communication or evidence derived therefrom may use such contents to the extent such use is appropriate to the proper performance of his official duties

(3) Any person who has received, by any means authorized by this chapter, any information concerning a wire, oral, or electronic communication, or evidence derived therefrom intercepted in accordance with the provisions of this chapter may disclose the contents of that communication or such derivative evidence while giving testimony under oath or affirmation in any proceeding held under the authority of the United States or of any State or political subdivision thereof.

(4) No otherwise privileged wire, oral, or electronic communication intercepted in accordance with, or in violation of, the provisions of this chapter shall lose its privileged character.

(5) When an investigative or law enforcement officer, while engaged in intercepting wire, oral, or electronic communications in the manner authorized herein, intercepts wire, oral, or electronic communications relating to offenses other than those specified in the order of authorization or approval, the contents thereof, and evidence derived therefrom, may be disclosed or used as provided in subsections (1) and (2) of this section. Such contents and any evidence derived therefrom may be used under subsection (3) of this section when authorized or approved by a judge of competent jurisdiction where such judge finds on subsequent application that the contents were otherwise intercepted in accordance with the provisions of this chapter. Such application shall be made as soon as practicable.

(6) Any investigative or law enforcement officer, or attorney for the Government, who by any means authorized by this chapter, has obtained knowledge of the contents of any wire, oral, or electronic communication, or evidence derived therefrom, may disclose such contents to any other Federal law enforcement, intelligence, protective, immigration, national defense, or national security official to the extent that such contents include foreign intelligence or counterintelligence (as defined in section 3 of the National Security Act of 1947 (50 U.S.C. 401a)), or foreign intelligence information (as defined in subsection (19) of section 2510 of this title), to assist the official who is to receive that information in the performance of his official duties. Any Federal official who receives information pursuant to this provision may use that information only as necessary in the conduct of that person's official duties subject to any limitations on the unauthorized disclosure of such information.

(7) Any investigative or law enforcement officer, or other Federal official in carrying out official duties as such Federal official, who by any means authorized by this chapter, has obtained knowledge of the contents of any wire, oral, or electronic communication, or evidence derived therefrom, may disclose such contents or derivative evidence to a foreign investigative or law enforcement officer to the extent that such disclosure is appropriate to the proper performance of the official duties of the officer making or receiving the disclosure, and foreign investigative or law enforcement officers may use or disclose such contents or derivative evidence to the extent such use or disclosure is appropriate to the proper performance of their official duties.

(8) Any investigative or law enforcement officer, or other Federal official in carrying out official duties as such Federal official, who by any means authorized by this chapter, has obtained knowledge of the contents of any wire, oral, or electronic communication, or evidence derived therefrom, may disclose such contents or derivative evidence to any appropriate Federal, State, local, or foreign government official to the extent that such contents or derivative evidence reveals a threat of actual or potential attack or other grave hostile acts of a foreign power or an agent of a foreign power, domestic or international sabotage, domestic or international terrorism, or clandestine intelligence gathering activities by an intelligence service or network of a foreign power or by an agent of a foreign power, within the United States or elsewhere, for the purpose of preventing or responding to such a threat. Any official who receives information pursuant to this provision may use that information only as necessary in the conduct of that person's official duties subject to any limitations on the unauthorized disclosure of such information, and any State, local, or foreign official who receives information pursuant to this provision may use that information only consistent with such guidelines as the Attorney General and Director of Central Intelligence shall jointly issue.

* * *

§ 2518. Procedure for interception of wire, oral or electronic communications

(1) Each application for an order authorizing or approving the interception of a wire, oral, or electronic communication under this chapter shall be made in writing upon oath or affirmation to a judge of competent jurisdiction and shall state the applicant's authority to make such application. Each application shall include the following information:

(a) the identity of the investigative or law enforcement officer making the application, and the officer authorizing the application;

(b) a full and complete statement of the facts and circumstances relied upon by the applicant, to justify his belief that an order should be issued, including (i) details as to the particular offense that has been, is being, or is about to be committed, (ii) except as provided in subsection (11)[permitting the authorization of "roving wiretaps" under certain conditions], a particular description of the nature and location of the facilities from which or the place where the communication is to be intercepted, (iii) a particular description of the type of communications sought to be intercepted, (iv) the identity of the person, if known, committing the offense and whose communications are to be intercepted;

(c) a full and complete statement as to whether or not other investigative procedures have been tried and failed or why they reasonably appear to be unlikely to succeed if tried or to be too dangerous;

(d) a statement of the period of time for which the interception is required to be maintained. If the nature of the investigation is such that the authorization for interception should not automatically terminate when the described type of communication has been first obtained, a particular description of facts establishing probable cause to believe that additional communications of the same type will occur thereafter;

(e) a full and complete statement of the facts concerning all previous applications known to the individual authorizing and making the application, made to any judge for authorization to intercept, or for approval of interceptions of, wire, oral, or electronic communications involving any of the same persons, facilities or places specified in the application, and the action taken by the judge on each such application; and

(f) where the application is for the extension of an order, a statement setting forth the results thus far obtained from the interception, or a reasonable explanation of the failure to obtain such results.

(2) The judge may require the applicant to furnish additional testimony or documentary evidence in support of the application.

(3) Upon such application the judge may enter an ex parte order, as requested or as modified, authorizing or approving interception of wire, oral or electronic communications within the territorial jurisdiction of the court in which the judge is sitting (and outside that jurisdiction but within the United States in the case of a mobile interception device authorized by a Federal court within such jurisdiction), if the judge determines on the basis of the facts submitted by the applicant that—

(a) there is probable cause for belief that an individual is committing, has committed, or is about to commit a particular offense enumerated in section 2516 of this chapter;

(b) * * * there is probable cause for belief that particular communications concerning that offense will be obtained through such interception;

(c) normal investigative procedures have been tried and have failed or reasonably appear to be unlikely to succeed if tried or to be too dangerous;[38]

(d) * * * there is probable cause for belief that the facilities from which, or the place where, the wire, oral or electronic communications are to be intercepted are being used, or are about to be used, in connection with the commission of such offense, or are leased to, listed in the name of, or commonly used by such person.

(4) Each order authorizing or approving the interception of any wire or oral communication shall specify—

(a) the identity of the person, if known, whose communications are to be intercepted;[39]

---

38. The statute's reference to other available investigative methods is known as the "necessity" requirement. But "it is not an 'exhaustion' requirement." United States v. Castillo–Garcia, 117 F.3d 1179 (10th Cir.1997). As the Court stated in United States v. Giordano, 416 U.S. 505 (1974), the statute was intended to ensure not that wiretaps are used only as a last resort, "but that they were not to be routinely employed as the initial step in a criminal investigation." Thus, the statute does not require that alternative investigative procedures have been tried and failed, "but only that the success of other methods of investigation appear unlikely." United States v. Thompson, 944 F.2d 1331 (7th Cir.1991) (wiretap

properly authorized where it was unlikely that infiltration by confidential informants would be successful). Compare *Castillo-Garcia,* supra (necessity requirement not satisfied where the government relies on conclusory assertions that investigative methods such as search warrants and standard surveillance will be unsuccessful).

39. In United States v. Kahn, 415 U.S. 143 (1974), the Court held that where the government knew of the existence of a person but did not know she was using the phone for illegal purposes, she was not a person whose identity must be disclosed under this section.

(b) the nature and location of the communications facilities as to which, or the place where, authority to intercept is granted;

(c) a particular description of the type of communication sought to be intercepted, and a statement of the particular offense to which it relates;

(d) the identity of the agency authorized to intercept the communications, and of the person authorizing the application; and

(e) the period of time during which such interception is authorized, including a statement as to whether or not the interception shall automatically terminate when the described communication has been first obtained.[40]

* * *

(5) No order entered under this section may authorize or approve the interception of any wire, oral, or electronic communication for any period longer than is necessary to achieve the objective of the authorization, nor in any event longer than thirty days. Extensions of an order may be granted, but only upon application for an extension * * * [with] the court making the findings required by subsection (3) of this section. The period of extension shall be no longer than the authorizing judge deems necessary to achieve the purposes for which it was granted and in no event for longer than thirty days. Every order and extension thereof shall contain a provision that the authorization to intercept shall be executed as soon as practicable, shall be conducted in such a way as to minimize the interception of communications not otherwise subject to interception under this chapter,[41] and must terminate upon attainment of the authorized objective, or in any event in thirty days. * * *

* * *

(7) Notwithstanding any other provision of this chapter, any investigative or law enforcement officer, specially designated by the Attorney General, the Deputy Attorney General, the Associate Attorney General or by the principal prosecuting attorney of any State or subdivision thereof acting pursuant to a statute of that State, who reasonably determines that—

(a) an emergency situation exists that involves—

40. In Dalia v. United States, 441 U.S. 238 (1979), the Supreme Court held that the electronic surveillance statute permits courts to authorize electronic surveillance that requires entry into private premises for installation of the necessary equipment. The Court also held that such authorization need not include a specific statement by the court indicating approval of the covert entry. Although the Court recognized that one of the purposes of a warrant is to reduce or eliminate executive discretion when it comes to intrusions into protected areas, the Court concluded that executive officers must have some leeway in deciding how best to execute a warrant.

41. In Scott v. United States, 436 U.S. 128 (1978), the Court held it irrelevant that officers had no subjective intent to comply with the minimization requirement. What is controlling, said the Court, is whether the agents actually intercepted conversations that were not otherwise subject to interception under the

Act. In this case, there was no violation of the requirement because the only calls made were those covered by the Act. Justice Brennan, joined by Justice Marshall, dissented and charged that the decision eviscerated the protection that Congress attempted to codify.

Courts have noted that the minimization requirement must be applied more flexibly at the early stages of an investigation. See United States v. Killingsworth, 117 F.3d 1159 (10th Cir.1997) ("[t]he conversations at issue were intercepted during the early stages of the investigation, when the officers had not yet identified the voices of the persons named in the authorization order and had not yet determined the scope of the Bustos Organization. More deference is owed with regard to such interceptions because it is difficult for investigating officers to determine which conversations are pertinent and which are impertinent early in an investigation.").

(i) immediate danger of death or serious physical injury to any person,

(ii) conspiratorial activities threatening the national security interest, or

(iii) conspiratorial activities characteristic of organized crime,

that requires a wire, oral, or electronic communication to be intercepted before an order authorizing such interception can, with due diligence, be obtained, and

(b) there are grounds upon which an order could be entered under this chapter to authorize such interception,

may intercept such wire, oral, or electronic communication if an application for an order approving the interception is made in accordance with this section within forty-eight hours after the interception has occurred, or begins to occur. In the absence of an order, such interception shall immediately terminate when the communication sought is obtained or when the application for the order is denied, whichever is earlier. In the event such application for approval is denied, or in any other case where the interception is terminated without an order having been issued, the contents of any wire, oral, or electronic communication intercepted shall be treated as having been obtained in violation of this chapter, and an inventory shall be served as provided for in subsection (d) of this section on the person named in the application.

* * *

(8)(d) Within a reasonable time but not later than ninety days after the filing of an application for an order of approval * * * which is denied or the termination of the period of an order or extensions thereof, the issuing or denying judge shall cause to be served, on the persons named in the order or the application, and such other parties to intercepted communications as the judge may determine in his discretion that is in the interest of justice, an inventory which shall include notice of—

(1) the fact of the entry of the order or the application;

(2) the date of the entry and the period of authorized, approved or disapproved interception, or the denial of the application; and

(3) the fact that during the period wire, oral or electronic communications were or were not intercepted.

The judge, upon the filing of a motion, may in his discretion make available to such person or his counsel for inspection such portions of the intercepted communications, applications and orders as the judge determines to be in the interest of justice. On an ex parte showing of good cause to a judge of competent jurisdiction the serving of the inventory required by this subsection may be postponed.[42]

* * *

---

42. In United States v. Donovan, 429 U.S. 413 (1977), the Court held that when the government inadvertently excluded persons from its list of those intercepted and thus deprived them of the inventory notice, suppression of evidence was not warranted because the requirements did not play a "substantive role" in the statutory scheme. The Court in United

(10)(a) Any aggrieved person in any trial, hearing, or proceeding in or before any court, department, officer, agency, regulatory body, or other authority of the United States, a State, or a political subdivision thereof, may move to suppress the contents of any wire or oral communication intercepted pursuant to this chapter, or evidence derived therefrom, on the grounds that—

(i) the communication was unlawfully intercepted;

(ii) the order of authorization or approval under which it was intercepted is insufficient on its face; or

(iii) the interception was not made in conformity with the order of authorization or approval.

* * *

(c) The remedies and sanctions described in this chapter with respect to the interception of electronic communications are the only judicial remedies and sanctions for nonconstitutional violations of this chapter involving such communications.

(11) The requirements of subsections (1)(b)(ii) and (3)(d) of this section relating to the specification of the facilities from which, or the place where, the communication is to be intercepted do not apply if—

(a) in the case of an application with respect to the interception of an oral communication—

(i) the application is by a Federal investigative or law enforcement officer and is approved by the Attorney General, the Deputy Attorney General, the Associate Attorney General, an Assistant Attorney General, or an acting Assistant Attorney General;

(ii) the application contains a full and complete statement as to why such specification is not practical and identifies the person committing the offense and whose communications are to be intercepted; and

(iii) the judge finds that such specification is not practical; and

(b) in the case of an application with respect to a wire or electronic communication—

(i) the application is by a Federal investigative or law enforcement officer and is approved by the Attorney General, the Deputy Attorney General, the Associate Attorney General, an Assistant Attorney General, or an acting Assistant Attorney General;

(ii) the application identifies the person believed to be committing the offense and whose communications are to be intercepted and the applicant makes a showing that there is probable cause to believe that the person's actions could have the effect of thwarting interception from a specified facility;

(iii) the judge finds that such showing has been adequately made; and

States v. Ojeda Rios, 495 U.S. 257 (1990), held that a failure to comply with the Title III requirement that tapes be immediately sealed would not result in suppression if the govern-ment's error was the result of a good faith, objectively reasonable misinterpretation of the statute.

(iv) the order authorizing or approving the interception is limited to interception only for such time as it is reasonable to presume that the person identified in the application is or was reasonably proximate to the instrument through which such communication will be or was transmitted.

* * *

———————

Do you believe the statute satisfies the concerns expressed by the *Berger* Court? For an attack on the statute, see Schwartz, The Legitimation of Electronic Eavesdropping: The Politics of "Law and Order," 67 Mich.L.Rev. 455 (1969). Are wiretaps and eavesdropping devices inherently unreasonable? See Spritzer, Electronic Surveillance by Leave of the Magistrate: The Case in Opposition, 118 U.Pa.L.Rev. 169 (1969). Does electronic surveillance remove some of the danger law enforcement officials face when using undercover techniques? The Supreme Court's handling of important questions under the statute is criticized in Goldsmith, The Supreme Court and Title III; Rewriting the Law of Electronic Surveillance, 74 J.Crim.L. & Crim. 1 (1983).

For an article analyzing the changes wrought to Title III by the PATRIOT ACT, including the authorization of "roving wiretaps", see Orin Kerr, Internet Surveillance After the USA PATRIOT ACT: The Big Brother That Isn't, 97 Nw.U. L.Rev. 603 (2003).

Application of Title III, as Amended, to Evidence Obtained From a Computer

The following case is an example of how Title III, as amended, does or does not apply to the surveillance of computer activities.

UNITED STATES v. STEIGER

United States Court of Appeals for the Eleventh Circuit, 2003.
318 F.3d 1039.

GOODWIN, CIRCUIT JUDGE:

Bradley Steiger appeals his convictions for sexual exploitation of children, possession of a computer containing child pornography, and receipt of child pornography through interstate and foreign commerce. He challenges the district court's conclusion that neither the Fourth Amendment nor Title III of the Omnibus Crime Control and Safe Streets Act of 1968, as amended by the Electronic Communications Privacy Act of 1986, (1986) ("ECPA"), codified at 18 U.S.C. § § 2510–2522 ("The Wiretap Act"),

warranted suppression of the evidence used to convict him. We affirm.

I.

The Montgomery, Alabama Police Department ("MPD") initiated an investigation of Steiger when an unidentified person ("anonymous source" or "source") sent the following e-mail on July 16, 2000:

I found a child molester on the net. I'm not sure if he is abusing his own child or a child he kidnaped. He is from Montgomery, Alabama. As you see he is torturing the kid. She is 5–6 y.o. His face is seen clearly on some of the pictures. I know his name, internet account, home address and I can see when he is on-line. What should I do? Can I send all the pics and info I have to these emails?

Regards

P.S. He is a doctor or a paramedic.

The anonymous source attached to this e-mail an electronic image file containing a picture of a white male sexually abusing a young white female who appeared to be approximately four to six years of age.

On July 17, 2000, Captain Kevin Murphy of the MPD replied, asking the anonymous source to call him at his office. The source responded that he was from Turkey and could not afford an overseas phone call, but could send everything by e-mail. Captain Murphy then sent an e-mail stating: "Please feel free to send the information that you have." The source next sent an e-mail with eight attached images showing an adult white male nude from the waist down fondling and pressing the young girl against his body in various positions and exposing her genitalia. * * * The girl was nude in several photographs and partially dressed in others. The anonymous e-mail again identified the molester as "Brad Steiger," and provided Steiger's Internet service account information with AT & T WorldNet, possible home address, telephone number used to connect to the Internet, and a fax number.

The anonymous source also informed Captain Murphy that he had Steiger's "i.p. number with local (Turkish) time." An IP number, also known as an Internet Protocol ("IP") address, "is the unique address assigned to a particular computer connected to the Internet. All computers connected to the Internet have an IP address." Daniel J. Solove, Digital Dossiers and the Dissipation of Fourth

Amendment Privacy, 75 S. Cal. L. Rev. 1083, 1145 (2002). "IP addresses are either static—associated with one computer—or dynamically assigned. The latter is usually the case for patrons of dial-up Internet Service Providers (ISP).... Static addresses are undoubtedly easier to trace, but ISPs generally log the assignments of their dynamic addresses." Elbert Lin, Prioritizing Privacy: A Constitutional Response to the Internet, 17 Berkeley Tech. L. J. 1085, 1104 n.101 (2002).

Captain Murphy viewed the eight images, and, on July 19, asked the source to send Steiger's IP address. The source sent three IP addresses used by Steiger on July 14 and 15; thus, it appears that Steiger's Internet Service Provider assigned dynamic IP addresses for each login. Apparently without being asked to do so, the source sent an e-mail to the MPD on July 19 providing Steiger's checking account records. On July 21, the source sent another e-mail that identified specific folders where pornographic pictures were stored on Steiger's computer.

Captain Murphy collected the information the source provided and referred it to Special Agent Margaret Faulkner of the FBI, who viewed the images and verified the details the anonymous source provided in his first two e-mails. She issued a subpoena to Security at AT & T Worldnet Service, who advised Agent Faulkner that the Internet account the anonymous source referred to was registered to a Brad Steiger at the home address the source provided. Agent Faulkner then performed an Alabama Driver's License check and obtained a "photo ID" copy of the license issued to a "Bradley Joseph Steiger." She concluded that the photo "appeared identical to the white male subject depicted in the photographs with the young girl." She also checked with the Alabama Medical Board and determined that a "Brad Steiger" had a license to dispense medicine as a practitioner in Alabama and had worked as an emergency room physician in Montgomery. Agent Faulkner went to the hospital where the Medical Board indicated Steiger had been working and showed one of the pictures of Steiger with the young girl. A security officer identified the man as Brad Steiger, a doctor who had been seen around the hospital on occasion. Agent Faulkner then learned that Steiger had become employed by a hospital in Selma, Alabama. She also discovered that Steiger then resided at an address different from the one the source supplied.

Agent Faulkner next prepared an affidavit in support of a search warrant in which she stated that "an anonymous source ... had located a child molester on the Internet." The affidavit described the pictures the anonymous source sent on July 17 without mentioning that the source had obtained the evidence by "hacking" into Steiger's computer. Agent Faulkner also described in the affidavit the steps she took to corroborate the information the anonymous source provided. After obtaining a warrant, law enforcement officers searched Steiger's home and seized his computer and related equipment, as well as leg restraints, clamps connected to a chain, and what appeared to be a blindfold.

* * *

An FBI agent stationed in Turkey attempted to interview the source at the end of November 2000 to determine how he had acquired the information regarding Steiger that he sent to the MPD. But the source was adamant about not revealing his identity, but explained in an e-mail on November 30, 2000 how he obtained that information:

> I will not tell you my name or meet you. . . . If I tell you my name and make an official interview with you, that guy and his lawyer will know all about me so I will have an overseas enemy.

> I'm not a computer freak. I'm a 33 years [sic] old professional. I have a family. I don't want to risk my peace because of a hobby. I'll answer some of your possible questions.

* * *

How did I get access to his pc?

> I used the well known trojan horse named subseven. . . . I made it undetectable so av softwares [sic] couldnt [sic] see it and bind it with a fake program. After this I posed it to the news group "alt.binaries.pictures.erotica.pre-teen" where one can find 1000s of sick people.

> If you have any more questions, just mail me. I tell you again "I WILL NEVER TELL YOU MY NAME AND NEVER MEET YOU."

After Steiger downloaded the fake picture the source posted to the news group, the Trojan Horse program permitted the source to enter into Steiger's computer via the Internet and find the images and identifying information he sent to the MPD.

[The district court denied Steiger's motions to suppress the information obtained by the computer hacker and referred to the authorities.]

II.

A. THE FOURTH AMENDMENT

Steiger claims that the search warrant was obtained in violation of his Fourth Amendment right against unreasonable searches and seizures because it was based in part on information from an anonymous source who hacked into his computer. * * *

A search by a private person does not implicate the Fourth Amendment unless he acts as an instrument or agent of the government. * * * The district court's finding of probable cause for the search warrant was based on the information provided in the anonymous source's first and second e-mails, together with Agent Faulkner's affidavit describing how she personally corroborated that information. The information conveyed in those two e-mails was limited to that which the source had acquired *before* making *any* contact with the MPD. Thus, even assuming *arguendo* that the MPD tacitly encouraged further nonconsensual searches, the information relied on in support of the warrant—graphic images showing Steiger sexually abusing a young child and identifying information regarding Steiger which Agent Faulkner thoroughly corroborated—more than sufficed to establish probable cause.

We also reject Steiger's argument for suppression based on Agent Faulkner's failure to advise the judge who issued the warrant *how* the source obtained the information he sent to the MPD. Steiger asserts that no judge would have found probable cause knowing that the source had hacked into his computer. But he supplies no authority for this assertion. * * * Because information obtained by a private person is not subject to the Fourth Amendment's exclusionary rule, a statement that the anonymous source had hacked into Steiger's computer to obtain that information would not have affected the magistrate's finding of probable cause.

B.   The Wiretap Act

Unlike the Fourth Amendment, the Wiretap Act applies to private conduct as well as to governmental agents. The Act denounces certain "interceptions." Steiger's argument that the district court should have granted his motion to suppress pursuant to the Wiretap Act presents two questions of first impression in this Circuit: (1) whether the anonymous source "intercepted" any "electronic communications" in violation of the Wiretap Act; and (2) if so, whether any of the Act's provisions require suppression. The district court declined to address the threshold issue and instead ruled that even if the source had intercepted electronic communications in violation of the Wiretap Act, the Act's provisions provide for suppression only with respect to unlawful interceptions of oral or wire communications. Steiger concedes that the Wiretap Act expressly provides for suppression only with respect to unlawfully intercepted *oral* and *wire* communications. *See* 18 U.S.C. § § 2515, 2518(10)(a). But he asserts that suppression of unlawfully seized *electronic* communications is available by negative implication under 18 U.S.C. § 2517(3), which authorizes disclosure of electronic evidence at trial if it was acquired in accordance with the Wiretap Act. * * *

We hold that the anonymous source did not intercept electronic communications in violation of the Wiretap Act. We also hold that while the Wiretap Act clearly provides criminal and civil sanctions for the unlawful interception of electronic communications, *see* 18 U.S.C. § § 2511(1), (4), (5), 2520, the Act provides no basis for moving to suppress such communications.

(1) The anonymous source did not intercept electronic communications in violation of the Wiretap Act when he hacked into Steiger's computer.

In 1986, Title I of the ECPA amended the federal Wiretap Act, which previously had addressed only interception of wire and oral communications, to also address interception of electronic communications. Konop v. Hawaiian Airlines, Inc., 302 F.3d 868, 874 (9th Cir. 2002). At the same time, Title II of the ECPA created the Stored Communications Act ("SCA") to cover access to stored communications and records. 18 U.S.C. § 2701(a); Konop, 302 F.3d at 874. We begin our analysis by agreeing with the Ninth Circuit that

> the intersection of these two statutes is a complex, often convoluted, area of the law. The difficulty is compounded by the fact that the ECPA was written prior to the advent of the Internet and the World Wide Web. As a result, the existing statutory framework is ill-suited to address modern forms of communication.... Courts have struggled to analyze problems involving modern technology within the confines of this statutory framework, often with unsatisfying results. Until Congress brings the laws in line with modern technology, protection of the Internet ... will remain a confusing and uncertain area of the law.

Konop, 302 F.3d at 874 (collecting law review articles criticizing judicial interpretations of the ECPA).

The Wiretap Act generally prohibits the intentional "interception" of "wire, oral, or electronic communications." See 18 U.S.C. § 2511(1). Thus, we must decide whether any information the source provided in his first two e-mails to the MPD falls within the definition of "electronic communications," and, if so, whether the source "intercepted" that information within the meaning of the Act.

"Electronic communications" are defined in the Wiretap Act as "any transfer of signs, signals, writing, images, sounds, data, or intelligence of any nature transmitted in whole or in part by a wire, radio, electromagnetic, photoelectronic or photooptical system that affects interstate or foreign commerce." 18 U.S.C. § 2510(12). At least one Circuit has held that information stored on a server and conveyed from a private website to users clearly falls within the definition of "electronic communications." Konop, 302 F.3d at 876. Here, the source penetrated Steiger's computer by using a "Trojan Horse" virus that enabled him to discover and download files stored on Steiger's hard drive. That information was transferred from Steiger's computer to the source over one of the specified media and thus falls within the Wiretap Act's definition of "electronic communications."

"Interception" is defined as "the aural or other acquisition of the contents of any wire, electronic, or oral communication through the use of any electronic, mechanical, or other device." 18 U.S.C. § 2510(4). The Circuits which have interpreted this definition as applied to electronic communications have held that it encompasses only acquisitions contemporaneous with transmission. See Konop, 302 F.3d at 878–89 (withdrawing previous panel opinion at 236 F.3d 1035 (9th Cir. 2001) holding to the contrary); Steve Jackson Games, Inc. v. United States Secret Serv., 36 F.3d 457 (5th Cir. 1994).

The Fifth Circuit observed in Steve Jackson Games that, before Congress enacted the ECPA, federal courts had read "intercept" to mean the acquisition of a communication contemporaneous with transmission. The Steve Jackson Games court further explained that in passing the ECPA, Congress intended to retain the previous definition of "intercept" while amending the Wiretap Act to cover interceptions of electronic communications. But the Fifth Circuit reasoned that the word "intercept" could not describe identical conduct with respect to both wire and electronic communications, because they were defined differently. Specifically the ECPA redefined the term "wire communication" to include electronic storage of the communication, but omitted reference to storage from its definition of "electronic communication." *See* 18 U.S.C. § 2510(1) (2000) (defining "wire communication"); 18 U.S.C. § 2510(12) (2000) (defining "electronic communication").

This textual difference illustrates Congress' intent that one could "intercept" a wire communication in storage, but could not "intercept" a similarly situated electronic communication:

> Congress' use of the word "transfer" in the definition of "electronic communication," and its omission in that definition of the phrase "any electronic storage of such communication" ... reflects that Congress did not intend for "intercept" to apply to "electronic communications" when those communications are in "electronic storage."

Steve Jackson Games, 36 F.3d at 461–62. * * *

The *Konop* court also noted that Congress' recent amendment to the Wiretap Act eliminating "storage" from the definition of "wire communication" provides further support to the analysis relied on in *Steve Jackson Games*:

> By eliminating storage from the definition of wire communication, Congress essentially reinstated the pre-ECPA definition of "intercept"—acquisition contemporaneous with transmission—with respect to wire communications. The purpose of the recent amendment was to reduce protection of voice mail messages to the lower level of protection provided other electronically stored communications. When Congress passed the USA PATRIOT Act,

it was aware of the narrow definition courts had given the term "intercept" with respect to electronic communications, but chose not to change or modify that definition. To the contrary, it modified the statute to make that definition applicable to voice mail messages as well. Congress, therefore, accepted and implicitly approved the judicial definition of "intercept" as acquisition contemporaneous with transmission.

Indeed, as *Konop* pointed out, this definition is "consistent with the ordinary meaning of 'intercept,' which is 'to stop, seize, or interrupt in progress or course before arrival.' " *Id.* (quoting *Webster's Ninth New Collegiate Dictionary* 630 (1985)).

The Fifth and Ninth Circuits' reasoning is persuasive and we hold that a contemporaneous interception—*i.e.*, an acquisition during "flight"—is required to implicate the Wiretap Act with respect to electronic communications.

The Ninth and Fifth Circuits also concluded that their reading of the Wiretap Act "is consistent with the structure of the ECPA, which created the SCA for the express purpose of addressing 'access to *stored* ... electronic communications and transactional records.' " *Konop*, 302 F.3d at 878–79; *Steve Jackson Games*, 36 F.3d at 463. These two cases reasoned that

> the level of protection provided stored communications under the SCA is considerably less than that provided by communications covered by the Wiretap Act.... [If] acquisition of a stored communication were an interception under the Wiretap Act, the government would have to comply with the more burdensome, more restrictive procedures of the Wiretap Act to do exactly what Congress apparent-

ly authorized it to do under the less burdensome procedures of the SCA. Congress could not have intended this result.

Konop, 302 F.3d at 879; *see also Steve Jackson Games*, 36 F.3d at 463.

Though we agree with the Fifth and Ninth Circuits' interpretation of the Wiretap Act, we do not rely on this particular reasoning in doing so. The SCA creates criminal and civil penalties, but no exclusionary remedy, for unauthorized access to a "facility through which an electronic communication service is provided" to "obtain[], alter[], or prevent[] authorized access to a wire or electronic communication *while it is in electronic storage in such system.*" 18 U.S.C. § 2701 (emphasis added); *see also* 18 U.S.C. § § 2707, 2708. "Electronic communication service" is defined as "any service which provides users thereof the ability to send or receive wire or electronic communications." 18 U.S.C. § 2510(15). The SCA also generally prohibits an entity providing an electronic communication service to the public from disclosing information absent an applicable exception. *See* 18 U.S.C. § 2702. Thus, the SCA clearly applies, for example, to information stored with a phone company, Internet Service Provider (ISP), or electronic bulletin board system (BBS).

The SCA, however, does not appear to apply to the source's hacking into Steiger's computer to download images and identifying information stored on his hard-drive because there is no evidence to suggest that Steiger's computer maintained any "electronic communication service" as defined in 18 U.S.C. § 2510(15). We note, however that the SCA may apply to the extent the source accessed and retrieved any information stored with Steiger's Internet service provider. In sum, our reading of the Wiretap Act to cover only real-time interception of electronic communications, together with the apparent non-applicability of the SCA to hacking into personal computers to retrieve information stored therein, reveals a legislative hiatus in the current laws purporting to protect privacy in electronic communications. This hiatus creates no remedy.

We now turn to the issue of whether the anonymous source acquired any electronic communications contemporaneously with their transmission. The Ninth Circuit in *Konop* held that viewing a private website by way of the Internet without authorization did not constitute an interception of electronic communications in violation of the Wiretap Act because such unauthorized viewing merely gained access to stored electronic communications. Similarly, the Fifth Circuit in *Steve Jackson Games* rejected an argument that seizure of a computer used to operate an electronic bulletin board system (BBS) constituted an interception of the stored but unread e-mail contained on that system, reasoning that e-mail stored on the BBS' computer hard drive was no longer in transmission and thus could not be intercepted within the meaning of the Wiretap Act.

Indeed, under the narrow reading of the Wiretap Act we adopt from the Fifth and Ninth Circuits, very few seizures of electronic communications from computers will constitute "interceptions."

There is only a narrow window during which an E-mail interception may occur—the seconds or mili-seconds before which a newly composed message is saved to any temporary location following a send command. Therefore, unless some type of automatic routing software is used (for example, a duplicate of all of an employee's messages are automatically sent to the employee's boss), interception of E-mail within the prohibition of [the Wiretap Act] is virtually impossible.

Jarrod J. White, E-Mail at Work.com: Employer Monitoring of Employee E-Mail, 48 Ala. L. Rev. 1079, 1083 (1997).

In this case, there is nothing to suggest that any of the information provided in the source's e-mails to the MPD was obtained through contemporaneous acquisition of electronic communications while in flight. Rather, the evidence shows that the source used a Trojan Horse virus that enabled him to access and download information stored on Steiger's personal computer. This conduct, while possibly tortious, does not constitute an interception of electronic communications in violation of the Wiretap Act.

(2) Suppression is not a remedy under the Wiretap Act with respect to unlawfully seized electronic communications.

Even if Steiger could demonstrate that the actions of the source constituted an "interception" in violation of the Wiretap Act, the suppression provision in the Act provides no basis for moving to suppress electronic communications. By its terms, 18 U.S.C. § 2515 applies *only* to "wire or oral communications," and not to "electronic communications":

> Whenever any *wire or oral communication* has been intercepted, no part of the contents of such communication and no evidence derived therefrom may be received in evidence in any trial, hearing, or other proceeding in or before any court, grand jury, department, officer,

agency, regulatory body, legislative committee, or other authority of the United States, a State, or a political subdivision thereof if the disclosure of that information would be in violation of this chapter.

18 U.S.C. § 2515. Despite the fact that the ECPA amended numerous sections of the Wiretap Act to include "electronic communications," the ECPA did not amend § 2515. Further, although, as noted by Steiger, Congress considered amending § 2515 in the USA Patriot Act to "extend[] the statutory exclusion rule in 18 U.S.C. § 2515 to electronic communications," the Act was passed without such an amendment.

* * *

Case law supports this conclusion. In United States v. Meriwether, the Sixth Circuit held that it could not "under the ECPA grant appellant's requested remedy—suppression because the ECPA does not provide an independent statutory remedy of suppression for interceptions of electronic communications." 917 F.2d 955, 960 (6th Cir. 1990).

* * *

The omission of "electronic communications" from section 2515 is dispositive. The Wiretap Act does not provide a suppression remedy for electronic communications unlawfully acquired under the Act.

IV.

Because this case implicates neither the Fourth Amendment nor the Wiretap Act, we AFFIRM the judgment of the district court.

VII. REMEDIES FOR FOURTH AMENDMENT VIOLATIONS

A. THE BACKGROUND OF THE EXCLUSIONARY RULE

Thus far we have suspended any discussion of the exclusionary rule, which is at the heart of most search and seizure disputes. Whether there is an exclusionary rule or not, virtually every problem presented up to this point in the Chapter still exists, because there is a Fourth Amendment. This is not an argument for the exclusionary rule. It is only recognition that one evil associated with it—i.e., it unduly complicates constitutional decisionmaking—may be over-stated. Of course, it would be possible to treat the Amendment as hortatory and to deny that there should be any remedy for its violation. The right that remained, however, hardly would be worth inclusion in a Bill of Rights. Some remedy is necessary, then. But what it should be is the subject of much dispute.

Once it has been determined that a violation of the Fourth Amendment has occurred, the usual remedy today is exclusion of any evidence gathered as a result of that violation—i.e., evidence seized in an illegal search and evidence directly associated with the illegal search (the "fruits" thereof). But the exclu-sionary rule was not born contemporaneously with the Fourth Amendment. The Bill of Rights is not explicit as to remedies. For over a century after the adoption of the Fourth Amendment, virtually the only remedies available to victims of illegal searches were suits in trespass for damages, or in replevin for return of the goods seized. The trespass alternative was usually impractical, and replevin had no chance of success if the goods seized were contraband, or the fruits or instrumentalities of crime, since these items were considered forfeited to the state regardless of the legality of the seizure.

Why did it take the Supreme Court so long to formulate the exclusionary rule? Did the first 100 years plus indicate that the Court believed that the Amendment did not require exclusion of evidence seized unconstitutionally? In a discussion of Fifth Amendment protections in United States v. Scott, 437 U.S. 82 (1978), the Supreme Court explained that one reason the earlier years provide little guidance to the remedial requirements of the Bill of Rights is that at the time the Bill of Rights was adopted, there was little opportunity for the Supreme Court to address criminal cases:

> [M]ost criminal prosecutions proceeded to final judgment, and neither the United States nor the defendant had any right to appeal an adverse verdict. The verdict in such a case was unquestionably final, and could be raised in bar against any further prosecution for the same offense.
>
> Soon thereafter, Congress made provision for review of certain criminal cases by this Court, but only upon a certificate of division from the Circuit Court, and not at the instigation of the defendant. It was not until 1889 that Congress permitted criminal defendants to seek a writ of error in this Court, and then only in capital cases. Only then did it become necessary for this Court to deal with the issues presented by the challenge of verdicts on appeal.

Exclusionary Rule for the Federal Courts:
Weeks v. United States

The exclusionary rule was applied to the federal courts in Weeks v. United States, 232 U.S. 383 (1914). Justice Day wrote for a unanimous court:

> The case in the aspect in which we are dealing with it involves the right of the court in a criminal prosecution to retain for the purposes of evidence the letters and correspondence of the accused, seized in his house in his absence and without his authority, by a United States Marshal holding no

warrant for his arrest and none for the search of his premises. * * * If letters and private documents can thus be seized and held and used in evidence against a citizen accused of an offense, the protection of the Fourth Amendment declaring his right to be secure against such searches and seizures is of no value, and, so far as those thus placed are concerned, might as well be stricken from the Constitution. The efforts of the courts and their officials to bring the guilty to punishment, praiseworthy as they are, are not to be aided by the sacrifice of those great principles established by years of endeavor and suffering which have resulted in their embodiment in the fundamental law of the land. The United States Marshal * * * acted without sanction of law, doubtless prompted by the desire to bring further proof to the aid of the Government, and under color of his office undertook to make a seizure of private papers in direct violation of the constitutional prohibition against such action. * * * To sanction such proceedings would be to affirm by judicial decision a manifest neglect if not an open defiance of the prohibitions of the Constitution intended for the protection of the people against such unauthorized action.

Weeks was limited to cases where the illegal search was conducted by federal officers and the evidence was sought to be admitted in a federal criminal proceeding. It was essentially an exercise of the Court's supervisory power over the federal courts.

Two themes articulated in *Weeks,* and finding recurrent expression in later cases dealing with the rationale for excluding evidence, were that the exclusionary rule is the only effective means of protecting Fourth Amendment rights, and that the interest in judicial integrity requires that the courts not sanction illegal searches by admitting the fruits of illegality into evidence. In Silverthorne Lumber Co. v. United States, 251 U.S. 385 (1920), these considerations were held to prohibit the copying of illegally seized documents, and their use as the basis for a subpoena of the originals, which had been returned pursuant to a motion by the defendant. The Court stressed that "[t]he essence of a provision forbidding the acquisition of evidence in a certain way is [not merely that] evidence so acquired shall not be used before the Court but that it shall not be used at all."

B. THE EXCLUSIONARY RULE AND THE STATES

During the next thirty years, the Supreme Court had several opportunities to discuss the Fourth Amendment in the context of the incorporation doctrine and federal-state relations. *Weeks* had explicitly rejected the notion that the exclusionary rule should apply to violations by state or local police. Dicta in Byars v. United States, 273 U.S. 28 (1927) and Gambino v. United States, 275 U.S. 310 (1927), established what came to be known as the "silver platter doctrine." This doctrine made evidence obtained in an illegal state search admissible in federal court as long as there was no federal participation in the search. While the definition of "federal participation" broadened considerably in the ensuing years so as to more readily trigger the exclusion of evidence, Lustig v. United States, 338 U.S. 74 (1949), the silver platter doctrine remained in force until 1960 when Elkins v. United States, 364 U.S. 206, abolished it. Shortly thereafter, the issue became largely academic with the application of the exclusionary rule to the states. Mapp v. Ohio, 367 U.S. 643 (1961).

The rationale underlying these developments in Fourth Amendment remedies can best be understood by contrasting two major opinions of that period: Wolf v. Colorado, where unreasonable state searches and seizures were held to violate the Due Process Clause of the Fourteenth Amendment, and Mapp v. Ohio, where such a violation was held to require the exclusion of evidence. As you study the two opinions, consider not only the debate over the efficacy of the exclusionary rule, but also the sensitive issues of federal-state relations.

WOLF v. COLORADO

Supreme Court of the United States, 1949.
338 U.S. 25.

MR. JUSTICE FRANKFURTER **delivered the opinion of the Court.**

* * *

The security of one's privacy against arbitrary intrusion by the police—which is at the core of the Fourth Amendment—is basic to a free society. It is therefore implicit in "the concept of ordered liberty" and as such enforceable against the States through the Due Process Clause. The knock at the door, whether by day or by night, as a prelude to a search, without authority of law but solely on the authority of the police, did not need the commentary of recent history to be condemned as inconsistent with the conception of human rights enshrined in the history and the basic constitutional documents of English-speaking peoples.

Accordingly, we have no hesitation in saying that were a State affirmatively to sanction such police incursion into privacy it would run counter to the guaranty of the Fourteenth Amendment. But the ways of enforcing such a basic right raise questions of a different order. How such arbitrary conduct should be checked, what remedies against it should be afforded, the means by which the right should be made effective, are all questions that are not to be so dogmatically answered as to preclude the varying solutions which spring from an allowable range of judgment on issues not susceptible of quantitative solution.

In Weeks v. United States, this Court held that in a federal prosecution the Fourth Amendment barred the use of evidence secured through an illegal search and seizure. This ruling * * * was not derived from the explicit requirements of the Fourth Amendment; it was not based on legislation expressing Congressional policy in the enforcement of the Constitution. The decision was a matter of judicial implication. Since then it has been frequently applied and we stoutly adhere to it. But the immediate question is whether the basic right to protection against arbitrary intrusion by the police demands the exclusion of logically relevant evidence obtained by an unreasonable search and seizure because, in a federal prosecution for a federal crime, it would be excluded. As a matter of inherent reason, one would suppose this to be an issue as to which men with complete devotion to the protection of the right of privacy might give different answers. When we find that in fact most of the English-speaking world does not regard as vital to such protection the exclusion of evidence thus obtained, we must hesitate to treat this remedy as an essential ingredient of the right. The contrariety of views of the States is particularly impressive in view of the careful reconsideration which they have given the problem in the light of the *Weeks* decision.

[Justice Frankfurter summarized state case law on the issue of admissibility of evidence, contrasting pre-and post-*Weeks* decisions. In 1949, 31 states had rejected the *Weeks* doctrine and 16 states were in agreement with it.]

The jurisdictions which have rejected the *Weeks* doctrine have not left the right to privacy without other means of protection. Indeed, the exclusion of evidence is a remedy which directly serves only to protect those upon whose person or premises something incriminating has been found. We cannot, therefore, regard it as a departure from basic standards to remand such persons, together with those who emerge scatheless from a search, to the remedies of private action and such protection as the internal discipline of the police, under the eyes of an alert public opinion, may afford. Granting that in practice the exclusion of evidence may be an effective way of deterring unreasonable searches, it is not for this Court to condemn as falling below the minimal standards assured by the Due Process Clause a State's reliance upon other methods which, if consistently enforced, would be equally effective. We cannot brush aside the experience of States which deem the incidence of such conduct by the police too slight to call for a deterrent remedy not by way of disciplinary measures but by overriding the relevant rules of evidence. There are, moreover, reasons for excluding evidence unreasonably obtained by the federal police which are less compelling in the case of police under State or local authority. The public opinion of a community can far more effectively be exerted against oppressive conduct on the part of police directly responsible to the community itself than can local opinion, sporadically aroused, be brought to bear upon remote authority pervasively exerted throughout the country.

We hold, therefore, that in a prosecution in a State court for a State crime the Fourteenth Amendment does not forbid the admission of evidence obtained by an unreasonable search and seizure. * * *

Mr. Justice Murphy, **with whom Mr.** Justice Rutledge **joins, dissenting.**

* * *

The conclusion is inescapable that but one remedy exists to deter violations of the search and seizure clause. That is the rule which excludes illegally obtained evidence. Only by exclusion can we impress upon the zealous prosecutor that violation of the Constitution will do him no good. And only when that point is driven home can the prosecutor be expected to emphasize the importance of observing constitutional demands in his instructions to the police.

* * *

[Justice Rutledge's separate dissent is omitted, as is Justice Douglas' dissent. Justice Black's concurring opinion, stating that the exclusionary rule "is not a command of the Fourth Amendment" also is omitted.]

Note on Wolf and the Road to Mapp

Although the Court was divided 6–3 in *Wolf,* the division was over the applicability of the exclusionary rule to the States. The Justices unanimously agreed that the prohibition against unreasonable searches and seizures applied to the States. They disagreed as to whether the exclusionary rule was a constitutionally required remedy.

In the next decade, the issue received the Court's attention twice more. In Rochin v. California, 342 U.S. 165 (1952), the shocking methods used by the State to obtain incriminating evidence were held to so offend "a sense of justice" as to require exclusion at a state trial. The evidence had been obtained by pumping the defendant's stomach. Two years later, in Irvine v. California, 347 U.S. 128 (1954), *Wolf* was reaffirmed, 5–4, and evidence was admitted where the search of a home, although shocking, did not involve a physical assault on the suspect's person.

In 1961, the Supreme Court once again considered the question in Mapp v. Ohio. *Mapp* appeared to be exclusively a First Amendment case; the exclusionary rule issue was neither briefed nor argued. Yet, *Wolf* was overruled 5–3. The change is partly explained by the fact that six members of the *Wolf* court were no longer on the Bench. Consider, however, whether other factors might account for the rejection of *Wolf* in that short period of time.

MAPP v. OHIO

Supreme Court of the United States, 1961.
367 U.S. 643.

MR. JUSTICE CLARK **delivered the opinion of the Court.**

* * *

[I]n the year 1914, in the *Weeks* case, this Court "for the first time" held that "in a federal prosecution the Fourth Amendment barred the use of evidence secured through an illegal search and seizure." This Court has ever since required of federal law officers a strict adherence to that command which this Court has held to be a clear, specific, and constitutionally required—even if judicially implied—deterrent safeguard without insistence upon which the Fourth Amendment would have been reduced to "a form of words." It meant, quite simply, that "conviction by means of unlawful seizures and enforced confessions * * * should find no sanction in the judgments of the courts * * *," Weeks v. United States, and that such evidence "shall not be used at all." Silverthorne Lumber Co. v. United States.

[Justice Clark considered the current validity of the factual grounds on which *Wolf* was based and found them to be no longer controlling. In particular, he noted that the trend among the States since *Wolf* had been toward acceptance of the exclusionary rule, and that experience had proved other remedies to be ineffective. However, these considerations "are not basically relevant to a decision that the exclusionary rule is an essential ingredient of the Fourth Amendment as the right it embodies is vouchsafed against the States by the Due Process Clause."]

III

Some five years after *Wolf,* in answer to a plea made here Term after Term that we overturn its doctrine on applicability of the *Weeks* exclusionary rule, this Court indicated that such should not be done until the States had "adequate opportunity to adopt or reject the [*Weeks*] rule." Irvine v. California. * * *

* * * Today we once again examine *Wolf's* constitutional documentation of the right to privacy free from unreasonable state intrusion, and, after its dozen years on our books, are led by it to close the only courtroom door remaining open to evidence secured by official lawlessness in flagrant abuse of that basic right, reserved to all persons as a specific guarantee against that very same unlawful conduct. We hold that all evidence obtained by searches and seizures in violation of the Constitution is, by that same authority, inadmissible in a state court.

IV

Since the Fourth Amendment's right of privacy has been declared enforceable against the States through the Due Process Clause of the Fourteenth, it is enforceable against them by the same sanction of exclusion as is used against the Federal Government. * * * [T]he admission of the new constitutional right by *Wolf* could not consistently tolerate denial of its most important constitutional privilege, namely, the exclusion of the evidence which an accused had been forced to give by reason of the unlawful seizure. To hold otherwise is to grant the right but in reality to withhold its privilege and enjoyment. Only last year the Court itself recognized that the purpose of the exclusionary rule "is to deter—to compel respect for the constitutional guaranty in the only effectively available way—by removing the incentive to disregard it." Elkins v. United States.

Indeed, we are aware of no restraint, similar to that rejected today, conditioning the enforcement of any other basic constitutional right. The right to privacy, no less important than any other right carefully and particularly reserved to the people, would stand in marked contrast to all other rights declared as basic to a free society. This Court has not hesitated to enforce as strictly against the States as it does against the Federal Government the rights of free speech and of a free press, the rights to notice and to a fair, public trial, including, as it does, the right not to be convicted by use of a coerced confession, however logically relevant it be, and without regard to its reliability. * * * Why should not the same rule apply to what is tantamount to coerced testimony by way of unconstitutional seizure of goods, papers, effects, documents, etc.? * * *

V

[The Court focuses on the incentives *Wolf* provided for federal officials to provide state courts unconstitutionally obtained evidence.]

There are those who say, as did Justice (then Judge) Cardozo, that under our constitutional exclusionary doctrine "[t]he criminal is to go free because the constable has blundered." People v. Defore, 242 N.Y. at 21, 150 N.E. at 587. In some cases this will undoubtedly be the result. But, as was said in *Elkins,* "there is another consideration—the imperative of judicial integrity." The criminal goes free, if he must, but it is the law that sets him free. Nothing can destroy a government more quickly than its failure to observe its own laws, or worse, its disregard of the charter of its own existence. * * *

The ignoble shortcut to conviction left open to the States tends to destroy the entire system of constitutional restraints on which the liberties of the people rest. Having once recognized that the right to privacy embodied in the Fourth Amendment is enforceable against the States, and that the right to be secure against rude invasions of privacy by state officers is, therefore, constitutional in origin, we can no longer permit that right to remain an empty promise. Because it is enforceable in the same manner and to like effect as other basic rights secured by the Due Process Clause, we can no longer permit it to be revocable at the whim of any police officer who, in the name of law enforcement itself, chooses to suspend its enjoyment. Our decision, founded on reason and truth, gives to the individual no more than that which the Constitution guarantees him, to the police officer no less than that to which honest law enforcement is entitled, and, to the courts, that judicial integrity so necessary in the true administration of justice. * * *

* * *

[Justice Black concurred in a separate opinion, arguing that the Constitutional basis for the majority rule was the Fourth Amendment in conjunction with the Fifth Amendment's ban against compelled self-incrimination.[a] The concurrences of Justices Douglas and Stewart have been omitted. Justice Stewart did not reach the Fourth Amendment question, preferring to decide the case on First Amendment grounds.]

MR. JUSTICE HARLAN, whom MR. JUSTICE FRANKFURTER and JUSTICE WHITTAKER join, dissenting.

* * *

I would not impose upon the States this federal exclusionary remedy. The reasons given by the majority for now suddenly turning its back on *Wolf* seem to me notably unconvincing.

* * *

[W]e are told that imposition of the *Weeks* rule on the States makes "very good sense," in that it will promote recognition by state and federal officials of their "mutual obligation to respect the same fundamental criteria" in their approach to law enforcement, and will avoid "needless conflict between state and federal courts." Indeed the majority now finds an incongruity in *Wolf's* discriminating perception between the demands of "ordered liberty" as respects the basic right of "privacy" and the means of securing it among the States. That perception, resting both on a sensitive regard for our federal system and a sound recognition of this Court's remoteness from particular state prob-

lems, is for me the strength of that decision.

An approach which regards the issue as one of achieving procedural symmetry or of serving administrative convenience surely disfigures the boundaries of this Court's functions in relation to the state and federal courts. * * *

Finally, it is said that the overruling of *Wolf* is supported by the established doctrine that the admission in evidence of an involuntary confession renders a state conviction Constitutionally invalid. Since such a confession may often be entirely reliable, and therefore of the greatest relevance to the issue of the trial, the argument continues, this doctrine is ample warrant in precedent that the way evidence was obtained, and not just its relevance, is Constitutionally significant to the fairness of a trial. I believe this analogy is not a true one. The "coerced confession" rule is certainly not a rule that any illegally obtained statements may not be used in evidence. * * *

The point, then, must be that in requiring exclusion of an involuntary statement of an accused, we are concerned not with an appropriate remedy for what the police have done, but with something which is regarded as going to the heart of our concepts of fairness in judicial procedure. * * * What is crucial is that the trial defense to which an accused is entitled should not be rendered an empty formality by reason of statements wrung from him, for then "a prisoner * * * [has been] made the deluded instrument of his own conviction." 2 Hawkins, Pleas of the Crown (8th ed., 1824), c. 46, § 34. That this is a *procedural right,* and that its violation occurs at the time his improperly obtained statement is ad-

a. A fascinating description of how Justice Clark fashioned a majority in *Mapp* and especially how he won the vote of Justice Black is

found in Dorin, "Seize the Time: Justice Tom Clark's Role in Mapp v. Ohio (1961)," in Law and the Legal Process (Swigert ed. 1982).

mitted at trial, is manifest. For without this right all the careful safeguards erected around the giving of testimony, whether by an accused or any other witness, would become empty formalities in a procedure where the most compelling possible evidence of guilt, a confession, would have already been obtained at the unsupervised pleasure of the police.

This, and not the disciplining of the police, as with illegally seized evidence, is surely the true basis for excluding a statement of the accused which was unconstitutionally obtained. In sum, I think the coerced confession analogy works strongly *against* what the Court does today.

* * *

Note on Mapp

Both the majority and dissent in *Mapp* stressed that the issue was not the effectiveness of the exclusionary rule or the ineffectiveness of alternative remedies, but whether the exclusion of evidence illegally obtained was constitutionally mandated. Are the two issues really distinct? What is the basis for the majority's conclusion that the exclusionary rule is required? Obviously, the texts of the Fourth and Fourteenth Amendments lend no support to the proposition. The recent origins of the rule likewise throw no historical weight behind its acceptance. In the final analysis, isn't the majority implicitly deciding that the exclusion of evidence is the only effective sanction, and that the right to be free from unreasonable searches is "a dead letter" without a sanction? If other alternatives had proved effective in deterring violations, would the Court have found exclusion to be a constitutional requirement?

Would a showing that exclusion of evidence has no deterrent effect whatsoever have required a different result? Professor Dripps, in Living with *Leon*, 95 Yale L.J. 906 (1986), argues that if no sanction attaches to a Fourth Amendment violation, the Amendment does not qualify as a law, thus betraying "the fundamental principle of constitutionalism, which is after all that the Constitution states the law." He argues that "even if the sanction does not deter, the refusal to apply it or anything else expresses the judgment that the underlying norm is of little importance." Do you agree? Dripps gives the following example: "Even if we were absolutely certain that a convicted murderer would never murder again, we would still feel obliged to impose a relatively severe sentence in order to vindicate the principle that life is dear and may not be unlawfully taken without paying a price." Is this example persuasive?

Both the majority and the dissent in *Mapp* discuss the constitutional rule of exclusion of coerced confessions. Who has the better of the argument on this point? As we will see in *Leon,* the Court has held that, despite its decision in *Mapp,* the exclusionary rule is not constitutionally required, in part because the violation of a Fourth Amendment right occurs at the time of the original police intrusion. The argument is that later exclusion from the trial has nothing to do with the already completed violation, and that introduction of the evidence at trial is not a separate violation of privacy. When does the constitutional violation occur if the police coerce a confession? See Schulhofer, Confessions and the Court, 79 Mich.L.Rev. 569 (1981) (violation of right to be free from coerced confession occurs when the confession is admitted at trial). Does this mean that the dissent in *Mapp* was right? For an argument that the Fourth Amendment violation is not complete at the time of the intrusion, and that the exclusionary rule is constitutionally required, see Heffernan, On Justifying Fourth Amendment Exclusion, 1989 Wis.L.Rev. 1193.

Arguments for and Against the Exclusionary Rule

Many judges are not enamoured of the exclusionary rule. For example, Judge Bowman had this to say about the exclusionary rule in United States v. Jefferson, 906 F.2d 346 (8th Cir.1990), a case in which the entire court agreed that evidence obtained during a stop without reasonable suspicion had to be excluded due to the exclusionary rule:

> This case vividly illustrates the perversity of the exclusionary rule. Here, an officer's educated hunch led to the discovery of evidence (nine kilograms of cocaine) of substantial criminal activity. This discovery occurred as a result of information the officer developed by asking questions and examining documents in the course of his routine check of a parked car and its occupants at a highway rest stop. The ordinary law-abiding citizen, I believe, would think the officer should be commended for his fine work, and the cocaine dealers punished. Instead, because we hold (as I agree, under the existing case law, we must) that a "seizure" within the meaning of the Fourth Amendment occurred before the officer had formed an objectively reasonable basis for suspecting the defendants of criminal activity, the exclusionary rule requires that the evidence be suppressed. The defendants thus exit unpunished, free to continue dealing illegal drugs to the pathetic addicts and contemptible scofflaws who comprise the national market for these substances. As for the officer, far from his being commended, it is judicially recorded that he blundered, and the point once again is driven home that legalistic observance of even the most technical of the judge-created rules of search and seizure—rules which, like the Fourth Amendment itself, seek to protect law-abiding citizens from intrusive conduct by officers of the state—is more important than intelligent, courageous, and vigorous initiative to expose criminal activity and bring those responsible for it to the bar of justice.

> It has been reported that since 1961, when [*Mapp* was decided], "the murder rate has doubled, rape has quadrupled and robbery has quintupled." *Wall St.J.*, May 7, 1990, at A14, Col. 1. While it would be foolish to blame the exclusionary rule for all of this alarming increase in violent crime, I believe it is equally foolish to pretend that the exclusionary rule, and the *zeitgeist* it has created, is to blame for none of it.

Judge Bowman's comments prompted Chief Judge Lay to respond as follows:

> If police are not deterred from illegal intrusions of privacy by excluding whatever evidence is seized, the fourth amendment will have no meaning or force. Surely an appreciation for the history and purpose of our basic freedoms will never allow emotional fear to justify an environment where there is no check on the abuse of police power.

> The fourth amendment protects the good guy as well as the bad. It would mean very little to anyone if it did not. The argument that since 1961 murders have doubled, rapes quadrupled, and robbery quintupled in part because of the exclusionary rule is a statement more fitting for headlines of the National Enquirer. It is irrational hyperbole totally unsupported in fact or in law.

Supporters of the exclusionary rule generally make four points in its favor: 1. The rule preserves judicial integrity, by insulating the courts from tainted evidence; 2. The rule prevents the government from profiting from its own wrong; 3. The rule is not costly, because it only excludes what should never have been obtained in the first place; and 4. The rule is necessary to deter police misconduct. See, e.g., Barnett, Resolving the Dilemma of the Exclusionary Rule: An Application of Restitutive Principles of Justice, 32 Emory L.J. 937 (1983).

Professor Amar, in Fourth Amendment First Principles, 107 Harv.L.Rev. 757 (1994), attacks each of the justifications listed by Judge Lay. As to the judicial integrity rationale, Amar responds: "we must remember that integrity and fairness are also threatened by excluding evidence that will help the justice system to reach a true verdict. Thus, the courts best affirm their integrity not by closing their eyes to truthful evidence, but by opening their doors to any civil suit brought against wayward government officials, even one brought by a convict."

Professor Amar continues his critique of the exclusionary rule as follows:

Consider next the nice-sounding idea that government should not profit from its own wrongdoing. Our society, however, also cherishes the notion that cheaters—or murderers or rapists, for that matter—should not prosper. When the murderer's bloody knife is introduced, it is not only the government that profits; the people also profit when those who truly do commit crimes against person and property are duly convicted on the basis of reliable evidence. * * *

The classic response is that setting criminals free is a cost of the Fourth Amendment itself, and not of the much-maligned exclusionary rule. If the government had simply obeyed the Fourth Amendment it would never have found the bloody knife. Thus, excluding the knife simply restores the status quo ante and confers no benefit on the murderer. The classic response is too quick.

In many situations, it is far from clear that the illegality of a search is indeed a but-for cause of the later introduction of an item found in the search. Suppose the police could easily get a warrant, but fail to do so because they think the case at hand falls into a judicially recognized exception to the warrant requirement. A court later disagrees—and so, under current doctrine, the search was unconstitutional. But if the court goes on to exclude the bloody knife, it does indeed confer a huge benefit on the murderer. The police could easily have obtained a warrant before the search, so the illegality is not a but-for cause of the introduction of the knife into evidence.

* * *

But even if a defendant could conclusively establish but-for causation, the bloody knife should still come in as evidence. Not all but-for consequences of an illegal search are legally cognizable. * * * [I]f an illegal search turns up a ton of marijuana, the government need not return the contraband even if the government's possession of the marijuana is clearly a but-for consequence of its illegal search. Indeed, the government may sell the marijuana (say, for legitimate medical uses) and use the proceeds to finance the continued war on drugs. In a very real way, the government *has* profited from its own wrong.

Finally, Professor Amar critiques the deterrence rationale of the exclusionary rule, and decries the fact that deterrence comes by way of benefit to criminal defendants.

> Deterrence is concerned with the government, it is concerned with systematic impact. It treats the criminal defendant merely as a surrogate for the larger public interest in restraining the government. The criminal defendant is a kind of private attorney general.

> But the worst kind. He is self-selected and self-serving. He is often unrepresentative of the larger class of law-abiding citizens. Indeed, he is often despised by the public, the class he implicitly is supposed to represent. He will litigate on the worst set of facts, heedless that the result will be a bad precedent for the Fourth Amendment generally. He cares only about the case at hand—his case—and has no long view. He is not a sophisticated repeat player. He rarely hires the best lawyer. He cares only about exclusion—and can get only exclusion—even if other remedies (damages or injunctions) would better prevent future violations. * * * He is, in short, an awkward champion of the Fourth Amendment.

> He is also overcompensated. * * * In a criminal case, if we insist on using criminal defendants as private attorneys general, why not give a defendant who successfully establishes a Fourth Amendment violation only a ten percent sentence discount—surely a tangible incentive—and substitute for the remaining ninety percent some other structural remedy, injunctive or damages, that will flow to the direct benefit of law-abiding citizens? * * *

> Put differently, if deterrence is the key, the idea is to make the government pay, in some way, for its past misdeeds, in order to discourage future ones. But why should that payment flow to the guilty? Under the exclusionary rule, the more guilty you are, the more you benefit. * * * In sum, when it comes to private attorneys general, the exclusionary rule's deterrence rationale looks in the wrong place—to paradigmatically guilty criminal defendants rather than to prototypically law-abiding civil plaintiffs.

Has Professor Amar convinced you? Are you concerned that if the exclusionary rule is abolished, there will be no effective remedy to take its place?

Professor Slobogin, in Why Liberals Should Chuck the Exclusionary Rule, 1999 Univ. Ill. L.Rev. 363, argues that the exclusionary rule should be replaced by an effective remedy of monetary damages.

> [I]f optimal deterrence of illegal searches and seizures is the goal, the exclusionary rule is a poor solution. Changing or suppressing behavior is a complex and difficult task. It is especially difficult when, as is true with many types of illegal searches and seizures, the behavior is implicitly or explicitly endorsed by peers, superiors, and a large segment of the general public. Without a strong disincentive to engage in such conduct, it will continue. Thus, a regime that directly sanctions officers and their departments is preferable to the [exclusionary] rule. Although there are many versions of such a regime, it should have several core components: (1) a liquidated damages/penalty for all unconstitutional actions, preferably based on the average officer's salary; (2) personal liability, at the liquidated

damages sum, of officers who knowingly or recklessly violate the Fourth Amendment; (3) entity liability, at the liquidated damages sum, for all other violations; (4) state-paid legal assistance for those with Fourth Amendment claims; and (5) a judicial decisionmaker.

That such a regime is a better deterrent than the rule does not establish that it should be adopted, of course. The exclusionary rule clearly does have some deterrent effect. If it proves to be considerably less costly than a damages regime, perhaps it should remain the sanction of choice. It is unlikely that the rule is significantly "cheaper," however, whether one looks at financial or other types of costs. To many, the primary "cost" of the exclusionary rule is the number of criminals who escape conviction because evidence against them has been suppressed. A conservative estimate is that approximately 10,000 felons and 55,000 misdemeanants evade punishment each year because of successful Fourth Amendment suppression motions. Other costs of the rule are more subtle. These include the threat to the Fourth Amendment posed by judges and prosecutors concerned with freeing criminals, the psychic and systemic costs of routine perjury by police officers, the distracting impact of suppression hearings on the quality of defense representation on other issues, and the damage to courts and government generally because of public outrage at the huge benefit criminals receive when the cases against them are dismissed or damaged by exclusion.

* * *

[A] favorite liberal argument on behalf of the rule has been * * * that the only difference between the exclusionary rule and an effective alternative is that the former flaunts before us the costs we must pay for fourth amendment guarantees. Put another way, the contention is that any alternative that truly works will result in at least as many lost convictions as the rule. A first response to this argument is that if we can avoid flaunting the costs of the Fourth Amendment and still achieve its goals, so much the better. More importantly, the assumption that an effective alternative prevents us from catching any criminal the exclusionary rule prevents us from convicting is wrong. The point of an effective deterrent is not only to discourage unconstitutional actions but to encourage constitutional ones. With an effective deterrent in place, police who lack probable cause will not necessarily give up; the more reasonable assumption is that they will simply get more cause. That is precisely the behavior a damages regime would systematically induce and what the exclusionary rule fails to encourage in any concerted way.

For more arguments about the value of the exclusionary rule, see Stuntz The Virtues and Vices of the Exclusionary Rule, 20 Harv.J.L and Pub.Pol. 443 (1997); Perrin et al., If It's Broken, Fix It: Moving Beyond the Exclusionary Rule—A New and Extensive Empirical Study of the Exclusionary Rule and a Call for a Civil Administrative Remedy to Partially Replace the Rule, 83 Iowa L.Rev. 669 (1998). For a debate over the exclusionary rule by two titans of the law, see Calabresi and Kamisar, Debate on the Search and Seizure Exclusionary Rule, 26 Harv. J. L. & Pub. Pol. 4 (2003). Judge Calabresi argues as an alternative to the exclusionary rule that defendants could object to illegally obtained evidence at sentencing, and would receive a sentence reduction if successful. In addition, Judge Calabresi would impose direct administrative sanctions on police officers for illegal searches and seizures. Professor Kamisar expresses doubt that administrative sanctions on wrongdoing police officers will be imposed in practice.

C. EVIDENCE SEIZED ILLEGALLY, BUT CONSTITUTIONALLY

1. *Violations of State Law*

Generally speaking, a violation of state law that is not itself a violation of the Fourth Amendment will not result in exclusion of evidence in federal court. Whether exclusion will occur in state court is a matter of state law. Some states require exclusion of evidence obtained in violation of nonconstitutional law; other states do not. The cases generally hold that in federal courts, state law need not be followed by either Federal or state officers. See, e.g., United States v. Vite-Espinoza, 342 F.3d 462 (6th Cir.2002) ("We conclude that in circumstances such as the present, where there was no violation of the United States Constitution, but there may have been a violation of the state constitution, the appropriate remedy is a civil action in state court, not evidentiary exclusion in federal court."); United States v. Bell, 54 F.3d 502 (8th Cir.1995)(arrest by state officers, in violation of state law, does not require exclusion). The reasoning is that Federal law governs the admissibility of evidence in a federal criminal action, so it is irrelevant that the evidence might be inadmissible under state law. Doesn't this result create a reverse "silver platter" doctrine? See, e.g., United States v. Appelquist, 145 F.3d 976 (8th Cir.1998), where state officers entered the defendant's house and obtained evidence in violation of a state law restricting nighttime searches. Appelquist was initially charged in state court and filed a motion to suppress. The state then ceased to prosecute and a federal prosecution was commenced. The Court found this sequence of events to be "irrelevant" because "the general rule applies even when a motion to suppress was *granted* in an earlier state prosecution."

State Standards as Part of the Fourth Amendment Analysis

Despite the general rule that a violation of state law will not result in exclusion in Federal court, there are a few instances in which state standards are effectively *incorporated* into Federal law. When that is the case, a violation of the state standard is actually a violation of the Fourth Amendment, and exclusion is warranted in a Federal (and state) trial. For example, in United States v. Wanless, 882 F.2d 1459 (9th Cir.1989), the court held that evidence obtained in an inventory search of a car by a Washington State Trooper was improperly admitted, because the Trooper did not follow state guidelines requiring him to ask for the owner's consent before impounding the car. The court distinguished other cases in which it found state law to be irrelevant, reasoning that "the federal law on inventory searches by state or local police officers is that they must be conducted in accordance with the official procedures of the relevant state or local police department." (Citing South Dakota v. Opperman and Colorado v. Bertine, supra). See also United States v. Bell, 54 F.3d 502 (8th Cir.1995)("to show the reasonableness of an inventory search, the Government must show officers complied with state standardized procedures").

State Ethical Standards

Should a violation of a state ethical standard by a Federal prosecutor result in the exclusion of evidence from a Federal trial? A statute commonly referred to as the "McDade amendment" (28 U.S.C. § 530(b)) provides that a lawyer for the federal government "shall be subject to State laws and rules, and local Federal court rules, governing attorneys in each State where such attorney engages in that attorney's duties, to the same extent and in the same manner as other attorneys in that State." This appears to mean that a federal prosecutor violates *federal* law if she violates a state rule of professional responsibility. For example, some states prohibit lawyers from contacting people who are represented by counsel, even before litigation has begun. As will be more fully developed in Chapter 3, a "no-contact" rule before litigation imposes a greater restriction on prosecutors than is imposed by the Constitution. The question is whether exclusion should result if a prosecutor violates a state no-contact rule and obtains evidence thereby, even though the evidence was obtained consistently with the Constitution.

The courts have held that the McDade amendment does not authorize exclusion of evidence obtained in violation of state standards of professional responsibility. As the court noted in United States v. Lowery, 166 F.3d 1119 (11th Cir.1999), the McDade amendment simply provides that state laws and rules governing attorney conduct shall apply to federal government attorneys "to the same extent and in the same manner as other attorneys in that State." On its face it appears directed toward controlling the conduct of federal prosecutors, and not toward whether evidence should be excluded. The *Lowery* Court concluded that "nothing in the language or legislative history of the Act that would support" the "radical notion" that a rule designed to control prosecutorial ethics should also be employed as a source for excluding evidence in federal court. Making state professional conduct rules applicable to federal attorneys is one thing. Letting those rules govern the admission of evidence in federal court is quite another. The *Lowery* Court concluded that "[i]f Congress wants to give state courts and legislatures veto power over the admission of evidence in federal court, it will have to tell us that in plain language using clear terms."

2. Violations of Federal Statutes, Regulations and Federal Rules of Criminal Procedure

The courts have been reluctant to impose exclusion as a judicial remedy for a violation of a federal statute or regulation, or a Federal Rule of Criminal Procedure. For example, violations of the procedural limitations on warrants contained in Fed.R.Crim.P. 41 ordinarily do not result in exclusion. As stated by the court in United States v. Schoenheit, 856 F.2d 74 (8th Cir.1988), exclusion is not required "unless the search would not have otherwise occurred or would not have been so abrasive if the Rule had been followed, or there was evidence of an intentional and deliberate disregard of Fed.R.Crim.P. 41." In *Schoenheit*, a search was made at 10:30 p.m.; the warrant provided for execution at night, but the application and affidavits did not establish reasonable cause authorizing execution at times other than between 6:00 a.m. and 10:00 p.m., as required by Rule 41. The court refused to suppress the evidence, finding that the search would have occurred anyway, and that no showing was made that the search would have been less abrasive if conducted before 10:00 p.m. See also United States v. Charles, 883 F.2d 355 (5th Cir.1989) (violation of Rule 41 provision requiring officer to conduct a search with the warrant in hand does not require exclusion where the search would have occurred anyway). Compare United States v. Gantt, 179 F.3d 782 (9th Cir.1999) (exclusion required where officers fail to serve the warrant upon on the owner of the premises, in violation of Fed.R.Crim.P. 41(d); officers intentionally disregarded this requirement, and failure to serve the warrant made the search more "abrasive", because if served, the owner "would not have been in doubt regarding the authority of the agents, and she might also have been able to point out to the agents that many of the items seized were beyond the scope of the warrant.").

With respect to statutes, Congress has in some cases provided expressly for exclusion, such as in the wiretapping statute, Title III, discussed supra. Where Congress has not so provided, the courts ordinarily have not imposed exclusion as a remedy. See United States v. Blue Diamond Coal Co., 667 F.2d 510 (6th Cir.1981)(no suppression required for violation of statute requiring consent or administrative warrant for seizure of lawfully inspected records). Similar results occur with violations of agency regulations or other non-constitutional law. See United States v. Caceres, 440 U.S. 741 (1979)(violation of IRS regulations concerning recording of conversations does not require suppression); United States v. Hensel, 699 F.2d 18 (1st Cir.1983)(no suppression even if international law and coast guard regulations were violated).

D. THE EXCLUSIONARY RULE IN DETAIL: PROCEDURES, SCOPE AND PROBLEMS

1. *Procedures for Return of Property and Motions to Suppress*

Before addressing the coverage of the exclusionary rule, it is helpful to understand the procedures that trigger its application. Previously, we have seen that a copy of the search warrant is either provided to the person whose premises are searched or left at unoccupied premises. Accompanying the copy of the warrant is a list of things seized. (The exception is for sneak and peak warrants, authorized by the USA PATRIOT Act and the accompanying amendment to Rule 41).

When the person whose property is taken wants to challenge the validity of the search, a motion to return the evidence can be made. See, e.g., Fed.R.Crim.P. 41(g). Also, a motion to suppress evidence can be made, even if the evidence seized is contraband, someone else's property, or otherwise not returnable. The motion to suppress is directed to the use of the evidence rather than its return. See, e.g., Fed.R.Crim.P. 41(h). Since it is usually more efficient for courts to hear suppression motions prior to trial, rather than in the midst of trying the merits (especially when a jury is used), court rules may encourage or require pretrial motions. Failure to make a pre-trial motion could in some jurisdictions result in the loss of the claim absent a good reason for the failure. See Fed.R.Crim.P 12 (b)(3)(C) (motion to suppress must be made before trial, though failure to move may be excused for good cause). If a motion at trial is permitted, generally it will have to be made when the evidence is offered.

Pre-trial hearings obviously are outside the presence of the jury. Generally, mid-trial hearings also will be outside the hearing of the jury. Whether a search and seizure is lawful is a question for the judge, but in some jurisdictions the judge who finds the search to be lawful will resubmit the issue to the jury with an instruction on search and seizure law. Naturally, the judge's determination will not be revealed to the jury.

2. Attacking the Warrant

If the search was pursuant to a warrant, the judge ruling on the motion to suppress will consider the sworn evidence presented to the magistrate who issued the warrant. The Fourth Amendment determination will be made on the basis of only this evidence. No after-acquired evidence can be considered because the issue is whether the magistrate properly issued the warrant on the basis of the information available to her. See generally Kaiser v. Lief, 874 F.2d 732 (10th Cir.1989)(magistrate may rely on affidavit, complaint, and other affidavits contemporaneously presented for other warrants).

Challenging the Truthfulness of the Warrant Application: Franks v. Delaware

In Franks v. Delaware, 438 U.S. 154 (1978), the Court held that a defendant has a limited right to attack the truthfulness of statements made in warrant applications. But the Court was clear that such challenges were not to be routine.

> * * * There is, of course, a presumption of validity with respect to the affidavit supporting the search warrant. To mandate an evidentiary hearing, the challenger's attack must be more than conclusory and must be supported by more than a mere desire to cross-examine. There must be allegations of deliberate falsehood or of reckless disregard for the truth, and those allegations must be accompanied by an offer of proof. They should point out specifically the portion of the warrant affidavit that is claimed to be false; and they should be accompanied by a statement of supporting reasons. Affidavits or sworn or otherwise reliable statements of witnesses should be furnished, or their absence satisfactorily explained. Allegations of negligence or innocent mistake are insufficient. The deliberate falsity or reckless disregard whose impeachment is permitted today is only that of the affiant, not of any nongovernmental informant. Finally, if these requirements are met, and if, when material that is the subject of the alleged falsity or reckless disregard is set to one side, there remains sufficient content in the warrant affidavit to support a finding of probable cause, no hearing is required. On the other hand, if the remaining content is insufficient, the defendant is entitled, under the Fourth Amendment, to his hearing. Whether he will prevail at that hearing is, of course, another issue.

The Court found that where defendants could make the required preliminary showing, the need to assure that the police act in good faith outweighed the drain on resources that the limited hearing requirement would necessitate. Justice Rehnquist, joined by Chief Justice Burger, dissented, arguing that, even if "some inaccurate or falsified information may have gone into the making of the determination" to issue a warrant, "I simply do not think the game is worth the candle in this situation." When you recall that the warrant application is made ex parte and the magistrate makes nothing like a credibility determination, what would become of the warrant clause of the Amendment if Justice Rehnquist's view had prevailed?

Scienter Requirement

The *Franks* deliberate falsity or reckless disregard standard is applicable to statements of the officer-affiant, but it is generally not applicable to statements of non-governmental informants. As one court stated, "the fact that a third party lied to the affiant, who in turn included the lies in a warrant affidavit, does not constitute a *Franks* violation. A *Franks* violation occurs only if the affiant knew the third party was lying, or if the affiant proceeded in reckless disregard for the truth." United States v. McAllister, 18 F.3d 1412 (7th Cir. 1994). Why is this so? Can probable cause be based on a deliberate, material misstatement from an informant? To answer this question it may be helpful to recall the Court's analysis in Illinois v. Gates, supra.

United States v. Johns, 851 F.2d 1131 (9th Cir.1988), provides an example of a showing sufficient to warrant a *Franks* hearing. In *Johns*, probable cause was based in material part on the officer's averment that he had detected the odor of methamphetamine emanating from the defendant's premises. The defendant submitted affidavits from two experts stating that in light of the way the methamphetamine was stored, it would have been impossible for the officer outside the premises to smell it. *Johns* was distinguished in United States v. Mueller, 902 F.2d 336 (5th Cir.1990), where the officer averred that he could smell methamphetamine emanating from the defendant's house while standing across the street. The defendant submitted an expert affidavit to the effect that it would have been unlikely to pick up such a smell given the officer's distance from the house and the prevailing winds. The court denied a *Franks* hearing, noting that Mueller's expert merely concluded that the officer's story was "unlikely," while the experts in *Johns* concluded that the officer's story was "impossible."

Materiality Requirement

An officer's misstatement is not material under *Franks* if probable cause would exist even without the misstatement. See United States v. Campbell, 878 F.2d 170 (6th Cir.1989), citing cases in every circuit applying this test. In *Campbell,* the court found the search warrant valid even though the affidavit included a statement attributed to an informant known by the affiant to be fictitious. The court found that untainted information in the affidavit from three reliable informants was sufficient to establish probable cause under Illinois v. Gates, supra. Essentially, the officer's deliberate falsehood constituted harmless error.

3. Challenging A Warrantless Search

The burden of producing evidence placed on the moving party in *Franks* is different from the burden placed on the moving party when a warrantless search is challenged. Once it is established that no warrant was obtained, the government must justify the search. Generally, the state must prove by a preponderance of the evidence that an exception to the warrant requirement was satisfied. See United States v. Matlock, 415 U.S. 164 (1974); United States v. Hurtado, 905 F.2d 74 (5th Cir.1990) (government must prove voluntariness of consent by a preponderance of the evidence). This allocation of the burden of proof reflects the Court's mild preference for warrants. See generally Saltzburg, Standards of Proof and Preliminary Questions of Fact, 27 Stan.L.Rev. 271 (1975).

4. *The Hearing and Judicial Review*

At the hearing on the motion to suppress evidence, the government will have a privilege to protect the identity of informants. See McCray v. Illinois, 386 U.S. 300 (1967)(holding that it is constitutional to withhold informant's identity on issue of probable cause). Of course, the judge can require the government to reveal the informant's identity if that is necessary "to decide whether the officer is a believable witness." State v. Burnett, 42 N.J. 377, 201 A.2d 39 (1964). "[T]he judge may in his discretion require the prosecution, *in camera,* to disclose to him the identity of the informant, or produce the informant for questioning. If the judge does so require, the information or testimony so obtained shall be kept securely under seal and, in the event of an appeal from the judge's disposition of the motion, transmitted to the appellate court." § 290.4, ALI Model Code of Pre–Arraignment Procedure.

In a suppression hearing in federal court, the ordinary rules of evidence are not applicable, with the exception of rules of privilege. A judge can, for example, rely on hearsay to determine the legality of a search or seizure. In United States v. Matlock, 415 U.S. 164 (1974), the Court reasoned that "in proceedings where the judge himself is considering the admissibility of evidence, the exclusionary rules, aside from rules of privilege, should not be applicable; and the judge should receive the evidence and give it such weight as his judgment and experience counsel." The *Matlock* Court concluded that at a suppression hearing "the judge should be empowered to hear any relevant evidence, such as affidavits or other reliable hearsay." See also United States v. Schaefer, 87 F.3d 562 (1st Cir.1996) ("a judge presiding at a suppression hearing may receive and consider any relevant evidence, including affidavits and unsworn documents that bear indicia of reliability.").

Sequestering Police Officers

Should police officers be sequestered before giving suppression hearing testimony? Why might that be necessary? In United States v. Brewer, 947 F.2d 404 (9th Cir.1991), the defendant moved to sequester a police officer who was scheduled to testify after another police officer at a suppression hearing. The defendant cited Federal Rule of Evidence 615, which requires the judge to sequester witnesses upon motion of one of the parties. The trial court held that Rule 615 was not applicable to suppression hearings, relying on the general principle that the Federal Rules of Evidence are not applicable to such hearings. The two police officers testified virtually identically. The Ninth Circuit reversed. The *Brewer* Court found that Rule 615 was a procedural rule designed to guarantee a fair proceeding, as opposed to a rule dealing with the admissibility of evidence. The Court distinguished the Supreme Court's decision in *Matlock,* which held specifically that the hearsay rule is inapplicable in suppression hearings. The *Brewer* Court stated that *Matlock* "does not support the notion that procedural rules designed to protect the integrity of the fact finding process are inapplicable in a suppression hearing." Will sequestration of police officers be effective in uncovering "testilying?"

Limitations on Use of Suppression Hearing Testimony at Trial: *Simmons v. United States*

At the hearing, the defendant may testify in support of his claim of a Fourth Amendment violation. Simmons v. United States, 390 U.S. 377 (1968), holds that when a defendant testifies on the question of "standing" (a subject discussed infra) at a suppression hearing, the government may not use his testimony against him on the question of guilt or innocence. So for example, the defendant can testify at the suppression hearing that the briefcase full of narcotics was his, and this statement cannot be used against him as an admission of guilt at trial. Justice Harlan's opinion for the 6–2 majority in *Simmons* reasoned that defendants would be unduly inhibited from making Fourth Amendment claims absent protection against automatic use of suppression hearing testimony at trial. In light of the way the opinion is written, it is likely that it extends to all Fourth Amendment questions (e.g., consent) considered at the hearing, not just to "standing" questions.

Can the testimony at the suppression hearing be used at trial to impeach a defendant who takes the stand and changes his testimony? *Simmons* left the impeachment question open. But lower courts have held that *Simmons* does not prevent the use of suppression hearing testimony for impeachment purposes. See, e.g., United States v. Beltran–Gutierrez, 19 F.3d 1287 (9th Cir.1994) (defendant's statements at a suppression hearing can be used to impeach him if his trial testimony is inconsistent with them). Thus, a defendant who testifies at the suppression hearing that he owned the briefcase full of drugs will run into difficulty if the evidence is not suppressed and he takes the stand at trial and testifies that the briefcase was not his. His suppression hearing testimony can be offered as a prior inconsistent statement to impeach him. He will be entitled to have the jury instructed that the prior statement is not to be used as substantive evidence that the briefcase was actually his, but only for its bearing on the defendant's credibility. But that limiting instruction is likely to have little practical effect.

If the defendant calls a witness to testify at the suppression hearing (e.g., a friend who testifies that the briefcase was the defendant's), the government may use that testimony against the defendant at trial. This is because *Simmons* was designed to protect defendants from sacrificing one constitutional right (the Fifth Amendment right against self-incrimination) for another (the Fourth Amendment right). When the defendant calls a witness at the suppression hearing, the defendant's Fifth Amendment rights are not implicated. As the court stated in United States v. Boruff, 870 F.2d 316 (5th Cir.1989):

> While a defendant's decision to call third-parties to corroborate his testimony at a suppression hearing might be affected by his knowledge that the government may subsequently utilize that testimony at trial, this dilemma does not rise to the level of a constitutional problem.

Appellate Review

If a motion to suppress is granted, federal law permits immediate appellate review of the ruling subject to certain conditions. 18 U.S.C. § 3731. Most states are in accord. The federal statute provides that three conditions must be satisfied before the government can appeal from a suppression order: 1. The government cannot appeal if the defendant has been put in jeopardy, within the meaning of the Double Jeopardy Clause; 2. An appeal must not be taken for the purpose of delay; and 3. The suppressed evidence must be substantial proof of a fact material to the proceedings. See United States v. Gantt, 179 F.3d 782 (9th Cir.1999), for an application of these factors.

A few states allow a defendant to appeal a denial of a motion to suppress immediately if the trial judge or appellate tribunal certifies that the issue is substantial and an immediate appeal would expedite litigation; but most jurisdictions deny the defendant the right to an immediate appeal. This includes the federal courts, where an appeal from the denial of a suppression motion must await a judgment of conviction. It must be kept in mind that prosecutors cannot appeal the merits of an acquittal; only defendants can. Thus, prosecutors have to get an immediate appeal or none at all. If the defendant is convicted, an issue on appeal may be the denial of a suppression motion.

Where the case stands or falls on admitting the challenged evidence, and the court has denied the motion to suppress, a defendant may wish to plead guilty on condition that he reserves the right to appeal the court's Fourth Amendment ruling. Fed.R.Crim.P. 11(a)(2) permits a defendant, with the approval of the court and the consent of the government, to enter a conditional plea of guilty, reserving the right to appeal the court's denial of a motion to suppress. A defendant who prevails on appeal "may then withdraw the plea."

Deferential Review

Great deference is paid by reviewing courts to magistrates who issue warrants and to judges who make suppression rulings. As to issuing magistrates, the Court in Illinois v. Gates, supra, stated that "after the fact scrutiny by courts of the sufficiency of an affidavit should not take the form of *de novo* review." The Court declared that the magistrate's determination was entitled to "great deference," and that the reviewing court should uphold the warrant so long as the magistrate had a "substantial basis" for issuing it. The Court found that this deferential review was necessary to further the Fourth Amendment's "strong preference" for warrants.

Should magistrates defer to each other? If one magistrate refuses to issue a warrant because of perceived inadequacies in the application, can another magistrate issue a warrant on the same showing? Some courts have found it problematic that an officer would seek another magistrate's review after having been rebuffed. See People v. Cocilova, 132 Misc.2d 106, 503 N.Y.S.2d 258 (1986)(suppressing evidence on grounds that "judge shopping" cannot be permitted). Other courts permit the practice, so long as the magistrate who ultimately issues the warrant is neutral and detached, and the warrant is sufficiently particular and supported by probable cause. See United States v. Pace, 898 F.2d 1218 (7th Cir.1990). If probable cause exists and the second magistrate is neutral and detached, why should it matter that prior magistrates refused to issue a warrant? What if the officer had been to 15 magistrates, all of whom denied the application, before a friendly magistrate was found?

5.   *Establishing a Violation of a Personal Fourth Amendment Right*

Fourth Amendment rights are personal rights. It therefore follows that for a defendant to be entitled to exclusion of evidence, he must establish that his own personal rights were implicated by the government's search or seizure. This has been characterized by many courts as a question of "standing"—though as will be seen below, the Supreme Court has chafed at this label. The question of "standing" is determined by whether the person seeking to suppress the evidence has had his own Fourth Amendment rights violated.

In the 1960's, the Court developed a generous view of a defendant's entitlement to invoke the exclusionary rule. Jones v. United States, 362 U.S. 257 (1960), held that a defendant had "automatic standing" to challenge the legality of the search that produced the very drugs that he was charged with possessing at the time of the search. The Court in *Jones* also stated that a search could be challenged by anyone "legitimately on the premises where a search occurs". In the following case the Court substantially cut back on *Jones* and, more importantly, recharacterized "standing" questions so that they are now resolved by substantive principles of Fourth Amendment law.

RAKAS v. ILLINOIS

Supreme Court of the United States, 1978.
439 U.S. 128.

JUSTICE REHNQUIST **delivered the opinion of the Court.**

[Officers received a radio call concerning a robbery and describing the getaway car. They stopped a vehicle which matched the description. Petitioners and two female companions were ordered out of the car. The officers searched the passenger compartment and found a box of rifle shells in the glove compartment and a sawed-off rifle under the front passenger seat. Petitioners had been passengers in the car; the owner of the car had been the driver when the car was stopped. The lower court denied the motion to suppress, reasoning that petitioners lacked standing, and the Illinois appellate courts affirmed. The Supreme Court found that petitioners had the burden of proof as to standing, and that they failed to meet their burden of showing ownership of the rifle or shells. The Court proceeded to consider whether standing could be established in the absence of ownership of the property seized].

* * *

II

Petitioners first urge us to relax or broaden the rule of standing enunciated in Jones v. United States, so that any criminal defendant at whom a search was "directed" would have standing to contest the legality of that search and object to the admission at trial of evidence obtained as a result of the search. Alternatively, petitioners argue that they have standing to object to the search under *Jones* because they were "legitimately on [the] premises" at the time of the search.

* * * Adoption of the so-called "target" theory advanced by petitioners would in effect permit a defendant to assert that a violation of the Fourth Amendment rights of a third party entitled him to have evidence suppressed at his trial. If we reject petitioners' request for a broadened rule of standing such as this, and reaffirm the holding of *Jones* and other cases that Fourth Amendment rights are personal rights that may not be asserted vicariously, we will have occasion to reexamine the "standing" terminology emphasized in *Jones.* For we are not at all sure that the determination of a motion to suppress is materially aided

by labeling the inquiry identified in *Jones* as one of standing, rather than simply recognizing it as one involving the substantive question of whether or not the proponent of the motion to suppress has had his own Fourth Amendment rights infringed by the search and seizure which he seeks to challenge. * * *

A

We decline to extend the rule of standing in Fourth Amendment cases in the manner suggested by petitioners. As we stated in Alderman v. United States, 394 U.S. 165, 174 (1969), "Fourth Amendment rights are personal rights which, like some other constitutional rights, may not be vicariously asserted." A person who is aggrieved by an illegal search and seizure only through the introduction of damaging evidence secured by a search of a third person's premises or property has not had any of his Fourth Amendment rights infringed. And since the exclusionary rule is an attempt to effectuate the guarantees of the Fourth Amendment, it is proper to permit only defendants whose Fourth Amendment rights have been violated to benefit from the rule's protections. There is no reason to think that a party whose rights have been infringed will not, if evidence is used against him, have ample motivation to move to suppress it. Even if such a person is not a defendant in the action, he may be able to recover damages for the violation of his Fourth Amendment rights, or seek redress under state law for invasion of privacy or trespass.

* * * In *Jones,* the Court set forth two alternative holdings: It established a rule of "automatic" standing to contest an allegedly illegal search where the same possession needed to establish standing is an essential element of the offense charged; and second, it stated that "anyone legitimately on

premises where a search occurs may challenge its legality by way of a motion to suppress." Had the Court intended to adopt the target theory now put forth by petitioners, neither of the above two holdings would have been necessary since Jones was the "target" of the police search in that case. * * *

In Alderman v. United States, * * * Mr. Justice Harlan * * * identified administrative problems posed by the target theory:

> "[T]he [target] rule would entail very substantial administrative difficulties. In the majority of cases, I would imagine that the police plant a bug with the expectation that it may well produce leads to a large number of crimes. A lengthy hearing would, then, appear to be necessary in order to determine whether the police knew of an accused's criminal activity at the time the bug was planted and whether the police decision to plant a bug was motivated by an effort to obtain information against the accused or some other individual. I do not believe that this administrative burden is justified in any substantial degree by the hypothesized marginal increase in Fourth Amendment protection."

When we are urged to grant standing to a criminal defendant to assert a violation, not of his own constitutional rights but of someone else's, we cannot but give weight to practical difficulties such as those foreseen by Mr. Justice Harlan in the quoted language.

Conferring standing to raise vicarious Fourth Amendment claims would necessarily mean a more widespread invocation of the exclusionary rule during criminal trials. * * * Each time the exclusionary rule is applied it exacts a substantial social cost for the vindication of Fourth Amendment rights. Relevant and reliable evidence is kept from the trier of fact and the

search for truth at trial is deflected.
* * *

B

* * * [H]aving rejected petitioners'
target theory and reaffirmed the principle that the "rights assured by the
Fourth Amendment are personal
rights, [which] ... may be enforced by
exclusion of evidence only at the instance of one whose own protection
was infringed by the search and seizure," the question necessarily arises
whether it serves any useful analytical
purpose to consider this principle a
matter of standing, distinct from the
merits of a defendant's Fourth Amendment claim. We can think of no decided cases of this Court that would have
come out differently had we concluded, as we do now, that the type of
standing requirement discussed in
Jones and reaffirmed today is more
properly subsumed under substantive
Fourth Amendment doctrine. Rigorous
application of the principle that the
rights secured by this Amendment are
personal, in place of a notion of
"standing," will produce no additional
situations in which evidence must be
excluded. The inquiry under either approach is the same. But we think the
better analysis forthrightly focuses on
the extent of a particular defendant's
rights under the Fourth Amendment,
rather than on any theoretically separate, but invariably intertwined concept of standing.

* * *

Analyzed in these terms, the question is whether the challenged search
and seizure violated the Fourth
Amendment rights of a criminal defendant who seeks to exclude the evidence obtained during it. That inquiry
in turn requires a determination of
whether the disputed search and seizure has infringed an interest of the
defendant which the Fourth Amend-

ment was designed to protect. We are
under no illusion that by dispensing
with the rubric of standing used in
Jones we have rendered any simpler
the determination of whether the proponent of a motion to suppress is
entitled to contest the legality of a
search and seizure. But by frankly
recognizing that this aspect of the
analysis belongs more properly under
the heading of substantive Fourth
Amendment doctrine than under the
heading of standing, we think the decision of this issue will rest on sounder
logical footing.

C

Here petitioners, who were passengers occupying a car which they neither owned nor leased, seek to anal-
ogize their position to that of the
defendant in Jones v. United States.
In *Jones,* petitioner was present at
the time of the search of an apartment which was owned by a friend.
The friend had given Jones permission to use the apartment and a key
to it, with which Jones had admitted
himself on the day of the search. He
had a suit and shirt at the apartment
and had slept there "maybe a night,"
but his home was elsewhere. At the
time of the search, Jones was the
only occupant of the apartment because the lessee was away for a period of several days. Under these circumstances, this Court stated that
while one wrongfully on the premises could not move to suppress evidence obtained as a result of searching them, "anyone legitimately on
premises where a search occurs may
challenge its legality." Petitioners argue that their occupancy of the automobile in question was comparable
to that of Jones in the apartment
and that they therefore have standing
to contest the legality of the
search—or as we have rephrased the
inquiry, that they, like Jones, had

their Fourth Amendment rights violated by the search.

We do not question the conclusion in *Jones* that the defendant in that case suffered a violation of his personal Fourth Amendment rights if the search in question was unlawful. Nonetheless, we believe that the phrase "legitimately on premises" coined in *Jones* creates too broad a gauge for measurement of Fourth Amendment rights. For example, applied literally, this statement would permit a casual visitor who has never seen, or been permitted to visit, the basement of another's house to object to a search of the basement if the visitor happened to be in the kitchen of the house at the time of the search. Likewise, a casual visitor who walks into a house one minute before a search of the house commences and leaves one minute after the search ends would be able to contest the legality of the search. * * *

We think that *Jones* on its facts merely stands for the unremarkable proposition that a person can have a legally sufficient interest in a place other than his own home so that the Fourth Amendment protects him from unreasonable governmental intrusion into that place. * * *

Katz v. United States, provides guidance in defining the scope of the interest protected by the Fourth Amendment. * * * [T]he Court in *Katz* held that capacity to claim the protection of the Fourth Amendment depends not upon a property right in the invaded place but upon whether the person who claims the protection of the Amendment has a legitimate expectation of privacy in the invaded place. Viewed in this manner, the holding in *Jones* can best be explained by the fact that Jones had a legitimate expectation of privacy in the premises he was using and therefore could claim the protection of the Fourth Amendment with respect to a governmental invasion of those premises, even though his "interest" in those premises might not have been a recognized property interest at common law.[a]

Our Brother WHITE in dissent expresses the view that by rejecting the phrase "legitimately on [the] premises" as the appropriate measure of Fourth Amendment rights, we are abandoning a thoroughly workable, "bright line" test in favor of a less certain analysis of whether the facts of a particular case give rise to a legitimate expectation of privacy. If "legitimately on premises" were the successful litmus test of Fourth Amendment rights that he assumes it is, his approach would have at least the merit of easy application, whatever it lacked in fidelity to the history and purposes of the Fourth Amendment. But a reading of lower court cases that have applied the phrase "legitimately on premises," and of the dissent itself, reveals that this expression is not a shorthand summary for a bright-line rule which somehow encapsulates the "core" of the Fourth Amendment's protections.

---

a. Obviously, however, a "legitimate" expectation of privacy by definition means more than a subjective expectation of not being discovered. A burglar plying his trade in a summer cabin during the off season may have a thoroughly justified subjective expectation of privacy, but it is not one which the law recognizes as "legitimate." His presence, in the words of *Jones*, 362 U.S., at 267, is "wrongful"; his expectation is not "one that society is prepared to recognize as 'reasonable.' "Katz v. United States, 389 U.S., at 361 (Harlan, J., concurring). And it would, of course, be merely tautological to fall back on the notion that those expectations of privacy which are legitimate depend primarily on cases deciding exclusionary-rule issues in criminal cases. Legitimation of expectations of privacy by law must have a source outside of the Fourth Amendment, either by reference to concepts of real or personal property law or to understandings that are recognized and permitted by society. * * *

* * * The dissenters concede that "there comes a point when use of an area is shared with so many that one simply cannot reasonably expect seclusion." But surely the "point" referred to is not one demarcating a line which is black on one side and white on another; it is inevitably a point which separates one shade of gray from another. We are likewise told by the dissent that a person "legitimately on *private* premises . . . , though his privacy is *not absolute,* is entitled to expect that he is sharing it only with those persons [allowed there] and that governmental officials will intrude only with *consent* or by complying with the Fourth Amendment." This single sentence describing the contours of the supposedly easily applied rule virtually abounds with unanswered questions: What are "private" premises? Indeed, what are the "premises?" It may be easy to describe the "premises" when one is confronted with a 1–room apartment, but what of the case of a 10–room house, or of a house with an attached garage that is searched?

* * * In abandoning "legitimately on premises" for the doctrine that we announce today, we are not forsaking a time-tested and workable rule, which has produced consistent results when applied, solely for the sake of fidelity to the values underlying the Fourth Amendment. Rather, we are rejecting blind adherence to a phrase which at most has superficial clarity and which conceals underneath that thin veneer all of the problems of line drawing which must be faced in any conscientious effort to apply the Fourth Amendment. Where the factual premises for a rule are so generally prevalent that little would be lost and much would be gained by abandoning case-by-case analysis, we have not hesitated to do so. See United States v. Robinson [discussed in the section on search incident to arrest, supra]. But

the phrase "legitimately on premises" has not been shown to be an easily applicable measure of Fourth Amendment rights so much as it has proved to be simply a label placed by the courts on results which have not been subjected to careful analysis. We would not wish to be understood as saying that legitimate presence on the premises is irrelevant to one's expectation of privacy, but it cannot be deemed controlling.

D

Judged by the foregoing analysis, petitioners' claims must fail. They asserted neither a property nor a possessory interest in the automobile, nor an interest in the property seized. And as we have previously indicated, the fact that they were "legitimately on [the] premises" in the sense that they were in the car with the permission of its owner is not determinative of whether they had a legitimate expectation of privacy in the particular areas of the automobile searched. * * *

Jones v. United States and Katz v. United States, involved significantly different factual circumstances. Jones not only had permission to use the apartment of his friend, but had a key to the apartment with which he admitted himself on the day of the search and kept possessions in the apartment. Except with respect to his friend, Jones had complete dominion and control over the apartment and could exclude others from it. Likewise in *Katz,* the defendant occupied the telephone booth, shut the door behind him to exclude all others and paid the toll, which "entitled [him] to assume that the words he utter[ed] into the mouthpiece [would] not be broadcast to the world." Katz and Jones could legitimately expect privacy in the areas which were the subject of the search and seizure each sought to contest. No such showing was made by these petitioners with respect to those portions of the automobile which were searched and from which incriminating evidence was seized.

* * *

JUSTICE POWELL, **with whom** CHIEF JUSTICE BURGER **joins, concurring.**

* * *

This is not an area of the law in which any "bright line" rule would safeguard both Fourth Amendment rights and the public interest in a fair and effective criminal justice system. The range of variables in the fact situations of search and seizure is almost infinite. Rather than seek facile solutions, it is best to apply principles broadly faithful to Fourth Amendment purposes.

JUSTICE WHITE, **with whom** JUSTICE BRENNAN, JUSTICE MARSHALL, **and** JUSTICE STEVENS **join, dissenting.**

* * * Insofar as passengers are concerned, the Court's opinion today declares an "open season" on automobiles. However unlawful stopping and searching a car may be, absent a possessory or ownership interest, no "mere" passenger may object, regardless of his relationship to the owner. * * *

* * * The *Jones* rule is relatively easily applied by police and courts; the rule announced today will not provide law enforcement officials with a bright line between the protected and the unprotected. Only rarely will police know whether one private party has or has not been granted a sufficient possessory or other interest by another private party. Surely in this case the officers had no such knowledge. * * *

More importantly, the ruling today undercuts the force of the exclusionary rule in the one area in which its use is most certainly justified—the deterrence of bad-faith violations of the Fourth Amendment. This decision invites police to engage in patently unreasonable searches every time an automobile contains more than one occupant. Should something be found, only the owner of the vehicle, or of the item, will have standing to seek suppression, and the evidence will presumably be usable against the other occupants. The danger of such bad faith is especially high in cases such as this one where the officers are only after the passengers and can usually infer accurately that the driver is the owner. * * *

Note on Rakas

The Court rejects the bright-line rule of *Jones*. In other cases in this Chapter, such as *Mimms*, *Robinson*, and *Belton*, the Court has adopted bright line rules for ease of administration and to provide necessary guidance to police officers. Has the Court been consistent in deciding when to draw a bright line and when not to draw one?

While the *Rakas* test for "standing" is identical to that applied under *Katz* to determine whether a search has occurred, the analysis for the two questions is often different. The question traditionally labelled as "standing"—whether the defendant's personal rights were violated—is not identical to the question of whether a Fourth Amendment search or seizure has occurred. For example, the police may have violated a legitimate expectation of privacy of *someone* (for instance by entering a house) and yet a particular defendant would not have have the right to object if he had no legitimate expectation of privacy in the premises. Thus, there will often be a search, but a particular defendant will have no right (no "standing") to object to it. In other cases, such as with an aerial overflight, there will be no search at all and therefore the court will never reach the question of "standing." It follows that the question of whether personal rights have been violated is still a separate question from whether a search has occurred, even though both questions are governed by the same test.

Abolition of Automatic Standing: United States v. Salvucci

Rakas was relied upon by the Supreme Court in United States v. Salvucci, 448 U.S. 83 (1980), which finally overruled *Jones* and abolished the automatic standing doctrine. The notion of automatic standing was that possession of property gave a person an automatic right to complain about the search or seizure of that property. Justice Rehnquist's majority opinion concluded that possession of a seized good should not be used as a substitute for a factual finding that the owner of the good had a legitimate expectation of privacy in the area searched. The automatic standing rule had been based on fairness concerns—that it would be unfair for the government to argue at the suppression hearing that the defendant did not possess the property sought to be suppressed, and then to turn around and argue at trial that the defendant did possess the same property. According to the *Salvucci* majority, however, *Rakas* and other cases "clearly establish that a prosecutor may simultaneously maintain that a defendant criminally possessed the seized good, but was not subject to a Fourth Amendment deprivation, without legal contradiction." This was because, after *Rakas,* a "person in legal possession of a good seized during an illegal search has not necessarily been subject to a Fourth Amendment deprivation."

Ownership of Seized Property Does Not Necessarily Confer Standing: Rawlings v. Kentucky

Rawlings v. Kentucky, 448 U.S. 98 (1980), demonstrated the significance of *Salvucci*. Rawlings was convicted of trafficking in and possession of various controlled substances. These substances were seized from the purse of a woman who, along with Rawlings, was visiting the premises when police arrived. The Supreme Court found that Rawlings had no right to object to the search of the purse because he had no legitimate expectation of privacy in the purse. The Court added that even assuming that the woman consented to have the drugs stored in the purse, "the precipitous nature of the transaction hardly supports a reasonable inference that petitioner took normal precautions to maintain his privacy." Ownership of the drugs was not enough to confer a right to object to the search, because the question was whether Rawlings had a legitimate expectation of privacy in the area that was searched, i.e., the purse. Justice Marshall, joined by Justice Brennan, dissented.

While ownership of the property seized does not necessarily provide the right to object to a search, it necessarily provides right to object to a *seizure* of that property. Of course, this did not help Rawlings, since the seizure of his property was completely reasonable—the officers searched the purse and found contraband. Neither Rawlings nor anyone else has a legitimate possessory interest in contraband.

Targets Without Standing: United States v. Payner

United States v. Payner, 447 U.S. 727 (1980), shows the consequences of the Court's rejection of the "target" theory of standing in *Rakas*. An IRS investigation of American citizens doing business in the Bahamas focused on a certain Bahamian bank. When an official of that bank visited the United States, IRS agents stole his briefcase and removed and photographed hundreds of documents. They did this to obtain evidence against Payner. Under *Rakas*, Payner had no right to object to the search of the briefcase, even though he was the target of the illegal search. Payner argued that the federal district court should exercise its supervisory power to exclude the evidence and thus to deter such purposefully illegal tactics. The district court agreed with Payner and excluded the evidence, but the Supreme Court held "that the supervisory power does not authorize a federal court to suppress otherwise admissible evidence on the ground that it was seized unlawfully from a third party not before the court." *Rakas* and *Rawlings* were relied upon. Justice Marshall, joined by Justices Brennan and Blackmun, dissented and argued that the government agents acted in bad faith by manipulating the standing rules in order to conduct an unconstitutional search; therefore, suppression of the illegally seized evidence was essential to protect the integrity of the judiciary whose rules were being manipulated.

Presence in the Home of Another

Assume that you are at a party and police officers enter and conduct a thorough search of the premises. Assume further that the officers do not search your person. If the search of the premises is illegal, do you, as a partygoer, have the right to complain that the search was a violation of your Fourth Amendment rights? Questions like this are determined, after *Rakas*, by whether you had a reasonable expectation of privacy in the areas that were searched. What follows is the Supreme Court's most recent opinion applying the *Rakas* analysis.

MINNESOTA v. CARTER

Supreme Court of the United States, 1998.
525 U.S. 83.

CHIEF JUSTICE REHNQUIST **delivered the opinion of the Court.**

Respondents and the lessee of an apartment were sitting in one of its rooms, bagging cocaine. While so engaged they were observed by a police officer, who looked through a drawn window blind. The Supreme Court of Minnesota held that the officer's viewing was a search which violated respondents' Fourth Amendment rights. We hold that no such violation occurred.

James Thielen, a police officer in the Twin Cities' suburb of Eagan, Minnesota, went to an apartment building to investigate a tip from a confidential informant. The informant said that he had walked by the window of a ground-floor apartment and had seen people putting a white powder into bags. The officer looked in the same window through a gap in the closed blind and observed the bagging operation for several minutes. He then notified headquarters, which began preparing affidavits for a search warrant while he returned to the apartment building. When two men left the building in a previously identified Cadillac, the police stopped the car. Inside were respondents Carter and Johns. As the police opened the door of the car to let Johns out, they observed a black zippered pouch and a handgun, later determined to be loaded, on the vehicle's floor. Carter and Johns were arrested, and a later police search of the vehicle the next day discovered pagers, a scale, and 47 grams of cocaine in plastic sandwich bags.

After seizing the car, the police returned to Apartment 103 and arrested the occupant, Kimberly Thompson, who is not a party to this appeal. A search of the apartment pursuant to a warrant revealed cocaine residue on the kitchen table and plastic baggies similar to those found in the Cadillac. Thielen identified Carter, Johns, and Thompson as the three people he had observed placing the powder into baggies. The police later learned that while Thompson was the lessee of the apartment, Carter and Johns lived in Chicago and had come to the apartment for the sole purpose of packaging the cocaine. Carter and Johns had never been to the apartment before and were only in the apartment for approximately 2 1/2 hours. In return for the use of the apartment, Carter and Johns had given Thompson one-eighth of an ounce of the cocaine.

Carter and Johns were charged with conspiracy to commit controlled substance crime in the first degree and aiding and abetting in a controlled substance crime in the first degree * * *. They argued that Thielen's initial observation of their drug packaging activities was an unreasonable search in violation of the Fourth Amendment and that all evidence obtained as a result of this unreasonable search was inadmissible as fruit of the poisonous tree. The Minnesota trial court held that since, unlike the defendant in Minnesota v. Olson, 495 U.S. 91 (1990), Carter and Johns were not overnight social guests but temporary out-of-state visitors, they were not entitled to claim the protection of the Fourth Amendment against the government intrusion into the apartment. * * *

A divided Minnesota Supreme Court reversed, holding that respondents had "standing" to claim the protection of the Fourth Amendment because they had " 'a legitimate expectation of privacy in the invaded place.' " * * * Based upon its conclusion that the respondents had "standing" to raise their Fourth Amendment claims, the court went on to hold that Thielen's observation constituted a search of the apartment under the Fourth Amendment, and that the search was unreasonable. We granted certiorari, and now reverse.

The Minnesota courts analyzed whether respondents had a legitimate expectation of privacy under the rubric of "standing" doctrine, an analysis which this Court expressly rejected 20 years ago in *Rakas*. In that case, we held that automobile passengers could not assert the protection of the Fourth Amendment against the seizure of incriminating evidence from a vehicle where they owned neither the vehicle nor the evidence. Central to our analysis was the idea that in determining whether a defendant is able to show the violation of his (and not someone else's) Fourth Amendment rights, the "definition of those rights is more properly placed within the purview of substantive Fourth Amendment law than within that of standing." Thus, we held that in order to claim the protection of the Fourth Amendment, a defendant must demonstrate that he personally has an expectation of privacy in the place searched, and that his expectation is reasonable; i.e., one which has "a source outside of the Fourth Amendment, either by reference to concepts of real or personal property law or to understandings that are recognized and permitted by society."

* * * We have held that "capacity to claim the protection of the Fourth Amendment depends . . . upon whether the person who claims the protection of the Amendment has a legitimate expectation of privacy in the invaded place." *Rakas*.

The text of the Amendment suggests that its protections extend only to people in "their" houses. But we have held that in some circumstances a person may have a legitimate expectation of privacy in the house of someone else. In Minnesota v. Olson, for example, we decided that an overnight guest in a house had the sort of expectation of privacy that the Fourth Amendment protects. We said:

> * * * From the overnight guest's perspective, he seeks shelter in another's home precisely because it provides him with privacy, a place where he and his possessions will not be disturbed by anyone but his host and those his host allows inside. We are at our most vulnerable when we are asleep because we cannot monitor our own safety or the security of our belongings. It is for this reason that, although we may spend all day in public places, when we cannot sleep in our own home we seek out another private place to sleep, whether it be a hotel room, or the home of a friend.

* * *

Respondents here were obviously not overnight guests, but were essentially present for a business transaction and were only in the home a matter of hours. There is no suggestion that they had a previous relationship with Thompson, or that there was any other purpose to their visit. Nor was there anything similar to the overnight guest relationship in *Olson* to suggest a degree of acceptance into the household. While the apartment was a dwelling place for Thompson, it was for these respondents simply a place to do business.

* * *

If we regard the overnight guest in Minnesota v. Olson as typifying those who may claim the protection of the Fourth Amendment in the home of another, and one merely "legitimately on the premises" as typifying those who may not do so, the present case is obviously somewhere in between. But the purely commercial nature of the transaction engaged in here, the relatively short period of time on the premises, and the lack of any previous connection between respondents and the householder, all lead us to conclude that respondents' situation is closer to that of one simply permitted on the premises. We therefore hold that any search which may have occurred did not violate their Fourth Amendment rights.

Because we conclude that respondents had no legitimate expectation of privacy in the apartment, we need not decide whether the police officer's observation constituted a "search." The judgment of the Supreme Court of Minnesota is accordingly reversed, and the cause is remanded for proceedings not inconsistent with this opinion.

JUSTICE SCALIA, with whom JUSTICE THOMAS joins, concurring.

I join the opinion of the Court because I believe it accurately applies our recent case law, including Minnesota v. Olson. I write separately to express my view that that case law—like the submissions of the parties in this case—gives short shrift to the text of the Fourth Amendment, and to the well and long understood meaning of that text. Specifically, it leaps to apply the fuzzy standard of "legitimate expectation of privacy"—a consideration that is often relevant to whether a search or seizure covered by the Fourth Amendment is "unreasonable"—to the threshold question whether a search or seizure covered by the Fourth Amendment has occurred. If that latter question is addressed first and analyzed under the text of the Constitution as traditionally understood, the present case is not remotely difficult.

The Fourth Amendment protects "[t]he right of the people to be secure in their persons, houses, papers, and effects, against unreasonable searches and seizures....". It must be acknowledged that the phrase "their ... houses" in this provision is, in isolation, ambiguous. It could mean "their respective houses," so that the protection extends to each person only in his own house. But it could also mean "their respective and each other's houses," so that each person would be protected even when visiting the house of someone else. As today's opinion for the Court suggests, however, it is not linguistically possible to give the provision the latter, expansive interpretation with respect to "houses" without giving it the same interpretation with respect to the nouns that are parallel to "houses"—"persons, ... papers, and effects"—which would give me a constitutional right not to have your person unreasonably searched. This is so absurd that it has to my knowledge never been contemplated. The obvious meaning of the provision is that each person has the right to be secure against unreasonable searches and seizures in his own person, house, papers, and effects.

* * *

That "their ... houses" was understood to mean "their respective houses" would have been clear to anyone who knew the English and early American law of arrest and trespass that underlay the Fourth Amendment. The people's protection against unreasonable search and seizure in their "houses" was drawn from the English common-law maxim, "A man's home is his castle." * * *

Of course this is not to say that the Fourth Amendment protects only the Lord of the Manor who holds his estate in fee simple. People call a house "their" home when legal title is in the bank, when they rent it, and even when they merely occupy it rent-free— so long as they actually live there. That this is the criterion of the people's protection against government intrusion into "their" houses is established by the leading American case of Oystead v. Shed, 13 Mass. 520 (1816), which held it a trespass for the sheriff to break into a dwelling to capture a boarder who lived there. * * *

* * * The text of the Fourth Amendment, the common-law background against which it was adopted, and the understandings consistently displayed after its adoption make the answer clear. We were right to hold in Chapman v. United States, 365 U.S. 610 (1961), that the Fourth Amendment protects an apartment tenant against an unreasonable search of his dwelling, even though he is only a leaseholder. And we were right to hold in Bumper v. North Carolina, 391 U.S. 543 (1968), that an unreasonable search of a grandmother's house violated her resident grandson's Fourth Amendment rights because the area searched "was his home." We went to the absolute limit of what text and tradition permit in Minnesota v. Olson, when we protected a mere overnight guest against an unreasonable search of his hosts' apartment. But whereas it is plausible to regard a person's overnight lodging as at least his "temporary" residence, it is entirely impossible to give that characterization to an apartment that he uses to package cocaine. Respondents here were not searched in "their ... hous[e]" under any interpretation of the phrase that bears the remotest relationship to the well understood meaning of the Fourth Amendment.

The dissent believes that "[o]ur obligation to produce coherent results" requires that we ignore this clear text and four-century-old tradition, and apply instead the notoriously unhelpful test adopted in a "benchmar[k]" decision that is 31 years old, citing Katz v. United States, 389 U.S. 347 (1967). In my view, the only thing the past three decades have established about the *Katz* test (which has come to mean the test enunciated by Justice Harlan's separate concurrence in *Katz*) is that, unsurprisingly, those "actual (subjective) expectation[s] of privacy" "that society is prepared to recognize as 'reasonable,'"bear an uncanny resemblance to those expectations of privacy that this Court considers reasonable. When that self-indulgent test is employed (as the dissent would employ it here) to determine whether a "search or seizure" within the meaning of the Constitution has occurred (as opposed to whether that "search or seizure" is an "unreasonable" one), it has no plausible foundation in the text of the Fourth Amendment. That provision did not guarantee some generalized "right of privacy" and leave it to this Court to determine which particular manifestations of the value of privacy society is prepared to recognize as reasonable. Rather, it enumerated ("persons, houses, papers, and effects") the objects of privacy protection to which the Constitution would extend, leaving further expansion to the good judgment, not of this Court, but of the people through their representatives in the legislature.

The dissent may be correct that a person invited into someone else's house to engage in a common business (even common monkey-business, so to speak) ought to be protected against government searches of the room in which that business is conducted; and that persons invited in to deliver milk or pizza * * * ought not to be protected against government searches of the rooms that they occupy. I am not sure of the answer to those policy questions. But I am sure that the answer is not remotely contained in the Constitution, which means that it is left—as many, indeed most, important questions are left—to the judgment of state and federal legislators. We go beyond our proper role as judges in a democratic society when we restrict the people's power to govern themselves over the full range of policy choices that the Constitution has left available to them.

JUSTICE KENNEDY, concurring.

I join the Court's opinion, for its reasoning is consistent with my view that almost all social guests have a legitimate expectation of privacy, and hence protection against unreasonable searches, in their host's home.

* * *

I would expect that most, if not all, social guests legitimately expect that, in accordance with social custom, the homeowner will exercise her discretion to include or exclude others for the guests' benefit. As we recognized in Minnesota v. Olson, where these social expectations exist—as in the case of an overnight guest—they are sufficient to create a legitimate expectation of privacy, even in the absence of any property right to exclude others. In this respect, the dissent must be correct that reasonable expectations of the owner are shared, to some extent, by the guest. This analysis suggests that, as a general rule, social guests will have an expectation of privacy in their host's home. That is not the case before us, however.

In this case respondents have established nothing more than a fleeting and insubstantial connection with Thompson's home. For all that appears in the record, respondents used Thompson's house simply as a convenient processing station, their purpose involving nothing more than the mechanical act of chopping and packing a substance for distribution. There is no suggestion that respondents engaged in confidential communications with Thompson about their transaction. Respondents had not been to Thompson's apartment before, and they left it even before their arrest. * * *

We cannot remain faithful to the underlying principle in *Rakas* without reversing in this case, and I am not persuaded that we need depart from it to protect the homeowner's own privacy interests. * * * With these observations, I join the Court's opinion.

JUSTICE BREYER, concurring in the judgment.

I agree with Justice GINSBURG that respondents can claim the Fourth Amendment's protection. Petitioner, however, raises a second question, whether under the circumstances Officer Thielen's observation made "from a public area outside the curtilage of the residence" violated respondents' Fourth Amendment rights. In my view, it did not.

* * *

Officer Thielen * * * stood at a place used by the public and from which one could see through the window into the kitchen. The precautions that the apartment's dwellers took to maintain their privacy would have

failed in respect to an ordinary passer-by standing in that place. Given this Court's well-established case law, I cannot say that the officer engaged in what the Constitution forbids, namely, an "unreasonable search."

* * *

For these reasons, while agreeing with Justice GINSBURG, I also concur in the Court's judgment reversing the Minnesota Supreme Court.

JUSTICE GINSBURG, with whom JUSTICE STEVENS and JUSTICE SOUTER join, dissenting.

The Court's decision undermines not only the security of short-term guests, but also the security of the home resident herself. In my view, when a homeowner or lessor personally invites a guest into her home to share in a common endeavor, whether it be for conversation, to engage in leisure activities, or for business purposes licit or illicit, that guest should share his host's shelter against unreasonable searches and seizures.

I do not here propose restoration of the "legitimately on the premises" criterion stated in Jones v. United States, 362 U.S. 257 (1960), for the Court rejected that formulation in Rakas v. Illinois, as it did the "automatic standing rule" in United States v. Salvucci, 448 U.S. 83 (1980). * * * Further, I would here decide only the case of the homeowner who chooses to share the privacy of her home and her company with a guest, and would not reach classroom hypotheticals like the milkman or pizza deliverer.

* * *

A home dweller places her own privacy at risk, the Court's approach indicates, when she opens her home to others, uncertain whether the duration of their stay, their purpose, and their "acceptance into the household" will earn protection. * * * Human frailty suggests that today's decision will tempt police to pry into private dwellings without warrant, to find evidence incriminating guests who do not rest there through the night. *Rakas* tolerates that temptation with respect to automobile searches. See Ashdown, The Fourth Amendment and the "Legitimate Expectation of Privacy," 34 Vand. L.Rev. 1289, 1321 (1981) (criticizing Rakas as "present[ing] a framework in which there may be nothing to lose and something to gain by the illegal search of a car that carries more than one occupant"). I see no impelling reason to extend this risk into the home. * * *

* * *

* * * The Court's decision in this case veers sharply from the path marked in *Katz*. I do not agree that we have a more reasonable expectation of privacy when we place a business call to a person's home from a public telephone booth on the side of the street, than when we actually enter that person's premises to engage in a common endeavor.

For the reasons stated, I dissent from the Court's judgment, and would retain judicial surveillance over the warrantless searches today's decision allows.

Note on Carter

When the votes are counted up in *Carter*, how would you answer the question whether you as a partygoer could object to the search of the room in which you were partying? Would it make any difference if you had only been at the party for five minutes before the police busted in? What if you had *crashed* the party?

Cars, Drivers, Passengers

Standing questions arise quite frequently when vehicles are stopped and searched. It is clear that the owner of a car has standing to object to a search. But there are several problematic questions, such as: 1. What if the owner is not present? 2. What if the owner is in the car but somebody else is driving? 3. Can a passenger ever have a protectible Fourth Amendment interest in the car? and 4. Who can object to the seizure of the car, as distinct from the search?

Some of these questions are discussed in United States v. Carter, 14 F.3d 1150 (6th Cir.1994). The facts are stated by the court as follows:

Memphis, Tennessee, police officers Charles Cox and Edward Hall were patrolling an interstate highway in Memphis at around 4:30 in the morning on Sunday, November 17, 1991, when a 1991 GMC van came by. The officers saw that instead of a normal license plate, the van displayed what looked like a temporary "drive-out" tag from North Carolina. The officers had no way to check the validity of the tag by radio, and they pulled the van over.

The driver, a man named Timmie Locklear, rushed out of the van and walked quickly back to the patrol car. At the request of one of the officers Locklear produced a driver's license and some paperwork showing that he had recently purchased the van. A radio check disclosed that the driver's license was valid, that there were no outstanding warrants in Locklear's name, and that the van had not been reported stolen.

Mr. Locklear, who sat in the back seat of the patrol car while the check was going on, told Officer Cox that he and a man who was traveling with him (defendant Leslie Carter) were returning from a week-long visit with Locklear's sister in Hope, Arkansas. Mr. Locklear said he did not know the name of the street on which his sister lived and did not know what direction he had taken once he got to Hope. Locklear spoke choppily and acted nervous, according to Officer Cox.

Officer Hall, meanwhile, had a roadside conversation with the passenger, defendant Carter. When Carter got out of the van, according to the officer, he kept trying to walk away from the vehicle. Officer Hall asked him to wait a minute and questioned him as to where he and the driver had been. Mr. Carter replied that they had been in Arkansas—he could not say where, specifically—visiting a cousin. The trip had taken a day and a half, according to Carter.

Although the officers were suspicious about the stories they had been told, Officer Cox advised Mr.Locklear that he was free to leave. Before Locklear could get back in the van, however, the officer asked him if he would agree to let the vehicle be searched for contraband. Locklear refused. * * * [T]he magistrate found as a fact that Mr. Locklear never consented in any way to the search of his vehicle.

* * * [T]he officers proceeded to search the van. When the back door of the vehicle was opened, they immediately smelled marijuana. The odor (which Officer Hall described as "very strong") emanated from five suitcases that proved to contain a total of 437 pounds of marijuana.

Locklear and Carter were both indicted by a federal grand jury. Each of the men subsequently filed a motion to suppress any and all evidence seized as a result of the search of Locklear's van. Although he had only been a passenger in the van, defendant Carter argued in a brief filed in support of his motion that he had agreed to accompany Locklear on a lengthy trip; that he (Carter) had taken toilet articles and a change of clothing with him in the van; that he had entertained an expectation of privacy in the vehicle throughout the duration of the trip; * * * [and] that he had been detained in violation of his Fourth Amendment rights * * *.

* * * Evidence presented at the hearing showed that Mr. Carter had no ownership interest in the van and no control over it; that he had no possessions in the van other than a change of clothes (a pair of jeans and a shirt) and a shaving kit found in the front of the vehicle; and that he claimed no possessory or other interest in the suitcases filled with marijuana.

The lower court found that Locklear had the right to object to the search of the car, because he was the owner. But Carter did not. It also found that the search was illegal. The government consented to dismissal of the indictment against Locklear, but Carter went to trial and was convicted. The lower court observed that "the result of suppressing the search for the driver and not the passenger is an unfortunate one, given that the progress of both driver and passenger [was] impeded by illegal actions of the police."

The court of appeals held that Carter had the right to challenge the *seizure* of his person that occurred when the car was stopped, but that he didn't have the right to contest the *search* of the car. Nor could the evidence be excluded as the fruit of Carter's seizure. It was the search of the car that uncovered the evidence, and that search was not connected to Carter's seizure.

A passenger, like anyone else, obviously has a right not to be detained illegally. * * * It follows, in the case before us, that Mr. Carter had standing to challenge the legality of his detention by the police. And whether or not the original traffic stop was unconstitutional * * * we shall assume, for purposes of analysis, not only that the subsequent arrest of the driver was unconstitutional, but also that the detention of Mr. Carter, if not illegal from the outset, became illegal when the driver was arrested.

It does not follow from any of this, however, that the discovery and seizure of the marijuana represented "fruit" of Mr. Carter's unlawful detention. Suppose that at the time of the driver's arrest the police had summoned a taxi cab for Mr. Carter and told him he was free to leave. The marijuana would still have been discovered, because it was located in a van owned and controlled by Mr. Locklear (who was not going anywhere until his vehicle had been searched) and not in a vehicle controlled by Mr. Carter.

* * *

* * * [T]he presence of the shaving kit and change of clothing in the front of the van [did not give] Carter a legitimate expectation that the police would not open the van's back door.

Would the result in *Carter* have been different if his shaving kit and change of clothing had been in the back of the van? What if he could show that he had been traveling in the van across country for a week before it was stopped by the police?

United States v. Lopez, 474 F.Supp. 943 (C.D.Cal.1979), holds that defendants who had been given keys to a truck, who had permission to use it and who did use it, had the right to challenge a search of the truck. Compare United States v. Tropiano, 50 F.3d 157 (2d Cir.1995)("a defendant who knowingly possesses a stolen car has no legitimate expectation of privacy in the car"). In United States v. Powell, 929 F.2d 1190 (7th Cir.1991), the court held that where the owner of a car was absent at the time the car was stopped and searched, he had the right to object to the search but not to the stop. Does this make sense?

The Time Runs Out on the Rental

As recognized in *Carter*, you don't have to own something to have a right to object to the search of that thing. For example, a person has the right to object to the search of a house where he lives, even though he rents rather than owns the house. The same would be true for those who rent or lease rather than own a car. But what if the rental period has run out? Does the termination of the rental period also terminate the right to object to a search? Consider the facts of United States v. Cooper, 133 F.3d 1394 (11th Cir.1998):

On January 6, 1996, appellant, Dwayne Cooper, rented a car from Budget Rent–A–Car (Budget) in West Palm Beach, Florida. The contract specified January 20 as the return due date and West Palm Beach as the return location. The contract also included the following terms and conditions:

* * *

16) FAILURE TO RETURN VEHICLE: If the Vehicle is not returned when due or within 24 hours after written or oral demand by
Budget, Renter will be in unlawful possession of the Vehicle, and
Budget may seek the issuance of a warrant for the arrest of anyone in
possession of the Vehicle (including Renter). Written demand is considered delivered 48 hours after Budget mails a certified letter to Renter at
the home or business address Renter provides at time of rental.

Budget's established policy, however, is that it will extend the due date
if the renter makes a request over the telephone and sufficient funds exist
on his or her credit card. Through his past course of dealings with Budget,
Cooper knew of this unwritten policy. It had also been Cooper's experience
that returning a rental car after the due date was "no problem" with
Budget as long he had "room" on his credit card for the extra days and
applicable fees.

On January 24, four days after the rental contract expired, Michael
King of the Florida Highway Patrol (FHP) saw the rental car on Interstate
95 in Jacksonville, Florida. * * * Intending to issue Cooper a citation for an
improper lane change, King signaled for Cooper to pull over into the exit's
emergency lane.

Complying with King's requests, Cooper identified himself, stepped out
of the car and proffered his driver's license and the rental contract. King
inquired about the rental car being four days overdue, and Cooper explained
that he had extended the due date. Using his car telephone, King directed
the FHP dispatcher to contact Budget and verify this information. Budget
informed the dispatcher that Cooper had not requested an extension past
January 20 and asked that the car be towed and returned. * * * The
dispatcher relayed this information to King, and he asked the dispatcher to
contact a private towing service.

Soon thereafter, a second FHP trooper, Michael Smith, arrived to assist
King. The troopers informed Cooper about Budget's plan to tow the car.
* * * King reached in through the passenger door, turned off the ignition,
"swept" under the car seats and opened the glove compartment. * * * King
found a loaded firearm in the glove compartment and arrested Cooper for
concealing a firearm.

The officers then thoroughly searched the car and found drugs hidden
in safes in the trunk. The car was eventually towed and returned to Budget.
In the ultimate indignity, Budget charged Cooper's credit card for use of the
car through January 25.

Cooper challenged the search of the car, and the case boiled down to
whether he had the right to make such a challenge, given the fact that the rental
period on the car had expired at the time of the search. The court found that
Cooper's expectation of privacy was reasonable under the circumstances. The
rental contract had not been expired for long. Cooper was in possession of the
car. Cooper paid Budget in full, in accordance with Budget's standard operating
procedure. And Budget never took any affirmative steps to repossess the car
prior to law enforcement officers' inquiries. The *Cooper* court concluded with the
following policy argument:

If we were to accept the government's position, a driver could not expect privacy in a rental car even one minute after the rental contract expired. In other words, the rental company's dormant right of repossession would govern the scope of the driver's Fourth Amendment protections. The Supreme Court, however, highly disfavors such hard-and-fast rules. See *Rakas*,(stating that "arcane distinctions developed in property and tort law . . . ought not . . . control" the reasonableness of an expectation of privacy). Declining to adopt this interpretation of the Fourth Amendment is especially appropriate where, as here, a simple phone call could have extended the rental contract past the date of the warrantless search. * * * In our view, Cooper retained a sufficient amount of control and possession over the rental car for it to fall within the zone of constitutional sanctity.

Disassociation from Property

If a person disassociates himself from certain property, then he loses standing to object to a search of that property. United States v. Boruff, 909 F.2d 111 (5th Cir.1990), provides an example. A pick-up truck driven by Taylor and a rented car driven by Boruff were involved in a drug-smuggling scheme. The truck had been purchased by Boruff, but title, registration and insurance were put in Taylor's name. Boruff added improvements to the truck, and it was understood that if the truck were sold, the money would go to Boruff. The car was rented by Boruff's girlfriend in her own name. The standard rental agreement signed by the girlfriend stated that only she would drive the car and that the car would not be used for any illegal purpose. Boruff and Taylor drove to Mexico, loaded marijuana into the pick-up truck, and started back. They travelled 100 yards apart on the highway. When a suspicious Border Patrol agent began to pursue the pick-up truck, Boruff did two u-turns in an effort to divert the agent's attention. A second agent pursued Boruff, while the first agent stopped the truck, searched it, found drugs, and placed Taylor under arrest. The second agent stopped Boruff, searched the rented car and found incriminating evidence. Boruff argued that both searches were illegal and moved to suppress all the evidence. As to the truck, the court held that Boruff had failed to establish an expectation of privacy, even though he paid for it.

> Despite his asserted ownership interest, Boruff did everything he could to disassociate himself from the truck in the event it was stopped by law enforcement officials. [Besides placing all documentation in Taylor's name], during the smuggling operation, Taylor, not Boruff, drove the truck. Boruff travelled in a separate vehicle, * * * and left his position in front of the truck after spotting the Border Patrol vehicle. * * * In addition, Boruff was not present when the truck was stopped or searched. See Rakas v. Illinois (legitimate presence at time of search an important factor). * * * Boruff also disavowed any knowledge of the truck and its contents after his own vehicle was stopped.

As to the rental car, the court found that Boruff had no standing to contest the search because his girlfriend was the only legal operator of the vehicle under the terms of the agreement and thus "had no authority to give control of the car to Boruff. The rental agreement also expressly forbade any use of the vehicle for illegal purposes." Do you agree with the court? Shouldn't Boruff have had some expectation of privacy somewhere?

For another case in which disavowal of ownership resulted in a loss of "standing", see United States v. Mangum, 100 F.3d 164 (D.C.Cir.1996). Mangum was a passenger in a car that was stopped by police. Mangum conceded that there was reasonable suspicion for the stop. A knapsack was removed from the trunk and Mangum, when asked, denied that it was his and said it belonged to the driver. The officer searched the bag and found that it contained a loaded handgun and Mangum's driver's license. The court held that because Mangum denied ownership, "he abandoned his property and waived any legitimate privacy interest in it. Courts have long held that, when a person voluntarily denies ownership of property in response to a police officer's question, he forfeits any privacy interest in the property; consequently, police may search it without a warrant."

Coconspirator "Standing" Rejected: United States v. Padilla

A unanimous Supreme Court held in United States v. Padilla, 508 U.S. 77 (1993)(per curiam), that a person does not have an automatic right to challenge a search or seizure simply because he is a member of the conspiracy that owned the property that was searched or seized. In *Padilla,* a highway patrol officer stopped a car because the driver acted suspiciously. After receiving consent to search the car, the officer found 560 pounds of cocaine and arranged for the driver to make a controlled delivery of the cocaine. The driver made a telephone call from a motel, and when two persons arrived in response to the call they were arrested as they attempted to drive away in the car. One of those arrested agreed to cooperate and led the police to the house where her husband was staying. When charges were brought, the defendants, including the husband, challenged the initial stop of the car. Relying on Ninth Circuit law, the district court held that conspirators who have joint control and supervision over drugs have the right to challenge a search or a seizure. Consequently, the district court held that the defendant could contest the legality of the stop of the car due to his supervisory role in the conspiracy, even though he was not present during the stop and did not own the car. But the Supreme Court reversed, explaining that a "coconspirator standing" rule "squarely contradicts" *Rakas,* under which each person must establish an individual expectation of privacy, or a legitimate possessory interest, intruded upon by the search or seizure.

The Court concluded: "Expectations of privacy and property interests govern the analysis of Fourth Amendment search and seizure claims. Participants in a criminal conspiracy may have such expectations or interests, but the conspiracy itself neither adds nor detracts from them." The Court remanded the case so that the lower court could consider "whether each respondent had either a property interest protected by the Fourth Amendment that was interfered with by the stop of the automobile" or "a reasonable expectation of privacy that was invaded by the search thereof."

On remand, the court of appeals held that the conspirators had no right to object to the seizure of the car. They did not own the car, and they were not driving it. The conspirators argued that they took steps to conceal the packages of cocaine that were placed in the car, but this was not enough to establish an interest in the car itself; and it was the stop of the car that the conspirators sought to challenge. United States v. Padilla, 111 F.3d 685 (9th Cir.1997).

6. The Fruits of the Search: Causation and Attenuation

Searches and Seizures That Produce No Evidence

The exclusionary rule is not applicable unless evidence is seized as a result of a search. If no evidence is obtained, there is nothing to exclude. United States v. Occhipinti, 998 F.2d 791 (10th Cir.1993)(legality of protective sweep need not be determined because no evidence was obtained). In Ker v. Illinois, 119 U.S. 436 (1886), and Frisbie v. Collins, 342 U.S. 519 (1952), the Supreme Court held that an illegal or unconstitutional arrest of a person did not deprive a court of jurisdiction to try the person—i.e., the body of the person, which is not being used as evidence, need not be released from the jurisdiction. *Ker* and *Frisbie* remain good law; the *Ker-Frisbie* doctrine has been invoked to uphold the abduction of suspects from foreign countries so that they may be tried in the United States. See United States v. Alvarez–Machain, 504 U.S. 655 (1992)(holding that because the U.S.-Mexican Extradition treaty did not explicitly prohibit abduction, "the rule in *Ker* applies, and the court need not inquire as to how respondent came before it").

When the Fourth Amendment Violation Produces Evidence

The exclusionary rule is potentially applicable to all evidence derived from an illegal search or seizure. But it is often difficult to determine whether a particular piece of evidence "derived from" a particular illegal search or seizure. The Supreme Court coined the term "fruit of the poisonous tree" as a tool with which to answer these derivation questions. See, e.g., Nardone v. United States, 308 U.S. 338 (1939) (noting that exclusionary rule prevents both the "direct" and the "indirect" use of illegally obtained evidence). Wong Sun v. United States, 371 U.S. 471 (1963) and the following case, Brown v. Illinois, are the Court's leading cases on whether there is a sufficient connection between proffered evidence and an illegal search or seizure to justify exclusion. In these cases, the defendant asserts that there is a direct link between the illegality and the proffered evidence. The government, while admitting at least for argument's sake that there was an illegal search or seizure, nonetheless argues that the relationship between the illegality and the proffered evidence is too attenuated to justify exclusion. *Wong Sun* is discussed in detail in *Brown*.

BROWN v. ILLINOIS

Supreme Court of the United States, 1975.
422 U.S. 590.

MR. JUSTICE BLACKMUN **delivered the opinion of the Court.**

* * *

I

As petitioner Richard Brown was climbing the last of the stairs leading to the rear entrance of his Chicago apartment in the early evening of May 13, 1968, he happened to glance at the window near the door. He saw, pointed at him through the window, a revolver held by a stranger who was inside the apartment. The man said: "Don't move, you are under arrest." Another man, also with a gun, came up behind Brown and repeated the statement that he was under arrest. It was about 7:45 p.m. The two men turned out to be Detectives William Nolan and William Lenz of the Chicago police force. * * * As both officers held him at gunpoint, the three entered the apartment. Brown was ordered to stand against the wall and was searched. No weapon was found. * * * Detective Lenz informed him that he was under arrest for the murder of Roger Corpus, handcuffed him, and escorted him to the squad car.

The two detectives took petitioner to the Maxwell Street police station. [While at the station, Brown was twice given *Miranda* warnings and twice confessed. The first confession occurred 90 minutes after the arrest, the second occurred seven hours after the arrest. Brown moved to suppress the confessions as the fruit of an arrest without probable cause. The trial court denied the motion, and Brown was convicted. The Illinois Supreme Court found that Brown had been arrested without probable cause, but nonetheless held that the motion to suppress was properly denied because the confessions were too attenuated from the illegal arrest to justify exclusion].

* * * The [Illinois] court appears to have held that the *Miranda* warnings in and of themselves broke the causal chain so that any subsequent statement, even one induced by the continuing effects of unconstitutional custody, was admissible so long as, in the traditional sense, it was voluntary and not coerced in violation of the Fifth and Fourteenth Amendments.

* * *

II

In *Wong Sun,* the Court pronounced the principles to be applied where the issue is whether statements and other evidence obtained after an illegal ar-

rest or search should be excluded. In that case, federal agents elicited an oral statement from defendant Toy after forcing entry at 6 a.m. into his laundry, at the back of which he had his living quarters. The agents had followed Toy down the hall to the bedroom and there had placed him under arrest. The Court of Appeals found that there was no probable cause for the arrest. This Court concluded that that finding was "amply justified by the facts clearly shown on this record." Toy's statement, which bore upon his participation in the sale of narcotics, led the agents to question another person, Johnny Yee, who actually possessed narcotics. Yee stated that heroin had been brought to him earlier by Toy and another Chinese known to him only as "Sea Dog." Under questioning, Toy said that "Sea Dog" was Wong Sun. Toy led agents to a multifamily dwelling where, he said, Wong Sun lived. Gaining admittance to the building through a bell and buzzer, the agents climbed the stairs and entered the apartment. One went into the back room and brought Wong Sun out in handcuffs. After arraignment, Wong Sun was released on his own recognizance. Several days later, he returned voluntarily to give an unsigned confession.

This Court ruled that Toy's declarations and the contraband taken from Yee were the fruits of the agents' illegal action and should not have been admitted as evidence against Toy. It held that the statement did not result from " 'an intervening independent act of a free will,' "and that it was not "sufficiently an act of free will to purge the primary taint of the unlawful invasion." With respect to Wong Sun's confession, however, the Court held that in the light of his lawful arraignment and release on his own recognizance, and of his return voluntarily several days later to make the statement, the connection between his unlawful arrest and the statement "had 'become so attenuated as to dissipate the taint.' "The Court said:

> "We need not hold that all evidence is 'fruit of the poisonous tree' simply because it would not have come to light but for the illegal actions of the police. Rather, the more apt question in such a case is 'whether, granting establishment of the primary illegality, the evidence to which instant objection is made has been come at by exploitation of that illegality or instead by means sufficiently distinguishable to be purged of the primary taint.' "

* * *

III

The Illinois courts refrained from resolving the question, as apt here as it was in *Wong Sun*, whether Brown's statements were obtained by exploitation of the illegality of his arrest. They assumed that the *Miranda* warnings, by themselves, assured that the statements (verbal acts, as contrasted with physical evidence) were of sufficient free will as to purge the primary taint of the unlawful arrest. *Wong Sun*, of course, preceded *Miranda*.

* * *

* * * In order for the causal chain, between the illegal arrest and the statements made subsequent thereto, to be broken, *Wong Sun* requires not merely that the statement meet the Fifth Amendment standard of voluntariness but that it be "sufficiently an act of free will to purge the primary taint." * * *

If *Miranda* warnings, by themselves, were held to attenuate the taint of an unconstitutional arrest, regardless of how wanton and purposeful the Fourth Amendment violation, the effect of the exclusionary rule would be substantially diluted. * * * Any incentive to avoid Fourth Amendment violations would be eviscerated by making the warnings, in effect, a "cure-all," and the constitutional guarantee against unlawful searches and seizures could be said to be reduced to "a form of words."

* * *

While we therefore reject the *per se* rule which the Illinois courts appear to have accepted, we also decline to adopt any alternative *per se* or "but for" rule. * * * The question whether a confession is the product of a free will under *Wong Sun* must be answered on the facts of each case. No single fact is dispositive. The workings of the human mind are too complex, and the possibilities of misconduct too diverse, to permit protection of the Fourth Amendment to turn on such a talismanic test. The *Miranda* warnings are an important factor, to be sure, in determining whether the confession is obtained by exploitation of an illegal arrest. But they are not the only factor to be considered. The temporal proximity of the arrest and the confession, the presence of intervening circumstances, and, particularly, the purpose and flagrancy of the official misconduct are all relevant. * * * And the burden of showing admissibility rests, of course, on the prosecution.

IV

* * * We conclude that the State failed to sustain the burden of showing that the evidence in question was admissible under *Wong Sun*.

Brown's first statement was separated from his illegal arrest by less than two hours, and there was no intervening event of significance whatsoever. In its essentials, his situation is remarkably like that of James Wah Toy in

Wong Sun.[a] We could hold Brown's first statement admissible only if we overrule *Wong Sun.* We decline to do so. And the second statement was clearly the result and the fruit of the first.

The illegality here, moreover, had a quality of purposefulness. The impropriety of the arrest was obvious; awareness of that fact was virtually conceded by the two detectives when they repeatedly acknowledged, in their testimony, that the purpose of their action was "for investigation" or for "questioning." The arrest, both in design and in execution, was investigatory. The detectives embarked upon this expedition for evidence in the hope that something might turn up. The manner in which Brown's arrest was effected gives the appearance of having been calculated to cause surprise, fright, and confusion.

* * *

[The concurring opinion of Justice White is omitted.]

MR. JUSTICE POWELL, with whom MR. JUSTICE REHNQUIST joins, concurring in part.

I join the Court insofar as it holds that the *per se* rule adopted by the Illinois Supreme Court for determining the admissibility of petitioner's two statements inadequately accommodates the diverse interests underlying the Fourth Amendment exclusionary rule. I would, however, remand the case for reconsideration under the general standards articulated in the Court's opinion and elaborated herein.

* * *

* * * If an illegal arrest merely provides the occasion of initial contact between the police and the accused,

and because of time or other intervening factors the accused's eventual statement is the product of his own reflection and free will, application of the exclusionary rule can serve little purpose: the police normally will not make an illegal arrest in the hope of eventually obtaining such a truly volunteered statement. * * * Bearing these considerations in mind, and recognizing that the deterrent value of the Fourth Amendment exclusionary rule is limited to certain kinds of police conduct, the following general categories can be identified.

Those most readily identifiable are on the extremes: the flagrantly abusive violation of Fourth Amendment rights, on the one hand, and "technical" Fourth Amendment violations, on the other. In my view, these extremes call for significantly different judicial responses.

I would require the clearest indication of attenuation in cases in which official conduct was flagrantly abusive of Fourth Amendment rights. * * * In such cases the deterrent value of the exclusionary rule is most likely to be effective, and the corresponding mandate to preserve judicial integrity most clearly demands that the fruits of official misconduct be denied. I thus would require some demonstrably effective break in the chain of events leading from the illegal arrest to the statement, such as actual consultation with counsel or the accused's presentation before a magistrate for a determination of probable cause, before the taint can be deemed removed.

At the opposite end of the spectrum lie "technical" violations of Fourth Amendment rights * * *.

* * * [In "technical" violation cases], with the exception of statements given in the immediate circum-

---

a. The situation here is thus in dramatic contrast to that of Wong Sun himself. Wong Sun's confession, which the Court held admis-

sible, came several days after the illegality, and was preceded by a lawful arraignment and a release from custody on his own recognizance.

stances of the illegal arrest—a constraint I think is imposed by existing exclusionary-rule law—I would not require more than proof that effective *Miranda* warnings were given and that the ensuing statement was voluntary in the Fifth Amendment sense. * * *

Between these extremes lies a wide range of situations that defy ready ca-

tegorization, and I will not attempt to embellish on the factors set forth in the Court's opinion other than to emphasize that the *Wong Sun* inquiry always should be conducted with the deterrent purpose of the Fourth Amendment exclusionary rule sharply in focus. * * *

Statements Tainted by an Illegal Arrest: Dunaway v. New York, Taylor v. Alabama, and Kaupp v. Texas

Brown is followed in Dunaway v. New York, 442 U.S. 200 (1979), where the defendant was arrested without probable cause, taken down to the station, and confessed after receiving *Miranda* warnings. The Court found that Dunaway's situation was "virtually a replica of the situation in *Brown*." As in *Brown*, the Court was concerned that officers would "violate the Fourth Amendment with impunity, safe in the knowledge that they could wash their hands in the procedural safeguards of the Fifth."

Brown and *Dunaway* were deemed to be dispositive in Taylor v. Alabama, 455 U.S. 1014 (1982). On the basis of a tip that was insufficient to provide probable cause, police arrested Taylor without a warrant for a grocery store robbery, searched him, took him to the station for questioning and gave him *Miranda* warnings. At the station, he was fingerprinted, re-advised of his rights, questioned and placed in a lineup. Police told Taylor that his fingerprints matched those on some grocery items that had been handled by a participant in the robbery, and after a short visit with his girlfriend and a male companion, Taylor signed a *Miranda* waiver and confessed. Although the length of time between the illegal arrests and the confessions in *Brown* and *Dunaway* was two hours and in this case it was six hours, the Court said that "a difference of a few hours is not significant where, as here, petitioner was in police custody, unrepresented by counsel, and he was questioned on several occasions, fingerprinted and subjected to a line-up." Although Taylor was given *Miranda* warnings three times, the Court found that this was insufficient to break the connection with the illegal arrest and detention. The Court declined to limit the prior cases to "flagrant or purposeful" illegal police conduct. Four dissenters agreed on the applicable law but disagreed on its application to the facts of the case.[43]

The Court applied *Brown*, *Dunaway* and *Taylor* in Kaupp v. Texas, 123 S.Ct. 1843 (2003) (per curiam) as it held that a suspect's confession was, on the record before it, the fruit of an arrest without probable cause. Police officers suspected Kaupp, an adolescent, of involvement in a murder, but did not have probable cause to arrest him. The officers entered Kaupp's house at 3 a.m., went to his bedroom, woke him up, placed him in handcuffs, and took him in his underwear in a patrol car. They stopped for 5 to 10 minutes at the site where the victim's body had been found, and then went on to the sheriff's headquarters, where they removed his handcuffs, gave him *Miranda* warnings, and told

---

43. Citing *Taylor,* the Supreme Court summarily vacated and remanded in Lanier v. South Carolina, 474 U.S. 25 (1985). The Court observed that even a voluntary confession is subject to suppression as the fruit of an illegal arrest.

him that the victim's brother had confessed to the crime and implicated him as an accomplice. Kaupp then admitted to some part in the crime.

The state courts held that Kaupp had not been arrested, because he voluntarily accompanied the officers. But the Court found this conclusion to be error, holding that the "evidence points to arrest even more starkly than the facts in *Dunaway*, where the petitioner was taken from a neighbor's home to a police car, transported to a police station, and placed in an interrogation room." On the question of admissibility of the confession, the Court declared as follows:

> Since Kaupp was arrested before he was questioned, and because the state does not even claim that the sheriff's department had probable cause to detain him at that point, well-established precedent requires suppression of the confession unless that confession was "an act of free will [sufficient] to purge the primary taint of the unlawful invasion." Wong Sun v. United States. Demonstrating such purgation is, of course, a function of circumstantial evidence, with the burden of persuasion on the state. Relevant considerations include observance of *Miranda*, the temporal proximity of the arrest and the confession, the presence of intervening circumstances, and, particularly, the purpose and flagrancy of the official misconduct.

> The record before us shows that only one of these considerations, the giving of *Miranda* warnings, supports the state, and we held in *Brown* that "*Miranda* warnings, *alone* and *per se*, cannot always ... break, for Fourth Amendment purposes, the causal connection between the illegality and the confession." All other factors point the opposite way. There is no indication from the record that any substantial time passed between Kaupp's removal from his home in handcuffs and his confession after only 10 or 15 minutes of interrogation. In the interim, he remained in his partially clothed state in the physical custody of a number of officers, some of whom, at least, were conscious that they lacked probable cause to arrest. In fact, the state has not even alleged "any meaningful intervening event" between the illegal arrest and Kaupp's confession. *Taylor.* Unless, on remand, the state can point to testimony undisclosed on the record before us, and weighty enough to carry the state's burden despite the clear force of the evidence shown here, the confession must be suppressed.

Statements Not Tainted by an Illegal Arrest: *Rawlings v. Kentucky*

Brown was distinguished in Rawlings v. Kentucky, 448 U.S. 98 (1980). The Court assumed that Rawlings and others were improperly detained in a house while police went to get a search warrant, but found that the improper detention did not require suppression of statements made by Rawlings after evidence was discovered. Justice Rehnquist's majority opinion observed that *Miranda* warnings were given (also true in *Brown*); that the 45 minute detention was in a congenial atmosphere; that the statements were apparently spontaneous reactions to the discovery of evidence rather than the product of the illegal detention; that the police action did not involve flagrant misconduct; and that no argument was made that the statements were involuntary. Justices White and Stewart would have remanded for consideration of the "fruit" question. Justices Marshall and Brennan thought that the statements "were obviously the fruit of the illegal detention."

Determining the Fruits of a Warrantless In–Home Arrest: New York v. Harris

Brown, Dunaway and *Taylor* each excluded confessions as the fruit of an arrest made without probable cause. In New York v. Harris, 495 U.S. 14 (1990), the defendant confessed at the station after police made a warrantless in-home arrest in violation of Payton v. New York, *supra* (holding that an arrest warrant is necessary for an in-home arrest in the absence of exigent circumstances). The challenged confession was made at the station an hour after the illegal arrest, and after Harris received *Miranda* warnings and waived his rights. Justice White concluded for the Court that the confession was not tainted, because unlike the prior cases, the defendant was not unlawfully in custody when he made the confession. Justice White reasoned that "the rule in *Payton* was designed to protect the physical integrity of the home; it was not intended to grant criminal suspects * * * protection for statements made outside their premises where the police have probable cause to arrest the suspect." Thus, a violation of *Payton* constitutes an illegal *search* of the home, but it does not result in an illegal arrest, so long as there is probable cause; and while evidence obtained in the warrantless search of the home is subject to exclusion, there is no automatic connection between that search and a subsequent confession outside the home.

Justice Marshall dissented in an opinion joined by Justices Brennan, Blackmun and Stevens. Justice Marshall contended that the rule adopted by the majority would give the police an incentive to violate *Payton*. He reasoned that the officer might find it beneficial to enter the arrestee's home illegally in order to save time, and perhaps to rattle the suspect and increase the likelihood of a confession. Excluding evidence found in the house would be no deterrent, since such suppression would make the officer no worse off than if he had waited outside to make the arrest.

In *Harris* the *Payton* violation turned up no evidence; nothing incriminating was seen in Harris' home. Would the fruit of the poisonous tree doctrine apply if the officers found incriminating evidence in Harris' house in the course of making a warrantless arrest, and subsequently used that evidence to obtain a stationhouse confession from Harris? In United States v. Beltran, 917 F.2d 641, 645 (1st Cir.1990), police arrested Beltran in her home without a warrant. During the arrest the police saw cocaine in plain view. They took the defendant to the stationhouse where she made incriminating statements. The court stated that "whether or the extent to which *Harris* applies may turn on questions of fact such as when the police seized the items in question or what motivated Ms. Beltran's statements" and remanded the case to the district court for a factual determination. Does this mean that if Beltran was rattled into a confession by the fact that the police saw the cocaine, rather than by the arrest, then *Harris* would not apply and the confession would be excluded?

Consent as Breaking the Chain of Causation

Police often argue that an illegal search or seizure should not result in exclusion of "fruits" because the suspect voluntarily consented to the search that uncovered the "fruits." Sometimes this argument is successful, sometimes not. The question is whether the voluntary consent is enough to break the chain of causation running from the illegal police activity to the evidence ultimately uncovered. As one court put it:

> To determine whether the defendant's consent was an independent act of free will, breaking the causal chain * * * we must consider three factors: 1) the temporal proximity of the illegal conduct and the consent; 2) the presence of intervening circumstances; and 3) the purpose and flagrancy of the initial misconduct.

United States v. Hernandez, 279 F.3d 302 (5th Cir. 2002). In *Hernandez*, the court found that the defendant voluntarily consented to a search of luggage, but that this voluntary act was not sufficient to break the chain of causation from the officer's initial illegal search. Hernandez was traveling on a bus when police seized her bag and manipulated it in such a way as to determine that a hard package was inside it. This manipulation constituted an illegal search under United States v. Bond, discussed earlier in this Chapter. The officer then immediately sought and obtained consent from Hernandez to open the suitcase. The Court found that there were no intervening circumstances, and therefore the opening of the suitcase was a fruit of the *Bond* violation. This was so even though the officer's misconduct was not flagrant, as it was conducted before the Supreme Court's decision in *Bond*. The Court noted that while not flagrant, the officer exploited the illegality as the officer's suspicions were aroused only after manipulating Hernandez's suitcase. As a result, "even though Hernandez voluntarily consented to Officer Ordaz's opening her suitcase and searching it, her consent did not cure the Fourth Amendment violation caused by Officer Ordaz's prior manipulation of the suitcase." For a contrary result, see United States v. Becker, 333 F.3d 858 (8th Cir. 2003)(voluntary consent cuts the chain of causation from illegal an illegal detention to the evidence obtained: consent was removed in time from the detention, and the officers were not engaged in flagrant misconduct).

Witness Testimony After Illegal Arrests and Searches

Courts are reluctant to suppress the testimony from a live witness that is alleged to be the "fruit" of an illegal search or arrest. In United States v. Ceccolini, 435 U.S. 268 (1978), an officer stopped to talk with a friend who was in Ceccolini's flower shop. While there, the officer illegally picked up and opened an envelope, and found money and gambling slips. He then learned from his friend, who did not know about this discovery, that the envelope belonged to Ceccolini. The officer relayed his information to detectives who in turn transmitted it to the FBI. Four months later, an FBI agent questioned the officer's friend who had been in the flower shop, without mentioning the illegally discovered gambling slips. The friend expressed a willingness to testify against Ceccolini, and did so before the grand jury and at Ceccolini's trial. Justice Rehnquist, writing for the Court, declined to adopt a rule that the testimony of a live witness should never be excluded. But he stated that "the exclusionary rule should be invoked with much greater reluctance where the claim is based on a causal relationship between a constitutional violation and the discovery of a live witness than when a similar claim is advanced to support suppression of an inanimate object." The Court noted that the willingness of the witness to testify is very likely, if not certain, to break the chain of causation under *Wong Sun*. Justice Rehnquist also noted that exclusion of a live witness would have a serious cost, since it would "perpetually disable a witness from testifying about relevant and material facts, regardless of how unrelated such testimony might be to the purpose of the originally illegal search or the evidence discovered thereby." Because of this cost, the Court concluded that the exclusionary rule should only apply if there is a very close and direct link between the illegality and the witness' testimony. The Court found no such close link under the facts in *Ceccolini,* where the witness was willing to testify, four months passed between the illegality and the agent's contact with the witness, and the witness was unaware of the illegality. Justice Marshall, in a dissent joined by Justice Brennan, found no meaningful distinction between live witnesses and inanimate evidence. He argued that "the same tree" cannot bear "two different kinds of fruit, with one kind less susceptible than the other to exclusion."

After *Ceccolini,* can you think of facts that would result in the exclusion of a live witness? For a case distinguishing *Ceccolini,* see United States v. Ramirez–Sandoval, 872 F.2d 1392 (9th Cir.1989)(witnesses' statements were tainted where illegally obtained information was used in questioning them, no time elapsed between the illegal search and the questioning, officer did not know the identity of the witnesses beforehand, and witnesses expressed no willingness to come forward).

In United States v. Crews, 445 U.S. 463 (1980), the question was whether the in-court identification of an armed robber should have been suppressed as the fruit of an illegal arrest. After the illegal arrest, the defendant was photographed by the police, who conducted a photo identification session with the victim and a court-ordered lineup. Justice Brennan, writing for the Court, identified three distinct elements of a victim's in-court identification: the presence of the victim to testify at trial; the ability of the victim to reconstruct the crime; and the physical presence of the defendant. He concluded "that none of these three elements 'has been come at by exploitation' of the violation of the defendant's Fourth Amendment rights." The majority concluded that a person brought to trial following an illegal arrest can be identified, as long as the in-court identification is free from any improper taint attributable to unconstitutional extra-judicial identification procedures.

Relationship Between the "Standing" Requirement and the Fruits Doctrine

A defendant can successfully challenge derivative evidence as tainted only if he has the right to object to the original illegal search or seizure. For example, in *Wong Sun,* police officers illegally entered Toy's apartment and extracted a statement from him. This statement led them to Yee, who turned over drugs. The Court held that the drugs were tainted by the entry into Toy's apartment, and thus that they could not be used against Toy. However, the narcotics were admissible against Wong Sun because Wong Sun did not have the right to object to the entry of Toy's apartment. As the Court stated, "the seizure of this heroin invaded no right of privacy of person or premises which would entitle Wong Sun to object to its use at his trial."

On the other hand, if the defendant is subject to an illegal search or seizure, and evidence is thereafter obtained in a subsequent search or seizure, the defendant can argue that this evidence is fruit of the poisonous tree even though he has no right to object to the subsequent intrusion. For example, in *Wong Sun*, Toy's rights were not violated when the officers searched and seized Yee. However, the drugs turned over by Yee were nonetheless excluded as to Toy, because they were tainted by the initial illegal entry into Toy's apartment. The exclusionary rule operated not because Yee's rights were violated but because Toy's rights were violated, and the evidence obtained from Yee was the fruit of that violation. In fact, it would not even matter if the search and seizure of Yee was perfectly legal. The "fruits" question is not about whether the search or seizure that uncovers evidence is legal, but whether it is sufficiently connected with a prior illegal search or seizure to justify exclusion.

7. Independent Source

In addition to the concept of attenuation, two additional doctrines soften the impact of the fruit of the poisonous tree rule. The first doctrine is that of the independent source. The independent source doctrine allows "the introduction of evidence discovered initially during an unlawful search if the evidence is discovered later through a source that is untainted by the initial illegality." United States v. Markling, 7 F.3d 1309 (7th Cir.1993).

In Segura v. United States, 468 U.S. 796 (1984), and in the following case, Murray v. United States, the Court considered whether an illegal search of premises could be cured when the officers later obtained a warrant, and where the probable cause supporting the warrant was not derived from information obtained in the illegal search. *Segura* is discussed in detail in *Murray*.

MURRAY v. UNITED STATES

Supreme Court of the United States, 1988.
487 U.S. 533.

JUSTICE SCALIA **delivered the opinion of the Court.**

In Segura v. United States, 468 U.S. 796 (1984), we held that police officers' illegal entry upon private premises did not require suppression of evidence subsequently discovered at those premises when executing a search warrant obtained on the basis of information wholly unconnected with the initial entry. In these consolidated cases we are faced with the question whether, again assuming evidence obtained pursuant to an independently obtained search warrant, the portion of such evidence that had been observed in plain view at the time of a prior illegal entry must be suppressed.

I

* * * Based on information received from informants, federal law enforcement agents had been surveilling petitioner Murray and several of his co-conspirators. At about 1:45 p.m. on April 6, 1983, they observed Murray drive a truck and Carter drive a green camper, into a warehouse in South Boston. When the petitioners drove the vehicles out about 20 minutes later, the surveilling agents saw within the warehouse two individuals and a tractor-trailer rig bearing a long, dark container. Murray and Carter later turned over the truck and camper to other drivers, who were in turn followed and ultimately arrested, and the vehicles lawfully seized. Both vehicles were found to contain marijuana.

After receiving this information, several of the agents converged on the

South Boston warehouse and forced entry. They found the warehouse unoccupied, but observed in plain view numerous burlap-wrapped bales that were later found to contain marijuana. They left without disturbing the bales, kept the warehouse under surveillance, and did not reenter it until they had a search warrant. In applying for the warrant, the agents did not mention the prior entry, and did not rely on any observations made during that entry. When the warrant was issued—at 10:40 p.m., approximately eight hours after the initial entry—the agents immediately reentered the warehouse and seized 270 bales of marijuana and notebooks listing customers for whom the bales were destined.

[The motion to suppress was denied and the Court of Appeals affirmed.]

II

* * *

Almost simultaneously with our development of the exclusionary rule, * * * we also announced what has come to be known as the "independent source" doctrine. That doctrine, which has been applied to evidence acquired not only through Fourth Amendment violations but also through Fifth and Sixth Amendment violations, has recently been described as follows:

"[T]he interest of society in deterring unlawful police conduct and the public interest in having juries receive all probative evidence of a crime are properly balanced by putting the police in the same, not a *worse,* position than they would have been in if no police error or misconduct had occurred. . . . When the challenged evidence has an independent source, exclusion of such evidence would put the police in a worse position than they would

have been in absent any error or violation." Nix v. Williams, 467 U.S. 431, 443 (1984).

The dispute here is over the scope of this doctrine. Petitioners contend that it applies only to evidence obtained for the first time during an independent lawful search. The Government argues that it applies also to evidence initially discovered during, or as a consequence of, an unlawful search, but later obtained independently from activities untainted by the initial illegality. We think the Government's view has better support in both precedent and policy.

Our cases have used the concept of "independent source" in a more general and a more specific sense. The more general sense identifies *all* evidence acquired in a fashion untainted by the illegal evidence-gathering activity. Thus, where an unlawful entry has given investigators knowledge of facts x and y, but fact z has been learned by other means, fact z can be said to be admissible because derived from an "independent source." This is how we used the term in Segura v. United States. In that case, agents unlawfully entered the defendant's apartment and remained there until a search warrant was obtained. The admissibility of what they discovered while waiting in the apartment was not before us, but we held that the evidence found for the first time during the execution of the valid and untainted search warrant was admissible because it was discovered pursuant to an "independent source."

The original use of the term, however, and its more important use for purposes of this case, was more specific. It was originally applied in the exclusionary rule context * * *, with reference to that particular category of evidence acquired by an untainted search *which is identical to the evi-*

dence unlawfully acquired—that is, in the example just given, to knowledge of facts *x* and *y* derived from an independent source.

* * *

We recently assumed this application of the independent source doctrine (in the Sixth Amendment context) in Nix v. Williams. There incriminating statements obtained in violation of the defendant's right to counsel had led the police to the victim's body. The body had not in fact been found through an independent source as well, and so the independent source doctrine was not itself applicable. We held, however, that evidence concerning the body was nonetheless admissible because a search had been under way which would have discovered the body, had it not been called off because of the discovery produced by the unlawfully obtained statements. This "inevitable discovery" doctrine obviously assumes the validity of the independent source doctrine as applied to evidence initially acquired unlawfully. It would make no sense to admit the evidence because the independent search, had it not been aborted, would have found the body, but to exclude the evidence if the search had continued and had in fact found the body. The inevitable discovery doctrine, with its distinct requirements, is in reality an extrapolation from the independent source doctrine: *Since* the tainted evidence would be admissible if in fact discovered through an independent

source, it should be admissible if it inevitably would have been discovered.

Petitioners' asserted policy basis for excluding evidence which is initially discovered during an illegal search, but is subsequently acquired through an independent and lawful source, is that a contrary rule will remove all deterrence to, and indeed positively encourage, unlawful police searches. As petitioners see the incentives, law enforcement officers will routinely enter without a warrant to make sure that what they expect to be on the premises is in fact there. If it is not, they will have spared themselves the time and trouble of getting a warrant; if it is, they can get the warrant and use the evidence despite the unlawful entry. We see the incentives differently. An officer with probable cause sufficient to obtain a search warrant would be foolish to enter the premises first in an unlawful manner. By doing so, he would risk suppression of all evidence on the premises, both seen and unseen, since his action would add to the normal burden of convincing a magistrate that there is probable cause the much more onerous burden of convincing a trial court that no information gained from the illegal entry affected either the law enforcement officers' decision to seek a warrant or the magistrate's decision to grant it. Nor would the officer *without* sufficient probable cause to obtain a search warrant have any added incentive to conduct an unlawful entry, since whatever he finds cannot be used to establish probable cause before a magistrate.[a]

---

a. * * To say that a district court must be satisfied that a warrant would have been sought without the illegal entry is not to give dispositive effect to police officers' assurances on the point. Where the facts render those assurances implausible, the independent source doctrine will not apply.

We might note that there is no basis for pointing to the present cases as an example of a "search first, warrant later" mentality. The District Court found that the agents entered the warehouse "in an effort to apprehend any participants who might have remained inside and to guard against the destruction of possibly critical evidence." While they may have

It is possible to read petitioners' briefs as asserting the more narrow position that the "independent source" doctrine does apply to independent acquisition of evidence previously derived *indirectly* from the unlawful search, but does not apply to what they call "primary evidence," that is, evidence acquired during the course of the search itself. In addition to finding no support in our precedent, this strange distinction would produce results bearing no relation to the policies of the exclusionary rule. It would mean, for example, that the government's knowledge of the existence and condition of a dead body, knowledge lawfully acquired through independent sources, would have to be excluded if government agents had previously observed the body during an unlawful search of the defendant's apartment; but not if they had observed a notation that the body was buried in a certain location, producing consequential discovery of the corpse.

III

To apply what we have said to the present cases: Knowledge that the marijuana was in the warehouse was assuredly acquired at the time of the unlawful entry. But it was also acquired at the time of entry pursuant to the warrant, and if that later acquisition was not the result of the earlier entry there is no reason why the independent source doctrine should not apply. Invoking the exclusionary rule would put the police (and society) not in the *same* position they would have occupied if no violation occurred, but in a *worse* one.

We think this is also true with respect to the tangible evidence, the bales of marijuana. It would make no more sense to exclude that than it

would to exclude tangible evidence found upon the corpse in *Nix,* if the search in that case had not been abandoned and had in fact come upon the body. * * * The independent source doctrine does not rest upon such metaphysical analysis, but upon the policy that, while the government should not profit from its illegal activity, neither should it be placed in a worse position than it would otherwise have occupied.

The ultimate question, therefore, is whether the search pursuant to warrant was in fact a genuinely independent source of the information and tangible evidence at issue here. This would not have been the case if the agents' decision to seek the warrant was prompted by what they had seen during the initial entry, or if information obtained during that entry was presented to the Magistrate and affected his decision to issue the warrant. * * * The District Court found that the agents did not reveal their warrantless entry to the Magistrate and that they did not include in their application for a warrant any recitation of their observations in the warehouse. It did not, however, explicitly find that the agents would have sought a warrant if they had not earlier entered the warehouse. * * * To be sure, the District Court did determine that the purpose of the warrantless entry was in part "to guard against the destruction of possibly critical evidence," and one could perhaps infer from this that the agents who made the entry already planned to obtain that "critical evidence" through a warrant-authorized search. That inference is not, however, clear enough to justify the conclusion that the District Court's findings amounted to a determination of independent source.

misjudged the existence of sufficient exigent circumstances to justify the warrantless entry * * * there is nothing to suggest that they

went in merely to see if there was anything worth getting a warrant for.

Accordingly, we vacate the judgment and remand these cases to the Court of Appeals with instructions that it remand to the District Court for determination whether the warrant-authorized search of the warehouse was an independent source of the challenged evidence in the sense we have described.

Justice Brennan and Justice Kennedy took no part in the consideration or decision of this litigation.

Justice Marshall, **with whom** Justice Stevens **and** Justice O'Connor **join, dissenting.**

* * * In holding that the independent source exception may apply to the facts of these cases, I believe the Court loses sight of the practical moorings of the independent source exception and creates an affirmative incentive for unconstitutional searches. * * *

* * * Obtaining a warrant is inconvenient and time consuming. Even when officers have probable cause to support a warrant application, therefore, they have an incentive first to determine whether it is worthwhile to obtain a warrant. Probable cause is much less than certainty, and many "confirmatory" searches will result in the discovery that no evidence is present, thus saving the police the time and trouble of getting a warrant. If contraband is discovered, however, the officers may later seek a warrant to shield the evidence from the taint of the illegal search. The police thus know in advance that they have little to lose and much to gain by forgoing the bother of obtaining a warrant and undertaking an illegal search.

Under the Court's view, today's decision does not provide an incentive for unlawful searches, because the officer undertaking the search would know that "his action would add to the normal burden of convincing a magistrate that there is probable cause the much more onerous burden of convincing a trial court that no information gained from the illegal entry affected either the law enforcement officers' decision to seek a warrant or the magistrate's decision to grant it." The Court, however, provides no hint of why this risk would actually seem significant to the officers. Under the circumstances of these cases, the officers committing the illegal search have both knowledge and control of the factors central to the trial court's determination. First, it is a simple matter, as was done in these cases, to exclude from the warrant application any information gained from the initial entry so that the magistrate's determination of probable cause is not influenced by the prior illegal search. Second, today's decision makes the application of the independent source exception turn entirely on an evaluation of the officers' intent. It normally will be difficult for the trial court to verify, or the defendant to rebut, an assertion by officers that they always intended to obtain a warrant, regardless of the results of the illegal search.[b] The testimony of the officers conducting the illegal search is the only direct evidence of intent, and the defendant will be relegated simply to arguing that the officers should not be believed. Under these circumstances, the litigation risk described by the Court seems hardly a risk at all; it does not significantly

---

b. * * * The Court fails to describe how a trial court will properly evaluate whether the law enforcement officers fully intended to obtain a warrant regardless of what they discovered during the illegal search. The obvious

question is whose intent is relevant? Intentions clearly may differ both among supervisory officers and among officers who initiate the illegal search.

dampen the incentive to conduct the initial illegal search.

[The dissenting opinion of Justice Stevens is omitted.]

* * *

Questions About Murray

The majority in *Murray* expresses concern about a "confirmatory" search, and states that the subsequent search will be invalidated if the officer's testimony denying a confirmatory motivation is "implausible." The officer denying a confirmatory motivation must explain why he or she made the original search without a warrant, and after *Murray* this explanation must rise only to the level of plausibility. In *Murray,* the explanation found plausible was that the officers thought they had exigent circumstances, even though in fact they did not. (If they did have exigent circumstances, *Murray* would not be a fruits case, because the original search would have been legal). Recall the discussion of exigent circumstances earlier in the Chapter. Under what facts could the officers be so wrong about exigent circumstances that their explanation on that point would not even be plausible? Could that ever happen in a narcotics case? Has the Court in *Murray* established a good faith exception for warrantless searches that are later sanitized by a warrant? As in *Leon,* discussed infra, the search, though illegal, does not result in exclusion so long as the officers are not totally unreasonable in believing that they were acting legally. For criticism of *Murray* on these points, see Bradley, Murray v. United States: The Bell Tolls for the Search Warrant Requirement, 64 Ind.L.J. 907 (1989). See also United States v. Johnson, 994 F.2d 980 (2d Cir.1993)(independent source doctrine applies where officers made an initial search under the mistaken impression that it was incident to an arrest; while mistaken, the officers were not totally unreasonable).

Is the primary purpose of the exclusionary rule to deter police misconduct, or to restore the situation as it existed before the illegal search? If the primary purpose is deterrence, can it be argued that it is sometimes necessary to place the government in a worse position than if the illegal search had not occurred? Is *Murray* one of those times?

The court in United States v. Curtis, 931 F.2d 1011 (4th Cir.1991), applied *Murray* where an undercover agent bought drugs in Curtis' house, and then the officers went to get a warrant, but while they were gone the officers remaining for surveillance purposes entered Curtis' house for an ostensible protective sweep. The court found that, assuming the protective sweep was illegal, it did not affect the officers' decision to get a warrant. Is *Curtis* an easier or harder case than *Murray?*

"Mixed" Warrant Applications

In *Murray,* the magistrate was not informed of the initial illegal search or of any evidence discovered in that search, so it was clear that the search did not affect the magistrate's decision to issue the warrant. But what if the warrant application includes information obtained in the illegal search? On the one hand, it could be argued that the independent source exception should never apply because the tainted information necessarily affects the warrant process. On the other hand, it could be argued that the independent source exception should apply so long as the untainted information in the warrant application rises to the level of probable cause. The untainted information could constitute the independent source for the warrant.

The lower courts after *Murray* have generally taken the latter view, i.e., "that a search warrant procured in part on the basis of illegally obtained information will still support a search if the untainted information supporting the warrant, considered alone, is sufficient to establish probable cause." United States v. Markling, 7 F.3d 1309 (7th Cir.1993). The court in *Markling* reasoned that this approach "is a logical application of the Supreme Court's reasoning in Franks v. Delaware," which is discussed supra in the section on attacking the warrant. As the *Markling* court put it:

> In *Franks*, the Court held that when a government agent deliberately or recklessly includes false information in a warrant application, the warrant is still valid if the other information in the application, standing alone, is sufficient to support probable cause. * * * If we may uphold a warrant based on an application including knowingly false information if other information in the application establishes probable cause, it is logical to conclude that we may uphold a warrant based on an application including illegally obtained information under the same circumstances.

Is this reasoning persuasive? Is it consistent with the deterrence rationale of the exclusionary rule as applied in *Murray*?

8. *Inevitable Discovery*

The inevitable discovery exception, discussed in *Murray,* has been termed the "hypothetical independent source" exception. See Note, The Inevitable Discovery Exception, Primary Evidence, and the Emasculation of the Fourth Amendment, 55 Fordham L.Rev. 1221 (1987). For the exception to apply, the government must show that the illegally obtained evidence would have been discovered through legitimate means independent of the official misconduct. Note that if the evidence is actually discovered through legitimate independent means, the independent source exception would apply. So the inevitable discovery exception is one step removed from the independent source exception.[44]

Establishing the Exception: Nix v. Williams

The Supreme Court approved the inevitable discovery limitation upon the exclusionary rule for the first time in Nix v. Williams, 467 U.S. 431 (1984), which is discussed in *Murray*. Seven years earlier, the Court had held by a 5–4 vote that Williams' conviction for murdering a 10–year-old girl was tainted when a police officer managed to obtain statements from Williams in violation of Williams' Sixth Amendment right to counsel. In the course of making statements, Williams led police to the girl's body. Although the Court held that the statements must be suppressed, it left open the question whether evidence as to the location and condition of the body might be admissible in a new trial.

At Williams' second trial, a state court judge found that the government proved by a preponderance of the evidence that a search party, which had suspended its activities once Williams agreed to lead the police to the body, would have found the body shortly afterwards anyway and that the body would have been found in essentially the same condition as when Williams led the police to it. Thus, the judge admitted evidence concerning the body's location

---

44. A variation on the inevitable discovery doctrine is the rule in most courts that, if an arrest warrant is invalid but the arrest could have been made without a warrant, evidence will not be suppressed. See, e.g., United States v. Hall, 348 F.2d 837 (2d Cir.1965). A few courts hold the arrest to be invalid and suppress. See, e.g., Isaacks v. State, 350 So.2d 1340 (Miss.1977). What are the opposing arguments?

and condition. The state supreme court affirmed, but a federal appellate court found that the inevitable discovery rule could not be invoked where a police officer acted in bad faith, as it found the officer had in dealing with Williams.

Chief Justice Burger wrote for a majority as it reversed the court of appeals. He treated the independent source and inevitable discovery doctrines as related, reasoning that both doctrines limit the exclusionary rule so that the government is not denied evidence it would have had even without its officers' overstepping constitutional boundaries. The Court indicated that the exclusionary rule works to assure that police do not believe they will benefit from constitutional violations, and that the inevitable discovery exception simply recognizes that the government actually obtains no advantage from illegal conduct *if* the government can prove that it would have obtained the evidence anyway. The Court declined to restrict the inevitable discovery limitation to situations in which an officer acts in good faith. It found that a "good faith" requirement is not needed to deter officers from violating constitutional rules, because officers seeking to gather evidence cannot know in advance whether the government will be able to prove that their evidence would have been discovered inevitably. Thus, sufficient deterrence flows from the uncertainty that any evidence would have been inevitably obtained legally. The Chief Justice found that excluding evidence that would have been inevitably discovered legally, on the ground that officers acted in bad faith, "would put the police in a *worse* position than they would have been if no unlawful conduct had transpired" and that the exclusionary rule could not be used to punish the state in that way.

The Court in *Nix* held that to invoke the inevitable discovery exception, the government must prove by a preponderance that the challenged evidence would have been discovered through independent legal means. Chief Justice Burger rejected the more stringent clear and convincing evidence standard, stating that "we are unwilling to impose added burdens on the already difficult task of proving guilt in criminal cases by enlarging the barrier to placing evidence of unquestioned truth before juries." Applying the preponderance of the evidence standard to the facts, the Chief Justice found that the government had established its burden that the body would have been found by the search team only a short time after Williams directed the officers there.

Justice Stevens concurred in the judgment. He expressed concern, however, that the majority emphasized the "societal costs" of the exclusionary rule without also emphasizing the "societal costs" of unconstitutional police conduct.

Although Justice Brennan, joined by Justice Marshall, dissented, he accepted the inevitable discovery doctrine. He emphasized, however, that inevitable discovery was a more hypothetical exception than independent source, and consequently would have required the government to prove inevitability by clear and convincing evidence.

Although *Williams* was a case involving Sixth Amendment violation, the Court discussed the exclusionary rules it has adopted to enforce Fourth, Fifth and Sixth Amendment standards. The Court's opinion strongly suggests that the inevitable discovery doctrine will limit the exclusionary rule under all three amendments. Both before and after *Nix,* lower courts have applied the inevitable discovery exception to Fourth Amendment violations. See, e.g., United States v. Jackson, 901 F.2d 83 (7th Cir.1990)(even if defendant did not give voluntary consent to a search of his person, officers would have inevitably conducted a

Terry frisk and uncovered crack cocaine in defendant's pockets); United States v. Kennedy, 61 F.3d 494 (6th Cir.1995) (evidence discovered by airport police in an illegal search of lost luggage was properly admitted, because if the police had not searched the suitcase, they would have returned it to the airline, and the airline's policy was to open lost luggage to determine the identity of the owner).

Primary and Derivative Evidence

In *Nix,* the inevitable discovery exception was applied to admit the evidence one step removed from the illegally obtained evidence, as opposed to the evidence that directly resulted from the illegality. That is, the condition of the body was admitted, but not the illegally obtained confession that led to the body. Questions have arisen whether the inevitable discovery exception can be applied to admit the illegally obtained evidence itself, which some have called "primary" as opposed to "derivative" evidence. See Capra, Independent Source and Inevitable Discovery, N.Y.L.J. Dec. 8, 1989, p. 4, col. 3; Bloom, Inevitable Discovery: An Exception Beyond the Fruits, 20 Am.J.Crim.L.79 (1992).

For example, in United States v. Andrade, 784 F.2d 1431 (9th Cir.1986), officers searched Andrade's bag and found cocaine after he was arrested for a drug violation. The search did not occur until an hour after the arrest. The court held that even if the search could not be justified as incident to arrest and was thus unlawful (see United States v. Chadwick, supra), "the cocaine was admissible because it would have been inevitably discovered through a routine inventory search." The court noted that it was normal DEA procedure to inventory the contents of bags held by arrestees, and that such a procedure was valid under Illinois v. Lafayette, supra. Judge Reinhardt, concurring, agreed that the "confluence" of *Nix* and *Lafayette* required this result, but concluded that "the result we are required to reach will serve only to encourage illegal and unconstitutional searches." See also United States v. Seals, 987 F.2d 1102 (5th Cir.1993)(evidence found in car held admissible where it "would have been discovered pursuant to an authorized inventory search").

If *Andrade* is correct that the existence of routine inventory procedures allows admission of the very evidence obtained from the illegal search of a car or container, then why would an officer ever have to comply with the rules that still limit searches of cars or containers? For example, probable cause is required to search the trunk of a car. But does the probable cause requirement mean anything if the inevitable discovery exception applies by way of the (hypothetical) inventory search of anything found in the trunk? Is there any reason for an officer even to follow the standardized inventory procedures themselves, given the fact that standards are in place to permit an argument that such an inventory would have been conducted? See United States v. Martin, 982 F.2d 1236 (8th Cir.1993) (improper inventory excused because a proper one would have been conducted under police guidelines).

In United States v. $639,558.00 in United States Currency, 955 F.2d 712 (D.C.Cir.1992), the court held that the exclusionary rule required exclusion of the primary evidence obtained in an illegal search (evidence obtained during the illegal search itself), even if that evidence inevitably would have been discovered in an inventory search. The court reasoned as follows:

If the evidence stemming from the violation is nevertheless admissible on the basis that the bags inevitably would have been opened when they were inventoried, the practical consequence is apparent. In the vast run of cases, there would be no incentive whatever for police to go to the trouble of seeking a warrant (or, we should add, of waiting for a lawful inventory to occur during normal processing). The police could readily make this assessment on their own. Contrary to what *Nix* supposed, they would almost invariably be in a position to calculate whether the evidence would inevitably have been discovered, because they would know that inventory procedures were in place.

The court in *United States Currency* distinguished primary evidence, which it thought not subject to the inevitable discovery exception, from secondary evidence derived from the illegal activity. For example, assume that in an illegal search of a car trunk, the officers find an address book. The address book is primary evidence of the illegal search. But the address book could indicate the location of a locker that contains drugs. The drugs found in that locker constitute derivative evidence. The *United States Currency* court would apply the inevitable discovery rule only to the drugs found in the locker, and not to the address book itself. Is this distinction persuasive? If the primary evidence found in the illegal search of a trunk would have been discovered in a lawful inventory search, doesn't exclusion put the officers in a worse position than they would have been if the illegal conduct had never occurred? Isn't that result contrary to *Nix* and *Murray*? Is it necessary to punish in order to deter illegality in cases like *United States Currency* and *Andrade?*

The D.C. Circuit's reasoning in *United States Currency* does not represent the majority view. In United States v. Zapata, 18 F.3d 971 (1st Cir.1994), the court criticized the D.C. Circuit's position in the following analysis:

> We decline to embrace the suggestion that courts should confine the inevitable discovery rule to cases in which the disputed evidence comprises a derivative, rather than primary, fruit of unlawful police conduct. Although the *Nix* case involved derivative evidence, we regard its rationale—that the exclusion of inevitably discovered evidence would put the government in a worse position than if no illegality had occurred—to be fully applicable to cases involving primary evidence. And we are thrice fortified in this conclusion: by the *Nix* Court's approving citation to cases that had applied the rule in the context of primary evidence; by the Court's subsequent endorsement [in *Murray*] of the closely related independent source rule in a case involving primary evidence; and by the fact that no fewer than seven other circuits have approved application of the inevitable discovery rule in primary evidence cases.

"We Would Have Obtained a Warrant"

If the inevitable discovery exception applies to the very evidence obtained in an illegal search, what is to stop the government from making the following argument:

> "We realize that we conducted an illegal warrantless search. Sorry. However, we had probable cause, and we would have obtained a warrant on that basis. Because we had probable cause, the warrant inevitably would have

issued, and we would have searched pursuant to it (if we had bothered to obtain it). So all the evidence we obtained is admissible under the inevitable discovery exception."

Do *Nix* and *Murray* require that such an argument must be accepted? If so, is there anything left of the warrant requirement?

Most courts have rejected government arguments that the inevitable discovery exception is met on the simple assertion that the officers had probable cause and would have obtained a warrant. Judge Easterbrook rejected that argument in United States v. Brown, 64 F.3d 1083 (7th Cir.1995):

What makes a discovery "inevitable" is not probable cause alone, * * * but probable cause plus a chain of events that would have led to a warrant (or another justification) independent of the search. Otherwise the requirement of a warrant for a residential entry will never be enforced by the exclusionary rule. A warrant requirement matters only when the police have probable cause, because otherwise they can't get one. (Under the second clause of the fourth amendment, "no Warrants shall issue, but upon probable cause".) To say that a warrant is required for a search is to say that the police must get judicial approval before acting. Yet if probable cause means that discovery is inevitable, then the prior-approval requirement has been nullified.

See also United States v. Johnson, 22 F.3d 674 (6th Cir.1994) ("to hold that simply because the police could have obtained a warrant, it was therefore inevitable that they would have done so would mean that there is inevitable discovery and no warrant requirement whenever there is probable cause"); United States v. Echegoyen, 799 F.2d 1271 (9th Cir.1986)("to excuse the failure to obtain a warrant merely because the officers had probable cause and could have inevitably obtained a warrant would completely obviate the warrant requirement of the fourth amendment"). But see Bradley, Murray v. United States: The Bell Tolls for the Search Warrant Requirement, 64 Ind.L.J. 907 (1989)(noting that the "we would have obtained a warrant" argument is creditable and persuasive in light of *Murray,* which applied the independent source exception to primary evidence, i.e., evidence discovered during the illegal search itself).

Some decisions can be found that appear to rely on *Nix* to hold that evidence found in an illegal warrantless search was admissible because a warrant could and would have been obtained. See, e.g., United States v. Buchanan, 910 F.2d 1571 (7th Cir.1990)(excusing an illegal search because police inevitably would have sought a search warrant and a magistrate would have issued one).

Establishing Inevitability

Nix holds that the government must prove by a preponderance that the illegally obtained evidence inevitably would have been discovered by legal means. For example, even if the exception applies to primary evidence that would have been discovered in an inventory, the government has the burden of showing that the inventory would have been conducted. See, e.g., United States v. Stern, 13 F.3d 489 (1st Cir.1994)(inevitable discovery exception inapplicable where government made no showing that "their actions were controlled by established procedures and standardized criteria," as required by the inventory cases).

In United States v. Feldhacker, 849 F.2d 293 (8th Cir.1988), the court cautioned that in deciding whether the inevitable discovery exception applies, courts must focus on what the officers actually would have done, not on what they could possibly have done.

There are reasonable limits to the scope that courts will impute to the hypothetical untainted investigation. An investigation conducted over an infinite time with infinite thoroughness will, of course, ultimately or inevitably turn up any and all pieces of evidence in the world. Prosecutors may not justify unlawful extractions of information post hoc where lawful methods present only a theoretical possibility of discovery. While the hypothetical discovery by lawful means need not be reached as rapidly as that actually reached by unlawful means, the lawful discovery must be inevitable through means that would actually have been employed.

Similar concerns arose in United States v. Allen, 159 F.3d 832 (4th Cir. 1998). The government sought to avoid exclusion after Officer Tackett illegally searched a bag in a bus sweep. The government argued, and Officer Tackett testified, that if she hadn't opened the bag and discovered drugs, she would have called the K–9 unit and had a dog sniff the bag. The government presented testimony that a dog unit was at the bus terminal that day, and that the dog would have had no problem alerting to the drugs in Allen's bag. Officer Tackett testified that if the dog alerted, she would have sought a search warrant to search the bag. But the court found this scenario speculative.

Our initial problem * * * lies in the lack of evidentiary support for the conclusion that Tackett would have used the dog. We have no doubt that Tackett *could* have used the dog, but whether she *would* have presents an entirely different question. Tackett testified specifically that if she had not conducted the illegal search and if she had thought the bag "could have been Allen's," she would have used the drug dog to sniff the bag. However, when Detective Kennedy (the dog's handler) testified, he did not so much as suggest that his dog had ever been used to sniff bags located inside the passenger compartment of a bus. Instead, he stated that his usual duty involved sending his dog into the undercarriage of the bus, as he had done that day. Furthermore, nothing in the record indicates that Tackett had ever previously called for a police dog to sniff baggage inside a bus, and Tackett conceded as much. * * *

A finding of inevitable discovery necessarily rests on facts that did not occur. However, by definition the occurrence of these facts must have been likely, indeed "inevitable," absent the government's misconduct. On the record here, * * * we cannot possibly conclude that the government inevitably would have discovered the cocaine by employing a drug dog to establish probable cause.

Active Pursuit Requirement

A few courts have held that in order to invoke the inevitable discovery exception, the police must be actively pursuing the lawful means at the time the illegal search is conducted. Thus, in United States v. Khoury, 901 F.2d 948 (11th Cir.1990), the court rejected the argument that evidence obtained in an illegal search of a car inevitably would have been discovered in an inventory search. Applying an "active pursuit" rule, the court concluded that at the time of the illegal search, an inventory had not yet begun. Other courts, such as the court in

Andrade, reject the "active pursuit" limitation on the inevitable discovery exception. Would an active pursuit limitation solve some of the concerns posed in applying the inevitable discovery exception to primary evidence?

9. Use of Illegally Seized Evidence Outside the Criminal Trial Context

Where it applies, the exclusionary rule operates to exclude evidence at a criminal trial. But in a series of cases, the Court has held that the exclusionary rule generally does not apply outside the context of a criminal trial. This is because, according to the Court, exclusion from the criminal prosecution's case-in-chief is all that is necessary to deter Fourth Amendment violations. The cost of exclusion in other contexts generally has been held to outweigh the benefits in deterrence that the rule provides.

Grand Jury Proceedings

In United States v. Calandra, 414 U.S. 338 (1974), agents illegally seized certain documents located at Calandra's place of business. The documents related to loansharking activities. A grand jury was convened to investigate these activities, and Calandra was subpoenaed to appear so that he might be questioned on the basis of the information obtained from the illegally seized documents. Calandra moved to suppress the documents and refused to answer the grand jury's questions. The Supreme Court held that Calandra had no right to refuse to answer the questions, because the exclusionary rule does not apply to grand jury proceedings. The Court concluded that the marginal deterrent effect of allowing a witness to raise a Fourth Amendment claim before the grand jury was outweighed by the disruption of investigations that exclusion of evidence would produce. The Court declared that sufficient deterrence flowed from exclusion of the illegally obtained evidence at trial. Justice Brennan, whose dissent was joined by Justices Douglas and Marshall, de-emphasized the deterrent rationale of the rule and focused instead on the benefits of keeping courts from lending their assistance to unconstitutional practices.

Justice Powell's majority opinion in *Calandra* fails to address the obvious question that arises from the Court's holding: i.e., if, as a direct result of using illegally seized evidence, the grand jury gathers all the evidence that the government can find, is all the evidence to be suppressed at trial? If so, the administrative inconvenience of allowing witnesses to challenge questions put by the grand jury may pale before the inconvenience of "untainting" evidence at trial.

The fact that indictments can be based on illegally seized evidence is another arrow in the government's quiver. One of the most obvious trends in the decisions of the Supreme Court and lower courts is to restrict the use of exclusion to the government's case-in-chief at trial. The end result is that police know that illegally seized evidence often can be used in a variety of proceedings. On the other hand, there is something to the *Calandra* Court's assertion that it will ordinarily be impractical to use tainted evidence to obtain an indictment; because that evidence would not be admissible at trial, it seems that the chances of obtaining a conviction would be remote. See United States v. Puglia, 8 F.3d 478 (7th Cir.1993)("Prosecutors will not waste their time seeking indictments of individuals against whom they do not have enough evidence to convict.").

Yet recently prosecutors have been quoted as saying that it is important to indict someone even if they are not convicted—that is, the indictment can be used as punishment in the public eye, and as a means of imposing inconvenience and distress on a suspected criminal. For example, the special prosecutor in the case against former Secretary of Agriculture Mike Espy was quoted as being content with Espy's acquittal, because law enforcement and deterrence interests were substantially furthered by the indictment itself. If prosecutors feel this way about indictments, did the Court get it right in *Calandra* when it reasoned that sufficient deterrence flows from excluding illegally obtained evidence at trial?

Civil Tax Proceedings

The Court has held that evidence illegally seized by state police could be used by federal tax officials in civil tax litigation, despite the fact that federal and local law enforcement personnel regularly provide federal tax officials with information. United States v. Janis, 428 U.S. 433 (1976). The Court in *Janis* found the deterrent effect of the exclusionary rule "attenuated when the punishment imposed upon the offending criminal enforcement officer is the removal of that evidence from a civil suit by or against a different sovereign." This attenuation, coupled with the "existing deterrence" effected by exclusion of the evidence from both state and federal criminal trials, tilted the cost-benefit analysis in favor of admitting the evidence.

The search in *Janis* was conducted by local officials and the evidence was ultimately used in a Federal tax proceeding. In a footnote in *Janis*, the Court intimated that the exclusionary rule might have more deterrent effect if the search were conducted by officials of the same sovereign that ultimately used the evidence. However, lower courts after *Janis* have generally refused to apply the exclusionary rule even where the search and the subsequent civil tax proceeding are both conducted by the same sovereign. For example, in Tirado v. Commissioner, 689 F.2d 307 (2d Cir.1982), the court found it "unsound to invoke the exclusionary rule on the assumption that officers of one federal agency have such a strong motivating interest in all federal law enforcement concerns that broad application of the rule will achieve significant marginal deterrence." The court thus found the Federal tax proceeding to be outside the "zone of primary interest" of a Federal narcotics officer who conducted an illegal search.

Civil Deportation Proceedings

In Immigration and Naturalization Service v. Lopez–Mendoza, 468 U.S. 1032 (1984), the question was whether illegally obtained statements could be used in deportation proceedings. INS officials had illegally obtained confessions from aliens concerning their status. Justice O'Connor's opinion for the Court recognized that "the deterrence value of applying the exclusionary rule in deportation proceedings would be higher than it was in *Janis*." This is because, unlike the searches by the police officers involved in *Janis*, INS law enforcement efforts are geared specifically toward deportation proceedings rather than toward criminal prosecutions. But the Court found that the social costs of exclusion would be much greater as well, since exclusion could mean that a person who is committing a criminal offense at the time of the proceeding would be allowed to go free. Applying the *Janis* balancing test, the Court held that illegally seized evidence may be used in a deportation proceeding.

Justice O'Connor reasoned as follows: 1) no matter how an arrest is made, deportation will still be possible when evidence derived independently of the arrest is available, and evidence of alienage alone might be sufficient to warrant deportation—thus, the use of illegally obtained evidence will ordinarily be harmless; 2) as a practical matter, it is highly unlikely that deportees will raise exclusionary rule claims and therefore unlikely that the rule would deter INS agents; 3) the INS has its own scheme for deterring Fourth Amendment violations by its agents; 4) declaratory relief is available to restrain institutional practices by the INS that violate the Fourth Amendment; 5) deportation currently requires only a simple hearing, and it would be inappropriate to add complex issues of exclusion to these hearings; 6) INS agents handle so many cases that they might have difficulty accounting for exactly how they handled each suspected alien; and 7) "[a]pplying the exclusionary rule in proceedings that are intended not to punish past transgressions but to prevent their continuance or renewal would require the courts to close their eyes to ongoing violations of the law."

Justice White dissented. He reasoned that INS agents seek to gather evidence specifically for use in deportation proceedings, and that their activities are closely analogous to those of police officers who seek evidence for criminal trials. Thus, the deterrent effect of the exclusionary rule is the same as it would be for criminal prosecutions.[45]

Habeas Corpus Proceedings

In Stone v. Powell, 428 U.S. 465 (1976), the Court, using its familiar cost-benefit analysis, held that the exclusionary rule could not be invoked in habeas corpus proceedings to challenge Fourth Amendment violations. The Court stated that in the context of habeas proceedings, "the contribution of the exclusionary rule, if any, to the effectuation of the Fourth Amendment is minimal and the substantial societal costs of application of the rule persist with special force." The consequence of *Stone* is that unless the Supreme Court grants certiorari, no federal court will ever review a state court ruling on a Fourth Amendment issue. Why is the deterrent effect of the exclusionary rule especially low and the cost especially high in the habeas context?

Sentencing Proceedings

The Supreme Court has not considered whether illegally obtained evidence can be used in sentencing proceedings. But the federal courts have found the exclusionary rule inapplicable to sentencing hearings under the Federal Sentencing Guidelines. United States v. Tejada, 956 F.2d 1256 (2d Cir.1992), is an example of the predominant approach. The *Tejada* court analyzed the costs and benefits of exclusion of illegally obtained evidence at sentencing as follows:

> [The defendants] posit that police and prosecutors with enough lawfully obtained evidence for a conviction of a relatively minor offense that has a broad sentencing range could guarantee a heavier sentence by seizing other evidence illegally and introducing it at sentencing. * * *

45. Justices Brennan, Marshall and Stevens each filed a short dissenting opinion in *Lopez-Mendoza.* Each agreed with most of Justice White's analysis, but declined to adopt his suggestion that INS agents acting in good faith would not have to fear exclusion of evidence.

Defendants * * * do not explain why this supposed incentive to violate the Fourth Amendment will prove incrementally stronger than the rewards that already exist. Illegally seized evidence long has played a role in our legal system, and many of its uses might motivate a police officer to violate the Fourth Amendment. [Citing *Lopez-Mendoza, Janis,* and *Calandra*]. The Supreme Court has held that these uses for illegally seized evidence do not diminish deterrence sufficiently to justify the exclusion of probative evidence. We see no reason why this additional use of illegally seized evidence justifies different treatment.

The *Tejada* court asserted that "[g]reat rewards still exist for following accepted police procedures." If evidence cannot be used at trial, the government may never get to the sentencing proceeding due to the weakness of its case. Against the perceived minimal deterrent effect of exclusion at the sentencing hearing, the court weighed the need for sentencing courts to have "as much information as possible at sentencing." The result:

We conclude that the benefits of providing sentencing judges with reliable information about the defendant outweigh the likelihood that allowing consideration of illegally seized evidence will encourage unlawful police conduct. Absent a showing that officers obtained evidence expressly to enhance a sentence, a district judge may not refuse to consider relevant evidence at sentencing, even if that evidence has been seized in violation of the Fourth Amendment.

The *Tejada* court reached this result even though it recognized that the Sentencing Guidelines remove a great deal of judicial discretion from sentencing and, in drug cases, impose a sentence based in large part on the quantity of the drug associated with the defendant—including amounts not proven at trial. Even though "consideration of illegally seized evidence at sentencing is likely to result in increased penalties," the court found the exclusionary rule inapplicable.

Note that the *Tejada* court held that courts *must* consider illegally obtained evidence at sentencing. It reasoned that only a mandatory rule would provide the uniformity in sentencing envisioned by the Federal Sentencing Guidelines. Note also that the court provided an exception for cases in which officials obtain evidence expressly to enhance a sentence. Presumably these are cases in which application of the exclusionary rule would have some deterrent effect. But how do you know when an officer has conducted an illegal search expressly to enhance a sentence? Do you ask him?

Parole Revocation Proceedings

The Court held that illegally obtained evidence can be admitted in parole revocation proceedings in Pennsylvania Board of Probation and Parole v. Scott, 524 U.S. 357 (1998). This meant that Scott's parole could be revoked and he could be imprisoned on the basis of evidence uncovered in an illegal search, even though the evidence could not be used against Scott in a criminal trial.

Justice Thomas wrote the majority opinion for five members of the Court. Applying the standard "cost-benefit" analysis, Justice Thomas found that the cost of applying the exclusionary rule in parole revocation proceedings outweighed the benefits in deterrence of official misconduct. His "cost" argument proceeded as follows:

The costs of excluding reliable, probative evidence are particularly high in the context of parole revocation proceedings. Parole is a "variation on imprisonment of convicted criminals," Morrissey v. Brewer, 408 U.S. 471, 477 (1972), in which the State accords a limited degree of freedom in return for the parolee's assurance that he will comply with the often strict terms and conditions of his release. In most cases, the State is willing to extend parole only because it is able to condition it upon compliance with certain requirements. The State thus has an "overwhelming interest" in ensuring that a parolee complies with those requirements and is returned to prison if he fails to do so. The exclusion of evidence establishing a parole violation, however, hampers the State's ability to ensure compliance with these conditions by permitting the parolee to avoid the consequences of his noncompliance. The costs of allowing a parolee to avoid the consequences of his violation are compounded by the fact that parolees (particularly those who have already committed parole violations) are more likely to commit future criminal offenses than are average citizens. * * *

The exclusionary rule, moreover, is incompatible with the traditionally flexible, administrative procedures of parole revocation. Because parole revocation deprives the parolee not "of the absolute liberty to which every citizen is entitled, but only of the conditional liberty properly dependent on observance of special parole restrictions," States have wide latitude under the Constitution to structure parole revocation proceedings. Most States * * * have adopted informal, administrative parole revocation procedures in order to accommodate the large number of parole proceedings. These proceedings generally are not conducted by judges, but instead by parole boards, members of which need not be judicial officers or lawyers. * * * Nor are these proceedings entirely adversarial, as they are designed to be predictive and discretionary as well as factfinding.

Application of the exclusionary rule would significantly alter this process. The exclusionary rule frequently requires extensive litigation to determine whether particular evidence must be excluded. Such litigation is inconsistent with the nonadversarial, administrative processes established by the States. Although States could adapt their parole revocation proceedings to accommodate such litigation, such a change would transform those proceedings from a predictive and discretionary effort to promote the best interests of both parolees and society into trial-like proceedings less attuned to the interests of the parolee. We are simply unwilling so to intrude into the States' correctional schemes. Such a transformation ultimately might disadvantage parolees because in an adversarial proceeding, "the hearing body may be less tolerant of marginal deviant behavior and feel more pressure to reincarcerate than to continue nonpunitive rehabilitation." And the financial costs of such a system could reduce the State's incentive to extend parole in the first place, as one of the purposes of parole is to reduce the costs of criminal punishment while maintaining a degree of supervision over the parolee.

The majority's "benefit" argument found little deterrence value to the exclusionary rule in the context of parole revocation proceedings:

The deterrence benefits of the exclusionary rule would not outweigh these costs. * * * [A]pplication of the exclusionary rule to parole revocation proceedings would have little deterrent effect upon an officer who is unaware that the subject of his search is a parolee. In that situation, the officer will likely be searching for evidence of criminal conduct with an eye toward the introduction of the evidence at a criminal trial. The likelihood that illegally obtained evidence will be excluded from trial provides deterrence against Fourth Amendment violations, and the remote possibility that the subject is a parolee and that the evidence may be admitted at a parole revocation proceeding surely has little, if any, effect on the officer's incentives.

Justice Thomas further rejected the lower court's position that the exclusionary rule should at least be applicable when the government official conducts an illegal search *for the specific purpose* of using illegally obtained evidence in the parole revocation proceeding, as opposed to a criminal trial. Despite the apparent deterrent effect of excluding the evidence in these circumstances, Justice Thomas was unpersuaded:

> We have never suggested that the exclusionary rule must apply in every circumstance in which it might provide marginal deterrence. Furthermore, such a piecemeal approach to the exclusionary rule would add an additional layer of collateral litigation regarding the officer's knowledge of the parolee's status.

> * * * Where the person conducting the search is a police officer, the officer's focus is not upon ensuring compliance with parole conditions or obtaining evidence for introduction at administrative proceedings, but upon obtaining convictions of those who commit crimes. The non-criminal parole proceeding "falls outside the offending officer's zone of primary interest." Thus, even when the officer knows that the subject of his search is a parolee, the officer will be deterred from violating Fourth Amendment rights by the application of the exclusionary rule to criminal trials.

> Even when the officer performing the search is a parole officer, the deterrence benefits of the exclusionary rule remain limited. Parole agents, in contrast to police officers, are not "engaged in the often competitive enterprise of ferreting out crime"; instead, their primary concern is whether their parolees should remain free on parole. Thus, their relationship with parolees is more supervisory than adversarial. * * * Although this relationship does not prevent parole officers from ever violating the Fourth Amendment rights of their parolees, it does mean that the harsh deterrent of exclusion is unwarranted, given such other deterrents as departmental training and discipline and the threat of damages actions.

Justice Stevens wrote a short dissenting opinion in *Scott*, emphasizing his continuing position that the Constitution requires exclusion of illegally obtained evidence. Justice Souter, joined by Justices Ginsburg and Breyer, took issue with the majority's assessment of the costs and benefits of the exclusionary rule in the parole revocation context. He argued that the costs of applying the exclusionary rule in parole revocation proceedings are certainly no greater than the costs of applying the rule in a criminal trial. As to the benefits of applying the rule, Justice Souter noted that the parole revocation proceeding often takes the place of a criminal trial, rendering it the only venue in which illegally obtained evidence would be used against a parolee, and consequently raising the deterrent value of exclusion. He reasoned as follows:

As to the benefit of an exclusionary rule in revocation proceedings, the majority does not see that in the investigation of criminal conduct by someone known to be on parole, Fourth Amendment standards will have very little deterrent sanction unless evidence offered for parole revocation is subject to suppression for unconstitutional conduct. * * * [P]arole revocation will frequently be pursued instead of prosecution as the course of choice, a fact recognized a quarter of a century ago when we observed in Morrissey v. Brewer that a parole revocation proceeding "is often preferred to a new prosecution because of the procedural ease of recommitting the individual on the basis of a lesser showing by the State."

The reasons for this tendency to skip any new prosecution are obvious. If the conduct in question is a crime in its own right, the odds of revocation are very high. Since time on the street before revocation is not subtracted from the balance of the sentence to be served on revocation, the balance may well be long enough to render recommitment the practical equivalent of a new sentence for a separate crime. And all of this may be accomplished without shouldering the burden of proof beyond a reasonable doubt; hence the obvious popularity of revocation in place of new prosecution.

The upshot is that without a suppression remedy in revocation proceedings, there will often be no influence capable of deterring Fourth Amendment violations when parole revocation is a possible response to new crime. Suppression in the revocation proceeding cannot be looked upon, then, as furnishing merely incremental or marginal deterrence over and above the effect of exclusion in criminal prosecution. Instead, it will commonly provide the only deterrence to unconstitutional conduct when the incarceration of parolees is sought, and the reasons that support the suppression remedy in prosecution therefore support it in parole revocation.

Question After Scott

The Court in *Scott* rejected exclusion even if it is apparent that the purposes of the illegal search was to obtain evidence to be used in a parole revocation proceeding. In light of this rejection, reconsider the Second Circuit's opinion in United States v. Tejada, supra, discussed in the section on sentencing proceedings. The *Tejada* court held that the exclusionary rule generally does not apply in sentencing proceedings, but that it would apply upon a showing "that officers obtained evidence expressly to enhance a sentence." Does this limited proviso survive the Court's analysis in *Scott*?

Forfeiture Proceedings

Forfeiture proceedings provide one exception to the Court's general rule that the exclusionary rule is inapplicable outside the criminal trial context. In One 1958 Plymouth Sedan v. Pennsylvania, 380 U.S. 693 (1965), the Court reasoned that if the exclusionary rule were inapplicable, the government would be obtaining a reward—the forfeiture of property—for carrying out an illegal search or seizure.

Note that *Plymouth Sedan* did not involve the forfeiture of contraband. If the government seizes contraband, there is no obligation to return it simply because it was illegally obtained. As the Court in *Plymouth Sedan* put it, "the express public policy against the possession of such objects" would be frustrated if the government were obligated to return contraband. The Court therefore held that the exclusionary rule is applicable only when the property is "not intrinsically illegal in character." See also United States v. Bagley, 899 F.2d 707 (8th Cir.1990)(convicted felon not entitled to return of guns illegally seized from him).

Finally, note that while illegally obtained non-contraband property cannot be used as evidence in the forfeiture proceeding, the government may still be able to prove through independent evidence that the illegally seized property is forfeitable. Forfeiture proceedings are not terminated merely because the government came by the property illegally, any more than criminal proceedings are terminated merely because the defendant was illegally arrested. See United States v. $191,910.00 in U.S. Currency, 16 F.3d 1051 (9th Cir.1994)(while an illegally seized res is subject to forfeiture, it may not be introduced as evidence in a forfeiture proceeding).

Other Proceedings

Certainly, there are arguments for holding the exclusionary rule inapplicable in some proceedings, sometimes even at trials. For example, in In re Diane P., 110 A.D.2d 354, 494 N.Y.S.2d 881 (1985), a 13–year–old girl went to the police and complained that her mother hit her with a broom. The officers went to the mother's apartment at 3 a.m. and did a warrantless search. They seized a broom and a shoe. These were offered not at a criminal trial but at a child protective proceeding. The court held that the exclusionary rule did not apply to child protective proceedings. It found that sufficient deterrence flowed from exclusion in a criminal prosecution, and that exclusion in a child protection proceeding would impose an extraordinary cost. Do you agree? See also Garrett v. Lehman, 751 F.2d 997 (9th Cir.1985)(exclusionary rule inapplicable to military discharge proceedings).

10.   Use of Illegally Obtained Evidence for Impeachment Purposes

Opening the Door on Direct Examination:
Walder v. United States

In Walder v. United States, 347 U.S. 62 (1954), Walder testified on direct examination in a trial on narcotics charges that he had never possessed or sold narcotics in his life. The Supreme Court held that he was properly impeached with evidence of heroin that had been illegally seized from his home in an earlier, unrelated case. The Court reasoned that Walder had "opened the door" to this evidence and that the exclusionary rule could not be used as a license for perjury.

Opening the Door on Cross–Examination:
United States v. Havens

United States v. Havens, 446 U.S. 620 (1980), extended the impeachment exception to the exclusionary rule that had been applied in *Walder*. Officers stopped McLeroth and Havens coming off a flight. They illegally searched Havens' suitcase and found a shirt from which the pocket had been torn out.

McLeroth was also searched, and officers found a pocket, matching the shirt found in Havens' bag, sewn into McLeroth's clothing. The officers found cocaine in the pocket. At his trial, Havens took the stand and denied being involved with McLeroth in the transportation of cocaine; he did not mention anything about the shirt or the pocket. On cross-examination, Havens was asked specifically whether he had been involved in sewing a pocket into McLeroth's clothing, and whether he had a shirt in his own suitcase from which that pocket had been torn out. Havens answered in the negative, and this testimony was impeached by introduction of the illegally seized shirt. The court of appeals held that the evidence was improperly admitted. It reasoned that *Walder* permitted impeachment only if the illegally obtained evidence contradicted the defendant's direct testimony, and that there was no such contradiction between the evidence and the direct testimony in this case—since Havens hadn't mentioned the shirt on direct.

But in a 5–4 decision written by Justice White, the Supreme Court held that illegally obtained evidence can be used to impeach the defendant's testimony no matter when it is elicited. Justice White argued that there was no difference of constitutional magnitude between impeachment of direct testimony and impeachment of testimony elicited on cross-examination, so long as the questions put to the defendant on cross-examination "are plainly within the scope" of the direct. He noted that a contrary rule would severely impede the normal function of cross-examination. Justice White concluded as follows:

> [T]he policies of the exclusionary rule no more bar impeachment here than they did in *Walder* * * *. [The incremental deterrence which occurs] by forbidding impeachment of the defendant who testifies was deemed [in *Walder*] insufficient to permit or require that false testimony go unchallenged, with the resulting impairment of the integrity of the fact-finding goals of the criminal trial. We reaffirm this assessment of the competing interests * * *.

Justice Brennan, joined by Justices Stewart, Marshall and Stevens, dissented. He complained that the majority had passed control of the impeachment exception to the government, "since the prosecutor can lay the predicate for admitting otherwise suppressible evidence with his own questioning." He argued that after *Havens,* a defendant who has been the victim of an illegal search will have to forego testifying on his own behalf, because it is impossible for the defendant to testify to anything on direct that would not open him up to impeachment through illegally obtained evidence on cross-examination.

The cost-benefit analysis as applied to the impeachment exception is argued as follows:

1) The officer is not motivated by a desire to obtain impeachment evidence, but rather by a desire to obtain substantive evidence of guilt; therefore exclusion of illegally obtained evidence when offered for impeachment purposes has minimal deterrent effect.

2) Against the minimal deterrence is the significant cost of excluding illegally obtained evidence for impeachment purposes; not only would the jury be deprived of reliable information, but the defendant would be able to commit perjury on the stand, secure in the knowledge that he is free from impeachment.

3) Therefore the costs of the rule outweigh the benefits in the impeachment context.

But does this analysis work when it is the defendant's testimony on cross-examination, rather than direct, that is being impeached?

Impeachment of Defense Witnesses: James v. Illinois

In James v. Illinois, 493 U.S. 307 (1990), the Court refused to extend the impeachment exception to allow impeachment of defense witnesses with illegally obtained evidence. James made a statement to police officers that he had changed his hair color and style the day after taking part in a shooting. The trial court suppressed this statement because it was the fruit of an arrest made without probable cause. Prosecution witnesses at trial identified James, though they admitted that his hair color at trial was different from that of the perpetrator at the time of the shooting. To rebut the identification testimony, James called a family friend, who testified that just before the shooting, James' hair color and style was the same as it was at trial. The trial court, relying on the impeachment exception to the exclusionary rule, allowed the prosecution to introduce James' suppressed statement to impeach the credibility of the defense witness.

The Supreme Court reversed in an opinion by Justice Brennan for five members of the Court. Justice Brennan found a compelling distinction between impeachment of a defendant's own testimony and that of defense witnesses. Despite his prior dissents on the impeachment exception, Justice Brennan argued that as applied to the defendant, the impeachment exception serves salutary purposes: it "penalizes defendants for committing perjury," and yet "leaves defendants free to testify truthfully on their own behalf." According to the Court, the impeachment exception keeps perjury out and allows truthful testimony in, thus furthering the search for truth.

In contrast, the Court found that expanding the impeachment exception to encompass the testimony of all defense witnesses would result in the loss of truthful testimony. Justice Brennan argued that the fear of impeachment of one's witnesses likely would discourage defendants from even presenting the testimony of others. He posited that the defendant could carefully limit his own truthful testimony to avoid reference to matters that could be impeached by illegally obtained evidence. But the defendant's witnesses could not be so easily controlled.

> Defendants might reasonably fear that one or more of their witnesses, in a position to offer truthful and favorable testimony, would also make some statement in sufficient tension with the tainted evidence to allow the prosecutor to introduce that evidence for impeachment * * *. As a result, an expanded impeachment exception likely would chill some defendants from calling witnesses who would otherwise offer probative evidence * * *.

> Given the potential chill created * * *, the conceded gains to the truthseeking process from discouraging or disclosing perjured testimony would be offset to some extent by the concomitant loss of probative witness testimony.

Justice Brennan also argued that impeachment was not needed to deter defense witnesses from offering perjurious testimony. Unlike the defendant, defense witnesses are sufficiently deterred by the threat of a perjury prosecution.

Justice Brennan concluded that the exclusionary rule would be robbed of significant deterrent effect if illegally obtained evidence could be used to impeach not only the defendant but the defendant's witnesses. He argued that illegally obtained evidence would have greater value to the government because it could be used to prevent defendants from calling witnesses to give truthful testimony. Justice Brennan asserted that a rule allowing impeachment of defense witnesses "would leave officers with little to lose and much to gain by overstepping constitutional limits on evidence gathering."

Justice Kennedy, joined by Chief Justice Rehnquist and Justices O'Connor and Scalia, dissented. The dissenters complained that the majority had granted the defendant "broad immunity to introduce whatever false testimony it can produce from the mouth of a friendly witness." Justice Kennedy was particularly concerned about the costs to the truthseeking process if defense witnesses could testify without fear of impeachment with probative though illegally obtained evidence. He argued that impeachment is even more vital for attacking untruthful testimony of a defense witness than it is for attacking the defendant's testimony:

> It is natural for jurors to be skeptical of self-serving testimony by the defendant. Testimony by a witness said to be independent has the greater potential to deceive. And if a defense witness can present false testimony with impunity, the jurors may find the rest of the prosecution's case suspect, for ineffective and artificial cross-examination will be viewed as a real weakness in the State's case. * * * The State must * * * suffer the introduction of false testimony and appear to bolster the falsehood by its own silence.

Justice Kennedy advocated a rule that illegally obtained evidence could be used to impeach defense witnesses, but only where there is a direct conflict between the evidence and the witness' testimony. According to Justice Kennedy, the requirement of a direct conflict would alleviate the majority's concern that the defendant would not present truthful witnesses for fear they would be impeached in virtually all cases.

The majority in *James* bases its decision on the assumption that the defendant can restrict his testimony to avoid impeachment, while the defendant's witnesses cannot be so controlled. After *Havens,* which allowed impeachment on cross-examination even though the direct testimony was carefully tailored to avoid any reference to the shirt, is it ever possible for the defendant to avoid impeachment with illegally obtained evidence? If not, isn't the majority's decision in *James* based on a faulty premise? Is Justice Brennan simply making the best of what he thinks is bad law? *James* is criticized in Note, The Pinocchio Defense Witness Impeachment Exception to the Exclusionary Rule: Combatting a Defendant's Right to Use with Impunity the Perjurious Testimony of Defense Witnesses, 1990 U.Ill.L.Rev. 375.

11. *Good Faith*

In the following case, the Court adopted a limited "good faith" exception for searches conducted pursuant to a warrant that is later found to be invalid. As you read the case, keep in mind that the Court is not promulgating an "absolute" exception. Rather, there are "exceptions to the exception," where a good faith argument will be rejected and the evidence excluded.[46]

UNITED STATES v. LEON

Supreme Court of the United States, 1984.
468 U.S. 897.

JUSTICE WHITE **delivered the opinion of the Court.**

This case presents the question whether the Fourth Amendment exclusionary rule should be modified so as not to bar the use in the prosecution's case-in-chief of evidence obtained by officers acting in reasonable reliance on a search warrant issued by a detached and neutral magistrate but ultimately found to be unsupported by probable cause. * * *

I

[On the basis of information from an informant and other investigation, Officer Rombach obtained a facially valid search warrant. The ensuing searches produced large quantities of drugs and related evidence that the government proffered against several alleged coconspirators.]

The respondents then filed motions to suppress the evidence seized pursuant to the warrant. The District Court held an evidentiary hearing and, while recognizing that the case was a close one, granted the motions to suppress in part. It concluded that the affidavit was insufficient to establish probable cause, but did not suppress all of the evidence as to all of the respondents because none of the respondents had standing to challenge all of the searches. In response to a request from the Government, the court made clear that Officer Rombach had acted in good faith, but it rejected the Government's suggestion that the Fourth Amendment exclusionary rule should not apply where evidence is seized in reasonable, good-faith reliance on a search warrant.

[The court of appeals affirmed the order of suppression, finding that Officer Rombach's affidavit failed to establish probable cause under the then-applicable *Spinelli* test. One court of appeals judge dissented from this ruling.]

The Government's petition for certiorari expressly declined to seek review of the lower courts' determinations that the search warrant was unsupported by probable cause and presented only the question "[w]hether the Fourth Amendment exclusionary rule should be modified so as not to bar the admission of evidence seized in reasonable, good-faith reliance on a search warrant that is subsequently held to be defective." We granted certiorari to consider the propriety of such a modification. Although it undoubtedly is within our power to consider the question whether probable cause existed under the "totality of the circumstances" test announced last Term in Illinois v. Gates, that question has not been briefed or argued; and it is also within our authority, which we choose to exercise, to take the case as it comes to us, accepting the Court of Appeals' conclusion that probable cause was lacking under the prevailing legal standards.

46. The companion case to *Leon*, Massachusetts v. Sheppard, is discussed in the Note following *Leon*.

We have concluded that, in the Fourth Amendment context, the exclusionary rule can be modified somewhat without jeopardizing its ability to perform its intended functions. Accordingly, we reverse the judgment of the Court of Appeals.

II

Language in opinions of this Court and of individual Justices has sometimes implied that the exclusionary rule is a necessary corollary of the Fourth Amendment, or that the rule is required by the conjunction of the Fourth and Fifth Amendments. These implications need not detain us long. The Fifth Amendment theory has not withstood critical analysis or the test of time, and the Fourth Amendment "has never been interpreted to proscribe the introduction of illegally seized evidence in all proceedings or against all persons."

A

The Fourth Amendment contains no provision expressly precluding the use of evidence obtained in violation of its commands, and an examination of its origin and purposes makes clear that the use of fruits of a past unlawful search or seizure "works no new Fourth Amendment wrong." The wrong condemned by the Amendment is "fully accomplished" by the unlawful search or seizure itself, and the exclusionary rule is neither intended nor able to "cure the invasion of the defendant's rights which he has already suffered." The rule thus operates as "a judicially created remedy designed to safeguard Fourth Amendment rights generally through its deterrent effect, rather than a personal constitutional right of the party aggrieved."

Whether the exclusionary sanction is appropriately imposed in a particular case, our decisions make clear, is "an issue separate from the question whether the Fourth Amendment rights of the party seeking to invoke the rule were violated by police conduct." Only the former question is currently before us, and it must be resolved by weighing the costs and benefits of preventing the use in the prosecution's case-in-chief of inherently trustworthy tangible evidence obtained in reliance on a search warrant issued by a detached and neutral magistrate that ultimately is found to be defective.

The substantial social costs exacted by the exclusionary rule for the vindication of Fourth Amendment rights have long been a source of concern. * * * An objectionable collateral consequence of this interference with the criminal justice system's truth-finding function is that some guilty defendants may go free or receive reduced sentences as a result of favorable plea bargains. Particularly when law enforcement officers have acted in objective good faith or their transgressions have been minor, the magnitude of the benefit conferred on such guilty defendants offends basic concepts of the criminal justice system. * * *

B

Close attention to those remedial objectives has characterized our recent decisions concerning the scope of the Fourth Amendment exclusionary rule.

[Justice White discusses some of the limitations that the Court has placed upon the exclusionary rule and notes that the Court had: confined the rule to criminal trials; required "standing" on the part of defendants who seek suppression; permitted impeachment use of illegally seized evidence; and allowed evidence to be admitted where its link to a violation is attenuated.]

As yet, we have not recognized any form of good-faith exception to the

Fourth Amendment exclusionary rule. But the balancing approach that has evolved during the years of experience with the rule provides strong support for the modification currently urged upon us. * * *

III

A

Because a search warrant provides the detached scrutiny of a neutral magistrate, which is a more reliable safeguard against improper searches than the hurried judgment of a law enforcement officer "engaged in the often competitive enterprise of ferreting out crime," we have expressed a strong preference for warrants and declared that "in a doubtful or marginal case a search under a warrant may be sustainable where without one it would fail." Reasonable minds frequently may differ on the question whether a particular affidavit establishes probable cause, and we have thus concluded that the preference for warrants is most appropriately effectuated by according "great deference" to a magistrate's determination.

* * *

* * * To the extent that proponents of exclusion rely on its behavioral effects on judges and magistrates in these areas, their reliance is misplaced. First, the exclusionary rule is designed to deter police misconduct rather than to punish the errors of judges and magistrates. Second, there exists no evidence suggesting that judges and magistrates are inclined to ignore or subvert the Fourth Amendment or that

lawlessness among these actors requires application of the extreme sanction of exclusion.

Third, and most important, we discern no basis, and are offered none, for believing that exclusion of evidence seized pursuant to a warrant will have a significant deterrent effect on the issuing judge or magistrate. * * * Judges and magistrates are not adjuncts to the law enforcement team; as neutral judicial officers, they have no stake in the outcome of particular criminal prosecutions. The threat of exclusion thus cannot be expected significantly to deter them. Imposition of the exclusionary sanction is not necessary to inform judicial officers of their errors, and we cannot conclude that admitting evidence obtained pursuant to a warrant while at the same time declaring that the warrant was somehow defective will in any way reduce judicial officers' professional incentives to comply with the Fourth Amendment, encourage them to repeat their mistakes, or lead to the granting of all colorable warrant requests.[a]

B

If exclusion of evidence obtained pursuant to a subsequently invalidated warrant is to have any deterrent effect, therefore, it must alter the behavior of individual law enforcement officers or the policies of their departments. One could argue that applying the exclusionary rule in cases where the police failed to demonstrate probable cause in the warrant application deters future inadequate presentations or

---

a. Limiting the application of the exclusionary sanction may well increase the care with which magistrates scrutinize warrant applications. We doubt that magistrates are more desirous of avoiding the exclusion of evidence obtained pursuant to warrants they have issued than of avoiding invasions of privacy.

Federal magistrates, moreover, are subject to the direct supervision of district courts. They may be removed for "incompetency, misconduct, neglect of duty, or physical or mental disability." 28 U.S.C.A. § 631(i). If a magistrate serves merely as a "rubber stamp" for the police or is unable to exercise mature judgment, closer supervision or removal provides a more effective remedy than the exclusionary rule.

"magistrate shopping" and thus promotes the ends of the Fourth Amendment. Suppressing evidence obtained pursuant to a technically defective warrant supported by probable cause also might encourage officers to scrutinize more closely the form of the warrant and to point out suspected judicial errors. We find such arguments speculative and conclude that suppression of evidence obtained pursuant to a warrant should be ordered only on a case-by-case basis and only in those unusual cases in which exclusion will further the purposes of the exclusionary rule.[b]

We have frequently questioned whether the exclusionary rule can have any deterrent effect when the offending officers acted in the objectively reasonable belief that their conduct did not violate the Fourth Amendment. * * * But even assuming that the rule effectively deters some police misconduct and provides incentives for the law enforcement profession as a whole to conduct itself in accord with the Fourth Amendment, it cannot be expected, and should not be applied, to deter objectively reasonable law enforcement activity. * * *[c]

This is particularly true, we believe, when an officer acting with objective good faith has obtained a search warrant from a judge or magistrate and acted within its scope. In most such cases, there is no police illegality and thus nothing to deter. It is the magistrate's responsibility to determine whether the officer's allegations establish probable cause and, if so, to issue a warrant comporting in form with the requirements of the Fourth Amendment. In the ordinary case, an officer cannot be expected to question the magistrate's probable cause determination or his judgment that the form of the warrant is technically sufficient. * * * Penalizing the officer for the magistrate's error, rather than his own, cannot logically contribute to the deterrence of Fourth Amendment violations.[d]

C

We conclude that the marginal or nonexistent benefits produced by suppressing evidence obtained in objectively reasonable reliance on a subsequently invalidated search warrant cannot justify the substantial costs of exclusion. We do not suggest, however, that exclusion is always inappropriate in cases where an officer has ob-

---

b. Our discussion of the deterrent effect of excluding evidence obtained in reasonable reliance on a subsequently invalidated warrant assumes, of course, that the officers properly executed the warrant and searched only those places and for those objects that it was reasonable to believe were covered by the warrant. * * *

c. We emphasize that the standard of reasonableness we adopt is an objective one. Many objections to a good-faith exception assume that the exception will turn on the subjective good faith of individual officers. "Grounding the modification in objective reasonableness, however, retains the value of the exclusionary rule as an incentive for the law enforcement profession as a whole to conduct themselves in accord with the Fourth Amendment." The objective standard we adopt, moreover, requires officers to have a reasonable knowledge of what the law prohibits.

d. To the extent that Justice Stevens' conclusions concerning the integrity of the courts, rest on a foundation other than his judgment, which we reject, concerning the effects of our decision on the deterrence of police illegality, we find his argument unpersuasive. "Judicial integrity clearly does not mean that the courts must never admit evidence obtained in violation of the Fourth Amendment." * * * Our cases establish that the question whether the use of illegally obtained evidence in judicial proceedings represents judicial participation in a Fourth Amendment violation and offends the integrity of the courts "is essentially the same as the inquiry into whether exclusion would serve a deterrent purpose. * * * The analysis showing that exclusion in this case has no demonstrated deterrent effect and is unlikely to have any significant such effect shows, by the same reasoning that the admission of the evidence is unlikely to encourage violations of the Fourth Amendment." * * *

tained a warrant and abided by its terms. * * * [T]he officer's reliance on the magistrate's probable-cause determination and on the technical sufficiency of the warrant he issues must be objectively reasonable, and it is clear that in some circumstances the officer[e] will have no reasonable grounds for believing that the warrant was properly issued.

Suppression therefore remains an appropriate remedy if the magistrate or judge in issuing a warrant was misled by information in an affidavit that the affiant knew was false or would have known was false except for his reckless disregard of the truth. The exception we recognize today will also not apply in cases where the issuing magistrate wholly abandoned his judicial role in the manner condemned in Lo–Ji Sales, Inc. v. New York [where the magistrate issued the warrant and then participated in the search]; in such circumstances, no reasonably well-trained officer should rely on the warrant. Nor would an officer manifest objective good faith in relying on a warrant based on an affidavit "so lacking in indicia of probable cause as to render official belief in its existence entirely unreasonable." Finally, depending on the circumstances of the particular case, a warrant may be so facially deficient—i.e., in failing to particularize the place to be searched or the things to be seized—that the executing officers cannot reasonably presume it to be valid.

In so limiting the suppression remedy, we leave untouched the probable-cause standard and the various requirements for a valid warrant. * * *

Nor are we persuaded that application of a good-faith exception to searches conducted pursuant to warrants will preclude review of the constitutionality of the search or seizure, deny needed guidance from the courts, or freeze Fourth Amendment law in its present state. * * *

If the resolution of a particular Fourth Amendment question is necessary to guide future action by law enforcement officers and magistrates, nothing will prevent reviewing courts from deciding that question before turning to the good-faith issue. Indeed, it frequently will be difficult to determine whether the officers acted reasonably without resolving the Fourth Amendment issue. Even if the Fourth Amendment question is not one of broad import, reviewing courts could decide in particular cases that magistrates under their supervision need to be informed of their errors and so evaluate the officers' good faith only after finding a violation. In other circumstances, those courts could reject suppression motions posing no important Fourth Amendment questions by turning immediately to a consideration of the officers' good faith. We have no reason to believe that our Fourth Amendment jurisprudence would suffer by allowing reviewing courts to exercise an informed discretion in making this choice. * * *

IV

When the principles we have enunciated today are applied to the facts of this case, it is apparent that the judgment of the Court of Appeals cannot stand. The Court of Appeals applied the prevailing legal standards to Offi-

e. References to "officer" throughout this opinion should not be read too narrowly. It is necessary to consider the objective reasonableness, not only of the officers who eventually executed a warrant, but also of the officers who originally obtained it or who provided information material to the probable-cause determina-

tion. Nothing in our opinion suggests, for example, that an officer could obtain a warrant on the basis of a "bare bones" affidavit and then rely on colleagues who are ignorant of the circumstances under which the warrant was obtained to conduct the search. See Whiteley v. Warden, 401 U.S. 560, 568 (1971).

cer Rombach's warrant application and concluded that the application could not support the magistrate's probable-cause determination. In so doing, the court clearly informed the magistrate that he had erred in issuing the challenged warrant. This aspect of the court's judgment is not under attack in this proceeding.

* * *

In the absence of an allegation that the magistrate abandoned his detached and neutral role, suppression is appropriate only if the officers were dishonest or reckless in preparing their affidavit or could not have harbored an objectively reasonable belief in the existence of probable cause. * * * Officer Rombach's application for a warrant clearly was supported by much more than a "bare bones" affidavit. The affidavit related the results of an extensive investigation and, as the opinions of the divided panel of the Court of Appeals make clear, provided evidence sufficient to create disagreement among thoughtful and competent judges as to the existence of probable cause. Under these circumstances, the officers' reliance on the magistrate's determination of probable cause was objectively reasonable, and application of the extreme sanction of exclusion is inappropriate.

Accordingly, the judgment of the Court of Appeals is

Reversed.

JUSTICE BLACKMUN, **concurring.**

* * * I believe that the rule announced today advances the legitimate interests of the criminal justice system without sacrificing the individual rights protected by the Fourth Amendment. I write separately, however, to underscore what I regard as the una-

voidably provisional nature of today's decisions.

* * *

* * * By their very nature, the assumptions on which we proceed today cannot be cast in stone. To the contrary, they now will be tested in the real world of state and federal law enforcement, and this Court will attend to the results. If it should emerge from experience that, contrary to our expectations, the good faith exception to the exclusionary rule results in a material change in police compliance with the Fourth Amendment, we shall have to reconsider what we have undertaken here. The logic of a decision that rests on untested predictions about police conduct demands no less.

* * *

JUSTICE BRENNAN, **with whom** JUSTICE MARSHALL **joins, dissenting.**[f]

* * *

I

* * *

At bottom, the Court's decision turns on the proposition that the exclusionary rule is merely a " 'judicially created remedy designed to safeguard Fourth Amendment rights generally through its deterrent effect, rather than a personal constitutional right.' " * * * The essence of this view * * * is that the sole "purpose of the Fourth Amendment is to prevent unreasonable governmental intrusions into the privacy of one's person, house, papers, or effects. The wrong condemned is the unjustified governmental invasion of these areas of an individual's life. That wrong * * * is *fully accomplished* by the original search without probable cause." * * * This view of the scope of the Amend-

---

f. The dissent addresses both *Leon* and the companion case, *Sheppard.*

ment relegates the judiciary to the periphery. * * * [T]he most the judge can do is wring his hands and hope that perhaps by excluding such evidence he can deter future transgressions by the police.

Such a reading appears plausible, because, as critics of the exclusionary rule never tire of repeating, the Fourth Amendment makes no express provision for the exclusion of evidence secured in violation of its commands. A short answer to this claim, of course, is that many of the Constitution's most vital imperatives are stated in general terms and the task of giving meaning to these precepts is therefore left to subsequent judicial decisionmaking. * * *

A more direct answer may be supplied by recognizing that the Amendment, like other provisions of the Bill of Rights, restrains the power of the government as a whole; * * *. The judiciary is responsible, no less than the executive, for ensuring that constitutional rights are respected.

* * * Because seizures are executed principally to secure evidence, and because such evidence generally has utility in our legal system only in the context of a trial supervised by a judge, it is apparent that the admission of illegally obtained evidence implicates the same constitutional concerns as the initial seizure of that evidence. Indeed, by admitting unlawfully seized evidence, the judiciary becomes a part of what is in fact a single governmental action prohibited by the terms of the Amendment. * * *

[I]f the Amendment is to have any meaning, police and the courts cannot be regarded as constitutional strangers to each other; because the evidence-gathering role of the police is directly linked to the evidence-admitting function of the courts, an individual's Fourth Amendment rights may be undermined as completely by one as by the other.

B

* * *

[T]he Court has frequently bewailed the "cost" of excluding reliable evidence. In large part, this criticism rests upon a refusal to acknowledge the function of the Fourth Amendment itself. If nothing else, the Amendment plainly operates to disable the government from gathering information and securing evidence in certain ways. * * * Thus, some criminals will go free *not*, in Justice (then Judge) Cardozo's misleading epigram, "because the constable has blundered," but rather because official compliance with Fourth Amendment requirements makes it more difficult to catch criminals. Understood in this way, the Amendment directly contemplates that some reliable and incriminating evidence will be lost to the government; therefore, it is not the exclusionary rule, but the Amendment itself that has imposed this cost.

* * * [T]he Court's decisions over the past decade have made plain that the entire enterprise of attempting to assess the benefits and costs of the exclusionary rule in various contexts is a virtually impossible task for the judiciary to perform honestly or accurately. Although the Court's language in those cases suggests that some specific empirical basis may support its analyses, the reality is that the Court's opinions represent inherently unstable compounds of intuition, hunches, and occasional pieces of partial and often inconclusive data. * * *

II

[Justice Brennan concluded that the warrant should not have issued in this case.]

III

Even if I were to accept the Court's general approach to the exclusionary rule, I could not agree with today's result. There is no question that in the hands of the present Court the deterrence rationale has proved to be a powerful tool for confining the scope of the rule. * * *

* * *

* * * The key to the Court's conclusion * * * is its belief that the prospective deterrent effect of the exclusionary rule operates only in those situations in which police officers, when deciding whether to go forward with some particular search, have reason to know that their planned conduct will violate the requirements of the Fourth Amendment. * * *

* * *

The flaw in the Court's argument, however, is that its logic captures only one comparatively minor element of the generally acknowledged deterrent purposes of the exclusionary rule. To be sure, the rule operates to some extent to deter future misconduct by individual officers who have had evidence suppressed in their own cases. But what the Court overlooks is that the deterrence rationale for the rule is not designed to be, nor should it be thought of as, a form of "punishment" of individual police officers for their failures to obey the restraints imposed by the Fourth Amendment. Instead, the chief deterrent function of the rule is its tendency to promote institutional compliance with Fourth Amendment requirements on the part of law enforcement agencies generally. * * *

If the overall educational effect of the exclusionary rule is considered, application of the rule to even those situations in which individual police officers have acted on the basis of a reasonable but mistaken belief that

their conduct was authorized can still be expected to have a considerable long-term deterrent effect. If evidence is consistently excluded in these circumstances, police departments will surely be prompted to instruct their officers to devote greater care and attention to providing sufficient information to establish probable cause when applying for a warrant, and to review with some attention the form of the warrant that they have been issued, rather than automatically assuming that whatever document the magistrate has signed will necessarily comport with Fourth Amendment requirements.

* * *

Although the Court brushes these concerns aside, a host of grave consequences can be expected to result from its decision to carve this new exception out of the exclusionary rule. A chief consequence of today's decision will be to convey a clear and unambiguous message to magistrates that their decisions to issue warrants are now insulated from subsequent judicial review. * * *

Moreover, the good faith exception will encourage police to provide only the bare minimum of information in future warrant applications. The police will now know that if they can secure a warrant, so long as the circumstances of its issuance are not "entirely unreasonable," all police conduct pursuant to that warrant will be protected from further judicial review. * * *

[E]ven if one were to believe, as the Court apparently does, that police are hobbled by inflexible and hypertechnical warrant procedures, today's decision cannot be justified. This is because, given the relaxed standard for assessing probable cause established just last Term in Illinois v. Gates, the Court's newly fashioned good faith exception, when applied in the warrant context, will rarely, if ever, offer any greater flexibility for police than the *Gates* standard already supplies. In *Gates,* the Court held that "the task of an issuing magistrate is simply to make a practical, common-sense decision whether, given all the circumstances set forth in the affidavit before him, * * * there is a fair probability that contraband or evidence of a crime will be found in a particular place." * * * Given such a relaxed standard, it is virtually inconceivable that a reviewing court, when faced with a defendant's motion to suppress, could first find that a warrant was invalid under the new *Gates* standard, but then, at the same time, find that a police officer's reliance on such an invalid warrant was nevertheless "objectively reasonable" under the test announced today. Because the two standards overlap so completely, it is unlikely that a warrant could be found invalid under *Gates* and yet the police reliance upon it could be seen as objectively reasonable; otherwise, we would have to entertain the mindboggling concept of objectively reasonable reliance upon an objectively unreasonable warrant.

This paradox * * * perhaps explains the Court's unwillingness to remand for reconsideration in light of *Gates,* for it is quite likely that on remand the Court of Appeals would find no violation of the Fourth Amendment, thereby demonstrating that the supposed need for the good faith exception in this context is more apparent than real. Therefore, although the Court's decisions are clearly limited to the situation in which police officers reasonably rely upon an apparently valid warrant in conducting a search, I am not at all confident that the exception unleashed today will remain so confined.

Indeed, the full impact of the Court's regrettable decision will not be felt until the Court attempts to extend this rule to situations in which the police have conducted a warrantless search solely on the basis of their own judgment about the existence of probable cause and exigent circumstances. When that question is finally posed, I for one will not be surprised if my colleagues decide once again that we simply cannot afford to protect Fourth Amendment rights.

* * *

JUSTICE STEVENS, concurring in the judgment in [*Sheppard*], and dissenting in [*Leon*].[g]

* * *

The Court assumes that the searches in these cases violated the Fourth Amendment, yet refuses to apply the exclusionary rule because the Court concludes that it was "reasonable" for the police to conduct them. In my opinion an official search and seizure cannot be both "unreasonable" and "reasonable" at the same time.

* * *

The notion that a police officer's reliance on a magistrate's warrant is automatically appropriate is one the Framers of the Fourth Amendment would have vehemently rejected. The precise problem that the Amendment was intended to address was *the unreasonable issuance of warrants.* As we have often observed, the Amendment was actually motivated by the practice of issuing general warrants—warrants which did not satisfy the particularity and probable cause requirements. * * *

* * *

g. Justice Stevens expressed the view that there was no constitutional violation in *Sheppard.*

Today's decisions do grave damage to [the exclusionary rule's] deterrent function. Under the majority's new rule, even when the police know their warrant application is probably insufficient, they retain an incentive to submit it to a magistrate, on the chance that he may take the bait. No longer must they hesitate and seek additional evidence in doubtful cases. * * *

* * * While, as the Court correctly notes, we have refused to apply the exclusionary rule to collateral contexts in which its marginal efficacy is questionable, until today every time the police have violated the applicable commands of the Fourth Amendment a court has been prepared to vindicate that Amendment by preventing the use of evidence so obtained in the prosecution's case-in-chief against those whose rights have been violated. Today, for the first time, this Court holds that although the Constitution has been violated, no court should do anything about it at any time and in any proceeding. In my judgment, the Constitution requires more. * * * Nor should we so easily concede the existence of a constitutional violation for which there is no remedy. To do so is to convert a Bill of *Rights* into an unenforced honor code that the police may follow in their discretion. The Constitution requires more; it requires a *remedy*. If the Court's new rule is to be followed, the Bill of Rights should be renamed.[h]

Questions About Leon

Recall the discussion in *Rakas*, where the Court declared that Fourth Amendment rights are personal rights—a person cannot invoke the exclusionary rule unless his personal rights are violated. Is this consistent with the Court's statements in *Leon* that the exclusionary rule serves only deterrence principles, and is not a personal right of the party aggrieved?

In *Leon,* the Court clearly holds that the exclusionary rule is not constitutionally required. Why then are the states required to exclude evidence? Has *Mapp* been overruled?

Note on Massachusetts v. Sheppard

Massachusetts v. Sheppard, 468 U.S. 981 (1984), is the companion case to *Leon*. In the course of a murder investigation in Roxbury, Officer O'Malley obtained probable cause to arrest Sheppard and to search his residence. Officer O'Malley's affidavit described in detail the property to be seized in the search of Sheppard's house, e.g., the victim's clothing. Detective O'Malley showed the affidavit to the district attorney, the district attorney's first assistant, and a sergeant, who all concluded that it set forth probable cause for the search and the arrest, and that a warrant based on the affidavit would particularly describe the things to be seized. The *Sheppard* Court described what happened next:

---

h. The Mississippi Supreme Court declined to adopt a good faith exception in Stringer v. State, 477 So.2d 1335 (Miss.1985). Relying on the state constitution, the court reasoned that "[t]he fundamental flaw in *Leon* is that its new 'insight'—that in the type of cases we are concerned with it is the issuing magistrate who violates the accused's Fourth Amendment rights, not the officer—suggests a *greater* need for the exclusionary rule, not a lesser one." It concluded that the exclusionary rule is "our only practicable means of getting the attention of issuing magistrates who disregard the rights of persons to be free of searches except under warrants issued upon probable cause."

People v. Bigelow, 66 N.Y.2d 417, 497 N.Y.S.2d 630, 488 N.E.2d 451 (1985), also rejects the good faith exception to the warrant requirement. Other state courts have followed *Leon*. See, e.g., Potts v. State, 300 Md. 567, 479 A.2d 1335 (1984).

Because it was Sunday, the local court was closed, and the police had a difficult time finding a warrant application form. Detective O'Malley finally found a warrant form previously in use in the Dorchester District. The form was entitled 'Search Warrant—Controlled Substance G.L. c. 276 §§ 1 through 3A.' Realizing that some changes had to be made before the form could be used to authorize the search requested in the affidavit, Detective O'Malley deleted the subtitle 'controlled substance' with a typewriter. He also substituted 'Roxbury' for the printed 'Dorchester' and typed Sheppard's name and address into blank spaces provided for that information. However, the reference to 'controlled substance' was not deleted in the portion of the form that constituted the warrant application and that, when signed, would constitute the warrant itself.

Detective O'Malley then took the affidavit and the warrant form to the residence of a judge who had consented to consider the warrant application. The judge examined the affidavit and stated that he would authorize the search as requested. Detective O'Malley offered the warrant form and stated that he knew the form as presented dealt with controlled substances. He showed the judge where he had crossed out the subtitles. After unsuccessfully searching for a more suitable form, the judge informed O'Malley that he would make the necessary changes so as to provide a proper search warrant. The judge then took the form, made some changes on it, and dated and signed the warrant. However, he did not change the substantive portion of the warrant, which continued to authorize a search for controlled substances; nor did he alter the form so as to incorporate the affidavit. The judge returned the affidavit and the warrant to O'Malley, informing him that the warrant was sufficient authority in form and content to carry out the search as requested. O'Malley took the two documents and, accompanied by other officers, proceeded to Sheppard's residence. The scope of the ensuing search was limited to the items listed in the affidavit, and several incriminating pieces of evidence were discovered. Sheppard was then charged with first degree murder.

The Court stated that "[t]here is no dispute that the officers believed that the warrant authorized the search that they conducted." The Court found that there was an objectively reasonable basis for the officers' mistaken belief. If an error of constitutional dimension was made, the Court found that it was the judge who made it, and the Court therefore declined to suppress the evidence. The Court concluded that the officers "took every step that could reasonably be expected of them," and that O'Malley was not required "to disbelieve a judge who has just advised him, by word and by action, that the warrant he possesses authorizes him to conduct the search he has requested." The Court refused to decide whether the warrant was in fact invalid for lack of particularity. It stated that this was "a fact-bound issue of little importance since similar situations are unlikely to arise with any regularity." Justice Stevens argued in his dissent that there was no error of constitutional dimension and therefore no need to suppress evidence.

For cases following *Sheppard*, see United States v. Kelley, 140 F.3d 596 (5th Cir.1998) (officers could reasonably rely on the warrant even though it was defective because the magistrate hadn't signed it:"The rare occasion when a magistrate accidentally fails to sign a warrant cannot be eliminated by suppressing the evidence" and "it is unlikely that police will wilfully and recklessly attempt to evade getting a warrant signed"); United States v. Russell, 960 F.2d 421 (5th Cir. 1992)(warrant fails to include an attachment of the items to be seized, but the officer specifically described the items in an affidavit; judge committed the "clerical error" of failing to incorporate the affidavit in the warrant); United States v. Maxwell, 920 F.2d 1028 (D.C.Cir.1990)(even though warrant did not incorporate the affidavit describing the property to be seized, the officer could reasonably believe that the scope of the warrant was limited to materials supporting the allegations in the affidavit).

Reasonable Reliance on Unreasonable Warrants

The *Leon* Court rejects a good faith test that would depend on the subjective state of mind of the officer. Instead, the Court establishes a concept of "reasonable" reliance on an invalid warrant. Does this make sense? Justice Stevens contends that it is impossible to rely reasonably on an unreasonable warrant. But, arguably, that is a simplistic conclusion. Reasonable minds can and often do differ as to what is reasonable. One person might think that a warrant is valid while two others might think it defective; certainly there could be a reasonable disagreement when it comes to Fourth Amendment standards that are sometimes ambiguous and fact-dependent. What the *Leon* Court appears to mean is that in cases where some or most people would think that a warrant is invalid—for lack of probable cause, or particularity, or other procedural details—the good faith exception will apply so long as reasonable minds can differ on the point. Where no reasonable argument can be made that the warrant is valid, then the good faith exception will not apply because no reasonable officer could rely on the magistrate's determination—it is at that point the officer's error in relying on the warrant, and officers can be deterred by the exclusionary rule.

Thus, the good faith exception is similar to the standard used for reviewing jury verdicts in civil cases—the standard is not whether the jury was correct or whether the reviewing court would have decided the case another way, but whether no reasonable person could have decided the way the jury did. So long as there is room for argument, then, the good faith exception will apply.

Another useful analogy comes from the qualified immunity cases decided under the civil rights statute, 42 U.S.C. § 1983. Even if the plaintiff's constitutional rights are violated, an official is not liable unless he violated clearly established law; if the law was not clearly established at the time of the officer's action, then there is room for argument as to whether the officer's conduct was lawful. The Supreme Court has equated the standards of qualified immunity with the objective reasonableness standard of the good faith exception to the exclusionary rule. See Anderson v. Creighton, 483 U.S. 635 (1987) (rejecting the argument that an officer may not reasonably act unreasonably). See also United States v. Baker, 894 F.2d 1144 (10th Cir.1990)(state officer who obtained a state search warrant located in Indian Country did not act in good faith in light of "clearly established law recognizing that such a warrant would be beyond the jurisdiction of the state court").

Because an officer can reasonably act unreasonably, there are three types of errors after *Leon:* (1) reasonable mistakes that are not a violation of the Fourth Amendment at all, such as a mistake of fact; (2) unreasonable mistakes that in fact violate the Fourth Amendment, but at the time of the conduct reasonable minds could have differed about whether the officer was acting lawfully; and (3) unreasonable mistakes where the officer violated clearly established law, so that no reasonable argument could be made that the action was lawful. Illinois v. Rodriguez, (discussed in the materials on third party consent), where the officers made a reasonable mistake concerning the authority of a third party to consent to a search, falls into the first category; *Leon* falls into the second; and reliance on a warrant issued on the basis of a barebones affidavit falls into the third.

Reasonable Search or Good Faith Exception: Maryland v. Garrison

As discussed above, there is a distinction to be made between a search that is reasonable despite an officer's mistake of fact and thus not a violation of the Fourth Amendment, and a search that is unreasonable but not so egregious as to warrant exclusion and thus is potentially within the good faith exception. In which category would you place Maryland v. Garrison, 480 U.S. 79 (1987)? Officers applied for a search warrant for a "third floor apartment" at a certain address. Utility records showed one bill being sent to the third floor at that address. There were seven apartments in the three story building. When the officers executed the warrant, they found one door on the third floor corridor. Inside the door was a foyer, and two open doorways led off from that. Officers went in each direction from the foyer, and it was not until they discovered a kitchen in each direction that they realized that they were searching two separate apartments. The Court held that the search warrant authorizing the search of the entire third floor, rather than a particular apartment, was valid when issued, because it was reasonable, though erroneous, to assume that there was only one apartment on that floor. The Court also found that the execution of the warrant up until the time the error was discovered was valid because "the officers' failure to realize the overbreadth of the warrant was objectively understandable and reasonable." The majority opinion was written by Justice Stevens, who dissented in *Leon*. Some have argued that the Court in *Garrison* applied the good faith exception to the exclusionary rule. See Note, Maryland v. Garrison, Extending the Good Faith Exception to Warrantless Searches, 40 Baylor L.Rev. 151 (1988). Do you agree?

Leon, Gates and Warrants Clearly Lacking in Probable Cause

In Justice Brennan's view, the good faith standard and the *Gates* standard for probable cause overlap completely, so that if a warrant is invalid under *Gates* it must be so deficient, so clearly lacking in probable cause, that it could not possibly be reasonably relied upon. This view has not been adopted by the courts after *Leon*, however. There are a number of cases in which courts have found the good faith exception applicable because reasonable minds could differ about whether the *Gates* standards were satisfied. These cases indicate that there is some grey area between the *Gates* standard and a warrant that clearly lacks probable cause. See, e.g., United States v. Johnson, 78 F.3d 1258 (8th Cir.1996) (officer was objectively reasonable in relying on a warrant even though the warrant was based on a tip from an anonymous caller that was not very strongly corroborated—this was close enough to provide a reasonable argument that the *Gates* standard was satisfied); United States v. Gibson, 928 F.2d 250 (8th Cir.1991)(*Gates* standard not satisfied because police only corroborated a few "innocent details," but good faith exception applies because reasonable minds could differ on whether *Gates* standard is satisfied on such minimal corroboration); United States v. Brunette, 256 F.3d 14 (1st Cir. 2001) (it was error for the magistrate to issue a warrant to search for internet child pornography where the magistrate relied solely on the officer's conclusion that the pictures posted by the defendant were pornographic; however, "although we hold that the omission of images or a description of them was a serious defect in the warrant application, the uncertain state of the law at the time made reliance on the warrant objectively reasonable.").

There are a fair number of cases in which probable cause is found lacking under *Gates*, and the court further finds that the officer was *not* objectively reasonable in relying on the warrant. See United States v. Weaver, 99 F.3d 1372 (6th Cir.1996) (barebones affidavit using boilerplate language, with no corroboration of the informant's assertions, cannot be relied upon in objective good faith); United States v. Baxter, 889 F.2d 731 (6th Cir.1989)(affidavit describing tip from anonymous informant, with corroboration only of defendant's address and prior conviction on drug charges, is a barebones affidavit, and officer was not objectively reasonable in relying on the warrant); United States v. Leake, 998 F.2d 1359 (6th Cir.1993)(warrant was defective where officer could not corroborate informant's statement that drugs were in the defendant's house: "Officer Murphy could not properly have placed objective good faith reliance on the warrant in light of his knowledge that corroboration was needed, and that none, of any significance, was obtained."); United States v. Helton, 314 F.3d 812 (6th Cir. 2003) ("A reasonable officer knows that evidence of three calls a month to known drug dealers from a house, a description of that house, and an allegation that a drug dealer stores drug proceeds with his bother and his brother's girlfriend (neither of whom live at or are known to visit that house) falls well short of establishing probable cause that the house contains evidence of a crime.").

For an example of reliance on the good faith exception when a warrant is lacking in probable cause, see United States v. Savoca, 761 F.2d 292 (6th Cir.1985). The court summarized the affidavit supporting a warrant for a search of a hotel room in Phoenix as follows:

> The affidavit, when read in a common sense and realistic fashion, indicated that (1) FBI agents in Phoenix had just arrested Thomas Savoca and James Carey pursuant to federal arrest warrants for a bank robbery which took place in Austinburg, Ohio at an unspecified prior date, (2) the two suspects had been seen in Room 135 on two prior occasions, and (3) the two suspects were allegedly responsible for several other bank robberies in northeast Ohio and northwest Pennsylvania.

Although the court had originally held that the affidavit failed to establish probable cause for a search of the hotel room in Phoenix, it concluded in light of *Leon* that a reasonably well-trained police officer who was reasonably aware of applicable judicial decisions might not have concluded that the warrant was invalid. A dissenting judge argued that "the warrant was based on an affidavit so lacking in indicia of probable cause as to render official belief in its existence entirely unreasonable." Who has the better of the argument?

Leon and Overbroad Warrants

Applying the *Leon* framework to particularity questions, it would appear that the good faith exception would apply to a search pursuant to an overbroad warrant, so long as reasonable minds could differ about whether the warrant is in fact overbroad. On the other hand, if all reasonable people would agree that the warrant is overbroad, then the officer cannot reasonably rely upon it.

United States v. Dahlman, 13 F.3d 1391 (10th Cir.1993), is an example of *Leon*-applicability. Officers searching for narcotics obtained a warrant to search two "lots" in a subdivision. As conducted, the search encompassed a camping trailer and a cabin on one of the lots, as well as the lots themselves. The court found that the warrant was defective as applied to the cabin: "a warrant authorizing the search of a lot of land without a more precise definition of the scope of the search is inconsistent with the particularity requirement of the Fourth Amendment, and does not suffice to authorize a search of a residence located on the land." Still, the court held that the evidence obtained in the cabin was admissible under the good faith exception. It noted that two other circuits had held similar warrants to be sufficiently particular, and therefore that reasonable minds could differ about whether the warrant was in fact overbroad.

In contrast, some cases have found a warrant to be so overbroad that it could not reasonably be relied upon. In United States v. Fuccillo, 808 F.2d 173 (1st Cir.1987), officers searched a clothing warehouse and retail clothing store, with search warrants authorizing the seizure of "women's clothing" believed to be stolen. They seized virtually all the clothing found at each of the premises (including men's clothing). The court ruled that the warrants were insufficiently particular, since the officers "could have obtained specific information for presentment to the magistrate and placement in the warrant which would have enabled the agents [executing the warrants] to differentiate contraband cartons of women's clothing from legitimate ones." In fact the officers had a detailed list of the stolen clothing, but they failed to include it in the warrant application. The court further held that the good faith exception could not justify the searches and seizures. It reasoned that the officers were "reckless in not including in the affidavit information which was known or easily accessible to them," and that the warrant was so overbroad that the executing officers could not reasonably presume it to be valid. See also United States v. Stubbs, 873 F.2d 210 (9th Cir.1989) (good faith exception unavailable where warrant authorizes seizure of virtually all business documents, and probable cause existed as to only one transaction).

Leon and Untrue or Omitted Statements in the Warrant Application

An exception to the good faith exception arises if the officer includes material information in the application that he "knew was false or would have known was false except for his reckless disregard of the truth." *Leon.* Exclusion also applies if the officer knowingly omits material information that would have resulted in the magistrate's refusing to issue the warrant. The good faith exception cannot apply in these instances because the error is the officer's not the magistrate's. Determining whether the officer has made such an error is sometimes difficult, however.

Consider United States v. Johnson, 78 F.3d 1258 (8th Cir.1996). A police officer received a call from an anonymous informant who stated that he had been present when marijuana had been delivered to Johnson's residence. The officer verified Johnson's address and discovered that Johnson had been arrested previously for marijuana possession. The officer then prepared an affidavit to obtain a search warrant of Johnson's address. The affidavit for search warrant had a printed form attached, Attachment B. This form had a section relating to whether the informant was anonymous or confidential, and a section with four printed reasons why the informant is reliable. The officer checked two reasons why the anonymous caller was reliable: "C. Information he has supplied has been corroborated by law enforcement personnel." and "D. He has not given false information in the past." The warrant was issued and a search turned up drugs. The government conceded that the tip was too conclusory and the corroboration too thin to support probable cause under *Gates*; but the government argued that the information provided was close enough that reasonable minds could differ about whether the *Gates* standards were satisfied.

Because the officer had corroborated at least some part of the informant's tip as asserted in the warrant application, the question was whether the officer had knowingly or recklessly disregarded the truth in checking the line stating that the informant had not given false information in the past. The Court held that the officer's assertion did not trigger the "officer misrepresentation" exception to *Leon*. The court reasoned as follows:

> The officer took the literal view of the phrase that the caller had not given false information in the past even though this was the informant's first call. We do not believe that checking this statement rises to the level of making a false statement knowingly or intentionally or with a reckless disregard for the truth. * * * [W]e do not subject law enforcement officers to absolute syllogistic precision.

Judge Arnold, in dissent, disagreed and argued that the affidavit was deceptive and outside the realm of *Leon* good faith:

> This is hardly a matter of requiring law enforcement officers to observe "syllogistic precision". It is, rather, a matter of common ordinary speech. A statement that an informant had not previously given false information is clearly calculated to influence the magistrate to whom the application for warrant was to be submitted. The statement could hardly have been other than deliberate. To read the statement absolutely literally seems disingenuous to me, and certainly not the way one would understand the statement under the circumstances. At the very least, it could have been explained that the informant had not, to the officers' knowledge, given false information in the past, for the simple reason that the officers, so far as they knew, had never heard from this particular informant before. For this reason, it seems to me that the affidavit falls clearly within one of the exceptions to the *Leon* "good faith" rule, and that the motion to suppress should have been granted.

Why did the form affidavit have a "fill in the blank" for whether the informant had ever given *false* information in the past? Why wasn't the issue phrased as whether the informant had ever given *truthful* information in the past? Isn't that the important question under *Gates*? If it is the form itself that is deceptive, should *Leon* apply?

For a case in which *Leon* was found inapplicable due to officer misrepresentations in the warrant application, see United States v. Vigeant, 176 F.3d 565 (1st Cir.1999). Officers filed a detailed affidavit, based in large part on a tip from a confidential informant (CI) alleging that Vigeant was engaged in money-laundering resulting from sales of drugs. Among the allegations was that Vigeant was unemployed, and yet had purchased a "pleasure boat"—the inference being that he must have done so with laundered funds. One problem with the case, however, was that Vigeant filed a proper Currency Transaction Report (CTR) for each of his financial transactions, and made no attempt to disguise the electronic or paper trail of any transaction. The court reviewed the affidavit and found it insufficient to establish probable cause; it also found the good faith exception inapplicable due to the various misrepresentations and omissions in the affidavit. It elaborated as follows:

We believe this is a case in which excluding the evidence will have a substantial deterrent effect on the police. Our conclusion rests on the fact that a finding of good faith is inconsistent with the numerous material omissions excluded from—and false and misleading statements included in—the underlying affidavit. * * * Officer Botelho's numerous omissions of material facts were at least reckless. An enumeration of Botelho's omissions follows.

First, and most important, Botelho neglected to mention the CI's long criminal history, his numerous aliases, his recent plea agreement, and other indicia of his unreliability. Second, Botelho failed to note that Vigeant had filed the necessary CTR, yet Botelho included in the affidavit such minute details about the transaction as that it involved "small bills"—a fact he presumably obtained from the CTR. Filing a CTR, like failing to "structure" the transaction to avoid the reporting requirement, is evidence manifestly inconsistent with money laundering. Third, Botelho mentioned an additional deposit by cashier's check, but neglected to say that Vigeant's grandmother, who was above suspicion in this case, was the purchaser of the check. Fourth, Botelho could have (but did not) obtain Vigeant's employment status from the probation office, apparently deciding instead to infer (without informing the magistrate that he had done so) Vigeant's present unemployment from a blank space marked "current employment" on a two-year-old bank application. Fifth, Botelho stated that "the evidence indicates that Robert Vigeant has created front companies," which implies the existence of underlying evidence not disclosed. Such evidence did not, in fact, exist. Sixth, the government failed to note that the supposed "pleasure boat" mentioned in the affidavit was, in fact, a stripped-down craft in poor condition in need of considerable repair and refurbishing before it could be sold at a profit. Seventh, the affidavit implies that the CI personally witnessed a marijuana transaction and personally received $10,000; neither is true. According to the contemporaneous DEA Report of Investigation on which the affidavit was based, the CI in fact said that Vigeant gave Vigneau approximately $4,000, which Vigneau then gave to the CI. The CI does not report witnessing an exchange of marijuana.

The government offers no rational explanation for these omissions and foundationless conclusions. Instead, the government argues in its brief—with information obtained after the search in question—that Vigeant is a bad person. Be that as it may, even unsavory persons have constitutional rights. We conclude that a reasonable officer in Botelho's position—that is, in possession of the omitted information—would have known that he should not have applied for the warrant, at least not without further investigation.

See also United States v. Zimmerman, 277 F.3d 426 (3rd Cir. 2002) ("Good faith is not a magic lamp for police officers to rub whenever they find themselves in trouble.").

Leon and the Abdicating Magistrate

The Supreme Court denied review over the dissent of Justice Brennan, joined by Justice Marshall, in McCommon v. Mississippi, 474 U.S. 984 (1985), a case involving the candid suppression hearing testimony of a state court "judge" who had issued a search warrant. The judge testified that "if Sheriff Jones walked in there and said, 'Judge, I need a Search Warrant to search John Doe for Marijuana,' or drugs or whatever—liquor or whatever it might be, I'm going to go on his word because he's—I take him to be an honest law enforcement officer and he needs my help to get in to search these places and it's my duty to help him fulfill that." Justice Brennan wrote that he found "the Court's refusal to take this case particularly disturbing in light of the good faith exception to the Fourth Amendment exclusionary rule created by United States v. Leon." See also United States v. Breckenridge, 782 F.2d 1317 (5th Cir.1986), where the court held that the good faith exception applied even though the judge who issued the warrant never read the officer's affidavit. The court reasoned that the officer could reasonably rely on the warrant because, while the judge did not read the affidavit, he "appeared to Agent Alexander to be doing so."

United States v. Decker, 956 F.2d 773 (8th Cir.1992), is a rare case in which the court held that Leon could not apply because the magistrate abdicated his neutral and detached role. Agents subjected a suspicious-looking UPS package to a canine sniff, and the dog positively alerted to drugs. The agents then made a controlled delivery, and followed the package to Decker's house. Decker was arrested when he received the package. A search of his person revealed a small amount of narcotics. An agent prepared an affidavit setting forth these facts and applying for permission to seize narcotics at Decker's house. The magistrate issued a warrant to search Decker's house, but the warrant failed to list any items to be seized other than the UPS package, which was already in the possession of the agents. The search warrant was a standard form relating to stolen property, not to drugs, and referred to the UPS package as "unlawfully stolen." The magistrate later admitted that the flaws in the warrant were his fault and attributed these errors "to the fact that he was intrigued by the manner in which Agent Hicks became suspicious of the package and the ensuing investigation and therefore did not focus on the language of the warrant." Pursuant to the warrant, the officers seized more than 300 items from Decker's house, including a clock radio, two lamps, a microwave oven, and a weed eater. The court found that the magistrate signed the warrant without reading it, that he acted as "a rubber stamp," and that the agents could not reasonably rely on the warrant. So the evidence had to be suppressed.

The Teaching Function

Whether the good faith rule permits police and magistrates too much free reign may well depend on whether appellate courts provide guidance as to what is acceptable and unacceptable. The concern of the dissenters in Leon was that appellate courts will routinely refuse to decide Fourth Amendment questions about the validity of a warrant, preferring instead to reach the easier holding that the officer was not totally unreasonable in relying on a magistrate's determination. There is some indication in the cases decided after *Leon* that the lower courts are doing what the dissenters thought they would do—i.e., they are avoiding decisions about substantive Fourth Amendment law and ruling instead on the easier question of good faith. For example, in United States v. Henderson, 746 F.2d 619 (9th Cir.1984), defendants convicted of drug offenses challenged an order authorizing beeper surveillance. Rather than rule on whether the order was valid, the court sustained the search by citing *Leon* and relying upon the good faith of the agents. Thus, in future cases, the agents have no guidance as to the validity of similar orders. Presumably, officers continue to act in good faith until a similar order actually is invalidated. Likewise, in United States v. Tedford, 875 F.2d 446 (5th Cir.1989), the court bypassed a probable cause question and proceeded directly to the issue of good faith. The court stated that the probable cause issue was fact-bound, and resolution would not provide important guidance on Fourth Amendment limitations.

Indeed, the Fifth Circuit has gone so far as to state that a court must *first* decide whether the good-faith exception applies, thus effectively pretermitting any questions of substantive Fourth Amendment law. United States v. Kleinebreil, 966 F.2d 945 (5th Cir.1992).

In United States v. Cancelmo, 64 F.3d 804 (2d Cir.1995), a warrant was issued on the basis of intercepted conversations between Cancelmo and a known narcotics dealer. The conversations contained nothing facially incriminating. For example, one conversation was about "chimneys" and another about "decks"—and both Cancelmo and the dealer were in the construction business. The affiants asserted, on the basis of their expertise, that Cancelmo was using code words for a drug transaction. A warrant was issued, drugs were found, and Cancelmo moved to suppress on the ground that probable cause cannot be found solely on the basis of an officer's interpretation that facially innocent conversations are actually coded drug-related conversations.

The *Cancelmo* court noted that it could be problematic to rest a probable cause determination solely on an officer's interpretation of a conversation, because the magistrate would be relying "solely on the opinion of an agent as to the true meaning of facially innocent words." However, the court ultimately used *Leon* as a bail-out:

> [A]lthough we are skeptical of the government's claim that probable cause existed, we need not resolve the close legal question presented. In a case such as this one, a reasonably well-trained agent could not be expected to know that the warrant issued" by the magistrate was invalid. Given that the issue presented is sufficiently difficult as to create disagreement among thoughtful and competent judges, we decline to hold that the agents acted unreasonably in accepting the magistrate's legal conclusion that probable cause existed. Requiring suppression in this case would disserve the deterrent function of the exclusionary rule.

Judge Calabresi concurred in *Cancelmo*. He agreed that the question was close enough that the officers had not acted unreasonably in relying on the warrant, and therefore *Leon* applied. He accused the majority, however, of abdicating the teaching function that the Court in *Leon* had bestowed on the lower courts.

Courts of appeals are the final deciders of the law in the vast majority of cases of this sort. This means that we owe a duty to define the boundaries of probable cause, so that affiants submitting applications for warrants, issuing magistrates, reviewing courts, and the executing officers on whose good faith we rely may have appropriate guidance. And these boundaries are best set, not by abstract statements, but by case-by-case decisions in real situations.

In this case, there was no probable cause. The supposedly coded conversations are fully consistent with the conduct of legitimate business. Cancelmo was employed in construction, and conversations about decks and chimneys are natural for one in that line of work. The idea that the parties were talking in code rests on very little more than a prejudgment, not itself based on probable cause, that since one of the parties was, on reliable information, a drug dealer, they had to be talking about drugs. * * * In the absence of evidence that more directly tied Cancelmo, and not the person with whom he was speaking, to drug-related activity, it was improper for the magistrate to issue a warrant in reliance on the intercepted phone calls.

Despite the general trend to avoid Fourth Amendment questions after *Leon*, there are some courts that have taken their teaching function seriously. Illustrative is United States v. Dahlman, 13 F.3d 1391 (10th Cir.1993), discussed above. In *Dahlman*, the court held that a warrant authorizing the search of a certain "lot", without mentioning a residence, was insufficiently particular to justify a search of the residence. Then the court found that the good faith exception applied to the search of the residence, because the law on particularity, as applied to the search of a "lot", was unsettled at the time of the search. The court had this to say about the teaching function after *Leon*:

This court could have simply affirmed the trial court on the good faith issue without first discussing the underlying Fourth Amendment issue, i.e., the validity of the warrant. Indeed, the rule set forth in *Leon* concerning the sequential order of analysis in good faith cases is primarily one of discretion. However, a close reading of *Leon* reveals that, while the Supreme Court intended to vest lower courts with discretion, the preferred sequence is to address the Fourth Amendment issues before turning to the good faith issue unless there is no danger of "freezing" Fourth Amendment jurisprudence or unless the case poses "no important Fourth Amendment questions."

The soundness of this practice is apparent from examining the facts of the case before us today. In this case, the officers acted in good faith because they relied on a warrant issued by a neutral magistrate and the officers genuinely believed that the word "lot" and the boilerplate language in the warrant allowed them to search the residence. This belief was reasonable in part because this practice had not been ruled unconstitutional prior to today. If we were to have avoided addressing the underlying Fourth Amendment question today, a magistrate could legitimately issue an identical warrant tomorrow and the officers could engage in the same conduct without consequence—since there would be no adverse ruling to guide the magistrate or the officers, the warrant would be issued and the search would once again be valid under principles of good faith. In effect, Fourth Amendment jurisprudence would be frozen on this issue because of this never-ending cycle. Thus, the policy of avoiding "freezing" Fourth Amendment jurisprudence, discussed by the Court in *Leon*, compels us in this case to resolve the constitutional issue so that magistrates and law enforcement officers do not continue to make the same mistake indefinitely.

Once a court, such as in *Dahlman*, declares a particular practice illegal, an officer who thereafter engages in the conduct is acting unreasonably, and the good faith exception will not apply. See United States v. Buck, 813 F.2d 588 (2d Cir.1987), where the court held that a warrant with a catch-all clause was insufficiently particular, but nonetheless applied the good faith exception because "what the officers failed to do was to anticipate our holding today that the particularity clause of the Fourth Amendment prohibits the use of a catch-all description in a search warrant, unaccompanied by any list of particular items or any other limiting language." However, the court stated in a footnote that "with respect to searches conducted hereafter, police officers may no longer invoke the reasonable-reliance exception to the exclusionary rule when they attempt to introduce as evidence the fruits of searches undertaken on the basis of warrants containing only a catch-all description of the property to be seized." And the court was true to its word. In United States v. George, 975 F.2d 72 (2d Cir.1992), the court invalidated a warrant similar to that in *Buck*, and refused to apply the good faith exception "in light of the settled nature of the law."

Exclusion for Bad Faith Searches?

Professor Burkoff, in Bad Faith Searches, 57 N.Y.U.L.Rev. 70 (1982), argues for a "bad faith" extension to the exclusionary rule. He proposes exclusion of evidence if the officer intended to violate the Fourth Amendment, even though the officer's conduct turned out to be objectively reasonable. So for example, if an officer thought he was searching a home without probable cause, evidence discovered in the search would be excluded even though probable cause in fact existed. Recall the discussion on pretext, supra. Do you think courts would be receptive to a bad faith extension? What problems of proof would it present? See United States v. George, 971 F.2d 1113 (4th Cir.1992)(lower court erred in suppressing evidence because officer acted in bad faith; the "inquiry into the subjective motivations of the officers was irrelevant to the applicability of *Leon*").

Thomas and Pollack, in Balancing the Fourth Amendment Scales: The Bad Faith "Exception" to Exclusionary Rule Limitations, 45 Hastings L.J.21 (1993), take a somewhat different approach. They argue that the exceptions to the exclusionary rule—e.g., impeachment, independent source, etc. should not apply if the officer has acted in bad faith. Thus, they do not argue that an officer's bad faith should turn an otherwise legal search into an illegal one. Rather, they contend that if there is a Fourth Amendment violation, the bad faith nature of that violation should result in an "expanded exclusionary rule." Does this position deal any more effectively with the Court's insistence on an objective approach to the Fourth Amendment?

12.   The Good Faith Exception and Warrantless Searches

The Court in *Leon* applied the good faith exception because an officer reasonably relied on the magistrate's decision. The Court reasoned that the magistrate, rather than the officer, made the error, and that magistrates cannot be deterred by the exclusionary rule. An important question is whether this reasoning can be applied to excuse illegal but "good faith," objectively reasonable searches *without a warrant*. In two cases after *Leon*, the Court extended the good faith exception to certain warrantless searches; but in each of the cases the officer was relying, as in *Leon*, on a person or entity whose mistakes, in the Court's view, could not be deterred by applying the exclusionary rule.

Reasonable Reliance on Legislative Acts: Illinois v. Krull

Leon was held to be controlling in Illinois v. Krull, 480 U.S. 340 (1987). Illinois had enacted a statute authorizing warrantless searches by state officials to inspect the records of dealers in motor vehicles, automobile parts, or automobile scrap metal. Officers searched Krull's premises without a warrant, under the authority of the statute. But after the search, the statute was found by the state court to be unconstitutional. The question for the Supreme Court was whether the good faith exception should apply, because the statute had not yet been invalidated at the time of the search.

Justice Blackmun's majority opinion reasoned that, as in *Leon*, the presence of an intermediary upon whom the officer could reasonably rely meant that the officer could not be deterred by the exclusionary rule. The error was that of the legislature that passed an unconstitutional law. Justice Blackmun concluded that a legislature could not be deterred from passing unconstitutional laws by application of the exclusionary rule, because legislators enact statutes for "broad programmatic purposes, not for the purpose of procuring evidence in particular criminal investigations." And the officer, who is subject to the deterrent effect of the rule, had done nothing wrong in reasonably relying on the legislative act.

The *Krull* Court decided, as in *Leon*, that a good faith claim must have an objective basis, so that "[a] statute cannot support objectively reasonable reliance if, in passing the statute, the legislature wholly abandoned its responsibility to enact constitutional laws," and "a law enforcement officer [cannot] be said to have acted in good-faith reliance upon a statute if its provisions are such that a reasonable officer should have known that the statute was unconstitutional." But neither of these exceptions were applicable to the facts of the case.

Justice O'Connor, joined by Justices Brennan, Marshall and Stevens, dissented. She distinguished legislators from magistrates, finding that "[t]he judicial role is particularized, fact-specific and nonpolitical," and argued that "[p]roviding legislatures a grace period during which the police may freely perform unreasonable searches in order to convict those who might have otherwise escaped creates a positive incentive to promulgate unconstitutional laws."

Clerical Errors and Reliance on Court Clerical Personnel: Arizona v. Evans

The Court continued to adhere to the *Leon* framework in Arizona v. Evans, 514 U.S. 1 (1995), a case that arose from a clerical error. Evans was stopped for a traffic violation. The officer entered Evans' name in a computer data terminal, and the computer inquiry indicated that there was an outstanding misdemeanor warrant for Evans' arrest. On the basis of that information, the officer arrested Evans, and in a search incident to the arrest, the officer found marijuana. Subsequently, it was discovered that the arrest warrant had been quashed well before Evans had been stopped by the officer, but that an entry to that effect had never been made in the computer records of outstanding warrants. Although no specific finding was made below, the Supreme Court assumed that the error was caused by court clerical personnel who, contrary to standard procedure, never called the Sheriff's office with notification that Evans' arrest warrant had been quashed.

Chief Justice Rehnquist, writing for a seven-person majority, held that the critical analysis under "the *Leon* framework" was whether the government official who makes a mistake that leads to an illegal search or seizure can be deterred by operation of the exclusionary rule. Applying this reasoning to errors of court clerical personnel, the Chief Justice stated as follows:

> If court employees were responsible for the erroneous computer record, the exclusion of evidence at trial would not sufficiently deter future errors so as to warrant such a severe sanction [as exclusion]. First, as we noted in *Leon*, the exclusionary rule was historically designed as a means of deterring police misconduct, not mistakes by court employees. Second, respondent offers no evidence that court employees are inclined to ignore or subvert the Fourth Amendment or that lawlessness among these actors requires application of the extreme sanction of exclusion. * * *

> Finally, and most important, there is no basis for believing that application of the exclusionary rule in these circumstances will have a significant effect on court employees responsible for informing the police that a warrant has been quashed. Because court clerks are not adjuncts to the law enforcement team engaged in the often competitive enterprise of ferreting out crime, they have no stake in the outcome of particular criminal prosecutions. The threat of exclusion of evidence could not be expected to deter such individuals from failing to inform police officials that a warrant had been quashed.

The next question under the *Leon* framework is whether application of the exclusionary rule would deter misconduct of police officers where the initial mistake was made by a different government official. The Chief Justice concluded that officers could not be deterred when they reasonably rely on erroneous computer records prepared and maintained by court clerical personnel:

> If it were indeed a court clerk who was responsible for the erroneous entry on the police computer, application of the exclusionary rule * * * could not be expected to alter the behavior of the arresting officer. As the trial court in this case stated: "I think the police officer [was] bound to arrest. I think he would [have been] derelict in his duty if he failed to arrest." * * * There is no indication that the arresting officer was not acting objectively reasonably when he relied upon the police computer record. Application of the *Leon* framework supports a categorical exception to the exclusionary rule for clerical errors of court employees.

Justice O'Connor, joined by Justices Souter and Breyer, wrote a concurring opinion emphasizing that the Court had not decided whether the good faith exception should apply if the computer error was caused by police personnel rather than court personnel. She also stated that the exclusionary rule should be applicable if police officers rely on a court recordkeeping system that is known to be rife with error. She elaborated as follows:

[T]he Court does not hold that the court employee's mistake in this case was necessarily the only error that may have occurred and to which the exclusionary rule might apply. While the police were innocent of the court employee's mistake, they may or may not have acted reasonably in their reliance on the recordkeeping system itself. Surely it would not be reasonable for the police to rely, say, on a recordkeeping system, their own or some other agency's, that has no mechanism to ensure its accuracy over time and that routinely leads to false arrests, even years after the probable cause for any such arrest has ceased to exist (if it ever existed).

In recent years, we have witnessed the advent of powerful, computer-based recordkeeping systems that facilitate arrests in ways that have never before been possible. The police, of course, are entitled to enjoy the substantial advantages this technology confers. They may not, however, rely on it blindly. With the benefits of more efficient law enforcement mechanisms comes the burden of corresponding constitutional responsibilities.

Justice Souter, joined by Justice Breyer, wrote a separate, short concurring opinion in which he left open the possibility that the exclusionary rule might be necessary as a last resort to combat erroneous computerized recordkeeping by non-police personnel. Justice Souter stated:

[W]e do not answer another question that may reach us in due course, that is, how far, in dealing with fruits of computerized error, our very concept of deterrence by exclusion of evidence should extend to the government as a whole, not merely the police, on the ground that there would otherwise be no reasonable expectation of keeping the number of resulting false arrests within an acceptable minimum limit.

Relying on Justice O'Connor's dissent in *Krull*, Justice Stevens dissented from the Court's opinion in *Evans*. Justice Stevens argued that even if deterrence is the sole basis for the exclusionary rule—a point with which he disagreed—the rationale of *Leon* could not apply to excuse errors of court clerical personnel that lead to illegal searches. He contended that court clerical personnel often "work in the same building with police officers and may have more regular and direct contact with police than with judges or magistrates." Justice Stevens expressed concern that the Court had not sufficiently considered the threat to the privacy of citizens that is presented by computerization and computer error. He found it "outrageous" for a citizen to be "arrested, handcuffed, and searched on a public street simply because some bureaucrat has failed to maintain an accurate computer data base."

Justice Ginsburg wrote a separate dissent that was joined by Justice Stevens. She argued that the Arizona Court had sufficiently relied on state law in excluding the evidence, and that the Supreme Court should therefore not have taken the case. While expressing no final view on the merits of the exclusionary rule question, Justice Ginsburg did note her concern with the risk to privacy that could result from errors in computer entries. She explained the scope of the problem in the following passage:

Widespread reliance on computers to store and convey information generates, along with manifold benefits, new possibilities of error, due to both computer malfunctions and operator mistakes. Most germane to this case, computerization greatly amplifies an error's effect, and correspondingly intensifies the need for prompt correction; for inaccurate data can infect not only one agency, but the many agencies that share access to the database. The computerized databases of the FBI's National Crime Information Center (NCIC), to take a conspicuous example, contain over 23 million records, identifying, among other things, persons and vehicles sought by law enforcement agencies nationwide. NCIC information is available to approximately 71,000 federal, state, and local agencies. Thus, any mistake entered into the NCIC spreads nationwide in an instant.

* * * Evans' case is not idiosyncratic. Rogan v. Los Angeles, 668 F.Supp. 1384 (C.D.Cal.1987), similarly indicates the problem. There, the Los Angeles Police Department, in 1982, had entered into the NCIC computer an arrest warrant for a man suspected of robbery and murder. Because the suspect had been impersonating Terry Dean Rogan, the arrest warrant erroneously named Rogan. Compounding the error, the Los Angeles Police Department had failed to include a description of the suspect's physical characteristics. During the next two years, this incorrect and incomplete information caused Rogan to be arrested four times, three times at gunpoint, after stops for minor traffic infractions in Michigan and Oklahoma.

Justice Ginsburg concluded that, in light of the enormity and relative recency of the problem arising from illegal searches based on computer error, the Court should have dismissed the grant of certiorari and allowed the issue to be developed and argued throughout the lower courts.

Good Faith Reliance on Court Decisions

So far, the Supreme Court has applied the good faith exception only where the officer is reasonably relying on an intermediary. But there is another intermediary that an officer relies upon, and that is the Court itself. If the officer relies on the law established by the Court at the time of the conduct, and the conduct is later found to be unconstitutional by the Supreme Court (as in *Chimel,* which overruled *Rabinowitz,* or as in *Katz,* which overruled *Olmstead*), should the good faith exception apply to admit the evidence? In these circumstances, the officer has not made an error; and the Court, which has made the error that it has now corrected, can hardly be considered deterrable by the exclusionary rule.

However, if the good faith exception applies to police activity that was lawful under Court precedent at the time, what does that do to the retroactivity doctrine? In Griffith v. Kentucky, 479 U.S. 314 (1987), discussed in Chapter One, the Court held that decisions overruling prior law must apply retroactively to all cases on direct review. Wouldn't application of the good faith exception to a change of law mean that Fourth Amendment law would be applied only prospectively? Is the argument that the *law* applies retroactively, but the *remedy* applies prospectively, very comforting? See United States v. Butz, 982 F.2d 1378 (9th Cir.1993)(applying the good faith exception to conduct arising before case law declared it unconstitutional, and therefore finding it unnecessary to determine whether the case law applies retroactively). If the good faith exception applies to changes of law, what incentive does a defendant have for arguing that the Court should reconsider one of its prior decisions? See United States v. Richardson, 848 F.2d 509 (5th Cir.1988)(good faith exception applied where searches were conducted in accordance with the law "as then reflected by our decisions" even though these decisions have since been overruled).

Good Faith Where the Officer Is at Fault?

The Supreme Court has not addressed the question whether the good faith exception applies to warrantless actions by police, where an officer is not relying on any intermediary, but only upon his or her own mistaken judgment.[47] If the exception is held not to apply to warrantless activity where an officer has miscalculated on whether a warrant is required, then the warrant clause of the Fourth Amendment might benefit from the Court's recognition of the good faith exception. Police will have an incentive to seek a warrant in doubtful cases, in order to obtain the benefit of the good faith exception.

Hasn't the Court in *Leon*, *Krull* and *Evans* painted itself into a corner by holding that while intermediary officials (such as magistrates and legislators) cannot be deterred by the exclusionary rule, an officer in the competitive enterprise of ferreting out crime *can* be deterred? How could the Court then turn around and say that officers cannot be deterred by the exclusionary rule when they wrongly, but reasonably, interpret Fourth Amendment law?

The consequences of extending the good faith exception to warrantless searches can be seen in the Fifth Circuit, where the exception has been applied to all searches and seizures since the court's en banc decision in United States v. Williams, 622 F.2d 830 (5th Cir.1980). The case of United States v. De Leon—Reyna, 930 F.2d 396 (5th Cir.1991), provides a good example of the difficulties inherent in applying the exception. An officer suspected the defendant of carrying drugs in his truck, but he had no probable cause or reasonable suspicion to support this belief. He took down the license plate number of the truck the defendant was driving and radioed it to the dispatcher. The officer relayed the number "WM–1438" to the dispatcher, but did not follow unit policy requiring the use of code words for communicating license plate letters. The dispatcher misunderstood the officer to say "WN–1438" and radioed back that the license check had (not surprisingly) revealed that the plates were issued to a different truck than the truck that the defendant was driving. On the basis of the dispatcher's information, the officer stopped the truck and found cocaine. The district court and a panel of the Fifth Circuit found that the officer had acted negligently in failing to use a well-accepted and simple method by which mistaken stops could be avoided, and held that the good faith exception could not apply to acts of negligence. On review en banc, the court reversed, concluding that even if negligent, the officer's "good faith reliance on the license report information * * * was objectively reasonable." The court reasoned that the failure to use code words does not mean that "*all* communications * * * are *wholly* unreliable." In dissent, Judge Thornberry objected to the application of the good faith exception to warrantless searches.

If a mistake is made by someone other than the law enforcement officer [as in *Leon* and *Krull*], it is possible for the officer to be reasonable in believing that he is justified in stopping a defendant even though the basis for his suspicions is not objectively reasonable, but when the officer is also the one who made the mistake, the reasonableness required by the good faith exception is analytically identical to the reasonableness required by the

---

47. Arguments against applying the good faith exception to warrantless conduct can be found in Greenhalgh, The Warrantless Good Faith Exception: Unprecedented, Indefensible, and Devoid of Necessity, 26 S.Tex.L.J. 129 (1985).

Fourth Amendment. Adding a good faith analysis to a Fourth Amendment analysis contributes nothing but confusion.

Does the result in *De Leon–Reyna* create any possibilities for abuse? Does the exclusionary rule deter officers from engaging in illegal conduct when reasonable minds can differ about whether the conduct was illegal?

Other courts have not been hesitant to apply the exclusionary rule to "good faith" errors by police officers. An example is United States v. Lopez–Soto, 205 F.3d 1101 (9th Cir. 2000). An officer stopped the defendant with a Baja California license plate. The vehicle had no registration sticker visible from the rear. The officer had been told at the police academy that this was a violation of the Baja California vehicle code, and that vehicles from Baja could therefore be stopped and ticketed for not having a registration sticker on the back. The police academy information was in error, however. In fact, the applicable Baja California code section directs that the registration sticker be displayed on the windshield. Thus, the officer stopped the vehicle on a mistaken, but "good faith" view of the law. In making the stop, the officer discovered marijuana in the car.

The court held that the exclusionary rule applied, rejecting the officer's "good faith" argument:

> We have no doubt that Officer Hill held his mistaken view of the law in good faith, but there is no good-faith exception to the exclusionary rule for police who do not act in accordance with the governing law. To create an exception here would defeat the purpose of the exclusionary rule, for it would remove the incentive for police to make certain that they properly understand the law that they are entrusted to enforce and obey.

13.   *Alternatives to Exclusion*

The most common argument in support of the exclusionary rule is the alleged absence of alternative means of enforcing Fourth Amendment protections. The efficacy of the alternatives are, however, as hotly debated as the rule itself. In this section, other possible remedies will be evaluated, both in terms of deterrent value and workability.

The most frequently cited replacements for the rule are damage remedies, criminal prosecution of the offending officers, and internal police discipline. It should be noted at the outset that any of these remedies could be used as *supplements* to rather than replacements for suppression of evidence. If effective as deterrents, these supplements might reduce the frequency with which the exclusionary rule must be relied upon.

Limitations of Current Tort Recovery

At present several forms of damage actions are available to the victim of an illegal search or seizure. Common law tort actions include false arrest, false imprisonment and trespass. In addition, a civil rights action under 42 U.S.C.A. § 1983 is available when state officers, acting under color of law, violate a constitutional right. In Bivens v. Six Unknown Named Agents of Federal Bureau of Narcotics, 403 U.S. 388 (1971), the Supreme Court created a federal common law counterpart to § 1983 for violations by federal officials. Chief Justice Burger dissented and proposed a legislative remedy that would replace the exclusionary rule. Features of the proposal would include waiver of sovereign immunity as to illegal acts committed in the performance of assigned duties, and the creation of a statutory right on the part of aggrieved persons to proceed against the government before a quasi-judicial body.

Tort remedies have seldom been invoked in the past 150 years for Fourth Amendment violations. The two major problems involved in a tort action against police are first, winning, and second, collecting on the judgment. Obstacles such as governmental immunity exist in many states. Magistrates who issue invalid warrants are immune from suit. Pierson v. Ray, 386 U.S. 547, 553–55 (1967). Police officers exercising discretion are entitled to qualified immunity, so that even if they violate the Fourth Amendment, the citizen does not recover unless the law was clearly established at the time of the conduct.[48] How much Fourth Amendment law can be considered clearly established?

Besides the daunting prospect of overcoming qualified immunity, the "moral aspects of the case" make recovery in a jury trial difficult. Many victims of illegal police practices are not very sympathetic plaintiffs. In a false arrest action, for example, proof of the plaintiff's prior convictions often can be used to impeach his credibility or to show that probable cause existed for the arrest. "Respectable" persons have the greatest chance of recovering, because they will not be tainted by their past, but the "respectable" person is probably least likely to be subject to arbitrary arrest and harassment, and thus least likely to require a tort remedy.

If a plaintiff succeeds in proving liability, the next obstacle is proving—and collecting—damages adequate to cover the costs of the suit. In a trespass action, where damages are limited to actual property loss, the award is usually small except in the most extreme search cases. Nominal damages provide no incentive for an aggrieved citizen to sue, and thus prevent private persons from effectively enforcing the public policy against police illegality. A § 1983 action, which provides for attorney fees for the prevailing party, avoids some of the drawbacks of common law tort remedies. However, proof of the requisite intent and measuring the value of constitutional rights impose additional problems.

If the plaintiff receives a substantial damage award, the final problem is collecting on the judgment. Where sovereign immunity prevents actions against the government, a plaintiff is left to attempt recovery from the offending officers, who are often unable to pay. In § 1983 actions, the governmental unit

---

48. In Malley v. Briggs, 475 U.S. 335 (1986), the Court adopted the good faith standard it had established in *Leon* in the context of liability of officers who seek a warrant without having probable cause. Justice White's opinion for the Court states that the question to be asked is "whether a reasonably well-trained officer * * * would have known that his affidavit failed to establish probable cause and that he should not have applied for the warrant." The opinion observes that "[i]t is true that in an ideal system an unreasonable request for a warrant would be harmless, because no judge would approve it," but that "ours is not an ideal system, and it is possible that a magistrate, working under docket pressures, will fail to perform as a magistrate should."

The Court specifically held in Anderson v. Creighton, 483 U.S. 635 (1987), that the qualified immunity doctrine applied to police officers who commit Fourth Amendment violations. The case arose when an FBI agent searched the Creightons' home without a warrant in the unsuccessful attempt to find a robbery suspect.

Justice Scalia wrote for the Court as it held that the officer is entitled to summary judgment on qualified immunity grounds if he can establish as a matter of law that a reasonable officer could have believed that the search comported with the Fourth Amendment, even though it did not. He rejected the Creightons' argument that qualified immunity should only protect reasonable official action and that an unreasonable search under the Fourth Amendment cannot be reasonable official action.

employing the officer is not liable simply because one of its officers has violated the plaintiff's Fourth Amendment rights. In order to hold the government entity liable, the plaintiff must show that his injury resulted from the entity's custom or policy; otherwise the plaintiff is left to recover against the individual officer. Monell v. Department of Social Services, 436 U.S. 658 (1978)(applying the custom or policy requirement for municipal liability in § 1983 actions).

Fortified Tort Remedy

Professor Amar, in Fourth Amendment First Principles, 107 Harv.L.Rev.757 (1994), recommends five steps that would strengthen the deterrent effects of the tort remedy. He contends that if these steps are employed, the damages remedy will provide effective deterrence against illegal police activity; the exclusionary rule can then be abolished. First, the government should be made liable for illegal police behavior. Not only would this provide a financially responsible defendant, but it would apply the deterrent at the level where policy is made. Second, damage multipliers and punitive damages should be made available— with some of the excess recovery going to a "Fourth Amendment Fund to educate Americans about the Amendment and comfort victims of crime and police brutality." Third, claims for small damage amounts should be entitled to reasonable attorney's fees and the possibility of class action consolidation. Fourth, the procedural limitations on injunctive relief for Fourth Amendment violations should be liberalized. Fifth, administrative channels should be established so that claims can be processed quickly and efficiently without the need for a court action.

Would this fortified tort remedy be more effective than the exclusionary rule? Does it make more sense than the exclusionary rule because it potentially provides compensation to innocent people, whereas the exclusionary rule can by definition be invoked only by guilty people?

Is it possible to argue that one of the costs of the exclusionary rule is that it results in judicial cutbacks on the Fourth Amendment's substantive protections? Do courts, when they see the consequences of exclusion of evidence, tend to hold that there is no Fourth Amendment violation under the circumstances? Would the courts be more prone to find Fourth Amendment violations if the only consequence was a monetary remedy, as opposed to allowing a guilty person to go free?

The Senate Proposal

Senator Hatch has often proposed legislation that would abrogate the exclusionary rule and replace it with a fortified tort remedy. As of yet, no such proposal has been enacted. In its typical form, the tort proposal provides that the United States shall be liable for damages resulting from an illegal search or seizure of an investigative or law enforcement officer. Punitive damages are capped at $10,000; awards to anyone convicted of an offense in which the illegally obtained evidence was used are, however, limited to damages for actual physical injury and property damage; and attorney's fees and costs are awarded to claimants who prevail.

The Committee on Federal Legislation of the Association of the Bar of the City of New York had this to say about the Hatch Proposal, which at the time was proposed as Senate Bill 3:

We believe that S. 3 might be worthy of consideration if the damage caps were lifted; a substantial liquidated damages provision were available as an option for the plaintiff; and reasonable attorney fees were guaranteed to prevailing plaintiffs. In the absence of these provisions, the tort remedy will not provide sufficient incentive to sue for constitutional violations. Correspondingly, it would not provide sufficient deterrence of police misconduct. And it would result in freezing Fourth Amendment law in its current state, because if cases are not brought, courts cannot interpret and develop the law of the Fourth Amendment.

Yet even if a tort remedy could be fashioned that would result in meaningful monetary recovery for the victims of Fourth Amendment violations, we would object to it as a replacement for (rather than a supplement to) the exclusionary rule. The tort remedy is based upon the premise that Fourth Amendment rights can and should be left to the marketplace—that the government can make an economic decision to violate a person's Fourth Amendment rights, so long as it is willing to pay its way out of it. We do not believe that Fourth Amendment rights are susceptible to such a market analysis. * * *

* * * We find it troubling that the government could establish a budget line for Fourth Amendment violations as part of its war on crime. It cannot be the case that a Fourth Amendment violation is truly remedied simply because the government cuts a check.

Finally, we fail to see how the proposed tort remedy can deter police misconduct, even presuming that claims are successfully brought against the government. The exclusionary rule operates directly upon law enforcement agencies, because illegal searches and seizures are rendered inefficient and wasteful. With a tort remedy, law enforcement agencies do not pay for violations of the Fourth Amendment. Rather, it is the citizens who pay, by way of a government budget line. * * * Given government compartmentalization, it is extremely unlikely that budgetary authorities could put meaningful pressure on law enforcement authorities to comply with the Fourth Amendment.

Proposed Changes to the Exclusionary Rule, 50 The Record of the Association of the Bar of the City of New York 385 (1995).

Does Congress even have the power under the Constitution to abrogate the exclusionary rule and replace it with another remedy?

Criminal Prosecutions

Criminal prosecution of offending officers is often suggested as the only real deterrent to police misconduct. A federal statute has been in existence since 1921 that makes federal officers who participate in illegal searches guilty of a misdemeanor and subject to substantial fines. 18 U.S.C.A. § 2236. To our knowledge, however, no officer has ever been convicted under the statute. Many states have similar statutes which remain dormant. A fair number of criminal actions have been brought under state and federal law for actions of police officers that have resulted in death or serious injury of persons who are arrested. The cases involving the beatings of Rodney King and Abner Louima are examples. But again, few criminal prosecutions are brought against police officers who simply make illegal searches.

Why has there been such a dearth of prosecutions? The most likely answer is that prosecutors are reluctant to press charges against the police, except in the most extreme cases involving physical injury, because they rely heavily on cooperation with the department. In addition, juries are reluctant to convict policemen of crime, unless the circumstances are egregious.

More fundamentally, it can be argued that the threat of a direct criminal sanction on the officer who conducts an illegal search is an over-deterrent. It may lead to an officer "second-guessing" himself in fast-developing situations, in such a way that effective law enforcement would be hindered and public safety endangered. Isn't the systemic deterrence provided by the exclusionary rule more appropriate in these circumstances?

Police Rulemaking and Other Administrative Solutions

A third alternative remedy for Fourth Amendment violations is police regulation and discipline. This model emphasizes the development of respect by officers for constitutional rights, rather than compensation of individual victims. These goals can be achieved through a number of processes: internal disciplinary measures, civilian review boards, or "rulemaking."

Internal discipline, while probably the preferred remedy among police administrators, has not yet proved an effective deterrent. In a study of the Chicago Police Department, J.E. Spiotto found that disciplinary action was taken against officers primarily for corrupt practices. Spiotto, An Empirical Study of the Exclusionary Rule and its Alternatives, 2 J. Legal Studies 243 (1973). Insofar as illegal searches are concerned, suspension or dismissal were used almost exclusively in cases where officers failed to inventory all they seized. A search that was neither brutal nor outrageous would not result in disciplinary action, even if a citizen's complaint was filed. In part, this was a reflection of the Department's view that the exclusionary rule was the mechanism for punishing overzealous searches. But it could also be indicative of what several commentators have found to be the fundamental flaw of using internal disciplinary processes to deter illegal searches: Much of the illegality occurs in the normal scope of police activity and is subtly condoned by administrators and prosecutors who ignore violations as a matter of practice.

These same aspects of bureaucratic organization and personality tend to limit the effectiveness of citizen review boards as watchdogs of Fourth Amendment rights. Like police disciplinary committees, the review boards deal primarily with police corruption and brutality, or other outrageous police conduct. They have neither the time nor the resources to investigate routine illegal searches. Furthermore, the hostility and distrust with which these boards are often viewed by police make it unlikely that any action they take would significantly influence police attitudes.

Another proposal that warrants consideration is the adoption of a constitutional requirement of "rulemaking." Rulemaking involves the publication of regulations and standards to govern the scope of searches and seizures. The rules could be formulated by either legislative or police committees, but the essence of the proposal is that the articulated standards are open to community scrutiny and input. The rules would necessarily meet all Fourth Amendment requirements and would be subject to judicial review. Promotions would be contingent on an officer's record of conformance to regulations.

The doctrinal and practical advantages of requiring rulemaking are discussed in Amsterdam, Perspectives on the Fourth Amendment, 58 Minn.L.Rev. 349 (1974). Amsterdam argues that rulemaking provides a safeguard against arbitrary search and seizure without requiring the creation of new exceptions to the warrant requirement. It allows for flexibility and local autonomy, and permits the Court to extend Fourth Amendment coverage to police activities which demand control against abuse, but do not lend themselves to regulation by warrants or probable cause standards—e.g., border searches and driver's license checks.

Amsterdam maintains that rulemaking also improves police performance. It enhances the quality of police decisions by focusing attention on the importance of making policy, rather than on case-by-case, after-the-fact line-drawing. Police actions are made fairer and more consistent because the rulemaking process, being subject to community scrutiny, is less influenced by bias than discretionary decisions by individual officers at the scene of a crime.

Rulemaking also increases the visibility of police policy decisions. Amsterdam concludes that the process offers the best possibility for changing police attitudes toward constitutional liberties because police-made rules are most likely to be understood, enforced and obeyed by the police.

Does rulemaking provide the answer to the problem of deterring illegal searches and seizures? If underlying attitudes remain the same, will rulemaking be seen as something other than an attempt to limit the power of the police? If the proposal successfully changed the attitudes of the public and the police, would the exclusionary rule still be necessary, or would internal discipline do the job?

Chapter Three

SELF–INCRIMINATION AND CONFESSIONS

I. THE PRIVILEGE AGAINST COMPELLED SELF–INCRIMINATION

A. THE POLICIES OF THE PRIVILEGE AGAINST COMPELLED SELF–INCRIMINATION

1. *The Need to Examine Policies*

The Fifth Amendment provides that no person "shall be compelled in any criminal case to be a witness against himself * * *." Judge Friendly pointed out the need for careful examination of this privilege in his oft-cited article, The Fifth Amendment Tomorrow: The Case For Constitutional Change, 37 U.Cin.L.Rev. 679–81, 698 (1968):

> Reexamination of the policies of the privilege is not a task undertaken with alacrity. * * * But it is indispensable to any reconsideration of the proper scope of the fifth amendment and peculiarly necessary because of the extent to which eloquent phrases have been accepted as a substitute for thorough thought. It is still true, as Bentham wrote 140 years ago, that the main obstacle to rational discussion of the privilege is
>
> > the *assumption of the propriety of the rule,* as a proposition too plainly true to admit of dispute * * *. By assuming it as true, you * * * represent all men * * * whose opinions are worth regarding, as joining in the opinion; and by this means * * * you present * * * the fear of incurring the indignation or contempt of all reasonable men, by presuming to disbelieve or doubt what all such reasonable men are assured of.
>
> A good way to start dissipating the lyricism now generally accompanying any reference to the privilege is to note how exceptional it is in the general setting of jurisprudence and morality. While it carries the burden of impeding ascertainment of the truth that is common to all testimonial privileges, it has uncommon burdens as well. Most other privileges, for example, communications between husband and wife, attorney and client, doctor and patient, priest and penitent, promote and preserve relationships possessing social value. Yet the law has rather steadfastly resisted their expansion, even to a profession having such strong claims as accountancy.

In contrast, the fifth amendment privilege extends, by hypothesis, only to persons who have been breakers of the criminal law or believe they may be charged as such.

Again, while the other privileges accord with notions of decent conduct generally accepted in life outside the court room, the privilege against self-incrimination defies them. No parent would teach such a doctrine to his children; the lesson parents preach is that while a misdeed, even a serious one, will generally be forgiven, a failure to make a clean breast of it will not be. Every hour of the day people are being asked to explain their conduct to parents, employers and teachers. Those who are questioned consider themselves to be morally bound to respond, and the questioners believe it proper to take action if they do not.

Finally, the privilege, at least in its pre-trial application, seriously impedes the state in the most basic of all tasks, "to provide for the security of the individual and his property," not only as against the individual asserting the privilege but as against others who it has reason to think were associated with him. The privilege not only stands in the way of convictions but often prevents restitution to the victim—of goods, of money, even of a kidnapped child. In contrast to the rare case where it may protect an innocent person, it often may do the contrary. A man in suspicious circumstances but not in fact guilty is deprived of official interrogation of another whom he knows to be the true culprit * * *.

One would suppose that such a collection of detriments would have led the Supreme Court to expound the basis for the privilege thoughtfully and carefully before asking the country to accept extensions in no way called for by the fifth amendment's words or history. It thus is strange how rarely one encounters in the Court's opinions on the privilege the careful weighing of *pros* and *cons,* the objective investigation of how rules of law actually work, and, above all, the consideration whether a less extreme position might not adequately meet the needs of the accused without jeopardizing other important interests, which ought to characterize constitutional adjudication before the Court goes beyond the ordinary meaning of the language.

See also Tague, The Fifth Amendment: If an Aid to the Guilty Defendant, an Impediment to an Innocent One, 78 Geo.L.J. 1 (1989)(Fifth Amendment "can shackle the innocent defendant from attempting to prove that another person committed the crime").

2. *A Chart to Assist Analysis*

The chart below lists the most commonly offered justifications for the privilege against self-incrimination, critical responses to those justifications, and sources wherein these arguments are discussed.[1] As you study the chart, consid-

---

1. Sources that are referred to several times are cited in shorthand form. The full citations follow:

Murphy v. Waterfront Comm., 378 U.S. 52 (1964).

Fortas, The Fifth Amendment: Nemo Tenetur Prodere Seipsum, 25 Clev.Bar Assn.J. 91 (1954).

Friendly, The Fifth Amendment Tomorrow: The Case for Constitutional Change, 37 U.Cin.L.Rev. 671 (1968).

McKay, Self–Incrimination and the New Privacy, 1967 Sup.Ct.Rev. 193.

L. Mayers, Shall We Amend the Fifth Amendment (1959).

8 J. Wigmore, Evidence in Trials at Common Law (McNaughten rev. 1961).

er which of the asserted policies are valid rationales for the privilege. Which responses adequately dispose of the policy arguments? Are there convincing responses to any of the criticisms? To all of them?

1. *Protection of the Innocent:* The privilege protects the innocent defendant from convicting himself by a bad performance on the witness stand. *Murphy,* 378 U.S. at 55 (quoting Quinn v. United States, 349 U.S. 155, 162 (1955)); Mayers, at 61.

1. The Supreme Court has explicitly disclaimed this rationale. Tehan v. United States ex rel. Shott, 382 U.S. 406, 415–16 (1966). There is no proof that it protects the innocent. In fact, juries are unlikely to give a defendant the benefit of an innocent explanation of his silence in the face of evidence against him. Mayers, at 26, 61–67. Nor should the innocent defendant fear taking the stand since jurors often sympathize with the defendant who is subjected to brutal questioning. A. Train, From the District Attorney's Office 97 (1939). It is admittedly possible that an innocent defendant will invoke the privilege to avoid impeachment with prior convictions. However, the problem of threatened impeachment does not require a constitutionally-based solution protecting all defendants. A better solution is to impose appropriate limitations on the use of prior convictions. See Montana Rule of Evidence 609 (prior convictions not admissible to attack credibility). Finally, the privilege historically—and by hypothesis—protects the guilty, i.e., those whose testimony would implicate them of a crime. Fortas, at 98–100.

2. *The Cruel Trilemma:* We are unwilling to subject those suspected of crime to the cruel trilemma of self-accusation, perjury, or contempt. Brown v. Walker, 161 U.S. 591, 637 (1896)(Field, J., dissenting).

2. First, this problem is not peculiar to self-incrimination: it exists whenever a witness is reluctant to testify for whatever reason. Any such witness is subject to the trilemma of testifying despite an interest in not doing so, perjury, or contempt. Why is the incrimination interest protected and other interests not? Wigmore, § 2251, at 316. Second, is it necessarily cruel to create a situation where perjury is an option? "The prevalence of per-

The usual rationales for the privilege against self-incrimination are found wanting in Dolinko, Is There a Rationale for the Privilege Against Self–Incrimination, 33 U.C.L.A.L.Rev.

1963 (1986). For a discussion of the debate on the privilege in England, see Gerstein, The Self–Incrimination Debate in Great Britain, 27 Am.J.Comp.L. 81 (1979).

3. *Deter Perjury:* If there were no privilege, people compelled to testify would commit perjury rather than incriminate themselves. Rampant perjury would burden the courts. Wigmore, § 2251, at 311.

4. *Unreliability of Coerced Statements:* We do not trust self-deprecatory statements, particularly when they are the product of coercion. *Murphy,* 378 U.S. at 55; Michigan v. Tucker, 417 U.S. 433, 448–49 (1974).

5. *Preference for Accusatorial System:* We prefer an accusatorial rather than inquisitorial system of criminal justice. *Murphy,* 378 U.S. at 55.

6. *Deter Improper Police Practices:* Self-incriminating statements are likely to be elicited by inhumane treatment and abuses. The privilege has historically protected against such forms of torture. *Murphy,* 378 U.S. at 55.

jury today leads one to doubt that it is thought by the average witness as a soul-destroying experience." Wigmore, § 2251, at 316–17. Finally, this argument can only justify the privilege at trial. Where police questioning is involved, false answers are not perjury and contempt cannot be used against one who refuses to answer. Wigmore, § 2252, n. 27. See also W. Schaefer, The Suspect and Society 17–18 (1967). We do subject friends, lovers, parents, teachers, and most people to the discomfort of having to testify against individuals about whom they might care the most.

3. Perjury is prevalent despite the existence of the privilege. Silence is also a burden on the truth-finding function of the criminal process. Friendly, at 680. There is no reason to believe that a defendant who concludes that perjury will succeed will not attempt it. Nor is there reason to believe that a defendant who concludes that perjury will fail will attempt it or succeed if an attempt is made.

4. If reliability is the primary concern, there is no need to exclude compelled evidence that can be independently corroborated, nor physical evidence extracted from a defendant. Moreover, testimony at trial is likely to be cast by the defense in its most favorable light. It will not always be self-deprecatory. Also, it is more likely to be reliable than statements obtained by police interrogation, which are admitted as evidence.

5. "Language like this, no matter how often repeated, no matter how eloquently intoned, is merely restatement of the privilege itself." McKay, at 209.

6. Torture is unacceptable on its own merits, regardless of the existence of a privilege. Wigmore, § 2251, at 315. The privilege is unnecessary to guard against objectionable police practices—adequate protection is afforded by the Due Process clauses of the Fifth and

7. *Fair State–Individual Balance:* "The privilege contributes towards a fair state-individual balance by requiring the government to leave the individual alone until good cause is shown for disturbing him and by requiring the government in its contest with the individual to shoulder the entire load." Wigmore, § 2251, at 317.

8. *Preservation of Official Morality:* "Any system * * * which permits the prosecution to trust habitually to compulsory self-disclosure as a source of proof must itself suffer morally thereby. 8 J. Wigmore, § 2251 (3d ed. 1940).

Fourteenth Amendments. Testimony in court is subject to the safeguards of the judicial process.

7. First, the probable cause requirements for search and arrest provide adequate protection against unwarranted governmental disturbance. Second, the argument depends on unprovable assumptions about the terms of the Lockian social contract upon which our government is based, i.e., did the sovereign individual yield to the sovereign state the power to extract evidence of his own guilt? *Compare* Friendly, at 692–93, *with* Fortas, at 98–100. Third, the argument relies on a notion of the criminal trial as "a jousting contest where the rules bear equally on both participants and neither is expected to be of the slightest help to the other"—a concept which bears no relation to reality. For example, the state and the defendant operate under different rules for discovery, appeal, and burdens of proof. Fourth, even assuming that the ideal balance between state and defendant could be determined, manipulating the scope of the privilege is not necessarily the best way to achieve that balance. Friendly, at 693–94. Finally, the fact is that the government is not required to "shoulder the entire load" in a criminal prosecution. For example, the government can compel the defendant to produce DNA samples, voice prints, and physical evidence. Compelled production of this evidence is not covered by the Fifth Amendment. So what is it about testimony that makes it free from compulsion?

8. Wigmore's statement was based on two debatable assumptions: First, he believed the privilege applied only in the courtroom. When extended to the stationhouse, this rationale would disallow most police questioning—an untenable proposition. Second, he assumed that the privilege developed historically because the bal-

9. *Privacy Rationale:* "Our respect for the inviolability of the human personality and of the right of each individual 'to a private enclave where he may lead a private life'" justifies the privilege. *Murphy,* 378 U.S. at 55 (quoting United States v. Grunewald, 233 F.2d 556, 581–82 (2d Cir.1956)(Frank, J., dissenting)). See also, Fried, Privacy, 77 Yale L.J. 475, 488–89 (1968); McKay, at 212.

ance struck by the English judicial system had become morally unacceptable. Friendly, at 691.

9. If the basis for the privilege is a general freedom of silence to protect one's privacy, it is inconsistent first, with immunity statutes which require testimony no matter how private the matter; second, with rules requiring information of a far more private nature in civil suits (e.g., annulment suits); and third, with the Fourth Amendment, which clearly does protect privacy, but only to the extent that intrusions are unreasonable. This privacy rationale enjoys historical support only when crimes of belief or association are involved. It is immoral to suggest that a murderer in a typical criminal case is justified in withholding his aid because he "prefers to remain in a 'private enclave.'" Friendly, at 689–90.

10. *First Amendment Rationale:* The privilege affords "a shelter against governmental snooping and oppression concerning political and religious beliefs." Friendly, at 696.

10. The First Amendment is the appropriate vehicle for dealing with this problem, as the Court implicitly recognized in cases such as NAACP v. Alabama, 357 U.S. 449 (1958). Furthermore, this justification, even if valid, would apply only in free speech, religion, or association situations, not in the typical criminal investigation and prosecution. Wigmore, § 2251, at 314.

Consider how one's choice of rationale necessarily affects one's view of the legitimate scope of the Amendment. For example, if the privilege is primarily intended to prevent "the cruel trilemma" and to deter perjury, then it should be applicable only when testimony under oath is involved. If one is concerned that the government bear its burden of proof without assistance, then voice or handwriting exemplars and other physical evidence extracted from a defendant would be protected. In the cases that follow, try to determine which policies underlie the Supreme Court's analysis of the privilege. Are those policies defensible? Do they emerge inexorably from the language or background of the privilege? Do the policies identified in particular cases support the result reached by the Court in these cases? Are the policies consistently applied?

Judge Friendly criticizes the Fifth Amendment as protecting only the guilty. Professors Seidmann and Stein argue to the contrary in The Right to Silence Helps the Innocent: A Game–Theoretic Analysis of the Fifth Amendment Privilege, 114 Harv. L.Rev. 430 (2000). They contend that the Fifth Amendment allows guilty defendants to remain silent; without the Fifth Amendment, guilty defendants would have to take the stand and concoct false alibis. The professors assume, probably correctly, that guilty defendants choose not to testify. Therefore, an innocent person who actually does have an alibi will testify and be believed by the jury. If there were no Fifth Amendment, juries would have difficulty distinguishing between all of the false and true alibis.

Professor Bibas, in The Right to Remain Silent Helps Only the Guilty, 88 Iowa L.Rev.421 (2003), disagrees with Seidmann and Stein. He states that their "elegant game-theoretic construct avails them little" because their premises do not mirror reality. Bibas points out that most guilty defendants do confess in an attempt to cooperate with the government, and very few go to trial. He also notes that juries are instructed to consider a witness's stake in the outcome in deciding their credibility.

B. SCOPE OF THE PRIVILEGE

1. *Proceedings in Which the Privilege Applies*

Read literally, the language of the Fifth Amendment would seem to indicate that the privilege against self-incrimination applies only to testimony sought to be compelled in a criminal case. However, the Supreme Court has consistently given the privilege a broader interpretation, holding that it

> not only protects the individual against being involuntarily called as a witness against himself in a criminal prosecution but also privileges him not to answer official questions put to him in any other proceeding, civil or criminal, formal or informal, where his answers might incriminate him in future criminal proceedings.

Lefkowitz v. Turley, 414 U.S. 70, 77 (1973).

Applicability to Non–Criminal Cases: Boyd v. United States and Counselman v. Hitchcock

This policy of liberal interpretation was first articulated in Boyd v. United States, 116 U.S. 616 (1886). *Boyd* involved a forfeiture proceeding, pursuant to a statute authorizing the government to appropriate any goods about which an owner had made false statements with intent to defraud the revenue. The trial court had ordered appellants to produce an invoice under the authority of a statute providing that failure to comply with such an order was tantamount to a confession of guilt. The appellants complied under protest and subsequently suffered a forfeiture judgment. After first holding that the use of the subpoena was an unreasonable seizure in violation of the Fourth Amendment, the Court turned to the applicability of the Fifth Amendment in non-criminal cases.

> We are * * * clearly of opinion that proceedings instituted for the purpose of declaring the forfeiture of a man's property by reason of offences committed by him, though they may be civil in form, are in their nature criminal. * * * As, therefore, suits for penalties and forfeitures incurred by the commission of offences against the law, are of this quasi-criminal nature, we think that they are within the reason of criminal proceedings for all the purposes of * * * that portion of the Fifth Amendment which declares that no person shall be compelled in any criminal case to be a witness against himself; and we are further of opinion that a compulsory

production of the private books and papers of the owner of goods sought to be forfeited in such a suit is compelling him to be a witness against himself, within the meaning of the Fifth Amendment to the Constitution * * *.

In *Boyd,* the Court took an expansive view of the privilege, finding not only that a forfeiture proceeding was a "criminal case," but that the subpoenaing of business records was equivalent to compelling a person to be a witness against himself. The latter point will be considered in detail later in this Chapter.

The broad construction of the "criminal case" requirement was reaffirmed a few years later in Counselman v. Hitchcock, 142 U.S. 547, 562 (1892). The issue in *Counselman* was whether a grand jury witness could claim the privilege. The Court held that a grand jury investigation of a criminal matter was a "criminal case," but the language and analysis of the opinion suggested that the privilege was available in *any* proceeding, whenever the testimony sought from a party or witness might later be *used* in a criminal prosecution against that person.

It is impossible that the meaning of the constitutional provision can only be, that a person shall not be compelled to be a witness against himself in a criminal prosecution against himself. It would doubtless cover such cases; but it is not limited to them. The object was to insure that a person should not be compelled, when acting as a witness in any investigation, to give testimony which might tend to show that he himself had committed a crime. The privilege is limited to criminal matters, but it is as broad as the mischief against which it seeks to guard.

Thus, *Boyd* and *Counselman* established that a person called as a witness in any federal proceeding could invoke the privilege against self-incrimination to avoid testifying to matters that could possibly tend to be damaging in a subsequent criminal prosecution. These decisions now bind the states as well as the federal government. See Malloy v. Hogan, 378 U.S. 1 (1964)(right to be free from compelled self-incrimination is incorporated by the Fourteenth Amendment to apply against the states).

2. Criminal Cases

Boyd and *Counselman* make clear that the privilege against compelled self-incrimination is available whenever the proceeding in which testimony is sought can itself be characterized as a criminal case, and also whenever the compelled testimony might be used against the witness in a later criminal proceeding. However, the actual *use* of compelled testimony other than in a criminal case does not itself implicate the Fifth Amendment. Thus, in Minnesota v. Murphy, 465 U.S. 420 (1984), the Court held that a person has no right to refuse to answer questions on the ground that they might be used against him in subsequent probation revocation proceedings, because those proceedings are civil and not criminal. See also Piemonte v. United States, 367 U.S. 556 (1961)(privilege does not prevent use of compelled testimony for purposes of private retribution).

What makes a proceeding a "criminal case?"[2] *Boyd* held that the potential penalties made a forfeiture proceeding criminal. In re Gault, 387 U.S. 1 (1967),

2. This question was asked in Chapter One. It is repeated here to demonstrate how courts have struggled to answer it with respect to a particular constitutional provision.

held that juvenile delinquency proceedings are criminal cases for Fifth Amendment purposes, even though they were labeled "civil" by most states.

Civil Penalties: United States v. L.O. Ward

When incarceration is not available as a penalty, a legislative determination that a proceeding is "civil" is more likely to be upheld today than when *Boyd* was decided. United States v. L. O. Ward, 448 U.S. 242 (1980), held, for example, that a statute imposing a "civil penalty" upon persons discharging hazardous material into navigable waters was not "quasi-criminal" so as to invalidate a reporting requirement imposed upon polluters. The Court distinguished *Boyd* and several other forfeiture cases, suggesting that they involved penalties that had no correlation with the damages sustained by society or the costs of enforcing the law. It also noted that in *Boyd* the forfeiture provision was listed along with fine and imprisonment as possible punishments for customs fraud. Finally, the Court noted that the applicable civil and criminal remedies are contained in separate statutes enacted 70 years apart and that the civil statute has a use immunity provision preventing reported information from being used in criminal prosecutions. Justice Stevens dissented.

Detention for "Treatment"

In Allen v. Illinois, 478 U.S. 364 (1986), the Court held 5–4 that proceedings under the Illinois Sexually Dangerous Persons Act were not criminal for self-incrimination purposes. Thus, the state court properly relied upon statements made by Allen to psychiatrists who subjected him to compulsory examination to determine whether he should be committed for treatment under the Act. The argument for applying the privilege focused on the fact that the state could not file a petition under the Act unless it had already filed criminal charges; the Act provided some of the same safeguards found in criminal proceedings; and a person committed for treatment was kept in a maximum security institution that also housed prisoners in need of psychiatric care. Justice Rehnquist's majority opinion stated that the question of whether a proceeding is criminal for Fifth Amendment purposes was "first of all a question of statutory construction." The majority relied heavily on the fact that the Illinois Legislature had expressly provided that proceedings under the Act would "be civil in nature." Justice Rehnquist concluded that the state's decision to limit proceedings under the Act to persons charged with criminal acts did not turn a civil proceeding into a criminal one. Nor did the presence of some safeguards also found in criminal cases do so. The majority found that the conditions of the institution were not incompatible with the state's interest in treatment. Finally, it held that due process did not require recognition of the privilege, because the privilege would decrease, not increase, the reliability of the fact finding.

Justice Stevens, joined by Justices Brennan, Marshall, and Blackmun, dissented. He argued that a treatment goal was insufficient to render the privilege inapplicable and that the Court was "permitting a State to create a shadow criminal law without the fundamental protection of the Fifth Amendment."

Does *Allen* look more like a civil or a criminal proceeding? Does it matter that only criminal defendants could be affected by the statute? For a case applying *Allen*, see United States v. Phelps, 955 F.2d 1258 (9th Cir. 1992)(insanity acquittee who seeks release from involuntary commitment has no Fifth Amendment right to refuse to speak to state psychiatrist; release proceeding is civil because the emphasis is on treatment rather than punishment, the acquittee bears the burden of proof, and there is no right to a jury determination).

Invoking the Privilege in a Civil Case to Prevent Use of Statements in a Criminal Case

As noted earlier, the privilege can be invoked in almost any proceeding, whether judicial, administrative, or legislative, in order to protect against the use of incriminating statements in subsequent criminal proceedings. Fifth Amendment claims have been upheld when asserted by a party in a bankruptcy case. McCarthy v. Arndstein, 266 U.S. 34 (1924). Fifth Amendment claims also can be asserted by the subject of an investigation into possible wrongdoing by public contractors, Lefkowitz v. Turley, 414 U.S. 70 (1973)(architect); by public employees, Garrity v. New Jersey, 385 U.S. 493 (1967) (policemen); by prisoners, Baxter v. Palmigiano, 425 U.S. 308 (1976); or by lawyers (in disbarment proceedings), Spevack v. Klein, 385 U.S. 511 (1967). In none of these cases, however, did the Court hold that the proceeding itself was a "criminal case," although substantial penalties—loss of professional status or even more severe incarceration in the case of prisoners—were often at stake.

3. *Foreign Prosecution*

As will be discussed below, a grant of use immunity allows the state to compel a witness's testimony. The immunity grant means that neither the statement nor its fruits can be used against the person in either a state or a federal prosecution. But what if there is a risk of foreign prosecution? It is clear that a grant of use immunity by an American prosecutor has no binding effect on a foreign government. Can the witness refuse to testify, regardless of a grant of domestic immunity, on the ground that the compelled testimony could incriminate him in a foreign prosecution? Is a foreign prosecution a "criminal" case within the meaning of the Fifth Amendment?

In United States v. Balsys, 524 U.S. 666 (1998), the Court held that "concern with foreign prosecution is beyond the scope of the Self–Incrimination Clause." Justice Souter wrote the majority opinion that was joined in full by four other Justices, and joined in substantial part by Justices Scalia and Thomas as well. Balsys had refused to answer questions in a deportation proceeding, in which the government alleged that he had committed atrocities during World War II. Balsys asserted the Fifth Amendment privilege on the ground that his testimony could be used against him in a criminal prosecution in either Israel or Lithuania.

Justice Souter analyzed the policies of the Fifth Amendment, as asserted by the Court in Murphy v. Waterfront Commission, 378 U.S. 52 (1964), to determine whether these policies demanded application of Fifth Amendment protection against the risk of foreign prosecution. In particular, *Murphy* had stated that the Fifth Amendment reflects "our unwillingness to subject those suspected of crime to the cruel trilemma of self-accusation, perjury or contempt; our preference for an accusatorial rather than an inquisitorial system of criminal justice; our fear that self-incriminating statements will be elicited by inhumane treatment and abuses; our sense of fair play which dictates a fair state-individual balance by requiring the government to leave the individual alone until good cause is shown for disturbing him and by requiring the government in its contest with the individual to shoulder the entire load; our respect for the inviolability of the human personality and of the right of each individual to a private enclave where he may lead a private life, our distrust of self-deprecatory statements; and our realization that the privilege, while sometimes a shelter to the guilty, is often a protection to the innocent." As to this articulation, Justice Souter declared:

> Some of the policies listed would seem to point no further than domestic arrangements and so raise no basis for any privilege looking beyond fear of domestic prosecution. Others, however, might suggest a concern broad enough to encompass foreign prosecutions and accordingly to support a more expansive theory of the privilege * * *.

* * *

> The most general of *Murphy's* policy items ostensibly suggesting protection as comprehensive as that sought by Balsys is listed in the opinion as "the inviolability of the human personality and ... the right of each individual to a private enclave where he may lead a private life." * * * If in fact these values were reliable guides to the actual scope of protection under the Clause, they would be seen to demand a very high degree of protection indeed * * *.

> The Fifth Amendment tradition, however, offers no such degree of protection. If the Government is ready to provide the requisite use and derivative use immunity, see *Kastigar v. United States* [discussed infra in the section on immunity], the protection goes no further: no violation of personality is recognized and no claim of privilege will avail. * * * [Moreover,] when a witness's response will raise no fear of criminal penalty, there is no protection for testimonial privacy at all.

> Thus, what we find in practice is not the protection of personal testimonial inviolability, but a conditional protection of testimonial privacy subject to basic limits recognized before the framing and refined through immunity doctrine in the intervening years. Since the Judiciary could not recognize fear of foreign prosecution and at the same time preserve the Government's existing rights to seek testimony in exchange for immunity (because domestic courts could not enforce the immunity abroad), it follows that extending protection as Balsys requests would change the balance of private and governmental interests that has seemingly been accepted for as long as there has been Fifth Amendment doctrine. * * *

Justice Souter then proceeded to address the lower court's argument that applying Fifth Amendment protection to the risk of foreign prosecution would not be very costly to government interests.

> That some testimony will be lost is highly probable, since the United States will not be able to guarantee immunity if testimony is compelled (absent some sort of cooperative international arrangement that we cannot assume will occur). While the Court of Appeals is doubtless correct that the expected consequences of some foreign prosecutions may be so severe that a

witness will refuse to testify no matter what, not every foreign prosecution may measure up so harshly as against the expectable domestic consequences of contempt for refusing to testify. We therefore must suppose that on Balsys's view some evidence will in fact be lost to the domestic courts, and we are accordingly unable to dismiss the position of the United States in this case, that domestic law enforcement would suffer serious consequences if fear of foreign prosecution were recognized as sufficient to invoke the privilege.

Finally, Justice Souter stated that the Fifth Amendment might indeed apply to protect against foreign self-incrimination if it could be shown that the domestic government, in compelling incriminating testimony, is simply acting as a surrogate or stalking horse for another country.

> If it could be said that the United States and its allies had enacted substantially similar criminal codes aimed at prosecuting offenses of inter-national character, and if it could be shown that the United States was granting immunity from domestic prosecution for the purpose of obtaining evidence to be delivered to other nations as prosecutors of a crime common to both countries, then an argument could be made that the Fifth Amend-ment should apply based on fear of foreign prosecution simply because that prosecution was not fairly characterized as distinctly "foreign." The point would be that the prosecution was as much on behalf of the United States as of the prosecuting nation, so that the division of labor between evidence-gatherer and prosecutor made one nation the agent of the other, rendering fear of foreign prosecution tantamount to fear of a criminal case brought by the Government itself.

However, no such level of cooperation was found on the facts of this case.

Justice Stevens wrote a short concurring opinion in *Balsys*, emphasizing that the costs of extending the privilege to protect against the risk of foreign prosecutions were too great to bear. If a person could refuse to testify due to a risk of foreign prosecution, "we would confer power on foreign governments to impair the administration of justice in this country. A law enacted by a foreign power making it a crime for one of its citizens to testify in an American proceeding against another citizen of that country would immunize those citizens from being compelled to testify in our courts."

Justice Ginsburg wrote a short dissenting opinion in *Balsys* and joined Justice Breyer's far more extensive opinion. Justice Breyer disagreed with the majority's assessment that applying the privilege to claims of foreign incrimina-tion would substantially impair law enforcement:

> [T]hat fear is overstated. After all, "foreign application" of the privilege would matter only in a case where an individual could not be prosecuted domestically but the threat of foreign prosecution is substantial. The Second Circuit points out that there have only been a handful of such cases. That is because relatively few witnesses face deportation or extradition, and a witness who will not be forced to enter a country disposed to prosecute him, cannot make the showing of "real and substantial" fear that the Fifth Amendment would require.

The majority in *Balsys* was clearly concerned about the costs to the government if the Fifth Amendment were held to protect against the risk of foreign prosecution. The government would never be able to compel testimony in such situations by granting use immunity; domestic law enforcement efforts against those other than the witness would depend upon the substantive criminal laws of foreign nations; and sophisticated lawbreakers could manufacture foreign contacts to bring domestic prosecutions to a halt. In the modern era of international transactions, it might be possible credibly to argue a risk of foreign prosecution for virtually everyone involved in organized crime. Or is all this an overreaction?

Cooperating Governments

The Court in *Balsys* leaves open the possibility that the Fifth Amendment will apply if the United States is cooperating with a foreign government to such an extent that the foreign prosecution is really a domestic prosecution as well. But courts after *Balsys* have found this "cooperation" exception to be a very limited one, if it exists at all. Thus, in In re Impounded, 178 F.3d 150 (3d Cir.1999), the government moved to hold immunized witnesses in contempt for refusing to testify before a grand jury investigating violations of the Sherman Antitrust Act. The witnesses argued that they had a constitutional right not to testify due to the risk of prosecution in Canada, Germany and England. The witnesses noted that they were being questioned by U.S. officials about foreign contacts; that the United States had entered into cooperative agreements with these other countries to investigate and prosecute violations of the antitrust laws of the respective countries; and that the criminal antitrust laws and penalties in these nations were similar to those in the United States. But the Court rejected all these connections as requiring a finding of a cooperative prosecution within the meaning of *Balsys.*

> The fact that a few instances of evidence gathering have occurred in other countries does not create an inferential leap that appellants' fear of foreign prosecution is "tantamount to a fear of a criminal case brought by the Government itself." In addition, the fact that other nations have enacted criminal antitrust laws does not dictate a conclusion that nations are acting in concert through a system of complementary substantive offenses * * *. [W]e view appellants' argument as urging a "what if" scenario rather than a true case of an ongoing or imminent international "cooperative prosecution" that would warrant our viewing foreign activity as part of a domestic prosecution.

4.   *Compulsion of Statements Never Admitted at a Criminal Trial*

In *Chavez v. Martinez,* 538 U.S. 760 (2003), the Court considered whether the Fifth Amendment is violated when police compel a statement from a suspect during interrogation but the statement is never admitted against the suspect in a criminal trial. Martinez brought a 1983 action for violation of his Fifth Amendment rights. Chavez was a police officer who interrogated Martinez after Martinez was shot in a fight with police officers. The interrogation session occurred while Martinez was in the hospital being treated for bullet wounds. Martinez made some inculpatory statements. For purposes of the appeal, all of the Justices on the Court assumed that the statements made by Martinez would have been excluded under the Fifth Amendment as compelled self-incrimination, had the statements been offered at a criminal trial. However, Martinez was never charged with a crime, and the statements were never used against him in a criminal prosecution.

A majority found that the Fifth Amendment does not protect against statements compelled during interrogation that are never admitted in a criminal case, but there was no opinion for the Court on this question. Justice Thomas, joined by Chief Justice Rehnquist and Justices O'Connor and Scalia, provided the broadest opinion, declaring that the Fifth Amendment simply did not apply because Martinez's confession was ever admitted against him in a criminal case. Justice Thomas reasoned as follows:

> Although Martinez contends that the meaning of "criminal case" should encompass the entire criminal investigatory process, including police interrogations, we disagree. In our view, a "criminal case" at the very least requires the initiation of legal proceedings. * * * Here, Martinez was never made to be a "witness" against himself in violation of the Fifth Amendment's Self–Incrimination Clause because his statements were never admitted as testimony against him in a criminal case. Nor was he ever placed under oath and exposed to the cruel trilemma of self-accusation, perjury or contempt. * * *

> We fail to see how Martinez was any more "compelled in any criminal case to be a witness against himself" than an immunized witness forced to testify on pain of contempt. One difference, perhaps, is that the immunized witness *knows* that his statements will not, and may not, be used against him, whereas Martinez likely did not. But this does not make the statements of the immunized witness any less "compelled" and lends no support to the Ninth Circuit's conclusion that coercive police interrogations, absent the use of the involuntary statements in a criminal case, violate the Fifth Amendment's Self–Incrimination Clause.

Justice Souter, joined by Justice Breyer, concurred in the judgment, agreeing with the general proposition that the Fifth Amendment does not protect against compulsion of statements that are never used in a criminal case. Justice Souter expressed concern over the stopping point for a rule of law providing that compelled confessions are actionable in themselves.

> The most obvious drawback inherent in Martinez's purely Fifth Amendment claim to damages is its risk of global application in every instance of interrogation producing a statement inadmissible under Fifth and Fourteenth Amendment principles, or violating one of the complementary rules we have accepted in aid of the privilege against evidentiary use. If obtaining Martinez's statement is to be treated as a stand-alone violation of the privilege subject to compensation, why should the same not be true whenever the police obtain any involuntary self-incriminating statement, or whenever the government so much as threatens a penalty in derogation of the right to immunity, or whenever the police fail to honor *Miranda?* Martinez offers no limiting principle or reason to foresee a stopping place short of liability in all such cases.

Justice Kennedy, joined by Justices Stevens and Ginsburg, dissented. He argued as follows:

> The conclusion that the Self–Incrimination Clause is not violated until the government seeks to use a statement in some later criminal proceeding

strips the Clause of an essential part of its force and meaning. This is no small matter. It should come as an unwelcome surprise to judges, attorneys, and the citizenry as a whole that if a legislative committee or a judge in a civil case demands incriminating testimony without offering immunity, and even imposes sanctions for failure to comply, that the witness and counsel cannot insist the right against compelled self-incrimination is applicable then and there. * * * To tell our whole legal system that when conducting a criminal investigation police officials can use severe compulsion or even torture with no present violation of the right against compelled self-incrimination can only diminish a celebrated provision in the Bill of Rights.
* * *

Justice Ginsburg added a separate dissenting opinion.

While a majority of the Court held that Martinez could claim no Fifth Amendment violation because the compelled statements were not admitted against him in a criminal case, a different majority of the Court voted to remand the case for a determination of whether the interrogation session so "shocked the conscience" as to constitute a violation of Martinez's right to substantive due process. The Justices agreed that if a police officer's misconduct rises to the level of a substantive due process violation, it would not matter whether the suspect's statements were ever admitted at trial. Justice Thomas, joined by the Chief Justice and Justice Scalia, declared that Chavez's conduct did not shock the conscience and therefore dissented from a remand on this question.

C. WHAT IS COMPULSION?

The Fifth Amendment protects against self-incrimination only if it is compelled by the government. But it is sometimes difficult to determine whether a particular pressure imposed by the government on a citizen rises to the level of compulsion.

1. Use of the Contempt Power

Use of the contempt power is the classic form of compulsion, because it imposes substantial punishment on the witness who is exercising the right to remain silent, and it presents the witness with a cruel trilemma: remain silent and face imprisonment; tell the truth and face imprisonment; or tell a lie and face imprisonment for perjury. Thus, a witness cannot be subjected to contempt for refusing to testify, if the testimony could create a risk of self-incrimination in a criminal case.

2. Other State–Imposed Sanctions

The Supreme Court has extended the concept of compulsion well beyond its original grounding in the contempt power. For example, the Court in Miranda v. Arizona, discussed infra, found compulsion in the setting of custodial interrogation. The Court has also found other state-imposed sanctions for silence, of less severity than contempt, to constitute compulsion. The following case provides an example of the Court's approach.

LEFKOWITZ v. TURLEY

Supreme Court of the United States, 1973.
414 U.S. 70.

MR. JUSTICE WHITE **delivered the opinion of the Court:**

[New York statutes required public contracts to provide that if a contractor refuses to waive immunity or to testify concerning state contracts, existing contracts could be canceled and future contracts could be denied for five years. Contractors refused to answer questions that could incriminate them, and were denied the right to future contracts under the statute.]

II

* * *

It is true that the State has a strong, legitimate interest in maintaining the integrity of its civil service and of its transactions with independent contractors furnishing a wide range of goods and services; and New York would have it that this interest is sufficiently strong to override the privilege. The suggestion is that the State should be able to interrogate employees and contractors about their job performance without regard to the Fifth Amendment, to discharge those who refuse to answer or to waive the privilege by waiving the immunity to which they would otherwise be entitled, and to use any incriminating answers obtained in subsequent criminal prosecutions. But claims of overriding interests are not unusual in Fifth Amendment litigation and they have not fared well.

* * *

[I]n almost the very context here involved, this court has only recently held that employees of the State do not forfeit their constitutional privilege and that they may be compelled to respond to questions about the performance of their duties but only if their answers cannot be used against them in subsequent criminal prosecutions. Garrity v. New Jersey, 385 U.S. 493 (1967); Gardner v. Broderick, 392 U.S. 273 (1968); Sanitation Men v. Sanitation Comm'r, 392 U.S. 280 (1968).

III

In Garrity v. New Jersey, certain police officers were summoned to an inquiry being conducted by the Attorney General concerning the fixing of traffic tickets. They were asked questions following warnings that if they did not answer they would be removed from office and that anything they said might be used against them in any criminal proceeding. No immunity of any kind was offered or available under state law. The questions were answered and the answers later used over their objections, in their prosecutions for conspiracy. The Court held that "protection of the individual under the Fourteenth Amendment against coerced statements prohibits use in subsequent criminal proceedings of statements obtained under threat of removal from office, and that it extends to all, whether they are policemen or other members of our body politic." * * *

The issue in Gardner v. Broderick, supra, was whether the State might discharge a police officer who, after he was summoned before a grand jury to testify about the performance of his official duties and was advised of his right against compulsory self-incrimination, then refused to waive that right as requested by the State. Conceding that appellant could be discharged for refusing to answer questions about the performance of his official duties, if not required to waive immunity, the Court held that the officer could not be terminated, as he was, for refusing to waive his constitutional privilege. * * *

The companion case, Sanitation Men v. Sanitation Com'r, supra, was to the same effect. * * *

These cases, and their predecessors, ultimately rest on a reconciliation of the well-recognized policies behind the privilege of self-incrimination, and the need of the State, as well as the Federal Government, to obtain information "to assure the effective functioning of government." Immunity is required if there is to be "rational accommodation between the imperatives of the privilege and the legitimate demands of government to compel citizens to testify." It is in this sense that immunity statutes have "become part of our constitutional fabric."

We agree with the District Court that *Garrity, Gardner,* and *Sanitation Men* control the issue now before us. The State sought to interrogate appellees about their transactions with the State and to require them to furnish possibly incriminating testimony by demanding that they waive their immunity and by disqualifying them as public contractors when they refused. It seems to us that the State intended to accomplish what *Garrity* specifically prohibited—to compel testimony that had not been immunized. The waiver sought by the State, under threat of loss of contracts, would have been no less compelled than a direct request for the testimony without resort to the waiver device. A waiver secured under threat of substantial economic sanction cannot be termed voluntary.

* * *

Threat of Disbarment as Compulsion

Spevack v. Klein, 385 U.S. 511 (1967), forbids disbarment of a lawyer for invoking the privilege during a bar investigation, where any statements could be used against the lawyer in a subsequent criminal prosecution. Can an applicant for the bar exam refuse to answer questions on an application and still insist on admission to the bar?

The Function of Immunity

If the contractor in *Lefkowitz* had been given immunity from criminal prosecution, could he then be denied public contracts for refusing to testify? If he spoke pursuant to a grant of immunity, could he then be denied public contracts on the basis of incriminating statements made in his testimony? The court explained the relevant principles in National Federation of Federal Employees v. Greenberg, 983 F.2d 286 (D.C.Cir.1993), a case in which government employees were subject to firing for refusing to answer questions, and relevant statutes prevented use of the compelled statements in a criminal prosecution:

> The government * * * may fire employees who refuse, on the basis of their Fifth Amendment privilege, to answer questions concerning the performance of their duties, so long as the employees' answers could not be used against them in a criminal prosecution. For purposes of the Fifth Amendment, the threat of firing or other economic sanctions may constitute compulsion. But the protection of the privilege extends only to criminal prosecutions. A government employee would not be incriminating himself

within the meaning of the Fifth Amendment if his answers could not be used against him in a criminal case.

The Benefit–Penalty Distinction

What if the government does not impose a penalty for silence, as in *Turley*, but instead conditions a benefit on the waiver of the privilege? Is this "compulsion" within the meaning of the Fifth Amendment?

The benefit/penalty distinction has often been applied when a defendant is required to provide incriminating information in order to receive a reduction in sentence. For example, in United States v. Cruz, 156 F.3d 366 (2d Cir.1998), the defendant was subject to a mandatory minimum sentence of ten years for a drug crime. However, a federal statute and Sentencing Guideline provide for "safety valve" relief from mandatory minimums in some narcotics cases if, among other things, the defendant "has truthfully provided to the Government all information and evidence the defendant has concerning the offense or offenses that were part of the same course of conduct or of a common scheme or plan". The defendant in *Cruz* argued that this disclosure provision compelled him to incriminate himself, because in order to receive the waiver of the mandatory minimum, he would have to implicate himself in other drug transactions for which he was not yet charged. But the Court found no compulsion, noting that the penalty cases "have all involved some kind of loss or reduction from the status quo", such as the loss of public employment or disbarment. "A defendant facing a particular sentence, however, with the option of obtaining a lower sentence if he or she waives the Fifth Amendment privilege is not presented with the same 'negative' sanction as presented in the penalty cases." The Court declared that "the choice confronting the defendant gives rise to no more compulsion than that present in a typical plea bargain." If the defendant had actually received an enhanced sentence for *not* cooperating, this would have amounted to compulsion. But conditioning a reduction of sentence on cooperation is a different matter.

The *Cruz* Court recognized that some defendants might be worse off by admitting to uncharged criminal conduct in trying to invoke the safety valve provision. That is, the benefit in reduced sentence from the safety valve would be outweighed by the risk of longer incarceration from admitting to the uncharged offenses. But this problem did not rise to the level of compulsion, because in such cases "the defendant effectively doesn't have the safety valve option open to him or her, and accordingly no Fifth Amendment issue arises."

Self-Incrimination and Clemency Proceedings: Ohio Adult Parole Authority v. Woodard

The Supreme Court considered the benefit-penalty distinction in Ohio Adult Parole Authority v. Woodard, 523 U.S. 272 (1998). The Parole Authority commenced a clemency proceeding in accordance with state law, after Woodard's appeal from his capital murder conviction had been denied. Under Ohio law, the Parole Authority must conduct a clemency hearing within 45 days of the scheduled date of execution. Prior to the hearing, the inmate may request an interview with one or more parole board members. The Authority must hold the hearing, complete its clemency review, and make a recommendation to the

Governor. Woodard did not request an interview. Instead, he brought a section 1983 action in federal court, arguing, among other things, that the clemency proceeding left him with a "Hobson's choice": to have any chance of clemency, he would have to subject himself to an interview, thereby opening himself up to incrimination both on the current charge (given the possibility of successful post-conviction proceedings) as well as on other charges.

The Supreme Court, in a unanimous opinion on this point, rejected Woodard's Fifth Amendment argument and held that the clemency procedure did not compel him to incriminate himself. Chief Justice Rehnquist, writing for the Court, reasoned as follows:

> It is difficult to see how a voluntary interview could "compel" respondent to speak. He merely faces a choice quite similar to the sorts of choices that a criminal defendant must make in the course of criminal proceedings, none of which has ever been held to violate the Fifth Amendment.

> Long ago we held that a defendant who took the stand in his own defense could not claim the privilege against self-incrimination when the prosecution sought to cross-examine him. Brown v. Walker, 161 U.S. 591 (1896); Brown v. United States, 356 U.S. 148 (1958). A defendant who takes the stand in his own behalf may be impeached by proof of prior convictions without violation of the Fifth Amendment privilege. Spencer v. Texas, 385 U.S. 554, 561 (1967). A defendant whose motion for acquittal at the close of the Government's case is denied must then elect whether to stand on his motion or to put on a defense, with the accompanying risk that in doing so he will augment the Government's case against him. McGautha v. California, 402 U.S. 183 (1971). In each of these situations, there are undoubted pressures—generated by the strength of the Government's case against him—pushing the criminal defendant to testify. But it has never been suggested that such pressures constitute "compulsion" for Fifth Amendment purposes.

* * *

> Here, respondent has the same choice of providing information to the Authority—at the risk of damaging his case for clemency or for postconviction relief—or of remaining silent. But this pressure to speak in the hope of improving his chance of being granted clemency does not make the interview compelled. We therefore hold that the Ohio clemency interview, even on assumptions most favorable to respondent's claim, does not violate the Fifth Amendment privilege against compelled self-incrimination.

The Benefit–Penalty Distinction and Penalties Imposed on Incarcerated Sex Offenders: McKune v. Lile

In the following case, a divided Court considers whether the benefit-penalty distinction works when applied to a program for rehabilitating incarcerated sex offenders.

McKUNE v. LILE

Supreme Court of the United States, 2002.
536 U.S. 24

JUSTICE KENNEDY announced the judgment of the Court and delivered an opinion, in which THE CHIEF JUSTICE, JUSTICE SCALIA, and JUSTICE THOMAS join.

Respondent Robert G. Lile is a convicted sex offender in the custody of the Kansas Department of Corrections (Department). A few years before respondent was scheduled to reenter society, Department officials recommended that he enter a prison treatment program so that he would not rape again upon release. * * * Kansas officials and officials who administer the United States prison system have made the determination that it is of considerable importance for the program participant to admit having committed the crime for which he is being treated and other past offenses. The first and in many ways most crucial step in the Kansas rehabilitation program thus requires the participant to confront his past crimes so that he can begin to understand his own motivations and weaknesses. As this initial step can be a most difficult one, Kansas offers sex offenders incentives to participate in the program.

Respondent contends this incentive system violates his Fifth Amendment privilege against self-incrimination. Kansas' rehabilitation program, however, serves a vital penological purpose, and offering inmates minimal incentives to participate does not amount to compelled self-incrimination prohibited by the Fifth Amendment.

I

In 1982, respondent lured a high school student into his car as she was returning home from school. At gun-point, respondent forced the victim to perform oral sodomy on him and then drove to a field where he raped her. After the sexual assault, the victim went to her school, where, crying and upset, she reported the crime. The police arrested respondent and recovered on his person the weapon he used to facilitate the crime. Although respondent maintained that the sexual intercourse was consensual, a jury convicted him of rape, aggravated sodomy, and aggravated kidnaping. * * *

In 1994, a few years before respondent was scheduled to be released, prison officials ordered him to participate in a Sexual Abuse Treatment Program (SATP). As part of the program, participating inmates are required to complete and sign an "Admission of Responsibility" form, in which they discuss and accept responsibility for the crime for which they have been sentenced. Participating inmates also are required to complete a sexual history form, which details all prior sexual activities, regardless of whether such activities constitute uncharged criminal offenses. A polygraph examination is used to verify the accuracy and completeness of the offender's sexual history.

While information obtained from participants advances the SATP's rehabilitative goals, the information is not privileged. Kansas leaves open the possibility that new evidence might be used against sex offenders in future criminal proceedings. * * *

Department officials informed respondent that if he refused to participate in the SATP, his privilege status would be reduced from Level III to Level I. As part of this reduction, respondent's visitation rights, earnings, work opportunities, ability to send money to family, canteen expenditures, access to a personal television, and other privileges automatically would be curtailed. In addition, respondent would be transferred to a maximum-security unit, where his movement would be more limited, he would be moved from a two-person to a four-person cell, and he would be in a potentially more dangerous environment.

Respondent refused to participate in the SATP on the ground that the required disclosures of his criminal history would violate his Fifth Amendment privilege against self-incrimination. He brought this action under 42 U.S.C. § 1983 against the warden and the secretary of the Department, seeking an injunction to prevent them from withdrawing his prison privileges and transferring him to a different housing unit.

[Both lower courts found that the Kansas plan constituted compelled self-incrimination.]

II

* * *.

Therapists and correctional officers widely agree that clinical rehabilitative programs can enable sex offenders to manage their impulses and in this way reduce recidivism. An important component of those rehabilitation programs requires participants to confront their past and accept responsibility for their misconduct. Research indicates that offenders who deny all allegations of sexual abuse are three times more likely to fail in treatment than those who admit even partial complicity.

The critical first step in the Kansas Sexual Abuse Treatment Program (SATP), therefore, is acceptance of responsibility for past offenses. This gives inmates a basis to understand why they are being punished and to identify the traits that cause such a frightening and high risk of recidivism. As part of this first step, Kansas requires each SATP participant to complete an "Admission of Responsibility" form, to fill out a sexual history form discussing their offending behavior, and to discuss their past behavior in individual and group counseling sessions.

* * *

As the parties explain, Kansas' decision not to offer immunity to every SATP participant serves two legitimate state interests. First, the professionals who design and conduct the program have concluded that for SATP participants to accept full responsibility for their past actions, they must accept the proposition that those actions carry consequences. * * * If inmates know society will not punish them for their past offenses, they may be left with the false impression that society does not consider those crimes to be serious ones. The practical effect of guaranteed immunity for SATP participants would be to absolve many sex offenders of any and all cost for their earlier crimes. This is the precise opposite of the rehabilitative objective.

Second, while Kansas as a rule does not prosecute inmates based upon information revealed in the course of the program, the State confirms its valid interest in deterrence by keeping open the option to prosecute a particularly dangerous sex offender. Kansas is not alone in declining to offer blanket use immunity as a condition of participation in a treatment program. The Federal Bureau of Prisons and other States conduct similar sex offender programs and do not offer immunity to the participants.

The mere fact that Kansas declines to grant inmates use immunity does not render the SATP invalid. Asking at the outset whether prison administrators can or should offer immunity skips the constitutional inquiry altogether. If the State of Kansas offered immunity, the self-incrimination privilege would not be implicated. * * * So the central question becomes whether the State's program, and the consequences for nonparticipation in it, combine to create a compulsion that encumbers the constitutional right. If there is compulsion, the State cannot continue the program in its present form; and the alternatives, as will be discussed, defeat the program's objectives.

The SATP does not compel prisoners to incriminate themselves in violation of the Constitution. * * * The consequences in question here—a transfer to another prison where television sets are not placed in each inmate's cell, where exercise facilities are not readily available, and where work and wage opportunities are more limited—are not ones that compel a prisoner to speak about his past crimes despite a desire to remain silent. The fact that these consequences are imposed on prisoners, rather than ordinary citizens, moreover, is important in weighing respondent's constitutional claim.

* * *

* * * The compulsion inquiry must consider the significant restraints already inherent in prison life and the State's own vital interests in rehabilitation goals and procedures within the prison system. A prison clinical rehabilitation program, which is acknowledged to bear a rational relation to a legitimate penological objective, does not violate the privilege against self-incrimination if the adverse consequences an inmate faces for not participating are related to the program objectives and do not constitute atypical and significant hardships in relation to the ordinary incidents of prison life.

* * *

In the present case, respondent's decision not to participate in the Kansas SATP did not extend his term of incarceration. Nor did his decision affect his eligibility for good-time credits or parole. Respondent instead complains that if he remains silent about his past crimes, he will be transferred from the medium-security unit—where the program is conducted—to a less desirable maximum-security unit. No one contends, however, that the transfer is intended to punish prisoners for exercising their Fifth Amendment rights. Rather, the limitation on these rights is incidental to Kansas' legitimate penological reason for the transfer: Due to limited space, inmates who do not participate in their respective programs will be moved out of the facility where the programs are held to make room for other inmates. As the Secretary of Corrections has explained, "it makes no sense to have someone who's not participating in a program taking up a bed in a setting where someone else who may be willing to participate in a program could occupy that bed and participate in a program."

It is well settled that the decision where to house inmates is at the core of prison administrators' expertise. For this reason the Court has not required administrators to conduct a hearing before transferring a prisoner to a bed in a different prison, even if "life in one prison is much more disagreeable than in another." The Court has considered the proposition that a prisoner in a more comfortable facility might begin to feel entitled to remain there throughout his term of incarceration. The Court has concluded, nevertheless, that this expectation "is too ephemeral and insubstantial to trigger procedural due process protections as long as prison officials have discretion to transfer him for whatever reason or for no reason at all." This logic has equal force in analyzing respondent's self-incrimination claim.

Respondent also complains that he will be demoted from Level III to Level I status as a result of his decision not to participate. This demotion means the loss of his personal television; less access to prison organizations and the gym area; a reduction in certain pay opportunities and canteen privileges; and restricted visitation rights. An essential tool of prison administration, however, is the authority to offer inmates various incentives to behave. The Constitution accords prison officials wide latitude to bestow or revoke these perquisites as they see fit. * * *

Respondent fails to cite a single case from this Court holding that the denial of discrete prison privileges for refusal to participate in a rehabilitation program amounts to unconstitutional compulsion. Instead, relying on the so-called penalty cases, respondent treats the fact of his incarceration as if it were irrelevant. See, e.g., Garrity v. New Jersey, 385 U.S. 493 (1967); Spevack v. Klein, 385 U.S. 511 (1967). Those cases, however, involved free citizens given the choice between invoking the Fifth Amendment privilege and sustaining their economic livelihood. Those principles are not easily extended to the prison context, where inmates surrender upon incarceration their rights to pursue a livelihood and to contract freely with the State, as well as many other basic freedoms. * * *

* * * There is no indication that the SATP is an elaborate attempt to avoid the protections offered by the privilege against compelled self-incrimination. Rather, the program serves an impor-

tant social purpose. It would be bitter medicine to treat as irrelevant the State's legitimate interests and to invalidate the SATP on the ground that it incidentally burdens an inmate's right to remain silent.

Determining what constitutes unconstitutional compulsion involves a question of judgment: Courts must decide whether the consequences of an inmate's choice to remain silent are closer to the physical torture against which the Constitution clearly protects or the *de minimis* harms against which it does not. [In the prison context, the question is] whether the response of prison administrators to correctional and rehabilitative necessities are so out of the ordinary that one could sensibly say they rise to the level of unconstitutional compulsion.

Prison context or not, respondent's choice is marked less by compulsion than by choices the Court has held give no rise to a self-incrimination claim. The criminal process, like the rest of the legal system, is replete with situations requiring the making of difficult judgments as to which course to follow. Although a defendant may have a right, even of constitutional dimensions, to follow whichever course he chooses, the Constitution does not by that token always forbid requiring him to choose. It is well settled that the government need not make the exercise of the Fifth Amendment privilege cost free. See, e.g., Jenkins v. Anderson, 447 U.S. 231, 238 (1980) (a criminal defendant's exercise of his Fifth Amendment privilege prior to arrest may be used to impeach his credibility at trial); Williams v. Florida, 399 U.S. 78, 84–85 (1970) (a criminal defendant may be compelled to disclose the substance of an alibi defense prior to trial or be barred from asserting it). * * * The Court likewise has held that plea bargaining does not violate the

Fifth Amendment, even though criminal defendants may feel considerable pressure to admit guilt in order to obtain more lenient treatment. See, e.g., Bordenkircher v. Hayes, 434 U.S. 357 (1978).

Nor does reducing an inmate's prison wage and taking away personal television and gym access pose the same hard choice faced by the [defendant in] Ohio Adult Parole Authority v. Woodard, 523 U.S. 272 (1998). * * * In *Woodard,* the plaintiff faced not loss of a personal television and gym access, but loss of life. In a unanimous opinion just four Terms ago, this Court held that a death row inmate could be made to choose between incriminating himself at his clemency interview and having adverse inferences drawn from his silence. The Court reasoned that it "is difficult to see how a voluntary interview could 'compel' respondent to speak. He merely faces a choice quite similar to the sorts of choices that a criminal defendant must make in the course of criminal proceedings, none of which has ever been held to violate the Fifth Amendment." As here, the inmate in *Woodard* claimed to face a Hobson's choice: He would damage his case for clemency no matter whether he spoke and incriminated himself, or remained silent and the clemency board construed that silence against him. Unlike here, the Court nevertheless concluded that the pressure the inmate felt to speak to improve his chances of clemency did not constitute unconstitutional compulsion.

* * *

Respondent is mistaken as well to concentrate on the so-called reward/penalty distinction and the illusory baseline against which a change in prison conditions must be measured. The answer to the question whether the government is extending a benefit or taking away a privilege rests entirely in the eye of the beholder. For this reason, emphasis of any baseline, while superficially appealing, would be an inartful addition to an already confused area of jurisprudence. The prison warden in this case stated that it is largely a matter of chance where in a prison an inmate is assigned. Even if Inmates A and B are serving the same sentence for the same crime, Inmate A could end up in a medium-security unit and Inmate B in a maximum-security unit based solely on administrative factors beyond their control. Under respondent's view, however, the Constitution allows the State to offer Inmate B the opportunity to live in the medium-security unit conditioned on his participation in the SATP, but does not allow the State to offer Inmate A the opportunity to live in that same medium-security unit subject to the same conditions. The consequences for Inmates A and B are identical: They may participate and live in medium security or refuse and live in maximum security. Respondent, however, would have us say the Constitution puts Inmate A in a superior position to Inmate B solely by the accident of the initial assignment to a medium-security unit.

This reasoning is unsatisfactory. * * * Respondent's reasoning would provide States with perverse incentives to assign all inmates convicted of sex offenses to maximum security prisons until near the time of release, when the rehabilitation program starts. The rule would work to the detriment of the entire class of sex offenders who might not otherwise be placed in maximum-security facilities. And prison administrators would be forced, before making routine prison housing decisions, to identify each inmate's so-called baseline and determine whether an adverse effect, however marginal, will result from the administrative decision. The easy alternatives that respondent predicts for prison administrators would turn out to be not so trouble free.

Respondent's analysis also would call into question the constitutionality of an accepted feature of federal criminal law: the downward adjustment for acceptance of criminal responsibility provided in § 3E1.1 of the United States Sentencing Guidelines (Nov. 2002). If the Constitution does not permit the government to condition the use of a personal television on the acceptance of responsibility for past crimes, it is unclear how it could permit the government to reduce the length of a prisoner's term of incarceration based upon the same factor. By rejecting respondent's theory, we do not, in this case, call these policies into question.

Acceptance of responsibility is the beginning of rehabilitation. And a recognition that there are rewards for those who attempt to reform is a vital and necessary step toward completion. The Court of Appeals' ruling would defeat these objectives. If the State sought to comply with the ruling by allowing respondent to enter the program while still insisting on his innocence, there would be little incentive for other SATP participants to confess and accept counseling; indeed, there is support for Kansas' view that the dynamics of the group therapy would be impaired. If the State had to offer immunity, the practical effect would be that serial offenders who are incarcerated for but one violation would be given a windfall for past bad conduct, a result potentially destructive of any public or state support for the program and quite at odds with the dominant goal of acceptance of responsibility. If the State found it was forced to graduate prisoners from its rehabilitation program without knowing what other offenses they may have commit-

ted, the integrity of its program would be very much in doubt. If the State found it had to comply by allowing respondent the same perquisites as those who accept counseling, the result would be a dramatic illustration that obduracy has the same rewards as acceptance, and so the program itself would become self-defeating, even hypocritical, in the eyes of those whom it seeks to help. The Fifth Amendment does not require the State to suffer these programmatic disruptions when it seeks to rehabilitate those who are incarcerated for valid, final convictions.

* * *

The judgment of the Court of Appeals is reversed, and the case is remanded for further proceedings.

JUSTICE O'CONNOR, concurring in the judgment.

* * *

I do not believe the consequences facing respondent in this case are serious enough to compel him to be a witness against himself. These consequences involve a reduction in incentive level, and a corresponding transfer from a medium-security to a maximum-security part of the prison. In practical terms, these changes involve restrictions on the personal property respondent can keep in his cell, a reduction in his visitation privileges, a reduction in the amount of money he can spend in the canteen, and a reduction in the wage he can earn through prison employment. These changes in living conditions seem to me minor. Because the prison is responsible for caring for respondent's basic needs, his ability to support himself is not implicated by the reduction in wages he would suffer as a result. While his visitation is reduced as a result of his failure to incriminate himself, he still retains the ability to see his attorney, his family, and members of the clergy. The limitation on the possession of personal items, as well as the amount that respondent is allowed to spend at the canteen, may make his prison experience more unpleasant, but seems very unlikely to actually compel him to incriminate himself.

* * *

JUSTICE STEVENS, **with whom** JUSTICE SOUTER, JUSTICE GINSBURG, **and** JUSTICE BREYER **join, dissenting.**

* * * Until today the Court has never characterized a threatened harm as "a minimal incentive." Nor have we ever held that a person who has made a valid assertion of the privilege may nevertheless be ordered to incriminate himself and sanctioned for disobeying such an order. This is truly a watershed case.

* * *

I

* * *

Not a word in our discussion of the privilege in Ohio Adult Parole Authority v. Woodard, requires a heightened showing of compulsion in the prison context to establish a Fifth Amendment violation. That case is wholly unlike this one because Woodard was not ordered to incriminate himself and was not punished for refusing to do so. * * *

Respondent was directly ordered by prison authorities to participate in a program that requires incriminating disclosures, whereas no one ordered Woodard to do anything. Like a direct judicial order to answer questions in the courtroom, an order from the State to participate in the SATP is inherently coercive. Moreover, the penalty for refusing to participate in the SATP is automatic. Instead of conjecture and speculation about the indi-

rect consequences that may flow from a decision to remain silent, we can be sure that defiance of a direct order carries with it the stigma of being a lawbreaker or a problem inmate, as well as other specified penalties. The penalty involved in this case is a mandated official response to the assertion of the privilege.

* * *

II

The plurality and Justice O'CONNOR hold that the consequences stemming from respondent's invocation of the privilege are not serious enough to constitute compulsion. The threat of transfer to Level I and a maximum-security unit is not sufficiently coercive in their view—either because the consequence is not really a penalty, just the loss of a benefit, or because it is a penalty, but an insignificant one. I strongly disagree.

* * *

The punitive consequences * * * include not only the dignitary and reputational harms flowing from the transfer, but a serious loss of tangible privileges as well. Because he refused to participate in the SATP, respondent's visitation rights will be restricted. He will be able to earn only $0.60 per day, as compared to Level III inmates, who can potentially earn minimum wage. His access to prison organizations and activities will be limited. He will no longer be able to send his family more than $30 per pay period. He will be prohibited from spending more than $20 per payroll period at the canteen, rather than the $140 he could spend at Level III, and he will be restricted in what property he can keep in his cell. In addition, because he will be transferred to a maximum-security unit, respondent will be forced to share a cell with three other inmates rather than one, and his movement outside the cell will be substantially curtailed. The District Court found that the maximum-security unit is "a more dangerous environment occupied by more serious offenders." Perhaps most importantly, respondent will no longer be able to earn his way back up to Level III status through good behavior during the remainder of his sentence.

The plurality's glib attempt to characterize these consequences as a loss of potential benefits rather than a penalty is wholly unpersuasive. The threatened transfer to Level I and to a maximum-security unit represents a significant, adverse change from the status quo. * * *

* * * We have recognized that the government can extend a benefit in exchange for incriminating statements, but cannot threaten to take away privileges as the cost of invoking Fifth Amendment rights. Based on this distinction, nothing that I say in this dissent calls into question the constitutionality of *downward* adjustments for acceptance of responsibility under the United States Sentencing Guidelines. Although such a reduction in sentence creates a powerful incentive for defendants to confess, it completely avoids the constitutional issue that would be presented if the Guidelines operated like the scheme here and authorized an *upward* adjustment whenever a defendant refused to accept responsibility. * * * By obscuring the distinction between penalties and incentives, it is the plurality that calls into question both the Guidelines and plea bargaining.

* * *

III

* * *

The plurality's willingness to sacrifice prisoners' Fifth Amendment rights is also unwarranted because available alternatives would allow the State to achieve the same objectives without impinging on inmates' privilege. The most obvious alternative is to grant participants use immunity. * * *

The plurality contends that requiring immunity will undermine the therapeutic goals of the program because once "inmates know society will not punish them for their past offenses, they may be left with the false impression that society does not consider those crimes to be serious ones." The idea that an inmate who is confined to prison for almost 20 years for an offense could be left with the impression that his crimes are not serious or that wrongdoing does not carry consequences is absurd. Moreover, the argument starts from a false premise. Granting use immunity does not preclude prosecution; it merely prevents the State from using an inmate's own words, and the fruits thereof, against him in a subsequent prosecution. The plurality's concern might be justified if the State were required to grant *transactional* immunity, but we have made clear since *Kastigar* that use immunity is sufficient to alleviate a potential Fifth Amendment violation. Nor is a State *required* to grant use immunity in order to have a sex offender treatment program that involves admission of responsibility.

* * *

Through its treatment program, Kansas seeks to achieve the admirable goal of reducing recidivism among sex offenders. In the process, however, the State demands an impermissible and unwarranted sacrifice from the participants. No matter what the goal, inmates should not be compelled to forfeit the privilege against self-incrimination simply because the ends are legitimate or because they have been convicted of sex offenses. Particularly in a case like this one, in which respondent has protested his innocence all along and is being compelled to confess to a crime that he still insists he did not commit, we ought to ask ourselves—what if this is one of those rare cases in which the jury made a mistake and he is actually innocent? And in answering that question, we should consider that even members of the Star Chamber thought they were pursuing righteous ends. I respectfully dissent.

3. Comment on the Invocation of the Privilege

The Griffin Rule

In Griffin v. California, 380 U.S. 609 (1965), the Court held that adverse comment to the jury, by either the judge or the prosecutor, on the defendant's election not to testify constitutes punishment for the invocation of silence, which is tantamount to compulsion and therefore violates the Fifth Amendment. Thus, the fact that the defendant did not take the stand cannot be used as information against him.[3]

The Court extended *Griffin* in Carter v. Kentucky, 450 U.S. 288 (1981). Carter asked the trial judge to instruct the jurors that they were not to draw an adverse inference from the fact that Carter did not testify. The trial judge denied the request, reasoning that such an instruction would only draw attention to the fact that the defendant had not testified. The Supreme Court held that the trial judge was required to give the instruction upon request, "to minimize the danger that the jury will give evidentiary weight to a defendant's failure to testify".

Then in Lakeside v. Oregon, 435 U.S. 333 (1978), the trial judge instructed the jury not to draw an adverse inference from Lakeside's failure to testify. Lakeside *objected* to the instruction and argued that he was being penalized for not testifying when the trial judge gave the instruction against his wishes. But the Court rejected Lakeside's argument. It reasoned that the instruction could not be compulsion, because the Court had held in *Carter* that the instruction was necessary to *dispel* the compulsion that would otherwise exist due to the negative inferences that could be drawn from the defendant's failure to testify. Why, do you think, did Lakeside's counsel object to the no-adverse-inference instruction?

The Court distinguished *Griffin* in United States v. Robinson, 485 U.S. 25 (1988), and held that a prosecutor properly pointed out in closing argument that the defendant had an opportunity to testify. The prosecutor was responding to defense counsel's argument that the defendant had not been permitted to explain his side of the story. How is this case distinguishable from *Griffin*?

How does an adverse inference "punish" a defendant who refuses to testify? Consider the assessment of Judge Posner, writing in United States v. Castillo, 965 F.2d 238 (7th Cir.1992). He argued that the "punishment" found impermis-

3. For a criticism of *Griffin*, see Ayer, The Fifth Amendment and the Inference of Guilt from Silence: Griffin v. California After Fifteen Years, 78 Mich.L.Rev. 841 (1980)(arguing that *Griffin* is an ill-advised exception to the rule that attorneys may draw any reasonable infer-ence from the facts legitimately within the jury's knowledge). For a defense of *Griffin*, see Saltzburg, Foreword: The Flow and Ebb of Constitutional Criminal Procedure in the War-ren and Burger Courts, 69 Geo.L.J. 151, 204 (1980).

sible in *Griffin* was "slight, because juries are perfectly capable of drawing an adverse inference from a defendant's refusal to testify on their own, without having to be told to do so." Do you agree?

Indirect References to the Defendant's Failure to Testify

Sometimes it is difficult to tell whether a prosecutor is commenting on the silence of the defendant or on the totality of the evidence in a case. The difficulty in distinguishing comments on the accused's failure to testify from permissible argument is apparent in United States v. Monaghan, 741 F.2d 1434 (D.C.Cir. 1984). The defendant was tried for taking indecent liberties with a minor. A majority of the court found that the prosecutor did not impermissibly comment on the defendant's silence by arguing that the government's evidence was "uncontradicted." A dissenting judge reasoned that the defendant was the only witness who could have contradicted the alleged victim, and that repeated emphasis on the absence of contradictory evidence was a clear signal to the jury to consider the defendant's failure to testify as evidence against him. See also United States v. McKenzie, 922 F.2d 1323 (7th Cir.1991)(statement that evidence was "uncontradicted" is permissible, where defendant was not the only person who could rebut the prosecution's case, and therefore the comment would not "naturally and necessarily" remind the jury that the defendant refused to testify); United States v. Mietus, 237 F.3d 866 (7th Cir. 2001) (prosecutor's statement that "we never heard evidence" from the defense on a certain point was not improper, where the codefendant testified and failed to mention anything on the point); Lent v. Wells, 861 F.2d 972 (6th Cir.1988) (statement that evidence was uncontradicted violates *Griffin* where defendant was the only person who could rebut the complainant's assertion that a sexual attack occurred).

Adverse Inferences at Sentencing: Mitchell v. United States

The defendant in Mitchell v. United States, 526 U.S. 314 (1999), pleaded guilty to federal charges of conspiring to distribute five or more kilograms of cocaine and of distributing cocaine. But she reserved the right to contest at sentencing the drug quantity attributable to her under the conspiracy count. Before accepting her plea, the District Court made the inquiries required by Fed.R.Crim.P. 11 (see Chapter 9); told petitioner that she faced a mandatory minimum of one year in prison for distributing cocaine, but a 10–year minimum for conspiracy if the Government could show that she was involved in a quantity more than 5 kilograms; and explained that by pleading guilty she would be waiving her right "at trial to remain silent." Indicating that she had done "some of" the proffered conduct, Mitchell confirmed her guilty plea. At her sentencing hearing, three codefendants testified that she had sold 1 1/2 to 2 ounces of cocaine twice a week for 1 1/2 years, and another person testified that Mitchell had sold her two ounces of cocaine. This was enough to take the quantity over the 5 kilogram threshold for an enhancement of Mitchell's sentence. Mitchell put on no evidence at the sentencing hearing, choosing instead to attack the credibility of the codefendant-witnesses. The sentencing court found that the codefendants' testimony put her over the 5–kilogram threshold, thus mandating the 10–year minimum, and noted specifically that Mitchell's failure to testify at sentencing was a factor in persuading the court to rely on the codefendants' testimony.

Thus, one question in *Mitchell* was whether the sentencing court was permitted to draw an adverse inference from Mitchell's silence. In a 5–4 opinion written by Justice Kennedy, the Court relied on *Griffin* and held that a defendant could not be subject to an adverse inference upon invoking the right to remain silent at a sentencing proceeding. Justice Kennedy's analysis of *Griffin*, and its applicability to sentencing, proceeded as follows:

> [A] sentencing hearing is part of the criminal case—the explicit concern of the self-incrimination privilege. In accordance with the text of the Fifth Amendment, we must accord the privilege the same protection in the sentencing phase of "any criminal case" as that which is due in the trial phase of the same case.
>
> The concerns which mandate the rule against negative inferences at a criminal trial apply with equal force at sentencing. Without question, the stakes are high: Here, the inference drawn by the District Court from petitioner's silence may have resulted in decades of added imprisonment.

* * *

> The rule against adverse inferences from a defendant's silence in criminal proceedings, including sentencing, is of proven utility. * * * [T]here can be little doubt that the rule prohibiting an inference of guilt from a defendant's rightful silence has become an essential feature of our legal tradition. * * * The rule against adverse inferences is a vital instrument for teaching that the question in a criminal case is not whether the defendant committed the acts of which he is accused. The question is whether the Government has carried its burden to prove its allegations while respecting the defendant's individual rights. The Government retains the burden of proving facts relevant to the crime at the sentencing phase and cannot enlist the defendant in this process at the expense of the self-incrimination privilege.

Justice Kennedy took pains to note that Fifth Amendment protection against an adverse inference applied only to the underlying facts of the crime that formed the basis of sentencing. Thus, the sentencing judge was not permitted to draw an adverse inference about the quantity of drugs from the fact that the defendant was silent about the quantity. It should be noted, however, that in determining the proper sentence under the Sentencing Guidelines, a sentencing judge considers many factors other than the facts underlying the conviction. For example, a judge will consider whether the defendant has accepted responsibility for his crime, and can reduce the sentence if she so finds. Conversely, if the defendant shows lack of remorse, this can result in an upward departure. (For the details, see Chapter 11). Can the defendant's silence be used as evidence that he has not accepted responsibility, or as evidence of lack of remorse? Justice Kennedy in *Mitchell* declared this "a separate question" on which the majority expressed no view. He concluded that "[b]y holding petitioner's silence against her in determining the facts of the offense at the sentencing hearing, the District Court imposed an impermissible burden on the exercise of the constitutional right against compelled self-incrimination."

Justice Scalia, joined by the Chief Justice and Justices O'Connor and Thomas, dissented from the Court's holding that an adverse inference cannot be drawn from the defendant's refusal to testify at her sentencing hearing. Justice Scalia analyzed the cogency and applicability of *Griffin* in the following passage:

> The Fifth Amendment provides that "[n]o person . . . shall be compelled in any criminal case to be a witness against himself." As an original matter, it would seem to me that the threat of an adverse inference does not "compel" anyone to testify. It is one of the natural (and not governmentally imposed) consequences of failing to testify—as is the factfinder's increased readiness to believe the incriminating testimony that the defendant chooses not to contradict. Both of these consequences are assuredly cons rather than pros in the "to testify or not to testify" calculus, but they do not compel anyone to take the stand. * * *
>
> * * *
>
> The majority muses that the no-adverse-inference rule has found "wide acceptance in the legal culture" and has even become "an essential feature of our legal tradition." Although the latter assertion strikes me as hyperbolic, the former may be true—which is adequate reason not to overrule these cases, a course I in no way propose. It is not adequate reason, however, to extend these cases into areas where they do not yet apply, since neither logic nor history can be marshaled in defense of them. The illogic of the *Griffin* line is plain, for it runs exactly counter to normal evidentiary inferences: If I ask my son whether he saw a movie I had forbidden him to watch, and he remains silent, the import of his silence is clear.

Justice Scalia then launched into an extensive historical analysis, concluding, on the basis of common-law cases and the understanding of the Framers, that *Griffin's* "pedigree" is "dubious." He asserted that "the text and history of the Fifth Amendment give no indication that there is a federal constitutional prohibition on the use of the defendant's silence as demeanor evidence." He explained as follows:

> Our hardy forebears, who thought of compulsion in terms of the rack and oaths forced by the power of law, would not have viewed the drawing of a commonsensical inference as equivalent pressure. And it is implausible that the Americans of 1791, who were subject to adverse inferences for failing to give unsworn testimony, would have viewed an adverse inference for failing to give sworn testimony as a violation of the Fifth Amendment.

Justice Scalia next contested the application of *Griffin* to sentencing proceedings:

> Our case law has long recognized a natural dichotomy between the guilt and penalty phases. The jury-trial right contained in the Sixth Amendment—whose guarantees apply "[i]n all criminal prosecutions," a term indistinguishable for present purposes from the Fifth Amendment's "in any criminal case"—does not apply at sentencing. Nor does the Sixth Amendment's guarantee of the defendant's right "to be confronted with the witnesses against him." (The sentencing judge may consider, for example, reports of probation officers and psychiatrists without affording any cross-examination.) See Williams v. New York, 337 U.S. 241 (1949). Likewise inapplicable at sentencing is the requirement of the Due Process Clause that

the prosecution prove the essential facts beyond a reasonable doubt. McMillan v. Pennsylvania, 477 U.S. 79 (1986).

Finally, Justice Scalia took issue with the majority's self-limitation—that an adverse inference could not be drawn with respect to the underlying facts of the conviction, with no opinion expressed as to whether an adverse inference could be drawn for other sentencing issues such as acceptance of responsibility:

> If the Court ultimately decides—in the fullness of time and after a decent period of confusion in the lower courts—that the "no inference" rule is indeed limited to "determining facts of the offense," then we will have a system in which a state court can increase the sentence of a convicted drug possessor who refuses to say how many ounces he possessed—not because that suggests he possessed the larger amount (to make such an inference would be unconstitutional!) but because his refusal to cooperate suggests he is unrepentant. Apart from the fact that there is no logical basis for drawing such a line within the sentencing phase (whereas drawing a line between guilt and sentencing is entirely logical), the result produced provides new support for Mr. Bumble's renowned evaluation of the law. Its only sensible feature is that it will almost always be unenforceable, since it will ordinarily be impossible to tell whether the sentencer has used the silence for either purpose or for neither.

> If, on the other hand, the Court ultimately decides—in the fullness of time and after a decent period of confusion in the lower courts—that the extension of *Griffin* announced today is not limited to "determining facts of the offense," then it will have created a system in which we give the sentencing judge access to all sorts of out-of-court evidence, including the most remote hearsay, concerning the character of the defendant, his prior misdeeds, his acceptance of responsibility and determination to mend his ways, but declare taboo the most obvious piece of first-hand evidence standing in front of the judge: the defendant's refusal to cooperate with the court. Such a rule orders the judge to avert his eyes from the elephant in the courtroom when it is the judge's job to size up the elephant.

Justice Thomas wrote a separate dissenting opinion in *Mitchell*, in which he stated that he was prepared to revisit the *Griffin* rule *in toto*. He attacked the analysis in *Griffin* in the following passage:

> *Griffin* relied partly on the premise that comments about a defendant's silence (and the inferences drawn therefrom) penalized the exercise of his Fifth Amendment privilege. As the dissenting Justices in *Griffin* rightly observed, such comments or inferences do not truly "penalize" a defendant. Prosecutorial comments on a defendant's decision to remain silent at trial surely impose no greater "penalty" on a defendant than threats to indict him on more serious charges if he chooses not to enter into a plea bargain— a practice that this Court previously has validated. See, e.g., Bordenkircher v. Hayes, 434 U.S. 357, 365 (1978) (finding no due process violation where plea negotiations "presented the defendant with the unpleasant alternatives of forgoing trial or facing charges on which he was plainly subject to prosecution"). Moreover, this so-called "penalty" lacks any constitutional significance, since the explicit constitutional guarantee has been fully honored—a defendant is not "compelled ... to be a witness against himself," merely because the jury has been told that it may draw an adverse inference

from his failure to testify. Therefore, at bottom, *Griffin* constitutionalizes a policy choice that a majority of the Court found desirable at the time. * * * This sort of undertaking is not an exercise in constitutional interpretation but an act of judicial willfulness that has no logical stopping point.

* * * Given their indefensible foundations, I would be willing to reconsider *Griffin* and *Carter* in the appropriate case. For purposes of this case, which asks only whether the principle established in *Griffin* should be extended, I agree that the Fifth Amendment does not prohibit a sentencer from drawing an adverse inference from a defendant's failure to testify and, therefore, join Justice SCALIA's dissent.

Adverse Inferences Drawn in Civil Cases

In Baxter v. Palmigiano, 425 U.S. 308 (1976), the Court declared that "the Fifth Amendment does not forbid inferences against parties to civil actions when they refuse to testify in response to probative evidence offered against them: the Amendment does not preclude the inference where the privilege is claimed by a party to a civil cause." Why is an adverse inference in a criminal case tantamount to punishment for electing the right to remain silent, whereas it is not punishment to draw the same inference in a civil case? The *Baxter* Court explained that in ordinary civil cases, the party confronted with the invocation of the privilege by the opposing side has no capacity to avoid it, say, by offering immunity from prosecution. Thus the rule allowing invocation of the privilege, though at the risk of suffering an adverse inference or even a default, accommodates the right not to be a witness against oneself while still permitting civil litigation to proceed. Another reason for treating civil and criminal cases differently is that "the stakes are higher" in criminal cases, where liberty or even life may be at stake, and where the Government's "sole interest is to convict."

For a discussion of what courts should do when the privilege against self-incrimination is raised in civil cases, see Heidt, The Conjurer's Circle, The Fifth Amendment Privilege in Civil Cases, 91 Yale L.J. 1062 (1982).

Adverse Inferences Against Non–Parties

In the O.J. Simpson case, Detective Mark Fuhrman declared the privilege when asked whether he had used racially derogatory terms and whether he had planted evidence in the case. Fuhrman's invocations came at a hearing outside the jury's presence. Defense counsel asked the trial court for an instruction that the jury could draw an adverse inference against Fuhrman, i.e., that the jury could conclude that by invoking the privilege, Fuhrman was admitting that the accusations inherent in the questions were true. The trial judge crafted a proposed instruction that Detective Fuhrman was "unavailable" to testify and that the jury could draw a negative inference about this unavailability. But the prosecution took an immediate appeal, and the California Court of Appeals held that the trial judge could not give the proposed instruction. An appeal by the defense to the California Supreme Court was unavailing. The appellate courts relied on a state statute that could be read to prohibit the drawing of adverse inferences from declaration of a privilege. The prosecution's brief implied that it would be inappropriate to "punish" Fuhrman for his invocation of the privilege.

How would Fuhrman, who was only a witness in the case, be "punished" by an instruction to draw an adverse inference?

Is the protection afforded by the California statute required by the Constitution? Should it apply to witnesses, as opposed to parties? Does it mean that a defendant cannot call as a witness the person who the defendant claims is the perpetrator, and have that witness invoke his privilege on the stand? Is the statute really based on evidentiary rather than constitutional principles? Do the rules of evidence support exclusion on the ground that when a witness invokes the privilege in response to a question, it is not really an admission of guilt or wrongdoing, and it may provide an invitation to baseless questions from inquiring counsel who knows that the "answers" will be an invocation of the privilege? See United States v. Griffin, 66 F.3d 68 (5th Cir. 1995) (holding that defendants were not entitled to call a witness who will invoke his privilege on the witness stand when asked questions about the crime for which the defendants were charged: "a claim of Fifth Amendment privilege is likely to be regarded by the jury as high courtroom drama and a focus of ineradicable interest, when in fact its probative force is weak and it cannot be tested by cross-examination"). Could these evidentiary concerns be handled by a requirement that all questions to the witness must have a substantial basis in fact?

For arguments that adverse inferences should be drawn against non-parties who invoke the privilege—both as a constitutional and as an evidentiary matter—see Nesson and Leotta, The Fifth Amendment Privilege Against Cross–Examination, 85 Geo.L.J. 1627 (1997); VanOort, Invocations as Evidence: Admitting Nonparty Witness Invocations of the Privilege Against Self–Incrimination, 65 Univ.Chi.L.Rev. 1435 (1998).

4. Compulsion and the "Exculpatory No" Doctrine

The Court in Brogan v. United States, 522 U.S. 398 (1998), considered whether the Fifth Amendment prohibited the government from criminalizing false statements to government investigators. Justice Scalia, writing for the Court, summarized the facts.

> While acting as a union officer during 1987 and 1988, petitioner James Brogan accepted cash payments from JRD Management Corporation, a real estate company whose employees were represented by the union. On October 4, 1993, federal agents from the Department of Labor and the Internal Revenue Service visited petitioner at his home. The agents identified themselves and explained that they were seeking petitioner's cooperation in an investigation of JRD and various individuals. * * *

> The agents then asked petitioner if he would answer some questions, and he agreed. One question was whether he had received any cash or gifts from JRD when he was a union officer. Petitioner's response was "no." At that point, the agents disclosed that a search of JRD headquarters had produced company records showing the contrary. They also told petitioner that lying to federal agents in the course of an investigation was a crime. Petitioner did not modify his answers, and the interview ended shortly thereafter.

> Petitioner was indicted for accepting unlawful cash payments from an employer * * *, and making a false statement within the jurisdiction of a federal agency in violation of 18 U.S.C. § 1001.

Section 1001, the false statement statute, provides that "whoever, in any matter within the jurisdiction of any department or agency of the United States knowingly and willfully falsifies, conceals or covers up by any trick, scheme, or device a material fact, or makes any false, fictitious or fraudulent statements or representations, or makes or uses any false writing or document knowing the same to contain any false, fictitious or fraudulent statement or entry, shall be fined not more than $10,000 or imprisoned not more than five years, or both." Brogan admitted that his denial of involvement was literally within the statute, but argued that he could not be convicted because of a doctrine developed under the case law called the "exculpatory no doctrine." The central feature of this doctrine is that a simple denial of guilt does not come within the statute. The rationale of the doctrine is that section 1001 does not criminalize simple denials of guilt to Government investigators, because to do so would violate the "spirit" of the Fifth Amendment.

Justice Scalia categorically rejected the "exculpatory no" doctrine. He dismissed the Fifth Amendment argument by noting that Brogan was not compelled, in any sense, to deny criminal responsibility when he said "no" to the agents. He could simply have remained silent without penalty. Justice Scalia addressed the Fifth Amendment argument as follows:

> [Brogan] argues that a literal reading of section 1001 violates the "spirit" of the Fifth Amendment because it places a "cornered suspect" in the "cruel trilemma" of admitting guilt, remaining silent, or falsely denying guilt. This "trilemma" is wholly of the guilty suspect's own making, of course. An innocent person will not find himself in a similar quandary (as one commentator has put it, the innocent person lacks even a "lemma," Allen, The Simpson Affair, Reform of the Criminal Justice Process, and Magic Bullets, 67 U. Colo. L.Rev. 989, 1016 (1996)). And even the honest and contrite guilty person will not regard the third prong of the "trilemma" (the blatant lie) as an available option. The bon mot "cruel trilemma" first appeared in Justice Goldberg's opinion for the Court in Murphy v. Waterfront Comm'n of N.Y. Harbor, 378 U.S. 52 (1964), where it was used to explain the importance of a suspect's Fifth Amendment right to remain silent when subpoenaed to testify in an official inquiry. Without that right, the opinion said, he would be exposed "to the cruel trilemma of self-accusation, perjury or contempt." In order to validate the "exculpatory no," the elements of this "cruel trilemma" have now been altered—ratcheted up, as it were, so that the right to remain silent, which was the liberation from the original trilemma, is now itself a cruelty. We are not disposed to write into our law this species of compassion inflation.
>
> Whether or not the predicament of the wrongdoer run to ground tugs at the heart strings, neither the text nor the spirit of the Fifth Amendment confers a privilege to lie. "[P]roper invocation of the Fifth Amendment privilege against compulsory self-incrimination allows a witness to remain silent, but not to swear falsely." United States v. Apfelbaum, 445 U.S. 115 (1980). Petitioner contends that silence is an "illusory" option because a suspect may fear that his silence will be used against him later, or may not even know that silence is an available option. As to the former: It is well established that the fact that a person's silence can be used against him— either as substantive evidence of guilt or to impeach him if he takes the stand—does not exert a form of pressure that exonerates an otherwise

unlawful lie. And as for the possibility that the person under investigation may be unaware of his right to remain silent: In the modern age of frequently dramatized "Miranda" warnings, that is implausible. * * *

Justice Scalia was equally skeptical of the "public policy" arguments that allegedly supported the "exculpatory no" doctrine.

> Petitioner repeats the argument made by many supporters of the "exculpatory no," that the doctrine is necessary to eliminate the grave risk that section 1001 will become an instrument of prosecutorial abuse. The supposed danger is that overzealous prosecutors will use this provision as a means of "piling on" offenses—sometimes punishing the denial of wrongdoing more severely than the wrongdoing itself. The objectors' principal grievance on this score, however, lies not with the hypothetical prosecutors but with Congress itself, which has decreed the obstruction of a legitimate investigation to be a separate offense, and a serious one. It is not for us to revise that judgment. Petitioner has been unable to demonstrate, moreover, any history of prosecutorial excess, either before or after widespread judicial acceptance of the "exculpatory no." And finally, if there is a problem of supposed "overreaching" it is hard to see how the doctrine of the "exculpatory no" could solve it. It is easy enough for an interrogator to press the liar from the initial simple denial to a more detailed fabrication that would not qualify for the exemption.

Justices Ginsburg, joined by Justice Souter, concurred only in the judgment in *Brogan*, inviting Congress to consider the possibility that section 1001 might be used for overreaching, i.e., to prosecute people who are not aware that denying criminal responsibility in a situation like Brogan's is in fact a criminal act. Justice Stevens, joined by Justice Breyer, dissented.

D. TO WHOM DOES THE PRIVILEGE BELONG?

The privilege against self-incrimination is personal, belonging only to the person who is himself incriminated by his own testimony. For example, an attorney may not claim the privilege on the ground that his testimony might incriminate his client. Which of the rationales for the privilege, discussed above, justify this limitation? Consider the Court's policy analysis in the following case.

FISHER v. UNITED STATES

Supreme Court of the United States, 1976.
425 U.S. 391.

MR. JUSTICE WHITE **delivered the opinion of the Court.**

[Taxpayers, who were under investigation for possible civil or criminal tax violations, obtained documents relating to the preparation of their tax returns from their accountants. Shortly thereafter, they transferred these documents to the lawyers handling their cases. The IRS served summonses on the attorneys directing them to pro-duce the records, but the attorneys refused to comply on Fifth Amendment grounds.]

II

All of the parties in these cases and the Court of Appeals for the Fifth Circuit have concurred in the proposition that if the Fifth Amendment would have excused a *taxpayer* from turning over the accountant's papers had he possessed them, the *attorney* to whom they are delivered for the purpose of obtaining legal advice should also be immune from subpoena. Although we agree with this proposition * * * we are convinced that, under our decision in Couch v. United States, 409 U.S. 322 (1973), it is not the taxpayer's Fifth Amendment privilege that would excuse the *attorney* from production.

The relevant part of that Amendment provides:

"No person * * * shall be *compelled* in any criminal case to be a *witness against himself.*" (Emphasis added.)

The taxpayer's privilege under this Amendment is not violated by enforcement of the summonses involved in these cases because enforcement against a taxpayer's lawyer would not "compel" the taxpayer to do anything—and certainly would not compel him to be a "witness" against himself. The Court has held repeatedly that the Fifth Amendment is limited to prohibiting the use of "physical or moral compulsion" exerted on the person asserting the privilege. In Couch v. United States, supra, we recently ruled that the Fifth Amendment rights of a taxpayer were not violated by the enforcement of a documentary summons directed to her accountant and requiring production of the taxpayer's own records in the possession of the accountant. We did so on the ground that in such a case "the ingredient of personal compulsion against an accused is lacking."

Here, the taxpayers are compelled to do no more than was the taxpayer in *Couch.* The taxpayers' Fifth Amendment privilege is therefore not violated by enforcement of the summonses directed toward their attorneys. This is true whether or not the Amendment would have barred a subpoena direct-ing the taxpayer to produce the documents while they were in his hands.

The fact that the attorneys are agents of the taxpayers does not change this result. *Couch* held as much, since the accountant there was also the taxpayer's agent, and in this respect reflected a longstanding view. In Hale v. Henkel, 201 U.S. 43, 69–70 (1906), the Court said that the privilege "was never intended to permit [a person] to plead the fact that some third person might be incriminated by his testimony, even though he were the agent of such person * * *. [T]he Amendment is limited to a person who shall be compelled in any criminal case to be a witness against *himself.*" (Emphasis in original.) "It is extortion of information from the accused himself that offends our sense of justice."

* * *

Nor is this one of those situations, which *Couch* suggested might exist, where constructive possession is so clear or relinquishment of possession so temporary and insignificant as to leave the personal compulsion upon the taxpayer substantially intact. * * *

* * *

The Court of Appeals for the Fifth Circuit suggested that because legally and ethically the attorney was required to respect the confidences of his client, the latter had a reasonable expectation of privacy for the records in the hands of the attorney and therefore did not forfeit his Fifth Amendment privilege with respect to the records by transferring them in order to obtain legal advice. It is true that the Court has often stated that one of the several purposes served by the constitutional privilege against compelled testimonial self-incrimination is that of protecting personal privacy. But the Court has never suggested that every invasion of privacy violates the privilege. Within the limits imposed by the language of the Fifth Amendment, which we necessarily observe, the privilege truly serves privacy interests; but the Court has never on any ground, personal privacy included, applied the Fifth Amendment to prevent the otherwise proper acquisition or use of evidence which, in the Court's view, did not involve compelled testimonial self-incrimination of some sort.

* * *

We cannot cut the Fifth Amendment completely loose from the moorings of its language, and make it serve as a general protector of privacy—a word not mentioned in its text and a concept directly addressed in the Fourth Amendment. We adhere to the view that the Fifth Amendment protects against "compelled self-incrimination, not [the disclosure of] private information."

Insofar as private information not obtained through compelled self-incriminating testimony is legally protected, its protection stems from other sources—the Fourth Amendment's protection against seizures without warrant or probable cause and against subpoenas which suffer from "too much indefiniteness or breadth in the things required to be 'particularly described,'"or evidentiary privileges such as the attorney-client privilege.

[In Part III, the Court held that the attorney-client privilege protects against disclosure of documents that would have been protected by the Fifth Amendment had they been in the taxpayer's possession. However, in Part IV it concluded that the documents in question would not be privileged even in the hands of the taxpayer. See infra section E, 2 of this chapter for the Court's discussion of the latter issue.]

Note on the Collective Entity Rule

Prior to *Fisher* the Court in Bellis v. United States, 417 U.S. 85 (1974), had applied the "personal compulsion" limitation to exclude partnerships from Fifth Amendment protection. The partnership in *Bellis* was a law firm with three partners and a handful of employees. Justice Marshall, writing for the Court, stated broadly that the privilege against compelled self-incrimination is a "purely personal" one, which applies "only to natural individuals." Therefore, "no artificial organization may utilize the personal privilege against compulsory self-incrimination." Justice Marshall concluded that the partnership in *Bellis* had "an established institutional identity independent of its individual partners."

In United States v. Doe, 465 U.S. 605 (1984), the Court distinguished *Bellis* and held that a sole proprietorship was entitled to Fifth Amendment protection. A sole proprietorship was not considered an entity distinct from the individual. However, in Braswell v. United States, 487 U.S. 99 (1988), the Court held that a corporation wholly owned and operated by a single individual was not itself entitled to Fifth Amendment protection.[4] Chief Justice Rehnquist, writing for the Court, distinguished *Doe* as follows:

> Had petitioner conducted his business as a sole proprietorship, *Doe* would require that he be provided the opportunity to show that his act of production would entail testimonial self-incrimination. But petitioner has operated his business through the corporate form, and we have long recognized that for

---

4. See also In re Grand Jury Subpoena, 973 F.2d 45 (1st Cir.1992)(trust established by two brothers for purposes of conducting real estate transactions held an entity not entitled to Fifth Amendment protection).

purposes of the Fifth Amendment, corporations and other collective entities are treated differently from individuals.

Corporations have Fourth Amendment rights (see Marshall v. Barlow's in Chapter Two); they have First Amendment rights (First National Bank v. Bellotti, 435 U.S. 765 (1978)); they have due process rights (International Shoe Co. v. Washington, 326 U.S. 310 (1945)); why don't they have Fifth Amendment rights? Why is it of constitutional importance that Braswell operated a business as a wholly owned corporation rather than as a sole proprietorship?

E. WHAT IS PROTECTED

The privilege only protects a person when that person is being compelled to be a "witness" against himself. Thus, it does not protect against all forms of compelled self-incrimination. If a person is forced to give information other than what a "witness" would provide, the privilege is inapplicable. In the cases that follow, the Court attempts to define the scope of information protected by the privilege.

1. Non-testimonial Evidence

SCHMERBER v. CALIFORNIA

Supreme Court of the United States, 1966.
384 U.S. 757.

MR. JUSTICE BRENNAN **delivered the opinion of the Court.**

Petitioner was convicted in Los Angeles Municipal Court of the criminal offense of driving an automobile while under the influence of intoxicating liquor. He had been arrested at a hospital while receiving treatment for injuries suffered in an accident involving the automobile that he had apparently been driving. At the direction of a police officer, a blood sample was then withdrawn from petitioner's body by a physician at the hospital. The chemical analysis of this sample revealed a percent by weight of alcohol in his blood at the time of the offense which indicated intoxication, and the report of this analysis was admitted in evidence at the trial. Petitioner object-

ed to receipt of this evidence of the analysis on the ground that the blood had been withdrawn despite his refusal, on the advice of his counsel, to consent to the test. He contended that in that circumstance the withdrawal of the blood and the admission of the analysis in evidence denied him * * * his privilege against self-incrimination under the Fifth Amendment * * *.

* * *

II

* * *. We hold that the privilege protects an accused only from being compelled to testify against himself, or otherwise provide the State with evidence of a testimonial or communicative nature,[a] and that the withdrawal

a. A dissent suggests that the report of the blood test was "testimonial" or "communicative," because the test was performed in order to obtain the testimony of others, communicating to the jury facts about petitioner's condition. Of course, all evidence received in court is "testimonial" or "communicative" if these words are thus used. But the Fifth Amendment relates only to acts on the part of the person to

whom the privilege applies, and we use these words subject to the same limitations. A nod or head-shake is as much a "testimonial" or "communicative" act in this sense as are spoken words. But the terms as we use them do not apply to evidence of acts noncommunicative in nature as to the person asserting the privilege, even though, as here, such acts are compelled to obtain the testimony of others.

of blood and use of the analysis in question in this case did not involve compulsion to these ends.

It could not be denied that in requiring petitioner to submit to the withdrawal and chemical analysis of his blood the State compelled him to submit to an attempt to discover evidence that might be used to prosecute him for a criminal offense. * * * The critical question, then, is whether petitioner was thus compelled "to be a witness against himself."

If the scope of the privilege coincided with the complex of values it helps to protect, we might be obliged to conclude that the privilege was violated. * * *

* * * [H]owever, the privilege has never been given the full scope which the values it helps to protect suggest. History and a long line of authorities in lower courts have consistently limited its protection to situations in which the State seeks to submerge those values by obtaining the evidence against an accused through "the cruel, simple expedient of compelling it from his own mouth. * * * In sum, the privilege is fulfilled only when the person is guaranteed the right 'to remain silent unless he chooses to speak in the unfettered exercise of his own will." * * *

It is clear that the protection of the privilege reaches an accused's communications, whatever form they might take * * *. On the other hand, both federal and state courts have usually held that it offers no protection against compulsion to submit to fingerprinting, photographing, or measurements, to write or speak for identification, to appear in court, to stand, to assume a stance, to walk, or to make a particular gesture. The distinction which has emerged, often expressed in different ways, is that the privilege is a bar against compelling "communications" or "testimony," but that compulsion which makes a suspect or accused the source of "real or physical evidence" does not violate it.

* * *

* * * Not even a shadow of testimonial compulsion upon or enforced communication by the accused was involved either in the extraction or in the chemical analysis. Petitioner's testimonial capacities were in no way implicated; indeed, his participation, except as a donor, was irrelevant to the results of the test, which depend on chemical analysis and on that alone. Since the blood test evidence, although an incriminating product of compulsion, was neither petitioner's testimony nor evidence relating to some communicative act or writing by the petitioner, it was not inadmissible on privilege grounds.

* * *

MR. JUSTICE BLACK **with whom MR.** JUSTICE DOUGLAS **joins, dissenting.**

* * * [I]t seems to me that the compulsory extraction of petitioner's blood for analysis so that the person who analyzed it could give evidence to convict him had both a "testimonial" and a "communicative nature." The sole purpose of this project which proved to be successful was to obtain "testimony" from some person to prove that petitioner had alcohol in his blood at the time he was arrested. And the purpose of the project was certainly "communicative" in that the analysis of the blood was to supply information to enable a witness to communicate to the court and jury that petitioner was more or less drunk.

* * *

[The concurring opinion of Justices Harlan and Stewart and the dissenting opinions of Chief Justice Warren and Justice Fortas are omitted.]

Note on Testimonial vs. Non–Testimonial Evidence

The holding of *Schmerber* has been reaffirmed and applied several times. One year after that decision, the Court held that requiring a suspect to participate in a police line-up did not violate the Fifth Amendment. In United States v. Wade, 388 U.S. 218 (1967), the defendant was arrested for robbing a bank. He was forced to stand in a line-up with several other prisoners, each of whom wore strips of tape on their faces, as had the actual robber. In addition, each man was required to utter the words allegedly spoken by the robber. The Court held:

> We have no doubt that compelling the accused merely to exhibit his person for observation by a prosecution witness prior to trial involves no compulsion of the accused to give evidence having testimonial significance. It is compulsion of the accused to exhibit his physical characteristics, not compulsion to disclose any knowledge he might have. It is no different from compelling Schmerber to provide a blood sample * * *. [C]ompelling Wade to speak within hearing distance of the witnesses, even to utter words purportedly uttered by the robber, was not compulsion to utter statements of a "testimonial" nature; he was required to use his voice as an identifying physical characteristic, not to speak his guilt.

Justice Black again dissented on the Fifth Amendment issue, because requiring a suspect to stand in a line-up and speak certain words is "forcing [that] person to supply proof of his own crime."

Justice Fortas filed a separate opinion challenging the constitutionality of forcing a suspect to speak in the line-up.

> * * * It is more than passive, mute assistance to the eyes of the victim or of witnesses. It is the kind of volitional act—the kind of forced cooperation by the accused—which is within the historical perimeter of the privilege against compelled self-incrimination.

> * * * *Schmerber,* which authorized the forced extraction of blood from the veins of an unwilling human being, did not compel the person actively to cooperate—to accuse himself by a volitional act which differs only in degree from compelling him to act out the crime, which, I assume, would be rebuffed by the Court. It is the latter feature which places the compelled utterance by the accused squarely within the history and noble purpose of the Fifth Amendment's commandment.

What other physical characteristics are excepted from Fifth Amendment protection? In Gilbert v. California, 388 U.S. 263 (1967), a companion case to *Wade,* the Court held that handwriting exemplars may be compelled from an unwilling defendant. In United States v. Dionisio, 410 U.S. 1 (1973), the same rule was applied to voice-prints. While one's voice and handwriting are means of communication, the Court's view is that the sample itself, in contrast to the content of the communication, is merely an identifying physical characteristic, outside the protection of the Fifth Amendment.

Of course, another view of voice and handwriting exemplars is that the suspect is saying "this is my real voice and handwriting." If, in fact, the suspect attempts to distort the exemplar, this may be considered as evidence of guilt. Viewed in this light, do the cases make sense? Note that your answer may depend upon the policy arguments that you accept as a valid basis for the privilege.

Testimonial Evidence and the Cruel Trilemma: Pennsylvania v. Muniz

The Court in Pennsylvania v. Muniz, 496 U.S. 582 (1990), finally articulated a rationale for understanding the *Schmerber* line of cases. It held that the line between testimonial and non-testimonial evidence must be determined by whether the witness faces the "cruel trilemma" in disclosing the evidence. After failing sobriety tests, police officers transported Muniz to a booking center. There they asked Muniz, among other things, the date of his sixth birthday. The officers did not give Muniz *Miranda* warnings. Muniz responded with slurred speech, stumbled over his answers, and said that he did not know the date of his sixth birthday. Both the manner of speech and the content of Muniz's answers were used at trial as evidence that he was under the influence of alcohol. In the Supreme Court, a violation of *Miranda* was assumed; this means that the police officer's questions operated as compulsion. However, the Fifth Amendment is applicable only if the government compels the defendant to be a "witness" against himself. The question therefore was whether any of the information derived from Muniz was testimonial.

Writing for eight members of the Court, Justice Brennan concluded that evidence of the slurred nature of Muniz's speech was not testimonial under *Schmerber* and its progeny. The slurred speech in *Muniz* was held to be physical evidence, because its relevance was divorced from the content of the words themselves. The Court stated that "[r]equiring a suspect to reveal the physical manner in which he articulates words, like requiring him to reveal the physical properties of the sound produced by his voice * * * does not, without more, compel him to provide a 'testimonial' response for purposes of the privilege." Only Justice Marshall dissented on this point.

The Court did not decide whether a person's performance on a sobriety test (e.g., standing on one leg for thirty seconds and counting) was testimonial, because Muniz did not challenge the lower court's decision that such evidence was non-testimonial under *Schmerber*. The Court noted, however, that many lower courts have held that such tests merely measure physical capacity such as reflex, dexterity, and balance, and consequently do not compel testimony under *Schmerber*. See People v. Hager, 69 N.Y.2d 141, 512 N.Y.S.2d 794, 505 N.E.2d 237 (1987)("physical performance tests do not reveal a person's subjective knowledge or thought processes but, rather, exhibit a person's degree of physical coordination.").

With respect to the answer to the sixth birthday question, Justice Brennan, writing on this point for five members of the court (including Justice Marshall), held that Muniz's response *was* testimonial, and therefore that the use of it as evidence at trial was error. The State argued that an answer to the sixth birthday question did not trigger Fifth Amendment protection because the only evidence derived would concern the physiological functioning of Muniz's brain, which the State contended was physical and not testimonial. Justice Brennan rejected this argument, reasoning "that the 'fact' to be inferred might be said to concern the physical status of Muniz's brain merely describes the way in which the inference is incriminating. The correct question * * * is whether the incriminating inference of mental confusion is drawn from a testimonial act or from physical evidence." Thus, when facts about a person's physical condition are obtained through testimonial evidence, the Fifth Amendment applies. For example, if police had compelled Schmerber to answer questions about the alcohol in his blood, his oral responses (e.g., "I am drunk") would be testimonial even though the fact proven would concern Schmerber's physical condition.

Justice Brennan found that Muniz's answer to the sixth birthday question was protected by the "core meaning" of the self-incrimination clause. He explained as follows:

> Because the privilege was designed primarily to prevent a recurrence of the Inquisition and the Star Chamber * * * it is evident that a suspect is compelled to be a witness against himself at least whenever he must face the modern day analog of the historic trilemma. * * * Whenever a suspect is asked for a response requiring him to communicate an express or implied assertion of fact or belief, the suspect confronts the trilemma of truth, falsity or silence and hence the response (whether based on truth or falsity) contains a testimonial component.

The State argued that Muniz did not face the cruel trilemma in answering the sixth birthday question, because the State was not interested in the actual date of Muniz's sixth birthday. Justice Brennan concluded, however, that Muniz was indeed "confronted with the trilemma." He reasoned as follows:

> By hypothesis, the inherently coercive environment created by the custodial interrogation precluded the option of remaining silent. * * * Muniz was left with the choice of incriminating himself by admitting that he did not then know the date of his sixth birthday, or answering untruthfully by reporting a date that he did not then believe to be accurate (an incorrect guess would be incriminating as well as untruthful). The content of his truthful answer supported an inference that his mental faculties were impaired, because his assertion (he did not know the date of his sixth birthday) was different from the assertion (he knew the date was [correct date]) that the trier of fact might reasonably have expected a lucid person to provide. Hence, the incriminating inference of impaired mental faculties stemmed, not just from the fact that Muniz slurred his response, but also from a testimonial aspect of that response.

Chief Justice Rehnquist, joined by Justices White, Blackmun, and Stevens, dissented from the Court's holding that the content of Muniz's answer to the sixth birthday question was testimonial. The Chief Justice argued that the question was designed to elicit the physical fact of Muniz's mental coordination. The dissenters reasoned that since the police could extract Schmerber's blood "to determine how much that part of his system had been affected by alcohol," the police could likewise "examine the functioning of Muniz's mental processes for the same purpose."

The dissenters also took issue with the Court's analysis of the "trilemma" facing Muniz. According to the Chief Justice, "the potential for giving a bad guess does not subject the suspect to the truth-falsity-silence predicament that renders a response testimonial." The Chief Justice reasoned by analogy that if the condition of Muniz's eyesight was relevant, a question concerning what Muniz saw on an eye chart would not require a testimonial response, even though Muniz might have to say "I don't know" or make a wrong guess. The dissenters could not see a distinction between oral responses to an eye chart and oral responses concerning defendant's mental faculties.

Consider Chief Justice Rehnquist's hypothetical case of the eye test where the defendant's poor eyesight is relevant to a prosecution. When compelled to read an eye chart during custodial interrogation, the suspect would appear to be subject to the modern analog of the cruel trilemma—the same one in which Muniz found himself. He cannot be silent due to the pressures of custodial interrogation. If he answers truthfully, that he cannot read the chart, such information can incriminate him where poor eyesight is relevant. If he answers untruthfully and ventures a guess about the chart, that information is incriminating as well. Much to the *Muniz* dissenters' chagrin, the risk of making a wrong guess appears to be the modern day analog of the Star Chamber.

Express or Implied Assertions of Fact: Doe v. United States

Muniz does not stand for the proposition that all compelled oral statements are testimonial. To be testimonial, the communication must be an express or implied assertion of fact that can be true or false: otherwise there is no risk of perjury, and no cruel trilemma (of punishment for truth, falsity, or silence) is presented. For example, in Doe v. United States, 487 U.S. 201 (1988), the Court held that a person's compelled signature on a bank consent form, directing the release of bank records—assuming such records existed—was not testimonial because there was no assertion of fact that the records did or did not exist. A simple authorization is not an implied assertion of fact—it cannot be false, and therefore cannot expose the citizen to the truth-falsity-silence trilemma. See In re Grand Jury Subpoena, 826 F.2d 1166 (2d Cir.1987)("the directives here * * * do not contain any assertions by appellants regarding the existence of, or control over, foreign bank accounts. They authorize disclosure of records and information only if such accounts exist."). Compare United States v. Davis, 767 F.2d 1025 (2d Cir.1985)(consent form may be testimonial if there is an implied assertion that bank records actually exist).

Psychological Evaluations

Estelle v. Smith, 451 U.S. 454 (1981), holds that a defendant who is to be interviewed by a government psychiatrist who will testify at sentencing (in this case the death penalty was involved) has a right to be warned that what he says may be used against him in the sentencing proceeding. Writing for the Court, Chief Justice Burger rejected the state's argument that the psychiatrist's assessment was not made on the basis of testimonial communications, but rather upon physical manifestations and demeanor. The Court found instead that the doctor based his testimony, at least in part, on the defendant's statements about the crime and omissions from his statements. Three Justices concurred in the judgment on right to counsel grounds.

In Jones v. Dugger, 839 F.2d 1441 (11th Cir.1988), Jones was arrested for sexually assaulting two women. He was questioned by Detective Holsberry, without *Miranda* warnings. In response to these questions, he answered that he had finished ninth grade and could read and write; he first denied involvement in the crime, then he confessed. Sanity was the central issue at trial. Holsberry testified as to his observations of Jones at the time, but he did not testify to the content of the statements. Holsberry stated that Jones appeared to be rational and well-oriented at the time of questioning, and appeared to know the difference between right and wrong. The court found that the Fifth Amendment was not violated because no testimonial communication of Jones had been used. The court distinguished *Estelle* as a case where the doctor based his conclusion on the details of the story that defendant told him, whereas Holsberry's testimony merely related "demeanor evidence." How could Holsberry have testified that Jones knew the difference between right and wrong without considering the details of Jones' statement? Moreover, couldn't demeanor either be true or false in the sense that one can "put on" a false demeanor? For a view contrary to *Jones*, see United States v. Hinckley, 672 F.2d 115 (D.C.Cir.1982), affirming the suppression of opinion testimony of FBI agents that John Hinckley was sane, on the basis of statements taken in violation of *Miranda*.

Drawing an Adverse Inference as to Non–Testimonial Evidence

When a suspect refuses to supply physical evidence or to participate in a line-up, what sanctions are available to the state? One possibility is an action for contempt. See Doss v. United States, 431 F.2d 601, 603 (9th Cir.1970). Contempt, while compulsion, is permissible because the suspect has no constitutional right to refuse production of non-testimonial evidence.

Another possibility is that an adverse inference could be drawn against the person who refuses to supply non-testimonial evidence. Justice O'Connor wrote for seven members of the Court in South Dakota v. Neville, 459 U.S. 553 (1983), and explained why an adverse inference permissibly could be drawn. Neville was stopped for drunken driving and was asked to submit to a blood-alcohol test. He refused, saying he was too drunk to pass the test. The state courts suppressed evidence of the refusal on self-incrimination grounds and the Supreme Court reversed. It reasoned as follows: *Schmerber* authorized a state to force a person to take such a test; South Dakota, therefore, had the power to administer a test to Neville without his consent; the state could agree to respect Neville's refusal to take the test; and in doing so the state could condition its agreement to refrain from doing what it lawfully could do by providing that Neville's refusal would result in certain disadvantages being imposed upon him. One such disadvantage is use of the defendant's refusal to take the test as evidence against him at trial. Nor was the officer required to inform Neville that his refusal might be used as evidence against him. The Court found no "implicit promise to forego use of evidence that would unfairly 'trick' " a person.

2. Documents

In *Boyd*, the Court held that a subpoena of one's private books and papers violates the Fifth Amendment, when the content of those papers are incriminating. In *Fisher*, the Court found that the privilege cannot be asserted to prevent the government from obtaining evidence from third parties. The rationale is that the incriminated person has not been *compelled* to do anything when the evidence is gathered from third parties. The same rationale served as a basis for the holding in Andresen v. Maryland, 427 U.S. 463 (1976)(discussed in the previous chapter), that the use at trial of the defendant's business records, seized pursuant to a valid warrant, did not violate the Fifth Amendment. The Court explained:

> [I]n this case, petitioner was not asked to say or to do anything. The records seized contained statements that petitioner had voluntarily commit-

ted to writing. The search for and seizure of these records were conducted by law enforcement personnel. Finally, when these records were introduced at trial, they were authenticated by a handwriting expert, not by petitioner. Any compulsion of petitioner to speak, other than the inherent psychological pressure to respond at trial to unfavorable evidence, was not present.

This case thus falls within the principle stated by Mr. Justice Holmes: "A party is privileged from producing the evidence but not from its production." Johnson v. United States, 228 U.S. 457, 458 (1913). * * *

Fisher and *Andresen* mean that the portion of *Boyd* holding that a person may rely on the privilege to resist a formal governmental demand for private papers in existence when the demand is made no longer will be followed. *Fisher* does suggest, however, that in some circumstances a person may properly refuse to respond to a subpoena because of the tendency of the response to incriminate.

FISHER v. UNITED STATES

Supreme Court of the United States, 1976.
425 U.S. 391.

* * *

IV

* * *

It is also clear that the Fifth Amendment does not independently proscribe the compelled production of every sort of incriminating evidence but applies only when the accused is compelled to make a *testimonial* communication that is incriminating. * * *

A subpoena served on a taxpayer requiring him to produce an accountant's workpapers in his possession without doubt involves substantial compulsion. But it does not compel oral testimony; nor would it ordinarily compel the taxpayer to restate, repeat, or affirm the truth of the contents of the documents sought. Therefore, the Fifth Amendment would not be violated by the fact alone that the papers on their face might incriminate the taxpayer, for the privilege protects a per-

son only against being incriminated by his own compelled testimonial communications.

The accountant's workpapers are not the taxpayer's. They were not prepared by the taxpayer, and they contain no testimonial declarations by him. Furthermore, as far as this record demonstrates, the preparation of all of the papers sought in these cases was wholly voluntary, and they cannot be said to contain compelled testimonial evidence, either of the taxpayers or of anyone else.[a] The taxpayer cannot avoid compliance with the subpoena merely by asserting that the item of evidence which he is required to produce contains incriminating writing, whether his own or that of someone else.

The act of producing evidence in response to a subpoena nevertheless has communicative aspects of its own, wholly aside from the contents of the

---

a. The fact that the documents may have been written by the person asserting the privilege is insufficient to trigger the privilege, and, unless the Government has compelled the subpoenaed person to write the document, the fact that it was written by him is not controlling with respect to the Fifth Amendment issue. Conversations may be seized and introduced in

evidence under proper safeguards, if not compelled. In the case of a documentary subpoena the only thing compelled is the act of producing the document and the compelled act is the same as the one performed when a chattel or document not authored by the producer is demanded.

papers produced. Compliance with the subpoena tacitly concedes the existence of the papers demanded and their possession or control by the taxpayer. It also would indicate the taxpayer's belief that the papers are those described in the subpoena. The elements of compulsion are clearly present, but the more difficult issues are whether the tacit averments of the taxpayer are both "testimonial" and "incriminating" for purposes of applying the Fifth Amendment. These questions perhaps do not lend themselves to categorical answers; their resolution may instead depend on the facts and circumstances of particular cases or classes thereof. In light of the records now before us, we are confident that however incriminating the contents of the accountant's workpapers might be, the act of producing them—the only thing which the taxpayer is compelled to do—would not itself involve testimonial self-incrimination.

It is doubtful that implicitly admitting the existence and possession of the papers rises to the level of testimony within the protection of the Fifth Amendment. The papers belong to the accountant, were prepared by him, and are the kind usually prepared by an accountant working on the tax returns of his client. Surely the Government is in no way relying on the "truthtelling" of the taxpayer to prove the existence of or his access to the documents. The existence and location of the papers are a foregone conclusion and the taxpayer adds little or nothing to the sum total of the Government's information by conceding that he in fact has the papers. Under these circumstances by enforcement of the summons no constitutional rights are touched. The question is not of testimony but of surrender.

When an accused is required to submit a handwriting exemplar he admits his ability to write and impliedly asserts that the exemplar is his writing. But in common experience, the first would be a near truism and the latter self-evident. In any event, although the exemplar may be incriminating to the accused and although he is compelled to furnish it, his Fifth Amendment privilege is not violated because nothing he has said or done is deemed to be sufficiently testimonial for purposes of the privilege. * * *

Moreover, assuming that these aspects of producing the accountant's papers have some minimal testimonial significance, surely it is not illegal to seek accounting help in connection with one's tax returns or for the accountant to prepare workpapers and deliver them to the taxpayer. At this juncture, we are quite unprepared to hold that either the fact of existence of the papers or of their possession by the taxpayer poses any realistic threat of incrimination to the taxpayer.

As for the possibility that responding to the subpoena would authenticate the workpapers, production would express nothing more than the taxpayer's belief that the papers are those described in the subpoena. The taxpayer would be no more competent to authenticate the accountant's workpapers or reports by producing them than he would be to authenticate them if testifying orally. The taxpayer did not prepare the papers and could not vouch for their accuracy. The documents would not be admissible in evidence against the taxpayer without authenticating testimony. Without more, responding to the subpoena in the circumstances before us would not appear to represent a substantial threat of self-incrimination.

Whether the Fifth Amendment would shield the taxpayer from producing his own tax records in his possession is a question not involved here; for the papers demanded here are not his "private papers." We do hold that compliance with a summons directing the taxpayer to produce the accountant's documents involved in these cases would involve no incrimi- nating testimony within the protection of the Fifth Amendment.

* * *

Application of the Fisher Analysis: United States v. Doe and the Act of Production

The Court applied *Fisher* in United States v. Doe, 465 U.S. 605 (1984), holding that the owner of several sole proprietorships properly invoked his privilege against self-incrimination in response to grand jury subpoenas for business documents and records. A district judge had found that the act of producing the documents would have required the owner to "admit that the records exist, that they are in his possession, and that they are authentic." Justice Powell's opinion for the Court stated that the privilege did not protect the content of records prepared voluntarily by Doe, because the government did not compel the owner to make incriminating records. Justice Powell recognized, however, that the privilege may be invoked when the *act of producing* documents involves "testimonial self-incrimination." All Justices agreed with him on this point. Justice O'Connor added a one paragraph concurring opinion stating "that the Fifth Amendment provides absolutely no protection for the contents of private papers of any kind." Justice Marshall, joined by Justice Brennan, offered a short opinion, arguing that the Court had not decided whether the content of some private papers might be protected by the privilege.

Private Papers

Both *Fisher* and *Doe* held that the Fifth Amendment does not protect the content of documents that were voluntarily prepared; even if production of these documents is compelled and the content would be incriminating, the Fifth Amendment is inapplicable because the government did not compel the preparation (as opposed to the production) of the documents. *Fisher* and *Doe* dealt with business papers. Does the rationale of those cases apply to private papers as well? For example, can the government compel a criminal defendant to turn over a diary in which the defendant has written an account of how he committed the crime? In such a case, the act of production itself is not incriminating, since by production the defendant is simply admitting that the diary exists, that he has it, and that it's the document the prosecution demanded. The existence of a diary is not an incriminating fact; having custody of your own diary is not incriminating; and so long as the government can prove that it is the diary in some way other than the act of production, the defendant's act of production itself is not incriminating. The only thing incriminating is the—voluntarily prepared—content of the diary.

Most courts have agreed with Justice O'Connor's concurring opinion in *Doe*, that the contents of voluntarily prepared documents are never protected by the Fifth Amendment. See In re Grand Jury Proceedings on February 4, 1982, 759 F.2d 1418 (9th Cir.1985)(no distinction between business and personal records); In re Grand Jury Subpoena Duces Tecum, 1 F.3d 87 (2d Cir.1993)("Self-incrimination analysis now focuses on whether the creation of the thing demanded was compelled and, if not, whether the act of producing it would constitute compelled testimonial communication."). See also Senate Select Committee v. Packwood, 845 F.Supp. 17 (D.D.C.1994)(denying motion to quash subpoena for Senator Bob Packwood's personal diaries). Other courts still draw a business/personal distinction, and hold that the contents of personal records are protected; this position obviously creates problems in determining which records are business and which are personal. United States v. Stone, 976 F.2d 909 (4th Cir.1992)(affirming a lower court finding, after a hearing, that beach house utility records were business-related and not personal). Given the rationale of *Fisher* and *Doe,* how can one validly distinguish between voluntarily prepared business records and voluntarily prepared personal records?

When is the Act of Production Incriminating?

In *Fisher,* the Court found that the act of producing documents is, to some extent, testimonial. By producing documents in response to a subpoena, the individual admits that the documents exist; that he has custody of the documents; and that the documents are those that are described in the subpoena. This last admission is pertinent to authenticating the documents. If the documents were to be admitted at a trial, the government would have to establish that the documents are authentic, meaning that the documents are what the government says they are, e.g., the defendant's diary and not a forgery. See Federal Rule of Evidence 901. One possible way of proving authenticity is through the defendant's own admission, by way of production in response to a subpoena, that the documents are authentic—at least this is so if the documents were prepared by him or are ones he is personally familiar with.

While every production of documents in response to a subpoena admits existence, control, and authenticity, it does not by any means follow that the Fifth Amendment prohibits every compelled act of document production. The Fifth Amendment applies only if the compelled testimonial act of production could incriminate the person responding to the subpoena. In *Fisher,* the testimonial aspects of the act of production were not incriminating, since existence and control of the documents was a "foregone conclusion", and since the defendant was not competent to authenticate the accountant's workpapers. (The *contents* of the documents were incriminating, but the Fifth Amendment provided no protection as to content, because the documents were voluntarily prepared.) In *Doe,* the Court accepted the finding of the District Court that the act of production would have incriminated the taxpayer. So just when is the act of production, independent of the contents of the documents, incriminating?

A simple admission of the mere existence of documents is rarely incriminating. For example, it is not incriminating for a business to have inventory records, so when someone turns them over to the government, a compelled admission of their existence is not protected by the Fifth Amendment. See United States v. Stone, 976 F.2d 909 (4th Cir.1992)(act of producing utility records for a beach house was not privileged, because there was nothing incriminating about the existence of such records). However, in certain cases the fact that records exist can itself tend to incriminate. Thus, if a corporation has a *second set* of books and records, that fact is incriminating independent of the content of the records. See In re Doe, 711 F.2d 1187 (2d Cir.1983), where a doctor was suspected of dispensing quaaludes without a proper medical purpose. A subpoena for patient files for a certain time period was served. The court found that there were an inordinate number of files for this time period, and that "simply turning over these files could constitute incriminating testimony by Doe that he treated this unrealistic number of patients during the specified periods." See also United States v. Argomaniz, 925 F.2d 1349 (11th Cir. 1991)(existence of documents would show that taxpayer had income for a year when he claimed not to have any). Similarly admission of existence of a document would be incriminating if a person had previously testified, under oath, that a document did not exist. The act of production of that document would be an admission of perjury.

The producer of documents in response to a subpoena admits not only existence but also that he has custody of the documents. Again, however, it is ordinarily not incriminating to control documents, independent of their content. See United States v. Stone, 976 F.2d 909 (4th Cir.1992)(act of producing utility records for a beach house was not privileged, because as the owner of the house, it was not incriminating for the defendant to have the utility bills for the house). For example, the fact that a records custodian has control of corporate records is not inherently incriminating. However, in some limited cases the admission of control creates an inference of affiliation with another person or business that itself tends to incriminate. Thus, in In re Sealed Case, 832 F.2d 1268 (D.C.Cir. 1987), a person allegedly involved in the Iran–Contra scandal was served with a subpoena to produce the records of eight foreign companies involved in covert and illegal activity. The court found that by producing the records, thus admitting custody of them, the person would be admitting that he was intimately involved with these corporations. See also Smith v. Richert, 35 F.3d 300 (7th Cir.1994)(defendant charged with not reporting income could be incriminated by act of production of W–2 forms: "by producing them Smith would have acknowledged having received them, foreclosing any defense of nonwilfulness").

Finally, while admission of authenticity is potentially incriminating, it is sometimes the case that the act of production is insufficient to authenticate the records. In *Fisher*, for example, the Court found that the taxpayer's admission could not be used to authenticate the documents, because they were prepared by the accountant. In such cases, there is no risk of an incriminating admission of authentication.

Even in the limited cases where the act of production would be incriminating, the Fifth Amendment will not apply if existence, control, and authentication are in *Fisher's* words, a "foregone conclusion." This will be the case when the government has substantial independent evidence that the records exist, that the witness controls them, and that the records produced are authentic. For example, existence and control can be shown through other witnesses, when the records have either been prepared by or shown to them. See United States v. Clark, 847 F.2d 1467 (10th Cir.1988)(existence and control of records that the defendant had once given to his accountant to prepare his tax return is proven by subpoenaing the accountant to testify; existence and control of bank records can be proven through testimony of bank officials). Persons in similar situations can testify that in their jobs, records such as those subpoenaed exist and they have custody over them. See U.S. S.E.C. v. First Jersey Securities, Inc., 843 F.2d 74 (2d Cir.1988)(possession of parallel documents by other branch managers). Existence and control is often admitted, though perhaps unwittingly, by the witness at some time before the subpoena is served. See United States v. Rue, 819 F.2d 1488 (8th Cir.1987)(dentist demurs to voluntary inspection on grounds that his records are too voluminous to produce); In re Grand Jury Subpoena Duces Tecum, 1 F.3d 87 (2d Cir.1993)("Since Doe produced a copy of the calendar to the SEC and testified about his possession and use of it, its existence and location are foregone conclusions, and his production of the original adds little or nothing to the sum total of the government's information."). Finally, authentication can be shown in a variety of ways other than through the act of production, such as by handwriting exemplars, testimony by those who prepared the documents, and comparison to similar documents. See In re Grand Jury Subpoena Duces Tecum, 1 F.3d 87 (2d Cir.1993)(noting that the defendant's "authentication is a foregone conclusion if someone else can verify that the records are in fact what they purport to be"); United States v. Stone, 976 F.2d 909 (4th Cir.1992)(defendant's authentication of utility records for a beach house was unnecessary to the government's case, because authentication "could easily be obtained from the utilities involved"). Given all these considerations, how much Fifth Amendment protection is left for documents after *Fisher* and *Doe?*

Act Of Production As A Roadmap For The Government: United States v. Hubbell

To the extent that an act of production of documents would be incriminating, the government can still obtain the documents by giving immunity to the party holding the documents. That immunity, as discussed later in the Chapter, will mean that the government cannot use the incriminating admissions in the act of production, and also cannot use any "fruits" of those incriminating admissions. In the following case, the Court found that the compelled act of production of personal documents was incriminating, because it provided the government information about a trail of documentation of which it had not been aware. This incrimination was not solved by a grant of use immunity. The concurring opinion is especially notable for its willingness to reconsider *Fisher* and restore the *Boyd* rule that the content of compelled documents is protected by the Fifth Amendment.

UNITED STATES v. HUBBELL

Supreme Court of the United States, 2000.
530 U.S. 27.

JUSTICE STEVENS **delivered the opinion of the Court.**

* * *

I

This proceeding arises out of the second prosecution of respondent, Webster Hubbell, commenced by the Independent Counsel appointed in August 1994 to investigate possible violations of federal law relating to the Whitewater Development Corporation.

The first prosecution was terminated pursuant to a plea bargain. In December 1994, respondent pleaded guilty to charges of mail fraud and tax evasion arising out of his billing practices as a member of an Arkansas law firm from 1989 to 1992, and was sentenced to 21 months in prison. In the plea agreement, respondent promised to provide the Independent Counsel with "full, complete, accurate, and truthful information" about matters relating to the Whitewater investigation.

The second prosecution resulted from the Independent Counsel's attempt to determine whether respondent had violated that promise. In October 1996, while respondent was incarcerated, the Independent Counsel served him with a subpoena duces tecum calling for the production of 11 categories of documents before a grand jury sitting in Little Rock, Arkansas. On November 19, he appeared before the grand jury and invoked his Fifth Amendment privilege against self-incrimination. In response to questioning by the prosecutor, respondent initially refused "to state whether there are documents within my possession, custody, or control responsive to the Subpoena." Thereafter, the prosecutor produced an order, which had previously been obtained from the District Court * * * directing him to respond to the subpoena and granting him immunity "to the extent allowed by law." Respondent then produced 13,120 pages of documents and records and responded to a series of questions that established that those were all of the documents in his custody or control that were responsive to the commands in the subpoena, with the exception of a few documents he claimed were shielded by the attorney-client and attorney work-product privileges.

The contents of the documents produced by respondent provided the Independent Counsel with the information that led to this second prosecution. On April 30, 1998, a grand jury in the District of Columbia returned a 10–count indictment charging respondent with various tax-related crimes and mail and wire fraud. The District Court dismissed the indictment relying, in part, on the ground that the Independent Counsel's use of the subpoenaed documents [was illegal] because all of the

evidence he would offer against respondent at trial derived either directly or indirectly from the testimonial aspects of respondent's immunized act of producing those documents. Noting that the Independent Counsel had admitted that he was not investigating tax-related issues when he issued the subpoena, and that he had learned about the unreported income and other crimes from studying the records' contents, the District Court characterized the subpoena as "the quintessential fishing expedition."

The Court of Appeals vacated the judgment and remanded for further proceedings. The majority concluded that the District Court had incorrectly relied on the fact that the Independent Counsel did not have prior knowledge of the contents of the subpoenaed documents. The question the District Court should have addressed was the extent of the Government's independent knowledge of the documents' existence and authenticity, and of respondent's possession or control of them.

* * *

On remand, the Independent Counsel acknowledged that he could not satisfy the * * * standard prescribed by the Court of Appeals and entered into a conditional plea agreement with respondent. In essence, the agreement provides for the dismissal of the charges unless this Court's disposition of the case makes it reasonably likely that respondent's "act of production immunity" would not pose a significant bar to his prosecution. * * *

II

* * *

[It is settled that] a person may be required to produce specific documents even though they contain incriminating assertions of fact or belief because the creation of those documents was not "compelled" within the meaning of the privilege. * * * It is clear, therefore, that respondent Hubbell could not avoid compliance with the subpoena served on him merely because the demanded documents contained incriminating evidence, whether written by others or voluntarily prepared by himself.

On the other hand, we have also made it clear that the act of producing documents in response to a subpoena may have a compelled testimonial aspect. We have held that the act of production itself may implicitly communicate "statements of fact." By producing documents in compliance with a subpoena, the witness would admit that the papers existed, were in his possession or control, and were authentic. Moreover, as was true in this case, when the custodian of documents responds to a subpoena, he may be compelled to take the witness stand and answer questions designed to determine whether he has produced everything demanded by the subpoena. The answers to those questions, as well as the act of production itself, may certainly communicate information about the existence, custody, and authenticity of the documents. Whether the constitutional privilege protects the answers to such questions, or protects the act of production itself, is a question that is distinct from the question whether the unprotected contents of the documents themselves are incriminating.

* * *

III

* * *

IV

The Government correctly emphasizes that the testimonial aspect of a response to a subpoena duces tecum does nothing more than establish the existence, authenticity, and custody of items that are produced. We assume that the Government is also entirely correct in its submission that it would not have to advert to respondent's act of production in order to prove the existence, authenticity, or custody of any documents that it might offer in evidence at a criminal trial; indeed, the Government disclaims any need to introduce any of the documents produced by respondent into evidence in order to prove the charges against him. It follows, according to the Government, that it has no intention of making improper "use" of respondent's compelled testimony.

The question, however, is not whether the response to the subpoena may be introduced into evidence at his criminal trial. That would surely be a prohibited "use" of the immunized act of production. But the fact that the Government intends no such use of the act of production leaves open the separate question whether it has already made "derivative use" of the testimonial aspect of that act in obtaining the indictment against respondent and in preparing its case for trial. It clearly has.

It is apparent from the text of the subpoena itself that the prosecutor needed respondent's assistance both to identify potential sources of information and to produce those sources. Given the breadth of the description of the 11 categories of documents called for by the subpoena, the collection and production of the materials demanded was tantamount to answering a series of interrogatories asking a witness to disclose the existence and location of particular documents fitting certain broad descriptions. The assembly of literally hundreds of pages of material in response to a request for "any and all documents reflecting, referring, or relating to any direct or indirect sources of money or other things of value received by or provided to" an individual or members of his family during a 3–year period, is the functional equivalent of the preparation of an answer to either a detailed written interrogatory or a series of oral questions at a discovery deposition. Entirely apart from the contents of the 13,120 pages of materials that respondent produced in this case, it is undeniable that providing a catalog of existing documents fitting within any of the 11 broadly worded subpoena categories could provide a prosecutor with a lead to incriminating evidence, or a link in the chain of evidence needed to prosecute.

Indeed, the record makes it clear that that is what happened in this case. The documents were produced before a grand jury sitting in the Eastern District of Arkansas in aid of the Independent Counsel's attempt to determine whether respondent had violated a commitment in his first plea agreement. The use of those sources of information eventually led to the return of an indictment by a grand jury sitting in the District of Columbia for offenses that apparently are unrelated to that plea agreement. What the District Court characterized as a "fishing expedition" did produce a fish, but not the one that the Independent Counsel expected to hook. It is abundantly clear that the testimonial aspect of respondent's act of producing subpoenaed documents was the first step in a chain of evidence that led to this prosecution. The documents did not magically appear in the prosecutor's office like "manna from heaven." They arrived there only after respondent asserted his constitutional privilege, received a grant of immunity, and—under the compulsion of the District Court's order—took the mental and physical steps necessary to provide the

prosecutor with an accurate inventory of the many sources of potentially incriminating evidence sought by the subpoena. It was only through respondent's truthful reply to the subpoena that the Government received the incriminating documents of which it made substantial use in the investigation that led to the indictment.

For these reasons, we cannot accept the Government's submission that respondent's immunity did not preclude its derivative use of the produced documents because its possession of the documents was the fruit only of a simple physical act—the act of producing the documents. It was unquestionably necessary for respondent to make extensive use of "the contents of his own mind" in identifying the hundreds of documents responsive to the requests in the subpoena. The assembly of those documents was like telling an inquisitor the combination to a wall safe, not like being forced to surrender the key to a strongbox. * * *

In sum, we have no doubt that the constitutional privilege against self-incrimination protects the target of a grand jury investigation from being compelled to answer questions designed to elicit information about the existence of sources of potentially incriminating evidence. That constitutional privilege has the same application to the testimonial aspect of a response to a subpoena seeking discovery of those sources. * * * [T]he Government has argued that the communicative aspect of respondent's act of producing ordinary business records is insufficiently "testimonial" to support a claim of privilege because the existence and possession of such records by any businessman is a "foregone conclusion" under our decision in Fisher v. United States. This argument both misreads *Fisher* and ignores our subsequent decision in United States v. Doe.

* * * *Fisher* involved summonses seeking production of working papers prepared by the taxpayers' accountants that the IRS knew were in the possession of the taxpayers' attorneys. * * *

Whatever the scope of this "foregone conclusion" rationale, the facts of this case plainly fall outside of it. While in *Fisher* the Government already knew that the documents were in the attorneys' possession and could independently confirm their existence and authenticity through the accountants who created them, here the Government has not shown that it had any prior knowledge of either the existence or the whereabouts of the 13,-

120 pages of documents ultimately produced by respondent. The Government cannot cure this deficiency through the overbroad argument that a businessman such as respondent will always possess general business and tax records that fall within the broad categories described in this subpoena. The *Doe* subpoenas also sought several broad categories of general business records, yet we upheld the District Court's finding that the act of producing those records would involve testimonial self-incrimination.

* * *

Accordingly, the indictment against respondent must be dismissed. The judgment of the Court of Appeals is affirmed.

CHIEF JUSTICE REHNQUIST dissents and would reverse the judgment of the Court of Appeals in part, for the reasons given by Judge Williams in his dissenting opinion in that court, 167 F.3d 552, 597 (C.A.D.C.1999).

JUSTICE THOMAS, **with whom** JUSTICE SCALIA **joins, concurring**.

Our decision today involves the application of the act-of-production doctrine, which provides that persons compelled to turn over incriminating papers or other physical evidence pursuant to a subpoena duces tecum or a summons may invoke the Fifth Amendment privilege against self-incrimination as a bar to production only where the act of producing the evidence would contain "testimonial" features. I join the opinion of the Court because it properly applies this doctrine, but I write separately to note that this doctrine may be inconsistent with the original meaning of the Fifth Amendment's Self–Incrimination Clause. A substantial body of evidence suggests that the Fifth Amendment privilege

protects against the compelled production not just of incriminating testimony, but of any incriminating evidence. In a future case, I would be willing to reconsider the scope and meaning of the Self–Incrimination Clause.

I

The Fifth Amendment provides that "[n]o person ... shall be compelled in any criminal case to be a witness against himself." The key word at issue in this case is "witness." The Court's opinion, relying on prior cases, essentially defines "witness" as a person who provides testimony, and thus restricts the Fifth Amendment's ban to only those communications that are "testimonial" in character. None of this Court's cases, however, has undertaken an analysis of the meaning of the term at the time of the founding. A review of that period reveals substantial support for the view that the term "witness" meant a person who gives or furnishes evidence, a broader meaning than that which our case law currently ascribes to the term. If this is so, a person who responds to a subpoena duces tecum would be just as much a "witness" as a person who responds to a subpoena ad testificandum.

Such a meaning of "witness" is consistent with, and may help explain, the history and framing of the Fifth Amendment. The 18th century common-law privilege against self-incrimination protected against the compelled production of incriminating physical evidence such as papers and documents. * * *

* * * James Madison penned the Fifth Amendment. In so doing, Madison substituted the phrase "to be a witness" for the proposed language "to give evidence" and "to furnish evidence." But it seems likely that Madison's phrasing was synonymous with that of the proposals. The definitions of the word "witness" and the background history of the privilege against self-incrimination * * * support this view. And this may explain why Madison's unique phrasing—phrasing that none of the proposals had suggested—apparently attracted no attention, much less opposition, in Congress, the state legislatures that ratified the Bill of Rights, or anywhere else. * * *

II

This Court has not always taken the approach to the Fifth Amendment that we follow today. The first case interpreting the Self–Incrimination Clause—Boyd v. United States—was decided, though not explicitly, in accordance with the understanding that "witness" means one who gives evidence. In *Boyd*, this Court unanimously held that the Fifth Amendment protects a defendant against compelled production of books and papers. And the Court linked its interpretation of the Fifth Amendment to the common-law understanding of the self-incrimination privilege.

But this Court's decision in Fisher v. United States, rejected this understanding, permitting the Government to force a person to furnish incriminating physical evidence and protecting only the "testimonial" aspects of that transfer. In so doing, *Fisher* not only failed to examine the historical backdrop to the Fifth Amendment, it also required—as illustrated by extended discussion in the opinions below in this case—a difficult parsing of the act of responding to a subpoena duces tecum.

None of the parties in this case has asked us to depart from *Fisher*, but in light of the historical evidence that the Self–Incrimination Clause may have a broader reach than *Fisher* holds, I remain open to a reconsideration of that decision and its progeny in a proper case.

Production of Corporate Documents: Braswell v. United States

Recall that in *Bellis* the Court held that business entities are not entitled to Fifth Amendment protection. But a business entity itself cannot be compelled to produce incriminating evidence, except through individual agents of the entity. If the act of production of an entity's documents would be personally incriminating to an agent of the entity, can the agent invoke his personal Fifth Amendment privilege? This was the question in Braswell v. United States, 487 U.S. 99 (1988). Braswell formed two corporations in which he was the sole shareholder. A grand jury issued a subpoena to him—in his capacity as agent—to produce the books and records of the two companies. Braswell invoked his personal privilege against self-incrimination on the ground that the act of production might be incriminating. Chief Justice Rehnquist, writing for the Court, relied on the "collective entity" rule to deny the Fifth Amendment claim. The Chief Justice described that rule as follows:

> The official records and documents of the organization that are held [by the agent] in a representative rather than in a personal capacity cannot be the subject of the personal privilege against self-incrimination, even though production of the papers might tend to incriminate [the agent] personally.

The Chief Justice expressed the following rationale for the collective entity rule:

> The custodian of corporate or entity records holds those documents in a representative rather than a personal capacity * * * and a custodian's assumption of his representative capacity leads to certain obligations, including the duty to produce corporate records on proper demand by the Government. Under those circumstances, the custodian's act of production is not deemed a personal act, but rather an act of the corporation.

Braswell sought support from Curcio v. United States, 354 U.S. 118 (1957), where Curcio was served with a subpoena to testify in his capacity as a secretary-treasurer of a local union. Curcio refused to answer any questions as to the whereabouts of the books and records of the union. The Court in *Curcio* held that the collective entity rule did not require "the giving of oral testimony by the custodian" where that testimony could incriminate him personally. The Chief Justice distinguished *Curcio* in *Braswell,* stating that a corporate agent assumes the risk of producing documents as part of the job, but not the risk of being compelled to give incriminating oral testimony.

The Chief Justice reasoned that recognizing a privilege on the part of records custodians would have a detrimental impact on the government's efforts to prosecute white collar crime; that the possibility of providing use immunity for the act of production so that it could not be used as evidence against the custodian posed a problem for the government because the act of production might taint other evidence; and that if the privilege were recognized, any subpoena to the corporation rather than to a particular custodian might not be honored because the custodian might refuse to cooperate with any other representative of the corporation if cooperation might be incriminating.

Although a custodian like Braswell is not permitted to claim the privilege in response to a subpoena for corporate records, the Court recognized that "certain consequences flow from the fact that the custodian's act of production is one in his representative rather than personal capacity." The Court noted that the government had conceded that "it may make no use of the 'individual act' against the individual," which means, "[f]or example, in a criminal prosecution the Government may not introduce into evidence before the jury the fact that the subpoena was served upon and the corporation's documents were delivered by one particular individual, the custodian."

This is not to say, however, that the government may not use the act of production as evidence; the *corporation's* act of production may be used as evidence against the custodian. The jury cannot be told that the individual defendant produced the records as a corporate agent, but it can be told that the corporation produced the records. The *Braswell* Court concluded that "the jury may draw from the corporation's act of production the conclusion that the records in question are authentic corporate records, which the corporation possessed, and which it produced in response to the subpoena, and if the defendant held a prominent position within the corporation that produced the records, the jury may, just as it would had someone else produced the documents, reasonably infer that he had possession of the documents or knowledge of their contents."

As a result of the limits on the use of the corporate agent's act of production, the Court concluded that Braswell was not incriminated by the fact of personal production, only by the fact of corporate production. The Court left "open the question whether the agency rationale supports compelling a custodian to produce corporate records when the custodian is able to establish, by showing for example that he is the sole employee and officer of the corporation, that the jury would inevitably conclude that he produced the records."

Justice Kennedy, joined by Justices Brennan, Marshall, and Scalia, dissented and argued that "[t]he Court today denies an individual his Fifth Amendment privilege against self-incrimination in order to vindicate the rule that a collective entity which employs him has no privilege itself." He concluded that the majority's approach to the privilege—i.e., holding that it did not apply to a corporate custodian but that the custodian's act of production could not be used as evidence—"avoided and manipulated" basic Fifth Amendment principles. He asserted that the only way to obtain corporate documents from an agent whose act of production would be personally incriminating was to grant use immunity to the agent.

It is easy to state the Court's holding with respect to the privilege but more difficult to understand what difference it would make if the dissenters had prevailed in *Braswell*. In order to understand the stakes in *Braswell,* it is important to know something about the law of immunity, discussed infra. At this point, it should suffice to state that a person loses the right to remain silent because of the privilege if the government, at a minimum, formally guarantees that no compelled testimony or evidence derived from it will be used against the person in a future criminal prosecution. This is called use immunity. The majority states that use immunity would pose problems for the government, therefore there is no privilege at all protecting the personal act of production; and the dissent disagrees.

Suppose that Braswell had been given use immunity for the act of production. The fact that he provided documents to the grand jury could not be used as evidence against him. But, it cannot be used in any event, because of the nonconstitutional agency analysis that the majority holds flows naturally from the logic of its approach. The difference, if any, between the majority and the dissenters must focus, then, on derivative evidence. If Braswell were given use immunity, the following facts might arguably be derived from the act of production: certain documents were prepared by or for the corporation, these documents still exist, and they are under the control of the corporation or its agent. The majority is concerned that the derivative use rule would cover these facts and that the government might have a difficult time proving that any other evidence of the same facts was not also derived from the production by the custodian. In the end, the majority permits the corporation's act of production to be used as evidence and implicitly recognizes that evidence derived from the corporation's act of production is also admissible.

The Difference Between a Corporate Agent's Compelled Oral Testimony and Compelled Document Production

In *Curcio*, the Court held that the corporate agent had a privilege to refuse to testify as to the whereabouts of corporate documents. But in *Braswell*, the Court held that the agent had no privilege to refuse their production. What is the difference between a corporate agent's compelled oral testimony and compelled document production? Judge Kravitch proffered this explanation in In re Grand Jury Subpoena Dated April 9, 1996 v. Smith, 87 F.3d 1198 (11th Cir.1996):

> In drawing a line between acts of production and oral testimony, the Court appears to have relied on one fact that distinguishes these two types of testimony: the corporation owns the documents. In contrast, to the extent that one's thoughts and statements can be said to "belong" to anyone, they belong to the witness herself. A custodian has no personal right to retain corporate books. Because the documents belong to the corporation, the state may exercise its right to review the records. For Fifth Amendment analysis, oral statements are different. The government has no right to compel a person to speak the contents of her mind when doing so would incriminate that person; to do so would be "contrary to the spirit and letter of the Fifth Amendment." *Curcio*, 354 U.S. at 126–28.

The corporate agent in *Grand Jury Subpoena* did not refuse to produce corporate documents. Rather, she claimed not to possess them, and refused to testify as to their location. The court stated that this case was controlled by *Curcio*, because the government was demanding oral testimony as to the location of records, and the answer could have personally incriminated the defendant (the answer probably being, "I destroyed them, that's where they are"). Accordingly, the subpoena demanding oral testimony was quashed.

Doesn't *Curcio* give corporate agents an incentive to destroy incriminating documents, so that the corporate agent won't have to produce them under *Braswell*, and can then remain silent as to their destruction?

Production of a Person in Response to a Court Order: Baltimore City Dept. of Social Services v. Bouknight

In Baltimore City Dept. of Social Services v. Bouknight, 493 U.S. 549 (1990), the Court relied in part upon the collective entity rule to find the Fifth Amendment inapplicable to an act of production of a child. Suspecting child abuse, the Department of Social Services obtained a court order removing Maurice Bouknight from his mother's control. The Department obtained a further order declaring Maurice to be a "child in need of assistance" under Maryland law. That court order gave the Department jurisdiction over Maurice. Maurice was returned to his mother, but only under extensive conditions imposed by a protective order. Ms. Bouknight did not comply with those conditions, and the Juvenile Court granted the Department's petition again to remove Maurice from his mother's control. Ms. Bouknight failed to produce Maurice, and Department officials feared that he might be dead. The case was referred to the police homicide division. The Juvenile Court directed that Ms.

Bouknight be held in contempt for failing to produce Maurice. That court rejected her argument that the Fifth Amendment protected her from any incrimination that might result from the act of producing Maurice.

Justice O'Connor wrote the majority opinion for the Supreme Court. She assumed, without deciding, that Bouknight's act of producing Maurice could be potentially incriminating, as an "implicit communication of control over Maurice at the moment of production." However, Justice O'Connor concluded that Bouknight could not invoke the privilege "because she has assumed custodial duties related to production and because production is required as part of a noncriminal regulatory regime."

Justice O'Connor found an analogy to *Braswell*. She argued that by "accepting care of Maurice subject to the custodial order's conditions," Bouknight accepted the consequent obligations of production. However, because the act of production would be that of a custodian, Justice O'Connor also relied upon *Braswell's* nonconstitutional agency analysis:

> We are not called upon to define the precise limitations that may exist upon the State's ability to use the testimonial aspect of Bouknight's act of production in subsequent criminal proceedings. But we note that imposition of such limitations is not foreclosed. The same custodial role that limited the ability to resist the production order may give rise to corresponding limitations upon the direct and indirect use of that testimony.

Justice Marshall, joined by Justice Brennan, dissented. He rejected the analogy to the collective entity rule. He reasoned that Bouknight "is not the agent for an artificial entity that possesses no Fifth Amendment privilege. Her role as Maurice's parent is very different from the role of a corporate custodian who is merely the instrumentality through whom the corporation acts."

In discussing the nonconstitutional agency analysis of *Braswell*, Justice O'Connor refers to the "direct and indirect" limitations upon the use of the act of production. Does she go farther than the Court did in *Braswell*? What protections after the fact are available to a custodian who is compelled to produce something? If Bouknight revealed the corpse of her son, would the body be admissible in evidence in a subsequent criminal case?

3. *Required Records*

Even if documents are not voluntarily prepared, their contents as well as the act of production will be unprotected if the government requires the documents to be kept for a legitimate administrative purpose that is not focused solely on those inherently suspect of criminal activity. This principle is embodied in the "required records" exception to the Fifth Amendment. Under the exception, the government can require records to be kept; it can punish those who do not keep the records; it can punish those who keep false records; and it can punish those who truthfully admit criminal activity in the compelled records.

In Shapiro v. United States, 335 U.S. 1 (1948), a 5–4 decision, Chief Justice Vinson wrote for the Court as it held that the compelled production of defendant's customary business records, which were required to be kept under the Emergency Price Control Act, did not implicate the Fifth Amendment:

> It may be assumed at the outset that there are limits which the Government cannot constitutionally exceed in requiring the keeping of

records which may be inspected by an administrative agency and may be used in prosecuting statutory violations committed by the record-keeper himself. But no serious misgiving that those bounds have been overstepped would appear to be evoked when there is a sufficient relation between the activity sought to be regulated and the public concern so that the Government can constitutionally regulate or forbid the basic activity concerned, and can constitutionally require the keeping of particular records, subject to inspection by the Administrator. It is not questioned here that Congress has constitutional authority to prescribe commodity prices as a war emergency measure, and that the licensing and record-keeping requirements of the Price Control Act represent a legitimate exercise of that power. * * *

In a dissenting opinion, Justice Frankfurter expressed concern about the scope of the required records exception.

> * * * The underlying assumption of the Court's opinion is that all records which Congress in the exercise of its constitutional powers may require individuals to keep in the conduct of their affairs, because those affairs also have aspects of public interest, become "public" records in the sense that they fall outside the constitutional protection of the Fifth Amendment. The validity of such a doctrine lies in the scope of its implications. The claim touches records that may be required to be kept by federal regulatory laws, revenue measures, labor and census legislation in the conduct of business which the understanding and feeling of our people still treat as private enterprise, even though its relations to the public may call for governmental regulation, including the duty to keep designated records.

Limitations on the Exception

The majority opinion in *Shapiro* refers to "limits which the Government cannot constitutionally exceed" in requiring that records be kept or produced for inspection. What are those limits? In 1968, the Court decided several cases in which the scope of the required records doctrine was an issue. Marchetti v. United States, 390 U.S. 39 (1968), involved a defendant who had been convicted for wilfully failing to register and to pay an occupational tax for engaging in the business of accepting wagers, as required by 26 U.S.C.A. §§ 4411 and 4412. Marchetti claimed that he failed to register and pay because to do so would provide an incriminating admission that he was involved in illegal gambling. While acknowledging Congress' authority to tax unlawful activities, the Court reversed the convictions, stating that "those who properly assert the constitutional privilege as to these provisions may not be criminally punished for failure to comply with their requirements."

Justice Harlan, writing for the Court in *Marchetti*, distinguished *Shapiro* and explained why the required records doctrine did not apply:

> Each of the three principal elements of the [required records] doctrine, as it is described in *Shapiro,* is absent from this situation. First, petitioner Marchetti was not, by the provisions now at issue, obliged to keep and preserve records "of the same kind as he has customarily kept"; he was required simply to provide information, unrelated to any records which he may have maintained, about his wagering activities. This requirement is not significantly different from a demand that he provide oral testimony. Sec-

ond, whatever "public aspects" there were to the records at issue in *Shapiro,* there are none to the information demanded from Marchetti. The Government's anxiety to obtain information known to a private individual does not without more render that information public; if it did, no room would remain for the application of the constitutional privilege. Nor does it stamp information with a public character that the Government has formalized its demands in the attire of a statute; if this alone were sufficient, the constitutional privilege could be entirely abrogated by any Act of Congress. Third, the requirements at issue in *Shapiro* were imposed in "an essentially non-criminal and regulatory area of inquiry" while those here are directed to a "selective group inherently suspect of criminal activities."

In Haynes v. United States, 390 U.S. 85 (1968), decided the same day, the Court reversed a conviction for failing to register a sawed-off shotgun as required by the National Firearms Act, 26 U.S.C.A. § 5841. Other sections of the Act provided that possession of a sawed-off shotgun was itself a criminal offense. The reversal was grounded on a finding that the registration statute created real and appreciable hazards of incrimination, because it was "directed principally at those persons who * * * are immediately threatened by criminal prosecution" under other sections of the Act.

Justice Harlan again found the required records doctrine to be inapplicable because the registration did not involve records of the kind "customarily kept," the statutory provisions were directed at "a highly selective group inherently suspect of criminal activities," they were not concerned essentially with noncriminal and regulatory inquiries, and the records involved were in no sense "public."

How does one distinguish between legislation that has a noncriminal or regulatory purpose, such as the production of tax revenue, and one that is essentially targeted at criminals? If both require self-reporting that may be incriminating, what is the basis for differential application of the Fifth Amendment?

Compelled Reporting of an Accident: California v. Byers

In California v. Byers, 402 U.S. 424 (1971), the constitutionality of California's "hit and run" statute was in issue. Byers was convicted of a misdemeanor for failure to stop at the scene of an accident and to leave his name and address. The California Supreme Court had upheld the statute, but inserted a use restriction on the information provided (i.e., the information provided by the driver could not be used in a criminal prosecution), because disclosure created "substantial hazards of self-incrimination." The United States Supreme Court vacated the state court's judgment, finding that the statute did not infringe the privilege against compelled self-incrimination and thus a use restriction was not constitutionally required. In a plurality opinion, Chief Justice Burger stressed that the statutory scheme was essentially regulatory and noncriminal; it was directed to the motoring public at large, rather than to "a highly selective group inherently suspect of criminal activities;" and self-reporting was indispensable to fulfillment of its purposes. On balance, the possibility of incrimination was not sufficiently certain as to justify invalidation of a statute that provided valuable protection to the public. Even if incrimination was a danger, Chief Justice

Burger argued, the Fifth Amendment was not implicated. The act of stopping at the scene of an accident was no more "testimonial" than standing in a line-up, and disclosure of identity "is an essentially neutral act." It would be an extravagant extension of the Fifth Amendment, the Chief Justice concluded, to hold that there is a constitutional right "to flee the scene of an accident in order to avoid the possibility of legal involvement."

Justice Harlan, in his opinion concurring in the result in *Byers,* disagreed with the Chief Justice's analysis. Justice Harlan was willing to call the information sought by the statute testimonial and he recognized that it was potentially incriminatory, but he argued that a use restriction would seriously undermine the state's legitimate interests in enforcing criminal sanctions to deter dangerous driving by making those sanctions unavailable in the most appropriate cases—those that involved accidents. A constitutionally mandated use restriction would thus deprive the government of its capacity to use all self-reporting schemes effectively.

Is the Target Group Inherently Suspect?

18 U.S.C. § 922(e) makes it a crime to knowingly fail to provide written notice to an airline before shipping firearms. Does a defendant who fails to comply have a Fifth Amendment defense? Courts have held that the statute is within the required records exception, as a legitimate exercise of regulatory activity. Therefore there is no privilege to refuse to comply, even if the report would be incriminating. See United States v. Alkhafaji, 754 F.2d 641 (6th Cir.1985); United States v. Wilson, 721 F.2d 967 (4th Cir.1983). Isn't the statute targeted toward a group inherently suspect of illegal activity? What legitimate, non-criminal purpose can be found in the statute?

The City of Seattle recently experimented with an ordinance requiring "crack houses" (premises where crack cocaine is sold) to file "neighborhood impact" statements with the City, and imposing criminal sanctions for failure to file such a statement. Can this ordinance be justified under the required records exception?

Recall the discussion of searches based on "special needs" beyond criminal law enforcement in Chapter Two. Do you see any analogy between the law governing those searches and the required records exception?

In Baltimore City Dept. of Social Services v. Bouknight, discussed supra, the Court relied in part upon the required records exception to find the Fifth Amendment inapplicable to an act of production of a child who was feared dead. The mother, upon whom the order to produce the child was served, claimed that the Fifth Amendment protected her from the incriminating aspects of the act of production. The Court held that the collective entity rule and the required records exception each applied, so that the mother was not protected from incrimination.

With regard to the required records exception, Justice O'Connor, writing for the majority, relied heavily on *Shapiro* and *Byers.* As in those cases, the State's demand for information was imposed in an "essentially non-criminal and regulatory area of inquiry" and was not "directed to a selective group inherently suspect of criminal activities." Justice O'Connor reasoned that the State's efforts to gain access to "children in need of assistance" did not focus solely on criminal conduct, and were motivated by the proper regulatory purpose of concern for the child's safety and welfare.

Justice Marshall, joined by Justice Brennan, dissented. He rejected the analogy to the required records exception. He noted that as a matter of fact, the State's scheme was "narrowly targeted at parents who through abuse or neglect deny their children the minimal reasonable level of care and attention," and argued that the State's goal of protecting children from abuse "inevitably intersects" with criminal provisions that serve the same goal.

Note that in *Bouknight,* the matter had been referred to criminal authorities, though the order to produce was issued in a child protective proceeding. Does it matter whether the state is pursuing a civil, protective course or a criminal investigation?

In Bionic Auto Parts and Sales, Inc. v. Fahner, 721 F.2d 1072 (7th Cir. 1983), the court held that the privilege against self-incrimination barred a state from enforcing a regulation requiring a record of any serial number or identifying mark that was removed from an auto or an auto part. It said that "[a]lthough there is a fine line between a regulatory purpose and the specific effort to root out criminal activity, we are hard pressed to articulate a regulatory rationale for the record-keeping requirement in question." Compare that same court's decision in United States v. Lehman, 887 F.2d 1328 (7th Cir.1989), which held that a statute requiring buyers and sellers of livestock to keep records was within the required records exception. The court stated that "there is nothing ordinarily criminally suspect in buying and selling livestock."

For a general approach to required records, see Saltzburg, The Required Records Doctrine: Its Lessons for the Privilege Against Self–Incrimination, 53 U.Chi.L.Rev. 6 (1986).

F. PROCEDURAL ASPECTS OF SELF–INCRIMINATION CLAIMS

1. *Determining the Risk of Incrimination*

If a criminal defendant decides not to take the stand, there is no need for the court to decide whether this exercise of the privilege is valid, for it clearly is. But when the privilege is invoked by someone who is testifying at a proceeding, it must be decided whether the privilege is properly invoked. The relevant test is whether the information requested of a witness might possibly tend to incriminate the witness in the future; and this determination must be made without compelling the witness to divulge the information that the witness claims is protected by the privilege. Thus, the task of determining the risk of incrimination is delicate and in most cases the claim is sustained. The Supreme Court has stated that the risk of incrimination is determined by whether it is

> *perfectly clear,* from a careful consideration of all the circumstances in the case, that the witness is mistaken, and that the answers *cannot possibly* have such tendency to incriminate.

Hoffman v. United States, 341 U.S. 479, 488 (1951). The Court in *Hoffman* detailed the standards for determining whether testimony could tend to incriminate a witness within the meaning of the Fifth Amendment:

> If a person cannot possibly be prosecuted in the future—e.g., a complete pardon has been issued, double jeopardy clearly bars future prosecution, or

immunity [as discussed infra] has been granted—then the privilege cannot be relied upon. If the privilege is applicable, it extends to answers that would in themselves support a conviction * * * but likewise embraces those which would furnish a link in the chain of evidence needed to prosecute * * *. [I]f the witness, upon interposing his claim, were required to prove the hazard * * * he would be compelled to surrender the very protection which the privilege is designed to guarantee. To sustain the privilege, it need only be evident from the implications of the question, in the setting in which it is asked, that a responsive answer to the question or an explanation of why it cannot be answered might be dangerous because injurious disclosure could result.

See also Malloy v. Hogan, 378 U.S. 1 (1964)(even after Malloy was convicted and served a prison sentence for gambling activities, he could not be compelled to identify his associates in those activities, because disclosure of these names "might furnish a link in a chain of evidence sufficient to connect the petitioner with a more recent crime for which he might still be prosecuted").

The Risk of Incrimination and Denial of Guilt: Ohio v. Reiner

Can a witness invoke the Fifth Amendment privilege if she denies guilt of any crime? This question was faced by the Court in Ohio v. Reiner, 532 U.S. 17 (2001) (per curiam). Reiner was charged with involuntary manslaughter in connection with the death of his infant son. He blamed it on the babysitter. The babysitter refused to testify, claiming a Fifth Amendment privilege. She was granted immunity, then testified as a prosecution witness that she had nothing to do with the infant's death or with other injuries to the infant's brother. Reiner was convicted but the state court reversed on the ground that the babysitter should not have been granted immunity. In the state court's view, the babysitter's testimony "did not incriminate her, because she denied any involvement in the abuse. Thus, she did not have a valid Fifth Amendment privilege."

The Supreme Court reinstated the conviction; it found that the babysitter faced a risk of self-incrimination even though she denied wrongdoing, and therefore the grant of immunity was not unlawful. The Court reasoned as follows:

> We have held that the privilege's protection extends only to witnesses who have "reasonable cause to apprehend danger from a direct answer." Hoffman v. United States. That inquiry is for the court; the witness' assertion does not by itself establish the risk of incrimination. A danger of "imaginary and unsubstantial character" will not suffice. But we have never held, as the Supreme Court of Ohio did, that the privilege is unavailable to those who claim innocence. To the contrary, we have emphasized that one of the Fifth Amendment's "basic functions * * * is to protect innocent men * * * who otherwise might be ensnared by ambiguous circumstances." Grunewald v. United States, 353 U.S. 391, 421 (1957). In *Grunewald,* we recognized that truthful responses of an innocent witness, as well as those of a wrongdoer, may provide the government with incriminating evidence from the speaker's own mouth.

> The Supreme Court of Ohio's determination that Batt [the babysitter] did not have a valid Fifth Amendment privilege because she denied any

involvement in the abuse of the children clearly conflicts with *Hoffman* and *Grunewald*. Batt had "reasonable cause" to apprehend danger from her answers if questioned at respondent's trial. Batt spent extended periods of time alone with [the infant in the weeks before his death]. She was with Alex within the potential timeframe of the fatal trauma. The defense's theory of the case was that Batt, not respondent, was responsible for Alex's death and his brother's uncharged injuries. In this setting, it was reasonable for Batt to fear that answers to possible questions might tend to incriminate her. Batt therefore had a valid Fifth Amendment privilege against self-incrimination.

2. *Immunity*

If a witness is guaranteed that no criminal prosecution having anything to do with statements given to the government will take place, then there is no possibility of incrimination and no right to refuse to testify because of the privilege. A broad guarantee against future prosecution is often called transactional immunity, to signify that no transaction about which a witness testifies can be the subject of a future prosecution against the witness. The Federal immunity statute, 18 U.S.C. § 6002, provides for a more limited kind of immunity known as use and derivative use immunity. That statute provides:

> Whenever a witness refuses, on the basis of his privilege against self-incrimination, to testify or provide other information in a proceeding before or ancillary to [a Federal court, grand jury, agency proceeding, or Congressional proceeding], and the person presiding over the proceeding communicates to the witness an order issued under this part, the witness may not refuse to comply with the order on the basis of his privilege against self-incrimination; but no testimony or other information compelled under the order (or any information directly or indirectly derived from such testimony or other information) may be used against the witness in any criminal case, except a prosecution for perjury, giving a false statement, or otherwise failing to comply with the order.

Thus, a person who receives immunity has no right to refuse to testify and may be punished (e.g., by imprisonment for contempt) for so refusing, or for lying. A person who receives immunity is not subject to the cruel trilemma of punishment for truth, silence and falsity—because there is no punishment for telling the truth when immunized.

The Constitutionality of Use Immunity:
Kastigar v. United States

At one time, it appeared that the Supreme Court might require transactional immunity (i.e., immunity from prosecution for the acts that are the subject of the compelled testimony) as the cost to the government of forcing a witness to testify. In Counselman v. Hitchcock, 142 U.S. 547 (1892), the Court held that a statute, providing that no "evidence obtained from a party or witness by means of a judicial proceeding * * * shall be given in evidence; or in any matter used against him * * * in any court of the United States," was insufficient to supplant the privilege against self-incrimination.

But, in the landmark case of Kastigar v. United States, 406 U.S. 441 (1972),[5] the Court explained that *Counselman* did not require transactional immunity; what it required was use and "derivative use" or "use-fruits" immunity. The defect in the statute rejected in *Counselman* was that it did not "prevent the use of his testimony to search out other testimony to be used in evidence against him [the immunized witness]." In *Kastigar*, the Court upheld 18 U.S.C.A. § 6002 and stated that use-fruits immunity was "a rational accommodation between the imperatives of the privilege and the legitimate demands of government to compel citizens to testify" and that it "leaves the witness and the prosecutorial authorities in substantially the same position as if the witness had claimed the Fifth Amendment privilege. The immunity therefore is coextensive with the privilege and suffices to supplant it."

The Court said that after immunity is granted and a witness is compelled to talk, the burden is on the government "to prove that the evidence it proposes to use is derived from a legitimate source wholly independent of the compelled testimony."

Justice Marshall dissented in *Kastigar*, arguing that the burden placed on the government was not adequate protection for the witness, "[f]or the paths of information through the investigative bureaucracy may well be long and winding, and even a prosecutor acting in the best of faith cannot be certain that somewhere in the depths of his investigative apparatus, often including hundreds of employees, there was not some prohibited use of the compelled testimony."[6]

Proving That Immunized Testimony Was Not Used

When a witness gives immunized testimony and is later prosecuted, the question of whether the government has used the fruits of the immunized testimony inevitably arises. One way for the government to satisfy its burden of showing that its evidence is not the fruit of immunized testimony is to establish a "Wall of Silence" between the prosecutors exposed to the testimony and the prosecutors who bring the case against the witness. See United States v. Schwimmer, 882 F.2d 22 (2d Cir.1989) (recommending the "Wall of Silence" approach); U.S. Dep't of Justice, U.S. Attorneys' Manual, § 1–11.–400 (1987) (to demonstrate that no use has been made of the compelled testimony, prosecution should be handled by an attorney unfamiliar with its substance). See also United States v. Harris, 973 F.2d 333 (4th Cir.1992)(while there is no per se rule requiring withdrawal of a prosecutor who was exposed to immunized testimony, "a prosecutor's failure to withdraw certainly makes it more difficult for the

---

5. Prior to *Kastigar*, the Court had held in Murphy v. Waterfront Comm., 378 U.S. 52 (1964), that a state grant of immunity prevented the federal government from using the compelled testimony or its fruits, and that this protection was sufficient to supplant the Fifth Amendment privilege against self-incrimination. Until *Kastigar*, no one was sure whether the *Murphy* rule applied when the same sovereign granted the immunity and subsequently sought to bring a criminal charge against an immunized witness.

6. Justice Douglas also dissented. Justices Brennan and Rehnquist did not participate. States may still require transactional immunity as a matter of state constitutional or statutory law. See, e.g., Attorney General v. Colleton, 387 Mass. 790, 444 N.E.2d 915 (1982); N.Y.C.P.L. 190.40. Even though a state gives transactional immunity, the witness can still be prosecuted in a federal court, so long as the testimony and its fruits are not used. United States v. Gallo, 863 F.2d 185 (2d Cir.1988).

government to prove that the compelled testimony did not contribute to the prosecution"). How likely is it that a "Wall of Silence" will be effective?

Tainted Witnesses: United States v. North

In United States v. North, 920 F.2d 940 (D.C.Cir.1990), North had been granted immunity by Congress to testify about his role in the Iran–Contra scandal. His testimony was nationally televised. The Independent Counsel (IC) who brought the case against North was not exposed to the testimony and did not use the immunized testimony at trial. The IC's documentary evidence was "canned" before the testimony began, i.e., placed in boxes and sealed with the date of sealing indicated. However, many of the IC's witnesses had seen North's testimony on their own. The court held that *Kastigar* is violated "whenever the prosecution puts on a witness whose testimony is shaped, directly or indirectly, by compelled testimony, regardless of *how or by whom* he was exposed to that compelled testimony." The court rejected the government's excuse that it had no involvement in the witnesses' access to immunized, televised testimony, and reasoned as follows:

> Were the rule otherwise, a private lawyer for a witness sympathetic to the government could listen to the compelled testimony and use it to prepare the witness for trial. The government would presumably thereby gain the advantage of use of the immunized testimony so long as it did not actually cooperate in that effort. This interpretation of *Kastigar*, ("Look ma, no hands") * * * if accepted, would enormously increase the risk of providing immunized testimony.

The *North* court was most concerned that the memory of the prosecution witnesses would be refreshed impermissibly by their exposure to the immunized testimony, and that therefore their testimony would carry more weight at trial than it otherwise would have. The court held that the prosecutor's burden of showing no use by the witnesses of the immunized testimony could be met by "canning the testimony beforehand, just as wise prosecutors meet their burden of showing independent investigation by canning the results of the investigation before the defendant gives immunized testimony."

Chief Judge Wald argued in dissent in *Jones* that witnesses who wish to frustrate prosecutions will "line up to testify before Congress" in exchange for immunity, and that prospective witnesses at a trial "may seek to frustrate the conviction of a target by exposing themselves to immunized testimony." Under *North*, is there any practical difference between transactional and use immunity?

Independent Source, Inevitable Discovery

In United States v. Gallo, 859 F.2d 1078 (2d Cir.1988), Gallo's immunized grand jury testimony was used along with other information to obtain a wiretap on another person's phone. Conversations were intercepted that incriminated Gallo, and these were used against him at trial. The court held that *Kastigar* was not violated, because the affidavit upon which the wiretap authorization was based contained sufficient information to support a wiretap even without the immunized testimony. Is this "independent source" analysis consistent with *Kastigar?* See also United States v. Streck, 958 F.2d 141 (6th Cir.1992) (no violation of use immunity where the government inevitably would have discovered the defendant's unlawful activity even if the immunized statements had never been made).

Impeachment, Perjury

The Supreme Court has made clear that once use immunity is granted, the testimony that is extracted from the immunized witness is coerced and cannot be used as evidence against the witness in a subsequent case against the witness, even for impeachment purposes. New Jersey v. Portash, 440 U.S. 450 (1979). However, the Court held in United States v. Apfelbaum, 445 U.S. 115 (1980), that an immunized witness has no right to lie, and that evidence of lying could be used in a subsequent prosecution for perjury, false statements, or obstruction of justice. Justice Rehnquist, writing for the Court, noted that if a person could not be punished for lying while immunized, an option would be created that would make a mockery of conferring immunity on a witness because the very purpose of granting immunity would be defeated. Justice Brennan and Justice Blackmun, joined by Justice Marshall, concurred in the result. The court in United States v. Veal, 153 F.3d 1233 (11th Cir.1998), put it this way:

> When an accused has been accorded immunity to preserve his right against self-incrimination, he must choose either to relinquish his Fifth Amendment right and testify truthfully, knowing that his statements cannot be used against him in a subsequent criminal prosecution regarding the matter being investigated, or continue to assert the privilege and suffer the consequences. There is no third option for testifying falsely without incurring potential prosecution for perjury or false statements.

For a discussion of *Apfelbaum* and *Portash,* see Hoffman, The Privilege Against Self–Incrimination and Immunity Statutes: Permissible Uses of Immunized Testimony, 16 Crim.L.Bull. 421 (1980).

Subsequent Statements

What happens if a witness testifies pursuant to a grant of immunity, then later makes a statement that is identical to the immunized statement? Can the later statement be used against the witness? Put another way, does a witness who testifies under a grant of immunity have a Fifth Amendment right to refuse to give an identical statement at a later point? In Pillsbury Co. v. Conboy, 459 U.S. 248 (1983), the Court upheld the right of a witness at a deposition in a civil case to claim the privilege against self-incrimination, even though he had previously been granted use immunity in related criminal proceedings. Conboy was a former executive of a company involved in an antitrust case. He testified before a grand jury after receiving use immunity. Subsequently, his grand jury testimony was provided to lawyers in related civil litigation. The lawyers decided to depose Conboy, and at the deposition, they read from the grand jury transcript in the course of asking questions. Conboy invoked his privilege against self-incrimination, but the district court found that the former immunity grant required him to answer and held him in contempt. A majority of the Court concluded that the prior grant of immunity was not sufficient protection to assure Conboy that nothing that he said at the deposition could be used against him in later criminal proceedings. It also reasoned that should the government ultimately decide to prosecute Conboy, it might have a difficult time proving that its evidence was not derived from the deposition in which the prior immunized testimony was used. To protect both the witness and the government, the Court held that a new immunity grant would be required before the witness could be forced to answer. Justice Marshall wrote a concurring opinion, and Justices Brennan and Blackmun concurred in the judgment. Justice Stevens, joined by Justice O'Connor, dissented.

Informal Immunity?

In United States v. Doe, 465 U.S. 605 (1984), the Court held that a sole proprietor could rely on the privilege against self-incrimination and decline to produce records if the act of production would tend to incriminate him. The government had stated that it would not use the act of production as evidence, but it did not seek a formal grant of immunity. The Court declined "to extend the jurisdiction of courts to include prospective grants of use immunity in the absence of the formal request that the statute requires."

3. *Waiver of the Privilege*

Determining the Scope of a Waiver

If a witness elects to testify, has the witness waived the privilege completely? On direct examination, the witness ordinarily can control what she says, but not on cross-examination. The usual rule is that a witness who takes the stand waives the privilege as to any subject matter within the scope of the direct examination. Therefore the witness might well have the right to refuse to testify even if her direct testimony would not be incriminating. The following suggestion has been made for a fair accommodation of the interests of the witness and the government:

> * * * We * * * recommend that the [witness] be subject to cross-examination only to the extent necessary to fairly test the statements made upon direct examination and inferences that might be drawn from such statements. In other words, a rule of "verbal completeness" would be an appropriate test with which to determine the scope of a waiver.
>
> This position respects the privilege, but insures that it does not give the [proponent] an extra tactical weapon not contemplated by the Constitution.

S. Saltzburg, M. Martin & D. Capra, Federal Rules of Evidence Manual 1091 (8th ed. 2002). Would you take the same or a different approach?

United States v. Hearst, 563 F.2d 1331 (9th Cir.1977), involved the scope of a waiver in a famous criminal trial. The defendant was charged with bank robbery. She admitted participation, but testified that at the time of the robbery, she was under duress from members of the Symbionese Liberation Army. The court held that by so testifying she waived the privilege with respect to questions on cross-examination concerning a later period in which she allegedly lived with SLA members voluntarily. The court found that the government's questions were "reasonably related" to the subjects covered by the direct testimony. Consequently, it was not error to allow the jury to hear Hearst invoke a privilege against self-incrimination in response to the questions: *Griffin* was not violated because Hearst's invocation of the privilege was invalid.

Hearst unsuccessfully relied on Calloway v. Wainwright, 409 F.2d 59 (5th Cir.1968), a case in which the defendant testified at trial that his confession was involuntarily obtained. The *Calloway* court held that the defendant had not waived the privilege concerning the substance of the charges against him, and therefore that the prosecutor's reference to Calloway's failure to testify on these matters violated *Griffin*. Why was *Calloway* not helpful to Hearst? See also Lesko v. Lehman, 925 F.2d 1527 (3d Cir.1991)(defendant who testifies at capital sentencing hearing concerning biographical information does not waive the privilege concerning the circumstances of the crime).

Waiver of the Privilege at a Guilty Plea Hearing? Mitchell v. United States

The defendant in Mitchell v. United States, 526 U.S. 314 (1999), pleaded guilty to federal charges of conspiring to distribute five or more kilograms of cocaine and of distributing cocaine. But she reserved the right to contest at sentencing the drug quantity attributable to her under the conspiracy count. Before accepting her plea, the District Court made the inquiries required by Federal Rule of Criminal Procedure 11 (see Chapter 9); told Mitchell that she faced a mandatory minimum of 1 year in prison for distributing cocaine, but a 10–year minimum for conspiracy if the Government could show that she was involved in a quantity more than 5 kilograms; and explained that by pleading guilty she would be waiving her right "at trial to remain silent." Indicating that she had done "some of" the proffered conduct, Mitchell confirmed her guilty plea. At her sentencing hearing, three codefendants testified that she had sold 1 1/2 to 2 ounces of cocaine twice a week for 1 1/2 years, and another person testified that Mitchell had sold her two ounces of cocaine. This was enough to take the quantity over the 5 kilogram threshold for an enhancement of Mitchell's sentence. Mitchell put on no evidence at the sentencing hearing, choosing to contest the credibility of the codefendant-witnesses. The sentencing court found that the codefendants' testimony put her over the 5–kilogram threshold, thus mandating the 10–year minimum; and the court noted specifically that Mitchell's failure to testify at sentencing was a factor in persuading it to rely on the codefendants' testimony.

One of the questions in *Mitchell* was whether the defendant had waived her Fifth Amendment privilege, insofar as sentencing was concerned, by pleading guilty and admitting to "some of" the conduct at her plea colloquy. If so, there would be no constitutional problem in penalizing her silence at sentencing. The Supreme Court, in an opinion by Justice Kennedy, held that Mitchell had not waived her privilege. Justice Kennedy's analysis of the waiver question proceeded as follows:

> It is well established that a witness, in a single proceeding, may not testify voluntarily about a subject and then invoke the privilege against self-incrimination when questioned about the details. The privilege is waived for the matters to which the witness testifies, and the scope of the "waiver is determined by the scope of relevant cross-examination." * * *

The justifications for the rule of waiver in the testimonial context are evident: A witness may not pick and choose what aspects of a particular subject to discuss without casting doubt on the trustworthiness of the statements and diminishing the integrity of the factual inquiry. * * * [A] contrary rule "would open the way to distortion of facts by permitting a witness to select any stopping place in the testimony." It would * * * "make of the Fifth Amendment not only a humane safeguard against judicially coerced self-disclosure but a positive invitation to mutilate the truth a party offers to tell." * * *

We may assume for purposes of this opinion, then, that if petitioner had pleaded not guilty and, having taken the stand at a trial, testified she did "some of it," she could have been cross-examined on the frequency of her drug deliveries and the quantity of cocaine involved. The concerns which justify the cross-examination when the defendant testifies are absent at a plea colloquy, however. The purpose of a plea colloquy is to protect the defendant from an unintelligent or involuntary plea. The Government would turn this constitutional shield into a prosecutorial sword by having the defendant relinquish all rights against compelled self-incrimination upon entry of a guilty plea, including the right to remain silent at sentencing.

There is no convincing reason why the narrow inquiry at the plea colloquy should entail such an extensive waiver of the privilege. Unlike the defendant taking the stand, * * * the defendant who pleads guilty puts nothing in dispute regarding the essentials of the offense. Rather, the defendant takes those matters out of dispute, often by making a joint statement with the prosecution or confirming the prosecution's version of the facts. Under these circumstances, there is little danger that the court will be misled by selective disclosure. In this respect a guilty plea is more like an offer to stipulate than a decision to take the stand. Here, petitioner's statement that she had done "some of" the proffered conduct did not pose a threat to the integrity of factfinding proceedings, for the purpose of the District Court's inquiry was simply to ensure that petitioner understood the charges and that there was a factual basis for the Government's case.

Justice Kennedy next addressed the Government's argument that Mitchell had no Fifth Amendment privilege at the time of her sentencing, because she had already been convicted (i.e., she suffered no risk of incrimination at that point).

Where the sentence has not yet been imposed a defendant may have a legitimate fear of adverse consequences from further testimony. * * * [I]t appears that in this case, as is often true in the criminal justice system, the defendant was less concerned with the proof of her guilt or innocence than with the severity of her punishment. Petitioner faced imprisonment from one year upwards to life, depending on the circumstances of the crime. To say that she had no right to remain silent but instead could be compelled to cooperate in the deprivation of her liberty would ignore the Fifth Amendment privilege at the precise stage where, from her point of view, it was most important.

Justice Scalia, joined by the Chief Justice and Justices O'Connor and Thomas, dissented in *Mitchell*. He agreed, however, with the majority's position that Mitchell could invoke her Fifth Amendment right to silence at the sentencing proceeding. In Justice Scalia's view, while Mitchell could invoke her privilege, there was nothing in the Fifth Amendment to prohibit the sentencing judge from drawing an adverse inference from her silence. This aspect of the decision in *Mitchell* is discussed *supra* in this Chapter.

Waiver by Interposing a Psychiatric Defense

In Buchanan v. Kentucky, 483 U.S. 402 (1987), the Court found no Fifth Amendment violation in the use of a psychiatric evaluation of the defendant to rebut a psychiatric defense. During his trial for murder and related crimes, Buchanan did not testify in support of the defense of "extreme emotional disturbance." He called a social worker, who formerly had been assigned to him, to read portions of evaluations of his mental state, which had been made when Buchanan had been arrested for an earlier offense. The prosecutor asked the social worker to read another report made during the period in which Buchanan was hospitalized as a result of the evaluation that had originally been made. The prosecutor also sought, over Buchanan's objection, to introduce a report of a psychological evaluation made when Buchanan's counsel and the prosecutor jointly requested a psychiatric examination for Buchanan pursuant to a state procedure for involuntary hospitalization. Justice Blackmun wrote for the Court that "if a defendant requests such an evaluation or presents psychiatric evidence, then, at the very least, the prosecution may rebut this presentation with evidence from the reports of the examination that the defendant requested." Thus, the Court found a waiver of Fifth Amendment rights in these circumstances.

Justice Marshall, joined by Justice Brennan, dissented and argued that when Buchanan agreed to an examination, he implicitly limited his consent to an examination for purposes of hospitalization and treatment.

Failure to Invoke the Privilege as a Waiver

When a person is compelled by the government to answer questions that might tend to incriminate that person in a subsequent criminal case, the person can refuse to answer and rely on the Fifth Amendment privilege against self-incrimination. However, if the person does answer, the privilege will be deemed waived and the answer can be used as evidence. For example, in Garner v. United States, 424 U.S. 648 (1976), the Court held that a taxpayer lost whatever privilege he might have had when he answered questions on a tax return, rather than invoking the privilege.

In Minnesota v. Murphy, 465 U.S. 420 (1984), the Court reiterated its view that generally a person who is asked to answer questions must invoke his privilege against self-incrimination or lose its protection. It held that a probationer lost the protection of the privilege when he answered questions of his probation officer concerning crimes for which he had not yet been charged. The state supreme court had held that the probation officer should have warned Murphy of his right to refuse to answer her questions, but a majority of the Supreme Court held that no warnings were required. This case is considered in connection with the *Miranda* cases, infra.

II. CONFESSIONS AND DUE PROCESS

A. INTRODUCTION

The United States Supreme Court has relied on three constitutional provisions in regulating the admissibility of confessions:

(1) From 1936 to the present, the due process clauses of the Fifth and Fourteenth Amendments have been used to exclude involuntary confessions.

(2) From 1964 to the present, the Sixth Amendment right to counsel has been applied in determining the admissibility of a confession obtained from a defendant who has been charged with a crime.

(3) From 1966 to the present, the Fifth Amendment's privilege against self-incrimination has been applied to statements made during custodial interrogation; a waiver analysis has prevailed, and the privilege must be shown to have been effectively waived before a confession is admissible.

These developments have not been as smooth as this brief description might suggest. The changing nature of coerced confession claims and of the Court's approach to them is an important part of the development of constitutionally-based criminal procedure. Thus, it warrants careful attention.

In 1884, the Court reviewed a federal criminal conviction in Hopt v. People of Territory of Utah, 110 U.S. 574.[7] It explicitly recognized that there was a common-law rule prohibiting the use of confessions obtained by inducements, promises and threats. The common-law rule was based on the premise that confessions resulting from promises or threats are unreliable—therefore they could not be admitted into evidence. The same desire to prevent erroneous convictions led the Court to cite treatises on evidence and to follow the common-law rule. (There is no indication that the Court was relying on any constitutional language.)

Thirteen years later, in Bram v. United States, 168 U.S. 532 (1897) (suspect in custody of police was stripped, searched, and questioned), the Court abruptly departed from an emphasis on the reliability of confessions, and relied on the self-incrimination clause of the Fifth Amendment to find that statements of an accused, which were introduced to establish his guilt, were made involuntarily and therefore violated the constitutional prohibition against compelled incrimination. This decision was sharply criticized by a number of legal scholars as an erroneous union of the right against self-incrimination and the common-law confessions rule.[8]

The proposition that the Fifth Amendment is the proper basis on which to assess the admissibility of confessions "was not itself developed in subsequent decisions," Miranda v. Arizona, 384 U.S. 436, 506 (1966) (Harlan, J., dissenting). This was so, even though the rule stated in Justice White's majority opinion in *Bram* was not challenged by Justice Brewer's dissent, in which Chief Justice Fuller and Justice Brown joined. Although it did not overrule *Bram,* for two-thirds of a century the Court never explicitly and exclusively relied on the

---

7. This section on the background of confessions law draws heavily from O. Stephens, The Supreme Court and Confessions of Guilt 19–26 (1973).

8. See, e.g., 3 J. Wigmore, Evidence § 823 (Chadbourn Rev. 1981).

privilege against self-incrimination to suppress the use of a confession in another federal case. It did assume in dicta, however, that *Bram* might have continued force. See generally, Developments in the Law: Confessions, 79 Harv.L.Rev. 935, 959–61 (1966).[9] After *Bram* and until 1964, the Court turned to the due process clauses of the Constitution to decide coerced confession cases.

B. THE DUE PROCESS CASES

The Involuntariness Test: Brown v. Mississippi

The Court made its first important decision on confessions under the due process clause of the Fourteenth Amendment in Brown v. Mississippi, 297 U.S. 278 (1936). Summarily reversing convictions obtained in the state court, the Supreme Court found that severe whippings, used to procure confessions from helpless defendants, made the confessions involuntary and violated basic due process rights. In reaching its decision, the Court emphasized the unreliability of confessions extracted by torture and referred to the confessions in *Brown* as "spurious."

The Court decided thirty-five confession cases between *Brown* in 1936 and Massiah v. United States, 377 U.S. 201, in 1964. It struggled in the ensuing cases, which involved more subtle and less physical methods of obtaining confessions, to define appropriate constitutional limitations on the interrogation methods used by police in light of the capacity of an individual possessed of free will to withstand coercion. Case-by-difficult-case, the Court attempted to describe the reach of the due process clauses, and their role in controlling the methods by which government agents seek evidence.

Circumstances Relevant to Involuntariness

A summary, by no means exhaustive, might convey the breadth of circumstances that the Court considered when it tried to determine the validity of confessions under the due process clauses. With respect to the personal characteristics of the accused, the Court was concerned not only with the youthfulness of the suspect, but also with the educational background of the accused in cases such as Payne v. Arkansas, 356 U.S. 560 (1958)(fifth grade education), and Fikes v. Alabama, 352 U.S. 191 (1957)(illiterate). In addition, the Court was sensitive to any mental deficiency of the defendant as illustrated by Culombe v. Connecticut, 367 U.S. 568, 620 (1961)(illiterate mental defective), and Blackburn v. Alabama, 361 U.S. 199, 207 (1960)(strong probability that the accused was insane at the time he allegedly confessed). Conversely, the Court was less likely to find undue coercion if the defendant was well-educated as in Crooker v. California, 357 U.S. 433 (1958)(accused had completed one year of law school), or was a hardened veteran of criminal proceedings as in Stein v. New York, 346 U.S. 156, 185 (1953)(defendants were not "young, soft, ignorant or timid").

In considering circumstances of physical deprivation or mistreatment, the Court not only disapproved of severe brutality like that found in *Brown,* supra, but also of the denial of food, *Payne,* supra (accused was given no food for

---

9. The Court could not rely on *Bram* in reviewing state confession cases until 1964 when the Fifth Amendment's self-incrimina-tion clause was incorporated into the Fourteenth Amendment and thereby made applicable to the states.

twenty-four hours), or sleep, Ashcraft v. Tennessee, 322 U.S. 143 (1944)(defendant was not permitted to sleep for thirty-six hours). If the accused was permitted certain amenities, the Court responded favorably. In *Crooker,* supra, for instance, the confession was found admissible and the Court pointed out that the defendant was provided with food and was permitted to smoke during interrogations.

A third factor, psychological influence, was also accorded great weight by the Court. Although the Court stated that a voluntary statement need not be volunteered, it refused to hold that only physical brutality was impermissible. In Watts v. Indiana, 338 U.S. 49, 53 (1949), the Court said that:

> if [the confession] is the product of sustained pressure by the police it does not issue from a free choice. When a suspect speaks because he is overborne, it is immaterial whether he has been subjected to a physical or mental ordeal. Eventual yielding to questioning under such circumstances is plainly the product of the suction process of interrogation and therefore the reverse of voluntary.

In *Watts,* as in Haley v. Ohio, 332 U.S. 596 (1948), and numerous other cases, the Court paid special attention to whether the accused was denied the aid of family, friends, or counsel.[10] Incommunicado confinement consistently was viewed as an element of coercion. Another form of psychological influence was trickery, though this was only one factor in the due process calculus. See generally White, Police Trickery in Inducing Confessions, 127 U.Pa.L.Rev. 581 (1979).

The Court also recognized the pressure inherent in such psychological techniques as sustained interrogation, *Ashcraft,* supra, and the threat of mob violence, *Payne,* supra (defendant was told thirty to forty people would be waiting to get him unless he confessed). The Court also was concerned about rewards and inducements to confess, which had been condemned in *Hopt,* supra. New techniques as well as old were carefully scrutinized. For example, in Leyra v. Denno, 347 U.S. 556 (1954), the Court took exception to the use of a trained psychiatrist to extract a confession through skillful and suggestive questioning.

Finally, as will be considered in more detail later, in applying the voluntariness standard, the Court considered whether the accused was aware or had been apprised of his constitutional right to counsel, as well as his right to remain silent.

It should be apparent from this overview that the voluntariness standard required a case-by-case scrutiny of the circumstances surrounding a particular confession to determine if the methods by which it was obtained comported with due process. The Court considered both the police conduct in procuring the confession and the defendant's ability to withstand coercion; therefore, the "totality of the circumstances" test that was set forth in Fikes v. Alabama, 352 U.S. 191 (1957), was determinative of the voluntariness of the confession. The question was whether the suspect confessed because his will was overborne.

10. Some other cases in which the accused was not permitted the support of friends or counsel include Chambers v. Florida, 309 U.S. 227 (1940); Ward v. Texas, 316 U.S. 547 (1942); Ashcraft v. Tennessee, 322 U.S. 143 (1944); Turner v. Pennsylvania, 338 U.S. 62 (1949); and Blackburn v. Alabama, 361 U.S. 199 (1960).

Criticism of the Involuntariness Test

Although the Court refined its analysis of the voluntariness test in the course of handing down over 30 full-length opinions under the due process standard, some members of the Court recognized the shortcomings of the voluntariness approach. Justice Frankfurter, a supporter of the due process standard, noted in *Culombe* that "[n]o single litmus-paper test for constitutionally impermissible interrogations has been evolved. * * * " The word "voluntary" hardly offered clear guidance to law enforcement officers and to lower court judges. It had to be defined anew in every case. Because the Court could not possibly pass on all of the state confession cases in which review was sought, usually certiorari was limited to death penalty cases or others of special concern. Thus, the confusion in the lower courts was not something with which the Supreme Court could concern itself. In fact, each totality of the circumstances decision, it might be argued, caused a greater division among lower trial and appellate courts. That the Justices themselves often disagreed on the proper application of the test compounded the problem.

The totality of circumstances test gave little guidance to the police. For example, the instruction "don't overbear the will of the suspect" has little defined content outside the realm of physical force. Professor Schulhofer has criticized the indeterminacy of the involuntariness test in the following passage:

> In theory, brutality is ruled out by the due process test * * * but in operation the due process test sends police a fatally mixed message. The job of the interrogator, of course, is to get the reticent suspect to "come clean." When a tired, confused, or shaky prisoner shows signs of starting to "crack," is the interrogator supposed to keep up the pressure, or back off to avoid breaking the suspect's will? In effect, under the due process test, the officer is expected to do both. Instances of overbearing coercion are bound to occur under such a system, not because some officers will deliberately flout the law but because even the best of professionals will inevitably misjudge the elusive psychological line.

Schulhofer, *Miranda's* Practical Effect: Substantial Benefits and Vanishingly Small Costs, 90 Nw. Univ.L.Rev. 500 (1996).

Increasing Emphasis on Assistance of Counsel: Spano v. New York

The growing dissatisfaction of certain members of the Court with the voluntariness standard became very apparent in Spano v. New York, 360 U.S. 315 (1959). Four concurring justices expressed greater concern about the fact that the defendant Spano had been indicted and was refused permission to see his attorney than about the voluntariness of the confession under the totality of the circumstances. Spano, a 25–year old immigrant with a junior high school education, shot a person after a bar fight. He left the scene and disappeared for a week or so, and was indicted for murder during this period. The facts surrounding Spano's confession were set forth by Chief Justice Warren as follows:

> On February 3, 1957, petitioner called one Gaspar Bruno, a close friend of 8 or 10 years' standing who had attended school with him. Bruno was a fledgling police officer, having at that time not yet finished attending police

academy. According to Bruno's testimony, petitioner told him "that he took a terrific beating, that the deceased hurt him real bad and he dropped him a couple of times and he was dazed; he didn't know what he was doing and that he went and shot at him." Petitioner told Bruno that he intended to get a lawyer and give himself up. Bruno relayed this information to his superiors.

The following day, February 4, at 7:10 p.m., petitioner, accompanied by counsel, surrendered himself to the authorities * * *. His attorney had cautioned him to answer no questions, and left him in the custody of the officers. He was promptly taken to the office of the Assistant District Attorney and at 7:15 p.m. the questioning began, being conducted by Assistant District Attorney Goldsmith, Lt. Gannon, Detectives Farrell, Lehrer and Motta, and Sgt. Clarke. The record reveals that the questioning was both persistent and continuous. Petitioner, in accordance with his attorney's instructions, steadfastly refused to answer. * * * He asked one officer, Detective Ciccone, if he could speak to his attorney, but that request was denied. Detective Ciccone testified that he could not find the attorney's name in the telephone book. He was given two sandwiches, coffee and cake at 11 p.m.

At 12:15 a.m. on the morning of February 5, after five hours of questioning in which it became evident that petitioner was following his attorney's instructions, on the Assistant District Attorney's orders petitioner was transferred to the 46th Squad, Ryer Avenue Police Station. The Assistant District Attorney also went to the police station and to some extent continued to participate in the interrogation. Petitioner arrived at 12:30 and questioning was resumed at 12:40. * * * But petitioner persisted in his refusal to answer, and again requested permission to see his attorney, this time from Detective Lehrer. His request was again denied.

It was then that those in charge of the investigation decided that petitioner's close friend, Bruno, could be of use. * * * Although, in fact, his job was in no way threatened, Bruno was told to tell petitioner that petitioner's telephone call had gotten him "in a lot of trouble," and that he should seek to extract sympathy from petitioner for Bruno's pregnant wife and three children. Bruno developed this theme with petitioner without success, and petitioner, also without success, again sought to see his attorney, a request which Bruno relayed unavailingly to his superiors. After this first session with petitioner, Bruno was again directed by Lt. Gannon to play on petitioner's sympathies, but again no confession was forthcoming. But the Lieutenant a third time ordered Bruno falsely to importune his friend to confess, but again petitioner clung to his attorney's advice. Inevitably, in the fourth such session directed by the Lieutenant, lasting a full hour, petitioner succumbed to his friend's prevarications and agreed to make a statement. Accordingly, at 3:25 a.m. the Assistant District Attorney, a stenographer, and several other law enforcement officials entered the room where petitioner was being questioned, and took his statement in question and answer form with the Assistant District Attorney asking the questions. The statement was completed at 4:05 a.m.

But this was not the end. At 4:30 a.m. three detectives took petitioner to Police Headquarters in Manhattan. On the way they attempted to find the bridge from which petitioner said he had thrown the murder weapon. They crossed the Triborough Bridge into Manhattan, arriving at Police Headquarters at 5 a.m., and left Manhattan for the Bronx at 5:40 a.m. via the Willis Avenue Bridge. When petitioner recognized neither bridge as the one from which he had thrown the weapon, they reentered Manhattan via the Third Avenue Bridge, which petitioner stated was the right one, and then returned to the Bronx well after 6 a.m. During that trip the officers also elicited a statement from petitioner that the deceased was always "on [his] back," "always pushing" him and that he was "not sorry" he had shot the deceased. All three detectives testified to that statement at the trial.

Spano argued that his Sixth Amendment right to counsel was violated when he was interrogated, despite his repeated request for counsel, after he had been formally charged with the crime. Chief Justice Warren found it unnecessary to decide the Sixth Amendment's applicability, because the use of Spano's confessions was "inconsistent with the Fourteenth Amendment under traditional principles." The Chief Justice surveyed the law governing involuntary confessions:

> The abhorrence of society to the use of involuntary confessions does not turn alone on their inherent untrustworthiness. It also turns on the deep-rooted feeling that the police must obey the law while enforcing the law; that in the end life and liberty can be as much endangered from illegal methods used to convict those thought to be criminals as from the actual criminals themselves. * * * The facts of no case recently in this Court have quite approached the brutal beatings in Brown v. Mississippi, 297 U.S. 278 (1936), or the 36 consecutive hours of questioning present in Ashcraft v. Tennessee, 322 U.S. 143 (1944). But as law enforcement officers become more responsible, and the methods used to extract confessions more sophisticated, our duty to enforce federal constitutional protections does not cease. It only becomes more difficult because of the more delicate judgments to be made.

In assessing the circumstances surrounding Spano's confessions, the Court the following factors in their totality constituted substantial police misconduct that caused an involuntary confession: 1) Spano was young, foreign-born, relatively uneducated, emotionally unstable, and inexperienced in the criminal justice system; 2) Spano "did not make a narrative statement, but was subject to the leading questions of a skillful prosecutor in a question and answer confession; 3) he was questioned virtually incessantly by a number of officers, throughout the night; 4) the questioning 'persisted' in the face of his repeated refusals to answer on the advice of his attorney;" 5) the officers "ignored his reasonable requests to contact the local attorney whom he had already retained and who had personally delivered him into the custody of these officers."; and 6) the use of Bruno, Spano's friend, and Bruno's false statements to Spano.

Chief Justice Warren closed his opinion as follows:

> We conclude that petitioner's will was overborne by official pressure, fatigue and sympathy falsely aroused, after considering all the facts in their post-indictment setting. Here a grand jury had already found sufficient cause to require petitioner to face trial on a charge of first-degree murder, and the police had an eyewitness to the shooting. The police were not therefore merely trying to solve a crime, or even to absolve a suspect. They

were rather concerned primarily with securing a statement from defendant on which they could convict him. The undeviating intent of the officers to extract a confession from petitioner is therefore patent.

Justice Douglas, joined by Justice Black and Justice Brennan, wrote a concurring opinion that emphasized the officers' denial of Spano's request for counsel:

> We have often divided on whether state authorities may question a suspect for hours on end when he has no lawyer present and when he has demanded that he have the benefit of legal advice. But here we deal not with a suspect but with a man who has been formally charged with a crime. The question is whether after the indictment and before the trial the Government can interrogate the accused *in secret* when he asked for his lawyer and when his request was denied. * * * Depriving a person, formally charged with a crime, of counsel during the period prior to trial may be more damaging than denial of counsel during the trial itself.

Justice Stewart, joined by Justice Douglas and Justice Brennan wrote a separate concurring opinion that also emphasized the right to counsel:

> Our Constitution guarantees the assistance of counsel to a man on trial for his life in an orderly courtroom, presided over by a judge, open to the public, and protected by all the procedural safeguards of the law. Surely a Constitution which promises that much can vouchsafe no less to the same man under midnight inquisition in the squad room of a police station.

The Importance of Spano

The concurring justices believed that once a person is formally charged by an indictment or information, his constitutional right to counsel begins, at least when counsel previously has been retained. Although the majority of the Court analyzed the confession under the traditional voluntariness standard, the majority did not reject the views expressed in the concurring opinions. It left the counsel question for another day, which was not long in coming, as we shall soon see. Thus, while *Spano* is a due process case, it provided a doctrinal bridge for the Court to consider the applicability of other constitutional limitations on police efforts to obtain confessions.

The Continuing Relevance of Due Process Protection

Despite the Court's regulation of confessions through the Sixth Amendment in *Massiah* and through the Fifth Amendment in *Miranda* (both discussed later in this Chapter), the totality of the circumstances voluntariness test is in some cases a suspect's only protection from police coercion. The Sixth Amendment does not apply until the suspect has been formally charged (Moran v. Burbine, infra). *Miranda* applies only during police "custodial interrogation," and that term does not cover all potentially coercive police practices (Rhode Island v. Innis, infra). See United States v. Murphy, 763 F.2d 202 (6th Cir.1985)(sending an attack dog to apprehend the suspect is not custodial interrogation, but confession made while dog was attacking held involuntary). Moreover, *Miranda* rights can be waived, while the right to be free from coercion cannot (nobody argues, for example, that the defendants in Brown v. Mississippi could have waived the right to be free from physical beating). Thus, if the defendant has made a valid waiver of *Miranda* rights, his only protection from police pressure is the due process involuntariness test. See, e.g., United States v. Astello, 241 F.3d 965 (8th Cir. 2001) (court considers whether confession was involuntary after the defendant made a valid waiver of *Miranda* rights). Finally, the Court has found several exceptions to *Miranda*, so that a *Miranda*–defective confession can be used for impeachment (Harris v. New York, infra), the fruits of such a confession are admissible (Oregon v. Elstad, infra), and the confession itself can be admitted if obtained under emergency circumstances (New York v. Quarles, infra). However, even where *Miranda* and *Massiah* are inapplicable, the confession is still excluded under the Due Process Clause if obtained through police coercion. Thus, the due process involuntariness test retains vitality today, and cases are still being decided under that doctrine.

Modern Due Process Cases

It is the rare case, however, in which a court will find that a suspect confessed involuntarily. See White, Interrogation Without Questions, 78 Mich. L.Rev. 1209 (1980). Examples of cases denying involuntariness claims are Sumpter v. Nix, 863 F.2d 563 (8th Cir.1988)(suspect with I.Q. of 89 and psychological problems, promised treatment, and interrogated for more than seven hours); McCall v. Dutton, 863 F.2d 454 (6th Cir.1988)(defendant was wounded, and officers interrogated with guns drawn); Moore v. Dugger, 856 F.2d 129 (11th Cir.1988)(suspect with an I.Q. of 62, who functioned at the level of an 11–year old, had been without food or sleep for 25 hours at the time he confessed); and United States v. Kelley, 953 F.2d 562 (9th Cir.1992)(suspect confessed while handcuffed and suffering from heroin withdrawal).

Grano, Voluntariness, Free Will, and the Law of Confessions, 65 Va.L.Rev. 859 (1979), argues that an involuntary confession is "any confession produced by interrogation pressures that a person of reasonable firmness, with some of the defendant's characteristics, would not resist." How would *Spano* be resolved under this standard?

Others have argued that a confession is involuntary only where police tactics are such as would force an innocent person to confess. This is a reflection of the premise of some scholars that "the Constitution seeks to protect the innocent." Amar, The Constitution and Criminal Procedure: First Principles 154 (1997). This would mean that threats and physical violence would be prohibited, but tactics that could be used to trick a person to confess (e.g., false expressions of sympathy, or understating the significance of the crime) would be permitted. Is this view of the involuntariness test a workable one? Would it allow the police too much leeway in extracting confessions on the assumption ground that the suspect is guilty anyway?

An example of permissible interrogation techniques is found in United States v. Astello, 241 F.3d 965 (8th Cir. 2001). Police interrogated an 18 year-old boy in a murder investigation in which he was one of several suspects. They refused to let him consult with his mother, and engaged in several tactics to get him to confess, which he did. The court described and analyzed those tactics in the following passage:

Astello argues that the agents improperly used several tactics to coerce him to confess. He argues that they placed time constraints on his decision whether to talk to them, thus subjecting him to psychological pressure * * * and they played on his emotions and used his respect for his family against him. Obviously, interrogation of a suspect will involve some pressure because its purpose is to elicit a confession. In order to obtain the desired result, interrogators use a laundry list of factors. See Richard A. Leo, Inside the Interrogation Room, 86 J.Crim.L. & Criminology 266 (1996). Numerous cases have held that questioning tactics such as a raised voice, deception, or a sympathetic attitude on the part of the interrogator will not render a confession involuntary * * *.

Here, the agents used a train analogy, telling Astello that the train was leaving the station and those who told the truth would be on the train while those left behind at the station would be charged with the crime. They said that the train was getting crowded, and that those who were on the train would testify against him. Certainly, these statements may have influenced Astello's decision to tell the truth. * * * [But] we conclude that the statements were not so coercive as to deprive Astello of his ability to make an unconstrained decision to confess.

* * *

The agents told Astello that he had disgraced his family and that his lies dishonored his family. They also told him that he had broken his father's heart. Astello did not seem to be affected in the least by this "family dishonor" interrogation tactic. Immediately after [the officer] said "why do you persist in bringing dishonor to your family by lying?" Astello commented "That's a shame, huh?" and laughed. Astello's response indicates that his will was not overborne.

Assessing the totality of circumstances, the *Astello* Court concluded as follows:

Astello knew his rights and understood the consequences of committing the crime for which he was arrested. He was questioned for less than three hours and was not mistreated in any way. Police interrogation tactics are designed to elicit a response, and the fact that the tactics produced the intended result does not make Astello's confession involuntary. This, of course, does not mean that we condone any of the tactics used by the agents in this case. We see no indication, however, that Astello's will was overborne and his capacity for self-determination critically impaired.

Deception and False Promises by the Police

What effect does the use of police deception and similar psychological ploys have on the voluntariness inquiry? The Court in *Bram* had stated that a confession induced by "any direct or implied promises, however slight" must be suppressed. But courts have not followed that language from *Bram*. For example, in Green v. Scully, 850 F.2d 894 (2d Cir.1988), Green was taken to the station by two New York detectives to be interrogated as a murder suspect. He waived his *Miranda* rights. Thereafter, Detective Byrnes threatened him with the electric chair, even though there was at that time no capital punishment in New York. Then Byrnes left the room. During a lengthy interrogation, Detective

Hazel consistently asserted that the police had all the evidence they needed to convict Green, stating that he had personally checked it out. This was false. When Green stated that he would never confess because he would not be able to face his and the victim's families, Hazel said he could help Green with that and suggested that Green must have been mentally ill when he committed the murder. Hazel referred to Green as "brother" and said that he would get psychiatric help for Green. Then Hazel took a different tack, appeared frustrated, and threatened to leave the interrogation over to the "bad cop," Byrnes. Byrnes then came in and stated that he had found Green's palm prints at the scene, with blood stains on them. This was not true. Byrnes told Green that he was lucky that Hazel was there, because Hazel cared about him while Byrnes did not. Green then began to consider cooperating, after again receiving assurance from Hazel that he would obtain psychiatric help and would avoid capital punishment. In the course of his confession, Green stated that he suffered from blackouts, that he was confessing out of fear that if he were not convicted of this crime he might kill someone else, and that confessing would be the only way to obtain psychiatric help.

The court held that the confession was voluntary. It concluded that despite *Bram,* "the presence of a direct or implied promise of help or leniency alone has not barred the admission of a confession" and that "promises do not require an analysis separate from or different than the totality of circumstances rule." The court found that Green was of above average intelligence and streetwise, that the interrogation session was only two hours long, and that Green was not handcuffed or in pain during that time. As to the psychological tactics, the court found the police conduct "troubling." But the use of these tactics was not enough to taint the confession, in part because Green had his own motivation for confessing.

> [T]he scare tactics, false representation as to the evidence, good cop/bad cop routine, and whatever hopes were instilled from the promises or fears from the reference to the "chair" considered together did not overbear Green's will and bring about his confession. He confessed—as he candidly admitted—because he was afraid that what he had done to the victims in a blackout would be something he was going to do to his own family—maybe even his mother.

Did the court overlook the fact that Green confessed not precisely to take himself "off the street," but because in doing so he would obtain psychiatric help? See generally White, Confessions Induced by Broken Government Promises, 43 Duke L.J.947 (1994). Suppose Green had been taken before a judge for a bail hearing, and the judge had offered to obtain psychiatric help for Green if he would confess. Would the confession be coerced? If so, is it true that a judge has more coercive power over a suspect than the officers had in *Green*? See also Clark v. Murphy, 331 F.3d 1062 (9th Cir. 2003)(no due process violation where the officer, "using his hands to illustrate the scales of justice, expressed his *opinion* that a judge and jury would weigh fear of punishment against remorse, and that in his *opinion*, remorse would outweigh the fear of punishment"; these opinions did not constitute an express or implied promise of leniency).

A leading interrogation manual, authored by Inbau, Reid and Buckley, argues the merits of deceptive interrogation techniques in leading to confessions. The techniques they recommend include: 1) showing fake sympathy for the suspect by acting like his friend (e.g., by falsely telling a rape suspect that the officer himself had once "roughed it up" with a girl in an attempt to have intercourse with her); 2) reducing the suspect's feelings of guilt through lies (e.g., by telling a person suspected of killing his wife that he was not as "lucky" as the officer, who at one time was just about to "pound" his wife when the doorbell rang); 3) exaggerating the crime in an effort to get the suspect to negotiate, or in hopes of obtaining a denial which will indirectly inculpate the suspect (e.g., accusing the suspect of stealing $40,000 when only $20,000 involved, or accusing the suspect of murder where the victim, while shot, survived the incident); 4) lying that implies that "the game is up" because the evidence is so strong (e.g., stating that the suspect was identified at the scene when in fact he was not); and 5) playing one codefendant against another (e.g., leading one to believe the other has confessed when no confession has occurred). Inbau, Reid & Buckley, Criminal Interrogation and Confessions 98–132 (3rd ed. 1986).

Most courts applying the involuntariness test prohibit false promises only when the officer makes a specific promise to provide a specific benefit to the defendant in exchange for him confessing, and then that promise is not kept. Thus, vague and general promises to get the suspect some help are considered permissible. See Miller v. Fenton, 796 F.2d 598 (3d Cir. 1986) (general statement that the person who committed the crime "needed help" and would undoubtedly get psychiatric help does not render confession involuntary).

Cases permitting deceptive techniques under the voluntariness test are numerous. See, e.g., Frazier v. Cupp, 394 U.S. 731 (1969) (use of "false friend" and "game is up" techniques, although relevant to the due process inquiry, were not sufficient to render the confession involuntary). Miller v. Fenton, 796 F.2d 598 (3d Cir. 1986) (use of "false friend" technique, together with a ruse that the victim had not died when in fact she had, does not render confession involuntary). See also Young, Unnecessary Evil: Police Lying in Interrogations, 28 Conn. L.Rev. 425 (1996) (providing citations to lower court cases refusing to exclude confessions obtained after the suspect was exposed to lies about matters such as the strength of the case, fabricated evidence, suggestions that the suspect was not at fault, and lies about the identity of the interrogator).

Are these techniques permitted because they are unlikely to overbear the will of the suspect? Are they permitted because they are unlikely to get an innocent person to confess? Compare United States v. LeBrun, 306 F.3d 545 (8th Cir. 2002) (confession was involuntary where officers told the defendant–falsely–that if he confessed to killing the victim as a spontaneous act, he could not be prosecuted because a spontaneous act was outside the statute of limitations: "a reasonable person in LeBrun's position would have perceived the statements of the agents as a promise of nonprosecution if LeBrun confessed to a spontaneous act").

Are deception techniques permitted because the courts tacitly assume that suspects are not naive enough to believe that police will tell them the absolute truth during an interrogation? After all, it is an interrogation, not a picnic, right? But if suspects anticipate police mendacity, what good are these deceptive practices? See Paris, Trust, Lies and Interrogation, 3 Va.J.Soc.Pol. & L. 3 (1995) (arguing for a rule prohibiting police from lying, on the ground that such a rule would lead to more reliable confessions, not less: "suspects would be able to relax their guard if assured that lying interrogators would be punished" and will be more prone "to trust their interrogators and confess in situations in which confessions will serve their interests").

False Documentary Evidence

In Florida v. Cayward, 552 So.2d 971 (Fla.App.1989), police fabricated a scientific report for use as a ploy in interrogating the defendant. The report was prepared on stationery of Lifecodes, Inc., a DNA testing service, and it indicated that DNA testing showed that bodily fluids on the victim came from the defendant. The defendant confessed when shown the false report. The court found the resulting confession involuntary, reasoning as follows:

> The reporters are filled with examples of police making false verbal assertions to a suspect, but * * * we perceive an intrinsic distinction between verbal assertions and manufactured documentation. * * * It may well be that a suspect is more impressed and thereby more easily induced to confess when presented with tangible, official-looking reports as opposed to merely being told that some tests have implicated him. In addition to our spontaneous distaste for the conduct we have reviewed in this matter, we have practical concerns regarding the use of the false reports beyond the inducement of a confession. Unlike oral misrepresentations, manufactured documents have the potential of indefinite life and the facial appearance of authenticity. * * * Such reports have the potential of finding their way into the courtroom.

Do you agree that there is a per se distinction between false verbal statements and false documentary evidence? Is the distinction that an innocent person may shrug off an officer's verbal statement that the suspect's DNA was found at the scene, whereas even an innocent person might have to think about confessing where the forensic test apparently incriminates him? Is this a reason to think about the voluntariness test in terms of prohibiting those actions and tactics that would cause an innocent person to confess?

Promises of Consideration

The fact that an officer makes a promise does not mean that it is necessarily a false promise. Judge Posner, in United States v. Baldwin, 60 F.3d 363 (7th Cir.1995), had this to say about a confession obtained after a police officer's promise to the defendant that any cooperation by him would be brought to the prosecutor's attention:

> A false promise of lenience would be an example of forbidden tactics, for it would impede the suspect in making an informed choice as to whether he was better off confessing or clamming up. But government is not forbidden to buy information with honest promises of consideration. And as it is well known that the suspect's cooperation, by lightening the government's burdens of investigation and prosecution, is looked upon favorably by prosecutors and judges, what the agent told the defendant was very close to a truism; * * * and the defendant was not a tyro or ignoramus, but a 39–year-old with a long history of involvement in the criminal justice system.

See also United States v. Fraction, 795 F.2d 12 (3d Cir. 1986) (officer promises to relate the fact of the suspect's cooperation to the prosecutor, but does not represent that he has authority to affect the outcome of the case; confession voluntary). Compare United States v. Walton, 10 F.3d 1024 (3d Cir. 1993)(confession involuntary where the officer, a long-time friend of the defendant, promises to keep a conversation "off the record" and then does not do so).

Threats of Physical Violence: Arizona v. Fulminante

Justice White wrote for a majority in Arizona v. Fulminante, 499 U.S. 279 (1991), as it found that a confession made by one prisoner to another was coerced and thus involuntary under the Fifth and Fourteenth Amendments. Fulminante was suspected of murdering his stepdaughter in Arizona, but had not been arrested or charged before he was incarcerated in New Jersey on an unrelated firearms conviction. He became friends with another inmate who was a paid informant for the FBI and who masqueraded as an organized crime figure. When the informant learned that Fulminante was suspected of killing a child, he suggested to Fulminante that he could protect him from other inmates, who did not look kindly upon suspected child killers. But this protection would be provided only if Fulminante told him the truth about what had occurred. This offer resulted in the confession to which the informant testified.

Justice White observed that the *Bram* standard, which condemned any confession obtained by any direct or implied promises, however slight, or by the exertion of any improper influence, had been replaced by a totality of the circumstances test. In applying that test, he concluded that a credible threat of physical violence had existed, and that Fulminante confessed due to his misplaced hope for protection from that violence. Therefore the confession was involuntary. Justice White stressed that "a finding of coercion need not depend upon actual violence by a government agent; a credible threat is sufficient." The majority analogized Fulminante's plight to that of the defendant in Payne v. Arkansas, supra, where the interrogating officer threatened that unless Payne confessed, the officer would leave him to an angry mob just outside the jailhouse door.

Chief Justice Rehnquist, joined by Justices O'Connor, Kennedy, and Souter, dissented. He emphasized that Fulminante offered no evidence that he believed his life was in danger or that he confessed to obtain protection; that the conversations between Fulminante and the informant were not lengthy; that Fulminante was free at all times to leave the informant's company; that the informant never threatened Fulminante and never demanded that he confess; and that Fulminante was "an experienced habitue of prisons." The Chief Justice asserted that the majority had embraced a "more expansive definition" of involuntariness than was warranted by previous case law.

After *Fulminante,* is a credible threat of physical violence a per se factor? If so, why is it different from a threat of the electric chair, as in *Green,* or an assertion that the suspect's fingerprints were found at the scene? Is the distinction that an innocent person might confess to avoid a beating?

Focus on Police Misconduct: Colorado v. Connelly

The Supreme Court held in Colorado v. Connelly, 479 U.S. 157 (1986), that the due process focus is primarily on police misconduct rather than the suspect's state of mind. Connelly approached a uniformed officer in downtown Denver and stated that he had murdered someone and wanted to talk about it. The officer warned Connelly that he had the right to remain silent, that anything he said could be used against him in court, and that he had a right to an attorney before any questioning. Connelly stated that he understood his rights and wanted to talk about the murder. A homicide detective arrived and repeated the warnings. Connelly then stated that he had come from Boston to confess to the murder of a young girl whom he had killed months earlier. The officers took him to the police station, examined their records, discovered that an unidentified female body had been found, talked with Connelly concerning the murder, and took Connelly in a police car to point out the location of the crime. The next morning Connelly began to appear disoriented, and he stated that "voices" had told him to come to Denver to confess. He was initially found incompetent to assist in his own defense, but later was declared fit to proceed to trial.

An expert witness testified in support of Connelly's motion to suppress his confessions that Connelly was experiencing "command hallucinations," which interfered with his ability to make free and rational choices. The state courts suppressed the confessions on the ground that Connelly did not confess of his own free will. But the Supreme Court reversed. Writing for the Court, Chief Justice Rehnquist reasoned that the police applied absolutely no pressure on Connelly to confess. The state courts failed "to recognize the essential link between coercive activity of the State, on the one hand, and a resulting confession by a defendant, on the other." The Court held that "coercive police activity is a necessary predicate to the finding that a confession is not 'voluntary' within the meaning of the Due Process Clause."

The Chief Justice asserted that suppressing a statement in the absence of police coercion "would serve absolutely no purpose in enforcing constitutional guarantees" because it would not deter future police conduct. The Court concluded as follows:

> Only if we were to establish a brand new constitutional right—the right of a criminal defendant to confess to his crime only when totally rational and properly motivated—could respondent's present claim be sustained. * * * Respondent would now have us require sweeping inquiries into the state of mind of a criminal defendant who has confessed, inquiries quite divorced from any coercion brought to bear on the defendant by the State. We think the Constitution rightly leaves this sort of inquiry to be resolved by state laws governing the admission of evidence * * *. A statement rendered by one in the condition of respondent might be proved to be quite unreliable, but this is a matter to be governed by the evidentiary laws of the forum.

Justice Brennan, joined by Justice Marshall, dissented from this holding. He argued that the absence of police wrongdoing was not conclusive and "[t]he requirement that a confession be voluntary reflects a recognition of the importance of free will and of reliability in determining the admissibility of a confession, and thus demands an inquiry into the totality of the circumstances surrounding the confession."

The effect of *Connelly* can be seen in such cases as United States v. Erving L., 147 F.3d 1240 (10th Cir.1998), where the suspect's mother coerced him into confessing to the authorities. The court relied on *Connelly* to find no due process violation. Courts have also held after *Connelly* that it is irrelevant that the suspect was drunk, on drugs, mentally impaired, emotionally vulnerable, etc., when he confessed. As one court put it, "*Connelly* makes it clear that personal characteristics of the defendant are constitutionally irrelevant absent proof of police coercion." United States v. Rohrbach, 813 F.2d 142 (8th Cir.1987).

Problems With a Test Based on Free Will

Is "free will" a workable standard for confession cases? Judge Posner in United States v. Rutledge, 900 F.2d 1127 (7th Cir.1990), had this to say about the "overbearing of free will" test:

> Taken seriously it would require the exclusion of virtually all fruits of custodial interrogation, since few choices to confess can be thought truly "free" when made by a person who is incarcerated and is being questioned by * * * officers without the presence of counsel or anyone else to give him moral support. The formula is not taken seriously. *Connelly* may have driven the stake through its heart by holding that a confession which is not a product of the defendant's free choice * * * is admissible so long as whatever it was that destroyed the defendant's power of choice was not police conduct. In any event, very few incriminating statements, custodial or otherwise, are held to be involuntary, though few are the product of a choice that the interrogators left completely free.

> An alternative approach, which is implied by *Connelly* and may well describe the courts' actual as distinct from articulated standard, is to ask whether the government has made it impossible for the defendant to make a *rational* choice as to whether to confess—has made it in other words impossible for him to weigh the pros and cons of confessing and go with the balance as it appears at the time. This approach * * * implies, for example, that if the government feeds the defendant false information that seriously distorts his choice, by promising him that if he confesses he will be set free, or if the government drugs him so that he cannot make a conscious choice at all, then the confession must go out. * * * The police are allowed to play on a suspect's ignorance, his anxieties, his fears, and his uncertainties; they just are not allowed to magnify those fears, uncertainties and so forth to the point where rational decision becomes impossible.

Is Judge Posner saying that confessions are involuntary only when police tactics are such as would cause an innocent person to confess (e.g., a statement "if you confess you go free")? Is his analysis consistent with *Fulminante*?

III. THE SPECIAL FEDERAL STANDARD FOR CONFESSIONS

Delay in Presentment: The McNabb/Mallory Rule

During the period that the state confession cases were decided exclusively under the voluntariness approach, federal cases were governed by an identical constitutional standard. A coerced confession that violated the Due Process Clause of the Fourteenth Amendment also violated the Due Process Clause of the Fifth Amendment. But in federal court, a confession might be rejected even without a finding of coercion. In 1943, in McNabb v. United States, 318 U.S.

332, the Court focused on the need to bring arrested suspects before a judicial officer in a timely fashion. The Court utilized its supervisory power over the federal judiciary to exclude confessions obtained during a period in which the officers delayed, without cause, in presenting the suspects to a judicial officer for a preliminary hearing. The Court noted that a prompt preliminary hearing was required by federal law; at that hearing, the suspect would be notified of his right to counsel and his right to remain silent. In order to preclude federal law enforcement agents from questioning suspects under their exclusive control in violation of federal law, a new exclusionary rule was created.[11] The idea was to deter federal officers from delaying a suspect's referral to a judge or magistrate, in the hope that the suspect would confess before the referral.

The *McNabb* decision was criticized for unduly handcuffing federal agents in their investigatory endeavors. But the Court unanimously reaffirmed the *McNabb* decision in Mallory v. United States, 354 U.S. 449 (1957). See generally Hogan & Snee, The McNabb–Mallory Rule: Its Rise, Rationale and Rescue, 47 Geo.L.J. 1 (1958). In *Mallory,* the Court found a confession of a rape suspect to be inadmissible, because obtained in violation of Rule 5(a) of the Federal Rules of Criminal Procedure (which were not yet adopted when *McNabb* was decided), requiring that an arrested person be taken before a committing magistrate without "unnecessary delay." The accused in *Mallory* had been arrested in the early afternoon and was detained at headquarters within the vicinity of numerous committing magistrates. However, the police did not try to arraign him until that night, after they had secured a confession. The accused was not actually taken before a magistrate until the following morning. The Court opined that "[i]t is not the function of the police to arrest, as it were at large and to use an interrogating process at police headquarters in order to determine whom they should charge before a committing magistrate * * *."

The Congressional Approach: 18 U.S.C. § 3501

Congress eventually became concerned that the Court in *McNabb* and *Mallory* had focused too much on delay in presentment to a judicial officer, and too little on whether the suspect's confession was in fact voluntary. Consequently, in 1968, Congress enacted 18 U.S.C.A. § 3501. It provides, in pertinent part, as follows:

(a) In any criminal prosecution brought by the United States or by the District of Columbia, a confession * * * shall be admissible in evidence if it is voluntarily given. Before such confession is received in evidence, the trial judge shall, out of the presence of the jury, determine any issue as to voluntariness. * * *

(b) The trial judge in determining the issue of voluntariness shall take into consideration all the circumstances surrounding the giving of the confession, including (1) the time elapsing between arrest and arraignment of the defendant making the confession, if it was made after arrest and before arraignment, (2) whether such defendant knew the nature of the

---

11. That *McNabb* was not based on any constitutional provision must be emphasized. In a state case, Gallegos v. Nebraska, 342 U.S. 55, 63 (1951), in which the accused was not brought before a magistrate for twenty-five days after his arrest and fourteen days after his arrival in Nebraska, the Court specifically noted that the Federal rule on prompt presentment was not constitutionally mandated and was not applicable to trials in state courts.

offense with which he was charged or of which he was suspected at the time of making the confession, (3) whether or not such defendant was advised or knew that he was not required to make any statement and that any such statement could be used against him, (4) whether or not such defendant had been advised prior to questioning of his right to the assistance of counsel; and (5) whether or not such defendant was without the assistance of counsel when questioned and when giving such confession. The presence or absence of any of the above-mentioned factors to be taken into consideration by the judge need not be conclusive on the issue of voluntariness of the confession.

(c) In any criminal prosecution by the United States or by the District of Columbia, a confession made or given by a person who is a defendant therein, while such person was under arrest or other detention in the custody of any law-enforcement officer or law-enforcement agency, shall not be inadmissible solely because of delay in bringing such person before a magistrate judge or other officer empowered to commit persons charged with offenses against the laws of the United States or of the District of Columbia if such confession is found by the trial judge to have been made voluntarily * * * and if such confession was made or given by such person within six hours immediately following his arrest or other detention: Provided, That the time limitation contained in this subsection shall not apply in any case in which the delay in bringing such person before such magistrate or other officer beyond such six-hour period is found by the trial judge to be reasonable considering the means of transportation and the distance to be traveled to the nearest available such magistrate or other officer.

(d) Nothing contained in this section shall bar the admission in evidence of any confession made or given voluntarily by any person to any other person without interrogation by anyone, or at any time at which the person who made or gave such confession was not under arrest or other detention.

Construing the Statute: United States v. Alvarez–Sanchez

In United States v. Alvarez–Sanchez, 511 U.S. 350 (1994), the Court, in an opinion by Justice Thomas, held that the protections of 18 U.S.C. § 3501 do not apply during a period when the suspect is being held by state authorities on state charges. Justice Thomas reasoned that the statute is triggered by "delay in bringing [a suspect] before a magistrate or other officer empowered to commit persons charged with offenses against the laws of the United States * * *." He concluded that "there can be no delay in bringing a person before a federal magistrate until, at a minimum, there is some obligation to bring the person before such a judicial officer in the first place. Plainly, a duty to present a person to a federal magistrate does not arise until the person has been arrested for a federal offense." Consequently, the Court found that section 3501 did not preclude the admission of Alvarez–Sanchez's otherwise voluntary confession made to federal officers while he was being detained on state charges, even though he had been in custody for three days at the time of the confession, and had not yet been brought before a judicial officer. Justice Thomas stated that "[a]s long as a person is arrested and held only on state charges by state or local authorities, the provisions of § 3501(c) are not triggered."

Justice Thomas mentioned that the provisions of § 3501 might be applicable if state officials were detaining a suspect in collusion with federal officials, but declined to rule on such a scenario because it did not occur in the instant case.

Relationship Between Section 3501 and the McNabb–Mallory Rule

Section 3501 has been held to mean that under certain conditions, voluntary confessions can be admitted even if they were made after the six-hour "safe harbor" period of delay in presenting the suspect to a magistrate has expired. Generally, voluntary statements made after the expiration of the six-hour "safe harbor" period will be admissible if voluntary and either:

1) The suspect was not interrogated after the safe harbor expires. United States v. Fullwood, 86 F.3d 27 (2d Cir.1996) (statement made after 24 hour delay was admissible where defendant asked to speak to an officer, even though the delay was unreasonable); or

2) The delay, though lengthy, was not completely unreasonable or in bad faith. United States v. Van Poyck, 77 F.3d 285 (9th Cir.1996) (weekend delay in presenting the suspect to a magistrate was not unreasonable, and therefore a statement made during that period was admissible: "An arraignment requires court personnel to randomly select a judge, requires pretrial services to process the defendant, and often requires an interpreter; this is simply not a task that can be performed in a magistrate's living room.").

In light of Congress' adoption of section 3501, is there anything left of the *McNabb-Mallory* rule? If so, it would appear that a court could exclude a confession solely on the basis of an unreasonable delay in presenting the suspect to a judicial officer under *McNabb-Mallory,* even though the delay would be excused under section 3501. For example, a delay of less than six hours in presenting the suspect to a magistrate might be unreasonable under some circumstances; that could result in exclusion under *McNabb-Mallory,* but it would be within the safe harbor provision for purposes of section 3501. The court in United States v. Pugh, 25 F.3d 669 (8th Cir.1994) held that the statute superseded the court-made supervisory rule:

Pugh's * * * contention is that even if suppression is not accomplished by § 3501(c), his statements should have been suppressed on the basis of *McNabb* and *Mallory.* Collectively, these two cases hold that, under a federal court's supervisory authority * * * a defendant's incriminating statements should be inadmissible at trial if the defendant made them during an unreasonable delay between his arrest and his presentment to a judicial officer. These two cases, however, no longer are the governing law for the determination whether incriminating statements are inadmissible due to a delay between a defendant's arrest and his initial appearance. Due to Congress' concern that *McNabb* and *Mallory* focused too much on delay and too little on a confession's voluntariness, the present rule of law is simply that a confession "shall be admissible in evidence if it is voluntarily given." Delay between arrest and presentment is only one of five factors a trial judge must consider when determining whether a confession was voluntary, but delay is not dispositive.

Isn't the best reading of the statute that the relevance of unnecessary delay in presentment to a magistrate increases with its length; that at some point, unnecessary delay in itself can give rise to a finding of involuntariness; but that a delay of less than six hours has less relevance, and can never in itself lead to exclusion of a confession?

IV. FIFTH AMENDMENT LIMITATIONS ON CONFESSIONS

As discussed above, the Court became dissatisfied with the due process-totality of the circumstances test as an exclusive means of regulating confessions. After *Spano*, the Court applied the Sixth Amendment right to counsel to exclude two confessions. Massiah v. United States, 377 U.S. 201 (1964); Escobedo v. Illinois, 378 U.S. 478 (1964). The problem with the Sixth Amendment, however, is that the Court came to see it as limited to the accusatory stage of the criminal process. The Sixth Amendment applies to all "criminal prosecutions," but the Court came to doubt whether that Amendment's protections could apply to the investigatory stage, before the defendant has been charged. And it is during the investigatory stage that most police interrogation occurs and most confessions are obtained. The Court therefore began to shift to a different constitutional amendment—the Fifth Amendment, which is not temporally limited to criminal prosecutions.[12]

A. MIRANDA v. ARIZONA

In 1964, the Court in Malloy v. Hogan, 378 U.S. 1, paved the way for its decision in *Miranda* by ruling that the Fifth Amendment privilege against self-incrimination is applicable to the states through the Fourteenth Amendment. Two years later, in *Miranda,* the Court declared that the Fifth Amendment is the touchstone for determining the admissibility of any statements obtained through custodial interrogation by government officials. The advantage seen in Fifth Amendment application was that the official pressure on a suspect required to trigger Fifth Amendment protections is substantially less than the pressure required to trigger due process protections.

MIRANDA v. ARIZONA
Supreme Court of the United States, 1966.
384 U.S. 436.

Mr. Chief Justice Warren **delivered the opinion of the Court.**

The cases before us raise questions which go to the roots of our concepts of American criminal jurisprudence: the restraints society must observe consistent with the Federal Constitution in prosecuting individuals for crime. More specifically, we deal with the admissibility of statements obtained from an individual who is subjected to custodial police interrogation and the necessity for procedures which assure that the individual is accorded his privilege under the Fifth Amendment to the Constitution not to be compelled to incriminate himself.

* * *

12. Eventually the Court was to return to the Sixth Amendment as an additional control over police interrogations. *Massiah* and its progeny are discussed after the materials on the *Miranda* doctrine.

Our holding will be spelled out with some specificity in the pages which follow but briefly stated it is this: the prosecution may not use statements, whether exculpatory or inculpatory, stemming from custodial interrogation of the defendant unless it demonstrates the use of procedural safeguards effective to secure the privilege against self-incrimination. By custodial interrogation, we mean questioning initiated by law enforcement officers after a person has been taken into custody or otherwise deprived of his freedom of action in any significant way. As for the procedural safeguards to be employed, unless other fully effective means are devised to inform accused persons of their right of silence and to assure a continuous opportunity to exercise it, the following measures are required. Prior to any questioning, the person must be warned that he has a right to remain silent, that any statement he does make may be used as evidence against him, and that he has a right to the presence of an attorney, either retained or appointed. The defendant may waive effectuation of these rights, provided the waiver is made voluntarily, knowingly and intelligently. If, however, he indicates in any manner and at any stage of the process that he wishes to consult with an attorney before speaking there can be no questioning. Likewise, if the individual is alone and indicates in any manner that he does not wish to be interrogated, the police may not question him. The mere fact that he may have answered some questions or volunteered some statements on his own does not deprive him of the right to refrain from answering any further inquiries until he has consulted with an attorney and thereafter consents to be questioned.

I

The constitutional issue we decide in each of these cases is the admissibility of statements obtained from a defendant questioned while in custody or otherwise deprived of his freedom of action in any significant way. In each, the defendant was questioned by police officers, detectives, or a prosecuting attorney in a room in which he was cut off from the outside world. In none of these cases was the defendant given a full and effective warning of his rights at the outset of the interrogation process. In all the cases, the questioning elicited oral admissions, and in three of them, signed statements as well which were admitted at their trials. They all thus share salient features—incommunicado interrogation of individuals in a police-dominated atmosphere, resulting in self-incriminating statements without full warnings of constitutional rights.

An understanding of the nature and setting of this in-custody interrogation is essential to our decisions today. The difficulty in depicting what transpires at such interrogations stems from the fact that in this country they have largely taken place incommunicado. From extensive factual studies undertaken in the early 1930's, including the famous Wickersham Report to Congress by a Presidential Commission, it is clear that police violence and the "third degree" flourished at that time. * * *

* * *

[T]he modern practice of in-custody interrogation is psychologically rather than physically oriented. * * * Interrogation still takes place in privacy. Privacy results in secrecy and this in turn results in a gap in our knowledge as to what in fact goes on in the interrogation rooms. A valuable source of information about present police practices, however, may be found in various police manuals and texts which document procedures employed with success in the past, and which recommend various other effective tactics. These texts are used by law enforcement agencies themselves as guides. It should be noted that these texts professedly present the most enlightened and effective means presently used to obtain statements through custodial interrogation. By considering these texts and other data, it is possible to describe procedures observed and noted around the country.

The officers are told by the manuals that the "principal psychological factor contributing to a successful interrogation is *privacy*—being alone with the person under interrogation." The efficacy of this tactic has been explained as follows:

"If at all practicable, the interrogation should take place in the investigator's office or at least in a room of his own choice. The subject should be deprived of every psychological advantage. In his own home he may be confident, indignant, or recalcitrant. He is more keenly aware of his rights and more reluctant to tell of his indiscretions or criminal behavior within the walls of his home. Moreover his family and other friends are nearby, their presence lending moral support. In his own office, the investigator possesses all the advantages. The atmosphere suggests the invincibility of the forces of the law."

To highlight the isolation and unfamiliar surroundings, the manuals instruct the police to display an air of confidence in the suspect's guilt and from outward appearance to maintain only an interest in confirming certain details. The guilt of the subject is to be posited as a fact. The interrogator should direct his comments toward the reasons why the subject committed the act, rather than court failure by asking the subject whether he did it. Like other men, perhaps the subject has had a bad family life, had an unhappy childhood, had too much to drink, had an unrequited desire for women. The officers are instructed to minimize the moral seriousness of the offense, to cast blame on the victim or on society. These tactics are designed to put the subject in a psychological state where his story is but an elaboration of what the police purport to know already—that he is guilty. Explanations to the contrary are dismissed and discouraged.

The texts thus stress that the major qualities an interrogator should possess are patience and perseverance. * * *

The manuals suggest that the suspect be offered legal excuses for his actions in order to obtain an initial admission of guilt. * * *

When the techniques described above prove unavailing, the texts recommend they be alternated with a show of some hostility. * * *

The interrogators sometimes are instructed to induce a confession out of trickery. The technique here is quite effective in crimes which require identification or which run in series. In the identification situation, the interrogator may take a break in his questioning to place the subject among a group of men in a line-up. "The witness or complainant (previously coached, if necessary) studies the line-up and confidently points out the subject as the guilty party." Then the questioning resumes "as though there were now no doubt about the guilt of the subject." A variation on this technique is called the "reverse line-up":

"The accused is placed in a line-up but this time he is identified by several fictitious witnesses or victims who associated him with different offenses. It is expected that the subject will become desperate and confess to the offense under investigation in order to escape from the false accusations."

* * *

Even without employing brutality, the "third degree" or the specific stratagems described above, the very fact of custodial interrogation exacts a heavy toll on individual liberty and trades on the weakness of individuals. * * *

In the cases before us today, given this background, we concern ourselves primarily with this interrogation atmosphere and the evils it can bring. In No. 759, Miranda v. Arizona, the police arrested the defendant and took him to a special interrogation room where they secured a confession. In No. 760, Vignera v. New York, the defendant made oral admissions to the police after interrogation in the afternoon, and then signed an inculpatory statement upon being questioned by an assistant district attorney later the same evening. In No. 761, Westover v. United States, the defendant was handed over to the Federal Bureau of Investigation by local authorities after they had detained and interrogated him for a lengthy period, both at night and the following morning. After some two hours of questioning, the federal officers had obtained signed statements from the defendant. Lastly, in No. 584, California v. Stewart, the local police held the defendant five days in the station and interrogated him on nine separate occasions before they secured his inculpatory statement.

In these cases, we might not find the defendants' statements to have been involuntary in traditional terms. Our concern for adequate safeguards to protect precious Fifth Amendment rights is, of course, not lessened in the slightest. In each of the cases, the defendant was thrust into an unfamiliar atmosphere and run through menacing police interrogation procedures.

The potentiality for compulsion is forcefully apparent, for example, in *Miranda,* where the indigent Mexican defendant was a seriously disturbed individual with pronounced sexual fantasies, and in *Stewart,* in which the defendant was an indigent Los Angeles Negro who had dropped out of school in the sixth grade. To be sure, the records do not evince overt physical coercion or patent psychological ploys. The fact remains that in none of these cases did the officers undertake to afford appropriate safeguards at the outset of the interrogation to insure that the statements were truly the product of free choice.

It is obvious that such an interrogation environment is created for no purpose other than to subjugate the individual to the will of his examiner. This atmosphere carries its own badge of intimidation. To be sure, this is not physical intimidation, but it is equally destructive of human dignity. The current practice of incommunicado interrogation is at odds with one of our Nation's most cherished principles—that the individual may not be compelled to incriminate himself. Unless adequate protective devices are employed to dispel the compulsion inherent in custodial surroundings, no statement obtained from the defendant can truly be the product of his free choice.

From the foregoing, we can readily perceive an intimate connection between the privilege against self-incrimination and police custodial questioning. It is fitting to turn to history and precedent underlying the Self–Incrimination Clause to determine its applicability in this situation.

II

[The Court briefly traces the roots of the Fifth Amendment and how the privilege against self-incrimination obtained constitutional status in the United States.]

The question in these cases is whether the privilege is fully applicable during a period of custodial interrogation. * * * We are satisfied that all the principles embodied in the privilege apply to informal compulsion exerted by law-enforcement officers during in-custody questioning. An individual swept from familiar surroundings into police custody, surrounded by antagonistic forces, and subjected to the techniques of persuasion described above cannot be otherwise than under compulsion to speak. As a practical matter, the compulsion to speak in the isolated setting of the police station may well be greater than in courts or other official investigations, where there are often impartial observers to guard against intimidation or trickery.

This question, in fact could have been taken as settled in federal courts almost 70 years ago, when, in Bram v. United States, 168 U.S. 532, 542 (1897), this Court held:

"In criminal trials, in the courts of the United States, wherever a question arises whether a confession is incompetent because not voluntary, the issue is controlled by that portion of the Fifth Amendment * * * commanding that no person 'shall be compelled in any criminal case to be a witness against himself.' "

* * *

III

Today, then, there can be no doubt that the Fifth Amendment privilege is available outside of criminal court proceedings and serves to protect persons in all settings in which their freedom of action is curtailed in any significant way from being compelled to incriminate themselves. We have concluded that without proper safeguards the process of in-custody interrogation of persons suspected or accused of crime contains inherently compelling pressures which work to undermine the individual's will to resist and to compel him to speak where he would not otherwise do so freely. In order to combat these pressures and to permit a full opportunity to exercise the privilege against self-incrimination, the accused must be adequately and effectively apprised of his rights and the exercise of those rights must be fully honored.

It is impossible for us to foresee the potential alternatives for protecting the privilege which might be devised by Congress or the States in the exercise of their creative rule-making capacities. Therefore we cannot say that the Constitution necessarily requires adherence to any particular solution for the inherent compulsions of the interrogation process as it is presently conducted. Our decision in no way creates a constitutional straitjacket which will handicap sound efforts at reform, nor is it intended to have this effect. We encourage Congress and the States to continue their laudable search for increasingly effective ways of protecting the rights of the individual while promoting efficient enforcement of our criminal laws. However, unless we are shown other procedures which are at least as effective in apprising accused persons of their right of silence and in assuring a continuous opportunity to exercise it, the following safeguards must be observed.

At the outset, if a person in custody is to be subjected to interrogation, he must first be informed in clear and unequivocal terms that he has the right to remain silent. For those unaware of the privilege, the warning is needed simply to make them aware of it—the threshold requirement for an intelligent decision as to its exercise.

More important, such a warning is an absolute prerequisite in overcoming the inherent pressures of the interrogation atmosphere. It is not just the subnormal or woefully ignorant who succumb to an interrogator's imprecations, whether implied or expressly stated, that the interrogation will continue until a confession is obtained or that silence in the face of accusation is itself damning and will bode ill when presented to a jury.[a] Further, the warning will show the individual that his interrogators are prepared to recognize his privilege should he choose to exercise it.

The Fifth Amendment privilege is so fundamental to our system of constitutional rule and the expedient of giving an adequate warning as to the availability of the privilege so simple, we will not pause to inquire in individual cases whether the defendant was aware of his rights without a warning being given. Assessments of the knowledge the defendant possessed, based on information as to his age, education, intelligence, or prior contact with authorities, can never be more than speculation; a warning is a clearcut fact. More important, whatever the background of the person interrogated, a warning at the time of the interrogation is indispensable to overcome its pressures and to insure that the individual knows he is free to exercise the privilege at that point in time.

The warning of the right to remain silent must be accompanied by the explanation that anything said can and will be used against the individual in court. This warning is needed in order to make him aware not only of the privilege, but also of the consequences of forgoing it. It is only through an awareness of these consequences that there can be any assurance of real understanding and intelligent exercise of the privilege. Moreover, this warning may serve to make the individual more acutely aware that he is faced with a phase of the adversary system— that he is not in the presence of persons acting solely in his interest.

The circumstances surrounding in-custody interrogation can operate very quickly to overbear the will of one merely made aware of his privilege by his interrogators. Therefore, the right to have counsel present at the interrogation is indispensable to the protection of the Fifth Amendment privilege under the system we delineate today. Our aim is to assure that the individual's right to choose between silence and speech remains unfettered throughout the interrogation process. A once-stated warning, delivered by those who will conduct the interrogation, cannot itself suffice to that end among those who most require knowledge of their rights. A mere warning given by the interrogators is not alone sufficient to accomplish that end. Prosecutors themselves claim that the admonishment of the right to remain silent without more "will benefit only the recidivist and the professional." Even preliminary advice given to the accused by his own attorney can be swiftly overcome by the secret interrogation process. Thus, the need for counsel to protect the Fifth Amendment privilege comprehends not merely a right to consult with counsel prior to questioning, but also to have counsel present during any questioning if the defendant so desires.

That presence of counsel at the interrogation may serve several significant subsidiary functions as well. If the accused decides to talk to his interro-

---

a. In accord with our decision today it is impermissible to penalize an individual for exercising his Fifth Amendment privilege when he is under police custodial interrogation. The prosecution may not, therefore, use at trial the fact that he stood mute or claimed his privilege in the face of accusation.

gators, the assistance of counsel can mitigate the dangers of untrustworthiness. With a lawyer present the likelihood that the police will practice coercion is reduced, and if coercion is nevertheless exercised the lawyer can testify to it in court. The presence of a lawyer can also help to guarantee that the accused gives a fully accurate statement to the police and that the statement is rightly reported by the prosecution at trial.

An individual need not make a pre-interrogation request for a lawyer. While such request affirmatively secures his right to have one, his failure to ask for a lawyer does not constitute a waiver. No effective waiver of the right to counsel during interrogation can be recognized unless specifically made after the warnings we here delineate have been given. The accused who does not know his rights and therefore does not make a request may be the person who most needs counsel. * * *

* * *

Accordingly we hold that an individual held for interrogation must be clearly informed that he has the right to consult with a lawyer and to have the lawyer with him during interrogation under the system for protecting the privilege we delineate today. As with the warnings of the right to remain silent and that anything stated can be used in evidence against him, this warning is an absolute prerequisite to interrogation. No amount of circumstantial evidence that the person may have been aware of this right will suffice to stand in its stead. Only through such a warning is there ascertainable assurance that the accused was aware of this right.

If an individual indicates that he wishes the assistance of counsel before any interrogation occurs, the authorities cannot rationally ignore or deny

his request on the basis that the individual does not have or cannot afford a retained attorney. The financial ability of the individual has no relationship to the scope of the rights involved here. The privilege against self-incrimination secured by the Constitution applies to all individuals. The need for counsel in order to protect the privilege exists for the indigent as well as the affluent. In fact, were we to limit these constitutional rights to those who can retain an attorney, our decisions today would be of little significance. The cases before us as well as the vast majority of confession cases with which we have dealt in the past involve those unable to retain counsel. While authorities are not required to relieve the accused of his poverty, they have the obligation not to take advantage of indigence in the administration of justice. Denial of counsel to the indigent at the time of interrogation while allowing an attorney to those who can afford one would be no more supportable by reason or logic than the similar situation at trial and on appeal. * * *

In order fully to apprise a person interrogated of the extent of his rights under this system then, it is necessary to warn him not only that he has the right to consult with an attorney, but also that if he is indigent a lawyer will be appointed to represent him. Without this additional warning, the admonition of the right to consult with counsel would often be understood as meaning only that he can consult with a lawyer if he has one or has the funds to obtain one. The warning of a right to counsel would be hollow if not couched in terms that would convey to the indigent—the person most often subjected to interrogation—the knowledge that he too has a right to have counsel present. As with the warnings of the right to remain silent and of the general right to counsel, only by effective and express explanation to the indigent of this right can there be assurance that he was truly in a position to exercise it.[b]

Once warnings have been given, the subsequent procedure is clear. If the individual indicates in any manner, at any time prior to or during questioning, that he wishes to remain silent, the interrogation must cease.[c] At this point he has shown that he intends to exercise his Fifth Amendment privilege; any statements taken after the person invokes his privilege cannot be other than the product of compulsion, subtle or otherwise. Without the right to cut off questioning, the setting of in-custody interrogation operates on the individual to overcome free choice in producing a statement after the privilege has been once invoked. If the individual states that he wants an attorney, the interrogation must cease until an attorney is present. At that time, the individual must have an opportunity to confer with the attorney and to have him present during any subsequent questioning. If the individual cannot obtain an attorney and he indicates that he wants one before speaking to police, they must respect his decision to remain silent.

This does not mean, as some have suggested, that each police station must have a "station house lawyer" present at all times to advise prisoners. It does mean, however, that if police propose to interrogate a person they must make known to him that he is entitled to a lawyer and that if he cannot afford one, a lawyer will be provided for him prior to any interrogation. If authorities conclude that they will not provide counsel during a reasonable period of time in which investigation in the field is carried out, they may refrain from doing so without violating the person's Fifth Amendment privilege so long as they do not question him during that time.

If the interrogation continues without the presence of an attorney and a statement is taken, a heavy burden rests on the government to demonstrate that the defendant knowingly and intelligently waived his privilege against self-incrimination and his right to retained or appointed counsel. This Court has always set high standards of proof for the waiver of constitutional rights, and we reassert these standards as applied to in-custody interrogation. Since the State is responsible for establishing the isolated circumstances under which the interrogation takes place and has the only means of making available corroborated evidence of warnings given during incommunicado interrogation, the burden is rightly on its shoulders.

An express statement that the individual is willing to make a statement and does not want an attorney followed closely by a statement could constitute a waiver. But a valid waiver will not be presumed simply from the silence of the accused after warnings are given or simply from the fact that a confession was in fact eventually obtained. * * *

* * * Moreover, where in-custody interrogation is involved, there is no

---

b. While a warning that the indigent may have counsel appointed need not be given to the person who is known to have an attorney or is known to have ample funds to secure one, the expedient of giving a warning is too simple and the rights involved too important to engage in *ex post facto* inquiries into financial ability when there is any doubt at all on that score.

c. If an individual indicates his desire to remain silent, but has an attorney present, there may be some circumstances in which further questioning would be permissible. In the absence of evidence of overbearing, statements then made in the presence of counsel might be free of the compelling influence of the interrogation process and might fairly be construed as a waiver of the privilege for purposes of these statements.

room for the contention that the privilege is waived if the individual answers some questions or gives some information on his own prior to invoking his right to remain silent when interrogated.

Whatever the testimony of the authorities as to waiver of rights by an accused, the fact of lengthy interrogation or incommunicado incarceration before a statement is made is strong evidence that the accused did not validly waive his rights. In these circumstances the fact that the individual eventually made a statement is consistent with the conclusion that the compelling influence of the interrogation finally forced him to do so. It is inconsistent with any notion of a voluntary relinquishment of the privilege. Moreover, any evidence that the accused was threatened, tricked, or cajoled into a waiver will, of course, show that the defendant did not voluntarily waive his privilege. The requirement of warnings and waiver of rights is a fundamental with respect to the Fifth Amendment privilege and not simply a preliminary ritual to existing methods of interrogation.

The warnings required and the waiver necessary in accordance with our opinion today are, in the absence of a fully effective equivalent, prerequisites to the admissibility of any statement made by a defendant. No distinction can be drawn between statements which are direct confessions and statements which amount to "admissions" of part or all of an offense. The privilege against self-incrimination protects the individual from being compelled to incriminate himself in any manner; it does not distinguish degrees of incrimination. Similarly, for precisely the same reason, no distinction may be drawn between inculpatory statements and statements alleged to be merely "exculpatory." If a statement made were in fact truly exculpatory it would,

of course, never be used by the prosecution. In fact, statements merely intended to be exculpatory by the defendant are often used to impeach his testimony at trial or to demonstrate untruths in the statement given under interrogation and thus to prove guilt by implication. These statements are incriminating in any meaningful sense of the word and may not be used without the full warnings and effective waiver required for any other statement. * * *

The principles announced today deal with the protection which must be given to the privilege against self-incrimination when the individual is first subjected to police interrogation while in custody at the station or otherwise deprived of his freedom of action in any significant way. * * * Under the system of warnings we delineate today or under any other system which may be devised and found effective, the safeguards to be erected about the privilege must come into play at this point.

Our decision is not intended to hamper the traditional function of police officers in investigating crime. When an individual is in custody on probable cause, the police may, of course, seek out evidence in the field to be used at trial against him. Such investigation may include inquiry of persons not under restraint. General on-the-scene questioning as to facts surrounding a crime or other general questioning of citizens in the fact-finding process is not affected by our holding. It is an act of responsible citizenship for individuals to give whatever information they may have to aid in law enforcement. In such situations the compelling atmosphere inherent in the process of in-custody interrogation is not necessarily present.

In dealing with statements obtained through interrogation, we do not purport to find all confessions inadmissible. Confessions remain a proper element in law enforcement. Any statement given freely and voluntarily without any compelling influences is, of course, admissible in evidence. * * *

* * *

IV

* * *

V

Because of the nature of the problem and because of its recurrent significance in numerous cases, we have to this point discussed the relationship of the Fifth Amendment privilege to police interrogation without specific concentration on the facts of the cases before us. We turn now to these facts to consider the application to these cases of the constitutional principles discussed above. In each instance, we have concluded that statements were obtained from the defendant under circumstances that did not meet constitutional standards for protection of the privilege.

* * *

MR. JUSTICE CLARK, dissenting in Nos. 759, 760, and 761, and concurring in the result in No. 584.

It is with regret that I find it necessary to write in these cases. However, I am unable to join the majority because its opinion goes too far on too little, while my dissenting brethren do not go quite far enough. Nor can I join in the Court's criticism of the present practices of police and investigatory agencies as to custodial interrogation. The materials it refers to as "police manuals" are, as I read them, merely writings in this field by professors and some police officers. * * *

I

* * * Such a strict constitutional specific inserted at the nerve center of crime detection may well kill the patient. Since there is at this time a paucity of information and an almost total lack of empirical knowledge on the practical operation of requirements truly comparable to those announced by the majority, I would be more restrained lest we go too far too fast.

[In parts II and III of his opinion, Justice Clark advocates a totality of the circumstances test.]

MR. JUSTICE HARLAN, whom MR. JUSTICE STEWART and MR. JUSTICE WHITE join, dissenting.

I believe the decision for the Court represents poor constitutional law and entails harmful consequences for the country at large. How serious these consequences may prove to be only time can tell. But the basic flaws in the Court's justification seem to me readily apparent now once all sides of the problem are considered.

I. INTRODUCTION

* * *

* * * The new rules are not designed to guard against police brutality or other unmistakably banned forms of coercion. Those who use third-degree tactics and deny them in court are equally able and destined to lie as skillfully about warnings and waivers. Rather, the thrust of the new rules is to negate all pressures, to reinforce the nervous or ignorant suspect, and ultimately to discourage any confession at all. The aim in short is toward "voluntariness" in a utopian sense, or to view it from a different angle, voluntariness with a vengeance.

* * *

II. CONSTITUTIONAL PREMISES

[Justice Harlan surveys the limits on confessions the Court evolved under the Due Process Clause of the Fourteenth Amendment.]

I turn now to the Court's asserted reliance on the Fifth Amendment, an approach which I frankly regard as a *trompe l'oeil.* The Court's opinion in my view reveals no adequate basis for extending the Fifth Amendment's privilege against self-incrimination to the police station. Far more important, it fails to show that the Court's new rules are well supported, let alone compelled, by Fifth Amendment precedents. Instead, the new rules actually derive from quotation and analogy drawn from precedents under the Sixth Amendment, which should properly have no bearing on police interrogation.

The Court's opening contention, that the Fifth Amendment governs police station confessions, is perhaps not an impermissible extension of the law but it has little to commend itself in the present circumstances. Historically, the privilege against self-incrimination did not bear at all on the use of extra-legal confessions, for which distinct standards evolved. * * * Even those who would readily enlarge the privilege must concede some linguistic difficulties since the Fifth Amendment in terms proscribes only compelling any person "in any criminal case to be a witness against himself."

* * *

Having decided that the Fifth Amendment privilege does apply in the police station, the Court reveals that the privilege imposes more exacting restrictions than does the Fourteenth Amendment's voluntariness test. * * *

The more important premise is that pressure on the suspect must be eliminated though it be only the subtle influence of the atmosphere and surroundings. The Fifth Amendment, however, has never been thought to forbid *all* pressure to incriminate one's self in the situations covered by it. * * * This is not to say that short of jail or torture any sanction is permissible in any case; policy and history alike may impose sharp limits. However, the Court's unspoken assumption that *any* pressure violates the privilege is not supported by the precedents and it has failed to show why the Fifth Amendment prohibits that relatively mild pressure the Due Process Clause permits.

The Court appears similarly wrong in thinking that precise knowledge of one's rights is a settled prerequisite under the Fifth Amendment to the loss of its protections. * * * No Fifth Amendment precedent is cited for the Court's contrary view. There might of course be reasons apart from Fifth Amendment precedent for requiring warning or any other safeguard on questioning but that is a different matter entirely.

A closing word must be said about the Assistance of Counsel Clause of the Sixth Amendment, which is never expressly relied on by the Court but whose judicial precedents turn out to be linchpins of the confession rules announced today. * * *

* * * The sound reason why [the Sixth Amendment] right is so freely extended for a criminal trial is the severe injustice risked by confronting an untrained defendant with a range of technical points of law, evidence, and tactics familiar to the prosecutor but not to himself. This danger shrinks markedly in the police station where indeed the lawyer in fulfilling his professional responsibilities of necessity may become an obstacle to truthfinding. * * *

[Justice Harlan points out that no state had imposed the newly announced interrogation rules on its own initiative, unlike cases such as Mapp v. Ohio, where more than half the states had already adopted the exclusionary rule before the Supreme Court approved it, and Gideon v. Wainwright, where 22 states filed an *amicus* brief in favor of the course taken by the court. By contrast, 27 states signed an *amicus* brief opposing the new restrictions on police interrogation not including the three other states which were parties. He also argued that other countries that strictly controlled confessions gave the prosecutor advantages not given in the United States. Finally, he applied his due process approach to the specific cases before the Court.]

MR. JUSTICE WHITE, **with whom** MR. JUSTICE HARLAN **and** MR. JUSTICE STEWART **join, dissenting.**

I

The proposition that the privilege against self-incrimination forbids in-custody interrogation without the warnings specified in the majority opinion and without a clear waiver of counsel has no significant support in the history of the privilege or in the language of the Fifth Amendment. As for the English authorities and the common-law history, the privilege, firmly established in the second half of the seventeenth century, was never applied except to prohibit compelled judicial interrogations. * * * Morgan, The Privilege Against Self–Incrimination, 34 Minn.L.Rev. 1, 18 (1949).

[Justice White surveyed the history of the Fifth Amendment and the Court's prior treatment of confession cases in support of this proposition.]

II

* * *

III

* * *

If the rule announced today were truly based on a conclusion that all confessions resulting from custodial interrogation are coerced, then it would simply have no rational foundation. * * * Even if one were to postulate that the Court's concern is not that all confessions induced by police interrogation are coerced but rather that some such confessions are coerced and present judicial procedures are believed to be inadequate to identify the confessions that are coerced and those that are not, it would still not be essential to impose the rule that the Court has now fashioned. Transcripts or observers could be required, specific time limits, tailored to fit the cause, could be imposed, or other devices could be utilized to reduce the chances that otherwise indiscernible coercion will produce an inadmissible confession.

On the other hand, even if one assumed that there was an adequate factual basis for the conclusion that all confessions obtained during in-custody interrogation are the product of compulsion, the rule propounded by the Court would still be irrational, for, apparently, it is only if the accused is also warned of his right to counsel and waives both that right and the right against self-incrimination that the inherent compulsiveness of interrogation disappears. But if the defendant may not answer without a warning a question such as "Where were you last night?" without having his answer be a compelled one, how can the Court ever accept his negative answer to the question of whether he wants to consult his retained counsel or counsel whom the court will appoint? And why if counsel is present and the accused nevertheless confesses, or counsel tells the accused to tell the truth, and that is what the accused does, is the situation any less coercive insofar as the accused is concerned? The Court apparently realizes its dilemma of foreclosing questioning without the necessary warnings but at the same time permitting the accused, sitting in the same chair in front of the same policemen, to waive his right to consult an attorney. It expects, however, that the accused will not often waive the right; and if it is claimed that he has, the State faces a severe, if not impossible burden of proof.

All of this makes very little sense in terms of the compulsion which the Fifth Amendment proscribes. That amendment deals with compelling the accused himself. It is his free will that is involved. Confessions and incriminating admissions, as such, are not forbidden evidence; only those which are compelled are banned. I doubt that the Court observes these distinctions today. * * *

* * *

IV

* * *

The obvious underpinning of the Court's decision is a deep-seated distrust of all confessions. As the Court declares that the accused may not be interrogated without counsel present, absent a waiver of the right to counsel, and as the Court all but admonishes the lawyer to advise the accused to remain silent, the result adds up to a judicial judgment that evidence from the accused should not be used against him in any way, whether compelled or not. This is the not so subtle overtone of the opinion—that it is inherently wrong for the police to gather evidence from the accused himself. And this is precisely the nub of this dissent. I see nothing wrong or immoral, and certainly nothing unconstitutional, in the police's asking a suspect whom they have reasonable cause to arrest whether or not he killed his wife or in confronting him with the evidence on which the arrest was based, at least where he has been plainly advised that he may remain completely silent * * *. Particularly when corroborated, as where the police have confirmed the accused's disclosure of the hiding place of implements or fruits of the crime, such confessions have the highest reliability and significantly contribute to the certitude with which we may believe the accused is guilty. Moreover, it is by no means certain that the process of confessing is injurious to the accused. To the contrary it may provide psychological relief and enhance the prospects for rehabilitation.

[Justice White argues that the due process test worked well enough; that the Court's holding will impair the swift and sure apprehension of criminals; that release of the guilty is not necessarily in their best interests, and certainly not in society's best interest; and that the innocent may be reluctant to talk to the police after the decision.]

Analysis of Miranda

Miranda merged self-incrimination and confession law and thus departed from the analytic framework of most of the Court's opinions in the Twentieth Century. Because of this, *Miranda* was viewed by many as a radical change in the law. The *Miranda* dissents nurtured this view. But it is not difficult to find the seeds of *Miranda* in Bram v. United States, discussed at the beginning of the section on confessions. Moreover, the history of the privilege against self-incrimination is ambiguous enough that reasonable people easily may reach different conclusions as to whether it should reach into the modern day station-house. For a defense of the majority's approach, see Kamisar, A Dissent From the Miranda Dissents: Some Comments on the "New" Fifth Amendment and the Old "Voluntariness" Test, 65 Mich.L.Rev. 59 (1966).

Miranda's importation of the Fifth Amendment into the stationhouse, and the Court's rationale for doing so, is explained by Professor Schulhofer in *Miranda's* Practical Effect: Substantial Benefits and Vanishingly Small Costs, 90 Nw.U.L.Rev. 500 (1996):

> Police do not have to violate KGB standards in order to violate the Fifth Amendment. * * * [W]hatever one may think of *Miranda*, it is clear—and uncontroversial—that pressure need not rise to the level of overbearing physical or psychological coercion, in the due process sense, before it is sufficiently compelling to violate the Fifth Amendment. Outside the context of police interrogation, the law has long been settled, before *Miranda* and since, that the Fifth Amendment is violated by any pressure or penalty deliberately imposed for the purpose of getting a criminal suspect to speak. [citing cases such as *Lefkowitz* and *Griffin*, discussed earlier in this Chapter]. As the Court stressed in Bram v. United States, in determining compulsion under the Fifth Amendment, "the law cannot measure the force of the influence used or decide its effect upon the mind of the prisoner, and, therefore, excludes the declaration if any degree of influence has been exerted." The opposing view, pressed so hard by *Miranda's* critics—that Fifth Amendment compulsion and due-process coercion are identical concepts—would, if taken seriously and applied to contexts other than police interrogation, make shreds of the entire fabric of Fifth Amendment doctrine and tradition.
>
> *Miranda's* innovation was to hold that police interrogation could no longer be treated as a world apart. Prior to *Miranda*, the courts had uniformly held that police interrogation, because it imposed no formal penalty for silence, was immune from the Fifth Amendment limitations that apply in every other context. Because there was no formal legal obligation to speak, and thus no duty against which a formal privilege of silence could be applied, there simply was no privilege for the arrested suspect to waive; interrogation was thus restricted only by the due process anticoercion principle that protects all individuals even after they waive the protections of the Fifth Amendment. *Miranda*, in a radical break with prior precedent, rejected that view. The Court's central holding was not the now-famous warnings, but the principle that Fifth Amendment standards would henceforth apply. And the two premises cited to support that conclusion, though hotly contested then, are surely uncontroversial now: that a formalistic showing of compulsion by legal process or official punishment cannot be essential, and that from every practical vantage point, once a suspect is isolated in police custody and deprived of his freedom to leave, interrogation involves pressures that can dwarf those that were decisive in cases like *Griffin* and *Lefkowitz*. The pressures are normally compelling in this practical sense, as even *Miranda's* most committed critics now acknowledge. * * * As a result, the typical custodial police interrogation, even if not brutally coercive in the due process sense, will readily (perhaps almost invariably) violate the Fifth Amendment bar on the use of compelling

pressure, at least in the absence of safeguards sufficient to dispel that pressure.

In thinking about *Miranda*, it might be useful to ask whether a suspect who is compelled to undergo interrogation in the police station might believe that the police have the power to keep him in custody and to ask questions until he confesses. If so, the warnings simply clarify that the suspect may be confined against his will but not compelled to speak. See Saltzburg, Miranda v. Arizona Revisited: Constitutional Law or Judicial Fiat, 26 Washburn L.Rev. 1 (1986).

Judicial Review and Education of the Public

The Court in *Miranda* appears to have tow distinct goals, and it is useful to consider them separately. First, the Court was clearly concerned that under the due process test it was all but impossible to have judicial review over police interrogation practices. It was difficult after an interrogation to determine how coercive it really was, especially when the usual witnesses were police officers and the suspect—all of whom may have tended to have a skewed view of the process. One purpose of *Miranda* is therefore to create a prophylactic rule to aid in judicial review: If the warnings are not given, then a confession is tainted. If they are given, then the confession still may not be voluntary, but at least courts have some greater confidence in any confession that is obtained. But, to the extent that *Miranda* was intended to ease the task of judicial review of confessions, it is subject to attack on the ground that taperecording of interrogations and the placement of a heavy burden on the government to demonstrate voluntariness would have been a sufficient, and perhaps a better, way to promote effective review. See Saltzburg, Standards of Proof and Preliminary Questions of Fact, 27 Stan.L.Rev. 271, 295–96 (1975). The wisdom of the Court's approach also is subject to challenge on the ground that the courts remain dependent on testimony (and perhaps "testilying") to determine in what manner the warnings were given and what happened afterwards.

Second, *Miranda* signifies that no person should be deemed to confess voluntarily and intelligently unless she knows of the right to remain silent and that statements made can be used as evidence against her. See generally Schrock, Welsh & Collins, Interrogational Rights: Reflections on Miranda v. Arizona, 52 So.Cal.L.Rev. 1 (1978). There is a powerful attraction in an argument that assumes, in a democracy like ours, that all persons should know what their rights are. If our educational process taught law like reading, writing, and arithmetic, *Miranda* might not have been necessary. But, prior to *Miranda* it was the rare, not the usual person, who could articulate her constitutional rights to refuse cooperation to the police. Although the Court could not compel that law be taught to all, it had a way of making the government the teacher in custody situations. Thus, part of *Miranda* involves educating suspects about the real choice they have to make in the interrogation process. See generally George Thomas, Separated at Birth but Siblings Nonetheless: *Miranda* and the Due Process Notice Cases, 99 U. Mich. L.Rev. 1081 (2001).

The educational aspect of *Miranda* has its own problems, however. The Court was depending on the very police officers about whom it was concerned to give the warnings. How effective could the Court have expected police officers to be as teachers of constitutional rights to their adversaries? We do not rely on an officer "in the competitive enterprise of ferreting out crime" to protect our

Fourth Amendment rights, but rather impose a judicial officer as an intermediary. Why do we rely on a police officer to protect our Fifth Amendment rights? On the other hand, what is the alternative—that no custodial interrogation can occur until the suspect is brought before a magistrate and given warnings? How would that rule affect the state's ability to obtain confessions? See Kamisar, Kauper's "Judicial Examination of the Accused" Forty Years Later—Some Comments on a Remarkable Article, 73 Mich.L.Rev. 15 (1974).

If knowledge of a choice is important before people say things that might incriminate them, why would the Court have required warnings only in custodial settings? In other words, custody would seem arguably relevant to a concern about judicial review and police pressure, but not to a concern about knowing actions by people. Finally, there is the most important question of all: did the framers of the Fifth and Fourteenth Amendments have any intent or purpose to make the government educate people so that they would not say damaging things; or, were the framers concerned with forcible government action directed at people who refuse to say anything?

Even as a set of warnings, *Miranda* is not wholly adequate. Despite the fact that Chief Justice Warren repeats the Court's holding in several places, it is arguable that there are subtle differences in different parts of the opinion. Test yourself on this by stating what you think the Court's required warning is. Then ask someone else to do the same. Compare your warnings. You may find some significant differences. Even if you do not, ask yourself what you have not told the suspect. For example, have you communicated what happens if the suspect remains silent? Have you invited the person to ask questions to assure an understanding of the warnings? Have you informed the suspect that if he wants to talk, he can change his mind at any time?

The Impact of Miranda

What effect has *Miranda* had? Some empirical evidence appears to indicate that the costs imposed by *Miranda* are limited. See generally Stephens, The Supreme Court and Confessions of Guilt 179–200 (1973), and authorities cited therein. See also Medalie, Leitz and Alexander, Custodial Police Interrogation in Our Nation's Capital: The Attempt to Implement *Miranda*, 66 Mich.L.Rev. 1347 (1968). In some instances warnings are not given to all suspects, the warnings are incomplete, they are given in an unhelpful way, or the suspect has less than full understanding of the available options. See Interrogations in New Haven: The Impact of *Miranda*, 76 Yale L.J. 1519 (1967); Griffiths & Ayres, A Postscript to the *Miranda* Project: Interrogation of Draft Protesters, 77 Yale L.J. 300 (1967). Although in some places the absolute number of confessions may have fallen after *Miranda,* it does not appear that the conviction rates of law enforcement agencies has suffered. See Seeburger & Wettick, *Miranda* in Pittsburgh—A Statistical Study, 29 U.Pitt.L.Rev. 1 (1967). Certainly the published cases in which confessions are excluded and convictions reversed under *Miranda*—when the confessions would not have been excluded anyway under the involuntariness test—are few. See Guy and Huckabee, Going Free on a Technicality: Another Look at the Effect of the *Miranda* Decision on the Criminal Justice Process, 4 Crim.J.Res.Bull. 1 (1988)(*Miranda* issue raised in 9% of appeals, but only 5.6% of those claims were successful, resulting in a reversal rate of .51% of all criminal appeals).

Debate continues over the effects of *Miranda*. Among the writings asserting that the decision has hurt law enforcement are Office of Legal Policy, Report on the Law of Pretrial Interrogation (Feb. 12, 1986), defended in Markman, The Fifth Amendment and Custodial Questioning: A Response to "Reconsidering *Miranda*," 54 U.Chi.L.Rev. 938 (1987), and Caplan, Questioning *Miranda*, 38 Vand.L.Rev. 1417 (1985). An attempt to reevaluate the empirical data to consider all relevant costs, including lost cases and more lenient plea bargains, can be found in Cassell, *Miranda's* Social Costs: An Empirical Reassessment, 90 Nw.U.L.Rev. 387 (1995). Professor Cassell finds the costs of *Miranda* significant, especially in light of less onerous alternatives that he asserts are available to deal with the concerns of the *Miranda* majority. In a later article, Professor Cassell argues that *Miranda* has imposed substantial harms on the innocent, including victims of criminals who are not caught due to the *Miranda* safeguards, and innocent people who are accused of crime because police are not permitted to obtain a confession from another suspect. See Cassell, Protecting the Innocent From False Confessions and Lost Confessions—and From *Miranda*, 88 J.Crim.L. & Crim. 497 (1998).

Contrary views are found in Schulhofer, The Fifth Amendment at Justice: A Reply, 54 U.Chi.L.Rev. 950 (1987); Schulhofer, Reconsidering *Miranda*, 54 U.Chi.L.Rev. 435 (1987); and White, Defending *Miranda*: A Reply to Professor Caplan, 39 Vand.L.Rev. 1 (1986). Professor White concludes that "the great weight of empirical evidence supports the conclusion that *Miranda's* impact on the police's ability to obtain confessions has not been significant." And a special committee of the ABA Criminal Justice Section reported that a "very strong majority of those surveyed—prosecutors, judges and police officers—agree that compliance with *Miranda* does not present serious problems for law enforcement." Special Committee on Criminal Justice in a Free Society, Criminal Justice Section, ABA, Criminal Justice In Crisis 28–29 (1988).

Professors Inbau and Manak assess another cost of *Miranda* in Miranda v. Arizona: Is It Worth the Cost? (A Sample Survey, with Commentary, of the Expenditure of Court Time and Effort), 24 Cal.Western L.Rev. 185 (1988). They conclude that *Miranda* questions take up a disproportionate amount of time in trial and appellate courts. They do not factor in, however, the amount of court time that would be expended if *Miranda* were overruled and the courts returned to the old case-by-case voluntariness test to regulate confessions.

If you agree with the supporters of *Miranda* that it has had no real effect on police officers' ability to obtain confessions, then you have to ask yourself, "what good is *Miranda* anyway?" Wasn't the point of *Miranda* to limit confessions? Professor Schulhofer addresses this question in *Miranda's* Practical Effect: Substantial Benefits and Vanishingly Small Costs, 90 Nw.U.L.Rev. 500 (1996):

> If *Miranda* really has so little impact on confession and conviction rates, why bother defending it? Isn't *Miranda* simply a hollow promise for civil libertarians and an inconvenient nuisance for law enforcement? If the *Miranda* Court's goal was to reduce or eliminate confessions, the decision was an abject failure. Plainly, however, the Warren Court had no such thought in mind; it explicitly structured *Miranda's* warning and waiver requirements to ensure that confessions could continue to be elicited and used. *Miranda's* stated objective was not to eliminate confessions, but to eliminate compelling pressure in the interrogation process.

Yet here, too, there is a paradox. If the flow of confessions has not slackened, it would seem plausible to infer that the pressures deployed to produce those confessions have not slackened either. But the dynamics of police interrogation are more complicated than that view implies. As recent observational studies of interrogation demonstrate, today's suspects typically confess not because of fear of mistreatment but primarily because of misplaced confidence in their own ability to talk their way out of trouble. Detectives are trained to reinforce the suspect's hope of finding what David Simon calls "the Out":

> Homicide detectives in Baltimore ... like to imagine their suspects imagining a small, open window at the top of the long wall. The open window is the escape hatch, the Out. It is the perfect representation of what every suspect believes when he opens his mouth during an interrogation. Every last one envisions himself parrying questions with the right combination of alibi and excuse; every last one sees himself coming up with the right words, then crawling out the window to go home and sleep in his own bed. More often than not, a guilty man is looking for the Out from his first moments in the interrogation room.... * * *

If there were an affirmative right not to incriminate oneself, analogous to the affirmative Sixth Amendment right to assistance of counsel at trial, then ill-informed, misguided waivers of the right would surely be invalid. But the Fifth Amendment protects suspects only against state-orchestrated compulsion, not against their own poor judgment.

For those concerned with the "bottom line," *Miranda* may appear to be a mere symbol. But the symbolic effects of criminal procedure safeguards are important. Those guarantees help shape the self-conception and define the role of conscientious police professionals; they underscore our constitutional commitment to restraint in an area in which emotions easily run uncontrolled.

Miranda is, in any event, more than a mere symbol. In a constitutional system, procedure matters; the means to the end are never irrelevant. *Miranda* does not protect suspects from conviction but only from a particular method of conviction. The rate of confessions has not changed, but those confessions are now mostly the result of persuasion and the suspect's overconfidence, not of pressure and fear. That difference in method is crucial.

Miranda's Costs on Habeas Review

In Withrow v. Williams, 507 U.S. 680 (1993), the Court downplayed the costs of deciding *Miranda* issues, as it held that *Miranda* claims can be pursued on collateral review of a state court conviction. Justice Souter, writing for five Justices, concluded that exclusion of *Miranda* claims on habeas "would not significantly benefit the federal courts." Justice Souter explained this assertion as follows:

> [E]liminating habeas review of *Miranda* issues would not prevent a state prisoner from simply converting his barred *Miranda* claim into a due process claim that his conviction rested on an involuntary confession. * * *

If that is so, the federal courts would certainly not have heard the last of *Miranda* on collateral review. Under the due process approach, * * * courts look to the totality of circumstances to determine whether a confession was voluntary. Those potential circumstances * * * include the failure of police to advise the defendant of his rights to remain silent and to have counsel present during custodial interrogation. We could lock the front door against *Miranda,* but not the back.

We thus fail to see how abdicating *Miranda's* bright line (or, at least, brighter line) rules in favor of an exhaustive totality-of-circumstances approach on habeas would do much of anything to lighten the burdens placed on busy federal courts.

Justice O'Connor wrote a dissenting opinion joined by the Chief Justice, while Justice Scalia wrote a dissenting opinion joined by Justice Thomas. *Withrow* is discussed more fully infra in the section on habeas corpus.

The Miranda Compromise

Part of the reason *Miranda* may not have much of an adverse effect on law enforcement is that the *Miranda* opinion is not as drastic as its opponents initially feared. *Miranda* does not put an end to confessions without counsel, nor to stationhouse interrogation. *Miranda* does impose a warning requirement, but these warnings are given by a police officer, not a judicial officer. *Miranda* provides a right to silence and to counsel, but the decision whether to invoke these rights (and conversely whether to waive them) is made by the suspect in the same coercive atmosphere that the Court was so concerned about. *Miranda* does not impose a videotaping requirement, and so what goes on in the stationhouse is as murky as under the old voluntariness test.

The Court in *Miranda* specifically rejected the suggestion—which would seem to flow from the premise that stationhouse interrogation is inherently coercive—that a suspect must have a nonwaivable right to an attorney before being interrogated. Thus, *Miranda* did not give significant advantages to suspects at the expense of law enforcement. Rather, it struck a compromise. See Benner, Requiem for *Miranda:* The Rehnquist Court's Voluntariness Doctrine in Historical Perspective, 67 Wash.U.L.Q. 59 (1989)("confronted with the storm of controversy that *Escobedo* [implying an absolute right to counsel] created, the Court retreated in *Miranda,* and struck a compromise" that "transformed the debate about self-incrimination into a debate about waiver"); Saltzburg, Miranda v. Arizona Revisited: Constitutional Law or Judicial Fiat, 26 Washburn L.J. 1 (1986)("*Miranda* is more of a compromise than most critics would care to admit").

For an argument that the *Miranda* Court did not go far enough and that "all suspects should have a nonwaivable right to consult with a lawyer before being interrogated by police," see Ogletree, Are Confessions Really Good for the Soul? A Proposal to Mirandize *Miranda,* 100 Harv.L.Rev. 1826 (1987). If *Miranda* had gone that far, would it have been overruled by now? Would a rule imposing an absolute right to counsel have garnered a majority of the *Miranda* Court?

Alternatives to Miranda

The *Miranda* Court emphasized that its system of warnings and waivers was not the exclusive means of regulating the problem of custodial interrogation. According to Professor Cassell, however, the Court's invitation to alternatives "was in reality empty because it did not specify what alternatives would be deemed acceptable." Consequently, since *Miranda*, "reform efforts have been virtually nonexistent." In Cassell's view, the lack of experimentation results from the reluctance of the states to spend resources on alternatives that the Court might simply strike down. Cassell, *Miranda's* Social Costs: An Empirical Reassessment, 90 Nw.U.L.Rev. 387 (1995). Professor Cassell proposes the following alternative to *Miranda*:

> Videotaping interrogations would be at least as effective as *Miranda* in preventing police coercion. The *Miranda* regime appears to have had little effect on what police misconduct exists. In contrast, videotaping, when it has been used, has often reduced claims of police coercion and probably real coercion as well. To be sure, police could conceivably alter tapes or deploy force off-camera. But if you were facing a police officer with a rubber hose, would you prefer a world in which he was required to mumble the *Miranda* warnings and have you waive your rights, all as reported by him in later testimony? Or a world in which the interrogation is videorecorded and the burden is on law enforcement to explain if it is not; where date and time are recorded on the videotape; where your physical appearance and demeanor during the interrogation are permanently recorded?

Do you agree that videotaping will be a better solution than *Miranda* to the problem of police coercion?[13] Professor Schulhofer, in *Miranda's* Practical Effect: Substantial Benefits and Vanishingly Small Social Costs, 90 Nw.U.L.Rev. 500 (1996), argues that a videotaping requirement would be a valuable *supplement* to, but a problematic replacement for, the *Miranda* safeguards.

> In effect, the proposal to substitute videotaping for *Miranda* amounts to a police offer in the form, "We'll stop lying about what we do, if you allow us to do it." No doubt a videotaped record would often prevent police abuse and manipulation of the "swearing contest." But without clear substantive requirements against which to test the police behavior that the videotape will reveal, the objective record will lack any specific legal implications. * * * Thus, videotaping, though an excellent idea, does not meet the constitutional concerns about compulsion to which the *Miranda* safeguards are addressed. Videotaping could provide a useful complement to the *Miranda* protections, but it cannot replace them.

Can you think of any other means by which police coercion can be controlled, without the loss of reliable evidence? Amar and Lettow, in Fifth

---

13. Some state courts have relied on their own constitutions to mandate videotaping of all custodial interrogations. See, e.g., Kane, No More Secrets: Minnesota State Due Process Requirement that Law Enforcement Officers Electronically Record Custodial Interrogation and Confessions, 77 Minn.L.Rev.983 (1993). These requirements are, however, in addition to and not in replacement of the *Miranda* safeguards. See also Leonard Post, Illinois to Tape Police Questioning, Nat'l L.J., 8/4/2003 p.1 (noting some police officers as critical of taping because "it absolutely hasn't shortened evidentiary hearings or the swearing contests" and that "When suspects have to go to the bathroom, we chase them with tape recorders.").

Amendment First Principles: The Self–Incrimination Clause, 93 Mich.L.Rev.857 (1995), suggest "a prophylactic rule that no police-station confession by a defendant is ever allowed in, unless volunteered by a suspect in the presence of an on-duty defense lawyer or ombudsman in the police station." In place of custodial interrogation, Amar and Lettow propose that at a pretrial hearing before a judge, the government would be permitted to compel a suspect to provide evidence against himself. The suspect would be given only "testimonial" immunity as opposed to use-fruits immunity, meaning that his statement could not be used as evidence against him, but the government could use the statement as a means of finding other information such as physical evidence and adverse witnesses. If the suspect refuses to make a statement at this pretrial hearing, Amar and Lettow propose that the suspect could be jailed for contempt, and that an adverse inference could be drawn at trial. Is this a better system than *Miranda*?

B. DID CONGRESS OVERRULE *MIRANDA*?

In 1968, Congress passed 18 U.S.C. § 3501, which provides, among other things, that a confession "shall be admissible in evidence if it is voluntarily given," and that the issue of voluntariness shall be determined on the basis of "all the circumstances surrounding the giving of the confession," including whether the defendant received warnings and counsel. Thus, warnings and counsel are simply factors in the voluntariness analysis—the absence of warnings or the failure to provide counsel do not themselves render a confession inadmissible. The apparent intent of Congress was to "overrule" *Miranda* in favor of a return to the "voluntariness" standard. The Supreme Court considered whether Congress has the power to overrule *Miranda* in the following case.

DICKERSON v. UNITED STATES

United States Supreme Court, 2000.
530 U.S. 428.

CHIEF JUSTICE REHNQUIST **delivered the opinion of the Court.**

In Miranda v. Arizona, we held that certain warnings must be given before a suspect's statement made during custodial interrogation could be admitted in evidence. In the wake of that decision, Congress enacted 18 U.S.C. § 3501, which in essence laid down a rule that the admissibility of such statements should turn only on whether or not they were voluntarily made. We hold that *Miranda*, being a constitutional decision of this Court, may not be in effect overruled by an Act of Congress, and we decline to overrule *Miranda* ourselves. We therefore hold that *Miranda* and its progeny in this Court govern the admissibility of state-

ments made during custodial interrogation in both state and federal courts.

Petitioner Dickerson was indicted for bank robbery, conspiracy to commit bank robbery, and using a firearm in the course of committing a crime of violence, all in violation of the applicable provisions of Title 18 of the United States Code. Before trial, Dickerson moved to suppress a statement he had made at a Federal Bureau of Investigation field office, on the grounds that he had not received "*Miranda* warnings" before being interrogated. The District Court granted his motion to suppress, and the Government took an interlocutory appeal to the United States Court of Appeals for the Fourth Circuit. That court, by a divided vote, reversed the District Court's suppression order. It agreed with the District Court's conclusion that petitioner had not received *Miranda* warnings before making his statement. But it went on to hold that § 3501, which in effect makes the admissibility of statements such as Dickerson's turn solely on whether they were made voluntarily, was satisfied in this case. It then concluded that our decision in *Miranda* was not a constitutional holding, and that therefore Congress could by statute have the final say on the question of admissibility.

Because of the importance of the questions raised by the Court of Appeals' decision, we granted certiorari, and now reverse.

* * * Prior to *Miranda*, we evaluated the admissibility of a suspect's confession under a voluntariness test. * * * [The Court discusses its cases decided under the due process, totality of circumstances test.]

We have never abandoned this due process jurisprudence, and thus continue to exclude confessions that were obtained involuntarily. But our decisions in Malloy v. Hogan, 378 U.S. 1 (1964), and *Miranda* changed the focus of much of the inquiry in determining the admissibility of suspects' incriminating statements. In *Malloy*, we held that the Fifth Amendment's Self–Incrimination Clause is incorporated in the Due Process Clause of the Fourteenth Amendment and thus applies to the States. We decided *Miranda* on the heels of *Malloy*.

* * *

Two years after *Miranda* was decided, Congress enacted § 3501. * * * Given § 3501's express designation of voluntariness as the touchstone of admissibility, its omission of any warning requirement, and the instruction for trial courts to consider a nonexclusive list of factors relevant to the circumstances of a confession, we agree with the Court of Appeals that Congress intended by its enactment to overrule *Miranda*. Because of the obvious conflict between our decision in *Miranda* and § 3501, we must address whether Congress has constitutional authority to thus supersede *Miranda*. If Congress has such authority, § 3501's totality-of-the-circumstances approach must prevail over *Miranda's* requirement of warnings; if not, that section must yield to *Miranda's* more specific requirements.

The law in this area is clear. This Court has supervisory authority over the federal courts, and we may use that authority to prescribe rules of evidence and procedure that are binding in those tribunals. * * * Congress retains the ultimate authority to modify or set aside any judicially created rules of evidence and procedure that are not required by the Constitution. But Congress may not legislatively supersede our decisions interpreting and applying the Constitution. This case therefore turns on whether the *Miranda* Court announced a constitutional rule or merely exercised its supervisory authority to regulate evidence in the absence of congressional direction.

Recognizing this point, the Court of Appeals surveyed *Miranda* and its progeny to determine the constitutional status of the *Miranda* decision. Relying on the fact that we have created several exceptions to *Miranda's* warnings requirement and that we have repeatedly referred to the *Miranda* warnings as "prophylactic," New York v. Quarles, 467 U.S. 649, 653 (1984), and "not themselves rights protected by the Constitution," Michigan v. Tucker, 417 U.S. 433, 444 (1974), [These cases are discussed immediately infra in the section on exceptions to *Miranda*.] the Court of Appeals concluded that the protections announced in *Miranda* are not constitutionally required.

We disagree with the Court of Appeals' conclusion, although we concede that there is language in some of our opinions that supports the view taken by that court. But first and foremost of the factors on the other side—that *Miranda* is a constitutional decision—is that both *Miranda* and two of its companion cases applied the rule to proceedings in state courts—to wit, Arizona, California, and New York. Since that time, we have consistently applied *Miranda's* rule to prosecutions arising in state courts. It is beyond dispute that we do not hold a supervisory power over the courts of the several States.

The *Miranda* opinion itself begins by stating that the Court granted certiorari "to explore some facets of the problems ... of applying the privilege against self-incrimination to in-custody interrogation, and to give concrete constitutional guidelines for law enforcement agencies and courts to follow." In fact, the majority opinion is replete with statements indicating that the majority thought it was announcing a constitutional rule. Indeed, the Court's ultimate conclusion was that the unwarned confessions obtained in the four cases before the Court in *Miranda* "were obtained from the defendant under circumstances that did not meet constitutional standards for protection of the privilege." Additional support for our conclusion that *Miranda* is constitutionally based is found in the *Miranda* Court's invitation for legislative action to protect the constitutional right against coerced self-incrimination. After discussing the "compelling pressures" inherent in custodial police interrogation, the *Miranda* Court concluded that, "[i]n order to combat these pressures and to permit a full opportunity to exercise

the privilege against self-incrimination, the accused must be adequately and effectively appraised of his rights and the exercise of those rights must be fully honored." However, the Court emphasized that it could not foresee "the potential alternatives for protecting the privilege which might be devised by Congress or the States," and it accordingly opined that the Constitution would not preclude legislative solutions that differed from the prescribed *Miranda* warnings but which were "at least as effective in apprising accused persons of their right of silence and in assuring a continuous opportunity to exercise it."

The Court of Appeals also relied on the fact that we have, after our *Miranda* decision, made exceptions from its rule in cases such as New York v. Quarles, 467 U.S. 649 (1984), and Harris v. New York, 401 U.S. 222 (1971)[also discussed immediately infra]. But we have also broadened the application of the *Miranda* doctrine in cases such as Doyle v. Ohio, 426 U.S. 610 (1976), and Arizona v. Roberson, 486 U.S. 675 (1988). These decisions illustrate the principle—not that *Miranda* is not a constitutional rule—but that no constitutional rule is immutable. No court laying down a general rule can possibly foresee the various circumstances in which counsel will seek to apply it, and the sort of modifications represented by these cases are as much a normal part of constitutional law as the original decision.

The Court of Appeals also noted that in Oregon v. Elstad, 470 U.S. 298 (1985), we stated that "[t]he Miranda exclusionary rule ... serves the Fifth Amendment and sweeps more broadly than the Fifth Amendment itself." Our decision in that case—refusing to apply the traditional "fruits" doctrine developed in Fourth Amendment cases—does not prove that *Miranda* is a nonconstitutional decision, but simply recognizes the fact that unreasonable searches under the Fourth Amendment are different from unwarned interrogation under the Fifth Amendment.

As an alternative argument for sustaining the Court of Appeals' decision, the court-invited amicus curiae contends that the section complies with the requirement that a legislative alternative to *Miranda* be equally as effective in preventing coerced confessions. See Brief for Paul G. Cassell as Amicus Curiae 28–39. We agree with the amicus' contention that there are more remedies available for abusive police conduct than there were at the time *Miranda* was decided. But we do not agree that these additional measures supplement § 3501's protections sufficiently to meet the constitutional minimum. *Miranda* requires procedures that will warn a suspect in custody of his right to remain silent and which will assure the suspect that the exercise of that right will be honored. As discussed above, § 3501 explicitly eschews a requirement of pre-interrogation warnings in favor of an approach that looks to the administration of such warnings as only one factor in determining the voluntariness of a suspect's confession. The additional remedies cited by amicus do not, in our view, render them, together with § 3501 an adequate substitute for the warnings required by *Miranda*.

The dissent argues that it is judicial overreaching for this Court to hold § 3501 unconstitutional unless we hold that the *Miranda* warnings are required by the Constitution, in the sense that nothing else will suffice to satisfy constitutional requirements. But we need not go farther than *Miranda* to decide this case. In *Miranda*, the Court noted that reliance on the traditional totality-of-the-circumstances test raised a risk of overlooking an involuntary custodial confession, a risk that the Court found unacceptably great when the confession is offered in the case in chief to prove guilt. The Court therefore concluded that something more than the totality test was necessary. As discussed above, § 3501 reinstates the totality test as sufficient. Section 3501 therefore cannot be sustained if *Miranda* is to remain the law.

Whether or not we would agree with *Miranda's* reasoning and its resulting rule, were we addressing the issue in the first instance, the principles of stare decisis weigh heavily against overruling it now. While stare decisis is not an inexorable command, particularly when we are interpreting the Constitution, even in constitutional cases, the doctrine carries such persuasive force that we have always required a departure from precedent to be supported by some 'special justification.'

We do not think there is such justification for overruling *Miranda*. *Miranda* has become embedded in routine police practice to the point where the warnings have become part of our national culture. While we have overruled our precedents when subsequent cases have undermined their doctrinal underpinnings, we do not believe that this has happened to the *Miranda* decision. If anything, our subsequent cases have reduced the impact of the *Miranda* rule on legitimate law enforcement while reaffirming the decision's core ruling that unwarned statements may not be used as evidence in the prosecution's case in chief.

The disadvantage of the *Miranda* rule is that statements which may be by no means involuntary, made by a defendant who is aware of his "rights," may nonetheless be excluded and a guilty defendant go free as a result. But experience suggests that the totality-of-the-circumstances test which § 3501 seeks to revive is more difficult than *Miranda* for law enforcement officers to conform to, and for courts to apply in a consistent manner. The requirement that *Miranda* warnings be given does not, of course, dispense with the voluntariness inquiry. But as we said in Berkemer v. McCarty, 468 U.S. 420 (1984), "[c]ases in which a defendant can make a colorable argument that a self-incriminating statement was 'compelled' despite the fact that the law enforcement authorities adhered to the dictates of *Miranda* are rare."

In sum, we conclude that *Miranda* announced a constitutional rule that Congress may not supersede legislatively. Following the rule of stare decisis, we decline to overrule *Miranda* ourselves. The judgment of the Court of Appeals is therefore

Reversed.

JUSTICE SCALIA, with whom JUSTICE THOMAS joins, dissenting.

* * * Justices whose votes are needed to compose today's majority are on record as believing that a violation of *Miranda* is not a violation of the Constitution. See Davis v. United States, 512 U.S. 452, 457–458 (1994) (opinion of the Court, in which Kennedy, J., joined); Duckworth v. Eagan, 492 U.S. 195, 203 (1989) (opinion of the Court, in which Kennedy, J., joined); Oregon v. Elstad, 470 U.S. 298 (1985) (opinion of the Court by O'Connor, J.); New York v. Quarles, 467 U.S. 649 (1984) (opinion of the Court by Rehnquist, J.). And so, to justify today's agreed-upon result, the Court must adopt a significant new, if not entirely comprehensible, principle of constitutional law. As the Court chooses to describe that principle, statutes of Congress can be disregarded, not only when what they prescribe violates the Constitution, but when what they prescribe

contradicts a decision of this Court that "announced a constitutional rule." * * *

I

* * *

It was once possible to characterize the so-called *Miranda* rule as resting (however implausibly) upon the proposition that what the statute here before us permits—the admission at trial of un-*Mirandized* confessions—violates the Constitution. That is the fairest reading of the *Miranda* case itself. * * *

So understood, *Miranda* was objectionable for innumerable reasons, not least the fact that cases spanning more than 70 years had rejected its core premise that, absent the warnings and an effective waiver of the right to remain silent and of the (hitherto unknown) right to have an attorney present, a statement obtained pursuant to custodial interrogation was necessarily the product of compulsion. Moreover, history and precedent aside, the decision in *Miranda*, if read as an explication of what the Constitution requires, is preposterous. There is, for example, simply no basis in reason for concluding that a response to the very first question asked, by a suspect who already knows all of the rights described in the *Miranda* warning, is anything other than a volitional act. And even if one assumes that the elimination of compulsion absolutely requires informing even the most knowledgeable suspect of his right to remain silent, it cannot conceivably require the right to have counsel present.* * * Thus, what is most remarkable about the *Miranda* decision—and what made it unacceptable as a matter of straightforward constitutional interpretation in the *Marbury* tradition—is its palpable hostility toward the act of confession per se, rather than toward what the Constitution abhors, compelled confession.

For these reasons, and others more than adequately developed in the *Miranda* dissents and in the subsequent works of the decision's many critics, any conclusion that a violation of the *Miranda* rules necessarily amounts to a violation of the privilege against compelled self-incrimination can claim no support in history, precedent, or common sense, and as a result would at least presumptively be worth reconsidering even at this late date. But that is unnecessary, since the Court has (thankfully) long since abandoned the notion that failure to comply with *Miranda's* rules is itself a violation of the Constitution.

II

As the Court today acknowledges, since *Miranda* we have explicitly, and repeatedly, interpreted that decision as having announced, not the circumstances in which custodial interrogation runs afoul of the Fifth or Fourteenth Amendment, but rather only "prophylactic" rules that go beyond the right against compelled self-incrimination. * * * The Court has squarely concluded that it is possible—indeed not uncommon—for the police to violate *Miranda* without also "violating the Constitution."

[Justice Scalia discusses cases in which the Court stated that the *Miranda* warnings are prophylactic safeguards rather than constitutional rights, including New York v. Quarles and Oregon v. Elstad, discussed infra in this Chapter.]

In light of these cases, * * * it is simply no longer possible for the Court to conclude, even if it wanted to, that a violation of *Miranda's* rules is a violation of the Constitution. * * * By disregarding congressional action that concededly does not vio-

late the Constitution, the Court flagrantly offends fundamental principles of separation of powers, and arrogates to itself prerogatives reserved to the representatives of the people.

The Court seeks to avoid this conclusion in two ways: First, by misdescribing these post-*Miranda* cases as mere dicta. The Court concedes only "that there is language in some of our opinions that supports the view" that *Miranda's* protections are not "constitutionally required." It is not a matter of language; it is a matter of holdings. The proposition that failure to comply with *Miranda's* rules does not establish a constitutional violation was central to the holdings of *Tucker, Hass, Quarles,* and *Elstad.*

The second way the Court seeks to avoid the impact of these cases is simply to disclaim responsibility for reasoned decisionmaking. It says:

These decisions illustrate the principle—not that *Miranda* is not a constitutional rule—but that no constitutional rule is immutable. No court laying down a general rule can possibly foresee the various circumstances in which counsel will seek to apply it, and the sort of modifications represented by these cases are as much a normal part of constitutional law as the original decision.

The issue, however, is not whether court rules are "mutable"; they assuredly are. It is not whether, in the light of "various circumstances," they can be "modifi[ed]"; they assuredly can. The issue is whether, as mutated and modified, they must make sense. The requirement that they do so is the only thing that prevents this Court from being some sort of nine-headed Caesar, giving thumbs-up or thumbs-down to whatever outcome, case by case, suits or offends its collective fancy. And if confessions procured in violation of *Miranda* are confessions "compelled" in violation of the Constitution, the post-*Miranda* decisions I have discussed do not make sense. The only reasoned basis for their outcome was that a violation of *Miranda* is not a violation of the Constitution. If, for example, as the Court acknowledges was the holding of *Elstad*, "the traditional 'fruits' doctrine developed in Fourth Amendment cases" (that the fruits of evidence obtained unconstitutionally must be excluded from trial) does not apply to the fruits of *Miranda* violations; and if the reason for the difference is not that *Miranda* violations are not constitutional violations (which is plainly and flatly what *Elstad* said); then the Court must come up with some other explanation for the difference. (That will take quite a bit of doing, by the way, since it is not clear on the face of the Fourth Amendment that evidence obtained in violation of that guarantee must be excluded from trial, whereas it is clear on the face of the Fifth Amendment that unconstitutionally compelled confessions cannot be used.) To say simply that "unreasonable searches under the Fourth Amendment are different from unwarned interrogation under the Fifth Amendment," is true but supremely unhelpful.

Finally, the Court asserts that *Miranda* must be a "constitutional decision" announcing a "constitutional rule," and thus immune to congressional modification, because we have since its inception applied it to the States. If this argument is meant as an invocation of stare decisis, it fails because, though it is true that our cases applying *Miranda* against the States must be reconsidered if *Miranda* is not required by the Constitution, it is likewise true that our cases (discussed above) based on the principle that *Miranda* is not required by the Constitution will have to be reconsidered if it

is. So the stare decisis argument is a wash. * * *

III

* * *

IV

Neither am I persuaded by the argument for retaining *Miranda* that touts its supposed workability as compared with the totality-of-the-circumstances test it purported to replace. *Miranda's* proponents cite ad nauseam the fact that the Court was called upon to make difficult and subtle distinctions in applying the "voluntariness" test in some 30–odd due process "coerced confessions" cases in the 30 years between Brown v. Mississippi, 297 U.S. 278 (1936), and *Miranda*. It is not immediately apparent, however, that the judicial burden has been eased by the "bright-line" rules adopted in *Miranda*. In fact, in the 34 years since *Miranda* was decided, this Court has been called upon to decide nearly 60 cases involving a host of *Miranda* issues, most of them predicted with remarkable prescience by Justice White in his *Miranda* dissent. * * * But even were I to agree that the old totality-of-the-circumstances test was more cumbersome, it is simply not true that *Miranda* has banished it from the law and replaced it with a new test. Under the current regime, which the Court today retains in its entirety, courts are frequently called upon to undertake both inquiries. That is because, as explained earlier, voluntariness remains the constitutional standard, and as such continues to govern the admissibility for impeachment purposes of statements taken in violation of *Miranda,* the admissibility of the "fruits" of such statements, and the admissibility of statements challenged as unconstitutionally obtained despite the interrogator's compliance with *Miranda*.

* * *

* * * I believe we cannot allow to remain on the books even a celebrated decision—especially a celebrated decision—that has come to stand for the proposition that the Supreme Court has power to impose extraconstitutional constraints upon Congress and the States. This is not the system that was established by the Framers, or that would be established by any sane supporter of government by the people.

I dissent from today's decision, and, until § 3501 is repealed, will continue to apply it in all cases where there has been a sustainable finding that the defendant's confession was voluntary.

Note on Dickerson

The Court in *Dickerson* seemed to be between a rock and a hard place: either hold one final time that the *Miranda* safeguards are not constitutionally guaranteed (thereby leaving the states to their own devices) or reject all of the exceptions to *Miranda* that had been based on the premise that the *Miranda* safeguards are not constitutionally required. As it turned out the Court, much to the dismay of Justice Scalia, appeared to have its cake and eat it too: the *Miranda* safeguards are constitutionally required, and yet all of the exceptions are retained, though now as exceptions to a constitutional rule. Is this a satisfactory solution? Does it mean that other exceptions to *Miranda* can be established? For more on *Dickerson* and its effect on the *Miranda* exceptions, see Susan R. Klein, *Miranda's* Exceptions in a Post-*Dickerson* World, 91 J.Crim.L. & Criminology 567 (2001).

Can a Miranda Violation Occur If the Statement Is Never Admitted? Chavez v. Martinez

In Chavez v. Martinez, 538 U.S. 760 (2003), the Court held that a person's *Miranda* rights are not violated if his confession is never admitted at trial. Martinez brought a federal civil rights action after Chavez, a police officer, questioned Martinez in a hospital after Martinez had been shot. Martinez received no *Miranda* warnings, and he made some incriminating admissions. But charges were never brought and these statements were never admitted against Martinez. Martinez nonetheless argued that his Fifth Amendment rights were violated by the custodial questioning itself. The Court, in a number of separate opinions, held that the *Miranda* rule is a trial right that is not implicated until the government offers *Miranda*-defective statements against the defendant at trial. The Court also held that the Fifth Amendment provided no protection because the statements were never admitted in a "criminal case."

Justice Thomas, in an opinion for four Justices in *Chavez*, declared that *Miranda* simply provides a "prophylactic safeguard." While this declaration seems at odds with the Court's ruling in *Dickerson*, it did not command a majority of the Court. For more extensive treatment of *Chavez*, see *supra* in the section on the Fifth Amendment.

C. EXCEPTIONS TO THE *MIRANDA* RULE OF EXCLUSION

In a number of cases after *Miranda*, the Court has held that a certain evidence that is the product of a *Miranda*-defective confession is nonetheless admissible at trial. These cases originally relied on the premise that the *Miranda* safeguards were merely prophylactic rules and not constitutionally required. After *Dickerson,* however, that analysis can no longer stand. Rather, these exceptions to the *Miranda* rule of exclusion are just that: exceptions to a constitutional rule.

1. Impeaching the Defendant–Witness

One of the most significant cases limiting the Court's decision in *Miranda* is Harris v. New York, 401 U.S. 222 (1971).[14] Harris was charged with selling heroin to undercover police officers, and he took the stand in his own defense. On cross-examination, he was asked if he had made statements to the police immediately after his arrest that partially contradicted his direct testimony. The statements were not admissible as substantive evidence under *Miranda,* because Harris was not warned of his right to counsel prior to his in-custody interrogation. However, Chief Justice Burger, writing for the Court, declared that the *Miranda* safeguards are not required by the Constitution, and therefore that Harris' *Miranda*-defective statements could be admitted for purposes of impeaching his credibility. While this "non-constitutional" analysis is no longer viable after *Dickerson*, the impeachment exception remains intact. Perhaps the reason for this retention stems from the Court's cost-benefit analysis in *Harris*. It found that the cost of excluding *Miranda*-defective confessions when offered for impeachment outweighed the benefit in deterring *Miranda* violations. The Court explained its cost-benefit balance as follows:

> * * * The impeachment process here undoubtedly provided valuable aid to the jury in assessing petitioner's credibility, and the benefits of this process should not be lost, in our view, because of the speculative possibility that impermissible police conduct will be encouraged thereby. Assuming that the exclusionary rule has a deterrent effect on proscribed police conduct, sufficient deterrence flows when the evidence in question is made unavailable to the prosecution in its case in chief.

> The shield provided by *Miranda* cannot be perverted into a license to use perjury by way of a defense, free from the risk of confrontation with prior inconsistent utterances. We hold, therefore, that petitioner's credibility was appropriately impeached by use of his earlier conflicting statements.

Can the decision in *Harris* be reconciled with the language in *Miranda*? Does it diminish the effectiveness of *Miranda*? If so, how?

The Court reaffirmed *Harris* in Oregon v. Hass, 420 U.S. 714 (1975).[15] In *Hass,* the defendant had received the full *Miranda* warnings and had said that he would like to call a lawyer. He was told that he could not telephone an attorney until he and the police officer reached the police station. Thereafter, the defendant made inculpatory statements before he was given an opportunity to call a lawyer. The Court stated that the only difference between the situations in *Harris* and *Hass* was that the *Miranda* warnings given in *Hass* were proper, whereas those given in *Harris* were defective. Finding that *Hass* was controlled by *Harris*, the Court held that the statements were admissible to impeach the defendant, who had taken the stand and offered direct testimony in conflict with

---

14. Justices Black, Brennan, Douglas, and Marshall dissented. Arguably, the Court strained, to the point of distorting the record, to use this case to cabin *Miranda*. See Ely & Dershowitz, Harris v. New York: Some Anxious Observations on the Candor and Logic of the Emerging Nixon Majority, 80 Yale L.J. 1198 (1971).

15. Justices Brennan and Marshall dissented. Justice Douglas took no part in the decision.

the incriminating information with knowledge that the inculpatory statements had been ruled inadmissible as substantive evidence.

The Court's decisions in *Harris* and *Hass* leave a defendant with a practical problem. The defendant may not want to take the stand, because if he does the jury may learn about a confession obtained from him in violation of *Miranda*. Even though the jury will be told that the confession can be used for impeachment purposes only, the Court has recognized that juries are likely to be swayed by confessions and to use them improperly, contrary to instructions. See Bruton v. United States, 391 U.S. 123 (1968). If the defendant does not take the stand, he loses the opportunity to testify in his own behalf, and the chance of conviction increases appreciably. See H. Kalven & H. Zeisel, The American Jury 160 (1960).

A police training tape entitled "Questioning Outside *Miranda*" provides a lecture from an Assistant District Attorney suggesting options that an officer might consider if the suspect, when given *Miranda* warnings, decides not to talk. The ADA suggests that the questioning continue "outside *Miranda*" because such questioning can help the police officer even if the confession is inadmissible at trial. The ADA notes, for example, that obtaining a confession "outside *Miranda*"

> forces the defendant to commit to a statement that will prevent him from pulling out some defense and using it at trial—that he's cooked up with some defense lawyer—that wasn't true. So if you get a statement "outside *Miranda*" and he tells you that he did it and how he did it or if he gives you a denial of some sort, he's tied to that, he's married to that, because * * * we can use statements outside *Miranda* to impeach or rebut. We can't use them for our case-in-chief. The D.A. can't trot them out to the jury before he says "I rest," but * * * we can use his "outside *Miranda*" statements to impeach him. * * * I mean we can't use them for any purpose if you beat them out of him, but if they're voluntary statements, the fact that they weren't Mirandized will mean that we cannot use them in the case-in-chief but it does not mean we can't use them to impeach or rebut. So you see you got all those legitimate purposes that could be served by statements taken "outside *Miranda*."

Given the value to the prosecution of a *Miranda*-defective confession after *Harris,* as emphasized again and again in the police training video, do you think the Chief Justice was correct in asserting that sufficient deterrence flows from exclusion of the confession in the case-in-chief? For a critique of *Harris*, see Weisselberg, Saving *Miranda*, 84 Cornell L.Rev. 109 (1998).

Involuntary Confessions and Impeachment

In Mincey v. Arizona, 437 U.S. 385 (1978), the Court distinguished *Harris* and *Hass* and held that if a confession is involuntary, as opposed to merely *Miranda*-defective, it cannot be admitted even for impeachment purposes. The Court reasoned that the Due Process Clause operates to prohibit the use of involuntary confessions for any purpose.

Impeachment With Prior Silence

Under standard evidentiary principles, a defendant can be impeached with prior silence if a reasonable person would have spoken at the time about the matter later testified to. For example, if Joe is sitting in his yard and his neighbor comes up to Joe and accuses him of stealing money from the neighbor's home, and Joe says nothing, Joe can be impeached at trial with this silence if he later testifies that he did not steal the money. The silence is considered inconsistent with the later testimony.

A different question arises, however, if the person has been given *Miranda* warnings and remains silent. In Doyle v. Ohio, 426 U.S. 610 (1976), the defendant had been given *Miranda* warnings at the time of his arrest and chose to remain silent. At his trial, he took the stand and related an exculpatory story that he had not told to the police when Mirandized. On cross-examination, he was asked why he had not given the exculpatory explanation before. Doyle appealed his conviction, arguing that the reference to post-*Mirandized* silence violated his constitutional rights.

The *Doyle* Court held that after *Miranda* warnings are given, the Due Process Clause prohibits the government from using the defendant's silence against him.[16] In reaching this conclusion, the Court said that "while it is true that the *Miranda* warnings contain no express assurance that silence will carry no penalty, such assurance is implicit to any person who receives the warnings. In such circumstances, it would be fundamentally unfair and a deprivation of due process to allow the arrested person's silence to be used to impeach an explanation subsequently offered at trial."[17]

---

16. Justices Stevens, Blackmun, and Rehnquist dissented. Prior to *Doyle*, the Court had limited the use of silence upon arrest for impeachment, but as an evidentiary, not a constitutional, ruling. See United States v. Hale, 422 U.S. 171 (1975).

The Court later held that a person who waived his rights after receiving *Miranda* warnings and who spoke to the police could be asked at trial why his pretrial statement differed from his trial testimony, even if the question focused on a relevant omission in the pretrial statement. Anderson v. Charles, 447 U.S. 404 (1980). This is because the *Miranda* promise that silence will not carry a penalty is inoperative where the defendant chose to speak.

17. Justice Stevens' majority opinion in Wainwright v. Greenfield, 474 U.S. 284 (1986), relied upon *Doyle* to hold that a defendant's silence after receiving *Miranda* warnings may not be used to rebut an insanity defense at trial. The Court indicated that the prosecution could have elicited testimony concerning the defendant's behavior at the time of his arrest as long as questions were carefully framed to avoid any reference to the defendant's assertion of his right to remain silent or his right to remain silent until appointment of counsel. Justice Rehnquist, joined by Chief Justice Burger, concurred in the judgment, but argued that a request for a lawyer after *Miranda* warnings should be treated differently from a decision to remain silent. He reasoned that the warnings do not imply that a defendant's request for counsel will not be used against him and that a request for counsel "may be highly relevant where the plea is based on insanity."

The Supreme Court found no violation of *Doyle* in Greer v. Miller, 483 U.S. 756 (1987). When Miller took the stand in his trial for kidnaping, robbery, and murder, he testified that he had taken no part in the criminal activity, and that two other defendants had come to his trailer and confessed to the crimes shortly after they occurred. The prosecutor asked Miller why he didn't tell his story to anyone after he was arrested. Miller's lawyer objected and moved for a mistrial. The trial judge denied the motion and instructed the jury to "ignore the question, for the time being." Justice Powell's opinion for the Court concluded that the trial judge in Miller's case, unlike the judge in *Doyle*, did not permit the inquiry into silence after receipt of warnings. Once objection was made, no further question or argument concerning silence was heard. Thus, the fact of Miller's post-arrest silence was not submitted to the jury as evidence, and no *Doyle* violation occurred.

Pre–Arrest Silence

In Jenkins v. Anderson, 447 U.S. 231 (1980), the Court considered whether the use of *pre*-arrest silence for impeachment purposes was prohibited by *Doyle*. Jenkins stabbed and killed Redding, and at his trial for murder he contended that the killing was in self-defense. Jenkins was not apprehended until he turned himself in two weeks after the killing. On cross-examination and in closing argument, the prosecutor emphasized that Jenkins' two-week waiting period was inconsistent with his later claim of self-defense, i.e., if he had really acted in self-defense, he would have come forward right away rather than remaining at large. Justice Powell, writing for the Court, found *Doyle* inapplicable, reasoning as follows:

> In this case, no governmental action induced petitioner to remain silent before arrest. The failure to speak occurred before the petitioner was taken into custody and given *Miranda* warnings. Consequently, the fundamental unfairness present in *Doyle* is not present in this case. We hold that impeachment by use of pre-arrest silence does not violate the Fourteenth Amendment.

Justice Stevens, joined by Justice Stewart, concurred in the judgment, stating that "the admissibility of petitioner's failure to come forward with the excuse of self-defense shortly after the stabbing raised a routine evidentiary question that turns on the probative significance of that evidence and presented no issue under the Federal Constitution." Justices Marshall and Brennan dissented.

Surely the *Jenkins* Court is correct in wanting to uphold fair cross-examination of a defendant who takes the witness stand. But does the Court mean that persons who may be involved in criminal activities must report their involvement to the police or risk having their failure to report used against them at trial, at least for impeachment purposes? Would this not be a penalty imposed on silence in violation of the Fifth Amendment? Assume you are a criminal lawyer and a client comes to you and tells you facts that might indicate possible criminal activity. What do you advise? If you tell your client to tell the police everything she knows, you are a more effective agent for the government than the police can be under *Miranda*. If you tell your client to do nothing, *Jenkins* suggests that the client may suffer as a result. Could you tell your client to send an anonymous letter to the police stating that she is not guilty of criminal activity and that her failure to come forward represents a decision not to risk misinterpretation of the facts and concomitant incrimination? Would this bar use of silence as evidence under *Jenkins*? What other advice could you give?

For a criticism of Jenkins, see Saltzburg, Foreword: The Flow and Ebb of Constitutional Criminal Procedure in the Warren and Burger Courts, 69 Geo. L.J. 151, 203–05 (1980).

Post-Arrest, Pre–Miranda Silence

In Fletcher v. Weir, 455 U.S. 603 (1982), the Court considered whether *Doyle* prohibited the use of a suspect's *post*-arrest silence for impeachment purposes, when that silence preceded *Miranda* warnings. Weir testified at trial

Justice Stevens filed an opinion concurring in the judgment. Justice Brennan filed a dissenting opinion, in which Justices Marshall and Blackmun joined.

that he acted in self-defense, and the prosecutor asked why he did not offer this explanation when he was arrested. The Court, per curiam, held that "in the absence of the sort of affirmative assurances embodied in the *Miranda* warnings," impeachment with post-arrest silence was constitutionally permissible. The Court stated that the arrest by itself does not implicitly induce a suspect to remain silent.[18]

2. Admitting the Fruits of a Miranda Violation

By its terms (and even after *Harris*), *Miranda* requires that if the police engage in custodial interrogation and give no warnings or incomplete warnings, the resulting confession must be excluded from the case-in-chief. But what about the fruits of that confession? Some possible fruits of a *Miranda*-defective confession are: investigative leads pursued as a result of the confession; physical evidence; and a second confession by the suspect. In Michigan v. Tucker, 417 U.S. 433 (1974), and Oregon v. Elstad, 470 U.S. 298 (1985), the Court severely limited the exclusionary impact of *Miranda* on the fruits of confessions, relying on two propositions: 1) that exclusion of the fruit of a poisonous tree is only justified if a constitutional right is violated (i.e., the "poison" must be a constitutional violation); and 2) that a violation of *Miranda* is not by itself a violation of the Fifth Amendment. This analysis is no longer valid after *Dickerson*. However, the Court in *Dickerson* specifically held that the "fruits" exception to *Miranda* retained validity even though the *Miranda* safeguards are constitutionally based.

Leads to Witnesses: Michigan v. Tucker

In *Tucker,* the defendant was arrested for rape. Before he was interrogated, he was advised of his right to remain silent and his right to counsel, but was not told that he had the right to appointed counsel if he was indigent. The defendant told the police that he was with his friend Henderson at the time the crime was committed. The police then went to talk to Henderson. But Henderson gave information tending to incriminate the defendant. Before trial, the defendant moved to exclude Henderson's expected testimony because the defendant's *Miranda*-defective statement had led them to Henderson. In Tucker's view, Henderson's statement was the fruit of the poisonous tree. The motion was denied and the defendant was convicted.

The Court found that the failure to give the full *Miranda* warnings required exclusion of Tucker's confession but not Henderson's testimony. The Court found "no reason to believe that Henderson's testimony is untrustworthy simply because [Tucker] was not advised of *his* right to appointed counsel." Justice Rehnquist, writing for the majority, declared that exclusion of this reliable evidence was not required simply because it proceeded from Tucker's *Miranda*-defective confession. He concluded that the *Miranda* warnings were "procedural safeguards" that "were not themselves rights protected by the Constitution but were instead measures to insure that the right against compulsory self-incrimination was protected." While this rationale is, again, no longer applicable after

---

18. Some state courts have rejected *Fletcher* as a matter of state law. See Nelson v. State, 691 P.2d 1056 (Alaska App.1984); State v. Davis, 38 Wash.App. 600, 686 P.2d 1143 (1984).

Dickerson, *the* Tucker *rule has been retained, perhaps because the Court still agrees with the cost-benefit analysis that the Court conducted in* Tucker.

Justice Rehnquist in *Tucker* considered whether the benefits of exclusion (deterring future *Miranda* violations) outweighed the costs of exclusion (the loss of reliable evidence). He reasoned that the deterrent effect of excluding Henderson's testimony would be minimal, because sufficient deterrence already existed by excluding Tucker's confession from the case-in-chief. The Court weighed the minimal incremental deterrence resulting from exclusion of derivative evidence, against the cost of excluding Henderson's reliable testimony, and found that the *Miranda* exclusionary rule should not apply.

Justice Rehnquist noted, however, that if Tucker's confession had been involuntary, the Due Process Clause would require exclusion of the confession as well as its fruits. Justices Brennan and Marshall concurred in the judgment.

Subsequent Confessions: Oregon v. Elstad

Justice O'Connor, writing for the Court in *Elstad,* extended the *Tucker* analysis to a case where a second confession resulted from a *Miranda*-defective confession. The facts were as follows: Police investigating a burglary of a home suspected Elstad, an 18–year–old neighbor. They obtained a warrant for his arrest and served it at his house. One officer asked Elstad if he knew someone by the name of Gross (the burglarized family), and Elstad said that he did and that he had heard the Gross house was burglarized. The officer indicated that he thought Elstad was involved in the burglary, and Elstad replied "Yes, I was there." Elstad had not received *Miranda* warnings at that point. The officers took Elstad from his home to the Sheriff's headquarters and approximately an hour later gave him *Miranda* warnings. Elstad then waived his rights and gave a full statement, which was typed, read back to him, initialed, and signed by Elstad and the officers. Only this second statement was used at the trial, in which Elstad was convicted of burglary. The state supreme court overturned the conviction, reasoning that because of Elstad's initial *Miranda*-defective statement, "the cat was sufficiently out of the bag to exert a coercive impact" on Elstad at the time he made his second statement.

Justice O'Connor rejected the argument that the second confession had to be excluded as tainted by the first. Again, the Court relied on its now-discredited premise that the *Miranda* safeguards are not constitutionally-grounded. The Court held that "since there was no actual infringement of the suspect's *constitutional* rights" the case was not controlled "by the doctrine expressed in *Wong Sun* that fruits of a *constitutional* violation must be suppressed."

While the "non-constitutional" rationale of *Elstad* is no longer viable, the *Dickerson* Court reaffirmed the result in *Elstad,* i.e., statements that are the "fruit" *Miranda*-defective confession are not excluded. Again, the Court's retention of the *Elstad* rule may be based on the cost-benefit analysis conducted in that case: even if *Miranda* is a constitutional rule, the costs of compliance by excluding fruits outweigh the benefits of deterrence. In *Elstad* Justice O'Connor applied the cost-benefit analysis as follows:

In deciding "how sweeping the judicially imposed consequences" of a failure to administer *Miranda* warnings should be, the *Tucker* Court noted that neither the general goal of deterring improper police conduct nor the Fifth Amendment goal of assuring trustworthy evidence would be served by suppression of the witness' testimony. * * *

We believe that this reasoning applies with equal force when the alleged "fruit" of a noncoercive *Miranda* violation is neither a witness nor an article of evidence but the accused's own voluntary testimony. As in *Tucker,* the absence of any coercion or improper tactics undercuts the twin rationales—trustworthiness and deterrence—for a broader rule. Once warned, the suspect is free to exercise his own volition in deciding whether or not to make a statement to the authorities.

* * * It is an unwarranted extension of *Miranda* to hold that a simple failure to administer the warnings, unaccompanied by any actual coercion or other circumstances calculated to undermine the suspect's ability to exercise his free will so taints the investigatory process that a subsequent voluntary and informed waiver is ineffective for some indeterminate period. Though *Miranda* requires that the unwarned admission must be suppressed, the admissibility of any subsequent statement should turn in these circumstances solely on whether it is knowingly and voluntarily made.

Was the First Confession Involuntary?

Justice O'Connor recognized that if Elstad's *first* confession was involuntary within the meaning of the Due Process Clause, then the second confession would have to be excluded if it were derived from the first. But she rejected Elstad's argument that his first confession was involuntary simply because it was not preceded by *Miranda* warnings.

There is a vast difference between the direct consequences flowing from coercion of a confession by physical violence or other deliberate means calculated to break the suspect's will and the uncertain consequences of disclosure of a "guilty secret" freely given in response to an unwarned but non-coercive question, as in this case. * * * We must conclude that, absent deliberately coercive or improper tactics in obtaining the initial statement, the mere fact that a suspect has made an unwarned admission does not warrant a presumption of compulsion. A subsequent administration of *Miranda* warnings to a suspect who has given a voluntary but unwarned statement ordinarily should suffice to remove the conditions that precluded admission of the earlier statement.

Criticism of Elstad

Justice Brennan, joined by Justice Marshall, dissented in *Elstad*. Justice Brennan argued that the majority had dealt a "crippling blow to *Miranda*," by allowing police officers to obtain an unwarned confession virtually secure in the knowledge that by giving warnings they could then obtain a second confession which would be admissible. He reasoned as follows:

For all practical purposes, the pre-warning and post-warning questioning are often but stages of one overall interrogation. Whether or not the authorities explicitly confront the suspect with his earlier illegal admissions makes no significant difference, of course, because the suspect knows that the authorities know of his earlier statements and most frequently will believe that those statements have already sealed his fate.

Justice Brennan concluded that "the correct approach, administered for almost 20 years by most courts with no untoward results, is to presume that an admission or confession obtained in violation of *Miranda* taints a subsequent confession unless the prosecution can show the taint is so attenuated as to justify [its] admission."

Justice Stevens wrote a separate dissent, arguing that the majority's distinction between "police misconduct that warrants a finding of actual coercion" and "police misconduct that establishes an irrebuttable presumption of coercion" was untenable as well as unfaithful to *Miranda.*

Do you agree with Justice Brennan that *Elstad* has dealt *Miranda* a "crippling blow"? Consider Bryant v. Vose, 785 F.2d 364 (1st Cir.1986), where officers obtained an unwarned confession, then gave warnings and obtained a second confession soon thereafter. *Both* confessions were admitted at trial. On review, the court found both confessions voluntary, and held that while the first confession should have been excluded under *Miranda,* its admission was harmless because the jury "learned no more from the improperly admitted confession than it did from the properly admitted one." Is this result consistent with *Elstad?*[19]

Physical Evidence Derived From Miranda–Defective Confessions

In New York v. Quarles, 467 U.S. 649 (1984), Justice O'Connor in a concurring opinion argued that physical evidence obtained as a fruit of a *Miranda*-defective confession should not be excluded. This concurrence, together with the reasoning in *Tucker* and *Elstad,* has persuaded most courts that all evidentiary fruits of a *Miranda*-defective confession are admissible. See United States v. Gonzalez–Sandoval, 894 F.2d 1043 (9th Cir.1990)(reasoning of *Tucker* and *Elstad* "applies as well to non-testimonial physical evidence obtained as a result of a *Miranda* violation").

Post-Dickerson Elstad Jurisprudence

The *Elstad* rule rests uneasily after *Dickerson.* Perhaps this is why the Supreme Court has granted certiorari in two cases that raise *Miranda*-fruits issues in the 2003–2004 term. Those two cases are:

1.　**United States v. Patane**, 304 F.3d 1013 (10th Cir. 2002):

Patane was arrested and when the officer started to give the *Miranda* warnings, Patane stopped him and said he knew his rights. Patane then made incriminating statements that led to the discovery of a gun. The Court

---

19.　In People v. Bethea, 67 N.Y.2d 364, 502 N.Y.S.2d 713, 493 N.E.2d 937 (1986), the court rejected *Elstad* as a matter of state constitutional law. It concluded that the state privilege against compelled self-incrimination "would have little deterrent effect if the police know that they can as part of a continuous chain of events question a suspect in custody without warning, provided only they thereafter question him or her again after warnings have been given."

of Appeals held that both the statements and the gun had to be excluded. The court distinguished Michigan v. Tucker and Oregon v. Elstad, both of which rejected the application of the fruits doctrine to *Miranda* violations based on the asserted prophylactic nature of *Miranda* rights. The Court of Appeals noted that lower courts have divided over the scope of the *Elstad* rule after *Dickerson*. The Tenth Circuit refused to adopt the Third and Fourth Circuit's blanket rule that the fruits doctrine never applies to *Miranda* violations—in other words, that *Elstad* survives in full force after *Dickerson*. The Tenth Circuit held that physical fruits of *Miranda* violations should be suppressed when suppression of the statement alone would not provide sufficient deterrence in order to protect *Miranda* rights. Applying a cost-benefit analysis, the Court of Appeals found exclusion of the physical evidence was required. The Supreme Court granted certiorari in *Patane* to address whether the failure to give *Miranda* warnings requires suppression of physical evidence derived from the unwarned but voluntary statements.

2. Missouri v. Seibert, 93 S.W.3d 700 (Sup. Ct. Mo. 2002): Seibert was arrested on suspicion of murder. Officers approached her interrogation with a two-step plan: 1) get a confession from her without giving *Miranda* warnings; 2) then give her *Miranda* warnings and get another confession, which would be admissible under *Elstad*. Their plan worked beautifully. But the State court held that the *Elstad* rule could not apply where the failure to give *Miranda* warnings is intentional. The Court reasoned that the exclusion of fruits of the confession would have an important deterrent effect where the violation is intentional. The Supreme Court granted review in *Seibert* to address whether the fruits of a Miranda-defective confession must be excluded when the failure to read the warnings is intentional.

The Supreme Court's decisions in *Seibert* and *Patane* will be found in the Supplement when they are handed down.

3. An Emergency Exception

New York v. Quarles

In New York v. Quarles, 467 U.S. 649 (1984), the Court concluded that "overriding considerations of public safety" can justify an officer's failure to provide *Miranda* warnings, and that an unwarned confession obtained under such circumstances is admissible despite *Miranda*. The Court relied on the now-discredited rationale that a violation of *Miranda* was not a violation of the Constitution. After *Dickerson*, the *Quarles* public safety exception to *Miranda* is apparently justified as a necessary exception to the constitutionally-based *Miranda* rule—much like the exigent circumstances exception to the constitutionally-based warrant requirement. See United States v. Talley, 275 F.3d 560 (6th Cir. 2001) ("the *Dickerson* majority expressly incorporated existing decisions, like *Quarles*, into the 'constitutional' right to a *Miranda* warning").

Justice Rehnquist wrote for the majority in *Quarles* and stated the facts as follows:

> On September 11, 1980, at approximately 12:30 a.m., Officer Frank Kraft and Officer Sal Scarring were on road patrol in Queens, New York, when a young woman approached their car. She told them that she had just

been raped by a black male, approximately six feet tall, who was wearing a black jacket with the name "Big Ben" printed in yellow letters on the back. She told the officers that the man had just entered an A & P supermarket located nearby and that the man was carrying a gun.

The officers drove the woman to the supermarket, and Officer Kraft entered the store while Officer Scarring radioed for assistance. Officer Kraft quickly spotted respondent, who matched the description given by the woman, approaching a check-out counter. Apparently upon seeing the officer, respondent turned and ran toward the rear of the store, and Officer Kraft pursued him with a drawn gun. When respondent turned the corner at the end of an aisle, Officer Kraft lost sight of him for several seconds, and upon regaining sight of respondent, ordered him to stop and put his hands over his head.

Although more than three other officers had arrived on the scene by that time, Officer Kraft was the first to reach respondent. He frisked him and discovered that he was wearing a shoulder holster which was then empty. After handcuffing him, Officer Kraft asked him where the gun was. Respondent nodded in the direction of some empty cartons and responded, "the gun is over there." Officer Kraft thereafter retrieved a loaded .38 caliber revolver from one of the cartons.

The Court agreed with the state courts that the facts demonstrated custodial interrogation and thus the confession would appear to fall within the exclusionary rule of *Miranda,* because Quarles never received the warnings. But it explained the need for an exception for emergency circumstances as follows:

The police in this case, in the very act of apprehending a suspect, were confronted with the immediate necessity of ascertaining the whereabouts of a gun which they had every reason to believe the suspect had just removed from his empty holster and discarded in the supermarket. So long as the gun was concealed somewhere in the supermarket, with its actual whereabouts unknown, it obviously posed more than one danger to the public safety: an accomplice might make use of it, a customer or employee might later come upon it.

In such a situation, if the police are required to recite the familiar *Miranda* warnings before asking the whereabouts of the gun, suspects in Quarles' position might well be deterred from responding. Procedural safeguards which deter a suspect from responding were deemed acceptable in *Miranda* in order to protect the Fifth Amendment privilege; when the primary social cost of those added protections is the possibility of fewer convictions, the *Miranda* majority was willing to bear that cost. Here, had *Miranda* warnings deterred Quarles from responding to Officer Kraft's question about the whereabouts of the gun, the cost would have been something more than merely the failure to obtain evidence useful in convicting Quarles. Officer Kraft needed an answer to his question not simply to make his case against Quarles but to insure that further danger to the public did not result from the concealment of the gun in a public area.

* * * We decline to place officers such as Officer Kraft in the untenable position of having to consider, often in a matter of seconds, whether it best serves society for them to ask the necessary questions without the *Miranda* warnings and render whatever probative evidence they uncover inadmissible, or for them to give the warnings in order to preserve the admissibility of evidence they might uncover but possibly damage or destroy their ability to obtain that evidence and neutralize the volatile situation confronting them.

Although the Court recognized that it had "to some degree * * * lessen[ed] the desirable clarity of" the *Miranda* rule, it stated that "we recognize here the importance of a workable rule to guide police officers, who have only limited time and expertise to reflect on and balance the social and individual interests involved in the specific circumstances they confront." It expressed the belief that "the exception we recognize today lessens the necessity of that on-the-scene balancing process." The Court held that the both the gun and the statement revealing its location were therefore admissible despite the *Miranda* violation.

Justice O'Connor concurred in part and dissented in part. She dissented from the public safety exception created by the Court on the ground that it would be confusing and contrary to *Miranda's* bright line approach. She offered the following criticism of the majority's public safety exception:

> In my view, a "public safety" exception unnecessarily blurs the edges of the clear line heretofore established and makes *Miranda's* requirements more difficult to understand. In some cases, police will benefit because a reviewing court will find that an exigency excused their failure to administer the required warnings. But in other cases, police will suffer because, though they thought an exigency excused their noncompliance, a reviewing court will view the "objective" circumstances differently and require exclusion of admissions thereby obtained. The end result will be a finespun new doctrine on public safety exigencies incident to custodial interrogation, complete with the hair-splitting distinctions that currently plague our Fourth Amendment jurisprudence. * * *

Justice O'Connor argued that *Miranda* does not prevent an officer from *asking* unwarned questions in order to protect public safety interests. It simply prohibits admission at trial of incriminating answers.

> *Miranda* has never been read to prohibit the police from asking questions to secure the public safety. Rather, the critical question *Miranda* addresses is who shall bear the cost of securing the public safety when such questions are asked and answered: the defendant or the State. *Miranda,* for better or worse, found the resolution of that question implicit in the prohibition against compulsory self-incrimination and placed the burden on the State. When police ask custodial questions without administering the required warnings, *Miranda* quite clearly requires that the answers received be presumed compelled and that they be excluded from evidence at trial.

While disagreeing with the majority's implementation of a public safety exception, and thus dissenting from the Court's ruling that Quarles' statement was admissible, Justice O'Connor concurred in the result as to the admission of the gun. In her view, the gun was admissible because *Miranda* does not require exclusion of the fruits of *Miranda*-defective confessions.

Justice Marshall dissented and was joined by Justices Brennan and Stevens. He disagreed as to the existence of an emergency in the case, describing the facts in the following way:

> [C]ontrary to the majority's intimations, no customers or employees were wandering about the store in danger of coming across Quarles'

discarded weapon. Although the supermarket was open to the public, Quarles' arrest took place during the middle of the night when the store was apparently deserted except for the clerks at the checkout counter. The police could easily have cordoned off the store and searched for the missing gun. Had they done so, they would have found the gun forthwith. The police were well aware that Quarles had discarded his weapon somewhere near the scene of the arrest.

The Scope of the Public Safety Exception

The Court in *Quarles* had no occasion to indicate the scope of the public safety exception to *Miranda*. Are the police permitted to keep a suspect in custody for an extended period without *Miranda* warnings if they claim to be seeking information to protect the public? For example, if a murder suspect is arrested and a firearm was used to commit the murder, may the police delay *Miranda* warnings for several hours so that they can interrogate the suspect about the whereabouts of the firearm? Or, is it critical that in *Quarles* the officer acted in the heat of the moment as he came upon a crime scene? See United States v. Mobley, 40 F.3d 688 (4th Cir.1994), where the court found that an officer's question concerning the location of a gun in a house was not within the public safety exception. The officers went to the defendant's house to arrest him for a narcotics violation, the defendant was naked when he answered the door, and before asking the question about the gun, the officers had already conducted a protective sweep and found that no other persons were present. The court found no "immediate need" to ask about a gun and declared that "[t]here is nothing that separates these facts from those of an ordinary arrest scenario." Therefore the defendant's statement about the location of the gun could not be admitted under *Miranda*.

Categorical Application of the Public Safety Exception

Can the public safety exception be applied categorically to certain arrest situations? Consider United States v. Carrillo, 16 F.3d 1046 (9th Cir.1994). Carrillo was arrested after a narcotics transaction, and transported to a detention facility. At that point, Officer Weeks decided to search Carrillo. Before beginning the search, however, the officer asked Carrillo if he had any drugs or needles on his person. Carrillo responded, "No, I don't use drugs, I sell them." This statement was used against Carrillo as an admission at trial. Carrillo argued that the statement should have been suppressed because it was made before he had been given a *Miranda* warning. But the court held that the statement was properly admitted under the "public safety" exception to *Miranda*. The court noted that at the suppression hearing, Officer Weeks testified that during past searches he had been poked by needles and suffered headaches and skin irritation from contact with illegal drugs. The court reasoned as follows:

> Officer Weeks's question stemmed from an objectively reasonable need to protect himself from immediate danger. Officer Weeks testified that he asks this question as a matter of policy before searching a prisoner to avoid contact with syringes and toxic substances. The risk differs from that presented by a gun, but the danger of transmission of disease or contact

with harmful substances is real and serious enough; a pressing need for haste is not essential.

Our conclusion is buttressed by the non-investigatory nature of the officer's question. The question called for a "yes" or "no," not a testimonial response. Ordinarily, a question framed in this manner would not elicit any incriminating evidence not produced by the search itself. After Carrillo gave the incriminating but unrequested response, the officer asked no more questions. Although the test is an objective one, the officer's deliberate refusal to pursue the subject heightens our confidence that, in this case, the narrowly tailored question was a reasonable attempt by a police officer to insure his personal safety in the midst of a search. Consequently, the spontaneous and unrequested response of the suspect was properly admitted under the *Quarles* public safety exception to *Miranda*.

Does the *Carrillo* holding mean that "public safety" permits an officer to dispense with *Miranda* warnings and ask *any* arrestee (e.g., those arrested for theft or white collar crime) whether they are carrying drugs or syringes? See also United States v. Lackey, 334 F.3d 1224 (10th Cir. 2003) (it was proper, under the public safety exception, to ask an arrestee whether he was carrying any guns or sharp objects, before conducting a search incident to the arrest; the defendant's response, "no I am not, but there is a gun in the car" was properly admitted under *Quarles*).

D. OPEN QUESTIONS AFTER *MIRANDA*

The Court in Miranda held broadly that warnings were required before the police could engage in custodial interrogation of the defendant. These broad parameters left many important questions for police and the courts. What does it mean for the suspect to be "in custody"? When is a suspect being "interrogated"? Must the warnings be given pursuant to a standard and precise script? These and other important questions are discussed in this section.

1. *What is Custody?*

The Supreme Court held in *Miranda* that the police must give an accused the *Miranda* warnings before commencing a custodial interrogation. If the defendant who confesses is not in custody, *Miranda* does not apply, and the admissibility of the confession is based on whether is was given voluntarily under the totality of the circumstances. As one court put it: "Because the presence of *both* a custodial setting and official interrogation is required to trigger the *Miranda* right * * * absent one or the other, *Miranda* is not implicated." Alston v. Redman, 34 F.3d 1237 (3d Cir.1994).

Arrest is Custody

An important question, therefore, is "what constitutes 'custody'?" According to *Miranda,* the test is whether a person is deprived of his freedom of action in any significant way. In several cases subsequent to *Miranda,* the Court specifically addressed the custody question. In Orozco v. Texas, 394 U.S. 324 (1969), it held that the defendant was in custody when four armed policemen entered his bedroom at 4:00 a. m. and tried to elicit incriminating information from him. In so deciding, the Court noted that one of the four officers had testified that the defendant was under arrest and not free to leave his bedroom. Clearly, if a person is arrested, he is in custody.

Conversely, in Beckwith v. United States, 425 U.S. 341 (1976), the Court found that the defendant was not in custody for purposes of receiving *Miranda* warnings where two I.R.S. agents arrived at his house at 8:00 p.m., were invited in, and sat with the defendant at his dining room table to discuss their investigation of his federal income tax returns. The agents were looking into the possibility of criminal tax fraud. The Court maintained that although Beckwith was the focus of a tax investigation, he was not in a custodial situation when he talked with the agents in his home. The Court stated that if the defendant is not in custody the inherently coercive atmosphere that triggers the need for *Miranda* warnings is not present.

Prisoners in Custody

In Mathis v. United States, 391 U.S. 1 (1968), the defendant was interrogated while in jail by I.R.S. agents about his alleged tax evasion. The Court found that although the defendant was in jail for reasons unrelated to the tax investigation, he was still in custody, and the failure to give him his *Miranda* warnings violated his constitutional rights.

Subsequent cases have refused to read *Mathis* as establishing a per se rule that prisoners are always in custody for *Miranda* purposes. Rather, the question is whether prison officials' conduct would cause "a reasonable person to believe his freedom of movement had been *further* diminished." Garcia v. Singletary, 13 F.3d 1487 (11th Cir.1994). In *Garcia*, an inmate had set fire to his cell, and a guard took him out of the cell and asked the inmate why he set the fire. The inmate gave an incriminating answer. The court held that *Miranda* did not apply:

> Because Garcia was the only person in the cell during the fire and failing to remove him would have endangered his safety, [the guard's] action added no further restraint on Garcia's freedom to depart. In fact, removing Garcia from his cell provided him with greater freedom of movement and significantly reduced those preexisting restrictions.

Compare United States v. Chamberlain, 163 F.3d 499 (8th Cir.1998) (prisoner was in custody for *Miranda* purposes when he was taken from his cell to an office and interrogated, and leaving the interrogation would have constituted a violation of prison rules).

Interrogation at the Police Station: Oregon v. Mathiason

In Oregon v. Mathiason, 429 U.S. 492 (1977), a per curiam opinion, the Court ruled that an individual questioned at a police station is not necessarily in custody. An officer told Mathiason over the phone that he wanted to discuss something with him and asked if they could meet somewhere. Mathiason had no preference, so the policeman asked if he could come down to the station house. Mathiason agreed, and arriving a short time later, was told that he was not under arrest. Mathiason was ushered into an office, the door was closed and the two sat across a desk. No *Miranda* warnings were given. The officer told Mathiason about the burglary he was investigating, that he believed Mathiason was involved, and that his fingerprints were found at the scene (which was not true). Mathiason confessed, and was then allowed to leave the police station.

The Court concluded that Mathiason's freedom was not restrained so as to render him in custody under *Miranda*. The Court stressed that Mathiason went down to the station voluntarily, was informed that he was not under arrest, and left the station without hindrance after he confessed. The dissenters, Justices Brennan, Marshall, and Stevens, stressed that Mathiason was a parolee and so it could not be truly said that he went down to the station of his own accord. Does *Mathiason* encourage suspects to be cooperative with the police? If it is important that a suspect is allowed to leave, can't that factor be manipulated by officers after *Mathiason*?

In California v. Beheler, 463 U.S. 1121 (1983), the Court extended *Mathiason* to find that the suspect was not in custody when he agreed to accompany police officers down to the station for questioning. He was told he was not under arrest and was released after confessing. Should there be a difference between going to the station unaccompanied and going to the station with police officers?

Meetings With a Probation Officer: Minnesota v. Murphy

Justice White wrote for six Justices in Minnesota v. Murphy, 465 U.S. 420 (1984), as the Court held that the privilege against self-incrimination was not violated when a probation officer called Murphy, a probationer, to her office and questioned him about the rape and murder of a teenage girl. Murphy had admitted the offenses to a counselor as part of the treatment prescribed as a condition of probation. The Court held that *Miranda* did not require the officer to warn Murphy of his rights prior to asking questions about crimes he might have committed, since Murphy was not arrested or otherwise in custody although he was required to meet with the officer. Although the Court recognized that the officer sought incriminating information, it reiterated its statement in *Beckwith* that warnings are not required simply because an investigation has focused upon a suspect.

Justice Marshall, joined by Justice Stevens and in part by Justice Brennan, dissented. He argued that a reasonable man in Murphy's position would have believed that his duty to answer questions honestly as a condition of probation required him to respond to the questions put by the officer.

Objective Test: Stansbury v. California

In Stansbury v. California, 511 U.S. 318 (1994)(per curiam), the Court held, "not for the first time, that an officer's subjective and undisclosed view concerning whether the person being interrogated is a suspect is irrelevant to the assessment whether the person is in custody." An officer questioned Stansbury about a murder, thinking that Stansbury was a potential witness. When the questioning began, the officer believed that another man was the prime suspect. But after Stansbury gave incriminating information in response to a few questions, it became clear to the officer that the defendant was the perpetrator. At that point, the officer gave Stansbury *Miranda* warnings. There was no indication that the officer's initial lack of suspicion had been imparted to Stansbury.

The question for the Court was whether Stansbury's initial statements had been obtained in violation of *Miranda*. Stansbury argued that he was in custody during the period of initial questioning because he was questioned in the jail part of the police station, by officers whose guns were visible. But the lower courts found that Stansbury was not in custody until the officer's suspicions shifted to him as a result of the initial questioning.

The Supreme Court unanimously held that the lower courts were incorrect in focusing on the officer's undisclosed state of mind. It reasoned as follows:

> It is well settled * * * that a police officer's subjective view that the individual under questioning is a suspect, if undisclosed, does not bear upon the question whether the individual is in custody for purposes of *Miranda*. The same principle obtains if an officer's undisclosed assessment is that the person being questioned is not a suspect. In either instance, one cannot expect the person under interrogation to probe the officer's innermost thoughts. * * *
>
> * * * [A]n officer's views concerning the nature of an interrogation, or beliefs concerning the potential culpability of the individual being questioned, may be one among many factors that bear upon the assessment whether that individual was in custody, but only if the officer's views or beliefs were somehow manifested to the individual under interrogation and would have affected how a reasonable person in that position would perceive his or her freedom to leave.

The Court remanded to the lower court to determine the question of custody without relying on the officer's subjective and undisclosed opinions.

Terry Stops: Berkemer v. McCarty

If a police officer interrogates a suspect during a *Terry* stop, must the officer give *Miranda* warnings? In Berkemer v. McCarty, 468 U.S. 420 (1984), the Court in an opinion by Justice Marshall held that *Terry* stops are not custodial for *Miranda* purposes. Justice Marshall noted that *Terry* stops are typically of brief duration; questioning is limited, because the officer can ask only a "moderate number of questions to determine identity and to try to obtain information confirming or dispelling the officer's suspicions;" the detainee is not obliged to respond; and unless probable cause arises in a short time, the detainee must be released. Justice Marshall concluded that *Terry* stops were "comparatively nonthreatening" and hence unlike the custodial situations required to trigger *Miranda*. If the stop escalates to an arrest, however, *Miranda* will apply.

Thus, the law distinguishing *Terry* stops from arrests discussed in Chapter Two (see, e.g., Dunaway v. New York, supra) also determines whether custody exists under *Miranda*. See Saltzburg, Foreword: The Flow and Ebb of Constitutional Criminal Procedure in the Warren and Burger Courts, 69 Geo.L.J. 151, 200–03 (1980). See also United States v. Ozuna, 170 F.3d 654 (6th Cir.1999) (limited interrogation at customs checkpoint is not custodial within the meaning of *Miranda:* "All persons attempting to enter the United States must anticipate detention while answering a few basic questions and this cuts against the potentially coercive aspect of the Customs inquiry.").

Summary on Custody: Relevant Factors

One court has set forth six indicia for determining whether a suspect is in custody for *Miranda* purposes:

(1) whether the suspect was informed at the time of questioning that the questioning was voluntary, that the suspect was free to leave or request the officers to do so, or that the suspect was not considered under arrest; (2) whether the suspect possessed unrestrained freedom of movement during questioning; (3) whether the suspect initiated contact with authorities or voluntarily acquiesced to official request to respond to questions; (4) whether strong arm tactics or deceptive stratagems were employed during questioning; (5) whether the atmosphere of the questioning was police dominated; and (6) whether the suspect was placed under arrest at the termination of the questioning.

United States v. Brown, 990 F.2d 397 (8th Cir.1993). The *Brown* court stated that "[t]he presence of the first three indicia tends to mitigate the existence of custody at the time of questioning" while "the presence of the last three indicia aggravate the existence of custody."

How would the above six-factor test apply to the following facts?

On February 25, 1989, the Twin Cities Federal Savings and Loan Association (TCF) was robbed by two men armed with a shotgun and possibly a handgun. [Eyewitness descriptions and other information led the officers to focus on Griffin as a suspect. The officers telephoned Griffin's house].

* * * Griffin's stepfather answered the phone and informed the agents that Griffin would be home early that evening. Agents Waldie and Tremper proceeded to Griffin's home, arriving at 7 p.m., and were invited into the living room by Griffin's stepfather. The purpose of the interview was to determine what Griffin knew of the bank robbery. The officers did not intend to arrest him at that time. The agents waited in the living room until 8:15 p.m. when Griffin was heard approaching the house outside. The agents moved to the hall near the front door to meet Griffin as he entered the house. Waldie and Tremper identified themselves as F.B.I. agents investigating a bank robbery and informed Griffin that they needed to speak with him. At that point, before any other words were spoken, Griffin stated, "The gun wasn't loaded."

The agents explained to Griffin's parents that it was necessary for them to speak to Griffin in private and, accordingly, the three went into the dining room and sat down. The agents did not draw their guns, handcuff Griffin, or place him under formal arrest. Griffin's parents retired to the upstairs of the house where they remained throughout the course of the questioning.

Neither of the agents informed Griffin that he was not under arrest, that he was free to request the agents to leave without speaking to them, nor did they inform him of his *Miranda* rights. Twice during the two-hour interview Griffin asked to obtain cigarettes from other places in the house and each time Agent Waldie required that Agent Tremper escort him.

Griffin was told he was to stay in their view at all times. The agents used this procedure to ensure their personal safety because a weapon had been used in the course of the robbery, although this was not explained to Griffin at the time.

During the interview, Griffin appeared nervous, "sort of choked up for words" and "fearful" of the agents. In the course of the questioning Griffin implicated himself and Chapman in the robbery. The agents questioned Griffin for approximately two hours. At the conclusion of the interview the agents placed Griffin under arrest. Griffin was then transported to the F.B.I. office where, three hours after his initial confrontation with the agents, he was advised of his *Miranda* rights for the first time.

In United States v. Griffin, 922 F.2d 1343 (8th Cir.1990), the Court analyzed the above facts and held that Griffin was in custody when he confessed. Do you agree? Which of the factors cut most strongly in Griffin's favor? Which cut most strongly in the government's favor? Compare United States v. Wyatt, 179 F.3d 532 (7th Cir.1999) (suspect was not in custody when he was escorted out of a bar with his consent, brought into a well-lighted parking lot, patted down, and questioned about his involvement in a bank robbery; court notes that the suspect was "never physically restrained"); United States v. Kim, 292 F.3d 969 (9th Cir. 2002) (suspect was in custody when she was detained inside her shop, the officers locked the door, and she was interrogated for about an hour about illegal drug sales, ordered to respond in English, and not informed that she was free to leave).

2. *What is Interrogation?*

In addition to the custody requirement, the police must also be interrogating the individual before the need for *Miranda* warnings arises. Thus, volunteered statements or "threshold" confessions (where the defendant walks into the police station and immediately confesses) are not barred by the fact that they were made without *Miranda* warnings.

The following case sets forth the Supreme Court's guidelines for determining when interrogation can be found.

RHODE ISLAND v. INNIS

Supreme Court of the United States, 1980.
446 U.S. 291.

Mr. Justice Stewart delivered the opinion of the Court.

In Miranda v. Arizona, the Court held that, once a defendant in custody asks to speak with a lawyer, all interrogation must cease until a lawyer is present. The issue in this case is whether the respondent was "interrogated" in violation of the standards promulgated in the *Miranda* opinion.

I

[Innis was identified as the perpetrator in the shooting death of a cab driver. Some time later, Innis was seen on the street and arrested by Patrolman Lovell. He was unarmed. Lovell gave Innis *Miranda* warnings.]

Within minutes, Sergeant Sears arrived at the scene of the arrest, and he also gave the respondent the *Miranda* warnings. Immediately thereafter, Captain Leyden and other police officers arrived. Captain Leyden advised the respondent of his *Miranda* rights. The respondent stated that he understood those rights and wanted to speak with a lawyer. Captain Leyden then directed that the respondent be placed in a "caged wagon," a four-door police car with a wire screen mesh between the front and rear seats, and be driven to the central police station. Three officers, Patrolmen Gleckman, Williams, and McKenna, were assigned to accompany the respondent to the central station. They placed the respondent in the vehicle and shut the doors. Captain Leyden then instructed the officers not to question the respondent or intimidate or coerce him in any way. The three officers then entered the vehicle, and it departed.

While enroute to the central station, Patrolman Gleckman initiated a conversation with Patrolman McKenna concerning the missing shotgun. As Patrolman Gleckman later testified:

"A. At this point, I was talking back and forth with Patrolman McKenna stating that I frequent this area while on patrol and [that because a school for handicapped children is located nearby,] there's a lot of handicapped children running around in this area, and God forbid one of them might find a weapon with shells and they might hurt themselves."

Patrolman McKenna apparently shared his fellow officer's concern:

"A. I more or less concurred with him [Gleckman] that it was a safety factor and that we should, you know, continue to search for the weapon and try to find it."

While Patrolman Williams said nothing, he overheard the conversation between the two officers:

"A. He [Gleckman] said it would be too bad if the little—I believe he said girl—would pick up the gun, maybe kill herself."

The respondent then interrupted the conversation, stating that the officers should turn the car around so he could show them where the gun was located. * * * At the time the respondent indicated that the officers should turn back, they had traveled no more than a mile, a trip encompassing only a few minutes.

The police vehicle then returned to the scene of the arrest where a search for the shotgun was in progress. There, Captain Leyden again advised the respondent of his *Miranda* rights. The respondent replied that he understood those rights but that he "wanted to get the gun out of the way because of the kids in the area in the school." The respondent then led the police to a nearby field, where he pointed out the shotgun under some rocks by the side of the road. [A motion to suppress was denied by the trial court and Innis was convicted. But the state appellate court found that Innis had been subject to interrogation about the gun.]

* * *

II

* * *

In the present case, the parties are in agreement that the respondent was fully informed of his *Miranda* rights and that he invoked his *Miranda* right to counsel when he told Captain Leyden that he wished to consult with a lawyer. It is also uncontested that the respondent was "in custody" while being transported to the police station.

The issue, therefore, is whether the respondent was "interrogated" by the police officers in violation of the respondent's undisputed right under *Miranda* to remain silent until he had consulted with a lawyer.[a] In resolving this issue, we first define the term "interrogation" under *Miranda* before turning to a consideration of the facts of this case.

A

The starting point for defining "interrogation" in this context is, of course, the Court's *Miranda* opinion. There the Court observed that "[b]y custodial interrogation, we mean *questioning* initiated by law enforcement officers after a person has been taken into custody or otherwise deprived of his freedom of action in any significant way." This passage and other references throughout the opinion to "questioning" might suggest that the *Miranda* rules were to apply only to those police interrogation practices that involve express questioning of a defendant while in custody.

We do not, however, construe the *Miranda* opinion so narrowly. The concern of the Court in *Miranda* was that the "interrogation environment" created by the interplay of interrogation and custody would "subjugate the individual to the will of his examiner" and thereby undermine the privilege against compulsory self-incrimination. The police practices that evoked this concern included several that did not involve express questioning. * * *

This is not to say, however, that all statements obtained by the police after a person has been taken into custody are to be considered the product of interrogation. * * * It is clear therefore that the special procedural safeguards outlined in *Miranda* are required not where a suspect is simply taken into custody, but rather where a suspect in custody is subjected to interrogation. "Interrogation," as conceptualized in the *Miranda* opinion, must reflect a measure of compulsion above and beyond that inherent in custody itself.[b] * * *

We conclude that the *Miranda* safeguards come into play whenever a person in custody is subjected to either express questioning or its functional equivalent. That is to say, the term "interrogation" under *Miranda* refers not only to express questioning, but also to any words or actions on the part of the police (other than those normally attendant to arrest and custody) that the police should know are reasonably likely to elicit an incriminating response[c] from the suspect. The latter portion of this definition focuses primarily upon the perceptions of the suspect, rather than the intent of the police. This focus reflects the fact that the *Miranda* safeguards were designed to vest a suspect in custody with an added measure of protection against

---

a. Since we conclude that the respondent was not "interrogated" for *Miranda* purposes, we do not reach the question whether the respondent waived his right under *Miranda* to be free from interrogation until counsel was present.

b. There is language in the opinion of the Rhode Island Supreme Court in this case suggesting that the definition of "interrogation" under *Miranda* is informed by this Court's decision in Brewer v. Williams [discussed infra in the section on the Sixth Amendment]. This suggestion is erroneous. Our decision in *Brewer* rested solely on the Sixth and Fourteenth Amendment right to counsel. That right, as we held in *Massiah*, prohibits law enforcement officers from "deliberately elicit[ing]" incriminating information from a defendant in the

absence of counsel after a formal charge against the defendant has been filed. Custody in such a case is not controlling; * * *. By contrast, the right to counsel at issue in the present case is based not on the Sixth and Fourteenth Amendments, but rather on the Fifth and Fourteenth Amendments as interpreted in the *Miranda* opinion. The definitions of "interrogation" under the Fifth and Sixth Amendments, if indeed the term "interrogation" is even apt in the Sixth Amendment context, are not necessarily interchangeable, since the policies underlying the two constitutional protections are quite distinct.

c. By "incriminating response" we refer to any response—whether inculpatory or exculpatory—that the *prosecution* may seek to introduce at trial. * * *

coercive police practices, without regard to objective proof of the underlying intent of the police. A practice that the police should know is reasonably likely to evoke an incriminating response from a suspect thus amounts to interrogation.[d] But, since the police surely cannot be held accountable for the unforeseeable results of their words or actions, the definition of interrogation can extend only to words or actions on the part of police officers that they *should have known* were reasonably likely to elicit an incriminating response.[e]

B

Turning to the facts of the present case, we conclude that the respondent was not "interrogated" within the meaning of *Miranda*. It is undisputed that the first prong of the definition of "interrogation" was not satisfied, for the conversation between Patrolmen Gleckman and McKenna included no express questioning of the respondent. Rather, that conversation was, at least in form nothing more than a dialogue between the two officers to which no response from the respondent was invited.

* * *

Moreover, it cannot be fairly concluded that the respondent was subjected to the "functional equivalent" of questioning. * * * There is nothing in the record to suggest that the officers were aware that the respondent was peculiarly susceptible to an appeal to his conscience concerning the safety of handicapped children, or that the police knew that the respondent was unusually disoriented or upset at the time of his arrest.

The case thus boils down to whether, in the context of a brief conversation, the officers should have known that the respondent would suddenly be moved to make a self-incriminating response. Given the fact that the entire conversation appears to have consisted of no more than a few off-hand remarks, we cannot say that the officers should have known that it was reasonably likely that Innis would so respond. This is not a case where the police carried on a lengthy harangue in the presence of the suspect. Nor does the record support the respondent's contention that, under the circumstances, the officers' comments were particularly "evocative."

* * *

[Justice White's concurring opinion, and Chief Justice Burger's opinion concurring in the judgment, are omitted].

Mr. Justice Marshall, **with whom** Mr. Justice Brennan **joins, dissenting.**

I am substantially in agreement with the Court's definition of "interrogation" within the meaning of Miranda v. Arizona. In my view, the *Miranda* safeguards apply whenever police conduct is intended or likely to produce a response from a suspect in custody. * * *

I am utterly at a loss, however, to understand how this objective stan-

---

d. This is not to say that the intent of the police is irrelevant, for it may well have a bearing on whether the police should have known that their words or actions were reasonably likely to evoke an incriminating response. In particular, where a police practice is designed to elicit an incriminating response from the accused, it is unlikely that the practice will not also be one which the police should have known was reasonably likely to have that effect.

e. Any knowledge the police may have had concerning the unusual susceptibility of a defendant to a particular form of persuasion might be an important factor in determining whether the police should have known that their words or actions were reasonably likely to elicit an incriminating response from the suspect.

dard as applied to the facts before us can rationally lead to the conclusion that there was no interrogation. * * *

One can scarcely imagine a stronger appeal to the conscience of a suspect—*any* suspect—than the assertion that if the weapon is not found an innocent person will be hurt or killed. And not just any innocent person, but an innocent child—a little girl—a helpless, handicapped little girl on her way to school. The notion that such an appeal could not be expected to have any effect unless the suspect were known to have some special interest in handicapped children verges on the ludicrous.

* * *

I firmly believe that this case is simply an aberration, and that in future cases the Court will apply the standard adopted today in accordance with its plain meaning.

JUSTICE STEVENS, **dissenting.**

* * *

* * * In my view any statement that would normally be understood by the average listener as calling for a response is the functional equivalent of a direct question, whether or not it is punctuated by a question mark. The Court, however, takes a much narrower view. It holds that police conduct is not the "functional equivalent" of direct questioning unless the police should have known that what they were saying or doing was likely to elicit an incriminating response from the suspect. This holding represents a plain departure from the principles set forth in *Miranda*.

* * *

[T]he Court's test creates an incentive for police to ignore a suspect's invocation of his rights in order to make continued attempts to extract information from him. If a suspect does not appear susceptible to a particular type of psychological pressure, the police are apparently free to exert that pressure on him despite his request for counsel, so long as they are careful not to punctuate their statements with question marks. And if, contrary to all reasonable expectations, the suspect makes an incriminating statement, that statement can be used against him at trial. * * *

Application of Innis: Arizona v. Mauro

Applying the *Innis* test to statements made by a suspect to his wife in the presence of a police officer who recorded the statements, the Supreme Court held, 5–4, in Arizona v. Mauro, 481 U.S. 520 (1987), that the police did not engage in interrogation. Police received a telephone call stating that a man had entered a store claiming to have killed his son. When officers reached the store, Mauro freely admitted that he had killed his son and directed officers to the body. The police arrested Mauro and gave him two sets of *Miranda* warnings. After the second set, given at the police station, Mauro indicated that he wished to say nothing more without a lawyer. Mrs. Mauro, who was being questioned separately, asked to speak with her husband. The police were reluctant to permit her to do so, but ultimately agreed to her request. An officer told the Mauros, however, that they could speak together only if an officer were present to observe and hear what was said. The officer placed a tape recorder in plain view. During the conversation between husband and wife, Mrs. Mauro expressed despair, and Mr. Mauro consoled her by saying that "You tried to stop me as best you can." Mauro's defense at trial was insanity, and the prosecutor played the tape at trial in rebuttal, arguing that it demonstrated that Mauro was sane.

Justice Powell wrote for the majority, as it concluded that there was no evidence that the officers sent Mrs. Mauro in to see her husband for the purpose of eliciting statements. Even though the officers conceded that they recognized a possibility that Mauro would incriminate himself while talking with his wife, Justice Powell concluded that "officers do not interrogate a suspect simply by hoping that he will incriminate himself." Justice Powell determined that "Mauro was not subjected to compelling influences, psychological ploys, or direct questioning," and "his volunteered statements cannot properly be considered the result of police interrogation." He added that "[p]olice departments need not adopt inflexible rules barring suspects from speaking with their spouses, nor must they ignore legitimate security concerns by allowing spouses to meet in private."

Justice Stevens, joined by Justices Brennan, Marshall, and Blackmun, dissented. He concluded that "it was not only likely, but highly probable, that one of the suspects would make a statement that the prosecutor might seek to introduce at trial," and that "[i]t follows that the police conduct in this case was the 'functional equivalent' of deliberate, direct interrogation."

Suppose the police officers refused to permit Mrs. Mauro to speak with her husband, and he had made a statement to the police. Wouldn't Mauro have argued that the refusal to permit contact was itself interrogation? If the dissenters are correct in *Mauro,* what advice would they give to police confronted with the *Mauro* facts?

Appeals to the Welfare of Others as Interrogation?

In *Innis*, the Court held that an average suspect would not likely be moved by an appeal based on harm to innocent children; the fact that Innis himself *was* so moved was not dispositive, because the test is whether an incriminating response would have been likely from an *average suspect*. Would an average suspect be affected by an appeal based on possible harm to a loved one? Consider United States v. Calisto, 838 F.2d 711 (3d Cir.1988), where officers searched Calisto's home and found large quantities of drugs in a bedroom. Calisto was placed under arrest by Officer McKeefry and invoked his right to silence. The officers knew that Calisto lived with his adult daughter. One of the searching officers came up to McKeefry and said that he had found both men's and women's clothing in the bedroom where the drugs had been located. Officer McKeefry responded, "Well, then we'll have to get an arrest warrant for the daughter." Calisto, who was a few feet away from McKeefry, said "Don't lock my daughter up. She has nothing to do with that stuff. That's mine. I'm the one you want." The court found that McKeefry's statement concerning the daughter was not interrogation, reasoning that his remark "was not directed at Calisto, was the kind of remark that an officer would normally make in carrying out his duties under the circumstances that confronted him, and was not made in a provocative manner." The court concluded that "even if it could be said that reasonable officers might have expected a protest of some kind from Calisto upon his hearing of his daughter's possible arrest, we do not think it was reasonable to expect an *inculpatory* response from Calisto." (emphasis added). Do you agree with the court? Why do the courts in *Innis* and *Calisto* take such a dim view of the character of an average suspect? Didn't the Court in *Miranda* specifically extend protection to elicitation of both inculpatory and exculpatory statements?

Confronting the Suspect With Incriminating Evidence

In Edwards v. Arizona, 451 U.S. 477 (1981), the Court found that Edwards had been interrogated when officers played for him a tape recorded statement of Edwards' associate, that implicated Edwards in the crime. See also People v. Ferro, 63 N.Y.2d 316, 482 N.Y.S.2d 237, 472 N.E.2d 13 (1984)(interrogation found where officers placed the fruits of Ferro's crime in front of his jail cell). Why does confronting the suspect with incriminating evidence constitute interrogation, while confronting the same suspect with a risk of harm to innocent children, as in *Innis*, does not?

It should be noted that despite the holding in *Edwards*, courts have not been uniform in finding interrogation whenever a suspect in custody is confronted with incriminating evidence. See Shedelbower v. Estelle, 885 F.2d 570 (9th Cir.1989)(lying to the defendant that he had just been identified by an eyewitness was not reasonably likely to elicit an incriminating response). The court in United States v. Payne, 954 F.2d 199 (4th Cir.1992), argued that it would be inappropriate to apply *Miranda* to every instance in which a person in custody is told about incriminating evidence against them:

> That no comment on the evidence in a case will ever issue in the presence of a criminal suspect seems to us neither realistic nor desirable as an absolute rule derived from the Fifth Amendment. Indeed, it may even be in the interest of a defendant to be kept informed about matters relating to the charges against him. * * * Information about the evidence against a suspect may also contribute to the intelligent exercise of his judgment regarding what course of conduct to follow.

> * * * It simply cannot be said that all such statements are objectively likely to result in incriminating responses by those in custody. The inquiry mandated by *Innis* into the perceptions of the suspect is necessarily contextual, and whether descriptions of incriminating evidence constitute the functional equivalent of interrogation will depend on circumstances that are too numerous to catalogue.

Of course it is true, as the *Payne* court states, that a suspect may have an interest in being apprised of the evidence against him. But does that mean that *Miranda* is inapplicable? *Miranda* does not prevent an officer from speaking to a suspect, it just requires that the information must be preceded by warnings and waiver in order for a resulting confession to be admissible. Hasn't the *Payne* court overlooked the fact that an officer who is trying to "help" the defendant by keeping him informed, can also help him by providing the warnings? If there is no per se rule, how does one tell whether confronting a suspect with incriminating evidence will constitute interrogation?

Direct vs. Indirect Statements

One factor mentioned in *Innis* as cutting against a finding of interrogation was that the officers were ostensibly talking among themselves; they did not direct their comments at Innis. Likewise, the officer's statement in *Calisto*, about arresting the defendant's daughter, was held not interrogation in part because it was not made in a "provocative" manner. The reasoning is that a comment not even directed at a suspect is less likely to produce an incriminating response. Conversely, if an officer is addressing the suspect directly, an incriminating response is presumably more likely. Illustrative is United States v. Soto, 953 F.2d 263 (6th Cir.1992). Soto was stopped for a traffic violation, gave suspicious answers to preliminary questions, and ultimately consented to a search of his car. The officer discovered narcotics in an opaque bag in the trunk, and Soto was placed under arrest. The officer continued to search the car, and came upon a photograph of Soto's wife and child. The officer pointed to the narcotics and said "What are you doing with crap like that when you have these two waiting for you at home?" Soto gave an incriminating answer. The court held that the officer's comment constituted impermissible interrogation. It reasoned that while the remark "was not couched in formal question and answer form, in substance it was a direct inquiry into Soto's reasons for committing the offense he appeared to have committed, and it elicited an incriminating response." Do you think the officer in *Soto* was trying to obtain an incriminating statement? Does that make any difference under *Innis*?

Questions Attendant to Custody: Pennsylvania v. Muniz

In *Innis,* the Court's definition of interrogation excludes questions "attendant to custody." Thus, officers can ask questions attendant to custody without *Miranda* warnings, and if the suspect's answer is incriminating, it is admissible at trial. This "booking exception" was further developed in Pennsylvania v. Muniz, 496 U.S. 582 (1990). Muniz was stopped on suspicion of drunk driving. He failed sobriety tests and was brought to a booking center, where he was asked, among other things, his name, address, height, weight, eye color, date of birth, and current age. Muniz stumbled over the answers and gave incorrect information on some points. His responses were admitted at his trial as evidence of drunkenness. Justice Brennan, writing for a plurality of four members of the Court, held that Muniz's answers to the questions were admissible, even though in response to custodial interrogation, because they fell within a "routine booking question exception which exempts from *Miranda's* coverage questions to secure the biographical data necessary to complete booking or pretrial services." The plurality noted that the booking exception would not apply if such questions were "designed to elicit incriminatory admissions."

Chief Justice Rehnquist, joined by Justices White, Blackmun, and Stevens, concurred in the result. The Chief Justice did not find it necessary to consider whether the questions to Muniz fell within a booking exception to *Miranda*. He found Muniz's answers to these questions to be non-testimonial, and hence not protected by the Fifth Amendment, since they were used at trial only to show that Muniz's mental processes were not operating properly. (This aspect of the case is discussed earlier in this Chapter). However, Chief Justice Rehnquist assumed that a booking exception to *Miranda* does exist.

Justice Marshall dissented. He argued that a booking exception would lead to difficult, time-consuming litigation concerning its scope and application, contrary to the *Miranda* bright-line approach.

Muniz may be important with respect to provision of pretrial services. In federal proceedings, an officer may inquire about a suspect's financial status before a magistrate rules on pretrial release. In some cases, this financial information might be relevant to prove guilt. It might show unexplained income for a tax violation, or that the defendant had money shortly after a crime occurred, or that the defendant had no money and thus a motive to commit a crime. Does *Muniz* mean that questions asked for routine administrative purposes never require *Miranda* warnings?

Determining the Scope of the Booking Questions Exception

How is a court able to tell whether an officer's question about biographical information is, as *Muniz* puts it, "designed to elicit incriminatory admissions?" Is it a subjective test? Lower courts have looked to objective factors such as whether there could be a proper administrative purpose for the question, whether the question is asked by an officer who routinely books suspects, and whether the officer would need to know the information for booking purposes. See, e.g., Gladden v. Roach, 864 F.2d 1196 (5th Cir.1989)("straightforward questions to secure the biographical data necessary to complete the booking process" are not covered by *Miranda*); United States v. Webb, 755 F.2d 382 (5th Cir.1985)(questions by classification officer concerning the nature of the defendant's crime were not booking questions where the classification officer already knew what the defendant was charged with, and such questions were not ordinarily asked by classification officers); United States v. Hinckley, 672 F.2d 115 (D.C.Cir.1982)(questions were not within the booking exception where they had a clear investigative purpose, and the interrogation was conducted by officers who did not ordinarily book suspects).

In United States v. Carmona, 873 F.2d 569 (2d Cir.1989), officers arresting Carmona asked his name, even though they knew who he was. He answered with a false name, and this answer was used as evidence of consciousness of guilt at his trial. The court held that the question "what's your name?" is *always* within the booking exception, even if the officer knows the information in advance. The court noted that it is prudent practice for officers to make sure that the person arrested is the correct person. Was the question in *Carmona* "designed to elicit incriminating information?" What kind of answer were they expecting?

Questions Pertinent to Custodial Procedures and Tests

After the booking questions, the defendant in *Muniz* was asked to perform certain sobriety tests and to submit to a breathalyzer test. These tests, as well as the consequences of refusal to take the tests, were explained to Muniz by officers, who never gave *Miranda* warnings. While attempting to comprehend the explanations, Muniz gave responses admitting that he was impaired by alcohol. Writing for eight members of the Court, Justice Brennan concluded that Muniz's responses were admissible since the instructions from the officers "were not likely to be perceived as calling for any verbal response" and thus were not interrogation. The Court reasoned that the officers' instructions were "limited and focused inquiries" which were "necessarily attendant to the legitimate police procedure."

Justice Marshall dissented from the Court's holding that questions and instructions attendant to sobriety tests and breathalyzer tests were not interrogation. He concluded that in light of Muniz's impaired state, these questions were reasonably likely to elicit an incriminating response.

After *Muniz,* explanations concerning custodial procedures such as fingerprinting, transportation, inventorying, etc. will probably not be considered interrogation even though the defendant may make incriminating statements during the explanation process. This is because such explanations cannot be considered to call for an incriminating response any more than did the explanations involved in *Muniz.* Moreover, even direct questions about the suspect's understanding of such explanations will not be interrogation, since they are considered "necessarily attendant to" such explanations. Statements and questions by police officers that go beyond the subject matter of the custodial procedure could still be considered interrogation after *Muniz,* since the Court emphasized that the officers strictly circumscribed the dialogue to the specific issues of a breathalyzer test and a sobriety test.

It should be noted, though, that extended discussions with much incriminating information can occur in these explanatory situations. See State v. Whitehead, 458 N.W.2d 145 (Minn.App.1990)(advisory interview concerning testing for alcohol under the state's implied consent law does not constitute interrogation under *Muniz,* even though the defendant and the officer each made more than 100 statements; while the discussion was unfocused, it was still within the scope of questioning attendant to the interview). See also United States v. Lemon, 550 F.2d 467 (9th Cir.1977) (asking for consent to search is not interrogation, even though it could give rise to incriminating statements). Do you see any room for abuse when an officer explains a police procedure to a suspect?

3.   *Does Miranda Apply to Undercover Activity?*

What if a suspect in custody does not know that he is speaking to a police officer or agent? In Illinois v. Perkins, 496 U.S. 292 (1990), authorities suspected that Perkins was involved in a murder. Perkins was in prison on charges unrelated to the murder. An undercover officer was placed as Perkins' cellmate, with the hope that he could obtain incriminating statements from Perkins about the murder. In the course of conversation concerning a planned escape, the undercover officer asked Perkins whether he had ever killed anybody. Perkins said yes and described the murder that was being investigated. For obvious reasons, Perkins had received no *Miranda* warnings. The Court held that Perkins' statement was admissible because "*Miranda* was not meant to protect suspects from boasting about their criminal activities in front of persons who they believe to be their cellmates." Justice Kennedy wrote the opinion for seven members of the Court. He reasoned that *Miranda* was concerned with the pressures upon a suspect in a police-dominated atmosphere. If the suspect does not even know that he is talking to a police officer, the problems with which the Court was concerned in *Miranda* do not exist. Justice Kennedy explained as follows:

> It is the premise of *Miranda* that the danger of coercion results from the interaction of custody and official interrogation. * * * Questioning by captors, who appear to control the suspect's fate, may create mutually reinforcing pressures that the Court has assumed will weaken the suspect's will, but where a suspect does not know that he is conversing with a government agent, these pressures do not exist.

One of the virtues of *Miranda,* often recognized by the Court, is its bright-line character. Perkins argued that the creation of an "undercover investigations exception" to *Miranda* would destroy the clarity of the rule. The majority rejected this argument, on the ground that the *Perkins* rule itself is a bright-line rule: if there is an undercover investigation (and it is easy to determine whether there is one) then *Miranda* is completely inapplicable. Justice Kennedy stated that "law enforcement officers will have little difficulty putting into practice our holding that undercover agents need not give *Miranda* warnings to incarcerated suspects."

Justice Brennan concurred in the judgment. He agreed that when a suspect does not know he is talking to a police agent, *Miranda* warnings are not required. Justice Brennan argued, however, that undercover activity constituted trickery, which could raise a "substantial claim that the confession was obtained in violation of the Due Process Clause."

Justice Marshall dissented. He argued that undercover questioning of an incarcerated suspect constituted both "custody" and "interrogation," and that the majority's opinion was thus an unjustified "exception" to *Miranda*. Justice Marshall also expressed concern that police would use the majority's decision to circumvent *Miranda* requirements by the use of undercover agents.

4. *Does Miranda Protection Depend on the Nature of the Offense?*

The Court in Berkemer v. McCarty, 468 U.S. 420 (1984), established that there is no distinction between felonies and misdemeanors insofar as *Miranda* is concerned.

Writing for the Court, Justice Marshall rejected the felony-misdemeanor distinction on the ground that it would remove one of *Miranda's* principal advantages—i.e., the clarity of the rule.

> The exception to *Miranda* proposed * * * would substantially undermine this crucial advantage of the doctrine. The police often are unaware when they arrest a person whether he may have committed a misdemeanor or a felony. * * * Indeed, the nature of his offense may depend upon circumstances unknowable to the police, such as whether the suspect has previously committed a similar offense or has a criminal record of some other kind. It may even turn upon events yet to happen, such as whether a victim of the accident dies. It would be unreasonable to expect the police to make guesses as to the nature of the criminal conduct at issue before deciding how they may interrogate the suspect.

> Equally importantly, the doctrinal complexities that would confront the courts if we accepted [the misdemeanor-felony distinction] would be byzantine. Difficult questions quickly spring to mind: For instance, investigations into seemingly minor offenses sometimes escalate gradually into investigations into more serious matters; at what point in the evolution of an affair of this sort would the police be obliged to give *Miranda* warnings to a suspect in custody? * * * The litigation necessary to resolve such matters would be time-consuming and disruptive of law enforcement. And the end result would be an elaborate set of rules, interlaced with exceptions and subtle distinctions, discriminating between different kinds of custodial interrogations. Neither the police nor criminal defendants would benefit from such a development.

If the bright-line aspect of *Miranda* is so important, why did the Court in *Quarles* establish a public safety exception? Is a public safety exception to *Miranda* any easier to apply than a misdemeanor exception?

5. *How Complete and Accurate Must the Warnings Be?*

The Court in *Miranda* promulgated a set of detailed warnings. Yet it left unclear whether something less than a verbatim transcription of the Court's warnings would suffice. In California v. Prysock, 451 U.S. 1301 (1981), the Court seemed to hold that police should be given some flexibility—so long as they provide the suspect with the gist of the warnings. Prysock was informed that he had "the right to talk to a lawyer before you are questioned, have him present while you are being questioned, and all during the questioning" and also that he had "the right to have a lawyer appointed to represent you at no cost to yourself." Prysock argued that he was never informed of his right to have an attorney appointed before being questioned. Thus, he was left with the impression that he could only have an attorney if he agreed to answer questions. The Court declared, however, that it had "never indicated that the rigidity of *Miranda* extends to the precise formulation of the warnings," and that "*Miranda* itself indicates that no talismanic incantation" is required. Under the circumstances, the warnings gave sufficient information, and were not misrepresentative. They didn't specifically say, for example, that Prysock had no right to an attorney unless he agreed to talk.

Chief Justice Rehnquist wrote for the Court in Duckworth v. Eagan, 492 U.S. 195 (1989), as it found no *Miranda* violation in a police officer's reading a printed waiver form to a suspect, which provided:

> "Before we ask you any questions, you must understand your rights. You have the right to remain silent. Anything you say can be used against you in court. *You have the right to talk to a lawyer for advice before we ask you any questions, and to have him with you during questioning.* You have this right to the advice and presence of a lawyer even if you cannot afford to hire one. We *have no way of giving you a lawyer, but one will be appointed for you, if you wish, if and when you go to court.* If you wish to answer questions now without a lawyer present, you have the right to stop answering questions at any time. You also have the right to stop answering at any time until you've talked to a lawyer." (emphasis added)

The Chief Justice noted that the Court has never insisted that *Miranda* warnings be given in the exact form described in Chief Justice Warren's opinion, and concluded that the inclusion of the "if and when you go to court" language accurately described state procedure and did not fail to apprise the defendant of his rights.

Justice Marshall, joined by Justices Brennan, Blackmun, and Stevens, dissented. He argued that the "if and when" language led the defendant to believe that a lawyer would not be appointed until some future time after questioning took place.

In United States v. Connell, 869 F.2d 1349 (9th Cir.1989), Connell received an oral warning that "you must make your own arrangements to obtain a lawyer, and this will be at no expense to the Government," and that "if you cannot afford to pay for a lawyer, one *may* be appointed to represent you." (emphasis added). He also received written warnings stating that if he could not afford a lawyer, "arrangements will be made for you to obtain one in accordance with the law." The court held that these warnings together were insufficient, and therefore that Connell's confession should have been excluded under *Miranda*. The court reasoned that the oral warning was "misleading" because it appeared that the right to appointed counsel was subject to government discretion. It found the written warning to be "ambiguous" because "Connell is not expected to know what the requirements of the law are. In fact, conveying to the person in custody the requirements of the law is the whole purpose of the warning." Is *Connell* inconsistent with *Prysock* and *Eagan*? See also United States v. Tillman, 963 F.2d 137 (6th Cir.1992)(warning insufficient where it fails to inform the suspect specifically that anything he says can be used against him *in court*: "By omitting this essential element from the *Miranda* warnings a person may not realize why the right to remain silent is so critical."). *Contra* United States v. Frankson, 83 F.3d 79 (4th Cir.1996) (warning that fails to specify that statements can be used in court is sufficient: "*Miranda* and its progeny simply do not require the police officers provide highly particularized warnings. Such a requirement would impose an onerous burden on police officers to accurately list all circumstances in which *Miranda* rights might apply. Given the common sense understanding that an unqualified statement lacks qualifications, all that police officers need to is convey the general rights enumerated in *Miranda*.").

6. Do the Miranda Safeguards Apply to Custodial Interrogations of Foreigners Conducted Abroad?

Since the rise in acts of terrorism against United States interests abroad, the question has arisen whether United States officials are bound by the *Miranda* requirements when interrogating suspects on foreign soil. (It is clear that *Miranda* does not apply to interrogation by foreign officials conducted abroad, at least when they are acting independently from United States officials.) The district court in United States v. Bin Laden, 132 F.Supp.2d 168 (S.D.N.Y. 2001), considered whether and how the *Miranda* safeguards applied to custodial interrogation of defendants who were suspected of (and ultimately charged with and convicted of) taking part in terrorist bombings of American Embassies in Africa.

The *Bin Laden* Court held that the privilege against self-incrimination protects foreigners who are interrogated abroad by American law enforcement officials. It also held that *Miranda* protections must be provided to replicate "to the maximum extent reasonably possible" the rights that a suspect would have when subject to custodial interrogation in America. The Court recognized that adaptations would have to be made to accommodate local conditions, such as the unavailability of counsel. If counsel was not available under foreign law, the suspect would have to be told of that fact, and also must be told that if counsel cannot be made available the suspect does not have to speak to the officers, and if he decides to speak, he can stop at any time. The Court suppressed statements that were made to American officials by the foreign defendant in the absence of these modified warnings.

For an argument that the *Bin Laden* Court went too far in protecting foreign suspects on foreign soil, see Mark Godsey, *Miranda's* Final Frontier–The International Arena: A Critical Analysis of United States v. Bin Laden and a Proposal for a New *Miranda* Exception Abroad, 51 Duke L.J. 1703 (2002). Professor Godsey argues that a warnings requirement will encourage American officials to leave the questioning to foreign officials–meaning that extending the *Miranda* requirements to American officials abroad will not be doing foreign suspects any favors.

E. WAIVER OF *MIRANDA* RIGHTS

1. Waiver and the Role of Counsel

The *Miranda* Court stated that the accused may waive the rights to silence and counsel, but only if, under all the circumstances, the rights are waived "voluntarily, knowingly, and intelligently." Thus, the validity of a waiver is a question of fact in any particular case. According to *Miranda,* a valid waiver will not be assumed from the silence of the accused after the warnings are given, nor from the fact that a confession is eventually obtained. However, the Court later held in North Carolina v. Butler, 441 U.S. 369 (1979), that neither an express statement of waiver nor a written waiver is required, so long as there is sufficient evidence to show that the suspect understood his rights and voluntarily waived them. The *Butler* Court stated that "the question is not one of form, but rather whether the defendant in fact knowingly and voluntarily waived the rights delineated in the *Miranda* case." Of course, while a written waiver is not required, it certainly supports the government's claim that a knowing and voluntary waiver was obtained.

Knowing and Voluntary

The Supreme Court in Moran v. Burbine, 475 U.S. 412 (1986), held that two requirements must be met before a suspect can be found to have waived his *Miranda* rights:

> First, the relinquishment of the right must have been voluntary in the sense that it was the product of a free and deliberate choice rather than intimidation, coercion, or deception. Second, the waiver must have been made with a full awareness both of the nature of the right being abandoned and the consequences of the decision to abandon it.

In Tague v. Louisiana, 444 U.S. 469 (1980)(per curiam), the Court held that a waiver of *Miranda* rights was not proven by an officer's testimony that he read a suspect his rights from a card and the suspect then confessed. The officer could not remember what the rights were, whether he asked the suspect if he understood them, or whether he made an effort to determine if the suspect "was literate or otherwise capable of understanding his rights." Thus, a valid waiver could not be found simply by the fact that the warnings are given and the suspect confesses.

On the other hand, a waiver can be found if it seems apparent from the giving of the warnings and the suspect's reaction that the suspect understood his *Miranda* rights and freely waived them. For example, in United States v. Frankson, 83 F.3d 79 (4th Cir.1996), the officer read Frankson his rights, asked him if he understood those rights, and Frankson said "yes." Immediately after that, Frankson answered a number of questions posed by the officer, providing extensive details on how he evaded detection for drug activity: he would find a house where no one was ordinarily home during the day, instruct his drug supplier to send a package of drugs via UPS to that house, and then pick up the package when it was left on the home's doorstep. The court held that the circumstances indicated a knowing and voluntary waiver:

> A defendant's subsequent willingness to answer questions after acknowledging his *Miranda* rights is sufficient to constitute an implied waiver. * * * Even though Frankson never "formally" waived his *Miranda* rights, such cooperation, when coupled with his acknowledgment of his *Miranda* rights, constituted a valid waiver.

See also United States v. Banks, 78 F.3d 1190 (7th Cir.1996) (waiver found, even though waiver form not signed, where defendant was familiar with the criminal justice system, and answered some questions and refused to answer others); United States v. Smith, 218 F.3d 777 (7th Cir. 2000)(waiver found where the defendant refused to sign a waiver form, but then immediately began to talk to police officers and continued to do so for an hour).

Often waiver issues turn on a "swearing contest" between police officers and defendants as to whether warnings were given and whether they were waived. Should there be a requirement that interrogations be videotaped with a sound recording? Even with videotaping, questions can arise as to the capacity of a defendant to understand and waive *Miranda* rights. But would a good tape help resolve most cases?

Relationship of Waiver Standards to the Test for Voluntary Confessions

It is important to keep in mind that even after *Miranda* warnings are given, a confession can still be coerced under traditional due process standards. For example, the suspect may make a valid waiver of his rights, but the subsequent confession may be involuntary due to overbearing police pressure; or it may be that warnings are given but the police pressure is so great that it cannot be said that the suspect voluntarily waived his *Miranda* rights. See, e.g., United States v. Syslo, 303 F.3d 860 (8th Cir. 2002) (statements were properly suppressed even though the defendant had voluntarily waived her *Miranda* rights, where the suspect had her young children at the police station and was informed that they could not be picked up by a relative until she confessed); Commonwealth v. Perry, 475 Pa. 1, 379 A.2d 545 (1977)(a confession was involuntary even when warnings were given, because the statement was taken while the defendant was in the hospital and in a great deal of pain).

The Supreme Court held in Colorado v. Connelly, 479 U.S. 157 (1986), (described supra), the decision holding that coercive police activity is a prerequisite to a finding that a confession is involuntary, that "[t]here is obviously no reason to require more in the way of a 'voluntariness' inquiry in the *Miranda* waiver context than in the Fourteenth Amendment confession context." Thus, "[t]he voluntariness of a waiver of this privilege [against self-incrimination] has always depended on the absence of police overreaching, not on 'free choice' in any broader sense of the word." The Court found that a defendant voluntarily waived his *Miranda* rights because he decided to confess after receiving warnings, without the police engaging in any coercive behavior: "Respondent's perception of coercion flowing from the 'voice of God,' however important or significant such a perception may be in other disciplines, is a matter to which the United States Constitution does not speak." Chief Justice Rehnquist's majority opinion did not address the question whether Connelly actually understood the warnings and thus made a knowing waiver. This question was left for the state courts on remand.

Understanding the Miranda Warnings

Subsequent to *Connelly* and its remand on the issue of whether Connelly *understood* his rights as well as voluntarily waived them, several courts have held that persons who are deranged or mentally defective cannot knowingly and intelligently waive their *Miranda* rights. In Smith v. Zant, 887 F.2d 1407 (11th

Cir.1989)(en banc), the court concluded that "the *Connelly* Court addressed only voluntariness," and noted the "continued vitality of the knowing and intelligent requirement." The court found that the state did not satisfy its burden of showing that the defendant in that case was capable of understanding his *Miranda* rights; the defendant had an I.Q. of 65, he was under extreme stress, and the warnings were read to him only once, very quickly.

Similarly, courts have held that a waiver might not be "knowing" if the suspect could not understand the *Miranda* warnings due to some language barrier. Thus, in United States v. Garibay, 143 F.3d 534 (9th Cir.1998), the suspect was given *Miranda* warnings in English and said he understood them. Nonetheless, the Court held that the government failed to satisfy its burden that Garibay actually understood the warnings. The court noted evidence at the suppression hearing that Garibay's primary language was Spanish; that he received D+ grades in English in high school, and only passed because those classes were taught in Spanish; that he was "borderline retarded with extremely low verbal-English comprehension skills"; and that he had no previous experience with the criminal justice system, so that his "personal life experiences do not indicate that he was familiar with his *Miranda* rights and with his option to waive those rights." The court concluded that its result would have changed if Garibay either had been given the warnings in Spanish, or if he had signed a waiver form in English. Why?

In *Garibay*, the government argued that it had no reason to know anything about Garibay's grades in English, and that Garibay had said "yes" when asked if he understood the warnings. But the court noted testimony at the suppression hearing from Garibay's teacher that when Garibay was under stress, he often claimed to understand English, when in fact he did not. So the court held that the test for a "knowing" waiver is whether the *suspect actually understood* the *Miranda* warnings. Why should the suspect's actual understanding be the focus? Isn't the government being penalized for not knowing something it had no reason to know? Shouldn't the focus be on police misconduct? That is what *Connelly* says with respect to the voluntariness component of waiver of *Miranda* rights—the waiver is voluntary in the absence of police misconduct. Why should it be different with respect to the "knowledge" component?

Judge Posner, in Rice v. Cooper, 148 F.3d 747 (7th Cir.1998), addressed the apparent inconsistency between a voluntariness standard premised on police misconduct and a knowledge standard premised on the suspect's actual knowledge without regard to police misconduct. In *Rice*, the suspect was a 16 year-old with a mental disability. He received the *Miranda* warnings, asked some questions about what they meant, and then confessed. Judge Posner analyzed the matter as follows:

> Whether the incriminating statements that Rice made at the time of his arrest after waiving his right to remain silent or consult a lawyer should have been suppressed because of his mental condition raises the interesting general question of the duty, if any, of the police to protect a mentally impaired person from incriminating himself. A confession or other admission is not deemed coerced or involuntary merely because it would not have been made had the defendant not been mentally defective or deranged. Colorado v. Connelly. The relevant constitutional principles are aimed not at protecting people from themselves but at curbing abusive practices by public

officers. From this it might be argued that officers are free to recite the standard *Miranda* warnings to anyone they arrest, regardless of the person's evident mental condition, and to accept the person's waiver. But this has to be wrong, though we cannot find a case that says so. If the suspect is a small child, or if it is apparent that he cannot speak English, then attempting to extract a waiver of *Miranda* rights is pretty obviously an abusive practice, as it is a calculated, conscious effort to extract a decision that is not the product of a rational choice. And likewise if it is apparent that because of illness, insanity, or mental retardation the suspect is incapable of rationally waiving his *Miranda* rights. The significance of the principle of *Connelly*, the principle that the Constitution doesn't protect the suspect against himself, is that if he understands the *Miranda* warnings yet is moved by a crazy impulse to blurt out a confession, the confession is admissible because it is not a product of coercion. The police have given him his *Miranda* warnings in an intelligible form; it is not their fault that he is impulsive. It is different, if perhaps only by a shade, if the police question him knowing that he does not understand his rights.

On this analysis, the knowledge of the police is vital. If they have no reason to think that the suspect doesn't understand them, there is nothing that smacks of abusive behavior. It would seem to follow that the question is not whether if Rice were more intelligent, informed, balanced, and so forth he would not have waived his *Miranda* rights, but whether the police believed he understood their explanation of those rights; * * *. The police testified that at the outset of the questioning Rice did not appear to be incapable of understanding what was going on. So there was no element of abuse in the giving of the *Miranda* warnings envisaged as the first stage of an interrogation. But it immediately appeared that Rice did have some problems understanding the warnings. The interrogating officer testified that he "told Mr. Rice first that he had a right to remain silent. And he asked me what that meant. I told him that meant that he didn't have to talk to me or anybody else about this case if he didn't want to. I asked him if he understood that and he told me that he did." This pattern was repeated throughout the giving of the Miranda warnings—Rice expressing a lack of understanding, the officer trying to explain, Rice then signifying his understanding. For example, "I told him he had the right to have an attorney present during any questioning. He asked me if an attorney was the same thing as a lawyer. I told him that it was. I asked him if he understood and he told me that he did."

This pattern is consistent with Rice's having, to the best of the police officers' knowledge, understood the warnings sufficiently to be able to waive them knowingly. He did not understand them at first, and when he signified his lack of understanding to the interrogating officer this put the latter on notice that if he wanted to obtain an effective waiver he had better explain the *Miranda* rights to Rice in the simplest possible manner. Which is what he tried to do. And the questions that Rice asked, such as whether an attorney is the same as a lawyer, while they indicate a lack of legal and intellectual sophistication, do not evince such a profound derangement as would require the suppression of his statements on the ground that there was no effective waiver—and the police knew it but persisted in questioning him.

Our emphasis on the absence of police abuse is, however, in tension with the conventional approach to waivers of the *Miranda* rights—that of asking simply whether the defendant had the maturity, competence, etc. to make a knowing waiver of his rights, without reference to what the police knew or should have known. * * * If Connelly's waiver of his Fifth Amendment right not to confess was effective even though the confession was induced by madness rather than by remorse or calculation, why should a waiver of *Miranda* rights be ineffective if prompted solely by the defendant's mental condition rather by anything the police did? Because "waiver" in law is defined as a knowing relinquishment of a right? * * * In neither case is there a responsible relinquishment of rights; in neither is there police misconduct; in both the government receives a windfall as a result of the suspect's mental abnormality.

Maybe the real difference between the two cases is that judges are more confident about being able to determine whether a suspect understands the *Miranda* warnings than about being able to determine whether he waived them because he was remorseful, calculating, or merely impulsive, on the one hand, or mentally ill or deficient on the other. It is generally easier to infer whether someone understands something—a type of inference we draw all the time, as it is fundamental to human communication—than it is to infer the motives that prompt a person to react in one way rather than another to particular information. It is a considerable mystery why people ever confess to a crime if they are not coerced; and deciding whether and in what sense a confession can be said to be "involuntary" when it is not the product of coercion may be beyond the practical competence of the courts. But we need not pursue this issue further; there was neither police abuse nor compelling evidence of Rice's incapacity to make a knowing waiver of his *Miranda* rights after the police explained in simple terms what those rights were.

Conditional Waivers: Connecticut v. Barrett

Is it possible for the suspect to give a limited or conditional waiver of *Miranda* rights? In Connecticut v. Barrett, 479 U.S. 523 (1987), Barrett received *Miranda* warnings and then signed a form indicating that he would talk to the police about a sexual assault investigation. He stated he had "no problem" in talking about the assault, but that he would not give a written statement. He was given *Miranda* warnings several times, and eventually gave an oral confession which was admitted at trial. In an opinion by Chief Justice Rehnquist, the Court held that Barrett had knowingly and voluntarily waived his *Miranda* rights. The Chief Justice reasoned that the police had complied with Barrett's conditions, because they never sought to obtain a written statement. He emphasized that Barrett gave affirmative indications that he was willing to make an oral statement. The fact that Barrett's decision may have been "illogical" was held irrelevant, "for we have never embraced the theory that a defendant's ignorance of the full consequences of his decisions vitiates their voluntariness."

Justice Brennan concurred in the judgment. He argued that if Barrett was laboring under the misimpression that oral statements could not be admitted against him at trial, his waiver would have been invalid. However, Barrett's testimony at trial that he understood the warnings (to the effect that *any* statement could be used against him) demonstrated a valid waiver. Justice Stevens, joined by Justice Marshall, dissented.

The court in Bruni v. Lewis, 847 F.2d 561 (9th Cir.1988), relied on *Barrett* to uphold a waiver when the defendant told the police to "ask your questions and I will answer those I see fit." Is this a limited waiver?

Another question of limited waiver arises when a suspect says he will talk about "x" but not about "y". If the police then question him on "y", they have violated *Miranda* because the suspect never waived his rights with respect to "y". For example, in United States v. Soliz, 129 F.3d 499 (9th Cir.1997), the defendant was arrested on suspicion of an immigration violation as well as smuggling activity. He agreed to talk to police officers about his citizenship. The police then began asking him about the smuggling and Soliz said "I thought this was just about my citizenship." The questioning continued about the smuggling and Soliz made admissions concerning the smuggling. The court held that those statements had to be excluded. It found that Soliz had made an unequivocal invocation of his right to remain silent on all issues other than citizenship. Accordingly, the officer's were required to respect the conditions Soliz placed on his waiver.

Information Needed for an Intelligent Waiver: The Scope of the Interrogation—Colorado v. Spring

How much information must a suspect have to make a "knowing and intelligent" waiver of *Miranda* rights? This question arose in three Supreme Court cases, in each of which defendants argued that the *Miranda* warnings did not give them enough information. The Court rejected this argument in each case.

In Colorado v. Spring, 479 U.S. 564 (1987), Spring was arrested in Missouri when he tried to sell stolen firearms to an undercover agent. Agents also had information that Spring had been involved in a killing in Colorado. Spring was given warnings and signed a waiver form. He was first questioned about the firearms. Then the agents asked him whether he had ever shot anyone. He said that he had "shot another guy once." Eventually Spring gave a complete confession to the killing. Spring argued that he had not knowingly and intelligently waived his *Miranda* rights concerning the Colorado shooting, because the agents had not warned him that he would be questioned about that matter. Justice Powell, writing for seven members of the Court, rejected Spring's argument. Justice Powell reasoned as follows:

> Spring understood that he had the right to remain silent and that anything he said could be used as evidence against him. The Constitution does not require that a criminal suspect know and understand every possible consequence of a waiver of the Fifth Amendment privilege. * * * The *Miranda* warnings protect this privilege by ensuring that a suspect knows that he may choose not to talk to law enforcement officers, to talk only with counsel present, or to discontinue talking at any time. * * * [A] suspect's awareness of all the possible subjects of questioning in advance of interrogation is not relevant to determining whether the suspect voluntarily, knowingly, and intelligently waived his Fifth Amendment privilege.

Spring also argued that his waiver was invalid because the agents "tricked" him into believing that they were only concerned with the firearms charge. Justice Powell rejected this argument as well, stating that while trickery could vitiate the voluntariness of a waiver, trickery could not be found through "mere silence" on the part of the police. Here, the agents had not affirmatively misrepresented the intended scope of their questioning; they simply said nothing about it.

Justice Marshall, joined by Justice Brennan, dissented. He argued that a suspect's decision to waive the privilege will "necessarily be influenced by his awareness of the scope and seriousness of the matters under investigation." He claimed that the majority's rule would allow officers to take "unfair advantage of the suspect's psychological state."

Note that Spring never invoked his *Miranda* rights. Thus, he was in a different situation than the defendant in *Soliz*, supra, who said that he would talk about one crime but not another. If Spring had imposed such a condition, the officers could not have asked him about the other crime.

Information Needed for an Intelligent Waiver:
The Inadmissibility of a Previous
Confession—Oregon v. Elstad

In Oregon v. Elstad, 470 U.S. 298 (1985), Elstad gave a *Miranda*-defective confession, then he received warnings, signed a waiver, and made a formal confession. Only this second confession was admitted at his trial. Elstad argued that the waiver he made before giving his second confession was not knowing and intelligent. Justice O'Connor described the argument, and rejected it, in the following passage:

> Respondent * * * has argued that he was unable to give a fully *informed* waiver of his rights because he was unaware that his prior statement could not be used against him. Respondent suggests that Deputy McAllister, to cure this deficiency, should have added an additional warning to those given him at the Sheriff's office. Such a requirement is neither practicable nor constitutionally necessary. In many cases, a breach of *Miranda* procedures may not be identified as such until long after full *Miranda* warnings are administered and a valid confession obtained. The standard *Miranda* warnings explicitly inform the suspect of his right to consult a lawyer before speaking. Police officers are ill equipped to pinch-hit for counsel, construing the murky and difficult questions of when "custody" begins or whether a given unwarned statement will ultimately be held admissible.

> This Court has never embraced the theory that a defendant's ignorance of the full consequences of his decisions vitiates their voluntariness. * * *

At the time *Miranda* was decided, it arguably signified the minimum showing required before the government could successfully claim that an individual had waived his privilege and voluntarily made a statement. Did the Court in *Miranda* intend to set the maximum requirements that will be imposed upon the government?

Information Needed for an Intelligent Waiver: Efforts of a Lawyer to Contact the Suspect—Moran v. Burbine

The Court in Moran v. Burbine, 475 U.S. 412 (1986), again considered whether the basic *Miranda* warnings were sufficient to establish the knowledge required for a knowing and intelligent waiver of *Miranda* rights. Justice O'Connor's majority opinion begins with a useful summary of the case:

> After being informed of his rights pursuant to Miranda v. Arizona, and after executing a series of written waivers, respondent confessed to the murder of a young woman. At no point during the course of the interrogation, which occurred prior to arraignment, did he request an attorney. While he was in police custody, his sister attempted to retain a lawyer to represent him. The attorney telephoned the police station and received assurances that respondent would not be questioned until the next day. In fact, the interrogation session that yielded the inculpatory statements began later that evening. The question presented is whether either the conduct of the police or respondent's ignorance of the attorney's efforts to reach him taints the validity of the waivers and therefore requires exclusion of the confessions.

Justice O'Connor concluded first that Burbine's waiver was valid despite the fact that he was not informed that an attorney sought to contact him. She reasoned as follows:

> The voluntariness of the waiver is not at issue. As the Court of Appeals correctly acknowledged, the record is devoid of any suggestion that police resorted to physical or psychological pressure to elicit the statements. * * * Nor is there any question about respondent's comprehension of the full panoply of rights set out in the *Miranda* warnings and of the potential consequences of a decision to relinquish them. * * *

> Events occurring outside of the presence of the suspect and entirely unknown to him surely can have no bearing on the capacity to comprehend and knowingly relinquish a constitutional right. [Accepting Burbine's argument would mean that] the same defendant, armed with the same information and confronted with precisely the same police conduct, would have knowingly waived his *Miranda* rights had a lawyer not telephoned the police station to inquire about his status. Nothing in any of our waiver decisions or in our understanding of the essential components of a valid waiver requires so incongruous a result. No doubt the additional information would have been useful to respondent; perhaps even it might have affected his decision to confess. But we have never read the Constitution to require that the police supply a suspect with a flow of information to help him calibrate his self interest in deciding whether to speak or stand by his rights. Once it is determined that a suspect's decision not to rely on his rights was uncoerced, that he at all times knew he could stand mute and request a lawyer, and that he was aware of the state's intention to use his statements to secure a conviction, the analysis is complete and the waiver is valid as a matter of law.

State of Mind of Police Irrelevant

In the *Burbine* majority's view, the fact that the police acted *deliberately* to deprive the suspect of information concerning counsel's attempt to reach him did not affect the validity of the waiver. Justice O'Connor reasoned as follows:

> [W]hether intentional or inadvertent, the state of mind of the police is irrelevant to the question of the intelligence and voluntariness of respondent's election to abandon his rights. Although highly inappropriate, even deliberate deception of an attorney could not possibly affect a suspect's decision to waive his *Miranda* rights unless he were at least aware of the incident. Nor was the failure to inform respondent of the telephone call the kind of "trick[ery]" that can vitiate the validity of a waiver. Granting that the "deliberate or reckless" withholding of information is objectionable as a matter of ethics, such conduct is only relevant to the constitutional validity of a waiver if it deprives a defendant of knowledge essential to his ability to understand the nature of his rights and the consequences of abandoning them. Because respondent's voluntary decision to speak was made with full awareness and comprehension of all the information *Miranda* requires the police to convey, the waivers were valid.

The Role of Counsel Under Miranda

The defendant in *Burbine* argued that apart from the waiver issue, *Miranda* should be read to prohibit the police from deliberately deceiving counsel, or from denying counsel's request to see the suspect. In other words, *Miranda* should be read to provide some protection of the right to counsel independent of the suspect's decision whether to invoke that right. The majority declined "to further extend *Miranda's* reach." Justice O'Connor explained the Court's position as follows:

> [W]hile we share respondent's distaste for the deliberate misleading of an officer of the court, reading *Miranda* to forbid police deception of an *attorney* would cut [the decision] completely loose from its own explicitly stated rationale. * * * Clearly, a rule that focuses on how the police treat an attorney—conduct that has no relevance at all to the degree of compulsion experienced by the defendant during interrogation—would ignore both *Miranda's* mission and its only source of legitimacy.

In other words, it is the suspect who has the right to counsel under *Miranda*; and that right does not come into effect until the suspect invokes the right. Because the defendant never asked for counsel in *Burbine*, counsel had no independent rights to assert.

No Requirement to Inform the Suspect of Counsel's Efforts

Finally, the *Burbine* Court declined to "extend" *Miranda* to require the police to inform the suspect of an attorney's efforts to reach him. Such a requirement would be inconsistent with *Miranda's* bright-line approach. Justice O'Connor explained as follows:

> As we have stressed on numerous occasions, "[o]ne of the principal advantages" of *Miranda* is the ease and clarity of its application. We have

little doubt that the approach urged by respondent * * * would have the inevitable consequence of muddying *Miranda's* otherwise relatively clear waters. The legal questions it would spawn are legion: To what extent should the police be held accountable for knowing that the accused has counsel? Is it enough that someone in the station house knows, or must the interrogating officer himself know of counsel's efforts to contact the suspect? Do counsel's efforts to talk to the suspect concerning one criminal investigation trigger the obligation to inform the defendant before interrogation may proceed on a wholly separate matter?

Justice O'Connor also argued that an extra warning requirement would be too costly to law enforcement interests, and thus inconsistent with the *Miranda* compromise:

> * * * [R]eading *Miranda* to require the police in each instance to inform a suspect of an attorney's efforts to reach him would work a substantial and, we think, inappropriate shift in the subtle balance struck in that decision. Custodial interrogations implicate two competing concerns. On the one hand, the need for police questioning as a tool for effective enforcement of criminal laws cannot be doubted. Admissions of guilt are more than merely desirable, they are essential to society's compelling interest in finding, convicting and punishing those who violate the law. On the other hand, the Court has recognized that the interrogation process is "inherently coercive" and that, as a consequence, there exists a substantial risk that the police will inadvertently traverse the fine line between legitimate efforts to elicit admissions and constitutionally impermissible compulsion.

> *Miranda* attempted to reconcile these opposing concerns by giving the *defendant* the power to exert some control over the course of the interrogation. Declining to adopt the more extreme position that the actual presence of a lawyer was necessary to dispel the coercion inherent in custodial interrogation, the Court found that the suspect's Fifth Amendment rights could be adequately protected by less intrusive means. Police questioning, often an essential part of the investigatory process, could continue in its traditional form, the Court held, but only if the suspect clearly understood that, at any time, he could bring the proceeding to a halt or, short of that, call in an attorney to give advice and monitor the conduct of his interrogators.

> The position urged by respondent would upset this carefully drawn approach in a manner that is both unnecessary for the protection of the Fifth Amendment privilege and injurious to legitimate law enforcement. Because, as *Miranda* holds, full comprehension of the rights to remain silent and request an attorney are sufficient to dispel whatever coercion is inherent in the interrogation process, a rule requiring the police to inform the suspect of an attorney's efforts to contact him would contribute to the protection of the Fifth Amendment privilege only incidentally, if at all. This minimal benefit, however, would come at a substantial cost to society's legitimate and substantial interest in securing admissions of guilt. * * * Because neither the letter nor purposes of *Miranda* require this additional handicap on otherwise permissible investigatory efforts, we are unwilling to

expand the *Miranda* rules to require the police to keep the suspect abreast of the status of his legal representation.

Dissent in Burbine

Justice Stevens, joined by Justices Brennan and Marshall, dissented in *Burbine*. He argued that the Court's holding "exalts incommunicado interrogation, sanctions police deception, and demeans the right to consult with an attorney." In his view, "[p]olice interference with communications between an attorney and his client is a recurrent problem." Justice Stevens responded to the majority's reliance on *Miranda's* careful balance with the observation that a rule requiring the police to inform a suspect of an attorney's call would serve *Miranda's* goal of dispelling the compulsion inherent in custodial interrogation. He responded to the majority's concern for clarity with the suggestion that no state that required the police to tell a suspect of an attorney's call had experienced problems. Justice Stevens argued that the police deliberately deceived the suspect's agent, his attorney, and that "as a matter of law, the police deception of Munson [the attorney] was tantamount to deception of Burbine himself."

Questions After Burbine

Is Moran v. Burbine consistent with *Miranda?* For a view that it is, see Kamisar, Remembering the "Old World" of Criminal Procedure: A Reply to Professor Grano, 23 U.Mich.J.L.Ref. 537 (1990).

Burbine never knew that counsel had been retained to represent him. Would it have made any difference if he had retained an attorney, and the officers never told him that the attorney was trying to contact him? In People v. Griggs, 152 Ill.2d 1, 178 Ill.Dec. 1, 604 N.E.2d 257 (1992), the defendant's sister informed him that she had retained counsel for him; but the police never told the defendant that counsel was at the stationhouse waiting to talk to him. The court distinguished *Burbine* and held that the defendant's waiver was not knowing and intelligent. What's the basis for the distinction?

The *Burbine* approach has been rejected as a matter of state constitutional law by some courts. See Haliburton v. Florida, 514 So.2d 1088 (Fla.1987). In Connecticut v. Stoddard, 206 Conn. 157, 537 A.2d 446 (1988), the court rejected *Burbine* and held that a waiver could not be knowing unless the suspect was informed of counsel's attempt to contact him. The court reasoned as follows:

> *Miranda* warnings refer only to an abstract right to counsel. That a suspect validly waives the presence of counsel only means that for the moment the suspect is forgoing the exercise of that conceptual privilege. Faced with a concrete offer of assistance, however, a suspect may well decide to reclaim his or her continuing right to legal assistance. We cannot therefore conclude that a decision to forgo the abstract offer contained in *Miranda* embodies an implied rejection of a specific opportunity to confer with a known lawyer.

Has the *Stoddard* court effectively addressed the concerns of the majority in *Burbine?*

2. Waiver After Invocation of Miranda Rights

In all the above cases, the suspect had never invoked his *Miranda* rights, and the government argued that the suspect waived his rights and confessed.

Can the government argue that waiver occurred if the suspect first invokes his *Miranda* rights and later confesses? Obviously it is a more difficult argument to make, because in the prior cases the suspects may have at all times wanted to speak with the police. Where the suspect has initially invoked his rights, however, something must have changed his mind. The government must show that this change of mind came from the suspect, and not from police harassment. Where the suspect has invoked his rights, the Supreme Court has shown far greater sensitivity to the waiver issue than in cases where there was no invocation.

A suspect can invoke two rights in response to the *Miranda* warnings—the right to silence, and the right to counsel. The Court has held that the rules on waiver differ depending on which right is invoked.

Invocation of the Right to Silence: Michigan v. Mosley

In Michigan v. Mosley, 423 U.S. 96 (1975), the defendant was arrested in connection with certain robberies, given *Miranda* warnings, and told that he could remain silent. Mosley said that he did not want to discuss the robberies, and the detective refrained from questioning him further. Approximately two hours later *Miranda* warnings were given again, and a different detective questioned Mosley about a murder that was not related to the robberies. Mosley signed a waiver form, and made an incriminating statement, which was admitted at his murder trial, in which he was convicted.

Justice Stewart, writing for the Court, found that the admission of the incriminating statements did not violate *Miranda*. In reaching this decision, the Court found it necessary to interpret the following language from *Miranda*:

> If the individual indicates in any manner, at any time prior to or during questioning, that he wishes to remain silent, the interrogation must cease. At this point he has shown that he intends to exercise his Fifth Amendment privilege; any statement taken after the person invokes his privilege cannot be other than the product of compulsion, subtle or otherwise.

The *Mosley* Court concluded that the *Miranda* Court could not have meant that interrogation is forever barred simply because the defendant invokes his right to silence. Justice Stewart concluded that the only sensible reading of the above language was that the suspect's right to cut off questioning must be "scrupulously honored." If the right to silence was scrupulously honored, then police interrogation could be permitted and a knowing and voluntary waiver could be found. Reviewing the circumstances of Mosley's second interrogation, the Court found:

> This is not a case * * * where the police failed to honor a decision of a person in custody to cut off questioning, either by refusing to discontinue the interrogation upon request or by persisting in repeated efforts to wear down his resistance and make him change his mind. In contrast to such practices, the police here immediately ceased the interrogation, resumed questioning only after the passage of a significant period of time and the provision of a fresh set of warnings, and restricted the second interrogation to a crime that had not been a subject of the earlier interrogation.

Justice Stewart indicated that the Court would not tolerate repetitive attempts, without respite, to interrogate a defendant who wanted to remain silent. But he concluded *Miranda* should not be a per se bar to resumption of questioning.

Scrupulously Honoring an Invocation of Silence

It may be wondered how an officer can "scrupulously honor" a suspect's right to remain silent and yet resume interrogation. Generally speaking, courts have found the most important factor to be whether the officers gave the suspect a "cooling off" period after he invoked the right to silence. See Charles v. Smith, 894 F.2d 718 (5th Cir.1990)(waiver invalid where suspect was asked whether he owned a certain hat and coat, two minutes after invoking the right to silence); United States v. Ramsey, 992 F.2d 301 (11th Cir.1993)(waiver invalid where defendant was given a last "opportunity to help himself", twenty minutes after invoking the right to silence); Grooms v. Keeney, 826 F.2d 883 (9th Cir. 1987)(waiver valid after four hour break in questioning); United States v. Wyatt, 179 F.3d 532 (7th Cir.1999) (permissible to provide the defendant with a summary of the evidence against him and to obtain a signed waiver form and a confession; after invoking the right to silence, the defendant was left alone for a day before the police re-approached him with the summary of the evidence).

Multiple attempts to get the suspect to speak are considered problematic. See Vujosevic v. Rafferty, 844 F.2d 1023 (3d Cir.1988)(waiver invalid where suspect was approached four times to determine whether he had changed his mind about not talking, and where officers had no reason to believe that he had changed his mind). If the officers give fresh *Miranda* warnings when they approach the suspect, this is evidence that they are scrupulously honoring the suspect's right to silence, as well as evidence that defendant knowingly and voluntarily waived his rights if a confession is obtained. See Otey v. Grammer, 859 F.2d 575 (8th Cir.1988) (waiver found where warnings were given frequently and defendant was allowed to control the subject matter of the questioning).

What if the officers use a tactic designed to impress upon the defendant the seriousness of the situation? Is this permissible when the defendant has invoked his right to silence? In United States v. Tyler, 164 F.3d 150 (3d Cir. 1998), the defendant was arrested for murdering a witness who was scheduled to testify at his brother's criminal trial. He invoked his right to silence, and was placed in a room at the police station. The walls of the room contained a time line of the murder investigation and crime scene photographs, including two photos of the body of the victim. Tyler remained in the room, alone, for hours. When the officers came to question him again, Tyler immediately confessed. The Court found that this confession had to be excluded under *Mosley*. Do you agree?

When Is the Right to Silence Invoked?

The *Mosley* standards presume that the suspect has invoked the right to silence after receiving *Miranda* warnings. If the suspect, in response to the warnings, says "I don't want to talk about anything," then he has clearly triggered the protections provided by *Mosley*. Not all invocations are so clear, however. What if the suspect says "If I knew what was good for me, I wouldn't be talking to you," or "I'd like to cooperate, but my brother would kill me if I did"? If it is unclear whether the suspect is invoking his right to silence, must the police stop the interrogation?

In Davis v. United States, 512 U.S. 452 (1994), the Court held that police questioning a suspect can continue the interrogation when the suspect has made an ambiguous or equivocal invocation of the *Miranda* right to *counsel*. The Court ruled further that police were not obligated to clarify the suspect's intent; rather, they could assume that in the absence of a clear invocation, the suspect was consenting to continued interrogation. While *Davis* concerned an ambiguous invocation of the right to counsel, is there any reason to think that the Court would rule differently with respect to an ambiguous invocation of the right to silence?

The court in United States v. Banks, 78 F.3d 1190 (7th Cir.1996), relied on *Davis* to hold that officers are not required to "scrupulously honor" the defendant's right to remain silent unless the suspect's invocation of that right is unequivocal. Mills, the defendant challenging his confession, was given a waiver form when he was arrested. He said "Get that out of my face. I don't got nothing to say." In response, the officer asked Mills if he knew the nicknames his co-conspirators had for him. He told Mills that they had been referring to him as "Big Dumbo" behind his back. Shortly thereafter the officer showed Mills a transcript of a telephone conversation between his co-conspirators to confirm that they were calling him "Big Dumbo" behind his back. Then Mills made incriminating statements. Mills argued that the officer was not "scrupulously honoring" his right to remain silent when he used the "Big Dumbo" ploy. But the court held that *Mosley* was inapplicable because Mills never unequivocally invoked his right to remain silent.

> Mr. Mills' response of "I don't got nothing to say," standing alone, could be construed as an invocation of his right to remain silent. Yet, when placed in the context of his other comments, the alternate interpretation—that it was merely an angry response to the form in front of him—is also possible. Given these two possible interpretations, the magistrate judge's determination that Mr. Mills' statement, when considered in context, was not a clear, unambiguous assertion of his right to remain silent cannot be disturbed by this court.

> Earlier case law from this circuit took the view that, when it is unclear whether a suspect has invoked his *Miranda* rights, the police have the obligation to cease questioning immediately, except for questions designed to clarify the ambiguity. Although this circuit has not had a recent opportunity to revisit the precise issue, the circuits and state supreme courts that have addressed the matter in the wake of the Supreme Court's decision in Davis v. United States, 512 U.S. 452 (1994), have held that an ambiguous invocation of the right to remain silent does not require that the police cease all questioning. Upon reflection, we have no reason to depart from the conclusion reached by these courts, * * *. If an ambiguous request for counsel—a request that, if it were more clear, would amount to a per se invocation of Fifth Amendment rights—does not require the cessation of all questioning, we do not believe that *Davis* permits our imposing such a rule on any other ambiguous invocation of the right to silence. Thus, in light of the ambiguous nature of Mr. Mills' initial statement when presented with the waiver form, the investigating officers were not barred from questioning him later. Mr. Mills cannot challenge the admission of his statement on this basis.

Note also that *Mosley's* requirement of "scrupulous honor" applies only if the defendant's invocation of the right to silence occurs in the context of custodial interrogation. For example, in United States v. Kelly, 329 F.3d 624 (8th Cir. 2003), the defendant argued that his confession had to be excluded under *Mosley* because he had previously invoked his right to silence when he spoke to police officers in an initial interview, and then confessed when the officers interrogated him later. The court, however, noted that the defendant was not in custody during the initial interview; accordingly, he had no *Miranda* rights to invoke. The court concluded that "Kelly's termination of the voluntary encounter posed no independent barrier to later questioning."

Invocation of the Right to Counsel: Edwards v. Arizona

In Edwards v. Arizona, 451 U.S. 477 (1981), the Court determined whether and under what circumstances a waiver can be found after the suspect invokes his right to counsel. The Court adopted a per se approach when it confronted the following facts:

On January 19, 1976, a sworn complaint was filed against Edwards in Arizona state court charging him with robbery, burglary, and first-degree murder. An arrest warrant was issued pursuant to the complaint, and Edwards was arrested at his home later that same day. At the police station, he was informed of his rights as required by Miranda v. Arizona. Petitioner stated that he understood his rights, and was willing to submit to questioning. After being told that another suspect already in custody had implicated him in the crime, Edwards denied involvement and gave a taped statement presenting an alibi defense. He then sought to "make a deal." The interrogating officer told him that he wanted a statement, but that he did not have the authority to negotiate a deal. The officer provided Edwards with the number of a county attorney. Petitioner made the call, but hung up after a few moments. Edwards then said, "I want an attorney before making a deal." At that point, questioning ceased and Edwards was taken to county jail.

At 9:15 the next morning, two detectives, colleagues of the officer who had interrogated Edwards the previous night, came to the jail and asked to see Edwards. When the detention officer informed Edwards that the detectives wished to speak with him, he replied that he did not want to talk to anyone. The guard told him that "he had" to talk and then took him to meet with the detectives. The officers identified themselves, stated they wanted to talk to him, and informed him of his *Miranda* rights. Edwards was willing to talk, but he first wanted to hear the taped statement of the alleged accomplice who had implicated him. After listening to the tape for several minutes, petitioner said that he would make a statement so long as it was not tape recorded. The detectives informed him that the recording was irrelevant since they could testify in court concerning whatever he said. Edwards replied "I'll tell you anything you want to know, but I don't want it on tape." He thereupon implicated himself in the crime.

The Court found that the defendant's waiver of *Miranda* rights was invalid, reasoning as follows:

[A]dditional safeguards are necessary when the accused asks for counsel; and we now hold that when an accused has invoked his right to have counsel present during custodial interrogation, a valid waiver of that right cannot be established by showing only that he responded to further police-initiated custodial interrogation even if he has been advised of his rights. We further hold that an accused, such as Edwards, having expressed his desire to deal with the police only through counsel, is not subject to further interrogation by the authorities until counsel has been made available to him, unless the accused himself initiates further communication, exchanges or conversations with the police.

Chief Justice Burger and Justices Powell and Rehnquist agreed with the result, but expressed concern about the seemingly per se aspects of the majority rule which they found to be an unnecessary embellishment on the standard knowing and intelligent waiver rule. In their view, Edwards had not made a knowing and voluntary waiver because the totality of circumstances indicated that he was directed to confess.[20]

Relationship Between Edwards and Innis

Edwards holds that a suspect cannot waive the right to counsel after invoking it, unless he initiates the conversation. But if police-renewed contact does not rise to the level of custodial interrogation, *Miranda* itself is inapplicable to a resulting confession, and therefore so is *Edwards*. This is shown by the facts of *Innis*. Innis invoked his right to counsel, but the Court found it unnecessary to reach the question of waiver, because the officers never interrogated him. They had *contact* with him—the officer's statement in the cruiser about the gun possibly being picked up by a handicapped child—but they did not interrogate him. So if the suspect invokes his right to counsel, what *Edwards* holds is that police may not *interrogate* him while in custody unless the suspect initiates the conversation and then knowingly and voluntarily waives his *Miranda* rights. See United States v. Ortiz, 177 F.3d 108 (1st Cir.1999) (officers who approached defendant after he invoked his right to counsel, and asked him whether he wanted to cooperate, violated *Edwards* because a request for cooperation constituted interrogation).

Defining Initiation: Oregon v. Bradshaw

Edwards requires that a suspect "initiate" further communication before a waiver can be found. Whether a suspect has initiated reinterrogation is often a difficult question. In Oregon v. Bradshaw, 462 U.S. 1039 (1983), Oregon police were investigating the death of Lowell Reynolds, who apparently died in the wreck of his pickup truck. Bradshaw was asked and consented to come to the

---

20. The Court found that *Edwards* did not require the suppression of statements in Wyrick v. Fields, 459 U.S. 42 (1982). Fields was suspected of rape, invoked his right to counsel and, on the advice of counsel, agreed to submit to a polygraph examination. At the conclusion of the examination, the examiner told Fields that there had been some deceit and asked whether Fields could explain why some of his answers were bothering him. Fields then made an incriminating statement to the examiner and, later, to police officers. The Court found no violation of *Edwards*. Fields had initiated the polygraph examination, and this constituted a waiver with respect to reasonable follow-up questions after the conclusion of the polygraph. The Court saw nothing to indicate that the circumstances after the polygraph examination "changed so seriously that his answers no longer were voluntary."

police station for questioning. Once there, he was advised of his rights and admitted providing liquor to Reynolds. He was arrested for furnishing liquor to a minor. When an officer suggested that Bradshaw might have been driving Reynolds' truck, Bradshaw invoked his right to an attorney. Questioning stopped. Thereafter, during or just before a 10 or 15 mile trip from the station to the jail, Bradshaw asked, "Well, what is going to happen to me now?" An officer answered that Bradshaw had requested an attorney and that Bradshaw should not be talking with the officer unless he desired to do so. The two had a conversation concerning where Bradshaw was being taken and with what he would be charged. The officer suggested that Bradshaw might help himself by taking a lie detector test, and Bradshaw agreed to take one. The next day, following new warnings, he took the test. The examiner expressed doubts that Bradshaw had told the truth and Bradshaw then admitted he was driving the vehicle in which Reynolds was killed. The trial court admitted Bradshaw's confession, and he was convicted of first degree manslaughter, driving while under the influence of intoxicants, and driving with a revoked license.

A plurality of the Supreme Court found that *Edwards* was satisfied, because Bradshaw initiated the contact with the police officer after invoking his right to counsel, and then made a knowing and voluntary waiver of his *Miranda* right. Justice Rehnquist's plurality opinion, joined by Chief Justice Burger and Justices White and O'Connor, found initiation by reasoning as follows:

> There can be no doubt in this case that in asking, "Well, what is going to happen to me now?", respondent "initiated" further conversation in the ordinary dictionary sense of that word. While we doubt that it would be desirable to build a superstructure of legal refinements around the word "initiate" in this context, there are undoubtedly situations where a bare inquiry by either a defendant or by a police officer should not be held to "initiate" any conversation or dialogue. There are some inquiries, such as a request for a drink of water or a request to use a telephone that are so routine that they cannot be fairly said to represent a desire on the part of an accused to open up a more generalized discussion relating directly or indirectly to the investigation. Such inquiries or statements, by either an accused or a police officer, relating to routine incidents of the custodial relationship, will not generally "initiate" a conversation in the sense in which that word was used in *Edwards*.

> Although ambiguous, the respondent's question in this case as to what was going to happen to him evinced a willingness and a desire for a generalized discussion about the investigation; it was not merely a necessary inquiry arising out of the incidents of the custodial relationship. It could reasonably have been interpreted by the officer as relating generally to the investigation. That the police officer so understood it is apparent from the fact that he immediately reminded the accused that "you do not have to talk to me," and only after the accused told him that he "understood" did they have a generalized conversation. On these facts we believe that there was not a violation of the *Edwards* rule.

The plurality clarified that a finding of initiation by the suspect was not enough to constitute a waiver under *Edwards*. Justice Rehnquist stated that even if the suspect initiates communication, "where reinterrogation follows, the burden remains upon the prosecution to show that subsequent events indicated a waiver of the Fifth Amendment right to have counsel present during the interrogation." Thus, the Court uses a two-step analysis to determine whether a suspect waives his rights after invoking the right to counsel. The first step is the bright-line prophylactic safeguard of the initiation requirement, and the second step is the familiar totality of circumstances test of a knowing and voluntary waiver. The plurality in *Bradshaw* found that after initiating communication, Bradshaw knowingly and voluntarily waived his *Miranda* rights, because he was given fresh warnings and it was clear he understood them and voluntarily waived them.

Justice Marshall, joined by Justices Brennan, Blackmun, and Stevens, dissented. The dissenters applied the same two-step approach as had the majority, but they differed as to the application of the threshold requirement of "initiation" to the facts. Justice Marshall argued that the plurality's definition of "initiation" was overbroad, and "drastically undermined" the protection erected in *Edwards*. In Justice Marshall's view, initiation could not be found unless the suspect expresses a willingness to discuss the specific subject matter of the investigation. He argued that Bradshaw's question was merely a response to his custodial surroundings, rather than an expression of willingness to discuss his crime.

The deciding vote in *Bradshaw* was cast by Justice Powell, who concurred in the judgment reversing the Oregon court. He expressed concern about the two step approach. He argued that this analysis, if followed literally, would be so rigid as to "frustrate justice as well as common sense." Justice Powell preferred to rely on the totality of the circumstances, which in this case indicated that Bradshaw had knowingly and voluntarily waived his *Miranda* rights.

Suppose the Supreme Court announced that once a suspect requested a lawyer, the police must be sure that any subsequent statements by the suspect are intended to initiate a discussion with the police concerning the offenses for which a suspect has been placed in custody. Would this unduly burden the police? What would police have to do to ascertain the intent of the suspect? Had they made an effort in *Bradshaw*, what would they have discovered?

Applications of Bradshaw

While the Court split 4–4 in *Bradshaw* as to the proper test for initiation, the lower courts have consistently followed Justice Rehnquist's broad view. The court in United States v. Velasquez, 885 F.2d 1076 (3d Cir.1989), relied on the *Bradshaw* plurality to hold that the suspect's statement "what is going to happen?" was an initiation under *Edwards*. The court stated that the plurality's test was a reasonable compromise between individual and state interests, and that Justice Marshall's test "might convert the prophylactic value of the initiation requirement * * * into an overly stringent substantive hurdle." Do you agree?

In Henderson v. Dugger, 925 F.2d 1309 (11th Cir.1991), Henderson was suspected of a string of murders, and he was being transported by Officers Hord and Bakker from one county to another. He invoked his right to counsel before getting into the police car. Upon arrival in the county of destination, Officer Bakker stopped the car and got out to make a phone call. Henderson asked officer Hord, "what's going to happen next?" Hord responded that Henderson was going to be placed in a county detention facility. At the suppression hearing, Hord testified that in response to this statement, Henderson "had a look on his face like 'you've got to be kidding. I know all these things, and all you're going to do is take me to jail.' " Hord took it that Henderson wanted to show the officers where bodies were buried. Henderson was given fresh warnings, and signed a waiver form, and after interrogation led the officers to the bodies of three previously undiscovered murder victims. The court, relying on the plurality opinion in *Bradshaw,* held that Henderson had initiated conversation when he asked what was going to happen next. However, the court added this cautionary note:

> We are careful to add that this holding is a result of our conclusion that Henderson himself asked a question initially that could have been taken as relating to his crimes, * * *. A holding that Henderson initiated his confession through nonverbal communication would allow police to interrogate suspects who have invoked their right to counsel on the basis of police interpretations of suspects' demeanors, facial expressions, and so on. A twitch of the cheek could be taken as a desire to confess. Such a rule would effectively wipe out the protections that cases such as *Edwards* provide.

Even under the plurality's broader view of initiation in *Bradshaw,* it does not follow that every statement from a suspect's mouth evinces a desire to "talk generally about his case." See, e.g., United States v. Soto, 953 F.2d 263 (6th Cir.1992)(indicating desire to keep belongings separate from those of co-defendant is not initiation); Desire v. Attorney General of California, 969 F.2d 802 (9th Cir.1992)(asking co-defendant, in front of police officer, whether he told the police officer everything is not initiation); Jacobs v. Singletary, 952 F.2d 1282 (11th Cir.1992)(asking officer "Where are my children?" is not initiation).

Ambiguous Invocation of the Right to Counsel: Davis v. United States

As with invocation of the right to silence, questions sometimes arise as to whether the suspect has in fact invoked a right to counsel. In Davis v. United States, 512 U.S. 452 (1994), the Court held that a suspect must clearly and unequivocally invoke the right to counsel in order to trigger the protections of *Edwards.* If the invocation is ambiguous or equivocal, police questioning can continue; and such questioning need not be limited to that necessary to clarify the suspect's desire with respect to counsel.

After waiving his *Miranda* rights, Davis answered questions about a killing; about 90 minutes into the interview, he said, "Maybe I should talk to a lawyer." The officers then asked clarifying questions to determine whether Davis wanted a lawyer. He said that he did not. A short break was taken, Davis was reminded of his rights, and the interview continued for another hour, until Davis said, "I think I want a lawyer before I say anything else." At that point, questioning ceased. In the Supreme Court, Davis argued that the statements he made after his first reference to counsel were improperly admitted at his trial.

The Supreme Court, in an opinion by Justice O'Connor for five Justices, rejected Davis' argument and held that the statements Davis made after referring to counsel were properly admitted at his trial. Justice O'Connor set forth the standards applicable to the invocation of the *Miranda* right to counsel, and the protections of *Edwards,* in the following analysis:

> [T]he suspect must unambiguously request counsel. Although a suspect need not "speak with the discrimination of an Oxford don," he must articulate his desire to have counsel present sufficiently clearly that a reasonable police officer in the circumstances would understand the statement to be a request for an attorney. If the statement fails to meet the requisite level of clarity, *Edwards* does not require that the officers stop questioning the suspect.

We decline petitioner's invitation to extend *Edwards* and require law enforcement officers to cease questioning immediately upon the making of an ambiguous or equivocal reference to an attorney. The rationale underlying *Edwards* is that the police must respect a suspect's wishes regarding his right to have an attorney present during custodial interrogation. But when the officers conducting the questioning reasonably do not know whether or not the suspect wants a lawyer, a rule requiring the immediate cessation of questioning would * * * needlessly prevent the police from questioning a suspect in the absence of counsel even if the suspect did not wish to have a lawyer present. Nothing in *Edwards* requires the provision of counsel to a suspect who consents to answer questions without the assistance of a lawyer.

Davis argued that if police were permitted to continue interrogation in the face of an ambiguous invocation of counsel, they could take unfair advantage of inarticulate and overmatched suspects. But Justice O'Connor held that these concerns were not of sufficient weight to prevent the continuation of police questioning:

> We recognize that requiring a clear assertion of the right to counsel might disadvantage some suspects who—because of fear, intimidation, lack of linguistic skills, or a variety of other reasons—will not clearly articulate their right to counsel although they actually want to have a lawyer present. But the primary protection afforded suspects subject to custodial interrogation is the *Miranda* warnings themselves. * * * A suspect who knowingly and voluntarily waives his right to counsel after having that right explained to him has indicated his willingness to deal with the police unassisted. Although *Edwards* provides an additional protection—if a suspect subsequently requests an attorney, questioning must cease—it is one that must be affirmatively invoked by the suspect.

Justice O'Connor further declared that the continued questioning after a suspect's ambiguous reference to counsel need not be limited to questions clarifying whether the suspect really wants a lawyer:

> Of course, when a suspect makes an ambiguous or equivocal statement it will often be good police practice for the interviewing officers to clarify whether or not he actually wants an attorney. That was the procedure followed by the [officers] in this case. Clarifying questions help protect the rights of the suspect by ensuring that he gets an attorney if he wants one, and will minimize the chance of a confession being suppressed due to subsequent judicial second-guessing as to the meaning of the suspect's statement regarding counsel. But we decline to adopt a rule requiring officers to ask clarifying questions. If the suspect's statement is not an

unambiguous or unequivocal request for counsel, the officers have no obligation to stop questioning him.

To recapitulate: We held in *Miranda* that a suspect is entitled to the assistance of counsel during custodial interrogation even though the Constitution does not provide for such assistance. We held in *Edwards* that if the suspect invokes the right to counsel at any time, the police must immediately cease questioning him until an attorney is present. But we are unwilling to create a third layer of prophylaxis to prevent police questioning when the suspect might want a lawyer. Unless the suspect actually requests an attorney, questioning may continue.

Finally, Justice O'Connor found no reason to disturb the rulings of the lower courts that Davis' statement—"Maybe I should talk to a lawyer"—was not a sufficiently explicit request for counsel.

Justice Souter, joined by Justices Blackmun, Stevens, and Ginsburg, concurred only in the judgment in *Davis*. He agreed with the Court that Davis' position—i.e., questioning must cease completely whenever the suspect invokes counsel, even if the invocation is ambiguous—was overprotective of suspects and too costly to law enforcement. He disagreed, however, with the Court's position that an ambiguous invocation was essentially irrelevant and placed no limits on subsequent questioning. Justice Souter preferred the view taken by the majority of courts prior to *Davis*—that questioning could continue, but that the questions must be limited to clarifying whether or not the suspect wanted to invoke the right to counsel. Because the officers in *Davis* asked only clarifying questions until it was determined that Davis did not desire counsel, Justice Souter concluded that Davis' subsequent confession was properly admitted. Justice Souter expressed concern that the majority's explicit invocation test, without a safety valve requirement that officers ask only clarifying questions, would fall hard on many criminal suspects:

> [C]riminal suspects who may (in *Miranda's* words) be "thrust into an unfamiliar atmosphere and run through menacing police interrogation procedures," would seem an odd group to single out for the Court's demand of heightened linguistic care. A substantial percentage of them lack anything like a confident command of the English language; many are "woefully ignorant;" and many more will be sufficiently intimidated by the interrogation process or overwhelmed by the uncertainty of their predicament that the ability to speak assertively will abandon them.

Questions After Davis

What is the difference between Davis' first statement—"Maybe I should talk to a lawyer"—and his second statement—"I think I want a lawyer before I say anything else"? Are you as convinced as the Court that the first one was an ambiguous statement that did not constitute a request for counsel, while the second one was a clear invocation of the right to counsel? The majority in *Davis* opted for the "clarity" of a bright-line rule. Are you convinced that the rule is as bright a line as the *Davis* Court suggests?

Ainsworth, In a Different Register: The Pragmatics of Powerlessness in Police Interrogation, 103 Yale L.J.259 (1993), argues that an explicit invocation requirement puts an unfair premium on direct and assertive speech patterns. She concludes that conditioning *Edwards* protection on an explicit request for counsel "is a gendered doctrine that privileges male speech norms" and thus "disadvantages women and other marginalized and relatively powerless groups in society, who are more likely to use less direct and assertive patterns of speech characteristic of the female register." Do you agree? Would Justice O'Connor, who wrote *Davis*, agree?

Consequences of Explicit Invocation: Smith v. Illinois

In Smith v. Illinois, 469 U.S. 91 (1984), a suspect who was asked whether he understood his right to have a lawyer present stated, "Uh, yeah, I'd like that." The Court rejected the state's argument that the invocation of counsel was too vague to trigger the protections of *Edwards*. It found that "with the possible exception of the word 'uh' the defendant's statement in this case was neither indecisive nor ambiguous." The Court concluded that "where nothing about the request for counsel or the circumstances leading up to the request would render it ambiguous, all questioning must cease."

When the officer questioned Smith after his "uh" response to the warnings, ostensibly to clarify the request, Smith did make ambiguous statements concerning his desire for counsel. But the Court dismissed this later ambiguity as irrelevant. It declared that "using an accused's subsequent responses to cast doubt on the adequacy of the initial request *itself* is * * * intolerable" and that a contrary rule would lead to abusive use of "clarifying" questions. Justice Rehnquist, joined by Chief Justice Burger and Justice Powell, dissented. He argued that Smith's statement was ambiguous under the circumstances, and that the majority's rule preventing consideration of post-request statements was overbroad.

Unrelated Crimes: Arizona v. Roberson

Does *Edwards* permit officers to initiate interrogation on crimes other than the one for which the suspect invoked his right to counsel? In Arizona v. Roberson, 486 U.S. 675 (1988), the Court answered this question in the negative and held that an invocation of the right to counsel under *Edwards* was not offense-specific. Such an invocation prevents police-initiated interrogation on any crime.

Roberson was arrested at the scene of a just-completed burglary. After he was given *Miranda* warnings, he stated that he wanted a lawyer before answering any questions. Three days later while the defendant remained in custody, a different officer, who was unaware of the previous request for a lawyer, gave new *Miranda* warnings and obtained a statement concerning another burglary. Justice Stevens wrote for the Court as it declared that "*Edwards* serves the purpose of providing clear and unequivocal guidelines to the law enforcement profession," and that "there is nothing ambiguous about the requirement that after a person in custody has expressed his desire to deal with the police only through counsel, he is not subject to further interrogation by the authorities until counsel has been made available to him, unless the accused himself initiates further communication, exchanges, or conversations with the police."

The Court concluded that "to a suspect who has indicated his inability to cope with the pressures of custodial interrogation by requesting counsel, any further interrogation without counsel having been provided will surely exacerbate whatever compulsion to speak the suspect may be feeling." In response to the suggestion of the United States as *amicus curiae* that a suspect might have good reason to want to speak to police about a new investigation, Justice Stevens wrote that "[t]he simple answer is that the suspect, having requested counsel, can determine how to deal with the separate investigations with counsel's advice." He added that "even if the police have decided temporarily not to provide counsel, they are free to inform the suspect of the facts of the second investigation as long as such communication does not constitute interrogation."

Justice Kennedy, joined by Chief Justice Rehnquist, dissented, complaining that the Court's ruling was unnecessary to protect a suspect's rights and unduly restricted legitimate investigations of crimes other than those for which a suspect has been arrested. He described the breadth of the Court's rule as follows: "The rule announced today will bar law enforcement officials, even those from some other city or other jurisdiction, from questioning a suspect about an unrelated matter if he is in custody and has requested counsel to assist in answering questions put to him about the crime for which he was arrested." Justice Kennedy attacked the Court's presumption "that a suspect has made the decision that he does not wish to talk about that [separate investigation] without counsel present, although that decision was made when the suspect was unaware of even the existence of a second investigation," and argued that "[a]llowing authorities who conduct a separate investigation to read the suspect his *Miranda* rights and ask him whether he wishes to invoke them strikes an appropriate balance."

Which Constitutional Right to Counsel is Invoked? McNeil v. Wisconsin

Besides the *Miranda* right to counsel, a defendant who has been formally charged with a crime (e.g., indicted) also has a Sixth Amendment right to counsel, as discussed later in this Chapter. When a formally charged defendant appears at an arraignment and invokes the right to counsel, is that an invocation of the *Miranda* right to counsel or the Sixth Amendment right to counsel? And why would it make any difference? The Court in McNeil v. Wisconsin, 501 U.S. 171 (1991), held that an accused who is arraigned and asks for counsel is invoking the Sixth Amendment, rather than the *Miranda*, right to counsel, and that there is a difference in the protections provided. The difference is that an invocation of Sixth Amendment rights is "offense-specific"; therefore police can initiate questioning on crimes other than the crime with which the defendant was charged.[21] This contrasts with the invocation of the *Miranda* right to counsel, which protects against police-initiated interrogation with respect to any crime.

McNeil was charged with armed robbery, and at his initial appearance before a judicial officer, he invoked his right to counsel. Police thereafter initiated questioning of McNeil concerning armed robbery and murder committed in another part of the state. McNeil waived his *Miranda* rights and confessed to those crimes; he argued that this waiver was invalid under *Edwards* and *Roberson*, because the police had initiated interrogation after he had invoked his right to counsel. Justice Scalia, writing for a six-person majority, stated that

---

21. The *McNeil* analysis of the offense-specific nature of an invocation of the Sixth Amendment right to counsel is considered in the section on Sixth Amendment protections, later in this Chapter.

McNeil's invocation of his offense-specific Sixth Amendment right at his initial appearance did not constitute an invocation of the non-offense specific *Miranda–Edwards–Roberson* right. Justice Scalia explained as follows:

> To invoke the Sixth Amendment interest is, as a matter of fact, not to invoke the *Miranda–Edwards* interest. One might be quite willing to speak to the police without counsel present concerning many matters, but not the matter under prosecution. It can be said, perhaps, that it is likely that one who has asked for counsel's assistance in defending against a prosecution would want counsel present for all custodial interrogation, even interrogation unrelated to the charge. * * * But even if that were true, the likelihood that a suspect would wish counsel to be present is not the test for applicability of *Edwards*. The rule of that case * * * requires, at a minimum, some statement that can reasonably be construed to be expression of a desire for the assistance of an attorney in dealing with custodial interrogation by the police. Requesting the assistance of an attorney at a bail hearing does not bear that construction.

Justice Scalia rejected the defendant's argument that a total prohibition on police-initiated questioning after any invocation of counsel (whether it is a Sixth or Fifth amendment invocation) would provide a clear guideline for the police. He responded that "the police do not need our assistance to establish such a guideline; they are free, if they wish, to adopt it on their own." Justice Scalia recognized that clear guidelines are nonetheless important for judicial review. He responded, however, that bright-line rules should be used "only when they guide sensibly, and in a direction we are authorized to go." Justice Scalia concluded that the defendant's proposed bright-line rule "would do much more harm than good, and is not contained within, or even in furtherance of, the Sixth Amendment's right to counsel or the Fifth Amendment's right against compelled self-incrimination."

Justice Kennedy wrote a concurring opinion, reiterating the views of his *Roberson* dissent that an invocation of the *Miranda* right to counsel should be offense-specific as well.

Justice Stevens, joined by Justices Marshall and Blackmun, dissented. The dissenters argued that the Court's offense-specific test for a Sixth Amendment invocation would lead to ambiguity and consequent abuse. Justice Stevens argued that police might "file charges selectively in order to preserve opportunities for custodial interrogation."

Can Edwards Protections Be Triggered in Advance of Interrogation?

The dissenters in *McNeil* contended that the majority's limited construction of a Sixth Amendment invocation (i.e., that it is offense-specific) would have little practical effect. Because *Roberson* held that an invocation of *Miranda* rights is *not* offense-specific, Justice Stevens asserted that "the entire offense-specific house of cards that the Court has erected" for the Sixth Amendment would collapse whenever defendant or counsel makes an explicit statement invoking *Miranda* rights at an initial appearance before a judge.

Is Justice Stevens correct that the holding in *McNeil* will affect very few cases, because a defendant can and will explicitly invoke his *Miranda* rights at the initial appearance before a judge? Note that no police officer was attempting to question McNeil at his preliminary appearance. Thus, Justice Stevens assumes that the *Miranda* right to counsel can be invoked in advance of police interrogation. This assumption was challenged by Justice Scalia in a footnote in the *McNeil* majority opinion. Justice Scalia asserted that "we have never held that a person can invoke his *Miranda* rights anticipatorily, in a context other than custodial interrogation—which a preliminary hearing will not always, or even usually, involve." He stated that such reasoning would lead to the unacceptable conclusion that *Miranda* rights could be invoked "in a letter prior to arrest, or indeed even prior to identification as a suspect." He concluded as follows:

> Most rights must be asserted when the government seeks to take the action they protect against. The fact that we have allowed the *Miranda* right to counsel, once asserted, to be effective with respect to future custodial interrogation does not necessarily mean that we will allow it to be asserted initially outside the context of custodial interrogation, with similar future effect.

In light of the footnote in the majority opinion in *McNeil*, the lower courts have held that the *Miranda* right to counsel cannot be invoked in advance of police interrogation. As the court explained in Alston v. Redman, 34 F.3d 1237 (3d Cir.1994):

> The *McNeil* footnote * * * reflects the general proposition * * * that the rights guaranteed by the Constitution of the United States are primarily negative in character, standing guard as vigilant sentinels at the perimeter of permissible state conduct. * * * To require that the Government first act to compel an individual to incriminate herself before that individual can assert her right to remain silent is merely to recognize that the privilege against self-incrimination acts as a shield against state action rather than as a sword, and that the shield may only be interposed when state action actually threatens.

See also United States v. Wyatt, 179 F.3d 532 (7th Cir.1999) (suspect could not invoke his *Miranda* right to counsel when he was not yet in custody; therefore there was no violation of *Edwards* when officers later initiated interrogation, gave warnings, and the defendant voluntarily confessed); United States v. Melgar, 139 F.3d 1005 (4th Cir.1998) ("[A]lthough Melgar invoked his right to counsel at his arraignment on state charges, the right invoked was grounded in the Sixth Amendment, not the Fifth. In order for the Fifth Amendment protection to arise, a suspect must be in a custodial interrogation context. Melgar's arraignment did not constitute an interrogation."); United States v. Wright, 962 F.2d 953 (9th Cir.1992)(suspect cannot invoke *Miranda* at an initial appearance, because it would "make it virtually impossible for any defendant charged with one crime ever to be questioned about unrelated criminal activity").

Where the Suspect Has Consulted With Counsel: Minnick v. Mississippi

Suppose the suspect properly invokes his *Miranda* right to counsel and then the police let him confer with counsel. After counsel leaves, can the police approach the suspect and ask him if he would now like to talk to them? This was the question in Minnick v. Mississippi, 498 U.S. 146 (1990). The Court in *Minnick* held that the protection of *Edwards* continues even after the suspect has consulted with an attorney. Justice Kennedy, who dissented in *Roberson,* wrote the majority opinion for six justices. Minnick committed murders in Mississippi, and was apprehended in California. After making inculpatory statements at an FBI interview (which were excluded from Minnick's trial as violative of *Edwards)* an appointed attorney met with Minnick on two or three occasions. The attorney told Minnick not to say anything, and not to sign any waiver forms. After these consultations, a Mississippi Deputy Sheriff initiated an interrogation of Minnick. Minnick was given *Miranda* warnings, refused to sign a waiver of rights form, and confessed. The trial court held that the confession to the Deputy Sheriff was not excluded by *Edwards,* reasoning that *Edwards* was inapplicable once counsel had been made available to Minnick.

Justice Kennedy declared that under *Edwards,* police-initiated interrogation after an invocation of counsel may occur only if counsel is actually present during the interrogation. The Court relied upon language in *Miranda, Edwards,* and the *Edwards* line of cases which stated that "the interrogation must cease until an attorney is present" and that the suspect has the right "to have counsel present during custodial interrogation." Justice Kennedy reasoned that two policies underlying *Edwards* rendered its application in this case "appropriate and necessary": (1) the bright line *Edwards* rule provides clarity and certainty, and (2) the rule guarantees that suspects will not be badgered by police officers and provides prophylactic protection against police coercion.

On the issue of clarity, the Court found that a rule allowing police-initiated interrogation after consultation with counsel "would undermine the advantages flowing from *Edwards'* clear and unequivocal character." Justice Kennedy observed that a rule denying *Edwards* protection after consultation with a lawyer would be vague because "consultation is not a precise concept, for it may encompass variations from a telephone call to say that the attorney is in route, to a hurried exchange, * * * to a lengthy in-person conference."

As to the *Edwards* policy of preventing badgering and coercion, the Court found that mere consultation with an attorney would be insufficient to protect against the risk of harassment and exploitation of the suspect by the police. Justice Kennedy stated that "a single consultation with an attorney does not remove the suspect from persistent attempts by officials to persuade him to waive his rights, or from the coercive pressures that accompany custody and that may increase as custody is prolonged."

In a vigorous dissent, Justice Scalia, joined by Chief Justice Rehnquist, attacked the Court's "irrebuttable presumption" that a suspect who has invoked his right to counsel "can never validly waive that right during any police-initiated encounter, even after the suspect has been provided multiple *Miranda* warnings and has actually consulted with his attorney." More fundamentally, Justice Scalia contended that *Edwards* itself was an unnecessary prophylactic rule. Even more fundamentally, Justice Scalia attacked what he thought was the underlying premise of *Miranda* and its progeny: that an honest confession is a "foolish mistake" which ought to be rejected as evidence.

Justice Scalia stated that, even if *Edwards* struck an appropriate balance between the need to protect the suspect and proper law enforcement objectives, the extension of *Edwards* promulgated by the majority did not. He contended that a suspect who has consulted with counsel knows "that he has an advocate on his side, and that the police will permit him to consult with that advocate. He almost certainly also has a heightened awareness (above what the *Miranda* warning itself will provide) of his right to remain silent."

Justice Scalia concluded with a broad attack on the prophylactic rules of *Edwards* and *Miranda* itself:

> It seems obvious to me that, even in *Edwards* itself but surely in today's decision, we have gone far beyond any genuine concern about suspects who do not know their right to remain silent, or who have been coerced to abandon it. Both holdings are explicable * * * only as an effort to protect suspects against what is regarded as their own folly. The sharp-witted criminal would know better than to confess; why should the dull-witted suffer for his lack of mental endowment? Providing him an attorney at every stage where he might be induced or persuaded (though not coerced) to incriminate himself will even the odds. Apart from the fact that this protective enterprise is beyond our authority under the Fifth Amendment * * * it is unwise. The procedural protections of the Constitution protect the guilty as well as the innocent, but it is not their objective to set the guilty free. That some clever criminals may employ those protections to their advantage is poor reason to allow criminals who have not done so to escape justice.

> Thus, even if I were to concede that an honest confession is a foolish mistake, I would welcome rather than reject it * * *. More fundamentally, however, it is wrong, and subtly corrosive of our criminal justice system, to regard an honest confession as a "mistake." While every person is entitled to stand silent, it is more virtuous for the wrongdoer to admit his offense and accept the punishment he deserves. * * * We should, then, rejoice at an honest confession, rather than pity the "poor fool" who has made it.[22]

The Continuous Custody Requirement

Lower courts have unanimously held that *Edwards* protections will not apply if, after invoking the right to counsel, the suspect is released from custody. Thus, officers can approach such a suspect when he is again brought into custody and interrogate him–no initiation by the suspect is required. The rationale for the continuous custody requirement is that a suspect who is released from custody is not being subject to the risk of harassment and pressure that the Court was concerned about in *Edwards*. See, e.g., United States v. Coleman, 208 F.3d 786 (9th Cir. 2000) ("Because Defendant had been released from custody for a significant period of time before investigators questioned him again, the district court's refusal to suppress those statements did not violate *Edwards*); United States v. Harris, 221 F.3d 1048 (8th Cir. 2000) ("Concern that a suspect will be 'badgered' is greatest when a suspect remains in confinement for the time he requests a lawyer until the time that police attempt to reinterrogate him. That concern is not present in cases such as this, however,

---

22. For an incisive discussion of the issues addressed by Justice Scalia in *Minnick*, see Rosenberg and Rosenberg, *Miranda, Minnick,* and the Morality of Confessions, 19 Am. J.Crim.L.1 (1991).

where a person is not in continuous custody and the coercive effects of confinement dissolve.'').

V. CONFESSIONS AND THE SIXTH AMENDMENT RIGHT TO COUNSEL

A. THE *MASSIAH* RULE

In addition to the Fifth Amendment and the Due Process Clause, the Court has also extended the protections of the Sixth Amendment to some police-induced confessions. Recall that in *Spano*, the concurring Justices heavily emphasized the fact that Spano had been formally charged with a crime, and yet was interrogated without his counsel being present. In the following case, the Supreme Court explicitly relied on the Sixth Amendment to exclude a confession.

MASSIAH v. UNITED STATES

Supreme Court of the United States, 1964.
377 U.S. 201.

Mr. Justice Stewart **delivered the opinion of the Court.**

* * *

[Massiah was a merchant seaman. Drugs were found on a ship and connected to Massiah. He was arrested, arraigned, and subsequently indicted for possession of narcotics aboard a United States vessel. Thereafter, a superseding indictment was returned, charging Massiah, Colson with narcotics offenses and conspiracy. Massiah, who had retained a lawyer, pleaded not guilty and was released on bail, along with Colson.]

A few days later, and quite without the petitioner's knowledge, Colson decided to cooperate with the government agents in their continuing investigation of the narcotics activities in which the petitioner, Colson, and others had allegedly been engaged. Colson permitted an agent named Murphy to install a Schmidt radio transmitter under the front seat of Colson's automobile, by means of which Murphy, equipped with an appropriate receiving device, could overhear from some distance away conversations carried on in Colson's car.

On the evening of November 19, 1959, Colson and the petitioner held a lengthy conversation while sitting in Colson's automobile, parked on a New York street. By prearrangement with Colson, and totally unbeknown to the petitioner, the agent Murphy sat in a car parked out of sight down the street and listened over the radio to the entire conversation. The petitioner made several incriminating statements during the course of this conversation. At the petitioner's trial these incriminating statements were brought before the jury through Murphy's testimony, despite the insistent objection of defense counsel. The jury convicted the petitioner of several related narcotics offenses, and the convictions were affirmed by the Court of Appeals.

* * * [I]t is said that the petitioner's Fifth and Sixth Amendment rights were violated by the use in evidence against him of incriminating statements which government agents had deliberately elicited from him after he had been indicted and in the absence of his retained counsel.

[The Court discusses *Spano,* paying more attention to the concurring opinions than to the majority opinion. It also discusses right to counsel precedents, which are discussed in Chapter Five, infra. The Court ultimately finds the Sixth Amendment right to counsel to be determinative.]

* * * We hold that the petitioner was denied the basic protections of that [Sixth Amendment] guarantee when there was used against him at his trial evidence of his own incriminating words, which federal agents had deliberately elicited from him after he had been indicted and in the absence of his counsel. It is true that in the *Spano* case the defendant was interrogated in a police station, while here the damaging testimony was elicited from the defendant without his knowledge while he was free on bail. But, as Judge Hays pointed out in his dissent in the Court of Appeals, "if such a rule is to have any efficacy it must apply to indirect and surreptitious interrogations as well as those conducted in the jailhouse. In this case, Massiah was more seriously imposed upon * * * because he did not even know that he was under interrogation by a government agent."

The Solicitor General * * * has strenuously contended that the federal law enforcement agents had the right, if not indeed the duty, to continue their investigation of the petitioner and his alleged criminal associates even though the petitioner had been indicted. He points out that the Government was continuing its investigation in order to uncover not only the source of narcotics found on the S. S. *Santa Maria,* but also their intended buyer. He says that the quantity of narcotics involved was such as to suggest that the petitioner was part of a large and well-organized ring, and indeed that the continuing investigation confirmed this suspicion, since it resulted in criminal charges against many defendants. Under these circumstances the Solicitor General concludes that the government agents were completely "justified in making use of Colson's cooperation by having Colson continue his normal associations and by surveilling them."

* * * We do not question that in this case, as in many cases, it was entirely proper to continue an investigation of the suspected criminal activities of the defendant and his alleged confederates, even though the defendant had already been indicted. All that we hold is that the defendant's own incriminating statements, obtained by federal agents under the circumstances here disclosed, could not constitutionally be used by the prosecution as evidence against *him* at his trial.

MR. JUSTICE WHITE, with whom MR. JUSTICE CLARK and MR. JUSTICE HARLAN join, dissenting.

* * *

Massiah was not prevented from consulting with counsel as often as he wished. No meetings with counsel were disturbed or spied upon. Preparation for trial was in no way obstructed. It is only a sterile syllogism—an unsound one, besides—to say that because Massiah had a right to counsel's aid before and during the trial, his out-of-court conversations and admissions must be excluded if obtained without counsel's consent or presence. The right to counsel has never meant as much before, and its extension in this case requires some further explanation, so far unarticulated by the Court.

* * *

[T]he Court's newly fashioned exclusionary principle goes far beyond the constitutional privilege against self-incrimination, which neither requires nor suggests the barring of voluntary pre-trial admissions. * * *

At the time of the conversation in question, petitioner was not in custody but free on bail. He was not ques- tioned in what anyone would call an atmosphere of official coercion.

* * *

The Rationale of Massiah

Massiah was certainly not pressured to confess in the same way that Spano was. Indeed, he suffered less pressure than Miranda, because he didn't even know that he was speaking with a government agent. So the Sixth Amendment protection established in *Massiah* must be directed toward something other than police-created pressure to confess. What is the rationale for Sixth Amendment regulation of confessions? Judge Higginbotham, in United States v. Johnson, 954 F.2d 1015 (5th Cir.1992), explained it this way:

> [The Sixth Amendment] recognizes that once the government has brought formal charges against an individual the adversary relationship between the parties is cemented. Once an accused has chosen to retain an attorney to act as his representative in the adversary process, the government may not try to circumvent the protection afforded by the presence of counsel during questioning. The vice is not deprivation of privacy, but interference with the parity required by the Sixth Amendment.

Thus, the *Massiah* right is basically a constitutionalized version of a rule of professional ethics: that an adverse party may be contacted only through her lawyer. This rule protects the attorney-client relationship and guards against overreaching by the adversary. See Model Rules of Professional Conduct 4.2; Model Code of Professional Responsibility DR 7–104.[23]

Note on Escobedo v. Illinois

In Escobedo v. Illinois, 378 U.S. 478 (1964), the Court undertook a short-lived experiment to extend the Sixth Amendment right to counsel to suspects who have not yet been formally charged. Escobedo was taken into custody on suspicion of murder. He asked for a lawyer several times, but his request was denied. His mother retained a lawyer for him, and the lawyer went to the police station, but the police would not let the lawyer speak to Escobedo. Escobedo was confronted with incriminating evidence, while handcuffed in a standing position, and was given false promises that if he confessed, he would be allowed to go home. While these facts established a strong case for holding Escobedo's confession involuntary, the Court, in this pre-*Miranda* case, relied explicitly on the Sixth Amendment to invalidate the confession. Justice Goldberg, writing for the Court, recognized that unlike Spano and Massiah, Escobedo had not been indicted at the time he confessed; but he argued that "in the context of this case, that fact should make no difference." This was because the police had focused on Escobedo as a prospective criminal defendant. Justice Goldberg stated that when Escobedo was denied his request for counsel, "the investigation had ceased to be a general investigation of an unsolved crime" and that Escobedo had become the "accused."

Justices Harlan, Stewart, White, and Clark dissented in *Escobedo*. The dissenters were concerned that the majority's "focus" test would result in an extravagant

---

23. For an eloquent defense of the *Massiah* doctrine, in response to an attack on that doctrine by the Justice Department, see Tomko- vicz, The Truth About *Massiah*, 23 U.Mich. J.L.Ref. 641 (1990).

extension of the Sixth Amendment right to counsel, which by its terms applies to criminal "prosecutions," not criminal "investigations." As Justice Stewart put it:

> [T]he institution of formal, meaningful judicial proceedings, by way of indictment, information, or arraignment, marks the point at which a criminal investigation has ended and adversary litigative proceedings have commenced. * * * [T]he Court today converts a routine police investigation of an unsolved murder into a distorted analogue of a judicial trial. It imports into this investigation constitutional concepts historically applicable only after the onset of formal prosecutorial proceedings.

As a Sixth Amendment case, *Escobedo* has little or no continuing relevance. In Moran v. Burbine, 475 U.S. 412 (1986), discussed in the section on *Miranda*, Burbine was being interrogated as a suspect in a murder. His family retained counsel for him, but police officers denied counsel's request to see Burbine. Burbine had not been formally charged at the time he confessed, but he was certainly the focus of the police investigation. Burbine relied on *Escobedo* to argue that his Sixth Amendment rights were violated, but Justice O'Connor, writing for the majority, rejected that argument. She stated that "subsequent decisions foreclose any reliance on *Escobedo* * * * for the proposition that the Sixth Amendment right, in any of its manifestations, applies prior to the initiation of adversary criminal proceedings." She concluded that *Escobedo* is in retrospect best understood as a Fifth Amendment case, because the prime purpose of the Court in *Escobedo* was not to vindicate the right to counsel as such but rather to guarantee "the full effectuation of the privilege against self-incrimination."

While *Escobedo* is therefore mainly of historical note on the Court's road to *Miranda*, the Sixth Amendment right to counsel has significant contemporary relevance where information is sought from a person who has been formally charged. After the Court decided *Miranda*, it returned to *Massiah* and gave it a very broad reading. These cases are discussed immediately below.

B. OBTAINING INFORMATION FROM FORMALLY CHARGED DEFENDANTS

After *Massiah*, the Supreme Court for several years virtually ignored the Sixth Amendment as a means of regulating confessions. As you know, the Court turned to the Fifth Amendment in *Miranda*. However, in 1977, the Court unexpectedly returned to the Sixth Amendment as an additional source for excluding confessions.

BREWER v. WILLIAMS

Supreme Court of the United States, 1977.
430 U.S. 387.[a]

MR. JUSTICE STEWART **delivered the opinion of the Court.**

I

On the afternoon of December 24, 1968, a 10–year-old girl named Pamela Powers went with her family to the YMCA in Des Moines, Iowa, to watch a wrestling tournament in which her brother was participating. When she failed to return from a trip to the washroom, a search for her began. The search was unsuccessful.

a. For an exhaustive analysis of this case, see Kamisar, Brewer v. Williams, Massiah and

Miranda: What is "Interrogation"? When Does it Matter? 67 Geo.L.J. 1 (1978).

Robert Williams, who had recently escaped from a mental hospital, was a resident of the YMCA. Soon after the girl's disappearance Williams was seen in the YMCA lobby carrying some clothing and a large bundle wrapped in a blanket. He obtained help from a 14–year-old boy in opening the street door of the YMCA and the door to his automobile parked outside. When Williams placed the bundle in the front seat of his car the boy "saw two legs in it and they were skinny and white." Before anyone could see what was in the bundle Williams drove away. His abandoned car was found the following day in Davenport, Iowa, roughly 160 miles east of Des Moines. A warrant was then issued in Des Moines for his arrest on a charge of abduction.

On the morning of December 26, a Des Moines lawyer named Henry McKnight went to the Des Moines police station and informed the officers present that he had just received a long distance call from Williams, and that he had advised Williams to turn himself in to the Davenport police. Williams did surrender that morning to the police in Davenport, and they booked him on the charge specified in the arrest warrant and gave him the warnings required by Miranda v. Arizona. The Davenport police then telephoned their counterparts in Des Moines to inform them that Williams had surrendered. McKnight, the lawyer, was still at the Des Moines police headquarters, and Williams conversed with McKnight on the telephone. In the presence of the Des Moines chief of police and a police detective named Leaming, McKnight advised Williams that Des Moines police officers would be driving to Davenport to pick him up, that the officers would not interrogate him or mistreat him, and that Williams was not to talk to the officers about Pamela Powers until after con-

sulting with McKnight upon his return to Des Moines. As a result of these conversations, it was agreed between McKnight and the Des Moines police officials that Detective Leaming and a fellow officer would drive to Davenport to pick up Williams, that they would bring him directly back to Des Moines, and that they would not question him during the trip.

In the meantime Williams was arraigned before a judge in Davenport on the outstanding arrest warrant. The judge advised him of his Miranda rights and committed him to jail. Before leaving the courtroom, Williams conferred with a lawyer named Kelly, who advised him not to make any statements until consulting with McKnight back in Des Moines.

Detective Leaming and his fellow officer arrived in Davenport about noon to pick up Williams and return him to Des Moines. Soon after their arrival they met with Williams and Kelly, who, they understood, was acting as Williams' lawyer. Detective Leaming repeated the Miranda warnings, and told Williams:

> "[W]e both know that you're being represented here by Mr. Kelly and you're being represented by Mr. McKnight in Des Moines, and * * * I want you to remember this because we'll be visiting between here and Des Moines."

Williams then conferred again with Kelly alone, and after this conference Kelly reiterated to Detective Leaming that Williams was not to be questioned about the disappearance of Pamela Powers until after he had consulted with McKnight back in Des Moines. When Leaming expressed some reservations, Kelly firmly stated that the agreement with McKnight was to be carried out—that there was to be no interrogation of Williams during the automobile journey to Des Moines.

Kelly was denied permission to ride in the police car back to Des Moines with Williams and the two officers.

The two detectives, with Williams in their charge, then set out on the 160–mile drive. At no time during the trip did Williams express a willingness to be interrogated in the absence of an attorney. Instead, he stated several times that "[w]hen I get to Des Moines and see Mr. McKnight, I am going to tell you the whole story." Detective Leaming knew that Williams was a former mental patient, and knew also that he was deeply religious.

The detective and his prisoner soon embarked on a wide-ranging conversation covering a variety of topics, including the subject of religion. Then, not long after leaving Davenport and reaching the interstate highway, Detective Leaming delivered what has been referred to in the briefs and oral arguments as the "Christian burial speech." Addressing Williams as "Reverend," the detective said:

> "I want to give you something to think about while we're traveling down the road. * * * Number one, I want you to observe the weather conditions, it's raining, it's sleeting, it's freezing, driving is very treacherous, visibility is poor, it's going to be dark early this evening. They are predicting several inches of snow for tonight, and I feel that you yourself are the only person that knows where this little girl's body is, that you yourself have only been there once, and if you get a snow on top of it you yourself may be unable to find it. And, since we will be going right past the area on the way into Des Moines, I feel that we could stop and locate the body, that the

parents of this little girl should be entitled to a Christian burial for the little girl who was snatched away from them on Christmas [E]ve and murdered. And I feel we should stop and locate it on the way in rather than waiting until morning and trying to come back out after a snow storm and possibly not being able to find it at all."

Williams asked Detective Leaming why he thought their route to Des Moines would be taking them past the girl's body, and Leaming responded that he knew the body was in the area of Mitchellville—a town they would be passing on the way to Des Moines.[b] Leaming then stated: "I do not want you to answer me. I don't want to discuss it any further. Just think about it as we're riding down the road."

As the car approached Grinnell, a town approximately 100 miles west of Davenport, Williams asked whether the police had found the victim's shoes. When Detective Leaming replied that he was unsure, Williams directed the officers to a service station where he said he had left the shoes; a search for them proved unsuccessful. As they continued towards Des Moines, Williams asked whether the police had found the blanket, and directed the officers to a rest area where he said he had disposed of the blanket. Nothing was found. The car continued towards Des Moines, and as it approached Mitchellville, Williams said that he would show the officers where the body was. He then directed the police to the body of Pamela Powers.

Williams was indicted for first-degree murder. Before trial, his counsel moved to suppress all evidence relating to or resulting from any statements Williams had made during the automo-

b. The fact of the matter, of course, was that Detective Leaming possessed no such knowledge.

bile ride from Davenport to Des Moines. After an evidentiary hearing the trial judge denied the motion. He found that "an agreement was made between defense counsel and the police officials to the effect that the Defendant was not to be questioned on the return trip to Des Moines," and that the evidence in question had been elicited from Williams during "a critical stage in the proceedings requiring the presence of counsel on his request." The judge ruled, however, that Williams had "waived his right to have an attorney present during the giving of such information."

* * * The jury found Williams guilty of murder. [The Iowa Supreme Court affirmed 4–3. But Williams was successful below in his federal habeas corpus action.]

II

A

* * *

B

[T]he District Court based its judgment in this case on three independent grounds. The Court of Appeals appears to have affirmed the judgment on two of those grounds. We have concluded that only one of them need be considered here.

Specifically, there is no need to review in this case the doctrine of Miranda v. Arizona, a doctrine designed to secure the constitutional privilege against compulsory self-incrimination. It is equally unnecessary to evaluate the ruling of the District Court that Williams' self-incriminating statements were, indeed, involuntarily made. For it is clear that the judgment before us must in any event be affirmed upon the ground that Williams was deprived of a different constitutional right—the right to the assistance of counsel.

* * *

There can be no doubt in the present case that judicial proceedings had been initiated against Williams before the start of the automobile ride from Davenport to Des Moines. A warrant had been issued for his arrest, he had been arraigned on that warrant before a judge in a Davenport courtroom, and he had been committed by the court to confinement in jail. The State does not contend otherwise.

There can be no serious doubt, either, that Detective Leaming deliberately and designedly set out to elicit information from Williams just as surely as—and perhaps more effectively than—if he had formally interrogated him. Detective Leaming was fully aware before departing for Des Moines that Williams was being represented in Davenport by Kelly and in Des Moines by McKnight. Yet he purposely sought during Williams' isolation from his lawyers to obtain as much incriminating information as possible. Indeed, Detective Leaming conceded as much when he testified at Williams' trial:

"Q. In fact, Captain, whether he was a mental patient or not, you were trying to get all the information you could before he got to his lawyer, weren't you?

"A. I was sure hoping to find out where that little girl was, yes, sir.

* * *

"Q. Well, I'll put it this way: You was [sic] hoping to get all the information you could before Williams got back to McKnight, weren't you?

"A. Yes, sir."

* * *

The circumstances of this case are thus constitutionally indistinguishable from those presented in Massiah v. United States. * * *

That the incriminating statements were elicited surreptitiously in the *Massiah* case, and otherwise here, is constitutionally irrelevant. Rather, the clear rule of *Massiah* is that once adversary proceedings have commenced against an individual, he has a right to legal representation when the government interrogates him.[c] It thus requires no wooden or technical application of the *Massiah* doctrine to conclude that Williams was entitled to the assistance of counsel guaranteed to him by the Sixth and Fourteenth Amendments.

III

The Iowa courts recognized that Williams had been denied the constitutional right to the assistance of counsel. They held, however, that he had waived that right during the course of the automobile trip from Davenport to Des Moines. * * *

* * *

[I]t was incumbent upon the State to prove "an intentional relinquishment or abandonment of a known right or privilege." That standard has been reiterated in many cases. We have said that the right to counsel does not depend upon a request by the defendant, and that courts indulge in every reasonable presumption against waiver. This strict standard applies equally to an alleged waiver of the right to counsel whether at trial or at a critical stage of pretrial proceedings.

* * * [J]udged by these standards, the record in this case falls far short of sustaining petitioner's burden. It is true that Williams had been informed

of and appeared to understand his right to counsel. But waiver requires not merely comprehension but relinquishment, and Williams' consistent reliance upon the advice of counsel in dealing with the authorities refutes any suggestion that he waived that right. He consulted McKnight by long distance telephone before turning himself in. He spoke with McKnight by telephone again shortly after being booked. After he was arraigned, Williams sought out and obtained legal advice from Kelly. Williams again consulted with Kelly after Detective Leaming and his fellow officer arrived in Davenport. Throughout, Williams was advised not to make any statements before seeing McKnight in Des Moines, and was assured that the police had agreed not to question him. His statements while in the car that he would tell the whole story *after* seeing McKnight in Des Moines were the clearest expressions by Williams himself that he desired the presence of an attorney before any interrogation took place. But even before making these statements, Williams had effectively asserted his right to counsel by having secured attorneys at both ends of the automobile trip, both of whom, acting as his agents, had made clear to the police that no interrogation was to occur during the journey. Williams knew of that agreement and, particularly in view of his consistent reliance on counsel, there is no basis for concluding that he disavowed it.

Despite Williams' express and implicit assertions of his right to counsel, Detective Leaming proceeded to elicit incriminating statements from Williams. Leaming did not preface this effort by telling Williams that he had a right to the presence of a lawyer, and

---

c. The only other significant factual difference between the present case and *Massiah* is that here the police had *agreed* that they would not interrogate Williams in the absence of his counsel. This circumstance plainly provides petitioner with no argument for distinguishing away the protection afforded by *Massiah*.

made no effort at all to ascertain whether Williams wished to relinquish that right. The circumstances of record in this case thus provide no reasonable basis for finding that Williams waived his right to the assistance of counsel.

The Court of Appeals did not hold, nor do we, that under the circumstances of this case Williams *could not,* without notice to counsel, have waived his rights under the Sixth and Fourteenth Amendments. It only held, as do we, that he did not.

IV

* * *

The judgment of the Court of Appeals is affirmed.[d]

Mr. Justice Marshall, concurring.

* * *

Leaming knowingly isolated Williams from the protection of his lawyers and during that period he intentionally "persuaded" him to give incriminating evidence. It is this intentional police misconduct—not good police practice—that the Court rightly condemns. * * *

* * *

Mr. Justice Powell, concurring.

* * *

I

* * *

I join the opinion of the Court which also finds that the efforts of Detective Leaming "to elicit information from Williams," as conceded by counsel for petitioner at oral argument, were a skillful and effective form of interrogation. Moreover, the entire setting was conducive to the psychological coercion that was successfully exploited. Williams was known by the police to be a young man with quixotic religious convictions and a history of mental disorders. The date was the day after Christmas, the weather was ominous, and the setting appropriate for Detective Leaming's talk of snow concealing the body and preventing a "Christian burial." * * *

Mr. Justice Stevens, concurring.

* * *

Underlying the surface issues in this case is the question, whether a fugitive from justice can rely on his lawyer's advice given in connection with a decision to surrender voluntarily. The defendant placed his trust in an experienced Iowa trial lawyer who in turn trusted the Iowa law enforcement authorities to honor a commitment made during negotiations which led to the apprehension of a potentially dangerous person. Under any analysis, this was a critical stage of the proceeding in which the participation of an independent professional was of vital importance to the accused and to society. * * * If, in the long run, we are seriously concerned about the individual's effective representation by coun-

---

d. The District Court stated that its decision "does not touch upon the issue of what evidence, if any, beyond the incriminating statements themselves must be excluded as 'fruit of the poisonous tree.'" We, too, have no occasion to address this issue, and in the present posture of the case there is no basis for the view of our dissenting Brethren (White, J., dissenting)(Blackmun, J., dissenting), that any attempt to retry the respondent would probably be futile. While neither Williams' incriminating statements themselves nor any testimo-

ny describing his having led the police to the victim's body can constitutionally be admitted into evidence, evidence of where the body was found and of its condition might well be admissible on the theory that the body would have been discovered in any event, even had incriminating statements not been elicited from Williams. [The evidence concerning the body was admitted at the retrial, and Williams' conviction was upheld. See Nix v. Williams in Chapter Two].

sel, the State cannot be permitted to dishonor its promise to this lawyer.

MR. CHIEF JUSTICE BURGER, **dissenting.**

The result in this case ought to be intolerable in any society which purports to call itself an organized society. It continues the Court—by the narrowest margin—on the much-criticized course of punishing the public for the mistakes and misdeeds of law enforcement officers, instead of punishing the officer directly, if in fact he is guilty of wrongdoing. It mechanically and blindly keeps reliable evidence from juries whether the claimed constitutional violation involves gross police misconduct or honest human error.

Williams is guilty of the savage murder of a small child; no member of the Court contends he is not. While in custody, and after no fewer than *five* warnings of his rights to silence and to counsel, he led police to the concealed body of his victim. The Court concedes Williams was not threatened or coerced and that he spoke and acted voluntarily and with full awareness of his constitutional rights. In the face of all this, the Court now holds that because Williams was prompted by the detective's statement—not interrogation but a statement—the jury must not be told how the police found the body.

* * *

The evidence is uncontradicted that Williams had abundant knowledge of his right to have counsel present and of his right to silence. Since the Court does not question his mental competence, it boggles the mind to suggest that Williams could not understand that leading police to the child's body would have other than the most serious consequences. All of the elements necessary to make out a valid waiver are shown by the record and acknowledged by the Court; we thus are left to guess how the Court reached its holding.

* * *

MR. JUSTICE WHITE, **with whom MR. JUSTICE BLACKMUN and MR. JUSTICE REHNQUIST join, dissenting.**

* * *

* * * That respondent knew of his right not to say anything to the officers without advice and presence of counsel is established on this record to a moral certainty. He was advised of the right by three officials of the State— telling at least one that he understood the right—and by two lawyers. * * * The issue in this case, then, is whether respondent relinquished that right intentionally.

Respondent relinquished his right not to talk to the police about his crime when the car approached the place where he had hidden the victim's clothes. Men usually intend to do what they do and there is nothing in the record to support the proposition that respondent's decision to talk was anything but an exercise of his own free will. * * * The statement by Leaming was not coercive; it was accompanied by a request that respondent not respond to it; and it was delivered hours before respondent decided to make any statement. Respondent's waiver was thus knowing and intentional.

* * *

MR. JUSTICE BLACKMUN, **with whom MR. JUSTICE WHITE and MR. JUSTICE REHNQUIST join, dissenting.**

* * *

First, the police did not deliberately seek to isolate Williams from his lawyers so as to deprive him of the assistance of counsel. The isolation in this case was a necessary incident of transporting Williams to the county where the crime was committed.

Second, Leaming's purpose was not solely to obtain incriminating evidence. The victim had been missing for only two days, and the police could not be certain that she was dead. Leaming, of course, and in accord with his duty, was "hoping to find out where that little girl was," but such motivation does not equate with an intention to evade the Sixth Amendment. Moreover, the Court seems to me to place an undue emphasis, and aspersion on what it and the lower courts have chosen to call the "Christian burial speech," and on Williams' "deeply religious" convictions.

Third, not every attempt to elicit information should be regarded as "tantamount to interrogation." I am not persuaded that Leaming's observations and comments, made as the police car traversed the snowy and slippery miles between Davenport and Des Moines that winter afternoon, were an interrogation, direct or subtle, of Williams.

In summary, it seems to me that the Court is holding that *Massiah* is violated whenever police engage in any conduct, in the absence of counsel, with the subjective desire to obtain information from a suspect after arraignment. Such a rule is far too broad.

* * *

Sixth Amendment Attaches at Formal Charge: United States v. Gouveia

Reaffirming that the Sixth Amendment right to counsel attaches only after adversarial proceedings have begun, the Supreme Court held in United States v. Gouveia, 467 U.S. 180 (1984), that prison officials did not violate the right to counsel of inmates suspected of two murders when the officials placed them in administrative detention for periods of 19 and 8 months prior to their being indicted. Justice Rehnquist's opinion for the Court stated that "both inside and outside the prison, it may well be true that in some cases pre-indictment investigation could help a defendant prepare a better defense. But, * * * our cases have never suggested that the purpose of the right to counsel is to provide a defendant with a pre-indictment private investigator, and we see no reason to adopt that novel interpretation of the right to counsel in this case." The majority opinion recognizes the possible prejudice that can result from delay in the filing of charges and cites statutes of limitations and general concepts of due process as protections against unfairness. Justice Marshall dissented and argued that administrative detention was part of an accusatorial process.

The Supreme Court held in Moran v. Burbine, supra, that there was no violation of a suspect's Sixth Amendment right to counsel when police failed to disclose to him that a lawyer had called and had been falsely told that the suspect would not be interrogated until the next day. Justice O'Connor's majority opinion observed that the suspect had not been formally charged, cited *Gouveia* as well as *Massiah, Brewer,* and other cases drawing a line between pre- and post-charge situations, and declined to adopt a rule that would make the right to counsel depend "on the fortuity of whether the suspect or his family happens to have retained counsel prior to interrogation."

On the Meaning of "Deliberate" Elicitation

The Sixth Amendment prohibits a government agent from "deliberately eliciting" incriminating information from an "accused" in the absence of counsel or a waiver. This means, does it not, that the officer must be *trying* to obtain incriminating information from the accused? For example, the Court found deliberate elicitation in Brewer v. Williams because Leaming actually admitted that he was trying to pump Williams for information about the location of the body. But what if the officer can plausibly argue that he was not trying to obtain incriminating information? Can there still be a violation of the Sixth Amendment?

The court in Bey v. Morton, 124 F.3d 524 (3d Cir. 1997), considered this question. Bey was on death row. The only people he was permitted to talk to were Corrections Officers. Bey struck up a relationship with Officer Pearson, and they engaged in a number of conversations, covering many different topics, including sports, women and the news. In the course of their extensive discourse, Bey confessed to the murder of two women—the murders for which he was sitting on death row. Then his convictions were reversed and he had to be retried. At the retrials, the Officer testified and related Bey's confessions. Bey argued that these confessions had to be excluded because Officer Pearson had deliberately elicited these confessions from him, clearly after he had been charged. But the court disagreed. It analyzed the deliberate elicitation question as follows:

> The critical distinction between this case and the *Massiah* [line of cases] is that Pearson, while a state actor, was not a state actor deliberately engaged in trying to secure information from the defendant for use in connection with the prosecution that was the subject matter of counsel's representation. * * *

> Ordinarily, when a state agent converses with an indicted defendant under circumstances in which the agent should expect that incriminating information might be disclosed and such information is disclosed and is subsequently used in the prosecution, it can be presumed that there was a deliberate elicitation of information for use in connection with the case. The undisputed facts in this case, however, are simply inconsistent with a deliberate plan on the part of Pearson to garner information for use against Bey.

> * * * First, Pearson had no responsibility for eliciting or reporting information for use in the prosecution of Bey's case and was not working with anyone who had such responsibility. Second, and most importantly, Pearson did not behave like someone who intended to secure incriminating statements from Bey. The record lacks evidence of any questions designed to elicit the statement that Bey had raped and beaten a woman to death on the beach, and merely reveals Pearson's asking "why" Bey had committed the act and seeking clarification "if it was something [he] didn't understand." Pearson did not take any notes or compile any reports of his conversations with Bey. In fact, Pearson disclosed the confession to no one for five years. It was only through the systematic efforts of the investigator that the prosecutor's office uncovered Bey's statements. Even Pearson's testimony in

Bey's case was "reluctantly given." Thus, the state's receipt of Bey's confession was not the result of any deliberate elicitation by Pearson for use in connection with Bey's prosecution, and the state's use of Bey's confession at trial did not violate the Sixth Amendment.

If the focus of the Sixth Amendment is on whether the officer is *trying* to get information from a person charged with a crime, won't it be difficult for a court to assess the intent of the officer?

Application of the Deliberate Elicitation Standard: Fellers v. United States

What follows is the Supreme Court's most recent application of the "deliberate elicitation" standard. Note that the Court makes a point of distinguishing Sixth Amendment "deliberate elicitation" from the Fifth Amendment standard of "interrogation."

FELLERS v. UNITED STATES

Supreme Court of the United States, 2004.
124 S.Ct. 1019.

JUSTICE O'CONNOR **delivered the opinion of the Court.**

After a grand jury indicted petitioner John J. Fellers, police officers arrested him at his home. During the course of the arrest, petitioner made several inculpatory statements. He argued that the officers deliberately elicited these statements from him outside the presence of counsel, and that the admission at trial of the fruits of those statements therefore violated his Sixth Amendment right to counsel. Petitioner contends that in rejecting this argument, the Court of Appeals for the Eighth Circuit improperly held that the Sixth Amendment right to counsel was "not applicable" because "the officers did not interrogate [petitioner] at his home." We granted the petition for a writ of certiorari, and now reverse.

I

On February 24, 2000, after a grand jury indicted petitioner for conspiracy to distribute methamphetamine, Lincoln Police Sergeant Michael Garnett and Lancaster County Deputy Sheriff Jeff Bliemeister went to petitioner's home in Lincoln, Nebraska, to arrest

him. The officers knocked on petitioner's door and, when petitioner answered, identified themselves and asked if they could come in. Petitioner invited the officers into his living room.

The officers advised petitioner they had come to discuss his involvement in methamphetamine distribution. They informed petitioner that they had a federal warrant for his arrest and that a grand jury had indicted him for conspiracy to distribute methamphetamine. The officers told petitioner that the indictment referred to his involvement with certain individuals, four of whom they named. Petitioner then told the officers that he knew the four people and had used methamphetamine during his association with them.

After spending about 15 minutes in petitioner's home, the officers transported petitioner to the Lancaster County jail. There, the officers advised petitioner for the first time of his rights under Miranda v. Arizona, and Patterson v. Illinois, 487 U.S. 285 (1988) [discussed infra and holding that a waiver of Sixth Amendment rights can be found if officers give *Miranda* warnings to an indicted suspect, and the defendant makes a knowing and voluntary waiver]. Petitioner and the two officers signed a *Miranda* waiver form, and petitioner then reiterated the inculpatory statements he had made earlier, admitted to having associated with other individuals implicated in the charged conspiracy, and admitted to having loaned money to one of them even though he suspected that she was involved in drug transactions.

* * *

The District Court suppressed the "unwarned" statements petitioner made at his house but admitted petitioner's jailhouse statements pursuant to Oregon v. Elstad, concluding petitioner had knowingly and voluntarily waived his *Miranda* rights before making the statements.

Following a jury trial at which petitioner's jailhouse statements were admitted into evidence, petitioner was convicted of conspiring to possess with intent to distribute methamphetamine. Petitioner appealed, arguing that his jailhouse statements should have been suppressed as fruits of the statements obtained at his home in violation of the Sixth Amendment. The Court of Appeals affirmed. With respect to petitioner's argument that the officers' failure to administer *Miranda* warnings at his home violated his Sixth Amendment right to counsel under *Patterson*, the Court of Appeals stated: "*Patterson* is not applicable here ... for the officers did not interrogate [petitioner] at his home." The Court of Appeals also concluded that the statements from the jail were properly admitted under the rule of *Elstad, supra.*

* * *

II

The Sixth Amendment right to counsel is triggered "at or after the time that judicial proceedings have been initiated ... 'whether by way of formal charge, preliminary hearing, indictment, information, or arraignment.' " Brewer v. Williams. We have held that an accused is denied "the basic protections" of the Sixth Amendment "when there [is] used against him at his trial evidence of his own incriminating words, which federal agents ... deliberately elicited from him after he had been indicted and in the absence of his counsel." Massiah v. United States; cf. Patterson v. Illinois, *supra* (holding that the Sixth Amendment does not bar postindictment questioning in the absence of counsel if a defendant waives the right to counsel).

We have consistently applied the deliberate-elicitation standard in subsequent Sixth Amendment cases, see United States v. Henry ("The question here is whether under the facts of this case a Government agent 'deliberately elicited' incriminating statements ... within the meaning of *Massiah*"); *Brewer, supra,* at 399 (finding a Sixth Amendment violation where a detective "deliberately and designedly set out to elicit information from [the suspect]"), and we have expressly distinguished this standard from the Fifth Amendment custodial-interrogation standard, see Michigan v. Jackson, 475 U.S. 625 (1986) ("The Sixth Amendment provides a right to counsel ... even when there is no interrogation and no Fifth Amendment applicability"); Rhode Island v. Innis ("The definitions of 'interrogation' under the Fifth and Sixth Amendments, if indeed the term 'interrogation' is even apt in the Sixth Amendment context, are not necessarily interchangeable").

The Court of Appeals erred in holding that the absence of an "interrogation" foreclosed petitioner's claim that the jailhouse statements should have been suppressed as fruits of the statements taken from petitioner at his home. First, there is no question that the officers in this case "deliberately elicited" information from petitioner. Indeed, the officers, upon arriving at petitioner's house, informed him that their purpose in coming was to discuss his involvement in the distribution of methamphetamine and his association with certain charged co-conspirators. Because the ensuing discussion took place after petitioner had been indicted, outside the presence of counsel, and in the absence of any waiver of petitioner's Sixth Amendment rights, the Court of Appeals erred in holding that the officers' actions did not violate the Sixth Amendment standards established in *Massiah, supra*, and its progeny.

Second, because of its erroneous determination that petitioner was not questioned in violation of Sixth Amendment standards, the Court of Appeals improperly conducted its "fruits" analysis under the Fifth Amendment. Specifically, it applied *El-stad, supra*, to hold that the admissibility of the jailhouse statements turns solely on whether the statements were "knowingly and voluntarily made." The Court of Appeals did not reach the question whether the Sixth Amendment requires suppression of petitioner's jailhouse statements on the ground that they were the fruits of previous questioning conducted in violation of the Sixth Amendment deliberate-elicitation standard. We have not had occasion to decide whether the rationale of *Elstad* applies when a suspect makes incriminating statements after a knowing and voluntary waiver of his right to counsel notwithstanding earlier police questioning in violation of Sixth Amendment standards. We therefore remand to the Court of Appeals to address this issue in the first instance.

Accordingly, the judgment of the Court of Appeals is reversed, and the case is remanded for further proceedings consistent with this opinion.

It is so ordered.

C.   USE OF UNDERCOVER OFFICERS AND STATE AGENTS

In one respect, the Sixth Amendment is less protective in regulating confessions than is the Fifth: it applies only to those who have been formally charged, whereas *Miranda* applies to all suspects facing custodial interrogation. In another respect, however, the Sixth Amendment is more protective than the Fifth: it limits the use of undercover tactics, whereas *Miranda* only applies when the suspect knows that he is speaking to a police officer.

Jailhouse Plant: United States v. Henry

Chief Justice Burger, who so vigorously dissented in *Brewer*, may have extended *Massiah* in his opinion for the Court in United States v. Henry, 447 U.S. 264 (1980).

Henry was convicted of armed bank robbery and sought collateral relief after he learned that a cellmate (Nichols) who testified at trial had been a paid government informant. Nichols had been paid in the past for expenses and services in connection with information he supplied. An FBI agent told Nichols, who was kept in the same jail as Henry, of the government's interest in several individuals who were housed in the jail, including Henry. The agent told Nichols not to initiate conversations with Henry, but to pay attention to anything Henry said about the robbery.

Citing both *Massiah* and *Brewer,* the Chief Justice wrote that "[t]he question here is whether * * * a government agent 'deliberately elicited' incriminating statements from Henry within the meaning of *Massiah.*" The Chief Justice found "deliberate" elicitation even though the state denied that the officers had the intent to elicit a confession from Henry. On the question of "deliberateness", the court reasoned as follows:

Three factors are important. First, Nichols was acting under instructions as a paid informant for the Government; second, Nichols was ostensibly no more than a fellow inmate of Henry; and third, Henry was in custody and under indictment at the time he was engaged in conversation by Nichols.

* * * Even if the agent's statement that he did not intend that Nichols would take affirmative steps to secure incriminating information is accepted, he must have known that such propinquity would lead to that result.

The Government argues that the federal agents instructed Nichols not to question Henry about the robbery. Yet according to his own testimony, Nichols was not a passive listener; rather, he had "some conversations with Mr. Henry" while he was in jail and Henry's incriminatory statements were "the product of this conversation." While affirmative interrogation, absent waiver, would certainly satisfy *Massiah,* we are not persuaded, as the Government contends, that Brewer v. Williams modified *Massiah's* "deliberately elicited" test. * * *

The Government argues that this Court should apply a less rigorous standard under the Sixth Amendment [to undercover activity] than where the accused is speaking in the hearing of persons he knows to be Government officers. That line of argument, however, seeks to infuse Fifth Amendment concerns * * * into the Sixth Amendment protection * * *.

Moreover, the concept of a knowing and voluntary waiver of Sixth Amendment rights does not apply in the context of communications with an undisclosed undercover informant acting for the Government. In that setting, Henry, being unaware that Nichols was a Government agent expressly commissioned to secure evidence, cannot be held to have waived his right to the assistance of counsel.

Finally, Henry's incarceration at the time he was engaged in conversation by Nichols is also a relevant factor. * * * [T]he mere fact of custody imposes pressures on the accused; confinement may bring into play subtle influences that will make him particularly susceptible to the ploys of undercover Government agents.

The Court concluded that "[b]y intentionally creating a situation likely to induce Henry to make incriminating statements without the assistance of counsel, the government violated Henry's Sixth Amendment's right to counsel."

Justice Blackmun, joined by Justice White, dissented. He argued that the Court purported to retain the "deliberately elicited" test, but that in reality it was extending *Massiah* to "cover even a 'negligent' triggering of events resulting in reception of disclosures." He concluded that a deliberateness standard "imposes the exclusionary sanction on that conduct that is most culpable, most likely to frustrate the purpose of having counsel, and most susceptible to being checked by a deterrent." He went on to criticize the Court's application of its own test to the facts, which in his view did not reveal that anything the government agent did was " 'likely to induce' Nichols' successful prompting of Henry."

Justice Rehnquist filed a separate dissent. He urged another look at the doctrinal underpinnings of the *Massiah* doctrine. After observing that in cases like this one the government has done nothing to impair the defendant's ability to consult with an attorney, Justice Rehnquist observed:

> The role of counsel in an adversary system is to offer advice and assistance in the preparation of a defense and to serve as a spokesman for the accused in technical legal proceedings. And the Sixth Amendment, of course, protects the confidentiality of communications between the accused and his attorney. But there is no constitutional or historical support for concluding that an accused has a right to have his attorney serve as a sort of guru who must be present whenever an accused has an inclination to reveal incriminating information to anyone who acts to elicit such information at the behest of the prosecution. To the extent the accused is protected from revealing evidence that may be incriminatory, the focus must be on the Fifth Amendment privilege against compulsory self-incrimination.

The Listening Post: Kuhlmann v. Wilson

The Court distinguished *Henry* in Kuhlmann v. Wilson, 477 U.S. 436 (1986), as it held that the Sixth Amendment was not violated when police put a jailhouse informant in close proximity to a defendant and the defendant made statements to the informant without any effort on the informant's part to elicit the statements. The Court stated that, to prove a Sixth Amendment violation, a defendant must show that the police took some action, beyond merely listening, that was deliberately designed to elicit incriminating remarks. No elicitation was found on the facts of the case.

The basic facts were the following: Prior to the defendant's arrival at a jail following an arraignment for robbery and murder, an officer entered into an agreement with inmate Lee under which Lee would listen to the defendant's conversations and report them, but Lee would ask no questions and would simply "keep his ears open." The defendant, without prompting, told Lee that he had been present during the robbery but denied knowing the robbers. Lee responded that the explanation "didn't sound too good." The defendant changed details over the next few days. Finally, after a visit from his brother, the defendant, again without prompting, admitted to Lee that he and two other men had committed the robbery and murder.

Justice Powell, writing for the Court, distinguished *Henry* on the ground that the informant in *Henry* had "stimulated" the conversations with Henry and that Lee had not done so in the instant case. The Court stated that a defendant does not show a Sixth Amendment violation "simply by showing that an informant, either through prior arrangement or voluntarily, reported his incriminating statements to the police." Justice Powell found it insignificant that Lee had said that the defendant's version of the crimes didn't sound too good. Just that one remark did not bring the case out of the realm of the "passive recording device"; that single remark did not constitute "elicitation".

Chief Justice Burger filed a short concurring opinion stating that "[t]here is a vast difference between placing an 'ear' in the suspect's cell and placing a voice in the cell to encourage conversation for the 'ear' to record." Justice Brennan, joined by Justice Marshall, dissented in *Wilson* and found the case to be virtually indistinguishable on its facts from *Henry*. Justice Stevens also dissented briefly and agreed with Justice Brennan. See also United States v. York, 933 F.2d 1343 (7th Cir.1991)(no deliberate elicitation where the informant responded with neutral comments when incriminating topics were brought up by the defendant; informants are not required to reveal their status by refusing to participate in the natural flow of conversation).

Is the Informant a State Agent?

Sixth Amendment protection under *Henry* requires that the informant must have been working for the government at the time the information was obtained from the accused—otherwise there is no state action implicated in the deliberate elicitation. Whether the informant is a state agent, or is simply working on his own account, is often a difficult question. For example, in United States v. Watson, 894 F.2d 1345 (D.C.Cir.1990), Watson argued that the jailhouse informant was working as a government agent at the time he elicited incriminating statements from Watson. He noted that the informant had worked for the DEA for two years and was in regular contact with the DEA while he was in jail. But the court found "no evidence that the DEA in any way encouraged" the informant to talk to Watson; that the informant was in contact with the DEA on unrelated cases, and did not mention Watson until after Watson made incriminating statements; and that the informant "was acting as an entrepreneur." The court stated that the informant "may have hoped to make a sale to the government when he spoke with Watson, but that does not make the government responsible for his actions, any more than a person who has bought an article from a salesman in the past is responsible if the salesman then steals something similar in the hope of making a second sale." Do you agree? See also United States v. Sampol, 636 F.2d 621 (D.C.Cir.1980)(Sixth Amendment violated where informant "had been accepted by the government as an informant at large whose reports about any criminal activity would be gratefully received"); United States v. York, 933 F.2d 1343 (7th Cir.1991)(jailhouse plant was a state agent as a matter of law, where he had been promised a reward for suitable information obtained from any source about any inmate, and the informant was motivated by a concern to obtain that reward); United States v. Johnson, 4 F.3d 904 (10th Cir.1993)("we decline to handicap legitimate investigations by assuming that any time the government is approached by a would-be informant, an implicit agency relationship is established").

D. CONTINUING INVESTIGATIONS

A defendant who is formally charged has a right to be free from deliberate attempts by state agents to elicit incriminating information in the absence of defendant's counsel. But defendants who have been formally charged are often suspected of committing crimes in addition to those charged. Does the Sixth Amendment prohibit an officer from obtaining information from the defendant concerning uncharged crimes?

Maine v. Moulton

That was the question in Maine v. Moulton, 474 U.S. 159 (1985). Moulton and a codefendant, Colson, were charged with theft of automobiles and parts. Colson, along with his lawyer, informed the Chief of Police of threatening telephone calls to his house and of the fact that Moulton had spoken of killing a key witness. Colson cooperated with the police. The police wired Colson with a transmitter when he agreed to meet with Moulton. The codefendants, at their meeting, spoke of eliminating witnesses. Moulton rejected the idea, and Colson led Moulton into talking about their theft activities, as well as burglaries that were related to the thefts. Both the recorded telephone statements and the recorded meeting were used as evidence at trial. Moulton was convicted.

Justice Brennan wrote for the Court as it reversed Moulton's conviction. He found it irrelevant that the meeting with the informant was initiated by Moulton, concluding that "knowing exploitation by the State of an opportunity to confront the accused without counsel being present is as much a breach of the State's obligation not to circumvent the right to the assistance of counsel as is the intentional creation of such an opportunity."

Justice Brennan also rejected the argument that Moulton's statements should be admissible because the police were investigating new crimes, including threats to the safety of witnesses. Justice Brennan recognized that police may investigate crimes separate from the crimes charged and may use statements made by a suspect in a later trial for those crimes. But he concluded that "incriminating statements pertaining to pending charges are inadmissible at the trial of those charges, notwithstanding the fact that the police were also investigating other crimes, if, in obtaining the evidence, the State violated the Sixth Amendment by knowingly circumventing the accused's right to the assistance of counsel." He stated that the Sixth Amendment guarantees the accused "the right to rely on counsel as a 'medium' between him and the State."

Justice Brennan was unpersuaded that the officers' instructions to the informant to limit the scope of discussion, (i.e., to the subject matter of killing witnesses), was sufficient to protect Moulton. He stated that the agents should have known that despite their instructions, the conversation between the informant and Moulton would be likely to turn to the crime for which both were charged. Justice Brennan noted that "direct proof of the State's knowledge will seldom be available," but that "proof that the State must have known that its agent was likely to obtain incriminating statements" suffices to establish a Sixth Amendment violation.

Thus, the officer's actions in *Moulton* constituted "deliberate" elicitation even though there was no showing of specific intent on the part of the officers to obtain information about the charged crime. "Deliberate" elicitation is found whenever the officers should have known that their investigative tactic would lead to incriminating information from a charged defendant in the absence of counsel.

Chief Justice Burger dissented in *Moulton*, joined by Justices White and Rehnquist and in part by Justice O'Connor. The Chief Justice argued that the Sixth Amendment term "deliberate elicitation" focuses upon a bad purpose—to use statements in connection with pending charges—and that suppression should not be required unless police institute the investigation of separate charges in bad faith to avoid the dictates of *Massiah*.

Questions After Moulton

Consider the impact of *Moulton* on police behavior. *Massiah* and subsequent cases taught that it was impermissible for the police deliberately to seek statements from a suspect who had been formally charged. *Moulton* holds that it is permissible to seek statements relating to crimes not charged, but that it is impermissible to seek statements regarding the crimes already charged. Suppose that the police use an undercover informant to seek the permissible statements, but the suspect changes the conversation to talk about the charged offenses. Are the statements admissible? Does it depend on the likelihood that the conversation would have gravitated toward the charged crime? Suppose that the statements made with respect to the uncharged offenses are relevant—e.g., to show intent, plan, etc.—in the prosecution of the charged offenses. May they be used in that prosecution if the realization of their relevance came only after they were obtained? See Mealer v. Jones, 741 F.2d 1451 (2d Cir.1984)(*Massiah* requires exclusion of the defendant's confessions to uncharged offenses offered as "other crimes" evidence, where the government "must have known" that any statements covering the uncharged offense would incriminate the accused on the charged crime as well). Suppose that it is impossible to seek evidence about additional crimes without eliciting statements about charges already brought. Why should the statements be suppressed, as in *Moulton*, in the prosecution of the pending charges? Under Fourth Amendment cases, police who come upon evidence in a legal search may use it in any prosecution. Why should it be different for the Sixth Amendment?

E. WAIVER OF SIXTH AMENDMENT PROTECTIONS

Under what circumstances can an accused be held to have waived his Sixth Amendment rights? Is the test for waiver similar or identical to that applied for waiver of *Miranda* violations? In the *Miranda* section, we noted two distinct waiver situations: 1) where the defendant receives warnings and waives his rights; and 2) where the defendant receives his warnings, invokes his rights, and then subsequently is argued to have waived his rights. Similar situations arise in the Sixth Amendment context.

Waiving Sixth Amendment Rights After Receiving
Miranda Warnings: Patterson v. Illinois

Where the defendant receives warnings and waives his rights, the question is simply whether the waiver was knowing and voluntary. The Court in Brewer v. Williams held that the government, to prove a waiver of Sixth Amendment rights, must show more than simply that the defendant received warnings and elected to speak. The majority in Brewer v. Williams found nothing to indicate that Williams had actually relinquished his rights. Analogizing from *Miranda*, evidence of relinquishment could be found in myriad ways, for example by the defendant's signing a waiver form; answering some questions but not others; showing a high level of cooperation; or providing an extremely detailed and lengthy confession. But none of this was shown to the majority's satisfaction in Brewer v. Williams.

Assuming that the government can show that the defendant voluntarily relinquished his Sixth Amendment rights, another question arises: whether the defendant was sufficiently informed of his rights to make a knowing waiver. In the *Miranda* context, the Court held that the *Miranda* warnings provide a suspect with all the information he needs to make a knowing waiver. Does the same hold true for a waiver of the Sixth Amendment right to counsel?

The Court's answer to this question came in Patterson v. Illinois, 487 U.S. 285 (1988). Patterson was indicted, received *Miranda* warnings, and signed the waiver form and confessed. He had never invoked his right to counsel. He argued that his waiver, while voluntary, was not knowing and intelligent, because he received only the *Miranda* warnings, and these warnings did not adequately inform him of his Sixth Amendment right to counsel. Justice White, writing for the Court, rejected this argument in the following analysis:

> By telling petitioner that he had a right to consult with an attorney, to have a lawyer present while he was questioned, and even to have a lawyer appointed for him if he could not afford to retain one on his own, [the officers] conveyed to petitioner the sum and substance of the rights that the Sixth Amendment provided him. * * * [The *Miranda*] warning also sufficed * * * to let petitioner know what a lawyer could do for him during the postindictment questioning; namely, advise petitioner to refrain from making any [incriminating] statements * * *

> Our conclusion is supported by petitioner's inability, in the proceedings before this Court, to articulate with precision what additional information should have been provided to him before he would have been competent to waive his right to counsel. * * * The State's decision to take an additional step and commence formal adversarial proceedings against the accused does not substantially increase the value of counsel to the accused at questioning, or expand the limited purpose that an attorney serves when the accused is questioned by authorities. With respect to this inquiry, we do not discern a substantial difference between the usefulness of a lawyer to a suspect during custodial interrogation, and his value to an accused at postindictment questioning. * * * Because the role of counsel at questioning is relatively simple and limited, we see no problem in having a waiver procedure at that stage which is likewise simple and limited.

Justice White distinguished Faretta v. California, 422 U.S. 806 (1975), where the Court required copious warnings to be conveyed to an accused before a waiver of the right to counsel *at trial* could be found.[24] Justice White explained that the "full dangers and disadvantages of self-representation during questioning are less substantial and more obvious to an accused than they are at trial."

Justice Stevens, joined by Justices Brennan, Marshall, and Blackmun dissented in *Patterson*. Justice Stevens argued that the majority had underplayed the significance of the initiation of formal proceedings and the multifaceted role of counsel after an indictment. He noted that the lawyer might examine the indictment for legal sufficiency, or might be able to negotiate a plea bargain, and that the *Miranda* warnings did not apprise the accused of these possibilities. Therefore, the person indicted is not fully aware of the value of an attorney if he simply receives the *Miranda* warnings.

---

24. The breadth and detail of the required *Faretta* warnings are discussed in Chapter Ten.

Two Situations in Which Sixth Amendment
Waiver Standards Might Be Different

In a footnote in *Patterson*, Justice White stressed that there are some limited situations in which a valid waiver might be found under *Miranda* but not under the Sixth Amendment. He gave two examples where Sixth Amendment waiver standards would be different from the standards applicable to *Miranda*. First,

> we have permitted a waiver to stand where a suspect was not told that his lawyer was trying to reach him during questioning [Moran v. Burbine]; in the Sixth Amendment context, this waiver would not be valid.

Second,

> a surreptitious conversation between an undercover police officer and an unindicted suspect would not give rise to any *Miranda* violation [Illinois v. Perkins]; however, once the accused is indicted, such questioning would be prohibited [and a waiver could not be found].

Why should these two circumstances preclude a finding of a knowing and voluntary waiver of Sixth Amendment rights?

Indictment Warnings

The Court in *Patterson* left open whether an indicted suspect is entitled to a warning that he has been indicted before a waiver of the Sixth Amendment right to counsel can be found; Patterson had been so informed. But the sweeping language in *Patterson*, to the effect that *Miranda* warnings impart the necessary information for a Sixth Amendment waiver, has led courts to hold that an "indictment warning" is not required. See United States v. Chadwick, 999 F.2d 1282 (8th Cir.1993) ("law enforcement officers need not inform an accused that he has been indicted before seeking a waiver of his right to counsel").

Waiving the Sixth Amendment Right to Counsel
After Invoking It: Michigan v. Jackson

In Michigan v. Jackson, 475 U.S. 625 (1986), the accused formally requested counsel at an arraignment. Later he was interrogated by police officers about the crime for which he had been charged. Jackson did not initiate the contact, but he signed a waiver form, and confessed. Justice Stevens wrote for the Court as it held that Jackson had not knowingly and voluntarily waived his Sixth Amendment rights. He stated that when an accused invokes his Sixth Amendment right to counsel, the standards of Edwards v. Arizona, supra, govern the waiver of Sixth Amendment rights. Accordingly, Jackson could only have waived his Sixth Amendment rights if he had initiated a later conversation and also knowingly and voluntarily waived his rights; this he had not done. Justice Stevens contended that "the reasons for prohibiting the interrogation of an uncounseled prisoner are even stronger after he has been formally charged with an offense than before."

Justice Rehnquist, joined by Justice Powell and Justice O'Connor, dissented in *Jackson* and argued that the majority had placed itself in "an analytical strait-jacket" because the Court's *Edwards*-like waiver rule did not apply unless the accused actually invoked his Sixth Amendment right to counsel. He explained as follows:

The problem with the limitation the Court places on the Sixth Amendment version of the *Edwards* rule is that, unlike a defendant's right to counsel under *Miranda*, which does not arise until affirmatively invoked by the defendant during custodial interrogation, a defendant's Sixth Amendment right to counsel does not depend at all on whether the defendant has requested counsel.

The Court provides no satisfactory explanation for its decision to extend the *Edwards* rule to the Sixth Amendment, yet limit that rule to those defendants foresighted enough, or just plain lucky enough, to have made an explicit request for counsel which we have always understood to be completely unnecessary for Sixth Amendment purposes.

Lower courts after *Jackson* have held what is implicit in that opinion: the protections of *Edwards* are not applicable in the Sixth Amendment context unless the accused unequivocally invokes his right to counsel. For example, in Wilcher v. Hargett, 978 F.2d 872 (5th Cir.1992), Wilcher was appointed counsel at his arraignment, but made no statement when counsel was appointed for him by the court. After arraignment, he was approached by police for a statement, waived his rights, and confessed. The court found the waiver valid, even though Wilcher had not initiated the contact with the police. It stated that "for purposes of *Jackson*, an 'assertion' means some kind of positive statement or other action that informs a reasonable person of the defendant's desire to deal with the police only through counsel." Simply remaining silent while counsel was appointed did not rise to the level of an "assertion." Thus, the police were not constrained by the suspect-initiation requirement of *Edwards*. They could approach Wilcher and interrogate him, so long as they gave him *Miranda* warnings and he understood the warnings and voluntarily waived his right to counsel. Such a waiver was shown on the facts.

Waiver as to Crimes Unrelated to the Crime Charged: McNeil v. Wisconsin

When the *Miranda* right to counsel is invoked, police are prohibited from initiating interrogation as to any crime, including crimes unrelated to that for which the suspect has been arrested. This was the holding in Arizona v. Roberson, supra. Does the same hold true if an accused has invoked his Sixth Amendment right to counsel? In McNeil v. Wisconsin, 501 U.S. 171 (1991), the Court held that an invocation of the Sixth Amendment right to counsel, unlike the *Miranda* right, is "offense-specific." The state had charged McNeil with armed robbery and at his initial appearance before a judicial officer, McNeil invoked his right to counsel. Police thereafter initiated questioning of McNeil concerning an armed robbery and murder committed in another part of the state. McNeil was given warnings, waived his rights and confessed to those crimes. He thereafter argued on the basis of Michigan v. Jackson that his waiver was not voluntary because, when he invoked his right to counsel at the initial appearance, it applied as well to unrelated charges. This would mean that police-initiated interrogation would preclude a finding of a waiver.

Justice Scalia, writing for a 6–3 majority, held that an invocation of Sixth Amendment rights gives *Jackson-Edwards* protection *only as to the crime with which the accused has been charged.* He concluded that "just as the right is offense-specific, so also its Michigan v. Jackson effect of invalidating subsequent waivers in police-initiated interviews is offense-specific." Accordingly, the rule of Arizona v. Roberson, prohibiting police-initiated interrogation as to unrelated crimes when a suspect invokes his *Miranda* right to counsel, does not apply when an accused invokes his Sixth Amendment right to counsel. Put another way, Michigan v. Jackson applied *Edwards* to Sixth Amendment invocations, but the Court in *McNeil* refused to apply the *Roberson* extension of *Edwards* to such invocations. Therefore the officers in *McNeil* were permitted to question McNeil on crimes unrelated to those on which he was charged. All they needed to show was that McNeil had been given warnings and knowingly and voluntarily waived his rights.

Justice Scalia recognized that an invocation of counsel at an initial appearance on a formal charge could, as held in *Jackson,* be construed as a desire not to be questioned without counsel concerning the crime charged. But he contended that the invocation could not be construed to imply a desire never to undergo custodial interrogation, about anything, without counsel present.

The Court further found that a broad construction of the scope of the invocation of counsel at an initial appearance would be unsound as a matter of policy. Justice Scalia asserted that such a broad rule would mean that "most persons in pretrial custody for serious offenses would be unapproachable by police officers suspecting them of involvement in other crimes, even though they have never expressed any unwillingness to be questioned." He concluded that "since the ready ability to obtain uncoerced confessions is not an evil but an unmitigated good, society would be the loser" from such a rule. Justice Scalia also stated that when a suspect invokes his Sixth Amendment right to counsel at an initial appearance, he does not thereby invoke a *Miranda/Roberson* right to counsel as to unrelated crimes. This aspect of *McNeil* is discussed in the section on *Miranda* waivers, supra.

Justice Kennedy wrote a concurring opinion in *McNeil*, reiterating his dissenting arguments in *Roberson,* to the effect that an invocation of the *Miranda* right to counsel should be considered offense-specific as well. He contended that "the Court should devote some attention to bringing its Fifth and Sixth Amendment jurisprudence into a logical alignment."

Justice Stevens, joined by Justices Marshall and Blackmun, dissented. He contended that the majority's offense-specific construction of a Sixth Amendment invocation "ignores the substance of the attorney-client relationship that the legal profession has developed over the years." He reasoned that the scope of the relationship between attorney and client "is as broad as the subject matter that might reasonably be encompassed by negotiations for a plea bargain or the contents of a presentence investigation report."

Which Crimes Are Related to the Crime Charged?

After *McNeil,* if a suspect invokes his Sixth Amendment rights, the police cannot initiate questioning about the crime charged, but they can initiate questioning about unrelated crimes so long as they obtain a knowing and voluntary waiver. How are the police to determine whether crimes are related or unrelated? What happens if the crime charged and the crime inquired into by the police arise out of the same fact situation? The Court considered these questions in the following case.

TEXAS v. COBB

Supreme Court of the United States, 2001.
532 U.S. 162.

CHIEF JUSTICE REHNQUIST **delivered the opinion of the Court.**

The Texas Court of Criminal Appeals held that a criminal defendant's Sixth Amendment right to counsel attaches not only to the offense with which he is charged, but to other offenses "closely related factually" to the charged offense. We hold that our decision in McNeil v. Wisconsin meant what it said, and that the Sixth Amendment right is "offense specific."

In December 1993, Lindsey Owings reported to the Walker County, Texas, Sheriff's Office that the home he shared with his wife, Margaret, and their 16–month-old daughter, Kori Rae, had been burglarized. He also informed police that his wife and daughter were missing. Respondent Raymond Levi Cobb lived across the street from the Owings. Acting on an anonymous tip that respondent was involved in the burglary, Walker County investigators questioned him about the events. He denied involvement. In July 1994, while under arrest for an unrelated offense, respondent was again questioned about the incident. Respondent then gave a written statement confessing to the burglary, but he denied knowledge relating to the disappearances. Respondent was subsequently indicted for the burglary, and Hal Ridley was appointed in August 1994 to represent respondent on that charge.

* * *

In November 1995, respondent, free on bond in the burglary case, was living with his father in Odessa, Texas. At that time, respondent's father contacted the Walker County Sheriff's Office to report that respondent had confessed to him that he killed Margaret Owings in the course of the burglary. Walker County investigators directed respondent's father to the Odessa police station, where he gave a statement. Odessa police then faxed the statement to Walker County, where investigators secured a warrant for respondent's arrest and faxed it back to Odessa. Shortly thereafter, Odessa police took respondent into custody and administered warnings pursuant to Miranda v. Arizona. Respondent waived these rights.

After a short time, respondent confessed to murdering both Margaret and Kori Rae. Respondent explained that when Margaret confronted him as he was attempting to remove the Owings' stereo, he stabbed her in the stomach with a knife he was carrying. Respondent told police that he dragged her body to a wooded area a few hundred yards from the house. Respondent then stated:

> "I went back to her house and I saw the baby laying on its bed. I took the baby out there and it was sleeping the whole time. I laid the baby down on the ground four or five feet away from its mother. I went back to my house and got a flat edge shovel. That's all I could find. Then I went back over to where they were and I started digging a hole between them. After I got the hole dug, the baby was awake. It started going toward its mom and it fell in the hole. I put the lady in the hole and I covered them up. I remember stabbing a different knife I had in the ground where they were. I was crying right then."

Respondent later led police to the location where he had buried the victims' bodies.

Respondent was convicted of capital murder for murdering more than one person in the course of a single criminal transaction. He was sentenced to death. On appeal to the Court of Criminal Appeals of Texas, respondent argued * * * that his confession [to the murders] should have been suppressed because it was obtained in violation of his Sixth Amendment right to counsel. Relying on Michigan v. Jackson, respondent contended that his right to counsel had attached when Ridley was appointed in the burglary case and that Odessa police were therefore required to secure Ridley's permission before proceeding with the interrogation.

The Court of Criminal Appeals reversed respondent's conviction by a divided vote and remanded for a new trial. * * * Finding the capital murder charge to be "factually interwoven with the burglary," the court concluded that respondent's Sixth Amendment right to counsel had attached on the capital murder charge even though respondent had not yet been charged with that offense. * * *

* * *

The Sixth Amendment provides that "[i]n all criminal prosecutions, the accused shall enjoy the right . . . to have the Assistance of Counsel for his defence." In McNeil v. Wisconsin, we explained when this right arises:

> "The Sixth Amendment right [to counsel] . . . is offense specific. It cannot be invoked once for all future prosecutions, for it does not attach until a prosecution is commenced, that is, at or after the initiation of adversary judicial criminal proceedings—whether by way of formal charge, preliminary hearing, indictment, information, or arraignment."

Accordingly, we held that a defendant's statements regarding offenses for which he had not been charged were admissible notwithstanding the attachment of his Sixth Amendment right to counsel on other charged offenses.

Some state courts and Federal Courts of Appeals, however, have read into McNeil's offense-specific definition an exception for crimes that are "factually related" to a charged offense. Several of these courts have interpreted Brewer v. Williams, and Maine v. Moulton–both of which were decided well before McNeil—to support this view, which respondent now invites us to approve. We decline to do so.

* * *

Respondent suggests that Brewer implicitly held that the right to counsel attached to the factually related murder when the suspect was arraigned on the abduction charge. The Court's opinion, however, simply did not address the significance of the fact that the suspect had been arraigned only on the abduction charge, nor did the parties in any way argue this question. Constitutional rights are not defined by inferences from opinions which did not address the question at issue.

Moulton is similarly unhelpful to respondent. That case involved two individuals indicted for a series of thefts, one of whom had secretly agreed to cooperate with the police investigation of his codefendant, Moulton. At the suggestion of police, the informant recorded several telephone calls and one face-to-face conversation he had with Moulton during which the two discussed their criminal exploits and possible alibis. In the course of those conversations, Moulton made various incriminating statements regarding both the thefts for which he had been charged and additional crimes. * * *

Respondent contends that, in affirming reversal of both the theft and burglary charges, the *Moulton* Court must have concluded that Moulton's Sixth Amendment right to counsel attached to the burglary charge. But the *Moulton* Court did not address the question now before us, and to the extent *Moulton* spoke to the matter at all, it expressly referred to the offense-specific nature of the Sixth Amendment right to counsel:

"The police have an interest in the thorough investigation of crimes for which formal charges have already been filed. They also have an interest in investigating new or additional crimes. Investigations of either type of crime may require surveillance of individuals already under indictment. Moreover, law enforcement officials investigating an individual suspected of committing one crime and formally charged with having committed another crime obviously seek to discover evidence useful at trial of either crime. In seeking evidence pertaining to pending charges, however, the Government's investigative powers are limited by the Sixth Amendment rights of the accused. . . . On the other hand, to exclude evidence pertaining to charges as to which the Sixth Amendment right to counsel had not attached at the time the evidence was obtained, simply because other charges were pending at that time, would unnecessarily frustrate the public's interest in the investigation of criminal activities."

Thus, respondent's reliance on *Moulton* is misplaced and, in light of the language employed there and subsequently in *McNeil,* puzzling.

Respondent predicts that the offense-specific rule will prove "disastrous" to suspects' constitutional rights and will "permit law enforcement officers almost complete and total license to conduct unwanted and uncounseled interrogations." Besides offering no evidence that such a parade of horribles has occurred in those jurisdictions that have not enlarged upon *McNeil,* he fails to appreciate the significance of two critical considerations. First, there can be no doubt that a suspect must be apprised of his rights against compulsory self-incrimination and to consult with an attorney before authorities may conduct custodial interrogation. In the present case, police scrupulously followed *Miranda's* dictates when questioning respondent. Second, it is critical to recognize that the Constitution does not negate society's interest in the ability of police to talk to witnesses and suspects, even those who have been charged with other offenses.

* * *

Although it is clear that the Sixth Amendment right to counsel attaches only to charged offenses, we have recognized in other contexts that the definition of an "offense" is not necessarily limited to the four corners of a charging instrument. In Blockburger v. United States, 284 U.S. 299 (1932), we explained that "where the same act or transaction constitutes a violation of two distinct statutory provisions, the test to be applied to determine whether there are two offenses or only one, is whether each provision requires proof of a fact which the other does not." We have since applied the *Blockburger* test to delineate the scope of the Fifth Amendment's Double Jeopardy Clause, which prevents multiple or successive prosecutions for the "same offence." We see no constitutional difference between the meaning of the term "offense" in the contexts of double jeopardy and of the right to counsel. Accordingly, we hold that when the Sixth Amendment right to counsel attaches, it does encompass offenses that, even if not formally charged, would be considered the same offense under the *Blockburger* test.

While simultaneously conceding that its own test "lacks the precision for which police officers may hope," the dissent suggests that adopting *Blockburger's* definition of "offense" will prove difficult to administer. But it is the dissent's vague iterations of the " 'closely related to' " or " 'inextricably intertwined with' " test that would defy simple application. The dissent seems to presuppose that officers will possess complete knowledge of the circumstances surrounding an incident, such that the officers will be able to tailor their investigation to avoid addressing factually related offenses. Such an assumption, however, ignores the reality that police often are not yet aware of the exact sequence and scope of events they are investigating—indeed, that is why police must investigate in the first place. Deterred by the possibility of violating the Sixth Amendment, police likely would refrain from questioning certain defendants altogether.

It remains only to apply these principles to the facts at hand. At the time he confessed to Odessa police, respondent had been indicted for burglary of the Owings residence, but he had not been charged in the murders of Margaret and Kori Rae. As defined by Texas law, burglary and capital murder are not the same offense under *Blockburger*. Compare Texas Penal Code Ann. § 30.02(a) (1994) (requiring entry into or continued concealment in a habitation or building) with § 19.03(a)(7)(A) (requiring murder of more than one person during a single criminal transaction). Accordingly, the Sixth Amendment right to counsel did not bar police from interrogating respondent regarding the murders, and respondent's confession was therefore admissible.

The judgment of the Court of Criminal Appeals of Texas is reversed.

JUSTICE KENNEDY, with whom JUSTICE SCALIA and JUSTICE THOMAS join, concurring.

* * *

As the facts of the instant case well illustrate, it is difficult to understand the utility of a Sixth Amendment rule that operates to invalidate a confession given by the free choice of suspects who have received proper advice of their *Miranda* rights but waived them nonetheless. The *Miranda* rule, and the related preventative rule of Edwards v. Arizona, 451 U.S. 477 (1981), serve to protect a suspect's voluntary choice not to speak outside his lawyer's presence. The parallel rule announced in *Jackson*, however, supersedes the suspect's voluntary choice to speak with investigators. * * *

* * *

The Sixth Amendment right to counsel attaches quite without reference to the suspect's choice to speak with investigators after a *Miranda* warning. It is the commencement of a formal prosecution, indicated by the initiation of adversary judicial proceedings, that marks the beginning of the Sixth Amendment right. These events may be quite independent of the suspect's election to remain silent, the interest which the *Edwards* rule serves to protect with respect to *Miranda* and the Fifth Amendment, and it thus makes little sense for a protective rule to attach absent such an election by the suspect. We ought to question the wisdom of a judge-made preventative rule to protect a suspect's desire not to speak when it cannot be shown that he had that intent.

Even if *Jackson* is to remain good law, its protections should apply only where a suspect has made a clear and unambiguous assertion of the right not to speak outside the presence of counsel, the same clear election required under *Edwards*. Cobb made no such assertion here, yet Justice BREYER's dissent rests upon the assumption that the *Jackson* rule should operate to exclude the confession no matter. There would be little justification for this extension of a rule that, even in a more limited application, rests on a doubtful rationale.

* * *

JUSTICE BREYER, **with whom** JUSTICE STEVENS, JUSTICE SOUTER, **and** JUSTICE GINSBURG **join, dissenting.**

This case focuses upon the meaning of a single word, "offense," when it arises in the context of the Sixth Amendment. Several basic background principles define that context.

First, the Sixth Amendment right to counsel plays a central role in ensuring the fairness of criminal proceedings in our system of justice. Second, the right attaches when adversary proceedings, triggered by the government's formal accusation of a crime, begin. Third, once this right attaches, law enforcement officials are required, in most circumstances, to deal with the defendant through counsel rather than directly, even if the defendant has waived his Fifth Amendment rights. Cf. ABA Model Rule of Professional Conduct 4.2 (2001) (lawyer is generally prohibited from communicating with a person known to be represented by counsel "about the subject of the representation" without counsel's "consent"); Green, A Prosecutor's Communications with Defendants: What Are the Limits?, 24 Crim. L. Bull. 283, 284, and n. 5 (1988) (version of Model Rule 4.2 or its predecessor has been adopted by all 50 States).

Fourth, * * * the right is "offense specific."

This case focuses upon the last-mentioned principle, in particular upon the meaning of the words "offense specific." These words appear in this Court's Sixth Amendment case law, not in the Sixth Amendment's text. See U.S. Const., Amdt. 6 (guaranteeing right to counsel "[i]n all criminal prosecutions"). The definition of these words is not self-evident. * * * This case requires us to determine whether an "offense"—for Sixth Amendment purposes—includes factually related aspects of a single course of conduct other than those few acts that make up the essential elements of the crime charged.

We should answer this question in light of the Sixth Amendment's basic objectives as set forth in this Court's case law. * * * * But the Court today decides that "offense" means the crime set forth within "the four corners of a charging instrument," along with other crimes that "would be considered the same offense" under the test established by Blockburger v. United States. In my view, this unnecessarily technical definition undermines Sixth Amendment protections while doing nothing to further effective law enforcement.

* * *

Jackson focuses upon a suspect—perhaps a frightened or uneducated suspect—who, hesitant to rely upon his own unaided judgment in his dealings with the police, has invoked his constitutional right to legal assistance in such matters. *Jackson* says that, once such a request has been made, the police may not simply throw that suspect—who does not trust his own unaided judgment—back upon his own devices by requiring him to rely for protection upon that same unaided judgment that he previously rejected as inadequate. In a word, the police may not force a suspect who has asked for legal counsel to make a critical legal choice without the legal assistance that he has requested and that the Constitution guarantees. The Constitution does not take away with one hand what it gives with the other.

* * *

[T]he majority would undermine [*Jackson*] by significantly diminishing the Sixth Amendment protections that the case provides. That is because criminal codes are lengthy and highly detailed, often proliferating "overlapping and related statutory offenses" to the point where prosecutors can easily spin out a startlingly numerous series of offenses from a single * * * criminal transaction. Thus, an armed robber who reaches across a store counter, grabs the cashier, and demands "your money or your life," may through that single instance of conduct have committed several "offenses," in the majority's sense of the term, including armed robbery, assault, battery, trespass, use of a firearm to commit a felony, and perhaps possession of a firearm by a felon, as well. A person who is using and selling drugs on a single occasion might be guilty of possessing various drugs, conspiring to sell drugs, being under the influence of illegal drugs, possessing drug paraphernalia, possessing a gun in relation to the drug sale, and, depending upon circumstances, violating various gun laws as well. A protester blocking an entrance to a federal building might also be trespassing, failing to disperse, unlawfully assembling, and obstructing Government administration all at one and the same time.

The majority's rule permits law enforcement officials to question those charged with a crime without first approaching counsel, through the simple device of asking questions about any other related crime not actually charged in the indictment. * * * In-

deed, the majority's rule would permit law enforcement officials to question anyone charged with any crime in any one of the examples just given about his or her conduct on the single relevant occasion without notifying counsel unless the prosecutor has charged every possible crime arising out of that same brief course of conduct. What Sixth Amendment sense—what common sense—does such a rule make? What is left of the "communicate through counsel" rule? The majority's approach is inconsistent with any common understanding of the scope of counsel's representation. * * *

In fact, under the rule today announced by the majority, two of the seminal cases in our Sixth Amendment jurisprudence would have come out differently. In Maine v. Moulton, * * * we treated burglary and theft as the same offense for Sixth Amendment purposes. Despite the opinion's clear statement that "[i]ncriminating statements pertaining to other crimes, as to which the Sixth Amendment right has not yet attached, are, of course, admissible at a trial of those offenses," the Court affirmed the lower court's reversal of both burglary and theft charges even though, at the time that the incriminating statements at issue were made, Moulton had been charged only with theft by receiving. Under the majority's rule, in contrast, because theft by receiving and burglary each required proof of a fact that the other did not, only Moulton's theft convictions should have been overturned. Compare Me.Rev.Stat. Ann., Tit. 17–A, § 359 (1981) (theft) (requiring knowing receipt, retention, or disposal of stolen property with the intent to deprive the owner thereof), with § 401 (burglary) (requiring entry of a structure without permission and with the intent to commit a crime).

In Brewer v. Williams, the effect of the majority's rule would have been even more dramatic. Because first-degree murder and child abduction each required proof of a fact not required by the other, and because at the time of the impermissible interrogation Williams had been charged only with abduction of a child, Williams' murder conviction should have remained undisturbed. Compare Iowa Code § 690.2 (1950 and Supp.1978) (first-degree murder) (requiring a killing) with Iowa Code § 706.2 (1950) (repealed 1978) (child-stealing) (requiring proof that a child under 16 was taken with the intent to conceal the child from his or her parent or guardian). This is not to suggest that this Court has previously addressed and decided the question presented by this case. Rather, it is to point out that the Court's conception of the Sixth Amendment right at the time that *Moulton* and *Brewer* were decided naturally presumed that it extended to factually related but uncharged offenses.

At the same time, the majority's rule threatens the legal clarity necessary for effective law enforcement. That is because the majority, aware that the word "offense" ought to encompass something beyond "the four corners of the charging instrument," imports into Sixth Amendment law the definition of "offense" set forth in Blockburger v. United States, 284 U.S. 299 (1932), a case interpreting the Double Jeopardy Clause of the Fifth Amendment, which Clause uses the word "offence" but otherwise has no relevance here. * * *

In theory, the test says that two offenses are the "same offense" unless each requires proof of a fact that the other does not. That means that most of the different crimes mentioned above are not the "same offense." * * *. Hence the extension of the definition of "offense" that is accomplished by the use of the *Blockburger*

test does nothing to address the substantial concerns about the circumvention of the Sixth Amendment right that are raised by the majority's rule.

But, more to the point, the simple-sounding *Blockburger* test has proved extraordinarily difficult to administer in practice. Judges, lawyers, and law professors often disagree about how to apply it. The test has emerged as a tool in an area of our jurisprudence that THE CHIEF JUSTICE has described as "a veritable Sargasso Sea which could not fail to challenge the most intrepid judicial navigator." Albernaz v. United States, 450 U.S. 333, 343 (1981). Yet the Court now asks, not the lawyers and judges who ordinarily work with double jeopardy law, but police officers in the field, to navigate *Blockburger* when they question suspects. The result, I believe, will resemble not so much the Sargasso Sea as the criminal law equivalent of Milton's "Serbonian Bog . . . Where Armies whole have sunk."

There is, of course, an alternative. We can, and should, define "offense" in terms of the conduct that constitutes the crime that the offender committed on a particular occasion, including criminal acts that are "closely related to" or "inextricably intertwined with" the particular crime set forth in the charging instrument. This alternative is not perfect. The language used lacks the precision for which police officers may hope; and it requires lower courts to specify its meaning further as they apply it in individual cases. Yet virtually every lower court in the United States to consider the issue has defined "offense" in the Sixth Amendment context to encompass such closely related acts. These courts have found offenses "closely related" where they involved the same victim, set of acts, evidence, or motivation. They have found offenses unrelated where time, location, or factual circumstances significantly separated the one from the other.

* * *

The Texas Court of Criminal Appeals, following this commonly accepted approach, found that the charged burglary and the uncharged murders were "closely related." All occurred during a short period of time on the same day in the same basic location. The victims of the murders were also victims of the burglary. Cobb committed one of the murders in furtherance of the robbery, the other to cover up the crimes. The police, when question-

ing Cobb, knew that he already had a lawyer representing him on the burglary charges and had demonstrated their belief that this lawyer also represented Cobb in respect to the murders by asking his permission to question Cobb about the murders on previous occasions. The relatedness of the crimes is well illustrated by the impossibility of questioning Cobb about the murders without eliciting admissions about the burglary. * * * The police officers ought to have spoken to Cobb's counsel before questioning Cobb. I would affirm the decision of the Texas court.

Consequently, I dissent.

F.   THE SIXTH AMENDMENT EXCLUSIONARY RULE

In *Moulton,* Chief Justice Burger argued in dissent that even if there were a Sixth Amendment violation, the exclusionary rule should not be used to exclude the evidence of Moulton's reliable incriminatory statements. Citing the good faith exception to the Fourth Amendment exclusionary rule (discussed in Chapter Two), the Chief Justice argued that "the Sixth Amendment claims at issue here closely parallel claims under the Fourth Amendment where we have found the exclusionary rule to be inapplicable by weighing the costs and benefits of its applications."

The Court has held that the Fourth Amendment exclusionary rule is not constitutionally required. In *Dickerson,* the Court held that exclusion of *Miranda*-defective confessions was required by the Fifth Amendment, but that there are certain exceptions to the exclusionary rule, such as for fruits, impeachment, and public safety. On the other hand, a violation of the Due Process Clause carries with it an automatic rule of exclusion, as the Court has consistently stated in cases such as Michigan v. Tucker, Oregon v. Elstad, and Mincey v. Arizona. Does the Constitution require exclusion of a confession obtained in violation of the Sixth Amendment, or is Chief Justice Burger correct in *Moulton*?

Despite the Chief Justice's assertions, several commentators have argued that the Constitution requires exclusion of evidence obtained as a result of a Sixth Amendment violation. They reason that a violation of the *Massiah* right to counsel is not complete until the confession is admitted at trial. It is only at that point that the effectiveness of counsel envisioned by *Massiah* is impaired. As such, a *Massiah* violation is unlike a Fourth Amendment violation, which occurs at the time of the intrusion. See Schulhofer, Confessions and the Court, 79 Mich.L.Rev. 865 (1981); Loewy, Police Obtained Evidence and the Constitution: Distinguishing Unconstitutionally Obtained Evidence from Unconstitutionally Used Evidence, 87 Mich.L.Rev. 907 (1989).

If the commentators are right, the question then is whether the exceptions to exclusion found for *Miranda*-defective confessions should also apply to confessions obtained in violation of the Sixth Amendment. Could a *Massiah*-defective confession be used for impeachment purposes? Could the fruits of *Massiah*-defective confessions—such as physical evidence or a second confession—be admitted? What if the officer had a "public safety" excuse for deliberately eliciting information from the accused?

The question of whether the Constitution requires exclusion of a confession obtained in violation of the Sixth Amendment was discussed but not decided in Michigan v. Harvey, 494 U.S. 344 (1990). The Court in *Harvey* held that a statement obtained in violation of Michigan v. Jackson could be used for impeachment purposes. Harvey confessed after invoking his right to counsel at arraignment. The confession resulted from police-initiation, but Harvey received warnings, understood them, and was not coerced into waiving his rights. Chief Justice Rehnquist's opinion for the Court stressed that the *Jackson* rule was merely a transposition of the prophylactic standards of Edwards v. Arizona to the Sixth Amendment context. Accordingly, a violation of the prophylactic safeguards of *Jackson* was not a violation of the Constitution itself. Rather, *Jackson* "established a presumption which renders invalid some waivers that would be considered voluntary, knowing and intelligent under the traditional case-by-case inquiry." As a result, the holding in Harris v. New York, allowing *Miranda*-defective confessions to be used for impeachment purposes, was fully applicable. The Chief Justice specifically left open the "admissibility for impeachment purposes of a voluntary statement obtained in the absence of a knowing and voluntary waiver of the right to counsel." However, the majority intimated that a "true" violation of the Sixth Amendment (as opposed to prophylactic safeguards) would result in exclusion for all purposes.

Though the issue has not been decided by the Supreme Court, lower courts have held that a *Massiah*-defective confession cannot be used for impeachment purposes. See United States v. Abdi, 142 F.3d 566 (2d Cir.1998)(noting that such a violation "transgresses the core constitutional right to counsel * * * and therefore should not be available to the prosecution for any purpose"). Courts have also held that the fruits of *Massiah*-defective confessions must be excluded from trial. See United States v. Kimball, 884 F.2d 1274 (9th Cir.1989). Do you agree that a violation of *Massiah* should be treated differently from a violation of *Miranda* or a violation of the Fourth Amendment?

Chapter Four

IDENTIFYING SUSPECTS

I. INTRODUCTION

Often it is easier for law enforcement officers to discover and prove that a crime has been committed and how it took place than it is to identify the perpetrator. At times, the failure or absence of witnesses leads prosecutors to seek other ways of establishing identity. The development of handwriting analysis and fingerprint evidence are, in part, responses to the felt need for better identification techniques.

One of the most important scientific breakthroughs has been the use of DNA profiling, in which body fluid samples are "lifted," like fingerprints, from the crime scene, the DNA is extracted from the body fluid, and then compared with the DNA extracted from body fluid taken from the defendant. Most courts have found DNA profiling to be sufficiently reliable to be admissible. See generally United States v. Bonds, 12 F.3d 540 (6th Cir.1993). A sample of the extensive legal literature on DNA identification evidence includes Developments in the Law—Confronting the New Challenges of Scientific Evidence, 108 Harv. L.Rev.1481 (1995); Giannelli, Criminal Discovery, Scientific Evidence, and DNA, 44 Vand.L.Rev. 791 (1991); and Burk, DNA Identification: Possibilities and Pitfalls Revisited, 31 Jurimetrics 53 (1990).

Unfortunately, science cannot replace identification by witnesses in all cases. In fact, most cases in which identity is disputed will turn on whether witnesses are believed. Yet, it is well known that eyewitness evidence is not very reliable and that police procedures may render identifications even less reliable than they otherwise would be. Circuit Judge McGowan has explained that many experts believe that erroneous identifications are "conceivably the greatest single threat to the achievement of our ideal that no innocent man shall be punished." Constitutional Interpretation and Criminal Identification, 12 Wm. & Mary L.Rev. 235, 238 (1970).[1] Another documented problem is that an identifica-

---

1. A shocking case in which two men were erroneously identified as the same "stocking mask" rapist before a third suspect was arrested is reported by Bauer, Two Wrongly Arrested Men Free; Third is Held in Staunton, Wash. Post., Jan. 23, 1980, at A1, col. 5. One man was kept nine months in the criminal ward of a state mental hospital before being released; the other was more fortunate, having been con-

fined 71 days in a local jail before being released.

For a description of a well publicized case of mistaken identification of a priest as a gentleman robber, see Winer, Pagano Case Points Finger at Lineups, Nat'l L.J., Sept. 10, 1979, at 1, col. 4.

For an excellent summary of the literature on eyewitness identification, see Special Issue

tion may be more in accord with the witness' expectation than with reality. This may be particularly so where a white witness identifies a black person as the perpetrator: a witness who has preconceptions of what a criminal "looks like" may subconsciously adjust their perceptions accordingly. See Johnson, Cross–Racial Identification Errors in Criminal Cases, 69 Cornell L.Rev. 934 (1984). The dangers of misidentification can be exacerbated by the police, through the use of suggestive identification procedures such as one-on-one showups.

This Chapter examines the very real dangers associated with identification evidence and the safeguards that the criminal justice system has fashioned to assure that, if we can help it, witness error will not irreparably taint criminal litigation.

II. THE JUDICIAL RESPONSE

A. IDENTIFICATIONS AND THE RIGHT TO COUNSEL

1. *The Wade–Gilbert Rule*

With so much evidence available casting doubt for so long on the identification techniques commonly used by the police, sooner or later the judiciary was going to have to examine them. Once the United States Supreme Court began to focus generally on police procedures in the 1960's, the time for an examination had come. One morning in June of 1967, the Court handed down three major opinions designed to protect those suspected and accused of crime from unfair identification tactics.

The first case was the following one:

UNITED STATES v. WADE

Supreme Court of the United States, 1967.
388 U.S. 218.

MR. JUSTICE BRENNAN **delivered the opinion of the Court.**

The question here is whether courtroom identifications of an accused at trial are to be excluded from evidence because the accused was exhibited to the witnesses before trial at a post-indictment lineup conducted for identification purposes without notice to and in the absence of the accused's appointed counsel.

The federally insured bank in Eustace, Texas, was robbed on September 21, 1964. A man with a small strip of tape on each side on his face entered the bank, pointed a pistol at the female cashier and the vice president, the only persons in the bank at the time, and forced them to fill a pillowcase with the bank's money. The man then drove away with an accomplice who had been waiting in a stolen car outside the bank. On March 23, 1965, an indictment was returned against respondent, Wade, and two others for conspiring to rob the bank, and against Wade and the accomplice for the robbery itself. Wade was arrested on April 2, and counsel was appointed

on Eyewitness Behavior, 4 L. & Hum.Behav. 237 (1980).

Two popular additions to the literature on eyewitness identification are E. Loftus, Eyewitness Testimony (1979) and A. Yarmey, The

Psychology of Eyewitness Testimony (1979). Both are reviewed by Circuit Court Judge David Bazelon in Psychology Today, March 1980, at 102.

to represent him on April 26. Fifteen days later an FBI agent, without notice to Wade's lawyer, arranged to have the two bank employees observe a lineup made up of Wade and five or six other prisoners and conducted in a courtroom of the local county courthouse. Each person in the line wore strips of tape such as allegedly worn by the robber and upon direction each said something like "put the money in the bag," the words allegedly uttered by the robber. Both bank employees identified Wade in the lineup as the bank robber.

At trial, the two employees, when asked on direct examination if the robber was in the courtroom, pointed to Wade. The prior lineup identification was then elicited from both employees on cross-examination. * * *

* * *

III

The Government characterizes the lineup as a mere preparatory step in the gathering of the prosecution's evidence, not different—for Sixth Amendment purposes—from various other preparatory steps, such as systematized or scientific analyzing of the accused's fingerprints, blood sample, clothing, hair, and the like. We think there are differences which preclude such stages being characterized as critical stages at which the accused has the right to the presence of his counsel. Knowledge of the techniques of science and technology is sufficiently available, and the variables in techniques few enough, that the accused has the opportunity for a meaningful confrontation of the Government's case at trial through the ordinary processes of cross-examination of the Government's expert witnesses and the presentation of the evidence of his own experts. The denial of a right to have his counsel present at such analy-

ses does not therefore violate the Sixth Amendment; they are not critical stages since there is minimal risk that his counsel's absence at such stages might derogate from his right to a fair trial.

IV

But the confrontation compelled by the State between the accused and the victim or witnesses to a crime to elicit identification evidence is peculiarly riddled with innumerable dangers and variable factors which might seriously, even crucially, derogate from a fair trial. The vagaries of eyewitness identification are well-known; the annals of criminal law are rife with instances of mistaken identification. * * * A major factor contributing to the high incidence of miscarriage of justice from mistaken identification has been the degree of suggestion inherent in the manner in which the prosecution presents the suspect to witnesses for pretrial identification. * * * Suggestion can be created intentionally or unintentionally in many subtle ways. And the dangers for the suspect are particularly grave when the witness' opportunity for observation was insubstantial, and thus his susceptibility to suggestion the greatest.

Moreover, "[i]t is a matter of common experience that, once a witness has picked out the accused at the lineup, he is not likely to go back on his word later on, so that in practice the issue of identity may (in the absence of other relevant evidence) for all practical purposes be determined there and then, before the trial."

The pretrial confrontation for purpose of identification may take the form of a lineup, also known as an "identification parade" or "showup," as in the present case, or presentation of the suspect alone to the witness. * * * It is obvious that risks of suggestion attend either form of confrontation and increase the dangers inhering in eyewitness identification. But as in the case with secret interrogations, there is serious difficulty in depicting what transpires at lineups and other forms of identification confrontations. * * * [T]he defense can seldom reconstruct the manner and mode of lineup identification for judge or jury at trial. Those participating in a lineup with the accused may often be police officers; in any event, the participants' names are rarely recorded or divulged at trial. The impediments to an objective observation are increased when the victim is the witness. Lineups are prevalent in rape and robbery prosecutions and present a particular hazard that a victim's understandable outrage may excite vengeful or spiteful motives. In any event, neither witnesses nor lineup participants are apt to be alert for conditions prejudicial to the suspect. And if they were, it would likely be of scant benefit to the suspect since neither witnesses nor lineup participants are likely to be schooled in the detection of suggestive influences.[a] Improper influences may go undetected by a suspect, guilty or not, who experiences the emotional tension which we might expect in one being confronted with potential accusers. Even when he does observe abuse, if he has a criminal record he may be reluctant to take the stand and open up the admission of prior convictions. Moreover, any protestations by the suspect of the fairness of the lineup made at trial are likely to be in vain; the jury's choice is between the accused's unsupported version and that of the police officers present. In short, the accused's inability effectively to reconstruct at trial any unfairness that occurred at the lineup may deprive him of his only opportunity meaning-

fully to attack the credibility of the witness' courtroom identification.

* * *

Insofar as the accused's conviction may rest on a courtroom identification in fact the fruit of a suspect pretrial identification which the accused is helpless to subject to effective scrutiny at trial, the accused is deprived of that right of cross-examination which is an essential safeguard to his right to confront the witnesses against him. And even though cross-examination is a precious safeguard to a fair trial, it cannot be viewed as an absolute assurance of accuracy and reliability. Thus in the present context, where so many variables and pitfalls exist, the first line of defense must be the prevention of unfairness and the lessening of the hazards of eyewitness identification at the lineup itself. The trial which might determine the accused's fate may well not be that in the courtroom but that at the pretrial confrontation, with the State aligned against the accused, the witness the sole jury, and the accused unprotected against the overreaching, intentional or unintentional, and with little or no effective appeal from the judgment there rendered by the witness—"that's the man."

Since it appears that there is grave potential for prejudice, intentional or not, in the pretrial lineup, which may not be capable of reconstruction at trial, and since presence of counsel itself can often avert prejudice and assure a meaningful confrontation at trial, there can be little doubt that for Wade the post-indictment lineup was a critical stage of the prosecution at which he was "as much entitled to such aid [of counsel] * * * as at the trial itself." Thus both Wade and his

a. An additional impediment to the detection of such influences by participants, including the suspect, is the physical conditions often surrounding the conduct of the lineup. In many, lights shine on the stage in such a way that the suspect cannot see the witness. In some a one-way mirror is used and what is said on the witness' side cannot be heard.

counsel should have been notified of the impending lineup, and counsel's presence should have been a requisite to conduct of the lineup, absent an "intelligent waiver." No substantial countervailing policy considerations have been advanced against the requirement of the presence of counsel. Concern is expressed that the requirement will forestall prompt identifications and result in obstruction of the confrontations. As for the first, we note that in the two cases in which the right to counsel is today held to apply, counsel had already been appointed and no argument is made in either case that notice to counsel would have prejudicially delayed the confrontations. Moreover, we leave open the question whether the presence of substitute counsel might not suffice where notification and presence of the suspect's own counsel would result in prejudicial delay. And to refuse to recognize the right to counsel for fear that counsel will obstruct the course of justice is contrary to the basic assumptions upon which this Court has operated in Sixth Amendment cases. * * * In our view counsel can hardly impede legitimate law enforcement; on the contrary, for the reasons expressed, law enforcement may be assisted by preventing the infiltration of taint in the prosecution's identification evidence. That result cannot help the guilty avoid conviction but can only help assure that the right man has been brought to justice.

* * *

V

We come now to the question whether the denial of Wade's motion to strike the courtroom identification by the bank witnesses at trial because of the absence of his counsel at the lineup required * * * the grant of a new trial at which such evidence is to be excluded. We do not think this disposition can be justified without first giving the Government the opportunity to establish by clear and convincing evidence that the in-court identifications were based upon observations of the suspect other than the lineup identification. Where, as here, the admissibility of evidence of the lineup identification itself is not involved, a *per se* rule of exclusion of courtroom identification would be unjustified. A rule limited solely to the exclusion of testimony concerning identification at the lineup itself, without regard to admissibility of the courtroom identification, would render the right to counsel an empty one. The lineup is most often used, as in the present case, to crystallize the witnesses' identification of the defendant for future reference. We have already noted that the lineup identification will have that effect. The State may then rest upon the witnesses' unequivocal courtroom identification, and not mention the pretrial identification as part of the State's case at trial. Counsel is then in the predicament in which Wade's counsel found himself—realizing that possible unfairness at the lineup may be the sole means of attack upon the unequivocal courtroom identification, and having to probe in the dark in an attempt to discover and reveal unfairness, while bolstering the government witness' courtroom identification by bringing out and dwelling upon his prior identification. Since counsel's presence at the lineup would equip him to attack not only the lineup identification but the courtroom identification as well, limiting the impact of violation of the right to counsel to exclusion of evidence only of identification at the lineup itself disregards a critical element of that right.

We think it follows that the proper test to be applied in these situations is that quoted in Wong Sun v. United States, 371 U.S. 471, 488, "[W]hether, granting establishment of the primary illegality, the evidence to which instant objection is made has been come at by exploitation of that illegality or instead by means sufficiently distinguishable to be purged of the primary taint." Application of this test in the present context requires consideration of various factors; for example, the prior opportunity to observe the alleged criminal act, the existence of any discrepancy between any pre-lineup description and the defendant's actual description, any identification prior to lineup of another person, the identification by picture of the defendant prior to the lineup, failure to identify the defendant on a prior occasion, and the lapse of time between the alleged act and the lineup identification. It is also relevant to consider those facts which, despite the absence of counsel, are disclosed concerning the conduct of the lineup.

* * *

On the record now before us we cannot make the determination whether the in-court identifications had an independent origin. * * * That inquiry is most properly made in the District Court. We therefore think the appropriate procedure to be followed is to vacate the conviction pending a hearing to determine whether the in-court identifications had an independent source, or whether, in any event, the introduction of the evidence was harmless error, and for the District Court to reinstate the conviction or order a new trial, as may be proper.

* * *

[Separate opinions by Justice Fortas (joined by Chief Justice Warren), Justice Black, Justice Clark, and Justice Douglas are omitted.]

MR. JUSTICE WHITE, whom MR. JUSTICE HARLAN and MR. JUSTICE STEWART join,

dissenting in part and concurring in part.

The Court has again propounded a broad constitutional rule barring use of a wide spectrum of relevant and probative evidence, solely because a step in its ascertainment or discovery occurs outside the presence of defense counsel. This was the approach of the Court in Miranda v. Arizona. I objected then to what I thought was an uncritical and doctrinaire approach without satisfactory factual foundation. * * *

The Court's opinion is far-reaching. It proceeds first by creating a new *per se* rule of constitutional law: a criminal suspect cannot be subjected to a pretrial identification process in the absence of his counsel without violating the Sixth Amendment. * * *

The rule applies to any lineup, to any other techniques employed to produce an identification and *a fortiori* to a face-to-face encounter between the witness and the suspect alone, regardless of when the identification occurs, in time or place, and whether before or after indictment or information. It matters not how well the witness knows the suspect, whether the witness is the suspect's mother, brother, or long-time associate, and no matter how long or well the witness observed the perpetrator at the scene of the crime. The kidnap victim who has lived for days with his abductor is in the same category as the witness who has had only a fleeting glimpse of the criminal. Neither may identify the suspect without defendant's counsel being present. The same strictures apply regardless of the number of other witnesses who positively identify the defendant and regardless of the corroborative evidence showing that it was the defendant who had committed the crime.

* * * The Court apparently believes that improper police procedures are so widespread that a broad prophylactic rule must be laid down, requiring the presence of counsel at all pretrial identifications, in order to detect recurring instances of police misconduct. I do not share this pervasive distrust of all official investigations. None of the materials the Court relies upon supports it.

* * *

Note on the Meaning of Wade

It is important to understand exactly what the result in *Wade* was. The lineup was held improper because of the absence of counsel, substitute counsel, or waiver of counsel. But, when Wade was tried, the lineup was not mentioned by the prosecution; its results were not a part of the evidence until brought up by the defense in cross-examination. Thus, the controlling question was whether the in-court identification was tainted by the unconstitutional lineup—i.e., whether the in-court identification, which the prosecutor used, would have been made had there been no lineup.

Evidence of an out-of-court identification, offered for its truth, was hearsay not subject to any exception at the time of the federal trial in *Wade*. Thus, the prosecution made no use of the prior identification until the defense "opened the door." A federal prosecutor would no longer be so constrained, because Rule 801(d)(1)(C) of the Federal Rules of Evidence provides for admissibility of prior identifications as "not hearsay" when the person who made the identification is "subject to cross-examination."

Evidence of the Prior Identification Itself: Gilbert v. California

In Gilbert v. California, 388 U.S. 263 (1967), one of the companion cases to *Wade,* the out-of-court identification made in the absence of counsel was actually admitted in the prosecution's case-in-chief under a state hearsay exception. Gilbert was convicted of armed bank robbery and the murder of a police officer who entered the bank during the course of the robbery. At the time of the challenged identification procedure, Gilbert had been indicted for robberies occurring in Alhambra. Justice Brennan, writing for the Court, noted that the lineup was on a stage behind bright lights which prevented those in the line from seeing the audience. Upwards of 100 persons were in the audience, each an eyewitness to one of the several robberies charged to Gilbert. Doubtful witnesses were allowed to call Gilbert out of the lineup to make him repeat a phrase in a particular way or to walk in a particular way. The witnesses talked to each other and made their identifications in each other's presence.

As in *Wade,* the Court held that the in-court identifications would be excluded unless they proceeded from a source independent of the tainted identification, such as a substantial opportunity to view the perpetrator at the time of the crime. As in *Wade,* the Court remanded for an independent source determination. However, as to the use of the out-of-court identifications as evidence, the Court adopted a per se rule of exclusion. Justice Brennan explained testimony concerning the fact that a pre-trial identification had been made, in the absence of counsel,

> is the direct result of the illegal lineup come at by exploitation of the primary illegality. The State is therefore not entitled to an opportunity to show that that testimony had an independent source. Only a *per se* exclusionary rule as to such testimony can be an effective sanction to assure that

law enforcement authorities will respect the accused's constitutional right to the presence of his counsel at the critical lineup. In the absence of legislative regulations adequate to avoid the hazards to a fair trial which inhere in lineups as presently conducted, the desirability of deterring the constitutionally objectionable practice must prevail over the undesirability of excluding relevant evidence. That conclusion is buttressed by the consideration that the witness' testimony of his lineup identification will enhance the impact of his in-court identification on the jury and seriously aggravate whatever derogation exists of the accused's right to a fair trial.

The Role of a Lawyer at a Lineup

The Court in *Wade* and *Gilbert* was concerned about inadequate identification procedures and the lasting effect they may have in some cases. But did the Court, in imposing a counsel requirement, fashion a suitable remedy for the problems it identified? The Court's counsel remedy is criticized in Read, Lawyers at Lineups: Constitutional Necessity or Avoidable Extravagance?, 17 U.C.L.A.L.Rev. 339, 362–67 (1969). Read makes the following arguments: *Wade* viewed counsel as essentially an observer, i.e., a passive participant. A passive observer is unlikely to be able to improve the quality of lineups. If the defendant is not a very good witness in a hearing on a lineup because of obvious bias, his lawyer is likely to be almost as biased and thus no better a witness. Moreover, various recording devices would depict the lineup more effectively than testimony by participants. And counsel is no more schooled than other participants in psychology and may be insensitive to lineup conditions that might be prejudicial to a defendant.

The presence of a lawyer at a lineup might do some good, however. Even a passive observer is not barred from making suggestions to police and prosecutors. A lawyer who is used to bargaining with law enforcement officials may be able to persuade them as to the unfairness of some procedures at lineups. Moreover, knowledge that a lawyer is present may tend to make officials more careful–something like is thought to occur with observers in elections. Lawyers may not be trained psychologists, but they should know the kinds of suggestive factors that make lineups vulnerable and can urge case law on police and prosecutors. Even without formal interdisciplinary training, lawyers may be careful listeners and should be able to identify certain forms of suggestiveness— e.g., leading questions to witnesses. Finally, cross-examination of identification witnesses is likely to be more effective when the lawyer has actually seen the identification process.

If the lawyer is inclined to be active, what can she do that will not work against her client's interests by calling attention to the client? If the lawyer is too passive, does she risk waiving her client's rights? Compare Gilligan, Eyewitness Identification, 58 Mil.L.Rev. 183, 201 (1972) with Panel Discussion, The Role of the Defense Lawyer at a Lineup in Light of the *Wade, Gilbert* and *Stovall* Decisions, 4 Crim.L.Bull. 273, 290 (1968).

If the lawyer is only a passive observer at the lineup, could police permissibly dispense with a lawyer's presence by simply videotaping the identification and giving the tape to counsel? In United States v. LaPierre, 998 F.2d 1460 (9th Cir.1993), the court refused to decide whether videotaping could ever be a substitute for the presence of counsel. It found, however, that videotaping was inadequate under the facts because the videotape showed only the people in the lineup, and did not record anything that occurred in the witness room. Why should that make any difference?

2. Limiting the Right to Counsel to Post–Charge Lineups

The Sixth Amendment right to counsel invoked in *Wade* applies to all "criminal prosecutions." As seen in the discussion of *Massiah* and *Escobedo* in Chapter Three, the Court has held that a criminal prosecution within the meaning of the Sixth Amendment does not begin until the suspect has been formally charged with a crime. In the following case, the Court applies that limitation to the *Wade-Gilbert* right to counsel.

KIRBY v. ILLINOIS

Supreme Court of the United States, 1972.
406 U.S. 682.

MR. JUSTICE STEWART **announced the judgment of the Court and an opinion in which** THE CHIEF JUSTICE, MR. JUSTICE BLACKMUN, **and** MR. JUSTICE REHNQUIST **join.**

* * * In the present case we are asked to extend the *Wade-Gilbert per se* exclusionary rule to identification testimony based upon a police station showup that took place *before* the defendant had been indicted or otherwise formally charged with any criminal offense.

[The defendants were arrested for robbery. The victim identified them at the police station. The defendants had no counsel present at the time of the identification. Some time after this identification, the defendants were indicted. The victim identified the defendants at trial and also testified to the fact of the previous identification.]

I

* * *

In a line of constitutional cases in this Court stemming back to the Court's landmark opinion in Powell v. Alabama, 287 U.S. 45, it has been firmly established that a person's Sixth and Fourteenth Amendment right to counsel attaches only at or after the time

that adversary judicial proceedings have been initiated against him.

This is not to say that a defendant in a criminal case has a constitutional right to counsel only at the trial itself. The *Powell* case makes clear that the right attaches at the time of arraignment, and the Court has recently held that it exists also at the time of a preliminary hearing. But the point is that, while members of the Court have differed as to existence of the right to counsel in the contexts of some of the above cases, *all* of those cases have involved points of time at or after the initiation of adversary judicial criminal proceedings—whether by way of formal charge, preliminary hearing, indictment, information, or arraignment.

* * *

The initiation of judicial criminal proceedings is far from a mere formalism. It is the starting point of our whole system of adversary criminal justice. For it is only then that the government has committed itself to prosecute, and only then that the adverse positions of government and defendant have solidified. It is then that a defendant finds himself faced with the prosecutorial forces of organized society, and immersed in the intricacies of substantive and procedural criminal law. It is this point, therefore, that marks the commencement of the "criminal prosecutions" to which alone the explicit guarantees of the Sixth Amendment are applicable.

In this case we are asked to import into a routine police investigation an absolute constitutional guarantee historically and rationally applicable only after the onset of formal prosecutorial proceedings. We decline to do so. Less than a year after *Wade* and *Gilbert* were decided, the Court explained the rule of those decisions as follows: "The rationale of those cases was that an accused is entitled to counsel at any 'critical stage of the *prosecution*,' and that a post-indictment lineup is such a 'critical stage.'" (Emphasis supplied.) Simmons v. United States, 390 U.S. 377, 382–383. * * *

II

What has been said is not to suggest that there may not be occasions during the course of a criminal investigation when the police do abuse identification procedures. Such abuses are not beyond the reach of the Constitution. * * * The Due Process Clause of the Fifth and Fourteenth Amendments forbids a lineup that is unnecessarily suggestive and conducive to irreparable mistaken identification. * * *

Mr. Chief Justice Burger, concurring.

I agree that the right to counsel attaches as soon as criminal charges are formally made against an accused and he becomes the subject of a "criminal prosecution." Therefore, I join in the plurality opinion and in the judgment.

Mr. Justice Powell, concurring in the result.

As I would not extend the *Wade-Gilbert per se* exclusionary rule, I concur in the result reached by the Court.

Mr. Justice Brennan with whom Mr. Justice Douglas and Mr. Justice Marshall join, dissenting.

* * *

While it should go without saying, it appears necessary, in view of the plurality opinion today, to re-emphasize that *Wade* did not require the presence of counsel at pretrial confrontations for identification purposes simply on the basis of an abstract consideration of the words "criminal prosecutions" in the Sixth Amendment. Counsel is required at those confrontations because "the dangers inherent in eyewitness identification and the suggestibility inherent in the context of the pretrial identification," mean that protection must be afforded to the "most basic right [of] a criminal defendant—his right to a fair trial at which the witnesses against him might be meaningfully cross-examined." * * * Hence, "the initiation of adversary judicial criminal proceedings," is completely irrelevant to whether counsel is necessary at a pretrial confrontation for identification in order to safeguard the accused's constitutional rights to confrontation and the effective assistance of counsel at his trial.

* * *

Mr. Justice White, dissenting.

United States v. Wade and Gilbert v. California govern this case and compel reversal of the judgment below.

Note on the Meaning of Kirby

It helps to remember that *Kirby* states that "[t]he Due Process Clause of the Fifth and Fourteenth Amendments forbids a lineup that is unnecessarily suggestive and conducive to irreparable mistaken identification." The cases reviewing claims of "unnecessary suggestiveness" under the Due Process Clause are examined in the next section.

As a practical matter, the Court in *Kirby* must have been concerned with the implications of extending the *Wade* right to counsel rule to all or virtually all identifications. Many identifications are made on the street only minutes after the event. Application of the *Wade* rule in these circumstances obviously presents problems; the delay resulting from waiting for counsel to arrive may perversely decrease the reliability of the identification due to the fading memory of witnesses. In light of these problems, the result in *Kirby* is understandable, so long as the Due Process Clause provides meaningful protection against mistaken identifications in cases where the *Wade* rule does not apply. As we will see, though, this has not always been the case.

The vast majority of identification procedures are conducted before a formal charge has been filed. Indeed lineups and other identifications are conducted to obtain evidence with which to bring a formal charge. Thus, *Kirby* strips the *Wade* counsel requirement of significant practical effect.

Does *Kirby* create an incentive for the government to delay an indictment in order to conduct an identification procedure in the absence of counsel? Does a suspect have a constitutional right to be indicted at a certain point? Courts have stated that if adversary proceedings are "deliberately delayed" in order to evade the *Wade* rule, the resulting identification will be invalidated. See United States ex rel. Burbank v. Warden, 535 F.2d 361 (7th Cir.1976). However, proving that an indictment was deliberately delayed is difficult, to say the least. See United States ex rel. Hall v. Lane, 804 F.2d 79 (7th Cir.1986)(no evidence that delay in obtaining indictment was caused by bad faith, therefore there was no right to counsel at the pre-indictment identification).

Post-Charge Photographic Identifications: United States v. Ash

In United States v. Ash, 413 U.S. 300 (1973), the Court again restricted the *Wade* rule, holding that a defendant has no right to counsel at a *photographic* identification, whether conducted before or after indictment or formal charge. Justice Blackmun's majority opinion described the right to counsel as a defendant's right to have a spokesperson or advisor. The Court noted that "the accused himself is not present at the time of the photographic display and asserts no right to be present" and therefore "no possibility arises that the accused might be misled by his lack of familiarity with the law or overpowered by his professional adversary." The Court noted that photo arrays are unlike lineups, because an "accurate reconstruction" of a photographic array is possible at trial. It concluded that "the opportunity to cure defects at trial causes the pretrial confrontation to cease to be critical." The Court also saw photo displays as a mere preparatory step in the gathering of evidence where the defense counsel had an "equal ability * * * to seek and interview witnesses himself." Justice Stewart concurred in the result, concluding that "[a] photographic identification is quite different from a lineup, for there are substantially fewer possibilities of impermissible suggestion when photographs are used, and those unfair influences can be readily reconstructed at trial."

Professor Grano, in *Kirby, Biggers*, and *Ash*: Do Any Constitutional Safeguards Remain Against the Danger of Protecting the Innocent?, 72 Mich.L.Rev. 717 (1974), suggests that there are myriad possibilities of suggestiveness in photographic identifications. While it might be true that the photograph array itself can be reproduced at trial, what about the conditions surrounding the identification of the photo—such as police suggestion as to whom to pick, whether the witness was completely certain in his choice, etc. Doesn't counsel need to know about all of these factors in order to effectively cross-examine the identifying witness? How can counsel know these factors if she wasn't there?

What if the defendant, who has already been charged, is identified in a photograph of a lineup? Does the lineup rule of *Wade* control, so that counsel is required? In United States v. Barker, 988 F.2d 77 (9th Cir.1993), the court held that *Ash* rather than *Wade* applied to such an identification. It explained as follows:

> This case is a hybrid: it involves a photograph of a lineup. The fact that the lineup is depicted in the photograph, though, does not call into question the reasoning behind the decision in *Ash*. Counsel must be present where there is a potential "that the accused might be misled by his lack of familiarity with the law or overpowered by his professional adversary," or where counsel would "produce equality in a trial-like adversary confrontation." Here, as in *Ash*, the defendant is not present when the photograph of the lineup is shown and thus cannot be "misled" or "overpowered," and the "adversary mechanism remains as effective for a photographic display as for other parts of a pretrial interview" whether the photos concerned are of a lineup or an array of suspects.

While it is probably true that the rationale of *Ash* is applicable to all photographic identifications, did the Court in *Ash* adequately state the rationale of *Wade*? Was counsel required in *Wade* in order to keep the defendant from being misled or overpowered? Or did the Court think that counsel was required in order to guarantee adequate cross-examination of the identification witnesses? If adequate cross-examination was the goal, why would counsel's presence not be required at a photographic identification?

B. DUE PROCESS LIMITATIONS ON IDENTIFICATION EVIDENCE

1. *The Foundations of a Due Process Test*

Stovall v. Denno

On the same day that it decided *Wade* and *Gilbert,* the Court made it clear that those decisions applied prospectively only. Stovall v. Denno, 388 U.S. 293 (1967). The Court in *Stovall* held that a due process-fundamental fairness approach would be used in assessing identification procedures that are not governed by *Wade* and *Gilbert*. This approach has continuing relevance, even though *Stovall* dealt specifically with identifications occurring before the date that *Wade* and *Gilbert* were decided. As stated above, after *Kirby* and *Ash*, the application of *Wade* and *Gilbert* is limited to post-indictment corporeal identifications. The due process test set forth in *Stovall,* and developed in later cases discussed below, therefore governs the admissibility of most identification evidence. Justice Brennan, again writing for the Court, described the relevant facts in *Stovall*:

> Dr. Paul Behrendt was stabbed to death in the kitchen of his home in Garden City, Long Island, about midnight August 23, 1961. Dr. Behrendt's wife, also a physician, had followed her husband to the kitchen and jumped at the assailant. He knocked her to the floor and stabbed her 11 times. The police found a shirt on the kitchen floor and keys in a pocket which they

traced to petitioner. They arrested him on the afternoon of August 24. An arraignment was promptly held but was postponed until petitioner could retain counsel.

Mrs. Behrendt was hospitalized for major surgery to save her life. The police, without affording petitioner time to retain counsel, arranged with her surgeon to permit them to bring petitioner to her hospital room about noon of August 25, the day after the surgery. Petitioner was handcuffed to one of five police officers who, with two members of the staff of the District Attorney, brought him to the hospital room. Petitioner was the only Negro in the room. Mrs. Behrendt identified him from her hospital bed after being asked by an officer whether he "was the man" and after petitioner repeated at the direction of an officer a "few words for voice identification." None of the witnesses could recall the words that were used. Mrs. Behrendt and the officers testified at the trial to her identification of the petitioner in the hospital room, and she also made an in-court identification of petitioner in the courtroom.

Petitioner was convicted and sentenced to death. * * *

After holding that *Wade* and *Gilbert* would not be applied retroactively to cases on habeas review, the Court considered Stovall's contention that "in any event the confrontation conducted in this case was so unnecessarily suggestive and conducive to irreparable mistaken identification that he was denied due process of law." Justice Brennan analyzed this question by focusing on whether it was necessary for the police to act as they did.

The practice of showing suspects singly to persons for the purpose of identification, and not as part of a lineup, has been widely condemned. However, a claimed violation of due process of law in the conduct of a confrontation depends on the totality of the circumstances surrounding it, and the record in the present case reveals that the showing of Stovall to Mrs. Behrendt in an immediate hospital confrontation was imperative.

Justice Brennan then quoted approvingly from the Court of Appeals' decision finding no due process violation:

"Here was the only person in the world who could possibly exonerate Stovall. Her words, and only her words, 'He is not the man' could have resulted in freedom for Stovall. The hospital was not far distant from the courthouse and jail. No one knew how long Mrs. Behrendt might live. Faced with the responsibility of identifying the attacker, with the need for immediate action and with the knowledge that Mrs. Behrendt could not visit the jail, the police followed the only feasible procedure and took Stovall to the hospital room. Under these circumstances, the usual police station lineup, which Stovall now argues he should have had, was out of the question."

Note that the Court in *Stovall* did not mention the possible unreliability of the identification, even though Stovall was handcuffed and was the only African-American man in the room. Does the Court mean that even unreliable identifications are constitutionally permissible so long as the police have a legitimate excuse for conducting a suggestive identification? Conversely, if the police had no good reason for acting as they did, would the Court then be concerned about whether the identification was reliable? These questions were taken up by the

Court in such cases as Neil v. Biggers and Manson v. Brathwaite, discussed below.

Note also that Mrs. Behrendt, the witness who made the identification in *Stovall*, survived her attack and testified at trial. Of course, her survival was a happy event; but could this lead you to question whether there was really such an emergency as to excuse the suggestive activity in *Stovall?* Part of the reason the hospital show-up was held permissible was that this was the only procedure that could have resulted in exoneration for Stovall. But if that is the case, why not let Stovall decide whether he wants to be subject to a show-up identification in handcuffs? If Stovall had been given the option to "exonerate" himself in this way, what do you think he would have done?

Permissible Suggestiveness?

Cases arise from time to time in which the government argues, as in *Stovall*, that there was a legitimate excuse for conducting a suggestive identification procedure. Usually these claims are rebuffed. For example, in Neil v. Biggers, 409 U.S. 188 (1972), Biggers was identified in a one-on-one showup by the victim of a rape. The government offered an excuse for conducting the one-on-one showup: the officers tried to conduct a lineup, but when they checked the city jail and the juvenile home for people who looked similar to Biggers, they found no one at either place fitting the suspect's "unusual physical description." The Court stated that it was "inclined to agree with the courts below that the police did not exhaust all possibilities in seeking persons physically comparable to respondent." Yet in *Biggers*, the unnecessarily suggestive identification was nonetheless held admissible. Cases such as Manson v. Brathwaite, infra, discuss how this could be so.

On the other hand, street identifications held immediately after the crime have often been excused as "necessarily" suggestive. A typical analysis is found in United States v. Bautista, 23 F.3d 726 (2d Cir.1994), a case in which the suspects were presented, in handcuffs, for an identification by a confidential informant (CI) immediately after a drug raid:

> We find that the presentation of the suspects to the CI immediately following the raid was not unnecessarily suggestive. * * * [A] prompt showing of a detained suspect at the scene of arrest has a very valid function: to prevent the mistaken arrest of innocent persons. Indeed, this court has instructed law enforcement officials that where an officer has or should have doubts whether a detained suspect is in fact the person sought, the officer must make immediate reasonable efforts to confirm the suspect's identity.

* * *

> The fact that the suspects were handcuffed, in the custody of law enforcement officers, and illuminated by flashlights * * * did not render the pretrial identification procedure unnecessarily suggestive. In this case, handcuffs, custody, and flashlights were all necessary incidents of an on-the-scene identification immediately following a night-time narcotics raid. Because the on-the-scene identification was necessary to allow the officers to release the innocent, the incidents of that identification were also necessary.

See also United States v. King, 148 F.3d 968 (8th Cir.1998) ("Police officers need not limit themselves to station house lineups when an opportunity for a quick, on-the-scene identification arises. Such identifications are essential to free innocent suspects and to inform the police if further investigation is necessary."). Compare People v. Johnson, 81 N.Y.2d 828, 595 N.Y.S.2d 385, 611 N.E.2d 286 (1993) (one-on-one show-up conducted several hours after the crime, with both the complainant and the defendant transported to the crime scene, could not be justified as necessary). How many innocent people do you think are released by these "necessary" on-the-scene identifications?

2. Applying the Due Process Test

Simmons v. United States

In Simmons v. United States, 390 U.S. 377 (1968), a Chicago Savings and Loan Association was robbed by two men. Andrews and Simmons were suspected. The FBI had shown the bank employees at least six pictures, mostly group photos of Andrews, Simmons, and others, and some individual snapshots of Simmons and Andrews. Simmons and Andrews were identified; the witnesses identified Simmons at his trial, but the prosecution made no mention of the pre-trial identification. Simmons challenged the identification procedures under the Due Process Clause. The Court stated that the due process test protects against identifications that are "so impermissibly suggestive as to give rise to a very substantial likelihood of irreparable misidentification." Applying that test to the facts, the Court emphasized the following factors: the officers had a pressing need for fast action; Simmons was readily identified by the witnesses, while Andrews was not, even though Andrews was in many of the same pictures as Simmons; the witnesses had an excellent opportunity to observe the robbery and the perpetrators; and the identification was made shortly after the robbery. The Simmons Court found no due process violation "even though the identification procedure employed may have in some respects fallen short of the ideal." The fact was that the witnesses' bases for making the identification was so strong that it was unaffected by any police suggestiveness.

Violation of Due Process: Foster v. California

In Foster v. California, 394 U.S. 440 (1969), the Court found for the first and so far the only time that a police procedure was so impermissibly suggestive as to create a substantial risk of mistaken identification. The eyewitness was called to the station to view a three-person lineup. Foster, who was six feet tall, was placed between two men who were both six inches shorter. Only Foster wore a jacket similar to that of the perpetrator. The witness could not positively identify Foster. Foster was then brought into an office for a one-on-one showup. The witness could still not make a positive identification. A week later, the witness viewed a second lineup. Only Foster remained from the first lineup. At this point, the witness positively identified Foster. This identification was admitted at trial pursuant to the California hearsay exception discussed in Gilbert, and the witness also identified Foster at trial. The Supreme Court stated that the "suggestive elements in this identification procedure made it all but inevitable that [the witness] would identify petitioner whether or not he was in fact the man," and that the procedure "so undermined the reliability of the eyewitness identification as to violate due process." The Court held that both the in-court and out-of-court identifications were improperly admitted, since both were tainted by the police suggestiveness.

The Independent Source: Neil v. Biggers

In Neil v. Biggers, 409 U.S. 188 (1972), the defendant was convicted of rape, after the victim identified him at trial and described her pretrial identification of Biggers. The latter was of concern to the Supreme Court. For seven months after the rape, the victim viewed lineups, one person showups, and photographs, but was unable to identify her assailant. One day the police arrested Biggers on an unrelated charge. They brought the victim to the police station, walked Biggers past her, and directed him to utter certain words. The victim identified Biggers. Justice Powell's opinion for the Court stated that "the primary evil to be avoided is 'a very substantial likelihood of irreparable misidentification.' "Thus, the question was whether the identification was reliable "even though the confrontation procedure was suggestive." On the facts, the Court found that the police suggestiveness did not cause the identification to be made, and therefore "the identification was reliable even though the confrontation procedure was suggestive." Essentially, the Court found that the witness had an independent source for the identification—her experience with the perpetrator at the time of the crime.

> The victim spent a considerable period of time with her assailant, up to half an hour. She was with him under adequate artificial light in her house and under a full moon outdoors, and at least twice, once in the house and later in the woods, faced him directly and intimately. She was no casual observer, but rather the victim of one of the most personally humiliating of all crimes. Her description to the police, which included the assailant's approximate age, height, weight, complexion, skin texture, build, and voice, might not have satisfied Proust but was more than ordinarily thorough. She had "no doubt" that respondent was the person who raped her. * * * The victim here, a practical nurse by profession, had an unusual opportunity to observe and identify her assailant. She testified * * * that there was something about his face "I don't think I could ever forget."

> There was, to be sure, a lapse of seven months between the rape and the confrontation. This would be a serious negative factor in most cases. Here, however, the testimony is undisputed that the victim made no previous identification at any of the showups, lineups, or photographic showings.

Thus, the question for admissibility under the Due Process Clause is whether the witness had a picture of the defendant in his or her mind *before* the police suggestiveness occurred, and whether that suggestiveness altered that picture in any way. To determine this question, a court must investigate how clear the witness' pre-identification picture was; this is determined by such factors as how good a look the witness got during or before the crime, how attentive the witness was, and whether memory loss has faded the picture in the witness' mind by the time of the identification. Inferences are drawn about the clarity of the picture in the witness' mind by descriptions given by the witness, by whether the witness has mistakenly identified another person as the criminal, by whether the witness' description fits the person that is identified, and by the certainty of the witness at the time the defendant is identified. Against all these factors, a court must look at the suggestive tactics used by the police and determine how likely they were to have had an effect on the witness. After *Biggers,* police suggestiveness is not the predominant inquiry that it may have appeared to be in *Stovall.* Rather, it is only one factor among the totality of circumstances to be considered. The following case makes this clear.

3. Reliability as the Linchpin

MANSON v. BRATHWAITE

Supreme Court of the United States, 1977.
432 U.S. 98.

MR. JUSTICE BLACKMUN **delivered the opinion of the Court.**

This case presents the issue as to whether the Due Process Clause of the Fourteenth Amendment compels the exclusion, in a state criminal trial, apart from any consideration of reliability, of pretrial identification evidence obtained by a police procedure that was both suggestive and unnecessary. This Court's decisions in Stovall v. Denno and Neil v. Biggers are particularly implicated.

I

Jimmy D. Glover, a full-time trooper of the Connecticut State Police, in 1970 was assigned to the Narcotics Division in an undercover capacity. On May 5 of that year, about 7:45 p.m., e.d.t., and while there was still daylight, Glover and Henry Alton Brown, an informant, went to an apartment building at 201 Westland, in Hartford, for the purpose of purchasing narcotics from "Dickie Boy" Cicero, a known narcotics dealer. Cicero, it was thought, lived on the third floor of that apartment building. Glover and Brown entered the building, observed by backup Officers D'Onofrio and Gaffey, and proceeded by stairs to the third floor. Glover knocked at the door of one of the two apartments served by the stairway. The area was illuminated by natural light from a window in the third floor hallway. The door was opened 12 to 18 inches in response to the knock. Glover observed a man standing at the door and, behind him, a woman. Brown identified himself. Glover then asked for "two things" of narcotics. The man at the door held out his hand, and Glover gave him two $10 bills. The door closed. Soon the man returned and handed Glover two glassine bags. While the door was open, Glover stood within two feet of the person from whom he made the purchase and observed his face. Five to seven minutes elapsed from the time the door first opened until it closed the second time.

Glover and Brown then left the building. This was about eight minutes after their arrival. Glover drove to headquarters where he described the seller to D'Onofrio and Gaffey. Glover at that time did not know the identity of the seller. He described him as being "a colored man, approximately five feet eleven inches tall, dark complexion, black hair, short Afro style, and having high cheekbones, and of heavy build. He was wearing at the time blue pants and a plaid shirt." D'Onofrio, suspecting from this description that respondent might be the seller, obtained a photograph of respondent from the Records Division of the Hartford Police Department. He left it at

Glover's office. D'Onofrio was not acquainted with respondent personally, but did know him by sight and had seen him "[s]everal times" prior to May 5. Glover, when alone, viewed the photograph for the first time upon his return to headquarters on May 7; he identified the person shown as the one from whom he had purchased the narcotics.

* * *

Respondent was charged, in a two-count information, with possession and sale of heroin * * *. At his trial in January 1971, the photograph from which Glover had identified respondent was received in evidence without objection on the part of the defense. Glover also testified that, although he had not seen respondent in the eight months that had elapsed since the sale, "there [was] no doubt whatsoever" in his mind that the person shown on the photograph was respondent. Glover also made a positive in-court identification without objection.

No explanation was offered by the prosecution for the failure to utilize a photographic array or to conduct a lineup.

* * *

The jury found respondent guilty on both counts of the information. * * *

[The Court discusses its precedents, all of which have been discussed, supra.]

II

* * *

IV

Petitioner at the outset acknowledges that "the procedure in the instant case was suggestive [because only one photograph was used] and unnecessary" [because there was no emergency or exigent circumstance].

The respondent, in agreement with the Court of Appeals, proposes a *per se* rule of exclusion that he claims is dictated by the demands of the Fourteenth Amendment's guarantee of due process. * * *

Since the decision in *Biggers,* the Courts of Appeals appear to have developed at least two approaches to [identification] evidence. The first, or *per se* approach, employed by the Second Circuit in the present case, focuses on the procedures employed and requires exclusion of the out-of-court identification evidence, without regard to reliability, whenever it has been obtained through unnecessarily suggestive confrontation procedures. The justifications advanced are the elimination of evidence of uncertain reliability, deterrence of the police and prosecutors, and the stated "fair assurance against the awful risks of misidentification."

The second, or more lenient, approach is one that continues to rely on the totality of the circumstances. It permits the admission of the confrontation evidence if, despite the suggestive aspect, the out-of-court identification possesses certain features of reliability. Its adherents feel that the *per se* approach is not mandated by the Due Process Clause of the Fourteenth Amendment. This second approach, in contrast to the other, is *ad hoc* and serves to limit the societal costs imposed by a sanction that excludes relevant evidence from consideration and evaluation by the trier of fact. See United States ex rel. Kirby v. Sturges, 510 F.2d 397, 407–408 (CA7)(opinion by Judge, now Mr. Justice, Stevens).

The respondent here stresses * * * the need for deterrence of improper identification practice, a factor he regards as pre-eminent. Photographic identification, it is said, continues to be needlessly employed. * * * He argues that a totality rule cannot be expected to have a significant deterrent impact; only a strict rule of exclusion will have direct and immediate impact on law enforcement agents. Identification evidence is so convincing to the jury that sweeping exclusionary rules are required. Fairness of the trial is threatened by suggestive confrontation evidence, and thus, it is said, an exclusionary rule has an established constitutional predicate.

There are, of course, several interests to be considered and taken into account. The driving force behind United States v. Wade and Gilbert v. California (right to counsel at a post-indictment lineup), and *Stovall,* all decided on the same day, was the Court's concern with the problems of eyewitness identification. Usually the witness must testify about an encounter with a total stranger under circumstances of emergency or emotional stress. The witness' recollection of the stranger can be distorted easily by the circumstances or by later actions of the police. Thus, *Wade* and its companion cases reflect the concern that the jury not hear eyewitness testimony unless that evidence has aspects of reliability. It must be observed that both approaches before us are responsive to this concern. The *per se* rule, however, goes too far since its application automatically and peremptorily, and without consideration of alleviating factors, keeps evidence from the jury that is reliable and relevant.

The second factor is deterrence. Although the *per se* approach has the more significant deterrent effect, the totality approach also has an influence on police behavior. The police will guard against unnecessarily suggestive procedures under the totality rule, as well as the *per se* one, for fear that their actions will lead to the exclusion of identifications as unreliable.

The third factor is the effect on the administration of justice. Here the *per se* approach suffers serious drawbacks. Since it denies the trier reliable evidence, it may result, on occasion, in the guilty going free. Also, because of its rigidity, the *per se* approach may make error by the trial judge more likely than the totality approach. And in those cases in which the admission of identification evidence is error under the *per se* approach but not under the totality approach—cases in which the identification is reliable despite an unnecessarily suggestive identification procedure—reversal is a Draconian sanction. Certainly, inflexible rules of exclusion, that may frustrate rather than promote justice, have not been viewed recently by this Court with unlimited enthusiasm.

* * *

We therefore conclude that reliability is the linchpin in determining the admissibility of identification testimony for both pre-and post-*Stovall* confrontations. The factors to be considered are set out in *Biggers.* These include the opportunity of the witness to view the criminal at the time of the crime, the witness' degree of attention, the accuracy of his prior description of the criminal, the level of certainty demonstrated at the confrontation, and the time between the crime and the confrontation. Against these factors is to be weighed the corrupting effect of the suggestive identification itself.

V

We turn, then, to the facts of this case and apply the analysis:

1. *The opportunity to view.* Glover testified that for two to three minutes he stood at the apartment door, within two feet of the respondent. The door opened twice, and each time the man

stood at the door. The moments passed, the conversation took place, and payment was made. Glover looked directly at his vendor. It was near sunset, to be sure, but the sun had not yet set, so it was not dark or even dusk or twilight. Natural light from outside entered the hallway through a window. There was natural light, as well, from inside the apartment.

2. *The degree of attention.* Glover was not a casual or passing observer, as is so often the case with eyewitness identification. Trooper Glover was a trained police officer on duty—and specialized and dangerous duty— when he called at the third floor of 201 Westland in Hartford on May 5, 1970. Glover himself was a Negro and unlikely to perceive only general features of "hundreds of Hartford black males," as the Court of Appeals stated. It is true that Glover's duty was that of ferreting out narcotics offenders and that he would be expected in his work to produce results. But it is also true that, as a specially trained, assigned, and experienced officer, he could be expected to pay scrupulous attention to detail, for he knew that subsequently he would have to find and arrest his vendor. In addition, he knew that his claimed observations would be subject later to close scrutiny and examination at any trial.

3. *The accuracy of the description.* Glover's description was given to D'Onofrio within minutes after the transaction. It included the vendor's race, his height, his build, the color and style of his hair, and the high cheekbone facial feature. It also included clothing the vendor wore. No claim has been made that respondent did not possess the physical characteristics so described. D'Onofrio reacted positively at once. Two days later, when Glover was alone, he viewed the photograph D'Onofrio produced and identified its subject as the narcotics seller.

4. *The witness' level of certainty.* There is no dispute that the photograph in question was that of respondent. Glover, in response to a question whether the photograph was that of the person from whom he made the purchase, testified: "There is no question whatsoever." This positive assurance was repeated.

5. *The time between the crime and the confrontation.* Glover's description of his vendor was given to D'Onofrio within minutes of the crime. The photographic identification took place only two days later. We do not have here the passage of weeks or months between the crime and the viewing of the photograph.

These indicators of Glover's ability to make an accurate identification are hardly outweighed by the corrupting effect of the challenged identification itself. Although identifications arising from single-photograph displays may be viewed in general with suspicion, we find in the instant case little pressure on the witness to acquiesce in the suggestion that such a display entails. D'Onofrio had left the photograph at Glover's office and was not present when Glover first viewed it two days after the event. There thus was little urgency and Glover could view the photograph at his leisure. And since Glover examined the photograph alone, there was no coercive pressure to make an identification arising from the presence of another. The identification was made in circumstances allowing care and reflection.

* * *

Surely, we cannot say that under all the circumstances of this case there is "a very substantial likelihood of irreparable misidentification." Short of that point, such evidence is for the jury to weigh. We are content to rely upon the good sense and judgment of American juries, for evidence with some element of untrustworthiness is customary grist for the jury mill. Juries are not so susceptible that they cannot measure intelligently the weight of identification testimony that has some questionable feature.

* * *

We conclude that the criteria laid down in *Biggers* are to be applied in determining the admissibility of evidence offered by the prosecution concerning a post-*Stovall* identification, and that those criteria are satisfactorily met and complied with here.

* * *

MR. JUSTICE STEVENS, **concurring.**

* * * [I]n evaluating the admissibility of particular identification testimony it is sometimes difficult to put other evidence of guilt entirely to one side. Mr. Justice Blackmun's opinion for the Court carefully avoids this pitfall and correctly relies only on appropriate indicia of the reliability of the identification itself. Although I consider the factual question in this case extremely close, I am persuaded that the Court has resolved it properly.

MR. JUSTICE MARSHALL, **with whom** MR. JUSTICE BRENNAN **joins, dissenting.**

Today's decision can come as no surprise to those who have been watching the Court dismantle the protections against mistaken eyewitness testimony erected a decade ago * * *. But it is still distressing to see the Court virtually ignore the teaching of experience embodied in those decisions and blindly uphold the conviction of a defendant who may well be innocent.

* * *

* * * [I]n determining the admissibility of the post-*Stovall* identification in this case, the Court considers two

alternatives, a *per se* exclusionary rule and a totality-of-the-circumstances approach. The Court weighs three factors in deciding that the totality approach, which is essentially the test used in *Biggers,* should be applied. In my view, the Court wrongly evaluates the impact of these factors.

First, the Court acknowledges that one of the factors, deterrence of police use of unnecessarily suggestive identification procedures, favors the *per se* rule. Indeed, it does so heavily, for such a rule would make it unquestionably clear to the police they must never use a suggestive procedure when a fairer alternative is available. I have no doubt that conduct would quickly conform to the rule.

Second, the Court gives passing consideration to the dangers of eyewitness identification recognized in the *Wade* trilogy. It concludes, however, that the grave risk of error does not justify adoption of the *per se* approach because that would too often result in exclusion of relevant evidence. In my view, this conclusion totally ignores the lessons of *Wade.* * * *

Finally, the Court errs in its assessment of the relative impact of the two approaches on the administration of justice. * * *

First, the *per se* rule here is not "inflexible." Where evidence is suppressed, for example, as the fruit of an unlawful search, it may well be forever lost to the prosecution. Identification evidence, however, can by its very nature be readily and effectively reproduced. The in-court identification, permitted under *Wade* and *Simmons* if it has a source independent of an uncounseled or suggestive procedure, is one example. Similarly, when a prosecuting attorney learns that there has been a suggestive confrontation, he can easily arrange another lineup conducted under scrupulously fair conditions. * * *

Second, other exclusionary rules have been criticized for preventing jury consideration of relevant and usually reliable evidence in order to serve interests unrelated to guilt or innocence, such as discouraging illegal searches or denial of counsel. Suggestively obtained eyewitness testimony is excluded, in contrast, precisely because of its unreliability and concomitant irrelevance. Its exclusion both protects the integrity of the truth-seeking function of the trial and discourages police use of needlessly inaccurate and ineffective investigatory methods.

* * *

[Justice Marshall applies the majority's "totality of circumstances" test to the facts of the case.]

I consider first the opportunity that Officer Glover had to view the suspect. Careful review of the record shows that he could see the heroin seller only for the time it took to speak three sentences of four or five short words, to hand over some money, and later after the door reopened, to receive the drugs in return. The entire face-to-face transaction could have taken as little as 15 or 20 seconds. But during this time, Glover's attention was not focused exclusively on the seller's face. He observed that the door was opened 12 to 18 inches, that there was a window in the room behind the door, and, most importantly, that there was a woman standing behind the man. Glover was, of course, also concentrating on the details of the transaction—he must have looked away from the seller's face to hand him the money and receive the drugs. The observation during the conversation thus may have been as brief as 5 or 10 seconds.

As the Court notes, Glover was a police officer trained in and attentive to the need for making accurate identifications. Nevertheless, both common sense and scholarly study indicate that while a trained observer such as a police officer is somewhat less likely to make an erroneous identification than the average untrained observer, the mere fact that he has been so trained is no guarantee that he is correct in a specific case. * * *

Another factor on which the Court relies—the witness' degree of certainty in making the identification—is worthless as an indicator that he is correct. Even if Glover had been unsure initially about his identification of respondent's picture, by the time he was called at trial to present a key piece of evidence for the State that paid his salary, it is impossible to imagine his responding negatively to such questions as "is there any doubt in your mind whatsoever" that the identification was correct. * * *

Next, the Court finds that because the identification procedure took place two days after the crime, its reliability is enhanced. While such temporal proximity makes the identification more reliable than one occurring months later, the fact is that the greatest memory loss occurs within hours after an event. After that, the dropoff continues much more slowly. Thus, the reliability of an identification is increased only if it was made within several hours of the crime. If the time gap is any greater, reliability necessarily decreases.

Finally, the Court makes much of the fact that Glover gave a description of the seller to D'Onofrio shortly after the incident. Despite the Court's assertion that because "Glover himself was a Negro and unlikely to perceive only general features of 'hundreds of Hartford black males,' as the Court of Appeals stated," the description given by Glover was actually no more than a general summary of the seller's appearance. We may discount entirely the seller's clothing, for that was of no significance later in the proceeding. Indeed, to the extent that Glover noticed clothes, his attention was diverted from the seller's face. Otherwise, Glover merely described vaguely the seller's height, skin color, hairstyle, and build. He did say that the seller had "high cheekbones," but there is no other mention of facial features, nor even an estimate of age. Conspicuously absent is any indication that the seller was a native of the West Indies, certainly something which a member of the black community could immediately recognize from both appearance and accent.

From all of this, I must conclude that the evidence of Glover's ability to make an accurate identification is far weaker than the Court finds it. In contrast, the procedure used to identify respondent was both extraordinarily suggestive and strongly conducive to error. * * *

* * *

Questions After Manson

In evaluating who has the better of the argument in *Manson,* consider the following hypothetical. A victim of a kidnaping, who lived in close quarters with the perpetrator for six months, finally escapes. He contacts the police and describes the kidnapper in perfect detail, including a distinctive scar on the kidnapper's forehead. The defendant is apprehended, and the victim views him in a one-on-one showup. He has the distinctive scar described by the victim. The victim immediately identifies the defendant with absolute certainty. The police had no reason for failing to conduct a lineup. Under the per se rule rejected in *Manson,* this identification would be inadmissible; but the in-court identification would be admissible because it proceeded from an independent source. Does this make sense? One could argue that it does because otherwise police will not be deterred from conducting suggestive identifications. Moreover, the cost of exclusion to the state is not significant because the in-court identification will still be admissible, and the police could always conduct a lineup *after* this suggestive procedure. The identification from that subsequent lineup, like the in-court identification, would proceed from an independent source and would therefore be admissible. But if the rule of exclusion can be so easily evaded, is it worth having? If the lineup would be *pro forma* in these circumstances, does it make sense to require one?

Ultimately, the question is whether the *per se* rule would be a more effective deterrent than the totality of circumstances test chosen by the Court. There is certainly strong evidence that the *Manson* test, at least as applied by the courts, does little to deter the police from using suggestive identification procedures. For example, the Court has denounced the use of showups in most of the cases you have read. Yet, in 1990, the court in Rodriguez v. Young, 906 F.2d 1153 (7th Cir.), noted with distress "that we continue to review cases both of showups and other suggestive procedures," and that "in few of these cases do we ever find an explanation, by the prosecution, for the failure to conduct a lineup." Of course, the court in *Rodriguez* held that the identification was admissible despite the police suggestiveness (because the witness had a good view of the suspect at the time of the crime), so it will continue to hear more such cases.

Independent Source for In–Court Identification?

If an out-of-court identification is excluded under *Manson,* can the witness identify the defendant in court? Recall that under *Wade,* the witness could make an in-court identification if it was free from the taint of the lineup conducted in the absence of counsel. But if the prior identification was caused by police suggestiveness, as required for exclusion after *Manson* (and as distinguished from a counsel-free lineup which may not have changed the picture of the perpetrator in the witness' mind) there can by definition be no independent source for the in-court identification. If there were an independent source, then the out-of-court identification itself would be admissible. See Marsden v. Moore, 847 F.2d 1536 (11th Cir.1988)(single photograph procedure creates substantial risk of mistaken identification where witness had only a fleeting glimpse of the perpetrator two years before the identification; in-court identification must be excluded as well); Dispensa v. Lynaugh, 847 F.2d 211 (5th Cir. 1988)(identification caused by police suggestiveness requires exclusion of both in-court and out-of-court identification).

Relevance of the Officers' State of Mind

Recall that *Stovall* implied that if police suggestiveness was *permissible,* an identification could be admitted even if it were unreliable. But after *Manson,* reliability is the "linchpin." Does that mean that defendants can actually benefit from application of the *Manson* test in cases where the police have a good excuse for obtaining an unreliable identification? Some courts have said yes. In United States v. Bouthot, 878 F.2d 1506 (1st Cir.1989), the witness happened by accident to see the defendant in the courthouse on an unrelated matter. He based his identification in defendant's trial on that viewing. The government argued that the identification should be admitted because "there was no impermissibly suggestive identification procedure conducted by the government." The court relied on *Manson* and rejected this argument.

> Because the due process focus in the identification context is on the fairness of the trial and not exclusively on police deterrence, it follows that federal courts should scrutinize all suggestive identification procedures, not just those orchestrated by the police, to determine if they would sufficiently taint the trial so as to deprive the defendant of due process.

See also Thigpen v. Cory, 804 F.2d 893 (6th Cir.1986)(citing *Biggers,* and stating that "the deterrence of police misconduct is not the basic purpose for excluding identification evidence" and that "only the effects of, and not the causes for, pre-identification encounters should be determinative of whether the confrontations were suggestive."); Dunnigan v. Keane, 137 F.3d 117 (2d Cir.1998) (rejecting the State's contention that no due process scrutiny of an identification was required on the theory that the person who showed the pictures was a private party: "the due process focus, in the identification context, is principally on the fairness of the trial, rather than on the conduct of the police").[2] Do these cases mean that

---

2. The court in United States v. Emanuele, 51 F.3d 1123 (3d Cir.1995), found police intent relevant in the following respect:

We hold that the government's intent may be one factor in determining the risk of misidentification, but it is not an essential element of defendant's burden of proof. A series of events that is suggestive and creates a substantial risk of misidentification is no less a due process violation, even absent evil intent on the part of the government. Stated differently, governmental intent is one of many factors in the totality of circumstances * * *. On the other hand, evidence that the government intended and arranged such an encounter would be a substantial factor in the court's analysis.

Is this analysis supported by *Manson*? Why should unreliability be easier to find if the government "intended and arranged" a suggestive identification?

an in-court identification cannot be made if the witness bases it on having seen the defendant alone on the street a week after the crime, or if he had happened to see the defendant driving by in the back of a police car? If so, the Court may want to re-think the implications of the totality of circumstances test.

4. Identifications In the Lower Courts After Manson

It is fair to state that, for better or worse, after *Kirby, Ash, Neil,* and *Manson,* many courts are not very careful in their handling of eyewitness evidence. Many lower courts view *Manson* as an invitation to ignore suggestiveness. Archuleta v. Kerby, 864 F.2d 709 (10th Cir.1989), is an example. Two men were eating in a restaurant when they saw a man break the window of their van with a tire iron. The van was parked across the street. The witnesses ran out of the restaurant, and one of them chased the perpetrator; when that witness and the perpetrator were about ten feet apart, the witness got an unobstructed look at the man's face. The witness lost the man after a two minute chase. The police arrived and the witnesses gave descriptions; the witness who chased the perpetrator described him as 5'9", Hispanic, with a mustache; the other witness said the man was 5'7". Based on these descriptions, the police detained Archuleta and brought him back to the scene of the crime thirty minutes after the incident. The police displayed Archuleta to both witnesses while he was in the back of the police car, handcuffed. Both witnesses made a positive identification. The state conceded that the identification procedure was unnecessarily suggestive.

Balancing the five *Manson* factors against the "corruptive effect" of the identification procedure, the *Archuleta* court found: (1) both witnesses had "ample opportunity to view the criminal;" (2) the attention of both witnesses was focused on the criminal, as evidenced by their ability to describe him; (3) while the witnesses overestimated Archuleta's height and did not tell the police that he had distinctive tattoos, "these appear to be minor errors;" (4) the witnesses were very certain about their identification; and (5) the identification occurred within a very short interval of time. The court cited cases in which identifications made over a year after the crime had been upheld.

Certainty of the Witness

How important is it that the witness is certain about an identification? The court in Rodriguez v. Young, 906 F.2d 1153 (7th Cir.1990), had this to say about the certainty factor relied upon in *Manson*:

> We are skeptical about equating certainty with reliability. Determinations of the reliability suggested by a witness's certainty after the use of suggestive procedures are complicated by the possibility that the certainty may reflect the corrupting effect of the suggestive procedures themselves. Also, the most certain witnesses are not invariably the most reliable ones. We consider certainty a relevant factor but consider it warily.

Character of the Witness

How important is the witness' character in determining whether police suggestiveness caused the witness to make an unreliable identification? Consider

United States ex rel. Hudson v. Brierton, 699 F.2d 917 (7th Cir.1983), where a witness pursued armed bank robbers, and engaged in a high speed car chase through city streets, while one of the robbers was shooting at him. For a part of the chase, the witness' car was within seven inches of the robbers' car. Eventually, the witness lost the robbers. The witness was later called down to the police station, and identified the defendant while he was handcuffed in a jail cell. The court found that this impermissible suggestiveness did not cause a mistaken identification. It noted that the witness had an opportunity to view the defendant at close quarters; he had a desire to seek out and retain an image of the defendant, because he knew that he could be a witness at a later criminal trial; he had not given a prior description, but this was just one factor; the witness was certain when he made the identification; and the identification was made within a few hours after the event. Most important for the court, however, was the character of the witness. The court found it extremely unlikely that the witness "would be affected by the suggestive identification procedure in light of his serious attitude and diligence with respect to the episode."[3]

Example of a Due Process Violation

Occasionally, a court will find a police identification procedure so suggestive, and the witness' pre-identification picture so vague, that the identification must be excluded under the Due Process Clause. An example is United States v. Eltayib, 88 F.3d 157 (2d Cir.1996). The facts surrounding the identification were described by the court as follows:

> As the Blue Crown [a freighter] proceeded north in the Atlantic [from Barbados to Newark], drug trafficker Peter Califano was in Brooklyn plotting cocaine importation strategy. As he did, Califano told his friend and commercial-fishing partner Thomas Van Salisbury that a large cocaine shipment arriving from South America by boat would be delivered to Califano in a mid-ocean transfer. Van Salisbury agreed to accompany Califano and to help with the transfer. As the transfer day approached, a nervous Van Salisbury contacted the FBI and told them that a July 20 late-evening rendezvous had been planned. * * *

> In the early hours of July 19–20, Califano's fishing boat, the Hunter, set sail from its berth near Coney Island. * * * At about 9:00 p.m., with Van Salisbury in the engine room, the Hunter approached the rendezvous point and came in sight of the delivering courier ship. * * * [T]he boats were tied off. Van Salisbury then left the wheelhouse and came on deck with Califano. For the next several hours, nearly five metric tons of cocaine were tossed off the courier ship in bales onto the deck of the Hunter. At several points during the cocaine transfer, Van Salisbury stood on the deck of the Hunter and saw crew members on the courier ship, one of whom he later identified in a photo array as Eltayib (captain of the Blue Crown). * * *

> When Van Salisbury left the wheelhouse and went on deck, the sea had a "slight roll"; the night was "fairly bright, [but][t]here was no [moon]

---

3. Conversely, if the witness is a person who could be easily led by the police to make an unreliable identification, this will be a relevant factor. See United States v. de Jesus–Rios, 990 F.2d 672 (1st Cir.1993) (identification un- reliable where the witness' boat had been seized, and officers told him that his boat would be released if he identified the person who was involved in the smuggling of drugs on the boat).

beams coming down." Standing on the Hunter's deck, Van Salisbury heard what he believed to be large metal plates scraping together on the courier ship, as if its hold was being opened. Just as he was asking Califano how the other boat's crew was going to transfer the cocaine to the Hunter, a bale of cocaine came flying onto the Hunter's deck, nearly bouncing off the deck into the ocean. Califano shouted to the courier ship crew expressing displeasure with the near-mishap. He and Van Salisbury then opened up the Hunter's fish hold where they were to store the cocaine, and Van Salisbury climbed down into it. * * *

As Van Salisbury entered the fish hold, a flying bale of cocaine hit him and broke the ladder he was standing on, dropping him eight to ten feet to the fish hold floor. Possibly dazed, he clambered back onto the deck. He testified that at this point he saw two men on the rail of the courier ship, 35–40 feet away, one of whom he "had a good look at":

Q: Could you describe what you were able to make out?

A: That man there, he had, seemed like a head full of hair, real bushy hair, afro-type hair, seemed like an awful lot of hair for the head. I don't know how to really describe it but he had a lot of hair.

This was the only time during Van Salisbury's direct examination that he mentioned seeing the bushy-haired man, and it was the only description that he gave. Just after this question, the government asked Van Salisbury to stand up, look around the courtroom, and try to identify the bushy-haired man. He could not.

* * * When pressed about the amount of time that he had spent looking at the bushy-haired man during the fifteen minutes he was on the deck, Van Salisbury's testimony indicates that (i) he saw very little of the bushy-haired man's face, and (ii) he may have been confused about whether this fifteen-minute interval during which he saw the man occurred before or after he had descended into the fish hold:

A: I didn't look directly at his face but for a few moments. I seen him up there. I didn't stare into his face. When I got out of the fish hold, I looked up and I seen the person.

Q: So when you say you saw the person, all you saw is that the person had bushy hair, is that right?

A: I remembered his face and bushy hair, yes.

Q: You remembered his face and what—what is it that you remembered about his face?

A: I can't recall right offhand.

Q: Would it be fair to say that anything you remembered that when you were debriefed by Agent Maher on the Coast Guard cutter, you told him at that time, isn't that right?

A: At that time that I remembered I told him, yes.

According to the record, the only information Van Salisbury provided to Agent Maher about the suspect's physical characteristics was that he had bushy hair. Later in his cross-examination, Van Salisbury testified that when he came out of the fish hold after getting hit with the bale, he looked at the bushy-haired man's face for only "[a] few moments . . . a few seconds or better."

Once Van Salisbury returned to the fish hold, he apparently stayed there for the remainder of the delivery, stacking the cocaine bales that passed continuously from courier ship deck to Hunter deck, and from Hunter deck into the fish hold. By about 2:00 a.m. on July 21, the transfer was complete, and the two boats separated. [The Blue Crown was eventually tracked down and Eltayib and others were arrested.]

Ten days after the high-seas transfer, Drug Enforcement Agency Agent Bradley Cheek showed Van Salisbury nine photo arrays. Each array contained a photo of a different crew member and seven filler photos. Van Salisbury identified * * * Eltayib (apparently the "bushy-haired" man).

The Court described the photo array that led to Van Salisbury's identification of Eltayib as the bushy-haired man.

The Eltayib photo array was presented to Van Salisbury by DEA Agent Bradley Cheek. We have examined it. The array's eight photos are cut roughly along the head and shoulders. The scissors line on Eltayib's photo travels slightly above his shoulders, a bit outside his neck, and then around and above his head, so that the full outline of the top and sides of his full head of hair can be clearly made out. As to each of the seven other photos, the line of the scissors defines the head with straight strokes that crop the head (and such of the hair as remains) into an irregular polygon. Because the tops and sides of the photos have been cropped in this way, it is impossible to tell what style or amount of hair these men may have had. However, the cropping gives all seven the appearance of short hair cut close to the head (albeit at strange angles). * * * Eltayib thus stands out as the only one of the eight who could remotely fit Van Salisbury's description of the man he saw at the rail of the courier ship.

In another apparent precaution, Eltayib is made to stand out by his skin color. He is a Sudanese man of apparent Arab descent with a light complexion. The other seven are all men of apparent sub-Saharan African descent with skin tones that range from medium brown to dark brown.

The court found that the photo array was unnecessarily suggestive, and that it caused an unreliable identification. It reasoned as follows:

A photo array is improperly suggestive if the picture of an accused, matching descriptions given by the witness, so stood out from all of the other photographs as to suggest to an identifying witness that that person was more likely to be the culprit. * * * [W]e believe that the picture of Eltayib so stood out from the other photographs as to make the array improperly suggestive.

Even if an array is improperly suggestive, the witness's identification of the suspect from among the array's filler photos is still admissible if the identification has independent reliability. The question is whether under the "totality of the circumstances" the identification was reliable even though the confrontation procedure was suggestive. * * * Van Salisbury's opportunity to make a genuine identification of the bushy-haired man was small. Van Salisbury stood on the deck of a bobbing ship in the middle of the night, nervous, and possibly dazed from falling off a ladder after being hit by flying cargo; he was in position to see the man in question on another moving ship at a distance of 35 to 40 feet for fifteen (or perhaps only a few) minutes, but he did not look directly at the man's face for more than a few moments. What little he could say about the man can hardly be called an "accurate description" of a suspect, and suggests that he really did not get "a good look" at the bushy-haired man. Van Salisbury may have had an incentive to pay close "attention" to the physical characteristics of the Blue Crown crew members (since he was a government informant), but he admitted that he did not take the opportunity to scrutinize the bushy-haired man's face for very long. There is no indication that Van Salisbury expressed uncertainty during his photo array identification, but that would seem to cut the other way given the suggestive nature of the array. The fact that the identification took place ten days after Van Salisbury first saw Eltayib does not seem probative one way or the other.

Thus, * * * the indicia of reliability are few and weak. When these circumstances are combined with Van Salisbury's failure to identify Eltayib at trial, there is no dependable evidence to support the conclusion that Van Salisbury ever knew what Eltayib's face looked like. We therefore conclude that Van Salisbury's photo array identification was not independently reliable, and that it violated Eltayib's due process rights to admit the identification.

But the court found the error to be harmless.

If it is difficult in most cases and impossible in some cases to know the extent to which suggestive procedures corrupt the identification process, does Kirby v. Illinois make sense? Does Manson v. Brathwaite?

5.   The Effect of Identification Procedures on Trials

Some of the defects in pre-trial lineups may even have an impact on trials aside from possibly tainting identification evidence. If the government uses "mug shots" in a photo identification, the suggestion to the witness will be that the mug shot reflects a prior criminal record of the person photographed. This may not be so bad before trial, if all the photos are mug shots. But if the photo identification is mentioned by the prosecution's witnesses and its reliability is challenged during trial by the defense, the government will offer the photographs as evidence. At this point the jury will learn that the defendant has a prior record. Although the courts will balance the need for the evidence against its possible prejudicial effect, in many cases the photos will be admitted. See, e.g., United States v. Stevens, 935 F.2d 1380 (3d Cir.1991)(submitting "wanted board," with which defendant was identified, to the jury, was permissible under Federal Rule of Evidence 403, even though others on the board were violent felons and defendant had no record of violent activity: "Allowing the jury to inspect the board in its unaltered condition would permit the jurors to determine what, if anything, drew the victims' attention to Stevens"). Thus, the defendant identified by mug shot may have to choose between challenging the identification and protecting against disclosure of a prior record. United States v. McCoy, 848 F.2d 743 (6th Cir.1988)(introducing mug shots prohibited by Rule 403 where the defendant never challenged the suggestiveness of the identification, and therefore did not "open the door").

Can the defendant call expert witnesses to testify to the unreliability of identification evidence? How will that testimony help the jury? What kind of people have expertise on this subject? See United States v. Rincon, 28 F.3d 921 (9th Cir.1994)(upholding trial court's exclusion of such evidence on the ground that the expert's testimony was not sufficiently scientific, but emphasizing that there is no per se rule of exclusion); United States v. Brien, 59 F.3d 274 (1st Cir.1995) (finding no abuse of discretion in the trial court's exclusion of the defense expert on the unreliability of identification evidence; the expert's proffered testimony was very general, and did not fit with many of the circumstances underlying the identifications in this case; nor did the expert explicate the methodology by which he concluded that the identifications were unreliable). Compare United States v. Smith, 122 F.3d 1355 (11th Cir. 1997) (expert testimony concerning the unreliability of identification procedures is inadmissible because it does not assist the jury; it is not needed, "because the jury [can] determine the reliability of identification with the tools of cross-examination.").

6. The Unreliability of In–Court Identifications

Speaking of unreliable identifications, what can be more suggestive than an identification that occurs *at the trial*? Courts have understandably held that *Manson* applies to identifications at trial, and they also recognize that in-court identifications are suggestive. But under *Manson*, this does not at all mean that in-court identification are inadmissible; it simply means that the witness must have an independent source for the in-court identification. An independent source is usually found in the witness' viewing of the perpetrator before or during the crime. In other words, the same considerations that determine the admissibility of a pre-trial identification under *Manson* will also determine the admissibility of an identification made at trial. See United States v. Hill, 967 F.2d 226 (6th Cir.1992)(holding that the *Manson* analysis applies to in-court identifications "for the same reasons that the analysis applies to impermissibly suggestive pre-trial identifications," but that the in-court identification was admissible in this case because the witness viewed the perpetrator head-on, at close quarters, during a robbery); United States v. Tucker, 169 F.3d 1115 (8th Cir.1999)(in-court identification of the defendant as the passenger in a car linked to a robbery was admissible because the witness "had an opportunity to view the passenger as he met the car while rounding a corner on his way to the scene, his attention was focused on the car because it was coming from the direction of the robbery shortly after it occurred, and when he spoke to investigators, he gave a description of the passenger which was the same as his trial testimony.").

Can anything be done about the suggestiveness inherent in an identification at trial? Defense counsel in United States v. Brien, 59 F.3d 274 (1st Cir.1995), moved for permission to have the defendant seated in the spectator section of the courtroom and asked leave to "salt the audience with three or four individuals of the same general description as the bank robber." The trial judge responded that he would agree to a "fairly staged courtroom lineup" but that he was concerned about the risk of unfairness to the prosecution in defense counsel's open-ended proposal. Defense counsel did not take the judge up on his offer, and the defendant appealed the conviction as based on an unfair in-court identification. The court of appeals responded as follows:

> If Brien had presented the court with a detailed plan for a fair in-court lineup, and the court had rejected the plan without a plausible justification,

then on the present facts we think that a significant issue would be presented. But Brien's motion is not within a country mile of such a proposal. As the trial court sensibly explained, Brien's plan left room for a scenario fully capable of misleading the jury. To alter the standard practice, it was up to Brien's counsel to propose a plan that would guard against unfairness to either side.

Why do you suppose Brien's counsel did not accept the trial judge's offer of a fairly staged courtroom lineup? Why was it Brien's obligation to propose a plan that would guard against unfairness to both sides? Isn't that the prosecution's obligation? See also United States v. Burdeau, 168 F.3d 352 (9th Cir.1999) (trial court has discretion to order an in-court lineup, but no obligation to do so).

7. Voice Identification

Do voice identifications raise problems that are different from those encountered in photograph identifications, lineups, show-ups, etc.? Courts use the *Manson* standards for voice identification.[4] But as discussed above, the *Manson* test gives only minimal protection against police suggestiveness for any identification procedure whether by sight or voice. For example, in United States v. Patton, 721 F.2d 159 (6th Cir.1983), the defendant was charged with making threatening phone calls. The witness identified the defendant's voice at a pretrial "show-up." The court held that the *Manson* test "applies with full force to aural identification." But then the court found that the show-up had not caused a mistaken identification. Applying the *Manson* factors, the court concluded that the witness had an opportunity to hear the defendant's voice during four phone calls; that the witness was attentive to these calls, as evidenced by her description of their content; that the time between the crime and the voice "show-up" was only three weeks; and that, upon hearing the defendant's voice at the "show-up" the witness "immediately recoiled, instantly recognizing the voice." Is the likelihood of mistaken identification any greater with voice identifications than with visual identifications?

---

4. For an interesting case on voice identification in which Manson v. Brathwaite was deemed applicable and an out-of-court identification was suppressed, see State v. Pendergrass, 179 Mont. 106, 586 P.2d 691 (Mont. 1978).

Chapter Five

THE RIGHT TO COUNSEL

I. THE BACKGROUND

The Sixth Amendment provides that "[i]n all criminal prosecutions, the accused shall enjoy the right * * * to have the Assistance of Counsel for his defence."[1] The right to counsel embodied in the Amendment deviated from the English common-law practice at the time of the American Revolution. Under English law, an accused had a right to have counsel in misdemeanor, but not felony, cases. Although Parliament granted special treatment to those accused under the Treason Act of 1695, and required the court to appoint counsel upon the request of the accused, in ordinary felony cases in England the defendant was not permitted to have counsel until 1836.[2]

When the Constitution was adopted, twelve of the thirteen original states had rejected the English common-law rule and had fully recognized the right to counsel in criminal prosecutions. Powell v. Alabama, 287 U.S. 45, 64–65 (1932). Adoption of the Sixth Amendment formalized this practice. As such, it conveyed the idea that the right to counsel was a grant of privilege—i.e., eliminating the prohibition on counsel—rather than a requirement that counsel be appointed. This can be contrasted with the Federal Crimes Act of 1790, which imposed a statutory *duty* on federal courts in capital cases to assign counsel. 1 Stat. 118 (1790). Although no statute required appointment of counsel in noncapital cases

---

1. The right to counsel is important in many stages of the criminal process. This is already apparent from the previous chapters. The *Massiah* rule, for example, governed attempts to elicit statements from an accused following an indictment or other formal charge. And the *Wade* and *Gilbert* rules governing lineups following a formal charge also involved a right to counsel. The chapters that follow this one involve the decision to bring formal charges against a suspect, the treatment of the suspect while charges are pending, trials and guilty pleas, and post-trial procedures. Counsel is important in most of the stages of the criminal process that will be examined. At some point it is useful to look at the development of the right to counsel. That look is provided in this Chapter. The discussion of counsel here is limited to establishing how the right to counsel developed and to examining the stages of the process to which the right extends. In Chapter Ten, which covers trial rights, the right to counsel at trial is more extensively examined. The doctrine of effective assistance will be discussed there, along with the right of self-representation.

2. See Faretta v. California, 422 U.S. 806, 821–826 (1975); W. Beaney, The Right to Counsel in American Courts 8–15 (1955); F. Heller, The Sixth Amendment (1951); Holtzoff, The Right of Counsel Under the Sixth Amendment, 20 N.Y.U.L.Rev. 1–22 (1944). Despite the absence of a right to counsel, in practice English courts frequently allowed counsel to argue points of law and to assume other defense functions. W. Beaney at 9–11.

and no one originally read the Sixth Amendment as so requiring, the practice developed of appointing counsel for indigents in serious federal cases.[3]

II. THE EARLY DEVELOPMENT OF THE RIGHT

In Johnson v. Zerbst, 304 U.S. 458 (1938), the Court held that the Sixth Amendment requires counsel in federal court in all criminal proceedings, unless the defendant waives the assistance of counsel. (At that point, the Sixth Amendment was not applicable to the States). The Court viewed counsel as a jurisdictional prerequisite to a federal court's authority to deprive an accused of life or liberty.

The right to counsel in state prosecutions for many years was determined exclusively by state law. In 1932, even before Johnson v. Zerbst, the famous "Scottsboro Case" raised the question of whether a failure to make an effective appointment of counsel to indigent defendants in a capital case could deprive the defendants of their rights to due process.

POWELL v. ALABAMA
Supreme Court of the United States, 1932.
287 U.S. 45.

MR. JUSTICE SUTHERLAND **delivered the opinion of the Court.**

These cases were argued together and submitted for decision as one case.

The petitioners, hereinafter referred to as defendants, are negroes charged with the crime of rape, committed upon the persons of two white girls. The crime is said to have been committed on March 25, 1931. The indictment was returned in a state court of first instance on March 31, and the record recites that on the same day the defendants were arraigned and entered pleas of not guilty. There is a further recital to the effect that upon the arraignment they were represented by counsel. But no counsel had been employed, and aside from a statement made by the trial judge several days later during a colloquy immediately preceding the trial, the record does not disclose when, or under what circumstances, an appointment of counsel was made, or who was appointed. During the colloquy referred to, the trial judge, in response to a question, said that he had appointed all the members of the bar for the purpose of arraigning the defendants and then of course anticipated that the members of the bar would continue to help the defendants if no counsel appeared. * * *

There was a severance upon the request of the state, and the defendants were tried in three several groups * * *. Each of the three trials was completed within a single day. Under the Alabama statute the punishment for rape is to be fixed by the jury, and in its discretion may be from ten years imprisonment to death. The juries found defendants guilty and imposed the death penalty upon all. * * *

* * *

The record shows that on the day when the offense is said to have been committed, these defendants, together with a number of other negroes, were upon a freight train on its way through Alabama. On the same train were sev-

---

3. Before 1938, some courts would appoint counsel for indigents, but the practice was not uniform. See W. Beaney, supra note 2, at 29–33; Holtzoff, supra note 2, at 8.

en white boys and the two white girls. A fight took place between the negroes and the white boys, in the course of which the white boys, with the exception of one named Gilley, were thrown off the train. A message was sent ahead, reporting the fight and asking that every negro be gotten off the train. The participants in the fight, and the two girls, were in an open gondola car. The two girls testified that each of them was assaulted by six different negroes in turn, and they identified the seven defendants as having been among the number. None of the white boys was called to testify, with the exception of Gilley, who was called in rebuttal.

Before the train reached Scottsboro, Alabama, a sheriff's posse seized the defendants and two other negroes. Both girls and the negroes then were taken to Scottsboro, the county seat. Word of their coming and of the alleged assault had preceded them, and they were met at Scottsboro by a large crowd. It does not sufficiently appear that the defendants were seriously threatened with, or that they were actually in danger of, mob violence; but it does appear that the attitude of the community was one of great hostility. The sheriff thought it necessary to call for the militia to assist in safeguarding the prisoners. * * * It is perfectly apparent that the proceedings, from beginning to end, took place in an atmosphere of tense, hostile and excited public sentiment. During the entire time, the defendants were closely confined or were under military guard. The record does not disclose their ages, except that one of them was nineteen; but the record clearly indicates that most, if not all, of them were youthful, and they are constantly referred to as "the boys." They were ignorant and illiterate. All of them were residents of other states, where all members of their families or friends resided.

* * *

First. * * *

It is hardly necessary to say that, the right to counsel being conceded, a defendant should be afforded a fair opportunity to secure counsel of his own choice. Not only was that not done here, but such designation of counsel as was attempted was either so indefinite or so close upon the trial as to amount to a denial of effective and substantial aid in that regard. * * *

* * * [U]ntil the very morning of the trial no lawyer had been named or definitely designated to represent the defendants. Prior to that time, the trial judge had "appointed all the members of the bar" for the limited "purpose of arraigning the defendants." Whether they would represent the defendants thereafter if no counsel appeared in their behalf, was a matter of speculation only, or, as the judge indicated, of mere anticipation on the part of the court. Such a designation, even if made for all purposes, would, in our opinion, have fallen far short of meeting, in any proper sense, a requirement for the appointment of counsel. How many lawyers were members of the bar does not appear; but, in the very nature of things, whether many or few, they would not, thus collectively named, have been given that clear appreciation of responsibility or impressed with that individual sense of duty which should and naturally would accompany the appointment of a selected member of the bar, specifically named and assigned.

* * *

The defendants, young, ignorant, illiterate, surrounded by hostile sentiment, haled back and forth under guard of soldiers, charged with an atrocious crime regarded with especial horror in the community where they were to be tried, were thus put in peril of their lives within a few moments after counsel for the first time charged with any degree of responsibility began to represent them.

It is not enough to assume that counsel thus precipitated into the case thought there was no defense, and exercised their best judgment in proceeding to trial without preparation. Neither they nor the court could say what a prompt and thoroughgoing investigation might disclose as to the facts. No attempt was made to investigate. No opportunity to do so was given. Defendants were immediately hurried to trial. * * * Under the circumstances disclosed, we hold that defendants were not accorded the right of counsel in any substantial sense.

* * *

Second. The Constitution of Alabama provides that in all criminal prosecutions the accused shall enjoy the right to have the assistance of counsel; and a state statute requires the court in a capital case, where the defendant is unable to employ counsel, to appoint counsel for him. The state supreme court held that these provisions had not been infringed, and with that holding we are powerless to interfere. The question, however, which it is our duty and within our power, to decide, is whether the denial of the assistance of counsel contravenes the due process clause of the Fourteenth Amendment to the federal Constitution.

[The Court discussed the historical development of the right to counsel in England and the colonies. One test for determining whether due process has been accorded is to examine whether the settled "usages and modes of proceeding" were followed. The Court concluded that the procedures em-

ployed in this case deviated from traditionally accepted practices.]

* * *

What, then, does a hearing include? Historically and in practice, in our own country at least, it has always included the right to the aid of counsel when desired and provided by the party asserting the right. The right to be heard would be, in many cases, of little avail if it did not comprehend the right to be heard by counsel. Even the intelligent and educated layman has small and sometimes no skill in the science of law. If charged with crime, he is incapable, generally, of determining for himself whether the indictment is good or bad. He is unfamiliar with the rules of evidence. Left without the aid of counsel he may be put on trial without a proper charge, and convicted upon incompetent evidence, or evidence irrelevant to the issue or otherwise inadmissible. He lacks both the skill and knowledge adequately to prepare his defense, even though he have a perfect one. He requires the guiding hand of counsel at every step in the proceedings against him. Without it, though he be not guilty, he faces the danger of conviction because he does not know how to establish his innocence. If that be true of men of intelligence, how much more true is it of the ignorant and illiterate, or those of feeble intellect.

* * *

In the light of the facts outlined in the forepart of this opinion—the ignorance and illiteracy of the defendants, their youth, the circumstances of public hostility, the imprisonment and the close surveillance of the defendants by the military forces, the fact that their friends and families were all in other states and communication with them necessarily difficult, and above all that they stood in deadly peril of their lives—we think the failure of the trial court to give them reasonable time and opportunity to secure counsel was a clear denial of due process.

* * * [W]e are of opinion that, under the circumstances just stated, the necessity of counsel was so vital and imperative that the failure of the trial court to make an effective appointment of counsel was likewise a denial of due process within the meaning of the Fourteenth Amendment. Whether this would be so in other criminal prosecutions, or under other circumstances, we need not determine. All that it is necessary now to decide, as we do decide, is that in a capital case,

where the defendant is unable to employ counsel, and is incapable adequately of making his own defense because of ignorance, feeble mindedness, illiteracy, or the like, it is the duty of the court, whether requested or not, to assign counsel for him as a necessary requisite of due process of law; and that duty is not discharged by an assignment at such a time or under such circumstances as to preclude the giving of effective aid in the preparation and trial of the case. * * *

* * *

[Justice Butler dissented.]

Note on Betts v. Brady

Although the defendants' due process rights were violated in *Powell*, the Court did not require counsel in all state prosecutions. Ten years later, in fact, the Court held explicitly that the Due Process Clause of the Fourteenth Amendment did not incorporate the specific guarantees of the Sixth Amendment. Betts v. Brady, 316 U.S. 455 (1942). Counsel for indigent defendants was not considered a fundamental right essential to a fair trial. The Court endorsed a case-by-case inquiry into the fundamental fairness of the proceeding, in light of the totality of the facts in a given case. The defendant's conviction for robbery was affirmed even though the judge refused to appoint counsel upon request. The Court considered the circumstances of the case and concluded as follows:

> [T]he accused was not helpless, but was a man forty-three years old, of ordinary intelligence, and ability to take care of his own interests on the trial of this narrow issue [alibi defense]. He had once before been in a criminal court, pleaded guilty to larceny and served a sentence and was not wholly unfamiliar with criminal procedure. It is quite clear that in Maryland, if the situation had been otherwise and it had appeared that the petitioner was, for any reason, at a serious disadvantage by reason of the lack of counsel, a refusal to appoint would have resulted in the reversal of judgment of conviction. * * *

The Court in *Betts* held that the Due Process Clause required appointment of counsel only where "special circumstances" indicated that the defendant could not perform adequately on his own.

Between Betts and Gideon

The case-by-case, "special circumstances" approach to appointment of counsel in *Betts* was undermined by a number of cases decided before *Betts* was overruled in Gideon v. Wainwright, 372 U.S. 335 (1963), set forth infra. The Court faced difficult problems in deciding in what circumstances due process required appointment of counsel. Two cases in particular, in which counsel was not appointed, effectively undercut *Betts*. In Hudson v. North Carolina, 363 U.S. 697 (1960), the Court held that the defendant needed a lawyer to protect against the prejudicial effect of his co-defendant's plea of guilty to a lesser charge in the presence of the jury. In Chewning v. Cunningham, 368 U.S. 443 (1962), the Court reversed the defendant's conviction under a recidivist statute. The defendant was denied due process because the difficult legal questions in the case presented too great a potential for prejudice to the defendant. As one commentator noted, "[a]s this history of the 'special circumstances' cases shows, the Court had consistently whittled away at the *Betts* rule until with *Chewning* and *Hudson* it was almost completely eroded." Israel, Gideon v. Wainwright: The "Art" of Overruling, 1963 Sup.Ct.Rev. 211, 260.

Furthermore, the Court held in Hamilton v. Alabama, 368 U.S. 52 (1961), that there was an unqualified right to counsel in state capital cases. The distinction between a case involving capital punishment, where counsel was mandated, and one involving a maximum punishment of life imprisonment, where counsel was not absolutely required, proved to be tenuous, at best. For a more extended discussion of the decisions following *Betts,* see generally Israel, supra, at 260; Kamisar, Betts v. Brady Twenty Years Later, 61 Mich.L.Rev. 219 (1962).

III. A NEW AND SWEEPING RIGHT AND ITS LIMITS

A. APPOINTED COUNSEL FOR INDIGENTS IN FELONY PROSECUTIONS

Application of the *Betts* rule was not easy for the Court. Nor was that rule entirely consistent with the language of *Powell. Thus, it was only a matter of time before the Court would call for a more sweeping approach to appointment of counsel. That call came as Gideon's trumpet sounded*[4] in 1963.

GIDEON v. WAINWRIGHT

Supreme Court of the United States, 1963.
372 U.S. 335.

MR. JUSTICE BLACK delivered the opinion of the Court.

Petitioner was charged in a Florida state court with having broken and entered a poolroom with intent to commit a misdemeanor. This offense is a felony under Florida law. Appearing in court without funds and without a lawyer, petitioner asked the court to appoint counsel for him, whereupon the following colloquy took place:

"The Court: Mr. Gideon, I am sorry, but I cannot appoint Counsel to represent you in this case. Under the laws of the State of Florida, the only time the Court can appoint Counsel to represent a Defendant is when that person is charged with a capital offense. I am sorry, but I will have to deny your request to appoint Counsel to defend you in this case.

"The Defendant: The United States Supreme Court says I am entitled to be represented by Counsel."

Put to trial before a jury, Gideon conducted his defense about as well as could be expected from a layman. He made an opening statement to the jury, cross-examined the State's witnesses, presented witnesses in his own

4. See A. Lewis, Gideon's Trumpet (1964).

defense, declined to testify himself, and made a short argument "emphasizing his innocence to the charge contained in the Information filed in this case." The jury returned a verdict of guilty, and petitioner was sentenced to serve five years in the state prison. * * * Since 1942, when Betts v. Brady was decided by a divided Court, the problem of a defendant's federal constitutional right to counsel in a state court has been a continuing source of controversy and litigation in both state and federal courts. To give this problem another review here, we granted certiorari. Since Gideon was proceeding *in forma pauperis,* we appointed counsel to represent him and requested both sides to discuss in their briefs and oral arguments the following: "Should this Court's holding in Betts v. Brady be reconsidered?"

I

* * *

[The Court discussed the facts of Betts v. Brady, which were virtually indistinguishable from those in *Gideon.* The Court noted that *Betts* addressed the circumstance of an indigent charged with a felony.]

* * * Upon full reconsideration we conclude that Betts v. Brady should be overruled.

II

* * *

We accept Betts v. Brady's assumption, based as it was on our prior cases, that a provision of the Bill of Rights which is "fundamental and essential to a fair trial" is made obligatory upon the States by the Fourteenth Amendment. We think the Court in *Betts* was wrong, however, in concluding that the Sixth Amendment's guarantee of counsel is not one of these fundamental rights. Ten years before Betts v. Brady, this Court, after full

consideration of all the historical data examined in *Betts,* had unequivocally declared that "the right to the aid of counsel is of this fundamental character." Powell v. Alabama. While the Court at the close of its *Powell* opinion did by its language, as this Court frequently does, limit its holding to the particular facts and circumstances of that case, its conclusions about the fundamental nature of the right to counsel are unmistakable.

* * *

* * * The fact is that in deciding as it did—that "appointment of counsel is not a fundamental right, essential to a fair trial"—the Court in Betts v. Brady made an abrupt break with its own well-considered precedents. In returning to these old precedents, sounder we believe than the new, we but restore constitutional principles established to achieve a fair system of justice. Not only these precedents but also reason and reflection require us to recognize that in our adversary system of criminal justice, any person haled into court, who is too poor to hire a lawyer, cannot be assured a fair trial unless counsel is provided for him. This seems to us to be an obvious truth. Governments, both state and federal, quite properly spend vast sums of money to establish machinery to try defendants accused of crime. Lawyers to prosecute are everywhere deemed essential to protect the public's interest in an orderly society. Similarly, there are few defendants charged with crime, few indeed, who fail to hire the best lawyers they can get to prepare and present their defenses. That government hires lawyers to prosecute and defendants who have the money hire lawyers to defend are the strongest indications of the widespread belief that lawyers in criminal courts are necessities, not luxuries. The right of one charged with crime to

counsel may not be deemed fundamental and essential to fair trials in some countries, but it is in ours. From the very beginning, our state and national constitutions and laws have laid great emphasis on procedural and substantive safeguards designed to assure fair trials before impartial tribunals in which every defendant stands equal before the law. This noble ideal cannot be realized if the poor man charged with crime has to face his accusers without a lawyer to assist him. * * *

The Court in Betts v. Brady departed from the sound wisdom upon which the Court's holding in Powell v. Alabama rested. Florida, supported by two other States, has asked that Betts

v. Brady be left intact. Twenty-two States, as friends of the Court, argue that Betts was "an anachronism when handed down" and that it should now be overruled. We agree.

The judgment is reversed and the cause is remanded to the Supreme Court of Florida for further action not inconsistent with this opinion.

[Justices Douglas, Clark, and Harlan wrote separate concurring opinions. Justice Harlan questioned whether Betts was an abrupt break with history. He viewed the Betts rule as one that did not work, but argued that it was "entitled to a more respectful burial than has been accorded."]

Establishing Indigency

Gideon requires the state to appoint counsel for indigents in felony cases, but what does it mean to be "indigent?" Consider Barry v. Brower, 864 F.2d 294 (3d Cir.1988), where the defendant was denied a request for the appointment of counsel on the ground that he and his wife had an $80,000 equity in their home and $7,500 in a money market fund. Barry claimed that his debts exceeded his assets, his wife opposed selling their property to pay for his legal expenses, and that he had consulted six attorneys recommended by the public defender, all of whom had refused to represent him without a substantial "up-front" payment. The court held that Barry was entitled to appointed counsel. It stated that "indigence is not equivalent to destitution," and that "if by their nature an accused's assets cannot be timely reduced to cash and cash is required, the present financial inability to obtain counsel which defines indigence for Sixth Amendment purposes appears." The court noted that the state may require reasonable reimbursement if the defendant's indigency is temporary.

In Fuller v. Oregon, 417 U.S. 40 (1974), the Court upheld a statute that conditioned probation on repayment to the state of the costs of a free legal defense, where the defendant had gained a subsequent ability to pay.

Many states have detailed statutes determining eligibility for appointed counsel. See, e.g., N.J.Stat.Ann. 2A:158A–14 (considering factors such as liquid assets, the ability to make bail, the projected costs of defense, and whether the defendant has made reasonable efforts to retain counsel). The federal standard for appointment of counsel "for any person financially unable to obtain adequate representation" is codified in the Criminal Justice Act, 18 U.S.C. § 3006A. For an application of the federal statute, see United States v. Bauer, 956 F.2d 693 (7th Cir.1992)("It is not enough to claim inability to hire a lawyer and back up the claim with an affidavit. The statute provides for 'appropriate inquiry' into the veracity of that claim."). The court in Bauer held that it is the defendant's burden to establish indigency, and that the defendant has no right to appointed counsel at a hearing to establish indigency.

At a hearing to establish indigency, the defendant will often testify about his financial circumstances. Can his statements at such a hearing be used against him at trial? For example, in United States v. Pavelko, 992 F.2d 32 (3d Cir.1993), a defendant charged with bank robbery requested court-appointed counsel, and in response to questions put by the court to determine whether he was indigent, stated that he had not been employed for a year and had received no income from any lawful source during that year. At trial, the government sought to prove that the defendant had made a number of cash purchases during the year, and that the funds for these purchases could not have come from lawful sources. The trial court permitted an FBI agent to testify about the statements the defendant made at his indigency hearing, as proof that the funds did not come from lawful sources. The court of appeals held that this was error, because admitting the statements "created a tension between [the defendant's] Fifth and Sixth Amendment rights. It in effect conditioned the free exercise of one constitutional right upon waiver of the other."

Money Talks

After the O.J. Simpson verdict, many pundits expressed the opinion that the quality of criminal justice depends on how much money the defendant has. Indeed, in the press conference after the verdict, Simpson's attorneys agreed that Simpson may well have been convicted had he not been able to mount a high-priced defense. What does this say about the chances of an indigent who is appointed counsel? What does this say about a person from the middle class, who has too much money to be entitled to appointed counsel, but too little money to mount an aggressive defense?

B. THE RIGHT TO APPOINTED COUNSEL IN MISDEMEANOR CASES

After *Gideon,* the Court was asked to determine whether a defendant charged with a misdemeanor was inherently more capable of self-representation than a felony defendant. The right to counsel grew with the answer.

ARGERSINGER v. HAMLIN

Supreme Court of the United States, 1972.
407 U.S. 25.

MR. JUSTICE DOUGLAS **delivered the opinion of the Court.**

Petitioner, an indigent, was charged in Florida with carrying a concealed weapon, an offense punishable by imprisonment up to six months, a $1,000 fine, or both. The trial was to a judge, and petitioner was unrepresented by counsel. He was sentenced to serve 90 days in jail, and brought this habeas corpus action in the Florida Supreme Court, alleging that, being deprived of his right to counsel, he was unable as an indigent layman properly to raise and present to the trial court good and sufficient defenses to the charge for which he stands convicted. The Florida Supreme Court * * * in ruling on the right to counsel, followed the line we marked out in Duncan v. Louisiana, 391 U.S. 145, 159, as respects the right to trial by jury and held that the right to court-appointed counsel extends only to trials "for non-petty offenses punishable by more than six months imprisonment."

[The Court noted that the Sixth Amendment was binding on the states through the Fourteenth Amendment and proceeded to examine the Amendment's requirements of a public trial, the right to be informed of the nature and cause of the accusation, the right of confrontation, and the right of compulsory process. These rights have never been limited to felonies or to serious offenses. Although Duncan v. Louisiana limited the right to trial by jury to trials where the potential punishment was imprisonment for six months or more, the Court concluded that "there is no support for a similar limitation on the right to assistance of counsel." The Court relied heavily on the rationale in *Powell* and *Gideon* and utilized lengthy quotations from both opinions.]

* * *

The requirement of counsel may well be necessary for a fair trial even in a petty-offense prosecution. We are by no means convinced that legal and constitutional questions involved in a case that actually leads to imprisonment even for a brief period are any less complex than when a person can be sent off for six months or more.

* * *

Beyond the problem of trials and appeals is that of the guilty plea, a problem which looms large in misdemeanor as well as in felony cases. Counsel is needed so that the accused may know precisely what he is doing, so that he is fully aware of the prospect of going to jail or prison, and so that he is treated fairly by the prosecution.

* * *

We must conclude, therefore, that the problems associated with misdemeanor and petty offenses often require the presence of counsel to insure the accused a fair trial. Mr. Justice Powell suggests that these problems are raised even in situations where there is no prospect of imprisonment. We need not consider the requirements of the Sixth Amendment as regards the right to counsel where loss of liberty is not involved, however, for here petitioner was in fact sentenced to jail. And, as we said in Baldwin v. New York, 399 U.S., at 73, "the prospect of imprisonment for however short a time will seldom be viewed by the accused as a trivial or 'petty' matter and may well result in quite serious repercussions affecting his career and his reputation." * * *

We hold, therefore, that absent a knowing and intelligent waiver, no person may be imprisoned for any offense, whether classified as petty, misdemeanor, or felony, unless he was represented by counsel at his trial.

* * *

[Justice Brennan filed a concurring opinion. Chief Justice Burger concurred in the result, and Justice Powell filed an opinion concurring in the result, in which Justice Rehnquist joined. Justice Brennan emphasized the availability of law students to assist indigents. The Chief Justice expressed concern that trial judges would have difficulty deciding whether to appoint counsel before hearing evidence in a case. He pointed out that the judge probably will rely on representations of the prosecutor. Justice Powell preferred an approach that, like Betts v. Brady, would have afforded counsel when necessary to a fair trial whether a defendant is faced with a fine or imprisonment. He was bothered by the fact that indigents would receive counsel in cases in which relatively poor non-indigents would be forced by circumstances to forego counsel. Also of concern to him was the lack of attorney resources available to courts in some areas and the increased burden that appointing counsel represented for overworked judges.]

The Actual Imprisonment Rule: Scott v. Illinois

Although *Argersinger* extended the right to appointed counsel to anyone actually imprisoned, the Court did not decide whether the right to counsel extends to one who is punished only with a fine. In Scott v. Illinois, 440 U.S. 367 (1979), the Court considered whether the Sixth Amendment requires appointed counsel when a defendant actually is fined, but the offense is punishable by fine or imprisonment.

In *Scott,* the Court stated that there was a line drawn in *Argersinger* between imprisonment and other forms of punishment. Even though the statute under which Scott was convicted authorized a year of incarceration, he was not entitled to counsel because he was not sentenced to prison. The majority reasoned as follows:

> Although the intentions of the *Argersinger* Court are not unmistakably clear from its opinion, we conclude today that *Argersinger* did indeed delimit the constitutional right to appointed counsel in state criminal proceedings. Even were the matter *res nova,* we believe that the central premise of *Argersinger*—that actual imprisonment is a penalty different in kind from fines or the mere threat of imprisonment—is eminently sound and warrants adoption of actual imprisonment as the line defining the constitutional right to appointment of counsel. *Argersinger* has proved reasonably workable, whereas any extension would create confusion and impose unpredictable, but necessarily substantial, costs on 50 quite diverse States. We therefore hold that the Sixth and Fourteenth Amendments to the United States Constitution require only that no indigent criminal defendant be sentenced to a term of imprisonment unless the State has afforded him the right to assistance of appointed counsel in his defense.

Justice Powell concurred, although he expressed reservations about the rule enunciated in *Argersinger* and reaffirmed in *Scott.* He argued that the constitution does not mandate the rule in *Argersinger,* and preferred a more flexible due process approach to the appointment of counsel. Nevertheless, in *Scott* he recognized a need to provide clear guidance to lower courts.

Justice Brennan, joined by Justices Marshall and Stevens, dissented. The dissenters focused on the need for counsel to defend against a charge, and concluded that counsel should be furnished whenever imprisonment is authorized for an offense. They noted that public defender systems are economically feasible, and that many states actually require counsel where any imprisonment is authorized.

Justice Brennan argued in *Scott* that the actual imprisonment approach was unworkable because it forces the judge to consider sentencing factors before the case has even begun. He explained as follows:

> [T]he judge will be forced to decide in advance of trial—and without hearing the evidence—whether he will forego entirely his judicial discretion to impose some sentence of imprisonment and abandon his responsibility to

consider the full range of punishments established by the legislature. His alternatives, assuming the availability of counsel, will be to appoint counsel and retain the discretion vested in him by law, or to abandon this discretion in advance and proceed without counsel.

Justice Brennan argued that a rule requiring appointment of counsel whenever imprisonment for conviction of crime is authorized "respects the allocation of functions between legislatures and courts in the administration of the criminal justice system." He noted that another salutary effect of the authorized imprisonment approach would be to encourage state legislatures to update criminal statutes. As Justice Brennan put it, "a state legislature or local government might determine that it no longer desired to authorize incarceration for certain minor offenses in light of the expense of meeting the requirements of the Constitution. In my view, this re-examination is long overdue."

Justice Blackmun also dissented in *Scott*. He agreed that *Argersinger* did not decide this question, but would have held that an indigent defendant must be given counsel in any prosecution for an offense punishable by more than six months imprisonment (or, under *Argersinger*, when the defendant is actually subjected to a term of imprisonment). This approach would make the right to counsel co-extensive with the right to a jury trial, also guaranteed by the Sixth Amendment and discussed in Chapter Ten, infra.

With which approach do you agree? For a critical analysis of *Scott*, see Herman & Thompson, Scott v. Illinois and the Right to Counsel: A Decision in Search of a Doctrine? 17 Am.Crim.L.Rev. 71 (1979).

One lower court had this to say about *Scott:*

> In essence, the *Scott* holding set up a trade-off whereby states could choose between providing indigent defendants with appointed counsel and foregoing jail time for convictions obtained without appointed counsel. *Scott* holds that, if the state wants to incarcerate an indigent defendant, the state must provide appointed counsel.

Moore v. Jarvis, 885 F.2d 1565 (11th Cir.1989). Does the "trade-off" approach described have anything to do with the Sixth Amendment right to counsel in "all criminal prosecutions?" Does it have anything to do with the right to due process, which extends to deprivations of both liberty and property?

Applying the Actual Imprisonment Approach

Recall that in Berkemer v. McCarty (Chapter Three) the Court held that the protections of Miranda v. Arizona applied to arrests for misdemeanors. Thus, an indigent person subject to custodial questioning for a misdemeanor has a right to appointed counsel during that questioning. But then at trial, he has no right to appointed counsel unless he receives a prison sentence. Is the *Miranda* right more important than the right to counsel at trial in misdemeanor cases?

If a defendant is not provided counsel at trial, can the court impose a suspended sentence and probation under *Scott*? The Court in Alabama v. Shelton, 535 U.S. 654 (2002), held in the negative. Justice Ginsburg, writing for the Court, declared that a suspended sentence is "a prison term imposed for the offense of conviction" upon the defendant's violation of probation and that once the prison term is triggered, "the defendant is incarcerated not for the probation violation, but for the underlying offense." Justice Scalia, joined by Chief Justice Rehnquist, Justice Kennedy, and Justice Thomas, dissented in *Shelton*. He argued that the threat of a suspended sentence could deter many probation violations.

Use of Uncounseled Convictions to Enhance a Sentence: Baldasar v. Illinois and Nichols v. United States

Suppose an indigent defendant is denied counsel and convicted of a misdemeanor. Under *Scott*, he can only be fined. Suppose further that the same defendant is later charged with another crime, given counsel, and convicted. Can the first uncounseled conviction be used to enhance his sentence for the second crime? In Baldasar v. Illinois, 446 U.S. 222 (1980), a divided Supreme Court held that a defendant was denied his right to counsel under *Argersinger* and *Scott* when his misdemeanor theft conviction was transformed into a felony because of a previous conviction for the same offense, where the defendant had not had counsel when previously convicted and fined. The Court reasoned that *Scott* was violated because Baldasar "was sentenced to an increased term of imprisonment *only* because he had been convicted in a previous prosecution in which he had *not* had the assistance of appointed counsel."

But the Court overruled *Baldasar* in Nichols v. United States, 511 U.S. 738 (1994). Nichols was sentenced under the Federal Sentencing Guidelines after pleading guilty to a federal drug felony. He had previously been convicted on a DUI offense, which was a misdemeanor for which he received no jail time; he was not provided counsel at that previous trial. The DUI conviction was used to place Nichols in a higher criminal history category for sentencing on the drug offense. As a consequence, Nichols received a sentence at least seventeen months longer than he could otherwise have received. Chief Justice Rehnquist, in an opinion for five members of the Court, declared that "an uncounseled misdemeanor conviction, valid under *Scott* because no prison term was imposed, is also valid when used to enhance punishment at a subsequent conviction."

The Chief Justice reasoned that "[e]nhancement statutes, whether in the nature of criminal history provisions such as those contained in the Sentencing Guidelines, or recidivist statutes which are commonplace in state criminal laws, do not change the penalty imposed for the earlier conviction." To the contrary, enhancement statutes penalize "only the last offense committed by the defendant." The Chief Justice also argued that the unrestricted use of valid uncounseled convictions was consistent with the "less exacting" standards applicable to the sentencing process. Under the Sentencing Guidelines, a defendant's prior bad acts can be taken into account as part of his criminal history, whenever the government can prove by a preponderance of the evidence that the defendant committed the acts. Thus, Nichols' DUI offense could have been used against him to enhance the sentence even if he had never been convicted. The Chief Justice concluded that "it must be constitutionally permissible to consider a prior uncounseled misdemeanor conviction based on the same conduct where that conduct must be proven beyond a reasonable doubt." Justice Souter concurred in the judgment.

Justice Blackmun, joined by Justices Stevens and Ginsburg, dissented. He contended that it was "more logical, and more consistent with the reasoning in *Scott*, to hold that a conviction that is invalid for imposing a sentence for the offense itself remains invalid for increasing the term of imprisonment imposed for a subsequent conviction." He concluded that "a rule that an uncounseled conviction *never* can form the basis for a term of imprisonment is faithful to the principle born of *Gideon* and announced in *Argersinger* that an uncounseled misdemeanor, like an uncounseled felony, is not reliable enough to form the basis for the severe sanction of incarceration."[5]

IV. THE SCOPE OF THE RIGHT

A. CRITICAL STAGES

Gideon, Argersinger, and *Scott* analyze the right of an indigent to appointed trial counsel. But as we have already seen in connection with confessions and identification procedures, counsel may be needed before a trial starts. And counsel may be needed after it ends. Other "critical stages"—stages where the presence of counsel is critical—are so labeled when it is said that counsel is constitutionally required to protect against substantial prejudice to a defendant's rights.

Definition of a Critical Stage: United States v. Wade

The justification for and development of the "critical stage" analysis is expressed in United States v. Wade, 388 U.S. 218 (1967), a case examined in the preceding chapter on identification. The *Wade* Court wrote as follows:

> * * * When the Bill of Rights was adopted, there were no organized police forces as we know them today. The accused confronted the prosecutor and the witnesses against him, and the evidence was marshalled, largely at the trial itself. In contrast, today's law enforcement machinery involves critical confrontations of the accused by the prosecution at pretrial proceedings where the results might well settle the accused's fate and reduce the trial itself to a mere formality. In recognition of these realities of modern criminal prosecution, our cases have construed the Sixth Amendment guarantee to apply to "critical" stages of the proceedings. * * *

> [The Court discusses *Powell, Escobedo, Massiah, Miranda,* and other cases.]

> In sum, the principle of Powell v. Alabama and succeeding cases requires that we scrutinize *any* pretrial confrontation of the accused to determine whether the presence of his counsel is necessary to preserve the defendant's basic right to a fair trial as affected by his right meaningfully to cross-examine the witnesses against him and to have effective assistance of counsel at the trial itself. It calls upon us to analyze whether potential

---

5. It must be remembered that Nichols' prior conviction, while uncounseled, was a *valid* conviction because Nichols received no jail time for it. In contrast, if the prior uncounseled conviction is invalid under *Gideon* and its progeny, the conviction cannot be used to enhance a later sentence. Thus, in Custis v. United States, 511 U.S. 485 (1994), the Court stated that, where a prior conviction is being used to enhance a sentence, the defendant can collaterally attack the prior conviction at the sentencing hearing if it was rendered in violation of *Gideon*. The Court held, in fact, that *Gideon* claims were the *only* claims that could be brought collaterally to attack prior convictions in a sentencing proceeding. The defendant in *Custis* was not permitted to challenge his prior convictions on the ground that his counsel was ineffective or that his guilty plea was invalid. See the discussion of *Custis* in Chapters Nine and Ten.

substantial prejudice to defendant's rights inheres in the particular confrontation and the ability of counsel to help avoid that prejudice.

The Court concluded, as Chapter Four revealed, that there was great potential for suggestiveness in a lineup, and "the accused's inability effectively to reconstruct at trial any unfairness that occurred at the lineup may deprive him of his only opportunity meaningfully to attack the credibility of the witness' courtroom identification."

Preliminary Hearings: Coleman v. Alabama

Using this "critical stage" method of analysis, the Court found in Coleman v. Alabama, 399 U.S. 1 (1970), that Alabama's preliminary hearing was a critical stage requiring the appointment of counsel for the indigent defendant. Although preliminary hearings have not yet been examined, it is sufficient for present purposes to note that the purposes of the preliminary hearing are to determine whether there is sufficient evidence against the accused to present the case to the grand jury, and to fix bail. The Court in *Coleman* declared as follows:

> Plainly the guiding hand of counsel at the preliminary hearing is essential to protect the indigent accused against an erroneous or improper prosecution. First, the lawyer's skilled examination and cross-examination of witnesses may expose fatal weaknesses in the State's case that may lead the magistrate to refuse to bind the accused over. Second, in any event, the skilled interrogation of witnesses by an experienced lawyer can fashion a vital impeachment tool for use in cross-examination of the State's witnesses at the trial, or preserve testimony favorable to the accused of a witness who does not appear at the trial. Third, trained counsel can more effectively discover the case the State has against his client and make possible the preparation of a proper defense to meet that case at the trial. Fourth, counsel can also be influential at the preliminary hearing in making effective arguments for the accused on such matters as the necessity for an early psychiatric examination or bail.

Other Pre–Trial Critical Stages

The right to counsel has not been extended to all pretrial phases of a criminal investigation. Kirby v. Illinois, 406 U.S. 682 (1972), for instance, limited the scope of the critical stage doctrine, in holding that a show-up identification before the defendant is charged with a criminal offense is not a critical stage. Unless counsel is provided to safeguard an independent constitutional right, as in *Miranda,* generally one can say that adversary proceedings must be formally initiated before a particular phase of a prosecution can be considered a critical stage requiring counsel. (Recall Massiah v. United States, and Moran v. Burbine). Adversary criminal proceedings plainly can be initiated by formal charge, preliminary hearing, indictment, information, or arraignment. It is not clear what the Supreme Court means by "formal charge," but presumably the Court is focusing on the filing of some statement with the court that expresses the government's belief that the criminal process leading to conviction should begin against a suspect. Before this formal filing, an investigation generally does not trigger counsel rights. Thus, counsel is not constitutionally required at the grand jury stage, because no charges have yet been filed. See, e.g., In re Grand Jury

Subpoenas, 906 F.2d 1485 (10th Cir.1990)(subpoenaing attorney to testify before the grand jury to give information against his client does not violate defendant's right to counsel, even though it may result in defense attorney's disqualification from representation; no Sixth Amendment rights attach prior to indictment).

Even where the criminal process has begun, there are limitations on the extension of the right to counsel to pre-trial proceedings. United States v. Ash, 413 U.S. 300 (1973), holding that a photographic identification at which the accused was not present was not a critical stage, illustrates this point. After reviewing the history and expansion of the Sixth Amendment counsel guarantee, the *Ash* Court redefined the approach used in extending the right to counsel: "[T]he test utilized by the Court has called for examination of the event in order to determine whether the accused required aid in coping with legal problems or assistance in meeting his adversary." The Court distinguished the lineup in *Wade* because in *Ash* there was no confrontation between the accused and the prosecution. After stating that there is no right to counsel because the accused has no right to be present at a photographic array, the Court went on to make the following argument:

> A substantial departure from the historical test would be necessary if the Sixth Amendment were interpreted to give Ash a right to counsel at the photographic identification in this case. Since the accused himself is not present at the time of the photographic display, and asserts no right to be present, no possibility arises that the accused might be misled by his lack of familiarity with the law or overpowered by his professional adversary. Similarly, the counsel guarantee would not be used to produce equality in a trial-like adversary confrontation. * * *

> Even if we were willing to view the counsel guarantee in broad terms as a generalized protection of the adversary process, we would be unwilling to go so far as to extend the right to a portion of the prosecutor's trial-preparation interviews with witnesses. * * * The traditional counterbalance in the American adversary system for these interviews arises from the equal ability of defense counsel to seek and interview witnesses himself.

After *Ash*, what kind of post-charge, pre-trial situations will be deemed critical stages? See, e.g., Commonwealth v. Holzer, 480 Pa. 93, 389 A.2d 101 (1978)(indigent has right to appointed counsel at search and seizure suppression hearing).

B. POST–TRIAL STAGES

The Court often talks about the test of whether a stage of the process is critical as if it involved only one question: is counsel's presence at the pre-trial stage necessary to assure a subsequent, fair trial? Might there be another aspect to the test, one that focuses on the skills a lawyer brings to trials and whether those kinds of skills are almost as important to a suspect at other stages? If attention is paid to this possible aspect of the critical stage test, it might help to explain how the right to counsel has been extended to certain stages of a criminal prosecution following trial.

MEMPA v. RHAY

Supreme Court of the United States, 1967.
389 U.S. 128.

MR. JUSTICE MARSHALL **delivered the opinion of the Court.**

These consolidated cases raise the question of the extent of the right to counsel at the time of sentencing where the sentencing has been deferred subject to probation.

Petitioner Jerry Douglas Mempa was convicted in the Spokane County Superior Court on June 17, 1959, of the offense of "joyriding." This conviction was based on his plea of guilty entered with the advice of court-appointed counsel. He was then placed on probation for two years on the condition, *inter alia,* that he first spend 30 days in the county jail, and the imposition of sentence was deferred * * *.

About four months later the Spokane County prosecuting attorney moved to have petitioner's probation revoked on the ground that he had been involved in a burglary on September 15, 1959. A hearing was held in the Spokane County Superior Court on October 23, 1959. Petitioner Mempa, who was 17 years old at the time, was accompanied to the hearing by his stepfather. He was not represented by counsel and was not asked whether he wished to have counsel appointed for him. Nor was any inquiry made concerning the appointed counsel who had previously represented him.

At the hearing Mempa was asked if it was true that he had been involved in the alleged burglary and he answered in the affirmative. A probation officer testified without cross-examination that according to his information petitioner had been involved in the burglary and had previously denied participation in it. * * * [T]he court immediately entered an order revoking petitioner's probation and then sentenced him to 10 years in the penitentiary, * * *.

* * *

In 1948 this Court held in Townsend v. Burke, 334 U.S. 736, that the absence of counsel during sentencing after a plea of guilty coupled with "assumptions concerning his criminal record which were materially untrue" deprived the defendant in that case of due process. Mr. Justice Jackson there stated in conclusion, "in this case, counsel might not have changed the sentence, but he could have taken steps to see that the conviction and sentence were not predicated on misinformation or misreading of court records, a requirement of fair play which absence of counsel withheld from this prisoner." [The Court discusses other pre-*Gideon* cases.]

There was no occasion in *Gideon* to enumerate the various stages in a criminal proceeding at which counsel was required, but [these earlier cases], when the *Betts* requirement of special circumstances is stripped away by *Gideon,* clearly stand for the proposition that appointment of counsel for an indigent is required at every stage of a criminal proceeding where substantial rights of a criminal accused may be affected. * * *

The State, however, argues that the petitioners were sentenced at the time they were originally placed on probation and that the imposition of sentence following probation revocation is, in effect, a mere formality constituting part of the probation revocation proceeding. It is true that sentencing in Washington offers fewer opportunities for the exercise of judicial discretion than in many other jurisdictions. The applicable statute requires the trial judge in all cases to sentence the convicted person to the maximum term provided by law for the offense of which he was convicted. The actual determination of the length of time to be served is to be made by the Board of Prison Terms and Paroles within six months after the convicted person is admitted to prison.

On the other hand, the sentencing judge is required by statute, together with the prosecutor, to furnish the Board with a recommendation as to the length of time that the person should serve, in addition to supplying it with various information about the circumstances of the crime and the character of the individual. We were informed during oral argument that the Board places considerable weight on these recommendations, although it is in no way bound by them. Obviously to the extent such recommendations are influential in determining the resulting sentence, the necessity for the aid of counsel in marshaling the facts, introducing evidence of mitigating circumstances and in general aiding and assisting the defendant to present his case as to sentence is apparent.

Even more important in a case such as this is the fact that certain legal rights may be lost if not exercised at this stage. For one, Washington law provides that an appeal in a case involving a plea of guilty followed by probation can only be taken after sentence is imposed following revocation of probation. Therefore in a case where an accused agreed to plead guilty, although he had a valid defense, because he was offered probation, absence of counsel at the imposi-

tion of the deferred sentence might well result in loss of the right to appeal. * * *

Likewise the Washington statutes provide that a plea of guilty can be withdrawn at any time prior to the imposition of sentence, if the trial judge in his discretion finds that the ends of justice will be served. Without undertaking to catalog the various situations in which a lawyer could be of substantial assistance to a defendant in such a case, it can be reiterated that a plea of guilty might well be improperly obtained by the promise to have a defendant placed on the very probation the revocation of which furnishes the occasion for desiring to withdraw the plea. An uncounseled defendant might very likely be unaware of this opportunity.

The two foregoing factors assume increased significance when it is considered that * * * the eventual imposition of sentence on the prior plea of guilty is based on the alleged commission of offenses for which the accused is never tried.

In sum, we do not question the authority of the State of Washington to provide for a deferred sentencing procedure coupled with its probation provisions. Indeed, it appears to be an enlightened step forward. All we decide here is that a lawyer must be afforded at this proceeding whether it be labeled a revocation of probation or a deferred sentencing. We assume that counsel appointed for the purpose of the trial or guilty plea would not be unduly burdened by being requested to follow through at the deferred sentencing stage of the proceeding.

* * *

Limitations on Mempa

Today, it is likely to come as no surprise that sentencing is treated as part of the trial process and as requiring the assistance of counsel. However, courts have held that *Mempa* does not mean that every step in the sentencing process is "critical" within the meaning of the Sixth Amendment. In United States v. Johnson, 935 F.2d 47 (4th Cir.1991), the defendant was sentenced in part on the basis of *ex parte* communications between his probation officer and the sentencing judge. The court rejected the argument that the right to counsel attached to those meetings. It found the communications to be "nonadversarial," reasoning that under the Federal Sentencing Guidelines, the probation officer is an agent of the court and assists the court in arriving at a just sentence. Do you agree that a conference between the probation officer and the judge is not a critical stage?

Right to Counsel on Appeal: Douglas v. California and Ross v. Moffitt

Before *Mempa,* the Court had ruled in Douglas v. California, 372 U.S. 353 (1963), that an indigent defendant has a right to appointed counsel for his first appeal of right from a criminal conviction. The Court relied on an equal protection rationale: since a person with means would retain counsel for an appeal of right, the denial of counsel to an indigent was discrimination that violated the Equal Protection Clause.

The problem with an equal protection rationale is that there would appear to be no limits to it; stated broadly, *Douglas* appeared to endorse a form of wealth equalization. See Harris, The Constitution and Truth Seeking: A New Theory on Expert Services for Indigent Defendants, 83 J.Crim.L. and Crim.469 (1992)("While the equality principle surely represents an earnest and well-intentioned effort to deal with the effect of poverty on criminal defendants, it is, if nothing else, too open-ended.").

Over time, the Court switched from an equal protection rationale to a due process rationale in assessing whether indigents had a right to appointed counsel in the appeal process. Under this approach, the state has an obligation to appoint counsel for an indigent whenever counsel would be necessary for adequate access to court relief. Thus, in Ross v. Moffitt, 417 U.S. 600 (1974), the Court refused to extend the *Douglas* reasoning to require counsel for discretionary appeals. Ross received counsel for his first appeal to the state's intermediate appellate court. But he was denied counsel for his subsequent appeal to the state supreme court. Justice Rehnquist, writing for the court, declared that the Fourteenth Amendment "does not require absolute equality or precisely equal advantages, nor does it require the State to equalize economic conditions." Applying the due process test of adequate access, Justice Rehnquist found that counsel was not reasonably necessary for discretionary appeals:

> [P]rior to his seeking discretionary review in the State Supreme Court, [respondent's] claims had once been presented by a lawyer and passed upon by an appellate court. Douglas v. California. We do not believe it can be said, therefore, that a defendant in respondent's circumstances is denied meaningful access to the North Carolina Supreme Court simply because the State

does not appoint counsel to aid him in seeking review in that court. At that stage he will have, at the very least, a brief on his behalf in the Court of Appeals setting forth his claims of error, and in many cases an opinion by the Court of Appeals disposing of his case. These materials, supplemented by whatever submission respondent may make *pro se,* would appear to provide the Supreme Court of North Carolina with an adequate basis on which to base its decision to grant or deny review. * * *

This is not to say, of course, that a skilled lawyer * * * would not prove helpful to any litigant able to employ him. * * * [But] the fact that a particular service might be of benefit to an indigent defendant does not mean that the service is constitutionally required. The duty of the State under our cases is not to duplicate the legal arsenal that may be privately retained by a criminal defendant in a continuing effort to reverse his conviction, but only to assure the indigent defendant an adequate opportunity to present his claims fairly in the context of the State's appellate process.

Applying Ross to Other Post–Trial Stages

Reasoning from Ross v. Moffitt, the Court held, in Wainwright v. Torna, 455 U.S. 586 (1982)(per curiam), that a defendant could not challenge his retained lawyer's failure to file a timely petition for discretionary review in the state supreme court. Torna argued that counsel had been ineffective. But since Torna had no right to counsel in his appeal to the state supreme court, there could be no claim of ineffective counsel. Justice Marshall, dissenting, argued that the defendant was denied due process. Can you identify reasons why counsel should be required in one appeal—as of right—and not another—discretionary appeal?

Chief Justice Rehnquist wrote for the Court in Pennsylvania v. Finley, 481 U.S. 551 (1987), as it relied on Ross v. Moffitt to hold that a defendant has no right to counsel in postconviction (habeas corpus) proceedings. Because such right is lacking, the Court held that a lawyer, who is appointed to represent a defendant in such a proceeding and who finds the defendant's claims to be frivolous, need not file a brief referring to anything in the record that would support the defendant's claims. Such a brief (or a similar showing by counsel) is required on direct appeal as of right under the Supreme Court's decision in Anders v. California, 386 U.S. 738 (1967), but the requirement is derived from the right to counsel itself. When the right is nonexistent, there is no requirement of an *Anders* brief or any other comparable effort by counsel. The Chief Justice also rejected due process and equal protection arguments made in support of a briefing requirement.

In Murray v. Giarratano, 492 U.S. 1 (1989), the Court relied on *Ross* and *Finley* to hold that the state was not required to provide counsel for death-row inmates pursuing post conviction habeas corpus remedies. The plurality opinion, written by Chief Justice Rehnquist, "declined to read either the Eighth Amendment or the Due Process Clause to require yet another distinction between the rights of capital case defendants and those in noncapital cases." The Chief Justice noted, however, that many states "automatically provide counsel to death-row inmates in state habeas corpus proceedings, as a matter of state law." Justice Kennedy concurred in the judgment "on the facts and record of this case" noting that "no prisoner on death row in Virginia has been unable to obtain counsel to represent him in postconviction proceedings." Justice Stevens, joined by Justices Blackmun, Marshall, and Brennan, dissented. He noted that under Virginia law, some claims that would ordinarily be brought on direct review are deferred until habeas corpus proceedings, such as claims concerning ineffective assistance of counsel. He concluded that review of those claims in a habeas proceeding is tantamount to a first appeal of right, as to which the defendant does have a right to counsel under *Douglas*. Justice Stevens also argued that capital litigation is more complex, and subject to a greater time pressure, than the postconviction proceedings considered in *Finley*.[6]

Right to Free Transcripts

The indigent appellant has the constitutional right to a relevant transcript or adequate substitute when challenging trial errors on an appeal as of right. Griffin v. Illinois, 351 U.S. 12 (1956). This is so even though the conviction is for an ordinance violation punishable by fine only. Mayer v. Chicago, 404 U.S. 189 (1971). And a state cannot require an indigent to pay a filing fee as a condition precedent to an appeal. Burns v. Ohio, 360 U.S. 252 (1959). Although the Court often uses equal protection language in these cases, Ross v. Moffitt and noncriminal cases like San Antonio Independent School Dist. v. Rodriguez, 411 U.S. 1 (1973), suggest that the Court is more concerned with establishing a system that permits all criminal defendants to take reasonable advantage of procedures that the structure of the system itself implies are fundamental checks against erroneous results. This helps to explain why a preliminary hearing transcript must be afforded free of charge to an indigent standing trial. Roberts v. LaVallee, 389 U.S. 40 (1967).

Parole and Probation Revocation Proceedings: Gagnon v. Scarpelli

Once the defendant has been properly convicted and sentenced, some constitutional protections diminish or disappear. A defendant has no absolute right to counsel at parole or probation revocation proceedings, for example. In Gagnon v. Scarpelli, 411 U.S. 778 (1973), the Court adopted a case-by-case approach to the appointment of counsel at these revocation hearings. Relying on Morrissey v. Brewer, 408 U.S. 471 (1972), which held that due process protections apply to parole revocation proceedings (in other words, that they have to be fundamentally fair because liberty interests are threatened), the *Gagnon* Court first determined that due process also applied to probation revocation hearings. However, the Court rejected the contention that states are under a constitutional duty to provide counsel for indigents in all probation and parole revocation cases. Acknowledging that its case-by-case approach to counsel is similar to the fundamental fairness approach of *Betts*, which was rejected in *Gideon*, the Court distinguished criminal trials from probation or parole revocation hearings, reasoning as follows:

> In a criminal trial, the State is represented by a prosecutor; formal rules of evidence are in force; a defendant enjoys a number of procedural rights which may be lost if not timely raised; and, in a jury trial, a defendant

6. 21 U.S C. § 848(q)(4)(B) entitles capital defendants to qualified legal representation in any "post conviction proceeding" brought under 28 U.S.C. § 2254 or § 2255, sections of the federal habeas corpus statute.

must make a presentation understandable to untrained jurors. In short, a criminal trial under our system is an adversary proceeding with its own unique characteristics. In a revocation hearing, on the other hand, the State is represented, not by a prosecutor, but by a parole officer with a different orientation; formal procedures and rules of evidence are not employed; and the members of the hearing body are familiar with the problems and practice of probation or parole. The need for counsel at revocation hearings derives, not from the invariable attributes of those hearings, but rather from the peculiarities of particular cases.

The Court in *Gagnon* articulated the relevant considerations:

> * * * Presumptively, it may be said that counsel should be provided in cases where, after being informed of his right to request counsel, the probationer or parolee makes such a request, based on a timely and colorable claim (i) that he has not committed the alleged violation of the conditions upon which he is at liberty; or (ii) that, even if the violation is a matter of public record or is uncontested, there are substantial reasons which justified or mitigated the violation and make revocation inappropriate, and that the reasons are complex or otherwise difficult to develop or present. In passing on a request for the appointment of counsel, the responsible agency also should consider, especially in doubtful cases, whether the probationer appears to be capable of speaking effectively for himself.

Juvenile Proceedings: In re Gault

When guilt is adjudicated at a particular stage, the Court has shown a special sensitivity to the need for counsel. This helps to explain In re Gault, 387 U.S. 1 (1967), which involved a fifteen-year-old who was confined to a State Industrial School until he reached majority. Before being committed as a juvenile delinquent, he was given a hearing without counsel. In holding that due process required that he be appointed counsel, the Court focused on the juvenile's need for assistance of counsel to cope with the problems of law. Underlying the majority's opinion is the concern that the proceeding, though civil in nature, involved the potential for incarceration that was as real as a similar threat in a criminal case.[7]

C. THE RIGHT EXTENDED TO EXPERTS

Using the principle of adequate access, the Court in Ake v. Oklahoma, 470 U.S. 68 (1985), held that an indigent defendant may in some cases be entitled to appointed expert assistance in addition to appointed counsel. Ake was arrested and charged with murdering a couple and wounding their two children. He was hospitalized after initially being found incompetent to stand trial. Subsequently, he responded sufficiently well to medication that he was declared fit to stand trial. At the guilt stage of the capital proceeding, he raised an insanity defense. Defense counsel called and questioned each psychiatrist who had examined Ake

---

7. In contrast, in Middendorf v. Henry, 425 U.S. 25 (1976), the Court refused to hold, on the basis of *Argersinger,* that a summary court-martial is a criminal prosecution because it results in a loss of liberty. The peculiarities of the military setting and its procedures led the Court to distinguish the summary court-martial from the traditional criminal trial. The Court was concerned that counsel would alter the nature of the proceeding, which is informal and flexible.

while he was hospitalized. But each doctor indicated on cross-examination that he had not diagnosed Ake's mental state at the time of the offense. The jury convicted. During the sentencing stage no new evidence was presented.

Justice Marshall's opinion for the Court reasoned that Ake should have had a psychiatrist appointed to assist his defense at both stages. The Court borrowed a procedural due process test it uses in civil cases to balance the defendant's need for help against the burden on the state of providing help. It found a strong "private interest" in life and liberty and the importance of avoiding an unjust conviction; no governmental interest in prevailing at trial if the result "is to cast a pall on the accuracy of the verdict obtained"; and a great value in providing expert assistance to a defendant when his sanity at the time of the offense is to be a significant factor at trial and when the government presents psychiatric evidence concerning future dangerousness in a capital sentencing proceeding. Thus, it held that Ake had been denied due process when he was not afforded access to a competent psychiatrist who might have conducted an appropriate examination and assisted in the evaluation, preparation, and presentation of the defense.

An indigent defendant's right to an appointed expert under *Ake* is not automatic. It is only triggered when the defendant will be deprived of a fair opportunity to present his defense without the expert assistance. For example, in Caldwell v. Mississippi, 472 U.S. 320 (1985), the defendant sought the appointment of several experts, including a ballistics expert. As support for his request, he stated only that the expert "would be of great necessarius [sic] witness." The trial court denied the request. The Supreme Court affirmed and stated that Caldwell's "undeveloped assertions" were not sufficient to require appointment of an expert. See also Bowden v. Kemp, 767 F.2d 761 (11th Cir. 1985)(appointment of psychiatrist not required where no showing was made that sanity would be a real issue at trial).

Generally speaking the courts have read *Ake* narrowly, and have refused to require appointment of an expert unless it is absolutely essential to the defense. See Harris, *Ake* Revisited: Expert Psychiatric Witnesses Remain Beyond Reach for the Indigent, 68 No.Car.L.Rev. 763 (1990). For a discussion of when and whether *Ake* mandates the appointment of a DNA expert in cases where DNA evidence is proffered, see Developments in the Law—Confronting the New Challenges of Scientific Evidence, 108 Harv.L.Rev.1481, 1559 (1995).

Chapter Six

THE SCREENING AND CHARGING PROCESS

I. INTRODUCTION

Once the police have made an arrest, or they have made the decision to arrest a person, the suspect's fate lies mainly in the hands of the prosecutor. The prosecutor has very broad discretion to decide whether to file a formal charge against the suspect, and if so, what crime to charge. As a practical matter, this is so even if the charge actually is made by a grand jury or is screened by a magistrate. The prosecutor's discretion continues even after the charging decision has been made, because a prosecutor usually can obtain a dismissal of a criminal case prior to trial or the entry of a guilty plea. The fact that a prosecutor chooses to bring a charge does not guarantee that a defendant will be convicted, but it does guarantee that the defendant will be significantly burdened as a result of the initiation of the criminal process.

A decision to charge a defendant with criminal activity puts into motion several formal and informal procedures. These will be considered in this Chapter. Two of the most important are the preliminary hearing and the grand jury investigation. These procedures and their relationship to the prosecutor's role in the screening of cases and the charging process receive most of the attention in the material that follows.

II. CHOICES AND THE CHARGING PROCESS

A. CONTROLLED AND UNCONTROLLED CHOICES

Choices must be made at all levels of our criminal justice system. The police must decide whether to arrest or to investigate. Prosecutors must decide whether to initiate cases, what charges to file, and whether to plea bargain. Magistrates issuing search and arrest warrants, or sitting in preliminary hearings, must decide whether probable cause exists or whether a suspect should be released on bail or pursuant to other conditions of pre-trial release. Grand juries must decide whether to indict, and prosecutors must decide whether to seek dismissal of indictments. Trial judges must decide whether there is enough evidence for cases to go to petit juries, and petit juries must decide whether to convict or acquit. Judges or juries must determine the sentences to be imposed on convicted offenders. Correctional authorities must decide how to treat incarcerated offenders, and parole or pardon authorities must determine whether to release offenders before their formal sentences have been served.

Some of these choices are controlled by standards—e.g., whether probable cause exists, whether there is enough evidence to go to a jury, and how convinced the jury must be before it convicts—and the task of government officials or jurors is to apply the standards to particular facts. Other choices— sentencing in some states is an example—might be controlled at the margin by minimum and maximum provisions but provide the decisionmaker some latitude in choosing where to settle within the permissible range. The standards channel decisionmaking to some extent, but not completely. Still other choices are virtually standardless; that is, the persons who make them are not bound to follow any constitutional, statutory, or other guidelines and have articulated none of their own to explain their actions.

The screening and charging process involves many uncontrolled choices, and these are a cause of concern. As you proceed in this chapter, keep in mind what choices are possible and what controls, if any, are placed upon them by the agency making the choice, or by some external agency.

B. LESS THAN FULL ENFORCEMENT OF THE LAW

One of the realities of law enforcement is that not all crimes are investigated, not all criminals are prosecuted, and not all laws are enforced. Nowhere in the United States is there a full enforcement policy—i.e, one that seeks to impose a sanction on every criminal act that occurs.

One compelling reason for underenforcement is that full enforcement is just too costly. We are not willing to pay for the police, the prosecutors, the public defenders, the judges, the courtrooms, and the penal institutions that would be required to punish all criminal acts that occur. Because we are not willing to pay for full enforcement, it is apparent that we expect that the people who administer the criminal justice system will be able to focus on important cases and to disregard less important ones.

Apart from economics, there are reasons why choices are made in the processing of cases. The notion of individualized justice runs deep in this country. Actions that technically fall under the same statutory proscription may not be equally reprehensible. Unlike the concern about economics, however, individualized justice need not depend on the exercise of discretion by a prosecutor or by a charging authority. Judges or juries could decide culpability after trial. Yet, the leveling of a charge can have such a devastating impact on a person that we probably have come to expect prosecutors to refuse to charge in some cases, even though it is possible that a conviction might be obtained.

Finally, legislative "overcriminalization" has resulted in criminal codes that, if they were fully enforced, might be intolerable. Laws are sometimes passed as "state-declared ideals," such as adultery statutes, which are "unenforced because we want to continue our conduct, and unrepealed because we want to preserve our morals."[1] Other laws, e.g., gambling laws, are drafted broadly for administrative convenience but are never fully enforced, because there is a general feeling that the legislature never really wanted to prohibit private poker

---

1. LaFave, The Prosecutor's Discretion in   (1970).
the United States, 18 J.Am.Comp.L. 532, 533

games among friends. Outdated laws, which would cause public outrage were they enforced, remain unrepealed, sometimes because legislators do not want to go on record as having repealed any criminal law for fear of being labelled as "soft on crime".[2]

It seems, then, that legislatures pass and refuse to repeal statutes that invite choices by those who screen cases and make charging decisions. See Misner, Recasting Prosecutorial Discretion, 86 J.Crim.L. & Crim. 717 (1996)(arguing that legislatures, "by creating too many policy choices, have effectively abdicated policy-making to the prosecutor since it is the prosecutor, and not the legislature, that has the final decision in determining which public policy, if any, is breached by an individual's conduct.").

It should be noted that the concept of individualized justice runs counter to another fundamental concept of American law: that all citizens should be treated equally under the law. When a legislature passes a broad statute and depends upon government officials who enforce the statute to exercise their discretion as to who should be prosecuted, the distinctions between classes of people and individuals are less visible. If the legislature were to write the distinctions into the statute, they would be more accessible to citizens, more easily subject to review, and undoubtedly more controversial. For a long time now, legislatures have been permitted to delegate to others the task of refining a statutory scheme through enforcement. Whether this is desirable is one question. Whether it is a permissible delegation of authority is another. Assuming that it is both desirable and permissible, there is yet a third question: Are there mechanisms available to provide some guarantee of equal treatment?

Some other countries purport to operate on the principle that the police and prosecutor have no discretion to exercise at all. If the case is one in which there is sufficient evidence to prosecute, it must be prosecuted. Whether these systems operate in practice as they are designed to in theory is questionable. Two observers make the following comment:

> The principle of compulsory prosecution which formally permeates the German and Italian systems, and informally the French, demands the impossible: full enforcement of the law in a time of rising crime and fierce competition for resources. Inevitably, adjustments must be made in the way in which the principle is to be applied; where formal law or ideology does not permit these adjustments, informal processes are created that do.[3]

This observation serves as a reminder that it may be more difficult to make a mandatory system of prosecutions work in practice than it is to posit such a system in theory.

Judge Miner, in The Consequences of Federalizing Criminal Law, 4 Crim. Just. 16 (1989) argues that a prosecutor's decision not to prosecute someone who is guilty of a crime invades the province of the jury and creates a public

---

2. An example of this problem is mentioned in Misner, Recasting Prosecutorial Discretion, 86 J.Crim.L. & Crim. 717 (1996). When the Arizona legislature adopted its revised criminal code, a majority of legislators refused to go on record as voting for a repeal of any sex offense statutes, even if they had become outmoded or superfluous. So now Arizona has two sets of sex offense statutes, using different terminology and imposing different punishment. This obviously gives prosecutors greater discretion in charging decisions.

3. Goldstein & Marcus, The Myth of Judicial Supervision in Three Inquisitorial Systems: France, Italy, and Germany, 87 Yale L.J. 240, 280 (1977).

perception of unfairness. Professor Green, in "Hare and Hounds": The Fugitive Defendant's Constitutional Right to be Pursued, 56 Brooklyn L.Rev. 439 (1990), disagrees with Judge Miner and argues that it makes sense that the prosecutor enjoys "virtually unfettered discretion in deciding how to allocate investigative and prosecutorial resources." Professor Green contends that the prosecution is in the "best position" to decide how to use the finite resources allocated to prosecuting crime. With whom do you agree?

III. SCREENING BY THE POLICE

A. THE NATURE OF POLICE CHOICES

Before reaching the question of what choices should be available to those responsible for charging suspects with criminal offenses, it is necessary to focus on the police. Generally, officials who have the ultimate responsibility for charging decisions do not themselves investigate criminal conduct.[4] The job of investigation is ordinarily left to the police. Obviously, then, if the police do not turn information over to the charging officials, it is unlikely that those officials will have any real choice to make.

In Chapter Two, the restrictions on police investigations, arrests, and searches were examined. The assumption there was that the police wanted to proceed against citizens, and the question was what limits, if any, should be placed on police activity. Sometimes, the police decide they do not want to take action against individuals, even though such action might be permissible under the rules previously discussed. When the police decide not to act, often they effectively screen cases from the criminal justice process.

The Choice Not to Arrest

The first level of screening may be done when the police decide whom to arrest. Although a decision to make an arrest must be reviewed by an impartial magistrate, either before or after the arrest is made, a decision not to arrest is essentially unreviewable.

The suggestion has been made that police cannot properly be given the choice whether or not to arrest, and that they must arrest when they have probable cause to do so.[5] In fact, it appears that the police in all American jurisdictions make decisions not to arrest people whom they could arrest. Several explanations can be offered for this phenomenon.

4. Prosecutors may be well advised not to become too active in investigating cases they will have to prosecute. It might create problems if the prosecutor would have to be called as a witness at trial. In United States v. Johnston, 690 F.2d 638 (7th Cir.1982), the court reversed a decision barring the prosecutor assigned to a case from testifying at a suppression hearing concerning a telephone conversation he had with the defendant about which the defendant had testified. The court noted that prosecutors should avoid interviewing prospective witnesses except in the presence of third parties and indicated that prosecutors generally ought to withdraw where they must

testify during a part of a case. But where the defendant placed the telephone call to the prosecutor and voluntarily chose to testify to its contents, the court concluded that the prosecutor should be permitted to testify and, if there was no reasonable likelihood that he would again be called as a witness, he could continue in the case. In other situations, it warned, the government would be required to show that its case would be prejudiced by substitution of counsel before a prosecutor would be permitted to continue after having testified.

5. Hall, Police and Law in a Democratic Society, 28 Ind.L.J. 133, 155 (1953).

Were the police to arrest every suspect who they reasonably believed committed a crime, an already overburdened judicial system would be further burdened. Thus, we tolerate choices by the police because we are not prepared to handle more cases. Actually, the police themselves are not prepared to handle more cases either. If they spent more time in processing cases, they would have less time to spend on the street to deal with crimes that they view as more serious than the ones they now choose to ignore. Also, police officers learn that courts and prosecutors will not proceed very far in processing certain kinds of cases. Rather than initiating a process that they know will be shortlived, the police may decide not to make arrests as to certain crimes and to devote their energies to other activities.

Some of these reasons should cause concern. A prosecutor may drop charges against an individual, who might be convicted were the charge pursued, because the arrest itself is a sufficient stigma and the prosecutor believes that conviction would be overkill. If no arrest is made, the deterrent impact of the law may be reduced. Thus, the fact that a prosecutor may choose to drop a case does not necessarily mean that no arrest should be made. As a practical matter, however, the police do not like to see their work end in a dismissal of a case. Whether or not they should refuse to arrest, they may do so when they know that a case will not go very far in the prosecutor's office. For an interesting discussion of the interrelationship between the police investigatory function and the prosecutor's function, see Richman, Prosecutors and Their Agents: Agents and Their Prosecutors, 103 Colum.L.Rev. 749 (2003).

Another reason that police will refrain from arresting is that the function they perform is more than initiating the criminal process; they also attempt to maintain order, and to do so they may need to maintain good relations with community elements who would resent the filing of criminal charges in some instances. The police officer may approach a disruptive incident "not in terms of enforcing the law but in terms of 'handling the situation.' "[6] Arrest is only one of several tools that the officer may use to maintain order. The officer may rely on personal qualities and an aura of authority to command respect, so that order may be restored. Once order is restored, the officer may decide that it would be unnecessary or inappropriate to make an arrest.

Police officers are also aware that enforcement of certain crimes by arrest would create a public backlash. If police officers arrested every driver who drove 56 miles per hour in a 55 mile per hour zone, it is clear that the police would hear about it. Upset drivers might raise the possibility of violence during the arrest for such a minimal offense. Requiring police officers to arrest whenever they have probable cause of a violation of any of the thousands of offenses that legislatures have enacted would simply be unworkable.

That said, there is an undeniable problem in the police having virtually unfettered discretion in determining who to arrest and who not to arrest. Professor Davis, in Prosecution and Race: The Power and Privilege of Discretion, 67 Fordham L.Rev. 13 (1998), notes the racial impact that such discretion can have:

> Because police officers are not required to make an arrest when they observe conduct creating probable cause, their discretion may result in the

6. J. Wilson, Varieties of Police Behavior 33 (1968).

discretia
concour
disparate
impach
of diff
races

failure to detain or arrest whites who commit acts for which their African American counterparts would often be detained or arrested.

As an illustration, Professor Davis notes an event in Prince George's County, Maryland, "where white officers observed three white adults smoking crack cocaine in a car with a baby and neither made arrest nor filed charges." Is there anything that can be done about underenforcement of the criminal law when motivated by racial considerations?

Post-September 11 Efforts at Prevention

After the terrorist attacks of September 11, a studied choice has been made by the Justice Department and many local law enforcement agencies to shift from arresting for completed crimes to prevention of acts of terrorism. See Dan Eggen, Ashcroft Plans to Reorganize Justice, Curtail Programs, Wash. Post, Nov. 9, 2001, at A17 (reporting that Attorney General Ashcroft declared "that the primary mission of federal prosecutors, FBI agents and immigration officers must become thwarting future terrorist strikes"). Because resources are not infinite, it is clear that the recent emphasis on security and prevention has resulted in a shift in which arrests for garden-variety crimes have become even less frequent.

B. SOME TYPICAL CASES

Consider the following situations, which a police officer might expect to confront, and in which a choice to arrest or not will be made.

1. An officer responds to a call from a woman who says her husband is going to beat her. When the officer arrives, the woman has a broken nose and several facial bruises, but she refuses to sign a complaint. Should the officer arrest the husband anyway? Should he suggest that the couple see a marriage counselor? Should his decision be affected by whether the couple has children who witnessed the beating?

2. An officer watches an adult sell an ounce of marijuana to a juvenile. When he apprehends the seller, the seller offers to work as an informant in exchange for favorable treatment, but only if no arrest is made. What should the officer do?

3. Suppose two officers are operating a speed trap and a car whizzes by at 20 miles per hour over the speed limit. They usually issue tickets to anyone speeding more than 8 miles over the limit. Should they issue a ticket if the driver is a parent rushing to the hospital to see an ill child? If the driver is an employee who is late to work and may be facing the loss of a job if tardy one more time? If the driver is a 17–year-old youth who has only a probationary license and will lose it automatically if a ticket is issued? If the driver is from out of town and did not realize that he was speeding?

4. An officer seizes drugs from a house, and it is questionable whether his entry into the house was permissible under the Fourth Amendment. Should he arrest the occupants and let the prosecution and the court figure it out? Or should he just seize and destroy the narcotics as an informal sanction?

5. An officer stationed at a security checkpoint in front of a courthouse witnesses a purse-snatching. Should he chase after the perpetrator in order to make an arrest?

Is police rulemaking a means by which an officer's discretion to arrest or not to arrest can be limited? Ironically, if police departments contemplate adopting rules that would indicate circumstances in which an arrest could be, but probably ought not be, made, they may be criticized. There would be no deterrent effect to a law that the police have advertised will not be enforced. Yet, without rules, decisions are left to individual officers at the lowest enforcement level.

IV. THE PROSECUTORIAL DECISION WHETHER TO CHARGE

A. THE POWER OF THE PROSECUTOR

While discretion runs through the criminal justice system, it is the discretionary decisions made by the prosecutor that have the most impact. Professor Misner, in Recasting Prosecutorial Discretion, 86 J.Crim.L. & Crim. 717 (1996), notes the awesome authority granted to prosecutors—authority that has increased over time.

Although the discretion given to the legislature, to the police, and to prison officials is broad and immensely important, the prosecutor has become the most powerful office in the criminal justice system. The prosecutor's authority is evident in bail hearings, grants of immunity, and in trial strategy. But in the areas of charging, bargaining, and sentencing, it has become clear that the prosecutor plays the pivotal role in the criminal justice process. Despite criticism, plea bargaining continues unabated. While a few courts have rather unsuccessfully attempted to formulate "a common law of prosecutorial discretion," the authority of the prosecutor continues to grow.

Three closely related trends have been at work to promote the authority of the prosecutor. First, current criminal codes contain so many overlapping provisions that the choice of how to characterize conduct as criminal has passed to the prosecutor. In many cases the legislature has effectively delegated its prerogative to define the nature and severity of criminal conduct to the prosecutor. Legislative mandates regarding sentencing maxima, sentencing minima, and sentencing guidelines are dependent upon the substantive charge chosen by the prosecutor. In addition, prosecutors have the untrammeled authority to select the number of separate criminal acts for which the defendant will be charged. The prosecutors also determine whether to seek sentencing enhancements.

Second, the increase in reported crime without a concomitant increase in resources dedicated to the prosecution and defense of criminal conduct has resulted in a criminal process highly dependent upon plea bargaining. There are very few restraints placed upon the prosecutor in the bargaining process.

Third, the development of sentencing guidelines and a growth of statutes with mandatory minimum sentences have increased the importance of the charging decision since the charging decision determines the range of sentences available to the court. * * *

* * * Whether one agrees with the critics of the role of the prosecutor, it appears that the future belongs to the prosecutor. Proposals to guarantee greater justice for defendants or more efficient use of scarce resources must accept the fact that the prosecutor has become, and will remain, the preeminent office in the criminal justice system.

Prosecutorial Discretion After 9/11

Prosecutorial discretion has, if anything, increased after the terrorist attacks of 9/11. The Federal government has taken the position that prosecutors have the discretion to decide whether suspected terrorists can be designated "enemy combatants", who will be tried in military as opposed to civilian courts– if they are to be tried at all. A discussion of "enemy combatant" designation can be found in Chapter 10. Prosecutors also have discretion to detain individuals virtually indefinitely on suspected association with acts of terrorism. This can be done under the material witness statute (discussed in Chapter 2) or, for foreign nationals, as an immigration detention outside the United States (specifically at Guantanamo, discussed in Chapter 7). Is this virtually unbridled discretion justified in light of the threat of terrorism?

B. THE NATURE OF THE CHARGING DECISION

The prosecutor's decision whether to charge a suspect with a crime is of a different character than the officer's decision whether to arrest. While the officer usually must make an on-the-spot decision, the prosecutor has time, a fuller knowledge of the facts, and the opportunity to consult with colleagues. The consequences of a decision to charge are far greater than those of the decision to arrest. A decision to charge constitutes a finding that the suspect should bear the monetary and social costs of trial and, in some cases, that the suspect's freedom should either be conditioned on payment of bail or suspended as a means of preventive detention. That the defendant may reduce some of these costs by pleading guilty to a lesser charge only makes the prosecutor's decision more consequential.

Professor Davis, in Prosecution and Race: The Power and Privilege of Discretion, 67 Fordham L.Rev. 13 (1998), well-describes the importance of the prosecutor's decision to charge a person with a crime:

> The first and most important function exercised by a prosecutor is the charging decision. Although police officers decide whether to arrest a suspect, the prosecutor decides whether he should be formally charged with a crime and what the charge should be. This decision is entirely discretionary. Even if there is probable cause to believe the suspect has committed a crime, the prosecutor may decide to dismiss the case and release the suspect. She may also file a charge that is either more or less serious than that recommended by the police officer, as long as there is probable cause to believe the suspect committed the crime. Other than a constitutional challenge by a criminal defendant, there is very little process for review of these decisions.

> The charging decision is one of the most important decisions a prosecutor makes. In conjunction with the plea bargaining process, the charging decision almost predetermines the outcome of a criminal case, because the

vast majority of criminal cases result in guilty pleas or guilty verdicts. The charge also often determines the sentence that the defendant will receive, particularly in federal court, where criminal sentences are governed by the federal sentencing guidelines, and in state cases involving mandatory sentences. Because the sentencing guidelines and mandatory sentencing laws virtually eliminate judicial discretion, the prosecutor often effectively determines the defendant's sentence at the charging stage of the process, if the defendant is eventually found guilty.

At the outset, does it trouble you that the prosecutor's decision to charge, carrying the grave consequences that it does, is largely discretionary? But if you think the prosecutor's unfettered discretion is a problem, what safeguards would you impose?

C. THE FACTORS THAT ARE CONSIDERED

The prosecutor must decide whether to charge and what crime to charge. The decision whether to charge depends on the prosecutor's belief that (1) the suspect is guilty, (2) the evidence is sufficient to secure conviction, and (3) it is in the community's best interest to prosecute the suspect. General criteria to be employed by the prosecutor are set forth in the ABA Standards for Criminal Justice: The Prosecution Function, approved by the ABA's House of Delegates in February, 1992:

Standard 3–3.9 Discretion in the Charging Decision

(a) A prosecutor should not institute, or cause to be instituted, or permit the continued pendency of criminal charges when the prosecutor knows that the charges are not supported by probable cause. A prosecutor should not institute, cause to be instituted, or permit the continued pendency of criminal charges in the absence of sufficient admissible evidence to support a conviction.

(b) The prosecutor is not obliged to present all charges which the evidence might support. The prosecutor may in some circumstances and for good cause consistent with the public interest decline to prosecute, notwithstanding that sufficient evidence may exist which would support a conviction. Illustrative of the factors which the prosecutor may properly consider in exercising his or her discretion are:

(i) the prosecutor's reasonable doubt that the accused is in fact guilty;

(ii) the extent of the harm caused by the offense;

(iii) the disproportion of the authorized punishment in relation to the particular offense or the offender;

(iv) possible improper motives of a complainant;

(v) reluctance of the victim to testify;

(vi) cooperation of the accused in the apprehension or conviction of others; and

(vii) availability and likelihood of prosecution by another jurisdiction.

* * *

(d) In making the decision to prosecute, the prosecutor should give no weight to the personal or political advantages or disadvantages which might be involved or to a desire to enhance his or her record of conviction.

(e) In cases which involve a serious threat to the community, the prosecutor should not be deterred from prosecution by the fact that in the jurisdiction juries have tended to acquit persons accused of the particular kind of criminal act in question.

(f) The prosecutor should not bring or seek charges greater in number or degree than can reasonably be supported with evidence at trial or than are necessary to fairly reflect the gravity of the offense.

must be supported by evidence

Sample Cases

Using the criteria from the ABA standards, consider whether the prosecutor should have brought the following cases:

yes?

1. Congressman Mel Reynolds, an African–American, was charged and convicted of statutory rape and obstruction of justice. The evidence showed that he had a long-term sexual relationship with a teenage girl, and that he tried to cover-up the relationship when an investigation began. The relationship was consensual and the girl was at best a reluctant witness against him.

yes

2. In the Southern District of New York, the U.S. Attorney promulgated a "Federal Tuesday" program, in which low-level drug dealers were arrested on the streets while making narcotics transactions. These low-level dealers were prosecuted under the federal narcotics laws, and given much harsher sentences than they would have received had they been prosecuted in the state system. No other prosecutions for these low-level crimes were brought.

yes bitch!

3. Leona Helmsley was charged and convicted of tax fraud. The government proved that she evaded taxes by charging renovations to her home as business expenses. On balance, however, Ms. Helmsley paid millions of dollars a year in taxes—the amount of evasion was a rather small percentage of the amount she paid.

yes

4. Los Angeles police officers Stacy Koon and Lawrence Powell were convicted in federal court for violating the civil rights of Rodney King. The convictions arose out of the use of excessive force after the officers had lawfully pursued King in a high-speed chase and stopped and arrested him. The Rodney King beating was on videotape. A state prosecution had already been brought, resulting in acquittal on most of the counts and a hung jury on one count.

No

5. The Independent Prosecutor, Kenneth Starr, brought obstruction of justice charges against Julia Hiatt Steele, a single mother, after she failed to corroborate Kathleen Willey's account that President Clinton had made unwanted sexual advances toward Willey. Steele was acquitted, after spending her life savings on a legal defense.

6. John Walker Lindh, the "American Taliban" was charged with treason against the United States after taking part in armed conflict against U.S. troops in Afghanistan. He was charged in a federal court and was allowed to plead guilty to a lesser offense. But the government has treated some (not all) suspected Al Quaeda supporters as "enemy combatants", meaning that they will

yes

be tried in secret military courts, with no pretrial access to counsel or witnesses. Is this a proper exercise of discretion?

y,s

7. The accused snipers, John Muhammad and Lee Malvo, were going to be tried in Maryland, where most of the sniper attacks occurred. But the Justice Department intervened to decide that the defendants should be prosecuted in Virginia. The apparent reason for this decision is that prosecutors could seek the death penalty for Malvo in Virginia but not in Maryland (because Malvo was a juvenile at the time of the crimes, and Maryland does not permit the use of the death penalty when the crime is committed by a juvenile).

Politics, and the Chance of a Favorable Outcome

Of course, an important factor in a prosecutor's decision to prosecute is whether the prosecutor thinks a case can be won. A prosecutor with a high conviction rate is not only more likely to be successful in a reelection bid (in jurisdictions where prosecutors are elected), but also will have enhanced credibility when she does file charges. Therefore, she is likely to want to carry all the way to trial only those cases that are supported by a great deal of evidence to which the judge and jury will be sympathetic.

That said, it is undeniably true that politics can often affect a charging decision. Attorney General Reno's decision to seek the death penalty in the prosecution of the bombing of the Federal Building in Oklahoma City is a prominent example. She announced that the death penalty would be sought even before the perpetrators were apprehended. And Attorney General Ashcroft has ordered United States attorneys to seek the death penalty in certain cases even though the attorneys initially exercised discretion not to do so.

Prosecution rates do not tell accurate story.

Problems can arise if charging decisions are dominated by politics and the goal of maintaining high conviction rates. Prosecutors could become less concerned about the danger of convicting innocent persons. Conviction rates could be reached by offering very favorable plea bargains to people against whom the evidence is quite weak and who might well be acquitted at trial. In short, it is not clear that a prosecutor's office should be judged on the basis of its rate of conviction. But the reality is that it probably will be.

Use of Private Prosecutors: Young v. United States ex rel Vuitton et Fils, S.A.

Is it possible for a prosecutor's charging decision to be affected by a conflict of interest? Justice Brennan wrote for the majority in Young v. United States ex rel. Vuitton et Fils S.A., 481 U.S. 787 (1987), as the Court held that district courts have the authority to appoint a private attorney to prosecute a criminal contempt case, but that ordinarily they should do so only as a last resort after requesting the appropriate prosecuting authority to initiate prosecution. The case arose as a result of the issuance of an injunction by a federal district court forbidding trademark infringement. Counsel for the company that obtained the injunction requested the district court to appoint them as special counsel to prosecute a criminal contempt action for violation of the injunction. The Supreme Court held that, under Fed.R.Crim.P. 42(b), a district court has the power to instigate contempt proceedings and to appoint counsel, but concluded that by affording the appropriate prosecuting authority an opportunity to initiate the proceeding, a district court enhances "the prospect that investigative activity will be conducted by trained prosecutors pursuant to Justice Department guidelines." The Court used its supervisory power to declare "that counsel for a party that is the beneficiary of a court order may not be appointed as prosecutor in a contempt action alleging a violation of that order." The Court observed that the prosecutor is expected to represent the interests of the government, not private litigants, and reasoned that "[i]n a case where a prosecutor represents an interested party, * * * the ethics of the legal profession *require* that an interest other than the government's be taken into account."

Justice Scalia concurred in the judgment reversing the conviction. He concluded that the United States Attorney might have exercised discretion and chosen not to prosecute the contempt, and that the convictions must be reversed because "[i]t would be impossible to conclude with any certainty that these prosecutions would have been brought had the court simply referred the matter to the Executive Branch."

Justice Powell, joined by Chief Justice Rehnquist and Justice O'Connor, concurred with most of the reasoning of the Court, but rejected the notion that an error in appointing an interested lawyer to prosecute always requires reversal. He argued for a remand to determine whether the error in this case was prejudicial. Justice White dissented.[7]

D. THE DECISION NOT TO PROSECUTE

A prosecutor's decision not to prosecute a suspect is generally protected from judicial review. This means that the effect of a prosecutor's decision not to charge a suspect is a final resolution of the case in favor of the suspect. Of course, the prosecutor may change her mind and decide to charge the suspect within the time prescribed by the applicable statute of limitations, but courts rarely attempt to compel the prosecutor to file charges.

Even when statutory language appears to make prosecution of all violations of a statute mandatory, courts have been extremely reluctant to require prosecution where the prosecutor has decided against it. See, e.g., Inmates of Attica v. Rockefeller, 477 F.2d 375 (2d Cir.1973)(statutory language that prosecutor is "required" to institute prosecutions "has never been thought to exclude the exercise of prosecutorial discretion"). The court in *Attica* relied on separation of powers principles and refused to order the prosecutor to instigate prosecutions against state officials.

Refusing to Prosecute a Certain Type of Crime

It is clear that prosecutors, with respect to some crimes, are not making case by case judgments. They are simply saying that a certain crime will not be prosecuted. A prosecutor's decision not to prosecute a certain type of crime is often based on a judgment that the violation of law involved is simply not worth the resources that would have to be expended in a prosecution. Prosecutors might also be concerned about a public backlash in prosecuting certain crimes. Local and cultural conditions might be involved as well.

7. For an interesting discussion of *Young*, see Meier, The "Right" to a Disinterested Prosecutor of Criminal Contempt: Unpacking Public and Private Interests, 70 Wash.U.L.Q. 85 (1992).

An example of the non-prosecution of a class of crime arose in Utah, as reported in an article in the National Law Journal, Aug. 10, 1998, p. A10:

> Facing criticism for suggesting that polygamy may fall under religious freedoms, Gov. Mike Leavitt turned to Utah's attorney general for advice on why the state fails to prosecute polygamists when the practice is widespread. * * * The Tapestry of Polygamy, a self-help group for former polygamist wives and children, held a news conference outside the governor's office July 27 and presented his chief of staff, Vicky Varela, a letter urging that the state constitutional ban on polygamy be enforced.

* * *

> Ms. Varela drew a distinction between prosecuting the act of polygamy itself and prosecuting crimes that may occur within plural marriages. "Polygamy is against the law in Utah," she said. "We do not know why prosecutors do not choose to prosecute it."

> There has not been a prosecution of anyone solely for practicing polygamy in Utah since 1952, when federal and state agents raided the border community of Short Creek * * *. The raid turned into a public-relations debacle as children were pulled from their parents' arms and husbands were jailed.

> Ms. Varela said the governor will ask Utah Attorney General Jan Graham for a "policy statement" on polygamy prosecutions. But Ms. Graham's chief deputy, Reed Richards, said the policy is simple: "Crimes are prosecuted when we know about them, and the vast majority of these relationships are consenting adults."

Does the explanation given by Chief Deputy Graham make any sense? If crimes are prosecuted when the prosecutor knows about them, and consent is no defense to polygamy, then why is the fact of consent an answer to non-prosecution?

Overriding the Grand Jury's Decision to Indict

No federal prosecutor can lawfully sign an indictment not approved by the grand jury, but it appears that he or she may decline to sign off on charges which the grand jury wishes to file. A few years ago, a dozen grand jurors in Colorado rebelled against a prosecutor's decision not to indict Rockwell International for polluting a site with nuclear waste. During its term, the grand jury heard from more than 100 witnesses and examined hundreds of thousands of documents. The evidence indicated that the cost of the clean-up at the site would be $2 billion. But the prosecutor pulled the plug on the grand jury by entering into a deal whereby Rockwell would pay an $18 million fine. The grand jurors made statements to the press that they wanted to indict Rockwell but were overruled by the prosecutor. They then wrote a report about their findings and sent it to a federal judge, requesting judicial intervention. The judge not only refused to intervene in the prosecutor's decision; he asked the U.S. Attorney General to determine whether criminal charges could be brought against the grand jurors for violation of grand jury secrecy. The foreman of the grand jury was quoted as saying: "The judge's instructions were very vivid and clear to us. He said that we were not to be a rubber stamp for the prosecutor. What we've done is in the best interest of the prosecutor and the nation." Do you agree? See Sachs, Rebellious Grand Jurors Hire Lawyer, A.B.A.J., Feb. 1993, p.31. In thinking about the prosecutor's role, can you see a difference between the failure to approve an indictment that the grand jury wishes to return and the filing of an indictment that the grand jury opposes?[8]

Limits on the Decision Not to Prosecute

There are several theoretical checks on the prosecutor's decision not to prosecute. None of them are widely used, however. In some states, a grand jury can return a valid indictment without the prosecutor's approval. In four states, citizens can petition for a grand jury to be formed to investigate a certain matter. See Conspiracy and Cover-up Will Be Probed By a Citizen Grand Jury, A.B.A.J., Sept. 1997, p. 34 (noting a successful petition to appoint a citizen grand jury to investigate whether the bombing of the Oklahoma City federal building was the work of a large-scale conspiracy). In some states, a grand jury that is dissatisfied with the performance of the local prosecutor may request the attorney general to appoint a special prosecutor. In some states, the attorney general or the governor may supersede the local prosecutor and initiate prosecution—as occurred in New York when Governor Pataki appointed a special prosecutor in a murder case in which the local prosecutor refused to seek the death penalty. Finally, a few jurisdictions permit private prosecution by allowing a citizen to present a claim to the grand jury where the prosecutor has failed to do so.[9] But if the grand jury indicts, the prosecutor may take over and quickly dispose of the case as she wishes.

Explaining the Decision Not to Prosecute

The public is rarely made aware of a prosecutor's decision not to bring charges. In highly publicized cases, however, prosecutors may have to worry about public opinion. Some prosecutors have found it necessary to explain their decisionmaking process when they decide not to charge in a high profile case.

For example, U.S. Attorney Otto Obermaier decided not to bring charges against Salomon Brothers, the Wall Street Brokerage house, in connection with Salomon's admission of submitting false bids in treasury securities auctions. He made a public statement explaining why he decided not to seek charges. Obermaier singled out four pertinent factors: (1) Salomon's extensive cooperation with the authorities; (2) Salomon's replacement of those senior management officials who had failed to promptly report the offenses to the authorities after first learning of it; (3) heavy fines and other punishments imposed as part

---

8. Morrison v. Olson, 487 U.S. 654 (1988), upheld a federal statute that required the Attorney General to conduct a preliminary investigation of allegations of criminal activity on the part of high-ranking federal officials and, unless the allegations are found to be insubstantial, to ask a three-judge federal panel to appoint an "independent counsel" to complete the investigation, to decide whether or not to prefer charges, and to conduct any trials. Seven justices voted to uphold the statute and rejected the dissenting argument of Justice

Scalia that the statute violates separation of powers principles. In 1999, Congress allowed the Independent Counsel law to expire, largely due to the controversy created by Kenneth Starr's investigation of President Clinton.

9. See, e.g., Brack v. Wells, 184 Md. 86, 40 A.2d 319 (1944). There is no private right of prosecution in federal courts. See United States v. Panza, 381 F.Supp. 1133 (W.D.Pa. 1974).

of Salomon's civil settlement with the SEC, the Federal Reserve Bank, and the Treasury Department; and (4) the "negative effect on the company's innocent employees and shareholders" that would have resulted from criminal charges against the corporation. Obermaier, Drafting Companies to Fight Crime, New York Times, May 24, 1992, sec. 3, p.11, col.2. Are these sufficient reasons to reject a criminal prosecution? Should there be a general practice of public notice of a decision not to prosecute, just as there is public notice for a decision to prosecute? What good can come out of a prosecutor's disclosure of why she chose not to prosecute? Could a publicized decision not to prosecute become a source of abuse, by casting public suspicion upon the target?

E. PROSECUTORIAL RULEMAKING

Just as there have been numerous calls for rulemaking by the police, there have been a number of suggestions that chief prosecutorial officers should formulate regulations to govern the conduct of their offices. See, e.g., ALI Model Code of Pre–Arraignment Procedure § 10.3 (calling for regulations); ABA Standards, The Prosecution Function § 3–3.4 (1992) (calling for policy guidelines to determine "whether criminal proceedings should be instituted").

Some guidelines have been drafted, but they leave much room for individualized charging judgment on the part of particular prosecutors. See, e.g., U.S. Dept. of Justice, Materials Relating to Prosecutorial Discretion. The arguments for prosecutorial rulemaking are similar to those made in favor of police rulemaking, but they are even stronger, because policy-making executive officials are likely to be trusted with greater power to make enforcement decisions than are lower level police officers.

Arguments against prosecutorial rulemaking have been made, however. They are the following: the application of rules in particular cases would be challenged, thus raising the costs of the criminal process; rules would reduce the deterrent efficacy of the criminal law by announcing which laws would not be vigorously enforced; individual treatment would be sacrificed in order to have uniformity; problems in law enforcement change rapidly (e.g., post-September 11) and rulemaking would inhibit a rapid prosecutorial response to new problems; and adequate rules cannot be devised.[10] Are these arguments persuasive?

F. SELECTIVE ENFORCEMENT

Whether by rules or by ad hoc decisions, prosecutors operating in a world of partial enforcement must somehow choose whom to prosecute. The selection of a certain type of case for emphasis may raise questions of arbitrariness and even equal protection. Understandably, however, courts are reluctant to regulate the traditional discretion of the prosecutor to charge. As Judge Posner has stated:

> A judge in our system does not have the authority to tell prosecutors which crimes to prosecute or when to prosecute them. Prosecutorial discre-

---

10. See generally, Beck, The Administrative Law of Criminal Prosecution: The Development of Prosecutorial Policy, 27 Am. U.L.Rev. 310, 337–80 (1978). See also, Vorenberg, Decent Restraint of Prosecutorial Discretion, 94 Harv.L.Rev. 1521 (1981), which suggests appropriate ways of controlling discretion. Frase, The Decision to File Federal Criminal Charges: A Quantitative Study of Prosecutorial Discretion, 47 U.Chi.L.Rev. 246 (1980), focuses on one United States Attorney's office and documents the tremendous discretion afforded federal prosecutors and the factors they most often consider in exercising it.

tion resides in the executive, not in the judicial, branch, and that discretion, though subject of course to judicial review, is not reviewable for a simple abuse of discretion.

United States v. Giannattasio, 979 F.2d 98 (7th Cir.1992).[11]

1. Emphasis on Career or Dangerous Criminals

It should be no surprise that a disproportionate number of prosecutions are brought against career offenders, members of organized crime, and suspected terrorists. Often prosecutors hunt to bring a charge that will "stick," even if the crime charged might be considered collateral to the central criminal activity of the defendant. The classic example is the successful prosecution of Al Capone for tax violations. Another example is the prosecution of the Muslim student Awadallah in San Diego for lying to the grand jury about knowing some of the 9/11 terrorists (as opposed to taking part in the 9/11 conspiracy).

Does disproportionate enforcement against these defendants violate equal protection of the law? Should a prosecutor be able to tell law enforcement officials to "go after X who I believe is an organized crime official. Check his tax records, his business dealings, everything"? As discussed below, selective prosecution claims are limited to charges based on impermissible motives such as race and religion. Is discriminatory enforcement the only evil that should be cognizable as a selective prosecution claim?

2. Constitutional Limitations

The following case sets forth strict requirements for proving a constitutional claim of selective prosecution.

UNITED STATES v. ARMSTRONG

Supreme Court of the United States, 1996.
517 U.S. 456.

CHIEF JUSTICE REHNQUIST delivered the opinion of the Court.

In this case, we consider the showing necessary for a defendant to be entitled to discovery on a claim that the prosecuting attorney singled him out for prosecution on the basis of his race. We conclude that respondents failed to satisfy the threshold showing: They failed to show that the Government declined to prosecute similarly situated suspects of other races.

In April 1992, respondents were indicted in the United States District Court for the Central District of California on charges of conspiring to possess with intent to distribute more than 50 grams of cocaine base (crack) and conspiring to distribute the same, in violation of 21 U.S.C. §§ 841 and 846, and federal firearms offenses. * * * On seven separate occasions * * * informants had bought a total of 124.3 grams of crack from respondents and witnessed respondents carrying firearms during the sales. The agents searched the hotel room in which the sales were transacted, ar

11. In Imbler v. Pachtman, 424 U.S. 409 (1976), the Court held that a prosecutor has absolute immunity from liability for all claims concerning the initiation of charges and the trying of the case. See also Buckley v. Fitzsimmons, 509 U.S. 259 (1993)(prosecutor entitled to absolute immunity for charging decisions, but receives only qualified immunity for statements to the media and for actions taken during the preliminary investigation of an uncharged crime).

rested respondents Armstrong and Hampton in the room, and found more crack and a loaded gun. The agents later arrested the other respondents as part of the ring.

In response to the indictment, respondents filed a motion for discovery or for dismissal of the indictment, alleging that they were selected for federal prosecution because they are black. In support of their motion, they offered only an affidavit by a "Paralegal Specialist," employed by the Office of the Federal Public Defender representing one of the respondents. The only allegation in the affidavit was that, in every one of the 24 §§ 841 or 846 cases closed by the office during 1991, the defendant was black. Accompanying the affidavit was a "study" listing the 24 defendants, their race, whether they were prosecuted for dealing cocaine as well as crack, and the status of each case.

The Government opposed the discovery motion, arguing, among other things, that there was no evidence or allegation "that the Government has acted unfairly or has prosecuted non-black defendants or failed to prosecute them." The District Court granted the motion. It ordered the Government (1) to provide a list of all cases from the last three years in which the Government charged both cocaine and firearms offenses, (2) to identify the race of the defendants in those cases, (3) to identify what levels of law enforcement were involved in the investigations of those cases, and (4) to explain its criteria for deciding to prosecute those defendants for federal cocaine offenses.

The Government moved for reconsideration of the District Court's discovery order. With this motion it submitted affidavits and other evidence to explain why it had chosen to prosecute respondents and why respondents' study did not support the inference that the Government was singling out blacks for cocaine prosecution. The federal and local agents participating in the case alleged in affidavits that race played no role in their investigation. An Assistant United States Attorney explained in an affidavit that the decision to prosecute met the general criteria for prosecution, because

"there was over 100 grams of cocaine base involved, over twice the threshold necessary for a ten year mandatory minimum sentence; there were multiple sales involving multiple defendants, thereby indicating a fairly substantial crack cocaine ring; ... there were multiple federal firearms violations intertwined with the narcotics trafficking; the overall evidence in the case was extremely strong, including audio and videotapes of defendants; ... and several of the defendants had criminal histories including narcotics and firearms violations."

The Government also submitted sections of a published 1989 Drug Enforcement Administration report which concluded that "large-scale, interstate trafficking networks controlled by Jamaicans, Haitians and Black street gangs dominate the manufacture and distribution of crack."

In response, one of respondents' attorneys submitted an affidavit alleging that an intake coordinator at a drug treatment center had told her that there are "an equal number of caucasian users and dealers to minority users and dealers." Respondents also submitted an affidavit from a criminal defense attorney alleging that in his experience many nonblacks are prosecuted in state court for crack offenses, and a newspaper article reporting that Federal "crack criminals ... are being punished far more severely than if they had been caught with powder cocaine, and almost every single one of them is black," Newton, Harsher Crack Sentences Criticized as Racial Inequity, Los Angeles Times, Nov. 23, 1992, p. 1.

The District Court denied the motion for reconsideration. When the Government indicated it would not comply with the court's discovery order, the court dismissed the case. A divided three-judge panel of the Court of Appeals for the Ninth Circuit reversed, holding that, because of the proof requirements for a selective-prosecution claim, defendants must "provide a colorable basis for believing that 'others similarly situated have not been prosecuted' "to obtain discovery. (Quoting United States v. Wayte, 710 F.2d 1385, 1387 (C.A.9 1983), aff'd, 470 U.S. 598 (1985)). The Court of Appeals voted to rehear the case en banc, and the en banc panel affirmed the District Court's order of dismissal, holding that "a defendant is not required to demonstrate that the government has failed to prosecute others who are similarly situated." We granted certiorari to determine the appropriate standard for discovery for a selective-prosecution claim.

[The Court held that Federal Rule of Criminal Procedure 16 did not mandate disclosure of material supporting a selective prosecution claim. That Rule requires disclosure of documents "material to the preparation of the defendant's defense" and the Court construed that phrase to refer to a defense that was responsive to the government's case-in-chief (e.g., that the defendant is not guilty). A selective prosecution attack was not material to the "defense" in this sense. See the discussion of this aspect of the opinion in Chapter Eight, infra.]

* * *

A selective-prosecution claim is not a defense on the merits to the criminal charge itself, but an independent assertion that the prosecutor has brought the charge for reasons forbidden by the Constitution. Our cases delineating the necessary elements to prove a claim of selective prosecution have taken great pains to explain that the standard is a demanding one. These cases afford a "background presumption" that the showing necessary to obtain discovery should itself be a significant barrier to the litigation of insubstantial claims.

A selective-prosecution claim asks a court to exercise judicial power over a "special province" of the Executive. The Attorney General and United States Attorneys retain broad discretion to enforce the Nation's criminal laws. They have this latitude because they are designated by statute as the President's delegates to help him discharge his constitutional responsibility to "take Care that the Laws be faithfully executed." U.S. Const., Art. II, § 3; see 28 U.S.C. §§ 516, 547. As a result, "the presumption of regularity supports" their prosecutorial decisions and "in the absence of clear evidence to the contrary, courts presume that they have properly discharged their official duties." In the ordinary case, "so long as the prosecutor has probable cause to believe that the accused committed an offense defined by statute, the decision whether or not to prosecute, and what charge to file or bring before a grand jury, generally rests entirely in his discretion." Bordenkircher v. Hayes, 434 U.S. 357, 364 (1978).

Of course, a prosecutor's discretion is "subject to constitutional constraints." One of these constraints, imposed by the equal protection component of the Due Process Clause of the Fifth Amendment, is that the decision whether to prosecute may not be based on "an unjustifiable standard such as race, religion, or other arbitrary classification," Oyler v. Boles, 368 U.S. 448, 456 (1962). A defendant may demonstrate that the administration of a criminal law is "directed so exclusively against a particular class of persons ... with a mind so unequal and oppressive" that the system of prosecution amounts to "a practical denial" of equal protection of the law. Yick Wo v. Hopkins, 118 U.S. 356, 373 (1886).

In order to dispel the presumption that a prosecutor has not violated equal protection, a criminal defendant must present "clear evidence to the contrary." We explained in *Wayte* why courts are "properly hesitant to examine the decision whether to prosecute." Judicial deference to the decisions of these executive officers rests in part on an assessment of the relative competence of prosecutors and courts. "Such factors as the strength of the case, the prosecution's general deterrence value, the Government's enforcement priorities, and the case's relationship to the Government's overall enforcement plan are not readily susceptible to the kind of analysis the courts are competent to undertake." It also stems from a concern not to unnecessarily impair the performance of a core executive constitutional function. "Examining the basis of a prosecution delays the criminal proceeding, threatens to chill law enforcement by subjecting the prosecutor's motives and decisionmaking to outside inquiry, and may undermine prosecutorial effectiveness by revealing the Government's enforcement policy."

The requirements for a selective-prosecution claim draw on ordinary equal protection standards. The claimant must demonstrate that the federal prosecutorial policy had a discriminatory effect and that it was motivated by a discriminatory purpose. To establish a discriminatory effect in a race case, the claimant must show that similarly situated individuals of a different race were not prosecuted. * * *

The similarly situated requirement does not make a selective-prosecution claim impossible to prove. [In Yick Wo v. Hopkins], we invalidated an ordinance, * * * adopted by San Francisco, that prohibited the operation of laundries in wooden buildings. The plaintiff in error successfully demonstrated that the ordinance was applied against Chinese nationals but not against other laundry-shop operators. The authorities had denied the applications of 200 Chinese subjects for permits to operate shops in wooden buildings, but granted the applications of 80 individuals who were not Chinese subjects to operate laundries in wooden buildings "under similar conditions."

* * *

Having reviewed the requirements to prove a selective-prosecution claim, we turn to the showing necessary to obtain discovery in support of such a claim. If discovery is ordered, the Government must assemble from its own files documents which might corroborate or refute the defendant's claim. Discovery thus imposes many of the costs present when the Government must respond to a prima facie case of selective prosecution. It will divert prosecutors' resources and may disclose the Government's prosecutorial strategy. The justifications for a rigorous standard for the elements of a selective-prosecution claim thus require a correspondingly rigorous standard for discovery in aid of such a claim.

The parties, and the Courts of Appeals which have considered the requisite showing to establish entitlement to discovery, describe this showing with a variety of phrases, like "colorable basis," "substantial threshold showing," "substantial and concrete basis," or "reasonable likelihood". However, the many labels for this showing conceal the degree of consensus about the evidence necessary to meet it. The Courts of Appeals "require some evidence tending to show the existence of the essential elements of the defense," discriminatory effect and discriminatory intent. United States v. Berrios, 501 F.2d 1207, 1211 (C.A.2 1974).

In this case we consider what evidence constitutes "some evidence tending to show the existence" of the discriminatory effect element. The Court of Appeals held that a defendant may establish a colorable basis for discriminatory effect without evidence that the Government has failed to prosecute others who are similarly situated to the defendant. We think it was mistaken in this view. The vast majority of the Courts of Appeals require the defendant to produce some evidence that similarly situated defendants of other races could have been prosecuted, but were not, and this requirement is consistent with our equal protection case law. As the three-judge panel explained,"selective prosecution implies that a selection has taken place."

The Court of Appeals reached its decision in part because it started "with the presumption that people of all races commit all types of crimes— not with the premise that any type of crime is the exclusive province of any particular racial or ethnic group." It cited no authority for this proposition, which seems contradicted by the most recent statistics of the United States Sentencing Commission. Those statistics show that: More than 90% of the persons sentenced in 1994 for crack cocaine trafficking were black, United States Sentencing Comm'n, 1994 Annual Report 107 (Table 45); 93.4% of convicted LSD dealers were white,

ibid.; and 91% of those convicted for pornography or prostitution were white, id., at 41 (Table 13). Presumptions at war with presumably reliable statistics have no proper place in the analysis of this issue.

The Court of Appeals also expressed concern about the "evidentiary obstacles defendants face." But all of its sister Circuits that have confronted the issue have required that defendants produce some evidence of differential treatment of similarly situated members of other races or protected classes. In the present case, if the claim of selective prosecution were well founded, it should not have been an insuperable task to prove that persons of other races were being treated differently than respondents. For instance, respondents could have investigated whether similarly situated persons of other races were prosecuted by the State of California, were known to federal law enforcement officers, but were not prosecuted in federal court. We think the required threshold—a credible showing of different treatment of similarly situated persons—adequately balances the Government's interest in vigorous prosecution and the defendant's interest in avoiding selective prosecution.

In the case before us, respondents' "study" did not constitute "some evidence tending to show the existence of the essential elements of" a selective-prosecution claim. The study failed to identify individuals who were not black, could have been prosecuted for the offenses for which respondents were charged, but were not so prosecuted. This omission was not remedied by respondents' evidence in opposition to the Government's motion for reconsideration. The newspaper article, which discussed the discriminatory effect of federal drug sentencing laws, was not relevant to an allegation of discrimination in decisions to prosecute. Respondents' affidavits, which recounted one attorney's conversation with a drug treatment center employee and the experience of another attorney defending drug prosecutions in state court, recounted hearsay and reported personal conclusions based on anecdotal evidence. The judgment of the Court of Appeals is therefore reversed, and the case is remanded for proceedings consistent with this opinion.

[The concurring opinions of Justices Souter, Ginsburg and Breyer are omitted.]

JUSTICE STEVENS, **dissenting**.

* * *

The District Judge's order should be evaluated in light of three circumstances that underscore the need for judicial vigilance over certain types of drug prosecutions. First, the Anti–Drug Abuse Act of 1986 and subsequent legislation established a regime of extremely high penalties for the possession and distribution of so-called "crack" cocaine. Those provisions treat one gram of crack as the equivalent of 100 grams of powder cocaine. The distribution of 50 grams of crack is thus punishable by the same mandatory minimum sentence of 10 years in prison that applies to the distribution of 5,000 grams of powder cocaine. The Sentencing Guidelines extend this ratio to penalty levels above the mandatory minimums: for any given quantity of crack, the guideline range is the same as if the offense had involved 100 times that amount in powder cocaine. These penalties result in sentences for crack offenders that average three to eight times longer than sentences for comparable powder offenders.

Second, the disparity between the treatment of crack cocaine and powder cocaine is matched by the disparity

between the severity of the punishment imposed by federal law and that imposed by state law for the same conduct. For a variety of reasons, often including the absence of mandatory minimums, the existence of parole, and lower baseline penalties, terms of imprisonment for drug offenses tend to be substantially lower in state systems than in the federal system. The difference is especially marked in the case of crack offenses. The majority of States draw no distinction between types of cocaine in their penalty schemes; of those that do, none has established as stark a differential as the Federal Government. For example, if respondent Hampton is found guilty, his federal sentence might be as long as a mandatory life term. Had he been tried in state court, his sentence could have been as short as 12 years, less worktime credits of half that amount.

Finally, it is undisputed that the brunt of the elevated federal penalties falls heavily on blacks. While 65% of the persons who have used crack are white, in 1993 they represented only 4% of the federal offenders convicted of trafficking in crack. Eighty-eight percent of such defendants were black. During the first 18 months of full guideline implementation, the sentencing disparity between black and white defendants grew from preguideline levels: blacks on average received sentences over 40% longer than whites. * * *

The extraordinary severity of the imposed penalties and the troubling racial patterns of enforcement give rise to a special concern about the fairness of charging practices for crack offenses. Evidence tending to prove that black defendants charged with distribution of crack in the Central District of California are prosecuted in federal court, whereas members of other races charged with similar offenses are prosecuted in state court, warrants close scrutiny by the federal judges in that District. In my view, the District Judge, who has sat on both the federal and the state benches in Los Angeles, acted well within her discretion to call for the development of facts that would demonstrate what standards, if any, governed the choice of forum where similarly situated offenders are prosecuted.

Critique of Armstrong

Professor Davis, in Prosecution and Race: The Power and Privilege of Discretion, 67 Fordham L.Rev. 13 (1998), provides the following critique on the intent-based test of selective prosecution set forth by the Court in *Armstrong*:

Like police officers, prosecutors often make decisions that discriminate against African American victims and defendants. These decisions may or may not be intentional or conscious. Although it may be difficult to prove intentional discrimination when it exists, unintentional discrimination poses even greater challenges. Prosecutors may not be aware that the seemingly harmless, reasonable, race-neutral decisions they make every day may have a racially discriminatory impact. This discriminatory impact may occur because of unconscious racism—a phenomenon that plays a powerful role in so many discretionary decisions in the criminal process—and because the lack of power and disadvantaged circumstances of so many African American defendants and victims make it more likely that prosecutors will treat them less well than whites.

If one acknowledges that African Americans experience both disparate and discriminatory treatment in the criminal justice system, the discussion ultimately turns to the issue of blame. Whose fault is it? Who has committed the invidious act or acts that have caused African Americans to experience this discriminatory treatment? It is this intent-focused analysis, sanctioned by the Supreme Court in its equal protection analysis, that has stymied legal challenges to discrimination in the criminal context. Instead of focusing on the harm experienced by African Americans as a result of actions by state actors, the Court has focused on whether the act itself is inherently invidious and whether the actor intended to cause the harm. In addition, the Court has placed the burden of proving intent on the shoulders of the victim. If the victim is unable to prove the actor's bad intent or, in certain contexts, if the actor can establish a nondiscriminatory explanation for his behavior, the Court offers no remedy for the harm experienced by the victim.

The main problem with this intent-focused analysis is that it is backward-looking. Although perhaps adequate in combating straightforward and explicit discrimination as it existed in the past, it is totally deficient as a remedy for the more complex and systemic discrimination that African Americans currently experience. When state actors openly expressed their racist views, it was easy to identify and label the invidious nature of their actions. But today, with some notable exceptions, most racist behavior is not openly expressed. More significantly, some racist behavior is committed unconsciously, and many who engage in this behavior are well-intentioned people who would be appalled by the notion that they would be seen as behaving in a racist or discriminatory manner.

[handwritten margin note: invidious discrimination]

Unconscious racism, although arguably less offensive than purposeful discrimination, is no less harmful. In fact, in many ways it is more perilous because it is often unrecognizable to the victim as well as the perpetrator. And the Court, by focusing on intent rather than harm, has refused to recognize, much less provide a remedy for, this most common and wide-spread form of racism. By focusing on blame rather than injury, the Court serves to satisfy the psychological needs of the uninjured party while leaving the victim without relief.

For another critique of the *Armstrong* standards, see McAdams, Race and Selective Prosecution: Discovering the Pitfalls of *Armstrong*, 73 Chicago–Kent L.Rev. 605 (1998).

Unprosecuted Similar Conduct

In United States v. Parham, 16 F.3d 844 (8th Cir. 1994), the defendants were African–Americans who were convicted of voting more than once in the same Arkansas election. The defendants elicited evidence of numerous voter irregularities attributable to whites that went unprosecuted. These included episodes where African–American disabled or elderly voters were refused assistance while whites were helped, and armed intimidation of African–American voters. While the court found that these acts warranted prosecution, they were held irrelevant to the defendants' selective prosecution claim. This is because the acts by whites were

> not sufficiently similar to the acts of voter fraud for which Parham and Johnson were prosecuted to constitute a prima facie case of selective prosecution. Parham and Johnson were in effect charged with forging names on absentee ballots. They presented no evidence that other's acts of absentee ballot forgery or fraud were tolerated without prosecution. Where a defendant cannot show anyone in a similar situation who was not prosecuted, he has not met the threshold point of showing that there has been selectivity in prosecution.

Judge Heaney dissented in *Parham*, reasoning that the defendant need only establish that unprosecuted crimes are similar, not that they are identical. With whom do you agree? And isn't armed intimidation of voters even a more serious crime than voting more than once? Shouldn't the former crime be prosecuted before the latter?

Selective Prosecution of Gang Activity?

In United States v. Turner, 104 F.3d 1180 (9th Cir.1997), defendants who were members of a street gang were convicted of crack cocaine violations. They claimed selective prosecution and offered the following hypothetical as proof: if the government set up a road block in Beverly Hills, it would end up catching and prosecuting Caucasian criminals. In this case, the government had set up the equivalent of a road block in South Central Los Angeles and so ended up catching and prosecuting African Americans. Thus, the defendants argued that selection of a particular community for a particular enforcement operation constitutes racial discrimination if it is foreseeable that because of the ethnic composition of the community one race will necessarily provide most of the government's targets.

The Court rejected the selective prosecution claim. Judge Noonan found that the hypothetical had "a superficial attraction" but that it was "seriously flawed" because its acceptance would actually harm the minority community. He explained as follows:

> In effect, as applied in this case, the defendants' hypothetical is an argument that the minorities of the inner city of Los Angeles must be denied the protection of law enforcement by the federal government because the likely suspects are overwhelmingly apt to be members of the minority living in that area. The defense is a grave perversion of proper sensitivity to the civil liberty of minorities. If any policy of government had a racially discriminatory effect, it would be to deny law enforcement on the grounds of a specious claim of racial discrimination.

Example of a Case in Which Discovery Was Ordered on a Selective Prosecution Claim

United States v. Jones, 159 F.3d 969 (6th Cir.1998), is one of the rare cases in which discovery was ordered to permit investigation of a selective prosecution claim, after the defendant was convicted of drugs and weapons offenses. The shocking facts were related by the court as follows:

> Jones argues on appeal that he was prosecuted based on his race, citing to the Government's decision to prosecute him in federal court instead of state court and the egregious and unprofessional conduct of the arresting local law enforcement officers, Kerry Nelson and Terry Spence.
>
> The conduct of officers Nelson and Spence was undeniably shameful. Prior to the planned arrest of Jones and his wife, the two officers had t-shirts made with Jones's picture emblazoned on the front accompanied by the printed words, "See ya, wouldn't want to be ya" above the picture, and below, "going back to prison." On the back of the t-shirts appeared a picture of Jones's wife, a co-defendant, with the words, "wait on me, Slow, [Jones' nickname was "Slow Motion"] I am coming, too." The two officers were wearing the t-shirts when they arrested Jones in August of 1995. Over one year later, while on a Caribbean cruise, Officer Spence mailed a postcard purchased in Jamaica to Jones while he was in custody awaiting trial. Jones regards Spence's mailing of the postcard, that pictured a black woman with a basket of bananas on her head, as a racial insult. On the postcard, postmarked from Cozumel, Mexico on October 24, 1996, appeared the following handwritten message:
>
> > Slow Motion. What's up? Haven't talked to you since you were in court and lost all your motions. Sorry, but life goes on. Just wanted to drop you a line and let you know that Cozumel, Mexico is beautiful. I'm on vacation and I'll be back Monday for trial, and chances are good you're going to jail for a long time. See ya, Officer Spence.

Spence testified that he sent the postcard to relieve "stress I was feeling while I was on the cruise." Regarding the t-shirts, Spence explained that "It was just—I took pride in arresting [Jones]." Nelson also testified that he wore the t-shirt to demonstrate "a great deal of pride in Mr. Jones's arrest."

In addition, there was testimony at the hearing with respect to Jones's claim that local law enforcement agents improperly referred his case for federal prosecution based on his race. The testimony showed that the Murfreesboro Police Department had referred fourteen defendants, including Jones and his Caucasian co-defendant, Donnie Billings, for federal prosecution in the preceding five years. Of those fourteen defendants, four were African–American, two were Columbian, two were Lebanese, one was Israeli and five were Caucasian. Of the cases referred for federal prosecution in the preceding five years, however, only Jones's and Billings's prosecutions involved crack cocaine. Further, Jones presented evidence of eight non-African–American defendants prosecuted for crack cocaine offenses who were not referred for federal prosecution.

The court found that Jones had established a prima facie case of discriminatory intent, which is the first part of the intent/impact test imposed by *Armstrong*. The court explained as follows:

> The conduct of Officers Spence and Nelson was not only outrageous and unprofessional, but also racially motivated. Although there were three individuals involved in this case (Jones, his wife and co-defendant Donnie Billings), only Jones and his wife were African–American. The officers made t-shirts for only those two. Moreover, any argument premised on the fact that Billings was not as involved in the crime as Jones fails, because Jones's wife was no more involved than Billings and yet a t-shirt was made with her picture. We also reject the officers' purported reason for making the t-shirts—that they took pride in the arrests. For some reason, this pride manifested itself in a way that the department had never done before, because this was the first time that such t-shirts were present at an arrest or a search scene.

> Additionally, Spence's mailing of the postcard evidences racial animus. Even if we were to discount the obvious impropriety of mailing a postcard, any postcard, to a criminal defendant awaiting trial, we could not so easily disregard the nature of the postcard mailed to Jones. The officer sent to an African–American man a postcard of an African–American woman with bananas on her head, and did not choose any other available postcards such as the sunset or the beach. * * * Given the history of racial stereotypes against African–Americans and the prevalent one of African–Americans as animals or monkeys, it is a reasonable—perhaps even an obvious—conclusion that Spence intended the racial insult that Jones perceived in receiving the postcard. In addition, Officer Spence's testimony that he sent the postcard to relieve stress is irrational, if not incredulous. It is far more likely that Spence sent the postcard to disparage Jones and his wife on the basis of their race. Accordingly, we believe that Jones has made the requisite showing of discriminatory intent.

The court found, however, that there was not enough evidence of discriminatory impact to require dismissal of the indictment. Yet there was enough to justify further discovery.

> The second prong of a selective prosecution claim—discriminatory effect—creates a greater challenge for Jones. As we have stated, to establish discriminatory effect, a defendant must show that similarly situated individuals of a different race were not similarly prosecuted. The evidence that Jones has presented to this point does not establish that law enforcement failed to refer similarly situated non-African–Americans for federal prosecu-

tion. Accordingly, Jones thus far has not established a prima facie case of discriminatory effect.

In *Armstrong*, the Supreme Court stated that in order for a defendant to obtain discovery in a selective prosecution case, there must be a showing of "some evidence tending to show the existence of the essential elements of the defense, discriminatory effect and discriminatory intent." As we have stated, Jones has established a showing of discriminatory intent. With respect to discriminatory effect, we believe that Jones has set forth some evidence "tending to show the existence of discriminatory effect," despite the fact that Jones was unable to establish a prima facie case of discriminatory effect on the merits of his selective prosecution claim. Obviously, a defendant need not prove his case in order to justify discovery on an issue.

No dismissal but order for further discovery.

Jones has presented evidence that law enforcement referred only him and his co-defendant Billings for a federal prosecution that involved crack cocaine, and failed to refer for federal prosecution eight non-African–Americans who were arrested and prosecuted for crack cocaine. The harshness of the crack cocaine guidelines in federal court is certainly a factor that may have been considered in referring defendants for federal prosecution. The fact that law enforcement never considered foregoing the prosecution of Billings, Jones's white co-defendant, in federal court does not change our analysis. It would have been beyond foolish for law enforcement to have done such a thing, considering that Jones's and Billings's cases involved the same events.

Accordingly, Jones has set forth "some evidence" tending to show the existence of discriminatory effect that warrants discovery on his selective prosecution claim. Thus, the district court abused its discretion in denying Jones's request for discovery. We therefore remand the case to the district court to compel discovery on Jones's selective prosecution claim. If Jones is able to obtain evidence that establishes a prima facie case of discriminatory effect, Jones may renew his motion to dismiss the indictment.

See also United States v. Bass, 266 F.3d 532 (6th Cir. 2001) (the stark discriminatory effect of the federal death penalty protocol, when coupled with official statements of members of the Department of Justice recognizing the possibility of intentional discrimination, constituted at least "some evidence" tending to show that race played a role in deciding which defendants to charge with death-eligible offenses; district court's order for discovery on the African–American defendant's selective prosecution claim in a death penalty case was therefore a proper exercise of discretion).

3. Choice of Forum

In the American system of dual sovereignty, the same criminal conduct is often prosecutable under either federal or state law. It is also possible for the choice of forum to be outcome-determinative. For example, in drug cases, the Federal Sentencing Guidelines generally provide for much harsher sentences than could be given for the same conduct in a state prosecution. Also, federal law has more and harsher mandatory minimum sentences than exist under state law. Finally, as discussed in Chapter One, state constitutions may provide more procedural protections to defendants than the federal constitution. Suppose that the defendant can show that a federal prosecution was brought in order to

No guarantee to leniency unless disc. motive is reason for harsh penalty

trigger the harsher sentences under the Guidelines, or to avoid state constitutional mandates. However, unlike in *Jones, supra,* there is no allegation that the decision was based on racial or other discriminatory grounds. Is the defendant entitled to relief?

A typical response to a challenge to the prosecutor's choice of forum is found in United States v. Jacobs, 4 F.3d 603 (8th Cir.1993), a case in which the defendant would have received probation had he been convicted on state charges, but instead received a five-year prison sentence after being convicted in federal court. As the court noted:

> Prosecutors have broad discretion in making prosecutive decisions. So long as the prosecutor has probable cause to believe that the accused committed an offense defined by statute, the decision whether or not to prosecute, and what charge to file, generally rests entirely in his discretion. In exercising this discretion, the prosecutor may take into account the penalties available upon conviction. The prosecutor may not, of course, base the decision to prosecute upon impermissible factors such as race, religion, or other arbitrary and unjustifiable classifications. Likewise the prosecutor may not file charges out of vindictiveness nor in retaliation for a defendant's exercise of legal rights.
>
> The fact that the federal government prosecutes a federal crime in a federal court that could have been or has been prosecuted as a state crime in a state court does not itself violate due process. Choice of forum lies within the realm of prosecutorial discretion.

See also United States v. Dockery, 965 F.2d 1112 (D.C.Cir.1992) (it was permissible for the U.S. Attorney in the District of Columbia to terminate prosecutions in the D.C. Superior Court and reinstitute them in the U.S. District Court a block away to take advantage of the sterner penalties set by the federal sentencing law and Sentencing Guidelines; defendant received a ten-year minimum sentence, which would have been 1–5 years in the Superior Court); United States v. Williams, 963 F.2d 1337 (10th Cir.1992)(defendant received 20 years under Federal Guidelines, and would have received 5 years under state law: "prosecution in a federal rather than a state court does not violate due process despite the absence of guidelines for such referral"); United States v. Ucciferri, 960 F.2d 953 (11th Cir.1992)(it was irrelevant that a federal prosecution was motivated by a desire to avoid more rigorous state constitutional protections).

Forum selection is not dispositive of selective enforcement unless proof of purposeful discriminatory motive plus lack of enforcement in other similar circ.

Of course, if the defendant can show that his case was referred to the federal system because of some racial, gender, or religious animus, then the referral will be unconstitutional. Thus, in United States v. Jones, supra, Jones was allowed discovery on his claim that his case was referred to federal authorities as the result of racial discrimination.

The above cases indicate that the courts are loathe to intrude into charging decisions, to the point that a significant disparity in outcome between the federal and state systems is tolerated. If consistency and fairness are legitimate concerns, is there another way to reach these goals without intruding into charging decisions?

4. Choice of Crime

What if two criminal statutes cover the same conduct—does the prosecutor have the discretion to charge under the statute resulting in the longer prison sentence? In United States v. Batchelder, 442 U.S. 114 (1979), Justice Marshall wrote for the Court as it held that a defendant who was convicted of receiving a firearm that had traveled in interstate commerce could be sentenced to five years' imprisonment, the maximum term under the statute, and that he was not entitled to be sentenced under another statute that punished felons for transporting firearms with a maximum penalty of two years. Justice Marshall reasoned that a wrongdoer has notice that more than one statute covers his conduct. Thus, the fact that conduct violates two statutes does not require a prosecution under the more lenient of them. The Court emphasized the deference due to the prosecutor in making a charging decision and reiterated that a defendant's sole complaint is against invidious discrimination.

Choice of charge is not prohibited unless discriminatory based on similar circ

Justice Marshall observed that a trial judge has discretion to make sentencing choices after a prosecution is brought and a conviction is obtained. But, under sentencing guidelines, those choices might be rather narrowly constrained today (see Chapter Eleven). Thus, the charging decision may be determinative of sentence except for a modest choice by the sentencing judge within a guidelines range. Should prosecutorial discretion be more circumscribed when judicial discretion in sentencing is reduced? If the same conduct is punishable under two or more statutes and there are no regulations governing the prosecutor's choice, how can it be "just" for a court to impose a sentence for whatever offense the prosecutor has chosen?

Prosecutors may be limited in their ability to charge a defendant in a certain way as punishment for a defendant's exercise of constitutional rights. The subject of vindictive prosecutions is considered in Chapter Twelve, infra.

V. THE GRAND JURY

The American criminal justice system, like the American political system, has checks and balances to prevent against too much centralized authority being placed in the hands of the executive. In some instances, depending on the jurisdiction and the seriousness of the crime, the grand jury operates as a check on the prosecutor's decision to charge. In other instances, the preliminary hearing serves this function. In some rare instances, both checks are available. Where a minor offense is charged, it is possible that no pretrial screening procedure will be utilized. This section will focus on the checks that exist and how they operate.

A. BACKGROUND ON THE GRAND JURY

Professor Younger, in The People's Panel, provides a good summary of the history and purpose of the grand jury:

Accusors

> The Grand Jury originated in England as the accusing body in the administration of criminal justice. At the Assize of Clarendon, in 1166, Henry II provided that twelve knights or twelve "good and lawful men" of every hundred and four lawful men of every will disclose under oath the names of those in the community believed guilty of criminal offenses. Members of this inquisitorial body were obliged to present to the judge sworn accusations against all suspected offenders. Unlike petit juries, grand juries were not to pass upon guilt or innocence but were to decide only whether an individual should be brought to trial. At first all accusations

originated with the members of the inquest themselves, but gradually the juries came to consider accusations made by outsiders as well. The jurors then heard only witnesses against the accused and, if they were convinced that there were grounds for trial, indicted him. They also passed upon indictments laid before them by crown prosecutors, returning a "true bill" if they found the accusation true or a "no bill" if they found it false. However, the juries never lost their power to accuse on their own knowledge. This they did by making a presentment to the court. The presentment represented an accusation on the jury's own initiative while an indictment represented a charge that originated outside the membership. Under their power of presentment English grand juries could and did investigate any matter that appeared to them to involve a violation of the law.

Slowly the character of the institution changed. Originally an important instrument of the Crown, it gradually became instead a strong independent power guarding the rights of the English people. The juries did not have to divulge to the court the evidence upon which they acted, and when royal officials abused their authority, they intervened to protect citizens from unfounded accusations. With the growth of royal absolutism in England the inquests became highly prized as defenders of the liberties of the people and shields against royal persecution. The refusal, in 1681, of a grand jury to indict Lord Shaftesbury on charges of treason, in spite of the insistence of Charles II, led Englishmen to look upon the grand jury system with increased respect. John Somers, Lord Chancellor of England, in his tract The Security of Englishmen's Lives, noted that "Grand juries are our only security, in as much as our lives cannot be drawn into jeopardy by all the malicious crafts of the devil, unless such a number of our honest countrymen shall be satisfied in the truth of the accusations." By the end of the seventeenth century the grand jury had become an important bulwark of the rights and privileges of English citizens.

Hafetz and Pellettieri, in Time to Reform the Grand Jury, The Champion, Jan. 1999 at 12, provide a helpful discussion of the historical use of the grand jury in America:

The first grand jury in the American Colonies sat in 1635. * * * It is not clear to what extent the grand jury consistently worked in its dual capacity to both investigate and screen cases but, as in England, the general tone was set by a few prominent cases. Most notable was that of John Peter Zenger, a newspaper publisher who was critical of the colonial New York Governor. In 1754, a grand jury refused to indict him for libel despite the existence of adequate supporting evidence under the law. * * * In Boston, * * * grand juries refused to indict those who led riots in protest against the Stamp Act, while indicting British soldiers for crimes against the colonists. Thus, the popular image of the grand jury that had developed in England was bolstered in America during the Revolutionary Period. As a result, there was very little resistance to its inclusion in the Bill of Rights.

So as a historical matter, the grand jury served two major functions. On one hand, it was a "buffer" protecting citizens from unjust prosecution by the state. On the other hand, it served an enforcement function by investigating incidents or offenses that the grand jurors thought suspicious. The buffer function of the grand jury was considered so fundamental that it was included in the Bill of Rights. The Fifth Amendment states in relevant part:

> No person shall be held to answer for a capital, or otherwise infamous crime, unless on a presentment or indictment of a Grand Jury, except in cases arising in the land or naval forces, or in the Militia, when in actual service in time of War or public danger; * * *.

The Supreme Court has stated that the grand jury's dual historic functions "survive to this day. Its responsibilities continue to include both the determination whether there is probable cause to believe a crime has been committed and the protection of citizens against unfounded criminal prosecutions." United States v. Calandra, 414 U.S. 338 (1974).

Many observers, however, see the modern grand jury as performing only the first (prosecutorial) function and ignoring the second (protective) function. For example, Hafetz and Pellettieri conclude that

> whatever its historic antecedents, the grand jury has long ceased to function as an independent entity acting both as shield for the citizenry as well as sword for the prosecutor. * * * [T]he grand jury functions as an investigative tool of the prosecutor. Employing the power of compulsory process in a secret proceeding the prosecutor investigates and determines with virtually no check by the grand jury who gets indicted and for what.

See also United States v. Marcucci, 299 F.3d 1156 (9th Cir. 2002) ("The history of independence of the grand jury as an indicting body is mixed. Refusals to indict have almost always been as much political as principled.").

As you read the materials in this Chapter, consider whether the assessment of the grand jury as only a tool for the prosecutor is correct, and if so, whether reforms can be instituted to return the grand jury to its role as protector of citizens from unfounded prosecutions.

A Right Not Incorporated

Unlike most other provisions of the Bill of Rights examined thus far, the right to a grand jury indictment does not extend to defendants accused of state crimes. In Hurtado v. California, 110 U.S. 516 (1884), the Supreme Court held that the right to a grand jury indictment is not incorporated in the Due Process Clause of the Fourteenth Amendment. Today, slightly less than half the states require prosecution by indictment for serious crimes as a matter of state constitutional or statutory law. The majority of the states use the alternatives of preliminary hearing and the filing of an information, methods of charging discussed later in this Chapter.

What Is an Infamous Crime?

The Fifth Amendment requires a grand jury indictment for the prosecution of an "infamous crime". Courts have held that a crime is "infamous" only if it can result in either hard labor or imprisonment in a penitentiary. Ex parte Wilson, 114 U.S. 417 (1885). Thus, the court in United States v. Armored Transport, Inc., 629 F.2d 1313 (9th Cir.1980), held that indictment was not constitutionally required to charge a corporation with an antitrust felony.

Because a corporation is subject only to a fine and a fine is not an infamous punishment, no indictment was required. See also United States v. Colt, 126 F.3d 981 (7th Cir.1997) (no right to grand jury indictment where statute authorized imprisonment in a federal prison camp, but not in a federal penitentiary: "The distinction between penitentiaries and other places of imprisonment survives in today's federal prison system. * * * Only eight of the Bureau of Prisons' institutions are designated as U.S. Penitentiaries, which feature the highest security and the closest control of prisoner actions.").

How the Grand Jury Works

The court in In re Motions of Dow Jones & Co., 142 F.3d 496 (D.C.Cir.1998), provided this summary of the operation of the grand jury:

> Grand juries summon witnesses and documents with subpoenas. Witnesses, including custodians of documents, report on the scheduled date not to a courtroom, but to a hallway outside the room where the grand jury is sitting. The witness must enter the grand jury room alone, without his or her lawyer. No judge presides and none is present. See Beale et al., Grand Jury Law and Practice § 4.10, at 4–44 (2d ed.1997). Inside the grand jury room are sixteen to twenty-three grand jurors, one or more prosecuting attorneys, and a court reporter. 18 U.S.C. § 3321; Fed.R.Crim.P. 6. The witness is sworn, and questioning commences, all to the end of determining whether "there is adequate basis for bringing a criminal charge." United States v. Williams, 504 U.S. 36 (1992). Other than witnesses, each person present in the grand jury room or otherwise assisting the prosecutor is forbidden from disclosing matters occurring before the grand jury, Fed. R.Crim.P. 6.

The court explained judicial oversight of the grand jury in the following paragraph:

> Although the grand jury normally operates, of course, in the courthouse and under judicial auspices, its institutional relationship with the Judicial Branch has traditionally been, so to speak, at arm's length. Still, at many points, from service of the subpoena through the completion of the witness's grand jury appearance, judicial proceedings relating to the grand jury may take place. The judge may be called upon to decide a witness's motion to postpone the date of testimony or to quash the subpoena. If a witness refuses to answer questions on the basis of a testimonial privilege, such as attorney-client or husband-wife, the grand jury may seek a court order compelling the witness to answer. This may be done forthwith, through an oral presentation to the court, or upon the filing of pleadings, followed by a hearing. A hearing will also be needed if a witness asserts his or her privilege against self-incrimination, and the prosecutor seeks an order from the court granting the witness immunity. See 18 U.S.C. § 6003(a).

B. THE CHARGE OF THE GRAND JURY

The following model instructions to the grand jury for New Jersey provide a useful introduction to the work of the grand jury and the expectations that the community has for this body. The charge is given by the judge who empanels and supervises the grand jury.

MODEL GRAND JURY CHARGE

* * *

Citizens in general have only a vague idea of what a grand jury is and what its functions are. Since you are now members of the grand jury * * * you should be clear as to the functions you fulfill and the responsibilities placed upon you under our law. The term "grand" jury is sometimes misunderstood. It must be differentiated from the term "petit" jury. Both expressions are French in origin. "Grand" means large; "petit" means small. The terms refer to the size of membership of each jury—not the importance of the respective functions. Both juries—grand and petit—are essential to our system of justice, although their size and function differ. The grand jury is composed of 23 members; the petit or trial jury is composed of 12 members.[12]

The function of the grand jury is not to determine whether someone is guilty or not guilty of a crime—that is the responsibility of a petit jury. Rather, the primary function of the grand jury is to make a determination whether there is probable cause to believe that a crime was committed and that the accused committed it. While I will shortly define your obligations in greater detail, suffice it to say at this point that the grand jury serves as a screening mechanism to protect citizens from having to respond to unfounded charges. * * *

As I have noted, your principal function will be to consider alleged violations of the criminal law. You will determine whether or not an indictment should be returned against a person accused of violating the law. Under our system of justice, it is not enough that someone simply accuses another of committing a crime. After the accusation and before the person is made to stand trial on the charge, there must be an inquiry made by a grand jury to determine whether there is a basis for the charge. If the grand jury determines that there is an adequate basis for the charge, it votes to return an indictment against the accused.[13] An indictment is a formal document brought in the name of the State * * *, naming the accused as defendant and setting forth in writing the specific date and place of the alleged offense; the name of the alleged victim; the facts

---

12. The federal system requires 16 to 23 grand jurors. Fed.R.Crim.P. 6(a). Other jurisdictions establish different numerical requirements for their grand juries. See, e.g., § 19.2–195 of the Code of Virginia.

When you examine the right to jury trial in Chapter Ten, you will see that more federal grand jurors are required than petit jurors; yet, the federal grand jury need not be unanimous, although the trial jury must be. Why would there be more grand jurors than petit jurors? Virginia provides for fewer grand jurors than petit jurors and still does not require unanimity among grand jurors. What does size tell you, if anything, about the role the grand jury is to play? What does the absence of a unanimity requirement tell you about the grand jury?

In most places, the grand jury is drawn from the same pool as the petit jury, as under the Jury Selection and Service Act of 1968, 28 U.S.C.A. § 1861 et seq. But in states like Virginia, random selection of trial jurors is required (with voting and other lists to be used)—see

Va.Code § 8.01–345—whereas grand jurors are selected differently.

13. Some states include an express instruction that grand jurors have the authority to nullify, that is, to refuse to indict even though the quantum of proof is sufficient.

The recommended federal instruction provides that "you *should* vote to indict where the evidence is sufficiently strong to warrant a reasonable person's believing that the accused is probably guilty or the crime charged." In United States v. Marcucci, 299 F.3d 1156 (9th Cir. 2002), the defendants argued that they had a constitutional right to have the grand jury instructed that it need not return an indictment even if it finds probable cause. The court rejected the argument, noting that the use of the word "should" in the standard instruction implies discretion not to return an indictment, and defendants had no right to a specific instruction that grand jurors could nullify the pertinent criminal laws.

and circumstances making the alleged conduct criminal and the specific section of the criminal statutes of this state violated by that alleged conduct. If the grand jury decides that there is not an adequate basis for the charge it votes not to return an indictment or, in legal parlance, "no bills" the charge.

Whether or not there is an adequate basis shown for an indictment is known in legal language as "probable cause." "Probable cause" is not a technical concept. It has a practical meaning. Probable cause exists where the evidence presented is sufficient to lead a reasonable person to believe that a crime has been committed and that the accused committed it. Again, be clear that your function is not to decide beyond a reasonable doubt whether the evidence presented indicates that the accused committed a crime. A full-blown trial is not conducted before you; the technical rules of evidence do not apply; lawyers for the accused are not present to present a defense; the accused and any witnesses he may produce at a trial are generally not heard. In short, an indictment is merely the mechanism by which the criminal trial process is commenced. What you have to decide, based on what is presented to you, is whether there is reasonable ground to believe that a crime has been committed and that the accused committed it. If you do not believe that to be so you should vote against returning an indictment.[14]

We have thus far limited our consideration of your function to criminal charges—to deciding whether or not to indict a person. But since the grand jury is that independent investigative body which represents the public concern of the community, you may also inquire into matters which, while not strictly of a criminal nature, still have overtones of wrongdoing. You may become aware of official acts or omissions which fall short of criminal conduct and yet those acts or omissions are not in the public interest. It is certainly in the public interest that such conduct be revealed in an effective, well-considered manner. To investigate such matters you have those broad, comprehensive and independent powers I have previously alluded to. If you feel, after a well considered investigation, that some problem of public concern or some aspect of public business or some evil ought to be brought to the attention of the general populace you may do so by way of a presentment. A presentment, then, is a formal document, presented by you to the public in which you set forth your findings as to some problem in public affairs or public concern or derelictions in duty of public officers.

A presentment requires the exercise of sensitive judgment on your part. It involves serious matters and may not be returned lightly. It cannot be used to single out persons in private or unofficial positions to impugn their motives or hold them up to scorn. A presentment has to do with matters of public concern, not idle curiosity. If there is a problem of which the public should be aware and if the problem is caused in whole or in part by the noncriminal misconduct of a public official that individual may be named and indeed criticized. But before

---

14. Since a grand jury indictment often will result in the arrest of the defendant, probable cause is a constitutional minimum. The grand jury is treated as though it were an independent magistrate, and no further finding of probable cause is necessary after the arrest is made to justify custody. In some jurisdictions, such as in federal courts, the grand jury is told to decide whether the evidence would warrant conviction by a reasonable juror. It is unclear whether the difference has an impact on grand jury deliberations. The difference in quantum of proof, if any, clearly has no effect on a reviewing court, because there is generally no appellate review of the sufficiency of the evidence before a grand jury. Costello v. United States, 350 U.S. 359 (1956).

such a presentment is voted you must be satisfied that the proof of such wrongdoing is conclusive for once the presentment is made public there is no reversing its effect. And so as a matter of fundamental fairness a presentment naming and censuring a specific individual in a position affected with a public interest will not be made public, after being handed up, until the assignment judge obtains and reviews the full record of the testimony and exhibits and determines that sufficient evidence has been presented to support such charges.[15]

With respect to both indictments and presentments, the proofs respecting the alleged offense or public condition will be presented to you in the grand jury room in the form of witnesses or documentation. For the orderliness of the proceeding the matters will be presented and the witnesses called, in the usual case, by the prosecuting attorney. If, after hearing those witnesses called you feel that you wish to hear from additional witnesses before deciding whether or not there is an adequate basis for an indictment or a presentment you have the right to ask the prosecutor to subpoena them and if he refuses you may request the assistance of the assignment judge.

As I have said, the prosecuting attorney will present the various matters to you for your consideration. But understand clearly that the grand jury is an independent legal institution. It is not the agent of the prosecutor. It functions under our Constitution as the representative of the community with its own separate and distinct powers. It may investigate matters of a criminal nature of which its members may be aware even though not presented by the prosecutor. The same is true with respect to a presentment. The prosecutor, as a lawyer, is available to advise you on legal questions and you should freely call upon him for such legal advice—as you may the Court if you deem it necessary. You may, if you wish, ask the prosecutor for his opinion as to the sufficiency or insufficiency of the evidence. However, the prosecutor is not the one who decides whether to indict or not, or whether to return a presentment or not.

The prosecutor is not entitled to be present during your discussions. If during your discussion you do not want the prosecutor present you may ask him to leave the room and he must comply. Such requests are requests of the grand jury not individual jurors, and are to be determined by a majority of the jurors present.

It should be obvious that because of the sensitive nature of the matters which may come before you, these proceedings must be conducted in complete confidence. It would be dereliction of your duty and a violation of your oath were you ever to discuss with anyone outside the grand jury room what you may have heard while there. Untold and irreversible harm could be done to individual reputations were it otherwise. Remember, one of the prime functions of a grand jury is to protect the good name of individuals from unfounded charges.

---

15. The word presentment is used in different ways. In New Jersey it means a report, not an indictment. In Virginia, "[a] presentment is a written accusation of crime prepared and returned by a grand jury from their knowledge or observation; without any bill of indictment laid before them." Va.Code § 19.2–216.

The idea of reports, not formal charges, by grand juries can be troublesome. When the reports criticize particular individuals, who have difficulty responding in an effective way, courts are most troubled. A federal statute grants individuals criticized in a report the opportunity to publish an official response. 18 U.S.C.A. § 3333(c). But that may not be nearly as powerful as the charge by the grand jury.

Therefore, all your deliberations and discussions must take place in the grand jury room while you are in session. It is wrong for jurors to confer or deliberate together privately or by telephone concerning grand jury matters outside the grand jury room. A grand jury must confer together and act as a body. Your deliberations must likewise be kept secret. Each juror has the right to expect that his or her communications with fellow jurors during deliberations will remain confidential. There must be the utmost freedom of expression and debate in the grand jury room uninhibited by fear on the part of any juror that his views or expressions will be revealed or "leaked" outside of the grand jury room.

If, during your service, anyone should attempt to influence you in the performance of your duties, it would be an unquestionable violation of the law on the part of that person. Bring any such conduct to my attention immediately. Such breach will be dealt with by me expeditiously.

* * *

Any indictments you vote to return shall be handed up to me as assignment judge in open court. If you vote not to indict, that is "no bill" a matter, that document should immediately be signed by your foreman and returned to the Court the same day it is voted upon so that the individual, if in custody on that pending charge, may be immediately released. If you decide to return a present-ment your foreman shall notify me ahead of time so that I may arrange to be present to receive it.

Now that you understand what is required of you we will ask the clerk to call the roll and administer to you your oath as grand jurors.

C. THE PROCEDURES OF THE GRAND JURY

The Federal Rule illustrates typical procedures of the grand jury.

FEDERAL RULES OF CRIMINAL PROCEDURE
Rule 6
The Grand Jury

(a) Summoning a Grand Jury.

(1) In General. When the public interest so requires, the court must order that one or more grand juries be summoned. A grand jury must have 16 to 23 members, and the court must order that enough legally qualified persons be summoned to meet this requirement.

* * *

(b) Objections to the Grand Jury or to a Grand Juror.

(1) Challenges. Either the government or a defendant may challenge the grand jury on the ground that it was not lawfully drawn, summoned, or selected, and may challenge an individual juror on the ground that the juror is not legally qualified.

(2) Motion to Dismiss. A party may move to dismiss the indictment based on an objection to the grand jury or on an individual juror's lack of legal qualification, unless the court has previously ruled on the same objection under Rule 6(b)(1). * * * The Court must not dismiss the indictment on the ground that a grand juror was not legally qualified if the record shows that at least 12 qualified jurors concurred in the indictment.[16]

(c) Foreperson and Deputy Foreperson. The court will appoint one juror as the foreperson and another as the deputy foreperson. In the foreperson's absence, the deputy foreperson will act as the foreperson. The foreperson may administer oaths and affirmations and will sign all indictments. The foreperson—or another juror designated by the foreperson—will record the number of jurors concurring in every indictment and will file the record with the clerk, but the record may not be made public unless the court so orders.

(d) Who May Be Present.

(1) While the Grand Jury Is in Session. The following persons may be present while the grand jury is in session: attorneys for the government,[17] the witness being questioned, interpreters when needed, and a court reporter or an operator of a recording device.

(2) During Deliberations and Voting. No person other than the jurors, and any interpreter needed to assist a hearing-impaired or speech-impaired juror, may be present while the grand jury is deliberating or voting.[18]

(e) Recording and Disclosure of Proceedings.

16. Because as many as 11 grand jurors could be disqualified without invalidating an indictment (so long as 12 remaining jurors vote to indict), such challenges rarely succeed. Most jurisdictions do not allow challenge to the bias of a grand jury, although some statutes and rules do allow particular forms of challenge. See, e.g., Me.R.Crim.P. 6(b). The Supreme Court has not ruled on whether an indictment by a biased grand jury is fundamentally unfair. It did not reach the question in Beck v. Washington, 369 U.S. 541 (1962). The fact that a state charges someone through a grand jury, which supposedly is an independent, impartial group of citizens, may enhance the significance of the charge. If so, should the grand jury at least have to have the votes of the designated number of unbiased jurors to charge an offense?

Most courts probably would not entertain a claim that a grand jury was influenced improperly by pre-trial publicity. See People ex rel. Sears v. Romiti, 50 Ill.2d 51, 277 N.E.2d 705 (1971). The reason is that grand jurors, unlike petit jurors, are allowed to consider inadmissible evidence and other inflammatory material that would be the subject of preindictment publicity. See LaFave and Israel, Criminal Procedure § 15.4(g)(2d ed.West 1992)(concluding that preindictment publicity claims are all but "inevitably doomed as a matter of law").

17. Note that there is no right to have defense counsel present, even when the target testifies before the grand jury. See Gollaher v. United States, 419 F.2d 520 (9th Cir.1969) Usually the prosecutor may be present when evidence is presented. But see Va.R.Crim.P. 3A:6(b). Virginia gives the prosecutor a greater

opportunity to be present before special grand juries. Va.Code § 19.2–210.

In United States v. Mechanik, 475 U.S. 66 (1986), the Supreme Court held that a violation of Rule 6(d) that occurred when two agents testified in tandem before a grand jury was harmless error that had no effect on the outcome of the trial. Justice O'Connor, joined by Justices Brennan and Blackmun, concurred in the judgment, reasoning that a Rule 6 violation affects the grand jury proceeding rather than the trial, and that dismissal of the indictment is an appropriate remedy "if it is established that the violation substantially influenced the grand jury's decision to indict, or if there is grave doubt as to whether it had such effect." Justice Marshall dissented.

Justice Kennedy, writing for the Court, cited *Mechanik* in Bank of Nova Scotia v. United States, 487 U.S. 250 (1988), which held that a federal court may not invoke its supervisory power to dismiss an indictment where the error was harmless. The Court concluded that a district court exceeds its powers in dismissing an indictment for prosecutorial misconduct not prejudicial to the defendant. For nonconstitutional errors, the Court adopted the standard of prejudice suggested by Justice O'Connor in her *Mechanik* concurrence.

18. If there is testimony by the prosecutor, some decisions say that the prosecutor can no longer remain as the legal advisor to the grand jury. See, e.g., United States v. Treadway, 445 F.Supp. 959 (N.D.Tex.1978). Does this make sense when a grand juror can testify and remain part of the grand jury?

(1) Recording of Proceedings. Except while the grand jury is deliberating or voting, all proceedings must be recorded by a court reporter or by a suitable recording device.[19] But the validity of a prosecution is not affected by the unintentional failure to make a recording. Unless the court orders otherwise, an attorney for the government will retain control of the recording, the reporter's notes, and any transcript prepared from those notes.

(2) Secrecy.

(A) No obligation of secrecy may be imposed on any person except in accordance with Rule 6(e)(2)(B).

(B) Unless these rules provide otherwise, the following persons must not disclose a matter occurring before the grand jury:

(i) a grand juror;

(ii) an interpreter;

(iii) a court reporter;

(iv) an operator of a recording device;

(v) a person who transcribes recorded testimony;

(vi) an attorney for the government; or

(vii) a person to whom disclosure is made under 6(e)(3)(A)(ii) or (iii).

(3) Exceptions.—

(A) Disclosure of a grand-jury matter—other than the grand jury's deliberations or any grand juror's vote—may be made to:

(i) an attorney for the government for use in performing that attorney's duty;

(ii) any government personnel—including those of a state or state subdivision or of an Indian tribe—that an attorney for the government considers necessary to assist in performing that attorney's duty to enforce federal criminal law; or

(iii) a person authorized by 18 U.S.C. § 3322.[20]

(B) A person to whom information is disclosed under Rule 6(e)(3)(A)(ii) may use that information only to assist an attorney for the government in performing that attorney's duty to enforce federal criminal law. An attorney for the government must promptly provide the court that impaneled the grand jury with the names of all persons to whom a disclosure has been made, and must certify that the attorney has advised those persons of their obligation of secrecy under this rule.

(C) An attorney for the government may disclose any grand-jury matter to another federal grand jury.

(D) An attorney for the government may disclose any grand-jury matter involving foreign intelligence, counterintelligence * * *, or foreign intelligence information * * * to any federal law enforcement, intelligence, protective, immi-

---

19. Not all states mandate recording of grand jury testimony. See Knodsen, Pretrial Disclosure of Federal Grand Jury Testimony, 48 Wash.L.Rev. 422 (1973).

20. 18 U.S.C. § 3322 makes a limited exception to grand jury secrecy to authorize disclosure to banking regulators to obtain information in certain cases involving civil forfeiture and civil banking laws.

gration, national defense, or national security official to assist the official receiving the information in the performance of that official's duties.

(i) Any federal official who receives information under Rule 6(e)(3)(D) may use the information only as necessary in the conduct of that person's official duties subject to any limitations on the unauthorized disclosure of such information.

(ii) Within a reasonable time after disclosure is made under Rule 6(e)(3)(D), an attorney for the government must file, under seal, a notice with the court in the district where the grand jury convened stating that such information was disclosed and the departments, agencies, or entities to which the disclosure was made.

(iii) As used in Rule 6(e)(3)(D), the term "foreign intelligence information" means:

(a) information, whether or not it concerns a United States person, that relates to the ability of the United States to protect against—

- actual or potential attack or other grave hostile acts of a foreign power or its agent;

- sabotage or international terrorism by a foreign power or its agent; or

- clandestine intelligence activities by an intelligence service or network of a foreign power or by its agent; or

(b) information, whether or not it concerns a United States person, with respect to a foreign power or foreign territory that relates to—

- the national defense or the security of the United States; or

- the conduct of the foreign affairs of the United States.[21]

(E) The court may authorize disclosure—at a time, in a manner, and subject to any other conditions that it directs—of a grand jury matter:

(i) preliminarily to or in connection with a judicial proceeding;[22]

(ii) at the request of a defendant who shows that a ground may exist to dismiss the indictment because of a matter that occurred before the grand jury;

(iii) at the request of the government if it shows that the matter may disclose a violation of state or Indian tribal criminal law, as long as the disclosure is to an appropriate state, state-subdivision, or Indian tribal official for the purpose of enforcing that law; or

(iv) at the request of the government if it shows that the matter may disclose a violation of military criminal law under the Uniform Code of Military Justice, as long as the disclosure is to an appropriate military official for the purpose of enforcing that law.

* * *

21. Rule 6(D) in its entirety was added by the USA PATRIOT Act, Section 203(a), to remove bars to sharing information concerning terrorism.

22. In United States v. Baggot, 463 U.S. 476 (1983), the Court held, 8–1, that an IRS tax audit is not conducted preliminarily to or in connection with a judicial proceeding. Thus, grand jury evidence could not be disclosed for use in such an audit. The Court found that disclosure is only permitted when there is pending or anticipated litigation, not where litigation is merely possible.

(4) Sealed Indictments. The magistrate judge to whom an indictment is returned may direct that the indictment be kept secret until the defendant is in custody or has been released pending trial. The clerk must then seal the indictment, and no person may disclose the indictment's existence except as necessary to issue or execute a warrant or summons.[23]

(5) Closed Hearing. Subject to any right to an open hearing in a contempt proceeding, the court must close any hearing to the extent necessary to prevent disclosure of matters occurring before a grand jury.

(6) Sealed Records. Records, orders and subpoenas relating to grand-jury proceedings must be kept under seal to the extent and for as long as necessary to prevent the unauthorized disclosure of a matter occurring before a grand jury.

(7) Contempt. A knowing violation of Rule 6 may be punished as a contempt of court.

(f) Indictment and Return. A grand jury may indict only if at least 12 jurors concur. The grand jury—or its foreperson or deputy foreperson—must return the indictment to a magistrate judge in open court. If a complaint or information is pending against the defendant and 12 jurors do not concur in the indictment, the foreperson must promptly and in writing report the lack of concurrence to the magistrate judge.

(g) Discharging the Grand Jury. A grand jury must serve until the court discharges it, but it may serve more than 18 months only if the court, having determined that an extension is in the public interest, extends the grand jury's service. An extension may be granted for no more than 6 months, except as otherwise provided by statute.[24]

(h) Excusing a Juror. At any time, for good cause, the court may excuse a juror either temporarily or permanently, and if permanently, the court may impanel an alternate juror in place of the excused juror.

* * *

Discriminatory Selection of Grand Jurors

It is clear that racial or ethnic discrimination in the selection of grand jurors will violate the Equal Protection Clause, and perhaps notions of fundamental fairness under the Due Process Clause as well. See Rose v. Mitchell, 443 U.S. 545 (1979)(racial discrimination in the selection of grand jurors is a valid ground for setting aside a criminal conviction, even where the defendant has been found guilty beyond a reasonable doubt by a properly constituted petit jury at a trial on the merits that was free from other constitutional error). In Castaneda v.

---

23. An indictment is properly sealed "when the government requests that the magistrate judge seal the indictment for any legitimate prosecutorial objective or where the public interest otherwise requires it." Permissible objectives include, but are not limited to, the need to prevent flight and the need to protect witnesses. See generally United States v. Richard, 943 F.2d 115 (1st Cir.1991).

Courts have held that a sealed indictment tolls the statute of limitations, unless the defendant can show that he was substantially prejudiced during the time period in which the indictment remained sealed. See United States v. Sharpe, 995 F.2d 49 (5th Cir.1993)(no prejudice where the indictment was sealed for six days—one day before the limitation period expired and five thereafter).

24. Some jurisdictions provide that a grand jury can only be discharged before its term expires for "legal" or good cause. E.g., N.J.Ct.R. 3, 6–10. Still others allow discharge when the grand jury's work is done. E.g., Cal.Penal Code § 915.

Partida, 430 U.S. 482 (1977), the Court established that statistics could be used to make out a prima facie case of discrimination against Mexican–Americans, even where a majority of a county's population were Mexican–Americans. Challenges under the Fourteenth Amendment are like all of the challenges to government action on the basis of suspect classifications. See also Jefferson v. Morgan, 962 F.2d 1185 (6th Cir.1992)(statistical evidence, adjusted by standard deviation, shows systematic exclusion of African–Americans from grand jury; conviction reversed and indictment dismissed; error was not harmless simply because the defendant was convicted at trial).

[handwritten margin note: racial exclusion is reversable error]

Discriminatory Selection of Grand Jury Forepersons

Chief Justice Burger wrote for the Court in Hobby v. United States, 468 U.S. 339 (1984), as it held that discrimination in the selection of grand jury forepersons and deputy forepersons in a federal district did not require reversal of a conviction. Chief Justice Burger condemned all discrimination in the selection of grand jurors, but found that the ministerial functions of the foreperson and the deputy added little to the role that any particular grand juror plays. Thus, as long as the grand jury itself was validly selected, discrimination in the selection of the two ministerial leaders did not prejudice the defendant.

[handwritten margin note: racial exclusion from fore person role not reversible]

The Court distinguished *Hobby* in Campbell v. Louisiana, 523 U.S. 392 (1998). Campbell alleged racial discrimination in the selection of grand jury foremen in Louisiana. In *Hobby,* the jury foreman was picked from the ranks of the already seated jurors, and performed only ministerial tasks. In Louisiana, by contrast, the judge selects the foreperson from the grand jury venire, and then the remaining members are chosen from the venire by lot. In addition to his other duties, the Louisiana foreperson has the same full voting powers as other grand jury members. As a result, when the Louisiana judge selected the foreperson, he also selected one member of the grand jury outside of the drawing system used to compose the balance of that body. Justice Kennedy, writing for the Court, held that Campbell's claim would therefore be treated "as one alleging discriminatory selection of grand jurors." Justice Kennedy further declared that Campbell, a white defendant, had third-party standing to complain that blacks were excluded from grand jury service on racial grounds in violation of the Equal Protection Clause. The Court relied on Powers v. Ohio, 499 U.S. 400 (1991), which held that a white defendant had third-party standing to bring an equal protection claim alleging race-based exclusion of blacks from the petit jury. The Court remanded for consideration of Thompson's equal protection and due process claims. Justice Thomas, joined by Justice Scalia, concurred in part and dissented in part.

[handwritten margin note: foreperson is selected from jury; jury is selected from whole pool]

Secrecy of Grand Jury Proceedings

The Supreme Court has consistently acknowledged the important interests that the grand jury secrecy requirement aims to protect.

First, if preindictment proceedings were made public, many prospective witnesses would be hesitant to come forward voluntarily, knowing that those against whom they testify would be aware of that testimony. Moreover, witnesses who appeared before the grand jury would be less likely to testify fully and frankly, as they would be open to retribution as well as to inducements. There also would be the risk that those about to be indicted would flee, or would try to influence individual grand jurors to vote against indictment. Finally, by preserving the secrecy of the proceedings, we assure that persons who are accused but exonerated by the grand jury will not be held up to public ridicule.

Douglas Oil Co. v. Petrol Stops N.W., 441 U.S. 211 (1979).

Of course, the importance of grand jury secrecy was seen in the course of the proceedings for impeachment of President Clinton, where allegations were made that Independent Counsel Kenneth Starr and his staff engaged in a practice of leaking grand jury information in an attempt to damage the President and influence public opinion. See In re Sealed Case No. 98–3077, 151 F.3d 1059 (D.C.Cir.1998), for a discussion of the issues and procedures arising from the alleged leaks by the Independent Counsel.

Grand Jury Witnesses and Secrecy

Note that Federal Rule 6 imposes no obligation of secrecy on grand jury witnesses. The argument has been made that a secrecy requirement for the witness's own testimony would be impractical. Do you agree with this? If witnesses are free to talk, how effective do you think the secrecy rule is likely to be?

In Butterworth v. Smith, 494 U.S. 624 (1990), the Court unanimously held that a Florida statute violated the First Amendment insofar as it prohibited a grand jury witness from disclosing his own testimony after the grand jury's term has ended. Chief Justice Rehnquist's opinion noted in contrast that Federal Rule of Criminal Procedure 6 exempts witnesses from the obligation of secrecy as to their own statements.

Rule 6 provides for certain exceptions to secrecy, among them the use of grand jury information by an attorney for the government for use in the performance of the attorney's duty. Despite this exception, the Court held in United States v. Sells Engineering, Inc., 463 U.S. 418 (1983), that lawyers in the civil division of the Justice Department may not obtain automatic disclosure of evidence presented to a grand jury. The majority reasoned that automatic disclosure would increase the risk of inadvertent or illegal disclosure of grand jury proceedings and discourage witnesses from cooperating with grand juries. Thus, to obtain disclosure, civil division lawyers, like private litigants, must make a strong showing of particularized need for disclosure for use in another proceeding, demonstrate that this need is greater than the need for secrecy in the grand jury proceeding, and structure requests for disclosure so as to obtain only what is really needed. Given the interests in grand jury secrecy, such a showing will be extremely rare.

The Supreme Court distinguished *Sells Engineering* in United States v. John Doe, Inc. I, 481 U.S. 102 (1987), as it held that attorneys in the antitrust division of the Justice Department who themselves conducted a grand jury investigation may make continued use of grand jury materials in the civil phase of a dispute, without obtaining a court order to do so. Justice Stevens' majority opinion reasoned that an attorney who conducted a grand jury investigation does not necessarily disclose any grand jury materials when continuing into a civil phase of a proceeding, and that the danger of abuse of the grand jury in the context of this case was small. Justice Brennan, joined by Justices Marshall and Blackmun, dissented and argued that the Court's approach to the word "disclosure" ignored the substantive concerns of Rule 6. Justice White did not participate in the case.

Courts have held that documents obtained by grand juries may more readily be disclosed than testimony, and more generally that the need for protection of documents depends upon the degree to which the material would reveal the inner workings of the grand jury. See, e.g., In re Grand Jury Investigation, 55 F.3d 350 (8th Cir.1995)(noting that the purpose of Rule 6 is to protect the inner workings of the grand jury, and that the more the requested information reveals about that work, "the greater protection it receives under the rule").

D. THE RELATIONSHIP OF THE GRAND JURY TO THE PROSECUTOR AND TO THE COURT

The roles played by the prosecutor, the court, and the grand jury are not exactly the same in all jurisdictions. However, it is common for courts to view the prosecutor's relationship to the grand jury as subject to little, if any, judicial scrutiny. United States v. Chanen, 549 F.2d 1306 (9th Cir.1977), illustrates this. The government presented its case three times to a federal grand jury. The first time the government did not ask for an indictment, and no vote was taken before the grand jury was discharged. A second grand jury indictment was dismissed because no transcript was made, and the government failed to present the jury with the evidence presented to the first grand jury. On the third attempt, the government secured an indictment against defendants for statutory fraud. The government presented its evidence to the third grand jury by reading testimony from its first grand jury presentation. The district court quashed the indictment because the judge felt that where the first grand jury failed to indict on the basis of live testimony, a subsequent grand jury should hear live testimony as well. The court of appeals reversed. It held that the prosecutor's action was not "fundamentally unfair" and therefore did not constitute a basis for dismissal. It reasoned as follows:

> Respecting the work of the grand jury, both court and prosecutor play supportive and complementary roles. As a practical matter, the grand jury generally relies on the prosecutor to determine what witnesses to call. Also, in practice the prosecutor conducts the examination of the witnesses and otherwise determines what evidence to present before the grand jury. In addition, it is the prosecutor who normally prepares the indictment, although of course the grand jury must review the indictment and adopt it as its own. Some of these functions—such as initiating a criminal case by presenting evidence before the grand jury—qualifies as "an executive function within the exclusive prerogative of the Attorney General." In re Persico, 522 F.2d 41, 54–55 (2d Cir.1975).
>
> The court, on the other hand, exercises its power to summon witnesses to attend and to give testimony before the grand jury. Also, "it is the court which must compel a witness to testify if, after appearing, he refuses to do so." In addition, the court exercises a form of authority over the grand jury when, for example, it dismisses an indictment for failure to charge all elements of the offense or to warn the defendant fairly of the charge against which he must defend. Likewise, the court exercises authority over the

prosecutor when it dismisses an indictment because of prosecutorial misconduct. * * *

Nevertheless, given the constitutionally-based independence of each of the three actors—court, prosecutor and grand jury—we believe a court may not exercise its "supervisory power" in a way which encroaches on the prerogatives of the other two unless there is a clear basis in fact and law for doing so. If the district courts were not required to meet such a standard, their "supervisory power" could readily prove subversive of the doctrine of separation of powers.

Application of this standard to the present case requires reversal. The asserted legal basis for the district court's interference with a standard prosecutorial decision—what evidence to present to the grand jury and how to present it—is the need to preserve the integrity of the judicial process and to avoid any fundamental unfairness. But it is far from clear that the prosecutor's decision in this case regarding the presentation of evidence to the third grand jury implicates any of those interests.

See also United States v. Strouse, 286 F.3d 767 (5th Cir. 2002)(federal court does not have supervisory power to dismiss a grand jury indictment based on perjured testimony, unless it is shown that the prosecutor knew that the testimony was perjurious: "a rule allowing dismissal of an indictment without a showing of government misconduct would open the door to attacks on grand jury evidence for which there are large incentives including discovery by the accused").[25]

Role of the Prosecutor

The role of the prosecutor does vary from place to place in grand jury proceedings, but generally she serves the following functions:

(a) She is the legal advisor to the grand jury. Many critics maintain that the grand jury should have separate counsel at its disposal to reduce the prosecutor's control over the grand jury. But traditionally the prosecutor is also the grand jury's counsel. See Mogul Bent on Grand Jury Reform, Nat.L.J. July 27, 1998, p. A10 (discussing an "Open Letter" sent to grand jurors suggesting that grand jurors should retain their own counsel, as "a simple way to the Grand Jury to reclaim its legal independence").

(b) She presents evidence to the grand jury. The grand jury can always hear any additional evidence that it requests, but as a practical matter grand juries usually rely on the prosecutor to explain criminal offenses and to present the evidence that the grand jury considers. The prosecutor can subpoena witnesses to attend grand jury hearings, and once the witnesses are present the grand jury will hear them.

---

25. United States v. McKenzie, 678 F.2d 629 (5th Cir.1982), indicates that an indictment will be quashed because of prosecutorial conduct before a grand jury "only when prosecutorial misconduct amounts to overbearing the will of the grand jury so that the indictment is, in effect, that of the prosecutor rather than the grand jury." The court indicated that a prosecutor could tell the grand jury that the evidence shows the defendant is guilty.

United States v. Udziela, 671 F.2d 995 (7th Cir.1982), holds that when a prosecutor discovers that perjured testimony has been presented to a grand jury, the government has the option of voluntarily withdrawing the tainted indictment and seeking a new one or appearing with defense counsel before the district court for an in camera inspection of the grand jury transcript to determine whether sufficient untainted evidence supports the indictment.

(c) The prosecutor usually may negate a grand jury's decision to return an indictment by refusing to sign the indictment, or by nolle prosequi, which dismisses the charges. And a grand jury decision not to indict can be circumvented if the prosecutor resubmits the case to another grand jury. In some jurisdictions such action requires court approval.

E. THE GRAND JURY AS A PROTECTION AGAINST UNJUST PROSECUTION

The traditional view of the grand jury as a protection against unwarranted prosecution has been described as follows:

> Historically, this body has been regarded as a primary security to the innocent against hasty, malicious and oppressive persecution; it serves the invaluable function in our society of standing between the accuser and the accused, whether the latter be an individual, minority group, or other, to determine whether a charge is founded upon reason or was dictated by an intimidating power or by malice and personal ill will.

Wood v. Georgia, 370 U.S. 375, 390 (1962).

In recent years this view has been challenged. Commentators and courts now see a grand jury indictment as little more than a rubber stamp for the prosecutor's decision to go forward. See Leipold, Why Grand Juries Do Not (And Cannot) Protect the Accused, 80 Cornell L.Rev.260 (1995) (noting that during 1984, federal grand juries returned 17,419 indictments and only sixty-eight no bills, a success rate of 99.6%). In Hawkins v. Superior Court, 22 Cal.3d 584, 150 Cal.Rptr. 435, 586 P.2d 916 (1978), the California Supreme Court expressed its somewhat cynical view of the modern grand jury:

> The prosecuting attorney is typically in complete control of the total process in the grand jury room: he calls the witnesses, interprets the evidence, states and applies the law, and advises the grand jury on whether a crime has been committed. The grand jury is independent only in the sense that it is not formally attached to the prosecutor's office; though legally free to vote as they please, grand jurors virtually always assent to the recommendations of the prosecuting attorney, a fact borne out by available statistical and survey data. Indeed, the fiction of grand jury independence is perhaps best demonstrated by the following fact to which the parties herein have stipulated: between January 1, 1974, and June 30, 1977, 235 cases were presented to the San Francisco grand jury and indictments were returned in all 235.

> The pervasive prosecutorial influence reflected in such statistics has led an impressive array of commentators to endorse the sentiment expressed by United States District Judge William J. Campbell, a former prosecutor: "Today, the grand jury is the total captive of the prosecutor who, if he is candid, will concede that he can indict anybody, at any time, for almost anything, before any grand jury." (Campbell, Eliminate the Grand Jury (1973) 64 J.Crim.L. & C. 174.) Another distinguished federal jurist, Judge Marvin E. Frankel, put it this way: "The contemporary grand jury investigates only those whom the prosecutor asks to be investigated, and by and large indicts those whom the prosecutor wants to be indicted." (Frankel & Naftalis, The Grand Jury: An Institution on Trial (1977) p. 100.) * * *

The domination of grand jury proceedings by the prosecuting attorney no doubt derives at least in part from the grand jury's institutional schizophrenia: it is expected to serve two distinct and largely inconsistent functions—accuser and impartial factfinder. * * *

Ex Parte Investigation

The high proportion of true bills (i.e., decisions to charge) compared to no bills is not surprising. The grand jury is a body that hears only one side of a case. And it reacts to that side. It is only natural that it agrees with the prosecutor in almost every case, because no opposition to the prosecutor appears before the grand jury. The principal function of the grand jury today probably is not to refuse indictment, but rather to force the prosecution to gather and to offer evidence in some systematic way before a charge is brought. What often is overlooked in discussions of grand juries is the fact that when the evidence, once put together, turns out to be weak, prosecutors sometimes decide not to ask for indictments or to seek indictments on lesser offenses than they might have charged on their own.

F.   THE EVIDENCE BEFORE THE GRAND JURY

One reason that the screening function of the grand jury does not work better than it otherwise could is that prosecutors often are permitted to offer evidence to grand juries that could not be offered at trials. The next case is an illustration.

COSTELLO v. UNITED STATES

Supreme Court of the United States, 1956.
350 U.S. 359.

Mr. Justice Black delivered the opinion of the Court.

We granted certiorari in this case to consider a single question: "May a defendant be required to stand trial and a conviction be sustained where only hearsay evidence was presented to the grand jury which indicted him?"

Petitioner, Frank Costello, was indicted for wilfully attempting to evade payment of income taxes due the United States for the years 1947, 1948 and 1949. The charge was that petitioner falsely and fraudulently reported less income than he and his wife actually received during the taxable years in question. Petitioner promptly filed a motion for inspection of the minutes of the grand jury and for a dismissal of the indictment. His motion was based on an affidavit stating that he was firm-

ly convinced there could have been no legal or competent evidence before the grand jury which indicted him since he had reported all his income and paid all taxes due. The motion was denied. At the trial which followed the Government offered evidence designed to show increases in Costello's net worth in an attempt to prove that he had received more income during the years in question than he had reported. To establish its case the Government called and examined 144 witnesses and introduced 368 exhibits. All of the testimony and documents related to business transactions and expenditures by petitioner and his wife. The prosecution concluded its case by calling three government agents. Their investigations had produced the evidence used against petitioner at the trial. They were allowed to summarize the vast amount of evidence already heard and to introduce computations showing, if correct, that petitioner and his wife had received far greater income than they had reported.

* * *

Counsel for petitioner asked each government witness at the trial whether he had appeared before the grand jury which returned the indictment. This cross-examination developed the fact that the three investigating officers had been the only witnesses before the grand jury. After the Government concluded its case, petitioner again moved to dismiss the indictment on the ground that the only evidence before the grand jury was "hearsay," since the three officers had no firsthand knowledge of the transactions upon which their computations were based. Nevertheless the trial court again refused to dismiss the indictment, and petitioner was convicted.

* * *

* * * [N]either the Fifth Amendment nor any other constitutional provision prescribes the kind of evidence upon which grand juries must act. * * * There is every reason to believe that our constitutional grand jury was intended to operate substantially like its English progenitor. The basic purpose of the English grand jury was to provide a fair method for instituting criminal proceedings against persons believed to have committed crimes. Grand jurors were selected from the body of the people and their work was not hampered by rigid procedural or evidential rules. * * *

* * * If indictments were to be held open to challenge on the ground that

there was inadequate or incompetent evidence before the grand jury, the resulting delay would be great indeed. The result of such a rule would be that before trial on the merits a defendant could always insist on a kind of preliminary trial to determine the competency and adequacy of the evidence before the grand jury. This is not required by the Fifth Amendment. An indictment returned by a legally constituted and unbiased grand jury, like an information drawn by the prosecutor, if valid on its face, is enough to call for trial of the charge on the merits. The Fifth Amendment requires nothing more.

Petitioner urges that this Court should exercise its power to supervise the administration of justice in federal courts and establish a rule permitting defendants to challenge indictments on the ground that they are not supported by adequate or competent evidence. No persuasive reasons are advanced for establishing such a rule. It would run counter to the whole history of the grand jury institution, in which laymen conduct their inquiries unfettered by technical rules. Neither justice nor the concept of a fair trial requires such a change. In a trial on the merits, defendants are entitled to a strict observance of all the rules designed to bring about a fair verdict. Defendants are not entitled, however, to a rule which would result in interminable delay but add nothing to the assurance of a fair trial.

MR. JUSTICE CLARK and MR. JUSTICE HARLAN took no part in the consideration or decision of this case.

[The concurring opinion of Justice Burton is omitted.]

Analysis of Costello

Aside from historical justifications, several arguments can be offered in support of *Costello*. First, inadmissible evidence often has probative value, and the grand jury's function is investigative, not adjudicative. Second, many evidentiary rules are designed to ensure fairness in an adversary proceeding, and the grand jury is not adversarial. See Federal Rule of Evidence 1101 (providing that the Rules of Evidence, except those related to privilege, are not applicable in grand jury proceedings). Related to this is the argument that a prosecutor cannot be expected to object to her own evidence, and that the general rule is that, even at trial, evidence that is technically inadmissible will be admitted if no objection is made. Third, any misleading effect of inadmissible evidence will be remedied at trial. Fourth, grand jury proceedings would be greatly burdened if the rules of evidence were applicable to them. The court would have to review decisions as to the admissibility of evidence, since defense counsel would not be there to object. In order to make relevance and other rulings, supervising courts would have to ask grand juries why they wanted certain evidence, and this might infringe upon the independence of the grand jury.

Note that the fact situation of *Costello* was rather unique because defense counsel was able, by questioning witnesses at trial, to determine that hearsay statements were the only evidence presented to the grand jury. More commonly, the defendant will never know the degree to which hearsay and other inadmissible evidence is considered by the grand jury. Grand jury minutes are exempt from disclosure under Fed.R.Crim.P. 6. And the witnesses who render hearsay and other inadmissible testimony might not, for that very reason, testify at trial. But doesn't this mean that the use of inadmissible testimony in the grand jury is by nature harmless error? Isn't this especially so if the defendant is convicted on the basis of admissible evidence? See United States v. Mechanik, 475 U.S. 66 (1986)(challenge to indictment based upon prosecutorial misconduct was rendered moot by conviction at a fairly conducted trial).

Use of Illegally Obtained Evidence

In Chapter Two, we saw that illegally seized evidence can be used in the grand jury proceeding. United States v. Calandra, 414 U.S. 338 (1974). The Court in *Calandra* reasoned that applying the exclusionary rule "would unduly interfere with the effective and expeditious discharge of the grand jury's duties" and that sufficient deterrence of illegal police activity would flow from the fact that the tainted evidence could not be used at trial.

Exculpatory Evidence: United States v. Williams

Does the prosecutor have an obligation to present all relevant evidence to the grand jury—including evidence that would exculpate the accused? Justice Scalia wrote for the Court in United States v. Williams, 504 U.S. 36 (1992), as it rejected a Tenth Circuit supervisory rule that required prosecutors to present "substantial exculpatory evidence" to the grand jury. He concluded that a rule requiring the prosecutor to present all substantially exculpatory evidence exceeded the courts' supervisory authority, because "the grand jury is an institution separate from the courts, over whose functioning the courts [do] not preside."

Justice Scalia stated that "any power federal courts may have to fashion, on their own initiative, rules of grand jury procedure is a very limited one, not remotely comparable to the power they maintain over their own proceedings." He asserted that the Tenth Circuit's rule was far from so limited, because it would result in the "judicial reshaping of the grand jury institution, substantially altering the traditional relationships between the prosecutor, the constituting court, and the grand jury itself." Justice Scalia reasoned that "requiring the prosecutor to present exculpatory as well as inculpatory evidence would alter the grand jury's historical role, transforming it from an accusatory to an adjudicatory body." He explained as follows:

> It is axiomatic that the grand jury sits not to determine guilt or innocence, but to assess whether there is adequate basis for bringing a criminal charge. That has always been so; and to make the assessment it has always been thought sufficient to hear only the prosecutor's side. * * *

> Imposing upon the prosecutor a legal obligation to present exculpatory evidence in his possession would be incompatible with this system. If a "balanced" assessment of the entire matter is the objective, surely the first thing to be done—rather than requiring the prosecutor to say what he knows in defense of the target of the investigation—is to entitle the target to tender his own defense. To require the former while denying (as we do) the latter would be quite absurd. It would also be quite pointless, since it would merely invite the target to circumnavigate the system by delivering his exculpatory evidence to the prosecutor, whereupon it would *have* to be passed on to the grand jury * * *

Justice Scalia observed that the grand jury itself might choose not to hear more evidence than that which suffices to support an indictment. That is, the grand jury is free on its own to refuse to consider evidence that exculpated the target. He reasoned that if "the grand jury has no obligation to consider all substantial exculpatory evidence, we do not understand how the prosecutor can be said to have a binding obligation to present it." The Court thus rejected "the attempt to convert a nonexistent duty of the grand jury itself into an obligation of the prosecutor."

Justice Stevens, joined by Justices Blackmun and O'Connor and in relevant part by Justice Thomas, dissented. Justice Stevens stated that he was "unwilling to hold that countless forms of prosecutorial misconduct must be tolerated—no matter how prejudicial they may be, or how seriously they may distort the legitimate function of the grand jury—simply because they are not proscribed by Rule 6 of the Federal Rules of Criminal Procedure or a statute that is applicable in grand jury proceedings."

As to the scope of the prosecutor's duty to disclose exculpatory evidence to the grand jury, the dissenters endorsed the position expressed in the Department of Justice's United States Attorneys' Manual, Title 9, ch. 7, par. 9–11.233,88: "When a prosecutor conducting a grand jury inquiry is personally aware of substantial evidence which directly negates the guilt of a subject of the investigation, the prosecutor must present or otherwise disclose such evidence to the grand jury before seeking an indictment against such a person."

G. THE GRAND JURY'S POWERS OF INVESTIGATION

The Supreme Court has emphasized that the role of the grand jury is to investigate into the existence of any and all criminal conduct, and that the scope of the inquiry is broad. See, e.g., Branzburg v. Hayes, 408 U.S. 665 (1972); United States v. Nixon, 418 U.S. 683 (1974). To understand how broadly the grand jury can sweep, it is helpful to think back to the search and seizure material in Chapter Two. You will recall that the government cannot obtain a search warrant to gather evidence unless it has probable cause. The same is true of an arrest warrant. And no warrantless arrest can validly take place without probable cause. This is in sharp contrast with the standards used by a grand jury. The grand jury can call anyone to testify before it upon the hint of suspicion or on the basis of a prosecutor's speculation about possible criminal activity. People called before the grand jury can be asked to bring documents and other tangible objects with them. Although the usual privileges can be raised before the grand jury, the burden is on the person called to raise them and sometimes to be willing to litigate in order to preserve them. Any aspect of a person's life that might shed light on some criminal activity by somebody is within the proper scope of a grand jury inquest. See, e.g., In re Grand Jury, 286 F.3d 153 (3d Cir. 2002) (grand jury has the power to demand the production of material even where it is covered by a protective order in a civil case).

Grand Jury Subpoena Power

The scope of the subpoena power of a federal grand jury is nationwide, which means that the burden of traveling to testify can be considerable. The state grand jury has no such nationwide reach, but it too can impose travel burdens on witnesses. When it is recognized that often the prosecutor subpoenas witnesses without prior consultation with the grand jurors, it is apparent that a prosecutor can call witnesses before grand juries who are considerably burdened by the duty of responding to a subpoena but who have little to tell the grand jury. Prosecutors can call witnesses who will add nothing to the grand jury's knowledge, but who suffer simply because they are called.

For example, one of the cases consolidated for hearing in Branzburg v. Hayes, supra, involved Earl Caldwell, a New York Times reporter who covered the Black Panther Party. Caldwell claimed that his appearance before the grand jury would compromise his relationship with the Party. The Supreme Court held that this risk of harm gave him neither the right to refuse to appear before the grand jury nor the right to refuse to answer questions based on information related to him in confidence. Under the Court's opinion, even if the grand jury did not have any significant need for answers to questions, and even if, by answering, Caldwell's ability to function as a reporter covering the Party would be destroyed, the grand jury had a right to the information. Justice Powell's concurring opinion suggested that some First Amendment protections might be afforded news reporters, but in light of the facts of the three consolidated cases, it appears that the power of the grand jury to subpoena the press is substantial and unregulated.

The breadth of grand jury power was evidenced once again in the grand jury investigation into charges of impropriety by President Clinton. The grand jury subpoenaed information from a bookstore concerning a purchase made by Monica Lewinsky. Despite the First Amendment ramifications, the subpoena was found valid. See Stout, Lewinsky's Bookstore Purchases Are Now Subject of a Subpoena, N.Y. Times, March 26, 1998, at A16 (quoting a legal director for the ACLU as stating that "people in this country ought to have the right to buy books without government scrutiny").

Any person who can demonstrate that a grand jury is harassing him may move to quash a subpoena.[26] In the absence of a valid claim of privilege, however, such motions are not likely to succeed. Early in this century the Supreme Court established the appropriate degree of deference to be accorded grand jury subpoenas by judicial officers.

> [I]t is clearly recognized that the giving of testimony and the attendance upon court or grand jury in order to testify are public duties which every person within the jurisdiction of the Government is bound to perform upon being properly summoned, and for performance of which he is entitled to no further compensation than that which the statutes provide. The personal sacrifice involved is a part of the necessary contribution of the individual to the welfare of the public. The duty, so onerous at times, yet so necessary to the administration of justice according to the forms and modes established in our system of government is subject to mitigation in exceptional circumstances; there is a constitutional exemption from being compelled in any criminal case to be a witness against oneself, entitling the witness to be excused from answering anything that will tend to incriminate him; some confidential matters are shielded from considerations of policy, and perhaps in other cases for special reasons a witness may be excused from telling all that he knows.

> But, aside from exceptions and qualifications—and none such is asserted in the present case—the witness is bound not only to attend but to tell what he knows in answer to questions framed for the purpose of bringing out the truth of the matter under inquiry.

* * *

> [The grand jury] is a grand inquest, a body with powers of investigation and inquisition, the scope of whose inquiries is not to be limited narrowly by questions of propriety or forecasts of the probable result of the investigation, or by doubts whether any particular individual will be found properly subject to an accusation of crime. As has been said before, the identity of the offender, and the precise nature of the offense, if there be one, normally are developed at the conclusion of the grand jury's labors, not at the beginning.

Blair v. United States, 250 U.S. 273 (1919).

Grand Jury Cattle Call: United States v. Dionisio

An objection to the breadth of a grand jury investigation, and correspondingly to the broad use of its subpoena power, is ordinarily dismissed out of hand. A case in point is United States v. Dionisio, 410 U.S. 1 (1973). The next excerpt contains the Court's description of the facts and its approach to grand jury subpoenas.

> A special grand jury was convened in the Northern District of Illinois in February 1971, to investigate possible violations of federal criminal statutes

---

26. If a grand jury witness refuses to answer a question or provide information requested by the grand jury, the government will request that the witness be held in contempt. A court could order the witness incarcerated until the witness cooperates or the grand jury dissolves, which would be civil contempt; the court could order the witness punished for failure to comply, which would be criminal contempt; or, the court could do both. If the witness is properly relying on a privilege, no contempt order can be imposed and the subpoena must be quashed.

relating to gambling. In the course of its investigation, the grand jury received in evidence certain voice recordings that had been obtained pursuant to court orders.

The grand jury subpoenaed approximately 20 persons, including the respondent Dionisio, seeking to obtain from them voice exemplars for comparison with the recorded conversations that had been received in evidence. Each witness was advised that he was a potential defendant in a criminal prosecution. Each was asked to examine a transcript of an intercepted conversation, and to go to a nearby office of the United States Attorney to read the transcript into a recording device. * * * Dionisio and other witnesses refused to furnish the voice exemplars * * *.

* * *

The Court of Appeals found critical significance in the fact that the grand jury had summoned approximately 20 witnesses to furnish voice exemplars. We think that fact is basically irrelevant to the constitutional issues here. The grand jury may have been attempting to identify a number of voices on the tapes in evidence, or it might have summoned the 20 witnesses in an effort to identify one voice. But whatever the case, a grand jury's investigation is not fully carried out until every available clue has been run down and all witnesses examined in every proper way to find if a crime has been committed * * *. The grand jury may well find it desirable to call numerous witnesses in the course of an investigation. It does not follow that each witness may resist a subpoena on the ground that too many witnesses have been called. Neither the order to Dionisio to appear nor the order to make a voice recording was rendered unreasonable by the fact that many others were subjected to the same compulsion.

* * *

In dissent, Justice Marshall argued that a stigma often attaches to witnesses called to testify before grand juries, and that some protection against prosecutorial control of the grand jury is necessary. Justice Marshall urged that the government should have to make a showing of reasonableness before real evidence is gathered by the grand jury over the objection of a witness.

Does Justice Marshall's argument have more resonance after the spectacle of the Clinton impeachment inquiry, where grand jury witnesses were paraded before the press, and swamped with legal bills, even though they were not the targets of the investigation? Or was the Starr grand jury inquiry a sui generis event?

Subpoenaing Criminal Defense Attorneys

Grand juries, guided by prosecutors, have sometimes sought to obtain information from criminal defense attorneys concerning monetary arrangements between the defense attorneys and their clients. Defense attorneys contend that fee-related information is protected by the attorney-client privilege, but this argument has been roundly rejected, with one limited exception: fee-related information is protected if disclosure of the fee arrangement would disclose the motive that the client had for seeking counsel in the first place. See, e.g., Vingelli v. DEA, 992 F.2d 449 (2d Cir.1993)(benefactor payment made by attorney on behalf of client, for legal services rendered on behalf of the client's associate, is not privileged; name of client and fee payment is not privileged except in exceptional circumstances where disclosure would indicate the client's confidential reason for seeking counsel; the fact that the attorney made a benefactor payment does not fully indicate why the client may have sought the attorney's advice). Nor is the Sixth Amendment right to counsel implicated when a grand jury subpoena is served, because the client has by definition not yet been formally charged with a crime. See Massiah v. United States, in Chapter Three.

Defense attorneys argue more broadly that serving a grand jury subpoena upon a defense attorney chills the attorney-client relationship, and might lead to disqualification because the attorney could be forced into being a witness against her own client. Yet this argument as well has generally fallen on deaf ears. Thus, in In re Grand Jury Proceeding (Schofield), 721 F.2d 1221 (9th Cir.1983), the court reversed an order requiring the government to make a preliminary showing of relevance before obtaining information concerning fees and expenses paid to a lawyer: "No preliminary affidavit, disclaiming ill intent, will be required of the government where a grand jury has subpoenaed testimony or material evidence in good faith." Accord, In re Grand Jury Subpoena Served Upon Doe, 781 F.2d 238 (2d Cir.1986)(en banc).

It should be noted, however, that ethical standards in some states, as well as in some federal district courts pursuant to local rulemaking, prohibit the prosecutor from subpoenaing defense attorneys without prior court approval. These rules require the prosecutor to make a showing of relevance and a lack of other reasonable alternative sources for the fee-related information. See ABA Model Rules of Professional Conduct, Rule 3.8(f) (providing that a prosecutor shall not subpoena a lawyer in a grand jury or other criminal proceeding for information concerning a past or present client unless the evidence sought is essential, there is no feasible alternative to obtain the information, and the prosecutor "obtains prior judicial approval after an opportunity for an adversarial proceeding"). Most courts have held, however, that these ethical standards cannot be enforced because to do so would impair the subpoena power of grand juries. See, e.g., Stern v. U.S. Dist. Court for Dist. of Mass., 214 F.3d 4 (1st Cir. 2000) (invalidating Rule 3.8(f)because it "encroaches on grand jury prerogatives").

Given the generally unregulated power of grand juries to compel the disclosure of information, why should criminal defense attorneys be given the special protection of prior approval by a court before a subpoena is issued?

No Probable Cause Requirement: United States v. R. Enterprises, Inc.

The Court in United States v. Nixon, 418 U.S. 683 (1974), held that a *trial* subpoena must satisfy a three pronged test of relevancy, admissibility, and specificity. However, in United States v. R. Enterprises, Inc., 498 U.S. 292 (1991), the Court rejected the application of the *Nixon* standards to grand jury subpoenas. Justice O'Connor, writing for a unanimous Court on this point, stressed the distinction between a grand jury investigation and a trial proceeding. She stated that "the Government cannot be required to justify the issuance of a grand jury subpoena by presenting evidence sufficient to establish probable cause because the very purpose of requesting the information is to ascertain whether probable cause exists." The Court also noted that the multifactor *Nixon* test would produce unacceptable procedural delays that would frustrate the grand jury's investigation.

Justice O'Connor noted, however, that the grand jury's investigatory powers are "not unlimited." Under Federal Rule of Criminal Procedure 17(c), subpoenas may be quashed if compliance would be "unreasonable or oppressive." The Court held that a subpoena would be unreasonable under Rule 17(c) only if "there is no reasonable possibility that the category of materials the Government seeks will produce information relevant to the general subject of the grand jury's investigation." Justice O'Connor recognized that this standard would be extraordinarily difficult to meet in practice, especially given the difficult position of subpoena recipients, who may have no knowledge of the government's purpose in seeking production of the requested information. The Court suggested that an *in camera* proceeding be employed in cases where the recipient of the subpoena is unaware of the nature of the investigation.

Regulating Abuses

While the Court in *R. Enterprises* set an extremely high threshold for quashing a grand jury subpoena, it pointedly left at least some room for court protection in egregious cases. When it becomes apparent that a grand jury is not acting in the course of a good faith investigation, but is rather attempting to harass or abuse citizens, courts will take action. See, e.g., Ealy v. Littlejohn, 569 F.2d 219 (5th Cir.1978)(holding that a state grand jury investigation into a citizens' association having no arguable or colorable relationship to a shooting death violated First Amendment rights). Similarly, when it appears that a grand jury is being used as a discovery device for civil litigation, a court will intervene, because it is unfair for the government to use the grand jury subpoena power simply to assist itself in obtaining a civil recovery. See, e.g., United States v. Gibbons, 607 F.2d 1320 (10th Cir.1979)(holding that it is improper to use a grand jury as a discovery device when an indictment already has been returned, although discovery may be an incidental benefit of investigation of additional crimes).

It is clearly improper for the prosecutor to call a person who already has been indicted by a grand jury to testify before that grand jury in order to gather evidence for the pending prosecution. One court has held that "[w]here a substantial purpose of calling an indicted defendant before a grand jury is to question him secretly and without counsel present without his being informed of the nature and cause of the accusation about a crime for which he stands already indicted, the proceeding is an abuse of process which violates both the right to counsel provision of the Sixth Amendment and the due process clause of the Fifth Amendment." United States v. Doss, 563 F.2d 265 (6th Cir.1977)(en banc). The *Doss* court held that a witness improperly called before a grand jury under such circumstances could not be prosecuted for perjury on the basis of false statements made. Note, however, that the grand jury may call an indicted person to investigate new charges.[27]

27. Sometimes it may be difficult for a court to know whether the government is pur-   suing a new investigation. But the court may indicate to the government that it will careful-

Warnings at the Grand Jury

The *Doss* case leads into what is perhaps the most significant charge made against the grand jury: it is an inherently unfair proceeding, because witnesses are called to testify without being told why they are being called, what the purpose of the inquiry is, and whether they are suspected of criminal wrongdoing. Ignorance of the nature of the proceeding is compounded by the absence of counsel in the federal grand jury room, as well as in many states, and by the legal inability of the individual witness to say "I do not wish to talk with you." The complaint that no one should be asked to give information without being told why has a ring to it like that which gave birth to the privilege against self-incrimination in England. Because grand jurors and prosecutors can ask leading questions, a witness who might be a target of the grand jury has good reason to fear that a slip of the tongue may come back to haunt her. Yet, the witness will have difficulty in answering carefully without knowledge of what the investigation is all about. Without a lawyer present to assist, vague or confusing questions may be asked, and a witness may later discover that what she said to the grand jury can be cast in a more negative light than she would have supposed while testifying.

In response to these complaints, the Department of Justice has added to the guidelines for United States Attorneys, found in the United States Attorney's Manual,[28] sections that require that a witness be advised of several things before testifying: of the general subject matter of the grand jury's inquiry (to the extent that an investigation would not be compromised); that the witness may refuse to answer questions that would tend to incriminate; that any answers may be used against the witness; and that the witness may step outside the grand jury room to consult with counsel. The guidelines provide that a target of an investigation may be subpoenaed, but known targets should be advised that they are targets and should be invited to testify voluntarily; if they refuse, a subpoena should be issued only after the grand jury and the responsible prosecutor have approved the subpoena. The prosecutor is encouraged to offer a target an opportunity to testify before the grand jury indicts.

It is notable, however, that there is no private right of action for violation of the warning requirements. Rather, the most that will occur is a referral by the court to the Justice Department for internal (and confidential) discipline. See United States v. Gillespie, 974 F.2d 796 (7th Cir.1992)(asserting that judicial enforcement might deter the DOJ from adopting such rules in the first place). It should also be noted that a witness before the grand jury is not entitled to *Miranda* warnings, even if he is a target or subject of the investigation; such a witness is not in custody within the meaning of *Miranda*. See United States v. Mandujano, 425 U.S. 564 (1976)(plurality opinion).

Counsel in the Grand Jury Room

As discussed above, under Federal practice, a witness has no right to counsel while in the grand jury room. The Supreme Court reaffirmed the nonexistence of

---

ly scrutinize the government's conduct when its use of the grand jury has been completed. See, e.g., United States v. Doe, 455 F.2d 1270 (1st Cir.1972).

28. United States Department of Justice, United States Attorneys' Manual, Title 9, Ch.11, ¶ 9–11.50.

any right to counsel in Conn v. Gabbert, 526 U.S. 286 (1999). The plaintiff in *Conn* was a criminal defense attorney. He sued prosecutors and others for subjecting him to a search while his client was testifying before a grand jury. Before the Supreme Court, the attorney did not press a Fourth Amendment claim. Rather, he argued that the search "interfered with his client's right to have him outside the grand jury room and available to consult with her." Chief Justice Rehnquist, writing for the Court, analyzed this claim in the following passage:

> A grand jury witness has no constitutional right to have counsel present during the grand jury proceeding, United States v. Mandujano, 425 U.S. 564 (1976), and no decision of this Court has held that a grand jury witness has a right to have her attorney present outside the jury room. We need not decide today whether such a right exists, because Gabbert clearly had no standing to raise the alleged infringement of the rights of his client Tracy Baker.

Justice Stevens concurred in the judgment in *Gabbert*.

Thus, the Court in *Conn* does not even admit that a grand jury witness has a right to have counsel *outside* the room, much less inside. In practice, counsel is permitted to park herself outside the grand jury room, and the witness can excuse himself for consultation.[29]

Thirteen of the 23 states employing the grand jury permit witnesses to be accompanied by counsel in the grand jury room. A subcommittee of the Judicial Conference Advisory Committee on Criminal Rules, however, has considered making such a change in federal procedure, and has decided against it. The Report of the Subcommittee reasons that allowing counsel to be present before the grand jury would create the following problems:

1. Loss of spontaneity of testimony.

2. Transformation of the grand jury into an adversary proceeding.

3. Loss of secrecy with resultant chilling effect on witness cooperation.

The Subcommittee also notes a "potential ancillary issue. Would an indigent witness summoned to the grand jury be entitled to the appointment of counsel at the obvious cost to the Treasury?"

To these concerns, the head of the Criminal Division of the Justice Department added another:

> [A]llowing defense counsel to accompany a witness before a grand jury would have adverse consequences for investigations of serious crimes by organizations, such as organized crime groups, corporations, or unions where typically a single lawyer represents all or several members of the organization. Currently, if a member of the organization wishes to cooperate with the grand jury secretly, the member may do so by appearing alone before the grand jury. But if the law allowed the member to bring the attorney, failure to do so would be a tip-off that the witness was likely

---

29. This limited opportunity to consult counsel probably reflects a practical consideration: if the witness refuses to answer, the grand jury would have to seek a contempt citation to make the witness answer; before going through that process, the grand jury may be better advised to let the witness discuss with counsel the question, because the witness may after consultation find that there is no Fifth Amendment or other privilege that is implicated.

cooperating, which would deter cooperation in many instances (or result in retaliation).

Letter from James K. Robinson to Subcommittee on Grand Jury Proceedings, Judicial Conference Advisory Committee on Criminal Rules, Dec. 22, 1998.

Despite these dire predictions, the evidence from the States that permit counsel in the grand jury room indicates that the presence of counsel can have a positive rather than negative effect. For example, Colorado passed a law in the late 1970's permitting a witness' counsel to be present in the jury room. Jeffrey Bayles, a former Denver deputy district attorney, explains the salutary effect of the law as follows:

> The presence of counsel has a definitely positive effect. Prosecutors who have worked under both the new and the old laws strongly prefer the new. Not only does the new law speed the process by eliminating the walk outside the room on every question, but it also reduces the number of questions requiring conferences between the witness and counsel. The educational process, which of necessity accompanies having counsel in the grand jury room, promotes a better understanding of the grand jury within the bar. The more the processes are known, the less is the aura of mystery surrounding the grand jury. When the mystery leaves, so does much of the fear and distrust of the institution. The demand for abolition of the grand jury will decrease in direct proportion to the number of counsel who attend grand jury sessions with their clients.

Bales, Grand Jury Reform: The Colorado Experience, A.B.A.J., May, 1981, at 568. See also Hixson, Bringing Down the Curtain on the Absurd Drama of Entrances and Exits—Witness Representation in the Grand Jury Room, 15 Am.Cr.L.Rev. 307 (1978)(given that the witness is allowed to go in and out of the room to get advice of counsel, it is more efficient to permit counsel to be present in the grand jury room.).

There probably is merit to the argument that the grand jury will get somewhat less cooperation from some witnesses if those witnesses are given greater access to counsel. The real question is whether we are willing to accept a procedure in which the prosecutor and a group of citizens advised by this trained lawyer can question a person in secret without giving that person the right to have somebody there to advise her when she wants advice.

Reforms and Limitations on Abuse

Many commentators suggest that the abuses seen in grand jury practice can be eliminated by imposing reforms on grand jury practice. The ABA Criminal Justice Section Committee on the Grand Jury proposed the following reforms:

> 1. A witness before the grand jury shall have the right to be accompanied by counsel in his or her appearance before the grand jury. Such counsel shall be allowed to be present in the grand jury room only during the questioning of the witness and shall be allowed to advise the witness. Such counsel shall not be permitted to address the grand jurors or otherwise take part in proceedings before the grand jury. The court shall have the power to remove such counsel from the grand jury room for conduct inconsistent with this principle.

[handwritten margin note: Proposals for counsel for witnesses in Grand jury - not adopted]

2.   No prosecutor shall knowingly fail to disclose to the grand jury evidence which will tend substantially to negate guilt.

3.   The prosecutor shall not present to the grand jury evidence which he or she knows to be constitutionally inadmissible at trial.

4.   A target of a grand jury investigation shall be given the right to testify before the grand jury. Prosecutors shall notify such targets of their opportunity to testify unless notification may result in flight, endanger other persons, or obstruct justice, or unless the prosecutor is unable to notify said persons with reasonable diligence. A target of the grand jury may also contact the foreperson in writing to offer information or evidence to the grand jury.

5.   Witnesses should have the right to receive a transcript (at their own expense) of grand jury testimony.

6.   The grand jury shall not name a person in an indictment as an unindicted coconspirator to a criminal conspiracy.[30]

The Criminal Justice Section report, proposing the above reforms, was issued in 1977. Congress held hearings on the proposals, but did not act on them. It is easy to see why no action was taken. The reforms would overrule Supreme Court doctrine, and would create a sea-change in the historically-ingrained federal grand jury practice. The reform proposals were staunchly opposed by the Justice Department. It is unlikely that the political climate will ever warm up enough for these proposals to be enacted. See, e.g., Rovella, Grand Jury Battle Begins, Nat'l L.J., May 29, 2000, p. A4 (discussing attempt by Congressman Delahunt to revive the 1977 proposals under the new title "Federal Grand Jury Bill of Rights"; no legislation resulted).

The Hyde Amendment

This is not to say that Congress is uninterested in regulating investigatory abuses by prosecutors (and by extension, grand juries). Recently Congress amended 18 U.S.C. § 3006A. The amendment, called the Hyde amendment, provides for recoupment of attorney fees by defendants who are subject to unwarranted criminal prosecution. Victorious defendants are entitled to their attorneys' fees unless the government can prove that the prosecution was "substantially justified." The right of recovery is not automatic upon acquittal; the defendant must show misconduct by the prosecutor that substantially affected the decision to proceed with the case or that infected the proceedings. Examples include personal animus or political motivation on the prosecutor's part. The monetary recovery runs against the government and not against the prosecutor personally.

The Justice Department opposed the Hyde amendment, stating that it "would have a chilling effect on prosecutorial discretion." And yet the bill passed by large majorities in both Houses of Congress. It remains to be seen whether

---

30.   See United States v. Briggs, 514 F.2d 794 (5th Cir.1975) ("the grand jury that returns an indictment naming a person as an unindicted coconspirator does not perform its shielding function but does exactly the reverse. If the charges are baseless, the named person should not be subjected to public branding, and if supported by probable cause, he should not be denied a forum.").

Congress' apparent concern with prosecutorial overreaching will translate into any kind of grand jury reform.

For a discussion of the Hyde amendment and the cases in which defendants have recovered attorney's fees, see Peter Henning, Prosecutorial Misconduct in Grand Jury Investigations, 51 S.Car. L.Rev. 1 (1999).

VI. THE PRELIMINARY HEARING AND ITS RELATIONSHIP TO INDICTMENTS AND INFORMATIONS

Federal Rule of Criminal Procedure 5 provides that when an arrest is made, the arrested person must be taken without unnecessary delay before the nearest available federal magistrate. You will recall that Gerstein v. Pugh, 420 U.S. 103 (1975), discussed in Chapter Two, requires that, if there has been no previous probable cause determination, one must be made promptly. Fed.R.Crim.P. 5 provides for such a determination when the person arrested is brought before the magistrate. The rule provides that a defendant is entitled to a preliminary examination for any crime except a petty offense. Fed.R.Crim.P. 5.1 governs preliminary examinations.

Note that an indictment cuts off the right to a preliminary hearing, because probable cause is held to be validly established by the indictment itself. It is common in some federal districts for prosecutors to avoid preliminary hearings by indicting as many defendants as possible. Rule 5 requires a preliminary hearing within a reasonable time, and it provides outer time limits. Whether a defendant's request for an examination as soon as the government can be ready must be granted is unclear. See Weinberg & Weinberg, The Congressional Invitation to Avoid a Preliminary Hearing, 67 Mich.L.Rev. 1361 (1969). But it would seem that the government can avoid a preliminary hearing if it presents its evidence to the grand jury as soon as it can.

Virtually every state that requires felony prosecutions to commence by indictment establishes some right to a preliminary examination. In most, the filing of the indictment cuts off the right to a preliminary hearing, just as does Federal Rule 5. About half the states do not require indictments in felony cases. In these states, prosecutors can begin felony cases by filing informations. A typical information procedure is to require a magistrate's determination of probable cause following a preliminary examination. In special cases prosecutors may utilize grand jury indictments, but usually they will use the information, since it is a less burdensome way of beginning a case.

Most states that permit the filing of an information in a felony case make a magistrate's decision to bind the defendant over for trial a prerequisite to the filing of the information. A few states do allow the prosecutor to file the information directly, however. The Supreme Court has upheld the direct filing of an information in Lem Woon v. Oregon, 229 U.S. 586 (1913), and Ocampo v. United States, 234 U.S. 91 (1914). Of course, after Gerstein v. Pugh, supra, a magistrate will have to make a probable cause determination, if the accused is deprived of freedom. But the *Gerstein* opinion indicates that the limited hearing it requires is to protect against erroneous detention; it is not a screening device to check the validity of the prosecutor's charges against a defendant.

Unsubstantiated Charges: Albright v. Oliver

In Albright v. Oliver, 510 U.S. 266 (1994), the Court held that there is no right under the Due Process Clause to be protected from a criminal prosecution in the absence of probable cause. State authorities issued a warrant for Albright's arrest. When he learned of the warrant, Albright surrendered. He was released after posting bond. At a preliminary hearing, on the basis of testimony of dubious reliability, the court found probable cause to bind Albright over for trial; but at a later hearing, the charges were dismissed on the ground that the charge did not state an offense under state law. Albright brought a civil rights action, alleging that state actors had violated his "substantive" due process right to be free from an arbitrary deprivation of liberty. In a number of separate opinions, a majority of Justices concluded that while a citizen might have a Fourth Amendment right to be free from arrest without probable cause, this right could not be supplemented by notions of "substantive due process." The plurality opinion authored by Chief Justice Rehnquist essentially treated Albright's claim as a Fourth Amendment claim and did not recognize an independent due process right to be free from prosecution in the absence of probable cause.

Justice Kennedy, joined by Justice Thomas in an opinion concurring in the judgment, argued that Albright's real claim was one for malicious prosecution, not false arrest. As to this claim, Justice Kennedy concluded that the Constitution neither imposes "a standard for the initiation of a prosecution" nor a requirement that a pretrial hearing must weigh the evidence according to a particular standard. He stated that the defendant's remedy for a baseless prosecution is a dismissal of the charges if the case is not proven at trial.[31] Justice Stevens, joined by Justice Blackmun, dissented.

In most criminal cases a probable cause determination is in fact made before the defendant proceeds to trial, because a person is indicted by a grand jury or provided with a post-arrest determination of probable cause. But it is possible that the state could provide for the filing of an information or complaint without any hearing, as long as the defendant was not subject to any extended incarceration pending trial—as was the case in *Albright*. In such a case, the question is whether the Constitution requires that a neutral decisionmaker find probable cause before trial. The alternative is that the charges will be dismissed at the trial; but should the defendant have to wait that long? The Court in *Albright* seems to answer yes.

Procedural Requirements for a Preliminary Hearing

Most states have time limits in which the preliminary hearing must be held. But other aspects of the hearing are often not covered by any rule. Even the standard to be used by the magistrate who conducts the preliminary hearing often is unclear. It is apparent that different judges sitting in the same jurisdiction have different ideas about what screening function the hearing is to serve. Some judges believe that their function is to determine probable cause, with the evidence viewed in the light most favorable to the government, ignoring

---

31. Justices Souter and Ginsburg wrote separate opinions concurring in the judgment. They concluded that Albright's damages, in- cluding those attendant to the charges, flowed from his arrest, and thus were compensable under the Fourth Amendment, if at all.

[Margin handwritten notes:] No right to bring action if proceed to trial and prob cause is found lacking or testimony used to indict fails.

[Margin handwritten notes:] All diff procedures because no one is sure what purpose the pre-lim hearing serves

credibility questions. This is the standard set forth in the federal system. See Fed.R.Crim.P. 5.1. Others take the view that there must be enough evidence for a trier of fact to find guilt beyond a reasonable doubt. Some magistrates probably consider whether a defendant should be burdened by going to trial in some cases, even if there is enough evidence to warrant a bindover.

The standard that is chosen indicates how much screening a jurisdiction wants its magistrates to do. It probably is true that if a prosecutor presents all her evidence to the magistrate and the magistrate concludes that no reasonable jury could convict, it is silly to bind the defendant over for trial, even if there technically is probable cause. But the question that may arise is whether the prosecutor should be required to present all of her evidence to the magistrate as a prerequisite to bringing charges. The more thorough the screening at the preliminary hearing, the more it resembles a trial, and the more duplicative and costly it is.

Although some jurisdictions require magistrates to follow the usual rules of evidence at preliminary hearings, most others provide that trial evidence rules need not be followed—which means in most cases that hearsay evidence can be used, as it can be used before grand juries. Again, the approach to the question whether evidence rules should be followed at the preliminary hearing depends on the kind of hearing that is to be held. Obviously, the more closely the evidence rules resemble the rules that will be used at trial, the more screening the magistrate is able to do. But the more screening that is done, the more time-consuming and duplicative the procedure is likely to be.

Another obvious difference among jurisdictions is in their approach to the hearing as a discovery device. If the hearing is not intended to serve a discovery purpose, as under Fed.R.Crim.P. 5.1, then questions asked for discovery reasons are unlikely to be permitted over objection.[32] If, however, a jurisdiction recognizes a discovery purpose, the scope of questioning may be quite broad.

Preclusive Effect of a Preliminary Determination

If the case is a felony case that will begin by a grand jury indictment, a decision by the magistrate at a preliminary hearing that there is no cause for bindover generally is not binding on a grand jury. The grand jury still can indict. See Fed.R.Crim.P. 5.1(f)("A discharge does not preclude the government from later prosecuting the defendant for the same offense."). Likewise, a decision by the magistrate that bindover should be limited to designated offenses also is not binding on the grand jury in most jurisdictions. The grand jury can charge any offense for which it finds probable cause.

If the prosecution can begin by information, generally the prosecutor is limited by the bindover in the charges that can be brought. In some states only those charges designated by the magistrate can be brought. In other states the offense for which the defendant is bound over or others supported by the evidence at the preliminary hearing may be charged. Still others use a transactional test, which allows all crimes related to the same transactions and facts adduced at the examination to be charged. See, e.g., Kirby v. State, 86 Wis.2d 292, 272 N.W.2d 113 (1978). Under all these approaches, the defendant can

---

32. The preliminary hearing may be used as a device to preserve testimony, and to pre-cipitate bargaining that will lead to a guilty plea.

challenge the information in the trial court, although it is likely that the trial court will defer to the preliminary hearing judge (and the absence of a formal record may make a challenge especially difficult). If the prosecutor is not satisfied with the bindover decision, she may drop the prosecution, file a new complaint, and hope for a better bindover ruling from another magistrate. If the magistrate refuses to bind over the defendant, the prosecutor usually can try again before another magistrate. See, e.g., Commonwealth v. Prado, 481 Pa. 485, 393 A.2d 8 (1978). Generally, the refusal to bind the defendant over is not appealable, although sometimes mandamus may be possible. If the prosecutor cannot get a favorable bindover decision, she might decide to present the case, even if it is a misdemeanor, to the grand jury, or decide to file charges directly against the defendant, if that is possible.

Harmless Error

In many instances an error at a preliminary hearing is likely to be considered harmless error once the defendant is tried and convicted. See, e.g., State v. McCloud, 357 So.2d 1132 (La.1978). For a defendant to preserve her rights, a prompt objection to the preliminary hearing should be made in the trial court. In some jurisdictions an adequate preliminary hearing is a jurisdictional prerequisite to prosecution, so that error cannot be harmless, if it renders the hearing inadequate.

VII. NOTICE OF CHARGES, CONSTRUCTIVE AMENDMENT, AND VARIANCE

In Stirone v. United States, 361 U.S. 212 (1960), the Supreme Court reversed a conviction for violation of the Hobbs Act (interfering with interstate commerce) because the government's proof of the defendants' effect on interstate commerce involved shipments of steel from inside Pennsylvania to points outside the state, whereas the indictment charged that the effect was on shipments from outside the state into Pennsylvania. The Court said that it could not permit a defendant to be tried on charges not made in the indictment, because to do so would threaten the protection afforded by grand jury scrutiny, and also would deny the defendant his constitutional right to be notified of the charges against him.[33]

Justice Marshall wrote for a unanimous Court (Justice Powell not participating) in United States v. Miller, 471 U.S. 130 (1985), holding that the Fifth Amendment's protection of indictment by grand jury is not violated "when a defendant is tried under an indictment that alleges a certain fraudulent scheme but is convicted based on trial proof that supports only a significantly narrower

---

33. Sometimes indictments are attacked on the ground that they are confusing and would be difficult for jurors to understand. Rarely do such attacks succeed. An exception is United States v. Gonsalves, 691 F.2d 1310 (9th Cir. 1982), where a district court used its supervisory power to dismiss an indictment as unmanageable. The indictment charged drug trafficking and contained two conspiracy counts. It named thirteen defendants and identified sev-

enteen alleged co-conspirators who were not named as defendants. The district court described the case as "a complex monstrosity" that was unmanageable. On appeal, the court affirmed and reasoned that "the degree of encroachment upon the prerogatives of the prosecutor that a dismissal entails in this case is minimal." The government remained free to break the case down into smaller, more manageable indictments.

and more limited, though included, fraudulent scheme." The government had charged Miller with fraudulent acts in consenting to a burglary of his business and lying to the insurer about the value of his loss. The proof focused only on the value of the loss and Miller's lying about it. Justice Marshall wrote that "[a]s long as the crime and the elements of the offense that sustain the conviction are fully and clearly set out in the indictment, the right to a grand jury is not normally violated by the fact that the indictment alleges more crimes or other means of submitting the same crime." He distinguished *Stirone* on the ground that the offense proved at Stirone's trial was *not* fully charged in the indictment.

Constructive Amendment or Variance?

In light of *Stirone* and *Miller*, courts have found two types of claims that arise when a grand jury indictment is allegedly altered during the trial. One claim is that the indictment was constructively amended; the other claim is that there has been a variance between the indictment and the proof elicited at trial. The court in Martin v. Kassulke, 970 F.2d 1539 (6th Cir.1992), discussed the difference between these two claims:

> An amendment of the indictment occurs when the charging terms of the indictment are altered, either literally or in effect, by prosecutor or court after the grand jury has last passed upon them. A variance occurs when the charging terms of an indictment are left unaltered, but the evidence offered at trial proves facts materially different from those alleged in the indictment. An amendment is per se prejudicial, as it directly infringes the defendant's right to know of the charges against him by effectively allowing the jury to convict the defendant of a different crime than that for which he was charged. * * *

> A variance, on the other hand, is not reversible error unless the accused has proved a prejudicial effect upon his defense, because it merely permits the prosecution to prove facts to establish the criminal charge materially different from the facts contained in the charging instrument. Although it is generally subject to the harmless error test, a variance infringes upon the apprisal function of the sixth amendment which requires that in all criminal prosecutions, the accused shall enjoy the right to be informed of the nature and cause of the accusation. If a variance infringes too strongly upon a defendant's sixth amendment rights, it is considered a constructive amendment, which is a variance that is accorded the per se prejudicial treatment of an amendment. * * * A constructive amendment occurs when the terms of an indictment are in effect altered by the presentation of evidence and jury instructions which so modify essential elements of the offense charged that there is a substantial likelihood that the defendant may have been convicted of an offense other than that charged in the indictment.

* * *

> A variance is not material, or does not rise to the level of a constructive amendment, unless the variance misleads the accused in making her defense or exposes her to the danger of double jeopardy.

In *Martin*, the defendant was charged with rape by engaging in sexual intercourse "by forcible compulsion." The evidence showed, and the prosecutor argued, that the rape occurred while the victim was "physically helpless"—i.e., while unconscious. The pertinent rape statute criminalized sexual intercourse either by forcible compulsion or when the victim was physically helpless. The *Martin* court found that the difference between the proof at trial and the charging instrument constituted a variance, but did not rise to the level of a constructive amendment of the indictment. Under the statute, rape was a single crime, which could be committed by two alternative methods. The defendant was not prejudiced by the prosecution's proof of a method other than that charged, because his defense was that the victim was a willing participant in whatever sex occurred. This defense "clearly negates any possibility that the victim was physically helpless and that her helplessness meant that he was not guilty of the crime with which he was charged." See also United States v. Moore, 198 F.3d 793 (10th Cir. 1999) (defendant was not prejudiced by a variance where he was charged with carjacking, and the victim named in the indictment was Brent Beyers, whereas the government proved that the car was owned by his wife, Anne Byers; no showing that the defendant was prejudiced).

A case that can be compared usefully with *Martin* is United States v. Lawton, 995 F.2d 290 (D.C.Cir.1993). Lawton was an official of a local union. He was charged with embezzling money from the Local. His defense was that he had an oral arrangement with the Local to write checks to himself to pay his salary. The federal labor embezzlement statute makes criminal only the embezzlement of the funds of a labor organization of which the defendant "is an officer, or by which he is employed, directly or indirectly." The trial court instructed the jury, however, that it could convict Lawton if it found that he embezzled the Local's funds, *or* the District Labor Council's funds, *or* the International Union's funds. It was clear that Lawton was neither an officer nor an employee of these latter two groups. The court found that the trial judge's charge constituted a constructive amendment of the indictment, which was per se reversible error:

> Under the Fifth Amendment, the infamous crimes on which a defendant must stand trial are limited by the charges contained in the grand jury's indictment. The district court's embezzlement instructions, however, allowed the petit jury to convict Lawton of additional charges. The trial court's instructions thus violated the Grand Jury Clause just as surely as if the court had written additional charges onto the grand jury's "true bill." Still worse, the instructions allowed the jury to convict on the basis of conduct that, on the face of the evidence, did not amount to a violation of [the labor embezzlement statute].

See also United States v. Floresca, 38 F.3d 706 (4th Cir.1994)(per se reversal where trial judge instructed on a different statute than that charged in the indictment); Lucas v. O'Dea, 169 F.3d 1028 (6th Cir.1999) (where the defendant was charged in the indictment with murder by shooting the victim with a pistol, it was a fatal variance for the jury to be instructed that the defendant could be convicted if his coconspirator fired the shot: the defendant was clearly prejudiced because his defense to the murder charge was that he was not the shooter: "Because it exposed Lucas to charges for which he had no notice and thus no opportunity to plan a defense, the variance from the indictment to the jury instruction constituted a constructive amendment that violated his Fifth Amendment rights.").

Inspecific Charges

The concern of *Stirone* and its progeny is that an amendment or variance at trial will effectively deprive the defendant of sufficient notice of the charges against him. Obviously, lack of adequate notice is likely to impair the defense. This problem can also arise at the outset—where the indictment is so general that it is difficult or impossible to prepare a defense.[34] One remedy for this inspecificity is a bill of particulars. Fed.R.Crim.P. 7(f) permits the court to direct the filing of a bill of particulars. The court in United States v. Salisbury, 983 F.2d 1369 (6th Cir.1993), described the function of a bill of particulars:

> A bill of particulars is meant to be used as a tool to minimize surprise and assist defendant in obtaining the information needed to prepare a defense and to preclude a second prosecution for the same crimes. * * * The decision to order a bill of particulars is within the sound discretion of the court. * * * A court does not abuse its discretion in light of a detailed indictment.

Whether or not supplemented by a bill of particulars, it is at least possible for an indictment to be so vague as to provide constitutionally inadequate notice. The test for constitutional sufficiency was stated by Judge Easterbrook in Fawcett v. Bablitch, 962 F.2d 617 (7th Cir.1992): "[A] charge is sufficiently specific when it contains the elements of the crime, permits the accused to plead and prepare a defense, and allows the disposition to be used as a bar in a subsequent prosecution." The *Fawcett* court rejected the argument that an indictment is constitutionally defective whenever the prosecution could have provided more specific information in the indictment. It declared that "the prosecutor's ability to do better does not vitiate the conviction."

In *Fawcett*, the defendant was charged with two events of unlawful sexual contact with a minor "during the six months preceding December 1985." Fawcett argued that the time period was impermissibly broad, because it was impossible for him to provide an alibi for the entire six month period. The court rejected this contention, finding that sufficient notice had been given, and noting that Fawcett was free to attack the complainant's veracity and to deny participation. Do you agree that sufficient notice was given? Would the indictment have been sufficient if it charged one act of sexual misconduct within a ten-year period? Compare United States v. Salisbury, 983 F.2d 1369 (6th Cir. 1993)(indictment insufficiently specific where it charges the defendant with "voting more than once," and that term is not defined in the criminal statute); United States v. Fassnacht, 332 F.3d 440 (7th Cir. 2003) (indictment is not insufficiently specific simply because it tracks the language of the statute under which the defendant was charged, "so long as those words expressly set forth all the elements necessary to constitute the offense intended to be punished.").

The Elements of the Crime: Apprendi v. New Jersey

Under *Stirone* an indictment that does not set forth all of the elements of the crime charged is constitutionally deficient. Sometimes it is difficult to determine what is an element of the crime and what is a sentencing factor that

---

34. Fed.R.Crim.P. 7(c)(1) requires the indictment to set out the essential facts constituting the offense charged, in order to inform the defendant of the offense against which he must defend.

can be left for the judge. This issue is discussed in detail in Chapters 10 and 11. At this point, it is sufficient to note that in Apprendi v. New Jersey, 530 U.S. 466 (2000), the Court held that a factual determination authorizing an increase in sentencing beyond a statutory maximum is an element of the crime, and therefore is a question for the jury that must be proved beyond a reasonable doubt. As such, it was an element of the crime that had to be set forth in the indictment. So for example, if the legislature has authorized a sentencing enhancement, beyond the statutory maximum, for possession of a certain amount of drugs, the jury must determine the amount that the defendant possessed, and that amount must be set forth in the indictment. *Apprendi* is discussed in detail in Chapters 10 and 11.

The Consequences of a Failure to Include All Elements of the Crime in the Indictment: United States v. Cotton

In the following case, the Court considered the consequences of an indictment that does not include an element of the crime, and specifically whether such a failure deprives a court of jurisdiction to hear the criminal case.

UNITED STATES v. COTTON

Supreme Court of the United States, 2002.
535 U.S. 625.

CHIEF JUSTICE REHNQUIST **delivered the opinion of the Court.**

In Apprendi v. New Jersey, 530 U.S. 466 (2000), we held that "[o]ther than the fact of a prior conviction, any fact that increases the penalty for a crime beyond the prescribed statutory maximum must be submitted to a jury, and proved beyond a reasonable doubt." In federal prosecutions, such facts must also be charged in the indictment. In this case, we address whether the omission from a federal indictment of a fact that enhances the statutory maximum sentence justifies a court of appeals' vacating the enhanced sentence, even though the defendant did not object in the trial court.

Respondent Stanley Hall, Jr., led a "vast drug organization" in Baltimore. The six other respondents helped run the operation. In October 1997, a federal grand jury returned an indictment charging respondents with conspiring to distribute and to possess with intent to distribute 5 kilograms or more of cocaine and 50 grams or more of

cocaine base, in violation of 21 U.S.C. §§ 846 and 841(a)(1). A superseding indictment returned in March 1998, which extended the time period of the conspiracy and added five more defendants, charged a conspiracy to distribute and to possess with intent to distribute a "detectable amount" of cocaine and cocaine base. The superseding indictment did not allege any of the threshold levels of drug quantity that lead to enhanced penalties under § 841(b).

In accord with the superseding indictment, the District Court instructed the jury that "as long as you find that a defendant conspired to distribute or posses[s] with intent to distribute these controlled substances, the amounts involved are not important." The jury found respondents guilty.

Congress established "a term of imprisonment of not more than 20 years" for drug offenses involving a detectable quantity of cocaine or cocaine base. § 841(b)(1)(C). But the

District Court did not sentence respondents under this provision. Consistent with the practice in federal courts at the time, at sentencing the District Court made a finding of drug quantity that implicated the enhanced penalties of § 841(b)(1)(A), which prescribes "a term of imprisonment which may not be … more than life" for drug offenses involving at least 50 grams of cocaine base. The District Court found, based on the trial testimony, respondent Hall responsible for at least 500 grams of cocaine base, and the other respondents responsible for at least 1.5 kilograms of cocaine base. The court sentenced respondents Hall and Powell to 30 years' imprisonment and the other respondents to life imprisonment. Respondents did not object in the District Court to the fact that these sentences were based on an amount of drug quantity not alleged in the indictment.

While respondents' appeal was pending in the United States Court of Appeals for the Fourth Circuit, we decided Apprendi v. New Jersey, *supra.* Respondents then argued in the Court of Appeals that their sentences were invalid under *Apprendi,* because the issue of drug quantity was neither alleged in the indictment nor submitted to the petit jury. The Court of Appeals noted that respondents "failed to raise this argument before the district court" and thus reviewed the argument for plain error. (citing Fed. Rule Crim. Proc. 52(b)). A divided court nonetheless vacated respondents' sentences on the ground that "because an indictment setting forth all the essential elements of an offense is both mandatory and jurisdictional, … a court is without jurisdiction to … *impose a sentence* for an offense not charged in the indictment." Such an error, the Court of Appeals concluded, "seriously affects the fairness, integrity or public reputation of judicial pro-

ceedings." We granted certiorari, and now reverse.

We first address the Court of Appeals' conclusion that the omission from the indictment was a "jurisdictional" defect and thus required vacating respondents' sentences. Ex parte Bain, 121 U.S. 1 (1887), is the progenitor of this view. In *Bain,* the indictment charged that Bain, the cashier and director of a bank, made false statements "with intent to deceive the Comptroller of the Currency and the agent appointed to examine the affairs" of the bank. Before trial, the court struck the words "the Comptroller of the Currency and," on the ground that they were superfluous. The jury found Bain guilty. Bain challenged the amendment to the indictment in a petition for a writ of habeas corpus. The Court concluded that the amendment was improper and that therefore "the jurisdiction of the offence [was] gone, and the court [had] no right to proceed any further in the progress of the case for want of an indictment."

Bain, however, is a product of an era in which this Court's authority to review criminal convictions was greatly circumscribed. At the time it was decided, a defendant could not obtain direct review of his criminal conviction in the Supreme Court. The Court's authority to issue a writ of habeas corpus was limited to cases in which the convicting "court had no jurisdiction to render the judgment which it gave." In 1887, therefore, this Court could examine constitutional errors in a criminal trial only on a writ of habeas corpus, and only then if it deemed the error "jurisdictional." The Court's desire to correct obvious constitutional violations led to a somewhat expansive notion of "jurisdiction."

Bain's elastic concept of jurisdiction is not what the term "jurisdiction" means today, *i.e.,* "the courts' statutory or constitutional *power* to adjudicate the case." Steel Co. v. Citizens for Better Environment, 523 U.S. 83, 89 (1998). This latter concept of subject-matter jurisdiction, because it involves a court's power to hear a case, can never be forfeited or waived. Consequently, defects in subject-matter jurisdiction require correction regardless of whether the error was raised in district court. In contrast, the grand jury right can be waived. See Fed. Rule Crim. Proc. 7(b).

* * *

[T]his Court some time ago departed from *Bain's* view that indictment defects are "jurisdictional." *Bain* has been cited in later cases such as Stirone v. United States, for the proposition that "an indictment may not be amended except by resubmission to the grand jury, unless the change is merely a matter of form." But in each of these cases proper objection had been made in the District Court to the sufficiency of the indictment. We need not retreat from this settled proposition of law decided in *Bain* to say that the analysis of that issue in terms of "jurisdiction" was mistaken in the light of later cases * * *. Insofar as it held that a defective indictment deprives a court of jurisdiction, *Bain* is overruled.

Freed from the view that indictment omissions deprive a court of jurisdiction, we proceed to apply the plain-error test of Federal Rule of Criminal Procedure 52(b) to respondents' forfeited claim

[The Court found that the failure to include the amount of drugs in the indictment was not plain error because there was substantial evidence of the amount of drugs presented at trial and so the defendant was not substantially prejudiced. See Chapter 13 for a discussion of the "plain error" analysis in *Cotton.*]

Chapter Seven

BAIL AND PREVENTIVE DETENTION

I. INTRODUCTION TO THE PROBLEMS OF PRETRIAL RESTRAINT

A. THE SUSPECT'S CONCERNS

Many defendants are released or convicted and sentenced within 24 hours of their arrest.[1] The remaining defendants await disposition of their cases for days, weeks, or months, depending on prosecutors' workloads, the gravity and complexity of the cases, the condition of court calendars, and the actions of defense attorneys. The magistrate must determine which defendants may and should be released pending trial.

At the time that the magistrate rules, the police have progressed sufficiently far in the investigatory process to have focused on an individual suspect. But there is some possibility that the suspect is innocent of all charges, or of most charges that are being considered or have been brought. In contrast to the final determination of guilt beyond a reasonable doubt at trial, the pretrial determination of probable cause, which forms the basis for arrest and detention pending trial, has the limited function of establishing only a fair probability that a suspect committed a crime. The claim is made that it is improper to deprive a person of liberty pending a finding of guilt. This claim has considerable appeal.

The suspect can certainly point to significant personal costs associated with pretrial detention.[2] The consequences of incarceration include deprivation of contacts with friends and family, absence from employment and possibly loss of job or a house, diminished ability to support family and to hire counsel, restrictions in the preparation of a defense, and stigmatizing effects on the prisoner's reputation and future employment prospects.[3] These factors, as well

---

1. The Challenge of Crime in a Free Society, Report of the President's Commission on Law Enforcement and the Administration of Justice (1968).

2. As Professor Caleb Foote noted in his seminal article, The Coming Constitutional Crisis in Bail, 113 U.Pa.L.Rev. 959, 964 (1965) (hereinafter, Crisis in Bail):

Any resolution of the detention problem involves an allocation of inescapable costs. Someone has to pay a price for the fact we have to

have a pretrial period between accusation and final adjudication. If defendants are kept locked up, the cost is borne by those among them who are innocent or prejudiced by the detention. If they are all released, society pays in those cases where the defendant flees or commits new crimes.

3. See Thaler, Punishing the Innocent: The Need for Due Process and the Presumption of Innocence Prior to Trial, 1978 Wis.L.Rev. 441.

as the poor conditions that characterize most pretrial detention facilities,[4] are imposed on a person who has yet to be proven guilty beyond a reasonable doubt, and who has not been afforded other rights associated with trial. If the defendant is ultimately convicted, it can be argued that the punishment of pretrial incarceration is *de minimis* because it can be treated as time served on the sentence. But for an acquitted defendant, or one who is never even tried, the deprivation of liberty resulting from pretrial detention is severe indeed. And this is particularly true if the trial is complex or protracted.

Moreover, studies indicate that pretrial imprisonment prejudices the actual adjudication of guilt or innocence when it finally occurs. By limiting the defendant's participation in investigation and trial preparation, incarceration may affect the verdict.[5] In addition, prior detention erodes the rehabilitative prospects of the accused, placing him at a disadvantage both in conviction and sentencing. The defendant's demeanor, recognized as an essential element of the fact-finding determination, will reflect recent imprisonment: He is apt to be unshaven, unwashed, unkempt, and unhappy as he enters the courtroom under guard.[6] The hopelessness, the lowered self-esteem, and a decline in respect for the criminal justice system may produce a tendency to plead guilty in detained suspects, who lose their incentives to prolong the adjudication process.

There are social costs to pretrial detention, as well. In addition to the significant costs of maintenance and support of the prisoners, society must bear the secondary welfare costs incident to the imprisonment of a member of a household. See Colbert, Thirty–Five Years After *Gideon*: The Illusory Right to Counsel at Bail Proceedings, 1998 Univ.Ill.L.Rev. 1 (noting that pretrial incarceration imposes "a hefty price on society" in the form of job loss, family dislocation, and emotional turmoil, and that when the charges are eventually dismissed or not prosecuted, "the economic, social, and emotional consequences incurred cannot be justified or remedied.").

The individual costs of pretrial incarceration fall most heavily on the underprivileged and indigent. A very high percentage of pretrial inmates are incarcerated because they cannot even post relatively modest cash bail. The Bar Association of the City of Baltimore has reported that almost half of Baltimore's pretrial detainees had a bail of $1,000 or less. See The Drug Crisis and Underfunding of the Justice System in Baltimore City 33 (1990). A study by the Department of Justice indicates that about one-third of pretrial detainees throughout the country are jailed on bail of less than $2,500. Bureau of Justice Statistics Bulletin, Pretrial Release of Felony Defendants, 1992, at 4.

"Pretrial" detention becomes even more of a concern if there is not even a certainty that there will ever be any trial. For example, after the 9/11 attacks, hundreds of people were rounded up on the basis of suspected ties to terrorism.

---

4. See President's Commission on Law Enforcement and the Administration of Justice, Task Force Report: Corrections (1967).

5. See Kinney v. Lenon, 425 F.2d 209 (9th Cir.1970), where the court held that the defendant's release was necessary so that he might track down witnesses essential to his defense.

6. See P. Wald, Pretrial Detention and Ultimate Freedom: A Statistical Study, 39 N.Y.U.L.Rev. 631, 632 (1964).

In Zeisel, Bail Revisited, 4 A.B.F.Res.J. 769, the argument is made that defendants who do not make bail on less serious offenses often serve more time than they would serve if they were released pending disposition of their cases; jailed defendants are likely to enter pleas for time served in order to obtain release, whereas freed defendants are less likely to accept just any deal that is offered.

Most were released after more than a year of incarceration, with no charges being filed. As of this writing, many foreigners rounded up after 9/11 are still incarcerated at the military installation at Guantanamo Bay, Cuba. Many are suspected terrorist operatives, but others have been found to have no connection to terrorism, and yet are still being detained. Obviously, these open-ended detentions, with no trial set or perhaps even planned, impose substantial hardships on the detainees.

B. COUNTERVAILING CONCERNS

On the other hand, there are compelling societal interests that militate in favor of pretrial detention of at least a good number of criminal suspects. The basic justification for imprisonment pending trial is to guarantee the presence of the suspect in order to ensure proper judicial disposition of the case. If the accused does not appear in court, the integrity of the criminal justice system suffers, the deterrent effect of the criminal law is undermined, and victims of crime are given no sense of vindication or closure.[7] Also, pretrial incarceration may protect the judicial processes by preventing the defendant from improperly interfering with evidence or witnesses. Detention may even serve to protect the accused from others who have a stake in the disposition of his case, or from himself, if the accused is violent or unstable or otherwise judged likely to harm himself.

Pretrial detention also has a preventive aspect. The state has an interest in the protection of the community that warrants imprisonment of at least some of those accused of criminal activity. Having established that there is probable cause to believe that the suspect committed a crime that is dangerous to society and for which he is likely to be punished, there is a legitimate concern that pretrial release will simply give the suspect an opportunity to commit more criminal acts. And this concern is obviously ratcheted up in the post–9/11 environment when the government apprehends a person with suspected ties to terrorism.

Courts, in determining whether a person should be released pending trial, are thus essentially balancing the individual's liberty interests against the legitimate interests of the state. What mechanism will operate to release those who pose no threat to the judicial process or the community at large, while detaining criminal suspects who are dangerous or likely to flee? How can the system protect the presumption of innocence and the right to be free pending adjudication, without hampering the law enforcement process? These are the questions posed in this Chapter as well as in the real world of processing criminal cases.

---

7. The New York Times, October 9, 1995, p.B1, col.2, reports that in New Jersey, more criminal defendants are currently at large, having failed to appear in court, than are incarcerated in the state. Police departments report a lack of resources to track down defendants who do not appear, especially if they have left the state. The article included an interview with a victim of child sexual abuse; the defendant in the case never appeared for trial, and had been at large in Florida for eight years, even though the victim had given the police his address.

II. BAIL: ITS HISTORY AND THE CONSTITUTION

A. THE COMMON LAW ORIGINS OF BAIL[8]

The traditional mechanism for pretrial release, the posting of bail, originated in medieval England, where prisoners could be confined in disease-ridden and insecure prisons for years awaiting trial by traveling justices, whose visits were infrequent.

Sheriffs welcomed the opportunity to place custodial responsibility in third parties. A prisoner would seek a friend or master, usually a property owner, who accepted custody or "bailment" of the accused, and promised to surrender himself if the defendant failed to appear. Of course, the law developed to permit the surety to forfeit property or money instead of his person, but the relationship remained a personal one, with a minimal risk of flight. Eventually Parliament specified which offenses were bailable, and the Habeas Corpus Act of 1679 provided procedures to free prisoners who were bailable by law. Some judges still circumvented these requirements by setting prohibitive levels of bail; so in 1689, Parliament responded with a Bill of Rights provision forbidding excessive bail.

B. THE CONSTITUTIONAL BASIS FOR PRETRIAL RELEASE: THE EIGHTH AMENDMENT

The American Constitution incorporated the right of a person in custody to seek a writ of habeas corpus in Article I § 9, and the ban on excessive bail in the Eighth Amendment. The third aspect of British law regarding bail, that is, the actual right to bail for specific offenses, was not included in the Constitution. Thus, the Amendment prohibits excessive bail, but it does not explicitly grant a right to bail. The Supreme Court described the provenance of the Bail Clause in Carlson v. Landon, 342 U.S. 524 (1952):

> The bail clause was lifted with slight changes from the Bill of Rights Act. In England that clause has never been thought to accord a right to bail in all cases, but merely to provide that bail shall not be excessive in those cases where it is proper to grant bail. When this clause was carried over in our Bill of Rights, nothing was said that indicated any different concept. The Eighth Amendment has not prohibited Congress from defining the classes of cases in which bail shall be allowed in this country. * * *

In *Carlson,* a civil case, the Court denied bail to alien communists awaiting deportation hearings. The *Carlson* majority held that the Eighth Amendment prohibits excessive bail in cases where statute and court decisions provide for bail, but that the clause itself does not require bail. Critics of the holding point out that this interpretation would subsume the Constitution to some other law. "It requires one to believe that a basic human right would be deliberately inserted in the Constitution in a form which permitted Congress to restrict it at will, or even to render the eighth amendment entirely moot by enacting legislation denying the right to bail in all cases." Foote, The Coming Constitutional Crisis in Bail, 113 U.Pa.L.Rev.959 (1965). Some states have resolved this dilemma by adding a bail requirement, usually for all but capital crimes, to their state constitutions.[9]

---

8. See D. Freed & P. Wald, Bail in the United States: 1964, Working Paper for the National Conference on Bail and Criminal Justice, Washington, D.C.

9. The Supreme Court has never held that the Eighth Amendment Bail Clause is binding on the states, though it has implied that a limitation on excessive bail is a fundamental

See United States v. Salerno, infra, for a further discussion of the constitutional and policy issues surrounding bail.

III. THE OPERATION OF A BAIL RELEASE SYSTEM

Before examining the scope of the right to bail that is recognized in most jurisdictions, an overview of bail procedures—the mechanics of the system—is in order.

A. THE ADMINISTRATION OF BAIL: THE PROCEDURES

The most frequently used procedure for obtaining one's pretrial release is through *cash bail*. Having learned of the bail figure, a defendant may raise the full amount of the bond through personal savings or those of his friends and family. If he shows up for all required court appearances and complies with all conditions of release, the entire amount posted is usually refunded to him. See Fed.R.Crim.P. 46(g) (providing for release of bail when bond conditions have been satisfied). Conditions of release may include not only appearance at all court dates, but other conditions such as refraining from criminal activity, retaining employment, drug treatment, avoiding association with certain individuals, etc.

If the defendant can't come up with money to post bail, he may seek the assistance of a bail bondsman, who has complete discretion in selecting clients. The bondsman's usual fee is 10 percent of bond amount; this fee is nonrefundable. The bondman places the entire bond with the court and the defendant gains pretrial freedom. If the defendant fails to comply with the conditions of pretrial release the bond is forfeited. It is therefore in the bondsman's interest to assure such compliance.

Personal bond is another method of release, which may be referred to as personal surety, nominal bond, or release on own recognizance. It is used when a judge determines that the defendant is sufficiently motivated to show up for his scheduled court appearance and can be released on his own signature without bail.

Defendants released on personal or surety bond by a nonjudicial officer, such as a police desk sergeant, have obtained freedom only until their first court appearance, which usually occurs the following day. At that time, unless the case is disposed of then and there, the judge reviews the bail amount and may revise it upward or downward. Similarly, bail set by a lower court for those accused of felonies may be reviewed and revised by the higher court which conducts the actual trial.

Judges might also exercise discretion to release the defendant into a third party's custody. The magistrate in such cases charges the third party with the responsibility of assuring that the defendant will appear and will not violate specified conditions of the release. Common candidates for third party responsibility include the defendant's relatives or friends, or social service agencies or pretrial release programs. See Torborg, Pretrial Release: A National Evaluation

right. Schilb v. Kuebel, 404 U.S. 357 (1971).   to bail.
Again, however, this does not establish a right

of Practices and Outcomes, National Institute of Justice (1981), for a further discussion of release mechanisms used throughout the country.

B. THE BONDSMAN

Free of most political and governmental restraints, the private bail bondsman lurks in the background of any discussion of bail, and is one of the most important players in the pretrial drama. When bail is set, the accused can pay a non-refundable premium—usually 10%—to a private bondsman, who then puts up the total amount of bail. Because the bondsman assumes the risk of forfeiture, he has traditionally been given much discretion in establishing collateral for bail, and in tracking down and retrieving a fleeing accused. The legal right of a bondsman to cancel the bond and keep the fee at any time that he surrenders the defendant to court gives the bondsman considerable leverage, especially when bail may be set anew at different stages of a trial. The threat of being "turned in" ties the defendant to his bondsman, who may demand new premiums as the trial progresses.

Proponents of the bond system point out that without the private bondsman, numerous defendants would remain in jail for lack of available assets.[10] Also, bondsmen are often on call 24 hours a day. The profit motive provides them with the incentive to enforce a defendant's appearance in court. Thus, the system encourages private enterprise to assume part of the cost of administering the criminal justice process. In theory, the bondsmen reinforce the law enforcement system by preventing flight and helping to return fugitives.

Critics, however, argue that the private bond system undercuts the purposes of bail and contravenes the ideals of the criminal justice system. Release from jail on commercial bond can minimize the possibility of pecuniary loss to a defendant, so that his bail is no longer a direct deterrent to flight. The defendant loses the same amount to the bondsman whether or not he appears at trial. Theoretically, the court aims to set bail at a level that will ensure the appearance of the accused, but the intervening role of the bondsman supersedes the judicial determination. Thus, magistrates may fix bail with knowledge that the defendant has found a bondsman to advance funds or has been unable to secure help. Should a magistrate, aware of the existence of the bondsman, increase the bail so that the premium (assuming it is a percentage of the bail set) will approximate the bail intended by the court? Should the magistrate lower the bail for a prisoner who is not accepted for bail by a private bondsman?

Discretion in choosing clients provides one explanation for the relatively low level of risk in the bonding business.[11] Bondsmen consider principally the type of crime for which the defendant was arrested, not necessarily the seriousness of the offense. Thus, those accused of organized crime or professional gambling are good risks, while a first time offender is considered a bad risk, unsophisticated as to the intricacies of the court system and prone to panic and jump bail. Narcotic addicts are considered good risks, prostitutes are not.[12] Bondsmen are free to

---

10. The Justice Department reports that in 1992, about half of the defendants for whom bail was set had to turn to a private bondsman to get released. Bureau of Justice Statistics, Pretrial Release of Felony Defendants, 1992.

11. See J. Campbell, J. Sahid, and D. Staing, Law and Order Reconsidered, Report of

the Task Force on Law & Law Enforcement to the National Commission on the Causes and Prevention of Violence, 462–466 (1970).

12. See A. Marticz, The Ups and Downs of a Bail Bondsman, L.A. Times, 8/2/76, reprinted

incorporate their own political or personal prejudices in the bonding decision. The result can be disturbing. For example, civil rights activists who were arrested in the South often were unable to obtain the services of a bondsman.[13]

On the other hand, there are numerous minor offenders for whom even temporary detention is not justified by the crime charged, who simply would have to stay in jail were it not for the private bondsman. When the bondsmen in New York went on strike in 1961 and 1964, refusing to write bonds except on 100% collateral in bankbooks or real estate, the population of the city jails swelled. The strikes were in retaliation for tighter collection policies enforced on forfeitures.[14]

If the defendant flees, some bondsmen use a system of informants and "skip tracers"—modern day bounty hunters, who often carry arms and have criminal records—to locate the fugitive. Recapture has been held to be a private remedy, arising from a private action, and thus freed from the constraints of due process[15] and constitutional criminal procedure. For example, a bondsman can seize a fugitive in another jurisdiction and present him to authorities, while the state must await extradition proceedings.

Bondsmen and bounty hunters are subject to local laws, however. See, e.g., Lund v. Seneca County Sheriff's Department, 230 F.3d 196 (6th Cir. 2000), where the court dismissed a claim for illegal arrest filed by a bondsman where the bondsman broke into a house to catch a woman who had skipped bail, and took her away, leaving her two young children unattended. The bondsman took the position that he had a federal constitutional right under the Extradition Clause, Article IV section 2, to "break the law to re-arrest his fugitive." The court rejected this rather outrageous assertion and held that the Extradition Clause "does not shield a bondsman under federal law from arrest and prosecution for violating [state law] in apprehending bail jumpers."

Noting that "the methods often employed by bondsmen are hardly likely to promote respect for the administration of justice," the ABA Standards on Pretrial Release set forth a standard prohibiting, or at least severely limiting, private bonding:

§ 5.4   Prohibition of Compensated Sureties

Compensated sureties should be abolished. Pending abolition, they should be licensed and carefully registered. The amount which a compensated surety can charge for writing a bond should be set by law. No licensed surety should be permitted to reject an applicant willing to pay the statutory fee or insist upon additional collateral other than specified by law.

Similar acts have been passed in a few states, although most states have hesitated to eliminate the private bondsman for fear that fewer persons would be released, and higher bonds would result for those who are released.[16]

---

in J. Snortum and I. Hader, Criminal Justice Allies and Adversaries (1978).

13. R. Goldfarb, Ransom 2–3 (1965).

14. Bail or Jail, 19 Record of the Ass'n of the N.Y. City Bar 13 (1964).

15. Bondsmen are not public officers and therefore are not bound by the constitutional restraints that were examined in Chapters Two and Three. Although they are not restrained by the Constitution, bondsmen rely

upon it to protest forfeitures. In Wilshire Ins. Co. v. State, 94 Nev. 546, 582 P.2d 372 (1978), the court held that due process requires that the bondsmen be given notice of bail forfeiture proceedings.

16. The Uniform Bail Bond Act, promulgated by the National Association of Insurance Commissioners, regulates the practices of bondsmen; however, it has only been adopted by a few jurisdictions.

Forfeiture

A bond can be forfeited if the terms of the release are violated. See Fed.R.Crim.P. 46. Forfeiture may occur even if the defendant appears for trial; this is because the bail bond can impose numerous obligations. For example, in United States v. Vaccaro, 51 F.3d 189 (9th Cir.1995), the defendant was charged with racketeering. His pretrial release was secured by a $100,000 bond provided by Bell Bail Bonds. As one of the conditions of his release, Vaccaro agreed that he would "not violate any local, state or federal laws or regulations." Vaccaro committed a crime while released, and the trial court ordered the bail bond forfeited. Bell argued that the forfeiture provision of Fed.R.Crim.P. 46(f)(1) was triggered only if the defendant failed to appear. But the court held that the "break no laws" provision was a material part of the release agreement, and reasoned that "a bail bond is a contract between the government and the defendant and his surety." See also United States v. Gigante, 85 F.3d 83 (2d Cir.1996) (upholding bail condition requiring forfeiture of bond if the defendant commits a federal, state or local crime while released on bail).

Bail bondsmen have appealed to Congress for an amendment to Rule 46 to allow forfeiture only "if the defendant fails to appear physically before the court." (This is the language of the proposed "Bail Bond Fairness Act of 2001," H.R. 2929). The Judicial Conference opposes such legislation, having surveyed magistrate judges who report that it is often important to impose other conditions of release as part of the bail bond, e.g., that the defendant refrain from drug use. Magistrate judges argue that if they are not permitted to impose extra conditions, they will be less likely to grant bail in the first place. The Judicial Conference, in a letter to Congress, concludes that Rule 46 "provides judges with the valuable flexibility to impose added safeguards ensuring a defendant's compliance with conditions of release." As of this writing, Rule 46 still permits magistrate judges to impose additional conditions on release, and bail can be forfeited for non-compliance with those conditions.

Remission of a Forfeiture

If the bond is forfeited when the defendant fails to appear, must it be remitted if the defendant is later apprehended? In United States v. Amwest Surety Ins. Co., 54 F.3d 601 (9th Cir.1995), two sureties, Amwest and Tito's, executed a $100,000 bond to secure the release of Johnny Nash, who was charged with drug violations. Nash fled, and four days later, the bond was ordered forfeited. Nash was apprehended a month later. The court analyzed the forfeiture/remission question as follows:

> A district court may consider six factors when deciding whether to remit the forfeiture of a bond. These factors are: 1) the defendant's willfulness in breaching the release condition; 2) the sureties' participation in apprehending the defendant; 3) the cost, inconvenience, and prejudice suffered by the government; 4) mitigating factors; 5) whether the surety is a professional or a member of the family or a friend; and 6) the appropriateness of the amount of the bond. Not all of the factors need to be resolved in the government's favor.

Applying these factors, the court found that: (1) the defendant had willfully absconded, having left a note that "there is just no way I can do twenty or more years for what I have done"; (2) the sureties had not assisted in Nash's apprehension; (3) the government incurred costs of more than $37,000 in apprehending Nash; (4) there were no mitigating factors warranting relief to the sureties; (5) the sureties were professional, rather than a family member or a friend; and (6) the amount of the bond, while higher than the government's cost of apprehension and delay, was appropriate "as a form of liquidated damages." The court concluded its opinion as follows:

> Amwest and Tito's are professional sureties who earn income by issuing bail bonds but who do not wish to pay off when things go wrong. To their surprise and regret things went wrong when Mr. Nash that he did not want to do twenty or more years. We see no reason to hold that the district court was required to relieve them from their obligation to do what they promised to do—pay the agreed upon amount if Mr. Nash did not appear. * * * In fine, their promise was *nudum pactum*; they must now perform it.

Will decisions such as *Amwest*, imposing a total forfeiture of the bond, make it more difficult for defendants to make bail?[17] Will it encourage more aggressive efforts on the part of bondsmen to apprehend their fugitives?

C. THE BAIL SETTING DECISION

In most places, the judiciary is entrusted with vast discretion in implementing the controlling statutes or court rules pertaining to bail. Bail criteria are not self-executing; it is the application of general criteria to particular cases that effectively determines which defendants are released. Often courts can choose among criteria in making bail decisions, and the choice often reflects a court's view of the purposes of bail.

Individualized Determinations: Stack v. Boyle

As stated previously, the Court has never held that bail or any form of pretrial release is constitutionally required. However, the Court in Stack v. Boyle, 342 U.S. 1 (1951) recognized that, if bail is set, then a federal court must set it at an amount that appropriately furthers the purposes of bail. Although the Court indicated that judicial discretion in non-capital cases is limited to the setting of amount, it recognized that the decision to release an individual accused is necessarily fact-specific, leaving ample room for judicial discretion. The Court held that bail fixed in uniform amounts of $50,000 for each of twelve defendants charged with violations of the Smith Act could not be justified in the absence of evidence relating to the particular untrustworthiness of each defendant. Three paragraphs from the Court's opinion follow:

> The right to release before trial is conditioned upon the accused's giving adequate assurance that he will stand trial and submit to sentence if found guilty. Like the ancient practice of securing the oaths of responsible persons

17. For a case in which individual guarantors were subject to forfeiture of a bond, see United States v. Gambino, 17 F.3d 572 (2d Cir.1994) (forfeiture of $2,000,000 bond posted by family members, and foreclosure of real property securing the bond, where organized crime figure failed to appear and was later apprehended: "We believe that the deterrence value served by total forfeiture is especially important in high-profile narcotics and racketeering cases like this one.").

to stand as sureties for the accused, the modern practice of requiring a bail bond or the deposit of a sum of money subject to forfeiture serves as additional assurance of the presence of an accused. Bail set at a figure higher than an amount reasonably calculated to fulfill this purpose is "excessive" under the Eighth Amendment.

Since the function of bail is limited, the fixing of bail for any individual defendant must be based upon standards relevant to the purpose of assuring the presence of that defendant. The traditional standards as expressed in the Federal Rules of Criminal Procedure are to be applied in each case to each defendant. In this case petitioners are charged with offenses under the Smith Act and, if found guilty, their convictions are subject to review with the scrupulous care demanded by our Constitution. Upon final judgment of conviction, petitioners face imprisonment of not more than five years and a fine of not more than $10,000. It is not denied that bail for each petitioner has been fixed in a sum much higher than that usually imposed for offenses with like penalties and yet there has been no factual showing to justify such action in this case. The Government asks the courts to depart from the norm by assuming, without the introduction of evidence, that each petitioner is a pawn in a conspiracy and will, in obedience to a superior, flee the jurisdiction. To infer from the fact of indictment alone a need for bail in an unusually high amount is an arbitrary act. Such conduct would inject into our own system of government the very principles of totalitarianism which Congress was seeking to guard against in passing the statute under which petitioners have been indicted.

If bail in an amount greater than that usually fixed for serious charges of crimes is required in the case of any of the petitioners, that is a matter to which evidence should be directed in a hearing so that the constitutional rights of each petitioner may be preserved. In the absence of such a showing, we are of the opinion that the fixing of bail before trial in these cases cannot be squared with the statutory and constitutional standards for admission to bail.

Relevant Factors in Setting Bail

The most important factor in setting bail is the seriousness of the offense charged. The rationale is that the more serious the offense, the more likely that the defendant presents a risk of flight or harm to others.[18]

A second factor in the bail-setting decision is the strength of the case against the defendant. This information is often relayed to the judge by prosecutors and police officers.[19]

---

18. In a study of pretrial release in New Haven, a Yale Law Student found that the offense charged was the primary consideration at bail hearings. His conclusion, based on interviews with 81 accused felons, was that nearly half of those who were held in jail because of inability to post bond had sufficient ties in the community to meet conditions of release. W. Brochett, Pre–Trial Detention: The Most Critical Period (Unpublished manuscript 1970), cit-ed in W. Thomas, Bail Reform in America 143 (1976).

19. Prosecutors may not be unbiased in their recommendations to judges. One study in King County, Washington, indicates that the bail system is used to protect prosecutors from public criticism. By suggesting a high bail amount with the expectation that the judge will lower it, prosecutors seek to shield themselves from responsibility if the accused fails to appear in court. The court, in turn, is under

A third, obviously relevant factor considered very relevant by the judiciary is the defendant's prior criminal record. *[margin: prior record]*

Other factors are the defendant's background, such as his community ties, financial status, and character references. *[margin: char.]*

Of course if the defendant's counsel is present at the bail hearing, she tries to supply facts in attempting to secure the client's release on the best conditions possible.[20]

It should be noted that there are public pressures exerted on the judiciary that may well influence the bail-setting decision. This has been particularly the case in high-profile crimes such as the charges against Michael Jackson for child molestation, and charges against suspected terrorists after 9/11.

D. FOUR SAMPLE CASES

In the following fact situations, consider what arguments you see for and against recommending bail for the accused. As judge, would you set bail? What conditions would you set, if any, in addition to a promise to appear? As a private bondsman, whose general practice is either to accept 10% of the bond as a non-refundable premium or to refuse the client, would you take the risk? *[margin: pro/con? bail. conditions? would bondsman accept risk?]*

1. The 39–year–old defendant was arrested 2 days ago for attempted murder and aggravated battery. He has a prior record of 10 armed robberies and one attempted jailbreak while awaiting an earlier trial. Yesterday, he threatened the life of a cellmate, and boasted that he always carried a loaded gun. He has an excellent record for his prior experience on parole, and a perfect attendance record while free on bond for a prior conviction. He has been working part-time, and for the past 6 months has lived with his mother. The maximum sentence is 10 years. Would your answer differ if he had no job, and no permanent address? If he were charged with burglary? With armed robbery? With vagrancy?

2. A 36–year–old defendant is charged with breaking and entering. She is a heroin addict, and has a record of seven prior convictions for breaking and entering, as well as two convictions for possession of narcotics. She lives with her three young children, and works part-time in the department store where she was arrested. Should she be released on bail? How much bail should be required?

3. A 65–year-old defendant is charged in an arson conspiracy. He owned and ran a diner in New York City for 25 years, until it burned to the ground. He has no passport and no family members who live in New York. He has a brother in Greece. This is his first offense. Should bail be set? How high? Would it make a difference if a person died in the fire? Would it make a difference if the defendant had a passport?

4. A Muslim student is charged with lying to the grand jury about knowing some of the individuals who took part in the 9/11 terrorist attacks. He is not charged with taking part in the attacks. He traveled extensively in the Middle

---

pressure to keep the prison population down. Cole, The Decision to Prosecute, 4 Law & Soc'y Rev. 331 (1970).

20. Federal Rule 44 provides that an indigent defendant has a right to counsel at the bail hearing. But the bail hearing has never been held to be a "critical stage" at which counsel must be provided as a matter of constitutional law. As a result, only eight states guarantee indigents the right to counsel at bail hearings. See Colbert, Thirty–Five Years After *Gideon*: The Illusory Right to Counsel at Bail Proceedings, 1998 Univ.Ill.L.Rev. 1.

East before settling in San Diego and becoming an American citizen. He has a brother in the United States. He has traveled back to the Middle East on several occasions, and the prosecutor submits a statement from a State Department official that the defendant has been contributed to Muslim charities "known to funnel monies to Al Qaeda." Do you set bail? Are you worried about a public outcry?

IV. BAIL REFORM AND PREVENTIVE DETENTION

A. THE FEDERAL BAIL REFORM ACTS

Congress, concerned about the arbitrariness and unfairness of a system of pretrial release that depended heavily on bail bondsmen, enacted the Bail Reform Act of 1966, a statute emulated by many states. The purpose of the 1966 Act was to encourage federal courts to release accused persons without requiring them to deal with bail bondsmen. Apparently, courts were to consider only whether pretrial release "will reasonably assure the appearance of the person for trial." No provision was made for confinement of an accused who might pose a "danger" to the community. The Act provided for alternative methods of assuring an appearance, including in-home detention and supervision by a designated person or organization.

Congress repealed the 1966 Bail Reform Act as part of its Comprehensive Crime Control Act of 1984, 18 U.S.C.A. §§ 3141–3150. The Bail Reform Act of 1984 was an important part of the comprehensive overhaul of federal criminal law and is much less generous to defendants than the prior act. The most important changes are the explicit recognition that potential dangerousness to the community may be considered in pretrial release decisions, and the possibility for preventive detention without bail. The heart of the Bail Reform Act of 1984 is found in 18 U.S.C. § 3142, which provides in part as follows:

§ 3142. Release or detention of a defendant pending trial

(a) In general. Upon the appearance before a judicial officer of a person charged with an offense, the judicial officer shall issue an order that, pending trial, the person be—

(1) Released on personal recognizance or upon execution of an unsecured appearance bond, under subsection (b) of this section;

(2) released on a condition or combination of conditions under subsection (c) of this section;

(3) temporarily detained to permit revocation of conditional release, deportation, or exclusion under subsection (d) of this section; or

(4) detained under subsection (e) of this section.

(b) Release on personal recognizance or unsecured appearance bond. The judicial officer shall order the pretrial release of the person on personal recognizance, or upon execution of an unsecured appearance bond in an amount specified by the court, subject to the condition that the person not commit a Federal, State, or local crime during the period of release, unless the judicial officer determines that such release will not reasonably assure the appearance of the person as required or will endanger the safety of any other person or the community.

(c) Release on conditions.

(1) If the judicial officer determines that the release described in subsection (b) of this section will not reasonably assure the appearance of the person as required or will endanger the safety of any other person or the community, such judicial officer shall order the pretrial release of the person—

(A) subject to the condition that the person not commit a Federal, State, or local crime during the period of release; and

(B) subject to the least restrictive further condition, or combination of conditions, that such judicial officer determines will reasonably assure the appearance of the person as required and the safety of any other person and the community, which may include the condition that the person—

(i) remain in the custody of a designated person, who agrees to assume supervision and to report any violation of a release condition to the court, if the designated person is able reasonably to assure the judicial officer that the person will appear as required and will not pose a danger to the safety of any other person or the community;

(ii) maintain employment, or, if unemployed, actively seek employment;

(iii) maintain or commence an educational program;

(iv) abide by specified restrictions on personal associations, place of abode, or travel;

(v) avoid all contact with an alleged victim of the crime and with a potential witness who may testify concerning the offense;

(vi) report on a regular basis to a designated law enforcement agency, pretrial services agency, or other agency;

(vii) comply with a specified curfew;

(viii) refrain from possessing a firearm, destructive device, or other dangerous weapon;

(ix) refrain from excessive use of alcohol, or any use of a narcotic drug or other controlled substance * * * without a prescription by a licensed medical practitioner;

(x) undergo available medical, psychological, or psychiatric treatment, including treatment for drug or alcohol dependency, and remain in a specified institution if required for that purpose;

(xi) execute an agreement to forfeit upon failing to appear as required, property of a sufficient unencumbered value, including money, as is reasonably necessary to assure the appearance of the person as required, and shall provide the court with proof of ownership and the value of the property along with information regarding existing encumbrances as the judicial office may require;

(xii) execute a bail bond with solvent sureties; who will execute an agreement to forfeit in such amount as is reasonably necessary to assure appearance of the person as required * * *;

(xiii) return to custody for specified hours following release for employment, schooling, or other limited purposes; and

(xiv) satisfy any other condition that is reasonably necessary to assure the appearance of the person as required and to assure the safety of any other person and the community.

(2) The judicial officer may not impose a financial condition that results in the pretrial detention of the person.

(3) The judicial officer may at any time amend the order to impose additional or different conditions of release.

(d) Temporary detention to permit revocation of conditional release, deportation, or exclusion. If the judicial officer determines that—

(1) such person—

(A) is, and was at the time the offense was committed, on—

(i) release pending trial for a felony under Federal, State, or local law;

(ii) release pending imposition or execution of sentence, appeal of sentence or conviction, or completion of sentence, for any offense under Federal, State, or local law; or

(iii) probation or parole for any offense under Federal, State, or local law; or

(B) is not a citizen of the United States or lawfully admitted for permanent residence * * *; and

(2) the person may flee or pose a danger to any other person or the community;

such judicial officer shall order the detention of the person, for a period of not more than ten days, excluding Saturdays, Sundays, and holidays, and direct the attorney for the Government to notify the appropriate court, probation or parole official, or State or local law enforcement official, or the appropriate official of the Immigration and Naturalization Service. * * *

(e) Detention. If, after a hearing pursuant to the provisions of subsection (f) of this section, the judicial officer finds that no condition or combination of conditions will reasonably assure the appearance of the person as required and the safety of any other person and the community, such judicial officer shall order the detention of the person before trial. In a case described in subsection (f)(1) of this section, a rebuttable presumption arises that no condition or combination of conditions will reasonably assure the safety of any other person and the community if such judicial officer finds that—

(1) the person has been convicted of a Federal offense that is described in subsection (f)(1) of this section, or of a State or local offense that would have been an offense described in subsection (f)(1) of this section if a circumstance giving rise to Federal jurisdiction had existed;

(2) the offense described in paragraph (1) of this subsection was committed while the person was on release pending trial for a Federal, State, or local offense; and

(3) a period of not more than five years has elapsed since the date of conviction, or the release of the person from imprisonment, for the offense described in paragraph (1) of this subsection, whichever is later.

Subject to rebuttal by the person, it shall be presumed that no condition or combination of conditions will reasonably assure the appearance of the person as required and the safety of the community if the judicial officer finds that there is probable cause to believe that the person committed an offense for which a maximum term of imprisonment of ten years or more is prescribed [for a violation of Federal narcotics laws].

(f) Detention hearing. The judicial officer shall hold a hearing to determine whether any condition or combination of conditions set forth in subsection (c) of this section will reasonably assure the appearance of the person as required and the safety of any other person and the community—

(1) upon motion of the attorney for the Government, in a case that involves—[violent crimes, capital crimes, certain specified drug crimes, and any felony if the person has been previously convicted of other specified crimes]

(2) upon motion of the attorney for the Government or upon the judicial officer's own motion, in a case that involves—

(A) a serious risk that such person will flee; or

(B) a serious risk that the person will obstruct or attempt to obstruct justice, or threaten, injure, or intimidate, or attempt to threaten, injure, or intimidate, a prospective witness or juror.

The hearing shall be held immediately upon the person's first appearance before the judicial officer unless that person, or the attorney for the Government, seeks a continuance. * * * At the hearing, the person has the right to be represented by counsel, and, if financially unable to obtain adequate representation, to have counsel appointed. The person shall be afforded an opportunity to testify, to present witnesses, to cross-examine witnesses who appear at the hearing, and to present information by proffer or otherwise. The rules concerning admissibility of evidence in criminal trials do not apply to the presentation and consideration of information at the hearing. The facts the judicial officer uses to support a finding pursuant to subsection (e) that no condition or combination of conditions will reasonably assure the safety of any other person and the community shall be supported by clear and convincing evidence. * * *

(g) Factors to be considered. The judicial officer shall, in determining whether there are conditions of release that will reasonably assure the appearance of the person as required and the safety of any other person and the community, take into account the available information concerning—

(1) the nature and circumstances of the offense charged, including whether the offense is a crime of violence or involves a narcotic drug;

(2) the weight of the evidence against the person;

(3) the history and characteristics of the person, including—

    (A) the person's character, physical and mental condition, family ties, employment, financial resources, length of residence in the community, community ties, past conduct, history relating to drug or alcohol abuse, criminal history, and record concerning appearance at court proceedings; and

    (B) whether, at the time of the current offense or arrest, the person was on probation, on parole, or on other release pending trial, sentencing, appeal, or completion of sentence for an offense under Federal, State, or local law; and

    (4) the nature and seriousness of the danger to any person or the community that would be posed by the person's release. * * *

    (j) Presumption of innocence. Nothing in this section shall be construed as modifying or limiting the presumption of innocence.

* * *

    Unlike the earlier Act, the 1984 Act specifically requires the court to take into account the risk to public safety posed by the accused's release. The court must select the least restrictive conditions that will assure the accused's appearance and protect public safety. If the court finds that no condition or combination of conditions is adequate, then the person must be detained before trial. A rebuttable presumption in favor of pretrial detention exists under certain circumstances, most importantly for most drug crimes and for crimes of violence.

    There is little doubt that the 1984 legislation makes it more difficult for some defendants to obtain release pending trial and for most defendants who are convicted to obtain release pending sentencing. Before the 1984 Act, only about 2% of federal defendants were detained without bail pending trial. In 1990, the figure rose to 29% of all federal defendants. The rate of detention in 1990 was 50% for those charged with violent crime, and 37% for those charged with drug crimes. Bureau of Justice Statistics, Pretrial Release of Federal Felony Defendants (1994).

    It would be wrong to conclude, however, that the statute represents a uniformly negative attitude toward pretrial release. As noted above, no accused may be detained pending trial without findings by the judicial officer. A defendant may seek review of these findings. [§ 3145]. Most importantly, the statute explicitly provides that a financial condition may not be imposed if it results in the pretrial detention of the person. This means that, unless the judicial officer finds that no condition or conditions of release will provide that an accused will appear and will protect the community, the officer must provide for release of the accused.[21]

---

21. Senate Report No. 98–225 explains the 1984 legislation as viewed by the Senate Judiciary Committee:

    The constraints of the Bail Reform Act [of 1966] fail to grant the courts the authority to impose conditions of release geared toward assuring community safety, or the authority to deny release to those defendants who pose an especially grave risk to the safety of the community.

* * *

    If a defendant is detained, he is logically precluded from engaging in criminal activity, and thus the correctness of the detention decision cannot be factually determined. However, the presence of certain combinations of offense and offender characteristics, such as the nature and seriousness of the offense charged, the extent of prior arrests and convictions, and a history of drug addiction, have been shown in studies to have a strong positive relationship to predicting the

Which system of pretrial release is preferable, the one established by the 1966 Act or the one established in 1984? Will magistrates consider dangerousness in making release decisions no matter what the governing statute or rule provides? If some magistrates might, is it desirable to have some criteria set forth to govern decisionmaking? If Congress concluded that federal courts took dangerousness into account without saying so prior to 1984, what guarantee is there that the courts will not actually use criteria other than those set forth in the 1984 statute when making decisions?

Applying the Bail Reform Act of 1984

The Bail Reform Act of 1984 has caused a number of interpretive problems for the courts. One question is how a court is to assess the risk of flight. In United States v. Jessup, 757 F.2d 378 (1st Cir.1985), the court sustained the presumption in the Bail Reform Act of 1984 that a defendant charged with a serious drug offense poses a serious risk of flight. It concluded that Congress shifted only the burden of production with respect to the flight issue to the defendant and that the government continued to bear the burden of persuasion with respect to likelihood of flight. The court also concluded, however, that the presumption did not disappear when the defendant offered rebuttal evidence. Instead, it adopted a "middle ground" which requires judges and magistrates to consider Congress' finding that suspects charged with serious drug offenses pose special risks of flight and to weigh that finding when deciding whether the government has satisfied its persuasion burden. See also United States v. Xulam, 84 F.3d 441 (D.C.Cir.1996) (in non-drug cases, when the government seeks pretrial detention of a defendant on the ground that he poses a risk of flight, the standard it must satisfy is a preponderance of the evidence).

Drug Cases

The court in United States v. Rueben, 974 F.2d 580 (5th Cir.1992), set forth the standards for pretrial detention in drug cases as follows: (1) probable cause as to a serious drug crime creates a rebuttable presumption that no conditions of release exist which would assure the defendant's appearance and the safety of the community; (2) where the defendant presents considerable evidence of longstanding ties to the community, the presumption of flight has been rebutted; (3) the risk of continued drug trafficking while on bail constitutes a safety risk to the community; (4) for pretrial detention to be imposed, it is enough for the court to find either the lack of a reasonable assurance of the defendant's appearance, or the safety risk to others or the community; (5) the rebuttable

probability that a defendant will commit a new offense while on release. While predictions which attempt to identify those defendants who will pose a significant danger to the safety of others if released are not infallible, the Committee believes that judges can, by considering factors such as those noted above, make such predictions with an acceptable level of accuracy.

* * *

Providing statutory authority to conduct a hearing focusing on the issue of a defendant's dangerousness, and to permit an order of detention where a defendant poses such a risk to others that no form of conditional release is sufficient, would allow the courts to address the issue of pretrial criminality honestly and effectively. It would also be fairer to the defendant than the indirect method of achieving detention through the imposition of financial conditions beyond his reach.

presumption against release shifts only the weight of producing evidence, not the burden of persuasion, but the mere production of some evidence does not completely rebut the presumption; and (6) in making its ultimate determination, "the court may still consider the finding by Congress that drug offenders pose a special risk of flight and dangerousness to society."

In *Rueben*, the court of appeals held that the district court erred in releasing two drug defendants on a $100,000 unsecured bond. The court found that the defendants' "alleged family ties was hardly more than a reflection of the drug conspiracy itself." Similarly, the fact that one defendant owned a house "is not compelling as a tie to the community when its loss through forfeiture is a possibility because of its use in drug trafficking." Nor had the defendants presented any evidence to "indicate that they will not continue to engage in drug trafficking if released on bail pending trial."

Has the court in *Reuben* in effect established an irrebuttable presumption of detention in drug cases? See also United States v. Smith, 79 F.3d 1208 (D.C.Cir. 1996) (indictment on drug charges creates a rebuttable presumption that no condition would reasonably assure the safety of the community; no error in ordering detention where the defendant was an "enforcer" in a drug conspiracy, and murdered a rival drug dealer in furtherance of the conspiracy); United States v. Cisneros, 328 F.3d 610 (10th Cir. 2003) (pretrial release properly denied where the defendant was charged with taking part in an international drug conspiracy, the weight of the evidence was significant, the defendant had the resources to abscond to Mexico, and the evidence suggested that the defendant was deeply involved in serious acts of violence). Compare United States v. Giampa, 755 F.Supp. 665 (W.D.Pa.1990)(presumption rebutted where drug defendant shows his long residence in the area, his close ties to his family, steady employment history, lack of resources or contacts that would enable him to flee the country with ease, and the fact that he had no record and did not appear to live the life of a serious drug dealer; court notes that the defendant was not the kind of "international narcotics trafficker" with whom Congress was most concerned when it enacted the Bail Reform Act).

Less Intrusive Alternatives

The ultimate statutory determination under the Bail Reform Act is whether "there are conditions of release that will reasonably assure the appearance of the [defendant] as required and the safety of any other person in the community." This statutory language is sometimes invoked by defendants to suggest less intrusive alternatives to pretrial detention. A typically suggested alternative is home detention and electronic monitoring. As to the effectiveness of this alternative to detention, consider the facts of United States v. Tortora, 922 F.2d 880 (1st Cir.1990):

> An alleged soldier in the Patriarca Family of the Mafia was indicted for violation of the RICO statute. His three predicate crimes in furtherance of the RICO enterprise were: extortion; violation of the Travel Act; and conspiracy to violate the Travel Act. Upon the grant of the government's motion for pretrial detention, the defendant proposed certain release conditions to assure the safety of the community. These conditions mandated, for example, that the defendant not violate the law, appear at scheduled

proceedings, eschew possession of weapons and substance abuse, restrict his travel, etc. In granting the release order, the [district] court required the defendant to (1) remain at home twenty-four hours a day, except for a reasonable number of visits to doctors and lawyers, wearing an electronic bracelet; (2) refrain from communicating with any person not approved by the prosecutor and defense counsel; (3) meet with codefendants only in the presence of counsel for the purpose of preparing a defense; (4) allow only one telephone line into his residence, hooking it up to a pen register; and (5) post the residence—a house owned by his brother—as security.

The court of appeals vacated the order releasing Tortora. It first agreed with the district court that Tortora was properly classified as dangerous. The court reasoned that membership in an Organized Crime Organization was clearly relevant to dangerousness, rejecting Tortora's argument that such "associational ties" could not be considered. It concluded that so long as the defendant was judged as an individual, his devotion to the Mafia was important evidence of his dangerous character, especially where Tortora, at a ritualistic Mafia ceremony, "threatened to kill his brother if the latter posed a danger to any member of the organization." The court also rejected Tortora's argument that devotion to his family precluded a finding of dangerousness. It responded that in light of Tortora's oath of fealty to the Mafia, "there is every reason to believe that he will prefer Family over family."

The *Tortora* court next held that the release conditions were not adequate to assure the community's safety in view of the fact that virtually all of the conditions hinged upon the defendant's good faith compliance. As such they could be too easily manipulated or circumvented. For instance, electronic monitoring "cannot be expected to prevent a defendant from committing crimes or deter him from participating in felonious activity within the monitoring radius"; and pen registers could be evaded by "the surreptitious introduction into his home of a cellular telephone." The court concluded that the "honor-dependent" nature of the restrictions took on great significance where "little about the defendant or his history suggests that good faith will be forthcoming." The court rejected the argument that the conditions of release could be amended to eliminate the risk of danger to the community:

> Given the breadth of human imagination, it will always be possible to envision some set of release conditions which might reasonably assure the safety of the community. For instance, agents could be posted by the government to watch Tortora at all times to ensure that he remains compliant; the guards could search all visitors, dog Tortora's footsteps en route to all appointments, and otherwise act as private jailers. But the Bail Reform Act, as we read it, does not require release of a dangerous defendant if the only combination of conditions that would reasonably assure societal safety consists of heroic measures beyond those which can fairly be said to have been within Congress' contemplation.

Tortora argued that the release conditions proposed by him and adopted by the lower court were sufficient because the alternative was incarceration—and if kept in prison, he would have at least as much ability to commit crimes as he would have if released. The court viewed this argument as "perverse" and stated:

The Bail Reform Act does not ordain that dangerousness upon release is to be measured relative to dangerousness if incarcerated, and for good reason: the ability of an incarcerated person to commit crimes while in jail is a problem for the Executive Branch to solve. The idea that someone who otherwise ought not to be released should be let loose by the courts because his jailers may not prevent him from committing crimes in prison comprises a classic non sequitur * * *.

See also United States v. Gotti, 776 F.Supp. 666 (E.D.N.Y.1991)(ordering pretrial detention and rejecting home detention as an alternative: "Home detention and electronic monitoring at best elaborately replicate a detention facility without the confidence of security such a facility instills."); United States v. Ciccone, 312 F.3d 535 (2d Cir. 2002) (rejecting alternatives of high amount of bail secured by real property, in-home detention, restricted visitation and telephone calls, and electronic monitoring).

The Right to a Prompt Hearing: United States v. Montalvo–Murillo

In United States v. Montalvo–Murillo, 495 U.S. 711 (1990), the government failed to comply with the provision in the Bail Reform Act of 1984 that a hearing to determine the propriety of pretrial release be held "immediately upon the person's first appearance before the judicial officer." The district court ultimately found that Montalvo–Murillo posed a risk of flight and a danger to the community, and that no condition of release could give reasonable assurances against these risks. The court nonetheless released Montalvo–Murillo due to the lack of a timely hearing. The government challenged the release order and argued that release was an unwarranted remedy.

Justice Kennedy, writing for six Justices, agreed with the government. He acknowledged the importance of a prompt hearing, but asserted that "neither the timing requirements nor any other part of the Act can be read to require, or even suggest, that a timing error must result in release of a person who should otherwise be detained." The majority reasoned as follows:

> The safety of society does not become forfeit to the accident of noncompliance with statutory time limits where the Government is ready and able to come forward with the requisite showing to meet the burden of proof required by the statute. * * * An order of release in the face of the Government's ability to prove at once that detention is required by the law has neither causal nor proportional relation to any harm caused by the delay in holding the hearing.

Justice Kennedy concluded that release of Montalvo–Murillo was an unwarranted remedy because he had not been prejudiced by the delay:

> In this case, it is clear that the noncompliance with the timing requirement had no substantial influence on the outcome of the proceeding. Because respondent was dangerous and likely to flee, he would have been detained if his hearing had been held upon his first appearance rather than a few days later. On these facts, the detention was harmless.

The majority did not decide what remedies would be appropriate for a failure to comply with the timely hearing requirement, nor what remedies would be available to a person detained beyond the statutory limit and later found to have been eligible for release.

Justice Stevens wrote a dissenting opinion joined by Justices Brennan and Marshall. The dissenters argued that the majority had undervalued the importance of a prompt hearing concerning pretrial detention. Justice Stevens concluded that "Congress has written detailed legislation in a sensitive area that requires the Government to turn square corners. The Court today, however, permits federal prosecutors to violate the law with impunity."

After *Montalvo–Murillo,* what incentive does the prosecutor have to comply with the timely hearing requirement? What remedies other than release can be imposed by the court? Does it follow that because a person is found dangerous and likely to flee at a *later* hearing, the failure to provide an earlier hearing was harmless?

Time Served and the Bail Reform Act: Reno v. Koray

Under the Bail Reform Act, it is possible that a defendant could be released pending trial and yet remain subject to substantial restrictions on liberty, such as confinement in a treatment center or under house arrest. Is such a defendant entitled to a reduction for pre-sentence "time served" if he is ultimately sentenced? Or must he actually be incarcerated to have credit for time served? This question is controlled by statute. 18 U.S.C. § 3585(b) provides that a defendant generally must "be given credit toward the service of a term of imprisonment for any time he has spent in official detention prior to the date the sentence commences." The limits of this provision in light of the Bail Reform Act are indicated by Reno v. Koray, 515 U.S. 50 (1995). Koray was convicted of money laundering. A federal magistrate judge "released" him on bail, pending sentencing, pursuant to the Bail Reform Act. The "release" order required that Koray be confined to a community treatment center, where he stayed for 150 days, leaving the center only once and under supervision. The Supreme Court, in an opinion by Chief Justice Rehnquist, held that since Koray was "released" by the magistrate judge's order under the terms of the Bail Reform Act, he could not be considered in "official detention" while confined in the treatment center so as to receive the credit provided by 18 U.S.C. § 3585(b). Chief Justice Rehnquist set forth the relationship between § 3585(b) and the Bail Reform Act in the following analysis:

> Section 3585(b) provides credit for time "spent in official detention prior to the date the sentence commences," thus making clear that credit is awarded only for presentence restraints on liberty. Because the Bail Reform Act of 1984 is the body of law that authorizes federal courts to place presentence restraints on a defendant's liberty, the "official detention" language of § 3585(b) must be construed in conjunction with that Act. * * *

> The Bail Reform Act of 1984 provides a federal court with two choices when dealing with a criminal defendant who has been "charged with an offense" and is awaiting trial, 18 U.S.C. § 3142(a), or who "has been found guilty of an offense and . . . is awaiting imposition or execution of sentence," § 3143(a)(1). The court may either (1) "release" the defendant on bail or (2) order him "detained" without bail. A court may "release" a defendant subject to a variety of restrictive conditions, including residence in a

community treatment center. If, however, the court "finds that no condition or combination of conditions will reasonably assure the appearance of the person as required and the safety of any other person and the community," the court "shall order the detention of the person," by issuing a "detention order" "directing that the person be committed to the custody of the Attorney General for confinement in a corrections facility." Thus, under the language of the Bail Reform Act of 1984, a defendant suffers "detention" only when committed to the custody of the Attorney General; a defendant admitted to bail on restrictive conditions, like respondent was, is "released."

The Chief Justice recognized that a defendant "released" to a community treatment center "could be subject to restraints which do not materially differ from those imposed on a 'detained' defendant committed to the custody of the Attorney General, and thence assigned to a treatment center." But this did not change the result mandated by the statute. The latter defendant would be entitled to a credit while the former would not.

Justice Ginsburg wrote a concurring opinion in *Koray*. She agreed with the majority's statutory construction, but added that "Koray has not argued before us that he did not elect bail intelligently, i.e., with comprehension that time in the halfway house, unlike time in jail, would yield no credit against his eventual sentence." Justice Ginsburg would not foreclose the possibility that a defendant has a due process right to "notice and a comprehension check" before accepting the terms of release under the Bail Reform Act. Justice Stevens was the lone dissenter in *Koray*. Does a statutory scheme make sense where "release" and "detention" can result in similar deprivations of liberty?

Application of the Bail Reform Act to Persons Charged With Acts of Terrorism

After the attacks of September 11, 2001, the Bail Reform Act has been used for preventive detention of a number of defendants charged with having ties to terrorism. [It should be noted that the Bail Reform Act applies only to those who are going to be tried in a civilian court; if the government decides to treat a suspected terrorist as an "enemy combatant" then preventive detention is argued to be justified on separation of powers grounds–see Chapter 10]. In the following case, the court applies the Bail Reform Act to suspected terrorists, with predictable results.

UNITED STATES v. GOBA

U.S. District Court, Western District of New York, 2003.
240 F.Supp.2d 242.

SKRETNY, **District Judge.**

I. INTRODUCTION

Defendants Yahya Goba, Shafal Mosed, Yasein Taher and Mukhtar Al–Bakri are presently detained pending trial pursuant to an order issued by United States Magistrate Judge H. Ken-

neth Schroeder, Jr. on October 8, 2002. Currently before me are motions filed on behalf of Defendants Goba, Mosed, Taher and Al–Bakri for revocation of the detention order.

As discussed more fully below, I will deny Defendants' motions. In doing so, I find that the charged offense, 18

U.S.C. § 2339B, is a "crime of violence," and that the Government has demonstrated by clear and convincing evidence that Defendants pose a danger to the community. Significantly, the Government has produced credible evidence that each defendant associated himself with al-Qaeda, a designated terrorist organization with the avowed aim of inflicting death and destruction on American citizens and interests. In reaching my decision, I note that the express purpose of a terrorist training camp such as al-Farooq is to make its participants more dangerous (and thus more useful to the terrorist group) than they were before they received the training. Given the well-known modus operandi of terrorist organizations such as al-Qaeda, the stated goals of Usama bin Ladin, and the evidence regarding the type of training that each Defendant received while at the camp, I find that no release condition or combination of release conditions will adequately safeguard the community.

In addition, I find that the Government has proven by a preponderance of the evidence that each defendant poses a risk of flight if released. The Government proffered evidence indicating that each defendant has the ability to sustain himself abroad, either with his own resources or through the use of an international support network. This ability, combined with Western New York's proximity to the Canadian border and the potential period of incarceration faced by each defendant, is sufficient to establish that no release condition or combination of conditions will assure the continued appearance of these Defendants.

Therefore, Defendants Goba, Mosed, Taher and Al–Bakri shall remain detained pending trial.

* * *

II. BACKGROUND

On October 21, 2002, a federal Grand Jury in the Western District of New York indicted each of the above-captioned defendants on two counts of violating 18 U.S.C. §§ 2339B. Count One charges each defendant with conspiring to knowingly provide material support and resources to al-Qaeda, a foreign terrorist organization. Count Two charges each defendant with the substantive offense of knowingly and unlawfully providing material support and resources to al-Qaeda.

Briefly, the Government alleges that during the spring and summer of 2001, Defendants traveled in two separate groups from the United States to Pakistan, and from Pakistan to Afghanistan, where they attended an al-Qaeda terrorist training camp. Defendants allegedly received firearms and other tactical training, underwent anti-American and anti-Israeli indoctrination, were lectured on martyrdom and the justification for using suicide as a weapon, and attended a speech personally given by Usama bin Ladin that, in part, emphasized the need to prepare and train for a "fight against the Americans." After several weeks, Defendants left the camp and returned to Lackawanna, New York. All resumed their regular lives until their arrests on or about September 13, 2002.

At their initial appearances after their arrests, the Government moved for the pretrial detention of each defendant. Defendants opposed the Government's motion, prompting Judge Schroeder to conduct a single, comprehensive detention hearing that ultimately spanned the course of four days—September 18, 19 and 20, 2002, and October 3, 2002. Defendants were present and represented by assigned counsel during the hearing, at which the Government and Defendants proceeded by way of proffer with exhibits.

On October 8, 2002, Judge Schroeder issued a widely publicized Decision and Order granting the Government's Motion to Detain in part and denying it in part. United States v. Goba, 220 F.Supp.2d 182 (W.D.N.Y. 2002). * * * Shortly after Judge Schroeder issued his Decision and Order, Defendants filed motions for revocation with this Court. * * *

III. DISCUSSION AND ANALYSIS

* * *

Bail Reform Act Overview

Under the Bail Reform Act, 18 U.S.C. §§ 3141, et seq., pretrial detention is available only pursuant to § 3142(e). That subsection expressly authorizes the pretrial detention of a defendant upon a judicial finding that "no condition or combination of conditions will reasonably assure the appearance of the person as required and the safety of any other person and the community."

Pretrial detention under § 3142(e), however, must be predicated on at least one of the six categories or entry points enumerated in § 3142(f). Satisfaction of any category triggers a mandatory detention hearing before a judicial officer. Three of the categories, §§ 3142(f)(1)(A)-(C), are based on the nature of the charged offense, including the potential term of incarceration; § 3142(f)(1)(D) is based on the nature of the charged offense and the defendant's prior criminal record; and the final categories, §§ 3142(f)(2)(A) and (B), are based on whether there is a serious risk that the defendant will either flee, or obstruct justice or threaten a prospective witness or juror. It is the government's burden to prove by a preponderance of the evidence that the defendant falls into one or more of the six categories.

Assuming satisfaction of one of the six entry points, the court must next examine the factors set forth in § 3142(g) in connection with its determination as to whether any condition or combination of conditions set forth in § 3142(c) will reasonably assure the defendant's appearance and the safety of other persons and the community. In this regard, the Government must establish risk of flight by a preponderance of the evidence, or danger to others and the community by clear and convincing evidence.

Defendants' Points of Argument

Defendants' points of argument can be distilled into five distinct areas: (1) the Government improperly proceeded by proffer, (2) 18 U.S.C. § 2339B is not a "crime of violence," (3) Defendants are not flight risks, (4) Defendants are not dangers to the community, and (5) there are conditions that this Court could impose to assure each defendant's future appearance and the safety of the community. Each point will be discussed in turn.

1. Proceeding by Proffer

The Bail Reform Act sets certain parameters within which detention proceedings must be held. For example, it requires that any detention hearing be held immediately upon the defendant's initial appearance and that the defendant be afforded an opportunity to testify, present witnesses, cross-examine witnesses, and present information by way of proffer or otherwise. 18 U.S.C. § 3142(f). Generally though, detention proceedings are informal: the Federal Rules of Evidence do not apply, and the Government is held to burdens of proof less than the customary criminal burden of proof beyond a reasonable doubt.

The Bail Reform Act remains silent, however, regarding how the Government must proceed in satisfaction of its burdens. In this Circuit it is well established that the Government may, at a minimum, proceed by way of proffer, just as the defendant is permitted to do under § 3142(f).

This seemingly low threshold is consistent with the informal nature of detention proceedings and the desire to keep them from morphing into "mini-trials," yet tempered by the court's obligation to ensure the reliability of proffered information. Whether presented by proffer or direct evidence, courts retain the responsibility for assessing the accuracy of the Government's proof. To that end, courts are vested with considerable discretion to determine, on a case-by-case basis, the appropriate method by which the Government must present its case.

* * * Defendants contend that in light of their challenges to portions of the Government's proffer, this Court should direct the Government to produce live witnesses subject to cross-examination, namely FBI Special Agent Edward Needham, who took Defendant Alwan's statement, and either Agent Gamal Abdel–Hafiz or Agent Rachel F. Pifer, one or both of whom took Defendant Al–Bakri's statement. Defendants argue that further inquiry into the reliability of these statements is crucial because they comprise the critical pieces of evidence supporting the Government's proffer. By Defendants' account, the absence of the agents' live testimony undermines the sufficiency of the Government's proffer in its totality. This Court disagrees.

The Government proffered a great deal of information during the proceedings before Judge Schroeder. Some of that information was drawn from the statements given by Defendants Alwan and Al–Bakri, while other information was presented by way of direct evidence, *e.g.,* passports, passport stamps, customs reports, airline boarding passes and the fruits of exe-

cuted search warrants. Further, the Government proffered additional information that was neither derived from the statements nor from the direct evidence identified above.

To be sure, the statements at issue are salient. Defendants Alwan and Al–Bakri admit that they traveled to Afghanistan and attended the al-Farooq training camp operated by al-Qaeda. Moreover, they expressly place Defendants Goba, Mosed, Galab and Taher at the al-Farooq camp. Further, Defendant Alwan's statement is proffered to support the Government's assertion that Defendants attended the camp because they wanted to receive the training.

The Government also proffered evidence of the tactical training offered at al-Farooq, which included training on a variety of firearms, as well as jihad and anti-American indoctrination. This proffer was derived directly from Defendant Alwan's and Defendant Al–Bakri's statements. Notably, information in the statements also indicates that each defendant attended a speech delivered by al-Qaeda leader Usama bin Ladin, wherein bin Ladin espoused anti-American and anti-Israeli sentiments, and addressed the importance of training and fighting for the cause of Islam.

At this stage, Defendants' stated purpose for seeking to examine Agents Needham, Abdel–Hafiz and Pifer is to test the reliability of Defendant Alwan's and Defendant Al–Bakri's statements. However, despite the serious implications that these statements may have for Defendants, this Court finds nothing in the record to suggest that they are unreliable. Indeed, Defendants do not proffer that the statements were made involuntarily or that Agents Needham, Abdel–Hafiz or Pifer exerted undue influence or otherwise acted in violation of Defendant Alwan's or Al–Bakri's rights. Rather, Defendants offer general denials of the substantive information contained in the statements, which this Court finds go to the ultimate weight afforded the statements, not to their reliability at the proffer stage. In this Court's view, Defendants articulate no serious challenge to the reliability of Defendant Alwan's and Defendant Al–Bakri's statements. Thus, this Court finds that Defendants' assertions of unreliability, standing alone, are insufficient to require the Government to produce live testimony from the agents in the absence of any other obligation to do so.

* * *

While Defendants' desire to gather additional information concerning the content and context of Defendant Alwan's and Defendant Al–Bakri's statements is understandable, a detention proceeding is not the proper forum for conducting discovery.

Accordingly, at this stage, this Court finds no cause for further inquiry into the reliability of the Government's proffer. The proceedings before Judge Schroeder comported with the Bail Reform Act's hearing requirements and the governing precedent in this Circuit. * * *

2. Entry Point: Crime of Violence

Turning now to the statutory framework, pretrial detention under § 3142(e) must be predicated on one of the six entry points enumerated in § 3142(f). The Government urges detention on two entry points: (1) crime of violence under § 3142(f)(1)(A), and (2) serious risk of flight under § 3142(f)(2)(A).

In this Circuit, a categorical analysis is employed to determine whether an offense constitutes a "crime of violence." The categorical analysis "focuses on the intrinsic nature of the offense, rather than on the factual cir-

cumstances surrounding any particular violation." This Court finds the categorical analysis applicable here.

The immediate issue is whether 18 U.S.C. § 2339B constitutes a "crime of violence" under 18 U.S.C. § 3156(a)(4)(B), which defines "crime of violence" as an offense "that is a felony and that, by its nature, involves a substantial risk that physical force against the person or property of another may be used in the course of committing the offense." This Court need not linger on this issue because it finds itself in agreement with the analysis employed by the Honorable T.S. Ellis, III, United States District Judge for the Eastern District of Virginia, who thoroughly addressed this point in United States v. Lindh, 212 F.Supp.2d 541, 580 (E.D.Va.2002).

In Lindh, Judge Ellis faced the issue of whether the substantive and conspiracy offenses of knowingly providing material resources and support to al-Qaeda in violation of § 2339B were "crimes of violence" within the meaning of 18 U.S.C. § 924(c)(3)(B). * * * Judge Ellis's application of the categorical analysis led him to conclude that both the conspiracy and substantive offenses of violating § 2339B are "crimes of violence." This Court agrees. As Judge Ellis noted: "When one provides material support or resources to a terrorist organization, there is a substantial risk that physical force against the person or property of another may be used in the course of committing the offense." * * * It takes little imagination to conclude that providing material support and resources to a terrorist organization creates a substantial risk that the violent aims of the terrorists will be realized. * * *

With the entry point requirement satisfied, this Court must now determine whether Defendants pose a risk of flight or danger to the community.

3. Risk of Flight

This Court finds, after considering the submitted evidence and thoroughly reviewing the 622–page transcript of the proceedings before Judge Schroeder, that each defendant poses a risk of flight if released. Specifically, this Court finds that each defendant has demonstrated the ability to sustain himself abroad for an extended period of time through his own or others' means. * * * Defendants Taher and Mosed paid $1309.20 in cash for their airline tickets, despite working in low-wage jobs. While that, in and of itself, is not determinative, this Court also notes that Defendants Taher and Mosed remained abroad for approximately two months. While it is unclear exactly how they supported themselves for the entire time they were outside of the United States, it is reasonable to conclude that they either had their own cash-on-hand or were supported by others in Pakistan and Afghanistan. In either case, whether Defendants Taher and Mosed have their own undisclosed financial resources or whether they may be the beneficiaries of others' support, the fact remains that they have demonstrated an ability to maintain themselves abroad for a considerable period of time.

The case is equally clear for Defendants Goba and Al–Bakri, whose pattern of travel more definitively indicates the existence of a support network. They traveled through six countries, sometimes by air, sometimes by ground. They had contact with unidentified co-conspirator "A," who coordinated their stay at the "guest house" in Quetta and their travel to al-Farooq. Moreover, Defendant Al–Bakri specifically told the FBI that the al-Qaeda members running the "guest house" financed his flight from Karachi to Quetta. Nothing in the record suggests that this type of assistance is no longer available.

Further, as for Defendants Goba and Al–Bakri, the proffered evidence demonstrates that they have the ability to travel internationally and cross borders without detection. Defendant Goba, for example, obtained Pakistani visas for himself, as well as for Defendants Al–Bakri and Alwan. Moreover, the passports seized from Defendants Goba, Al–Bakri and Alwan do not contain entrance or exit stamps from Afghanistan, indicating each defendant's ability to travel, at least to and from Afghanistan, undetected.

In each defendant's case, this Court finds that the evidence discussed above, as well as Western New York's proximity to the Canadian border and the potential period of incarceration that each defendant faces under the statute, provide evidence sufficient to conclude, by a preponderance of the evidence, that each Defendant presents a risk of flight if released pretrial.

4. Dangerousness to the Community

Again, having thoroughly reviewed the record in this case, this Court finds, by clear and convincing evidence, that each defendant attended and was trained at the al-Farooq training camp. More specifically, this Court finds that each defendant's attendance and training at the al-Farooq camp, as described in the Government's proffer, in and of itself, renders each defendant a danger to the community. The following recitation, mined from the proffers and direct evidence submitted, constitutes this Court's factual findings on the element of dangerousness.

Within a few days of arriving in Karachi, Pakistan, Defendants Goba, Al–Bakri and Alwan met unidentified co-conspirator "A." Unidentified co-conspirator "A" informed the group that they were going to meet "The Most Wanted," who they understood to be Usama bin Ladin. In his statement to the FBI, Defendant Al–Bakri declared that he knew making the trip was wrong. However, he and Defendants Goba and Alwan ultimately traveled to al-Farooq.

Prior to attending the camp, however, Defendants Goba, Al–Bakri and Alwan spent approximately one week at an al-Qaeda operated "guest house" in Quetta, Pakistan. Trainers at the "guest house" espoused anti-American and anti-Israeli sentiments and lectured on the justification for using suicide as a weapon. The trainers also showed videos about the terrorist attack on the USS Cole that detailed the method by which al-Qaeda carried out the attack. Attendees were also issued uniforms to be worn at the al-Farooq training camp. Defendants Goba, Al–Bakri and Alwan all went through this indoctrination.

After approximately twenty individuals had arrived at the "guest house," the group, including Defendants Goba, Al–Bakri and Alwan, traveled by automobile to the al-Farooq training camp, a camp maintained and financed by the al-Qaeda terrorist organization for the purpose of training and producing fighters for its cause.

While the record is not a model of clarity as it pertains to the exact dates that each defendant was at al-Farooq, the Government proffers that Defendant Alwan remained for ten days and that the rest of the Defendants—Goba, Mosed, Taher, Al–Bakri and Galab—remained for a total of five or six weeks of training, although not all of these Defendants were trained together. * * *

In their statements to the FBI, Defendants Alwan and Al–Bakri described * * * the military training provided at al-Farooq, and stated that each of them, as well as Defendants Goba, Mosed, Taher, and Galab received the same military and tactical training. Defendants received firearms training on a variety of weapons, including the Kalishnokov automatic weapon, handguns, and long-range rifles. In addition, Defendants Goba, Al–Bakri and Alwan received training or attended demonstrations in the use of C–4, TNT and other explosives, while Defendants Taher, Mosed and Galab received mountain climbing training.

Also while at al-Farooq, each defendant attended a speech delivered by Usama bin Ladin, who appeared in person under heavy guard. Bin Ladin spoke of the need to prepare and train for the upcoming fight against Americans, and spoke of the importance of fighting for the cause of Islam. Bin Ladin also espoused general anti-American and anti-Israeli sentiments. Moreover, trainers at al-Farooq supplemented bin Laden's remarks by speaking about jihad, the justification for using suicide, and how people who commit suicide attacks are martyrs.

Based on this proffered evidence, the Government urges this Court to recognize a *per se* rule linking attendance and training at a terrorist camp with dangerousness. However, outside the confines of this case, this Court is reluctant to adopt the Government's *per se* rule. Other cases may present factual circumstances that would not fit the Government's rule. In addition, the adoption of a *per se* rule, at least facially, connotes an evisceration of the individual consideration that each defendant is entitled to under the Bail Reform Act.

That said, this Court has little difficulty finding that in this case, each individual defendant's attendance and training at the al-Farooq camp makes him a danger to the community. The extent of the weapons and explosives training, as well as the indoctrination that each Defendant underwent, combined with this Court's recognition of the well known fact that terrorist organizations have a modus operandi of training unassuming individuals and then activating them at a later date, cause this Court to conclude that Defendants' attendance and training at the al-Farooq camp, in and of itself, is more than sufficient to establish by clear and convincing evidence that each defendant poses a danger to the community. After all, the express purpose of attending a terrorist training camp is to increase one's dangerousness. That is, al-Qaeda's goal in running the camp is to make individuals more dangerous coming out than they were going in. Otherwise, there is simply no reason to attend or run a terrorist training camp.

Moreover, this Court finds the fact that each of these defendants was able to personally attend a speech by Usama bin Ladin, a man who is wanted worldwide, to be indicative of their significant connection to the al-Qaeda organization. * * * This Court finds that the available evidence to date regarding Defendants' connection to al-Qaeda leads to the conclusion that each defendant, at least at the time of the alleged offense conduct, supported the terrorist organization. * * * Moreover, the Government proffered that al-Qaeda and bin Ladin's directives impose a continuing obligation on their followers to perpetrate violence against Americans in the furtherance of al-Qaeda's cause. While this Court recognizes that each Defendant currently disavows allegiance to al-Qaeda, it nonetheless finds that, at this stage, the Government has established, by clear and convincing evidence, that each individual defendant poses a danger to the community.

Further, if each defendant's attendance and training at the al-Farooq camp and connection to al-Qaeda were not enough, each defendant also possesses individual characteristics that, taken in combination with his attendance and training at al-Farooq, leave no doubt that he poses a danger to the community.

For example, upon a search of Defendant Al–Bakri's last known residence, the Government discovered an illegal .22 caliber, single shot Derringer with a spent shell casing in the chamber and a single bullet bolt-action rifle with a telescopic sight In addition, the Government found a cassette tape entitled "Call to Jihad" or "Invitation to Jihad." Still further, Defendant Al–Bakri admitted to sending an e-mail regarding a planned attack by al-Qaeda on Americans. That e-mail message, which has commonly been referred to in these proceedings as the "Big Meal" e-mail, has been translated as follows:

> "How are you my beloved, God willing you are fine. I would like to remind you of obeying God and keeping him in your heart because the next meal will be very huge. No one will be able to withstand it except those with faith. There are people here who had visions and their visions were explained that this thing will be very strong. No one will be able to bare [sic] it."

While a search of Defendant Goba's residence did not reveal any weapons, it did reveal three Arabic audiotapes. However, this Court is not convinced that these tapes are anything but wholly innocuous musical recordings and recitations of the Koran. This Court notes, however, that Defendant Al–Bakri described Defendant Goba as the "emir" and leader of the group, who collected money for the trip and secured visas to Pakistan for himself and Defendants Alwan and Al–Bakri.

The search of Defendant Mosed's last known residence revealed an illegal Panther stun gun, still in its original package. In a search of Defendant Taher's wife's apartment, the Government discovered a nine-page document, which included a discussion of the justification of suicide as a form of martyrdom under Islam.

In fairness, this Court notes that each Defendant offers innocuous explanations and excuses for his possession of weapons or indoctrination material. If it were simply the possession of these items, this Court might be persuaded to delve deeper into an examination of the nature of the weapons and materials. Certainly, possession of the written materials seized from Defendants alone cannot be held against them, and in fact, each defendant has an affirmative right under the First Amendment to possess such materials. Innocuous explanations or not, taken in the context of each defendant's travel abroad for the purposes of undergoing terrorist training at an al-Qaeda camp where Usama bin Ladin personally appeared, this Court need not be blind to the implications that Defendants' possession of these materials suggests.

Accordingly, for the reasons discussed above, this Court first finds, by clear and convincing evidence, that each defendant attended and was trained at the al-Farooq training camp as described in the Government's proffer. In addition, this Court finds that each defendant's attendance and training at the al-Farooq camp described in the Government's proffer, in and of itself, renders each defendant a danger to the community. Moreover, the fact that each defendant attended an al-Qaeda training camp and was able to sit as an audience for Usama bin Laden supports a finding of dangerousness as it indicates the existence of a significant connection to the al-Qaeda terror-

ist network. Finally, the discovery of weapons or indoctrination materials, or both, through searches of Defendants' residences, as described above, further supports a finding of dangerousness in this case.

5. Release Condition or Combination of Release Conditions

Having found that § 2339B is a "crime of violence" and that each defendant is a flight risk and danger to the community, the final stage of analysis under the Bail Reform Act requires resolution of the ultimate statutory issue: whether a release condition or set of release conditions exist that, if imposed, will eliminate these risks. This Court concludes that there are not.

In so finding, this Court has considered the factors outlined in § 3142(g) and has afforded them due weight. As this Court's previous discussion foreshadows, it finds that the grave nature and circumstances of the crimes of violence charged in the Indictment, the considerable weight of the Government's proffered evidence against each defendant, and the nature and seriousness of the danger to the community that each defendant poses by virtue of his attendance and training at al-Qaeda's al-Farooq terrorist training camp, lead to the impregnable conclusion that no release condition or combination of release conditions set forth in § 3142(c), or otherwise, could assure Defendants' future appearance or the safety of the community.

In reaching this conclusion, this Court has considered each individual defendants' personal history and characteristics. Each defendant shares the common factors of being a United States citizen, having long-standing ties to Lackawanna, NY, having family and friends living in and around Western New York, and having no significant criminal history. Each also possesses individual characteristics that this Court has considered.

This Court has weighed the fact that Defendant Goba is regarded as a leader of the Yemeni community in Lackawanna, NY, and is involved in the daily practice of teaching language and religion to children in his community. Defendant Goba is married and his wife is expecting their first child. Moreover, this Court acknowledges that Defendant Goba is in good physical and mental condition and is not a drug or alcohol user.

This Court is also cognizant of the fact that Defendant Al–Bakri is married, although his wife currently resides in Bahrain, and that he is only twenty-two years old. Defendant Al–Bakri has no prior arrests and is not a drug user.

Moreover, this Court has considered that Defendant Taher is twenty-four years old and was fairly steadily employed prior to his arrest. He is married under the Muslim faith to one Nicole Frick, and together, they have a three-year-old son. Defendant Taher lives part-time with his mother and part-time with Ms. Frick. He has been arrested twice, but has no criminal convictions, and he does not use alcohol or drugs.

Finally, this Court recognizes that Defendant Mosed is twenty-four years old, is married, and lives with his wife and son in an apartment in Lackawanna, N.Y. He, along with his three brothers and two sisters, helps take care of his mother, who suffers from mental health difficulties. Defendant Mosed is an avid sports fan and was enrolled at Erie Community College prior to his arrest.

Nonetheless, this Court finds that each individual defendant's background is significantly outweighed by the risk of flight and danger to the community that each poses as a result of his demonstrated ability to live abroad for an extended period of time and by his attendance and training at al-Qaeda's al-Farooq terrorist training camp.

In light of these facts, the inescapable conclusion is that no set of release conditions will adequately guard against the inherent risks that each defendant presents. In this Court's view, the electronic surveillance suggested by defense counsel is simply insufficient. Here, defending against the danger that each of these four men present would require institution of four replica detention facilities, a measure not required by the caselaw. "Home detention and electronic monitoring at best elaborately replicate a detention facility without the confidence of security such a facility instills." *United States v. Gotti*, 776 F.Supp. 666, 672 (E.D.N.Y.1991). Thus, Defendants' future appearance and the safety of the community can only be reasonably assured by Defendants' continued pretrial detention.

IV. CONCLUSION

In conclusion, I find the following: (1) that the Government's presentation by proffer with evidence before Judge Schroeder satisfied the requirements of the Bail Reform Act, (2) that 18 U.S.C. § 2339B is a "crime of violence" as that phrase is defined in 18 U.S.C. § 3156(a)(4)(B), and (3) that no release condition or combination of release conditions could be imposed to eliminate the risk that Defendants may flee the District or the danger that Defendants pose to the community. Accordingly, Defendants' Motions for Revocation of Judge Schroeder's Detention Order are denied.

B. THE CONSTITUTIONALITY OF PREVENTIVE DETENTION

Preventive detention results in a loss of liberty, before an adjudication has been made that a person is guilty of a criminal defense. How can this be squared with the detainee's right to due process? This question is explored in the following case.

UNITED STATES v. SALERNO

Supreme Court of the United States, 1987.
481 U.S. 739.

CHIEF JUSTICE REHNQUIST delivered the opinion of the Court.

The Bail Reform Act of 1984 allows a federal court to detain an arrestee pending trial if the government demonstrates by clear and convincing evidence after an adversary hearing that no release conditions "will reasonably assure . . . the safety of any person and the community." The United States Court of Appeals for the Second Circuit struck down this provision of the Act as facially unconstitutional, because, in that court's words, this type of pretrial detention violates "substantive due process." We granted certiorari because of a conflict among the Courts of Appeals regarding the validity of the Act. We hold that, as against the facial attack mounted by these respondents, the Act fully comports with constitutional requirements. We therefore reverse.

I

Responding to "the alarming problem of crimes committed by persons on release," Congress formulated the Bail Reform Act of 1984, as the solution to a bail crisis in the federal courts. * * *

Respondents Anthony Salerno and Vincent Cafaro were arrested on March 21, 1986, after being charged in a 29–count indictment alleging various Racketeer Influenced and Corrupt Organizations Act (RICO) violations, mail and wire fraud offenses, extortion, and various criminal gambling viola-

tions. The RICO counts alleged 35 acts of racketeering activity, including fraud, extortion, gambling, and conspiracy to commit murder. At respondents' arraignment, the Government moved to have Salerno and Cafaro detained * * * on the ground that no condition of release would assure the safety of the community or any person. The District Court held a hearing at which the Government made a detailed proffer of evidence. The Government's case showed that Salerno was the "boss" of the Genovese Crime Family of La Cosa Nostra and that Cafaro was a "captain" in the Genovese Family. According to the Government's proffer, based in large part on conversations intercepted by a court-ordered wiretap, the two respondents had participated in wide-ranging conspiracies to aid their illegitimate enterprises through violent means. The Government also offered the testimony of two of its trial witnesses, who would assert that Salerno personally participated in two murder conspiracies. Salerno opposed the motion for detention, challenging the credibility of the Government's witnesses. He offered the testimony of several character witnesses as well as a letter from his doctor stating that he was suffering from a serious medical condition. Cafaro presented no evidence at the hearing, but instead characterized the wiretap conversations as merely "tough talk."

The District Court granted the Government's detention motion, concluding that the Government had established by clear and convincing evidence that no condition or combination of conditions of release would ensure the safety of the community or any person * * *.

Respondents appealed, contending that to the extent that the Bail Reform Act permits pretrial detention on the ground that the arrestee is likely to commit future crimes, it is unconstitutional on its face. Over a dissent, the United States Court of Appeals for the Second Circuit agreed. Although the court agreed that pretrial detention could be imposed if the defendants were likely to intimidate witnesses or otherwise jeopardize the trial process, it found "§ 3142(e)'s authorization of pretrial detention [on the ground of future dangerousness] repugnant to the concept of substantive due process, which we believe prohibits the total deprivation of liberty simply as a means of preventing future crimes." * * * It reasoned that our criminal law system holds persons accountable for past actions, not anticipated future actions. Although a court could detain an arrestee who threatened to flee before trial, such detention would be permissible because it would serve the basic objective of a criminal system— bringing the accused to trial. * * * The Court of Appeals also found our decision in Schall v. Martin, 467 U.S. 253 (1984), upholding postarrest pretrial detention of juveniles, inapposite because juveniles have a lesser interest in liberty than do adults. * * *

II

A facial challenge to a legislative Act is, of course, the most difficult challenge to mount successfully, since the challenger must establish that no set of circumstances exists under which the Act would be valid. The fact that the Bail Reform Act might operate unconstitutionally under some conceivable set of circumstances is insufficient to render it wholly invalid, since we have not recognized an "overbreadth" doctrine outside the limited context of the First Amendment. We think respondents have failed to shoulder their heavy burden to demonstrate that the Act is "facially" unconstitutional.[a]

* * *

A

* * *

Respondents first argue that the Act violates substantive due process because the pretrial detention it authorizes constitutes impermissible punishment before trial. The Government, however, has never argued that pretrial detention could be upheld if it were "punishment." The Court of Appeals assumed that pretrial detention under the Bail Reform Act is regulatory, not penal, and we agree that it is.

As an initial matter, the mere fact that a person is detained does not inexorably lead to the conclusion that the government has imposed punishment. To determine whether a restriction on liberty constitutes impermissible punishment or permissible regulation, we first look to legislative intent. Unless Congress expressly intended to impose punitive restrictions, the punitive/regulatory distinction turns on " 'whether an alternative purpose to which [the restriction] may rationally be connected is assignable for it, and whether it appears excessive in relation to the alternative purpose assigned [to it].' "

We conclude that the detention imposed by the Act falls on the regulatory side of the dichotomy. The legislative history of the Bail Reform Act clearly indicates that Congress did not formulate the pretrial detention provisions as punishment for dangerous individuals. Congress instead perceived pretrial detention as a potential solution to a pressing societal problem. There is no doubt that preventing danger to the community is a legitimate regulatory goal.

Nor are the incidents of pretrial detention excessive in relation to the regulatory goal Congress sought to achieve. The Bail Reform Act carefully limits the circumstances under which detention may be sought to the most serious of crimes. See 18 U.S.C. § 3142(f)(detention hearings available if case involves crimes of violence, offenses for which the sentence is life imprisonment or death, serious drug offenses, or certain repeat offenders). The arrestee is entitled to a prompt detention hearing, and the maximum length of pretrial detention is limited by the stringent time limitations of the Speedy Trial Act.[b] See 18 U.S.C. § 3161 et seq. Moreover, as in Schall v. Martin, the conditions of confinement envisioned by the Act "appear to reflect the regulatory purposes relied upon by the government." As in *Schall* the statute at issue here requires that detainees be housed in a "facility separate, to the extent practicable, from persons awaiting or serving sentences or being held in custody pending appeal." 18 U.S.C. § 3142(i)(2). We conclude, therefore, that the pretrial detention contemplated by the Bail Reform Act is regulatory in nature, and does not constitute punishment before trial in violation of the Due Process Clause.

The Court of Appeals nevertheless concluded that "the Due Process Clause prohibits pretrial detention on the ground of danger to the community as a regulatory measure, without regard to the duration of the detention." Respondents characterize the Due Process Clause as erecting an impenetrable "wall" in this area that "no governmental interest—rational, important, compelling or otherwise—may surmount."

We do not think the Clause lays down any such categorical imperative. We have repeatedly held that the government's regulatory interest in community safety can, in appropriate circumstances, outweigh an individual's liberty interest. For example, in times of war or insurrection, when society's interest is at its peak, the government may detain individuals whom the government believes to be dangerous. Even outside the exigencies of war, we have found that sufficiently compelling governmental interests can justify detention of dangerous persons. Thus, we have found no absolute constitutional barrier to detention of potentially dangerous resident aliens pending deportation proceedings. We have also held that the government may detain mentally unstable individuals who present a danger to the public, and dangerous defendants who become incompetent to stand trial. We have approved of postarrest regulatory detention of juveniles when they present a continuing danger to the community. Even competent adults may face substantial liberty restrictions as a result of the operation of our criminal justice system. If the police suspect an individual of a crime, they may arrest and hold him until a neutral magistrate determines whether probable cause

b. We intimate no view as to the point at which detention in a particular case might become excessively prolonged, and therefore

punitive, in relation to Congress' regulatory goal.

exists. Finally, respondents concede and the Court of Appeals noted that an arrestee may be incarcerated until trial if he presents a risk of flight, or a danger to witnesses.

These are exceptions to gen rule no detention w/o crim trial.

Respondents characterize all of these cases as exceptions to the "general rule" of substantive due process that the government may not detain a person prior to a judgment of guilt in a criminal trial. Such a "general rule" may freely be conceded, but we think that these cases show a sufficient number of exceptions to the rule that the congressional action challenged here can hardly be characterized as totally novel. Given the well-established authority of the government, in special circumstances, to restrain individuals' liberty prior to or even without criminal trial and conviction, we think that the present statute providing for pretrial detention on the basis of dangerousness must be evaluated in precisely the same manner that we evaluated the laws in the cases discussed above.

The government's interest in preventing crime by arrestees is both legitimate and compelling. In *Schall*, supra, we recognized the strength of the State's interest in preventing juvenile crime. This general concern with crime prevention is no less compelling when the suspects are adults. * * * The Bail Reform Act of 1984 responds to an even more particularized governmental interest than the interest we sustained in *Schall*. The statute we upheld in *Schall* permitted pretrial detention of any juvenile arrested on any charge after a showing that the individual might commit some undefined further crimes. The Bail Reform Act, in contrast, narrowly focuses on a particularly acute problem in which the government interests are overwhelming. The Act operates only on individuals who have been arrested for a specific category of extremely serious offenses. 18 U.S.C. § 3142(f). Congress specifi-

Narrowly tailored

cally found that these individuals are far more likely to be responsible for dangerous acts in the community after arrest. Nor is the Act by any means a scattershot attempt to incapacitate those who are merely suspected of these serious crimes. The government must first of all demonstrate probable cause to believe that the charged crime has been committed by the arrestee, but that is not enough. In a full-blown adversary hearing, the government must convince a neutral decisionmaker by clear and convincing evidence that no conditions of release can reasonably assure the safety of the community or any person. 18 U.S.C.A. § 3142(f). While the government's general interest in preventing crime is compelling, even this interest is heightened when the government musters convincing proof that the arrestee, already indicted or held to answer for a serious crime, presents a demonstrable danger to the community. Under these narrow circumstances, society's interest in crime prevention is at its greatest.

Safe-guards 2 hearings 1 - prob cause 2 - clear + convincing of no less restrictive means.

On the other side of the scale, of course, is the individual's strong interest in liberty. We do not minimize the importance and fundamental nature of this right. But, as our cases hold, this right may, in circumstances where the government's interest is sufficiently weighty, be subordinated to the greater needs of society. * * * When the government proves by clear and convincing evidence that an arrestee presents an identified and articulable threat to an individual or the community, we believe that, consistent with the Due Process Clause, a court may disable the arrestee from executing that threat. Under these circumstances, we cannot categorically state that pretrial detention "offends some principle of justice so rooted in the traditions and conscience of our people as to be ranked as fundamental."

individual rt is subordinate to greater needs

Finally, we may dispose briefly of respondents' facial challenge to the procedures of the Bail Reform Act. To sustain them against such a challenge, we need only find them "adequate to authorize the pretrial detention of at least some [persons] charged with crimes," whether or not they might be insufficient in some particular circumstances. We think they pass that test. As we stated in *Schall,* "there is nothing inherently unattainable about a prediction of future criminal conduct."

Under the Bail Reform Act, the procedures by which a judicial officer evaluates the likelihood of future dangerousness are specifically designed to further the accuracy of that determination. Detainees have a right to counsel at the detention hearing. 18 U.S.C. § 3142(f). They may testify in their own behalf, present information by proffer or otherwise, and cross-examine witnesses who appear at the hearing. The judicial officer charged with the responsibility of determining the appropriateness of detention is guided by statutorily enumerated factors, which include the nature and the circumstances of the charges, the weight of the evidence, the history and characteristics of the putative offender, and the danger to the community. § 3142(g). The government must prove its case by clear and convincing evidence. § 3142(f). Finally, the judicial officer must include written findings of fact and a written statement of reasons for a decision to detain. § 3142(i). The Act's review provisions, § 3145(c), provide for immediate appellate review of the detention decision.

We think these extensive safeguards suffice to repel a facial challenge. * * *

B

Respondents also contend that the Bail Reform Act violates the Excessive Bail Clause of the Eighth Amendment. The Court of Appeals did not address this issue because it found that the Act violates the Due Process Clause. We think that the Act survives a challenge founded upon the Eighth Amendment.

The Eighth Amendment addresses pretrial release by providing merely that "Excessive bail shall not be required." This Clause, of course, says nothing about whether bail shall be available at all. Respondents nevertheless contend that this Clause grants them a right to bail calculated solely upon considerations of flight. They rely on Stack v. Boyle, 342 U.S. 1, 5 (1951), in which the Court stated that "Bail set at a figure higher than an amount reasonably calculated [to ensure the defendant's presence at trial] is 'excessive' under the Eighth Amendment." In respondents' view, since the Bail Reform Act allows a court essentially to set bail at an infinite amount for reasons not related to the risk of flight, it violates the Excessive Bail Clause. Respondents concede that the right to bail they have discovered in the Eighth Amendment is not absolute. A court may, for example, refuse bail in capital cases. And, as the Court of Appeals noted and respondents admit, a court may refuse bail when the defendant presents a threat to the judicial process by intimidating witnesses. Respondents characterize these exceptions as consistent with what they claim to be the sole purpose of bail—to ensure integrity of the judicial process.

While we agree that a primary function of bail is to safeguard the courts' role in adjudicating the guilt or innocence of defendants, we reject the proposition that the Eighth Amendment categorically prohibits the government from pursuing other admittedly compelling interests through regulation of pretrial release. The above-quoted *dicta* in Stack v. Boyle is far too slender a reed on which to rest this argument. The Court in *Stack* had no occasion to consider whether the Excessive Bail Clause requires courts to admit all defendants to bail, because the * * * Court had to determine only whether bail, admittedly available in that case, was excessive if set at a sum greater than that necessary to ensure the arrestees' presence at trial.

The holding of *Stack* is illuminated by the Court's holding just four months later in Carlson v. Landon, 342 U.S. 524 (1952). In that case, remarkably similar to the present action, the detainees had been arrested and held without bail pending a determination of deportability. The Attorney General refused to release the individuals, "on the ground that there was reasonable cause to believe that [their] release would be prejudicial to the public interest and *would endanger the welfare and safety of the United States.*" The detainees brought the same challenge that respondents bring to us today: The Eighth Amendment required them to be admitted to bail. The Court squarely rejected this proposition * * *.

Carlson v. Landon was a civil case, and we need not decide today whether the Excessive Bail Clause speaks at all to Congress' power to define the classes of criminal arrestees who shall be admitted to bail. For even if we were to conclude that the Eighth Amendment imposes some substantive limitations on the National Legislature's powers in this area, we would still hold that the Bail Reform Act is valid. Nothing in the text of the Bail Clause limits permissible government considerations solely to questions of flight. The only arguable substantive limitation of the Bail Clause is that the government's proposed conditions of

release or detention not be "excessive" in light of the perceived evil. Of course, to determine whether the government's response is excessive, we must compare that response against the interest the government seeks to protect by means of that response. Thus, when the government has admitted that its only interest is in preventing flight, bail must be set by a court at a sum designed to ensure that goal, and no more. We believe that when Congress has mandated detention on the basis of a compelling interest other than prevention of flight, as it has here, the Eighth Amendment does not require release on bail.

III

* * *

Reversed.

JUSTICE MARSHALL with whom **JUSTICE BRENNAN** joins, dissenting.

* * *

The statute does not authorize the government to imprison anyone it has evidence is dangerous; indictment is necessary. But let us suppose that a defendant is indicted and the government shows by clear and convincing evidence that he is dangerous and should be detained pending a trial, at which trial the defendant is acquitted. May the government continue to hold the defendant in detention based upon its showing that he is dangerous? The answer cannot be yes, for that would allow the government to imprison someone for uncommitted crimes based upon "proof" not beyond a reasonable doubt. The result must therefore be that once the indictment has failed, detention cannot continue. But our fundamental principles of justice declare that the defendant is as innocent on the day before his trial as he is on the morning after his acquittal. Under this statute an untried indictment somehow acts to permit a detention, based on other charges, which after an acquittal would be unconstitutional.

* * *

There is a connection between the peculiar facts of this case and the evident constitutional defects in the statute which the Court upholds today. Respondent Cafaro was originally incarcerated for an indeterminate period at the request of the Government, which believed (or professed to believe) that his release imminently threatened the safety of the community. That threat apparently vanished, from the Government's point of view, when Cafaro agreed to act as a covert agent of the Government. There could be no more eloquent demonstration of the coercive power of authority to imprison upon prediction, or of the dangers which the almost inevitable abuses pose to the cherished liberties of a free society.

* * *

Throughout the world today there are men, women and children interned indefinitely, awaiting trials which may never come or which may be a mockery of the word, because their governments believe them to be "dangerous." Our Constitution, whose construction began two centuries ago, can shelter us forever from the evils of such unchecked power. Over two hundred years it has slowly, through our efforts, grown more durable, more expansive, and more just. But it cannot protect us if we lack the courage, and the self-restraint, to protect ourselves. Today a majority of the Court applies itself to an ominous exercise in demolition. Theirs is truly a decision which will go forth without authority, and come back without respect.

I dissent.

[The dissenting opinion of Justice Stevens is omitted.]

Unconstitutional Applications

The Court in *Salerno* left open the possibility that the federal statute might be unconstitutionally applied. But after *Salerno*, courts have upheld extensive pretrial detentions. For example, in United States v. Infelise, 934 F.2d 103 (7th Cir.1991), the court held that continued detention for two years pending trial did not violate due process. The court noted that the Government cannot delay a trial in order to use preventive detention as a surrogate for punishment. But the court found the delay to be due to the complexity of the case, the presence of multiple defendants, and pre-trial motions by the defendants. In United States v. Millan, 4 F.3d 1038 (2d Cir.1993), the court upheld a 30 month pretrial detention of a defendant who was the head of a large heroin distribution network. It noted that the prosecution was not solely responsible for the delay in the trial, and that the evidence of risk of flight and dangerousness to the community was compelling. The court stated that "the constitutional limits on a detention period based on dangerousness to the community may be looser than the limits on a detention period based solely on risk of flight. In the former case, release risks injury to others, which in the latter case, release risks only the loss of a conviction." Do cases like these give defendants a disincentive to file pretrial motions?

Is it possible for a pretrial detention to be so prolonged that it violates due process regardless of any risk of flight or danger to the community? In *Millan*, the court stated that the length of detention "will rarely by itself offend due process" and that the prospective detention of thirty months, "while weighing in favor of release, does not, standing alone, establish that pretrial confinement has exceeded constitutional limits." Rather, the court must balance "(i) the length of the detention; (ii) the extent of the prosecution's responsibility for the delay of the trial; and (iii) the strength of the evidence upon which the detention was based." Of course, the longer the detention, the more likely it is that some of the delay is attributable to the prosecution.

Constitutionality of Other Forms of Preventive Detention— Insanity Acquittees: Foucha v. Louisiana

Salerno was distinguished by the Court in Foucha v. Louisiana, 504 U.S. 71 (1992). Foucha was tried for a violent crime and was acquitted by reason of insanity. Under Louisiana law he was committed to a psychiatric hospital. Hospital officials subsequently recommended his release on the ground that he was not currently, and probably never had been, insane. However, Louisiana law provided that commitment would continue, even in the absence of mental illness, unless the acquittee could prove that he was not dangerous to himself or others; and hospital officials, noting Foucha's "anti-social" personality, refused to attest to his non-dangerousness. The State relied heavily on *Salerno* to justify Foucha's continuing commitment on grounds of dangerousness, but a five-person majority, in an opinion by Justice White, held that the Louisiana scheme violated Foucha's right to due process. Justice White rejected *Salerno's* applicability in the following passage:

> Unlike the sharply focused scheme at issue in *Salerno,* the Louisiana scheme of confinement is not carefully limited. Under the state statute, Foucha is not now entitled to an adversary hearing at which the State must prove by clear and convincing evidence that he is demonstrably dangerous to the community. Indeed, the State need prove nothing to justify continued detention, for the statute places the burden on the detainee to prove that he is not dangerous. * * *

> It was emphasized in *Salerno* that the detention we found constitutionally permissible was strictly limited in duration. Here, in contrast, the State asserts that because Foucha once committed a criminal act and now has an antisocial personality that sometimes leads to aggressive conduct, a disorder for which there is no effective treatment, he may be held indefinitely. This rationale would permit the State to hold indefinitely any other insanity acquittee not mentally ill who could be shown to have a personality disorder that may lead to criminal conduct. The same would be true of any convicted criminal, even though he has completed his prison term. It would also be only a step away from substituting confinements for dangerousness for our present system which, with only narrow exceptions and aside from permissible confinements for mental illness, incarcerates only those who are proved beyond reasonable doubt to have violated a criminal law.

Justice O'Connor wrote a concurring opinion stating that, under *Salerno,* it might "be permissible for Louisiana to confine an insanity acquittee who has regained sanity if, unlike the situation in this case, the nature and duration of detention were tailored to reflect pressing public safety concerns related to the acquittee's continuing dangerousness."

Justice Thomas wrote a dissenting opinion and was joined by Chief Justice Rehnquist and Justice Scalia. He agreed that *Salerno* was readily distinguishable from the instant case, but argued that the distinction cut in favor of the Louisiana commitment scheme. He noted that insanity acquittees, unlike pretrial detainees subject to the Bail Reform Act, "have had their day in court. Although they have not been convicted of crimes, neither have they been exonerated * * *." Justice Kennedy also dissented in a separate opinion in which the Chief Justice joined.

Constitutionality of Other Forms of Preventive Detention— Sexual Predators: Kansas v. Hendricks

Responding to the rising public alarm over sex crimes, several states have enacted "sexual predator" laws. These laws typically allow preventive detention of defendants who have been convicted of sex crimes and have completed their sentences. The Supreme Court considered the constitutionality of preventive detention of sexual predators in Kansas v. Hendricks, 521 U.S. 346 (1997). Kansas' Sexually Violent Predator Act establishes procedures for the civil commitment of persons who, due to a "mental abnormality" or a "personality disorder," are likely to engage in "predatory acts of sexual violence." Kansas filed a petition under the Act to commit Hendricks, who had a long history of sexually molesting children and who was scheduled for release from prison after serving time for a series of convictions for sexual assault of minors. After Hendricks testified that he agreed with the state physician's diagnosis that he suffered from pedophilia and was not cured and that he continued to harbor sexual desires for children that he could not control when he got "stressed out," the jury determined that he was a sexually violent predator. Finding that pedophilia qualifies as a mental abnormality under the Act, the court ordered him committed. On appeal, the State Supreme Court invalidated the Act on the ground that the precommitment condition of a "mental abnormality" did not satisfy what it perceived to be the "substantive" due process requirement that involuntary civil commitment must be predicated on a "mental illness" finding.

The Supreme Court reversed the State Supreme Court. The Justices unanimously agreed that civil detention of sex offenders, based on a finding of "mental abnormality", did not violate any guarantee of substantive due process. Justice Thomas, writing for five members of the Court on this question, stated as follows:

> Although freedom from physical restraint "has always been at the core of the liberty protected by the Due Process Clause from arbitrary governmental action," Foucha v. Louisiana, that liberty interest is not absolute. The Court has recognized that an individual's constitutionally protected interest in avoiding physical restraint may be overridden even in the civil context. * * * We have consistently upheld such involuntary commitment statutes provided the confinement takes place pursuant to proper procedures and evidentiary standards. See *Foucha,* supra; Addington v. Texas, 441 U.S. 418 (1979). It thus cannot be said that the involuntary civil confinement of a limited subclass of dangerous persons is contrary to our understanding of ordered liberty.

> The challenged Act unambiguously requires a finding of dangerousness either to one's self or to others as a prerequisite to involuntary confinement.

Commitment proceedings can be initiated only when a person "has been convicted of or charged with a sexually violent offense," and "suffers from a mental abnormality or personality disorder which makes the person likely to engage in the predatory acts of sexual violence." The statute thus requires proof of more than a mere predisposition to violence; rather, it requires evidence of past sexually violent behavior and a present mental condition that creates a likelihood of such conduct in the future if the person is not incapacitated. * * * A finding of dangerousness, standing alone, is ordinarily not a sufficient ground upon which to justify indefinite involuntary commitment. We have sustained civil commitment statutes when they have coupled proof of dangerousness with the proof of some additional factor, such as a "mental illness" or "mental abnormality." * * * These added statutory requirements serve to limit involuntary civil confinement to those who suffer from a volitional impairment rendering them dangerous beyond their control. The Kansas Act is plainly of a kind with these other civil commitment statutes: It requires a finding of future dangerousness, and then links that finding to the existence of a "mental abnormality" or "personality disorder" that makes it difficult, if not impossible, for the person to control his dangerous behavior. The precommitment requirement of a "mental abnormality" or "personality disorder" is consistent with the requirements of these other statutes that we have upheld in that it narrows the class of persons eligible for confinement to those who are unable to control their dangerousness.

Focusing on the facts of the case, the Court found that Hendricks' mental abnormality justified preventive detention:

The mental health professionals who evaluated Hendricks diagnosed him as suffering from pedophilia, a condition the psychiatric profession itself classifies as a serious mental disorder. Hendricks even conceded that, when he becomes "stressed out," he cannot "control the urge" to molest children. This admitted lack of volitional control, coupled with a prediction of future dangerousness, adequately distinguishes Hendricks from other dangerous persons who are perhaps more properly dealt with exclusively through criminal proceedings. Hendricks' diagnosis as a pedophile, which qualifies as a "mental abnormality" under the Act, thus plainly suffices for due process purposes.

Justice Kennedy wrote a short concurring opinion. Justice Breyer, joined by Justices Stevens, Souter, and Ginsburg, dissented. He argued that the statute operated as an ex post facto law on Hendricks, because the State sought to punish him retroactively for an act that had been committed before the effective date of the statute. He agreed with Justice Thomas, however, that the civil commitment of sexually dangerous persons, on the basis of a finding of mental abnormality, did not violate the Due Process Clause. He summarized his views on this point as follows:

Because (1) many mental health professionals consider pedophilia a serious mental disorder; and (2) Hendricks suffers from a classic case of irresistible impulse, namely he is so afflicted with pedophilia that he cannot "control the urge" to molest children; and (3) his pedophilia presents a serious danger to those children; I believe that Kansas can classify Hendricks as "mentally ill" and "dangerous" as this Court used those terms in *Foucha*.

If the sexual predator law were struck down, couldn't the state respond by imposing mandatory sentences of life in prison without parole for every person convicted of an act of sexual violence? Would it be a better system to confine such an offender in prison for life, rather than in a hospital for treatment? See In re Blodgett, 510 N.W.2d 910 (Minn.1994)(upholding indefinite civil commitment of sexual predators: "If the state were denied the ability to hospitalize the sexual predator, rather than let the offender out on the street, the state will counter by increasing the length of the prison sentence. * * * Arguably, then, the question is not whether the sexual predator can be confined, but where? Should it be in prison or in a security hospital?").

Constitutionality of Other Forms of Preventive Detention– Persons Subject to Deportation: Zadvydas v. Davis

In Zadvydas v. Davis, 533 U.S. 678 (2001), the Court considered the plight of an alien ordered removed from the United States but who could not be deported to a receiving country. A statute, 8 U.S.C. § 1231(a)(6), provides for detention for certain categories of aliens who have been ordered removed but who cannot be removed within 90 days of the deportation order. Those aliens subject to continued detention are: inadmissible aliens, criminal aliens, aliens who have violated their nonimmigrant status conditions, and aliens removable for certain national security or foreign relations reasons, as well as any alien "who has been determined by the Attorney General to be a risk to the community or unlikely to comply with the order of removal." The statute states that an alien who falls into one of these categories "may be detained beyond the removal period and, if released, shall be subject to [certain] terms of supervision."

The Government in Zadvydas argued that the statute means literally what it says, setting no limit on the length of time that an alien subject to the statute may be detained if they cannot be removed within 90 days. Justice Stevens, writing for five members of the Court, refused to read the statute to provide for indefinite detention, reasoning that to so read the statute would result in a serious constitutional question under the Due Process Clause. Justice Stevens discussed the constitutional concerns in the following passage:

> Freedom from imprisonment—from government custody, detention, or other forms of physical restraint—lies at the heart of the liberty that Clause protects. See Foucha v. Louisiana. And this Court has said that government detention violates that Clause unless the detention is ordered in a criminal proceeding with adequate procedural protections, see United States v. Salerno, or, in certain special and "narrow" non-punitive "circumstances," where a special justification, such as harm-threatening mental illness, outweighs the "individual's constitutionally protected interest in avoiding physical restraint." Kansas v. Hendricks. The proceedings at issue here are civil, not criminal, and we assume that they are nonpunitive in purpose and effect. There is no sufficiently strong special justification here for indefinite civil detention—at least as administered under this statute. The statute, says the Government, has two regulatory goals: "ensuring the appearance of aliens at future immigration proceedings" and "preventing danger to the community." But by definition the first justification—preventing flight—is weak or nonexistent where removal seems a remote possibility at best. * * * The second justification—protecting the community—does not necessarily

diminish in force over time. But we have upheld preventive detention based on dangerousness only when limited to specially dangerous individuals and subject to strong procedural protections. In cases in which preventive detention is of potentially indefinite duration, we have also demanded that the dangerousness rationale be accompanied by some other special circumstance, such as mental illness, that helps to create the danger. See *Hendricks*.

The civil confinement here at issue is not limited, but potentially permanent. The provision authorizing detention does not apply narrowly to "a small segment of particularly dangerous individuals," *Hendricks*, say suspected terrorists, but broadly to aliens ordered removed for many and various reasons, including tourist visa violations. And, once the flight risk justification evaporates, the only special circumstance present is the alien's removable status itself, which bears no relation to a detainee's dangerousness. * * * The serious constitutional problem arising out of a statute that, in these circumstances, permits an indefinite, perhaps permanent, deprivation of human liberty without any such protection is obvious.

The majority in *Zadvydas* construed the statute to avoid the constitutional problem that it perceived. It held that an alien who is not removed within the 90–day period can bring a habeas corpus action to challenge his continued detention as unreasonable. In that action,

the habeas court must ask whether the detention in question exceeds a period reasonably necessary to secure removal. It should measure reasonableness primarily in terms of the statute's basic purpose, namely assuring the alien's presence at the moment of removal. Thus, if removal is not reasonably foreseeable, the court should hold continued detention unreasonable and no longer authorized by statute. In that case, of course, the alien's release may and should be conditioned on any of the various forms of supervised release that are appropriate in the circumstances, and the alien may no doubt be returned to custody upon a violation of those conditions. And if removal is reasonably foreseeable, the habeas court should consider the risk of the alien's committing further crimes as a factor potentially justifying confinement within that reasonable removal period.

The Court emphasized that it did not deny "the right of Congress to remove aliens, to subject them to supervision with conditions when released from detention, or to incarcerate them where appropriate for violation of those conditions."

Justice Kennedy wrote a dissenting opinion joined by Chief Justice Rehnquist and joined in part by Justices Scalia and Thomas.

Constitutionality of Other Forms of Preventive Detention–
Detention of Aliens During Removal Proceedings:
Demore v. Kim

In the following case, the Court considered the constitutionality of detaining a deportable alien during the pendency of removal proceedings. In doing so, the Court distinguishes *Zadvydas, supra,* much to the chagrin of the dissenters. Note that this case was decided after the terrorist attacks of September 11, 2001, while *Zadvydas* was decided before those attacks.

DEMORE v. KIM

Supreme Court of the United States, 2003.
538 U.S. 510.

CHIEF JUSTICE REHNQUIST **delivered the opinion of the Court.**

Section 236(c) of the Immigration and Nationality Act, 66 Stat. 200, as amended, 8 U.S.C. § 1226(c), provides that "the Attorney General shall take into custody any alien who" is removable from this country because he has been convicted of one of a specified set of crimes. Respondent is a citizen of the Republic of South Korea. He entered the United States in 1984, at the age of six, and became a lawful permanent resident of the United States two years later. In July 1996, he was convicted of first-degree burglary in state court in California and, in April 1997, he was convicted of a second crime, "petty theft with priors." The Immigration and Naturalization Service (INS) charged respondent with being deportable from the United States in light of these convictions, and detained him pending his removal hearing. We hold that Congress, justifiably concerned that deportable criminal aliens who are not detained continue to engage in crime and fail to appear for their removal hearings in large numbers, may require that persons such as respondent be detained for the brief period necessary for their removal proceedings.

Respondent does not dispute the validity of his prior convictions, which were obtained following the full procedural protections our criminal justice system offers. Respondent also did not dispute the INS' conclusion that he is subject to mandatory detention under § 1226(c). In conceding that he was deportable, respondent forwent a hearing at which he would have been entitled to raise any nonfrivolous argument available to demonstrate that he was not properly included in a mandatory detention category. Respondent instead filed a habeas corpus action pursuant to 28 U.S.C. § 2241 in the United States District Court for the Northern District of California challenging the constitutionality of § 1226(c) itself. He argued that his detention under § 1226(c) violated due process because the INS had made no determination that he posed either a danger to society or a flight risk.

The District Court agreed with respondent that § 1226(c)'s requirement of mandatory detention for certain criminal aliens was unconstitutional. The District Court therefore granted respondent's petition subject to the INS' prompt undertaking of an individualized bond hearing to determine whether respondent posed either a flight risk or a danger to the community. Following that decision, the District Director of the INS released respondent on $5,000 bond.

The Court of Appeals for the Ninth Circuit affirmed. That court held that § 1226(c) violates substantive due process as applied to respondent because he is a permanent resident alien. It noted that permanent resident aliens constitute the most favored category of aliens and that they have the right to reside permanently in the United States, to work here, and to apply for citizenship. * * * Relying upon our recent decision in Zadvydas v. Davis, 533 U.S. 678 (2001), the Court of Appeals concluded that the INS had not provided a justification "for no-bail civil detention sufficient to overcome a lawful permanent resident alien's liberty interest."

I

[The Court determined that it had jurisdiction to review a constitutional challenge to the detention statute.]

II

* * * Section 1226(c) mandates detention during removal proceedings for a limited class of deportable aliens—including those convicted of an aggravated felony. Congress adopted this provision against a backdrop of wholesale failure by the INS to deal with increasing rates of criminal activity by aliens. Criminal aliens were the fastest growing segment of the federal prison population, already constituting roughly 25% of all federal prisoners, and they formed a rapidly rising share of state prison populations as well. Congress' investigations showed, however, that the INS could not even *identify* most deportable aliens, much less locate them and remove them from the country. One study showed that, at the then-current rate of deportation, it would take 23 years to remove every criminal alien already subject to deportation. Making matters worse, criminal aliens who were deported swiftly reentered the country illegally in great numbers.

The agency's near-total inability to remove deportable criminal aliens imposed more than a monetary cost on the Nation. First, as Congress explained, "aliens who enter or remain in the United States in violation of our law are effectively taking immigration opportunities that might otherwise be extended to others." S. Rep. No. 104–249, p. 7 (1996). Second, deportable criminal aliens who remained in the United States often committed more crimes before being removed. One 1986 study showed that, after criminal aliens were identified as deportable, 77% were arrested at least once more and 45%—nearly half—were arrested multiple times before their deportation proceedings even began.

Congress also had before it evidence that one of the major causes of the INS' failure to remove deportable criminal aliens was the agency's failure to detain those aliens during their deportation proceedings. The Attorney General at the time had broad discretion to conduct individualized bond hearings and to release criminal aliens from custody during their removal proceedings when those aliens were determined not to present an excessive flight risk or threat to society. Despite this discretion to conduct bond hearings, however, in practice the INS faced severe limitations on funding and detention space, which considerations affected its release determinations.

Once released, more than 20% of deportable criminal aliens failed to appear for their removal hearings. * * * [The information before Congress] strongly supports Congress' concern that, even with individualized screening, releasing deportable criminal aliens on bond would lead to an unacceptable rate of flight.

* * *

During the same period in which Congress was making incremental changes to the immigration laws, it was also considering wholesale reform of those laws. Some studies presented to Congress suggested that detention of criminal aliens during their removal proceedings might be the best way to ensure their successful removal from this country. It was following those Reports that Congress enacted 8 U.S.C. § 1226, requiring the Attorney General to detain a subset of deportable criminal aliens pending a determination of their removability.

* * *

Aliens get due process in deportation hearings

It is well established that the Fifth Amendment entitles aliens to due process of law in deportation proceedings. At the same time, however, this Court has recognized detention during deportation proceedings as a constitutionally valid aspect of the deportation process. As we said more than a century ago, deportation proceedings "would be vain if those accused could not be held in custody pending the inquiry into their true character." Wong Wing v. United States, 163 U.S. 228, 235 (1896).

In Carlson v. Landon, 342 U.S. 524 (1952), the Court considered a challenge to the detention of aliens who were deportable because of their participation in Communist activities. The detained aliens did not deny that they were members of the Communist Party or that they were therefore deportable. Instead, like respondent in the present case, they challenged their detention on the grounds that there had been no finding that they were unlikely to appear for their deportation proceedings when ordered to do so. Although the Attorney General ostensibly had discretion to release detained Communist aliens on bond, the INS had adopted a policy of refusing to grant bail to those aliens in light of what Justice Frankfurter viewed as the mistaken "conception that Congress had made [alien Communists] in effect unbailable." 342 U.S., at 559, 568 (dissenting opinion).

The Court rejected the aliens' claims that they were entitled to be released from detention if they did not pose a flight risk, explaining "detention is necessarily a part of this deportation procedure." The Court noted that Congress had chosen to make such aliens deportable based on its "understanding of [Communists'] attitude toward the use of force and violence . . . to accomplish their political aims." And it concluded that the INS could

can detain for deportation b/c of leg desire to deport more effectively

deny bail to the detainees "by reference to the legislative scheme" even without any finding of flight risk.

* * *

Despite this Court's longstanding view that the Government may constitutionally detain deportable aliens during the limited period necessary for their removal proceedings, respondent argues that the narrow detention policy reflected in 8 U.S.C. § 1226(c) violates due process. Respondent * * * relies heavily upon our recent opinion in Zadvydas v. Davis. * * *

But *Zadvydas* is materially different from the present case in two respects.

First, in *Zadvydas*, the aliens challenging their detention following final orders of deportation were ones for whom removal was "no longer practically attainable." The Court thus held that the detention there did not serve its purported immigration purpose. * * * The Court observed that where, as there, "detention's goal is no longer practically attainable, detention no longer bears a reasonable relation to the purpose for which the individual was committed."

In the present case, the statutory provision at issue governs detention of deportable criminal aliens *pending their removal proceedings*. Such detention necessarily serves the purpose of preventing deportable criminal aliens from fleeing prior to or during their removal proceedings, thus increasing the chance that, if ordered removed, the aliens will be successfully removed. * * *

Zadvydas is materially different from the present case in a second respect as well. While the period of detention at issue in *Zadvydas* was "indefinite" and "potentially permanent," the detention here is of a much shorter duration.

detention here serves a purpose effective deportation; leg 2 concern. detention serves to assist deportation

Zadvydas distinguished the statutory provision it was there considering from § 1226 on these very grounds, noting that "post-removal-period detention, *unlike detention pending a determination of removability* . . . , has no obvious termination point." (emphasis added). Under 1226(c), not only does detention have a definite termination point, in the majority of cases it lasts for less than the 90 days we considered presumptively valid in *Zadvydas*. The Executive Office for Immigration Review has calculated that, in 85% of the cases in which aliens are detained pursuant to § 1226(c), removal proceedings are completed in an average time of 47 days and a median of 30 days. In the remaining 15% of cases, in which the alien appeals the decision of the Immigration Judge to the Board of Immigration Appeals, appeal takes an average of four months, with a median time that is slightly shorter.

* * *

For the reasons set forth above, respondent's claim must fail. Detention during removal proceedings is a constitutionally permissible part of that process. * * * The judgment of the Court of Appeals is

Reversed.

[Justice O'Connor, joined by Justices Scalia and Thomas, wrote a separate opinion contending that the Court had no jurisdiction over the case. She agreed, however, with the Court's resolution of the challenge on the merits. Justice Kennedy's concurring opinion is omitted.]

JUSTICE SOUTER, **with whom** JUSTICE STEVENS **and** JUSTICE GINSBURG **join, concurring in part and dissenting in part.**

* * *

I join Part I of the Court's opinion, which upholds federal jurisdiction in this case, but I dissent from the Court's disposition on the merits. The Court's holding that the Constitution permits the Government to lock up a lawful permanent resident of this country when there is concededly no reason to do so forgets over a century of precedent acknowledging the rights of permanent residents, including the basic liberty from physical confinement lying at the heart of due process.

* * *

I

* * *

[Justice Souter contests the majority's assertion that Kim had conceded his removability.]

II

A

* * *

The constitutional protection of an alien's person and property is particularly strong in the case of aliens lawfully admitted to permanent residence (LPRs). The immigration laws give LPRs the opportunity to establish a life permanently in this country by developing economic, familial, and social ties indistinguishable from those of a citizen. In fact, the law of the United States goes out of its way to encourage just such attachments by creating immigration preferences for those with a citizen as a close relation, and those with valuable professional skills or other assets promising benefits to the United States.

* * *

B

Kim's claim is a limited one: not that the Government may not detain LPRs to ensure their appearance at removal hearings, but that due process under the Fifth Amendment conditions a po-

tentially lengthy detention on a hearing and an impartial decisionmaker's finding that detention is necessary to a governmental purpose. He thus invokes our repeated decisions that the claim of liberty protected by the Fifth Amendment is at its strongest when government seeks to detain an individual. THE CHIEF JUSTICE wrote in 1987 that "in our society liberty is the norm, and detention prior to trial or without trial is the carefully limited exception." United States v. Salerno, 481 U.S. 739, 755. See also Foucha v. Louisiana, 504 U.S. 71, 80 (1992) ("Freedom from bodily restraint has always been at the core of the liberty protected by the Due Process Clause from arbitrary governmental action").

* * * In deciding in *Salerno* that this principle did not categorically bar pretrial detention of criminal defendants without bail under the Bail Reform Act of 1984, it was crucial that the statute provided that, "in a full-blown adversary hearing, the Government must convince a neutral decisionmaker by clear and convincing evidence that no conditions of release can reasonably assure the safety of the community or any person." * * *

* * * Due process calls for an individual determination before someone is locked away. In none of the cases cited did we ever suggest that the government could avoid the Due Process Clause by doing what § 1226(c) does, by selecting a class of people for confinement on a categorical basis and denying members of that class any chance to dispute the necessity of putting them away. * * *

C

We held as much just two Terms ago in Zadvydas v. Davis, which stands for the proposition that detaining an alien requires more than the rationality of a general detention statute; any justification must go to the alien himself. * * * Our individualized analysis and disposition in *Zadvydas* support Kim's claim for an individualized review of his challenge to the reasons that are supposed to justify confining him prior to any determination of removability. In fact, aliens in removal proceedings have an additional interest in avoiding confinement, beyond anything considered in *Zadvydas:* detention prior to entry of a removal order may well impede the alien's ability to develop and present his case on the very issue of removability. * * *

III

* * *

IV

This case is not about the National Government's undisputed power to detain aliens in order to avoid flight or prevent danger to the community. The issue is whether that power may be exercised by detaining a still lawful permanent resident alien when there is no reason for it and no way to challenge it. The Court's holding that the Due Process Clause allows this under a blanket rule is devoid of even ostensible justification in fact and at odds with the settled standard of liberty. I respectfully dissent.

[The dissenting opinion of Justice Breyer is omitted.]

C. THE CONSTITUTIONALITY OF QUASI–PERMANENT PREVENTIVE DETENTION OF FOREIGNERS SUSPECTED OF TERRORISM

The Court in *Salerno, Zadvydas,* and even in *Kim* emphasized the relatively short-term nature of the preventive detentions permitted in those cases. But in each of those cases, there is also language that could be read to allow longer (perhaps permanent?) preventive detention of those suspected of acts of terrorism against United States interests. The Court in *Salerno* refers favorably to extended detentions during wartime, and the United States has indeed declared a war on terror. And in *Zadvydas,* Justice Stevens noted that the objectionable civil confinement was potentially permanent and did not apply narrowly to "a small segment of particularly dangerous individuals, say suspected terrorists."

In light of these cases, is the government permitted to permanently detain, pending (or without) trial, foreigners suspected of involvement with terrorism? This question has arisen after 9/11 in light of the detention of scores of foreign nationals at the military base at Guantanamo Bay, Cuba. The opinion in *Al Odah v. United States,* 321 F.3d 1134 (D.C. Cir. 2003) concerned a consolidated challenge to some of these detentions. The action was brought by next friends of aliens captured abroad and currently detained at the Guantanamo Bay Naval Base. Some of the detainees are Kuwaiti nationals. The complaint alleged that these detainees were in Afghanistan and Pakistan as humanitarian aid volunteers and that local villagers seized them and handed them over to United States forces, who transferred them to Guantanamo Bay between January and March 2002. The plaintiffs' attorneys have not communicated with any of the Kuwaiti detainees. A consolidated action involves an Australian detainee, and two British detainees. The petition claims that the Australian detainee was living in Afghanistan when the Northern Alliance captured him in early December 2001; that one of the British detainees traveled to Pakistan for an arranged marriage after September 11, 2001; and that the other British detainee went to Pakistan after that date to visit relatives and continue his computer education. The respective governments informed the next friends in this action of the detainment of these aliens. Another consolidated action was brought on behalf of an Australian citizen and alleges that the detainee traveled to Pakistan to look for employment and a school for his children when he was arrested by Pakistani authorities in October 2001 and eventually handed over to the United States military and transferred to Guantanamo Bay in May 2002. All of the detainees in these cases deny that they are enemy combatants or enemy aliens of the United States, except for the father of one detainee who admitted that his son had joined the Taliban forces.

These consolidated cases involve claims of denial of due process under the Fifth Amendment and Fourteenth Amendments, and due process under international law, as well as violations of the War Powers Clause and Article I of the Constitution because of the President's alleged suspension of the writ of habeas corpus. Some detainees sought a declaratory judgment and an injunction ordering that they be informed of any charges against them and requiring that they be permitted to consult with counsel and meet with their families. Others sought a writ of habeas corpus, release from unlawful custody, access to counsel, an end to interrogations, and other relief.

The district court held that no United States court could have jurisdiction over these claims and dismissed the actions with prejudice. The court relied on Johnson v. Eisentrager, 339 U.S. 763 (1950). *Eisentrager* arose out of the time period between Germany's surrender and Japan's surrender during WWII, when twenty-one German nationals in China assisted Japanese forces fighting against the United States. The Germans were captured and placed in a prison under the control of the United States Army. *Eisentrager* was a petition for a writ of habeas corpus on behalf of the twenty-one Germans in the United States District

Court for the District of Columbia, claiming, among other things, violation of the Unites States Constitution. These prisoners were considered "enemy aliens." The Supreme Court held that "the privilege of litigation" had not been extended to the German prisoners and thus, the prisoners had no right to petition for a writ of habeas corpus:

> [T]hese prisoners at no relevant time were within any territory over which the United States is sovereign, and the scenes of their offense, their capture, their trial and their punishment were all beyond the territorial jurisdiction of any court of the United States.

The *Eisentrager* court also noted the burden that these trials would place on the war effort due to witnesses traveling from overseas as well as the potential diversion of the attention military commanders "from the military offensive abroad to their legal defensive at home."

The Court of Appeals in *Al Odah* agreed with the district court that the Guantanamo detainees were in a similar situation as the detainees in *Eisentrager*:

> [The Guantanamo detainees] too are aliens, they too were captured during military operations, they were in a foreign country when captured, they are now abroad, they are in the custody of the American military, and they have never had any presence in the United States. * * * [W]e believe that under *Eisentrager* these factors preclude the detainees from seeking habeas relief in the courts of the United States.

The D.C. Circuit read Supreme Court decisions following *Eisentrager* as stating that constitutional rights, such as due process under the Fifth Amendment, are not held by aliens outside the sovereign territory of the United States, regardless of whether or not they have been adjudicated as enemy aliens. The court went on to say:

> The consequence is that no court in this country has jurisdiction to grant habeas relief . . . to the Guantanamo detainees, even if they have not been adjudicated enemies of the United States. We cannot see why, or how, the writ may be made available to aliens abroad when basic constitutional protections are not. . . . If the Constitution does not entitle the detainees to due process, and it does not, they cannot invoke the jurisdiction of our courts to test the constitutionality or the legality of restraints on their liberty.

Eisentrager noted that "the privilege of litigation has been extended to aliens, whether friendly or enemy, only because permitting their presence in the country implied protection." The *Al Odah* court considered whether Guantanamo Bay was in fact a sovereign territory of the United States. The United States leases Guantanamo Bay from Cuba and, quoting the text of the lease, the court found that Cuba, not the United States has sovereignty over Guantanamo Bay. "Control," which the United States does assert over the area, did not in the court's view rise to the level of sovereignty.

The Supreme Court granted certiorari in *Al Odah*, limited to the question of "whether United States courts lack jurisdiction to consider challenges to the legality of the detention of foreign nationals captured abroad in connection with hostilities and incarcerated at the Guantanamo Bay Naval Base, Cuba." The Court's opinion will be reproduced in the Supplement.

V. SPECIAL PROBLEMS IN THE OPERATION OF BAIL

A. CAPITAL OFFENSES

Historically, statutes recognizing a right to bail have excluded capital crimes "where the proof is evident, or the presumption great" from those offenses for which bail is required. The granting or denial of bail is traditionally a matter of judicial discretion where a capital offense is charged, though some states by statute prohibit bail for these offenses. Is there any justification for distinguishing between capital and non-capital offenses?

If a distinction in bail treatment is preserved for capital offenses, what considerations are relevant to judicial discretion? Most statutes withhold pretrial release in capital cases only when the "proof is evident" or the "presumption is great." The states differ over the allocation of the burden of proof on these issues. State v. Konigsberg, 33 N.J. 367, 164 A.2d 740 (1960), discusses the various approaches that are used.

B. JUVENILE OFFENDERS

In the legislative effort to afford complete treatment for juvenile offenders, many states do not provide a right to bail for juveniles charged with offenses that would be crimes if committed by an adult. These courts seem to suggest that if the juvenile offender wants to be treated like an adult he has to take the bad with the good—he can only have bail if his offense is adjudicated as a crime. Other courts have noted the possibility of release into parental custody, and have held that the existence of such an option precludes bail, even in a case when the possibility is foreclosed by a judicial determination that release into parental custody would be inappropriate. In line with the general predilection against awarding bail after conviction (discussed infra), most courts disallow bail for juveniles after adjudication of their delinquency, pending appeal. See, e.g., City of Warwick v. Robalewski, 120 R.I. 119, 385 A.2d 669 (1978). The courts adopt the view that the juvenile is a "ward" of the state, subject to "treatment," regardless of the existence or adequacy of such treatment.

C. BAIL AFTER CONVICTION

As early as 1894, the Supreme Court held that there is no constitutional right to bail pending appeal from a conviction. McKane v. Durston, 153 U.S. 684 (1894). The courts reason that "since there is no constitutional right to appeal, there is no constitutional right to be free pending appeal." United States v. Sine, 461 F.Supp. 565 (D.S.C.1978). The fundamental rights of the convicted defendant differ in other respects, as well. "[T]he presumption of innocence and the right to participate in the preparation of a defense to ensure a fair trial—are obviously not present where the defendant has already been convicted." Gallie v. Wainwright, 362 So.2d 936, 941 (Fla.1978). At the same time, the risk of flight is arguably greater for a defendant who has already been convicted and who may have little hope of a reversal. For these reasons, the standards for postconviction release are stricter, and different criteria may be applied from those used prior to trial. After conviction, the court may consider factors such as the likelihood of reversal, the substantiality of issues on appeal, the length of the sentence imposed, future dangerousness, and the seriousness of the conviction.

The Bail Reform Act of 1984 provides that a defendant may be released pending appeal only if the court finds "by clear and convincing evidence that the person is not likely to flee or pose a danger to the safety of any other person or the community" and "the appeal is not for purpose of delay and raises a substantial question of law or fact likely to result in reversal or an order for a new trial." If the defendant has been convicted of a crime of violence he must show, in addition to the above factors, that there are "exceptional reasons" why detention is not appropriate. 18 U.S.C. §§ 3143(b)(2) and 3145(c). Thus, detention pending appeal is mandatory in the vast majority of cases. See United States v. Marshall, 78 F.3d 365 (8th Cir.1996) (intent of the Bail Reform Act was "bluntly, that fewer convicted persons remain at large while pursuing their appeals"; bail properly denied where the defendant could not show a "close question, so integral to the merits of the conviction that it is more probable than not that reversal or a new trial will occur if the question is decided in the defendant's favor"); United States v. Garcia, 340 F.3d 1013 (9th Cir. 2003) ("exceptional reasons" can include a meritorious appeal and "circumstances that would render the hardships of prison unusually harsh for a particular defendant").

The court in United States v. Koon, 6 F.3d 561 (9th Cir.1993), considered the "exceptional circumstances" language in an appeal by the two officers convicted in the beating of Rodney King. Officers Koon and Powell advanced several reasons in their request for release pending appeal which they argued qualified as "exceptional," including: their offense was "highly situational"; they had been acquitted in a state court before being prosecuted and convicted for the same activity in a federal court; the victim's conduct contributed to the offense; there would be difficulty in assuring the officers' safety during detention pending appeal; and their sentences were relatively short in comparison to the relatively long process for appeal. But the court held that none of these reasons was "exceptional" because "each is an ordinary corollary of being a law enforcement officer convicted of violating another's civil rights under 18 U.S.C. § 242." Do you agree? Is it fair to require a defendant convicted of a crime of violence to in effect serve his sentence before his appeal is decided, assuming that his release poses no risk and his appeal raises a substantial question?

Chapter Eight

DISCOVERY

I. CRIMINAL DISCOVERY: UNLIKE CIVIL DISCOVERY

It is common knowledge that the promulgation of the Federal Rules of Civil Procedure in 1938 marked an important change in the theory and practice of civil litigation. Before those Rules were adopted

> a diligent lawyer could come into court well prepared on his own case, but he was frequently in the dark as to the exact nature of his opponent's case, and consequently unprepared to meet it. Surprise was a legitimate trial tactic. A lawsuit was viewed as a game or joust in which counsel for each side strove mightily for his client, and the theory was that justice would emerge triumphant when the dust of combat settled in the judicial arena.

M. Green, The Business of the Trial Courts, in The Courts, the Public and the Law Explosion 7, 21–22 (1965).

This "sporting theory of justice" gave way to the belief that a trial should be a "quest for truth." The federal civil rules, as well as the civil discovery rules in the states, provide opposing counsel and litigants with tools, such as depositions and interrogatories, for discovery of information prior to trial; they permit each party to discover much of the evidence that is in the exclusive control of the other.

In theory at least, civil discovery means that one side rarely has monopoly power over the facts. In contrast, criminal discovery remains decidedly limited— despite the almost universal condemnation of the "sporting theory" of litigation. This raises obvious questions: Are the arguments in favor of broad discovery for civil litigants any less persuasive in the criminal context? Is the "quest for truth" inherently different in civil and criminal cases? If not, are there counter-vailing considerations in criminal cases that justify a different approach to discovery?

Within the criminal law, the wide range of possible cases makes it difficult to predict the need for discovery or its possible abuses in particular cases. Opponents of discovery tend to focus on violent criminals, citing the danger of revealing prosecutorial information to them.[1] Adherents of more liberal discov-

---

1. * * * A criminal trial is as different from a civil trial as night is from day. In a civil trial the parties are ordinarily law-abiding citizens who are peacefully seeking to have the

ery often point to white collar crimes in order to align the accused with the civil defendant.[2] In truth, one may wonder whether a "white collar" defendant is more of a threat to criminal than to civil proceedings.[3] One may also wonder whether those charged with violent crimes are more likely to abuse discovery than other defendants. Although there is little evidence to suggest that defendants convicted of crimes of violence actually would abuse discovery, there is a widespread, and reasonable, belief that certain defendants—those with organized crime or terrorist connections, for example—pose the greatest threat to witnesses and evidence. When a system of discovery is established, the most important issue is whether or not to presume that most defendants and most defense lawyers will abuse discovery or to presume that most will use discovery as it should be used—i.e., to prepare for trial or plea negotiations.[4]

The Role of Constitutional Law

Most of the discovery questions considered in this chapter involve nonconstitutional issues. The Supreme Court has repeatedly stated that "there is no general constitutional right to discovery in a criminal case." Weatherford v. Bursey, 429 U.S. 545, 559 (1977). On the other hand, it is clear that constitutional considerations are implicated when a jurisdiction establishes a discovery system. Some sharing of information by the government may be necessary in order to guarantee a fair trial. And even though an accused may have to give the government notice of certain claims, if it is to have a fair chance to meet them, the accused must be permitted to preserve her privilege against self-incrimination, which can be a complicating factor.

court resolve a dispute involving money or property. In a criminal trial, on the other hand, the stakes are much higher than mere money or property. The defendant's liberty, and sometimes his very life, depends on the outcome. Many defendants are desperate, vicious criminals who are guilty of most serious crimes against society and who would stop at nothing to win an acquittal.

Flannery, Prosecutor's Case Against Liberal Discovery, 33 F.R.D. 74, 78 (1963).

2. [T]he range of civil and criminal substantive law is too broad to permit the generalization that one involved in civil litigation is far less likely to suborn perjury or intimidate witnesses. It is difficult to believe that the defendant to charges of income tax evasion, false advertising, mail fraud, et cetera, will regularly tamper with justice on the criminal side of the court but that he will not do so when defending against the same or comparable charges on the civil side.

A. Goldstein; The State & The Accused: Balance of Advantage 69 Yale L.J. 1149 (1960).

3. See generally Statement of Harris Steinberg, in Discovery in Criminal Cases, 44 F.R.D. 481, 508–510 (1968):

Discovery, of course, is only one part of the criminal trial process, and it cannot do, nor should it be blamed for not doing, nor should

it be judged in the light of whether it does, anything about crooked lawyers, perjurers or suborners. Crooked lawyers should be summarily dealt with, but that should be done by disbarment proceedings, and not by withholding from a presumptively innocent man, on trial for his liberty, information bearing on the issues of his case, which will enable him to defend himself. Perjurers and suborners should be sent to jail, but defendants on trial should not be deprived of discovery about their own cases, because we fear that tailor-made perjured evidence will be concocted to bolster the defense, if the facts are revealed.

4. The federal discovery framework is discussed at some length herein. A number of states have used it as a model. Some states still regulate discovery by common-law decision-making, in which appellate decisions and past practice tend to control basic approaches. In such jurisdictions, it is not uncommon to find variances among cities or counties and differences in attitudes among trial judges. Most states have court rules or statutes that regulate discovery. Some states provide broader discovery for defendants than that granted in the Federal Rules of Criminal Procedure.

II. THE BASIC ISSUES

A. ARGUMENTS AGAINST CRIMINAL DISCOVERY

Arguments against criminal discovery focus primarily on the risks involved in the defendant's access to prosecutorial information. Judge Learned Hand set the framework for such arguments in his oft-quoted opinion in United States v. Garsson, 291 Fed. 646, 649 (S.D.N.Y.1923):

> * * * Under our criminal procedure the accused has every advantage. While the prosecution is held rigidly to the charge, he need not disclose the barest outline of his defense. He is immune from question or comment on his silence; he cannot be convicted when there is the least fair doubt in the minds of any one of the twelve. Why in addition he should in advance have the whole evidence against him to pick over at his leisure, and make his defense, fairly or foully, I have never been able to see. No doubt grand juries err and indictments are calamities to honest men, but we must work with human beings and we can correct such errors only at too large a price. Our dangers do not lie in too little tenderness to the accused. Our procedure has been always haunted by the ghost of the innocent man convicted. It is an unreal dream.

Opponents of discovery argue that expansion would tip the balance too much on the side of the accused. Prosecutors already face a heavy burden of proof and the defendant has the benefit of a privilege against self-incrimination which allows her not to testify at all. Neither of these elements is found in a civil trial. As one prosecutor explained:

> A civil trial is a search for the truth by both sides. But is a criminal trial a search for the truth? As far as the Government is concerned, it certainly is, for the Government prosecutor has just as great a duty to protect the innocent as he has to prosecute the guilty. The defense lawyer, however, has no duty to reveal the truth. His responsibility is to insure that the defendant receives a fair trial and to require the Government to prove his client's guilt beyond a reasonable doubt. He may be convinced that his client is guilty; but if the defendant insists on a trial, the defense lawyer must require the Government to prove him guilty beyond a reasonable doubt. * * * There is, therefore, a vast difference between a civil and criminal case in that a civil case is a search for the truth and there can be a mutual exchange of information so that the truth may be ascertained, whereas in a criminal case involving a guilty defendant, there is a one-sided search for the truth and there can be no equal exchange of information due to the very nature of the proceedings.

Statement of Thomas A. Flannery, The Prosecutor's Case Against Liberal Discovery, 33 F.R.D. 74, 78–79 (1963).

Opponents of discovery in criminal cases seem to argue that the accused can be treated poorly in some respects if she is treated well in other respects. But what does this say about our attitude toward constitutional rights? It is true that the privilege against self-incrimination as interpreted by the Supreme Court makes it more difficult for the prosecutor to gather evidence from a defendant than if no such broad privilege were recognized. It is true that the restrictions on evidence-gathering attributable to the Fourth Amendment and the right to counsel under the Sixth Amendment sometimes impair the government's ability to gather evidence. But does this mean that defendants should not get information that might be necessary for them to prepare a defense or enter into a plea agreement?

A related argument against broad discovery is that it will enable the defendant to prepare a perjured defense.[5] For example, if informed in advance of what the government witnesses will say, the defendant may concoct a defense to explain and rebut that testimony. But is the danger of perjury appreciably greater in criminal than in civil cases? Assuming that it is, doesn't the government have opportunities to "freeze" evidence in criminal cases that are virtually unknown in civil cases and that make the danger of perjury attributable to discovery slight? For example, the government can obtain a search warrant to seize tangible evidence and hold it for trial. This tangible evidence will often limit the defendant's ability to concoct a defense. Similarly, the government can use sophisticated electronic eavesdropping pursuant to court order. The government can call witnesses to testify before a secret grand jury and obtain statements that are made under oath. The government can call witnesses to testify in a preliminary hearing to pin down their testimony before the defendant's very eyes. With such evidence-gathering devices available, does the government have to worry much about manufactured evidence? It is true that the government does not know what the defendant herself will say in many instances. But the defendant has the constitutional right to attend the trial; and the government will disclose all its evidence at trial before the defendant testifies in any event, so is discovery much of an incremental inducement to perjury? See Brooks v. Tennessee, 406 U.S. 605 (1972)(invalidating a statute requiring the defendant to testify as the first witness at trial or not at all).

In a classic opinion, Judge Vanderbilt described the specific dangers that he perceived with rules providing for liberal discovery in criminal cases:

> In criminal proceedings long experience has taught the courts that often discovery will lead not to honest factfinding, but on the contrary to perjury and the suppression of evidence. Thus the criminal who is aware of the whole case against him will often procure perjured testimony in order to set up a false defense * * *. Another result of full discovery would be that the criminal defendant who is informed of the names of all of the State's witnesses may take steps to bribe or frighten them into giving perjured testimony or into absenting themselves so that they are unavailable to testify. Moreover, many witnesses, if they know that the defendant will have knowledge of their names prior to trial, will be reluctant to come forward with information during the investigation of the crime. * * * All these dangers are more inherent in criminal proceedings where the defendant has much more at stake, often his own life, than in civil proceedings.

State v. Tune, 13 N.J. 203, 210–11, 98 A.2d 881, 884 (1953).

The danger to witnesses may be the strongest argument against extensive discovery on behalf of criminal defendants. Whether the threat to witnesses and

(margin note: Problems with full disclosure of ev to crim Δ)

---

5. The search for truth may also be impaired if prosecutors, who know they will have to reveal information, are discouraged from making records and rely on memory instead. See Louisell, Criminal Discovery: Dilemma Real or Apparent? 49 Calif.L.Rev. 56 (1961). Do you think this really would happen?

to the administration of justice is as great as the quote suggests is subject to fair debate, but it certainly is the case that many experienced prosecutors believe the threat to be real, as some of the material that follows will demonstrate. The question is whether this danger justifies a blanket limitation on discovery in a criminal case.

Another argument against broad defense discovery is that it will result in fishing expeditions into government records. This argument probably can be addressed by providing in discovery rules that only relevant information can be requested and by indicating the classes of information that generally should be discoverable. The use of protective orders and sanctions for discovery abuse can also go far to limit excessive discovery demands—as they do in civil cases. The fact that the same prosecutors' offices appear in all criminal cases means that prosecutors should be able to learn quickly what material courts will require them to turn over to defendants.

Case–By–Case Approach?

One thing that you might want to ponder as you proceed in the chapter is whether it is necessary to take an all or nothing approach to various discovery issues. Opponents of liberal discovery claim that it poses dangers, but surely they would concede that the dangers do not exist in all cases. Advocates of discovery reform argue that the dangers are overstated in the run of the mine case, but surely they would concede that danger is real in some cases. Why should a rule be written to deny or grant discovery for all criminal cases? An alternative would be to permit discovery in some but not all cases. It is possible, for example, either to presume that discovery is to be permitted, but to allow the government to oppose it in a particular case, or to presume that it is not to be permitted absent a showing by the defendant of specialized need. Indeed, this is something like the approach of Fed.R.Crim.P. 16(d), which provides: "At any time the court may, for good cause, deny, restrict or defer discovery of inspection, or grant other appropriate relief."

One of the problems with a case-by-case approach, however, is that it may result in hearings when one side or the other tries to overcome the presumption. Early in a criminal case it may be hard for the side against whom the presumption operates to offer proof—for the very reason that there has been limited access to pertinent information. Also, the hearing itself may tend to produce the discovery that the government opposes. But another tack might be taken. Discovery of relevant material could be presumed proper, but the prosecutor could be empowered to deny discovery if an affidavit were submitted under seal to the trial court explaining why discovery in a particular case might threaten the fair administration of justice. See Fed.R.Crim.P. 16(d) (providing that the party opposing discovery may "show good cause by a written statement that the court will inspect ex parte"). The natural response of a defendant would be to protest against any ex parte procedure. But if the choice is to deny all defendants discovery to protect against some defendants, or to grant discovery to all except those against whom an affidavit is submitted, isn't there a good argument that the latter procedure is the better one?

B. ARGUMENTS FAVORING CRIMINAL DISCOVERY

Proponents of more liberal discovery hold that the gravity of the liberty and reputation interests at stake in criminal cases argues for liberalized discovery. In a dissent in *Tune,* supra, State Court Justice (later Supreme Court Justice) Brennan said:

> It shocks my sense of justice that in these circumstances counsel for an accused facing a possible death sentence should be denied inspection of his confession which, were this a civil case, could not be denied.

In a later article, The Criminal Prosecution: Sporting Event or Quest for Truth? 1963 Wash.U.L.Q. 279, Justice Brennan addressed the arguments against discovery. He pointed out that the privilege against self-incrimination has not prevented prosecutors from securing confessions or incriminating non-testimonial evidence from the criminally accused; that the best protections against manipulation and perjury are early exposure of the facts and emphasis on the ethical responsibilities of defense counsel; and that the trial judge can act to protect witnesses shown to be in danger. Justice Brennan and others have pointed out that, without discovery, indigent defendants are seriously handicapped in the preparation of a defense. In addition, as Dean Pye has noted:

> Most criminal cases result in a plea of guilty. The principal role of the capable advocate in many circumstances is to advise that his client plead guilty. For this advice to be meaningful, it must be based upon knowledge of the facts and the consequences. One of these consequences is the probability of conviction if the client goes to trial. It may be impossible for counsel to make any intelligent evaluation of the alternatives if he knows only what his client has told him and what he has discovered on his own.

The Defendant's Case for More Liberal Discovery, 33 F.R.D. 82, 83 (1963).

Finally, proponents seek to dispel the arguments against discovery by pointing to jurisdictions where it works. In many states, where discovery is a matter of prosecutorial discretion, there has been a general "open-file" policy, at least in particular cases, and the prosecutors take into account the same considerations discussed above. In still other states, legislatures have expanded criminal discovery, without apparent detriment to the criminal justice process. See, e.g., Langrock, Vermont's Experiment in Criminal Discovery, 53 A.B.A.J. 732 (1967); Fletcher, Pretrial Discovery in State Criminal Cases, 12 Stan.L.Rev. 293 (1960). Even in Federal practice, many U.S. Attorneys provide broader discovery than the minimum required by the Federal Rules. Seventy-six percent of U.S. Attorneys who responded to an ABA survey stated that they provided "extensive informal discovery beyond the dictates" of the Federal Rules of Criminal Procedure. Middlekauf, What Practitioners Say About Broad Criminal Discovery, Criminal Justice, Spring 1994. This broader discovery has had no apparent deleterious effect, especially because U.S. Attorneys state that they do not grant additional discovery in cases where there is a substantial risk of witness intimidation.

C. OBJECTIVES OF CRIMINAL DISCOVERY

In 1994, the ABA adopted discovery standards that emphasized the advantages to the courts of broad discovery:

Standard 11–1.1. Objectives of pretrial procedures

(a) Procedures prior to trial should, consistent with the constitutional rights of the defendant:

(i) promote a fair and expeditious disposition of the charges, whether by diversion, plea, or trial;

(ii) provide the defendant with sufficient information to make an informed plea;

(iii) permit thorough preparation for trial and minimize surprise at trial;

(iv) reduce interruptions and complications during trial and avoid unnecessary and repetitious trials by identifying and resolving prior to trial any procedural, collateral, or constitutional issues;

(v) minimize the procedural and substantive inequities among similarly situated defendants;

(vi) effect economies in time, money, judicial resources, and professional skills by minimizing paperwork, avoiding repetitious assertions of issues, and reducing the number of separate hearings; and

(vii) minimize the burden upon victims and witnesses.

(b) These needs can be served by:

(i) full and free exchange of appropriate discovery;

(ii) simpler and more efficient procedures; and

(iii) procedural pressures for expediting the processing of cases.

The ABA standards urge trial courts to promote discovery, to encourage automatic disclosure of information, and to develop procedural devices to assist the litigants in discovery. Counsel are urged to engage in discovery without judicial supervision to the greatest possible extent. Wouldn't these standards require a sea change in federal criminal practice? Which constituency would benefit the most from such a change—prosecutors, defendants, or the courts?

III.   DISCOVERY ON BEHALF OF THE DEFENDANT

A.   THE STATE OF THE LAW

In most jurisdictions, criminal discovery remains strictly circumscribed either by statute or court action.

> Most of the states have * * * limited a defendant's discovery by a variety of doctrines that had their origins in the halting and cautious growth of discovery. The most common of these doctrines holds that the question of whether to grant discovery is in the discretion of the trial court. A second limiting doctrine confines discovery to evidence that would be admissible in court. Another such doctrine requires the defendant to establish a foundation for discovery by demonstrating a particularized need for the information he requests. Some states surprisingly refuse discovery of evidence about which the defendant already knows on the ground that he has no need of it. * * * In addition, many states deny discovery of particular categories of information—for example, the defendant's confession, the confessions of co-

defendants, the statements of prospective witnesses, and the transcript or minutes of grand jury testimony.[6]

On the other hand,

> in many jurisdictions, there is considerable discovery by grace—i.e., discovery provided by the prosecutor although not compelled by statute, rule, or decision. * * * While it is dangerous to generalize too much about the form and scope of this informal discovery * * *, it seems that the sine qua non of defense discovery is defense cooperation. If the defense attorney is willing to provide information, he may usually obtain access to information in return.

> Some might think such discovery by grace adequately protects the legitimate interests of criminal defendants. But clearly any system that relies wholly on discretion entrusted to one side is open to abuse and unfairness. The ability to withhold or grant information is one form of control that prosecutors hold over the defense bar. Information may be given selectively to encourage a guilty plea; a defense counsel who has "unreasonably" refused to plead certain clients guilty may find that his access to information has been shut off, and in the "big case" normal channels of communication may close. It is, of course, the client who suffers when an attorney falls from grace, or when the prosecutor, for other reasons, disregards usual procedures for trading information.

R. Lempert & S. Saltzburg, A Modern Approach to Evidence 127–28 (2d ed.1982).

B. SOME SPECIFICS OF DEFENSE DISCOVERY

The federal system, like many of the states, grants only very limited discovery to criminal defendants. Fed.R.Crim.P. 16 is the basic rule providing for discovery in federal criminal cases. Subdivision (a)(1) of the Rule sets forth seven categories of information that *must* be disclosed by the government "upon a defendant's request." They are: (A) the defendant's own oral statements made in response to official interrogation, if the government intends to offer the statements at trial; (B) the defendant's own written or recorded statements of which the government has custody; (C) for organizational defendants, such as corporations, statements of agents that are legally attributable to the organization; (D) the defendant's prior criminal record; (E) documents and other tangible objects that are material to the defense, or intended for use by the government in its case in chief, or that were obtained from or belong to the defendant; (F) reports of physical or mental examinations, as well as scientific tests, that are material to the defense or intended for use by the government in its case in chief; and (G) a summary of testimony of expert witnesses that the government intends to call in its case in chief, including a description of the bases and reasons for the expert's opinion, and a description of the witness' qualifications.

By making discovery of certain materials a matter of right upon request, Rule 16 places primary responsibility on defense attorneys and prosecutors, instead of on the court.

By examining the rule's approach to various aspects of discovery and by comparing it to other approaches that have been recommended or adopted, we can outline the current state of discovery in most American criminal cases.

---

6. Nakell, Criminal Discovery for the Defense and the Prosecution—The Developing Constitutional Considerations, 50 N.C.L.Rev. 437, 474–75 (1972).

1. *The Defendant's Statements*

The Federal Rule gives the defendant the right to discover any oral statement made by the defendant in response to interrogation by a person known by the defendant to be a government agent; the defendant also has the right to discover any relevant written or recorded statement within the custody or control of the government. The Rule provides a corresponding right to collective entities, such as corporations and labor organizations, to obtain the statements of their agents. The government must exercise due diligence in obtaining such statements upon request. Such discovery may not seem very controversial, but the fact that it has been indicates the kind of opposition to defense discovery that has existed for some time.

The argument has been made that if the defendant's prior statements are disclosed, she can tailor her testimony at trial to eliminate any discrepancies and the prosecution will not be able to impeach her by way of prior inconsistent statement. This advantage, however, is already available for prosecution witnesses, who are "prepped" for cross-examination. Moreover, revelation of prior incriminating statements may persuade the defendant to plead guilty and avoid trial—which provides an advantage not just for the defendant but for the system itself. Finally, the government will ordinarily offer the defendant's statements during its case-in-chief. There, the defendant often will hear it before testifying anyway. So the opposition to disclosure of the defendant's own statements seems to make little sense.

Perhaps the most significant argument for disclosure is that the defendant should know what the government claims she told its agents, since the government can always use the defendant's statements in some fashion, and the importance of the defendant's words makes it imperative that she should know exactly what it is she may have to explain or deny. For example, in United States v. Camargo–Vergara, 57 F.3d 993 (11th Cir.1995), the defendant prepared a trial strategy emphasizing that he had no experience with drugs. In the middle of trial, the government called an agent who said that the defendant made a post-arrest statement to her that indicated substantial knowledge of the drug trade. This statement had not been disclosed previously to the defendant. The court found this a violation of Rule 16 and reversed the defendant's conviction, reasoning that the disclosure at trial "attacked the very foundation of the defense strategy." But didn't the defendant know that he had made this statement to the agent? And why is the court concerned about impairing a defense strategy that is belied by the facts? Does the defendant have the right to present a false defense? See also United States v. Alvarez, 987 F.2d 77 (1st Cir.1993)(failure to disclose defendant's statement to government agent was reversible error where disclosure at trial undermined the defendant's innocent bystander defense).

What Is a "Statement"?

There has been some controversy over the meaning of the word "statement" in Rule 16. The difficulty arises where the defendant's words have been paraphrased or summarized in a writing. Must the writing be disclosed? The Jencks Act, discussed infra, defines statements of *government witnesses* discoverable for cross-examination purposes as:

(1) a written statement made by said witness and signed or otherwise adopted or approved by him;

(2) a stenographic, mechanical, electrical, or other recording, or a transcription thereof, which is a substantially verbatim recital of an oral statement made by said witness and recorded contemporaneously with the making of such oral statement; or

(3) a statement, however taken or recorded, or a transcription thereof, if any, made by said witness to a grand jury.

The courts have read the Jencks Act to limit discovery to statements that reproduce exact words or are substantially verbatim. The drafters of Rule 16 provided no definition; but courts construe the term "statement" under Rule 16 in accordance with the Jencks Act definition. See United States v. Malone, 49 F.3d 393 (8th Cir.1995)(holding that the definition of "statement" under Rule 16 is the same as that under the Jencks Act: agent's notes do not qualify as Rule 16 material because the notes "constitute the agent's impression of his interview with Luckett, not a statement by Luckett"). Compare ABA Standard 11–1.3, defining "statement" as: "the substance of a 'statement' of any kind made by that person that is embodied or summarized in any writing or recording, whether or not specifically signed or adopted by that person."

Notice that oral statements made by the defendant to undercover agents are not subject to disclosure, nor are oral statements made to those who are not government agents. See United States v. Byrne, 83 F.3d 984 (8th Cir.1996) (statements made by defendant to an undercover informant during the course of a conspiracy are not subject to disclosure under Rule 16(a)(1)(A)). Can you figure out why the rule is drafted as it is?

Have you any problem with turning over to the defendant her own statements?

2. Co–defendants' Statements

Rule 16 does not require that a defendant be given a copy of a codefendant's statements, but ABA Standard § 11–2.1(a)(i) does. The rationale for the ABA version rests in part on Bruton v. United States, 391 U.S. 123 (1968). *Bruton* held that it is constitutional error to hold a joint trial where one defendant has confessed and implicated his codefendant, and the statement is not admissible against that codefendant. Thus, knowledge of a codefendant's confession in advance is necessary to allow defense counsel to move for appropriate remedies such as severance or redaction of the confession. But the ABA Standards go further and note that even if it is clear that the confessing defendant will testify, so that there is no *Bruton* concern, there is still good reason to allow one defendant a look at the other's statement. Defense counsel cannot prepare properly without knowing what each defendant has previously said. Under the Federal Rule, each defendant could obtain her own statement and share it—but that depends on whether the defendants are making a common defense. In cases where the defendants are pointing fingers at each other, it would seem very helpful for a defendant to have pretrial access to inculpatory statements made by a codefendant, wouldn't it? Would any harm be done by providing for discovery directly by each defendant of all statements by all codefendants?

3. Discovery of Prior Criminal Records

As the Advisory Committee on the Federal Rules noted in its comment to Fed.R.Crim.P. 16(a):

> A defendant may be uncertain of the precise nature of his prior record and it seems therefore in the interest of efficient and fair administration to make it possible to resolve prior to trial any disputes as to the correctness of the relevant criminal record of the defendant.

> Disclosure of prior convictions should enable the defendant to seek pretrial rulings on the admissibility of such convictions to impeach her if she should choose to testify. Rules like Fed.R.Evid. 609(a)(1), which permit the trial judge some discretion in admitting and rejecting some convictions as impeachment evidence, often invite such motions, and these motions often save time once trial commences.

4. Documents and Tangible Objects

Few discovery disputes arise concerning evidence obtained from or belonging to the defendant. And the government knows that it must disclose upon request material that it plans to use at trial. More difficult to apply is the language in Rule 16(a)(1)(D) requiring disclosure of documents and tangible objects "material to preparing the defense." Consider United States v. Phillip, 948 F.2d 241 (6th Cir.1991). Phillip was on trial for murder and child abuse of one of his sons, Jamal. Jamal died after falling down a flight of stairs. The government contended that Phillip hit Jamal so hard that he fell down the steps. Phillip admitted that he had beaten Jamal for a period of weeks, but contended that Jamal had fallen down the steps accidentally while Phillip had his back turned. The government videotaped an interview with the defendant's six-year-old son, Roderick. Roderick stated that Phillip had not hit Jamal at the time of the dispute, but also stated that his mother had coached him; he also made several statements inculpating Phillip and describing acts of abuse. The court of appeals rejected Phillip's argument that the videotape was "material to preparing" his defense:

> Phillip asserts in conclusory fashion that access to the videotape * * * would have aided him in the preparation of his defense, but he does not state convincingly how the videotape would have assisted him. He does suggest that viewing the videotape would have allowed him to reach a more informed decision concerning whether or not to depose Roderick or to subpoena him as a defense witness. However, since Roderick was his son, Phillip was aware of Roderick's potential availability to testify concerning Phillip's battering of Jamal. Moreover, early access to the videotape certainly could not have enlightened Phillip with respect to the *wisdom* of deposing Roderick or calling him as a witness. * * * On the whole, the videotape is inculpatory in nature and reveals a highly impressionable young child making highly inconsistent statements within a short period of time. * * *

> [E]arly access to the videotape would have informed Phillip that if deposed or placed on the witness stand, Roderick might 1) make exculpatory statements, 2) make inculpatory statements, 3) make both exculpatory and inculpatory statements, and/or 4) have little memory of relevant events. After viewing the videotape, Phillip would have been in no better position to evaluate the wisdom of deposing Roderick or calling him as a witness.

tape not material to trial prep.

Accordingly, we conclude that the videotape was not material to the preparation of Phillip's defense * * *.

See also United States v. Stevens, 985 F.2d 1175 (2d Cir.1993)(document is not material "merely because it would have persuaded the defendant from proffering easily impeached testimony"). Compare United States v. Cedano–Arellano, 332 F.3d 568 (9th Cir. 2003) (where the defendant was attacking the reliability of a drug-sniffing dog, the dog's training materials and certification records were material to preparing the defense, and should have been disclosed under Fed. R.Crim.P. 16(a)(1)(E)).

Defenses Not Going to the Merits

Doc discovered bb only
① Δ's prop?
② Gov intends to use in case
③ mat to defense

Fed.R.Crim.P. 16(a)(1)(E) authorizes discovery of documents only when 1) they are the defendant's property; 2) the government intends to use them in its case-in-chief; or 3) they are "material to preparing the defense." In United States v. Armstrong, 517 U.S. 456 (1996), the defendants were African–Americans charged with crack cocaine offenses. They claimed that they were being prosecuted because of their race. The defendants argued that they were entitled under Rule 16 to discovery of documents relevant to their claim of selective prosecution, e.g., charging criteria, the number of unprosecuted crack violators who are white, etc. These materials were obviously not the property of the defendants. Nor did the government intend to use the documents at trial. Thus, discovery therefore hinged on whether materials supporting a claim of selective prosecution could be considered "material to preparing the defense."

mat to Δ means - that which is responsive to Pros case in Chief.

The Court, in an opinion by Chief Justice Rehnquist, held that the term "material to preparing the defense" covered only those documents and objects that are responsive to the government's case-in-chief, i.e., those documents and objects that are pertinent to the defendant's guilt or innocence. The Chief Justice reasoned as follows:

Respondents argue that the Rule applies because any claim that "results in nonconviction" if successful is a "defense" for the Rule's purposes, and a successful selective-prosecution claim has that effect.

We reject this argument, because we conclude that in the context of Rule 16 "the defendant's defense" means the defendant's response to the Government's case-in-chief. While it might be argued that as a general matter, the concept of a "defense" includes any claim that is a "sword," challenging the prosecution's conduct of the case, the term may encompass only the narrower class of "shield" claims, which refute the Government's arguments that the defendant committed the crime charged. Rule 16 * * * tends to support the "shield-only" reading. If "defense" means an argument in response to the prosecution's case-in-chief, there is a perceptible symmetry between documents "material to the preparation of the defendant's defense," and, in the very next phrase, documents "intended for use by the government as evidence in chief at the trial."

* * *

We hold that Rule 16(a) * * * authorizes defendants to examine Government documents material to the preparation of their defense against the

Government's case-in-chief, but not to the preparation of selective-prosecution claims.

Justices Souter and Ginsburg concurred, with the reservation that the application of Rule 16(a)(1)(E) to other non-merits defenses (e.g., speedy trial, or affirmative defenses unrelated to the merits) had not been decided. Justice Stevens dissented on the ground that discovery was warranted under the district court's equitable power, but he agreed with the Chief Justice's Rule 16 analysis. Justice Breyer concurred in the judgment on the ground that a sufficient preliminary showing of selective prosecution had not been made in order to justify discovery. He disagreed, however, with the Chief Justice's construction of Rule 16, and argued that the Rule authorized discovery of any document material to dismissal of the prosecution on any grounds.

The Court in *Armstrong* did not hold that defendants *never* have a right to inspect documents and other information that pertain to matters other than the government's case-in-chief. Rather, the holding was that defendants are not *entitled* to these materials under Rule 16. A defendant is free to argue, for example, that notwithstanding Rule 16, discovery of certain materials is necessary to protect a constitutional right. This constitutional argument of selective prosecution was indeed made in *Armstrong,* but the Court held that mere allegations of selective prosecution are not enough to warrant discovery. See the discussion of this aspect of *Armstrong* in Chapter 6.

Fishing Expeditions

Under Rule 16(d)(1), the judge has discretion to quash discovery requests that are vague or overbroad. The courts are properly concerned with preventing "fishing expeditions"; thus it has been held that a request for "anything exculpatory" is equivalent to no request at all, and the "trial judge need not accord the slightest heed to such shotgun approach." United States v. Weiner, 578 F.2d 757 (9th Cir.1978).

Because documents cannot be intimidated and cannot easily be tampered with if the government retains the original, the fear of misuse by the defendant is not great. The limits of discovery here are to protect the government from having to respond to overbroad requests. If the documents would reveal the names of witnesses or other information not discoverable, such as work product, then they will not be disclosed.

Too Much Disclosure?

In complex criminal cases, especially white collar crime cases, document production under Rule 16(a)(1)(E) can be voluminous. Indeed, the defendant may complain that he is receiving *too much* production. Abramowitz, in Judicial Intervention in the Discovery Process, N.Y.L.J., March 2, 1993, p.3, discusses this problem in the context of a particular white collar crime prosecution:

> Counsel in white-collar cases are often faced with the daunting task of sifting through reams of documents made available by the government in an attempt to find the proverbial needle in the haystack. Not only is this unfair, but when such a task becomes so onerous that the defense cannot make meaningful inroads into the material provided to find relevant information, excessive trial delays can occur.

The extent of the government's obligations under Rule 16, however, is far from clear. Does the government fulfill its obligations by merely giving the defense access to discovery materials, or is greater specificity required?

E.D.P.A Said specify what is poignent in the volums of info.

A judge for the U.S. District Court for the Eastern District of Pennsylvania recently decided that defense counsel, who was given access to several rooms full of documents and 2,400 hours of tape-recorded conversations, was entitled to learn from the government which portions of the materials would not be used at trial. [The case is United States v. McDade, 1992 WL 382351 (E.D.Pa.1992)].

* * * The defense cried foul because the government, by delivering so much documentation, rendered the defense incapable of distilling what was germane and relevant. * * *

Pros said that would divulge work prod

The government countered that the defense had no right to discover what the government intended to produce and prove at trial because such information is its attorney work product. The government contended that to grant the defense request would, in effect, force the government to disgorge a blueprint of its trial strategy * * *.

The district court judge, finding that "both sides' arguments ... have some logical, legal and equitable bases," decided to exercise his discretion and apply a negative-identification approach to the problem. He directed the government, "to the best of its good-faith ability, to tell the defense of any discrete parcels of materials that it does not plan to use at trial." He concluded that to force the government to set forth its trial plans by disclosing its * * * lists of exhibits and other documents it intends to rely on at trial * * * "would be to compel too much."

ok - only state what you do not plan on using

On the other hand, recognizing the difficulty the defense was having in sifting through the discovery material, he determined that "if the government does in fact know that of ... 27 empirical haystacks which it has forked over to the defense, there are 11 haystacks, for example, which the government views as being so far afield from the focus of the trial that it does not intend to use them, then the cause of speedy and efficient justice would be furthered by the government's telling the defense about those 11 haystacks which contain no needles."

Did the trial judge reach a proper compromise? Compare United States v. Poindexter, 727 F.Supp. 1470 (D.D.C.1989)(requiring the government to identify, in advance, and with specificity, the documents that it intends to use at trial).

Assume that documents number in the thousands and they are all located and maintained at a private company under contract with the government. The government arranges for defense counsel to sift through the documents in the company's headquarters. Can the prosecuting attorney sit in the room during this sifting process? Can he instruct agents of the private company to send a copy to the prosecutor of each document copied by the defense? See United States v. Horn, 811 F.Supp. 739 (D.N.H.1992)(prosecutor disqualified and referred to disciplinary authorities for instructing corporate agent to send him a copy of all materials copied by defense counsel; such conduct constituted a breach of defense counsel's work product immunity).

5. Experts, Examinations, and Tests

Many jurisdictions, even those with restrictive discovery rules, allow discovery of results of examinations and tests such as autopsy reports, reports of medical or psychiatric examinations, blood tests, handwriting or fingerprinting comparisons, ballistic tests, and so forth. Because of its factual nature, such evidence is unlikely to be misused or distorted by disclosure. There is virtually no risk of witness intimidation. And the need for such discovery is apparent—it is practically impossible for the defense to test or rebut scientific or expert evidence without opportunities to examine that evidence before the trial. Federal Rule 16(a)(1)(F) requires disclosure of all such reports that are "material to preparing the defense" or that the government intends to use in its case-in-chief at trial.

Oral reports are not discoverable under Rule 16, as the Rule requires the government to "permit a defendant to inspect and to copy or photograph the results" and this cannot be done with oral reports. Professor Giannelli, in Criminal Discovery, Scientific Evidence, and DNA, 44 Vand.L.Rev. 791 (1991), notes that when the was drafted in 1966, "most scientific evidence consisted of autopsy reports and crime laboratory reports." However, "today experts have developed many new categories of scientific evidence." Examples include expert testimony on DNA identification, blood spatter testimony, rape trauma syndrome, child sexual abuse accommodation syndrome, battered woman syndrome, and bite mark comparisons. "Neither custom nor regulation requires these experts to write reports. Indeed * * * the prosecution loses the element of surprise by preparing the report."

The ability to challenge a scientific expert's report has become especially critical after the Supreme Court's decision in Daubert v. Merrell Dow Pharmaceuticals, Inc., 509 U.S. 579 (1993). In Daubert, the Court held that the trial court must act as a "gatekeeper" to assure that an expert's testimony is based on "good science" and comports with the scientific method. Obviously it would be difficult for the defendant to challenge a prosecution expert's scientific reasoning, without prior information about the expert's basis, methodology, and conclusion.[7] Accordingly, Rule 16(a)(1)(G) was added shortly after Daubert, to provide that at the defendant's request, the government must provide a written summary of the testimony of any expert who the government intends to call in its case-in-chief. The summary must "describe the witness's opinions, the bases and the reasons for those opinions, and the witness's qualifications."

Note that the disclosure requirement applies to any witness that the government intends to call as an expert, even if the expert is not going to testify on a scientific subject. Discovery of the opinions of non-scientific experts is made more critical after the Supreme Court's decision in Kumho Tire Co. v. Carmichael, 526 U.S. 137 (1999). The Court in Kumho held that the Daubert gatekeeping requirement applies to non-scientific experts. Thus, the trial judge must determine that non-scientific experts are using a reliable methodology and are applying that methodology properly to the facts of the case. So it is crucial for defendants to obtain discovery of reports and opinions of non-scientific experts

---

7. For further discussion of Daubert and its progeny, see Capra, The Daubert Puzzle, 32 Ga.L.Rev. 699 (1998).

such as experts on handwriting identification; only with advance notice can defendants make a proper challenge to the reliability of this expert testimony.

6. Names, Addresses, and Statements of Witnesses

Most of the states require disclosure of the names and the written or recorded statements of witnesses that the government intends to call. See Clennon, Pre–Trial Discovery of Witness Lists: A Modest Proposal to Improve the Administration of Justice in the Superior Court of the District of Columbia, 38 Cath.U.L.Rev. 641 (1989) (noting that "twenty-eight states grant the defendant as a matter of right pre-trial disclosure of the trial witnesses the prosecutor expects to call"). Some states by statute ban disclosure of witnesses' statements.

Federal courts have traditionally refused such advance discovery of witnesses, relying on the rationale underlying the Jencks Act, 18 U.S.C.A. § 3500. In Jencks v. United States, 353 U.S. 657 (1957), the Court exercised its supervisory power to require disclosure *during the trial* of the prior statements of prosecution witnesses. The Court rejected the notion that pretrial statements should only be made available where the defense could show a probable inconsistency between the witness' pretrial statements and his in-court testimony. The Court recognized that it would be very difficult for a defendant to prove that the statement was inconsistent without having access to the statement.

Jencks Act Particulars

The Jencks Act codified the *Jencks* Court's basic requirement that the government disclose pretrial statements made by its witnesses, whether or not the statements are inconsistent with trial testimony.[8] However, the *timing* of the disclosure requirement is critical. The Act *does not* provide for advance notification. Rather, a statement covered by the Act must be disclosed, on the defendant's motion, *after* the witness testifies on direct examination. "Statements" within the meaning of the Act include only written statements approved by the witness, stenographic or mechanical transcripts that purport to be almost verbatim accounts of oral statements, and any statements, however recorded, made to a grand jury. See United States v. Farley, 2 F.3d 645 (6th Cir.1993)(a summary of a witness' account is not Jencks Act material unless it is a verbatim account or unless it has been adopted by the witness); United States v. Crowley, 285 F.3d 553 (7th Cir. 2002) ("The Jencks Act does not obligate the government to disclose investigative or trial preparation material; rather, it requires only the disclosure of pretrial statements a government witness signed, adopted, or otherwise approved.").[9]

A witness's prior statement need not be disclosed under the Jencks Act unless it relates to the subject matter of the witness's direct testimony. See United States v. Susskind, 4 F.3d 1400 (6th Cir.1993) (witness' statement, even

---

8. In Goldberg v. United States, 425 U.S. 94 (1976), the Court held that statements made to government lawyers otherwise producible under the Act are not barred from production by the work product doctrine.

9. United States v. Hinton, 719 F.2d 711 (4th Cir.1983), canvasses the cases that analyze whether the government has an obligation to preserve the rough notes used to prepare formal reports. Although it recognized that some courts have required that rough notes be preserved and made available, the court concluded that these notes were not statements within the meaning of the Jencks Act and that the government was not obliged to produce them.

though relevant to the case, was not Jencks Act material when it was not related to the subject of the witness's direct testimony); United States v. Byrne, 83 F.3d 984 (8th Cir.1996) (where witness testifies to acts occurring during the conspiracy, there was no violation of the Jencks Act when the government failed to disclose the witness's prior statement concerning acts committed before the conspiracy—this was collateral or background information that did not relate to the subject matter of the direct testimony). The Jencks Act provides for *in camera* review for the purpose of separating portions of statements relating to the witness' trial testimony from unrelated portions. Fed.R.Crim.P. 26.2, which was promulgated after the Jencks Act, largely tracks the provisions of the Act, with the exception that the Rule requires defense production of defense witness statements as well. See the discussion after United States v. Nobles, infra.

The Objections to Advance Disclosure of Witness Names and Statements

At one time, the Supreme Court proposed an amendment to Rule 16 that would have required the government to provide advance disclosure of names, addresses and prior statements of witnesses. The Department of Justice vigorously opposed the amendment and mustered the support of numerous United States Attorneys, so that the amendment was never adopted. A typical complaint was expressed by the United States Attorney for the Western District of Pennsylvania at the congressional hearings on the amendment:

> It seems clear that we have a hard enough time securing the cooperation of civilian witnesses who don't want to get involved without putting them in a situation in which, months before trial, they become subject to such degradation and harassment as may occur to an ingenious defendant, who will have far more to gain under the new rules than the present post-conviction satisfaction of revenge. Indeed, we are of the view that the law should not, in the name of "enlightened" discovery procedures, expose innocent members of the public, who have had the misfortune to be victims of or witnesses to criminal conduct, to the mercy of defendants any more than the confrontation clause presently requires.[10]

In contrast, ABA Standard 11–2.1 provides that the prosecution must provide advance disclosure of names, addresses, and prior statements of witnesses. The reasoning is that disclosure is necessary so that defense counsel can prepare adequately to cross-examine witnesses and test their credibility.

Are there more direct ways to eliminate the problems of witness intimidation and harassment perceived by the U.S. Attorney? Earl Silbert testified at the hearings and suggested the following alternative:

> Alternatively, we would recommend that in the event witness disclosure is to be permitted, some burden be placed on the party seeking disclosure to show a reasonable need for the information sought, and that whatever disclosure in this regard is permitted, no party be required to disclose earlier than three days in advance of trial. Finally, it is particularly critical that in this area the trial Court retain discretion as to whether or not to grant the discovery sought.

---

10. Statement of W. Vincent Rakestraw, Ass't Att'y Gen'l, in House Hearings on Federal Rules of Criminal Procedure, 93rd Cong., 2nd Sess. (1974).

Would this have been a preferable approach?

It is on this question, whether witnesses' names, addresses, and statements should be disclosed, that the debate about discovery becomes most heated. Would this be an appropriate place to invoke the presumption of discovery, but to permit the prosecutor in any case to state in writing reasons for nondisclosure that would not be revealed to the defense, but that would be reviewed by the court? For example, would it be workable for the government to get a protective order on a case-by-case basis where it can be shown that the witness might be in danger if their identity or statement is disclosed in advance?

7. Grand Jury Minutes and Transcripts

Rule 16(a)(3) precludes defense discovery of grand jury proceedings, with two exceptions: 1) the defendant is entitled to a copy of his own grand jury testimony under Rule 16(a)(1)(A); and 2) the Jencks Act requires production of a trial witness' grand jury testimony after she has testified on direct examination. And, of course, the prosecution is required to disclose any information obtained by the grand jury that is materially exculpatory to the defendant. But there is no right to more general disclosure of grand jury minutes and transcripts.

Once an indictment is returned, do arguments for secrecy still hold? Will secrecy protect the reputations of those accused? Will secrecy inhibit flight once a defendant is formally charged? Will secrecy deter collusion among witnesses after an investigation is completed and charges have been brought? Will secrecy protect the identity of witnesses who will appear at trial? Will secrecy prevent tampering with a grand jury following a charge?

8. Work Product

Fed.R.Crim.P. 16(a)(2) protects against disclosure of "reports, memoranda, or other internal government documents made by an attorney for the government or other government agent in connection with investigating or prosecuting the case." What theory justifies protecting police or FBI reports under the Federal Rule? If it is true that the government has easier access to information than the defendant in many situations, why should that information not be shared with the defense?

Work product is one of those areas in which prosecutors complain that discovery would be one-sided, because the privilege against self-incrimination or the attorney-client privilege will in most cases bar the government from finding out what the defendant or her attorney has done to prepare a defense. Assume that the government could not force disclosure of much of the work product of the defense. Does that mean that one-sided disclosure of the government's work product is undesirable? Since the government has the power of the grand jury and the prosecutor has subpoena power, is there any information that the government will want to reach—other than that protected by the privilege against self-incrimination—that it cannot reach as easily as the defense? There will be many times when the converse is untrue—i.e., the defense will not have the same ease of access to information as the prosecutor. Is this important?

C. MECHANISMS FOR DISCOVERY

The predominant means for discovery in civil cases are depositions and interrogatories. In criminal cases the defense is not permitted to discover prosecutorial information through interrogatories, and if a bill of particulars is requested as a pretext for discovery, it is likely to be denied.

Depositions are authorized in criminal cases, although usually they are not permitted as a matter of right at the instance of any party as they are in civil cases. In fact, depositions are not permitted to be used as discovery devices in criminal cases. Rather, they are allowed only where necessary to preserve testimony for trial. Federal Rule 15 illustrates the restrictions on the use of depositions in federal criminal cases.

(a) When Taken.

(1) **In General.** A party may move that a prospective witness be deposed in order to preserve testimony for trial. The court may grant the motion because of exceptional circumstances and in the interest of justice. If the court orders the deposition to be taken, it may also require the deponent to produce at the deposition any designated material that is not privileged, including any book, paper, document, record, recording, or data.

* * *

Assume that somehow a defendant learns the names of witnesses. There is little that she can do in most jurisdictions to get the witnesses to talk with her or with counsel. It now seems clear that the prosecutor cannot advise the witnesses not to talk with the defendant or with defense counsel. See, e.g., Gregory v. United States, 369 F.2d 185 (D.C.Cir.1966). But many witnesses may want to have nothing to do with the defense. Should there be some mechanism for the defense to find out what the witnesses know? Two possibilities exist. The first is that a preliminary hearing can be made a discovery hearing in part, so that witnesses can be called by the defense. The trouble with this approach is that at the time the hearing is held, the defense may not know what questions to ask. More importantly, if the defense is not careful, it will preserve the testimony of an unfavorable witness who may become unavailable, and the witness's preliminary hearing testimony will be admitted at trial under a hearsay exception, even though the defense really did not effectively examine the witness. Also, early in the case, the defense may not have discovered the identities of all the witnesses. On the other hand, the advantage of the preliminary hearing approach is that discovery takes place in one place, at one time, and under the supervision of the court.

The alternative is the one used in civil cases: to allow depositions to be taken for discovery. Do you believe that such a rule would threaten legitimate government interests? Would it add substantially to the cost of criminal cases?[11] Does this depend on how many fewer motions and how much less abuse of preliminary hearings and other procedures would result by permitting direct discovery?

Computerized Information

In complex cases, computer technology is critical to the success of an investigation and prosecution. The use of computer technology creates signifi-

---

11. Some jurisdictions have adopted the approach and are staying with it. See, e.g., Alaska R.Crim.P. 15(a).

cant discovery problems, however. Is the defendant entitled to a relevant report generated by the government? To the data underlying the report? To the computer program? For an interesting discussion of these problems, see Garcia, "Garbage In, Gospel Out": Criminal Discovery, Computer Reliability, and the Constitution, 38 UCLA L.Rev. 1043 (1991). Professor Garcia concludes that defense counsel should have access to computerized information as well as the "underlying information, programs, computers, manuals, procedures, tests and personnel, in order to protect a client against the use of unreliable information during plea discussions, at pretrial hearings, at trial, and at sentencing."

IV. THE PROSECUTOR'S CONSTITUTIONAL DUTY TO DISCLOSE

A. THE *BRADY* RULE

Pros has const duty to disclose to Δ + Ct.

The Supreme Court has established that, above and beyond the (minimal) obligations imposed by discovery rules, the prosecution has a constitutional duty to disclose certain information to both the defendant and the trial court. The nature of the information required to be disclosed, and the scope of the prosecutor's obligation, are the subjects of this section.

Disclosure of False Evidence: *Mooney* v. Holohan *and Its Progeny*

The first case establishing a prosecutor's constitutional obligations in the discovery process was Mooney v. Holohan, 294 U.S. 103 (1935). The defendant sought habeas corpus relief, claiming "that the sole basis of his conviction was perjured testimony, which was knowingly used by the prosecuting authorities in order to obtain that conviction and also that the prosecution knowingly suppressed evidence that the defense could have used to impeach the perjured testimony." The Court said that the Due Process Clause is violated if the government engages in "a deliberate deception of court and jury by the presentation of testimony known to be perjured." Seven years later, in Pyle v. Kansas, 317 U.S. 213 (1942), a habeas petitioner charged the prosecution with knowing use of perjured testimony and the deliberate suppression of evidence favorable to the defense by threats made to witnesses. The Court cited *Mooney* and held that the "allegations * * *, if proven, would entitle petitioner to release from his present custody."

Δ - Pros knowingly suppressed evidence that their wit-nesses purjured

It • due proces violation if knowingly suppressed

Alcorta v. Texas, 355 U.S. 28 (1957), applied and invigorated the *Mooney* principle. The defendant was convicted of first degree murder; a defense claim of "sudden passion" was rejected after a witness answered the prosecutor's questions by saying that he had not kissed the defendant's wife (the victim) on the night of the murder and that he had only a casual relationship with her. Although the witness had previously told the prosecution that he had sexual intercourse with the victim on several occasions, the prosecution did not disclose this. The Supreme Court reversed because the prosecutor knowingly allowed an important witness to create a false impression at trial. Napue v. Illinois, 360 U.S. 264 (1959), further developed the principle that prevents the prosecutor from knowingly presenting false evidence. There, the principal government witness testified that he had received no promises of special consideration in exchange for his testimony. The prosecutor elicited the information from the witness and

Δ charged w/ murder

Δ: crime of passion

witness denied sleeping w/ Δ's wife
• Pros knew it was a lie

It: reversed ρ conviction

made no effort to correct it, although he knew the testimony was false. The Court found that the resulting conviction was invalid.

Mandatory Disclosure of Materially Exculpatory Evidence: The Brady Rule

In 1963, the Court decided one of its most important disclosure cases, Brady v. Maryland, 373 U.S. 83. Brady and a companion, Boblit, were charged with first degree murder, a capital offense. Brady was tried first; he admitted participation in the crime, but claimed that Boblit did the actual killing. Prior to trial Brady's lawyer asked the prosecutor to allow him to see Boblit's statements. Several statements were shown to counsel, but one in which Boblit admitted the homicide was not revealed. The defense did not learn about that statement until after Brady's conviction and death sentence were affirmed. Brady's state court post-conviction claim produced a victory in the Maryland Court of Appeals. Since Brady admitted participation, the victory resulted only in a resentencing. The Supreme Court affirmed. It said that "[a] prosecution that withholds evidence on demand of an accused which, if made available, would tend to exculpate him or reduce the penalty helps shape a trial that bears heavily on the defendant. That casts the prosecutor in the role of an architect of a proceeding that does not comport with standards of justice * * *."

Knowledge Attributable to the Prosecutor: Giglio v. United States

In Giglio v. United States, 405 U.S. 150 (1972), the Court found a violation of due process when a key witness testified that he had not been given a deal for testifying for the government. Promises had in fact been made by a predecessor in the prosecutor's office and the trial attorney for the government did not know it. Even though the prosecutor was not aware that the witness' testimony was false, the Court reversed the conviction; it said that a promise by one attorney would be attributed to the government and suggested that procedures and regulations could be developed to avoid future problems of the Giglio type.

———————

The next case develops the Brady rule and answers important questions about the materiality of suppressed evidence and the relationship between a defense request for information and a prosecutor's suppression.

UNITED STATES v. AGURS

Supreme Court of the United States, 1976.
427 U.S. 97.

MR. JUSTICE STEVENS **delivered the opinion of the Court**.

After a brief interlude in an inexpensive motel room, respondent repeatedly stabbed James Sewell, causing his death. She was convicted of second- degree murder. The question before us is whether the prosecutor's failure to provide defense counsel with certain background information about Sewell, which would have tended to support the argument that respondent acted in self-defense, deprived her of a fair trial under the rule of Brady v. Maryland.

* * *

I

At about 4:30 p.m. on September 24, 1971, respondent, who had been there before, and Sewell, registered in a motel as man and wife. They were assigned a room without a bath. Sewell was wearing a bowie knife in a sheath, and carried another knife in his pocket. Less than two hours earlier, according to the testimony of his estranged wife, he had had $360 in cash on his person.

About 15 minutes later three motel employees heard respondent screaming for help. A forced entry into their room disclosed Sewell on top of respondent struggling for possession of the bowie knife. She was holding the knife; his bleeding hand grasped the blade; according to one witness he was trying to jam the blade into her chest. The employees separated the two and summoned the authorities. Respondent departed without comment before they arrived. Sewell was dead on arrival at the hospital.

Circumstantial evidence indicated that the parties had completed an act of intercourse, that Sewell had then gone to the bathroom down the hall, and that the struggle occurred upon his return. The contents of his pockets were in disarray on the dresser and no money was found; the jury may have inferred that respondent took Sewell's money and that the fight started when Sewell re-entered the room and saw what she was doing.

On the following morning respondent surrendered to the police. She was given a physical examination which revealed no cuts or bruises of any kind, except needle marks on her upper arm. An autopsy of Sewell disclosed that he had several deep stab wounds in his chest and abdomen, and a number of slashes on his arms and hands, characterized by the pathologist as "defensive wounds."

Respondent offered no evidence. Her sole defense was the argument made by her attorney that Sewell had initially attacked her with the knife, and that her actions had all been directed toward saving her own life. The support for this self-defense theory was based on the fact that she had screamed for help. Sewell was on top of her when help arrived, and his possession of two knives indicated that he was a violence-prone person. It took the jury about 25 minutes to elect a foreman and return a verdict.

Three months later defense counsel filed a motion for a new trial asserting that he had discovered (1) that Sewell had a prior criminal record that would have further evidenced his violent character; (2) that the prosecutor had failed to disclose this information to the defense; and (3) that a recent opinion of the United States Court of Appeals for the District of Columbia Circuit made it clear that such evidence was admissible even if not known to the defendant. Sewell's prior record included a plea of guilty to a charge of assault and carrying a deadly weapon in 1963, and another guilty plea to a charge of carrying a deadly weapon in 1971. Apparently both weapons were knives.

The Government opposed the motion, arguing that there was no duty to tender Sewell's prior record to the defense in the absence of an appropriate request; that the evidence was readily discoverable in advance of trial and hence was not the kind of "newly discovered" evidence justifying a new trial; and that, in all events, it was not material.

The District Court denied the motion. * * *

The Court of Appeals reversed. The court found no lack of diligence on the part of the defense and no misconduct by the prosecutor in this case. It held, however, that the evidence was material, and that its nondisclosure required a new trial because the jury might have returned a different verdict if the evidence had been received.

The decision of the Court of Appeals represents a significant departure from this Court's prior holding; because we believe that that court has incorrectly interpreted the constitutional requirement of due process, we reverse.

II

The rule of Brady v. Maryland, arguably applies in three quite different situations. Each involves the discovery, after trial, of information which had been known to the prosecution but unknown to the defense.

In the first situation, typified by Mooney v. Holohan, the undisclosed evidence demonstrates that the prosecution's case includes perjured testimony and that the prosecution knew, or should have known, of the perjury. In a series of subsequent cases, the Court has consistently held that a conviction obtained by the knowing use of perjured testimony is fundamentally unfair, and must be set aside if there is any reasonable likelihood that the false testimony could have affected the judgment of the jury. It is this line of cases on which the Court of Appeals placed primary reliance. In those cases the Court has applied a strict standard of materiality, not just because they involve prosecutorial misconduct, but more importantly because they involve a corruption of the truth-seeking function of the trial process. Since this case involves no misconduct, and since there is no reason to question the

veracity of any of the prosecution witnesses, the test of materiality followed in the Mooney line of cases is not necessarily applicable to this case.

The second situation, illustrated by the Brady case itself, is characterized by a pretrial request for specific evidence. In that case defense counsel had requested the extrajudicial statements made by Brady's accomplice, one Boblit. This Court held that the suppression of one of Boblit's statements deprived Brady of due process, noting specifically that the statement had been requested and that it was "material." A fair analysis of the holding in Brady indicates that implicit in the requirement of materiality is a concern that the suppressed evidence might have affected the outcome of the trial.

* * *

In Brady the request was specific. It gave the prosecutor notice of exactly what the defense desired. Although there is, of course, no duty to provide defense counsel with unlimited discovery of everything known by the prosecutor, if the subject matter of such a request is material, or indeed if a substantial basis for claiming materiality exists, it is reasonable to require the prosecutor to respond either by furnishing the information or by submitting the problem to the trial judge. When the prosecutor receives a specific and relevant request, the failure to make any response is seldom, if ever, excusable.

In many cases, however, exculpatory information in the possession of the prosecutor may be unknown to defense counsel. In such a situation he may make no request at all, or possibly ask for "all Brady material" or for "anything exculpatory." Such a request really gives the prosecutor no better notice than if no request is made. If there is a duty to respond to a general request of that kind, it must derive from the obviously exculpatory character of certain evidence in the hands of the prosecutor. But if the evidence is so clearly supportive of a claim of innocence that it gives the prosecution notice of a duty to produce, that duty should equally arise even if no request is made. Whether we focus on the desirability of a precise definition of the prosecutor's duty or on the potential harm to the defendant, we conclude that there is no significant difference between cases in which there has been merely a general request for exculpatory matter and cases, like the one we must now decide, in which there has been no request at all. The third situation in which the *Brady* rule arguably applies, typified by this case, therefore embraces the case in which only a general request for "*Brady* material" has been made.

We now consider whether the prosecutor has any constitutional duty to volunteer exculpatory matter to the defense, and if so, what standard of materiality gives rise to that duty.

III

* * *

The Court of Appeals appears to have assumed that the prosecutor has a constitutional obligation to disclose any information that might affect the jury's verdict. That statement of a constitutional standard of materiality approaches the "sporting theory of justice" which the Court expressly rejected in *Brady*. For a jury's appraisal of a case "might" be affected by an improper or trivial consideration as well as by evidence giving rise to a legitimate doubt on the issue of guilt. If everything that might influence a jury must be disclosed, the only way a prosecutor could discharge his constitutional duty would be to allow complete discovery of his files as a matter of routine practice.

Whether or not procedural rules authorizing such broad discovery might be desirable, the Constitution surely does not demand that much. * * * The mere possibility that an item of undisclosed information might have helped the defense, or might have affected the outcome of the trial, does not establish "materiality" in the constitutional sense.

Nor do we believe the constitutional obligation is measured by the moral culpability, or the willfulness, of the prosecutor. If evidence highly probative of innocence is in his file, he should be presumed to recognize its significance even if he has actually overlooked it. Conversely, if evidence actually has no probative significance at all, no purpose would be served by requiring a new trial simply because an inept prosecutor incorrectly believed he was suppressing a fact that would be vital to the defense. If the suppression of evidence results in constitutional error, it is because of the character of the evidence, not the character of the prosecutor.

As the District Court recognized in this case, there are situations in which evidence is obviously of such substantial value to the defense that elementary fairness requires it to be disclosed even without a specific request. For though the attorney for the sovereign must prosecute the accused with earnestness and vigor, he must always be faithful to his client's overriding interest that "justice shall be done." He is the "servant of the law, the twofold aim of which is that guilt shall not escape or innocence suffer." Berger v. United States, 295 U.S. 78, 88. This description of the prosecutor's duty illuminates the standard of materiality that governs his obligation to disclose exculpatory evidence.

* * *

The proper standard of materiality must reflect our overriding concern with the justice of the finding of guilt.[a] Such a finding is permissible only if supported by evidence establishing guilt beyond a reasonable doubt. It necessarily follows that if the omitted evidence creates a reasonable doubt that did not otherwise exist, constitutional error has been committed. This means that the omission must be evaluated in the context of the entire record. If there is no reasonable doubt about guilt whether or not the additional evidence is considered, there is no justification for a new trial. On the other hand, if the verdict is already of questionable validity, additional evidence of relatively minor importance might be sufficient to create a reasonable doubt.

This statement of the standard of materiality describes the test which courts appear to have applied in actual cases although the standard has been phrased in different language. It is also the standard which the trial judge applied in this case. He evaluated the significance of Sewell's prior criminal record in the context of the full trial which he recalled in detail. Stressing in particular the incongruity of a claim that Sewell was the aggressor with the evidence of his multiple wounds and respondent's unscathed condition, the trial judge indicated his unqualified opinion that respondent was guilty.

He noted that Sewell's prior record did not contradict any evidence offered by the prosecutor, and was largely cumulative of the evidence that Sewell was wearing a bowie knife in a sheath and carrying a second knife in his pocket when he registered at the motel.

Since the arrest record was not requested and did not even arguably give rise to any inference of perjury, since after considering it in the context of the entire record the trial judge remained convinced of respondent's guilt beyond a reasonable doubt, and since we are satisfied that his firsthand appraisal of the record was thorough and entirely reasonable, we hold that the prosecutor's failure to tender Sewell's record to the defense did not deprive respondent of a fair trial as guaranteed by the Due Process Clause of the Fifth Amendment. * * *

MR. JUSTICE MARSHALL with whom MR. JUSTICE BRENNAN joins, dissenting.

* * *

* * * [The majority's] rule creates little, if any, incentive for the prosecutor conscientiously to determine whether his files contain evidence helpful to the defense. Indeed, the rule reinforces the natural tendency of the prosecutor to overlook evidence favorable to the defense, and creates an incentive for the prosecutor to resolve close questions of disclosure in favor of concealment.

* * * I would hold that the defendant in this case had the burden of

---

a. It has been argued that the standard should focus on the impact of the undisclosed evidence on the defendant's ability to prepare for trial, rather than the materiality of the evidence to the issue of guilt or innocence. See Note, The Prosecutor's Constitutional Duty to Reveal Evidence to the Defense, 74 Yale L.J. 136 (1964). Such a standard would be unacceptable for determining the materiality of what has been generally recognized as "Brady material" for two reasons. First, that standard

would necessarily encompass incriminating evidence as well as exculpatory evidence, since knowledge of the prosecutor's entire case would always be useful in planning the defense. Second, such an approach would primarily involve an analysis of the adequacy of the notice given to the defendant by the State, and it has always been the Court's view that the notice component of due process refers to the charge rather than the evidentiary support for the charge.

demonstrating that there is a significant chance that the withheld evidence, developed by skilled counsel,
would have induced a reasonable
doubt in the minds of enough jurors
to avoid a conviction. * * *

Refining the Test of Materiality: United States v. Bagley

Justice Blackmun wrote for the Court in United States v. Bagley, 473 U.S.
667 (1985), as the Court declined to overturn a conviction because of nondisclosure of exculpatory evidence. Bagley was charged with narcotics and firearms
offenses and convicted in a bench trial only on the narcotics charges. Thereafter
he learned that, despite his motion to discover any deals or promises between
the government and its witnesses, the government had not disclosed that its two
principal witnesses had signed contracts with the Bureau of Alcohol, Tobacco
and Firearms to be paid for their undercover work. Although the trial judge
ruled that the contracts would not have affected the outcome because the
principal witnesses testified primarily concerning the firearms charges on which
Bagley was acquitted, the court of appeals disagreed. The Supreme Court agreed
with the trial judge and found that nondisclosure of impeachment evidence, like
nondisclosure of other exculpatory evidence, requires reversal only if the evidence was material in the sense that it might have affected the outcome of the
trial. No such showing was made on the facts of this case.

Justice Blackmun's opinion set forth a single "standard of materiality"
applicable to nondisclosed exculpatory evidence. Justice Blackmun borrowed
from the Court's ineffective assistance of counsel cases (discussed in Chapter 10)
and derived the following standard:

> [Suppressed evidence] is material only if there is a reasonable probability
> that, had the evidence been disclosed to the defense, the result of the
> proceeding would have been different. A reasonable probability is a probabil-
> ity sufficient to undermine confidence in the outcome.

Justice Blackmun noted that this test was "sufficiently flexible" to cover no
request, general request, and specific request cases. In a part of the opinion
joined only by Justice O'Connor, Justice Blackmun reasoned that "the more
specifically the defense requests certain evidence * * * the more reasonable it is
for the defense to assume from the nondisclosure that the evidence does not
exist and to make pretrial and trial decisions on the basis of this assumption."
Thus, specific request cases present special considerations in applying the single
"reasonable probability" standard of materiality. The more specific the request,
the more likely the suppression will be "material" in the Brady sense.

Justice White, joined by Chief Justice Burger and Justice Rehnquist, concurred in the judgment in Bagley. Although he expressed agreement with the
single materiality standard developed by Justice Blackmun, he saw "no reason
to attempt to elaborate on the relevance to the inquiry of the specificity of the
defense's request for disclosure."

Justice Marshall, joined by Justice Brennan, dissented and argued that
"when the Government withholds from a defendant evidence that might impeach the prosecution's only witnesses, that failure to disclose cannot be deemed
harmless error." Justice Stevens, who authored Agurs, also dissented. He argued
that, unlike Agurs, the instant case involved a specific request and that Brady
requires reversal for failure to disclose evidence favorable to an accused upon a

specific request if the evidence is material either to guilt or punishment. Thus, he would have remanded for a determination of whether there was "any reasonable likelihood" that the nondisclosure could have affected the judgment of the trier of fact.

Comments on Brady–Agurs–Bagley

Professor Stacy, in The Search for the Truth in Constitutional Criminal Procedure, 91 Colum.L.Rev. 1369, 1392 (1991), has this to say about the *Bagley* standard of materiality:

> The *Bagley* standard, which focuses on the likely impact of evidence on the ultimate result in the case, suffers from two interrelated deficiencies. The first problem is that the standard will frequently be misapplied. A prosecutor's lack of information about the planned defense and partisan inclinations impede her from making an accurate and objective assessment of the evidence's effect on the outcome. The second problem is that many misapplications of the *Bagley* standard will never be detected and remedied. Because the prosecution has exclusive possession of the evidence subject to the duty to disclose and a clear incentive to withhold it, the defense or a court will sometimes never learn of evidence wrongly withheld.

In short, the Court has interpreted the prosecution's duty to disclose exculpatory evidence more narrowly than a true concern for accurate factfinding implies. For a Court genuinely interested in the search for the truth, neither the adversarial system, prosecutorial burdens, nor the constitutional text can justify the *Bagley* standard, which will result in important exculpatory evidence not being disclosed in a significant number of cases.

As a prosecutor, would you now be entitled to refuse to turn over evidence that appears to be exculpatory but not sufficiently so to require a new trial under *Bagley-Agurs–Bagley?* Should prosecutors be trusted with this authority? What would be wrong with requiring the prosecutor to turn over all evidence that a defense counsel would conclude *might tend* to exculpate the defendant?

Capra, Access to Exculpatory Evidence: Avoiding the Agurs Problems of Prosecutorial Discretion and Retrospective Review, 53 Ford.L.Rev. 391 (1984), argues that a per se right to an in camera hearing, at which the court would examine a prosecutor's files for *Brady* material, would be more effective than retrospective review of claims that exculpatory evidence was suppressed.

The Relevance of a Specific Request

While the combination of the Blackmun and White opinions in *Bagley* produce a single standard of materiality for all nondisclosure cases, *Bagley* leaves ambiguity about the relevance of a specific defense request for the evidence. In *Agurs,* Justice Stevens emphasized that the specific request increased the level of prosecutorial responsibility. In *Bagley,* Justice Blackmun emphasized the greater prejudicial impact of a denied specific request due to the possibility that defense counsel will be misled. Justice White thought it appropriate to leave the precise impact of a specific request for another day. Where a case involves a specific request, lower courts after *Bagley* have continued to take account of that factor, although not always stating why it is significant. See, e.g.,

Jean v. Rice, 945 F.2d 82 (4th Cir.1991)(recordings and reports indicating that the prosecution's star witness had been hypnotized were *Brady* material: "We are persuaded that the audio recordings and accompanying reports—twice requested—should have been disclosed to defense counsel."). As the Fifth Circuit stated in Lindsey v. King, 769 F.2d 1034 (5th Cir.1985): "Viewing the [*Bagley*] opinions as a whole, it is fair to say that all the participating Justices agreed on one thing at least: that reversal for suppression of evidence by the government is most likely where the request for it was specific."

B. APPLYING THE *BRADY* RULE

Fact-Intensive Application: Kyles v. Whitley

The Court reaffirmed its *Brady-Agurs–Bagley* line of cases in *Kyles v. Whitley*, 514 U.S. 419 (1995), and applied those cases in an intensely fact-specific manner to reverse a conviction and death sentence. Kyles was convicted (after his first trial ended in a hung jury) of murdering a woman during the course of a robbery outside Schwegmann's grocery store. There was evidence that the killer left his car in the parking lot and drove away in the victim's car. The prosecution presented four eyewitnesses who identified Kyles unequivocally both before and at the trial. Kyles argued that an acquaintance, Beanie, committed the murders and framed him by planting the murder weapon (a gun) and the victim's purse and other items at Kyles' house. Beanie had originally approached the police with information that Kyles was the killer, and received a reward for his information. Beanie was not called by either side to testify at Kyles' trial. The prosecution suppressed many pieces of evidence, including: 1. pretrial statements from two of the eyewitnesses, which were markedly inconsistent with their later identifications, and one of which appeared to point to Beanie rather than Kyles as the perpetrator; 2. a series of statements by Beanie which were inconsistent, and which inconsistencies were ignored by the investigating officer; and 3. a police report indicating that Kyles' car was not on the list of cars found at the Schwegmann's shortly after the murder.

Justice Souter, writing for five Justices, made the following general points about the Court's *Brady-Agurs–Bagley* materiality standard:

> Four aspects of materiality under *Bagley* bear emphasis. * * * *Bagley's* touchstone of materiality is a "reasonable probability" of a different result, and the adjective is important. The question is not whether the defendant would more likely than not have received a different verdict with the evidence, but whether in its absence he received a fair trial, understood as a trial resulting in a verdict worthy of confidence. A "reasonable probability" of a different result is accordingly shown when the Government's evidentiary suppression "undermines confidence in the outcome of the trial."

> The second aspect of *Bagley* materiality bearing emphasis here is that it is not a sufficiency of evidence test. * * * The possibility of an acquittal on a criminal charge does not imply an insufficient evidentiary basis to convict. One does not show a *Brady* violation by demonstrating that some of the inculpatory evidence should have been excluded, but by showing that the favorable evidence could reasonably be taken to put the whole case in such a different light as to undermine confidence in the verdict.

Third, we note that * * * once a reviewing court applying *Bagley* has found constitutional error there is no need for further harmless-error review. Assuming arguendo that a harmless error enquiry were to apply, a *Bagley* error could not be treated as harmless, since "a reasonable probability that, had the evidence been disclosed to the defense, the result of the proceeding would have been different," necessarily entails the conclusion that the suppression must have had "substantial and injurious effect or influence in determining the jury's verdict." * * *

The fourth and final aspect of *Bagley* materiality to be stressed here is its definition in terms of suppressed evidence considered collectively, not item-by-item. * * * [T]he Constitution is not violated every time the government fails or chooses not to disclose evidence that might prove helpful to the defense. We have never held that the Constitution demands an open file policy * * *.

Justice Souter stressed that suppression of exculpatory evidence implicates *Brady* rights even if the suppression is by police officers and the prosecutor is unaware of it. He explained this point as follows:

> * * * In the State's favor it may be said that no one doubts that police investigators sometimes fail to inform a prosecutor of all they know. But neither is there any serious doubt that procedures and regulations can be established to carry the prosecutor's burden and to insure communication of all relevant information on each case to every lawyer who deals with it. Since, then, the prosecutor has the means to discharge the government's *Brady* responsibility if he will, any argument for excusing a prosecutor from disclosing what he does not happen to know about boils down to a plea to substitute the police for the prosecutor, and even for the courts themselves, as the final arbiters of the government's obligation to ensure fair trials.

The State in *Kyles* argued that the *Brady-Bagley* standard of materiality should be made more rigorous (i.e., harder for the defendant to meet) because the current standard places a prosecutor in the uncomfortable position of having to predict the materiality of evidence before the trial. The State asked for "a certain amount of leeway in making a judgment call" as to the disclosure of any given piece of evidence. But the majority rejected the State's argument, and adhered to the *Brady-Bagley* standard of materiality, in the following analysis:

> [W]ith or without more leeway, the prosecution cannot be subject to any disclosure obligation without at some point having the responsibility to determine when it must act. Indeed, even if due process were thought to be violated by every failure to disclose an item of exculpatory or impeachment evidence (leaving harmless error as the government's only fallback), the prosecutor would still be forced to make judgment calls about what would count as favorable evidence, owing to the very fact that the character of a piece of evidence as favorable will often turn on the context of the existing or potential evidentiary record. Since the prosecutor would have to exercise some judgment even if the State were subject to this most stringent disclosure obligation, it is hard to find merit in the State's complaint over the responsibility for judgment under the existing system, which does not tax the prosecutor with error for any failure to disclose, absent a further showing of materiality. * * *

This means, naturally, that a prosecutor anxious about tacking too close to the wind will disclose a favorable piece of evidence. This is as it should be. Such disclosure will serve to justify trust in the prosecutor * * * [and] will tend to preserve the criminal trial, as distinct from the prosecutor's private deliberations, as the chosen forum for ascertaining the truth about criminal accusations. The prudence of the careful prosecutor should not therefore be discouraged.

Applying these principles to the case, Justice Souter concluded that the cumulative effect of the suppressed evidence satisfied the materiality standard of *Brady-Agurs–Bagley*. In the majority's view, the suppressed evidence would have caused the jury to doubt the statements of two eyewitnesses, due to their inconsistent prior statements, and would further have caused the jury to doubt the integrity of the lead investigator, who trusted Beanie completely and never considered him as a suspect, even though Beanie's statements were often inconsistent and implausible. The majority concluded:

> [T]he question is not whether the State would have had a case to go to the jury if it had disclosed the favorable evidence, but whether we can be confident that the jury's verdict would have been the same. Confidence that it would have been cannot survive a recap of the suppressed evidence and its significance for the prosecution. The jury would have been entitled to find

> (a) that the investigation was limited by the police's uncritical readiness to accept the story and suggestions of an informant [Beanie] whose accounts were inconsistent to the point, for example, of including four different versions of the discovery of the victim's purse, and whose own behavior was enough to raise suspicions of guilt;

> (b) that the lead police detective who testified was either less than wholly candid or less than fully informed;

> (c) that the informant's behavior raised suspicions that he had planted both the murder weapon and the victim's purse in the places they were found;

> (d) that one of the four eyewitnesses crucial to the State's case had given a description that did not match the defendant and better described the informant;

> (e) that another eyewitness had been coached, since he had first stated that he had not seen the killer outside the getaway car, or the killing itself, whereas at trial he claimed to have seen the shooting, described the murder weapon exactly, and omitted portions of his initial description that would have been troublesome for the case;

> (f) that there was no consistency to eyewitness descriptions of the killer's height, build, age, facial hair, or hair length.

Since all of these possible findings were precluded by the prosecution's failure to disclose the evidence that would have supported them, "fairness" cannot be stretched to the point of calling this a fair trial. Perhaps, confidence that the verdict would have been the same could survive the evidence impeaching even two eyewitnesses if the discoveries of gun and purse were above suspicion. * * * But confidence that the verdict would have been unaffected cannot survive when suppressed evidence would have entitled a jury to find that the eyewitnesses were not consistent in describing the killer, that two out of the four eyewitnesses testifying were unreliable, that the most damning physical evidence was subject to suspicion [of having been planted], that the investigation that produced it was insufficiently probing, and that the principal police witness was insufficiently informed or candid.[12]

Justice Scalia, joined by Chief Justice Rehnquist and Justices Kennedy and Thomas, dissented in *Kyles*. The dissenters did not disagree with the majority's restatement of the principles derived from *Brady*, *Agurs* and *Bagley*. Rather, they argued that reversal was unwarranted because the suppressed evidence, even considered cumulatively, was not materially exculpatory. Justice Scalia stated that even with the suppressed evidence, Kyles could not have overcome the implausibility of his own defense, which was that the witnesses misidentified him and that Beanie framed him. Justice Scalia explained as follows:

> [P]etitioner's theory was that he was the victim of a quadruple coincidence, in which four eyewitnesses to the crime mistakenly identified him as the murderer—three picking him out of a photo-array without hesitation, and all four affirming their identification in open court after comparing him with Beanie. The extraordinary mistake petitioner had to persuade the jury these four witnesses made was not simply to mistake the real killer, Beanie, for the very same innocent third party (hard enough to believe), but in addition to mistake him for the very man Beanie had chosen to frame—the last and most incredible level of coincidence. However small the chance that the jury would believe any one of those improbable scenarios, the likelihood that it would believe them all together is far smaller. The Court concludes that it is "reasonably probable" the undisclosed witness interviews would have persuaded the jury of petitioner's implausible theory of mistaken eyewitness testimony, and then argues that it is "reasonably probable" the undisclosed information regarding Beanie would have persuaded the jury of petitioner's implausible theory regarding the incriminating physical evidence [i.e., that Beanie had planted it in Kyles' house]. I think neither of those conclusions is remotely true, but even if they were the Court would still be guilty of a fallacy in declaring victory on each implausibility in turn, and thus victory on the whole, without considering the infinitesimal probability of the jury's swallowing the entire concoction of implausibility squared.

Suppressed Evidence That Would Have Been Inadmissible at Trial: Wood v. Bartholemew

If the evidence suppressed by the prosecution could not have been admitted at the defendant's trial, could it ever be considered materially exculpatory? The Supreme Court considered this question in Wood v. Bartholomew, 516 U.S. 1 (1995), a per curiam opinion, in which exculpatory polygraph results were suppressed. The Court set forth the facts as follows:

> On August 1, 1981, respondent Dwayne Bartholomew robbed a laundromat in Tacoma, Washington. In the course of the robbery, the laundromat

---

12. Justice Stevens wrote a short concurring opinion, defending the Court's role in engaging in fact-intensive review of capital cases, especially where the record points to the possibility that the defendant did not commit the crime.

attendant was shot and killed. Two shots were fired: one hit the attendant in the head, the second lodged in a counter near the victim's body. From the beginning, respondent admitted that he committed the robbery and that the shots came from his gun. The only issue at trial was whether respondent was guilty of aggravated first-degree murder, which requires proof of premeditation; or of first-degree (felony) murder, which does not. Respondent's defense was that the gun, a single action revolver (one that must be cocked manually before each shot), discharged by accident—twice.

In addition to the physical evidence concerning the operation of the gun, the prosecution's evidence consisted of the testimony of respondent's brother, Rodney Bartholomew, and of Rodney's girlfriend, Tracy Dormady. Both Rodney and Tracy testified that on the day of the crime they had gone to the laundromat in question to do their laundry, and that respondent was sitting in his car in the parking lot when they arrived. While waiting for their laundry, Rodney sat with his brother in the car. Rodney testified that respondent told him that he intended to rob the laundromat and "leave no witnesses." According to their testimony, Rodney and Tracy left the laundromat soon after the conversation and went to Tracy's house. Respondent arrived at the house a short time later, and when Tracy asked respondent if he had killed the attendant respondent said "he had put two bullets in the kid's head." Tracy also testified that she had heard respondent say that he intended to leave no witnesses. Both Rodney and Tracy's testimony was consistent with their pretrial statements to the police.

Respondent testified in his own defense. He admitted threatening the victim with his gun and forcing him to lie down on the floor. Respondent said, however, that while he was removing money from the cash drawer his gun accidently fired, discharging a bullet into the victim's head. Respondent further claimed that the gun went off a second time while he was running away. Respondent denied telling Rodney or Tracy that he intended to leave no witnesses. According to his testimony, moreover, Rodney had assisted in the robbery by convincing the attendant to open the laundromat's door after it had closed for the night, although Rodney left before the crime was committed. In closing argument the defense sought to discredit Rodney and Tracy's testimony by suggesting that they were lying about the extent of Rodney's participation in the crime.

* * *

Before trial, the prosecution requested that Rodney and Tracy submit to polygraph examinations. The answers of both witnesses to the questions asked by the polygraph examiner were consistent with their testimony at trial. As part of the polygraph examination, the examiner asked Tracy whether she had helped respondent commit the robbery and whether she had ever handled the murder weapon. Tracy answered in the negative to both questions. The results of the testing as to these questions were inconclusive, but the examiner noted his personal opinion that her responses were truthful. The examiner also asked Rodney whether he had assisted his brother in the robbery and whether at any time he and his brother were in the laundromat together. Rodney responded in the negative to both questions, and the examiner concluded that the responses to the questions indicated deception. Neither examination was disclosed to the defense.

The Ninth Circuit Court of Appeals found that suppression of the polygraph results constituted a *Brady* violation, even though it recognized that polygraph evidence is inadmissible in Washington state courts, even for impeachment purposes. That court reasoned that if defense counsel had known about the polygraph results, he would have attacked Rodney's story more aggressively; that he "likely would have taken Rodney's deposition"; that in that deposition defense counsel "might well have succeeded in obtaining an admission that Rodney was lying about his participation in the crime"; and that defense counsel "would likely have uncovered a variety of conflicting statements which could have been used quite effectively in cross-examination at trial."

The Supreme Court rejected this reasoning as speculative and inconsistent with the *Brady-Agurs–Bagley* materiality requirement. The Court elaborated as follows:

> The information at issue here * * * is not "evidence" at all. Disclosure of the polygraph results, then, could have had no direct effect on the outcome of trial, because respondent could have made no mention of them either during argument or while questioning witnesses. To get around this problem, the Ninth Circuit reasoned that the information, had it been disclosed to the defense, might have led respondent's counsel to conduct additional discovery that might have led to some additional evidence that could have been utilized. Other than expressing a belief that in a deposition Rodney might have confessed to his involvement in the initial stages of the crime—a confession that itself would have been in no way inconsistent with respondent's guilt—the Court of Appeals did not specify what particular evidence it had in mind. Its judgment is based on mere speculation, in violation of the standards we have established.

The Court noted that Bartholemew's counsel, at the habeas hearing, testified that he made the strategic decision not to cross-examine Rodney aggressively at trial, for fear that Rodney would reiterate his brother's statement that he would "leave no witnesses." Thus, the Ninth Circuit's judgment on what could have been done with the polygraph responses was inconsistent with the approach actually taken by Bartholemew's own trial counsel. Finally, the Court noted that the polygraph responses could not have been material in light of the overwhelming evidence of Bartholemew's guilt:

> To acquit of aggravated murder, the jury would have had to believe that respondent's single action revolver discharged accidently, not once but twice, by tragic coincidence depositing a bullet to the back of the victim's head, execution-style, as the victim lay face down on the floor. In the face of this physical evidence, as well as Rodney and Tracy's testimony—to say nothing of the testimony by Bell that the State likely could introduce on retrial—it should take more than supposition on the weak premises offered by respondent to undermine a court's confidence in the outcome.[13]

Does *Bartholomew* mean that inadmissible evidence can *never* be *Brady* material?

---

13. Four Justices in *Bartholomew* dissented from the summary disposition of the case.

The Power of Impeachment Evidence

The Court in *Bagley* specifically held that evidence that would impeach government witnesses can be "material" within the meaning of *Brady*. Of course, a case-by-case approach must be employed to determine whether suppressed impeachment evidence is material. Factors bearing on the materiality inquiry include the importance of the witness, whether the witness has been impeached with other evidence, and the nature and quality of the suppressed impeachment evidence. Ordinarily, impeachment evidence is not as likely to be "material" as is substantive evidence such as, say, a forensic test indicating that the defendant could not have committed the crime. But it is not unheard of for an appellate court to reverse a conviction on *Brady* grounds when the government has suppressed impeachment evidence of an important government witness. See United States v. Smith, 77 F.3d 511 (D.C.Cir.1996) (prosecutor's failure to disclose the fact that two charges against a prosecution witness had been dismissed in exchange for cooperation constituted a *Brady* violation warranting reversal).

United States v. Boyd, 55 F.3d 239 (7th Cir.1995), is an example of suppression of important impeachment evidence that constitutes a *Brady* violation. Judge Posner set forth the rather astounding facts as follows:

> The defendants, six leaders and one close associate of the "El Rukns," a notorious Chicago street gang formerly known as the "Blackstone Rangers" and the "Black P Stone Nation," were convicted by a jury after a four-month trial of a variety of very serious federal crimes. * * * The evidence showed that during the 1980s the El Rukns had trafficked in heroin and cocaine on a large scale in the southern and western areas of the city and to protect their lucrative turf had committed many murders, attempted murders, kidnapings, and acts of intimidation. * * *

> The government's case depended heavily on the testimony of six former gang leaders, including Harry Evans and Henry Harris. The ground for the motion for a new trial was that the government had knowingly allowed Evans and Harris to perjure themselves at the trial and had withheld from the defense evidence that during the trial all six, who were being held at the Metropolitan Correctional Center (near the federal courthouse where the trial was held), had used illegal drugs and received unlawful favors from government prosecutors and their staffs. The district judge granted the motion for a new trial * * * after he had taken testimony at a post-trial evidentiary hearing from 29 witnesses. The testimony convinced him that prosecutors and staff in the office of the U.S. Attorney for the Northern District of Illinois had engaged in misconduct far more serious than anything involved in typical cases in which a prosecutor is accused of the knowing use of perjured testimony or of the violation of a defendant's right under Brady v. Maryland, to be shown exculpatory evidence that is in the prosecution's possession.

> * * *

> Witness Evans, jailed in 1988 on numerous charges, had been held in the Metropolitan Correctional Center (MCC) ever since. He thus was there throughout the trial of the defendants, which was held in 1991, except of course when he was testifying or meeting with prosecutors or prosecution staff in the courthouse or in the federal building across the street. Through-

out the entire period Evans used illegal drugs and the prosecutors knew it. The question of his drug use came up at trial. He was asked by the prosecutor, "You used and abused drugs from the seventies until the time you went to jail in 1988, isn't that correct?" "Yes, sir," replied Evans. The prosecutor then asked, "How many years would you say you have been using and abusing drugs?" Answer: "You just said it." "From '74 to '88, or earlier?" "That's a good figure." Judge Aspen interpreted Evans's last answer to mean that he had stopped using drugs in 1988. This is not an inevitable interpretation, but we cannot call it unreasonable; and so interpreted Evans's answer was a lie, and the government knew it.

Judge Posner noted that while the Supreme Court has granted relief when the prosecutor used "perjured testimony", the question is not whether a witness has perjured himself in a legal sense:

> Whether the question was precise enough that Evans could actually be convicted of perjury may be doubted; but the wrong of knowing use by prosecutors of perjured testimony does not require a determination that the witness could have been successfully prosecuted. Successful prosecution would require proof beyond a reasonable doubt not only that the witness's testimony had been false but also that it had been knowingly false (and hence perjury). The wrong of knowing use by prosecutors of perjured testimony is different, and misnamed—it is knowing use of false testimony. It is enough that the jury was likely to understand the witness to have said something that was, as the prosecution knew, false. * * * Shortly after the exchange that we just quoted, Evans said, "But I'm not on drugs now." We do not know whether he was high when he said this, so probably, again, he could not be successfully prosecuted for perjury. But given the context, Judge Aspen was entitled to infer that Evans would have been understood by the jury to have meant that he was no longer using drugs, which was false.

Besides the knowing use of false testimony, the court in *Boyd* noted several egregious instances of suppression of exculpatory evidence relating to impeachment.

> The prisoner witnesses, not only Harris and Evans but the four other ex-El Rukns, received a continuous stream of unlawful, indeed scandalous, favors from staff at the U.S. Attorney's office while jailed at the MCC awaiting the trial of the defendants. Disclosure of these benefits, of course known to the prosecution (the source of the benefits), would have helped the defendants by undermining the credibility of key witnesses against them. * * *

> * * * Bizarrely, the prosecutors permitted the prisoner witnesses—hardened and dangerous criminals all—to entertain their visitors in the U.S. Attorney's office in the federal courthouse and in the office of the Bureau of Alcohol, Tobacco, and Firearms in the federal building across the street from the courthouse. Security for these visits was so lax that the visitors, almost always women, were able not only to pass drugs to the witnesses but also to have sexual intercourse with them. Evans's most frequent visitor was a woman politely described as his "common law wife" (there is no common law marriage in Illinois). Evans had been caught having sex with her in the MCC and had been disciplined for this violation of the MCC's rules, as the prosecutors well knew. The prosecutors nevertheless allowed her to visit

him in the government offices in circumstances in which a repetition of his offense was certain. Evans's "common law wife" also appears to have been the principal source for the drugs that he obtained and used—and sold— throughout the period of the trial. The government, while not aware of the details of these visits, was well aware of the opportunity that the visits afforded for shenanigans involving sex and drugs. It also knew that the witnesses used their opportunity to roam about in government offices unsupervised to steal numerous documents (some highly confidential), later found back in the MCC whither they had carried them.

The prosecutors also gave the witnesses unlimited and unsupervised telephone privileges available to no other federal prisoners. Members of the prosecution team would routinely accept collect calls from the witnesses at the MCC and then at the witness's request would forward the calls to outside numbers. The telephoning was incessant, reaching a point at which two of the prosecutors complained to the head of the prosecution team about the cost to the government. Some witnesses, on their visits to the office of the Bureau of Alcohol, Tobacco, and Firearms, were permitted to answer the phones in the office, and they would often answer "ATF." Some of the calls they answered were from other inmates, and they would forward these calls to outside numbers at the request of the caller. The witnesses also used their phone privileges to order drugs. * * *

A government paralegal named Luchetta, a member of the prosecution team, developed personal relationships with the prisoner witnesses. These relationships involved phone sex and assistance in smuggling contraband into the MCC. Luchetta gave witness Harris a number of presents [and] she threw two birthday parties for him. Harris and other witnesses received presents from other members of the prosecution team as well. The head of the team, Hogan, developed a personal relationship with Harris. Hogan accepted gifts from Harris, who in turn made Hogan a legatee in his will. Harris took a fancy to a female paralegal (not Luchetta), and apparently told Hogan about this, for Hogan approached the paralegal's supervisor and asked her whether the paralegal would accept phone calls from Harris. (The supervisor replied, "Absolutely not.") The government did not disclose any of these goings on to the defendants.

Judge Posner assessed the "difficult question" of whether the false testimony and the suppression of the favors received by the witnesses collectively constituted "material" evidence that warranted reversal of the convictions.

As the perjured testimony and the concealed evidence went only to the credibility of the prisoner witnesses, the question of prejudicial impact can be * * * decomposed into two questions: Is there some reasonable probability that the jury would have acquitted the defendants on at least some of the counts against them had the jury disbelieved the essential testimony of these witnesses? And might the jury have disbelieved that testimony if the witnesses hadn't perjured themselves about their continued use of drugs and (or) if the government had revealed to the defense the witnesses' continued use of drugs and the favors that the prosecution had extended to them?

The answer to the first question is clearly "yes." Although the testimony of the six prisoner witnesses for the prosecution was corroborated, had their testimony been disbelieved the defendants would have had to be acquitted on most counts. It is true that the government introduced a number of taped conversations that were highly incriminating of the defendants, but these tapes were translated by witness Harris and their meaning was thus conveyed to the jury through his testimony. If the jury hadn't believed him, it would not have been impressed by the tapes. And without the tapes, the testimony of the prisoner witnesses was essential on most of the counts of which the defendants were convicted.

* * * The government argues that the witnesses had already been so thoroughly impeached that additional impeachment could have made no difference. The witnesses were cross-examined extensively about their criminal activities while they were members of the El Rukns. These activities covered the full gamut of the El Rukns' crimes and thus included drug trafficking and murder, not to mention the intimidation of witnesses. The jury could not have doubted that the witnesses would lie if they thought it in their interest and that their only hope of avoiding life imprisonment or, in the case of one witness, capital punishment lay with the prosecution. The argument is that if the jury believed that such scoundrels notwithstanding such pressures were telling the truth, additional impeachment could not have shaken that belief. * * *

Judge Posner found that the impeachment evidence suppressed was of a different character than that presented at trial, and therefore met the *Brady* standard of materiality:

If the evidence that was not revealed had consisted of one more crime, or for that matter ten more crimes, committed by each of the witnesses when he was an El Rukn, we have no doubt that Judge Aspen would have denied the motion for a new trial; for extending the list of past crimes would not have made a difference to the jury's evaluation of the witnesses' credibility. The reason the concealed evidence might well have made a difference was that the witnesses had claimed to have "seen the light" when, having been arrested and sentenced or threatened with severe punishment for their activities as El Rukns, they had decided to cooperate with the government. That had been in 1985. Six years later they were still dealing drugs, stealing, smuggling, violating jail rules, and lying on the stand. Had these things been known to the jury it might have doubted their testimony that they had "seen the light." * * * And this is not all. Had the jury known that the prisoner witnesses were receiving favors, including sexual favors, the equivalent of a free telephone credit card, and illegal drugs, all with the permission or connivance of the U.S. Attorney's office, the jury might have wondered whether the witnesses were not receiving implicit assurances of compensation for their testimony going far beyond anything promised in their plea agreements, the terms of which had been revealed to the jury. If a prisoner is treated by officers of the United States Government as if he had the sexual and other privileges of a free man, treated indeed as a friend (even as a potential lover), may it not occur to him that if he plays ball with his powerful friend the friend will not just get his death sentence reduced to natural life or his natural-life sentence reduced to thirty years but will somehow arrange to restore his freedom to him in the near future? Do you throw a birthday party for a man who you think deserves to spend his life behind bars? Might not a reasonable jury have concluded, had they known all the facts, that the prosecution team must have had desperate doubts about the testimonial reliability of these witnesses to have lavished such extraordinary personal attentions upon them? In short, might not the prosecution's case have collapsed entirely had the truth come out about the behavior and the treatment of these witnesses?

We do not know, of course. An alternative hypothesis is that the witnesses were simply very good bargainers, who obtained more consideration from the prosecution in exchange for their testimony than most witnesses do. The issue is judgmental. The responsibility for the exercise of the requisite judgment is the district judge's and we are to intervene only if strongly convinced that he judged wrong. We are not strongly convinced. The grant of the new trial must therefore stand.

Has the Court in *Boyd* simply punished the prosecution for outrageous misconduct?

Impeachment Evidence That Does Not Raise a Reasonable Probability of a Different Result: *Strickler v. Greene*

In Strickler v. Greene, 527 U.S. 263 (1999), the Court considered the effect of suppressed impeachment evidence in a prosecution for capital murder. Strickler and Henderson murdered Whitlock after abducting her at a shopping center and commandeering her car; Whitlock was killed by a blow to the head from a 69–pound rock. There was abundant evidence connecting Strickler to the murder—among other things, he was seen driving the victim's car near the scene of the murder, he gave away some of the victim's valuables as presents, and both he and Henderson made inculpatory statements to friends. However, the only witness who testified to the abduction itself was a bystander named Stoltzfus. She gave detailed testimony indicating that Strickler took the lead in breaking into Whitlock's car and forcing her into the passenger seat, while Henderson and Strickler's girlfriend "hung back." Throughout her testimony, she referred to Strickler as "Mountain Man" and Henderson as "Shy Guy." She had no doubt about her testimony and offered that she had an excellent memory. In fact, however, Stoltzfus had been unable to identify Strickler during several meetings with a police officer, and generally indicated that she hadn't thought that the event she witnessed was very serious, in that it seemed like a college prank. This information about Stoltzfus' prior uncertainty was never disclosed to Strickler's defense counsel. Strickler was convicted and sentenced to death. In a separate trial, Henderson was also convicted, but did not receive a death sentence.

The District Court granted a writ of habeas corpus on Strickler's *Brady* claim. The Fourth Circuit reversed, finding no merit in the *Brady* claim on the ground that Stoltzfus' testimony related only to the abduction, and was therefore essentially irrelevant to the capital murder charges. The Supreme Court, in an opinion by Justice Stevens, agreed with the Fourth Circuit, though it found the *Brady* "prejudice" question much more difficult than the Court of Appeals had.

Justice Stevens analyzed the *Brady* "prejudice" claim in the following passage:

The Court of Appeals' [ruling that the suppressed impeachment evidence was not "material"] rested on its conclusion that, without considering Stoltzfus' testimony, the record contained ample, independent evidence of guilt, as well as evidence sufficient to support the findings of vileness and future dangerousness that warranted the imposition of the death penalty. The standard used by that court was incorrect. As we made clear in *Kyles*, the materiality inquiry is not just a matter of determining whether, after discounting the inculpatory evidence in light of the undisclosed evidence, the remaining evidence is sufficient to support the jury's conclusions. Rather, the question is whether "the favorable evidence could reasonably be taken to put the whole case in such a different light as to undermine confidence in the verdict."

* * *

The District Court was surely correct that there is a reasonable *possibility* that either a total, nor just a substantial, discount of Stoltzfus' testimony might have produced a different result, either at the guilt or sentencing phases. Petitioner did, for example, introduce substantial mitigating evidence about abuse he had suffered as a child at the hands of his stepfather. As the District Court recognized, however, petitioner's burden is to establish a reasonable *probability* of a different result.

Even if Stoltzfus and her testimony had been entirely discredited, the jury might still have concluded that petitioner was the leader of the criminal enterprise because he was the one seen driving the car * * * near the location of the murder and the one who kept the car for the following week. In addition, [Strickler's girlfriend] testified that petitioner threatened Henderson with a knife later in the evening.

* * *

We recognize the importance of eyewitness testimony; Stoltzfus provided the only disinterested, narrative account of what transpired on January 5, 1990. However, Stoltzfus' vivid description of the events at the mall was not the only evidence that the jury had before it. Two other eyewitnesses, the security guard and Henderson's friend, placed petitioner and Henderson at the Harrisonburg Valley Shopping Mall on the afternoon of Whitlock's murder. One eyewitness later saw petitioner driving Dean's car near the scene of the murder.

The record provides strong support for the conclusion that petitioner would have been convicted of capital murder and sentenced to death, even if Stoltzfus had been severely impeached. The jury was instructed on two predicates for capital murder: robbery with a deadly weapon and abduction with intent to defile. * * * [A]rmed robbery still would have supported the capital murder conviction. * * *

Petitioner also maintains that he suffered prejudice from the failure to disclose the Stoltzfus documents because her testimony impacted on the jury's decision to impose the death penalty. * * * With respect to the jury's discretionary decision to impose the death penalty, it is true that Stoltzfus described petitioner as a violent, aggressive person, but that portrayal surely was not as damaging as either the evidence that he spent the evening of the murder dancing and drinking * * * or the powerful message conveyed by the 69–pound rock that was part of the record before the jury. Notwithstanding the obvious significance of Stoltzfus' testimony, petitioner has not convinced us that there is a reasonable probability that the jury would have returned a different verdict if her testimony had been either severely impeached or excluded entirely.

Justice Souter, joined by Justice Kennedy, dissented in part. He agreed with the Court that the suppressed impeachment information was not "material", in a *Brady* sense, to the defendant's guilt or innocence. But he argued that the impeachment material did create a reasonable probability that the jury would have recommended a life sentence rather than the death penalty. He explained as follows:

> I could not regard Stoltzfus's colorful testimony as anything but significant on the matter of sentence. It was Stoltzfus alone who described Strickler as the initiator of the abduction, as the one who broke into Whitlock's car, who beckoned his companions to follow him, and who violently subdued the victim while 'Shy Guy' sat in the back seat. The bare content of this testimony, important enough, was enhanced by one of the inherent hallmarks of reliability, as Stoltzfus confidently recalled detail after detail. The withheld documents would have shown, however, that many of the details Stoltzfus confidently mentioned on the stand * * * had apparently escaped her memory in her initial interviews with the police. Her persuasive account did not come, indeed, until after her recollection had been aided by further conversations with the police and with the victim's boyfriend. I therefore have to assess the likely havoc that an informed cross-examiner could have wreaked upon Stoltzfus as adequate to raise a significant possibility of a different recommendation [of sentence], as sufficient to undermine confidence that the death recommendation would have been the choice. All it would have taken, after all, was one juror to hold out against death to preclude the recommendation actually given.

* * *

Brady and Guilty Pleas

If the prosecutor has materially exculpatory evidence, must it be disclosed before the defendant enters into a guilty plea? Or is the *Brady* right simply a trial right? The question arises in the following procedural context: the defendant pleads guilty, later learns of exculpatory evidence that was suppressed, and moves to vacate his guilty plea as insufficiently knowing and voluntary.[14]

In United States v. Ruiz, 536 U.S. 622 (2002), the Court held that during guilty plea negotiations the government is not required to disclose information that could impeach government witnesses, nor information that could be used by the defendant on an affirmative defense. Ruiz was offered a deal whereby she would waive the right to disclosure of any information that could be used to impeach government witnesses or for any affirmative defenses she might have; however, the agreement acknowledged the government's continuing obligation

14. See Chapter Nine for a more complete discussion of the voluntariness standards attendant to guilty pleas.

to disclose "information establishing the factual innocence of the defendant." The lower court had held that a defendant pleading guilty has a constitutional right to disclosure of materially exculpatory impeachment information as well as information the defendant could use to prove affirmative defenses, and that a plea agreement requiring waiver of these rights could not be voluntary. But the Court, in an opinion by Justice Breyer, unanimously rejected the lower court's reasoning.

Justice Breyer noted that "impeachment information is special in relation to the *fairness of a trial,* not in respect to whether a plea is *voluntary.*" He stated that the Constitution "permits a court to accept a guilty plea, with its accompanying waiver of various constitutional rights, despite various forms of misapprehension under which a defendant might labor." [See Chapter Nine for the cases discussing knowing and voluntary waiver of guilty pleas.] Justice Breyer expressed concern that requiring disclosure of impeachment information during guilty plea negotiations "could seriously interfere with the Government's interest in securing those guilty pleas that are factually justified, desired by defendants, and help to secure the efficient administration of justice." Specifically, early disclosure of impeachment evidence "could disrupt ongoing investigations and expose prospective witnesses to serious harm."

As to required disclosure of impeachment evidence, Justice Breyer concluded that it

> could force the Government to abandon its general practice of not disclosing to a defendant pleading guilty information that would reveal the identities of cooperating informants, undercover investigators, or other prospective witnesses. It could require the Government to devote substantially more resources to trial preparation prior to plea bargaining, thereby depriving the plea-bargaining process of its main resource-saving advantages. Or it could lead the Government instead to abandon its heavy reliance upon plea bargaining in a vast number—90% or more—of federal criminal cases. We cannot say that the Constitution's due process requirement demands so radical a change in the criminal justice process in order to achieve so comparatively small a constitutional benefit.

As to required disclosure of information bearing on an affirmative defense, the Court concluded as follows:

> We do not believe the Constitution here requires provision of this information to the defendant prior to plea bargaining—for most (though not all) of the reasons previously stated. That is to say, in the context of this agreement, the need for this information is more closely related to the *fairness* of a trial than to the *voluntariness* of the plea; the value in terms of the defendant's added awareness of relevant circumstances is ordinarily limited; yet the added burden imposed upon the Government by requiring its provision well in advance of trial (often before trial preparation begins) can be serious, thereby significantly interfering with the administration of the plea bargaining process.

It should be noted that *Ruiz* could be read narrowly as dealing only with the enforceability of a provision under which the defendant waives his right to disclosure of information bearing on impeachment of government witnesses and affirmative defenses. In other words, the case could be looked at as holding that there *is* a right to this information under *Brady,* but that the right can be waived by the defendant. Thus, a guilty plea might still be invalid, *in the absence of a waiver clause*, if the government has failed to disclose materially exculpatory information concerning impeachment or affirmative defenses. Obviously, the government now has an incentive to include such waiver provisions as boiler-plate in its plea agreements.

Another point of limitation on the *Ruiz* holding is that the Court recognized the government's duty to disclose information bearing on the defendant's "factual innocence" during guilty plea negotiations, as well as a continuing duty to disclose such information throughout the plea proceedings. Indeed, the government recognized this obligation by including it in the plea agreement in *Ruiz*. See also Sanchez v. United States, 50 F.3d 1448 (9th Cir.1995)(guilty plea vacated because evidence material to innocence was suppressed, noting that otherwise "prosecutors may be tempted to deliberately withhold exculpatory information as part of an attempt to elicit guilty pleas").

Test for need to disclose or prejudiced pled is

What is the test of materiality in a guilty plea context? The court in *Sanchez, supra* declared that suppressed evidence is material if "there is a reasonable probability that but for the failure to disclose the *Brady* material, the defendant would have refused to plead and would have gone to trial." How is a court to determine this question? Does it rely on the defendant's assertions? On the power of the suppressed evidence? On a comparison between the deal that the defendant received and the sentence that he would have faced if convicted? See Miller v. Angliker, 848 F.2d 1312 (2d Cir.1988)(test of materiality, in the guilty plea context, is an objective one that centers on "the likely persuasiveness of the withheld information"). For a discussion of the relationship between *Brady* material and guilty pleas, see Corrina Lain, Accuracy Where It Matters: Brady v. Maryland in the Plea Bargaining Context, 80 Wash.U. L.Q. 1 (2002)(noting that "*Brady's* importance in the plea bargaining context is clear in part just because so many cases are resolved there"); John Douglass, Fatal Attraction? The Uneasy Courtship of *Brady* and Plea Bargaining, 50 Emory L.J.437 (2001)("If we are serious about better-informed guilty pleas, then we should address the problem when it matters most: before the plea.").

but for failure to disclose Δ would have refused to plead and gone to trial

C.   IS THERE A DUTY TO PRESERVE EXCULPATORY EVIDENCE?

Brady prohibits the government from *suppressing* materially exculpatory evidence. But is there a constitutional right to have such evidence *preserved*? And how do you know if it was materially exculpatory unless it is preserved in the first place?

No duty to preserve breath samples for use by Δ at trial

Justice Marshall wrote for a unanimous Supreme Court in California v. Trombetta, 467 U.S. 479 (1984), declaring that law enforcement officers are not required by the Due Process Clause to preserve breath samples of suspected drunk drivers for potential use by defendants at trial. A device called an Intoxilyzer was used to test these samples. Suspects, including those challenging the police procedures in the instant case, breathed into the device and infrared light sensed their blood alcohol level. California officers purge the device after each test, thus destroying the breath samples. Although the state health department had approved a kit which officers could use to preserve breath samples, it was not standard practice for officers to use the kit.

In his opinion in *Trombetta*, Justice Marshall declared that "[w]hatever duty the Constitution imposes on the States to preserve evidence, that duty must be limited to evidence that might be expected to play a significant role in the suspect's defense." The Court found that the chances were extremely low that preserved samples would have assisted defendants; that the state had developed procedures to protect against machine malfunctions; and that some alternative attacks were possible when a defendant raised one of the limited number of claims available to challenge the functioning of a testing machine.

Chief Justice Rehnquist wrote for the Court in Arizona v. Youngblood, 488 U.S. 51 (1988), as it expanded upon *Trombetta* and held that "unless a criminal defendant can show bad faith on the part of the police, failure to preserve potentially useful evidence does not constitute a denial of due process of law." Youngblood was convicted of sexually assaulting a young boy. Although investigative authorities attempted to analyze semen obtained from the victim's clothing, they did not refrigerate the clothing and because of this they were unable to conduct an analysis. The Supreme Court found that the failure to preserve the evidence for testing was, at worst, negligent. The Chief Justice noted that there was no evidence that the police had any reason to believe that the semen samples might have exonerated the accused when they handled the clothing at the outset of the investigation. Nor was there any indication of bad faith on the part of the police. Indeed, the evidence, had it not been destroyed, could have helped the police to find the perpetrator, who at that point was unknown.

Chief Justice Rehnquist recognized that the *Brady* cases made the good or bad faith of the police irrelevant when material exculpatory evidence is *suppressed*, but he concluded that "the Due Process Clause requires a different result when we deal with the failure of the State to preserve evidentiary material of which no more can be said than that it could have been subjected to tests, the results of which might have exonerated the defendant." With suppression, the evidence still exists, and so the court and the parties can determine whether it is materially exculpatory; but such is not the case with evidence that has been destroyed. The Chief Justice reasoned "that requiring a defendant to show bad faith on the part of the police both limits the extent of the police's obligation to preserve evidence to reasonable bounds and confines it to that class of cases where the interests of justice most clearly require it, i.e., those cases in which the police themselves by their conduct indicate that the evidence could form a basis for exonerating the defendant."

The Chief Justice commented on language in the state appellate court's opinion, which indicated that newer tests could not be performed on the clothing as follows: "If the court meant * * * that the Due Process Clause is violated when the police fail to use a particular investigatory tool, we strongly disagree. The situation here is no different than a prosecution for drunk driving that rests on police observation alone; the defendant is free to argue to the finder of fact that a breathalyzer test might have been exculpatory, but the police do not have a constitutional duty to perform any particular tests."

Justice Blackmun, joined by Justices Brennan and Marshall, dissented. He suggested that the bad faith test was less than clear and might create more questions than it answers. Justice Blackmun stated his due process test as follows: "[W]here no comparable evidence is likely to be available to the defendant, police must preserve physical evidence of a type that they reasonably should know has the potential, if tested, to reveal immutable characteristics of the criminal, and hence to exculpate a defendant charged with the crime."

Is There a Duty to Look for Exculpatory Evidence?

The Court in *Youngblood* clearly implies that while the prosecution has a duty to *disclose* exculpatory evidence, it has no duty to seek out or to investigate information that would lead to exculpatory evidence. That is, the government has no obligation to act as an investigator for the defense. If the government fails to follow leads, or to seek an alternative explanation for the crime, then this can be brought out to the jury at trial. Should the government have a duty to investigate on the defendant's behalf? See Fisher, "Just the Facts, Ma'am": Lying and the Omission of Exculpatory Evidence in Police Reports, 28 New Eng.L.Rev.1 (1993), for a discussion of this and other problems of police investigations that fail to develop exculpatory evidence.

V. DISCOVERY BY THE PROSECUTION

A. DISCLOSURE OF DEFENSE INFORMATION BEFORE TRIAL

1. *Constitutional Implications*

Any attempt to force defendants to comply with government discovery requests runs into Fifth Amendment and due process concerns. The next case disposes of some of these.

WILLIAMS v. FLORIDA

Supreme Court of the United States, 1970.
399 U.S. 78.

Mr. Justice White delivered the opinion of the Court.

Prior to his trial for robbery in the State of Florida, petitioner filed a "Motion for a Protective Order," seeking to be excused from the requirements of Rule 1.200 of the Florida Rules of Criminal Procedure. That rule required a defendant, on written demand of the prosecuting attorney, to give notice in advance of trial if the defendant intends to claim an alibi, and to furnish the prosecuting attorney with information as to the place where he claims to have been and with the names and addresses of the alibi witnesses he intends to use. In his motion petitioner openly declared his intent to claim an alibi, but objected to the further disclosure requirements on the ground that the rule "compels the Defendant in a criminal case to be a witness against himself" in violation of his Fifth and Fourteenth Amendment rights. The motion was denied. * * * [The other aspect of the case involved a challenge to the six man jury provided by Florida. It also was unsuccessful. The jury issue is discussed in Chapter Ten]. Petitioner was convicted as charged and was sentenced to life imprisonment. * * *

I

Florida's notice-of-alibi rule is in essence a requirement that a defendant submit to a limited form of pretrial discovery by the State whenever he intends to rely at trial on the defense of alibi. In exchange for the defendant's disclosure of the witnesses he proposes to use to establish that defense, the State in turn is required to notify the defendant of any witnesses it proposes to offer in rebuttal to that defense. Both sides are under a continuing duty promptly to disclose the names and addresses of additional witnesses bearing on the alibi as they become available. The threatened sanction for failure to comply is the exclusion at trial of the defendant's alibi evidence—except for his own testimony—or, in the case of the State, the exclusion of the State's evidence offered in rebuttal of the alibi.

In this case, following the denial of his Motion for a Protective Order, petitioner complied with the alibi rule and gave the State the name and address of one Mary Scotty. Mrs. Scotty was summoned to the office of the State Attorney on the morning of the trial, where she gave pretrial testimony. At the trial itself, Mrs. Scotty, petitioner, and petitioner's wife all testified that the three of them had been in Mrs. Scotty's apartment during the time of the robbery. On two occasions during cross-examination of Mrs. Scotty, the prosecuting attorney confronted her with her earlier deposition in which she had given dates and times that in some respects did not correspond with the dates and times given at trial. Mrs. Scotty adhered to her trial story, insisting that she had been mistaken in her earlier testimony. The State also offered in rebuttal the testimony of one of the officers investigating the robbery who claimed that Mrs. Scotty had asked him for directions on the afternoon in question during the time when she claimed to have been in her apartment with petitioner and his wife.

We need not linger over the suggestion that the discovery permitted the State against petitioner in this case deprived him of "due process" or a "fair trial." Florida law provides for liberal discovery by the defendant against the State, and the notice-of-

alibi rule is itself carefully hedged with reciprocal duties requiring state disclosure to the defendant. Given the ease with which an alibi can be fabricated, the State's interest in protecting itself against an eleventh-hour defense is both obvious and legitimate. Reflecting this interest, notice-of-alibi provisions, dating at least from 1927, are now in existence in a substantial number of States.[a] The adversary system of trial is hardly an end in itself; it is not yet a poker game in which players enjoy an absolute right always to conceal their cards until played. We find ample room in that system, at least as far as "due process" is concerned, for the instant Florida rule, which is designed to enhance the search for truth in the criminal trial by insuring both the defendant and the State ample opportunity to investigate certain facts crucial to the determination of guilt or innocence.

Petitioner's major contention is that he was "compelled * * * to be a witness against himself" contrary to the commands of the Fifth and Fourteenth Amendments because the notice-of-alibi rule required him to give the State the name and address of Mrs. Scotty in advance of trial and thus to furnish the State with information useful in convicting him. No pretrial statement of petitioner was introduced at trial; but armed with Mrs. Scotty's name and address and the knowledge that she was to be petitioner's alibi witness, the State was able to take her deposition in advance of trial and to find rebuttal testimony. Also, requiring him to reveal the elements of his defense is claimed to have interfered with his right to wait until after the State had

---

a. In addition to Florida, at least 15 States appear to have alibi-notice requirements of one sort or another. * * * [See also Fed.R.Crim.P. 12.1.]

We do not, of course, decide that each of these alibi-notice provisions is necessarily valid

in all respects; that conclusion must await a specific context and an inquiry, for example, into whether the defendant enjoys reciprocal discovery against the State.

presented its case to decide how to defend against it. We conclude, however, as has apparently every other court that has considered the issue, that the privilege against self-incrimination is not violated by a requirement that the defendant give notice of an alibi defense and disclose his alibi witnesses.

The defendant in a criminal trial is frequently forced to testify himself and to call other witnesses in an effort to reduce the risk of conviction. When he presents his witnesses, he must reveal their identity and submit them to cross-examination which in itself may prove incriminating or which may furnish the State with leads to incriminating rebuttal evidence. That the defendant faces such a dilemma demanding a choice between complete silence and presenting a defense has never been thought an invasion of the privilege against compelled self-incrimination. The pressures generated by the State's evidence may be severe but they do not vitiate the defendant's choice to present an alibi defense and witnesses to prove it, even though the attempted defense ends in catastrophe for the defendant. However, "testimonial" or "incriminating" the alibi defense proves to be, it cannot be considered "compelled" within the meaning of the Fifth and Fourteenth Amendments.

Very similar constraints operate on the defendant when the State requires pretrial notice of alibi and the naming of alibi witnesses. Nothing in such a rule requires the defendant to rely on an alibi or prevents him from abandoning the defense; these matters are left to his unfettered choice. That choice must be made, but the pressures that bear on his pretrial decision are of the same nature as those that would induce him to call alibi witnesses at the trial: the force of histori-

cal fact beyond both his and the State's control and the strength of the State's case built on these facts. Response to that kind of pressure by offering evidence or testimony is not compelled self-incrimination transgressing the Fifth and Fourteenth Amendments.

* * *

* * * We decline to hold that the privilege against compulsory self-incrimination guarantees the defendant the right to surprise the State with an alibi defense.

* * *

[Justice Blackmun did not participate in the case. The Chief Justice filed a short concurring opinion on the alibi point. Justice Marshall dissented on the jury issue, but concurred in the alibi ruling.]

MR. JUSTICE BLACK, with whom MR. JUSTICE DOUGLAS joins, concurring in part and dissenting in part.

* * *

On the surface this case involves only a notice-of-alibi provision, but in effect the decision opens the way for a profound change in one of the most important traditional safeguards of a criminal defendant. The rationale of today's decision is in no way limited to alibi defenses, or any other type or classification of evidence. The theory advanced goes at least so far as to permit the State to obtain under threat of sanction complete disclosure by the defendant in advance of trial of all evidence, testimony, and tactics he plans to use at that trial. In each case the justification will be that the rule affects only the "timing" of the disclosure, and not the substantive decision itself. * * *

* * *

Reciprocality Requirement

In Wardius v. Oregon, 412 U.S. 470 (1973), the Court struck down a notice of alibi provision that was not reciprocal—i.e., that did not require the prosecution to disclose in advance its rebuttal evidence. The Court suggested "that if there is to be any unbalance in discovery rights, it should work in the defendant's favor."

Other Notice Requirements

Besides a notice of alibi defense, the Federal Rules of Criminal Procedure also require the defendant to give advance notice of an insanity defense (Rule 12.2) and a notice of intent to assert "a defense of actual or believed exercise of public authority on behalf of a law enforcement agency or federal intelligence agency at the time of the offense" (Rule 12.3). Failure to follow the notice requirements, without good cause, results in preclusion of witnesses who would testify to these defenses.

2. *General Discovery*

The general federal discovery rule covering the defense is Rule 16(b), which provides for discovery of: (A) documents and tangible objects within the control of the defendant and which the defendant intends to use at trial; (B) reports of examinations and tests within the control of the defendant and which the defendant either intends to use at trial or which were prepared by a witness whom the defendant intends to call at trial; and (C) a written summary of the testimony of an expert the defendant intends to call at trial, describing the opinions, bases, and qualifications of the expert. Protections are provided for privileged materials and work product. See Rule 16(b)(2).

The Federal Rule conditions government discovery on a prior request by a defendant for discovery of similar information from the government and government compliance with that request. The ABA standards, in contrast, would give the government a right to discovery even without a defense request. The ABA approach recognizes that each side in a criminal case has a right to prepare for trial and that discovery is a necessary part of that preparation. By conditioning the government's right to discovery on a defense request, the Federal Rule is probably intended to avoid constitutional problems. But if it would violate a defendant's self-incrimination right to seek discovery directly, can the government avoid the constitutional problem so easily by providing for reciprocal discovery?

If you were establishing a discovery system, would you give each side a right to discovery irrespective of what the other side did or would you condition the government's right to discovery on a prior defense request?

Justice Black in *Williams* was plainly correct in foreseeing that notice requirements would not be limited to alibi defenses. Mosteller, Discovery Against the Defense: Tilting the Adversarial Balance, 74 Cal.L.Rev. 1567 (1986), describes a discovery "revolution" in the states. Mosteller found that in addition to prosecutorial discovery with respect to alibi and insanity, which is available in the great majority of states, 25 states grant the prosecution an independent (non-reciprocal) right to discover at least one of the following: "defenses, witness names, statements of witnesses, reports of experts, or documents and tangible evidence." Seven states require broad defense disclosure upon a request for discovery from the prosecution. Twelve states give the prosecution an independent right to obtain the statements of all defense witnesses, and three more permit this discovery when the defendant seeks discovery from the government. Some states require a defendant to summarize the expected testimony of defense witnesses and to create a statement summarizing oral statements of witnesses. Other states require the defense to furnish the government with statements taken from government witnesses. Two questions naturally arise. Does this discovery, going as it does beyond *Williams,* violate the privilege against self-incrimination? If it does not, are defendants and prosecutors equally treated as required by *Wardius?*

3. Sanctions for Nondisclosure

In Taylor v. Illinois, 484 U.S. 400 (1988) and Michigan v. Lucas, 500 U.S. 145 (1991), the Court considered whether the Sixth Amendment right to an adequate defense prohibits trial courts from precluding evidence proffered by criminal defendants who violate legitimate discovery obligations. In *Taylor,* defense counsel wilfully violated a state procedural rule by failing to identify a particular defense witness in response to a pretrial discovery request. The trial court sanctioned this violation by refusing to allow the undisclosed witness to testify. The Court rejected the argument that, under the Sixth Amendment, preclusion is never a permissible sanction for a discovery violation. The Court did not find it problematic to in effect sanction the defendant for his counsel's discovery violation; it reasoned that in most cases it would be quite difficult to determine whether the defense counsel or the defendant (or both) was responsible for the violation. Moreover, the Court did not consider it novel that a client would suffer due to the misstep of his counsel. Therefore, the trial court had discretion to determine whether to sanction defense counsel directly, or to use the sanction of preclusion. Justice Stevens wrote the majority opinion for six members of the Court. Justice Brennan, joined by Justices Marshall and Blackmun, dissented.

In *Lucas,* the defendant in a rape case proffered a defense of consent based in part upon the defendant's prior sexual relationship with the victim. The Michigan rape shield statute required that the defense give notice to the prosecution, within 10 days of the arraignment, of the intent to present evidence of past sexual conduct with the victim. The defendant did not comply with that notice requirement. As a discovery sanction, the trial court precluded any evidence of the sexual relationship at trial; but the State Supreme Court held that such preclusion violated the defendant's constitutional right to an effective defense. Justice O'Connor, writing for a majority of six justices, treated the case as presenting a limited question: whether the State Supreme Court had erred in adopting a per se rule that preclusion of evidence of a rape victim's prior sexual relationship with a criminal defendant violates the constitution. The majority held that such a per se rule of unconstitutionality was inappropriate, because the notice requirement could serve a legitimate state purpose in some cases, and a defendant's violation of the notice requirement could be so egregious as to warrant the sanction of preclusion. The Court did not decide whether the Michigan notice period (the shortest in the nation, requiring notice to be given well before trial) was in fact "arbitrary or disproportionate" in light of the State's interests. Justice O'Connor left room for a defendant to argue that a minimal violation of a notice requirement should result in some remedy short of preclusion of the evidence, e.g., a continuance, and that a rigid rule of preclusion might be unconstitutional. The Court remanded to determine whether preclusion was appropriate under the circumstances of the case. Justice Blackmun concurred in the judgment. Justice Stevens, joined by Justice Marshall, dissented, contending that the State Supreme Court had not in fact gone so far "as to adopt the per se straw man that the Court has decided to knock down today." In their view, the State Court had simply held that preclusion was unjustified under the circumstances.

Taylor and *Lucas* do not hold that exclusion of evidence is permitted every time the defense violates a discovery obligation. Those cases do hold that the Constitution does not absolutely prohibit the sanction of exclusion of defense-proffered evidence in all cases. What factors should a court take into account in determining whether a sanction of exclusion is warranted? See the next case for further discussion of the constitutionality of a preclusion sanction.

B. DISCOVERY AT TRIAL

UNITED STATES v. NOBLES

Supreme Court of the United States, 1975.
422 U.S. 225.

MR. JUSTICE POWELL delivered the opinion of the Court.

In a criminal trial, defense counsel sought to impeach the credibility of key prosecution witnesses by testimony of a defense investigator regarding statements previously obtained from the witnesses by the investigator. The question presented here is whether in these circumstances a federal trial court may compel the defense to reveal the relevant portions of the investigator's report for the prosecution's use in cross-examining him. The United States Court of Appeals for the Ninth Circuit concluded that it cannot. We granted certiorari, and now reverse.

I

Respondent was tried and convicted on charges arising from an armed robbery of a federally insured bank. The only significant evidence linking him to the crime was the identification testimony of two witnesses, a bank teller

and a salesman who was in the bank during the robbery. Respondent offered an alibi but, as the Court of Appeals recognized, his strongest defense centered around attempts to discredit these eyewitnesses. Defense efforts to impeach them gave rise to the events that led to this decision.

In the course of preparing respondent's defense, an investigator for the defense interviewed both witnesses and preserved the essence of those conversations in a written report. When the witnesses testified for the prosecution, respondent's counsel relied on the report in conducting their cross-examination. Counsel asked the bank teller whether he recalled having told the investigator that he had seen only the back of the man he identified as respondent. The witness replied that he did not remember making such a statement. He was allowed, despite defense counsel's initial objection, to refresh his recollection by referring to a portion of the investigator's report. The prosecutor also was allowed to see briefly the relevant portion of the report. The witness thereafter testified that although the report indicated that he told the investigator he had seen only respondent's back, he in fact had seen more than that and continued to insist that respondent was the bank robber.

The other witness acknowledged on cross-examination that he too had spoken to the defense investigator. Respondent's counsel twice inquired whether he told the investigator that "all blacks looked alike" to him, and in each instance the witness denied having made such a statement. The prosecution again sought inspection of the relevant portion of the investigator's report, and respondent's counsel again objected. The court declined to order disclosure at that time, but ruled that it would be required if the investigator testified as to the witnesses' alleged statements from the witness stand. The court further advised that it would examine the investigator's report *in camera* and would excise all reference to matters not relevant to the precise statements at issue.

After the prosecution completed its case, respondent called the investigator as a defense witness. The court reiterated that a copy of the report, inspected and edited *in camera,* would have to be submitted to Government counsel at the completion of the investigator's impeachment testimony. When respondent's counsel stated that he did not intend to produce the report, the court ruled that the investigator would not be allowed to testify about his interviews with the witnesses.

The Court of Appeals for the Ninth Circuit, while acknowledging that the trial court's ruling constituted a "very limited and seemingly judicious restriction," nevertheless considered it reversible error. * * *

II

* * *

* * * Decisions of this Court repeatedly have recognized the federal judiciary's inherent power to require the prosecution to produce the previously recorded statements of its witnesses so that the defense may get the full benefit of cross-examination and the truth-finding process may be enhanced. Jencks v. United States. At issue here is whether, in a proper case, the prosecution can call upon that same power for production of witness statements that facilitate "full disclosure of all the [relevant] facts."

In this case, the defense proposed to call its investigator to impeach the identification testimony of the prosecution's eyewitnesses. * * * The investigator's contemporaneous report might provide critical insight into the issues of credibility that the investigator's testimony would raise. It could assist the jury in determining the extent to which the investigator's testimony actually discredited the prosecution's witnesses. If, for example, the report failed to mention the purported statement of one witness that "all blacks looked alike," the jury might disregard the investigator's version altogether. On the other hand, if this statement appeared in the contemporaneously recorded report, it would tend strongly to corroborate the investigator's version of the interview and to diminish substantially the reliability of that witness' identification.[a]

---

a. Rule 612 of the * * * Federal Rules of Evidence entitles an adverse party to inspect a writing relied on to refresh the recollection of a witness while testifying. The Rule also author-

izes disclosure of writings relied on to refresh recollection before testifying if the court deems it necessary in the interests of justice. The party obtaining the writing thereafter can use

It was therefore apparent to the trial judge that the investigator's report was highly relevant to the critical issue of credibility. In this context, production of the report might substantially enhance "the search for truth." We must determine whether compelling its production was precluded by some privilege available to the defense in the circumstances of this case.

III

A

The Court of Appeals concluded that the Fifth Amendment renders criminal discovery "basically a one-way street." Like many generalizations in constitutional law, this one is too broad. The relationship between the accused's Fifth Amendment rights and the prosecution's ability to discover materials at trial must be identified in a more discriminating manner.

* * *

In this instance disclosure of the relevant portions of the defense investigator's report would not impinge on the fundamental values protected by the Fifth Amendment. The court's order was limited to statements allegedly made by third parties who were available as witnesses to both the prosecution and the defense. Respondent did not prepare the report, and there is no suggestion that the portions subject to the disclosure order reflected any information that he conveyed to the investigator. The fact that these statements of third parties were elicited by a defense investigator on respondent's behalf does not convert them into respondent's personal communications. Requiring their production from the investigator therefore would not in any sense compel respondent to be a

witness against himself or extort communications from him.

* * *

B

The Court of Appeals also held that Fed.Rule Crim.Proc. 16 deprived the trial court of the power to order disclosure of the relevant portions of the investigator's report. * * *

Both the language and history of Rule 16 indicate that it addresses only pretrial discovery. * * *

* * * We conclude, therefore, that Rule 16 imposes no constraint on the District Court's power to condition the impeachment testimony of respondent's witness on the production of the relevant portions of his investigative report. In extending the Rule into the trial context, the Court of Appeals erred.

IV

Respondent contends further that the work-product doctrine exempts the investigator's report from disclosure at trial. While we agree that this doctrine applies to criminal litigation as well as civil, we find its protection unavailable in this case.

The work-product doctrine, recognized by this court in Hickman v. Taylor, 329 U.S. 495 (1947), reflects the strong "public policy underlying the orderly prosecution and defense of legal claims." * * * The Court therefore recognized a qualified privilege for certain materials prepared by an attorney "acting for his client in anticipation of litigation."

Although the work-product doctrine most frequently is asserted as a bar to discovery in civil litigation, its role in

---

it in cross-examining the witness and can introduce into evidence those portions that relate to the witness' testimony. As the Federal Rules of Evidence were not in effect at the time of

respondent's trial, we have no occasion to consider them or their applicability to the situation here presented.

assuring the proper functioning of the criminal justice system is even more vital. The interests of society and the accused in obtaining a fair and accurate resolution of the question of guilt or innocence demand that adequate safeguards assure the thorough preparation and presentation of each side of the case.

At its core, the work-product doctrine shelters the mental processes of the attorney, providing a privileged area within which he can analyze and prepare his client's case. But the doctrine is an intensely practical one, grounded in the realities of litigation in our adversary system. One of those realities is that attorneys often must rely on the assistance of investigators and other agents in the compilation of materials in preparation for trial. It is therefore necessary that the doctrine protect material prepared by agents for the attorney as well as those prepared by the attorney himself. Moreover, the concerns reflected in the work-product doctrine do not disappear once trial has begun. Disclosure of an attorney's efforts at trial, as surely as disclosure during pretrial discovery, could disrupt the orderly development and presentation of his case. We need not, however, undertake here to delineate the scope of the doctrine at trial, for in this instance it is clear that the defense waived such right as may have existed to invoke its protections.

The privilege derived from the work-product doctrine is not absolute. Like other qualified privileges, it may be waived. Here respondent sought to adduce the testimony of the investigator and contrast his recollection of the contested statements with that of the prosecution's witnesses. Respondent, by electing to present the investigator as a witness, waived the privilege with respect to matters covered in his testimony.[b] Respondent can no more advance the work-product doctrine to sustain a unilateral testimonial use of work-product materials than he could elect to testify in his own behalf and thereafter assert his Fifth Amendment privilege to resist cross-examination on matters reasonably related to those brought out in direct examination.

V

Finally, our examination of the record persuades us that the District Court properly exercised its discretion in this instance. The court authorized no general "fishing expedition" into the defense files or indeed even into the defense investigator's report. Rather, its considered ruling was quite limited in scope, opening to prosecution scrutiny only the portion of the report that related to the testimony the investigator would offer to discredit the witnesses' identification testimony. The court further afforded respondent the maximum opportunity to assist in avoiding unwarranted disclosure or to exercise an informed choice to call for the investigator's testimony and thereby open his report to examination.

The court's preclusion sanction was an entirely proper method of assuring compliance with its order. Respondent's argument that this ruling deprived him of the Sixth Amendment rights to compulsory process and cross-examination misconceives the issue. The District Court did not bar the investigator's testimony. It merely pre-

---

b. What constitutes a waiver with respect to work-product materials depends, of course, upon the circumstances. Counsel necessarily makes use throughout trial of the notes, documents, and other internal materials prepared to present adequately his client's case, and often relies on them in examining witnesses.

When so used, there normally is no waiver. But where, as here, counsel attempts to make a testimonial use of these materials the normal rules of evidence come into play with respect to cross-examination and production of documents.

vented respondent from presenting to the jury a partial view of the credibility issue by adducing the investigator's testimony and thereafter refusing to disclose the contemporaneous report that might offer further critical insights. * * *

Mr. Justice Douglas took no part in the consideration or decision of this case.

[Justice White's concurring opinion, which was joined by Justice Rehnquist, is omitted.]

Post-Testimonial Disclosure Under the Federal Rules of Criminal Procedure, the Federal Rules of Evidence, and the Jencks Act

Following *Nobles*, the Supreme Court adopted Fed.R.Crim.P. 26.2, which requires production of witness statements "after a witness other then the defendant has testified on direct examination." The production requirement is triggered by motion of a party who did not call the witness, and applies to any party (government or defendant) who has any statement in their possession that relates to the subject matter of the witness' testimony. Failure to comply can result in the striking of the witness' testimony from the record, or, in the case of a refusal by the government, a mistrial.

There is some question about how the Jencks Act, Fed.R.Crim.P. 26.2 and Fed.R.Evid. 612 relate to one another. The Jencks Act was the first to be adopted and covers only the prosecution. Fed.R.Crim.P. 26.2 covers both sides in a criminal case and largely supersedes the Act. Fed.R.Evid. 612 applies in civil and criminal cases and establishes that, except where the Jencks Act dictates otherwise, a judge, prior to trial, must give one party access to material used to refresh recollection. Because the criminal procedure rule was adopted after the evidence rule, it is not mentioned along with the Jencks Act in the evidence rule. However, it would seem that under Fed.R.Evid. 612 statements covered by either the Jencks Act or the criminal procedure rule ought to receive similar treatment and that, since the procedure rule supersedes the Jencks Act, the evidence rule should defer to the procedure rule in the same way it defers to the statute.

It is important to note that none of these provisions authorizes disclosure of "work product" or other material in the files of counsel unless a witness testifies. Once a witness finishes direct examination, the Jencks Act and Fed. R.Crim.P. 26.2 compel disclosure, upon request, of the witness' prior statements, but of nothing else.

The evidence rule covers all material, not just witness statements, that a witness uses to refresh recollection. When the evidence rule defers to the Jencks Act and the criminal procedure rule, a trial judge should not order disclosure of a witness' prior statements until the conclusion of direct examination. This means there will never be pretrial disclosure of these statements. Other material used to refresh recollection may be disclosed prior to the end of direct examination, and in the case of material reviewed by a witness before trial, even before the witness testifies.

For a slightly different view, see Foster, The Jencks Act: Rule 26.2—Rule 612 Interface—"Confusion Worse Confounded," 34 Okla.L.Rev. 679 (1981).

Two Nobles Problems

To test the implications of *Nobles* and Fed.R.Crim.P. 26.2, consider the following two hypotheticals. Ask how the *Nobles* Court would have resolved the issues prior to the adoption of Rule 26.2, and then compare your answer to the resolution under the rule.

1. A fight occurs on a street corner between the defendant and the "victim," during which the latter is stabbed. In a trial charging the defendant with assault with a deadly weapon, the defendant's claim is self-defense. The victim testifies for the prosecution on direct that the assault was unprovoked. On cross-examination, he is asked whether it is not true that he told a passerby, just seconds before the fight began, that he intended to kill the defendant. The victim denies ever speaking with the passerby. In its case-in-chief, the defense calls the passerby who testifies to two things: first, that the conversation with the victim did occur, and second, that he, the passerby, actually saw the victim strike the initial blow. Previously, this defense witness had given the defense counsel a statement to the effect that (1) before the fight the victim had stated to the passerby that he intended to kill the defendant; (2) there was another witness to the fight; (3) the defendant admitted to the passerby after the fight that he overreacted; (4) it was actually too dark for the passerby to see what happened; and (5) the passerby had been a good friend of the defendant for years. [Must the statement be turned over to the government? If so, the whole statement, or only parts of it?]

Scheininger, United States v. Nobles: A Prosecutor's Perspective, 14 Am.Cr. L.Rev. 1, 7 (1976). Compare Scheininger with Rosenbleet, United States v. Nobles: A Defense View, 14 Am.Cr.L.Rev. 17 (1976).

2. Powell is appointed by a state trial court to represent Jarv in a criminal case. Jarv is charged with robbing a convenience store and with unlawful possession of a firearm. Powell talks with Sharp, the store clerk and only eyewitness. Powell makes an accurate written record of everything Sharp has to say. Trial is delayed a year and a half due to the illness of Jarv. At trial Sharp has difficulty recalling details of the crime. The prosecution is worried because of Sharp's problems on the stand and defense evidence that Sharp is reputed to be a liar. At a recess Sharp tells the prosecutor that defense counsel has a written record of a statement made by Sharp shortly after Jarv's arrest. Sharp and the prosecutor believe the statement will bolster Sharp's testimony. The prosecutor demands its production. Should the Court accede to the demand? Is it important that Powell made the record, or would your answer be the same if Sharp gave a written statement in his own hand? Is there any force to a contention by Powell that the posture of the case required that he seek a statement and that it is unfair to use the statement against the defense?

R. Lempert & S. Saltzburg, A Modern Approach to Evidence 146, Problem II–20 (2d ed.1982).

Chapter Nine

GUILTY PLEAS AND BARGAINING

I. THE GENERAL ISSUES

Once the determination to press charges is made and a case survives pre-trial motions or preliminary screening, the government becomes committed to the idea that the accused should be punished. The accused, even if innocent, must be concerned with how the case will ultimately be resolved. Questions like "Will I be convicted?" and "What kind of sentence will be imposed on me if I am convicted?" become increasingly important. Uncertainty about how these and other questions would be answered by going to trial often leads an accused to respond favorably to, or to initiate, "settlement" discussions with the government. By agreeing to plead guilty (or nolo contendere perhaps) the accused accepts punishment for some criminal activity. In exchange for this acceptance, the system—i.e., the prosecutor and the court—permits the accused to avoid some of the uncertainty endemic in any litigation system in which human beings must decide crucial questions of fact and law and often can exercise broad discretion in implementing social policy.

The extent to which settlement negotiations actually take place, the nature of most settlements reached, the legitimacy of any settlements in criminal cases and the role of the various participants—i.e., the prosecutor, the trial judge, the defense counsel, the defendant, the victim, etc.—are all subjects that have been debated in the literature.

Although it is not possible in one chapter to capture all of the nuances of the debate, at least the surface of some of the principal issues can be scratched. A good place to start is with an overview of the system of plea bargaining, and some commentary from supporters and critics.

But before that, a note on the scope of plea bargaining. Plea bargains vastly outnumber jury trials, especially in the federal system. More than 90% of defendants charged with crime in the federal system, as well as in most state systems, end up pleading guilty rather than going to trial. See Joseph Colquitt, Ad Hoc Plea Bargaining, 75 Tulane L. Rev. 695 (2001) ("Despite the fact that there is no right to a negotiated plea, most–if not virtually all–criminal cases result in a guilty plea"). Plea bargaining permeates the system. And as will be seen in this Chapter, it is largely unregulated by legal standards–it is essentially a marketplace for defendants and prosecutors, with sentencing parameters set by the Sentencing Guidelines and charging decisions, and governed by basic principles of contract. Much of this Chapter considers whether this is any way to run a criminal justice system. is

A. OVERVIEW OF THE PLEA BARGAINING SYSTEM

Professor Joseph Colquitt provides this overview of the plea bargaining process in Ad Hoc Plea Bargaining, 75 Tulane L.Rev. 695 (2001) (footnotes omitted):

> Plea bargaining typically is defined as an explicit or implicit exchange of concessions by the parties. Usually, the accused agrees to plead guilty and the government agrees to some form of reduction in charges or sentence. However, not all successful plea bargaining ends in a guilty plea. Some negotiations end in dismissal of the charges, perhaps after a deferral. Several types of negotiated settlements exist. First, the prosecution may agree to recommend to the court that one or more charges be dismissed in return for a plea of guilty by the defendant to another charge or other charges. The charges to which the defendant may agree to plead might include lesser offenses rather than the original charges. This approach is known as charge bargaining.

> Alternatively, the prosecution might agree simply to recommend a particular sentence in return for the plea. This approach frequently is called sentence bargaining. Sometimes the agreement includes both a reduction in the charge or a dismissal of other charges and a recommendation on the sentence. In all of these cases, in return for the prosecution's recommendation, the defendant waives the privilege against self-incrimination and the right to a trial, including the attendant rights to confront accusers, to present witnesses on the question of guilt or innocence, and to testify in his or her own behalf.

> Plea negotiation has gained its prominence in recent times even though it has been a part of the American criminal justice system for almost 200 years. Yet, despite its age and prominence, plea bargaining is controversial. As late as 1973, major governmental and legal task forces and study commissions were calling for the total elimination of negotiated pleas. Moreover, many Americans are opposed to the disposition of cases through plea bargaining. Why, then, does it continue to be the predominant method of case disposition? As then-Justice William H. Rehnquist noted in 1973:

>> It should be recognized at the outset that the process of plea bargaining is not one which any student of the subject regards as an ornament to our system of criminal justice. Up until now its most resolute defenders have only contended that it contains more advantages than disadvantages, while others have been willing to endure or sanction it only because they regard it as a necessary evil.

> Actually, some of plea bargaining's most resolute defenders believe that the court system needs plea bargaining in order to avoid a disastrous failure of the system as a result of the overwhelming number of cases that courts otherwise would have to try. However, it is more likely that plea bargaining endures because courts and prosecutors routinely rely on the process to dispose of their caseloads in an efficient and timely fashion. Moreover, bargaining reduces the time lag between the offense and the punishment, which potentially benefits not only the State, but also defendants, particu-

larly those incarcerated. Reducing the time between crime and punishment also potentially enhances the deterrent effect of both conviction and punishment.

In addition to faster and more efficient case disposition, plea bargaining reduces costs, uncertainty, and risks. It allows courts and prosecutors to direct their resources more effectively, mitigates potentially severe punishment, provides flexibility, and, in the view of some, delivers justice. In sum, plea bargaining exists to a large extent because its supporters believe that the alternative, the criminal trial, is much more costly and time-consuming and no more likely to provide a just result.

Despite its widespread use and asserted benefits, the scheme is frequently criticized. * * * One of the principal arguments against plea bargaining is that those who plea bargain their cases are likely to be punished less severely than are those who insist on their constitutional right to trial. Some argue that the process abdicates control to the parties, relies too heavily on the prosecutor, or favors defense attorneys who carry favor with the prosecutor. Others fear that plea bargaining results in the conviction and punishment of innocent defendants at times. Some critics dislike the private, sometimes secret nature of the bargaining process or believe that the process causes the public to lose confidence in the criminal justice system.

* * *

Despite all of the arguments advanced against plea bargaining, and, perhaps supporting the view that plea bargaining is virtually inevitable, only a limited number of jurisdictions have been willing to confront their criminal caseloads without negotiated pleas. Four examples of such attempts warrant a brief review.

Alaska. In 1975, Alaska's Attorney General announced the demise of plea bargaining in that state, in part to ensure fairness, to restore public confidence in the criminal justice system, and to improve the trial skills of his prosecutorial staff. The new policy prohibited both charge and sentence bargaining. The implementation of the new policy did not bring about the disaster commonly predicted by those who opposed discarding plea bargaining. By 1985, though, only ten years after the ban, the policy was supported by written guidelines, but the guidelines did not include the original prohibition of plea bargaining.

Some attorneys in Alaska continue to profess ignorance of the prohibitions of plea bargaining. Others contend that exceptions to the policy are rare and that most pleas occur without specific, agreed-upon concessions from the prosecutor. However, the most general understanding of the policy, even among prosecutors, is that, despite the mid-eighties change, sentence bargains are prohibited absent special circumstances, but charge bargaining is allowed.

California. The State of California also attempted to abandon plea bargaining. In 1982, the voters of California approved a referendum which sought to abolish plea bargaining in serious felonies and other enumerated crimes. The resulting statute prohibits plea bargaining in any case involving a serious felony, a felony in which the accused personally used a firearm, or any offense of driving while under the influence of alcohol or any drug. It permits plea bargaining if the evidence is inadequate to prove the charge, the testimony of a material witness cannot be obtained, or the negotiated settlement does not result in a substantial change in the sentence. Despite these restrictions, plea bargaining continues to exist in California's courts.

El Paso, Texas. A third attempt to ban plea bargaining occurred in El Paso, Texas. * * * [T]wo state district judges initiated the policy on the local level in El Paso. Their policy resulted from their dissatisfaction with the local prosecutor's unwillingness to recommend probation in some plea bargained cases. The judges prohibited all plea negotiations in their courts as a way to ensure equal treatment for similarly situated defendants. Moreover, they instituted sentencing guidelines. The immediate result gives credence to the argument espoused by opponents of the abolition of plea bargaining: they experienced increased jury trials, increased time for case disposition and increased backlogs. Furthermore, plea bargaining and guilty pleas did not cease to exist in El Paso. Even under the new policy, a guilty plea assured each defendant of his sentence at arraignment. If the accused chose to go to trial, the sentence upon conviction frequently was longer than the sentence that would have been imposed had there been a guilty plea. The acknowledgment by assistant district attorneys that they and others often circumvented the policy also demonstrates that plea bargaining in El Paso continued to exist.

Maricopa County, Arizona. A fourth effort, this one an attempt to abandon stipulated sentence bargaining, surfaced in Maricopa County, Arizona. Five Maricopa County Superior Court judges adopted a policy that prohibited settlements based on stipulated sentences. The policy provided, with two exceptions, that plea "[a]greements may not stipulate to any term of years ... or to any non-mandatory terms or conditions of probation ... or to sentences running concurrently or consecutively." Thus, the judges effectively agreed not to accept a plea package that included a negotiated sentence, nonstatutory conditions of probation, or an agreement about whether the sentence would run consecutive to or concurrent with other sentences. When the policy came before the Supreme Court of Arizona, the court decided that the policy actually constituted an invalid effort to establish a local rule of procedure. The judges in Maricopa County were left with Arizona Rule of Criminal Procedure 17.4, which provides that "parties may negotiate concerning, and reach an agreement on, any aspect of the case," including the sentence to be imposed. Although the parties may stipulate the sentence to be imposed, the judge may reject the proposed sentence and permit the defendant to withdraw the plea.

In sum, many practitioners and scholars view plea bargaining as inevitable. Plea negotiation is simply too important and too ingrained in our criminal justice system to abandon it without identifying and providing a suitable replacement. That replacement has not been forthcoming, and it probably is the absence of a suitable replacement, rather than enthusiasm for plea bargaining, that supports its retention.

* * *

Cooperating Witnesses

As will be seen in this Chapter, a major reason that plea bargaining is here to stay is that prosecutors find it necessary to enter into cooperation agreements with criminals in order to get the testimony necessary to convict other criminals. Without plea bargaining–specifically the "carrots" of reduced charges and a further reduction in sentence for "substantial cooperation"–there would be little reason for criminal associates to "flip" and become a prosecution witness. Without turncoat witnesses, many prosecutions of major criminals would become virtually impossible.

Sentencing Differential Between Guilty Plea and Trial

It has been alleged that judges induce guilty pleas by imposing more severe sentences when a defendant chooses a trial rather than pleading guilty. Some studies suggest that differential sentencing exists at the misdemeanor and felony levels.

There is a split as to the propriety of differential sentencing. Proponents believe leniency is proper for those who accept responsibility for their conduct by pleading guilty and contribute to the efficient and economical administration of the law. They assert that those submitting themselves to prompt correctional measures should be granted sentence concessions, and that differential sentences for those demanding trial is not undue punishment if it is not excessive. Those opposed believe that guilty pleas have no direct relevance to the appropriate disposition of an offender and that the constitutional right to trial should not be the cause of enhanced punishment.

Support for Plea Bargaining: Brady v. United States

The leading case in the Supreme Court on plea bargaining is Brady v. United States, 397 U.S. 742 (1970). In *Brady*, the Court rejected the defendant's argument that a guilty plea is invalid "whenever motivated by the defendant's desire to accept the certainty or probability of a lesser penalty rather than face a wider range of possibilities extending from acquittal to conviction and a higher penalty authorized by law for the crime charged." The Court provided support for the system of plea bargaining in the following passage:

> The issue we deal with is inherent in the criminal law and its administration because guilty pleas are not constitutionally forbidden, because the criminal law characteristically extends to judge or jury a range of choice in setting the sentence in individual cases, and because both the State and the defendant often find it advantageous to preclude the possibility of the maximum penalty authorized by law. For a defendant who sees slight possibility of acquittal, the advantages of pleading guilty and limiting the probable penalty are obvious—his exposure is reduced, the correctional processes can begin immediately, and the practical burdens of a trial are eliminated. For the State there are also advantages—the more promptly imposed punishment after an admission of guilt may more effectively attain the objectives of punishment; and with the avoidance of trial, scarce judicial and prosecutorial resources are conserved for those cases in which there is a

substantial issue of the defendant's guilt or in which there is substantial doubt that the State can sustain its burden of proof. It is this mutuality of advantage that perhaps explains the fact that at present well over three-fourths of the criminal convictions in this country rest on pleas of guilty, a great many of them no doubt motivated at least in part by the hope or assurance of a lesser penalty than might be imposed if there were a guilty verdict after a trial to judge or jury.

B. SUPPORT FOR PLEA BARGAINING

Judge Easterbrook, in Plea Bargaining as Compromise, 101 Yale L.J. 1969 (1992), sets forth the following eloquent defense of plea bargaining, even though he recognizes that the system of plea bargaining is not as efficient as it might be:

On the economic side, plea bargains do not represent Pareto improvements. Instead of engaging in trades that make at least one person better off and no one worse off, the parties dicker about how much worse off one side will be. In markets persons can borrow to take advantage of good deals or withdraw from the market, wait for a better offer, and lend their assets for a price in the interim. By contrast, both sides to a plea bargain operate under strict budget constraints, and they cannot bide their time. They bargain as bilateral monopolists (defendants can't shop in competitive markets for prosecutors) in the shadow of legal rules that work suspiciously like price controls. Judges, who do not join the bargaining, set the prices, increasingly by reference to a table of punishments that looks like something the Office of Price Administration would have promulgated. Plea bargaining is to the sentencing guidelines as black markets are to price controls.

Black markets are better than no markets. Plea bargains are preferable to mandatory litigation—not because the analogy to contract is overpowering, but because compromise is better than conflict. Settlements of civil cases make both sides better off; settlements of criminal cases do so too. Defendants have many procedural and substantive rights. By pleading guilty, they sell these rights to the prosecutor, receiving concessions they esteem more highly than the rights surrendered. Rights that may be sold are more valuable than rights that must be consumed, just as money (which may be used to buy housing, clothing, or food) is more valuable to a poor person than an opportunity to live in public housing. Defendants can use or exchange their rights, whichever makes them better off. So plea bargaining helps defendants. Forcing them to use their rights at trial means compelling them to take the risk of conviction or acquittal; risk-averse persons prefer a certain but small punishment to a chancy but large one. Defendants also get the process over sooner, and solvent ones save the expense of trial. Compromise also benefits prosecutors and society at large. In purchasing procedural entitlements with lower sentences, prosecutors buy that most valuable commodity, Time. With time they can prosecute more criminals. When eight percent of defendants plead guilty, a given prosecutorial staff obtains five times the number of convictions it could achieve if all went to trial. Even so, prosecutors must throw back the small fish. The ratio of prosecutions (and convictions) to crimes would be extremely low if compromises were forbidden. Sentences could not be raised high enough to maintain deterrence, especially not when both economics and principles of desert call for proportionality between crime and punishment.

* * *

Plea bargains are compromises. Autonomy and efficiency support them. "Imperfections" in bargaining reflect the imperfections of an anticipated trial. To improve plea bargaining, improve the process for deciding cases on the merits. When we deem that process adequate, there will be no reason to prevent the person most affected by the criminal process from improving his situation through compromise.

C. CRITIQUE OF PLEA BARGAINING

Professor Schulhofer, in Plea Bargaining as Disaster, 101 Yale L.J. 1979 (1992), argues that plea bargaining should be abolished because, among other things, it gives an innocent defendant a choice of pleading guilty and avoiding a trial—a choice that Professor Schulhofer argues should not be permitted:

> I have suggested three reasons why we cannot assume that voluntary contracting will necessarily enhance the welfare of affected parties in plea bargaining. First, condemnation, punishment, and litigation time are public goods with powerful social effects that the prosecution and defense counsel cannot fully internalize in a two-party contractual situation. Second, pervasive conflicts of interest introduce additional agency costs into the negotiating process. Third, no contractual mechanisms permit monitoring or ensure that gains from trade outweigh the agency costs of bargaining through intermediaries.

* * *

> * * * [T]he innocent defendant, facing a small possibility of conviction on a serious charge, [often] considers it in his interest to accept conviction and a small penalty. The defendant's choice to plead guilty can be rational from his private perspective, but it imposes costs on society by undermining public confidence that criminal convictions reflect guilt beyond a reasonable doubt. An "efficient" system of voluntary contracting for pleas would convict large numbers of defendants who had a high probability of acquittal at trial; indeed, to the extent that innocent defendants are likely to be more risk averse than guilty ones, the former are likely to be overrepresented in the pool of "acquittable" defendants who are attracted by prosecutorial offers to plead guilty. To deal seriously with these problems we must consider complete abolition of plea bargaining. * * * The social interest in not punishing defendants who are factually innocent justifies a bar on compromise, low-sentence settlements, even if individual defendants would prefer to have that option.

Professor Schulhofer also argues that a system of plea bargaining imposes significant disadvantages on indigent defendants, because appointed counsel are underpaid, thus giving them an incentive to plead a case at the first opportunity, whether the plea agreement is fair or not. Abolishing plea bargaining would mean that an appointed attorney's performance would be more closely monitored:

The single most serious agency problem on the defense side is that the attorney incurs a severe financial penalty if the case goes to trial. That prospect can powerfully skew his appraisal of the value of a prosecutor's plea offer and the advice he provides to his client. A prohibition on bargaining protects defendants who would accept a plea offer that was not in their interest, even if the attorney, once forced to trial, would give the same indifferent assistance that he would provide in plea negotiations.

* * *

In plea bargaining, the attorney's role is virtually immune from scrutiny or control. The quality of attorney performance is difficult for both clients and peers to assess; the formal obligations of effective assistance do not, even in theory, require investigation of factual or legal defenses; and retrospective control by suits for malpractice or ineffective assistance are precluded by nearly insuperable doctrinal hurdles.

The shift from plea bargaining to trial renders the attorney's performance highly visible to peers in the courtroom. This shift also enlarges both the attorney's formal legal obligations of effective assistance and the practical likelihood that they will be taken seriously. The institutional environment of the trial process thus limits the consequences of the agency problem in ways that are precluded when disposition occurs in a low-visibility plea. The visibility of trial also tends to generate pressure to alleviate the worst inadequacies of indigent defense funding. Indigents are far more likely to receive conscientious representation when cases are tried in open court than when the attorneys are permitted to settle on the basis of an uninformed guess about the likelihood of conviction.

Thus, even if deeply flawed systems for indigent defense remain common, abolishing bargaining and conducting more trials would not hurt poor defendants. Indeed, the more that indigents face acute problems of involuntary representation, inadequate funding, and pervasive conflicts of interests, the more that abolition remains necessary to permit better monitoring of the attorney-client relationship. The mission of the criminal justice system is to ascertain guilt and appropriate punishment. Structural flaws only increase the importance of resolving these issues in the sunlight of open, adversarial proceedings before a neutral decisionmaker, rather than permitting them to be settled behind closed doors by agents who have few incentives to act in the interests of their principals.

Professor Schulhofer argues that one alternative for the current system of plea bargaining is a structured system in which defendants receive some automatic, non-negotiable concessions for pleading guilty.

By abolishing bargaining but not abolishing concessions, a jurisdiction could retain control over its guilty plea rate and preserve its existing low level of resources committed to trials. Such a system has frequently been proposed; it was adopted by Italy when it transformed its criminal procedure into an adversary system in 1988; and it is approximated, though imperfectly, under the guilty plea provisions of the federal sentencing guidelines. [The Guidelines provide for a reduction in sentence for acceptance of responsibility, with a guilty plea being a strong indicator of that acceptance]. In such a system, the proportion of defendants pleading guilty would be similar to the present number, but the composition of the guilty plea pool presumably would change. Those who elect trial in the present system do not necessarily have the greatest chance of acquittal because such defendants are also the ones most likely to win the best sentence concessions in negotiation. Rather, those who now go to trial tend to be those who are least risk averse, a group that may include disproportionate numbers of those who are actually guilty. In contrast, in a system of nonnegotiable sentence concessions, defendants who elect trial are most likely to be those with the greatest likelihood of acquittal, a group that should include disproportionate numbers of the innocent. The normative premise of this approach is that the trial process, however infrequently used, should be reserved for cases where guilt is most in doubt.

As another alternative, Professor Schulhofer simply proposes that plea bargaining be abolished. He argues that a system without plea bargaining would provide greater protection for innocent defendants:

> Because processing each case would be more costly, and because innocents would be more difficult to convict, the prosecutor's incentives (both personal and public) to screen carefully at the charging stage would be enhanced. The total number of defendants charged might decrease if prosecutorial resources were held constant. But even if the number charged did not decline, the proportion of innocents in the pool of defendants would tend to decrease. * * * Because abolition would make it harder to convict the innocent, it would benefit defendants convicted in the plea bargaining process who would not be convicted, and perhaps would not even be charged, in a no-concessions world.

Professor Schulhofer concludes as follows:

> With trials in open court and deserved sentences imposed by a neutral factfinder, we protect the due process right to an adversarial trial, minimize the risk of unjust conviction of the innocent, and at the same time further the public interest in effective law enforcement and adequate punishment of the guilty. But plea negotiation simultaneously undercuts all of these interests. The affected parties are represented by agents who have inadequate incentives for proper performance; prospects for effective monitoring are limited or nonexistent; and the dynamics of negotiation can create irresistible pressure for defendants falsely to condemn themselves. As a result, plea agreements defeat the public interest in effective law enforcement at the same time that they deny defendants the benefits of a vigorous defense and inflict undeserved punishment on innocents who could win acquittal at trial. Plea bargaining is a disaster. It can be, and should be, abolished.[1]

Who has the better of the argument, Judge Easterbrook or Professor Schulhofer? Professor Schulhofer's position is that innocent defendants should not be permitted to bargain away their rights. Do you agree? Does Professor Schulhofer underestimate the costs to the system that would arise (especially in the form of underdeterrence) if plea bargaining is abolished? Is his argument undermined by

---

1. Similar views are found in Parnas and Atkins, Abolishing Plea Bargaining: A Proposal, 14 Crim.L.Bull. 101 (1978); Langbein, Torture and Plea Bargaining, 46 Chi.L.Rev. 3 (1978). Professor Langbein argues that because of the panoply of trial rights owed to a defendant, the prosecutor has a strong incentive to coerce a guilty plea.

the fact that several jurisdictions have tried to abolish plea bargaining and failed in the attempt?

The Federal Initiative to Limit Plea Bargaining

In September, 2003, Attorney General Ashcroft issued a memorandum to federal prosecutors instructing them not to charge defendants with an eye toward plea bargaining. With few exceptions, prosecutors are instructed to pursue the toughest sentences possible under the Federal Sentencing Guidelines. The memo states that prosecutors "must charge and pursue the most serious, readily provable offenses that are supported by the facts." The purpose of the policy is to assure consistency in charging decisions across the country. The exceptions to the "highest charge" policy are limited to: 1) cases in which problems with witnesses lead to a "post-indictment reassessment"; 2) cases in which the defendant decides to provide "substantial assistance" in prosecution of other criminals; and 3) "other exceptional circumstances" where a single case might place an extraordinary burden on a local U.S. attorney's office or reduce "the total number of cases disposed of by the office."

Professor George Fisher, in an op-ed piece in the New York Times, argues that Attorney General Ashcroft's new policy is doomed to fail. Fisher, A Practice as Old as Justice Itself, N.Y. Times, Sept.28, 2003, at WK 11. He argues that plea bargaining reaches just results and that any attempt to regulate the practice simply drives it "underground". He elaborates as follows:

There are good reasons to dislike plea bargains. Justice is dealt behind closed doors rather than in the open air of a courtroom. Prosecutors can hijack sentencing authority from judges, and criminals can get off with less than they deserve.

Just as it survived the Massachusetts legislature, however, plea bargaining will survive Mr. Ashcroft. Most prosecutors like plea bargaining; a sound bargain means an easy victory and more time to prosecute the next serious case.

* * *

Today the entire criminal justice system depends for its survival on plea bargaining. Last year 95 percent of criminal cases adjudicated in federal courts ended with pleas of guilty or no contest. To try even one-quarter of all cases would mean five times as many trials, with a comparable increase in public expense. One wonders if Mr. Ashcroft wishes to preside over such an expansion.

It's hardly likely. His new policy claiming to clamp down on plea bargaining leaves lots of bargaining room [given the built-in exceptions.] * * *

And even if Mr. Ashcroft actually tries to limit plea bargaining, many judges will conspire with prosecutors to evade the rules. Judges know that the hundreds of new appointees needed to preside over an avalanche of new trials won't take the bench for years, if ever. Moreover, many judges resent the rigidity of the federal sentencing guidelines and will gladly help to undermine them. Defense lawyers will also help elude the policy. Private counsel often demand full payment up front and enjoy a rich payday when a case ends in an effortless plea bargain. Public defenders have limited resources and know they cannot try all or most cases.

Still, Mr. Ashcroft's new rule, while pointless as policy, makes good politics. To many, less plea bargaining sounds like more justice. But don't be fooled. Once everyone in the system finds the loopholes, plea bargaining will march on the same as before.

D. THE LINE BETWEEN REWARDING A GUILTY PLEA AND PUNISHING THE DECISION TO GO TO TRIAL

The trial judge in United States v. Medina–Cervantes, 690 F.2d 715 (9th Cir.1982), indicated concern that the defendant, convicted of entering the United States illegally and of reentering the United States after having been deported, was "thumbing his nose at our judicial system" by insisting on a trial and the exercise of the full panoply of trial rights. He imposed a fine that was intended to reimburse the government for the costs of the trial. The court of appeals stated that it did not doubt the good faith of the trial judge, but remanded for resentencing, observing that "[i]t is well settled that an accused may not be subjected to more severe punishment simply because he exercised his right to stand trial." It directed the trial judge to state the reasons for the sentence imposed upon remand.

Had the trial judge said nothing, and simply imposed a higher sentence within a permissible range, the court of appeals presumably would have sustained the sentence. Do you think that a system that "encourages" pleas is likely to penalize those who insist on going to trial? Could a judge identify a lack of remorse as a basis for increasing the penalty? Should the judge do so? See Scott v. United States, 419 F.2d 264 (D.C.Cir.1969)(while a defendant may receive a longer sentence after going to trial, no part of that sentence can be attributable to punishing the defendant for having gone to trial).

Acceptance of Responsibility

These questions are no longer of merely theoretical interest. The United States Sentencing Guidelines, discussed at much greater length in Chapter Eleven, provide for a reduced sentence for defendants who accept responsibility for their criminal conduct. Section 3E1.1. Acceptance of responsibility does not require a guilty plea, but the Sentencing Commission envisioned, and the courts have held, that a defendant who goes to trial rarely will be able to qualify for the reduction.

Would the Guidelines be unconstitutional if they conditioned acceptance of responsibility on a plea of guilty? See, e.g., United States v. White, 869 F.2d 822 (5th Cir.1989)(Section 3E1.1 does not impinge on defendant's Sixth Amendment right to trial: "It is not unconstitutional for the Government to bargain for a guilty plea in exchange for a reduced sentence. The fact that a more lenient sentence is imposed on a contrite defendant does not establish a corollary that those who elect to stand trial are penalized.").

The Sentencing Commission's approach does not focus in the slightest on the probability of conviction or the strength of the government's evidence. Nor does it focus on the seriousness of the offense charged. All defendants are treated equally. This is consistent with the mandate of the Commission to reduce unjustified disparities in sentencing, but arguably it may result in disparity. A defendant against whom the evidence is weak might well have negotiated a more favorable plea arrangement prior to the adoption of guidelines than a defendant against whom the evidence is strong. Does it make sense to treat these two defendants as though they were similarly situated? On these questions, see O'Hear, Remorse, Cooperation, and "Acceptance of Responsibility": The Structure, Implementation, and Reform of Section 3E1.1 of the Federal Sentencing Guidelines, 91 Nw.U.L.Rev. 1507 (1997).

E. GUILTY PLEAS, CHARGING DECISIONS, AND THE FEDERAL SENTENCING GUIDELINES

The Federal Sentencing Guidelines purport to limit "plea bargaining" to the extent that the amount of the reduction in sentence is fixed. The Guidelines cannot control the charges brought against a defendant, however. Some have asserted that prosecutors at times evade the guidelines by their charging decisions. See, e.g., Schulhofer & Nagel, Negotiated Pleas Under the Federal Sentencing Guidelines: The First Fifteen Months, 27 Am.Crim.L.Rev. 231 (1989) (noting that prosecutors have at times certified that a defendant has "substantially assisted" an investigation, even when he hasn't, in order to permit a sympathetic defendant to obtain a reduction and avoid what is perceived as a harsh sentence under the Guidelines).

1. Controls on Discretion

During the Reagan Administration, the Department of Justice attempted to control plea bargaining under the Guidelines. A memorandum of Attorney General Dick Thornburgh stated that charges were to reflect the most serious conduct of an offender that could be proven, and that plea arrangements were not to subvert the Guidelines. Thus, charging decisions were to be based on what was readily provable by the government, as opposed to what the prosecutor thought was the appropriate charge under the circumstances of the case.

Subsequently, however, Attorney General Reno rescinded the Thornburgh Memorandum in an amendment to the United States Attorney's Manual. See Amendment to 9–27.000, United States Attorney's Manual, October 12, 1993. The effect of this amendment is described by Liebman and Snyder in Joint Guilty Pleas: "Group Justice" In Federal Plea Bargaining, N.Y.L.J. Sept. 8, 1994, p.1, col.1:

The Reno Amendment states that "a faithful and honest application of the Sentencing Guidelines is not incompatible with selecting charges or entering into plea agreements on the basis of an individualized assessment of the extent to which particular charges fit the specific circumstances of a case, are consistent with the federal criminal code, and maximize the impact of federal resources on crime." * * * In other words, liberated from the rigid constraints of the Thornburgh Memo, federal prosecutors arguably are now authorized to import their views of what is "just" into the plea bargaining process.

But is all this discretion in deciding what to charge and bargain over a good thing? Doesn't it give the prosecutor essentially unregulated authority to force a defendant into a guilty plea, for example, by overcharging and then obtaining a plea on a lesser charge? Consider Professor Standen's comments in Plea Bargaining in the Shadow of the Guidelines, 81 Calif.L.Rev.1471 (1993):

> Historically, the prosecutor's extraordinary bargaining power over defendants was constrained by independent judicial sentencing. The bargains that prosecutors offered and struck with criminal defendants were confined to a range representing a discount of the likely judicial sentencing outcome. Thus, regardless of the extent of the prosecutor's potentially exploitative bargaining power or the paucity of plea concessions offered by the prosecutor, the defendant retained the option of proceeding to trial. In effect, the defendant could always reject the prosecutor's offer for the judge's. As a result, prosecutors' plea offers were necessarily fashioned in response to likely judicial sentences.

> Judicial sentencing no longer limits prosecutorial power in federal courts. The United States Sentencing Guidelines have substantially eliminated the discretion of federal judges to determine final sentences and have thus curtailed judges' ability to constrain prosecutors. Today it is the sentencing guidelines, rather than judge-determined sentences, that supply the parameters of plea bargaining.

> The sentencing guidelines, however, fail to constrain prosecutorial power. Because the sentencing guidelines are largely "charge-offense based," the eventual sentencing outcome is determined primarily by the crime with which the prosecutor charges the defendant. By determining sentencing outcomes as a function of charging decisions, the sentencing guidelines have had the unintended effect of giving more control over the sentencing outcome to the person who controls charging, the prosecutor. Instead of constraining prosecutors, the sentencing guidelines further empower them. The prosecutor's new power to shape the outcomes of criminal trials radically alters the nature of plea bargaining. Rather than being constrained to shape bargains according to judge-determined sentencing parameters, the prosecutor now determines with little inhibition the sentencing parameters. Because the prosecutor now sets the range from which the prosecutor and defense counsel discount to reflect the likelihood of conviction and the costs of trial, full exercise of the prosecutor's monopsony power [i.e., the position of being the only possible buyer] is now possible. Indeed, full exploitation of the monopsony power by prosecutors constitutes faithful service to their principals, using public resources to maximum effect. Further, except in cases of gross overcharging, neither the judge nor the jury can gainsay the prosecutor's selection of the bargaining parameters. If a defendant opts not to accept the prosecutor's offer and is convicted as charged, the guidelines sentence is typically an automatic function of the charge. Consequently, the prosecutor's control over the charge is effectively control of the sentence. Plea bargaining, traditionally understood as a process of bargaining over neutral sentencing outcomes, is a thing of the past.

Professor Standen concludes that "effective dispersement of discretion can be achieved only by abrogating the requirement that judges adhere to the sentencing guidelines."[2]

---

2. Professor Alschuler ultimately concludes that "neither a transfer of discretion to the prosecutor's office nor an increase in prosecutorial bargaining power is inevitable" under

A more positive view of plea bargaining under the Guidelines is set forth by Judge Easterbrook in Plea Bargaining as Compromise, 101 Yale L.J. 1969 (1992):

> Plea bargaining is easier to justify today than ever before. * * * [T]he federal sentencing guidelines serve a valuable function by establishing benchmark sentences, derived from normal judicial practices in the years before 1987. A "price" so established, known to any defendant who elects trial, squelches one of the perennial attacks on plea bargaining: that the bargain sentence is the norm, and the higher sentence imposed after trial a penalty heaped on persons who dare to exercise their constitutional rights. Formally, the guidelines limit the discount for "acceptance of responsibility" to * * * roughly fifteen percent of the sentence. This discount, significantly less than the historical reduction, could have discouraged pleas. Curtailing the discount for pleading guilty has been justified in the name of equality. Yet the greatest disparity in sentencing is between those convicted at trial and those not prosecuted. A reduction in the number of convictions attributable to a decline in the number of pleas would dramatically increase the effective disparity in the treatment of persons suspected of crime, the opposite of the effect the guidelines' authors sought to achieve. As it turns out, however, bargaining has continued in other ways—for example, by reduction in charges, which takes the matter out of the hands of judges, or by awarding of additional reductions for assistance to the prosecutor. The percentage of guilty pleas in federal criminal cases accordingly has been stable.

It should also be noted that some of the Sentencing Guidelines provisions can frustrate the intent of the bargaining parties, thus impacting the efficiency of the bargaining system. For example, Guideline Section 1B1.3 provides that a judge may consider "relevant conduct" in increasing the sentence—this includes charges that are dismissed by agreement of the parties, where the charges are related to the offense of conviction. See United States v. Barber, 119 F.3d 276 (4th Cir.1997). Thus, the benefit of the bargain is diminished by the possibility of the judge's enhancing the sentence on the basis of relevant conduct.

Finally, note that, as discussed above, the Attorney General pendulum has swung once again. Attorney General Ashcroft's memo to prosecutors instructs them that they "must charge and pursue the most serious, readily provable offenses that are supported by the facts." But this standard is flexible enough that prosecutors, in cahoots with judges and defense counsel, will still be able to reap the rewards of charge bargaining under the Guidelines.

2. The Impact of Mandatory Minimum Sentencing and Substantial Assistance Motions

There can be circumstances in which the pressure on a federal defendant to plead can be tremendous even without regard to the sentence reduction for acceptance of responsibility. This pressure results from two factors: (1) the existence of mandatory minimum sentencing statutes; and (2) the possibility of a

Guidelines sentencing, but suggests that the Guidelines "permit the judicial control of prosecutorial power—again if judges will do the job." Alschuler, Departures and Plea Agreements Under the Sentencing Guidelines, 117 F.R.D. 459 (1988).

reduction in sentence below a mandatory minimum for substantial assistance to the prosecution in the investigation and prosecution of other defendants.

Congress has provided substantial mandatory minimum sentences for a number of crimes, particularly those involving drugs and firearms. The Sentencing Commission provided Congress in August, 1991 with a "Special Report" entitled "Mandatory Minimum Penalties in the Federal Criminal Justice System." This lengthy document observes that at that time there were more than 60 criminal statutes in the federal criminal code that contain mandatory minimum penalties, and that only four of the 60 frequently result in convictions. All four relate to drug and weapon offenses. The Commission found that, despite the expectation that the mandatory minimum would be applied in all cases in which the defendant seemed eligible for the penalty, a considerable number of cases resulted in a lesser sentence. Indeed, the Commission found that in 35% of these cases, defendants pled guilty to offenses carrying either nonmandatory or reduced mandatory minimum penalties. The Commission was unable to determine whether the pleas were justified by evidentiary concerns or other legitimate governmental interests. But it seems clear that there is a lot of room for a prosecutor to offer a deal by charging something other than an offense that would carry a mandatory minimum term–and this is so despite the efforts from the Attorney General to limit the practice.

The presence of a mandatory minimum penalty can produce great pressure on a defendant to plead guilty in such a way as to escape the minimum. In a number of instances, the Guidelines do not impose a sentence as strict as required by a mandatory minimum statute. If a prosecutor is willing to charge under a nonmandatory or reduced mandatory statute, the defendant may leap at a plea offer, particularly if the mandatory penalty that is avoided by the plea is 10 years or more. See DeBenedectis, Mandatory Minimum Sentences Hit, A.B.A.J. Dec. 1991, p. 36 (noting that "mandatory minimums give federal prosecutors wide discretion over sentencing through the crimes they charge and bargains they accept").

Additionally, section 5K1.1 of the Guidelines contains a policy statement recognizing that where a defendant provides substantial assistance, a trial court may depart from the Guidelines. Because Congress has provided in 18 U.S.C. § 3553(e) that a substantial assistance departure may go below a mandatory minimum, the defendant who can provide substantial assistance may be able to avoid a very high penalty even if he or she cannot persuade a prosecutor to reduce or amend charges. The defendant may be encouraged to plead to obtain the benefits of the substantial assistance rule.

The higher the mandatory minimum and the greater the reduction associated with cooperation, the more pressure there is for the defendant to abandon a defense and to cooperate. Should mandatory minimum penalties be permitted to go hand in hand with plea bargaining? If not, which should be abolished? For a discussion of the impact of the Guidelines and mandatory minimum sentences on the decision to cooperate, see Richman, Cooperating Clients, 56 Ohio State L.J. 69 (1995). Professor Richman points out that clients are often caught between the pressures of severe sentencing under federal law on the one hand, and defense counsel's financial, institutional, and emotional interest in preventing the client from cooperating with the government on the other.

F. EFFICIENCY AT WHAT PRICE?

Plea bargaining is almost certain to produce disturbing results in some cases. Consider, for example, the following problem:

Problem

A defendant is charged with first degree murder, and he pleads self-defense. The two witnesses for the state are the daughter and wife of the deceased. Both claim that the defendant fired a gun without provocation. At a preliminary hearing the magistrate believes that the question of sufficiency of the evidence to hold the defendant is a close one because the eyewitnesses are less believable than the defendant, but ultimately binds the defendant over because a jury could believe them and return a guilty verdict. The grand jury charges first degree murder.

Assume that the prosecutor says to the defense lawyer in the course of plea bargaining, "I agree with the magistrate. The greater probability is self-defense here, but I figure that there is about a 40% chance that the defendant will be convicted of first degree murder. This surely is a case of premeditated murder or self-defense. It was one or the other, pure and simple." The prosecutor goes on to say: "If I am right, the expected minimum penalty from your client's perspective is 40% multiplied by the minimum sentence he can receive which is twenty years, or 8 years as the bottom line. In other words, your client will be found innocent and serve no time in 6 out of 10 cases, and in 4 out of 10 cases your client will serve a minimum of twenty years. The way I see it the jury either believes my witnesses or yours and that kind of case is always unpredictable. Like the magistrate implied, reasonable juries have leeway in determining whom to believe. Since your client has a 40% chance of serving a minimum of 20 years, a conservative, but impartial, observer would say that your client should be looking to reduce his exposure to jail. Here is what I am prepared to do: I will let your client plead to negligent homicide and recommend a two year sentence. Because your client has no prior record, the court will probably accept that recommendation, though I cannot guarantee that." The defense lawyer takes this offer back to the client who is afraid of the possibility of a minimum twenty year sentence.

If the defense lawyer agrees on the odds and so informs the defendant, should the defendant be permitted to plead to the negligent homicide charge? Does it matter that the defendant could not possibly have committed negligent homicide under either side's version of the facts? If a factual basis requirement is in effect, must there be a factual basis for negligent homicide, or is it sufficient that there is a basis for the greater offense? If a basis for the lesser offense must be shown, can the prosecutor ethically permit the defendant to state to the court a distorted version of the facts? Could the prosecutor put on only part of the state's evidence in an effort to create for the court an appearance of negligent homicide? If the answer to either or both of the last two questions is "no," what incentive does the system provide for anyone to challenge an improper plea? If the defense lawyer agrees with the prosecutor about the odds but, in fact, better lawyers would calculate the chance of conviction as 20%, is ineffective assistance of counsel demonstrated? Is it ethical for the prosecutor to prosecute a case where the odds of getting a guilty verdict are less than even? Does it matter whether the prosecutor has a subjective belief in the guilt of the defendant?

If the illustration uses numbers that you believe are unrealistic, change them so that there is a 60% chance of conviction. Should the defendant accept an offer to plead to second degree murder with an 8–year sentence recommendation? Could a rational lawyer advise against such a plea? If you like plea bargaining, consider whether there is any prosecutorial offer that would be so coercive as to be unreasonable. If you don't like plea bargaining, consider whether there is any offer that you would deem proper.

Inverted Sentencing

Another disturbing phenomenon of plea bargaining is that in multi-defendant cases, those more culpable might have a chance at receiving a lighter sentence than those less culpable. This is because prosecutors often need cooperation from some criminals in order to convict others, and plea bargaining is about the only tool that the prosecutor can legitimately employ to encourage cooperation. This results in what Professor Richman terms "inverted sentencing": "The more serious the defendant's crimes, the lower the sentence— because the greater his wrongs, the more information and assistance he has to offer a prosecutor." Richman, Cooperating Clients, 56 Ohio St.L.J. 69 (1995). Judge Bright, dissenting in United States v. Griffin, 17 F.3d 269 (8th Cir.1994), had this to say about the phenomenon of inverted sentencing:

> What kind of a criminal justice system rewards the drug kingpin or near-kingpin who informs on all the criminal colleagues he or she has recruited, but sends to prison for years and years the least knowledgeable or culpable conspirator, one who knows very little about the conspiracy and is without information for the prosecution?

Is inverted sentencing an indictment of the plea bargaining system? Or is it an inevitable consequence of the prosecutor's need for cooperation from criminals? If plea bargaining were abolished, what incentive would a criminal have to cooperate with the government by giving away information about his confederates?

G. PROBLEMS OF OVERCHARGING

Timing Questions: Bordenkircher v. Hayes

Not all plea bargaining involves settlements that look like a wonderful deal for the defendant. Consider, for example, Bordenkircher v. Hayes, 434 U.S. 357 (1978). Hayes was indicted by a Kentucky grand jury on a charge of uttering a forged instrument in the amount of $88.30, an offense punishable by 2–10 years imprisonment. During pre-trial negotiations, the prosecutor told Hayes that if he did not plead guilty and "save the court the inconvenience and necessity of a trial," the prosecutor would seek a new indictment under the then existing Kentucky Habitual Criminal Act, which carried a mandatory life sentence. Hayes chose not to plead guilty, was indicted under the Act and received a life sentence. The Supreme Court affirmed, holding that the decision whether to charge an offense rests with prosecutors and grand juries and that "a rigid constitutional rule that would prohibit a prosecutor from acting forthrightly in his dealings with the defense could only invite unhealthy subterfuge that would drive the practice of plea bargaining back into the shadows from which it has so recently emerged." In sum, the Court concluded that "this case would be no different if the grand jury had indicted Hayes as a recidivist from the outset, and the prosecutor had offered to drop that charge as part of the plea bargain."[3]

---

3. Although the government can use a bargain to induce a defendant to go to trial, it cannot use one to induce a witness' silence. See

Jones v. United States, 386 A.2d 308 (D.C.App. 1978). Can you see a distinction that you can defend?

Justice Blackmun, joined by Justices Brennan and Marshall, dissented. He disagreed with the Court's analysis that the timing of the indictment made no difference and suggested that prior to *Hayes* the Court "ha[d] never openly sanctioned such deliberate overcharging or taken such a cynical view of the bargaining process." He added that "[e]ven if overcharging is to be sanctioned, there are strong reasons of fairness why the charge should be presented at the beginning of the bargaining process, rather than as a filliped thread at the end." Justice Powell also dissented on the ground that the prosecutor effectively conceded that his strategy did not reflect the public interest in an appropriate sentence, but simply a desire to avoid trial even if the means of doing so was the imposition of an unreasonable sentence. Which view, if any, would you support?[4]

Three Strikes

Under federal law and the law of many states, a mandatory life sentence is imposed on a conviction for a specified felony, if the defendant has been twice previously convicted of certain specified felonies. How do these "three strikes and you're out" provisions affect plea bargaining for the first, second, and third offenses? Is the bargaining dynamic different at each offense? Some states structure their three strikes laws so that the prosecution *must* charge a "strike" felony if the facts support it. In these states, will more defendants refuse to plead guilty and go to trial on the assumption that they have nothing to lose? Or can the parties work "underground" by fudging the facts and agreeing to a charge that does not qualify as a strike?

II.   THE REQUIREMENTS FOR A VALID GUILTY PLEA

A.   DISTINGUISHING BARGAINING FROM THE PLEA PROCEDURE

Courts tend to distinguish the bargaining that takes place, which is largely unregulated as Bordenkircher v. Hayes illustrates, from the procedures surrounding the judicial acceptance of a guilty plea. These procedures have grown more formal over time. See, e.g., United States v. Livorsi, 180 F.3d 76 (2d Cir.1999) ("we examine critically even slight procedural deficiencies to ensure that the defendant's guilty plea was a voluntary and intelligent choice, and that none of the defendant's substantial rights have been compromised"). The unanswered question is whether the formality provides realistic protection for defendants or only trappings to persuade a watchful public that justice is being done.

B.   THE REQUIREMENT OF SOME KIND OF A RECORD

The Boykin Requirements

In two cases decided in 1969, McCarthy v. United States, 394 U.S. 459, and Boykin v. Alabama, 395 U.S. 238, the Supreme Court made it clear that a valid

---

4. In Corbitt v. New Jersey, 439 U.S. 212 (1978), the Court upheld a New Jersey statute that mandated life sentences for defendants convicted by a jury, but permitted lesser terms for those who pleaded guilty. The Court relied on Bordenkircher v. Hayes.

guilty plea requires "an intentional relinquishment or abandonment of a known right or privilege." This is because a defendant who pleads guilty is giving up the constitutional right to a fair trial before a jury, the right to be proven guilty of all elements of the crime beyond a reasonable doubt, the right to silence, and the right to confront adverse witnesses. The Court said that "[c]onsequently, if a defendant's guilty plea is not equally voluntary and knowing, it has been obtained in violation of due process and is therefore void."

In *McCarthy,* the Court set aside the guilty plea of a defendant who had pleaded to one count of a three count indictment charging wilful and knowing attempts to evade federal income tax payments. After discussing in dictum the constitutional requirements for a valid plea, the Court based its decision on Fed.R.Crim.P. 11, which sets forth procedural requirements for obtaining a valid guilty plea. The trial judge did not comply with the rule, because he failed both to ask the defendant whether he understood the nature of the charges against him and to inquire adequately into the voluntariness of the plea. The Court concluded that the defendant had to be afforded the opportunity to plead anew. Rule 11 was viewed as an attempt to avoid post-plea hearings on waiver, and the Court refused to remand the case for such a hearing into the intelligent and voluntary nature of McCarthy's plea. See also United States v. Andrades, 169 F.3d 131 (2d Cir.1999) (guilty plea invalidated where trial judge did not inform the defendant of the elements of the crime to which he pled guilty; it is not enough to simply read the barebones charge); United States v. Villalobos, 333 F.3d 1070 (9th Cir. 2003) (guilty plea invalidated where the defendant was not informed that the government at trial would have to prove to the jury beyond a reasonable doubt any quantity of drugs that would expose the defendant to a higher statutory maximum sentence, as such an amount of drugs constitutes an element of the crime).

Boykin v. Alabama overturned death sentences imposed on a 27 year old black man who pleaded guilty to five indictments charging common-law robbery. The Supreme Court said that "[i]t was error, plain on the face of the record, for the trial judge to accept petitioner's guilty plea without an affirmative showing that it was intelligent and voluntary." The Court held that it was impermissible to presume, on the basis of a silent record, a waiver of constitutional rights as important as the privilege against self-incrimination, trial by jury, and confrontation. Justice Harlan, joined by Justice Black, would have remanded for a hearing, apparently because the absence of a good record showing waiver did not establish that no constitutionally valid waiver took place.

Application of Boykin

Justice Harlan's dissent voices concern that *Boykin* "in effect fastens upon the States, as a matter of federal constitutional law, the rigid prophylactic requirements of Rule 11 of the Federal Rules of Criminal Procedure." *Boykin* itself did not tell the states exactly what to do, other than to develop a record relating to a guilty plea. Arguably, the *Boykin* majority at least wanted the judge to give the defendant a specific warning about the constitutional trial rights that the defendant will forego by pleading guilty. This interpretation often has been rejected by lower courts, however. See, e.g., United States v. Henry, 933 F.2d 553 (7th Cir.1991)(guilty plea held valid even though the defendant was not precisely informed of rights listed in *Boykin*; literal compliance with *Boykin* is not required, so long as the defendant understands that by pleading guilty, he waives his right to trial); United States v. Colston, 936 F.2d 312 (7th Cir. 1991)(when the judge described what would occur at trial, defendant who pleaded guilty must have known that he was waiving his right to confrontation).

Boykin's requirement of an explicit record has also been applied with some flexibility. Absence of an explicit record creates a presumption that the plea is invalid; but that presumption can be overcome by the government. See, e.g., United States v. Ferguson, 935 F.2d 862 (7th Cir.1991)(absence of transcript of guilty plea hearing is not fatal; the court relies on the custom, practice, and law applicable to guilty pleas in Illinois state courts, warranting a presumption that the defendant was informed of the necessary rights under *Boykin*).

Guilty Pleas Used for Enhancement of Sentence: Parke v. Raley

In Parke v. Raley, 506 U.S. 20 (1992), the Court considered the applicability of *Boykin* standards where guilty plea convictions are used to enhance punishment in subsequent cases. Raley was charged in 1986 with robbery and with being a repeat offender because he had pleaded guilty in 1979 and 1981 to two burglaries. Under Kentucky law, a presumption of regularity attaches to prior convictions resulting from guilty pleas, and an accused recidivist must produce evidence that his rights were infringed or that some other procedural irregularity occurred to render the conviction invalid. If the defendant produces such evidence, the burden shifts to the state to prove the actual validity of the prior conviction by a preponderance of the evidence. Raley argued that this procedure violated *Boykin* because it resulted in a presumption of a valid guilty plea from a silent record.

Justice O'Connor's opinion for the Court concluded that there was no tension between the Kentucky procedure and *Boykin*. She explained as follows:

> *Boykin* involved direct review of a conviction allegedly based upon an uninformed guilty plea. Respondent, however, never appealed his earlier convictions. They became final years ago, and he now seeks to revisit the question of their validity in a separate recidivism proceeding. To import *Boykin's* presumption of invalidity into this very different context would, in our view, improperly ignore another presumption deeply rooted in our jurisprudence: the "presumption of regularity" that attaches to final judgments, even when the question is waiver of constitutional rights.

Justice O'Connor also rejected Raley's policy argument that it was unfair to place on the defendant the burden of producing evidence that prior guilty pleas are invalid. Raley contended that a defendant would find it inordinately difficult to obtain information concerning a dated guilty plea hearing. Justice O'Connor responded that a rule placing the entire burden on the state to prove the validity of a conviction would force the state "to expend considerable effort and expense attempting to reconstruct records from far-flung states where procedures are unfamiliar and memories are unreliable." Justice O'Connor noted that federal courts of appeals have allocated the full burden of proof (not just a burden of production) on defendants who claim that an invalid guilty plea renders a prior conviction invalid for purposes of calculating criminal history under the Federal Sentencing Guidelines. See United States v. Boyer, 931 F.2d 1201 (7th Cir.1991).

Attacking a State Guilty Plea Conviction in
Federal Court: Custis v. United States

When a federal defendant's sentence would be enhanced due to a prior guilty plea conviction rendered in state court, can the defendant attack the state conviction in federal court on the ground that it was obtained in violation of *Boykin*? This question was addressed by the Court in *Custis v. United States*, 511 U.S. 485 (1994). Custis was given an enhanced sentence under the Armed Career Criminal Act (18 U.S.C. § 924(e)) on the basis of having three previous state convictions "for a violent felony or a serious drug offense." At the sentencing hearing, Custis sought to collaterally attack one of his prior state convictions on the ground that his guilty plea was not knowing and intelligent as required by *Boykin*. The Court, in an opinion by Chief Justice Rehnquist, held that Custis had no statutory or constitutional right to collaterally attack a prior state conviction at his federal sentencing hearing, unless the prior conviction was obtained in the complete absence of counsel in violation of Gideon v. Wainright. The Chief Justice distinguished a collateral attack for absence of counsel from a collateral attack for an invalid guilty plea on the basis that the former defect is "jurisdictional" while the latter is not. He also noted that "ease of administration" and principles of finality supported the distinction:

> [F]ailure to appoint counsel at all will generally appear from the judgment roll itself, or from an accompanying minute order. But determination of claims of * * * failure to assure that a guilty plea was voluntary, would require sentencing courts to rummage through frequently nonexistent or difficult to obtain state court transcripts or records that may date from another era, and may come from any one of the 50 States.

Justice Souter, joined by Justices Blackmun and Stevens, dissented in *Custis*. He saw no constitutional distinction between a collateral attack based on the absence of counsel and a collateral attack based on an invalid guilty plea. He noted that the guilty plea claim, "if meritorious, would mean that the defendant was convicted despite invalid waivers of at least one of two Sixth Amendment rights (to trial by jury and to confront adverse witnesses) or of a Fifth Amendment right (against compulsory self-incrimination)."

C. VOLUNTARY AND INTELLIGENT PLEAS AND THE ADVANTAGES OF A COMPLETE RECORD

1. A Voluntary Plea

To be valid, a guilty plea must be voluntary; that is, it must not be the product of improper coercion by government officials. The standard of voluntariness is similar to that employed in connection with confessions, a standard that was examined in Chapter Three, supra. As the Supreme Court said in Brady v. United States, discussed supra, "the agents of the State may not produce a plea by actual or threatened physical harm or by mental coercion overbearing the will of the defendant." Thus, it is clear that if a defendant were threatened with physical torture or actually harmed as part of an effort to get him to plead guilty, any resulting plea would be involuntary. Most challenges to guilty pleas do not raise these kinds of claims, however. Unlike the interrogation process, the procedure for accepting pleas affords opportunities for trial judges to see whether a defendant is apparently exercising free will in choosing to plead. Still, some sophisticated questions of validity of guilty pleas have arisen under the rubric of voluntariness.

Package Deals

Suppose a prosecutor in a multi-defendant case proposes a global settlement: all the defendants can plead to specified crimes, but that they must plead guilty as a group; if all the defendants do not agree, the deal is off.[5] Does a "wired" plea or "package deal" present a greater risk of coercion than an individual plea? In United States v. Pollard, 959 F.2d 1011 (D.C.Cir.1992), the defendant pleaded guilty to one count of conspiracy to deliver national defense information to the Government of Israel. He later claimed that the government coerced his guilty plea by linking his wife's plea to his own, especially since his wife was seriously ill at the time. But the court rejected his argument:

> To say that a practice is "coercive" or renders a plea "involuntary" means only that it creates improper pressure that would be likely to overbear the will of some innocent persons and cause them to plead guilty. Only physical harm, threats of harassment, misrepresentation, or promises that are by their nature improper as having no proper relationship to the prosecutor's business (e.g., bribes) render a guilty plea legally involuntary. * * *

> * * * We must be mindful * * * that if the judiciary were to declare wired pleas unconstitutional, the consequences would not be altogether foreseeable and perhaps would not be beneficial to defendants. Would Pollard, for instance, have been better off had he not been able to bargain to aid his wife? Would his wife have been better off? Would the bargaining take place in any event, but with winks and nods rather than in writing?

> Nor do we believe that Mrs. Pollard's medical condition makes an otherwise acceptable linkage of their pleas unconstitutional. The appropriate dividing line between acceptable and unconstitutional plea wiring does not depend upon the physical condition or personal circumstances of the defendant; rather, it depends upon the conduct of the government. Where, as here, the government had probable cause to arrest and prosecute both defendants in a related crime, and there is no suggestion that the government conducted itself in bad faith in an effort to generate additional leverage over the defendant, we think a wired plea is constitutional.

Pollard considered the problem of a defendant "pressured" because of feelings toward the person to whom his plea is linked. The court in United States v. Caro, 997 F.2d 657 (9th Cir.1993), considered a different problem that might be created by wired pleas—the possibility of coercion by other defendants. Caro moved to set aside his guilty plea on the ground that he was pressured by his codefendants into going along with the deal. At the hearing in which his plea

5. Such a package plea bargain was employed in a case in which Aldrich Ames, the CIA agent turned spy, and his wife pleaded guilty; Ames received life in prison without parole, while his wife received less than 5 years and got to keep much of the couple's property. See Liebman and Snyder, Joint Guilty Pleas:

"Group Justice" In Federal Plea Bargaining, N.Y.L.J., Sept.8, 1994, p.1, col.1 (discussing the Ames case and noting that for the government, "group pleas dispose of cases in one fell swoop and thereby conserve scarce prosecutorial resources and, in some cases, avoid lengthy, costly or potentially embarrassing trials").

was entered, the judge was never informed that Caro's plea was part of a group settlement. Judge Kozinski analyzed the problem as follows:

> Though package deal plea agreements are not per se impermissible, they pose an additional risk of coercion not present when the defendant is dealing with the government alone. Quite possibly, one defendant will be happier with the package deal than his codefendants; looking out for his own interests, the lucky one may try to force his codefendants into going along with the deal. * * * We * * * have recognized that the trial court should make a more careful examination of the voluntariness of a plea when it might have been induced by threats or promises from a third party. We make it clear today that, in describing a plea agreement * * * the prosecutor must alert the district court to the fact that codefendants are entering into a package deal.[6]

The court, holding that the trial court's error was not harmless, vacated Caro's guilty plea and remanded. Compare United States v. Carr, 80 F.3d 413 (10th Cir.1996) (pressures of cohorts to accept a package deal "might have been palpable" to the defendant, but they did not vitiate the voluntariness of his plea because "it was still his choice to make").

Also note that the court in *Pollard* emphasized that a package plea would be coercive if the case against one of the defendants was especially weak and that person was indicted in order to put pressure on the other defendants (e.g., indicting the defendant, against whom the evidence is strong, and his child, against whom the evidence is particularly weak, and offering a package plea bargain).

Can the Defendant Voluntarily Waive the Right to Disclosure of Information That Could Be Used to Impeach Government Witnesses or for Affirmative Defenses? United States v. Ruiz

In the following case, the Court adhered to its position that the free market principles behind plea bargaining generally permit criminal defendants to voluntarily waive rights that could be invoked at trial.

UNITED STATES v. RUIZ

Supreme Court of the United States, 2002.
536 U.S. 622.

JUSTICE BREYER delivered the opinion of the Court.

In this case we primarily consider whether the Fifth and Sixth Amendments require federal prosecutors, before entering into a binding plea agreement with a criminal defendant, to disclose "impeachment information relating to any informants or other witnesses." We hold that the Constitution does not require that disclosure.

I

After immigration agents found 30 kilograms of marijuana in Angela Ruiz's luggage, federal prosecutors offered her what is known in the Southern District of California as a "fast

---

6. Professor Green, in "Package" Plea Bargaining and the Prosecutor's Duty of Good Faith, 25 Crim.L.Bull. 507 (1989), argues that prosecutors who offer multi-defendant deals have an ethical responsibility to avoid overreaching.

track" plea bargain. That bargain—standard in that district—asks a defendant to waive indictment, trial, and an appeal. In return, the Government agrees to recommend to the sentencing judge a two-level departure downward from the otherwise applicable United States Sentencing Guidelines sentence. In Ruiz's case, a two-level departure downward would have shortened the ordinary Guidelines-specified 18–to–24–month sentencing range by 6 months, to 12–to–18 months.

The prosecutors' proposed plea agreement contains a set of detailed terms. Among other things, it specifies that "any [known] information establishing the factual innocence of the defendant" "has been turned over to the defendant," and it acknowledges the Government's "continuing duty to provide such information." At the same time it requires that the defendant "waiv[e] the right" to receive "impeachment information relating to any informants or other witnesses" as well as the right to receive information supporting any affirmative defense the defendant raises if the case goes to trial. Because Ruiz would not agree to this last-mentioned waiver, the prosecutors withdrew their bargaining offer. The Government then indicted Ruiz for unlawful drug possession. And despite the absence of any agreement, Ruiz ultimately pleaded guilty.

At sentencing, Ruiz asked the judge to grant her the same two-level downward departure that the Government would have recommended had she accepted the "fast track" agreement. The Government opposed her request, and the District Court denied it, imposing a standard Guideline sentence instead.

* * * Ruiz appealed her sentence to the United States Court of Appeals for the Ninth Circuit. The Ninth Circuit vacated the District Court's sentencing determination. The Ninth Circuit

pointed out that the Constitution requires prosecutors to make certain impeachment information available to a defendant before trial. It decided that this obligation entitles defendants to receive that same information before they enter into a plea agreement. The Ninth Circuit also decided that the Constitution prohibits defendants from waiving their right to that information. And it held that the prosecutors' standard "fast track" plea agreement was unlawful because it insisted upon that waiver. * * *

The Government sought certiorari. It stressed what it considered serious adverse practical implications of the Ninth Circuit's constitutional holding. And it added that the holding is unique among courts of appeals. We granted the Government's petition.

II

* * *

III

The constitutional question concerns a federal criminal defendant's waiver of the right to receive from prosecutors exculpatory impeachment material—a right that the Constitution provides as part of its basic "fair trial" guarantee. * * *

In this case, the Ninth Circuit in effect held that a guilty plea is not "voluntary" (and that the defendant could not, by pleading guilty, waive his right to a fair trial) unless the prosecutors first made the same disclosure of material impeachment information that the prosecutors would have had to make had the defendant insisted upon a trial. We must decide whether the Constitution requires that preguilty plea disclosure of impeachment information. We conclude that it does not.

First, impeachment information is special in relation to the *fairness of a trial,* not in respect to whether a plea is *voluntary* ("knowing," "intelligent," and "sufficient[ly] aware"). Of course, the more information the defendant has, the more aware he is of the likely consequences of a plea, waiver, or decision, and the wiser that decision will likely be. But the Constitution does not require the prosecutor to share all useful information with the defendant. And the law ordinarily considers a waiver knowing, intelligent, and sufficiently aware if the defendant fully understands the nature of the right and how it would likely apply *in general* in the circumstances—even though the defendant may not know the *specific detailed* consequences of invoking it. A defendant, for example, may waive his right to remain silent, his right to a jury trial, or his right to counsel even if the defendant does not know the specific questions the authorities intend to ask, who will likely serve on the jury, or the particular lawyer the State might otherwise provide.

It is particularly difficult to characterize impeachment information as critical information of which the defendant must always be aware prior to pleading guilty given the random way in which such information may, or may not, help a particular defendant. The degree of help that impeachment information can provide will depend upon the defendant's own independent knowledge of the prosecution's potential case—a matter that the Constitution does not require prosecutors to disclose.

Second, we have found no legal authority embodied either in this Court's past cases or in cases from other circuits that provide significant support for the Ninth Circuit's decision. To the contrary, this Court has found that the Constitution, in respect to a defendant's awareness of relevant circumstances, does not require complete knowledge of the relevant circumstances, but permits a court to accept a guilty plea, with its accompanying waiver of various constitutional rights, despite various forms of misapprehension under which a defendant might labor. See Brady v. United States, (defendant "misapprehended the quality of the State's case", misapprehended "the likely penalties" and failed to "anticipate a change in the law regarding" relevant "punishments"); McMann v. Richardson, 397 U.S. 759, 770 (1970) (counsel "misjudged the admissibility" of a "confession"); United States v. Broce, 488 U.S. 563, 573 (1989) (counsel failed to point out a potential defense); Tollett v. Henderson, 411 U.S. 258, 267 (1973) (counsel failed to find a potential constitutional infirmity in grand jury proceedings). It is difficult to distinguish, in terms of importance, (1) a defendant's ignorance of grounds for impeachment of potential witnesses at a possible future trial from (2) the varying forms of ignorance at issue in these cases.

Third, due process considerations, the very considerations that led this Court to find trial-related rights to exculpatory and impeachment information, argue against the existence of the "right" that the Ninth Circuit found here. This Court has said that due process considerations include not only (1) the nature of the private interest at stake, but also (2) the value of the additional safeguard, and (3) the adverse impact of the requirement upon the Government's interests. Here, as we have just pointed out, the added value of the Ninth Circuit's "right" to a defendant is often limited, for it depends upon the defendant's independent awareness of the details of the Government's case. And in any case, as the proposed plea agreement at issue here specifies, the Government will provide "any information establishing the factual innocence of the defendant" regardless. That fact, along with other guilty-plea safeguards, see Fed. Rule Crim. Proc. 11, diminishes the force of Ruiz's concern that, in the absence of impeachment information, innocent individuals, accused of crimes, will plead guilty.

At the same time, a constitutional obligation to provide impeachment information during plea bargaining, prior to entry of a guilty plea, could seriously interfere with the Government's interest in securing those guilty pleas that are factually justified, desired by defendants, and help to secure the efficient administration of justice. The Ninth Circuit's rule risks premature disclosure of Government witness information, which, the Government tells us, could "disrupt ongoing investigations" and expose prospective witnesses to serious harm. Cf. Amendments to Federal Rules of Criminal Procedure: Hearings before the Subcommittee on Criminal Justice of the House Committee on the Judiciary, 94th Cong., 1st Sess., 92 (1975) (statement of John C. Keney, Acting Assistant Attorney General, Criminal Div., Dept. of Justice) (opposing mandated witness disclosure three days before trial because of documented instances of witness intimidation). And the careful tailoring that characterizes most legal Government witness disclosure requirements suggests recognition by both Congress and the Federal Rules Committees that such concerns are valid.

Consequently, the Ninth Circuit's requirement could force the Government to abandon its "general practice" of not "disclos[ing] to a defendant pleading guilty information that would reveal the identities of cooperating informants, undercover investigators, or other prospective witnesses." It could require the Government to devote substantially more resources to trial preparation prior to plea bargaining, thereby depriving the plea-bargaining process of its main resource-saving advantages. Or it could lead the Government instead to abandon its heavy reliance upon plea bargaining in a vast number—90% or more—of federal criminal cases. We cannot say that the Constitution's due process requirement demands so radical a change in the criminal justice process in order to achieve so comparatively small a constitutional benefit.

These considerations, taken together, lead us to conclude that the Constitution does not require the Government to disclose material impeachment evidence prior to entering a plea agreement with a criminal defendant.

In addition, we note that the "fast track" plea agreement requires a defendant to waive her right to receive information the Government has regarding any "affirmative defense" she raises at trial. We do not believe the Constitution here requires provision of this information to the defendant prior to plea bargaining—for most (though not all) of the reasons previously stated. That is to say, in the context of this agreement, the need for this information is more closely related to the *fairness* of a trial than to the *voluntariness* of the plea; the value in terms of the defendant's added awareness of relevant circumstances is ordinarily limited; yet the added burden imposed upon the Government by requiring its provision well in advance of trial (often before trial preparation begins) can be serious, thereby significantly interfering with the administration of the plea bargaining process.

For these reasons the decision of the Court of Appeals for the Ninth Circuit is

Reversed.

[The opinion of Justice Thomas, concurring in the judgment, is omitted.]

2. A Knowing and Intelligent Plea

Knowledge of the Elements of the Crime: Henderson v. Morgan

In Henderson v. Morgan, 426 U.S. 637 (1976), a 19 year old defendant, with substantially less than average intelligence, pleaded guilty to second degree murder after he was advised by counsel that a 25 year sentence would be imposed. The defendant had been indicted for first degree murder as a result of stabbing to death a woman who employed him while he was on release from a state school for the mentally disabled. The stabbing took place when she discovered him in her room at night trying to get his wages so that he could leave the premises unnoticed. The defendant was never informed that an intent to cause the victim's death was an element of second degree murder. The Court held the plea involuntary, even though it assumed that the defendant's lawyers would have given the defendant the same advice—i.e., to plead guilty—and even if, having been informed of the elements of the crime, he would have pleaded anyway. The Court declared that a guilty plea cannot be valid unless the defendant knows the nature of the offense to which he pleads. In its footnote 18, the Court assumed that notice of a charge did not always require a description of every element of an offense, but said that "intent is such a critical element of the offense of second-degree murder that notice of that element is required."[7]

Applying Henderson v. Morgan

Under Henderson, it is normally presumed that the defendant is informed by his attorney of the charges against him and the elements of those charges. See Oppel v. Meachum, 851 F.2d 34 (2d Cir.1988). Furthermore, testimony of an accused's counsel that it is his standard practice to advise his clients of the elements of the charged offense and potential defenses has been held sufficient to defeat a due process challenge. United States v. Butcher, 926 F.2d 811 (9th Cir.1991).

Henderson establishes that a defendant must know about some "crucial" elements of the offense to which the guilty plea is addressed. What else must a defendant know? Generally, a defendant must know the penalty that can be imposed. See, e.g., United States v. Goins, 51 F.3d 400 (4th Cir.1995)(guilty plea invalid where defendant was not made aware that he was subjecting himself to a mandatory minimum sentence of five years). Is a general idea of the maximum penalty enough? If the defendant is to understand the potential consequences of pleading, the general rule should be that a defendant must know whether several counts or indictments will produce concurrent or consecutive sentences. See ABA Standards, Pleas of Guilty, § 11–1.4 (requiring such an understanding).

On the other hand, a guilty plea can be voluntary even though the defendant has not been informed with precision of potential punishments under

---

7. Justice White, joined by Justices Stewart, Blackmun, and Powell, concurred and emphasized that the decision whether or not to plead to a specific offense is the defendant's alone, not his lawyer's. Justice Rehnquist, joined by Chief Justice Burger, dissented.

[Handwritten margin note top: But con be voluntary w/o accurate penalty if Pros does not have enough evi. to determine]

the Sentencing Guidelines. This is because, at the time of the plea allocution, the court "frequently has too little information available to provide defendant with an accurate sentencing range. For example, probation department officials often have not scored or researched defendant's criminal history, and the court is unaware of upward of downward departure motions that the government or defense counsel may pursue." United States v. Andrades, 169 F.3d 131 (2d Cir.1999).

[Handwritten margin note: here held Δ knew elements when Judge read Δ elements of more serious offense than pled.]

Is a plea knowing and voluntary when the judge explains the elements of a more severe offense but the defendant pleads to a lesser offense? In United States v. Wildes, 910 F.2d 1484 (7th Cir.1990), the court held that the defendant's guilty plea to aiding and abetting delivery of marijuana was not rendered invalid when the trial court recited more complex elements of the party to crime offense rather than the elements of the aiding and abetting offense prior to accepting the defendant's guilty plea. The court emphasized that the defendant never stated that he did not know the elements of an aiding and abetting offense. Did the defendant really know the crucial elements of the offense?

Most decisions distinguish knowledge of sentence possibilities from knowledge of "collateral consequences." For example, most courts do not require that a defendant be told of the possibility (or even of a mandatory requirement) of deportation following conviction. See Vizcarra–Delgadillo v. United States, 395 F.2d 70 (9th Cir.1968) (Browning, J., dissenting). Most do not require that a defendant be told about the possibility of future prosecution under a multiple offender (or habitual or repeat offender) law, of the loss of driver's license, of the loss of business opportunities, of parole revocation, or of parole generally. See generally Note, Guilty Plea Bargains and Compromises By Prosecutor to Secure Guilty Pleas, 112 U.Pa.L.Rev. 865 (1964). Can you see any practical problems that would arise if a guilty plea could be invalidated whenever the defendant did not receive information about collateral consequences?

Pleading to Something That Is Not a Crime: Bousley v. United States

[Handwritten margin note: plead to drugs + using gun during drug crime. Gov interp of using was wide @ time. S.C. interps using as brandish or shoot. Δ challenged plea]

The Court in Bousley v. United States, 523 U.S. 614 (1998), considered the problem of a defendant who pleaded guilty to a violation of a criminal statute that was later held not to cover his conduct. Bousley pleaded guilty to drug crimes, as well as to a violation of a federal statute that prohibited "using" a firearm during the course of a drug transaction. At the time he pleaded guilty to the firearms offense, the local federal courts had construed "using" expansively to cover basically any situation in which a defendant possessed a gun during the course of a drug offense. Bousley appealed his sentence, but did not challenge his guilty plea on direct appeal. His sentence was affirmed. Thereafter, the Supreme Court determined that the term "using" in the statute meant some kind of active use, such as brandishing or shooting. Bousley sought a writ of habeas corpus challenging the factual basis for his guilty plea on the ground that neither the "evidence" nor the "plea allocution" showed a "connection between the firearms in the bedroom of the house, and the garage, where the drug trafficking occurred."

The Supreme Court, in an opinion by Chief Justice Rehnquist for six Justices, held that Bousley would be entitled to a hearing on the merits of his

[Handwritten footer note: neither evidence nor plea allocution showed connection to using gun.]

involuntary guilty plea claim, if he could make the showing necessary to relieve the procedural default resulting from his failure to directly appeal his guilty plea. (On the question of procedural default, see the discussion of this case in Chapter 13). Addressing the question of whether Bousley's guilty plea could be considered voluntary and intelligent under the circumstances, the Chief Justice declared:

> A plea of guilty is constitutionally valid only to the extent it is "voluntary" and "intelligent." Brady v. United States, 397 U.S. 742 (1970). We have long held that a plea does not qualify as intelligent unless a criminal defendant first receives "real notice of the true nature of the charge against him, the first and most universally recognized requirement of due process." Smith v. O'Grady, 312 U.S. 329 (1941). [It is contended] that petitioner's plea was intelligently made because, prior to pleading guilty, he was provided with a copy of his indictment, which charged him with "using" a firearm. Such circumstances, standing alone, give rise to a presumption that the defendant was informed of the nature of the charge against him. Henderson v. Morgan. Petitioner nonetheless maintains that his guilty plea was unintelligent because the District Court subsequently misinformed him as to the elements of [the firearms] offense. In other words, petitioner contends that the record reveals that neither he, nor his counsel, nor the court correctly understood the essential elements of the crime with which he was charged. Were this contention proven, petitioner's plea would be * * * constitutionally invalid.

> Our decisions in Brady v. United States, supra, McMann v. Richardson, 397 U.S. 759 (1970), and Parker v. North Carolina, 397 U.S. 790 (1970) * * * are not to the contrary. Each of those cases involved a criminal defendant who pleaded guilty after being correctly informed as to the essential nature of the charge against him. Those defendants later attempted to challenge their guilty pleas when it became evident that they had misjudged the strength of the Government's case or the penalties to which they were subject. For example, Brady, who pleaded guilty to kidnaping, maintained that his plea was neither voluntary nor intelligent because it was induced by a death penalty provision later held unconstitutional. We rejected Brady's voluntariness argument, explaining that a "plea of guilty entered by one fully aware of the direct consequences" of the plea is voluntary in a constitutional sense "unless induced by threats ..., misrepresentation ..., or perhaps by promises that are by their nature improper as having no proper relationship to the prosecutor's business." We further held that Brady's plea was intelligent because, although later judicial decisions indicated that at the time of his plea he "did not correctly assess every relevant factor entering into his decision," he was advised by competent counsel, was in control of his mental faculties, and "was made aware of the nature of the charge against him." In this case, by contrast, petitioner asserts that he was misinformed as to the true nature of the charge against him.

The Court remanded for a determination of whether Bousley could overcome his procedural default, whereupon he would receive a hearing on the merits of his invalid guilty plea claim.

Justice Stevens wrote a separate opinion concurring on the guilty plea question. He elaborated upon the Court's analysis in the following passage:

> [W]hen petitioner was advised by the trial judge, by his own lawyer, and by the prosecutor that mere possession of a firearm would support a conviction under [the firearms statute], he received critically incorrect legal advice. The fact that all of his advisers acted in good-faith reliance on existing precedent does not mitigate the impact of that erroneous advice. Its consequences for petitioner were just as severe, and just as unfair, as if the court and counsel had knowingly conspired to deceive him in order to induce him to plead guilty to a crime that he did not commit. Our cases make it perfectly clear that a guilty plea based on such misinformation is constitutionally invalid.

Justice Scalia, joined by Justice Thomas, dissented, arguing that procedural defaults in the context of guilty pleas should never be excusable. In Justice Scalia's view, Bousley's failure to appeal his guilty plea was fatal to his claim for habeas relief. The procedural default questions arising in *Bousley* are taken up in detail in Chapter 13.

3. Competency to Plead Guilty

The validity of a guilty plea is also dependent on whether the defendant is competent to make a plea. That the "competence" factor is distinct from the "knowing and intelligent" factor was made plain by the Court in Godinez v. Moran, 509 U.S. 389 (1993). One question in *Moran* was whether the competency standard for pleading guilty is higher than the competency standard for standing trial. The competency standard for standing trial is met when the defendant is able to consult with his lawyer "with a reasonable degree of rational understanding" and has "a rational as well as factual understanding of the proceedings against him." Dusky v. United States, 362 U.S. 402 (1960). The lower court in *Moran* had held that this "rational understanding" test was insufficient to determine whether Moran was competent to plead guilty, because the decision to plead guilty required the appreciation of alternatives; that court concluded that a person cannot be competent to plead guilty unless he has the capacity to make a "reasoned choice" among the alternatives available to him.

The Supreme Court, in an opinion by Justice Thomas, rejected the lower court's position and held that the "rational understanding" test that defines competency to stand trial also defines competency to plead guilty. The Court found that the decisionmaking process attendant to standing trial was at least as complex and demanding as that required to plead guilty. Justice Thomas explained as follows:

> A defendant who stands trial is likely to be presented with choices that entail relinquishment of the same rights that are relinquished by a defendant who pleads guilty. He will ordinarily have to decide whether to waive his privilege against compulsory self-incrimination, by taking the witness stand; if the option is available, he may have to decide whether to waive his right to trial by jury; and in consultation with counsel, he may have to decide whether to waive his right to face his accusers, by declining to cross-examine witnesses for the prosecution. In consultation with his attorney, he may be called upon to decide, among other things, whether (and how) to put on a defense and whether to raise one or more affirmative defenses. In sum,

all criminal defendants—not merely those who plead guilty—may be required to make important decisions once criminal proceedings have been initiated. And while the decision to plead guilty is undeniably a profound one, it is no more complicated than the sum total of decisions that a defendant may be called upon to make during the course of a trial. * * * This being so, we can conceive of no basis for demanding a higher level of competence for those defendants who plead guilty. If the *Dusky* standard is adequate for defendants who plead not guilty, it is necessarily adequate for those who plead guilty.

Justice Thomas stressed, however, that competence was not the only requirement for a valid guilty plea. He explained as follows:

> A finding that a defendant is competent to stand trial, however, is not all that is necessary before he may be permitted to plead guilty * * * [A] trial court must [also] satisfy itself that the waiver of his constitutional rights is knowing and voluntary. In this sense there is a "heightened" standard for pleading guilty * * *, but it is not a heightened standard of competence.

Justice Kennedy, joined by Justice Scalia, concurred in part and in the judgment. He noted the difficulty that would result from applying different standards of competency at various stages of a criminal proceeding:

> The standard applicable at a given point in a trial could be difficult to ascertain. For instance, if a defendant decides to change his plea to guilty after a trial has commenced, one court might apply the competency standard for undergoing trial while another court might use the standard for pleading guilty. In addition, the subtle nuances among different standards are likely to be difficult to differentiate, as evidenced by the lack of any clear distinction between a "rational understanding" and a "reasoned choice" in this case.[8]

4. Secret Promises

Blackledge v. Allison, 431 U.S. 63 (1977), illustrates the problems that can arise when the court does not follow strict procedures in reviewing a plea bargain. Allison pleaded guilty to attempted robbery in a North Carolina state court. The trial court judge read questions to Allison from a printed form.

Three days after answering the questions, Allison was sentenced to 17–21 years in prison. He sought habeas corpus relief to attack his conviction, alleging that he was told by counsel that the trial judge told counsel that Allison would only get 10 years if he pleaded guilty. The Court noted that "[t]he litany of form questions * * * nowhere indicated to Allison (or indeed to the lawyers involved) that plea bargaining was a legitimate practice that could be freely disclosed in open court. * * * The process thus did nothing to dispel a defendant's belief that any bargain struck must remain concealed." Thus, the Court held that Allison had a right to have his claim heard. Justice Powell concurred and stated that the case was "an example * * * of how finality can be frustrated by failure to adhere to proper procedures at the trial court level."[9]

---

8. Justice Blackmun, joined by Justice Stevens, dissented in *Morrow.*

9. Chief Justice Burger concurred in the judgment. Justice Rehnquist did not participate in the decision of the case.

D. REGULATING GUILTY PLEAS UNDER FEDERAL RULE 11

1. Procedural Requirements of the Rule

Fed.R.Crim.P. 11 sets forth detailed procedural requirements to assure that defendants who plead guilty are informed of their rights and that the guilty plea is fairly rendered.[10] Subdivision (b)(1) provides that the court must "address the defendant personally in open court and inform the defendant" of, and determine that the defendant understands, the following:

(A) the government's right, in a prosecution for perjury or false statement, to use against the defendant any statement that the defendant gives under oath;

(B) the right to plead not guilty, or having already so pleaded, to persist in that plea;

(C) the right to a jury trial;

(D) the right to be represented by counsel—and if necessary have the court appoint counsel—at trial and at every other stage of the proceeding;

(E) the right at trial to confront and cross-examine adverse witnesses, to be protected from compelled self-incrimination, to testify and present evidence, and to compel the attendance of witnesses;

(F) the defendant's waiver of these trial rights if the court accepts a plea of guilty or nolo contendere;

(G) the nature of each charge to which the defendant is pleading;

(H) any maximum possible penalty, including imprisonment, fine, and term of supervised release;

(I) any mandatory minimum penalty;

(J) any applicable forfeiture;

(K) the court's authority to order restitution;

(L) the court's obligation to impose a special assessment;

(M) the court's obligation to apply the Sentencing Guidelines, and the court's discretion to depart from those guidelines under some circumstances; and

(N) the terms of any plea-agreement provision waiving the right to appeal or to collaterally attack the sentence.

Subdivision (b)(2) of Rule 11 requires the court to "determine that the plea is voluntary and did not result from force, threats or promises (other than promises in a plea agreement)." See United States v. Smith, 184 F.3d 415 (5th Cir.1999) (Rule 11 violation where judge did not specifically inform the defendant of the elements of the crime and did not personally ask the defendant if his plea was voluntary); United States v. Damon, 191 F.3d 561 (4th Cir. 1999) (Rule 11 violation where the judge, after being informed that the defendant was under medication after a suicide attempt, failed to inquire into the effect that the medication may have had on the defendant's ability to make a voluntary plea and to understand the consequences: "The plea colloquy required by Rule 11

---

10. In United States v. Timmreck, 441 U.S. 780 (1979), Justice Stevens' opinion for a unanimous court established that a conviction based on a guilty plea cannot be collaterally attacked for a Rule 11 violation, unless the violation is constitutional or jurisdictional.

must be conducted with some flexibility. If a defendant's response to a court's question indicates the need for clarification, follow-up questions must be asked. Otherwise, the Rule 11 colloquy would be reduced to a formalistic ritual, stripped of its purpose.'').

Rule 11(b)(3) provides that the court must assure itself that there is a factual basis for the guilty plea. See, e.g., United States v. Camacho, 233 F.3d 1308 (11th Cir. 2000) (district court satisfied its obligation of ensuring that there was an adequate factual basis for the defendant's guilty plea to a charge of possessing cocaine with intent to distribute, even though it did not explain or discuss directly the significance of the aiding and abetting theory set forth in the indictment; the court could conclude from the proffered facts that someone had knowingly possessed cocaine with intent to distribute and that the defendant had intentionally arranged for the acquisition of the cocaine, thereby committing an act that contributed to and furthered the unlawful possession.).

Rule 11(c) provides that the prosecution and the defendant can enter into any of three agreements: (A) agreement not to bring or to dismiss charges; (B) recommendation, or agreement not to oppose the defendant's request, to the judge, "that a particular sentence or sentencing range is appropriate or that a particular provision of the Sentencing Guidelines, or policy statement, or sentencing factor does or does not apply"–with the understanding that the recommendation or request *does not bind the court*; or (C) agreement between the parties "that a specific sentence or sentencing range is the appropriate disposition of the case." Rule 11(c) provides further that the court "must not participate" in the discussions leading to a plea agreement.

Plea Colloquies Under Rule 11

United States v. Bachynsky, 934 F.2d 1349 (5th Cir.1991)(en banc), analyzes the various approaches taken by federal circuits to plea colloquies that fail to satisfy Rule 11. It defined the issue before it and summarized its conclusion as follows:

> Today we consider whether there may be circumstances under which the harmless error provision of Rule 11(h), * * * obviates the need to vacate a plea of guilty or nolo contendere even though, during the plea colloquy specified in Rule 11 for determining the defendant's understanding of the maximum possible penalty provided by law, the district court fails totally to mention or explain the effect of any supervised release term to which the defendant is exposed. For the reasons set forth below, we respond affirmatively, concluding that a district court's total failure during the plea colloquy to mention or explain the effect of supervised release does not constitute a total failure to address a Rule 11 core concern, and thus does not automatically mandate reversal. Consequently, when a total failure to address supervised release is determined to constitute only a partial failure to address a core concern of Rule 11, the door is open to a determination of whether the district court's failure to explain the effects of supervised release affected the substantial rights of the defendant. * * *

The defendant was a Ph.D.–M.D. who pleaded guilty to racketeering and a tax conspiracy. The scheme giving rise to the convictions involved weight loss and smoking cessation clinics in which unnecessary medical tests were conducted for which insurance companies were billed. The defendant's plea agreement stated that he was aware of the maximum sentences for both charges to which he pleaded and that he could be sentenced to the maximum sentence allowable under the law. At the plea hearing, the district court explained the nature of the charges and the maximum penalties, but did not explain supervised release or advise the defendant that his sentence could or would include a term of supervised release. The defendant was sentenced to 121 months imprisonment and three years of supervised release.

The court of appeals reasoned that, even if supervised release were considered to be the equivalent of prison, and even if it assumed that the three years or 36 months of such release could be extended to five years and would be revoked so that the defendant would spend every day of the sentence (including the supervised release portion) incarcerated, the total sentence was less than the maximum sentence that could have been imposed. It concluded that "the core concern * * * is that the defendant understand the consequences of his plea," and that, once the district court explains the statutory maxima for offenses, a failure to inform a defendant of supervised release is a partial failure to address a core concern.

On the facts of the case, the en banc court found harmless error. It warned that "[o]ur decision today should be viewed by this circuit's criminal defense bar as a caution not to 'lie behind the log' in hopes of getting a second bite at the plea bargain apple when and if counsel should notice an inadvertent omission in the district court's plea colloquy," and that "our decision should not be interpreted by prosecutors or district courts as a signal to relax their dedication to total compliance with all provisions of Fed.R.Crim.P. 11, particularly those of section (b)(1)." It added that "this court has no intention of abdicating its obligation to scrutinize plea colloquies for adherence to Rule 11."

Later, in United States v. Bounds, 943 F.2d 541 (5th Cir.1991), the court was presented with the problem that did not exist in Bachynsky: the aggregate amount of supervised release and actual prison sentence imposed exceeded the statutory maximum explained to the defendant. The lower court informed the defendant of a twenty-five year maximum, whereas he actually received a twenty-five year prison sentence plus three years of supervised release. Accordingly, the Court of Appeals found a violation of a "core concern" of Rule 11. The question was what remedy to apply. The court noted that one possible remedy would be to remove the supervised release period and uphold the plea. But the court found that not possible where, as here, the statute under which the defendant pleaded required the imposition of supervised release. Therefore, the court reversed the conviction and vacated the sentence, giving the defendant leave to plead anew. See also United States v. Hekimain, 975 F.2d 1098 (5th Cir.1992)(plea vacated where court fails to tell the defendant that he is subject to an upward departure under the Sentencing Guidelines).

Should defense counsel be required in all cases to submit to the court a statement declaring that the defendant has been informed of all possible consequences of a guilty plea and to state what those consequences are? This would permit both the prosecution and the trial court to focus on any misunderstandings or omissions which might later serve as the basis for challenging a plea. Would such a requirement violate the attorney-client privilege? Is there any argument that it would be unfair to impose such a burden on counsel? If such a burden were imposed, should the prosecutor be required to submit in writing a statement of the possible consequences so that it could be compared with that submitted by the defense?

Transcript of a Plea Colloquy Under Rule 11

The following is a transcript of a plea colloquy in an armed bank robbery case conducted by Hon. Milton I. Shadur, Senior District Judge of the Northern District of Illinois, one of the most distinguished judges in the country. It shows how good judges are careful to make sure that the defendant has knowingly and voluntarily entered into a guilty plea.

THE CLERK: This Is 02 CR 611, United States of America vs. Walter Turner.

MS. EGAN: Good afternoon, your Honor. Christina Egan on behalf of the United States.

MR. WHITNEY: Good afternoon, Judge. Doug Whitney on behalf of Walter Turner, who is present in court.

THE COURT: Good afternoon.

* * *

THE COURT: Well, I just had left on the desk for me here a signed copy of a plea agreement, and I had had a draft delivered the other day. So as always, my first question is whether the signed document is in the same form as the draft?

MS. EGAN: Your Honor, there is one change and that appears in the very first paragraph, line 4 in the draft that you saw. It referenced paragraph 16. The corrected version of the final signed copy correctly references paragraph 17.

THE COURT: Okay. So you mean you didn't catch, I gather, over on page 3 in the first complete paragraph where it refers to having—to Mr. Turner having—"waived the gun." It's actually lawyers who waive and not defendants, right?

MS. EGAN: I did not, your Honor.

THE COURT: You know they have the phrase, as you know, in the state court system about "swallowing the gun," but this is the first time I ever heard of waiving the gun.

Anyway—

MS. EGAN: Neither I nor Mr. Whitney caught that, your Honor.

THE COURT: Neither here nor there.

Mr. Turner, as I am sure Mr. Whitney has explained to you, whenever I have a proposed plea agreement in which somebody wants to change from a not guilty plea to a guilty plea or to start out by pleading guilty, the Court has really some independent responsibilities. And those are not answered just by the fact that somebody happens to have signed a document that says, "I am pleading guilty." Because a proper guilty plea, one that meets all of the legal tests, has to have a number of things that the Court has to make sure of, one being that you are pleading guilty voluntarily. Nobody is—I don't want to use a bad pun—you know, nobody is putting a gun to your head, you know. All right? The second thing is that I have to make sure that you are pleading guilty with a full understanding of what's involved when you plead guilty. And the third part is that we have to make sure that the reason that you are pleading guilty is because you are really acknowledging that you did what it is that the government charged.

And because I have to do that, that means that I have got to ask you a number of questions. Lawyers, as you've learned from all of this stuff, talk a different kind of language, and judges are no different on that score. So what I don't think is technical you might think is technical. And so if there is any question that you are wondering about, you are not sure you understand what it means, or maybe you are not even sure that you ought to be answering, our procedure is one under which you can say: "Wait a minute," and you can talk to your lawyer, because it's very important that you understand each question before you answer.

Do you follow all of that?

DEFENDANT TURNER: Yes, your Honor.

Sandy, would you administer the oath, then, to Mr. Turner?

* * *

THE COURT: Now one reason for my emphasizing your need for you to understand is that you should recognize that once Sandy administers the oath, all of the answers that you give to these questions become subject to the penalties of perjury or making a false statement. So it is very important that you give truthful answers.

Is that all right, too?

DEFENDANT TURNER: Yes.

THE COURT: How old are you?

DEFENDANT TURNER: 25.

THE COURT: And how far did you go in school?

DEFENDANT TURNER: The 11th grade.

THE COURT: Before you were taken into custody here, were you working?

DEFENDANT TURNER: No, sir, I wasn't.

THE COURT: Had you been working before that, or have you ever had employment?

DEFENDANT TURNER: Yes, I worked at several jobs here in the downtown area in '97 and '98.

THE COURT: What kind of jobs were those?

DEFENDANT TURNER: I was a messenger service—I mean I worked at a messenger service called Eagle Services.

And I also worked at a Burger King that's on 200 Monroe—Monroe and Walls.

THE COURT: At any time in the past or now—and whenever I ask this question I always try to make it clear that I am not just talking about professional help, the kind of thing that, for example, a psychologist or psychiatrist provides, but also sometimes people get involved in voluntary programs having the same goal—have you ever had any such things relating to mental health?

DEFENDANT TURNER: No, sir.

THE COURT: A similar kind of question about what we call substance abuse. That is, either use of narcotics or any excessive use of alcohol. Have you ever had any kind of treatment or have you ever been involved in any kind of a program having to do with any of those things?

DEFENDANT TURNER: No, sir, I haven't.

THE COURT: In the last few days have you had occasion, either under a doctor's prescription or otherwise, to take any kind of medicine or pills or drugs of any kind?

DEFENDANT TURNER: No, sir.

THE COURT: Mr. Whitney, based on your discussions with Mr. Turner and what you know about the case, do you have any question at all as to his competence to change his plea?

MR. WHITNEY: I do not, Judge.

THE COURT: Ms. Egan, anything from your perspective?

MS. EGAN: I do not, your Honor.

THE COURT: I will find then that Mr. Turner is competent to plead at this time.

Have you received a copy of this indictment that we have here? You know, you are proposing according to this plea agreement to enter a plea of guilty to Counts 1 and 3 of the indictment here. You are—wait just a minute. You are also named in Count 2 and in Count 4. But the understanding as I get it is that those things at the time of sentencing are going to get dismissed, because the conduct that's referred to there is also included as part of the conduct that's here in your plea agreement.

Do you understand that?

DEFENDANT TURNER: Yes.

THE COURT: Have you had a chance to read over these two counts, Count 1 and Count 3, and to discuss the charges and your case entirely with your lawyer?

DEFENDANT TURNER: Yes I have.

THE COURT: Are you happy, are you fully satisfied, with the work that your lawyer is doing for you?

DEFENDANT TURNER: Yes, I am.

THE COURT: I had referred to this plea agreement as having been signed. Let me make sure about this one. Is this your signature up here–

DEFENDANT TURNER: Yes, sir, it is.

THE COURT:–on the plea agreement?

Mr. Whitney, it's yours?

MR. WHITNEY: It is, Judge.

THE COURT: And Ms. Egan, it's yours?

MS. EGAN: Yes, it is, your Honor.

THE COURT: * * *

Did you have an opportunity to read this over and to discuss it with your lawyer before you signed it?

DEFENDANT TURNER: Yes.

THE COURT: So far as you know, does this plea agreement contain everything in the way of understandings–formal, informal, written, unwritten– everything as between you and your lawyer on the one hand and the government on the other hand?

DEFENDANT: Yes, it does.

THE COURT Mr. Whitney, any side agreements of any kind, formal,infor- mal, written, unwritten?

MR. WHITNEY: Not that I am aware of, Judge.

THE COURT: Ms. Egan?

MS. EGAN: No, your Honor.

THE COURT: Do you think you understand the terms of the plea agree- ment?

DEFENDANT TURNER: Yes, sir, I do.

THE COURT: Did anybody make any different kind of a promise to you that's not contained in here in order to try to persuade you to plead guilty?

DEFENDANT TURNER: No, sir.

THE COURT: Did anybody threaten you or threaten anybody else or try in any way to force you?

DEFENDANT TURNER: No, sir.

THE COURT: Leaving aside these other two counts that as I said are anticipated to go away at the time of sentencing, did anybody tell you that you if you didn't plead guilty the government was going to take any other unfavorable action, either by bringing any other charge or doing do anything else against you, if you didn't agree to plead guilty?

DEFENDANT TURNER: No, sir.

THE COURT: Just to summarize all of these things, would it be accurate to say that you pleading guilty of your own free will because you believe that you are guilty?

DEFENDANT TURNER: Yes, sir, I do.

THE COURT: Do you know what the maximum possible penalty is that the law provides for the offenses that are involved here? And if you don't, if you want to take a look, that's over here on page 6 in paragraph 9. Do you see that?

DEFENDANT TURNER: Yes, sir.

THE COURT: Do you see what that says is that the first count has a maximum possible sentence of 5 years. And Count 3 has a minimum penalty, a required penalty of–unless there is a change in that because of the agreement–of at least 7 years. And that has to be tacked on, that has to be served consecutive- ly, to any sentence that would be assigned on Count 1.

Do you see that?

DEFENDANT TURNER: Yes, sir.

* * *

THE COURT: You also understand that there is a maximum fine which could be as much as a quarter of a million dollars?

DEFENDANT TURNER: Yes.

THE COURT: Then there is a period of supervised release that would follow any time that you have to spend in custody, which would be at least 2 years, not more than 3 years.

Now my reason for mentioning particularly supervised release is, you understand the way that works is that conditions get imposed for supervised release?

DEFENDANT TURNER: Yes.

THE COURT: And if you were to violate any of the conditions of supervised release, what that would mean is that you could be sent back for additional time in prison without the government having to go ahead and bring a brand new indictment because of whatever that conduct was.

Do you understand that?

DEFENDANT TURNER: Yes, sir, I do.

THE COURT: Do you also understand that whether or not I impose any kind of a fine, there is what we call a "special assessment"? And because you are proposing to plead guilty to two counts, that special assessment means there must be a $200 paid in connection with these charges?

Do you understand that?

DEFENDANT TURNER: Yes, sir, I do.

THE COURT: Have you talked to Mr. Whitney about how the guidelines operate in your case?

DEFENDANT TURNER: Yes, sir, I have. And I also did some work myself on it.

THE COURT: Yes.

Well, I am sure if you've done work on it yourself that's confirmed that it is a very complicated system.

DEFENDANT TURNER: Yes, sir.

THE COURT: And the thing that I want to emphasize is that what's included here represents a kind of best judgment on the part of the lawyers about how the guidelines work. And that's dependent on their having looked at the nature of the charges and also what they know about your criminal background, or the lack of any criminal background. And those are estimates. Okay?

DEFENDANT TURNER: Yes, sir.

THE COURT: Now what happens is that a probation officer gets assigned to your case. And the probation officer has the responsibility to work up his or her own guideline calculations, including what the facts are. Now the probation officer could come up, for example, with a different answer from the one that the lawyers have talked about in this plea agreement. And if that's true anybody has got a right to object to what the probation officer has come up with, and then everything comes in front of me, so that if there are differing versions I have to decide that. And then I can impose, subject to the thing that we are going to be talking about afterwards this specific plea agreement, but if that weren't the case, I would be in a position to impose a sentence that would be within those guidelines, or sometimes impose a tougher sentence or sometimes a weaker sentence, although that's kind of limited.

My decision, you should understand, is also not the last word, because anybody could take the position that I have made a mistake, so that could be taken up to a higher court. Do you understand that's generally how the guidelines work?

DEFENDANT TURNER: Yes.

THE COURT: Okay. Let's talk about what happens if you don't plead guilty. All right?

DEFENDANT TURNER: Yes.

THE COURT: What that involves is the right, both under our Constitution and under our law, to a jury trial. A jury trial is a system in which the people who decide cases actually are not just the judge, but they are people, the citizens, who are taken at random off of the voting lists. And what happens is every couple of weeks, because we have got a lot of courtrooms in our building, the jury people downstairs bring in a large number of possible jurors who would be in a position to be involved in our cases.

DEFENDANT TURNER: Uh-huh.

THE COURT: And if your case were to come up for a trial, Sandy, the young woman who swore you in here, calls downstairs and says, "We need a criminal jury." So they send somewhere in the range of 35 to 40 people up here, and those are chosen at random from this bigger random group. And then to make sure that everything about the system is random, there is a computer that scrambles the names and prints them out in a way that gives the priority in which Sandy calls off the names. So she gets this sheet, and she calls off the first 12 names, and they go over there and they sit in the jury box. We ask them a lot of questions. Your lawyer may suggest questions after talking with you. The prosecutor can suggest questions. I ask questions that I think are important and useful to ask to make sure that we have people who are going to be fair.

If anybody has any kind of a bias or prejudice or anything that we can see represents a really good cause for excusing them, we do that automatically. Suppose for example we find out from questioning a prospective juror that somebody in their family has been a teller at a bank that got robbed. Okay? It would be very different for somebody like that to look at a case that has a similar charge, and sometimes that gets in the way of their being able to decide, "Did you really do the same kind of thing", which after all is the only thing that jurors are supposed to do. So we would disqualify anybody who showed an inability to deal fairly with the case.

But besides that, you and your lawyer and the government get a chance to exercise what are called "peremptory challenges." That's one of those fancy terms that simply means that you can ask that people be excused without having to give any reasons. You don't even have to have any reasons with a couple of exceptions. You might not like the way somebody is answering a question or you might not like the way they are looking at you. And any of those things can be used as a basis for saying, "I don't want that person".

The only exceptions are that nobody can be excused on one of those challenges because of that person's race or color. Nobody can be excused because of that person's sex, because it is a man or because it's a woman. But outside of that, it's open season. Okay?

Now whenever anybody is excused for any reason, Sandy calls off the next names that show up on the list and they fill in the vacated spots. We go through the question and answer business again and again, and we finally end up with 12 people nobody has objected to. And they are your jury. And that means in an important way they are your judges. They decide, not I, whether you are to be found guilty or not guilty. And all 12 have to agree, it has to be a unanimous decision before you can be found guilty. If you go to trial on more than one charge, they have to make a separate decision on each one of the charges. And if you were to go to trial with one of the co-defendants, the jury would have to make a separate decision about you and a separate decision about each of the co-defendants. So it is just as though there are a whole group of mini-trials going on at the same time.

Do you understand that's what we mean by jury trial?

DEFENDANT TURNER: Yes.

THE COURT: In our system a defendant can't say, "I don't want a jury, I'd rather have a judge decide the case." In the federal system, unlike over in the states courts, if a defendant would rather not have a jury, a defendant has got to ask for that, and the prosecutor has a right to say, "No." If the prosecutor agrees and if the Court agrees, then the case could go ahead in what we call a bench trial, where it is the judge and not a jury who decides guilt or not guilt.

state does not allow bench trial

Do you understand that?

DEFENDANT TURNER: Yes, I do.

THE COURT: Either way, though, with or without a jury, the trials are always public. They are in this public courtroom. Members of the public can come in, they can listen, they can watch. It's always what we call a speedy trial. Nobody can just keep these charges sitting there indefinitely and hanging over your head. It's always a trial in which in which you have a right to a lawyer. The same way that Mr. Whitney is here for you today * * * he would be here for you in connection with a trial. * * *

public trial

It's always a trial, and this is very important, in which you are presumed to be innocent. That means that it's the government's burden to prove you guilty beyond a reasonable doubt and by proper evidence before you could ever be found guilty. And you don't have to prove that you are innocent. You and your lawyer can say to the prosecutor, "Go ahead and prove it if you can." Of course you have a right to offer evidence, but the point is that you don't have an obligation to do it.

presumed innocent

Now whenever we have a trial the government witnesses have to come into open court. They sit on the witness stand over there. They are sworn just as you have been. Your lawyer gets a right to cross-examine them. You and your lawyer

w. witnesses

have a right to listen and to watch them. Your lawyer has the right on your behalf to object to any government evidence, and, as I said, to offer evidence for you. And if for example you wanted to call a witness who was reluctant to show up, your lawyer could get a court order, a subpoena, to require them to come in.

trial

But in a trial you are in a very special position. We have what the law calls the presumption of innocence and the privilege against self-incrimination. What that means is that you can decide absolutely "I do or I do not want to testify." If you decided no, nobody could suggest there was something wrong about that. Nobody could suggest, "Uh oh, you know if Mr. Turner was really innocent he would get on the stand." That isn't the way it works. We always tell juries, if we have a jury in any criminal case, that one thing they may not consider at all is the fact that the defendant didn't testify.

Then I guess the last thing about the trial is that if you want to go to trial and if you were found guilty, that's also something that could be taken up to a higher court. You could say "Mistakes were made, I shouldn't have been convicted." So all of these things together make up we summarize in this very short phrase, "the right to a trial."

Do you understand that?

DEFENDANT TURNER: Yes, sir, I do.

understand what waiver of rts means

THE COURT: My reason for giving this very lengthy explanation is to make sure you understand that none of these things are going to happen. That is, if you plead guilty to these counts and if I accept your plea, what will happen is that you waive your right to a trial. You waive the other rights that I have talked about. There is no trial. And what happens instead is that later on I would sentence you on the basis of this guilty plea after I have considered a presentence report from the same probation officer who works up this guideline calculation.

Do you understand that?

DEFENDANT TURNER: Yes, sir.

THE COURT: Most particularly, as I mentioned at the very beginning, the privilege against self-incrimination, the idea of saying that you don't have to testify, that's gone by the boards this afternoon, because the minute that you started to answer the questions after you had been sworn you are testifying.

DEFENDANT TURNER: Yes.

THE COURT: And because I am going to have to ask you in a few minutes what you really did about the thing, and you are going to have to admit what you did if you did it in fact, that's a privilege you are giving up right now.

Do you understand that?

DEFENDANT TURNER: Yes, I do.

THE COURT: Knowing all of these things, knowing that by pleading guilty you are expressing your willingness to give up all of these other rights, is it still your intention to plead guilty?

DEFENDANT TURNER: Yes, sir, it is.

THE COURT: Okay. Let's take a look at the two charges so that we are on the same page in terms of what they say. The first charge and the third charge are related, because both of them talk about May 21st of this year. And both of them talk about events that are said to have occurred here in Chicago in this Northern District of Illinois. And what both of them say is that you were acting with three other people: Marcal Grant, Narada Abrahams and Robert Bell.

The first count says that the four of you were involved in a conspiracy to violate the law. And conspiracy is kind of a shorthand term for the idea that if two or more people agree to do something that's illegal knowing that it's illegal, that's what we call a conspiracy. And when I say "agree", that doesn't mean sitting down and signing a contract. You know that doesn't mean that there is anything that has to be formal about it. Just the understanding that people have is enough to qualify as this conspiracy. And the one that's charged here in Court 1 is a bank robbery, in which it was agreed to rob the First Commercial Bank up on Howard Street, right on the border between Chicago and Evanston.

And what's charged is that the four of you drove up there, talked about how you were to go about the offense, and it was agreed that you and Grant would go into the bank to do the robbery and that the other two would stay in the car for purposes of a getaway. And it's also provided by this charge that you in fact carried out the plan of going in there in order to rob the bank, and in fact ended up taking a little over $3,600 from it.

What's charged in Count 3 relates to the same bank robbery. And what's said is, it says that all four of you, although it doesn't have to be this way, carried and brandished a firearm and possessed a firearm in furtherance of this crime. So that's basically what's charged.

Now when I mention–you understand that's what the charges are sort of in summary form?

DEFENDANT TURNER: Yes.

THE COURT: Now when I talked earlier about the possible sentence, you understand that what is said there in the plea agreement when we talked about the 7 years, is that in order for that to operate you have to be at least one of the people who actually brandished–had a weapon and brandished it.

Do you understand that's the nature of the charge in that regard?

DEFENDANT TURNER: Yes.

THE COURT: Now I do want to, before asking you what you actually did, make sure that you understand what the understanding is that's expressed in this plea agreement, and that's this. That because of the fact that you are willing to have changed to a guilty plea at this point, and if you want to turn to this it's over here at page 9 in paragraph 17, what it says that if in fact you have cooperated, it's the government's expectation that they will come in and ask for what's called a departure from what the guidelines call for, but also to knock out this mandatory minimum sentence. And instead of imposing that it would involve a sentence that would be two-thirds of the combined amount of the low end of what the guidelines call for on Count 1, which is this conspiracy count, plus the 7–year period on Count 3. So that if the conditions of this thing are satisfied, you would end up with instead of all of 7 plus whatever the guidelines say on Count 1, you would end up with two-thirds of that total.

Do you understand that?

DEFENDANT TURNER: Yes, sir.

THE COURT: Now what I want to emphasize about that is that whether the government does this is really the government's call. The Court can't force that. That is, the government has to make a judgment about whether it believes that you are qualifying for that. And if the government does that, as indicated here, then this agreement is binding. You can't back out of this understanding.

Do you follow that?

DEFENDANT TURNER: Yes, sir.

* * *

THE COURT: Okay. Now tell me, if you would, what you actually did in connection with this charged offense?

DEFENDANT TURNER: I was at home on May 21st, and the three co-defendants came to my house and asked me did I have a lick for them, which means someone or someplace that they can rob.

* * *

THE COURT: By the way, where was home? In Chicago?

DEFENDANT TURNER: Yes.

THE COURT: Go ahead. I didn't mean to interrupt. Go ahead.

DEFENDANT TURNER: They came to me and asked me about robbing someone or someplace.

THE COURT: Yes.

DEFENDANT TURNER: We later drove to the north side of Chicago and circled the bank. I was told that that's where we was going. The gun was got for me by Narada Abrahams out of the trunk of his car. He gave it to his cousin, which is Marcel Grant. Marcel Grant gave to it me. It had been agreed that Narada and Robert Bell wasn't going in. Robert had a breathing problem and couldn't run. And Narada was the only one that was in the car that knew how to drive a stick.

THE COURT: Okay.

DEFENDANT TURNER: And it was agreed that me and Marcel would go in. I would carry the gun and he would jump over the counter. We walked through an alley approaching the bank, we went into the bank, I stepped into the doorway and held the gun up and told everybody to get on the floor, it was a robbery. Marcel Grant later jumped back over the counter after me noticing that the security guard was laying on the floor, and I could see his badge and gun, and I said "He's got a gun. Let's go." And we left the bank and ran to the car. Upon reaching the car, it was a van riding past with an older gentleman in it. Once the van left, we got in the car—

THE COURT: Well, I don't need you to get to that part. It seems to me that—I appreciate your wanting to give the whole story, but my main purpose on this one is to make sure that you are admitting the things that what we call the elements of the offense, the things that are necessary here. I did have one question then for the prosecutor. Let me just make sure here.

(Pause)

Well, wait a minute. Okay. What would the government be in a position to prove? And Mr. Whitney, listen carefully to this, as to the fact that the object of the robbery was indeed a bank. Okay?

MS. EGAN: Is your Honor asking us what the defendants intent was, or are you asking as to the federally insured?

THE COURT: The charge, remember, brings into play 2113—

MS. EGAN: Right, exactly.

THE COURT: 2113 talks about robbery of a "bank".

MS. EGAN: Exactly.

THE COURT: It doesn't use the term, as we have in other situations, of "insured deposits" and so on. But the government does have to prove that the target was a bank. And therefore what I am asking you is what you would be in a position to establish for proving that element of the offense?

MS. EGAN: Your Honor, we would put forth the testimony of Mr. Turner with respect to the discussions among him and his co-defendants that they intended to rob a bank.

THE COURT: And you are saying that the target was this First Commercial Bank up on Howard Street, is that right?

MS. EGAN: Exactly, your Honor. That was the bank that they selected to rob.

THE COURT: Okay. Unless–and he's already confirmed both the place and the date. So I think that all those things together establish each of the elements of the offense. Unless counsel believes that there is some omission, right?

MR. WHITNEY: I don't, Judge.

MS. EGAN: No, your Honor.

THE COURT: All right. I am going to make the findings then that Mr. Turner is fully competent. That he's capable of entering an informal plea. That he is aware of both the nature of the two charges, Counts 1 and 3, and also the consequences of the plea. And I further make the finding that the guilty plea is both knowing and voluntary, and that in each instance it's supported by an independent basis in fact that contains each of the elements of the offenses in both Count 1 and Count 3. And all of that being true, I will accept the plea agreement, and I am now going to adjudge Mr. Turner guilty of both of those charges.

Now Mr. Turner, I mentioned early, you know, about the presentence report.

DEFENDANT TURNER: Yes.

THE COURT: And the probation officer has the responsibility for preparing that.

Now you are going to be asked to provide information for that. And that's because the presentence investigation report tells us all about a person, a person's background, a person's family, health, financial condition, any prior criminal activity, any matters having to do with anything that could bear and cast light on what kind of sentence to impose.

Now a couple of things I want to mention about that. The first one is that you have a right to have your lawyer along with you whenever you are asked to meet with the probation officer.

* * *

The second thing which is very important is this: We have been talking about the guidelines. And one of the things that enters into the guideline determination has to do with what's called "acceptance of responsibility."

Now from the way you have conducted yourself today, not just by pleading guilty but the way you have outlined what happened and what your involvement was, you are certainly accepting responsibility. But the thing that I want to caution you about is that sometimes people start out by doing something that accepts responsibility and then later on or for some reason might create problems by not giving correct information to the probation officer, engaging in other inappropriate activity and lose the benefit of it. And that's very important because under your agreement the sentence that would be imposed is going to be in part directly affected by the guidelines. And in this instance we are talking about three levels [reduction for acceptance of responsibility], right?

MS. EGAN: Yes, your Honor.

THE COURT: In this instance, whether you get credit for acceptance of responsibility or not makes about a one-third difference in the part of a sentence that gets tacked onto whatever is attributable to the weapon charge. So it's something that you should talk to your lawyer about in that regard whenever it comes to the idea of meeting with the probation officer. You don't want to stonewall. You don't want to create roadblocks or problems.

Do you understand that?

DEFENDANT TURNER: Yes, sir.

THE COURT: Now as you know we have–Ms. Egan, we have the cases as to the other defendants set for trial–

MS. EGAN: Yes, your Honor. November 8th.

THE COURT:–on November 8th. Are you anticipating that Mr. Turner would be a witness in the trial?

MS. EGAN: Yes, your Honor, we are anticipating that.

* * *

THE COURT: All right. So sentencing is December 12th at 1:15.

Now the only other thing I wanted to mention is you know the Court unfortunately can't control what the MCC [the federal detention center] does as far as housing people. You know they are overcrowded, and we try to get cooperation from them in terms of keeping defendants here rather than farming them out, especially during the time period when it's important for the defendant to meet with the probation officer and during the time that the defendant has to meet with counsel for that purpose or anything else. Again all I can say about that is that I can't control it. So I would hope, Mr. Whitney, that [you] will monitor that, so that there is not extra awkwardness that's created because of the idea of well, maybe now they can send him out to Dodge County, Wisconsin, or you know, someplace else while the process is ongoing. Okay?

I think that covers everything, doesn't it?

MS. EGAN: Thank you, Judge.

THE COURT: Thank you all.

MR. WHITNEY: Thank you.

2. The Role of the Court

The Judge's Power to Review the Agreement

Fed.R.Crim.P. 11 (c)(3) permits the trial judge to reject the plea agreement that was reached between the prosecution and the defense. The rejection power must be considered, however, in light of the three agreements that can be made between the parties. These are set forth in Rule 11(c)(1)(A), (B), and (C), and are explained by the court in United States v. Bennett, 990 F.2d 998 (7th Cir.1993):

> If the plea agreement includes the dismissal of any charges (a type "A" plea agreement), or if the agreement includes a specific sentence (a type "C" plea agreement), the district court may accept or reject the plea agreement, or it may defer its decision regarding acceptance or rejection until it considers the presentence investigation report. In contrast, if the plea agreement includes sentencing recommendations or the government's promise not to oppose the defendant's sentencing requests (a type "B" plea agreement), the district court must advise the defendant of the nonbinding effect the recommendations have on the court and must also inform the defendant that he may not withdraw his guilty plea, even if the court does not adopt the recommendations. The district court does not need to make such an admonition when dealing with a type "A" or "C" plea agreement.

The court in *Bennett* found that the agreement was a type "B" agreement, which did not bind the court in any respect. Thus, it refused to allow Bennett to vacate his plea when the court imposed a sentence significantly higher than that suggested in the agreement. If the agreement in *Bennett* had been a "C" agreement, the court could not have imposed a higher sentence than that agreed to between the parties. If the court objects to the terms of an "A" or "C" agreement, its only recourse is to reject the agreement, thus sending the prosecution and defendant back to the bargaining table.[11] See, e.g., United States v. Greener, 979 F.2d 517 (7th Cir.1992)(district court properly rejected a type "C" agreement where the sentence would not have sufficiently reflected the seriousness of the defendant's conduct); United States v. Brown, 331 F.3d 591 (8th Cir. 2003) (there is no absolute right to have a guilty plea accepted and a district court may reject a plea in the exercise of sound discretion).

Given the uncertain results, why would defense counsel ever agree to a type "B" agreement? Are you satisfied that a defendant is adequately informed when he has reached a type "B" agreement, and is told at the plea colloquy that it

---

11. Note how this effectively makes the judge a participant in bargaining. At some point the judge may accept a bargain and both the prosecutor and the defendant must realize this.

A trial judge's blanket policy of rejecting plea agreements that permit a defendant charged with multiple counts to plead to only one was condemned in United States v. Miller, 722 F.2d 562 (9th Cir.1983). The court of appeals reasoned that trial judges must exercise their discretion in particular cases rather than establish blanket rules regarding acceptable pleas.

does not bind the judge and that he cannot withdraw his plea if he pleads guilty? Is it right to allow the defendant to "roll the dice" in this way?[12] See United States v. Livorsi, 180 F.3d 76 (2d Cir.1999) (conviction vacated where defendant and prosecution reach a "B" agreement, and judge fails to inform the defendant that such an agreement is not binding on the court).

Intrusion Into the Negotiations

Federal Rule 11(c) prohibits the judge from taking part in plea negotiations. The reasons for this rule are set forth in United States v. Barrett, 982 F.2d 193 (6th Cir.1992):

> When a judge becomes a participant in plea bargaining he brings to bear the full force and majesty of his office. His awesome power to impose a substantially longer or even maximum sentence in excess of that proposed is present whether referred to or not. * * *

> It is not only a court's sentencing power which gives coercive potential to its participation in the plea bargaining process, but also the court's control over the conduct of a trial. The defendant must view the judge as the individual who conducts the trial and whose rulings will affect what the jury is to consider in determining guilt or innocence. The defendant may be reluctant to reject such a proposition offered by one who wields such immediate power. * * * There is also a real danger that a judge's neutrality can be compromised.

See also United States v. Daigle, 63 F.3d 346 (5th Cir.1995) (judicial participation increases the possibility of coerced guilty pleas, and may impair judicial impartiality because the judge "seems more like an advocate for the agreement than a neutral arbiter if he joins the negotiations").

If the judge rejects a plea on the ground that it is too lenient, has she participated in the negotiations? If she rejects a plea and states what terms would be acceptable to her, has she participated in the negotiations? See United States v. Miles, 10 F.3d 1135 (5th Cir.1993)(plea vacated due to judicial participation, where the trial judge rejected a plea and suggested the terms that would be acceptable to him). If she rejects the plea without giving an explanation, is her action subject to attack as arbitrary? If she tells the defendant at a bail hearing, "you'd better see what you can get from the prosecutor because you have no defense as far as I can see," has she participated in the negotiations? If she tells the defendant, before the agreement is filed, that she accepts the government's recommendations in most cases, has she engaged in improper participation? See United States v. Daigle, 63 F.3d 346 (5th Cir.1995) (judge who so informs the defendant has improperly participated in negotiations).

3. *Harmless Error and Plain Error*

Fed.R.Crim.P. 11(h) provides that any error under Rule 11 "that does not affect substantial rights" will be disregarded as harmless. This is the classic

---

12. In United States v. Benchimol, 471 U.S. 453 (1985), the Court held that the government did not breach its plea agreement when it recommended, as promised, probation without restitution for a defendant convicted of mail fraud, but it made no effort to explain its reason for agreeing to recommend a lenient sentence. The Court found that it was error for the court of appeals to imply a condition—i.e., explanation of the recommendation—that the parties had not made part of their agreement. Justice Stevens concurred in the judgment. Justice Brennan, joined by Justice Marshall, dissented.

definition of harmless error that is also found in Fed.R.Crim.P. 52(a). But what if the defendant does not object to an error under Rule 11? Should the same harmless error standard apply as if he did? With respect to trial errors, Rule 52(b) provides that a defendant who fails to object has the burden of showing "plain error" that affected substantial rights. [See the discussion of plain error in Chapter 13]. But Rule 11(h) does not include a plain-error provision comparable to Rule 52(b).

[handwritten margin: stand for R52]

The Court in United States v. Vonn, 535 U.S. 55 (2002), held that a defendant who does not object to an error under Rule 11 has the burden of showing "plain error." Justice Souter wrote for eight Justices. Justice Souter was not persuaded that there was any intent to differentiate by including a plain error provision in Rule 52 but not in Rule 11. He found that the lack of a plain error standard in Rule 11 would create an anomalous result, in that a defendant would be able to stand by and do nothing to correct an obvious Rule 11 error, and would lose nothing in doing so. The Court reasoned that Rule 52(b) implicitly applied to Rule 11 errors, and declared that the policy of the plain error rule is sound: "the value of finality requires defense counsel to be on his toes, not just the judge, and the defendant who just sits there when a mistake can be fixed cannot just sit there when he speaks up later on." Justice Stevens dissented from the Court's holding on plain error.

[handwritten margin: if Δ does not object to an error under R 11 - burden of proof is "plain error"]

The *Vonn* Court also held, unanimously, that in assessing whether a Rule 11 error affected the defendant's substantial rights, a reviewing court may look at information outside the record of the plea proceeding. In this case, the defendant was not told at his plea hearing that by pleading guilty, he would be giving up the right to assistance of counsel at trial. He did not raise this Rule 11 error until he appealed the conviction resulting from his guilty plea. Transcripts indicated, however, that Vonn was informed of his right to trial counsel at his initial appearance before the magistrate and at his first arraignment. The Court remanded for the lower court to determine whether, in light of this extra information, Vonn could meet his burden of showing plain error from the failure to inform him of his right to trial counsel at the plea hearing.

[handwritten margin: in assessing whether R 11 error affected sub ct look at inform outside the record of plea proceeding]

E. CLAIMS OF INNOCENCE

The Model Code of Pre–Arraignment Procedure § 350.4(4) addresses a subject not explicitly covered by Rule 11. It provides that "[t]he court may accept the defendant's guilty plea even though the defendant does not admit that he is in fact guilty if the court finds that it is reasonable for someone in the defendant's position to plead guilty. The court shall advise the defendant that if he pleads guilty he will be treated as guilty whether he is guilty or not." This approach is consistent with North Carolina v. Alford, 400 U.S. 25 (1970).

[handwritten margin: MPC allows Δ to plead guilty w/ ct assuring itself of actual guilty]

[handwritten left margin: if reasonable for someone in Δ's pos to do so.]

Alford was indicted by North Carolina for the capital crime of first-degree murder. He pleaded guilty to second-degree murder, but at the plea hearing he took the stand and testified in part as follows:

> I pleaded guilty on second degree murder because they said there is too much evidence, but I ain't shot no man, but I take the fault for the other man. We never had an argument in our life and I just pleaded guilty because they said if I didn't they would gas me for it, and that is all.

Subsequently, Alford sought post-conviction relief on the ground that his plea was produced by fear and coercion. After noting that "[s]tate and lower federal courts are divided upon whether a guilty plea can be accepted when it is accompanied by protestations of innocence and hence contains only a waiver of trial but no admission of guilt," the Court concluded that "[i]n view of the strong factual basis for the plea demonstrated by the State and Alford's clearly expressed desire to enter it despite his professed belief in his innocence, we hold that the trial judge did not commit constitutional error in accepting it."[13]

One of the reasons for sustaining the plea in *Alford* was the factual basis for it. Under Rule 11 there must always be a "factual basis" for the plea to be valid, but it is not necessary that the defendant actually admit his guilt. See Cranford v. Lockhart, 975 F.2d 1347 (8th Cir.1992)(*Alford* plea upheld where information in prosecutor's file establishes a factual basis for the guilty plea).

In the federal system, a defendant who enters an *Alford* plea is all but certain to be denied a reduction in sentence for acceptance of responsibility. See United States v. Harlan, 35 F.3d 176 (5th Cir.1994)("A defendant's refusal to acknowledge essential elements of an offense is incongruous with the guideline's commentary that truthful admission of the conduct comprising an offense is relevant in determining whether a defendant qualifies for this reduction.").

For an attack on the very concept of *Alford* pleas as well as nolo contendere pleas, see Stephanos Bibas, Harmonizing Substantive–Criminal–Law Values and Criminal Procedure: The Case of Alford and Nolo Contendere Pleas, 88 Cornell L. Rev. 1361 (2003). Professor Bibas argues that these pleas

> undermine the procedural values of accuracy and public confidence in accuracy and fairness by convicting innocent defendants and creating the perception that innocent defendants are being pressured into pleading guilty. More basically, they allow guilty defendants to avoid accepting responsibility for their wrongs. Guilty defendants' refusals to admit guilt impede their repentance, education, and reform, as well as victims' healing process. In addition, pleas without confessions muddy the criminal law's moral message. Both kinds of pleas, but especially *Alford* pleas, equivocate; one might call them "guilty-but-not-guilty" pleas. * * * Sacrificing these substantive goals is too high a price for an efficient plea procedure. * * *. Thus, guilty pleas should be reserved for those who confess. * * * Because criminal law's norms include honesty and responsibility for one's actions, criminal procedure should not let guilty defendants dishonestly dodge responsibility and the truth.

F. FACTUAL BASIS FOR PLEAS

As seen in Judge Shadur's plea colloquy, supra, the court's determination of the factual basis for a plea can help to assure that defendants who are innocent do not plead guilty. The advantages of a judicial determination are analyzed in Barkai, Accuracy Inquiries for All Felony and Misdemeanor Pleas: Voluntary Pleas But Innocent Defendants, 126 U.Pa.L.Rev. 88 (1977).

As stated above, Federal Rule 11(b)(3) requires the judge to determine that there is a factual basis for the plea. Such a factual basis can be found through statements by the defendant, factual assertions in the indictment, or informa-

---

13. Justice Brennan, joined by Justices Douglas and Marshall, dissented. Justice Black concurred in "substantially all of the opinion in this case."

The Indiana Supreme Court held that an Indiana judge may not accept an *Alford* plea in Ross v. Indiana, 456 N.E.2d 420 (Ind.1983).

tion in the prosecutor's file. See generally United States v. Adams, 961 F.2d 505 (5th Cir.1992)(insufficient factual basis where defendant did not admit facts in plea colloquy, and no other factual information was provided; but the error was harmless because there was sufficient factual information in the presentence report filed after the plea was taken).

Would you require a determination that the facts support a guilty plea? Thinking back to the problem of the defendant charged with murder who is offered a chance to plead to involuntary manslaughter, would you reject pleas that appear to represent compromises that cannot fairly be said to fit the facts? Would you permit a defendant to plead guilty notwithstanding a defect in the facts presented?

Lack of Factual Basis for a Forfeiture: Libretti v. United States

In Libretti v. United States, 516 U.S. 29 (1995), the defendant challenged a forfeiture order that was entered after he pleaded guilty to participating in a continuing criminal enterprise. He had stipulated the terms of the forfeiture with the government when he entered into the plea agreement. But he argued that the stipulation was invalid because there was no factual basis for the forfeiture. In Libretti's view, Rule 11 prevented the entry of the forfeiture order because the trial judge had never determined that the forfeiture had a factual basis. But the Court, in an opinion by Justice O'Connor, rejected this argument and held that Rule 11 was not applicable to the terms of a forfeiture agreement. She reasoned that, by its terms, the Rule applies only to a "plea of guilty." She concluded that a "forfeiture provision embodied in a plea agreement is of an entirely different nature. Forfeiture is an element of the sentence imposed following conviction or, as here, a plea of guilty, and thus falls outside the scope of Rule 11." Justice Stevens dissented.

G.   THE FINALITY OF GUILTY PLEAS

1.   Withdrawal of a Plea

The criminal justice system abides and promotes plea bargaining because it is efficient. But in order to be efficient, plea bargains must carry some measure of finality. The system of plea bargaining could be disrupted if defendants could withdraw their pleas unilaterally and demand a trial. In effect this would create a system more inefficient than an "all trial" system. On the other hand, some safety valve must be in place to protect defendants from plea bargains that are completely unfair and unjust; a safety valve is especially in order when it is remembered that the performance of appointed counsel for indigents often leaves much to be desired (as will be seen in Chapter 10).

Many jurisdictions limit the period in which a plea can be withdrawn. Some bar any attempt at withdrawal after sentence is imposed; others make the day the judgment is entered the final day for any withdrawal attempt. Fed.R.Crim.P. 11(d) provides that a court may allow the defendant to withdraw a guilty plea before sentence is imposed for any reason if the judge has not yet accepted the plea. But if the judge has accepted the plea, it may be withdrawn only if the court has rejected the terms of the plea agreement or if the defendant provides the court with a fair and just reason for withdrawal. It has been declared that a motion to withdraw a guilty plea before sentencing should be "freely allowed, viewed with favor, treated with liberality, and given a great deal of latitude." United States v. Jones, 168 F.3d 1217 (10th Cir.1999) (nonetheless finding no abuse of discretion in the trial court's denial of a motion to withdraw a guilty plea before sentence). But in fact courts are relatively strict about allowing withdrawal of a guilty plea once the court accepts it. See United States v. Abreu, 964 F.2d 16 (D.C.Cir.1992)(pre-sentence withdrawal of plea was properly denied where motion to withdraw was based upon the defendant's "reevaluation of the strength of the government's case"); United States v. Doyle, 981 F.2d 591 (1st Cir.1992)(defendant had no right to renounce his plea simply because "of a dawning awareness of what the likely sentence would be").

Rule 11(e) prohibits the withdrawal of a guilty plea after sentence is imposed: the defendant's only recourse is appeal or collateral attack.[14] Of course, if a guilty plea was not knowing and voluntary, or was not rendered with sufficient knowledge, then it can be withdrawn or vacated under the standards discussed earlier in this Chapter.

Withdrawal of Plea Before the Agreement Is Accepted: United States v. Hyde

As stated above, Rule 11 permits withdrawal of a guilty plea after it has been accepted by the court only "if the defendant can show a fair and just reason for requesting the withdrawal". In United States v. Hyde, 520 U.S. 670 (1997), a defendant reached a plea agreement with the government. At the guilty plea hearing, the defendant pleaded guilty to four counts of an eight-count indictment. The trial judge accepted the plea, but *deferred* decision on whether to accept the plea agreement, in which the government had agreed to dismiss the remaining four charges. So at this point the court had upheld the defendant's part of the agreement, while deferring consideration on the government's part of the agreement (as opposed to rejecting it). The defendant then sought to withdraw his plea—he did not proffer any "fair and just reason" for doing so. The lower court permitted the withdrawal, reasoning that a defendant has an absolute right to withdraw a guilty plea until it has been accepted; that the agreement and the plea itself are inextricably intertwined; and therefore that the guilty plea is not really accepted until the agreement as a whole is accepted by the trial judge.

The Supreme Court, in a unanimous opinion by Chief Justice Rehnquist, rejected this reasoning and held that when a plea is accepted and the acceptance of the plea *agreement* deferred, the defendant cannot withdraw his plea unless he satisfies the "fair and just reason" requirement of Rule 11. The Chief Justice argued that if the defendant were permitted an absolute right to withdraw his plea after the court had actually accepted or rejected it, it would debase the judicial proceeding at which a defendant pleads and the court accepts his plea:

> After the defendant has sworn in open court that he actually committed the crimes, after he has stated that he is pleading guilty because he is guilty, after the court has found a factual basis for the plea, and after the court has explicitly announced that it accepts the plea, the Court of Appeals would allow the defendant to withdraw his guilty plea simply on a lark. * * * We

14. If a defendant starts a trial, has a change of heart and pleads guilty, and then seeks to withdraw the plea, courts are not inclined to allow withdrawal. See, e.g., Commonwealth v. Whelan, 481 Pa. 418, 392 A.2d 1362 (1978). Do you see why?

think the Court of Appeals' holding would degrade the otherwise serious act of pleading guilty into something akin to a move in a game of chess.

The Chief Justice addressed the Court of Appeals' premise that a plea and a plea agreement are inextricably intertwined:

> The guilty plea and the plea agreement are "bound up together" in the sense that a *rejection* of the agreement simultaneously frees the defendant from his commitment to plead guilty. See And since the guilty plea is but one side of the plea agreement, the plea is obviously not wholly independent of the agreement.

> But the Rules nowhere state that the guilty plea and the plea agreement must be treated identically. Instead, they explicitly envision a situation in which the defendant performs his side of the bargain (the guilty plea) before the Government is required to perform its side (here, the motion to dismiss four counts). If the court accepts the agreement and thus the Government's promised performance, then the contemplated agreement is complete and the defendant gets the benefit of his bargain. But if the court rejects the Government's promised performance, then the agreement is terminated and the defendant has the right to back out of his promised performance (the guilty plea), just as a binding contractual duty may be extinguished by the non-occurrence of a condition subsequent.

Thus, if the agreement were to be rejected by the judge, it would be void. But the defendant could not, before the judge accepted the plea, move to withdraw the plea without providing a fair and just reason for doing so. The Court reversed and remanded for a determination of whether Hyde had a "fair and just" reason for withdrawing his guilty plea under the circumstances presented.

If judge rejected agreement it would be void
• here he deferred on Pros obligation

2. *Breach of a Plea Agreement*

K law

H: Remand for findings for fair + just.

Breach by the Prosecution: Santobello v. New York

A plea agreement between the government and the defendant is treated as a contract and is enforceable under contract principles. The leading case on enforceability of plea agreements is Santobello v. New York, 404 U.S. 257 (1971). Charged with two gambling felonies, Santobello agreed to plead guilty to a lesser included offense and the prosecutor agreed to make no recommendation as to sentence. Thereafter, a second prosecutor took over the case and, ignorant of the terms of the bargain, made a sentence recommendation. In an opinion by Chief Justice Burger, the Court held that even an inadvertent breach of a plea agreement was unacceptable. The Court remanded to afford the state courts the option of allowing Santobello to withdraw the plea or to have a new sentencing proceeding before a different judge. Justice Marshall, joined by Justices Brennan and Stewart, argued that Santobello "must be permitted to withdraw his guilty plea." Justice Douglas said that "[i]n choosing a remedy, * * * a court ought to accord a defendant's preference considerable, if not controlling, weight inasmuch as the fundamental rights flouted by a prosecutor's breach of a plea bargain are those of the defendant, not of the state."

Pros 1 makes deal
Pros 2 takes over unaware
• breaches violation of K

Remedies for Prosecutorial Breach

If the prosecutor reneges on a bargain, should the defendant have a choice of starting all over again by withdrawing the plea or of specific enforcement of the promise? If you are inclined to answer that specific performance leaves the defendant in as good a position as she otherwise would have been in, ask yourself whether this is really the case. Is the defendant no worse off when she had to bear the burden of obtaining performance of a promise? Sometimes the defendant will want specific performance. If courts are reluctant to allow defendants to withdraw pleas, should they be any more willing to let prosecutors out of their bargains?

If a defendant manages to set aside a guilty plea and decides to go to trial, is the prosecutor entitled to charge a higher offense than the one to which the defendant pleaded? Most courts treat the withdrawal of the plea as an erasure that allows both sides to proceed anew. See, e.g., United States ex rel. Williams v. McMann, 436 F.2d 103 (2d Cir.1970). However, the *Williams* court acknowledged that although general principles of fundamental fairness do not bar every prosecution, certain allegations such as prosecutorial vindictiveness could pose a reasonable challenge on the basis of due process. Nonetheless, "no presumption of vindictiveness arises when the prosecutor simply reinstates the indictment that was in effect before the plea agreement was entered." Taylor v. Kincheloe, 920 F.2d 599 (9th Cir.1990), citing Blackledge v. Perry, 417 U.S. 21 (1974). Would you require that the defendant be permitted to plead again pursuant to the original bargain whenever the prosecutor changes or raises the charges? See Borman, The Chilled Right to Appeal from a Plea Bargain Conviction: A Due Process Cure, 69 Nw.U.L.Rev. 663 (1974).

Is There a Breach?

Sometimes it is difficult to determine whether a bargain has been breached. For example, if a prosecutor agrees to drop two counts of a three count indictment in exchange for a plea to the remaining count, and the sentencing judge relies on the fact that three offenses were committed, has the bargain been breached? In deciding how to answer, would you view an objective or subjective test of the bargain as more appropriate? See United States v. Hayes, 946 F.2d 230 (3d Cir.1991)(where government promised to "make no recommendation as to the specific sentence to be imposed" and then emphasized the seriousness of the offense at the sentencing hearing, the government breached the terms of the plea agreement; principles of contract control whether plea agreement has been breached); United States v. Johnson, 187 F.3d 1129 (9th Cir.1999) (where plea agreement required the prosecution to recommend a certain sentence, the prosecutor violated the agreement by recommending the sentence and then introducing a victim impact statement: "We see no way to view the introduction of McDonald's statement other than as an attempt by the prosecutor to influence the court to give a higher sentence than the prosecutor's recommendation.").

Questions of breach often arise when the government, as part of a plea agreement, agrees to recommend a certain sentence. Defendants often object that the government at the sentencing hearing might have recommended the agreed-upon sentence, but made clear to the judge that it was doing so only reluctantly, and wouldn't mind at all if the judge were to impose a higher sentence. Under such circumstances the Court in United States v. Benchimol, 471 U.S. 453 (1985), found no breach. The Court reasoned that the agreement called only for the prosecutor to recommend a certain sentence, and the prosecutor did make the recommendation—there was nothing in the agreement specifically requiring the prosecutor to make an enthusiastic recommendation. See also United States v. Johnson, 187 F.3d 1129 (9th Cir.1999) ("unless specifically required in the agreement, the government need not make the agreed-upon recommendation enthusiastically").

It is clear that if the government is to be held to an obligation, it must be in the plea agreement. Thus, in United States v. Austin, 255 F.3d 593 (8th Cir. 2001), the defendant argued that the government breached its agreement when it sought a sentencing enhancement based on the defendant's leadership role in the offense. The defendant argued that the prosecutor had promised during negotiations not to seek such an enhancement. But the agreement itself was silent on the issue of enhancement, and a clause in the agreement provided that the agreement reflected "all promises, agreements, and conditions between the parties." The court therefore found that the government did not breach the agreement by arguing for enhancement at sentencing.

Δ alleges oral promise · not written in k · k terms were to b final — No breach

Cooperation Agreements

The question of prosecutorial breach becomes particularly difficult when the agreement imposes cooperation obligations on the defendant in exchange for the government's agreement to recommend a lesser sentence. Generally the prosecution prefers that its obligations under such an agreement remain vague, and contingent on its own view of the quality of the defendant's cooperation. When the defendant claims that the prosecution breached the agreement by failing to recommend a certain sentence or a sentence reduction, the prosecution responds that its duty was contingent on the defendant's cooperation, and in its opinion the defendant failed to comply with his contractual obligations. Professor Richman, in Cooperating Clients, 56 Ohio St.L.J. 69 (1995), describes this phenomenon:

When Pros claims their breach was based on Δ's failure to cooperate fully.

> Typically, the defendant will broadly promise to testify truthfully, and to truthfully disclose all information concerning matters covered by the government's inquiries. Any effort to bind a cooperator to a particular "story" would be unseemly, and probably illegal. The government will reserve for itself the right to determine, prior to sentencing, whether the defendant has in fact cooperated fully and told the truth. * * * The Federal Sentencing Guidelines have strengthened the government's hand even more * * * by providing that cooperation generally cannot be a basis for a departure below the Guidelines range or a statutory minimum *except* when the government makes an explicit motion certifying that the defendant has indeed rendered "substantial assistance." [See Federal Sentencing Guideline § 5K1.1]. * * * If the government determines that a cooperator has not lived up to his obligations, it will thus generally be able to prevent the sentencing judge from showing the defendant any significant leniency based on his cooperation.

Professor Richman notes that while a government's obligations under a cooperation agreement are thus difficult to enforce in court, there is some discipline that is imposed by the marketplace. "The prosecutor who mistreats snitches risks not being able to attract such assets in the future."

One defense attorney became so frustrated at what he perceived as a failure of a United States Attorney's office to live up to its obligations under a cooperation agreement, that he was moved to publish an open letter in a full-page advertisement in the National Law Journal:

> [Despite the client's cooperation], your office broke two written promises to make a 5K.1 motion [for reduction in sentence due to cooperation]. The reasons given by your office were pure bovine do-do. Even the district judge was appalled.

> During the sentence proceedings I stated that I was going to tell every defense lawyer in our nation not to enter any plea agreement with your office. Your office cannot be trusted. Your office cares nothing about promises and agreements. I am surprised that the eagle in the Great Seal of the United States didn't fly from the wall in horror. * * * Like some sleazy insurance company who refuses to pay the widow because it wants the premiums but doesn't want to honor its obligations, your office will go to any length to renege on its solemn promises.

Michael Metzger, Advertisement, Nat'l L.J., May 24, 1993, at 26. Metzger was complaining about the U.S. Attorney's office in the Southern District of Florida. If you were a defense attorney practicing in Miami, would this advertisement affect the advice that you would give to a client who wishes to cooperate? Can you write a cooperation agreement that would bind the prosecution to its promises?

For a case in which a breach was found when the government failed to move for a sentence reduction in a cooperation agreement, see United States v. Lukse, 286 F.3d 906 (6th Cir. 2002), where the government was required in the agreement to file a downward departure motion if the defendant provided the government with substantial assistance. At the sentencing hearing, the government conceded that the defendant had provided substantial assistance, but argued that the defendant had breached the agreement because he was caught smoking marijuana in jail after providing the assistance. Because the defendant made no promises in the agreement that were breached by this conduct, the agreement was found fully enforceable against the government. The court remanded and ordered the government to file a downward departure motion at a new sentencing proceeding.

Breach by the Defendant: Ricketts v. Adamson

In Ricketts v. Adamson, 483 U.S. 1 (1987), the Court held that the Double Jeopardy Clause did not bar a state from filing capital charges against a defendant who had entered a guilty plea in return for a specific prison term and subsequently violated the terms of the plea agreement. Adamson was one of three individuals charged with first-degree murder in the dynamiting of a reporter's car. He agreed to plead guilty to second-degree murder and to testify against the other defendants in exchange for a designated prison sentence. Although Adamson testified as promised and the other defendants were convicted, the State Supreme Court reversed the convictions and remanded their cases for new trials. Adamson's lawyer informed the prosecutor that Adamson would only testify at second trials if certain conditions were met, including his release from prison following his testimony. The state took the position that Adamson's refusal to testify would put him in breach of the agreement. Adamson nevertheless invoked his privilege against self-incrimination when called to testify at a pretrial proceeding. Thereafter, the state filed a new information and convicted Adamson of first-degree murder. He was sentenced to death. An en banc court of appeals found that Adamson was placed in jeopardy twice, but the Supreme Court disagreed.

Justice White wrote for the Court. The Court assumed that jeopardy attached when Adamson was sentenced pursuant to his guilty plea and that absent special circumstances, Adamson could not have been retried for first-degree murder. Justice White agreed with the state that special circumstances arose from the plea agreement which specifically provided that the entire agreement would be null and void if Adamson refused to testify. He was unimpressed with the court of appeals' reasoning that Adamson acted in good faith. Justice White concluded that Adamson knew that if he breached the agreement he could be retried, "it is incredible to believe that he did not anticipate that the extent of his obligation would be decided by a court," and the end "result was that respondent was returned to the position that he occupied prior to execution of the plea bargain; he stood charged with first-degree murder."

Justice White reasoned that it was "of no moment" that Adamson offered to comply with the agreement after the state supreme court decision interpreting it, since "[t]he parties did not agree that respondent would be relieved of the consequences of his refusal to testify if he were able to advance a colorable argument that a testimonial obligation was not owing." Justice White ended his opinion with the observation that "[t]he parties could have struck a different bargain, but permitting the State to enforce the agreement the parties actually made does not violate the Double Jeopardy Clause."

Justice Brennan, joined by Justices Marshall, Blackmun, and Stevens, dissented. He disagreed that Adamson ever breached the plea agreement and argued that, assuming such a breach occurred, Adamson never made a conscious decision to violate the agreement. Justice Brennan focused on the provision of the agreement stating that Adamson was to be sentenced at the conclusion of his promised testimony, and noted that Adamson was sentenced after he had provided extensive testimony. Thus, Justice Brennan found that Adamson reasonably could have concluded that he had met his contractual obligations. After observing that "[t]he Court has yet to address in any comprehensive way the rules of construction appropriate for disputes involving plea agreements," Justice Brennan suggested that "the law of commercial contract may in some cases prove useful as an analogy or point of departure in construing a plea agreement, or in framing the terms of the debate." Relying on commercial law, he reasoned that the state failed to explain why a letter from Adamson's lawyer to the state, which indicated that the lawyer concluded that Adamson did not have to testify at re-trials of the other defendants, was a breach of contract.

Is a prosecutor who breaches a plea agreement treated more favorably than a defendant who breaches? How useful is the contract analogy in these cases?

3. Appeal and Collateral Attack

Jurisdictions that do not like to see guilty pleas withdrawn or vacated often also do not like to see them challenged on appeal or collaterally attacked.[15] Thus, they generally establish a regime in which a voluntary and intelligent guilty plea is a waiver of all claims that the pleader has. The Supreme Court has promoted this approach in four cases: the *Brady* trilogy—Brady v. United States, 397 U.S. 742 (1970); McMann v. Richardson, 397 U.S. 759 (1970); Parker v. North Carolina, 397 U.S. 790 (1970)—and Tollett v. Henderson, 411 U.S. 258 (1973).

The defendant in *Brady* was charged with kidnaping under a federal statute that authorized the death penalty if a jury recommended it but not in a bench trial. Brady pleaded guilty when it appeared that the trial judge would not try the case without a jury, but Brady sought to challenge his guilty plea via habeas corpus on the ground that the statute unconstitutionally infringed his right to jury trial. The Supreme Court held that even if Brady would not have pleaded guilty but for the death penalty provision, he pleaded voluntarily and intelligently with the advice of counsel. Thus, he was not entitled to withdraw his plea collaterally, even if a Supreme Court decision rendered after his plea was entered suggested that the kidnaping statute was invalid in burdening the right to jury trial.

In *Parker,* the Court reached a similar result with respect to a state court defendant who was charged with first-degree burglary and who pleaded guilty to avoid a possible jury-imposed death sentence. The Court also said in *Parker* and in *McMann* that a defendant who pleaded guilty could not attack the plea in a subsequent collateral proceeding on the ground that it was motivated by a prior coerced confession. Following this trilogy, the Court held in *Tollett* that a defendant who pleaded guilty to first-degree murder could not challenge in subsequent habeas corpus proceedings the racial composition of the grand jury that indicted him.

The four cases appeared to hold that a guilty plea represents acceptance by a defendant of his conviction and that the conviction was valid unless the defendant was not adequately represented by counsel. But, the Court soon muddied the waters in Blackledge v. Perry, 417 U.S. 21 (1974), as it held that a prison inmate who pleaded guilty to a felony charge in a North Carolina court after seeking a trial de novo following a conviction on a misdemeanor charge could attack his plea on the ground that the prosecutor acted improperly in retaliating against the defendant by raising the charge to a felony from a misdemeanor (a ground discussed in Chapter Twelve, infra). Thereafter, the Court held in Menna v. New York, 423 U.S. 61 (1975), that a defendant who pleaded guilty did not lose the right to challenge the plea as a violation of double jeopardy rights.

The Court held in United States v. Broce, 488 U.S. 563 (1989), that defendants, who pleaded guilty to two separate counts charging bidrigging conspiracies, could not successfully move to vacate their sentences on the ground that they actually were involved in a single, large conspiracy. Justice Kennedy

15. For a discussion of the defendant's right to appeal a guilty plea conviction, see Borman, The Hidden Right to Direct Appeal from a Federal Plea Conviction, 64 Cornell L.Rev. 319 (1979); United States v. Melancon, 972 F.2d 566 (5th Cir.1992)(defendant may, as part of his plea agreement, waive the right to appeal his sentence; finding a knowing and intelligent waiver under the circumstances).

reasoned for the Court that the indictments charged two conspiracies and that the defendants conceded by their pleas that they committed two separate crimes. He observed that *Blackledge* and *Menna* were resolved on the basis of the existing record and did not require an inquiry into evidence outside the record; in contrast, the instant case involved indictments which on their face charged separate offenses—the only way to determine whether it was a single conspiracy would be to conduct a detailed inquiry into the facts. Thus, Justice Kennedy concluded that the defendants could not make a double jeopardy claim without contradicting their pleas and, therefore, it was not necessary to "consider the degree to which the decision by an accused to enter into a plea bargain which incorporates concessions by the Government, such as the one agreed to here, heightens the already substantial interest the Government has in the finality of the plea."

It is clear that the Supreme Court has attempted to promote plea bargaining. Yet, the Court has identified a narrow range of cases in which guilty pleas cannot bar a subsequent collateral attack. Can you think of any rule that would rationalize the cases?[16]

4. Conditional Pleas

Although many jurisdictions do everything possible to make a guilty plea as final as possible, others have found that plea bargaining can be promoted if defendants who plead guilty are permitted to raise some post-plea claims. For example, Fed.R.Crim. P. 11(a)(2) provides that with the approval of the court and with the consent of the government, "a defendant may enter a conditional plea of guilty * * * reserving in writing the right to have an appellate court review an adverse determination of a specified pretrial motion." If the defendant prevails on appeal, he has the right to withdraw the plea. A typical example of the use of a conditional plea is where the defendant moves to suppress evidence on the ground that it was obtained as a result of an illegal search and seizure, and the court denies the motion to suppress. At that point, the defendant could go to trial to preserve the right to appeal the suppression motion, but this might make little sense to a defendant who is actually guilty. So the defendant pleads guilty on condition that he can appeal the judge's suppression ruling. Thus, a defendant need not go to trial just to preserve a search and seizure or confession challenge.[17] If the defendant prevails on appeal, he is then allowed to withdraw the plea.[18]

[handwritten margin note: when such a plea might be needed]

16. For two attempts at stating such a rule, see Saltzburg, Pleas of Guilty and the Loss of Constitutional Rights: The Current Price of Pleading Guilty, 76 Mich.L.Rev. 1265 (1978); Westen, Away from Waiver: A Rationale for the Forfeiture of Constitutional Rights in Criminal Procedure, 75 Mich.L.Rev. 1214 (1977). See also Alschuler, The Supreme Court, the Defense Attorney, and the Guilty Plea, 47 U.Colo.L.Rev. 1 (1975); Dix, Waiver in Criminal Procedure: A Brief for More Careful Analysis, 55 Tex.L.Rev. 193 (1977).

17. United States v. Burns, 684 F.2d 1066 (2d Cir.1982), urges trial courts to consent to the reservation of issues only where they can be reviewed without a full trial and are likely to be dispositive of the case.

18. Note, Conditional Guilty Pleas, 93 Harv.L.Rev. (1980), argues that a defendant has a constitutional right to enter a conditional guilty plea.

Chapter Ten

TRIAL AND TRIAL–RELATED RIGHTS

In the previous Chapter we found that almost all criminal prosecutions in the United States end in a guilty plea. Why, then, is it worth it to spend much time studying criminal trials? The answer is that trials and trial rights remain important because the decision to plead guilty or not is dependent on the parties' view of how a trial would unfold. Moreover, prosecutions of extremely serious or high profile crimes usually go to trial. Finally, the explication and development of constitutional rights at trial indicates our attitude toward civil rights in this country. So we proceed to an in-depth discussion of trial rights in America.

I. THE RIGHT TO A SPEEDY TRIAL

A. THE BACKGROUND OF AND POLICIES SUPPORTING THE RIGHT

The Sixth Amendment provides that "[i]n all criminal prosecutions, the accused shall enjoy the right to a speedy and public trial * * * "It is a guarantee of deliberate speed in the prosecution of a case and a protection against several evils associated with delayed litigation. The Supreme Court has long recognized that "[t]he right of a speedy trial is necessarily relative. It is consistent with delays and depends upon circumstances." Beavers v. Haubert, 198 U.S. 77 (1905). Careful analysis of the facts of each case, rather than bright line tests, has been, and is still, the preferred approach of the Court to constitutionally-based speedy trial claims.

Fundamental Right: Klopfer v. North Carolina

In Klopfer v. North Carolina, 386 U.S. 213 (1967), the Court established that the right to a speedy trial is fundamental and part of the bundle of rights binding upon the states through the Due Process Clause of the Fourteenth Amendment. In *Klopfer*, the Court found a speedy trial violation when a Duke University professor, who was indicted for criminal trespass for participation in a sit-in at a restaurant, saw the prosecutor obtain a "nolle prosequi with leave" following a trial that ended in a hung jury. The nolle prosequi permitted the prosecutor to reinstate the case without further order. Because the procedure indefinitely prolonged the anxiety and concern accompanying public accusation, the Court found that it violated the defendant's right to a speedy trial.

Interests Protected by the Speedy Trial Right

There are three interests protected by the right to a speedy trial. First is the interest of an accused person in avoiding prolonged detention prior to trial. Innocent persons are never compensated for the losses that result from such detention. Those who are convicted following trial may have been confined for long periods in inadequate jails. Some who receive probation would never have spent time incarcerated except for pretrial delay. Second is the interest of the accused in avoiding prolonged anxiety concerning the charges made and public suspicion while charges are pending. Third is the accused's interest in litigating a case before evidence disappears and memories fade. Not all of these concerns are present in all cases, but they can be. See generally Godbold, Speedy Trial— Major Surgery for a National Ill, 24 Ala.L.Rev. 265 (1972).

Imprisonment on Other Offenses: Smith v. Hooey and Dickey v. Florida

In Smith v. Hooey, 393 U.S. 374 (1969), the Court held that speedy trial rights extend to people imprisoned on other offenses. The Court reasoned as follows:

> At first blush it might appear that a man already in prison under a lawful sentence is hardly in a position to suffer from "undue and oppressive incarceration prior to trial." But the fact is that delay in bringing such a person to trial on a pending charge may ultimately result in as much oppression as is suffered by one who is jailed without bail upon an untried charge. First, the possibility that the defendant already in prison might receive a sentence at least partially concurrent with the one he is serving may be forever lost if trial of the pending charge is postponed. Secondly, under procedures now widely practiced, the duration of his present imprisonment may be increased, and the conditions under which he must serve his sentence greatly worsened, by the pendency of another criminal charge outstanding against him.

> And while it might be argued that a person already in prison would be less likely than others to be affected by "anxiety and concern accompanying public accusation," there is reason to believe that an outstanding untried charge (of which even a convict may, of course, be innocent) can have fully as depressive an effect upon a prisoner as upon a person who is at large.

> * * *

> Finally, it is self-evident that "the possibilities that long delay will impair the ability of an accused to defend himself" are markedly increased when the accused is incarcerated in another jurisdiction. * * * And, while "evidence and witnesses disappear, memories fade, and events lose their perspective," a man isolated in prison is powerless to exert his own investigative efforts to mitigate these erosive effects of the passage of time.

One year later, in Dickey v. Florida, 398 U.S. 30 (1970), the Court ordered a prosecution dismissed when a federal prisoner made persistent requests for a speedy trial on an armed robbery charge, and for seven years Florida took no action to bring him to trial. In the interim, potential defense witnesses had died or disappeared. Chief Justice Burger wrote the opinion for a unanimous court, stating that "[s]tale claims have never been favored by the law, and far less so in criminal cases. Although a great many accused persons seek to put off the confrontation as long as possible, the right to a prompt inquiry into criminal charges is fundamental and the duty of the charging authority is to provide a prompt trial."[1]

B. DELAY IN ARRESTING OR CHARGING THE DEFENDANT

Klopfer, Smith, and Dickey all wanted the charges against them disposed of promptly. Because each was charged in some fashion or other with an offense, speedy trial rights attached. If no formal charge is made against a person but it is clear that one might be forthcoming at some future time, what protection, if any, can be claimed? That is the issue in the next two cases.

1. Speedy Trial Clause Analysis

UNITED STATES v. MARION

Supreme Court of the United States, 1971.
404 U.S. 307.

MR. JUSTICE WHITE delivered the opinion of the Court.

This appeal requires us to decide whether dismissal of a federal indictment was constitutionally required by reason of a period of three years between the occurrence of the alleged criminal acts and the filing of the indictment.

* * *

Appellees * * * claim that their rights to a speedy trial were violated by the period of approximately three years between the end of the criminal scheme charged and the return of the indictment * * *. In our view, however, the Sixth Amendment speedy trial provision has no application until the putative defendant in some way becomes an "accused," an event that occurred in this case only when the appellees were indicted on April 21, 1970.

The Sixth Amendment provides that "[i]n all criminal prosecutions, the accused shall enjoy the right to a speedy and public trial * * *." On its face, the protection of the Amendment is activated only when a criminal prosecution has begun and extends only to those persons who have been "accused" in the course of that prosecution. These provisions would seem to afford no protection to those not yet accused, nor would they seem to require the Government to discover, investigate, and accuse any person within any particular period of time. * * *

III

It is apparent also that very little support for appellees' position emerges from a consideration of the purposes of the Sixth Amendment's

1. Almost every state has adopted the Interstate Agreement on Detainers (IAD), which means that states can provide speedy trials to persons incarcerated in other states. The IAD provides that a prisoner of one state who is the subject of a detainer lodged by another state must be brought to trial within 180 days "after he shall have caused to be delivered" to the prosecuting officer and the appropriate court of the latter state a request for final disposition of the charges on which the detainer was based. For a discussion of the IAD, see Fex v. Michigan, 507 U.S. 43 (1993) (the 180–day clock provided in the IAD began to run when the prisoner's request was received by the jurisdiction lodging the detainer against him, not when the prisoner delivered the request to the authorities of his state of incarceration).

speedy trial provision, a guarantee that this Court has termed "an important safeguard to prevent undue and oppressive incarceration prior to trial, to minimize anxiety and concern accompanying public accusation and to limit the possibilities that long delay will impair the ability of an accused to defend himself." Inordinate delay between arrest, indictment, and trial may impair a defendant's ability to present an effective defense. But the major evils protected against by the speedy trial guarantee exist quite apart from actual or possible prejudice to an accused's defense. * * * Arrest is a public act that may seriously interfere with the defendant's liberty, whether he is free on bail or not, and that may disrupt his employment, drain his financial resources, curtail his associations, subject him to public obloquy, and create anxiety in him, his family and his friends. * * * So viewed, it is readily understandable that it is either a formal indictment or information or else the actual restraints imposed by arrest and holding to answer a criminal charge that engage the particular protections of the speedy trial provision of the Sixth Amendment.

Invocation of the speedy trial provision thus need not await indictment, information, or other formal charge. But we decline to extend the reach of the amendment to the period prior to arrest. Until this event occurs, a citizen suffers no restraints on his liberty and is not the subject of public accusation; his situation does not compare with that of a defendant who has been arrested and held to answer. Passage of time, whether before or after arrest, may impair memories, cause evidence to be lost, deprive the defendant of witnesses, and otherwise interfere with his ability to defend himself. But this possibility of prejudice at trial is not itself sufficient reason to wrench the Sixth Amendment from its proper

context. Possible prejudice is inherent in any delay, however short; it may also weaken the Government's case.

The law has provided other mechanisms to guard against possible as distinguished from actual prejudice resulting from the passage of time between crime and arrest or charge. [T]he applicable statute of limitations is the primary guarantee against bringing overly stale criminal charges. * * * These statutes provide predictability by specifying a limit beyond which there is an irrebuttable presumption that a defendant's right to a fair trial would be prejudiced. * * * There is thus no need to press the Sixth Amendment into service to guard against the mere possibility that pre-accusation delays will prejudice the defense in a criminal case since statutes of limitation already perform that function.

Since appellees rely only on potential prejudice and the passage of time between the alleged crime and the indictment, * * * we perhaps need go no further to dispose of this case, for the indictment was the first official act designating appellees as accused individuals and that event occurred within the statute of limitations. Nevertheless, since a criminal trial is the likely consequence of our judgment and since appellees may claim actual prejudice to their defense, it is appropriate to note here that the statute of limitations does not fully define the appellees' rights with respect to the events occurring prior to indictment. Thus, the Government concedes that the Due Process Clause of the Fifth Amendment would require dismissal of the indictment if it were shown at trial that the pre-indictment delay in this case caused substantial prejudice to appellees' rights to a fair trial and that the delay was an intentional device to gain tactical advantage over the accused. * * * However, we need not, and could not now, determine when and in what circumstances actual prejudice resulting from preaccusation delays requires the dismissal of the prosecution. * * *

IV

[The Court found no denial of a speedy trial or of due process.]

[Justice Douglas, joined by Justices Brennan and Marshall concurred in the result on the ground that the case against the defendants was complex and required extensive investigation, so that the government's three-year delay in bringing the prosecution was permissible under the circumstances.]

Second Indictment: United States v. MacDonald

In United States v. MacDonald, 456 U.S. 1 (1982), military charges had been brought against the defendant for murdering his wife and children. Those charges were dismissed without prejudice and MacDonald was honorably discharged. Four years later the Justice Department presented the case against MacDonald to a grand jury, and MacDonald was indicted on murder charges. MacDonald brought an interlocutory appeal alleging a speedy trial violation, based on an assertion that the speedy trial clock started ticking as of the initial indictment. The Supreme Court held that a defendant could not bring an appeal from the denial of a motion to dismiss on speedy trial grounds until after completion of the trial. 435 U.S. 850 (1978). MacDonald was tried and convicted. On appeal, the court of appeals found a speedy trial violation because the long delay allowed the prosecution to refresh the memory of its witnesses, and the defense could not adequately probe the recollection of the witnesses whose memories were refreshed. The Supreme Court rejected these concerns as irrelevant and held that the time between the dropping of charges and a later indictment does not count toward the speedy trial determination.

The *MacDonald* Court noted that the speedy trial guarantee is designed to "minimize the possibility of lengthy incarceration prior to trial" and that after charges are dismissed, the citizen, as in *Marion,* suffers no restraints on his liberty. Chief Justice Burger, writing for the majority, concluded that once charges are dismissed, "the formerly accused is, at most, in the same position as any other subject of a criminal investigation." Justice Marshall, joined by Justices Brennan and Blackmun dissented, arguing that MacDonald suffered continuous anxiety, disruption of employment, financial strain, and public obloquy while the same government that arrested him continued to investigate him from the time that formal charges were dropped in 1970 until he was indicted in 1975. Justice Stevens concurred in the judgment. He agreed with the dissenters that the Speedy Trial Clause applied, but he found no violation because the government had a need "to proceed cautiously and deliberately before making a final decision to prosecute for such a serious offense."

Reinstated Indictment: United States v. Loud Hawk

A majority of the Court relied upon *MacDonald* in United States v. Loud Hawk, 474 U.S. 302 (1986), which held that the time after a district court dismissed an indictment, and before the dismissal was reversed on appeal, should be excluded from the length of delay considered under the Speedy Trial Clause where defendants were not subject to any restraints during this time period. Justice Powell's opinion for the Court reasoned that even if the defendants remained under public suspicion, their liberty was not impaired, and impairment of liberty is the "core concern" of the Clause. Justice Marshall, joined by Justices Brennan, Blackmun, and Stevens, dissented. He argued that the defendants' position during the time that the government appealed "is most closely analogous to that of a defendant who has been arrested but not yet indicted."

Inconsistent Attachment of Sixth Amendment Rights?

The Sixth Amendment begins "In all criminal prosecutions" and then lists the rights protected, including the right to speedy trial and the right to counsel. United States v. Gouveia, 467 U.S. 180 (1984), and Kirby v. Illinois (Chapter Four, supra) construe the term "criminal prosecutions" and conclude that the right to counsel does not begin until a formal charge has been filed. In contrast, *Marion* construes the term "criminal prosecutions" and holds that the right to speedy trial attaches at *arrest*. How can the same term mean something different depending on the right invoked? Are you persuaded that there is a good reason to distinguish pre-charge and post-charge rights to speedy process?[2]

[margin handwritten notes: inconsistent application · rt to counsel starts at formal charges · rt to speedy trial begins at arrest - both 6th Am]

2. Due Process Clause Analysis

UNITED STATES v. LOVASCO

Supreme Court of the United States, 1977.
431 U.S. 783.

Mr. Justice Marshall delivered the opinion of the Court.

* * *

I

On March 6, 1975, respondent was indicted for possessing eight firearms stolen from the United States mails, and for dealing in firearms without a license. The offenses were alleged to have occurred between July 25 and August 31, 1973, more than 18 months before the indictment was filed. Respondent moved to dismiss the indictment due to the delay.

The District Court conducted a hearing on respondent's motion at which the respondent sought to prove that the delay was unnecessary and that it had prejudiced his defense. In an effort to establish the former proposition, respondent presented a Postal Inspector's report on his investigation that was prepared one month after the crimes were committed, and a stipulation concerning the post-report progress of the probe. The report stated, in brief, that within the first month of the investigation respondent had admitted to Government agents that he had possessed and then sold five of the stolen guns, and that the agents had developed strong evidence linking respondent to the remaining three weapons. The report also stated, however, that the agents had been unable to confirm or refute respondent's claim that he had found the guns in his car when he returned to it after visiting his son, a mail handler, at work. The stipulation into which the Assistant United States Attorney entered indicated that little additional in-

[margin handwritten notes: charge of possession of firearms stolen from mail + dealing in firearms w/o license; 18 mo b/f being charged; report showed: Gov agents could not prove/disprove Δ's claims that he found guns in his car when visiting his son a mail handler]

2. A comprehensive analysis of delay between criminal activity and the filing of a charge is found in Townsend, Pre–Accusation Delay, 24 S.Tex.L.Rev. 69 (1983).

formation concerning the crimes was uncovered in the 17 months following the preparation of the Inspector's report.

To establish prejudice to the defense, respondent testified that he had lost the testimony of two material witnesses due to the delay. The first witness, Tom Stewart, died more than a year after the alleged crimes occurred. At the hearing respondent claimed that Stewart had been his source for two or three of the guns. The second witness, respondent's brother, died in April 1974, eight months after the crimes were completed. Respondent testified that his brother was present when respondent called Stewart to secure the guns, and witnessed all of respondent's sales. Respondent did not state how the witnesses would have aided the defense had they been willing to testify.

* * *

II

* * *

* * * *Marion* makes clear that proof of prejudice is generally a necessary but not sufficient element of a due process claim, and that the due process inquiry must consider the reasons for the delay as well as the prejudice to the accused.

The Court of Appeals found that the sole reason for the delay here was "a hope on the part of the Government that others might be discovered who may have participated in the theft * * *." It concluded that this hope did not justify the delay, and therefore affirmed the dismissal of the indictment. But the Due Process Clause does not permit courts to abort criminal prosecutions simply because they disagree with a prosecutor's judgment as to when to seek an indictment.
* * *

It requires no extended argument to establish that prosecutors do not deviate from "fundamental conceptions of justice" when they defer seeking indictments until they have probable cause to believe an accused is guilty; indeed it is unprofessional conduct for a prosecutor to recommend an indictment on less than probable cause. It should be equally obvious that prosecutors are under no duty to file charges as soon as probable cause exists but before they are satisfied they will be able to establish the suspect's guilt beyond a reasonable doubt. To impose such a duty "would have a deleterious effect both upon the rights of the accused and upon the ability of society to protect itself." From the perspective of potential defendants, requiring prosecutions to commence when probable cause is established is undesirable because it would increase the likelihood of unwarranted charges being filed, and would add to the time during which defendants stand accused but untried. * * * From the perspective of law enforcement officials, a requirement of immediate prosecution upon probable cause is equally unacceptable because it could make obtaining proof of guilt beyond a reasonable doubt impossible by causing potentially fruitful sources of information to evaporate before they are fully exploited. And from the standpoint of the courts, such a requirement is unwise because it would cause scarce resources to be consumed on cases that prove to be insubstantial, or that involve only some of the responsible parties or some of the criminal acts. Thus, no one's interests would be well served by compelling prosecutors to initiate prosecutions as soon as they are legally entitled to do so.

It might be argued that once the Government has assembled sufficient evidence to prove guilt beyond a reasonable doubt, it should be constitutionally required to file charges promptly, even if its investigation of the entire criminal transaction is not complete. Adopting such a rule, however, would have many of the same consequences as adopting a rule requiring immediate prosecution upon probable cause.

First, compelling a prosecutor to file public charges as soon as the requisite proof has been developed against one participant on one charge would cause numerous problems in those cases in which a criminal transaction involves more than one person or more than one illegal act. In some instances, an immediate arrest or indictment would impair the prosecutor's ability to continue his investigation, thereby preventing society from bringing lawbreakers to justice. In other cases, the prosecutor would be able to obtain additional indictments despite an early prosecution, but the necessary result would be multiple trials involving a single set of facts. Such trials place needless burdens on defendants, law enforcement officials, and courts.

Second, insisting on immediate prosecution once sufficient evidence is developed to obtain a conviction would pressure prosecutors into resolving doubtful cases in favor of early—and possibly unwarranted—prosecutions. * * * In the instant case, for example, since respondent admitted possessing at least five of the firearms, the primary factual issue in dispute was whether respondent knew the guns were stolen as required by 18 U.S.C.A. § 1708. Not surprisingly, the Postal Inspector's report contained no direct evidence bearing on this issue. The decision whether to prosecute, therefore, required a necessarily subjective evaluation of the strength of the circumstantial evidence available and the credibility of respondent's denial. Even if a prosecutor concluded

that the case was weak and further investigation appropriate, he would have no assurance that a reviewing court would agree. To avoid the risk that a subsequent indictment would be dismissed for preindictment delay, the prosecutor might feel constrained to file premature charges, with all the disadvantages that would entail.

Finally, requiring the Government to make charging decisions immediately upon assembling evidence sufficient to establish guilt would preclude the Government from giving full consideration to the desirability of not prosecuting in particular cases. The decision to file criminal charges, with the awesome consequences it entails, requires consideration of a wide range of factors in addition to the strength of the Government's case, in order to determine whether prosecution would be in the public interest. Prosecutors often need more information than proof of a suspect's guilt, therefore, before deciding whether to seek an indictment. Again the instant case provides a useful illustration. Although proof of the identity of the mail thieves was not necessary to convict respondent of the possessory crimes with which he was charged, it might have been crucial in assessing respondent's culpability, as distinguished from his legal guilt. If, for example, further investigation were to show that respondent had no role in or advance knowledge of the theft and simply agreed, out of paternal loyalty, to help his son dispose of the guns once respondent discovered his son had stolen them, the United States Attorney might have decided not to prosecute, especially since at the time of the crime respondent was over 60 years old and had no prior criminal record. Requiring prosecution once the evidence of guilt is clear, however, could prevent a prosecutor from awaiting the information necessary for such a decision.

We would be most reluctant to adopt a rule which would have these consequences absent a clear constitutional command to do so. We can find no such command in the Due Process Clause of the Fifth Amendment. In our view, investigative delay is fundamentally unlike delay undertaken by the Government solely "to gain tactical advantage over the accused," precisely because investigative delay is not so one-sided. Rather than deviating from elementary standards of "fair play and decency," a prosecutor abides by them if he refuses to seek indictments until he is completely satisfied that he should prosecute and will be able

promptly to establish guilt beyond a reasonable doubt. Penalizing prosecutors who defer action for these reasons would subordinate the goal of "orderly expedition" to that of "mere speed." This the Due Process Clause does not require. We therefore hold that to prosecute a defendant following investigative delay does not deprive him of due process, even if his defense might have been somewhat prejudiced by the lapse of time.

* * *

[The dissenting opinion of Justice Stevens is omitted.]

Comment on Lovasco

If *Lovasco* had come out the other way, consider the oddity of the arguments that the parties would have to make. The defendant would have to argue that his case was indictment-worthy—he would point to the strength of the evidence against him. Then he would have to turn around and argue, to prove prejudice, that his important witnesses had been lost, thus impairing his strong defense. The government would have to argue that its case was weak, justifying delay for more investigation. This all seems reason enough to reject the idea that pre-accusation delay is actionable in the absence of bad faith on the part of the government.

Dismissal of indictments for pre-accusation delay, in the absence of bad faith, would also raise separation of powers problems. For example, in United States v. Crouch, 84 F.3d 1497 (5th Cir.1996) (en banc), the defendants, who were charged with bank fraud, argued that their indictments should be dismissed due to pre-accusation delay of seven years. They attributed the delay in their case to "lack of manpower and the low priority which this investigation was assigned." This resulted from "the failure of the Executive Branch and the Department of Justice to request sufficient funding and to assign appropriate priorities." The court responded to these contentions as follows:

> What are we to make of all this? Are we to say that there would be no due process violation if the President had vigorously and timely requested additional funds to investigate and prosecute these cases, but Congress had refused? Or, that even so we will find a due process violation because Congress shouldn't have refused? Of course, funds must come from somewhere. Are we to say that such additional funding is better than increasing taxes or the deficit or decreasing funding for some other programs? Are we to judge whether financial institution fraud should be assigned a higher priority than drug or other offenses? It seems to us that all those decisions are quintessentially the business of either the legislative or the executive branch, or both, rather than the judiciary. * * *

Accordingly, we * * * hold that for preindictment delay to violate the due process clause it must not only cause the accused substantial, actual prejudice, but the delay must also have been intentionally undertaken by the government for the purpose of gaining some tactical advantage over the accused in the contemplated prosecution or for some other impermissible, bad faith purpose. We need not now attempt to catalogue all possible "other" impermissible, bad faith purposes of intentional delay, although *Marion* indicates that a purpose "to harass" the defendant would be included. As suggested by *Marion* and *Lovasco*, we leave that to further case-by-case development.

C. ASSESSING SPEEDY TRIAL CLAIMS

BARKER v. WINGO

Supreme Court of the United States, 1972.
407 U.S. 514.

MR. JUSTICE POWELL delivered the opinion of the Court.

* * *

I

On July 20, 1958, in Christian County, Kentucky, an elderly couple was beaten to death by intruders wielding an iron tire tool. Two suspects, Silas Manning and Willie Barker, the petitioner, were arrested shortly thereafter. The grand jury indicted them on September 15. Counsel was appointed on September 17, and Barker's trial was set for October 21. The Commonwealth had a stronger case against Manning, and it believed that Barker could not be convicted unless Manning testified against him. Manning was naturally unwilling to incriminate himself. Accordingly, on October 23, the day Silas Manning was brought to trial, the Commonwealth sought and obtained the first of what was to be a series of 16 continuances of Barker's trial. Barker made no objection. By first convicting Manning, the Commonwealth would remove possible problems of self-incrimination and would be able to assure his testimony against Barker.

The Commonwealth encountered more than a few difficulties in its prosecution of Manning. The first trial ended in a hung jury. A second trial resulted in a conviction, but the Kentucky Court of Appeals reversed because of the admission of evidence obtained by an illegal search. At his third trial, Manning was again convicted, and the Court of Appeals again reversed because the trial court had not granted a change of venue. A fourth trial resulted in a hung jury. Finally, after five trials, Manning was convicted, in March 1962, of murdering one victim, and after a sixth trial, in December 1962, he was convicted of murdering the other.

The Christian County Circuit Court holds three terms each year—in February, June, and September. Barker's initial trial was to take place in the September term of 1958. The first continuance postponed it until the February 1959 term. The second continuance was granted for one month only. Every term thereafter for as long as the Manning prosecutions were in process, the Commonwealth routinely moved to continue Barker's case to the next term. When the case was continued from the June 1959 term until the following September, Barker, having spent 10 months in jail, obtained his release by posting a $5,000 bond.

He thereafter remained free in the community until his trial. Barker made no objection, through his counsel, to the first 11 continuances.

When on February 12, 1962, the Commonwealth moved for the twelfth time to continue the case until the following term, Barker's counsel filed a motion to dismiss the indictment. The motion to dismiss was denied two weeks later, and the Commonwealth's motion for a continuance was granted. The Commonwealth was granted further continuances in June 1962 and September 1962, to which Barker did not object.

In February 1963, the first term of court following Manning's final conviction, the Commonwealth moved to set Barker's trial for March 19. But on the day scheduled for trial, it again moved for a continuance until the June term. It gave as its reason the illness of the ex-sheriff who was the chief investigating officer in the case. To this continuance, Barker objected unsuccessfully.

The witness was still unable to testify in June, and the trial, which had been set for June 19, was continued again until the September term over Barker's objection. This time the court announced that the case would be dismissed for lack of prosecution if it were not tried during the next term. The final trial date was set for October 9, 1963. On that date, Barker again moved to dismiss the indictment, and this time specified that his right to a speedy trial had been violated. The motion was denied; the trial commenced with Manning as the chief prosecution witness; Barker was convicted and given a life sentence.

* * *

II

The right to a speedy trial is generically different from any of the other rights enshrined in the Constitution for the protection of the accused. In addition to the general concern that all accused persons be treated according to decent and fair procedures, there is a societal interest in providing a speedy trial which exists separate from, and at times in opposition to, the interests of the accused. The inability of courts to provide a prompt trial has contributed to a large backlog of cases in urban courts which, among other things, enables defendants to negotiate more effectively for pleas of guilty to lesser offenses and otherwise manipulate the system. In addition, persons released on bond for lengthy periods awaiting trial have an opportunity to commit other crimes. It must be of little comfort to the residents of Christian County, Kentucky, to know that Barker was at large on bail for over four years while accused of a vicious and brutal murder of which he was ultimately convicted. Moreover, the longer an accused is free awaiting trial, the more tempting becomes his opportunity to jump bail and escape. Finally, delay between arrest and punishment may have a detrimental effect on rehabilitation.

If an accused cannot make bail, he is generally confined, as was Barker for 10 months, in a local jail. This contributes to the overcrowding and generally deplorable state of those institutions. Lengthy exposure to these conditions has a destructive effect on human character and makes the rehabilitation of the individual offender much more difficult. * * * Finally, lengthy pretrial detention is costly. * * * In addition, society loses wages which might have been earned, and it must often support families of incarcerated breadwinners.

A second difference between the right to speedy trial and the accused's other constitutional rights is that deprivation of the right may work to the accused's advantage. Delay is not an uncommon defense tactic. As the time between the commission of the crime and trial lengthens, witnesses may become unavailable or their memories may fade. If the witnesses support the prosecution, its case will be weakened, sometimes seriously so. And it is the prosecution which carries the burden of proof. Thus, unlike the right to counsel or the right to be free from compelled self-incrimination, deprivation of the right to speedy trial does not *per se* prejudice the accused's ability to defend himself.

Finally, and perhaps most importantly, the right to speedy trial is a more vague concept than other procedural rights. It is, for example, impossible to determine with precision when the right has been denied. * * * As a consequence, there is no fixed point in the criminal process when the State can put the defendant to the choice of either exercising or waiving the right to a speedy trial. * * *

The amorphous quality of the right also leads to the unsatisfactorily severe remedy of dismissal of the indictment when the right has been deprived. This is indeed a serious consequence because it means that a defendant who may be guilty of a serious crime will go free, without having been tried. Such a remedy is more serious than an exclusionary rule or a reversal for a new trial, but it is the only possible remedy.

III

Perhaps because the speedy trial right is so slippery, two rigid approaches are urged upon us as ways of eliminating some of the uncertainty which courts experience in protecting the right. The first suggestion is that we hold that the Constitution requires a criminal defendant to be offered a trial within a specified time period. The result of such a ruling would have the virtue of clarifying when the right is infringed and of simplifying courts' application of it. * * *

But such a result would require this Court to engage in legislative or rule-making activity, rather than in the adjudicative process to which we should confine our efforts. * * * We find no constitutional basis for holding that the speedy trial right can be quantified into a specified number of days or months. The States, of course, are free to prescribe a reasonable period consistent with constitutional standards, but our approach must be less precise.

The second suggested alternative would restrict consideration of the right to those cases in which the accused has demanded a speedy trial. * * *

Such an approach, by presuming waiver of a fundamental right from inaction, is inconsistent with this Court's pronouncements on waiver of constitutional rights. * * *

The nature of the speedy trial right does make it impossible to pinpoint a precise time in the process when the right must be asserted or waived, but that fact does not argue for placing the burden of protecting the right solely on defendants. A defendant has no duty to bring himself to trial; the State has that duty as well as the duty of insuring that the trial is consistent with due process. Moreover, for the reasons earlier expressed, society has a particular interest in bringing swift prosecutions, and society's representatives are the ones who should protect that interest.

* * *

We reject, therefore, the rule that a defendant who fails to demand a speedy trial forever waives his right. This does not mean, however, that the defendant has no responsibility to assert his right. We think the better

[margin note: failure to exercise rt → factor in determining prejudice]

rule is that the defendant's assertion of or failure to assert his right to a speedy trial is one of the factors to be considered in an inquiry into the deprivation of the right. Such a formulation * * * allows the trial court to exercise a judicial discretion based on the circumstances, including due consideration of any applicable formal procedural rule. It would permit, for example, a court to attach a different weight to a situation in which the defendant knowingly fails to object from a situation in which his attorney acquiesces in long delay without adequately informing his client, or from a situation in which no counsel is appointed. It would also allow a court to weigh the frequency and force of the objections as opposed to attaching significant weight to a purely *pro forma* objection.

[margin note: Ct + pros bear burden of bringing (cases) in timely manner]

* * * We have shown above that the right to a speedy trial is unique in its uncertainty as to when and under what circumstances it must be asserted or may be deemed waived. But the rule we announce today, which comports with constitutional principles, places the primary burden on the courts and the prosecutors to assure that cases are brought to trial. We hardly need add that if delay is attributable to the defendant, then his waiver may be given effect under standard waiver doctrine, the demand rule aside.

* * *

IV

A balancing test necessarily compels courts to approach speedy trial cases on an *ad hoc* basis. We can do little more than identify some of the factors which courts should assess in determining whether a particular defendant has been deprived of his right. Though some might express them in different ways, we identify four such factors:

[margin note: 4 factors to consider to determine rights]

Length of delay, the reason for the delay, the defendant's assertion of his right, and prejudice to the defendant.

The length of the delay is to some extent a triggering mechanism. Until there is some delay which is presumptively prejudicial, there is no necessity for inquiry into the other factors that go into the balance. Nevertheless, because of the imprecision of the right to speedy trial, the length of delay that will provoke such an inquiry is necessarily dependent upon the peculiar circumstances of the case. To take but one example, the delay that can be tolerated for an ordinary street crime is considerably less than for a serious, complex conspiracy charge.

Closely related to length of delay is the reason the government assigns to justify the delay. Here, too, different weights should be assigned to different reasons. A deliberate attempt to delay the trial in order to hamper the defense should be weighted heavily against the government. A more neutral reason such as negligence or overcrowded courts should be weighted less heavily but nevertheless should be considered since the ultimate responsibility for such circumstances must rest with the government rather than with the defendant. Finally, a valid reason, such as a missing witness, should serve to justify appropriate delay.

We have already discussed the third factor, the defendant's responsibility to assert his right. Whether and how a defendant asserts his right is closely related to the other factors we have mentioned. The strength of his efforts will be affected by the length of the delay, to some extent by the reason for the delay, and most particularly by the personal prejudice, which is not always readily identifiable, that he experiences. The more serious the deprivation, the more likely a defendant is to complain. The defendant's assertion of his speedy trial right, then, is entitled to strong evidentiary weight in determining whether the defendant is being deprived of the right. We emphasize that failure to assert the right will make it difficult for a defendant to prove that he was denied a speedy trial.

A fourth factor is prejudice to the defendant. Prejudice, of course, should be assessed in the light of the interests of defendants which the speedy trial right was designed to protect. This Court has identified three such interests: (i) to prevent oppressive pretrial incarceration; (ii) to minimize anxiety and concern of the accused; and (iii) to limit the possibility that the defense will be impaired. Of these, the most serious is the last, because the inability of a defendant adequately to prepare his case skews the fairness of the entire system. If witnesses die or disappear during a delay, the prejudice is obvious. There is also prejudice if defense witnesses are unable to recall accurately events of the distant past. * * *

We have discussed previously the societal disadvantages of lengthy pretrial incarceration, but obviously the disadvantages for the accused who cannot obtain his release are even more serious. The time spent in jail awaiting trial has a detrimental impact on the individual. It often means loss of a job; it disrupts family life; and it enforces idleness. * * * The time spent in jail is simply dead time. Moreover, if a defendant is locked up, he is hindered in his ability to gather evidence, contact witnesses, or otherwise prepare his defense. Imposing those consequences on anyone who has not yet been convicted is serious. It is especially unfortunate to impose them on those persons who are ultimately found to be innocent. Finally, even if an accused is not incarcerated prior to trial, he is still disadvantaged by restraints on his liberty and by living under a cloud of anxiety, suspicion, and often hostility.

We regard none of the four factors identified above as either a necessary or sufficient condition to the finding of a deprivation of the right of speedy trial. Rather, they are related factors and must be considered together with such other circumstances as may be relevant. * * *

V

The difficulty of the task of balancing these factors is illustrated by this case, which we consider to be close. It is clear that the length of delay between arrest and trial—well over five years—was extraordinary. Only seven months of that period can be attributed to a strong excuse, the illness of the ex-sheriff who was in charge of the investigation. Perhaps some delay would have been permissible under ordinary circumstances, so that Manning could be utilized as a witness in Barker's trial, but more than four years was too long a period, particularly since a good part of that period was attributable to the Commonwealth's failure or inability to try Manning under circumstances that comported with due process.

Two counterbalancing factors, however, outweigh these deficiencies. The first is that prejudice was minimal. Of course, Barker was prejudiced to some extent by living for over four years under a cloud of suspicion and anxiety. Moreover, although he was released on bond for most of the period, he did spend 10 months in jail before trial. But there is no claim that any of Barker's witnesses died or otherwise became unavailable owing to the delay. The trial transcript indicates only two very minor lapses of memory—one on the part of a prosecution witness—which were in no way significant to the outcome.

More important than the absence of serious prejudice, is the fact that Barker did not want a speedy trial. * * * Instead the record strongly suggests that while he hoped to take advantage of the delay in which he had acquiesced, and thereby obtain a dismissal of the charges, he definitely did not want to be tried.

* * *

The probable reason for Barker's attitude was that he was gambling on Manning's acquittal. The evidence was not very strong against Manning, as the reversals and hung juries suggest, and Barker undoubtedly thought that if Manning were acquitted, he would never be tried.

* * *

We do not hold that there may never be a situation in which an indictment may be dismissed on speedy trial grounds where the defendant has failed to object to continuances. There

may be a situation in which the defendant was represented by incompetent counsel, was severely prejudiced, or even cases in which the continuances were granted *ex parte*. But barring extraordinary circumstances, we would be reluctant indeed to rule that a defendant was denied this constitutional right on a record that strongly indicates as does this one, that the defendant did not want a speedy trial. We hold, therefore, that Barker was not deprived of his due process right to a speedy trial.

The judgment of the Court of Appeals is affirmed.

Mr. Justice White, with whom Mr. Justice Brennan joins, concurring.

Although the Court rejects petitioner's speedy trial claim * * *, it is apparent that had Barker not so clearly acquiesced in the major delays * * * the result would have been otherwise. * * *

Application of the Barker Test: Doggett v. United States

In Doggett v. United States, 505 U.S. 647 (1992), the Court applied and elaborated upon the *Barker* factors. It found that an eight and one half year delay between Doggett's indictment and trial violated his Sixth Amendment right to a speedy trial, even though Doggett knew nothing about the indictment during that delay. Doggett was indicted on federal drug charges, but he left the country before he could be informed of the indictment. Two years after leaving, he returned to the United States, passed unhindered through Customs, married, went to college, found a job, lived openly under his own name, and engaged in no further criminal misconduct. Six years after his return, the Marshal's Service ran a credit check on several thousand people subject to outstanding arrest warrants and, within minutes, found where Doggett lived and worked. He was arrested within days of the credit check. Up to the time of his arrest, Doggett was never aware of the fact that he had been indicted more than eight years earlier.

Justice Souter wrote the majority opinion for five Justices. He addressed the first *Barker* factor—whether delay before trial was "uncommonly long"—as a "double enquiry." He explained as follows:

Simply to trigger a speedy trial analysis, an accused must allege that the interval between accusation and trial has crossed the threshold dividing ordinary from "presumptively prejudicial" delay, * * *. If the accused makes this showing, the court must then consider, as one factor among several, the extent to which the delay stretches beyond the bare minimum needed to trigger judicial examination of the claim. This latter enquiry is significant to the speedy trial analysis because * * * the presumption that pretrial delay has prejudiced the accused intensifies over time.

So to trigger a *Barker* enquiry, the defendant must show that the delay was presumptively prejudicial. The *Doggett* majority stated that lower courts have generally undertaken the *Barker* enquiry when the period of postaccusation delay "approaches one year."[3] The Court therefore had no trouble finding that the "extraordinary" delay in Doggett's case was sufficient "to trigger the speedy trial enquiry."

As to the second *Barker* factor, concerning responsibility for the delay, Justice Souter relied on the findings of the lower court that the delay occurring after Doggett returned to the United States was attributable to the government. He concluded that "while the Government's lethargy may have reflected no more than Doggett's relative unimportance in the world of drug trafficking, it was still findable negligence, and the finding stands."

As to the third *Barker* factor, concerning the defendant's diligence in asserting his speedy trial rights, Justice Souter again relied on the findings of the lower court that Doggett was unaware of his indictment until he was arrested. Had that not been the case, the third factor would have been "weighed heavily against him." Thus, Justice Souter implied that a person who knows he is indicted, and who is at large, will lose his speedy trial claim because of his failure to timely assert it, even if he is not being diligently pursued by the authorities.

The fourth *Barker* factor, that of prejudice due to the delay, presented the most difficult problem for the majority, because Doggett was neither incarcerated nor aware of his indictment during the delay. Justice Souter noted that there was more to the "prejudice" factor than incarceration and anxiety over the indictment:

> We have observed in prior cases that unreasonable delay between formal accusation and trial threatens to produce more than one sort of harm, including * * * the possibility that the accused's defense will be impaired by dimming memories and loss of exculpatory evidence. * * * [T]he inability of a defendant adequately to prepare his case skews the fairness of the entire system.

After holding that the defendant could be prejudiced by the delay even though he was not incarcerated or under any anxiety during that time, the majority addressed the Government's argument that Doggett's claim should fail because he had "failed to make any affirmative showing that the delay weakened his ability to raise specific defenses, elicit specific testimony, or produce specific items of evidence." Justice Souter responded to this argument by stating that "consideration of prejudice is not limited to the specifically demonstrable" and that "affirmative proof of particularized prejudice is not essential to every speedy trial claim." He elaborated as follows:

3. See also Joseph, Speedy Trial Rights in Application, 48 Fordham L.Rev. 611 (1980)(quoted in *Doggett*, noting a general consensus that a delay is presumptively prejudicial if it is longer than eight months, and that there is general agreement that a delay of less than five months is not presumptively prejudicial).

[T]hough time can tilt the case against either side, one cannot generally be sure which of them it has prejudiced more severely. Thus, we generally have to recognize that excessive delay presumptively compromises the reliability of a trial in ways that neither party can prove or, for that matter, identify. While such presumptive prejudice cannot alone carry a Sixth Amendment claim without regard to the other *Barker* criteria, it is part of the mix of relevant facts, and its importance increases with the length of delay.

* * * Our speedy trial standards recognize that pretrial delay is often both inevitable and wholly justifiable. The government may need time to collect witnesses against the accused, oppose his pretrial motions, or, if he goes into hiding, track him down. We attach great weight to such considerations when balancing them against the costs of going forward with a trial whose probative accuracy the passage of time has begun by degrees to throw into question. Thus, in this case, if the Government had pursued Doggett with reasonable diligence from his indictment to his arrest, his speedy trial claim would fail. * * *

* * * [O]n the other hand, Doggett would prevail if he could show that the Government had intentionally held back in its prosecution of him to gain some impermissible advantage at trial. * * *

Between diligent prosecution and bad-faith delay, official negligence in bringing an accused to trial occupies the middle ground. While not compelling relief in every case where bad-faith delay would make relief virtually automatic, neither is negligence automatically tolerable simply because the accused cannot demonstrate exactly how it has prejudiced him. * * *

Although negligence is obviously to be weighed more lightly than a deliberate intent to harm the accused's defense, it still falls on the wrong side of the divide between acceptable and unacceptable reasons for delaying a criminal prosecution once it has begun. And such is the nature of the prejudice presumed that the weight we assign to official negligence compounds over time as the presumption of evidentiary prejudice grows. Thus, our toleration of such negligence varies inversely with its protractedness, and its consequent threat to the fairness of the accused's trial. Condoning prolonged and unjustifiable delays in prosecution would both penalize many defendants for the state's fault and simply encourage the government to gamble with the interests of criminal suspects assigned a low prosecutorial priority. * * *

To be sure, to warrant granting relief, negligence unaccompanied by particularized trial prejudice must have lasted longer than negligence demonstrably causing such prejudice. But even so, the Government's egregious persistence in failing to prosecute Doggett is clearly sufficient.

Applying these factors, Justice Souter concluded that Doggett was entitled to dismissal of the indictment because the Government's negligence caused a delay "six times as long as that generally sufficient to trigger judicial review" and the presumption of prejudice was "neither extenuated, as by the defendant's acquiescence, nor persuasively rebutted."

Justice O'Connor wrote a short dissenting opinion. She would have required a showing of actual prejudice. She also noted that "delay is a two-edged sword" because the Government bears the burden of proof beyond a reasonable doubt, and "the passage of time may make it difficult or impossible for the Government to carry this burden."

Justice Thomas, joined by Chief Justice Rehnquist and Justice Scalia, wrote a lengthy dissent in which he argued that the Speedy Trial Clause provides direct protection against only two "evils": 1) "oppressive and undue incarceration;" and 2) the "anxiety and concern accompanying public accusation." Because Doggett suffered neither of these burdens during the delay, Justice Thomas would have dismissed the speedy trial claim even if Doggett had proven that the passage of time had prejudiced his defense. In Justice Thomas' view, any possibility that a defendant may not be able to defend himself due to a pretrial delay was adequately protected by the Due Process Clause and by statutes of limitations.

Justice Thomas argued that the Speedy Trial Clause could not logically be concerned with prejudice to the defense resulting from pretrial delay. He explained as follows:

> [P]rejudice to the defense stems from the interval between crime and trial, which is quite distinct from the interval between accusation and trial. * * * A defendant prosecuted 10 years after a crime is just as hampered in his ability to defend himself whether he was indicted the week after the crime or the week before the trial—but no one would suggest that the Clause protects him in the latter situation, where the delay did not substantially impair his liberty, either through oppressive incarceration or the anxiety of known criminal charges. * * * The initiation of a formal criminal prosecution is simply irrelevant to whether the defense has been prejudiced by delay.

Justice Thomas concluded with an argument that the majority's decision would allow excessive judicial intrusion into law enforcement decisionmaking. He explained as follows:

> Today's opinion, I fear, will transform the courts of the land into boards of law-enforcement supervision. For the Court compels dismissal of the charges against Doggett not because he was harmed in any way by the delay between his indictment and arrest, but simply because the Government's efforts to catch him are found wanting. * * * By divorcing the Speedy Trial Clause of all considerations of prejudice to an accused, the Court positively invites the Nation's judges to indulge in an ad hoc and result-driven second-guessing of the government's investigatory efforts.

Questions After Doggett

Before *Doggett*, lower courts had held that with respect to sealed (secret) indictments, the protections of the Speedy Trial Clause are triggered not when the indictment is filed, but when it is unsealed. See, e.g., United States v. Hay, 527 F.2d 990 (10th Cir.1975). Are these decisions good law after *Doggett*?

Who suffers more from a pretrial delay: a person who knows he is being investigated but has not been arrested, or a person like Doggett who has been indicted but knows nothing about it? If you think that a person who is being investigated suffers more than a person like Doggett, does that mean that

Justice Thomas is correct in concluding that *Barker's* prejudice analysis is flawed? Or does it mean that the Court in *Marion* was wrong when it denied the protection of the Speedy Trial Clause to persons who have not yet been arrested or charged?

*Rule: When Gov has excusible delay
∆ has burden to prove prejudice
substantially increased.*

Excusable Delay

What is excusible delay?

Doggett holds that when the government has a good reason for a post-charge delay, the defendant's burden of showing prejudice is substantially increased. What constitutes excusable delay? In United States v. Vassell, 970 F.2d 1162 (2d Cir.1992), the court held that a seven-month delay did not amount to a Speedy Trial Clause violation where the government spent most of that time trying to get Vassell's co-defendant to take a deal and testify against Vassell. The court stated:

○ getting ○ co-∆ to take deal + testify during 7mo.

> A guilty plea takes time to negotiate. A defendant may initially reject the plea offered by the government. Because prosecutors must obtain approval of a plea from their superiors, negotiations may drag on almost interminably. At some point the process may become so extreme as to prejudice co-defendants who are either not offered a plea, or who reject the plea offer. However, we are not called upon to establish a rigid time table prescribing how long the government may take to procure a guilty plea. Rather, consistent with the ad hoc balancing required by *Barker*, we hold only that a seven-month delay in a complex case is not transformed into a Sixth Amendment violation just because the government sought the delay to encourage a co-defendant to testify against a remaining defendant at trial.

Do you think that the *Vassell* court imposed a meaningful limitation on government-induced delay in multi-defendant cases?

○ interlocutory is excusible delay

In United States v. Loud Hawk, 474 U.S. 302 (1986), a majority of the Supreme Court concluded that "an interlocutory appeal by the Government [an appeal on a judge's ruling before a verdict has been rendered] ordinarily is a valid reason that justifies delay." Justice Powell's opinion observed that in assessing whether the delay is justifiable, the factors that might be examined "include the strength of the Government's position on the appealed issue, the importance of the issue in the posture of the case, and—in some cases—the seriousness of the crime." The opinion also stated that defendants ordinarily cannot use the delay caused by their own interlocutory appeals to support a speedy trial claim, although they might be able to do so if they "bear the heavy burden of showing an unreasonable delay caused by the prosecution in that appeal, or a wholly unjustifiable delay by the appellate court." Justice Marshall's dissenting opinion, joined by Justices Brennan, Blackmun, and Stevens, argued that the court of appeals, which took over five years to decide two interlocutory appeals, one of which was expedited, delayed a "patently unreasonable" amount of time and that the prosecutor's good faith could not discharge the responsibility of a court to decide an appeal within a reasonable period of time.

Defendant's Diligence

Under *Barker* and *Doggett*, a defendant's diligence in asserting his speedy trial right is a critical factor. Exemplary is United States v. Aguirre, 994 F.2d 1454 (9th Cir.1993). Aguirre knew about his indictment during the five-year period before he was arrested. While the five-year delay was presumptively prejudicial under *Doggett*, the court noted that the government had diligently pursued the defendant during that period. Because the delay was not attributable to the government but to Aguirre's evasive actions, Aguirre was required to show prejudice, and this he could not do. But the court said that even if Aguirre had shown prejudice, his speedy trial claim would have been denied:

> Where, as here, the government diligently pursues the defendant and the defendant is aware that the government is trying to find him, even severe prejudice would still not be enough to tip the balance in his favor. Here Aguirre knew his charges were pending, but [chose not to appear]; the government, on the other hand, conducted a reasonably diligent investigation to find him. It's true that prejudice can arise with time, but it's equally true in situations like Aguirre's that the defendant, not the government, is in the best position to stop the clock and avoid the damage.

Is the *Aguirre* court really saying that delay, no matter how long and no matter how prejudicial, is irrelevant if the defendant knows about the charges and fails to appear? Would the case be different if the government had not been diligently pursuing Aguirre? How does the *Barker–Doggett* balance come out if neither the prosecution nor the defendant is acting diligently? See United States v. Juarez–Fierro, 935 F.2d 672 (5th Cir.1991)(four month delay due to negligent failure to procure attendance of a witness did not violate the right to a speedy trial, where the defendant's speedy trial claim was made for the first time on appeal).

It goes without saying that to the extent the trial is delayed because the defendant is making pre-trial motions that are being considered and disposed of, this will count against the defendant in the *Barker/Doggett* calculus. See United States v. Munoz–Amado, 182 F.3d 57 (1st Cir.1999) (rejecting a speedy trial claim and noting that the defendant "ignores the role his many pretrial motions played in causing the nineteen month delay between his indictment and the jury trial").

Delay and Prejudice

The Court in *Doggett* stated that, at some point, delay attributable to the government will be so extended that prejudice will be presumed, i.e., the defendant will not have to show, specifically, how he was prejudiced by the delay. The need to find prejudice thus diminishes as the delay mounts. The eight-year delay in *Doggett* went beyond the point of presumptive prejudice; but where is that point exactly? In United States v. Beamon, 992 F.2d 1009 (9th Cir.1993), the government was responsible for a 17 month delay. While this was long enough to trigger a *Barker-Doggett* inquiry, the court held that it was not long enough "to relieve the defendant of the burden of coming forward with any showing of actual prejudice." Thus forced to show prejudice, the defendant argued that the delay impaired his ability to negotiate a deal with the government. But the court held that "a diminished plea bargaining position does not amount to impairment of defense."[4] Because the defendant could not show that

---

4. For another case on the meaning of "prejudice" under *Barker* and *Doggett*, see United States v. Mundt, 29 F.3d 233 (6th Cir. 1994)(in a tax prosecution, the defendant suffered no prejudice from a long delay where his "position was and continues to be that he is not subject to the federal tax laws"; such defense is not dependent on witnesses or fresh recollections).

he suffered any form of prejudice pursuant to trial presentation, his appeal was dismissed. Compare United States v. Shell, 974 F.2d 1035 (9th Cir.1992)(no showing of prejudice required when government negligence caused a five year delay).

Thus, under *Doggett*, the term "presumptive prejudice" has two distinct meanings. First, the delay must be so long as to trigger the *Barker-Doggett* inquiry in the first place. In this sense, the delay is presumptively prejudicial when it approaches one year. Second, if the delay is attributable to the government, it can be so extended as to be presumptively prejudicial—meaning in this context that the defendant does not need to show specifically how the delay prejudiced him. In *Beamon*, the 17 month delay was presumptively prejudicial in the first (threshold, triggering) sense, but not in the second (balancing) sense. In *Doggett*, the delay was presumptively prejudicial as to both the threshold and the balancing inquiries. See also United States v. Brown, 169 F.3d 344 (6th Cir. 1999) (five year delay between indictment and trial; the fact that the defendant was evading the authorities was irrelevant because he was not aware of the indictment; because the delay was so lengthy, the defendant was not required to indicate the prejudice that he suffered due to the delay: "Given the extraordinary delay in this case combined with the fact that the delay was attributable to the government's negligence in pursuing Brown, we conclude that the government did not sufficiently rebut the presumption that its delay did not prejudice Brown's case."); United States v. Graham, 128 F.3d 372 (6th Cir.1997) (eight year delay, much of it due to the trial court's failure to move discovery along and to appoint new counsel for one of the co-defendants; prejudice in *Barker-Doggett* balancing inquiry was presumed due to the length of the delay).

Won't it almost always be the prosecution, rather than the defense, that suffers actual prejudice from a delay in the trial? See Green, "Hare and Hounds": The Fugitive Defendant's Constitutional Right to be Pursued, 56 Brooklyn L.Rev. 439, 507 (1990)("the passage of time is more likely to hurt the prosecution than the defense which, after all, has no obligation to call witnesses or present evidence, but need only, and in many cases does only, put the government to its proof").

D. REMEDIES FOR SPEEDY TRIAL VIOLATIONS

In Strunk v. United States, 412 U.S. 434 (1973), the Court considered what remedies are properly available when the defendant's right to a speedy trial has been violated. The court of appeals had found a speedy trial violation, but declared that the "extreme" remedy of dismissal of the charges with prejudice was unwarranted. The court of appeals thought that a more appropriate remedy would be reduction in Strunk's sentence to compensate for the period of unnecessary delay. But Chief Justice Burger's opinion for a unanimous Court rejected this alternative. The Chief Justice wrote that "[i]n light of the policies which underlie the right to a speedy trial, dismissal must remain, as *Barker* noted, the only possible remedy."

Can you imagine situations in which you might find a speedy trial violation but not require dismissal? For example, if the only form of prejudice suffered by delay was incarceration, would it make sense to simply reduce the sentence of a defendant who was convicted after a delayed trial? Why is dismissal necessary in such a case?

If *Strunk* really means that there is only one remedy for all speedy trial violations and that remedy is dismissal, how likely is it that the courts will find such violations? Professor Arkin, in Speedy Criminal Appeal: A Right Without a Remedy, 74 Minn.L.Rev. 437, 482 (1990), states that because of the extreme, exclusive remedy provided by *Barker* and *Strunk,* courts have "refused to find speedy trial violations except in the most outlandish cases" and that the *Barker-Strunk* remedy "effectively gutted the right."

E.　BEYOND THE CONSTITUTION: STATUTORY AND JUDICIAL TIME LIMITS

Although not required by the Sixth Amendment, a large number of jurisdictions have, by statute or court rule, set time limits for bringing cases to trial. The statutes and rules that have been adopted differ greatly, since each jurisdiction is free to set up any protective system that it wishes. Because of these statutes and rules, there has been "a shift from the amorphousness of constitutional litigation to the relative certainty of legislative enforcement. The final outcome is a more effective protection of the right to a speedy trial." Arkin, supra, at 440. It should be noted, however, that these enactments do not in all cases ensure prompt adjudication of criminal cases. See R. Misner, Speedy Trial: Federal and State Practice § 17.13 (1983).

The Speedy Trial Act

One important statute is the Speedy Trial Act of 1974. 18 U.S.C.A. §§ 3161–74. The Act provides definite time periods for bringing an accused to trial. For example, any indictment or information must be filed within 30 days of arrest (or, if no grand jury is in session, 60 days);[5] arraignment of a defendant pursuant to Fed.R.Crim.P. 10 must be within ten days of either the public filing date of the indictment or information or the date a defendant has been ordered held to answer and has appeared before a judicial officer of the court in which the charge is pending, whichever date is later; and trial must commence within 70 days of arraignment. The Act also provides for a number of periods of delay that do not count in computing the time periods between various events. Examples of "excludible delay" include: time needed to determine the competency of the defendant; delay resulting from other trials of the defendant; delay resulting from interlocutory appeals; delay resulting from pre-trial motions; and delay made necessary by the "interests of justice."[6]

Dismissal With or Without Prejudice

If the applicable time limits of the Speedy Trial Act are not adhered to, charges against the defendant are to be dismissed *either with or without*

5.　See United States v. Orbino, 981 F.2d 1035 (9th Cir.1992)(30–day clock does not begin to run when a defendant, under suspicion of a crime for which he is later convicted, is in the meantime arrested on an unrelated charge).

6.　See, e.g., United States v. Drapeau, 978 F.2d 1072 (8th Cir.1992)(8–week continuance was excludible delay within the "interests of justice" exception, where delay was necessary to obtain results of DNA testing).

prejudice.[7] See 18 U.S.C.A. § 3162(a)(1)(2). Some of the factors that are to be considered, in determining whether dismissal should be with or without prejudice, include: the seriousness of the offense; the facts and circumstances which led to the dismissal; and the impact of a reprosecution on the administration of the Act and the administration of justice. Some commentators have discussed these and other factors and have analyzed how the Act has been implemented by federal judges.[8]

In United States v. Taylor, 487 U.S. 326 (1988), the Supreme Court reversed the dismissal of an indictment with prejudice where the defendant failed to appear for his trial on federal narcotics charges, which was scheduled one day prior to expiration of the statutory period, and subsequently the government exceeded by 15 days the period permitted between the defendant's arrest and the filing of a superseding indictment. Justice Blackmun wrote for the court and reasoned that the statute provides no preference for whether a dismissal should be with or without prejudice; it permits district courts to exercise sound discretion. The Court noted that the statute sets forth specific factors—seriousness of the offense, facts and circumstances leading to dismissal, and the impact of a reprosecution on the speedy trial process and the administration of justice—as being "among others" that the Court may consider in ruling on a motion to dismiss. The Court determined that prejudice to the defendant was also a factor. It observed that the district court did not explain why these factors justified a dismissal with prejudice and that it had ignored the "brevity of the delay" as well as Taylor's own "illicit contribution to the delay" (i.e., his failure to appear).

Where the defendant has already served a good part of his sentence by the time of appeal, the preferred remedy for a Speedy Trial Act violation is a dismissal of the indictment. The court applied this preference in United States v. Blackwell, 12 F.3d 44 (5th Cir.1994):

> [W]hile the maximum time of incarceration Blackwell could receive for committing the offense of impersonating a federal officer is three years, he has already been incarcerated for over two years. * * * [A] reprosecution would work a manifest injustice upon Blackwell, given the time he has already effectively "served" for this conviction which we reverse today due to the Speedy Trial Act violation in this case.

F. THE RIGHT TO A SPEEDY APPEAL

Does the Sixth Amendment right to speedy trial include a right to speedy appeal? The court in Rheuark v. Shaw, 477 F.Supp. 897 (N.D.Tex.1979), said yes. Is the right determined by resort to the *Barker* factors? If so, it would seem that all speedy appeal claims would founder on the prejudice prong of *Barker,* unless the appeal itself was meritorious. Delay of an appeal does not result in

---

7. Some states require dismissals to be with prejudice. See, e.g., Alaska Crim.R. 45(g); Wash.Sup.Ct.Rule 33(i).

In United States v. Blackwell, 12 F.3d 44 (5th Cir.1994), the court held that the provisions of the Speedy Trial Act are not waivable by the defendant, because the Act is intended to protect the public as well as the defendant, by ensuring that criminal trials are quickly resolved.

8. See, e.g., Steinberg, Dismissal With or Without Prejudice Under the Speedy Trial Act: A Proposed Interpretation, 68 J.Crim.L. & Cr. 1 (1977).

Misner, Speedy Trial: Federal and State Practice (1983), analyzes speedy trial statutes and rules throughout the United States.

the loss of evidence that would be relevant for the appeal; nor is incarceration problematic if the defendant has been justly convicted. Is the result of this reasoning that a defendant with an unmeritorious appeal has no right to a speedy appeal? See United States v. Tucker, 8 F.3d 673 (9th Cir.1993)(because the defendant's appeal lacked merit, his incarceration pending appeal was not "oppressive" and his appeal was not impaired by delay).

What is the remedy for a defendant with a meritorious appeal—an order that the appeal be heard? Professor Arkin, in Speedy Criminal Appeal: A Right Without a Remedy, 74 Minn.L.Rev. 437 (1990), argues that the *Barker* prejudice factor is inapposite in the appellate context, and that remedies for a denial of the right to speedy appeal should include reduction of sentence or discharge from custody in egregious cases.

[handwritten margin note: remedy for lack of speedy appeal should be reduction not dismissal]

In Simmons v. Reynolds, 898 F.2d 865 (2d Cir.1990), the court held that the defendant, a state prisoner, was not entitled to be released from custody, even though a six year delay in hearing his state appeal violated his due process rights. The court found that the disposition of his state appeal while his habeas corpus petition was pending transformed the prisoner's custody from illegal to legal. The Court concluded that any prejudice the prisoner suffered from the delay did not harm his ability to have a fair review of his conviction. It noted that the prisoner could seek redress through a federal civil rights action for damages. See also Muwwakkil v. Hoke, 968 F.2d 284 (2d Cir.1992)(13 year delay in appeal was a violation of due process, but no remedy is warranted where the defendant cannot show that the result of the appeal would have been different but for the delay).

[handwritten margin note: No dismissal for 6 yr delay. Ct could still adequately review conviction]

II. JOINDER AND SEVERANCE

A. SOME GENERAL RULES AND PROBLEMS

The outcome of a criminal case can be affected by the number and nature of charges and defendants joined together. There was a time when the government could only charge one offense in an indictment and was greatly restricted in trying defendants jointly over objection. But that time is long past, largely because of the perceived economies of joinder in an era of scarce resources. In Richardson v. Marsh, 481 U.S. 200 (1987), Justice Scalia, writing for the Court, had this to say about the advantages of joining defendants:

> Joint trials play a vital role in the criminal justice system, accounting for almost one third of federal criminal trials in the past five years. Many joint trials—for example, those involving large conspiracies to import and distribute illegal drugs—involve a dozen or more codefendants. * * * It would impair both the efficiency and the fairness of the criminal justice system to require * * * that prosecutors bring separate proceedings, presenting the same evidence again and again, requiring victims and witnesses to repeat the inconvenience (and sometimes trauma) of testifying, and randomly favoring the last-tried defendants who have the advantage of knowing the prosecution's case beforehand. Joint trials generally serve the interests of justice by avoiding inconsistent verdicts and enabling more accurate assessment of relative culpability—advantages which sometimes operate to the defendant's benefit. Even apart from these tactical consider-

ations, joint trials generally serve the interests of justice by avoiding the scandal and inequity of inconsistent verdicts.

Similar benefits, especially from the government's point of view, can flow from joining multiple counts against a single defendant. But there also are dangers when joinder is effected—most obviously, that defendants will suffer prejudice from the jury's possible tendency to merge defendants and charges into one big guilty verdict. The Federal Rules of Criminal Procedure attempt to strike a balance through three separate but related rules. Rule 8 governs the charges and defendants that can be joined. The Rule provides that charges against a single defendant can be joined if the offenses "are of the same or similar character or are based on the same act or transaction, or are connected with or constitute parts of a common scheme or plan." The Rule further provides that defendants can be joined "if they are alleged to have participated in the same act or transaction, or in the same series of acts or transactions, constituting an offense or offenses." Rule 13 permits the court to consolidate separate actions if they could have been joined under Rule 8. Rule 14 gives the court discretion to sever or to provide other relief if prejudice would result from joinder.

The principal arguments respecting joinder center around two competing assertions: (1) The defense contends that the government is seeking an unfair advantage by having charges combined in order to brand the defendant as a bad person, to show that "birds of a feather flock together," to reduce a jury's regret at convicting the defendant in a world of imperfect proof, or to establish a "where there's smoke, there's fire" attitude in the trier of fact.[9] (2) The government contends that the defense is trying to separate out issues to wear down the government, to compartmentalize a case in order to weaken it, to increase the odds that witnesses and evidence will become unavailable, or to increase the odds of winning at least one case.[10]

The competing policy considerations—efficiency in the presentation of evidence versus a fair trial on each charge made against a defendant—are best understood in the context of actual cases.

B. JOINDER OF CLAIMS

United States v. Holloway, 1 F.3d 307 (5th Cir.1993), illustrates a simple problem of joinder of claims. Holloway was identified as a culprit in two armed bank robberies. When he was arrested for these robberies, he was found to be carrying a firearm. Holloway had been convicted previously of a felony. The government joined the bank robbery counts with an additional count for felon firearm possession. The government never contended that the gun found on Holloway when he was arrested was the same gun used in the bank robberies. Holloway requested a severance of the felon firearm possession count from the other counts, but this was denied. The court of appeals, however, found that the firearms count was improperly joined under Rule 8(a), and therefore that the trial court abused its discretion in failing to sever it. The court analyzed the severance question in light of the standards of Rule 8(a):

9. Conversely, the defendant sometimes may want weak charges combined with strong ones in the hope that reasonable doubts as to the weak ones will carry over to the others.

10. Usually the government wants to win at least one case. But defendants may believe that their best strategy is "divide and conquer."

Δ claim
felony possession diff than is not same or similar char as underlying offense
- no sev Joinder

Holloway argues that the mere possession of a weapon when one is arrested, which is unrelated to the crime for which he is arrested, is not a charge that is of "the same or similar character" as the commission of the underlying offense. Furthermore, Holloway argues that the government's allegation that he possessed a weapon nearly two months after the last alleged robbery occurred is not "based on the same act or transaction" as any of the robberies; nor can it be said to constitute part of "a common scheme or plan" connected to the earlier completed robberies.

Δ - he possed weapon 2 mo after crime · no common scheme

* * *

* * * Plainly speaking, we can see no basis for the United States Attorney to have included this weapons charge in the indictment in the first place unless he was seeking to get before the jury evidence that likely would be otherwise inadmissible, i.e., that Holloway was a convicted felon and that he had a weapon on his person when arrested. * * *

No basis for Joinder · no admission in trial

We thus conclude that this remote weapons charge should never have been joined with the other counts of Holloway's indictment in the first place. [By joining] the weapons charge with the robbery charges, the jury emphatically was told that Holloway was a bad and dangerous person "by his very nature" and that a felon who carried a gun was just the sort of character who was most likely to have committed the robberies charged in the indictment. In short, Holloway was unjustifiably tried, at least in part, on the basis of who he was, and not on the basis of the material evidence presented against him.

The *Holloway* court noted, however, that if evidence of the gun possession had been admissible as proof on the robbery charges, or if the gun had been used in the robbery, it would have been a different case and joinder would have been permitted. Under Rule 404(b) of the Federal Rules of Evidence, evidence of the defendant's uncharged bad acts cannot be admitted to show he is a bad person, but they can be admitted where relevant to prove intent, knowledge, identity, or any other "non-character" issue.[11] Thus, if evidence of a criminal act would be admissible to prove a different crime, there is no prejudice in joining charges as to both crimes in a single trial. See United States v. Windom, 19 F.3d 1190 (7th Cir.1994)(gun charge was properly joined with a narcotics charge, "for the same reasons that allow the government to introduce weapons into evidence at narcotics trials"). Compare United States v. Randazzo, 80 F.3d 623 (1st Cir. 1996) (charges of filing false tax returns could not be joined with charges for introducing misbranded or adulterated food into interstate commerce; crimes were completely unrelated and evidence as to one could not be admitted to prove the other).

if gun had been brought in evidence as proof of Robbery or used in robbery than its inclusion meritorious

It is notable that the trial court in *Holloway* failed to instruct the jury to refrain from using evidence concerning the firearms charge as proof on the robbery charge. Where the judge makes an effort to protect the defendant from prejudicial misjoinder, the risks of reversal are substantially diminished. See Leach v. Kolb, 911 F.2d 1249 (7th Cir.1990)(improper joinder of attempted murder, armed robbery, and attempted armed robbery charges arising from

---

11. Complete coverage of Rules like 404(b) is left for a course in evidence. For an extensive discussion of that Rule, see Saltzburg, Martin and Capra, Federal Rules of Evidence Manual § 404.02 (8th ed. 1998).

separate incidents did not deprive defendant of a fair trial, where evidence of the defendant's guilt on each charge was overwhelming, and the trial court gave explicit limiting instructions requiring the jury to determine guilt or innocence on each count without reference to guilt or innocence on other charged counts).

Declaring the Privilege as to One Count But Not the Other

In United States v. Dixon, 184 F.3d 643 (7th Cir.1999), the defendant objected to joinder of two counts of sexual abuse. The counts related to two different victims on two separate occasions. The defendant argued that joinder was improper (and severance should have been granted) because he wanted to testify in his own defense as to one of the counts but not the other. But the court held that this was not in itself a reason to prohibit joinder of the counts. If the defendant's wish to testify on only one count were enough to require severance, "a court would be divested of all control over the matter of severance and the choice would be entrusted to the defendant." The court held that severance is not required in such circumstances "until the defendant makes a convincing showing that he has (1) important testimony to give concerning one count and (2) a strong need to refrain from testifying on the other." A defendant fails to make a convincing showing of a strong need to refrain from testifying on a particular count when "without the defendant's testimony, the government offered sufficient evidence to support the jury's verdict on that count." That is, if the government has sufficient evidence on the count, the defendant should have a need to testify, not a need to refrain from doing so. In Dixon, the court found the evidence sufficient to convict on both counts, and consequently found no error in their joinder. Under the analysis in Dixon, doesn't the question of joinder and severance devolve into a question of sufficiency of the evidence?

C. JOINDER OF DEFENDANTS

It is common to find joinder of defendants in several classes of cases, especially conspiracy cases. Generally, courts express sympathy for the plight of defendants joined in conspiracy cases, but find the Government interest in efficiency to be paramount. The general rule of thumb is that "persons who are indicted together should be tried together." United States v. O'Bryant, 998 F.2d 21 (1st Cir.1993). For example, in Schaffer v. United States, 362 U.S. 511 (1960), defendants were joined on the basis of a conspiracy charge, though the substantive counts charged each defendant with different acts of theft. At the close of the government's case, the trial court dismissed the conspiracy count for lack of proof. But the substantive counts were submitted to the jury and the defendants were convicted. The Supreme Court found that defendants had not suffered any prejudice warranting severance, since the proof at trial was "carefully compartmentalized" as to each defendant. It noted that as of the beginning of the trial, the joinder was authorized by Rule 8(b), and it refused to adopt "a hard-and-fast formula that, when a conspiracy count fails, joinder is error as a matter of law." Justice Douglas, joined by Chief Justice Warren and Justices Black and Brennan, in dissent, found "implicit prejudice" in trying separate offenses in a joint trial, because "a subtle bond is likely to be created between the several defendants even though they have never met nor acted in unison."

Exculpatory Testimony From a Codefendant

The courts have recognized that joinder can be prejudicial in some situations, however. One situation is where one or more of the defendants would, if separately tried, offer testimony that would exculpate the defendant who complains about joinder. The complaint is that the witness/codefendant will not testify if he is joined, for fear that he will injure his own defense. This is a legitimate ground for arguing prejudice. But in order to trigger severance on this ground, a defendant "must establish a bona fide need for the codefendant's testimony, the substance of the testimony, the exculpatory nature and effect of the testimony, and that the codefendant would in fact testify." United States v. Neal, 27 F.3d 1035 (5th Cir.1994)(severance should have been granted where codefendant would have taken the stand in a separate trial to exculpate the complaining defendants); United States v. Cobb, 185 F.3d 1193 (11th Cir.1999) (finding a "rare case" in which severance should have been granted, because the codefendant's testimony would have been critical to the defendant's defense, and the codefendant stated unequivocally that he would testify at the defendant's trial if his case were severed). Compare United States v. Tolliver, 937 F.2d 1183 (7th Cir.1991)(joint trial permissible where codefendant with exculpatory information stated that he would not testify for the defendant even if the cases were severed; the fact that the codefendant often changed his mind was irrelevant, because the mere possibility of exculpatory testimony is not sufficient to require a severance). The defendant must show that the prospective testimony is substantially exculpatory. See United States v. Gonzalez, 933 F.2d 417 (7th Cir.1991) (severance not required where codefendant would testify that the defendant took a certain trip for a legitimate business purpose; the testimony would not exclude the possibility that the defendant took trips for drug-related purposes on other occasions).

Disparity in the Evidence

Another, limited exception to the general rule of joinder is where there is a gross disparity in the evidence against the joined defendants. In these cases, "the danger is that the bit players may not be able to differentiate themselves in the jurors' minds from the stars." United States v. Zafiro, 945 F.2d 881 (7th Cir.1991), aff'd 506 U.S. 534 (1993). In order to obtain a severance on this ground, the defendant will have to show a disparity in the evidence so great that the jury will not be able to follow limiting instructions. See, e.g., United States v. Farmer, 924 F.2d 647 (7th Cir.1991)(defendants arguing gross disparity were not prejudiced from a joint trial, where the record showed that the jury meticulously considered the evidence against each defendant; the jury returned 62 findings of guilty and 38 findings of not guilty, and all defendants but one were acquitted on at least one count); United States v. Gonzalez, 933 F.2d 417 (7th Cir.1991)(some disparity between defendants is permissible if it is within the jury's capacity to follow the court's limiting instructions). Given the institutional interest in trying all participants in a crime together, the gross disparity argument is rarely successful. And it is particularly unlikely to be successful on appeal if the jury returned acquittals as to some defendants and/or some charges. See United States v. Neal, 27 F.3d 1035 (5th Cir.1994)("the jury's not guilty verdicts as to some defendants demonstrate that the jurors followed the district court's instructions and considered the evidence separately as to each defendant").

Antagonistic Defenses

While courts are reluctant to grant severances that result in multiple trials, some cases hold that severance must be granted where the defendants have defenses so antagonistic that the defense of each is substantially impaired by joinder. United States v. Walters, 913 F.2d 388 (7th Cir.1990), is an example. Walters and Bloom sought to represent professional athletes. They enticed football players who were still in college to sign contracts by providing cash bonuses and other incentives. These contracts were dated as of a future date, beyond the date of the athlete's prospective graduation, so that the athlete would retain his college eligibility; the agreements were in violation of National Collegiate Athletic Association ("NCAA") rules. The athletes would then have to lie to their colleges on eligibility forms (i.e., assert that they had not signed any professional contracts) in order to continue to receive scholarships. Prior to their enterprise, Walters and Bloom consulted a noted sports attorney to obtain advice concerning the legal ramifications of these agreements. The attorney opined that Walters and Bloom were violating NCAA rules, but that they were not violating any laws. It was unclear whether the attorney factored in that the athletes would be lying on the college eligibility forms. Walters and Bloom were charged with mail fraud, RICO violations, and conspiracy. Walters defended on the ground that his actions were taken in good faith on the advice of the sports counsel, which, of course, was Bloom's counsel as well. Bloom's motion to sever was denied, and both Bloom and Walters were convicted. On appeal, Bloom argued that Walters' pursuit of an advice of counsel defense required Bloom to assert the same defense, and also to waive his attorney-client privilege. The court of appeals analyzed this claim as follows:

> [S]everances are called for where the defenses of codefendants are mutually antagonistic or irreconcilable, such that the acceptance of one party's defense will preclude the acquittal of the other. Even where defenses are not mutually antagonistic, a severance may be granted if the actual conduct of one defendant's defense unduly prejudices his or her codefendant. * * *

> When Walters pursued his advice-of-counsel defense, Bloom was forced to observe his own attorneys testify about the intimate discussions to which he had been a party. Bloom could not pursue his own defense, but was forced to skittle along behind that of Walters. * * * Bloom's counsel did not wish to pursue the advice of counsel gambit with Walters. In fact, Bloom's counsel stated to the court that Walters' theory had "gone over like a lead balloon" with the jury. * * *

> We recognize that joint trials are an essential element of the quick administration of justice. If every defendant who wanted a severance was given one, the slow pace of our court system would go from a crawl to paralysis; any motion for severance must be balanced against the need for judicial economy. Here, no such balance can be reasonably struck. * * * Once Walters pursued his advice of counsel defense, as was his right, Bloom must have been provided the option of a separate trial. Any other course of action forced Bloom to waive his attorney-client privilege. We cannot tolerate such devil's bargains.

Is it important that the court in *Walters* never describes what Bloom's defense would have been if not for Bloom's advice of counsel gambit, nor whether that defense would have been more viable than the advice of counsel defense? Is it important that in another part of the opinion, the court reversed Walters' conviction on the ground that he had presented sufficient evidence to the jury on the advice of counsel defense to be entitled to a jury instruction on that issue? Aren't antagonistic defenses something that the jury can sort out? See United States v. Neal, 27 F.3d 1035 (5th Cir.1994)(severance not required where one defendant admits taking part in the conspiracy but claims entrapment, while other defendants claim that they were not members of any conspiracy; in order to believe the "core" of the entrapment defense, the jury was "not required to disbelieve the core of the other defendants' claims of innocence").

Finger-Pointing: Zafiro v. United States

In *Walters*, severance was held required because Walters' defense deprived Bloom of the ability to choose a different defense. Is severance required if defendants are "pointing fingers" at each other, such that if one defense is believed the other cannot be? This was the question in *Zafiro v. United States*, 506 U.S. 534 (1993), a case in which four defendants were tried for a narcotics conspiracy. Officers discovered a large amount of cocaine at a residence to which all four defendants were connected. Soto and Garcia argued lack of knowledge and that Martinez and Zafiro were the drug dealers. Martinez and Zafiro argued lack of knowledge and that Soto and Garcia were the drug dealers. Justice O'Connor, writing for eight members of the Court, held that all of the defendants were properly tried together. She declared that "[t]here is a preference in the federal system for joint trials of defendants who are indicted together" and rejected the defendants' proposed bright line test that severance is required whenever defendants have mutually antagonistic defenses. She concluded that severance might be required in only a few exceptional circumstances:

> Mutually antagonistic defenses are not prejudicial *per se*. Moreover, Rule 14 does not require severance even if prejudice is shown; rather, it leaves the tailoring of the relief to be granted, if any, to the district court's sound discretion.

> We believe that, when defendants properly have been joined under Rule 8(b), a district court should grant a severance under Rule 14 only if there is a serious risk that a joint trial would compromise a specific trial right of one of the defendants, or prevent the jury from making a reliable judgment about guilt or innocence. Such a risk might occur when evidence that the jury should not consider against a defendant and that would not be admissible if a defendant were tried alone is admitted against a codefendant. For example, evidence of a codefendant's wrongdoing in some circumstances erroneously could lead a jury to conclude that a defendant was guilty. When many defendants are tried together in a complex case and they have markedly different degrees of culpability, this risk of prejudice is heightened. Evidence that is probative of a defendant's guilt but technically admissible only against a codefendant also might present a risk of prejudice. Conversely, a defendant might suffer prejudice if essential exculpatory evidence that would be available to a defendant tried alone were unavailable in a joint trial.

Justice O'Connor noted that the defendants in *Zafiro* did not articulate any specific instances of prejudice, but merely argued that "the very nature of their defenses, without more, prejudiced them." She responded that "it is well settled that defendants are not entitled to severance merely because they may have a better chance of acquittal in separate trials."

The defendants in *Zafiro* argued that they suffered a risk of prejudice from the possibility that the jury could conclude, in light of the finger-pointing defenses, that *some* defendant must be guilty without regard to whether the evidence proved so beyond a reasonable doubt. But Justice O'Connor responded that "the short answer is that petitioners' scenario did not occur here" because the "Government argued that all four petitioners were guilty and offered sufficient evidence as to all four petitioners; the jury in turn found all four petitioners guilty of various offenses." She further stated that "even if there were some risk of prejudice, here it is of the type that can be cured with proper instructions." Justice O'Connor noted that the trial court instructed the jury to give separate consideration to each defendant, and also warned the jury that each defendant was entitled to have his or her case judged only on the basis of the evidence applicable to the individual defendant. She concluded that these instructions "sufficed to cure any possibility of prejudice."

Justice Stevens concurred in the judgment, observing that he did not share the majority's preference for joint trials. He pointed out two ways in which joinder is problematic in cases involving mutually antagonistic defenses:

> First, joinder may introduce what is in effect a second prosecutor into a case, by turning each codefendant into the other's most forceful adversary. Second, joinder may invite a jury confronted with two defendants, at least one of whom is almost certainly guilty, to convict the defendant who appears the more guilty of the two regardless of whether the prosecutor has proven guilt beyond a reasonable doubt as to that particular defendant.

The Problem of the Megatrial

In United States v. Andrews, 754 F.Supp. 1161 (N.D.Ill.1990), the court encountered the phenomenon of a "megatrial." Thirty-eight defendants were charged in a 175 count indictment under the RICO statute. See 18 U.S.C. § 1962. The government alleged that the defendants were involved in a street gang, and the indictment related over 250 factually separate criminal acts committed over a 23 year period. The court held that joinder of these claims and parties was permissible under Fed.R.Crim.P. 8, because the defendants were each alleged members of a single and unified RICO conspiracy. The court commented that substantive criminal law statutes like RICO vastly expand the possibilities of joinder of claims and defendants:

> This case provides a vivid example of the broad charging authority that RICO has conferred to the government. Prior to RICO, the scope of a proper indictment under Rule 8(b) was largely restricted to the number of individuals who could conspire to commit a single substantive crime. RICO removes this natural ceiling by making it a crime to agree to the commission of a pattern of racketeering, which can include a limitless number of substantive crimes and, consequently, a limitless number of conspirators. Thus, RICO evades the practical limitations of group conduct that Rule 8(b) places on the scope of an indictment.

The court found, however, that though joinder was technically proper under Rule 8, severance was required under Rule 14 because the defendants would be prejudiced by the megatrial. As a remedy, the court divided various actors and charges into five trial units. It expressed general concern about megatrials, and doubted their efficiency. Following the lead of several other courts, the judge adopted a "presumption *against* a joint trial and *for* severance when faced with the prospect of a mega-trial." It defined a "megatrial" as one in which the prosecution estimates the length of trial to be greater than four months, and ten or more defendants are joined. The court noted that a megatrial, as so defined, would often be more costly than a number of individual trials:

> [A]t some point, the oft-cited advantages of a joint trial are outweighed by the manifest disadvantages of a large and protracted trial. * * * One disadvantage * * * is the significant exacerbation of the public cost of providing defense counsel to each defendant. All but one of the defense attorneys currently representing a defendant in this case are being federally funded. Testimony directly implicating most of their clients is projected to last not more than a few weeks, and, for many, not more than a few days. Thus, in a single trial, [the attorneys] would be compelled to sit idly by for the duration of a lengthy trial where the vast majority of evidence deals solely with the criminal activities of other attorneys' clients. * * * The cost of twenty-one court-appointed attorneys for a one-year trial is at least $1.6 million. Here, a significant majority of this total would be wasted as compensation to defense counsel for idle time.

The court also noted other disadvantages of a megatrial: 1) the management aspect of the case would wreak havoc upon an already overburdened docket; 2) the trial would place "enormous personal burdens on the jurors, the defendants, defense counsel and the Court"; and 3) the search for truth would be impaired due to the "massive and complex evidence making it almost impossible for the jury to separate evidence as it relates to each defendant." The court concluded that these costs were "too high a price to pay for the government's ill-conceived desire to prosecute all these defendants in one spectacular trial extravaganza." See also United States v. Casamento, 887 F.2d 1141 (2d Cir.1989)(where trial includes more than 10 defendants and will exceed four months, the prosecution is obligated to make a compelling justification that joinder will further the ends of justice; consideration should be given to limiting the prosecution of peripheral defendants to easily proveable charges that carry adequate penalties).

D. MISJOINDER

Violation of Rule 8: United States v. Lane

The Supreme Court held in United States v. Lane, 474 U.S. 438 (1986), that misjoinder of counts in violation of Fed.R.Crim.P. 8(b) does not automatically compel reversal of convictions. A father and son were charged with various offenses arising out of an arson conspiracy. They persuaded a court of appeals that one count, brought solely against the father, was improperly joined with four counts naming them both and another count charging the son with perjury. The court of appeals concluded that misjoinder is prejudicial per se. Chief Justice Burger's opinion for the Court disagreed, reasoning that misjoinder surely can be harmless in light of decisions holding that even constitutional errors do not

[handwritten margin note: reviewed under harmless error]

inevitably require reversal of convictions. The question in cases of misjoinder, then, is whether the error is harmless under Fed.R.Crim.P. 52(a).

The Bruton Problem

[handwritten margin notes: 2 def / 1 Δ makes post-custodial confession / • can be used against 1 Δ / • hearsay against other / Jury instruction insufficient / severance needed / post Bruton sep trial not needed.]

While the misjoinder in *Lane* was not of constitutional dimension, constitutional error can occur in a joint trial that would not arise if the defendants were tried separately. For example, in Bruton v. United States, 391 U.S. 123 (1968), the Court found constitutional error when Bruton's codefendant made a post-custodial confession implicating both himself and Bruton, and this confession was admitted into evidence at the joint trial. The confession was admissible against the codefendant as a party admission, but it was inadmissible hearsay as to Bruton. The trial judge gave a limiting instruction that the statement could only be used against the codefendant. But the Court held that in light of the "powerfully incriminating" nature of the confession, the instruction was insufficient to protect Bruton's constitutional right to confront his accuser.

The Court suggested separate trials to avoid a *"Bruton"* problem, but courts after *Bruton* have often used means short of separate trials to protect against the use of the confession of one codefendant against another. The Supreme Court has approved redaction of a confession as a permissible substitute for severance, so long as all reference to the existence of the non-confessing defendant is excised from the confession. See Richardson v. Marsh, 481 U.S. 200 (1987). In *Marsh*, the confession was redacted to refer only to the confessing codefendant and another perpetrator who had absconded. In contrast, in Gray v. Maryland, 523 U.S. 185 (1998), redaction was held insufficient to protect the defendant where the confession was changed, in essence, from "Gray and I did it" to "deleted and I did it." The *Gray* Court held that the redaction provided no protection, because the jury would know that "deleted" would have to be the other defendant sitting there at the trial.

Some courts have experimented with empaneling two juries in a single trial as a way of resolving the *Bruton* problem short of severing the trials. The jury hearing the case against the non-confessing codefendant is excused when the other defendant's confession is introduced or referred to. A judge who tried such a case stated that before the confession was introduced, she excused both juries, and then called the confessing defendant's jury back to hear the confession. In that way, the jurors for the non-confessing defendant would not think that they were missing anything. See Santagata, One Trial, Two Juries—It Works in Extraordinary Cases, N.Y.L.J., May 11, 1988, p. 1. In People v. Ricardo B., 73 N.Y.2d 228, 538 N.Y.S.2d 796, 535 N.E.2d 1336 (1989), the court held that the use of multiple juries to avoid a *Bruton* problem "does not deny defendants their constitutional right to a jury trial or, in the absence of identified prejudice, to due process of law." The court noted, however, that multiple juries should be used sparingly, because their use "can only magnify the problems inherent in joint trials because of the need to insulate the juries from inadmissible evidence or argument."

[handwritten margin note: ct used multiple juries to avoid problem]

Bruton has been held inapplicable to a bench trial of joined defendants, because the problem that the Court was concerned about in *Bruton* was the jury's inability to follow the judge's instruction not to use one codefendant's confession against another. Rogers v. McMackin, 884 F.2d 252 (6th Cir.1989).

III. CONSTITUTIONALLY BASED PROOF REQUIREMENTS

A. PROOF BEYOND A REASONABLE DOUBT GENERALLY

Constitutional Requirement: In re Winship

In re Winship, 397 U.S. 358 (1970), decided that the Due Process Clause requires the government in a criminal case to prove every *element* of the crime beyond a reasonable doubt. Samuel Winship, a 12–year–old boy, was brought before a juvenile court and charged with delinquency for taking $112 from a woman's pocketbook in a locker. The judge acknowledged that the conduct might not have been proved beyond a reasonable doubt, but determined that Winship could be adjudged a delinquent by a preponderance of the evidence. The Court in *Winship* held that the requirement of proof beyond a reasonable doubt is one of the "essentials of due process and fair treatment" required during the adjudicatory stage when a juvenile is charged with an act that would constitute a crime if committed by an adult. Justice Brennan's majority opinion traced the history of proof in American criminal trials and found "virtually unanimous" authority supporting the reasonable doubt standard for all elements of the crime. He concluded that the criminal defendant has a transcendent liberty interest in criminal trials that requires the narrowest margin for error.

> * * * [U]se of the reasonable-doubt standard is indispensable to command the respect and confidence of the community in applications of the criminal law. It is critical that the moral force of the criminal law not be diluted by a standard of proof that leaves people in doubt whether innocent men are being condemned. It is also important in our free society that every individual going about his ordinary affairs have confidence that his government cannot adjudge him guilty of a criminal offense without convincing a proper factfinder of his guilt with utmost certainty.

> Lest there remain any doubt about the constitutional stature of the reasonable-doubt standard, we explicitly hold that the Due Process Clause protects the accused against conviction except upon proof beyond a reasonable doubt of every fact necessary to constitute the crime with which he is charged.

Justice Harlan wrote an influential concurring opinion, stressing the policy arguments that support the reasonable doubt standard.

> [E]ven though the labels used for alternative standards of proof are vague and not a very sure guide to decisionmaking, the choice of the standard for a particular variety of adjudication does, I think, reflect a very fundamental assessment of the comparative social costs of erroneous factual determinations. * * * [A] standard of proof represents an attempt to instruct the factfinder concerning the degree of confidence our society thinks he should have in the correctness of factual conclusions for a particular type of adjudication. Although the phrases "preponderance of the evidence" and "proof beyond a reasonable doubt" are quantitatively imprecise, they do communicate to the finder of fact different notions concerning the degree of

confidence he is expected to have in the correctness of his factual conclusions.

* * * If * * * the standard of proof for a criminal trial were a preponderance of the evidence rather than proof beyond a reasonable doubt, there would be a smaller risk of factual errors that result in freeing guilty persons, but a far greater risk of factual errors that result in convicting the innocent. Because the standard of proof affects the comparative frequency of these two types of erroneous outcomes, the choice of the standard to be applied in a particular kind of litigation should, in a rational world, reflect an assessment of the comparative social disutility of each.

When one makes such an assessment, the reason for different standards of proof in civil as opposed to criminal litigation becomes apparent. In a civil suit between two private parties for money damages, for example, we view it as no more serious in general for there to be an erroneous verdict in the defendant's favor than for there to be an erroneous verdict in the plaintiff's favor. * * *

In a criminal case, on the other hand, we do not view the social disutility of convicting an innocent man as equivalent to the disutility of acquitting someone who is guilty. * * *

In this context, I view the requirement of proof beyond a reasonable doubt in a criminal case as bottomed on a fundamental value determination of our society that it is far worse to convict an innocent man than to let a guilty man go free.

B. REASONABLE DOUBT AND JURY INSTRUCTIONS

"Presumed Innocent" Instructions

In Taylor v. Kentucky, 436 U.S. 478 (1978), the Court reversed a conviction where the judge refused to give a requested instruction that the defendant was presumed innocent. Later, however, in Kentucky v. Whorton, 441 U.S. 786 (1979), the Court held that a presumption of innocence instruction was not constitutionally required in every case. It stressed the facts of *Taylor,* where the trial judge's instructions were "spartan," the prosecutor made improper remarks, and the evidence against the defendant was weak. The Court concluded that the failure to give a requested instruction on the presumption of innocence "must be evaluated in light of the totality of the circumstances—including all the instructions to the jury, the arguments of counsel, whether the weight of the evidence was overwhelming, and other relevant factors—to determine whether the defendant received a constitutionally fair trial." See also United States v. Payne, 944 F.2d 1458 (9th Cir.1991)(underlying purposes of a presumption of innocence instruction were "served adequately by other instructions which squarely placed the burden on the government of proving its case beyond a reasonable doubt, defined beyond a reasonable doubt, and clearly confined the scope of the evidence properly before the jury").

Reasonable Doubt Instructions: Cage v. Louisiana and Victor v. Nebraska

What should the judge say to the jury about the meaning of reasonable doubt? The instruction in Cage v. Louisiana, 498 U.S. 39 (1990), defined reasonable doubt as one creating "a grave uncertainty" and "an actual substantial doubt." The trial court elaborated that a "moral certainty" was required to convict. The Supreme Court in a per curiam opinion held that the words "grave" and "substantial" "suggest a higher degree of doubt than is required for acquittal under the reasonable doubt standard." The Court concluded that the instruction was constitutionally defective; the references to grave and substantial doubt, combined with the reference to moral certainty, as opposed to evidentiary certainty, could have led a reasonable juror to find guilt on a lesser standard than that required by *Winship*.

In Sullivan v. Louisiana, 508 U.S. 275 (1993), the Court unanimously held that a constitutionally-defective reasonable doubt instruction cannot be harmless error. At Sullivan's trial, the judge gave a reasonable doubt instruction substantially identical to the instruction found defective in *Cage*. Justice Scalia, writing for the Court, stated that because of the instruction, Sullivan was deprived of his Sixth Amendment right to a jury verdict of guilt beyond a reasonable doubt. Under these circumstances, an appellate court cannot determine that the error was harmless, because "the wrong entity" would be judging the defendant guilty. *Sullivan* is discussed in more detail, infra, in the Chapter 13 discussion of harmless error.

In the consolidated cases of Sandoval v. California and Victor v. Nebraska, 511 U.S. 1 (1994), the Court considered the constitutionality of two reasonable doubt instructions in light of *Cage*. In *Sandoval,* the trial court defined reasonable doubt as follows:

> It is not a mere possible doubt; because everything relating to human affairs, and depending on *moral evidence,* is open to some possible or imaginary doubt. It is that state of the case which, after the entire comparison and consideration of all the evidence, leaves the minds of the jurors in that condition that they cannot say they feel *an abiding conviction, to a moral certainty*, of the truth of the charge. [Emphasis added.]

Justice O'Connor, writing for the Court, found that while the instruction lacked clarity, there was no "reasonable likelihood" that the jury understood it to allow conviction to be based on proof less than the *Winship* standard. She rejected Sandoval's argument that the trial judge's reference to "moral certainty" would be understood by modern jurors to mean a standard of proof less stringent than that of reasonable doubt. She recognized that while the reference to moral certainty was "ambiguous in the abstract," the rest of the instruction sufficiently corrected any ambiguity by requiring "an abiding conviction" as to guilt. She stated that "we are satisfied that the reference to moral certainty, in conjunction with the abiding conviction language, impressed upon the factfinder the need to reach a subjective state of near certitude of the guilt of the accused."

While the Court found that the "moral certainty" language was not fatal, it stressed that it did not "condone the use of the phrase" and noted that the pattern jury instructions for federal courts do not refer to moral certainty.

The instruction defining reasonable doubt given by the trial court in *Victor* was as follows:

> Reasonable doubt is such a doubt as would cause a reasonable and prudent person, in one of the graver and more important transactions of life, to *pause and hesitate* before taking the represented facts as true and relying and acting thereon. It is such a doubt as will not permit you, after full, fair, and impartial consideration of all the evidence, to have an *abiding conviction, to a moral certainty*, of the guilt of the accused. At the same time, absolute or mathematical certainty is not required. You may be convinced of the truth of a fact beyond a reasonable doubt and yet be fully aware that possibly you may be mistaken. You may find an accused guilty upon the strong probabilities of the case, provided such probabilities are strong enough to exclude any doubt of his guilt that is reasonable. A reasonable doubt is an *actual and substantial doubt* arising from the evidence, or from the lack of evidence on the part of the state, *as distinguished from a doubt arising from mere possibility, from bare imagination, or from fanciful conjecture*. [Emphasis added.]

As with the instruction in *Sandoval*, Justice O'Connor found that the instruction in *Victor* adequately conveyed the concept of reasonable doubt to the jury. Justice O'Connor rejected Victor's argument that the reference to "substantial doubt" overstated the degree of doubt necessary for acquittal. She noted that the trial court had distinguished "substantial doubt" from "a doubt rising from mere possibility, from bare imagination, or from fanciful conjecture." This was enough to distinguish the instruction in *Victor* from that in *Cage*, where the "substantial doubt" language was also used. According to Justice O'Connor:

> This explicit distinction between a substantial doubt and a fanciful conjecture was not present in the *Cage* instruction. * * * [In *Cage*] we were concerned that the jury would interpret the term "substantial doubt" in parallel with the preceding reference to "grave uncertainty," leading to an overstatement of the doubt necessary to acquit. In the instruction given in Victor's case, the context makes clear that "substantial" is used in the sense of existence rather than magnitude of the doubt, so the same concern is not present.

Justice O'Connor noted in the alternative that the trial court's "hesitate to act" instruction cured whatever defect might have existed in the reference to substantial doubt. She concluded that "to the extent the word 'substantial' denotes the quantum of doubt necessary for acquittal, the hesitate to act standard gives a common-sense benchmark for just how substantial such a doubt must be."

Justice Kennedy wrote a short concurring opinion, in which he stated that a reference to moral certainty might once have made sense to jurors, but that it has "long since become archaic."

Justice Ginsburg wrote a concurring opinion, agreeing with the Court's suggestion that the term "moral certainty," "while not in itself so misleading as to render the instructions unconstitutional, should be avoided as an unhelpful way of explaining what reasonable doubt means." Unlike the Court, however, she also criticized the "hesitate to act" instruction as providing a "misplaced analogy." She reasoned that important decisions in one's life "generally involve a very heavy element of uncertainty and risk-taking" and thus are "wholly unlike the decisions jurors ought to make in criminal cases."[12]

Justice Ginsburg took issue with the position of some federal circuit courts that have held that a reasonable doubt instruction should never be given. See, e.g., United States v. Adkins, 937 F.2d 947 (4th Cir.1991) (arguing that such instructions "tend to impermissibly lessen the burden of proof"); Seventh Circuit Committee on Federal Jury Instructions ("The phrase 'reasonable doubt' is self-explanatory and is its own best definition. Further elaboration tends to misleading refinements which weaken and make imprecise the existing phrase."). Justice Ginsburg noted studies indicating that "jurors are often confused about the meaning of reasonable doubt when that term is left undefined."

Justice Ginsburg approved of the reasonable doubt instruction proposed by the Federal Judicial Center. That instruction reads as follows:

> Proof beyond a reasonable doubt is proof that leaves you *firmly convinced* of the defendant's guilt. There are very few things in this world that we know with absolute certainty, and in criminal cases the law does not require proof that overcomes every possible doubt. If, based on your consideration of the evidence, you are firmly convinced that the defendant is guilty of the crime charged, you must find him guilty. If on the other hand, you think there is a *real possibility* that he is not guilty, you must give him the benefit of the doubt and find him not guilty. [Emphasis added.]

Justice Ginsburg concluded that the above instruction is "clear, straightforward and accurate" and that it avoids a choice between two potential sources of jury confusion: "on one hand, the confusions that may be caused by leaving reasonable doubt undefined, and on the other, the confusion that might be induced by the anachronism of 'moral certainty,' the misplaced analogy of 'hesitation to act,' or the circularity of 'doubt that is reasonable.'"

How meaningful are the distinctions set forth by the Court between the instructions in *Cage, Sandoval,* and *Victor?* Do you think that any of these distinctions would be grasped by jurors receiving a rather long-winded, oral instruction? Remember that a reasonable doubt instruction is merely one among many long-winded, oral instructions given to the jury in a criminal trial. Is it better to leave well enough alone and assume that the jury knows what reasonable doubt means? See Newman, Beyond Reasonable Doubt, 68 N.Y.U.L.Rev. 979 (1984) (arguing that the concept of reasonable doubt "will become less clear the more we explain it"). If jurors are confused about reasonable doubt in the absence of an instruction, as Justice Ginsburg contends, is their confusion cleared up by the instructions given in *Sandoval* or *Victor?* Does the instruction proposed by the Federal Judicial Center clear up any confusion? For a critical view of *Victor* and *Sandoval,* see Dery, The Atrophying of the Reasonable Doubt Standard: The United States Supreme Court's Missed

---

12. See also Vargas v. Keane, 86 F.3d 1273 (2d Cir.1996) (Weinstein, J., concurring) (criticizing a "hesitate to act" instruction: "It could be misunderstood since many of us recognize that in the most important affairs of our lives—such as choice of mate, careers and conception—we tend to be largely emotional. Were we to require proof beyond a reasonable doubt that our important decisions are correct, few of us would marry, choose law as a career or have children. Most of us are probably comfortable with more risk-taking when making important personal decisions than we would be in declaring as criminals people who may be innocent.").

Opportunity in Victor v. Nebraska and Its Implications in the Courtroom, 99 Dick.L.Rev.613 (1995).

C. THE SCOPE OF THE REASONABLE DOUBT REQUIREMENT: WHAT IS AN ELEMENT OF THE CRIME?

Winship requires the government to prove all elements of the crime beyond a reasonable doubt. But does this leave the government with an unfettered discretion to determine just what the elements of a crime are? What if the government changes what was once an element of the crime into an affirmative defense—thus shifting the burden of proof? What if the government shifts what might be considered an element of the crime into a sentencing consideration, thus lessening the burden of proof? Does any of this violate *Winship*? These questions have been the subject of much Supreme Court and lower court case law.

1. Element of the Crime or Affirmative Defense?

Impermissible Burden–Shifting: *Mullaney v. Wilbur*

The Court's first attempt to identify *Winship's* scope came in Mullaney v. Wilbur, 421 U.S. 684 (1975). Maine required a defendant charged with murder to prove that he acted "in the heat of passion on sudden provocation" in order to reduce the homicide to manslaughter. Under the Maine system, the prosecutor had to show beyond a reasonable doubt that a homicide was both intentional and unlawful. Unless the defendant proved heat of passion or sudden provocation by a preponderance of the evidence, the defendant was convicted of murder. The Maine statute defined murder as the killing of a person "with malice afore-thought." After briefly tracing the history of homicide statutes in the United States, Justice Powell's majority opinion stated the Court's holding "that the Due Process Clause requires the prosecution to prove beyond a reasonable doubt the absence of the heat of passion or sudden provocation when the issue is properly presented in a homicide case."[13] In other words, the absence of heat of passion or provocation was an element of the crime, and could not be shifted to an affirmative defense. The Court reasoned as follows:

> [T]he criminal law of Maine, like that of other jurisdictions, is con-cerned not only with guilt or innocence in the abstract but also with the degree of criminal culpability. Maine has chosen to distinguish those who kill in the heat of passion from those who kill in the absence of this factor. * * * By drawing this distinction, while refusing to require the prosecution to establish beyond a reasonable doubt the fact upon which it turns, Maine denigrates the interests found critical in *Winship*.

> The safeguards of due process are not rendered unavailing simply because a determination may already have been reached that would stigma-

---

13. In contrast to the burden of persuasion is the burden of production. Many jurisdictions put the burden on a defendant to raise suffi-cient evidence to bring a defense into a case, at which time the prosecutor must disprove the defense beyond a reasonable doubt. Even if the Constitution permits a jurisdiction to impose the persuasion burden on a defendant, a juris-diction may be satisfied with imposing the pro-duction burden instead. Whenever it is consti-tutional to put a burden of persuasion on a defendant, it will be constitutional to impose the lesser burden of production. *Mullaney* es-tablishes that in some cases only a production burden may be imposed.

tize the defendant and that might lead to a significant impairment of personal liberty. The fact remains that the consequences resulting from a verdict of murder, as compared with a verdict of manslaughter, differ significantly. Indeed, when viewed in terms of the potential difference in restrictions of personal liberty attendant to each conviction, the distinction established by Maine between murder and manslaughter may be of greater importance than the difference between guilt or innocence for many lesser crimes.

Moreover, if *Winship* were limited to those facts that constitute a crime as defined by state law, a State could undermine many of the interests that decision sought to protect without effecting any substantive change in its law. It would only be necessary to redefine the elements that constitute different crimes, characterizing them as factors that bear solely on the extent of punishment.

Justice Rehnquist, joined by Chief Justice Burger, concurred and noted that he saw no inconsistency between *Mullaney* and Leland v. Oregon, 343 U.S. 790 (1952)(upholding placement upon defendant of burden of persuasion beyond a reasonable doubt on issue of insanity).[14]

One obvious problem with *Mullaney* is that the state appeared to get into a constitutional difficulty because it tried to give certain less culpable defendants a break. The Court apparently saw no constitutional problem if the state were to have a single crime of murder, without providing any differentiation for those who murdered in the heat of passion or under provocation. Why is this a better system than that chosen by the state in *Mullaney*?

Flexibility to Determine Affirmative Defenses:
Patterson v. New York

In Patterson v. New York, 432 U.S. 197 (1977), Justice White wrote for the majority as it upheld a New York statute that placed the burden on the defendant to prove extreme emotional disturbance by a preponderance of the evidence—after the prosecutor proved an intentional homicide beyond a reasonable doubt—in order to reduce second degree murder to manslaughter. After citing Leland v. Oregon, the majority reasoned as follows:

> We cannot conclude that Patterson's conviction under the New York law deprived him of due process of law. The crime of murder is defined by the statute * * * as causing the death of another person with intent to do so. The death, the intent to kill, and causation are the facts that the State is required to prove beyond a reasonable doubt if a person is to be convicted of murder. No further facts are either presumed or inferred in order to constitute the crime. The statute does provide an affirmative defense—that the defendant acted under the influence of extreme emotional disturbance for which there was a reasonable explanation—which, if proved by a

---

14. Nor did the majority of the Court. In Rivera v. Delaware, 429 U.S. 877 (1976), over the dissent of Justice Brennan joined by Justice Marshall, the Court dismissed, for want of a substantial federal question, an appeal from the Delaware Supreme Court's holding that it was constitutional to put the burden of persuasion on insanity on the defendant. The federal statute, passed after the prosecution of John Hinckley, imposes the burden of persuasion of proving insanity on the defendant.

preponderance of the evidence, would reduce the crime to manslaughter, an offense defined in a separate section of the statute. * * *

* * * This affirmative defense, which the Court of Appeals described as permitting "the defendant to show that his actions were caused by a mental infirmity not arising to the level of insanity, and that he is less culpable for having committed them," does not serve to negative any facts of the crime which the State is to prove in order to convict of murder. It constitutes a separate issue on which the defendant is required to carry the burden of persuasion; * * *

* * * Here, in revising its criminal code, New York provided the affirmative defense of extreme emotional disturbance, a substantially expanded version of the older heat-of-passion concept; but it was willing to do so only if the facts making out the defense were established by the defendant with sufficient certainty. The State was itself unwilling to undertake to establish the absence of those facts beyond a reasonable doubt, perhaps fearing that proof would be too difficult and that too many persons deserving treatment as murderers would escape that punishment if the evidence need merely raise a reasonable doubt about the defendant's emotional state. It has been said that the new criminal code of New York contains some 25 affirmative defenses which exculpate or mitigate but which must be established by the defendant to be operative. The Due Process Clause, as we see it, does not put New York to the choice of abandoning those defenses or undertaking to disprove their existence in order to convict of a crime which otherwise is within its constitutional powers to sanction by substantial punishment.

* * *

We thus decline to adopt as a constitutional imperative, operative countrywide, that a State must disprove beyond a reasonable doubt every fact constituting any and all affirmative defenses related to the culpability of an accused. * * *

Justice White noted that there are limits to shifting the burden of proof to the defendant–the state could not transmute an element of the crime into an affirmative defense:

This view may seem to permit state legislatures to reallocate burdens of proof by labeling as affirmative defenses at least some elements of the crimes now defined in their statutes. But there are obviously constitutional limits beyond which the States may not go in this regard. It is not within the province of a legislature to declare an individual guilty or presumptively guilty of a crime. The legislature cannot validly command that the finding of an indictment, or mere proof of the identity of the accused, should create a presumption of the existence of all the facts essential to guilt.

In a footnote, Justice White quoted extensively from Chief Judge Breitel's concurring opinion in the New York Court of Appeals:

In the absence of affirmative defenses the impulse to legislators, especially in periods of concern about the rise of crime, would be to define particular crimes in unqualifiedly general terms, and leave only to sentence the adjustment between offenses of lesser and greater degree. * * *

* * * Absent the affirmative defense, the crime of murder or manslaughter could legislatively be defined simply to require an intent to kill, unaffected by the spontaneity with which that intent is formed or the provocative or mitigating circumstances which should legally or morally lower the grade of crime. The placing of the burden of proof on the defense, with a lower threshold, however, is fair because of defendant's knowledge or access to the evidence other than his own on the issue. * * *

In sum, the appropriate use of affirmative defenses enlarges the ameliorative aspects of a statutory scheme for the punishment of crime, rather than the other way around—a shift from primitive mechanical classifications based on the bare antisocial act and its consequences, rather than on the nature of the offender and the conditions which produce some degree of excuse for his conduct, the mark of an advanced criminology.

Thus, the Court adopted Judge Breitel's reasoning that the state should be allowed to provide for affirmative defenses, because otherwise the state would simply legislate a single crime, making no attempt to differentiate levels of culpability.

Justice Powell's dissent in *Patterson* was joined by Justices Brennan and Marshall. He was plainly correct in arguing that the distinction between the Maine law invalidated in *Mullaney* and the New York law upheld in *Patterson* was "formalistic rather than substantive."

After *Patterson*, can the state define murder as causing a death, and shift the burden of persuasion to the defendant to prove lack of intent? If not, why not? See also Mason v. Gramley, 9 F.3d 1345 (7th Cir.1993)(upholding Illinois murder statute, which requires the state to prove first degree murder, then permits the defendant to establish, by a preponderance, mitigating evidence to reduce the crime to second degree murder).[15]

Burden of Persuasion on Self–Defense: Martin v. Ohio

The Court chose *Patterson* over *Mullaney* in Martin v. Ohio, 480 U.S. 228 (1987). Justice White again wrote for the Court as it sustained an Ohio rule placing the burden of persuasion on self-defense on the defendant. Martin was charged with aggravated murder. The trial judge instructed the jury that the prosecution was required by state law to prove beyond a reasonable doubt that the defendant purposefully, and with prior calculation and design, caused the death of her husband. The defendant was required to establish self-defense by a preponderance of the evidence.

The *Martin* majority recognized that evidence offered to prove self-defense may also negate a purposeful killing by prior calculation and design. But it rejected the claim that this factual overlap, together with the defendant's burden to prove self-defense, would in effect mean that the defendant would have the burden of disproving his guilt of the crime itself. Justice White explained that a

---

15. The Court relied heavily on *Patterson* in Medina v. California, 505 U.S. 437 (1992), as it upheld a state statute that established a presumption of competency to stand trial, and required the defendant to prove his incompetency by a preponderance of the evidence. Justice Kennedy wrote the opinion for the Court.

He stated that under *Patterson,* it is appropriate to give "substantial deference to legislative judgments" allocating the burden of proof, because "the States have considerable expertise in matters of criminal procedure and the criminal process is grounded in centuries of common-law tradition."

jury would be required to acquit a defendant if it had a reasonable doubt about the defendant's calculation and design; but a jury might believe beyond a reasonable doubt that the defendant purposefully killed someone with prior calculation and design and still excuse the killing as having been done in self-defense. Thus, even though Ohio and South Carolina were the only two states that imposed the burden of proving self-defense on a defendant, their allocation of the burden was constitutionally sound.

Justice Powell, joined by Justices Brennan and Marshall and in large part by Justice Blackmun, dissented. He argued that "[t]he reason for treating a defense that negates an element of the crime differently from other affirmative defenses is plain. If the jury is told that the prosecution has the burden of proving all of the elements of a crime, but then also is instructed that defendant has the burden of *dis*proving one of those same elements, there is a danger that the jurors will resolve the inconsistency in a way that lessens the presumption of innocence." Justice Powell expressed concern that "[t]oday's decision could be read to say that virtually all state attempts to shift the burden of proof for affirmative defenses will be upheld, regardless of the relationship between the elements of the defense and the elements of the crime" and complained that "[t]he Court today fails to discuss or even cite *Mullaney,* despite our unanimous agreement in that case that this danger [of unchecked discretion to shift burdens] would justify judicial intervention in some cases."

Intoxication as a Defense

In *Montana v. Egelhoff*, 518 U.S. 37 (1996), the Court, without a majority opinion, upheld a state statute that prohibited the defendant from offering evidence of intoxication as a defense to the mental state necessary to commit homicide. Justice Scalia, writing for a plurality, relied on *Patterson* for the proposition that states are generally free to construct the elements of a crime, and reasoned that precluding proof of intoxication was simply one way of defining the "mental state" element of homicide; to the plurality, it made no difference that Montana had essentially redefined an element of a crime by way of rendering proof of intoxication irrelevant through a rule of evidence. Justice Scalia's reasoning is summed up in the following passage:

> The doctrines of actus reus, mens rea, insanity, mistake, justification, and duress have historically provided the tools for a constantly shifting adjustment of the tension between the evolving aims of the criminal law and changing religious, moral, philosophical, and medical views of the nature of man. This process of adjustment has always been thought to be the province of the States. The people of Montana have decided to resurrect the rule of an earlier era, disallowing consideration of voluntary intoxication when a defendant's state of mind is at issue. Nothing in the Due Process Clause prevents them from doing so, and the judgment of the Supreme Court of Montana to the contrary must be reversed.

Justice Ginsburg wrote an opinion concurring in the judgment in *Egelhoff*. She characterized the Montana statute not as an exclusionary rule of evidence, but rather as a redefinition of the mental-state element of the offense of murder. She described the operation of the Montana statute as follows:

> [The statute] extracts the entire subject of voluntary intoxication from the mens rea inquiry, thereby rendering evidence of voluntary intoxication

logically irrelevant to proof of the requisite mental state. * * *Comprehended as a measure redefining mens rea, [the Montana statute] encounters no constitutional shoal. States enjoy wide latitude in defining the elements of criminal offenses, see, e.g., Martin v. Ohio, particularly when determining the extent to which moral culpability should be a prerequisite to conviction of a crime. When a State's power to define criminal conduct is challenged under the Due Process Clause, we inquire only whether the law "offends some principle of justice so rooted in the traditions and conscience of our people as to be ranked as fundamental." *Patterson*. Defining mens rea to eliminate the exculpatory value of voluntary intoxication does not offend a "fundamental principle of justice," given the lengthy common-law tradition, and the adherence of a significant minority of the States to that position today.

In referring to Justice Ginsburg's opinion, the plurality opinion dropped the following footnote:

[W]e are in complete agreement with the concurrence that § 45–2–203 "embodies a legislative judgment regarding the circumstances under which individuals may be held criminally responsible for their actions." We also agree that the statute "extracts the entire subject of voluntary intoxication from the mens rea inquiry." We believe that this judgment may be implemented, and this effect achieved, with equal legitimacy by amending the substantive requirements for each crime, or by simply excluding intoxication evidence from the trial. We address this as an evidentiary statute simply because that is how the Supreme Court of Montana chose to analyze it.

Justices O'Connor, Stevens, Souter and Breyer dissented in *Egelhoff*.

2. *Element of the Crime or Sentencing Factor?*

While the government has the burden of proving an element of the crime beyond a reasonable doubt, facts determined at sentencing have traditionally been subject to the preponderance of the evidence standard. Thus, if the defendant's criminal history is a sentencing factor (as it is), the government need not prove that the defendant committed a prior crime beyond a reasonable doubt. The preponderance of the evidence standard is sufficient. [See Chapter 11 for a discussion of the rationale for this lesser standard of proof at sentencing].

Given the difference between the standard of proof at trial and sentencing, it is possible that a legislature might try to allocate certain facts to sentencing factors rather than to an element of the crime. Such a shift to sentencing factors implicates not only the reasonable doubt requirement of *Winship*, but also the defendant's constitutional right to a trial by jury on all elements of the crime. This is because sentencing factors are tried to the judge, not the jury.

In a series of important cases, the Court has sought to distinguish between what is a permissible sentencing factor and what must be part of the element of a crime. It is fair to state that the Court's journey down this path has been a winding one.

Preponderance of the Evidence at Sentencing:
McMillan v. Pennsylvania

At issue in McMillan v. Pennsylvania, 477 U.S. 79 (1986), was a state statute providing that anyone convicted of certain enumerated felonies is subject to a mandatory minimum sentence of five years' imprisonment if the sentencing judge finds by a preponderance of the evidence that the defendant "visibly possessed a firearm" during the commission of the offense. If the aggravating factor of possessing a firearm were an element of the crime, it would of course have to be proven beyond a reasonable doubt—but the state chose instead to make it a sentencing factor.

The Court upheld the statute against a due process challenge. Justice Rehnquist wrote for the Court and stated that it was permissible for the state to treat visible possession of a firearm as a sentencing factor rather than as an element of the crime. The state statute did not create a new offense, nor did it change the maximum punishment that could be imposed for an offense. Instead, it limited judicial discretion in sentencing. The Court found no problem with permitting a higher sentence to be based on proof of a fact by preponderance of the evidence, noting that the beyond the reasonable doubt standard had never been applied to sentencing factors. In support of Pennsylvania's delineation of sentencing factors and elements of the crime, Justice Rehnquist stated that "*Patterson* stressed that in determining what facts must be proved beyond a reasonable doubt the state legislature's definition of the elements of the offense is usually dispositive," and that the Pennsylvania statute did not go beyond the minimal limitations set by *Patterson*: it did not create a presumption of guilt, and did not relieve the prosecution of its burden of proving guilt of the underlying crime. The statute's applicability depended on the conviction of the defendant on charges other than visible possession of a firearm.

Justice Rehnquist addressed the argument that if Pennsylvania could have free reign in deciding what was a sentencing factor and what was an element of the crime, it would shift virtually all of the elements of the crime to sentencing factors in order to avoid having to establish proof beyond a reasonable doubt:

> Finally, we note that the spectre raised by petitioners of States restructuring existing crimes in order to evade the commands of *Winship* just does not appear in this case. * * * The Pennsylvania Legislature did not change the definition of any existing offense. It simply took one factor that has always been considered by sentencing courts to bear on punishment—the instrumentality used in committing a violent felony—and dictated the precise weight to be given that factor if the instrumentality is a firearm. Pennsylvania's decision to do so has not transformed a sentencing factor into an element of some hypothetical offense.

Justice Stevens dissented, arguing that "a state legislature may not dispense with the requirement of proof beyond a reasonable doubt for conduct that it targets for severe criminal penalties." He concluded that under *Patterson* "the Due Process Clause requires proof beyond a reasonable doubt of conduct which exposes a criminal defendant to greater stigma or punishment * * *." Justice Marshall, joined by Justices Brennan and Blackmun, also dissented. He agreed with Justice Stevens that the Pennsylvania statute operated to create a special stigma and a special punishment upon a finding of specific conduct, and this was enough to mandate that the prosecution prove the conduct beyond a reasonable doubt.

Applying the preponderance of the evidence standard to sentencing means that society is saying that the problem of having sentences that are too long is about as serious as the problem of having sentences that are too short—the costs of error are equal. But if that is the case, why is the problem of convicting an innocent person so much more serious than the problem of acquitting a guilty one?

Recidivism as a Sentencing Factor or as an Element of the Crime?

In Almendarez–Torres v. United States, 523 U.S. 224 (1998), the Court considered the meaning of *McMillan* in the context of a statute that provided a higher maximum sentence for a recidivist. Almendarez–Torres was convicted under a statute with two provisions. The first provision prohibits a deported alien from returning to the United States, and authorizes a maximum prison term of two years. The second provision authorizes a maximum prison term of 20 years if the initial "deportation was subsequent to a conviction for commission of an aggravated felony." The defendant was convicted under the second provision and was sentenced to 85 months' imprisonment. The defendant argued that he could not be subject to such a serious sentence, as his indictment did not mention his aggravated felony convictions. Because an indictment must recite all elements of the crime charged, the defendant argued that he could not be convicted under the statute's second provision. The government argued that the second provision of the statute did not set forth a separate crime, but was rather a provision mandating an enhanced sentence for recidivism; thus, in the government's view, the first provision of the statute defined the elements of the crime, and the second provision established a sentencing enhancement for felons who committed the crime. The case therefore turned on whether the legislature could authorize the use of recidivism as a sentencing factor, or instead whether the Constitution requires the legislature to treat recidivism as an element of the crime.

In a 5–4 decision written by Justice Breyer, the Court held that the legislature had the constitutional authority to treat recidivism as a sentencing factor rather than as an element of the crime. Therefore it was not necessary to include the defendant's prior felony record in the indictment. The Court found that the most pertinent case on the subject was *McMillan,* and discussed that case in the following passage:

> The Court [in *McMillan*] considered a Pennsylvania statute that set forth a sentencing factor—"visibly possessing a firearm"—the presence of which required the judge to impose a minimum prison term of five years. The Court held that the Constitution did not require the State to treat the factor as an element of the crime. In so holding, the Court said that the State's "linking the 'severity of punishment' to 'the presence or absence of an identified fact' "did not automatically make of that fact an "element." * * * It said that it would not "define precisely the constitutional limits" of a legislature's power to define the elements of an offense. And it held that, whatever those limits might be, the State had not exceeded them. Petitioner

must therefore concede that "firearm possession" (in respect to a mandatory minimum sentence) does not violate those limits. And he must argue that, nonetheless, "recidivism" (in respect to an authorized maximum) does violate those limits.

In assessing petitioner's claim, we have examined *McMillan* to determine the various features of the case upon which the Court's conclusion arguably turned. The *McMillan* Court pointed out: ① that the statute plainly "does not transgress the limits expressly set out in *Patterson*"; ② that the defendant (unlike *Mullaney's* defendant) did not face "a differential in sentencing ranging from a nominal fine to a mandatory life sentence"; ③ that the statute did not "alter the maximum penalty for the crime" but "operates solely to limit the sentencing court's discretion in selecting a penalty within the range already available to it"; ④ that the statute did not "create a separate offense calling for a separate penalty"; and ⑤ that the statute gave "no impression of having been tailored to permit the visible possession finding to be a tail which wags the dog of the substantive offense," but, to the contrary, "simply took one factor that has always been considered by sentencing courts to bear on punishment . . . and dictated the precise weight to be given that factor".

This case resembles *McMillan* in respect to most of these factors. But it is different in respect to the third factor, for it does "alter the maximum penalty for the crime"; and, it also creates a wider range of appropriate punishments than did the statute in *McMillan*. We nonetheless conclude that these differences do not change the constitutional outcome for several basic reasons.

First, the sentencing factor at issue here—recidivism—is a traditional, if not the most traditional, basis for a sentencing court's increasing an offender's sentence. * * * [T]o hold that the Constitution requires that recidivism be deemed an "element" of petitioner's offense would mark an abrupt departure from a longstanding tradition of treating recidivism as "going to the punishment only."

Second, the major difference between this case and *McMillan* consists of the circumstance that the sentencing factor at issue here (the prior conviction) triggers an increase in the maximum permissive sentence, while the sentencing factor at issue in *McMillan* triggered a mandatory minimum sentence. Yet that difference—between a permissive maximum and a mandatory minimum—does not systematically, or normally, work to the disadvantage of a criminal defendant. To the contrary, a statutory minimum binds a sentencing judge; a statutory maximum does not. A mandatory minimum can * * * mandate a minimum sentence of imprisonment more than twice as severe as the maximum the trial judge would otherwise have imposed. It can eliminate a sentencing judge's discretion in its entirety. And it can produce unfairly disproportionate impacts on certain kinds of offenders. In sum, the risk of unfairness to a particular defendant is no less, and may well be greater, when a mandatory minimum sentence, rather than a permissive maximum sentence, is at issue.

* * *

* * * The relevant statutory provisions do not change a pre-existing definition of a well-established crime, nor is there any more reason here, than in *McMillan*, to think Congress intended to "evade" the Constitution, either by "presuming" guilt or "restructuring" the elements of an offense.

For these reasons, we cannot find in *McMillan* (a case holding that the Constitution permits a legislature to require a longer sentence for gun possession) significant support for the proposition that the Constitution forbids a legislature to authorize a longer sentence for recidivism.

Justice Scalia, joined by Justices Stevens, Souter and Ginsburg, dissented. He argued that the question of whether recidivism must be an element of the crime was at least close enough that the statute should be construed as treating recidivism as an element of the crime. He contended that it could violate the defendant's right to jury trial to take from the jury factual issues that affect the penalty to which a defendant is exposed.

Sentencing Factors Extending the Sentence Beyond the Statutory Maximum Penalty: Apprendi

In the following case, the Court limited *McMillan* to its facts, and established a broad principle that prohibits the state and federal governments from using sentencing enhancements to increase a sentence beyond the statutory maximum. Where a factor is used in that way, it is an element of the crime that must be set forth in the indictment and the defendant has the right to have the factor proved beyond a reasonable doubt to a jury. In reaching this ruling, the Court relies on a case decided between *Almendarez-Torres* and this one–Jones v. United States, 526 U.S. 227 (1999), which questioned whether serious bodily injury could be considered a sentencing factor when it raised the sentence for the crime of car-jacking beyond the statutory maximum imposed for the simple offense.

APPRENDI v. NEW JERSEY

Supreme Court of the United States, 2000.
530 U.S. 466.

Justice Stevens delivered the opinion of the Court.

A New Jersey statute classifies the possession of a firearm for an unlawful purpose as a "second-degree" offense. N. J. Stat. Ann. § 2C:39–4(a) (West 1995). Such an offense is punishable by imprisonment for "between five years and 10 years." § 2C:43–6(a)(2). A separate statute, described by that State's Supreme Court as a "hate crime" law, provides for an "extended term" of imprisonment if the trial judge finds, by a preponderance of the evidence, that "[t]he defendant in

committing the crime acted with a purpose to intimidate an individual or group of individuals because of race, color, gender, handicap, religion, sexual orientation or ethnicity." N. J. Stat. Ann. § 2C:44–3(e) (West Supp. 2000). The extended term authorized by the hate crime law for second-degree offenses is imprisonment for "between 10 and 20 years." § 2C:43–7(a)(3).

The question presented is whether the Due Process Clause of the Fourteenth Amendment requires that a factual determination authorizing an increase in the maximum prison sentence for an offense from 10 to 20 years be made by a jury on the basis of proof beyond a reasonable doubt.

I

[Apprendi pleaded guilty to a shooting, and at sentencing the government brought evidence that the shooting was racially motivated. The sentencing court found evidence of racial bias by a preponderance of the evidence, and imposed an enhanced sentence on the basis of the hate crime law. That sentence was well above what Apprendi could have received for the crime to which he pled guilty. The sentence was upheld by the New Jersey court, which concluded that the state had the authority to define racial motivation as a sentencing factor rather than as an element of the crime.]

We granted certiorari, and now reverse.

II

* * * The constitutional question * * * is whether the 12–year sentence imposed on count 18 was permissible, given that it was above the 10–year maximum for the offense charged in that count. The finding is legally significant because it increased—indeed, it doubled—the maximum range within which the judge could exercise his discretion, converting what otherwise was a maximum 10–year sentence on that count into a minimum sentence. * * * The question whether Apprendi had a constitutional right to have a jury find such bias on the basis of proof beyond a reasonable doubt is starkly presented.

Our answer to that question was foreshadowed by our opinion in Jones v. United States, 526 U.S. 227 (1999), construing a federal statute. We there noted that "under the Due Process Clause of the Fifth Amendment and the notice and jury trial guarantees of the Sixth Amendment, any fact (other

than prior conviction) that increases the maximum penalty for a crime must be charged in an indictment, submitted to a jury, and proven beyond a reasonable doubt." The Fourteenth Amendment commands the same answer in this case involving a state statute.

III

* * *

At stake in this case are constitutional protections of surpassing importance: the proscription of any deprivation of liberty without "due process of law," Amdt. 14, and the guarantee that "[i]n all criminal prosecutions, the accused shall enjoy the right to a speedy and public trial, by an impartial jury," Amdt. 6. Taken together, these rights indisputably entitle a criminal defendant to "a jury determination that [he] is guilty of every element of the crime with which he is charged, beyond a reasonable doubt."

As we have * * * explained, the historical foundation for our recognition of these principles extends down centuries into the common law. "[T]o guard against a spirit of oppression and tyranny on the part of rulers," and "as the great bulwark of [our] civil and political liberties," 2 J. Story, Commentaries on the Constitution of the United States 540–541 (4th ed. 1873), trial by jury has been understood to require that "the truth of every accusation, whether preferred in the shape of indictment, information, or appeal, should afterwards be confirmed by the unanimous suffrage of twelve of [the defendant's] equals and neighbours...." 4 W. Blackstone, Commentaries on the Laws of England 343 (1769).

Equally well founded is the companion right to have the jury verdict based on proof beyond a reasonable doubt.

"The demand for a higher degree of persuasion in criminal cases was recurrently expressed from ancient times, [though] its crystallization into the formula 'beyond a reasonable doubt' seems to have occurred as late as 1798. It is now accepted in common law jurisdictions as the measure of persuasion by which the prosecution must convince the trier of all the essential elements of guilt." C. McCormick, Evidence § 321, pp. 681–682 (1954).

Any possible distinction between an "element" of a felony offense and a "sentencing factor" was unknown to the practice of criminal indictment, trial by jury, and judgment by court as it existed during the years surrounding our Nation's founding. As a general rule, criminal proceedings were submitted to a jury after being initiated by an indictment containing "all the facts and circumstances which constitute the offence, ... stated with such certainty and precision, that the defendant ... may be enabled to determine the species of offence they constitute, in order that he may prepare his defence accordingly ... and that there may be no doubt as to the judgment which should be given, if the defendant be convicted." J. Archbold, Pleading and Evidence in Criminal Cases 44 (15th ed. 1862). The defendant's ability to predict with certainty the judgment from the face of the felony indictment flowed from the invariable linkage of punishment with crime.

* * *

The historic link between verdict and judgment and the consistent limitation on judges' discretion to operate within the limits of the legal penalties provided highlight the novelty of a legislative scheme that removes the jury from the determination of a fact that, if found, exposes the criminal defendant to a penalty exceeding the maximum he would receive if punished according to the facts reflected in the jury verdict alone.

We do not suggest that trial practices cannot change in the course of centuries and still remain true to the principles that emerged from the Framers' fears "that the jury right could be lost not only by gross denial, but by erosion." But practice must at least adhere to the basic principles undergirding the requirements of trying to a jury all facts necessary to constitute a statutory offense, and proving those facts beyond reasonable doubt. As we made clear in *Winship*, the "reasonable doubt" requirement "has a vital role in our criminal procedure for cogent reasons." Prosecution subjects the criminal defendant both to "the possibility that he may lose his liberty upon conviction and ... the certainty that he would be stigmatized by the conviction." We thus require this, among other, procedural protections in order to "provid[e] concrete substance for the presumption of innocence," and to reduce the risk of imposing such deprivations erroneously. * * *

Since *Winship*, we have made clear beyond peradventure that *Winship's* due process and associated jury protections extend, to some degree, "to determinations that [go] not to a defendant's guilt or innocence, but simply to the length of his sentence." This was a primary lesson of Mullaney v. Wilbur, 421 U.S. 684 (1975), in which we invalidated a Maine statute that presumed that a defendant who acted with an intent to kill possessed the "malice aforethought" necessary to constitute the State's murder offense (and therefore, was subject to that crime's associated punishment of life imprisonment). The statute placed the burden on the defendant of proving, in rebutting the statutory presumption, that he acted with a lesser degree of culpability, such as in the heat of passion, to win a reduction in the offense from murder to manslaughter (and thus a reduction of the maximum punishment of 20 years).

* * *

IV

It was in McMillan v. Pennsylvania, 477 U.S. 79 (1986), that this Court, for the first time, coined the term "sentencing factor" to refer to a fact that was not found by a jury but that could affect the sentence imposed by the judge. That case involved a challenge to the State's Mandatory Minimum Sentencing Act. According to its provisions, anyone convicted of certain felonies would be subject to a mandatory minimum penalty of five years imprisonment if the judge found, by a preponderance of the evidence, that the person "visibly possessed a firearm" in the course of committing one of the specified felonies. Articulating for the first time, and then applying, a multifactor set of criteria for determining whether the *Winship* protections applied to bar such a system, we concluded that the Pennsylvania statute did not run afoul of our previous admonitions against relieving the State of its burden of proving guilt, or tailoring the mere form of a criminal statute solely to avoid *Winship's* strictures.

We did not, however, there budge from the position that (1) constitutional limits exist to States' authority to define away facts necessary to constitute a criminal offense, and (2) that a state scheme that keeps from the jury facts that "expos[e] [defendants] to greater or additional punishment,"

may raise serious constitutional concern. As we explained:

> Section 9712 neither alters the maximum penalty for the crime committed nor creates a separate offense calling for a separate penalty; it operates solely to limit the sentencing Court's discretion in selecting a penalty within the range already available to it without the special finding of visible possession of a firearm.... The statute gives no impression of having been tailored to permit the visible possession finding to be a tail which wags the dog of the substantive offense. Petitioners' claim that visible possession under the Pennsylvania statute is "really" an element of the offenses for which they are being punished—that Pennsylvania has in effect defined a new set of upgraded felonies—would have at least more superficial appeal if a finding of visible possession exposed them to greater or additional punishment, cf. 18 U.S.C. § 2113(d) (providing separate and greater punishment for bank robberies accomplished through "use of a dangerous weapon or device"), but it does not.[a]

Finally, as we made plain in *Jones* last Term, Almendarez–Torres v. United States, represents at best an exceptional departure from the historic practice that we have described. * * * Because Almendarez–Torres had admitted the three earlier convictions for aggravated felonies—all of which had been entered pursuant to proceedings with substantial procedural safeguards of their own—no question concerning the right to a jury trial or the standard of proof that would apply to a contested issue of fact was before the Court.

---

a. The principal dissent accuses us of today "overruling *McMillan*." We do not overrule *McMillan*. We limit its holding to cases that do not involve the imposition of a sentence more severe than the statutory maximum for the offense established by the jury's verdict—a limitation identified in the *McMillan* opinion itself. Conscious of the likelihood that legislative decisions may have been made in reliance on *McMillan*, we reserve for another day the question whether *stare decisis* considerations preclude reconsideration of its narrower holding.

* * *. More important, as *Jones* made crystal clear, our conclusion in *Almendarez-Torres* turned heavily upon the fact that the additional sentence to which the defendant was subject was "the prior commission of a serious crime." 523 U.S., at 243 (explaining that "recidivism . . . is a traditional, if not, the most traditional, basis for a sentencing Court's increasing an offender's sentence"). Both the certainty that procedural safeguards attached to any "fact" of prior conviction, and the reality that Almendarez–Torres did not challenge the accuracy of that "fact" in his case, mitigated the due process and Sixth Amendment concerns otherwise implicated in allowing a judge to determine a "fact" increasing punishment beyond the maximum of the statutory range.

Even though it is arguable that *Almendarez-Torres* was incorrectly decided, and that a logical application of our reasoning today should apply if the recidivist issue were contested, Apprendi does not contest the decision's validity and we need not revisit it for purposes of our decision today to treat the case as a narrow exception to the general rule we recalled at the outset. Given its unique facts, it surely does not warrant rejection of the otherwise uniform course of decision during the entire history of our jurisprudence.

In sum, our reexamination of our cases in this area, and of the history upon which they rely, confirms the

opinion that we expressed in *Jones*. Other than the fact of a prior conviction, any fact that increases the penalty for a crime beyond the prescribed statutory maximum must be submitted to a jury, and proved beyond a reasonable doubt. With that exception, we endorse the statement of the rule set forth in the concurring opinions in that case: "[I]t is unconstitutional for a legislature to remove from the jury the assessment of facts that increase the prescribed range of penalties to which a criminal defendant is exposed. It is equally clear that such facts must be established by proof beyond a reasonable doubt." 526 U.S., at 252–253 (opinion of Stevens, J.); see also id., at 253 (opinion of Scalia, J.).[b]

V

The New Jersey statutory scheme that Apprendi asks us to invalidate allows a jury to convict a defendant of a second-degree offense based on its finding beyond a reasonable doubt that he unlawfully possessed a prohibited weapon; after a subsequent and separate proceeding, it then allows a judge to impose punishment identical to that New Jersey provides for crimes of the first degree, N. J. Stat. Ann. § 2C:43–6(a)(1) (West 1999), based upon the judge's finding, by a preponderance of the evidence, that the defendant's "purpose" for unlawfully possessing the weapon was "to intimidate" his victim on the basis of a par-

---

b. The principal dissent would reject the Court's rule as a "meaningless formalism," because it can conceive of hypothetical statutes that would comply with the rule and achieve the same result as the New Jersey statute. While a State could, hypothetically, undertake to revise its entire criminal code in the manner the dissent suggests—extending all statutory maximum sentences to, for example, 50 years and giving judges guided discretion as to a few specially selected factors within that range—this possibility seems remote. Among other reasons, structural democratic constraints exist to discourage legislatures from enacting penal statutes that expose every defendant convicted

of, for example, weapons possession, to a maximum sentence exceeding that which is, in the legislature's judgment, generally proportional to the crime. This is as it should be. Our rule ensures that a State is obliged to make its choices concerning the substantive content of its criminal laws with full awareness of the consequence, unable to mask substantive policy choices of exposing all who are convicted to the maximum sentence it provides. So exposed, "the political check on potentially harsh legislative action is then more likely to operate.

* * *

ticular characteristic the victim possessed. In light of the constitutional rule explained above, and all of the cases supporting it, this practice cannot stand.

* * *

New Jersey would * * * point to the fact that the State did not, in placing the required biased purpose finding in a sentencing enhancement provision, create a "separate offense calling for a separate penalty." [But] because the state legislature placed its hate crime sentence "enhancer" "within the sentencing provisions" of the criminal code "does not mean that the finding of a biased purpose to intimidate is not an essential element of the offense." Indeed, the fact that New Jersey, along with numerous other States, has also made precisely the same conduct the subject of an independent substantive offense makes it clear that the mere presence of this "enhancement" in a sentencing statute does not define its character.

New Jersey's reliance on *Almendarez-Torres* is also unavailing. The reasons supporting an exception from the general rule for the statute construed in that case do not apply to the New Jersey statute. Whereas recidivism "does not relate to the commission of the offense" itself, New Jersey's biased purpose inquiry goes precisely to what happened in the "commission of the offense." Moreover, there is a vast difference between accepting the validity of a prior judgment of conviction entered in a proceeding in which the defendant had the right to a jury trial and the right to require the prosecutor to prove guilt beyond a reasonable doubt, and allowing the judge to find the required fact under a lesser standard of proof.

* * *

The New Jersey procedure challenged in this case is an unacceptable departure from the jury tradition that is an indispensable part of our criminal justice system. Accordingly, the judgment of the Supreme Court of New Jersey is reversed, and the case is remanded for further proceedings not inconsistent with this opinion.

JUSTICE SCALIA, concurring.

I feel the need to say a few words in response to Justice Breyer's dissent. It sketches an admirably fair and efficient scheme of criminal justice designed for a society that is prepared to leave criminal justice to the State. (Judges, it is sometimes necessary to remind ourselves, are part of the State—and an increasingly bureaucratic part of it, at that.) The founders of the American Republic were not prepared to leave it to the State, which is why the jury-trial guarantee was one of the least controversial provisions of the Bill of Rights. It has never been efficient; but it has always been free.

As for fairness, which Justice Breyer believes "[i]n modern times," the jury cannot provide: I think it not unfair to tell a prospective felon that if he commits his contemplated crime he is exposing himself to a jail sentence of 30 years—and that if, upon conviction, he gets anything less than that he may thank the mercy of a tenderhearted judge (just as he may thank the mercy of a tenderhearted parole commission if he is let out inordinately early, or the mercy of a tenderhearted governor if his sentence is commuted). Will there be disparities? Of course. But the criminal will never get more punishment than he bargained for when he did the crime, and his guilt of the crime (and hence the length of the sentence to which he is exposed) will be determined beyond a reasonable doubt by the unanimous vote of 12 of his fellow citizens.

In Justice Breyer's bureaucratic realm of perfect equity, by contrast, the facts that determine the length of sentence to which the defendant is exposed will be determined to exist (on a more-likely-than-not basis) by a single employee of the State. It is certainly arguable (Justice Breyer argues it) that this sacrifice of prior protections is worth it. But it is not arguable that, just because one thinks it is a better system, it must be, or is even more likely to be, the system envisioned by a Constitution that guarantees trial by jury. * * *

JUSTICE THOMAS, with whom JUSTICE SCALIA joins as to Parts I and II, concurring.

I join the opinion of the Court in full. I write separately to explain my view that the Constitution requires a broader rule than the Court adopts.

I

This case turns on the seemingly simple question of what constitutes a "crime" * * * that is, which facts are the "elements" or "ingredients" of a crime. In order for an accusation of a crime (whether by indictment or some other form) to be proper under the common law, and thus proper under the codification of the common-law rights in the Fifth and Sixth Amendments, it must allege all elements of that crime; likewise, in order for a jury trial of a crime to be proper, all elements of the crime must be proved to the jury (and, under *Winship*, proved beyond a reasonable doubt).

Thus, it is critical to know which facts are elements. This question became more complicated following the Court's decision in McMillan v. Pennsylvania, which spawned a special sort of fact known as a sentencing enhancement. Such a fact increases a defendant's punishment but is not subject to the constitutional protections to which elements are subject. * * *

Sentencing enhancements may be new creatures, but the question that they create for courts is not. Courts have long had to consider which facts are elements in order to determine the sufficiency of an accusation (usually an indictment). The answer that courts have provided regarding the accusation tells us what an element is, and it is then a simple matter to apply that answer to whatever constitutional right may be at issue in a case—here, *Winship* and the right to trial by jury. A long line of essentially uniform authority addressing accusations, and stretching from the earliest reported cases after the founding until well into the 20th century, establishes that the original understanding of which facts are elements was even broader than the rule that the Court adopts today.

This authority establishes that a "crime" includes every fact that is by law a basis for imposing or increasing punishment (in contrast with a fact that mitigates punishment). Thus, if the legislature defines some core crime and then provides for increasing the punishment of that crime upon a finding of some aggravating fact—of whatever sort, including the fact of a prior conviction—the core crime and the aggravating fact together constitute an aggravated crime, just as much as grand larceny is an aggravated form of petit larceny. The aggravating fact is an element of the aggravated crime. * * *

II

[Justice Thomas undertakes a long disquisition into the common-law cases interpreting the elements of a crime.]

III

The consequence of the above discussion for our decisions in *Almendarez-Torres* and *McMillan* should be plain enough, but a few points merit special mention.

* * *

[O]neof the chief errors of *Almendarez-Torres*—an error to which I succumbed—was to attempt to discern whether a particular fact is traditionally (or typically) a basis for a sentencing court to increase an offender's sentence. * * * What matters is the way by which a fact enters into the sentence. If a fact is by law the basis for imposing or increasing punishment—for establishing or increasing the prosecution's entitlement—it is an element. * * *. One reason frequently offered for treating recidivism differently, a reason on which we relied in *Almendarez-Torres*, is a concern for prejudicing the jury by informing it of the prior conviction. But this concern, of which earlier courts were well aware, does not make the traditional understanding of what an element is any less applicable to the fact of a prior conviction.

* * *

For the foregoing reasons, as well as those given in the Court's opinion, I agree that the New Jersey procedure at issue is unconstitutional.

JUSTICE O'CONNOR, with whom THE CHIEF JUSTICE, JUSTICE KENNEDY, and JUSTICE BREYER join, dissenting.

* * *

I

Our Court has long recognized that not every fact that bears on a defendant's punishment need be charged in an indictment, submitted to a jury, and proved by the government beyond a reasonable doubt. Rather, we have held that the "legislature's definition of the elements of the offense is usually dispositive." Although we have recognized that "there are obviously constitutional limits beyond which the States may not go in this regard," and that "in certain limited circumstances *Winship's* reasonable-doubt requirement applies to facts not formally identified as elements of the offense charged," we have proceeded with caution before deciding that a certain fact must be treated as an offense element despite the legislature's choice not to characterize it as such. * * *

In one bold stroke the Court today casts aside our traditional cautious approach and instead embraces a universal and seemingly bright-line rule limiting the power of Congress and state legislatures to define criminal offenses and the sentences that follow from convictions thereunder.

* * *

* * * The Court * * * cites our decision in Mullaney v. Wilbur, 421 U.S. 684 (1975), to demonstrate the "lesson" that due process and jury protections extend beyond those factual determinations that affect a defendant's guilt or innocence. The Court explains *Mullaney* as having held that the due process proof-beyond-a-reasonable-doubt requirement applies to those factual determinations that, under a State's criminal law, make a difference in the degree of punishment the defendant receives. The Court chooses to ignore, however, the decision we issued two years later, Patterson v. New York, 432 U.S. 197 (1977), which clearly rejected the Court's broad reading of *Mullaney*.

majority ignores Patterson who's reject Mullaney

* * *

Patterson is important because it plainly refutes the Court's expansive reading of *Mullaney*. * * *. We explained *Mullaney* instead as holding only "that a State must prove every ingredient of an offense beyond a reasonable doubt, and that it may not shift the burden of proof to the defendant by presuming that ingredient upon proof of the other elements of the offense." Because nothing had been presumed against Patterson under New York law, we found no due process violation. Ever since our decision in *Patterson*, we have consistently explained the holding in *Mullaney* in these limited terms and have rejected the broad interpretation the Court gives *Mullaney* today.

* * *

II

* * *

Any discussion of either the constitutional necessity or the likely effect of the Court's rule must begin, of course, with an understanding of what exactly that rule is. As was the case in *Jones*, however, that discussion is complicated here by the Court's failure to clarify the contours of the constitutional principle underlying its decision. In fact, there appear to be several plausible interpretations of the constitutional principle on which the Court's decision rests.

For example, under one reading, the Court appears to hold that the Constitution requires that a fact be submitted to a jury and proved beyond a reasonable doubt only if that fact, as a formal matter, extends the range of punishment beyond the prescribed statutory maximum. A State could, however, remove from the jury (and subject to a standard of proof below "beyond a reasonable doubt") the assessment of those facts that define narrower ranges of punishment, within the overall statutory range, to which the defendant may be sentenced. Thus, apparently New Jersey could cure its sentencing scheme, and achieve virtually the same results, by drafting its weapons possession statute in the following manner: First, New Jersey could prescribe, in the weapons

possession statute itself, a range of 5 to 20 years' imprisonment for one who commits that criminal offense. Second, New Jersey could provide that only those defendants convicted under the statute who are found by a judge, by a preponderance of the evidence, to have acted with a purpose to intimidate an individual on the basis of race may receive a sentence greater than 10 years' imprisonment. * * * It is difficult to understand, and the Court does not explain, why the Constitution would require a state legislature to follow such a meaningless and formalistic difference in drafting its criminal statutes.

Under another reading of the Court's decision, it may mean only that the Constitution requires that a fact be submitted to a jury and proved beyond a reasonable doubt if it, as a formal matter, increases the range of punishment beyond that which could legally be imposed absent that fact. A State could, however, remove from the jury (and subject to a standard of proof below "beyond a reasonable doubt") the assessment of those facts that, as a formal matter, decrease the range of punishment below that which could legally be imposed absent that fact. Thus, consistent with our decision in *Patterson*, New Jersey could cure its sentencing scheme, and achieve virtually the same results, by drafting its weapons possession statute in the following manner: First, New Jersey could prescribe, in the weapons possession statute itself, a range of 5 to 20 years' imprisonment for one who commits that criminal offense. Second, New Jersey could provide that a defendant convicted under the statute whom a judge finds, by a preponderance of the evidence, not to have acted with a purpose to intimidate an individual on the basis of race may receive a sentence no greater than 10 years' imprisonment. * * * Again, it is difficult to understand, and neither the Court nor Justice Thomas explains, why the Constitution would require a state legislature to follow such a meaningless and formalistic difference in drafting its criminal statutes.

If either of the above readings is all that the Court's decision means, the Court's principle amounts to nothing more than chastising the New Jersey Legislature for failing to use the approved phrasing in expressing its intent as to how unlawful weapons possession should be punished. If New Jersey can, consistent with the Constitution, make precisely the same differences in punishment turn on precisely the same facts, and can remove the assessment of those facts from the jury and subject them to a standard of proof below "beyond a reasonable doubt," it is impossible to say that the Fifth, Sixth, and Fourteenth Amendments require the Court's rule.

* * *

Prior to the most recent wave of sentencing reform, the Federal Government and the States employed indeterminate-sentencing schemes in which judges and executive branch officials (e.g., parole board officials) had substantial discretion to determine the actual length of a defendant's sentence. Studies of indeterminate-sentencing schemes found that similarly situated defendants often received widely disparate sentences. Although indeterminate sentencing was intended to soften the harsh and uniform sentences formerly imposed under mandatory-sentencing systems, some studies revealed that indeterminate sentencing actually had the opposite effect.

In response, Congress and the state legislatures shifted to determinate-sentencing schemes that aimed to limit judges' sentencing discretion and, thereby, afford similarly situated of-

fenders equivalent treatment. The most well known of these reforms was the federal Sentencing Reform Act of 1984, 18 U.S.C. § 3551 et seq. In the Act, Congress created the United States Sentencing Commission, which in turn promulgated the Sentencing Guidelines that now govern sentencing by federal judges. Whether one believes the determinate-sentencing reforms have proved successful or not—and the subject is one of extensive debate among commentators—the apparent effect of the Court's opinion today is to halt the current debate on sentencing reform in its tracks and to invalidate with the stroke of a pen three decades' worth of nationwide reform, all in the name of a principle with a questionable constitutional pedigree. Indeed, it is ironic that the Court, in the name of constitutional rights meant to protect criminal defendants from the potentially arbitrary exercise of power by prosecutors and judges, appears to rest its decision on a principle that would render unconstitutional efforts by Congress and the state legislatures to place constraints on that very power in the sentencing context.

* * *

III

Because I do not believe that the Court's "increase in the maximum penalty" rule is required by the Constitution, I would evaluate New Jersey's sentence-enhancement statute, N. J. Stat. Ann. § 2C:44–3 (West Supp. 2000), by analyzing the factors we have examined in past cases. First, the New Jersey statute does not shift the burden of proof on an essential ingredient of the offense by presuming that ingredient upon proof of other elements of the offense. Second, the magnitude of the New Jersey sentence enhancement, as applied in petitioner's

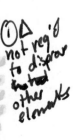

(handwritten margin notes: ② sentence enhancement is consti valid in range

③ not obviously trying to evade consti req'mt of proving an element of charged crime by mobthly if sentence factor

too many sentencing factors to put to jury)

case, is constitutionally permissible. Under New Jersey law, the weapons possession offense to which petitioner pleaded guilty carries a sentence range of 5 to 10 years' imprisonment. The fact that petitioner, in committing that offense, acted with a purpose to intimidate because of race exposed him to a higher sentence range of 10 to 20 years' imprisonment. The 10–year increase in the maximum penalty to which petitioner was exposed falls well within the range we have found permissible. Third, the New Jersey statute gives no impression of having been enacted to evade the constitutional requirements that attach when a State makes a fact an element of the charged offense. For example, New Jersey did not take what had previously been an element of the weapons possession offense and transform it into a sentencing factor.

* * * New Jersey, therefore, has done no more than what we held permissible in *McMillan*; it has taken a traditional sentencing factor and dictated the precise weight judges should attach to that factor when the specific motive is to intimidate on the basis of race.

* * *

Justice Breyer, **with whom** Chief Justice Rehnquist **joins, dissenting.**

The majority holds that the Constitution contains the following requirement: "any fact [other than recidivism] that increases the penalty for a crime beyond the prescribed statutory maximum must be submitted to a jury, and proved beyond a reasonable doubt." This rule would seem to promote a procedural ideal—that of juries, not judges, determining the existence of those facts upon which increased punishment turns. But the real world of criminal justice cannot hope to meet any such ideal. It can function only with the help of procedural compro-

mises, particularly in respect to sentencing. And those compromises, which are themselves necessary for the fair functioning of the criminal justice system, preclude implementation of the procedural model that today's decision reflects. At the very least, the impractical nature of the requirement that the majority now recognizes supports the proposition that the Constitution was not intended to embody it.

I

* * * There are, to put it simply, far too many potentially relevant sentencing factors to permit submission of all (or even many) of them to a jury. As the Sentencing Guidelines state the matter, "[a] bank robber with (or without) a gun, which the robber kept hidden (or brandished), might have frightened (or merely warned), injured seriously (or less seriously), tied up (or simply pushed) a guard, a teller or a customer, at night (or at noon), for a bad (or arguably less bad) motive, in an effort to obtain money for other crimes (or for other purposes), in the company of a few (or many) other robbers, for the first (or fourth) time that day, while sober (or under the influence of drugs or alcohol), and so forth." Sentencing Guidelines, Part A, at 1.2.

The Guidelines note that "a sentencing system tailored to fit every conceivable wrinkle of each case can become unworkable and seriously compromise the certainty of punishment and its deterrent effect." To ask a jury to consider all, or many, such matters would do the same.

At the same time, to require jury consideration of all such factors—say, during trial where the issue is guilt or innocence—could easily place the defendant in the awkward (and conceivably unfair) position of having to deny he committed the crime yet offer proof about how he committed it, e.g., "I did not sell drugs, but I sold no more than 500 grams." And while special postverdict sentencing juries could cure this problem, they have seemed (but for capital cases) not worth their administrative costs. * * *

* * * A sentencing system in which judges have discretion to find sentencing-related factors is a workable system and one that has long been thought consistent with the Constitution; why, then, would the Constitution treat sentencing statutes any differently?

II

* * *

III

* * * The majority raises no objection to traditional pre-Guidelines sentencing procedures under which judges, not juries, made the factual findings that would lead to an increase in an individual offender's sentence. How does a legislative determination differ in any significant way? For example, if a judge may on his or her own decide that victim injury or bad motive should increase a bank robber's sen-

tence from 5 years to 10, why does it matter that a legislature instead enacts a statute that increases a bank robber's sentence from 5 years to 10 based on this same judicial finding?

* * *

IV

I certainly do not believe that the present sentencing system is one of "perfect equity," and I am willing, consequently, to assume that the majority's rule would provide a degree of increased procedural protection in respect to those particular sentencing factors currently embodied in statutes. I nonetheless believe that any such increased protection provides little practical help and comes at too high a price. For one thing, by leaving mandatory minimum sentences untouched, the majority's rule simply encourages any legislature interested in asserting control over the sentencing process to do so by creating those minimums. That result would mean significantly less procedural fairness, not more.

* * *

I respectfully dissent.

Note on Apprendi

Professor Jacqueline Ross points out that the Court's ruling in *Apprendi* does not do defendants any favors. In fact, defendants may be put to disadvantages after *Apprendi*, as Justice Breyer intimates in his dissent. Professor Ross elaborates as follows:

> Turning sentencing factors into offense elements to be tried to a jury will put defendants under pressure to produce evidence on an increasing range of issues. If the government must prove racial animus, drug amounts, relative culpability of different participants, or similar aggravating factors that may increase the maximum penalty for certain crimes, the government's presentation of evidence on these issues will put pressure on defendants to rebut the government's prima facie case by presenting their own evidence. Reallocating factual determinations from the sentencing judge to the jury in effect shifts the burden of production onto defendants, while the burden of proof remains formally on the government. * * * If he wishes to rebut the government's evidence on the disputed aggravating circumstances, a defendant may have to forego the benefits of the presumption of innocence (a) by presenting evidence and (b) by admitting some level of

guilt or criminal involvement as the price of disagreeing with the degree of imputed culpability.

For example, if the government were required to prove to the jury the amount of drugs sold by co-conspirators in furtherance of a narcotics conspiracy, government evidence that the conspirators sold at least 100 grams of heroin would potentially raise the maximum prison term from twenty to forty years' imprisonment. Defendants wanting to deny their identification as members of the conspiracy, or their presence at a drug transaction, may have to choose between presenting no evidence on the issue of drug amounts, in effect solidifying the often circumstantial inferences raised by the government's evidence, or producing evidence [of smaller than 100 gram drug amounts, which is] inconsistent with putting the government to its proof on the issues of defendant's identity and presence at the drug deal.

Ross, Unanticipated Consequences of Turning Sentencing Factors Into Offense Elements: The *Apprendi* Debate, 12 Federal Sentencing Reporter 197 (2000). As a juror, how would you react to the defendant's argument that "I wasn't there at the drug deal, but if I was there, the deal involved a lot less than 100 grams."?

Apprendi and Sentencing Factors That Do Not Increase the Statutory Maximum Penalty: Harris v. United States

In the following case, the Court considered, and substantially limited, the implications of its decision in *Apprendi*.

HARRIS v. UNITED STATES

United States Supreme Court, 2002.
536 U.S. 545.

JUSTICE KENNEDY **announced the judgment of the Court and delivered the opinion of the Court with respect to Parts I, II, and IV, and an opinion with respect to Part III, in which the** CHIEF JUSTICE, JUSTICE O'CONNOR, **and** JUSTICE SCALIA **join.**

Once more we consider the distinction the law has drawn between the elements of a crime and factors that influence a criminal sentence. Legislatures define crimes in terms of the facts that are their essential elements, and constitutional guarantees attach to these facts. In federal prosecutions, "[n]o person shall be held to answer for a capital, or otherwise infamous crime, unless on a presentment or indictment of a Grand Jury" alleging all the elements of the crime. U.S. Const., Amdt. 5. "In all criminal prosecutions," state and federal, "the accused

shall enjoy the right to . . . trial . . . by an impartial jury," U.S. Const., Amdt. 6, at which the government must prove each element beyond a reasonable doubt, see In re Winship.

Yet not all facts affecting the defendant's punishment are elements. After the accused is convicted, the judge may impose a sentence within a range provided by statute, basing it on various facts relating to the defendant and the manner in which the offense was committed. Though these facts may have a substantial impact on the sentence, they are not elements, and are thus not subject to the Constitution's indictment, jury, and proof requirements. Some statutes also direct judges to give specific weight to certain facts when choosing the sentence. The statutes do not require these facts, sometimes referred to as sentencing factors, to be alleged in the indictment, submitted to the jury, or established beyond a reasonable doubt.

The Constitution permits legislatures to make the distinction between elements and sentencing factors, but it imposes some limitations as well. For if it did not, legislatures could evade the indictment, jury, and proof requirements by labeling almost every relevant fact a sentencing factor. The Court described one limitation in this respect two Terms ago in *Apprendi v. New Jersey,* 530 U.S. 466, 490 (2000): "Other than the fact of a prior conviction, any fact that increases the penalty for a crime beyond the prescribed statutory maximum," whether the statute calls it an element or a sentencing factor, "must be submitted to a jury, and proved beyond a reasonable doubt." Fourteen years before, in *McMillan v. Pennsylvania,* 477 U.S. 79 (1986), the Court had declined to adopt a more restrictive constitutional rule. *McMillan* sustained a statute that increased the minimum penalty for a crime, though not beyond the statutory maximum, when the sentencing judge found, by a preponderance of the evidence, that the defendant had possessed a firearm.

The principal question before us is whether *McMillan* stands after *Apprendi.*

I

Petitioner William Joseph Harris sold illegal narcotics out of his pawnshop with an unconcealed semiautomatic pistol at his side. He was later arrested for violating federal drug and firearms laws, including 18 U.S.C. § 924(c)(1)(A). That statute provides in relevant part:

> [A]ny person who, during and in relation to any crime of violence or drug trafficking crime ... uses or carries a firearm, or who, in further-

ance of any such crime, possesses a firearm, shall, in addition to the punishment provided for such crime of violence or drug trafficking crime—

> (i) be sentenced to a term of imprisonment of not less than 5 years;

> (ii) if the firearm is brandished, be sentenced to a term of imprisonment of not less than 7 years; and

> (iii) if the firearm is discharged, be sentenced to a term of imprisonment of not less than 10 years.

The Government proceeded on the assumption that § 924(c)(1)(A) defines a single crime and that brandishing is a sentencing factor to be considered by the judge after the trial. For this reason the indictment said nothing of brandishing and made no reference to subsection (ii). Instead, it simply alleged the elements from the statute's principal paragraph: that "during and in relation to a drug trafficking crime," petitioner had "knowingly carr[ied] a firearm." At a bench trial the United States District Court for the Middle District of North Carolina found petitioner guilty as charged.

Following his conviction, the presentence report recommended that petitioner be given the 7–year minimum because he had brandished the gun. Petitioner objected, * * * arguing that, as a matter of statutory interpretation, brandishing is an element of a separate offense, an offense for which he had not been indicted or tried. At the sentencing hearing the District Court overruled the objection, found by a preponderance of the evidence that petitioner had brandished the gun, and sentenced him to seven years in prison.

In the Court of Appeals for the Fourth Circuit petitioner again pressed his statutory argument. He added that if brandishing is a sentencing factor as a statutory matter, the statute is unconstitutional in light of *Apprendi*—even though, as petitioner acknowledged, the judge's finding did not alter the maximum penalty to which he was exposed. Rejecting these arguments, the Court of Appeals affirmed. Like every other Court of Appeals to have addressed the question, it held that the statute makes brandishing a sentencing factor. The court also held that the constitutional argument was foreclosed by *McMillan*.

We granted certiorari, and now affirm.

II

[The Court finds that Congress intended to make brandishing a sentencing factor rather than an element in § 924(c)(1)(A)].

III

Confident that the statute does just what *McMillan* said it could, we consider petitioner's argument that § 924(c)(1)(A)(ii) is unconstitutional because *McMillan* is no longer sound authority. * * * [Petitioner argues that *Apprendi*] cannot be reconciled with *McMillan*. We do not find the argument convincing. As we shall explain, *McMillan* and *Apprendi* are consistent because there is a fundamental distinction between the factual findings that were at issue in those two cases. *Apprendi* said that any fact extending the defendant's sentence beyond the maximum authorized by the jury's verdict would have been considered an element of an aggravated crime—and thus the domain of the jury—by those who framed the Bill of Rights. The same cannot be said of a fact increasing the mandatory minimum (but not extending the sentence beyond the statutory maximum), for the jury's verdict has authorized the judge to im-

pose the minimum with or without the finding As *McMillan* recognized, a statute may reserve this type of factual finding for the judge without violating the Constitution.

Though defining criminal conduct is a task generally "left to the legislative branch," *Patterson v. New York*, 432 U.S. 197, 210 (1977), Congress may not manipulate the definition of a crime in a way that relieves the Government of its constitutional obligations to charge each element in the indictment, submit each element to the jury, and prove each element beyond a reasonable doubt. *McMillan* and *Apprendi* asked whether certain types of facts, though labeled sentencing factors by the legislature, were nevertheless "traditional elements" to which these constitutional safeguards were intended to apply.

McMillan's answer stemmed from certain historical and doctrinal understandings about the role of the judge at sentencing. The mid–19th century produced a general shift in this country from criminal statutes "providing fixed-term sentences to those providing judges discretion within a permissible range." Under these statutes, judges exercise their sentencing discretion through an inquiry broad in scope, largely unlimited either as to the kind of information they may consider, or the source from which it may come. The Court has recognized that this process is constitutional—and that the facts taken into consideration need not be alleged in the indictment, submitted to the jury, or proved beyond a reasonable doubt. * * *

In sustaining the statute the *McMillan* Court placed considerable reliance on the similarity between the sentencing factor at issue and the facts judges contemplate when exercising their discretion within the statutory range. * * * In response to the argument that the Act evaded the Constitution's procedural guarantees, the Court noted that the statute "simply took one factor that has always been considered by sentencing courts to bear on punishment ... and dictated the precise weight to be given that factor.

That reasoning still controls. If the facts judges consider when exercising their discretion within the statutory range are not elements, they do not become as much merely because legislatures require the judge to impose a minimum sentence when those facts are found—a sentence the judge could have imposed absent the finding. * * * These facts, though stigmatizing and punitive, have been the traditional domain of judges; they have not been alleged in the indictment or proved beyond a reasonable doubt. There is no reason to believe that those who framed the Fifth and Sixth Amendments would have thought of them as the elements of the crime.

* * *

McMillan was on firm historical ground, then, when it held that a legislature may specify the condition for a mandatory minimum without making the condition an element of the crime. The fact of visible firearm possession was more like the facts considered by judges when selecting a sentence within the statutory range—facts that, as the authorities from the 19th century confirm, have never been charged in the indictment, submitted to the jury, or proved beyond a reasonable doubt:

* * *

Since sentencing ranges came into use, defendants have not been able to predict from the face of the indictment precisely what their sentence will be; the charged facts have simply made them aware of the heaviest punishment they face if convicted. Judges, in turn, have always considered un-

charged aggravating circumstances that, while increasing the defendant's punishment, have not "swell[ed] the penalty above what the law has provided for the acts charged." Because facts supporting a mandatory minimum fit squarely within that description, the legislature's choice to entrust them to the judge does not implicate the "competition ... between judge and jury over ... their respective roles," *Jones,* 526 U.S., at 245, that is the central concern of the Fifth and Sixth Amendments.

At issue in *Apprendi,* by contrast, was a sentencing factor that did "swell the penalty above what the law has provided," and thus functioned more like a traditional element. * * *

Apprendi's conclusions do not undermine *McMillan*'s. There was no comparable historical practice of submitting facts increasing the mandatory minimum to the jury, so the *Apprendi* rule did not extend to those facts. Indeed, the Court made clear that its holding did not affect *McMillan* at all:

> We do not overrule *McMillan*. We limit its holding to cases that do not involve the imposition of a sentence more severe than the statutory maximum for the offense established by the jury's verdict—a limitation identified in the *McMillan* opinion itself. 530 U.S., at 487, n. 13.

The sentencing factor in *McMillan* did not increase "the penalty for a crime beyond the prescribed statutory maximum." * * *. As the *Apprendi* Court observed, the *McMillan* finding merely required the judge to impose "a specific sentence *within the range* authorized by the jury's finding that the defendant [was] guilty."

* * *

Petitioner argues * * * that the concerns underlying *Apprendi* apply with equal or more force to facts increasing

[Handwritten margin note, top left: Δ claims - increasing the mand min is more detrimental + effective to Δ than increasing max]

the defendant's minimum sentence. Those factual findings, he contends, often have a greater impact on the defendant than the findings at issue in *Apprendi*. This is so because when a fact increasing the statutory maximum is found, the judge may still impose a sentence far below that maximum; but when a fact increasing the minimum is found, the judge has no choice but to impose that minimum, even if he or she otherwise would have chosen a lower sentence. Why, petitioner asks, would fairness not also require the latter sort of fact to be alleged in the indictment and found by the jury under a reasonable-doubt standard? The answer is that because it is beyond dispute that the judge's choice of sentences within the authorized range may be influenced by facts not considered by the jury, a factual finding's practical effect cannot by itself control the constitutional analysis. The Fifth and Sixth Amendments ensure that the defendant "will never get *more* punishment than he bargained for when he did the crime," but they do not promise that he will receive "anything less" than that. *Apprendi, supra,* at 498 (SCALIA, J., concurring). If the grand jury has alleged, and the trial jury has found, all the facts necessary to impose the maximum, the barriers between government and defendant fall. The judge may select any sentence within the range, based on facts not alleged in the indictment or proved to the jury—even if those facts are specified by the legislature, and even if they persuade the judge to choose a much higher sentence than he or she otherwise would have imposed. That a fact affects the defendant's sentence, even dramatically so, does not by itself make it an element.

[Handwritten margin note, left: protection of 5th + 6th guarantees that Δ will never get more than max penalty - not that they get anything less]

* * * The factual finding in *Apprendi* extended the power of the judge, allowing him or her to impose a punishment exceeding what was author-ized by the jury. The finding in *McMillan* restrained the judge's power, limiting his or her choices within the authorized range. It is quite consistent to maintain that the former type of fact must be submitted to the jury while the latter need not be.

Read together, *McMillan* and *Apprendi* mean that those facts setting the outer limits of a sentence, and of the judicial power to impose it, are the elements of the crime for the purposes of the constitutional analysis. Within the range authorized by the jury's verdict, however, the political system may channel judicial discretion—and rely upon judicial expertise—by requiring defendants to serve minimum terms after judges make certain factual findings. It is critical not to abandon that understanding at this late date. Legislatures and their constituents have relied upon *McMillan* to exercise control over sentencing through dozens of statutes like the one the Court approved in that case. Congress and the States have conditioned mandatory minimum sentences upon judicial findings that, as here, a firearm was possessed, brandished, or discharged, * * * or among other examples, that the victim was over 60 years of age, that the defendant possessed a certain quantity of drugs, that the victim was related to the defendant, and that the defendant was a repeat offender. We see no reason to overturn those statutes or cast uncertainty upon the sentences imposed under them.

[Handwritten margin note, right: The factors that set the outer most limits of sentence are the elements]

IV

Reaffirming *McMillan* and employing the approach outlined in that case, we conclude that the federal provision at issue, 18 U.S.C. § 924(c)(1)(A)(ii), is constitutional. Basing a 2–year increase in the defendant's minimum sentence on a judicial finding of brandishing does not evade the requirements of the Fifth and Sixth

[Handwritten margin note, right: H: Consti • adding a higher min mandatory penalty that does not exceed mand max does not violate 5/6]

Amendments. Congress "simply took one factor that has always been considered by sentencing courts to bear on punishment . . . and dictated the precise weight to be given that factor." *McMillan,* 477 U.S., at 89–90. That factor need not be alleged in the indictment, submitted to the jury, or proved beyond a reasonable doubt.

The Court is well aware that many question the wisdom of mandatory minimum sentencing. Mandatory minimums, it is often said, fail to account for the unique circumstances of offenders who warrant a lesser penalty. See, *e.g.,* Brief for Families Against Mandatory Minimums Foundation as *Amicus Curiae* 25, n. 16. These criticisms may be sound, but they would persist whether the judge or the jury found the facts giving rise to the minimum. We hold only that the Constitution permits the judge to do so, and we leave the other questions to Congress, the States, and the democratic processes.

The judgment of the Court of Appeals is affirmed.

It is so ordered.

[The concurring opinion of Justice O'Connor is omitted.]

JUSTICE BREYER, concurring in part and concurring in the judgment.

I cannot easily distinguish Apprendi v. New Jersey from this case in terms of logic. For that reason, I cannot agree with the plurality's opinion insofar as it finds such a distinction. At the same time, I continue to believe that the Sixth Amendment permits judges to apply sentencing factors—whether those factors lead to a sentence beyond the statutory maximum (as in *Apprendi*) or the application of a mandatory minimum (as here). And because I believe that extending *Apprendi* to mandatory minimums would have adverse practical, as well as legal, consequences, I cannot yet accept its

rule. I therefore join the Court's judgment, and I join its opinion to the extent that it holds that *Apprendi* does not apply to mandatory minimums.

In saying this, I do not mean to suggest my approval of mandatory minimum sentences as a matter of policy. During the past two decades, as mandatory minimum sentencing statutes have proliferated in number and importance, judges, legislators, lawyers, and commentators have criticized those statutes, arguing that they negatively affect the fair administration of the criminal law, a matter of concern to judges and to legislators alike.

Mandatory minimum statutes are fundamentally inconsistent with Congress' simultaneous effort to create a fair, honest, and rational sentencing system through the use of Sentencing Guidelines. Unlike Guideline sentences, statutory mandatory minimums generally deny the judge the legal power to depart downward, no matter how unusual the special circumstances that call for leniency. They rarely reflect an effort to achieve sentencing proportionality—a key element of sentencing fairness that demands that the law punish a drug "kingpin" and a "mule" differently. They transfer sentencing power to prosecutors, who can determine sentences through the charges they decide to bring, and who thereby have reintroduced much of the sentencing disparity that Congress created Guidelines to eliminate. They rarely are based upon empirical study. And there is evidence that they encourage subterfuge, leading to more frequent downward departures (on a random basis), thereby making them a comparatively ineffective means of guaranteeing tough sentences.

Applying *Apprendi* in this case would not, however, lead Congress to abolish, or to modify, mandatory minimum sentencing statutes. Rather, it would simply require the prosecutor to charge, and the jury to find beyond a reasonable doubt, the existence of the "factor," say, the amount of unlawful drugs, that triggers the mandatory minimum. In many cases, a defendant, claiming innocence and arguing, say, mistaken identity, will find it impossible simultaneously to argue to the jury that the prosecutor has overstated the drug amount. How, the jury might ask, could this "innocent" defendant know anything about that matter? The upshot is that in many such cases defendant and prosecutor will enter into a stipulation before trial as to drug amounts to be used at sentencing (if the jury finds the defendant guilty). To that extent, application of *Apprendi* would take from the judge the power to make a factual determination, while giving that power not to juries, but to prosecutors. And such consequences, when viewed through the prism of an open, fair sentencing system, are seriously adverse.

JUSTICE THOMAS, with whom JUSTICE STEVENS, JUSTICE SOUTER, and JUSTICE GINSBURG join, dissenting.

* * *

I agree with the Court that a legislature is free to decree, within constitutional limits, which facts are elements that constitute a crime. But when the legislature provides that a particular fact shall give rise both to a special stigma and to a special punishment, the constitutional consequences are clear. * * * We made clear in *Apprendi* that if a statute "annexes a higher degree of punishment based on certain circumstances, exposing a defendant to that higher degree of punishment requires that those circumstances be charged in the indictment and proved beyond a reasonable doubt."

* * *

It is true that *Apprendi* concerned a fact that increased the penalty for a crime beyond the prescribed statutory maximum, but the principles upon which it relied apply with equal force to those facts that expose the defendant to a higher mandatory minimum * * *. Whether one raises the floor or raises the ceiling it is impossible to dispute that the defendant is exposed to greater punishment than is otherwise prescribed.

* * *

Because, like most Members of this Court, I cannot logically distinguish the issue here from the principles underlying the Court's decision in *Apprendi*, I respectfully dissent.

Apprendi and the Death Penalty: Ring v. Arizona

In Ring v. Arizona, 536 U.S. 584 (2002), the Court held that the Arizona capital sentencing statute was constitutionally infirm after *Apprendi*. Arizona provided that the judge would determine whether sufficient aggravating factors existed to justify the death penalty. Thus, if the judge found the factors to exist, she would impose a sentence–death–greater than that which could be authorized by the jury, because the jury's verdict could only justify a sentence of life imprisonment. Justice Ginsburg, writing for the Court, held that such a system could not be squared with *Apprendi*. She declared that "[c]apital defendants, no less than non-capital defendants * * * are entitled to a jury determination of any fact on which the legislature conditions an increase in their maximum punishment". Justice Ginsburg concluded as follows:

The right to trial by jury guaranteed by the Sixth Amendment would be senselessly diminished if it encompassed the factfinding necessary to increase a defendant's sentence by two years, but not the factfinding necessary to put him to death. We hold that the Sixth Amendment applies to both.

The Court in *Ring* overruled its prior holding in Walton v. Arizona, 497 U.S. 639 (1990), which held that it was permissible for a judge to sentence the defendant to death on the basis of judicial findings of aggravating circumstances. The holding in *Walton* could not be squared with *Apprendi*.

Justice Scalia wrote a concurring opinion joined by Justice Thomas, in which he declared that "the accelerating propensity of both state and federal legislatures to adopt 'sentencing factors' determined by judges that increase punishment beyond what is authorized by the jury's verdict * * * cause me to believe that our people's traditional belief in the right of trial by jury is in perilous decline. That decline is bound to be confirmed, and indeed accelerated, by the repeated spectacle of a man's going to his death because *a judge* found that an aggravating factor existed. We cannot preserve our veneration for the protection of the jury in criminal cases if we render ourselves callous to the need for that protection by regularly imposing the death penalty without it."

Justice Kennedy wrote a short concurring opinion in *Ring* noting that while he disagreed with *Apprendi,* that case "is now the law, and its holding must be implemented in a principled way. * * *. It is beyond question that during the penalty phase of a first-degree murder prosecution in Arizona, the finding of an aggravating circumstance exposes the defendant to a greater punishment than that authorized by the jury's guilty verdict. When a finding has this effect, *Apprendi* makes clear, it cannot be reserved for the judge."

Justice Breyer concurred in the judgment, continuing to reject *Apprendi,* but concluding that jury sentencing in capital cases is mandated by the Eighth Amendment.

Justice O'Connor wrote a dissenting opinion joined by Chief Justice Rehnquist. She agreed that *Walton* could not be squared with *Apprendi*. But forced to choose one case or the other to overrule, she would overrule *Apprendi*. She elaborated as follows:

> Not only was the decision in *Apprendi* unjustified in my view, but it has also had a severely destabilizing effect on our criminal justice system. I predicted in my dissent that the decision would "unleash a flood of petitions by convicted defendants seeking to invalidate their sentences in whole or in part on the authority of [*Apprendi*]." As of May 31, 2002, less than two years after *Apprendi* was announced, the United States Courts of Appeals had decided approximately 1,802 criminal appeals in which defendants challenged their sentences, and in some cases even their convictions, under *Apprendi*. These federal appeals are likely only the tip of the iceberg, as federal criminal prosecutions represent a tiny fraction of the total number of criminal prosecutions nationwide. The number of second or successive habeas corpus petitions filed in the federal courts also increased by 77% in 2001, a phenomenon the Administrative Office of the United States Courts attributes to prisoners bringing *Apprendi* claims. * * * It is simply beyond dispute that *Apprendi* threw countless criminal sentences into doubt and thereby caused an enormous increase in the workload of an already overburdened judiciary.

The decision today is only going to add to these already serious effects. The Court effectively declares five States' capital sentencing schemes unconstitutional. [Colorado, Idaho, Montana and Nebraska have capital sentencing schemes similar to Arizona.] There are 168 prisoners on death row in these States * * * each of whom is now likely to challenge his or her death sentence. I believe many of these challenges will ultimately be unsuccessful, either because the prisoners will be unable to satisfy the standards of harmless error or plain error review, or because, having completed their direct appeals, they will be barred from taking advantage of today's holding on federal collateral review. Nonetheless, the need to evaluate these claims will greatly burden the courts in these five States. In addition, I fear that the prisoners on death row in Alabama, Delaware, Florida, and Indiana, which [have] hybrid sentencing schemes in which the jury renders an advisory verdict but the judge makes the ultimate sentencing determination may also seize on today's decision to challenge their sentences. There are 529 prisoners on death row in these States.

By expanding on *Apprendi*, the Court today exacerbates the harm done in that case. Consistent with my dissent, I would overrule *Apprendi* rather than *Walton*.

D. PROOF OF ALTERNATIVE MEANS OF COMMITTING A SINGLE CRIME

The requirement of proof beyond a reasonable doubt of all elements of a crime raises another question: whether it is constitutionally acceptable to define a "crime" so broadly as to permit jurors to reach one verdict based on any combination of alternative findings of fact. The Court considered this question in Schad v. Arizona, 501 U.S. 624 (1991). Schad was charged with first-degree murder. In Arizona, the crime of first-degree murder encompasses both premeditated murder and felony murder. At trial, the prosecutor advanced both premeditated and felony murder theories, and offered proof under both theories. The jury returned a general verdict of guilty of first degree murder. Schad complained that this procedure was invalid, because it excused the state from having to prove all of the elements of one specific crime beyond a reasonable doubt.

Justice Souter, writing for a plurality of four Justices, stated that it was constitutionally permissible to define first-degree murder in such a way that it could be committed by alternative means, so long as those means "reasonably reflect notions of equivalent blameworthiness or culpability." Justice Souter recognized that the Due Process Clause would not permit a state "to convict anyone under a charge of 'Crime' so generic that any combination of jury findings of embezzlement, reckless driving, murder, burglary, tax evasion, or littering, for example, would suffice for conviction." However, the Arizona statute did not create such a disparate collection of alternative means to commit first degree murder. Justice Souter concluded that felony murder and premeditated murder were of sufficient "moral equivalence" to be grouped together as two ways of committing the same crime, and that therefore the general verdict of guilt was constitutionally permissible.

Justice Souter found it highly relevant that many states have traditionally considered felony murder and premeditated murder as alternative means of committing first degree murder. He stated that the "historical and contemporary acceptance of Arizona's definition of the offense and verdict practice is a strong indication" that it did not violate due process, because "legal definitions, and the practices comporting with them, are unlikely to endure for long, or to retain wide acceptance, if they are at odds with notions of fairness and rationality sufficiently fundamental to be comprehended in due process."

Justice Scalia concurred in the judgment. In his view, the fact that the Arizona statutory definition of first-degree murder is traditionally and currently accepted in most states was dispositive of the due process issue. He concluded as follows:

> Submitting killing in the course of a robbery and premeditated killing to the jury under a single charge is not some novel composite that can be subjected to the indignity of fundamental fairness review. It was the norm when this country was founded, * * * and remains the norm today. Unless we are here to invent a Constitution rather than enforce one, it is impossible that a practice as old as the common law and still in existence in the vast majority of States does not provide that process which is due.

Justice White, joined by Justices Marshall, Blackmun, and Stevens, dissented. He noted that felony murder and premeditated murder contain separate elements of conduct and state of mind and argued that these elements could not "be mixed and matched at will." He asserted that "it is particularly fanciful to equate an intent to do no more than rob with a premeditated intent to murder."

The prosecution in *Schad* was required to prove all elements beyond a reasonable doubt, and the defendant was not required to prove anything. So how does the *Schad* issue relate to the *Mullaney-Patterson–Apprendi* line of cases, which deals with the state's power to define the elements of a crime? The answer lies in the possibility that by combining alternative theories of guilt, a prosecutor may manage to convict a defendant without proving beyond a reasonable doubt all of the elements of any one theory to a constitutionally adequate number of jurors. At the logical limit of the analysis, for example, a prosecutor could argue twelve alternatives to a twelve-person jury and persuade only one juror beyond a reasonable doubt of each theory. Were the theories set forth in separate counts, a defendant would never be convicted. In fact, the vote would be 11–1 for acquittal on each count. But, by combining the theories, all twelve jurors would agree that the defendant is "guilty" of a "crime." All members of the Court in *Schad* agreed that at some point this tactic would be impermissible under the Due Process Clause. They disagreed, however, on where that point lies. Four Justices gave traditional and current acceptance significant weight, and one found traditional and current acceptance dispositive. How important is it that states traditionally gave, and currently give, alternative theories of first-degree murder to a jury in a single count with a general verdict form? For a cogent criticism of Schad, see Howe, Jury Fact–Finding in Criminal Cases: Constitutional Limits on Factual Disagreements Among Convicting Jurors, 58 Missouri L.Rev.1 (1993).

Distinction Between Means and Elements: Richardson v. United States

Under *Schad*, the means by which a defendant commits a crime need not be proven beyond a reasonable doubt, if there are alternative means to commit the crime. Under *Winship*, the elements of the crime must be proven beyond a reasonable doubt. The distinction between means and elements is often less than clear. The Supreme Court encountered a problem of delineation between means and elements in Richardson v. United States, 526 U.S. 813 (1999). Richardson was convicted under the Continuing Criminal Enterprise statute. The statute defines "continuing criminal enterprise" (CCE) as involving a "violat[ion]" of the drug statutes where "such violation is a part of a continuing series of violations." The definitional problem arising under the statute was set forth in the majority opinion by Justice Breyer:

> The question before us arises out of the trial court's instruction about the statute's "series of violations" requirement. The judge rejected Richardson's proposal to instruct the jury that it must "unanimously agree on which three acts constituted [the] series of violations." Instead, the judge instructed the jurors that they "must unanimously agree that the defendant committed at least three federal narcotics offenses," while adding, "[y]ou do not ... have to agree as to the particular three or more federal narcotics offenses committed by the defendant." * * *

> The question before us arises because a federal jury need not always decide unanimously which of several possible sets of underlying brute facts make up a particular element, say, which of several possible means the defendant used to commit an element of the crime. Schad v. Arizona. Where, for example, an element of robbery is force or the threat of force, some jurors might conclude that the defendant used a knife to create the threat; others might conclude he used a gun. But that disagreement—a disagreement about means—would not matter as long as all 12 jurors unanimously concluded that the Government had proved the necessary related element, namely that the defendant had threatened force.

> In this case, we must decide whether the statute's phrase "series of violations" refers to one element, namely a "series," in respect to which the "violations" constitute the underlying brute facts or means, or whether those words create several elements, namely the several "violations," in respect to each of which the jury must agree unanimously and separately. Our decision will make a difference where, as here, the Government introduces evidence that the defendant has committed more underlying drug crimes than legally necessary to make up a "series." (We assume, but do not decide, that the necessary number is three, the number used in this case.) If the statute creates a single element, a "series," in respect to which individual violations are but the means, then the jury need only agree that the defendant committed at least three of all the underlying crimes the Government has tried to prove. The jury need not agree about which three. On the other hand, if the statute makes each "violation" a separate element, then the jury must agree unanimously about which three crimes the defendant committed.

The majority held that the underlying illegal activity constituted an element of the crime, and not the means. Thus, the jury in order to convict the defendant would have to agree unanimously that the defendant committed at least three underlying drug transactions—*and* they would have to agree on the specific transactions in order for them to count toward the "series." Justice Breyer explained the majority's decision in the following passage:

The CCE statute's breadth * * * argues against treating each individual violation as a means, for that breadth aggravates the dangers of unfairness that doing so would risk. Cf. Schad v. Arizona. The statute's word "violations" covers many different kinds of behavior of varying degrees of seriousness. * * * At the same time, the Government in a CCE case may well seek to prove that a defendant, charged as a drug kingpin, has been involved in numerous underlying violations. The first of these considerations increases the likelihood that treating violations simply as alternative means, by permitting a jury to avoid discussion of the specific factual details of each violation, will cover-up wide disagreement among the jurors about just what the defendant did, or did not, do. The second consideration significantly aggravates the risk (present at least to a small degree whenever multiple means are at issue) that jurors, unless required to focus upon specific factual detail, will fail to do so, simply concluding from testimony, say, of bad reputation, that where there is smoke there must be fire.

Finally, this Court has indicated that the Constitution itself limits a State's power to define crimes in ways that would permit juries to convict while disagreeing about means, at least where that definition risks serious unfairness and lacks support in history or tradition. Schad v. Arizona, 501 U.S., at 632–633 (plurality opinion); id., at 651 (SCALIA, J., concurring) ("We would not permit ... an indictment charging that the defendant assaulted either X on Tuesday or Y on Wednesday ..."). We have no reason to believe that Congress intended to come close to, or to test, those constitutional limits when it wrote this statute.

Justice Kennedy, joined by Justices O'Connor and Ginsburg, dissented in *Richardson*. He argued that the majority had drummed up a constitutional question that did not exist:

The CCE statute does not in any way implicate the suggestion in *Schad* that an irrational single crime consisting of, for instance, either robbery or failure to file a tax return would offend due process. Although the continuing series may consist of different drug crimes, the mere proof of a series does not suffice to convict. The Government must also prove action in concert with five or more persons, a leadership role for the defendant with respect to those persons, and substantial income or resources derived from the continuing series. The presence of these additional elements distinguishes the CCE statute from a simple recidivism statute * * *.

E. PRESUMPTIONS

An alternative to placing a burden of persuasion on a defendant in order to reduce the burden on the government of presenting evidence is to utilize a presumption or a judicially recognized inference.[16] Few aspects of procedural law can be more confusing than presumptions, since the word "presumption" is used to mean several different things in different contexts.

The following case illustrates how the Supreme Court has approached many criminal presumptions, and indicates the importance of jury instructions in

---

16. In this section, the word presumption will be used to cover situations in which the court instructs a jury that proof of one fact entitles the jury to infer, assume, or presume the existence of another fact.

assessing the permissibility of presumptions. The extensive footnotes provided by the Court are particularly helpful.

COUNTY COURT v. ALLEN

Supreme Court of the United States, 1979.
442 U.S. 140.

MR. JUSTICE STEVENS delivered the opinion of the Court.

A New York statute provides that, with certain exceptions, the presence of a firearm in an automobile is presumptive evidence of its illegal possession by all persons then occupying the vehicle. The United States Court of Appeals for the Second Circuit held that respondents may challenge the constitutionality of this statute in a federal habeas corpus proceeding and that the statute is "unconstitutional on its face." * * *

Four persons, three adult males (respondents) and a 16–year-old girl (Jane Doe, who is not a respondent here), were jointly tried on charges that they possessed two loaded handguns, a loaded machinegun, and over a pound of heroin found in a Chevrolet in which they were riding when it was stopped for speeding on the New York Thruway shortly after noon on March 28, 1973. The two large-caliber handguns, which together with their ammunition weighed approximately six pounds, were seen through the window of the car by the investigating police officer. They were positioned crosswise in an open handbag on either the front floor or the front seat of the car on the passenger side where Jane Doe was sitting. Jane Doe admitted that the handbag was hers. The machinegun and the heroin were discovered in the trunk after the police pried it open. The car had been borrowed from the driver's brother earlier that day; the key to the trunk could not be found in the car or on the person of any of its occupants, although there was testimony that two

of the occupants had placed something in the trunk before embarking in the borrowed car. The jury convicted all four of possession of the handguns and acquitted them of possession of the contents of the trunk.

Counsel for all four defendants objected to the introduction into evidence of the two handguns, the machinegun, and the drugs, arguing that the State had not adequately demonstrated a connection between their clients and the contraband. The trial court overruled the objection, relying on the presumption of possession created by the New York statute. Because that presumption does not apply if a weapon is found "upon the person" of one of the occupants of the car, the three male defendants also moved to dismiss the charges relating to the handguns on the ground that the guns were found on the person of Jane Doe. * * *

At the close of the trial, the judge instructed the jurors that they were entitled to infer possession from the defendants' presence in the car. He did not make any reference to the "on the person" exception in his explanation of the statutory presumption, nor did any of the defendants object to this omission or request alternative or additional instructions on the subject.

* * *

Inferences and presumptions are a staple of our adversary system of fact-finding. It is often necessary for the trier of fact to determine the existence of an element of the crime—that is, an "ultimate" or "elemental" fact—from the existence of one or more "evidentiary" or "basic" facts. The value of these evidentiary devices, and their validity under the Due Process Clause, vary from case to case, however, depending on the strength of the connection between the particular basic and elemental facts involved and on the degree to which the device curtails the factfinder's freedom to assess the evidence independently. Nonetheless, in criminal cases, the ultimate test of any device's constitutional validity in a given case remains constant; the device must not undermine the factfinder's responsibility at trial, based on evidence adduced by the State, to find the ultimate facts beyond a reasonable doubt.

The most common evidentiary device is the entirely permissive inference or presumption, which allows—but does not require—the trier of fact to infer the elemental fact from proof by the prosecutor of the basic one and that places no burden of any kind on the defendant. In that situation the basic fact may constitute prima facie evidence of the elemental fact. When

reviewing this type of device, the Court has required the party challenging it to demonstrate its invalidity as applied to him. Because this permissive presumption leaves the trier of fact free to credit or reject the inference and does not shift the burden of proof, it affects the application of the "beyond a reasonable doubt" standard only if, under the facts of the case, there is no rational way the trier could make the connection permitted by the inference. For only in that situation is there any risk that an explanation of the permissible inference to a jury, or its use by a jury, has caused the presumptively rational factfinder to make an erroneous factual determination.

A mandatory presumption is a far more troublesome evidentiary device. For it may affect not only the strength of the "no reasonable doubt" burden but also the placement of that burden; it tells the trier that he or they must find the elemental fact upon proof of the basic fact, at least unless the defendant has come forward with some evidence to rebut the presumed connection between the two facts.[a] In this

---

a. This class of more or less mandatory presumptions can be subdivided into two parts; presumptions that merely shift the burden of production to the defendant, following the satisfaction of which the ultimate burden of persuasion returns to the prosecution; and presumptions that entirely shift the burden of proof to the defendant. The mandatory presumptions examined by our cases have almost uniformly fit into the former subclass, in that they never totally removed the ultimate burden of proof beyond a reasonable doubt from the prosecution. E.g., Tot v. United States, 319 U.S. 463 (1943) [requiring a "rational connection between the fact proved and the ultimate fact presumed"].

To the extent that a presumption imposes an extremely low burden of production—e.g., being satisfied by "any" evidence—it may well be that its impact is no greater than that of a permissive inference, and it may be proper to analyze it as such.

In deciding what type of inference or presumption is involved in a case, the jury instructions will generally be controlling, although their interpretation may require recourse to

the statute involved and the cases decided under it. * * *

The importance of focusing attention on the precise presentation of the presumption to the jury and the scope of that presumption is illustrated by a comparison of United States v. Gainey, 380 U.S. 63 (1965), with United States v. Romano, 382 U.S. 136 (1965). Both cases involved statutory presumptions based on proof that the defendant was present at the site of an illegal still. In *Gainey* the Court sustained a conviction "for carrying on" the business of the distillery in violation of 26 U.S.C. § 5601(a)(4), whereas in *Romano*, the Court set aside a conviction for being in "possession, or custody, or * * * control" of such a distillery in violation of § 5601(a)(1). The difference in outcome was attributable to two important differences between the cases. Because the statute involved in *Gainey* was a sweeping prohibition of almost any activity associated with the still, whereas the *Romano* statute involved only one narrow aspect of the total undertaking, there was a much higher probability that mere presence could support an inference of guilt in the former case than in the latter.

situation, the Court has generally examined the presumption on its face to determine the extent to which the basic and elemental facts coincide. To the extent that the trier of fact is forced to abide by the presumption, and may not reject it based on an independent evaluation of the particular facts presented by the State, the analysis of the presumption's constitutional validity is logically divorced from those facts and based on the presumption's accuracy in the run of cases.[b] It is for this reason that the Court has held it irrelevant in analyzing a mandatory presumption, but not in analyzing a purely permissive one, that there is ample evidence in the record other than the presumption to support a conviction.

* * *

The trial judge's instructions [in this case] make it clear that the presump-

tion * * * gave rise to a permissive inference available only in certain circumstances, rather than a mandatory conclusion of possession, and that it could be ignored by the jury even if there was no affirmative proof offered by defendants in rebuttal. The judge explained that possession could be actual or constructive, but that constructive possession could not exist without the intent and ability to exercise control or dominion over the weapons. He also carefully instructed the jury that there is a mandatory presumption of innocence in favor of the defendants that controls unless it, as the exclusive trier of fact, is satisfied beyond a reasonable doubt that the defendants possessed the handguns in the manner described by the judge. In short, the instructions plainly directed the jury to consider all the circumstances tending to support or contradict the inference that all four occu-

Of perhaps greater importance, however, was the difference between the trial judge's instructions to the jury in the two cases. In *Gainey*, the judge had explained that the presumption was permissive; it did not require the jury to convict the defendant even if it was convinced that he was present at the site. On the contrary, the instructions made it clear that presence was only "a circumstance to be considered along with all the other circumstances in the case." As we emphasized, the "jury was thus specifically told that the statutory inference was not conclusive." In *Romano*, the trial judge told the jury that the defendant's presence at the still "shall be deemed sufficient evidence to authorize conviction." Although there was other evidence of guilt, that instruction authorized conviction even if the jury disbelieved all of the testimony except the proof of presence at the site. This Court's holding that the statutory presumption could not support the *Romano* conviction was thus dependent, in part, on the specific instructions given by the trial judge. Under those instructions it was necessary to decide whether, regardless of the specific circumstances of the particular case, the statutory presumption adequately supported the guilty verdict.

b. * * * [T]his point is illustrated by Leary v. United States, 395 U.S. 6 (1969). In that case, Dr. Timothy Leary, a professor at Harvard University, was stopped by customs inspectors in Laredo, Tex., as he was returning

from the Mexican side of the international border. Marihuana seeds and a silver snuffbox filled with semirefined marihuana and three partially smoked marihuana cigarettes were discovered in his car. He was convicted of having knowingly transported marihuana which he knew had been illegally imported into this country in violation of 21 U.S.C. § 176a (1964 ed.) That statute included a mandatory presumption: "possession shall be deemed sufficient evidence to authorize conviction [for importation] unless the defendant explains his possession to the satisfaction of the jury." Leary admitted possession of the marihuana and claimed that he had carried it from New York to Mexico and then back.

* * *

Despite the fact that the defendant was well educated and had recently traveled to a country that is a major exporter of marihuana to this country, the Court found the presumption of knowledge of importation from possession irrational. It did so, not because Dr. Leary was unlikely to know the source of the marihuana, but instead because "a majority of possessors" were unlikely to have such knowledge. Because the jury had been instructed to rely on the presumption even if it did not believe the Government's direct evidence of knowledge of importation (unless, of course, the defendant met his burden of "satisfying" the jury to the contrary), the Court reversed the conviction.

[margin note, top left: It says the jury instruction instructed the jury to determine all the facts pro/com about possession of gun and decide for themself]

[margin note, top center: than why create presumption?]

pants of the car had possession of the two loaded handguns and to decide the matter for itself without regard to how much evidence the defendants introduced.

Our cases considering the validity of permissive statutory presumptions such as the one involved here have rested on an evaluation of the presumption as applied to the record before the Court. None suggests that a court should pass on the constitutionality of this kind of statute "on its face." It was error for the Court of Appeals to make such a determination in this case.

III

[margin note, left: From the facts it is not unreasonable to infer possession by everyone]

As applied to the facts of this case, the presumption of possession is entirely rational. * * * [R]espondents were not "hitch-hikers or other casual passengers," and the guns were neither "a few inches in length" nor "out of [respondents'] sight." The argument against possession by any of the respondents was predicated solely on the fact that the guns were in Jane Doe's pocketbook. But several circumstances * * * made it highly improbable that she was the sole custodian of those weapons.

Even if it was reasonable to conclude that she had placed the guns in her purse before the car was stopped by police, the facts strongly suggest that Jane Doe was not the only person able to exercise dominion over them. The two guns were too large to be concealed in her handbag. The bag was consequently open, and part of one of the guns was in plain view, within easy access of the driver of the car and even, perhaps, of the other two respondents who were riding in the rear seat.

Moreover, it is highly improbable that the loaded guns belonged to Jane Doe or that she was solely responsible

for their being in her purse. As a 16–year-old girl in the company of three adult men she was the least likely of the four to be carrying one, let alone two, heavy handguns. It is far more probable that she relied on the pocket-knife found in her brassiere for any necessary self-protection. Under these circumstances, it was not unreasonable for her counsel to argue and for the jury to infer that when the car was halted for speeding, the other passengers in the car anticipated the risk of a search and attempted to conceal their weapons in a pocketbook in the front seat. The inference is surely more likely than the notion that these weapons were the sole property of the 16–year-old girl.

Under these circumstances, the jury would have been entirely reasonable in rejecting the suggestion—which, incidentally, defense counsel did not even advance in their closing arguments to the jury—that the handguns were in the sole possession of Jane Doe. Assuming that the jury did reject it, the case is tantamount to one in which the guns were lying on the floor or the seat of the car in plain view of the three other occupants of the automobile. In such a case, it is surely rational to infer that each of the respondents was fully aware of the presence of the guns and had both the ability and the intent to exercise dominion and control over the weapons.

[margin note, right: H: presumption is allowed when permissive + not interfering w/ brd]

MR. JUSTICE POWELL, with whom MR. JUSTICE BRENNAN, MR. JUSTICE STEWART, and MR. JUSTICE MARSHALL join, dissenting.

* * *

Undeniably, the presumption charged in this case encouraged the jury to draw a particular factual inference regardless of any other evidence presented: to infer that respondents possessed the weapons found in the automobile "upon proof of the presence of the machine gun and the hand weapon" and proof that respondents "occupied the automobile at the time such instruments were found." I believe that the presumption thus charged was unconstitutional because it did not fairly reflect what common sense and experience tell us about

passengers in automobiles and the possession of handguns. People present in automobiles where there are weapons simply are not "more likely than not" the possessors of those weapons.

* * *

Comment on Presumption Cases

The presumption cases establish two rules: "[T]he first rule is that where the prosecution bears the burden of persuasion, a trial judge may not encourage the jury to make logical jumps not supported by the evidence. Otherwise the persuasion burden would be compromised." The second rule, which would apply where a persuasion burden could be shifted to a defendant, is that any "instruction must be a fair statement about evidence actually produced in the case." Saltzburg, Burdens of Persuasion in Criminal Cases: Harmonizing the Views of the Justices, 20 Am.Cr.L.Rev. 393 (1983).[17]

Shifting the Burden on Intent: Sandstrom
v. Montana and Francis v. Franklin

After deciding *Allen*, the Court held in Sandstrom v. Montana, 442 U.S. 510 (1979), that an instruction to the jury in a homicide case that "the law presumes that a person intends the ordinary consequences of his voluntary acts" violated the Constitution, because it may have removed from the prosecution some of its burden to prove beyond a reasonable doubt all elements of the crime charged. The Court observed that unlike in *Allen*, a reasonable jury could have interpreted the instruction as a legal command that was not rebuttable. Alternatively, the jury may have interpreted the instruction as a direction to find intent once voluntary action was proven unless the defendant proved the lack of intent. Finally, the jury could have read the instruction as authorizing it to draw a permissive inference. Because the first two interpretations would have shifted a constitutionally required burden from the prosecutor, and since the Court could not be sure how the jury treated the instruction, the Court found that reversal of the conviction was required.

Justice Brennan, who authored *Sandstrom*, wrote for five members of the Court in Francis v. Franklin, 471 U.S. 307 (1985), as it held invalid the following jury instructions:

> A crime is a violation of a statute of this State in which there shall be a union of joint operation of act or omission to act, and intention or criminal

---

17. An excellent discussion of problems with County Court v. Allen is found in Lushing, Faces Without Features: The Surface Validity of Criminal Inferences, 72 J.Crim.L. & Crim. 82 (1981).

For a discussion of the Supreme Court's presumption cases as applied to the federal bank robbery statute, see Ponsoldt, A Due Process Analysis of Judicially–Authorized Pre-

sumptions in Federal Aggravated Bank Robbery Cases, 74 J.Crim.L. & Crim. 363 (1983). See also Glenn v. Bartlett, 98 F.3d 721 (2d Cir.1996) (upholding New York statute providing that the presence of drugs in a car constitutes "presumptive evidence of knowing possession thereof by each and every person in the automobile at the time such controlled substance was found.").

mand, lang

negligence. A person shall not be found guilty of any crime committed by misfortune or accident where it satisfactorily appears there was no criminal scheme or undertaking or intention or criminal negligence. *The acts of a person of sound mind and discretion are presumed to be the product of the person's will, but the presumption may be rebutted. A person of sound mind and discretion is presumed to intend the natural and probable consequences of his acts but the presumption may be rebutted.* A person will not be presumed to act with criminal intention but the trier of facts, that is, the jury, may find criminal intention upon a consideration of the words, conduct, demeanor, motive and all other circumstances connected with the act for which the accused is prosecuted. [Emphasis added.]

The defendant escaped from custody and attempted to obtain a car to speed his flight. He pounded on the door of a house until a 72–year-old resident opened the door. When the defendant pointed a gun and demanded the keys to the resident's car, the resident slammed the door and the gun fired and killed him. The defendant claimed that he did not intend to kill and that the firing was accidental. The jury found him guilty.

Justice Brennan began his analysis by restating the principles the Court had laid down for determining the constitutionality of presumptions:

The court must determine whether the challenged portion of the instruction creates a mandatory presumption or merely a permissive inference. A mandatory presumption instructs the jury that it must infer the presumed fact if the State proves certain predicate facts. A permissive inference suggests to the jury a possible conclusion to be drawn if the State proves predicate facts, but does not require the jury to draw the conclusion.

Mandatory presumptions must be measured against the standards of *Winship* as elucidated in *Sandstrom*. Such presumptions violate the Due Process Clause if they relieve the State of the burden of persuasion on an element of an offense. A permissive inference does not relieve the State of its burden of persuasion because it still requires the State to convince the jury that the suggested conclusion should be inferred based on the predicate facts involved. Such inferences do not necessarily implicate the concerns of *Sandstrom*. A permissive inference violates the Due Process Clause only if the suggested conclusion is not one that reason and common sense justify in light of the proven facts before the jury. County Court v. Allen.

Justice Brennan concluded that the challenged instruction created a mandatory presumption, because it was "cast in the language of command." The fact that the judge said the presumption "may be rebutted" did not affect the mandatory nature of the presumption itself. According to Justice Brennan, a mandatory rebuttable presumption can be just as constitutionally infirm as a mandatory irrebuttable presumption.

A mandatory rebuttable presumption does not remove the presumed element from the case if the State proves the predicate facts, but it nonetheless relieves the State of the affirmative burden of persuasion on the presumed element by instructing the jury that it must find the presumed element unless the defendant persuades the jury not to make such a finding. A mandatory rebuttable presumption is perhaps less onerous from the defendant's perspective, but it is no less unconstitutional.

Justice Brennan reasoned that a reasonable jury could have concluded that it had to find an intent to kill unless the defendant persuaded it that intent should not be inferred. Although the presumption in this case was plainly rebuttable, whereas the *Sandstrom* presumption was subject to several interpretations, Justice Brennan found that it might have led the jury to place a burden of persuasion as to the element of intent upon the defendant.

Justice Powell dissented and argued that the combination of the trial court's instructions on reasonable doubt, the presumption of innocence, and interpretation of circumstantial evidence, and the portion of the challenged instructions stating that "criminal intention" cannot be presumed sufficiently removed any danger that a reasonable jury would have imposed a persuasion burden on the defendant. Justice Rehnquist also dissented, joined by the Chief Justice and Justice O'Connor. He suggested that instead of focusing on what a reasonable jury *might* have interpreted the instructions to mean, the Court should find it *likely* that a juror so understood the charge before finding constitutional error.[18]

Observations About Sandstrom, et al.

Sandstrom and *Francis* are cases in which the trial court impermissibly shifted a burden of persuasion through a jury instruction imposing a mandatory presumption. Remember, however, that such an impermissible shift can occur by way of statute as well. See also Government of Virgin Islands v. Parrilla, 7 F.3d 1097 (3d Cir.1993)(statute criminalizing maiming, which provides that the infliction of injury is presumptive evidence of intent, constitutes an impermissible mandatory presumption, invalid on its face).

After *Sandstrom, Francis,* and *Allen,* why would a trial court choose to instruct the jury with a presumption, unless the defendant stipulated to it? If the presumption is mandatory, it runs the risk of violating *Winship* and *Mullaney.* If the instruction is permissive, it must be in accord with reason and common sense and as such it would seem to be superfluous to a jury of reasonable people. Since the prosecutor could argue to the jury that it should draw reasonable inferences from the evidence, do you see any value to the judge giving an instruction on presumptions? Does it matter that the permissible inference is explained by the judge?

IV.   TRIAL BY JURY

A.   THE FUNDAMENTAL RIGHT

Article III, Section 2, clause 3 of the Constitution provides that "[t]he trial of all Crimes, except in Cases of Impeachment, shall be by Jury; and such Trial shall be held in the State where the said Crimes shall have been committed; but when not committed within any State, the Trial shall be at such Place or Places as the Congress may by Law have directed." The Sixth Amendment is, in part, redundant; it provides that "[i]n all criminal prosecutions, the accused shall

---

18. See also United States v. Johnson, 71 F.3d 139 (4th Cir.1995) (defendant charged with armed robbery of a credit union; trial judge instructs jury that the institution was a credit union within the meaning of the statute; reversal required because the instruction was a mandatory, irrebuttable presumption, and the status of the victim institution as a credit union was an element of the crime).

enjoy the right to a speedy and public trial, by an impartial jury of the State and district wherein the crime shall have been committed, which district shall have been previously ascertained by law * * *." Certainly, a right found in two places in the Constitution is likely to be regarded as fundamental. And that is just how the Supreme Court viewed it when it incorporated the Sixth Amendment through the Fourteenth and made it binding on the states.

It should be remembered that we have already discussed the right to a jury trial in one context–its interrelationship with the right to require the state to prove every element of the crime beyond a reasonable doubt. Thus, in *Apprendi*, *supra*, the Court held that the state violated both *Winship* and the constitutional right to a jury trial when it treated an element of a crime as a sentencing factor. The importance of jury determination of all elements of the crime was set out most forcefully in the following case.

DUNCAN v. LOUISIANA

Supreme Court of the United States, 1968.
391 U.S. 145.

MR. JUSTICE WHITE **delivered the opinion of the Court.**

Appellant, Gary Duncan, was convicted of simple battery in the Twenty-fifth Judicial District Court of Louisiana. Under Louisiana law simple battery is a misdemeanor, punishable by a maximum of two years' imprisonment and a $300 fine. Appellant sought trial by jury, but because the Louisiana Constitution grants jury trials only in cases in which capital punishment or imprisonment at hard labor may be imposed, the trial judge denied the request. Appellant was convicted and sentenced to serve 60 days in the parish prison and pay a fine of $150.
* * *

* * *

Appellant was 19 years of age when tried. While driving on Highway 23 in Plaquemines Parish on October 18, 1966, he saw two younger cousins engaged in a conversation by the side of the road with four white boys. Knowing his cousins, Negroes who had recently transferred to a formerly all-white high school, had reported the occurrence of racial incidents at the school, Duncan stopped the car, got out, and approached the six boys. At trial the white boys and a white onlooker testified, as did appellant and his cousins. The testimony was in dispute on many points, but the witnesses agreed that appellant and the white boys spoke to each other, that appellant encouraged his cousins to break off the encounter and enter his car, and that appellant was about to enter the car himself for the purpose of driving away with his cousins. The whites testified that just before getting in the car appellant slapped Herman Landry, one of the white boys, on the elbow. The Negroes testified that appellant had not slapped Landry, but had merely touched him. The trial judge concluded that the State had proved beyond a reasonable doubt that Duncan had committed simple battery, and found him guilty.

I

[The Court discusses its prior incorporation tests.]

* * * The claim before us is that the right to trial by jury guaranteed by the Sixth Amendment meets these tests. The position of Louisiana, on the other hand, is that the Constitution imposes upon the State no duty to give a jury trial in any criminal case, regardless of the seriousness of the crime or the size of the punishment which may be imposed. Because we believe that trial by jury in criminal cases is fundamental to the American scheme of justice, we hold that the Fourteenth Amendment guarantees a right of jury trial in all criminal cases which—were they to be tried in a federal court— would come within the Sixth Amendment's guarantee. Since we consider the appeal before us to be such a case, we hold that the Constitution was violated when appellant's demand for jury trial was refused.

The guarantees of jury trial in the Federal and State Constitutions reflect a profound judgment about the way in which law should be enforced and justice administered. A right to a jury trial is granted to criminal defendants in order to prevent oppression by the Government. Those who wrote our constitutions knew from history and experience that it was necessary to protect against unfounded criminal charges brought to eliminate enemies and against judges too responsive to the voice of higher authority. The framers of the constitutions strove to create an independent judiciary but insisted upon further protection against arbitrary action. Providing an accused with the right to be tried by a jury of his peers gave him an inestimable safeguard against the corrupt or overzealous prosecutor and against the compliant, biased, or eccentric judge. If the defendant preferred the common-sense judgment of a jury to the more tutored but perhaps less sympathetic reaction of the single judge, he was to have it. Beyond this, the jury trial provisions in the Federal and State Constitutions reflect a fundamental decision about the exercise of official power—a reluctance to entrust plenary powers over the life and liberty of the citizen to one judge or to a group of judges. Fear of unchecked power, so typical of our State and Federal Governments in other respects, found expression in the criminal law in this insistence upon community participation in the determination of guilt or innocence. The deep commitment of the Nation to the right of jury trial in serious criminal cases as a defense against arbitrary law enforcement qualifies for protection under the Due Process Clause of the Fourteenth Amendment, and must therefore be respected by the States.

Of course jury trial has "its weaknesses and the potential for misuse," Singer v. United States, 380 U.S. 24, 35 (1965). We are aware of the long debate, especially in this century, among those who write about the administration of justice, as to the wisdom of permitting untrained laymen to determine the facts in civil and criminal proceedings. * * *

The State of Louisiana urges that holding that the Fourteenth Amendment assures a right to jury trial will cast doubt on the integrity of every trial conducted without a jury. Plainly, this is not the import of our holding. Our conclusion is that in the American States, as in the federal judicial system, a general grant of jury trial for serious offenses is a fundamental right, essential for preventing miscarriages of justice and for assuring that fair trials are provided for all defendants. We would not assert, however, that every criminal trial—or any particular trial—held before a judge alone is unfair or that a defendant may never be as fairly treated by a judge as he would be by a jury. Thus we hold no constitutional doubts about the practices common in both federal and state courts, of accepting waivers of jury trial and prosecuting petty crimes without extending a right to jury trial. However, the fact is that in most places more trials for serious crimes are to juries than to a court alone; a great many defendants prefer the judgment of a jury to that of a court. Even where defendants are satisfied with bench trials, the right to a jury trial very likely serves its intended purpose of making judicial or prosecutorial unfairness less likely.

II

Louisiana's final contention is that even if it must grant jury trials in serious criminal cases, the conviction before us is valid and constitutional because here the petitioner was tried for simple battery and was sentenced to only 60 days in the parish prison. We are not persuaded. It is doubtless true that there is a category of petty crimes or offenses which is not subject to the Sixth Amendment jury trial provision and should not be subject to the Fourteenth Amendment jury trial requirement here applied to the States. Crimes carrying possible penalties up to six months do not require a jury trial if they otherwise qualify as petty offenses, Cheff v. Schnackenberg, 384 U.S. 373 (1966). But the penalty authorized for a particular crime is of major relevance in determining whether it is serious or not and may in itself, if severe enough, subject the trial to the mandates of the Sixth Amendment. * * * In the case before us the Legislature of Louisiana has made simple battery a criminal offense punishable by imprisonment for up to two years and a fine. The question, then, is whether a crime carrying such a penalty is an offense which Louisiana may insist on trying without a jury.

We think not. * * * Of course the boundaries of the petty offense category have always been ill-defined, if not ambulatory. * * * [I]t is necessary to draw a line in the spectrum of crime, separating petty from serious infractions. This process, although essential, cannot be wholly satisfactory, for it requires attaching different consequences to events which, when they lie near the line, actually differ very little.

In determining whether the length of the authorized prison term or the seriousness of other punishment is enough in itself to require a jury trial, we * * * refer to objective criteria, chiefly the existing laws and practices in the Nation. In the federal system, petty offenses are defined as those punishable by no more than six months in prison and a $500 fine. In 49 of the 50 States crimes subject to trial without a jury, which occasionally include simple battery, are punishable by no more than one year in jail. * * * We need not, however, settle in this case the exact location of the line between petty offenses and serious crimes. It is sufficient for our purposes to hold that a crime punishable by two years in prison is, based on past and contemporary standards in this country, a serious crime and not a petty offense. Consequently, appellant was entitled to a jury trial and it was error to deny it.

* * *

[The concurring opinions of Justice Fortas, and Justice Black (who was joined by Justice Douglas), and the dissenting opinion by Justice Harlan, joined by Justice Stewart, are all omitted.]

Note on the Definition of Petty Offenses

Duncan's declaration that "petty offenses" may be tried without a jury was subsequently affirmed in Baldwin v. New York, 399 U.S. 66 (1970). In *Baldwin* the Court defined "petty" by considering the severity of the maximum penalty and concluded that "no offense can be deemed petty for purposes of the right to trial by jury where imprisonment for more than six months is authorized."

Recall Scott v. Illinois, Chapter Five, supra, where the Court held that Scott was not entitled to appointed counsel because he was not imprisoned after his conviction. The offense for which Scott was convicted *authorized* imprisonment for up to a year. Apparently Scott had the right to a jury trial under *Baldwin*. Does it make sense to have a right to jury trial but no right to appointed counsel?

Joinder of Multiple Petty Offenses: Lewis v. United States

In Lewis v. United States, 518 U.S. 322 (1996), the defendant was charged with two misdemeanor counts of obstructing the mails. Each count carried a maximum prison term of six months, and thus each was a "petty offense" within the meaning of the Supreme Court's jury trial jurisprudence. However, the defendant could have been subject to consecutive sentences if convicted of both counts. The lower court denied the defendant's motion for a jury trial and also stated for the record that it would not impose a sentence of more than six months, even if the defendant were convicted of both counts.

Lewis appealed the denial of jury trial, arguing that petty offenses, when they are joined in a single trial, must be aggregated to determine the seriousness of the charges for purposes of the jury trial right. But the Supreme Court rejected this aggregation argument in an opinion by Justice O'Connor. Justice O'Connor analyzed the problem as follows:

> The Sixth Amendment reserves the jury-trial right to defendants accused of serious crimes. * * * [W]e determine whether an offense is serious by looking to the judgment of the legislature, primarily as expressed in the maximum authorized term of imprisonment. Here, by setting the maximum authorized prison term at six months, the legislature categorized the offense of obstructing the mail as petty. The fact that the petitioner was charged with two counts of a petty offense does not revise the legislative judgment as to the gravity of that particular offense, nor does it transform the petty offense into a serious one, to which the jury-trial right would apply. We note that there is precedent at common law that a jury trial was not provided to a defendant charged with multiple petty offenses.

> * * *

> Certainly the aggregate potential penalty faced by petitioner is of serious importance to him. But to determine whether an offense is serious for Sixth Amendment purposes, we look to the legislature's judgment, as evidenced by the maximum penalty authorized. Where the offenses charged are petty, and the deprivation of liberty exceeds six months only as a result of the aggregation of charges, the jury-trial right does not apply. As petitioner acknowledges, even if he were to prevail, the Government could properly circumvent the jury-trial right by charging the counts in separate informations and trying them separately.

Justice Kennedy, joined by Justice Breyer, concurred only in the judgment. He agreed that Lewis had no right to jury trial, but only because the lower court had stated that it would not sentence Lewis to more than six months even if he were convicted of both counts. In the absence of this self-imposed limitation, Justice Kennedy would have found a violation of the jury trial right. Justice Kennedy attacked the majority's analysis in the following passage:

The primary purpose of the jury in our legal system is to stand between the accused and the powers of the State. Among the most ominous of those is the power to imprison. * * * Providing a defendant with the right to be tried by a jury gives "him an inestimable safeguard against the corrupt or overzealous prosecutor and against the compliant, biased, or eccentric judge." These considerations all are present when a judge in a single case sends a defendant to prison for years, whether the sentence is the result of one serious offense or several petty offenses.

On the Court's view of the case, however, there is no limit to the length of the sentence a judge can impose on a defendant without entitling him to a jury, so long as the prosecutor carves up the charges into segments punishable by no more than six months apiece. Prosecutors have broad discretion in framing charges, for criminal conduct often does not arrange itself in neat categories. In many cases, a prosecutor can choose to charge a defendant with multiple petty offenses rather than a single serious offense, and so prevent him under today's holding from obtaining a trial by jury while still obtaining the same punishment.

Justice Kennedy expressed concern about the far-reaching consequences of the denial of jury trial in cases involving multiple petty offenses:

> * * * The decision affects more than repeat violators of traffic laws, persons accused of public drunkenness, persons who persist in breaches of the peace, and the wide range of eccentrics capable of disturbing the quiet enjoyment of life by others. Just as alarming is the threat the Court's holding poses to millions of persons in agriculture, manufacturing, and trade who must comply with minute administrative regulations, many of them carrying a jail term of six months or less. Violations of these sorts of rules often involve repeated, discrete acts which can result in potential liability of years of imprisonment. Still, under the Court's holding it makes no difference whether a defendant is sentenced to a year in prison or for that matter to 20 years: As long as no single violation charged is punishable by more than six months, the defendant has no right to a jury.

Justice Stevens wrote a short dissenting opinion in *Lewis*.

Penalties Other Than Incarceration

Justice Marshall wrote for a unanimous Court in Blanton v. City of North Las Vegas, 489 U.S. 538 (1989), rejecting the jury trial claim of a defendant charged under Nevada law with driving under the influence (DUI). Under the Nevada law, a convicted defendant is subject to a minimum term of two days' imprisonment and a maximum term of six months' imprisonment. Alternatively, a trial court may order the defendant to perform 48 hours of community work while wearing distinctive garb which identifies him as a DUI offender. A convicted defendant may also be fined from $200 to $1,000, he automatically loses his license for 90 days, and he must attend an alcohol abuse education class at his own expense.

Justice Marshall relied upon prior cases for the proposition that the primary emphasis in assessing the right to jury trial is on the maximum authorized possible period of incarceration. Although he recognized that a legislature's view of the seriousness of an offense might also be reflected in other penalties, he reasoned that incarceration is intrinsically different from other penalties and is the most powerful indication of whether an offense is "serious." Justice Marshall wrote that it is appropriate to presume for Sixth Amendment purposes that an offense is petty if it carries a maximum prison term of six months or less, and that "[a] defendant is entitled to a jury trial in such circumstances only if he can demonstrate that any additional statutory penalties, viewed in conjunction with the maximum authorized period of incarceration, are so severe that they clearly reflect a legislative determination that the offense in question is a 'serious' one." The Nevada penalties other than incarceration were not onerous enough to overcome the presumption that the offense was "petty."

The Court relied on its decision in *Blanton* in deciding United States v. Nachtigal, 507 U.S. 1 (1993)(per curiam). Nachtigal was charged with operating a motor vehicle in a national park while under the influence of alcohol. The maximum punishment was six months imprisonment and a $5,000 fine, and the sentencing court had the authority to impose a five year probationary sentence as an alternative to incarceration. A unanimous Supreme Court held that *Blanton* was controlling. Under *Blanton,* offenses for which the maximum period of incarceration is six months or less are presumptively "petty." The Court in *Nachtigal* stated that "a defendant can overcome this presumption, and become entitled to a jury trial, only by showing that the additional penalties, viewed together with the maximum prison term, are so severe that the legislature clearly determined that the offense is a serious one." It also noted that "it is a rare case where a legislature packs an offense it deems serious with onerous penalties that nonetheless do not puncture the 6–month incarceration line." The Court emphasized that under *Blanton,* "the statutory penalties in other States are irrelevant to the question whether a particular legislature deemed a particular offense serious."

As to the DUI offense at issue in *Nachtigal,* the Court reasoned that Congress limited penalties to six months and thereby made a legislative judgment as to the non-seriousness of such offenses, and that the possibility of a probationary sentence or a fine of $5,000 were not sufficiently severe to overcome the *Blanton* presumption.

B. WHAT THE JURY DECIDES

Are there any questions of fact that should or can be decided by the court rather than the jury? This question underlies much of the law concerning the use of presumptions, supra. Another question is whether factual issues can be allocated to the judge rather than the jury as part of a sentencing determination. This issue was discussed in the section of constitutional proof requirements, supra.

We have seen that all elements of a crime must be left for the jury and must be proved beyond a reasonable doubt. When courts occasionally forget this principle, they are reminded by the Supreme Court. Thus, in United States v. Gaudin, 515 U.S. 506 (1995), the defendant was charged with violating 18 U.S.C. § 1001, which prohibits the making of false "material" statements to government agencies. The trial judge instructed the jury that the defendant's statements were material within the meaning of the statute. The Court, in a unanimous opinion by Justice Scalia, held that the question of materiality was for the jury. Therefore, the defendant's rights to jury trial and due process were violated when the judge rather than the jury decided whether the statements were material. Justice Scalia declared:

> The Constitution gives a criminal defendant the right to demand that a jury find him guilty of all the elements of the crime with which he is charged; one of the elements in the present case is materiality; respondent therefore had a right to have the jury decide materiality.

Justice Scalia rejected the government's argument that the Sixth Amendment permits judges to decide whether elements of the crime have been proved when those elements present mixed questions of law and fact. He noted that juries typically decide mixed questions of law and fact, including the ultimate question of whether the defendant is guilty of the crime charged.

In Apprendi v. New Jersey, 530 U.S. 466 (2000), the Court held that "it is unconstitutional for a legislature to remove from the jury the assessment of facts that increase the prescribed range of penalties to which a criminal defendant is exposed." The Court invalidated a statute that allowed the judge to increase a sentence for a weapons crime, beyond the statutory maximum, if the judge found at sentencing that the crime was committed with a racial bias. The question of racial bias had to be submitted to the jury. When the judge at sentencing increased the defendant's punishment beyond the statutory maximum for the crime determined by the jury, this factfinding deprived the defendant of his constitutional right to a jury trial on the question of racial bias. Apprendi is set forth in detail supra, in the section on constitutionally-based proof requirements.

In Harris v. United States, 536 U.S. 545 (2002), the Court held that Apprendi does not prevent the judge from finding a fact that forms the basis of a mandatory minimum sentence, so long as the sentence imposed does not exceed the statutory maximum punishment for the crime of which the jury found the defendant guilty. The Court reasoned that so long as the sentence was within the prescribed sentencing range, the protection of a jury determination was not required by the Constitution. Harris is set forth in detail in the section on constitutionally-based proof requirements.

If an issue is collateral to the resolution of an element of the crime, it is generally resolved by the judge rather than the jury. For example, it is the judge who decides whether evidence was illegally obtained and should be excluded. Also, the admissibility of evidence is generally a question for the judge, while the jury decides the weight to be given to evidence that is admitted. See Federal Rule of Evidence 104.

C. REQUISITE FEATURES OF THE JURY

1. Size

WILLIAMS v. FLORIDA

Supreme Court of the United States, 1970.
399 U.S. 78.

Mr. Justice White delivered the opinion of the court.

[Petitioner filed a pretrial motion to impanel a 12–person jury instead of the six-person jury provided by Florida law in all but capital cases. The motion was denied and petitioner was convicted of robbery and sentenced to life imprisonment. In Part I of the opinion, the Court rejected the petitioner's attack on a state rule requiring the defendant to give notice of an alibi defense. See Chapter Eight for a discussion of that point.]

II

* * * The question in this case then is whether the constitutional guarantee of a trial by "jury" necessarily requires trial by exactly 12 persons, rather than some lesser number—in this case six. We hold that the 12–man panel is not a necessary ingredient of "trial by jury," and that respondent's refusal to impanel more than the six members provided for by Florida law did not violate petitioner's Sixth Amendment rights as applied to the States through the Fourteenth.

We had occasion in Duncan v. Louisiana to review briefly the oft-told history of the development of trial by jury in criminal cases. That history revealed a long tradition attaching great importance to the concept of relying on a body of one's peers to determine guilt or innocence as a safeguard against arbitrary law enforcement. That same history, however, affords little insight into the considerations that gradually led the size of that body to be generally fixed at 12. Some have suggested that the number 12 was fixed upon simply because that was the number of the presentment jury from the hundred, from which the petit jury developed. Other, less circular but more fanciful reasons for the number 12 have been given, "but they were all brought forward after the number was fixed," and rest on little more than mystical or superstitious insights into the significance of "12." Lord Coke's explanation that the "*number of twelve is much respected in holy writ*, as 12 *apostles,* 12 *stones,* 12 *tribes, etc.,*" is typical. In short, while sometime in the 14th century the size of the jury at common law came to be fixed generally at 12, that particular feature of the jury system appears to have been a historical accident, unrelated to the great purposes which gave rise to the jury in the first place. The question before us is whether this accidental feature of the jury has been immutably codified into our Constitution.

* * *

While "the intent of the Framers" is often an elusive quarry, the relevant constitutional history casts considerable doubt on the easy assumption in our past decisions that if a given feature existed in a jury at common law in 1789, then it was necessarily preserved in the Constitution. Provisions for jury trial were first placed in the Constitution in Article III's provision that "[t]he Trial of all Crimes * * * shall be by Jury; and such Trial shall be held in the State where the said Crimes shall have been committed." The "very scanty history [of this provision] in the records of the Constitutional Convention" sheds little light either way on the intended correlation between Article III's "jury" and the features of the jury at common law. Indeed, pending and after the adoption of the Constitution, fears were expressed that Article III's provision failed to preserve the common-law right to be tried by a "jury of the vicinage." That concern, as well as the concern to preserve the right to jury in civil as well as criminal cases, furnished part of the impetus for introducing amendments to the Constitution that ultimately resulted in the jury trial provisions of the Sixth and Seventh Amendments. As introduced by James Madison in the House, the Amendment relating to jury trial in criminal cases would have provided that:

"The trial of all crimes * * * shall be by an impartial jury of free-hold-ers of the vicinage, with the requisite of unanimity for conviction, of the right of challenge, and other accustomed requisites * * *."

The Amendment passed the House in substantially this form, but after more than a week of debate in the Senate it returned to the House considerably altered. * * * [The Court discusses more history, including appointment of a Conference committee.] The version that finally emerged from the Committee was the version that ultimately became the Sixth Amendment, ensuring an accused:

> "the right to a speedy and public trial, by an impartial jury of the State and district wherein the crime shall have been committed, which district shall have been previously ascertained by law * * *."

Gone were the provisions spelling out such common-law features of the jury as "unanimity," or "the accustomed requisites." And the "vicinage" requirement itself had been replaced by wording that reflected a compromise between broad and narrow definitions of that term, and that left Congress the power to determine the actual size of the "vicinage" by its creation of judicial districts.

Three significant features may be observed in this sketch of the background of the Constitution's jury trial provisions. First, even though the vicinage requirement was as much a feature of the common-law jury as was the 12–man requirement, the mere reference to "trial by jury" in Article III was not interpreted to include that feature. * * * Second, provisions that would have explicitly tied the "jury" concept to the "accustomed requisites" of the time were eliminated. * * * Finally, contemporary legislative and constitutional provisions indicate that where Congress wanted to leave no doubt that it was incorporating ex-

isting common-law features of the jury system, it knew how to use express language to that effect. * * *

* * * Nothing in this history suggests, then, that we do violence to the letter of the Constitution by turning to other than purely historical considerations to determine which features of the jury system, as it existed at common law, were preserved in the Constitution. The relevant inquiry, as we see it, must be the function that the particular feature performs and its relation to the purposes of the jury trial. Measured by this standard, the 12–man requirement cannot be regarded as an indispensable component of the Sixth Amendment.

The purpose of the jury trial, as we noted in *Duncan,* is to prevent oppression by the Government. * * * Given this purpose, the essential feature of a jury obviously lies in the interposition between the accused and his accuser of the commonsense judgment of a group of laymen, and in the community participation and shared responsibility that results from that group's determination of guilt or innocence. The performance of this role is not a function of the particular number of the body that makes up the jury. To be sure, the number should probably be large enough to promote group deliberation, free from outside attempts at intimidation, and to provide a fair possibility for obtaining a representative cross-section of the community. But we find little reason to think that these goals are in any meaningful sense less likely to be achieved when the jury numbers six, than when it numbers 12—particularly if the requirement of unanimity is retained. And, certainly the reliability of the jury as a factfinder hardly seems likely to be a function of its size.

It might be suggested that the 12–man jury gives a defendant a greater advantage since he has more "chances" of finding a juror who will insist on acquittal and thus prevent conviction. But the advantage might just as easily belong to the State which also needs only one juror out of twelve insisting on guilt to prevent acquittal. What few experiments have occurred—usually in the civil area—indicate that there is no discernible difference between the results reached by the two different-sized juries. In short, neither currently available evidence nor theory suggests that the 12–man jury is necessarily more advantageous to the defendant than a jury composed of fewer members.

Similarly, while in theory the number of viewpoints represented on a randomly selected jury ought to increase as the size of the jury increases, in practice the difference between the 12–man and the six-man jury in terms of the cross-section of the community represented seems likely to be negligible. Even the 12–man jury cannot insure representation of every distinct voice in the community, particularly given the use of the peremptory challenge. * * *

* * *

[Justice Harlan, concurring in the result reiterated his concern expressed in *Duncan*, that incorporation of the Sixth Amendment dilutes federal guarantees in order to reconcile the logic of "incorporation" with the reality of federalism.]

[The Chief Justice concurred. Justice Black and Justice Douglas concurred in part and dissented in part. Justice Marshall dissented in part. Justice Stewart concurred in the result. Justice Blackmun took no part in the decision of the case.]

BALLEW v. GEORGIA

Supreme Court of the United States, 1978.
435 U.S. 223.

MR. JUSTICE BLACKMUN announced the judgment of the court and delivered an opinion in which MR. JUSTICE STEVENS joined.

[Petitioner was convicted on two misdemeanor counts of distributing obscene material by a five-person jury impaneled according to Georgia law. The opinion recites the facts and describes *Williams*].

* * *

III

When the Court in *Williams* permitted the reduction in jury size * * * it expressly reserved ruling on the issue whether a number smaller than six

passed constitutional scrutiny. The Court refused to speculate when this so-called "slippery slope" would become too steep. We face now, however, the two-fold question whether a further reduction in the size of the state criminal trial jury does make the grade too dangerous, that is, whether it inhibits the functioning of the jury as an institution to a significant degree, and, if so, whether any state interest counterbalances and justifies the disruption so as to preserve its constitutionality.

Williams v. Florida * * * generated a quantity of scholarly work on jury size.[a] These writings do not draw or

---

a. E.g., M. Saks, Jury Verdicts (1977); Bogue & Fritz, The Six–Man Jury, 17 S.D.L.Rev. 285 (1972); Davis Kerr, Atkin, Holt & Mech, The Decision Processes of 6–and 12–Person

Mock Juries Assigned Unanimous and Two–Thirds Majority Rules, 32 J. of Personality & Soc. Psych. 1 (1975); Diamond, A Jury Experiment Reanalyzed, 7 U.Mich.J.L. Reform 520

identify a bright line below which the number of jurors would not be able to function as required by the standards enunciated in *Williams*. On the other hand, they raise significant questions about the wisdom and constitutionality of a reduction below six. We examine these concerns:

First, recent empirical data suggest that progressively smaller juries are less likely to foster effective group deliberation. At some point, this decline leads to inaccurate fact-finding and incorrect application of the common sense of the community to the facts. Generally, a positive correlation exists between group size and the quality of both group performance and group productivity. A variety of explanations have been offered for this conclusion. Several are particularly applicable in the jury setting. The smaller the group, the less likely are members to make critical contributions necessary for the solution of a given problem. Because most juries are not permitted to take notes, memory is important for accurate jury deliberations. As juries decrease in size, then, they are less likely to have members who remember each of the important pieces of evidence or argument. Furthermore, the smaller the group, the less likely it is to overcome the biases of its members to obtain an accurate result. When in-

dividual and group decisionmaking were compared, it was seen that groups performed better because prejudices of individuals were frequently counterbalanced, and objectivity resulted. Groups also exhibited increased motivation and self-criticism. All of these advantages, except, perhaps, self-motivation, tend to diminish as the size of the group diminishes.* * *

Second, the data now raise doubts about the accuracy of the results achieved by smaller and smaller panels. Statistical studies suggest that the risk of convicting an innocent person rises as the size of the jury diminishes * * *. [The studies posit that by considering the risk of not convicting a guilty party, an optimal jury size between six and eight is identified.] As the size diminished to five and below, the weighted sum of errors increased because of the enlarging risk of the conviction of innocent defendants.

Another doubt about progressively smaller juries arises from the increasing inconsistency that results from the decreases. [Several studies suggest that 12–person panels considering the same case will reach the same result, or compromise to the same result, with greater consistency than a six-person panel.]

(1974); Friedman, Trial by Jury: Criteria for Convictions, Jury Size and Type I and Type II Errors, 26–2 Am.Stat. 21 (April 1972); Institute of Judicial Administration, A Comparison of Six-and Twelve–Member Civil Juries in New Jersey Superior and County Courts (1972); Lempert, Uncovering "Nondiscernible" Differences: Empirical Research and the Jury–Size Cases, 73 Mich.L.Rev. 643 (1975); Nagel & Neef, Deductive Modeling to Determine an Optimum Jury Size and Fraction Required to Convict, 1975 Wash.U.L.Q. 933 (hereinafter cited as Nagel & Neef); Pabst, Statistical Studies of the Cost of Six–Man versus Twelve–Man Juries, 14 Wm. & Mary L.Rev. 326 (1972); Zeisel, * * * And Then There Were None: The Diminution of the Federal Jury, 38 U.Chi. L.Rev. 710 (1971); Zeisel, The Waning of the American Jury, 58 A.B.A.J. 367 (1972); Zeisel

& Diamond, "Convincing Empirical Evidence" on the Six Member Jury, 41 U.Chi.Rev. 281 (1974); Note, Six–Member and Twelve–Member Juries: An Empirical Study of Trial Results, 6 U.Mich.J.L.Ref. 671 (1973); Note, An Empirical Study of Six-and Twelve–Member Jury Decision–Making Processes, 6 U.Mich. J.L.Ref. 712 (1973).

We have considered them carefully because they provide the only basis, besides judicial hunch, for a decision about whether smaller and smaller juries will be able to fulfill the purpose and functions of the Sixth Amendment. Without an examination about how juries and small groups actually work, we would not understand the basis for the conclusion of Mr. Justice Powell that "a line has to be drawn somewhere."

Third, the data suggest that the verdicts of jury deliberation in criminal cases will vary as juries become smaller, and that the variance amounts to an imbalance to the detriment of one side, the defense. [The Court noted that hung juries will diminish because a person in the minority is less likely to have an ally on the six-person panel, and thus is less likely to speak up.]

Fourth, what has just been said about the presence of minority viewpoint as juries decrease in size foretells problems not only for jury decisionmaking, but also for the representation of minority groups in the community. * * * Further reduction in size will erect additional barriers to representation.

Fifth, several authors have identified in jury research methodological problems tending to mask differences in the operation of smaller and larger juries. Nationwide, however, these small percentages will represent a large number of cases. And it is with respect to those cases that the jury trial right has its greatest value. When the case is close, and the guilt or innocence of the defendant is not readily apparent, a properly functioning jury system will insure evaluation by the sense of the community and will also tend to insure accurate fact-finding. * * *

IV

While we adhere to, and reaffirm our holding in Williams v. Florida, these studies, most of which have been made since *Williams* was decided in 1970, lead us to conclude that the purpose and functioning of the jury in a criminal trial is seriously impaired, and to a constitutional degree, by a reduction in size to below six members. We readily admit that we do not pretend to discern a clear line between six members and five. But

the assembled data raise substantial doubt about the reliability and appropriate representation of panels smaller than six. Because of the fundamental importance of the jury trial to the American system of criminal justice, any further reduction that promotes inaccurate and possibly biased decisionmaking, that causes untoward differences in verdicts, and that prevents juries from truly representing their communities, attains constitutional significance.

* * *

V

* * * We find no significant state advantage in reducing the number of jurors from six to five. * * *

[The concurring opinion of Justice Stevens is omitted.]

MR. JUSTICE WHITE **concurring in the judgment.**

Agreeing that a jury of fewer than six persons would fail to represent the sense of the community and hence not satisfy the fair cross-section requirement of the Sixth and Fourteenth Amendments, I concur in the judgment of reversal.

MR. JUSTICE POWELL, **with whom** THE CHIEF JUSTICE **and** MR. JUSTICE REHNQUIST **join, concurring in the judgment.**

I concur in the judgment, as I agree that use of a jury as small as five members, with authority to convict for serious offenses, involves grave questions of fairness. As the opinion of Mr. Justice Blackmun indicates, the line between five-and six-member juries is difficult to justify, but a line has to be drawn somewhere if the substance of jury trial is to be preserved.

I do not agree, however, that every feature of jury trial practice must be the same in both federal and state courts. * * * Also, I have reservations as to the wisdom—as well as the necessity—of Mr. Justice Blackmun's heavy reliance on numerology derived from statistical studies. Moreover, neither the validity nor the methodology employed by the studies cited was subjected to the traditional testing mechanisms of the adversary process. The studies relied on merely represent unexamined findings of persons interested in the jury system.

2. Unanimity

APODACA v. OREGON

Supreme Court of the United States, 1972.
406 U.S. 404.

Mr. Justice White **announced the judgment of the Court and an opinion in which** The Chief Justice, Mr. Justice Blackmun **and** Mr. Justice Rehnquist **joined.**

[The three petitioners were convicted of various criminal charges by three separate, less than unanimous Oregon juries. Two juries returned 11–1 votes, the third returned the minimum (under state law) 10–2 verdict.]

In Williams v. Florida, 399 U.S. 78 (1970), we had occasion to consider a related issue: whether the Sixth Amendment's right to trial by jury requires that all juries consist of 12 men. After considering the history of the 12–man requirement and the functions it performs in contemporary society, we concluded that it was not of constitutional stature. We reach the same conclusion today with regard to the requirement of unanimity.

* * *

Our inquiry must focus upon the function served by the jury in contemporary society. As we said in *Duncan*, the purpose of trial by jury is to prevent oppression by the Government by providing a "safeguard against the corrupt or overzealous prosecutor and against the compliant, biased, or eccentric judge." "Given this purpose, the essential feature of a jury obviously lies in the interposition between the accused and his accuser of the commonsense judgment of a group of laymen * * *." A requirement of unanimity, however, does not materially contribute to the exercise of this commonsense judgment. As we said in *Williams*, a jury will come to such a judgment as long as it consists of a group of laymen representative of a cross section of the community who have the duty and the opportunity to deliberate, free from outside attempts at intimidation, on the question of a defendant's guilt. In terms of this function we perceive no difference between juries required to act unanimously and those permitted to convict or acquit by votes of 10 to two or 11 to one. Requiring unanimity would obviously produce hung juries in some situations where nonunanimous juries will convict or acquit. But in either case, the interest of the defendant in having the judgment of his peers interposed between himself and the officers of the State who prosecute and judge him is equally well served.

For these reasons I concur only in the judgment.

Mr. Justice Brennan, **with whom** Mr. Justice Stewart **and** Mr. Justice Marshall **join.**

I join Mr. Justice Blackmun's opinion insofar as it holds that the Sixth and Fourteenth Amendments require juries in criminal trials to contain more than five persons. * * *

III

Petitioners nevertheless argue that unanimity serves other purposes constitutionally essential to the continued operation of the jury system. Their principal contention is that a Sixth Amendment "jury trial" made mandatory on the States by virtue of the Due Process Clause of the Fourteenth Amendment, should be held to require a unanimous jury verdict in order to give substance to the reasonable-doubt standard otherwise mandated by the Due Process Clause.

6 th suggests unanim reqd to give merit to reasonable doubt standard

We are quite sure, however, that the Sixth Amendment itself has never been held to require proof beyond a reasonable doubt in criminal cases. The reasonable-doubt standard developed separately from both the jury trial and the unanimous verdict. As the Court noted in the *Winship* case, the rule requiring proof of crime beyond a reasonable doubt did not crystallize in this country until after the Constitution was adopted. And in that case, which held such a burden of proof to be constitutionally required, the Court purported to draw no support from the Sixth Amendment.

But bord not a constitutnl figure

* * *

IV

Petitioners also cite quite accurately a long line of decisions of this Court upholding the principle that the Fourteenth Amendment requires jury panels to reflect a cross section of the community. They then contend that unanimity is a necessary precondition for effective application of the cross-section requirement, because a rule permitting less than unanimous verdicts will make it possible for convictions to occur without the acquiescence of minority elements within the community.

Unanimity reqd to serve goal of having each elem in communy find guilt

w/o unanimity min voices never heard

There are two flaws in this argument. One is petitioners' assumption that every distinct voice in the community has a right to be represented on every jury and a right to prevent conviction of a defendant in any case. All that the Constitution forbids, however, is systematic exclusion of identifiable segments of the community from jury panels * * *.

every voice not reqd is every Jury in every trial

We also cannot accept petitioners' second assumption—that minority groups, even when they are represented on a jury, will not adequately represent the viewpoint of those groups simply because they may be outvoted in the final result. They will be present during all deliberations, and their views will be heard. We cannot assume that the majority of the jury will refuse to weigh the evidence and reach a decision upon rational grounds, just as it must now do in order to obtain unanimous verdicts, or that a majority will deprive a man of his liberty on the basis of prejudice when a minority is presenting a reasonable argument in favor of acquittal. We simply find no proof for the notion that a majority will disregard its instructions and cast its votes for guilt or innocence based on prejudice rather than the evidence.

H: Unanimy is not reqd

*Jury delibrtns fair
• lack of representatn does not mean prejudce*

* * *

MR. JUSTICE POWELL, concurring in the judgment.

[Justice Powell, subscribing to the views of Justice Harlan, rejected the theory that all elements of the jury trial within the meaning of the Sixth Amendment are incorporated into the Due Process Clause of the Fourteenth Amendment and applied against the states. Using a due process analysis, he agreed with the plurality that unanimity is not required in state trials, even though he believed that the Sixth Amendment requires unanimity in federal trials.][a]

MR. JUSTICE DOUGLAS, **with whom MR.** JUSTICE BRENNAN **and** MR. JUSTICE MARSHALL **concur, dissenting.**

* * *

The plurality approves a procedure which diminishes the reliability of a jury. * * *

The diminution of verdict reliability flows from the fact that nonunanimous juries need not debate and deliberate as fully as must unanimous juries. As soon as the requisite majority is attained, further consideration is not required * * * even though the dissident jurors might, if given the chance, be able to convince the majority. * * * The Court now extracts from the jury room this automatic check against hasty factfinding by relieving jurors of the duty to hear out fully the dissenters.

It is said that there is no evidence that majority jurors will refuse to listen to dissenters whose votes are unneeded for conviction. Yet human experience teaches that polite and academic conversation is no substitute for the earnest and robust argument necessary to reach unanimity. * * *

* * *

* * * *Williams* requires that the change be neither more nor less advantageous to either the State or the defendant. It is said that such a show-

ing is satisfied here since a [non-unanimous verdict can] result in acquittal. Yet experience shows that the less-than-unanimous jury overwhelmingly favors the States.

Moreover, even where an initial majority wins the dissent over to its side, the ultimate result in unanimous-jury States may nonetheless reflect the reservations of uncertain jurors. I refer to many compromise verdicts on lesser-included offenses and lesser sentences. Thus, even though a minority may not be forceful enough to carry the day, their doubts may nonetheless cause a majority to exercise caution. * * *

It is my belief that a unanimous jury is necessary if the great barricade known as proof beyond a reasonable doubt is to be maintained. * * *

Suppose a jury begins with a substantial minority but then in the process of deliberation a sufficient number changes to reach the required 9:3 or 10:2 for a verdict. Is not there still a lingering doubt about that verdict? Is it not clear that the safeguard of unanimity operates in this context to make it far more likely that guilt is established beyond a reasonable doubt?

* * *

[Justice Blackmun filed a concurring opinion. Justices Brennan, Stewart, and Marshall filed dissenting opinions.]

Note on Unanimity

Go back to *Duncan* and examine the reasons that the Court gave for holding that the right to jury trial is fundamental and binding on the states. Do these reasons suggest that the Court should be more concerned with the punishment that triggers the right or with the manner in which the jury is selected? If protection against eccentric or biased judges and vindictive prosecutions underlies the right, what would common sense tell you about the likelihood that a six-person, as opposed

a. Note the split of the Court in *Apodaca.* Eight Justices agreed that the Fourteenth Amendment incorporated all aspects of the Sixth Amendment jury trial right. Justice Powell alone advanced the theory of a different conception of jury trials for federal and state courts. Five Justices (the dissenters and Justice Powell) agreed that the Sixth Amendment requires unanimity. So why didn't Apodaca win?

to a twelve-person jury, would provide such protection? If a 10–2 verdict is acceptable, can you think of any good reason why a 7–5 verdict would not be acceptable? Do you think that conviction or acquittal by a divided jury is consistent with the values that make the jury trial right fundamental? If a state provided a five-person jury but required unanimity, are you as sure as the *Ballew* Court that this would have been worse than a 10–2 verdict?

One of the strongest arguments against unanimous verdicts is that it forces compromises. For example, if ten jurors decide a defendant is guilty of first degree murder and two believe that the defendant is innocent, the jury if required to be unanimous might compromise on second degree murder as an alternative to continued deliberation. Critics of unanimity argue that such compromise is acceptable in ordinary political life, but not in litigation.[19] Do you find this criticism persuasive? If so, re-examine what happens when a 9–3 or 10–2 jury verdict is accepted. Does the absence of a unanimity requirement promote deliberation? It does remove the need for some compromises. But is a compromise by a jury that follows the instructions of a court (requiring each juror to support the verdict) an evil? Is it arguable that any compromise by a unanimous jury is a final agreement by all jurors on a just verdict?

Remember that *Apodaca* dealt only with state jury verdicts. Fed.R.Crim.P. 31(a) requires jury verdicts in federal criminal cases to be unanimous. Most states still require unanimous verdicts as well. Recently, however, some mistrials due to hung juries in high profile prosecutions have spurred a movement in some states to permit non-unanimous verdicts.

Waiver

In unanimity jurisdictions, should the prosecution and defense be able to stipulate in advance that they agree to be bound by a non-unanimous verdict? The court in United States v. Ullah, 976 F.2d 509 (9th Cir.1992), declared that "the right to a unanimous verdict is so important that it is one of the few rights of a criminal defendant that cannot, under any circumstances, be waived." But if the parties can agree to opt for a bench trial and dispense with the jury entirely, why can't they agree to a non-unanimous verdict? See Sanchez v. United States, 782 F.2d 928 (11th Cir.1986)(permitting waiver of unanimity, but only in situations where the jury has been deliberating and is unable to come to an agreement).

Unanimity About What? Schad v. Arizona

In federal courts and in most state courts, jurors have to be unanimous, but it is sometimes difficult to determine what they have to be unanimous about. For example, if two findings could each lead to the same guilty verdict, must the jury be unanimous about at least one of the findings, or only about the ultimate conclusion that the defendant is guilty? In Schad v. Arizona, 501 U.S. 624 (1991), Schad was charged with first-degree murder. In Arizona, the crime of first-degree murder encompasses both premeditated murder and felony murder. At trial, the prosecutor advanced both premeditated and felony murder theories, and offered proof under both theories. The jury returned a general verdict of guilty of first degree murder. Schad argued that there was no showing that the

---

19. For an argument against unanimity premised on political theory, see Jacobson, The
     Unanimous Verdict: Politics and the Jury Trial, 1977 Wash.U.L.Q. 39.

jury had agreed unanimously that he had committed felony murder, nor could it be determined that the jurors were unanimous about premeditated murder. The Court reasoned that Schad's argument was really addressed to whether the state could permissibly characterize several alternative actions and mental states as a single crime. The Court stated that the issue "is one of the permissible limits in defining criminal conduct, * * * not one of jury unanimity." The Court held that Arizona did not violate defendant's due process rights by grouping felony murder and premeditated murder as two alternative means of committing the single crime of first-degree murder.

Thereafter, in Richardson v. United States, 526 U.S. 813 (1999), the Court construed the Continuing Criminal Enterprise statute in light of the unanimity requirement. The CCE statute defines "continuing criminal enterprise" as involving a "violat[ion]" of the drug statutes where "such violation is a part of a continuing series of violations." Three violations are considered to be a "series." The trial judge refused Richardson's proposal to instruct the jury that it must "unanimously agree on which three acts constituted [the] series of violations." Instead, the judge instructed the jurors that they "must unanimously agree that the defendant committed at least three federal narcotics offenses," while adding, "[y]ou do not ... have to agree as to the particular three or more federal narcotics offenses committed by the defendant." The Supreme Court, in a 6–3 opinion by Justice Breyer, held that the statute's phrase "series of violations" did not refer to one element, but rather created several elements, namely the several "violations," with respect to each of which the jury must agree unanimously. In other words, the statute unlike that in *Schad* did not provide for alternative means of violating a single element, but rather set forth separate elements, on which the jury of course must be unanimous. Justice Kennedy, joined by Justices O'Connor and Ginsburg, dissented.

Suppose that a court gave a twelve-person jury a special verdict form and six jurors agreed that a defendant was guilty of premeditation but not of felony murder, while the other six agreed that the defendant was guilty of felony murder but not of premeditation. Could the court add six votes on one theory with six votes on the other to find that the jury had found the defendant guilty? A general verdict form permits a jury to aggregate votes in just this way. At what point must a jury agree on basic elements before finding a defendant guilty? Which elements are basic? See Viveros v. State, 606 P.2d 790 (Alaska 1980)(court reverses where it is uncertain whether jury agreed on one finding).

In United States v. Holley, 942 F.2d 916 (5th Cir.1991), the defendant was tried on a perjury count that set forth several statements, each alleged to be perjurious. The jury was not instructed that it had to agree unanimously that at least one particular statement in the count was perjurious. A general verdict of guilty was returned. The court of appeals reversed the conviction on the ground that the defendant had been deprived of his right to a unanimous verdict: each juror found that the defendant had committed perjury, but there was no indication that they had all agreed that any particular statement was an act of perjury. The court distinguished *Schad* as a case in which the jury was allowed to choose among alternative means of committing a crime, whereas the prosecution in *Holley* sought to group several different acts in a single count; in *Schad* it could at least be said that the jury was unanimous that the defendant, when he acted on a certain occasion, was committing a crime. Is the court in *Holley* relying on the distinction between *actus reus* and *mens rea*? Why should that distinction make a difference in terms of unanimity?

3. The Interplay Between Size and Unanimity

The interplay between the constitutionally sufficient six-person jury, and the issue of unanimity was delineated in Burch v. Louisiana, 441 U.S. 130 (1979). In an opinion by Justice Rehnquist, the Court held that "conviction by a nonunanimous six-person jury in a state criminal trial for a nonpetty offense deprives an accused of his constitutional right to trial by jury." The Court conceded that drawing lines was difficult, but found it essential to draw the line somewhere. It concluded that use of nonunanimous six-person juries violated the right to jury trial. There were no dissents.

In *Burch,* Justice Rehnquist stated that the "near-uniform judgment of the Nation," as reflected by the fact that only two states permitted non-unanimous verdicts by a six-person jury, "provides a useful guide in delimiting the line between those jury practices that are constitutionally permissible and those that are not." But when *Apodaca* was decided, the vast majority of states required unanimous verdicts, and still do. How, then, did *Apodaca* get decided the way it did?

D. JURY SELECTION AND COMPOSITION

1. The Jury Pool

The Sixth Amendment assures the defendant "an impartial jury of the State and district wherein the crime shall have been committed." This language, with its emphasis on both the impartial and community character of the jury, has served as a touchstone in the regulation of the pool from which the petit jury is drawn. (The body of candidates from which the petit jury is drawn is also known as the "venire"). Another constitutional regulation on selection of the jury pool is the Equal Protection Clause, which prohibits exclusion from the jury pool on the basis of suspect classification such as race.

In Glasser v. United States, 315 U.S. 60, 85–86 (1942), the Court observed as follows:

> [The jury selection process] must always accord with the fact that the proper functioning of the jury system, and, indeed, our democracy itself, requires that the jury be a "body truly representative of the community," and not the organ of any special group or class. If that requirement is observed, the officials charged with choosing federal jurors may exercise some discretion to the end that competent jurors may be called. But they must not allow the desire for competent jurors to lead them into selections which do not comport with the concept of the jury as a cross-section of the community.

Thus, the selection of the jury panel must be unbiased; it must generate a panel representing a cross-section of the community. Selection of jurors cannot violate principles of equal protection. And finally, each individual juror must be impartial, unbiased and free from outside influences.

2. The Fair Cross–Section Requirement and the Equal Protection Clause

Two Separate Rights

As stated above, there are two separate constitutional provisions that can impact on selection of the pool from which a jury is drawn. The Equal Protection Clause prohibits the selection of jurors on the basis of race, sex, or any other suspect classification. Application of equal protection standards to jury selection is similar to the equal protection law applied in other contexts. See, e.g., Castaneda v. Partida, 430 U.S. 482 (1977) (in order to establish a prima facie equal protection violation, the defendant "must show that the procedure employed resulted in substantial underrepresentation of his race or of the identifiable group to which he belongs"; the burden then shifts to the state to rebut the inference of discrimination by showing neutral selection criteria); United States v. Esquivel, 75 F.3d 545 (9th Cir.1996) (rejecting a challenge that selection of jury panel violated equal protection due to underrepresentation of Hispanics; defendant failed to show statistical disparity or intent to discriminate).[20] The Sixth Amendment independently requires that the jury be chosen from a fair cross-section of the community. The Supreme Court has used both constitutional protections to attempt to assure representative jury selection procedures.

The goals of the two constitutional guarantees are somewhat different, though overlapping, in the context of selection of the jury pool. The goal of the Equal Protection Clause is of course to prevent government discrimination on the basis of race, sex, or other suspect classification. The goal of the fair cross-section requirement is to assure that the defendant get the benefit of an impartial jury. As one court put it, the purposes of the fair cross-section requirement include "ensuring that the common sense judgment of the community will act as a hedge against overzealous prosecutions; preserving public confidence in the criminal justice system; and furthering the notion that participation in the administration of justice is a part of one's civic responsibility." United States v. Raszkiewicz, 169 F.3d 459 (7th Cir.1999).

Early Cases Establishing the Rights

The first challenges to the selection of the jury developed under the rubric of the Fourteenth Amendment in response to race-related exclusions. In Strauder v. West Virginia, 100 U.S. 303 (1879), the Court struck down a state statute that excluded African–Americans from grand and petit jury service as violative of the Fourteenth Amendment's Equal Protection Clause.

In subsequent challenges to state systems that were administered so as to preclude African–Americans from jury service, the Court ruled that a system that provides the opportunity to discriminate, and that generates a low number of participating African–Americans (evidencing discrimination) is invalid. See, e.g., Smith v. Texas, 311 U.S. 128 (1940)(grand jury lists of sixteen people were drawn by 3–5 jury commissioners; few African–Americans served as jurors).

---

20. Equal protection standards also regulate the use of peremptory challenges to prospective jurors. See the discussion of Batson v.   Kentucky and its progeny, infra in this Chapter.

The Court first recognized the impact of the exclusion of a non-race-related class in a civil case, Thiel v. Southern Pacific Co., 328 U.S. 217 (1946). The Court held that the deliberate and intentional exclusion of daily wage earners from a federal court jury panel violated the fair cross-section requirement—no violation of equal protection could be found in the exclusion of daily wage earners. See, e.g., United States v. Esquivel, 75 F.3d 545 (9th Cir.1996) (in contrast to an equal protection violation, "a prima facie case for establishing a Sixth Amendment, fair cross section violation does not require the appellant to prove discriminatory intent or require that the appellant be a member of the distinct, excluded group").

In *Thiel*, the jury commissioner and clerk used a city directory to identify and exclude daily wage earners from a federal court jury panel. The Court ruled that although a judge may exclude a person from jury service when participation entails a financial hardship, complete exclusion in the absence of such a finding is forbidden.

In the same year, the Court ruled in Ballard v. United States, 329 U.S. 187 (1946), that women constitute a cognizable class that could not be excluded intentionally and systematically from federal jury service in a state in which women were eligible for jury service. Then in Hernandez v. Texas, 347 U.S. 475 (1954), the Court relied upon the fair cross-section requirement to strike down a selection process that discriminated on a non-racial basis.

Fair Cross–Section Requirement Does Not Apply to Petit Jury

In recognizing the existence of cognizable classes other than race under the Fair Cross–Section Clause, the Court has been careful to delineate the scope of the defendant's challenge. Both *Thiel* and *Ballard* emphasized that a defendant has no right to challenge a particular jury as failing to represent all social, economic, and political groups. Rather, the defendant is restricted to challenging the selection *procedure* as systematically excluding a cognizable group. That is, the fair cross-section requirement is applicable to the jury *pool*, but not to the ultimate petit jury that hears the defendant's case. This was confirmed in Holland v. Illinois, 493 U.S. 474 (1990), where a five-person majority explicitly held that the fair cross-section requirement does not apply to the petit jury. Consequently, the Sixth Amendment did not protect the defendant, who was white, from the prosecutor's discriminatory use of peremptory challenges to exclude African–Americans from the petit jury. Justice Scalia, writing for the Court, stressed that it would be all but impossible to form a petit jury that mirrored the community.[21]

Standing to Object to a Fair Cross–Section Violation

TAYLOR v. LOUISIANA

Supreme Court of the United States, 1975.
419 U.S. 522.

Mr. Justice White **delivered the opinion of the Court.**

[The Louisiana Code provided that a woman should not be selected for jury

21. The impact of *Holland* has been severely curtailed by the Court's use of the Equal Protection Clause to limit the exercise of peremptory challenges. Thus, the Equal Protec-

tion Clause, and not the Fair Cross–Section Clause, imposes restrictions on the composition of the petit jury. See the discussion of Batson v. Kentucky, infra.

service unless she had previously filed a written declaration of her desire to be subject to jury service. Appellant, a male, alleged that the statute violated his Sixth and Fourteenth Amendment right to a jury drawn from a fair cross-section of the community.]

II

The Louisiana jury-selection system does not disqualify women from jury service, but in operation its conceded systematic impact is that only a very few women, grossly disproportionate to the number of eligible women in the community, are called for jury service. In this case, no women were on the venire from which the petit jury was drawn. The issue we have, therefore, is whether a jury-selection system which operates to exclude from jury service an identifiable class of citizens constituting 53% of eligible jurors in the community comports with the Sixth and Fourteenth Amendments.

The State first insists that Taylor, a male, has no standing to object to the exclusion of women from his jury. But Taylor's claim is that he was constitutionally entitled to a jury drawn from a venire constituting a fair cross section of the community and that the jury that tried him was not such a jury by reason of the exclusion of women. Taylor was not a member of the excluded class; but there is no rule that claims such as Taylor presents may be made only by those defendants who are members of the group excluded from jury service. Taylor, in the case before us, was similarly entitled to tender and have adjudicated the claim that the exclusion of women from jury service deprived him of the kind of factfinder to which he was constitutionally entitled.

III

The background against which this case must be decided includes our holding in Duncan v. Louisiana that the Sixth Amendment's provision for jury trial is made binding on the States by virtue of the Fourteenth Amendment. Our inquiry is whether the presence of a fair cross section of the community on venires, panels, or lists from which petit juries are drawn is essential to the fulfillment of the Sixth Amendment's guarantee of an impartial jury trial in criminal prosecutions.

* * *

We accept the fair-cross-section requirement as fundamental to the jury trial guaranteed by the Sixth Amendment and are convinced that the requirement has solid foundation. The purpose of a jury is to guard against the exercise of arbitrary power—to make available the commonsense judgment of the community as a hedge against the overzealous or mistaken prosecutor and in preference to the professional or perhaps over-conditioned or biased response of a judge. This prophylactic vehicle is not provided if the jury pool is made up of only special segments of the populace or if large, distinctive groups are excluded from the pool. Community participation in the administration of the criminal law, moreover, is not only consistent with our democratic heritage but is also critical to public confidence in the fairness of the criminal justice system. Restricting jury service to only special groups or excluding identifiable segments playing major roles in the community cannot be squared with the constitutional concept of jury trial. * * *

IV

We are also persuaded that the fair-cross-section requirement is violated by the systematic exclusion of women, who in the judicial district involved here amounted to 53% of the citizens eligible for jury service. This conclusion necessarily entails the judgment that women are sufficiently numerous and distinct from men and that if they are systematically eliminated from jury panels, the Sixth Amendment's fair-cross-section requirement cannot be satisfied. * * *

* * *

V

There remains the argument that women as a class serve a distinctive role in society and that jury service would so substantially interfere with that function that the state has ample justification for excluding women from service unless they volunteer, even though the result is that almost all jurors are men. * * *

The States are free to grant exemptions from jury service to individuals in case of special hardship or incapacity and to those engaged in particular occupations the uninterrupted performance of which is critical to the community's welfare. * * * A system excluding all women, however, is a wholly different matter. It is untenable to suggest these days that it would be a special hardship for each and every woman to perform jury service or that society cannot spare *any* women from their present duties. This may be the case with many, and it may be burdensome to sort out those who should be exempted from those who should serve. But that task is performed in the case of men, and the administrative convenience in dealing with women as a class is insufficient justification for diluting the quality of community judgment represented by the jury in criminal trials.

* * *

Standards for Prima Facie Violation: Duren v. Missouri

In Duren v. Missouri, 439 U.S. 357 (1979), the Court held that in order to establish a prima facie violation of the fair cross-section requirement, a defendant must show three things: (1) the group excluded from the jury array is a distinctive group within the community; (2) the representation of the group in the venire from which jurors are selected is not fair and reasonable in relation to the number of such persons in the community; and (3) this underrepresentation is the result of a systematic exclusion of the group in the jury selection process. At that point, the burden shifts to the state to show that the inclusion of the underrepresented group would be "incompatible with a significant state interest." On the facts, the Court found that Duren had made out a prima facie case by showing that 54% of the adult inhabitants of the county were women, while only 15% of the persons placed on venires were women, and a woman could decline jury service by simply not reporting for jury duty while a man did not have the same option. Justice White, writing for the Court, stated that an exemption tailored to women who could not leave their children might effectuate a state interest sufficient to satisfy the fair cross-section requirement, but that no such limited exemption was operative in this case.

Distinctive Groups for Fair Cross–Section Purposes

Consider again the Court's holding in *Thiel,* forbidding the systematic exclusion of daily wage earners from a federal jury. *Thiel* relied on the federal supervisory power, not on the Sixth Amendment. After *Duren,* is a constitutional challenge alleging that blue collar workers are excluded from state juries likely to succeed? Do blue collar workers comprise a cognizable class for purposes of constitutional analysis? Would you distinguish blue collar workers from women? From young adults? See Anaya v. Hansen, 781 F.2d 1 (1st Cir.1986)(neither young adults nor blue collar workers constituted a cognizable group for cross-section analysis).

The court in United States v. Fletcher, 965 F.2d 781 (9th Cir.1992), set forth a test, followed by many courts, for determining whether a group is "distinctive" under *Duren*:

> [A] defendant must show (1) that the group is defined and limited by some factor (i.e., that the group has a definite composition such as by race or sex); (2) that a common thread or basic similarity in attitude, ideas, or experience runs through the group; and (3) that there is a community of interests among members of the group such that the group's interest cannot be adequately represented if the group is excluded from the jury selection process.

Applying this three-factor test, the *Fletcher* court held that college students are not a distinctive group for fair cross-section purposes:

> The group of individuals we call "college students" is no more capable of fitting into a pigeon hole than the group we call "young adults." The group is not defined by any "limiting factor"—anyone may be a college student. Nor is there a common thread of "attitude" or "experience" that runs through the group, beyond the fact that every member spends a certain percentage of his or her time in a classroom. It is true that the privilege of a college education continues to be enjoyed only by a minority of our citizens. Nevertheless, the variety of groups that are represented in college classrooms is vast and growing, so that the economic, geographic, racial, sexual, political, and religious demographics of that minority are nearly as diverse as those of the nation itself. It is farfetched to suggest that the college experience could coalesce the diverse points of view that are the necessary product of such divergent experiences into a single "community of interest" that will go unrepresented on a jury if there are no "college students" among its members.[22]

While college students do not have a sufficient community of interest to be distinctive, what about Grateful Dead fans? Catholics? See also Brewer v. Nix, 963 F.2d 1111 (8th Cir.1992)(people over 65 are not a distinctive group for cross-section purposes); United States v. Raszkiewicz, 169 F.3d 459 (7th Cir.1999) (exclusion from jury venires of Native Americans who live on reservations did not violate the fair-cross section requirement because they are not a distinctive group). Would a blue ribbon jury pool—i.e., one composed of specially trained people—be constitutional today?

22. See also People v. Bartolomeo, 126 A.D.2d 375, 513 N.Y.S.2d 981 (1987) (18–20 year-olds are not a distinctive group for fair cross-section analysis).

Proper Sources for the Jury Pool

If a state can show a truly random selection process, and if the state uses a source (or sources) of jury names—e.g., driver's license lists as well as voting lists—that is likely to include most members of a community, most challenges to selection of the jury pool can be avoided.[23]

Some citizens may decline to register to vote to avoid jury service. Contentions have been made that certain groups are especially likely not to register to vote and therefore that voter lists do not produce a cross-section of the community. However, as long as voter lists do not have racial identifications, and are used as part of some non-discriminatory selection scheme, their use is likely to be sustained. See United States v. Lewis, 10 F.3d 1086 (4th Cir. 1993)(use of voter lists is presumptively proper).[24] See also People v. Hicks, 59 A.D.2d 251, 399 N.Y.S.2d 316 (1977)(persons who do not register to vote are not a cognizable class of qualified jurors, and no proof was shown that the jury selection system based on voter lists was the product of intentional and systematic exclusion of African–Americans); United States v. Di Pasquale, 864 F.2d 271 (3d Cir.1988)(even if there is statistical underrepresentation of distinctive groups, the use of voter and drivers lists to obtain a jury pool is permissible and does not constitute systematic exclusion). In fact, underrepresentation should be rare if voting lists are used. But if a state refuses to follow clear, visible selection procedures, invalidation on fair cross-section grounds becomes far more likely.[25]

23. The Federal Jury Selection and Service Act of 1968, 28 U.S.C.A. §§ 1861–69, provides that Federal district courts must devise a plan for random selection of grand and petit jurors, and sets forth procedures for drawing names from a master wheel and summoning, qualifying, and impaneling jurors for service. The Act calls for the use of voter registration lists or lists of actual voters and "some other source or sources of names in addition to voter lists where necessary to foster the policy and protect the rights" set forth in the Act. The Act permits criminal defendants to move to dismiss the indictment or stay proceedings "on the ground of substantial failure to comply" with the provisions of the Act.

An en banc court held in United States v. Gometz, 730 F.2d 475 (7th Cir.1984), that the federal statute did not require a district court clerk to take steps to assure that the jury pool is a representative cross-section of the community when a large percentage of the prospective jurors who are sent qualification forms fail to return the forms. The court reasoned that nothing in the statute indicates a congressional intent to compel inclusion of "anti-authoritarian" personalities in a jury pool, and that as long as the number of responses is high enough to generate a sufficient number of names for the jury wheel, the clerk need not take measures to correct a low response rate. See also United States v. Barry, 71 F.3d 1269 (7th Cir.1995) (upholding the federal statute's exclusion from service of persons who have felony charges pending against them: "We are not convinced that alleged felons comprise a distinctive group. They have in common that they may have run afoul of the criminal justice system. However, there are many and varied ways to do that * * *. It is possible that an alleged tax evader may have something in common with a charged kidnapper, but the remote chance that he might, does not support a finding that the group is distinct.").

24. For an argument that the Constitution requires multiple source lists, see Kairys, Kadane & Lehoczky, Jury Representativeness: A Mandate for Multiple Source Lists, 65 Calif.L.Rev. 776 (1977).

25. Jurisdictions vary on whether a defendant has a right to inspect and copy jury lists. In Test v. United States, 420 U.S. 28 (1975), the Court held that a federal criminal defendant has the right to inspect in order to prepare challenges to petit and grand jury selection procedures. In some cases—e.g., treason or capital cases—statutes may require that the defendant be served with a list. See 18 U.S.C.A. § 3432.

Generally a defendant has not been given access to "jury books" or information on juries prepared by the government. See, e.g., Hamer v. United States, 259 F.2d 274 (9th Cir.1958). Should the *Brady* doctrine—which requires the prosecutor to disclose exculpatory information, as discussed in the discovery chapter, supra,— be read as requiring the government to share its information on jurors with the defense?

Everybody Is Dead in Hartford

United States v. Jackman, 46 F.3d 1240 (2d Cir.1995), was a notable case in which the use of voter lists failed to provide a fair cross-section in the jury pool. Hartford, Connecticut is a city with a large minority population. However, for some reason, the use of voter registration lists resulted in no resident of Hartford being included in the jury wheel used by the federal district court in Connecticut. Not surprisingly, there was a substantial underrepresentation of minorities in the jury venires in the district court. Subsequently, it was discovered that no jury questionnaires were sent to Hartford residents because a computer programming error had caused the letter "d" in "Hartford" to communicate to the computer that all potential jurors from Hartford were deceased and thus unavailable for jury service. The court in *Jackman* reversed the defendant's conviction because the procedure used to select the venire from which the defendant's jury was drawn violated the fair cross-section requirement. The court emphasized that a violation of the cross-section guarantee can be found even if the government operated its selection procedures in good faith.

Exemptions

Assuming that random selection procedures are used to call jurors, the questions that almost surely will arise will involve who can be excused from jury service on hardship grounds. Can all lawyers be excused? Can all wage earners? Can all single parents? Remember that exclusion of these people would be at their request only. Thus, their rights to serve would be unimpaired. But would the criminal defendant be permitted to complain about the diminishment of chances to have a real cross-section of the community? How would you approach the problem of excusing jurors upon request?

3. *Voir Dire and Court Control*

The establishment of a jury venire representing a fair cross-section of the community, and selected without violating principles of equal protection, is only the first stage in the jury selection procedure. The second stage, also regulated by these constitutional guarantees, is to assure that the actual trial jury is impartial and fairly chosen. Because preconceived notions about the case at issue threaten impartiality, each juror must be free of bias. Accordingly, in a process called voir dire, meaning "to speak the truth," prospective jurors are subject to two kinds of challenges: an unlimited number of challenges for cause based on a "narrowly specified, provable and legally cognizable basis of partiality," and a specified (by statute or rule) number of peremptory challenges which, at least until 1986, could be exercised for any reason or no reason—though as we will see the use of peremptory challenges has been limited by Batson v. Kentucky and its progeny, infra.

Voir dire may be conducted in any of several methods: 1) by addressing all questions to the panel at one time, or by addressing each juror individually; 2) by having the judge put questions to the jurors or by allowing counsel to ask the questions; and 3) by allowing a broad inquiry into juror attitudes or by limiting the number and scope of questions that may be asked to the narrow issues presented in a specific case. Voir dire vests broad authority in the trial judge.[26] In many jurisdictions the manner in which voir dire is conducted is left up to the judge.[27] In all jurisdictions, the judge has discretion to consider the relevance of the questions in a particular case, and has the right to refuse to allow and to strike questions deemed irrelevant or inappropriate. The judge's relevance determinations are fact-specific; they frequently turn on the particular aspects of the case to be tried. In most instances the appellate court will defer to the trial court, believing that the trial judge has a better feel than an appellate court for the need to put questions to prospective jurors. But the Constitution requires that some inquiries be made at the request of a defendant if there is to be effective voir dire.

Questions Concerning Prejudice: Ham v. South Carolina

In Ham v. South Carolina, 409 U.S. 524 (1973), a young, bearded African–American, active in the civil rights movement, was charged with possession of marijuana. He alleged, in defense, that police officials had framed him because of his civil rights activities. During voir dire, he requested that the trial judge ask four questions relating to potential juror prejudice: two related to prejudice against African–Americans, the third related to prejudice against individuals with beards, and the fourth related to pretrial publicity. The trial judge refused to ask any of the questions. The Supreme Court granted review to consider whether the refusal violated Ham's constitutional rights.

Justice Rehnquist, writing for the Court, declared as follows:

[W]e think that the Fourteenth Amendment required the judge in this case to interrogate the jurors upon the subject of racial prejudice. South Carolina law permits challenges for cause, and authorizes the trial judge to conduct *voir dire* examination of potential jurors. The State having created this statutory framework for the selection of juries, the essential fairness required by the Due Process Clause of the Fourteenth Amendment requires that under the facts

---

26. See, e.g., Fed.R.Crim.P. 24(a)(court *may* allow attorneys to question jurors). Some jurisdictions give parties or their counsel a right to conduct voir dire. See State v. Burns, 173 Conn. 317, 377 A.2d 1082 (1977).

United States v. Ible, 630 F.2d 389 (5th Cir.1980), expresses concern that "voir dire may have little meaning if it is not conducted at least in part by counsel. The 'federal' practice of almost exclusive voir dire examination by the court does not take into account the fact that it is parties, rather than the court, who have a full grasp of the nuances and the strength and weaknesses of the case." The court added in a footnote the following thought:

During the past fifteen to twenty years there has been a trend by federal district judges to conduct the voir dire questioning themselves. Such a course was a result of many abuses by counsel including the consumption of excessive time periods and delving into improper areas during voir dire examination. More recently, records reviewed in this court reflect a new pattern by trial courts. The trial judge will explain the nature of the case in general terms,

point out the parties and counsel, cover the most basic points of law (burden of proof, presumption of innocence, right to remain silent, etc.), explain the procedures and schedule to be followed and then turn the questioning over to trial counsel. We encourage this approach. Trial judges have a duty to control this and every other aspect of the trial, but all proper areas of inquiry must be covered fairly.

See McMillion, Advocating Voir Dire Reform, 77 A.B.A.J., Nov. 1991, p. 114 (discussing legislation proposed in the Senate to give attorneys a limited right to conduct questioning of jurors in the federal courts).

27. Although the trial judge exercises control over voir dire, certain subjects, such as the physical or mental capacity of persons to serve as jurors, must be the subject of inquiry where it appears from the information supplied by the prospective jurors themselves that there may be a problem. See United States v. Rucker, 557 F.2d 1046 (4th Cir.1977).

Voir dire is important enough that the defendant has a right to have his lawyer present. See Eason v. State, 563 S.W.2d 945 (Tex.Cr. App.1978).

Basic fairness of due process req'd Δ to be permitted to question potential Jurors about race.

shown by this record the petitioner be permitted to have the jurors interrogated on the issue of racial bias.

* * * [T]he trial judge was not required to put the question in any particular form, or to ask any particular number of questions on the subject, simply because requested to do so by petitioner. * * * In this context, either of the brief, general questions urged by the petitioner would appear sufficient to focus the attention of prospective jurors on any racial prejudice they might entertain.

The third of petitioner's proposed questions was addressed to the fact that he wore a beard. While we cannot say that prejudice against people with beards might not have been harbored by one or more of the potential jurors in this case, this is the beginning and not the end of the inquiry as to whether the Fourteenth Amendment required the trial judge to interrogate the prospective jurors about such possible prejudice. Given the traditionally broad discretion accorded to the trial judge in conducting *voir dire,* and our inability to constitutionally distinguish possible prejudice against beards from a host of other possible similar prejudices, we do not believe the petitioner's constitutional rights were violated when the trial judge refused to put this question. The inquiry as to racial prejudice derives its constitutional stature from * * * a principal purpose as well as from the language of those who adopted the Fourteenth Amendment. The trial judge's refusal to inquire as to particular bias against beards, after his inquiries as to bias in general, does not reach the level of a constitutional violation.

Δ did not have rt to question potential jurors about their prejudices about people w/ beards

* * *

Ham's holding, that due process required the judge to inquire into the prospective jurors' possible racial prejudice, was distinguished in the following case.

RISTAINO v. ROSS

Supreme Court of the United States, 1976.
424 U.S. 589.

[An African–American, charged in a state court with violent crimes against a white security guard, requested the trial court to ask during voir dire a question specifically directed to possible racial prejudice on the part of any prospective jurors. The trial court refused and was affirmed on appeal. The Supreme Court was reviewing a federal court of appeals' decision granting habeas relief on the basis of *Ham.*]

Δ desired to question potential jurors about racial prejudice.

T.C refused
A.C affirmed
S.C reversed reversed
A.C

Mr. Justice Powell delivered the opinion of the Court.

* * *

II

The Constitution does not always entitle a defendant to have questions posed during *voir dire* specifically directed to matters that conceivably might prejudice veniremen against him. *Voir dire* is conducted under the supervision of the court, and a great deal must, of necessity, be left to its sound discretion. This is so because the determination of impartiality, in which demeanor plays such an important part, is particularly within the province of the trial judge. Thus, the State's obligation to the defendant to impanel an impartial jury generally can be satisfied by less than an inquiry into a specific prejudice feared by the defendant.

Ct must get wide discretion to run voir dire

In *Ham,* however, we recognized that some cases may present circumstances in which an impermissible threat to the fair trial guaranteed by due process is posed by a trial court's refusal to question prospective jurors specifically about racial prejudice during *voir dire*. *Ham* involved a Negro tried in South Carolina courts for possession of marihuana. He was well known in the locale of his trial as a civil rights activist, and his defense was that law enforcement officials had framed him on the narcotics charge to "get him" for those activities. Despite the circumstances, the trial judge denied Ham's request that the court-conducted *voir dire* include questions specifically directed to racial prejudice. We reversed * * *.

By its terms *Ham* did not announce a requirement of universal applicability. * * *

The circumstances in *Ham* strongly suggested the need for *voir dire* to include specific questioning about racial prejudice. Ham's defense was that he had been framed because of his civil rights activities. His prominence in the community as a civil rights activist, if not already known to veniremen, inevitably would have been revealed to the members of the jury in the course of his presentation of that defense. Racial issues therefore were inextricably bound up with the conduct of the trial. Further, Ham's reputation as a civil rights activist and the defense he interposed were likely to intensify any prejudice that individual members of the jury might harbor. In such circumstances we deemed a *voir dire* that included questioning specifically directed to racial prejudice, when sought by Ham, necessary to meet the constitutional requirement that an impartial jury be impaneled.

a. Although we hold that *voir dire* questioning directed to racial prejudice was not constitutionally required, the wiser course generally is to propound appropriate questions de-

We do not agree with the Court of Appeals that the need to question veniremen specifically about racial prejudice also rose to constitutional dimensions in this case.[a] The mere fact that the victim of the crimes alleged was a white man and the defendants were Negroes was less likely to distort the trial than were the special factors involved in *Ham*. The victim's status as a security officer, also relied upon by the Court of Appeals, was cited by respective defense counsel primarily as a separate source of prejudice, not as an aggravating racial factor, and the trial judge dealt with it by his question about law-enforcement affiliations. The circumstances thus did not suggest a significant likelihood that racial prejudice might infect Ross' trial. This was made clear to the trial judge when Ross was unable to support his motion concerning *voir dire* by pointing to racial factors such as existed in *Ham* or others of comparable significance. In these circumstances, the trial judge acted within the Constitution in determining that the demands of due process could be satisfied by his more generalized but thorough inquiry into the impartiality of the veniremen.

* * *

Mr. Justice Stevens took no part in the consideration or decision of this case.

[The opinion of Justice White, concurring in the result, is omitted.]

Mr. Justice Marshall, with whom Mr. Justice Brennan joins, dissenting.

* * * Today, in reversing the Court of Appeals' affirmance of the District Court's grant of a writ of habeas corpus, the Court emphatically confirms that the promises inherent in *Ham* * * * will not be fulfilled. * * * I can-

signed to identify racial prejudice if requested by the defendant. Under our supervisory power we would have required as much of a federal court faced with the circumstances here. * * *

not join in this confirmation. Accordingly, I respectfully dissent.

Limits on Mandatory Inquiry Into Race:
Rosales–Lopez v. United States

A divided Supreme Court held that there was no reversible error in a
district court's refusal to voir dire prospective jurors on their racial prejudices in
Rosales–Lopez v. United States, 451 U.S. 182 (1981). The defendant was a
Mexican National charged with smuggling aliens into the United States. The
trial judge asked jurors about attitudes toward "the alien problem" and aliens,
but not about racial or ethnic prejudices. Justice White, writing for a plurality
(Justices Stewart, Blackmun, and Powell) concluded that "it is usually best to
allow the defendant * * * to have the inquiry into racial or ethnic prejudice
pursued," but refused to require deference to defendants in all cases, reasoning
that an inquiry into racial matters may create an impression that justice turns
on race. The plurality said that prior cases "fairly imply that federal trial courts
must make such an inquiry when requested by a defendant accused of a violent
crime and where the defendant and the victim are members of different racial or
ethnic groups." The plurality said this was a supervisory rule for federal courts
and might be extended to other circumstances that suggest a reasonable possibility that racial or ethnic prejudice will affect the jury. Justice Rehnquist, joined
by Chief Justice Burger, concurred in the judgment, noting that the scope of voir
dire was necessarily dependent on the discretion of trial judges. Justice Stevens,
joined by Justices Brennan and Marshall, dissented and argued that "[m]uch as
we wish it were otherwise, we should acknowledge the fact that there are many
potential jurors who harbor strong prejudices against all members of certain
racial, religious or ethnic groups for no reason other than hostility to the group
as a whole."

Capital Defendants and Interracial Crime: Turner v. Murray

The Supreme Court departed from *Ristaino* in capital cases as it held in
Turner v. Murray, 476 U.S. 28 (1986), that a death sentence was invalid where a
trial judge refused an African–American defendant's request to question prospective jurors on racial prejudice in a prosecution charging him with murdering a
white man. Justice White wrote for the Court as it held that "a capital
defendant accused of an interracial crime is entitled to have prospective jurors
informed of the race of the victim and questioned on the issue of racial bias." He
noted that the trial judge retains discretion as to the form and number of
questions, including whether to question jurors individually or collectively, and
that a defendant cannot complain unless he has specifically asked for voir dire
questions concerning race.

Voir Dire and the Need to Screen for Prejudicial
Pretrial Publicity: Mu'Min v. Virginia

Chief Justice Rehnquist relied on *Ristaino* in his opinion for the Court in
Mu'Min v. Virginia, 500 U.S. 415 (1991), holding that a state trial judge is not
obliged to question prospective jurors individually about the contents of pretrial
publicity to which they may have been exposed. Mu'Min was a state prisoner

serving time for first-degree murder when he was charged with capital murder while on a work detail. The case was widely publicized, as it arose during the 1988 presidential campaign in which another case of a murder by a prisoner on furlough became an issue of national debate. Articles in the newspapers revealed details of the prior murder for which Mu'Min was incarcerated; the fact that the death penalty was unavailable at the time he committed the first murder; the denial of parole six times to Mu'Min; his confession to the crime charged; and criticism of the supervision of work gangs in Virginia.

Prior to trial, the defendant submitted proposed voir dire questions and asked for individual voir dire concerning the content of the publicity to which each prospective juror had been exposed. The trial judge rejected this request. The judge instead asked jurors whether they had heard or read anything about the case and whether they could be fair. Jurors who indicated that they had received information about the case were examined in panels of four; they were asked to respond if they had an opinion about the case, and if they could not enter the Jury box with an open mind. Prospective jurors who remained silent were considered to have asserted that they could remain fair.

As the Court had done in *Ristaino,* Chief Justice Rehnquist distinguished the requirements of the Due Process Clause concerning voir dire in state trials from the more extensive supervisory power of federal courts over federal trials. He reasoned that the need to weed out prejudicial pretrial publicity through voir dire was certainly no greater than the need to protect against racial or ethnic prejudice. He observed that if the contents of pretrial publicity must be the subject of inquiry, each juror would have to be voir dired individually, in order to prevent jurors from infecting each other with the publicity giving rise to the inquiry. In the Chief Justice's view, such a substantial burden on the system was not justified. He rejected the less burdensome alternative of written questions concerning the content of publicity to which each juror had been exposed, reasoning that written answers would not give counsel or the court access to the demeanor of jurors. Thus, because efforts to fully protect the defendant from jurors infected by pretrial publicity were too onerous, the constitution did not require the court to take less effective efforts.

Justice O'Connor wrote a concurring opinion. She concluded that a trial judge could realistically assess whether jurors could be fair without knowing what each juror had heard about a case. Justice O'Connor agreed with Justice Marshall's dissenting view that the trial judge could have done more, but ultimately concluded that "content" questions are not so indispensable to a fair trial that it violates the Constitution for a trial court to evaluate jurors without asking them.

Justice Marshall's dissenting opinion was joined by Justice Blackmun and Justice Stevens. His basic principle was that "[w]hen a prospective juror has been exposed to prejudicial pretrial publicity, a trial court cannot realistically assess the juror's impartiality without first establishing what the juror already has learned about the case."

Justice Kennedy also dissented. He contended that "the trial judge should have substantial discretion in conducting the voir dire, but, in my judgment, findings of impartiality must be based on something more than the mere silence of the individual in response to questions asked *en masse.*"

Voir Dire and Jurors' Feelings About the Death Penalty

The Court in Morgan v. Illinois, 504 U.S. 719 (1992), departed from its deferential analysis in *Mu'Min*. Morgan was sentenced to death under an Illinois procedure that first requires the jury unanimously to find at least one aggravating circumstance. After the jury determines that the defendant is death-eligible, it is instructed that it "should consider" all mitigating circumstances, and that it should impose the death sentence if "there are no mitigating factors sufficient to preclude" the death penalty in light of the aggravating factors.

During jury selection, Morgan requested that the judge ask prospective jurors whether they would automatically—regardless of any mitigating circumstances—impose the death penalty upon a finding that the defendant was death-eligible. The trial judge refused Morgan's request on the ground that each prospective juror had already been asked whether they would be able to follow the instructions on the law, and they were also asked whether they would be fair and impartial. Justice White, writing for the majority, found that this general questioning was insufficient under the Due Process Clause. He first noted the defendant's stake in voir dire:

> We deal here with petitioner's ability to exercise his * * * challenge for cause against those biased persons on the venire who as jurors would unwaveringly impose death after a finding of guilt. Were voir dire not available to lay bare the foundation of petitioner's challenge for cause against those prospective jurors who would always impose death following conviction, his right not to be tried by such jurors would be rendered * * * nugatory and meaningless * * *.

Justice White rejected the State's argument that general "fairness" and "follow the law" questions were sufficient to satisfy Morgan's right to inquire about a prospective juror's bias in favor of the death penalty:

> As to general questions of fairness and impartiality, such jurors could in all truth and candor respond affirmatively, personally confident that such dogmatic views are fair and impartial, while leaving the specific concern unprobed. More importantly, however, the belief that death should be imposed ipso facto upon conviction of a capital offense reflects directly on that individual's inability to follow the dictates of law. It may be that a juror could, in good conscience, swear to uphold that law and yet be unaware that maintaining such dogmatic beliefs about the death penalty would prevent him or her from doing so. A defendant on trial for his life must be permitted on voir dire to ascertain whether his prospective jurors function under such misconception. The risk that such jurors may have been empaneled in this case and infected petitioner's capital sentencing is unacceptable in light of the ease with which that risk could have been minimized. Petitioner was entitled, upon his request, to inquiry discerning those jurors who, even prior to the State's case-in-chief, had predetermined * * * whether to impose the death penalty.

Justice Scalia, joined by Chief Justice Rehnquist and Justice Thomas, dissented, accusing the majority of ignoring the deferential standard of review of voir dire in state courts, established in cases such as *Mu'Min*. He asserted that under *Mu'Min*, a defendant in a state trial is entitled to specific questions on voir dire "only if the failure to ask them would render his trial fundamentally unfair." He concluded that "[t]aking appropriate account of the opportunity for the trial court to observe and evaluate the demeanor of the veniremen, I see no basis for concluding that its finding that the 12 jurors were impartial was manifestly erroneous."

Voir Dire and the Federal Supervisory Power

As indicated in *Mu'Min,* the regulation of voir dire under the federal supervisory power is more rigorous than that required by the Constitution. Generally speaking, voir dire of jurors individually has been required in three situations in the Federal courts, although trial judges have significant discretion as to how to frame the questions. These three situations are: 1) where a case has racial overtones; 2) where the case involves matters concerning which the local community is known to harbor strong feelings, that may stop short of a need for a change of venue but may nonetheless affect the trial—such as child abuse or narcotics distribution; and 3) where testimony from law enforcement agents is important in the case and is likely to be overvalued. See generally United States v. Contreras–Castro, 825 F.2d 185 (9th Cir.1987), where the trial court's failure to inquire about a bias in favor of law enforcement officers was held reversible error because the government's entire case rested on the testimony of government agents. But see United States v. Lancaster, 96 F.3d 734 (4th Cir.1996) (en banc) (no per se right to have jurors questioned on whether they would lend greater credibility to the testimony of law enforcement officers based solely on their status: "If the district court must, on pain of reversal, ask the venire whether they would give heightened credibility to the testimony of a police officer when the Government's case depends on law enforcement testimony, logic compels that a similar question be asked whenever the Government's case depends on the testimony of any identifiable class of witnesses that might conceivably be thought by jurors to be inherently credible, be they firefighters, priests, physicians, attorneys, butchers, bakers, or candlestick makers.").

4. *Illustrative Voir Dire Problems*

The cases discussed above indicate that the Constitution and the supervisory power impose only minimal limits on the voir dire process. The policy question remains, however: how much voir dire should be permitted? Consider the scope of voir dire permitted in three specific situations. Is the scope sufficient? Too restrictive?

    a.   The facts in this case are brutal, but unfortunately such cases arise.

        The record discloses that early on the morning of July 9, 1974, a seventy-nine year old resident was forcibly removed from her home and taken to a nearby isolated swamp where she was raped and sodomized. Her body was discovered later the same day, face down in the swampy area. The medical evidence established that the cause of death was drowning. Christian was arrested and charged with the murder and rape on September 27, 1974.

The appellant, an African–American man, was convicted on the basis of circumstantial evidence that included testimony from a white woman neighbor, alleging that he had made sexual advances to her, which she refused, the morning of the crime. During voir dire, the trial court denied the appellant's request to ask questions relating to each venireperson's beliefs about the difference, if any, in the sexual drives of African–American and white men, and their attitudes toward interracial sexual relations. The appellate court reversed, holding that the circumstances established a need for inquiry into possible racial prejudices and that the defense questions were "suited to elicit the prospective jurors' racial prejudices in a manner germane to issues which would crystallize at trial." Commonwealth v. Christian, 480 Pa. 131, 389 A.2d 545, 549 (1978). Would you have permitted the inquiry? Was it required under *Ham?* Would you have permitted a question to female jurors, asking whether the prospective juror had ever been raped? Would you have permitted a question to all the prospective jurors about whether a family member had ever been raped? Are the privacy interests of the prospective jurors entitled to respect in the voir dire process?

b. If a defendant is contemplating an insanity defense, does she have a right to ask the prospective jurors whether they would be hostile to such a defense? See United States v. Allsup, 566 F.2d 68 (9th Cir.1977). Should we be concerned that counsel might be trying to argue her case during voir dire?

c. In a drug case, should the trial court permit inquiry into whether a prospective juror had ever used drugs? Or whether a family member had ever used drugs? Or whether the juror feels that drugs should be legalized?

d. In a white collar prosecution, should the jurors be questioned about whether they believe that rich people can "buy justice" or have some other unfair advantage in the criminal justice system?

5. Challenges for Cause

The scope of voir dire, discussed above, is intricately related to the possibility of challenging prospective jurors for cause. The rationale for expansive voir dire is that counsel needs information in order to make challenges for cause possible and meaningful.

The cognizable, specific biases that permit a challenge for cause are defined by statute. The typical statute permits such a challenge where the juror is of unsound mind or lacks the qualifications required by law; is related to a party; has served in a related case or on the indicting grand jury; or "is unable or unwilling to hear the case at issue fairly or impartially." ABA Standards for Criminal Justice, Trial by Jury 15–2.5 (1993). See 28 U.S.C. § 1866 (district court may exclude any person summoned for jury service "on the ground that such person may be unable to render impartial jury service").

a. *Jurors Who Cannot Be Excused for Cause*

Willingness and Ability to Follow Instructions as to the Death Penalty: Witherspoon v. Illinois and Adams v. Texas

Usually the question is whether a person *must* be excused for cause. However, one line of cases focuses on when persons may not be so excused. In Witherspoon v. Illinois, 391 U.S. 510 (1968), a statute provided that the prosecutor could challenge a juror for cause if the prospective juror stated "that he has conscientious scruples against capital punishment, or that he is opposed to the same." At Witherspoon's trial 47 veniremen, referred to by the trial court as "conscientious objectors," were successfully challenged on the basis of their negative attitude toward the death penalty. These jurors were not asked whether their scruples would invariably compel them to vote against capital punishment. Justice Stewart, writing for the Court, found that Witherspoon's death sentence was invalid because "in its role as arbiter of the punishment to be imposed, this jury fell woefully short of that impartiality to which the petitioner was entitled under the Sixth and Fourteenth Amendments." Justice Stewart reasoned as follows:

> A man who opposes the death penalty, no less than one who favors it, can make the discretionary judgment entrusted to him by the State and can thus obey the oath he takes as a juror. But a jury from which all such men have been excluded cannot perform the task demanded of it. * * *

> If the State had excluded only those prospective jurors who stated in advance of trial that they would not even consider returning a verdict of death, it could argue the resulting jury was simply neutral with respect to the penalty. But when it swept from the jury all who expressed conscientious or religious scruples against capital punishment and all who opposed it in principle, the State crossed the line of neutrality. In its quest for a jury capable of imposing the death penalty, the State produced a jury uncommonly willing to condemn a man to die. * * *

> [W]e hold that a sentence of death cannot be carried out if the jury that imposed or recommended it was chosen by excluding veniremen for cause simply because they voiced general objections to the death penalty or expressed conscientious or religious scruples against its infliction.

The Court in *Witherspoon* emphasized the narrowness of its holding. It did not prohibit the State from impanelling a "death-qualified" jury. It simply prohibited the exclusion for cause of a juror who expresses reservations about the death penalty but states that these reservations would not preclude a vote for the death penalty in the proper case.

Adams v. Texas, 448 U.S. 38 (1980), held unconstitutional a Texas procedure that excluded jurors in a capital case who were unable to take an oath that the mandatory penalty of death or imprisonment for life would not "affect [their] deliberations on any issue of fact." The Court said that *Witherspoon* and subsequent cases establish "the general proposition that a juror may not be challenged for cause based on his views about capital punishment unless those views would prevent or substantially impair the performance of his duties as a juror in accordance with his instructions and his oath. The State may insist, however, that jurors will consider and decide the facts impartially and conscientiously apply the law as charged by the court." In order to exclude a juror for cause, the state must show that the juror's beliefs about capital punishment would lead him to violate his oath or ignore the law, not simply that a juror might be affected by the possibility of the death penalty.

Death-Qualified Juries and Guilty Verdicts: Lockhart v. McCree and Buchanan v. Kentucky

In *Witherspoon*, the Court invalidated the defendant's death sentence, but it did not reverse the guilty verdict. The Court rejected the defendant's argument that a "death-qualified" jury would be biased in favor of the prosecution and therefore more likely to convict the defendant at the guilt phase. The basis for this rejection was that Witherspoon's empirical evidence was tentative and sketchy. The defendant in Lockhart v. McCree, 476 U.S. 162 (1986), made a similar argument with updated empirical evidence, and met a similar fate. The Court held that the Constitution does not prohibit the removal for cause, prior to the guilt phase of a bifurcated trial, of prospective jurors whose opposition to the death penalty is so strong that it would prevent or substantially impair the performance of their duties as jurors at the sentencing phase of the trial.

Writing for the Court, Justice Rehnquist found fault with various empirical studies relied upon by the lower courts. But, even assuming that the studies supported the argument that "death qualified" juries were more prone to convict than juries on which persons were not excluded because of their opposition to capital punishment, he reasoned that the Constitution does not bar exclusion of jurors who are unwilling or unable to perform one of their duties as jurors.

The Court refused to find that a jury is biased when it is "death qualified." Justice Rehnquist reasoned that an impartial jury is one that will conscientiously apply the law and find the facts, and there was no showing that any of the twelve jurors in the case under review was partial. Finally, the Court distinguished Witherspoon and Adams, finding that they involved a deliberate attempt to slant a jury to make the death penalty more likely, whereas the removal of "Witherspoon-excludables" serves the proper interest of attaining a jury that could impartially decide all of the issues in a case.

Justice Marshall, joined by Justices Brennan and Stevens, dissented. He argued that "the Court upholds a practice that allows a State a special advantage in those prosecutions where the charges are the most serious and the possible punishments, the most severe." The advantage is that "[t]he State's mere announcement that it intends to seek the death penalty if the defendant is found guilty of a capital offense will give the prosecution a license to empanel a jury especially likely to return that very verdict." Justice Blackmun concurred in the judgment without opinion.

Relying on McCree, the Supreme Court held, in Buchanan v. Kentucky, 483 U.S. 402 (1987), that a defendant as to whom the capital portion of an indictment was dismissed was not denied an impartial jury when he was tried together with another defendant facing a capital charge, by a jury from which prospective jurors unalterably opposed to the death penalty were excluded. Justice Blackmun's opinion for the Court reasoned that "McCree requires rejection of petitioner's claim that 'death qualification' violated his right to a jury selected from a representative cross-section of the community." He added that the state had not excluded the jurors opposed to the death penalty for arbitrary reasons unrelated to their ability to serve as jurors. Finally, he concluded that the state's interest in a joint trial is as compelling an interest as that recognized in McCree as sufficient to justify exclusion of jurors.

Justice Marshall, joined by Justices Brennan and Stevens, argued in dissent that the additional costs to a state of implementing a system of separate juries, or of providing alternate jurors who would replace those who opposed the death penalty after the guilt determination had been made, are minimal in comparison to a defendant's interest in an impartial jury at the guilt determination stage.

Limitation on Witherspoon: Wainwright v. Witt

The Court limited the impact of *Witherspoon* and *Adams* in Wainwright v. Witt, 469 U.S. 412 (1985). One of the prospective jurors in Witt's capital murder trial indicated that personal beliefs concerning the death penalty would "interfere" with her judging the guilt or innocence of the defendant. That juror was excluded for cause and Witt argued that *Witherspoon* was violated because the juror did not state that she would automatically vote against the death penalty, nor that she would be prevented from making an impartial decision as to guilt. Justice Rehnquist, writing for the Court, stated that *Witherspoon* did not require a "ritualistic adherence" to a requirement that a prospective juror make it "unmistakably clear that he would automatically vote against the death penalty." Justice Rehnquist set forth the following standard for determining whether a juror could be excluded for cause due to a negative attitude about the death penalty:

> [The] standard is whether the juror's views would prevent or substantially impair the performance of his duties as a juror in accordance with his instructions and his oath. We note that, in addition to dispensing with *Witherspoon's* reference to automatic decisionmaking, this standard likewise does not require that a juror's bias be proved with unmistakable clarity. * * * What common sense should have realized experience has proved: many veniremen simply cannot be asked enough questions to reach the point where their bias has been made "unmistakably clear"; these veniremen may not know how they will react when faced with imposing the death sentence, or may be unable to articulate, or may wish to hide their true feelings. Despite this lack of clarity in the printed record, however, there will be situations where the trial judge is left with the definite impression that a prospective juror would be unable to faithfully and impartially apply the law. * * * [T]his is why deference must be paid to the trial judge who sees and hears the juror.

Justice Rehnquist concluded that, giving proper deference to the trial judge, the juror in Witt's case was properly excused for cause. Despite the fact that the juror had stated only that her beliefs might "interfere" with her impartiality, Justice Rehnquist stated that "whatever ambiguity respondent may find in this record, we think that the trial court, aided as it undoubtedly was by its assessment of [the juror's] demeanor, was entitled to resolve it in favor of the State."

Justice Stevens concurred in the judgment. Justice Brennan, joined by Justice Marshall, dissented and argued that "the inevitable result of the quest for such purity in the jury room in a capital case is not a neutral jury drawn from a fair cross-section of the community but a jury biased against the defendant, at least with respect to penalty, and a jury from which an identifiable segment of the community has been excluded."

Effect of a Witherspoon Violation: Gray v. Mississippi

The Court found a *Witherspoon* violation in Gray v. Mississippi, 481 U.S. 648 (1987), and effectively established a per se rule requiring the invalidation of a death sentence imposed by a jury from which a potential juror was improperly excluded as a result of such a violation. In *Gray*, the prosecutor essentially

[Handwritten margin note: Pros claims error was harmless b/c he would have used preemptory]

argued that a *Witherspoon* violation was harmless because he would have exercised a peremptory strike on the juror if she had not been (improperly) excused for cause. But Justice Blackmun concluded that "[t]he nature of the jury selection process defies any attempt to establish that an erroneous *Witherspoon-Witt* exclusion of a juror is harmless."

[Handwritten margin note: Ct said harmless error not factor]

Justice Blackmun was concerned with the practical implications of the prosecutor's argument that a *Witherspoon* violation should be deemed harmless whenever the prosecutor has an unexercised peremptory challenge that she said she would have exercised on the juror improperly excused for cause:

[Handwritten margin note: would insulate from appellate review any time a juror exclusion made]

> The practical result of this unexercised peremptory argument would be to insulate jury-selection error from meaningful appellate review. By simply stating during voir dire that the State is prepared to exercise a peremptory challenge if the court denies its motion for cause, a prosecutor would ensure that a reviewing court would consider any erroneous exclusion harmless.

Justice Scalia, joined by Chief Justice Rehnquist and Justices White and O'Connor, dissented in *Gray*.

Failure to Excuse for Cause, Corrected By a Peremptory Challenge: Ross v. Oklahoma

[Handwritten margin note: poss juror stated he would auto vot for death]

Ross v. Oklahoma, 487 U.S. 81 (1988), presented the opposite situation from *Gray*: the challenged juror stated that he would automatically vote for capital punishment, and so should have been excluded for cause, but the defendant exercised a peremptory challenge at any rate. The state conceded that the juror should have been disqualified under *Witt*, but argued that the defendant's use of one of his nine peremptory challenges rectified the trial court's error. The defendant responded that he ultimately exhausted all of his peremptories, and would have used the one that he expended due to the trial court's error to excuse another juror who ultimately sat on his panel.

[Handwritten margin notes: ∆ excluded him; Ct should have excluded but didn't; ∆ claims that he exhausted his preemptory + would have used that one on a jury member]

Chief Justice Rehnquist, writing for the Court, concluded that Ross had not been denied an impartial jury because the juror who would have automatically imposed the death penalty was "removed from the jury as effectively as if the trial court excused him for cause." The Chief Justice rejected the argument that the loss of a peremptory challenge constitutes a violation of the right to be tried by an impartial jury, reasoning that "peremptory challenges are not of constitutional dimension." He declared that the state may define the purpose and manner of exercise of peremptory challenges, and that Oklahoma had properly qualified its grant of such challenges "by the requirement that the defendant must use those challenges to cure erroneous refusal by the trial court to excuse jurors for cause." He concluded that Ross made no claim that any of the jurors who convicted him and sentenced him to death was biased or partial, and that an error with respect to a juror who did not sit did not mandate reversal.

[Handwritten margin notes: H: ① removal – preemptory challenges not consti; – Ok defines them as to cure erroneous refusal by ct to exclude juror; – so preemptory properly used; ② ∆ did not make claim that jury was not impartial; H.W. violation]

Justice Marshall, joined by Justices Brennan, Blackmun, and Stevens, wrote that "[a] man's life is at stake," and "[w]e should not be playing games." He argued as follows:

> [T]he loss of a peremptory challenge in this case affected the composition of the jury panel in precisely the same way as the trial court's error in *Gray* itself. In *Gray*, the defendant was deprived of a juror who, although inexcusable for cause, seemed to be sympathetic to the defense in that she

had expressed reservations about the death penalty. The defense in the instant case was deprived of an opportunity to remove an otherwise qualified juror whom it perceived to be sympathetic to the prosecution.

From the perspective of the defendants in *Gray* and *Ross,* was the trial judge's error obviously more detrimental in one case than the other? What difference, if any, is there between the harm suffered by the defendant in the two cases? See also United States v. Martinez–Salazar, 528 U.S. 304 (2000) (a defendant's exercise of peremptory challenges pursuant to Fed.R.Crim.P. 24 is not denied or impaired when the defendant chooses to use such a challenge to remove a juror who should have been excused for cause).

Life-Qualified Juries: Morgan v. Illinois

Under *Witherspoon* and its progeny, the State is not permitted to exclude jurors for cause merely because they are reluctant to impose the death penalty, but the State is permitted to exclude jurors who would not impose death under any circumstances. The question in Morgan v. Illinois, 504 U.S. 719 (1992), was the reverse of *Witherspoon:* whether the defendant has a right to exclude a juror who would automatically *impose* the death penalty without regard to mitigating circumstances. Justice White, writing for the majority, held that the defendant had a due process right to have a prospective juror excused for cause if the juror would impose death regardless of the mitigating circumstances. He concluded that while the prosecutor has the right to seek a "death-qualified" jury, the defendant has the right to seek a "life-qualified" jury. Justice White relied on *Witt* and *Adams* (cases which established that the *state* had the right to exclude jurors who would automatically *reject* the death penalty) and concluded as follows:

> A juror who will automatically vote for the death penalty in every case will fail in good faith to consider the evidence of aggravating and mitigating circumstances as the instructions require him to do. Indeed, because such a juror has already formed an opinion on the merits, the presence or absence of either aggravating or mitigating circumstances is entirely irrelevant to such a juror. Therefore, based on the requirement of impartiality embodied in the Due Process Clause of the Fourteenth Amendment, a capital defendant may challenge for cause any prospective juror who maintains such views. If even one such juror is empaneled and the death sentence is imposed, the State is disentitled to execute the sentence.

Justice Scalia, joined by Chief Justice Rehnquist and Justice Thomas, dissented. Justice Scalia distinguished *Witherspoon* on the ground that under Illinois law, a finding of aggravating circumstances must be considered by the jury, whereas the consideration of mitigating evidence "is left up to the judgment of each juror." He therefore concluded that a *Witherspoon*-excludible—one who says he will never vote for the death penalty and thus that he will never consider aggravating factors—is "saying that he will not apply the law" whereas the juror who says he will not consider mitigating evidence "is not promising to be lawless, since there is no case in which he is by law *compelled* to find a mitigating fact sufficiently mitigating."

b. *Jurors Who Must Be Excused for Cause*

Courts often face the question of whether a juror must be excused for cause. It is fair to state that judges vary in aggressiveness in striking jurors for cause.

Generally, the judge has considerable discretion in these matters, because it is the judge who sees and hears the suspect juror, and who knows the impact that any problems with the juror will have on the case. The most frequently invoked grounds for excusal for cause are: 1) bias; 2) taint from trial publicity; 3) preconceived notions inconsistent with a presumption of innocence; 4) inability or refusal to follow instructions from the court. But with respect to these and other grounds, the question is not only whether some disability exists but whether the prospective juror, despite the disability, can fairly assess the evidence. The following cases illustrate the kinds of challenges for cause that are attempted.

a.   The defendant was convicted on two counts of aggravated bank robbery and attempted bank robbery. The government's case indicated that the defendant participated in three bank robberies and engaged in a shootout with police at a residence. During the voir dire, one venireman stated he was "not interested in convicting anybody," and when asked if he would be prejudiced against conviction, he said there was a "reasonable doubt in my mind, [and] it would take an awful lot." He was removed for cause, over the defendant's objection. The trial court thereafter denied the defendant's two motions to strike for cause. One was directed at a juror who was a senior vice-president of another bank and had previously served on a grand jury. The other was directed at a juror whose daughter had been robbed and raped. Both jurors said they believed they could give the defendant a fair trial.[28] The appellate court sustained the trial court's rulings in both instances. United States v. Young, 553 F.2d 1132 (8th Cir.1977). How would you have ruled as a trial judge? As an appellate court?

b.   The defendant was convicted for robbery and sentenced to twelve years' imprisonment. During the trial court voir dire, the following exchange took place.

Mr. Pickard (Defense Counsel): Has anybody been robbed? Due to the fact that you have recently been robbed do you think you might be a little bit more inclined to convict regardless of the evidence?

Juror Spencer: Yes sir, I probably would.

Mr. Pickard: You think you may be a little biased?

Juror Spencer: Yes sir.

Mr. Pickard: You're saying in all probability you wouldn't be able to give him a fair trial and view the evidence objectively?

Juror Spencer: Yes sir.

Mr. Pickard: We challenge for cause.

The Court: In spite of your experience a couple of weeks ago, could you still listen to the evidence that comes from this witness stand, and this evidence

---

28.   One commentator has suggested that "[c]ourts, feeling helpless before questions of human psychology, are unable to decide whether a person can be fair in spite of having an opinion on the matter at issue—thus the technique of 'just asking her.' Once having asked, however, the court cannot easily impugn the credibility of a citizen who has professed her impartiality." B. Babcock, Voir Dire: Preserving "Its Wonderful Power", 27 Stan.L.Rev. 545, 550 (1975).

Allowing jurors with preconceived ideas about guilt to sit simply because they state they will be fair is a practice that is vigorously attacked in Yount v. Patton, 710 F.2d 956 (3d Cir.1983)(Stern, J., concurring).

alone, and render a fair and impartial decision concerning the defendant, Beauford Harold Johnson?[29]

Juror Spencer: Yes sir, I believe I could.

The Court: You wouldn't let that experience that you had affect you?

Juror Spencer: No sir.

The Court: Challenge denied.

Juror Spencer became the foreman of the jury. (Emphasis added.)

The appellate court sustained the trial court's denial of challenge. Johnson v. State, 356 So.2d 769 (Ala.Cr.App.1978). Would you have sustained the lower court?

c.   Is a juror who is a county commissioner and also a part-time deputy sheriff subject to a challenge for cause? See State v. Radi, 176 Mont. 451, 578 P.2d 1169 (1978)(statute does not permit challenge). How does a decision like this affect the impartial appearance of the jury? In Dennis v. United States, 339 U.S. 162 (1950), the Court held that where the government was a party in a litigation, jurors could not be excused for cause merely because they were government employees. The Court stated that actual bias must be shown. Should the result in *Dennis* have been affected by the fact that the defendant was charged with failure to comply with a subpoena issued by the House Un–American Activities Committee? Would jurors who are government employees be less impartial in cases where the substantive offense is a wrong done to the government itself?

[handwritten margin note: if gov party cannot excuse jurors b/c they are gov employees]

d.   Juror Brogan had a connection to law enforcement. Her son was a police officer, her brother was the Chief of Police in a nearby town, and her husband was a dispatcher for the state police. The voir dire of Juror Brogan went as follows:

The Court: Ms. Brogan, I think you have a brother who's a police chief and a son who's a police officer. Do you talk shop?

Prospective Juror Brogan: Occasionally.

The Court: And do you talk about—I mean not necessarily using those terms, but do you talk about bad guys and the problems that your brother and son have?

Prospective Juror Brogan: We talk about the problems, but I like to think I have an open mind about things like this. And I form my own opinions.

The Court: Okay.

The trial judge denied the defendant's motion to strike Juror Brogan for cause. The appellate court stated that "a trial judge has discretion to find that a juror's mere relationship to a law enforcement officer is insufficient to strike for cause." United States v. Beasley, 48 F.3d 262 (7th Cir.1995). It stated that since Juror Brogan was under oath, there was no reason to doubt her declaration that she had an "unbiased mind." But did Juror Brogan have a "mere" relationship with law enforcement? Are you troubled by the fact that the trial judge never asked about her husband, who was a dispatcher for the state police? Is saying that you

[handwritten margin note: mere relationship to law officer not enough to strike for cause]

29.   Worthington v. State, 273 Ind. 499, 405 N.E.2d 913 (1980), held that a challenge for cause was properly rejected even though a witness said she had an opinion about the defendant's guilt, since she also said she would decide the case on the evidence presented.

"form your own opinions" the same as saying that you will approach the case with an unbiased mind?

e. The defendant worked as a Spanish language radio announcer for the San Francisco Giants. He was charged with cocaine distribution. During jury selection, the court asked the prospective jurors whether they or anyone to whom they were close had any experience with illegal drugs. Juror Camacho responded affirmatively. She said that her ex-husband, the father of her five-year-old daughter, had both used and dealt cocaine during their marriage. His involvement in cocaine was one of the reasons for their divorce. Upon questioning by the court, Camacho admitted that the experience was painful. The court, apparently concerned by her answers, asked Camacho three times whether she could put her personal experience aside and serve impartially. Each time, she responded" "I'll try."

The trial judge denied the defendant's motion to strike Camacho for cause. But the Court of Appeals reversed. It reasoned as follows:

> Camacho was asked three times whether she could be fair, and each time she responded equivocally. Not *once* did she affirmatively state that she could or would serve fairly or impartially. * * *

> * * * When a juror is unable to state that she will serve fairly and impartially despite being asked repeatedly for such assurances, we can have no confidence that the juror will law aside her biases or her prejudicial personal experiences and render a fair and impartial verdict. Given Camacho's responses to the court's questions and the similarity between her traumatic familial experience and the defendant's alleged conduct, we conclude that the failure to excuse her for cause * * * requires reversal.

United States v. Gonzalez, 214 F.3d 1109 (9th Cir. 2000). What if Camacho responded to the court's inquiries by saying "I am pretty sure I can" rather than "I'll try"? Would you excuse her for cause? Would you reverse a trial court's decision not to excuse her for cause?

f. Is the trial judge permitted to disqualify a juror during the deliberations? Fed.R.Crim.P. 23(b) provides: "After a jury has retired to deliberate, the court may permit a jury of 11 persons to return a verdict, even without a stipulation by the parties, if the court finds good cause to excuse a juror." See United States v. Ruggiero, 928 F.2d 1289 (2d Cir.1991)(proper to excuse juror during deliberations when it was disclosed that the juror had been threatened by associates of the defendant). One of the most notable instances of a strike for cause during deliberations occurred in the trial in Los Angeles arising out of the beating of Reginald Denny. After eight days of deliberations, the jurors wrote a note to the judge that one of the jurors wasn't using "common sense" and could not comprehend "anything that we have been trying to accomplish." The judge interviewed the juror. In the course of the interview, the juror suggested that the case may have been better decided by the judge. The judge struck the juror for cause, for "failing to deliberate as the law defines it." See Hansen, Juror's Dismissal Debated, A.B.A.J., Jan. 1994, p. 26. Was this juror incompetent, or just obstinate? If the juror seems to have no grasp of the facts during deliberations, should or must he be struck for cause? See also United States v. Geffrard, 87 F.3d 448 (11th Cir.1996) (trial judge acted properly in excusing a juror for cause during the deliberations and proceeding to verdict with 11 jurors; the juror wrote a note to the judge which stated that she could not convict the defendants because of her beliefs in Swedenborgianism). Shouldn't jurors presenting these problems during deliberations have been rooted out during the voir dire process? Does this tell you anything about the voir dire process?

6. The Use of Peremptory Challenges

a. The Purpose and Function of the Peremptory Challenge

The Supreme Court has described the peremptory challenge as follows:

> The essential nature of the peremptory challenge is that it is one exercised without a reason stated, without inquiry, and without being subject to the court's control. While challenges for cause permit rejection of jurors on a narrowly specified, provable and legally cognizable basis of partiality, the peremptory permits rejection for a real or imagined partiality that is less easily designated or demonstrable.

Swain v. Alabama, 380 U.S. 202 (1965). The Court in *Swain* stated that the peremptory challenge serves salutary purposes in the adversary system:

> The function of the challenge is not only to eliminate extremes of partiality on both sides, but to assure the parties that the jurors before whom they try the case will decide on the basis of the evidence placed before them, and not otherwise. * * * Indeed the very availability of peremptories allows counsel to ascertain the possibility of bias through probing questions on the *voir dire* and facilitates the exercise of challenges for cause by removing the fear of incurring a juror's hostility through examination and challenge for cause.

Another purpose for the peremptory is to encourage a litigant to accept the jury and its decision because it belongs to him in a vivid sense: he picked it and was able to exclude those he feared. See Babcock, Voir Dire: Preserving "Its Wonderful Power," 27 Stan.L.Rev. 545, 552 (1975). Finally, as Ross v. Oklahoma, supra, points out, the peremptory challenge serves as a "safety valve" when the trial judge erroneously refuses to excuse a juror for cause.

Voir Dire and the Peremptory Challenge

The relationship between peremptory challenges and voir dire should be apparent. In cases like Mu'Min v. Virginia, supra, the defendant argues that extensive voir dire is essential not only to determine whether a juror should be excluded for cause, but also to give defense counsel the information necessary to decide whether to expend a peremptory. As you go through the materials on peremptory challenges, see if the Court has been consistent in protecting peremptories at the same time as it has, in cases like *Mu'Min*, accepted trial court limitations of voir dire. Note also that the Court in *Mu'Min* and Ross v. Oklahoma, supra, stressed that there is no constitutional right to peremptory challenges. Does this explain how the Court can approve of limitations on voir dire?

Number of Peremptories

In felony cases, Fed.R.Crim.P. 24(b) gives all of the defendants together ten peremptory challenges (20 in capital cases) and the prosecution six. Most states allocate equal numbers of challenges to prosecutors and defendants. In multiple defendant cases, the court will allocate challenges to defendants if they cannot agree on how to use them. Fed.R.Crim.P. 24(b) states that in multiple defendant cases "the court may allow the parties additional peremptory challenges and may allow the defendants to exercise those challenges separately or jointly."

Procedure for Exercising Peremptories

There are several different procedural approaches to the exercise of peremptory challenges. Some jurisdictions use the strike system, in which the parties get to see the entire panel and to strike the least desirable (from their viewpoints) jurors first. Some use the challenge system, where a party will not be sure who will take the seat of a challenged juror. In many courts, the defendant must strike all jurors to whom she objects and then give the prosecutor a chance to do the same. Once a juror is "passed" (that is, not struck) the juror remains. See, e.g., United States v. Anderson, 562 F.2d 394 (6th Cir.1977). Other courts permit challenges to any member of the panel until challenges are exhausted. Can you see a problem with the system prohibiting a challenge after a pass?

United States v. Warren, 982 F.2d 287 (8th Cir.1992), considered an interesting question of peremptory challenge procedure. During voir dire, the trial judge, as was his custom, excused the prospective jurors from the courtroom before the parties made their peremptory challenges. The trial court's purpose was to protect the prospective jurors from the humiliation of rejection in open court. But the defense counsel argued that this procedure took him by surprise. He was not prepared to strike potential jurors by name alone, without being able to see their faces. As a result, counsel had to guess at the names of the people he wanted to challenge. He guessed wrong as to two jurors who went on to be part of the jury that convicted the defendant; one of the jurors who slipped through became the foreman. The court of appeals found no error in the trial court's procedure:

> Trial judges have broad discretion in the jury-selection procedure they use in their courtrooms. * * * The District Court did not abuse its discretion here. There is nothing improper in excusing potential jurors from the courtroom before the parties make their challenges. To avoid being surprised, the parties need only ask in advance what the Court's practice is. The usual way to keep track of who the jurors are is to make a seating chart. Counsel can then go over the chart with the client before making strikes. Sufficient note-taking by the attorney and discussion with the client will avoid surprise.

Using a Peremptory to Strike a Juror Who Should Have Been Struck for Cause: United States v. Martinez–Salazar

In United States v. Martinez–Salazar, 528 U.S. 304 (2000), a prospective juror indicated that he would favor the prosecution; he assumed "people are on trial because they did something wrong", though he understood the presumption of innocence "in theory". The defendant moved to strike the juror for cause, but the trial judge refused. So the defendant exercised a peremptory challenge to strike the juror. Eventually he expended all his peremptories. On appeal, the parties agreed that the juror should have been struck for cause. The defendant claimed a violation of Fed.R.Crim.P. 24(b), under which the defense was entitled to 10 peremptory challenges. He argued that he did not receive his full complement of peremptories, because he was forced to expend a challenge on a juror who should have been struck for cause.

The Supreme Court, in an opinion by Justice Ginsburg, held that Rule 24(b) was not violated. She reasoned that the trial court's mistake did not force the defendant to expend a peremptory challenge. She stated that a "hard choice is not the same as no choice" and concluded as follows:

> After objecting to the District Court's denial of his for-cause challenge, Martinez–Salazar had the option of letting Gilbert sit on the petit jury and, upon conviction, pursuing a Sixth Amendment challenge on appeal. Instead, Martinez–Salazar elected to use a challenge to remove Gilbert because he did not want Gilbert to sit on his jury. This was Martinez–Salazar's choice. The District Court did not demand—and Rule 24(b) did not require—that Martinez–Salazar use a peremptory challenge curatively.
>
> In choosing to remove Gilbert rather than taking his chances on appeal, Martinez–Salazar did not lose a peremptory challenge. Rather, he used the challenge in line with a principal reason for peremptories: to help secure the constitutional guarantee of trial by an impartial jury.

Justice Ginsburg observed that it would have been a different matter if the trial court's ruling resulted in the seating of any juror who should have been dismissed for cause. Justice Souter wrote a short concurring opinion. Justice Scalia, joined by Justice Kennedy, wrote a short opinion concurring in the judgment. He agreed that the defendant had not been denied any peremptories, but disagreed with the majority's intimation that the defendant could have permitted the juror to sit on the jury and then pursue a Sixth Amendment challenge on appeal. In Justice Scalia's view, it was probable that "normal principles of waiver *.* * disable a defendant from objecting on appeal to the seating of a juror he was entirely able to prevent."

b. Constitutional Limits on Peremptory Challenges

While the peremptory challenge ostensibly allows the litigant to exclude a prospective juror on any grounds, the Equal Protection Clause imposes some limits on this choice. In Swain v. Alabama, supra, the defendant argued that the prosecutor exercised peremptories to exclude African–Americans from serving on petit juries. The Court held that if this allegation could be proven, the prosecutor's action would violate the Equal Protection Clause. However, in the Court's view, such a violation could not be proven by the discriminatory use of peremptory challenges in a single case. Rather, the defendant would have to show that the prosecutor "in case after case, whatever the circumstances" was responsible for the removal of prospective jurors who survived challenges for cause "with the result that no Negroes ever serve on petit juries."

It should be apparent that the proof requirement set forth in Swain is all but impossible to meet. See People v. Wheeler, 22 Cal.3d 258, 148 Cal.Rptr. 890, 583 P.2d 748 (1978)(noting that data on such practices is inaccessible, and that at the time a peremptory is exercised, trial judges would be reluctant to allow a continuance for an investigation into a pattern of discrimination in other cases). Moreover, Swain did nothing to protect the first several victims of discrimination in the use of peremptories. As the court in *Wheeler* stated, "each and every defendant, not merely the last in this artificial sequence," ought to be entitled to the same constitutional protection.

The following case reconsiders *Swain* and finds that its proof requirements are too stringent. Who is the Court trying to protect? And what kind of costs are involved in this protection?

BATSON v. KENTUCKY

Supreme Court of the United States, 1986.
476 U.S. 79.

JUSTICE POWELL **delivered the opinion of the Court.**

This case requires us to reexamine that portion of Swain v. Alabama, 380 U.S. 202 (1965), concerning the evidentiary burden placed on a criminal defendant who claims that he has been denied equal protection through the State's use of peremptory challenges to exclude members of his race from the petit jury.

I

Petitioner, a black man, was indicted in Kentucky on charges of second-degree burglary and receipt of stolen goods. * * * The prosecutor used his peremptory challenges to strike all four black persons on the venire, and a jury composed only of white persons was selected. Defense counsel moved to discharge the jury before it was sworn on the ground that the prosecutor's removal of the black veniremen violated petitioner's rights under the * * * Fourteenth Amendment to equal protection of the laws. * * * The judge then denied petitioner's motion * * *.

The jury convicted petitioner on both counts. On appeal to the Supreme Court of Kentucky, petitioner pressed, among other claims, the argument concerning the prosecutor's use of peremptory challenges. * * *

The Supreme Court of Kentucky affirmed. * * * We granted certiorari, and now reverse.

II

In Swain v. Alabama, this Court recognized that a "State's purposeful or deliberate denial to Negroes on account of race of participation as jurors in the administration of justice violates the Equal Protection Clause." * * * We reaffirm the principle today.

A

* * *

Purposeful racial discrimination in selection of the venire violates a defendant's right to equal protection because it denies him the protection that a trial by jury is intended to secure. * * * The petit jury has occupied a central position in our system of justice by safeguarding a person accused of crime against the arbitrary exercise of power by prosecutor or judge. Duncan v. Louisiana. Those on the venire must be "indifferently chosen," to secure the defendant's right under the Fourteenth Amendment to "protection of life and liberty against race or color prejudice."

Racial discrimination in selection of jurors harms not only the accused whose life or liberty they are summoned to try. Competence to serve as a juror ultimately depends on an assessment of individual qualifications and ability impartially to consider evidence presented at a trial. A person's race simply "is unrelated to his fitness as a juror." * * * [B]y denying a person participation in jury service on account of his race, the State unconstitutionally discriminated against the excluded juror.

The harm from discriminatory jury selection extends beyond that inflicted on the defendant and the excluded juror to touch the entire community. Selection procedures that purposefully exclude black persons from juries undermine public confidence in the fairness of our system of justice. * * *

B

* * * While decisions of this Court have been concerned largely with discrimination during selection of the venire, the principles announced there also forbid discrimination on account of race in selection of the petit jury. Since the Fourteenth Amendment protects an accused throughout the proceedings bringing him to justice, the State may not draw up its jury lists pursuant to neutral procedures but then resort to discrimination at "other stages in the selection process."

Accordingly, the component of the jury selection process at issue here, the State's privilege to strike individual jurors through peremptory challenges, is subject to the commands of the Equal Protection Clause. Although a prosecutor ordinarily is entitled to exercise permitted peremptory challenges "for any reason at all, as long as that reason is related to his view concerning the outcome" of the case to be tried, the Equal Protection Clause forbids the prosecutor to challenge potential jurors solely on account of their race or on the assumption that black jurors as a group will be unable impartially to consider the State's case against a black defendant.

III

* * *

A

* * * To preserve the peremptory nature of the prosecutor's challenge, the Court in *Swain* declined to scrutinize his actions in a particular case by relying on a presumption that he properly exercised the State's challenges.

* * *

A number of lower courts following the teaching of *Swain* reasoned that proof of repeated striking of blacks over a number of cases was necessary to establish a violation of the Equal Protection Clause. Since this interpretation of *Swain* has placed on defendants a crippling burden of proof, prosecutors' peremptory challenges are now largely immune from constitutional scrutiny. For reasons that follow, we reject this evidentiary formulation as inconsistent with standards that have been developed since *Swain* for assessing a prima facie case under the Equal Protection Clause.

B

[Justice Powell discusses and relies on general equal protection cases outside the peremptory challenge context].

[S]ince *Swain,* we have recognized that a black defendant alleging that members of his race have been impermissibly excluded from the venire may make out a prima facie case of purposeful discrimination by showing that the totality of the relevant facts gives rise to an inference of discriminatory purpose. Once the defendant makes the requisite showing, the burden shifts to the State to explain adequately the racial exclusion. The State cannot meet this burden on mere general assertions that its officials did not discriminate or that they properly performed their official duties. Rather, the State must demonstrate that "permissible racially neutral selection criteria and procedures have produced the monochromatic result."[a]

* * *

[T]his Court has recognized that a defendant may make a prima facie showing of purposeful racial discrimination in selection of the venire by relying solely on the facts concerning its selection *in his case.* * * * "A single invidiously discriminatory governmental act" is not "immunized by the absence of such discrimination in the making of other comparable decisions." For evidentiary requirements to dictate that "several must suffer discrimination" before one could object, would be inconsistent with the promise of equal protection to all.

The standards for assessing a prima facie case in the context of discriminatory selection of the venire have been fully articulated since *Swain.* These principles support our conclusion that a defendant may establish a prima facie case of purposeful discrimination in selection of the petit jury solely on evidence concerning the prosecutor's exercise of peremptory challenges at the defendant's trial. To establish such a case, the defendant first must show that he is a member of a cognizable racial group, and that the prosecutor has exercised peremptory challenges to remove from the venire members of the defendant's race. Second, the defendant is entitled to rely on the fact, as to which there can be no dispute, that peremptory challenges constitute a jury selection practice that permits "those to discriminate who are of a mind to discriminate." Finally, the de-

fendant must show that these facts and any other relevant circumstances raise an inference that the prosecutor used that practice to exclude the veniremen from the petit jury on account of their race. This combination of factors in the empaneling of the petit jury, as in the selection of the venire, raises the necessary inference of purposeful discrimination.

In deciding whether the defendant has made the requisite showing, the trial court should consider all relevant circumstances. For example, a "pattern" of strikes against black jurors included in the particular venire might give rise to an inference of discrimination. Similarly, the prosecutor's questions and statements during *voir dire* examination and in exercising his challenges may support or refute an inference of discriminatory purpose. These examples are merely illustrative. We have confidence that trial judges, experienced in supervising *voir dire,* will be able to decide if the circumstances concerning the prosecutor's use of peremptory challenges creates a prima facie case of discrimination against black jurors.

Once the defendant makes a prima facie showing, the burden shifts to the State to come forward with a neutral explanation for challenging black jurors. Though this requirement imposes a limitation in some cases on the full peremptory character of the historic challenge, we emphasize that the prosecutor's explanation need not rise to the level justifying exercise of a challenge for cause. But the prosecutor may not rebut the defendant's prima facie case of discrimination by stating merely that he challenged jurors of

a. Our decisions concerning "disparate treatment" under Title VII of the Civil Rights Act of 1964 have explained the operation of prima facie burden of proof rules. See McDonnell Douglas Corp. v. Green, 411 U.S. 792 (1973); Texas Dept. of Community Affairs v. Burdine, 450 U.S. 248 (1981); United States

Postal Service Board of Governors v. Aikens, 460 U.S. 711 (1983). The party alleging that he has been the victim of intentional discrimination carries the ultimate burden of persuasion. Texas Dept. of Community Affairs v. Burdine, supra, at 252–256.

the defendant's race on the assumption—or his intuitive judgment—that they would be partial to the defendant because of their shared race. * * * The core guarantee of equal protection, ensuring citizens that their State will not discriminate on account of race, would be meaningless were we to approve the exclusion of jurors on the basis of such assumptions, which arise solely from the jurors' race. Nor may the prosecutor rebut the defendant's case merely by denying that he had a discriminatory motive or "affirm[ing] [his] good faith in making individual selections." If these general assertions were accepted as rebutting a defendant's prima facie case, the Equal Protection Clause "would be but a vain and illusory requirement." The prosecutor therefore must articulate a neutral explanation related to the particular case to be tried. The trial court then will have the duty to determine if the defendant has established purposeful discrimination.

IV

The State contends that our holding will eviscerate the fair trial values served by the peremptory challenge. Conceding that the Constitution does not guarantee a right to peremptory challenges and that *Swain* did state that their use ultimately is subject to the strictures of equal protection, the State argues that the privilege of unfettered exercise of the challenge is of vital importance to the criminal justice system.

While we recognize, of course, that the peremptory challenge occupies an important position in our trial procedures, we do not agree that our decision today will undermine the contribution the challenge generally makes to the administration of justice. The reality of practice, amply reflected in many state-and federal-court opinions, shows that the challenge may be, and

unfortunately at times has been, used to discriminate against black jurors. By requiring trial courts to be sensitive to the racially discriminatory use of peremptory challenges, our decision enforces the mandate of equal protection and furthers the ends of justice. * * *

Nor are we persuaded by the State's suggestion that our holding will create serious administrative difficulties. * * * We decline, however, to formulate particular procedures to be followed upon a defendant's timely objection to a prosecutor's challenges.

V

In this case, petitioner made a timely objection to the prosecutor's removal of all black persons on the venire. Because the trial court flatly rejected the objection without requiring the prosecutor to give an explanation for his action, we remand this case for further proceedings. If the trial court decides that the facts establish, prima facie, purposeful discrimination and the prosecutor does not come forward with a neutral explanation for his action, our precedents require that petitioner's conviction be reversed.

[Justice White's concurring opinion is omitted].

JUSTICE MARSHALL, concurring.

I join JUSTICE POWELL'S eloquent opinion for the Court, which takes a historic step toward eliminating the shameful practice of racial discrimination in the selection of juries. The Court's opinion cogently explains the pernicious nature of the racially discriminatory use of peremptory challenges, and the repugnancy of such discrimination to the Equal Protection Clause. The Court's opinion also ably demonstrates the inadequacy of any burden of proof for racially discriminatory use of peremptories that requires that "justice ... sit supinely by" and be flouted in case after case before a remedy is available. I nonetheless write separately to express my views. The decision today will not end the racial discrimination that peremptories inject into the jury-selection process. That goal can be accomplished only by eliminating peremptory challenges entirely.

* * *

* * * Merely allowing defendants the opportunity to challenge the racially discriminatory use of peremptory challenges in individual cases will not end the illegitimate use of the peremptory challenge.

* * * First, defendants cannot attack the discriminatory use of peremptory challenges at all unless the challenges are so flagrant as to establish a prima facie case. * * * [W]here only one or two black jurors survive the challenges for cause, the prosecutor need have no compunction about striking them from the jury because of their race. Prosecutors are left free to discriminate against blacks in jury selection provided that they hold that discrimination to an "acceptable" level.

Second, when a defendant can establish a prima facie case, trial courts face the difficult burden of assessing prosecutors' motives. Any prosecutor can easily assert facially neutral reasons for striking a juror, and trial courts are ill equipped to second-guess those reasons. How is the court to treat a prosecutor's statement that he struck a juror because the juror had a son about the same age as defendant, or seemed "uncommunicative," or "never cracked a smile" and, therefore "did not possess the sensitivities necessary to realistically look at the issues and decide the facts in this case"? If such easily generated explanations are sufficient to discharge the prosecutor's obligation to justify his strikes on nonracial grounds, then the

protection erected by the Court today may be illusory.

Nor is outright prevarication by prosecutors the only danger here. * * * A prosecutor's own conscious or unconscious racism may lead him easily to the conclusion that a prospective black juror is "sullen," or "distant," a characterization that would not have come to his mind if a white juror had acted identically. A judge's own conscious or unconscious racism may lead him to accept such an explanation as well supported. * * * Even if all parties approach the Court's mandate with the best of conscious intentions, that mandate requires them to confront and overcome their own racism on all levels—a challenge I doubt all of them can meet. * * *

The inherent potential of peremptory challenges to distort the jury process by permitting the exclusion of jurors on racial grounds should ideally lead the Court to ban them entirely from the criminal justice system. * * *

Some authors have suggested that the courts should ban prosecutors' peremptories entirely, but should zealously guard the defendant's peremptory as "essential to the fairness of trial by jury," and "one of the most important of the rights secured to the accused." I would not find that an acceptable solution. Our criminal justice system "requires not only freedom from any bias against the accused, but also from any prejudice against his prosecution. Between him and the state the scales are to be evenly held." We can maintain that balance, not by permitting both prosecutor and defendant to engage in racial discrimination in jury selection, but by banning the use of peremptory challenges by prosecutors and by allowing the States to eliminate the defendant's peremptories as well.

* * *

[The concurring opinion of Justice Stevens, joined by Justice Brennan, and the concurring opinion of Justice O'Connor, are omitted.]

Chief Justice Burger, joined by Justice Rehnquist, dissenting.

* * *

Our system permits two types of challenges: challenges for cause and peremptory challenges. Challenges for cause obviously have to be explained; by definition, peremptory challenges do not. * * * Analytically, there is no middle ground: A challenge either has to be explained or it does not. It is readily apparent, then, that to permit inquiry into the basis for a peremptory challenge would force the peremptory challenge to collapse into the challenge for cause. * * *

Confronted with the dilemma it created, the Court today attempts to decree a middle ground. To rebut a prima facie case, the Court requires a "neutral explanation" for the challenge, but is at pains to "emphasize" that the "explanation need not rise to the level justifying exercise of a challenge for cause." I am at a loss to discern the governing principles here. * * * Apparently the Court envisions permissible challenges short of a challenge for cause that are just a little bit arbitrary—but not too much. While our trial judges are "experienced in supervising *voir dire*," they have no experience in administering rules like this.

* * *

Today we mark the return of racial differentiation as the Court accepts a positive evil for a perceived one. Prosecutors and defense attorneys alike will build records in support of their claims that peremptory challenges have been exercised in a racially discriminatory fashion by asking jurors to state their racial background and na-

tional origin for the record, despite the fact that "such questions may be offensive to some jurors and thus are not ordinarily asked on voir dire." This process is sure to tax even the most capable counsel and judges since determining whether a prima facie case has been established will "require a continued monitoring and recording of the 'group' composition of the panel present and prospective."

* * *

Justice Rehnquist, with whom The Chief Justice joins, dissenting.

* * *

I cannot subscribe to the Court's unprecedented use of the Equal Protection Clause to restrict the historic scope of the peremptory challenge, which has been described as "a necessary part of trial by jury." In my view, there is simply nothing "unequal" about the State's using its peremptory challenges to strike blacks from the jury in cases involving black defendants, so long as such challenges are also used to exclude whites in cases involving white defendants, Hispanics in cases involving Hispanic defendants, Asians in cases involving Asian defendants, and so on. This case-specific use of peremptory challenges by the State does not single out blacks, or members of any other race for that matter, for discriminatory treatment. Such use of peremptories is at best based upon seat-of-the-pants instincts, which are undoubtedly crudely stereotypical and may in many cases be hopelessly mistaken. But as long as they are applied across-the-board to jurors of all races and nationalities, I do not see—and the Court most certainly has not explained—how their use violates the Equal Protection Clause.

* * *

Open Questions Left By Batson

Batson left a number of open questions, including: Is *Batson* only applicable to exclusion of African–Americans? Does it apply to discriminatory use of peremptories by parties other than the prosecutor? Must the defendant be a member of the excluded group? What kind of neutral explanation, short of a challenge for cause, will suffice? The Court has decided several cases in an attempt to answer some of these questions.

Standing to Assert a Batson Violation: Powers v. Ohio

In *Powers v. Ohio*, 499 U.S. 400 (1991), the defendant, a white man, alleged that the prosecutor exercised peremptory challenges to exclude African–American jurors on the basis of race. Powers was not asserting that his own equal protection rights were violated. Rather, he asserted that the equal protection rights of the jurors excluded on racial grounds were violated. The question boiled down to one of standing. In a 7–2 decision, the Court held that Powers had standing to bring an equal protection claim on behalf of the excluded African–American jurors. The case was remanded to determine whether the prosecutor had in fact excluded African–Americans on the basis of race.

The majority opinion, written by Justice Kennedy, downplayed the numerous references in *Batson* to the racial identity between the defendant and the excused prospective juror. Justice Kennedy asserted that "*Batson* was designed to serve multiple ends, only one of which was to protect individual defendants from discrimination in the selection of jurors. * * * *Batson* recognized that a prosecutor's discriminatory use of peremptory challenges harms the excluded jurors and the community at large."[30]

Justice Kennedy noted three requirements for third party standing, based on the Court's previous cases: (1) the litigant must have suffered an "injury in fact;" (2) the litigant must have a "close relation to the third party;" and (3) there must exist some hindrance to the third party's ability to protect his or her own interests.

As to the first requirement of injury in fact, Justice Kennedy argued that a criminal defendant suffers injury in fact from exclusion of jurors of a different race because "racial discrimination in the selection of jurors casts doubt on the integrity of the judicial process * * * and places the fairness of a criminal proceeding in doubt."

As to the second requirement of a close relationship between the litigant and the third party, the Court stated that "the excluded juror and the criminal defendant have a common interest in eliminating racial discrimination from the courtroom. * * * The rejected juror may lose confidence in the court and its verdicts, as may the defendant if his or her objections cannot be heard." Justice Kennedy also asserted that "*voir dire* permits a party to establish a relation, if not a bond of trust, with the jurors."

Concerning the third requirement for third party standing, the majority found that it was very unlikely that the excluded prospective juror would assert

30. Does this mean that the community at large has a cause of action when prospective jurors are excluded on account of race? What if a defendant intentionally decides not to object to race-based strikes? Does the defendant waive the community's right to challenge exclusion?

his or her own equal protection rights. Justice Kennedy noted that the barriers to bringing an individual action are "daunting," and concluded that "the reality is that a juror dismissed because of his race probably will leave the courtroom possessing little incentive to set in motion the arduous process needed to vindicate his own rights."

Justice Scalia, joined by Chief Justice Rehnquist, filed a stinging dissent. Justice Scalia contended that the majority had misapplied the holding and reasoning of *Batson:*

> This case * * * involves not a clarification of *Batson,* but the creation of an additional, *ultra-Batson* departure from established law. * * * Notwithstanding history, precedent, and the significant benefits of the peremptory challenge system, it is intolerably offensive for the State to imprison a person on the basis of a conviction rendered by a jury from which members of that person's minority race were carefully excluded. I am unmoved, however, and I think most Americans would be, by this white defendant's complaint that he was sought to be tried by an all-white jury * * *.

Consider the result in *Powers* in light of the Court's absolute denial of third party standing in Fourth Amendment cases such as United States v. Payner and Rakas v. Illinois (Chapter Two, supra). Is there some difference between a Fourth Amendment violation and an Equal Protection Clause violation that can account for such disparate treatment?

Recall that in Holland v. Illinois, supra, the Court held that a white defendant could not challenge the exclusion of African–Americans from the petit jury under the fair cross-section requirement of the Sixth Amendment. The Court reasoned that the fair cross-section requirement was not applicable to the petit jury. After *Powers,* does *Holland* have any practical effect?

Peremptory Strikes in Civil Cases: Edmonson v. Leesville Concrete Co.

After *Powers,* the fact that the objecting party is not of the same race as the excluded juror is irrelevant. However, in *Powers,* the party exercising the peremptory challenge was a government actor. If the party exercising the peremptory is a private actor, the issue is whether the private actor's challenge, even though racially discriminatory, constitutes state action. In Edmonson v. Leesville Concrete Co., 500 U.S. 614 (1991), the Court held that a private litigant in a civil case may not use peremptory challenges to exclude jurors on account of race. Justice Kennedy, writing for six members of the Court, found the necessary state action in the trial judge's excusing of the juror once a peremptory challenge is exercised: "By enforcing a discriminatory peremptory challenge, the court has not only made itself a party to the biased act, but has elected to place its power, property and prestige behind the alleged discrimination."

Justice O'Connor, joined by Chief Justice Rehnquist and Justice Scalia, dissented. She asserted that "not everything that happens in a courtroom is state action" and that "the peremptory is, by design, an enclave of private action in a government-managed proceeding." She concluded that "it is antithetical to the nature of our adversarial process * * * to say that a private attorney acting on behalf of a private client represents the government for constitutional purposes."

Peremptory Challenges by Criminal Defense Counsel: Georgia v. McCollum

In Georgia v. McCollum, 505 U.S. 42 (1992), two white defendants were charged with assault and battery of two African–Americans. The incident had sparked racial conflict in the community. The prosecution moved to prohibit the defendants from using their peremptory strikes in a racially discriminatory manner. This motion was denied by the Georgia trial and appellate courts.

Justice Blackmun wrote for the majority and relied heavily on *Edmonson*. He first found that "a criminal defendant's exercise of peremptory challenges in a racially discriminatory manner inflicts the harms addressed by *Batson*." He noted that regardless of who exercises the challenge, the harm to the excluded juror is the same, in that the juror is "subjected to open and public racial discrimination." He also noted that the need for public confidence in the judicial system, addressed by *Batson* and *Edmonson*, is at stake when a criminal defendant exercises a peremptory challenge on racial grounds, and especially so in cases involving race-related crimes. On this point, he concluded as follows:

> Be it at the hands of the State or the defense, if a court allows jurors to be excluded because of group bias, it is a willing participant in a scheme that could only undermine the very foundation of our system of justice—our citizens' confidence in it. Just as public confidence in criminal justice is undermined by a conviction in a trial where racial discrimination has occurred in jury selection, so is public confidence undermined where a defendant, assisted by racially discriminatory peremptory strikes, obtains an acquittal.

On the question of state action, Justice Blackmun concluded that no matter who exercises the peremptory, "the perception and the reality in a criminal trial will be that the court has excused jurors based on race, an outcome that will be attributed to the State."

Justice Blackmun further relied on *Edmonson* and *Powers* to conclude that the prosecution had third-party standing to assert the equal protection rights of jurors excluded on racial grounds. On this point he concluded that "the State's relation to potential jurors in this case is closer than the relationships approved in *Powers* and *Edmonson*" because "[a]s the representative of all its citizens, the State is the logical and proper party to assert the invasion of the constitutional rights of the excluded jurors in a criminal trial."

Finally, Justice Blackmun concluded that prohibiting a defendant from exercising race-based peremptory challenges does not violate any constitutional or other right afforded to criminal defendants. Justice Blackmun made the following points: 1) "peremptory challenges are not constitutionally protected fundamental rights"; 2) "it is an affront to justice to argue that a fair trial includes the right to discriminate against a group of citizens based on their race"; 3) to the extent that a required explanation for challenges might intrude upon the attorney-client privilege, "an in camera discussion can be arranged"; 4) the criminal defendant has no right "to carry out through counsel an unlawful course of conduct"; and 5) the right to an impartial jury is sufficiently protected by voir dire, challenges for cause, and peremptory strikes of those jurors who are actually racially biased.

Chief Justice Rehnquist wrote a short concurring opinion, stating that while he disagreed with *Edmonson,* it "controls the disposition of this case."

Justice Thomas concurred in the judgment. Like the Chief Justice, he agreed that *Edmonson* logically prohibited the exercise of race-based challenges by a criminal defendant. Having not been on the Court when the previous cases were decided, however, he took the opportunity to express his "general dissatisfaction with our continuing attempts to use the Constitution to regulate peremptory challenges." He asserted that "black criminal defendants will rue the day that this Court ventured down this road that inexorably will lead to the elimination of peremptory strikes." In his view, the Court had inverted its priorities and had "exalted the right of citizens to sit on juries over the rights of the criminal defendant, even though it is the defendant, not the jurors, who faces imprisonment or even death."

this path is bad b/c peremptories will be gone soon

Justice O'Connor dissented from what she termed "the remarkable conclusion that criminal defendants being prosecuted by the State act on behalf of their adversary when they exercise peremptory challenges during jury selection."

Justice Scalia dissented in a separate opinion. He agreed with the Chief Justice and Justice Thomas that *Edmonson* logically applied to the exercise of race-based peremptory challenges by a criminal defendant. However, he asserted that "a bad decision should not be followed logically to its illogical conclusion." He argued that the Court should not, in the interest of promoting race relations, "use the Constitution to destroy the ages-old right of criminal defendants to exercise peremptory challenges as they wish, to secure a jury that they consider fair."

Questions After McCollum

Would the result in *McCollum* have been different if the defendant had been African–American, and had exercised race-based peremptory challenges against prospective white jurors? The NAACP filed an amicus brief in *McCollum,* which argued that "whether white defendants can use peremptory challenges to purge minority jurors presents quite different issues from whether a minority defendant can strike majority group jurors." In his separate opinion, Justice Thomas commented that while this issue "technically remains open, it is difficult to see how the result could be different if the defendants here were black." Do you agree? The courts have read *McCollum* to prohibit minority defendants from challenging majority jurors on racial grounds. See, e.g., State v. Knox, 609 So.2d 803 (La.1992)(relying on *McCollum,* the court holds that the State "may properly object to a minority criminal defendant's racially discriminatory exercise of peremptory challenges" and "require the defendant to assert a racially neutral explanation for the peremptory challenge").

Now that *Batson* applies to peremptory challenges by criminal defendants, what happens if the trial judge rejects defense counsel's peremptory strike, on the assumption that it is discriminatory, when in fact defense counsel has an appropriate race-neutral explanation for the strike? In these circumstances, there is no *Batson* violation—because there has been no discriminatory exclusion, indeed no exclusion at all—but there is an erroneous denial of a peremptory strike. What's the remedy? In United States v. Annigoni, 57 F.3d 739 (9th Cir.1995), the court held that the trial court's erroneous reliance on *Batson* to reject the defendant's peremptory strike was harmless error. The court reasoned that there is no constitutional right to a peremptory challenge, and that the defendant could not show that the juror who he tried to strike was biased or removable for cause. Do you agree with this analysis? Is it consistent with the Court's reversal of convictions in *Batson* and *Powers*? Compare United States v. Blotcher, 142 F.3d 728 (4th Cir.1998) (where trial court refused to honor defendant's peremptory strike on the ground that it was racially-based, conviction had to be reversed because defendant had a race-neutral explanation for the strike).

Making Your Own Batson Violation

After *McCollum*, can a defendant who strikes jurors on the basis of race complain on appeal about his own *Batson* violation? Why not? After all, such a defendant is not claiming that his own rights were violated, but is claiming third party standing for the rights of the jurors he excluded. Believe it or not, defendants have argued that their convictions should be reversed because of their own racially discriminatory peremptory strikes. Judge Easterbrook, in United States v. Boyd, 86 F.3d 719 (7th Cir.1996), rejected such a claim for reversal, reasoning that the defendant by his own action (together with his agent, the defense counsel) had forfeited any right to object to the racially-based exclusions. Judge Easterbrook concluded as follows:

> Giving a defendant a new trial because of his own violation of the Constitution would make a laughingstock of the process. If a decision of the Supreme Court gave the accused the right to bootstrap his own violation of *Batson* into a new trial, we would be obliged to uphold it. But there is no such decision, and the principle that no one is entitled to profit from his own wrong governs the conduct of trials as well as the imposition of punishment.

But see United States v. Huey, 76 F.3d 638 (5th Cir.1996) (in a joint trial, where one defendant exercised a peremptory challenge on racial grounds, the other defendant objected, and the trial judge overruled the objection, both defendants were entitled to a new trial).

Applying Batson Beyond Racial Exclusions: J.E.B. v. Alabama

Even a quick reading of *Batson* shows that the Court was concerned with exclusion of jurors on racial grounds. The Court in Hernandez v. New York, 500 U.S. 352 (1991), held, not surprisingly, that Hispanics also have a right under the Equal Protection Clause to be free from discrimination in jury selection. Can the *Batson* principle be logically extended beyond racially discriminatory peremptory strikes?

In J.E.B. v. Alabama, 511 U.S. 127 (1994), the Court extended *Batson* and held that the Equal Protection Clause prohibits the exercise of a peremptory challenge on the basis of the gender of a prospective juror. The case involved a child support action brought by the State against a father. The State used 9 of its 10 strikes to remove male jurors; as a result, all the selected jurors were female. Justice Blackmun, writing for five members of the Court, applied the "heightened scrutiny" test that the Court ordinarily applies to gender-based classifications in other contexts. Justice Blackmun stated that under that test, the question was whether gender-based peremptory challenges "substantially further the State's legitimate interest in achieving a fair and impartial trial." He found that gender-based challenges could not meet this strict test, because there was no substantial correlation between sex and impartiality.

Justice Blackmun rejected the State's argument that the Equal Protection Clause was not violated in this case because it was men, and not women, who were excluded in the action. He reasoned as follows:

> All persons, when granted the opportunity to serve on a jury, have the right not to be excluded summarily because of discriminatory and stereotypical presumptions that reflect and reinforce patterns of historical discrimination. Striking individuals on the assumption that they hold particular views simply because of their gender is practically a brand upon them, affixed by law, an assertion of their inferiority.

Justice Blackmun also found it irrelevant that women and men, unlike racial minorities, are found in such numbers in the jury pool that they are likely to be represented on the jury even if each side uses all of its peremptory challenges on one gender or another. He explained as follows:

> Because the right to nondiscriminatory jury selection procedures belongs to the potential jurors, as well as to the litigants, the possibility that members of both genders will get on the jury despite the intentional discrimination is beside the point. The exclusion of even one juror for impermissible reasons harms that juror and undermines public confidence in the fairness of the system.[31]

Justice Blackmun concluded the majority opinion by contending that it was of limited scope:

> Our conclusion that litigants may not strike potential jurors solely on the basis of gender does not imply the elimination of all peremptory challenges. * * * Parties still may remove jurors whom they feel might be less acceptable than others on the panel; gender simply may not serve as a proxy for bias. Parties may also exercise their peremptory challenges to remove from the venire any group or class of individuals normally subject to "rational basis" review. Even strikes based on characteristics that are disproportionately associated with one gender could be appropriate, absent a showing of pretext.

As an explanation of the last sentence in the above quote, Justice Blackmun wrote the following footnote:

> For example, challenging all persons who have had military experience would disproportionately affect men at this time, while challenging all persons employed as nurses would disproportionately affect women. Without a showing of pretext, however, these challenges may well not be unconstitutional, since they are not gender or race-based.

Justice O'Connor wrote a reluctant concurring opinion, reasoning that the Court's *Batson* jurisprudence led to a conclusion that gender-biased peremptory challenges are unconstitutional. But she emphasized the cost of the application of *Batson* to gender-classification, and argued that the majority's holding "should be limited to the *government's* use of gender-based peremptory challenges." She also noted that "[i]n extending *Batson* to gender we have added an

---

31. See also Alvarado v. United States, 497 U.S. 543 (1990)(per curiam), holding that a *Batson* violation could be found even if the resulting jury represented a fair cross-section of the community. The Court noted that a *Batson* claim is not premised on the actual makeup of the jury, but rather on the striking of prospective jurors on discriminatory grounds.

additional burden to the state and federal trial process, taken a step closer to eliminating the peremptory challenge, and diminished the ability of litigants to act on sometimes accurate gender-based assumptions about juror attitudes."

Chief Justice Rehnquist wrote a dissenting opinion in *J.E.B.*, arguing that "there are sufficient differences between race and gender discrimination such that the principle of *Batson* should not be extended to peremptory challenges to potential jurors based on sex." He declared that the "two sexes differ, both biologically and, to a diminishing extent, in experience. It is not merely stereotyping to say that these differences may produce a difference in outlook which is brought to the jury room." He concluded that the State had therefore shown that "jury strikes on the basis of gender substantially further the State's legitimate interest in achieving a fair and impartial trial through the venerable practice of peremptory challenges."

Justice Scalia also dissented in an opinion joined by the Chief Justice and Justice Thomas. He declared as follows:

> In order, it seems to me, not to eliminate any real denial of equal protection, but simply to pay conspicuous obeisance to the equality of the sexes, the Court imperils a practice [the peremptory challenge] that has been considered an essential part of fair jury trial since the dawn of the common law. The Constitution of the United States neither requires nor permits this vandalizing of our people's traditions.

In Davis v. Minnesota, 511 U.S. 1115 (1994), the Court denied certiorari from a decision by the Minnesota Supreme Court which held that *Batson* does not prevent exclusion of prospective jurors on the basis of religious affiliation. The Minnesota Supreme Court decision was handed down before *J.E.B.*, and the Minnesota Court at the time had reasoned that *Batson* had been confined by the Supreme Court to the context of racial exclusions. Justice Thomas, joined by Justice Scalia, dissented from the Supreme Court's disposition in *Davis,* arguing that the case should be remanded for reconsideration in light of *J.E.B.* Justice Thomas had this to say about the scope of *Batson* after *J.E.B.*:

> [G]iven the Court's rationale in *J.E.B.*, no principled reason immediately appears for declining to apply *Batson* to any strike based on a classification that is accorded heightened scrutiny under the Equal Protection Clause. * * * In breaking the barrier between classifications that merit strict equal protection scrutiny and those that receive what we have termed "heightened" or "intermediate" scrutiny, *J.E.B.* would seem to have extended *Batson's* equal protection analysis to all strikes based on the latter category of classifications—a category which presumably would include classifications based on religion. * * *[32]

32. Some groups, while probably protected by *Batson,* will often be so difficult to delineate that a prima facie case of discrimination will not be made. For example, in United States v. Di Pasquale, 864 F.2d 271 (3d Cir.1988), the defendant challenged the exclusion of prospective Italian–American jurors. The court held that a prima facie case had not been made, because the defendant's only proof was that the excluded jurors had Italian surnames. What should Di Pasquale have done to prove a prima facie case of discrimination? See also United States v. Maxwell, 160 F.3d 1071 (6th Cir.1998) (*Batson* does not apply to peremptory strikes made on the basis of age).

Prima Facie Case of Discrimination

What exactly constitutes a prima facie case of discrimination under *Batson?* What if the prosecutor strikes three of six prospective African–American jurors? What if five of six are struck, but the prosecutor still has a peremptory to use and does not use it against the sixth African–American? Is it relevant that the prosecutor exercised peremptory challenges against non-minorities? Are questions asked on voir dire relevant? See generally United States v. Esparsen, 930 F.2d 1461 (10th Cir.1991)(courts have looked to questions asked on voir dire, the answers of those included as compared to those who were struck, the number of challenges used on a certain group, whether members of the group actually sat on the jury, whether the litigant had unexpended peremptories, the rate at which members of the group were struck compared to the rate at which non-members were struck, and other factors particular to the case).

While no single factor is usually dispositive, a prima facie case of discrimination will ordinarily be found if the litigant strikes all prospective jurors belonging to a protected group. As the court in *Esparsen* put it, "the striking of a single juror will not always constitute a prima facie case, but when no members of a racial group remain because of that strike, it does." See also Fernandez v. Roe, 286 F.3d 1073 (9th Cir. 2002) (prima facie showing of a *Batson* violation was made where the prosecutor struck four out of seven Hispanics, 21% of his strikes were made against Hispanics, Hispanics constituted only 12% of the venire, 29% of the strikes against Hispanics were made before the trial judge warned the prosecutor not to strike any more Hispanics, and the prosecutor thereafter struck the only two prospective African–American jurors; the court noted that the prosecutor had failed to engage in meaningful questioning of any of the minority jurors, and that a prima facie case was found even though one Hispanic juror was ultimately seated); Morse v. Hanks, 172 F.3d 983 (7th Cir.1999) (prima facie case of discrimination found where the prosecutor struck the only African–American venireman on the panel, and the voir dire was perfunctory, giving no indication of any other reason to exercise a peremptory challenge: "It might be different, we think, if the excused black juror had given an answer that would expose a clear basis for the state to want to remove him from the pool."); People v. James, 132 A.D.2d 932, 518 N.Y.S.2d 266 (1987)(prima facie case of discrimination where the prosecutor challenged five out of six African–Americans, which constituted half of his peremptory challenges); United States v. Hughes, 864 F.2d 78 (8th Cir.1988)(questioning on voir dire did not reveal sufficient independent reasons, other than race, for the striking of two African–Americans). The court in *Hughes* also found it relevant that there had been frequent charges of systematic exclusion of African–Americans from juries in the judicial district.

Neutral Explanations: Purkett v. Elem

A *Batson* violation is not found every time that prima facie proof of a discriminatory peremptory challenge is established. A prima facie case of discrimination simply requires the party exercising the peremptory to provide a neutral explanation. The Court emphasized the minimal nature of the neutral explanation requirement in Purkett v. Elem, 514 U.S. 765 (1995), a per curiam opinion joined by seven Justices. The prosecutor in Elem's trial excluded two African–American jurors, and offered as an explanation that the two prospective jurors each had long unkempt hair, a mustache, and a goatee-type beard. The

Court of Appeals, on review of the denial of Elem's habeas petition, ordered that the writ be granted because of a *Batson* violation. The Court of Appeals reasoned that a prosecutor must give some explanation for exclusion that might be related to the prospective juror's performance in the case. It found that the prosecutor's explanations had nothing to do with juror performance and therefore were pretextual.

But the Supreme Court reversed, reasoning that the Court of Appeals had not properly applied the three-step analysis required by *Batson*. The Court explained as follows:

Under our *Batson* jurisprudence, once the opponent of a peremptory challenge has made out a prima facie case of racial discrimination (step 1), the burden of production shifts to the proponent of the strike to come forward with a race-neutral explanation (step 2). If a race-neutral explanation is tendered, the trial court must then decide (step 3) whether the opponent of the strike has proved purposeful racial discrimination. The second step of this process does not demand an explanation that is persuasive, or even plausible. * * *

The Court of Appeals erred by combining *Batson's* second and third steps into one, requiring that the justification tendered at the second step be not just neutral but also at least minimally persuasive, i.e., a plausible basis for believing that the person's ability to perform his or her duties as a juror will be affected. It is not until the third step that the persuasiveness of the justification becomes relevant—the step in which the trial court determines whether the opponent of the strike has carried his burden of proving purposeful discrimination. At that stage, implausible or fantastic justifications may (and probably will) be found to be pretexts for purposeful discrimination. But to say that a trial judge may choose to disbelieve a silly or superstitious reason at step 3 is quite different from saying that a trial judge must terminate the inquiry at step 2 when the race-neutral reason is silly or superstitious. The latter violates the principle that the ultimate burden of persuasion regarding racial motivation rests with, and never shifts from, the opponent of the strike.

Because the prosecutor's explanation in *Purkett* was neutral—in that long, unkempt hair and mustaches and goatees are not indicative of any race—the Court held that the state had met its obligation under the second step of *Batson*. The state court had concluded that Elem failed to prove purposeful racial discrimination, and the Court remanded to allow the lower federal court to determine, on habeas review, whether the state court's conclusion was fairly supported by the record.[33]

Justice Stevens, joined by Justice Breyer, dissented. He contended that the Court had watered down the race-neutral explanation requirement of *Batson* to the point where it had no meaning at all. He elaborated as follows:

In my opinion, preoccupation with the niceties of a three-step analysis should not foreclose meaningful judicial review of prosecutorial explanations that are entirely unrelated to the case to be tried. * * * The Court's

---

33. On remand, the court of appeals found no *Batson* violation, reasoning that the prosecutor proffered reasons for striking the juror that were facially race-neutral, and the defen- dant made no attempt to persuade the state trial court that the prosecutor's reasons for striking the juror were pretextual. Elem v. Purkett, 64 F.3d 1195 (8th Cir.1995).

unnecessary tolerance of silly, fantastic, and implausible explanations, together with its assumption that there is a difference of constitutional magnitude between a statement that "I had a hunch about this juror based on his appearance," and "I challenged this juror because he had a mustache," demeans the importance of the values vindicated by our decision in *Batson*.

Neutral Explanations and Bilingual Jurors: Hernandez v. New York

In Hernandez v. New York, 500 U.S. 352 (1991), the defendant claimed that the prosecutor struck Latino jurors on account of race. The prosecutor did not wait for the trial court's ruling on whether a prima facie case of discrimination had been established. Rather, the prosecutor defended his strikes on the ground that the prospective jurors were bilingual and many witnesses would be Spanish-speaking; therefore he "was very uncertain that they would be able to listen and follow the interpreter." The prosecutor based his assertion on the answers given by the prospective jurors to whether they could accept the interpreter as the final arbiter of what was said by the Spanish-speaking witnesses. According to the prosecutor, the excluded prospective jurors "looked away from me and said with some hesitancy that they would try * * * to follow the interpreter." The trial court and the State appellate courts found that this explanation was race-neutral and sufficient to rebut the defendant's prima facie case. The Supreme Court agreed, but there was no majority opinion.

Justice Kennedy wrote an opinion joined by Chief Justice Rehnquist, Justice White, and Justice Souter. Justice Kennedy defined a race-neutral explanation as one "based on something other than the race of the juror. * * * Unless a discriminatory intent is inherent in the prosecutor's explanation, the reason offered will be deemed race neutral." Justice Kennedy found that the prosecutor's explanation "rested neither on the intention to exclude Latino or bilingual jurors, nor on stereotypical assumptions about Latinos or bilinguals." According to Justice Kennedy, the prosecutor properly divided jurors into two potential classes: "those whose conduct during *voir dire* would persuade him they might have difficulty in accepting the translator's rendition of Spanish-language testimony and those potential jurors who gave no reason for such doubt. Each category would include both Latinos and non-Latinos."

Justice Kennedy recognized that the prosecutor's criterion for exclusion would have a disparate impact on prospective Latino jurors, because they were more likely to be fluent in Spanish than non-Latino jurors. He responded, however, that while disparate impact was relevant in determining whether the prosecutor acted with discriminatory intent, "it will not be conclusive in the preliminary race-neutrality step of the *Batson* inquiry. * * * Unless the government actor adopted a criterion with the intent of causing the impact asserted, that impact itself does not violate the principle of race-neutrality. Nothing in the prosecutor's explanation shows that he chose to exclude jurors * * * *because* he wanted to prevent bilingual Latinos from serving on the jury."[34]

---

34. See also United States v. Uwaezhoke, 995 F.2d 388 (3d Cir.1993)(in a drug prosecution, the prosecutor gave a neutral explanation when he excluded an African–American juror on the ground that she lived in public housing in Newark, an area known for drugs and crime; exclusion was permissible even though

Justice Kennedy cautioned that his opinion did not imply that the prosecutor had untrammeled discretion to exclude bilingual jurors. He noted that the case would be different if the prosecutor had merely stated that he did not want Spanish-speaking jurors. Justice Kennedy concluded:

> It may well be, for certain ethnic groups and in some communities, that proficiency in a particular language, like skin color, should be treated as a surrogate for race under an equal protection analysis. * * * And, as we make clear, a policy of striking all who speak a given language without regard to the particular circumstances of the trial or the individual responses of the jurors, may be found by the trial judge to be a pretext for racial discrimination. But that case is not before us.

Justice O'Connor, joined by Justice Scalia, concurred in the judgment. She agreed with much of Justice Kennedy's opinion, but felt that the plurality went "farther than it needs to in assessing the constitutionality of the prosecutor's asserted justification for his peremptory strikes." According to Justice O'Connor, "if the trial court believes the prosecutor's nonracial justification, and that finding is not clearly erroneous, that is the end of the matter." Justice O'Connor stressed that disparate impact was no substitute for a finding of intentional discrimination.

Justice Stevens, joined by Justices Marshall and Blackmun, dissented in *Hernandez*. He argued that the prosecutor's explanation was insufficient to overcome the prima facie case of discrimination because, among other things, "the justification would inevitably result in a disproportionate disqualification of Spanish-speaking venirepersons." According to Justice Stevens "an explanation that is race-neutral on its face is nonetheless unacceptable if it is merely a proxy for a discriminatory practice."[35]

What limitations are placed on a prosecutor's explanation for exercising peremptory challenges after *Hernandez* and *Purkett*? Will a prosecutor who is intentionally discriminating on the basis of race always be able to assert some credible race-neutral explanation? See, e.g., Jordan v. Lefevre, 293 F.3d 587 (2d Cir. 2002) (race-neutral explanation sufficient where African–American juror did not know the occupations or whereabouts of her children, and prosecutor explained that she lacked the common sense he was looking for in a juror; it was also permissible to exclude an African–American juror who lived with her mother, worked only part-time, and spent the rest of her time watching television; prosecutor explained that she seemed to lack both maturity and experience in making important decisions); Stubbs v. Gomez, 189 F.3d 1099 (9th Cir. 1999) (prosecutor's reasons for striking African–American juror were race-neutral under *Batson*: the prosecutor felt that the juror's demeanor and lack of eye contact showed disinterest in being a juror, and she had no employment record); United States v. Nichols, 937 F.2d 1257 (7th Cir.1991)(neutral explanation found where the prospective juror was young and living with a man to whom she was not married); United States v. Biaggi, 853 F.2d 89 (2d Cir. 1988)(*Batson* limits exclusion of Italian–Americans, but prosecutor gave neutral

the prosecutor's justification resulted in a disparate impact on African–Americans).

35. Professor Perea, in Hernandez v. New York: Courts, Prosecutors, and the Fear of Spanish, 21 Hofstra L.Rev. 1 (1992), states that the *Hernandez* opinion "reveals that the

Court's discourse and its understanding with respect to the ethnic and linguistic differences between Americans are inadequate for the Court to render appropriate decisions when it considers discrimination based on these traits."

explanation for exclusion; prospective jurors had displayed angry, arrogant, or flippant demeanors). Commentators have argued that the Court has rendered *Batson* a nullity, because any prosecutor worth his salt can come up with a facially neutral explanation for what is really a race-based challenge. See Cavise, The *Batson* Doctrine: The Supreme Court's Utter Failure to Meet the Challenge of Discrimination in Jury Selection, 1999 Wis.L.Rev. 501; Charlow, Tolerating Deception and Discrimination After *Batson*, 50 Stan.L.Rev. 9 (1997).

c. *The Future of Peremptory Challenges*

Consider Judge Gee's comments about *Batson*, which were made in dissent in the court of appeals decision in *Edmonson*, 860 F.2d 1308 (5th Cir.1988), the case in which the Court ultimately extended *Batson* to civil cases:

> What remains after [*Batson*] is not the peremptory challenge which our procedure has known for decades—or not one which can be freely exercised against all jurors in all cases, at any rate. Justice Marshall would dispense with strikes entirely, and perhaps this will be the final outcome. In this much at least he is surely correct, that we must go on or backward; to stay here is to rest content with a strange procedural creature indeed: a challenge for semi-cause, * * * a skewed and curious device, exercisable without giving reasons in some cases but not in others, all depending on race.

After *Batson* and its progeny, does retaining the system of peremptory challenges make any sense? Many commentators have agreed with Justice Marshall that peremptory challenges should be scrapped. See Ogletree, Just Say No!: A Proposal to Eliminate Racially Discriminatory Uses of Peremptory Challenges, 31 Am.Crim.L.Rev. 1099 (1994); Broderick, Why the Peremptory Challenge Should Be Abolished, 65 Temple L.Rev. 369 (1992).

Given the difficulty of establishing a challenge for cause, can a defendant get an impartial jury if he can't make peremptory challenges? How easy is it to dismiss the complaint of Justice Thomas in *McCollum*, i.e., that a prohibition on racially-based peremptories by the defendant can in fact lead to a biased verdict? See Nunn, Rights Held Hostage: Race, Ideology and the Peremptory Challenge, 28 Harv.Civ.Rts.Civ. Lib.L.Rev. 63 (1993)("The use of colorblind principles to govern the ability of criminal defendants to affect the use of peremptory challenges masks the continuing racial oppression that Black defendants face and prevents those defendants from doing anything about it."). For a view in favor of peremptory challenges, at least when exercised by criminal defendants, see Goldwasser, Limiting the Criminal Defendant's Use of Peremptory Challenges: On Symmetry and the Jury in a Criminal Trial, 102 Harv.L.Rev. 808 (1989).

E. PRESERVING THE INTEGRITY OF JURY DELIBERATIONS

Many devices are employed to assure that the jury process works as smoothly and as fairly as possible. Sometimes, however, efforts to protect the jury's deliberation process are in tension with the rights of the defendant or the interest in judicial efficiency.

1. *Anonymous Juries*

Ordinarily, the names of jurors are made known to counsel and the defendant during the voir dire process. However, in some cases prosecutors make the argument that juror anonymity is required to preserve the integrity of deliberations. Why would anonymity ever be needed? What are the risks involved in preventing disclosure of the jurors' identity?

In United States v. Barnes, 604 F.2d 121 (2d Cir.1979), a divided court approved the trial judge's decision to keep the names and addresses of jurors secret from counsel and to bar defense counsel from inquiring into the jurors' ethnic and religious backgrounds. The defendant was charged with being a drug kingpin and the government made a preliminary showing that the defendant engaged in acts of violence and intimidation. The trial judge permitted an inquiry of prospective jurors only as to their county and length of residence and certain family history. The limitations on voir dire were intended to protect the jurors from harassment and threats to themselves and their families. Do you believe that it is necessary for a party to know where a juror lives in order to make an intelligent decision whether to challenge the juror?

In United States v. Tutino, 883 F.2d 1125 (2d Cir.1989), the judge permitted the empanelling of an anonymous jury in a trial alleging a heroin distribution conspiracy when presented with the following submission from the government:

> The government requested an anonymous jury for five reasons: (1) the defendants faced serious penalties, including substantial prison terms and a possible parole revocation, and, according to the government, were therefore likely to bribe or threaten the jury; (2) [defendant] Tutino had attempted to tamper with a jury in a prior trial; (3) [defendants] Tutino and Guarino were known associates of organized crime figures; (4) Tutino had a prior extortion conviction and Guarino and [defendant] Larca had prior narcotics convictions; and (5) the jury had to be protected from the media.

In affirming the decision to use an anonymous jury, the court of appeals noted that the trial court issued instructions regarding the presumption of innocence more than once. The court believed that "these instructions were carefully framed to avoid any risk that the anonymous procedures would appear extraordinary or reflect adversely on the defendants." Do you believe that *any* instructions would suffice to protect the presumption of innocence when a jury is anonymous? See also United States v. Vario, 943 F.2d 236 (2d Cir.1991)(pre-trial publicity, and co-conspirator's tampering with grand jury, warrant anonymous jury). In *Vario,* the court took pains to note that "the invocation of the words 'organized crime,' 'mob' or 'Mafia,' unless there is something more, does not warrant an anonymous jury."

In United States v. Sanchez, 74 F.3d 562 (5th Cir.1996), the defendant, a police officer, was charged with coercing prostitutes to engage in sex acts with him. The trial judge ordered that the jury remain anonymous, reasoning that "I don't think there's anything more frightening to the populace than having a rogue cop on their hands." The court of appeals reversed the conviction. It noted that 1) the defendant was not involved in organized crime; 2) there was no evidence that the defendant had ever attempted to interfere with the judicial process; and 3) there was no indication that the case would receive extensive publicity that would enhance the possibility that the jurors' names would become public and expose them to intimidation or harassment. The court emphasized that anonymous juries are an extraordinary remedy that could only be used as a device of last resort.

The government in *Sanchez* argued that the error, if any, in empanelling an anonymous jury was harmless, because the trial court conducted extensive voir dire and permitted the defendant to pick an impartial jury. But the court held that this argument missed the point:

> The defendant has a right to a jury of known individuals not just because information such as was redacted here yields valuable clues for purposes of jury selection, but also because the verdict is both personalized and personified when rendered by 12 known fellow citizens. [Unless strong factors supporting anonymity exist, the defendant] should receive a verdict not from anonymous decisionmakers, but from people he can name as responsible for their actions.

Thus, the court held that the impermissible use of an anonymous jury could never be harmless.

2.   Protecting Against Judicial Influence on Jury Deliberations

Once the jury retires to deliberate, there is good reason to be concerned about any further contact with the judge.

Answering Jurors' Questions

In United States v. Neff, 10 F.3d 1321 (7th Cir.1993), the defendant was tried for possession of a firearm by a felon. The contested question was whether Neff possessed the gun that was found at his sister's house after his arrest; the gun had been found in a bag containing the defendant's clothing, in a room in which the defendant had been staying. Some time after beginning deliberations, the jury sent a note to the judge asking him to "please clarify some events for us." The jury asked about the time of the arrest, whether the defendant had been released after being arrested, and the time of the search. None of these facts had been the subject of proof at trial, apparently because neither side found them to be very relevant. The judge gave factual answers to each question. The jury then returned a guilty verdict. The court of appeals found reversible error:

> These questions from the jury were not the usual run-of-the-mill jury requests asking either that they be reinstructed on a point of law or be allowed to rehear evidence that had previously been introduced and developed at trial. Instead, these questions were really requests for evidence which had not been presented at trial, and which the jury apparently thought was necessary in reaching its determination * * *
>
> * * * Surely it is not a stretch of the imagination to assume that when a judge conclusively establishes certain nonexisting facts as a matter of record, a jury would feel free to accept the judge's word on the matter without ever going back to the evidence they had before them and decide if what the judge said was correct. Therefore, we find that by answering the jury's questions with facts not in evidence, the judge violated Neff's Sixth Amendment right to trial by jury.

What should the judge have done when confronted with these questions from the jury? Should he have said "those facts did not come out in the case"? Or, "those facts are not relevant to your determination"? Or, "it is up to you to decide the facts"?

Breaking a Deadlock: The Allen Charge

Assume that a jury has been deliberating for a day when it reports back that it is deadlocked. One possibility for the judge at this point is to consider granting a mistrial; but either or both parties might object to a mistrial, for their own strategic reasons, and moreover, a mistrial usually leads to the substantial cost of a retrial. Therefore, the trial judge may want to encourage the jury to deliberate further in the hopes of reaching a verdict. But just what should the judge tell the jury at this point? One such charge was considered in Allen v. United States, 164 U.S. 492 (1896), and is commonly referred to as the "Allen charge" or the "dynamite" charge:

In a large proportion of cases absolute certainty cannot be expected. Although your verdict must be the verdict of each of you individually and not a mere acquiescence in the conclusion of your fellows, yet you should examine the question submitted with candor and with a proper regard for and deference to the opinions of each other. It is your duty to decide the case if you can conscientiously do so. You should listen, with a disposition to be convinced, to each other's arguments. If much the larger number are for conviction, a dissenting juror should consider whether his doubts are reasonable ones when they make no impression upon the minds of so many others, equally honest and equally intelligent. If, upon the other hand, the majority is for acquittal, the minority ought to ask themselves whether they might not reasonably doubt the correctness of a judgment which was not concurred in by the majority.

The concern with an *Allen* charge is that it will coerce the minority into agreeing with the majority, simply to reach a verdict. See, e.g., United States v. Robinson, 953 F.2d 433 (8th Cir.1992)(impermissible coercion where judge implied that deadlock would be wasteful and unpatriotic, and instructed the minority to give special consideration to the majority's position).

To limit the possibility of coercion, courts have generally required an *Allen* charge to include the following: 1) a recognition that a majority of jurors may favor acquittal; 2) a reminder that the government has the burden of proof beyond a reasonable doubt; 3) a statement that both the majority and the minority should reexamine their views; 4) a statement that no juror should abandon his or her conscientiously held view; and 5) a statement that the jury is free to deliberate as long as necessary. These propositions go beyond the charge given in *Allen* itself, reproduced above. An instruction containing these five propositions is referred to as a "modified *Allen* charge." See United States v. Webb, 816 F.2d 1263 (8th Cir.1987)(finding reversible error where an *Allen* charge did not contain these five elements). Courts have generally not required the trial judge to instruct the jury that they are free to hang, i.e., that a deadlock is an acceptable resolution. United States v. Arpan, 887 F.2d 873 (8th Cir. 1989)(en banc). What is the problem with including such an instruction?

Even if a coercive deadlock charge is given, it does not necessarily mean that the verdict is tainted. Whether a coercive charge actually affected the jury depends on the circumstances. Thus, in United States v. Ajiboye, 961 F.2d 892 (9th Cir.1992), the judge gave a deadlock instruction which did not include all the protective elements of a modified *Allen* charge. The defendant was tried on two counts, and the jury was deadlocked 9–3 for acquittal on one count and 9–3 for conviction on the other. After receiving the charge, the jury deliberated for two more days, and asked to review some of the evidence. The jury then returned a guilty verdict on both counts. The court found that the *Allen* charge did not coerce the jury into rendering guilty verdicts. Why not?

Successive Allen Charges

Some courts have found reversible error where the trial judge gives successive *Allen* charges—i.e., the jury reports a deadlock, a deadlock charge is given, the jury comes back deadlocked again, and the judge gives another deadlock charge. The concern is that the dissenting jurors are being worn down, and are getting the message that they will never be able to leave so long as they are deadlocked. This concern exists even if the charge contains the ameliorative language of a modified *Allen* charge. See United States v. Seawell, 550 F.2d 1159 (9th Cir.1977)(reversible error when successive *Allen* charges are given). However, even multiple *Allen* charges may be permissible or at least not coercive, depending on the circumstances. Thus, in United States v. Nickell, 883 F.2d 824 (9th Cir.1989), the judge gave one modified *Allen* charge on Friday immediately before the jurors recessed for the weekend, and another when they resumed deliberations on Monday. The court found no error and reasoned as follows:

> In this case the danger of reproof and coercive disapproval of further deliberations inherent in a second instruction after a second report of deadlock does not exist. There was no intervening deliberation by the jury after the *Allen* charge was first given before the weekend recess. There was no second deadlock. In these circumstances there could have been no suggestion of criticism of intervening behavior by the jury in the second supplemental instruction, since the judge addressed the jury the second time only as a reminder of the instructions given before the break. In this case, the remarks of the judge before the jury resumed its deliberations after the break can be viewed not as a second modified *Allen* charge, but as a continuation of the first.

See also United States v. Ruggiero, 928 F.2d 1289 (2d Cir.1991)("we do not regard a repeated *Allen* charge as inevitably coercive").

Capital Punishment and the Allen Charge

The Supreme Court held, 5–3, in Lowenfield v. Phelps, 484 U.S. 231 (1988), that the trial judge did not act improperly in a capital case in giving a modified *Allen* charge during the sentencing phase of the case. When the jury indicated to the trial judge that it was unable to reach a decision on sentence, the judge gave each juror a piece of paper and asked each to indicate whether further deliberations would be helpful in obtaining a verdict. Eight jurors initially answered affirmatively, and three others subsequently indicated that they had misunderstood the question. The judge then asked each to indicate whether further deliberations would enable the jury to reach a verdict, and eleven jurors responded affirmatively. At this point, the judge told the jurors that they should consider each other's views with the objective of reaching a verdict without surrendering their honest beliefs in doing so, and that the court would impose a sentence of life imprisonment without possibility of probation, parole, or suspension of sentence if the jury failed to agree on a sanction. Shortly thereafter, the jury voted for the death penalty. Chief Justice Rehnquist's majority opinion reasoned that the trial judge had not coerced the jury into reaching a decision and distinguished Brasfield v. United States, 272 U.S. 448 (1926), which had used the Court's supervisory powers to condemn judicial inquiry into the numerical division of jurors. The Court also distinguished Jenkins v. United States, 380 U.S. 445 (1965), where the trial judge told the jury that "you have got to reach a decision in this case." Justice Marshall, joined by Justices Brennan and Stevens, dissented and argued that the two polls of the jury whittled the minority jurors from four to one. He condemned the fact that in the instant case, as in *Brasfield,* the jurors were asked to identify themselves by name in the polls. He also expressed doubts as to the wisdom of the *Allen* charge, especially in a case in which a hung jury would produce a life sentence rather than a new proceeding, and therefore the costs of a deadlock were not so substantial.

3. Protecting Against Jury Misconduct and Outside Influence

The conduct of the individual jurors during the trial proceedings and the subsequent deliberations must comport with the requirement of impartiality. The trial judge must deal with any particular action that could undermine a juror's impartiality. Where jurors learn of highly inflammatory information that will not be brought out in evidence, they may be disqualified. See, e.g., United States v. Martinez, 14 F.3d 543 (11th Cir.1994)(juror saw newscast); People v. Honeycutt, 20 Cal.3d 150, 141 Cal.Rptr. 698, 570 P.2d 1050 (1977)(information and advice from an attorney friend of the foreman was prejudicial.) Even if the juror is adversely affected by events outside her control, she may have to be excused. See, e.g., United States v. Angulo, 4 F.3d 843 (9th Cir.1993) (juror excused after receiving threatening phone call).

Additionally, a juror must remain able and qualified to perform his duty. See United States v. Smith, 550 F.2d 277 (5th Cir.1977)(sleeping juror and juror whose conduct suggests that tampering has occurred are disqualified). Of course, the trial judge must be careful not to excuse a juror too quickly, and to excuse jurors in a way that does not prejudice either of the parties. See, e.g., United States v. Hernandez, 862 F.2d 17 (2d Cir.1988) (finding error in the trial court's decision to dismiss a juror where "the record seemed to reflect that the cause of the removal was as much to avoid a mistrial because of a hung jury as to excuse an incompetent juror").

Habeas corpus relief was granted in Phillips v. Smith, 485 F.Supp. 1365 (S.D.N.Y.1980), affirmed, 632 F.2d 1019 (2d Cir.), on the ground that the defendant was denied a fair trial when the prosecutor learned during the trial that one juror's employment application was pending in his office, and the prosecutor did not disclose this fact to the court or the defense until after the jury returned its guilty verdict. The Supreme Court reversed, 455 U.S. 209 (1982), holding that due process does not require a new trial every time a juror is placed in a potentially compromising situation, and reasoning that where a post-trial hearing resulted in a finding that the juror was not actually biased, a federal court should not set aside a state conviction.

Sequestration

During the course of trial, the judge has discretion to sequester the jury. Some jurisdictions require sequestration, unless it is waived by the parties. See N.Y.C.P.L. § 310.10; Davidson v. Commonwealth, 555 S.W.2d 269 (Ky.1977). One famous trial lawyer believes that sequestration is usually prejudicial to the defendant:

> Every trial lawyer knows that a sequestered jury behaves radically differently from one whose members can go home at night. The jurors react to confinement with resentment. Sometimes they resent their captors. More often, they come to identify with the cops who are guarding them. And as the trial wears on, and the defense case threatens to lengthen their confinement, jurors begin to look at defense counsel with baleful eyes.

Tigar, Television and the Jury, Nat'l L.J., Aug. 21, 1995, p. A19.

Sequestration—as in the O.J. Simpson case, where the jurors were sequestered for more than a year—is ordinarily a response to the risk of prejudicial trial publicity. Is there a less onerous means of protecting the jurors from hearing about extrajudicial information? Would court orders preventing the jurors from reading newspapers, watching television, etc. be sufficient? Can we trust the jurors to close their eyes and ears if they are not sequestered?

Sequestration During Deliberations

It is more likely that a judge will exercise her discretion to sequester the jury once deliberations begin. The court in Hunley v. Godinez, 975 F.2d 316 (7th Cir.1992), considered a hopefully unique problem that arose with a jury that was sequestered during deliberations. The defendant was charged with murder and burglary, the prosecution contending that the murder occurred when the defendant was discovered by the victim while burgling her apartment. After the first day of deliberations, the jury stood 8 to 4 in favor of conviction. The jurors were then sequestered overnight in a hotel. That night, a burglar made an unforced entry into the rooms of four jurors, and stole several items. The jurors talked about the burglary among themselves the next day. The jury reached a guilty verdict after one hour of deliberations that day. Two of the four jurors who changed their minds from the previous day had been victims of the burglary. The trial judge held an in camera hearing, and each of the jurors said that the burglary had not affected their verdict. Nonetheless, the court of appeals reversed the conviction. It reasoned that "[t]he burglary placed the jurors in the shoes of the victim just before she was murdered." What should the trial judge have done?

Ex Parte Communications With the Jury

In Rushen v. Spain, 464 U.S. 114 (1983), the Court reversed lower federal courts that had granted habeas corpus relief to a petitioner who complained about ex parte communications between a trial judge and a juror. The juror had indicated to the judge that she was an acquaintance of a woman who had been murdered by one of the defense witnesses, although she expressed the view that she could be fair to the defendants. The lower courts had reasoned that the contact between judge and juror could not be deemed harmless, since no

H :
presumed
no
influence

contemporaneous record had been made. But the Supreme Court ruled that the lower federal courts should have deferred to the "presumptively correct" state court finding that the jury's deliberations had not been affected by the ex parte contact. See also United States v. Strickland, 935 F.2d 822 (7th Cir.1991)(a juror acted improperly when he asked a question of a government witness outside of court; but this was not prejudicial because the witness did not answer, curative instructions were given, and the trial judge determined after questioning that the juror could remain impartial).

Evidentiary Limitations on Proof of Jury Misconduct: Tanner v. United States

The Supreme Court held, 5–4, in Tanner v. United States, 483 U.S. 107 (1987), that two defendants, who were convicted of conspiring to defraud the United States and of mail fraud, were properly denied a hearing concerning juror misconduct. The defendants called to the trial judge's attention one juror's statement that several jurors had consumed alcohol at lunch throughout the trial, causing them to sleep during the afternoons. The only other evidence offered in the trial court in support of a hearing was defense counsel's testimony that he had observed one of the jurors "in a sort of giggly mood" during the trial, something not called to the judge's attention. While the case was pending on appeal, the defendants presented a second juror's affidavit indicating that numerous members of the jury, including the affiant, consumed alcohol during the trial and some jurors used illegal drugs.

Writing for the majority in *Tanner*, Justice O'Connor relied upon Rule 606(b) of the Federal Rules of Evidence, which generally prohibits an inquiry into the course of the jury's deliberations. Rule 606(b) does permit proof of "extraneous prejudicial information" that was brought to the jury's attention, and it also permits proof that an "outside influence was improperly brought to bear upon any juror." But Justice O'Connor declared that these exceptions did not apply to allegations of substance abuse by the jurors—rather, these exceptions covered matters such as threats or bribes to jurors from outside sources, or exposure to prejudicial trial publicity. Justice O'Connor also rejected the argument that the failure to inquire into juror intoxication denies a defendant a fair trial before an impartial and competent jury, reasoning that other aspects of the trial process—voir dire of jurors, observations by the trial judge and courtroom participants, and observations and reports by fellow jurors—are adequate to assure defendants fair trials. Justice O'Connor expressed concern that routine impeachment of jury verdicts, by inquiring into what went on in the deliberations, would have a negative effect on finality and on jury deliberations.

There is little doubt that post-verdict investigation into juror misconduct would in some instances lead to the invalidation of verdicts reached after irresponsible or improper behavior. It is not at all clear, however, that the jury system could survive such efforts to perfect it. Allegations of juror misconduct, incompetency, or inattentiveness, raised for the first time days, weeks, or months after the verdict seriously disrupt the finality of the process. Moreover, full and frank discussion in the jury room, jurors' willingness to return an unpopular verdict, and the community's trust in a system that relies on the decisions of laypeople would all be undermined by a barrage of post-verdict scrutiny of juror conduct.

Justice Marshall, joined by Justices Brennan, Blackmun, and Stevens, dissented. He concluded that "[e]very criminal defendant has a constitutional right to be tried by competent jurors," and that "[i]f, as charged, members of petitioners' jury were intoxicated as a result of their use of drugs and alcohol to the point of sleeping through material portions of the trial, the verdict in this case must be set aside." Justice Marshall contended that the evidence of alcohol and drug use was an outside influence about which jurors may testify under Rule 606(b), since it was unrelated to juror deliberations. He concluded that voir dire of jurors prior to trial cannot disclose whether they will use drugs during the trial, and the type of misconduct alleged would not have been verified easily by courtroom personnel.[36]

Examples of alleged jury misconduct that have been held immune from inquiry under Rule 606(b) after *Tanner* include: intimidation of one juror by another (United States v. Stansfield, 101 F.3d 909 (3d Cir.1996)); unfair inferences drawn from the evidence (United States v. DiSalvo, 34 F.3d 1204 (3d Cir.1994)); assumptions that if the defendant failed to take the stand, he must be guilty (United States v. Voigt, 877 F.2d 1465 (10th Cir.1989)); and a vote for conviction because extended deliberation would cut into the juror's vacation (United States v. Murphy, 836 F.2d 248 (6th Cir.1988)). The Court in United States v. Ruggiero, 56 F.3d 647, 652 (5th Cir.1995), summed it up by stating that Rule 606(b) bars juror testimony on "at least four topics: (1) the methods or arguments of the jury's deliberations, (2) the effect of any particular thing upon an outcome in the deliberations, (3) the mindset or emotions of any juror during deliberations, and (4) the testifying juror's own mental process during deliberations."

Despite the salutary policies against disclosure of jury deliberations, courts in criminal cases are understandably reluctant to limit their inquiry when there are good faith allegations that jurors relied on racial prejudices during their deliberations. As the Second Circuit has stated, courts "have hesitated to apply the rule precluding inquiry dogmatically" in the face of the defendant's Sixth Amendment right to an impartial jury. Wright v. United States, 732 F.2d 1048 (2d Cir.1984). While the court must remain sensitive to the policies of finality and protection of the jury, these policies must be tempered by the criminal defendant's right to a fair trial.

Lies on Voir Dire

Tanner states that the voir dire process is preferable to post-conviction review for determining whether jurors are competent and impartial. But what if the witness lies at the voir dire? In United States v. Colombo, 869 F.2d 149 (2d Cir.1989), the defendant submitted a post-conviction affidavit from an alternate juror, averring that a juror deliberately failed to reveal on voir dire that her brother-in-law was an attorney for the government. Her motivation for concealment was that she thought it would hurt her chances to sit on the case. The court held that if it could be shown that the juror's brother-in-law was a government attorney, "the conviction cannot stand, because such conduct obstructed the voir dire and indicated an impermissible partiality on the juror's

---

36. For an application of *Tanner*, see United States v. Straach, 987 F.2d 232 (5th Cir. 1993)(evidence that jury reached a compromise verdict is inadmissible under Rule 606(b) as it is not evidence of extraneous information or outside influence).

part." The court rejected as irrelevant the argument that merely having a government attorney as a brother-in-law would not have been enough to challenge the juror for cause.

> The point is not that her relationship with her brother-in-law tainted the proceedings but that her willingness to lie about it exhibited an interest strongly suggesting partiality. * * * [C]ourts cannot administer justice in circumstances in which a juror can commit a federal crime in order to serve as a juror in a criminal case and do so with no fear of sanction so long as a conviction results.

See also Dyer v. Calderon, 151 F.3d 970 (9th Cir.1998) (en banc) (conviction must be reversed where juror lies in answering voir dire question as to whether a family member had ever been a victim of a crime: "[T]here is a fine line between being willing to serve and being anxious, between accepting the grave responsibility for passing judgment on a human life and being so eager that you court perjury to avoid being struck. The individual who lies in order to improve his chances of serving has too much of a stake in the matter to be considered indifferent.").

Presuming the truth of the allegations in *Tanner* and *Colombo,* which case presents the more serious threat to the defendant's right to an impartial jury? Should a conviction be automatically reversed whenever it is discovered that the juror told a lie on voir dire? See United States v. Langford, 990 F.2d 65 (2d Cir.1993), where a juror failed to admit that she had been arrested three times for prostitution fifteen years earlier. At the time of voir dire, the juror worked as a mental health assistant, had just taken a test to be a nurse, had a six-year-old daughter, and taught Sunday School. The court found that the juror had deliberately lied, but that her motivation was embarrassment. Unlike the juror in *Colombo,* she "had no interest in being on that particular jury." Accordingly, the defendant suffered no prejudice. Do you agree? Could the juror have been challenged for cause if the defendant had known about her prior record?

4. *The Use and Function of Alternate Jurors*

Federal Rule of Criminal Procedure 24(c) provides that the court may empanel up to six alternate jurors, to provide for the possibility that one or more of the regular jurors may become unable or unqualified to serve as the trial progresses. The Federal Rule further provides that alternate jurors may be retained after the jury retires to consider its verdict; but the court must ensure that a retained alternate does not discuss the case with anyone until that alternate replaces a juror or is discharged. Thus, the alternate who is retained, but does not replace a juror, is not permitted to take an active part in the jury deliberations. The Federal Rule further provides that if "an alternate replaces a juror after deliberations have begun, the court must instruct the jury to begin its deliberations anew."

F. THE TRIAL JUDGE AND THE RIGHT TO JURY TRIAL

1. *The Role of the Judge Generally*

If the right to jury trial is to work as intended—i.e., to provide protection against eccentric, biased, overreaching or bureaucratic judges and public officials—it is necessary that the judge not take action that unduly invades the independence of the jury.

In any trial system with evidence and procedural rules like those found in the United States, it is almost certain that the trial judge will be called upon to decide what evidence will get to a jury and what will be excluded. To some extent, the development of modern evidence codes may control the judge's decisionmaking power, but even under codes judges are left with broad discretion. See Saltzburg, The Federal Rules of Evidence and the Quality of Practice in Federal Courts, 27 Cleve.St.L.Rev. 173 (1978). Appellate review of decisions in individual cases and careful selection of judges provide some assurance that evidentiary and procedural decisions will be fair, but the fact is that appellate courts reviewing a cold record are likely to defer on "judgment calls" to trial judges, and the selection of judges is neither careful, nor apolitical in many instances. Thus, there is little doubt that trial judges have an impact on jury decisions through their decisions on questions of evidence and procedure.

There is no doubt that judges have enormous powers reserved to them, powers that are exercised more or less independently of juries. For example, trial judges decide whether or not to accept guilty pleas and plea bargains; there is no right to jury trial on the advisability of any contract between the prosecutor and the defendant. Earlier in this Chapter, we saw that judges rule on questions of joinder and severance, that judges rule on speedy trial questions and that judges even control the selection process of the jury. It is not difficult, then, to demonstrate that the meaningfulness of the jury trial right will depend in large part on the role played by the trial judge.

2. *Selection of Judges*

Who are these trial judges and how are they selected? Federal trial judges are, of course, nominated by the President and confirmed, with life tenure as long as there is good behavior, by the Senate. Nominees are screened by an ABA Committee on the Federal Judiciary, although the ABA can do no more than make a judgment that may or may not be accepted by the President and the Senate. See Miller, The ABA's Role in Judicial Selection, 65 A.B.A.J. 516 (1979).

State judges are selected by a variety of different methods; often they must win elections to continue in office. See generally, Winters, Selection of Judges— An Historical Introduction, 44 Tex.L.Rev. 1081 (1966). The quality of judges may differ at different stages of the criminal process and in different geographical areas. For example, one commentator concluded that "[m]unicipal court judges in most urban centers are chosen neither because they have demonstrated great legal talent nor for their compassion. On the contrary, they are chosen by partisan political machines for their faithfulness to the party and their past work on behalf of the party." Katz, Municipal Courts—Another Urban Ill, 20 Case W.Res.L.Rev. 87, 119–39 (1968). The differences among judges sitting on the same court often are well known. See Smith & Blumberg, The Problem of Objectivity in Judicial Decisionmaking, 46 Social Forces 96 (1967).

Proposals are often made to make judicial selection and retention decisions less political. See, e.g., Nat'l Advisory Comm'n on Criminal Justice Standards and Goals: Courts, Standards 7.1 and 7.2 (1973), and authorities cited therein. But, in many states, political officials resist any attempt to limit the use of judicial positions as patronage or to remove the political constraints on the day-to-day actions of trial judges.

3. *Peremptory and Other Challenges*

Some jurisdictions recognize the potential impact that a judge can have on the ultimate disposition of any case, even one tried to a jury, by providing for a right of either the prosecution or defense to challenge one judge peremptorily— i.e., as a matter of right. See, e.g., Alaska Stat. 22.20.022. And all allow judges to be challenged for cause, although the standards by which such challenges are measured differ.

Where peremptory challenges of judges are permitted, can a judge be struck for discriminatory reasons? In People v. Williams, 8 Cal.App.4th 688, 10 Cal. Rptr.2d 873 (1992), the court held that the principles set forth in *Batson*, prohibiting discrimination in peremptory challenges of jurors, were applicable by analogy to peremptory challenges of judges. Isn't there a difference between excluding a juror and excluding a judge?

Biased Judge

If the judge is biased, he is subject to a challenge for cause, and if the bias is not discovered until after the verdict, the verdict is subject to reversal. See Ward v. Village of Monroeville, 409 U.S. 57 (1972)(traffic offense; judge not impartial where he is also the Mayor, responsible for village finances); Tumey v. Ohio, 273 U.S. 510 (1927)(judge was paid only if the defendant was convicted).

In the following case, the Supreme Court considered claims of judicial bias due to the corruption of the judge.

BRACY v. GRAMLEY

Supreme Court of the United States, 1997.
520 U.S. 899.

CHIEF JUSTICE REHNQUIST **delivered the opinion for the Court.**

Petitioner William Bracy was tried, convicted, and sentenced to death before then-Judge Thomas J. Maloney for his role in an execution-style triple murder. Maloney was later convicted of taking bribes from defendants in criminal cases. Although he was not bribed in this case, he "fixed" other murder cases during and around the time of petitioner's trial. Petitioner contends that Maloney therefore had an interest in a conviction here, to deflect suspicion that he was taking bribes in other cases, and that this interest violated the fair-trial guarantee of the Fourteenth Amendment's Due Process Clause. We hold that petitioner has made a sufficient factual showing to establish "good cause," as re-

quired by Habeas Corpus Rule 6(a), for discovery on his claim of actual judicial bias in his case.

Maloney was one of many dishonest judges exposed and convicted through "Operation Greylord," a labyrinthine federal investigation of judicial corruption in Chicago. Maloney served as a judge from 1977 until he retired in 1990, and it appears he has the dubious distinction of being the only Illinois judge ever convicted of fixing a murder case. Before he was appointed to the bench, Maloney was a criminal-defense attorney with close ties to organized crime who often paid off judges in criminal cases. Once a judge, Maloney exploited many of the relationships and connections he had developed while bribing judges to solicit bribes for himself. For example, Lucius

Robinson, a bailiff through whom Maloney had bribed judges while in practice, and Robert McGee, one of Maloney's former associates, both served as "bag men," or intermediaries, between Maloney and lawyers looking for a fix. Two such lawyers, Robert J. Cooley and William A. Swano, were key witnesses against Maloney at his trial.

Maloney was convicted in Federal District Court of conspiracy, racketeering, extortion, and obstructing justice in April 1993. Four months later, petitioner filed this habeas petition in the United States District Court for the Northern District of Illinois, claiming, among other things, that he was denied a fair trial because "in order to cover up the fact that [Maloney] accepted bribes from defendants in some cases, [he] was prosecution oriented in other cases." Petitioner also sought discovery in support of this claim. Specifically, he requested (1) the sealed transcript of Maloney's trial; (2) reasonable access to the prosecution's materials in Maloney's case; (3) the opportunity to depose persons associated with Maloney; and (4) a chance to search Maloney's rulings for a pattern of pro-prosecution bias. The District Court rejected petitioner's fair-trial claim and denied his supplemental motion for discovery, concluding that "[petitioner's] allegations contain insufficient specificity or good cause to justify further discovery."

The Court of Appeals affirmed by a divided vote. The court conceded the "appearance of impropriety" in petitioner's case but reasoned that this appearance did not require a new trial because it "provided only a weak basis for supposing the original trial an unreliable test of the issues presented for decision in it." Next, the court agreed that petitioner's theory—that Maloney's corruption "permeated his judicial conduct"—was "plausible," but

found it not "sufficiently compelling [an] empirical proposition" to justify presuming actual judicial bias in petitioner's case. Finally, the court held that petitioner had not shown "good cause" for discovery to prove his claim, as required by * * * [Habeas Corpus] Rule 6(a). This was because, in the court's view, even if petitioner were to uncover evidence that Maloney sometimes came down hard on defendants who did not bribe him, "it would not show that he followed the practice in this case." * * * We now reverse.

* * *

Before addressing whether petitioner is entitled to discovery under [the Habeas Corpus rules] to support his judicial-bias claim, we must first identify the "essential elements" of that claim. Of course, most questions concerning a judge's qualifications to hear a case are not constitutional ones, because the Due Process Clause of the Fourteenth Amendment establishes a constitutional floor, not a uniform standard. Instead, these questions are, in most cases, answered by common law, statute, or the professional standards of the bench and bar. But the floor established by the Due Process Clause clearly requires a "fair trial in a fair tribunal," before a judge with no actual bias against the defendant or interest in the outcome of his particular case.

The facts of this case are, happily, not the stuff of typical judicial-disqualification disputes. A judge who accepts bribes from a criminal defendant to fix that defendant's case is "biased" in the most basic sense of that word, but his bias is directed against the State, not the defendant. Petitioner contends, however, that Maloney's taking of bribes from some criminal defendants not only rendered him biased against the State in those cases, but also induced a sort of compensatory bias against defendants who did not bribe Maloney. Maloney was biased in this latter, compensatory sense, petitioner argues, to avoid being seen as uniformly and suspiciously "soft" on criminal defendants. The Court of Appeals, in its opinion, pointed out that this theory is quite speculative; after all, it might be equally likely that a judge who was "on the take" in some criminal cases would be careful to at least appear to favor all criminal defendants, so as to avoid apparently wild and unexplainable swings in decisions and judicial philosophy. In any event, difficulties of proof aside, there is no question that, if it could be proved, such compensatory, camouflaging bias on Maloney's part in petitioner's own case would violate the Due Process Clause of the Fourteenth Amendment. We now turn to the question whether petitioner has shown "good cause" for appropriate discovery to prove his judicial-bias claim.

* * *

[P]etitioner's attorney at trial was a former associate of Maloney's, and Maloney appointed him to defend this case in June 1981. The lawyer announced that he was ready for trial just a few weeks later. He did not request additional time to prepare penalty-phase evidence in this death-penalty case even when the State announced at the outset that, if petitioner were convicted, it would introduce petitioner's then-pending Arizona murder charges as evidence in aggravation. At oral argument before this Court, counsel for petitioner suggested, given that at least one of Maloney's former law associates—Robert McGee—was corrupt and involved in bribery, that petitioner's trial lawyer might have been appointed with the understanding that he would not object to, or interfere with, a prompt trial, so that petitioner's case could be tried before,

and camouflage the bribe negotiations in, [a fixed] murder case. This is, of course, only a theory at this point; it is not supported by any solid evidence of petitioner's trial lawyer's participation in any such plan. It is true, however, that McGee was corrupt and that petitioner's trial coincided with bribe negotiations in the [fixed] case and closely followed the Rosario murder case, which was also fixed.

We conclude that petitioner has shown "good cause" for discovery under Rule 6(a). * * * Ordinarily, we presume that public officials have " 'properly discharged their official duties.' "Were it possible to indulge this presumption here, we might well agree with the Court of Appeals that petitioner's submission and his compensatory-bias theory are too speculative to warrant discovery. But, unfortunately, the presumption has been soundly rebutted: Maloney was shown to be thoroughly steeped in corruption through his public trial and conviction. We emphasize, though, that petitioner supports his discovery request by pointing not only to Maloney's conviction for bribe-taking in other cases, but also to additional evidence, discussed above, that lends support to his claim that Maloney was actually biased in petitioner's own case. That is, he presents "specific allegations" that his trial attorney, a former associate of Maloney's in a law practice that was familiar and comfortable with corruption, may have agreed to take this capital case to trial quickly so that petitioner's conviction would deflect any suspicion the rigged * * * cases might attract. It may well be, as the Court of Appeals predicted, that petitioner will be unable to obtain evidence sufficient to support a finding of actual judicial bias in the trial of his case, but we hold that he has made a

sufficient showing * * * to establish
"good cause" for discovery.

Note on Bracy

On remand, the Court of Appeals found that Bracy, after getting discovery, did not show that the judge was biased against him but rather that the claim was "hopelessly speculative."

> For all that appears, Maloney was a prosecution-minded judge for reasons unrelated to his taking bribes. That he would accept payment to acquit criminals does not imply any affection for criminal defendants or their lawyers such that he *must* have been acting against character when he ruled in favor of the prosecution in cases in which he was not bribed. That is a possibility, but no more than a possibility. Maloney's conduct was appalling, his character depraved, but the bridge to the trial of Bracy * * * is missing. He was certainly capable of dreaming up and acting on compensatory bias, but there is no evidence that he did.

Bracy v. Shomig, 248 F.3d 604 (7th Cir. 2001). See also Mann v. Thalacker, 246 F.3d 1092 (8th Cir. 2001) (due process did not require state trial judge to recuse himself in a bench trial on charges involving sexual abuse of a child, even though the judge had been sexually abused by his father when he was a child; the record did not reveal any statements or actions by the judge that indicated actual bias; and the judge's personal history did not make bias so likely that it should be presumed).

4. Limitations on Judicial Powers

Although it is clear that the trial judge can influence the outcome of a jury trial, the constitutional right to a jury trial means that there are some things that are beyond the power of trial judges.

No Directed Verdict of Guilt

One constitutionally based rule is that the trial judge may not direct a verdict of guilty in a criminal jury trial, even if the defendant admits every material element of an offense. This is because a directed verdict deprives the defendant of the right to a jury trial. See Sullivan v. Louisiana, 508 U.S. 275 (1993)(recognizing that trial judges are constitutionally prohibited from directing a verdict against the defendant).

Jury Nullification

Because a trial judge cannot direct a verdict against the defendant, the jury is essentially given the power to nullify the application of the law to the facts of a case by refusing to convict.[37] Discussion of the phenomenon of jury nullification reached a new level after the O.J. Simpson case, in which the defense counsel arguably encouraged the jury to acquit Simpson even if they thought him guilty, in order to send a message to the Los Angeles Police Department. The nullifica-

---

37. A famous instance of jury nullification occurred in the trial of John Peter Zenger in 1735. He was acquitted of charges for seditious libel, even though he admitted the facts charged. See Scheflin, Jury Nullification: The Right to Say No, 45 S.Cal.L.Rev. 168 (1972). Less high-minded examples of jury nullification include juries in the South who would not convict white supremacists accused of racial crimes.

tion question has also arisen in cases where abused wives have been charged with murdering their abusive husbands, as well as in cases alleging drug possession or distribution of minor amounts of narcotics.

While jurors apparently have the power to nullify, should they be encouraged to do so? Aren't jurors expected to follow the instructions of the trial judge? Indeed, in the cases discussing voir dire, and challenges for cause, wasn't one of the controlling questions whether the juror would follow instructions? Does nullification create chaos, or is the nullification power necessary to enforce the jury's role as the conscience of the community and the shield against abuse of power? See Weinstein, Considering Jury Nullification: When May and Should a Jury Reject the Law and Do Justice?, 30 Am.Crim.L.Rev. 239 (1993).

The Second Circuit had this to say about the concept of jury nullification in United States v. Thomas, 116 F.3d 606 (2d Cir.1997):

> We are mindful that the term "nullification" can cover a number of distinct, though related, phenomena, encompassing in one word conduct that takes place for a variety of different reasons; jurors may nullify, for example, because of the identity of a party, a disapprobation of the particular prosecution at issue, or a more general opposition to the applicable criminal law or laws. We recognize, too, that nullification may at times manifest itself as a form of civil disobedience that some may regard as tolerable. The case of John Peter Zenger, the publisher of the New York Weekly Journal acquitted of criminal libel in 1735, and the nineteenth-century acquittals in prosecutions under the fugitive slave laws, are perhaps our country's most renowned examples of "benevolent" nullification. * * *

> * * * [T]he power of juries to "nullify" or exercise a power of lenity is just that—a power; it is by no means a right or something that a judge should encourage or permit if it is within his authority to prevent. * * * A jury has no more "right" to find a "guilty" defendant "not guilty" than it has to find a "not guilty" defendant guilty, and the fact that the former cannot be corrected by a court, while the latter can be, does not create a right out of the power to misapply the law. Such verdicts are lawless, a denial of due process and constitute an exercise of erroneously seized power. * * *

> Moreover, although the early history of our country includes the occasional Zenger trial or acquittals in fugitive slave cases, more recent history presents numerous and notorious examples of jurors nullifying—cases that reveal the destructive potential of a practice Professor Randall Kennedy of the Harvard Law School has rightly termed a "sabotage of justice." Consider, for example, the two hung juries in the 1964 trials of Byron De La Beckwith in Mississippi for the murder of NAACP field secretary Medgar Evers, or the 1955 acquittal of J.W. Millam and Roy Bryant for the murder of fourteen-year-old Emmett Till—shameful examples of how nullification has been used to sanction murder and lynching.

> Inasmuch as no juror has a right to engage in nullification—and, on the contrary, it is a violation of a juror's sworn duty to follow the law as instructed by the court—trial courts have the duty to forestall or prevent such conduct, whether by firm instruction or admonition or, where it does not interfere with guaranteed rights or the need to protect the secrecy of jury deliberations, by dismissal of an offending juror from the venire or the

jury. * * * Although nullification may sometimes succeed—because, among other things, it does not come to the attention of a presiding judge before the completion of a jury's work, and jurors are not answerable for nullification after the verdict has been reached—it would be a dereliction of duty for a judge to remain indifferent to reports that a juror is intent on violating his oath. * * *

Accordingly, every day in courtrooms across the length and breadth of this country, jurors are dismissed from the venire "for cause" precisely because they are unwilling or unable to follow the applicable law. * * *

So also, a presiding judge possesses both the responsibility and the authority to dismiss a juror whose refusal or unwillingness to follow the applicable law becomes known to the judge during the course of trial.

But how, exactly, is the judge to control the possibility of jury nullification once the jury has been empaneled? The facts of *Thomas* indicate the difficulty of the problem. After the jury retired to deliberate, the trial judge was informed by many of the jurors that Juror No. 5 was adamant in his opposition to a guilty verdict, rude to other jurors, and essentially refused to deliberate. There was a difference of views, however, on whether Juror No. 5 was basing his view on the evidence, or rather upon some moral objection to convicting the defendant. The trial court interviewed all the jurors in camera, and concluded that Juror No. 5 was purposely refusing to apply the law given in the judge's instructions. So the juror was excused for cause, and the remainder of the jury found the defendant guilty.

The Second Circuit reversed in *Thomas*. It noted that inquiries into jury nullification during deliberations were especially sensitive, and necessarily truncated, because of the need to protect jury secrecy, and to avoid intimidation of the jury. The court held that the trial court essentially did not have enough information to conclude, without any doubt, that Juror No. 5 was refusing to follow instructions or to consider the evidence. The court recognized, however, that the trial judge could not have obtained any more information without treading upon the secrecy of the jury deliberations. So essentially, the court held that a trial judge has a duty to inquire into allegations of juror nullification, but not to inquire so deeply that the judge would be able to find, without doubt, that a juror was actually engaged in nullification. The power to control jury nullification during deliberations was essentially limited to situations, undoubtedly rare, where the trial court asks jurors a few preliminary questions and a juror blurts out that he is engaged in nullification. The *Thomas* court summed up this way.

[A] court may not delve deeply into a juror's motivations because it may not intrude on the secrecy of the jury's deliberations. Thus, unless the initial request for a juror's dismissal is transparent, the court will likely prove unable to establish conclusively the reasons underlying it. Given these circumstances, we must hold that if the record evidence discloses any possibility that the request to discharge stems from the juror's view of the sufficiency of the government's evidence, the court must deny the request. * * *

Where the duty and authority to prevent defiant disregard of the law or evidence comes into conflict with the principle of secret jury deliberations, we are compelled to err in favor of the lesser of two evils—protecting the secrecy of jury deliberations at the expense of possibly allowing irresponsible juror activity. * * *

We are required to vacate these judgments because the court dismissed Juror No. 5 largely on the ground that the juror was acting in purposeful disregard of the court's instructions on the law, when the record evidence raises a possibility that the juror was simply unpersuaded by the Government's case against the defendants.

So the bottom line is that a juror bent on nullification might not have a right to nullify, but basically has an unreviewable power to do so.

Racially Based Jury Nullification

Marion Barry, the former Mayor of Washington, D.C., was caught on tape by federal agents while smoking crack cocaine. However, the African–American jury convicted Barry of only one minor count in a fourteen count indictment, despite the trial judge's post-verdict comment that he had "never seen a stronger government case." Is this an example of jury nullification? If so, should jury nullification by minority jurors be treated or considered differently from jury nullification in general? Professor Paul Butler, in Racially Based Jury Nullification: Black Power in the Criminal Justice System, 105 Yale L.J. 677 (1995), provides this analysis:

> My thesis is that, for pragmatic and political purposes, the black community is better off when some nonviolent lawbreakers remain in the community rather than go to prison. The decision as to what kind of conduct by African–Americans ought to be punished is better made by African–Americans themselves, based on the costs and benefits to their community, than by the traditional criminal justice process, which is controlled by white lawmakers and white law enforcers. Legally, the doctrine of jury nullification gives the power to make this decision to African–American jurors who sit in judgment on African–American defendants. Considering the costs of law enforcement to the black community and the failure of white lawmakers to devise significant nonincarcerative responses to black antisocial conduct, it is the moral responsibility of black jurors to emancipate some guilty black outlaws.

* * *

> At this point, every African–American should ask herself whether the operation of the criminal law in the United States advances the interests of black people. If it does not, the doctrine of jury nullification affords African–American jurors the opportunity to control the authority of the law over some African–American criminal defendants. In essence, black people can "opt out" of American criminal law.

Applying this thesis to specific crimes, Professor Butler makes the following conclusions:

> In cases involving violent *malum in se* crimes like murder, rape, and assault, jurors should consider the case strictly on the evidence presented, and, if they have no reasonable doubt that the defendant is guilty, they should convict. For nonviolent *malum in se* crimes such as theft or perjury, nullification is an option that the juror should consider, although there

should be no presumption in favor of it. A juror might vote for acquittal, for example, when a poor woman steals from Tiffany's, but not when the same woman steals from her next door neighbor. Finally, in cases involving nonviolent, *malum prohibitum* offenses, including "victimless" crimes like narcotics offenses, there should be a presumption in favor of nullification.

This approach seeks to incorporate the most persuasive arguments of both the racial critics and the law enforcement enthusiasts. If my model is faithfully executed, the result would be that fewer black people would go to prison; to that extent, the proposal ameliorates one of the most severe consequences of law enforcement in the African–American community. At the same time, the proposal, by punishing violent offenses and certain others, preserves any protection against harmful conduct that the law may offer potential victims.

If Butler's proposal were to be adopted, it would mean that there would be more deadlocked juries in cases where a few minority jurors were on a jury deciding the fate of a minority defendant. Is it possible that over time the legislature would react by passing a law permitting nonunanimous verdicts in criminal cases? Would that development be to the benefit or detriment of defendants who are members of minority groups?

Professor Nancy Marder, in The Myth of the Nullifying Jury, 93 Nw. U.L.Rev. 877 (1999), states that nullification can provide important benefits to the judicial system by operating as a device to curb overzealous prosecution or the application of bad laws. She takes issue, however, with Professor Butler's proposal for race-based nullification.

Under Butler's proposal, the jury would become a mini-legislature in which jurors represent constituencies based on race and try to change social policy through their vote of not guilty. According to Butler, African–American jurors should vote in accordance with the interests of African–American defendants. Their vote of not guilty is set even before they hear the evidence. In fact, they could ignore the trial and deliberations because they already know how they will vote. Not only does Butler's plan for the jury compromise a basic tenet of due process—the need for an impartial decisionmaker—but it does so in a particularly cynical and divisive way. Butler's proposal is cynical because it seeks to replicate in the jury the politics of the legislature, in which politicians vote according to the interests of their constituents and because it reduces all African–American jurors to one view based upon their race. Butler's plan is divisive because it pits African–American jurors against jurors of all other races and backgrounds.

* * *

Finally, Butler's plan contains the seeds of its own undoing. If African–American jurors take Butler's advice seriously and vote to acquit in all cases of nonviolent African–American defendants as a way of protesting social conditions, then African–American jurors will no longer be seated on juries. Judges could excuse such jurors with for cause challenges on the theory that these jurors could not be impartial. Prosecutors could also use their peremptory challenges to remove these jurors, and even if they could not remove them on the basis of race, they could probably offer various seemingly unrelated reasons, as they are already able to do, such as lack of eye contact or poor rapport. Ironically, as the different barriers to jury service for

African Americans have been lifted, from exclusionary venire lists to the use of racially discriminatory peremptories, Butler would lay the groundwork for a new barrier to service.

Instructions on the Power to Nullify

United States v. Dougherty, 473 F.2d 1113 (D.C.Cir.1972), was a prosecution brought against Vietnam War protesters, who broke into property owned by Dow Chemical, the manufacturer of napalm. The defendants argued that the trial judge erred in refusing to instruct the jury that it had the power to nullify. Judge Leventhal responded that the jury should not be told that it may refuse to apply the law given it by the court.

> What makes for health as an occasional medicine would be disastrous as a daily diet. The fact that there is widespread existence of the jury's prerogative, and approval of its existence as a "necessary counter to case-hardened judges and arbitrary prosecutors," does not establish as an imperative that the jury must be informed by the judge of that power. On the contrary, it is pragmatically useful to structure instructions in such wise that the jury must feel strongly about the values involved in the case, so strongly that it must itself identify the case as establishing a call of high conscience, and must independently initiate and undertake an act in contravention of the established instructions. This requirement of independent jury conception confines the happening of the lawless jury to the occasional instance that does not violate, and viewed as an exception may even enhance, the over-all normative effect of the rule of law.

Judge Bazelon disagreed.

> If, as the Court appears to concede, awareness is preferable to ignorance, then I simply do not understand the justification for relying on a haphazard process of informal communication whose effectiveness is likely to depend, to a large extent, on whether or not any of the jurors are so well-educated and astute that they are able to receive the message. If the jury should know of its power to disregard the law, then the power should be explicitly described by instruction of the court or argument of counsel.

See also United States v. Trujillo, 714 F.2d 102 (11th Cir.1983)(defense counsel is not permitted to argue that the jury should nullify); United States v. Edwards, 101 F.3d 17 (2d Cir.1996) (defendant has no right to a jury instruction alerting jurors of the power to nullify, because this power is in contravention of their duty to follow jury instructions).

An interesting use of nullification arose in United States v. Datcher, 830 F.Supp. 411 (M.D.Tenn.1993). In a drug and firearms case, the trial judge permitted the defendant to inform the jury of the sentence that he would receive if found guilty. Under the Federal Sentencing Guidelines, the jury has no role in setting a sentence. However, the court reasoned that the Guidelines, as applied to the defendant, were so harsh that the jury should be given the information necessary to decide whether a "sentencing law should be nullified." The judge noted that the "remedy is one that should be reserved for only those cases where criminal law and community norms greatly diverge." But is it better to acquit a guilty person than it is to impose a sentence that some members of society would think too harsh?

Commenting on the Evidence and Questioning Witnesses

Most states will not allow a trial judge to comment on the weight of the evidence or on the credibility of witnesses, although some of these states will allow the judge to sum up the evidence presented by both sides.

The federal courts and a minority of the states give much more power to the trial judge and allow comment and summation. Because they do not allow unlimited comment and find it difficult to demarcate when the limits of permissible comment are exceeded, it is difficult to know how much leeway the trial judge actually has. It appears that the practice is less expansive than the theory.

Virtually all jurisdictions allow the trial judge to call and to question witnesses, but none provides unlimited authority to the judge. See Federal Rule of Evidence 614. Again, drawing lines is difficult. See Saltzburg, Martin and Capra, Federal Rule of Evidence Manual § 614.02 (8th ed. 2002), for a discussion of the dangers of trial court questioning of witnesses, and the limitations imposed on the practice.

It is sufficient here to note that the more active the judge is, the greater the threat to the independence of the jury. See, e.g., People v. Cook, 33 Cal.3d 400, 189 Cal.Rptr. 159, 658 P.2d 86 (1983)(trial court's comments on evidence after jury failed to reach a verdict interfered with defendant's right to jury trial). See generally Saltzburg, The Unnecessarily Expanding Role of the American Trial Judge, 64 Va.L.Rev. 1 (1978).

In commenting on the evidence and questioning witnesses, the judge is expected to be neutral and not to assume the role of prosecutor. Gratuitous comments and interruptions by the judge are disfavored.[38] See Keane v. State, 357 So.2d 457 (Fla.Ct.App.1978). If the judge distorts important testimony in commenting to the jury on the evidence, reversal may be required. See Owens v. State, 561 S.W.2d 167 (Tenn.Cr.App.1977). But appellate courts will try to avoid reversals where the trial judge has a slip of the tongue. See generally Varela v. State, 561 S.W.2d 186 (Tex.Cr.App.1978)(comment must be reasonably calculated to prejudice defendant's rights to be prejudicial).

Instructing the Jury

The most important aspect of judicial control may be the judge's instructions to the jury and responses to their inquiries after instructions are given. Since in most jurisdictions the judge instructs the jury on the law and binds them to follow the instructions, what the judge says is critical to the disposition of the case by the jurors. It is common to find provisions like Fed.R.Crim.P. 30, which requires the court to accept or reject proposed instructions by counsel before closing argument, and before the instructions as a whole are given.[39]

---

38. It may be difficult to control nonverbal messages from the judge to the jury. See Note, Judges' Nonverbal Behavior in Jury Trials: A Threat to Judicial Impartiality, 61 Va.L.Rev. 1266 (1975).

39. Aside from instructing the jurors on the law, the trial judge controls the jury in many ways. For example, some judges do not allow note-taking by jurors, while others do. See United States v. Maclean, 578 F.2d 64 (3d Cir.1978). Trial judges differ in their attitude

G. THE JURY VERDICT

Generally the verdict that the jury returns must be in writing. It must be returned by the jury in open court. See Fed.R.Crim.P. 31(a). "If there are multiple defendants, the jury may return a verdict at any time during its deliberations as to any defendant about whom it has agreed." Fed.R.Crim.P. 31(b). Some jurisdictions provide that unless the parties waive the right to a poll, the clerk will ask each juror individually whether the verdict announced is his verdict. Others require polling on request or if the judge demands a poll. See, e.g., Fed.R.Crim.P. 31(d). See also United States v. Randle, 966 F.2d 1209 (7th Cir.1992)(reversible error for denying the defendant the opportunity to poll the jury). Verdicts are usually general verdicts of guilty or not guilty (or not guilty by reason of insanity) on each count. In rare instances a special interrogatory is used.

Inconsistent Verdicts

Generally speaking, jury verdicts are valid even if they are inherently inconsistent. See Dunn v. United States, 284 U.S. 390 (1932). The idea is that the inconsistent jury may be attempting to mitigate the force of its verdicts—the jury may be engaging in a form of nullification, as they have the power to do. Of course, if a verdict is not supported by sufficient evidence, it is subject to attack on post-trial review; but sufficiency and inconsistency are not identical concepts.

Justice Rehnquist, writing for a unanimous Court in United States v. Powell, 469 U.S. 57 (1984), applied the general rule that a defendant convicted on one count of an indictment cannot attack the verdict as being inconsistent with acquittal on another count. Powell was convicted of using the telephone in connection with a cocaine conspiracy and possession charges but was acquitted of the conspiracy and possession counts. The Court recognized that the verdict could not be reconciled, but reasoned that it is always uncertain as to why the jury returns such a verdict and that it is unclear "whose ox has been gored." Because the government may not appeal an inconsistent acquittal, the Court declined to give the defendant a new trial on the inconsistent conviction as a matter of course. Moreover, the Court expressed the view that inconsistent verdicts are often a matter of lenity and rejected as unworkable a rule that would permit criminal defendants to challenge verdicts by arguing that in particular cases they are not the product of lenity. The Court noted that the defendant received sufficient protection against jury irrationality "by the independent review of the sufficiency of the evidence undertaken by the trial and appellate courts."

In a footnote in *Powell*, Justice Rehnquist stated that "[n]othing in this opinion is intended to decide the proper resolution of a situation where a defendant is convicted of two crimes, where a guilty verdict on one count logically excludes a finding of guilt on the other." Why is this inconsistency different from the inconsistency accepted by the Court in *Powell*? See State v. Moore, 458 N.W.2d 90 (Minn.1990)(vacating convictions for first degree murder and manslaughter because, as instructed, jury necessarily found that the defen-

toward questions by the jurors to witnesses during the trial. For a suggested procedure, see Saltzburg, The Unnecessarily Expanding Role of the American Trial Judge, 64 Va.L.Rev. 1, 63–65 (1978).

dant's act was both intentional and reckless, mental states that are mutually exclusive).

Applying *Powell,* courts have held that a defendant can be properly convicted of conspiracy even if all of the other named co-conspirators are acquitted. See United States v. Zuniga–Salinas, 952 F.2d 876 (5th Cir.1992).

Inconsistent Defenses

While verdicts can be inconsistent, does it follow that defendants ought to be allowed to assert inconsistent defenses, such as "I wasn't there and if I was, it was self-defense"? Or, "I didn't do it but if I did, I was entrapped"? In Mathews v. United States, 485 U.S. 58 (1988), Chief Justice Rehnquist wrote for the Court as it held that "even if the defendant denies one or more elements of the crime, he is entitled to an entrapment instruction whenever there is sufficient evidence from which a reasonable jury could find entrapment." The Court rejected the government's argument "that allowing a defendant to rely on inconsistent defenses will encourage perjury" and confuse a jury. Justice White, joined by Justice Blackmun, dissented.

Use of Interrogatories

The question whether special interrogatories can and should be used in a criminal case is touched upon in United States v. Ruggiero, 726 F.2d 913 (2d Cir.1984). In a complicated prosecution for racketeering and other offenses, the government alleged various predicate acts to support its racketeering charges. (A minimum number of predicate acts must be proved to support a conviction.) The court of appeals found that one of the predicate acts alleged was improper. Because it was impossible to determine whether the jury relied upon this particular act in returning its guilty verdict on the racketeering charges, the court found that reversal was required. The majority opinion stated that "in a complex RICO [racketeering] trial such as this one, it can be extremely useful for a trial judge to request the jury to record their specific dispositions of the separate predicate acts charged, in addition to their verdict of guilt or innocence on the RICO charge."

Judge Newman wrote a separate opinion analyzing the subject of special interrogatories at greater length. He explained the reasons for judicial reluctance to use interrogatories in criminal cases: "There is apprehension that eliciting 'yes' or 'no' answers to questions concerning the elements of an offense may propel a jury toward a logical conclusion of guilt, whereas a more generalized assessment might have yielded an acquittal"; and "[t]he possibility also exists that fragmenting a single count into the various ways an offense may be committed affords a divided jury an opportunity to resolve its differences to the defendant's disadvantage by saying 'yes' to some means and 'no' to others, although unified consideration of the count might have produced an acquittal or at least a hung jury." He noted that "[i]nterrogatories are especially objectionable when they make resolution of a single fact issue determinative of guilt or innocence, without regard to the elements of an offense, * * * or when their wording shifts the burden of proof to the defendant." On balance, he concluded that a trial judge "should have the discretion to use a jury interrogatory in cases where risk of prejudice to the defendant is slight and the advantage of securing particularized factfinding is substantial."[40]

Lesser Included Offenses

The jury may find the defendant guilty of the crime charged or of any lesser included offense. The doctrine of lesser included offense was described in United States v. King, 567 F.2d 785, 790 (8th Cir.1977):

> This Court has held that a defendant is entitled to a lesser-included offense instruction when the following five elements are present: (1) a proper request is made; (2) the elements of the lesser offense are identical to part of the elements of the greater offense; (3) there is some evidence that would justify conviction of the lesser offense; (4) the proof on the element or elements differentiating the two crimes is sufficiently in dispute so that the jury may consistently find the defendant innocent of the greater and guilty of the lesser-included offense; and (5) there is mutuality, i.e., a charge may be demanded by either the United States or the defense.

> It does not follow that a lesser included offense instruction is mandatory every time a lesser offense is included within the offense charged in the indictment. The instruction need not be given when from the evidence adduced at the trial there is no rational basis upon which the jury could find the defendant guilty of the lesser offense.

In People v. Geiger, 35 Cal.3d 510, 199 Cal.Rptr. 45, 674 P.2d 1303 (1984), the court reversed a defendant's conviction for second-degree burglary because the trial judge refused to give an instruction on a related, but not lesser-included, offense of vandalism. It emphasized the importance of giving the jury a choice when a defendant's actions might arguably fall within the definitions of several different offenses, stating that the benefit of an instruction on lesser related offenses flows to the government as well as to the defendant. A similar ruling was made in the O.J. Simpson case, where the judge, over the defendant's objection, instructed the jury on second-degree murder as well as first-degree murder. Why do you think Simpson objected to the instruction on the lesser included offense? Is the defendant's strategic decision entitled to respect?

The Elements Test: Schmuck v. United States

In Schmuck v. United States, 489 U.S. 705 (1989), the Court adopted the "elements" test for determining whether a trial court must give a lesser included offense instruction under Fed.R.Crim.P. 31(c). Under this test, a lesser included offense is one in which each statutory element is also present in the more serious offense. For example, the elements required to prove involuntary manslaughter in most states are also required to prove the more serious offense

---

40. In Harris v. Rivera, 454 U.S. 339 (1981), the Court concluded that the Federal Constitution places no burden on a state trial judge in a bench trial to explain why he acquits one defendant and convicts another even when the verdicts appear to be inconsistent. Should a presumption that the trial judge may have been drawing fine lines between defendants be employed?

Rarely, if ever, do we ask criminal juries to make specific findings of fact. Under rules like Fed.R.Crim.P. 23, trial judges must make special findings in bench trials upon request. See United States v. Silberman, 464 F.Supp. 866 (M.D.Fla.1979).

of murder. Murder, of course, has additional elements, which is why manslaughter is referred to as "lesser included." The Court in *Schmuck* rejected the broader "inherent relationship" test, under which an offense is included within another when the facts proven at trial support the inference that the defendant committed the less serious offense, and an inherent relationship exists between the two offenses. Under this "inherent relationship" test, the lower court held that Schmuck was entitled to an instruction concerning odometer tampering, when he was charged with mail fraud arising from a scheme to sell cars with turned-back odometers. However, under the elements test, an instruction on odometer tampering was not required, since Schmuck could have been convicted of mail fraud without a showing that he actually turned back any odometers; thus, the elements of odometer tampering were not a "subset" of the elements of mail fraud.

In adopting the elements approach to Rule 31(c), the *Schmuck* Court noted that it was "grounded in the language and history of the Rule and provides greater certainty in its application." The Court also reasoned that the inherent relationship test may create notice problems where the prosecutor asks for a jury charge on an offense whose elements were not charged in the indictment. In contrast, the elements approach, which "involves a textual comparison of criminal statutes and does not depend on inferences that may be drawn from evidence introduced at trial * * * permits both sides to know in advance what jury instructions will be available and to plan their trial strategy accordingly." The Court found the inherent relationship approach to be "rife with the potential for confusion."

For an application of *Schmuck*, see Carter v. United States, 530 U.S. 255 (2000). Carter entered a bank, confronted an exiting customer, and pushed her back inside. She screamed, startling others in the bank. Undeterred, Carter ran inside and leaped over a counter and through one of the teller windows. A teller rushed into the manager's office. Meanwhile, Carter opened several teller drawers and emptied the money into a bag. After removing almost $16,000, he jumped back over the counter and fled. He was charged with violating 18 U.S.C. § 2113(a), which punishes "[w]hoever, by force and violence, or by intimidation, takes ... any ... thing of value [from a] bank." While not contesting the basic facts, Carter pleaded not guilty on the theory that he had not taken the bank's money "by force and violence, or by intimidation," as § 2113(a) requires. Before trial, he moved for a jury instruction on the offense described by § 2113(b) as a lesser included offense of the offense described by § 2113(a). Section 2113(b) entails less severe penalties than § 2113(a), punishing "[w]hoever takes and carries away, with intent to steal or purloin, any ... thing of value exceeding $1,000 [from a] ... bank." The District Court denied the motion. The jury, instructed on § 2113(a) alone, returned a guilty verdict.

The Supreme Court, in an opinion by Justice Thomas for five members of the Court, held that subsection (b) was not a lesser included offense of subsection (a), because it contains three elements that are not required by subsection (a). Those three elements are: (1) specific intent to steal; (2) asportation; and (3) valuation exceeding $1,000. Justice Thomas applied a "textual comparison" of the elements of the two offenses and concluded as follows:

First, whereas subsection (b) requires that the defendant act "with intent to steal or purloin," subsection (a) contains no similar requirement. Second, whereas subsection (b) requires that the defendant "tak[e] and carr[y] away" the property, subsection (a) only requires that the defendant "tak[e]" the property. Third, whereas the first paragraph of subsection (b) requires that the property have a "value exceeding $1,000," subsection (a) contains no valuation requirement. These extra clauses in subsection (b) cannot be regarded as mere surplusage; they mean something.

Justice Ginsburg, joined by Justices Stevens, Souter and Breyer, dissented in *Carter*. She relied on common law traditions rather than strict textual comparison. She explained as follows:

> At common law, robbery meant larceny plus force, violence, or putting in fear. Because robbery was an aggravated form of larceny at common law, larceny was a lesser included offense of robbery. Congress, I conclude, did not depart from that traditional understanding when it rendered "Bank robbery and incidental crimes" federal offenses. Accordingly, I would hold that petitioner Carter is not prohibited as a matter of law from obtaining an instruction on bank larceny as a lesser included offense. The Court holds that Congress, in 18 U.S.C. § 2113, has dislodged bank robbery and bank larceny from their common-law mooring. I dissent from that determination. [41]

H. WAIVER OF JURY TRIAL; TRIAL BY THE COURT

Even though a defendant has a right to a jury trial, she may desire to be tried by a judge. Certain crimes—e.g., child abuse—may be difficult for lay jurors to view dispassionately. See generally H. Kalven and H. Zeisel, The American Jury (1966). Defendants with prior records may believe that in reaching a decision on the merits of a case, a judge can discount prior convictions offered for impeachment purposes somewhat better than a jury can. Jurisdictions differ on whether the defendant can waive a jury trial at all, on whether the prosecutor can force a jury trial when the defendant prefers a judge trial, and on whether the court can try a case with a jury when neither side wants one.

In Singer v. United States, 380 U.S. 24 (1965), the Supreme Court rebuffed a constitutional attack on Fed.R.Crim.P. 23(a), which permits the defendant to waive a jury trial only with the consent of both the government and the court. The Court rejected the argument that the Sixth Amendment's right to jury trial implies a correlative, unilateral right to waive a jury trial. The Court did say that it would not "assume that federal prosecutors would demand a jury trial for an ignoble purpose." And it left open the possibility that in some circumstances the defendant's reasons for wanting to avoid a jury would be so compelling that the government would deny "an impartial trial" if it insisted on a jury.[42] See also United States v. Clark, 943 F.2d 775 (7th Cir.1991) (no violation of the Constitution where "the result is simply that the defendant is subject to an impartial trial by jury—the very thing that the Constitution guarantees him"; in

---

41. The concept of lesser included offense is also discussed in Chapter Twelve, in connection with double jeopardy rules.

42. For a discussion of the proper procedure for a court to use in accepting a waiver of jury trial in federal court, see Marone v. United States, 10 F.3d 65 (2d Cir.1993)("This court urges that at a minimum the district courts inform each defendant that a jury is composed of twelve members of the community, that the defendant may participate in the selection of the jurors, that the jury's verdict must be unanimous, and that a judge alone will decide guilt or innocence if the defendant waives the right to a jury trial.").

dictum, the court states that a defendant may have a right to a bench trial in a case involving "very complex facts").

Why would the prosecution ever object to the defendant's request for a bench trial? Consider United States v. Sun Myung Moon, 718 F.2d 1210 (2d Cir.1983). The Rev. Sun Myung Moon, the leader of the Unification Church, was charged with criminal tax violations. After his indictment, he made a speech and declared that the only reason he was being prosecuted was that he had "yellow skin" and was the head of the Unification Church. The government opposed Moon's request for a bench trial, arguing that in light of Moon's charges of governmental abuse, a "single factfinder would be put in an untenable position." The government contended that there was an overriding public interest in the appearance of a fair trial, that could be achieved only by a jury verdict. The court upheld the trial court's denial of the request for a bench trial. But how fair does the trial appear if the defendant is made a prisoner of his own right to a jury trial? By the way, why did Moon want a bench trial rather than a jury trial? Could there be any reason, other than the articulated one, for the government to oppose Moon's request?[43]

Nonlawyer Judges

The defendant who faces a trial by judge has the right to an impartial judge. Does the defendant have a right to a judge who knows much about the law? In North v. Russell, 427 U.S. 328 (1976), the Supreme Court held that an accused is not denied due process "when tried before a nonlawyer police court judge with a later trial de novo available under a State's two-tier court system." The Court, per Chief Justice Burger, recognized that the accused had the right to counsel at the first trial, but concluded that because lay magistrates can issue warrants, they could try cases in the first instance. Justice Stewart, joined by Justice Marshall, dissented, taking the view that "the essential presupposition of this basic constitutional right [of counsel] is that the judge conducting the trial will be able to understand what the defendant's lawyer is talking about." Can you reconcile *North* with the right-to-counsel cases?

V.　THE IMPARTIALITY OF THE TRIBUNAL AND THE INFLUENCE OF THE PRESS

We have already seen one way of protecting against a biased jury—i.e., voir dire of prospective jurors in order to eliminate those whose partiality would threaten the integrity of the jury as factfinder. Another way of preventing or inhibiting jury bias is to control the flow of information to the potential pool of jurors in a community and, even more importantly, to control the flow of information to those selected as jurors.

Whenever any government agency wants to control the flow of information to the public, it is likely to be resisted by the press and many willing recipients of information. Efforts to afford all parties a fair trial can threaten some of the interests served by a free press. How to accommodate the competing interests

---

43. For a critical view of the Federal Rule, see Kurland, Providing a Defendant With a Unilateral Right to a Bench Trial: A Renewed Call to Amend Federal Rule of Criminal Procedure 23(a), 26 U.C.D.L.Rev. 309 (1993).

has become known as the "fair trial—free press" issue and is the subject of this section of the Chapter.

A. THE IMPACT OF PRESS COVERAGE ON LITIGATION

1. *Prejudicial Pretrial Publicity*

Pervasive Prejudice: Irvin v. Dowd

In Irvin v. Dowd, 366 U.S. 717 (1961), a unanimous Supreme Court struck down for the first time a state conviction because of the effect of pretrial publicity.[44] Irvin had been convicted of murder and sentenced to death. The charge arose after six murders were committed in the vicinity of Evansville, Indiana. Police issued press releases saying that Irvin had confessed to murder. Although one change of venue was granted, it was from Evansville to an adjoining rural county that had received some of the publicity concerning the crimes and Irvin's arrest. A second change of venue was denied. Justice Clark's opinion for the Court stressed that the Constitution does not require a jury that is completely untouched by pretrial publicity:

> It is not required * * * that jurors be totally ignorant of the facts and issues involved. In these days of swift, widespread and diverse methods of communication, an important case can be expected to arouse the interest of the public in the vicinity, and scarcely any of those best qualified to serve as jurors will not have formed some impression or opinion as to the merits of the case. * * * To hold that the mere existence of any preconceived notion as to the guilt or innocence of the accused, without more, is sufficient to rebut the presumption of a prospective juror's impartiality would be to establish an impossible standard. It is sufficient if the juror can lay aside his impression or opinion and render a verdict based on the evidence presented in court.

The Court described the publicity that accompanied the case, and evaluated its effect on Irvin's trial, in the following passage:

> Here the build-up of prejudice is clear and convincing. * * * A reading of the 46 exhibits which petitioner attached to his motion indicates that a barrage of newspaper headlines, articles, cartoons and pictures was unleashed against him during the six or seven months preceding his trial. The motion further alleged that the newspapers in which the stories appeared were delivered regularly to approximately 95% of the dwellings in Gibson County and that, in addition, the Evansville radio and TV stations, which likewise blanketed that county, also carried extensive newscasts covering the same incidents. These stories revealed the details of his background, including a reference to crimes committed when a juvenile, his convictions for arson almost 20 years previously, for burglary and by a court-martial on AWOL charges during the war. He was accused of being a parole violator. The headlines announced his police line-up identification, that he faced a lie detector test, had been placed at the scene of the crime and that the six murders were solved but petitioner refused to confess. Finally, they announced his confession to the six murders and the fact of his indictment for

---

44. Prior to *Irvin*, the Court set aside a conviction in Marshall v. United States, 360 U.S. 310 (1959), under its supervisory powers because of news articles the jurors had read.

four of them in Indiana. They reported petitioner's offer to plead guilty if promised a 99–year sentence, but also the determination, on the other hand, of the prosecutor to secure the death penalty, and that petitioner had confessed to 24 burglaries (the modus operandi of these robberies was compared to that of the murders and the similarity noted). One story dramatically relayed the promise of a sheriff to devote his life to securing petitioner's execution by the State of Kentucky, where petitioner is alleged to have committed one of the six murders, if Indiana failed to do so. Another characterized petitioner as remorseless and without conscience but also as having been found sane by a court-appointed panel of doctors. In many of the stories petitioner was described as the "confessed slayer of six," a parole violator and fraudulent-check artist.

* * *

Here the "pattern of deep and bitter prejudice" shown to be present throughout the community, was clearly reflected in the sum total of the voir dire examination of a majority of the jurors finally placed in the jury box. Eight out of the 12 thought petitioner was guilty. With such an opinion permeating their minds, it would be difficult to say that each could exclude this preconception of guilt from his deliberations. * * * With his life at stake, it is not requiring too much that petitioner be tried in an atmosphere undisturbed by so huge a wave of public passion and by a jury other than one in which two-thirds of the members admit, before hearing any testimony, to possessing a belief in his guilt.

Thus, the Court set aside the conviction. Justice Frankfurter's concurring opinion suggested both that the problem of undue publicity was not isolated in Evansville, and that its impact on the *Irvin* case was not atypical.

Televised Confession: Rideau v. Louisiana

The Court overturned another state conviction in Rideau v. Louisiana, 373 U.S. 723 (1963). The Court began its opinion with a description of the facts of the case.

On the evening of February 16, 1961, a man robbed a bank in Lake Charles, Louisiana, kidnapped three of the bank's employees, and killed one of them. A few hours later the petitioner, Wilbert Rideau, was apprehended by the police and lodged in the Calcasieu Parish jail in Lake Charles. The next morning a moving picture film with a sound track was made of an "interview" in the jail between Rideau and the Sheriff of Calcasieu Parish. This "interview" lasted approximately 20 minutes. It consisted of interrogation by the sheriff and admissions by Rideau that he had perpetrated the bank robbery, kidnaping, and murder. Later the same day the filmed "interview" was broadcast over a television station in Lake Charles, and some 24,000 people in the community saw and heard it on television. The sound film was again shown on television the next day to an estimated audience of 53,000 people. The following day the film was again broadcast by the same television station, and this time approximately 29,000 people saw and heard the "interview" on their television sets. Calcasieu Parish has a population of approximately 150,000 people.

Some two weeks later, Rideau was arraigned on charges of armed robbery, kidnaping, and murder, and two lawyers were appointed to represent him. His lawyers promptly filed a motion for a change of venue, on the ground that it would deprive Rideau of rights guaranteed to him by the United States Constitution to force him to trial in Calcasieu Parish after the three television broadcasts there of his "interview" with the sheriff. After a hearing, the motion for change of venue was denied, and Rideau was accordingly convicted and sentenced to death on the murder charge in the Calcasieu Parish trial court.

Three members of the jury which convicted him had stated on voir dire that they had seen and heard Rideau's televised "interview" with the sheriff on at least one occasion. Two members of the jury were deputy sheriffs of Calcasieu Parish. Rideau's counsel had requested that these jurors be excused for cause, having exhausted all of their peremptory challenges, but these challenges for cause had been denied by the trial judge.

The Court held that "it was a denial of due process of law to refuse the request for a change of venue, after the people of Calcasieu Parish had been exposed repeatedly and in depth to the spectacle of Rideau personally confessing in detail to the crimes with which he was later to be charged." The Court stated that the televised confession "in a very real sense *was* Rideau's trial—at which he pleaded guilty to murder," and that a later trial in a community so pervasively exposed to the confession "could be but a hollow formality." Justice Clark, joined by Justice Harlan, dissented, complaining that the defendant had not established any "substantial nexus" between the televised confession and any prejudice suffered at the trial.

Questions About Rideau

In *Rideau,* there was no indication that the confession was coerced, and therefore it was undoubtedly admissible against Rideau at trial. Since the jurors would hear the confession at trial, what prejudice could Rideau have suffered from the pretrial publicity? Isn't the case really about the failure to strike the two law enforcement officers for cause? In terms of pretrial publicity, the demonstrated effect on the jury ultimately chosen was substantially less than that in *Irvin,* was it not? If the facts of *Rideau* suffice to establish constitutional error, how many trials are tainted in these days of extensive media coverage of high profile trials? Compare Fetterly v. Paskett, 163 F.3d 1144 (9th Cir.1998) (pretrial publicity not prejudicial where it focuses on facts and evidence that was ultimately presented at trial).

Delay Between Publicity and the Trial: Patton v. Yount

Irvin and *Rideau* seem to indicate that the Court would find prejudicial pretrial publicity in any number of cases. But the Court cut back in Patton v. Yount, 467 U.S. 1025 (1984), where it reinstated a state defendant's murder conviction that had been overturned due to prejudicial trial publicity. Justice Powell's opinion for the Court emphasized that the court of appeals' reliance on *Irvin* was misplaced because the trial in *Irvin* took place six or seven months after extensive publicity began, whereas Yount was convicted in a second trial four years after most of the publicity occurred in connection with his first trial. That most jurors remembered the case was not decisive. The Court stated that "[t]he relevant question is not whether the community remembered the case, but whether the jurors at Yount's trial had such fixed opinions that they could not judge impartially the guilt of the defendant." Justice Powell reasoned as follows:

> It is not unusual that one's recollection of the fact that a notorious crime was committed lingers long after the feelings of revulsion that create prejudice have passed. It would be fruitless to attempt to identify any particular lapse of time that in itself would distinguish the situation that existed in *Irvin*. But it is clear that the passage of time between a first and a second trial can be a highly relevant fact. In the circumstances of this case, we hold that it clearly rebuts any presumption of partiality or prejudice that existed at the time of the initial trial.

Justice Stevens, joined by Justice Brennan, dissented. Justice Marshall did not participate.

Limited Protection: Mu'Min v. Virginia

In Mu'Min v. Virginia, 500 U.S. 415 (1991), the defendant was a state prisoner serving time for first-degree murder when he was charged with capital murder while on a work detail. The case was widely publicized. Articles in the newspapers revealed details of the prior murder for which Mu'Min was incarcerated, the fact that the death penalty was unavailable at the time of his earlier murder trial, the denial of parole six times to Mu'Min, his confession to the crime charged, and criticism of the supervision of work gangs in Virginia. Mu'Min claimed that the jurors could not be impartial in such a setting, despite the judge's finding on voir dire that the jurors had not been substantially affected by the publicity.

The Chief Justice held that a trial court's finding of juror impartiality may be overturned only where there is manifest error. He stated that "particularly with respect to pretrial publicity, we think this primary reliance on the judgment of the trial court makes good sense. The judge of that court sits in the locale where the publicity is said to have had its effect, and brings to his evaluation of any such claim his own perception of the depth and extent of news stories that might influence a juror." This was so even though the judge in this case had not questioned jurors individually to determine whether they had been affected by pre-trial publicity.

The majority rejected Mu'Min's reliance on Irvin v. Dowd on the ground that the pretrial publicity in the instant case was not of the same kind or extent as in *Irvin*.

Justice O'Connor wrote a concurring opinion. She cited Patton v. Yount for the proposition that even jurors who had read about inadmissible confessions are not disqualified as a matter of law, and concluded that a trial judge could realistically assess whether jurors could be fair without knowing what each juror had heard about a case. Justices Marshall, Blackmun, Stevens, and Kennedy dissented.

Lower Court Cases

It should be no surprise that, after *Mu'Min*, the lower courts have been reluctant to find that prejudicial pretrial publicity has tainted a trial. See, e.g.,

Swindler v. Lockhart, 885 F.2d 1342 (8th Cir.1989) (substantial publicity, 98 out of 120 jurors had heard about the case, no reversal); Simmons v. Lockhart, 814 F.2d 504 (8th Cir.1987)(55 of 56 members of the venire had heard about the case, but "[t]he accused is not entitled to an ignorant jury, just a fair one"); United States v. Lehder–Rivas, 955 F.2d 1510 (11th Cir.1992)(extensive media coverage describing the defendant as a "drug kingpin" and a "narco-terrorist"; but the trial judge conducted extensive voir dire and the jurors credibly asserted that they could remain impartial).

2. *Television in the Courtroom*

In the wake of the O.J. Simpson trial, there has been extensive discussion about the use of cameras in the courtroom. Those who denigrate the practice argue that television simply encourages the lawyers, and maybe the judge as well, to play to the cameras; they contend that the Simpson trial could have been completed in half the time if it had not been televised. As one famous defense lawyer states:

> In the O.J. Simpson trial, the TV personae from the courtroom are seeking to capitalize on their televised court appearances, with consequent distortion of their participation in the trial process. Witnesses who otherwise might come forward may be deterred by the courtroom coverage.

Tigar, Television and the Jury, Nat'l L.J., Aug. 21, 1995, p.A19.

Those who support cameras in the courtroom argue that television provides the public a crucial viewpoint into the workings of the criminal justice system. They argue that the Simpson case was an aberration:

> The purpose of making a trial available to the public is neither to increase nor to decrease the people's confidence in the criminal justice system. It is to give the people a chance to observe and judge for themselves whether the system is working as it should.

* * *

> I would urge all trial judges who are deeply troubled by the impression left by the Simpson case, who believe that they could have done better and who recognize the importance of restoring public confidence, to invite the camera into their courtrooms and demonstrate how a proper trial is conducted. This is the only path to redemption for the criminal justice system.

Reiner, Cameras Keep Justice System in Focus, Nat'l L.J., Oct. 23, 1995, p. A23.

With whom do you agree? Assuming that the camera in the court had a distortive effect on the Simpson trial, could the solution be to exclude cameras from high profile trials, but to allow them in ordinary trials? Who would watch? Apparently people *would* watch–that's why we have Court TV.

Media Invades the Courtroom: Estes v. Texas

Billy Sol Estes was one of the first "subjects" of a high profile, televised trial. In Estes v. Texas, 381 U.S. 532 (1965), the Court held that Estes was denied a fair trial due to the pervasive and disruptive media presence in the courtroom. Justice Clark, writing for the Court, described the effect that the media had on the courtroom during both pre-trial hearings and at the trial:

[A]tleast 12 cameramen were engaged in the courtroom throughout the hearing taking motion and still pictures and televising the proceedings. Cables and wires were snaked across the courtroom floor, three microphones were on the judge's bench and others were beamed at the jury box and the counsel table. It is conceded that the activities of the television crews and news photographers led to considerable disruption of the hearings. * * * The trial witnesses present at the hearing, as well as the original jury panel, were undoubtedly made aware of the peculiar public importance of the case by the press and television coverage being provided, and by the fact that they themselves were televised live and their pictures rebroadcast on the evening show. * * *

The Court held that the First Amendment did not extend a right to the news media to televise from the courtroom, and that the disruption of the proceedings created by television coverage required a new trial, even though Estes had not made a showing of actual prejudice. Justice Clark concluded with these critical comments about televised coverage of courtroom proceedings:

[T]he chief function of our judicial machinery is to ascertain the truth. The use of television, however, cannot be said to contribute materially to this objective. Rather its use amounts to the injection of an irrelevant factor into court proceedings. In addition experience teaches that there are numerous situations in which it might cause actual unfairness—some so subtle as to defy detection by the accused or control by the judge. We enumerate some in summary:

1. The potential impact of television on the jurors is perhaps of the greatest significance. * * *

2. The quality of the testimony in criminal trials will often be impaired. * * * Embarrassment may impede the search for the truth, as may a natural tendency toward overdramatization. * * *

* * *

3. A major aspect of the problem is the additional responsibilities the presence of television places on the trial judge. His job is to make certain that the accused receives a fair trial. This most difficult task requires his undivided attention. Still when television comes into the courtroom he must also supervise it. * * *

* * *

4. Finally, we cannot ignore the impact of courtroom television on the defendant. * * * The inevitable close-ups of his gestures and expressions during the ordeal of his trial might well transgress his personal sensibilities, his dignity, and his ability to concentrate on the proceedings before him—

sometimes the difference between life and death—dispassionately, freely and without the distraction of wide public surveillance. A defendant on trial for a specific crime is entitled to his day in court, not in a stadium, or a city or nationwide arena. * * *. Furthermore, telecasting may also deprive an accused of effective counsel. The distractions, intrusions into confidential attorney-client relationships and the temptation offered by television to play to the public audience might often have a direct effect not only upon the lawyers, but the judge, the jury and the witnesses.

* * *

Chief Justice Warren, joined by Justices Douglas and Goldberg, wrote a concurring opinion concluding that "televising of criminal proceedings is inherently a denial of due process." Justice Harlan wrote a separate opinion, agreeing with the Court that the First Amendment does not require that television be allowed in the courtroom, but disagreeing with the Court that televised proceedings were per se prohibited by the constitution. He suggested a case-by-case approach. Justice Stewart's dissent, joined by Justices Black, Brennan, and White concluded that "in the present state of the art" televised judicial proceedings were unwise, but found no denial of Estes' constitutional rights. Justice White's short dissent noted that advances in technology might make televised judicial proceedings more acceptable. Justice Brennan's separate statement noted that because of Justice Harlan's vote, *Estes* could not be read as an absolute bar to televised trials. In the next case, the Court clearly agreed with Justice Brennan's view.

CHANDLER v. FLORIDA

Supreme Court of the United States, 1981.
449 U.S. 560.

CHIEF JUSTICE BURGER **delivered the opinion of the Court.**

The question presented on this appeal is whether, consistent with constitutional guarantees, a state may provide for radio, television, and still photographic coverage of a criminal trial for public broadcast, notwithstanding the objection of the accused.

I

A

* * *

[The Florida Supreme Court established a pilot program permitting electronic media to cover all judicial proceedings, without reference to the consent of the participants. After the pilot program ended, the Florida Supreme Court sought comments and

reviewed camera-in-the-courts projects in other states. The court concluded that "on balance there [was] more to be gained than lost by permitting electronic media coverage of judicial proceedings subject to standards for such coverage."]

The Florida court was of the view that because of the significant effect of the courts on the day-to-day lives of the citizenry, it was essential that the people have confidence in the process. It felt that broadcast coverage of trials would contribute to wider public acceptance and understanding of decisions. Consequently, after revising the 1977 guidelines to reflect its evaluation of the pilot program, the Florida Supreme Court promulgated a revised Canon 3A(7). The canon provides:

"Subject at all times to the authority of the presiding judge to (i) control the conduct of proceedings before the court, (ii) ensure decorum and prevent distractions, and (iii) ensure fair administration of justice in the pending cause, electronic media and still photography coverage of public judicial proceedings in the appellate and trial courts of this state shall be allowed in accordance with standards of conduct and technology promulgated by the Supreme Court of Florida."

* * *

B

In July 1977, appellants were charged with conspiracy to commit burglary, grand larceny, and possession of burglary tools. The counts covered breaking and entering a well-known Miami Beach restaurant.

The details of the alleged criminal conduct are not relevant to the issue before us, but several aspects of the case distinguish it from a routine burglary. At the time of their arrest, appellants were Miami Beach policemen. The State's principal witness was John Sion, an amateur radio operator who, by sheer chance, had overheard and recorded conversations between the appellants over their police walkie-talkie radios during the burglary. Not surprisingly, these novel factors attracted the attention of the media.

By pretrial motion, counsel for the appellants sought to have Experimental Canon 3A(7) declared unconstitutional on its face and as applied. The trial court denied relief but certified the issue to the Florida Supreme Court. However, the Supreme Court declined to rule on the question. * * *

After several additional fruitless attempts by the appellants to prevent electronic coverage of the trial, the jury was selected. At *voir dire*, the appellants' counsel asked each prospective juror whether he or she would be able to be "fair and impartial" despite the presence of a television camera during some, or all, of the trial. Each juror selected responded that such coverage would not affect his or her consideration in any way. A television camera recorded the *voir dire*.

A defense motion to sequester the jury because of the television coverage was denied by the trial judge. However, the court instructed the jury not to watch or read anything about the case in the media and suggested that jurors "avoid the local news and watch only the national news on television." * * *

A television camera was in place for one entire afternoon, during which the state presented the testimony of Sion, its chief witness. No camera was present for the presentation of any part of the case for the defense. The camera returned to cover closing arguments. Only two minutes and fifty-five seconds of the trial below were broadcast—and those depicted only the prosecution's side of the case.

The jury returned a guilty verdict on all counts. [The conviction was upheld on appeal.]

II

* * *

III

Appellants * * * argue that the televising of criminal trials is inherently a denial of due process, and they read *Estes* as announcing a *per se* constitutional rule to that effect.

* * *

Parsing the six opinions in *Estes*, one is left with a sense of doubt as to precisely how much of Justice Clark's opinion was joined in, and supported by, Justice Harlan. In an area charged with constitutional nuances, perhaps more should not be expected. Nonetheless, it is fair to say that Justice Harlan viewed the holding as limited to the proposition that *"what was done in this case* infringed the fundamental right to a fair trial assured by the Due Process Clause of the Fourteenth Amendment * * *."

* * *

IV

Since we are satisfied that *Estes* did not announce a constitutional rule that all photographic or broadcast coverage of criminal trials is inherently a denial of due process, we turn to consideration, as a matter of first impression, of the petitioner's suggestion that we now promulgate such a *per se* rule.

A

* * *

An absolute constitutional ban on broadcast coverage of trials cannot be justified simply because there is a danger that, in some cases, prejudicial broadcast accounts of pretrial and trial events may impair the ability of jurors to decide the issue of guilt or innocence uninfluenced by extraneous matter. The risk of juror prejudice in some cases does not justify an absolute ban on news coverage of trials by the printed media; so also the risk of such prejudice does not warrant an absolute constitutional ban on all broadcast coverage. * * *

B

* * *

Not unimportant to the position asserted by Florida and other states is the change in television technology since 1962, when Estes was tried. It is urged, and some empirical data are presented, that many of the negative factors found in *Estes*—cumbersome equipment, cables, distracting lighting, numerous camera technicians—are less substantial factors today than they were at that time.

It is also significant that safeguards have been built into the experimental programs in state courts, and into the Florida program, to avoid some of the most egregious problems envisioned by the six opinions in the *Estes* case. Florida admonishes its courts to take special pains to protect certain witnesses—for example, children, victims of sex crimes, some informants, and even the very timid witness or party—from the glare of publicity and the tensions of being "on camera."

* * * Inherent in electronic coverage of a trial is the risk that the very awareness by the accused of the coverage and the contemplated broadcast may adversely affect the conduct of the participants and the fairness of the trial, yet leave no evidence of how the conduct or the trial's fairness was affected. Given this danger, it is significant that Florida requires that objections of the accused to coverage be heard and considered on the record by the trial court. In addition to providing a record for appellate review, a pretrial hearing enables a defendant to advance the basis of his objection to broadcast coverage and allows the trial court to define the steps necessary to minimize or eliminate the risks of prejudice to the accused. * * *

Whatever may be the "mischievous potentialities [of broadcast coverage] for intruding upon the detached atmosphere which should always surround the judicial process," at present no one has been able to present empirical data sufficient to establish that the mere presence of the broadcast media inherently has an adverse effect on that process. The appellants have offered nothing to demonstrate that their trial was subtly tainted by broadcast coverage—let alone that all broadcast trials would be so tainted.

The concurring opinion of Chief Justice Warren joined by Justices Douglas and Goldberg in *Estes* can fairly be read as viewing the very broadcast of some trials as potentially a form of punishment in itself—a punishment before guilt. This concern is far from trivial. But, whether coverage of a few trials will, in practice, be the equivalent of a "Yankee Stadium" setting—which Justice Harlan likened to the public pillory long abandoned as a barbaric perversion of decent justice—must also await the continuing experimentation.

D

To say that the appellants have not demonstrated that broadcast coverage

is inherently a denial of due process is not to say that the appellants were in fact accorded all of the protections of due process in their trial. As noted earlier, a defendant has the right on review to show that the media's coverage of his case—printed or broadcast—compromised the ability of the jury to judge him fairly. Alternatively, a defendant might show that broadcast coverage of his particular case had an adverse impact on the trial participants sufficient to constitute a denial of due process. Neither showing was made in this case.

To demonstrate prejudice in a specific case a defendant must show something more than juror awareness that the trial is such as to attract the attention of broadcasters.

* * *

[The Court affirmed the convictions.]

3. *Protecting the Integrity of Judicial Proceedings*

Circus Atmosphere: Sheppard v. Maxwell

The Sam Sheppard murder trial was the O.J. Simpson trial of its day. The Supreme Court considered the effect of media coverage of the trial in Sheppard v. Maxwell, 384 U.S. 333 (1966). Sheppard was tried and convicted for murdering his wife. He claimed that she was killed by an intruder.[45] Apparently because Sheppard was a well-to-do doctor, the case received substantial media coverage. In his opinion for the Court, Justice Clark noted the pervasive pre-trial publicity and the circus media coverage during the trial. Pretrial publicity included newspaper coverage indicating that other suspects had been cleared and that the defendant had been having an affair. Newspapers called for Sheppard's arrest. The media invaded the courtroom. Pictures of the jury were published. During the nine week murder trial the courtroom "remained crowded to capacity with representatives of news media. Their movement in and out of the courtroom often caused so much confusion that, despite the loud-speaker system installed in the courtroom, it was difficult for the witnesses and counsel to be heard." Sheppard and counsel found it almost impossible to confer confidentially.

The *Sheppard* Court held that the trial judge's failure to control the media coverage of the judicial proceedings deprived Sheppard of his right to a fair trial, requiring a reversal of his conviction. Justice Clark reasoned as follows:

45. The television show "The Fugitive" was loosely based on the Sheppard case.

The fact is that bedlam reigned at the courthouse during the trial and newsmen took over practically the entire courtroom, hounding most of the participants in the trial, especially Sheppard. * * * The erection of a press table for reporters inside the bar is unprecedented. The bar of the court is reserved for counsel, providing them a safe place in which to keep papers and exhibits, and to confer privately with client and co-counsel. It is designed to protect the witness and the jury from any distractions, intrusions or influences, and to permit bench discussions of the judge's rulings away from the hearing of the public and the jury. Having assigned almost all of the available seats in the courtroom to the news media, the judge lost his ability to supervise that environment. * * *

Justice Clark emphasized that the trial court had substantial authority to control media coverage in order to protect the defendant's right to a fair trial, and that the trial court in *Sheppard* should have exercised this authority. The Court gave the following suggestions as to what could and should have been done:

The carnival atmosphere at trial could easily have been avoided since the courtroom and courthouse premises are subject to the control of the court. * * * Bearing in mind the massive pretrial publicity, the judge should have adopted stricter rules governing the use of the courtroom by newsmen, as Sheppard's counsel requested. The number of reporters in the courtroom itself could have been limited at the first sign that their presence would disrupt the trial. They certainly should not have been placed inside the bar. Furthermore, the judge should have more closely regulated the conduct of newsmen in the courtroom. For instance, the judge belatedly asked them not to handle and photograph trial exhibits lying on the counsel table during recesses.

Secondly, the court should have insulated the witnesses. All of the newspapers and radio stations apparently interviewed prospective witnesses at will, and in many instances disclosed their testimony. * * * Although the witnesses were barred from the courtroom during the trial the full verbatim testimony was available to them in the press. This completely nullified the judge's imposition of the rule [sequestering witnesses].

Thirdly, the court should have made some effort to control the release of leads, information, and gossip to the press by police officers, witnesses, and the counsel for both sides. * * *

* * *

More specifically, the trial court might well have proscribed extrajudicial statements by any lawyer, party, witness, or court official which divulged prejudicial matters, such as the refusal of Sheppard to submit to interrogation or take any lie detector tests; any statement made by Sheppard to officials; the identity of prospective witnesses or their probable testimony; any belief in guilt or innocence; or like statements concerning the merits of the case. * * * Being advised of the great public interest in the case, the mass coverage of the press, and the potential prejudicial impact of publicity, the court could also have requested the appropriate city and county officials to promulgate a regulation with respect to dissemination of information about the case by their employees. In addition, reporters who wrote or broadcast prejudicial stories, could have been warned as to the impropriety of publishing material not introduced in the proceedings.

Justice Clark concluded that "where there is a reasonable likelihood that prejudicial news prior to trial will prevent a fair trial, the judge should continue the case until the threat abates, or transfer it to another county not so permeated with publicity." With respect to publicity during the proceedings, he concluded that "courts must take such steps by rule and regulation that will protect their processes from prejudicial outside interferences."

A Different Approach

Taking a cue from *Estes* and *Sheppard*, many courts exercise considerable control over the use of media in and around the courtroom today. Consider, for example, the order entered in the case of James Earl Ray, accused and convicted upon his plea of guilty, of killing Dr. Martin Luther King, Jr.

In the Criminal Court of Shelby County, Tennessee
Order on Courthouse and Courtroom Procedures and Publicity

* * *

From the worldwide attention attracted to this case at bar resulting in massive and pervasive publicity in the news media, the Court is of the opinion that the following rules are necessary to a constitutionally guaranteed, orderly and fair trial by an impartial jury, and therefore orders:

I

* * *

All entrance ways, corridors, and approaches to courtrooms, offices, and other rooms in the Criminal Courts Buildings will be kept clear at all times for free access thereto by those using them in the course of their employment or those having business to transact therein.

II

No cameras, photographic, television, radio or sound equipment, including tape recorders, will be permitted in the Criminal Courts Buildings or upon the alley-ways, parking lots, yards or grounds immediately surrounding said buildings. No photographs will be taken of the Jury, nor will they be televised. No sketches will be made in the Criminal Courts Buildings.

III

All persons seeking admission to the courtroom will submit voluntarily to a search of his person before being admitted.

IV

No one will enter the courtroom after a session has begun without permission of the Court, but must wait until the next recess. No one will leave the courtroom except at recess or adjournment except in an emergency. At noon recess and adjournment, and at any other time the Jury is retiring from the second floor, or the prisoner is being removed to the jail, the spectators shall remain seated in the courtroom until the Jury and prisoner have had ample time to withdraw, and said spectators have been given permission to disperse.

V

The bar of the Court within the rail is reserved for the defendant, counsel, members of the Bar, court personnel and such witnesses as counsel may desire to be within the bar for consultation purposes. No one else will enter without permission of the Court.

VI

No one except attorneys of record, their agents, court personnel, witnesses and jurors may handle exhibits except by order of the Court.

VII

All lawyers participating in this case, their assistants, office associates, staff members, investigators and employees under their supervision and control are forbidden to take part in interviews for publicity and from making extrajudicial statements about this case from this date until such time as a verdict is returned in this case in open Court.

VIII

The County Medical Examiner, Jury Commissioners, Criminal Court Clerk, County Sheriff, Police Officials and other law enforcement officers, employees of this Court, all other persons employed in the "Criminal Courts Buildings," their associates, deputies, assistants, staff members and personnel under their supervision and control are forbidden to participate in interviews for publicity and from making extrajudicial statements about this case from this date and until such time as a verdict in this case is returned in open Court.

IX

All witnesses, persons subpoenaed to Grand Jury or Court, jurors, and those persons summoned but excused from serving as jurors, are forbidden to participate in interviews for publicity and from making extrajudicial statements about this case from this date and until such time as a verdict in this case is returned in open Court.

X

Nothing in this order shall prohibit any witness from discussing any matter in connection with the case with any of the attorneys representing the defendant or the State, or any representative of such attorneys.

* * *

Gag Orders

Following the suggestion of the *Sheppard* Court, the trial judge in the *Ray* case barred lawyers, their employees, law enforcement and court personnel, and witnesses from making extrajudicial statements prior to the entry of a verdict.

Similar "gag" orders are common today. An example arose in United States v. Cutler, 58 F.3d 825 (2d Cir.1995), where the lawyer for Mafia boss John Gotti was convicted of criminal contempt for violating a gag order entered in Gotti's murder prosecution. The order incorporated a local rule of court prohibiting statements from counsel that would create a reasonable likelihood of interfering with a fair trial. Despite the order, Cutler gave numerous interviews to the press and television. In these interviews, he claimed, among other things, that: the government was persecuting John Gotti; John Gotti was "anti-drugs" and a legitimate businessman; government witnesses were liars; and the Mafia does not exist. Cutler also mischaracterized important parts of the government's evidence.

Cutler argued that he did not violate the gag order because his statements were not reasonably likely to interfere with a fair trial. He contended that he was simply responding to the "veritable firestorm of anti-Gotti publicity." The court was not persuaded, however, by Cutler's "Uriah Heep pose." It stated that Cutler could be found in contempt for statements *likely* to impair a fair trial, even if the statements in fact had no effect. (Indeed, Cutler's p.r. campaign had no effect; almost all members of the venire panel had heard about Gotti, but most thought he was guilty; apparently none had heard about Cutler's statements).

Cutler argued, finally, that he had not wilfully violated the gag order. But the court found what it termed a "smoking gun" in a statement Cutler had made, while speaking at a seminar at Brooklyn Law School, about contacts with the press. At the seminar, Cutler said:

> I have honest reasons why I don't want to alienate [the press], that I want the prospective veniremen out there to feel that I mean what I say and say what I mean, and if that can spill over and help my client, then I feel its important for me to do that.

The court upheld Cutler's sentence of 90 days' house arrest, three years' probation, and a six month suspension from the practice of law. It concluded as follows:

> In some quarters, doubtless, this affirmance will elicit thunderbolts that we are chilling effective advocacy. Obviously, that is neither our intention nor our result. The advocate is still entitled—indeed encouraged—to strike hard blows, but not unfair blows. Trial practice, whether civil or criminal, is not a contact sport. And its tactics do not include eye-gouging or shin-kicking.

> In this case, a conscientious trial judge tried mightily to limit the lawyers to press statements that were accurate and fair. The defendant's statements were dipped in venom and were deliberately couched to poison the well from which the jury would be selected. Such conduct goes beyond the pale, by any reasonable standard, and cannot be condoned under the rubric of "effective advocacy."

What kind of "fair blows" could Cutler have struck, given the anti-Gotti publicity that pervaded New York when the prosecution began? What's wrong with Cutler's desire to shape the opinions of the jury venire? It should be noted that the prosecutor gave an interview shortly after the indictment against Gotti was handed down. In the interview, he said that Gotti was "a murderer, not a folk hero," and expressed pleasure that the evidence he had was much stronger than the evidence in prior prosecutions in which Gotti had been acquitted. These statements were made before the trial judge imposed the gag order. Are they relevant to Cutler's contempt prosecution? Do you think the *prosecutor* would have been found guilty of criminal contempt if he had made those statements after the trial judge imposed a gag order?

Overbroad Gag Orders

United States v. Salameh, 992 F.2d 445 (2d Cir.1993), was a prosecution of defendants accused of bombing the World Trade Center. It was obviously a high profile case, and the judge was concerned about trial publicity in general and extrajudicial statements by lawyers in particular. So he imposed the following gag order:

> There will be no more statements in the press, on TV, in radio, or in any other electronic media, issued by either side or their agents. The next time I pick up a paper and see a quotation from any of you, you had best be prepared to have some money. The first fine will be $200. Thereafter, the fines will be squared.

After the order was entered, defense counsel had some questions for the judge about the scope of the order, such as, could counsel make a statement that his client had been tortured in Egypt? Could the lawyer talk to reporters about the client's background and family? The trial judge responded that the gag order applied to "what we are dealing with here."

The court of appeals vacated the gag order, on the ground that it violated the first amendment principle that an order limiting speech "should be no broader than necessary to protect the integrity of the judicial system and the defendant's right to a fair trial." The court concluded as follows:

> The order imposed by the district court in the present case does not meet these standards. The restraint on the attorneys' speech is not narrowly tailored; rather, it is a blanket prohibition that extends to any statements that * * * may have something to do with the case. The court did not make a finding that alternatives to this blanket prohibition would be inadequate to protect defendants' rights to a fair trial before an impartial jury. There is no indication in the record that the court explored any alternatives or at all considered imposing any less broad proscription * * *. The record does not support a conclusion that no reasonable alternatives to a blanket prohibition exist.

Why was the order in *Salameh* any more problematic than the order at issue in *Cutler*, which prohibited counsel from making a statement that had a "reasonable likelihood of impairing a fair trial"?

Ethical Proscriptions: Gentile v. State Bar of Nevada

To the extent that prejudicial trial publicity is caused by lawyers, codes of ethics impose limitations even if no gag order is in place. DR 7–107 of the ABA Code of Professional Responsibility and Rule 3.6 of the Model Rules of Professional Conduct make disclosure of information by lawyers an ethical violation under some circumstances. See, e.g., United States v. Bingham, 769 F.Supp.

1039 (N.D.Ill.1991)(defense attorneys' conduct was referred to disciplinary committee, where attorneys criticized the empanelment of an anonymous jury in televised interviews the night before jury selection).

Like gag orders, lawyer disciplinary rules limiting speech raise first amendment issues. In Gentile v. State Bar of Nevada, 501 U.S. 1030 (1991), the Supreme Court rebuffed a first amendment challenge to a state disciplinary rule proscribing "an extrajudicial statement that a reasonable person would expect to be disseminated by means of media communication if the lawyer knows or reasonably should know that it will have a substantial likelihood of materially prejudicing an adjudicative proceeding." Chief Justice Rehnquist's opinion upholding this standard was joined by Justices White, O'Connor, Scalia, and Souter. However, Justice Kennedy wrote for the Court, joined by Justices Marshall, Blackmun, Stevens, and O'Connor, as it held that one aspect of the particular Nevada rule was void for vagueness. Consequently, the Court held that the rule could not support a private reprimand of counsel for remarks made at a press conference following the indictment of his client.

The case arose after cocaine and traveler's checks used in an undercover police operation were found missing from a vault, and an investigation led to the indictment of Gentile's client. Gentile held a press conference in which he suggested that the thief was a police officer, not his client, and that his client was not guilty. Gentile's main purpose in holding the press conference was to counter the adverse publicity that had been aired concerning his client. Gentile's client was ultimately acquitted.

Gentile argued that the disciplinary rule was unconstitutional because it precluded speech that created only a substantial likelihood of materially prejudicing a trial. In Gentile's view, an attorney's speech could not be regulated unless it created a "clear and present danger" of prejudicing the trial—this "clear and present danger" standard is the test applied to prior restraints of the press. Justice Kennedy found it unnecessary to address the constitutionality of the "substantial likelihood of material prejudice" standard, or to determine whether the First Amendment provides less protection for lawyers than for the press. He reasoned instead that the Nevada rule was vague because of its safe harbor provision, which set forth examples of some statements that would not violate the rule. He stated that a lawyer seeking to avail himself of the Nevada safe harbor provision "must guess at its contours." The safe harbor provision gave defense counsel the right to "explain the general nature of the defense" but "without elaboration." Justice Kennedy concluded that this provision was unconstitutionally vague because "general and elaboration are both classic terms of degree" with "no settled usage or tradition of interpretation in law." According to Justice Kennedy, Gentile was given "no principle for determining when his remarks pass from the safe harbor of the general to the forbidden sea of the elaborated." Justice Kennedy noted that Gentile had spent several hours researching the requirements of the Nevada rule, and that at his press conference his remarks were guarded and general. Yet still the Nevada courts had found that he violated the disciplinary rule. Justice Kennedy asserted that "the fact Gentile was found in violation of the Rules after studying them and making a conscious effort at compliance demonstrates that [the Nevada Rule] creates a trap for the wary as well as the unwary."

Justice O'Connor, who wrote a brief concurring opinion, agreed with Justice Kennedy's void for vagueness analysis. She also agreed, however, with Chief Justice Rehnquist's opinion that the "substantial likelihood of prejudice" standard set forth in the Nevada rule was indeed constitutional, even though it provided less protection to lawyers than the "clear and present danger" standard applicable to the press.

Chief Justice Rehnquist's opinion for the Court on the relevant standard held that lawyers are entitled to less First Amendment protection than the press. The Chief Justice reasoned that "lawyers representing clients in pending cases are key participants in the criminal justice system, and the State may demand some adherence to the precepts of that system in regulating their speech as well as their conduct." He noted that a lawyer's extrajudicial statements can have significant impact on the trial "since lawyers' statements are likely to be received as especially authoritative." He concluded that the "substantial likelihood of material prejudice" test was an appropriate balance of the interests of the lawyer and the state, since it imposes "only narrow and necessary limitations on lawyers' speech," and "it merely postpones the attorney's comments until after the trial." A more rigorous "clear and present danger" standard was therefore not required.

In the end, the Court invalidated the sanction imposed upon Gentile, indicated that state rules providing ambiguous examples may be invalidated as a result of vagueness, and yet upheld the standard that lawyers in pending cases may not make public comments when they know or should know that such comments will have a substantial likelihood of materially prejudicing an adjudicative proceeding.[46] The Court emphasized that lawyers pose a greater risk of

---

46. After *Gentile*, the ABA amended Model Rule of Professional Conduct 3.6 to provide as follows:

(a) A lawyer who is participating or has participated in the investigation or litigation of a matter shall not make an extrajudicial statement that a reasonable person would expect to be disseminated by means of public communication if the lawyer knows or reasonably should know that it will have a substantial likelihood of materially prejudicing an adjudicative proceeding in the matter.

(b) Notwithstanding paragraph (a), a lawyer may state:

(1) the claim, offense or defense involved and, except where prohibited by law, the identity of the persons involved;

(2) information contained in a public record;

(3) that an investigation of a matter is in progress;

(4) the scheduling or result of any step in litigation;

(5) a request for assistance in obtaining evidence and information necessary thereto;

(6) a warning of danger concerning the behavior of a person involved, when there is reason to believe that there exists the likelihood of substantial harm to an individual or to the public interest; and

(7) in a criminal case, in addition to subparagraphs (1) through (6):

(i) the identity, residence, occupation and family status of the accused;

(ii) if the accused has not been apprehended, information necessary to aid in apprehension of that person;

(iii) the fact, time and place of arrest;

(iv) the identity of investigating and arresting officers of agencies and the length of investigation.

(c) Notwithstanding paragraph (a), a lawyer may make a statement that a reasonable lawyer would believe is required to protect a client from the substantial undue prejudicial effect of recent publicity not initiated by the lawyer or the lawyer's client. A statement made pursuant to this paragraph shall be limited to such information as is necessary to mitigate the recent adverse publicity.

(d) No lawyer associated in a firm or government agency with a lawyer subject to paragraph (a) shall make a statement prohibited by paragraph (a).

The amended rule includes a "fight fire with fire" provision in paragraph (c). Could Cutler have been disciplined under this rule for his responsive comments about his client John Gotti? Could Gentile have been disciplined under this rule?

tainting the trial because their extrajudicial comments are likely to be taken as authoritative; and conversely, the Court noted that comments likely to prejudice the trial are sanctionable even if an untainted jury is ultimately found. That is, a disciplinary rule can be based on the *likelihood* of prejudice to the trial, even if no prejudice actually occurs.

Questions About Gentile

Justice Kennedy questioned whether, as an empirical matter, statements by defense counsel in all but a few cases could realistically threaten to prejudice a trial, especially when, as in *Gentile*, the statements are made shortly after charges are brought and well before the trial is to be held. What types of prejudice might a state reasonably fear when public comments are made by a trial counsel? Is a defense lawyer as capable as a prosecutor of creating a prejudicial environment? Suppose that police officers or witnesses who are not lawyers have made public statements. Should a defendant have a right to respond through counsel? When it is common practice for prosecutors to draft "speaking indictments," i.e., charging instruments that set forth in detail the crime charged, should a defendant be permitted to make a public response through counsel and to set forth the defense position in as much detail as is found in the indictment?

Chief Justice Rehnquist's opinion in *Gentile* stresses the state's legitimate concern that jurors will be affected by pretrial publicity, and that Gentile was properly disciplined for making general comments well before trial. Yet in Mu'Min v. Virginia, supra, the community had been barraged with newspaper and television reports prejudicial to the defendant, and the Chief Justice stated that the publicity did not rise even to a level requiring questioning of individual jurors about the content of the publicity. How can the two cases be reconciled?

B.   CONTROLLING THE MEDIA'S IMPACT

Many participants in and observers of the criminal justice system have argued that undue or unfair press coverage can be remedied by limiting the information disseminated to the public. This can be accomplished in two ways: by controlling press access to information and by restricting what the press prints. The Supreme Court and lower courts have often been confronted with whether and under what circumstances media access to trials can be controlled.

1.   Controlling Access to Courts; Public Trials

Pretrial Proceedings: Gannett Co., Inc. v. DePasquale

In Gannett Co., Inc. v. DePasquale, 443 U.S. 368 (1979), a state trial judge had granted two defendants' motions to exclude the press and public from a pretrial hearing on a motion to suppress confessions and physical evidence. A newspaper owner challenged the judge's decision, which was upheld in the Supreme Court. The Court stated that the Framers of the Sixth Amendment did not intend "to create a constitutional right in strangers to attend a pretrial proceeding, when all that they actually did was to confer upon the accused an explicit right to demand a public trial." The Court also noted that, assuming the First Amendment granted a right of access to pretrial proceedings, the trial court had appropriately balanced the First Amendment interests with the defendant's right to be free from prejudicial pretrial publicity. Justice Powell's concurring opinion suggested that he would recognize some such right, but Justice Rehnquist's concurring opinion indicated that he thought the Court's prior decisions had rejected the idea that the First Amendment guaranteed access to government facilities. Chief Justice Burger also concurred, noting that a pretrial hearing was not a "trial" within the meaning of the Sixth Amendment. Justice Blackmun's dissenting opinion was joined by Justices Brennan, White and Marshall.

Gannett left its readers confused as to its precise scope. See, e.g., Goodale, Gannett Means What It Says; But Who Knows What It Says? Nat'l L.J., Oct. 15, 1979, at 20, col. 1. Despite the fact that the Court had before it a pretrial proceeding, the reasoning of the majority opinion was not necessarily confined to such proceedings. Did *Gannett* mean to allow any and all exclusions of the public from any and all parts of trials? If not, what limitations does the Constitution place on the closing of proceedings?

Limited Right of Access to Criminal Trials: Richmond Newspapers, Inc. v. Virginia

In Richmond Newspapers, Inc. v. Virginia, 448 U.S. 555 (1980), the Supreme Court held that the First Amendment does give the public and the press a limited right of access to criminal trials. Chief Justice Burger's plurality opinion commanded the most votes in the case. Only Justices White and Stevens joined the opinion, however. Justice Stevens also added a separate concurrence, and Justice White added a concurring statement. The Chief Justice distinguished *Gannett* as dealing with pretrial proceedings, looked to the history of American criminal trials, and found that they had long been conducted in public places in which the public and the media were welcome. He observed that the presence of the public added something of importance to the proceedings. The Chief Justice concluded that the right of the public and the press to be present was not absolute and would give way to overriding governmental interests articulated in findings of a court. He suggested, however that alternatives must be explored before closure is ordered. Justice Brennan, joined by Justice Marshall, concurred in the judgment and would have held the underlying Virginia statute unconstitutional for giving trial judges too much discretion. Justice Brennan was reluctant to specify the countervailing government interests that might justify overriding the presumption of open trials. Justices Stewart and Blackmun wrote separate opinions concurring in the result. Justice Stewart distinguished the trial setting from places like jails not generally open to the public. Justice Blackmun had some extremely harsh words for the *Gannett* opinion. Justice Rehnquist dissented. Justice Powell did not participate in the decision.

Richmond Newspapers provides some answers to questions left open in *Gannett*, but it raised some new and difficult problems: What showing of governmental interest will satisfy a court that proceedings should be closed?[47]

---

47. People v. Martinez, 82 N.Y.2d 436, 604 N.Y.S.2d 932, 624 N.E.2d 1027 (1993), holds that the public may be excluded from testimony by an undercover informant, but only if a factual showing is made that continued confidentiality is necessary for the informant's safe-ty or to preserve the integrity of an ongoing investigation. In contrast, see People v. Kin Kan, 78 N.Y.2d 54, 571 N.Y.S.2d 436, 574 N.E.2d 1042 (1991), where error was found when the trial court excluded the public, including the defendant's family, during the tes-

Does the First Amendment right extend to pretrial proceedings? If so, must the government make the same showing of overriding interest to close those proceedings? What procedures must be employed before any proceeding is closed?[48]

One court has read *Richmond Newspapers* to articulate six societal interests advanced by open court proceedings. They are:

> promotion of informed discussion of governmental affairs by providing the public with the more complete understanding of the judicial system; promotion of the public perception of fairness which can be achieved only by permitting full public view of the proceedings; providing a significant community therapeutic value as an outlet for community concern, hostility and emotion; serving as a check on corrupt practices by exposing the judicial process to public scrutiny; enhancement of the performance of all involved; and discouragement of perjury.

United States v. Simone, 14 F.3d 833 (3d Cir.1994). Are these interests as valid today as when *Richmond Newspapers* was decided?

Closure to Protect Witnesses: Globe Newspaper Co. v. Superior Court

The Court relied on *Richmond Newspapers* in Globe Newspaper Co. v. Superior Court, 457 U.S. 596 (1982), to invalidate a state statute that required exclusion of the press and general public from the courtroom during the testimony of a sex offense victim under the age of 18. Justice Brennan's opinion for the Court observed that where "the State attempts to deny the right of access in order to inhibit the disclosure of sensitive information, it must be shown that the denial is necessitated by a compelling governmental interest, and is narrowly tailored to serve that interest." Although the Court agreed that safeguarding the physical and psychological well-being of a minor is a compelling state interest, it found that this could be accomplished on a case-by-case basis with the trial judge weighing "the minor victim's age, psychological maturity and understanding, the nature of the crime, the desires of the victim, and the interests of parents and relatives."[49] It rejected the assertion that the statute was necessary to encourage minor victims to come forward and to provide accurate testimony, saying that "[n]ot only is the claim speculative in empirical terms, but it is also open to serious question as a matter of logic and common sense."

timony of the key cooperating witness-accomplice to the defendant's crime. The witness stated that he feared retaliation from testifying in open court, but not from the defendant's family, who knew him already anyway. The court found that "the expulsion of everyone during this accomplice's testimony was broader than constitutionally tolerable and constituted a violation of Kan's overriding right to a public trial." See also Brown v. Andrews, 180 F.3d 403 (2d Cir.1999) (error to permit closure during testimony of undercover agent; the government failed to make a specific showing of why the agent might have a legitimate fear of testifying in an open courtroom).

48. In United States v. Criden, 648 F.2d 814 (3d Cir.1981), a case arising out of one of the Abscam prosecutions, the court relied on *Richmond Newspapers* to hold that the trial judge erred in denying an application by television networks for permission to copy for broadcasting purposes those video and audio tapes admitted into evidence and played to the jury in open court.

49. United States v. Sherlock, 962 F.2d 1349 (9th Cir.1989), upheld a trial court order excluding the defendant's family in a rape case. The victim, a child, became upset when the defendant's family began giggling and making faces at her during her testimony. The court held that a partial closure (excluding only certain people) was easier to justify than a total closure of a criminal proceeding.

Chief Justice Burger, joined by Justice Rehnquist, dissented in *Globe Newspapers*. He argued that there was historical support for exclusion of the public from trials involving sexual assaults, particularly those against minors; that it was paradoxical to permit states to close trials of juveniles to protect defendants but not to permit them to protect victims; that the law was a rational response to the undisputed problem of the underreporting of rapes and other sexual offenses; and that the states should have room to experiment before a court demands empirical data to justify a law permitting closure. Justice O'Connor concurred in the judgment, emphasizing that *Richmond Newspapers* applies only to criminal trials. Justice Stevens dissented on procedural grounds.

Globe Newspaper Co. answered some of the questions raised by *Richmond Newspapers*, but did not decide whether the First Amendment right of access applied in pretrial proceedings.

Closure of Voir Dire: Press Enterprise I

Richmond Newspapers was the authority that Chief Justice Burger cited in his opinion for the Court in Press–Enterprise Co. v. Superior Court, 464 U.S. 501 (1984)("Press–Enterprise I"). The important facts were as follows: Jury selection in a capital prosecution for rape and murder took six weeks. Only three days of the voir dire of the jury was open to the public, since the trial judge was concerned about the privacy of the jurors. After the jury was selected, the trial judge denied a request by Press–Enterprise to release a transcript of the voir dire. A state appellate court sustained the trial judge and the state supreme court denied review.

Citing neither the First nor the Sixth Amendment, the Court stated that "how we allocate the 'right' to openness as between the accused and the public, or whether we view it as a component inherent in the system benefitting both, is not crucial. No right ranks higher than the right of the accused to a fair trial. But the primacy of the accused's right is difficult to separate from the right of everyone in the community to attend the voir dire which promotes fairness." It reasoned that openness has "a community therapeutic value" and that secret proceedings would deny an outlet for community reaction to serious crime.

Openness, while prized, was not absolutely required, however. "The presumption of openness may be overcome only by an overriding interest based on findings that closure is essential to preserve higher values and is narrowly tailored to serve that interest. The interest is to be articulated along with findings specific enough that a reviewing court can determine whether the closure order was properly entered." As an example of proper closure, the Court suggested that in a rape trial a prospective juror might privately inform the judge that she or a member of her family had been raped, but had declined to seek prosecution because of the associated emotional trauma. It also suggested that "[b]y requiring the prospective juror to make an affirmative request, the trial judge can ensure that there is in fact a valid basis for a belief that disclosure infringes a significant interest in privacy," and that "[w]hen limited closure is ordered, the constitutional values sought to be protected by holding open proceedings may be satisfied later by making a transcript of the closed proceedings available within a reasonable time, if the judge determines that disclosure can be accomplished while safeguarding the juror's valid privacy interests." On the facts presented, the Court found that the closure order and the sealing of the transcript were unwarranted. It observed that there were less onerous alternatives than a total preclusion of media access to the voir dire transcript. For example, parts of the transcript might have been sealed and other parts disclosed; also, the judge could have considered revealing the substance of answers without disclosing the identity of jurors. The Court remanded for further proceedings.

Justice Blackmun concurred, stating that he saw no need to decide whether privacy interests of jurors might outweigh a defendant's need for information about jurors. Justice Marshall, who concurred in the judgment, also expressed concern about denying the public and the press private information about jurors. He argued that before closing proceedings the trial judge "should be obliged to show that the order in question constitutes *the least restrictive means available* for protecting compelling state interests" and that some transcript of proceedings should be available in all but the most extraordinary cases. Justice Stevens also concurred. He explicitly relied upon a First Amendment right of access.

Procedural Requirements for Determining the Propriety of Closure: Waller v. Georgia

Justice Powell wrote for a unanimous Court in Waller v. Georgia, 467 U.S. 39 (1984). An indictment charged a number of people with racketeering and other offenses. Prior to the trial of one group of defendants, a motion was made to suppress evidence obtained through wiretaps and searches of homes. The prosecution moved to have the suppression hearing closed to all persons other than those involved in the prosecution on the ground that the taps would "involve" some persons who were indicted but not on trial in this case and other persons not indicted at all. Over the objection of some defendants, the trial judge granted the motion. The suppression hearing lasted seven days, although only two and a half hours were devoted to playing tapes of intercepted conversations. The trial judge suppressed some, but not all, evidence. At trial the defendants were acquitted of racketeering and convicted on gambling charges. Thereafter, but before other persons named in the indictment were tried, a transcript of the suppression hearing was released. The Georgia Supreme Court found that the trial judge had properly balanced the defendants' right to a public hearing against the privacy rights of other persons. The United States Supreme Court disagreed.

Justice Powell cited the Court's First Amendment decisions and included *Press-Enterprise I* in his discussion of these cases. He reasoned that "there can be little doubt that the explicit Sixth Amendment right of the accused is no less protective than the implicit First Amendment right of the press and public." He also observed that "suppression hearings often are as important as the trial itself. In *Gannett*, as in many cases, the suppression hearing was the *only* trial, because the defendants thereafter pleaded guilty pursuant to a plea bargain." And he concluded that a suppression hearing often resembles a bench trial in which witnesses are sworn and testify, making the need for an open proceeding especially strong. Thus, the Court held "that under the Sixth Amendment any closure of a suppression hearing over the objections of the accused must meet the tests set out in *Press-Enterprise* and its predecessors."

The Court found that the trial judge erred in not considering alternatives to closing the entire hearing and in not requiring the government to provide more details about its need for closure. One option the Court cited was to close only the part of the hearing—e.g., the playing of the tapes—that jeopardized the interests articulated by the government. Rather than reverse the convictions, the Court remanded the case for a new suppression hearing to be conducted in accordance with the constitutional standards articulated in this and prior cases.

Lower courts have read *Waller* as articulating a four-prong test by which to assess the propriety of closure:

> (1) The party seeking to close the hearing must advance an overriding interest that is likely to be prejudiced; (2) the closure must be no broader than necessary to protect that interest; (3) the trial court must consider reasonable alternatives to closing the proceeding; and (4) the trial court must make findings adequate to support the closure.

People v. Kan, 78 N.Y.2d 54, 571 N.Y.S.2d 436, 574 N.E.2d 1042 (1991).

Preliminary Hearings: Press–Enterprise II

In Press–Enterprise Co. v. Superior Court, 478 U.S. 1 (1986) ("*Press–Enterprise II*"), Chief Justice Burger wrote for the majority as it concluded "that the qualified First Amendment right of access to criminal proceedings applies to preliminary hearings as they are conducted in California." He reasoned that preliminary hearings have usually been open, and that preliminary hearings are sufficiently like trials in California to justify the conclusion that public access is essential. Thus, the Chief Justice focused on two factors in determining the applicability of the First Amendment right of access to proceedings other than trials: 1) whether there has been a tradition of openness at such proceedings, and 2) whether the proceeding is "trial-like". Chief Justice Burger concluded that preliminary hearings may only be closed "if specific findings are made demonstrating that, first, there is a substantial probability that the defendant's right to a fair trial will be prejudiced by publicity that closure would prevent and, second, reasonable alternatives to closure cannot adequately protect the defendant's free trial rights."

Justice Stevens, joined in part by Justice Rehnquist, dissented. He challenged the majority's observation that pretrial proceedings are generally open, by citing *Gannett*, which had noted that the public had no general right to attend pretrial proceedings, and by pointing out that states differed in the ways they approached these proceedings. He also challenged the reliance on the value of openness as proving too much, because the same argument could be made with respect to grand jury proceedings, even though these proceedings have historically been secret. In the end, Justice Stevens found the test adopted by the majority to be inconsistent with *Gannett*.[50]

50. *Press–Enterprise II* was found controlling in El Vocero de Puerto Rico v. Puerto Rico, 508 U.S. 147 (1993)(per curiam). Under Puerto Rican law, an accused felon is entitled to a hearing to determine if he shall be held for trial. Both sides may introduce evidence and cross-examine witnesses, and the defendant has the right to counsel. Puerto Rican law provided that the hearing is private unless the defendant requests otherwise. The Supreme Court held that the privacy provision of the Puerto Rican law was unconstitutional. As in *Press–Enterprise II*, the Court found that the Puerto Rican hearing was "sufficiently like a trial" to require public access. The Court rejected the notion that the unique history and traditions of Puerto Rican culture were at all relevant to whether the press and public could have access to the hearing. The Court concluded that any concerns that the defendant might not receive a fair trial must be addressed on a case-by-case basis.

Deportation Proceedings After 9/11

After 9/11, many deportation proceedings have raised issues of national security, and the government has sought to exclude the press from some of these proceedings. In North Jersey Media Group, Inc. v. Ashcroft, 308 F.3d 198 (3d Cir. 2002), media groups sought access to "special interest" deportation proceedings involving persons whom the Attorney General listed as persons who might have connection to or knowledge of the 9/11 attacks. The Attorney General listed security risks that would be at stake if these proceedings were open to the press—concerns included the use of media to send coded messages; the hearings themselves could be targeted by terrorists; potential witnesses could be threatened; and terrorist organizations could use the published information to alter attack plans. Using the analysis of *Press Enterprise II,* the court held that the denial of media access to these special deportation proceedings was constitutional. Judge Becker, writing the opinion, concluded as follows:

> Deportation proceedings' history of openness is quite limited, and the presumption of openness is quite week. * * * We do not decide that there is no right to attend administrative proceedings, or even that there is no right to attend any immigration proceeding. Our judgment is confined to the extremely narrow class of deportation cases that are determined by the Attorney General to present significant national security concerns. In recognition of his experience in this field (and our lack of experience) in this field, we will defer to his judgment. We note that although there may be no judicial remedy for these closures, there is, as always, the powerful check of political accountability on Executive discretion.

For a contrary view, holding that these special deportation proceedings must be opened to the press, see Detroit Free Press v. Ashcroft, 303 F.3d 681 (6th Cir. 2002).

2. *Controlling What Is Printed*

Once information about judicial proceedings is discovered by observers, including the press, do courts have authority to control dissemination of the information to the public? The next case addresses this question.

NEBRASKA PRESS ASS'N v. STUART

Supreme Court of the United States, 1976.
427 U.S. 539.

Mr. Chief Justice Burger delivered the opinion of the court.

* * *

I

On the evening of October 18, 1975, local police found the six members of

the Henry Kellie family murdered in their home in Sutherland, Neb., a town of about 850 people. Police released the description of a suspect, Erwin Charles Simants, to the reporters who had hastened to the scene of the crime. Simants was arrested and arraigned in Lincoln County Court the

See also United States v. Simone, 14 F.3d 833 (3d Cir.1994)(relying on *Press-Enterprise II* and holding that the First Amendment qualified right of access applies to a post-trial investigation of juror misconduct).

following morning, ending a tense night for this small rural community.

The crime immediately attracted widespread news coverage, by local, regional, and national newspapers, radio and television stations. Three days after the crime, the County Attorney and Simants' attorney joined in asking the County Court to enter a restrictive order relating to "matters that may or may not be publicly reported or disclosed to the public," because of the "mass coverage by news media" and the "reasonable likelihood of prejudicial news which would make difficult, if not impossible, the impaneling of an impartial jury and tend to prevent a fair trial." The County Court heard oral argument but took no evidence; no attorney for members of the press appeared at this stage. The County Court granted the prosecutor's motion for a restrictive order and entered it the next day, October 22. The order prohibited everyone in attendance from "releas[ing] or authoriz[ing] the release for public dissemination in any form or manner whatsoever any testimony given or evidence adduced" * * *.

Simants' preliminary hearing was held the same day, open to the public but subject to the order. The County Court bound over the defendant for trial to the State District Court. The charges, as amended to reflect the autopsy findings, were that Simants had committed the murders in the course of a sexual assault.

Petitioners—several press and broadcast associations, publishers, and individual reporters—moved on October 23 for leave to intervene in the District Court, asking that the restrictive order imposed by the County Court be vacated. [The trial judge essentially affirmed the findings of the County Court, and entered an order restraining coverage; after extensive proceedings and appellate review, the Nebraska Supreme Court modified the order of the lower court.]

* * *

The Nebraska Supreme Court * * * modified the District Court's order to accommodate the defendant's right to a fair trial and the petitioners' interest in reporting pretrial events. The order as modified prohibited reporting of only three matters: (a) the existence and nature of any confessions or admissions made by the defendant to law enforcement officers, (b) any confessions or admissions made to any third parties, except members of the press, and (c) other facts "strongly implicative" of the accused. * * *

[Much of the procedural history is deleted, as is the Court's discussion of mootness.]

The state trial judge in the case before us acted responsibly, out of a legitimate concern, in an effort to protect the defendant's right to a fair trial. What we must decide is not simply whether the Nebraska courts erred in seeing the possibility of real danger to the defendant's rights, but whether in the circumstances of this case the means employed were foreclosed by another provision of the Constitution.

V

[The Court discusses its prior restraint cases: E.g., Near v. Minnesota ex rel. Olson, 283 U.S. 697, 707 (1931); Organization for a Better Austin v. Keefe, 402 U.S. 415 (1971); New York Times Co. v. United States, 403 U.S. 713 (1971).]

The thread running through all these cases is that prior restraints on speech and publication are the most serious and the least tolerable infringement on First Amendment rights. * * *

A prior restraint * * * has an immediate and irreversible sanction. If it can be said that a threat of criminal or civil sanctions after publication "chills" speech, prior restraint "freezes" it at least for the time.

The damage can be particularly great when the prior restraint falls upon the communication of news and commentary on current events. Truthful reports of public judicial proceedings have been afforded special protection against subsequent punishment. * * *

* * *

The authors of the Bill of Rights did not undertake to assign priorities as between First Amendment and Sixth Amendment rights, ranking one as superior to the other. In this case, the petitioners would have us declare the right of an accused subordinate to their right to publish in all circumstances. But if the authors of these guarantees, fully aware of the potential conflicts between them, were unwilling or unable to resolve the issue by assigning to one priority over the other, it is not for us to rewrite the Constitution by undertaking what they declined to do. It is unnecessary, after nearly two centuries, to establish a priority applicable in all circumstances. Yet it is nonetheless clear that the barriers to prior restraint remain high unless we are to abandon what the Court has said for nearly a quarter of our national existence and implied throughout all of it. * * *

* * *

VI

* * *

A

* * *

Our review of the pretrial record persuades us that the trial judge was justified in concluding that there would be intense and pervasive pretrial publicity concerning this case. He could also reasonably conclude, based on common human experience, that publicity might impair the defendant's right to a fair trial. He did not purport to say more, for he found only "a clear and present danger that pre-trial publicity *could* impinge upon the defendant's right to a fair trial." (Emphasis added.) His conclusion as to the impact of such publicity on prospective jurors was of necessity speculative, dealing as he was with factors unknown and unknowable.

B

* * *

Most of the alternatives to prior restraint of publication in these circumstances were discussed with obvious approval in Sheppard v. Maxwell: (a) change of trial venue to a place less exposed to the intense publicity that seemed imminent in Lincoln County; (b) postponement of the trial to allow public attention to subside; (c) searching questioning of prospective jurors, as Mr. Chief Justice Marshall used in the [Aaron] Burr case, to screen out those with fixed opinions as to guilt or innocence; (d) the use of emphatic and clear instructions on the sworn duty of each juror to decide the issues only on evidence presented in open court. Sequestration of jurors is, of course, always available. Although that measure insulates jurors only after they are sworn, it also enhances the likelihood of dissipating the impact of pretrial publicity and emphasizes the elements of the jurors' oaths.

* * *

We have noted earlier that pretrial publicity, even if pervasive and concentrated, cannot be regarded as leading automatically and in every kind of criminal case to an unfair trial. * * * Appellate evaluations as to the impact of publicity take into account what other measures were used to mitigate the adverse effects of publicity. The more difficult prospective or predictive assessment that a trial judge must make also calls for a judgment as to whether other precautionary steps will suffice.

We have therefore examined this record to determine the probable efficacy of the measures short of prior restraint on the press and speech. There is no finding that alternative measures would not have protected Simants' rights, and the Nebraska Supreme Court did no more than imply that such measures might not be adequate. Moreover, the record is lacking in evidence to support such a finding.

C

We must also assess the probable efficacy of prior restraint on publication as a workable method of protecting Simants' right to a fair trial, and we cannot ignore the reality of the problems of managing and enforcing pretrial restraining orders. The territorial jurisdiction of the issuing court is limited by concepts of sovereignty. The need for in personam jurisdiction also presents an obstacle to a restraining order that applies to publication at large as distinguished from restraining publication within a given jurisdiction. * * *

The Nebraska Supreme Court * * * opinion reflects awareness of the tensions between the need to protect the accused as fully as possible and the need to restrict publication as little as possible. The dilemma posed underscores how difficult it is for trial judges to predict what information will in fact undermine the impartiality of jurors, and the difficulty of drafting an order that will effectively keep prejudicial in-

formation from prospective jurors. When a restrictive order is sought, a court can anticipate only part of what will develop that may injure the accused. But information not so obviously prejudicial may emerge, and what may properly be published in these "gray zone" circumstances may not violate the restrictive order and yet be prejudicial.

Finally, we note that the events disclosed by the record took place in a community of 850 people. It is reasonable to assume that, without any news accounts being printed or broadcast, rumors would travel swiftly by word of mouth. One can only speculate on the accuracy of such reports, given the generative propensities of rumors; they could well be more damaging than reasonably accurate news accounts. But plainly a whole community cannot be restrained from discussing a subject intimately affecting life within it.

Given these practical problems, it is far from clear that prior restraint on publication would have protected Simants' rights.

D

* * *

E

* * *

Our analysis ends as it began, with a confrontation between prior restraint imposed to protect one vital constitutional guarantee and the explicit command of another that the freedom to speak and publish shall not be abridged. We reaffirm that the guarantees of freedom of expression are not an absolute prohibition under all circumstances, but the barriers to prior restraint remain high and the presumption against its use continues intact. We hold that, with respect to the order entered in this case prohibiting reporting or commentary on judicial proceedings held in public, the barriers have not been overcome; to the extent that this order restrained publication of such material, it is clearly invalid. To the extent that it prohibited publication based on information gained from other sources, we conclude that the heavy burden imposed as a condition to securing a prior restraint was not met and the judgment of the Nebraska Supreme Court is therefore reversed.

MR. JUSTICE WHITE, concurring.

Technically there is no need to go farther than the Court does to dispose of this case, and I join the Court's opinion. I should add, however, that for the reasons which the Court itself canvasses there is grave doubt in my mind whether orders with respect to the press such as were entered in this case would ever be justifiable. * * *

MR. JUSTICE POWELL, concurring.

* * *

In my judgment a prior restraint properly may issue only when it is shown to be necessary to prevent the dissemination of prejudicial publicity that otherwise poses a high likelihood of preventing, directly and irreparably, the impaneling of a jury meeting the Sixth Amendment requirement of impartiality. This requires a showing that (i) there is a clear threat to the fairness of trial, (ii) such a threat is posed by the actual publicity to be restrained, and (iii) no less restrictive alternatives are available. Notwithstanding such a showing, a restraint may not issue unless it also is shown that previous publicity or publicity from unrestrained sources will not render the restraint inefficacious. * * *

I believe these factors are sufficiently addressed in the Court's opinion to demonstrate beyond question that the prior restraint here was impermissible.

MR. JUSTICE BRENNAN, with whom MR. JUSTICE STEWART and MR. JUSTICE MARSHALL join, concurring in the judgment.

* * * The right to a fair trial by a jury of one's peers is unquestionably one of the most precious and sacred safeguards enshrined in the Bill of Rights. I would hold, however, that resort to prior restraints on the freedom of the press is a constitutionally impermissible method for enforcing that right; judges have at their disposal a broad spectrum of devices for ensuring that fundamental fairness is accorded the accused without necessitating so drastic an incursion on the equally fundamental and salutary constitutional mandate that discussion of public affairs in a free society cannot depend on the preliminary grace of judicial censors.

* * *

[Justice Stevens' opinion concurring in the judgment is omitted.]

Prior Restraints After Stuart

After *Stuart*, it is doubtful that a prior restraint would be upheld in any but the most exceptional case. The separate opinions support the assertion that it is difficult to imagine a case in which none of the alternatives to prior restraint would work, and in which the press will not have covered the case so fully before any restraint is ordered that it would be likely to work effectively.

On the subject of the right of the press to print the information that it obtains, see Landmark Communications, Inc. v. Virginia, 435 U.S. 829 (1978); Cox Broadcasting Corp. v. Cohn, 420 U.S. 469 (1975); Oklahoma Publishing Co.

v. District Court, 430 U.S. 308 (1977). The first two cases involved attempts to impose sanctions on newspapers for violating state laws prohibiting publication of certain facts bearing upon investigations or cases. *Landmark Communications, Inc.* upholds the right of the press to publish truthful information concerning "confidential proceedings" of a commission investigating the conduct of a judge. *Cohn* upheld the right of a publisher to reveal the name of a deceased rape victim once it was revealed in the courtroom. Citing *Cohn* and *Stuart,* the Court held in *Oklahoma Publishing* that publication of the name of a minor child obtained in the course of a juvenile hearing open to the public, and a picture obtained outside the courthouse, could not be prohibited.

In United States v. Noriega, 752 F.Supp. 1045 (S.D.Fla.1990), the defendant, a deposed Panamanian dictator being tried on drug charges, made telephone calls to his attorney from the correctional center where he was awaiting trial. These calls were recorded by correctional facility officials, and obtained by the Cable News Network (CNN) from an undisclosed source. Noriega moved to enjoin CNN from broadcasting the recordings insofar as they disclosed privileged communications. The court, citing *Stuart,* refused to grant the injunction, reasoning that less intrusive alternatives could be used to protect the defendant. Specifically the court imposed "sequestration" on the prosecuting attorneys and prosecution witnesses, so that Noriega's communications would not be revealed to them and could not be used against him. The court noted that the danger of prejudicial pretrial publicity could also be controlled through change of venue, continuance, careful voir dire, and emphatic jury instructions.

3. Change of Venue and Continuance

Press coverage on a crime is often greater in the place where the crime occurred. And coverage often is greater immediately after a crime is committed or an arrest takes place than later. By transferring a case, or by continuing a trial until passions cool, some of the ill effects of pretrial publicity might be avoided.

Transfer of Venue

Fed.R.Crim.P. 21(a) provides for transfer of proceedings to another district if the judge is "satisfied that so great a prejudice against the defendant exists in the transferring district that the defendant cannot obtain a fair and impartial trial there." In *Sheppard* the Court said that "where there is a *reasonable likelihood* that the prejudicial news prior to trial will prevent a fair trial, the judge should continue the case until the threat abates, or transfer it to another county not so permeated with publicity." (Emphasis added.) However, most courts require much more than a reasonable likelihood of prejudice from pretrial publicity before transfer of venue is mandated. A defendant must ordinarily make a showing of actual and substantial prejudice before change of venue is required.

For example, in United States v. Faul, 748 F.2d 1204 (8th Cir.1984), a widely publicized case in which two defendants—tax protesters and members of an organization known as the Posse Comitatus—were charged with murdering United States Marshals and assaulting other officials, a divided court of appeals held that the trial judge had not erred in refusing to grant a change of venue. The judges agreed that publicity had been widespread, but they disagreed on its nature. The majority found the publicity to be largely factual while the dissenting judge argued that "[t]he emotionalism running through this rural district caused even 'factual' reporting to fan the flames of the community's shock and anger."

Martinez v. Superior Court, 29 Cal.3d 574, 174 Cal.Rptr. 701, 629 P.2d 502 (1981), is one of the few cases that takes the reasonable likelihood of prejudice standard seriously. The court granted a mandamus petition and ordered a change of venue in a murder prosecution. It emphasized extensive publicity over the course of a year, the small size of the county, and the gravity of the charge. It also observed that the status of the victim and the accused in the community are significant, but not controlling, factors in ruling on a venue change request.

The more typical approach, demanding a showing of actual prejudice, is evident in cases such as United States v. Angiulo, 897 F.2d 1169 (1st Cir.1990), a widely publicized Mafia/RICO case, in which the court denied the defendant's motion for change of venue. The court, relying on Patton v. Yount, supra, held that the mere fact that a majority of the empaneled jurors had been exposed to the Patriarca–Angiulo names, or that some linked the Angiulo name with the Mafia, was not sufficient to support a finding of actual prejudice requiring a change of venue. The court deferred to the trial court's conclusion that the jurors could lay aside their impressions and render a verdict based on the evidence in court.

Because courts focus more on actual prejudice than on the likelihood of prejudice, it is common for the ruling on a change of venue motion to be reserved until jury selection, because it at that point in which the effect of trial publicity on potential jurors can be best assessed. But what happens then is predictable. Courts invest resources in voir dire of potential jurors, and the more they invest the more they want to get a return—to go ahead and try the case. It is the rare case in which a change of venue is granted once the jury is empaneled.

The hostility of some courts to change of venue motions can be attributed to feelings that trial at a distant location will burden witnesses, that the community in which the crime was committed has a substantial interest in seeing the law enforced against wrongdoers by means of the criminal justice system, and that a change of prosecutors may be required, which may be disruptive to the legitimate interests of the government.[51] Courts may also be concerned that the selection of the transferee jurisdiction may be viewed as unfair to one side or the other. These interests in not changing venue are usually found to outweigh the benefits to the defendant of a venue change—less onerous alternatives such as

---

51. Sometimes the government wants a change of venue despite the burden it may place on prosecutors. Because the defendant generally has a right to be tried in the jurisdiction where the crime was committed, courts are most reluctant to recognize change of venue requests by the government. See State v. Mendoza, 80 Wis.2d 122, 258 N.W.2d 260 (1977). Some states have upheld the prosecutor's right to seek a venue change. Others have limited the right to defendants. An alternative to a change of venue is a change of prospective jurors. If publicity in parts of a jurisdiction is much less than in the place where the crime was committed, jurors could be brought from the other parts to the original venue. There are obvious advantages to witnesses and to the prosecution from such a procedure. Are there disadvantages to the defendant? Are the attitudes of jurors brought into a courtroom outside their localities likely to differ from those that would exist in their home courthouse? If so, how? Once the point is reached at which a local jury cannot be trusted, can the local judge be trusted? The local prosecutor?

careful voir dire and strong jury instructions are usually held sufficient to protect the defendant's interests, whether that is actually true or not.

Famous Cases and Change of Venue

Two of the most famous cases in recent years have involved controversy about change of venue motions. In the state trial in California involving the beating of Rodney King by Los Angeles police officers, the trial judge granted a motion for change of venue from Los Angeles to Simi Valley. Most observers thought that the change of venue was unfairly beneficial to the defendants, because Simi Valley is a largely white community, and the home of many police officers. Obviously, a change of venue motion is intended to be outcome-determinative in some sense. But did the trial court go too far in the Rodney King beating case? Another controversial change of venue question arose in the prosecutions for the bombing of the Federal Building in Oklahoma City. Defense counsel did not argue that a change of venue was necessary due to prejudicial publicity. Rather, counsel successfully argued that the defendants would be substantially prejudiced by a trial in Oklahoma City, given the impact that the bombing had on virtually every person in the locality; all local jurors would essentially have to be struck for cause. Is there an argument that the community has the right to judge the defendants precisely *because* of the impact of the crime on the community? Is the judge entitled or required to take community interests into account in ruling on a change of venue motion?

With some cases, a change of venue will not be an effective weapon to control media exposure. For example, the media exposure in the O.J. Simpson case was unparalleled in American history, but obviously a change of venue— except perhaps to another planet—would not have done much good.

Continuance

A continuance may be less disruptive than a change of venue, because it does not change the place where trial is held. In Patton v. Yount, supra, the Supreme Court emphasized that the passage of time would go far to dissipate the taint of prejudicial pretrial publicity. 18 U.S.C.A. § 316(b)(8)(A) indicates that a continuance can be granted if the judge determines that "the ends of justice served by taking such action outweigh the best interest of the public and the defendant in a speedy trial." What this apparently means is that the defendant's right to a speedy trial must be balanced against his right to a fair trial free of prejudicial publicity. Does that make any sense? Query also whether a continuance is a proper solution if the defendant is subject to pretrial incarceration.

VI. THE DEFENDANT'S RIGHT TO PARTICIPATE IN THE TRIAL

A. THE RIGHT OF THE DEFENDANT TO BE PRESENT

6th Amendment

One aspect of the Sixth Amendment's right to a fair trial involves the defendant's right to be present during the trial. This right and its limits are discussed in the next case.

ILLINOIS v. ALLEN

Supreme Court of the United States, 1970.
397 U.S. 337.

MR. JUSTICE BLACK **delivered the opinion of the Court.**

The Confrontation Clause of the Sixth Amendment to the United States Constitution provides that: "In all criminal prosecutions, the accused shall enjoy the right * * * to be confronted with the witnesses against him * * *." * * * One of the most basic of the rights guaranteed by the Confrontation Clause is the accused's right to be present in the courtroom at every stage of his trial. The question presented in this case is whether an accused can claim the benefit of this constitutional right to remain in the courtroom while at the same time he engages in speech and conduct which is so noisy, disorderly, and disruptive that it is exceedingly difficult or wholly impossible to carry on the trial.

[Allen lost an appeal but won relief on federal habeas corpus in the Court of Appeals on his claim that his rights were violated when he was removed from the courtroom following disruptive behavior.]

* * *

It is essential to the proper administration of criminal justice that dignity, order, and decorum be the hallmarks of all court proceedings in our country. The flagrant disregard in the courtroom of elementary standards of proper conduct should not and cannot be tolerated. We believe trial judges confronted with disruptive, contumacious, stubbornly defiant defendants must be given sufficient discretion to meet the circumstances of each case. No one formula for maintaining the appropriate courtroom atmosphere will be best in all situations. We think there are at least three constitutionally permissible ways for a trial judge to handle an obstreperous defendant like Allen: (1) bind and gag him, thereby keeping him present; (2) cite him for contempt; (3) take him out of the courtroom until he promises to conduct himself properly.

I

Trying a defendant for a crime while he sits bound and gagged before the judge and jury would to an extent comply with that part of the Sixth Amendment's purposes that accords the defendant an opportunity to confront the witnesses at the trial. But even to contemplate such a technique, much less see it, arouses a feeling that no person should be tried while shackled and gagged except as a last resort. Not only is it possible that the sight of shackles and gags might have a significant effect on the jury's feelings about the defendant, but the use of this technique is itself something of an affront to the very dignity and decorum of judicial proceedings that the judge is seeking to uphold. Moreover, one of the defendant's primary advantages of being present at the trial, his ability to communicate with his counsel, is greatly reduced when the defendant is in a condition of total physical restraint. It is in part because of these inherent disadvantages and limitations in this method of dealing with disorderly defendants that we decline to hold with the Court of Appeals that a defendant cannot under any possible circumstances be deprived of his right to be present at trial. However, in some situations which we need not attempt to foresee, binding and gagging might possibly be the fairest and most reasonable way to handle a defendant * * *.

* * *

Allen's behavior was clearly of such an extreme and aggravated nature as to justify either his removal from the courtroom or his total physical restraint. Prior to his removal he was repeatedly warned by the trial judge that he would be removed from the courtroom if he persisted in his unruly conduct, and * * * the record demonstrates that Allen would not have been at all dissuaded by the trial judge's use of his criminal contempt powers. Allen was constantly informed that he could return to the trial when he would agree to conduct himself in an orderly manner. Under these circumstances we hold that Allen lost his right guaranteed by the Sixth and Fourteenth Amendments to be present throughout his trial.

* * *

Shackling, Courtroom Security, and Prejudice to the Defendant

Are you satisfied with the Court's directions to trial judges as to the proper response to cases of disruption? Some courts require that the shackling of a defendant be reserved for cases in which a clear showing of necessity—to prevent escape in exceptional circumstances, for example—is made. See, e.g., Kennedy v. Cardwell, 487 F.2d 101 (6th Cir.1973). Would you take this approach? Is there a hierarchy of appropriate responses to disruption that you would urge on trial judges? Harrell v. Israel, 672 F.2d 632 (7th Cir.1982), recommends a hearing to determine the need for shackling before a defendant is restrained.

The Supreme Court held in Holbrook v. Flynn, 475 U.S. 560 (1986), that deployment of uniformed law enforcement officers in a courtroom during a trial for security reasons is not inherently prejudicial to a defendant. It found no denial of due process or equal protection when four uniformed state troopers sat in the spectator section of the courtroom behind the defense table. Justice Marshall's unanimous opinion for the Court stated that it would never be possible "to eliminate from trial procedures every reminder that the State has chosen to marshal its resources against a defendant to punish him for allegedly criminal conduct." According to Justice Marshall, the Due Process Clause prohibits only such procedures which are so inherently prejudicial that they "brand the defendant with an unmistakable mark of guilt." The use of security officers was not considered inherently prejudicial because "the presence of guards at a defendant's trial need not be interpreted as a sign that he is particularly dangerous or culpable." Justice Marshall concluded that four troopers, sitting in the first row of the spectator's section, "are unlikely to have been taken as a sign of anything other than a normal official concern for the safety and order of the proceedings." The Court distinguished Estelle v. Williams, 425 U.S. 501 (1976), where it had found a due process violation when the defendant was forced to wear prison garb at the trial. Justice Marshall concluded that even if the presence of the guards was somewhat prejudicial, "sufficient cause for this level of security could be found in the State's need to maintain custody over defendants who had been denied bail after an individualized determination that their presence at trial could not otherwise be ensured." In contrast, there was no need in Williams to dress the defendant in prison garb for trial.

What about forcing the defendant to wear an electronic "stun belt" during trial proceedings? This can be hidden under the defendant's clothes, so it wouldn't seem to be the badge of guilt that the Court was concerned about in

stun belt(?)

Holbrook. But the courts have been–understandably–wary. See Gonzalez v. Pliler, 341 F.3d 897 (9th Cir. 2003) (forcing defendant to wear an electronic "stun belt" during trial proceedings was improper where the only justification was that the court heard from the bailiff that the defendant had a "bit of an attitude"); United States v. Durham, 287 F.3d 1297 (11th Cir. 2002) (use of stun belt improper where court did not inquire into the possibility that the belt might be activated accidentally, and the defendant was already shackled during the trial).

Commenting on the Defendant's Presence at Trial: Portuondo v. Agard

Witnesses are ordinarily sequestered before they testify in a criminal trial. See Federal Rule of Evidence 615. Sequestration addresses the concern that if a witness knows the evidence already presented, he may tailor his testimony to fit the evidence. But a criminal defendant who chooses to testify cannot be sequestered, because he has a constitutional right to attend the trial. In Portuondo v. Agard, 529 U.S. 61 (2000), the prosecutor in summation sought to draw this fact to the jury's attention. The case presented a credibility determination between the defendant Agard and the victims. The prosecutor argued as follows:

> You know, ladies and gentlemen, unlike all the other witnesses in this case the defendant has a benefit and the benefit that he has, unlike all the other witnesses, is he gets to sit here and listen to the testimony of all the other witnesses before he testifies. * * * That gives you a big advantage, doesn't it. You get to sit here and think what am I going to say and how am I going to say it? How am I going to fit it into the evidence? * * * He's a smart man. I never said he was stupid.... He used everything to his advantage.

Pros stated that Δ's rt to be present at trial gave him an advantage

Agard contended that the prosecutor's argument placed an impermissible burden on his right to be present at trial. The trial court rejected this claim, reasoning that Agard's status as the last witness in the case was simply a matter of fact, and held that his presence during the entire trial, and the advantage that this afforded him, "may fairly be commented on." The Supreme Court, in an opinion by Justice Scalia for five Justices, agreed with the trial court. Justice Scalia analyzed, and rejected, Agard's argument in the following passage:

Δ claims burdened the rt to be present

*S.C. Affirmed rejection of claim
• it is a matter of fact + can be commented upon*

> Respondent's argument boils down to a request that we extend to comments of the type the prosecutor made here the rationale of Griffin v. California, 380 U.S. 609 (1965), which involved comments upon a defendant's refusal to testify [see Chapter 3 for a discussion of *Griffin*.]. In that case, the trial court instructed the jury that it was free to take the defendant's failure to deny or explain facts within his knowledge as tending to indicate the truth of the prosecution's case. This Court held that such a comment, by "solemniz[ing] the silence of the accused into evidence against him," unconstitutionally "cuts down on the privilege [against self-incrimination] by making its assertion costly." We decline to extend *Griffin* to the present context. * * *

> That case is a poor analogue * * * for several reasons. What we prohibited the prosecutor from urging the jury to do in *Griffin* was something the jury is not permitted to do. The defendant's right to hold the

prosecution to proving its case without his assistance is not to be impaired by the jury's counting the defendant's silence at trial against him—and upon request the court must instruct the jury to that effect. It is reasonable enough to expect a jury to comply with that instruction since, as we observed in *Griffin*, the inference of guilt from silence is not always "natural or irresistible." A defendant might refuse to testify simply out of fear that he will be made to look bad by clever counsel, or fear "that his prior convictions will prejudice the jury." By contrast, it is natural and irresistible for a jury, in evaluating the relative credibility of a defendant who testifies last, to have in mind and weigh in the balance the fact that he heard the testimony of all those who preceded him. It is one thing (as *Griffin* requires) for the jury to evaluate all the other evidence in the case without giving any effect to the defendant's refusal to testify; it is something else (and quite impossible) for the jury to evaluate the credibility of the defendant's testimony while blotting out from its mind the fact that before giving the testimony the defendant had been sitting there listening to the other witnesses. Thus, the principle respondent asks us to adopt here differs from what we adopted in *Griffin* in one or the other of the following respects: It either prohibits inviting the jury to do what the jury is perfectly entitled to do; or it requires the jury to do what is practically impossible.

Second, *Griffin* prohibited comments that suggest a defendant's silence is "evidence of guilt." The prosecutor's comments in this case, by contrast, concerned respondent's credibility as a witness, and were therefore in accord with our longstanding rule that when a defendant takes the stand, his credibility may be impeached and his testimony assailed like that of any other witness. When a defendant assumes the role of a witness, the rules that generally apply to other witnesses—rules that serve the truth-seeking function of the trial—are generally applicable to him as well.

Justice Scalia was not troubled by the fact that the prosecutor's comments were made in summation, leaving the defendant no opportunity to reply. Justice Scalia stated that "[o]ur trial structure, which requires the defense to close before the prosecution, regularly forces the defense to predict what the prosecution will say." Justice Scalia concluded as follows:

In sum, we see no reason to depart from the practice of treating testifying defendants the same as other witnesses. A witness's ability to hear prior testimony and to tailor his account accordingly, and the threat that ability presents to the integrity of the trial, are no different when it is the defendant doing the listening. Allowing comment upon the fact that a defendant's presence in the courtroom provides him a unique opportunity to tailor his testimony is appropriate—and indeed, given the inability to sequester the defendant, sometimes essential—to the central function of the trial, which is to discover the truth.

Justice Stevens, joined by Justice Breyer, concurred in the judgment in *Agard*. Justice Stevens found no constitutional violation in the prosecutor's tailoring argument. He wrote, however, to express his "disagreement with the Court's implicit endorsement of her summation" and concluded that such arguments should be discouraged as a matter of fair trial practice.

Justice Ginsburg, joined by Justice Souter, dissented in *Agard*. She focused on the fact that the prosecutor's tailoring argument was "generic", i.e., it could

Consider whether they have proven this case fully

be applied in any case in which the defendant testified. Such an "automatic burden" on the defendant's credibility resulted, in her view, in an unfair penalty for the defendant's exercise of his constitutional right to be present.

B. THE REQUIREMENT OF COMPETENCY TO STAND TRIAL

The premise of the constitutional right to be present is that the defendant has the right to participate in his own defense. Indeed, participation by the defendant is ordinarily essential to assure that witnesses are fully cross-examined, exculpatory facts are presented, jurors are challenged when necessary, etc. But if the defendant is mentally incapable of participating in his defense, the right to be present is a nullity. Not surprisingly, then, the Supreme Court has often held that the Due Process Clause prohibits the criminal prosecution of a defendant who is not competent to stand trial. Drope v. Missouri, 420 U.S. 162 (1975); Pate v. Robinson, 383 U.S. 375 (1966).

In Dusky v. United States, 362 U.S. 402 (1960), the Court held that a defendant is competent to stand trial when he has "sufficient present ability to consult with his lawyer with a reasonable degree of rational understanding" and has a "rational as well as factual understanding of the proceedings against him." See also Drope v. Missouri, supra (a person "whose mental condition is such that he lacks the capacity to understand the nature and object of the proceedings against him, to consult with counsel, and to assist in preparing his defense may not be subjected to a trial").

A criminal prosecution must be delayed during the time that a defendant is incompetent, and a verdict rendered against an incompetent defendant is voidable. As a practical matter, it is often in the state's interest to press for a trial of a defendant who claims incompetency, and it is often in the defendant's interest to seek to delay such a trial. Predictably, many legal issues arise concerning whether a defendant is actually incompetent, and whether the state can use certain methods to assure that the defendant is competent to stand trial.

One thing is clear: a defendant is not incompetent simply because he has weird beliefs. Consider United States v. James, 328 F.3d 953 (7th Cir. 2003), where the defendant was charged with drug transactions, and his defense was "that his ancestors came from Africa, that he is therefore a Moorish national, and that as a result he need obey only those laws mentioned in an ancient treaty between the United States and Morocco." One of his tenets was that strangers were obliged to pay hefty sums for using his name, which he claimed to be copyrighted by his private legal system. Accordingly, James refused to recognize the authority of the court or court personnel until they entered into a compensation agreement with him for the use of his name. James refused to submit to a mental exam because, as might be expected, he demanded that the medical examiner compensate him for the use of his name. After all this, the court declared James mentally fit to stand trial, and the Court of Appeals agreed. The Court noted that James was actually a member of the Moorish Science Temple, all of whom held these beliefs. Judge Easterbrook noted:

> One person with a fantastic view may be suspected of delusions; two people with the identical view are just oddballs. That James was obstreperous likewise does not cast doubt on his mental acumen; many a person with no defense would rather play games, and try to goad the judge into error, than face the music politely. We do not doubt James' ability to understand the

proceedings and thus have no reason to instruct the judge to hold another hearing about his competence.

Forced Medication to Assure Competence: *Riggins v. Nevada*

What should the state do if a defendant's competency to stand trial is dependent on anti-psychotic medication, and the defendant refuses to take that medication? In Riggins v. Nevada, 504 U.S. 127 (1992), the defendant moved to terminate use of Mellaril, an anti-psychotic drug. His proposed defense at trial was insanity, and he argued that continued administration of the drug would deprive him of the right to show the jury his true mental state. The trial court held a hearing at which experts disagreed about whether Riggins would be competent to stand trial in the absence of medication. The experts also disagreed about the effects of the medication upon Riggins' demeanor at trial and upon his ability to participate in his defense. The trial court denied Riggins' motion. At the trial, Riggins testified while under medication. He was eventually convicted and sentenced to death.

The Supreme Court, in an opinion by Justice O'Connor, reversed the conviction. Justice O'Connor noted that a person has a liberty interest in being free from unwanted medication, citing Washington v. Harper, 494 U.S. 210 (1990). She recognized that the state could compel medication in certain circumstances—such as when the person presented a risk of harm to himself or to others—but concluded that the trial court had erred when it "allowed the administration of Mellaril to continue without making *any* determination of the need for this course or *any* findings about reasonable alternatives." She also noted that the trial court had not specifically acknowledged Riggins' liberty interest in freedom from unwanted anti-psychotic drugs. Relying on scientific literature, Justice O'Connor asserted that the side effects of Mellaril may have affected Riggins' demeanor, his testimony at trial, his ability to follow the proceedings, and his ability to communicate with counsel. She concluded that the forced medication created "a strong possibility that Riggins' defense was impaired due to the administration of Mellaril." Justice O'Connor recognized that under *Holbrook* and *Allen,* "trial prejudice can sometimes be justified by an essential state interest." But because the record contained no finding that forced medication was necessary to accomplish an essential state policy, the majority held that there was no basis "for saying that the substantial probability of trial prejudice in this case was justified."

Justice Kennedy concurred in the judgment and argued that by forcing medication at trial, the state was "manipulating the evidence." He concluded that "if the State cannot render the defendant competent without involuntary medication, then it must resort to civil commitment, if appropriate, unless the defendant becomes competent through other means."

Justice Thomas, joined by Justice Scalia, dissented. He noted that the trial court had allowed defense experts to testify as to the effects of Mellaril on Riggins' demeanor, and that insofar as his ability to participate in his defense was concerned, "the record indicates that Riggins' mental capacity was *enhanced* by his administration of Mellaril." Accordingly, Justice Thomas concluded that Riggins had suffered no trial prejudice from the forced medication. See also Sell v. United States, 539 U.S. 166 (2003) (Due Process Clause permits the Government to administer antipsychotic drugs to a mentally ill defendant facing serious criminal charges in order to render that defendant competent to stand trial, but only if the treatment is medically appropriate, is substantially unlikely to have side effects that may undermine the fairness of the trial, and, taking account of less intrusive alternatives, is necessary significantly to further important governmental trial-related interests; assuming that the defendant was not dangerous to himself or others, he could not be ordered involuntarily to take antipsychotic drugs solely to render him competent to stand trial without consideration of other factors).

Burden of Proof as to Competency: Medina v. California

Shortly after its decision in *Riggins,* the Court held in Medina v. California, 505 U.S. 437 (1992), that the Due Process Clause permits a state to allocate to the defendant the burden of proving that he is not competent to stand trial. On the basis of conflicting psychiatric testimony, Medina was found competent to stand trial and he was ultimately sentenced to death. Justice Kennedy wrote the majority opinion for five Justices. He cited *Riggins* and recognized that a criminal defendant has a constitutional right to be tried only if competent, and that this fundamental right is the foundation for other trial rights such as the right to be present and to assist in the defense. However, he asserted that the Due Process Clause does not "require a state to adopt one procedure over another on the basis that it may produce results more favorable to the accused." He concluded that "it is enough that the State affords the criminal defendant on whose behalf a plea of incompetence is asserted a reasonable opportunity to demonstrate that he is not competent to stand trial."

Justice Kennedy rejected the argument that the defendant's impairment may itself make it all but impossible to satisfy a burden of proof at the incompetency hearing. He explained that "although an impaired defendant might be limited in his ability to assist counsel in demonstrating incompetence, the defendant's inability to assist counsel can, in and of itself, constitute probative evidence of incompetence, and defense counsel will often have the best-informed view of the defendant's ability to participate in his defense."

Justice O'Connor, joined by Justice Souter, concurred in the judgment. Justice Blackmun dissented in an opinion joined by Justice Stevens. He concluded that the constitutional prohibition against convicting incompetent defendants is severely diminished "if the State is at liberty to go forward with a trial when the evidence of competency is inconclusive."

Requiring the Defendant to Prove Competency by Clear and Convincing Evidence: Cooper v. Oklahoma

The State of Oklahoma sought to extend the *Medina* principle in Cooper v. Oklahoma, 517 U.S. 348 (1996). The Oklahoma competency statute established a presumption that the defendant was competent to stand trial, and required the defendant to prove his incompetence by clear and convincing evidence. The trial court found it more likely than not that Cooper was incompetent, but nonetheless proceeded with the trial on the ground that Cooper had not shown incompetence by clear and convincing evidence. Cooper was convicted and sentenced to death, but his conviction was reversed in a unanimous opinion written by Justice Stevens.

Justice Stevens declared that the result in *Medina* (permitting the state to require the defendant to prove incompetence by a preponderance of the evidence) rested in part on the fact that a preponderance of the evidence standard "affects the outcome only in a narrow class of cases where the evidence is in equipoise." In contrast, Oklahoma's practice of requiring the defendant to prove incompetence by clear and convincing evidence "poses a significant risk of an erroneous determination that the defendant is competent" and "affects a class of cases in which the defendant has already demonstrated that he is more likely than not incompetent."

Justice Stevens reasoned that "while the difficulty of ascertaining where the truth lies may make it appropriate to place the burden of proof on the proponent of an issue, it does not justify the additional onus of a high standard of proof," and that a heightened standard of proof "does not decrease the risk of error, but simply reallocates that risk between the parties." Given the balance of interests at stake in the risk of a mistaken determination of a defendant's competence to stand trial, the Court found it unjust to allocate such a heavy burden to the defendant. The risk to the defendant of an erroneous determination of competence is that he will be unable to participate in his defense, thus impairing "the basic fairness of the trial itself." In contrast, the risk to the state of an erroneous determination of incompetence is "modest." While the state's interest in swift justice is implicated, the defendant can still be detained while incompetent, and a trial at a later date is possible if the defendant becomes competent. Justice Stevens concluded that where the defendant has proven his incompetence by a preponderance of the evidence, "the defendant's fundamental right to be tried only while competent outweighs the State's interest in the efficient operation of its criminal justice system."

C. THE RIGHT TO BE PRESENT AT ALL STAGES OF THE PROCEEDINGS

Fed.R.Crim.P. 43 provides that the defendant must be present be present at the arraignment, at the plea, at every trial stage, including jury impanelment and the return of the verdict, and at sentencing. Rogers v. United States, 422 U.S. 35 (1975), indicates the importance of the words "every trial stage" in the Federal Rule. Rogers' conviction for threatening the President was overturned because the jury sent a note to the trial judge inquiring whether the court would accept the Verdict—'Guilty as charged with extreme mercy of the Court,'" and the judge answered in the affirmative without notifying Rogers or his counsel. Despite the fact that Rogers did not know of the judge's action until after certiorari was granted and therefore never questioned it, the Court, in a unanimous opinion by Chief Justice Burger, concluded that Rule 43 was violated and that the error was not harmless.[52] The Court reasoned that the response that the judge gave the jury could have been improved considerably and might have induced unanimity among jury members.

---

52. The Supreme Court reversed a court of appeals summarily in United States v. Gagnon, 470 U.S. 522 (1985), and found that four defendants waived a right to be present when a trial judge questioned a juror in chambers concerning his statement of concern to a bailiff about one defendant's drawing pictures of the jury. The Court held that the presence of counsel and the defendants was not necessary to ensure fundamental fairness and that the defendants waived any right to be present under Fed.R.Crim.P. 43 by not objecting to the procedure used by the trial judge.

In United States v. Alikpo, 944 F.2d 206 (5th Cir.1991), a defendant charged with heroin distribution was over an hour late for scheduled jury selection. The judge began the jury selection process without him, and the defendant arrived just before the parties began to exercise peremptory challenges. The court of appeals found that conducting jury selection in the defendant's absence violated Rule 43 as well as the defendant's constitutional right to be present at all stages of the trial. The court refused to find waiver on the basis of the defendant's tardiness; it rejected the argument that the error was harmless because the defendant was present for the exercise of peremptory challenges. The court reasoned that the defendant's presence at the challenge stage is of diminished utility if he does not hear a prospective juror's response on voir dire. The court also relied upon the prejudice that could arise because the veniremembers would be adversely affected by "an accused heroin smuggler cavalierly walking in late for his trial." Would it have been less prejudicial to delay the jury selection process until the defendant saw fit to come to court? Compare United States v. Moore, 936 F.2d 1508 (7th Cir.1991)(defendant had no absolute right to be present at a conference in which his counsel advised the court that he would call a co-defendant to testify, the co-defendant's counsel advised the court that his client would declare the privilege, and the judge found a reasonable basis for the exercise of the privilege; the defendant's presence was not required to assure "a reasonable opportunity to defend against the charge").

Exclusion from Hearing as to Competency of Witnesses: Kentucky v. Stincer

The Supreme Court held in Kentucky v. Stincer, 482 U.S. 730 (1987), that a defendant was not denied his right of confrontation when he was barred from an in-chambers hearing to determine the competency to testify of two minors who allegedly were sodomized by the defendant. Justice Blackmun reasoned in his majority opinion that there was no indication that the defendant's presence at the hearing would have promoted a more reliable competency determination. The defendant was represented at the hearing by counsel, who was permitted to question the victims on competency issues. After the judge found the victims to be competent, they testified in open court in the presence of the defendant and were asked by defense counsel questions about their memory and understanding of the difference between the truth and a lie.

Justice Blackmun declined to decide whether a competency hearing is a trial or pretrial proceeding and stated that "it is more useful to consider whether excluding the defendant from the hearing interferes with his opportunity for effective cross-examination." He emphasized that state law permitted the defendant to cross-examine the victims completely at trial and to address their competency, even to the point of repeating questions asked at the competency hearing.

Justice Blackmun placed great weight on the fact that at the competency hearing "[n]o question regarding the substantive testimony that the two girls would have given during trial was asked," and stated that "although a competency hearing in which a witness is asked to discuss upcoming substantive testimony might bear a substantial relationship to a defendant's opportunity better to defend himself at trial, that kind of inquiry is not before us in this case."

Justice Marshall, joined by Justices Brennan and Stevens, dissented. Justice Marshall reasoned that "[p]hysical presence of the defendant enhances the reliability of the fact-finding process"; the findings that the trial judge must make concerning a witness' competency "often concern matters about which the defendant, and not his counsel, possesses the knowledge needed to expose the inaccuracies in the witness' answers"; and "[i]t is both functionally inefficient and fundamentally unfair to attribute to the defendant's attorney complete knowledge of the facts which the trial judge, in the defendant's involuntary absence, deems relevant to the competency determination."

D. TRIAL IN ABSENTIA

Federal Rule 43(c) provides that a defendant loses his right to be present by disruptive conduct or by voluntarily absenting himself after the trial starts. In Crosby v. United States, 506 U.S. 255 (1993), Justice Blackmun wrote for a unanimous Court as it held that Rule 43 does not permit the trial *in absentia* of a defendant who absconds *prior* to trial and is absent at its beginning. Crosby, charged with mail fraud, was released on bond pending his trial. He failed to appear for trial while three codefendants and a pool of 54 jurors waited for him. The trial judge found that his absence was deliberate and that the trial should commence. The Supreme Court recognized that Rule 43 permits a trial to continue if a defendant absconds *after* it begins, but held that the Rule means what it says and that it does not permit a trial to be started when a defendant is absent.

Justice Blackmun stated that the distinction in the Rule between pretrial and mid-trial flight was not "so farfetched as to convince us that Rule 43 cannot mean what it says." He noted the following reasons for making such a distinction: 1) "the costs of suspending a proceeding already under way will be greater than the cost of postponing a trial not yet begun;" 2) "the defendant's initial presence assures that any waiver is indeed knowing," whereas it could not as easily be assumed that a defendant not yet at trial would know that a trial could occur in his absence; and 3) "a rule that allows an ongoing trial to continue when a defendant disappears deprives the defendant of the option of gambling on an acquittal knowing that he can terminate the trial if it seems that the verdict will go against him—an option that might otherwise appear preferable to the costly, perhaps unnecessary, path of becoming a fugitive from the outset." The Court did not decide whether trying Crosby *in absentia* violated his constitutional right to be present, as well as Rule 43.

VII. THE RIGHT TO EFFECTIVE ASSISTANCE OF COUNSEL

In Chapter Five we saw that the accused is guaranteed the right to counsel. Here we examine the kind of counsel that the accused has a right to expect.

A. INEFFECTIVENESS AND PREJUDICE

Although counsel is constitutionally required at trial and at many pre-and post-trial stages of a criminal prosecution, the quality of representation afforded defendants is uneven. A defendant who is acquitted has little reason to complain, even if her lawyer made serious errors at trial. But a defendant who is convicted may believe that her lawyer did not provide sufficiently competent representation. If so, she may challenge her conviction on the theory that she was denied "effective" assistance of counsel.

The notion that counsel must provide at least some minimal level of representation first appeared in Powell v. Alabama, 287 U.S. 45 (1932). Justice Sutherland's opinion concluded that the trial judge's failure to make an effective appointment of counsel resulted in the "denial of effective and substantial aid. * * * [D]efendants were not accorded the right of counsel in any substantial sense." The Court in *Powell* concluded that the right to counsel means the right to a reasonably effective counsel.

[handwritten margin note: rt to counsel means the rt to effective counsel]

1. The Strickland Two–Pronged Test

In the following case, the Court set forth the standards that a defendant must meet to justify the reversal of a conviction or sentence for ineffective assistance of counsel.

STRICKLAND v. WASHINGTON

Supreme Court of the United States, 1984.
466 U.S. 668.

JUSTICE O'CONNOR **delivered the opinion of the Court.**

[handwritten margin note: How do you review a claim of ineffective assistance of counsel?]

This case requires us to consider the proper standards for judging a criminal defendant's contention that the Constitution requires a conviction or death sentence to be set aside because counsel's assistance at the trial or sentencing was ineffective.

I

A

During a ten-day period in September 1976, respondent planned and committed three groups of crimes, which included three brutal stabbing murders, torture, kidnapping, severe assaults, attempted murders, attempted extortion, and theft. After his two accomplices were arrested, respondent surrendered to police and voluntarily gave a lengthy statement confessing to the third of the criminal episodes. The State of Florida indicted respondent for kidnapping and murder and appointed an experienced criminal lawyer to represent him.

[handwritten margin note: murder, attempt, torture, kidnap, severe assault, attempted extortion, + theft; 2 accomplices captured; Δ surrendered; gave a voluntary confession]

Counsel actively pursued pretrial motions and discovery. He cut his efforts short, however, and he experienced a sense of hopelessness about the case, when he learned that, against his specific advice, respondent had also confessed to the first two murders. By the date set for trial, respondent was subject to indictment for three counts of first degree murder and multiple counts of robbery, kidnapping for ransom, breaking and entering and assault, attempted murder, and conspiracy to commit robbery. Respondent waived his right to a jury trial, again acting against counsel's advice, and pleaded guilty to all charges, including the three capital murder charges.

[handwritten margin note: Δ attny pursued pre-trial motions; cut efforts when Δ confessed to the first 2 murders against counsel's advice; Δ waived jury; against counsel; Δ plead guilty]

In the plea colloquy, respondent told the trial judge that, although he had committed a string of burglaries, he had no significant prior criminal record and that at the time of his criminal spree he was under extreme stress caused by his inability to support his family. He also stated, however, that he accepted responsibility for the crimes. The trial judge told respondent that he had "a great deal of respect for people who are willing to

[handwritten margin note: Δ admitted guilt; Judge promised no leniency for confession]

step forward and admit their responsibility" but that he was making no statement at all about his likely sentencing decision.

Counsel advised respondent to invoke his right under Florida law to an advisory jury at his capital sentencing hearing. Respondent rejected the advice and waived the right. He chose instead to be sentenced by the trial judge without a jury recommendation.

In preparing for the sentencing hearing, counsel spoke with respondent about his background. He also spoke on the telephone with respondent's wife and mother, though he did not follow up on the one unsuccessful effort to meet with them. He did not otherwise seek out character witnesses for respondent. Nor did he request a psychiatric examination, since his conversations with his client gave no indication that respondent had psychological problems.

Counsel decided not to present and hence not to look further for evidence concerning respondent's character and emotional state. That decision reflected trial counsel's sense of hopelessness about overcoming the evidentiary effect of respondent's confessions to the gruesome crimes. It also reflected the judgment that it was advisable to rely on the plea colloquy for evidence about respondent's background and about his claim of emotional stress: the plea colloquy communicated sufficient information about these subjects, and by foregoing the opportunity to present new evidence on these subjects, counsel prevented the State from cross-examining respondent on his claim and from putting on psychiatric evidence of its own.

Counsel also excluded from the sentencing hearing other evidence he thought was potentially damaging. He successfully moved to exclude respon-

dent's "rap sheet." Because he judged that a presentence report might prove more detrimental than helpful, as it would have included respondent's criminal history and thereby undermined the claim of no significant history of criminal activity, he did not request that one be prepared.

At the sentencing hearing, counsel's strategy was based primarily on the trial judge's remarks at the plea colloquy as well as on his reputation as a sentencing judge who thought it important for a convicted defendant to own up to his crime. Counsel argued that respondent's remorse and acceptance of responsibility justified sparing him from the death penalty. Counsel also argued that respondent had no history of criminal activity and that respondent committed the crimes under extreme mental or emotional disturbance, thus coming within the statutory list of mitigating circumstances. He further argued that respondent should be spared death because he had surrendered, confessed, and offered to testify against a co-defendant and because respondent was fundamentally a good person who had briefly gone badly wrong in extremely stressful circumstances. The State put on evidence and witnesses largely for the purpose of describing the details of the crimes. Counsel did not cross-examine the medical experts who testified about the manner of death of respondent's victims.

The trial judge found several aggravating circumstances with respect to each of the three murders. He found that all three murders were especially heinous, atrocious, and cruel, all involving repeated stabbings. All three murders were committed in the course of at least one other dangerous and violent felony, and since all involved robbery, the murders were for pecuniary gain. All three murders were committed to avoid arrest for the accompanying crimes and to hinder law enforcement. In the course of one of the murders, respondent knowingly subjected numerous persons to a grave risk of death by deliberately stabbing and shooting the murder victim's sisters-in-law, who sustained severe— in one case, ultimately fatal—injuries.

With respect to mitigating circumstances, the trial judge made the same findings for all three capital murders. First, although there was no admitted evidence of prior convictions, respondent had stated that he had engaged in a course of stealing. In any case, even if respondent had no significant history of criminal activity, the aggravating circumstances "would still clearly far outweigh" that mitigating factor. Second, the judge found that, during all three crimes, respondent was not suffering from extreme mental or emotional disturbance and could appreciate the criminality of his acts. Third, none of the victims was a participant in, or consented to, respondent's conduct. Fourth, respondent's participation in the crimes was neither minor nor the result of duress or domination by an accomplice. Finally, respondent's age (26) could not be considered a factor in mitigation, especially when viewed in light of respondent's planning of the crimes and disposition of the proceeds of the various accompanying thefts.

In short, the trial judge found numerous aggravating circumstances and no (or a single comparatively insignificant) mitigating circumstance. * * * He therefore sentenced respondent to death on each of the three counts of murder and to prison terms for the other crimes. The Florida Supreme Court upheld the convictions and sentences on direct appeal.

B

Respondent subsequently sought collateral relief in state court on nu-

merous grounds, among them that counsel had rendered ineffective assistance at the sentencing proceeding. Respondent challenged counsel's assistance in six respects. He asserted that counsel was ineffective because he failed to move for a continuance to prepare for sentencing, to request a psychiatric report, to investigate and present character witnesses, to seek a presentence investigation report, to present meaningful arguments to the sentencing judge, and to investigate the medical examiner's reports or cross-examine the medical experts. In support of the claim, respondent submitted fourteen affidavits from friends, neighbors, and relatives stating that they would have testified if asked to do so. He also submitted one psychiatric report and one psychological report stating that respondent, though not under the influence of extreme mental or emotional disturbance, was "chronically frustrated and depressed because of his economic dilemma" at the time of his crimes.

The trial court denied relief without an evidentiary hearing, finding that the record evidence conclusively showed that the ineffectiveness claim was meritless. Four of the assertedly prejudicial errors required little discussion. First, there were no grounds to request a continuance, so there was no error in not requesting one when respondent pleaded guilty. Second, failure to request a presentence investigation was not a serious error because the trial judge had discretion not to grant such a request and because any presentence investigation would have resulted in admission of respondent's rap sheet and thus undermined his assertion of no significant history of criminal activity. Third, the argument and memorandum given to the sentencing judge were "admirable" in light of the overwhelming aggravating circumstances and absence of mitigat-

(4) Why X experts when Δ admitted he murdered them in the way they described.

ing circumstances. Fourth, there was no error in failure to examine the medical examiner's reports or to cross-examine the medical witnesses testifying on the manner of death of respondent's victims, since respondent admitted that the victims died in the ways shown by the unchallenged medical evidence.

Psychiatric report?

• report done after arraignment

• no mental illness

• no extreme distress)

The trial court dealt at greater length with the two other bases for the ineffectiveness claim. The court pointed out that a psychiatric examination of respondent was conducted by state order soon after respondent's initial arraignment. That report states that there was no indication of major mental illness at the time of the crimes. Moreover, both the reports submitted in the collateral proceeding state that, although respondent was "chronically frustrated and depressed because of his economic dilemma," he was not under the influence of extreme mental or emotional disturbance. All three reports thus directly undermine the contention made at the sentencing hearing that respondent was suffering from extreme mental or emotional disturbance during his crime spree. Accordingly, counsel could reasonably decide not to seek psychiatric reports; indeed, by relying solely on the plea colloquy to support the emotional disturbance contention, counsel denied the State an opportunity to rebut his claim with psychiatric testimony. In any event, the aggravating circumstances were so overwhelming that no substantial prejudice resulted from the absence at sentencing of the psychiatric evidence offered in the collateral attack.

Counsel was ok in not pursuing a medical exam

Char evidence?

The court rejected the challenge to counsel's failure to develop and to present character evidence for much the same reasons. The affidavits submitted in the collateral proceeding showed nothing more than that certain persons would have testified that respondent was basically a good person who was worried about his family's financial problems. Respondent himself had already testified along those lines at the plea colloquy. Moreover, respondent's admission of a course of stealing rebutted many of the factual allegations in the affidavits. For those reasons, and because the sentencing judge had stated that the death sentence would be appropriate even if respondent had no significant prior criminal history, no substantial prejudice resulted from the absence at sentencing of the character evidence offered in the collateral attack.

Char witnesses would only support Δ's claim of good person not enough to outweigh aggravators

* * *

The Florida Supreme Court affirmed the denial of relief.

H: S.C. FL Affirmed

C

Respondent next filed a petition for a writ of habeas corpus in the United States District Court for the Southern District of Florida. * * *

The District Court disputed none of the state court factual findings concerning trial counsel's assistance and made findings of its own that are consistent with the state court findings. * * * On the legal issue of ineffectiveness, the District Court concluded that, although trial counsel made errors in judgment in failing to investigate nonstatutory mitigating evidence further than he did, no prejudice to respondent's sentence resulted from any such error in judgment. * * *

Counsel failed to investigate non-statutory mitigators but no prejudice to sentence

[The Court of Appeals, en banc, reversed the judgment of the District Court and remanded].

H: reversed & remanded

* * *

II

* * *

The Sixth Amendment recognizes the right to the assistance of counsel because it envisions counsel's playing a role that is critical to the ability of the adversarial system to produce just results. An accused is entitled to be assisted by an attorney, whether retained or appointed, who plays the role necessary to ensure that the trial is fair.

For that reason, the Court has recognized that "the right to counsel is the right to the effective assistance of counsel." Government violates the right to effective assistance when it interferes in certain ways with the ability of counsel to make independent decisions about how to conduct the defense. See, e.g., Geders v. United States, 425 U.S. 80 (1976)(bar on attorney-client consultation during overnight recess); Herring v. New York, 422 U.S. 853 (1975)(bar on summation at bench trial); Brooks v. Tennessee, 406 U.S. 605, 612–613 (1972)(requirement that defendant be first defense witness); Ferguson v. Georgia, 365 U.S. 570, 593–596 (1961) (bar on direct examination of defendant). Counsel, however, can also deprive a defendant of the right to effective assistance, simply by failing to render "adequate legal assistance," Cuyler v. Sullivan, [446 U.S. 335] at 344. (Actual conflict of interest adversely affecting lawyer's performance renders assistance ineffective).

The Court has not elaborated on the meaning of the constitutional requirement of effective assistance in the latter class of cases—that is, those presenting claims of "actual ineffectiveness." In giving meaning to the requirement, however, we must take its purpose—to ensure a fair trial—as the guide. The benchmark for judging any claim of ineffectiveness must be whether counsel's conduct so undermined the proper functioning of the adversarial process that the trial cannot be relied on as having produced a just result.

The same principle applies to a capital sentencing proceeding such as that provided by Florida law. * * *

III

A convicted defendant's claim that counsel's assistance was so defective as to require reversal of a conviction or death sentence has two components. First, the defendant must show that counsel's performance was deficient. This requires showing that counsel made errors so serious that counsel was not functioning as the "counsel" guaranteed the defendant by the Sixth Amendment. Second, the defendant must show that the deficient performance prejudiced the defense. This requires showing that counsel's errors were so serious as to deprive the defendant of a fair trial, a trial whose result is reliable. Unless a defendant makes both showings, it cannot be said that the conviction or death sentence resulted from a breakdown in the adversary process that renders the result unreliable.

A

As all the Federal Courts of Appeals have now held, the proper standard for attorney performance is that of reasonably effective assistance. * * * When a convicted defendant complains of the ineffectiveness of counsel's assistance, the defendant must show that counsel's representation fell below an objective standard of reasonableness.

* * *

Representation of a criminal defendant entails certain basic duties. Counsel's function is to assist the defendant, and hence counsel owes the client a duty of loyalty, a duty to avoid conflicts of interest. From counsel's function as assistant to the defendant derive the overarching duty to advocate the defendant's cause and the more particular duties to consult with the defendant on important decisions and to keep the defendant informed of important developments in the course of the prosecution. Counsel also has a duty to bring to bear such skill and knowledge as will render the trial a reliable adversarial testing process.

These basic duties neither exhaustively define the obligations of counsel nor form a checklist for judicial evaluation of attorney performance. In any case presenting an ineffectiveness claim, the performance inquiry must be whether counsel's assistance was reasonable considering all the circumstances. * * * No particular set of detailed rules for counsel's conduct can satisfactorily take account of the variety of circumstances faced by defense counsel or the range of legitimate decisions regarding how best to represent a criminal defendant. Any such set of rules would interfere with the constitutionally protected independence of counsel and restrict the wide latitude counsel must have in making tactical decisions. Indeed, the existence of detailed guidelines for representation could distract counsel from the overriding mission of vigorous advocacy of the defendant's cause. * * *

Judicial scrutiny of counsel's performance must be highly deferential. It is all too tempting for a defendant to second-guess counsel's assistance after conviction or adverse sentence, and it is all too easy for a court, examining counsel's defense after it has proved unsuccessful, to conclude that a particular act or omission of counsel was unreasonable. A fair assessment of attorney performance requires that every effort be made to eliminate the distorting effects of hindsight, to reconstruct the circumstances of counsel's challenged conduct, and to evaluate the conduct from counsel's perspective at the time. Because of the difficulties

inherent in making the evaluation, a court must indulge a strong presumption that counsel's conduct falls within the wide range of reasonable professional assistance; that is, the defendant must overcome the presumption that, under the circumstances, the challenged action "might be considered sound trial strategy." There are countless ways to provide effective assistance in any given case. Even the best criminal defense attorneys would not defend a particular client in the same way.

The availability of intrusive post-trial inquiry into attorney performance or of detailed guidelines for its evaluation would encourage the proliferation of ineffectiveness challenges. * * *

Thus, a court deciding an actual ineffectiveness claim must judge the reasonableness of counsel's challenged conduct on the facts of the particular case, viewed as of the time of counsel's conduct. A convicted defendant making a claim of ineffective assistance must identify the acts or omissions of counsel that are alleged not to have been the result of reasonable professional judgment. The court must then determine whether, in light of all the circumstances, the identified acts or omissions were outside the wide range of professionally competent assistance. * * * [T]he court should recognize that counsel is strongly presumed to have rendered adequate assistance and made all significant decisions in the exercise of reasonable professional judgment.

These standards require no special amplification in order to define counsel's duty to investigate, the duty at issue in this case. As the Court of Appeals concluded, strategic choices made after thorough investigation of law and facts relevant to plausible options are virtually unchallengeable; and strategic choices made after less than complete investigation are reasonable precisely to the extent that reasonable professional judgments support the limitations on investigation. * * *

The reasonableness of counsel's actions may be determined or substantially influenced by the defendant's own statements or actions. Counsel's actions are usually based, quite properly, on informed strategic choices made by the defendant and on information supplied by the defendant. In particular, what investigation decisions are reasonable depends critically on such information. For example, when the facts that support a certain potential line of defense are generally known to counsel because of what the defendant has said, the need for further investigation may be considerably diminished or eliminated altogether. And when a defendant has given counsel reason to believe that pursuing certain investigations would be fruitless or even harmful, counsel's failure to pursue those investigations may not later be challenged as unreasonable. * * *

B

An error by counsel, even if professionally unreasonable, does not warrant setting aside the judgment of a criminal proceeding if the error had no effect on the judgment. * * * Accordingly, any deficiencies in counsel's performance must be prejudicial to the defense in order to constitute ineffective assistance under the Constitution.

In certain Sixth Amendment contexts, prejudice is presumed. Actual or constructive denial of the assistance of counsel altogether is legally presumed to result in prejudice. So are various kinds of state interference with counsel's assistance. Prejudice in these circumstances is so likely that case by case inquiry into prejudice is not

worth the cost. Moreover, such circumstances involve impairments of the Sixth Amendment right that are easy to identify and, for that reason and because the prosecution is directly responsible, easy for the government to prevent.

One type of actual ineffectiveness claim warrants a similar, though more limited, presumption of prejudice. In Cuyler v. Sullivan [discussed infra], the Court held that prejudice is presumed when counsel is burdened by an actual conflict of interest. In those circumstances, counsel breaches the duty of loyalty, perhaps the most basic of counsel's duties. Moreover, it is difficult to measure the precise effect on the defense of representation corrupted by conflicting interests. Given the obligation of counsel to avoid conflicts of interest and the ability of trial courts to make early inquiry in certain situations likely to give rise to conflicts, see, *e.g.*, Fed.Rule Crim.Proc. 44(c), it is reasonable for the criminal justice system to maintain a fairly rigid rule of presumed prejudice for conflicts of interest. Even so, the rule is not quite the *per se* rule of prejudice that exists for the Sixth Amendment claims mentioned above. Prejudice is presumed only if the defendant demonstrates that counsel "actively represented conflicting interests" and "that an actual conflict of interest adversely affected his lawyer's performance."

Conflict of interest claims aside, actual ineffectiveness claims alleging a deficiency in attorney performance are subject to a general requirement that the defendant affirmatively prove prejudice. The government is not responsible for, and hence not able to prevent, attorney errors that will result in reversal of a conviction or sentence. Attorney errors come in an infinite variety and are as likely to be utterly harmless in a particular case as they are to be prejudicial. * * * Representation is an art, and an act or omission that is unprofessional in one case may be sound or even brilliant in another. * * *

It is not enough for the defendant to show that the errors had some conceivable effect on the outcome of the proceeding. Virtually every act or omission of counsel would meet that test, and not every error that conceivably could have influenced the outcome undermines the reliability of the result of the proceeding. Respondent suggests requiring a showing that the errors "impaired the presentation of the defense." That standard, however, provides no workable principle. * * *

On the other hand, we believe that a defendant need not show that counsel's deficient conduct more likely than not altered the outcome in the case. This outcome-determinative standard has several strengths. It defines the relevant inquiry in a way familiar to courts, though the inquiry, as is inevitable, is anything but precise. The standard also reflects the profound importance of finality in criminal proceedings. Moreover, it comports with the widely used standard for assessing motions for new trial based on newly discovered evidence. Nevertheless, the standard is not quite appropriate.

Even when the specified attorney error results in the omission of certain evidence, the newly discovered evidence standard is not an apt source from which to draw a prejudice standard for ineffectiveness claims. The high standard for newly discovered evidence claims presupposes that all the essential elements of a presumptively accurate and fair proceeding were present in the proceeding whose result is challenged. An ineffective assistance claim asserts the absence of one of the crucial assurances that the result of the proceeding is reliable, so finality concerns are somewhat weaker and

the appropriate standard of prejudice should be somewhat lower. * * *

Accordingly, the appropriate test for prejudice finds its roots in the test for materiality of exculpatory information not disclosed to the defense by the prosecution, United States v. Agurs, [set forth in Chapter Eight, *supra*] * * *. The defendant must show that there is a reasonable probability that, but for counsel's unprofessional errors, the result of the proceeding would have been different. A reasonable probability is a probability sufficient to undermine confidence in the outcome.

In making the determination whether the specified errors resulted in the required prejudice, a court should presume, absent challenge to the judgment on grounds of evidentiary insufficiency, that the judge or jury acted according to law. * * *

The governing legal standard plays a critical role in defining the question to be asked in assessing the prejudice from counsel's errors. When a defendant challenges a conviction, the question is whether there is a reasonable probability that, absent the errors, the factfinder would have had a reasonable doubt respecting guilt. When a defendant challenges a death sentence such as the one at issue in this case, the question is whether there is a reasonable probability that, absent the errors, the sentencer—including an appellate court, to the extent it independently reweighs the evidence—would have concluded that the balance of aggravating and mitigating circumstances did not warrant death.

In making this determination, a court hearing an ineffectiveness claim must consider the totality of the evidence before the judge or jury. * * *

IV

* * *

Although we have discussed the performance component of an ineffectiveness claim prior to the prejudice component, there is no reason for a court deciding an ineffective assistance claim to approach the inquiry in the same order or even to address both components of the inquiry if the defendant makes an insufficient showing on one. * * *

V

* * *

Application of the governing principles is not difficult in this case. The facts as described above make clear that the conduct of respondent's counsel at and before respondent's sentencing proceeding cannot be found unreasonable. They also make clear that, even assuming the challenged conduct of counsel was unreasonable, respondent suffered insufficient prejudice to warrant setting aside his death sentence.

With respect to the performance component, the record shows that respondent's counsel made a strategic choice to argue for the extreme emotional distress mitigating circumstance and to rely as fully as possible on respondent's acceptance of responsibility for his crimes. Although counsel understandably felt hopeless about respondent's prospects, nothing in the record indicates, as one possible reading of the District Court's opinion suggests, that counsel's sense of hopelessness distorted his professional judgment. Counsel's strategy choice was well within the range of professionally reasonable judgments, and the decision not to seek more character or psychological evidence than was already in hand was likewise reasonable.

* * *

With respect to the prejudice component, the lack of merit of respondent's claim is even more stark. The evidence that respondent says his trial counsel should have offered at the sentencing hearing would barely have altered the sentencing profile presented to the sentencing judge. * * *

* * *

Failure to make the required showing of either deficient performance or sufficient prejudice defeats the ineffectiveness claim. Here there is a double failure. More generally, respondent has made no showing that the justice of his sentence was rendered unreliable by a breakdown in the adversary process caused by deficiencies in counsel's assistance. * * *

* * *

JUSTICE MARSHALL, dissenting.

* * *

My objection to the performance standard adopted by the Court is that it is so malleable that, in practice, it will either have no grip at all or will yield excessive variation in the manner in which the Sixth Amendment is interpreted and applied by different courts. * * *

The debilitating ambiguity of an "objective standard of reasonableness" in this context is illustrated by the majority's failure to address important issues concerning the quality of representation mandated by the Constitution. It is an unfortunate but undeniable fact that a person of means, by selecting a lawyer and paying him enough to ensure he prepares thoroughly, usually can obtain better representation than that available to an indigent defendant, who must rely on appointed counsel, who, in turn, has limited time and resources to devote to a given case. Is a "reasonably competent attorney" a reasonably competent adequately paid retained lawyer or a reasonably competent appointed attorney? It is also a fact that the quality of representation available to ordinary defendants in different parts of the country varies significantly. Should the standard of performance mandated by the Sixth Amendment vary by locale? The majority offers no clues as to the proper responses to these questions.

* * * I agree that counsel must be afforded "wide latitude" when making "tactical decisions" regarding trial strategy, but many aspects of the job of a criminal defense attorney are more amenable to judicial oversight. For example, much of the work involved in preparing for a trial, applying for bail, conferring with one's client, making timely objections to significant, arguably erroneous rulings of the trial judge, and filing a notice of appeal if there are colorable grounds therefor could profitably be made the subject of uniform standards.

* * *

I object to the prejudice standard adopted by the Court for two independent reasons. First, it is often very difficult to tell whether a defendant convicted after a trial in which he was ineffectively represented would have fared better if his lawyer had been competent. Seemingly impregnable cases can sometimes be dismantled by good defense counsel. On the basis of a cold record, it may be impossible for a reviewing court confidently to ascertain how the government's evidence and arguments would have stood up against rebuttal and cross-examination by a shrewd, well prepared lawyer. The difficulties of estimating prejudice after the fact are exacerbated by the possibility that evidence of injury to the defendant may be missing from the record precisely because of the incompetence of defense counsel. * * *

Second and more fundamentally, the assumption on which the Court's holding rests is that the only purpose of the constitutional guarantee of effective assistance of counsel is to reduce the chance that innocent persons will be convicted. In my view, the guarantee also functions to ensure that convictions are obtained only through fundamentally fair procedures. * * *

* * *

[The separate opinion of Justice Brennan, concurring in part and dissenting in part, is omitted.]

Scope of the Right to Effective Assistance of Counsel

The Court held that Washington had the right to an appointed counsel who would perform effectively during the sentencing proceedings in a capital case. Questions have arisen as to the extent of a defendant's right to effective assistance. Does it apply to retained counsel? Does it apply to later stages such as appeal and collateral attack?

Retained Counsel

In Cuyler v. Sullivan, 446 U.S. 335 (1980), the Court held that persons who retain counsel are entitled to the same standards of effectiveness as persons for whom the State appoints counsel. The Court reasoned that "[s]ince the State's conduct of a criminal trial itself implicates the State in the defendant's conviction, we see no basis for drawing a distinction between retained and appointed counsel that would deny equal justice to defendants who must choose their own lawyers."

First Appeal of Right: Evitts v. Lucey and Roe v. Flores–Ortega

Justice Brennan wrote for the majority in Evitts v. Lucey, 469 U.S. 387 (1985), which holds that criminal defendants have the right to effective assistance of counsel on their first appeal of right. Lucey had been convicted of trafficking in drugs. He appealed, but his counsel failed to file a "statement of appeal," as required by state law, along with the appellate brief. For this reason, the state appellate courts refused to review the conviction. Justice Brennan reasoned that cases holding that a defendant has a right to counsel on a first appeal as of right, and that the right to counsel includes such things as a right to a necessary transcript for an indigent, dispositively established that a defendant also has a right to *effective* counsel on a first appeal as of right. He noted that an ineffective attorney may be sanctioned by the state or a state may establish a postconviction substitute for an appeal that a defendant lost as a result of ineffective assistance of counsel. But, he concluded that "[a] State may not extinguish this right [of appeal] because another right of the appellant—the right to effective assistance of counsel—has been violated." The Court recognized that it had held that there is no constitutional right to appeal from a criminal conviction; however, the Court reasoned that "when a State opts to act in a field where its action has significant discretionary elements, it must nonetheless act in accord with the dictates of the Constitution—and, in particular, in accord with the Due Process Clause." Thus, because the state had instituted an appeal of right, it was required to comport with the constitutional standards for effective assistance of counsel. The Court affirmed lower court rulings that a conditional writ of habeas corpus should issue, requiring the state to release the defendant unless it either reinstated his appeal or granted him a new trial. Justice Rehnquist, joined by Chief Justice Burger, dissented. The Chief Justice added two short dissenting paragraphs of his own.

In Roe v. Flores–Ortega, 528 U.S. 470 (2000), the Court considered whether it was automatically ineffective assistance for counsel to fail to file a notice of appeal without the defendant's consent. The Court set forth the following standard:

> [C]ounsel has a constitutionally-imposed duty to consult with the defendant about an appeal when there is reason to think either (1) that a rational defendant would want to appeal (for example, because there are non-frivolous grounds for appeal), or (2) that this particular defendant reasonably demonstrated to counsel that he was interested in appealing.

If counsel fails to comply with this standard, then the Court determined that prejudice would be found if the defendant can show that he would have filed an appeal if not for counsel's failure to file a notice. This standard does not require the defendant to show that his appeal would have been successful.

Appeals Without Merit: Anders v. California

The Court in Anders v. California, 386 U.S. 738 (1967), determined how appointed counsel should proceed if she believes that an appeal lacks merit. The

Court held that if, after a "conscientious examination" of the case, counsel finds an appeal to be "wholly frivolous," counsel should advise the court and request permission to withdraw. However, that request must be accompanied by a brief (now called an "*Anders* brief") "referring to anything in the record that might arguably support the appeal." If the court thereafter finds that there are non-frivolous arguments to be made, counsel must be appointed to bring the appeal. In McCoy v. Court of Appeals of Wisconsin, 486 U.S. 429 (1988), the Court upheld a state rule that required an *Anders* brief to include a discussion of why the appeal lacks merit. The Court noted that the point of an *Anders* brief is to inform the court that the defendant's right to counsel has been satisfied, and a requirement of stated reasons would further that goal. The Court rejected the argument that it would be unethical for counsel to explain why she thought the appeal was frivolous. It stated that "if an attorney can advise the court of his or her conclusion that an appeal is frivolous without impairment of the client's fundamental rights, it must follow that no constitutional deprivation occurs when the attorney explains the basis for that conclusion."[53]

Other Methods to Determine Whether an Appeal Is Frivolous: Smith v. Robbins

The Court in *Anders* required counsel who thought his client's appeal frivolous to file a brief with the court, directing the court to anything in the record "that might arguably support the appeal." After *Anders*, California instituted a different procedure for dealing with appeals that a lawyer believes to be without merit. In California, a lawyer who believes the client's appeal to be frivolous must file a brief with the court that summarizes the procedural and factual history of the case, with citations to the record. He also attests that he has reviewed the record, explained his evaluation of the case to his client, provided the client with a copy of the brief, and informed the client of his right to file a pro se supplemental brief. He further requests that the court independently examine the record for arguable issues. Unlike under the *Anders* procedure, counsel neither explicitly states that his review has led him to conclude that an appeal would be frivolous nor requests leave to withdraw. Instead, he is silent on the merits of the case and expresses his availability to brief any issues on which the court might desire briefing. The appellate court, upon receiving the brief, must conduct a review of the entire record. If the appellate court after its review of the record also finds the appeal to be frivolous, it may affirm. If, however, it finds an arguable (i.e., nonfrivolous) issue, it orders briefing on that issue.

In Smith v. Robbins, 528 U.S. 259 (2000), the Court in a 5–4 decision by Justice Thomas held that the California procedure provided sufficient protection of the defendant's constitutional right to effective assistance of counsel on the first appeal of right. While the procedure differed from that set forth in *Anders* (most importantly in the fact that a lawyer in California is not required to direct the court to matters that might arguably support the appeal), Justice Thomas stated that the *Anders* procedure is only one method of satisfying the Constitu-

---

53. In Penson v. Ohio, 488 U.S. 75 (1988), the Court held that no showing of prejudice is required by a defendant whose counsel fails to file an *Anders* brief. The Court concluded that judicial scrutiny of the record is not an ade-quate substitute for a complete lack of counsel. It noted that "the denial of counsel in this case left petitioner completely without representation during the appellate court's actual decisional process."

tion's requirement for indigent criminal appeals; the States are free to adopt different procedures, so long as those procedures adequately safeguard a defendant's right to effective counsel on the first appeal. In Justice Thomas' view, the California procedure adequately assured that non-frivolous issues would be discovered and considered by counsel and the reviewing court.

Justice Souter, joined by Justice Stevens, Ginsburg, and Breyer, dissented. The dissenters complained that arguably non-frivolous issues on appeal would be unlikely to be discovered by the court, if counsel is not required to direct the court to those issues.

Subsequent Appeals and Collateral Attack

It is important to note that the right to effective assistance of counsel on appeal, of which *Anders* is a part, extends only to the first appeal of right. It is not applicable to any subsequent attacks on the judgment. This is because, as seen in Chapter Five, there is no constitutional right to counsel at these later stages. The Court has held that where there is no constitutional right to counsel, there can be no right to effective assistance of counsel. See Pennsylvania v. Finley, 481 U.S. 551 (1987)(no right to *Anders* brief in postconviction proceedings, therefore no claim of ineffective assistance of counsel is cognizable); Wainwright v. Torna, 455 U.S. 586 (1982)(no right to counsel at certiorari stage, therefore no claim of ineffective assistance can be asserted, even though defendant had retained counsel); Murray v. Giarratano, 492 U.S. 1 (1989)(no right to effective assistance of counsel in collateral attack of conviction of capital offense).

In Coleman v. Thompson, 501 U.S. 722 (1991), Coleman filed a habeas petition in state superior court, claiming that his counsel had been ineffective at his state trial for murder. State law required that claims of ineffectiveness of trial counsel be brought on collateral attack rather than on appeal. The state superior court denied Coleman's habeas petition. An appeal from such a denial was provided by state law. However, Coleman's appeal from the denial of the habeas petition was dismissed because no notice of appeal had been timely filed. Coleman claimed that his counsel's failure to file a timely appeal from the denial of state habeas petition constituted *another* act of ineffective assistance of counsel. Justice O'Connor, writing for the Court, held that Coleman had no right to counsel on appeal from a denial of a state habeas petition, citing Pennsylvania v. Finley. The Court concluded that because Coleman had no right to counsel, he had no right to claim constitutionally ineffective assistance of counsel.

Coleman argued that the appeal from the state habeas proceeding was tantamount to a first appeal of right, and thus was controlled by Evitts v. Lucey, because of the state law mandate that claims of ineffective assistance of trial counsel could only be asserted on habeas. Justice O'Connor responded that, presuming a state collateral proceeding could be treated as a first appeal of right in those cases where collateral review is the first place that a challenge can be presented, Coleman had that "appeal" of right when he petitioned the state superior court and that court denied habeas relief. His appeal from the superior court's denial of habeas was therefore not a first appeal of right under *Evitts*.

Justice Blackmun, joined by Justices Marshall and Stevens, dissented. The dissenters argued that "fundamental fairness dictates that the State, having removed certain claims from the process of direct review, bear the burden of ineffective assistance of counsel in the proceeding to which the claim has been removed."

Strickland Procedures

Ordinarily, ineffectiveness claims are not considered on direct appeal, because the trial record and the appellate briefs rarely provide sufficient information with which to evaluate counsel's performance and its impact on the trial. For example, it is hard to determine whether counsel made a strategic decision to forego cross-examination of a witness simply by looking at the record; ordinarily it would be necessary to take testimony from counsel as to what he was thinking at the time. Thus, *Strickland* claims are almost always deferred to a collateral attack in which an evidentiary hearing is conducted—at which the defense counsel is a prime witness. See United States v. Bounds, 943 F.2d 541 (5th Cir.1991)(declining to address ineffectiveness claim on appeal, where the only information in the record is the defendant's own assertions in his brief).

2. Assessing Counsel's Effectiveness

In *Strickland*, the Court found that counsel was not constitutionally ineffective, because he undertook sufficient investigation, made reasonable strategic choices, and generally made the best out of a bad situation. *Strickland* was a fairly easy case, however, especially in light of the stringent standards imposed for proving counsel's ineffectiveness. Since *Strickland*, hundreds of dissatisfied defendants have charged that their counsel acted ineffectively. How does a court go about applying the intentionally harsh *Strickland* standards to a lawyer's performance in a particular case?

Concerns About Prosecutorial Rebuttal: Darden v. Wainright

In Darden v. Wainwright, 477 U.S. 168 (1986), the Court held that a defendant convicted of murder and sentenced to death failed to demonstrate that his trial lawyers' performance fell below an objective standard of reasonableness. At the sentencing hearing, defense counsel failed to introduce any evidence in mitigation and relied solely on a simple plea for mercy from Darden himself. The Court, emphasizing the deference to defense counsel required by *Strickland*, noted several reasons why counsel may have made this strategic decision. If Darden's non-violence were introduced in mitigation, it would have opened the door to Darden's prior convictions. Any evidence of psychological impairment could have been rebutted by a state psychiatric report in which the expert concluded that Darden was a sociopath. Evidence that Darden was a family man could have been rebutted by his extramarital affairs. The Court concluded that Darden had failed to "overcome the presumption that, under the circumstances, the challenged action might be considered sound trial strategy." See also Stewart v. Dugger, 847 F.2d 1486 (11th Cir.1988)(counsel's decision to reargue innocence at capital sentencing hearing, rather than to present mitigating evidence, held reasonable strategy under *Strickland*: "Trial counsel cannot be faulted for attempting to make the best of a bad situation."). Compare Caro v. Calderon, 165 F.3d 1223 (9th Cir.1999) (failure to notify evaluating psychiatrist that defendant suffered organic brain damage from exposure to toxic chemicals was ineffective; information was critical to a psychiatric analysis, and disclosure did not present a risk of prosecutorial rebuttal).

Ignorance of the Law: Kimmelman v. Morrison

The Court finally found that a lawyer had acted ineffectively in Kimmelman v. Morrison, 477 U.S. 365 (1986). Justice Brennan's opinion for the Court noted that the defendant's trial counsel "failed to file a timely suppression motion, not due to strategic considerations, but because, until the day of trial, he was unaware of the search and of the State's intention to introduce the * * * evidence," "because he had conducted no pretrial discovery." Counsel mistakenly believed that the State was required to turn over all inculpatory evidence to the defense. Although the Court indicated that generally a reviewing court should assess counsel's overall performance in order to determine whether identified acts or omissions overcome the presumption that reasonable professional assistance was provided, it found that the total failure to conduct pretrial discovery was sufficient to justify the conclusion that the lawyer had not acted in accordance with standards of reasonable competence. Justice Brennan noted that "the justifications Morrison's attorney offered for his omission betray a startling ignorance of the law—or a weak attempt to shift blame for inadequate preparation," and that "such a complete lack of pre-trial preparation puts at risk both the defendant's right to meet the case of the prosecution and the reliability of the adversarial testing process." The Court remanded for an examination of possible prejudice. It noted that if the error alleged is counsel's failure to move to suppress evidence, the defendant must show both a reasonable probability of a successful suppression motion and a reasonable probability that without the suppressed evidence, the fact finder would have had a reasonable doubt as to guilt. Justice Powell, joined by Chief Justice Burger and Justice Rehnquist, concurred in the judgment. He noted that a strong argument, neither made by the parties nor discussed by the lower courts, could be made that the admission of illegally seized but reliable evidence could not constitute prejudice—this is because the admission of illegally obtained evidence does not impeach the integrity of a guilty verdict.

While courts are deferent to defense counsel's claims of strategy, they are less forgiving if, as in *Kimmelman*, defense counsel betrays an ignorance of controlling legal standards. Thus, in Cave v. Singletary, 971 F.2d 1513 (11th Cir.1992), the defendant was charged with felony-murder, arising out of a robbery at a convenience store. In her closing argument, defense counsel told the jury that the defendant was guilty of armed robbery of the convenience store, and that the jury would be justified in convicting him of that offense, but that they should not convict him of felony-murder since he never shot anybody. The court held that, "given the instructions by the state judge on the law of felony-murder, [counsel's] statements amounted to a concession by defense counsel to the jury that the State had proven its case." The court rejected defense counsel's contention, made at the habeas hearing, that she deliberately misstated the law of felony-murder throughout the trial in an attempt to confuse the jury. The court was convinced that defense counsel "completely misunderstood the law of felony murder, which is a concept that often confuses laypeople, but should be within the grasp of lawyers, especially those defending a client charged with a capital offense." But the court found that counsel's ineffectiveness was not prejudicial under *Strickland*, since the defendant had confessed to the robbery and thus "sealed his conviction for felony murder."

Strategy or Not?

Strickland indicated that the performance prong will be satisfied if, using appropriate deference, counsel's actions fall within the realm of reasonable trial strategy. Consider the following cases. Has counsel been ineffective, or has counsel used a reasonable, albeit unsuccessful, strategy?

1. Martin was charged with sexual abuse of his two stepdaughters. He denied the charges, and claimed that he had a witness who would testify that the children had been encouraged to falsify their charges. Martin's counsel, appointed shortly before trial, filed a motion for a continuance, alleging that he was unprepared to try the case. This motion was denied. Counsel was convinced that the denial of a continuance was error. So he decided to "rely on his motion"; by design, he did not put on any proof in defense, and did not cross-examine or participate in the trial, other than to make an opening statement to the jury. This opening statement indicated that the defense was relying on its motion for continuance, and that the jury should not think "that my lack of participation is, uh, that I'm a dummy over here, and I don't know what's going on." The court of appeals stated that "even deliberate trial tactics may constitute ineffective assistance of counsel if they fall outside the wide range of professionally competent assistance." The court asserted that by calling the defendant and his witness to testify, the attorney could have presented a strong defense "without compromising" the motion for continuance. The court concluded that "the decision of Martin's attorney not to participate cannot be considered sound trial strategy," and that the failure of counsel to put on a defense was prejudicial as well. Is the court second-guessing defense counsel? Is that permissible after *Strickland*? See also United States v. Wolf, 787 F.2d 1094 (7th Cir.1986), where the court criticized defense counsel's "tactic of no objections" and held it ineffective:

> It is true that lawyers will frequently not object to objectionable questions, believing either that the witness will give an answer helpful to the defense (or at least not harmful to it) or that too-frequent objecting will irritate the jury or make it think the defendant is trying to hide the truth. But to have a *policy* of never objecting to improper questions is forensic suicide. It shifts the main responsibility for the defense from defense counsel to the judge. It would make no sense in a case like this where the prosecutor was intent on bringing in extraneous and at times unfounded charges in order to blacken the defendant's character.

Compare Warner v. Ford, 752 F.2d 622 (11th Cir.1985)(strategy of silence not ineffective in multi-defendant trial, where other defendants were defending aggressively and evidence was overwhelming; under these circumstances, it was reasonable to keep a "low profile"). Moore v. Deputy Commissioners, 946 F.2d 236 (3d Cir.1991)(proper strategy to fail to object to the introduction of inadmissible inculpatory evidence; defense counsel decided that "the less said about it the better").

2. Chambers was tried for the murder of Oestricker. Chambers was a small man and his victim was large. The prosecution called Ieppert, who testified that

Chambers and Oestricker had a fight in a bar, that they decided to take the argument outside, and that Ieppert thereupon moved from his chair to the door of the bar to watch the fight, taking a few seconds to do so. At that point he saw Chambers point a gun at Oestricker and shoot him in the chest. After that, Chambers pistol-whipped his victim and said "take that, tough guy" and ran away. Another witness, Jones, had been outside the bar trying to start his car. He testified that Chambers came out of the bar first and waited for Oestricker. Then Oestricker hit Chambers in the face and knocked him to the ground. Chambers then got up, pulled a gun, shot Oestricker, pistol-whipped him, said "take that, tough guy," yelled into the bar "Do any of you want any of this?" and ran to a parked car that had its engine running; the car sped quickly away. Chambers' attorney requested that a self-defense instruction be submitted to the jury. The trial court refused, and Chambers was found guilty of capital murder and sentenced to death. On appeal, the state supreme court reversed the conviction, holding that there was sufficient evidence to justify a self-defense instruction; the court pointed specifically to Jones' testimony that the victim hit Chambers first, and that the victim was a foot taller and 100 pounds heavier than the defendant. On re-trial, Chambers had newly appointed counsel. Defense counsel did not call Jones (the witness outside the bar) to testify, and neither did the state. Other than that, the second trial proceeded much as the first. Chambers' defense counsel proceeded on a self-defense theory, and his questions to government witnesses on cross-examination were focused solely on the issue of self-defense. He pointed out that the victim was a foot taller and 100 pounds heavier than Chambers. As in the first trial, the trial court refused to give a self-defense instruction, and Chambers was found guilty of capital murder. Chambers' attorney later stated at the ineffectiveness hearing that, after reading the transcript of the first trial, he decided not to call Jones because much of Jones' testimony was "damaging" and because Jones "lacked credibility," although counsel admitted that he had never spoken to Jones. The court in Chambers v. Armontrout, 907 F.2d 825 (8th Cir.1990) (en banc), held that the failure to call Jones at the second trial deprived Chambers of effective assistance of counsel. The dissenters argued that "*Strickland* is not violated when a counsel, in the exercise of professional judgment, decides not to produce mitigating evidence that could reasonably be considered more damaging than helpful." With whom do you agree?

The majority's decision in *Chambers* may give you the impression that courts are receptive to claims that counsel acted ineffectively. This is not at all the case. Most courts appear to bend over backwards to justify defense counsel's actions as proper strategy. See, e.g., Stringer v. Jackson, 862 F.2d 1108 (5th Cir.1988)(failure to present mitigating evidence is not ineffective); People v. Russell, 71 N.Y.2d 1016, 530 N.Y.S.2d 101, 525 N.E.2d 747 (1988)(failure to move to suppress evidence is a strategic decision); Brown v. Dixon, 891 F.2d 490 (4th Cir.1989) (not ineffective to argue inconsistent defenses); Bean v. Calderon, 163 F.3d 1073 (9th Cir.1998) (not ineffective for failing to pursue a diminished capacity defense, since counsel reasonably pursued an alibi defense, and arguing diminished capacity "would have contradicted the primary defense theory"); Rogers–Bey v. Lane, 896 F.2d 279 (7th Cir.1990)(proper strategy to inculpate the defendant in order to impeach a prosecution witness); United States v. Guerrero, 938 F.2d 725 (7th Cir.1991)(in light of overwhelming evidence of the defendant's involvement with narcotics, it was not ineffective to argue that the defendant was involved in a drug conspiracy different from that which was charged).

3. Willis was charged with murdering his son. At trial, the victim's wife testified that Willis came to his son's home to get a deer rifle. She then saw Willis shoot his son with a handgun. Willis denied this claim. No handgun was ever found or linked with the killing. No autopsy was ever performed. No bullet or bullet fragments were ever found. The medical examiner was unable to identify the caliber or type of gun used. Upon his arrest, Willis had stated with respect to his son "it was either him or me," and that statement was introduced at trial. The prosecution also introduced a trace metal test which showed that Willis had fired a gun on the day of his son's death. Willis' first trial ended in a deadlocked jury. He was convicted at the second trial. He claimed ineffective assistance because counsel failed to have an autopsy performed on the victim, so as to determine whether the victim was shot with a handgun or not. The court held that the failure to obtain an autopsy was a "reasonable tactical decision." It explained as follows:

> Appellant's defense was built entirely on the theory that the state had failed to prove appellant guilty beyond a reasonable doubt. Appellant's counsel decided that it was better for there to be uncertainty concerning the weapon used than to chance that an autopsy would reveal that a handgun was the murder weapon, thereby confirming the daughter-in-law's testimony. In their arguments to the jury, his defense attorneys played on this uncertainty regarding the murder weapon to establish reasonable doubt in the minds of the jurors. Appellant's counsel also thought that an attempt to exhume the body and perform an autopsy would have been opposed by appellant's ex-wife and daughters, who were also the victim's mother and sisters. Counsel feared that pursuit of an exhumation would have prompted them to reveal to the prosecution very damaging evidence regarding the appellant.

Willis v. Newsome, 771 F.2d 1445 (11th Cir.1985). Are you convinced? Consider that defense counsel's explanation for making a certain decision is given at a hearing long after the trial, and that counsel has been charged at that point with ineffectiveness. Is there a risk that counsel will "color" his or her testimony under these circumstances?

4. In the penalty phase of the defendant's capital murder trial, the defendant wanted to bring in mitigating evidence through testimony of his girlfriend, Laurie Elam. Ms. Elam arrived at the sentencing hearing adorned with a necklace that displayed the word "B–I–T–C–H" in clearly visible letters. The lawyer was unable to persuade Elam to remove the necklace. He therefore refused to call her as a witness. Was this a reasonable strategic decision? See Jones v. Page, 76 F.3d 831 (7th Cir.1996) (appellate court will not second-guess counsel's assessment of how a witness will play to the jury).

5. John Wayne Gacy was a notorious mass murderer. At the penalty phase of his capital murder trial, defense counsel argued to the jury that Gacy should not be executed. The argument was not based on an appeal for mercy, nor on proof of mitigating circumstances. Rather, defense counsel argued "that Gacy should be sentenced to life imprisonment so that he could be studied to find out why he committed the murders." Is this "spare him for science" argument ineffective, or is it proper strategy? See Gacy v. Welborn, 994 F.2d 305 (7th

Cir.1993)("spare him for science" argument does not violate *Strickland* perform-ance prong). See also Waters v. Thomas, 46 F.3d 1506 (11th Cir.1995), upholding a death sentence where a "spare him for science" argument was made. The court stated: "It was not unreasonable for counsel to have thought at least one juror in this case might have been persuaded that, given all the harm Waters had done it was time to get some good out of him, and that the way to do that was to keep him alive for study." The dissent in *Waters* stated that defense counsel "concluded the case for his client—not with a plea for mercy for a human being, but with a dehumanizing request to allow a specimen to be studied." Who has the better of this argument?

No Strategy at All

Cases have arisen in which counsel cannot even come up with a reason for acting (or not acting) as they did at trial. In these cases, courts have not been hesitant to find ineffectiveness. See, e.g., Jones v. Thigpen, 788 F.2d 1101 (5th Cir.1986)(no explanation for failure to argue mental retardation in mitigation at a capital sentencing hearing; defendant had an I.Q. of 41); Harding v. Davis, 878 F.2d 1341 (11th Cir.1989)(failure to object to judge's entry of directed guilty verdict is ineffective and per se prejudicial); Burley v. Cabana, 818 F.2d 414 (5th Cir.1987)(failure to inform trial court of sentencing alternatives for a defendant who was a minor); Nixon v. Newsome, 888 F.2d 112 (11th Cir.1989)(failure to introduce prior inconsistent statement of star prosecution witness, made at another trial, that someone else did the shooting for which defendant was charged, held ineffective and prejudicial, given the lack of overwhelming evidence).

Closing Argument: Yarborough v. Gentry

In the following case, the Court, giving deference to defense counsel, finds that counsel's closing argument was not constitutionally ineffective. The case shows that lawyers can have different opinions about how to approach a jury in closing argument.

YARBOROUGH, WARDEN v. GENTRY

Supreme Court of the United States, 2003.
124 S.Ct. 1.

PER CURIAM.

Respondent Lionel Gentry was convicted in California state court of assault with a deadly weapon for stabbing his girlfriend, Tanaysha Handy. Gentry claimed he stabbed her accidentally during a dispute with a drug dealer.

Handy testified for the prosecution. She stated that she recalled being stabbed but could not remember the details of the incident. The prosecu-

tion then confronted Handy with her testimony from a preliminary hearing that Gentry had placed his hand around her throat before stabbing her twice.

Albert Williams, a security guard in a neighboring building, testified that he saw Gentry, Handy, and another man from his third-floor window. According to Williams, Gentry swung his hand into Handy's left side with some object, causing her to lean forward

Security guard inconsistent about lighting

and scream. Williams was inconsistent about the quality of light at the time, stating variously that it was "pretty dark" or "getting dark," that "it wasn't that dark," and that the area of the stabbing was "lighted up."

A says it was on accident

· also lied about priors - stated 1 conviction - many more

Gentry testified in his own defense that he had stabbed Handy accidentally while pushing her out of the way. When asked about prior convictions, he falsely stated that he had been convicted only once; evidence showed he had been separately convicted of burglary, grand theft, battery on a peace officer, and being a felon in possession of a firearm. He attributed his error to confusion about whether a plea bargain counted as a conviction.

In her closing argument, the prosecutor expressed sympathy for Handy's plight as a pregnant, drug-addicted mother of three and highlighted her damaging preliminary hearing testimony. She accused Gentry of telling the jury a "pack of lies." Defense counsel responded with the following closing argument:

I don't have a lot to say today. Just once I'd like to find a prosecutor that doesn't know exactly what happened. Just once I'd like to find a D. A. that wasn't there and that can tell and they can stand up here and be honest and say I don't know who is lying and who is not 'cause she wasn't there, ladies and gentlemen. [I] wasn't there. None of the 12 of you were there. None of the other people in this courtroom were there except those two people and that one guy who saw parts of it, or saw it all. Pretty dark. Dark. It was light. Those are the three versions of his testimony with regard to what he saw and what he saw. I don't know what happened. I can't tell you. And if I sit here and try to tell you what happened, I'm lying to you. I don't know. I wasn't there. I don't have to judge. I don't have to decide. You

heard the testimony come from the truth chair. You heard people testify. You heard good things that made you feel good. You heard bad things that made you feel bad.

I don't care that Tanaysha is pregnant. I don't care that she has three children. I don't know why that had to be brought out in closing. What does that have to do with this case? She was stabbed. The question is, did he intend to stab her? He said he did it by accident. If he's lying and you think he's lying then you have to convict him. If you don't think he's lying, bad person, lousy drug addict, stinking thief, jail bird, all that to the contrary, he's not guilty. It's as simple as that. I don't care if he's been in prison. And for the sake of this thing you ought not care because that doesn't have anything to do with what happened on April 30th, 1994.

· lied priors

He doesn't know whether or not he's been convicted. Didn't understand the term conviction. That is not inconsistent with this whole thing of being spoken and doing all this other crime stuff as opposed to going to school. I don't know. I can't judge the man. The reason that they bring 12 jurors from all different walks of life, let them sit here and listen to people testify, and the reason that the court will give you instructions with regard to not having your life experience, leaving it at the door, is because you can't just assume that because a guy has done a bunch of bad things that he's now done this thing.

I don't know if thievery and stabbing your girlfriend are all in the same pot. I don't know if just because of the fact that you stole some things in the past that means you must have stabbed your girlfriend. That sounds like a jump to me, but that's just [me]. I'm not one of the 12 over there. All I ask you to do is to look at the evidence and listen to everything you've heard and then make a decision. Good decision or bad decision, it's still a decision. I would like all 12 of you to agree; but if you don't, I can't do anything about that either.

You heard everything just like all of us have heard it. I don't know who's lying. I don't know if anybody is lying. And for someone to stand here and tell you that they think someone is lying and that they know that lying goes on, ladies and gentlemen, if that person was on the witness stand I'd be objecting that they don't have foundation because they weren't there. And that's true. The defense attorney and the prosecutor, no different than 12 of you.

So I'd ask you to listen to what you've heard when you go back, ask you to take some time to think about it, and be sure that's what you want to do, then come out and do it. Thank you.

After deliberating for about six hours, the jury convicted.

On direct appeal, Gentry argued that his trial counsel's closing argument deprived him of his right to effective assistance of counsel. The California Court of Appeal rejected that contention, and the California Supreme Court denied review. Gentry's petition for federal habeas relief was denied by the District Court, but the Court of Appeals for the Ninth Circuit reversed. We grant the State's petition for a writ of certiorari * * * and reverse.

II

* * * If a state court has already rejected an ineffective-assistance claim, a federal court may grant habeas relief if the decision was "contrary to, or involved an unreasonable application of, clearly established Federal law, as determined by the Supreme Court of the United States." 28 U.S.C. § 2254(d)(1). Where, as here, the state court's application of governing federal law is challenged, it must be shown to be not only erroneous, but objectively unreasonable. [See Chapter 13 for a discussion of the standard of review on habeas corpus.].

The right to effective assistance extends to closing arguments. Nonetheless, counsel has wide latitude in deciding how best to represent a client, and deference to counsel's tactical decisions in his closing presentation is particularly important because of the broad range of legitimate defense strategy at that stage. Closing arguments should sharpen and clarify the issues for resolution by the trier of fact, but which issues to sharpen and how best to clarify them are questions with many reasonable answers. Indeed, it might sometimes make sense to forgo closing argument altogether. Judicial review of a defense attorney's summation is therefore highly deferential—and doubly deferential when it is conducted through the lens of federal habeas.

In light of these principles, the Ninth Circuit erred in finding the California Court of Appeal's decision objectively unreasonable. The California court's opinion cited state case law setting forth the correct federal standard for evaluating ineffective-assistance claims and concluded that counsel's performance was not ineffective. That conclusion was supported by the record. The summation for the defense made several key points: that Williams's testimony about the quality of light was inconsistent; that Handy's personal circumstances were irrelevant to Gentry's guilt; that the case turned on whether the stabbing was accidental, and the jury had to acquit if it believed Gentry's version of events; that Gentry's criminal history was irrelevant to his guilt, particularly given the seriousness of the charge compared to his prior theft offenses; and that Gentry's misstatement of the number of times he had been convicted could be explained by his lack of education. Woven through these issues was a unifying theme—that the jury, like the prosecutor and defense counsel himself, were not at the scene of the crime and so could only speculate about what had happened and who was lying.

The Ninth Circuit rejected the state court's conclusion in large part because counsel did not highlight various other potentially exculpatory pieces of evidence: that Handy had used drugs on the day of the stabbing and during the early morning hours of the day of her preliminary hearing; that Williams's inability to see the stabbing clearly was relevant to the issue of intent; that Gentry's testimony was consistent with Williams's in some respects; that the government did not call as a witness Williams's co-worker, who also saw the stabbing; that the stab wound was only one inch deep, suggesting it may have been accidental; that Handy testified she had been stabbed twice, but only had one wound; and that Gentry, after being confronted by Williams, did not try to retrieve his weapon but instead moved toward Handy while repeating, "she's my girlfriend."

These other potential arguments do not establish that the state court's decision was unreasonable. Some of the omitted items, such as Gentry's reaction to Williams, are thoroughly ambiguous. Some of the others might well have backfired. For example, although Handy claimed at trial she had used drugs before the preliminary hearing, she testified at the hearing that she was not under the influence

and could remember exactly what had happened the day of the stabbing. And, although Handy's wound was only one inch deep, it still lacerated her stomach and diaphragm, spilling the stomach's contents into her chest cavity and requiring almost two hours of surgery. These are facts that the prosecutor could have exploited to great advantage in her rebuttal.

Even if some of the arguments would unquestionably have supported the defense, it does not follow that counsel was incompetent for failing to include them. Focusing on a small number of key points may be more persuasive than a shotgun approach. As one expert advises: "The number of issues introduced should definitely be restricted. Research suggests that there is an upper limit to the number of issues or arguments an attorney can present and still have persuasive effect." R. Matlon, Opening Statements/Closing Arguments 60 (1993). Another authority says: "The advocate is not required to summarize or comment upon all the facts, opinions, inferences, and law involved in a case. A decision not to address an issue, an opponent's theory, or a particular fact should be based on an analysis of the importance of that subject and the ability of the advocate and the opponent to explain persuasively the position to the fact finder." R. Haydock & J. Sonsteng, Advocacy: Opening and Closing § 3.10, p. 70 (1994). In short, judicious selection of arguments for summation is a core exercise of defense counsel's discretion.

When counsel focuses on some issues to the exclusion of others, there is a strong presumption that he did so for tactical reasons rather than through sheer neglect. That presumption has particular force where a petitioner bases his ineffective-assistance claim solely on the trial record, creating a situation in which a court may have no way of knowing whether a seemingly unusual or misguided action by counsel had a sound strategic motive. Moreover, even if an omission is inadvertent, relief is not automatic. The Sixth Amendment guarantees reasonable competence, not perfect advocacy judged with the benefit of hindsight. To recall the words of Justice (and former Solicitor General) Jackson: "I made three arguments of every case. First came the one that I planned—as I thought, logical, coherent, complete. Second was the one actually presented—interrupted, incoherent, disjointed, disappointing. The third was the utterly devastating argument that I thought of after going to bed that night." Advocacy Before the Supreme Court, 37 A. B. A. J. 801, 803 (1951). Based on the record in this case, a state court could reasonably conclude that Gentry had failed to rebut the presumption of adequate assistance. Counsel plainly put to the jury the centerpiece of his case: that the only testimony regarding what had happened that the jury heard "come from the truth chair" was conflicting; that none of his client's testimony was demonstrably a lie; and that the testimony contradicting his client came in "three versions." The issues counsel omitted were not so clearly more persuasive than those he discussed that their omission can only be attributed to a professional error of constitutional magnitude.

The Ninth Circuit found other flaws in counsel's presentation. It criticized him for mentioning "a host of details that hurt his client's position, none of which mattered as a matter of law." Of course the reason counsel mentioned those details was precisely to remind the jury that they *were* legally irrelevant. That was not an unreasonable tactic. See F. Bailey & H. Rothblatt, Successful Techniques for Criminal

Trials § 19:23, p. 461 (2d ed. 1985) ("Face up to [the defendant's] defects . . . [and] call upon the jury to disregard everything not connected to the crime with which he is charged"). The Ninth Circuit singled out for censure counsel's argument that the jury must acquit if Gentry was telling the truth, even though he was a "bad person, lousy drug addict, stinking thief, jail bird." It apparently viewed the remark as a gratuitous swipe at Gentry's character. While confessing a client's shortcomings might remind the jury of facts they otherwise would have forgotten, it might also convince them to put aside facts they would have remembered in any event. This is precisely the sort of calculated risk that lies at the heart of an advocate's discretion. By candidly acknowledging his client's shortcomings, counsel might have built credibility with the jury and persuaded it to focus on the relevant issues in the case. See J. Stein, Closing Argument § 204, p. 10 (1992–1996) ("If you make certain concessions showing that you are earnestly in search of the truth, then your comments on matters that are in dispute will be received without the usual apprehension surrounding the remarks of an advocate"). As Judge Kleinfeld pointed out in dissenting from denial of rehearing en banc, the court's criticism applies just as well to Clarence Darrow's closing argument in the Leopold and Loeb case: "I do not know how much salvage there is in these two boys. . . . Your Honor would be merciful if you tied a rope around their necks and let them die; merciful to them, but not merciful to civilization, and not merciful to those who would be left behind."

The Ninth Circuit rebuked counsel for making only a passive request that the jury reach some verdict, rather than an express demand for acquittal. But given a patronizing and overconfident summation by a prosecutor, a low-key strategy that stresses the jury's autonomy is not unreasonable. One treatise recommends just such a technique: "Avoid challenging the jury to find for your client, or phrasing your argument in terms suggesting what their finding must be. . . . Scientific research indicates that jurors will react against a lawyer who they think is blatantly trying to limit their freedom of thought." Stein, *supra,* § 206, at 15.

The Ninth Circuit faulted counsel for not arguing explicitly that the government had failed to prove guilt beyond a reasonable doubt. Counsel's entire presentation, however, made just that point. He repeatedly stressed that no one—not the prosecutor, the jury, nor even himself—could be sure who was telling the truth. This is the very essence of a reasonable-doubt argument. To be sure, he did not insist that the existence of a reasonable doubt would *require* the jury to acquit—but he could count on the judge's charge to remind them of that requirement, and by doing so he would preserve his strategy of appearing as the friend of jury autonomy.

Finally, the Ninth Circuit criticized counsel's approach on the ground that, by confessing that he too could not be sure of the truth, counsel "implied that even he did not believe Gentry's testimony." But there is nothing wrong with a rhetorical device that personalizes the doubts anyone but an eyewitness must necessarily have. Winning over an audience by empathy is a technique that dates back to Aristotle. See P. Lagarias, Effective Closing Argument § § 2.05–2.06, pp. 99–101 (1989) (citing Aristotle's Rhetoric for the point that "[a] speech should indicate to the audience that the speaker shares the attitudes of the listener, so that, in turn, the listener will respond positively to the views of the speaker").

To be sure, Gentry's lawyer was no Aristotle or even Clarence Darrow. But the Ninth Circuit's conclusion—not only that his performance was deficient, but that any disagreement with that conclusion would be objectively unreasonable—gives too little deference to the state courts that have primary responsibility for supervising defense counsel in state criminal trials.

The judgment of the Ninth Circuit is reversed.

The Duty to Investigate

According to *Strickland,* pre-trial investigation is one component of effective assistance. Courts have found that a complete failure to investigate cannot be considered strategic, because a counsel who has done no investigation will lack the information necessary to make a strategic decision. See Holsomback v. White, 133 F.3d 1382 (11th Cir.1998) (in a case alleging child sex abuse, counsel was ineffective in failing to proffer medical records showing no indication that the victim had been abused; failure to bring in this evidence could not have been strategic: "Having conducted no investigation into the significance of the lack of medical evidence that Jeffrey had been sexually abused, Holsomback's counsel could not have made an informed tactical decision that the risk that the doctors might equivocate on the stand outweighed what potential benefit might come from their testimony."); United States v. Gray, 878 F.2d 702 (3d Cir. 1989)(counsel ineffective where he failed to contact 25 neutral eyewitnesses identified by the defendant, in a case in which the jury was required to make a credibility determination between the defendant and the complainant); Foster v.

Lockhart, 9 F.3d 722 (8th Cir.1993)(defense counsel in a rape case was ineffective for failing to discover, and develop at trial, the fact that the defendant was impotent).

In the following case the Court amplifies on counsel's duty to investigate, in the context of a capital sentencing proceeding.

WIGGINS v. SMITH

Supreme Court of the United States, 2003.
123 S.Ct. 2527.

JUSTICE O'CONNOR delivered the opinion of the Court.

Petitioner, Kevin Wiggins, argues that his attorneys' failure to investigate his background and present mitigating evidence of his unfortunate life history at his capital sentencing proceedings violated his Sixth Amendment right to counsel. In this case, we consider whether the United States Court of Appeals for the Fourth Circuit erred in upholding the Maryland Court of Appeals' rejection of this claim.

I

A

On September 17, 1988, police discovered 77-year-old Florence Lacs drowned in the bathtub of her ransacked apartment in Woodlawn, Maryland. The State indicted petitioner for the crime on October 20, 1988, and later filed a notice of intention to seek the death penalty. Two Baltimore County public defenders, Carl Schlaich and Michelle Nethercott, assumed responsibility for Wiggins' case. In July 1989, petitioner elected to be tried before a judge in Baltimore County Circuit Court. On August 4, after a 4-day trial, the court found petitioner guilty of first-degree murder, robbery, and two counts of theft.

After his conviction, Wiggins elected to be sentenced by a jury, and the trial court scheduled the proceedings to begin on October 11, 1989. On September 11, counsel filed a motion for bifurcation of sentencing in hopes of presenting Wiggins' case in two phases. Counsel intended first to prove that Wiggins did not act as a "principal in the first degree,"—i.e., that he did not kill the victim by his own hand. See Md. Ann. Code, Art. 27, § 413 (1996) (requiring proof of direct responsibility for death eligibility). Counsel then intended, if necessary, to present a mitigation case. In the memorandum in support of their motion, counsel argued that bifurcation would enable them to present each case in its best light; separating the two cases would prevent the introduction of mitigating evidence from diluting their claim that Wiggins was not directly responsible for the murder.

On October 12, the court denied the bifurcation motion, and sentencing proceedings commenced immediately thereafter. In her opening statement, Nethercott told the jurors they would hear evidence suggesting that someone other than Wiggins actually killed Lacs. Counsel then explained that the judge would instruct them to weigh Wiggins' clean record as a factor against a death sentence. She concluded: "You're going to hear that Kevin Wiggins has had a difficult life. It has not been easy for him. But he's worked. He's tried to be a productive citizen, and he's reached the age of 27 with no convictions for prior crimes of violence and no convictions, period.... I think that's an important thing for you to consider." During the proceedings themselves, however, counsel introduced no evidence of Wiggins' life history.

Before closing arguments, Schlaich made a proffer to the court, outside the presence of the jury, to preserve bifurcation as an issue for appeal. He detailed the mitigation case that counsel would have presented had the court granted their bifurcation motion. He explained that they would have introduced psychological reports and expert testimony demonstrating Wiggins' limited intellectual capacities and childlike emotional state on the one hand, and the absence of aggressive patterns in his behavior, his capacity for empathy, and his desire to function in the world on the other. At no point did Schlaich proffer any evidence of petitioner's life history or family background. On October 18, the court instructed the jury on the sentencing task before it, and later that afternoon, the jury returned with a sentence of death. A divided Maryland Court of Appeals affirmed.

B

In 1993, Wiggins sought postconviction relief in Baltimore County Circuit Court. With new counsel, he challenged the adequacy of his representation at sentencing, arguing that his attorneys had rendered constitutionally defective assistance by failing to investigate and present mitigating evidence of his dysfunctional background. To support his claim, petitioner presented testimony by Hans Selvog, a licensed social worker certified as an expert by the court. Selvog testified concerning an elaborate social history report he had prepared containing evidence of the severe physical and sexual abuse petitioner suffered at the hands of his mother and while in the care of a series of foster parents. Relying on state social services, medical, and school records, as well as interviews with petitioner

and numerous family members, Selvog chronicled petitioner's bleak life history.

According to Selvog's report, petitioner's mother, a chronic alcoholic, frequently left Wiggins and his siblings home alone for days, forcing them to beg for food and to eat paint chips and garbage. Mrs. Wiggins' abusive behavior included beating the children for breaking into the kitchen, which she often kept locked. She had sex with men while her children slept in the same bed and, on one occasion, forced petitioner's hand against a hot stove burner—an incident that led to petitioner's hospitalization. At the age of six, the State placed Wiggins in foster care. Petitioner's first and second foster mothers abused him physically, and, as petitioner explained to Selvog, the father in his second foster home repeatedly molested and raped him. At age 16, petitioner ran away from his foster home and began living on the streets. He returned intermittently to additional foster homes, including one in which the foster mother's sons allegedly gang-raped him on more than one occasion. After leaving the foster care system, Wiggins entered a Job Corps program and was allegedly sexually abused by his supervisor.

During the postconviction proceedings, Schlaich testified that he did not remember retaining a forensic social worker to prepare a social history, even though the State made funds available for that purpose. He explained that he and Nethercott, well in advance of trial, decided to focus their efforts on "retry[ing] the factual case" and disputing Wiggins' direct responsibility for the murder. In April 1994, at the close of the proceedings, the judge observed from the bench that he could not remember a capital case in which counsel had not compiled a social history of the defendant, explaining, "[n]ot to do a social history, at least to see what you have got, to me is absolute error. I just—I would be flabbergasted if the Court of Appeals said anything else." In October 1997, however, the trial court denied Wiggins' petition for postconviction relief. The court concluded that "when the decision not to investigate ... is a matter of trial tactics, there is no ineffective assistance of counsel."

The Maryland Court of Appeals affirmed the denial of relief, concluding that trial counsel had made "a deliberate, tactical decision to concentrate their effort at convincing the jury" that appellant was not directly responsible for the murder. The court observed that counsel knew of Wiggins' unfortunate childhood. * * * As a result, the court concluded, Schlaich and Nethercott "made a reasoned choice to proceed with what they thought was their best defense."

C

In September 2001, Wiggins filed a petition for writ of habeas corpus in Federal District Court. The trial court granted him relief, holding that the Maryland courts' rejection of his ineffective assistance claim "involved an unreasonable application of clearly established federal law." The court rejected the State's defense of counsel's "tactical" decision to retry guilt, concluding that for a strategic decision to be reasonable, it must be "based upon information the attorney has made after conducting a reasonable investigation." The court found that though counsel were aware of some aspects of Wiggins' background, that knowledge did not excuse them from their duty to make a "fully informed and deliberate decision" about whether to present a mitigation case. In fact, the court concluded, their knowledge triggered an obligation to look further.

Reviewing the District Court's decision de novo, the Fourth Circuit reversed, holding that counsel had made a reasonable strategic decision to focus on petitioner's direct responsibility. * * * The court acknowledged that counsel likely knew further investigation "would have resulted in more sordid details surfacing," but agreed with the Maryland Court of Appeals that counsel's knowledge of the avenues of mitigation available to them "was sufficient to make an informed strategic choice" to challenge petitioner's direct responsibility for the murder. * * *

We granted certiorari, and now reverse.

II

A

Petitioner renews his contention that his attorneys' performance at sentencing violated his Sixth Amendment right to effective assistance of counsel. The amendments to 28 U.S.C. § 2254, enacted as part of the Antiterrorism and Effective Death Penalty Act of 1996 (AEDPA), circumscribe our consideration of Wiggins' claim and require us to limit our analysis to the law as it was clearly established by our precedents at the time of the state court's decision. Section 2254 provides:

(d) An application for a writ of habeas corpus on behalf of a person in custody pursuant to the judgment of a State court shall not be granted with respect to any claim that was adjudicated on the merits in State court proceedings unless the adjudication of the claim—

(1) resulted in a decision that was contrary to, or involved an unreasonable application of, clearly established Federal law, as determined by the Supreme Court of the United States; or

(2) resulted in a decision that was based on an unreasonable determination of the facts in light of the evidence presented at the State court proceeding.

We have made clear that the "unreasonable application" prong of § 2254(d)(1) permits a federal habeas court to "grant the writ if the state court identifies the correct governing legal principle from this Court's decisions but unreasonably applies that principle to the facts" of petitioner's case. * * * In order for a federal court to find a state court's application of our precedent "unreasonable," the state court's decision must have been more than incorrect or erroneous. The application must have been "objectively unreasonable."

[The Court reiterates the *Strickland* standards.]

In light of these standards, our principal concern in deciding whether Schlaich and Nethercott exercised "reasonable professional judgmen[t]" is not whether counsel should have presented a mitigation case. Rather, we focus on whether the investigation supporting counsel's decision not to introduce mitigating evidence of Wiggins' background was itself reasonable. In assessing counsel's investigation, we must conduct an objective review of their performance, measured for "reasonableness under prevailing professional norms" which includes a context-dependent consideration of the challenged conduct as seen "from counsel's perspective at the time."

B

1

The record demonstrates that counsel's investigation drew from three sources. Counsel arranged for William Stejskal, a psychologist, to conduct a number of tests on petitioner. Stejskal concluded that petitioner had an IQ of 79, had difficulty coping with demanding situations, and exhibited features of a personality disorder. These reports revealed nothing, however, of petitioner's life history.

With respect to that history, counsel had available to them the written PSI, which included a one-page account of Wiggins' personal history noting his "misery as a youth," quoting his description of his own background as "disgusting," and observing that he spent most of his life in foster care. Counsel also tracked down records kept by the Baltimore City Department of Social Services (DSS) documenting petitioner's various placements in the State's foster care system. In describing the scope of counsel's investigation into petitioner's life history, both the Fourth Circuit and the Maryland Court of Appeals referred only to these two sources of information.

Counsel's decision not to expand their investigation beyond the PSI and the DSS records fell short of the professional standards that prevailed in Maryland in 1989. As Schlaich acknowledged, standard practice in Maryland in capital cases at the time of Wiggins' trial included the preparation of a social history report. Despite the fact that the Public Defender's office made funds available for the retention of a forensic social worker, counsel chose not to commission such a report. * * *

The scope of their investigation was also unreasonable in light of what counsel actually discovered in the DSS records. The records revealed several facts: Petitioner's mother was a chronic alcoholic; Wiggins was shuttled from foster home to foster home and displayed some emotional difficulties while there; he had frequent, lengthy absences from school; and, on at least one occasion, his mother left him and his siblings alone for days without food. As the Federal District Court emphasized, any reasonably competent attorney would have realized that pursuing these leads was necessary to making an informed choice among possible defenses, particularly given the apparent absence of any aggravating factors in petitioner's background. Indeed, counsel uncovered no evidence in their investigation to suggest that a mitigation case, in its own right, would have been counterproductive, or that further investigation would have been fruitless; this case is therefore distinguishable from our precedents in which we have found limited investigations into mitigating evidence to be reasonable. See, e.g., Burger v. Kemp, 483 U.S. 776, 794 (1987) (concluding counsel's limited investigation was reasonable because he interviewed all witnesses brought to his attention, discovering little that was helpful and much that was harmful); Darden v. Wainwright, 477 U.S. 168, 186 (1986) (concluding that counsel engaged in extensive preparation and that the decision to present a mitigation case would have resulted in the jury hearing evidence that petitioner had been convicted of violent crimes and spent much of his life in jail). Had counsel investigated further, they may well have discovered the sexual abuse later revealed during state postconviction proceedings.

The record of the actual sentencing proceedings underscores the unreasonableness of counsel's conduct by suggesting that their failure to investigate thoroughly resulted from inattention, not reasoned strategic judgment. Counsel sought, until the day before sentencing, to have the proceedings bifurcated into a retrial of guilt and a mitigation stage. On the eve of sentencing, counsel represented to the court that they were prepared to come forward with mitigating evidence, and that they intended to present such evidence in the event the court granted their motion to bifurcate. In other words, prior to sentencing, counsel never actually abandoned the possibility that they would present a mitigation defense. Until the court denied their motion, then, they had every reason to develop the most powerful mitigation case possible.

What is more, during the sentencing proceeding itself, counsel did not focus exclusively on Wiggins' direct responsibility for the murder. After introducing that issue in her opening statement, Nethercott entreated the jury to consider not just what Wiggins "is found to have done," but also "who [he] is." Though she told the jury it would "hear that Kevin Wiggins has had a difficult life," counsel never followed up on that suggestion with details of Wiggins' history. At the same time, counsel called a criminologist to testify that inmates serving life sentences tend to adjust well and refrain from further violence in prison—testimony with no bearing on whether petitioner committed the murder by his own hand. Far from focusing exclusively on petitioner's direct responsibility, then, counsel put on a halfhearted mitigation case, taking precisely the type of "shotgun" approach the Maryland Court of Appeals concluded counsel sought to avoid. When viewed in this light, the "strategic decision" the state courts and respondents all invoke to justify counsel's limited pursuit of mitigating evidence resembles more a post-hoc rationalization of counsel's conduct than an accurate description of their deliberations prior to sentencing.

In rejecting petitioner's ineffective assistance claim, the Maryland Court of Appeals appears to have assumed that because counsel had some information with respect to petitioner's background—the information in the PSI and the DSS records—they were in a position to make a tactical choice not to present a mitigation defense. In assessing the reasonableness of an attorney's investigation, however, a court must consider not only the quantum of evidence already known to counsel, but also whether the known evidence would lead a reasonable attorney to investigate further. Even assuming Schlaich and Nethercott limited the scope of their investigation for strategic reasons, Strickland does not establish that a cursory investigation automatically justifies a tactical decision with respect to sentencing strategy. Rather, a reviewing court must consider the reasonableness of the investigation said to support that strategy.

The Maryland Court of Appeals' application of *Strickland's* governing legal principles was objectively unreasonable. Though the state court acknowledged petitioner's claim that counsel's failure to prepare a social history "did not meet the minimum standards of the profession," the court did not conduct an assessment of whether the decision to cease all investigation upon obtaining the PSI and the DSS records actually demonstrated reasonable professional judgment. The state court merely assumed that the investigation was adequate. In light of what the PSI and the DSS records actually revealed, however, counsel chose to abandon their investigation at an unreasonable juncture, making a fully informed decision with respect to sentencing strategy impossible. * * *.

* * *

2

* * *

3

In finding that Schlaich and Nethercott's investigation did not meet *Strickland's* performance standards, we emphasize that *Strickland* does not require counsel to investigate every conceivable line of mitigating evidence no matter how unlikely the effort would be to assist the defendant at sentencing. Nor does *Strickland* require defense counsel to present mitigating evidence at sentencing in every case. Both conclusions would interfere with the constitutionally protected independence of counsel at the heart of *Strickland*. We base our conclusion on the much more limited principle that "strategic choices made after less than complete investigation are <u>reasonable</u>" only to the extent that "reasonable professional judgments support the limitations on investigation." A decision not to investigate thus "must be directly assessed for reasonableness in all the circumstances."

Counsel's investigation into Wiggins' background did not reflect reasonable professional judgment. Their decision to end their investigation when they did was neither consistent with the professional standards that prevailed in 1989, nor reasonable in light of the evidence counsel uncovered in the social services records—evidence that would have led a reasonably competent attorney to investigate further. Counsel's pursuit of bifurcation until the eve of sentencing and their partial presentation of a mitigation case suggest that their incomplete investigation was the result of inattention, not reasoned strategic judgment. In deferring to counsel's decision not to pursue a mitigation case despite their unreasonable investigation, the Maryland Court of Appeals unreasonably applied *Strickland*. * * * The requirements for habeas relief established by 28 U.S.C. § 2254(d) are thus satisfied.

III

In order for counsel's inadequate performance to constitute a Sixth

Amendment violation, petitioner must show that counsel's failures prejudiced his defense. In *Strickland*, we made clear that, to establish prejudice, a "defendant must show that there is a reasonable probability that, but for counsel's unprofessional errors, the result of the proceeding would have been different. A reasonable probability is a probability sufficient to undermine confidence in the outcome." In assessing prejudice, we reweigh the evidence in aggravation against the totality of available mitigating evidence. In this case, our review is not circumscribed by a state court conclusion with respect to prejudice, as neither of the state courts below reached this prong of the *Strickland* analysis.

The mitigating evidence counsel failed to discover and present in this case is powerful. As Selvog reported based on his conversations with Wiggins and members of his family, Wiggins experienced severe privation and abuse in the first six years of his life while in the custody of his alcoholic, absentee mother. He suffered physical torment, sexual molestation, and repeated rape during his subsequent years in foster care. The time Wiggins spent homeless, along with his diminished mental capacities, further augment his mitigation case. * * *

Given both the nature and the extent of the abuse petitioner suffered, we find there to be a reasonable probability that a competent attorney, aware of this history, would have introduced it at sentencing in an admissible form. While it may well have been strategically defensible upon a reasonably thorough investigation to focus on Wiggins' direct responsibility for the murder, the two sentencing strategies are not necessarily mutually exclusive. Moreover, given the strength of the available evidence, a reasonable attorney may well have chosen to prioritize the mitigation case

over the direct responsibility challenge, particularly given that Wiggins' history contained little of the double edge we have found to justify limited investigations in other cases.

* * *

We further find that had the jury been confronted with this considerable mitigating evidence, there is a reasonable probability that it would have returned with a different sentence. * * *

Wiggins' sentencing jury heard only one significant mitigating factor—that Wiggins had no prior convictions. Had the jury been able to place petitioner's excruciating life history on the mitigating side of the scale, there is a reasonable probability that at least one juror would have struck a different balance. Cf. Borchardt v. Maryland, 367 Md. 91, 139–140, 786 A.2d 631, 660 (2001) (noting that as long as a single juror concludes that mitigating evidence outweighs aggravating evidence, the death penalty cannot be imposed).

Moreover, * * * Wiggins does not have a record of violent conduct that could have been introduced by the State to offset this powerful mitigating narrative. * * * We thus conclude that the available mitigating evidence, taken as a whole, "might well have influenced the jury's appraisal" of Wiggins' moral culpability. Accordingly, the judgment of the United States Court of Appeals for the Fourth Circuit is reversed, and the case is remanded for further proceedings consistent with this opinion.

JUSTICE SCALIA, with whom JUSTICE THOMAS joins, dissenting.

The Court today vacates Kevin Wiggins' death sentence on the ground that his trial counsel's investigation of potential mitigating evidence was "incomplete." Wiggins' trial counsel testified under oath, however, that he was aware of the basic features of Wiggins' troubled childhood that the Court claims he overlooked. The Court chooses to disbelieve this testimony for reasons that do not withstand analysis. Moreover, even if this disbelief could plausibly be entertained, that would certainly not establish (as 28 U.S.C. § 2254(d) requires) that the Maryland Court of Appeals was unreasonable in believing it, and in therefore concluding that counsel adequately investigated Wiggins' background. The Court also fails to observe § 2254(e)(1)'s requirement that federal habeas courts respect state-court factual determinations not rebutted by "clear and convincing evidence." * * * I respectfully dissent.

Question on Wiggins

Does the Court's decision in *Wiggins* indicate a more liberal attitude to claims of ineffectiveness than was found in *Strickland*? Or is *Wiggins* an outrageous, one-of-a-kind fact situation?

3. Assessing Prejudice

In *Strickland,* the Court held that lower courts could proceed directly to the prejudice prong if that would dispose of the case, and thereby avoid having to evaluate defense counsel's performance. Many lower courts have done so. See, e.g., United States ex. rel. Cross v. DeRobertis, 811 F.2d 1008 (7th Cir. 1987)(performance issue requires "a particularly subtle assessment," so court proceeds directly to prejudice prong). Is it important for courts to provide guidance on effectiveness standards? If so, is it acceptable for a court to proceed directly to the prejudice prong of *Strickland?*

The Strength of the Case Against the Defendant

Concerning the prejudice prong of *Strickland,* it is obvious that the defendant is more likely to prove prejudice if the prosecution's evidence is weak. For example, in Atkins v. Attorney General of Alabama, 932 F.2d 1430 (11th Cir.1991), counsel failed to object to the introduction of a fingerprint card offered to make a comparison between Atkins' fingerprints and those found at the scene of the crime. The card included a printed notation of a prior arrest that would not have been admissible. The court found that the failure to object constituted ineffectiveness, and that without the error there was a reasonable probability that the outcome of the trial would have been different. Atkins' fingerprints had been found at the scene, but the victim testified that Atkins had worked for him at the house two days prior to the crime; no other physical evidence tied Atkins to the crime. The court asserted that "the introduction of a previous arrest can have an almost irreversible impact on the minds of the jurors" and that the evidence against Atkins was "not overwhelming." See also Hart v. Gomez, 174 F.3d 1067 (9th Cir.1999)(where trial was basically a credibility determination between the defendant's witness and the complainant, the defendant's counsel's failure to introduce record evidence corroborating the defense witness' account was ineffective and prejudicial); Burnett v. Collins, 982 F.2d 922 (5th Cir.1993)("a verdict strongly supported by the record is less likely to have been affected by counsel's errors than one with only weak support").

Prejudice Assessed at Time of Review: Lockhart v. Fretwell

In *Lockhart v. Fretwell*, 506 U.S. 364 (1993), the Court made it clear that prejudice under *Strickland* is not always found simply because effective assistance would have changed the outcome. Fretwell was tried for capital murder in an Arkansas state court. His trial counsel at the sentencing phase failed to object to the use of an aggravating factor that was unconstitutional under then-existing precedent of the United States Court of Appeals for the Eighth Circuit. The jury relied solely on this aggravating factor and sentenced Fretwell to death. Subsequent to Fretwell's trial, and in a different case, the Eighth Circuit Court of Appeals overruled its precedent and held that it was constitutional to use the Arkansas aggravating factor that had been relied upon by the jury in Fretwell's trial. Fretwell argued on habeas that trial counsel had acted ineffectively in failing to object to the use of the aggravating factor that the Court of Appeals had originally (and as of the time of his trial) declared unconstitutional, even though the Court of Appeals subsequently reversed itself. He argued further that counsel's ineffectiveness prejudiced him, because if counsel had made the objection, the jury could not have used the aggravating factor at that time, and Fretwell could not have been sentenced to death. In the Supreme Court, the State conceded that Fretwell's trial counsel's performance was deficient, and also conceded that the trial court would not have allowed the use of the aggravating factor if defense counsel had objected and cited the then-current Eighth Circuit authority. Thus the State admitted that Fretwell would not have been sentenced to death if his trial counsel had made an appropriate objection. Nonetheless, the State argued that Fretwell was not prejudiced by his counsel's performance, because the case on which the objection would have been made was later overruled, and Fretwell had no right under *Strickland* to have the trial court "make an error in his favor."

Chief Justice Rehnquist wrote for seven Justices as the Court held that "counsel's failure to make an objection in a state criminal sentencing proceeding—an objection that would have been supported by a decision which subsequently was overruled—" could not constitute prejudice, since "the result of the sentencing proceeding * * * was rendered neither unreliable nor fundamentally unfair as a result of counsel's failure to make the objection." The Chief Justice reasoned that the right to effective assistance of counsel is intended to provide a fair trial. "Thus, an analysis focusing solely on mere outcome determination, without attention to whether the result of the proceeding was fundamentally unfair or unreliable, is defective. To set aside a conviction or sentence solely because the outcome would have been different but for counsel's error may grant the defendant a windfall to which the law does not entitle him."

The Chief Justice relied heavily on *Nix v. Whiteside*, 475 U.S. 157 (1986), where the Court held that the defendant was not prejudiced under *Strickland* when counsel refused to cooperate in presenting perjured testimony. Even though Whiteside might well have swayed the jury with perjurious testimony, the Court in *Whiteside* held that "in judging prejudice and the likelihood of a different outcome, a defendant has no right to the luck of a lawless decisionmaker." The Chief Justice interpreted *Whiteside* as establishing that "sheer outcome determination" is not sufficient to make out a claim of prejudice under *Strickland*.

Fretwell argued that a finding of prejudice on the basis of case law arising after a defendant's trial would result in "hindsight" determination, and that this was inappropriate in light of *Strickland*, where the Court specifically precluded a hindsight-oriented review of counsel's conduct. But Chief Justice Rehnquist responded that the preclusion of hindsight-oriented review in *Strickland* was limited to the performance prong of the two-pronged test. He explained as follows:

> [F]rom the perspective of hindsight there is a natural tendency to speculate as to whether a different trial strategy might have been more successful. We adopted the rule of contemporary assessment of counsel's conduct [in *Strickland*] because a more rigid requirement "could dampen the ardor and impair the independence of defense counsel, discourage the acceptance of assigned cases, and undermine the trust between attorney and client." But the "prejudice" component of the *Strickland* test does not implicate these concerns. It focuses on the question whether counsel's deficient performance renders the result of the trial unreliable or the proceeding fundamentally unfair.

The Chief Justice concluded that since counsel's deficient performance resulted only in the failure to object on the basis of an erroneously decided case (though the "error" was determined subsequent to the trial), Fretwell was not deprived of any "substantive or procedural right to which the law entitles him." Therefore Fretwell suffered no prejudice from counsel's deficient performance.

Justice O'Connor wrote a concurring opinion, describing the Court's holding in specific terms as follows: "the court making the prejudice determination may not consider the effect of an objection it knows to be wholly meritless under current governing law, even if the objection might have been considered meritorious at the time of its omission." Justice Thomas also wrote a brief concurring opinion.

Justice Stevens, joined by Justice Blackmun, dissented and argued that "the Court today reaches the astonishing conclusion that deficient performance by counsel does not prejudice a defendant even when it results in the erroneous imposition of a death sentence," and "[t]he Court's aversion to windfalls seems to disappear * * * when the State is the favored recipient." He criticized the fact that "the State, through the coincidence of inadequate representation and fortuitous timing, may carry out a death sentence that was invalid when imposed." Justice Stevens declared that "[h]indsight has no place in a Sixth Amendment jurisprudence that focuses, quite rightly, on protecting the adversarial balance at trial." He argued that *Whiteside* could not "perform the heavy duty the court assigns it." He explained that "reliance on perjured testimony and reliance on current Court of Appeals case law are not remotely comparable, and that to suggest otherwise is simply disingenuous."

Prejudice From an Increased Sentence: Glover v. United States

In Glover v. United States, 531 U.S. 198 (2001), Glover argued that his trial counsel was ineffective for failing to challenge a sentence that was allegedly set in violation of the Federal Sentencing Guidelines. The Court of Appeals assumed that counsel was ineffective, but denied relief on the ground that any ineffectiveness did not prejudice Glover within the meaning of *Strickland*. The Court of

Appeals read Lockhart v. Fretwell, *supra*, to require a finding of "significant" prejudice. In this case, counsel's ineffectiveness resulted in an increased sentence somewhere between 6 and 21 months; the Court of Appeals did not view this increase as "significant".

The Supreme Court unanimously reversed in an opinion by Justice Kennedy. The Court assumed, as did the lower court, that counsel had been ineffective. Justice Kennedy criticized the lower court's analysis of prejudice in the following passage:

> The Seventh Circuit was incorrect to rely on *Lockhart* to deny relief to persons attacking their sentence who might show deficient performance in counsel's failure to object to an error of law affecting the calculation of a sentence because the sentence increase does not meet some baseline standard of prejudice. Authority does not suggest that a minimal amount of additional time in prison cannot constitute prejudice. Quite to the contrary, our jurisprudence suggests that any amount of actual jail time has Sixth Amendment significance.

> The Seventh Circuit's rule is not well considered in any event, because there is no obvious dividing line by which to measure how much longer a sentence must be for the increase to constitute substantial prejudice. Indeed, it is not even clear if the relevant increase is to be measured in absolute terms or by some fraction of the total authorized sentence. Although the amount by which a defendant's sentence is increased by a particular decision may be a factor to consider in determining whether counsel's performance in failing to argue the point constitutes ineffective assistance, under a determinate system of constrained discretion such as the Sentencing Guidelines it cannot serve as a bar to a showing of prejudice.

Prejudice From Ineffective Assistance at the Guilty Plea Stage

It is certainly possible for defense counsel to perform ineffectively at the guilty plea stage. The most common example is giving wrong advice about the consequences of a plea, e.g., telling the defendant that by accepting the plea, he would be eligible for work release or parole within a certain time, when in fact that is not the case; or telling the defendant that he is not subject to a mandatory minimum sentence, when in fact he is. See Ostrander v. Green, 46 F.3d 347 (4th Cir.1995)(incorrect advice as to eligibility for work release "falls well below the range of competence we must expect from defense lawyers"). Compare Moreland v. Scott, 175 F.3d 347 (5th Cir.1999) (it was not ineffective to advise the defendant to reject a guilty plea and go to trial, on the ground that trial court's advance rulings on the evidence were erroneous and would be reversed on appeal; the defendant lost the evidentiary issues on appeal, but it was a close case). The difficult question is: how does a defendant show that he was prejudiced by counsel's incorrect advice?

The Court considered the applicability of the *Strickland* prejudice prong to guilty pleas in Hill v. Lockhart, 474 U.S. 52 (1985). Hill's counsel told him that if he accepted a plea bargain, he would be eligible for parole after serving one-third of his sentence. A two-year old Arkansas statute provided, however, that individuals with prior convictions such as Hill were not eligible for parole until they served one-half of their sentence. This meant that by accepting the plea,

Hill would have to serve nine years, rather than six, before parole eligibility. The Supreme Court refused to decide whether counsel failed the performance prong of *Strickland,* since it found that Hill had not shown that he had been prejudiced. The Court stated that to prove prejudice in the guilty plea context, the defendant must show that "but for counsel's errors, he would not have pleaded guilty and would have insisted on going to trial."

In a subsequent habeas petition, Hill prevailed. See Hill v. Lockhart, 877 F.2d 698 (8th Cir.1989). The court of appeals found that Hill's counsel was clearly ineffective, due to his failure "to ascertain, through minimal research, the applicable statute governing parole eligibility for second offenders," and that parole eligibility "is normally one of the most important factors to a criminal client." The court concluded that but for the misadvice, Hill would have proceeded to trial. Hill had previously rejected a deal in which he would have been eligible for parole in nine years; and the court credited his testimony that if he had been correctly informed by counsel, he would have "rolled the dice" and gone to trial because he believed that he would have "just as good a chance on a life sentence imposed at trial of getting out after nine years." The court stated that "to succeed under *Strickland,* Hill need not show prejudice in the sense that he probably would have been acquitted or given a shorter sentence at trial." Compare Czere v. Butler, 833 F.2d 59 (5th Cir.1987), where the court found that the defendant had not shown prejudice when counsel advised him that by accepting a plea he would be eligible for parole in forty years, when in fact the applicable statute provided that he would not be eligible for parole for eighty years. The court found that in accepting the plea, Czere was concerned more with avoiding the electric chair than he was about parole, and that the difference between parole eligibility in eighty rather than forty years could not have affected Czere's decision.

Hill is a case of ineffectiveness where counsel advised the defendant to accept a plea on erroneous information. The opposite situation can also implicate *Strickland.* See Toro v. Fairman, 940 F.2d 1065 (7th Cir.1991), where counsel was found ineffective for advising the defendant to reject a plea. The court noted that the defendant had no defense to the charges, and that he received a much longer sentence after being tried and found guilty. According to the court, counsel's judgment was clouded by his emotional involvement in the case. Interestingly, though, the court found no prejudice from this bad advice, finding that the defendant did not prove that but for counsel's error, he would have accepted the plea and *not* gone to trial. The defendant's conclusory statements on this point were held insufficient. But if the defendant had no case, as the court admits, why would he have gone to trial only to obtain a more severe sentence? Isn't this a case where bad advice is per se prejudicial?

Prejudice Due to Ineffectiveness on Appeal

Dispute has arisen concerning application of the prejudice prong of *Strickland* to claims of ineffective assistance of counsel on appeal. For example, in Lozada v. Deeds, 498 U.S. 430 (1991), the defendant alleged that his counsel failed to inform him of his right to appeal or of the procedures and time limitations for an appeal, and that counsel had misled him into thinking that his case had been forwarded to the public defender's office. The district court dismissed Lozada's habeas corpus petition on the ground that Lozada had not indicated what issues he would have raised on appeal and had not demonstrated that the appeal might have succeeded. Both the district court and the court of appeals denied a certificate of probable cause to appeal the denial of habeas relief under 28 U.S.C. § 2253. The Supreme Court in a per curiam opinion held that the certificate of probable cause should have been granted. The standard for granting such a certificate is that a court "could resolve the issues" in petitioner's favor. The Court held that Lozada had met that standard, because the issue of prejudice "could be resolved in a different manner than the one followed by the District Court."

Subsequently, in Roe v. Flores–Ortega, 528 U.S. 470 (2000), the Court considered the circumstances under which defense counsel's failure to file a notice of appeal would be prejudicial within the meaning of *Strickland*. The Court declared that "to show prejudice in these circumstances, a defendant must demonstrate that there is a reasonable probability that, but for counsel's deficient failure to consult with him about an appeal, he would have timely appealed." The defendant did not have to show that the appeal would be likely to result in a reversal of the conviction–though obviously the merits of an appeal bear somewhat on whether the defendant would have pursued it.

4. Per Se Ineffectiveness and Prejudice

In the following case, the Court recognizes that there might be some situations in which counsel's ineffectiveness and prejudice could be presumed and therefore reversal would be automatic. But such an extreme situation was not presented under the facts.

UNITED STATES v. CRONIC

Supreme Court of the United States, 1984.
466 U.S. 648.

JUSTICE STEVENS delivered the opinion of the Court.

Respondent and two associates were indicted on mail fraud charges involving the transfer of over $9,400,000 in checks between banks in Tampa, Florida, and Norman, Oklahoma, during a four-month period in 1975. Shortly before the scheduled trial date, respondent's retained counsel withdrew. The court appointed a young lawyer with a real estate practice to represent respondent, but allowed him only 25 days for pretrial preparation, even though it had taken the Government over four and one-half years to investigate the case and it had reviewed thousands of documents during that investigation. The two codefendants agreed to testify for the Government; respondent was convicted on 11 of the 13 counts in the indictment and received a 25–year sentence.

The Court of Appeals reversed the conviction because it concluded that respondent did not "have the Assistance of Counsel for his defence" that is guaranteed by the Sixth Amendment to the Constitution. This conclusion was not supported by a determination that respondent's trial counsel had made any specified errors, that his actual performance had prejudiced the defense, or that he failed to exercise "the skill, judgment, and diligence of a reasonably competent defense attorney"; instead the conclusion rested on the premise that no such showing is necessary "when circumstances hamper a given lawyer's preparation of a defendant's case." The question presented by the Government's petition for certiorari is whether the Court of Appeals has correctly interpreted the Sixth Amendment.

I

The indictment alleged a "check kiting" scheme. At the direction of respondent, his codefendant Cummings opened a bank account in the name of Skyproof Manufacturing, Inc. (Skyproof), at a bank in Tampa, Florida, and codefendant Merritt opened two accounts, one in his own name and one in the name of Skyproof, at banks in Norman, Oklahoma. Knowing that there were insufficient funds in either account, the defendants allegedly drew a series of checks and wire transfers on the Tampa account aggregating $4,841,073.95, all of which were deposited in Skyproof's Norman bank account during the period between June 23, 1975, and October 16, 1975; during approximately the same period they drew checks on Skyproof's Norman account for deposits in Tampa aggregating $4,600,881.39. The process of clearing the checks involved the use of the mails. By "kiting" insufficient funds checks between the banks in those two cities, defendants allegedly created false or inflated balances in the accounts.

* * *

At trial the Government proved that Skyproof's checks were issued and deposited at the times and places, and in the amounts, described in the indictment. Having made plea bargains with defendants Cummings and Merritt, who had actually handled the issuance and delivery of the relevant written instruments, the Government proved through their testimony that respondent had conceived and directed the entire scheme, and that he had deliberately concealed his connection with Skyproof because of prior financial and tax problems.

After the District Court ruled that a prior conviction could be used to impeach his testimony, respondent decided not to testify. Counsel put on no defense. By cross-examination of Government witnesses, however, he established that Skyproof was not merely a sham, but actually was an operating company with a significant cash flow, though its revenues were not sufficient to justify as large a "float" as the record disclosed. Cross-examination also established the absence of written evidence that respondent had any control over Skyproof, or personally participated in the withdrawals or deposits.

The four-day jury trial ended on July 17, 1980, and respondent was sentenced on August 28, 1980. * * *

The Court of Appeals reversed the conviction because it inferred that respondent's constitutional right to the effective assistance of counsel had been violated. That inference was based on its use of five criteria: "[T]he time afforded for investigation and preparation; the experience of counsel; the gravity of the charge; the complexity of possible defenses; and the accessibility of witnesses to counsel." Under the test employed by the Court of Appeals, reversal is required even if the lawyer's actual performance was flawless. By utilizing this inferential approach, the Court of Appeals erred.

II

* * *

III

While the Court of Appeals purported to apply a standard of reasonable competence, it did not indicate that there had been an actual breakdown of the adversarial process during the trial of this case. Instead it concluded that the circumstances surrounding the representation of respondent mandated an inference that counsel was unable to discharge his duties.

* * * [B]ecause we presume that the lawyer is competent to provide the guiding hand that the defendant needs, the burden rests on the accused to demonstrate a constitutional violation. There are, however, circumstances that are so likely to prejudice the accused that the cost of litigating their effect in a particular case is unjustified.

Most obvious, of course, is the complete denial of counsel. The presumption that counsel's assistance is essential requires us to conclude that a trial is unfair if the accused is denied counsel at a critical stage of his trial. Similarly, if counsel entirely fails to subject the prosecution's case to meaningful adversarial testing, then there has been a denial of Sixth Amendment rights that makes the adversary process itself presumptively unreliable. * * *

Circumstances of that magnitude may be present on some occasions when although counsel is available to assist the accused during trial, the likelihood that any lawyer, even a fully competent one, could provide effective assistance is so small that a presumption of prejudice is appropriate without inquiry into the actual conduct of the trial. Powell v. Alabama, 287 U.S. 45 (1932), [set forth in Chapter Five] was such a case.

* * *

But every refusal to postpone a criminal trial will not give rise to such a presumption. * * *

The Court of Appeals did not find that respondent was denied the presence of counsel at a critical stage of the prosecution. Nor did it find, based on the actual conduct of the trial, that

there was a breakdown in the adversarial process that would justify a presumption that respondent's conviction was insufficiently reliable to satisfy the Constitution. The dispositive question in this case therefore is whether the circumstances surrounding respondent's representation—and in particular the five criteria identified by the Court of Appeals—justified such a presumption.

IV

The five factors listed in the Court of Appeals' opinion are relevant to an evaluation of a lawyer's effectiveness in a particular case, but neither separately nor in combination do they provide a basis for concluding that competent counsel was not able to provide this respondent with the guiding hand that the Constitution guarantees.

Respondent places special stress on the disparity between the duration of the Government's investigation and the period the District Court allowed to newly appointed counsel for trial preparation. The lawyer was appointed to represent respondent on June 12, 1980, and on June 19, filed a written motion for a continuance of the trial that was then scheduled to begin on June 30. Although counsel contended that he needed at least 30 days for preparation, the District Court reset the trial for July 14—thus allowing 25 additional days for preparation.

Neither the period of time that the Government spent investigating the case, nor the number of documents that its agents reviewed during that investigation, is necessarily relevant to the question whether a competent lawyer could prepare to defend the case in 25 days. The Government's task of finding and assembling admissible evidence that will carry its burden of proving guilt beyond a reasonable doubt is entirely different from the defendant's task in preparing to deny or rebut a criminal charge. Of course, in some cases the rebuttal may be equally burdensome and time consuming, but there is no necessary correlation between the two. In this case, the time devoted by the Government to the assembly, organization, and summarization of the thousands of written records evidencing the two streams of checks flowing between the banks in Florida and Oklahoma unquestionably simplified the work of defense counsel in identifying and understanding the basic character of the defendants' scheme. When a series of repetitious transactions fit into a single mold, the number of written exhibits that are needed to define the pattern may be unrelated to the time that is needed to understand it.

The significance of counsel's preparation time is further reduced by the nature of the charges against respondent. Most of the Government's case consisted merely of establishing the transactions between the two banks. A competent attorney would have no reason to question the authenticity, accuracy or relevance of this evidence—there could be no dispute that these transactions actually occurred. As respondent appears to recognize, the only *bona fide* jury issue open to competent defense counsel on these facts was whether respondent acted with intent to defraud. When there is no reason to dispute the underlying historical facts, the period of 25 days to consider the question whether those facts justify an inference of criminal intent is not so short that it even arguably justifies a presumption that

no lawyer could provide the respondent with the effective assistance of counsel required by the Constitution.

That conclusion is not undermined by the fact that respondent's lawyer was young, that his principal practice was in real estate, or that this was his first jury trial. Every experienced criminal defense attorney once tried his first criminal case. Moreover, a lawyer's experience with real estate transactions might be more useful in preparing to try a criminal case involving financial transactions than would prior experience in handling, for example, armed robbery prosecutions. The character of a particular lawyer's experience may shed light in an evaluation of his actual performance, but it does not justify a presumption of ineffectiveness in the absence of such an evaluation.

The three other criteria—the gravity of the charge, the complexity of the case, and the accessibility of witnesses—are all matters that may affect what a reasonably competent attorney could be expected to have done under the circumstances, but none identifies circumstances that in themselves make it unlikely that respondent received the effective assistance of counsel.

* * *

[The Court remanded for a determination of whether defense counsel's performance was in fact ineffective and prejudicial under the *Strickland* standards. Justice Marshall concurred in the judgment.]

Cronic on Remand

Note that the Court in *Cronic* did not hold that Cronic had received effective assistance of counsel. Rather, it rejected the per se rule of reversal applied by the lower court. On remand in *Cronic,* the court of appeals reviewed counsel's actual performance and held that it was ineffective and that Cronic was prejudiced. See United States v. Cronic, 839 F.2d 1401 (10th Cir.1988). The court found that defense counsel ignored the issues of the defendant's intent and good faith, which were, as the Supreme Court had recognized, the only issues of dispute in the case. Cronic's attorney testified at the hearing on ineffectiveness that the defense he used was one seeking to "cloud the issues." The court of appeals held that "this cannot be a satisfactory explanation under *Strickland* or any other authority for a selection of a defense." The court also noted that defense counsel failed to object to evidence due to a misunderstanding of the statute under which Cronic was tried.

Denial of "Counsel" Within the Meaning of the Sixth Amendment

Cronic holds that in some limited cases, ineffectiveness and prejudice will be presumed without having to investigate counsel's performance. But it is clear that this rule of per se reversal is rarely applicable. If it did not apply under the facts of *Cronic,* where could it apply? Consider *Solina v. United States,* 709 F.2d 160 (2d Cir.1983), where the court concluded that per se reversal was required because defendant's trial counsel had held himself out as an attorney, but had never passed a bar exam. The evidence against Solina was overwhelming, and Solina could point to no error of judgment on the part of his counsel at trial. Yet the court reasoned as follows:

> The problem of representation by [one not admitted to the bar] is not simply one of competence * * * but that he was engaging in a crime. Such a person cannot be wholly free from fear of what might happen if a vigorous defense should lead the prosecutor or the trial judge to inquire into his background and discover his lack of credentials.

The court found that Solina had been denied "counsel," as that term is used in the Sixth Amendment, and that this total denial of counsel was per se prejudicial. *Solina* preceded *Cronic,* but it has been followed by lower courts even after *Cronic.* See, e.g., *United States v. Novak,* 903 F.2d 883 (2d Cir.1990)(per se reversal where defense counsel had obtained admission to the bar by fraud). Do you think that the Supreme Court would require per se reversal in a case like *Solina?* Compare *Reese v. Peters,* 926 F.2d 668 (7th Cir.1991)(*Solina* distinguished; no per se reversal where attorney's license had been suspended for failure to pay dues: "mountebanks, as in *Solina,* and persons who obtain credentials by fraud, are classes apart from persons who satisfied the court of their legal skills but later ran afoul of some technical legal rule."). See also *Pilchak v. Camper,* 935 F.2d 145 (8th Cir.1991) (per se reversal where defense counsel was suffering from Alzheimer's disease at the time of trial).

Sleeping Defense Counsel

In *Tippins v. Walker,* 77 F.3d 682 (2d Cir.1996), Tippins argued for per se reversal of his conviction on the ground that his trial counsel slept through major portions of the trial. Testimony at the ineffectiveness hearing from the trial judge, court reporter, prosecutor, jurors and other defendants and defense counsel corroborated Tippins' account. Tippins' counsel slept every day of the trial; he could often be heard snoring; he slept through the testimony of several critical witnesses; and he was admonished by the trial judge for sleeping throughout the trial. The court held that this was a sufficient showing to trigger per se reversal under *Cronic.* It was careful to state, however, that not every instance of apparent sleeping on the part of defense counsel would be ineffective or cause for reversal. But the facts of this case were special:

> [T]he appearance of "sleeping" may cover a range of behavior. Lawyers may sometimes affect a drowsy or bored look to downplay an adversary's presentation of evidence. We are also mindful * * * that a per se rule would give unscrupulous attorneys a delayed-trigger weapon to be sprung at some later strategic phase of the proceeding if events developed very badly for a defendant. However, [the government] has not contended that Tirelli's sleeping was a charade or a tactical device. And it would be difficult for [the government] to make that claim, given the testimony that the trial prosecutor acknowledged his adversary's snoring by exchanging knowing looks with the court reporter. In any event, trial judges are well-positioned to detect, guard against, and penalize such a tactical abuse of the right to counsel.

* * *

The court concluded as follows:

> In short, there is simply no basis for the hope that Tirelli was functioning as a lawyer during critical times at trial. The trial judge was so alarmed by Tirelli's sleeping during damaging testimony by Stokes that he interrupted proceedings to reprimand him in the hall. The prosecutor recalls that there were two such reprimands. It may be that such an awakening would have been curative if the sleeping was an isolated event. But we cannot count on a trial judge to serve as the defense lawyer's alarm clock whenever matters arise that touch the client's interest. A judge is not privy to the tactics or strategy of the defense, however evident they may appear to be. Indeed, it would be an inversion of the attorney-client relationship to require the defendant to alert the lawyer to important events in the proceedings. In these circumstances, the steps taken by the trial judge evidenced the dangerous character of the problem without curing it. We therefore conclude that Tippins was deprived of effective assistance of counsel during his trial, in violation of his Sixth Amendment right to counsel.

Application of Per Se Prejudice Standard Not Warranted: Bell v. Cone

In the following case, the Court found that defense counsel in a capital case did not perform so poorly as to justify a ruling of *per se* prejudice under *Cronic*.

BELL v. CONE

Supreme Court of the United States, 2002.
535 U.S. 685.

CHIEF JUSTICE REHNQUIST **delivered the opinion of the Court**

The Tennessee Court of Appeals rejected respondent's claim that his counsel rendered ineffective assistance during his sentencing hearing under principles announced in Strickland v. Washington. The Court of Appeals for the Sixth Circuit concluded that United States v. Cronic, should have controlled the state court's analysis and granted him a conditional writ of habeas corpus. We hold that respondent's claim was governed by *Strickland*, and that the state court's decision neither was "contrary to" nor involved "an unreasonable application of clearly established Federal law" under the provisions of 28 U.S.C. § 2254(d)(1).

In 1982, respondent was convicted of, and sentenced to death for, the murder of an elderly couple in Memphis, Tennessee. The killings culminated a 2–day crime rampage that began when respondent robbed a Memphis jewelry store of approximately $112,000 in merchandise on a Saturday in August 1980. Shortly after the 12:45 p.m. robbery, a police officer in an unmarked vehicle spotted respondent driving at a normal speed and began to follow him. After a few blocks, respondent accelerated, prompting a high-speed chase through midtown Memphis and into a residential neighborhood where respondent abandoned his vehicle. Attempting to flee, respondent shot an officer who tried to apprehend him, shot a citizen who confronted him, and, at gunpoint, demanded that another hand over his car keys. As a police helicopter hovered overhead, respondent tried to shoot the fleeing car owner, but was frustrated because his gun was out of ammunition.

Throughout the afternoon and into the next morning, respondent managed to elude detection as police combed the surrounding area. In the meantime, officers inventorying his car found an array of illegal and prescription drugs, the stolen merchandise, and more than $2,400 in cash. Respondent reappeared early Sunday morning when he drew a gun on an elderly resident who refused to let him in to use her telephone. Later that afternoon, respondent broke into the home of Shipley and Cleopatra Todd, aged 93 and 79 years old, and killed

them by repeatedly beating them about the head with a blunt instrument. He moved their bodies so that they would not be visible from the front and rear doors and ransacked the first floor of their home. After shaving his beard, respondent traveled to Florida. He was arrested there for robbing a drugstore in Pompano Beach. He admitted killing the Todds and shooting the police officer.

A Tennessee grand jury charged respondent with two counts of first-degree murder in the perpetration of a burglary in connection with the Todds' deaths, three counts of assault with intent to murder in connection with the shootings and attempted shooting of the car owner, and one count of robbery with a deadly weapon for the jewelry store theft. At a jury trial in the Criminal Court of Shelby County, the prosecution adduced overwhelming physical and testimonial evidence showing that respondent perpetrated the crimes and that he killed the Todds in a brutal and callous fashion.

The defense conceded that respondent committed most of the acts in question, but sought to prove that he was not guilty by reason of insanity. A clinical psychologist testified that respondent suffered from substance abuse and posttraumatic stress disorders related to his military service in Vietnam. A neuropharmacologist recounted at length respondent's history of illicit drug use, which began after he joined the Army and escalated to the point where he was daily consuming "rather horrific" quantities. That drug use, according to the expert, caused chronic amphetamine psychosis, hallucinations, and ongoing paranoia, which affected respondent's mental capacity and ability to obey the law. Defense counsel also called respondent's mother, who spoke of her son coming back from Vietnam in 1969 a changed person, his honorable discharge from service, his graduation with honors from college, and the deaths of his father and fiancee while he was in prison from 1972–1979 for robbery. Although respondent did not take the stand, defense counsel was able to elicit through other testimony that he had expressed remorse for the killings. Rejecting his insanity defense, the jury found him guilty on all charges.

Punishment for the first-degree murder counts was fixed in a separate sentencing hearing that took place the next day and lasted about three hours. Under then-applicable Tennessee law, a death sentence was required if the jury found unanimously that the State proved beyond a reasonable doubt the existence of at least one statutory aggravating circumstance that was not outweighed by any mitigating circumstance. In making these determinations, the jury could (and was instructed that it could) consider evidence from both the guilt and punishment phases.

During its opening statement, the State said it would prove four aggravating factors: that (1) respondent had previously been convicted of one or more felonies involving the use or threat of violence to a person; (2) he knowingly created a great risk of death to two or more persons other than the victim during the act of murder; (3) the murder was especially heinous, atrocious, or cruel; and (4) the murder was committed for the purpose of avoiding unlawful arrest. In his opening statement, defense counsel called the jury's attention to the mitigating evidence already before them. He suggested that respondent was under the influence of extreme mental disturbance or duress, that he was an addict whose drug and other problems stemmed from the stress of his military

service, and that he felt remorse. Counsel urged the jury that there was a good reason for preserving his client's life if one looked at "the whole man." He asked for mercy, calling it a blessing that would raise them above the State to the level of God.

The prosecution then called a records custodian and fingerprint examiner to establish that respondent had three armed robbery convictions and two officers who said they tried unsuccessfully to arrest respondent for armed robbery after the jewelry store heist. Through cross-examination of the records custodian, respondent's attorney brought out that his client had been awarded the Bronze Star in Vietnam. After defense counsel successfully objected to the State's proffer of photos of the Todds' decomposing bodies, both sides rested. The junior prosecuting attorney on the case gave what the state courts described as a "low-key" closing. Defense counsel waived final argument, preventing the lead prosecutor, who by all accounts was an extremely effective advocate, from arguing in rebuttal. The jury found in both murder cases four aggravating factors and no mitigating circumstances substantial enough to outweigh them. The Tennessee Supreme Court affirmed respondent's convictions and sentence on appeal, and we denied certiorari.

[On habeas review, the Court of Appeals] held that respondent suffered a Sixth Amendment violation for which prejudice should be presumed under United States v. Cronic, because his counsel, by not asking for mercy after the prosecutor's final argument, did not subject the State's call for the death penalty to meaningful adversarial testing. The state court's adjudication of respondent's Sixth Amendment claim, in the Court of Appeals' analysis, was therefore an unreasonable application of the clearly established law * * *. We granted certiorari, and now reverse the Court of Appeals.

II

The Antiterrorism and Effective Death Penalty Act of 1996 [discussed in Chapter Thirteen] modified a federal habeas court's role in reviewing state prisoner applications in order to prevent federal habeas "retrials" and to ensure that state-court convictions are given effect to the extent possible under law. To these ends, § 2254(d)(1) provides:

> "(d) An application for a writ of habeas corpus on behalf of a person in custody pursuant to the judgment of a State court shall not be granted with respect to any claim that was adjudicated on the merits in State court proceedings unless the adjudication of the claim—

> "(1) resulted in a decision that was contrary to, or involved an unreasonable application of, clearly established Federal law, as determined by the Supreme Court of the United States."

* * * A federal habeas court may issue the writ under the "contrary to" clause if the state court applies a rule different from the governing law set forth in our cases, or if it decides a case differently than we have done on a set of materially indistinguishable facts. The court may grant relief under the "unreasonable application" clause if the state court correctly identifies the governing legal principle from our decisions but unreasonably applies it to the facts of the particular case. The focus of the latter inquiry is on whether the state court's application of clearly established federal law is objectively unreasonable, and * * * an unreasonable application is different from an incorrect one.

Petitioner contends that the Court of Appeals exceeded its statutory authority to grant relief under § 2254(d)(1) because the decision of the Tennessee courts was neither contrary to nor an unreasonable application of the clearly established law of *Strickland*. Respondent counters that he is entitled to relief under § 2254(d)(1)'s "contrary to" clause because the state court applied the wrong legal rule. In his view, *Cronic*, not *Strickland,* governs the analysis of his claim that his counsel rendered ineffective assistance at the sentencing hearing. * * *.

* * *

The aspects of counsel's performance challenged by respondent—the failure to adduce mitigating evidence and the waiver of closing argument— are plainly of the same ilk as other specific attorney errors we have held subject to *Strickland's* performance and prejudice components. In Darden v. Wainwright, 477 U.S. 168, 184 (1986), for example, we evaluated under *Strickland* a claim that counsel was ineffective for failing to put on any mitigating evidence at a capital sentencing hearing. In Burger v. Kemp, 483 U.S. 776, 788 (1987), we did the same when presented with a challenge to counsel's decision at a capital sentencing hearing not to offer any mitigating evidence at all.

We hold, therefore, that the state court correctly identified the principles announced in *Strickland* as those governing the analysis of respondent's claim. Consequently, we find no merit in respondent's contention that the state court's adjudication was contrary to our clearly established law.

III

The remaining issue, then, is whether respondent can obtain relief on the ground that the state court's adjudication of his claim involved an "unreasonable application" of *Strickland*. * * * For respondent to succeed, however, he must do more than show that he would have satisfied *Strickland's* test if his claim were being analyzed in the first instance, because under § 2254(d)(1), it is not enough to convince a federal habeas court that, in its independent judgment, the state-court decision applied *Strickland* incorrectly. Rather, he must show that the Tennessee Court of Appeals applied *Strickland* to the facts of his case in an objectively unreasonable manner. This, we conclude, he cannot do.

Respondent's counsel was faced with the formidable task of defending a client who had committed a horribly brutal and senseless crime against two elderly persons in their home. He had just the day before shot a police officer and an unarmed civilian, attempted to shoot another person, and committed a robbery. The State had near conclusive proof of guilt on the murder charges as well as extensive evidence demonstrating the cruelty of the killings. Making the situation more onerous were the facts that respondent, despite his high intelligence and relatively normal upbringing, had turned into a drug addict and had a history of robbery convictions.

Because the defense's theory at the guilt phase was not guilty by reason of insanity, counsel was able to put before the jury extensive testimony about what he believed to be the most compelling mitigating evidence in the case—evidence regarding the change his client underwent after serving in Vietnam; his drug dependency, which apparently drove him to commit the robbery in the first place; and its effects. Before the state courts, respondent faulted his counsel for not recalling his medical experts during the sentencing hearing. But we think counsel reasonably could have con-

cluded that the substance of their testimony was still fresh to the jury. Each had taken the stand not long before, and counsel focused on their testimony in his guilt phase closing argument, which took place the day before the sentencing hearing was held. Respondent's suggestion that the jury could not fully consider the mental health proof as potentially mitigating because it was adduced during the guilt phase finds no support in the record. Defense counsel advised the jury that the testimony of the experts established the existence of mitigating circumstances, and the trial court specifically instructed the jury that evidence of a mental disease or defect insufficient to establish a criminal defense could be considered in mitigation.

Respondent also assigned error in his counsel's decision not to recall his mother. While counsel recognized that respondent's mother could have provided further information about respondent's childhood and spoken of her love for him, he concluded that she had not made a good witness at the guilt stage, and he did not wish to subject her to further cross-examination. Respondent advances no argument that would call his attorney's assessment into question.

In his trial preparations, counsel investigated the possibility of calling other witnesses. He thought respondent's sister, who was closest to him, might make a good witness, but she did not want to testify. And even if she had agreed, putting her on the stand would have allowed the prosecutor to question her about the fact that respondent called her from the Todds' house just after the killings. After consulting with his client, counsel opted not to call respondent himself as a witness. And we think counsel had sound tactical reasons for deciding against it. Respondent said he was very angry with the prosecutor and thought he might lash out if pressed on cross-examination, which could have only alienated him in the eyes of the jury. There was also the possibility of calling other witnesses from his childhood or days in the Army. But counsel feared that the prosecution might elicit information about respondent's criminal history. He further feared that testimony about respondent's normal youth might, in the jury's eyes, cut the other way.

Respondent also focuses on counsel's decision to waive final argument. He points out that counsel could have explained the significance of his Bronze Star decoration and argues that his counsel's failure to advocate for life in closing necessarily left the jury with the impression that he deserved to die. The Court of Appeals "reject[ed] out of hand" the idea that waiving summation could ever be considered sound trial strategy. In this case, we think at the very least that the state court's contrary assessment was not "unreasonable." * * *

When the junior prosecutor delivered a very matter-of-fact closing that did not dwell on any of the brutal aspects of the crime, counsel was faced with a choice. He could make a closing argument and reprise for the jury, perhaps in greater detail than his opening, the primary mitigating evidence concerning his client's drug dependency and posttraumatic stress from Vietnam. And he could plead again for life for his client and impress upon the jurors the importance of what he believed were less significant facts, such as the Bronze Star decoration or his client's expression of remorse. But he knew that if he took this opportunity, he would give the lead prosecutor, who all agreed was very persuasive, the chance to depict his client as a heartless killer just before the jurors began deliberation. Al-

ternatively, counsel could prevent the lead prosecutor from arguing by waiving his own summation and relying on the jurors' familiarity with the case and his opening plea for life made just a few hours before. Neither option, it seems to us, so clearly outweighs the other that it was objectively unreasonable for the Tennessee Court of Appeals to deem counsel's choice to waive argument a tactical decision about which competent lawyers might disagree.

We cautioned in *Strickland* that a court must indulge a "strong presumption" that counsel's conduct falls within the wide range of reasonable professional assistance because it is all too easy to conclude that a particular act or omission of counsel was unreasonable in the harsh light of hindsight. Given the choices available to respondent's counsel and the reasons we have identified, we cannot say that the state court's application of *Strickland's* attorney-performance standard was objectively unreasonable. The judgment of the Court of Appeals is therefore reversed, and the case is remanded for further proceedings consistent with this opinion.

JUSTICE STEVENS, dissenting.

In my judgment, the Court of Appeals correctly concluded that during the penalty phase of respondent's capital murder trial, his counsel "entirely fail [ed] to subject the prosecution's case to meaningful adversarial testing." United States v. Cronic, 466 U.S. 648, 659 (1984). Counsel's shortcomings included a failure to interview witnesses who could have provided mitigating evidence; a failure to introduce available mitigating evidence; and the failure to make any closing argument or plea for his client's life at the conclusion of the penalty phase. Furthermore, respondent's counsel was, subsequent to trial, diagnosed with a mental illness that rendered him unqualified to practice law, and that apparently led to his suicide. These circumstances "justify a presumption that respondent's conviction was insufficiently reliable to satisfy the Constitution."

* * *

Although the state courts did not have the benefit of evidence concerning Dice's mental health, it appears from Dice's medical records that he suffered from a severe mental impairment. He began treatment for this illness a couple of years after trial, and he committed suicide approximately six months after the postconviction hearing in this case. The symptoms of his disorder included "confused thinking, impaired memory, inability to concentrate for more than a short period of time, paranoia, grandiosity, [and] inappropriate behavior." While these mental health problems may have onset after Cone's trial, a complete reading of the trial transcript and an assessment of Dice's actions at trial suggest this not to be the case.

A theme of fear of possible counterthrusts by his adversaries permeates Dice's loquacious explanations of his tactical decisions. But fear of the opponent cannot justify such absolute dereliction of a lawyer's duty to the client—especially a client facing death. * * * There may be cases in which such timidity is consistent with a "meaningful adversarial testing" of the prosecution's case, but my examina-

tion of the record has produced a firm conviction that this is not such a case.

* * *

* * * [P]resuming prejudice when counsel has entirely failed to function as an adversary makes sense, for three reasons. First, counsel's complete failure to advocate, coupled here with his likely mental illness, undermines *Strickland's* basic assumption: that counsel has "made all significant decisions in the exercise of reasonable professional judgment." Second, a proper *Strickland* inquiry is difficult, if not impossible, to conduct when counsel has completely abdicated his role as advocate, because the abdication results in an incomplete trial record from which a court cannot properly evaluate whether a defendant has or has not suffered prejudice from the attorney's conduct. Finally, counsel's total failure as an adversary renders "the likelihood that the verdict is unreliable" to be "so high that a case-by-case inquiry is unnecessary."

* * * Effective representation provides "the means through which the other rights of the person on trial are secured." For that reason, there is "a denial of Sixth Amendment rights that makes the adversary process itself presumptively unreliable" whenever defense counsel "entirely fails to subject the prosecution's case to meaningful adversary testing." That is exactly what happened in the penalty phase of Gary Cone's trial.

I respectfully dissent.

B. THE RIGHT TO CONFLICT–FREE REPRESENTATION

The right to effective assistance of counsel may be denied because defense counsel has a conflict of interest, and cannot or does not properly protect her client's interests. One situation of potential conflict arises when counsel represents multiple defendants. Codefendants may have divergent interests at all stages of a prosecution. A plea bargain advantageous to one defendant may produce testimony adverse to another defendant. Defendants may have inconsistent defenses, or wish to testify in ways that incriminate codefendants. See, e.g.,

United States v. Hall, 200 F.3d 962 (6th Cir. 2000) (conflict of interest where defense counsel represents two brothers, and one has a public authority defense while the other does not). Evidence inculpating one defendant might exculpate another, forcing counsel to make unsatisfactory choices in response to offered testimony. Separate counsel also might choose differing approaches to closing argument. Conflicts also might arise because defense counsel has a personal interest that could be negatively affected by aggressive representation of the defendant. Another possibility is that the interests of the defendant may be in conflict with the interests of defense counsel's client in another matter, or with the interests of a former client. See Green, "Through a Glass, Darkly": How the Court Sees Motions to Disqualify Criminal Defense Lawyers, 89 Colum.L.Rev. 1202 (1989), for an extensive discussion of conflicts of interest that can arise in the course of representation of criminal defendants.

The rules adopted by the Supreme Court for assessing claims of defense counsel conflict of interest have been helpfully summarized by the court in United States v. Kliti, 156 F.3d 150 (2d Cir.1998):

> A defendant's right to counsel under the Sixth Amendment includes the right to be represented by an attorney who is free from conflicts of interest. When the trial court knows or reasonably should know of the possibility of a conflict of interest, it has a threshold obligation to determine whether the attorney has an actual conflict, a potential conflict, or no conflict. In fulfilling this initial obligation to inquire into the existence of a conflict of interest, the trial court may rely on counsel's representations. If a district court ignores a possible conflict and does not conduct this initial inquiry, reversal of a defendant's conviction is automatic. If, through this inquiry, the court determines that the attorney suffers from an actual or potential conflict of interest, the court has a "disqualification/waiver" obligation. (An attorney has an actual, as opposed to a potential, conflict of interest when during the course of the representation, the defendants' interests diverge with respect to a material fact or legal issue or to a course of action. A potential conflict of interest exists if the interests of the defendant may place the attorney under inconsistent duties at some time in the future.) If the conflict is so severe that no rational defendant would waive it, the court must disqualify the attorney. If it is a lesser conflict, the court must conduct a * * * hearing to determine whether the defendant will knowingly and intelligently waive his right to conflict-free representation. (Before a defendant can knowingly and intelligently waive a conflict, the court must: (1) advise the defendant about potential conflicts; (2) determine whether the defendant understands the risks of those conflicts; and (3) give the defendant time to digest and contemplate the risks, with the aid of independent counsel if desired.) If, as a result of its inquiry, the court concludes that there is no conflict, and therefore no need to disqualify the attorney or to hold a * * * hearing, a defendant's claim that such a conclusion was in error will not establish a violation of the Sixth Amendment right to effective assistance of counsel unless the defendant can demonstrate that the attorney had either (1) a potential conflict of interest that resulted in prejudice to the defendant, or (2) an actual conflict of interest that adversely affected the attorney's performance.

1. The Duty of Court Inquiry

Per Se Reversal: Holloway v. Arkansas

In Holloway v. Arkansas, 435 U.S. 475 (1978), the Court made it clear that joint representation of codefendants by a single attorney is not a per se violation of the right to effective assistance of counsel. The Court noted that a common defense often gives strength against a common attack. Under some circumstances, however, joint representation may create a conflict that can deny a defendant effective assistance of counsel. In *Holloway,* the defense counsel made pretrial motions for appointment of separate counsel for each defendant because of possible conflicts of interest. The trial court denied the motion, and refused defense counsel's renewed request, during the trial, for separate counsel when the three codefendants each wished to testify. Counsel felt that he would be unable to examine or cross-examine any defendant to protect the interests of the others.

Without ever reaching the issue of whether there was an actual conflict of interest, the Supreme Court reversed the defendants' convictions. Reversal was required because the judge, after timely motions, erred in failing to "either appoint separate counsel, or to take adequate steps to ascertain whether the risk was too remote to warrant separate counsel." The Court held that in these circumstances, prejudice to the defendants must be presumed:

> Joint representation of conflicting interests is suspect because of what it tends to prevent the attorney from doing. For example, in this case it may well have precluded defense counsel for [one of the codefendants] from exploring possible plea negotiations and the possibility of an agreement to testify for the prosecution, provided a lesser charge or a favorable sentencing recommendation would be acceptable. Generally speaking a conflict may also prevent an attorney from challenging the admission of evidence prejudicial to one client but perhaps favorable to another, or from arguing at the sentencing hearing the relative involvement and culpability of his clients in order to minimize the culpability of one by emphasizing that of another. Examples can be readily multiplied. The mere physical presence of an attorney does not fulfill the Sixth Amendment guarantee when the advocate's conflicting obligations have effectively sealed his lips on crucial matters.

> Finally, a rule requiring a defendant to show that a conflict of interests—which he and his counsel tried to avoid by timely objections to the joint representation—prejudiced him in some specific fashion would not be susceptible to intelligent, evenhanded application. In the normal case where a harmless error rule is applied, the error occurs at trial and its scope is readily identifiable. Accordingly, the reviewing court can undertake with some confidence its relatively narrow task of assessing the likelihood that the error materially affected the deliberations of the jury. But in a case of joint representation of conflicting interests the evil—it bears repeating—is in what the advocate finds himself compelled to *refrain* from doing, not only at trial but also as to possible pretrial plea negotiations and in the sentencing process. It may be possible in some cases to identify from the record the prejudice resulting from an attorney's failure to undertake certain trial tasks, but even with a record of the sentencing hearing available it would be

difficult to judge intelligently the impact of a conflict on the attorney's representation of a client. And to assess the impact of a conflict of interests on the attorney's options, tactics and decisions in plea negotiations would be virtually impossible. Thus, an inquiry into a claim of harmless error here would require, unlike most cases, unguided speculation.

Question About Holloway

Holloway was decided before *Strickland*. How does *Holloway's* rule of per se reversal square with *Strickland's* holding that a defendant must show that counsel was ineffective and that the ineffectiveness was prejudicial? In Selsor v. Kaiser, 22 F.3d 1029 (10th Cir.1994), the court concluded that the per se reversal rule of *Holloway* was unaffected by the Court's later requirement of a showing of prejudice in *Strickland*. It reasoned as follows:

> *Strickland's* requirement of a showing of actual conflict presupposes that trial courts conduct an appropriate inquiry when the defendant properly raises the issue. *Holloway*, however, addresses the situation where the trial court *fails* to make such inquiry in the face of the defendant's timely objection. As a result, the *Strickland* rule requiring a defendant to demonstrate an actual conflict of interest in order to obtain a presumption of prejudice is inapplicable in a *Holloway*-type case.

Federal Rule 44

Fed.R.Crim.P. 44 attempts to address the problem of joint representation that the Court was concerned with in *Holloway*:[54]

Rule 44. Right to and assignment of counsel

* * *

(c)(2) Court's Responsibilities in Cases of Joint representation.–The court must promptly inquire about the propriety of joint representation and must personally advise each defendant of the right to the effective assistance of counsel, including separate representation. Unless there is good cause to believe that no conflict of interest is likely to arise, the court must take appropriate measure to protect each defendant's right to counsel.

It should be apparent that Rule 44 does not address all the conflict situations that can arise in a criminal case. Rule 44 addresses only questions of multiple representation in the same criminal proceeding. It does not apply if defense counsel has previously represented a person who is now a government witness in the case against the defendant. It does not apply if the lawyer has a personal conflict, such as that he is suspected of being the defendant's coconspirator. It doesn't apply if the lawyer has accepted the case on a contingent fee. It does not apply if the lawyer is representing two related defendants in separate proceedings. Do these examples even present questions of conflict of interest? Presuming that they do, how can they be regulated by the trial court?

---

54. For an argument in favor of a per se rule against joint representation, see Lowenthal, Joint Representation in Criminal Cases: A Critical Appraisal, 64 Va.L.Rev. 939 (1978).

For an argument against such a rule see Margolin & Coliver, Pretrial Disqualification of Criminal Defense Counsel, 20 Am.Crim.L.Rev. 227 (1982).

2. Active Conflict Impairing the Representation

A Different Kind of Prejudice Test: Cuyler v. Sullivan

In Cuyler v. Sullivan, 446 U.S. 335 (1980), the considered the propriety of relief where defense counsel operated under a conflict of interest that was not brought to the attention of the trial judge. Justice Powell's opinion for the Court rejected the petitioner's claim that *Holloway* requires a trial judge to inquire in every case into the propriety of joint representation, even in the absence of the defendant's timely motion. He reasoned as follows:

> Defense counsel have an ethical obligation to avoid conflicting representations and to advise the court promptly when a conflict of interest arises during the course of a trial. Absent special circumstances, therefore, trial courts may assume that multiple representation entails no conflict or that the lawyer and his clients knowingly accept such risk of conflict as may exist.

The opinion reiterated the suggestion in *Holloway* that multiple representation does give rise to a possibility of an improper conflict of interest and that a defendant "must have the opportunity to show that potential conflicts impermissibly imperil his right to a fair trial." But, said the Court, "a defendant who raised no objection at trial must demonstrate that an actual conflict of interest adversely affected his lawyer's performance." Thus, the Court created a limited presumption of prejudice in cases where a defendant fails to make a timely objection to conflicted representation: prejudice is presumed, but only if the defendant demonstrates that counsel "actively represented conflicting interests" and that "an actual conflict of interest adversely affected his lawyer's performance."[55]

The *Cuyler* prejudice standard applies when a defendant fails to bring a potential conflict to the trial court's attention. But it also applies when the defendant notifies the trial court of a potential conflict and the trial court, after a full hearing, finds that there is no actual or potential conflict and orders the multiple representation to continue. See Freund v. Butterworth, 165 F.3d 839 (11th Cir.1999) (en banc). *Holloway* applies when the court refuses to hold a hearing after the defendant brings a potential conflict to its attention.

Application of the Cuyler Standard: Burger v. Kemp

The Supreme Court found no ineffective assistance of counsel under the *Cuyler* standards in Burger v. Kemp, 483 U.S. 776 (1987), a capital case in which Burger and a codefendant were represented by law partners. The defendants were soldiers charged with the murder of a fellow soldier who worked part-time driving a taxi. Each defendant confessed, and Burger took military police to the place where the victim had been drowned. Leaphart, an experienced lawyer, was

---

55. When the Supreme Court remanded *Cuyler*, the court of appeals found that there was an actual conflict of interest that required reversal of Sullivan's conviction. Sullivan v. Cuyler, 723 F.2d 1077 (3d Cir.1983). Counsel, representing both a prospective witness and Sullivan, admitted at an evidentiary hearing that he did not call the witness on Sullivan's behalf because he had to take the witness' interests into account as well as those of Sullivan. See also Sanders v. Ratelle, 21 F.3d 1446 (9th Cir.1994)(actual conflict impairs defense where counsel represents two brothers, and puts forth alibi defense for one brother, where the stronger defense would have been that the other brother was the perpetrator).

appointed to represent Burger, and he insisted that his law partner represent the codefendant. The two defendants were tried separately, and at their trials each defendant sought to avoid the death penalty by emphasizing the other's culpability. Burger was sentenced to death, and attacked his representation in a habeas corpus proceeding on the ground that Leaphart's partnership relationship created a conflict of interest for him. A federal district court denied relief, and the court of appeals affirmed.

Justice Stevens wrote for the Court as it affirmed the denial of relief. He conceded that "[t]here is certainly much substance to petitioner's argument that the appointment of two partners to represent coindictees in their respective trials creates a possible conflict of interest that could prejudice either or both clients," and that "the risk of prejudice is increased when the two lawyers cooperate with one another in planning and conduct of trial strategy." He observed, however, that the Court's decisions do not presume prejudice in all cases, and he concluded that "the overlap of counsel, if any, did not so infect Leaphart's representation as to constitute an active representation of competing interests." Justice Stevens added that "[p]articularly in smaller communities where the supply of qualified lawyers willing to accept the demanding and unrewarding work of representing capital prisoners is extremely limited, the two defendants may actually benefit from the joint efforts of two partners who supplement one another in their preparation." He noted that "we generally presume that the lawyer is fully conscious of the overarching duty of complete loyalty to his or her client," and that trial courts "appropriately and necessarily rely in large measure upon the good faith and good judgment of defense counsel." Justice Stevens also emphasized that each defendant was tried separately, and that separate trials significantly reduce the risk of a conflict of interest. The Court declined to disturb the lower courts' findings that there was no actual conflict of interest.

Justice Stevens added that, even if an actual conflict had been established, counsel's advocacy was unaffected by it. He concluded that there was no evidence that the prosecutor would have been receptive to a plea bargain and no doubt that Leaphart sought to negotiate for a life sentence, there was no reason to believe that Leaphart attempted to protect the other defendant who was not on trial with Burger, and the decision not to offer mitigating evidence and open the door to cross-examination about Burger's background was not unreasonable even if it was erroneous. Although Justice Stevens stated that the evidence at the habeas corpus hearing "does suggest that Leaphart could well have made a more thorough investigation than he did," he added that "counsel's decision not to mount an all-out investigation into petitioner's background in search of mitigating circumstances was supported by reasonable professional judgment." Counsel had interviewed all potential witnesses who were called to his attention, and "there was a reasonable basis for his strategic decision that an explanation of petitioner's history would not have minimized the risk of the death penalty."[56]

56. Justice Blackmun filed a dissenting opinion, in which Justices Brennan and Marshall joined, and in which Justice Powell joined in part. Justice Powell filed a separate dissenting opinion, in which Justice Brennan joined.

A comprehensive discussion of the problems that can result when one lawyer, firm, or public agency represents successive defendants is found in Lowenthal, Successive Representation By Criminal Lawyers, 93 Yale L.J. 1 (1983).

Relationship Between the Holloway Automatic Reversal Rule and the Cuyler Rule Regulating Active Representation of Conflicting Interests: Mickens v. Taylor

In the following case, the Court divided over whether the *Holloway* rule–requiring automatic reversal when the trial court fails to inquire into a multiple representation conflict raised by defense counsel–applies when the trial court becomes aware of a conflict that is *not* raised by defense counsel.

MICKENS v. TAYLOR

Supreme Court of the United States, 2002.
535 U.S. 162.

JUSTICE SCALIA **delivered the opinion of the Court.**

The question presented in this case is what a defendant must show in order to demonstrate a Sixth Amendment violation where the trial court fails to inquire into a potential conflict of interest about which it knew or reasonably should have known.

I

In 1993, a Virginia jury convicted petitioner Mickens of the premeditated murder of Timothy Hall during or following the commission of an attempted forcible sodomy. Finding the murder outrageously and wantonly vile, it sentenced petitioner to death. In June 1998, Mickens filed a petition for writ of habeas corpus, * * * alleging, inter alia, that he was denied effective assistance of counsel because one of his court-appointed attorneys had a conflict of interest at trial. Federal habeas counsel had discovered that petitioner's lead trial attorney, Bryan Saunders, was representing Hall (the victim) on assault and concealed-weapons charges at the time of the murder. Saunders had been appointed to represent Hall, a juvenile, on March 20, 1992, and had met with him once for 15 to 30 minutes some time the following week. Hall's body was discovered on March 30, 1992, and four days later a juvenile court judge dismissed the charges against him, noting on the docket sheet that Hall was de-

ceased. The one-page docket sheet also listed Saunders as Hall's counsel. On April 6, 1992, the same judge appointed Saunders to represent petitioner. Saunders did not disclose to the court, his co-counsel, or petitioner that he had previously represented Hall. Under Virginia law, juvenile case files are confidential and may not generally be disclosed without a court order, but petitioner learned about Saunders' prior representation when a clerk mistakenly produced Hall's file to federal habeas counsel.

The District Court held an evidentiary hearing and denied petitioner's habeas petition.* * * On the merits, the Court of Appeals assumed that the juvenile court judge had neglected a duty to inquire into a potential conflict, but rejected petitioner's argument that this failure either mandated automatic reversal of his conviction or relieved him of the burden of showing that a conflict of interest adversely affected his representation. Relying on Cuyler v. Sullivan, the court held that a defendant must show "both an actual conflict of interest and an adverse effect even if the trial court failed to inquire into a potential conflict about which it reasonably should have known." Concluding that petitioner had not demonstrated adverse effect, it affirmed the District Court's denial of habeas relief. We granted a stay of execution of petitioner's sentence and granted certiorari.

II

Δ must
prove
a reasonable
probability
but-for
counsel
errors
result would
be different

* * * As a general matter, a defendant alleging a Sixth Amendment violation must demonstrate "a reasonable probability that, but for counsel's unprofessional errors, the result of the proceeding would have been different."

There is an exception to this general rule. We have spared the defendant the need of showing probable effect upon the outcome, and have simply presumed such effect, where assistance of counsel has been denied entirely or during a critical stage of the proceeding. When that has occurred, the likelihood that the verdict is unreliable is so high that a case-by-case inquiry is unnecessary. See *Cronic*. But only in "circumstances of that magnitude" do we forgo individual inquiry into whether counsel's inadequate performance undermined the reliability of the verdict.

We have held in several cases that "circumstances of that magnitude" may also arise when the defendant's attorney actively represented conflicting interests. The nub of the question before us is whether the principle established by these cases provides an exception to the general rule of *Strickland* under the circumstances of the present case. To answer that question, we must examine those cases in some detail.

In Holloway v. Arkansas, defense counsel had objected that he could not adequately represent the divergent interests of three codefendants. Without inquiry, the trial court had denied counsel's motions for the appointment of separate counsel and had refused to allow counsel to cross-examine any of the defendants on behalf of the other two. The *Holloway* Court deferred to the judgment of counsel regarding the existence of a disabling conflict, recognizing that a defense attorney is in the best position to determine when a conflict exists, that he has an ethical obligation to advise the court of any problem, and that his declarations to the court are "virtually made under oath." *Holloway* presumed, moreover, that the conflict, "which [the defendant] and his counsel tried to avoid by timely objections to the joint representation," undermined the adversarial process. The presumption was justified because joint representation of conflicting interests is inherently suspect, and because counsel's conflicting obligations to multiple defendants "effectively sea[l] his lips on crucial matters" and make it difficult to measure the precise harm arising from counsel's errors. *Holloway* thus creates an automatic reversal rule only where defense counsel is forced to represent codefendants over his timely objection, unless the trial court has determined that there is no conflict. ("[W]henever a trial court improperly requires joint representation over timely objection reversal is automatic").

In Cuyler v. Sullivan, the respondent was one of three defendants accused of murder who were tried separately, represented by the same counsel. Neither counsel nor anyone else objected to the multiple representation, and counsel's opening argument at Sullivan's trial suggested that the interests of the defendants were aligned. We declined to extend *Holloway's* automatic reversal rule to this situation and held that, absent objection, a defendant must demonstrate that "a conflict of interest actually affected the adequacy of his representation." In addition to describing the defendant's burden of proof, *Sullivan* addressed separately a trial court's duty to inquire into the propriety of a multiple representation, construing *Holloway* to require inquiry only when "the trial court knows or reasonably should know that a particular conflict exists"—which is not to be confused with when the trial court is aware of a vague, unspecified possibility of conflict, such as that which "inheres in almost every instance of multiple representation." In *Sullivan*, no "special circumstances" triggered the trial court's duty to inquire.

* * *

Petitioner's proposed rule of automatic reversal when there existed a conflict that did not affect counsel's performance, but the trial judge failed to make the *Sullivan*-mandated inquiry, makes little policy sense. As discussed, the rule applied when the trial judge is not aware of the conflict (and thus not obligated to inquire) is that prejudice will be presumed only if the conflict has significantly affected counsel's performance—thereby rendering the verdict unreliable, even though *Strickland* prejudice cannot be shown. The trial court's awareness of a potential conflict neither renders it more likely that counsel's performance was significantly affected nor in any other way renders the verdict unreliable. Nor does the trial judge's failure to make the *Sullivan*-mandated inquiry often make it harder for reviewing courts to determine conflict and effect, particularly since those courts may rely on evidence and testimony whose importance only becomes established at the trial.

Nor, finally, is automatic reversal simply an appropriate means of enforcing *Sullivan's* mandate of inquiry. Despite Justice SOUTER's belief that there must be a threat of sanction (to-wit, the risk of conferring a windfall upon the defendant) in order to induce "resolutely obdurate" trial judges to follow the law we do not presume that judges are as careless or as partial as those police officers who need the incentive of the exclusionary rule. And in any event, the *Sullivan* standard, which requires proof of effect upon representation but (once such effect is shown) presumes prejudice, already creates an "incentive" to inquire into a potential conflict. In those cases where the potential conflict is in fact an actual one, only inquiry will enable the judge to avoid all possibility of reversal by either seeking waiver or replacing a conflicted attorney. We doubt that the deterrence of "judicial dereliction" that would be achieved by an automatic reversal rule is significantly greater.

Since this was not a case in which (as in *Holloway*) counsel protested his inability simultaneously to represent multiple defendants; and since the trial court's failure to make the *Sullivan*-mandated inquiry does not reduce the petitioner's burden of proof; it was at least necessary, to void the conviction, for petitioner to establish that the conflict of interest adversely affected his counsel's performance. The Court of Appeals having found no such effect, the denial of habeas relief must be affirmed.

III

Lest today's holding be misconstrued, we note that the only question presented was the effect of a trial court's failure to inquire into a potential conflict upon the *Sullivan* rule that deficient performance of counsel must be shown. The case was presented and argued on the assumption that (absent some exception for failure to inquire) *Sullivan* would be applicable—requiring a showing of defective performance, but not requiring in addition (as *Strickland* does in other ineffectiveness-of-counsel cases), a showing of probable effect upon the outcome of trial. That assumption was not unreasonable in light of the holdings of Courts of Appeals, which have applied *Sullivan* "unblinkingly" to "all kinds of alleged attorney ethical conflicts," Beets v. Scott, 65 F.3d 1258, 1266 (C.A.5 1995) (en banc). They have invoked the *Sullivan* standard not only when (as here) there is a conflict rooted in counsel's obligations to former clients, but even when representation of the defendant somehow implicates counsel's personal or financial interests, including a book deal, United States v. Hearst, 638 F.2d 1190, 1193 (C.A.9 1980), a job with the prosecutor's office, Garcia v. Bunnell, 33 F.3d 1193, 1194–1195, 1198, n. 4 (C.A.9 1994), the teaching of classes to Internal Revenue Service agents, United States v. Michaud, 925 F.2d 37, 40–42 (C.A.1 1991), a romantic "entanglement" with the prosecutor, Summerlin v. Stewart, 267 F.3d 926, 935–941 (C.A.9 2001), or fear of antagonizing the trial judge, United States v. Sayan, 968 F.2d 55, 64–65 (C.A.D.C.1992).

It must be said, however, that the language of *Sullivan* itself does not clearly establish, or indeed even support, such expansive application. "[U]ntil," it said, "a defendant shows that his counsel actively represented conflicting interests, he has not established the constitutional predicate for his claim of ineffective assistance." Both *Sullivan* itself, and *Holloway*, stressed the high probability of prejudice arising from multiple concurrent representation, and the difficulty of proving that prejudice. Not all attorney conflicts present comparable difficulties. Thus, the Federal Rules of Criminal Procedure treat concurrent representation and prior representation differently, requiring a trial court to inquire into the likelihood of conflict whenever jointly charged defendants are represented by a single attorney (Rule 44(c)), but not when counsel previously represented another defendant in a substantially related matter, even where the trial court is aware of the prior representation.

This is not to suggest that one ethical duty is more or less important than another. The purpose of our *Holloway* and *Sullivan* exceptions from the ordinary requirements of *Strickland*, however, is not to enforce the Canons of Legal Ethics, but to apply needed prophylaxis in situations where *Strickland* itself is evidently inadequate to assure vindication of the defendant's Sixth Amendment right to counsel. In resolving this case on the grounds on which it was presented to us, we do not rule upon the need for the *Sullivan* prophylaxis in cases of successive representation. Whether *Sullivan* should be extended to such cases remains, as far as the jurisprudence of this Court is concerned, an open question.

* * *

For the reasons stated, the judgment of the Court of Appeals is

Affirmed.

JUSTICE KENNEDY, **with whom** JUSTICE O'CONNOR **joins, concurring.**

* * *

At petitioner's request, the District Court conducted an evidentiary hearing on the conflict claim and issued a thorough opinion, which found that counsel's brief representation of the victim had no effect whatsoever on the course of petitioner's trial. * * * The District Court found that Saunders did not believe he had any obligation to his former client, Timothy Hall, that would interfere with the litigation. Although the District Court concluded that Saunders probably did learn some matters that were confidential, it found that nothing the attorney learned was relevant to the subsequent murder case. Indeed, even if Saunders had learned relevant information, the District Court found that he labored under the impression he had no continuing duty at all to his deceased client. While Saunders' belief may have been mistaken, it establishes that the prior representation did not influence the choices he made during the course of the trial. This conclusion is a good example of why a case-by-case inquiry is required, rather than simply adopting an automatic rule of reversal.

* * *

The District Court said the same for counsel's alleged dereliction at the sentencing phase. Saunders' failure to attack the character of the 17–year-old victim and his mother had nothing to do with the putative conflict of interest. This strategy was rejected as likely to backfire, not only by Saunders, but also by his co-counsel, who owed no duty to Hall. These facts, and others relied upon by the District Court, provide compelling evidence that a theoretical conflict does not establish a constitutional violation, even when the conflict is one about which the trial judge should have known.

* * *

JUSTICE STEVENS, **dissenting.**

* * *

Mickens had a constitutional right to the services of an attorney devoted solely to his interests. That right was violated. The lawyer who did represent him had a duty to disclose his prior representation of the victim to Mickens and to the trial judge. That duty was violated. When Mickens had no counsel, the trial judge had a duty to "make a thorough inquiry and to take all steps necessary to insure the fullest protection of" his right to counsel. Despite knowledge of the lawyer's prior representation, she violated that duty.

* * *

Setting aside Mickens' conviction is the only remedy that can maintain public confidence in the fairness of the procedures employed in capital cases. Death is a different kind of punishment from any other that may be imposed in this country. * * * A rule that allows the State to foist a murder victim's lawyer onto his accused is not only capricious; it poisons the integrity of our adversary system of justice.

I respectfully dissent.

JUSTICE SOUTER, **dissenting**

* * *

The different burdens on the *Holloway* and *Cuyler* defendants are consistent features of a coherent scheme for dealing with the problem of conflicted defense counsel; a prospective risk of conflict subject to judicial notice is treated differently from a retrospective claim that a completed proceeding was tainted by conflict, although the trial judge had not been derelict in any duty to guard against it. When the problem comes to the trial court's attention before any potential conflict has become actual, the court has a duty to act prospectively to assess the risk and, if the risk is not too remote, to eliminate it or to render it acceptable through a defendant's knowing and intelligent waiver.

* * *

Since the District Court in this case found that the state judge was on notice of a prospective potential conflict, this case calls for nothing more than the application of the prospective notice rule announced and exemplified by *Holloway* * * *. The remedy for the judge's dereliction of duty should be an order vacating the conviction and affording a new trial.

* * *

II

* * *

The irrationality of taxing defendants with a heavier burden for silent lawyers naturally produces an equally irrational scheme of incentives operating on the judges. The judge's duty independent of objection * * * is made concrete by reversal for failure to honor it. The plain fact is that the specter of reversal for failure to enquire into risk is an incentive to trial judges to keep their eyes peeled for lawyers who wittingly or otherwise play loose with loyalty to their clients and the fundamental guarantee of a fair trial. That incentive is needed least when defense counsel points out the risk with a formal objection, and needed most with the lawyer who keeps risk to himself, quite possibly out of self-interest. Under the majority's rule, however, it is precisely in the latter situation that the judge's incentive to take care is at its ebb. With no objection on record, a convicted defendant can get no relief without showing adverse effect, minimizing the possibility of a later reversal and the consequent inducement to judicial care. This makes no sense.

* * *

JUSTICE BREYER, **with whom** JUSTICE GINSBURG **joins, dissenting.**

The Commonwealth of Virginia seeks to put the petitioner, Walter Mickens, Jr., to death after having appointed to represent him as his counsel a lawyer who, at the time of the murder, was representing the very person Mickens was accused of killing. I believe that, in a case such as this one, a categorical approach is warranted and automatic reversal is required.

* * *

The Commonwealth complains that this argument "relies heavily on the immediate visceral impact of learning that a lawyer previously represented the victim of his current client."And that is so. The "visceral impact," however, arises out of the obvious, unusual nature of the conflict. It arises from the fact that the Commonwealth seeks to execute a defendant, having provided that defendant with a lawyer who, only yesterday, represented the victim. In my view, to carry out a death sentence so obtained would invariably diminish faith in the fairness and integrity of our criminal justice system. That is to say, it would diminish that public confidence in the criminal justice system upon which the successful functioning of that system continues to depend.

I therefore dissent.

The Risk of Coercion in Multiple Representation

The facts of United States v. Laura, 667 F.2d 365 (3d Cir.1981), illustrate why many judges are uncomfortable with joint representation. A husband and wife indicted for cocaine importation jointly hired counsel. The district judge ordered them to retain separate lawyers, but their lawyer prepared affidavits stating they desired that he continue to represent them both. Both spouses indicated that they did not wish to consider plea bargaining and saw no other conflict of interest. The district judge permitted the defendants to waive their right to separate counsel and ultimately they pleaded guilty. Subsequently, the wife moved to withdraw her guilty plea and alleged a conflict of interest on counsel's part. She stated that she had only met with the lawyer for 10 minutes outside the presence of her husband before signing her affidavit; that before she pleaded guilty the lawyer had indicated to her that the government would only accept a plea bargain that covered both spouses; and that he told her she probably could be acquitted at trial, but her husband would be worse off without the plea agreement. A majority of the court of appeals rejected her claims. A dissenting judge argued for a one-lawyer, one-client rule and persuasively demonstrated that the lawyer never clearly explained that there was a real conflict of interest between the spouses and that there was no waiver of her right to be advised by a lawyer loyal to her.

The difficult question raised by cases like *Laura* is whether a trial judge can ever be confident that codefendants have a full and complete understanding of the risks of joint representation. Because of the attorney-client privilege, there is a definite limit to how far the court can go in examining the advice the attorney has given to joint clients. This and the privilege against self-incrimination force judges to rely on the lawyer, who may have a personal stake in joint representation, or who may have been retained by one defendant (the husband in *Laura*) and thus may have a special loyalty to him. A judge can warn a defendant in the abstract about the ills associated with sharing a lawyer, but do defendants faced with a criminal prosecution understand? Can the judge trust the lawyer to help the defendants understand?

In cases involving "organized criminal activity," a lawyer may be selected by one defendant for all, or even by someone not charged. Such counsel may be more a screen to protect the organization than an advocate for an individual defendant. Even if a judge orders defendants to obtain separate counsel, it is uncertain whether counsel will be independent and not tied in some way to the organization. In some cases there may be nothing the judge can do to assure that the lawyers hired for defendants truly have their clients' best interest at heart. By ordering separate counsel, however, the judge does all that she can to protect the defendant, even if the protection ultimately is not successful.

One problem with a one-client-per-lawyer rule is that it can increase the financial hardship on criminal defendants who are not indigent. If criminal defendants are in fact voluntarily pursuing a common defense, should they automatically be denied the economies of scale that joint representation can bring?

Conflict With the Attorney's Personal Interests

Conflicts of interest can arise even where counsel is representing a single client. In some cases, counsel's personal interests may be in conflict with the duty of loyalty owed the client. Courts have applied the *Cuyler* standards in such situations–though the Supreme Court in *Mickens, supra* appears to cast doubt on using the *Cuyler* test for conflicts other than those resulting from multiple representation.

United States v. Cancilla, 725 F.2d 867 (2d Cir.1984), is an example of a pre-*Mickens* analysis of a lawyer conflicted by personal interests. It turned out that the defendant's counsel was engaged in criminal conduct with the defendant's coconspirators. The court reasoned that "with the similarity of counsel's criminal activities to Cancilla's schemes and the link between them, it must have occurred to counsel that a vigorous defense might uncover evidence or prompt testimony revealing his own crimes." The court found an actual conflict of interest that adversely affected the representation. See also United States ex rel.

Duncan v. O'Leary, 806 F.2d 1307 (7th Cir.1986) (reversal under *Cuyler* where defense counsel is the prosecutor's campaign manager and the prosecutor is running on a "law and order" ticket).

In Winkler v. Keane, 7 F.3d 304 (2d Cir.1993), the court found an actual conflict of interest where counsel represented a criminal defendant on a contingent fee basis; under the agreement, defense counsel would receive a fee of $25,000, but only if the defendant was found not guilty. The court reasoned that counsel had "a disincentive to seek a plea agreement, or to put forth mitigating defenses that would result in conviction of a lesser included offense." But the court held that the conflict of interest did not adversely affect the defense, because the defendant steadfastly maintained his innocence throughout, rejected all attempts to plea bargain, and vetoed any attempt of defense counsel to argue the partial defense of intoxication. Thus, there was no reason to believe that defense counsel's representation would have been any different "if a proper fee arrangement had been utilized."[57]

Sex

Are the *Cuyler* standards (or at least the ineffectiveness standards after *Mickens*) violated if the attorney is having a sexual affair with the defendant's spouse? This question arose in Hernandez v. State, 750 So.2d 50 (Fla.App.1999). Miami City Commissioner Hernandez retained Quinon to defend him against charges of election fraud. Hernandez was acquitted of the most serious charges, but was found guilty for being an accessory and sentenced to 364 days in jail. After he was sentenced, the Miami Herald broke the story that Hernandez's wife confessed to having had a sexual relationship with Quinon that began just before jury selection and continued throughout Hernandez's trial. Hernandez challenged his conviction, claiming that Quinon was operating under a conflict of interest. The court did not dispute that Quinon was operating under a conflict. But it noted that, under the *Cuyler* standards, Hernandez had to show that the conflict had an adverse effect upon Quinon's representation. This Hernandez could not do. The court noted that everything in the record indicated that Quinon did a good job; after all, Hernandez was acquitted on the most serious charges.

Dissenting Judge Huffman argued that Hernandez should not have to show an adverse effect on the attorney's performance in these circumstances; he would have presumed prejudice. He noted that even the most diligent lawyer would "hold back a bit at trial" or alter strategy in subtle ways to assure that the client would be out of the way while the affair continued. He concluded as follows:

> Requiring proof by a defendant that his attorney not only cuckolded him, but reduced his trial performance, leaves that defendant with an impossible task, and thus no remedy.

Should Quinon be disciplined for his conduct? If so, why isn't that enough to warrant relief for Hernandez? How would the *Cuyler* standards apply, if at all, if

---

57. Professor Karlan, in Contingent Fees and Criminal Cases, 93 Colum.L.Rev. 595 (1993), challenges the standard explanation for the ban against contingent fees and argues that such arrangements might be appropriate in certain white-collar cases or in regimes where the bonus comes from the government.

defense counsel is having a sexual affair with the *defendant*, rather than with the defendant's spouse?

3. Waiver of the Right to Conflict–Free Counsel

The premise of Federal Rule 44 is that if the defendant is properly warned of the possible conflicts that could arise, then he can knowingly and voluntarily waive the right to conflict-free representation. Generally speaking, a knowing and voluntary waiver of conflict-free representation can be found if the trial court informs the defendant about the ways in which conflicted counsel can impair the representation—particularly that one client could shift blame to another, or testify against another, and defense counsel would be impaired in representing the multiple interests. The trial court must assure itself that the defendant understands the consequences, and has made a rational decision to proceed with counsel despite the conflict. Examples of typical colloquies can be found in United States v. Fan, 36 F.3d 240 (2d Cir.1994) and United States v. Flores, 5 F.3d 1070 (7th Cir.1993). What would you want to tell a defendant about the right to conflict-free counsel?

Non-Waivable Conflicts?

The courts in *Fan* and *Flores* held, not surprisingly, that where warnings are adequate and the defendant knowingly and voluntarily waived the right to conflict-free counsel, then the defendant could not challenge the verdict on appeal. Some courts have held, however, that certain conflicts are so egregious as to be non-waivable—even if the defendant is warned and makes a knowing and voluntary waiver. An example is United States v. Fulton, 5 F.3d 605 (2d Cir.1993), a drug prosecution. In the middle of Fulton's trial, the government informed the court in an ex parte conference that the government witness then on the stand had previously stated that he once imported heroin for Fulton's defense counsel. The trial judge informed defense counsel and the defendant of this development, and explained to Fulton that the witness' accusation "makes your attorney personally involved in this trial" and that defense counsel "may be to some degree distracted from doing his best job representing you." Fulton was also warned that counsel would not be able to cross-examine the witness on these matters, because to do so would result in disclosure of the confidences of defense counsel's former client. Fulton nonetheless agreed to continue with counsel, and he was convicted. The court reversed Fulton's conviction, finding the conflict so pervasive as to be unwaivable:

> Where a government witness implicates defense counsel in a related crime, the resultant conflict so permeates the defense that no meaningful waiver can be obtained. In such a case, we must assume that counsel's fear of, and desire to avoid, criminal charges, or even the reputational damage from an unfounded but ostensibly plausible accusation, will affect virtually every aspect of his or her representation of the defendant. At the pre-trial stage, counsel's ability to advise the defendant as to whether he or she should seek to cooperate with the government is impaired. Cooperation almost always entails a promise to answer truthfully all questions put by the government. Because the government knows of the allegations against defense counsel, questions concerning those allegations seem inevitable, and counsel may have good reason to be apprehensive about what the client

knows or has heard from co-conspirators. In such circumstances, counsel is hardly an appropriate negotiator of a plea and cooperation agreement. Counsel's judgments about potential defense strategies may be affected by the fear that evidence concerning counsel's involvement might come out. The cross-examination of the witness who implicated counsel will be affected (because counsel is also in effect a witness) but so too may the cross-examination of other witnesses who could provide corroborating evidence. Advice as to whether the defendant should take the stand may be affected by the fear or knowledge that the defendant knows of counsel's criminal activities. Finally, the government's precise knowledge of the conflict may affect its conduct of the trial.

What if the witness in *Fulton* was lying about defense counsel's drug activity? The court found that the government was in no position to argue this, since it had presented the witness at trial and argued in favor of the witness' credibility to the jury. However, the *Fulton* court was concerned that a non-waivable conflict could be manufactured in future cases by unreliable witnesses (perhaps called by the defendant?) who would implicate the defense counsel in criminal activity. It therefore held that "if a district court holds a full hearing and can definitively rule out the possibility that the allegations are true, a meaningful waiver is possible since the falsely accused attorney is conflicted only to the extent that she cannot cross-examine the witness regarding the false allegations." In such a situation, the defendant may give a valid waiver of conflict-free counsel.

C. INEFFECTIVE ASSISTANCE WITHOUT FAULT ON THE PART OF DEFENSE COUNSEL

Impairing Defense Strategy

Governmental or prosecutorial action also can deprive a defendant of effective assistance of counsel. For example in Brooks v. Tennessee, 406 U.S. 605 (1972), a Tennessee rule required the defendant to testify first or not at all. The Court held that the rule violated the defendant's right to remain silent, and deprived him of the aid of counsel in planning his defense, particularly in the decision to testify or remain silent.

> By requiring the accused and his lawyer to make that choice without an opportunity to evaluate the actual worth of their evidence, the state restricts the defense—particularly counsel—in the planning of its case. Furthermore, the penalty for not testifying first is to keep the defendant off the stand entirely, even though as a matter of professional judgment his lawyer might want to call him later in the trial. The accused is thereby deprived of the "guiding hand of counsel" in the timing of this critical element of his defense.

The Court reversed the conviction and ordered a new trial. Similarly, in Herring v. New York, 422 U.S. 853 (1975), a New York statute giving a judge in a nonjury criminal trial the power to deny absolutely the opportunity for defense counsel to make a closing argument was held to be unconstitutional. New York denied Herring the effective assistance of counsel by permitting the judge to dispense with his counsel's summation.[58]

Limiting Consultation Between Defendant and Counsel

In Geders v. United States, 425 U.S. 80 (1976), the defendant was prohibited from consulting with counsel during a 17–hour overnight recess between the direct and cross-examination of the defendant. Although recognizing the problem of "coached" witnesses, the Court decided that this method of preventing coaching violated the defendant's right to the effective assistance of counsel.

Justice Stevens wrote for a majority in Perry v. Leeke, 488 U.S. 272 (1989), as it distinguished *Geders* and held that a state trial judge did not commit constitutional error in declaring a 15 minute recess after the defendant's direct testimony in his murder trial and in ordering that the defendant talk to no one, including his lawyer, during the recess. Although Justice Stevens recognized that "[t]here is merit in petitioner's argument that a showing of prejudice is not an essential component of a violation of the rule announced in *Geders*," he reasoned that "when a defendant becomes a witness, he has no constitutional right to consult with his lawyer while he is testifying." Justice Stevens recognized that nondiscussion orders can prevent coaching of witnesses that might interfere with the search for truth. He described *Geders* as a case involving an overnight recess in which matters that go beyond a defendant's own testimony would be discussed with counsel and stated that "in a short recess in which it is appropriate to presume that nothing but the testimony will be discussed, the testifying defendant does not have a constitutional right to advice."

Justice Marshall, joined by Justices Brennan and Blackmun, dissented. He argued that a defendant cannot be prevented from consulting with counsel during a recess and that the defendant was not arguing for a right to interrupt cross-examination in order to consult with his lawyer.

Interference With the Attorney–Client Relationship

State intrusion into attorney-client consultations can be a problem outside the trial context as well. The Supreme Court addressed one such problem in Weatherford v. Bursey, 429 U.S. 545 (1977). The defendant claimed a Sixth Amendment violation when an undercover agent and informant attended two meetings between the defendant and counsel; the undercover informant was ostensibly a codefendant. The Court concluded that despite this intrusion, the defendant received effective assistance of counsel. Those meetings resulted in no tainted evidence, and no communication of defense strategy to the government. Thus, there was indication of prejudice that would require reversal. Justices Marshall and Brennan dissented, because they believed that when the prosecution acquires information about the defense, the fairness and integrity of the adversary system are impaired. Concerned with the potential chilling effect on freedom of communication between lawyer and client, they maintained that the essence of the Sixth Amendment right to counsel is the privacy of communications with counsel.

58. See also United States v. Bohn, 890 F.2d 1079 (9th Cir.1989)(exclusion of counsel from hearing to assess validity of defendant's Fifth Amendment claim required per se reversal; such a hearing is a critical stage of the proceedings).

In United States v. Morrison, 449 U.S. 361 (1981), the Supreme Court unanimously concluded that "absent demonstrable prejudice, or substantial threat thereof, dismissal of the indictment is plainly inappropriate, even though the [Sixth Amendment] violation may have been deliberate," and even though the conduct of drug investigators in meeting with a defendant, after she was indicted and had counsel, outside of counsel's presence and suggesting that her lawyer might not be adequate and that she should cooperate with the government was "egregious." See also United States v. Noriega, 752 F.Supp. 1045 (S.D.Fla.1990), which held that despite outrageous, unconscionable conduct of law enforcement officers in eavesdropping on two conversations between the defendant and his counsel, dismissal of the prosecution was not warranted where there was no showing that trial strategy was revealed or that the defendant's ability to work in confidence with his attorney was impaired.

D. THE PERJURY PROBLEM

When a defense attorney believes that her client is about to commit perjury, she faces a particularly difficult dilemma.

Applying Strickland to Client Perjury: Nix v. Whiteside

In a highly publicized case, Nix v. Whiteside, 475 U.S. 157 (1986), the defendant pleaded self-defense, but in his initial statement to defense counsel, he did not mention that the victim had a gun. In a later interview, the defendant stated that he now remembered that he saw the victim with "something metallic" in his hand. When challenged about the discrepancy by defense counsel, the defendant referred to a case in which an acquaintance was acquitted after testifying that his victim wielded a gun. In apparent comparison with that case, the defendant concluded: "If I don't say I saw a gun, I'm dead." The defense counsel told the client that any statement about a gun would be perjury; that if the defendant testified about a gun at trial, the lawyer would advise the court of the perjury, would probably be permitted to impeach the testimony, and would seek to withdraw. The client succumbed to the threats. He testified at trial that he believed the victim was reaching for a gun, but he had not seen one. The client challenged his second degree murder conviction on an ineffective assistance of counsel ground. Although the state courts commended the lawyer's integrity, a federal court of appeals granted habeas corpus relief.

The Supreme Court unanimously reversed in an opinion by Chief Justice Burger. He reasoned that no defendant has a right to commit perjury, so that no defendant has a right to rely upon counsel to assist in the development of false testimony. The Court noted that under *Strickland,* the defendant must prove prejudice, and Whiteside "has no valid claim that confidence in the result of his trial has been diminished by his desisting from the contemplated perjury." Even if the jury would have been persuaded by the perjury, the Court concluded that under *Strickland,* "a defendant has no entitlement to the luck of a lawless decisionmaker." The Chief Justice also rejected Whiteside's argument that the *Cuyler* limited presumption of prejudice should apply. Whatever conflict existed between Whiteside and his counsel "was imposed on the attorney by the client's proposal to commit the crime of fabricating testimony." The Chief Justice reasoned that "if a 'conflict' between a client's proposal and counsel's ethical obligation gives rise to a presumption that counsel's assistance was prejudicially ineffective, every guilty criminal's conviction would be suspect if the defendant had sought to obtain an acquittal by illegal means."

Although this was enough to decide the case, the Chief Justice went further and held that Whiteside's counsel had not been ineffective in discouraging his client from committing perjury. He concluded that for the purposes of this case, effectiveness could be determined by reference to the prevailing rules of professional responsibility governing the conduct of lawyers. He noted that Disciplinary Rule 7–102(A)(4) of the ABA Code of Professional Responsibility (in effect in Iowa and in a minority of states) provides that a lawyer shall not "knowingly use perjured testimony or false evidence;" and that Rule 3.3 of the more recent Model Rules of Professional Conduct (in effect in a majority of states) requires disclosure of client perjury to the tribunal as a last resort. The Chief Justice found that the prevailing ethical standards "confirm that the legal profession has accepted that an attorney's ethical duty to advance the interests of his client is limited by an equally solemn duty to comply with the law and standards of professional conduct." He concluded as follows:

> [U]nder no circumstances may a lawyer either advocate or passively tolerate a client's giving false testimony. * * * The rule adopted by the Court of Appeals, which seemingly would require an attorney to remain silent while his client committed perjury, is wholly incompatible with the established standards of ethical conduct and the laws of Iowa and contrary to professional standards promulgated by that State. The position advanced by the [Government], on the contrary, is wholly consistent with the Iowa standards of professional conduct and law, with the overwhelming majority of courts, and with codes of professional ethics. Since there has been no breach of any recognized professional duty, it follows that there can be no deprivation of the right to assistance of counsel under the *Strickland* standard.

Justice Brennan wrote an opinion concurring in the judgment. He agreed with the majority's analysis on the prejudice prong of *Strickland*. As to the performance prong, however, he argued that the Court "has no constitutional authority to establish rules of ethical conduct for lawyers practicing in the state courts," and that "the Court's essay regarding what constitutes the correct response to a criminal client's suggestion that he will perjure himself is pure discourse without force of law." Justice Blackmun wrote an opinion concurring in the judgment, joined by Justices Brennan, Marshall, and Stevens. He agreed that Whiteside had not shown prejudice from his lawyer's conduct, and saw no need to "grade counsel's performance." He argued, however, that the client perjury problem could not be solved by a simple reference to lawyers' ethics codes:

> Whether an attorney's response to what he sees as a client's command to commit perjury violates a defendant's Sixth Amendment rights may depend on many factors: how certain the attorney is that the proposed testimony is false, the stage of the proceedings at which the attorney discovers the plan, or the ways in which the attorney may be able to dissuade his client, to name just three. The complex interaction of factors, which is likely to vary from case to case, makes inappropriate a blanket rule that defense attorneys must reveal, or threaten to reveal, a client's anticipated perjury to the court. Except in the rarest of cases, attorneys who

adopt the role of the judge or jury to determine the facts, pose a danger of depriving their clients of the zealous and loyal advocacy required by the Sixth Amendment.

Justice Stevens also wrote an opinion concurring in the judgment, emphasizing that it is often difficult to determine whether the client's proposed testimony is perjurious.

> From the perspective of an appellate judge, after a case has been tried and the evidence has been sifted by another judge, a particular fact may be as clear and certain as a piece of crystal or a small diamond. A trial lawyer, however, must often deal with mixtures of sand and clay. Even a pebble that seems clear enough at first glance may take on a different hue in a handful of gravel. * * *

> A lawyer's certainty that a change in his client's recollection is a harbinger of intended perjury—as well as judicial review of such apparent certainty—should be tempered by the realization that, after reflection, the most honest witness may recall (or sincerely believe he recalls) details that he previously overlooked.

Whiteside Was Too Easy

Even if the propriety of counsel's performance is considered, *Whiteside* is an easy case. Most lawyers would think it entirely appropriate to try to discourage the client from a planned course of perjury. Indeed, discouragement of perjury is effective advocacy, because the jury may disbelieve the lie, the prosecutor may easily tear it apart on cross-examination, and obviously the client may subject himself to a perjury charge. Moreover, if the trial judge believes that a defendant lied on the stand, this will be taken into account at sentencing. See United States v. Dunnigan, 507 U.S. 87 (1993)(upholding a Sentencing Guideline requiring an enhancement of sentence when the trial judge finds by a preponderance of the evidence that the defendant has committed perjury). So it certainly makes sense to do everything reasonable to discourage a client from committing perjury on the witness stand.

Harder Questions

The difficult questions, not presented by *Whiteside,* are three. First, what if the client refuses to be dissuaded from a course of perjury and demands to testify? Second, what if the client appears to have been dissuaded from testifying falsely, but then commits perjury after taking the stand? Third, what if the lawyer discovers after the testimony that the client has perjured himself? See Freedman, Client Confidences and Client Perjury: Some Unanswered Questions, 136 U.Pa.L.Rev. 1939 (1988)(arguing that all of these problems should be left to the adversary system and to cross-examination by the prosecutor). After *Whiteside,* the A.B.A. Standing Committee on Ethics issued Formal Opinion 87–353 (1987), to suggest an appropriate response to these problems under the Code of Professional Responsibility and the Model Rules of Professional Conduct. Portions of that opinion follow.[59]

---

59. In the opinion, the reference to "DR" means one of the Disciplinary Rules of the Code of Professional Responsibility, adopted by the A.B.A. in 1969 and in effect in a minority of states. The reference to "Rule" means one of the Model Rules of Professional Conduct, adopted by the A.B.A. in 1983 and in effect in most of the states. See generally Gillers, Regulation of Lawyers (6th ed. 2002).

Formal Opinion 87–353

April 20, 1987

Lawyer's Responsibility with Relation to Client Perjury

Model Rule 3.3(a) and (b) represent a major policy change with regard to the lawyer's duty * * * when the client testifies falsely. It is now mandatory, under these Model Rule provisions, for a lawyer, who knows the client has committed perjury, to disclose this knowledge to the tribunal if the lawyer cannot persuade the client to rectify the perjury.

The relevant provisions of Rule 3.3(a) are: "(a) A lawyer shall not knowingly: ... (2) fail to disclose a material fact to a tribunal when disclosure is necessary to avoid assisting a criminal or fraudulent act by the client; ... (4) offer evidence that the lawyer knows to be false. If a lawyer has offered material evidence and comes to know of its falsity, the lawyer shall take reasonable remedial measures."

* * *

[Contrary to] the exception provided in DR 7–102(B)(1) of the Model Code [preventing disclosure of client perjury if the information is a confidence or a secret] the disclosure requirement of Model Rule 3.3(a)(2) and (4) is not excused because of client confidences. Rule 3.3(b) provides in pertinent part: "The duties stated in paragraph (a) ... apply even if compliance requires disclosure of information otherwise protected by Rule 1.6." Thus, the lawyer's responsibility to disclose client perjury to the tribunal under Rule 3.3(a)(2) and (4) supersedes the lawyer's responsibility to the client under [the confidentiality requirements of] Rule 1.6.

* * *

Without doubt, the vitality of the adversary system, certainly in criminal cases, depends upon the ability of the lawyer to give loyal and zealous service to the client. And this, in turn, requires that the lawyer have the complete confidence of the client and be able to assure the client that the confidence will be protected and honored. However, the ethical rules of the bar which have supported these basic requirements of the adversary system have emphasized from the time they were first reduced to written form that the lawyer's duties to the client in this regard must be performed within the bounds of law.

For example, these ethical rules clearly recognize that a lawyer representing a client who admits guilt in fact, but wants to plead not guilty and put the state to its proof, may assist the client in entering such a plea and vigorously challenge the state's case at trial through cross-examination, legal motions and argument to the jury. However, neither the adversary system nor the ethical rules permit the lawyer to participate in the corruption of the judicial process by assisting the client in the introduction of evidence the lawyer knows is false. * * *

On the contrary, the lawyer, as an officer of the court, has a duty to prevent the perjury, and if the perjury has already been committed, to prevent its playing any part in the judgment of the court. This duty the lawyer owes the court is not inconsistent with any duty owed to the client. More particularly, it is not inconsistent with the lawyer's duty to preserve the client's confidences. For that duty is based on the lawyer's need for information from the client to obtain for the client all that the law and lawful process provide. Implicit in the promise of confidentiality is its nonapplicability where the client seeks the unlawful end of corrupting the judicial process by false evidence.

It must be emphasized that this opinion does not change the professional relationship the lawyer has with the client and require the lawyer now to judge, rather than represent, the client. The lawyer's obligation to disclose client perjury to the tribunal, discussed in this opinion, is strictly limited by Rule 3.3 to the situation where the lawyer *knows* that the client has committed perjury, ordinarily based on admissions the client has made to the lawyer. (The Committee notes that some trial lawyers report that they have avoided the ethical dilemma posed by Rule 3.3 because they follow a practice of not questioning the client about the facts in the case and, therefore, never "know" that a client has given false testimony. Lawyers who engage in such practice may be violating their duties under Rule 3.3 and their obligation to provide competent representation under Rule 1.1.) * * *.

So far, this opinion has discussed the duty of the lawyer when the lawyer learns that the client has committed perjury. The lawyer is presented with a different dilemma when, prior to trial, the client states an intention to commit perjury at trial. * * *

* * * Ordinarily, after warning the client of the consequences of the client's perjury, including the lawyer's duty to disclose it to the court, the lawyer can reasonably believe that the client will be persuaded not to testify falsely at trial. That is exactly what happened in Nix v. Whiteside. Under these circumstances, the lawyer may permit the client to testify and may examine the client in the normal manner. If the client does in fact testify falsely, the lawyer's obligation to make disclosure to the court is covered by Rule 3.3(a)(2) and (4).

In the unusual case, where the lawyer does know, on the basis of the client's clearly stated intention, that the client will testify falsely at trial, and the lawyer is unable to effectively withdraw from the representation, the lawyer cannot examine the client in the usual manner. Under these circumstances, when the client has not yet committed perjury, the Committee believes that the lawyer's conduct should be guided in a way that is consistent, as much as possible, with the confidentiality protections provided in Rule 1.6, and yet not violative of Rule 3.3. This may be accomplished by the lawyer's refraining from calling the client as a witness when the lawyer knows that the only testimony the client would offer is false; or, where there is some testimony, other than the false testimony, the client can offer in the client's defense, by the lawyer's examining the client on only those matters and not on the subject matter which would produce the false testimony. Such conduct on the part of the lawyer would serve as a way for the lawyer to avoid assisting the fraudulent or criminal act of the client without having to disclose the client's confidences to the court. However, if the lawyer does not offer the client's testimony, and, on inquiry by the court into whether the client has been fully advised as to the client's right to testify, the client states a desire to testify, but is being prevented by the lawyer from testifying, the lawyer may have no other choice than to disclose to the court the client's intention to testify falsely.

This approach must be distinguished from the solution offered in the initially ABA-approved Defense Function Standard 7.7 (1971). This proposal, no longer applicable, permitted a lawyer, who could not dissuade the client from committing perjury and who could not withdraw, to call the client solely to give the client's own statement, without being questioned by the lawyer and without the lawyer's arguing to the jury any false testimony presented by the client.

The Committee believes that under Model Rule 3.3(a)(2) and the recent Supreme Court decision of Nix v. Whiteside, the lawyer can no longer rely on the narrative approach to insulate the lawyer from a charge of assisting the client's perjury. Despite differences on other issues in Nix v. Whiteside, the Justices were unanimous in concluding that a criminal defendant does not have the constitutional right to testify falsely. * * *

———

Can you think of anything more destructive to the attorney-client relationship than the lawyer ratting out her client? Can the perjury problem instead be handled through cross-examination? When a District Attorney was asked what the defense lawyer should do when a client intends to commit perjury, he responded "Do me a favor. Let him try it." (Quoted in Freedman, Client Confidences and Client Perjury: Some Unanswered Questions, 136 U.Pa.L.Rev. 1939 (1988)). Would most prosecutors respond the same way? Is the existence of a lawyer-client relationship a sufficient reason to permit defense lawyers but not prosecutors to offer perjured testimony? See Saltzburg, Lawyers, Clients, and the Adversary System, 37 Mercer L.Rev. 674 (1986).

One problem with the ABA solution is that criminal defendants have a constitutional right to testify. They don't of course have a constitutional right to commit perjury; but perjury occurs only when the defendant actually testifies. A common scenario proceeds like this: defense counsel believes that the client is adamant about committing perjury, even after counsel gives the defendant *Whiteside* warnings. According to the ABA, counsel must now inform the trial judge that his client intends to commit perjury. The trial judge cannot at this point, on defense counsel's word alone, prevent the defendant from testifying. To do so would risk almost certain reversal for violating the defendant's constitutional right to testify. So the trial judge would have to hold some kind of hearing. At that hearing, the defendant will not admit that he is going to commit perjury if he is permitted to testify. The trial judge will be most reluctant to get into a quagmire of confidential communications between client and counsel in determining who is right about whether perjury is planned. It is very likely in most cases that a trial judge will be uncertain as to whether the defendant is going to commit perjury. The judge will not risk violating the constitutional right to testify by keeping the defendant off the stand. So in the vast majority of cases, defense counsel will have accomplished nothing by informing the tribunal of the client's planned perjury—the defendant will be permitted to testify anyway. The only thing accomplished is the destruction of the attorney-client relationship.

Compare the solutions proposed by the A.B.A. Ethics Committee with that proposed by Professor Monroe Freedman, who addressed the perjury problem in Lawyer's Ethics in an Adversary System 31–37 (1985).

In my opinion, the attorney's obligation in such a situation would be to advise the client that the proposed testimony is unlawful, but to proceed in the normal fashion in presenting the testimony and arguing the case to the jury if the client makes the decision to go forward. Any other course would be a betrayal of the assurances of confidentiality given by the attorney in order to induce the client to reveal everything, however damaging it might appear.[60]

Professor Friedman argues that none of the other alternatives are workable:

> The most obvious way to avoid the ethical difficulty is for the lawyer to withdraw from the case, at least if there is sufficient time before trial for the client to retain another attorney. The client will then go to the nearest law office, realizing that the obligation of confidentiality is not what it has been represented to be, and withhold incriminating information or the fact of guilt from the new attorney. In terms of professional ethics, the practice of withdrawing from a case under such circumstances is difficult to defend, since the identical perjured testimony will ultimately be presented. Moreover, the new attorney will be ignorant of the perjury and therefore will be in no position to attempt to discourage the client from presenting it. Only the original attorney, who knows the truth, has that opportunity, but loses it in the very act of evading the ethical problem.

* * *

> [Freedman describes the "Free Narrative" proposal, in which defense counsel lets the defendant tell his story on the stand, without asking questions and without referring to the statement in closing argument.]

> There are at least two critical flaws in that proposal. The first is purely practical: The prosecutor might well object to testimony from the defendant in narrative form rather than in the conventional manner, because it would give the prosecutor no opportunity to object to inadmissible evidence prior to the jury's hearing it. * * *

> More importantly, experienced trial attorneys have often noted that jurors assume that the defendant's lawyer knows the truth about the case, and that the jury will frequently judge the defendant by drawing inferences from the attorney's conduct in the case. There is, of course, only one inference that can be drawn if the defendant's own attorney turns his or her back on the defendant at the most critical point in the trial, and then, in closing argument, sums up the case with no reference to the fact that the defendant has given exculpatory testimony.

Despite the rejection of the "free narrative" solution by the A.B.A., the Court in *Whiteside,* and Professor Freedman, the narrative "continues to be a commonly accepted method of dealing with client perjury." Shockley v. State, 565 A.2d 1373 (Del.1989)(holding that use of free narrative was ethically permissible and did not constitute ineffective assistance of counsel). See also Florida Bar v. Rubin, 549 So.2d 1000 (Fla.1989)(lawyer jailed for thirty days for

---

60. The National Association of Criminal Defense Lawyers has issued an ethics opinion in support of Professor Freedman's view. See The Champion, March, 1993, p. 23:

In the relatively small number of cases in which the client who has contemplated perjury rejects the lawyer's advice and decides to proceed to trial, to take the stand, and to give false testimony, the lawyer should go forward at trial in the ordinary way. That is,

the lawyer should examine the client in the normal professional manner and should argue the client's testimony to the jury in summation to the extent that sound tactics justify doing so.

The NACDL also emphasizes that the "perjury dilemma" does not arise unless the lawyer *knows* that the client committed perjury, and concludes that counsel in *Whiteside* did not have actual knowledge.

refusing to defend client who intended to commit perjury; proper solution would have been to use a free narrative). Can the free narrative be prohibited in practice? Suppose a defendant volunteers perjured testimony that goes beyond the scope of defense counsel's questions. Would it constitute ineffective assistance for defense counsel to move to strike the volunteered testimony as unresponsive? Should defense counsel be required to inform the judge that the volunteered testimony is perjurious? Does anyone tell the jury?[61]

E.   INEFFECTIVENESS AND SYSTEMS OF APPOINTED COUNSEL

Inadequate Funding

The overall quality and effectiveness of court-appointed attorneys may be limited by low compensation for services. For example, in South Carolina, a statute provided the following payment for appointed counsel in capital cases: $15/hour for in-court work, $10 for out-of-court time, with a $5,000 cap for trial work and a $2,500 cap for investigative and expert services. The South Carolina Supreme Court, in Bailey v. State, 309 S.C. 455, 424 S.E.2d 503 (1992), found that these statutory limits imposed a "gross and fundamental unfairness" on defense attorneys, and "do not provide compensation adequate to ensure effective assistance of counsel." The court remanded to determine what compensation would be reasonable. See also Smith v. New Hampshire, 118 N.H. 764, 394 A.2d 834 (1978) (invalidating similar statutory limits).

Cases like *Bailey* raise the question whether there are systemic flaws in the process of appointing counsel for indigents. Public defenders often have enormous caseloads and, like prosecutors, may have to choose to dispose of cases in ways that maximize the overall output of the agency, rather than the welfare of any one client. Private appointed attorneys are often so poorly compensated that talented counsel are discouraged from taking on a representation; and even the best counsel become so financially strapped that it becomes impossible to put on a defense. The O.J. Simpson case presented an excellent example of the value of a well-funded defense; but it also illustrated the disparity between wealthy defendants and indigent ones. At a press conference after the verdict, Simpson's attorneys freely admitted that money buys justice, and that most people can't afford justice in America. Who could argue?

Overwork

Is an overworked public defender ineffective per se? In State v. Peart, 621 So.2d 780 (La.1993), a public defender in Orleans parish launched a broad attack on Louisiana's system for providing defense services to indigents. The court found that the defender was handling 70 active felony cases, and that in a period of eight months, he represented 418 defendants. His clients were incarcerated an average of 70 days before he even saw them. The defender office in Orleans parish had funds to hire only three investigators, who were responsible for rendering assistance in over 7,000 cases. There were no funds for expert witnesses, and the library was not up to date. The court concluded that "not even a lawyer with an **S** on his chest could effectively handle this docket." The

---

61. For more on the "perjury dilemma," see Rutherglen, Dilemmas and Disclosures: A   Comment on Client Perjury, 19 Am.J.Crim.L. 219 (1992).

court found that indigent defendants in the parish are "provided with counsel who are so overburdened as to be effectively unqualified" and "are generally not provided with the effective assistance of counsel that the constitution requires."

The court's remedy in *Peart*, however, was somewhat ironic. The court deferred to the legislature to come up with a plan for better funding of public defender services, and, in the interim, imposed a presumption of ineffective representation as to defendants represented by the public defender's office in Orleans parish. The court reasoned that questions of counsel's adequacy must be answered on an individual basis; therefore, each indigent in the parish would be entitled to a hearing, at which the presumption of ineffectiveness would apply. Doesn't this ruling simply force the overburdened public defender to prepare for another set of hearings? What does the public defender argue at these hearings—that he is ineffective, again and again and again?[62]

Systematic Inadequacy in Capital Cases

Justice Blackmun, in his last term on the Court, took the occasion of the Court's denial of certiorari in a death penalty case to express concern about the system of appointed counsel in capital cases. Dissenting from denial of certiorari in McFarland v. Scott, 512 U.S. 1256 (1994), Justice Blackmun declared as follows:

> Without question, "the principal failings of the capital punishment review process today are the inadequacy and inadequate compensation of counsel at trial and the unavailability of counsel in state post-conviction proceedings." Robbins, Toward a More Just and Effective System of Review in State Death Penalty Cases, Report of the American Bar Association's Recommendations Concerning Death Penalty Habeas Corpus, 40 Am. U.L.Rev. 1, 16 (1990). The unique, bifurcated nature of capital trials and the special investigation into a defendant's personal history and background that may be required, the complexity and fluidity of the law, and the high, emotional stakes involved all make capital cases more costly and difficult to litigate than ordinary criminal trials. Yet, the attorneys assigned to represent indigent capital defendants at times are less qualified than those appointed in ordinary criminal cases. See Green, Lethal Fiction: The Meaning of "Counsel" in the Sixth Amendment, 78 Iowa L.Rev. 433, 434 (1993); Coyle, et al., Fatal Defense, 12 Nat'l L.J. 30, 44 (June 11, 1990)(Capital-defense attorneys in eight States were disbarred, suspended, or disciplined at rates 3 to 46 times higher than the general attorney-discipline rates).

> * * * [C]ompensation for attorneys representing indigent capital defendants often is perversely low. Although a properly conducted capital trial can involve hundreds of hours of investigation, preparation, and lengthy trial proceedings, many States severely limit the compensation paid for capital defense. * * * See generally Klein, The Eleventh Commandment: Thou Shalt Not be Compelled to Render the Ineffective Assistance of Counsel, 68 Ind.L.J. 363, 364–375 (1993).

62. The court in *Peart* did state that if the legislature was not forthcoming with a remedy in a reasonable period of time, "this Court, in the exercise of its constitutional and inherent power and supervisory jurisdiction, may find it necessary to employ the more intrusive and specific measures it has thus far avoided to ensure that indigent defendants receive reasonably effective assistance of counsel."

    Court-awarded funds for the appointment of investigators and experts often are either unavailable, severely limited, or not provided by state courts. As a result, attorneys appointed to represent capital defendants at the trial level frequently are unable to recoup even their overhead costs and out-of-pocket expenses, and effectively may be required to work at minimum wage or below while funding from their own pockets their client's defense. * * * The prospect that hours spent in trial preparation or funds expended hiring psychiatrists or ballistics experts will be uncompensated unquestionably chills even a qualified attorney's zealous representation of his client.

    The practical costs of such ad hoc systems of attorney selection and compensation are well documented. Capital defendants have been sentenced to death when represented by counsel who never bothered to read the state death penalty statute, e.g., Smith v. State, 581 So.2d 497 (Ala.Crim.App. 1990), slept through or otherwise were not present during trial, or failed to investigate or present any mitigating evidence at the penalty phase, Mitchell v. Kemp, 483 U.S. 1026 (1987)(Marshall, J., dissenting from denial of certiorari). * * * One Louisiana defendant was convicted of capital murder following a one-day trial and 20–minute penalty phase proceeding, in which his counsel stipulated to the defendant's age at the time of the crime and rested. State v. Messiah, 538 So.2d 175, 187 (La.1988). When asked to cite the criminal cases he knew, one defense attorney who failed to challenge his client's racially unrepresentative jury pool, could name only two cases: *Miranda* and *Dred Scott*. See Bright, Counsel for the Poor: The Death Sentence Not for the Worst Crime but for the Worst Lawyer, 103 Yale L.J. 1835, 1839.

Justice Blackmun contended that the *Strickland* test for reviewing the effectiveness of counsel provides insufficient protection for capital defendants, in light of the systemic underfunding and underregulation of appointed counsel in capital cases. He elaborated as follows:

    The impotence of the *Strickland* standard is perhaps best evidenced in the cases in which ineffective assistance claims have been denied. John Young, for example, was represented in his capital trial by an attorney who was addicted to drugs and who a few weeks later was incarcerated on federal drug charges. The Court of Appeals for the Eleventh Circuit rejected Young's ineffective assistance of counsel claim on federal habeas, Young v. Zant, 727 F.2d 1489 (11th Cir.1984), and this Court denied review. Young was executed in 1985. John Smith and his codefendant Rebecca Machetti were sentenced to death by juries selected under the same Georgia statute. Machetti's attorneys successfully challenged the statute under a recent Supreme Court decision, Taylor v. Louisiana, 419 U.S. 522 (1975), winning Machetti a new trial and ultimately a life sentence. Smith's counsel was unaware of the Supreme Court decision, however, and failed similarly to object at trial. Smith v. Kemp, 715 F.2d 1459 (C.A.11 1983). Smith was executed in 1983.

    Jesus Romero's attorney failed to present any evidence at the penalty phase and delivered a closing argument totalling 29 words. Although the attorney later was suspended on unrelated grounds, Romero's ineffective assistance claim was rejected by the Court of Appeals for the Fifth Circuit, Romero v. Lynaugh, 884 F.2d 871, 875 (1989), and this Court denied certiorari. Romero was executed in 1992. Larry Heath was represented on direct appeal by counsel who filed a 6–page brief before the Alabama Court of Criminal Appeals. The attorney failed to appear for oral argument before the Alabama Supreme Court and filed a brief in that court containing a 1–page argument and citing a single case. The Eleventh Circuit found no prejudice, Heath v. Jones, 941 F.2d 1126, 1131 (11th Cir.1991), and this Court denied review. Heath was executed in Alabama in 1992.

James Messer, a mentally impaired capital defendant, was represented by an attorney who at the trial's guilt phase presented no defense, made no objections, and emphasized the horror of the capital crime in his closing statement. At the penalty phase, the attorney presented no evidence of mental impairment, failed to introduce other substantial mitigating evidence, and again repeatedly suggested in closing that death was the appropriate punishment. The Eleventh Circuit refused to grant relief, Messer v. Kemp, 760 F.2d 1080 (11th Cir.1985), and this Court denied certiorari. Messer was executed in 1988. * * *

Justice Blackmun concluded with the hope that the system of appointed counsel in capital cases would be improved:

> Our system of justice is adversarial and depends for its legitimacy on the fair and adequate representation of all parties at all levels of the judicial process. * * * My 24 years of overseeing the imposition of the death penalty from this Court have left me in grave doubt whether this reliance is justified and whether the constitutional requirement of competent legal counsel for capital defendants is being fulfilled. * * * [W]e must have the courage to recognize the failings of our present system of capital representation and the conviction to do what is necessary to improve it.

Once you recognize these problems with appointing lawyers, what sort of a system would you set up to provide incentives for good lawyering?

F. LIMITATIONS ON THE RIGHT TO COUNSEL OF CHOICE

Gideon guarantees an absolute right to counsel for all serious crimes. But there is no absolute right to choose a particular counsel. Whether there is any right at all to choose a particular counsel depends on whether the defendant can afford it. The Supreme Court has held that so long as an indigent receives effective representation, he has no right to choose a particular counsel. In Morris v. Slappy, 461 U.S. 1 (1983), Slappy was appointed counsel whom he trusted, but that counsel became ill before trial, and another was substituted. Slappy argued that a continuance should have been granted until trusted counsel could return. He did not contend that substitute counsel was ineffective. Chief Justice Burger, writing for the Court, interpreted Slappy's request, and the lower court's holding, as assuming that the indigent had the right to a "meaningful attorney-client relationship." He rejected this argument in no uncertain terms.

> No authority was cited for this novel ingredient of the Sixth Amendment guarantee, and of course none could be. No court could possibly guarantee that a defendant will develop the kind of rapport with his attorney * * * that the Court of Appeals thought part of the Sixth Amendment guarantee of counsel.

See also United States v. Pina, 844 F.2d 1 (1st Cir.1988) (court has no obligation to appoint a lawyer outside the public defender's office, simply because the defendant believes that all lawyers from that office are incompetent).

1. Disqualification of Defendant's Counsel of Choice

If the defendant can afford it, there is a *qualified* right to retain counsel of choice. The following case indicates one type of qualification.

WHEAT v. UNITED STATES

Supreme Court of the United States, 1988.
486 U.S. 153.

CHIEF JUSTICE REHNQUIST **delivered the opinion of the Court.**

The issue in this case is whether the District Court erred in declining petitioner's waiver of his right to conflict-free counsel and by refusing to permit petitioner's proposed substitution of attorneys.

I

Petitioner Mark Wheat, along with numerous codefendants, was charged with participating in a farflung drug distribution conspiracy. * * *

Also charged in the conspiracy were Juvenal Gomez–Barajas and Javier Bravo, who were represented in their criminal proceedings by attorney Eugene Iredale. Gomez–Barajas was tried first and was acquitted on drug charges overlapping with those against petitioner. To avoid a second trial on other charges, however, Gomez–Barajas offered to plead guilty to tax evasion and illegal importation of merchandise. At the commencement of petitioner's trial, the District Court had not accepted the plea; Gomez–Barajas was thus free to withdraw his guilty plea and proceed to trial.

Bravo, evidently a lesser player in the conspiracy, decided to forgo trial and plead guilty to one count of transporting approximately 2,400 pounds of marijuana from Los Angeles to a residence controlled by Victor Vidal. At the conclusion of Bravo's guilty plea

proceedings on August 22, 1985, Iredale notified the District Court that he had been contacted by petitioner and had been asked to try petitioner's case as well. In response, the Government registered substantial concern about the possibility of conflict in the representation. * * *

* * * The Government's position was premised on two possible conflicts. First, the District Court had not yet accepted the plea and sentencing arrangement negotiated between Gomez–Barajas and the Government; in the event that arrangement were rejected by the court, Gomez–Barajas would be free to withdraw the plea and stand trial. He would then be faced with the prospect of representation by Iredale, who in the meantime would have acted as petitioner's attorney. Petitioner, through his participation in the drug distribution scheme, was familiar with the sources and size of Gomez–Barajas' income, and was thus likely to be called as a witness for the Government at any subsequent trial of Gomez–Barajas. This scenario would pose a conflict of interest for Iredale, who would be prevented from cross-examining petitioner and thereby from effectively representing Gomez–Barajas.

Second, and of more immediate concern, Iredale's representation of Bravo would directly affect his ability to act as counsel for petitioner. The Government believed that a portion of the marijuana delivered by Bravo to Vidal's residence eventually was transferred to petitioner. In this regard, the Government contacted Iredale and asked that Bravo be made available as a witness to testify against petitioner, and agreed in exchange to modify its position at the time of Bravo's sentencing. In the likely event that Bravo were called to testify, Iredale's position in representing both men would become untenable, for ethical proscriptions would forbid him to cross-examine Bravo in any meaningful way. By failing to do so, he would also fail to provide petitioner with effective assistance of counsel. Thus because of Iredale's prior representation of Gomez–Barajas and Bravo and the potential for serious conflict of interest, the Government urged the District Court to reject the substitution of attorneys.

In response, petitioner emphasized his right to have counsel of his own choosing and the willingness of Gomez–Barajas, Bravo, and petitioner to waive the right to conflict-free counsel. Petitioner argued that the circumstances posited by the Government that would create a conflict for Iredale were highly speculative and bore no connection to the true relationship between the co-conspirators. If called to testify, Bravo would simply say that he did not know petitioner and had no dealings with him; no attempt by Iredale to impeach Bravo would be necessary. Further, in the unlikely event that Gomez–Barajas went to trial on the charges of tax evasion and illegal importation, petitioner's lack of involvement in those alleged crimes made his appearance as a witness highly improbable. Finally, and most importantly, all three defendants agreed to allow Iredale to represent petitioner and to waive any future

claims of conflict of interest. In petitioner's view, the Government was manufacturing implausible conflicts in an attempt to disqualify Iredale, who had already proved extremely effective in representing Gomez–Barajas and Bravo.

[The District Court found for the Government and rejected the substitution of Iredale. Wheat was convicted and the court of appeals affirmed the conviction.]

II

* * * We have * * * recognized that the purpose of providing assistance of counsel "is simply to ensure that criminal defendants receive a fair trial," and that in evaluating Sixth Amendment claims, "the appropriate inquiry focuses on the adversarial process, not on the accused's relationship with his lawyer as such." Thus, while the right to select and be represented by one's preferred attorney is comprehended by the Sixth Amendment, the essential aim of the Amendment is to guarantee an effective advocate for each criminal defendant rather than to ensure that a defendant will inexorably be represented by the lawyer whom he prefers. See Morris v. Slappy.

The Sixth Amendment right to choose one's own counsel is circumscribed in several important respects. Regardless of his persuasive powers, an advocate who is not a member of the bar may not represent clients (other than himself) in court.[a] Similarly, a defendant may not insist on representation by an attorney he cannot afford or who for other reasons declines to represent the defendant. Nor may a defendant insist on the counsel of an attorney who has a previous or ongoing relationship with an opposing par-

---

a. Our holding in Faretta v. California, [discussed infra], that a criminal defendant has a Sixth Amendment right to represent *himself*

if he voluntarily elects to do so, does not encompass the right to choose any advocate if the defendant wishes to be represented by counsel.

ty, even when the opposing party is the Government. The question raised in this case is the extent to which a criminal defendant's right under the Sixth Amendment to his chosen attorney is qualified by the fact that the attorney has represented other defendants charged in the same criminal conspiracy.

* * *

Petitioner insists that the provision of waivers by all affected defendants cures any problems created by the multiple representation. But no such flat rule can be deduced from the Sixth Amendment presumption in favor of counsel of choice. Federal courts have an independent interest in ensuring that criminal trials are conducted within the ethical standards of the profession and that legal proceedings appear fair to all who observe them. * * * Not only the interest of a criminal defendant but the institutional interest in the rendition of just verdicts in criminal cases may be jeopardized by unregulated multiple representation.

For this reason, the Federal Rules of Criminal Procedure direct trial judges to investigate specially cases involving joint representation. * * *

To be sure, this need to investigate potential conflicts arises in part from the legitimate wish of district courts that their judgments remain intact on appeal. As the Court of Appeals accurately pointed out, trial courts confronted with multiple representations face the prospect of being "whipsawed" by assertions of error no matter which way they rule. If a district court agrees to the multiple representation, and the advocacy of counsel is thereafter impaired as a result, the defendant may well claim that he did not

receive effective assistance. On the other hand, a district court's refusal to accede to the multiple representation may result in a challenge such as petitioner's in this case. Nor does a waiver by the defendant necessarily solve the problem, for we note, without passing judgment on, the apparent willingness of Courts of Appeals to entertain ineffective-assistance claims from defendants who have specifically waived the right to conflict-free counsel.

Thus, where a court justifiably finds an actual conflict of interest, there can be no doubt that it may decline a proffer of waiver, and insist that defendants be separately represented.

* * *

Unfortunately for all concerned, a district court must pass on the issue of whether or not to allow a waiver of a conflict of interest by a criminal defendant not with the wisdom of hindsight after the trial has taken place,[b] but in the murkier pre-trial context when relationships between parties are seen through a glass, darkly. The likelihood and dimensions of nascent conflicts of interest are notoriously hard to predict, even for those thoroughly familiar with criminal trials. It is a rare attorney who will be fortunate enough to learn the entire truth from his own client, much less be fully apprised before trial of what each of the Government's witnesses will say on the stand. A few bits of unforeseen testimony or a single previously unknown or unnoticed document may significantly shift the relationship between multiple defendants. These imponderables are difficult enough for a lawyer to assess, and even more difficult to convey by way of explanation to a criminal defendant untutored in the niceties of legal eth-

---

b. Pretrial disqualification of defense counsel is not immediately appealable. Flanagan v.

United States, 465 U.S. 259 (1984).

ics. Nor is it amiss to observe that the willingness of an attorney to obtain such waivers from his clients may bear an inverse relation to the care with which he conveys all the necessary information to them.

For these reasons we think the district court must be allowed substantial latitude in refusing waivers of conflicts of interest not only in those rare cases where an actual conflict may be demonstrated before trial, but in the more common cases where a potential for conflict exists which may or may not burgeon into an actual conflict as the trial progresses. In the circumstances of this case, with the motion for substitution of counsel made so close to the time of trial the District Court relied on instinct and judgment based on experience in making its decision. We do not think it can be said that the court exceeded the broad latitude which must be accorded it in making this decision. Petitioner of course rightly points out that the Government may seek to "manufacture" a conflict in order to prevent a defendant from having a particularly able defense counsel at his side; but trial courts are undoubtedly aware of this possibility, and must take it into consideration along with all of the other factors which inform this sort of a decision.

Here the District Court was confronted not simply with an attorney who wished to represent two coequal defendants in a straightforward criminal prosecution; rather, Iredale proposed to defend three conspirators of varying stature in a complex drug distribution scheme. The Government intended to call Bravo as a witness for the prosecution at petitioner's trial.[c] The Government might readily have tied certain deliveries of marijuana by Bravo to petitioner, necessitating vigorous cross-examination of Bravo by

petitioner's counsel. Iredale, because of his prior representation of Bravo, would have been unable ethically to provide that cross-examination.

Iredale had also represented Gomez–Barajas, one of the alleged kingpins of the distribution ring, and had succeeded in obtaining a verdict of acquittal for him. Gomez–Barajas had agreed with the Government to plead guilty to other charges, but the District Court had not yet accepted the plea arrangement. If the agreement were rejected, petitioner's probable testimony at the resulting trial of Gomez–Barajas would create an ethical dilemma for Iredale from which one or the other of his clients would likely suffer.

Viewing the situation as it did before trial, we hold that the District Court's refusal to permit the substitution of counsel in this case was within its discretion and did not violate petitioner's Sixth Amendment rights. Other district courts might have reached differing or opposite conclusions with equal justification, but that does not mean that one conclusion was "right" and the other "wrong." The District Court must recognize a presumption in favor of petitioner's counsel of choice, but that presumption may be overcome not only by a demonstration of actual conflict but by a showing of a serious potential for conflict. The evaluation of the facts and circumstances of each case under this standard must be left primarily to the informed judgment of the trial court.

The judgment of the Court of Appeals is accordingly affirmed.

JUSTICE MARSHALL, with whom JUSTICE BRENNAN joins, dissenting.

* * *

---

c. Bravo was in fact called as a witness at petitioner's trial. His testimony was elicited to

demonstrate the transportation of drugs that the prosecution hoped to link to petitioner.

At the time of petitioner's trial, Iredale's representation of Gomez–Barajas was effectively completed. * * * Gomez–Barajas was not scheduled to appear as a witness at petitioner's trial; thus, Iredale's conduct of that trial would not require him to question his former client. The only possible conflict this Court can divine from Iredale's representation of both petitioner and Gomez–Barajas rests on the premise that the trial court would reject the negotiated plea agreement and that Gomez–Barajas then would decide to go to trial. In this event, the Court tells us, "petitioner's probable testimony at the resulting trial of Gomez–Barajas would create an ethical dilemma for Iredale."

This argument rests on speculation of the most dubious kind. * * * The most likely occurrence at the time petitioner moved to retain Iredale as his defense counsel was that the trial court would accept Gomez–Barajas' plea agreement, as the court in fact later did. Moreover, even if Gomez–Barajas had gone to trial, petitioner probably would not have testified. The record contains no indication that petitioner had any involvement in or information about crimes for which Gomez–Barajas might yet have stood trial. The only alleged connection between petitioner and Gomez–Barajas sprang from the conspiracy to distribute marijuana, and a jury already had acquitted Gomez–Barajas of that charge. It is therefore disingenuous to say that representation of both petitioner and Gomez–Barajas posed a serious potential for a conflict of interest.

Similarly, Iredale's prior representation of Bravo was not a cause for concern. * * * As all parties were aware at the time, Bravo did not know and could not identify petitioner; indeed, prior to the commencement of legal proceedings, the two men never had heard of each other. Bravo's eventual testimony at petitioner's trial related to a shipment of marijuana in which petitioner was not involved; the testimony contained not a single reference to petitioner. Petitioner's counsel did not cross-examine Bravo, and neither petitioner's counsel nor the prosecutor mentioned Bravo's testimony in closing argument. All of these developments were predictable when the District Court ruled on petitioner's request that Iredale serve as trial counsel; the contours of Bravo's testimony were clear at that time. Given the insignificance of this testimony to any matter that petitioner's counsel would dispute, the proposed joint representation of petitioner and Bravo did not threaten a conflict of interest.[d]

Moreover, even assuming that Bravo's testimony might have "necessitat[ed] vigorous cross-examination," the District Court could have insured against the possibility of any conflict of interest without wholly depriving petitioner of his constitutional right to the counsel of his choice. Petitioner's motion requested that Iredale either be substituted for petitioner's current counsel or be added to petitioner's defense team. Had the District Court allowed the addition of Iredale and then ordered that he take no part in

---

d. The very insignificance of Bravo's testimony, combined with the timing of the prosecutor's decision to call Bravo as a witness, raises a serious concern that the prosecutor attempted to manufacture a conflict in this case. The prosecutor's decision to use Bravo as a witness was an 11th–hour development. * * * Only after the prosecutor learned of the substitution motion and decided to oppose it did he arrange for Bravo's testimony by agree-ing to recommend to the trial court a reduction in Bravo's sentence. Especially in light of the scarce value of Bravo's testimony, this prosecutorial behavior very plausibly may be viewed as a maneuver to prevent Iredale from representing petitioner at trial. Iredale had proved to be a formidable adversary; he previously had gained an acquittal for the alleged kingpin of the marijuana distribution scheme. * * *

the cross-examination of Bravo, any possibility of a conflict would have been removed. Especially in light of the availability of this precautionary measure, the notion that Iredale's prior representation of Bravo might well have caused a conflict of interest at petitioner's trial is nothing short of ludicrous.

* * *

[The dissenting opinion of Justice Stevens, joined by Justice Blackmun, is omitted.]

Analysis of Wheat

Wheat is criticized in Green, "Through a Glass, Darkly": How the Court Sees Motions to Disqualify Criminal Defense Lawyers, 89 Colum.L.Rev. 1201 (1989). Among other criticisms, Professor Green notes that "the Court relied on an unwarranted assumption that if the defendant is willing to waive potential conflict of interest claims his attorney probably has not complied with the ethical standards governing the investigation and disclosure of potential conflicts." Professor Green also contends that the Court in *Wheat* "inexplicably retreated from the concern expressed in previous cases for the attorney-client relationship and for the defendant's autonomy," and that it "exaggerated the significance of judicial interests" which justify disqualification of counsel despite a client's waiver.

Wheat is defended in Stuntz, Waiving Rights in Criminal Procedure, 75 Va.L.Rev. 761 (1989). Professor Stuntz argues that clients jointly represented by a single counsel may or may not have improper motives. It may be that joint counsel is retained to deter conspirators from cutting an individual deal and cooperating with the government. Thus, some defendants may be coerced into accepting a joint counsel relationship. On the other hand, it may be that the clients have proper motives—they all want the same lawyer because that lawyer is excellent. Stuntz argues that the capability of the lawyer is likely to be known by the trial judge; if the lawyer is known to be merely average, bad motives for the multiple representation can be inferred, and disqualification should be ordered because the client's waiver of conflict-free counsel is not really voluntary. Therefore a broad grant of discretion to the trial judge is necessary to allow the judge to separate good from bad motives in joint representation. Professor Stuntz's arguments are not borne out by the facts in *Wheat,* however, where it appeared that a number of the defendants came to Iredale fairly far along in the proceedings, because he had been so successful in defending other defendants. The trial judge specifically noted that Iredale was an excellent and highly successful defense attorney, and disqualified him nonetheless.

Why must a lawyer be disqualified if he has represented one client who is now testifying against another? Of course, the lawyer cannot cross-examine the witness-client with confidential information without client consent. But if the lawyer cross-examines the witness-client with only non-confidential information, as she must, who does the cross-examination hurt? How is that cross-examination different from that would be conducted by substitute counsel, who would not have access to the confidential information in the first place? And if there is some limited impairment in the cross-examination, why can't the defendant consent to it? And what was wrong with Justice Marshall's point that Wheat was asking for Iredale to be *cocounsel,* thus permitting his other attorney to conduct the cross-examination of Iredale's former client? Professor Green asserts that "the Court in *Wheat* upheld the denial of Wheat's choice of counsel in a case where the ethical rules plainly would have permitted that choice." See United States v. Cunningham, 672 F.2d 1064 (2d Cir.1982)(no disqualification required where defense attorney would need to use only public information in cross-examining the witness).

Cases Applying Wheat

After *Wheat*, appellate courts have usually upheld trial court disqualifications of defense counsel. For example, in United States v. Stites, 56 F.3d 1020 (9th Cir.1995), Stites and his sister Cheryl Dark were charged with RICO violations resulting from a scheme of insurance fraud. Stites fled the state, and Cheryl was represented by Juanita Brooks. Cheryl pleaded guilty and at the sentencing hearing, Brooks argued that Cheryl was a pawn of Stites; that Stites was "the mastermind," "a thief and a fraud," and a "cheap con artist." She added for good measure that "as an officer of the court and attorney myself, it makes me angry to see that people are able to so pervert our system of justice." Brooks won a light sentence for Dark. Two years later, Stites finally turned up for trial—and retained Brooks. When the prosecution objected, both Stites and Dark waived any conflict. But the trial judge—who happened to be the same judge who sentenced Dark—disqualified Brooks. The court of appeals upheld the disqualification. The court noted that Dark would be a witness at Stites' trial, and that the trial court was right to question the voluntariness of Dark's waiver. Most importantly, though, the court found that Brooks was properly disqualified because "[s]he could not, in the very same criminal prosecution, tell the court that Stites was a liar, a thief, and the mastermind of the massive fraud charged by the government and then represent the same person contending that he was innocent of the crimes charged." The court concluded as follows:

> Students of the classics may recall Cicero's comment that speeches at trials are for "the case and the occasion," they do not disclose "the man himself." But even if a certain insincerity may accompany the filling of an advocate's role, nothing in our professional ethics permits an advocate to tell a court one set of facts today and a contradictory set of facts tomorrow.

Aren't lawyers expected to represent a client, clean the slate, and then represent another? Do hired guns act unethically? Was Brooks supposed to have a conscience when she represented Stites?

One of the more notable disqualifications of counsel occurred in the prosecution of former Mafia boss John Gotti. United States v. Locascio, 6 F.3d 924 (2d Cir.1993). The trial court disqualified Gotti's long-time counsel, Bruce Cutler, on two grounds: (1) The government had proof that Cutler served as house counsel to the Mafia, representing various conspirators who had not personally retained him—thus his representation would actually be proof of conspiratorial activity at trial; and (2) The government had tapes in which Cutler was present while criminal activity was being discussed—thus, in challenging the government's interpretation of the tapes, Cutler would be acting as an unsworn witness. The court of appeals upheld the disqualification, and noted in particular with respect to Cutler's status as an unsworn witness, that Gotti's waiver of conflict was irrelevant:

When an attorney is an unsworn witness * * * the detriment is to the government, since the defendant gains an unfair advantage, and to the court, since the factfinding process is impaired. Waiver by the defendant is ineffective in such situations, since he is not the party prejudiced.

* * * The government was legitimately concerned that, when Cutler argued before the jury for a particular interpretation of the tapes, his interpretation would be given added credibility due to his presence in the room when the statements were made. This would have given Gotti an unfair advantage, since Cutler would not have had to take an oath in presenting his interpretation, but could merely frame it in the form of legal argument.

Professor Karlan, in Discrete and Relational Criminal Representation: The Changing Vision of the Right to Counsel, 105 Harv.L.Rev. 670 (1992), contends that decisions such as *Locascio* reflect a negative reaction to "relational" criminal representation, where an attorney's ongoing relationship with a client allows the client to continue to pursue criminal goals. In her view, disqualification is less likely to occur for "discrete", i.e., singular representations. See also United States v. Register, 182 F.3d 820 (11th Cir.1999) (no error in disqualifying counsel over the defendant's objections, where a government informant might testify that the defendant paid the attorney with drugs from the conspiracy: "It would have been virtually impossible for the attorney to question the informant without being concerned to a significant degree about his own interests rather than those of his client").

2. *Rendering the Defendant Unable to Pay for Counsel of Choice*

CAPLIN & DRYSDALE v. UNITED STATES

Supreme Court of the United States, 1989.
491 U.S. 617.

JUSTICE WHITE **delivered the opinion of the Court.**

We are called on to determine whether the federal drug forfeiture statute includes an exemption for assets that a defendant wishes to use to pay an attorney who conducted his defense in the criminal case where forfeiture was sought. Because we determine that no such exemption exists, we must decide whether that statute, so interpreted, is consistent with the Fifth and Sixth Amendments. We hold that it is.

a. The forfeiture statute provides, in relevant part, that any person convicted of a particular class of criminal offenses

"shall forfeit to the United States, irrespective of any provision of State law—

I

In January 1985, Christopher Reckmeyer was charged in a multi-count indictment with running a massive drug importation and distribution scheme. The scheme was alleged to be a continuing criminal enterprise (CCE), in violation of 21 U.S.C. § 848. Relying on a portion of the CCE statute that authorized forfeiture to the Government of "property constituting, or derived from ... proceeds ... obtained" from drug-law violations, § 853(a),[a] the indictment sought for-

"(1) any property constituting, or derived from, any proceeds the person obtained, directly or indirectly, as the result of such violation;

. . . . .

feiture of specified assets in Reckmeyer's possession. At this time, the District Court, acting pursuant to § 853(e)(1)(A),[b] entered a restraining order forbidding Reckmeyer to transfer any of the listed assets that were potentially forfeitable.

Sometime earlier, Reckmeyer had retained petitioner, a law firm, to represent him in the ongoing grand jury investigation which resulted in the January 1985 indictments.

* * * Reckmeyer moved to modify the District Court's earlier restraining order to permit him to use some of the restrained assets to pay petitioner's fees; Reckmeyer also sought to exempt from any postconviction forfeiture order the assets that he intended to use to pay petitioner. However, one week later, before the District Court could conduct a hearing on this motion, Reckmeyer entered a plea agreement with the Government. Under the agreement, Reckmeyer pleaded guilty to the drug-related CCE charge, and agreed to forfeit all of the specified assets listed in the indictment. * * * Subsequently, an order forfeiting virtually all of the assets in Reckmeyer's possession was entered by the District Court in conjunction with his sentencing.

After this order was entered, petitioner filed a petition under § 853(n), which permits third parties with an interest in forfeited property to ask the sentencing court for an adjudication of their rights to that property; specifically, § 853(n)(6)(B) gives a third party

who entered into a bona fide transaction with a defendant a right to make claims against forfeited property, if that third party was "at the time of [the transaction] reasonably without cause to believe that the [defendant's assets were] subject to forfeiture." * * * Petitioner argued alternatively that assets used to pay an attorney were exempt from forfeiture under § 853, and if not, the failure of the statute to provide such an exemption rendered it unconstitutional. The District Court granted petitioner's claim for a share of the forfeited assets.

[The Court of Appeals reversed in an en banc decision.]

II

[The Court, relying on the companion case of United States v. Monsanto, 491 U.S. 600, held that the statute did not exempt attorney's fees from forfeiture.]

III

We therefore address petitioner's constitutional challenges to the forfeiture law. Petitioner contends that the statute infringes on criminal defendants' Sixth Amendment right to counsel of choice, and upsets the "balance of power" between the Government and the accused in a manner contrary to the Due Process Clause of the Fifth Amendment. We consider these contentions in turn.

A

Petitioner's first claim is that the forfeiture law makes impossible, or at

---

"The court, in imposing sentence on such person, shall order, in addition to any other sentence imposed ..., that the person forfeit to the United States all property described in this subsection." 21 U.S.C. § 853(a). * * *

b. The pretrial restraining order provision states that

"[u]pon application of the United States, the court may enter a restraining order or injunction ... or take any other action to

preserve the availability of property described in subsection (a) of [§ 853] for forfeiture under this section—

"(A) upon the filing of an indictment or information charging a violation ... for which criminal forfeiture may be ordered under [§ 853] and alleging that the property with respect to which the order is sought would, in the event of conviction, be subject to forfeiture under this section." § 853(e)(1).

least impermissibly burdens, a defendant's right "to select and be represented by one's preferred attorney." Petitioner does not, nor could it defensibly do so, assert that impecunious defendants have a Sixth Amendment right to choose their counsel. The Amendment guarantees defendants in criminal cases the right to adequate representation, but those who do not have the means to hire their own lawyers have no cognizable complaint so long as they are adequately represented by attorneys appointed by the courts. * * * The forfeiture statute does not prevent a defendant who has nonforfeitable assets from retaining any attorney of his choosing. Nor is it necessarily the case that a defendant who possesses nothing but assets the Government seeks to have forfeited will be prevented from retaining counsel of choice. Defendants like Reckmeyer may be able to find lawyers willing to represent them, hoping that their fees will be paid in the event of acquittal, or via some other means that a defendant might come by in the future. The burden placed on defendants by the forfeiture law is therefore a limited one.

Nonetheless, there will be cases where a defendant will be unable to retain the attorney of his choice, when that defendant would have been able to hire that lawyer if he had access to forfeitable assets, and if there was no risk that fees paid by the defendant to his counsel would later be recouped under § 853(c).[c] It is in these cases, petitioner argues, that the Sixth Amendment puts limits on the forfeiture statute.

This submission is untenable. Whatever the full extent of the Sixth Amendment's protection of one's right to retain counsel of his choosing, that protection does not go beyond "the individual's right to spend his own money to obtain the advice and assistance of . . . counsel." A defendant has no Sixth Amendment right to spend another person's money for services rendered by an attorney, even if those funds are the only way that that defendant will be able to retain the attorney of his choice. A robbery suspect, for example, has no Sixth Amendment right to use funds he has stolen from a bank to retain an attorney to defend him if he is apprehended. The money, though in his possession, is not rightfully his; the Government does not violate the Sixth Amendment if it seizes the robbery proceeds and refuses to permit the defendant to use them to pay for his defense. * * *

* * *

There is no constitutional principle that gives one person the right to give another's property to a third party, even where the person seeking to complete the exchange wishes to do so in order to exercise a constitutionally protected right. * * *

Petitioner's "balancing analysis" to the contrary rests substantially on the view that the Government has only a modest interest in forfeitable assets that may be used to retain an attorney. Petitioner takes the position that, in large part, once assets have been paid over from client to attorney, the principal ends of forfeiture have been achieved: dispossessing a drug dealer

---

c. That section of the statute, which includes the so-called "relation back" provision, states:

"All right, title, and interest in property described in [§ 853] vests in the United States upon the commission of the act giving rise to forfeiture under this section. Any such property that is subsequently trans-

ferred to a person other than the defendant may be the subject of a special verdict of forfeiture and thereafter shall be forfeited to the United States, unless the transferee establishes" his entitlement to such property pursuant to § 853(n), discussed supra. 21 U.S.C. § 853(c).

or racketeer of the proceeds of his wrongdoing. We think that this view misses the mark for three reasons.

First, the Government has a pecuniary interest in forfeiture that goes beyond merely separating a criminal from his ill-gotten gains; that legitimate interest extends to recovering all forfeitable assets, for such assets are deposited in a Fund that supports law-enforcement efforts in a variety of important and useful ways. The sums of money that can be raised for law-enforcement activities this way are substantial,[d] and the Government's interest in using the profits of crime to fund these activities should not be discounted.

Second, the statute permits "rightful owners" of forfeited assets to make claims for forfeited assets before they are retained by the Government. The Government's interest in winning undiminished forfeiture thus includes the objective of returning property, in full, to those wrongfully deprived or defrauded of it. * * *

Finally, as we have recognized previously, a major purpose motivating congressional adoption and continued refinement of the racketeer influenced and corrupt organizations (RICO) and CCE forfeiture provisions has been the desire to lessen the economic power of organized crime and drug enterprises. This includes the use of such economic power to retain private counsel. As the Court of Appeals put it: "Con-

gress has already underscored the compelling public interest in stripping criminals such as Reckmeyer of their undeserved economic power, and part of that undeserved power may be the ability to command high-priced legal talent." The notion that the Government has a legitimate interest in depriving criminals of economic power, even insofar as that power is used to retain counsel of choice, may be somewhat unsettling. But when a defendant claims that he has suffered some substantial impairment of his Sixth Amendment rights by virtue of the seizure or forfeiture of assets in his possession, such a complaint is no more than the reflection of "the harsh reality that the quality of a criminal defendant's representation frequently may turn on his ability to retain the best counsel money can buy." Again, the Court of Appeals put it aptly: "The modern day Jean Valjean must be satisfied with appointed counsel. Yet the drug merchant claims that his possession of huge sums of money ... entitles him to something more. We reject this contention, and any notion of a constitutional right to use the proceeds of crime to finance an expensive defense."[e]

It is our view that there is a strong governmental interest in obtaining full recovery of all forfeitable assets, an interest that overrides any Sixth Amendment interest in permitting

---

d. For example, just one of the assets which Reckmeyer agreed to forfeit, a parcel of land known as "Shelburne Glebe," was recently sold by federal authorities for $5.3 million. The proceeds of the sale will fund federal, state, and local law-enforcement activities.

e. We also reject the contention, advanced by amici, see, e.g., Brief for American Bar Association as Amicus Curiae 20–22, * * * that a type of "per se" ineffective assistance of counsel results—due to the particular complexity of RICO or drug-enterprise cases—when a defendant is not permitted to use assets in his possession to retain counsel of choice, and in-

stead must rely on appointed counsel. If such an argument were accepted, it would bar the trial of indigents charged with such offenses, because those persons would have to rely on appointed counsel—which this view considers per se ineffective.

If appointed counsel is ineffective in a particular case, a defendant has resort to the remedies discussed in Strickland v. Washington. But we cannot say that the Sixth Amendment's guarantee of effective assistance of counsel is a guarantee of a privately retained counsel in every complex case, irrespective of a defendant's ability to pay.

criminals to use assets adjudged forfeitable to pay for their defense. * * *

We therefore reject petitioner's claim of a Sixth Amendment right of criminal defendants to use assets that are the Government's—assets adjudged forfeitable, as Reckmeyer's were—to pay attorney's fees, merely because those assets are in their possession.[f] See also *Monsanto,* which rejects a similar claim with respect to pretrial orders and assets not yet judged forfeitable.

B

Petitioner's second constitutional claim is that the forfeiture statute is invalid under the Due Process Clause of the Fifth Amendment because it permits the Government to upset the "balance of forces between the accused and his accuser." We are not sure that this contention adds anything to petitioner's Sixth Amendment claim, because, while "[t]he Constitu-

tion guarantees a fair trial through the Due Process Clauses ... it defines the basic elements of a fair trial largely through the several provisions of the Sixth Amendment." * * * Even if, however, the Fifth Amendment provides some added protection not encompassed in the Sixth Amendment's more specific provisions, we find petitioner's claim based on the Fifth Amendment unavailing.

Forfeiture provisions are powerful weapons in the war on crime; like any such weapons, their impact can be devastating when used unjustly. But due process claims alleging such abuses are cognizable only in specific cases of prosecutorial misconduct (and petitioner has made no such allegation here) or when directed to a rule that is inherently unconstitutional. * * * Petitioner's claim—that the power available to prosecutors under the statute *could* be abused—proves too much,

---

f. Petitioner advances three additional reasons for invalidating the forfeiture statute, all of which concern possible ethical conflicts created for lawyers defending persons facing forfeiture of assets in their possession.

Petitioner first notes the statute's exemption from forfeiture of property transferred to a bona fide purchaser who was "reasonably without cause to believe that the property was subject to forfeiture." 21 U.S.C. § 853(n)(6)(B). This provision, it is said, might give an attorney an incentive not to investigate a defendant's case as fully as possible, so that the lawyer can invoke it to protect from forfeiture any fees he has received. Yet given the requirement that any assets which the Government wishes to have forfeited must be specified in the indictment, see Fed.Rule Crim.Proc. 7(c)(2), the only way a lawyer could be a beneficiary of § 853(n)(6)(B) would be to fail to read the indictment of his client. In this light, the prospect that a lawyer might find himself in conflict with his client, by seeking to take advantage of § 853(n)(6)(B), amounts to very little. * * *

The second possible conflict arises in plea bargaining: petitioner posits that a lawyer may advise a client to accept an agreement entailing a more harsh prison sentence but no forfeiture—even where contrary to the client's interests—in an effort to preserve the lawyer's fee. Following such a strategy, however, would

surely constitute ineffective assistance of counsel. We see no reason why our cases such as Strickland v. Washington are inadequate to deal with any such ineffectiveness where it arises. * * *

Finally, petitioner argues that the forfeiture statute, in operation, will create a system akin to "contingency fees" for defense lawyers: only a defense lawyer who wins acquittal for his client will be able to collect his fees, and contingent fees in criminal cases are generally considered unethical. See ABA Model Rule of Professional Conduct 1.5(d)(2)(1983); ABA Model Code of Professional Responsibility DR 2–106(C)(1979). But there is no indication here that petitioner, or any other firm, has actually sought to charge a defendant on a contingency basis; rather the claim is that a law firm's prospect of collecting its fee may turn on the outcome at trial. This, however, may often be the case in criminal defense work. Nor is it clear why permitting contingent fees in criminal cases—if that is what the forfeiture statute does—violates a criminal defendant's Sixth Amendment rights. The fact that a federal statutory scheme authorizing contingency fees—again, if that is what Congress has created in § 853 (a premise we doubt)—is at odds with model disciplinary rules or state disciplinary codes hardly renders the federal statute invalid.

for many tools available to prosecutors can be misused in a way that violates the rights of innocent persons.

* * * Cases involving particular abuses can be dealt with individually by the lower courts, when (and if) any such cases arise.

JUSTICE BLACKMUN, **with whom** JUSTICES BRENNAN, MARSHALL **and** STEVENS **join, dissenting. [Dissent also applicable to** *Monsanto***].**

* * *

I

[JUSTICE BLACKMUN argues that the statute exempts attorney's fees from forfeiture.]

II

* * *

Had it been Congress' express aim to undermine the adversary system as we know it, it could hardly have found a better engine of destruction than attorney's-fee forfeiture. The main effect of forfeitures under the Act, of course, will be to deny the defendant the right to retain counsel, and therefore the right to have his defense designed and presented by an attorney he has chosen and trusts.[g] If the Government restrains the defendant's assets before trial, private counsel will be unwilling to continue, or to take on, the defense. Even if no restraining order is entered, the possibility of forfeiture after conviction will itself substantially diminish the likelihood that private counsel will agree to take the case. * * *

Even if the defendant finds a private attorney who is "so foolish, ignorant, beholden or idealistic as to take the

business," the attorney-client relationship will be undermined by the forfeiture statute. Perhaps the attorney will be willing to violate ethical norms by working on a contingent-fee basis in a criminal case. But if he is not—and we should question the integrity of any criminal-defense attorney who would violate the ethical norms of the profession by doing so—the attorney's own interests will dictate that he remain ignorant of the source of the assets from which he is paid. Under § 853(c), a third-party transferee may keep assets if "the transferee establishes . . . that he is a bona fide purchaser for value of such property who at the time of purchase was reasonably without cause to believe that the property was subject to forfeiture under this section." The less an attorney knows, the greater the likelihood that he can claim to have been an "innocent" third party. The attorney's interest in knowing nothing is directly adverse to his client's interest in full disclosure. * * * Other conflicts of interest are also likely to develop. The attorney who fears for his fee will be tempted to make the Government's waiver of fee forfeiture the sine qua non for any plea agreement, a position which conflicts with his client's best interests.

Perhaps most troubling is the fact that forfeiture statutes place the Government in the position to exercise an intolerable degree of power over any private attorney who takes on the task of representing a defendant in a forfeiture case. * * * The Government will be ever tempted to use the forfeiture weapon against a defense attorney who is particularly talented or aggres-

---

g. There is reason to fear that, in addition to depriving a defendant of counsel of choice, there will be circumstances in which the threat of forfeiture will deprive the defendant of *any* counsel. If the Government chooses not to restrain transfers by employing § 853(e)(1), it is

likely that the defendant will not qualify as "indigent" under the Criminal Justice Act. Potential private counsel will be aware of the threat of forfeiture, and, as a result, will likely refuse to take the case. * * *

sive on the client's behalf—the attorney who is better than what, in the Government's view, the defendant deserves. The specter of the Government's selectively excluding only the most talented defense counsel is a serious threat to the equality of forces necessary for the adversarial system to perform at its best. * * *

The long-term effects of the fee-for-feiture practice will be to decimate the private criminal-defense bar. As the use of the forfeiture mechanism expands to new categories of federal crimes and spreads to the States, only one class of defendants will be free routinely to retain private counsel: the affluent defendant accused of a crime that generates no economic gain. As the number of private clients diminishes, only the most idealistic and the least skilled of young lawyers will be attracted to the field, while the remainder seek greener pastures elsewhere.

* * *

Analysis of Caplin

Isn't the forfeitability of the assets the very point to be decided at trial? Hasn't the majority, by presuming the assets are ill-gotten and thus not the defendant's, begged the question? Maybe not, because according to the dissenters, it is the risk that assets will later be adjudicated forfeitable at trial that prevents the defendant from being able to retain an attorney, i.e., an attorney will not take the case given the risk that all of the assets will be forfeited at the end. Thus, even if the government only relied on post-trial forfeitures, defense counsel would be deterred from the representation due to the relation-back provision in the statute, which takes forfeited assets out of the hands of third parties.

Forfeiture Hearings

Still, where assets are restrained prior to trial, as in *Monsanto* (the companion case to *Caplin & Drysdale*), an argument can be made that the defendant is entitled at a minimum to notice and an opportunity to defend against the restraining order. See Mitchell v. W.T. Grant Co., 416 U.S. 600 (1974), requiring a hearing promptly after a seizure made pursuant to a pre-judgment remedy. The forfeiture statute does not provide for a hearing if assets are restrained after the defendant has been indicted on a forfeiture count (though there is a hearing requirement for pre-indictment restraint on assets). The statute provides that the fact of indictment is enough to show that the government is entitled to an order restraining the defendant's assets. How significant is this protection?

On remand in *Monsanto,* the court of appeals held that defendants subject to pre-trial restraint of assets are entitled to a hearing at which the government must show evidence independent of the indictment itself. This evidence must indicate that the restrained assets are likely to be found forfeitable by the jury. A hearing is not required before a temporary restraining order is issued, however, since the very point of a TRO is to surprise the defendant and prevent his disposition of forfeitable assets. See 924 F.2d 1186 (2d Cir.1991). How can a defendant whose assets have been restrained afford to pay counsel for the hearing provided by *Monsanto?*

3. *Other Limitations on the Right to Counsel of Choice*

There are other situations in which the right to chosen counsel has been trumped by a state interest. For example, defense attorneys have been subpoenaed before grand juries, as well as after indictment, to provide non-privileged evidence against their client, such as information concerning fee arrangements. This may result in disqualification of the attorney under relevant ethical codes. See Disciplinary Rule 5–102 of the Code of Professional Responsibility and Rule 3.7 of the Model Rules of Professional Conduct (both disqualifying the lawyer when he may be called as a witness against the client). In these cases, the qualified right to chosen counsel has usually been held outweighed by the state's interest in investigating and prosecuting crime. See In re Grand Jury Subpoena Served Upon John Doe, 781 F.2d 238 (2d Cir.1986)(en banc). Prosecutors are not allowed to subpoena defense counsel solely to create a disqualification, but it is the rare case where such bad intent will be found. See In re Antitrust Grand Jury Investigation, 714 F.2d 347 (4th Cir.1983)(where subpoena might aid in the investigation or prosecution, "the subpoena should issue even though there is also the possibility that the prosecutor will use it for some purpose other than obtaining evidence"). Compare In re Grand Jury Matters, 751 F.2d 13 (1st Cir.1984)(subpoena on defense attorney quashed where it was issued right before trial in circumstances indicating that the prosecutor was retaliating for successful motions by defense counsel). Problems created when defense attorneys are subpoenaed are discussed in Capra, Deterring the Formation of the Attorney–Client Relationship: Disclosure of Client Identity, Payment of Fees, and Communications by Fiduciaries, 4 Geo.J.Leg.Eth. 235 (1990).

If the defendant's chosen counsel is from out-of-state, counsel must apply for *pro hac vice* admission. In Leis v. Flynt, 439 U.S. 438 (1979), the Court held that the attorney had no due process right to be admitted *pro hac vice*. But the Court in *Leis* did not consider whether a criminal defendant's right to chosen counsel would be violated if out-of-state counsel is denied *pro hac vice* admission. Generally, courts have found that the state has a legitimate interest in regulating the practice of out-of-state lawyers who want to try cases in local courts, and that *pro hac vice* admission can be denied so long as the exclusion is not arbitrary. See Panzardi–Alvarez v. United States, 879 F.2d 975 (1st Cir.1989) (denial of *pro hac vice* admission does not violate right to chosen counsel where counsel had previously represented joint clients with conflicting interests). Compare Fuller v. Diesslin, 868 F.2d 604 (3d Cir.1989), where the trial court denied *pro hac vice* admission of the defendant's chosen counsel on the following grounds: 1) that local lawyers were always better prepared on local practice rules; 2) that out-of-state attorneys created delays due to traveling; and 3) that there were many local attorneys who could effectively represent the defendant. The court of appeals found that the right to chosen counsel had been violated:

> [T]he trial court's wooden approach and its failure to make record-supported findings balancing the right to [chosen] counsel with the demands of the administration of justice resulted in an arbitrary denial [that] constituted per se constitutional error * * *. We conclude that [the argument that if there is adequate local counsel, then *pro hac vice* admission can be denied] is without merit, because it collapses the right to counsel of choice into the right to effective assistance of counsel. * * * [A]lthough the core value in the sixth amendment is effective assistance of counsel, the

amendment also comprehends other related rights, such as the right to select and be represented by one's preferred attorney.

VIII. SELF–REPRESENTATION

A. THE CONSTITUTIONAL RIGHT

Although a defendant has a right to the assistance of counsel in all criminal prosecutions, sometimes she may prefer to defend herself. Beginning with the Judiciary Act of 1789, the right of self-representation in federal courts has been protected by statute.[63] Before Faretta v. California, 422 U.S. 806 (1975), established that a defendant in a state criminal trial has a constitutional right to proceed pro se, most states also granted that right. But California, where Anthony Faretta was convicted of grand theft, did not. It allowed a judge to appoint counsel over Faretta's objection and despite his knowing and voluntary waiver of his right to counsel.

FARETTA v. CALIFORNIA

Supreme Court of the United States, 1975.
422 U.S. 806.

MR. JUSTICE STEWART delivered the opinion of the Court.

* * *

I

Anthony Faretta was charged with grand theft in an information filed in the Superior Court of Los Angeles County, Cal. At the arraignment, the Superior Court Judge assigned to preside at the trial appointed the public defender to represent Faretta. Well before the date of trial, however, Faretta requested that he be permitted to represent himself. Questioning by the judge revealed that Faretta had once represented himself in a criminal prosecution, that he had a high school education, and that he did not want to be represented by the public defender because he believed that that office was "very loaded down with * * * a heavy case load." The judge responded that he believed Faretta was "making a mistake" and emphasized that in further proceedings Faretta would re-

ceive no special favors. Nevertheless, after establishing that Faretta wanted to represent himself and did not want a lawyer, the judge, in a "preliminary ruling," accepted Faretta's waiver of the assistance of counsel. The judge indicated, however, that he might reverse this ruling if it later appeared that Faretta was unable adequately to represent himself.

Several weeks thereafter, but still prior to trial, the judge *sua sponte* held a hearing to inquire into Faretta's ability to conduct his own defense, and questioned him specifically about both the hearsay rule and the state law governing the challenge of potential jurors. After consideration of Faretta's answers, and observation of his demeanor, the judge ruled that Faretta had not made an intelligent and knowing waiver of his right to the assistance of counsel, and also ruled that Faretta had no constitutional right to conduct his own defense. The judge, accordingly, reversed his earlier ruling per-

63. Section 35 of the Judiciary Act of 1789, 1 Stat. 73, 92 (1789)(current version at 28 U.S.C.A. § 1654) provided that "in all courts of

the United States, the parties may plead and manage their own causes personally or by the assistance of * * * counsel. * * *"

mitting self-representation and again appointed the public defender to represent Faretta. * * * Throughout the subsequent trial, the judge required that Faretta's defense be conducted only through the appointed lawyer from the public defender's office. At the conclusion of the trial, the jury found Faretta guilty as charged, and the judge sentenced him to prison.

[The appellate court affirmed Faretta's conviction.]

II

[The Court reviewed federal and state statutes according the right of self-representation, and decisions supporting such a right.]

* * * We confront here a nearly universal conviction, on the part of our people as well as our courts, that forcing a lawyer upon an unwilling defendant is contrary to his basic right to defend himself if he truly wants to do so.

III

This consensus is soundly premised. The right of self-representation finds support in the structure of the Sixth Amendment, as well as in the English and colonial jurisprudence from which the Amendment emerged.

A

* * *

The Sixth Amendment does not provide merely that a defense shall be made for the accused; it grants to the accused personally the right to make his defense. It is the accused, not counsel, who must be "informed of the nature and cause of the accusation," who must be "confronted with the witnesses against him," and who must be accorded "compulsory process for obtaining witnesses in his favor." Although not stated in the Amendment in so many words, the

right to self-representation—to make one's own defense personally—is thus necessarily implied by the structure of the Amendment. The right to defend is given directly to the accused; for it is he who suffers the consequences if the defense fails.

The counsel provision supplements this design. It speaks of the "assistance" of counsel, and an assistant, however expert, is still an assistant. The language and spirit of the Sixth Amendment contemplate that counsel, like the other defense tools guaranteed by the Amendment, shall be an aid to a willing defendant—not an organ of the State interposed between an unwilling defendant and his right to defend himself personally. To thrust counsel upon the accused, against his considered wish, thus violates the logic of the Amendment. In such a case, counsel is not an assistant, but a master; and the right to make a defense is stripped of the personal character upon which the Amendment insists. It is true that when a defendant chooses to have a lawyer manage and present his case, law and tradition may allocate to the counsel the power to make binding decisions of trial strategy in many areas. This allocation can only be justified, however, by the defendant's consent, at the outset, to accept counsel as his representative. An unwanted counsel "represents" the defendant only through a tenuous and unacceptable legal fiction. Unless the accused has acquiesced in such representation, the defense presented is not the defense guaranteed him by the Constitution, for, in a very real sense, it is not *his* defense.

* * *

[The Court explored in detail the historical development of the right to counsel in England and in the United States. It found that both English and colonial legal history support interpreting the Sixth Amendment to imply a right of self-representation].

* * *

IV

There can be no blinking the fact that the right of an accused to conduct his own defense seems to cut against the grain of this Court's decisions holding that the Constitution requires that no accused can be convicted and imprisoned unless he has been accorded the right to the assistance of counsel. For it is surely true that the basic thesis of those decisions is that the help of a lawyer is essential to assure the defendant a fair trial. And a strong argument can surely be made that the whole thrust of those decisions must inevitably lead to the conclusion that a State may constitutionally impose a lawyer upon even an unwilling defendant.

But it is one thing to hold that every defendant, rich or poor, has the right to the assistance of counsel, and quite another to say that a State may compel a defendant to accept a lawyer he does not want. The value of state-appointed counsel was not unappreciated by the Founders, yet the notion of compulsory counsel was utterly foreign to them. And whatever else may be said of those who wrote the Bill of Rights, surely there can be no doubt that they understood the inestimable worth of free choice.

It is undeniable that in most criminal prosecutions defendants could better defend with counsel's guidance than by their own unskilled efforts.

But where the defendant will not voluntarily accept representation by counsel, the potential advantage of a lawyer's training and experience can be realized, if at all, only imperfectly. To force a lawyer on a defendant can only lead him to believe that the law contrives against him. Moreover, it is not inconceivable that in some rare instances, the defendant might in fact present his case more effectively by conducting his own defense. Personal liberties are not rooted in the law of averages. The right to defend is personal. The defendant, and not his lawyer or the State, will bear the personal consequences of a conviction. It is the defendant, therefore, who must be free personally to decide whether in his particular case counsel is to his advantage. And although he may conduct his own defense ultimately to his own detriment, his choice must be honored out of "that respect for the individual which is the lifeblood of the law."[a]

V

When an accused manages his own defense, he relinquishes, as a purely factual matter, many of the traditional benefits associated with the right to counsel. For this reason, in order to represent himself, the accused must "knowingly and intelligently" forego those relinquished benefits. Although a defendant need not himself have the skill and experience of a lawyer in order competently and intelligently to choose self-representation, he should be made aware of the dangers and disadvantages of self-representation,

---

a. Of course, a State may—even over objection by the accused—appoint a "standby counsel" to aid the accused if and when the accused requests help, and to be available to represent the accused in the event that termination of the defendant's self-representation is necessary.

The right of self-representation is not a license to abuse the dignity of the courtroom.

Neither is it a license not to comply with relevant rules of procedural and substantive law. Thus, whatever else may or may not be open to him on appeal, a defendant who elects to represent himself cannot thereafter complain that the quality of his own defense amounted to a denial of "effective assistance of counsel."

so that the record will establish that "he knows what he is doing and his choice is made with eyes open."

Here, weeks before trial, Faretta clearly and unequivocally declared to the trial judge that he wanted to represent himself and did not want counsel. The record affirmatively shows that Faretta was literate, competent, and understanding, and that he was voluntarily exercising his informed free will. The trial judge had warned Faretta that he thought it was a mistake not to accept the assistance of counsel, and that Faretta would be required to follow all the "ground rules" of trial procedure. We need make no assessment of how well or poorly Faretta had mastered the intricacies of the hearsay rule and the California code provisions that govern challenges of potential jurors on *voir dire*. For his technical legal knowledge, as such, was not relevant to an assessment of his knowing exercise of the right to defend himself.

In forcing Faretta, under these circumstances, to accept against his will a state-appointed public defender, the California courts deprived him of his constitutional right to conduct his own defense. Accordingly, the judgment before us is vacated, and the case is remanded for further proceedings not inconsistent with this opinion.

MR. CHIEF JUSTICE BURGER, **with whom** MR. JUSTICE BLACKMUN **and** MR. JUSTICE REHNQUIST **join, dissenting.**

* * *

This case * * * is an example of the judicial tendency to constitutionalize what is thought "good." That effort fails on its own terms here, because there is nothing desirable or useful in permitting every accused person, even the most uneducated and inexperienced, to insist upon conducting his own defense to criminal charges. Moreover, there is no constitutional

basis for the Court's holding, and it can only add to the problems of an already malfunctioning criminal justice system. I therefore dissent.

The most striking feature of the Court's opinion is that it devotes so little discussion to the matter which it concedes is the core of the decision, that is, discerning an independent basis in the Constitution for the supposed right to represent oneself in a criminal trial. Its ultimate assertion that such a right is tucked between the lines of the Sixth Amendment is contradicted by the Amendment's language and its consistent judicial interpretation.

* * *

Society has the right to expect that, when courts find new rights implied in the Constitution, their potential effect upon the resources of our criminal justice system will be considered. However, such considerations are conspicuously absent from the Court's opinion in this case.

It hardly needs repeating that courts at all levels are already handicapped by the unsupplied demand for competent advocates, with the result that it often takes far longer to complete a given case than experienced counsel would require. If we were to assume that there will be widespread exercise of the newly discovered constitutional right to self-representation, it would almost certainly follow that there will be added congestion in the courts and that the quality of justice will suffer. * * *

* * *

[Justice Blackmun also wrote a dissenting opinion in which the Chief Justice and Justice Rehnquist joined. He argued that the procedural problems spawned by the case "will far outweigh whatever tactical advantage the defendant may feel he has gained by electing to represent himself." Referring to the old proverb that "one who is his own lawyer has a fool for a client," Justice Blackmun opined that "the Court * * * now bestows a *constitutional* right on one to make a fool of himself."]

Competency to Waive the Right to Counsel and Proceed Pro Se: Godinez v. Moran

As discussed earlier in the Chapter, the Due Process Clause provides that a defendant may not be tried unless he is competent to stand trial. It follows that a defendant cannot validly waive his right to counsel and proceed to trial *pro se* unless he is competent to do so. The competency standard for standing trial is whether the defendant is able to consult with his lawyer "with a reasonable degree of rational understanding" and has "a rational as well as factual understanding of the proceedings against him." Dusky v. United States, 362 U.S. 402 (1960). In Godinez v. Moran, 509 U.S. 389 (1993), the Court considered whether this "rational understanding" test was also a sufficient standard for determining a defendant's competency to waive counsel and proceed *pro se*. The lower court in *Moran* had concluded that competency to waive the right to counsel "requires a higher level of mental functioning than that required to stand trial," and that a person cannot competently waive counsel unless he has the capacity to make a "reasoned choice" among the alternatives available to him. The lower court reasoned that a defendant who represents himself at trial must have greater powers of comprehension and judgment than would be required to stand trial with the aid of an attorney.

The Supreme Court, in an opinion by Justice Thomas, rejected the lower court's position and held that the "rational understanding" test, which defines competency to stand trial, also defines competency to waive counsel and proceed to trial. The Court stated that the lower court's reasoning had "a flawed premise." Citing *Faretta,* Justice Thomas declared that "the competence that is required of a defendant seeking to waive his right to counsel is the competence to waive the right, not the competence to represent himself."

Justice Thomas stressed, however, that competence was not the only requirement for a valid waiver of the right to counsel. He explained that a trial court must also "satisfy itself that the waiver of his constitutional rights is knowing and voluntary." In this sense there is a heightened standard for waiving the right to counsel, "but it is not a heightened standard of competence."

Justice Kennedy, joined by Justice Scalia, concurred in part and in the judgment. He stated that if a defendant "elects to stand trial and to take the foolish course of acting as his own counsel, the law does not for that reason require any added degree of competence."

Justice Blackmun, joined by Justice Stevens, dissented. He declared that "a defendant who is utterly incapable of conducting his own defense" cannot be considered competent to waive the right to counsel at trial, "any more than a person who chooses to leap out of a window in the belief that he can fly can be considered 'competent' to make such a choice."

Judge Lewis, concurring in Government of the Virgin Islands v. Charles, 72 F.3d 401 (3d Cir. 1995), took the *Godinez* majority to task for ignoring the possibility that a minimally competent defendant might waive his right to counsel and yet be simply incapable of conducting a defense. Charles was diagnosed as paranoid and delusional. He wanted to dismiss appointed counsel because counsel favored an insanity defense. Charles thought counsel and the government were out to get him because they were afraid of him. The trial judge engaged in an extensive colloquy about the dangers and risks of self-representation, and Charles made known throughout his desire to represent himself. Judge Lewis found himself constrained to uphold Charles' waiver of counsel. But he criticized the *Godinez* holding in the following passage:

> This difficult case presents us with a window through which to view the real-world effects of the Supreme Court's decision in Godinez v. Moran, and it is not a pretty sight. Charles' behavior at a hearing before the district court left little doubt that he was prone to paranoid delusions and was unstable. * * *

> In this case, it is abundantly clear from the record that Charles was not competent to conduct his own defense. This man has had a well documented history of mental illness. Indeed, it appears that Charles' decision to waive counsel, reject a possibly valid defense and proceed on his own may itself have been the product of mental illness. * * * Under the *Godinez* Court's reasoning, * * * it doesn't matter that Charles obviously is not competent to actually represent himself; the only question is whether he is lucid enough to make it through a colloquy and to waive his right to counsel. So long as he is, according to the Court, he is ready and able to try his case. There is no need to look any deeper because, after all, during the colloquy Charles was able to punctuate his random incoherences with a few moments of apparent lucidity and to answer the right questions satisfactorily. This, according to the Court, automatically renders him fit to try his murder case * * *. It is hardly surprising, then, that Charles and many others similarly situated—some of whom might have reasonable insanity defenses or other avenues of defense to pursue—usually wind up either on death row or serving life sentences. * * * Given that the Supreme Court has determined that a defendant's competency to conduct his or her own defense is not relevant to whether a defendant has knowingly and voluntarily waived his or her right to counsel, district courts ought to be particularly vigilant in assuring that a defendant understands exactly what he or she is waiving in a *Faretta* hearing. The *Faretta* hearing, in this case and in many future cases, was and will be the last procedural safeguard available to a mentally unstable but "competent" defendant who mistakenly believes he or she can effectively try his or her own case. Through its holdings in *Faretta* and *Godinez*, the Court has defined [the right to self-representation] in such a way that requires us to allow a paranoid, delusional defendant to elect to represent himself at trial, pursue an ill-advised defense, and ultimately be sentenced to life imprisonment. That this result is constitutionally permissible is deeply disturbing and ultimately impugns the integrity of our criminal justice system.

Is the solution to the problem seen by Judge Lewis stricter standards of competency to waive *Faretta* rights? Or is the solution to reverse *Faretta*, a decision that didn't seem to do Charles much good?

Knowing and Intelligent Waiver

In order to exercise the independent right of self-representation, a defendant must not only be competent; he must know and understand the consequences of waiving the assistance of counsel. A criminal defendant usually is untrained and unskilled in law and trial procedures. Studies indicate that representation by an attorney substantially improves an accused's chances of receiving a preliminary hearing and release on bail. A defendant represented by an attorney more frequently receives a jury trial, dismissal, or acquittal and, if convicted, more frequently receives a suspended sentence, a relatively short sentence, or probation. See Nagel, Effects of Alternative Types of Counsel on Criminal Procedure Treatment, 48 Ind.L.J. 404 (1972–73). Should a defendant be advised of these and other dangers of self-representation before he waives the assistance of counsel? See United States v. Robinson, 913 F.2d 712 (9th Cir. 1990)(for a knowing and intelligent waiver, "a criminal defendant must be aware of the nature of the charges against him, the possible penalties, and the dangers and disadvantages of self-representation").

A model inquiry for Federal District Judges to use with defendants who wish to proceed *pro se* is contained in 1 Bench Book for United States District Judges 1.02–2 to–5:

When a defendant states that he wishes to represent himself, you should ask questions similar to the following:

(a) Have you ever studied law?

(b) Have you ever represented yourself or any other defendant in a criminal action?

(c) You realize, do you not, that you are charged with these crimes: (Here state the crimes with which the defendant is charged.)

(d) You realize, do you not, that if you are found guilty of the crime charged in Count I the court must impose an assessment of at least _____ and could sentence you to as much as _____ years in prison and fine you as much as $_____?

(Then ask him a similar question with respect to each other crime with which he may be charged in the indictment or information.)

(e) You realize, do you not, that if you are found guilty of more than one of those crimes this court can order that the sentences be served consecutively, that is, one after another?

(f) You realize, do you not, that if you represent yourself, you are on your own? I cannot tell you how you should try your case or even advise you as to how to try your case.

(g) Are you familiar with the Federal Rules of Evidence?

(h) You realize, do you not, that the Federal Rules of Evidence govern what evidence may or may not be introduced at trial and, in representing yourself, you must abide by those rules?

(i) Are you familiar with the Federal Rules of Criminal Procedure?

(j) You realize, do you not, that those rules govern the way in which a criminal action is tried in federal court?

(k) You realize, do you not, that if you decide to take the witness stand, you must present your testimony by asking questions of yourself? You cannot just take the stand and tell your story. You must proceed question by question through your testimony.

(*l*) (Then say to the defendant something to this effect):

I must advise you that in my opinion you would be far better defended by a trained lawyer than you can be by yourself. I think it is unwise of you to try to represent yourself. You are not familiar with the law. You are not familiar with court procedure. You are not familiar with the rules of evidence. I would strongly urge you not to try to represent yourself.

(m) Now, in light of the penalty that you might suffer if you are found guilty and in light of all of the difficulties of representing yourself, is it still your desire to represent yourself and to give up your right to be represented by a lawyer?

(n) Is your decision entirely voluntary on your part?

(*o*) If the answers to the two preceding questions are in the affirmative, [and in your opinion the waiver of counsel *is* knowing and voluntary,] you should then say something to the following effect:

"I find that the defendant has knowingly and voluntarily waived his right to counsel. I will therefore permit him to represent himself."

(p) You should consider the appointment of standby counsel to assist the defendant and to replace him if the court should determine during trial that the defendant can no longer be permitted to represent himself.

Failure to conduct a waiver inquiry at least similar to that suggested in the Bench Book has been held reversible error. See United States v. McDowell, 814 F.2d 245 (6th Cir.1987); United States v. Balough, 820 F.2d 1485 (9th Cir. 1987)(noting "limited exception" to per se reversal where the record on the whole reveals a knowing and intelligent waiver of counsel).

Faretta Warning?

Invoking the right to self-representation means a waiver of the right to counsel. Conversely, invoking the right to counsel means a waiver of the right to self-representation. The defendant must receive detailed warnings, as discussed above, before a waiver of the right to counsel will be found. Is the defendant invoking a right to counsel entitled to be notified of his right to proceed *pro se* before a waiver of *that* right can be found? In United States v. Martin, 25 F.3d 293 (6th Cir.1994), the court answered this question as follows:

While the right to self-representation is related to the right to counsel, [it] is grounded more in considerations of free choice than in fair trial concerns. Thus, the right to self-representation does not implicate constitutional fair trial concerns to the same extent as does an accused's right to counsel. As the constitutional basis of the right to self-representation does not require a knowing and intelligent waiver of that right, the district court need not advise a defendant of her right to proceed pro se prior to assertion of such a right.

Accord Munkus v. Furlong, 170 F.3d 980 (10th Cir.1999) (right to counsel is absolute while right to self-representation is subject to many conditions; given the constraints on the right to self-representation, a criminal defendant does not have to be informed of this right).

Why is a right grounded in free choice considered subordinate to a right grounded in fair trial concerns? What would happen if all defendants were notified of their right to proceed *pro se*?

Requirement of Unequivocal Invocation

Courts have held that a defendant's waiver of the right to assistance of counsel must be "unequivocal." Courts are justifiably concerned that if the *Faretta* right is not clearly invoked, a defendant who ends up representing himself and losing will appeal on the ground that he never really waived his right to counsel. For example, in Meeks v. Craven, 482 F.2d 465 (9th Cir.1973), the defendant argued in a petition for habeas corpus that he was denied his right to proceed *pro se*. The court refused habeas corpus relief:

> Meeks' demand in this case was certainly not "unequivocal." He made no demand to proceed without counsel at the beginning of his trial. It is during the afternoon session that there appear in the record three statements which could be construed as demands by Meeks to proceed *pro se:*

> "The Defendant: Your Honor, I have a motion before me. I got a hernia. Motion is whether or not I can proceed on pro per status, and my motion is based on points and authorities if you'd like to hear them.

> "The Court: Why do you want to proceed in pro per?

> "The Defendant: Well, there is another motion I would like to make after this one and counsel is against it."

> * * *

> "The Defendant: * * * I do believe in this case, as the Federal right points out, that I be allowed to conduct my own defense due to the fact that counsel feels very, very strongly about a motion that I would like to present before the Court this afternoon. If it was not for this motion, I would be more than willing to let counsel proceed. But I believe that this motion should be entered into the record because I believe it has, in effect, law that has been overlooked."

> * * *

> "The Court: * * * Motion denied. You still want to represent yourself?"

> "The Defendant: Yes, Your Honor, I think I will."

> The first two demands were conditional: Meeks stated that he wished to waive counsel only in order to present his motion and that he had no objection to counsel otherwise. The judge permitted Meeks to represent himself for purposes of making his motion. Meeks' "I think I will" is a prototype of equivocation. His so-called "demands" are not made more effective by the intervening discussion about Meeks' inability to present a defense. All this discussion was prior to the second "demand"; none of it was calculated to make the judge believe that Meeks wished anything more

than to present his motion. Meeks made no further requests to proceed *pro se.*

An "unequivocal" demand to proceed *pro se* should be, at the very least, sufficiently clear that if it is granted the defendant should not be able to turn about and urge that he was improperly denied counsel. "I think I will" hardly meets the constitutional criteria for waiver of counsel.

See also Stano v. Dugger, 921 F.2d 1125 (11th Cir.1991)(en banc)("trial courts are not required to divine when a criminal defendant is proceeding pro se * * *. The right of self-representation must be manifested to the trial court by an oral or written request in order to be recognized and to trigger the requisite examination by the court.").

Dissatisfaction With Appointed Counsel

In Adams v. Carroll, 875 F.2d 1441 (9th Cir.1989), Public Defender Carroll was appointed to represent Adams. Their relationship deteriorated quickly. Citing "lack of trust and communication with Mr. Carroll", Adams requested the appointment of a different attorney. He said that "if I can't have another lawyer, I will have to go pro per." Eventually, the court granted Adams' motion and reappointed the Public Defender's office. To Adams' "evident astonishment" the Public Defender's office promptly reassigned Carroll to the case! Adams objected, saying that while he didn't think himself competent to defend himself, he would have to do so if representation by Carroll was his only other choice. The trial court refused to appoint another substitute counsel, and refused to allow Adams to represent himself, on the ground that Adams had declared himself not competent to do so. The case proceeded to trial with Carroll as defense counsel, and Adams was convicted. The court found that Adams had made an unequivocal request to proceed *pro se* and that Adams' conviction therefore had to be reversed. The court first noted that the "unequivocal request" requirement served two purposes:

First, it acts as a backstop for the defendant's right to counsel, by ensuring that the defendant does not inadvertently waive that right through occasional musings on the benefits of self-representation. Because a defendant normally gives up more than he gains when he elects self-representation, we must be reasonably certain that he in fact wishes to represent himself.

The requirement that a request for self-representation be unequivocal also serves an institutional purpose: It prevents a defendant from taking advantage of the mutual exclusivity of the rights to counsel and self-representation. A defendant who vacillates at trial between wishing to be represented by counsel and wishing to represent himself could place the trial court in a difficult position: If the court appoints counsel, the defendant could, on appeal, rely on his intermittent requests for self-representation in arguing that he had been denied the right to represent himself; if the court permits self-representation, the defendant could claim he had been denied the right to counsel. The requirement of unequivocality resolves this dilemma by forcing the defendant to make an explicit choice. If he equivocates, he is presumed to have requested the assistance of counsel.[64]

---

64. See also United States v. Singleton, 107 F.3d 1091 (4th Cir.1997) (noting that a trial court evaluating a defendant's request to represent himself must "traverse a thin line be-

According to the court, Adams had consistently expressed his desire to represent himself if Carroll was the only alternative. The court reasoned that "while his requests were *conditional,* they were not equivocal" and that "none of the purposes served by the [unequivocality] requirement would be furthered by treating a conditional request for self-representation as equivocal." Compare Burton v. Collins, 937 F.2d 131 (5th Cir.1991)(a defendant who expressed dissatisfaction with defense counsel, and asked whether he could represent himself, had not made a clear and unequivocal invocation of his right to self-representation; the colloquy with the judge was reasonably construed as an inquiry into alternatives rather than a waiver of counsel).

The reverse situation from *Adams* is where the defendant is allowed to proceed *pro se* because he doesn't like the counsel he was appointed and the court refuses to appoint a substitute counsel. Can the defendant argue that under these circumstances, his waiver of the right to counsel was not voluntary? Since there is no constitutional right to choose a particular counsel to be appointed, courts have rejected the notion that an election of *pro se* status is involuntary merely because of dissatisfaction with appointed counsel. See United States v. Robinson, 913 F.2d 712 (9th Cir.1990). On the other hand, when the defendant's only choice is between self-representation and *incompetent* counsel, choice of *pro se* status does not indicate a voluntary waiver of the right to counsel, and reversal is required. Therefore, if the defendant states that he wishes to defend himself because he believes appointed counsel to be incompetent, the trial court must conduct a thorough inquiry into the allegations, and must appoint substitute counsel if the counsel has, up to that point, given ineffective representation under the standards of Strickland v. Washington. See United States v. Silkwood, 893 F.2d 245 (10th Cir.1989)(trial court erred when it failed to conduct inquiry to ensure that the defendant was not forced to make the "Hobson's choice * * * between incompetent or unprepared counsel and appearing *pro se*"); Crandell v. Bunnell, 144 F.3d 1213 (9th Cir.1998)(where counsel did nothing to prepare a defense for two months, his representation fell below an objective standard of reasonableness; the defendant's choice to represent himself, after the court refused to appoint substitute counsel, was therefore involuntary). Compare United States v. Webster 84 F.3d 1056 (8th Cir.1996) (no "Hobson's choice" between self-representation and incompetent counsel; defendant was unhappy with counsel, but made no assertion that counsel was incompetent).

Remedy for a Faretta Violation

What is the remedy for the denial of the right to self-representation? Is reversal required even where counsel did a better job at trial than the defendant would have done? In McKaskle v. Wiggins, 465 U.S. 168 (1984), the Court held that the denial of the right to proceed *pro se* was a violation of the defendant's right to personal autonomy. It had nothing to do with the likelihood of a successful outcome at trial. The Court therefore concluded that "the right is either respected or denied; its deprivation cannot be harmless."

tween improperly allowing the defendant to proceed pro se, thereby violating his right to counsel, and improperly having the defendant proceed with counsel, thereby violating his right to self-representation"; noting also that "a skillful defendant could manipulate this dilemma to create reversible error.").

Thus, per se reversal is required for a violation of *Gideon,* and for the opposite violation of *Faretta.* Suppose that the defendant's *Faretta* rights are violated by the trial court's appointment of counsel. The conviction is therefore reversed. On re-trial, the defendant changes his mind and *demands* counsel. Can the trial judge refuse this demand and require the defendant to represent himself, because that is what he wanted to do in the first place? Why should the state have to give him what he so strongly objected to in the first trial? In Johnstone v. Kelly, 812 F.2d 821 (2d Cir.1987), the court stated that counsel must be provided on retrial unless the defendant makes an unequivocal invocation of the right of self-representation. The court explained as follows:

> If Johnstone elects to be represented by counsel at a retrial, it is not quite true, as the State contends, that he will again receive what the State once provided him. Though the State previously provided him with counsel, it denied him the choice whether to have counsel or proceed *pro se.* It is that choice that must be accorded at a retrial * * *.

B. LIMITS ON THE RIGHT OF SELF–REPRESENTATION

The Court in *Faretta* was careful to note that the right to self-representation is not absolute. It is fair to state that courts after *Faretta* have not given the right to self-representation preferred status. Many qualifications on the right have been found reasonable.

1. *Timeliness*

If the defendant waits until trial, or just before it, to invoke his right to self-representation, then the trial court has the discretion to deny it. See Horton v. Dugger, 895 F.2d 714 (11th Cir.1990)(request to proceed *pro se,* made on first day of trial, held untimely). Why can't the right be invoked at any time?

2. *Disruption of the Court*

The majority in *Faretta* recognized that "the right to self-representation is not a license to abuse the dignity of the courtroom." What type of acts can be considered so "obstructionist" that the right to self-representation is lost? In United States v. Flewitt, 874 F.2d 669 (9th Cir.1989), the trial court appointed counsel, against the Flewitts' wishes, because the Flewitts were unprepared at the time of trial, had made excessive and "poorly formulated" discovery motions, and had refused to cooperate with the government in utilizing discovery opportunities. On appeal, they argued that their right to self-representation had been violated, and the government argued that the Flewitts had lost their right due to their "obstructionist" tactics. The court found that the reference in *Faretta* to obstructionist tactics spoke of "disruption in the courtroom." The court noted that the Flewitts' pretrial activity may have been ill-advised and detrimental to them, but "that was their choice to make." Compare Savage v. Estelle, 924 F.2d 1459 (9th Cir.1990)(defendant with a severe speech impediment is found unable to "abide by rules of procedure and courtroom protocol"; therefore, the right to self-representation was properly denied).

Is the defendant "disruptive" when he makes ridiculous arguments in court, tries to introduce clearly irrelevant evidence, concocts outlandish defenses, and proffers long-winded questions on cross-examination? If such conduct at the trial is enough to be considered "disruptive" under *Faretta*, how many defendants will be permitted to invoke the right to self-representation?

3. *Protection of Witnesses*

In many cases, the defendant's self-representation is especially unsettling to prosecution witnesses. For example, in the case on Long Island where Colin Ferguson was tried for shooting commuters on a Long Island Railroad train, Ferguson demanded to represent himself. The shooting victims who survived were therefore subjected to the ordeal of having to be questioned directly in court by the very person who shot them. Can the interests of witnesses ever outweigh the defendant's qualified right to self-representation?

The Fourth Circuit, in Fields v. Murray, 49 F.3d 1024 (4th Cir.1995)(en banc), explored the limitations on a defendant's *Faretta* right to personally question witnesses in the context of a sex crimes prosecution. Fields sought to act, in his words, as "co-counsel" in order to question the alleged sex abuse victims himself, because he "firmly believed these kids cannot look me in the eye and lie to me." The state trial court did not permit Fields to personally cross-examine the young girls who were witnesses against him, but did permit him to write out his questions and give them to his appointed lawyer. Fields was convicted. His *Faretta* claim was rejected by the state appellate courts, on the ground that since he only wanted to cross-examine the prosecution witnesses, and not to represent himself in any other respect, he had failed to unequivocally invoke his right to self-representation.

On habeas review, the court of appeals agreed with the state courts that Field had not unequivocally invoked his right to self-representation. But the court held further that even if Fields had represented himself, he would have had no right under the circumstances to cross-examine the witnesses personally. The court relied on Maryland v. Craig, 497 U.S. 836 (1990), where the Supreme Court held that a defendant's right to face-to-face confrontation could be restricted where such confrontation would traumatize a child-witness. The court of appeals reasoned as follows:

> If a defendant's Confrontation Clause right can be limited in the manner provided in *Craig*, we have little doubt that a defendant's self-representation right can be similarly limited. While the Confrontation Clause right is guaranteed explicitly in the Sixth Amendment, * * * the self-representation right is only implicit in that Amendment. The self-representation right was only firmly established in 1975 in *Faretta,* and then only over the dissent of three justices. Moreover, it is universally recognized that the self-representation right is not absolute.

> The State's interest here in protecting child sexual abuse victims from the emotional trauma of being cross-examined by their alleged abuser is at least as great as, and likely greater than, the State's interest in *Craig* of protecting children from the emotional harm of merely having to testify in their alleged abuser's presence. We have little trouble determining, therefore, that the State's interest here was sufficiently important to outweigh Fields' right to cross-examine personally witnesses against him if denial of this cross-examination was necessary to protect the young girls from emotional trauma.

4. *Standby Counsel*

Faretta indicates that a state may appoint standby counsel, even over the defendant's objection, to aid the defendant and to be available to represent him if self-representation is for some reason terminated. The limits of standby counsel's role were explored in McKaskle v. Wiggins, 465 U.S. 168 (1984), where the Court found that advisory counsel's conduct did not unconstitutionally interfere with Wiggins' right to self-representation. Wiggins first waived counsel, then requested counsel, and finally decided to represent himself. The trial court appointed, at his request, two counsel to advise him. Disagreements between counsel and Wiggins occurred and at times counsel quarreled openly with Wiggins. From time-to-time throughout the trial, Wiggins would give in and let standby counsel take over the defense.

Justice O'Connor wrote for the majority and stated that *Faretta* requires that a defendant be given more than just the chance to be heard along with others: he must be given control over the defense. *Faretta* held that the right to self-representation was based on two factors: first, the defendant has the right grounded in personal autonomy to choose to control his own defense; second, self-representation may in some cases be an effective strategy, because it would allow the jury to sympathize with a defendant matched up against overwhelming prosecutorial forces. Accordingly, standby counsel cannot seize actual control over the defendant's case, or else the first, "core" aspect of the right to self-representation would be violated. And standby counsel cannot without the defendant's consent "destroy the jury's perception that the defendant is representing himself," or else the strategy aspect of the right to self-representation would be undermined. The Court noted that "participation by standby counsel outside the presence of the jury engages only the first of these two limitations." It further noted that "*Faretta* rights are adequately vindicated in proceedings outside the presence of the jury if the *pro se* defendant is allowed to address the court freely" and if "all disagreements between counsel and the *pro se* defendant are resolved in the defendant's favor whenever the matter is one that would normally be left to the discretion of counsel." It found that most of the incidents of which Wiggins complained occurred outside the jury's presence. And it emphasized that all conflicts between Wiggins and his counsel were resolved in Wiggins' favor, although it opined that several incidents in which counsel engaged in acrimonious exchanges with their client were "regrettable."

The majority also found that Wiggins' problems largely occurred because he frequently changed his mind about the role he wanted counsel to play. Justice O'Connor reasoned that once Wiggins asked counsel to participate, the trial judge could assume that subsequent appearances were with his acquiescence unless he indicated otherwise. The Court concluded as follows:

> *Faretta* affirmed the defendant's constitutional right to appear on stage at his trial. We recognize that a *pro se* defendant may wish to dance a solo, not a *pas de deux*. Standby counsel must generally respect that preference. But counsel need not be excluded altogether, especially when the participation is outside the presence of the jury or is with the defendant's express consent. The defendant in this case was allowed to make his own appearances as he saw fit. In our judgment counsel's unsolicited involvement was held within reasonable limits.

In dissent, Justice White, joined by Justices Brennan and Marshall, argued that the court of appeals correctly found that standby counsel continuously participated in the trial, disrupted the proceedings, and turned the trial into an ordeal for the jury. He expressed concern about the subtle influences that squabbles between counsel and client can have on the outcome of a case and about the defendant's (not the jury's) perception of fairness, observing that *Faretta* is premised on the importance of the appearance of justice to the accused.

It is worth noting that in later proceedings, Wiggins maintained that he was impermissibly *denied* his right to counsel at his trial, because he had not unequivocally invoked his right to self-representation. The court in Wiggins v. Procunier, 753 F.2d 1318 (5th Cir.1985), rejected his claim. Does this give you some perspective on why courts require the right of self-representation to be unequivocally invoked?

In United States v. Flewitt, 874 F.2d 669 (9th Cir.1989), the court held that the defendants' failure to cooperate with standby counsel was not sufficient reason to deny them the right of self-representation. The court stated that "it indeed would be a paradox to justify revoking a defendant's *pro se* status on the basis that the defendant failed to consult counsel." But isn't that the very "paradox" that the Court imposed in *Wiggins* when it held that standby counsel could have significant input into the defense even over the defendant's objection?

In United States v. Pollani, 146 F.3d 269 (5th Cir.1998), the Court held that the trial court erred in allowing the defendant to proceed pro se, because the defendant had not unequivocally waived his right to counsel. The government responded that there was no error, because the trial court provided standby counsel to assist Pollani at the trial. But the court rejected this as a solution to a *Faretta* violation. It stated that the appointment of standby counsel "is a tactic for assisting a pro se litigant in vindicating his Sixth Amendment right of self-representation, not a substitute for representation by counsel for a defendant who seeks to exercise his right to counsel."

For a discussion on standby counsel's proper role and how standby counsel can be most effective, see Poulin, The Role of Standby Counsel in Criminal Cases: In the Twilight Zone of the Criminal Justice System, 75 N.Y.U. L.Rev. 676 (2000).

5. *Hybrid Counsel and Control of the Defense*

Frequently a defendant wants to appear as "co-counsel" or to defend partially *pro se* and partially by counsel. The Court in *Wiggins* held that there is no constitutional right to "hybrid representation," but stated that a court could allow it in the exercise of its discretion. Only a few courts have exercised their discretion and permitted hybrid representation. See, e.g., State v. McCleary, 149 N.J.Super. 77, 373 A.2d 400 (1977). See also United States v. Turnbull, 888 F.2d 636 (9th Cir.1989)("if the defendant assumes any of the 'core functions' of the lawyer, the hybrid scheme is acceptable only if the defendant has voluntarily waived counsel"). What arguments support and oppose hybrid representation? When should a judge permit it? If the costs of the representation do not increase, what purpose, other than to discourage the exercise of *Faretta* rights, is served by denying hybrid representation? See generally Note, The Accused as Co–

Counsel: The Case for the Hybrid Defense, 12 Valparaiso L.Rev. 329 (1978). Does *Wiggins* suggest an answer?

Ceding Control Over the Defense

Unless hybrid representation is granted, a defendant who chooses the right to counsel over the right to self-representation gives up substantial control over the defense. Strategic choices are left to the lawyer; the lawyer can veto the client's wishes as to what defenses can be raised, what arguments will be made, how to cross-examine a witness, etc. See, e.g., United States v. Padilla, 819 F.2d 952 (10th Cir.1987), where the court found no constitutional violation even though counsel refused to structure a defense as the defendant directed. The court stated that "the Sixth Amendment provides no right to counsel blindly following a defendant's instructions."

There are three notable exceptions to counsel's control over the defense. It is ultimately the defendant's decision (1) whether to waive a jury trial, (2) whether to testify, and (3) whether to plead guilty. See, e.g., Stano v. Dugger, 921 F.2d 1125 (11th Cir.1991)(counsel cannot be deemed ineffective where defendant pleads guilty against counsel's advice). See also Rule 1.2 of the Model Rules of Professional Conduct (lawyer shall abide by client's decision "after consultation with the lawyer" as to these three matters).

In Jones v. Barnes, 463 U.S. 745 (1983), the Court held that the Sixth Amendment does not require appointed appellate counsel to raise all nonfrivolous claims on appeal. The Court reasoned that a contrary rule would seriously undermine "the ability of counsel to present the client's case in accord with counsel's professional evaluation." The Court stated that the right of personal autonomy recognized in *Faretta* did not extend to strategic choices once the right to counsel has been invoked. Justice Brennan, joined by Justice Marshall, dissented and argued that the defendant's right to "the assistance of counsel" requires that counsel raise all issues of arguable merit that his client insists upon raising. Justice Blackmun concurred in the result, reasoning that an attorney should, as an ethical, not a constitutional, requirement, raise all nonfrivolous claims upon which his client insists.

Retained Hybrid Counsel?

Does the defendant have the right to hybrid representation if he *retains* counsel? The Court in United States v. Singleton, 107 F.3d 1091 (4th Cir.1997), stated that there was no such right—if the defendant is asking for a constitutional right to control the "lawyer" aspects of the defense, then he must represent himself. The court reasoned as follows:

> [W]e believe the court acted well within its broad discretion in denying, absent a constitutional requirement, an arrangement under which retained counsel would play a supportive role to a pro se defendant during trial. A trial judge has broad supervisory power over his courtroom and may within that discretion insist that a trial before him, if orchestrated or guided by an attorney, be presented in accordance with the ethical, professional, and prudential rules of trial conduct. And in order to be so satisfied, the judge has discretion to insist that in the courtroom counsel, not the client, take

over completely and act as the spokesperson of the defense's case. Thus, the district court, having properly recognized no constitutional right to have advisory counsel support Singleton in the courtroom during trial, had discretion, should Singleton have retained counsel, to insist that Singleton's case be presented in court either by his attorney or by himself, but not by a combination of the two.

6. *Non–Lawyer Representation*

It is generally recognized that there is no constitutional right to non-lawyer representation. See, e.g., United States v. Turnbull, 888 F.2d 636 (9th Cir. 1989)("'Counsel' means 'attorney'"); Comment, Denial of Defendant's Request for Representation by a Nonattorney Does Not Abuse Sixth Amendment, 26 Emory L.J. 457, 459 n. 26 (1977). The reasoning of the court in United States v. Kelley, 539 F.2d 1199 (9th Cir.1976), is typical. Kelley wanted his friend Hurd, a roofer, to serve as trial counsel, but the district court denied that request and appointed "standby counsel." The court of appeals held that a defendant has no Sixth Amendment right to delegate his power of self-representation to a non-lawyer.

> An independent right to the assistance of a non-lawyer cannot be mechanically inferred from the right to waive the assistance of a lawyer and to represent oneself, even though self-representation will usually result in advocacy by a non-lawyer. * * * The Court in *Faretta* did not mechanically infer the right to self-representation from the power to waive the assistance of counsel. It held that the right has an independent source in the structure and history of the Constitution. No such independent source can be found for the alleged right to the assistance of a non-lawyer.

> The personal autonomy protected by the right of self-representation does not require that a delegation of this right to a non-lawyer be respected. It is true that autonomy is to some extent vindicated by allowing a right to be exercised by a designated proxy. However, such an interpretation of autonomy is at odds with the whole tenor of the *Faretta* opinion and runs counter to the competing institutional interest in seeing that justice is administered fairly and efficiently with the assistance of competent lawyers.

A judge may, in her discretion, permit hybrid representation, but may she allow representation by a layperson?[65] Some courts would say "no," since they would be concerned about unauthorized practice of law problems. Can monopolistic bar practices stand in the way of a defendant's choice of counsel?

7. *Self–Representation on Appeal*

Does a defendant have the right to proceed pro se on appeal? The Court answered "no" in Martinez v. Court of Appeal of California, 528 U.S. 152 (2000). Justice Stevens, writing for the Court, distinguished the *Faretta* right to self-representation as grounded in the structure of the Sixth Amendment; he reasoned that Sixth Amendment rights are trial rights, and that the Amendment "does not include any right to appeal." Because the right to appeal is "a

---

65. For an argument in favor of a defendant's right to elect lay representation, see Comment, The Criminal Defendant's Sixth Amendment Right to Lay Representation, 52 U.Chi.L.Rev. 460 (1985).

creature of statute", it followed that the Sixth Amendment "does not provide any basis for finding a right to self-representation on appeal."

Justice Stevens also noted that even at trial, the right to self-representation is not absolute. The autonomy-based right of self-representation is sometimes outweighed by "the government's interest in ensuring the integrity and efficiency of the trial." Justice Stevens applied this balancing of interests in the appellate context in the following passage:

> In the appellate context, the balance between the two competing interests surely tips in favor of the State. The status of the accused defendant, who retains a presumption of innocence throughout the trial process, changes dramatically when a jury returns a guilty verdict. * * * In the words of the *Faretta* majority, appellate proceedings are simply not a case of "hal[ing] a person into its criminal courts."
>
> The requirement of representation by trained counsel implies no disrespect for the individual inasmuch as it tends to benefit the appellant as well as the court. Courts, of course, may still exercise their discretion to allow a lay person to proceed pro se. We already leave to the appellate courts' discretion, keeping "the best interests of both the prisoner and the government in mind," the decision whether to allow a pro se appellant to participate in, or even to be present at, oral argument. Considering the change in position from defendant to appellant, the autonomy interests that survive a felony conviction are less compelling than those motivating the decision in *Faretta*. Yet the overriding state interest in the fair and efficient administration of justice remains as strong as at the trial level. Thus, the States are clearly within their discretion to conclude that the government's interests outweigh an invasion of the appellant's interest in self-representation.

Justice Stevens seemed to go out of his way to cast doubt on the wisdom of the *Faretta* decision. He criticized the *Faretta* Court's reliance on the historical grounding of the right to self-representation; he contended that self-representation was an absolute necessity in Colonial times, given the scarcity and widespread incompetence of counsel. He stated that the original reasons for protecting the right to self-representation "do not have the same force when the availability of competent counsel for every indigent defendant has displaced the need–though not always the desire–for self-representation." Justice Stevens also stated that "[n]o one * * * attempts to argue as a rule pro se representation is wise, desirable or efficient" and that "it is representation by counsel that is the standard, not the exception."

Justice Kennedy wrote a short concurring opinion. Justice Breyer also concurred in a short opinion, noting that judges "have sometimes expressed dismay about the practical consequences" of *Faretta*. He cited United States v. Farhad, 190 F.3d 1097 (9th Cir. 1999), in which Judge Reinhardt stated that the right to self-representation frequently "conflicts squarely and inherently with the right to a fair trial". Justice Breyer stated, however, that he had "found no empirical research * * * that might help determine whether, in general, the right to represent oneself furthers, or inhibits, the Constitution's basic guarantee of fairness. And without some strong factual basis for believing that *Faretta's* holding has proved counterproductive in practice, we are not in a position to reconsider the constitutional assumptions that underlie that case."

Justice Scalia concurred in the judgment. He objected to what he viewed as an inference in the majority opinion that *Faretta* itself was wrongly decided:

I do not share the apparent skepticism of today's opinion concerning the judgment of the Court (often curiously described as merely the judgment of "the majority") in Faretta v. California. I have no doubt that the Framers of our Constitution, who were suspicious enough of governmental power—including judicial power—that they insisted upon a citizen's right to be judged by an independent jury of private citizens, would not have found acceptable the compulsory assignment of counsel by the Government to plead a criminal defendant's case. While I might have rested the decision upon the Due Process Clause rather than the Sixth Amendment, I believe it was correct.

That asserting the right of self-representation may often, or even usually, work to the defendant's disadvantage is no more remarkable—and no more a basis for withdrawing the right—than is the fact that proceeding without counsel in custodial interrogation, or confessing to the crime, usually works to the defendant's disadvantage. Our system of laws generally presumes that the criminal defendant, after being fully informed, knows his own best interests and does not need them dictated by the State. Any other approach is unworthy of a free people. * * *

In any event, *Faretta* is relevant to the question before us only to the limited extent that we must decide whether its holding applies to self-representation on appeal. It seems to me that question is readily answered by the fact that there is no constitutional right to appeal. Since a State could, as far as the federal Constitution is concerned, subject its trial-court determinations to no review whatever, it could a fortiori subject them to review which consists of a nonadversarial reexamination of convictions by a panel of government experts. Adversarial review with counsel appointed by the State is even less questionable than that.

IX. NO RIGHT TO TRIAL OR COUNSEL: THE STATUS OF ENEMY COMBATANTS AFTER SEPTEMBER 11, 2001

This Chapter has concerned itself with the rights that a criminal defendant has that are bound up in the basic right to trial. Since the terrorist attacks of September 11, 2001, however, the Executive has taken the position that certain people suspected of terrorist activity are not entitled to any of the rights delineated in this Chapter. The rationale expressed is that such persons are "enemy combatants" and therefore can be treated as prisoners of war. At most, therefore, they would be entitled to trial at some point in front of a military tribunal.

The question of treatment of suspected terrorists after 9/11 is addressed in two previous parts of this Casebook. Chapter Two discussed the detention of those with information concerning terrorism under the Material Witness statute. Chapter Seven discussed the preventive detention of persons captured in a foreign country and detained at the Guantanamo base in Cuba. This section concerns the treatment of suspected terrorists that the Executive has designated as "enemy combatants."

As of this writing, the Supreme Court has not reviewed the designation of certain individuals as enemy combatants, with a corresponding loss of the right to a jury trial and the right to counsel. Two thoughtful circuit court opinions have been written however, and they are set forth below. It appears inevitable that the Supreme Court will weigh in on the practice, and when that occurs, the Court's opinions will be set forth in the Supplement.

A. ENEMY COMBATANT CAPTURED ABROAD

HAMDI v. RUMSFELD

United States Court of Appeals for the Fourth Circuit, 2003.
316 F.3d 450.

WILKINSON, CHIEF JUDGE:

Yaser Esam Hamdi filed a petition under 28 U.S.C. § 2241 challenging the lawfulness of his confinement in the Norfolk Naval Brig. On this third and latest appeal, the United States challenges the district court's order requiring the production of various materials regarding Hamdi's status as an alleged enemy combatant. The district court certified for appeal the question of whether a declaration by a Special Advisor to the Under Secretary of Defense for Policy setting forth what the government contends were the circumstances of Hamdi's capture was sufficient by itself to justify his detention. Because it is undisputed that Hamdi was captured in a zone of active combat in a foreign theater of conflict, we hold that the submitted declaration is a sufficient basis upon which to conclude that the Commander in Chief has constitutionally detained Hamdi pursuant to the war powers entrusted to him by the United States Constitution. No further factual inquiry is necessary or proper, and we remand the case with directions to dismiss the petition.

I.

As recounted in earlier appeals regarding Hamdi's detention, Hamdi v. Rumsfeld, 294 F.3d 598 (4th Cir. 2002) ("Hamdi I"), and Hamdi v. Rumsfeld, 296 F.3d 278 (4th Cir.

2002) ("Hamdi II"), the al Qaida terrorist network, utilizing commercial airliners, launched massive attacks on the United States on September 11, 2001, successfully striking the World Trade Center in New York City, and the Pentagon, the military headquarters of our country, near Washington, D.C. A third unsuccessful attack upon at least one additional target, most likely within Washington, D.C., was foiled by the efforts of the passengers and crew on the highjacked airliner when it crashed in Somerset County, Pennsylvania, southeast of Pittsburgh. In total, over 3,000 people were killed on American soil that day.

In the wake of this atrocity, Congress authorized the President "to use all necessary and appropriate force against those nations, organizations, or persons he determines planned, authorized, committed, or aided the terrorist attacks" or "harbored such organizations or persons." Authorization for Use of Military Force, Pub. L. No. 107–40, 115 Stat. 224 (Sept. 18, 2001). The President responded by ordering United States armed forces to Afghanistan to subdue al Qaida and the governing Taliban regime supporting it. During this ongoing military operation, thousands of alleged enemy combatants, including Hamdi, have been captured by American and allied forces.

The present case arises out of Hamdi's detention by the United States military in Norfolk, Virginia. Hamdi apparently was born in Louisiana but left for Saudi Arabia when he was a small child. Although initially detained in Afghanistan and then Guantanamo Bay, Hamdi was transferred to the Norfolk Naval Station Brig after it was discovered that he may not have renounced his American citizenship. He has remained in Norfolk since April 2002.

In June 2002, Hamdi's father, Esam Fouad Hamdi, filed a petition for writ of habeas corpus, naming as petitioners both Hamdi and himself as next friend. The petition alleged that Hamdi is a citizen of the United States who was residing in Afghanistan when he was seized by the United States government. According to the petition, "in the course of the military campaign, and as part of their effort to overthrow the Taliban, the United States provided military assistance to the Northern Alliance, a loosely-knit coalition of military groups opposed to the Taliban Government," and thereby "obtained access to individuals held by various factions of the Northern Alliance." The petition further alleges that "Hamdi was captured or transferred into the custody of the United States in the Fall of 2001" in Afghanistan, transported from Afghanistan to Camp X–Ray at the United States Naval Base in Guantanamo Bay, Cuba, in January 2002, and ultimately transferred to the Norfolk Naval Station Brig in Norfolk, Virginia, in April 2002.

Although acknowledging that Hamdi was seized in Afghanistan during a time of active military hostilities, the petition alleges that "as an American citizen, ... Hamdi enjoys the full protections of the Constitution," and that the government's current detention of him in this country without charges, access to a judicial tribunal, or the right to counsel, "violates the Fifth and Fourteenth Amendments to the United States Constitution." By way of relief, the petition asks, inter alia, that the district court: (1) "Order Respondents to cease all interrogations of Yaser Esam Hamdi, direct or indirect, while this litigation is pending"; (2) "Order and declare that Yaser Esam Hamdi is being held in violation of the Fifth and Fourteenth Amendments to the United States Constitution"; (3) "To the extent Respondents contest any material factual allegations in the Petition, schedule an evidentiary hearing, at which Petitioners may adduce proof in support of their allegations"; and (4) "Order that Petitioner Yaser Esam Hamdi be released from Respondents' unlawful custody."

On June 11, before the government had time to respond to the petition, the district court appointed Public Defender Frank Dunham as counsel for the detainee and ordered the government to allow the Defender unmonitored access to Hamdi. On July 12, we reversed the district court's order granting counsel immediate access to Hamdi. We cautioned that Hamdi's petition involved complex and serious national security issues and found that the district court had not shown proper deference to the government's legitimate security and intelligence interests. We did not order the petition dismissed outright, however, noting our reluctance to "embrace [the] sweeping proposition ... that, with no meaningful judicial review, any American citizen alleged to be an enemy combatant could be detained indefinitely without charges or counsel on the government's say-so." Rather, we sanctioned a limited and deferential inquiry into Hamdi's status, noting "that if Hamdi is indeed an 'enemy combatant' who was captured during hostilities in Afghanistan, the government's present detention of him is a lawful one." (citing Ex parte Quirin, 317 U.S. 1 (1942)). We also instructed that, in conducting the inquiry, "the district court must consider the most cautious procedures first, conscious of the prospect that the least drastic procedures may promptly resolve Hamdi's case and make more intrusive measures unnecessary."

Following this remand, the district court held a hearing on July 18. During this hearing, the court expressed its concern over possible violations of Hamdi's rights as an American citizen. The court also questioned the government's most basic contentions regarding the ongoing hostilities, asking "with whom is the war I should suggest that we're fighting?" and "will the war never be over as long as there is any member [or] any person who might feel that they want to attack the United States of America or the citizens of the United States of America?" The court directed that "all of these [answers should] be provided in the answer that the government is to file to the petition" and directed the United States to file such a response to Hamdi's petition by July 25.

On July 25, the government filed a response to, and motion to dismiss, the petition for a writ of habeas corpus. Attached to its response was an affidavit from the Special Advisor to the Under Secretary of Defense for Policy, Michael Mobbs, which confirms the material factual allegations in Hamdi's petition—specifically, that Hamdi was seized in Afghanistan by allied military forces during the course of the sanctioned military campaign, designated an "enemy combatant" by our Government, and ultimately transferred to the Norfolk Naval Brig for detention. Thus, it is undisputed that Hamdi was captured in Afghanistan during a time of armed hostilities there. It is further undisputed that the executive branch has classified him as an enemy combatant.

In addition to stating that Hamdi has been classified as an enemy combatant, the Mobbs declaration went on further to describe what the government contends were the circumstances surrounding Hamdi's seizure, his transfer to United States custody, and his placement in the Norfolk Naval Brig. According to Mobbs, the military determined that Hamdi "traveled to Afghanistan in approximately July or August of 2001" and proceeded to "affiliate[] with a Taliban military unit and receive[] weapons training." While serving with the Taliban in the wake of September 11, he was captured when his Taliban unit surrendered to Northern Alliance forces with which it had been engaged in battle. He was in possession of an AK–47 rifle at the time of surrender. Hamdi was then transported with his unit from Konduz, Afghanistan to the Northern Alliance prison in Mazar-e-Sharif, Afghanistan and, after a prison uprising there, to a prison at Sheberghan, Afghanistan. Hamdi was next transported to the U.S. short term detention facility in Kandahar, and then transferred again to Guantanamo Bay and eventually to the Norfolk Naval Brig. According to Mobbs, interviews with Hamdi confirmed the details of his capture and his status as an enemy combatant.

In keeping with our earlier instruction that the district court should proceed cautiously in reviewing military decisions reached during sanctioned military operations, we directed the district court to first "consider the sufficiency of the Mobbs declaration as an independent matter before proceeding further." Following this order, the district court held a hearing on August 13 to review the sufficiency of the Mobbs declaration.

During this hearing, the district court recognized that "the government is entitled to considerable deference in detention decisions during hostilities." The court also noted that it did not "have any doubts [Hamdi] had a firearm [or] any doubts he went to Afghanistan to be with the Taliban." Despite these observations, however, the court asserted that it was "challenging everything in the Mobbs' declaration" and that it intended to "pick it apart" "piece by piece." The court repeatedly referred to information it felt was missing from the declaration, asking "Is there anything in here that said Hamdi ever fired a weapon?" The court questioned whether Mr. Mobbs was even a government employee and intimated that the government was possibly hiding disadvantageous information from the court.

The district court filed an opinion on August 16, finding that the Mobbs declaration "falls far short" of supporting Hamdi's detention. The court ordered the government to turn over, among other things, copies of Hamdi's statements and the notes taken from any interviews with him; the names and addresses of all interrogators who have questioned Hamdi; statements by members of the Northern Alliance regarding the circumstances of Hamdi's surrender; and a list of the date of Hamdi's capture and all of the dates and locations of his subsequent detention.

Upon the Government's motion to certify the August 16 production order for immediate appeal, the district court certified the following question: "Whether the Mobbs Declaration, standing alone, is sufficient as a matter of law to allow a meaningful judicial review of Yaser Esam Hamdi's classification as an enemy combatant?" We then granted the Government's petition for interlocutory review pursuant to 28 U.S.C.A. § 1292(b).

II.

Yaser Esam Hamdi is apparently an American citizen. He was also captured by allied forces in Afghanistan, a zone of active military operations. This dual status—that of American citizen and that of alleged enemy combatant—raises important questions about the role of the courts in times of war.

A.

The importance of limitations on judicial activities during wartime may be inferred from the allocation of powers under our constitutional scheme. "Congress and the President, like the courts, possess no power not derived from the Constitution." Ex parte Quirin, 317 U.S. 1 (1942). * * *

The war powers * * * invest "the President, as Commander in Chief, with the power to wage war which Congress has declared, and to carry into effect all laws passed by Congress for the conduct of war and for the government and regulation of the Armed Forces, and all laws defining and punishing offences against the law of nations, including those which pertain to the conduct of war." *Quirin*, 317 U.S. at 26. These powers include the authority to detain those captured in armed struggle. These powers likewise extend to the executive's decision to deport or detain alien enemies during the duration of hostilities, and to confiscate or destroy enemy property.

Article III contains nothing analogous to the specific powers of war so carefully enumerated in Articles I and II. "In accordance with this constitutional text, the Supreme Court has shown great deference to the political branches when called upon to decide cases implicating sensitive matters of foreign policy, national security, or military affairs."

The reasons for this deference are not difficult to discern. Through their departments and committees, the executive and legislative branches are organized to supervise the conduct of overseas conflict in a way that the judiciary simply is not. The Constitution's allocation of the warmaking powers reflects not only the expertise and experience lodged within the executive, but also the more fundamental truth that those branches most accountable to the people should be the ones to undertake the ultimate protection and to ask the ultimate sacrifice from them. * * *

* * * For the judicial branch to trespass upon the exercise of the warmaking powers would be an infringement of the right to self-determination and self-governance at a time when the care of the common defense is most critical. This right of the people is no less a right because it is possessed collectively.

These interests do not carry less weight because the conflict in which Hamdi was captured is waged less against nation-states than against scattered and unpatriated forces. * * * Nor does the nature of the present conflict render respect for the judgments of the political branches any less appropriate. We have noted that the "political branches are best positioned to comprehend this global war in its full context," and neither the absence of set-piece battles nor the intervals of calm between terrorist assaults suffice to nullify the warmaking authority entrusted to the executive and legislative branches.

B.

Despite the clear allocation of war powers to the political branches, judicial deference to executive decisions made in the name of war is not unlimited. The Bill of Rights which Hamdi invokes in his petition is as much an instrument of mutual respect and tolerance as the Fourteenth Amendment is. It applies to American citizens regardless of race, color, or creed. And as we become a more diverse nation, the Bill of Rights may become even more a lens through which we recognize ourselves. To deprive any American citizen of its protections is not a step that any court would casually take.

Drawing on the Bill of Rights' historic guarantees, the judiciary plays its distinctive role in our constitutional structure when it reviews the detention of American citizens by their own government. Indeed, if due process means anything, it means that the courts must defend the fundamental principles of liberty and justice which lie at the base of all our civil and political institutions. The Constitution is suffused with concern about how the state will wield its awesome power of forcible restraint.* * *

The duty of the judicial branch to protect our individual freedoms does not simply cease whenever our military forces are committed by the political branches to armed conflict. * * *

It is significant, moreover, that the form of relief sought by Hamdi is a writ of habeas corpus. In war as in peace, habeas corpus provides one of the firmest bulwarks against unconstitutional detentions. As early as 1789, Congress reaffirmed the courts' common law authority to review detentions of federal prisoners, giving its explicit blessing to the judiciary's power to "grant writs of habeas corpus for the purpose of an inquiry into the cause of commitment" for federal detainees. While the scope of habeas review has expanded and contracted over the succeeding centuries, its essential function of assuring that restraint accords with the rule of law, not the whim of authority, remains unchanged. Hamdi's petition falls squarely within the Great Writ's purview, since he is an American citizen challenging his summary detention for reasons of state necessity.

C.

As the foregoing discussion reveals, the tensions within this case are significant. Such circumstances should counsel caution on the part of any court. Given the concerns discussed in the preceding sections, any broad or categorical holdings on enemy combatant designations would be especially inappropriate. We have no occasion, for example, to address the designation as an enemy combatant of an American citizen captured on American soil or the role that counsel might play in such a proceeding. We shall, in fact, go no further in this case than the specific context before us—that of the undisputed detention of a citizen during a combat operation undertaken in a foreign country and a determination by the executive that the citizen was allied with enemy forces.

The safeguards that all Americans have come to expect in criminal prosecutions do not translate neatly to the arena of armed conflict. In fact, if deference to the executive is not exercised with respect to military judgments in the field, it is difficult to see where deference would ever obtain. For there is a well-established power of the military to exercise jurisdiction over members of the armed forces, those directly connected with such forces, and enemy belligerents, prisoners of war, and others charged with violating the laws of war. As we emphasized in our prior decision, any judicial inquiry into Hamdi's status as an alleged enemy combatant in Afghanistan must reflect this deference as well as "a recognition that government has no more profound responsibility" than the protection of American

citizens from further terrorist attacks. Hamdi II, 296 F.3d at 283.

In this regard, it is relevant that the detention of enemy combatants serves at least two vital purposes. First, detention prevents enemy combatants from rejoining the enemy and continuing to fight against America and its allies. "The object of capture is to prevent the captured individual from serving the enemy. He is disarmed and from then on he must be removed as completely as practicable from the front. . . ." In re Territo, 156 F.2d 142, 145 (9th Cir. 1946). In this respect, "captivity is neither a punishment nor an act of vengeance," but rather "a simple war measure." W. Winthrop, Military Law and Precedents 788 (2d ed. 1920). And the precautionary measure of disarming hostile forces for the duration of a conflict is routinely accomplished through detention rather than the initiation of criminal charges. To require otherwise would impose a singular burden upon our nation's conduct of war.

Second, detention in lieu of prosecution may relieve the burden on military commanders of litigating the circumstances of a capture halfway around the globe. This burden would not be inconsiderable and would run the risk of "saddling military decision-making with the panoply of encumbrances associated with civil litigation" during a period of armed conflict. Hamdi II, 296 F.3d at 283–84. As the Supreme Court has recognized, "it would be difficult to devise more effective fettering of a field commander than to allow the very enemies he is ordered to reduce to submission to call him to account in his own civil courts and divert his efforts and attention from the military offensive abroad to the legal defensive at home." Johnson v. Eisentrager, 339 U.S. 763, 779 (1950).

The judiciary is not at liberty to eviscerate detention interests directly derived from the war powers of Articles I and II. As the nature of threats to America evolves, along with the means of carrying those threats out, the nature of enemy combatants may change also. In the face of such change, separation of powers doctrine does not deny the executive branch the essential tool of adaptability. * * * If anything, separation of powers bears renewed relevance to a struggle whose unforeseeable dangers may demand significant actions to protect untold thousands of American lives.

The designation of Hamdi as an enemy combatant thus bears the closest imaginable connection to the President's constitutional responsibilities during the actual conduct of hostilities. We therefore approach this case with sensitivity to both the fundamental liberty interest asserted by Hamdi and the extraordinary breadth of war-making authority conferred by the Constitution and invoked by Congress and the executive branch.

III.

* * *

On this appeal, it is argued that Hamdi's detention is invalid even if the government's assertions were entirely accurate. If that were clearly the case, there would be no need for further discovery such as that detailed in the August 16 production order, because Hamdi's detention would be invalid for reasons beyond the scope of any factual dispute. Indeed, any inquiry into the August 16 production order or any discussion of the certified question would be unnecessary, because neither could suffice to justify a detention that, as a threshold matter, was otherwise unlawful. Moreover, the burden of the August 16 order would necessarily outweigh any benefits if, quite independent of the disputed factual issues, Hamdi were already entitled to relief. For that reason, any purely legal challenges to Hamdi's detention are fairly includable within the scope of the certified order.

In this vein, Hamdi and amici have in fact pressed two purely legal grounds for relief: 18 U.S.C. § 4001(a) and Article 5 of the Geneva Convention. We now address them both.

A.

18 U.S.C. § 4001 regulates the detentions of United States citizens. It states in full:

(a) No citizen shall be imprisoned or otherwise detained by the United States except pursuant to an Act of Congress.

(b)(1) The control and management of Federal penal and correctional institutions, except military or naval institutions, shall be vested in the Attorney General, who shall promulgate rules for the government thereof, and appoint all necessary officers and employees in accordance with the civil-service laws, the Classification Act, as amended[,] and the applicable regulations.

(2) The Attorney General may establish and conduct industries, farms, and other activities and classify the inmates; and provide for their proper government, discipline, treatment, care, rehabilitation, and reformation.

18 U.S.C. § 4001 (2002). Hamdi argues that there is no congressional sanction for his incarceration and that § 4001(a) therefore prohibits his continued detention. We find this contention unpersuasive.

Even if Hamdi were right that § 4001(a) requires Congressional authorization of his detention, Congress has, in the wake of the September 11 terrorist attacks, authorized the President to "use all necessary and appropriate force against those nations, organizations, or persons he determines planned, authorized, committed, or aided the terrorist attacks" or "harbored such organizations or persons." Authorization for Use of Military Force, Pub. L. No. 107–40, 115 Stat. 224 (Sept. 18, 2001). As noted above, capturing and detaining enemy combatants is an inherent part of warfare; the "necessary and appropriate force" referenced in the congressional resolution necessarily includes the capture and detention of any and all hostile forces arrayed against our troops. Furthermore, Congress has specifically authorized the expenditure of funds for "the maintenance, pay, and allowances of prisoners of war [and] other persons in the custody of the [military] whose status is determined . . . to be similar to prisoners of war." 10 U.S.C. § 956(5) (2002). It is difficult if not impossible to understand how Congress could make appropriations for the detention of persons "similar to prisoners of war" without also authorizing their detention in the first instance.

* * *

It is likewise significant that § 4001(a) functioned principally to repeal the Emergency Detention Act. That statute had provided for the preventive "apprehension and detention" of individuals inside the United States "deemed likely to engage in espionage or sabotage" during "internal security emergencies." H.R. Rep. 92–116, at 2 (Apr. 6, 1971). Proponents of the repeal were concerned that the Emergency Detention Act might, inter alia, "permit[] a recurrence of the round ups which resulted in the detention of Americans of Japanese ancestry in 1941 and subsequently during World War II." Id. There is no indication that § 4001(a) was intended to overrule the longstanding rule that an armed

and hostile American citizen captured on the battlefield during wartime may be treated like the enemy combatant that he is. We therefore reject Hamdi's contention that § 4001(a) bars his detention.

B.

Hamdi and amici also contend that Article 5 of the Geneva Convention applies to Hamdi's case and requires an initial formal determination of his status as an enemy belligerent "by a competent tribunal." Geneva Convention Relative to the Treatment of Prisoners of War, Aug. 12, 1949, art. 5, 6 U.S.T. 3316, 75 U.N.T.S. 135.

This argument falters also because the Geneva Convention is not self-executing. Courts will only find a treaty to be self-executing if the document, as a whole, evidences an intent to provide a private right of action. The Geneva Convention evinces no such intent. * * * If two warring parties disagree about what the Convention requires of them, Article 11 instructs them to arrange a "meeting of their representatives" with the aid of diplomats from other countries, "with a view to settling the disagreement." Geneva Convention, at art. 11. Similarly, Article 132 states that "any alleged violation of the Convention" is to be resolved by a joint transnational effort "in a manner to be decided between the interested Parties." We therefore agree with other courts of appeals that the language in the Geneva Convention is not "self-executing" and does not "create private rights of action in the domestic courts of the signatory countries."

* * * This is not to say, of course, that the Geneva Convention is meaningless. Rather, its values are vindicated by diplomatic means and reciprocity, as specifically contemplated by Article 132. There is a powerful and self-regulating national interest in observing the strictures of the Convention, because prisoners are taken by both sides of any conflict. This is the very essence of reciprocity and, as the drafters of the Convention apparently decided, the most appropriate basis for ensuring compliance. * * *

* * *

For all these reasons, we hold that there is no purely legal barrier to Hamdi's detention. We now turn our attention to the question of whether the August 16 order was proper on its own terms.

IV.

As we will discuss below, we conclude that Hamdi's petition fails as a matter of law. It follows that the government should not be compelled to produce the materials described in the district court's August 16 order.

We also note that the order, if enforced, would present formidable practical difficulties. The district court indicated that its production request might well be only an initial step in testing the factual basis of Hamdi's enemy combatant status. The court plainly did not preclude making further production demands upon the government, even suggesting that it might "bring Hamdi before [the court] to inquire about [his] statements."

Although the district court did not have "any doubts [that Hamdi] had a firearm" or that "he went to Afghanistan to be with the Taliban," the court ordered the government to submit to the court for in camera, ex parte review: (1) "copies of all Hamdi's statements, and the notes taken from any interviews with Hamdi, that relate to his reasons for going to Afghanistan, his activities while in Afghanistan, or his participation in the military forces of the Taliban or any other organization in that country"; (2) "[a] list of all

the interrogators who have questioned Hamdi, including their names and addresses, and the dates of the interviews"; (3) "copies of any statements by members of the Northern Alliance" regarding Hamdi's surrender; (4) "[a] list that includes the date of Hamdi's capture, and that gives all the dates and locations of his subsequent detention"; (5) "the name and title of the individual within the United States Government who made the determination that Hamdi was an illegal enemy combatant"; (6) "the name and title of the individual within the United States Government who made the decision to move Hamdi from Guantanamo Bay, Cuba to the Norfolk Naval Station"; and (7) "the screening criteria utilized to determine the status of Hamdi." The court's order allows the government to redact "intelligence matters" from its responses, but only to the extent that those intelligence matters are outside the scope of inquiry into Hamdi's legal status.

Hamdi argues vigorously that this order should be affirmed. Because of the alleged "breadth with which Respondents construe their authority to imprison American citizens whom they consider to be enemy combatants," Hamdi argues we must allow the district court to subject the government's classification of him to a searching review. * * *

A review of the court's August 16 order reveals the risk of "standing the warmaking powers of Articles I and II on their heads," *Hamdi II*, 296 F.3d at 284. The district court, for example, ordered the government to produce all Hamdi's statements and notes from interviews. Yet it is precisely such statements, relating to a detainee's activities in Afghanistan, that may contain the most sensitive and the most valuable information for our forces in the field. The risk created by this order is that judicial involvement would proceed, increment by increment, into an area where the political branches have been assigned by law a preeminent role.

The district court further ordered the government to produce a list of all interrogators who have questioned Hamdi, including their names and addresses and the dates of the interviews, copies of any statements by members of the Northern Alliance regarding Hamdi's surrender, and a list that includes the date of Hamdi's capture and all the dates and locations of his subsequent detention. Once again, however, litigation cannot be the driving force in effectuating and recording wartime detentions. The military has been charged by Congress and the executive with winning a war, not prevailing in a possible court case. Complicating the matter even further is the fact that Hamdi was originally captured by Northern Alliance forces, with whom American forces were generally allied. The district court's insistence that statements by Northern Alliance members be produced cannot help but place a strain on multilateral efforts during wartime. The court also expressed concern in its order that the Northern Alliance did not "identify the unit [to which Hamdi was affiliated]," "where or by whom [Hamdi] received weapons training or the nature and extent thereof," or "who commanded the unit or the type of garb or uniform Hamdi may have worn. . . ." In demanding such detail, the district court would have the United States military instruct not only its own personnel, but also its allies, on precise observations they must make and record during a battlefield capture.

Viewed in their totality, the implications of the district court's August 16 production order could not be more serious. The factual inquiry upon which Hamdi would lead us, if it did

not entail disclosure of sensitive intelligence, might require an excavation of facts buried under the rubble of war. The cost of such an inquiry in terms of the efficiency and morale of American forces cannot be disregarded. Some of those with knowledge of Hamdi's detention may have been slain or injured in battle. Others might have to be diverted from active and ongoing military duties of their own. The logistical effort to acquire evidence from far away battle zones might be substantial. And these efforts would profoundly unsettle the constitutional balance.

For the foregoing reasons, the court's August 16 production request cannot stand.

V.

The question remains, however, whether Hamdi's petition must be remanded for further proceedings or dismissed.

Hamdi's American citizenship has entitled him to file a petition for a writ of habeas corpus in a civilian court to challenge his detention, including the military's determination that he is an "enemy combatant" subject to detention during the ongoing hostilities. Thus, as with all habeas actions, we begin by examining the precise allegations presented to us by the respective parties. In this case, there are two allegations that are crucial to our analysis. First, Hamdi's petition alleges that he was a resident of and seized in Afghanistan, a country in which hostilities were authorized and ongoing at the time of the seizure, but that his continued detention in this country without the full panoply of constitutional protections is unlawful. Second, the Government's response asserts that Hamdi is being detained pursuant to the Commander-in-Chief's Article II war powers and that the circumstances underlying Hamdi's detention, as reflected primarily in the Mobbs declaration, establish that Hamdi's detention is lawful.

Generally speaking, in order to fulfill our responsibilities under Article III to review a petitioner's allegation that he is being detained by American authorities in violation of the rights afforded him under the United States Constitution, we must first determine the source of the authority for the executive to detain the individual. Once the source of the authority is identified, we then look at the justification given to determine whether it constitutes a legitimate exercise of that authority.

A.

Here the government has identified the source of the authority to detain Hamdi as originating in Article II, Section 2 of the Constitution, wherein the President is given the war power. We have already emphasized that the standard of review of enemy combatant detentions must be a deferential one when the detainee was captured abroad in a zone of combat operations. The President "is best prepared to exercise the military judgment attending the capture of alleged combatants." *Hamdi II*, 296 F.3d at 283. Thus, in *Quirin*, the Supreme Court stated in no uncertain terms that detentions "ordered by the President in the declared exercise of his powers as Commander in Chief of the Army in time of war and of grave public danger" should not "be set aside by the courts without the clear conviction that they are in conflict with the Constitution or laws of Congress constitutionally enacted."

This deferential posture, however, only comes into play after we ascertain that the challenged decision is one legitimately made pursuant to the war powers. It does not preclude us from determining in the first instance whether the factual assertions set forth by the government would, if accurate, provide a legally valid basis for Hamdi's detention under that power. Otherwise, we would be deferring to a decision made without any inquiry into whether such deference is due. For these reasons, it is appropriate, upon a citizen's presentation of a habeas petition alleging that he is being unlawfully detained by his own government, to ask that the government provide the legal authority upon which it relies for that detention and the basic facts relied upon to support a legitimate exercise of that authority. Indeed, in this case, the government has voluntarily submitted—and urged us to review—an affidavit from Michael Mobbs, Special Advisor to the Under Secretary of Defense for Policy, describing what the government contends were the circumstances leading to Hamdi's designation as an enemy combatant under Article II's war power.

The Mobbs affidavit consists of two pages and nine paragraphs in which Mobbs states that he was "substantially involved with matters related to the detention of enemy combatants in the current war against the al Qaeda terrorists and those who support and harbor them." In the affidavit, Mobbs avers that Hamdi entered Afghanistan in July or August of 2001 and affiliated with a Taliban military unit. Hamdi received weapons training from the Taliban and remained with his military unit until his surrender to Northern Alliance forces in late 2001. At the time of his capture, Hamdi was in possession of an AK–47 rifle. After his capture, Hamdi was transferred first from Konduz, Afghanistan to the prison in Mazar-e-Sharif, and then to a prison in Sheberghan, Afghanistan where he was questioned by a United States interrogation team. This interrogation team determined that Hamdi met "the criteria for enemy combatants over whom the United States was taking control." Hamdi was then transported to the U.S. short term detention facility in Kandahar, and then transferred again to Guantanamo Bay and eventually to the Norfolk Naval Brig. According to Mobbs, a subsequent interview with Hamdi confirmed the details of his capture and his status as an enemy combatant.

* * *

To be sure, a capable attorney could challenge the hearsay nature of the Mobbs declaration and probe each and every paragraph for incompleteness or inconsistency, as the district court attempted to do. The court's approach, however, had a signal flaw. We are not here dealing with a defendant who has been indicted on criminal charges in the exercise of the executive's law enforcement powers. We are dealing with the executive's assertion of its power to detain under the war powers of Article II. To transfer the instinctive skepticism, so laudable in the defense of criminal charges, to the review of executive branch decisions premised on military determinations made in the field carries the inordinate risk of a constitutionally problematic intrusion into the most basic responsibilities of a coordinate branch.

The murkiness and chaos that attend armed conflict mean military actions are hardly immune to mistake. Yet these characteristics of warfare have been with us through the centuries and have never been thought sufficient to justify active judicial supervision of combat operations overseas. To inquire, for example, whether Hamdi actually fired his weapon is to demand a clarity from battle that often is not there. The district court, after reviewing the Mobbs affidavit, did not "have any doubts [Hamdi] had a firearm [or] any doubts he went to Af-

ghanistan to be with the Taliban." To delve further into Hamdi's status and capture would require us to step so far out of our role as judges that we would abandon the distinctive deference that animates this area of law.

For these reasons, and because Hamdi was indisputably seized in an active combat zone abroad, we will not require the government to fill what the district court regarded as gaps in the Mobbs affidavit. The factual averments in the affidavit, if accurate, are sufficient to confirm that Hamdi's detention conforms with a legitimate exercise of the war powers given the executive by Article II, Section 2 of the Constitution and, as discussed elsewhere, that it is consistent with the Constitution and laws of Congress. Asking the executive to provide more detailed factual assertions would be to wade further into the conduct of war than we consider appropriate and is unnecessary to a meaningful judicial review of this question.

B.

We turn then to the question of whether, because he is an American citizen currently detained on American soil by the military, Hamdi can be heard in an Article III court to rebut the factual assertions that were submitted to support the "enemy combatant" designation. We hold that no evidentiary hearing or factual inquiry on our part is necessary or proper, because it is undisputed that Hamdi was captured in a zone of active combat operations in a foreign country and because any inquiry must be circumscribed to avoid encroachment into the military affairs entrusted to the executive branch.

* * *

As we have emphasized throughout these appeals, we cannot set aside executive decisions to detain enemy combatants "without the clear conviction that they are in conflict with the Constitution or laws of Congress constitutionally enacted." *Quirin,* 317 U.S. at 25. We cannot stress too often the constitutional implications presented on the face of Hamdi's petition. The constitutional allocation of war powers affords the President extraordinarily broad authority as Commander in Chief and compels courts to assume a deferential posture in reviewing exercises of this authority. And, while the Constitution assigns courts the duty generally to review executive detentions that are alleged to be illegal, the Constitution does not specifically contemplate any role for courts in the conduct of war, or in foreign policy generally.

Indeed, Article III courts are ill-positioned to police the military's distinction between those in the arena of combat who should be detained and those who should not. Any evaluation of the accuracy of the executive branch's determination that a person is an enemy combatant, for example, would require courts to consider, first, what activities the detainee was engaged in during the period leading up to his seizure and, second, whether those activities rendered him a combatant or not. The first question is factual and, were we called upon to delve into it, would likely entail substantial efforts to acquire evidence from distant battle zones. The second question may require fine judgments about whether a particular activity is linked to the war efforts of a hostile power—judgments the executive branch is most competent to make.

Hamdi's petition places him squarely within the zone of active combat and assures that he is indeed being held in accordance with the Constitution and Congressional authorization for use of military force in the wake of al Qaida's attack. Any effort to as-

certain the facts concerning the petitioner's conduct while amongst the nation's enemies would entail an unacceptable risk of obstructing war efforts authorized by Congress and undertaken by the executive branch.

Hamdi contends that, although international law and the laws of this country might generally allow for the detention of an individual captured on the battlefield, these laws must vary in his case because he is an American citizen now detained on American soil. As an American citizen, Hamdi would be entitled to the due process protections normally found in the criminal justice system, including the right to meet with counsel, if he had been charged with a crime. But as we have previously pointed out, Hamdi has not been charged with any crime. He is being held as an enemy combatant pursuant to the well-established laws and customs of war. Hamdi's citizenship rightfully entitles him to file this petition to challenge his detention, but the fact that he is a citizen does not affect the legality of his detention as an enemy combatant.

Indeed, this same issue arose in *Quirin.* In that case, petitioners were German agents who, after the declaration of war between the United States and the German Reich, were trained at a German sabotage school where they "were instructed in the use of explosives and in methods of secret writing." The petitioners then journeyed by submarine to the beaches of New York and Florida, carrying large quantities of explosives and other sabotage devices. All of them were apprehended by FBI agents, who subsequently learned of their mission to destroy war industries and facilities in the United States. All of the petitioners were born in Germany but had lived in the United States at some point. One petitioner claimed American citizenship by virtue of the naturalization of his parents during his youth. The Court, however, did not need to determine his citizenship because it held that the due process guarantees of the Fifth and Sixth Amendments were inapplicable in any event. It noted that "citizenship in the United States of an enemy belligerent does not relieve him from the consequences of a belligerency which is unlawful." The petitioner who alleged American citizenship was treated identically to the other German saboteurs.

The *Quirin* principle applies here. One who takes up arms against the United States in a foreign theater of war, regardless of his citizenship, may properly be designated an enemy combatant and treated as such. The privilege of citizenship entitles Hamdi to a limited judicial inquiry into his detention, but only to determine its legality under the war powers of the political branches. At least where it is undisputed that he was present in a zone of active combat operations, we are satisfied that the Constitution does not entitle him to a searching review of the factual determinations underlying his seizure there.

* * * Hamdi contends that his petition does not implicate military concerns because "the underlying claims in this case are designed to test the legality of Hamdi's imprisonment in a naval brig in Norfolk, Virginia, not a military determination made overseas on the basis of caution rather than accuracy." But the fact that Hamdi is presently being detained in the United States—as opposed to somewhere overseas—does not affect the legal implications of his status as an enemy combatant. For the same reason that courts are ill-positioned to review the military's distinction between those who should or should not be detained in an arena of combat, courts are not in the position to overturn the military's decision to detain those persons

in one location or another. It is not clear why the United States should be precluded from exercising its discretion to move a detainee to a site within this country, nor do we see what purpose would be served by second guessing the military's decision with respect to the locus of detention.

To conclude, we hold that, despite his status as an American citizen currently detained on American soil, Hamdi is not entitled to challenge the facts presented in the Mobbs declaration. Where, as here, a habeas petitioner has been designated an enemy combatant and it is undisputed that he was captured in an zone of active combat operations abroad, further judicial inquiry is unwarranted when the government has responded to the petition by setting forth factual assertions which would establish a legally valid basis for the petitioner's detention. Because these circumstances are present here, Hamdi is not entitled to habeas relief on this basis.

C.

Finally, we address Hamdi's contention that even if his detention was at one time lawful, it is no longer so because the relevant hostilities have reached an end. In his brief, Hamdi alleges that the government "confuses the international armed conflict that allegedly authorized Hamdi's detention in the first place with an on-going fight against individuals whom Respondents refuse to recognize as 'belligerents' under international law." Whether the timing of a cessation of hostilities is justiciable is far from clear. The executive branch is also in the best position to appraise the status of a conflict, and the cessation of hostilities would seem no less a matter of political competence than the initiation of them. In any case, we need not reach this issue here. The government notes that American troops are still on the ground in Afghanistan, dismantling the terrorist infrastructure in the very country where Hamdi was captured and engaging in reconstruction efforts which may prove dangerous in their own right. Because under the most circumscribed definition of conflict hostilities have not yet reached their end, this argument is without merit.

VI.

It is important to emphasize that we are not placing our imprimatur upon a new day of executive detentions. We earlier rejected the summary embrace of "a sweeping proposition—namely that, with no meaningful judicial review, any American citizen alleged to be an enemy combatant could be detained indefinitely without charges or counsel on the government's say-so." *Hamdi II*, 296 F.3d at 283. But, Hamdi is not "any American citizen alleged to be an enemy combatant" by the government; he is an American citizen captured and detained by American allied forces in a foreign theater of war during active hostilities and determined by the United States military to have been indeed allied with enemy forces.

Cases such as Hamdi's raise serious questions which the courts will continue to treat as such. The nation has fought since its founding for liberty without which security rings hollow and for security without which liberty cannot thrive. The judiciary was meant to respect the delicacy of the balance, and we have endeavored to do so.

The events of September 11 have left their indelible mark. It is not wrong even in the dry annals of judicial opinion to mourn those who lost their lives that terrible day. Yet we speak in the end not from sorrow or anger, but from the conviction that separation of powers takes on special significance when the nation itself comes under attack. Hamdi's status as a citizen, as important as that is, cannot displace our constitutional order or the place of the courts within the Framer's scheme. Judicial review does not disappear during wartime, but the review of battlefield captures in overseas conflicts is a highly deferential one. That is why, for reasons stated, the judgment must be reversed and the petition dismissed. It is so ordered.

B. ENEMY COMBATANT CAPTURED IN THE UNITED STATES

PADILLA v. RUMSFELD

United States Court of Appeals for the Second Circuit, 2003.
352 F.3d 695.

Pooler, Circuit Judge:

Introduction

This habeas corpus appeal requires us to consider a series of questions raised by Secretary of Defense Donald Rumsfeld and by Donna R. Newman, Esq., on behalf of Jose Padilla, an American citizen held by military authorities as an enemy combatant. Padilla is suspected of being associated with al Qaeda and planning terrorist

attacks in this country. The questions were certified by the United States District Court for the Southern District of New York (Michael B. Mukasey, *C.J.*) and involve, among others: whether * * * the President has the authority to detain Padilla as an enemy combatant. We conclude that the Secretary of Defense is a proper respondent and that the District Court had jurisdiction. We also conclude that Padilla's detention was not authorized by Congress, and absent such authorization, the President does not have the power under Article II of the Constitution to detain as an enemy combatant an American citizen seized on American soil outside a zone of combat.

As this Court sits only a short distance from where the World Trade Center once stood, we are as keenly aware as anyone of the threat al Qaeda poses to our country and of the responsibilities the President and law enforcement officials bear for protecting the nation. But presidential authority does not exist in a vacuum, and this case involves not whether those responsibilities should be aggressively pursued, but whether the President is obligated, in the circumstances presented here, to share them with Congress.

Where, as here, the President's power as Commander-in-Chief of the armed forces and the domestic rule of law intersect, we conclude that clear congressional authorization is required for detentions of American citizens on American soil because 18 U.S.C. § 4001(a) (2000) (the "Non–Detention Act") prohibits such detentions absent specific congressional authorization. Congress's Authorization for Use of Military Force Joint Resolution, Pub. L. No. 107–40, 115 Stat. 224 (2001) ("Joint Resolution"), passed shortly after the attacks of September 11, 2001, is not such an authorization, and no exception to section 4001(a) otherwise exists. In light of this express prohibition, the government must undertake to show that Padilla's detention can nonetheless be grounded in the President's inherent constitutional powers. We conclude that it has not made this showing. In reaching this conclusion, we do not address the detention of an American citizen seized within a zone of combat in Afghanistan, such as the court confronted in Hamdi v. Rumsfeld, 316 F.3d 450 (4th Cir. 2003) ("*Hamdi III*"). Nor do we express any opinion as to the hypothetical situation of a congressionally authorized detention of an American citizen.

Accordingly, we remand to the District Court with instructions to issue a writ of habeas corpus directing Secretary Rumsfeld to release Padilla from military custody within 30 days, at which point the government can act within its legislatively conferred authority to take further action. For example, Padilla can be transferred to the appropriate civilian authorities who can bring criminal charges against him. If appropriate, he can also be held as a material witness in connection with grand jury proceedings. *See* United States v. Awadallah, 349 F.3d 42 (2d Cir. 2003) [discussed in Chapter Two, *supra*]. Under any scenario, Padilla will be entitled to the constitutional protections extended to other citizens.

BACKGROUND

I. The Initial Detention

On May 8, 2002, Jose Padilla, an American citizen, flew on his American passport from Pakistan, via Switzerland, to Chicago's O'Hare International Airport. There he was arrested by FBI agents pursuant to a material witness warrant issued by the Chief Judge of the Southern District of New York in connection with a grand jury investigation of the terrorist attacks of September 11. Padilla carried no weapons or explosives.

The agents brought Padilla to New York where he was held as a civilian material witness in the maximum security wing of the Metropolitan Correctional Center (MCC). At that point, Padilla was under the control of the Bureau of Prisons and the United States Marshal Service. Any immediate threat he posed to national security had effectively been neutralized. On May 15, 2002, he appeared before Chief Judge Mukasey, who appointed Donna R. Newman, Esq., to represent Padilla. * * *

On May 22, Newman moved to vacate the material witness warrant. By June 7, the motion had been submitted for decision. A conference on the motion was scheduled for June 11. However, on June 9, the government notified the court ex parte that (1) it wished to withdraw its subpoena and (2) the President had issued an Order (the "June 9 Order") designating Padilla as an enemy combatant and directing Secretary Rumsfeld to detain him. Chief Judge Mukasey vacated the warrant, and Padilla was taken into custody by Department of Defense (DOD) personnel and transported from New York to the high-security Consolidated Naval Brig in Charleston, South Carolina. At the scheduled June 11 conference, Newman, unable to secure Padilla's signature on a habeas corpus petition, nonetheless filed one on his behalf as "next friend."

For the past eighteen months, Padilla has been held in the Brig in Charleston. He has not been permitted any contact with his counsel, his family or any other non-military personnel. During this period he has been the subject of ongoing questioning regarding the al Qaeda network and its terrorist activities in an effort to obtain intelligence.

II. The Order Authorizing the Detention

In his June 9 Order, the President directed Secretary Rumsfeld to detain Padilla based on findings that Padilla was an enemy combatant who (1) was "closely associated with al Qaeda, an international terrorist organization with which the United States is at war"; (2) had engaged in "war-like acts, including conduct in preparation

for acts of international terrorism" against the United States; (3) had intelligence that could assist the United States to ward off future terrorist attacks; and (4) was a continuing threat to United States security. As authority for the detention, the President relied on "the Constitution and . . . the laws of the United States, including the [Joint Resolution]."

In an unsealed declaration submitted to the District Court, Michael H. Mobbs, a special advisor to the Under Secretary of Defense for Policy (who claims no direct knowledge of Padilla's actions or of the interrogations that produced the information discussed in his declaration), set forth the information the President received before he designated Padilla as an enemy combatant. According to the declaration, Padilla was born in New York, was convicted of murder in 1983, and remained incarcerated until his eighteenth birthday. In 1991, he was convicted on a handgun charge and again sent to prison. He moved to Egypt in 1998 and traveled to several countries in the Middle East and Southwest Asia between 1999 and 2000. During this period, he was closely associated with known members and leaders of al Qaeda. While in Afghanistan in 2001, Padilla became involved with a plan to build and detonate a "dirty bomb" within the United States, and went to Pakistan to receive training on explosives from al Qaeda operatives. There he was instructed by senior al Qaeda officials to return to the United States to conduct reconnaissance and/or other attacks on behalf of al Qaeda. He then traveled to Chicago, where he was arrested upon arrival into the United States on May 8, 2002. Notwithstanding Padilla's extensive contacts with al Qaeda members and his actions under their direction, the government does not allege that Padilla was a member of al Qaeda.

The government also offered for the District Court's review Mobbs' sealed declaration, which the District Court characterized as "identifying one or more of the sources referred to only in cryptic terms in the [unsealed] Mobbs Declaration" and "setting forth objective circumstantial evidence that corroborates the factual allegations in the [unsealed] Mobbs Declaration.

III. District Court Proceedings on the Habeas Petition

On June 26, 2002, the government moved to dismiss Padilla's habeas petition on the grounds that Newman lacked standing to act as Padilla's next friend, that Secretary Rumsfeld was not a proper respondent, and that, in any event, the District Court lacked personal jurisdiction over him. On the merits, the government contended that each Mobbs declaration contained sufficient evidence of Padilla's association with al Qaeda and his intention to engage in terrorist acts in this country on behalf of al Qaeda to establish the legality of holding Padilla in military custody as an enemy combatant. Padilla contended that the President lacked authority to detain an American citizen taken into custody in the United States. At a minimum, he sought access to counsel.

In a comprehensive and thorough opinion, the District Court determined that (1) Newman could bring the habeas petition as Padilla's next friend; (2) Secretary Rumsfeld was a proper respondent and the District Court had jurisdiction over him; (3) the Constitution and statutory law give the President authority to detain American citizens as enemy combatants; (4) Padilla was entitled to consult with counsel to pursue his habeas petition "under conditions that will minimize the likelihood that he [could] use his lawyers as unwilling intermediaries for the transmission of information to oth-

ers"; (5) Padilla could present facts and argument to the court to rebut the government's showing that he was an enemy combatant; and (6) the court would "examine only whether the President had some evidence to support his finding that Padilla was an enemy combatant, and whether that evidence has been mooted by events subsequent to his detention."

The District Court's order directed the parties to set conditions under which Padilla could meet with his counsel, but Secretary Rumsfeld declined to do so. Instead, more than a month after the *Padilla I* decision, the government moved for reconsideration of the portion of *Padilla I* that allowed him access to counsel, on the ground that no conditions could be set that would protect the national security. [The District Judge rejected the motion for reconsideration.]

* * *

On June 10, 2003, this Court granted the parties' application for an interlocutory appeal.

DISCUSSION

I. Preliminary Issues

A. Next Friend Status

[The Court holds that Padilla's attorney has standing as a "next friend" to bring a habeas petition on Padilla's behalf.]

B. Jurisdictional Issues

[The Court holds that Secretary Rumsfeld is a proper respondent and that the Court has personal jurisdiction over him.]

II. Power to Detain

A. Introduction

The District Court concluded, and the government maintains here, that the indefinite detention of Padilla was a proper exercise of the President's power as Commander-in-Chief. The power to detain Padilla is said to derive from the President's authority, settled by Ex parte Quirin, 317 U.S. 1 (1942), to detain enemy combatants in wartime—authority that is argued to encompass the detention of United States citizens seized on United States soil. This power, the court below reasoned, may be exercised without a formal declaration of war by Congress and "even if Congressional authorization were deemed necessary, the Joint Resolution, passed by both houses of Congress, ... engages the President's full powers as Commander in Chief." Specifically, the District Court found that the Joint Resolution acted as express congressional authorization under 18 U.S.C. § 4001(a), which prohibits the detention of American citizens absent such authorization. In addition, the government claims that 10 U.S.C. § 956(5), a statute that allows the military to use authorized funds for certain detentions, grants authority to detain American citizens.

These alternative arguments require us to examine the scope of the President's inherent power and, if this is found insufficient to support Padilla's detention, whether Congress has authorized such detentions of American citizens. We reemphasize, however, that our review is limited to the case of an American citizen arrested in the United States, not on a foreign battlefield or while actively engaged in armed conflict against the United States.

* * *

[The Court notes that in the landmark *Youngstown Steel* case, the Court created three categories of executive power. The third category was where the President acts on his own authority and Congress denies he has that authority. In that category, presidential power is at its "lowest ebb."]

Here, we find that the President lacks inherent constitutional authority as Commander-in-Chief to detain American citizens on American soil outside a zone of combat. We also conclude that the Non–Detention Act serves as an explicit congressional "denial of authority" within the meaning of *Youngstown,* thus placing us in *Youngstown*'s third category. Finally, we conclude that because the Joint Resolution does not authorize the President to detain American citizens seized on American soil, we remain within *Youngstown*'s third category.

i. Inherent Power

The government contends that the President has the inherent authority to detain those who take up arms against this country pursuant to Article II, Section 2, of the Constitution, which makes him the Commander-in-Chief, and that the exercise of these powers domestically does not require congressional authorization. Moreover, the argument goes, it was settled by *Quirin* that the military's authority to detain enemy combatants in wartime applies to American citizens as well as to foreign combatants. There the Supreme Court explained that "universal agreement and practice" under "the law of war" holds that "lawful combatants are subject to capture and detention as prisoners of war by opposing military forces" and "unlawful combatants are likewise subject to capture and detention, but in addition they are subject to trial and punishment by military tribunals for acts which render their belligerency unlawful." Finally, since the designation of an enemy combatant bears the closest imaginable connection to the President's constitutional responsibilities, principles of judicial deference are said by the government to assume heightened significance.

We agree that great deference is afforded the President's exercise of his authority as Commander-in-Chief. We also agree that whether a state of armed conflict exists against an enemy to which the laws of war apply is a political question for the President, not the courts. Because we have no authority to do so, we do not address the government's underlying assumption that an undeclared war exists between al Qaeda and the United States. * * *

However, it is a different proposition entirely to argue that the President even in times of grave national security threats or war, whether declared or undeclared, can lay claim to any of the powers, express or implied, allocated to Congress. The deference due to the Executive in its exercise of its war powers therefore only starts the inquiry; it does not end it. Where the exercise of Commander-in-Chief powers, no matter how well intentioned, is challenged on the ground that it collides with the powers assigned by the Constitution to Congress, a fundamental role exists for the courts. To be sure, when Congress and the President act together in the conduct of war, "it is not for any court to sit in review of the wisdom of their action or substitute its judgment for theirs." Hirabayashi v. United States, 320 U.S. 81 (1943). But when the Executive acts, even in the conduct of war, in the face of apparent congressional disapproval, challenges to his authority must be examined and resolved by the Article III courts. See Youngstown, 343 U.S. at 638 (Jackson, J., concurring).

These separation of powers concerns are heightened when the Commander-in-Chief's powers are exercised in the domestic sphere. The Supreme Court has long counseled that while the Executive should be "indulged the widest latitude of in-terpretation to sustain his exclusive function to command the instruments of national force, at least when turned against the outside world for the security of our society," he enjoys "no such indulgence" when "it is turned inward." Youngstown, 343 U.S. at 645 (Jackson, J., concurring). * * * "Congress, not the Executive, should control utilization of the war power as an instrument of domestic policy." Youngstown, 343 U.S. at 644 (Jackson, J., concurring). Thus, we do not concern ourselves with the Executive's inherent wartime power, generally, to detain enemy combatants on the battlefield. Rather, we are called on to decide whether the Constitution gives the President the power to detain an American citizen seized in this country until the war with al Qaeda ends.

The government contends that the Constitution authorizes the President to detain Padilla as an enemy combatant as an exercise of inherent executive authority. Padilla contends that, in the absence of express congressional authorization, the President, by his June 9 Order denominating Padilla an enemy combatant, has engaged in the "lawmaking" function entrusted by the Constitution to Congress in violation of the separation of powers. In response, no argument is made that the Constitution expressly grants the President the power to name United States citizens as enemy combatants and order their detention. Rather, the government contends that the Commander-in-Chief Clause implicitly grants the President the power to detain enemy combatants domestically during times of national security crises such as the current conflict with al Qaeda. U.S. Const. art. II, § 2.

* * *

The Constitution entrusts the ability to define and punish offenses against the law of nations to the Congress, not the Executive. U.S. Const. art. II, § 8, cl. 10. Padilla contends that the June 9 Order mandating his detention as an "enemy combatant" was not the result of congressional action defining the category of "enemy combatant." He also argues that there has been no other legislative articulation of what constitutes an "enemy combatant," what circumstances trigger the designation, or when it ends. As in *Youngstown*, Padilla maintains that "the President's order does not direct that a congressional policy be executed in a manner prescribed by Congress—it directs that a presidential policy be executed in a manner prescribed by the President." *Youngstown*, 343 U.S. at 588.

The Constitution envisions grave national emergencies and contemplates significant domestic abridgements of individual liberties during such times. Here, the Executive lays claim to the inherent emergency powers necessary to effect such abridgements, but we agree with Padilla that the Constitution lodges these powers with Congress, not the President. *See Youngstown*, 343 U.S. at 649–50 (Jackson, *J.*, concurring).

The Constitution's explicit grant of the powers authorized in the Offenses Clause, the Suspension Clause, and the Third Amendment, to Congress is a powerful indication that, absent express congressional authorization, the President's Commander-in-Chief powers do not support Padilla's confinement. The level of specificity with which the Framers allocated these domestic powers to Congress and the lack of any even near-equivalent grant of authority in Article II's catalogue of executive powers compels us to decline to read any such power into the Commander-in-Chief Clause. In sum, while Congress—otherwise acting consistently with the Constitution—may

have the power to authorize the detention of United States citizens under the circumstances of Padilla's case, the President, acting alone, does not.

The government argues that *Quirin* established the President's inherent authority to detain Padilla. In *Quirin*, the Supreme Court reviewed the habeas petitions of German soldiers captured on United States soil during World War II. All of the petitioners had lived in the United States at some point in their lives and had been trained in the German Army in the use of explosives. These soldiers, one of whom would later claim American citizenship, landed in the United States and shed their uniforms intending to engage in acts of military sabotage. They were arrested in New York and Chicago, tried by a military commission as "unlawful combatants," and sentenced to death. The Court denied the soldiers' petitions for habeas corpus, holding that the alleged American citizenship of one of the saboteurs was immaterial to its judgment: "Citizenship in the United States of an enemy belligerent does not relieve him from the consequences of a belligerency which is unlawful because in violation of the law of war." * * *

We do not agree that *Quirin* controls. First, and most importantly, the *Quirin* Court's decision to uphold military jurisdiction rested on express congressional authorization of the use of military tribunals to try combatants who violated the laws of war. Specifically, the Court found it "unnecessary for present purposes to determine to what extent the President as Commander in Chief has constitutional power to create military commissions without the support of Congressional legislation." Accordingly, *Quirin* does not speak to whether, or to what degree, the President may impose military authority upon United States citizens domestically without clear congressional authorization. * * *

Moreover, there are other important distinctions between *Quirin* and this case. First, when *Quirin* was decided in 1942, section 4001(a) had not yet been enacted. The *Quirin* Court consequently had no occasion to consider the effects of legislation prohibiting the detention of American citizens absent statutory authorization. As a result, *Quirin* was premised on the conclusion—indisputable at the time—that the Executive's domestic projection of military authority had been authorized by Congress. Because the *Quirin* Court did not have to contend with section 4001(a), its usefulness is now sharply attenuated.

Second, the petitioners in *Quirin* admitted that they were soldiers in the armed forces of a nation against whom the United States had formally declared war. The *Quirin* Court deemed it unnecessary to consider the dispositive issue here—the boundaries of the Executive's military jurisdiction—because the *Quirin* petitioners "upon the conceded facts, were plainly within those boundaries." Padilla makes no such concession. To the contrary, he, from all indications, intends to dispute his designation as an enemy combatant, and points to the fact that the civilian accomplices of the *Quirin* saboteurs—citizens who advanced the sabotage plots but who were not members of the German armed forces—were charged and tried as civilians in civilian courts, not as enemy combatants subject to military authority.

* * *

The government's argument for the legality of Padilla's detention also relies heavily on the Fourth Circuit's decisions in *Hamdi II* and *Hamdi III*. These decisions are inapposite. The Fourth Circuit directly predicated its holdings on the undisputed fact that Hamdi was captured in a zone of active combat in Afghanistan.

* * *

Based on the text of the Constitution and the cases interpreting it, we reject the government's contention that the President has inherent constitutional power to detain Padilla under the circumstances presented here. n27 Therefore, under *Youngstown*, we must now consider whether Congress has authorized such detentions.

The Non–Detention Act

[T]he Non–Detention Act provides: "No citizen shall be imprisoned or otherwise detained by the United States except pursuant to an Act of Congress." 18 U.S.C. § 4001(a). * * * We read the plain language of section 4001(a) to prohibit all detentions of citizens—a conclusion first reached by the Supreme Court. Howe v. Smith, 452 U.S. 473 (1981) (characterizing the Non–Detention Act as "proscribing detention *of any kind* by the United States" (emphasis in original)). Not only has the government not made an extraordinary showing of contrary intentions, but the legislative history of the Non–Detention Act is fully consistent with our reading of it. Both the sponsor of the Act and its primary opponent repeatedly confirmed that the Act applies to detentions by the President during war and other times of national crisis. The legislative history is replete with references to the detentions of American citizens of Japanese descent during World War II, detentions that were authorized both by congressional acts and by orders issued pursuant to the President's war power. This context convinces us that military detentions were intended to be covered.

[The Court discusses the legislative history of the Non–Detention Act.]

Specific Statutory Authorization

Since we conclude that the Non–Detention Act applies to military detentions such as Padilla's, we would need to find specific statutory authorization in order to uphold the detention. The government claims that both the Joint Resolution, which authorized the use of force against the perpetrators of the September 11 terrorist attacks, and 10 U.S.C. § 956(5), passed in 1984, which provides funding for military detentions, authorize the detention of enemy combatants. It is with respect to the Joint Resolution that we disagree with the District Court, which held that it must be read to confer authority for Padilla's detention. It found that the "language [of the Joint Resolution] authorizes action against not only those connected to the subject organizations who are directly responsible for the September 11 attacks, but also against those who would engage in 'future acts of international Terrorism' as part of 'such . . . organizations.' " *Padilla I*, 233 F. Supp. 2d at 598–99.

We disagree with the assumption that the authority to use military force against these organizations includes the authority to detain American citizens seized on American soil and not actively engaged in combat. First, we note that the Joint Resolution contains no language authorizing detention. It provides:

That the President is authorized to use all necessary and appropriate force against those nations, organizations, or persons he determines planned, authorized, committed, or aided the terrorist attacks that occurred on September 11, 2001, or harbored such organizations or persons, in order to prevent any future acts of international terrorism against the United States by such nations, organizations or persons.

Joint Resolution § 2 (a).

* * *

The plain language of the Joint Resolution contains nothing authorizing the detention of American citizens captured on United States soil, much less the express authorization required by section 4001(a) * * *. While it may be possible to infer a power of detention from the Joint Resolution in the battlefield context where detentions are necessary to carry out the war, there is no reason to suspect from the language of the Joint Resolution that Congress believed it would be authorizing the detention of an American citizen already held in a federal correctional institution and not "arrayed against our troops" in the field of battle.

* * *

Next, the Secretary argues that Padilla's detention is authorized by 10 U.S.C. § 956(5), which allows the use of appropriated funds for "expenses incident to the maintenance, pay, and allowances of prisoners of war, other persons in the custody of the Army, Navy or Air Force whose status is determined by the Secretary concerned to be similar to prisoners of war, and persons detained in the custody of [the Armed Services] pursuant to Presidential proclamation." 10 U.S.C. § 956(5). The Fourth Circuit found that section 956(5) along with the Joint Resolution sufficed to authorize Hamdi's detention. *Hamdi III*, 316 F.3d at 467–68. With respect to Section 956(5), the court said: "It is difficult if not impossible to understand how Congress could make appropriations for the detention of persons 'similar to prisoners of war' without also authorizing their detention in the first instance."

At least with respect to American citizens seized off the battlefield, we disagree. Section 956(5) authorizes nothing beyond the expenditure of money. * * * In light of the Non–Detention Act's requirement that Congress specifically authorize detentions of American citizens, and the guarantees of the Fourth and Fifth Amendments to the Constitution, we decline to impose on section 956(5) loads it cannot bear.

Conclusion

In sum, we hold that (1) Donna Newman, Esq., may pursue habeas relief on behalf of Jose Padilla; (2) Secretary of Defense Rumsfeld is a proper respondent to the habeas petition and the District Court had personal jurisdiction over him; (3) in the domestic context, the President's inherent constitutional powers do not extend to the detention as an enemy combatant of an American citizen seized within the country away from a zone of combat; (4) the Non–Detention Act prohibits the detention of American citizens without express congressional authorization; and (5) neither the Joint Resolution nor 10 U.S.C. § 956(5) constitutes such authorization under section 4001(a). These conclusions are compelled by the constitutional and statutory provisions we have discussed above. The offenses Padilla is alleged to have committed are heinous crimes severely punishable under the criminal laws. Further, under those laws the Executive has the power to protect national security and the classified information upon which it depends. And if the President believes this authority to be insufficient, he can ask Congress-which has shown its responsiveness-to authorize additional powers. To reiterate, we remand to the District Court with instructions to issue a writ of habeas corpus directing the Secretary of Defense to release Padilla from mili-

tary custody within 30 days. The government can transfer Padilla to appropriate civilian authorities who can bring criminal charges against him. Also, if appropriate, Padilla can be held as a material witness in connection with grand jury proceedings. In any case, Padilla will be entitled to the constitutional protections extended to other citizens.

Wesley, Circuit Judge, concurring in part, dissenting in part:

I respectfully dissent from that aspect of the majority's opinion that concludes the President is without authority from Congress or the Constitution to order the detention and interrogation of Mr. Padilla. In my view, the President as Commander in Chief has the inherent authority to thwart acts of belligerency at home or abroad that would do harm to United States citizens. But even if Mr. Padilla's status as a United States citizen on United States soil somehow changes the constitutional calculus, I cannot see how the Non–Detention Act precludes an affirmance.

* * *

My disagreement with the majority is two-fold. In my view, the President, as Commander in Chief, has inherent authority to thwart acts of belligerency on U.S. soil that would cause harm to U.S. citizens, and, in this case, Congress through the Joint Resolution specifically and directly authorized the President to take the actions herein contested.

* * *

It is quite clear from the President's Order of June 9, 2002 that Mr. Padilla falls within the Joint Resolution's intended sweep. As relevant here, the Joint Resolution authorizes the President (1) to use appropriate and necessary force—detention would seem to be an appropriate level of force in Mr.

Padilla's situation, (2) against those organizations that planned, authorized, or committed the terrorist attacks of 9–11—none of us disputes al Qaeda is responsible for the carnage of that day, (3) in order to prevent future attacks of terrorism against the United States—Padilla is alleged to be closely associated with an al Qaeda plan to carry out an attack in the United States and to possess information that if obtained by the U.S. would prevent future terrorist attacks.

The Joint Resolution has limits; it applies only to those subsets of persons, organizations and nations "[the President] determines planned, authorized, committed, or aided the terrorist attacks." The President is not free to detain U.S. citizens who are merely sympathetic to al Qaeda. Nor is he broadly empowered to detain citizens based on their ethnic heritage. Rather, the Joint Resolution is a specific and direct mandate from Congress to stop al Qaeda from killing or harming Americans here or abroad. The Joint Resolution is quite clear in its mandate. Congress noted that the 9–11 attacks made it "both necessary and appropriate that the United States exercise its rights to self-defense and to protect Unites States citizens both at home and abroad." It seems clear to me that Congress understood that in light of the 9–11 attacks the United States had become a zone of combat.

* * *

Organizations such as al Qaeda are comprised of people. Congress could not have intended to limit the President's authority to only those al Qaeda operatives who actually planned or took part in 9–11. That would do little to prevent future attacks. The fate of the participants is well known. And surely Congress did not intend to limit the President to pursue only those individuals who were al Qaeda opera-

tives as of September 11, 2001. But even if it did, Mr. Padilla fits within the class for by September of 2001, he had already been under the tutelage and direction of senior al Qaeda officers for three years. Clearly, Congress recognized that al Qaeda and those who now do its bidding are a continuing threat to the United States. Thus, the Joint Resolution does have teeth and whether Padilla is a loaded weapon of al Qaeda would appear to be a fact question. A hearing, as ordered by the district court, would have settled the matter.

The majority suggests, however, that the President's actions are ultra vires because "the Joint Resolution does not specifically authorize detentions." To read the resolution as the majority suggests would create a false distinction between the use of force and the ability to detain. It would be curious if the resolution authorized the interdiction and shooting of an al Qaeda operative but not the detention of that person.

* * *

The President's authority to detain an enemy combatant in wartime is undiminished by the individual's U.S. citizenship. Consequently, Padilla's citizenship here is irrelevant. Moreover, the fact that he was captured on U.S. soil is a distinction without a difference. While Mr. Padilla's conduct may have been criminal, it was well within the threat identified in the Joint Resolution. The resolution recognizes the painful reality of 9–11; it seeks to protect U.S. citizens from terrorist attacks at home and abroad.

Congress presumably was aware of § 4001(a) when it passed the Joint Resolution. The resolution was congressional confirmation that the nation was in crisis. Congress called upon the President to utilize his Article II war powers to deal with the emergency. By authorizing the President to use necessary and appropriate force against al Qaeda and its operatives, Congress had to know the President might detain someone who fell within the categories of identified belligerents in carrying out his charge. A different view requires a strained reading of the plain language of the resolution and cabins the theater of the President's powers as Commander in Chief to foreign soil. If that was the intent of Congress it was masked by the strong and direct language of the Joint Resolution. * * *

Sadly, the majority's resolution of this matter fails to address the real weakness of the government's appeal. Padilla presses to have his day in court to rebut the government's factual assertions that he falls within the authority of the Joint Resolution. The government contends that Mr. Padilla can be held incommunicado for 18 months with no serious opportunity to put the government to its proof by an appropriate standard. The government fears that to do otherwise would compromise its ability both to gather important information from Mr. Padilla and to prevent him from communicating with other al Qaeda operatives in the United States.

While those concerns may be valid, they cannot withstand the force of another clause of the Constitution on which all three of us could surely agree. No one has suspended the Great Writ. Padilla's right to pursue a remedy through the writ would be meaningless if he had to do so alone. I therefore would extend to him the right to counsel as Chief Judge Mukasey did. *See Padilla*, 233 F. Supp. 2d at 599–609. At the hearing, Padilla, assisted by counsel, would be able to contest whether he is actually an enemy combatant thereby falling within the President's constitutional and statutory authority.

One of the more troubling aspects of Mr. Padilla's detention is that it is undefined by statute or Presidential Order. Certainly, a court could inquire whether Padilla continues to possess information that was helpful to the President in prosecuting the war against al Qaeda. Presumably, if he does not, the President would be required to charge Padilla criminally or delineate the appropriate process by which Padilla would remain under the President's control.

* * *

Chapter Eleven

SENTENCING

I. INTRODUCTION

A. THE IMPORTANCE OF SENTENCING

Before and during trial, the constitutional and other protections afforded one accused of crime are various and important. The most striking thing about the criminal process following a conviction is the relative absence of constitutional and nonconstitutional safeguards to assure evenhanded, fair, and accurate decisionmaking. One veteran attorney has noted that American lawyers have been pre-occupied with the pre-verdict stages of the criminal process: "[O]ur almost total emphasis on the pre-trial and trial phases of the criminal process, important as they are, reflects the romantic image of the criminal trial contest and the freeing of innocent defendants." Dash, The Defense Lawyer's Role at the Sentencing Stage of a Criminal Case, 54 F.R.D. 315 (1972). Yet, the consequences of a sentence are obviously of critical importance. If too short or of the wrong type, it can deprive the law of its effectiveness and result in the premature release of a dangerous criminal. If too severe or improperly conceived, it can lead to injustice, and even criminal activity that the defendant might otherwise not have done.

B. THE RESPONSIBILITY FOR SENTENCING

Who does sentencing in American courts? The usual answer is that in the federal courts and in most states, judges sentence convicted defendants, while in a minority of jurisdictions the jury sentences those who are convicted.

But this is a most misleading answer, because the sentencing function hardly is confined to judges and juries. The prosecutor plainly has the power to affect the sentence that will be imposed on an offender through sentence and charge bargaining. Although the prosecutor never will pronounce the sentence in the sense of making it official, the power of the prosecutor to choose the charge upon which to proceed before a judge or jury and to press for either harsh or lenient treatment is substantial. And, of course, because most prosecutions end in a guilty plea, the sentencing power is in effect shifted to prosecutors (and defendants) through plea bargaining.

Prosecutorial Discretion and the Federal Sentencing Guidelines

At the federal level, the power of the prosecutor over the sentencing process has been expanded by the implementation of the Federal Sentencing Guidelines. The Guidelines, as will be discussed infra, are designed to limit judicial discretion in setting a sentence. This is done by holding irrelevant certain individualized factors and calculating sentences by objective factors such as criminal history, acceptance of responsibility, weight of drug in drug cases, etc. These factors are put into a grid, and a sentence within a very limited range is derived. Judges are limited in their ability to depart from the sentencing range imposed by the Guidelines. The Guidelines were promulgated due to a perceived disparity in sentencing from defendant to defendant and judge to judge. But as Judge Cabranes has written, the Guidelines simply shift the discretion in sentencing from judge to prosecutor:

> The problem with the 258–box grid is not merely that it reduces sentencing to computation, but rather, that it does not even come close to achieving the asserted objectives of confining discretion and eliminating the bogeyman of disparity. Indeed, disparity is not only alive and well, it is now probably more common than before and certainly more hidden than before. This is true in part because the Guidelines have sub silentio moved the locus of discretion from the judge to the prosecutor. It is largely the prosecutor, for example, who determines the quantity of drugs that will be charged or urged as the appropriate measure in calculating the Guidelines score; it is the prosecutor who will press or ignore the probation officer's calculation of the defendant's criminal history score; it is the prosecutor who will choose whether to stipulate facts dramatically increasing or decreasing the defendant's Guidelines range.

Cabranes, Sentencing Guidelines: A Dismal Failure, N.Y.L.J., February 11, 1992, p. 2.

Other Actors

But even the prosecutor and the courts (judges and juries, that is) together do not set "final" sentences in many jurisdictions. If they collectively impose a prison sentence on a defendant, then a parole board often will determine the time which a prisoner actually will serve in prison and when the prisoner should be released on parole—i.e., released upon conditions. If parole is granted, parole boards decide whether conditions are satisfied and, if not, whether to revoke parole. If probation is imposed in lieu of a prison term, probation officers will work with the courts to decide whether the terms of probation have been satisfied by offenders. If not, probation may be revoked. Similarly, a sentence may be reduced for good behavior while incarcerated. Thus, administrative officials play a significant role in the sentencing scheme.

Despite the real power exercised by these participants in the sentencing process, there undoubtedly is one more force, potentially the most powerful of all, to consider—namely, the legislature. Because the legislature prescribes punishments and sentencing ranges, it can narrow the choices available to judges and juries. In theory, it can abolish plea bargaining, although it is unclear that the legislature ever could totally eliminate prosecutorial discretion. The legislature can expand or contract parole schemes, and it can raise or lower overall punishment levels. The United States Congress has acted in this area by imposing mandatory minimum sentences for a number crimes (especially drug and firearms crimes). These mandatory minimums limit judicial discretion because they set a floor under which the judge cannot go. Correspondingly, they increase the opportunity of the prosecutor to exercise discretion—a prosecutor can avoid a mandatory minimum through charge bargaining.

C. THE DETERMINATION OF SENTENCES

How are sentences determined? The answer to this question reveals why the legislative potential to control sentencing in order to promote fairness and equality is rarely realized in American jurisdictions. For much of this century, American jurisdictions selected the penalty for any particular crime that the legislature, acting at the time a statute was enacted, thought appropriate. Little effort was made to make the punishments for different crimes consistent with one another or to explain how minimum and maximum punishments were chosen, and the range between the minimum and maximum often was considerable. There was an absence of "disciplined restriction on the size and number of discriminations * * * taken at the legislative level * * *." Wechsler, Sentencing, Correction and the Model Penal Code, 109 U.Pa.L.Rev. 465 (1961). In 1962, the Model Penal Code endeavored to fashion a more orderly system. It divided felonies into three degrees and specified two kinds of sentencing ranges for each degree—one for ordinary felony offenders, and one for persistent, professional, multiple, or specially dangerous offenders.[1] Numerous states have followed the lead of the Code and classified their crimes, although they may have used a different classification scheme than that proposed in the Code. See, e.g., Code of Virginia § 18.2–9 (6 classes of felonies and 4 classes of misdemeanors). But many jurisdictions have a variety of statutes that define crimes and prescribe punishment levels. Often, the result is a system in which particular, albeit haphazard, punishments are prescribed in particular sections of the criminal code. Although there has been a tendency to prescribe particular penalties for common law offenses that previously permitted unlimited punishment, the penalties prescribed for various offenses may not reflect a consistent approach to punishment.

Indeterminate Sentencing

Whether a classification or a more ad hoc system is used to prescribe punishments, many state legislatures have left the sentencing authority, judge or jury, with enormous flexibility in setting a sentence—subject of course to the influence of the prosecutor, parole board, etc. Sentencing ranges for offenses are often wide, e.g., first degree murder might be punishable by 20 years to life, and arson by 5 to 20 years. If no plea bargain has been made or accepted, a judge or jury doing the sentencing in these states has uncontrolled discretion to choose a sentence within the prescribed range. Actually, the choice of sentence is somewhat broader, because a trial judge can in many states grant probation, almost without limitation. In addition, judges can suspend portions of sentences, a procedure that is tantamount to partial probation after some time is served.

---

1. Many jurisdictions have habitual offender statutes, that raise maximum punishments, often dramatically, for repeat offenders.

They also can impose additional sanctions, such as fines or restitution, in many instances. All this describes a system known as one of *"indeterminate sentencing."* A report by the National Council on Crime and Delinquency (March 1998) indicates that nearly three fourths of the states use a system of indeterminate sentencing, including a wide range for discretionary sentencing, and discretionary authority to release an offender and revoke parole.

Federal Rejection of Indeterminate Sentencing

The Sentencing Reform Act of 1984 established the U.S. Sentencing Commission. The Act and the Commission's Guidelines are discussed later in the Chapter. In theory, the Guidelines limit disparity in sentencing. In practice, as noted in Judge Cabranes' comment, supra, there is concern that they actually shift greater control over sentencing to prosecutors. The charges that are brought limit the sentencing court's power, because the Guidelines severely circumscribe judicial discretion in setting the length of a sentence. Yet the Guidelines leave the prosecutor considerable room to pick a precise sentence by way of charging decisions and suggestions for upward and certain downward departures (such as for cooperation). See United States v. Kikumura, 918 F.2d 1084 (3d Cir.1990)(the Guidelines have "replaced judicial discretion over sentencing with prosecutorial discretion"). With greater prosecutorial discretion comes the risk of disparity in sentencing that the Guidelines ostensibly sought to avoid. See Heaney, The Reality of Guidelines Sentencing: No End to Disparity, 28 Am.Crim.L.Rev. 161 (1991). See the discussion in Chapter Nine concerning the process of plea bargaining in the shadow of the Guidelines.

Also discussed in Chapter Nine were mandatory minimum penalties. These penalties "trump" the Guidelines and require that courts impose what are often stiff penalties for various offenses, the most important of which are for firearm and narcotics offenses. Some states have guidelines fashioned by courts, or imposed by the legislature, that are similar to the Federal Guidelines. Again, the motive is to control judicial discretion, while the criticism is that guidelines solve one problem (judicial discretion) while creating another (prosecutorial discretion).

The federal approach is a reminder of the power the legislature has to influence sentencing by increasing or decreasing prescribed penalties, providing mandatory minimums, requiring the Sentencing Commission to fix guidelines above or below legislatively prescribed levels, and abolishing parole. The federal approach is a reminder also of the influence that prosecutors may have over sentencing. Although judges are thought of as having the most direct role in sentencing, in the federal system, their power is considerably less at the current time than it was before enactment of the 1984 statute. Where should power to determine sentences reside? The answer may depend on how important a value individualization is, and how vital it is to do away with allegedly unjustified disparities. The choices are explored as the Chapter continues.

D. CONSTITUTIONAL LIMITATIONS ON PUNISHMENT

The Constitution places few limitations on the choice of penalty ranges. As we shall see in the next section of the chapter on sentencing procedures, due process challenges to sentencing are unlikely to succeed. The only other challenges likely to be made are grounded in one of the following constitutional protections: 1) the Eighth Amendment; 2) the First Amendment; 3) the Equal Protection Clause.

1. *Cruel and Unusual Punishment*

Three Strikes and You're Out: *Rummell v. Estelle*

Most cruel and unusual punishment attacks on sentencing stand little chance of succeeding after Rummel v. Estelle, 445 U.S. 263 (1980). Justice Rehnquist's majority opinion concluded that it was unnecessary to decide whether a life sentence for obtaining $120.75 by false pretenses would be cruel and unusual punishment, since Rummel was sentenced for a third felony (the other two were fraudulent use of a credit card to obtain $80, and passing a forged check in the amount of $28.36). The fact of the third offense and the possibility of parole after 12 years made the punishment justifiable and not necessarily as severe as it might first appear, said the Court. Justice Powell dissented and was joined by Justices Brennan, Marshall, and Stevens. He argued that the possibility of parole should not be considered in deciding the cruel and unusual punishment question because it was not guaranteed, and that the penalty for the offense was unconstitutionally disproportionate in view of the nonviolent nature of the offenses.

Three–Pronged Test for Disproportionality: *Solem v. Helm*

The Court departed somewhat from *Rummel* in Solem v. Helm, 463 U.S. 277 (1983), as it struck down a life sentence without parole for a seventh nonviolent felony. Helm's crimes were of the same variety—relatively petty and nonviolent (e.g., burglary and driving under the influence). His seventh crime was uttering a "no account" check for $100. Because of his criminal record, Helm was subject to South Dakota's recidivist statute, resulting in a life sentence without parole.

Justice Powell, writing for the Court, rejected the state's argument that the Eighth Amendment proportionality principle was completely inapplicable to felony prison sentences. He explained as follows:

> The constitutional language itself suggests no exception for imprisonment. We have recognized that the Eighth Amendment imposes "parallel limitations" on bail, fines, and other punishments, and the text is explicit that bail and fines may not be excessive. It would be anomalous indeed if the lesser punishment of a fine and the greater punishment of death were both subject to proportionality analysis, but the intermediate punishment of imprisonment were not. * * *
>
> In sum, we hold as a matter of principle that a criminal sentence must be proportionate to the crime for which the defendant has been convicted. Reviewing courts, of course, should grant substantial deference to the broad authority that legislatures necessarily possess in determining the types and limits of punishments for crimes, as well as to the discretion that trial courts possess in sentencing convicted criminals. But no penalty is *per se* constitutional.

Justice Powell declared that proportionality review should be guided by three "objective" factors:

[Handwritten margin notes: Factors to det proportionality — (1) gravity of offense and harshness of the penalty — (2) how does penalty relate comparatively to penalties of same crime in the juris — (3) compare penalty for same offense in other juris.]

First, we look to the gravity of the offense and the harshness of the penalty. * * * Of course, a court must consider the severity of the penalty in deciding whether it is disproportionate.

Second, it may be helpful to compare the sentences imposed on other criminals in the same jurisdiction. If more serious crimes are subject to the same penalty, or to less serious penalties, that is some indication that the punishment at issue may be excessive. * * *

Third, courts may find it useful to compare the sentences imposed for commission of the same crime in other jurisdictions. * * *

Applying the three-pronged test to Helm's life sentence without parole, the Court found it constitutionally disproportionate:

[Handwritten margin notes: passive crime — bouncing check — • past crimes petty — • life imprisonment w/o parole]

Helm's crime was "one of the most passive felonies a person could commit." It involved neither violence nor threat of violence to any person. * * * His prior offenses, although classified as felonies, were all relatively minor. All were nonviolent and none was a crime against a person. * * * Helm's present sentence is life imprisonment without possibility of parole. Barring executive clemency, Helm will spend the rest of his life in the state penitentiary. This sentence is far more severe than the life sentence we considered in Rummel v. Estelle. Rummel was likely to have been eligible for parole within 12 years of his initial confinement, a fact on which the Court relied heavily. * * * Helm has been treated in the same manner as, or more severely than, criminals who have committed far more serious crimes. * * * Helm could not have received such a severe sentence in 48 of the 50 States.

Chief Justice Burger, joined by Justices White, Rehnquist, and O'Connor, dissented in *Solem.* The dissenters objected to the majority's three-pronged test. The Chief Justice viewed the test as unduly intrusive into legislative judgments, and impermissibly subjective:

[Handwritten margin note: ct imposing its own values over Legislature's]

* * * Today's conclusion by five Justices that they are able to say that one offense has less "gravity" than another is nothing other than a bald substitution of individual subjective moral values for those of the legislature.

* * *

By asserting the power to review sentences of imprisonment for excessiveness the Court launches into uncharted and unchartable waters. Today it holds that a sentence of life imprisonment, without the possibility of parole, is excessive punishment for a seventh allegedly "nonviolent" felony. How about the eighth "nonviolent" felony? The ninth? The twelfth? Suppose one offense was a simple assault? Or selling liquor to a minor? Or statutory rape? Or price-fixing? The permutations are endless and the Court's opinion is bankrupt of realistic guiding principles. * * * I can see no limiting principle in the Court's holding.[2]

2. On remand, Helm received a 20 year sentence. Is it constitutionally valid? Would 25 years have been too much? Does *Solem* offer much guidance to lower courts in cases that raise similar questions?

Limiting Proportionality Review: Harmelin v. Michigan

The Court substantially limited the application of the *Solem* three-factor test of disproportionality in Harmelin v. Michigan, 501 U.S. 957 (1991), although there was no majority opinion for the Court. Harmelin received a life sentence without parole for possession of 672 grams of cocaine. The Michigan statute was unique in the United States in the severity of punishment for possession of large amounts of cocaine. Moreover, the statute prescribed the same penalty, life without parole, for possession as well as for distribution of a large amount of cocaine. Harmelin argued that under the *Solem* three-factor test, his sentence was constitutionally disproportionate.

The Scalia Opinion in Harmelin

Justice Scalia, joined by Chief Justice Rehnquist, engaged in an extensive historical analysis of the Eighth Amendment, and concluded that "there is no proportionality requirement in the Eighth Amendment." Justice Scalia noted that the proportionality principle in the Eighth Amendment is derived from the term "excessive"; the term "excessive" is used in the Amendment in reference to bail and to fines, but is pointedly not used to modify the term "punishment."

Justice Scalia concluded that *Solem* should be overruled. He argued that the *Solem* factors were indeterminate, and led to judicial subjectivity.

Justice Scalia recognized that the Court had previously invalidated death sentences because of disproportionality. He stated, however, that proportionality review "is one of several respects in which we have held that death is different, and have imposed protections that the Constitution nowhere else provides."

The Kennedy Opinion in Harmelin

Justice Kennedy, joined by Justices O'Connor and Souter, stated that "stare decisis counsels our adherence to the narrow proportionality principle that has existed in our Eighth Amendment jurisprudence for 80 years." He saw the Eighth Amendment's relationship to sentencing to be governed by four principles: (1) the fixing of prison terms, as a general matter, is properly within the province of the legislature; (2) the Eighth Amendment "does not mandate adoption of any one penological theory;" (3) divergences in the length of prison terms "are the inevitable, often beneficial, result of the federal structure;" and (4) proportionality review should be informed by objective factors, such as consideration of the type of punishment imposed (especially the objective line between capital punishment and noncapital punishment).

From the above factors, Justice Kennedy concluded that the Eighth Amendment "forbids only extreme sentences that are grossly disproportionate to the crime." He stated that the second and third factors of *Solem*—which mandate an intra- and inter-jurisdictional comparative analysis—are appropriate "only in the rare case in which a threshold comparison of the crime committed and the sentence imposed leads to an inference of gross disproportionality."

In Justice Kennedy's view, a comparative analysis was not required for Harmelin's sentence, because life imprisonment without parole was not grossly disproportionate to the crime. Justice Kennedy emphasized the pernicious effects of the drug epidemic, and stated that "the Michigan Legislature could with reason conclude that the threat imposed to the individual and society by possession of this large an amount of cocaine—in terms of violence, crime, and social displacement—is momentous enough to warrant the deterrence and retribution of a life sentence without parole."

The White Dissent in Harmelin

Justice White, joined by Justices Marshall, Blackmun, and Stevens, dissented. Justice White reasoned that the Framers would not have included an excessive fines clause in the Eighth Amendment (which specifically refers to proportionality) without also intending to prevent excessive sentences that could be imposed in lieu of fines. He argued that Justice Scalia's view failed to explain why the words "cruel and unusual punishment" would impose a proportionality requirement in capital cases but not in noncapital cases. He contended that the *Solem* analysis "has worked well in practice" and stated that "Justice Kennedy's abandonment of the second and third factors set forth in *Solem* makes any attempt at an objective proportionality analysis futile."

Applying the *Solem* analysis to Harmelin's sentence, Justice White found it to be disproportionate. On the first factor—the gravity of the offense and the severity of the punishment—he found that mere possession of drugs, even in a large quantity, "is not so serious an offense that it will always warrant, much less mandate, life imprisonment without possibility of parole." He noted that the statute was undifferentiated in that it applied to first-time offenders as well as to recidivists. Justice White was also concerned that Michigan imposed the same sentence for possession and distribution of large amounts of cocaine. He stated that "the State succeeded in punishing Harmelin as if he had been convicted of the more serious crime without being put to the test of proving his guilt on those charges."

On the second *Solem* factor of intra-jurisdictional comparison, Justice White noted that Michigan imposed a life sentence without parole for three crimes: first-degree murder, possession or manufacture with intent to distribute 650 grams or more of narcotics, and the possession offense for which Harmelin was convicted. Justice White concluded that Harmelin had been treated the same as "criminals who have committed far more serious crimes."

On the third factor of inter-jurisdictional comparison, Justice White emphasized that "no other jurisdiction imposes a punishment nearly as severe as Michigan's for possession of the amount of drugs at issue here." Justice White pointed out that under the Federal Sentencing Guidelines, Harmelin would have received a ten-year sentence.

Suppose a state mandates a life sentence without parole for possession of *any* amount of cocaine. Would Justice Scalia find such a sentence to be constitutionally disproportionate? Would Justice Kennedy?

The Mandatory Sentencing Issue in Harmelin

Harmelin also attacked the constitutionality of his sentence on the ground that, even if it was not disproportionate, it was cruel and unusual to impose a mandatory life sentence without any consideration of mitigating factors. Justice Scalia, writing for five members of the Court on this question, held that if a sentence is not otherwise cruel and unusual, it cannot become so simply because it is mandatory. Justice Scalia recognized that in capital cases, the Eighth Amendment requires individualized sentencing and consideration of all relevant mitigating evidence. He stated, however, that "we have drawn the line of required individualized sentencing at capital cases, and see no basis for extending it further." Justices White, Marshall, Blackmun, and Stevens did not find it necessary to consider Harmelin's mandatory sentencing issue in light of their view that the sentence was constitutionally disproportionate at any rate.

Three Strikes Legislation: California v. Ewing

In the following case, the Court applies its *Rummel-Harmelin* line of Eighth Amendment jurisprudence to the California "Three Strikes" law.

EWING v. CALIFORNIA

Supreme Court of the United States, 2003.
538 U.S. 11.

JUSTICE O'CONNOR announced the judgment of the Court and delivered an opinion in which THE CHIEF JUSTICE and JUSTICE KENNEDY join.

In this case, we decide whether the Eighth Amendment prohibits the State of California from sentencing a repeat felon to a prison term of 25 years to life under the State's "Three Strikes and You're Out" law.

I

A

California's three strikes law reflects a shift in the State's sentencing policies toward incapacitating and deterring repeat offenders who threaten the public safety. The law was designed "to ensure longer prison sentences and greater punishment for those who commit a felony and have been previously convicted of serious and/or violent felony offenses." Cal. Penal Code Ann. § 667(b) (West 1999). * * * Between 1993 and 1995, 24 States and the Federal Government enacted three strikes laws. Though the three strikes laws vary from State to State, they share a common goal of protecting the public safety by providing lengthy prison terms for habitual felons.

B

* * * When a defendant [in California] is convicted of a felony, and he has previously been convicted of one or more prior felonies defined as "serious" or "violent" in Cal. Penal Code Ann. § § 667.5 and 1192.7 (West Supp. 2002), sentencing is conducted pursuant to the three strikes law. Prior convictions must be alleged in the charging document, and the defendant has a right to a jury determination that the prosecution has proved the prior convictions beyond a reasonable doubt. If the defendant has one prior "serious" or "violent" felony conviction, he must be sentenced to "twice the term otherwise provided as punishment for the current felony conviction." If the defendant has two or more prior "serious" or "violent" felony convictions, he must receive "an indeterminate term of life imprisonment." Defendants sentenced to life under the three strikes law become eligible for parole on a date calculated by reference to a "minimum term," which is the greater of (a) three times the term otherwise provided for the current conviction, (b) 25 years, or (c) the term determined by the court pursuant to § 1170 for the underlying conviction, including any enhancements.

Under California law, certain offenses may be classified as either felonies or misdemeanors. These crimes are known as "wobblers." Some crimes that would otherwise be misdemeanors become "wobblers" because of the defendant's prior record. For example, petty theft, a misdemeanor, becomes a "wobbler" when the defendant has previously served a prison term for committing specified theft-related crimes. Other crimes, such as grand theft, are "wobblers" regardless of the defendant's prior record. Both types of "wobblers" are triggering offenses under the three strikes law only when they are treated as felonies. Under California law, a "wobbler" is presumptively a felony and remains a felony except when the discretion is actually exercised to make the crime a misdemeanor.

In California, prosecutors may exercise their discretion to charge a "wobbler" as either a felony or a misdemeanor. Likewise, California trial courts have discretion to reduce a "wobbler" charged as a felony to a misdemeanor either before preliminary examination or at sentencing to avoid imposing a three strikes sentence. In exercising this discretion, the court may consider "those factors that direct similar sentencing decisions," such as "the nature and circumstances of the offense, the defendant's appreciation of and attitude toward the offense, ... [and] the general objectives of sentencing." California trial courts can also vacate allegations of prior "serious" or "violent" felony convictions, either on motion by the prosecution or *sua sponte*. In ruling whether to vacate allegations of prior felony convictions, courts consider whether, "in light of the nature and circumstances of [the defendant's] present felonies and prior serious and/or violent felony convictions, and the particulars of his background, character, and

prospects, the defendant may be deemed outside the [three strikes'] scheme's spirit, in whole or in part." Thus, trial courts may avoid imposing a three strikes sentence in two ways: first, by reducing "wobblers" to misdemeanors (which do not qualify as triggering offenses), and second, by vacating allegations of prior "serious" or "violent" felony convictions.

C

On parole from a 9-year prison term, petitioner Gary Ewing walked into the pro shop of the El Segundo Golf Course in Los Angeles County on March 12, 2000. He walked out with three golf clubs, priced at $399 apiece, concealed in his pants leg. A shop employee, whose suspicions were aroused when he observed Ewing limp out of the pro shop, telephoned the police. The police apprehended Ewing in the parking lot.

Ewing is no stranger to the criminal justice system. In 1984, at the age of 22, he pleaded guilty to theft. The court sentenced him to six months in jail (suspended), three years' probation, and a $300 fine. In 1988, he was convicted of felony grand theft auto and sentenced to one year in jail and three years' probation. After Ewing completed probation, however, the sentencing court reduced the crime to a misdemeanor, permitted Ewing to withdraw his guilty plea, and dismissed the case. In 1990, he was convicted of petty theft with a prior and sentenced to 60 days in the county jail and three years' probation. In 1992, Ewing was convicted of battery and sentenced to 30 days in the county jail and two years' summary probation. One month later, he was convicted of theft and sentenced to 10 days in the county jail and 12 months' probation. In January 1993, Ewing was convicted of burglary and sentenced to 60 days in the county jail and one year's summary probation. In February 1993, he was convicted of possessing drug paraphernalia and sentenced to six months in the county jail and three years' probation. In July 1993, he was convicted of appropriating lost property and sentenced to 10 days in the county jail and two years' summary probation. In September 1993, he was convicted of unlawfully possessing a firearm and trespassing and sentenced to 30 days in the county jail and one year's probation.

In October and November 1993, Ewing committed three burglaries and one robbery at a Long Beach, California, apartment complex over a 5–week period. He awakened one of his victims, asleep on her living room sofa, as he tried to disconnect her video cassette recorder from the television in that room. When she screamed, Ewing ran out the front door. On another occasion, Ewing accosted a victim in the mailroom of the apartment complex. Ewing claimed to have a gun and ordered the victim to hand over his wallet. When the victim resisted, Ewing produced a knife and forced the victim back to the apartment itself. While Ewing rifled through the bedroom, the victim fled the apartment screaming for help. Ewing absconded with the victim's money and credit cards.

On December 9, 1993, Ewing was arrested on the premises of the apartment complex for trespassing and lying to a police officer. The knife used in the robbery and a glass cocaine pipe were later found in the back seat of the patrol car used to transport Ewing to the police station. A jury convicted Ewing of first-degree robbery and three counts of residential burglary. Sentenced to nine years and eight months in prison, Ewing was paroled in 1999.

Only 10 months later, Ewing stole the golf clubs at issue in this case. He was charged with, and ultimately convicted of, one count of felony grand theft of personal property in excess of $400. As required by the three strikes law, the prosecutor formally alleged, and the trial court later found, that Ewing had been convicted previously of four serious or violent felonies for the three burglaries and the robbery in the Long Beach apartment complex. At the sentencing hearing, Ewing asked the court to reduce the conviction for grand theft, a "wobbler" under California law, to a misdemeanor so as to avoid a three strikes sentence. Ewing also asked the trial court to exercise its discretion to dismiss the allegations of some or all of his prior serious or violent felony convictions, again for purposes of avoiding a three strikes sentence. Before sentencing Ewing, the trial court took note of his entire criminal history, including the fact that he was on parole when he committed his latest offense. The court also heard arguments from defense counsel and a plea from Ewing himself. In the end, the trial judge determined that the grand theft should remain a felony. The court also ruled that the four prior strikes for the three burglaries and the robbery in Long Beach should stand. As a newly convicted felon with two or more "serious" or "violent" felony convictions in his past, Ewing was sentenced under the three strikes law to 25 years to life.

The California Court of Appeal affirmed in an unpublished opinion. Relying on our decision in Rummel v. Estelle, 445 U.S. 263 (1980), the court rejected Ewing's claim that his sentence was grossly disproportionate under the Eighth Amendment. Enhanced sentences under recidivist statutes like the three strikes law, the court reasoned, serve the "legitimate goal" of deterring and incapacitating repeat offenders. The Supreme Court of California denied Ewing's petition for review, and we granted certiorari. We now affirm.

II

A

The Eighth Amendment, which forbids cruel and unusual punishments, contains a "narrow proportionality principle" that "applies to noncapital sentences." Harmelin v. Michigan, 501 U.S. 957, 996–997 (1991) (KENNEDY, J., concurring in part and concurring in judgment). We have most recently addressed the proportionality principle as applied to terms of years in a series of cases beginning with Rummel v. Estelle.

[Justice O'Connor discusses the facts and analyses in Rummel v Estelle and Solem v. Helm.]

Eight years after *Solem*, we grappled with the proportionality issue again in *Harmelin, supra. Harmelin* was not a recidivism case, but rather involved a first-time offender convicted of possessing 672 grams of cocaine. He was sentenced to life in prison without possibility of parole. A majority of the Court rejected Harmelin's claim that his sentence was so grossly disproportionate that it violated the Eighth Amendment. The Court, however, could not agree on why his proportionality argument failed. Justice Scalia, joined by The Chief Justice, wrote that the proportionality principle was "an aspect of our death penalty jurisprudence, rather than a generalizable aspect of Eighth Amendment law." He would thus have declined to apply gross disproportionality principles except in reviewing capital sentences.

Justice Kennedy, joined by two other Members of the Court, concurred in part and concurred in the judgment. Justice Kennedy specifically recognized that "the Eighth Amendment proportionality principle also applies to non-

capital sentences." He then identified four principles of proportionality review—"the primacy of the legislature, the variety of legitimate penological schemes, the nature of our federal system, and the requirement that proportionality review be guided by objective factors"—that "inform the final one: The Eighth Amendment does not require strict proportionality between crime and sentence. Rather, it forbids only extreme sentences that are 'grossly disproportionate' to the crime." Justice Kennedy's concurrence also stated that *Solem* "did not mandate" comparative analysis "within and between jurisdictions."

The proportionality principles in our cases distilled in Justice Kennedy's concurrence guide our application of the Eighth Amendment in the new context that we are called upon to consider.

B

* * * Though three strikes laws may be relatively new, our tradition of deferring to state legislatures in making and implementing such important policy decisions is longstanding.

* * *

When the California Legislature enacted the three strikes law, it made a judgment that protecting the public safety requires incapacitating criminals who have already been convicted of at least one serious or violent crime. Nothing in the Eighth Amendment prohibits California from making that choice. To the contrary, our cases establish that States have a valid interest in deterring and segregating habitual criminals. Recidivism has long been recognized as a legitimate basis for increased punishment.

California's justification is no pretext. Recidivism is a serious public safety concern in California and throughout the Nation. According to a recent report, approximately 67 percent of former inmates released from state prisons were charged with at least one "serious" new crime within three years of their release. See U.S. Dept. of Justice, Bureau of Justice Statistics, P. Langan & D. Levin, Special Report: Recidivism of Prisoners Released in 1994, p. 1 (June 2002). In particular, released property offenders like Ewing had higher recidivism rates than those released after committing violent, drug, or public-order offenses. Approximately 73 percent of the property offenders released in 1994 were arrested again within three years, compared to approximately 61 percent of the violent offenders, 62 percent of the public-order offenders, and 66 percent of the drug offenders. * * *

The State's interest in deterring crime also lends some support to the three strikes law. We have long viewed both incapacitation and deterrence as rationales for recidivism statutes. Four years after the passage of California's three strikes law, the recidivism rate of parolees returned to prison for the commission of a new crime dropped by nearly 25 percent. California Dept. of Justice, Office of the Attorney General, "Three Strikes and You're Out"— Its Impact on the California Criminal Justice System After Four Years 10 (1998). Even more dramatically:

[handwritten: law works!]

"an unintended but positive consequence of 'Three Strikes' has been the impact on parolees leaving the state. More California parolees are now leaving the state than parolees from other jurisdictions entering California. This striking turnaround started in 1994. It was the first time more parolees left the state than entered since 1976. This trend has continued and in 1997 more than 1,000 net parolees left California." *Ibid.*

See also Janiskee & Erler, Crime, Punishment, and Romero: An Analysis of the Case Against California's Three Strikes Law, 39 Duquesne L. Rev. 43, 45–46 ("Prosecutors in Los Angeles routinely report that 'felons tell them they are moving out of the state because they fear getting a second or third strike for a nonviolent offense.' ").

To be sure, California's three strikes law has sparked controversy. Critics have doubted the law's wisdom, cost-efficiency, and effectiveness in reaching its goals. This criticism is appropriately directed at the legislature, which has primary responsibility for making the difficult policy choices that underlie any criminal sentencing scheme. We do not sit as a "superlegislature" to second-guess these policy choices. It is enough that the State of California has a reasonable basis for believing that dramatically enhanced sentences for habitual felons advances the goals of its criminal justice system in any substantial way.

[handwritten: defer to leg; goal is deter; means reasonably]

III

Against this backdrop, we consider Ewing's claim that his three strikes sentence of 25 years to life is unconstitutionally disproportionate to his offense * * *. We first address the gravity of the offense compared to the harshness of the penalty. At the threshold, we note that Ewing incorrectly frames the issue. * * *. Even standing alone, Ewing's theft should not be taken lightly. His crime was certainly not "one of the most passive felonies a person could commit." *Solem, supra,* at 296. To the contrary, the Supreme Court of California has noted the "seriousness" of grand theft in the context of proportionality review. Theft of $1,200 in property is a felony under federal law, and in the vast majority of States. * * *

[handwritten: claim is 25 life is unconst. & disproportional; gravity of offense compared to harshness of penalty; theft was not passive; grand theft serious felony]

In weighing the gravity of Ewing's offense, we must place on the scales not only his current felony, but also his long history of felony recidivism. Any other approach would fail to accord proper deference to the policy judgments that find expression in the legislature's choice of sanctions. * * *

Ewing's sentence is justified by the State's public-safety interest in incapacitating and deterring recidivist felons, and amply supported by his own long, serious criminal record. * * * His prior "strikes" were serious felonies including robbery and three residential burglaries. To be sure, Ewing's sentence is a long one. But it reflects a rational legislative judgment, entitled to deference, that offenders who have committed serious or violent felonies and who continue to commit felonies must be incapacitated. * * * Ewing's is not "the rare case in which a threshold comparison of the crime committed and the sentence imposed leads to an inference of gross disproportionality." _Harmelin_, 501 U.S., at 1005 (KENNEDY, J., concurring in part and concurring in judgment).

We hold that Ewing's sentence of 25 years to life in prison, imposed for the offense of felony grand theft under the three strikes law, is not grossly disproportionate and therefore does not violate the Eighth Amendment's prohibition on cruel and unusual punishments. The judgment of the California Court of Appeal is affirmed.

It is so ordered.

JUSTICE SCALIA, concurring in the judgment.

In my concurring opinion in Harmelin v. Michigan, I concluded that the Eighth Amendment's prohibition of "cruel and unusual punishments" was aimed at excluding only certain _modes_ of punishment, and was not a "guarantee against disproportionate sentences." Out of respect for

the principle of _stare decisis_, I might nonetheless accept the contrary holding of Solem v. Helm—that the Eighth Amendment contains a narrow proportionality principle—if I felt I could intelligently apply it. This case demonstrates why I cannot.

Proportionality—the notion that the punishment should fit the crime—is inherently a concept tied to the penological goal of retribution. It becomes difficult even to speak intelligently of "proportionality," once deterrence and rehabilitation are given significant weight—not to mention giving weight to the purpose of California's three strikes law: incapacitation. In the present case, the game is up once the plurality has acknowledged that "the Constitution does not mandate adoption of any one penological theory," and that a "sentence can have a variety of justifications, such as incapacitation, deterrence, retribution, or rehabilitation." * * * Perhaps the plurality should revise its terminology, so that what it reads into the Eighth Amendment is not the unstated proposition that all punishment should be reasonably proportionate to the gravity of the offense, but rather the unstated proposition that all punishment should reasonably pursue the multiple purposes of the criminal law. That formulation would make it clearer than ever, of course, that the plurality is not applying law but evaluating policy.

Because I agree that petitioner's sentence does not violate the Eighth Amendment's prohibition against cruel and unusual punishments, I concur in the judgment.

JUSTICE THOMAS, concurring in the judgment.

I agree with JUSTICE SCALIA's view that the proportionality test announced in Solem v. Helm, 463 U.S. 277 (1983), is incapable of judicial application. Even were _Solem_'s test perfectly clear, however, I would not feel compelled by *stare decisis* to apply it. In my view, the Cruel and Unusual Punishments Clause of the Eighth Amendment contains no proportionality principle.

Because the plurality concludes that petitioner's sentence does not violate the Eighth Amendment's prohibition on cruel and unusual punishments, I concur in the judgment.

JUSTICE STEVENS, **with whom** JUSTICE SOUTER, JUSTICE GINSBURG **and** JUSTICE BREYER **join, dissenting.**

* * * Faithful to the Amendment's text, this Court has held that the Constitution directs judges to apply their best judgment in determining the proportionality of fines, bail, and other forms of punishment, including the imposition of a death sentence. It "would be anomalous indeed" to suggest that the Eighth Amendment makes proportionality review applicable in the context of bail and fines but not in the context of other forms of punishment, such as imprisonment. Rather, by broadly prohibiting excessive sanctions, the Eighth Amendment directs judges to exercise their wise judgment in assessing the proportionality of all forms of punishment.

* * *

* * * I think it clear that the Eighth Amendment's prohibition of "cruel and unusual punishments" expresses a broad and basic proportionality principle that takes into account all of the justifications for penal sanctions. It is this broad proportionality principle that would preclude reliance on any of the justifications for punishment to support, for example, a life sentence for overtime parking.

Accordingly, I respectfully dissent.

JUSTICE BREYER, **with whom** JUSTICE STEVENS, JUSTICE SOUTER, **and** JUSTICE GINSBURG **join, dissenting.**

The constitutional question is whether the "three strikes" sentence imposed by California upon repeat-offender Gary Ewing is "grossly disproportionate" to his crime. The sentence amounts to a real prison term of at least 25 years. The sentence-triggering criminal conduct consists of the theft of three golf clubs priced at a total of $1,197. The offender has a criminal history that includes four felony convictions arising out of three separate burglaries (one armed). In Solem v. Helm, the Court found grossly disproportionate a somewhat longer sentence imposed on a recidivist offender for triggering criminal conduct that was somewhat less severe. In my view, the differences are not determinative, and the Court should reach the same ultimate conclusion here.

* * *

Ewing's sentence on its face imposes one of the most severe punishments available upon a recidivist who subsequently engaged in one of the less serious forms of criminal conduct. I do not deny the seriousness of shoplifting, which an *amicus curiae* tells us costs retailers in the range of $30 billion annually. But consider that conduct in terms of the factors that this Court mentioned in *Solem*—the "harm caused or threatened to the victim or society," the "absolute magnitude of the crime," and the offender's "culpability." In respect to all three criteria, the sentence-triggering behavior here ranks well toward the bottom of the criminal conduct scale. * * *

The Three Strikes Law on Habeas Corpus Review: Lockyer v. Andrade

Lockyer v. Andrade, 538 U.S. 63 (2003), was a companion case to *Ewing*, in which the Court considered a habeas corpus challenge to the constitutionality of the California three strikes law. Under the AEDPA (discussed in Chapter 13), a constitutional challenge on habeas corpus will be successful only if the state court's ruling was "contrary to" or "an unreasonable application of clearly established federal law" as determined by the Supreme Court. The California courts found that it did not violate the Eighth Amendment to sentence Andrade to two consecutive terms of 25 years to life for stealing videotapes worth about $150 from two stores. Andrade had been convicted previously of three counts of residential burglary. The Supreme Court, in an opinion by Justice O'Connor for five members of the Court, held that the state court's interpretation of the Eighth amendment was neither "contrary to" nor "an unreasonable application of clearly established federal law."

Justice O'Connor first analyzed the question of what had been "clearly established" in the *Rummell-Harmelin* line of cases:

> * * * "[C]learly established Federal law" under § 2254(d)(1) [the habeas corpus statute, as amended by AEDPA] is the governing legal principle or principles set forth by the Supreme Court at the time the state court renders its decision. In most situations, the task of determining what we have clearly established will be straightforward. The difficulty with Andrade's position, however, is that our precedents in this area have not been a model of clarity. * * * Through this thicket of Eighth Amendment jurisprudence, one governing legal principle emerges as "clearly established" under § 2254(d)(1): A gross disproportionality principle is applicable to sentences for terms of years.

> * * * [I]n this case, the only relevant clearly established law amenable to the "contrary to" or "unreasonable application of" framework is the gross disproportionality principle, the precise contours of which are unclear, applicable only in the "exceedingly rare" and "extreme" case.

Justice O'Connor then analyzed whether the state court's ruling was "contrary to" or an "unreasonable application of" the gross disproportionality principle that had been "clearly established" by the Supreme Court.

> First, a state court decision is "contrary to our clearly established precedent if the state court applies a rule that contradicts the governing law set forth in our cases" or "if the state court confronts a set of facts that are materially indistinguishable from a decision of this Court and nevertheless arrives at a result different from our precedent." In terms of length of sentence and availability of parole, severity of the underlying offense, and the impact of recidivism, Andrade's sentence implicates factors relevant in both *Rummel* and *Solem*. Because *Harmelin* and *Solem* specifically stated that they did not overrule *Rummel*, it was not contrary to our clearly established law for the California Court of Appeal to turn to *Rummel* in deciding whether a sentence is grossly disproportionate. Indeed, *Harmelin* allows a state court to reasonably rely on *Rummel* in determining whether a sentence is grossly disproportionate. The California Court of Appeal's decision was therefore not "contrary to" the governing legal principles set forth in our cases.

> Andrade's sentence also was not materially indistinguishable from the facts in *Solem*. The facts here fall in between the facts in *Rummel* and the facts in *Solem*. *Solem* involved a sentence of life in prison without the possibility of parole. The defendant in *Rummel* was sentenced to life in

prison with the possibility of parole. Here, Andrade retains the possibility of parole. *Solem* acknowledged that *Rummel* would apply in a "similar factual situation." And while this case resembles to some degree both *Rummel* and *Solem*, it is not materially indistinguishable from either. Consequently, the state court did not "confront a set of facts that are materially indistinguishable from a decision of this Court and nevertheless arrive at a result different from our precedent." * * *

Second, "under the 'unreasonable application' clause, a federal habeas court may grant the writ if the state court identifies the correct governing legal principle from this Court's decisions but unreasonably applies that principle to the facts of the prisoner's case." The "unreasonable application" clause requires the state court decision to be more than incorrect or erroneous. The state court's application of clearly established law must be objectively unreasonable. * * *

Section 2254(d)(1) permits a federal court to grant habeas relief based on the application of a governing legal principle to a set of facts different from those of the case in which the principle was announced. Here, however, the governing legal principle gives legislatures broad discretion to fashion a sentence that fits within the scope of the proportionality principle—the "precise contours" of which "are unclear." Harmelin v. Michigan, 501 U.S., at 998 (KENNEDY, J., concurring in part and concurring in judgment). And it was not objectively unreasonable for the California Court of Appeal to conclude that these "contours" permitted an affirmance of Andrade's sentence.

* * *

The gross disproportionality principle reserves a constitutional violation for only the extraordinary case. In applying this principle for § 2254(d)(1) purposes, it was not an unreasonable application of our clearly established law for the California Court of Appeal to affirm Andrade's sentence of two consecutive terms of 25 years to life in prison.

Justice Souter, joined by Justices Stevens, Ginsburg and Breyer, dissented in *Lockyer*. Justice Souter compared Andrade's 50 years to life sentence to that in the companion case of *Ewing*, noting that Andrade's criminal history was less grave than Ewing's, and yet Andrade received a prison term twice as long for a less serious triggering offense. Justice Souter also argued that the state court's sentence was an "unreasonable application" of the law that he contended to be "clearly established" in Solem v. Helm.

The facts here are on all fours with those of *Solem* and point to the same result. Andrade, like the defendant in *Solem*, was a repeat offender who committed theft of fairly trifling value, some $150, and their criminal records are comparable, including burglary (though Andrade's were residential), with no violent crimes or crimes against the person. The respective sentences, too, are strikingly alike. * * * The results under the Eighth Amendment should therefore be the same in each case. The only ways to reach a different conclusion are to reject the practical equivalence of a life sentence without parole and one with parole eligibility at 87, or to discount the continuing authority of *Solem*'s example, as the California court did. The former is unrealistic; an 87-year-old man released after 50 years behind bars will have no real life left, if he survives to be released at all. And the latter, disparaging *Solem* as a point of reference on Eighth Amendment analysis, is wrong as a matter of law.

Note on the Death Penalty

As the Court recognized in *Harmelin*, the Eighth Amendment does impose limitations on the use of the death penalty. The complexities of the death penalty are often considered in a separate law school course. A full treatment of the Supreme Court's complicated jurisprudence on the subject is beyond the scope of this Book. What follows is a short, and obviously incomplete, summary of the framework that the Court has established for regulating the death penalty under the Eighth Amendment.

1. A death sentence cannot be imposed arbitrarily. Furman v. Georgia, 408 U.S. 238 (1972). The Eighth Amendment requires each defendant to be considered individually, and that the death penalty be "narrowed" to apply only to those who truly merit such severe and final punishment. Gregg v. Georgia, 428 U.S. 153 (1976) (statute upheld where it provided that the sentencer could not impose a death sentence without stating in writing that it found an aggravating circumstance beyond a reasonable doubt).

2. A death sentence cannot be imposed on the basis of aggravating circumstances that are vague, overbroad, or ill-defined. See Maynard v. Cartwright, 486 U.S. 356 (1988), where the Court struck down death sentences based on a finding that the defendant had committed a murder in an "especially heinous, atrocious or cruel" manner. The Court held that this aggravating circumstance was impermissibly broad and vague. It did not sufficiently channel the sentencer's discretion, and thus presented the risk of arbitrary enforcement of the death penalty. Overbroad statutory aggravators can be "narrowed", however, by judicial construction that provides more definition. See Walton v. Arizona, 497 U.S. 639 (1990), where a death sentence was upheld where the statutory aggravating circumstance was that the murder was committed in a heinous, atrocious and cruel manner. While this statutory factor was vague and overbroad, the Court found that the Arizona Supreme Court "has sought to give substance to the operative terms" of the broad aggravating circumstance, and that the Arizona Supreme Court's construction of the statute sufficiently channeled the discretion of the factfinder

3. Another line of cases concerns a different "narrowing" principle—that the death penalty should only be applied to the most egregious types of crime. See, e.g., Enmund v. Florida, 458 U.S. 782 (1982)(imposition of a capital sanction for aiding and abetting a murder without regard to the intent of the defendant was cruel and unusual punishment); Coker v. Georgia, 433 U.S. 584 (1977) (rape not resulting in death could not be punished by death).

4. The *Furman-Gregg* line of cases deals with arbitrary imposition of the death penalty. The concern is that the sentencer will have too much discretion to choose among similarly situated defendants. The solution to the *Gregg* problem is to control the sentencer by guiding discretion through particularized aggravating circumstances that the sentencer must follow. In Lockett v. Ohio, 438 U.S. 586 (1978), the Court expressed a different concern about the death penalty—that the sentencer would not consider the individual *mitigating* characteristics of each defendant. *Lockett* requires that a defendant in a capital sentencing proceeding must have reasonably free reign to introduce, and to require the sentencer to consider, relevant evidence in mitigation of a death sentence. The Court declared that the sentencer "in all but the rarest kind of capital case, [must] not be precluded from considering *as a mitigating factor*,

any aspect of a defendant's character or record and any of the circumstances of the offense that the defendant proffers as a basis for a sentence less than death." However, the state is permitted to structure the sentencer's consideration of mitigating evidence in reasonable ways. Compare Saffle v. Parks, 494 U.S. 484 (1990) (no Eighth Amendment violation in permitting judge to instruct jury to caution against giving undue sympathy to the defendant), with McKoy v. North Carolina, 494 U.S. 433 (1990) (Eighth Amendment prohibits a state from requiring mitigating circumstances to be found unanimously). See also Walton v. Arizona, 497 U.S. 639 (1990) (Eighth Amendment does not prevent the state from allocating to the defendant the burden to prove mitigating factors).

Justice Stevens provides a useful summary of the Court's basic death penalty jurisprudence in his opinion in Graham v. Collins, 506 U.S. 461 (1993):

> In recent years, the Court's capital punishment cases have erected four important safeguards against arbitrary imposition of the death penalty. First, * * * we have concluded that death is an impermissible punishment for certain offenses. Specifically, neither the crime of rape nor the crime of unintentional homicide * * * may now support a death sentence. See Enmund v. Florida; Coker v. Georgia.

> Second, as a corollary to the proportionality requirement, the Court has demanded that the States narrow the class of individuals eligible for the death penalty, either through statutory definitions of capital murder, or through statutory specification of aggravating circumstances. This narrowing requirement, like the categorical exclusion of the offense of rape, has significantly minimized the risk of racial bias in the sentencing process. * * *

> Third, the Court has condemned the use of aggravating factors so vague that they actually enhance the risk that unguided discretion will control the sentencing determination. See, e.g., Maynard v. Cartwright (invalidating "especially heinous, atrocious, or cruel" aggravating circumstance); Godfrey v. Georgia (invalidating "outrageously or wantonly vile, horrible or inhuman" aggravating circumstance). An aggravating factor that invites a judgment as to whether a murder committed by a member of another race is especially "heinous" or "inhuman" may increase, rather than decrease, the chance of arbitrary decision-making, by creating room for the influence of personal prejudices. * * *

> Finally, at the end of the process, when dealing with the narrow class of offenders deemed death-eligible, we insist that the sentencer be permitted to give effect to all relevant mitigating evidence offered by the defendant, in making the final sentencing determination. See, e.g., Lockett v. Ohio. * * * [O]nce the class of death-eligible offenders is sufficiently narrowed, consideration of relevant, individual mitigating circumstances in no way compromises the rationalizing principle of Furman v. Georgia. To the contrary, the requirement that sentencing decisions be guided by consideration of relevant mitigating evidence reduces still further the chance that the decision will be based on irrelevant factors such as race. *Lockett* itself illustrates this point. A young black woman, Lockett was sentenced to death because the Ohio statute "did not permit the sentencing judge to consider, as mitigating factors, her character, prior record, age, lack of specific intent to cause death, and her relatively minor part in the crime." When such relevant facts are excluded from the sentencing determination, there is more, not less, reason to believe that the sentencer will be left to rely on irrational considerations like racial animus.

There is much more to the Court's death penalty jurisprudence than this thumbnail sketch can provide. For more on this difficult subject, see the Symposium on the death penalty, 83 Cornell L.Rev. 1431–1820 (1998); Steiker and Steiker, Sober Second Thoughts: Reflections on Two Decades of Constitutional Regulation of Capital Punishment, 109 Harv.L.Rev. 355 (1995); Sundby, The *Lockett* Paradox: Reconciling Guided Discretion and Unguided Mitigation in Capital Sentencing, 38 UCLA L.Rev. 1147 (1991).

For recent developments in death penalty jurisprudence, *see, e.g.,* Atkins v. Virginia, 536 U.S. 304 (2002) (execution of a mentally retarded defendants is a cruel and unusual punishment prohibited by the Eighth Amendment); Ring v. Arizona, 536 U.S. 584 (2002) (Sixth Amendment right to jury trial requires that statutory aggravating factors must be determined by the jury, not the judge).

2. The First Amendment

Enhancement for Hate Crimes: Wisconsin v. Mitchell

In Wisconsin v. Mitchell, 508 U.S. 476 (1993), the Court explored the extent of First Amendment limitations on punishment. Mitchell, an African–American, was convicted of aggravated battery for his part in the beating of a young white boy. The maximum sentence for aggravated battery was two years' imprisonment. However, the jury found that Mitchell intentionally selected his victim on account of the victim's race. Under a Wisconsin "hate crime" law, this finding resulted in an enhanced sentence of up to seven years' imprisonment; Mitchell received a four-year prison term for the aggravated battery. Mitchell argued that the enhancement statute violated his First Amendment rights because it resulted in punishment for his bigoted beliefs. But his argument was rejected by a unanimous Court in an opinion by Chief Justice Rehnquist.

The Chief Justice noted that "[t]raditionally, sentencing judges have considered a wide variety of factors in addition to evidence bearing on guilt in determining what sentence to impose," and that the defendant's "motive for committing the offense is one important factor." He observed that the First Amendment would prohibit a sentencer from taking a defendant's "abstract beliefs" into consideration in imposing a sentence. However, he declared that the enhancement of Mitchell's sentence was not based merely on his abstract beliefs. Rather, Mitchell received an enhanced sentence because Wisconsin had made an assessment that *conduct* motivated by racial animus was more harmful than conduct that was not. Citing Rummel v. Estelle, the Chief Justice declared that "the primary responsibility for fixing criminal penalties lies with the legislature."

Mitchell also argued that the enhancement statute was unconstitutional because it chilled free speech. His argument proceeded as follows: the prosecution may use statements made by the defendant on occasions unrelated to the crime charged (e.g., at meetings), in order to prove a racial animus in committing the charged crime; therefore, a person concerned about the possibility of an enhanced sentence, should they commit a crime in the future, would have to refrain from expressing ideas reflecting a racial bias. The Court rejected Mitchell's argument, concluding that the "chill" he envisioned was "attenuated and unlikely." The Chief Justice also declared that the First Amendment "does not prohibit the evidentiary use of speech to establish the elements of a crime or to prove motive or intent."

Proceeds of Book Sales Written by Criminals

In response to several celebrated cases in which convicted defendants made money by publishing books about their criminal activity, many states enacted statutes requiring payment of the proceeds from the sale of such books to the state's Crime Victims Board. The law in New York was known as the "Son of Sam" Law. In Simon & Schuster, Inc. v. Members of New York State Crime Victims Board, 502 U.S. 105 (1991), the Court invalidated the Son of Sam Law as inconsistent with the First Amendment. Justice O'Connor, writing for the Court, explained that the Son of Sam law was a "content-based statute" that "singles out income derived from expressive activity for a burden the State places on no other income, and it is directed only at works with a specified content." Because the law was content-based, the State was required to show, under the Court's First Amendment jurisprudence, that the law served a compelling state interest and was narrowly drawn to achieve that interest.

Justice O'Connor noted that while the State had a compelling interest in compensating victims from the fruits of crime, "the Son of Sam law is significantly overinclusive." She stressed that the statute "applies to works on *any* subject, provided that they express the author's thoughts or recollections about his crime, however tangentially or incidentally." She noted that the statute would have covered works such as "The Autobiography of Malcolm X" and the "Confessions of St. Augustine." The Court emphasized that a more narrowly tailored statute—such as a statute covering works predominantly rather than tangentially about the author's criminal activity—could possibly pass constitutional muster. Narrower statutes have been drawn and enforced according to the standards set forth in Justice O'Connor's opinion.

3. *The Equal Protection Clause*

Individual sentencing determinations are rarely the subject of equal protection claims—if for no other reason than they would be virtually impossible to prove. Some broad attacks have been launched at certain statutes or guidelines that are perceived to have a disproportionate effect on racial minorities. The most notable target of attack is the federal statute and accompanying Sentencing Guideline providing for a far higher sentence for crack distribution than for distribution of a similar amount of powder cocaine. The equal protection arguments were addressed in United States v. Thurmond, 7 F.3d 947 (10th Cir.1993), a case in which the defendants were sentenced to 87 months and 97 months of imprisonment respectively, for distributing six grams of crack cocaine:

> Defendants argue that their national statistics, which indicate that 95% of federal cocaine base prosecutions are brought against African–Americans while 40% of federal cocaine powder prosecutions are brought against whites, are so stark, that this case is one of those rare cases * * * wherein statistical evidence alone is enough to prove that Congress had a racially discriminatory purpose in enacting the provisions, as well as in leaving them intact. * * *

> In the Anti–Drug Abuse Act of 1986, Congress amended 21 U.S.C. 841(b)(1) to provide for enhanced penalties for offenses involving specified amounts of controlled substances. As a result, 21 U.S.C. 841(b)(1) and the

corresponding Sentencing Guideline, U.S.S.G. 2D1.1, impose a significantly greater penalty for offenses involving cocaine base than for offenses involving other forms of cocaine. Under the sentencing scheme * * *, one gram of cocaine base is treated the same as one hundred grams of cocaine powder.

* * *

Every Circuit that has addressed the issue has upheld the constitutionality of 21 U.S.C. 841(b)(1) and U.S.S.G. 2D1.1 against race-based equal protection challenges. [Citing cases from other circuits]. In light of the defendant's lack of evidence of a racially discriminatory purpose on the part of Congress or the Sentencing Commission, we [find the] statistics unpersuasive. * * *

* * * Defendants rely on statistics which * * * clearly demonstrate that the cocaine base enhanced penalty scheme has impacted African–Americans to a greater extent than other groups. However, * * * there is ample evidence of Congress's reasons, other than race, for providing harsher penalties for offenses involving cocaine base. * * * [T]he government offered evidence that Congress provided for enhanced penalties for cocaine base offenses because cocaine base (1) has a more rapid onset of action, (2) is more potent, (3) is more highly addictive, (4) is less expensive than cocaine powder, and (5) has widespread availability. [Citing to legislative history]. * * * Finally, cocaine base is simply a different drug than cocaine powder, with a different chemical composition; as a result, Congress can justifiably provide for different penalties for each. Therefore, because reasons exist, other than race, for enhanced penalties for cocaine base offenses, we conclude that Defendants' statistics of disproportionate impact are not sufficient * * * to demonstrate that Congress or the Sentencing Commission had a discriminatory purpose in enacting 21 U.S.C. 841(b)(1)(B) and U.S.S.G. 2D1.1, or in leaving them intact.

It should be noted that the Sentencing Commission proposed a reduction of the 100 to 1 quantity ratio, on the ground that "the high percentage of Blacks convicted of crack cocaine offenses is a matter of great concern to the Sentencing Commission." See U.S. Sentencing Commission: Executive Summary of Special Report on Cocaine and Federal Sentencing Policy, 56 Cr.L.Rep.2159 (1995). The Sentencing Commission also argued that as a matter of policy the 100 to 1 ratio was unwise, because among other things it "creates anomalous results by potentially punishing low-level (retail) crack dealers far more severely than their high-level (wholesale) suppliers of the powder cocaine that served as the product for conversion into crack." However, the Sentencing Commission's proposal to reduce sentences for crack was rejected by Congress. See P.L. 104–38, 109 Stat. 334 (1995) (rejecting proposed amendments to Guidelines relating to lowering of crack sentences). Apparently, nobody in Congress wanted to be on record as having voted for reduction of sentences in drug cases. It appears that Congress is now considering narrowing the ratio not by lowering the sentences for crack, but by increasing the sentences for powder.

For a discussion of the inability of current equal protection doctrine to regulate disparities in cocaine and crack sentencing, see Sklansky, Cocaine, Race, and Equal Protection, 47 Stan.L.Rev. 1283 (1995).

E. OPTIONS OTHER THAN INCARCERATION

What sentencing options other than traditional imprisonment are available? The answer is that a number of options exist; some are substitutes for imprisonment, and others amount to punishment in addition to imprisonment.

1. Fines and Forfeitures

Problems in Using a Fine as a Sanction

One of the most familiar alternatives is the fine. But there are several problems with the fine as a sanction. One problem is that it works better for middle-class or wealthier defendants who might be better able to pay the fine than poorer defendants.[3] Should ability to pay dictate the choice between jail and an alternative such as a fine? Should a fine be added to a prison sentence as punishment simply because the defendant can afford to pay it? Another problem is that judges often are not well enough informed about a defendant's ability to pay or to earn money to arrive at a realistic fine. Many defendants find that they are unable to pay the fine that the judge sets. A related problem is what to do with the defendant who attempts to pay the fine, but is unable to do so. A fourth problem is designating the kinds of offenses that are appropriately punished by fines. Is it ever appropriate to respond to violent crime with a fine? Are fines more appropriate for nonviolent theft crimes? A fifth problem is that the proceeds of a fine go to the government, usually to defray the expenses of law enforcement. Is there a concern that the government may have an economic incentive to seek an unduly harsh fine? Finally, there is the question whether corporations should be penalized by fine in a different and harsher manner than natural persons, on the ground that corporations cannot be incarcerated. In many jurisdictions, the fine is provided as an option, but there is little in the way of statutes or rules to guide judges in choosing or rejecting the option.

An interesting study of the use of fines is the National Institute of Justice's Executive Summary "Fines in Sentencing" (Nov. 1984), by Hillsman, Sichel, and Mahoney. The study finds that a number of courts frequently impose fines upon offenders of limited means and manage to collect them. The study also finds that some courts use fines extensively in felony cases. Judges impose these fines according to the gravity of the offense and the resources of the defendant. The report concludes that use of such fines results in a dramatic drop in the number of short-term custodial sentences that courts impose.

Should wealthy defendants be fined more than poor defendants? Does the answer depend on whether both wealthy and poor defendants are incarcerated as well as fined? See, e.g., United States v. Salerno, 937 F.2d 797 (2d Cir. 1991)(in a racketeering case, the trial judge sentenced the defendant to 70 years in prison and ordered him to pay a fine of $376,000 plus twice the gross profits of his racketeering activities).

---

3. For contrasting views on the relative benefits of imprisonment and fines for white-collar criminals, compare Posner, Optimal Sentences for White–Collar Criminals, 17 Am. Crim.L.Rev. 409 (1980) with Coffee, Corporate Crime and Punishment: A Non–Chicago View of the Economics of Criminal Sanctions, 17 Am.Crim.L.Rev. 419 (1980).

Indigents and Fines

Williams v. Illinois, 399 U.S. 235 (1970), and Tate v. Short, 401 U.S. 395 (1971), protect indigents against oppressive fine systems. In *Williams,* the Court held that an indigent defendant was denied equal protection when he was imprisoned beyond the maximum term authorized by statute because of an inability to pay a fine and court costs. Tate v. Short held that an indigent defendant could not be imprisoned for failure to pay a fine when the state statute made traffic offenses punishable by fine only. Thus, imposing a fine is not the problem—imprisonment for inability to pay the fine is the problem. How would you achieve deterrence for indigent offenders when jail is not an appropriate sanction?

[margin note: Δ denied e.p when imprisoned]

The Supreme Court again considered the permissible treatment of indigents unable to pay fines in Bearden v. Georgia, 461 U.S. 660 (1983). Bearden was convicted of burglary and theft by receiving stolen property. Under the state's first offender statute, the trial judge did not enter a judgment of guilt, but deferred further proceedings and sentenced Bearden to three years on probation for the burglary charge and a concurrent one year on probation for the theft charge. As a condition of probation he ordered Bearden to pay a $500 fine and $250 restitution. Bearden borrowed $200 to make the initial payments required by the order, but was unable to make further payments. Subsequently, the court revoked Bearden's probation for failure to pay the balance of the fine and restitution, entered a judgment of conviction, and sentenced him to serve the remaining portion of the probationary period (more than two years) in prison.

[margin note: charged + convicted burglary + theft by receiving stolen property • levied a fine]

[margin note: Δ could not pay so ct sentenced Δ to serve remaining portion of sentence]

Justice O'Connor's opinion for the Court observed that "[a] defendant's poverty in no way immunizes him from punishment." Thus, a state court may consider a defendant's entire background including employment and financial resources in arriving at a sentence. She reasoned further that "[t]he decision to place the defendant on probation * * * reflects a determination by the sentencing court that the State's penological interests do not require imprisonment"; that a state could imprison a probationer who wilfully refused to pay a fine or restitution or to make bona fide efforts to seek employment or borrow money to pay a fine; and that "if the probationer has made all reasonable efforts to pay the fine or restitution, and yet cannot do so through no fault of his own, it is fundamentally unfair to revoke probation automatically without considering whether adequate alternative methods of punishing the defendant are available." Alternatives might include an extension of time to make payments, a reduction of the fine, or a requirement of some form of public service. "Only if the sentencing court determines that alternatives to imprisonment are not adequate in a particular situation to meet the State's interest in punishment and deterrence may the State imprison a probationer who has made sufficient bona fide efforts to pay."

[margin note: Poverty is not a defense]

[margin note: But when Δ cannot pay ct must examine alternative methods of punishment]

[margin note: If it is not Δ's fault he pay • ct could look to extend time to pay • or public service]

Justice White, joined by Chief Justice Burger and Justices Powell and Rehnquist, concurred in the judgment. He argued that nothing in the Constitution prohibited a state from making "a good-faith effort to impose a jail sentence that in terms of the state's sentencing objectives will be roughly equivalent to the fine and restitution that the defendant failed to pay." He found no such effort by the trial court in this case.

[margin note: cannot]

[margin note: if Alt to imprisonment not appropriate ct can sentence to jail.]

Forfeiture of the Proceeds of Crime

A variation on the fine is forfeiture of property used in or the proceeds of criminal activity. It is increasingly common for both federal and state laws to provide for forfeiture upon conviction and also for civil forfeiture, which does not require a conviction. Congress has provided that a court shall order forfeiture where appropriate in addition to imposing other sanctions upon a defendant. 18 U.S.C. § 3554. As part of its Comprehensive Crime Control Act of 1984, Congress enacted the Comprehensive Forfeiture Act of 1984, which expands the forfeiture provisions in racketeering and drug cases. See 28 U.S.C. § 881. For a discussion of how these forfeiture provisions operate, see Caplin & Drysdale v. United States, discussed in Chapter Ten.

The government's economic interest in forfeiture is undeniable. At the federal level, all assets seized by the Department of Justice go into its Asset Forfeiture Fund, which the Attorney General is authorized to use for law enforcement purposes. 28 U.S.C. § 524(c). This led the Attorney General in 1990 to urge United States attorneys to increase the volume of forfeitures in order to meet the Department of Justice's annual budget target. As one court put it: "Forfeitures, in effect, impose an impressive levy on wrongdoers to finance, in part, the law enforcement efforts of both the state and national governments." United States v. Real Property Located in El Dorado, 59 F.3d 974 (9th Cir. 1995).[4]

Constitutional Limitations on Forfeiture: Alexander v. United States

In Alexander v. United States, 509 U.S. 544 (1993), the Court considered some constitutional questions arising from an application of the RICO forfeiture statute, 18 U.S.C. § 1963. Alexander was found guilty of 17 counts of obscenity and three counts of violating RICO, arising from the sale of obscene magazines and tapes. Alexander owned more than a dozen stores and theaters dealing in sexually explicit materials; the jury found that four magazines and three videotapes sold through Alexander's retail stores were obscene. Alexander was sentenced to six years in prison, fined $100,000, and ordered to pay the costs of prosecution, incarceration, and supervised release. The District Court then reconvened the same jury and conducted a forfeiture proceeding pursuant to 18 U.S.C. § 1963(a)(2). At this proceeding, the government sought forfeiture of the entirety of Alexander's interest in the stores and theaters. The jury found that Alexander had an interest in 10 pieces of commercial real estate and 31 current or former businesses, all of which had been used to conduct his racketeering enterprise. The District Court ultimately ordered Alexander to forfeit his wholesale and retail businesses, and all the assets thereof, as well as almost $9 million dollars acquired through racketeering activity. The government eventually destroyed the entire inventory of magazines and tapes, the vast majority of which had not been found obscene.

---

4. The federal government's annual net gain from all types of forfeitures grew from $27 million in 1985 to $531 million in 1992. Between 1985 and 1993, the Department of Justice seized $3.2 billion worth of assets. A 1993 estimate by the General Accounting Office put the federal government's forfeiture inventory at $1.9 billion. Assets seized have included cars, homes, land, businesses, money, planes, yachts, and even livestock. See Horowitz, What Can Government Take From You? Even Innocent People Can Have Property Seized, Investor's Daily, December 9, 1993, at 1.

First Amendment Questions in Alexander

Alexander argued that the forfeiture violated his First Amendment rights, because it "imposed a complete ban on his future expression because of previously unprotected speech" and thus operated as an impermissible prior restraint. But the Court, in an opinion by Chief Justice Rehnquist, rejected this argument. The Chief Justice reasoned as follows:

prior restraint

> [T]he forfeiture order in this case imposes no legal impediment to—no prior restraint on—petitioner's ability to engage in any expressive activity he chooses. He is perfectly free to open an adult bookstore or otherwise engage in the production and distribution of erotic materials; he just cannot finance these enterprises with assets derived from his prior racketeering offenses.

The Chief Justice concluded that "the RICO forfeiture order was not a prior restraint on speech, but a punishment for past criminal conduct." He also rejected Alexander's argument that the threat of forfeiture of businesses dealing with expressive materials constituted an impermissible chilling effect on speech. The Chief Justice recognized that "the monetarily large forfeiture in this case may induce cautious booksellers to practice self-censorship and remove marginally protected materials from their shelves out of fear that those materials could be found obscene and thus subject them to forfeiture." But he concluded that "the threat of forfeiture has no more of a chilling effect on free expression than the threat of a prison term or a large fine," and that "our cases have long recognized the practical reality that any form of criminal obscenity statute applicable to a bookseller will induce some tendency to self-censorship and have some inhibitory effect on the dissemination of material not obscene." The Chief Justice saw no reason to distinguish forfeitures from the stiff fines and long prison sentences for obscenity violations that had been found constitutional in previous cases. See, e.g., Fort Wayne Books v. Indiana, 489 U.S. 46 (1989)(10 years imprisonment and $20,000 fine under state version of RICO).

RICO not prior restraint but punishment for past crimes

Forfeiture equal to fines

Justice Kennedy, joined by Justices Blackmun and Stevens and in large part by Justice Souter, dissented from the majority's disposition of the First Amendment issue in *Alexander*. He criticized the majority's analysis in the following passage:

> The Court today embraces a rule that would find no affront to the First Amendment in the government's destruction of a book and film business and its entire inventory of legitimate expression as punishment for a single past speech offense. Until now I had thought one could browse through any book or film store in the United States without fear that the proprietor had chosen each item to avoid risk to the whole inventory and indeed to the business itself. This ominous, onerous threat undermines free speech and press principles essential to our personal freedom.

Eighth Amendment Questions in Alexander

Alexander also argued that the forfeiture order, considered together with his six-year prison term and $100,000 fine, was disproportionate to the gravity of his offenses and thus violated the Eighth Amendment. The lower court dismissed this claim by reasoning that the Eighth Amendment does not require any proportionality review of a sentence less than life imprisonment without the possibility of parole. But the Chief Justice rejected the lower court's analysis as misdirected to the Cruel and Unusual Punishments Clause of the Eighth Amendment, whereas Alexander's claim was more properly based in the Excessive Fines Clause. The Chief Justice explained as follows:

Δ also raised 8th - proportionality of offense to harm

- excessive fines

Unlike the Cruel and Unusual Punishments Clause, which is concerned with matters such as the duration or conditions of confinement, the Excessive Fines Clause limits the Government's power to extract payments, whether in cash or kind, as punishment for some offense. The in personam criminal forfeiture at issue here is clearly a form of monetary punishment no different, for Eighth Amendment purposes, from a traditional "fine."

The Court remanded for a determination of whether the forfeiture in combination with the other penalties was constitutionally disproportionate under the Excessive Fines Clause. On remand, the court of appeals found no constitutional infirmity in the forfeiture. It distinguished forfeiture of the proceeds of a crime from property that is used for criminal activity. The forfeiture of proceeds from an illegal enterprise "is not considered punishment subject to the excessive fines analysis because the forfeiture of proceeds simply deprives the owner of the fruits of his criminal activity." The court found that the amount of proceeds from Alexander's racketeering activity amounted to almost $9 million; that amount was excluded from to the proportionality analysis. The remainder of the property forfeited was not considered disproportionate in light of Alexander's racketeering crimes. United States v. Alexander, 108 F.3d 853 (8th Cir.1997).

Excessive Forfeiture: United States v. Bajakajian

In United States v. Bajakajian, 524 U.S. 321 (1998), the Court struck down an in personam criminal forfeiture as excessive under the Eighth Amendment. Justice Thomas wrote the majority opinion for five members of the Court. Bajakajian was found trying to leave the country with more than $350,000. He was charged with, and pleaded guilty to, failure to report the currency. The government sought forfeiture of all the currency, under a statute permitting forfeiture of property "involved" in a criminal offense. The majority found that forfeiture of the entire amount was disproportionate to Bajakajian's offense. Justice Thomas analyzed the proportionality question in the following passage:

Respondent's crime was solely a reporting offense. It was permissible to transport the currency out of the country so long as he reported it. Section 982(a)(1) orders currency to be forfeited for a "willful" violation of the reporting requirement. Thus, the essence of respondent's crime is a willful failure to report the removal of currency from the United States. Furthermore, as the District Court found, respondent's violation was unrelated to any other illegal activities. The money was the proceeds of legal activity and was to be used to repay a lawful debt. Whatever his other vices, respondent does not fit into the class of persons for whom the statute was principally designed: He is not a money launderer, a drug trafficker, or a tax evader. And under the Sentencing Guidelines, the maximum sentence that could have been imposed on respondent was six months, while the maximum fine was $5,000. Such penalties confirm a minimal level of culpability.

The harm that respondent caused was also minimal. Failure to report his currency affected only one party, the Government, and in a relatively minor way. There was no fraud on the United States, and respondent caused no loss to the public fisc. Had his crime gone undetected, the Government would have been deprived only of the information that $357,144 had left the country. * * * There is no inherent proportionality in such a forfeiture. * * *

Justice Kennedy, joined by Chief Justice Rehnquist and Justices O'Connor and Scalia, dissented. He argued that the forfeiture of the entire sum of smuggled cash was a reasonable means of deterring criminals such as money launderers and drug dealers.

Proportionality Limitations on in Rem Forfeitures: Austin v. United States

On the same day that the Court decided *Alexander,* the Court also handed down Austin v. United States, 509 U.S. 602 (1993), which dealt with a different type of forfeiture known as in rem forfeiture, i.e., a forfeiture proceeding brought against the property rather than against the owner. After a state court sentenced Austin on his guilty plea to one count of possessing cocaine with intent to distribute, the United States filed an in rem civil forfeiture action against his mobile home and auto body shop under 21 U.S.C. § 881, which provides for the forfeiture of property used, or intended to be used, to facilitate the commission of certain drug-related crimes. The government presented evidence that Austin had brought two ounces of cocaine from his mobile home to his body shop in order to consummate a pre-arranged sale there. The lower court ordered the properties to be forfeited to the government. Austin objected that forfeiture of the properties, in light of the relatively minor offense, constituted a violation of the Eighth Amendment's Excessive Fines Clause. The lower court rejected this argument by reasoning that when the government is proceeding in rem—against the property rather than its owner—the guilt or innocence of the owner is "constitutionally irrelevant" and therefore such a forfeiture could not be considered excessive in relationship to any offense.

The Supreme Court, in an opinion by Justice Blackmun, rejected the lower court's reasoning and held that the forfeiture was subject to review for proportionality under the Excessive Fines Clause. The Court rejected the government's argument that the Eighth Amendment is not applicable to a civil proceeding. Justice Blackmun noted that the text of the Eighth Amendment contained no specific limitation to criminal cases—unlike the Sixth Amendment, for example. Justice Blackmun elaborated as follows:

> The purpose of the Eighth Amendment, putting the Bail Clause to one side, was to limit the government's power to punish. The Cruel and Unusual Punishments Clause is self-evidently concerned with punishment. The Excessive Fines Clause limits the Government's power to extract payments, whether in cash or kind, as punishment for some offense. The notion of punishment, as we commonly understand it, cuts across the division between the civil and the criminal law. It is commonly understood that civil proceedings may advance punitive and remedial goals, and, conversely, that both punitive and remedial goals may be served by criminal penalties. Thus, the question is not, as the United States would have it, whether forfeiture under [the provisions for in rem forfeiture] is civil or criminal, but rather whether it is punishment.

The government in *Austin* argued further that the forfeiture of the property was not punishment because it was in rem—the forfeiture operated against the property, on the ground that the property had a nexus to criminal activity, rather than against the owner. The government noted that this in rem forfeiture was unlike the in personam forfeiture in *Alexander,* where forfeiture was based on the fact that Alexander had violated criminal laws. The government pointed out that under common law, the culpability of the owner was irrelevant in an in rem forfeiture action. But Justice Blackmun reviewed the common-law of in rem forfeiture and responded that "even though this Court has rejected the innocence of the owner as a common-law defense to [in rem] forfeiture, it consistently has recognized that forfeiture serves, at least in part, to punish the owner."

Justice Blackmun further stressed that—whatever the status of in rem forfeiture under the common-law—the statutory forfeiture provisions applicable to drug cases provide an "innocent owner" defense. He reasoned that these exemptions "serve to focus the provisions on the culpability of the owner in a way that makes them look more like punishment, not less" and concluded that the inclusion of innocent owner defenses revealed a "congressional intent to punish only those involved in drug trafficking." In other words, the statutory "in rem" forfeiture at issue in *Austin* was operating against the owner, not just against the property.

The Court remanded to determine whether the forfeiture was constitutionally excessive in light of the offense. It refused to set forth a particular test for determining proportionality in forfeiture actions.

Justice Kennedy, joined by Chief Justice Rehnquist and Justice Thomas, wrote an opinion concurring in part and in the judgment. He doubted whether, at common-law, all in rem forfeitures were imposed because of the owner's blameworthy conduct. He concluded that "at some point, we may have to confront the constitutional question whether forfeiture is permitted when the owner has committed no wrong of any sort, intentional or negligent. That for me would raise a serious question."[5]

Due Process Limitations on Forfeiture: United States v. James Daniel Good Real Property

The Court considered procedural due process limitations on civil forfeiture of real property in United States v. James Daniel Good Real Property, 510 U.S. 43 (1993). Police found a large quantity of drugs in Good's home, and Good pled guilty to state drug offenses. Over four years later, the United States filed a civil in rem action against Good's house and land, alleging that the property had been used to commit or facilitate a drug transaction. Following an ex parte proceeding, a Magistrate Judge issued a warrant authorizing the seizure of the property, and the government executed the warrant without prior notice to Good or an adversary hearing. The Supreme Court held that this procedure did not pass constitutional muster. It declared that absent exigent circumstances, a property owner has a due process right to notice and an opportunity to be heard before the government seizes real property subject to civil forfeiture.

Justice Kennedy, writing for a five-person majority, distinguished prior cases upholding the seizure of forfeitable personal property without prior notice. Those cases were based on the exigent circumstance that, if notice were given before the seizure, the property might be moved. But this consideration was not applicable to real property. Justice Kennedy concluded that seizure of real property without prior notice, simply on the basis that there will be an ultimate

---

5. But see Bennis v. Michigan, 516 U.S. 442 (1996) (forfeiture of automobile was permissible even though the owner was unaware of illegal activity occurring in the automobile).

judicial determination of forfeiture, "affords little or no protection to the innocent owner." He held that the ex parte warrant procedure set forth in the civil forfeiture statute was an insufficient protection, because at such a proceeding the government "is not required to offer any evidence on the question of innocent ownership or other potential defenses a claimant might have." He noted that a neutral adversary hearing was particularly required where, as in forfeiture proceedings, "the Government has a direct pecuniary interest in the outcome of the proceeding." Finally, he concluded that the state interest in seizures without notice was minimal compared to the individual ownership interest at stake. This was because the government could prevent the sale of forfeitable property through alternatives less onerous than outright seizure—for example, by obtaining a lis pendens.

In a footnote the Court stressed that it had not decided "what sort of procedures are required for preforfeiture seizures of real property in the context of criminal forfeiture."

Chief Justice Rehnquist dissented in an opinion joined by Justice Scalia and in large part by Justice O'Connor. The Chief Justice argued that legitimate state interests would be impaired by a pre-seizure notice requirement because, once notified, the owner could "destroy or otherwise damage the buildings on the property."

Justice O'Connor, in a separate dissent, contended that a pre-seizure notice requirement would do little to protect the interests of innocent property owners. She stated that "[a]t any hearing—adversary or not—the Government need only show probable cause that the property has been used to facilitate a drug offense in order to seize it [pending a final determination of forfeiture]; it will be unlikely that giving the property owner an opportunity to respond will affect the probable cause determination."

Justice Thomas, in a separate dissent, argued that the forfeiture statute's provision for seizure without notice was not unconstitutional as applied to Good's case. He noted that Good could not be considered an innocent owner because he had already been convicted of a drug offense. Justice Thomas saw no purpose in a pre-seizure hearing requirement in such circumstances, since notice had already been provided "by the conviction itself." He concluded that "seizure of the property without more formalized notice and an opportunity to be heard is simply one of the many unpleasant collateral consequences that follows from conviction of a serious drug offense."[6]

2. Probation

Another option to incarceration is probation—called "supervised release" in the federal system. Probation means that a prison sentence is held in abeyance and the defendant is released subject to terms and conditions. If the defendant fails to meet those conditions, then the sentence can be reinstated upon proof by a preponderance of evidence at a probation revocation hearing. Familiar condi-

---

6. In a case of statutory construction, the Court considered the scope of the innocent owner defenses that it discussed in *Good*. In United States v. A Parcel of Land, etc., 507 U.S. 111 (1993), the Court held that an owner was an "innocent owner" where she had been given money to purchase a home and lacked knowledge of the fact that the money was the proceeds of illegal drug transactions. Hence the property was not forfeitable under the statute. Justice Stevens wrote for a plurality of four, and Justice Scalia concurred in the result, joined by Justice Thomas.

tions for probation are that the probationer meet his family obligations, pay a fine if possible, keep a job, undergo medical (including psychiatric) treatment, submit to drug testing, follow a prescribed course of study or training, report regularly to a probation officer, and remain within a specified geographical area. Community service requirements may also be imposed today by some judges.

More controversial conditions are those that call upon probationers to forego personal liberties that the unconvicted citizen may claim under the Bill of Rights. For example, in United States v. Smith, 972 F.2d 960 (8th Cir.1992), the court imposed as a condition of supervised release that "the defendant shall not cause the conception of another child other than to his wife, unless he can demonstrate he is fully providing support to the three children presently in existence, and the two en ventre sa mere." The sentencing judge was concerned that the defendant if released would father children who would not be supported and sustained. But the court of appeals held that the sentencing court had no authority to impose this condition. Under the Federal Probation Act, 18 U.S.C. § 3563, conditions imposed on liberty or property must be reasonably necessary to foster rehabilitation of the defendant or the protection of the public.[7] The court held that restricting Smith's right to have offspring did not meet this test, and also noted that the right to have children is a "sensitive and important area of human rights." What conditions should the court have imposed to allay its concerns? If the judge cannot impose what she feels to be effective conditions, she can presumably deny probation and incarcerate the defendant. Is this a better result for the defendant? See also United States v. Smith, 332 F.3d 455 (7th Cir. 2003) ("A district court may impose special conditions of supervised release that it deems appropriate so long as the conditions are reasonably related to 1) the nature and circumstances of the offense and the history and characteristics of the defendant; 2) the need for the sentence imposed to afford adequate deterrence to criminal conduct; 3) the need to protect the public from further crimes of the defendant; and 4) the need to provide the defendant with needed educational or vocational training, medical care or other correctional treatment in the most effective manner.").

The trial judge usually has broad discretion to select a probation period. In United States v. Thomas, 934 F.2d 840 (7th Cir.1991), the defendant thought the conditions and length of the imposed probation to be onerous, and argued that he had an absolute right to reject probation and opt for a prison sentence— which would not have been as long as the probation period. The court of appeals held that the defendant had no such option. It reasoned that it is the court, not the defendant, who is given the task of determining the sentence for a crime. The court was concerned that giving defendants the option to choose one form of sentence over another would have a negative effect on the sentencing process. On the other hand, couldn't the defendant simply violate the terms of his probation to get where he wants to go (i.e., prison)?

3. Restitution

A third option to incarceration (or a penalty in addition to incarceration) is restitution. There is increasing concern in the United States with the plight of

---

7. As part of the Sentencing Reform Act of 1984, Congress elaborated upon and modified the law governing probation. The relevant statutory sections are 18 U.S.C. §§ 3561–3566, and 3601–3607. The statute now explicitly empowers and sometimes requires judges to make payment of a fine or restitution as a condition of probation.

victims of crime. Hence, it is not surprising that courts are ordering more defendants to make financial restitution to victims.[8] Several states have statutes that make restitution a "policy" of criminal sentencing. See, e.g., Iowa Code Ann. § 910.2; Pa.Const.Stat.Ann., tit. 42, § 9721(C). The interest in providing restitution for crime victims is explored in Harland, Monetary Remedies for the Victims of Crime: Assessing the Role of the Criminal Courts, 30 U.C.L.A.L.Rev. 52 (1982).

The Victim and Witness Protection Act of 1982 ("VWPA") amended Title 18 of the United States Code in significant respects. Two new sections on restitution, 18 U.S.C.A. §§ 3663 and 3664, provide for restitution for victims of certain offenses and require a court to justify a sentence that does not include restitution. 18 U.S.C.A. § 3664(c) requires that the defendant and the government be informed of provisions of the presentence report relating to restitution. The prosecution must bear the burden of persuasion as to the victim's loss, while the defendant has the burden of persuasion as to his financial resources.

Congress again demonstrated its concern for crime victims and its interest in promoting restitution in the Sentencing Reform Act of 1984. The Act recognizes that restitution may be a condition of probation, 18 U.S.C. § 3563, provides that a defendant may have to give notice to victims of fraud or deception in connection with sentencing, 18 U.S.C. § 3555, provides that a court may order portions of a fine remitted if a defendant makes restitution, 18 U.S.C. § 3572, and states that restitution may be imposed in addition to other sanctions, 18 U.S.C. § 3556. As part of the Comprehensive Crime Control Act of 1984, Congress also enacted the Victims of Crime Act of 1984, which creates a crime victims fund and provides for crime victim compensation.[9]

In 1996 Congress enacted the Mandatory Victim's Restitution Act (MVRA). The MVRA further amended 18 U.S.C. §§ 3663 and 3664, and added new section 3663A, all with the view to fortifying the remedy of restitution for victims of crime. As discussed above, the VWPA provided a presumption in favor of restitution. The MVRA goes much further by providing that restitution is *mandatory* for crimes of violence, offenses against property, and for the crime of tampering with consumer products. With respect to these crimes, an order of restitution is mandatory even if the defendant has no ability to pay. See, e.g., United States v. Nichols, 169 F.3d 1255 (10th Cir.1999) (upholding order requiring defendant, convicted of conspiracy to bomb the Federal building Oklahoma City, to pay restitution in the amount of $14.5 million: "The district court was not required to consider Mr. Nichols' financial condition under 18 U.S.C. 3664(f)(1)(A)."). The Act does provide, however, that an indigent defendant cannot be incarcerated "solely on the basis of inability" to make restitution payments. And for the crimes not covered by the MVRA amendments, a restitution order must be structured within the defendant's ability to pay. See

---

8. One experienced criminal defense counsel has written that prosecutors often prefer to seek a criminal fine rather than an order of restitution. See Morvillo, Restitution for Victims, N.Y.L.J., April 5, 1994, p. 3. Why do you think that is?

9. The Crime Victim's Fund is supported in part by monies derived from 18 U.S.C. § 3013, which requires courts to impose a monetary special assessment on any person convicted of

a federal misdemeanor. The Court in United States v. Munoz–Flores, 495 U.S. 385 (1990), upheld this statute against a challenge that it was passed in violation of the Origination Clause of the Constitution. Justice Marshall, writing for the majority, concluded that the statute was not a "Bill for raising Revenue." Justice Stevens (joined by Justice O'Connor) and Justice Scalia wrote opinions concurring in the judgment.

United States v. Dunigan, 163 F.3d 979 (6th Cir.1999) (defendant convicted of defrauding the United States; restitution order in the amount of $311,000 was vacated because defendant was indigent).

The MVRA specifically provides for restitution to victims who suffer bodily injury, essentially applying tort damages principles. Another innovation of the MVRA is to provide restitution for drug crimes. The money is allocated 65% to the government's crime assistance fund, and 35% to fund for substance abuse block grants. The Act also contains special provisions for compensation of victims of terrorism.

Who is a Victim of the Crime?

The VWPA as amended by the MVRA authorizes a court to order the defendant to make restitution to any "victim" of his criminal conduct. The term "victim" has raised some questions of statutory interpretation. One problem arises where a defendant has been charged with a massive scheme, but then is indicted for or pleads guilty to only a part of his criminal activity. In 1990, Congress amended § 3663 to cover this situation. This section now provides that for purposes of restitution, "a victim means a person directly and proximately harmed as a result of the commission of an offense for which restitution may be ordered including, in the case of an offense that involves as an element of a scheme, conspiracy, or pattern of criminal activity, any person directly harmed by the defendant's criminal conduct in the course of the scheme, conspiracy or pattern." Under this amended provision, all victims of the scheme are qualified to receive restitution, even if the indictment or guilty plea did not cover all of the victims. United States v. Jewett, 978 F.2d 248 (6th Cir.1992).

The term "victim" can include business entities as well as local, state, and federal governments. See United States v. Helmsley, 941 F.2d 71 (2d Cir. 1991)(in a tax prosecution, upholding a restitution order for payment of funds to the IRS and the State of New York); United States v. Nichols, supra (restitution to be paid to the government for destruction of government building). However, the government is not considered a "victim" to the extent that it paid money to investigate or prosecute the defendant. See United States v. Gibbens, 25 F.3d 28 (1st Cir.1994)(VWPA does not authorize recovery of money spent by government in a sting operation).

4. Pretrial Diversion and Partial Confinement

Pretrial diversion programs may encourage some offenders, especially drug addicts and alcoholics, to seek treatment instead of contesting charges. Successful completion of a treatment program usually results in the dismissal of charges. The federal program is discussed in Marshall v. United States, 414 U.S. 417 (1974), which holds that Congress can permissibly distinguish from other addicts those with two or more felony convictions and deny those with prior convictions the benefit of diversion programs.

Even if incarceration is used as a sanction, there are alternatives to the typical prison sentence. For example, a sentence of partial confinement—for selected periods—may be imposed. Or, an offender might serve a sentence on nights and weekends. The growth in the prison and jail populations of many jurisdictions has greatly increased the costs of running the criminal justice system and has led to a search for less expensive forms of incarceration. Some jurisdictions have experimented with "house arrest," a sentence imposed by the court in which offenders are legally ordered to remain confined in their own residences. See Petersilia, A Man's Home is His Prison, 2 Criminal Justice, No. 4, 16, 17 (1988).

5. *Young Offenders*

Special detention provisions are often made for juvenile offenders. One statutory scheme "designed to provide a better method for treating young offenders convicted in federal courts in that vulnerable age bracket [16–22], to rehabilitate them and restore normal behavior patterns," Dorszynski v. United States, 418 U.S. 424, 432 (1974), was the Federal Youth Corrections Act, which provided the trial judge with special sentencing options for offenders under 22 years of age. Although the result of sentencing under the Act could have been a longer sentence than would be served by an adult, there was greater emphasis on treatment under the Act. More treatment facilities were made available to youth offenders; more individualized treatment for youth offenders was expected; and special release provisions (in lieu of parole) applied to youth offenders. In the Comprehensive Crime Control Act of 1984, Congress decided to replace the Youth Corrections Act with its general guideline approach to sentencing. In United States v. R.L.C., 503 U.S. 291 (1992), the Court held that the maximum permissible sentence in federal juvenile-delinquency proceedings must be limited to that which could have been imposed upon an adult under the Sentencing Guidelines.[10]

6. *Insanity Acquittees and Civil Commitment*

In Jones v. United States, 463 U.S. 354 (1983), Justice Powell's opinion for the Court upheld District of Columbia laws that required a defendant found not guilty by reason of insanity to prove by a preponderance of the evidence that he is no longer insane in order to obtain release from a mental hospital. Although other persons may be civilly committed only if the government proves by clear and convincing evidence that they are mentally ill and likely to injure themselves or others, the Court found that insanity acquittees constituted a special class who could be treated differently and who could be kept in a mental hospital beyond the maximum periods prescribed as penalties in criminal statutes. Jones had been charged with a misdemeanor, attempted petit larceny, punishable by a

---

10. What is often a crucial question to a juvenile is whether he will be treated as a "child" or as an adult. See, e.g., Kent v. United States, 383 U.S. 541 (1966). Perhaps no advantage is more significant than the limit on incarceration to a designated age. If a person is transferred to the typical criminal court, the potential range of prison sentences may increase, so the transfer decision is of critical importance. 18 U.S.C. § 5032 provides that if a person between 15 and 18 commits a federal crime, he can be tried as an adult "in the interest of justice." In determining whether trying the defendant as an adult is in the interest of justice, the judge must consider the defendant's age and social background, the nature of the offense, any prior acts of delinquency, the juvenile's intellectual development and

emotional maturity, the nature of past treatment efforts, if any, and the juvenile's response to such treatment, and the availability of juvenile programs. See United States v. Nelson, 68 F.3d 583 (2d Cir.1995)(trial court erred in refusing to try the defendant as an adult, where he was 19 at the time of trial, charged with murder, and had committed previous acts of delinquency).

For a suggestion that juvenile courts should be abolished and that all juveniles should be tried as adults (where they would, on balance, obtain greater protection), see Ainsworth, Reimagining Childhood and Reconstructing the Legal Order: The Case for Abolishing the Juvenile Court, 69 N.C.L.Rev. 1083 (1991).

maximum prison sentence of one year. He raised insanity as a defense and proved it by a preponderance of the evidence as required by local law. The Court reasoned that because there had been proof beyond a reasonable doubt that Jones committed a crime, and he himself proved insanity, it was permissible to presume that he continued to be mentally ill.

In Foucha v. Louisiana, 504 U.S. 71 (1992), the Court, in an opinion by Justice White, held that *Jones* did not allow the continuing commitment of an insanity acquittee who had recovered his sanity. The Court invalidated a statute that allowed continuing commitment in a mental hospital until such time as the acquittee could prove that he was not dangerous to himself or to others. *Foucha* is discussed more fully in Chapter Seven.

The NGI Verdict

In the Insanity Defense Reform Act of 1984 ("IDRA"), Congress made insanity an affirmative defense, created a special verdict of "not guilty only by reason of insanity" ("NGI"), and established a comprehensive civil commitment procedure. See 18 U.S.C. §§ 17, 4241–4247. Under that procedure, a defendant found NGI is held in custody pending a court hearing, which must occur within 40 days of the verdict. At the conclusion of the hearing, the court determines whether the defendant should be hospitalized or released. Provisions similar to IDRA exist in many states.

One question that has arisen under IDRA is whether the defendant has the right to have the jury instructed that an NGI verdict will result in his involuntary commitment. In Shannon v. United States, 512 U.S. 573 (1994), Shannon argued that such an instruction was necessary to prevent a possible misconception among the jurors that he would be quickly set free after an NGI verdict. But the trial court refused to give the instruction and Shannon was found guilty.

The Supreme Court, in an opinion written by Justice Thomas for seven members of the Court, held that Shannon had no right to an instruction concerning the consequences of an NGI verdict. Justice Thomas relied on the "well established" principle that "when a jury has no sentencing function, it should be admonished to reach its verdict without regard to what sentence might be imposed." He argued that "providing jurors sentencing information invites them to ponder matters that are not within their province, distracts them from their factfinding responsibilities, and creates a strong possibility of confusion."

Justice Thomas noted that it would be difficult to limit a rule that would require the judge to instruct the jury about the consequences of an NGI verdict:

> Shannon offers us no principled way to limit the availability of instructions detailing the consequences of a verdict to cases in which an NGI defense is raised. Jurors may be as unfamiliar with other aspects of the criminal sentencing process as they are with NGI verdicts. But, as a general matter, jurors are not informed of mandatory minimum or maximum sentences, nor are they instructed regarding probation, parole, or the sentencing range accompanying a lesser included offense. Because it is conceivable that some jurors might harbor misunderstandings with regard to these sentencing options, a district court, under Shannon's reasoning, might be obligated to give juries information regarding these possibilities as well. In short, if we

pursue the logic of Shannon's position, the rule against informing jurors of the consequences of their verdicts would soon be swallowed by the exceptions.

Justice Thomas noted, however, that a clarifying instruction about an NGI verdict might be required if "a witness or prosecutor states in the presence of the jury that a particular defendant would 'go free' if found NGI." Justice Stevens, joined by Justice Blackmun, dissented in *Shannon*. He contended that "[t]here is no reason to keep this information from the jurors and every reason to make them aware of it."

II. GUIDELINES SENTENCING

A. THE PERCEIVED NEED FOR DETERMINATE SENTENCING

Judge Marvin Frankel conducted a study of sentencing and published his results in 1972. See Frankel, Criminal Sentences: Law Without Order. In that influential study, Judge Frankel found significant disparities in federal sentencing decisions. He attributed the disparities to "the almost wholly unchecked and sweeping powers we give to judges in the fashioning of sentences"—powers that Judge Frankel himself had exercised and found "terrifying and intolerable for a society that professes devotion to the rule of law." The solution, for Judge Frankel, was "concrete agreement on concrete factors capable of being stated, discussed and thought about in the style of a legal system for rational people rather than a lottery." He posited the possibility of "scientific sentencing." Judge Frankel's views eventually bore fruit in Congress, with a statute sponsored by Senators Kennedy and Thurmond, designed to replace "our haphazard approach to sentencing."

Professor Robinson provides the following perspective about the drive away from indeterminate sentencing and toward guidelines sentencing:

> Although almost ubiquitous in state and federal systems by the 1960's, the indeterminate sentence became the subject of intense criticism. Prisoners complained of the uncertainty of their situation and disparate sentences proposed by judges. Law and order advocates worried about the possibility of quick parole. Libertarians expressed concern with the length of time inmates spent prior to parole. Social scientists complained about the lack of empirical support for the proposition that prisons were rehabilitative institutions. Other critics pointed out that prison behavior correlated poorly with post-release recidivism and that the best predictors were factors known at the time of the original sentences. Thus, if guidelines could be directed at the courts, rather than the parole boards, the uncertainty and potential deceptiveness of indeterminate sentences could be avoided.

Robinson, The Decline and Potential Collapse of Federal Guideline Sentencing, 74 Wash.U.L.Q 881 (1996).

Congress enacted the Sentencing Reform Act of 1984 as part of the Comprehensive Crime Control Act of 1984. The Sentencing Reform Act makes a number of important changes in Federal sentencing. Among other changes, the Act 1) classifies federal criminal offenses and designates the sentencing range for the new classes; 2) states the purposes to be served by any sentence; 3) establishes a Sentencing Commission to promulgate guidelines binding on sentencing courts;

4) requires judges to give reasons for sentencing and for departing from the Guidelines; and 5) provides for appellate review when judges depart from the guidelines or from the sentence provided in a plea agreement.

Most importantly, the Reform Act abolishes parole in the Federal system. The rationale for abolishing parole is that the discretion exercised by parole boards was one of the major causes of disparity in sentencing. As Professor Robinson, supra, puts it:

> To achieve the goal of minimizing judge-created disparities, the danger of merely shifting discretion from the district court judges to other actors in the criminal justice process had to be faced. One such actor was the United States Parole Commission, which had authority to release inmates prior to completion of their maximum terms of confinement. The Sentencing Reform Act addressed this problem by abolishing parole for persons sentenced under the guidelines to be established by the Sentencing Commission.

The Goals of the Sentencing Commission

The U.S. Sentencing Commission found that adoption of guidelines satisfactory to legislators, prosecutors, defense lawyers, and judges was no simple task. As a result of the circulation of various drafts and extensive debate within the Commission, the Commission finally agreed to the following principles:

> (1) Similar offense categories—e.g., for various kinds of fraud—would be grouped together under a single generic heading.

> (2) The base sentence for each offense would be determined by a discussion process, *"anchored, but not bound by,"* estimates of the average time served in past years by offenders convicted of that offense and the percentage of offenders given a nonincarceration sentence.

> (3) For articulated policy reasons—e.g., to increase deterrence—sentences could be raised or lowered with respect to past practice.

> (4) Base offense sentences would be modified by a set of specific offense characteristics that would be determined by looking to past sentencing practices, to statutory aggravating or mitigating factors, to factors that are taken into consideration in similar offenses, to the vulnerability of victims, the offender's role in an offense, acceptance of responsibility, and the criminal history of the offender.

Thus, the Commission began with past practice, emphasized the importance of rationalizing sentences, and adopted an approach that focuses on the charges actually brought and the real offense behavior of the offender. It decided that conspiracies and attempts would generally be treated the same as the object offense, with a modest downward adjustment.

B. HOW THE FEDERAL SENTENCING GUIDELINES WORK

The process of sentencing under the Federal Guidelines has been described succinctly as follows:

> Under the federal guidelines, sentences are based on a mathematical equation that begins with an offense level depending on its seriousness. Murder, for instance, is at level 43, while robbery is at 20, altering or

removing a motor vehicle identification number is at level 8 and obscenity is at 6.

That offense level is then reduced or increased depending on factors such as a defendant's criminal history, level of cooperation, use of a deadly weapon and role in the offense. Other key factors are the quantities of drugs or money involved, injury to a victim and vulnerability of the victim.

The sum of factors leads to a box on a grid that suggests a sentencing range such as 0 to 6 months at the low end or 292 to 365 months at the high end. A judge must articulate the reasons for imposing a sentence outside the calculated range. Generally, the judge must cite an aggravating or mitigating circumstance of a "kind or to a degree not adequately taken into consideration" by the guidelines' drafters.

Pines, After Five Years, No One Loves Federal Sentencing Guidelines, N.Y.L.J., November 4, 1992, p. 3.

Base Offense Level

To understand how the Guidelines work, it is useful to consider a hypothetical case.[11] Suppose that a defendant is convicted of obstruction of justice. The Guidelines describe offenses generically and contain an index indicating which Guidelines cover various code sections. Obstruction of justice is governed by Guideline § 2J1.2. The base offense level is 14 (raised from 12 after the Enron scandal); but the level increases to 16 if the obstruction involved destruction or alteration of either a substantial number of records or an especially probative record.[12]

Relevant Conduct

Section 1B1.3 of the Guidelines provides that "conduct which is not formally charged or is not an element of the offense of conviction may enter into the determination of the applicable sentencing range." Under this section, the sentencing range can be based not only on evidence with which the defendant was convicted, but also on evidence that is *related* to the conduct forming the basis of the conviction. See, e.g., United States v. Santiago, 906 F.2d 867 (2d Cir.1990)(in a drug distribution case, quantities and types of drugs not specified in the count of conviction are to be included in determining the base offense level if they were part of the same course of conduct or part of a common scheme or plan as the count of conviction; court properly considered previous, uncharged sales to the same buyer). "Relevant conduct" must be proven by a preponderance of the evidence—*not* beyond a reasonable doubt. United States v. Mourning, 914 F.2d 699 (5th Cir.1990)(trial court properly considered uncharged acts of money laundering, proven by a preponderance of the evidence). Thus, in our obstruction of justice hypothetical, if the government could show by a preponder-

---

11. Citations to and quotations of particular Guidelines in the following discussion may not be definitive at the time you read this. To date, the Sentencing Commission has promulgated over 700 amendments to the Sentencing Guidelines! (More by the time you read this). The discussion that follows is therefore intended merely to give you a general impression of how the Guidelines work.

12. Similarly, with drug crimes, the base offense level increases as the quantity increases, and with financial crimes the base level increases as the amount of money involved increases.

ance that the defendant engaged in related acts of fraud or perjury, these acts would be considered in setting the base offense level. And they would *count as much for sentencing purposes as the acts for which the defendant was convicted.*

However, to be considered as relevant conduct, the criminal activity must be part of the same course of conduct or common scheme as the crime for which the defendant was convicted. "Factors useful in determining whether the two offenses are severable and distinct are temporal and geographical proximity, common victims, common scheme, charge in the indictment, and whether the prior conviction is used to prove the instant offense." United States v. Stone, 325 F.3d 1030 (8th Cir. 2003) (DWI could not be considered as relevant conduct where the defendant pleaded guilty to a drug conspiracy). Compare United States v. Mayle, 334 F.3d 552 (6th Cir. 2003) (court had discretion to increase the defendant's offense level by 23 levels, in sentencing the defendant from crimes related to fraudulent forgery and cashing of the victim's Social Security checks, based on relevant conduct that the defendant murdered the victim in order to obtain the checks).

Adjustments

Certain adjustments of sentence must be considered. There are victim-related adjustments—e.g., adjustments that increase punishment when the victim is a child or especially vulnerable, § 3A1.1, or when the victim is a law enforcement officer. § 3A1.2. See, e.g., United States v. Wright, 160 F.3d 905 (2d Cir.1998) (two-step enhancement upheld under vulnerable victim provision, based on defendant's embezzlement of funds from mentally retarded individuals). Adjustments are provided when the defendant had an aggravating or mitigating role in an offense. §§ 3B1.1, 3B1.2. The offense level is increased by two steps if the defendant is found to have "abused a position of public or private trust * * * in a manner that significantly facilitated the commission or concealment of the offense." § 3B1.3. That same Guideline authorizes a two-level increase if the defendant committed the crime by exploiting a "special skill." See, e.g., United States v. Smith, 332 F.3d 455 (7th Cir. 2003) (conviction for theft of interstate freight raised by two levels because the defendant exploited his "special skills" in operating a tractor-trailer). Another adjustment increases punishment by two levels for obstruction of justice with respect to the investigation or prosecution of the offense charged. § 3C1.1. See United States v. Thompson, 944 F.2d 1331 (7th Cir.1991)(enhancement for obstruction of justice not permitted where the defendant merely denies wrongdoing); United States v. Dunnigan, 507 U.S. 87 (1993)(obstruction adjustment required if court finds that defendant committed perjury while testifying at trial). Another upward adjustment can be made if the trial judge finds, by a preponderance of the evidence, that the defendant committed perjury at the trial.

Aggregation

If the defendant is convicted on several counts, the calculation is usually made separately for each count, and a set of rules is applied to the totality. But there are special rules that aggregate some conduct. §§ 3D1.1–3D1.5. See generally Alschuler, The Failure of Sentencing Guidelines: A Plea for Less Aggregation, 58 U.Chi.L.Rev. 901 (1991). Assume, for example, that a securities fraud defendant was convicted of defrauding three victims whose estimated losses were $250,000, $100,000, and $500,000. For crimes in which offense level is determined primarily on the basis of the amount of the loss, the three estimated losses are added together for a total of $850,000. The addition would result in a punishment increase of 11 levels above the base offense level.

Acceptance of Responsibility

The final determinant of the offense level is the defendant's acceptance of responsibility. § 3E1.1. A defendant who clearly demonstrates recognition and affirmative acceptance of personal responsibility for his crime may receive a reduction of two levels. The defendant receives a further one level reduction if his offense level is 16 or above and his acceptance of responsibility includes assistance to the government in the investigation or prosecution of his own misconduct. Thus, if the obstruction of justice defendant cooperates with the government and promises to institute corrective measures, his level might drop from 14 to 12. It could not drop to 11, however, even if he supplies the government complete information concerning his involvement in the crime, or promptly notifies the government of his intent to plead guilty (because the offense level started below 16). See, e.g., United States v. Phillip, 948 F.2d 241 (6th Cir.1991)(defendant not entitled to reduction for acceptance of responsibility where he gave a false alibi to the investigating officers); United States v. Burns, 925 F.2d 18 (1st Cir.1991)(defendant who enters *Alford* plea—pleading guilty while protesting his innocence—is not entitled to reduction for acceptance of responsibility); United States v. Boos, 329 F.3d 907 (7th Cir. 2003) (defendant who pleaded guilty to drug activity was not entitled to reduction for acceptance of responsibility where sentencing judge enhanced the sentence for obstruction of justice).

Criminal History Category

Once the offense level is fixed, the sentencing judge, with the assistance of the probation officer, must determine the defendant's criminal history. §§ 4A1.1–4A1.3. Criminal history points are determined by a defendant's prior convictions. Three points are allocated, for example, for each prior sentence of imprisonment exceeding one year and one month, and two points are added for each sentence of imprisonment of at least 60 days but less than one year and one month. Some offenses are excluded, and time periods are designated to exclude stale convictions. The sentencing judge is permitted to depart from the computational approach if reliable information indicates that the criminal history category understates the seriousness of the defendant's past criminal conduct. See, e.g., United States v. Thornberg, 326 F.3d 1023 (8th Cir. 2003) (upward departure permitted from criminal history category III to category V because the defendant's criminal history was far more extensive than that of a typical person in category III: such a departure is appropriate "where there is evidence of obvious incorrigibility"). Special provision is made for "career offenders"—i.e., defendants at least 18 at the time they commit the crime of conviction, which is a crime of violence or trafficking in a controlled substance, and the defendant has at least two prior felony convictions for violent crimes or trafficking in controlled substances. § 4B1.1. Using this formula, an obstruction of justice defendant with no prior criminal record would have a criminal history of 0. A prior conviction for non-violent crime would put him in category I.

Using the 258–Box Sentencing Grid

Using the sentencing table, and assuming no prior criminal history, an obstruction of justice defendant convicted of one count involving extensive destruction of documents, but was able to obtain all possible credit for acceptance of responsibility, he would fall within a guideline for offense level 13 calling for a sentence of 12–18 months.

If instead of no criminal record, a defendant had a category III criminal record, the sentence for a level 13 offense increases to 18–24 months and for a level 16 offense to 30–37 months. Defendants in the worst criminal category (VI) would face a Guideline of 33–41 months at level 13 and 51–63 months at level 16.

Each row of the sentencing table contains levels that overlap with the levels in the preceding and succeeding rows. By overlapping the levels, the Commission intended to discourage unnecessary litigation. Both the prosecutor and the defendant are expected to realize that the difference between one level and another will not necessarily make a difference in sentencing.

Authorized Departures

The Guidelines contain a section on "departures." They authorize departures from the Guidelines when a defendant has provided substantial assistance to authorities (downward departure), death or serious injury has resulted from conduct (upward departure), the defendant's conduct was unusually extreme or cruel (upward departure), and in other circumstances. §§ 5K1, 5K2. See, e.g., United States v. Orchard, 332 F.3d 1133 (8th Cir. 2003) (the defendant was convicted of knowingly distributing a controlled substance analogue to a person under 21; the seriousness of the psychological harm to victim, the defendant's abuse of a relationship of trust, and his facilitation of a sex crime on the victim justified an upward departure); United States v. Phillip, 948 F.2d 241 (6th Cir.1991)(three-level upward departure under § 5K2.8 for extreme cruelty inflicted by the defendant on his four-year-old son); United States v. Williams, 937 F.2d 979 (5th Cir.1991)(defendant's advantageous social background does not justify an upward departure).

The Court in Koon v. United States, 518 U.S. 81 (1996), described the system of departures under the Sentencing Guidelines as follows:

> Congress allows district courts to depart from the applicable Guideline range if "the court finds that there exists an aggravating or mitigating circumstance of a kind, or to a degree, not adequately taken into consideration by the Sentencing Commission in formulating the guidelines that should result in a sentence different from that described." 18 U.S.C. § 3553(b). To determine whether a circumstance was adequately taken into consideration by the Commission, Congress instructed courts to "consider only the sentencing guidelines, policy statements, and official commentary of the Sentencing Commission."

Turning our attention, as instructed, to the Guidelines Manual, we learn that the Commission did not adequately take into account cases that are, for one reason or another, "unusual." The Introduction to the Guidelines explains:

> "The Commission intends the sentencing courts to treat each guideline as carving out a 'heartland,' a set of typical cases embodying the conduct that each guideline describes. When a court finds an atypical case, one to which a particular guideline linguistically applies but where conduct significantly differs from the norm, the court may consider whether a departure is warranted."

The Commission lists certain factors which never can be bases for departure (race, sex, national origin, creed, religion, socio-economic status, 1995 USSG § 5H1.10; lack of guidance as a youth, § 5H1.12; drug or alcohol dependence, § 5H1.4; and economic hardship, § 5K2.12), but then states that with the exception of those listed factors, it "does not intend to limit the kinds of factors, whether or not mentioned anywhere else in the guidelines, that could constitute grounds for departure in an unusual case." 1995 USSG ch. 1, pt. A, intro. comment. 4(b).

* * *

So the Act authorizes district courts to depart in cases that feature aggravating or mitigating circumstances of a kind or degree not adequately taken into consideration by the Commission. The Commission, in turn, says it has formulated each Guideline to apply to a heartland of typical cases. Atypical cases were not "adequately taken into consideration," and factors that may make a case atypical provide potential bases for departure. Potential departure factors "cannot, by their very nature, be comprehensively listed and analyzed in advance," 1995 USSG § 5K2.0, of course. Faced with this reality, the Commission chose to prohibit consideration of only a few factors, and not otherwise to limit, as a categorical matter, the considerations which might bear upon the decision to depart.

Sentencing courts are not left adrift, however. The Commission provides considerable guidance as to the factors that are apt or not apt to make a case atypical, by listing certain factors as either encouraged or discouraged bases for departure. Encouraged factors are those "the Commission has not been able to take into account fully in formulating the guidelines." § 5K2.0. Victim provocation, a factor relied upon by the District Court in this case, is an example of an encouraged downward departure factor, § 5K2.10, whereas disruption of a governmental function is an example of an encouraged upward departure factor, § 5K2.7. Even an encouraged factor is not always an appropriate basis for departure, for on some occasions the applicable Guideline will have taken the encouraged factor into account. For instance, a departure for disruption of a governmental function "ordinarily would not be justified when the offense of conviction is an offense such as bribery or obstruction of justice; in such cases interference with a government function is inherent in the offense." A court still may depart on the basis of such a factor but only if it "is present to a degree substantially in excess of that which ordinarily is involved in the offense." § 5K2.0.

Discouraged factors, by contrast, are those "not ordinarily relevant to the determination of whether a sentence should be outside the applicable guideline range." 1995 USSG ch. 5, pt. H, intro. comment. Examples include the defendant's family ties and responsibilities, 1995 USSG § 5H1.6, his or her education and vocational skills, § 5H1.2, and his or her military, civic, charitable, or public service record, § 5H1.11. The Commission does not view discouraged factors "as necessarily inappropriate" bases for departure but says they should be relied upon only "in exceptional cases." 1995 USSG ch. 5, pt. H, intro. comment.

The Commission's treatment of departure factors led then-Chief Judge [of the First Circuit] Breyer to explain that a sentencing court considering a departure should ask the following questions:

"1) What features of this case, potentially, take it outside the Guidelines 'heartland' and make of it a special, or unusual, case?"

"2) Has the Commission forbidden departures based on those features?"

"3) If not, has the Commission encouraged departures based on those features?"

"4) If not, has the Commission discouraged departures based on those features?"

United States v. Rivera, 994 F.2d 942, 949 (1st Cir. 1993).

We agree with this summary. If the special factor is a forbidden factor, the sentencing court cannot use it as a basis for departure. If the special factor is an encouraged factor, the court is authorized to depart if the applicable Guideline does not already take it into account. If the special factor is a discouraged factor, or an encouraged factor already taken into account by the applicable Guideline, the court should depart only if the factor is present to an exceptional degree or in some other way makes the case different from the ordinary case where the factor is present. If a factor is unmentioned in the Guidelines, the court must, after considering the "structure and theory of both relevant individual guidelines and the Guidelines taken as a whole," decide whether it is sufficient to take the case out of the Guideline's heartland. The court must bear in mind the Commission's expectation that departures based on grounds not mentioned in the Guidelines will be "highly infrequent."

Too Many Downward Departures?

By 2003, many members of Congress came to the belief that some district judges had been using downward departures too frequently to evade what those departing judges thought was an improper limitation on their sentencing discretion. These members of Congress thought that discretionary downward departures were leading to inconsistent sentencing in the federal judiciary, which struck at the very point of the Sentencing Guidelines. Congressman Feeney, addressing this concern, proposed an amendment to a piece of legislation that was designed to protect children from sex crimes and other exploitation. The Feeney amendment was passed as part of the PROTECT Act, and while it specifically limits downward departures in child exploitation cases, it goes on to regulate downward departures more generally. Among other things, the Feeney Amendment: 1) provides that appellate review of district court downward departures are de novo, rather than for abuse of discretion; 2) requires written reasons for downward departures other than those involving substantial assistance to the government or so-called "fast track" plea bargains in illegal alienage cases; 3) institutes a registry in which judges are monitored for downward departures; 4) requires the Sentencing Commission to promulgate Guideline amendments that would "ensure that the incidence of downward departures is substantially reduced."

In response to the Feeney Amendment, the Sentencing Commission adopted amendments that do the following:

1) Downward departures are not permitted based solely on the existence of a plea agreement.

2) Downward departures are not permitted for acceptance of responsibility (that reduction can only be made as an adjustment under Guideline 3E.1, supra), minor role in the offense, gambling addiction, and legally-required restitution.

3) Downward departures on the basis of family ties and responsibilities and aberrant behavior are basically prohibited.

4) Downward departures for anything other than substantial assistance to the government are basically prohibited for career offenders.

5) Generally speaking, downward departures are permitted only for truly exceptional cases.

Note that the Feeney Amendment imposes no additional limit on *upward* departures. Nor does it limit downward departures based on the defendant cooperating in the prosecution of other defendants (known as "substantial assistance).

Former Prosecutor and now Professor Frank Bowman, in the Legal Times, April 21, 2003, has this to say about the Feeney Amendment and the attempt to limit downward departures—noting that the Amendment was pushed heavily by the Justice Department:

To appreciate the significance of the battle over the Feeney Amendment, one must understand the roles of judges, prosecutors, defense attorneys, the Sentencing Commission, and Congress in making and administering federal sentencing law. In 1984, Congress created the Sentencing Commission. Lawmakers were reacting, in large part, to the perception that the previous system gave too much play to the personal idiosyncrasies of judges and produced unjustifiable disparities between the sentences of similar offenders. Therefore, the first Sentencing Commission produced a system in which each offender's sentence is determined primarily by his placement on a grid measuring the seriousness of the offense and the offender's criminal history. Judges determine offense seriousness by making findings of fact regarding offense characteristics specified in the guidelines, such as the amount of money stolen, the quantity of drugs possessed, and so forth.

On the other hand, the reformers recognized that no rigid set of national rules could prescribe the "correct" sentence for every person. While the guidelines restrict judicial discretion, they also depend on the wisdom and good sense of judges to ensure that general rules are applied sensibly in particular cases. Therefore, each position on the grid is a sentence range stated in months. The trial judge may sentence the defendant anywhere within the range.

In addition, since the inception of the guidelines the judge has had the power to "depart"—to sentence a defendant above or below the guideline range if the judge finds aggravating or mitigating factors of a kind or degree not considered by the commission. The guidelines also provide for "substantial assistance" departures, in which the government seeks a reduced sentence for a defendant who has cooperated against others. In theory, both judge-initiated downward departures and prosecution-requested substantial assistance departures should be relatively rare.

Thus, the guidelines system envisions different roles for different actors. The Sentencing Commission is to be a politically neutral body of expert rule-makers accountable to Congress. Prosecutors are to bring charges, establish guilt, and prove facts relevant to sentencing. They may request downward departures to encourage cooperation or achieve a just sentence. Judges have the dual role of finding the facts necessary to apply the guidelines and exercising their discretion to choose sentences within the guidelines range or to depart appropriately. Prosecutors, judges, and the defense bar are all to be consulted by the Sentencing Commission, but no group is to dictate the rules.

The Feeney Amendment stems from Justice Department complaints that in recent years judges have exercised their downward departure power too promiscuously. Sentencing statistics make this complaint superficially plausible. The percentage of defendants receiving downward departures for reasons other than "substantial assistance" to the government rose from less than 6 percent of federal cases in 1991 to 18.8 percent in 2001.

However, the bulk of this increase stemmed not from liberal judges run amok but from government plea-bargaining. Beginning around 1995, U.S. attorneys in the five Mexican-border districts, faced with rising caseloads, began recommending downward departures to induce fast pleas. By 2001, 59 percent of all non-substantial-assistance departures occurred in the Mexican-border districts. Substantial assistance departures requested by the government have also risen, from roughly 12 percent of federal cases in 1991 to 17 percent in 2001. By 2001, roughly 79 percent of all downward departures were requested by the Justice Department, either for substantial assistance or as part of a fast-track plea bargain.

Through the original Feeney Amendment, the Justice Department sought to eliminate the fewer than 20 percent of downward departures initiated by judges, while retaining the more than 80 percent requested by the Justice Department. * * *

Even more troubling than the department's objectives were its methods. First, the Feeney Amendment was a deliberate end run around the Sentencing Commission. The department made no effort to work through the commission to address judicial departures. Second, the department showed utter disregard for the federal judiciary. It made no effort to consult directly with the judges. And by end-running the commission and introducing the

Feeney Amendment as a floor amendment to another bill, it ensured that the judges would have no forum in which to respond to the allegations about excessive departures.

Finally, the Justice Department manipulated Congress itself, using slanted statistics, alarmist rhetoric, and the procedural dodge of a floor amendment to avoid the scrutiny of legislative hearings and debate.

In its final form, the Feeney Amendment does not directly eliminate judicial discretion. But it does direct the Sentencing Commission to study departures and to pass guideline amendments ensuring that downward departures will be "substantially reduced."

* * *

In truth, the Justice Department's concerns about judicial departures are not entirely unfounded. Judicial departures have increased, and some judges seem to delight in proclaiming their disdain for the guidelines. Nonetheless, the overall rise in departure rates has been driven primarily by prosecutorial choices. * * *

For the moment at least, the Justice Department appears to have lost sight of the fact that it is only one among a group of institutions whose views must be respected in the making of sentencing policy. The other institutions, notably the judiciary and Congress, must provide a counterweight until the Justice Department rediscovers a sense of restraint.

Probation and Supervised Release

The Sentencing Guidelines also indicate when probation is authorized and the method for fixing the term of probation. § 5B1.1–4. Recommended conditions of probation and supervised release, and recommended "special conditions" are set forth.[13] The Guidelines classify as serious offenses, which require a prison term, some offenses for which probation has been common—e.g., tax evasion and antitrust offenses. However, the Guidelines permit the sentencing judge to impose a short prison term in such cases, together with a suspended sentence.

Guidelines for Corporate Sentencing

In 1991, the Sentencing Guidelines were amended to include a chapter on "Organizational Sentencing Guidelines." The report of the Sentencing Commission summarizes the governing principles of these Guidelines:

Because an organization is vicariously liable for actions taken by its agents, the Commission determined that the base fine, which measures the seriousness of the offense, should not be the sole basis for determining an appropriate sentence. Rather, the applicable culpability score, which is determined primarily by "the steps taken by the organization prior to the offense to prevent and detect criminal conduct, the level and extent of

---

13. Gozlon–Peretz v. United States, 498 U.S. 395 (1991), emphasized that Congress in the Sentencing Reform Act replaced most forms of parole with a new system of supervised release, in which the sentencing court rather than the Parole Commission would oversee the defendant's post-confinement monitoring.

involvement in or tolerance of the offense by certain personnel, and the organization's actions after an offense has been committed'' also influences the determination of a fine range.

Specifically, the organization's culpability is determined by the level or extent of involvement in or tolerance of the offense by certain personnel, the organization's prior history, whether an order was violated when the organization committed the offense, whether the organization obstructed or attempted to obstruct justice, whether the organization had an effective program to prevent and detect violations of law, and whether the organization reported the offense, cooperated fully in the investigation, and accepted responsibility for its criminal conduct. The guidelines increase the fine range when organizations are more culpable and reduce the fine range when organizations are less culpable.

The Organizational Guidelines treat all organizations similarly, but provide certain offsets for fines imposed on owners of closely held corporations. The Commission concluded that as a general rule the greater of pecuniary loss or gain should be used in setting a fine, provided that pecuniary loss should only be used if the loss was caused intentionally, knowingly, or recklessly.

Some lawyers and economists have criticized the Commission's approach. The approach plainly relies less on past practice than the approach taken in the individual Guidelines. This is largely the result of major increases in fine maxima and little experience on the part of courts in imposing fines under the higher statutory figures. (It should also be noted that the penalties for corporate wrongdoing have been ratcheted up after the Enron and Worldcom scandals.) To the extent that the criticism focuses on the Commission's writing on a blank slate, the Commission has responded by relying on the language Congress chose in its sentencing statute and the recognition that vicarious liability offenses require that some principles be recognized that may not have been fully recognized in the past when fine levels were much lower. The criticism is not limited to the absence of empirical support for the Guidelines; it rests also on a notion that the sanctions are too severe and that they may deter lawful and desirable economic activity.

One thing is clear under the Organizational Guidelines—cooperation is a good thing. Implementation of a compliance program, to prevent and detect criminal conduct before it is charged, is an even better thing. A corporation with an effective compliance program in place, and which promptly reports criminal activity and accepts responsibility, can reduce its culpability score by as much as eight points. This could mean a savings of tens of millions of dollars.

What are the arguments for punishing corporations and other organizations? Should they be punished if individuals who committed offenses are identifiable and can also be prosecuted? Should deterrence play a more significant role in organizational sentencing than in individual sentencing? The Guidelines clearly encourage corporate cooperation, but isn't it likely that this will come at the expense of "ratting out" corporate employees involved in the alleged wrongdoing? Does corporate counsel have a conflict of interest in advising the corporation to cooperate and accept responsibility, when that could mean that directors and other corporate agents will be incriminated? See generally Saltzburg, The Control of Criminal Conduct in Organizations, (Symposium on Sentencing of the Corporation), 71 B.U.L.Rev. 189, 421 (1991); Nagel and Swenson,

The Federal Sentencing Guidelines for Corporations: Their Development, Theoretical Underpinnings, and Some Thoughts About Their Future, 71 Wash.U.L.Q. 205 (1993).

The Effect of Mandatory Minimum Sentences on Guidelines Sentencing

The Sentencing Guidelines establish sentencing ranges to be considered by judges. But Congress has set mandatory minimum sentences for certain crimes—especially drug and firearms offenses—and has required that these sentences be incorporated into the Guidelines structure. What this means is that if the Guidelines calculation is lower than the minimum sentence statutorily provided, the mandatory minimum controls. See United States v. Stoneking, 60 F.3d 399 (8th Cir.1995)(where a statutorily required minimum sentence is greater than the maximum of the Guidelines range, the statute controls). In these circumstances, mandatory minimum sentences operate to limit judicial discretion even further than the Guidelines already do. In 1991, the Sentencing Commission released a report concluding that mandatory minimum sentences clash with the concept of sentencing guidelines, lead to unduly harsh sentences, and are responsible for increased racial disparities in sentencing. The report had little effect on Congress, however. See McMillion, Hard Time, A.B.A.J., March, 1993, p. 100. See also Hansen, Mandatories Going, Going, Gong, ABAJ, April, 1999, p. 14 ("More and more people who once supported mandatory minimums have realized that they have done nothing to reduce crime or put big-time drug dealers out of business. What they have done, critics say, is fill prisons with young, nonviolent, low-level drug offenders serving long sentences at enormous and growing cost to taxpayers.").

C. CRITICISM OF THE FEDERAL SENTENCING GUIDELINES

Many judges and commentators view the Guidelines as a failure. Some of the major criticisms are: 1. In the desire to bring mathematical precision to sentencing, the Commission has turned judges into accountants, and has turned sentencing proceedings into highly technical and burdensome ordeals for all concerned; 2. The Guidelines replace the discretion of an unbiased judge with the discretion of a prosecutor who is, obviously, an advocate for the government; 3. The Guidelines are unduly harsh, especially in drug cases;[14] and 4. The Guidelines punish equally for charged and uncharged "relevant conduct" even though the latter need only be proven by a preponderance of the evidence.

The following is a sampling of some of the criticism:

Judge Edwards, concurring in United States v. Harrington, 947 F.2d 956 (D.C.Cir.1991):

> We are told that the Guidelines are fair because they ensure "uniformity" in sentencing. Equally guilty persons receive equally stringent sentences, so it is said. But, as we have come to learn, the Guidelines are rigid in formulation and, thus, often produce harsh results that are patently unfair

---

14. See Richman, Cooperating Clients, 56 Ohio St.L.J. 69 (1995)(citing federal statistics showing a significant increase in both incarceration and in the average length of prison sentences since 1984, and an increase in mean prison terms for drug offenses from 27 months to 67 months).

because they fail to take account of individual circumstances that might militate in favor of a properly "tailored" sentence.

We also have come to understand that the Guidelines do not, by any stretch of the imagination, ensure uniformity in sentencing. Assistant U.S. Attorneys have been heard to say, with open candor, that there are many "games to be played," both in charging defendants and in plea bargaining, to circumvent the Guidelines. Because of this reality, sentences under the Guidelines often bear no relationship to what the Sentencing Commission may have envisioned as appropriate to any given case.

The first "game" to be played under the Guidelines occurs in connection with the charging decision. The confluence of the Guidelines' restriction of judicial discretion and the enactment of mandatory minimum sentences for many drug crimes has placed enormous power in the hands of the AUSA, effectively replacing judicial discretion over sentencing with prosecutorial discretion. Consider the case of a defendant who is charged with possessing ten grams of crack cocaine with intent to distribute—an offense carrying a Guideline sentence of 63–78 months for a defendant with no criminal record, and a mandatory minimum sentence of five years. If the prosecutor elects to add a weapons charge in connection with the drug offense, the Guideline range goes to 78–97 months and the mandatory minimum rises to ten years. * * * The only way for the defendant to escape these lengthy minimum terms is to cooperate with the government in the hope that his assistance will be "substantial" enough to induce the prosecutor to make a motion for downward departure; that decision, however, rests in the prosecutor's discretion.

The second disparity-creating game to be played—this one by prosecutors and defense attorneys in collaboration—is the plea bargaining process. By offering a plea, defense counsel may be able to cut a deal with the prosecutor to "bend the rules." However, whether the rules actually get bent may depend upon the luck of the draw in judicial assignment: if the trial judge is willing to look the other way, the facts can be manipulated and the Guidelines ignored because no appeal will be taken by the prosecutor.

* * *

Yet another glitch in the process is the Probation Officer, the person assigned to "characterize" the defendant so that "points" for upward and downward adjustments can be assigned pursuant to the Guidelines. Under the Guidelines, the Probation Officer acts as both investigator and fact-finder. Enormous potential power rests in his or her hands, for how the Probation Officer chooses to characterize the defendant may add years of confinement to a jail term. For example, the Probation Officer may find that the defendant was a ring-leader in the offense (which adds four offense levels); that he abused a position of trust (adding two levels); or that he is not contrite (foreclosing the possibility of a downward adjustment for acceptance of responsibility).

Perhaps most importantly, the Probation Officer determines and evaluates the defendant's "relevant conduct"—that is, conduct (often uncharged) that is related to, but not part of, the offense for which conviction has been sought. This determination can have a substantial impact on the applicable sentencing range. See, e.g., United States v. Kikumura, 918 F.2d 1084 (3d Cir.1990)(concluding that departure from 27–33 month Guideline range to 210–262 month range would be reasonable, based primarily upon defendant's relevant conduct).

* * *

I address the gamesmanship of the Guidelines and the problematic roles of the AUSA's and Probation Officers only to emphasize that the Guidelines have not eliminated sentencing discretion. Rather, they have merely transferred it from district judges—who, whatever their perceived failings, are at least impartial arbiters who make their decisions on the record and subject to public scrutiny and appellate review—to less neutral parties who are rarely called to account for the discretion they wield. Thus, the discretion and disparity game continues; it is only the players who have changed.

Viewed in this light, the Guidelines bring to mind the story *The Emperor's New Clothes*. We continue to enforce the Guidelines as if, by magic, they have produced uniformity and fairness, when in fact we know it is not so. * * * Nonetheless we * * * are forced to press on—through contorted computations, lengthy sentencing hearings and endless appeals—in the service of a sovereign who can be neither clothed nor dethroned.

Judge Bright, concurring in United States v. Baker, 961 F.2d 1390 (8th Cir.1992), a case in which the court upheld a sentence of almost 20 years for a "career offender" convicted of cocaine distribution and money laundering:

This sentence demonstrates yet again the vagaries of Guideline sentencing. A similar offender, who would have been under age eighteen when the prior offenses occurred, would not be a career offender, and would not have received this lengthy sentence but one no longer than eleven years and five months. This sort of gross disparity in sentencing often occurs under the Guidelines. * * * This case is another example of rigid guidelines sentencing producing inequity and injustice in sentencing, and demonstrates a need for the reformation, if not the abolishment, of Guideline sentencing.

Professor Raeder, Gender and Sentencing: Single Moms, Battered Women, and Other Sex–Based Anomalies in the Gender–Free World of the Federal Sentencing Guidelines, 20 Pepp.L.Rev.905 (1993):

[T]he Guidelines explicitly mandate that sex is not relevant in the determination of a sentence. However, such legislated equality poses difficulties for many women whose criminal behavior and history, as well as family responsibilities, cannot easily be shoehorned into a punitive pro-prison model for sentencing males assumed to be violent and/or major drug dealers. For example, female offenders are often mothers who have sole or primary responsibility for the care of their children, a consideration virtually ignored by the current Guidelines. Many women * * * may find themselves involved in criminal activity because of social and cultural pressures or occasionally as a result of more obvious means of coercion such as battering. Harsh mandatory minimums combined with the inflexible Guidelines regime result in lengthy incarceration of such women whose actual role in drug cases is often quite limited. Similarly, although property offenses, which constitute a significant percentage of female crime, result in lower average sentences than other types of offenses, Guidelines sentencing requires some incarceration for women who pre-Guidelines would have been sentenced to straight probation.

For more academic commentary critical of the Guidelines, see, e.g., Miller and Free, Honoring Judicial Discretion Under the Sentencing Reform Act, 3 Fed.Sent.Rep. 235 (1991)(arguing that by formulating a set of guidelines different from the general instructions set out by Congress in 18 U.S.C.§ 3553(a), the Sentencing Commission has "seemingly reversed the sentencing sequence intended by Congress"); Cabranes, Sentencing Guidelines: A Dismal Failure, N.Y.L.J., February 11, 1992, p. 2 ("We should face the possibility that the basic premise of the Guidelines—that the human element should be wiped away from the sentencing process and replaced by the clean, sharp edges of a sentencing slide rule—is itself highly questionable."); Yellen, Illusion, Illogic, and Injustice: Real–Offense Sentencing and the Federal Sentencing Guidelines, 78 Minn.L.Rev. 403 (1993); Parent, What Did the United States Sentencing Commission Miss?, 101 Yale L.J. 1773 (1992).

For more judicial commentary on the Guidelines, see United States v. Farah, 991 F.2d 1065 (2d Cir.1993)(Pratt, J., dissenting in part)(complaining of government's appeal of a one-level reduction in a defendant's offense level: "This case is not atypical of the apparent lack of judgment often revealed when inexperienced prosecutors flex their newfound power under the guidelines."); United States v. Andruska, 964 F.2d 640 (7th Cir.1992)(Will, J., concurring)(complaining about a harsh sentence and lack of discretion to impose a "reasonable sentence"); United States v. Concepcion, 983 F.2d 369 (2d Cir. 1992)(Newman, J., concurring)(complaining that because the Guidelines treat relevant conduct equally with conduct that is the subject of the conviction, the defendant who was charged with two crimes, and acquitted of one, received the same sentence as if he were convicted of both!); Bonin v. Calderon, 59 F.3d 815 (9th Cir.1995) (Kozinski, J., concurring)(criticizing the fact that the Guidelines often provide harsher sentences for small-time drug offenders than for murderers and rapists); Liptak, Opposition Rises to Crime Bill's Curb on Judicial Power in Sentencing, N.Y. Times, April 18, 2003, at A10 (noting that judges often defend their need for judicial discretion by citing cases involving minor participants in the drug trade and quoting one judge who imposed a long Guidelines sentence in such a case as saying "It was harrowing. You really felt like a total instrument of injustice.").

D. SUPREME COURT CONSTRUCTION OF THE FEDERAL SEN-TENCING GUIDELINES

The Supreme Court has to date not taken part in the policy arguments that have been spurred by Guidelines sentencing. But it has decided a number of important questions concerning the application of the Guidelines.

1. General Premises

Constitutionality of the Guidelines: Mistretta v. United States

Justice Blackmun wrote for an 8–1 majority in Mistretta v. United States, 488 U.S. 361 (1989), which upheld the constitutionality of the Guidelines promulgated by the United States Sentencing Commission. The Court rejected claims that Congress delegated excessive legislative power to the Commission, and that the statute violated separation of powers principles by requiring federal judges to serve on the Commission or by having them serve with non-judges on a Commission whose members were removable by the President for cause. Justice Scalia dissented.

Authoritative Commentary: Stinson v. United States

Justice Kennedy wrote for a unanimous Court in Stinson v. United States, 508 U.S. 36 (1993), as it held that a commentary in the Guidelines Manual published by the U.S. Sentencing Commission that explains or interprets a Guideline is authoritative unless it violates the Constitution or a federal statute, or is inconsistent with, or a plainly erroneous reading, of that Guideline. The Court reasoned that the commentary should be treated similarly to an agency's interpretation of its own legislative rule.

Intercircuit Conflicts: Braxton v. United States

In Braxton v. United States, 500 U.S. 344 (1991), the Court served notice that it may not need to resolve intercircuit conflicts on the meaning of the Guidelines. Justice Scalia, writing for the Court, stated that Congress contemplated that the Sentencing Commission would periodically review the work of the courts, and would make "whatever clarifying revisions to the Guidelines conflicting judicial decisions might suggest." Justice Scalia therefore concluded that the Court would be "more restrained and circumspect in using our certiorari power as the primary means of resolving such conflicts." The Court declined to resolve whether, under Guideline section 1B1.2(a), a stipulation must be part of a formal plea agreement in order to permit application of the sentence appropriate to the more serious offense stipulated. Justice Scalia noted that the Sentencing Commission had issued a call for public comment on whether the Guideline should be amended to resolve the ambiguity which had created a conflict among the circuits.

2. The Principle of Relevant Conduct

Relevant Conduct and Subsequent Convictions: Witte v. United States

As discussed above, the Sentencing Guidelines assess the sentence on the basis not only of the charge for which the defendant is convicted, but also on the basis of relevant uncharged conduct. If a defendant ends up with a longer sentence as a result of uncharged "relevant conduct," what happens if the defendant is subsequently convicted of that uncharged conduct? Does he, in effect, get sentenced twice for the same conduct? This question arose in Witte v.

United States, 515 U.S. 389 (1995), where Witte pleaded guilty to a marijuana offense. His uncharged cocaine transactions were considered as relevant conduct, and he received a longer sentence for the marijuana offense than he would otherwise have received. He was then charged with the cocaine transactions. He moved to dismiss the charges on double jeopardy grounds. The Court, in an opinion by Justice O'Connor, rejected Witte's double jeopardy attack, reasoning that he had not been punished previously for the cocaine transactions. Those transactions were simply a basis for "a stiffened penalty for the [marijuana] crime, which is considered to be an aggravated offense because a repetitive one." However, in a section of the opinion written for five members of the Court, Justice O'Connor noted that the Sentencing Guidelines provide some protection for a defendant who is convicted of conduct that had been previously used as "relevant conduct" under the Guidelines:

> Because the concept of relevant conduct under the Guidelines is recipro-
> cal, § 5G1.3 operates to mitigate the possibility that the fortuity of two
> separate prosecutions will grossly increase a defendant's sentence. If a
> defendant is serving an undischarged term of imprisonment "resulting from
> offense(s) that have been fully taken into account [as relevant conduct] in
> the determination of the offense level for the instant offense," § 5G1.3(b)
> provides that "the sentence for the instant offense shall be imposed to run
> concurrently to the undischarged term of imprisonment." And where
> § 5G1.3(b) does not apply, an accompanying policy statement provides, "the
> sentence for the instant offense shall be imposed to run consecutively to the
> prior undischarged term of imprisonment to the extent necessary to achieve
> a reasonable incremental punishment for the instant offense." USSG
> § 5G1.3(c)(policy statement). * * *

3. *Construction Problems in Drug Cases*

Carrier Mediums: Chapman v. United States

In Chapman v. United States, 500 U.S. 453 (1991), the Court considered whether the Sentencing Guidelines pertaining to LSD (§ 2D1.1(c)) allowed consideration of the weight of the carrier medium in determining the base offense level. Defendants argued that the carrier medium should not be included, because LSD is sold by dosage, not by weight, and the same dosage could be put on carrier mediums of various weights. If the carrier medium is considered in determining the base offense level, a person who sells five doses of LSD on sugar cubes could be subject to a greater sentence than a person caught with 20,000 doses in pure form. Chief Justice Rehnquist, writing for six members of the Court, noted that Congress had determined that sentences for trafficking in LSD should be based on the weight of the "mixture or substance"; and that the LSD together with the carrier medium could properly be termed a "mixture." The majority therefore held that the weight of the carrier medium should be included in determining the base offense level. The Court rejected the argument that inclusion of the carrier medium would result in arbitrary punishment. The Chief Justice stated that it was rational to increase the penalty for persons who possess large quantities of drugs, regardless of their purity. Justice Stevens, joined by Justice Marshall, dissented.

After *Chapman*, the Sentencing Guidelines were amended to provide that carrier mediums cannot be included in assessing the weight pertinent to an LSD offense. See Amendment 488 (instructing courts to give each dose of LSD on a carrier medium a constructive or presumed weight of 0.4 milligrams). However, defendants sentenced for distribution of LSD are still subject to the statutory minimum prescribed in 21 U.S.C. § 841(b)(1)—ten years for an offense involving more than ten grams of a "mixture or substance" containing LSD. Obviously, it is up to Congress and not the Sentencing Commission to change that statute. Thus, courts have held that under *Chapman*, the courts *must* consider the carrier medium in assessing the applicability of the mandatory minimum sentence; but under Amendment 488, courts *cannot* consider the carrier medium in determining the correct sentence under the Guidelines. If the mandatory minimum is applicable and is higher than the Guidelines, the mandatory minimum controls. In Neal v. United States, 516 U.S. 284 (1996), the Court held "that § 841(b)(1) directs a sentencing court to take into account the actual weight of the blotter paper with its absorbed LSD, even though the Sentencing Guidelines requires a different method of calculating the weight of an LSD mixture or substance." The Court rejected the contention that a two-tiered LSD sentencing scheme for LSD is arbitrary and irrational.

Sentencing Determinations in Combined Drugs Cases: United States v. Edwards

As discussed above, the Sentencing Guidelines impose a much harsher sentence for distributing crack as opposed to powder cocaine. What if the jury finds the defendants guilty of *either* crack or powder distribution? This question arose in Edwards v. United States, 523 U.S. 511 (1998). Pursuant to the pertinent criminal statute, the jury was instructed that the Government had to prove that the conspiracy involved measurable amounts of cocaine or crack. The jury returned a general verdict of guilty, and the District Judge imposed sentences based on his finding that each defendant's illegal conduct involved both cocaine and crack. The defendants argued that the sentence was unlawful insofar as it was based on crack, given the fact that the jury might have found the defendants guilty of powder cocaine offenses and not crack. The Supreme Court, in a unanimous opinion by Justice Breyer, held that the jury's belief on the matter made no difference. The Court analyzed the question as follows:

> [I]n the circumstances of this case the judge was authorized to determine for sentencing purposes whether crack, as well as cocaine, was involved in the offense-related activities. The Sentencing Guidelines instruct the judge in a case like this one to determine both the amount and the kind of "controlled substances" for which a defendant should be held accountable—and then to impose a sentence that varies depending upon amount and kind. See United States v. Watts, 519 U.S. 148 (1997) (per curiam) (judge may consider drug charge of which offender has been acquitted by jury in determining Guidelines sentence); Witte v. United States, 515 U.S. 389 (1995) (judge may impose higher Guidelines sentence on offender convicted of possessing marijuana based on judge's finding that offender also engaged in uncharged cocaine conspiracy). Consequently, regardless of the jury's actual, or assumed, beliefs about the conspiracy, the Guidelines nonetheless require the judge to determine whether the "controlled substances" at issue—and how much of those substances—consisted of cocaine, crack, or both. And that is what the judge did in this case.

Justice Breyer further noted that the defendants would not be entitled to relief even if the jury had specifically found that the defendants trafficked only in powder cocaine with respect to the crime charged. This is because the Trial Judge at the sentencing proceeding would have found the defendants' crack cocaine offenses to be "relevant conduct" under the Guidelines. Justice Breyer explained:

> [T]he Guidelines instruct a sentencing judge to base a drug-conspiracy offender's sentence on the offender's "relevant conduct." USSG § 1B1.3. And "relevant conduct," in a case like this, includes both conduct that constitutes the "offense of conviction," id.,§ 1B1.3(a)(1), and conduct that is "part of the same course of conduct or common scheme or plan as the offense of conviction," id., § 1B1.3(a)(2). Thus, the sentencing judge here would have had to determine the total amount of drugs, determine whether the drugs consisted of cocaine, crack or both, and determine the total amount of each—regardless of whether the judge believed that petitioners' crack-related conduct was part of the "offense of conviction," or the judge believed that it was "part of the same course of conduct, or common scheme or plan." The Guidelines sentencing range—on either belief—is identical.

4. Reductions for Substantial Assistance to the Government

Substantial Assistance Motions: Wade v. United States

Sentencing Guideline 5K1.1 provides for a possible reduction in sentence if the government files a motion to reduce the sentence on the basis of the defendant's substantial assistance in the prosecution of other defendants. In Wade v. United States, 504 U.S. 181 (1992), the Court held that a reduction for substantial assistance was, by the terms of the Guideline, contingent on a Government motion. Thus, the district court has no discretion to reduce the sentence for the defendant's assistance in other cases, unless the prosecution moves for such a reduction. The Court stated that the Government's decision not to make a substantial-assistance motion was reviewable only under two limited conditions: 1) if the prosecutor was acting pursuant to an unconstitutional motive such as to discriminate on the basis of race or religion; or 2) if the prosecutor's decision was totally arbitrary.

Note, however, that the government can obligate itself in a plea agreement to make a substantial assistance motion; and if the government has so agreed, the failure to do so would be a breach of the plea agreement, entitling the defendant either to specific performance or invalidation of the agreement. See United States v. Garcia–Bonilla, 11 F.3d 45 (5th Cir.1993)(government can obligate itself in a plea agreement to make a substantial assistance motion; such an agreement is not controlled by *Wade,* and is enforceable). Wade's problem was that his counsel failed to ask for such a promise in the plea agreement.

For more on the problems arising under cooperation agreements and substantial assistance motions, see Lee, Prosecutorial Discretion, Substantial Assistance, and the Federal Sentencing Guidelines, 42 UCLA L.Rev. 105 (1994) ("While the government motion requirement appears to serve the values of equality and reliance by restricting judicial sentencing discretion, it in fact undermines these goals because the government motion requirement merely replaces extremely broad judicial discretion with extremely broad prosecutorial discretion.").

Substantial Assistance Motions and Mandatory Minimums: Melendez v. United States

In Melendez v. United States, 518 U.S. 120 (1996), the defendant entered into a plea agreement under which the government agreed to make a substantial assistance motion for reduction of the applicable Guideline sentence. As discussed above, such a motion is provided for under § 5K1.1 of the Guidelines. However, the defendant pleaded guilty to a drug crime that was also subject to a mandatory minimum sentence of 10 years. The government moved, in accordance with the agreement, for a reduction of the applicable sentence under the Guidelines, which would have resulted in a sentence of less than 10 years. The government did not move, as it could have done (but not obligated to do by the plea agreement), for a reduction of the statutory minimum—there was no requirement in the agreement that the government make such a motion. The sentencing court held itself bound by the statutory minimum, and sentenced the defendant to 10 years.

Justice Thomas, writing for the Court, held that the trial court acted appropriately. Justice Thomas relied on 18 U.S.C. § 3553(e), which requires a specific government motion to depart from an applicable mandatory minimum sentence on the basis of the defendant's substantial assistance. Justice Thomas referred to this system as "binary". Thus, if the defendant is to receive a reduction from an applicable statutory minimum as well as from the Sentencing Guideline, the government must specifically move for reduction from both—and defense counsel must seek an agreement from the government for two substantial assistance motions rather than being content with one. Could Melendez argue that he received ineffective assistance of counsel in this case?

5. Sentencing Factors vs. Elements of the Crime

As seen above, the Sentencing Guidelines permit and sometimes require a judge to enhance a sentence on the basis of findings made at the sentencing hearing, e.g., obstruction of justice, perjury, relevant conduct, amount of drugs. These so-called "sentencing factors" are determined by the preponderance of the evidence. On the other hand, as seen in Chapter 10, the defendant has a constitutional right to have the prosecution prove him guilty beyond a reasonable doubt of all of the "elements" of the crime. How does one draw the line between an "element", which must be proven at trial beyond a reasonable doubt (and alleged in the indictment) and a "sentencing factor"?

In two recent cases—both set forth in detail in Chapter 10 in the section on constitutionally-based proof requirements—the Supreme Court decided that an "element" of the crime is any fact the finding of which would lead to a sentence higher than the statutory maximum for the crime with which the defendant is actually charged. Thus, in Apprendi v. New Jersey, 530 U.S. 466 (2000), the Court invalidated a conviction where the sentence was enhanced upon a finding that the crime was racially motivated. That factual question had to be proven beyond a reasonable doubt because the finding led to a sentence higher than the maximum sentence authorized by the legislature for the crime with which Apprendi was charged. In contrast, in Harris v. United States, 536 U.S. 545

(2002), the Court held that *Apprendi* does not prohibit sentences based on findings by the judge at sentencing so long as the sentence imposed does not exceed the maximum authorized by the statute under which the defendant was convicted.

After *Harris*, lower courts have held that *Apprendi* does not prohibit a judge from imposing consecutive sentences, even though the aggregated sentence is greater than the statutory maximum authorized for any one of the charges. See United States v. Chorin, 322 F.3d 274 (3d Cir. 2003) (noting that defendants were "comparing apples to oranges by comparing their aggregate consecutive sentences to the statutory maximum authorized for individual counts" and that "the Supreme Court's concern in *Apprendi* is with whether the sentencing court exceeds the statutory maximum sentence for a particular count; it ignores the effect of consecutive sentencing.").

With the possibilities of consecutive sentencing, charging discretion, and legislative initiative, it is apparent that *Apprendi's* limitation on judicial factfinding at sentencing can be evaded fairly easily. Professor Stephanos Bibas, in *Apprendi and the Dynamics of Guilty Pleas*, 54 Stan. L.Rev. 311 (2001) puts it this way:

> The only limit on using uncharged conduct at sentencing to circumvent the reasonable-doubt standard at trial is set by the statutory maximum. So where the statutory maxima are already high, this rule does little good. Legislatures can get around *Apprendi's* rule simply by raising maxima, which renders *Apprendi* toothless. And * * * prosecutors can get around this rule as well. They need only charge the same transaction as a conspiracy plus multiple substantive counts, then stack maxima by asking judges to impose multiple consecutive sentences. Any halfway-clever prosecutor can do so.

E. CONCLUSION ON THE FEDERAL SENTENCING GUIDELINES

In thinking about the Commission's approach to sentencing individuals and the tradeoff between preventing unjustified disparities and recognizing justifiable distinctions among offenders, consider the policy statements which the Commission has adopted with respect to individual offenders. Do you agree with the Commission as to the factors that should and should not be taken into consideration?

§ 5H1.1. *Age* (Policy Statement)

Age is not ordinarily relevant in determining whether a sentence should be outside the guidelines. Neither is it ordinarily relevant in determining the type of sentence to be imposed when the guidelines provide sentencing options. Age may be a reason to go below the guidelines when the offender is elderly *and* infirm and where a form of punishment (*e.g.,* home confinement) might be equally efficient as and less costly than incarceration. If, independent of the consideration of age, a defendant is sentenced to probation or supervised release, age may be relevant in the determination of the length and conditions of supervision.

§ 5H1.2. *Education and Vocational Skills* (Policy Statement)

Education and vocational skills are not ordinarily relevant in determining whether a sentence should be outside the guidelines, but the extent to which a defendant may have misused special training or education to facilitate criminal activity is an express guideline factor. * * * Neither are education and vocational skills relevant in determining the type of sentence to be imposed when the guidelines provide sentencing options. If, independent of consideration of education and vocational skills, a defendant is sentenced to probation or supervised release, these considerations may be relevant in the determination of the length and conditions of supervision for rehabilitative purposes, for public protection by restricting activities that allow for the utilization of a certain skill, or in determining the type or length of community service.

§ 5H1.3. *Mental and Emotional Conditions* (Policy Statement)

Mental and emotional conditions are not ordinarily relevant in determining whether a sentence should be outside the applicable guideline range * * *. Mental and emotional conditions, whether mitigating or aggravating, may be relevant in determining the length and conditions of probation or supervised release.

§ 5H1.4. *Physical Condition, Including Drug Dependence and Alcohol Abuse* (Policy Statement)

Physical condition is not ordinarily relevant in determining whether a sentence should be outside the guidelines or where within the guidelines a sentence should fall. However, an extraordinary physical impairment may be a reason to impose a sentence other than imprisonment.

Drug dependence or alcohol abuse is not a reason for imposing a sentence below the guidelines. Substance abuse is highly correlated to an increased propensity to commit crime. Due to this increased risk, it is highly recommended that a defendant who is incarcerated also be sentenced to supervised release with a requirement that the defendant participate in an appropriate substance abuse program. If participation in a substance abuse program is required, the length of supervised release should take into account the length of time necessary for the supervisory body to judge the success of the program.

This provision would also apply in cases where the defendant received a sentence of probation. The substance abuse condition is strongly recommended and the length of probation should be adjusted accordingly. Failure to comply would normally result in revocation of probation.

§ 5H1.5. *Previous Employment Record* (Policy Statement)

Employment record is not ordinarily relevant in determining whether a sentence should be outside the guidelines or where within the guidelines a sentence should fall. Employment record may be relevant in determining the type of sentence to be imposed when the guidelines provide for sentencing options. If, independent of the consideration of employment record, a defendant is sentenced to probation or supervised release, considerations of employment record may be relevant in the determination of the length and conditions of supervision.

§ 5H1.6. *Family Ties and Responsibilities, and Community Ties* (Policy Statement)

* * * [F]amily ties and responsibilities and community ties are not ordinarily relevant in determining whether a sentence should be outside the guidelines.

Family responsibilities that are complied with are relevant in determining whether to impose restitution and fines.

§ 5H1.8. *Criminal History* (Policy Statement)

A defendant's criminal history is relevant in determining the appropriate sentence. * * *

§ 5H1.9. *Dependence upon Criminal Activity for a Livelihood* (Policy Statement)

The degree to which a defendant depends upon criminal activity for a livelihood is relevant in determining the appropriate sentence. * * *

§ 5H1.10. *Race, Sex, National Origin, Creed, Religion, and Socio–Economic Status* (Policy Statement)

These factors are not relevant in the determination of a sentence.

Concluding Case: United States v. Pullen

Judge Posner, in United States v. Pullen, 89 F.3d 368 (7th Cir.1996), considered the structure of Guidelines sentencing, and the allocation of discretion between the judiciary and the Sentencing Commission, in a case in which it would appear that the defendant should have received a break on his sentence. Judge Posner describes the sentencing background as follows:

> The defendant pleaded guilty to armed robbery of a federally insured credit union and was sentenced to 188 months in prison. * * * The defendant's father was a drunkard and a gambler. He beat his wife and children and threatened them with guns and knives. When the defendant was five years old, his father abused him sexually over a period of several months. His parents divorced and the defendant lived with his mother, but when he was 15, and drinking, smoking marijuana, and having scrapes with the law, his mother could no longer control him and the juvenile court sent him to live with his father. The two would go out drinking together and once after a bout of drinking his father raped him. He ran away. His troubles with the law escalated. At the age of nineteen he committed his first bank robbery. He committed his second at the age of twenty-three. A year after he was released from prison, where he was serving a sentence for the second robbery, he robbed the credit union. A psychologist evaluated the defendant and concluded that as a result of the history of abuse that we have sketched the defendant "has a need to punish himself, hence his illegal acts and the relative ease with which he is caught." The psychologist also found that the defendant suffers from "schizoid disorder" and "borderline personality disorder," and that these conditions, too, are both "clinically linked to the history of abusive treatment by his father" and causative of his criminal activity because they "reduce impulse and behavioral controls" and impair "his ability to think and act clearly." The district judge concluded that he lacked authority to base a downward departure on the history and evaluation that we have summarized.

Judge Posner analyzed whether a departure on the basis of a history of abuse as a child was warranted under the Guidelines:

The Sentencing Reform Act authorizes sentencing below the guidelines if the judge finds a "mitigating circumstance of a kind, or to a degree, not adequately taken into consideration by the Sentencing Commission in formulating the guidelines." § 18 U.S.C. 3553(b). [A] departure from the guidelines range, in order to be allowable, must be consistent with the statutory sentencing goals, which are deterrence, incapacitation, retribution, and correction. § 18 U.S.C. 3553(a)(2). * * *

* * * The defendant argues not that his history of childhood abuse by his father warrants a reduction in sentence the better to serve the goals of deterrence, incapacitation, or correction—indeed it could well be argued that the lack of self-control that the psychologist attributes to his history would make an even longer sentence necessary to serve the first two of these goals—but that the history shows that a shorter sentence would be more apt to the retributive goal of punishment.

The obvious objection to this argument and the one emphasized by the government is that the framers of the guidelines appear not to have failed to take adequate account of the bearing of a history of childhood abuse that results in a diminished capacity to comply with the law. If this is right, the judge indeed lacked authority to depart. Section 5H1.3 (policy statement) of the guidelines provides that "mental and emotional conditions are not ordinarily relevant in determining whether a sentence should be outside the applicable guideline range, except as provided in" subpart 5K2 of the guidelines. In the word "ordinarily" there is some wiggle room for the defendant, but it appears to be taken away by section 5H1.12 (policy statement), which provides that "lack of guidance as a youth and similar circumstances indicating a disadvantaged upbringing are not relevant grounds for imposing a sentence outside the applicable guideline range." If we go to subpart 5K2, moreover, to which section 5H1.3 refers us, we find a section which states that diminished mental capacity is a basis for a downward departure only in the case of nonviolent crimes, § U.S.S.G. 5K2.13 (policy statement), and the defendant's crime was one of violence. § 4B1.2(1).

Judge Posner reasoned that the policies of determinate sentencing prohibited departure in cases such as Pullen:

These qualifications ("exceptional," out of "the ordinary") are important to the fundamental goal of the Sentencing Reform Act, which is to place federal sentencing on an objective, uniform, and rational (or at least articulable, nonintuitive) basis. If a miserable family history were in an average case a permissible basis for leniency (and a happy family history therefore a permissible basis for severity?), this would resurrect the pre-guidelines regime of discretionary sentencing. Just as in capital cases today, defense lawyers in run-of-the-mill federal criminal cases would hire psychologists, social workers, and other "mitigation specialists," to comb the defendant's personal and family history for evidence of adversity. The government would counter with its own expert witnesses. Not only would the sentencing process be encumbered, but the disagreement between experts would create a space in which a judge could defend any departure, upward or downward, from the sentencing guidelines. The result might be a better system of sentencing than we have under the guidelines; it would not be the system ordained by the Sentencing Reform Act.

> At argument the defendant's able and vigorous counsel kept trying to get us to listen to the defendant's "story." A skillful lawyer, aided by psychologists hired as expert witnesses, can often tell an arresting story about the concatenation of circumstances that brought the defendant to commit the crime of which he has been convicted. The richer the causal history that the lawyer can trace—the more the crime can be made to seem the inevitable consequence of circumstances external to the defendant's character, or rather the more the defendant's character can be made to seem the product of external circumstances—the less responsible the defendant can be made to seem, and therefore the less deserving, under the retributive rationale of punishment, of punishment of average severity. By this means the guidelines can be unraveled before the eyes of the judge.

Judge Posner concluded that arguments about the relevance of the defendant's background to the severity of punishment should be addressed to the Sentencing Commission, not to the courts.

> The proper way for lawyers and social scientists who believe that the guidelines give insufficient weight to the causal history of criminal activity to proceed is to submit their views to the Sentencing Commission. * * * It can assimilate, evaluate, and balance the findings of criminological research on the causes of particular forms of criminal behavior. The individual judge cannot.

Note that *Pullen* was decided before the Feeney Act's further limitation on downward departures—meaning that the sentencing judge would have even less discretion to downwardly depart in a case like *Pullen* than previously.

F. SENTENCING DEVELOPMENTS IN THE STATES

The United States Sentencing Commission has served as a model for some states that have created similar commissions. Other states have adopted sentencing guidelines without establishing a standing sentencing commission. As states have considered sentencing reform, the debates often intermingle the concepts of determinate sentencing, sentencing commissions, guideline sentencing, and truth in sentencing.

Both before and after the adoption of federal sentencing guidelines, there was a move in many states toward some form of determinate sentencing. This move often reflected cynicism toward the concept of parole and doubts about the ability of prisons to rehabilitate inmates. Determinate sentencing is often discussed in conjunction with "truth in sentencing." Truth in sentencing is frequently the mantra of sentencing advocates who believe that offenders and the public should know when a sentence is announced how long the offender will serve.

It seems clear that the federal government has influenced sentencing practices in a number of states through a grant program to promote truth in sentencing administered by the Department of Justice. The federal requirement for funding for state truth in sentencing programs requires only that five categories of violent crime be included in such a program. *See* 42 U.S.C.A. § 13701 (1)(B)(2) (violent crime "means murder and nonnegligent manslaughter, forcible rape, robbery, and aggravated assault as reported to the Federal Bureau of Investigation for purposes of the Uniform Crime Reports"). States may claim to be truth in sentencing states for federal funding purposes as long as they require offenders to serve 85% of sentences for the five categories of serious violent crime set forth above. Thus, states remain free, even after accepting federal funds, to retain parole and indeterminate sentences for other categories of crime. Approximately a third of the states can be viewed as qualifying as truth in sentencing states under the federal definition.

Not all truth in sentencing states are alike. Most states use between 75% and 85% of a pre-determined "benchmark" as their standard to implement a truth in sentencing program, but the states differ in how they implement the program. For example, Virginia requires a mandatory 85% of an offender's effective sentence (which is the imposed sentence minus any suspended portion) to be served. Thus, judges in Virginia retain some freedom to individualize sentences at the time of sentence. Other states—Utah, for example—have guideline sentencing and require an offender to serve 85% of a guideline sentence before any release is considered.

There is no necessary correlation between truth in sentencing and sentencing commissions. Although states like Utah have guideline sentencing, a sentencing commission and truth in sentencing, Delaware has truth in sentencing but no sentencing commission. Alaska has presumptive sentencing but no sentencing commission or movement toward truth in sentencing.

Some states—Florida and North Carolina, for example—have abolished parole completely. Other states retain some form of parole system. It may be misleading, however, to view the abolition of parole as meaning that offenders will serve their entire sentences in prison. In Virginia, for example, it is very common for judges to suspend large parts of a sentence of incarceration, which results in an offender serving a determinate time in prison and then being under supervision for the suspended portion of incarceration. The difference between this and parole is that the judge makes the decision to suspend a sentence at the time of sentencing, rather than having a parole board make a decision after sentence is imposed. But, the resulting punishment may be a shorter period of incarceration followed by a longer period of supervision, which may resemble a parole system and may be quite similar to a probationary system.

Virginia's sentencing system is one of several that demonstrate that there is no single conception of either truth in sentencing or determinate sentencing. A state may move toward what it regards as truth in sentencing and/or determinate sentences and adopt a model that includes both incarceration supervision and that uses the threat of revoking a suspended sentence and returning an offender to prison as a means of controlling behavior.

States may choose to adopt guideline sentencing whether or not they abolish parole, favor some form of truth in sentencing and utilize a sentencing commission. All states with guidelines appear to have the same basic goal, which is to reduce sentencing disparity and to provide guidance to judges (and in rare instances to juries) as to appropriate sentences for particular crimes and types of offenders. This is the basic rationale for guideline sentencing. This rationale has spawned two apparent trends, one stronger and more readily identified than the other. The first and stronger trend is that most jurisdictions with guidelines have made some effort to examine the pre-guideline sentences imposed by all judges in a state and to tailor the guidelines to the average or typical sentence previously imposed. The second and more subtle trend is to increase deliberately sentences for some violent offenders and to depart upward from the sentences imposed prior to the adoption of guidelines.

In drafting guidelines some sentencing commissions have considered the effect of sentences on prison populations. This may be viewed as consistent with the basic goal of reducing disparity. It may also be necessary for a state to consider adjusting some guidelines downward if the state desires to raise sentences for some violent offenders without creating additional prison space.

III.   SENTENCING PROCEDURES

A.   GENERAL PROCEDURES

One might suppose that a part of the criminal justice system as important as sentencing would carry with it extensive procedural protections to guard against abuse of authority. But that supposition would be largely unfounded. Due process rights in sentencing have been hard to establish since 1949.

WILLIAMS v. NEW YORK

Supreme Court of the United States, 1949.
337 U.S. 241.

MR. JUSTICE BLACK delivered the opinion of the court.

A jury in a New York state court found appellant guilty of murder in the first degree. The jury recommended life imprisonment, but the trial judge imposed sentence of death. In giving his reason for imposing the death sentence the judge discussed in open court the evidence upon which the jury had convicted stating that this evidence had been considered in the light of additional information obtained through the court's "Probation Department, and through other sources." * * *

The Court of Appeals of New York affirmed the conviction and sentence over the contention that * * * "the sentence of death was based upon information supplied by witnesses with whom the accused had not been confronted and as to whom he had no opportunity for cross-examination or rebuttal" [and accordingly was in violation of due process].

The narrow contention here makes it unnecessary to set out the facts at length. The record shows a carefully conducted trial lasting more than two weeks in which appellant was represented by three appointed lawyers who conducted his defense with fidelity and zeal. The evidence proved a wholly indefensible murder committed by a person engaged in a burglary. * * *

The case presents a serious and difficult question. The question relates to the rules of evidence applicable to the manner in which a judge may obtain information to guide him in the imposition of sentence upon an already convicted defendant. * * * To aid a judge in exercising * * * discretion intelligently the New York procedural policy encourages him to consider information about the convicted person's past life, health, habits, conduct, and mental and moral propensities. The sentencing judge may consider such information even though obtained outside the courtroom from persons whom a defendant has not been permitted to confront or cross-examine. It is the consideration of information obtained by a sentencing judge in this manner that is the basis for appellant's broad constitutional challenge * * *.

* * *

Tribunals passing on the guilt of a defendant always have been hedged in by strict evidentiary procedural limitations. But both before and since the American colonies became a nation, courts in this country and in England practiced a policy under which a sentencing judge could exercise a wide discretion in the sources and types of evidence used to assist him in determining the kind and extent of punishment to be imposed within limits fixed by law. Out-of-court affidavits have been used frequently, and of course in the smaller communities sentencing judges naturally have in mind their knowledge of the personalities and backgrounds of convicted offenders. * * *

In addition to the historical basis for different evidentiary rules governing trial and sentencing procedures there are sound practical reasons for the distinction. In a trial before verdict the issue is whether a defendant is guilty of having engaged in certain criminal conduct of which he has been specifically accused. Rules of evidence have been fashioned for criminal trials which narrowly confine the trial contest to evidence that is strictly relevant to the particular offense charged. These rules rest in part on a necessity to prevent a time-consuming and confusing trial of collateral issues. They were also designed to prevent tribunals concerned solely with the issue of guilt of a particular offense from being influenced to convict for that offense by evidence that the defendant had habitually engaged in other misconduct. A sentencing judge, however, is not confined to the narrow issue of guilt. His task within fixed statutory or constitutional limits is to determine the type and extent of punishment after the issue of guilt has been determined. Highly relevant—if not essential—to his selection of an appropriate sentence is the possession of the fullest information possible concerning the defendant's life and characteristics. And modern concepts individualizing punishment have made it all the more necessary that a sentencing judge not be denied an opportunity to obtain pertinent information by a requirement of rigid adherence to restrictive rules of evidence properly applicable to the trial.

* * *

Modern changes in the treatment of offenders makes it more necessary now than a century ago for observance of the distinctions in the evidential procedure in the trial and sentencing processes. For indeterminate sentences and probation have resulted in an increase in the discretionary powers exercised in fixing punishments. * * *

Under the practice of individualizing punishments, investigational techniques have been given an important role. Probation workers making reports of their investigations have not been trained to prosecute but to aid offenders. Their reports have been given a high value by conscientious judges who want to sentence persons on the best available information rather than on guesswork and inadequate information. * * * We must recognize that most of the information now relied upon by judges to guide them in the intelligent imposition of sentences would be unavailable if information were restricted to that given in open court by witnesses subject to cross-examination. And the modern probation report draws on information concerning every aspect of a defendant's life. The type and extent of this information make totally impractical if not impossible open court testimony with cross-examination. * * *

* * * New York criminal statutes set wide limits for maximum and minimum sentences. Under New York statutes a state judge cannot escape his grave responsibility of fixing sentence. In determining whether a defendant shall receive a one-year minimum or a twenty-year maximum sentence, we do not think the Federal Constitution restricts the view of the sentencing judge to the information received in open court.

* * *

MURPHY, J., dissenting:

* * *

Due process of law includes at least the idea that a person accused of crime shall be accorded a fair hearing through all the stages of the proceedings against him. I agree with the Court as to the value and humaneness of liberal use of probation reports as developed by modern penologists, but, in a capital case, against the unanimous recommendation of a jury where the report would concededly not have been admissible at the trial, and was not subject to examination by the defendant, I am forced to conclude that the high commands of due process were not obeyed.

Pre-Sentence Reports and the Sentencing Guidelines

In the Sentencing Reform Act of 1984, Congress provided that when guidelines are used to sentence offenders, Fed.R.Cr.P. 32 will require that a presentence report inform the defendant of the guidelines which govern his case and of pertinent policy statements by the Sentencing Commission.[15] Ordinarily the presentence report is prepared by a probation officer. The goal of Rule 32 is to focus "on preparation of the presentence report as a means of identifying and narrowing the issues to be decided at the sentencing hearing." Advisory Committee's Note to 1994 amendment to Rule 32. Some of the procedural requirements in the Rule are: (1) defense counsel is entitled to notice and a reasonable opportunity to be present at any interview of the defendant conducted by the probation officer who is preparing the presentence report; (2) the probation officer must present the presentence report to the parties not later than 35 days before the sentencing hearing, in order to provide additional time for the parties and the probation officer to attempt to resolve any objections to the report; (3) parties must provide the probation officer with a written list of objections to the presentence report within 14 days of receiving it; (4) provision is made for the probation officer to meet with the defendant, defense counsel, and an attorney for the Government, in order to go over objections to the report and to arrange for additional investigation and revisions to the report if necessary; and (5) the sentencing court may treat the presentencing report as its findings of fact, except for material subject to the parties' unresolved objections.

Notice of Intended Departure: Burns v. United States

In Burns v. United States, 501 U.S. 129 (1991), the district court departed upward from the prescribed sentencing range without first notifying the parties

---

15. The Supreme Court held in United States Department of Justice v. Julian, 486 U.S. 1 (1988), that prison inmates may obtain access to the nonconfidential aspects of their presentence reports pursuant to the Freedom of Information Act.

of its intent to depart. Justice Marshall, writing for a five-person majority, held that Fed.R.Crim.P. 32 requires that the district court give the parties reasonable notice that it is contemplating an upward or downward departure. Justice Souter, joined by Chief Justice Rehnquist and Justices White and O'Connor, dissented.

B.   PROCEDURES FOR DETERMINATE SENTENCING SYSTEMS

The sentencing system reviewed in *Williams* was a non-adversarial, indeterminate, individualized system granting unfettered discretion to trial judges. Do the procedural requirements need to be more stringent if the judge is given less (or no) discretion in deciding on the appropriate sentence, as is the case under the Federal Sentencing Guidelines?

Preponderance of the Evidence Standard: McMillan v. Pennsylvania and the Sentencing Guidelines

In McMillan v. Pennsylvania, 477 U.S. 79 (1986), the Court held that it was permissible for a state to impose a mandatory minimum sentence upon a defendant found by the trial judge to have "visibly possessed a firearm" during the commission of a specified offense. It rejected the defendant's argument that the finding of visible possession had to be supported by at least clear and convincing evidence; it concluded that there was no constitutional infirmity in the state's use of a preponderance of the evidence standard to determine a sentencing factor. The Court relied on *Williams* and the need for flexibility at the sentencing proceeding; it noted that procedures at a sentencing proceeding need not be as protective as at a trial, because the defendant at sentencing no longer carries the presumption of innocence. It also distinguished between sentencing factors and elements of the crime, as discussed in the materials in Chapter 10's section on constitutionally-based proof requirements.

Applying *McMillan*, the Court in United States v. Watts, 519 U.S. 148 (1997), held that defendants can be sentenced under the Guidelines on the basis of relevant conduct for which they have been acquitted, so long as the conduct is shown at sentencing by a preponderance of the evidence.

Sentencing Factors vs. Elements of the Crime: Apprendi v. New Jersey and Harris v. United States

McMillan upheld a statute that allowed the judge to impose a mandatory minimum sentence, on a showing of a particular fact by a preponderance of the evidence. The question of visible possession of a firearm was a sentencing factor rather than an element of the crime that had to be submitted to a jury. However, the defendant in *McMillan* did not receive a sentence that was higher than the prescribed range of penalties for the crime of which he was convicted—the sentencing enhancement factor established a higher "floor" for the sentence, but it did not create a higher "ceiling". In Apprendi v. New Jersey, 530 U.S. 466 (2000), a state statute permitted the judge to enhance a sentence for a weapons offense upon a finding (by a preponderance of the evidence) that the crime was committed with a racial bias. The difference from *McMillan* was that the sentence authorized, and imposed by the judge, was beyond the statutory maximum otherwise authorized for the weapons offense. The Supreme Court, in a 5–4 opinion written by Justice Stevens, struck down the statute as a violation of the defendant's constitutional right to a jury trial, as well as his constitutional right to proof beyond a reasonable doubt of every element of the crime.

Justice Stevens concluded that "it is unconstitutional for a legislature to remove from the jury the assessment of facts that increase the prescribed range of penalties to which a criminal defendant is exposed. It is equally clear that such facts must be established by proof beyond a reasonable doubt." Justice Stevens had this to say about *McMillan:*

> We do not overrule *McMillan.* We limit its holding to cases that do not involve the imposition of a sentence more severe than the statutory maximum for the offense established by the jury's verdict—a limitation identified in the *McMillan* opinion itself. Conscious of the likelihood that legislative decisions may have been made in reliance on *McMillan,* we reserve for another day the question whether *stare decisis* considerations preclude reconsideration of its narrower holding.

The dissenters in *Apprendi* argued that its rationale would lead to invalidating all upward adjustments and departures that are made under the Sentencing Guidelines. But the Court stepped back from that precipice in Harris v. United States, 536 U.S. 545 (2002). In *Harris* the Court reaffirmed *McMillan* and held that *Apprendi* does not prevent a judge from determining a fact that is the basis for a mandatory minimum sentence—so long as the sentence does not exceed the range established in the statute. By logical extension, *Harris* therefore preserves any factfinding at sentencing that enhances a sentence—including drug quantity, amount of loss, relevant conduct, obstruction of justice, and all factors for upward departure—so long as the sentence imposed does not exceed the maximum authorized by Congress for the offense of which the defendant was actually convicted. *Apprendi* and *Harris* are set forth in full in the section in Chapter 10 on constitutionally-based proof requirements.

Perjury at Trial as a Sentencing Factor:
United States v. Dunnigan

Federal Sentencing Guideline § 3C1.1 requires an enhancement of sentence when a defendant commits perjury at the trial. The Court in United States v. Dunnigan, 507 U.S. 87 (1993), unanimously upheld the Guideline, rejecting the defendant's argument that it violated her privilege against self-incrimination and her constitutional right to testify. The Court reasoned that the right to testify "does not include a right to commit perjury."

Dunnigan argued that if a sentence could be enhanced for perjury under the Guidelines, the government could use sentencing as a surrogate for a perjury prosecution. She pointed out that the standard of proof for upward adjustment sentencing factors under the Guidelines is a preponderance of the evidence. She argued that where perjury is suspected, the government should not be relieved of the burden of obtaining an indictment for perjury and a verdict of guilt beyond a reasonable doubt. Justice Kennedy, writing for the Court, rejected Dunnigan's argument and concluded that there was sufficient justification to permit enhancement of a sentence for perjury:

> A sentence enhancement based on perjury does deter false testimony in much the same way as a separate prosecution for perjury. But the enhance-

ment is more than a mere surrogate for a perjury prosecution. It furthers legitimate sentencing goals relating to the principal crime, including the goals of retribution and incapacitation. It is rational for a sentencing authority to conclude that a defendant who commits a crime and then perjures herself in an unlawful attempt to avoid responsibility is more threatening to society and less deserving of leniency than a defendant who does not so defy the trial process.

The Court emphasized, however, that "not every accused who testifies at trial and is convicted will incur an enhanced sentence under § 3C1.1 for committing perjury." Justice Kennedy explained that "an accused may give inaccurate testimony due to confusion, mistake or faulty memory." He concluded that "if a defendant objects to a sentence enhancement resulting from her trial testimony, a district court must review the evidence and make independent findings necessary to establish a wilful impediment to or obstruction of justice, or an attempt to do the same, under the perjury definition we have set out."

Of course, after Apprendi v. New Jersey, supra, a sentencing court could not impose an enhancement for perjury if it would increase the term of imprisonment beyond the maximum authorized by Congress for the underlying offense.

Consideration of Prior Convictions at the Sentencing Proceeding

In many cases, the prosecution offers evidence of the defendant's prior convictions at the sentencing proceeding. Under the Federal Sentencing Guidelines, a defendant's prior convictions, both state and federal, are relevant to the criminal history category that is part of the sentencing matrix. Moreover, many specific sentencing statutes provide for enhancement if the defendant has been convicted of certain specified state or federal crimes—such as the "Three Strikes and You're Out" provisions in current vogue.

One question that arises with the use of these prior convictions for sentencing purposes is whether the defendant has a right to challenge their validity at the sentencing proceeding. This is a particular problem in federal sentencing proceedings where the defendant wishes to attack prior state convictions. For example, in Custis v. United States, 511 U.S. 485 (1994), the defendant was given an enhanced sentence under the Armed Career Criminal Act (18 U.S.C. § 924(e)) on the basis of having three previous state convictions "for a violent felony or a serious drug offense." At the sentencing hearing, Custis sought to attack his prior state convictions collaterally on the ground that one was based on an invalid guilty plea and another was tainted by ineffective assistance of counsel.

The Court, in an opinion by Chief Justice Rehnquist, held that Custis had no statutory or constitutional right to collaterally attack a prior state conviction at his federal sentencing hearing. The only exception would be if the state conviction was obtained in the complete absence of counsel in violation of Gideon v. Wainwright. The Chief Justice distinguished a collateral attack for absence of counsel from a collateral attack for an invalid guilty plea or ineffective assistance of counsel, on the basis that a *Gideon* defect is "jurisdictional" while the other defects are not. He expressed concern about upsetting the finality of convictions, and about the costliness of having to investigate the effectiveness of counsel or the voluntariness of a guilty plea in a long-completed state proceeding. Justice Souter, joined by Justices Blackmun and Stevens, dissented in *Custis*. He saw no constitutional distinction between a collateral attack based on the absence of counsel and a collateral attack based on ineffective assistance of counsel or an invalid guilty plea.

Use of Hearsay at Sentencing Under the Guidelines

Williams permitted the use of hearsay by a sentencing judge. But again, the sentencing regime in *Williams* was highly discretionary, not based on structured findings of fact. Should the rationale of *Williams* apply to Guidelines sentencing? In United States v. Silverman, 945 F.2d 1337 (6th Cir.1991)(later vacated for rehearing en banc), the panel opinion held that the Confrontation Clause applied to the determination of disputed facts in adversary sentencing hearings conducted under the Federal Sentencing Guidelines. The court reasoned as follows:

> [T]he new system completely changes the discretionary, nonadversary, nonfactual nature of the sentencing process by introducing the adversary sentencing hearing and the need for precise and accurate findings of disputed facts. * * * The existence or nonexistence of a particular fact—for example, the amount of money involved or drugs possessed * * *—may automatically double or even in some cases multiply tenfold the particular sentence that judges are required to impose under the code.

The panel declared that "when the sentencing system changes, the nature of the applicable constitutional limitations may also change." But on en banc review, the court in United States v. Silverman, 976 F.2d 1502 (6th Cir.1992), reversed the panel and held that the right to confrontation was *not* applicable to sentencing proceedings involving disputed facts under the Federal Sentencing Guidelines. Thus, the sentencing court is permitted to use hearsay in assessing a sentence under the Guidelines. The court rejected the contention that sentencing under the Guidelines is substantially different from the discretionary sentencing procedures reviewed in *Williams*. The court asserted that procedural requirements for establishing the "factual basis of sentencing, akin to the real offense aspects of pre-guideline sentencing, continue from former sentencing practices." It concluded that "[s]o long as the evidence in the presentence report bears some minimal indicia of reliability in respect of defendant's right to due process, the district court may still continue to consider and rely on hearsay evidence without any confrontation requirement."

Chief Judge Merritt, in dissent, complained that the defendants' sentences were increased substantially on the basis of "relevant conduct" proven at the sentencing hearing through "unreliable double, triple, and quadruple hearsay information provided by the prosecution." See also United States v. Wise, 976 F.2d 393 (8th Cir.1992)(en banc), also finding no right to confrontation in Guidelines sentencing: "Because the sentencing judge still considers information not strictly relevant to a defendant's guilt and needs to conduct a broad inquiry to obtain that information, the Guidelines have not fundamentally transformed the search for information at the sentencing phase."

The *Wise* court, however, recognized that "in certain instances a sentence may so overwhelm or be so disproportionate to the punishment that would otherwise be imposed absent the sentencing factors mandated by the Guidelines that due process concerns must be addressed." According to the court, constitutional protections such as confrontation would be necessary where "a defendant's sentence is so greatly increased as a result of considering relevant conduct that the conduct essentially becomes an element of the offense for which the defendant is being punished." In other words, where the tail of sentencing wags the dog of conviction, the sentencing phase could be considered as a separate criminal proceeding, to which the constitutional trial protections would apply. But the court found that this limited exception was inapplicable where the defendant received "only" a two-fold increase in his sentence as a result of factual findings (i.e., that he had a leadership role in the offense) made in the sentencing process.

Chief Judge Arnold, dissenting in *Wise*, argued that the procedural flexibility authorized by *Williams* was inapposite to Guideline sentencing because "the deck of available facts seems a bit more stacked against the defendant under this regime." He elaborated as follows:

> Before, both the defendant and the prosecution contributed information to the process. The defendant played his cards—employment history, mental, physical, and emotional state, potential for rehabilitation, and other favorable policy arguments—and the prosecutor played his. The judge would then consider all of the information and impose a sentence which was fair and reasonable under those particular circumstances. The court now says there is no need to change the rules, even though the prosecutor has all the cards and the judge is required by law to impose a sentence depending not upon his independent analysis of the facts, but upon what cards the prosecutor chooses to play.

See also United States v. Petty, 982 F.2d 1365 (9th Cir.1993)(joining all other circuits in holding that the Confrontation Clause does not apply to Guidelines sentencing and declaring that "the procedural protections afforded a convicted defendant at sentencing are traditionally less stringent than the protections afforded a presumptively innocent defendant at trial"). For a further discussion of the limits on procedural protections applied in Guidelines sentencing, see Saltzburg, Sentencing Procedures: Where Does Responsibility Lie?, 4 Fed. Sen.Rep. 248 (1992). For a suggestion that the Federal Rules of Evidence should be amended so that they would be applicable to federal sentencing proceedings, see Young, Fact–Finding at Federal Sentencing: Why the Guidelines Should Meet the Rules, 79 Cornell L.Rev.299 (1994). See also Michaels, Trial Rights at Sentencing, 81 N.C. L.Rev. 1771 (2003) (reviewing case law and concluding that rights directed primarily at guaranteeing an accurate result have been made applicable to sentencing proceedings, whereas rights designed to protect the defendant's liberty or autonomy interests do not).

C. PAROLE AND PROBATION PROCEDURES

1. *Probation and Parole Denials; Classification Decisions*

A person is placed on probation as part of the usual sentencing process, and the *Williams* attitude toward procedural rights prevails. In People v. Edwards, 18 Cal.3d 796, 135 Cal.Rptr. 411, 557 P.2d 995 (1976), for example, the court held that a trial judge need not state reasons for denying probation. But parole is a different concept altogether. The parole board makes a determination whether someone who has been sentenced should be released before the sentence is fully served (though as we have seen, this is no longer the case under the Federal Sentencing Guidelines, which have abolished parole). For some time courts differed over the question of what, if any, procedural protections are constitutionally required in parole-release decisionmaking. The threshold question was whether a constitutionally protected liberty interest was at stake; if so, then certain procedural protections would be constitutionally mandated under the Due Process Clause. The Supreme Court considered the due process questions in a series of cases.

In Greenholtz v. Inmates, 439 U.S. 817 (1978), the Court, per Chief Justice Burger, held that the possibility of parole does not create an entitlement to due process protections. The Court did conclude that some parole systems, including Nebraska's which were at issue in the case, create legitimate expectations of release that require some procedural protections. But these are confined to some opportunity to be heard and some indication of the reasons why parole is not granted. Justice Marshall's dissenting opinion was joined by Justices Brennan and Stevens. Justice Powell agreed with these dissenters that parole decisionmaking triggered due process safeguards, but was unwilling to provide as many safeguards as the others would have. However, he concluded that Nebraska provided an inadequate opportunity for prisoners to present information to parole authorities. The Court relied upon *Greenholtz* in Board of Pardons v. Allen, 482 U.S. 369 (1987), which held, 6–3, that Montana parole law created a liberty interest.

No constitutionally protected expectancy interest was found in an explicitly discretionary pardon system despite the frequency with which pardons were granted. Connecticut Bd. of Pardons v. Dumschat, 452 U.S. 458 (1981). See also Jago v. Van Curen, 454 U.S. 14 (1981)(inmate told that he was being paroled had no protected interest that was violated when parole was rescinded before release from custody).

The Court reasoned in Hewitt v. Helms, 459 U.S. 460 (1983), that a prisoner has no right to procedural protections with respect to terms of confinement "ordinarily contemplated by a prison sentence" and that ordinarily "administrative segregation" is one of these terms. The Court rejected the claim that when a state provides procedural safeguards in connection with the use of administrative segregation it thereby recognizes a protected liberty interest. However, in this case the Court concluded that the state had gone beyond simple procedural guidelines and used "language of an unmistakably mandatory character," thus creating a liberty interest. Such an interest required, in the Court's view, only an informal, nonadversary review of evidence.[16]

2. *Probation and Parole Revocations*

MORRISSEY v. BREWER
Supreme Court of the United States, 1972.
408 U.S. 471.

Mr. Chief Justice Burger **delivered the opinion of the Court.**

[Morrisey and Booher both were paroled from Iowa state prisons. Each

---

16. See also Olim v. Wakinekona, 461 U.S. 238 (1983)(no liberty interest in confinement in one state rather than another); Meachum v. Fano, 427 U.S. 215 (1976)(no liberty interest in confinement in particular prison within a state); Montanye v. Haymes, 427 U.S. 236

(1976)(same as *Meachum*). For a thorough discussion of this line of cases, see Herman, The New Liberty: The Procedural Due Process Rights of Prisoners and Others under the Burger Court, 59 N.Y.U.L.Rev. 482 (1984).

subsequently had his parole revoked because of violations of parole conditions, and each sued, challenging the revocation procedures. One principal line of attack was that the absence of a revocation hearing violated due process.]

I

* * *

To accomplish the purpose of parole, those who are allowed to leave prison early are subjected to specified conditions for the duration of their terms. These conditions restrict their activities substantially beyond the ordinary restrictions imposed by law on an individual citizen. * * * Additionally, parolees must regularly report to the parole officer to whom they are assigned and sometimes they must make periodic written reports of their activities.

* * *

The enforcement leverage which supports the parole conditions derives from the authority to return the parolee to prison to serve out the balance of his sentence if he fails to abide by the rules. In practice not every violation of parole conditions automatically leads to revocation. * * * It has been estimated that 35–45% of all parolees are subjected to revocation and return to prison. Sometimes revocation occurs when the parolee is accused of another crime; it is often preferred to a new prosecution because of the procedural ease of recommitting the individual on the basis of a lesser showing by the State.

Implicit in the system's concern with parole violations is the notion that the parolee is entitled to retain his liberty

as long as he substantially abides by the conditions of his parole. The first step in a revocation decision thus involves a wholly retrospective factual question: whether the parolee has in fact acted in violation of one or more conditions of his parole. Only if it is determined that the parolee did violate the conditions does the second question arise: should the parolee be recommitted to prison or should other steps be taken to protect society and improve chances of rehabilitation? The first step is relatively simple; the second is more complex. The second question involves the application of expertise by the parole authority in making a prediction as to the ability of the individual to live in society without committing antisocial acts. This part of the decision, too, depends on facts, and therefore it is important for the Board to know not only that some violation was committed but also to know accurately how many and how serious the violations were. Yet this second step, deciding what to do about the violation once it is identified, is not purely factual but also predictive and discretionary.

If a parolee is returned to prison, he often receives no credit for the time "served" on parole. Thus the returnee may face a potential of substantial imprisonment.

II

We begin with the proposition that the revocation of parole is not part of a criminal prosecution and thus the full panoply of rights due a defendant in such a proceeding does not apply to parole revocations. Parole arises after the end of the criminal prosecution, including imposition of sentence.* * * Revocation deprives an individual not of the absolute liberty to which every citizen is entitled, but only of the conditional liberty properly dependent on observance of special parole restrictions.

We turn therefore to the question whether the requirements of due process in general apply to parole revocations. * * *

I (does Due Process apply?) [handwritten margin note]

* * * The liberty of a parolee enables him to do a wide range of things open to persons who have never been convicted of any crime. * * * Subject to the conditions of his parole, he can be gainfully employed and is free to be with family and friends and to form the other enduring attachments of normal life. Though the State properly subjects him to many restrictions not applicable to other citizens, his condition is very different from that of confinement in a prison. * * * The parolee has relied on at least an implicit promise that parole will be revoked only if he fails to live up to the parole conditions. * * *.

We see, therefore, that the liberty of a parolee, although indeterminate, includes many of the core values of unqualified liberty and its termination inflicts a "grievous loss" on the parolee and often on others. * * * Its termination calls for some orderly process, however informal.

Turning to the question what process is due, we find that the State's interests are several. The State has found the parolee guilty of a crime against the people. That finding justifies imposing extensive restrictions on the individual's liberty. * * * Given the previous conviction and the proper imposition of conditions, the State has an overwhelming interest in being able to return the individual to imprisonment without the burden of a new adversary criminal trial if in fact he has failed to abide by the conditions of his parole.

Yet the State has no interest in revoking parole without some informal procedural guarantees. Although the parolee is often formally described as being "in custody," the argument cannot even be made here that summary treatment is necessary as it may be with respect to controlling a large group of potentially disruptive prisoners in actual custody. Nor are we persuaded by the argument that revocation is so totally a discretionary matter that some form of hearing would be administratively intolerable. A simple factual hearing will not interfere with the exercise of discretion. * * *

simple factual hearing due to revoke parole [handwritten margin note]

This discretionary aspect of the revocation decision need not be reached unless there is first an appropriate determination that the individual has in fact breached the conditions of parole.

* * * What is needed is an informal hearing structured to assure that the finding of a parole violation will be based on verified facts and that the exercise of discretion will be informed by an accurate knowledge of the parolee's behavior.

III

We now turn to the nature of the process that is due, bearing in mind that the interest of both State and parolee will be furthered by an effective but informal hearing. In analyzing what is due, we see two important stages in the typical process of parole revocation.

(a) Arrest of Parolee and Preliminary Hearing. The first stage occurs when the parolee is arrested and detained, usually at the direction of his parole officer. The second occurs when parole is formally revoked. There is typically a substantial time lag between the arrest and the eventual determination by the parole board whether parole should be revoked. Additionally, it may be that the parolee is arrested at a place distant from the state institution, to which he may be returned before the final decision is made concerning revocation. Given these factors, due process would seem to require that some minimal inquiry be conducted at or reasonably near the place of the alleged parole violation or arrest and as promptly as convenient after arrest while information is fresh and sources are available. Such an inquiry should be seen as in the nature of a "preliminary hearing" to determine whether there is probable cause or reasonable grounds to believe that the arrested parolee has committed acts which would constitute a violation of parole conditions.

In our view due process requires that after the arrest, the determination that reasonable grounds exist for revocation of parole should be made by someone not directly involved in the case. * * * The officer directly involved in making recommendations cannot always have complete objectivity in evaluating them. * * *

This independent officer need not be a judicial officer. The granting and revocation of parole are matters traditionally handled by administrative officers. * * * It will be sufficient, therefore, in the parole revocation context, if an evaluation of whether reasonable cause exists to believe that conditions of parole have been violated is made by someone such as a parole officer other than the one who has made the report of parole violations or has recommended revocation. A State could certainly choose some other independent decisionmaker to perform this preliminary function.

With respect to the preliminary hearing before this officer, the parolee should be given notice that the hearing will take place and that its purpose is to determine whether there is probable cause to believe he has committed a parole violation. The notice should state what parole violations have been alleged. At the hearing the parolee may appear and speak in his own behalf; he may bring letters, documents, or individuals who can give relevant information to the hearing officer. On request of the parolee, persons who have given adverse information on which parole revocation is to be based are to be made available for questioning in his presence. However, if the hearing officer determines that the informant would be subjected to risk of harm if his identity were disclosed, he need not be subjected to confrontation and cross-examination.

The hearing officer * * * should determine whether there is probable cause to hold the parolee for the final decision of the parole board on revocation. Such a determination would be sufficient to warrant the parolee's continued detention and return to the state correctional institution pending the final decision. * * *

(b) The Revocation Hearing. There must also be an opportunity for a hearing, if it is desired by the parolee, prior to the final decision on revocation by the parole authority. This hearing must be the basis for more than determining probable cause; it must lead to a final evaluation of any contested relevant facts and consideration of whether the facts as determined warrant revocation. The parolee must have an opportunity to be heard and to show, if he can, that he did not violate the conditions, or, if he did, that circumstances in mitigation suggest the violation does not warrant revocation. The revocation hearing must be tendered within a reasonable time after the parolee is taken into custody. A lapse of two months, as the State suggests occurs in some cases, would not appear to be unreasonable.

* * * Our task is limited to deciding the minimum requirements of due process. They include (a) written notice of the claimed violations of parole;

(b) disclosure to the parolee of evidence against him; (c) opportunity to be heard in person and to present witnesses and documentary evidence; (d) the right to confront and cross-examine adverse witnesses (unless the hearing officer specifically finds good cause for not allowing confrontation); (e) a "neutral and detached" hearing body such as a traditional parole board, members of which need not be judicial officers or lawyers; and (f) a written statement by the factfinders as to the evidence relied on and reasons for revoking parole. We emphasize that there is no thought to equate this second stage of parole revocation to a criminal prosecution in any sense; it is a narrow inquiry; the process should be flexible enough to consider evidence including letters, affidavits, and other material that would not be admissible in an adversary criminal trial.

We do not reach or decide the question whether the parolee is entitled to the assistance of retained counsel or to appointed counsel if he is indigent.

We have no thought to create an inflexible structure for parole revocation procedures. The few basic requirements set out above, which are applicable to future revocations of parole, should not impose a great burden on any State's parole system. Control over the required proceedings by the hearing officers can assure that delaying tactics and other abuses sometimes present in the traditional adversary trial situation do not occur.

* * *

[Justice Brennan, joined by Justice Marshall, concurred in the result. He expressed his view that prisoners who can afford to retain and wish to retain counsel must be permitted to do so. He left open the question of whether counsel must be appointed for indigents. Justice Douglas dissented in part; although his view was not very different from the majority's, he would not as readily allow revocation upon a preliminary showing.]

Consideration of Alternatives: Black v. Romano

A unanimous Supreme Court held in Black v. Romano, 471 U.S. 606 (1985), that the Due Process Clause does not require a sentencing court to indicate that it has considered alternatives to incarceration before revoking probation. Romano pleaded guilty to two counts of transferring and selling a controlled substance. The trial judge imposed two concurrent twenty-year sentences, suspended execution of the sentences, and placed Romano on probation for five years. Two months later Romano was arrested for leaving the scene of an accident after he had run over a pedestrian. The trial judge held a probation revocation hearing during which no suggestion was made by Romano or his two lawyers that an alternative to incarceration be considered. Instead, Romano's argument was that he had not violated his probation conditions.

Justice O'Connor's opinion for the Court analyzed *Morrissey* and Gagnon v. Scarpelli, 411 U.S. 778 (1973)(providing right to counsel in certain parole and probation revocation proceedings) and concluded that although the Court did "not question the desirability of considering possible alternatives to imprisonment before probation is revoked," the "decision to revoke probation is generally predictive and subjective in nature" and "incarceration for violation of a probation condition is not constitutionally limited to circumstances where that sanction represents the only means of promoting the State's interest in punishment and deterrence." A statement of reasons for revocation is not required because "[t]he written statement required by *Gagnon* and *Morrissey* helps to insure accurate factfinding with respect to any alleged violation and provides an adequate basis for review to determine if the decision rests on permissible grounds supported by the evidence."

3. The Relationship Between Supervised Release and Imprisonment

In *Johnson v. United States*, 529 U.S. 694 (2000), the defendant was convicted on a number of narcotics and firearm counts. He was sentenced to a lengthy prison term on all these sentences, as well as a mandatory 3–year term of supervised release on the narcotics offenses. But because the firearms offenses were based on an incorrect interpretation of the law, they were vacated, and the court reduced the prison sentence. By the time this happened, Johnson had already served 30 months longer than the valid sentence. He was immediately released, and filed a motion to have his term of supervised release reduced by the amount of extra prison time he had served. The district court refused to grant this motion; that court's ruling was upheld in a unanimous opinion written by Justice Kennedy. The Court held that a period of supervised release is not altered by the fact that a defendant serves excess prison time.

Justice Kennedy parsed 18 U.S.C. § 3624(e), the statutory provision governing the time at which a period of supervised release can begin. That statute provides explicitly that the term of supervised release "commences on the day the person is released from imprisonment". Justice Kennedy reasoned that "released" means what it says, and to say that Johnson "was released while still imprisoned diminishes the concept the word intends to convey."

Justice Kennedy also noted that beginning the period of supervised release upon actual release from imprisonment is consistent with Congress' purpose in establishing a system of supervised release. He explained that the "objectives of supervised release would be unfulfilled if excess prison time were to offset and reduce terms of supervised release." He noted that "Congress intended supervised release to assist individuals in their transition to community life. Supervised release fulfills rehabilitative ends, distinct from those served by incarceration." Therefore, it would be error to treat time in prison as interchangeable with a period of supervised release.

D. APPELLATE REVIEW OF SENTENCING GENERALLY

Not only is enormous discretion vested in the sentencing authority in most states, but there is little review in many jurisdictions of how that discretion is exercised. The absence of much effective appellate supervision cannot be very surprising. To the extent that a rehabilitative or personalized sentence is imposed upon an offender, and to the extent we believe that trial judges can pierce the offender's soul to judge moral worth, an appellate court which sits away from the real life trial or plea proceedings and has little, if any, opportunity to see the participants will defer to the sentencing authority at trial.

With respect to the Federal Sentencing Guidelines, the Court in *Koon v. United States*, 518 U.S. 81 (1996), held that appellate review of sentencing determinations in the district court was to be governed by an abuse of discretion standard. But *Koon* was legislatively overruled in part by the Feeney amendment, which provides for de novo review of downward departures.

One of the most controversial aspects of appellate review is whether the state should be permitted to appeal a sentence. Many states forbid the raising of a sentence on appeal by the government. Cf. Alaska Stat. § 12.55.120(b)(allowing a government appeal of sentence to provide guidance to lower courts, but not to raise sentence). In the Williams v. New York type of sentencing system, unfettered as it is by guidelines, you can see why one would fear that, if the opportunity presented itself, prosecutors would threaten to appeal sentences in order to discourage defendants from taking appeals or challenging sentences. In a system of unchecked discretion, risk-averse defendants might well choose not to subject themselves to an unguided appellate tribunal's sentence. If a guideline or presumptive system of sentences is adopted, the factual inquiries and the importance of applying fact to law are increased, and arguably, the case for permitting the prosecutor to have some appellate review (at least where the guidelines are not followed by the trial court) may be more attractive.

Under the Federal Sentencing Guidelines, either party may appeal if (1) the sentence was imposed in violation of law; (2) the sentence was based on an incorrect application of the Guidelines; or (3) the sentence was imposed for an offense that lacked a Guideline and was plainly unreasonable. In addition, the defendant may appeal an upward departure and the government may appeal a downward departure. In the absence of the above circumstances, neither party may obtain review. United States v. DiFrancesco, 449 U.S. 117 (1980), upholds the constitutionality of appellate review of sentences at the request of the government.

Chapter Twelve

DOUBLE JEOPARDY

I. INTRODUCTION

The Double Jeopardy Clause of the Fifth Amendment provides: "[N]or shall any person be subject for the same offense to be twice put in jeopardy of life or limb."[1] Made applicable to the states in Benton v. Maryland, 395 U.S. 784 (1969), the clause provides three basic related protections: "It protects against a second prosecution for the same offense after acquittal. It protects against a second prosecution for the same offense after conviction. And it protects against multiple punishments for the same offense." North Carolina v. Pearce, 395 U.S. 711, 717 (1969). As you will see, interpretation and application of the Double Jeopardy Clause have resulted in an accommodation between the finality interests of the defendant and the government's interest in having one fair opportunity to prosecute and convict.

Protects 2nd Pros for same offense after acquittal
2nd Pros after conviction
multi-punishments for same offense

Like many of the constitutional provisions examined previously, the Double Jeopardy Clause is not easily understood. Although its history suggests some answers to a few questions, most hard questions were not debated, perhaps not even contemplated, during the drafting and discussion of the Bill of Rights and the Fourteenth Amendment. And when the words of the Double Jeopardy Clause are parsed, it appears that the language offers few clues as to the intent of its drafters.

II. THE EFFECT OF AN ACQUITTAL

Traditionally, the government has been unable to initiate a second prosecution on the theory that an acquittal was mistaken, and it has been forbidden to appeal from an acquittal or legal rulings that produced the acquittal, even if the rulings underlying an acquittal were erroneous.[2] And if a jury acquits a defendant, the trial judge cannot grant the government a second trial, even if she believes the jury erred badly. The government cannot appeal from an acquittal,

---

1. The Double Jeopardy Clause originated with the common-law pleas of autrefois acquit, autrefois convict, and pardon. The clause adopts the traditional language of "jeopardy." For a history of the Double Jeopardy Clause, see J. Sigler, Double Jeopardy (1969); United States v. Wilson, 420 U.S. 332, 339–42 (1975). For a discussion of the meaning of "life or

limb", see Amar, Double Jeopardy Law Made Simple, 106 Yale L.J. 1807 (1997).

2. When the prosecution is appealing a question of law that will not result in a retrial after a finding of innocence, an appeal may not be barred by the Double Jeopardy Clause. Whether an appeal will be permitted depends on local law.

even if it has a reasonable claim that the jury would have convicted but for errors committed by the trial judge, since the defendant's interest in finality is held to preclude a retrial. See *Sanabria v. United States*, 437 U.S. 54 (1978); *Fong Foo v. United States*, 369 U.S. 141 (1962). In *Sanabria*, for example, discussed infra, the trial court erroneously excluded evidence of the alleged crime and then granted an acquittal based on the insufficiency of the remaining evidence. The Double Jeopardy Clause barred retrial.

In view of the preclusive effect of an acquittal on future adjudication, it is important to know what constitutes an acquittal and when the government can appeal an adverse ruling or dismissal of a case on the ground that the trial court did something other than acquit the defendant. The Supreme Court considered these questions in United States v. Scott. Note carefully the Court's discussion of the history of the Double Jeopardy Clause and the basic double jeopardy principles in Part II of the opinion. The mistrial cases noted in Part III are discussed later in this Chapter.

UNITED STATES v. SCOTT

Supreme Court of the United States, 1978.
437 U.S. 82.

MR. JUSTICE REHNQUIST **delivered the opinion of the Court.**

On March 5, 1975, respondent, a member of the police force in Muskegon, Mich., was charged in a three-count indictment with distribution of various narcotics. Both before his trial in the United States District Court for the Western District of Michigan, and twice during the trial, respondent moved to dismiss the two counts of the indictment which concerned transactions that took place during the preceding September, on the ground that his defense had been prejudiced by preindictment delay. At the close of all the evidence, the court granted respondent's motion. Although the court did not explain its reasons for dismissing the second count, it explicitly concluded that respondent had "presented sufficient proof of prejudice with respect to Count I." The court submitted the third count to the jury, which returned a verdict of not guilty.

The Government sought to appeal the dismissals of the first two counts to the United States Court of Appeals for the Sixth Circuit. That court, relying on our opinion in United States v.

Jenkins, 420 U.S. 358 (1975), concluded that any further prosecution of respondent was barred by the Double Jeopardy Clause of the Fifth Amendment, and therefore dismissed the appeal. The Government has sought review in this Court only with regard to the dismissal of the first count. * * * We now reverse.

I

The problem presented by this case could not have arisen during the first century of this Court's existence. The Court has long taken the view that the United States has no right of appeal in a criminal case, absent explicit statutory authority. Such authority was not provided until the enactment of the Criminal Appeals Act, Act of Mar. 2, 1907, which permitted the United States to seek a writ of error in this Court from any decision dismissing an indictment on the basis of "the invalidity, or construction of the statute upon which the indictment is founded." Our consideration of Government appeals over the ensuing years ordinarily focused upon the intricacies of the Act and its amendments. In 1971, however, Congress adopted the current language of the Act, permitting Government appeals from any decision dismissing an indictment, "except that no appeal shall lie where the Double Jeopardy Clause of the United States Constitution prohibits further prosecution." 18 U.S.C.A. § 3731. Soon thereafter, this Court remarked in a footnote with more optimism than prescience that "[t]he end of our problems with this Act is finally in sight." United States v. Weller, 401 U.S. 254, 255 n. 1 (1971). For in fact the 1971 amendment did not end the debate over appeals by the Government in criminal cases; it simply shifted the focus of the debate from issues of statutory construction to issues as to the scope and meaning of the Double Jeopardy Clause.

In our first encounter with the new statute, we concluded that "Congress intended to remove all statutory barriers to Government appeals and to allow appeals whenever the Constitution would permit." United States v. Wilson, 420 U.S. 332, 337 (1975). Since up to that point Government appeals had been subject to statutory restrictions independent of the Double Jeopardy Clause, our previous cases construing the statute proved to be of little assistance in determining when the Double Jeopardy Clause of the Fifth Amendment would prohibit further prosecution. A detailed canvass of the history of the double jeopardy principles in English and American law led us to conclude that the Double Jeopardy Clause was primarily "directed at the threat of multiple prosecutions," and posed no bar to Government appeals "where those appeals would not require a new trial." We accordingly held in *Jenkins*, that, whether or not a dismissal of an indictment after jeopardy had attached amounted to an acquittal on the merits, the Government had no right to appeal, because "further proceedings of some sort, devoted to the resolution of factual issues going to the elements of the offense charged, would have been required upon reversal and remand."[a]

If *Jenkins* is a correct statement of the law, the judgment of the Court of Appeals relying on that decision, as it was bound to do, would in all likelihood have to be affirmed. Yet, though our assessment of the history and meaning of the Double Jeopardy Clause in *Wilson, Jenkins,* and Serfass v. United States, 420 U.S. 377 (1975),[b]

---

a. The rule established in *Wilson* and *Jenkins* was later described in the following terms:

"[D]ismissals (as opposed to mistrials) if they occurred at a stage of the proceeding after which jeopardy had attached, but prior to the factfinder's conclusion as to guilt or innocence, were final so far as the accused defendant was concerned and could not be appealed by the Government because retrial was barred by double jeopardy. This made the issue of double jeopardy turn very largely on temporal considerations—if the Court granted an order of dismissal during the factfinding stage of the proceedings, the defendant could not be reprosecuted, but if the dismissal came later, he could." Lee v. United States, 432 U.S. 23, 36 (1977) (Rehnquist, J., concurring).

[Editor's Note: In *Lee*, a defendant, after the prosecutor's opening statement, moved to dismiss an information because it failed to allege specific intent. Following a two hour trial, the court noted that the defendant had been proved guilty beyond a reasonable doubt, but granted the motion to dismiss the information. Subsequently, the defendant was charged again with the same crime and convicted. The Court held that retrial was not barred by the double jeopardy clause. The Court reasoned that the trial court granted the motion to dismiss in contemplation of a second prosecution, and that it was permissible under the circumstances to delay a ruling on the motion to dismiss until the trial was completed.]

b. [Editor's Note: In *Serfass*, the Court held that the government could appeal a pretrial dismissal of an indictment, because the defendant, having never been subjected to factfinding on the guilt and innocence question, could be tried if the trial judge erred in dismissing the indictment.]

occurred only three Terms ago, our vastly increased exposure to the various facets of the Double Jeopardy Clause has now convinced us that *Jenkins* was wrongly decided. It placed an unwarrantedly great emphasis on the defendant's right to have his guilt decided by the first jury empaneled to try him so as to include those cases where the defendant himself seeks to terminate the trial before verdict on grounds unrelated to factual guilt or innocence. We have therefore decided to overrule *Jenkins*, and thus to reverse the judgment of the Court of Appeals in this case.[c]

II

The origin and history of the Double Jeopardy Clause are hardly a matter of dispute. The constitutional provision had its origin in the three common-law pleas of *autrefois acquit, autrefois convict,* and pardon. These three pleas prevented the retrial of a person who had previously been acquitted, convicted, or pardoned for the same offense. As this Court has described the purpose underlying the prohibition against double jeopardy:

> "The underlying idea, one that is deeply ingrained in at least the Anglo–American system of jurisprudence, is that the State with all its resources and power should not be allowed to make repeated attempts to convict an individual for an alleged offense, thereby subjecting

him to embarrassment, expense and ordeal and compelling him to live in a continuing state of anxiety and insecurity, as well as enhancing the possibility that even though innocent he may be found guilty." *Green* [v. United States, 355 U.S. 184] at 187–188.

These historical purposes are necessarily general in nature, and their application has come to abound in often subtle distinctions which cannot by any means all be traced to the original three commonlaw pleas referred to above.

Part of the difficulty arises from the development of other protections for criminal defendants in the years since the adoption of the Bill of Rights. At the time the Fifth Amendment was adopted, its principles were easily applied, since most criminal prosecutions proceeded to final judgment, and neither the United States nor the defendant had any right to appeal an adverse verdict. See Act of Sept. 24, 1789, ch. 20, § 22, 1 Stat. 84. The verdict in such a case was unquestionably final, and could be raised in bar against any further prosecution for the same offense.

* * * It was not until 1889 that Congress permitted criminal defendants to seek a writ of error in this Court, and then only in capital cases.[d] Only then did it become necessary for this Court to deal with the issues pre-

---

c. [Editor's Note: The appellate scheme in the federal courts is described in this opinion. Note that there can be no appeal in circumstances where new trial court proceedings would be necessary for there to be a valid conviction and those proceedings are barred by the Double Jeopardy Clause. For purposes of this chapter, it is not critical to master the federal statute governing appeals; it is sufficient to remember that when the Supreme Court holds that there can be no appeal because of the jeopardy clause, the Supreme Court is saying that there can be no further trial proceedings. The Court would say the same thing if the government tried to bring a

second action instead of appealing, and the defendant complained.

Arizona v. Manypenny, 451 U.S. 232 (1981), holds that in a state criminal proceeding removed to a federal court (see 28 U.S.C. § 1442, removal by federal officers), a state may appeal under 28 U.S.C. § 1291 a district court's entry of judgment of acquittal following a jury verdict of guilty when state law would have permitted such an appeal in state court.]

d. Two years later, review was provided for all "infamous" crimes. Act of Mar. 3, 1891, ch. 517, § 5, 26 Stat. 827.

sented by the challenge of verdicts on appeal.

And, in the very first case presenting the issues, United States v. Ball, 163 U.S. 662 (1896), the Court established principles that have been adhered to ever since. Three persons had been tried together for murder; two were convicted, the other acquitted. This Court reversed the convictions, finding the indictment fatally defective, Ball v. United States, 140 U.S. 118 (1891), whereupon all three defendants were tried again. This time all three were convicted and they again sought review here. This Court held that the Double Jeopardy Clause precluded further prosecution of the defendant who had been *acquitted* at the original trial but that it posed no such bar to the prosecution of those defendants who had been *convicted* in the earlier proceeding. The Court disposed of their objection almost peremptorily:

> "Their plea of former conviction cannot be sustained, because upon a writ of error sued out by themselves the judgment and sentence against them were reversed, and the indictment ordered to be dismissed. * * * [I]t is quite clear that a defendant, who procures a judgment against him upon an indictment to be set aside, may be tried anew upon the same indictment, or upon another indictment, for the same offence of which he had been convicted."

Although *Ball* firmly established that a successful appeal of a conviction precludes a subsequent plea of double jeopardy, the opinion shed no light on whether a judgment of acquittal could be reversed on appeal consistently with the Double Jeopardy Clause. Because of the statutory restrictions upon Government appeals in criminal

If indictment fails Gov can try anew

cases, this Court in the years after *Ball* was faced with that question only in unusual circumstances, such as were present in Kepner v. United States, 195 U.S. 100 (1904). That case arose out of a criminal prosecution in the Philippine Islands, to which the principles of the Double Jeopardy Clause had been expressly made applicable by Act of Congress. Although the defendant had been acquitted in his original trial, traditional Philippine procedure provided for a trial *de novo* upon appeal. This Court, in reversing the resulting conviction, remarked:

> "The court of first instance, having jurisdiction to try the question of the guilt or innocence of the accused, found Kepner not guilty; to try him again upon the merits, even in an appellate court, is to put him a second time in jeopardy for the same offense * * * "

More than 50 years later, in Fong Foo v. United States, 369 U.S. 141 (1962), this Court reviewed the issuance of a writ of mandamus by the Court of Appeals for the First Circuit instructing a District Court to vacate certain judgments of acquittal. Although indicating its agreement with the Court of Appeals that the judgments had been entered erroneously, this Court nonetheless held that a second trial was barred by the Double Jeopardy Clause. Only last Term, this Court relied upon these precedents in United States v. Martin Linen Supply Co., 430 U.S. 564 (1977), and held that the Government could not appeal the granting of a motion to acquit pursuant to Fed.Rule Crim.Proc. 29 where a second trial would be required upon remand.[e] The Court, quoting language in *Ball* stated: "Perhaps the most fundamental rule in the history of double jeopardy juris-

---

e. [Editor's Note: In *Martin* the jury was hopelessly deadlocked and was discharged. Subsequently, the trial judge entered a judg-

ment of acquittal. The Court held that any retrial would violate the double jeopardy clause.]

prudence has been that a verdict of acquittal * * * could not be reviewed, on error or otherwise, without putting [a defendant] twice in jeopardy, and thereby violating the Constitution."

These, then, at least, are two venerable principles of double jeopardy jurisprudence. The successful appeal of a judgment of conviction, on any ground other than the insufficiency of the evidence to support the verdict, Burks v. United States, 437 U.S. 1, poses no bar to further prosecution on the same charge. A judgment of acquittal, whether based on a jury verdict of not guilty or on a ruling by the court that the evidence is insufficient to convict, may not be appealed and terminates the prosecution when a second trial would be necessitated by a reversal. What may seem superficially to be a disparity in the rules governing a defendant's liability to be tried again is explainable by reference to the underlying purposes of the Double Jeopardy Clause. As *Kepner* and *Fong Foo* illustrate, the law attaches particular significance to an acquittal. To permit a second trial after an acquittal, however mistaken the acquittal may have been, would present an unacceptably high risk that the Government, with its vastly superior resources, might wear down the defendant so that "even though innocent he may be found guilty." On the other hand, to require a criminal defendant to stand trial again after he has successfully invoked a statutory right of appeal to upset his first conviction is not an act of governmental oppression of the sort against which the Double Jeopardy Clause was intended to protect. * * *

III

Although the primary purpose of the Double Jeopardy Clause was to protect the integrity of a final judgment, this Court has also developed a body of law guarding the separate but related interest of a defendant in avoiding multiple prosecutions even where no final determination of guilt or innocence has been made. Such interests may be involved in two different situations: the first, in which the trial judge declares a mistrial; the second, in which the trial judge terminates the proceedings favorably to the defendant on a basis not related to factual guilt or innocence.

Mistrial

When a trial court declares a <u>mistrial</u>, it all but invariably contemplates that the prosecutor will be permitted to proceed anew notwithstanding the defendant's plea of double jeopardy. See Lee v. United States, 432 U.S. 23, 30 (1977). Such a motion may be granted upon the initiative of either party or upon the court's own initiative. The fact that the trial judge contemplates that there will be a new trial is not conclusive on the issue of double jeopardy; in passing on the propriety of a declaration of mistrial granted at the behest of the prosecutor or on the court's own motion, this Court has balanced "the valued right of a defendant to have his trial completed by the particular tribunal summoned to sit in judgment on him," Downum v. United States, 372 U.S. 734, 736 (1963), against the public interest in insuring that justice is meted out to offenders.

Our very first encounter with this situation came in United States v. Perez, 9 Wheat. 579 (1824), in which the trial judge had on his own motion declared a mistrial because of the jury's inability to reach a verdict. The Court said that trial judges might declare mistrials "whenever, in their opinion, taking all the circumstances into consideration, there is a manifest necessity for the act, or the ends of public justice would otherwise be defeated." In our recent decision in Arizona v. Washington, 434 U.S. 497

(1978), we reviewed this Court's attempts to give content to the term "manifest necessity." That case, like *Downum*, supra, arose from a motion of the prosecution for a mistrial, and we noted that the trial court's discretion must be exercised with a careful regard for the interests first described in United States v. Perez.

Where, on the other hand, a *defendant* successfully seeks to avoid his trial prior to its conclusion by a motion for mistrial, the Double Jeopardy Clause is not offended by a second prosecution. * * * Such a motion by the defendant is deemed to be a deliberate election on his part to forego his valued right to have his guilt or innocence determined before the first trier of fact. * * *[f]

[handwritten: Consensual termination of trial bef verdict]

We turn now to the relationship between the Double Jeopardy Clause and reprosecution of a defendant who has successfully obtained not a mistrial but a termination of the trial in his favor before any determination of factual guilt or innocence. * * *

In the present case, the District Court's dismissal of the first count of the indictment was based upon a claim of preindictment delay and not on the court's conclusion that the Government had not produced sufficient evidence to establish the guilt of the defendant. Respondent Scott points out quite correctly that he had moved to dismiss the indictment on this ground prior to trial, and that had the District Court chosen to grant it at that time the Government could have appealed the ruling under our holding in Serfass v. United States, 420 U.S.

377 (1975). He also quite correctly points out that jeopardy had undeniably "attached" at the time the District Court terminated the trial in his favor; since a successful Government appeal would require further proceedings in the District Court leading to a factual resolution of the issue of guilt or innocence, *Jenkins* bars the Government's appeal. However, our growing experience with Government appeals convinces us that we must re-examine the rationale of *Jenkins* in light of *Lee, Martin Linen,* and other recent expositions of the Double Jeopardy Clause.

IV

Our decision in *Jenkins* was based upon our perceptions of the underlying purposes of the Double Jeopardy Clause * * *. Upon fuller consideration, we are now of the view that this language from *Green* [referring to the impermissibility of repeated attempts to prosecute the defendant], while entirely appropriate in the circumstances of that opinion,[g] is not a principle which can be expanded to include situations in which the defendant is responsible for the second prosecution. It is quite true that the Government with all its resources and power should not be allowed to make repeated attempts to convict an individual for an alleged offense. This truth is expressed in the three common-law pleas of *autrefois acquit, autrefois convict*, and pardon, which lie at the core of the area protected by the Double Jeopardy Clause. As we have recognized * * * a defendant once acquitted may not be again subjected to trial without violating the Double Jeopardy Clause.

[handwritten margin note: Only acquitted no more prosecution]

f. [Editor's Note: But see the limited exception to this principle, established in the later case of Oregon v. Kennedy, discussed infra.]

g. [Editor's Note: The *Green* Court held that a conviction on a lesser included offense was the equivalent of an acquittal on the great-

er offense and barred retrial on the greater offense even if the defendant appealed and obtained a reversal of the conviction on the lesser offense. Of course, the defendant could be prosecuted again for the lesser crime of which he was convicted.]

But that situation is obviously a far cry from the present case, where the Government was quite willing to continue with its production of evidence to show the defendant guilty before the jury first empaneled to try him, but the defendant elected to seek termination of the trial on grounds unrelated to guilt or innocence. This is scarcely a picture of an all-powerful state relentlessly pursuing a defendant who had either been found not guilty or who had at least insisted on having the issue of guilt submitted to the first trier of fact. It is instead a picture of a defendant who chooses to avoid conviction and imprisonment, not because of his assertion that the Government has failed to make out a case against him, but because of a legal claim that the Government's case against him must fail even though it might satisfy the trier of fact that he was guilty beyond a reasonable doubt.

We have previously noted that "the trial judge's characterization of his own action cannot control the classification of the action." Despite respondent's contentions, an appeal is not barred simply because a ruling in favor of a defendant "is based upon facts outside the face of the indictment," or because it "is granted on the ground * * * that the defendant simply cannot be convicted of the offense charged." Rather, a defendant is acquitted only when "the ruling of the judge, whatever its label, actually represents a resolution [in the defendant's favor], correct or not, of some or all of the factual elements of the offense charged." Where the court, before the jury returns a verdict, enters a judgment of acquittal pursuant to Fed. Rule Crim.Proc. 29, appeal will be barred only when "it is plain that the District Court * * * evaluated the Government's evidence and deter-

mined that it was legally insufficient to sustain a conviction."

* * *

We think that in a case such as this the defendant, by deliberately choosing to seek termination of the proceedings against him on a basis unrelated to factual guilt or innocence of the offense of which he is accused, suffers no injury cognizable under the Double Jeopardy Clause if the Government is permitted to appeal from such a ruling of the trial court in favor of the defendant. We do not thereby adopt the doctrine of "waiver" of double jeopardy rejected in *Green*. Rather, we conclude that the Double Jeopardy Clause, which guards against Government oppression, does not relieve a defendant from the consequences of his voluntary choice. In *Green* the question of the defendant's factual guilt or innocence of murder in the first degree was actually submitted to the jury as a trier of fact; in the present case, respondent successfully avoided such a submission of the first count of the indictment by persuading the trial court to dismiss it on a basis which did not depend on guilt or innocence. He was thus neither acquitted nor convicted, because he himself successfully undertook to persuade the trial court not to submit the issue of guilt or innocence to the jury which had been empaneled to try him.

* * * [W]here the defendant, instead of obtaining a reversal of his conviction on appeal, obtains the termination of the proceedings against him in the trial court without any finding by a court or jury as to his guilt or innocence [h]e has not been "deprived" of his valued right to go to the first jury; only the public has been deprived of its valued right to one complete opportunity to convict those who have violated its laws. No interest protected by the Double Jeopardy

Clause is invaded when the Government is allowed to appeal and seek reversal of such a midtrial termination of the proceedings in a manner favorable to the defendant.[h]

* * *

MR. JUSTICE BRENNAN, with whom MR. JUSTICE WHITE, MR. JUSTICE MARSHALL, and MR. JUSTICE STEVENS join, dissenting.

* * *

* * * The Court's attempt to draw a distinction between "true acquittals" and other final judgments favorable to the accused, quite simply, is unsupportable in either logic or policy. * * *

* * *

It is manifest that the reasons that bar a retrial following an acquittal are equally applicable to a final judgment entered on a ground "unrelated to factual innocence." The heavy personal strain of the second trial is the same in either case. So too is the risk that, though innocent, the defendant may be found guilty at a second trial. If the appeal is allowed in either situation, the Government will, following any reversal, not only obtain the benefit of the favorable appellate ruling but also be permitted to shore up any other weak points of its case and obtain all the other advantages at the second trial that the Double Jeopardy Clause was designed to forbid.

[The dissenters also objected to the difficulties in applying the Court's approach. They questioned the difference between a dismissal based on the defenses of insanity and entrapment and a dismissal for pre-indictment delay. The decision, in their view, needlessly complicates an area of law which was "crystal clear."]

Problem: What is an Acquittal?

In Sanabria v. United States, 437 U.S. 54 (1978), the defendant was charged with the federal offense of conducting an illegal gambling business, in violation of the law of Massachusetts, the place where the business was located. The single count indictment alleged that Sanabria and his codefendants engaged in both numbers betting and betting on horse races. At the end of the defense presentation, the judge concluded that the Massachusetts statute cited in the indictment did not prohibit numbers betting and excluded all evidence of numbers betting. This was error, because the government only had to show that the gambling operation violated state law. Once this was demonstrated, any evidence that showed participation in the gambling operation was admissible. The evidentiary error led the trial judge to erroneously grant a defense motion for an acquittal, because there was insufficient evidence admitted to connect the

h. We should point out that it is entirely possible for a trial court to reconcile the public interest in the Government's right to appeal from an erroneous conclusion of law with the defendant's interest in avoiding a second prosecution. In *Wilson,* supra, the court permitted the case to go to the jury, which returned a verdict of guilty, but it subsequently dismissed the indictment for preindictment delay on the basis of evidence adduced at trial. More recently in United States v. Ceccolini, 435 U.S. 268 (1978), we described similar action with approval: "The District Court had sensibly first made its finding on the factual question of guilt or innocence, and then ruled on the motion to suppress; a reversal of these rulings would require no further proceedings in the District Court, but merely a reinstatement of the finding of guilt."

We, of course, do not suggest that a midtrial dismissal of a prosecution, in response to a defense motion on grounds unrelated to guilt or innocence, is necessarily improper. Such rulings may be necessary to terminate proceedings marred by fundamental error. But where a defendant prevails on such a motion, he takes the risk that an appellate court will reverse the trial court.

defendant with the horse-betting activities, as opposed to the overall gambling business. Seeking a new trial only on the part of the indictment related to numbers betting, the government appealed, urging that the district court's action should be construed as a dismissal of the numbers betting part of the case, rather than as an acquittal. The Court of Appeals accepted this characterization and remanded for a new trial because Sanabria voluntarily had moved to terminate the trial.

The Supreme Court reversed and held that a new trial was barred. It held that the district court acquitted the defendant, and that the action could not be characterized as a dismissal, since the trial judge believed that he was construing the indictment and ruling on the merits. Moreover, the indictment alleged one offense, with two theories of liability: numbers betting and horse betting. Thus, the Court said that even if the action could be characterized as a "dismissal," a retrial would subject the defendant to two trials for the same offense, after the defendant had been acquitted of the offense.

Assume that after the government offered its evidence, the following colloquy took place: the trial judge asked: "Do you claim that the defendant was involved in horse betting?" The prosecutor answered: "No, only in numbers betting, but as part of the same gambling operation as the horse betting." The trial judge said: "Well, you have not charged an offense under the statute then, because there can be no offense without a violation of a specific state gambling statute by this defendant himself. Thus, I am dismissing the indictment because there is no offense charged."

Would a reversal and a retrial be permissible if an appellate court concluded that an offense was properly charged? See generally Cooper, Government Appeals in Criminal Cases: The 1978 Decisions, 81 F.R.D. 539 (1979). For a thoughtful and scholarly discussion of double jeopardy problems generally, see Westen & Drubel, Toward a General Theory of Double Jeopardy, 1978 Sup.Ct. Rev. 81.

Entry of a Judgment of Acquittal

If a trial judge enters a judgment of acquittal, before the jury reaches a verdict, that determination is final. United States v. Martin Linen Supply, 430 U.S. 564 (1977), so indicates. In fact, it holds that a judgment of acquittal following a mistrial is as final as a directed verdict.[3]

In Smalis v. Pennsylvania, 476 U.S. 140 (1986), Justice White wrote for a unanimous Court as it found that a husband and wife, charged with various crimes in connection with a fire in a building they owned that killed two tenants, were acquitted for double jeopardy purposes when a state trial judge sustained a demurrer at the close of the prosecution's case in a bench trial. Since the state trial judge determined that the state's evidence was insufficient to establish factual guilt, the Double Jeopardy Clause barred a post-judgment appeal by the

---

3. Compare *Martin Linen Supply* with United States v. Sanford, 429 U.S. 14 (1976)(no double jeopardy problem where trial court dismissed indictment after mistrial was declared, even though based on evidence presented at trial). See also United States v. Maddox, 944 F.2d 1223 (6th Cir.1991)(no double jeopardy violation where the trial judge granted a post-trial motion for acquittal, then changed his mind and reinstated the conviction; *Martin Linen* distinguished as a case in which the jury never reached a verdict, and therefore further proceedings would have been necessary).

government. Even if the state trial court was incorrect, jeopardy had attached and was terminated by the acquittal. The Court held that an acquittal would be found not only where the judge assessed the evidence as a matter of credibility and found it insufficient, but also where the judge determined that evidence was insufficient "as a matter of law." For a discussion of *Smalis* and other cases concerning government appeals, see Strazzella, The Relationship of Double Jeopardy to Prosecution Appeals, 73 Notre Dame L.Rev. 1 (1997).

In *Price v. Vincent*, 538 U.S. 634 (2003), the Court distinguished *Smalis* and *Martin Linen* and held that a trial judge's ruling was not sufficiently final to terminate jeopardy. The defendant was charged with murder. At the close of the government's case, defense counsel moved for a directed verdict of acquittal as to first degree murder, arguing that there was insufficient evidence of deliberation and premeditation. The trial judge stated:

> "My impression at this time is that there's not been shown premeditation or planning in the, in the alleged slaying. That what we have at the very best is Second Degree Murder.... I think that Second Degree Murder is an appropriate charge as to the defendants. Okay."

The prosecutor asked to make a brief statement regarding first-degree murder, but the defendant objected, arguing that his motion for directed verdict had been granted, and that further consideration of that charge would violate the Double Jeopardy Clause. The trial judge responded that he had "granted a motion" but had not directed a verdict. The judge noted that the jury had not been informed of his statements, and that his language indicated that he was going to reserve a ruling on the matter. Subsequently, the trial judge submitted the charge of first-degree murder to the jury and the defendant was convicted on that charge. The state courts, on review, concluded that the trial judge's comments on the directed verdict motion were not sufficiently final to constitute a judgment of acquittal terminating jeopardy.

The defendant sought habeas corpus relief, arguing that his rights under the Double Jeopardy Clause had been violated. Chief Justice Rehnquist, in an opinion for a unanimous Court, noted first that to obtain habeas relief the petitioner must show that the state court's adjudication of his claim was "contrary to, or involved an unreasonable application of, clearly established Federal law, as determined by the Supreme Court of the United States." [See the discussion of the habeas corpus statute in Chapter 13]. Thus, if reasonable minds could differ about whether the state courts were correct in finding insufficient finality to the trial court's ruling in this case, habeas relief must be denied. On the question of finality, the Court noted that in *Smalis* and *Martin Linen*, unlike in the present case, "the trial courts not only rendered statements of clarity and finality but also entered formal orders from which appeals were taken." No such order was entered in the instant case. Under these circumstances, the Michigan courts were not unreasonable in concluding that the trial judge's oral ruling was insufficiently final to terminate jeopardy.

oral ruling insufficiently final to terminate jeopardy

Acquittal After a Jury Convicts

If a judge waits until after a jury convicts to enter a judgment of acquittal, may the government appeal that ruling? A footnote in *Scott* suggests that an appeal in those circumstances is permissible. The lower courts have agreed,

If there is jury verdict, the gov can appeal the directed verdict

reasoning that if the government is successful on appeal, the verdict can simply be reinstated and further proceedings are unnecessary. See United States v. Maddox, 944 F.2d 1223 (6th Cir.1991). Does this suggest that it is best for a trial judge to allow a case to be decided by a jury before she rules on a motion to dismiss? This approach would benefit both the defendant and the government, would it not?

A Second Trial Is Sometimes Permitted

Scott indicates that a defendant is not necessarily placed twice in jeopardy simply because he is subjected to two trials.[4] Sometimes a second trial is permissible, and sometimes it is not. Drawing lines between permissible and impermissible attempts by the government to litigate a case that has been litigated once previously is the Court's task under the Double Jeopardy Clause. *Scott* indicates that the Court has not found it to be easy.

Which approach—that of *Jenkins* or that of *Scott*—makes more sense? *Jenkins* focused on whether further factfinding would be necessary in a case. *Scott* focuses on whether there has been some determination by judge or jury relating to factual guilt or innocence. *Jenkins* attempted to prevent repetitive litigation. *Scott* attempts to protect an unimpaired statement by the trial court (judge or jury) that the government has not proved its case. Which is the more justifiable protection?

In thinking about this, it might be helpful to consider what happens when the defendant is convicted in the trial court and appeals.

III. THE CONVICTED DEFENDANT APPEALS

When a defendant successfully appeals a conviction, may he be retried? United States v. Ball, 163 U.S. 662 (1896), mentioned in *Scott* and discussed in the following case, established that a retrial following a reversal of a conviction is permissible. In the next case, the Court considered whether a defendant may be retried when the reversal was based on insufficiency of the evidence rather than on trial error.

---

4. The Court has recognized the importance of not making a defendant with a good double jeopardy claim stand trial twice. In Abney v. United States, 431 U.S. 651 (1977), for example, the Court held that under 18 U.S.C.A. § 1291 a defendant could appeal a denial of a pre-trial motion to dismiss on double jeopardy grounds.

In Justices v. Lydon, 466 U.S. 294 (1984), the Court reaffirmed *Abney* and emphasized that a defendant who has a claim that a second trial would place him in jeopardy twice is entitled to seek federal habeas corpus relief to bar the second trial. In a case such as Lydon's, which arose in state court, the defendant must exhaust state remedies before seeking federal relief. The Court found that Lydon had done so and therefore that he was entitled to federal review of his double jeopardy claim. On the merits, the Court rejected the claim.

Abney led the Court to conclude in Richardson v. United States, 468 U.S. 317 (1984), that a defendant could appeal the denial of his motion for a judgment of acquittal where a jury indicated that it was unable to agree on a verdict and the trial judge granted a mistrial and scheduled a second trial. Justice Rehnquist's opinion for the Court reasoned that the first trial was over and the defendant was not seeking to interrupt or delay that trial by filing his appeal. The opinion reiterated that an immediate appeal requires a showing of a colorable, non-frivolous claim. On the merits, the Court held that a defendant is not placed in jeopardy twice when a mistrial is declared due to a genuinely deadlocked jury and he is re-tried, irrespective of the sufficiency of the evidence in the first proceeding.

A. INSUFFICIENT EVIDENCE TO CONVICT

BURKS v. UNITED STATES

Supreme Court of the United States, 1978.
437 U.S. 1.

MR. CHIEF JUSTICE BURGER delivered the opinion of the Court.

We granted certiorari to resolve the question of whether an accused may be subjected to a second trial when conviction in a prior trial was reversed by an appellate court solely for lack of sufficient evidence to sustain the jury's verdict.

I

Petitioner Burks was tried in the United States District Court for the crime of robbing a federally insured bank by use of a dangerous weapon * * *. Burks' principal defense was insanity. To prove this claim petitioner produced three expert witnesses who testified, albeit with differing diagnoses of his mental condition, that he suffered from a mental illness at the time of the robbery, which rendered him substantially incapable of conforming his conduct to the requirements of the law. In rebuttal the Government offered the testimony of two experts, one of whom testified that although petitioner possessed a character disorder, he was not mentally ill. The other prosecution witness acknowledged a character disorder in petitioner, but gave a rather ambiguous answer to the question of whether Burks had been capable of conforming his conduct to the law. Lay witnesses also testified for the Government, expressing their opinion that petitioner appeared to be capable of normal functioning and was sane at the time of the alleged offense.

Before the case was submitted to the jury, the court denied a motion for a judgment of acquittal. The jury found Burks guilty as charged. There-

after, he filed a timely motion for a new trial, maintaining, among other things, that "[t]he evidence was insufficient to support the verdict." The motion was denied by the District Court, which concluded that petitioner's challenge to the sufficiency of the evidence was "utterly without merit."

On appeal petitioner narrowed the issues by admitting the affirmative factual elements of the charge against him, leaving only his claim concerning criminal responsibility to be resolved. With respect to this point, the Court of Appeals agreed with petitioner's claim that the evidence was insufficient to support the verdict and reversed his conviction. * * *

[The Court of Appeals, rather than terminating the case, remanded to the District Court for a determination of whether a directed verdict of acquittal should be entered or a new trial ordered.]

* * *

[In Part II of the opinion, the Court examined several prior decisions—Bryan v. United States, 338 U.S. 552 (1950); Sapir v. United States, 348 U.S. 373 (1955); Yates v. United States, 354 U.S. 298 (1957); Forman v. United States, 361 U.S. 416 (1960)—which indicated that a defendant who requests a new trial, as did Burks, may be required to stand trial even when his conviction is reversed for failure of proof.]

III

It is unquestionably true that the Court of Appeals' decision "represented a resolution, correct or not, of some or all of the factual elements of the offense charged." United States v. Martin Linen Supply Co., 430 U.S. 564, 571 (1977). By deciding that the Government had failed to come forward with sufficient proof of petitioner's capacity to be responsible for criminal acts, that court was clearly saying that Burks' criminal culpability had not been established. If the District Court had so held in the first instance, as the reviewing court said it should have done, a judgment of acquittal would have been entered and, of course, petitioner could not be retried for the same offense. Consequently * * * it should make no difference that the *reviewing* court, rather than the trial court, determined the evidence to be insufficient. The appellate decision unmistakably meant that the District Court had erred in failing to grant a judgment of acquittal. To hold otherwise would create a purely arbitrary distinction between those in petitioner's position and others who would enjoy the benefit of a correct decision by the District Court.

The Double Jeopardy Clause forbids a second trial for the purpose of affording the prosecution another opportunity to supply evidence which it failed to muster in the first proceeding. This is central to the objective of the prohibition against successive trials. * * *

Nonetheless, as the discussion in Part II, supra, indicates, our past holdings do not appear consistent with what we believe the Double Jeopardy Clause commands. A close reexamination of those precedents, however, persuades us that they have not prop-

erly construed the Clause, and accordingly should no longer be followed.

* * *

[Reconsideration of the prior cases involves an examination of United States v. Ball, 163 U.S. 662 (1896), which permitted a new trial when the accused successfully sought review of a conviction.]

* * *

Ball came before the Court twice, the first occasion being on writ of error from federal convictions for murder. On this initial review, those defendants who had been found guilty obtained a reversal of their convictions due to a fatally defective indictment. On remand after appeal, the trial court dismissed the flawed indictment and proceeded to retry the defendants on a new indictment. They were again convicted and the defendants came once more to this Court, arguing that their second trial was barred because of former jeopardy. The Court rejected this plea in a brief statement * * *. The reversal in *Ball* was therefore based not on insufficiency of evidence but rather on trial error, i.e., failure to dismiss a faulty indictment. Moreover, the cases cited as authority by *Ball* were ones involving trial errors.

We have no doubt that *Ball* was correct in allowing a new trial to rectify *trial error* * * *.

Various rationales have been advanced to support the policy of allowing retrial to correct trial error,[a] but in our view the most reasonable justification is that advanced by [United States v.] *Tateo*,[b] 377 U.S., at 466:

---

a. It has been suggested, for example, that an appeal from a conviction amounts to a "waiver" of double jeopardy protections, or that the appeal somehow continues the jeopardy which attached at the first trial.

b. [Editor's Note: United States v. Tateo, 377 U.S. 463 (1964), held that a defendant

could be retried after pleading guilty in the middle of a trial following a statement by the trial judge as to the sentence he would impose if the defendant were convicted and then setting aside the guilty plea.]

"It would be a high price indeed for society to pay were every accused granted immunity from punishment because of any defect sufficient to constitute reversible error in the proceedings leading to conviction."

* * * In short, reversal for trial error, as distinguished from evidentiary insufficiency, does not constitute a decision to the effect that the government has failed to prove its case. As such, it implies nothing with respect to the guilt or innocence of the defendant. Rather, it is a determination that a defendant has been convicted through a judicial process which is defective in some fundamental respect, e.g., incorrect receipt or rejection of evidence, incorrect instructions, or prosecutorial misconduct. When this occurs, the accused has a strong interest in obtaining a fair readjudication of his guilt free from error, just as society maintains a valid concern for insuring that the guilty are punished. * * *

The same cannot be said when a defendant's conviction has been overturned due to a failure of proof at trial, in which case the prosecution cannot complain of prejudice, for it has been given one fair opportunity to offer whatever proof it could assemble. Moreover, such an appellate reversal means that the government's case was so lacking that it should not have even been *submitted* to the jury. Since we necessarily afford absolute finality to a jury's *verdict* of acquittal—no matter how erroneous its decision—it is difficult to conceive how society has any greater interest in retrying a defendant when, on review, it is decided as a matter of law that the jury could not properly have returned a verdict of guilty.

The importance of a reversal on grounds of evidentiary insufficiency for purposes of inquiry under the Double Jeopardy Clause is underscored by the fact that a federal court's role in deciding whether a case should be considered by the jury is quite limited. * * * Obviously a federal appellate court * * * must sustain the verdict if there is substantial evidence, viewed in the light most favorable to the Government, to uphold the jury's decision. * * * Given the requirements for entry of a judgment of acquittal, the purposes of the Clause would be negated were we to afford the government an opportunity for the proverbial "second bite at the apple."

In our view it makes no difference that a defendant has sought a new trial as one of his remedies, or even as the sole remedy. It cannot be meaningfully said that a person "waives" his right to a judgment of acquittal by moving for a new trial. * * * Since we hold today that the Double Jeopardy Clause precludes a second trial once the reviewing court has found the evidence legally insufficient, the only "just" remedy available for that court is the direction of a judgment of acquittal. To the extent that our prior decisions suggest that by moving for a new trial, a defendant waives his right to a judgment of acquittal on the basis of evidentiary insufficiency, those cases are overruled.

* * *

[The Court reversed the order of the court of appeals remanding to determine whether a new trial should be ordered. It concluded that a new trial would violate the Double Jeopardy Clause.]

Mr. Justice Blackmun took no part in the consideration or decision of this case.

B. INSUFFICIENT EVIDENCE AND TRIAL COURT ERROR

Clarifying the Appellate Court's Reason for Reversal: Greene v. Massey

In Greene v. Massey, 437 U.S. 19 (1978), the per curiam opinion of the Florida Supreme Court and the concurrence of three judges did not make clear whether the reversal was for insufficiency of the evidence or for trial error. The United States Supreme Court remanded the case for reconsideration consistent with *Burks*, making clear that *Burks* applied to state cases. The Court noted that the concurring state court justices may have thought that once inadmissible hearsay evidence was discounted, there was insufficient evidence to permit the jury to convict.[5]

Erroneously Admitted Evidence: Lockhart v. Nelson

Does *Burks* apply when the evidence actually introduced at trial is sufficient to sustain the convictions, but the legally competent evidence (i.e., excluding from consideration evidence erroneously admitted by the trial court) is insufficient? The Court in Lockhart v. Nelson, 488 U.S. 33 (1988), answered that *Burks* does not apply and that the defendant can be retried after a successful appeal. The prosecutor used Nelson's prior convictions at a sentencing hearing, to prove that Nelson should receive an enhanced sentence as a habitual offender. This was error under state law as to one of the convictions, for which Nelson had been pardoned. On habeas review, the district court found the sentence invalid. The State announced its intention to resentence Nelson as a habitual offender, by using a prior conviction not offered or admitted at the initial sentencing hearing. Nelson interposed a claim of double jeopardy. Chief Justice Rehnquist, writing for the Court, concluded that the *Burks* exception was inapplicable and that Nelson's resentencing would not implicate Double Jeopardy concerns.

> *Burks* was based on the view that an appellate court's reversal for insufficiency of the evidence is in effect a determination that the government's case against the defendant was so lacking that the trial court should have entered a judgment of acquittal, rather than submitting the case to the jury. * * *

> *Burks* was careful to point out that a reversal based solely on evidentiary insufficiency has fundamentally different implications * * * than a reversal based on such ordinary 'trial errors' as the 'incorrect receipt or rejection of evidence.' While the former is in effect a finding 'that the government has failed to prove its case' against the defendant, the latter 'implies nothing with respect to the guilt or innocence of the defendant,' but is simply 'a determination that [he] has been convicted through a judicial *process* which is defective in some fundamental respect.'

> It appears to us to be beyond dispute that this is a situation described in *Burks* as reversal for 'trial error' * * *. The basis for the *Burks* exception to the general rule is that a reversal for insufficiency of the evidence should be

---

5. For a case applying the *Burks* rule, see United States v. Londono–Villa, 930 F.2d 994 (2d Cir.1991)(evidence insufficient to find that defendant knew or intended that cocaine would be imported into the United States, thus indictment dismissed).

treated no differently than a trial court's granting a judgment of acquittal at the close of all the evidence. A trial court in passing on such a motion considers all the evidence it has admitted, and to make the analogy complete it must be this same quantum of evidence which is considered by the reviewing court. * * *

Justice Marshall, joined by Justices Brennan and Blackmun, dissented. Justice Marshall argued that if the State had produced a "blank piece of paper" at the sentencing hearing "no one would doubt that Arkansas had produced insufficient evidence and that the Double Jeopardy Clause barred retrial." He concluded that "there is no constitutionally significant difference between that hypothetical and this case."

How did the Court know that the State would have introduced another prior conviction if the judge had properly excluded the inadmissible conviction at Nelson's sentencing hearing? If the State is prepared to introduce the admissible conviction on resentencing, why didn't the State introduce that conviction the first time around? Consider the explanation in State v. Boone, 284 Md. 1, 393 A.2d 1361 (1978):

> The prosecution, we believe, in proving its case is entitled to rely upon the correctness of the rulings of the court and proceed accordingly. If the evidence offered by the State is received after challenge and is legally sufficient to establish the guilt of the accused, the State is not obligated to go further and adduce additional evidence that would be, for example, cumulative. Were it otherwise, the State, to be secure, would have to consider every ruling by the court on the evidence to be erroneous and marshal and offer every bit of relevant and competent evidence. The practical consequences of this would seriously affect the orderly administration of justice, if for no other reason, because of the time which would be required to prepare for trial and try the case. Furthermore, if retrial were precluded because discounting erroneously admitted evidence results in evidentiary insufficiency, there would be no opportunity to correct an error by the court as distinguished from the mistaken belief by the prosecution that it had proved its case.

Do you agree? Should the government, in order to get a new trial, at least have to show that it had additional evidence that it did not offer at the first trial? Is *Nelson* consistent with *Burks'* focus on whether a rational jury should have acquitted?

Charged With the Wrong Crime: Montana v. Hall

In Montana v. Hall, 481 U.S. 400 (1987), the Supreme Court summarily reversed a state supreme court decision that a defendant whose conviction was overturned could not be retried on another charge. Hall was originally charged with sexual assault of the daughter of his ex-wife. He successfully moved to dismiss the charge, persuading the trial court that he could only be prosecuted for incest. After his conviction for incest, he persuaded the state supreme court that the incest statute did not apply on the facts of the case because the statute had not been in effect on the date of the charged criminal act. That court concluded that Hall could not be retried on the original charge because sexual assault and incest were the same offense, so that a retrial after a conviction for committing a nonexistent crime (incest under these circumstances) would violate double jeopardy. The Supreme Court disagreed, finding no constitutional bar to Hall's reprosecution for sexual assault, because a reversal of a conviction on grounds other than insufficiency of the evidence such as, in this case, a "defect in the charging instrument," does not bar a retrial. Justice Marshall dissented from the summary handling of the case, and Justice Stevens filed a separate dissent suggesting that the state supreme court may have rested its decision on state law. See also United States v. Dalton, 990 F.2d 1166 (10th Cir.1993)(new trial permitted where defendant's conviction was reversed because the statute under which he was charged had been implicitly repealed; reversal was due to a "defect in the charging instrument," not insufficiency of evidence).

Reversal of Convictions Rendered Against the Weight of the Evidence: Tibbs v. Florida

When *Scott, Burks,* and *Hall* are put together, they establish that the defendant has a right to one conclusive disposition of the merits of a case. But the government also may get an opportunity to challenge rulings that prevent it from obtaining a decision on the guilt or innocence of the defendant.

Hudson v. Louisiana, 450 U.S. 40 (1981), held that *Burks* was violated when a second trial was held after the trial judge at the first trial granted a motion for a new trial on the ground that the evidence was insufficient to support the jury's guilty verdict. The basis for the trial judge's ruling was insufficiency of the evidence, and under *Burks,* that ruling terminates the proceedings. But in Tibbs v. Florida, 457 U.S. 31 (1982), the Supreme Court held 5–4 that a defendant could be retried after an appellate court overturned an initial conviction on the ground that it was *against the weight* of the evidence. Writing for the majority, Justice O'Connor reasoned that "[a] reversal based on the weight of the evidence * * * can occur only after the State both has presented sufficient evidence to support conviction and has persuaded the jury to convict. The reversal simply affords the defendant a second opportunity to seek a favorable judgment." That is, there is a distinction for reversal based on insufficiency of the evidence and reversals based on a finding that the guilty verdict was against the weight of the evidence—under applicable legal standards, the prosecution's case is stronger in the latter instance, indeed it is legally sufficient to support a conviction. Thus, Justice O'Connor's opinion distinguished cases in which reviewing courts find that a defendant is entitled to a not guilty verdict as a matter of law from those in which the defendant is convicted on the basis of sufficient evidence but is given a second chance nonetheless.

Justice White's dissent in *Tibbs,* joined by Justices Brennan, Marshall, and Blackmun, argued that whether a reversal is based on insufficiency or weight of the evidence, a retrial gives the prosecution a second chance to do what it was unable to do in the first trial—i.e., put on stronger evidence. The dissenters suggested that appellate judges might use weight-of-the-evidence reasoning to permit retrial where it ought to be prohibited under *Burks*. In response, the majority observed that "trial and appellate judges commonly distinguish between the weight and the sufficiency of the evidence. We have no reason to believe that today's decision will erode the demonstrated ability of judges to distinguish legally insufficient evidence from evidence that rationally supports a verdict."

Insufficiency or Weight?

Despite the optimism expressed by the majority in *Tibbs,* it has not always been easy to determine whether a dismissal is based on insufficiency rather than weight. Thus, in Freer v. Dugger, 935 F.2d 213 (11th Cir.1991), the defendant was found guilty. After the verdict, he moved for a judgment of acquittal. The trial judge remarked that no evidence placed the defendant at the scene at the time of the crime, and that witnesses had in fact testified that he was not there. Evidence that the defendant's palm print was found at the scene was discounted by the fact that he had been there earlier. The judge ruled that he was "going to set aside the verdict;" in response to the government's request, the judge stated that he would grant its motion for a new trial, "because I'm not satisfied the evidence proves guilt beyond a reasonable doubt." The defendant was convicted on retrial, but the court of appeals relied on *Burks* and *Hudson* and held that the second trial violated the defendant's double jeopardy rights. The court stated that the question is whether "the substance of the court's judgment was an acquittal, even though, in form, the court granted a new trial." It noted that the trial judge's comments and rulings were made in response to a motion for acquittal, and that the judge apparently felt that the state had failed to prove identity beyond a reasonable doubt. Therefore, only the form, and not the substance of the trial court's ruling changed when the judge attempted to modify the effect of his ruling by granting a new trial rather than entering a judgment of acquittal.

The court noted that it was irrelevant whether, in fact, the evidence was sufficient to sustain a conviction. The question is whether the trial court, correctly or not, found the evidence to be insufficient. If so, there was a functional acquittal, which is final for purposes of the Double Jeopardy Clause— and having made that ruling, the trial judge had no authority to grant a new trial. But if the trial judge's ruling was an acquittal, why did the judge grant the government's motion for a new trial? Was the judge simply confused about the meaning of double jeopardy, like most everyone else? Shouldn't we presume that the judge knew double jeopardy law and that by granting a new trial, he was really saying that he found the evidence sufficient to convict?

Recap of Dismissals, Reversals and Double Jeopardy

A jury decision that the defendant is not guilty cannot be set aside by any judge, nor can a trial judge's decision in a bench trial that the defendant is not guilty be set aside by a higher court. However, once a judge or jury finds the defendant guilty and thereafter the trial judge attempts to eradicate the verdict on some legal ground, review is possible at the request of the government.

If a judgment of guilty is challenged by the defendant and the appellate court holds that no reasonable trier of fact could have convicted, then the appellate court will reverse the conviction and bar a new trial because the defendant is deemed as a matter of law to be proved not guilty. If the defendant's conviction is reversed because of a trial error not amounting to a misestimation of the sufficiency of the evidence, the government can try again because neither it nor the defendant has had a final judgment on the merits.

The *Ball* case, discussed in *Burks,* indicates that a defendant who is convicted and who successfully appeals may be tried again. One difference between *Ball* and *Scott* is that the trier of fact never reached the merits in the latter case. Hence, it is arguable that the trier of fact may have acquitted, whereas in *Ball* the trier's decision to convict in the first trial actually was made. Arguably, then, the *Scott* trial judge denied the defendant a decision on the merits in the first litigation. But as long as the defendant acquiesced in the judge's approach, the majority saw no bar to retrial. The majority may have been treating the case as if the trial judge had said this to the defendant: "You have moved to dismiss this case. I am inclined to grant your motion, but I don't want to deny the government a chance to litigate the merits in the event that my decision to dismiss on a technical, legal ground is wrong. Thus, I shall give you a choice: I'll dismiss now before the verdict is returned if you want, but if I do this, you must understand that there will be a second trial if I am reversed. Or, I'll let the motion to dismiss remain undecided until after the verdict is in. If you are acquitted, you will be free. If you are convicted, I'll dismiss the case and the government can appeal and seek to have the conviction reinstated without further ado." Is this a fair characterization of the majority's approach in *Scott*? Is this a defensible approach?

C. TRIAL DE NOVO AND CONTINUING JEOPARDY

Two-Tiered System: Justices v. Lydon

The Court distinguished *Burks* in Justices v. Lydon, 466 U.S. 294 (1984). Lydon was arrested after breaking into an automobile in Boston. Under state procedure, Lydon had a right to choose a jury trial or an initial trial to the bench. An acquittal before either a judge or a jury would have been final; but a guilty verdict was final only if rendered by a jury; a defendant who elected a bench trial had an absolute right to a trial de novo if convicted.

Lydon, like most Massachusetts defendants, opted for the bench trial. (Why not?). He was convicted. He then requested a trial de novo to a jury, but he attempted in state court, and then in federal court, to bar the second trial on the ground that there had been insufficient evidence to warrant a conviction in the bench trial. He claimed that *Burks* barred retrial. The Court disagreed.

Justice White wrote for the Court and recognized that *Burks* prohibited a second trial after a court found that a conviction was based on insufficient evidence. However, under the Massachusetts system, no such determination had been made. The policies underlying *Burks* did not apply, he said, because this was not a case in which the prosecution had an incentive to offer a weak case first, in order to discover the defendant's evidence and theories, since an acquittal would be a final victory for the defendant; and the prosecutor received no education as to how to present a better case from reviewing judges, since there had been no review. Justice White explained that the two-tiered option granted to a defendant offered benefits not generally available in a single-tiered system. He noted that if the defendant were convicted on insufficient evidence at the trial de novo, *Burks* would apply at that point.

Event Necessary to Terminate Jeopardy:
Richardson v. United States

Justice Rehnquist relied on the Court's reasoning in *Lydon* in his majority opinion in Richardson v. United States, 468 U.S. 317 (1984). The Court held that a defendant was not placed in jeopardy twice when a mistrial was declared due to a genuine jury deadlock, Richardson's motion for judgment of acquittal was denied and the trial judge scheduled a second trial. The Court held that neither a hung jury nor a subsequent order granting a mistrial was the type of event that terminated the original jeopardy that attached when the jury was sworn. Since the defendant had never been acquitted, he had no valid double jeopardy claim that a second trial was barred because of the failure to introduce legally sufficient evidence to go to the jury, regardless of the actual sufficiency of evidence at first trial.

As it had in *Lydon,* the Court read *Burks* as holding only that "once a defendant obtained an unreversed * * * ruling that the Government had failed to introduce sufficient evidence to convict him at trial, a second trial was barred by the Double Jeopardy Clause." Examining Richardson's claim, the Court said that "[w]here, as here, there has been only a mistrial resulting from a hung jury, *Burks* simply does not require that an appellate court rule on the sufficiency of the evidence because retrial might be barred by the Double Jeopardy Clause." The Court found that the declaration of a mistrial was not the equivalent of an acquittal, it did not terminate jeopardy, and that "[r]egardless of the sufficiency of the evidence at petitioner's first trial, he has no valid double jeopardy claim to prevent his retrial." Justice Brennan, joined by Justice Marshall, dissented. He agreed with the majority that a new trial is not barred simply because a jury could not reach a verdict, but urged that "[w]hen the prosecution has failed to present constitutionally sufficient evidence, it cannot complain of unfairness in being denied a second chance, and the interests in finality, shared by the defendant and society, strongly outweigh the reasons for a retrial." See also see United States v. Trigg, 988 F.2d 1008 (9th Cir.1993)(jeopardy continues where district court replaced jurors prior to trial: this was "but a temporary delay on the way to final judgment").

For a critical view of *Richardson*, see Thomas and Pollack, Rethinking Guilt, Juries, and Jeopardy, 91 Mich.L.Rev.1 (1992). The authors argue that if the jury is deadlocked in favor of the defendant by a vote of at least 9–3, the deadlock should be treated as an acquittal for double jeopardy purposes, and that *Richardson* should not stand in the way. The authors choose the 9–3 number because that is the constitutional minimum for a conviction, under the cases discussed in Chapter Ten.

IV. MULTIPLE PROSECUTIONS OF CONVICTED DEFENDANTS

A. THE SAME OFFENSE

Double jeopardy bars not only the retrial of a defendant who is acquitted; it also bars the reprosecution of a defendant who is convicted.[6] Here the policies are obvious. Of course, the defendant may be forced to defend, but not repeti-

---

6. Two Supreme Court cases consider the application of the Double Jeopardy Clause to juvenile proceedings. In Breed v. Jones, 421 U.S. 519 (1975), the defendant committed an

tively. Once the government gets the conviction it originally sought, further proceedings might well be vexatious, and they will certainly subject to the defendant to the inconvenience, anxiety and expense of having to defend again. Thus, there is no doubt that after a valid conviction, the same offense cannot be prosecuted again. But what constitutes the same offense?

Lesser Included Offenses: Brown v. Ohio and the Blockburger Test

In Brown v. Ohio, 432 U.S. 161 (1977), the defendant stole a car in East Cleveland, Ohio. Nine days later, he was arrested in another city and charged with joyriding. He pled guilty and served his sentence. After his release, he was returned to East Cleveland and charged with auto theft and joyriding. He pled guilty to auto theft, but reserved his double jeopardy claim for a motion to withdraw his plea. The court overruled his double jeopardy objection and sentenced him. The Supreme Court concluded that the conviction violated the Double Jeopardy Clause, because joyriding is a lesser included offense of auto theft under Ohio law. Adhering to the test of different offenses established in Blockburger v. United States, 284 U.S. 299 (1932), for the purpose of determining whether it is permissible to cumulate punishment, the Court asked whether each statutory provision contains an element which the other does not. The Court noted that "[w]here the judge is forbidden to impose cumulative punishment for two crimes at the end of a single proceeding, the prosecutor is forbidden to strive for the same result in successive proceedings." Because the Ohio statute defined auto theft as joyriding with the intent to permanently deprive the owner of possession, the only difference in proof between the two crimes was the intent. (i.e., only one crime—auto theft—required something that the other—joy riding—did not). The government argued that Brown could be tried twice because the second charge covered a different *part* of the joy ride than that considered in the first trial. But the Court disagreed. The nine-day joyride could not be divided into a series of temporal or spatial units, because Ohio law did not create separate offenses for each day someone was joyriding. Justices Blackmun, Burger, and Rehnquist argued in dissent that Brown committed a separate offense when he operated the car nine days after stealing it.

It is important under *Blockburger* that *each* statutory crime must require an element that the other does not for there to be separate offenses. In Illinois v. Vitale, 447 U.S. 410 (1980), the Court cited the *Blockburger* test as the appropriate one to use in judging whether a driver of an automobile that struck and killed two children could be prosecuted for involuntary manslaughter following his conviction for failing to reduce speed to avoid the collision. The

armed robbery and was adjudicated a delinquent in juvenile court. At a subsequent disposition hearing, the judge found him unfit for treatment as a juvenile and ordered him to be prosecuted as an adult. His trial and conviction as an adult violated the Double Jeopardy Clause, because he was subjected to the burden of two trials. The judge could and should have transferred the defendant to adult court before holding the factfinding adjudicatory hearing.

In Swisher v. Brady, 438 U.S. 204 (1978), the Court found that allowing the state to file exceptions to proposed nondelinquency findings made by juvenile court masters does not violate the prohibition against double jeopardy. The nature of the proceeding was crucial. Pursuant to a Maryland rule of procedure, a master makes preliminary findings and proposals at a hearing. The judge, who makes the final adjudication, retains the power to accept, reject, or modify the master's proposals, to remand for further hearings, and to supplement the record in some circumstances.

Court remanded the case for further development of state law, observing that "if manslaughter by automobile does not always entail proof of a failure to slow, then the two offenses are not the 'same' under the *Blockburger* test," but cautioning also that if the state would "find it necessary to prove a failure to slow or to rely on conduct necessarily involving such failure" Vitale's double jeopardy claim "would be substantial." Four dissenters argued that no further proceedings were appropriate.

The Grady v. Corbin "Same Conduct" Test

The Court held that the *Blockburger* test of "same offense" was not sufficient to protect double jeopardy rights in Grady v. Corbin, 495 U.S. 508 (1990)—though the holding proved to be short-lived, as demonstrated in *Dixon*, infra. Justice Brennan, writing for a five-Justice majority in *Grady*, stated that "the Double Jeopardy Clause bars a subsequent prosecution if, to establish an essential element of an offense charged in that prosecution, the government will prove conduct that constitutes an offense for which the defendant has already been prosecuted." The case involved Corbin, who was at fault in a car accident resulting in fatal injuries, and was also intoxicated. He was served with traffic tickets charging him with the misdemeanor of driving while intoxicated and with failing to keep right of the median in violation of § 1120(a). He pleaded guilty to the two traffic tickets, with the presiding judge being unaware of the fatality stemming from the accident. He was sentenced to a $350 fine, a $10 surcharge, and a 6–month license revocation. Thereafter he was indicted for reckless manslaughter, second-degree vehicular manslaughter, and criminally negligent homicide, third-degree reckless assault, and driving while intoxicated.

Justice Brennan held that a trial on manslaughter and homicide charges was barred by the Double Jeopardy Clause, if the government sought to prove the crimes through evidence of drunk driving or failure to keep to the right of the median. He recognized that the prosecution for these crimes would not be barred under the *Blockburger* test, because each of the minor crimes to which Corbin pled guilty contained elements that the more serious crimes did not, and vice versa. (For example, reckless manslaughter does not include an element of driving, or driving while intoxicated, and driving while intoxicated does not contain an element of reckless disregard for human life). Justice Brennan reasoned, however, that the *Blockburger* test was insufficient to protect against the risk of multiple prosecutions:

> If *Blockburger* constituted the entire double jeopardy inquiry in the context of successive prosecutions, the State could try Corbin in four consecutive trials: for failure to keep right of the median, for driving while intoxicated, for assault, and for homicide. The State could improve its presentation of proof with each trial, assessing which witnesses gave the most persuasive testimony, which documents had the greatest impact, which opening and closing arguments most persuaded the jurors. Corbin would be forced either to contest each of these trials or to plead guilty to avoid the harassment and expense.

Justice Brennan applied the "same conduct" test to Corbin's situation, and held that prosecution on the serious charges was barred, because the state had admitted that it would use the conduct for which he was convicted (i.e., driving carelessly and while drunk) to prove the more serious charges.

Justice O'Connor wrote a dissent. Justice Scalia also wrote a dissent, in which Chief Justice Rehnquist and Justice Kennedy joined. Justice Scalia "would adhere to the *Blockburger* rule that successive prosecutions under two different statutes do not constitute double jeopardy if each statutory crime contains an element that the other does not, regardless of the overlap between the proof required for each prosecution in the particular case." He argued that the "same conduct" test was an impermissible expansion from the common-law jurisprudence that spawned the Double Jeopardy Clause, and that it was inconsistent with precedent, which had relied solely on the *Blockburger* test.

Return to the Blockburger Test

The expansive *Grady* test was not the law for long.[7] Only three years later, the Court, in the following case, overruled *Grady* and returned to the *Blockburger* test as the sole benchmark for determining the permissibility of successive prosecutions. However, the case indicates that there is dispute among the Justices as to how to apply *Blockburger*.

UNITED STATES v. DIXON

Supreme Court of the United States, 1993.
509 U.S. 688.

JUSTICE SCALIA **announced the judgment of the Court and delivered the opinion of the Court with respect to Parts I, II, and IV, and an opinion with respect to Parts III and V, in which** JUSTICE KENNEDY **joins.**

In both of these cases, respondents were tried for criminal contempt of court for violating court orders that prohibited them from engaging in conduct that was later the subject of a criminal prosecution. We consider whether the subsequent criminal prosecutions are barred by the Double Jeopardy Clause.

I

Respondent Alvin Dixon was arrested for second-degree murder and was

released on bond. * * * Dixon's release form specified that he was not to commit "any criminal offense," and warned that any violation of the conditions of release would subject him "to revocation of release, an order of detention, and prosecution for contempt of court."

While awaiting trial, Dixon was arrested and indicted for possession of cocaine with intent to distribute. The court issued an order requiring Dixon to show cause why he should not be held in contempt or have the terms of his pretrial release modified. At the show-cause hearing, four police officers testified to facts surrounding the alleged drug offense; Dixon's counsel

---

[7.] In United States v. Felix, 503 U.S. 378 (1992), the defendant was prosecuted for conspiracy, manufacture and possession with intent to distribute narcotics. Of the nine overt acts supporting the conspiracy charge against Felix, two were based on conduct for which he had been previously prosecuted. Chief Justice Rehnquist, waiting for the majority, declared that the Court in *Grady* had not disturbed the time-honored rule that "a substantive crime, and a conspiracy to commit that crime, are not

the 'same offense' for double jeopardy purposes." The Chief Justice concluded that the essence of a conspiracy offense "is in the agreement or confederation to commit a crime" and that "the agreement to do the act is distinct from the act itself."

See also Garrett v. United States, 471 U.S. 773 (1985)(defendant can be successively prosecuted for criminal enterprise and predicate acts).

cross-examined these witnesses and introduced other evidence. The court concluded that the Government had established " 'beyond a reasonable doubt that [Dixon] was in possession of drugs and that those drugs were possessed with the intent to distribute.' " The court therefore found Dixon guilty of criminal contempt under D.C.Code Ann. § 23–1329(c) * * *. Dixon was sentenced to 180 days in jail. He later moved to dismiss the cocaine indictment on double jeopardy grounds; the trial court granted the motion.

Respondent Michael Foster's route to this Court is similar. Based on Foster's alleged physical attacks upon her in the past, Foster's estranged wife Ana obtained a civil protection order (CPO) in Superior Court of the District of Columbia. See D.C.Code Ann. § 16–1005(c)(1989)(CPO may be issued upon a showing of good cause to believe that the subject "has committed or is threatening an intrafamily offense"). The order, to which Foster consented, required that he not " 'molest, assault, or in any manner threaten or physically abuse' " Ana Foster * * *.

Over the course of eight months, Ana Foster filed three separate motions to have her husband held in contempt for numerous violations of the CPO. Of the 16 alleged episodes, the only charges relevant here are three separate instances of threats (on November 12, 1987, and March 26 and May 17, 1988) and two assaults (on November 6, 1987, and May 21, 1988), in the most serious of which Foster "threw [his wife] down basement stairs, kicking her body[,] * * * pushed her head into the floor causing head injuries, [and Ana Foster] lost consciousness."

After issuing a notice of hearing and ordering Foster to appear, the court held a 3–day bench trial. Counsel for Ana Foster * * * prosecuted the action; the United States was not represented at trial, although the United States Attorney was apparently aware of the action, as was the court aware of a separate grand jury proceeding on some of the alleged criminal conduct. As to the assault charges, the court stated that Ana Foster would have "to prove as an element, first that there was a Civil Protection Order, and then [that] . . . the assault as defined by the criminal code, in fact occurred." At the close of the plaintiffs' case, the court granted Foster's motion for acquittal on various counts, including the alleged threats on November 12 and May 17. Foster then took the stand and generally denied the allegations. The court found Foster guilty beyond a reasonable doubt of four counts of criminal contempt including the November 6, 1987 and May 21, 1988 assaults, but acquitted him on other counts, including the March 26 alleged threats. He was sentenced to an aggregate 600 days' imprisonment.

The United States Attorney's Office later obtained an indictment charging Foster with simple assault on or about November 6, 1987 (Count I, violation of § 22–504); threatening to injure another on or about November 12, 1987, and March 26 and May 17, 1988 (Counts II–IV, violation of § 22–2307); and assault with intent to kill on or about May 21, 1988 (Count V, violation of § 22–501). Ana Foster was the complainant in all counts; the first and last counts were based on the events for which Foster had been held in contempt, and the other three were based on the alleged events for which Foster was acquitted of contempt. Like Dixon, Foster filed a motion to dismiss, claiming a double jeopardy bar to all counts, and also collateral estoppel as to Counts II–IV. The trial court denied the double-jeopardy claim and did not rule on the collateral-estoppel assertion.

The Government appealed the double jeopardy ruling in *Dixon*, and Foster appealed the trial court's denial of his motion. The District of Columbia Court of Appeals * * * relying on our recent decision in Grady v. Corbin, ruled that both subsequent prosecutions were barred by the Double Jeopardy Clause. In its petition for certiorari, the Government presented the sole question "[w]hether the Double Jeopardy Clause bars prosecution of a defendant on substantive criminal charges based upon the same conduct for which he previously has been held in criminal contempt of court."

II

The Double Jeopardy Clause * * * provides that no person shall "be subject for the same offence to be twice put in jeopardy of life or limb." This protection applies both to successive punishments and to successive prosecutions for the same criminal offense. It is well established that criminal contempt, at least the sort enforced through nonsummary proceedings, is "a crime in the ordinary sense."

* * *

In both the multiple punishment and multiple prosecution contexts, this Court has concluded that where the two offenses for which the defendant is punished or tried cannot survive the "same-elements" test, the double jeopardy bar applies. See, e.g., Blockburger v. United States (multiple punishment); Gavieres v. United States, 220 U.S. 338, 342 (1911)(successive prosecutions). The same-elements test, sometimes referred to as the *"Blockburger"* test, inquires whether each offense contains an element not contained in the

other; if not, they are the "same offence" and double jeopardy bars additional punishment and successive prosecution. * * *

We recently held in *Grady* that in addition to passing the *Blockburger* test, a subsequent prosecution must satisfy a "same-conduct" test to avoid the double jeopardy bar. The *Grady* test provides that, "if, to establish an essential element of an offense charged in that prosecution, the government will prove conduct that constitutes an offense for which the defendant has already been prosecuted," a second prosecution may not be had.

III

A

The first question before us today is whether *Blockburger* analysis permits subsequent prosecution in [the] criminal contempt context, where judicial order has prohibited criminal act. If it does, we must then proceed to consider whether *Grady* also permits it.

We begin with *Dixon*. The statute applicable in Dixon's contempt prosecution provides that "[a] person who has been conditionally released . . . and who has violated a condition of release shall be subject to . . . prosecution for contempt of court." § 23–1329(a). * * *

In this situation, in which the contempt sanction is imposed for violating the order through commission of the incorporated drug offense, the later attempt to prosecute Dixon for the drug offense resembles the situation that produced our judgment of double jeopardy in Harris v. Oklahoma, 433 U.S. 682 (1977)(*per curiam*). There we held that a subsequent prosecution for robbery with a firearm was barred by the Double Jeopardy Clause, because the defendant had already been tried for felony-murder based on the same underlying felony. We have described our terse *per curiam* in *Harris* as standing for the proposition that, for double jeopardy purposes, "the crime generally described as felony murder" is not "a separate offense distinct from its various elements." Illinois v. Vitale, 447 U.S. 410, 420–421 (1980). So too here, the "crime" of violating a condition of release cannot be abstracted from the "element" of the violated condition. The *Dixon* court order incorporated the entire governing criminal code in the same manner as the *Harris* felony-murder statute incorporated the several enumerated felonies. Here, as in *Harris*, the underlying substantive criminal offense is "a species of lesser-included offense."

Dixon's drug offense did not include elements not contained in previous contempt offense · *violates Double jeopardy*

* * * Because Dixon's drug offense did not include any element not contained in his previous contempt offense, his subsequent prosecution violates the Double Jeopardy Clause. The foregoing analysis obviously applies as well to Count I of the indictment against Foster, charging assault in violation of § 22–504, based on the same event that was the subject of his prior contempt conviction for violating the provision of the CPO forbidding him to commit simple assault under § 22–504. The subsequent prosecution for assault fails the *Blockburger* test, and is barred.

Foster too · *both fail blockberg*

B

The remaining four counts in *Foster*, assault with intent to kill (Count V; § 22–501) and threats to injure or kidnap (Counts II–IV; § 22–2307), are not barred under *Blockburger*. As to Count V: Foster's conduct on May 21, 1988 was found to violate the Family Division's order that he not "molest, assault, or in any manner threaten or physically abuse" his wife. At the contempt hearing, the court stated that Ana Foster's attorney, who prosecuted the contempt, would have to prove

first, knowledge of a CPO, and second, a willful violation of one of its conditions, here simple assault as defined by the criminal code. On the basis of the same episode, Foster was then indicted for violation of § 22–501, which proscribes assault with intent to kill. Under governing law, that offense requires proof of specific intent to kill; simple assault does not. Similarly, the contempt offense required proof of knowledge of the CPO, which assault with intent to kill does not. Applying the *Blockburger* elements test, the result is clear: These crimes were different offenses and the subsequent prosecution did not violate the Double Jeopardy Clause.

Some of Foster's crimes are not same elements thus do not violate double jeopardy

Counts II, III, and IV of Foster's indictment are likewise not barred. These charged Foster under § 22–2307 (forbidding anyone to "threate[n] * * * to kidnap any person or to injure the person of another or physically damage the property of any person") for his alleged threats on three separate dates. Foster's contempt prosecution included charges that, on the same dates, he violated the CPO provision ordering that he not "in any manner threaten" Ana Foster. Conviction of the contempt required willful violation of the CPO—which conviction under § 22–2307 did not; and conviction under § 22–2307 required that the threat be a threat to kidnap, to inflict bodily injury, or to damage property—which conviction of the contempt (for violating the CPO provision that Foster not "in any manner threaten") did not. Each offense therefore contained a separate element, and the *Blockburger* test for double jeopardy was not met.

IV

Having found that at least some of the counts at issue here are not barred by the *Blockburger* test, we must consider whether they are barred by the new, additional double jeopardy test we announced three Terms ago in Grady v. Corbin. They undoubtedly are, since *Grady* prohibits "a subsequent prosecution if, to establish an essential element of an offense charged in that prosecution [here, assault as an element of assault with intent to kill, or threatening as an element of threatening bodily injury], the government will prove conduct that constitutes an offense for which the defendant has already been prosecuted [here, the assault and the threatening, which conduct constituted the offense of violating the CPO]."

We have concluded, however, that *Grady* must be overruled. Unlike *Blockburger* analysis, whose definition of what prevents two crimes from being the "same offence," U.S. Const., Amdt. 5, has deep historical roots and has been accepted in numerous precedents of this Court, *Grady* lacks constitutional roots. The "same-conduct" rule it announced is wholly inconsistent with earlier Supreme Court precedent and with the clear common-law understanding of double jeopardy. See, e.g., Gavieres v. United States, 220 U.S., at 345 (in subsequent prosecution, "[w]hile it is true that the conduct of the accused was one and the same, two offenses resulted, each of which had an element not embraced in the other"). We need not discuss the many proofs of these statements, which were set forth at length in the

Grady dissent. See 495 U.S., at 526 (Scalia, J., dissenting). * * *

* * *

* * * *Grady* * * * has already proved unstable in application. Less than two years after it came down, in United States v. Felix, we were forced to recognize a large exception to it. There we concluded that a subsequent prosecution for conspiracy to manufacture, possess, and distribute methamphetamine was not barred by a previous conviction for attempt to manufacture the same substance. We offered as a justification for avoiding a "literal" (i.e., faithful) reading of *Grady* "longstanding authority" to the effect that prosecution for conspiracy is not precluded by prior prosecution for the substantive offense. Of course the very existence of such a large and longstanding "exception" to the *Grady* rule gave cause for concern that the rule was not an accurate expression of the law. * * *

A hypothetical based on the facts in *Harris* reinforces the conclusion that *Grady* is a continuing source of confusion and must be overruled. Suppose the State first tries the defendant for felony-murder, based on robbery, and then indicts the defendant for robbery with a firearm in the same incident. Absent *Grady,* our cases provide a clear answer to the double-jeopardy claim in this situation. Under *Blockburger,* the second prosecution is not barred—as it clearly was not barred at common law * * *.[a]

---

a. * * * Justice Souter's concern that prosecutors will bring separate prosecutions in order to perfect their case seems unjustified. They have little to gain and much to lose from such a strategy. Under Ashe v. Swenson, 397 U.S. 436 (1970), an acquittal in the first prosecution might well bar litigation of certain facts essential to the second one—though a conviction in the first prosecution would not excuse the Government from proving the same facts the second time. Surely, moreover, the Government must be deterred from abusive, repeated

prosecutions of a single offender for similar offenses by the sheer press of other demands upon prosecutorial and judicial resources. Finally, even if Justice Souter's fear were well founded, no double-jeopardy bar short of a same-transaction analysis will eliminate this problem; but that interpretation of the Double Jeopardy Clause has been soundly rejected, and would require overruling numerous precedents, the latest of which is barely a year old * * *.

Having encountered today yet another situation in which the pre-*Grady* understanding of the Double Jeopardy Clause allows a second trial, though the "same-conduct" test would not, we think it time to acknowledge what is now, three years after *Grady,* compellingly clear: the case was a mistake. We do not lightly reconsider a precedent, but, because *Grady* contradicted an "unbroken line of decisions," contained "less than accurate" historical analysis, and has produced "confusion,"[b] we do so here. Although stare decisis is the "preferred course" in constitutional adjudication, "when governing decisions are unworkable or are badly reasoned, this Court has never felt constrained to follow precedent." We would mock stare decisis and only add chaos to our double jeopardy jurisprudence by pretending that *Grady* survives when it does not.

V

Dixon's subsequent prosecution, as well as Count I of Foster's subsequent prosecution, violate the Double Jeopardy Clause.[c] For the reasons set forth in Part IV, the other Counts of Foster's subsequent prosecution do not violate the Double Jeopardy Clause.[d] * * *

CHIEF JUSTICE REHNQUIST, with whom JUSTICE O'CONNOR and JUSTICE THOMAS join, concurring in part and dissenting in part.

The Court today concludes that the Double Jeopardy Clause prohibits the subsequent prosecutions of Foster for assault and Dixon for possession with intent to distribute cocaine, but does not prohibit the subsequent prosecutions of Foster for threatening to injure another or for assault with intent to kill. After finding that at least some of the charges here are not prohibited by the "same-elements" test set out in *Blockburger,* the Court goes on to consider whether there is a double-jeopardy bar under the "same-conduct" test set out in *Grady,* and determines that there is. However, because the same-conduct test is inconsistent with the text and history of the Double Jeopardy Clause, was a departure from our earlier precedents, and has proven difficult to apply, the Court concludes that *Grady* must be overruled. I do not join Part III of Justice Scalia's opinion because I think that none of the criminal prosecutions in this case were barred under *Blockburger.* I must then confront the expanded version of double jeopardy embodied in *Grady.* For the reasons set forth in the *Grady* dissent, and in Part IV of the Court's opinion, I, too, think that *Grady* must be overruled. I therefore join Parts I, II, and IV of the Court's opinion, and write separately to express my disagreement with Justice Scalia's application of *Blockburger* in Part III.

In my view, *Blockburger*'s same-elements test requires us to focus not on the terms of the particular court orders involved, but on the elements of contempt of court in the ordinary sense. Relying on *Harris,* a three-paragraph *per curiam* in an unargued case, Justice Scalia concludes otherwise today, and thus incorrectly finds in Part III–A of his opinion that the subsequent prosecutions of Dixon for drug distribution and of Foster for assault violated the Double Jeopardy Clause.

---

b. See, e.g., Sharpton v. Turner, 964 F.2d 1284, 1287 (CA2)(*Grady* formulation "has proven difficult to apply" and "whatever difficulties we have previously encountered in grappling with the *Grady* language have not been eased by" *Felix*); Ladner v. Smith, 941 F.2d 356, 362, 364 (C.A.5 1991)(a divided court adopts a four-part test for application of *Grady*

and notes that *Grady,* "even if carefully analyzed and painstakingly administered, is not easy to apply"). * * *

c. Justices White, Stevens, and Souter concur in this portion of the judgment.

d. Justice Blackmun concurs only in the judgment with respect to this portion.

* * * Because the generic crime of contempt of court has different elements than the substantive criminal charges in this case, I believe that they are separate offenses under *Blockburger*. I would therefore limit *Harris* to the context in which it arose: where the crimes in question are analogous to greater and lesser included offenses. The crimes at issue here bear no such resemblance.

[In *Blockburger*] we stated that two offenses are different for purposes of double jeopardy if "each *provision* requires proof of a fact which the other does not." Applying this test to the offenses at bar, it is clear that the elements of the governing contempt *provision* are entirely different from the elements of the substantive crimes. Contempt of court comprises two elements: (i) a court order made known to the defendant, followed by (ii) willful violation of that order. Neither of those elements is necessarily satisfied by proof that a defendant has committed the substantive offenses of assault or drug distribution. Likewise, no element of either of those substantive offenses is necessarily satisfied by proof that a defendant has been found guilty of contempt of court.

* * * Justice Scalia * * * concludes that *Harris* somehow requires us to look to the facts that must be proven under the particular court orders in question (rather than under the general law of criminal contempt) in determining whether contempt and the related substantive offenses are the same for double jeopardy purposes. This interpretation of *Harris* is both unprecedented and mistaken.

Our double jeopardy cases applying *Blockburger* have focused on the statutory elements of the offenses charged, not on the facts that must be proven under the particular indictment at issue—an indictment being the closest analogue to the court orders in this

case. By focusing on the facts needed to show a violation of the specific court orders involved in this case, and not on the generic elements of the crime of contempt of court, Justice Scalia's double-jeopardy analysis bears a striking resemblance to that found in *Grady*—not what one would expect in an opinion that overrules *Grady*.

Close inspection of the crimes at issue in *Harris* reveals, moreover, that our decision in that case was not a departure from *Blockburger*'s focus on the *statutory* elements of the offenses charged. In *Harris*, we held that a conviction for felony murder based on a killing in the course of an armed robbery foreclosed a subsequent prosecution for robbery with a firearm. Though the felony-murder statute in *Harris* did not require proof of armed robbery, it did include as an element proof that the defendant was engaged in the commission of *some* felony. We construed this generic reference to some felony as incorporating the statutory elements of the various felonies upon which a felony-murder conviction could rest. The criminal contempt provision involved here, by contrast, contains no such generic reference which by definition incorporates the statutory elements of assault or drug distribution.

* * *

The following analogy * * * helps illustrate the absurd results that Justice Scalia's *Harris/Blockburger* analysis could in theory produce. Suppose that the offense in question is failure to comply with a lawful order of a police officer, and that the police officer's order was, "Don't shoot that man." Under Justice Scalia's flawed reading of *Harris*, the elements of the offense of failure to obey a police officer's lawful order would include, for purposes of *Blockburger*'s same-elements test, the elements of, perhaps, murder or manslaughter, in effect converting those felonies into a lesser included offense of the crime of failure to comply with a lawful order of a police officer.

In sum, I think that the substantive criminal prosecutions in this case, which followed convictions for criminal contempt, did not violate the Double Jeopardy Clause, at least before our decision in *Grady*. Under *Grady*, "the Double Jeopardy Clause bars a subsequent prosecution if, to establish an essential element of an offense charged in that prosecution, the government will prove conduct that constitutes an offense for which the defendant has already been prosecuted." As the Court points out, this case undoubtedly falls within that expansive formulation: To secure convictions on the substantive criminal charges in this case, the Government will have to prove conduct that was the basis for the contempt convictions. Forced, then, to confront *Grady*, I join the Court in overruling that decision.

JUSTICE WHITE, with whom JUSTICE STEVENS joins, and with whom JUSTICE SOUTER joins as to Part I, concurring in the judgment in part and dissenting in part.

* * * I concur in the judgment of the Court in Part III–A which holds that Dixon's subsequent prosecution and Count I of Foster's subsequent prosecution were barred. I disagree with Justice Scalia's application of *Blockburger* in Part III–B. From Part IV of the opinion, in which the majority decides to overrule *Grady*, I dissent.

JUSTICE SOUTER, with whom JUSTICE STEVENS joins, concurring in the judgment in part and dissenting in part.

* * *

The Double Jeopardy Clause prevents the government from "mak[ing] repeated attempts to convict an individual for an alleged offense, thereby subjecting him to embarrassment, expense and ordeal and compelling him to live in a continuing state of anxiety and insecurity." The Clause addresses a further concern as well, that the government not be given the opportunity to rehearse its prosecution, "honing its trial strategies and perfecting its evidence through successive attempts at conviction" * * *.

If a separate prosecution were permitted for every offense arising out of the same conduct, the government could manipulate the definitions of offenses, creating fine distinctions among them and permitting a zealous prosecutor to try a person again and again for essentially the same criminal conduct. * * * The limitation on successive prosecution is thus a restriction on the government different in kind from that contained in the limitation on multiple punishments, and the government cannot get around the restriction on repeated prosecution of a single individual merely by precision in the way it defines its statutory offenses. * * *

[Justice Souter reviewed Harris v. Oklahoma and Illinois v. Vitale and concluded that "we clearly understood *Harris* to stand for the proposition that when one has already been tried for a crime comprising certain conduct, a subsequent prosecution seeking to prove the same conduct is barred by the Double Jeopardy Clause."]

[A]ny debate should have been settled by our decision three Terms ago in Grady v. Corbin, 495 U.S. 508 (1990), that "the Double Jeopardy Clause bars a subsequent prosecution if, to establish an essential element of an offense charged in that prosecution, the government will prove con-

[Margin handwritten note: Apply Grady]

duct that constitutes an offense for which the defendant has already been prosecuted." *Grady* did nothing more than apply a version of the [traditional] rule.

* * * Whatever may have been the merits of the debate in *Grady,* the decision deserves more respect than it receives from the Court today. Although adherence to precedent is not rigidly required in constitutional cases, any departure from the doctrine of *stare decisis* demands special justification.

[Margin handwritten note: departure from Stare decisis requires more analysis]

The search for any justification fails to reveal that *Grady*'s conclusion was either "unsound in principle," or "unworkable in practice." *Grady* 's rule is straightforward, and a departure from it is not justified by the fact that two Court of Appeals decisions have described it as difficult to apply * * *. [If *Blockburger* is the only protection against multiple prosecutions, the gov-

ernment] by defining its offenses with care, * * * could not merely add punishment to punishment (within Eighth and Fourteenth Amendment limits), but could bring a person to trial again and again for that same conduct, violating the principle of finality, subjecting him repeatedly to all the burdens of trial, rehearsing its prosecution, and increasing the risk of erroneous conviction, all in contravention of the principles behind the protection from successive prosecution included in the Fifth Amendment. The protection of the Double Jeopardy Clause against successive prosecutions is not so fragile that it can be avoided by finely drafted statutes and carefully planned prosecutions.

* * *

[Justice Blackmun's opinion, concurring in the judgment in part and dissenting in part, is omitted.]

Questions After Dixon

What are the arguments for and against a transactional test of the "same offence"? In civil cases, the plaintiff is required by the doctrine of res judicata to join in one case all claims against a single defendant arising from the same transaction. See Restatement, Second of Judgments, § 24 (1980). Why should we demand any less of a prosecutor?

Dispute About the Blockburger Test

The Justices in *Dixon*, especially Justice Scalia and Chief Justice Rehnquist, are in obvious disagreement about how to apply the *Blockburger* test. In determining the elements of various crimes, do you look at the statute itself (the Rehnquist view) or to the factual allegations in the indictment, at least when the crime covers a wide range of conduct (the Scalia view)? The different approaches are discussed by the court in United States v. Liller, 999 F.2d 61 (2d Cir.1993). Liller was charged with interstate transportation of a stolen firearm, and was acquitted, apparently on the basis of his testimony that he had taken the gun from its owner in order to prevent her from committing suicide. The government then discovered that Liller had been convicted of felonies under a different name. Liller was then charged with being a felon in possession of a firearm—the same firearm that was the subject of the first prosecution. The district court dismissed the indictment, relying on *Grady*; by the time the case reached the Second Circuit, *Dixon* had been decided. The court analyzed the double jeopardy question as follows:

[Margin handwritten note: gun charge acquitted then gov brings felony w/ gun charge]

While the District Court's application of *Grady* to the facts of the pending case would present several interesting questions, the analysis after

Dixon is straightforward. Normally we would apply *Blockburger* by examining the facts required to be proved for conviction under the provisions supporting Liller's prior and pending charges. However, in certain circumstances, including where one of the statutes covers a broad range of conduct, it is appropriate under *Blockburger* to examine the allegations of the indictment rather than only the terms of the statutes. * * * [I]n *Dixon*, at least four Justices, see (Scalia, J., joined by Kennedy, J.), (White, J., joined by Stevens, J.), and perhaps five, see (Souter, J., joined by Stevens, J.), examined the content of the particular Court order violated by the defendants rather than the more general statutory elements of the criminal contempt provision under which they were charged. But see (Rehnquist, C.J., joined by O'Connor, J., and Thomas, J.).

The *Liller* court found that it did not have to decide whether the more narrow "elements" test or the broader "facts in the indictment" test of *Blockburger* was controlling:

> In this case, whether we examine only the statutes or broaden the inquiry to include the facts alleged in the indictments, Liller's offenses are separate. Only the new charge under [the felon-firearm-possession statute] requires proof that the possessor is a felon, and only the old charge under [the interstate transportation of a stolen firearm statute] requires proof that the firearm was stolen and was transported interstate. Thus, each charge requires proof of a fact not required for the other. Therefore, the Double Jeopardy Clause does not bar the Government from prosecuting Liller for possession of a firearm by a felon despite his prior prosecution for transporting the same weapon in interstate commerce knowing it was stolen.

See also United States v. Bennett, 44 F.3d 1364 (8th Cir.1995)("[W]e note that courts are split on whether the test is to be applied by looking solely to the statutory elements of the offense, or by going beyond the statute and looking at the underlying facts or averments in the indictment."—citing cases and noting that there is "disagreement on this issue among members of the Supreme Court").

Chief Justice Rehnquist accuses Justice Scalia of resurrecting *Grady* by employing a "facts of the indictment" approach to the *Blockburger* test. Is this a fair criticism? What is the difference between a "facts of the indictment" approach and the *Grady* "same conduct" test? Should the Court be concerned that a "statutory elements" test might allow the government to charge a defendant with violation of a broad statute in one prosecution, and violations of more narrow statutes in successive prosecutions, even though the conduct at issue is identical in all cases?

Application of Blockburger to Criminal Enterprises: Rutledge v. United States

The Court applied the *Blockburger* test to a case of conspiracy and continuing criminal enterprise in Rutledge v. United States, 517 U.S. 292 (1996). The defendant was convicted of a conspiracy to distribute controlled substances in violation of 21 U.S.C. § 846, and one count of conducting a continuing criminal enterprise (CCE) "in concert" with others in violation of 21 U.S.C. § 848. Rutledge contended that the conspiracy count was a lesser included offense of the CCE count, and that therefore he had been punished twice for the same offense. The Supreme Court agreed. Justice Stevens, writing for a unanimous Court, reasoned that the elements of conspiracy were precisely the same as the "in concert" element of CCE. Thus, proof of the CCE offense requires proof of a conspiracy that would also violate 21 U.S.C. § 846. While the CCE offense required proof of several elements other than conspiracy, (such as the derivation of substantial income), the *Blockburger* test requires that *each* crime contain an element that the other does not. Accordingly, one of the defendant's convictions was unauthorized punishment, and had to be vacated.

Criticism of Blockburger

Amar and Marcus, in Double Jeopardy Law After Rodney King, 95 Colum.L.Rev.1 (1995), criticize the *Blockburger* test as inconsistent with the "same offence" language in the Double Jeopardy Clause. Under *Blockburger*, two offenses, such as robbery and armed robbery, are treated as the "same" offense, even though they plainly are not. The authors propose a due process solution to the "same offence" problem:

> In the end, *Blockburger* ordinarily reaches the right result—but not always. And even where *Blockburger* gets it right, it gives the wrong reason, insisting that day is night and that different offences are really the same.

> To reach the right results for the right reasons, we have proposed three simple rules: (1) the Double Jeopardy Clause means what it says—"same" means "same"; (2) the Due Process Clause generally gives a criminal defendant who prevails on any issue a right to collaterally estop the government from relitigating that issue; (3) the Due Process Clause also counsels that even where two different offences are involved, the government must have good, nonvexatious reasons for prosecuting these offences in two separate trials rather than one.

> Taken together, these three principles explain almost all of what the Court has done under *Blockburger*; but where our rules and *Blockburger* diverge—* * * [in] *Dixon*, for example—our approach is better as a matter of text, logic, and common sense. Our principles also have one happy side effect. By moving some issues out of double jeopardy and into due process, they can help courts craft rules that place special emphasis on protecting innocent defendants. The formal rules of double jeopardy require symmetry between *autrefois acquit* and *autrefois convict*—between those defendants who have been proved innocent, and those proved guilty in (presumptively) fair trials. The more flexible norm of due process need not demand strict symmetry, and may enable judges to craft stronger rules protecting acquitted defendants.

> Although our analytic assault on *Blockburger* might seem idiosyncratic and our fist-pounding insistence that "same" means "same" might look naive, we would invite skeptics to read with care an important but often overlooked 1985 case, Garrett v. United States. [471 U.S. 773]. In *Garrett* the Supreme Court upheld a prosecution for a greater offence—a federal "continuing criminal enterprise" (CCE) charge—after defendant had already been convicted of a predicate, lesser included drug charge. This result plainly violated a strict application of *Blockburger*, but the Court * * * said

in *Garrett*: "Quite obviously the CCE offense is not, in any common-sense or literal meaning of the term, the 'same' offense as one of the [lesser included] predicate offenses."

Though it went virtually unnoticed in *Dixon*, *Garrett* seems inconsistent with that 1993 case in language and result. For those, like Justice Souter, who particularly value precedent, it should be noted that *Garrett* was an opinion of the Court authored by now Chief Justice Rehnquist, whereas in *Dixon* no opinion commanded a majority on how *Blockburger* should be understood. For those, like Justice Scalia, who place a premium on "common sense" and "literal meaning," it should, upon further reflection, seem preposterous that cocaine possession is the "same offence" as contempt of court. *Dixon* was a windfall to the guilty, supported by neither the text of the Double Jeopardy Clause nor the common sense underlying due process.

Guilty Plea Problems Under the Blockburger Test

However, the *Blockburger* test is conceived, it obviously gives the prosecution a good deal of discretion in bringing successive prosecutions on related conduct. There are a lot of criminal statutes out there, with different elements, that could cover some aspect of a defendant's pattern of criminal conduct. Professor Richman, in Bargaining About Future Jeopardy, 49 Vand. L.Rev. 1181 (1996), notes the problems created by the *Blockburger* test that must be encountered by defendants who are engaged in bargaining with prosecutors.

Consider the plight of a savings and loan executive who finds herself facing a federal indictment in one district, charging her with several offenses relating to a fraudulent loan scheme. She would like to dispose of the pending charges but worries that whatever sentencing concessions she gains in exchange for her guilty plea would be effectively nullified if she were prosecuted for the other loan scams she engineered, some of which involved real estate in other federal districts. The pending indictment—and her limited knowledge of the investigation—give her no reason to think that the government knows of these other crimes. Yet she cannot be sure of what the future will hold. Should she bring the uncharged crimes to the government's attention and seek to reach a global settlement, or should she discount the value of the sentencing concessions offered on the pending indictment? If she fails to volunteer this information, to what extent would a plea agreement reached with respect to the charged counts bar the government from prosecuting on the uncharged counts?

This dilemma is not confined to the white-collar context. Consider the drug defendant charged with a single count of narcotics distribution who, upon arrest, confesses to having sold cocaine on thirty other occasions at the same street corner.

In neither case will the Double Jeopardy Clause, as currently interpreted [in *Blockburger*], be of much help.

Professor Richman concludes that because *Blockburger* provides so little in the way of protection against multiple prosecutions, defendants in the plea bargaining process may be forced to disclose information to the prosecution that they would not otherwise wish to without some corresponding concessions. He criticizes a system "that frequently works to extract private information from defendants as the price of repose."

Remedy for Multiple Prosecutions in Violation of the Double Jeopardy Clause: Morris v. Mathews

The Court found that an adequate remedy for a double jeopardy violation was provided by the state in Morris v. Mathews, 475 U.S. 237 (1986). The defendant pleaded guilty to aggravated robbery of a bank. Subsequently, he was charged with and convicted of aggravated murder, which was defined as causing the death of another while fleeing immediately after committing aggravated robbery. A state appellate court concluded that the Double Jeopardy Clause barred the conviction for aggravated murder under the *Vitale* decision. But the court held that the jury had properly found the defendant guilty of murder (a crime not barred by the Double Jeopardy Clause), and it reduced his sentence accordingly.

Justice White's opinion for the Court reasoned that there is no per se rule requiring a new trial following a double jeopardy violation and that "when a jeopardy-barred conviction is reduced to a conviction for a lesser included offense which is not jeopardy barred, the burden shifts to the defendant to demonstrate a reasonable probability that he would not have been convicted of the non-jeopardy-barred offense absent the presence of the jeopardy-barred offense."[8] See also Daniels v. Bronson, 932 F.2d 102 (2d Cir.1991)(reduction of the greater inclusive jeopardy-barred count to a non-duplicative lesser offense avoids double jeopardy without prejudice to the defendant).

B. DEFENSE RESPONSIBILITY FOR MULTIPLE TRIALS

Opposing Consolidation: Jeffers v. United States

The constitutional limitation on multiple prosecutions does not apply if the defendant is responsible for the multiplicity. In Jeffers v. United States, 432 U.S. 137 (1977), the defendant was charged with conspiracy to distribute drugs and with engaging in a continuing criminal enterprise to violate the drug laws. Jeffers opposed a government motion to consolidate the indictments. He successfully argued that his Sixth Amendment right to a fair trial would be endangered because much of the evidence that would be admitted against him and his codefendants on the conspiracy charge would be inadmissible in his trial for

---

8. He cited *Strickland v. Washington,* an ineffective assistance of counsel case, discussed in connection with Chapter Ten. Justice White explained that a reasonable probability is one that is "sufficient to undermine confidence in the outcome." Later, he added that "[t]o prevail in a case like this, the defendant must show that, but for the improper inclusion of the jeopardy-barred charge, the result of the proceeding would have been different." The Court remanded the case for further proceedings.

Justice Blackmun, joined by Justice Powell, concurred in the judgment. He argued that the usual harmless error test should apply and

that reversal should be required unless the error was harmless beyond a reasonable doubt. He objected to the test set forth by the majority, since the threshold question in ineffective assistance of counsel cases is whether the Constitution was violated. In the instant case, a violation was found, so the harmless error test should be used.

Justice Brennan dissented. He agreed with Justice Blackmun's argument that the harmless error test should apply, but found the error harmful. Justice Marshall also agreed that the harmless error test should apply, but argued that the court of appeals properly found the error to be prejudicial.

conducting a continuing criminal enterprise. Jeffers requested and obtained a severance. Subsequently, he maintained that his prosecution for engaging in a continuing criminal enterprise violated the Double Jeopardy Clause because the conspiracy charge was a lesser included offense. The Supreme Court rejected the claim.

> In this case, trial together of the conspiracy and continuing criminal enterprise charges could have taken place without undue prejudice to petitioner's Sixth Amendment right to a fair trial. If the two charges had been tried in one proceeding, it appears that petitioner would have been entitled to a lesser-included-offense instruction. * * * Nevertheless, petitioner did not adopt that course. Instead, he was solely responsible for the successive prosecutions for the conspiracy offense and the continuing-criminal-enterprise offense. Under the circumstances, we hold that his action deprived him of any right that he might have had against consecutive trials.

Guilty Plea to a Lesser Offense Over Government Objection: Ohio v. Johnson

If a trial judge accepts a guilty plea to a lesser offense over the objection of a prosecutor who seeks to convict on a greater offense, the fact that the trial judge dismisses the greater charges does not bar reprosecution on those charges. So the Supreme Court held in Ohio v. Johnson, 467 U.S. 493 (1984).

Johnson was charged with four offenses, including murder. He offered to plead guilty to involuntary manslaughter and grand theft, but not to murder and aggravated robbery. The trial judge accepted his offer and dismissed the remaining charges on the ground that to prosecute him on these charges would place him in jeopardy twice. The prosecutor objected to this procedure and appealed from the dismissals. Two state appellate courts upheld the trial judge, but the Supreme Court, in an opinion by Justice Rehnquist, reversed.

The Court accepted, as it was required to, the Ohio courts' interpretation of state law as not intending cumulative punishment for murder and manslaughter. Thus, it stated that should Johnson be convicted on the more serious charges, the trial court would have to confront the question of cumulative punishments and assure that state law was followed. The Court rejected, however, the claim that the Federal Constitution barred a trial on the more serious charges. It was the defendant who made the choice, over government objection, to split the offenses. For an analysis of the problems created by Ohio v. Johnson, see Ohio v. Johnson: Prohibiting the Offensive Use of Guilty Pleas to Invoke Double Jeopardy Protection, 19 Ga.L.Rev. 159 (1984). See also Taylor v. Whitley, 933 F.2d 325 (5th Cir.1991)(defendant waives a double jeopardy attack by pleading guilty, unless the double jeopardy violation is apparent on the face of the indictment; relying on United States v. Broce, 488 U.S. 563 (1989)(discussed in Chapter Nine)).

C.   SUBSEQUENT DEVELOPMENTS AND JEOPARDY

Continuing Violations: Garrett v. United States

In Garrett v. United States, 471 U.S. 773 (1985), the Court held that a defendant who had pleaded guilty to importing marijuana could be prosecuted thereafter and punished for engaging in a "continuing criminal enterprise," even though the marijuana importation to which he had pleaded was used as evidence of the enterprise. The enterprise charged had not been completed when the defendant was indicted for importing marijuana. The Court stated that "one who insists that the music stop and the piper be paid at a particular point must at least have stopped dancing himself before he may seek such an accounting." See also United States v. Paternostro, 966 F.2d 907 (5th Cir.1992)(permissible to bring multiple prosecutions for violating the terms of a Corps of Engineers use permit, since the defendant continued to violate the terms after his conviction, and thus the violation is a continuing one; citing *Garrett*, the court stated that "[i]n this case, Paternostro has not stopped dancing").

Post-Charge Changes of Fact

In Diaz v. United States, 223 U.S. 442 (1912), the defendant was convicted of assault and battery. Then his victim died. He was then tried for homicide, and moved to dismiss the charges on double jeopardy grounds. But the Court held that the homicide prosecution was permissible, because the government could not possibly have brought homicide charges in the original prosecution.

D.   SENTENCING ENHANCEMENTS AND SUBSEQUENT PROSECUTION

If criminal conduct is used to enhance a sentence, can that same conduct be charged in a subsequent prosecution? This question was addressed by the Court in Witte v. United States, 515 U.S. 389 (1995). After Witte pleaded guilty to a federal marijuana charge, a presentence report calculated the base offense level under the Sentencing Guidelines by aggregating the total quantity of drugs involved not only in Witte's offense of conviction but also in uncharged cocaine transactions in which he had engaged with several coconspirators. Under the Sentencing Guidelines, the sentencing range for a particular offense is determined on the basis of all "relevant conduct" in which the defendant was engaged, not just the conduct underlying the offense of conviction. See Sentencing Guidelines, § 1B1.3; see also the discussion in Chapter Eleven. The Sentencing Commission has noted that, "with respect to offenses involving contraband (including controlled substances), the defendant is accountable for all quantities of contraband with which he was directly involved and, in the case of a jointly undertaken criminal activity, all reasonably foreseeable quantities of contraband that were within the scope of the criminal activity that he jointly undertook." Witte's resulting sentencing range on the marijuana offense was higher than it would have been if only the drugs involved in his conviction had been considered, but it still fell within the scope of the legislatively authorized penalty. The district court accepted the presentence report's calculation in sentencing Witte, concluding that the other offenses were part of a continuing conspiracy that should be taken into account under the Guidelines as "relevant conduct." When

Witte was subsequently indicted for conspiring and attempting to import cocaine, he moved to dismiss the charges, arguing that he had already been punished for those offenses because that cocaine had been considered as "relevant conduct" at his marijuana sentencing.

The Supreme Court, in an opinion by Justice O'Connor, held that the Double Jeopardy Clause would not prevent prosecution of Witte for the subsequently charged cocaine offenses, because he had not been prosecuted for these offenses previously. The prior sentence was imposed only for the marijuana offense for which Witte was convicted. Consideration of uncharged relevant conduct was not prosecution for that conduct, but rather a basis for "a stiffened penalty for the [charged] crime, which is considered to be an aggravated offense because a repetitive one."

Justice Stevens dissented in *Witte*. He argued that from the defendant's point of view, it was clear that he was being punished twice for the relevant conduct used to enhance his sentence on the marijuana conviction.

V. CIVIL PENALTIES AS PUNISHMENT

In several cases, the Court has considered whether civil sanctions may constitute "punishment" under the Double Jeopardy Clause. If a civil sanction triggers the Double Jeopardy Clause, the state cannot bring multiple actions to enforce both the civil sanction and a criminal sanction for the same conduct.

Does the Double Jeopardy Clause Regulate Civil Penalties? United States v. Halper

The first in the line of cases was United States v. Halper, 490 U.S. 435 (1989). The facts involved a manager of a medical service company who was convicted of submitting 65 false claims for government reimbursement and fined $5,000. Thereafter, the government sought summary judgment under the False Claims Act, which provided for a civil penalty of $2,000 on each claim, as well as a penalty for twice the amount of the government's actual damages of $585 and the costs of the action. Thus, the government sought a sanction of $130,000 for a $585 fraud.

Justice Blackmun wrote as follows:

What we announce now is a rule for the rare case, the case such as the one before us, where a fixed-penalty provision subjects a prolific but small-gauge offender to a sanction overwhelmingly disproportionate to the damages he has caused. The rule is one of reason: Where a defendant previously has sustained a criminal penalty and the civil penalty sought in the subsequent proceeding bears no rational relation to the goal of compensating the Government for its loss, but rather appears to qualify as "punishment" in the plain meaning of the word, then the defendant is entitled to an accounting of the Government's damages and costs to determine if the penalty sought in fact constitutes a second punishment. * * * [T]he defendant is protected from a sanction so disproportionate to the damages caused that it constitutes a second punishment.

The scope of *Halper* is potentially broad. Criminal law violators often suffer substantial civil sanctions for the same conduct. For example, a defendant convicted of drunk driving will often lose his license; a lawyer convicted of stealing from clients will usually be disbarred; and a defendant convicted of a drug crime may also face civil charges for failure to pay taxes. Are all of these civil consequences barred by the Double Jeopardy Clause? In subsequent cases, the Court has taken pains to shy away from the implication in *Halper* that the Double Jeopardy Clause imposes some significant limitation on civil penalties.

Taxation of Illegal Activity as Punishment: Department of Revenue of Montana v. Kurth Ranch

In *Department of Revenue of Montana v. Kurth Ranch*, 511 U.S. 767 (1994), the Court considered whether the Double Jeopardy Clause prohibited a state's taxation of illegal activity that had been the subject of a previous conviction. The defendants pleaded guilty to marijuana offenses, and in their subsequent bankruptcy proceedings, they objected to Montana's attempt to collect a tax of $181,000 on 1,811 ounces of marijuana that they had harvested. This tax was imposed pursuant to Montana's Dangerous Drug Tax Act, which provides for taxation on "the possession and storage of dangerous drugs."

In a 5–4 decision, the Court held that the tax constituted a multiple punishment in violation of the Double Jeopardy Clause. Justice Stevens, writing for the majority, recognized that "[a]s a general matter, the unlawfulness of an activity does not prevent its taxation" and that it would have been permissible to assess the tax on any of the defendants "in the same proceeding that resulted in his conviction." However, Justice Stevens concluded that "a tax is not immune from double jeopardy scrutiny simply because it is a tax." He declared that the Double Jeopardy Clause is violated if a tax constitutes a de facto punishment and the conduct giving rise to the tax has already been punished under the criminal law.

Justice Stevens relied on a combination of four factors to conclude that Montana's Dangerous Drug Tax was punishment within the meaning of the Double Jeopardy Clause: 1. The tax imposed was more than eight times the market value of the drugs; 2. The legislature "intended the tax to deter people from possessing marijuana"; 3. The tax was conditioned on the commission of a crime and was exacted "only after the taxpayer has been arrested for the precise conduct that gives rise to the tax obligation in the first place"; and 4. The tax was levied on goods (i.e., the marijuana) that the taxpayers no longer possessed and that in fact had been destroyed by the State.

Chief Justice Rehnquist wrote a dissenting opinion in *Kurth Ranch*. He noted that the Court had often upheld taxation of unlawful activity, and that many taxes are designed at least in part to deter undesirable activity. He recognized that Montana's tax was conditioned on the making of an arrest, but concluded that "this characteristic simply reflects the reality of taxing an illegal enterprise," because Montana could not expect individuals who were subject to the tax to identify themselves voluntarily. The Chief Justice concluded that "the Montana tax has a nonpenal purpose of raising revenue, as well as the legitimate purpose of deterring conduct, such that it should be regarded as a genuine tax for double jeopardy purposes." Justice O'Connor wrote a separate dissent.

Justice Scalia also wrote a separate dissenting opinion, joined by Justice Thomas. He contended that *Halper* was wrongly decided and should be overruled. In Justice Scalia's view, "the Double Jeopardy Clause does not prohibit multiple punishments" and by its terms protects only against multiple prosecutions. Since the state's attempt to collect the tax was civil in nature, it was not a successive prosecution and therefore it did not implicate the concerns of the Double Jeopardy Clause. Justice Scalia noted some of the problems that have arisen from the Court's extension of the Double Jeopardy Clause to subsequent civil cases:

> Can a prison inmate who has been disciplined for an altercation with a guard subsequently be punished criminally for the same incident? Can a person who has paid a $75,000 fine and been permanently disbarred from commodity trading because of trading violations subsequently be sent to jail for the same violations? Can a person who has suffered civil forfeiture for violation of law later be prosecuted criminally for the same violation?

Justice Scalia concluded as follows:

> It is time to put the *Halper* genie back in the bottle, and to acknowledge what the text of the Constitution makes perfectly clear: the Double Jeopardy Clause prohibits successive prosecution, not successive punishment. Multiple punishment is of course restricted by the Cruel and Unusual Punishments Clause insofar as its nature is concerned, and by the Excessive Fines Clause insofar as its cumulative extent is concerned. Its multiplicity qua multiplicity, however, is restricted only by the Double Jeopardy Clause's requirement that there be no successive criminal prosecution, and by the Due Process Clause's requirement that the cumulative punishments be in accord with the law of the land, i.e., authorized by the legislature.

Lower Court Cases After Kurth Ranch

Kurth Ranch has been construed narrowly by the lower courts. Generally speaking, taxation schemes on criminal activity will be upheld against double jeopardy attacks unless they share *all* of the infirmities of the Montana taxing scheme at issue in *Kurth Ranch*. For example, in Padavich v. Thalacker, 162 F.3d 521 (8th Cir.1998), Padavich was convicted of possession of marijuana with intent to deliver, and was also assessed taxes and penalties for failing to pay Iowa's drug stamp tax. The court held that the tax was not punitive under *Kurth Ranch* because it was not conditioned on the commission of a crime, but rather was due and payable immediately upon possession of the drugs. The tax was not punitive even though the court recognized that the Iowa statute "has both a high rate of taxation and an obvious deterrent purpose." See also Bickham Lincoln–Mercury Inc. v. United States, 168 F.3d 790 (5th Cir.1999) (civil penalty for failing to report currency transactions can be imposed after the defendant paid a criminal fine for the same conduct).

Civil in rem Forfeiture: United States v. Ursery

In United States v. Ursery, 518 U.S. 267 (1996), the Court held that civil in rem forfeitures generally do not constitute punishment within the meaning of the Double Jeopardy Clause. *Ursery* was a consolidated appeal by the government from two separate lower court decisions that precluded civil in rem forfeitures after the respective property owners had been convicted of criminal offenses. In one case, the government sought forfeiture of the proceeds of drug and money-laundering activity that was the subject of the criminal prosecution. In the other case, the government sought forfeiture of the house of a person convicted of marijuana offenses. In this latter case, the government argued that the house was used as an instrumentality of the crime for which the defendant had been convicted.

Chief Justice Rehnquist, writing for the Court, relied heavily on previous cases involving civil in rem forfeitures and noted the precedent indicating "a sharp distinction between in rem civil forfeitures and in personam civil penalties such as fines: Though the latter could, in some circumstances, be punitive, the former could not." The Chief Justice analyzed a previous case drawing a distinction between in rem forfeitures and in personam penalties:

> In United States v. One Assortment of 89 Firearms, 465 U.S. 354 (1984), the owner of the defendant weapons was acquitted of charges of dealing firearms without a license. The Government then brought a forfeiture action against the firearms under 18 U.S.C. § 924(d), alleging that they were used or were intended to be used in violation of federal law.

> In another unanimous decision, we held that the forfeiture was not barred by the prior criminal proceeding. * * *

> Our inquiry proceeded in two stages. In the first stage, we looked to Congress' intent, and concluded that "Congress designed forfeiture under § 924(d) as a remedial civil sanction." * * * [W]e found it significant that "actions in rem have traditionally been viewed as civil proceedings, with jurisdiction dependent upon the seizure of a physical object." Second, we found that the forfeiture provision, because it reached both weapons used in violation of federal law and those "intended to be used" in such a manner, reached a broader range of conduct than its criminal analogue. Third, we concluded that the civil forfeiture "furthered broad remedial aims," including both "discouraging unregulated commerce in firearms," and "removing from circulation firearms that have been used or intended for use outside regulated channels of commerce."

> In the second stage of our analysis, we looked to "whether the statutory scheme was so punitive either in purpose or effect as to negate Congress' intention to establish a civil remedial mechanism." Considering several factors that we had used previously in order to determine whether a civil proceeding was so punitive as to require application of the full panoply of constitutional protections required in a criminal trial, we found only one of those factors to be present in the § 924(d) forfeiture. By itself, however, the fact that the behavior proscribed by the forfeiture was already a crime proved insufficient to turn the forfeiture into a punishment subject to the Double Jeopardy Clause. Hence, we found that the petitioner had "failed to establish by the clearest proof that Congress has provided a sanction so punitive as to transform what was clearly intended as a civil remedy into a criminal penalty." We concluded our decision by restating that civil forfeiture is "not an additional penalty for the commission of a criminal act, but rather is a separate civil sanction, remedial in nature."

Applying the "non-punitive" presumption to the in rem forfeitures at issue, the Chief Justice found no violation of the Double Jeopardy Clause. The claimants had not come close to establishing the "clearest proof" that the forfeitures were punitive rather than civil in nature. While "perhaps having punitive aspects", the forfeiture statutes at issue served significant nonpunitive goals, such as: encouraging property owners to use their property legally; abating a nuisance; and preventing drug dealers and money launderers from profiting. The Court also noted that the procedural requirements for establishing forfeitability in the relevant statutes tracked civil rather than criminal law. For example, the government was not required to establish scienter for purposes of civil in rem forfeiture. The Court also disregarded the fact that forfeiture statutes serve a deterrent purpose, reasoning that deterrence is a proper motive of both civil and criminal laws.

Justice Kennedy wrote a concurring opinion in *Ursery*. Justice Scalia, joined by Justice Thomas, concurred in the judgment. Justice Stevens concurred in part and dissented in part.

Repudiating Halper: Hudson v. United States

The Court finally repudiated the *Halper* analysis in *Hudson v. United States*, 522 U.S. 93 (1997). The Office of the Comptroller of the Currency (OCC) imposed monetary penalties and occupational debarment on Hudson, a bank official, for violating Federal banking laws by making improper loans. When the Government later indicted Hudson for essentially the same conduct, he moved to dismiss under the Double Jeopardy Clause. The Court of Appeals rejected the double jeopardy claims; it applied *Halper* and concluded that the monetary and other penalties were not disproportionate to the harm caused by Hudson. The Supreme Court, in an opinion by Chief Justice Rehnquist, affirmed the result in the Court of Appeals but rejected the *Halper* analysis.

The Chief Justice's analysis of the relationship between ostensibly civil penalties and the Double Jeopardy Clause proceeded as follows:

> Whether a particular punishment is criminal or civil is, at least initially, a matter of statutory construction. A court must first ask whether the legislature, "in establishing the penalizing mechanism, indicated either expressly or impliedly a preference for one label or the other." [United States v.] Ward, 448 U.S. at 248. Even in those cases where the legislature "has indicated an intention to establish a civil penalty, we have inquired further whether the statutory scheme was so punitive either in purpose or effect," as to "transform what was clearly intended as a civil remedy into a criminal penalty,"

> In making this latter determination, the factors listed in Kennedy v. Mendoza–Martinez, 372 U.S. 144 (1963), provide useful guideposts, including: (1) "whether the sanction involves an affirmative disability or restraint"; (2) "whether it has historically been regarded as a punishment"; (3) "whether it comes into play only on a finding of scienter"; (4) "whether its operation will promote the traditional aims of punishment—retribution and deterrence"; (5) "whether the behavior to which it applies is already a crime"; (6) "whether an alternative purpose to which it may rationally be connected is assignable for it"; and (7) "whether it appears excessive in relation to the alternative purpose assigned." It is important to note, however, that "these factors must be considered in relation to the statute on its face," and "only the clearest proof" will suffice to override legislative

intent and transform what has been denominated a civil remedy into a criminal penalty.

Our opinion in United States v. Halper marked the first time we applied the Double Jeopardy Clause to a sanction without first determining that it was criminal in nature. * * * As the *Halper* Court saw it, the imposition of "punishment" of any kind was subject to double jeopardy constraints, and whether a sanction constituted "punishment" depended primarily on whether it served the traditional "goals of punishment," namely "retribution and deterrence." Any sanction that was so "overwhelmingly disproportionate" to the injury caused that it could not "fairly be said solely to serve [the] remedial purpose" of compensating the government for its loss, was thought to be explainable only as "serving either retributive or deterrent purposes."

The analysis applied by the *Halper* Court deviated from our traditional double jeopardy doctrine in two key respects. First, the *Halper* Court bypassed the threshold question: whether the successive punishment at issue is a "criminal" punishment. Instead, it focused on whether the sanction, regardless of whether it was civil or criminal, was so grossly disproportionate to the harm caused as to constitute "punishment." In so doing, the Court elevated a single *Kennedy* factor—whether the sanction appeared excessive in relation to its nonpunitive purposes—to dispositive status. But as we emphasized in *Kennedy* itself, no one factor should be considered controlling as they "may often point in differing directions." The second significant departure in *Halper* was the Court's decision to "assess the character of the actual sanctions imposed," rather than, as *Kennedy* demanded, evaluating the "statute on its face" to determine whether it provided for what amounted to a criminal sanction.

We believe that *Halper's* deviation from longstanding double jeopardy principles was ill considered. As subsequent cases have demonstrated, *Halper's* test for determining whether a particular sanction is "punitive," and thus subject to the strictures of the Double Jeopardy Clause, has proved unworkable. We have since recognized that all civil penalties have some deterrent effect. See Department of Revenue of Mont. v. Kurth Ranch; United States v. Ursery. If a sanction must be "solely" remedial (i.e., entirely nondeterrent) to avoid implicating the Double Jeopardy Clause, then no civil penalties are beyond the scope of the Clause. Under *Halper's* method of analysis, a court must also look at the "sanction actually imposed" to determine whether the Double Jeopardy Clause is implicated. Thus, it will not be possible to determine whether the Double Jeopardy Clause is violated until a defendant has proceeded through a trial to judgment. But in those cases where the civil proceeding follows the criminal proceeding, this approach flies in the face of the notion that the Double Jeopardy Clause forbids the government from even attempting a second time to punish criminally.

Applying "traditional double jeopardy principles" to the facts, the Chief Justice found that the OCC penalties and debarment sanctions were clearly civil rather than criminal, and therefore the subsequent prosecution of Hudson did not violate the Double Jeopardy Clause. The monetary penalties were explicitly designated as civil, and the fact that debarment proceedings were conducted

[handwritten note in margin: If it is a civ proceed prob not double punishment]

administratively was a strong indication that they were civil rather than criminal. The Chief Justice also noted "that there is little evidence, much less the clearest proof that we require, suggesting that either OCC money penalties or debarment sanctions are so punitive in form and effect as to render them criminal despite Congress' intent to the contrary." Neither money penalties nor debarment have historically been viewed as punishment. Nor did the sanctions involve an "affirmative disability or restraint," as that term is normally understood. While Hudson was prohibited from further participating in the banking industry, this is "certainly nothing approaching the 'infamous punishment' of imprisonment." Furthermore, neither sanction came into play "only" on a finding of scienter. The regulatory provisions under which the monetary penalties were imposed allow for the assessment of a penalty against any person "who violates" any of the underlying banking statutes, without regard to the violator's state of mind.

The Chief Justice recognized that the imposition of both monetary penalties and debarment sanctions will deter others from engaging in similar conduct, a traditional goal of criminal punishment. "But the mere presence of this purpose is insufficient to render a sanction criminal, as deterrence may serve civil as well as criminal goals." The Chief Justice noted that the monetary and debarment sanctions, "while intended to deter future wrongdoing, also serve to promote the stability of the banking industry. To hold that the mere presence of a deterrent purpose renders such sanctions criminal for double jeopardy purposes would severely undermine the Government's ability to engage in effective regulation of institutions such as banks." The Court concluded that "there simply is very little showing, to say nothing of the 'clearest proof' required by *Ward*, that OCC money penalties and debarment sanctions are criminal. The Double Jeopardy Clause is therefore no obstacle to their trial on the pending indictments, and it may proceed."

Justice Stevens concurred in the judgment. He found it unnecessary to consider the viability of *Halper*, since it was clear to him that even if the civil sanctions were punishment, the statute under which they were imposed did not constitute the "same offense" as the criminal charge. This was because, under *Blockburger*, each statute contained an element that the other did not. Justice Souter, and Justice Breyer joined by Justice Ginsburg, also wrote separate opinions concurring in the judgment.

VI. MULTIPLE PUNISHMENTS IN A SINGLE CASE

A. PROHIBITION ON TWO PUNISHMENTS WHEN ONLY ONE IS AUTHORIZED

So far we have considered the application of the Double Jeopardy Clause to multiple actions brought against the defendant for the "same offence". Another line of cases indicates that the Double Jeopardy Clause has some relevance when the defendant is subject to multiple punishments for the same offense *in a single case*. However, if there is no multiple prosecution, only multiple punishment, the reach of the Double Jeopardy Clause is limited—the Clause does not prohibit the legislature from imposing multiple punishment in a single case. Rather, it prohibits the prosecution from charging and the court from sentencing a defendant to multiple punishments in the absence of statutory authorization.

The limitations on multiple punishment in a single case were first explored by the Court in Ex parte Lange, 85 U.S. (18 Wall.) 163 (1873). In *Lange*, the defendant was sentenced to both a fine and imprisonment for the same conduct. After the defendant fully paid the fine, the judge realized that the statute allowed only a fine *or* imprisonment. He vacated the sentence and imposed a new sentence of imprisonment. But since the defendant had suffered complete punishment for the crime by paying the fine, the Supreme Court held that no further punishment could be imposed. To do so would be outside the punishment authorized by the legislature. Thus the Double Jeopardy Clause in this context works (somewhat superfluously) as a means of keeping sentencing courts within the range authorized by the legislature.

The Court distinguished *Lange* in Jones v. Thomas, 491 U.S. 376 (1989). Thomas had been convicted of attempted robbery and of first-degree felony murder for a killing during the commission of a felony and was sentenced to 15 years and life respectively, with the 15 years to be served first. He sought state postconviction relief, arguing that the legislature did not authorize separate punishment for the enhanced murder and the underlying felony. After the state supreme court accepted this argument in another case, the Governor commuted Thomas' sentence, and he remained in custody pursuant to the murder conviction with credit for the time served on the underlying felony. The Supreme Court held that the Double Jeopardy Clause did not require that Thomas be released simply because he had completed his sentence on the underlying felony offense.

Justice Kennedy wrote for the Court and acknowledged that the Double Jeopardy Clause protects against "additions to a sentence in a subsequent proceeding that upset a defendant's legitimate expectation of finality." He nonetheless concluded that the state had properly cured the double jeopardy problem, since in effect the defendant was being subject to a single prison sentence (for the murder) that was authorized by the legislature. He distinguished *Lange* as involving more punishment than the legislature authorized. Justice Scalia, joined by Justices Stevens, Brennan and Marshall, dissented.

B. LEGISLATIVE INTENT TO IMPOSE MULTIPLE PUNISHMENTS FOR THE SAME OFFENSE

The protection against multiple punishments in a single case is directed against prosecutors and trial courts, not against legislators. If a legislature decides that it wants a robber or burglar to serve twice as much time for an offense, it can increase the maximum sentence (and raise the minimum also, if necessary)—subject to the Eighth Amendment's almost-nonexistent proportionality requirements. But a prosecutor who wants someone to serve more time than the legislature has prescribed may try to charge the same offense more than once. Generally, a legislature that establishes a hierarchy of lesser and greater offenses increases the punishment for each greater offense. The increased punishment represents punishment for the additional elements that distinguish the greater from the lesser offense. For example, if the legislature imposes a five year sentence for robbery and a ten year sentence for armed robbery, it can reasonably be assumed that the armed robbery penalty includes the robbery penalty, and adds on five years for the use of a weapon. Courts properly assume that prosecutors and trial courts cannot add together sentences for greater and lesser offenses, because to do so would constitute double-counting.

While there is a presumption that the legislature did not intend multiple punishment for the same conduct, the Supreme Court has emphasized that a legislature may provide separate, cumulative penalties for the same offense if it wishes to do so. It is a matter of legislative intent.

Felony Murder and the Underlying Felony:
Whalen v. United States

In Whalen v. United States, 445 U.S. 684 (1980), Justice Stewart's opinion for the Court held that the federal defendant was improperly sentenced when he was given one sentence for felony (first-degree) murder and another for the underlying offense of rape. Justice Stewart found that Congress had not authorized multiple sentences for these crimes. He stated that "[t]he Double Jeopardy Clause at the very least precludes federal courts from imposing consecutive sentences unless authorized by Congress to do so. * * * If a federal court exceeds its own authority by imposing multiple punishments not authorized by Congress, it violates not only the specific guarantee against double jeopardy, but also the constitutional principle of separation of powers in a manner that trenches particularly harshly on individual liberty." Separate opinions by Justice Blackmun and Justice White emphasized that their votes turned solely on the intent of Congress, not on double jeopardy principles—though that is really the same thing in this branch of Double Jeopardy law. Justice Rehnquist dissented and was joined by Chief Justice Burger.

Conspiracy to Import and Conspiracy to Distribute:
Albernaz v. United States

In Albernaz v. United States, 450 U.S. 333 (1981), the defendants received consecutive sentences for conspiracy to import and conspiracy to distribute marijuana. Both convictions were under the Comprehensive Drug Abuse and Control Act of 1970. The lower court focused on Congressional intent and found no double jeopardy problem, reasoning that "the Double Jeopardy Clause imposes no limits on Congress' power to define the allowable unit of prosecution and punishment, at least so long as all charges are brought in a single proceeding." The Supreme Court affirmed this analysis, saying that "the question of what punishments are constitutionally permissible is not different from the question of what punishment the Legislative Branch intended to be imposed." Justice Stewart, joined by Justices Marshall and Stevens, concurring in the judgment, agreed that there were two offenses under the scheme but argued that "[n]o matter how clearly it spoke, Congress could not constitutionally provide for cumulative punishments unless each statutory offense required proof of a fact that the other did not. * * *."

Overcoming the Presumption That Multiple Punishments for
the Same Offense Are Not Intended: Missouri v. Hunter

Justice Stewart's argument in *Albernaz* was based on Blockburger v. United States, discussed in detail, supra. In the context of multiple punishments in a single prosecution (as opposed to multiple prosecutions in cases like *Dixon*), the *Blockburger* test is used by the Court as a tool to divine legislative intent. The *Blockburger* test provides that offenses are separate if each contains an element that the other does not. If two offenses do not satisfy this test, the presumption is that the legislature did not intend for multiple punishments to be imposed. However, the Court in Missouri v. Hunter, 459 U.S. 359 (1983), held that *Blockburger* is, in this context, merely a rule of statutory construction, which can be overcome by a clear showing that the legislature intended multiple punishments. The Court stated that where "a legislature specifically authorizes cumulative punishments under two statutes, regardless of whether those two statutes proscribe the same conduct under *Blockburger,* a court's task of statutory construction is at an end" and cumulative punishments can be imposed so long as it is done in a single trial.

Hunter was convicted of first degree robbery of a grocery store, which meant that he used a dangerous and deadly weapon in the robbery, and also of armed criminal action, which meant that he committed a felony with a dangerous or deadly weapon. The state supreme court held that the state legislature intended to provide two punishments for what it found to be the same offense. Writing for the majority, Chief Justice Burger observed that Hunter had not been subjected to two trials, only to two punishments. He reasoned that there is nothing in the Double Jeopardy Clause to prohibit a state from punishing conduct by means of cumulative statutes. Justice Marshall, joined by Justice Stevens, dissented. The dissent argued that where multiple charges for the same conduct are brought, the prosecution obtains an unfair advantage because a jury is more likely to convict on one count, even as a compromise; that several convictions, rather than one, mean greater collateral consequences for the defendant; and that the stigma resulting from more than one conviction for the same conduct would be excessive.

For an application of *Blockburger* and *Hunter,* see United States v. Holloway, 905 F.2d 893 (5th Cir.1990)(cumulative punishment for the same offense in a single case is not prohibited by the Double Jeopardy Clause, so long as legislative intent is clear; under the Crime Control Act of 1984, the defendant can be punished both for armed bank robbery and for use of a firearm in a crime of violence, because Congress intended that offenses committed with firearms should be subject to cumulative punishment). For a critique of *Hunter* and a call for less deference to the legislature, see Susan Klein, Double Jeopardy's Demise, 88 Calif. L.Rev. 1001 (2000).

In United States v. York, 888 F.2d 1050 (5th Cir.1989), the defendant was cumulatively sentenced under 18 U.S.C. § 1001 and 18 U.S.C. § 1014. Both crimes concern the use of fraudulent documents to mislead the government. Section 1014 specifically applies to intent to influence a financial institution, while section 1001 generally prohibits lying on forms submitted to government officials. The court applied the *Blockburger* test and found that section 1014 has an element (influencing a financial institution) that section 1001 does not. The court had more trouble finding an element in section 1001 that is not included in section 1014. But the court held that even if all of the section 1001 elements were included in section 1014, and thus the *Blockburger* test was not met (because *each* crime must have an element that the other does not under that test), multiple punishment was still permissible. The court relied on *Hunter* and found a clear Congressional intent to punish these crimes separately. It reasoned that if multiple punishments were not intended, section 1014 would be superfluous: section 1001 crimes are easier to prove and carry a higher sentence. Also, the statutes were passed at different times and were in response to different problems. Does *York* mean that if the elements are different, multiple punishments are permissible under *Blockburger,* and if the elements are the same, multiple punishments are permissible under *Hunter* because otherwise one of the statutes would be superfluous?

Charged With Two, Sentenced for One: Ball v. United States

Chief Justice Burger wrote for the Court in Ball v. United States, 470 U.S. 856 (1985), as it found that Congress did not intend that a felon could be convicted and concurrently sentenced for both receiving a firearm and possessing it in violation of federal law. The Court concluded, however, that a defendant could be *charged* with two of the same offenses in a single prosecution. Should the defendant be found guilty of both, the trial judge may enter a judgment as to only one offense. Justice Stevens concurred in the judgment. He suggested that, since Ball was not only tried but was also convicted of both offenses, it was unnecessary for the Court to decide whether a defendant could be charged with the two offenses as long as he was convicted of only one. He added that "I see no reason why this Court should go out of its way to encourage prosecutors to tilt the scales of justice against the defendant by employing such tactics."

VII.   COLLATERAL ESTOPPEL

The same offense definition also applies when the defendant is acquitted and the government seeks to reprosecute. Separate offenses generally may be tried separately. But even where separate trials on distinct offenses are held, the Double Jeopardy Clause still may be important.

Closely related to the double jeopardy prohibition against retrial after an acquittal is the collateral estoppel bar to relitigation of any ultimate fact determined in favor of the defendant in a prior prosecution. In the following case, which holds that the rule of collateral estoppel is a constitutional requirement of the Double Jeopardy Clause, note what the prosecutor was trying to do.

ASHE v. SWENSON

Supreme Court of the United States, 1970.
397 U.S. 436.

MR. JUSTICE STEWART **delivered the opinion of the Court.**

* * *

Sometime in the early hours of the morning of January 10, 1960, six men were engaged in a poker game in the basement of the home of John Gladson at Lee's Summit, Missouri. Suddenly three or four masked men, armed with a shotgun and pistols, broke into the basement and robbed each of the poker players of money and various articles of personal property. The robbers—and it has never been clear whether there were three or four of them—then fled in a car belonging to one of the victims of the robbery. Shortly thereafter the stolen car was discovered in a field, and later that morning three men were arrested by a state trooper while they were walking on a highway not far from where the abandoned car had been found. The petitioner was arrested by another officer some distance away.

The four were subsequently charged with seven separate offenses—the armed robbery of each of the six poker players and the theft of the car. In May 1960 the petitioner went to trial on the charge of robbing Donald Knight, one of the participants in the poker game. At the trial the State called Knight and three of his fellow poker players as prosecution witnesses. Each of them described the circumstances of the holdup and itemized his own individual losses. The proof that an armed robbery had occurred and that personal property had been taken from Knight as well as from each of the others was unassailable. The testimony of the four victims in this regard was consistent both internally and with that of the others. But the State's evidence that the petitioner had been one of the robbers was weak. Two of the witnesses thought that there had been only three robbers altogether, and could not identify the petitioner as one of them. Another of the victims, who was the petitioner's uncle by marriage, said that at the "patrol station" he had positively identified each of the other three men accused of the holdup, but could say only that the petitioner's voice "sounded very much like" that of one of the robbers. The fourth participant in the poker game did identify the petitioner, but only by his "size and height, and his actions."

The cross-examination of these witnesses was brief, and it was aimed primarily at exposing the weakness of their identification testimony. Defense counsel made no attempt to question their testimony regarding the holdup itself or their claims as to their losses. Knight testified without contradiction that the robbers had stolen from him his watch, $250 in cash, and about

$500 in checks. His billfold, which had been found by the police in the possession of one of the three other men accused of the robbery, was admitted in evidence. The defense offered no testimony and waived final argument.

The trial judge instructed the jury that if it found that the petitioner was one of the participants in the armed robbery, the theft of "any money" from Knight would sustain a conviction. He also instructed the jury that if the petitioner was one of the robbers, he was guilty under the law even if he had not personally robbed Knight. The jury—though not instructed to elaborate upon its verdict—found the petitioner "not guilty due to insufficient evidence."

Six weeks later the petitioner was brought to trial again, this time for the robbery of another participant in the poker game, a man named Roberts. The petitioner filed a motion to dismiss, based on his previous acquittal. The motion was overruled, and the second trial began. The witnesses were for the most part the same, though this time their testimony was substantially stronger on the issue of the petitioner's identity. For example, two witnesses who at the first trial had been wholly unable to identify the petitioner as one of the robbers, now testified that his features, size, and mannerisms matched those of one of their assailants. Another witness who before had identified the petitioner only by his size and actions now also remembered him by the unusual sound of his voice. The State further refined its case at the second trial by declining to call one of the participants in the poker game whose identification testimony at the first trial had been conspicuously negative. The case went to the jury on instructions virtually identical to those given at the first trial. This time the jury found the petitioner guilty, and he was sentenced to a 35–year term in the state penitentiary.

* * *

"Collateral estoppel" is an awkward phrase, but it stands for an extremely important principle in our adversary system of justice. It means simply that when an issue of ultimate fact has once been determined by a valid and final judgment, that issue cannot again be litigated between the same parties in any future lawsuit. * * *

The federal decisions have made clear that the rule of collateral estoppel in criminal cases is not to be applied with the hypertechnical and archaic approach of a 19th century pleading book, but with realism and rationality. Where a previous judgment of acquittal was based upon a general verdict, as is usually the case, this approach requires a court to "examine the record of a prior proceeding, taking into account the pleadings, evidence, charge, and other relevant matter, and conclude whether a rational jury could have grounded its verdict upon an issue other than that which the defendant seeks to foreclose from consideration." * * * Any test more technically restrictive would, of course, simply amount to a rejection of the rule of collateral estoppel in criminal proceedings, at least in every case where the first judgment was based upon a general verdict of acquittal.

Straightforward application of the federal rule to the present case can lead to but one conclusion. For the record is utterly devoid of any indication that the first jury could rationally have found that an armed robbery had not occurred, or that Knight had not been a victim of that robbery. The single rationally conceivable issue in dispute before the jury was whether the petitioner had been one of the robbers. And the jury by its verdict found that he had not. The federal rule of law, therefore, would make a second prosecution for the robbery of Roberts wholly impermissible.

The ultimate question to be determined, then, is whether this established rule of federal law is embodied in the Fifth Amendment guarantee against double jeopardy. We do not hesitate to hold that it is. For whatever else that constitutional guarantee may embrace, it surely protects a man who has been acquitted from having to "run the gantlet" a second time.

The question is not whether Missouri could validly charge the petitioner with six separate offenses for the robbery of the six poker players. It is not whether he could have received a total of six punishments if he had been convicted in a single trial of robbing the six victims. It is simply whether, after a jury determined by its verdict that the petitioner was not one of the robbers, the State could constitutionally hale him before a new jury to litigate that issue again.

After the first jury had acquitted the petitioner of robbing Knight, Missouri could certainly not have brought him to trial again upon that charge. Once a jury had determined upon conflicting testimony that there was at least a reasonable doubt that the petitioner was one of the robbers, the State could not present the same or different identification evidence in a second prosecution for the robbery of Knight in the hope that a different jury might find that evidence more convincing. The situation is constitutionally no different here, even though the second trial related to another victim of the same robbery. For the name of the victim, in the circumstances of this case, had no bearing whatever upon the issue of whether the petitioner was one of the robbers.

In this case the State in its brief has frankly conceded that following the petitioner's acquittal, it treated the first trial as no more than a dry run for the second prosecution: "No doubt the prosecutor felt the state had a provable case on the first charge and, when he lost, he did what every good attorney would do—he refined his presentation in light of the turn of events at the first trial." But this is precisely what the constitutional guarantee forbids.

[JUSTICES BLACK and HARLAN concurred separately. JUSTICE BRENNAN, joined by JUSTICES DOUGLAS and MARSHALL, wrote a concurring opinion. CHIEF JUSTICE BURGER dissented.]

The Problem of General Verdicts

Ashe provides some protection for a defendant who is acquitted and then subject to prosecution on a crime that is related, but not the "same offence." However, collateral estoppel applies only to facts that were actually and necessarily decided by the jury in the defendant's favor. Juries usually return general verdicts. The defense of collateral estoppel may not be available because any number of issues might have been the basis for the acquittal; what issues the jury necessarily decided often cannot be determined.[9]

The Court in *Ashe* suggests a functional approach to determine what the jury decided. An easy case in this regard is Wright v. Whitley, 11 F.3d 542 (5th Cir.1994). Wright was charged with a firearm offense based on an alleged gunfight in which he participated in March, 1986. He testified that he was unarmed, and presented corroborating witnesses. The jury acquitted. Subsequently, Wright was indicted for a triple murder by firearm, occurring in May, 1986. The court held that the first acquittal had no preclusive effect on any issue in the second prosecution. The fact that Wright did not possess a firearm in one conflagration was not determinative of whether he possessed a firearm two months later. Compare United States v. Seley, 957 F.2d 717 (9th Cir.1992), where the defendant was acquitted of knowingly importing marijuana across the border. The court held that the government was precluded from proving in a subsequent prosecution that the defendant was involved in a conspiracy to import that same marijuana. See also United States v. Ruhbayan, 325 F.3d 197 (4th Cir. 2003) (defendant's acquittal of gun possession does not preclude a prosecution that he committed perjury in testifying that he had no knowledge of the gun; the jury could have ignored his testimony and acquitted him anyway).

Actual and Certain Determination of Fact: Schiro v. Farley

The application of collateral estoppel is dependent upon an actual and certain determination of an issue of fact. It is up to the party seeking preclusion to establish that the factfinder actually and certainly determined the issue of fact in the initial proceeding. Schiro v. Farley, 510 U.S. 222 (1994), illustrates this principle. Schiro admitted to raping and killing a woman. He was charged in separate counts with intentional murder and felony murder; the State sought the death penalty for the felony murder count. The State of Indiana, where Schiro was tried, does not require a showing of intent to kill for felony murder.

---

9. See United States v. Clark, 613 F.2d 391 (2d Cir.1979)(placing a heavy burden on a defendant claiming collateral estoppel to show that the fact he seeks to foreclose was actually resolved in his favor in previous litigation).

The jury was given verdict forms for both charges. The jury found Schiro guilty of felony murder, but left the other verdict forms blank. In the capital sentencing phase, the jury recommended against the death penalty, but the trial judge rejected this recommendation—a decision permitted under Indiana law. The trial judge sentenced Schiro to death on the basis of the aggravating circumstance that Schiro had "intentionally" murdered his victim. In the Supreme Court, Schiro argued that the double jeopardy principle of collateral estoppel precluded a death sentence based on intentional murder. He contended that the jury had necessarily acquitted him of intentional murder in the guilt phase of the trial.

Justice O'Connor, writing for seven members of the Court, held that "Schiro has not met his burden of establishing the factual predicate for the application of the doctrine [of collateral estoppel], * * * namely that an issue of ultimate fact has once been determined in his favor." She stated that the jury verdict did not necessarily amount to an acquittal on the intentional murder count, since the jury "could have grounded its verdict on an issue other than Schiro's intent to kill." She reasoned that the jury could have reached a guilty verdict on the felony murder count without ever deliberating on the intentional murder count. She noted that the jury was not instructed to return verdicts on all counts, and she relied on indications in the record that the jury "might have believed it could only return one verdict."

Finally, Justice O'Connor noted that the trial judge's charge could have been interpreted to require a finding of intent to kill for felony murder, and that the proof of Schiro's intent to kill was virtually uncontested. Therefore, it may well have been that the jury actually did find intent to kill when it rendered a guilty verdict on the felony murder count, even though they were not required to find intent under State law. Justice O'Connor concluded as follows:

> We have in some circumstances considered jury silence as tantamount to an acquittal for double jeopardy purposes. The failure to return a verdict does not have collateral estoppel effect, however, unless the record establishes that the issue was actually and necessarily decided in the defendant's favor. * * * [O]ur cases require an examination of the entire record to determine whether the jury could have grounded its verdict upon an issue other than that which the defendant seeks to foreclose from consideration. In view of Schiro's confession to the killing, the instruction requiring the jury to find intent to kill, and the uncertainty as to whether the jury believed it could return more than one verdict, we find Schiro has not met his burden * * *.

Justice Stevens, joined by Justice Blackmun, dissented. He argued among other things that the jury's recommendation against the death penalty was a further indication, ignored by the majority, that the jury believed Schiro had not acted with intent to kill.

In a case like *Schiro*, should defense counsel request the submission of special interrogatories to the jury, so that it will be easier to determine which questions of fact were actually decided? Why might defense counsel not wish to do that?

Identity of Party Requirement

Only a party to the prior criminal proceeding may take advantage of the collateral estoppel rule against the government in criminal cases. A unanimous Court in Standefer v. United States, 447 U.S. 10 (1980), held that a defendant accused of aiding and abetting in the commission of a federal offense may be convicted after the named principal has been acquitted of that offense. Chief Justice Burger's opinion rejected the attempt to extend the concept of "nonmutual collateral estoppel," developed in civil cases, into constitutional criminal procedure. Among the special attributes of criminal cases relied upon were the following: the government's limited discovery rights; the impossibility of a directed verdict for the government; the limitations on the government's right to appeal; the existence of exclusionary rules that may exclude evidence as to one defendant but not another; and the governmental interest in enforcement of the criminal law.

Non-parties cannot be bound by a prior adjudication of facts. See Vestal, Issue Preclusion and Criminal Prosecutions, 65 Iowa L.Rev. 281 (1980). So, for example, the suppression of evidence in a state prosecution does not automatically prevent the United States from using that evidence in a federal proceeding against the same defendant. "Since the United States was not a party to the state action, and had no way of making its views on the issue known to the state judge, it cannot be fairly considered to have had its day in court." United States v. Davis, 906 F.2d 829 (2d Cir.1990). The same principles would apply to a subsequent prosecution in a different state.

There is an exception to this rule if "the relationship between federal and state prosecutors is so close that it placed the federal government in privity with the state prosecution." Id. If that kind of close relationship is found, a determination in the defendant's favor rendered against one sovereign can be used by that defendant against the other sovereign. To find a privity relationship, some courts have required the defendant to show that "the state proceeding was merely a sham and a cover for a federal prosecution." United States v. Ng, 699 F.2d 63 (2d Cir.1983)(state must be the tool of the federal government). Other courts have required the lesser showing that the federal government "actively participated" in the state prosecution. United States v. Nasworthy, 710 F.Supp. 1353 (S.D.Fla.1989)(federal government had a "laboring oar" in the state court litigation). How much participation would you require before finding that one sovereign was bound by an adjudication against another? It should be noted that even if privity is found, "collateral estoppel would be inappropriate unless the issue resolved in the first proceeding was the same as the issue sought to be relitigated." United States v. Davis, supra. So if, for instance, a state court's suppression order is based on state law rather than the Fourth Amendment, collateral estoppel will not apply in the federal proceeding, or in a proceeding in another state. Id. See the material on the exclusionary rule in Chapter Two.

Collateral Estoppel Against the Defendant

Most courts have held that collateral estoppel cannot be used by the government to preclude a defendant from relitigating a fact found against him in a prior criminal proceeding. See, e.g., United States v. Harnage, 976 F.2d 633 (11th Cir.1992). The reasoning is that the use of collateral estoppel against the defendant would violate the defendant's constitutional right to a jury trial in the later prosecution. United States v. Pelullo, 14 F.3d 881 (3d Cir.1994)("applying collateral estoppel against the defendant in a criminal case interferes with the power of the jury to determine every element of the crime, impinging upon the accused's right to a jury trial").

Preclusive Effect of an Acquittal in a Subsequent Civil Case

May an acquittal on a substantive charge ever be used by a defendant as a bar to a subsequent civil forfeiture case? In One Lot Emerald Cut Stones v. United States, 409 U.S. 232, 233 (1972), the Court concluded that a prior acquittal for "willfully and knowingly, with intent to defraud the United States, smuggling * * * articles into the United States without submitting to the required customs procedures" did not bar a civil forfeiture action. The civil action only required proof that the property was brought into the United States without the required customs declaration. Collateral estoppel could not apply because the acquittal might have been based on the lack of the requisite intent. The Court also noted that the difference in burden of proof in the civil and criminal cases precluded the application of collateral estoppel. When the defendant is acquitted, it means that the jury has not found him guilty beyond a reasonable doubt. The jury in a criminal case thus makes no finding about whether facts could be proven against the defendant by a preponderance of the evidence.[10]

Relitigation of Facts Offered as Uncharged Misconduct: Dowling v. United States

In Dowling v. United States, 493 U.S. 342 (1990), the Court refused to apply the collateral estoppel doctrine when facts underlying a prior acquittal were used as evidence of an unrelated offense. Dowling was charged with bank robbery. On the issue of identification, the prosecution offered evidence that the defendant had participated in a different robbery, that was conducted similarly to the robbery with which Dowling was charged. Evidence of the prior robbery was admitted under Federal Rule of Evidence 404(b), which permits proof of the defendant's uncharged misconduct when offered to show intent, knowledge, identity, or any purpose other than to show that the defendant is a bad person. Dowling had been acquitted of the prior robbery. He argued that its introduction at the later trial was prohibited by *Ashe*. Justice White's majority opinion distinguished *Ashe* on the ground that Dowling's prior acquittal "did not determine the ultimate issue in the present case." The Court further noted that, to introduce evidence of an unrelated crime, the prosecution was not required to show that the defendant committed that crime beyond a reasonable doubt. Under the Federal Rules of Evidence, similar act evidence is admissible if the jury could reasonably conclude by a preponderance of the evidence that the act occurred and the defendant was the actor. Justice White therefore found support

---

10. Chief Justice Burger wrote for a unanimous Court in United States v. One Assortment of 89 Firearms, 465 U.S. 354 (1984), holding that a gun owner's acquittal on criminal charges involving firearms does not preclude a subsequent in rem forfeiture proceeding. The Court reasoned that since a lesser burden of proof applies in the forfeiture proceeding, collateral estoppel was no bar.

in the cases permitting civil forfeiture actions after an acquittal on a criminal conviction.

Justice Brennan, joined by Justices Marshall and Stevens, dissented. Justice Brennan argued that the majority took insufficient account of the burdens imposed upon a defendant if facts are relitigated in a subsequent criminal prosecution.

Use of Acquitted Conduct for Sentencing Purposes

The "relevant conduct" provisions of the Federal Sentencing Guidelines require the district court to consider all of the defendant's criminal acts that were part of the offense of conviction, whether those acts were the basis of the conviction or not. All that is required is that the government prove that the relevant conduct occurred by a preponderance of the evidence. Suppose the defendant is charged in a multiple count indictment. He is acquitted on some counts and convicted on others. Assume further that while the government could not prove the acquitted counts beyond a reasonable doubt, it can prove them by a preponderance of the evidence. Under these circumstances, the relevant conduct provisions require the district court to consider the conduct for which the defendant was acquitted in determining the appropriate sentence for the crime of which he was convicted. What's more, the acquitted conduct must be given *the same weight in sentencing* as the conduct for which the defendant was convicted. See United States v. Concepcion, 983 F.2d 369 (2d Cir.1992) (defendant acquitted on one count and convicted on another receives the same sentence as if he had been convicted of both).

Does *Ashe* prevent the use of acquitted conduct to increase the defendant's sentence? The courts have held that collateral estoppel does not protect the defendants from such enhancements. A typical analysis is found in United States v. Averi, 922 F.2d 765 (11th Cir.1991):

Acquitted conduct may be considered by a sentencing court because a verdict of acquittal demonstrates a lack of proof sufficient to meet a beyond-a-reasonable-doubt standard—a standard of proof higher than that required for consideration of relevant conduct at sentencing.

In the per curiam opinion in United States v. Watts, 519 U.S. 148 (1997), the Court relied on *Dowling* and *Ashe* and held that it was permissible for defendants to be sentenced in part on the basis of conduct for which they had been acquitted. Watts was charged with drug and firearms offenses. He was convicted of the former and acquitted of the latter. But the trial judge, using the preponderance of the evidence standard mandated by the Federal Sentencing Guidelines, found that Watts had in fact possessed guns in connection with the drug offenses, and added two points to his base offense level. The Court found that this did not violate the Double Jeopardy Clause. The Court declared that "sentencing enhancements do not punish a defendant for crimes of which he was not convicted, but rather increase his sentence because of the manner in which he committed the crime of conviction." The Court also noted that an acquittal could have no preclusive effect on a sentencing determination, because of the lesser standard of proof involved in sentencing. Justice Stevens dissented.

Note that use of acquitted conduct for enhancement *would* be prohibited if it resulted in a sentence greater than that authorized by the legislature for the crime on which the defendant was convicted. That is the rule of Apprendi v. New Jersey, 530 U.S. 466 (2000), discussed in both Chapters 10 and 11. The reason for this limitation lies not in the Double Jeopardy Clause but rather in the constitutional right to demand proof of guilt beyond a reasonable doubt of all the elements of a crime.

Isn't the use of acquitted conduct at sentencing tantamount to judicial nullification of a jury verdict? See United States v. Boney, 977 F.2d 624 (D.C.Cir.1992)(Randolph, J., concurring)(recognizing that consideration of acquitted conduct was required under the Sentencing Guidelines, but expressing concern that this result "has worked a significant erosion of the jury's dispensing power").

VIII. DUAL SOVEREIGNS

The Double Jeopardy Clause prohibits successive prosecutions only if brought by the same "sovereign." The dual sovereignty doctrine is well-explained by the court in United States v. Davis, 906 F.2d 829 (2d Cir.1990):

> One of the by-products of our nation's federal system is the doctrine of "dual sovereignty." Under this well-established principle, a federal prosecution does not bar a subsequent state prosecution of the same person for the same acts, and a state prosecution does not bar a federal one. This doctrine rests upon the basic structure of our polity. The states and the national government are distinct political communities, drawing their separate sovereign power from different sources, each from the organic law that established it. Each has the power, inherent in any sovereign, independently to determine what shall be an offense against its authority and to punish such offenses. When a single act violates the laws of two sovereigns, the wrongdoer has committed two distinct offenses. See generally United States v. Wheeler, 435 U.S. 313 (1978).

> In practice, successive prosecutions for the same conduct remain rarities. In the normal exercise of prosecutorial discretion, one sovereign usually defers to the other. For example, as a matter of policy the federal government ordinarily will not pursue criminal charges against a defendant who has already been prosecuted in state court. See United States Department of Justice, United States Attorneys' Manual, Tit. 9, § 2.142. However, this is no limitation on the government's sovereign right to vindicate its interests and values, and nothing prevents a federal prosecution whenever the state proceeding has not adequately protected the federal interest.

> The only legally binding exception to the dual sovereignty doctrine is a narrow one carved out by the Supreme Court in Bartkus v. Illinois, 359 U.S. 121 (1959). Successive prosecutions will be barred where one prosecuting sovereign can be said to be acting as a "tool" of the other, or where one prosecution is merely a "sham and a cover" for another. Except for this extraordinary type of case, successive state and federal prosecutions may, in fact as well as form, be brought by different sovereigns and the outcome in a state proceeding is not binding upon the later prosecution.

As implied by the discussion in *Davis,* the dual sovereignty principle also allows two different states to prosecute the defendant for the same conduct. Heath v. Alabama, 474 U.S. 82 (1985)(discussed below). Also, it does not matter that the defendant is acquitted by one sovereign, because another sovereign is not bound by the prior adjudication. See Bartkus v. Illinois, 359 U.S. 121 (1959)(upholding state conviction for robbery where defendant had been acquitted of federal charges stemming from the same robbery); United States v. Farmer, 924 F.2d 647 (7th Cir.1991)(previous acquittal on predicate acts in state court does not prohibit subsequent RICO prosecution in federal court).

The Petite Policy

In Abbate v. United States, 359 U.S. 187 (1959), the Court upheld a federal prosecution following a state conviction based upon the same criminal act. The Court reaffirmed *Bartkus*, and expressed concern that without the dual sovereignty doctrine, one sovereign could hinder the law enforcement efforts of another. Shortly after the decision in *Abbate*, the Justice Department established the "Petite Policy" of not prosecuting an individual after a state prosecution for the same act, unless there are "compelling interests of federal law enforcement" at stake. The policy is set forth in the United States Attorneys' Manual, § 9–2.142. United States Attorneys must obtain approval from an Assistant Attorney General before instituting the second prosecution.[11]

One of the most famous examples of the "compelling interests" exception to the Petite Policy arose in the federal prosecution of the Los Angeles police officers who beat Rodney King, an African–American arrestee. Two officers were convicted of federal civil rights violations, after an all-white state jury had acquitted them of most charges of excessive force, and deadlocked on one charge. While many applauded the federal prosecution, others argued that the Justice Department's decision to prosecute was essentially a political one. See Ricker, Double Exposure, A.B.A.J., August, 1993, p. 66.[12] Interestingly, the district court set a sentence that was below the Federal Sentencing Guidelines. The court departed downward, in part on the ground that the defendants had unfairly (though not unlawfully) suffered from having been twice placed in jeopardy. In Koon v. United States, 518 U.S. 81 (1996), the Court held that the District Court did not abuse its discretion in departing downward in part on the basis of the

11. The policy has resulted in the dismissal of convictions at the government's request when the policy has inadvertently been violated and a conviction has resulted. See, e.g., Petite v. United States, 361 U.S. 529 (1960).

In Rinaldi v. United States, 434 U.S. 22 (1977), the district court rejected the government's motion to dismiss an indictment after trial when the government represented before trial that it had authority to proceed with the case. Although the court of appeals affirmed, the Supreme Court reversed. It noted that the policy involved efficiency considerations for the government and fairness considerations for the defendant. Because the government's post-trial efforts to dismiss the indictment were not "tainted with impropriety," a majority of the Court concluded that the most important thing was to protect the individual defendant from unfairness associated with needless multiple prosecutions and that "[t]he defendant * * * should receive the benefit of the policy whenever its application is urged by the Government."

The court held in United States v. Renfro, 620 F.2d 569 (6th Cir.1980), that the decision whether or not to prosecute was left to the government and a defendant could not challenge the government's failure to comply with its Petite policy. See also United States v. Lester, 992 F.2d 174 (8th Cir.1993)(Petite policy does not grant substantive rights to the defendant; distinguishing *Rinaldi* as a case in which the government moved for dismissal).

12. The federal prosecution in the Rodney King case receives support in Amar and Marcus, Double Jeopardy After Rodney King, 95 Colum.L.Rev. 1 (1995). The authors argue that the dual sovereignty doctrine is generally insupportable in light of the incorporation of the Bill of Rights protections under the Fourteenth Amendment. However, the doctrine "still has a narrow but crucial role to play in enforcing the Reconstruction values [i.e., protecting against abuses of power by state actors] of that same Amendment against state officials."

hardships suffered by the defendants due to successive prosecutions. But the Court's deference to the lower court on the question of downward departures has been legislatively overruled by the Feeney Amendment, discussed in Chapter 11.

Municipality Is Not a Separate Sovereign: Waller v. Florida

In Waller v. Florida, 397 U.S. 387 (1970), the Court refused to consider a municipality a separate sovereign from the state of which it is a part. The defendant, who removed a mural from a wall in the St. Petersburg city hall, was convicted in municipal court of violating a city ordinance prohibiting destruction of city property and of disorderly breach of the peace. The State of Florida subsequently charged him with grand larceny. The Court refused to permit successive municipality-state prosecutions, and analogized the relationship to that of the federal government and a federal territory.[13]

[handwritten margin note: Municipality is part of the state]

The States as Dual Sovereigns: Heath v. Alabama

In Heath v. Alabama, 474 U.S. 82 (1985), the Supreme Court affirmed an Alabama capital murder conviction of a man who had pleaded guilty in Georgia to murder based on the same homicide. Heath was found guilty of hiring two men to kill his wife, who was nine months pregnant at the time of her death. The men kidnaped her in Alabama and apparently killed her in Georgia. Heath pleaded guilty in Georgia and received a life sentence. Thereafter, Alabama indicted him and convicted him of a murder during a kidnaping.

[handwritten margin note: Murder, 2 states • AL • GA]

Justice O'Connor wrote for the Court and stated that "in applying the dual sovereignty doctrine * * * the crucial determination is whether the two entities that seek successively to prosecute a defendant for the same course of conduct can be termed separate sovereigns. This determination turns on whether the two entities draw their authority to punish the offender from distinct sources of power." She cited Waller as confirmation that "it is the presence of independent authority to prosecute, not the relation between the States and the Federal Government in our federalist system, that constitutes the basis for the dual sovereignty doctrine."

[handwritten margin note: In applying dual sovereignty ask whether entities are both sovereign? distinct + separate power?]

Justice O'Connor asserted that "to deny a State its power to enforce its criminal laws because another state won the race to the courthouse would be a shocking and untoward deprivation of the historic right and obligation of the States to maintain peace and order within their confines." She rejected the argument that a state's interest could be vindicated by a prosecution in another state, asserting that "a State's interest in vindicating its sovereign authority through enforcement of its laws by definition can never be satisfied by another State's enforcement of its own laws." She concluded that "[t]he States are no less sovereign with respect to each other than they are with respect to the Federal Government." Thus, the Court assumed that the crimes charged in the two states were essentially the same, but found that each state may independently decide whether and how to prosecute a defendant for violations of its laws.

[handwritten margin note: Sep. states are separate sovereigns]

---

13. In United States v. Wheeler, 435 U.S. 313 (1978), federal prosecution of a Native American for statutory rape was permitted even though he had been convicted of a lesser offense by a tribal court.

Justice Marshall, joined by Justice Brennan, dissented and argued that the fact that the federal government and the states have differing interests in criminal prosecutions does not necessarily mean that two states have differing interests in prosecuting the same crime. He argued that "in contrast to the federal-state context, barring the second prosecution would still permit one government to act upon the broad range of sovereign concerns that have been reserved to the States by the Constitution."

Heath's Supreme Court lawyer has criticized the reasoning of the Supreme Court. See Allen & Ratnaswamy, Heath v. Alabama: A Case Study of Doctrine and Rationality in the Supreme Court, 76 J.Crim.L. & Crim. 801 (1985). The article predicts that ambitious prosecutors will abuse the authority conferred upon them in noteworthy cases in order to further their political advancement.[14]

Joint Efforts in the War on Drugs

In recent years there has been significant cooperation between State and Federal law enforcement in combating the drug trade. Apparently this cooperation has not resulted in any limitation on the power of both sovereigns to prosecute the same defendant for the same drug activity. Professor Sandra Guerra, in The Myth of Dual Sovereignty: Multijurisdictional Drug Law Enforcement and Double Jeopardy, 73 No.Car.L.Rev.1159 (1995), found over 100 federal drug prosecutions in the last 20 years that took place after a state prosecution on the same conduct. She draws the following conclusions:

> Times have changed in law enforcement; successive and dual prosecutions are not uncommon, especially in drug cases. Ironically, the dual sovereignty doctrine rests on a federalist theory that envisions two separate and independent sovereigns, each of which has its respective laws that reflect its unique priorities and interests. The doctrine shows respect for each sovereign's right to vindicate its own interests without interference from another sovereign. The irony lies in the fact that it is precisely in drug cases where this theory least reflects reality. In drug cases, multijurisdictional drug task forces bring the sovereigns together in a united effort against a common foe. * * * To insist that the cooperating governments make a choice of forum for criminal prosecutions resulting from their joint efforts would neither infringe the sovereign rights of the participating governments, nor create incentives for defendants to race to the courthouse of the jurisdiction offering the best plea bargain.

IX. ABORTED PROCEEDINGS

A. THE RIGHT TO A DETERMINATION FROM THE FIRST JURY IMPANELED

As noted earlier, the Double Jeopardy Clause is derived from English law, which provided that a defendant was put in jeopardy only after a conviction or

---

14. States are free to provide greater double jeopardy protection than the Federal Constitution provides.

Several states have rejected the dual sovereignty theory, at least in some circumstances. In State v. Hogg, 118 N.H. 262, 385 A.2d 844 (1978), the New Hampshire Supreme Court construed the state Double Jeopardy Clause to prohibit a state prosecution for robbery after a federal court acquittal on charges arising from the same criminal transaction. In Commonwealth v. Mills, 447 Pa. 163, 286 A.2d 638 (1971), the Supreme Court of Pennsylvania barred second prosecutions for the same offense unless the interests of the state and the other jurisdiction are substantially different.

an acquittal. The protection was afforded to a defendant only after a complete trial. The notion that a defendant may be put in jeopardy in a prosecution that does not terminate in a conviction or acquittal was incorporated gradually into the Double Jeopardy Clause. The Court determined that the defendant's interest in finality could be undermined if the prosecution could terminate a trial before the verdict, and institute a new proceeding. This protection, like other double jeopardy guarantees, becomes operative when jeopardy "attaches." In Crist v. Bretz, 437 U.S. 28 (1978), the Court concluded that the federal rule that jeopardy attaches when the jury is impaneled and sworn is an integral part of the constitutional guarantee against double jeopardy, and applies in state proceedings. The rule reflects and protects the defendant's interest in retaining a chosen jury, which the Court found to be one of the core principles of double jeopardy protection. See United States v. Juarez–Fierro, 935 F.2d 672 (5th Cir.1991)(pre-voir dire oath to the venire does not constitute attachment of jeopardy; a jury is not empaneled until all parties have exercised their challenges, and jurors have been selected to serve on the petit jury). In a non-jury trial, jeopardy attaches when the court begins to hear evidence.

B. MISTRIAL DECLARED OVER DEFENDANT'S OBJECTION

The following cases consider when a retrial is permissible following a mistrial. The next case discusses the major prior cases.

1. *The Requirement of Manifest Necessity for a Mistrial Granted Over the Defendant's Objection*

ILLINOIS v. SOMERVILLE

Supreme Court of the United States, 1973.
410 U.S. 458.

Mr. Justice Rehnquist **delivered the opinion of the Court.**

We must here decide whether declaration of a mistrial over the defendant's objection, because the trial court concluded that the indictment was insufficient to charge a crime, necessarily prevents a State from subsequently trying the defendant under a valid indictment. We hold that the mistrial met the "manifest necessity" requirement of our cases, since the trial court could reasonably have concluded that the "ends of public justice" would be defeated by having allowed the trial to continue. Therefore, the Double Jeopardy Clause of the Fifth Amendment, made applicable to the States through the Due Process Clause

of the Fourteenth Amendment, did not bar retrial under a valid indictment.

[The defendant was indicted for theft. After the jury was sworn, but before any evidence was presented, the trial court granted the State's motion for a mistrial despite the defendant's objection, because the indictment was fatally defective for failure to allege the requisite intent. After a new trial and conviction, the defendant sought a writ of habeas corpus. He alleged that the new trial violated his rights under the Double Jeopardy Clause.]

II

The fountainhead decision construing the Double Jeopardy Clause in the context of a declaration of a mistrial over a defendant's objection is United States v. Perez, 9 Wheat. 579 (1824). Mr. Justice Story, writing for a unanimous Court, set forth the standards for determining whether a retrial, following a declaration of a mistrial over a defendant's objection, constitutes double jeopardy within the meaning of the Fifth Amendment. In holding that the failure of the jury to agree on a verdict of either acquittal or conviction did not bar retrial of the defendant, Mr. Justice Story wrote:

> "We think that in all cases of this nature, the law has invested Courts of justice with the authority to discharge a jury from giving any verdict, whenever, in their opinion, taking all the circumstances into consideration, there is a manifest necessity for the act, or the ends of public justice would otherwise be defeated. They are to exercise a sound discretion on the subject; and it is impossible to define all the circumstances, which would render it proper to interfere. To be sure, the power ought to be used with the greatest caution, under urgent circumstances, and for very plain and obvious causes * * *. But, after all, they have the right to order the discharge * * *."

This formulation, consistently adhered to by this Court in subsequent decisions, abjures the application of any mechanical formula by which to judge the propriety of declaring a mistrial in the varying and often unique situations arising during the course of a criminal trial. The broad discretion reserved to the trial judge in such circumstances has been consistently reiterated in decisions of this Court. * * *

While virtually all of the cases turn on the particular facts and thus escape meaningful categorization, it is possible to distill from them a general approach, premised on the "public justice" policy enunciated in United States v. Perez, to situations such as that presented by this case. A trial judge properly exercises his discretion to declare a mistrial if an impartial verdict cannot be reached, or if a verdict of conviction could be reached but would have to be reversed on appeal due to an obvious procedural error in the trial. If an error would make reversal on appeal a certainty, it would not serve "the ends of public justice" to require that the Government proceed with its proof when, if it succeeded before the jury, it would automatically be stripped of that success by an appellate court. * * * While the declaration of a mistrial on the basis of a rule or a defective procedure that would lend itself to prosecutorial manipulation would involve an entirely different question, such was not the situation * * * in the instant case.

In Downum v. United States [372 U.S. 734 (1963)], the defendant was charged with six counts of mail theft, and forging and uttering stolen checks. A jury was selected and sworn in the morning, and instructed to return that afternoon. When the jury returned, the Government moved for the discharge of the jury on the ground that a key prosecution witness, for two of the six counts against defendant, was not present. The prosecution knew, prior to the selection and swearing of the jury, that this witness could not be found and had not been served with a subpoena. The trial judge discharged the jury over the defendant's motions to dismiss two counts for failure to prosecute and to continue the other four. This Court, in reversing the convictions on the ground of double jeopardy, emphasized that "[e]ach case must turn on its facts," and held that the second prosecution constituted double jeopardy, because the absence of the witness and the reason therefore did not there justify, in terms of "manifest necessity," the declaration of a mistrial.

In United States v. Jorn [400 U.S. 470 (1971)], the Government called a taxpayer witness in a prosecution for wilfully assisting in the preparation of fraudulent income tax returns. Prior to his testimony, defense counsel suggested he be warned of his constitutional right against compulsory self-incrimination. The trial judge warned him of his rights, and the witness stated that he was willing to testify and that the Internal Revenue Service agent who first contacted him warned him of his rights. The trial judge, however, did not believe the witness' declaration that the IRS had so warned him, and refused to allow him to testify until after he had consulted with an attorney. After learning from the Government that the remaining four witnesses were "similarly situated," and after surmising that they, too, had not been properly informed of their rights, the trial judge declared a mistrial to give the witnesses the opportunity to consult with attorneys. In sustaining a plea in bar of double jeopardy to an attempted second trial of the defendant, the plurality opinion of the Court, emphasizing the importance to the defendant of proceeding before the first jury sworn, concluded:

"It is apparent from the record that no consideration was given to the possibility of a trial continuance; indeed, the trial judge acted so abruptly in discharging the jury that, had the prosecutor been disposed to suggest a continuance, or the defendant to object to the discharge of the jury, there would have been no opportunity to do so. When one examines the circumstances surrounding the discharge of this jury, it seems abundantly apparent that the trial judge made no effort to

exercise a sound discretion to assure that, taking all the circumstances into account, there was a manifest necessity for the *sua sponte* declaration of this mistrial. Therefore, we must conclude that in the circumstances of this case, appellee's reprosecution would violate the double jeopardy provision of the Fifth Amendment."

* * *

[The Court rejected Somerville's argument that any trial on a defective indictment precludes retrial, and then considered whether the circumstances of the case justified the mistrial.]

In the instant case, the trial judge terminated the proceeding because a defect was found to exist in the indictment that was, as a matter of Illinois law, not curable by amendment. The Illinois courts have held that even after a judgment of conviction has become final, the defendant may be released on habeas corpus, because the defect in the indictment deprives the trial court of "jurisdiction." * * * The trial judge was faced with a situation * * * in which a procedural defect might or would preclude the public from either obtaining an impartial verdict or keeping a verdict of conviction if its evidence persuaded the jury. If a mistrial were constitutionally unavailable in situations such as this, the State's policy could only be implemented by conducting a second trial after verdict and reversal on appeal, thus wasting time, energy, and money for all concerned. Here, the trial judge's action was a rational determination designed to implement a legitimate state policy, with no suggestion that the implementation of that policy in this manner could be manipulated so as to prejudice the defendant. This situation is thus unlike *Downum*, where the mistrial entailed not only a delay for the defendant, but also operated as a post-jeopardy con-

[handwritten margin notes:]

Judge did not take in all circumstance to decide it was manifest necessity

Procedural defect precluded impartial verdict *and keeping the verdict if jury persuaded

2nd trial manifest so why go on?

[handwritten margin note: Mistrial was required by manifest necessity or the ends of public justice]

tinuance to allow the prosecution an opportunity to strengthen its case. Here, the delay was minimal, and the mistrial was, under Illinois law, the only way in which a defect in the indictment could be corrected. Given the established standard of discretion * * *, we cannot say that the declaration of a mistrial was not required by "manifest necessity" or the "ends of public justice."

Our decision in *Jorn*, relied upon by the court below and respondent, does not support the opposite conclusion. * * * That opinion dealt with action by a trial judge that can fairly be described as erratic. The Court held that the lack of apparent harm to the defendant from the declaration of a mistrial did not itself justify the mistrial, and concluded that there was no "manifest necessity" for the mistrial, as opposed to less drastic alternatives. The Court emphasized that the absence of any manifest need for the mistrial had deprived the defendant of his right to proceed before the first jury, but it did not hold that that right may never be forced to yield, as in this case, to "the public's interest in fair trials designed to end in just judgments." * * *.

The determination by the trial court to abort a criminal proceeding where jeopardy has attached is not one to be lightly undertaken, since the interest of the defendant in having his fate determined by the jury first impaneled is itself a weighty one. Nor will the lack of demonstrable additional prejudice preclude the defendant's invocation of the double jeopardy bar in the absence of some important countervailing interest of proper judicial administration. But where the declaration of a mistrial implements a reasonable state policy and aborts a proceeding that at best would have produced a verdict that could have been upset at will by one of the parties, the defendant's interest in proceeding to verdict is outweighed by the competing and equally legitimate demand for public justice.

[Justice White, joined by Justices Douglas and Brennan, dissented. Relying on *Downum* and *Jorn*, Justice White argued that even when prosecutorial misconduct consists of a mistake or oversight, the defendant's interest in having the trial completed by the first tribunal prevails. This should be true even when no specific prejudice to the defendant is shown. In this case, the reason for the mistrial was the state's error.

Justice Marshall dissented separately. Also relying on *Downum* and *Jorn*, he argued that the court's "balancing" approach underemphasized the defendant's interest in continuing with the trial. Continuation, under the circumstances of the case, was a viable alternative to a mistrial in his view.]

Note on the Impact of Somerville

Somerville generally has been considered a retreat from the heightened scrutiny of mistrials granted without the defendant's consent in *Downum* and *Jorn*. It is clear that after *Somerville*, the term "manifest necessity" is no longer an accurate description of what constitutes a proper ground for a mistrial. What factors are relevant to the Court's "balancing" approach? Consider the Court's treatment of the following issues in both *Somerville* and in Arizona v. Washington, the next case: Whose conduct or what event is responsible for the mistrial? What is the purpose, nature, and effect of that conduct? Is there prosecutorial overreaching or harassment? Does the potential for prosecutorial manipulation exist? Is there any actual prejudice to the defendant from the mistrial? Has the court considered all viable alternatives to a mistrial? For cases relying on *Downum* and *Jorn* and distinguishing

Somerville, see Randall v. Rothwax, 78 N.Y.2d 494, 577 N.Y.S.2d 211, 583 N.E.2d 924 (1991)(where the defendant pleaded guilty during jury deliberations due to misadvice from the judge that the jury was leaning toward conviction, when in fact they were leaning toward acquittal, the guilty plea must be vacated and double jeopardy bars a retrial; the trial court, without manifest necessity, eliminated the defendant's right to have a resolution from the jury); United States v. Meza–Soria, 935 F.2d 166 (9th Cir.1991)(trial court declares a mistrial over the defendant's objection, on the ground that evidence admitted on defendant's behalf should not have been introduced; retrial barred by double jeopardy because the evidence was in fact admissible).

2. *Manifest Necessity as a Flexible Test*

ARIZONA v. WASHINGTON

Supreme Court of the United States, 1978.
434 U.S. 497.

MR. JUSTICE STEVENS delivered the opinion of the Court.

An Arizona trial judge granted the prosecutor's motion for a mistrial predicated on improper and prejudicial comment during defense counsel's opening statement. In a subsequent habeas corpus proceeding, a Federal District Court held that the Double Jeopardy Clause protected the defendant from another trial. The Court of Appeals for the Ninth Circuit affirmed. The questions presented are whether the record reflects the kind of "necessity" for the mistrial ruling that will avoid a valid plea of double jeopardy, and if so, whether the plea must nevertheless be allowed because the Arizona trial judge did not fully explain the reasons for his mistrial ruling.

I

In 1971 respondent was found guilty of murdering a hotel night clerk. In 1973, the Superior Court of Pima County, Ariz., ordered a new trial because the prosecutor had withheld exculpatory evidence from the defense. The Arizona Supreme Court affirmed the new trial order in an unpublished opinion.

Respondent's second trial began in January 1975. During the *voir dire* examination of prospective jurors, the prosecutor made reference to the fact that some of the witnesses whose testimony the jurors would hear had testified in proceedings four years earlier. Defense counsel told the prospective jurors "that there was evidence hidden from [respondent] at the last trial." In his opening statement, he made this point more forcefully:

"You will hear testimony that notwithstanding the fact that we had a trial in May of 1971 in this matter, that the prosecutor hid those statements and didn't give those to the lawyer for George saying the man was Spanish speaking, didn't give those statements at all, hid them.

"You will hear that that evidence was suppressed and hidden by the prosecutor in that case. You will hear that that evidence was purposely withheld. You will hear that because of the misconduct of the County Attorney at that time and because he withheld evidence, that the Supreme Court of Arizona granted a new trial in this case."

[The prosecutor moved for a mistrial, because there was no theory on which the basis for the new trial ruling could be admissible, and the prejudice to the jury could not be repaired by any cautionary instruction. The judge granted the motion, but did not expressly find that there was "manifest necessity" for a mistrial, and did not expressly state that he had considered and found alternative solutions to be inadequate.]

II

* * *

Because jeopardy attaches before the judgment becomes final, the constitutional protection * * * embraces the defendant's "valued right to have his trial completed by a particular tribunal." The reasons why this "valued right" merits constitutional protection are worthy of repetition. Even if the first trial is not completed, a second prosecution may be grossly unfair. It increases the financial and emotional burden on the accused, prolongs the period in which he is stigmatized by an unresolved accusation of wrongdoing, and may even enhance the risk that an innocent defendant may be convicted. The danger of such unfairness to the defendant exists whenever a trial is aborted before it is completed. Consequently, as a general rule, the prosecutor is entitled to one, and only one, opportunity to require an accused to stand trial.

Unlike the situation in which the trial has ended in an acquittal or conviction, retrial is not automatically barred when a criminal proceeding is terminated without finally resolving the merits of the charges against the accused. Because of the variety of circumstances that may make it necessary to discharge a jury before a trial is concluded, and because those circumstances do not invariably create unfairness to the accused, his valued right to have the trial concluded by a particular tribunal is sometimes subordinate to the public interest in affording the prosecutor one full and fair opportunity to present his evidence to an impartial jury. Yet in view of the importance of the right, and the fact that it is frustrated by any mistrial, the prosecutor must shoulder the burden of justifying the mistrial if he is to avoid the double jeopardy bar. His burden is a heavy one. The prosecutor must demonstrate "manifest necessity" for any mistrial declared over the objection of the defendant.

The words "manifest necessity" appropriately characterize the magnitude of the prosecutor's burden. * * * Nevertheless, those words do not describe a standard that can be applied mechanically or without attention to the particular problem confronting the trial judge. Indeed, it is manifest that the key word "necessity" cannot be interpreted literally; instead, contrary to the teaching of Webster, we assume that there are degrees of necessity and we require a "high degree" before concluding that a mistrial is appropriate.

The question whether that "high degree" has been reached is answered more easily in some kinds of cases than in others. At one extreme are cases in which a prosecutor requests a mistrial in order to buttress weaknesses in his evidence. * * * Thus, the strictest scrutiny is appropriate when the basis for the mistrial is the unavailability of critical prosecution evidence,[a] or when there is reason to believe that the prosecutor is using the superior resources of the State to harass or to achieve a tactical advantage

---

a. If, for example, a prosecutor proceeds to trial aware that key witnesses are not available to give testimony and a mistrial is later granted for that reason, a second prosecution is barred. Downum v. United States, 372 U.S.

734. The prohibition against double jeopardy unquestionably "forbids the prosecutor to use the first proceeding as a trial run of his case." Note, Twice in Jeopardy, 75 Yale L.J. 262, 287–288 (1965).

over the accused.[b]

At the other extreme is the mistrial premised upon the trial judge's belief that the jury is unable to reach a verdict, long considered the classic basis for a proper mistrial. The argument that a jury's inability to agree establishes reasonable doubt as to the defendant's guilt, and therefore requires acquittal, has been uniformly rejected in this country. Instead, without exception, the courts have held that the trial judge may discharge a genuinely deadlocked jury and require the defendant to submit to a second trial. This rule accords recognition to society's interest in giving the prosecution one complete opportunity to convict those who have violated its laws.

if jury unable to deliver verdict another trial is warranted b/c of strong public interest in justice

Moreover, in this situation there are especially compelling reasons for allowing the trial judge to exercise broad discretion in deciding whether or not "manifest necessity" justifies a discharge of the jury. On the one hand, if he discharges the jury when further deliberations may produce a fair verdict, the defendant is deprived of his "valued right to have his trial completed by a particular tribunal." But if he fails to discharge a jury which is unable to reach a verdict after protracted and exhausting deliberations, there exists a significant risk that a verdict may result from pressures inherent in the situation rather than the considered judgment of all the jurors. If retrial of the defendant were barred whenever an appellate court views the

"necessity" for a mistrial differently from the trial judge, there would be a danger that the latter, cognizant of the serious societal consequences of an erroneous ruling, would employ coercive means to break the apparent deadlock. Such a rule would frustrate the public interest in just judgments. The trial judge's decision to declare a mistrial when he considers the jury deadlocked is therefore accorded great deference by a reviewing court.[c]

We are persuaded that, along the spectrum of trial problems which may warrant a mistrial and which vary in their amenability to appellate scrutiny, the difficulty which led to the mistrial in this case also falls in an area where the trial judge's determination is entitled to special respect.

In this case the trial judge ordered a mistrial because the defendant's lawyer made improper and prejudicial remarks during his opening statement to the jury. * * * We therefore start from the premise that defense counsel's comment was improper and may have affected the impartiality of the jury.

Δ improperly influenced jury

We recognize that the extent of the possible bias cannot be measured, and that the District Court was quite correct in believing that some trial judges might have proceeded with the trial after giving the jury appropriate cautionary instructions. In a strict, literal sense, the mistrial was not "necessary." Nevertheless, the overriding interest in the evenhanded administra-

---

b. * * * The "particular tribunal" principle is implicated whenever a mistrial is declared over the defendant's objection and without regard to the presence or absence of governmental overreaching. If the "right to go to a particular tribunal is valued, it is because, independent of the threat of bad-faith conduct by judge or prosecutor, the defendant has a significant interest in the decision whether or not to take the case from the jury." United States v. Jorn, 400 U.S., at 485.

c. It should be noted, however, that the rationale for this deference in the "hung" jury

situation is that the trial court is in the best position to assess all the factors which must be considered in making a necessarily discretionary determination whether the jury will be able to reach a just verdict if it continues to deliberate. If the record reveals that the trial judge has failed to exercise the "sound discretion" entrusted to him, the reason for such deference by an appellate court disappears. Thus, if the trial judge acts for reasons completely unrelated to the trial problem which purports to be the basis for the mistrial ruling, close appellate scrutiny is appropriate.

tion of justice requires that we accord the highest degree of respect to the trial judge's evaluation of the likelihood that the impartiality of one or more jurors may have been affected by the improper comment.

[The Court concluded that the mistrial was proper because the judge did not act irrationally or irresponsibly.]

* * * We are therefore persuaded by the record that the trial judge acted responsibly and deliberately, and accorded careful consideration to respondent's interest in having the trial concluded in a single proceeding. Since he exercised "sound discretion" in handling the sensitive problem of possible juror bias created by the improper comment of defense counsel, the mistrial order is supported by the "high degree" of necessity which is required in a case of this kind. Neither party has a right to have his case decided by a jury which may be tainted by bias; in these circumstances, "the public's interest in fair trials designed to end in just judgments" must prevail over the defendant's "valued right" to

have his trial concluded before the first jury impaneled.

IV

One final matter requires consideration. The absence of an explicit finding of "manifest necessity" appears to have been determinative for the District Court and may have been so for the Court of Appeals. If those courts regarded that omission as critical, they required too much. Since the record provides sufficient justification for the state-court ruling, the failure to explain that ruling more completely does not render it constitutionally defective.

* * *

[Justice White argued in dissent that the case should have been remanded to the district court for a new determination of manifest necessity for the mistrial. Justice Marshall, joined by Justice Brennan, dissented on the ground that in this case a finding of manifest necessity must be explicit, rather than implied from the record.]

Applying the Manifest Necessity Test

In Arizona v. Washington, the Court suggests that different levels of scrutiny are appropriate for mistrials granted for different reasons. Does the "manifest necessity" requirement for a mistrial have any identifiable meaning? Lower court decisions are inconsistent. For an extensive survey of mistrials under different circumstances, see Schulhofer, Jeopardy and Mistrials, 125 U.Pa.L.Rev. 449 (1977). The inquiry into the permissibility of a retrial following a mistrial is largely fact specific. How should the following situations be analyzed?

Weighing the Alternatives

1. The defendant's primary defense in a murder case was insanity. Prospective jurors were questioned carefully about their views of the defense and knowledge of the case. After the jurors were selected, but before they were sworn, one juror made a "passing comment" to his friend, the bailiff, that after seeing the defendant he thought "the poor man was crazy" and "didn't know what he was doing." The bailiff told the prosecutor about the incident, but did not notify the judge or defense counsel. The jurors were sworn, but before any evidence was introduced the prosecutor moved for a mistrial, arguing that the

juror's opinion would preclude a fair trial. The judge examined the juror, who maintained that he had no prejudgment or fixed opinion on the defendant's sanity. The judge also heard argument on the motion before granting the mistrial. Should the retrial have been barred? Why or why not? See Smith v. Mississippi, 478 F.2d 88 (5th Cir.1973), which held that retrial was not barred. The court stated that "what is of controlling importance is that the state trial judge first painstakingly weighed all the factors present and thereupon exercised the discretion invested in him. His declaration of a mistrial was not unreasonable." See also United States v. Melius, 123 F.3d 1134 (8th Cir.1997) (manifest necessity for a mistrial was found where the judge was informed that jurors had been improperly contacted by a member of the public, who tried to give them inadmissible information about the case). But compare Weston v. Kernan, 50 F.3d 633 (9th Cir.1995)(no manifest necessity for a mistrial where defendant's prior convictions were erroneously admitted; trial court did not explore the possibility that limiting instructions may have cured the prejudice).

[handwritten margin notes: Judge weighed factors / exercised discretion / No bar to new trial]

Deadlocked Juries

2. In Arizona v. Washington, the Court indicated that great deference should be given to a judge's determination to declare a mistrial when the jury is hopelessly deadlocked. In United States v. Horn, 583 F.2d 1124 (10th Cir.1978), after a two-day trial the jury deliberated for three or four hours. The jury then notified the judge that it was deadlocked. The judge recessed for the night. The following morning, the judge talked with the jury about their duty to agree, if possible, "without violence to individual judgment." He then gave a formal *Allen* charge (discussed in Chapter Ten). After the jury deliberated for a little more than an hour, they were brought back into court. Without further inquiry, the court declared a mistrial. The court of appeals held that a retrial was impermissible because there was no manifest necessity for the mistrial. Did the appellate court rule correctly?

What factors should a court consider in determining whether a judge properly exercised his discretion to declare a deadlocked jury? One court has isolated seven criteria:

[handwritten margin notes: Time / Complexity / Communication of judge to jurors]

(1) a timely objection by defendant, (2) the jury's collective opinion that it cannot agree, (3) the length of the deliberations of the jury, (4) the length of the trial, (5) the complexity of the issues presented to the jury, (6) any proper communications which the judge has had with the jury, and (7) the effects of possible exhaustion and the impact which coercion of further deliberations might have on the verdict.

[handwritten margin notes: What factors to consider declaring deadlock + new trial / 7]

See Arnold v. McCarthy, 566 F.2d 1377 (9th Cir.1978). Are these the factors that you would use? See also Escobar v. O'Leary, 943 F.2d 711 (7th Cir. 1991)(manifest necessity existed for mistrial, where the jury was deadlocked after three days of deliberations in a short trial posing relatively simple issues; the fact that the jury was actually split eleven to one in favor of acquittal does not show that the judge believed this to be the case when he granted the mistrial); United States v. Keene, 287 F.3d 229 (1st Cir. 2002) (declaration of mistrial due to deadlocked jury was a manifest necessity; when the jury notified the judge that it was deadlocked, the judge conferred with counsel and allowed them to be heard, considered all available options, tried to nudge the jury toward resolution through supplemental instructions, and sent the jury back to deliberate twice before declaring a mistrial).

Multi-Defendant Trials

3.   In a multi-defendant trial, one of the defendants had retained counsel who had a series of "scheduling conflicts" requiring several delays in setting a trial date. Eventually, the trial judge offered the codefendant the immediate services of an attorney who had worked with him previously on the case. The codefendant refused. The trial judge, sensing bad faith, proceeded with the trial. The codefendant disrupted the proceedings with continual requests for counsel during the testimony of government witnesses. Two days into trial, the judge received word that the attorney for another codefendant had been arrested in an unrelated case for aggravated perjury. This was widely publicized. The judge consulted with counsel for each defendant, but they offered "no uniform curative measure" for any prejudice that they would suffer from these various problems. Some wanted a mistrial, some (defendants Talamas and Cary) a severance, some a continuance. The judge interviewed the jury, but did not make direct reference to the news stories concerning the arrest of the defense counsel. Three jurors admitted to hearing media reports about the case. Over the objections of defendants Talamas and Cary, the judge declared a mistrial.

Should the retrial have been barred? In United States v. Bauman, 887 F.2d 546 (5th Cir.1989), the court held that retrial was permitted because there was a manifest necessity to grant the mistrial. It stated that the doctrine of manifest necessity frees the trial court from the Hobson's Choice of continuing with an unfair trial or permanently ending the prosecution of the defendant. The court recognized that the Supreme Court has left the "manifest necessity" standard deliberately ambiguous, but that the term sounds more onerous than it really is. The court concluded that a trial court has the discretion to order a mistrial even though severance may be a possible alternative. It rejected the argument "that the trial court must always agree to sever certain defendants if possible." The court noted that "reasonable judges may differ on the proper curative measure" in such circumstances and that under Arizona v. Washington "appellate courts are not meant to second-guess the sound discretion of the trial judge in declaring a mistrial for juror prejudice when that judge is closest to the compromising events." The court was satisfied that the trial court "evaluated, with due deliberation, whether a mistrial or some other curative measure was appropriate." Are you satisfied? What interests, if any, would not have been served by a severance of the defendants who objected to a mistrial?

Timing of the Declaration of Mistrial

4.   The defendant was charged with murder and his defense was self-defense. When the jury was deliberating, a juror knocked on the jury room door and asked the sheriff who opened the door how far 92 feet was. The evidence at trial had indicated that the defendant shot the victim from that distance. The sheriff began pacing off the distance down the hallway while some jurors watched. After learning about this incident, the trial judge gave a curative instruction to the jury and they returned to their deliberations. The judge had a conference with the attorneys to decide what to do about this incident. The judge

decided that a mistrial had to be declared. As the lawyers and the judge were preparing to return to the court, the jury reported that it had reached a verdict. The judge stated that since he had declared the mistrial he would have the verdict reported only for the purpose of completing the record. The jury reported a verdict of not guilty. Would a retrial violate the Double Jeopardy Clause?

In the actual case, Corey v. District Court of Vermont, Unit No. 1, Rutland Circuit, 917 F.2d 88 (2d Cir.1990), the court held that there was no manifest necessity to declare a mistrial, once the trial judge learned that the jury had reached a verdict and that the verdict was not guilty. The court recognized that the sheriff acted improperly in demonstrating the distance to the jury and that the judicial response to it was appropriate. However, it reasoned that the trial judge should have refrained from immediately declaring a mistrial because: (1) an acquittal would reveal the absence of prejudice to the defendant; and (2) if the verdict were guilty, the court, concluding that the sheriff's conduct could have prejudiced the defendant, could have ordered a new trial. Thus, there was no manifest necessity and Double Jeopardy barred a new prosecution. Did the reviewing court give the proper deference to the trial court under Arizona v. Washington?

C.　MISTRIAL DECLARED UPON DEFENDANT'S MOTION

Goading the Defendant Into Moving for a Mistrial: Oregon v. Kennedy

Under what circumstances, if any, can the defendant who *moves* for a mistrial invoke double jeopardy protections against a retrial? This question was considered in Oregon v. Kennedy, 456 U.S. 667 (1982). After defense counsel had brought out during cross-examination of the state's expert witness that the expert had previously filed a criminal complaint against the defendant, the prosecutor suggested on redirect examination that the reason for the filing was that the defendant was "a crook." Kennedy moved for a mistrial, and the trial court granted Kennedy's motion. When the state sought to retry Kennedy, he moved to dismiss the charges because of double jeopardy. Justice Rehnquist, writing for the Court, concluded that a retrial was not barred. He reasoned as follows:

> Where the trial is terminated over the objection of the defendant, the classical test for lifting the double jeopardy bar to a second trial is the 'manifest necessity' standard * * *. But in the case of a mistrial declared at the behest of the defendant, quite different principles come into play. Here the defendant himself has elected to terminate the proceedings against him, and the manifest necessity standard has no place in the application of the Double Jeopardy Clause. * * *

> Our cases, however, have indicated that even where the defendant moves for a mistrial, there is a narrow exception to the rule that the Double Jeopardy Clause is no bar to retrial. * * *

> Since one of the principal threads making up the protection embodied in the Double Jeopardy Clause is the right of the defendant to have his trial completed before the first jury empaneled to try him, it may be wondered as a matter of original inquiry why the defendant's election to terminate the

first trial by his own motion should not be deemed a renunciation of that right for all purposes. We have recognized, however, that there would be great difficulty in applying such a rule where the prosecutor's actions giving rise to the mistrial were done in order to goad the defendant into requesting a mistrial. In such a case, the defendant's valued right to complete his trial before the first jury would be a hollow shell if the inevitable motion for mistrial were held to prevent a later invocation of the bar of double jeopardy in all circumstances. But the precise phrasing of the circumstances which *will* allow a defendant to interpose the defense of double jeopardy * * * have been stated with less than crystal clarity * * *.

Justice Rehnquist rejected the argument that double jeopardy should apply whenever the prosecutor's conduct at the first trial indicated "overreaching." He argued that such a test offered "virtually no standards" for application. He opted for an approach that examined the intent of the prosecutor:

> [A] standard that examines the intent of the prosecutor, though certainly not entirely free from practical difficulties, is a manageable standard to apply. It merely calls for the court to make a finding of fact. Inferring the existence or nonexistence of intent from objective facts and circumstances is a familiar process in our criminal justice system. * * *
>
> Prosecutorial conduct that might be viewed as harassment or overreaching, even if sufficient to justify a mistrial on defendant's motion, therefore, does not bar retrial absent intent on the part of the prosecutor to subvert the protections afforded by the Double Jeopardy Clause. * * * Only where the governmental conduct in question is intended to "goad" the defendant into moving for a mistrial may a defendant raise the bar of double jeopardy. * * *
>
> * * * [W]e hold that the circumstances under which * * * a defendant may invoke the bar of double jeopardy to try him are limited to those cases in which the conduct giving rise to the successful motion for a mistrial was intended to provoke the defendant into moving for a mistrial. Since the Oregon trial court found, and the Oregon Court of Appeals accepted, that the prosecutorial conduct culminating in the termination of the first trial in this case was not so intended by the prosecutor, that is the end of the matter * * *.

Justice Powell's concurring opinion emphasized that a court determining the intent of the prosecutor "should rely primarily upon the objective facts and circumstances of the particular case." He noted that in the instant case, the prosecutor had made only a single comment, and that the prosecutor was surprised by and resisted the defendant's motion for a mistrial. Justice Stevens, joined by Justices Brennan, Marshall, and Blackmun, concurred in the judgment. He argued that "[i]t is almost inconceivable that a defendant could prove that the prosecutor's deliberate misconduct was motivated by an intent to provoke a mistrial," and asserted that an "overreaching" standard was preferable even though it would be a "rare and compelling case" in which retrial would be barred.[15] For an application of *Kennedy*, see United States v. Curry, 328 F.3d

---

15. When Oregon v. Kennedy returned to state court, the state supreme court relied upon the state constitution to find that Kennedy's rights were violated. State v. Kennedy, 295 Or. 260, 666 P.2d 1316 (1983). It reasoned that retrial should be barred when the prosecution "either intends or is indifferent to the resulting mistrial or reversal."

970 (8th Cir. 2003) (defendant was not entitled to dismissal of indictment on grounds of double jeopardy violation, following grant of mistrial on the basis of prosecutorial misconduct in suppressing impeachment evidence and in making improper comments during closing argument; the prosecutor did not engage in this conduct with the intent to goad the defendant into declaring a mistrial).

The Rationale of Oregon v. Kennedy

Judge Easterbrook, writing for the court in United States v. Jozwiak, 954 F.2d 458 (7th Cir.1992), provides an excellent explication and application of the Oregon v. Kennedy rationale. Judge Easterbrook set forth the facts of the case as follows:

> Nine of the twenty-six defendants in this case charging a conspiracy to distribute cocaine went to trial on November 4, 1991. A prosecutor—whose first trial this was—told the jury during his opening statement that five of the original defendants were cooperating with the government and would appear as witnesses and that four others had also pleaded guilty. The mention that some of the defendants had entered pleas of guilty led the defendants to seek a mistrial. A senior prosecutor from the United States Attorney's office confessed error and apologized. As everyone wanted a mistrial, the district judge sent the jury home. There was no point conducting a long trial with a built-in error.

> All nine defendants then insisted that the double jeopardy clause bars further prosecution. The district court denied the motion, observing that the defendants had requested the mistrial.

Judge Easterbrook analyzed the double jeopardy question, and the applicability of Oregon v. Kennedy, as follows:

> The double jeopardy clause gives the defendant a right to "get a verdict if he wants one and keep it if he gets it." A right to obtain implies a right to relinquish. Defendants may choose whether to proceed with the first jury; if they elect not to, they have not been "deprived" of any entitlement. To honor a choice is not to dishonor the underlying rule. The alternative to honoring the defendant's choice is forcing the parties to verdict in the first trial, then reversing the conviction and holding another trial—something neither side wants.

> * * * [A] motion for a mistrial is not an invariable sign of the accused's choice to forego decision by the first tribunal. Perhaps things have been going well for the defense but the prosecutor does something exceedingly prejudicial, so much so that the balance suddenly (and improperly) shifts in the prosecutor's favor. Even though the defense then moves for a mistrial, termination of the trial is properly attributed to the prosecutor's conniving rather than to the accused's preference. In Oregon v. Kennedy, the Court held that, if "the conduct giving rise to the successful motion for a mistrial was intended to provoke the defendant into moving for a mistrial", a second trial is impermissible. So our defendants asked for a hearing at which they could probe the prosecutor's intent, including "the actual circumstances surrounding the making of the statements by [the prosecutor] and his being designated to give the opening statement in this trial." The district judge

declined to hold a hearing. This decision provides the foundation for the defendants' arguments to us.

Doubtless every lawyer would like to have his adversary's counsel at his mercy. Put the prosecutor on the stand; ask him why he chose one strategy and rejected another; inquire what weakness in the evidence led to a given remark. Attractive to the defense, certainly; compelled by the Constitution, certainly not. To say that intent is an element of the constitutional rule is not to say that intent is to be proved by testimony and cross-examination. * * * [A] judge may evaluate the prosecutor's informal explanation for an action that leads to a mistrial. Here the prosecutor attributed the reference to guilty pleas to his inexperience, and the judge believed him.

Any search for steps intended to goad defendants into seeking mistrials encounters a problem. Because intent is a matter of characterization, you cannot even know what indicia to look for unless you know the direction toward which the (forbidden) intent would be bent. Prosecutors intend to secure convictions, intend to secure all advantages the adversary system allows. An overstep (sometimes even a correct step) may lead to howls from the defense, and next to an argument that the overstep was intended to goad the adversary into howling. Yet a search for intent that leads only to a conclusion that the prosecutor wanted to win is pointless. We must be looking for intent to do something that undercuts the interests protected by the double jeopardy clause. *Kennedy* distinguishes intent to improve the chance that the trier of fact will return a favorable decision from the forbidden intent to avoid decision by the trier of fact.

Judge Easterbrook provided a rule of thumb for determining prosecutorial intent in these murky circumstances:

A defendant's interest in preserving the benefits of a trial that has been going well enables us to distinguish these two characterizations of prosecutorial intent. Only a prosecutor who thinks the trial going sour—or who seeks to get just far enough into the trial to preview the defense—would want to precipitate a mistrial. Otherwise the mistrial means a waste for both sides, injuring the prosecutor along with the defense. (Trying one defendant twice means, for a prosecutor with limited resources, letting some other defendant go.) Unless there is reason to believe that the prosecutor set out to rescue a case on the path to acquittal or filch a road map of the defense, a court may cut off the inquiry; whatever may have been in the prosecutor's head was not the kind of intent with which the Double Jeopardy Clause is concerned.

Applying these standards to the facts, Judge Easterbrook concluded that the prosecutor had no intent to goad the defendant into asking for a mistrial when he referred, in opening argument, to the fact that some of the conspirators had entered guilty pleas.

The prosecutor's case against these nine defendants was not going downhill; it was not going, period. It ended within minutes after the prosecutor rose to speak. * * * Defense counsel did not tip their hands; they barely had time to tip their hats. Scuttling a trial at dockside poses few if any risks to the defendant's legitimate interests. It is no surprise that the Court is willing to find early terminations supported by "manifest necessity" even though deferred action might be unjustifiable. See Arizona v. Washington; Illinois v.

Somerville. When the early termination comes at the defendant's behest, there is no constitutional obstacle to a new trial.

Why Should Defendant's Motion Make a Difference?

As we have seen, if the prosecution moves for a mistrial, double jeopardy bars a new trial unless the "manifest necessity" standard is met. However, if the defendant moves for a mistrial, double jeopardy only bars a new trial in the very rare case in which the prosecutor has intentionally goaded the defendant into moving for a mistrial. Why should it matter, for double jeopardy purposes, whether it is the prosecutor or the defendant who moves for the mistrial? Judge Easterbrook, in Miller v. Indiana Dept. of Corrections, 75 F.3d 330 (7th Cir. 1996), posits that if double jeopardy would routinely bar a mistrial whenever the defendant moved for one in good faith, such a rule would in the long run harm defendants. He reasoned that the threat of double jeopardy in such circumstances would mean that "judges would be even more reluctant to grant mistrials than they are already." Assuming that a defendant's motion for a mistrial is meritorious, do you believe that a trial judge would be more likely to deny it if there was a greater risk that a retrial would be barred? Wouldn't the judge be worried about being reversed on appeal as to the denial of the defendant's motion for mistrial?

Failure to Object, or Consent, to a Mistrial

Under Oregon v. Kennedy, the manifest necessity standard is inapplicable if the defendant moves for a mistrial. Is the failure to object to the trial judge's order of a mistrial tantamount to consent or a motion for a mistrial? In United States v. Buljubasic, 808 F.2d 1260 (7th Cir.1987), the court looked at several factors to determine whether the defendant's silence creates an inference of consent to a mistrial—thus triggering the "goading" test of Oregon v. Kennedy as opposed to the "manifest necessity" test of Arizona v. Washington. The factors bearing on consent include (1) whether the defendant previously requested a mistrial; (2) whether there was sufficient time to object; (3) whether the trial court indicated that it would declare a mistrial no matter what; and (4) whether the trial to that point had been "going the defendant's way." On the facts, the court found that the defendant had consented to a mistrial—he had moved for a mistrial on several occasions before the court actually granted one, the court had held an hour-long hearing on the propriety of a mistrial, and the defense had not gone well to that point. Therefore, Oregon v. Kennedy was applicable, and because the defendant could not show that the prosecutor had "baited" him into seeking a mistrial, a retrial was not barred by the Double Jeopardy Clause.

In contrast, in Corey v. District Court of Vermont, Unit No. 1, Rutland Circuit, 917 F.2d 88 (2d Cir.1990), discussed in the Note after Arizona v. Washington, defense counsel did not object to the mistrial, but specifically stated that the defendant intended to assert his double jeopardy rights if there was a retrial. The court found that this action was sufficient to trigger the application of the manifest necessity standard. See also Escobar v. O'Leary, 943 F.2d 711 (7th Cir.1991)(the defendant sufficiently objected to a mistrial, which was granted by the court on the ground of jury deadlock; the defendant had raised a strong defense, had repeatedly requested more jury deliberations, and asked for an *Allen* charge, after the possibility of a mistrial arose); United States v. Huang, 960 F.2d 1128 (2d Cir.1992)(defendant found to object to a mistrial, where he moved for a mistrial "with prejudice", and objected when the trial court granted mistrial without prejudice).

Waiving the Double Jeopardy Claim

In Beringer v. Sheahan, 934 F.2d 110 (7th Cir.1991), the prosecutor engaged in intentional misconduct, but the defendant never moved for a mistrial. The defendant was convicted, and his conviction was reversed on appeal due to the prosecutorial misconduct. The defendant claimed that a retrial would be impermissible under Oregon v. Kennedy, but the court found that case inapplicable to a situation where the defendant fails to move for a mistrial; it held that the right to claim double jeopardy was waived, so that neither the "manifest necessity" standard nor the "intentional goading" standard were applicable. The court was concerned that a contrary result would allow defendants to refuse to move for a mistrial (thus avoiding the stricter Oregon v. Kennedy test) in the hope of obtaining a reversal and a double jeopardy bar on appeal. See also United States v. Gantley, 172 F.3d 422 (6th Cir.1999) (waiver of Double Jeopardy claim where defense counsel took no action after trial judge invited an objection to his plan to order a mistrial).

Multiple Defendants

Multi-defendant trials present intricate double jeopardy problems when some event occurs that raises the possibility of a mistrial. The complexity arises because there are two tests for determining the double jeopardy claim after a mistrial—the "manifest necessity" test and the "goading test"—and the applicability of these tests depends on whether the defendant opposes or moves for a mistrial. United States v. Huang, 960 F.2d 1128 (2d Cir.1992), is an example. After the star prosecution witness had testified in the Mandarin dialect of Chinese, it was discovered that the court translator was not properly certified, and moreover that he had made a summary of parts of the testimony, rather than a verbatim translation. Two defendants moved for a mistrial, and two defendants opposed a mistrial.

The *Huang* court separately analyzed the double jeopardy question as to each group of defendants. It rejected the double jeopardy claims of the defendants who moved for a mistrial, finding no indication that the prosecutor even knew about the translation problem, much less that it was used as a device to goad the defendants into moving for a mistrial.

In contrast, the court held that the two defendants who objected to the mistrial could not be retried. The court found no manifest necessity for declaring a mistrial. The court concluded that deviations from the ideal translation are not so fundamental as to constitute plain error. Nor had the trial court explored the alternative of severing the defendants who wanted to continue from those who wanted a mistrial. The government's interest in trying the defendants together could not outweigh the constitutionally-based interest of the two objecting defendants in having a verdict from the first jury that is impaneled.

X. CONTROLS ON JUDICIAL AND PROSECUTORIAL VINDICTIVENESS

In the following cases, the Court held that the Double Jeopardy Clause is not applicable to control judicial vindictiveness in sentencing or to prosecutorial vindictiveness in charging. However, the Due Process Clause is held to impose some limitations on those practices.

A. JUDICIAL VINDICTIVENESS

NORTH CAROLINA v. PEARCE

Supreme Court of the United States, 1969.
395 U.S. 711.

MR. JUSTICE STEWART **delivered the opinion of the Court.**

When at the behest of the defendant a criminal conviction has been set aside and a new trial ordered, to what extent does the Constitution limit the imposition of a harsher sentence after conviction upon retrial? That is the question presented by these two cases.

In No. 413 the respondent Pearce was convicted in a North Carolina court upon a charge of assault with intent to commit rape. The trial judge sentenced him to prison for a term of 12 to 15 years. Several years later he initiated a state post-conviction proceeding which culminated in the reversal of his conviction by the Supreme Court of North Carolina, upon the ground that an involuntary confession had unconstitutionally been admitted in evidence against him. He was retried, convicted, and sentenced by the trial judge to an eight-year prison term, which, when added to the time Pearce had already spent in prison, the parties agree amounted to a longer total sentence than that originally imposed. * * *

In No. 418 the respondent Rice pleaded guilty in an Alabama trial court to four separate charges of second-degree burglary. He was sentenced to prison terms aggregating 10 years. Two and one-half years later the judgments were set aside in a state * * * proceeding, upon the ground that Rice had not been accorded his constitutional right to counsel. He was retried upon three of the charges, convicted, and sentenced to prison on terms aggregating 25 years. No credit was given for the time he had spent in prison on the original judgments.

* * *

The problem before us involves two related but analytically separate issues. One concerns the constitutional limitations upon the imposition of a more severe punishment after conviction for the same offense upon retrial. * * *[a]

* * *

II

* * *

A

Long-established constitutional doctrine makes clear that * * * the guarantee against double jeopardy imposes no restrictions upon the length of a sentence imposed upon reconvic-

---

a. [Editor's Note: The other issue was whether credit must be given for time served, and the Court held that it must be given.]

tion. At least since 1896, when United States v. Ball, 163 U.S. 662, was decided, it has been settled that this constitutional guarantee imposes no limitations whatever upon the power to *retry* a defendant who has succeeded in getting his first conviction set aside. * * * And at least since 1919, when Stroud v. United States, 251 U.S. 15, was decided, it has been settled that a corollary of the power to retry a defendant is the power, upon the defendant's reconviction, to impose whatever sentence may be legally authorized, whether or not it is greater than the sentence imposed after the first conviction.[b] * * *

Although the rationale for this "well-established part of our constitutional jurisprudence" has been variously verbalized, it rests ultimately upon the premise that the original conviction has, at the defendant's behest, been wholly nullified and the slate wiped clean. As to whatever punishment has actually been suffered under the first conviction, that premise is, of course, an unmitigated fiction * * *. But, so far as the conviction itself goes, and that part of the sentence that has not yet been served, it is no more than a simple statement of fact to say that the slate *has* been wiped clean. The conviction *has* been set aside, and the unexpired portion of the original sentence will never be served. A new trial may result in an acquittal. But if it does result in a conviction, we cannot say that the constitutional guarantee against double jeopardy of its own weight restricts the imposition of an otherwise lawful single punishment for the offense in question. To hold to the contrary would be to cast doubt upon the whole validity of the basic principle enunciated in United States

v. Ball, supra, and upon the unbroken line of decisions that have followed that principle for almost 75 years. We think those decisions are entirely sound, and we decline to depart from the concept they reflect.

B

[The Court rejected an argument that the Equal Protection Clause forbids the imposition of a more severe sentence upon retrial.]

C

We hold, therefore, that neither the double jeopardy provision nor the Equal Protection Clause imposes an absolute bar to a more severe sentence upon reconviction. A trial judge is not constitutionally precluded, in other words, from imposing a new sentence, whether greater or less than the original sentence, in the light of events subsequent to the first trial that may have thrown new light upon the defendant's "life, health, habits, conduct, and mental and moral propensities." Such information may come to the judge's attention from evidence adduced at the second trial itself, from a new presentence investigation, from the defendant's prison record, or possibly from other sources. * * *

To say that there exists no absolute constitutional bar to the imposition of a more severe sentence upon retrial is not, however, to end the inquiry. There remains for consideration the impact of the Due Process Clause of the Fourteenth Amendment.

It can hardly be doubted that it would be a flagrant violation of the Fourteenth Amendment for a state trial court to follow an announced practice of imposing a heavier sentence upon every reconvicted defendant for the

---

b. In *Stroud* the defendant was convicted of first-degree murder and sentenced to life imprisonment. After reversal of this conviction, the defendant was retried, reconvicted of the

same offense, and sentenced to death. This Court upheld the conviction against the defendant's claim that his constitutional right not to be twice put in jeopardy had been violated.

explicit purpose of punishing the defendant for his having succeeded in getting his original conviction set aside. Where, as in each of the cases before us, the original conviction has been set aside because of a constitutional error, the imposition of such a punishment, "penalizing those who choose to exercise" constitutional rights, "would be patently unconstitutional." United States v. Jackson, 390 U.S. 570, 581. And the very threat inherent in the existence of such a punitive policy would, with respect to those still in prison, serve to "chill the exercise of basic constitutional rights." But even if the first conviction has been set aside for nonconstitutional error, the imposition of a penalty upon the defendant for having successfully pursued a statutory right of appeal or collateral remedy would be no less a violation of due process of law. * * *

Due process of law, then, requires that vindictiveness against a defendant for having successfully attacked his first conviction must play no part in the sentence he receives after a new trial. And since the fear of such vindictiveness may unconstitutionally deter a defendant's exercise of the right to appeal or collaterally attack his first conviction, due process also requires that a defendant be freed of apprehension of such a retaliatory motivation on the part of the sentencing judge.

In order to assure the absence of such a motivation, we have concluded that whenever a judge imposes a more severe sentence upon a defendant after a new trial, the reasons for his doing so must affirmatively appear. Those reasons must be based upon objective information concerning identifiable conduct on the part of the defendant occurring after the time of the original sentencing proceeding. And the factual data upon which the

increased sentence is based must be made part of the record, so that the constitutional legitimacy of the increased sentence may be fully reviewed on appeal.

We dispose of the two cases before us in the light of these conclusions. In No. 418 Judge Johnson noted that "the State of Alabama offers no evidence attempting to justify the increase in Rice's original sentences * * *." He found it "shocking that the State of Alabama has not attempted to explain or justify the increase in Rice's punishment—in these three cases, over threefold." And he found that "the conclusion is inescapable that the State of Alabama is punishing petitioner Rice for his having exercised his post-conviction right of review * * *." In No. 413 the situation is not so dramatically clear. Nonetheless, the fact remains that neither at the time the increased sentence was imposed upon Pearce, nor at any stage in this habeas corpus proceeding, has the State offered any reason or justification for that sentence beyond the naked power to impose it.

[The Court upheld the relief granted to Pearce and Rice by the lower courts. Justices Douglas and Marshall concurred, but would have held that the Double Jeopardy Clause bars a higher penalty upon reconviction in every case. Justice Harlan's separate opinion largely agreed with the view of Justices Douglas and Marshall.

Justice Black wrote a concurring and dissenting opinion. He concluded that due process prohibited a higher sentence imposed on appeal for the purpose of punishing a defendant for appealing, but that the detailed procedure mandated by the Court was not required. Justice White wrote an opinion concurring in part.]

Determining Vindictiveness After Pearce

That *Pearce* was decided as a due process and not a double jeopardy case is of great importance. The more flexible due process approach produced subsequent rulings that narrowed the potential reach of *Pearce*, rulings that would have been more difficult had *Pearce* rested on the more absolutist double jeopardy language of the Fifth Amendment.

More Convictions in the Interim: Wasman v. United States

The Supreme Court explained in Wasman v. United States, 468 U.S. 559 (1984), that *Pearce* did not prevent the imposition of a higher sentence upon reconviction of a defendant who had been convicted of additional offenses between the first and second trials. The trial judge who sentenced Wasman carefully explained that he gave him a greater sentence after the second trial than he had after the first because he had additional convictions at the time of the second trial. The Court found this explanation sufficient to rebut the presumption of vindictiveness established by *Pearce*.

Discovery of Events Occurring Prior to the Initial Proceeding: Texas v. McCullough

Chief Justice Burger wrote for the Court in Texas v. McCullough, 475 U.S. 134 (1986), as it upheld a trial judge's imposition of a 50–year sentence in a second trial necessitated by the judge's granting a mistrial after a jury had imposed a 20–year sentence in the first trial. The Court held that the *Pearce* presumption of vindictiveness was inapplicable because the second trial occurred only "because the trial judge herself concluded that the prosecutor's misconduct required it" and "because different sentencers assessed the varying sentences that McCullough received." Moreover, the Court found that even if *Pearce* were to apply, the trial judge's findings—i.e., two new witnesses testified in the second case concerning the murder, and the judge learned for the first time that the defendant had been released from prison only four months before the murder—rebutted the presumption. It rejected the argument that *Pearce* permitted consideration only of events occurring subsequent to the original sentencing. The Chief Justice recognized that "a defendant may be more reluctant to appeal if there is a risk that new, probative evidence supporting a longer sentence may be revealed on retrial." But he stated that "this Court has never recognized this 'chilling effect' as sufficient reason to create a constitutional prohibition against considering relevant information in assessing sentences."

Justice Marshall, joined by Justices Blackmun and Stevens, dissented, arguing that "the mere grant of a new trial motion can in no way be considered a guarantee, or even an indication, that the judge will harbor no resentment toward defendant as a result of his decision to exercise his statutory right to make such a motion." Thus, he would have applied the *Pearce* presumption. Justice Brennan concurred in the judgment on the ground that "the possibility that an increased sentence upon retrial resulted from judicial vindictiveness is sufficiently remote that the presumption * * * should not apply here."

No Presumption of Vindictiveness When There Are Two Separate Decisionmakers: Colten v. Kentucky and Chaffin v. Stynchcombe

In Colten v. Kentucky, 407 U.S. 104 (1972), the Court held that *Pearce* did not apply when a second sentence was handed down by a higher court in a two-tiered trial court system. The Court emphasized that the de novo court "was not the court that is asked to do over what it thought it had already done correctly," and that therefore a presumption of vindictiveness would be unwarranted.

In Chaffin v. Stynchcombe, 412 U.S. 17 (1973), the Court held that due process does not require the extension of *Pearce* to jury sentencing. In *Chaffin* the defendant was tried for and convicted of robbery by force or violence. The jury sentenced him to fifteen years, but his appeal was successful. Thereafter, he was retried, convicted, and sentenced to life imprisonment. The jury knew that he had been tried previously on the same charge but did not know of his prior conviction or sentence. The following excerpt represents the Court's treatment of *Pearce*:

> Petitioner seeks the extension of the *Pearce* rationale to jury resentencing. That decision, as we have said, was premised on the apparent need to guard against *vindictiveness* in the resentencing process. *Pearce* was not written with a view to protecting against the mere possibility that, once the slate is wiped clean and the prosecution begins anew, a fresh sentence may be higher for some valid reason associated with the need for flexibility and discretion in the sentencing process. The possibility of a higher sentence was recognized and accepted as a legitimate concomitant of the retrial process.

> * * *

> This case, then, is controlled by the inquiry into possible vindictiveness counseled by *Pearce* * * *. The potential for such abuse of the sentencing process by the jury is, we think, *de minimis* in a properly controlled retrial. The first prerequisite for the imposition of a retaliatory penalty is knowledge of the prior sentence. It has been conceded in this case that the jury was not informed of the prior sentence. We have no reason to suspect that this is not customary in a properly tried jury case. * * * Other distinguishing factors between jury and judicial sentencing further diminish the possibility of impropriety in jury sentencing. As was true in *Colten*, the second sentence is not meted out by the same judicial authority whose handling of the prior trial was sufficiently unacceptable to have required a reversal of the conviction. Thus, the jury, unlike the judge who has been reversed, will have no personal stake in the prior conviction and no motivation to engage in self-vindication. Similarly, the jury is unlikely to be sensitive to the institutional interests that might occasion higher sentences by a judge desirous of discouraging what he regards as meritless appeals.

> In light of these considerations, and where improper and prejudicial information regarding the prior sentence is withheld, there is no basis for holding that jury resentencing poses any real threat of vindictiveness.

Trial After a Guilty Plea: Alabama v. Smith

In Alabama v. Smith, 490 U.S. 794 (1989), the defendant pleaded guilty and was sentenced; he appealed to have his guilty plea vacated and was successful. He was thereupon tried on the original charges before the judge who had sentenced him under the vacated guilty plea. He was found guilty after trial, and the judge imposed a sentence more severe than the one he rendered after the guilty plea. Chief Justice Rehnquist, writing for eight Justices, held that the *Pearce* presumption of vindictiveness does not apply when a sentence imposed after a trial is greater than that previously imposed after a guilty plea that was subsequently found invalid. The Court asserted that post-*Pearce* cases had established that the *Pearce* presumption should apply only to circumstances where there is "a reasonable likelihood that the increase in sentence is the product of actual vindictiveness." The Chief Justice observed that "when a greater penalty is imposed after trial than was imposed after a prior guilty plea, the increase in sentence is not more likely than not attributable to the vindictiveness on the part of the sentencing judge." He reasoned that "[e]ven when the same judge imposes both sentences, the relevant sentencing information available to the judge after the plea will usually be considerably less than that available after a trial," and "after trial, the factors that may have indicated leniency as consideration for the guilty plea are no longer present." The Court distinguished *Pearce* as a situation in which the sentencing judge, who presided at both trials, could be "expected to operate in the context of roughly the same sentencing considerations after the second trial as he does after the first; any unexplained change in the sentence is therefore subject to a presumption of vindictiveness." Justice Marshall dissented.

B. PROSECUTORIAL VINDICTIVENESS

Prosecutor's Conduct After the Defendant Exercises the Right to Appeal: Blackledge v. Perry

Although the arguments about prosecutorial vindictiveness did not carry the day in *Chaffin*, they were more successful in Blackledge v. Perry, 417 U.S. 21 (1974). Perry, an inmate in a North Carolina prison, was involved in a fight with another inmate and was charged with misdemeanor assault with a deadly weapon. After he was convicted in the lower trial court, he appealed as of right to the higher trial court where he was entitled to a trial de novo. After the filing of the notice of appeal, the prosecutor obtained an indictment from a grand jury, charging Perry with felonious assault with intent to kill or inflict serious bodily injury. Perry pleaded guilty to the felony charge and received a sentence that was less favorable than that imposed by the lower trial court on the misdemeanor conviction. The Supreme Court held that a person who is convicted of an offense and who has an opportunity for a trial de novo has a right to avail himself of the opportunity without apprehension that the prosecutor will substitute a more serious charge for the one brought in the lower court. The Court found that where a prosecutor brings more serious charges after a trial has been completed, a presumption of vindictiveness arises. The Court reasoned as follows:

> The question is whether the opportunities for vindictiveness [on the part of the prosecutor] are such as to impel the conclusion that due process

of law requires a rule analogous to that of the *Pearce* case. We conclude that the answer must be in the affirmative.

A prosecutor clearly has a considerable stake in discouraging [appeals which] will clearly require increased expenditures of prosecutorial resources before the defendant's conviction becomes final, and may even result in a formerly convicted defendant going free. And, if the prosecutor has the means readily at hand to discourage such appeals—by "upping the ante" through a felony indictment * * * the state can insure that only the most hardy defendants will brave the hazards of a de novo trial.

There is, of course, no evidence that the prosecutor in this case acted in bad faith or maliciously in seeking a felony indictment against Perry. The rationale of [*Pearce*], however, was not grounded upon the proposition that actual retaliatory motivation must inevitably exist. Rather, we emphasized that since the fear of such vindictiveness may unconstitutionally deter a defendant's exercise of the right to appeal * * * due process also requires that a defendant be freed of apprehension of such a retaliatory motivation on the part of the sentencing judge. We think it clear that the same considerations apply here.

The Court noted that the presumption of vindictiveness would be overcome if the State could show "that it was impossible to proceed on the more serious charge at the outset" and cited Diaz v. United States, 223 U.S. 442 (1912), discussed supra. In *Diaz*, the Double Jeopardy Clause was held not to bar a later murder trial where the victim did not die until after the defendant's trial for assault and battery. See also United States v. York, 933 F.2d 1343 (7th Cir.1991), where the defendant was subjected to an additional charge of obstruction of justice after a successful appeal of his murder conviction. The court concluded that the testimony required to support the obstruction charge came from the defendant's son, who had expressed an unwillingness to testify against his father at the first trial. When the son changed his mind and approached the authorities two years later, the prosecution could not be presumed vindictive when it added the obstruction charge.[16]

Prosecutor's Conduct After the Defendant Invokes a Trial Right: United States v. Goodwin

In United States v. Goodwin, 454 U.S. 1138 (1982), the Court distinguished *Blackledge* and refused to apply a presumption of vindictiveness to a prosecutor's decisions in the pretrial setting. Goodwin was charged with several misdemeanors, including assault, following an incident in which a police officer stopped his car for speeding. After he invoked his right to a jury trial, an Assistant United States Attorney obtained a four count indictment against Goodwin that included a felony charge of forcibly assaulting a federal officer. Goodwin was convicted on the felony count and one misdemeanor count. The

---

16. The Court found that *Blackledge* clearly controlled in Thigpen v. Roberts, 468 U.S. 27 (1984). The defendant was convicted in a lower level court of several misdemeanors, he sought a de novo trial in a higher level court, and he was indicted for a felony offense arising out of the same conduct. Finding that the same prosecutor was involved in both prosecutions, the Court stated that it "need not determine the correct rule when two independent prosecutors are involved." It observed that the *Blackledge* presumption of vindictiveness is rebuttable, but that no attempt at rebuttal had been made in the lower courts.

Supreme Court, in an opinion by Justice Stevens, reversed a court of appeals' holding that the Due Process Clause prohibits the government from bringing more serious charges against a defendant after he has exercised his right to jury trial. Distinguishing *Pearce* and *Blackledge* as decisions reflecting "a recognition by the Court of the institutional bias inherent in the judicial system against the retrial of issues that have already been decided," Justice Stevens' opinion reasoned as follows:

> There is good reason to be cautious before adopting an inflexible presumption of prosecutorial vindictiveness in a pre-trial setting. In the course of preparing for trial, the prosecutor may uncover additional information that suggests a basis for further prosecution or he simply may come to realize that information possessed by the State has a broader significance. At this stage of the proceedings, the prosecutor's assessment of the proper extent of prosecution may not have crystallized. In contrast, once a trial begins—and certainly by the time a conviction has been obtained—it is much more likely that the State has discovered and assessed all of the information against an accused and has made a determination, on the basis of that information, of the extent to which he should be prosecuted. Thus, a change in the charging decision made after an initial trial is completed is much more likely to be improperly motivated than is a pretrial decision.

Although Justice Stevens declined to adopt a presumption of vindictiveness in the circumstances presented, he stated that "we of course do not foreclose the possibility that a defendant in an appropriate case might prove objectively that the prosecutor's decision was motivated by a desire to punish him for doing something that the law plainly allowed him to do." Justice Blackmun would have presumed vindictiveness but found that the prosecutor's reasons for seeking a felony indictment adequately rebutted the presumption. Justice Brennan, joined by Justice Marshall, dissented.[17]

Applications of Goodwin

The presumption of prosecutorial vindictiveness has not been found readily by lower courts. For example, in United States v. Sinigaglio, 942 F.2d 581 (9th Cir.1991), the court stated that "when increased charges are filed in the routine course of prosecutorial review or as a result of continuing investigation, there is no realistic likelihood of prosecutorial abuse, and therefore no appearance of vindictive prosecution arises merely because the prosecutor's action was taken after a defense right was exercised." It has also been held that the increase in charges due to the prosecutor's discovery of a new law does not warrant a presumption of vindictiveness. United States v. Austin, 902 F.2d 743 (9th Cir.1990). In United States v. Muldoon, 931 F.2d 282 (4th Cir.1991), the court held that a presumption of vindictiveness "does not arise from plea negotiations when the prosecutor threatens to bring additional charges if the accused refuses to plead guilty to pending charges. The Due Process Clause does not bar the

---

17. Recognizing that *Goodwin* makes a presumption of vindictiveness impossible, State v. Halling, 66 Or.App. 180, 672 P.2d 1386 (1983), nevertheless upholds a trial judge who found actual vindictiveness in the filing of two indictments against a defendant who refused to plead guilty to attempted murder. The prosecutor had not mentioned additional offenses during a pretrial conference and had phoned defense counsel to say that she had found a way "to cause further evil" to the defendant.

prosecutor from carrying out his threat." See also United States v. Williams, 47 F.3d 658 (4th Cir.1995)(no presumption of vindictiveness where prosecutor increases the charges when the defendant refuses to become a cooperating witness and undercover informant).

Vindictiveness in Bringing Related Charges After an Acquittal?

If a defendant is acquitted, should a presumption of vindictiveness apply if the prosecutor then charges the defendant with a related crime on the basis of the same conduct? Of course, the prosecutor cannot charge the "same offence". But under the *Blockburger* test, the prosecutor may be able to prosecute on the same conduct by charging a crime with somewhat different elements than the crime first charged. While this is permissible under the Double Jeopardy Clause, does it raise a presumption of vindictiveness?

Consider United States v. Johnson, 171 F.3d 139 (2d Cir.1999). Johnson was arrested by officers of the New York City Police Department for possession of a loaded handgun, and indicted by a state grand jury on two weapons possession charges. While the state weapons prosecution was pending, a federal grand jury indicted Johnson on substantive RICO and RICO conspiracy charges. After a jury trial in federal court, Johnson was acquitted of all outstanding RICO charges. Two months later, a federal prosecutor obtained an indictment against Johnson for possession of a firearm and ammunition by a felon, and for obliteration or alteration of a firearm's serial number. Shortly thereafter, the state weapons charges were dismissed. Johnson filed a pre-trial motion seeking dismissal of the weapons charges due to vindictive prosecution. The trial judge granted the dismissal on the ground that "nothing had occurred that would have prompted the government to submit the instant charges to the grand jury EXCEPT that Johnson had been acquitted of the RICO charges after having demanded a jury trial on those charges." The judge reasoned that the prosecution obviously knew about the weapons offenses before the RICO case arose, could have included them as part of the RICO case, and only decided to bring the weapons charges after Johnson had been acquitted.

The court of appeals reversed and reinstated the weapons charges. It analyzed the question of vindictiveness as follows:

> A presumption of vindictiveness arises when the circumstances of the case create a "realistic likelihood" of prosecutorial vindictiveness. Because the Government did not assert any reason why the prosecution of Johnson on federal weapons charges could not, as a practical matter, have been initiated at an earlier time, the district court assumed (appropriately, in our view) that the new charges were attributable to the acquittal on the RICO charges, which followed Johnson's exercise of his right to a jury trial. In these circumstances, it is conceivable that the weapons charges were brought in retaliation for Johnson's exercise of his rights. However, the Government also might have decided from the outset that it was unnecessary for Johnson to be convicted and sentenced for both sets of charges; under this line of thinking, the weapons prosecution was superfluous unless the RICO prosecution proved unsuccessful. This rationale does not eliminate the "but for" causal connection between Johnson's exercise of his right to a jury trial and the weapons prosecution, but it nevertheless is entirely legitimate, and certainly cannot be considered vindictive. The relevant

question, therefore, is whether there is a "realistic likelihood" that the Government acted out of a vindictive motivation, rather than a legitimate one such as that described above.

* * * [W]e join the other courts of appeals that have held that a new federal prosecution following an acquittal on separate federal charges does not, without more, give rise to a presumption of vindictiveness. Simply put, when a State brings another indictment supported by evidence against a defendant after an acquittal, the acquittal is a legitimate prosecutorial consideration because the State is not levying punishment for a right exercised but rather for the crimes the defendant committed. Accordingly, those circumstances do not present a "realistic likelihood" of prosecutorial vindictiveness.

The court noted the adverse consequences that might flow if a presumption of vindictiveness arose whenever charges on separate offenses were brought after a defendant's acquittal:

Furthermore, adoption of a presumption of vindictiveness in these circumstances would encourage prosecutors to overcharge defendants, a result we do not wish to promote.

The court rejected "a new constitutional rule that requires prosecutors to bring all possible charges in an indictment or forever hold their peace".

XI. DOUBLE JEOPARDY AND REVIEW OF SENTENCING

A. GOVERNMENT APPEALS GENERALLY

We have previously seen that an appellate court cannot set aside a jury or judge verdict of not guilty (except where the trial judge attempts to set aside a prior jury verdict of guilt), and a judge generally may not increase the sentence imposed upon a defendant who successfully appeals from a conviction. But can the prosecutor ask an appellate court to increase the sentence imposed by a trial court?

Seeking a Harsher Sentence: United States v. DiFrancesco

Justice Blackmun wrote for the majority in United States v. DiFrancesco, 449 U.S. 117 (1980), upholding the government's right to appeal the sentence imposed upon a "dangerous special offender." The majority said that the prohibition against multiple trials is the controlling constitutional principle in double jeopardy cases and that the problem with appellate review of acquittals is the necessity of a second trial if relief is granted. In contrast, appellate review of sentencing need not require a second trial. Moreover, the majority noted that "the pronouncement of sentence has never carried the finality that attaches to an acquittal." The Court also observed that the defendant is not subjected to multiple sentences when resentenced following an appeal, since the defendant understands that an initial sentence is not final. Justice Brennan, joined by Justices White, Marshall, and Stevens, dissented and argued that "[i]n both acquittals and sentences, the trier of fact makes a factual adjudication that removes from the defendant's burden of risk the charges of which he was acquitted and the potential sentence which he did not receive." The dissent argued "that most defendants are more concerned with how much time they must spend in prison than with whether their record shows a conviction" and that the anxiety associated with multiple trials is equally present when the government can take an appeal from sentencing. Justice Stevens also filed a separate dissent.[18]

B. REVIEW IN CAPITAL CASES

Death Is Different: Bullington v. Missouri

The Supreme Court distinguished *DiFrancesco* in Bullington v. Missouri, 451 U.S. 430 (1981), and held that it would violate the Double Jeopardy Clause to impose a death penalty at a second trial when the jury in the first trial returned a verdict of life imprisonment, in which the prosecution had the burden in the separate sentencing proceeding of proving certain elements beyond a reasonable doubt. The majority noted that the capital sentencing procedure was more like a trial on guilt or innocence than are most sentencing proceedings and that the prior jury determination was tantamount to an acquittal on the death sentence. Four dissenters argued that the purpose of double jeopardy protection is to protect the innocent from wrongful conviction and that sentencing procedures present no danger of convicting the innocent.

Trial Court Error in Favor of the Defendant:
Arizona v. Rumsey

Bullington proved to be controlling in Arizona v. Rumsey, 467 U.S. 203 (1984), as the Supreme Court held that a state judge's finding that there were no aggravating factors warranting imposition of capital punishment had the same effect as an "acquittal" and that the state supreme court violated the Double Jeopardy Clause when it remanded a defendant's case back for resentencing and a death sentence was then imposed. Like Missouri, Arizona placed on the prosecution the burden of proving aggravating circumstances beyond a reasonable doubt. The Court declined to distinguish Missouri's jury findings from Arizona's judge findings. Even though the state supreme court held that the trial judge had erred as a matter of law in construing one of the statutory aggravating circumstances and thus prejudiced the government, the Supreme Court held that "[r]eliance on an error of law * * * does not change the double jeopardy effects of a judgment that amounts to an acquittal on the merits." Justice O'Connor wrote for the Court. Justice Rehnquist dissented and was joined by Justice White. He argued that the implied acquittal analysis of *Bullington* ought not to apply to a case in which the state proved an aggravating circumstance but the trial judge improperly applied state law to the state's proof.

---

18. For a scholarly debate on the appeal question, see Stern, Government Appeals of Sentences: A Constitutional Response to Arbitrary and Unreasonable Sentences, 18 Am. Crim.L.Rev. 51 (1980); Freeman & Early, United States v. DiFrancesco: Government Appeal of Sentences, 18 Am.Cr.L.Rev. 91 (1980). See also Westen, The Three Faces of Double Jeopardy: Reflections on Government Appeals of Criminal Sentences, 78 Mich.L.Rev. 1001 (1980).

Review of Individual Issues After a Death Sentence Is Imposed: Poland v. Arizona

The Supreme Court distinguished *Bullington* and *Rumsey* in Poland v. Arizona, 476 U.S. 147 (1986). The defendants were convicted of robbing a bank van and killing its guards. The trial court, making the same error made in *Rumsey*, found that the offense was not committed for "pecuniary gain," because the statutory aggravating circumstance applied only to contract killings. But, the court found that the crime was committed in "an especially heinous" circumstance and imposed death sentences. On appeal, the state supreme court, reversing and remanding on another ground, held both that there was insufficient evidence of heinousness and that the trial judge erred in ruling that the crime was not for pecuniary gain under the statute.

Justice White's majority opinion found that both *Bullington* and *Rumsey* involved the equivalent of acquittals during sentencing, while there was no finding in the instant case that the prosecution failed to prove its case. The Court rejected the argument that a capital sentencer's failure to find a particular aggravating circumstance constitutes an acquittal of that circumstance for double jeopardy purposes and held instead that the proper inquiry is whether the sentencer or reviewing court has decided that the prosecution has failed to prove that death is an appropriate sentence. Thus, the Court ruled that the state supreme court acted properly in reviewing the "pecuniary gain" ruling by the trial judge and in permitting the judge to consider this aggravating circumstance once again upon retrial.

Justice Marshall, joined by Justices Brennan and Blackmun, dissented and argued that the only difference between this case and *Rumsey* was that the sentencing judge made two errors of state law while the *Rumsey* judge made only one. The dissent reasoned that the state supreme court effectively held that the defendants were entitled to acquittals on the only aggravating circumstance that the trial court found to have been validly proved.

Capital Sentencing Proceeding Is Not a Successive Prosecution: Schiro v. Farley

The Court once again distinguished *Bullington* in Schiro v. Farley, 510 U.S. 222 (1994). Schiro admitted to raping and killing a woman and was subsequently charged in separate counts with intentional murder and felony murder. The State sought the death penalty for the felony murder count. The State of Indiana, where Schiro was tried, does not require a showing of intent to kill for felony murder. The jury was given verdict forms for both charges and found Schiro guilty of felony murder, but left the other verdict forms blank. In the capital sentencing phase, the jury recommended against the death penalty, but the trial judge rejected their recommendation—a decision permitted by Indiana law. The trial judge sentenced Schiro to death on the basis of the aggravating circumstance that Schiro had "intentionally" murdered his victim. In the Supreme Court, Schiro argued that the imposition of the death sentence, on the basis of the intentional murder aggravating circumstance, violated the Double Jeopardy Clause. He reasoned that the sentencing proceeding became a successive prosecution for intentional murder, in light of the jury's failure to find an intent to kill at trial.

Justice O'Connor, writing for seven members of the Court, rejected Schiro's argument and concluded that an initial sentencing proceeding cannot constitute a successive prosecution for purposes of the Double Jeopardy Clause. She distinguished *Bullington* as follows:

> In *Bullington* we recognized the general rule that "the Double Jeopardy Clause imposes no absolute prohibition against the imposition of a harsher sentence at retrial." Nonetheless, we recognized a narrow exception to this general principle because the capital sentencing scheme at issue "differed significantly from those employed in any of the Court's cases where the Double Jeopardy Clause has been held inapplicable to sentencing." Because the capital sentencing proceeding "was itself a trial on the issue of punishment," requiring a defendant to submit to a second, identical proceeding was tantamount to permitting a second prosecution of an acquitted defendant.
>
> This case is manifestly different. Neither the prohibition against a successive trial on the issue of guilt, nor the *Bullington* prohibition against a second capital sentencing proceeding, is implicated here—the State did not reprosecute Schiro for intentional murder, nor did it force him to submit to a second death penalty hearing. It simply conducted a single sentencing hearing in the course of a single prosecution. The state is entitled to "one fair opportunity" to prosecute a defendant, and that opportunity extends not only to prosecution at the guilt phase, but also to present evidence at an ensuing sentencing proceeding.

Justice Blackmun, in dissent, argued that the "sentencing proceeding at issue here is indistinguishable from that confronted in *Bullington*." Justice Stevens wrote a separate dissent in which Justice Blackmun joined.

Jury Deadlock on the Death Penalty and Death Penalty on a Retrial: Sattazahn v. Pennsylvania

The Court applied its *Bullington-Rumsey* line of cases in Sattazahn v. Pennsylvania, 537 U.S. 101 (2003), and found that the state could permissibly impose the death penalty on a retrial, after the defendant appealed a conviction in which life imprisonment was imposed. The jury at Sattazahn's first trial convicted him of first degree murder but then deadlocked on the death penalty. Under Pennsylvania law, if the jury deadlocks on a penalty of death, the judge must sentence the defendant to life imprisonment. Sattazahn appealed his conviction, alleging that the jury in the guilt phase had received improper instructions on certain matters. The state court agreed with Sattazahn, reversing his conviction and remanding. On retrial, the defendant was found guilty; the state again sought the death penalty, and this time (in part based on facts not presented previously) the jury unanimously agreed on a death sentence.

Justice Scalia, joined by the Chief Justice, Justice Thomas, and in most respects by Justice Kennedy, reasoned that Satterzahn's double jeopardy rights were not violated because he had never been "acquitted" of a death sentence. Justice Scalia addressed the defendant's argument that a jury deadlock should trigger double jeopardy protection in the death penalty context:

> Under the *Bullington* line of cases * * *, the touchstone for double-jeopardy protection in capital-sentencing proceedings is whether there has been an "acquittal." Petitioner here cannot establish that the jury or the court "acquitted" him during his first capital-sentencing proceeding. As to

the jury: The verdict form returned by the foreman stated that the jury deadlocked 9-to-3 on whether to impose the death penalty; it made no findings with respect to the alleged aggravating circumstance. That result— or more appropriately, that non-result—cannot fairly be called an acquittal "based on findings sufficient to establish legal entitlement to the life sentence." *Rumsey.*

The entry of a life sentence by the judge was not "acquittal," either. As the Pennsylvania Supreme Court explained:

> " 'Under Pennsylvania's sentencing scheme, the judge has no discretion to fashion sentence once he finds that the jury is deadlocked. The statute directs him to enter a life sentence. The judge makes no findings and resolves no factual matter. Since judgment is not based on findings which resolve some factual matter, it is not sufficient to establish legal entitlement to a life sentence. A default judgment does not trigger a double jeopardy bar to the death penalty upon retrial.' "

Justice Ginsburg, joined by Justices Stevens, Souter and Breyer, dissented. She argued that the policies of the Double Jeopardy Clause are at stake when the defendant is sentenced to life imprisonment rather than death and is then subject to the death penalty on retrial. She explained as follows:

> I recognize that this is a novel and close question: Sattazahn was not "acquitted" of the death penalty, but his case was fully tried and the court, on its own motion, entered a final judgment—a life sentence—terminating the trial proceedings. I would decide the double jeopardy issue in Satta-zahn's favor [because the] Court's holding confronts defendants with a perilous choice * * * . Under the Court's decision, if a defendant sentenced to life after a jury deadlock chooses to appeal her underlying conviction, she faces the possibility of death if she is successful on appeal but convicted on retrial. If, on the other hand, the defendant loses her appeal, or chooses to forgo an appeal, the final judgment for life stands. In other words, a defendant in Sattazahn's position must relinquish either her right to file a potentially meritorious appeal, or her state-granted entitlement to avoid the death penalty.

C. RESENTENCING FOLLOWING PARTIAL REVERSAL

The Supreme Court cited *DiFrancesco* in its per curiam opinion in Pennsylvania v. Goldhammer, 474 U.S. 28 (1985), which held that the Double Jeopardy Clause did not prevent a state court from resentencing a defendant after some of his convictions had been overturned on appeal. Goldhammer had been convicted on 56 counts of forgery and 56 counts of theft, but he was sentenced to 2-5 years on a single theft count and five years of probation on a single forgery count with sentence on all other counts suspended. The state supreme court overturned 34 of the theft convictions, including the one count on which Goldhammer had been sentenced to prison, because the statute of limitations had run. The Supreme Court remanded the case for a determination of whether state law permitted resentencing.

Chapter Thirteen

POST–CONVICTION CHALLENGES

I. INTRODUCTION

Because of the Double Jeopardy Clause and the constitutional right to a jury trial, the prosecutor generally will be unable to seek review of an acquittal unless it occurs in a case in which there has been a verdict of guilty that was set aside by the trial judge whose decision, if erroneous, can be reversed so that the original verdict can be reinstated without an additional trial.[1] The criminal defendant who is convicted has greater opportunities to challenge the trial court's judgment.[2] This Chapter addresses the opportunities most likely to be made available in the typical criminal case.

Three types of proceedings will be examined in this chapter: trial court motions, direct appellate review of convictions, and collateral attacks on convictions. The assumption is made that everyone has a basic familiarity with the following facts: criminal cases are tried in both federal and state courts; an appeal of one sort or another generally is provided a convicted defendant; the decision whether to appeal is the client's and, in order to render effective assistance of counsel, a lawyer must inform the client of the right to appeal (see, e.g., Evitts v. Lucey, 469 U.S. 387 (1985)); the defendant may raise claims concerning almost any trial errors, defects in trial procedure, problems with the substantive law or the overall fairness of the results on appeal; but crowded appellate courts may screen some appeals and decide them on the basis of written briefs, reserving oral argument for special cases. Questions concerning the right to counsel and to the effective assistance of counsel in post-conviction proceedings are addressed in Chapters Five and Ten. The special aspects of

---

1. This Chapter addresses only claims by persons who have litigated; it does not examine the status of those who have pleaded guilty. That has been taken up, supra, in Chapter Nine. Also not considered here are problems of when a decision becomes final for purposes of appeal. See, e.g., United States v. Nixon, 418 U.S. 683, 690–92 (1974). Nor are special techniques of avoiding review examined—e.g., the concurrent sentence doctrine, see, e.g., Benton v. Maryland, 395 U.S. 784 (1969) (discretion to avoid review of one of concurrent judgments); the mootness doctrine, see, e.g., Sibron v. New York, 392 U.S. 40 (1968)(case not moot on direct appeal where adverse collateral conse-

quences are possible); Dove v. United States, 423 U.S. 325 (1976), (certiorari petition dismissed when petitioner dies).

2. As noted in the previous chapter on double jeopardy, not all government appeals are constitutionally barred. Generally, if the prosecutor is not challenging an acquittal or seeking a second adjudication on the guilt-innocence question, the Constitution will not stand in the way of an appeal. While Congress has acted to open the doors to government appeals virtually to the limits of the Constitution in 18 U.S.C.A. § 3731, not all states permit the government such review.

appellate review of sentences have been examined in Chapters Eleven and Twelve.

II. GROUNDS FOR DIRECT ATTACKS ON A CONVICTION

If the defendant has been convicted, there are several procedural avenues by which he can attack the judgment "directly", i.e., through motions to the trial judge or by way of direct appeal. This section considers some possible grounds for a direct attack, and some defenses that the government might have against a remedy that would vacate the judgment.

A. INSUFFICIENT EVIDENCE

1. *The General Standard*

A defendant may move during trial or after a verdict is returned for an acquittal on the ground that the evidence is insufficient to sustain a conviction. Federal Rule of Criminal Procedure 29 indicates the opportunities available to a defendant to make and repeat such a motion. The same legal standard is used in judging post-verdict as mid-trial motions. Courts have wisely adopted the general rule that a guilty verdict can only stand if there is sufficient evidence to support a finding beyond a reasonable doubt of all necessary elements of the government's case.[3] See American Tobacco Co. v. United States, 328 U.S. 781 (1946); United States v. Mariani, 725 F.2d 862 (2d Cir.1984). After In re Winship, discussed in Chapter Ten, supra, this standard of review is probably required by the Constitution. When the burden of persuasion as to a defense is placed upon the defendant, a guilty verdict will be set aside if no reasonable jury could have rejected the defendant's evidence, when measured under the appropriate standard of proof. For example, if a defendant bears the burden of proving insanity by a preponderance of the evidence, a jury verdict of guilty will be set aside if the defendant's evidence is so strong that any *reasonable* jury would have found the proof of insanity to be preponderant.

Circumstantial Evidence

At one time, some courts held that acquittal is required in a circumstantial evidence case unless the evidence excludes every reasonable hypothesis except guilt. Wisely, the United States Supreme Court held that such a rule is confusing and incorrect. Holland v. United States, 348 U.S. 121, 139–40 (1954). Today it is clear that "circumstantial evidence alone can sustain a guilty verdict and to do so, circumstantial evidence need not remove every reasonable hypothesis except that of guilt." United States v. White, 932 F.2d 588 (6th Cir.1991).

Review by Trial Judge for Insufficiency

The standard for review by a trial judge upon a motion for acquittal is well-stated by the court in United States v. Mariani, 725 F.2d 862 (2d Cir.1984):

---

3. In conspiracy cases, an ill-defined and objectionable "slight evidence" standard has been utilized by some courts, but it never has been justified. See, e.g., United States v. Shoffner, 71 F.3d 1429 (8th Cir.1995) ("Once the existence of a conspiracy is established, even slight evidence connecting a defendant to the conspiracy may be sufficient to prove the defendant's involvement.").

When a defendant moves for a judgment of acquittal, the court must determine whether upon the evidence, giving full play to the right of the jury to determine credibility, weigh the evidence, and draw justifiable inferences of fact, a reasonable mind might fairly conclude guilt beyond a reasonable doubt. If it concludes that upon the evidence there must be such a doubt in a reasonable mind, it must grant the motion; or, to state it another way, if there is no evidence upon which a reasonable mind might fairly conclude guilt beyond a reasonable doubt, the motion must be granted. If it concludes that either of the two results, a reasonable doubt or no reasonable doubt, is fairly possible, it must let the jury decide the matter.

Mere Presence

In *Mariani,* the court held that the trial court had used the correct standard but applied it improperly. Mariani was charged with conspiracy to steal money from the United States. An undercover agent had arranged a narcotics transaction with Mariani's friend, Miller. Mariani was parked at the scene where the deal was to be made. Miller went to the undercover agent, pointed toward Mariani and said "my man's over there, wait here and I'll get the package." Miller then went to Mariani's car, spoke to Mariani through the driver's side window, got into the car through the door on the passenger's side, and came out of the car carrying a package. Miller brought the package to the undercover agent, and received money. Miller and Mariani were then arrested. After their arrest, Miller stated that the agents should check the package because it did not contain drugs. Mariani then said, "you guys don't got what you think you got." Subsequent tests showed that the package did not contain drugs; hence the charge of stealing money from the United States. Mariani claimed that though he was present at the scene, he knew nothing about the transaction and was merely giving his friend a ride. After the jury returned a guilty verdict, the trial judge granted Mariani's motion for acquittal; he found that the evidence showed only that Mariani was present at the scene, and that mere presence was not sufficient to convict. He discounted Mariani's post-arrest statement as "merely echoing what he had heard Miller say earlier."

The court of appeals agreed that mere presence at the scene of a criminal transaction is not sufficient for a conviction. But it held that the trial court had erred in discounting the post-arrest statement, and in refusing to draw reasonable inferences from the fact that Miller spoke with Mariani before taking the package from Mariani's car. The court concluded that "the district court substituted its own determination of the weight of the evidence and the reasonable inferences to be drawn for that of the jury." The court of appeals noted that "conspiracy can be proven circumstantially," that "seemingly innocent acts taken individually may indicate complicity when viewed collectively and with reference to the circumstances in general," and that "the evidence is to be viewed not in isolation but in conjunction." Compare Mikes v. Borg, 947 F.2d 353 (9th Cir.1991)(in a case in which fingerprints are the only evidence against the defendant, the prosecution must establish that the defendant could only have left his fingerprints at the scene during the commission of the crime; post-trial relief granted because the prosecution offered no evidence to exclude the possibility that the defendant may have been at the scene at a different time).

Preserving the Right to Appeal on Grounds of Insufficiency of Evidence

Generally, a trial judge will rule on the sufficiency of evidence only if a motion for judgment of acquittal is made, but she does have the power to enter a judgment of acquittal *sua sponte*. See Fed. R.Crim.P. 29. Appellate courts, however, will not assess the sufficiency of the evidence absent a proper challenge. Generally, an appellate court will not review the sufficiency of the evidence in a jury trial if no motion for judgment of acquittal was made below. See, e.g., United States v. Stauffer, 922 F.2d 508 (9th Cir.1990). But appellate courts generally will consider the sufficiency of the evidence in bench trials whether or not any motion was made in the trial court for judgment of acquittal. This is because the trial judge in such circumstances acts as the trier of both fact and law, and implicitly rules on the sufficiency of the evidence by rendering a guilty verdict. "A motion to acquit is superfluous because the plea of not guilty has already brought the question of the sufficiency of the evidence to the court's attention." United States v. Atkinson, 990 F.2d 501 (9th Cir.1993).

Timing of a Motion for Acquittal

Fed.R.Crim.P. 29 provides, as does the law of most states, that a motion for judgment of acquittal must be granted after the evidence of either side is concluded if the evidence against the defendant is insufficient to warrant conviction. If the defendant makes a motion for acquittal at the close of the government's case, the trial court may reserve a ruling on the motion until the end of the case. If the defendant, after making the motion, puts on evidence, the trial court in subsequently ruling on the motion for acquittal is to consider only the evidence presented as of the time "the ruling was reserved." Therefore, the defendant who puts on evidence after the judge reserves a ruling on the motion avoids the risk that the evidence and the government's rebuttal will be considered as favorable to the government for purposes of the dismissal motion. That is, the defendant does not waive the right to have the acquittal motion judged solely on the basis of the government's evidence, without reference to the evidence offered after the government rests. While Rule 29 specifically limits only the trial court and not the appellate court, the Advisory Committee's comment to the Rule states that "in reviewing a trial court's ruling, the appellate court would be similarly limited" to the evidence presented as of the time the motion was made.

Fed.R.Crim.P. 29(c) provides that a motion for judgment of acquittal can be made after the jury returns a verdict, but it sets a time limit for such a motion—it must be made "within 7 days after a guilty verdict or after the court discharges the jury, whichever is later, or within any other time the court sets during the 7–day period." In Carlisle v. United States, 517 U.S. 416 (1996), the defendant's motion for acquittal was made 8 days after the jury was discharged, and the trial court had not fixed any later time period within which to make the motion. The Court, in an opinion by Justice Scalia, held that the district court has no jurisdiction to entertain a motion for acquittal made outside the time limit of Rule 29(c)—even if the defendant is innocent. Justice Scalia declared that the Rule is "plain and unambiguous" and that there is "simply no room in the text * * * for the granting of an untimely post-verdict motion for judgment of acquittal, regardless of whether the motion is accompanied by a claim of legal innocence, is filed before sentencing, or was filed late because of attorney error."

Justice Scalia rejected the defendant's argument that the district court could exercise inherent authority to grant an untimely motion for acquittal. He reasoned that "[w]hatever the scope of this inherent power, * * * it does not include the power to develop rules that circumvent or conflict with the Federal Rules of Criminal Procedure." Justice Souter wrote a short concurring opinion, as did Justice Ginsburg, joined by Justices Souter and Breyer. Justice Ginsburg argued that the Rule 29 time bar might be lifted if defense counsel were somehow misled by the trial court. But Carlisle's counsel was not misled; rather, he neglected to follow plain instructions as set forth in the Rule. She also observed that Carlisle was not bereft of protection at this point, because he could still challenge his conviction on appeal, and could also bring a collateral attack on grounds of ineffective assistance of counsel.

Justice Stevens, joined by Justice Kennedy, dissented in *Carlisle*. He contended that there was nothing in Rule 29(c) that "withdraws the court's pre-existing authority to refrain from entering judgment of conviction against a defendant whom it knows to be legally innocent."

2. The Standard of Appellate Review of Sufficiency of the Evidence

Rational Trier of Fact Test: Jackson v. Virginia

At one time, there was a tendency among appellate courts to uphold verdicts supported by *any* evidence. Only "no evidence" cases produced reversals. But in Jackson v. Virginia, 443 U.S. 307 (1979), the Supreme Court rejected the "no evidence" test. Writing for the Court, Justice Stewart opined that the "no evidence" rule was inadequate to protect against misapplication of the proof beyond a reasonable doubt requirement, and that the critical question on review of a criminal conviction is whether the record evidence could reasonably support a finding of guilt beyond a reasonable doubt. He also wrote that the standard should be utilized by federal courts hearing habeas corpus attacks on state convictions. Justice Stewart elaborated on the appropriate test for review of sufficiency claims:

> After *Winship* the critical inquiry on review of the sufficiency of the evidence to support a criminal conviction must be not simply to determine whether the jury was properly instructed, but to determine whether the record evidence could reasonably support a finding of guilt beyond a reasonable doubt. But this inquiry does not require a court to ask itself whether *it* believes that the evidence at the trial established guilt beyond a reasonable doubt. Instead, the relevant question is whether, after viewing the evidence in the light most favorable to the prosecution, *any* rational trier of fact could have found the essential elements of the crime beyond a reasonable doubt. This familiar standard gives full play to the responsibility of the trier of fact fairly to resolve conflicts in the testimony, to weigh the evidence, and to draw reasonable inferences from basic facts to ultimate facts. * * * The criterion thus impinges upon jury discretion only to the extent necessary to guarantee the fundamental protection of due process of law.

Thus, the standard for appellate review of sufficiency of the evidence under *Jackson* is the same as the standard used by the trial court in ruling on a motion for acquittal.[4] See United States v. Mariani, supra.

Ironically, Jackson, who was convicted of first degree murder, did not benefit from his victory. Jackson was convicted of premeditated murder and claimed that he shot the victim by accident. The Court found that because Jackson, among other things, admitted firing several shots into the ground and reloading his gun before killing the deceased, a rational trier of fact could have found beyond a reasonable doubt that the killing was premeditated.

Jackson was a habeas corpus case, but the standards set forth in *Jackson* apply for direct appeals as well. See, e.g., See also United States v. Aina–Marshall, 336 F.3d 167 (2d Cir. 2003) ("A defendant challenging a conviction based on insufficient evidence bears a heavy burden. * * * A conviction will be affirmed so long as any rational trier of fact could have found the essential elements of the crime beyond a reasonable doubt.").

Application of Jackson: Wright v. West

In Wright v. West, 505 U.S. 277 (1992), West was convicted of grand larceny on the basis of possession of stolen goods. The theft occurred several weeks before the items were found in West's house; only a few of the stolen items were found there; West had made no attempt to conceal the items; and West testified that he had bought the items at a flea market. West challenged his conviction on sufficiency grounds, arguing that his was a "mere possession" case, and that a rational trier of fact could not conclude that West had the intent to commit grand larceny. The court of appeals held in favor of West, but the Supreme Court concluded that the lower court had misapplied the standards of *Jackson* in reversing West's conviction.

Justice Thomas, in a plurality opinion joined by Chief Justice Rehnquist and Justice Scalia, concluded that "the case against West was strong." He stressed the following points: 1) over 15 of the stolen items were recovered from West's home; 2) West had failed to offer specific information about how he came to possess the stolen items, saying only that he frequently bought and sold items at various flea markets; 3) West contradicted himself repeatedly on the witness stand as to where he had bought the stolen goods; 4) West had no explanation whatsoever for the presence of some of the stolen goods in his home; 5) West failed to produce any other supporting evidence, such as testimony of the person from whom he claimed to have purchased some of the goods, even though he stated that he had known this person for years; and 6) the jury was entitled to disbelieve West's "uncorroborated and confused" testimony, and "was further entitled to consider whatever it concluded to be perjured testimony as affirmative evidence of guilt." Justice Thomas concluded as follows:

> In *Jackson*, we emphasized repeatedly the deference owed to the trier of fact and, correspondingly, the sharply limited nature of constitutional sufficiency review. We said that "all of the evidence is to be considered in the light most favorable to the prosecution"; that the prosecution need not

---

4. Justice Stevens dissented and was joined by Chief Justice Burger and Justice Rehnquist.   Justice Powell did not participate.

affirmatively "rule out every hypothesis except that of guilt"; and that a reviewing court "faced with a record of historical facts that supports conflicting inferences must presume—even if it does not appear affirmatively in the record—that the trier of fact resolved any such conflicts in favor of the prosecution, and must defer to that resolution." Under these standards, we think it clear that the trial record contained sufficient evidence to support West's conviction.[5]

General Verdict With Insufficient Evidence on One Ground: Griffin v. United States

Is reversal required where a defendant is charged with multiple acts or means of committing a crime in a single count, and the evidence is insufficient as to one of the acts or means? In Griffin v. United States, 502 U.S. 46 (1991), the Court relied on the common-law rule that a general verdict is valid so long as it is legally supportable on one of the submitted grounds—"even though that gave no assurance that a valid ground, rather than an invalid one, was actually the basis for the jury's action."

Griffin was charged, with others, in a conspiracy that was alleged to have two objects: (1) impairing the efforts of the Internal Revenue Service to ascertain income taxes (the "IRS object"); and (2) impairing the efforts of the Drug Enforcement Administration to ascertain forfeitable assets (the "DEA object"). The evidence introduced at trial implicated Griffin's codefendants in both conspiratorial objects, but it did not sufficiently connect Griffin with the DEA object. The trial court over objection instructed the jury that it could return a guilty verdict if it found Griffin to have participated in either one of the two objects of the conspiracy. The jury returned a general verdict of guilty. The court of appeals found the evidence tying Griffin to the DEA object insufficient, but nonetheless affirmed Griffin's conviction on the ground that sufficient evidence existed to tie her to the IRS object. Griffin argued that this result violated her right to due process, because the jury might not actually have found her guilty of the IRS crime. But the Supreme Court disagreed in an opinion by Justice Scalia.

Justice Scalia recognized that despite the general common-law rule upholding an ambiguous general verdict, the Court had held in Stromberg v. California, 283 U.S. 359 (1931), that "where a provision of the Constitution forbids conviction on a particular ground, the constitutional guarantee is violated by a general verdict that may have rested on that ground." He also recognized that in Yates v. United States, 354 U.S. 298 (1957), the Court used a similar principle to void a conviction in which one means alleged in a single count was insufficient in law because barred by the statute of limitations. But Justice Scalia found these precedents to be exceptions to the general rule, and inapposite to a case where one of the objects in a single count was void not because of a legal error but rather due to factual insufficiency. He explained the *Stromberg–Yates* exception, and distinguished it from the general rule, as follows:

> Jurors are not generally equipped to determine whether a particular theory of conviction submitted to them is contrary to law—whether, for

---

5. Justices White, O'Connor, Blackmun, Stevens, and Kennedy all concurred in the judgment, in three separate opinions. They all agreed that under *Jackson*, there was suffi-cient evidence to convince a rational factfinder of West's guilt beyond a reasonable doubt. Justice Souter, also concurred in the judgment, but did not reach the sufficiency issue.

example, the action in question is protected by the Constitution, is time barred, or fails to come within the statutory definition of the crime. When, therefore, jurors have been left the option of relying upon a legally inadequate theory, there is no reason to think that their own intelligence and expertise will save them from that error. Quite the opposite is true, however, when they have been left the option of relying upon a factually inadequate theory, since jurors *are* well equipped to analyze the evidence. * * * It is one thing to negate a verdict that, while supported by evidence, may have been based on an erroneous view of the law; it is another to do so merely on the chance—remote, it seems to us—that the jury convicted on a ground that was not supported by adequate evidence when there existed alternative grounds for which the evidence was sufficient.

Thus, the Court found it fair to presume from the general verdict that the jury convicted on the factually sufficient ground.[6] Compare United States v. Garcia, 992 F.2d 409 (2d Cir.1993)(*Griffin* distinguished where three legal theories were submitted to the jury, and two of them were legally erroneous: "If the challenge is evidentiary, as long as there was sufficient evidence to support one of the theories presented, then the verdict should be affirmed. However, if the challenge is legal and any of the theories was legally insufficient, then the verdict must be reversed.").

B. MOTION FOR NEW TRIAL

Federal Rule of Criminal Procedure 33, providing for a new trial on motion "if the interest of justice so requires", affords another avenue for direct attack on a conviction. Note that, as was true of motions for acquittal, post-verdict new trial motions are defendants' remedies.

One might expect that the same trial judge who erred once is unlikely to be quick to change her mind, but it sometimes happens. Today, the trial judge knows that it is likely that a convicted defendant will appeal, and the post-trial motion enables the trial judge to correct any error that an appellate court would correct. There is no doubt that, to avoid an unnecessary appeal, the trial judge should grant a new trial to correct any mistake that would result in reversal on appeal. In close cases, the trial judge has authority to grant a new trial even if an appellate court, acting on the basis of a cold record, would not, since the trial judge should be particularly well situated to see or feel the prejudicial impact of an error that on paper does not appear to be significant.

One ground on which a motion for a new trial might be granted is that the trial judge is convinced that a verdict is against the weight of the evidence. "Against the weight of the evidence" is not the same as "insufficient evidence." The standards governing a trial judge's ruling on a motion for a new trial on "weight of the evidence" grounds are well-stated by the court in United States v. Martinez, 763 F.2d 1297 (11th Cir.1985):

[A] motion for new trial on the ground that the verdict is contrary to the weight of the evidence raises issues very different from a motion for judgment of acquittal [for insufficient evidence]. On a motion for judgment of acquittal, the court must view the evidence in the light most favorable to the verdict, and, under that light, determine whether the evidence is sufficient to support the verdict. Thus, on this motion, the court assumes

---

6. Justice Blackmun concurred in the judgment. Justice Thomas did not participate.

the truth of the evidence offered by the prosecution. On a motion for a new trial based on the weight of the evidence, the court need not view the evidence in the light most favorable to the verdict. It may weigh the evidence and consider the credibility of the witnesses. If the court concludes that despite the abstract sufficiency of the evidence to sustain the verdict, the evidence preponderates sufficiently heavily against the verdict that a serious miscarriage of justice may have occurred, it may set aside the verdict, grant a new trial, and submit the issues for determination by another jury.

* * * While the district court's discretion is quite broad, there are limits to it. The court may not reweigh the evidence and set aside the verdict simply because it feels some other result would be more reasonable. The evidence must preponderate heavily against the verdict, such that it would be a miscarriage of justice to let the verdict stand. Motions for new trials based on weight of the evidence are not favored. Courts are to grant them sparingly and with caution, doing so only in those really exceptional cases.

Applying these principles trial courts, generally speaking, have granted new trial motions on weight of the evidence only where the credibility of the government's witnesses has been impeached and the government's case has been marked by uncertainties and discrepancies.

The court in *Martinez* reversed the trial court's order granting a new trial after the jury rendered a guilty verdict in a narcotics case. The disputed issue was whether the government could prove that the defendant knew there was cocaine on board a boat. To establish this knowledge, the government showed that the defendant was the captain of the boat, that 454 pounds of cocaine were found on board, that the boat had made a long journey from Colombia to Miami, and that there were only a few crew members. The court found that "the government's case against [the defendant] was not marked by uncertainties and discrepancies. It was not based on compound inferences. It was not presented through the testimony of impeached and suspect witnesses." The court concluded that this was not "one of those exceptional cases in which the court had the power to interfere with the jury's factual findings."

C. NEWLY DISCOVERED EVIDENCE CLAIMS

It is understandable that American judges, both trial and appellate, would be reluctant to overturn verdicts supported by sufficient evidence to amount to proof beyond a reasonable doubt. Reluctance to retry cases that are technically correct after the government has shouldered the load of a criminal prosecution also helps to explain the strict limitations on newly discovered evidence claims. If courts readily accepted newly discovered evidence claims, litigants who discovered that a tactical judgment made in one trial did not work would ask for another chance to litigate, and litigation would become interminable. The line between discovery of new evidence and discovery of new theories of how to use evidence is fuzzy, but rarely must it be sharpened in light of the reluctance of courts to take seriously either claim.

Requirements for a Newly Discovered Evidence Claim

A defendant must meet a four prong test before a court will grant him a retrial based on any newly discovered evidence. As stated in United States v. Seago, 930 F.2d 482 (6th Cir.1991), the defendant must establish the following: (1) the new evidence was discovered after the trial; (2) the evidence could not have been discovered earlier with due diligence; (3) the evidence is material and not merely cumulative or impeaching; and (4) the evidence would likely produce an acquittal. In *Seago,* the court concluded that evidence of ineffective assistance of counsel is not newly discovered evidence for purposes of a motion for a new trial where the facts supporting the claim were within the defendant's knowledge at the time of the trial. See also United States v. Gonzalez, 933 F.2d 417 (7th Cir.1991)(defendants were not entitled to a new trial on the basis of newly discovered evidence where the evidence would merely impeach a government witness' testimony that he had never had anything to do with cocaine, and evidence of the defendants' guilt was overwhelming).

There is a distinction between newly *discovered* and newly *available.* For example, there is a line of cases in which a defendant's accomplice invokes the Fifth Amendment and refuses to testify when called by the defendant. After the defendant is convicted, he asserts that his accomplice has now changed his mind and would be happy to testify on the defendant's behalf. Courts have uniformly held that this is not newly discovered evidence. See, e.g., United States v. Turns, 198 F.3d 584 (6th Cir. 2000) (the defendant was obviously aware of the witness's existence at the time of trial, so the witness's alleged change of heart makes her newly available, not newly discovered). See also United States v. Montilla–Rivera, 171 F.3d 37 (1st Cir.1999) (exculpatory testimony of the defendant's associates, who were not available at the time of trial because they declared their Fifth Amendment privileges, did not warrant a new trial on the basis of newly discovered evidence: "this sort of blanket exoneration of Montilla by two alleged coconspirators who had pled guilty and been sentenced is untrustworthy and * * * these statements do not lead to a reasonable probability that Montilla would be acquitted on retrial.").

Evidence Available Before the Conviction

Evidence is not "new" merely because it has been generated after the conviction. For example, in Harris v. Vasquez, 913 F.2d 606 (9th Cir.1990), a death penalty case, the court concluded that the defendant's new psychiatric reports did not justify another penalty hearing. Because defense counsel possessed evidence of the defendant's brain damage at the original hearing, and no new psychiatric techniques or theories were alleged to have arisen in the interim, the court concluded that the new reports were not new evidence but merely new opinions from new psychiatrists.

New Forensic Techniques

Advances in forensic testing techniques have occasionally given rise to new evidence claims—e.g., exculpatory DNA tests. But they are not always successful. When the forensic testing is conducted long after the crime, it will sometimes not be sufficiently conclusive to show that the defendant would probably be acquitted on retrial. See Dumond v. Lockhart, 911 F.2d 104 (8th Cir.1990), where the court held that evidence of a genetic marker test done on a semen sample, showing that the sample was unlikely to be the defendant's, was treated as newly discovered evidence. Yet the defendant's motion for a new trial was denied because it was not probable that the evidence would produce an acquittal on retrial.

Second Thoughts of Witnesses and Jurors

Once a verdict is rendered and judgment is imposed, experienced judges know that the participants in the trial process might have second thoughts after sending a person to prison, or even to death. See, e.g., Mastrian v. McManus, 554 F.2d 813 (8th Cir.1977)(recantation by star witness does not warrant new trial). Most second thoughts are treated as routine and ignored. For example, jurors cannot attack their verdicts by raising questions about the quality of the deliberations or the firmness of their votes. See Fed.R.Evid. 606(b). Similarly, witnesses who recant their trial testimony and change stories are viewed with utmost suspicion, not only because of the commonness of feelings of remorse, but also because of a judicial fear that improper post-trial influence may be encouraged by ready judicial acceptance of recantations. Third party confessions exculpating the defendant, which are viewed with suspicion even if offered during a trial, see, e.g., Fed.R.Evid. 804(b)(3), are scrutinized with great care.[8] See, e.g., United States v. Kamel, 965 F.2d 484 (7th Cir.1992)(third party "repeatedly and firmly denied involvement in the crime for a period of three years. [The third party's] purported confession, coming after his conviction and shortly before sentencing, when he has relatively little to lose by accepting sole responsibility * * * is far less credible.").

Time Limits

The Advisory Committee on Criminal Rules had suggested that newly discovered evidence motions could be made "at any time before or after final judgment," but the Federal Rule imposes a three-year time limit. See Herrera v. Collins, 506 U.S. 390 (1993), upholding, against a constitutional attack, a Texas procedure that requires a new trial motion based on newly discovered evidence to be made within 30 days of judgment.

D. THE EFFECT OF AN ERROR ON THE VERDICT

In order to preserve a right to complain in a post-trial motion or on direct appeal, a defendant must raise all appropriate claims in a timely manner. For example, certain suppression claims must be raised before trial or they are deemed waived, unless good cause for delay in raising them is shown. See, e.g., Fed.R.Crim.P. 12(b). If the defense wishes to object at trial to other evidence offered by the government, a timely and specific objection must be made. See

---

8. One of the rare cases in which a motion for a new trial on newly discovered evidence grounds was denied and an appellate court reversed is State v. Shannon, 388 So.2d 731 (La.1980). The new evidence consisted of the testimony of an eye-witness to a shooting, a friend of the victim, who contradicted the government's other witnesses and corroborated the defendant. On the question of the defendant's due diligence, the court observed that there was no way for the defendant to suspect prior to trial that an eyewitness was available, that during the seven hour trial the information that the defendant obtained could not have been verified in time to be of any use to the defense, and that a request for a recess would have been premature since the defendant's information was tenuous.

Fed.R.Evid. 103(a). And, if the defendant wants to complain about the rejection of defense evidence, an appropriate offer of proof is required. See id. Failure to raise claims in an appropriate and timely manner generally bars review by post-conviction motion and direct appeal. However, if plain error is committed, a court may take cognizance of a claim not properly raised before or during trial. See, e.g., Fed.R.Crim.P. 52(b); Fed.R.Evid. 103(d). Courts are reluctant to allow parties to raise claims belatedly for many of the same reasons that they do not welcome newly discovered evidence claims. Here too, the door is not entirely closed to post-verdict challenges, but the threshold showing needed to trigger the court's concern is high.

1. Harmless Error

If constitutional error has occurred at a trial (e.g., introduction of confession in violation of the Sixth Amendment), should reversal be automatic? The next case considers this question.

CHAPMAN v. CALIFORNIA

Supreme Court of the United States, 1967.
386 U.S. 18.

MR. JUSTICE BLACK delivered the opinion of the Court.

[Two petitioners were convicted in a California state court on charges that they robbed, kidnaped, and murdered a bartender. One was sentenced to life imprisonment and the other to death. At trial the prosecutor commented on the petitioners' failure to testify and the trial court told the jury it could draw adverse inferences from their silence. The comment and the instruction violated petitioners' privilege against self-incrimination under Griffin v. California, 380 U.S. 609 (1965). Although it recognized this, the California Supreme Court held that the error was harmless. Justice Black indicated at the outset of his opinion that two questions were presented: (1) whether a *Griffin* error could ever be harmless, and (2) if so, was the error harmless in this case?]

I

Before deciding the two questions here—whether there can ever be harmless constitutional error and whether the error here was harmless— we must first decide whether state or federal law governs. The application of a state harmless-error rule is, of course, a state question where it involves only errors of state procedure or state law. But the error from which these petitioners suffered was a denial of rights guaranteed against invasion by the Fifth and Fourteenth Amendments, rights rooted in the Bill of Rights * * *. Whether a conviction for crime should stand when a State has failed to accord federal constitutionally guaranteed rights is every bit as much of a federal question as what particular federal constitutional provisions themselves mean, what they guarantee, and whether they have been denied. * * * We have no hesitation in saying that the right of these petitioners not to be punished for exercising their Fifth and Fourteenth Amendment right to be silent—expressly created by the Federal Constitution itself—is a federal right which, in the absence of appropriate congressional action, it is our responsibility to protect by fashioning the necessary rule.

II

We are urged by petitioners to hold that all federal constitutional errors, regardless of the facts and circumstances, must always be deemed harmful. Such a holding, as petitioners correctly point out, would require an automatic reversal of their convictions and make further discussion unnecessary. We decline to adopt any such rule. All 50 States have harmless-error statutes or rules, and the United States long ago through its Congress established for its courts the rule that judgments shall not be reversed for "errors or defects which do not affect the substantial rights of the parties." 28 U.S.C.A. § 2111. * * * All of these rules, state or federal, serve a very useful purpose insofar as they block setting aside convictions for small errors or defects that have little, if any, likelihood of having changed the result of the trial. We conclude that there may be some constitutional errors which in the setting of a particular case are so unimportant and insignificant that they may, consistent with the Federal Constitution, be deemed harmless, not requiring the automatic reversal of the conviction.

III

In fashioning a harmless-constitutional-error rule, we must recognize that harmless-error rules can work very unfair and mischievous results when, for example, highly important and persuasive evidence, or argument, though legally forbidden, finds its way into a trial in which the question of guilt or innocence is a close one. What harmless-error rules all aim at is a rule that will save the good in harmless-error practices while avoiding the bad, so far as possible.

The federal rule emphasizes "substantial rights" as do most others. The California constitutional rule emphasizes "a miscarriage of justice," but the California courts have neutralized this

to some extent by emphasis, and perhaps overemphasis, upon the court's view of "overwhelming evidence." We prefer the approach of this Court in deciding what was harmless error in our recent case of Fahy v. Connecticut, 375 U.S. 85. There we said: "The question is whether there is a reasonable possibility that the evidence complained of might have contributed to the conviction." Although our prior cases have indicated that there are some constitutional rights so basic to a fair trial that their infraction can never be treated as harmless error,[a] this statement in *Fahy* itself belies any belief that all trial errors which violate the Constitution automatically call for reversal. At the same time, however, like the federal harmless-error statute, it emphasizes an intention not to treat as harmless those constitutional errors that "affect substantial rights" of a party. An error in admitting plainly relevant evidence which possibly influenced the jury adversely to a litigant cannot, under *Fahy,* be conceived of as harmless. Certainly error, constitutional error, in illegally admitting highly prejudicial evidence or comments, casts on someone other than the person prejudiced by it a burden to show that it was harmless. * * * There is little, if any, difference between our statement in Fahy v. Connecticut about "whether there is a reasonable possibility that the evidence complained of might have contributed to the conviction" and requiring the beneficiary of a constitutional error to prove beyond a reasonable doubt that the error complained of did not contribute to the verdict obtained. We, therefore, do no more than adhere to the meaning of our *Fahy* case when we hold, as we now do, that before a federal constitutional error can be held harmless, the court must be able to declare a belief that it was harmless

---

a. See, e.g., Payne v. Arkansas, 356 U.S. 560 (coerced confession); Gideon v. Wainwright, 372 U.S. 335 (right to counsel); Tumey v. Ohio, 273 U.S. 510 (impartial judge).

beyond a reasonable doubt. While appellate courts do not ordinarily have the original task of applying such a test, it is a familiar standard to all courts, and we believe its adoption will provide a more workable standard, although achieving the same result as that aimed at in our *Fahy* case.

* * *

[The Court went on to hold that the error was not harmless. Justice Stewart concurred in the result and opted for automatic reversal for *Griffin* violations. Justice Harlan dissented on the ground that application of a state harmless error rule was an independent state ground barring Supreme Court review.]

Errors Subject to the Chapman Analysis

The Court has invoked *Chapman* in several cases to hold errors harmless. See Harrington v. California, 395 U.S. 250 (1969)(holding harmless the improper introduction of confessions of non-testifying codefendants); Milton v. Wainwright, 407 U.S. 371 (1972)(declaring that any error in obtaining statements of accused in violation of right to counsel was harmless); Brown v. United States, 411 U.S. 223 (1973) (similar to *Harrington*, supra).[9]

Reversal as a Deterrent

Note that it is permissible for a court to refuse to consider the merits of a constitutional claim on the ground that even if error, it would be harmless in any event. This use of harmless error is taken to task by Professor Sam Kamin in Harmless Error and the Rights/Remedies Split, 88 Va. L.Rev. 1 (2002). Professor Kamin argues that excessive use of the harmless error will fail to deter official misconduct. He therefore suggests that the "harmlessness of an alleged error should never be used as a threshold question; that is, courts should determine whether or not the conduct alleged was error, and should turn to the impact of that error only after determining that it occurred." Professor Kamins also suggests that "where a state official should have known that her conduct was error, the state should be denied the benefit of the harmless error rule." He concludes that "it is only by applying the harmless error rule in these ways * * * that the rule can be kept from stifling the development of constitutional law and can become a tool for changing the behaviors of prosecutors and law enforcement."

Professor Landes and Judge Posner put an economics spin on the deterrence argument in, Harmless Error, 30 J.Legal Studies 161 (2001):

> The prosecutor's incentive to induce or avoid errors at the trial that make it more likely that the defendant will be convicted depends on the sanctions the appellate court imposes on him if he commits an error. If the appellate court reverses a conviction when error occurs, a prosecutor will have a greater incentive both to refrain from committing intentional and deliberate errors and to invest resources in preventing inadvertent errors from occurring than if the court, invoking the harmless error rule, declines to reverse.

9. The harmless error rule employed in habeas corpus cases is stricter (i.e., reversal less likely) than the *Chapman* standard that is applied to constitutional errors on direct review. See the discussion of habeas corpus later in this Chapter.

Constitutional Errors Not Subject to Harmless Error Review

The Supreme Court has held that most constitutional violations are subject to the harmless error rule, but, as it recognized in the footnote in *Chapman,* some errors can never be harmless. The question is how to determine which errors can be harmless and which cannot.

The Court has held that certain errors require automatic reversal and a new trial. These errors include: (1) total deprivation of the right to counsel (*Gideon,* cited in the footnote in *Chapman*); (2) a biased judge (Tumey v. Ohio, cited in the footnote in *Chapman*); (3) unlawful exclusion of members of the defendant's race from the grand jury (Vasquez v. Hillery, 474 U.S. 254 (1986)); (4) violation of the right to a public trial (Waller v. Georgia, 467 U.S. 39 (1984)); (5) violation of the right of self-representation (McKaskle v. Wiggins, discussed in Chapter Ten); (6) improper exclusion of a juror who is reluctant to impose the death penalty (Gray v. Mississippi, discussed in Chapter Ten); and (7) improper instruction on the prosecution's burden of proof (Sullivan v. Louisiana, discussed infra).

In addition, harmless error analysis cannot apply if a new trial would in itself be the harm. Thus, violations of the right to speedy trial and a multiple prosecution in violation of the Double Jeopardy Clause have never been considered harmless error. Finally, some errors require a showing of prejudice before a constitutional violation can even be found. This is so, for example, under the *Strickland* standard for ineffective assistance of counsel and under the *Brady* standard for disclosure of exculpatory evidence by the prosecution. In these two areas, a court that finds a constitutional violation has by definition determined that the error is harmful, and the *Chapman* standard becomes superfluous. See Capra, Access to Exculpatory Evidence: Resolving the *Agurs* Problems of Prosecutorial Discretion and Retrospective Review, 53 Ford.L.Rev. 391 (1984); Kyles v. Whitley, discussed in Chapter Eight (harmless error analysis redundant after *Brady* violation has been found).

Involuntary Confessions: Arizona v. Fulminante

In Arizona v. Fulminante, 499 U.S. 279 (1991), the Court retreated from the *Chapman* footnote insofar as it implied that admission of an involuntary confession could never be harmless error. Chief Justice Rehnquist, writing for five members of the Court, explained the *Chapman* footnote as a "historical reference." He asserted that Payne v. Arkansas, cited in *Chapman* for the proposition that admission of an involuntary confession could never be harmless, did not in fact reject the harmless error test of *Chapman* but rather rejected "a much more lenient rule which would allow affirmance of a conviction if the evidence other than the confession was sufficient to sustain the verdict."

The Chief Justice distinguished a trial error, "error which occurred during the presentation of the case to the jury, and which may therefore be quantitatively assessed in the context of other evidence presented in order to determine whether its admission was harmless beyond a reasonable doubt," from an error that is not subject to such an assessment, "a structural defect affecting the framework in which the trial proceeds * * *." A structural defect can never be harmless, because by definition the error infects the entirety of the trial. In contrast, a trial error can be harmless, because it is a more discrete violation and its harm can be more easily pinpointed. According to the majority, admission of an involuntary confession falls into the category of trial error, while total deprivation of counsel as in *Gideon,* or a biased judge as in *Tumey,* falls into the category of structural defect.

For purposes of harmless error analysis, the Chief Justice saw no reason to distinguish admission of coerced confessions from admissions of confessions obtained in violation of the defendant's Sixth Amendment rights or in violation of *Miranda.* Since these latter violations could be harmless, admission of a coerced confession could also be harmless. The Chief Justice noted, however, that due to the substantial impact that a confession has on the trial, it would be the rare case in which admission of a coerced confession would be harmless on the facts. On the merits, the Court found that the admission of Fulminante's involuntary confession was not harmless error.

Questions About Fulminante

Does Chief Justice Rehnquist's reference to "structural" error fully explain why certain errors can never be harmless? Could it also be that in some cases, the harmless error analysis is simply not responsive to the error that occurred? Consider the defendant who is deprived of the right to proceed *pro se.* It is no answer to say that at his trial, his counsel performed very well and the evidence against him was overwhelming. The right to self-representation is not based upon an effective defense and a correct verdict, but rather upon personal autonomy. Is a violation of this right a structural defect, or is the harmless error doctrine simply irrelevant to the wrong suffered?

Is it possible that the application of the harmless error standard to coerced confessions will make a reviewing court more likely to find certain police tactics impermissible? Is anyone better off when a court holds that a confession was coerced but that its introduction at trial harmless, where if automatic reversal were required, a court concerned about the cost of retrial might hold the confession voluntary?

Error in a Burden of Proof Instruction: Sullivan v. Louisiana

In Sullivan v. Louisiana, 508 U.S. 275 (1993), the Court unanimously held that a constitutionally deficient beyond-a-reasonable-doubt instruction can never be harmless error. At Sullivan's trial, the judge gave an instruction as to reasonable doubt that was virtually identical to the instruction held constitutionally defective in Cage v. Louisiana, 498 U.S. 39 (1990)(instruction defining reasonable doubt in terms of grave and substantial doubt suggests "a higher degree of doubt than is required for acquittal under the reasonable doubt standard"). The state appellate court determined that the evidence against Sullivan was overwhelming and that therefore the erroneous instruction was harmless beyond a reasonable doubt.

Justice Scalia, writing for the Court, noted that the Sixth Amendment right to jury trial means an entitlement to a jury verdict; so, for example, the trial judge may not direct a verdict for the State, no matter how overwhelming the evidence. He stated further that "the jury verdict required by the Sixth Amendment is a jury verdict of guilty beyond a reasonable doubt." Justice Scalia explained why, under *Chapman,* an erroneous reasonable doubt instruction could not be harmless:

Consistent with the jury-trial guarantee, the question [*Chapman*] instructs the reviewing court to consider is not what effect the constitutional error might generally be expected to have upon a reasonable jury, but rather what effect it had upon the guilty verdict in the case at hand. Harmless-error review looks, we have said, to the basis on which "the jury actually rested its verdict." The inquiry, in other words, is not whether, in a trial that occurred without the error, a guilty verdict would surely have been rendered, but whether the guilty verdict actually rendered in *this* trial was surely unattributable to the error. This must be so, because to hypothesize a guilty verdict that was never in fact rendered—no matter how inescapable the findings to support that verdict might be—would violate the jury trial guarantee.

Once the proper role of an appellate court engaged in the *Chapman* inquiry is understood, the illogic of harmless-error review in the present case becomes evident. Since there has been no jury verdict within the meaning of the Sixth Amendment, the entire premise of *Chapman* review is simply absent. * * * There is no *object,* so to speak, upon which harmless-error scrutiny can operate. * * * The Sixth Amendment requires more than appellate speculation about a hypothetical jury's action, or else directed verdicts for the State would be sustainable on appeal; it requires an actual jury verdict of guilty.

Justice Scalia also found that the analysis in *Fulminante* led to the conclusion that an erroneous beyond-a-reasonable-doubt instruction can never be harmless. He stated that the denial of the right to a jury verdict of guilt beyond a reasonable doubt is a "structural" error in *Fulminante* terms, because the jury verdict guarantee is "a basic protection whose precise effects are unmeasurable, but without which a criminal trial cannot function."

Justice Scalia distinguished cases where the trial court gives an erroneous instruction that erects a presumption regarding an element of the offense, upon the jury's finding of a predicate fact (e.g., that malice can be presumed if the jury finds that the defendant possessed a deadly weapon). See Yates v. Evatt, 500 U.S. 391 (1991)(erroneous burden-shifting presumption can be assessed for harmlessness). While such an instruction may impermissibly relieve the State of having to prove all elements of the offense, the jury is still instructed that it must find the existence of the predicate facts supporting the presumption beyond a reasonable doubt. In contrast, where the instructional error consists of a misdescription of the burden of proof, this "vitiates *all* of the jury's findings," and a reviewing court can only engage in "pure speculation," which would mean that "the wrong entity judges the defendant guilty."

Erroneous Instructions on the Elements of a Crime: Neder v. United States

The trial judge in Neder v. United States, 527 U.S. 1 (1999) erroneously instructed the jury that it would not have to decide whether his false statements on tax forms were "material." In the trial judge's view, the question of materiality was for the judge, not the jury. Neder was convicted. But subsequently it was held that materiality is an element of the crime of tax fraud, and therefore the question of materiality was for the jury. On appeal, the government agreed with the defendant that the erroneous instruction was error, but argued that the error was harmless. Neder argued that depriving the jury of the power to decide an element of the crime can never be harmless. The Supreme Court, in an opinion by Chief Justice Rehnquist, held that such an error was subject to harmless error review. He analyzed the harmless error question in the following passage:

We have recognized that "most constitutional errors can be harmless." *Fulminante.* If the defendant had counsel and was tried by an impartial adjudicator, there is a strong presumption that any other constitutional errors that may have occurred are subject to harmless-error analysis. Indeed, we have found an error to be "structural," and thus subject to automatic reversal, only in a "very limited class of cases." Johnson v. United States, 520 U.S. 461 (1997) (citing Gideon v. Wainwright, 372 U.S. 335 (1963) (complete denial of counsel); Tumey v. Ohio, 273 U.S. 510 (1927) (biased trial judge); Vasquez v. Hillery, 474 U.S. 254 (1986) (racial discrimination in selection of grand jury); McKaskle v. Wiggins, 465 U.S. 168 (1984) (denial of self-representation at trial); Waller v. Georgia, 467 U.S. 39 (1984) (denial of public trial); Sullivan v. Louisiana, 508 U.S. 275 (1993) (defective reasonable-doubt instruction)).

The error at issue here—a jury instruction that omits an element of the offense—differs markedly from the constitutional violations we have found to defy harmless-error review. Those cases, we have explained, contain a "defect affecting the framework within which the trial proceeds, rather than simply an error in the trial process itself." Such errors "infect the entire trial process," and "necessarily render a trial fundamentally unfair". Put another way, these errors deprive defendants of "basic protections" without which "a criminal trial cannot reliably serve its function as a vehicle for determination of guilt or innocence . . . and no criminal punishment may be regarded as fundamentally fair."

Unlike such defects as the complete deprivation of counsel or trial before a biased judge, an instruction that omits an element of the offense does not necessarily render a criminal trial fundamentally unfair or an unreliable vehicle for determining guilt or innocence. * * * In fact, as this case shows, quite the opposite is true: Neder was tried before an impartial judge, under the correct standard of proof and with the assistance of counsel; a fairly selected, impartial jury was instructed to consider all of the evidence and argument in respect to Neder's defense against the tax charges. Of course, the court erroneously failed to charge the jury on the element of materiality, but that error did not render Neder's trial "fundamentally unfair," as that term is used in our cases.

The defendant in *Neder* relied heavily on the Court's decision in Sullivan v. Louisiana, where the Court held that a defective reasonable doubt instruction could not be harmless, because such an error "vitiates all the jury's findings" and produces "consequences that are necessarily unquantifiable and indeterminate." But the Chief Justice distinguished *Sullivan* on the ground that a defective instruction as to one element of a crime did not vitiate *all* of the jury's findings. He also relied on prior case law finding defective instructions on issues other than reasonable doubt to be harmless error. On the applicability of *Sullivan*, the Chief Justice concluded as follows:

It would not be illogical to extend the reasoning of *Sullivan* from a defective "reasonable doubt" instruction to a failure to instruct on an element of the crime. But, as indicated in the foregoing discussion, the matter is not res nova under our case law. And if the life of the law has not been logic but experience, see O. Holmes, The Common Law 1 (1881), we are entitled to stand back and see what would be accomplished by such an extension in this case. The omitted element was materiality. Petitioner underreported $5 million on his tax returns, and did not contest the element of materiality at trial. Petitioner does not suggest that he would introduce any evidence bearing upon the issue of materiality if so allowed. Reversal without any consideration of the effect of the error upon the verdict would send the case back for retrial—a retrial not focused at all on the issue of materiality, but on contested issues on which the jury was properly instructed. We do not think the Sixth Amendment requires us to veer away from settled precedent to reach such a result.

Justice Stevens concurred in the judgment in *Neder*. Justice Scalia, joined by Justices Souter and Ginsburg, dissented and argued that a Trial Judge's taking an element of the crime away from the jury could never be harmless. He noted that cases such as *Sullivan* indicate that if the entire case is taken away from the jury, this cannot be harmless error. If that is so, how could it be harmless error to take an element of the case away from the jury? Justice Scalia stated that

> we do not know, when the Court's opinion is done, how many elements can be taken away from the jury with impunity, so long as appellate judges are persuaded that the defendant is surely guilty. What if, in the present case, besides keeping the materiality issue for itself, the District Court had also refused to instruct the jury to decide whether the defendant signed his tax return? If Neder had never contested that element of the offense, and the record contained a copy of his signed return, would his conviction be automatically reversed in that situation but not in this one, even though he would be just as obviously guilty? We do not know. We know that all elements cannot be taken from the jury, and that one can. How many is too many (or perhaps what proportion is too high) remains to be determined by future improvisation.

Harmlessness Standard for Non–Constitutional Error: The Kotteakos–Lane Rule

In Kotteakos v. United States, 328 U.S. 750 (1946), the Court established a test of harmlessness for trial errors of a nonconstitutional dimension: reversal is not required if the appellate court "is sure that the error did not influence the jury or had but very slight effect." Conversely, reversal is required for a nonconstitutional error if it "had substantial and injurious effect or influence in determining the jury's verdict." United States v. Lane, 474 U.S. 438 (1986)(applying the *Kotteakos* standard to a misjoinder under Fed.R.Crim.P. 8(b)). See also Fed.R.Crim.P. 52(a). The *Kotteakos–Lane* standard is clearly less protective of defendants than the harmless error rule applied to constitutional errors under *Chapman*. See United States v. Owens, 789 F.2d 750 (9th Cir. 1986)(if admission of prior identification was merely a violation of the hearsay rule, it was harmless under the *Kotteakos–Lane* standard; but if admission also violated the defendant's constitutional right to confrontation, the error was harmful under the *Chapman* standard and reversal was required).

Some state courts utilize the *Chapman* test for assessing the impact of state constitutional errors. See, e.g., Aldridge v. State, 584 P.2d 1105 (Alaska 1978). But others use a less demanding standard that is intended to save more convictions from reversal. Saltzburg, The Harm of Harmless Error, 59 Va.L.Rev. 988 (1973), argues that the *Chapman* test should be utilized generally in criminal cases. This approach has been followed in several jurisdictions. See, e.g., Commonwealth v. Story, 476 Pa. 391, 383 A.2d 155 (1978); Dorsey v. State, 276 Md. 638, 350 A.2d 665 (1976).

2. *Plain Error*

The harmless error standards discussed above are applied when the defendant makes an appropriate objection at trial. A more stringent standard for reversal is applied when the defendant fails to make an objection at trial, and then argues on appeal that the trial court was in error. The appellate court in such a situation reviews for "plain error." The rationale for the more stringent standard is that if a defendant does not properly object at trial, he deprives the trial judge of the opportunity to focus on the problem and perhaps correct the error at that point. The distinction between harmful error and plain error is set forth in Federal Rule of Criminal Procedure 52, which states as follows:

(a) Harmless Error. Any error, defect, irregularity or variance that does not affect substantial rights must be disregarded.

(b) Plain Error. A plain error that affects substantial rights may be considered even though it was not brought to the court's attention.

Thus, Rule 52(a), by negative implication, states that reversal is required if the error affected substantial rights.[10] However, if the defendant did not bring the error to the attention of the court, then a reversal *may* be granted if the error affected substantial rights.

Application of the Plain Error Standard: *United States v. Olano*

The Supreme Court had occasion to review the concept of "plain error," and its distinction from harmful error, in United States v. Olano, 507 U.S. 725 (1993). The Court held that the presence of alternate jurors during deliberations was not, under the circumstances of the case, an error that the court of appeals was authorized to correct under Fed.R.Crim.P. 52(b). The defendants had not objected to the presence of the alternate jurors during the deliberations, even though this practice at the time violated the plain terms of Fed.R.Crim.P. 24(c). [The current Rule 24 allows the court to retain alternate jurors even after the jury retires to deliberate].

Writing for the Court, Justice O'Connor reasoned that Rule 52(b) "defines a single category of forfeited-but-reversible error." She identified three limitations on a court's power to reverse because of errors that were not properly preserved

---

10. This is the harmless error standard applied for non-constitutional errors. For constitutional errors on direct review, the more de- fendant-friendly *Chapman* standard requires reversal unless the error was harmless beyond a reasonable doubt.

for review in the trial court. First there must be an error, i.e., deviation from a legal rule absent a waiver by a defendant. Justice O'Connor distinguished waiver of a right from forfeiture of a right, stating that "[w]hereas forfeiture is the failure to make the timely assertion of a right, waiver is the intentional relinquishment of a known right." Thus, if the defendant knowingly and voluntarily waives a right—such as the right to a jury trial—there is no error in the proceedings and the plain error rule is inapplicable. If, on the other hand, the defendant fails to object to an erroneous ruling by the trial court, then the plain error standard is potentially applicable.

The second limitation on a court's power to correct forfeited errors is that the error must be plain, which means it must be clear or obvious—so obvious that the judge should have seen it even though it was not flagged by defense counsel. Finally, the plain error must affect substantial rights, which means that it must have been prejudicial in the sense of affecting the outcome of the case. Justice O'Connor reasoned further that the language of Rule 52(b) is permissive, not mandatory. She stated that "the Court of Appeals should correct a plain forfeited error affecting substantial rights if the error seriously affects the fairness, integrity or public reputation of judicial proceedings." However, a "plain error affecting substantial rights, does not, without more" mandate reversal, "for otherwise the discretion afforded by Rule 52(b) would be rendered illusory."

Justice O'Connor compared Rule 52(a), which defines harmless error, with Rule 52(b). She concluded that the rules were different in the manner in which they allocated the burden of persuasion in showing prejudice. She analyzed the difference between the rules as follows:

> When the defendant has made a timely objection to an error and Rule 52(a) applies, the Court of Appeals normally engages in a specific analysis of the District Court record—a so-called "harmless error" inquiry—to determine whether the error was prejudicial. Rule 52(b) normally requires the same kind of inquiry, with one important difference: It is the defendant rather than the Government who bears the burden of persuasion with respect to prejudice. In most cases, the Court of Appeals cannot correct the forfeited error unless the defendant shows that the error was prejudicial. This burden-shifting is dictated by a subtle but important difference in language between the two parts of Rule 52: while Rule 52(a) precludes error-correction only if the error "does *not* affect substantial rights" (emphasis added), Rule 52(b) authorizes no remedy unless the error *does* "affec[t] substantial rights."

Justice O'Connor left open the possibility that "[t]here may be a special category of forfeited errors that can be corrected regardless of their effect on the outcome," and declined to address the errors that should be presumed prejudicial. She concluded that normally, the defendant must make a "specific showing of prejudice" under Rule 52(b).

In *Olano,* the Court held that the defendants had failed to show that their substantial rights had been affected by any error. Justice O'Connor noted that the trial judge instructed the alternates that they were not to participate in deliberations, and that the defendants had made no showing that the presence of the alternates affected deliberations in any way.[11]

Error "Plain" at the Time of Appellate Review: Johnson v. United States

Can an error be "plain" when the trial court rules correctly at the time of trial, but then the law changes while the case is on direct appeal? This was one of the questions in Johnson v. United States, 520 U.S. 461 (1997). At Johnson's trial for perjury, the trial judge rather than the jury decided the question of whether Johnson's false statement to a grand jury was "material." This practice was in accord with Circuit precedent at the time. However, in United States v. Gaudin, 515 U.S. 506 (1995), the Court held that the jury and not the judge must decide whether a false statement is material in cases such as Johnson's. *Gaudin* was decided after Johnson's trial, but while Johnson's case was on direct appeal—therefore *Gaudin* was applicable retroactively to Johnson's case. (See the discussion on retroactivity in Chapter One). However, Johnson had not objected at trial to the trial judge taking the materiality question away from the jury. Indeed, Johnson complained at trial about the prosecution's proffer of evidence of materiality; he argued that the evidence was irrelevant, on the ground that materiality was a question for the judge rather than the jury.

Chief Justice Rehnquist, writing for a unanimous Court, noted that because of *Gaudin*, an "error" had occurred at Johnson's trial. He also noted, however, that because *Gaudin* was decided after Johnson's trial, it was difficult to determine whether the error complained of was "plain" within the meaning of *Olano*:

> In the case with which we are faced today, the error is certainly clear under "current law," but it was by no means clear at the time of trial.
>
> The Government contends that for an error to be "plain," it must have been so both at the time of trial and at the time of appellate consideration. In this case, it says, petitioner should have objected to the court's deciding the issue of materiality, even though near-uniform precedent both from this Court and from the Courts of Appeals held that course proper. Petitioner, on the other hand, urges that such a rule would result in counsel's inevitably making a long and virtually useless laundry list of objections to rulings that were plainly supported by existing precedent. We agree with petitioner on this point, and hold that in a case such as this—where the law at the time of trial was settled and clearly contrary to the law at the time of appeal—it is enough that an error be "plain" at the time of appellate consideration. Here, at the time of trial it was settled that the issue of materiality was to be decided by the court, not the jury; by the time of appellate consideration, the law had changed, and it is now settled that materiality is an issue for the jury. The second part of the *Olano* test is therefore satisfied.

It must be remembered, though, that under *Olano* plain error does not give rise to relief unless the error affected "substantial rights" and "seriously affects the fairness, integrity or public reputation of judicial proceedings." The Chief

---

11. Justice Kennedy wrote a short concurring opinion. Justice Stevens, joined by Justices White and Blackmun, dissented.

Justice concluded that it was not necessary to decide whether the error at Johnson's trial affected substantial rights, because it was clear that the error did not affect the fairness or integrity of the proceedings. He found that the evidence indicating that statements were material was "overwhelming," and that the question of materiality was "essentially uncontroverted at trial and remains so on appeal." Therefore, "no miscarriage of justice will occur if we do not notice the error."

Plain Error Review of an Apprendi Violation: United States v. Cotton

In Apprendi v. New Jersey, 530 U.S. 466 (2000), the Court held that "[o]ther than the fact of a prior conviction, any fact that increases the penalty for a crime beyond the prescribed statutory maximum must be submitted to a jury, and proved beyond a reasonable doubt." [*Apprendi* is set forth in full in the Chapter 10 discussion of constitutionally-based proof requirements]. In federal prosecutions, such facts must also be charged in the indictment. In United States v. Cotton, 535 U.S. 625 (2002), the Court reviewed an *Apprendi* violation for plain error. The defendants in *Cotton* received a sentence beyond the statutory maximum, after the trial judge (rather than the jury) found that the drug offenses involved more than 50 grams of cocaine base. The indictment made no allegation as to any amount of drugs. Under *Apprendi*, the amount of drugs that triggers an enhanced sentence beyond the statutory maximum is an element of the crime that must be set forth in the indictment and proved to the jury. The government conceded that the defendants' enhanced sentence was erroneous under *Apprendi*, but pointed out that the defendants had failed to raise the *Apprendi* argument before the district court.

The Supreme Court, in an opinion by Chief Justice Rehnquist, held that the defendants were not entitled to relief because they could not meet their burden of showing plain error under the circumstances. Chief Justice Rehnquist analyzed the plain error question as follows:

> [W]e proceed to apply the plain-error test of Federal Rule of Criminal Procedure 52(b) to respondents' forfeited claim. See United States v. Olano, 507 U.S. 725, 731 (1993). "Under that test, before an appellate court can correct an error not raised at trial, there must be (1) 'error,' (2) that is 'plain,' and (3) that 'affect[s] substantial rights.' " Johnson v. United States, 520 U.S. 461, 466–467 (1997). "If all three conditions are met, an appellate court may then exercise its discretion to notice a forfeited error, but only if (4) the error seriously affect[s] the fairness, integrity, or public reputation of judicial proceedings." 520 U.S., at 467. The Government concedes that the indictment's failure to allege a fact, drug quantity, that increased the statutory maximum sentence rendered respondents' enhanced sentences erroneous under the reasoning of *Apprendi*. The Government also concedes that such error was plain.
>
> The third inquiry is whether the plain error "affect[ed] substantial rights." This usually means that the error "must have affected the outcome of the district court proceedings." *Olano, supra,* at 734. Respondents argue that an indictment error falls within the "limited class" of "structural errors," *Johnson, supra,* at 468–469 that "can be corrected regardless of their effect on the outcome," *Olano, supra,* at 735. * * *

As in *Johnson*, we need not resolve whether respondents satisfy this element of the plain-error inquiry, because even assuming respondents' substantial rights were affected, the error did not seriously affect the fairness, integrity, or public reputation of judicial proceedings. The error in *Johnson* was the District Court's failure to submit an element of the false statement offense, materiality, to the petit jury. The evidence of materiality, however, was "overwhelming" and "essentially uncontroverted." We thus held that there was "no basis for concluding that the error 'seriously affect[ed] the fairness, integrity or public reputation of judicial proceedings.'"

The same analysis applies in this case to the omission of drug quantity from the indictment. The evidence that the conspiracy involved at least 50 grams of cocaine base was "overwhelming" and "essentially uncontroverted." Much of the evidence implicating respondents in the drug conspiracy revealed the conspiracy's involvement with far more than 50 grams of cocaine base. Baltimore police officers made numerous state arrests and seizures between February 1996 and April 1997 that resulted in the seizure of 795 ziplock bags and clear bags containing approximately 380 grams of cocaine base. A federal search of respondent Jovan Powell's residence resulted in the seizure of 51.3 grams of cocaine base. A cooperating co-conspirator testified at trial that he witnessed respondent Hall cook one-quarter of a kilogram of cocaine powder into cocaine base. Another cooperating co-conspirator testified at trial that she was present in a hotel room where the drug operation bagged one kilogram of cocaine base into ziplock bags. Surely the grand jury, having found that the conspiracy existed, would have also found that the conspiracy involved at least 50 grams of cocaine base.

E. DISENTITLEMENT FROM THE RIGHT TO APPEAL

The Fugitive Dismissal Rule: Ortega–Rodriguez v. United States

If a defendant flees during the pendency of his appeal, the appellate court has the authority to dismiss the appeal. See Molinaro v. New Jersey, 396 U.S. 365 (1970). This "fugitive dismissal" rule is based upon two justifications: 1) the appellate court should not render a judgment that may prove unenforceable; and 2) a defendant who takes flight disentitles himself from the right to call upon the resources of the appellate court.

In Ortega–Rodriguez v. United States, 507 U.S. 234 (1993), the Court considered whether the justifications behind the fugitive dismissal rule apply when a defendant flees the jurisdiction of a district court and is recaptured *before* he invokes the jurisdiction of the appellate court. The Court, in a 5–4 decision, held that "when a defendant's flight and recapture occur before appeal, the defendant's former fugitive status may well lack the kind of connection to the appellate process that would justify an appellate sanction of dismissal." Justice Stevens, writing for the Court, explained as follows:

> [T]he justifications we have advanced for allowing appellate courts to dismiss pending fugitive appeals all assume some connection between a defendant's fugitive status and the appellate process, sufficient to make an appellate sanction a reasonable response. These justifications are necessarily

attenuated when applied to a case in which both flight and recapture occur while the case is pending before the district court, so that a defendant's fugitive status at no time coincides with his appeal.

* * * Absent some connection between a defendant's fugitive status and his appeal, as provided when a defendant is at large during the ongoing appellate process, the justifications advanced for dismissal of fugitives' appeals generally will not apply.

Justice Stevens pointed out that the enforceability concerns behind the fugitive dismissal rule are not applicable to a defendant who has been returned before the appellate process has begun. He further claimed that flight while the case is pending in the district court was a sign of disrespect for the authority of that court, not of the appellate court; therefore the disentitlement justification of the fugitive dismissal rule would ordinarily not apply to pre-appeal flight, and the defendant's act of flight "is best sanctioned by the district court itself."

The Court refused, however, to adopt a bright-line rule that pre-appeal flight could never result in dismissal of an appeal. Justice Stevens noted that "some actions by a defendant, though they occur while his case is before the district court, might have an impact on the appellate process sufficient to warrant an appellate sanction." For example, the government may be prejudiced in locating witnesses for retrial if the appeal is significantly delayed; or the appellate court may be inconvenienced due to the inability to consolidate the fugitive defendant's appeal with other related appeals. The Court ruled that if such circumstances existed, "a dismissal rule could properly be applied."[12] The Court remanded the case to determine whether the defendant's pre-appeal flight imposed consequences on the appellate system sufficient to justify dismissal of his appeal.

Chief Justice Rehnquist, joined by Justices White, O'Connor, and Thomas, dissented. He stated that the "only difference between a defendant who absconds preappeal and one who absconds postappeal is that the former has filed a notice of appeal while the latter has not." He claimed that "there is as much of a chance that flight will disrupt the proper functioning of the appellate process if it occurs before the court of appeals obtains jurisdiction as there is if it occurs after the court of appeals obtains jurisdiction."[13]

III. COLLATERAL ATTACK

A. REMEDIES GENERALLY

1. *Collateral Attacks*

After new trial motions have been made and all appeals are exhausted (or lost, perhaps for failure to comply with an appellate rule, such as a time limit on

---

12. See United States v. Reese, 993 F.2d 254 (D.C.Cir.1993)(applying *Ortega-Rodriguez* and dismissing an appeal where the defendant became a fugitive after the trial and before sentencing; the defendant's flight precluded the court from consolidating his appeal with that of his co-defendant); United States v. Rosales, 13 F.3d 1461 (11th Cir.1994)(dismissing an appeal where flight caused such a significant delay that the prosecution would be prejudiced in locating witnesses if a new trial were granted).

13. In a per curiam opinion, the Court in Goeke v. Branch, 514 U.S. 115 (1995), emphasized that its decision in *Ortega–Rodriguez* was

based on its supervisory power over the Federal courts. The Court stated that the Due Process Clause would not necessarily prohibit the state from applying a fugitive dismissal rule, even where there is no demonstrated adverse effect on the state's appellate process. The due process question was considered at best one on which reasonable minds could differ. Since *Goeke* was a habeas action, the Court concluded that the doctrine of Teague v. Lane, 489 U.S. 288 (1989)(new rules may not be considered in a habeas action), prohibited it from considering whether the Due Process Clause imposed any limits on the fugitive dismissal rule.

filing a notice of appeal), a defendant whose conviction emerges unscathed has a natural incentive to attempt additional attacks on the conviction.

Post-conviction remedies, of which habeas corpus is the most common, have always been regarded as *collateral* remedies, "providing an avenue for upsetting judgments that have become otherwise final." Mackey v. United States, 401 U.S. 667 (1971)(Harlan, J., separate opinion). They are not designed to substitute for direct review of convictions, nor can all the questions properly subject to appeal be raised collaterally. Because collateral attacks collide with principles of finality, there are substantial limitations imposed on persons who want to bring such attacks.

2.   *Coram Nobis*

One rarely used form of collateral attack is for the petitioner to obtain a writ of coram nobis. This is a remedy of last resort, available only to one otherwise remediless. Given the availability of a habeas corpus petition for those in custody, the coram nobis remedy has only very limited applicability. See Lowery v. United States, 956 F.2d 227 (11th Cir.1992)(coram nobis relief is not available where the defendant is still in custody and can petition for habeas relief). As the court in Telink, Inc. v. United States, 24 F.3d 42 (9th Cir.1994), put it:

> The writ of error coram nobis affords a remedy to attack an unconstitutional or unlawful conviction in cases when the petitioner has already served a sentence. The petition fills a very precise gap in federal criminal procedure. A convicted defendant in federal custody may petition to have a sentence or conviction vacated, set aside or corrected under the federal habeas statute, 28 U.S.C. § 2255. However, if the sentence has been served, there is no statutory basis to remedy the lingering collateral consequences of the unlawful conviction. Recognizing this statutory gap, the Supreme Court has held that the common law petition for writ of error coram nobis is available in such situations * * *.

Availability of the Writ in Federal Courts: United States
v. Morgan and Korematsu v. United States

The writ of error coram nobis can be used to attack convictions on the basis of an error in fact, or a defense in fact, that does not appear on the face of the record that produced the judgment. But the petitioner must show 1) that his failure to raise the factual claim was not negligent and 2) the errors complained of are constitutional errors of sufficient magnitude to have significantly affected the verdict of the trier of fact. The United States Supreme Court held that the writ is available in federal courts in United States v. Morgan, 346 U.S. 502 (1954). After Morgan was convicted in federal court and served his sentence, he was convicted in a state court and sentenced to a longer term as a second offender on the basis of the federal conviction. Collateral attack on the federal conviction under 28 U.S.C.A. § 2255, discussed infra, was not possible because Morgan was not in federal custody. But the Court held that an attack in the nature of coram nobis—in *Morgan* the challenge was that he had not been represented by counsel—was available. The burden of proving a right to relief was placed upon the convicted person. The Court stated that the grant of relief "should be allowed through this extraordinary remedy only under circumstances compelling such action to achieve justice."

Subsequently the Court recognized "the obvious fact of life that most criminal convictions do in fact entail adverse collateral legal consequences." Sibron v. New York, 392 U.S. 40, 55 (1968). Coram nobis, in the absence of other remedies, will allow a convicted person to attempt to avoid these consequences, for example, disentitlement from the right to vote.

One of the most celebrated uses of the writ of coram nobis is Korematsu v. United States, 584 F.Supp. 1406 (N.D.Cal.1984), in which the court vacated the notorious conviction of an American citizen of Japanese ancestry for being in a place where all persons of Japanese ancestry had been excluded following the declaration of war by the United States against Japan in 1941. The conviction had been sustained by the Supreme Court in 1944. 323 U.S. 214 (1944). The district court relied upon a Report of the Commission on Wartime Relocation and Internment of Civilians (1982), which concluded that military necessity did not warrant the exclusion and detention of ethnic Japanese. It also relied upon internal government documents that demonstrated that the government knowingly withheld information from the courts when they were considering the critical question of military necessity in this case.

3. *Habeas Corpus*

In many instances coram nobis will not lie because habeas corpus or a remedy in the nature of habeas corpus exists. Habeas corpus is a remedy for those who are in custody; the petitioner seeks a writ to be served against the official holding him in custody—usually the warden. Most recently, after the terrorist attacks of 9/11 and the detention of suspected Taliban and Al Qaeda sympathizers in military installations, these petitions have been directed toward the Secretary of Defense. (See the discussion of enemy combatants at the end of Chapter 10). The justification for the writ is that some error occurred that makes the custody illegal.

History of the Great Writ

"The early function of the writ of habeas corpus, say from 1150, was simply to get an unwilling party into court regardless of the kind of case involved." R. Sokol, Federal Habeas Corpus § B, at 4. It did not begin a proceeding; rather, it assured that once a proceeding was otherwise begun, it would not be futile because of the absence of a party. In the fourteenth century, the writ, in addition to its earlier function, also became an independent action to test the cause of a detention. With the development of this aspect of the writ, it took its place in the struggle between the common-law and the chancery courts. "Time and again * * * the common-law judges through habeas corpus released from custody persons committed by other courts," and thus undercut the authority of the Chancellor. D. Meador, Habeas Corpus and Magna Carta: Dualism of Power and Liberty 12 (1966).

Darnel's Case, 3 St.Trials 1, arose in 1627 and probably accounts significantly for the development of the writ. Darnel and four other knights were sent to prison for refusing to "loan" money to a demanding monarch. They sought habeas corpus to inquire into the power of the monarch to imprison them. Unsuccessful though they were, they invoked the concept of "due process of law," and they relied on Magna Carta in a way that led parliament to modify the decision by providing in its Petition of Right that no person should be imprisoned without being charged in some way that allowed an opportunity for an answer. Fifty years later the writ of habeas corpus was the established vehicle for challenging confinement as denying due process of law. In the famous decision in Bushell's Case, 124 Eng.Rep. 1006, 6 St.Trials 999 (1670), the court utilized habeas corpus to order the release of a juror committed for contempt for returning a not guilty verdict in the trial of William Penn and others. A century later Blackstone would call the writ "the most celebrated in the English law." R. Sokol, supra, at 15. But the writ was far from a perfect remedy for all illegal detentions. It developed that one court would not order the release of a person held by order of another court if the latter had proper jurisdiction. And, with respect to detentions ordered by the King, it was generally sufficient that the King asserted a right to detain a person despite the Petition of Right.

With the utilization of English common-law in the American colonies, the writ of habeas corpus became a part of American law. See generally Oaks, Habeas Corpus in the States—1776–1865, 32 U.Chi.L.Rev. 243 (1965). At the time of the constitutional convention, 4 of the 12 states with written constitutions had provisions regarding habeas corpus. Id. In Article I of the Constitution, which sets forth the powers of Congress and restrictions upon those powers, clause 2 of section 9 provides that "[t]he Privilege of the Writ of Habeas Corpus shall not be suspended, unless when in Cases of Rebellion or Invasion the public Safety may require it."[14]

Congressional Power to Restrict Habeas Corpus

It is unclear how far Congress could go in restricting the habeas corpus power of federal courts. If, for example, Congress did not authorize lower federal courts to hear any habeas corpus cases, would the anti-suspension clause be violated? That Congress need not create federal courts at all might suggest that no habeas power necessarily must be placed in lower courts. See generally Developments in the Law—Federal Habeas Corpus, 83 Harv.L.Rev. 1038, 1049–50, 1263–66 (1970). Some suggestions have been made that even without statutory authority federal courts could grant writs of habeas corpus. See, e.g., Chafee, The Most Important Human Right in the Constitution, 32 B.U.L.Rev. 143 (1952). This question has never been tested, however. Congress has passed statutes that authorize collateral attack by a petition for habeas corpus. Most recently, Congress has acted to limit the availability of the habeas corpus remedy—this legislative cutback has been fully enforced by the federal courts, as will be seen below.

State Habeas Provisions

At one time the Supreme Court granted certiorari to decide whether state courts are obliged under the Federal Constitution to provide persons convicted

---

14. After the adoption of the Constitution, it became more common for states to include habeas corpus provisions in their own constitutions.

in state court with some post-conviction process to correct judgments of conviction obtained in violation of federal law. But the Court remanded the case to the Nebraska Supreme Court when the state legislature passed a post-conviction statute. Case v. Nebraska, 381 U.S. 336 (1965). Since then, all states appear to have recognized some form of post-conviction attack after direct appeal in the state courts has been exhausted. See generally Whitmore v. State, 299 Ark. 55, 771 S.W.2d 266 (1989), for a discussion of the costs of allowing state post-conviction proceedings and the problems involved in integrating state and federal post-conviction proceedings.

The extent to which claims can be raised and the procedures that must be followed in raising the claims in state court depend upon state law, just as 28 U.S.C.A. § 2255 covers federal defendants in federal courts. If a convicted person wins collateral relief in state court, further proceedings will be unnecessary. But failure to win in state court often will not bar a subsequent federal action to set aside a state conviction. The remainder of this Chapter will focus on federal actions and two basic questions: (1) What issues should be cognizable in collateral actions? (2) Should it matter (and if so, why) whether the collateral action is brought by a person convicted in a state or federal court? Because this material involves, in part, complex questions of federal-state relations, only the surface is scratched here. An in-depth look at the problem is available in the standard course in Federal Courts or Federal Procedure.

B. THE FEDERAL HABEAS CORPUS SCHEME: THE PROCEDURAL FRAMEWORK

1. *The Statutes*

Federal habeas corpus remedies are available to challenge convictions rendered by both state and federal courts. The challenge must be brought by a person in custody—that person, who was originally the defendant in a criminal proceeding, is the "petitioner" in the habeas proceeding. The petitioner files a civil action in federal court, seeking a writ of habeas corpus on the ground that he is in custody in violation of federal law. Generally speaking, petitions for habeas corpus filed by state prisoners are governed by 28 U.S.C. § 2254 and are often referred to as section 2254 actions. Petitions for habeas corpus filed by federal prisoners are governed by 28 U.S.C. § 2255 and are often referred to as section 2255 actions.

On April 24, 1996, the President signed into law the Antiterrorism and Effective Death Penalty Act (hereinafter referred to as the AEDPA). The AEDPA imposes significant limitations on the habeas corpus remedy in federal courts. Some of these limitations are directed specifically to state death-row claimants, and are conditioned on the state's implementation of a mechanism for appointing competent counsel for state post-conviction proceedings. Other limitations are directed more generally toward any state claimant seeking relief in the federal district court under the provisions of 28 U.S.C. § 2254. Limitations similar to these are imposed on federal prisoners seeking collateral relief under 28 U.S.C. § 2255.

What follows are the statutory provisions that are pertinent to the habeas corpus remedy, as amended by AEDPA. AEDPA amendments are italicized.

Section 2241

28 U.S.C.A. § 2241 et seq. sets forth the powers of federal judges to issue writs of habeas corpus and the procedures to be utilized in habeas corpus actions. Section 2241 sets forth the reach of the writ and identifies the courts from which it may be sought.

§ 2241. Power to grant writ

(a) Writs of habeas corpus may be granted by the Supreme Court, any justice thereof, the district courts and any circuit judge within their respective jurisdictions. The order of a circuit judge shall be entered in the records of the district court of the district wherein the restraint complained of is had.

(b) The Supreme Court, any justice thereof, and any circuit judge may decline to entertain an application for a writ of habeas corpus and may transfer the application for hearing and determination to the district court having jurisdiction to entertain it.

(c) The writ of habeas corpus shall not extend to a prisoner unless—

(1) He is in custody under or by color of the authority of the United States or is committed for trial before some court thereof; or

(2) He is in custody for an act done or omitted in pursuance of an Act of Congress, or an order, process, judgment or decree of a court or judge of the United States; or

(3) He is in custody in violation of the Constitution or laws or treaties of the United States; * * *

* * *

Section 2244

Section 2244, as amended by AEDPA, essentially provides that a habeas petitioner gets one collateral attack. Successive petitions are virtually always to be dismissed. It also provides for a statute of limitations on habeas petitions.

28 U.S.C. § 2244. Finality of determination

(a) No circuit or district judge shall be required to entertain an application for a writ of habeas corpus to inquire into the detention of a person pursuant to a judgment of a court of the United States if it appears that the legality of such detention has been determined by a judge or court of the United States on a prior application for a writ of habeas corpus *except as provided in Section 2255.*

(b)(1) A claim presented in a second or successive Habeas Corpus application under section 2254 that was presented in a prior application shall be dismissed.

(2) A claim presented in a second or successive Habeas Corpus application under section 2254 that was not presented in a prior application shall be dismissed unless—

(A) The applicant shows that the claim relies on a new rule of Constitutional law, made retroactive to cases on collateral review by the Supreme Court, that was previously unavailable; or

(B)(i) the factual predicate for the claim could not have been discovered previously through the exercise of due diligence; and

(ii) the facts underlying the claim, if proven and viewed in light of the evidence as a whole, would be sufficient to establish by clear and convincing evidence that, but for constitutional error, no reasonable factfinder would have found the applicant guilty of the underlying offense.

(3)(A) Before a second or successive application permitted by this section is filed in the district court, the applicant shall move in the appropriate court of appeals for an order authorizing the district court to consider the application.

(B) A motion in the court of appeals for an order authorizing the district court to consider a second or successive application shall be determined by a three-judge panel of the court of appeals.

(C) The court of appeals may authorize the filing of a second or successive application only if it determines that the application makes a prima facie showing that the application satisfies the requirements of this subsection.

(D) The court of appeals shall grant or deny the authorization to file a second or successive application not later than 30 days after the filing of the motion.

(E) The grant or denial of an authorization by a court of appeals to file a second or successive application shall not be appealable and shall not be the subject of a petition for rehearing or for a Writ of Certiorari.

(4) A district court shall dismiss any claim presented in a second or successive application that the court of appeals has authorized to be filed unless the applicant shows that the claim satisfies the requirements of this section.

(c) In a habeas corpus proceeding brought in behalf of a person in custody pursuant to the judgment of a State court, a prior judgment of the Supreme Court of the United States on an appeal or review by a writ of certiorari at the instance of the prisoner of the decision of such State court, shall be conclusive as to all issues of fact or law with respect to an asserted denial of a Federal right which constitutes ground for discharge in a habeas corpus proceeding, actually adjudicated by the Supreme Court therein, unless the applicant for the writ of habeas corpus shall plead and the court shall find the existence of a material and controlling fact which did not appear in the record of the proceeding in the Supreme Court and the court shall further find that the applicant for the writ of habeas corpus could not have caused such fact to appear in such record by the exercise of reasonable diligence.

(d)(1) A 1–year period of limitation shall apply to an application for a writ of habeas corpus by a person in custody pursuant to the judgment of a State court. The limitation period shall run from the latest of—

(A) the date on which the judgment became final by the conclusion of direct review or the expiration of the time for seeking such review;

(B) the date on which the impediment to filing an application created by State action in violation of the Constitution or laws of the United States is removed, if the applicant was prevented from filing by such State action;

(C) the date on which the constitutional right asserted was initially recognized by the Supreme Court, if the right has been newly recognized by the Supreme Court and made retroactively applicable to cases on collateral review; or

(D) the date on which the factual predicate of the claim or claims presented could have been discovered through the exercise of due diligence.

(2) The time during which a properly filed application for State post-conviction or other collateral review with respect to the pertinent judgment or claim is pending shall not be counted toward any period of limitation under this subsection.

Section 2253

Section 2253 limits the right of appeal from a district court's denial of a writ of habeas corpus.

22 U.S.C. § 2253. Appeal

(a) In a habeas corpus proceeding or a proceeding under section 2255 before a district judge, the final order shall be subject to review, on appeal, by the court of appeals for the circuit in which the proceeding is held.

(b) There shall be no right of appeal from a final order in a proceeding to test the validity of a warrant to remove to another district or place for commitment or trial a person charged with a criminal offense against the United States, or to test the validity of such person's detention pending removal proceedings.

(c)(1) Unless a circuit justice or judge issues a certificate of appealability, an appeal may not be taken to the court of appeals from—

(A) the final order in a habeas corpus proceeding in which the detention complained of arises out of process issued by a State court; or

(B) the final order in a proceeding under section 2255.

(2) A certificate of appealability may issue under paragraph (1) only if the applicant has made a substantial showing of the denial of a constitutional right.

(3) The certificate of appealability under paragraph (1) shall indicate which specific issue or issues satisfy the showing required by paragraph (2).

Section 2254

Section 2254 is the basic section governing review of state court convictions by a federal district court in a habeas corpus action. The AEDPA requires substantial deference to be given to state court determinations of federal law. And it requires the petitioner to exhaust state remedies before seeking a habeas corpus petition in federal court. It also limits the ability of a state petitioner to receive an evidentiary hearing in the federal court.

28 U.S.C. § 2254. State custody; remedies in Federal courts

(a) The Supreme Court, a Justice thereof, a circuit judge, or a district court shall entertain an application for a writ of habeas corpus in behalf of a person in custody pursuant to the judgment of a State court only on the ground that he is in custody in violation of the Constitution or laws or treaties of the United States.

(b)*(1) An application for a writ of habeas corpus on behalf of a person in custody pursuant to the judgment of a State court shall not be granted unless it appears that—*

> *(A) the applicant has exhausted the remedies available in the courts of the State; or*

> *(B) (i) there is an absence of available State corrective process; or*

>> *(ii) circumstances exist that render such process ineffective to protect the rights of the applicant.*

(2) An application for a writ of habeas corpus may be denied on the merits, notwithstanding the failure of the applicant to exhaust the remedies available in the courts of the State.

(3) A State shall not be deemed to have waived the exhaustion requirement or be estopped from reliance upon the requirement unless the State, through counsel, expressly waives the requirement.

(c) An applicant shall not be deemed to have exhausted the remedies available in the courts of the State, within the meaning of this section, if he has the right under the law of the State to raise, by any available procedure, the question presented.

(d) An application for a writ of habeas corpus on behalf of a person in custody pursuant to the judgment of a State court shall not be granted with respect to any claim that was adjudicated on the merits in State court proceedings unless the adjudication of the claim—

> *(1) resulted in a decision that was contrary to, or involved an unreasonable application of, clearly established Federal law, as determined by the Supreme Court of the United States; or*

> *(2) resulted in a decision that was based on an unreasonable determination of the facts in light of the evidence presented in the State court proceeding.*

(e)*(1) In a proceeding instituted by an application for a writ of habeas corpus by a person in custody pursuant to the judgment of a State court, a determination of a factual issue made by a State court shall be presumed to be correct. The applicant shall have the burden of rebutting the presumption of correctness by clear and convincing evidence.*

(2) If the applicant has failed to develop the factual basis of a claim in State court proceedings, the court shall not hold an evidentiary hearing on the claim unless the applicant shows that—

(A) the claim relies on—

(i) a new rule of constitutional law, made retroactive to cases on collateral review by the Supreme Court, that was previously unavailable; or

(ii) a factual predicate that could not have been previously discovered through the exercise of due diligence; and

(B) the facts underlying the claim would be sufficient to establish by clear and convincing evidence that but for constitutional error, no reasonable factfinder would have found the applicant guilty of the underlying offense.; and

(f) If the applicant challenges the sufficiency of the evidence adduced in such State court proceeding to support the State court's determination of a factual issue made therein, the applicant, if able, shall produce that part of the record pertinent to a determination of the sufficiency of the evidence to support such determination. If the applicant, because of indigency or other reason is unable to produce such part of the record, then the State shall produce such part of the record and the Federal court shall direct the State to do so by order directed to an appropriate State official. If the State cannot provide such pertinent part of the record, then the court shall determine under the existing facts and circumstances what weight shall be given to the State court's factual determination.

(g) A copy of the official records of the State court, duly certified by the clerk of such court to be a true and correct copy of a finding, judicial opinion, or other reliable written indicia showing such a factual determination by the State court shall be admissible in the Federal court proceeding.

(h) Except as provided in section 408 of the Controlled Substances Act, in all proceedings brought under this section, and any subsequent proceedings on review, the court may appoint counsel for an applicant who is or becomes financially unable to afford counsel, except as provided by a rule promulgated by the Supreme Court pursuant to statutory authority. * * *

(i) The ineffectiveness or incompetence of counsel during Federal or State collateral post-conviction proceedings shall not be a ground for relief in a proceeding arising under section 2254.

Section 2255

Section 2255 is the main provision regulating habeas petitions by those who have been convicted in federal court. The AEDPA imposes a one-year statute of limitations on such petitions, and generally precludes successive petitions.

28 U.S.C. § 2255. Federal custody; remedies on motion attacking sentence

A prisoner in custody under sentence of a court established by Act of Congress claiming the right to be released upon the ground that the sentence was imposed in violation of the Constitution or laws of the United States, or that the court was without jurisdiction to impose such sentence, or that the sentence was in excess of the maximum authorized by law, or is otherwise subject to collateral attack, may move the court which imposed the sentence to vacate, set aside or correct the sentence.

Unless the motion and the files and records of the case conclusively show that the prisoner is entitled to no relief, the court shall cause notice thereof to be served upon the United States attorney, grant a prompt hearing thereon, determine the issues and make findings of fact and conclusions of law with respect thereto. If the court finds that the judgment was rendered without jurisdiction, or that the sentence imposed was not authorized by law or otherwise open to collateral attack, or that there has been such a denial or infringement of the constitutional rights of the prisoner as to render the judgment vulnerable to collateral attack, the court shall vacate and set the judgment aside and shall discharge the prisoner or resentence him or grant a new trial or correct the sentence as may appear appropriate.

A court may entertain and determine such motion without requiring the production of the prisoner at the hearing.

An appeal may be taken to the court of appeals from the order entered on the motion as from the final judgment on application for a writ of habeas corpus.

An application for a writ of habeas corpus in behalf of a prisoner who is authorized to apply for relief by motion pursuant to this section, shall not be entertained if it appears that the applicant has failed to apply for relief, by motion, to the court which sentenced him, or that such court has denied him relief, unless it also appears that the remedy by motion is inadequate or ineffective to test the legality of his detention.

A 1-year period of limitation shall apply to a motion under this section. The limitation period shall run from the latest of—

(1) the date on which the judgment of conviction becomes final;

(2) the date on which the impediment to making a motion created by governmental action in violation of the Constitution or laws of the United States is removed, if the movant was prevented from making a motion by such governmental action;

(3) the date on which the right asserted was initially recognized by the Supreme Court, if that right has been newly recognized by the Supreme Court and made retroactively applicable to cases on collateral review; or

(4) the date on which the facts supporting the claim or claims presented could have been discovered through the exercise of due diligence.

Except as provided in section 408 of the Controlled Substances Act, in all proceedings brought under this section, and any subsequent proceedings on review, the court may appoint counsel, except as provided by a rule promulgated by the Supreme Court pursuant to statutory authority. * * *

A second or successive motion must be certified as provided in section 2244 by a panel of the appropriate court of appeals to contain—

(1) newly discovered evidence that, if proven and viewed in light of the evidence as a whole, would be sufficient to establish by clear and convincing evidence that no reasonable factfinder would have found the movant guilty of the offense; or

(2) a new rule of constitutional law, made retroactive to cases on collateral review by the Supreme Court, that was previously unavailable.

Sections 2261–68

28 U.S.C. §§ 2261–68 are provisions added by AEDPA to limit collateral attacks by state death row inmates. Among other things, these sections: 1) limit the ability of death row inmates to obtain more than one stay of execution; 2) generally preclude considerations of claims that were not heard in state court because of the petitioner's failure to comply with a state procedural rule; 3) provide a "rocket docket" for expedited consideration of death penalty claims on habeas. To invoke these provisions, the state must prove that it has established "by statute, rule of its court of last resort, or by another agency authorized by State law, a mechanism for the appointment, compensation, and payment of reasonable litigation expenses of competent counsel in State post-conviction proceedings brought by indigent prisoners whose capital convictions and sentences have been upheld on direct appeal to the court of last resort in the State or have otherwise become final for State law purposes. The rule of court or statute must provide standards of competency for the appointment of such counsel."

It appears that no state has yet been found qualified to opt in to the "rocket docket" provisions of AEDPA. See, e.g., Ashmus v. Calderon, 123 F.3d 1199 (9th Cir.1997) (California does not qualify for the benefits of the rocket docket in death penalty cases, because it has no rule of court establishing a system for appointing counsel, only guidelines, and because its competency standards for capital counsel are nonbinding); Mata v. Johnson, 99 F.3d 1261 (5th Cir.1996) (Texas does not qualify, because it has not established explicit competency standards for counsel in capital cases). For a thorough discussion of the opting-in requirements and compliance, see Judge Graber's opinion in Spears v. Stewart, 283 F.3d 992 (9th Cir. 2002).

2. General Principles Concerning Habeas Relief After AEDPA

The innovations of AEDPA have raised some important questions about the nature of habeas corpus relief.

Statute of Limitations

An important provision in the AEDPA is the imposition of a statute of limitations for habeas corpus petitions: a petition must be filed within one year after the conviction becomes final, for most petitioners. There is potentially an even stricter period for death row petitioners—if it is determined, under criteria provided in the statute, that the state provides competent counsel for state post-conviction proceedings, then a death row claimant must file a habeas petition within 180 days of the date his conviction becomes final, with a possible 30–day extension for cause. As recently as March 1996, the Supreme Court, in Lonchar v. Thomas, 517 U.S. 314 (1996), held that there was no time limitation on an initial habeas petition, other than the equitable principle of laches. The Court in *Lonchar* denied the dismissal of an initial petition filed just before the petitioner was scheduled to be executed, and six years after his conviction became final. But under the AEDPA, such a petition would have to be dismissed as untimely.

Note that there are tolling provisions in the 1996 Act, applicable to section 2254 actions, for the time taken to pursue state collateral relief. See Duncan v. Walker, 533 U.S. 167 (2001) (action for federal relief does not toll the AEDPA statute of limitations; section 2254 refers only to "state" collateral proceedings as tolling the limitations period); Carey v. Saffold, 536 U.S. 214 (2002) (petition for state collateral review in California was "pending" in the time between the lower state court's decision and the filing of a new petition in a higher court, tolling the period for filing a federal habeas petition).

Courts have held that the limitation provisions in AEDPA are not jurisdictional and are subject to equitable tolling. See, e.g., Calderon v. United States District Court, 128 F.3d 1283 (9th Cir.1997) (one-year period tolled because counsel moved out of state); Rouse v. Lee, 314 F.3d 698 (4th Cir. 2003) (one-year period for habeas relief should have been equitably tolled for a petitioner sentenced to death, who missed the deadline by one day based on counsel's plausible but incorrect calculation of the limitations period, where the petitioner presented a strong claim of racial and personal juror bias that had not received a hearing in any state or federal court, and where the state could show no prejudice from the delay).

Effect on Supreme Court's Appellate Jurisdiction: Felker v. Turpin

The AEDPA requires dismissal of a claim presented in a state prisoner's federal habeas application if the claim was also presented in a prior application. The Act also compels dismissal of a claim that could have been but was not presented in a prior federal application, unless certain extremely rigorous conditions are met. These limitations are directed at the perceived problem of successive habeas petitions. To effectuate these strict standards, the Act creates a "gatekeeping" mechanism, whereby a petitioner must make a motion in the court of appeals for leave to file a second or successive habeas application in the district court, and a three-judge panel determines whether the petitioner has made a prima facie showing that the strict substantive requirements for successive applications have been met. The Act further declares that a panel's grant or denial of authorization to file "shall not be appealable and shall not be the subject of a petition for ... writ of certiorari." Thus, the Act limits the appellate jurisdiction of the Supreme Court over successive habeas applications.

In Felker v. Turpin, 518 U.S. 651 (1996), the Court unanimously rejected a constitutional attack on this statutory limitation of Supreme Court appellate jurisdiction. Chief Justice Rehnquist, writing for the Court, declared that the Act did not alter the Supreme Court's power to exercise *original* jurisdiction over a habeas petition, as provided for by 28 U.S.C. §§ 2241 and 2254. (It should be noted, however, that the Supreme Court has not granted relief on original jurisdiction over a habeas petition in more than 100 years.). On the jurisdictional question, Chief Justice Rehnquist concluded as follows:

The critical language of Article III, § 2, of the Constitution provides that, apart from several classes of cases specifically enumerated in this Court's original jurisdiction, "in all the other Cases . . . the supreme Court shall have appellate Jurisdiction, both as to Law and Fact, with such Exceptions, and under such Regulations as the Congress shall make." Previous decisions construing this clause have said that while our appellate powers "are given by the constitution," "they are limited and regulated by the [Judiciary Act of 1789], and by such other acts as have been passed on the subject." The [AEDPA] does remove our authority to entertain an appeal or a petition for a writ of certiorari to review a decision of a court of appeals exercising its "gatekeeping" function over a second petition. But since it does not repeal our authority to entertain a petition for habeas corpus, there can be no plausible argument that the Act has deprived this Court of appellate jurisdiction in violation of Article III, § 2.

On the merits, the Court refused, as an exercise of its original jurisdiction, to entertain Felker's claim for habeas relief on a successive petition. Felker challenged his conviction on the grounds of a *Brady* violation and an erroneous instruction on reasonable doubt. The Chief Justice set forth the standards for original jurisdiction, and the resolution of Felker's claims, in the following passage:

[W]e now dispose of the petition for an original writ of habeas corpus. Our Rule 20.4(a) delineates the standards under which we grant such writs:

"* * * To justify the granting of a writ of habeas corpus, the petitioner must show exceptional circumstances warranting the exercise of the Court's discretionary powers and must show that adequate relief cannot be obtained in any other form or from any other court. These writs are rarely granted."

Reviewing petitioner's claims here, they do not materially differ from numerous other claims made by successive habeas petitioners which we have had occasion to review on stay applications to this Court. Neither of them satisfies the requirements of the relevant provisions of the [AEDPA], let alone the requirement that there be "exceptional circumstances" justifying the issuance of the writ.

Certificate of Appealability

The AEDPA limits the right to appeal from a district court's denial of a state defendant's petition for a writ of habeas corpus. The Act requires that the petitioner must obtain a "certificate of appeal" from a circuit judge. In Slack v. McDaniel, 529 U.S. 473 (2000), the Court set forth the standard that circuit judges are to apply in deciding whether to issue a certificate of appealability. It declared as follows:

Where a district court has rejected the constitutional claims on the merits, the showing required to satisfy § 2253(c) is straightforward: The petitioner must demonstrate that reasonable jurists would find the district court's assessment of the constitutional claims debatable or wrong. The issue becomes somewhat more complicated where, as here, the district court dismisses the petition based on procedural grounds. We hold as follows: When the district court denies a habeas petition on procedural grounds without reaching the prisoner's underlying constitutional claim, a COA should issue when the prisoner shows, at least, that jurists of reason would find it debatable whether the petition states a valid claim of the denial of a constitutional right and that jurists of reason would find it debatable whether the district court was correct in its procedural ruling. This construction gives meaning to Congress' requirement that a prisoner demonstrate substantial underlying constitutional claims and is in conformity with the meaning of the "substantial showing" standard * * * adopted by Congress in AEDPA. Where a plain procedural bar is present and the district court is correct to invoke it to dispose of the case, a reasonable jurist could not conclude either that the district court erred in dismissing the petition or that the petitioner should be allowed to proceed further. In such a circumstance, no appeal would be warranted.

See also Miller–El v. Cockrell, 537 U.S. 322 (2003) (finding that the petitioner met the *Slack* standard by providing circumstantial evidence that the prosecutor excused jurors on racial grounds in violation of Batson v. Kentucky and remanding for a hearing of the appeal on the merits).

3. *Factual Findings and Mixed Questions of Law and Fact*

In a section 2254 action, what deference does a federal court owe to the state court's determinations of law and fact? Before the AEDPA, there was a good deal of dispute over how much deference should be given. While it was generally agreed that the statute required federal courts to give deference to state court factual determinations, the Court had held that federal habeas courts were not required to defer to a state court's interpretations of federal law, nor to mixed questions of fact and law. See, e.g., Miller v. Fenton, 474 U.S. 104 (1985) (state court's decision that a confession was voluntary is a mixed question of fact and law which federal courts do not presume to be correct).

As amended by the AEDPA, section 2254 resolves any dispute. It requires habeas courts to give substantial deference to *all* state court rulings in the case. The AEDPA makes no definite distinction, in terms of deference, between questions of law and mixed questions of law and fact. The pertinent provision states as follows:

(d) An application for a writ of habeas corpus on behalf of a person in custody pursuant to the judgment of a State court shall not be granted with respect to any claim that was adjudicated on the merits in State court proceedings unless the adjudication of the claim—

(1) resulted in a decision that was contrary to, or involved an unreasonable application of, clearly established Federal law, as determined by the Supreme Court of the United States; or

(2) resulted in a decision that was based on an unreasonable determination of the facts in light of the evidence presented in the State court proceeding.

Guidelines on the Deferential Standard of Review in Section 2254(d): Williams v. Taylor

In Williams v. Taylor, 529 U.S. 362 (2000), the Court construed section 2254(d) as amended by the AEDPA, and set forth the standard for federal review of state court determinations, as mandated by that section. The case involved a claim on habeas that Williams' counsel had been ineffective at the penalty phase of his capital trial by failing to introduce evidence that Williams had been abused as a child and was borderline retarded. The State Supreme Court, applying Strickland v. Washington and subsequent Supreme Court cases, rejected Williams' ineffectiveness claim on the ground that Williams had not been prejudiced. Justice O'Connor, writing for the Court, set forth and analyzed the statutory language of the AEDPA in the following passage:

Section 2254 now provides:

(d) An application for a writ of habeas corpus on behalf of a person in custody pursuant to the judgment of a State court shall not be granted with respect to any claim that was adjudicated on the merits in State court proceedings unless the adjudication of the claim—

(1) resulted in a decision that was contrary to, or involved an unreasonable application of, clearly established Federal law, as determined by the Supreme Court of the United States.

Accordingly, for Williams to obtain federal habeas relief, he must first demonstrate that his case satisfies the condition set by § 2254(d)(1). That provision modifies the role of federal habeas courts in reviewing petitions filed by state prisoners.

* * *

The word "contrary" is commonly understood to mean "diametrically different," "opposite in character or nature," or "mutually opposed." The text of § 2254(d)(1) therefore suggests that the state court's decision must be substantially different from the relevant precedent of this Court. * * * A state-court decision will certainly be contrary to our clearly established precedent if the state court applies a rule that contradicts the governing law set forth in our cases. Take, for example, our decision in Strickland v. Washington, 466 U.S. 668 (1984). If a state court were to reject a prisoner's claim of ineffective assistance of counsel on the grounds that the prisoner had not established by a preponderance of the evidence that the result of his criminal proceeding would have been different, that decision would be "diametrically different," "opposite in character or nature," and "mutually opposed" to our clearly established precedent because we held in *Strickland* that the prisoner need only demonstrate a "reasonable probability that . . . the result of the proceeding would have been different." A state-court decision will also be contrary to this Court's clearly established precedent if the state court confronts a set of facts that are materially indistinguishable from a decision of this Court and nevertheless arrives at a result different from our precedent. Accordingly, in either of these two scenarios, a federal court will be unconstrained by § 2254(d)(1) because the state-court decision falls within that provision's "contrary to" clause.

On the other hand, a run-of-the-mill state-court decision applying the correct legal rule from our cases to the facts of a prisoner's case would not fit comfortably within § 2254(d)(1)'s "contrary to" clause. Assume, for example, that a state-court decision on a prisoner's ineffective-assistance claim correctly identifies *Strickland* as the controlling legal authority and, applying that framework, rejects the prisoner's claim. Quite clearly, the state-court decision would be in accord with our decision in *Strickland* as to the legal prerequisites for establishing an ineffective-assistance claim, even assuming the federal court considering the prisoner's habeas application might reach a different result applying the *Strickland* framework itself. It is difficult, however, to describe such a run-of-the-mill state-court decision as "diametrically different" from, "opposite in character or nature" from, or "mutually opposed" to *Strickland*, our clearly established precedent. Although the state-court decision may be contrary to the federal court's conception of how *Strickland* ought to be applied in that particular case, the decision is not "mutually opposed" to *Strickland* itself.

Thus, in Justice O'Connor's view, a state court decision cannot be overturned on habeas simply because it is incorrect—under the "contrary to" clause, the state court decision must be diametrically opposed to Supreme Court precedent in order to justify habeas relief. Justice O'Connor next took issue with the broader view of the statute posited by Justice Stevens in dissent. Justice O'Connor summarized, and criticized, Justice Stevens' view in the following passage:

Justice Stevens would instead construe § 2254(d)(1)'s "contrary to" clause to encompass such a routine state-court decision. That construction, however, saps the "unreasonable application" clause of any meaning. If a federal habeas court can, under the "contrary to" clause, issue the writ whenever it concludes that the state court's application of clearly established federal law was incorrect, the "unreasonable application" clause becomes a nullity. We must, however, if possible, give meaning to every clause of the statute. Justice Stevens not only makes no attempt to do so, but also construes the "contrary to" clause in a manner that ensures that the "unreasonable application" clause will have no independent meaning. We reject that expansive interpretation of the statute. Reading § 2254(d)(1)'s "contrary to" clause to permit a federal court to grant relief in cases where a state court's error is limited to the manner in which it applies Supreme Court precedent is suspect given the logical and natural fit of the neighboring "unreasonable application" clause to such cases.

Justice O'Connor next construed the "unreasonable application" clause of § 2254(d)(1):

First, a state-court decision involves an unreasonable application of this Court's precedent if the state court identifies the correct governing legal rule from this Court's cases but unreasonably applies it to the facts of the particular state prisoner's case. Second, a state-court decision also involves an unreasonable application of this Court's precedent if the state court either unreasonably extends a legal principle from our precedent to a new context where it should not apply or unreasonably refuses to extend that principle to a new context where it should apply.

A state-court decision that correctly identifies the governing legal rule but applies it unreasonably to the facts of a particular prisoner's case certainly would qualify as a decision "involv[ing] an unreasonable application of . . . clearly established Federal law."

Justice O'Connor noted that some lower courts had defined "unreasonable application of law" by determining whether any reasonable jurist would agree with the state court's determination—if so, this would preclude habeas relief. Justice O'Connor, however, rejected the "reasonable jurist" standard:

There remains the task of defining what exactly qualifies as an "unreasonable application" of law under § 2254(d)(1). The [lower court] held * * * that a state-court decision involves an "unreasonable application of . . . clearly established Federal law" only if the state court has applied federal law "in a manner that reasonable jurists would all agree is unreasonable." * * *

Defining an "unreasonable application" by reference to a "reasonable jurist" * * * is of little assistance to the courts that must apply § 2254(d)(1) and, in fact, may be misleading. Stated simply, a federal habeas court making the "unreasonable application" inquiry should ask whether the state court's application of clearly established federal law was objectively unreasonable. The federal habeas court should not transform the inquiry into a subjective one by resting its determination instead on the simple fact that at least one of the Nation's jurists has applied the relevant federal law in the same manner the state court did in the habeas petitioner's case. The "all reasonable jurists" standard would tend to mislead federal habeas courts by focusing their attention on a subjective inquiry rather than on an objective one. For example, the Fifth Circuit appears to have applied its "reasonable jurist" standard in just such a subjective manner. See Drinkard v. Johnson, 97 F.3d 751, 769 (1996) (holding that state court's application of federal law was not unreasonable because the Fifth Circuit panel split 2–1 on the underlying mixed constitutional question). * * *

The term "unreasonable" is no doubt difficult to define. That said, it is a common term in the legal world and, accordingly, federal judges are familiar with its meaning. For purposes of today's opinion, the most important point is that an unreasonable application of federal law is different from an incorrect application of federal law. * * * In § 2254(d)(1), Congress specifically used the word "unreasonable," and not a term like "erroneous" or "incorrect." Under § 2254(d)(1)'s "unreasonable application" clause, then, a federal habeas court may not issue the writ simply because that court concludes in its independent judgment that the relevant state-court decision applied clearly established federal law erroneously or incorrectly. Rather, that application must also be unreasonable.

Justice O'Connor concluded as follows:

In sum, § 2254(d)(1) places a new constraint on the power of a federal habeas court to grant a state prisoner's application for a writ of habeas corpus with respect to claims adjudicated on the merits in state court. Under § 2254(d)(1), the writ may issue only if one of the following two conditions is satisfied—the state-court adjudication resulted in a decision that (1) "was contrary to . . . clearly established Federal law, as determined by the Supreme Court of the United States," or (2) "involved an unreasonable application of . . . clearly established Federal law, as determined by the Supreme Court of the United States." Under the "contrary to" clause, a federal habeas court may grant the writ if the state court arrives at a conclusion opposite to that reached by this Court on a question of law or if the state court decides a case differently than this Court has on a set of materially indistinguishable facts. Under the "unreasonable application" clause, a federal habeas court may grant the writ if the state court identifies the correct governing legal principle from this Court's decisions but unreasonably applies that principle to the facts of the prisoner's case.

On the merits, a majority of the Court held that the state court's decision was both "contrary to" and an "unreasonable application" of *Strickland*. The state court held that the *Strickland* prejudice prong did not focus on what the outcome might have been had defense counsel acted effectively—when in fact that is the very focus of the prejudice prong. The state court also ignored the impact that the substantial mitigating evidence might have had on the jury at the penalty phase.

The mandated deference to state court determinations of fact and law poses a substantial hurdle for petitioners who are seeking habeas relief from a state conviction. Several recent cases in the previous chapters apply this deferential standard in habeas actions, among them Bell v. Cone and Wiggins v. Smith, two cases in the Chapter 10 section on ineffective assistance.

4. *Retroactivity*

As discussed in Chapter One, in a habeas action, a state court's determination of federal law is assessed as of the time the state conviction was finalized. Once the defendant's conviction has been finalized, he is not entitled to subsequent changes in legal doctrine that might work to his advantage. The Court established this principle in Teague v. Lane. The AEDPA essentially codified Teague v. Lane in section 2254(d), set forth above. The AEDPA's innovation is to treat the *Teague* concept not as one of retroactive application, but rather as a matter of deference to state court determinations. If the petitioner argues that a new rule should work to his benefit, this argument would be dismissed because new section 2254(d) requires a federal court to defer to a state court's determination of "clearly established" federal law. Arguing for a new rule on habeas is by definition prohibited because the state court decision is judged by whether it was contrary to clearly established law at the time of the state court ruling.

C. CLAIMS COGNIZABLE IN COLLATERAL PROCEEDINGS

Section 2254(a) makes it clear that a district court can only entertain an application for habeas corpus relief on behalf of a state prisoner if the prisoner alleges that state custody "is in violation of the Constitution or laws or treaties of the United States." In almost every case the prisoner claims that the state conviction was obtained in violation of the Federal Constitution. Section 2255 allows an attack on a federal conviction alleged to be in violation of the Constitution or laws of the United States and adds other grounds for attack. But not every claim of a violation of federal law is cognizable on habeas. If it were, the collateral remedy might serve as a substitute for appeal.

1. Non–Constitutional Claims

Federal Defendants

The courts have limited section 2255 relief to "substantial" violations of federal law that have resulted in significant harm to the petitioner. See Hill v. United States, 368 U.S. 424 (1962)(defendant denied opportunity to make a statement before sentencing; no attack permitted); United States v. Timmreck, 441 U.S. 780 (1979)(technical violation of rule establishing procedures for accepting guilty pleas; no attack permitted). As the Court in *Hill* put it, habeas review for federal statutory violations is not available for federal defendants under section 2255 unless the statutory violation qualifies as a "fundamental defect which inherently results in a complete miscarriage of justice, or an omission inconsistent with the rudimentary demands of fair procedure."

The Court applied the principles of *Hill* and *Timmreck* in Peguero v. United States, 526 U.S. 23 (1999). Peguero sought habeas relief from a federal conviction because the district court at sentencing failed to inform him of his right to appeal the sentence. This failure to notify was a violation of Fed.R.Crim.P. 32(a)(2). The Court, in an opinion by Justice Kennedy, relied on *Hill* and *Timmreck* and declared that as a general rule, "a court's failure to give a defendant advice required by the Federal Rules is a sufficient basis for collateral relief only when the defendant is prejudiced by the court's error." In this case, no prejudice could be found, because Peguero in fact had full knowledge of his right to appeal the sentence. Accordingly, he was not entitled to habeas relief.

State Defendants

In Reed v. Farley, 512 U.S. 339 (1994), the Court extended the "fundamental defect" test of *Hill* to claims of federal statutory violations brought by state defendants under section 2254. The statutory violation at issue in *Reed* concerned the Interstate Agreement on Detainers ("IAD"), a compact among 48 States, the District of Columbia, and the Federal Government. Article IV(c) of the IAD provides, among other things, that the trial of a prisoner transferred from one participating jurisdiction to another shall commence within 120 days of the prisoner's arrival in the receiving State, and directs dismissal with prejudice when trial does not occur within the time prescribed. Reed's trial did not begin within this time limit. The trial court denied Reed's petition for discharge on the ground that the judge had previously been unaware of the 120–day limitation and that Reed had not earlier objected to the trial date or requested a speedier trial. Reed was convicted, and after unsuccessful appeals in the Indiana courts, he petitioned for a federal writ of habeas corpus under section 2254.

Justice Ginsburg, in an opinion for five Justices, rejected Reed's argument that the "fundamental defect" standard of *Hill* was limited to federal defendants under section 2255, and should not be applicable to habeas claims of state defendants brought under section 2254. She analyzed the issue as follows:

> [I]t is scarcely doubted that, at least where mere statutory violations are at issue, § 2255 was intended to mirror § 2254 in operative effect. Far from suggesting that the *Hill* standard is inapplicable to § 2254 cases, our decisions assume that *Hill* controls collateral review—under both §§ 2254

and 2255—when a federal statute, but not the Constitution, is the basis for the postconviction attack. * * *

We see no reason to afford habeas review to a state prisoner like Reed, who let a time clock run without alerting the trial court, yet deny collateral review to a federal prisoner similarly situated.

The question remained whether the statutory violation suffered by Reed (i.e., the violation of the time limits of the IAD) rose to the level of a "fundamental defect" under *Hill*. Five members of the Court concluded that there was no "fundamental defect," but there was no majority opinion on this point. Justice Ginsburg, joined by Chief Justice Rehnquist and Justice O'Connor on this question, emphasized that Reed had not asserted his rights under the IAD in a timely manner. She did not, however, preclude the possibility that some violation of the IAD might be cognizable on section 2254 habeas review under the "fundamental defect" standard. She noted that the IAD's purpose of providing a nationally uniform means of transferring prisoners between jurisdictions "would be undermined if a State's courts resisted steadfast enforcement, with total insulation from § 2254 review."

Justice Scalia, in an opinion joined by Justice Thomas, concurred in Justice Ginsburg's determination that the "fundamental defect" standard was applicable to claims brought for federal statutory violations by state defendants under section 2254. He concurred only in the result, however, on the question of whether the IAD violation suffered by Reed rose to the level of a "fundamental defect." He argued, more broadly than Justice Ginsburg, that a violation of the IAD could never result in a "fundamental defect" warranting habeas review, and he implied even more broadly that there could never be a federal statutory violation that would justify review under the "fundamental defect" standard. He elaborated as follows:

> Most statutory violations, at least when they do not occur in the context of other aggravating circumstances, are simply not important enough to invoke the extraordinary habeas jurisdiction. * * *

> * * * The class of procedural rights that are not guaranteed by the Constitution (which includes the Due Process Clauses), but that nonetheless are inherently necessary to avoid "a complete miscarriage of justice," or numbered among "the rudimentary demands of fair procedure," is no doubt a small one, if it is indeed not a null set. The guarantee of trial within 120 days of interjurisdictional transfer unless good cause is shown—a provision with no application to prisoners involved with only a single jurisdiction or incarcerated in one of the two States that do not participate in the voluntary IAD compact—simply cannot be among that select class of statutory rights.

Justice Blackmun dissented in *Reed* in an opinion joined by Justices Stevens, Kennedy, and Souter. He argued that the "fundamental defect" test of *Hill* was too stringent to be applied to federal statutory claims brought by state prisoners under section 2254. He analyzed the difference between section 2255 actions and section 2254 actions as follows:

> For the federal prisoner claiming statutory violations, habeas courts serve less to guarantee uniformity of federal law or to satisfy a threshold need for a federal forum than to provide a backstop to catch and correct certain nonconstitutional errors that evaded the trial and appellate courts.

* * * The *Hill* principle, in short, is that where the error is not egregious, the habeas court need not cover the ground already covered by other federal courts.

For the state prisoner, by contrast, a primary purpose of § 2254 is to provide a federal forum to review a state prisoner's claimed violations of federal law, claims that were, of necessity, addressed to the state courts. Thus, § 2254 motions anticipate that the federal court will undertake an independent review of the work of the state courts, even where the federal claim was fully and fairly litigated. Even if we recognize valid reasons for limiting this review to claims of serious or substantial error, where no federal court previously has addressed the § 2254 petitioner's federal claims, there is less reason to sift these claims through so fine a screen as *Hill* and *Timmreck* provide.

State Law Violations as Due Process Violations: Estelle v. McGuire

Federal due process claims are clearly cognizable under §§ 2254 and 2255. State defendants are often therefore tempted to characterize a violation of some state law as tantamount to a due process violation. This ploy is not often successful, however. For example, in Estelle v. McGuire, 502 U.S. 62 (1991), McGuire was convicted in state court of the murder of his infant daughter. At the trial, the state offered medical evidence indicating that the infant had suffered severe injuries several weeks before her death. This evidence was offered to prove "battered child syndrome." The Ninth Circuit granted McGuire's habeas petition, reasoning that evidence of the child's prior injury was "incorrectly admitted pursuant to California law," and that the violation of a California rule of evidence also violated McGuire's due process rights.

The Supreme Court, in an opinion by Chief Justice Rehnquist, held that the alleged error did not "rise to the level of a due process violation" and reversed the granting of habeas relief. The Chief Justice concluded that "it is not the province of a federal habeas court to reexamine state court determinations on state law questions," and that "in conducting habeas review, a federal court is limited to deciding whether a conviction violated the Constitution, laws, or treaties of the United States." Thus it was irrelevant that the evidence of prior injuries may have been inadmissible under state law. The only question was whether admission of the evidence violated McGuire's right to due process, and the Court held that it did not. The Chief Justice reasoned that the prior injuries were admissible even if they were not linked to McGuire, because they tended to show that the infant's death "was the result of an intentional act by *someone,* and not an accident." The Court concluded that evidence tending to prove lack of accident was relevant even though the defendant never claimed at trial that the infant's death was an accident. The Chief Justice noted that the prosecution was required to prove the element of intent beyond a reasonable doubt, and by eliminating the possibility of accident "the evidence regarding battered child syndrome was clearly probative of that element." As the evidence met the low threshold of relevance, any due process inquiry was at an end. The Chief Justice stated that "we need not explore further the apparent assumption of the court of appeals that it is a violation of the due process guaranteed by the Fourteenth Amendment for evidence that is not relevant to be received at a criminal trial."

2. *Constitutional Claims Generally*

From the foregoing it is apparent that federal habeas review is generally limited to constitutional claims. The next question is whether all constitutional claims can be raised in § 2254 and § 2255 proceedings. On the face of the statutes, the answer might appear to be "yes," but that would not be a correct statement of the current state of the law. Nor would it reflect the status of the writ through most of our history.

In the early days, as our brief historical exegesis noted, the writ was used most frequently to attack the jurisdiction of the court imposing judgment. However, in cases like Ex parte Lange, 85 U.S. (18 Wall.) 163 (1873)(permitting a challenge to a court's authority to impose sentence) and Ex parte Siebold, 100 U.S. 371 (1879)(permitting a challenge to the constitutionality of a statute), the writ was used more broadly for consideration of constitutional claims on the merits.

Limitation of Review to Jurisdictional Defects Only?

The first Judiciary Act gave the Supreme Court habeas corpus jurisdiction, but only as to federal prisoners. And the Court had no general appellate jurisdiction in criminal cases. The Court construed the habeas jurisdiction narrowly. Subsequently, the 1867 statute expanded habeas corpus jurisdiction to reach state prisoners and used language that was quite different from that used in the first Judiciary Act. The argument has been made that even after the adoption of the 1867 statute, the Supreme Court considered habeas corpus as extending only to jurisdictional defects in a proceeding. Bator, Finality in Criminal Law and Federal Habeas Corpus for State Prisoners, 76 Harv.L.Rev. 441 (1963). This argument has been challenged and it has been asserted that all constitutional claims have been cognizable in habeas corpus proceedings. Peller, In Defense of Federal Habeas Corpus Relitigation, 16 Harv.Civ.Rights & Civ. Lib.Rev. 579 (1982). In Saltzburg, Habeas Corpus: The Supreme Court and the Congress, 44 Ohio St.L.J. 367 (1983), the Court's opinions are described as confusing and the assessment is that the Court itself was not clear as to the scope of habeas corpus jurisdiction.

Consideration of Constitutional Claims: Brown v. Allen

In Brown v. Allen, 344 U.S. 443 (1953), claims of racial injustice in the South were at the heart of three consolidated cases. Brown, convicted of rape and sentenced to death, alleged racial discrimination in the selection of the grand and petit juries and also the use of a coerced confession. Speller, also convicted of rape and sentenced to death, charged racial discrimination in the selection of the jury array in his case. Bernie and Lloyd Daniels were sentenced to death upon convictions for murder. They claimed that coerced confessions were used against them, that the procedure to determine the voluntariness of their confessions was invalid, and that there was racial bias in the selection of both grand and petit juries. Justice Reed delivered the opinion of the Court on most issues. The Reed opinion assumed that the lower federal courts had the power to issue writs of habeas corpus, even though there was no allegation of a jurisdictional defect in the state proceedings: "A way is left open to redress violations of the Constitution." The Court considered the merits of the Brown and Speller claims in affirming the denial of habeas corpus relief. But the Daniels' claims were barred because of the noncompliance with state procedures and the petitioners' failure to file a timely appeal: "A failure to use a state's available remedy in the absence of some interference or incapacity * * * bars federal habeas corpus."

After Brown v. Allen, it appeared that all constitutional claims were cognizable in habeas corpus cases. No Justice actually argued otherwise in *Brown*. Kaufman v. United States, 394 U.S. 217 (1969), established that the same scope of review was available to § 2255 litigants.

Fourth Amendment Claims Not Cognizable on Habeas: Stone v. Powell

In the landmark case of Stone v. Powell, 428 U.S. 465 (1976), the Court held that Fourth Amendment claims are generally not cognizable on habeas review. Justice Powell, writing for the Court, reasoned that the primary purpose of the Fourth Amendment exclusionary rule is deterrence of illegal police conduct; as such, the rule operates to exclude reliable evidence and has nothing to do with protecting innocent people from unjust convictions. Justice Powell concluded that the benefits of extending the exclusionary rule to collateral review of Fourth Amendment claims were outweighed by the costs—not only the costs of losing reliable evidence, but also the dislocation costs associated with upsetting finalized criminal convictions and thereby increasing (1) the prosecutorial burdens on the government, (2) the sense of frustration of state and federal judges whose decisions are set aside, and (3) the general uncertainty costs associated with non-final judgments. Justice Powell concluded as follows:

> [W]here the State has provided an opportunity for full and fair litigation of a Fourth Amendment claim, a state prisoner may not be granted federal habeas relief on the ground that evidence obtained in an unconstitutional search or seizure was introduced at his trial. In this context the contribution of the exclusionary rule, if any, to the effectuation of the Fourth Amendment is minimal and the societal costs of the application of the rule persist with special force.

Thus, collateral review of Fourth Amendment questions is generally limited to whether the state provided the petitioner a "full and fair" opportunity to litigate the Fourth Amendment claim. If no "full and fair" opportunity was provided, and all other procedural requirements attendant to a habeas action are met, the federal court may consider the merits of the Fourth Amendment question.

Justice Brennan, joined by Justice Marshall, dissented. He urged that the Court was rewriting jurisdictional statutes, those governing § 2254 and § 2255 cases, and arrogating Congressional power into itself. Justice White also dissented and argued that "[u]nder the amendments to the habeas corpus statute, which * * * represented an effort by Congress to lend a modicum of finality to state criminal judgments, I cannot distinguish between Fourth Amendment and other constitutional issues."[15]

15. The Court refused to apply *Stone* in Rose v. Mitchell, 443 U.S. 545 (1979)(permitting habeas challenge to racial discrimination in selection of grand jury). The Supreme Court reaffirmed in Vasquez v. Hillery, 474 U.S. 254 (1986), the position that commanded a majority in *Rose*: a defendant may challenge his state court conviction in a

Ineffective Assistance of Counsel: Kimmelman v. Morrison

In Kimmelman v. Morrison, 477 U.S. 365 (1986), Justice Brennan wrote for the Court as it held that Stone v. Powell did not bar a habeas petitioner from claiming ineffective assistance of counsel based upon his trial counsel's failure to file a timely motion to suppress evidence. The Court declined "to hold either that the guarantee of effective assistance of counsel belongs solely to the innocent or that it attaches only to matters affecting the determination of actual guilt." Instead, it stated that "federal courts may grant habeas relief in appropriate cases, regardless of the nature of the underlying attorney error." Justice Brennan reasoned as follows:

> Were we to extend Stone and hold that criminal defendants may not raise ineffective assistance claims that are based primarily on incompetent handling of Fourth Amendment issues on federal habeas, we would deny most defendants whose trial attorneys performed incompetently in this regard the opportunity to vindicate their right to effective trial counsel. We would deny all defendants whose appellate counsel performed inadequately with respect to Fourth Amendment issues the opportunity to protect their right to effective appellate counsel. * * * Thus, we cannot say, as the Court was able to say in Stone, that restriction of federal habeas review would not severely interfere with the protection of the constitutional right asserted by the habeas petitioner.

Justice Brennan also noted that unlike Fourth Amendment claims, there is usually no full and fair opportunity to bring ineffective assistance claims at trial or on direct review.

It should be noted, however, that Kimmelman creates a certain anomaly when juxtaposed with Stone. If two defendants have the same meritorious Fourth Amendment claim, and both are prejudiced by the admission of the tainted evidence at trial, the defendant with the incompetent lawyer can reap the benefit of exclusion on habeas while the defendant with the competent lawyer cannot. See Friedman, A Tale of Two Habeas, 73 Minn.L.Rev. 247 (1988).

Miranda Claims: Withrow v. Williams

In Withrow v. Williams, 507 U.S. 680 (1993), the Court held that "Stone's restriction on the exercise of federal habeas jurisdiction does not extend to a state prisoner's claim that his conviction rests on statements obtained in violation of the safeguards mandated by Miranda v. Arizona." Justice Souter wrote for the Court and began by noting that "Stone's limitation on federal habeas relief was not jurisdictional in nature, but rested on prudential concerns counseling against the application of the Fourth Amendment exclusionary rule on collateral review." He stressed that cases decided after Stone had read that case narrowly:

federal habeas corpus proceeding on the ground that a grand jury was selected in a racially discriminatory manner. Thus, the Court affirmed the grant of habeas corpus relief to a petitioner who had been convicted of murder in 1963. Justice Marshall's majority opinion observed that the rule invalidating a conviction because of racial discrimination in selection of the grand jury had stood since Strauder v. West Virginia, 100 U.S. 303 (1880), and reasoned that reversal of conviction is the only effective remedy against discrimination. Justice Powell, joined by Chief Justice Burger and Justice Rehnquist, dissented, and would have found the constitutional error harmless. Justice O'Connor concurred in the judgment.

Over the years, we have repeatedly declined to extend the rule in *Stone* beyond its original bounds. In Jackson v. Virginia, 443 U.S. 307 (1979), for example, we denied a request to apply *Stone* to bar habeas reconsideration of a Fourteenth Amendment due process claim of insufficient evidence to support a state conviction. We stressed that the issue was "central to the basic question of guilt or innocence," unlike a claim that a state court had received evidence in violation of the Fourth Amendment exclusionary rule, and we found that to review such a claim on habeas imposed no great burdens on the federal courts.

Justice Souter concluded that with respect to *Miranda* claims, "the argument for extending *Stone* again falls short." He explained this conclusion by stressing the difference between Fourth Amendment claims and *Miranda* claims:

As we explained in *Stone,* the *Mapp* rule "is not a personal constitutional right," but serves to deter future constitutional violations; * * * the exclusion of evidence at trial can do nothing to remedy the completed and wholly extrajudicial Fourth Amendment violation. Nor can the *Mapp* rule be thought to enhance the soundness of the criminal process by improving the reliability of evidence introduced at trial. * * *

Miranda differs from *Mapp* in both respects. * * * [I]n protecting a defendant's Fifth Amendment privilege against self-incrimination *Miranda* safeguards a fundamental *trial* right. * * *

Nor does the Fifth Amendment "trial right" protected by *Miranda* serve some value necessarily divorced from the correct ascertainment of guilt. * * * By bracing against the possibility of unreliable statements in every instance of in-custody interrogation, *Miranda* serves to guard against the use of unreliable statements at trial.

According to Justice Souter, the most important consideration counselling against extending *Stone* to *Miranda* claims was that such an extension "would not significantly benefit the federal courts in their exercise of habeas jurisdiction, or advance the cause of federalism in any substantial way." Justice Souter explained this assertion as follows:

[E]liminating habeas review of *Miranda* issues would not prevent a state prisoner from simply converting his barred *Miranda* claim into a due process claim that his conviction rested on an involuntary confession. * * *

If that is so, the federal courts would certainly not have heard the last of *Miranda* on collateral review. Under the due process approach, * * * courts look to the totality of circumstances to determine whether a confession was voluntary. Those potential circumstances * * * include the failure of police to advise the defendant of his rights to remain silent and to have counsel present during custodial interrogation. We could lock the front door against *Miranda,* but not the back.

Justice O'Connor, joined by the Chief Justice, dissented on the *Stone* issue and reasoned that confessions obtained in violation of *Miranda* are not necessarily untrustworthy. She recognized that reversal of a conviction on direct review because of a violation of the *Miranda* rule may be "an acceptable sacrifice for the deterrence and respect for constitutional values that the *Miranda* rule brings." But she concluded that "once a case is on collateral review, the balance between the costs and benefits shifts; the interests of federalism, finality, and fairness compel *Miranda*'s exclusion from habeas."

Justice O'Connor concluded that the *Miranda* rule is "at war" with the quest for truth and therefore a claimed violation of the rule is not appropriate for habeas review. Finally, she argued that, even if exclusion of *Miranda* claims from habeas review resulted in prisoners' recasting their claims in terms of due process, such exclusion would at least avoid the need for habeas courts to struggle with the various lines of *Miranda* issues that have developed.

Justice Scalia, joined by Justice Thomas, also dissented on the *Stone* issue. Justice Scalia argued broadly that "[p]rior opportunity to litigate an issue should be an important equitable consideration in *any* habeas case, and should ordinarily preclude the court from reaching the merits of a claim, unless it goes to the fairness of the trial process or to the accuracy of the ultimate result."

Full and Fair Opportunity

It is truly a rare case in which the State fails to meet the *Stone* requirement that it provide a full and fair opportunity for litigation of Fourth Amendment claims.[16] The requirement has been held to mean that on factual issues the defendant had an opportunity to offer evidence, and that some appellate review was provided. See generally Willett v. Lockhart, 37 F.3d 1265 (8th Cir.1994)(en banc)(the only questions after *Stone* are whether the state has provided any corrective procedures at all, and whether an "unconscionable procedural breakdown" prevented the petitioner from using the corrective mechanism). For a collection of lower court cases on this subject, see C. Wright, Federal Practice and Procedure § 4263. See also Capellan v. Riley, 975 F.2d 67 (2d Cir. 1992)(summary affirmance of Fourth Amendment ruling, which was probably wrong on the merits, did not constitute an unconscionable breakdown in the state appellate process; claim barred on habeas).

D. LIMITATIONS ON OBTAINING HABEAS RELIEF

Even if the petitioner's claim is cognizable in a federal habeas proceeding, there are several important procedural limitations that must be overcome before habeas relief can be granted.

1. *The Custody Requirement*

Whether relief is sought under § 2254 or under § 2255, the applicant must be in custody. "Custody" is a term of art. Clearly if the petitioner is incarcerated at the time the habeas action is brought, as a result of the conviction that he is challenging, he is in custody for purposes of the habeas statutes. But difficult questions arise where the petitioner has been released, or where he has completed his sentence for one crime and is serving a sentence on another.

In 1963, the Court found that parole was a custody status. Jones v. Cunningham, 371 U.S. 236 (1963). Subsequently, in Peyton v. Rowe, 391 U.S. 54 (1968), the Court held that habeas corpus could be used by a prisoner serving

---

16. Halpern, Federal Habeas Corpus and the Mapp Exclusionary Rule After Stone v. Powell, 82 Colum.L.Rev. 1 (1982), suggests that "habeas corpus relief should be available under *Stone's* exception to correct judicial er- rors which, if otherwise uncorrected, could lead to diminished police adherence to fourth amendment values," errors that are "likely to become widespread among the courts of a particular state."

one sentence who wished to attack a consecutive sentence. In Carafas v. LaVallee, 391 U.S. 234 (1968), the Court held that a petitioner was in custody within the meaning of the statutes, when he was incarcerated at the time the petition was filed, but released before his case was heard on the merits by the Supreme Court. Thus, discharge of a prisoner once properly before the court will not result in a finding of "no custody." Subsequently, the Court found custody in Hensley v. Municipal Court, 411 U.S. 345 (1973), where a defendant sentenced to prison for one year had his sentence stayed pending appellate and post-conviction attacks. After *Hensley*, release on bail has been held to constitute custody for purposes of federal habeas corpus. See. e.g., Campbell v. Shapp, 385 F.Supp. 305 (E.D.Pa.1974), affirmed, 521 F.2d 1398 (3d Cir.1975). If a person is in custody in one jurisdiction and wishes to attack a conviction mandating future custody in another jurisdiction, Braden v. 30th Judicial Circuit Ct., 410 U.S. 484 (1973), suggests that any "detainer" or formal demand for custody by the expectant jurisdiction is "custody."

Collateral Harm

The first case in many years to restrict the "collateral harm" concept and to find a habeas corpus action moot was Lane v. Williams, 455 U.S. 624 (1982). Two defendants pleaded guilty to burglary charges. Each was incarcerated, released on parole, found to be a parole violator, and reincarcerated. When parole was revoked each challenged his plea on the ground that he had not known of the mandatory parole requirement when he pleaded. But before the case reached the Supreme Court, each was released from custody. Since the parole terms had expired, Justice Stevens' opinion for the Court concluded that the case was moot. "No civil disabilities such as those present in *Carafas* result from a finding that an individual has violated parole. At most, certain non-statutory consequences may occur; employment prospects, or the sentence imposed in a future criminal proceeding, could be affected." Justice Marshall, joined by Justices Brennan and Blackmun, dissented, arguing that federal courts should presume the existence of collateral consequences to avoid the necessity of predicting how a state might use a conviction or parole revocation in future proceedings.

The Court reaffirmed the Lane v. Williams mootness principle in Spencer v. Kemna, 523 U.S. 1 (1998). Spencer's parole was revoked due to charges that he committed a rape. He attacked the parole revocation unsuccessfully in state courts, then brought a habeas proceeding. Largely due to state delay, the habeas petition was not considered until after Spencer's sentence had expired and he was released. Relying heavily on Lane v. Williams, the Court, in an opinion by Justice Scalia for eight Justices, held that the habeas petition was moot. The Court declared: "We adhere to the principles announced in *Lane*, and decline to presume that collateral consequences adequate to meet Article III's injury-in-fact requirement resulted from petitioner's parole revocation."

The Court rejected, as speculative, all the collateral harms asserted by Spencer. Spencer argued (1) that his parole revocation could be used to his detriment in a future parole proceeding; (2) that the revocation could be used to increase his sentence in a future sentencing proceeding should he violate the law and be caught and convicted; (3) that the parole revocation could be used to impeach him should he appear as a witness in future proceedings; and (4) that it could be used directly against him should he appear as a defendant in a criminal proceeding. According to the Court, none of these asserted harms were concrete enough to create a case or controversy.

Finally, Justice Scalia rejected the notion that an exception to the mootness limitation should apply when the delay leading to mootness is caused by the State. He reasoned as follows:

> [M]ootness, however it may have come about, simply deprives us of our power to act; there is nothing for us to remedy, even if we were disposed to do so. We are not in the business of pronouncing that past actions which have no demonstrable continuing effect were right or wrong. As for petitioner's concern that law enforcement officials and district judges will repeat with impunity the mootness-producing abuse that he alleges occurred here: We are confident that, as a general matter, district courts will prevent dilatory tactics by the litigants and will not unduly delay their own rulings; and that, where appropriate, corrective mandamus will issue from the courts of appeals.

Justice Stevens dissented.

Custody and AEDPA

As seen above, custody questions have usually arisen after the petitioner has been released and is arguing that his conviction is causing him some collateral harm. The AEDPA has put a damper on such claims by imposing a one-year statute of limitations on habeas petitions. The year basically runs from the date on which a conviction becomes final. It is the rare habeas petitioner who has been freed from incarceration (and yet is still arguably in custody) within the one year AEDPA statutory period. Thus it can be expected that many difficult custody questions will evaporate under the AEDPA.

Custody, Habeas, and Section 1983 Actions

In Preiser v. Rodriguez, 411 U.S. 475 (1973), prisoners challenging the method by which good time credit was taken from them brought a civil rights suit under 42 U.S.C.A. § 1983. But the Court held that because the prisoners were in custody and seeking release, they were really seeking a habeas corpus remedy and that, therefore, they had to exhaust state remedies.

In Heck v. Humphrey, 512 U.S. 477 (1994), the Court decided a question left open in *Preiser*: whether an action could be brought for damages (as opposed to release) under 42 U.S.C. § 1983, where the action was dependent on establishing the invalidity of a state court conviction. The Court held that in order to recover damages for allegedly unconstitutional conviction or imprisonment, or for other harm caused by actions whose unlawfulness would render a conviction or sentence invalid, a § 1983 plaintiff must prove that the conviction or sentence has been reversed on direct appeal, expunged by executive order, declared invalid by a state tribunal authorized to make such determination, or called into question by a federal court's issuance of a writ of habeas corpus under 28 U.S.C. § 2254. Justice Scalia, writing for the Court, emphasized that section 1983 should not be used as an end-run around the principles of Federalism that Congress had imparted under section 2254. Justice Thomas wrote a concurring opinion. Justice Souter wrote an opinion concurring in the result, joined by Justices Blackmun, Stevens and O'Connor.

2. Exhaustion of State Remedies

A petitioner challenging a state conviction on habeas must establish that he has exhausted his state remedies before proceeding to federal court. The exhaustion requirement originated in Ex parte Royall, 117 U.S. 241 (1886),[17] and it is now codified in 28 U.S.C.A. § 2254(b)–(c).

The Purpose of the Exhaustion Requirement

As the Supreme Court pointed out in Darr v. Burford, 339 U.S. 200 (1950), the exhaustion requirement is rooted in federal-state comity. It allows the states the first opportunity to apply controlling legal principles to the facts bearing on the constitutional claim of a defendant in a state criminal action. It thereby preserves for state courts a role in the application and enforcement of federal law and prevents interruption of state adjudication by federal habeas proceedings. Consequently, it is not enough that the petitioner has been to the state courts; he must have presented there the same ground he seeks to advance in his federal habeas corpus petition. See Byrnes v. Vose, 969 F.2d 1306 (1st Cir.1992) ("considerations of comity require that state courts be afforded the opportunity, in the first instance, to correct a constitutional violation before a federal court intervenes").[18]

Which "Grounds" Have Been Exhausted?

In Sanders v. United States, 373 U.S. 1, 16 (1963), the Supreme Court explained what is meant by the same "ground" for purposes of the exhaustion requirement:

> By "ground" we mean simply a sufficient legal basis for granting the relief sought by the applicant. * * * [I]dentical grounds may often be proved by different factual allegations. So also, identical grounds may often be supported by different legal arguments, * * * or be couched in different language, * * * or vary in immaterial respects. * * * Should doubts arise in particular cases as to whether two grounds are different or the same, they should be resolved in favor of the applicant.

Subsequently, the Court refined the test by stating that "the substance of a federal habeas corpus claim must first be presented to the state courts." Picard v. Connor, 404 U.S. 270, 278 (1971). Connor challenged the legality of an indictment, which had originally named John Doe, and then was amended to name him. In the state courts, he contended that the amending procedure did not comply with the Massachusetts statute, and therefore that he had not been lawfully indicted. In his habeas petition, he alleged a violation of equal protection. Justice Black, writing for the Court, concluded that the equal protection claim had not been exhausted in the state courts. He stated as follows:

---

17. Royall sought to challenge a Virginia statute before trial. The Court recognized discretion on the part of federal courts to defer to a state court in the first instance.

18. To fully exhaust state remedies, the petitioner must utilize all state remedies available, including appellate remedies, but he is not required to petition the United States Supreme Court for certiorari. See Fay v. Noia, 372 U.S. 391, 435–38 (1963).

It would be unseemly in our dual system of government for a federal district court to upset a state court conviction without an opportunity to the state courts to correct a constitutional violation. It follows, of course, that once the federal claim has been fairly presented to the state courts, the exhaustion requirement is satisfied.

We emphasize that the federal claim must be fairly presented to the state courts. If the exhaustion doctrine is to prevent unnecessary conflict between courts equally bound to guard and protect rights secured by the Constitution, it is not sufficient merely that the federal habeas applicant has been through the state courts. The rule would serve no purpose if it could be satisfied by raising one claim in the state courts and another in the federal courts. * * *

Until he reached this Court, respondent never contended that the method by which he was brought to trial denied him equal protection of the laws. * * * To be sure, respondent presented all the facts. Yet the constitutional claim * * * in those facts was never brought to the attention of the state courts. * * * [We] do not imply that respondent could have raised the equal protection claim only by citing book and verse on the federal constitution. We simply hold that the substance of a federal habeas corpus claim must first be presented to the state courts. The claim that an indictment is invalid is not the substantial equivalent of a claim that it results in an unconstitutional discrimination.[19]

In Duncan v. Henry, 513 U.S. 364 (1995), Henry was convicted in a state court for child molestation, and on his state appeal he argued that the admission of testimony concerning an uncharged act of molestation was a violation of the California evidence code and was also a "miscarriage of justice" under the California Constitution. The state appellate courts denied relief. Subsequently, in his federal habeas petition, Henry argued that the admission of the challenged testimony resulted in a fundamentally unfair trial in violation of his federal due process rights. Relying on *Picard*, the Court, in a per curiam opinion, held that Henry had not exhausted that federal claim in the state courts. The Court concluded that Henry "did not apprise the state court of his claim that the evidentiary ruling of which he complained was not only a violation of state law, but denied him the due process of law guaranteed by the Fourteenth Amendment." While recognizing that the state law "miscarriage of justice" claim and the federal law "fundamental fairness" claim were *similar*, the Court stated that "mere similarity of claims is insufficient to exhaust." The Court noted that the state appellate court had "confined its analysis to the application of state law."

Justice Stevens dissented, accusing the majority of imposing "an exact labeling requirement." He called the majority's opinion "hypertechnical and unwise" because the state and Federal claims were substantially similar. Justice Stevens argued that where the state court has already denied a claim of fundamental unfairness, "nothing is to be gained by requiring the prisoner to present the same claim under a different label to the same courts that have already found it insufficient."

---

19. In Anderson v. Harless, 459 U.S. 4 (1982), six Justices concluded that a state prisoner had not exhausted state remedies where he challenged a jury instruction in state court by citing state law and in federal court raised a constitutional challenge for the first time. Three dissenters agreed with the court of appeals that the "substance" of the federal claim had been put before the state courts.

Mixed Petitions: Rose v. Lundy

What if a habeas petition contains a number of claims, some of which have been considered and denied by the state courts, and some of which have not? Such petitions are referred to as "mixed petitions", containing both exhausted and unexhausted claims. The AEDPA provides that a district court faced with a mixed petition has two options: 1) it can dismiss the entire petition without prejudice, requiring the petitioner to exhaust the unexhausted claims in state court, and holding the exhausted claims in abeyance—this procedure was set forth by the Court in the pre-AEDPA case of Rose v. Lundy, 455 U.S. 509 (1982); 2) if the exhausted claims lack merit, the court can consider and dismiss them on the merits, then dismiss the unexhausted claims without prejudice so that the petitioner can bring them to state court. Under the AEDPA, the district court does not have discretion to *grant* relief on the merits of exhausted claims that are included in mixed petitions. It only has discretion to deny relief on the merits. See Alexander v. Johnson, 163 F.3d 906 (5th Cir.1998).

As the Court in Rose v. Lundy made clear, the exhaustion requirement does not *preclude* habeas review; it merely *delays* habeas review. The exhaustion requirement is therefore unlike other limitations on collateral review, such as the bar of procedural default in the state court, or the related bar of adequate state ground, both of which prevent claims from ever being heard on habeas.[20]

Exhaustion and Multiple Habeas Petitions

What would happen if a petitioner wanted to split his claims, i.e., pursue the exhausted claims right now in federal court, then bring another habeas petition on the remaining claims once they were exhausted in the state court? This would not work, because the petitioner would run afoul of the severe limitations on multiple habeas petitions that are found in the AEDPA. See Burris v. Parke, 72 F.3d 47 (7th Cir.1995) ("A prisoner who decides to proceed only with his exhausted claims and deliberately sets aside his unexhausted claims risks dismissal of subsequent federal petitions.").

What happens if a habeas petition is dismissed because it contains unexhausted claims, then the petitioner exhausts the claims in state court and brings another federal habeas petition? Is this petition of now-exhausted claims considered "successive", and thus dismissed, within the meaning of the AEDPA? In Stewart v. Martinez–Villareal, 523 U.S. 637 (1998), the Court, in an opinion by the Chief Justice, held that such a petition setting forth claims previously dismissed as unexhausted could not be considered "successive" within the meaning of the AEDPA, and therefore such a petition could be considered on the merits. The Chief Justice declared that "[t]o hold otherwise would mean that a dismissal of a first habeas petition for technical procedural reasons would bar the prisoner from ever obtaining federal habeas review." Justice Scalia and Justice Thomas dissented.

---

20. These doctrines are discussed later in this Chapter.

Procedural Bars

A petition is not a mixed petition within the meaning of Rose v. Lundy if the unexhausted claims are procedurally barred on other grounds. For example, if a petitioner fails to make an objection in the trial court, and state rules of procedure treat that failure as barring consideration on appeal, the defendant's claim is probably procedurally barred from consideration on habeas. (See the discussion of state procedural bars later in this Chapter). If the unexhausted claim is procedurally barred, "exhaustion is not possible because the state court would find the claims procedurally defaulted. The district court may not go to the merits of the barred claims, but must decide the merits of the claims that are exhausted and not barred." Toulson v. Beyer, 987 F.2d 984 (3d Cir.1993).

Waiver by the State

Before the AEDPA, the state had to invoke the exhaustion requirement before a court would have the authority to dismiss unexhausted claims. Granberry v. Greer, 481 U.S. 129 (1987). But this is no longer the case. Under the AEDPA the exhaustion requirement is not waived unless it is waived expressly by the state through counsel.

The Futility Exception to the Exhaustion Requirement

A habeas petitioner is not required to bring his claims in the state court if to do so would be futile—this futility exception, which was established by case law, has been retained in the AEDPA. A good example of the futility exception is Harris v. DeRobertis, 932 F.2d 619 (7th Cir.1991). The district court dismissed Harris' habeas petition, hold that Harris had not exhausted the state post-conviction remedy established by an Illinois statute. Harris had failed to assert his constitutional claim in his state appeal. An Illinois statute allowed claims such as Harris' to be brought on collateral attack; but if the proceedings were commenced more than ten years after final judgment, the petitioner had to prove that the delay was for some reason other than "culpable negligence." Harris' petition was filed twenty years after his conviction. The district court held that Harris could have tried to invoke the state remedy by demonstrating a lack of culpable negligence, and therefore his claim was unexhausted. The court of appeals disagreed. It noted that the Illinois statute had been in effect for more than forty years, and in that time "the Illinois courts have failed to produce even a single published opinion in which the court found a lack of culpable negligence." Based on the Illinois case law, the court found that "the culpable negligence standard is an exceptional means of relief which will be unavailable to virtually all prisoners." The court concluded as follows:

> We believe the better approach is to forego resort to the Illinois post-conviction process if a petition would be untimely, absent judicial precedent indicating that the culpable negligence exception would be met. Such a holding avoids the 'merry-go-round procedure' * * * by which prisoners are shuttled back and forth between the state and federal courts before any decision on the merits is ever reached in order to exhaust meaningless remedies.

If, however, a state remedy is futile because the petitioner has failed to comply with a rule of procedure, the question is no longer one of exhaustion or futility. The question is then whether the habeas petition is barred by the petitioner's failure to comply with the state rule. See Jones v. Jones, 163 F.3d 285 (5th Cir.1998).

Inexhaustible State Review and the Exhaustion Requirement: Castille v. Peoples

Suppose the state provides for collateral review without limitation as to number of petitions or the time in which they may be brought. Would it follow that a federal habeas petition could never be brought because the state post-conviction remedy is never exhausted? The Court in Castille v. Peoples, 489 U.S. 346 (1989), addressed this question. Justice Scalia wrote for a unanimous Court as follows:

> Title 28 U.S.C. § 2254(c) provides that a claim shall not be deemed exhausted so long as a petitioner "has the right under the law of the State to raise, by any available procedure, the question presented." Read narrowly, this language appears to preclude a finding of exhaustion if there exists any possibility of further state-court review. We have, however, expressly rejected such a construction, holding instead that once the state courts have ruled upon a claim, it is not necessary for the petitioner to ask the state for collateral relief, based upon the same evidence and issues already decided by direct review. It would be inconsistent * * * to mandate recourse to state collateral review whose results have effectively been predetermined, or permanently to bar from federal habeas prisoners in States whose post-conviction procedures are technically inexhaustible.

> Thus, the rule is that state collateral review is relevant for exhaustion purposes only if direct appeal has been bypassed and only if the collateral review process is meaningful and not itself inexhaustible.

On the facts in *Peoples,* the Court held that the petitioner had not exhausted state court remedies. Peoples presented his constitutional claim for the first time by filing a petition for allocatur with the Pennsylvania Supreme Court. Under Pennsylvania law, allocatur review is only allowed where there are "special and important reasons therefor." Justice Scalia found that in rejecting the petition for allocatur, the state court had not actually passed upon the claim so as to render further state proceedings useless. He noted the limitations on allocatur review in Pennsylvania and concluded that "raising the claim in such a fashion does not, for the relevant purpose, constitute fair presentation" to the state courts within the meaning of the exhaustion requirement. He recognized, however, that "the requisite exhaustion may nonetheless exist, of course, if it is clear that respondent's claims are now procedurally barred under Pennsylvania law." Note, however, that if his claims were procedurally barred, Peoples has jumped from the exhaustion frying pan into the procedural bar fire, and so federal habeas review is probably precluded at any rate. See Wainwright v. Sykes, infra.

Exhaustion and Discretionary Review in the State Supreme Court: O'Sullivan v. Boerckel

If the habeas petitioner has failed to include a constitutional claim in his petition for leave to appeal to the state supreme court, must the claim be dismissed in a federal habeas action for lack of exhaustion? This was the question addressed by the Court in O'Sullivan v. Boerckel, 526 U.S. 838 (1999). Boerckel appealed his state conviction to an intermediate appellate court, asserting six constitutional claims. After the claims were denied, Boerckel sought leave to appeal to the Supreme Court of Illinois. Review in that Court, as in the United States Supreme Court, is discretionary. In his leave to appeal, Boerckel included only three of his constitutional claims. He then sought habeas review for the three claims that he did not include in his petition to the Illinois Supreme Court. If Boerckel was required to bring those claims before the Illinois Supreme Court in order to satisfy the exhaustion requirement, his habeas petition would have to be dismissed. Moreover, it would have to be dismissed with prejudice, because the time to bring those claims to the Illinois Supreme Court had long since run out—meaning that he had committed a procedural default disentitling him from habeas review. However, if the exhaustion doctrine did not require him to bring those claims to the Illinois Supreme Court, then there was no bar to hearing them on habeas.

The Supreme Court, in an opinion by Justice O'Connor for six Justices, held that Boerckel had failed to exhaust his claims when he failed to bring them before the Illinois Supreme Court. She analyzed the rationale and application of the exhaustion requirement as follows:

> Section 2254(c) requires only that state prisoners give state courts a fair opportunity to act on their claims. State courts, like federal courts, are obliged to enforce federal law. Comity thus dictates that when a prisoner alleges that his continued confinement for a state court conviction violates federal law, the state courts should have the first opportunity to review this claim and provide any necessary relief. This rule of comity reduces friction between the state and federal court systems by avoiding the unseemliness of a federal district court's overturning a state court conviction without the state courts having had an opportunity to correct the constitutional violation in the first instance.

> Because the exhaustion doctrine is designed to give the state courts a full and fair opportunity to resolve federal constitutional claims before those claims are presented to the federal courts, we conclude that state prisoners must give the state courts one full opportunity to resolve any constitutional issues by invoking one complete round of the State's established appellate review process. Here, Illinois's established, normal appellate review procedure is a two-tiered system. Comity, in these circumstances, dictates that Boerckel use the State's established appellate review procedures before he presents his claims to a federal court. * * * [A] petition for discretionary review in Illinois's Supreme Court is a normal, simple, and established part of the State's appellate review process. In the words of the statute, state prisoners have "the right . . . to raise" their claims through a petition for discretionary review in the state's highest court. § 2254(c). Granted, as Boerckel contends, he has no right to review in the Illinois Supreme Court, but he does have a "right . . . to raise" his claims before that court. That is all § 2254(c) requires.

Boerckel argued that if he were forced to bring all his constitutional claims before the Illinois Supreme Court, that Court would be inundated by claims that it could not meaningfully review and would have no interest in reviewing—thus undercutting the very comity interests that are behind the exhaustion requirement. Justice O'Connor responded to this argument in the following passage:

We acknowledge that the rule we announce today—requiring state prisoners to file petitions for discretionary review when that review is part of the ordinary appellate review procedure in the State—has the potential to increase the number of filings in state supreme courts. We also recognize that this increased burden may be unwelcome in some state courts because the courts do not wish to have the opportunity to review constitutional claims before those claims are presented to a federal habeas court. Under these circumstances, Boerckel may be correct that the increased, unwelcome burden on state supreme courts disserves the comity interests underlying the exhaustion doctrine. In this regard, we note that nothing in our decision today requires the exhaustion of any specific state remedy when a State has provided that that remedy is unavailable. * * * We hold today only that the creation of a discretionary review system does not, without more, make review in the Illinois Supreme Court unavailable.

Justice Souter concurred in *Boerckel*, with the following proviso:

I understand the Court to have left open the question (not directly implicated by this case) whether we should construe the exhaustion doctrine to force a State, in effect, to rule on discretionary review applications when the State has made it plain that it does not wish to require such applications before its petitioners may seek federal habeas relief. The Supreme Court of South Carolina, for example, has declared:

"[I]n all appeals from criminal convictions or post-conviction relief matters, a litigant shall not be required to petition for rehearing and certiorari following an adverse decision of the Court of Appeals in order to be deemed to have exhausted all available state remedies respecting a claim of error. Rather, when the claim has been presented to the Court of Appeals or the Supreme Court, and relief has been denied, the litigant shall be deemed to have exhausted all available state remedies." In re Exhaustion of State Remedies in Criminal and Post–Conviction Relief Cases, 321 S.C. 563, 471 S.E.2d 454 (1990).

Justice Stevens, joined by Justices Ginsburg and Breyer, dissented in *Boerckel*. Justice Stevens concluded that the majority's application of the exhaustion requirement to state appellate court discretionary review "will impose unnecessary burdens on habeas petitioners; it will delay the completion of litigation that is already more protracted than it should be; and, most ironically, it will undermine federalism by thwarting the interests of those state supreme courts that administer discretionary dockets."

Justice Breyer wrote a separate dissenting opinion in *Boerckel*, joined by Justice Ginsburg. He noted that discretionary review is rarely granted by any of the State Supreme Courts, and "would presume, on the basis of Illinois's own rules and related statistics, and in the absence of any clear legal expression to the contrary, that Illinois does not mind if a state prisoner does not ask its Supreme Court for discretionary review prior to seeking habeas relief in federal court."

3. *Procedural Default*

Like the exhaustion requirement, the procedural default doctrine is rooted in principles of federalism and comity. If the habeas remedy were always available despite the transgression of a procedural rule, state procedures (such as the requirement of a timely objection and the requirement of a timely notice of appeal) could be routinely disregarded. Unlike the exhaustion requirement, however, which merely delays a collateral attack, the procedural default doctrine precludes it. The question, then, is whether and under what circumstances a habeas petitioner can be excused from a procedural default that was made in the state courts.

While the bar of procedural default is usually applied against state defendants, it is also applicable to federal defendants seeking habeas relief under section 2255. The reason is obvious: if the defendant violated a procedural rule that would bar *direct* review in the federal court of appeal (e.g., failure to file timely notice of appeal), it would make no sense to excuse that default and allow collateral relief. This result is not, of course, due to federalism, but rather to the respect for federal rules of procedure.

a. *Deliberate Bypass*

In Fay v. Noia, 372 U.S. 391 (1963), the Court created a very permissive test for lifting a state procedural bar to habeas relief. Noia brought a habeas petition, arguing that the confession admitted against him at trial was coerced. However, Noia had not brought an appeal on this or any other issue in the state courts; he had failed to a file a timely notice of appeal. Justice Brennan, writing for the Court, held that a procedural bar would be lifted unless it could be shown that the petitioner had deliberately bypassed a state procedural rule. Justice Brennan argued that lifting a procedural bar in all other cases—including where the default was caused by inadvertence or neglect—was necessary to effectuate federal interests. He asserted that petitioners would be unlikely to flaunt state procedural requirements and that state interests would not be unduly impaired. He reasoned as follows:

> A man under conviction for crime has an obvious inducement to do his very best to keep his state remedies open, and not stake his all on the outcome of a federal habeas proceeding which, in many respects, may be less advantageous to him than a state court proceeding. And if because of inadvertence or neglect he runs afoul of a state procedural requirement, and thereby forfeits his state remedies, appellate and collateral, as well as direct review thereof in this Court, those consequences should be sufficient to vindicate the State's valid interest in orderly procedure. Whatever residuum of state interest there may be under such circumstances is manifestly insufficient in the face of the federal policy, drawn from the ancient principles of the writ of habeas corpus, * * * of affording an effective remedy for restraints contrary to the Constitution.

Justice Clark dissented in *Fay,* contending that a deliberate bypass test was insufficient to protect legitimate state interests. He argued that the majority had in effect substituted federal habeas corpus review for an appeal in state court. Justice Harlan also dissented, in an opinion joined by Justices Clark and Stewart. He contended that the deliberate bypass standard "amounts to no limitation at all."

b.   A Required Showing of Cause and Prejudice

Soon the Court began to cut back on Fay v. Noia, and ultimately it was overruled. In Francis v. Henderson, 425 U.S. 536 (1976), the petitioner challenged the make-up of his grand jury; but he had failed to comply with a state rule of procedure requiring that an objection to the composition of the grand jury must be made by motion prior to trial. The Court held that habeas corpus relief was barred, and expressed deference to state procedures. It distinguished *Fay* as a case where the petitioner had defaulted on his entire appeal (by failing to file a timely notice of appeal), rather than a specific claim.

The majority in *Francis* stated that the procedural bar could be lifted only if the petitioner 1) could show good "cause" (i.e., a legitimate excuse) for the procedural default, and 2) could establish that the alleged violation of federal law had actually prejudiced his case.[21] *Francis* paved the way for the next case.

WAINWRIGHT v. SYKES

Supreme Court of the United States, 1977.
433 U.S. 72.

Mr. Justice Rehnquist **delivered the opinion of the Court.**

* * *

Respondent Sykes was convicted of third-degree murder after a jury trial in the Circuit Court of DeSoto County. He testified at trial that on the evening of January 8, 1972, he told his wife to summon the police because he had just shot Willie Gilbert. Other evidence indicated that when the police arrived at respondent's trailer home, they found Gilbert dead of a shotgun wound, lying a few feet from the front porch. Shortly after their arrival, respondent came from across the road, and volunteered that he had shot Gilbert, and a few minutes later respondent's wife approached the police and told them the same thing. Sykes was immediately arrested and taken to the police station.

Once there, it is conceded that he was read his *Miranda* rights, and that he declined to seek the aid of counsel and indicated a desire to talk. He then made a statement, which was admitted into evidence at trial through the testimony of the two officers who heard it,

to the effect that he had shot Gilbert from the front porch of his trailer home. * * * At no time during the trial * * * was the admissibility of any of respondent's statements challenged by his counsel on the ground that respondent had not understood the *Miranda* warnings. Nor did the trial judge question their admissibility on his own motion or hold a factfinding hearing bearing on that issue.

Respondent appealed his conviction, but apparently did not challenge the admissibility of the inculpatory statements. [He was successful in obtaining habeas relief on *Miranda* grounds in the lower federal courts.]

* * *

[The Court of Appeals held that noncompliance with Florida's contemporaneous objection rule did not bar review by way of habeas corpus.] Concluding that "[t]he failure to object in this case cannot be dismissed as a trial tactic, and thus a deliberate by-pass," the court affirmed the District Court order that the State hold a hearing on whether respondent knowingly waived

---

21. Justices Marshall and Stevens did not participate. Justice Brennan dissented.

his *Miranda* rights at the time he made the statements.

* * *

To the extent that the dicta of Fay v. Noia may be thought to have laid down an all-inclusive rule rendering state timely objection rules ineffective to bar review of underlying federal claims in federal habeas proceedings—absent a "knowing waiver" or a "deliberate bypass" of the right to so object—its effect was limited by *Francis*, which applied a different rule and barred a habeas challenge to the make-up of a grand jury. Petitioner Wainwright in this case urges that we further confine its effect by applying the principle enunciated in *Francis* to a claimed error in the admission of a defendant's confession.

* * *

* * * [I]t has been the rule that the federal habeas petitioner who claims he is detained pursuant to a final judgment of a state court in violation of the United States Constitution is entitled to have the federal habeas court make its own independent determination of his federal claim, without being bound by the determination on the merits of that claim reached in the state proceedings. This rule * * * is in no way changed by our holding today. Rather, we deal only with contentions of federal law which were *not* resolved on the merits in the state proceeding due to respondent's failure to raise them there as required by state procedure. We leave open for resolution in future decisions the precise definition of the "cause"-and-"prejudice" standard, and note here only that it is

narrower than the standard set forth in dicta in Fay v. Noia, which would make federal habeas review generally available to state convicts absent a knowing and deliberate waiver of the federal constitutional contention. It is the sweeping language of Fay v. Noia, going far beyond the facts of the case eliciting it, which we today reject.[a]

The reasons for our rejection of it are several. The contemporaneous-objection rule itself is by no means peculiar to Florida, and deserves greater respect than *Fay* gives it, both for the fact that it is employed by a coordinate jurisdiction within the federal system and for the many interests which it serves in its own right. A contemporaneous objection enables the record to be made with respect to the constitutional claim when the recollections of witnesses are freshest, not years later in a federal habeas proceeding. It enables the judge who observed the demeanor of those witnesses to make the factual determinations necessary for properly deciding the federal constitutional question. * * *

A contemporaneous-objection rule may lead to the exclusion of the evidence objected to, thereby making a major contribution to finality in criminal litigation. Without the evidence claimed to be vulnerable on federal constitutional grounds, the jury may acquit the defendant, and that will be the end of the case; or it may nonetheless convict the defendant, and he will have one less federal constitutional claim to assert in his federal habeas petition. If the state trial judge admits the evidence in question after a full hearing, the federal habeas court * * * will gain significant guidance

---

a. The Court in *Fay* stated its knowing-and-deliberate-waiver rule in language which applied not only to the waiver of the right to appeal, but to failures to raise individual substantive objections in the state trial. Then, with a single sentence in a footnote, the Court swept aside all decisions of this Court "to the

extent that [they] may be read to suggest a standard of discretion in federal habeas corpus proceedings different from what we lay down today * * *." 372 U.S., at 439 n. 44. We do not choose to paint with a similarly broad brush here.

from the state ruling in this regard. Subtler considerations as well militate in favor of honoring a state contemporaneous-objection rule. An objection on the spot may force the prosecution to take a hard look at its hole card, and even if the prosecutor thinks that the state trial judge will admit the evidence he must contemplate the possibility of reversal by the state appellate courts or the ultimate issuance of a federal writ of habeas corpus based on the impropriety of the state court's rejection of the federal constitutional claim.

We think that the rule of Fay v. Noia, broadly stated, may encourage "sandbagging" on the part of defense lawyers, who may take their chances on a verdict of not guilty in a state trial court with the intent to raise their constitutional claims in a federal habeas court if their initial gamble does not pay off. The refusal of federal habeas courts to honor contemporaneous-objection rules may also make state courts themselves less stringent in their enforcement. Under the rule of Fay v. Noia, state appellate courts know that a federal constitutional issue raised for the first time in the proceeding before them may well be decided in any event by a federal *habeas* tribunal. Thus, their choice is between addressing the issue notwithstanding the petitioner's failure to timely object, or else face the prospect that the federal habeas court will decide the question without the benefit of their views.

* * *

We believe that the adoption of the *Francis* rule in this situation will have the salutary effect of making the state trial on the merits the "main event," so to speak, rather than a "tryout on the road" for what will later be the determinative federal habeas hearing. There is nothing in the Constitution or in the language of § 2254 which requires that the state trial on the issue of guilt or innocence be devoted largely to the testimony of fact witnesses directed to the elements of the state crime, while only later will there occur in a federal habeas hearing a full airing of the federal constitutional claims which were not raised in the state proceedings. If a criminal defendant thinks that an action of the state trial court is about to deprive him of a federal constitutional right there is every reason for his following state procedure in making known his objection.

The "cause"-and-"prejudice" exception of the *Francis* rule will afford an adequate guarantee, we think, that the rule will not prevent a federal habeas court from adjudicating for the first time the federal constitutional claim of a defendant who in the absence of such an adjudication will be the victim of a miscarriage of justice. Whatever precise content may be given those terms by later cases, we feel confident in holding without further elaboration that they do not exist here. Respondent has advanced no explanation whatever for his failure to object at trial, and, as the proceeding unfolded, the trial judge is certainly not to be faulted for failing to question the admission of the confession himself. The other evidence of guilt presented at trial, moreover, was substantial to a degree that would negate any possibility of actual prejudice resulting to the respondent from the admission of his inculpatory statement.

* * *

[The concurring opinions of CHIEF JUSTICE BURGER and MR. JUSTICE STEVENS are omitted].

[The opinion of JUSTICE WHITE, concurring in the judgment, is omitted].

MR. JUSTICE BRENNAN, **with whom** MR. JUSTICE MARSHALL **joins, dissenting.**

* * *

Punishing a lawyer's unintentional errors by closing the federal courthouse door to his client is both a senseless and misdirected method of deterring the slighting of state rules. It is senseless because unplanned and unintentional action of any kind generally is not subject to deterrence; and, to the extent that it is hoped that a threatened sanction addressed to the defense will induce greater care and caution on the part of trial lawyers, thereby forestalling negligent conduct or error, the potential loss of all valuable state remedies would be sufficient to this end. And it is a misdirected sanction because even if the penalization of incompetence or carelessness will encourage more thorough legal training and trial preparation, the habeas applicant, as opposed to his lawyer, hardly is the proper recipient of such a penalty. Especially with fundamental constitutional rights at stake, no fictional relationship of principal-agent or the like can justify holding the criminal defendant accountable for the naked errors of his attorney. This is especially true when so many indigent defendants are without any realistic choice in selecting who ultimately represents them at trial. * * *

Fay Overruled: Coleman v. Thompson

The Court finally overruled Fay v. Noia and its deliberate bypass standard in Coleman v. Thompson, 501 U.S. 722 (1991). Cases such as *Sykes* had limited *Fay* to its facts, so that the deliberate bypass standard essentially applied only when a state prisoner defaulted his entire appeal. That was the situation in *Coleman,* where the prisoner, by filing a late notice of appeal, defaulted his entire state post-conviction remedy. Justice O'Connor, writing for six members of the Court, recognized that the error in filing a late notice was "inadvertent" and the State admitted that Coleman had not deliberately bypassed his state post-conviction review. The Court nonetheless held that Coleman's habeas petition was barred in the absence of a showing of cause and prejudice. Justice O'Connor reasoned that the cause and prejudice standard was more compatible with interests of comity and finality than the deliberate bypass standard. She concluded as follows:

> In all cases in which a state prisoner has defaulted his federal claims in state court pursuant to an independent and adequate state procedural rule, federal habeas review of the claims is barred unless the prisoner can demonstrate cause for the default and actual prejudice as a result of the alleged violation of federal law, or demonstrate that failure to consider the claims will result in a fundamental miscarriage of justice. *Fay* was based on a conception of federal/state relations that undervalued the importance of state procedural rules. The several cases after *Fay* that applied the cause and prejudice standard to a variety of state procedural defaults represent a different view. We now recognize the important interest in finality served by state procedural rules, and the significant harm to the States that results from the failure of federal courts to respect them.

Justices Blackmun, Stevens, and Marshall dissented.

Cause and Prejudice for Federal Habeas Petitioners: United States v. Frady

United States v. Frady, 456 U.S. 152 (1982), holds that on collateral attack under § 2255 a petitioner convicted in federal court may not rely on the "plain error" doctrine of Fed.R.Crim.P. 52(b) to challenge an error as to which there was a procedural default. Frady, convicted of a vicious killing in 1963, moved to vacate his sentence on the ground that the jury instructions erroneously equated intent with malice and told the jury that the law presumes malice from the use of a weapon. He did not object to the instructions at trial. For the majority, Justice O'Connor wrote that the plain error standard, which is applicable on direct review and "was intended to afford a means for the prompt redress of miscarriages of justice," "is out of place when a prisoner launches a collateral attack against a criminal conviction after society's legitimate interest in the finality of the judgment has been perfected by the expiration of the time allowed for direct review or by the affirmance of the conviction on appeal." To prevail, Frady would have to meet the stricter standards of cause and prejudice under Wainwright v. Sykes.

The *Frady* majority found, without reaching the question of cause, that Frady could not show prejudice. The Court noted that Frady had admitted the killing for which he had been convicted. Justice O'Connor stated that prejudice does not follow simply from the fact that a jury instruction was erroneous. Rather, prejudice must be evaluated by the effect of the error in the context of the whole trial. She concluded that a petitioner must show that errors at the trial "worked to his *actual* and substantial disadvantage, infecting his entire trial with error of constitutional dimensions." Frady had failed to contradict strong evidence in the record that he had acted with malice, and therefore the instruction was not prejudicial.[22] See also United States v. Shaid, 937 F.2d 228 (5th Cir.1991)(en banc), where the court in a section 2255 case, citing *Frady*, held that the cause and prejudice standard is "designed to be significantly more difficult than the plain error test that we employ on direct appeal." The court concluded that "Shaid's argument that the jury may have misinterpreted the trial court's instruction on *mens rea* * * * suggests only the *possibility* that he was prejudiced by the erroneous instruction. Shaid has not challenged the sufficiency of the *mens rea* evidence at his trial, and he has not presented new evidence indicating his actual innocence." After *Frady*, is a procedural bar lifted only for those who can establish their actual innocence?

Federal Defendant's Failure to Raise an Ineffective Assistance Claim on Direct Appeal; Is That a Procedural Default?: Massaro v. United States.

In the following case, the Court considered whether a federal defendant had procedurally defaulted an ineffective assistance of counsel claim by failing to assert it on direct review of his conviction.

22. Justice Stevens concurred. Justice Blackmun concurred in the judgment. Justice Brennan dissented and argued that the Court obscured the distinction between § 2254, a civil proceeding, and § 2255, which he saw as a part of a criminal case. Justices Blackmun and Brennan both appeared to agree that federalism concerns were not present in a § 2255 proceeding. Chief Justice Burger and Justice Marshall did not participate in the case.

MASSARO v. UNITED STATES

Supreme Court of the United States, 2003.
538 U.S. 500.

JUSTICE KENNEDY delivered the opinion of the Court.

Petitioner, Joseph Massaro, was indicted on federal racketeering charges, including murder in aid of racketeering, in connection with the shooting death of Joseph Fiorito. He was tried in the United States District Court for the Southern District of New York. The day before Massaro's trial was to begin, prosecutors learned of what appeared to be a critical piece of evidence: a bullet allegedly recovered from the car in which the victim's body was found. They waited for several days, however, to inform defense counsel of this development. Not until the trial was underway and the defense had made its opening statement did they make this disclosure. After the trial court and the defense had been informed of the development but still during the course of trial, defense counsel more than once declined the trial court's offer of a continuance so the bullet could be examined. Massaro was convicted and sentenced to life imprisonment.

On direct appeal new counsel for Massaro argued the District Court had erred in admitting the bullet in evidence, but he did not raise any claim relating to ineffective assistance of trial counsel. The Court of Appeals for the Second Circuit affirmed the conviction.

Massaro later filed a motion under 28 U.S.C. § 2255, seeking to vacate his conviction. As relevant here, he claimed that his trial counsel had rendered ineffective assistance in failing to accept the trial court's offer to grant a continuance. The United States District Court for the Southern District of New York found this claim procedurally defaulted because Massaro could have raised it on direct appeal.

The Court of Appeals for the Second Circuit affirmed. The court acknowledged that ineffective-assistance claims usually should be excused from procedural default rules because an attorney who handles both trial and appeal is unlikely to raise an ineffective-assistance claim against himself. Nevertheless, it adhered to its decision in Billy–Eko v. United States, 8 F.3d 111 (1993). Under *Billy-Eko*, when the defendant is represented by new counsel on appeal and the ineffective assistance claim is based solely on the record made at trial, the claim must be raised on direct appeal; failure to do so results in procedural default unless the petitioner shows cause and prejudice. * * *

We granted certiorari. Petitioner now urges us to hold that claims of ineffective assistance of counsel need not be raised on direct appeal, whether or not there is new counsel and whether or not the basis for the claim is apparent from the trial record. The Federal Courts of Appeals are in conflict on this question, with the Seventh Circuit joining the Second Circuit, see Guinan v. United States, 6 F.3d 468 (CA7 1993), and 10 other Federal Courts of Appeals taking the position that there is no procedural default for failure to raise an ineffective-assistance claim on direct appeal. We agree with the majority of the Courts of Appeals, and we reverse.

The background for our discussion is the general rule that claims not raised on direct appeal may not be raised on collateral review unless the petitioner shows cause and prejudice.

The procedural default rule is neither a statutory nor a constitutional requirement, but it is a doctrine adhered to by the courts to conserve judicial resources and to respect the law's important interest in the finality of judgments. We conclude that requiring a criminal defendant to bring ineffective-assistance-of-counsel claims on direct appeal does not promote these objectives.

As Judge Easterbrook has noted, "rules of procedure should be designed to induce litigants to present their contentions to the right tribunal at the right time." *Guinan, supra,* at 474 (concurring opinion). Applying the usual procedural-default rule to ineffective-assistance claims would have the opposite effect, creating the risk that defendants would feel compelled to raise the issue before there has been an opportunity fully to develop the factual predicate for the claim. Furthermore, the issue would be raised for the first time in a forum not best suited to assess those facts. * * * The better-reasoned approach is to permit ineffective-assistance claims to be brought in the first instance in a timely motion in the district court under § 2255. We hold that an ineffective-assistance-of-counsel claim may be brought in a collateral proceeding under § 2255, whether or not the petitioner could have raised the claim on direct appeal.

* * * When an ineffective-assistance claim is brought on direct appeal, appellate counsel and the court must proceed on a trial record not developed precisely for the object of litigating or preserving the claim and thus often incomplete or inadequate for this purpose. Under Strickland v. Washington [discussed in Chapter 10], a defendant claiming ineffective counsel must show that counsel's actions were not supported by a reasonable strategy and that the error was prejudi-

cial. The evidence introduced at trial, however, will be devoted to issues of guilt or innocence, and the resulting record in many cases will not disclose the facts necessary to decide either prong of the *Strickland* analysis. If the alleged error is one of commission, the record may reflect the action taken by counsel but not the reasons for it. * * * The trial record may contain no evidence of alleged errors of omission, much less the reasons underlying them. And evidence of alleged conflicts of interest might be found only in attorney-client correspondence or other documents that, in the typical criminal trial, are not introduced. Without additional factual development, moreover, an appellate court may not be able to ascertain whether the alleged error was prejudicial.

Under the rule we adopt today, ineffective-assistance claims ordinarily will be litigated in the first instance in the district court, the forum best suited to developing the facts necessary to determining the adequacy of representation during an entire trial. The court may take testimony from witnesses for the defendant and the prosecution and from the counsel alleged to have rendered the deficient performance. In addition, the § 2255 motion often will be ruled upon by the same district judge who presided at trial. The judge, having observed the earlier trial, should have an advantageous perspective for determining the effectiveness of counsel's conduct and whether any deficiencies were prejudicial.

The Second Circuit's rule creates inefficiencies for courts and counsel, both on direct appeal and in the collateral proceeding. On direct appeal it puts counsel into an awkward position vis-a-vis trial counsel. Appellate counsel often need trial counsel's assistance in becoming familiar with a lengthy record on a short deadline, but trial counsel will be unwilling to help appellate counsel familiarize himself with a record for the purpose of understanding how it reflects trial counsel's own incompetence.

Subjecting ineffective-assistance claims to the usual cause-and-prejudice rule also would create perverse incentives for counsel on direct appeal. To ensure that a potential ineffective assistance claim is not waived—and to avoid incurring a claim of ineffective counsel at the appellate stage—counsel would be pressured to bring claims of ineffective trial counsel, regardless of merit.

* * *

On collateral review, the Second Circuit's rule would cause additional inefficiencies. Under that rule a court on collateral review must determine whether appellate counsel is "new." Questions may arise, for example, about whether a defendant has retained new appellate counsel when different lawyers in the same law office handle trial and appeal. The habeas court also must engage in a painstaking review of the trial record solely to determine if it was sufficient to support the ineffectiveness claim and thus whether it should have been brought on direct appeal. A clear rule allowing these claims to be brought in a proceeding under § 2255, by contrast, will eliminate these requirements. Although we could "require the parties and the district judges to search for needles in haystacks—to seek out the

rare claim that could have been raised on direct appeal, and deem it waived," *Guinan*, 6 F.3d at 475 (Easterbrook, J., concurring)—we do not see the wisdom in requiring a court to spend time on exercises that, in most instances, will produce no benefit. It is a better use of judicial resources to allow the district court on collateral review to turn at once to the merits.

* * * We do not hold that ineffective-assistance claims must be reserved for collateral review. There may be cases in which trial counsel's ineffectiveness is so apparent from the record that appellate counsel will consider it advisable to raise the issue on direct appeal. There may be instances, too, when obvious deficiencies in representation will be addressed by an appellate court *sua sponte*. In those cases, certain questions may arise in subsequent proceedings under § 2255 concerning the conclusiveness of determinations made on the ineffective-assistance claims raised on direct appeal; but these matters of implementation are not before us. We do hold that failure to raise an ineffective-assistance-of-counsel claim on direct appeal does not bar the claim from being brought in a later, appropriate proceeding under § 2255.

The judgment of the Court of Appeals is reversed, and the case is remanded for further proceedings consistent with this opinion.

It is so ordered.

c.　The Meaning of "Cause and Prejudice"

An Objection That Could Have Been Brought: Engle v. Isaac

One of the Court's first attempts to explain the "cause" part of the cause and prejudice standard is Engle v. Isaac, 456 U.S. 107 (1982). The Court in *Engle* held that three habeas corpus petitioners, who had failed to comply with an Ohio rule mandating contemporaneous objections to jury instructions, could not collaterally challenge those instructions in federal court. The petitioners contended that Ohio had impermissibly shifted the burden of persuasion on self-defense issues to them, but none had objected at trial to the trial court's instructions. Justice O'Connor observed for the majority that "[c]ollateral review of a conviction extends the ordeal of trial for both society and the accused," that "liberal allowance of the writ * * * degrades the prominence of the trial itself," and that "writs of habeas corpus frequently cost society the right to punish admitted offenders" as a result of "passage of time, erosion of memory and dispersion of witnesses."

Without reaching the question of prejudice, the *Engle* Court found that there was no good cause for the petitioners' failure to object to the instructions in the state trial. The petitioners contended that their failure to raise the claim should be excused because the legal basis for an objection to the instructions was "novel" or unknown to them at the time of their trial. But Justice O'Connor found that the basis of petitioners' constitutional claim (i.e., impermissible burden-shifting) had been apparent since *In re Winship,* decided before the petitioners were tried. (The Court in *Winship* held that due process requires the prosecution to prove every element of the crime beyond a reasonable doubt.) The petitioners argued that the failure to invoke *Winship* had been justifiable, because *Winship* concerned the prosecution's burden to prove the *elements* of the crime, and did not specifically consider whether it was permissible to allocate to the defendant the burdens of proof on affirmative defenses. But Justice O'Connor rejected this argument. She noted that *Winship* had been relied on by some lawyers making similar claims at that time, even before the Supreme Court in Mullaney v. Wilbur (discussed in Chapter Ten) had specifically applied the *Winship* analysis to affirmative defenses. Thus, it could not be said that the petitioners had "lacked the tools to construct" an argument based on *Winship,* and consequently there was no good cause for failing to bring the argument. So long as the claim was "reasonably available" at the time of trial, there was no cause for the petitioners' failure to comply with the state's contemporary objection requirement. Justice O'Connor recognized that not "every astute counsel" would have made a constitutional objection in these circumstances. However, she concluded that the Constitution "does not insure that defense counsel will recognize and raise every constitutional claim."

Finally, Justice O'Connor rejected the petitioners' argument that an objection would have been "futile," because Ohio courts had routinely given the instruction shifting the burden of proving self-defense to the defendant. She stated that "the futility of presenting an objection to the state courts cannot alone constitute cause for a failure to object at trial." Justice O'Connor reasoned that a contemporary objection was required because "a state court that has previously rejected a constitutional argument may decide, upon reflection, that the contention is valid." Thus, the question for determining cause is not whether an objection would be "futile" but rather whether the objection was "reasonably available."[23]

Failure to Bring a Novel Claim as Cause: Reed v. Ross

The Court examined the concept of "cause" again in Reed v. Ross, 468 U.S. 1 (1984). Ross was convicted of first-degree murder in 1969, prior to the

---

23. Justice Blackmun concurred in the result without opinion, and Justice Stevens concurred in part and dissented in part in a brief opinion. Justice Brennan, joined by Justice Marshall, dissented.

Supreme Court's holding in *Winship* that the Due Process Clause requires the state to prove beyond a reasonable doubt all of the elements necessary to constitute the crime with which a defendant is charged. (Thus, the case differed from *Engle*, where *Winship* had already been decided at the time of the state trial). Jury instructions had imposed upon Ross the burden of showing that he lacked malice and that he acted in self-defense. Ross did not contemporaneously object to the instructions, since state law did not require an objection. His appeal did not challenge the instructions either, and it was his failure to raise any objection on direct appeal that led the state courts to rule that he could not pursue a challenge to his convictions on collateral attack. Ross then sought federal habeas corpus relief.

The Supreme Court held, 5–4, in an opinion by Justice Brennan, that Ross had established cause for his failure to challenge the instructions on appeal. Since the state conceded that Ross had been prejudiced by the claimed violation, the Court concluded that the state procedural bar was lifted.

On the question of cause, Justice Brennan stated that "[c]ounsel's failure to raise a claim for which there was no reasonable basis in existing law does not seriously implicate any of the concerns that might otherwise require deference to a State's procedural bar" and that "if we were to hold that the novelty of a constitutional question does not give rise to cause for counsel's failure to raise it, we might actually disrupt state-court proceedings by encouraging defense counsel to include any and all remotely plausible constitutional claims that could, some day, gain recognition." The Court held, therefore, "that where a constitutional claim is so novel that its legal basis is not reasonably available to counsel, a defendant has cause for his failure to raise the claim in accordance with applicable state procedures." He concluded as follows:

> Whether an attorney had a reasonable basis for pressing a claim challenging a practice that this Court has arguably sanctioned depends on how direct this Court's sanction of the prevailing practice had been, how well entrenched the practice was in the relevant jurisdiction at the time of defense counsel's failure to challenge it, and how strong the available support is from sources opposing the prevailing practice.

Applying those standards to Ross' case, the Court looked to the law as it existed prior to *Winship* and found only scant, indirect support for the challenge that Ross mounted in his habeas corpus petition. So while Ross' claim of error was similar to that of the petitioners in *Engle*, those petitioners had the benefit of *Winship* in constructing their arguments at trial, while Ross did not. Therefore, Ross had cause for his procedural fault while the petitioners in *Engle* did not.

Justice Rehnquist dissented, joined by the Chief Justice and Justices Blackmun and O'Connor. He reasoned as follows:

> [T]his equating of novelty with cause pushes the Court into a conundrum which it refuses to recognize. The more "novel" a claimed constitutional right, the more unlikely a violation of that claimed right undercut the fundamental fairness of the trial.

Limited View of "Novel" Claims: Bousley v. United States

The Court in Bousley v. United States, 523 U.S. 614 (1998), considered the problem of a habeas petitioner who had pleaded guilty to a criminal statute that was later held not to cover his conduct. Bousley pleaded guilty to drug crimes, as well as to a violation of a federal statute that prohibited "using" a firearm during the course of a drug transaction. At the time he pleaded guilty to the firearms offense, the local federal courts had construed "using" expansively, to cover basically any situation in which a defendant possessed a gun during the course of a drug offense. Bousley appealed his sentence, but did not challenge his guilty plea on direct appeal. His sentence was affirmed. Thereafter, the Supreme Court determined that the term "using" in the firearms statute meant some kind of active use, such as brandishing or, of course, shooting. Bousley sought a writ of habeas corpus challenging the factual basis for his guilty plea on the firearms charge, on the ground that neither the "evidence" nor the "plea allocution" showed a "connection between the firearms in the bedroom of the house, and the garage, where the drug trafficking occurred."

The Supreme Court, in an opinion by Chief Justice Rehnquist for six Justices, held that Bousley would be entitled to a hearing on the merits of his involuntary guilty plea claim, *if* he could make the showing necessary to relieve the procedural default resulting from his failure to appeal his guilty plea. The Court noted, however, that the procedural default presented a substantial hurdle to Bousley's claim. The Chief Justice specifically rejected Bousley's claim that he had "cause" for his procedural default because his claim was "novel":

> Petitioner offers two explanations for his default in an attempt to demonstrate cause. First, he argues that "the legal basis for his claim was not reasonably available to counsel" at the time his plea was entered. This argument is without merit. While we have held that a claim that "is so novel that its legal basis is not reasonably available to counsel" may constitute cause for a procedural default, Reed v. Ross, petitioner's claim does not qualify as such. The argument that it was error for the District Court to misinform petitioner as to the statutory elements of [the firearms statute] was most surely not a novel one. Indeed, at the time of petitioner's plea, the Federal Reporters were replete with cases involving challenges to the notion that "use" is synonymous with mere "possession." Petitioner also contends that his default should be excused because, "before *Bailey* [the Supreme Court decision construing the firearms statute in Bousley's favor], any attempt to attack [his] guilty plea would have been futile." This argument too is unavailing. As we clearly stated in Engle v. Isaac, "futility cannot constitute cause if it means simply that a claim was 'unacceptable to that particular court at that particular time.'" Therefore, petitioner is unable to establish cause for his default.

The Court remanded for a determination of whether Bousley could establish actual innocence, thereby justifying relief from his procedural default. On the actual innocence question in *Bousley,* see the discussion *infra.* Justice Stevens and Justice Scalia (joined by Justice Thomas) wrote separate opinions in *Bousley.* Neither of the separate opinions disagreed with the Chief Justice's conclusion that Bousley had failed to establish "cause" for his procedural default.

The Reed–Engle/AEDPA Whipsaw

Reed v. Ross holds that if a development in the law could not have been reasonably anticipated by the petitioner, then there is cause for not invoking the rule in the state proceedings. But can the petitioner then rely on the rule in habeas proceedings to show a violation of the Constitution? Recall the discussion of nonretroactivity of new rules on habeas, and particularly Teague v. Lane, in Chapter One. Under *Teague,* new rules are generally inapplicable to habeas cases. A new rule is defined as any rule as to which reasonable minds could have differed before it was adopted, i.e., a rule that was not dictated by existing precedent. That standard has now been codified in the AEDPA, which essentially prohibits federal courts from finding constitutional error if the state courts reasonably construed then-existing federal law as determined by the Supreme Court. How can the petitioner establish cause on grounds of "novelty" and yet argue that the state court decision was completely unreasonable because it failed to consider an admittedly novel federal law? The "whipsaw" effect of *Ross* and the *Teague* principle is described by Professor Arkin in The Prisoner's Dilemma: Life in the Lower Federal Courts After Teague v. Lane, 69 No.Car.L.Rev. 371, 408 (1991):

> [I]f a petitioner is able to show that his claim is based on a "new" rule of law, the habeas court will excuse his state procedural default, assuming petitioner can show actual prejudice. But, having shown that the rule under which he seeks relief was not available to him at the time he should have raised it in the state courts, the petitioner may well have won the battle under *Wainwright* [v. Sykes] only to lose the war to *Teague.* Under most circumstances, the petitioner will have just shown that the very rule under which he seeks relief is not retroactive * * *.

While this is a pre-AEDPA analysis, the same result occurs under the AEDPA's requirement of deference to state court applications of federal law. See also Hopkinson v. Shillinger, 888 F.2d 1286 (10th Cir.1989)("a holding that a claim is so novel that there is no reasonably available basis for it, thus establishing cause, must also mean that the claim was too novel to be dictated by past precedent"); Selvage v. Collins, 975 F.2d 131 (5th Cir.1992)("This interaction of *Teague* and the cause standard supplied by *Engle* and *Reed* leads to a result that is as ineluctable as it is potent: claims not finally resolved at trial and on appeal are almost always gone forever.").

Unavailability of Facts: Amadeo v. Zant

The *Ross* "reasonable availability" definition of cause can still have utility where the failure to assert a claim is due to a lack of *facts* that were not reasonably available to the defendant at the time of the state proceedings. A unanimous Supreme Court held in Amadeo v. Zant, 486 U.S. 214 (1988), that a state defendant who was convicted of murder and sentenced to death showed cause for a late challenge to the racial composition of the grand jury by demonstrating that local officials had concealed a handwritten memorandum from the District Attorney to jury commissioners, which indicated that under-representation of black members of the grand jury was intentional. The memorandum was discovered by a lawyer for the plaintiffs in a civil suit challenging voting procedures and was the basis for a federal district court's finding of intentional discrimination. The defendant's lawyer relied upon the finding on the defendant's direct appeal, but the state supreme court found that the challenge to the grand jury's composition came too late under state procedures.

The defendant obtained habeas corpus relief from a federal district judge, only to have a divided appellate panel reverse.

Justice Marshall wrote for the Court as it held that the federal district court's findings that there had been discrimination in the selection of the grand jury and that the defendant had raised the discrimination claim as soon as the memorandum surfaced were not clearly erroneous. In articulating the meaning of "cause," the Court cited *Ross* and reasoned as follows:

> If the District Attorney's memorandum was not reasonably discoverable because it was concealed by Putnam County officials, and if that concealment, rather than tactical considerations, was the reason for the failure of petitioner's lawyers to raise the jury challenge in the trial court, then petitioner established cause to excuse his procedural default under this Court's precedents.

Attorney Error Is Not Cause Unless It Constitutes Ineffective Assistance: Murray v. Carrier and Smith v. Murray

In Murray v. Carrier, 477 U.S. 478 (1986), Justice O'Connor wrote for the Court as it held that a federal habeas petitioner cannot show cause for a procedural default by establishing that competent defense counsel's failure to raise a substantive claim of error was inadvertent rather than deliberate. In a rape and abduction case, the defendant's trial counsel had twice unsuccessfully requested an opportunity to review the victim's statements. Counsel failed to attack the trial judge's rulings in his petition for appeal, thus defaulting on a state court rule limiting judicial consideration on appeal to errors raised in the petition. The Court held that this failure barred federal habeas corpus review even if it resulted from ignorance or inadvertence. It declined to distinguish failures to raise a claim on appeal from failures to raise them at trial. Justice O'Connor wrote that "we discern no inequity in requiring [the defendant] to bear the risk of attorney error that results in a procedural default" by "counsel whose performance is not constitutionally ineffective." To establish cause for a procedural default, a prisoner must ordinarily "show that some objective factor external to the defense impeded counsel's efforts to comply with the State's procedural rule." Justice O'Connor elaborated as follows:

> Without attempting an exhaustive catalog * * *, we note that a showing that the factual or legal claim was not reasonably available to counsel * * *, or that some interference by officials * * * made compliance impracticable, would constitute cause under this standard.

> Similarly, if the procedural default is the result of ineffective assistance of counsel, the Sixth Amendment itself requires that responsibility for the default be imputed to the State [and it is therefore] cause for a procedural default.

Justice O'Connor further declared that claims of ineffective assistance should ordinarily be brought in the first instance in a state collateral proceeding—consistent with the exhaustion requirement, the state should have the first opportunity to rectify any error.

Justice Stevens, joined by Justice Blackmun, concurred in the judgment. He argued that the cause and prejudice formula "is not dispositive when the fundamental fairness of a prisoner's conviction is at issue" and advocated an "overall inquiry into justice." Justice O'Connor responded that the Stevens approach would actually replace the cause requirement with a manifest injustice standard. She observed that the relationship of this standard to prejudice was uncertain. But in recognition of the fact that the cause and prejudice standard might produce a miscarriage of justice in some cases, Justice O'Connor stated that "in an extraordinary case, where a constitutional violation has probably resulted in the conviction of one who is actually innocent, a federal habeas corpus court may grant the writ even in the absence of a showing of cause for the procedural default." Thus, the Court remanded for an inquiry into whether the victim's statements contained material that would establish the defendant's innocence.

Justice Brennan, joined by Justice Marshall, dissented and argued that the cause and prejudice limitation, a judicial form of abstention not required by the language of the habeas corpus statute, should permit federal consideration of claims not raised because of inadvertence or ignorance.

Decided with Murray v. Carrier was Smith v. Murray, 477 U.S. 527 (1986), a capital case. Once again Justice O'Connor found no cause for a procedural default. A psychiatrist who examined Smith was called to testify by the state at the sentencing phase of the trial. He described, over Smith's objection, an incident that Smith had related to him. On appeal, Smith's counsel did not claim error in the use of the testimony, and so the claim was procedurally defaulted. In his habeas corpus petition, Smith claimed that the use of the statements violated his constitutional rights under the Fifth and Sixth Amendments. Justice O'Connor found that a deliberate decision had been made not to put the claim before the state supreme court and that, even if the decision was made out of ignorance of the claim's strength, this was not sufficient to demonstrate cause. She also concluded that the application of the cause and prejudice standard would not result in a fundamental miscarriage of justice, because "the alleged constitutional error neither precluded the development of true facts nor resulted in the admission of false ones." Justice Stevens dissented, joined in full by Justices Marshall and Blackmun, and in part by Justice Brennan. He disagreed with the idea that only a claim implicating "actual innocence" could rise to the level of a miscarriage of justice, and argued that accuracy is not the only value protected by the Constitution.[24]

Default in Making a Timely Claim of Ineffective Assistance: Edwards v. Carpenter

Suppose a state defendant fails to bring a claim on direct appeal. That claim is procedurally defaulted unless the defendant can establish "cause and prejudice". Suppose the reason for failing to bring the claim on direct appeal is that appellate counsel was constitutionally ineffective. Under *Carrier*, this is enough to establish "cause." But suppose the state also has a procedural rule that all

---

24. Seidman, Factual Guilt and the Burger Court: An Examination of Continuity and Change in Criminal Procedure, 80 Colum.L.Rev. 436, 469 (1980), argues that the *Carrier* Court's "reluctance to look behind the presumption [of lawyer client identity] and its willingness to enforce procedural forfeitures undermine the reliability of our declarations of criminal responsibility in two ways: they mean that factually innocent defendants will nonetheless be punished because of procedural defaults, and they mean that defendants not even responsible for the procedural defaults will be punished because of the misconduct of their attorney."

claims of ineffective assistance must be brought within a certain time period, and the defendant fails to make a timely claim. At that point he has run into another procedural bar in his attempt to establish "cause" for his failure to comply with the first procedural bar. What happens then? Must the defendant establish "cause and prejudice" for his failure to meet the state time period? Must he prove, for instance, that his counsel was constitutionally ineffective for failing to comply with the state time period that mandates a timely complaint about an ineffective counsel?

These were the complicated questions addressed by the Court in Edwards v. Carpenter, 529 U.S. 446 (2000). Justice Scalia, writing for the Court, held that "an ineffective-assistance-of-counsel claim asserted as cause for the procedural default of another claim can itself be procedurally defaulted." Therefore, the petitioner was required to establish cause and prejudice for his failure to comply with the state procedural rule requiring ineffective assistance of counsel claims within a certain time period. Justice Scalia reasoned that this result is required by *Carrier's* holding that ineffective assistance of counsel claims must be exhausted at the state level before they can be heard by a federal habeas court. With the exhaustion requirement comes the need for the petitioner to comply with state procedural bars. Thus, the procedural default rule and the exhaustion requirement work together to assure respect for state interests. Justice Scalia explained the interrelationship as follows:

> The purposes of the exhaustion requirement * * * would be utterly defeated if the prisoner were able to obtain federal habeas review simply by "letting the time run" so that state remedies were no longer available. Those purposes would be no less frustrated were we to allow federal review to a prisoner who had presented his claim to the state court, but in such a manner that the state court could not, consistent with its own procedural rules, have entertained it. In such circumstances, though the prisoner would have concededly exhausted his state remedies, it could hardly be said that, as comity and federalism require, the State had been given a fair opportunity to pass upon his claims.

The Court remanded for a determination of whether counsel was ineffective for failing to file a timely claim of ineffective assistance of counsel.

Justice Breyer, joined by Justice Stevens, concurred in the judgment. He agreed that the case had to be remanded, but argued that the only determination necessary was whether the initial counsel was ineffective in failing to bring a claim on direct appeal. He argued that the majority was adding needless complexity to an already complex area of the law. He elaborated as follows:

> The added complexity resulting from the Court's opinion is obvious. Consider a prisoner who wants to assert a federal constitutional claim (call it FCC). Suppose the State asserts as a claimed "adequate and independent state ground" the prisoner's failure to raise the matter on his first state-court appeal. Suppose further that the prisoner replies by alleging that he had "cause" for not raising the matter on appeal (call it C). After *Carrier*, if that alleged "cause" (C) consists of the claim "my attorney was constitutionally ineffective," the prisoner must have exhausted C in the state courts first. And after today, if he did not follow state rules for presenting C to the state courts, he will have lost his basic claim, FCC, forever. But, I overstate. According to the opinion of the Court, he will not necessarily have lost FCC

forever if he had "cause" for not having followed those state rules (i.e., the rules for determining the existence of "cause" for not having followed the state rules governing the basic claim, FCC) (call this "cause" C*). The prisoner could therefore still obtain relief if he could demonstrate the merits of C*, C, and FCC.

I concede that this system of rules has a certain logic, indeed an attractive power for those who like difficult puzzles. But I believe it must succumb to this question: Why should a prisoner, who may well be proceeding pro se, lose his basic claim because he runs afoul of state procedural rules governing the presentation to state courts of the "cause" for his not having followed state procedural rules for the presentation of his basic federal claim? And, in particular, why should that special default rule apply when the "cause" at issue is an "ineffective-assistance-of-counsel" claim, but not when it is any of the many other "causes" or circumstances that might excuse a failure to comply with state rules? I can find no satisfactory answer to these questions.

Ineffectiveness of Counsel Where There Is No Constitutional Right to Counsel: Coleman v. Thompson

Carrier held that constitutionally ineffective assistance of counsel would establish the "cause" requirement that is part of the showing necessary to excuse a procedural default. In Coleman v. Thompson, 501 U.S. 722 (1991), Coleman had been convicted of capital murder; his direct appeals had been unsuccessful; he brought a petition in state court for relief under the *state* habeas corpus provisions; this petition was denied, and Coleman's counsel failed to file a notice of appeal from the denial. The failure to file the notice of appeal imposed a procedural bar to further relief. Coleman argued that his counsel's failure constituted ineffective assistance, therefore that the procedural bar was lifted after Murray v. Carrier. Justice O'Connor, writing for the Court, rejected this argument. She relied on the line of right to counsel cases (discussed in Chapters Five and Ten), which hold that the defendant has no constitutional right to appointed counsel beyond the first appeal of right. She reasoned that because Coleman had no constitutional right to counsel in the state habeas proceedings, there could be no claim of constitutionally ineffective counsel. She concluded that "Coleman must bear the risk of attorney error that results in a procedural default."

Justice O'Connor also rejected the argument that cause to excuse a procedural default should be found whenever counsel was so ineffective as to violate the standards of Strickland v. Washington (discussed in Chapter Ten), even though no Sixth Amendment claim is possible because the ineffectiveness did not occur at a stage of the proceedings in which there is a constitutional right to counsel. She stated that this argument "is inconsistent not only with the language of *Carrier,* but the logic of that opinion as well." She reasoned that "cause" must be something "external to the petitioner, something that cannot be fairly attributed to him." She asserted that the only type of attorney error for which the State must take responsibility independent of the petitioner is where the Sixth Amendment has been violated, i.e., where ineffectiveness occurs before or during the trial or in the first appeal. She explained as follows:

Where a petitioner defaults a claim as a result of the denial of the right to effective assistance of counsel, the State, which is responsible for the denial as a constitutional matter, must bear the cost of any resulting default and the harm to state interests that federal habeas review entails. A different allocation of costs is appropriate in those circumstances where the State has no responsibility to ensure that the petitioner was represented by competent counsel. As between the State and the petitioner, it is the petitioner who must bear the burden of a failure to follow state procedural rules.

Justice Blackmun, joined by Justices Marshall and Stevens in dissent, attacked the majority's holding as "patently unfair." He argued that to permit a procedural default to preclude habeas review, when it was caused by attorney error egregious enough to constitute ineffective assistance of counsel, "in no way serves the State's interest in preserving the integrity of its rules and proceedings."

Cause and Prejudice in the Context of a Brady Violation: Strickler v. Greene

The Court considered how the cause and prejudice standards apply to *Brady* violations in Strickler v. Greene, 527 U.S. 263 (1999). One of the major prosecution witnesses in Strickler's capital murder trial had made several statements to police that were flatly inconsistent with her very evocative trial testimony. The prosecutor had an open file policy, but despite this, the witness' statements were not turned over to the defense. Defense counsel, in light of the open file policy, made no pretrial request for *Brady* material. Nor did defense counsel pursue a *Brady* claim at trial or on state appellate and collateral review—this was understandable, however, because defense counsel had no reason to think that any exculpatory information had been suppressed.

Strickler conceded that he had procedurally defaulted the *Brady* claim; but he argued that the very suppression of the witness' statements constituted cause. As to prejudice, he argued that in order for information to be "material" under *Brady*, it has to be information strong enough to undermine confidence in the outcome of the trial. (See Chapter Eight, supra, for a full discussion of this standard). So if suppression of information violates *Brady*, it should by definition satisfy the standard for "prejudice" under the procedural default doctrine.

Justice Stevens, writing for the Court, agreed in principle with Strickler that the factors supporting the finding of a *Brady* violation could also be the factors that would lead to a finding of cause. He focused on three factors in the case at bar:

> The documents were suppressed by the Commonwealth; the prosecutor maintained an open file policy; and trial counsel were not aware of the factual basis for the claim. The first and second factors—i.e., the non-disclosure and the open file policy—are both fairly characterized as conduct attributable to the State that impeded trial counsel's access to the factual basis for making a *Brady* claim. As we explained in Murray v. Carrier it is just such factors that ordinarily establish the existence of cause for a procedural default.

Justice Stevens found it unnecessary to decide, however, whether "cause" for a procedural default would be found if the prosecutor did not maintain an open file policy, and the defendant failed to make a *Brady* request before trial, or a *Brady* claim on state court appeal.

On the question of prejudice, Justice Stevens agreed with Strickler that suppressing information important enough to rise to the level of *Brady* material would by definition satisfy the standard for prejudice under the procedural default doctrine. On the merits, however, the Court found that the suppression of the witness' statements did not constitute a *Brady* violation. Justice Stevens found that Strickler could not show that there was "a reasonable probability that his conviction or sentence would have been different had these materials been disclosed. He therefore cannot show materiality under *Brady* or prejudice from his failure to raise the claim earlier."

d. The Actual Innocence Exception

The Court in *Smith* and *Carrier* acknowledged that a procedural default could be lifted even in the absence of cause and prejudice, if the petitioner can show "actual innocence". This exception to the cause and prejudice requirement was described by the court in Johnson v. Singletary, 940 F.2d 1540 (11th Cir.1991)(en banc):

> [A]lthough factual inaccuracy in the guilt or sentencing context may well be *necessary* to a claim of actual innocence, factual inaccuracy is not *sufficient* unless the inaccuracy demonstrates, at least colorably, that the petitioner is * * * ineligible for either an adjudication of guilt or the sentence imposed. If prejudicial factual inaccuracy alone is enough to warrant review of a defaulted claim, then the actual innocence standard is meaningless.

Actual Innocence and the Death Penalty: Sawyer v. Whitley

In Sawyer v. Whitley, 505 U.S. 333 (1992), the Court applied the "actual innocence" exception to the cause and prejudice requirement in the context of a challenge to the death penalty. Chief Justice Rehnquist, writing for the Court, stated that in a habeas challenge to a death penalty, the petitioner will establish "actual innocence" only if he shows "by clear and convincing evidence that but for a constitutional error, no reasonable juror would have found the petitioner eligible for the death penalty under the applicable state law."

Sawyer and his accomplice Lane brutally murdered a woman; they beat her, scalded her with water, poured lighter fluid on her, and ignited the fluid. The victim died of her injuries two months later. At the sentencing phase, Sawyer's sister testified to Sawyer's mistreatment as a child. The jury found aggravating factors—that Sawyer was engaged in aggravated arson and that the murder was committed in an especially atrocious manner. It found no mitigating factors and sentenced Sawyer to death.

Sawyer brought two claims on habeas, both of which were procedurally barred, and neither of which satisfied the cause and prejudice requirement. One claim, a *Brady* claim, concerned exculpatory evidence relating to Sawyer's role in the offense, including evidence impeaching the credibility of a star prosecution witness, and an affidavit claiming that a child who witnessed the event had stated that Sawyer's accomplice had poured lighter fluid on the victim and ignited it, and that Sawyer had tried to stop him. The second claim was that Sawyer's trial lawyer had erred in failing to introduce at the sentencing phase the medical records from Sawyer's stays as a teenager in two mental hospitals.

The Chief Justice determined that there were three possible ways in which "actual innocence" might be defined in the death penalty context. The "strictest definition" would be to require the petitioner to show that the constitutional error negated an essential element of the capital offense of which he was convicted. The Chief Justice rejected this definition because the Court in Smith v. Murray had "suggested a more expansive meaning to the term of actual innocence in a capital case than simply innocence of the capital offense itself."

The "most lenient of the three possibilities" would be to allow the showing of actual innocence to extend to three factors: 1) the elements of the crime; 2) the existence of all aggravating factors; and 3) mitigating evidence "which bore, not on the defendant's eligibility to receive the death penalty, but only on the ultimate discretionary decision between the death penalty and life imprisonment." Put another way, "actual innocence" would be found under this view if the sentencer was presented with "a factually inaccurate sentencing profile." The Chief Justice rejected this definition, however, as too permissive. He reasoned that under this test, "actual innocence amounts to little more than what is already required to show prejudice." According to the Chief Justice, "if a showing of actual innocence were reduced to actual prejudice, it would allow the evasion of the cause and prejudice standard which we have held also acts as an exception to a defaulted, abusive or successive claim. In practical terms a petitioner would no longer have to show cause, contrary to our prior cases."

The majority therefore opted for a middle ground, and defined "innocent of the death penalty" as allowing a showing not only pertaining to innocence of the capital crime itself, but also permitting "a showing that there was no aggravating circumstance or that some other condition of eligibility had not been met." The Court noted that this test "hones in on the objective factors or conditions which must be shown to exist before a defendant is eligible to have the death penalty imposed." The Chief Justice concluded as follows:

> [T]he "actual innocence" requirement must focus on those elements which render a defendant eligible for the death penalty, and not on additional mitigating evidence which was prevented from being introduced as a result of claimed constitutional error.

Applying this test to Sawyer's claims, Chief Justice Rehnquist found that the medical records that Sawyer's attorney failed to introduce were not pertinent to actual innocence, as they were in the nature of mitigating evidence and so did not affect his death-eligibility. The fact that Sawyer had spent time in mental hospitals as a teenager was not relevant to an aggravating factor nor to an element of the crime.

As to the *Brady* material, the affidavit relating the statement of the child-eyewitness, to the effect that Sawyer had tried to stop the burning of the victim, was pertinent both to the crime and to the aggravating factor of arson. The Court concluded, however, that the affidavit, "in view of all the other evidence in the record, does not show that no rational juror would find that petitioner committed both of the aggravating circumstances found by the jury." The Court noted that the murder was atrocious and cruel "based on the undisputed evidence of torture before the jury quite apart from the arson" and that at any rate a reasonable juror could have discredited the affidavit in light of the other evidence. Thus, Sawyer had not established clear and convincing proof of his ineligibility for the death penalty.

Justice Stevens, joined by Justices Blackmun and O'Connor, concurred in the judgment. While agreeing that Sawyer had failed to establish "actual innocence," Justice Stevens took issue with the majority's definition of that standard. He argued that the majority's clear and convincing evidence standard imposed too severe a burden on the capital defendant. Justice Stevens found "no basis for requiring a federal court to be virtually certain that the defendant is actually ineligible for the death penalty, before merely entertaining his claim."

Justice Blackmun wrote a separate opinion concurring in the judgment. He launched a broad attack on the Court's habeas corpus jurisprudence. He criticized the "actual innocence" exception as assuming erroneously "that the only value worth protecting through federal habeas review is the accuracy and reliability of the guilt determination." He elaborated as follows:

> The accusatorial system of justice adopted by the Founders affords a defendant certain process-based protections that do not have accuracy of truth-finding as their primary goal. These protections * * * are debased, and indeed, rendered largely irrelevant, in a system that values the accuracy of the guilt determination above individual rights. Nowhere is this single-minded focus on actual innocence more misguided than in a case where a defendant alleges a constitutional error in the sentencing phase of a capital trial. * * *

Actual Innocence of the Crime Itself: Schlup v. Delo

The Court distinguished *Sawyer,* and applied a more permissive standard to claims of actual innocence of the crime itself (as opposed to the death penalty), in Schlup v. Delo, 513 U.S. 298 (1995). Schlup was subject to the cause and prejudice requirements, which would have barred his *Brady* and *Strickland* claims. He argued, however, that the bar should be lifted because he had discovered new evidence that established his innocence of the crime. The lower courts held that Schlup's new evidence did not provide "clear and convincing" proof of his innocence as required by *Sawyer.* But the Supreme Court, in an opinion by Justice Stevens for a five-person majority, held that *Sawyer* was limited to challenges to the petitioner's sentence, and that "actual innocence" claims must be treated more permissively when the petitioner's challenge is to the conviction itself.

Justice Stevens explained the need to provide a more permissive standard of proof to claims of innocence of the crime:

> Claims of actual innocence pose less of a threat to scarce judicial resources and to principles of finality and comity than do claims that focus solely on the erroneous imposition of the death penalty. Though challenges to the propriety of imposing a sentence of death are routinely asserted in capital cases, experience has taught us that a substantial claim that constitutional error has caused the conviction of an innocent person is extremely rare. To be credible, such a claim requires petitioner to support his allegations of constitutional error with new reliable evidence—whether it be

exculpatory scientific evidence, trustworthy eyewitness accounts, or critical physical evidence—that was not presented at trial. Because such evidence is obviously unavailable in the vast majority of cases, claims of actual innocence are rarely successful. * * *

Of greater importance, the individual interest in avoiding injustice is most compelling in the context of actual innocence. The quintessential miscarriage of justice is the execution of a person who is entirely innocent. * * *

The overriding importance of this greater individual interest merits protection by imposing a somewhat less exacting standard of proof on a habeas petitioner alleging a fundamental miscarriage of justice than on one alleging that his sentence is too severe. * * * Though the *Sawyer* standard was fashioned to reflect the relative importance of a claim of an erroneous sentence, application of that standard to petitioners such as Schlup would give insufficient weight to the correspondingly greater injustice that is implicated by a claim of actual innocence.

Justice Stevens concluded that in order to lift a procedural bar relating to a conviction as opposed to a sentence, in the absence of cause and prejudice, "the petitioner must show that it is more likely than not that no reasonable juror would have convicted him in the light of the new evidence." He noted that a habeas petitioner "is thus required to make a stronger showing than that needed to establish prejudice" but that, at the same time, the showing of "more likely than not" imposes a lower burden of proof than the "clear and convincing" standard required under *Sawyer*. The Court remanded for a determination of whether Schlup's new evidence met the more permissive standard.

Chief Justice Rehnquist wrote a dissenting opinion joined by Justices Kennedy and Thomas. The Chief Justice complained that the Court had added to the complexity of habeas corpus jurisprudence by creating two standards of proof for "actual innocence"—one for attacks on a conviction and one for attacks on a sentence. Justice Scalia wrote a separate dissent joined by Justice Thomas.

Actual Innocence and Invalid Guilty Pleas: Bousley v. United States

The Court in Bousley v. United States, 523 U.S. 614 (1998), considered whether the actual innocence exception could apply to a procedurally defaulted attack on the validity of a guilty plea. Bousley pleaded guilty to drug crimes, as well as to a violation of a federal statute that prohibited "using" a firearm during the course of a drug transaction. At the time he pleaded guilty to the firearms offense, the local federal courts had construed "using" expansively, to cover basically any situation in which a defendant possessed a gun during the course of a drug offense. Bousley appealed his sentence, but did not challenge his guilty plea on direct appeal. His sentence was affirmed. Thereafter, the Supreme Court determined that the term "using" in the statute meant some kind of active use, such as brandishing or, of course, shooting. Bousley sought a writ of habeas corpus challenging the factual basis for his guilty plea to the firearms charge, on the ground that neither the "evidence" nor the "plea allocution" showed a "connection between the firearms in the bedroom of the house, and the garage, where the drug trafficking occurred."

The Supreme Court, in an opinion by Chief Justice Rehnquist for six Justices, held that Bousley would be entitled to a hearing on the merits of his involuntary guilty plea claim, if he could make the showing necessary to relieve the procedural default resulting from his failure to appeal his guilty plea. While he could not establish "cause" and "prejudice" under the circumstances (see the discussion of this part of the opinion in this Chapter, supra), the Court held that Bousley would be entitled to relief if he could establish his actual innocence of the gun charge. However, the Court noted that the question of actual innocence was somewhat different in the context of an attack on a guilty plea. The Chief Justice elaborated:

> It is important to note in this regard that "actual innocence" means factual innocence, not mere legal insufficiency. See Sawyer v. Whitley. In other words, the Government is not limited to the existing record to rebut any showing that petitioner might make. Rather, on remand, the Government should be permitted to present any admissible evidence of petitioner's guilt even if that evidence was not presented during petitioner's plea colloquy and would not normally have been offered before our decision in *Bailey* [the Supreme Court decision construing the firearms statute in Bousley's favor]. In cases where the Government has forgone more serious charges in the course of plea bargaining, petitioner's showing of actual innocence must also extend to those charges.

The Chief Justice rejected the argument made by Justice Scalia, in dissent, that the actual innocence inquiry will be unduly complicated by the absence of a trial transcript in the guilty plea context. He found this concern "overstated," because in federal courts, where this case arose, "guilty pleas must be accompanied by proffers, recorded verbatim on the record, demonstrating a factual basis for the plea."

Justice Stevens wrote a separate opinion dissenting from the majority's application of the actual innocence standard. He argued that it was unnecessary for Bousley to establish actual innocence, since in light of the Supreme Court's subsequent construction of the firearms statute, he had never been found guilty of any criminal conduct. This in itself was enough to require that his guilty plea be vacated.

Justice Scalia, joined by Justice Thomas, dissented. He argued that actual innocence could not excuse a procedural default in the context of a guilty plea, because it would be impossible to determine on the record whether the habeas petitioner was in fact actually innocent. He asked: "How is the court to determine 'actual innocence' upon our remand in the present case, where conviction was based upon an admission of guilt? Presumably the defendant will introduce evidence (perhaps nothing more than his own testimony) showing that he did not 'use' a firearm in committing the crime to which he pleaded guilty, and the Government, eight years after the fact, will have to find and produce witnesses saying that he did. This seems to me not to remedy a miscarriage of justice, but to produce one."

Cause and Prejudice, Actual Innocence, and the AEDPA in Capital Cases

It must be noted that the AEDPA contains provisions that could potentially be employed to impose even stricter limitations on habeas relief for capital defendants who have procedurally defaulted their claims. Recall that the AEDPA has special provisions restricting the habeas corpus remedy for state death row inmates; however, these provisions do not come into play until the state has demonstrated that it has a system for appointing counsel in death penalty cases and regulating their competence. So far, it appears that no state has qualified. But if a state does qualify, then the state gets two major advantages in dealing with procedurally defaulted claims.

1) For capital defendants in qualifying states, the actual innocence exception to the cause and prejudice requirements, set forth in Sawyer v. Whitley and Schlup v. Delo, has been abrogated. The capital defendant in such a state must establish cause for procedural default, and prejudice, without exception.

2) The acceptable excuses constituting "cause" have been limited to three. The petitioner's failure to satisfy a procedural bar will only be excused: a) if the failure was caused by unconstitutional state action; b) if the petitioner can rely on retroactive application of a new rule (which, as the Court held in Teague v. Lane, is essentially never the case); or 3) if the failure to satisfy the procedural bar was based on a factual predicate that could not have been discovered at the time of the default (as with the suppressed information in Amedeo v. Zant, supra).

The above limitations on the cause-prejudice-actual innocence standards apply only to capital defendants in qualifying states.

4. Adequate and Independent State Grounds

A federal court is precluded from considering a habeas petition from a state prisoner if the state decision rests on an adequate and independent state ground, such as a state procedural bar. Where the state decision rests on a state law ground there is no federal issue to decide in a habeas corpus petition. The Supreme Court has stated that "in the habeas context, the application of the independent and adequate state ground doctrine is grounded in concerns of comity and federalism" and that without this doctrine "habeas petitioners would be able to avoid the exhaustion requirement by defaulting their federal claims in state court." Coleman v. Thompson, 501 U.S. 722 (1991).

The Court has recognized that it is often difficult to determine whether a state court has in fact relied on an adequate and independent state ground that would preclude review of any constitutional claim. In another context—to determine whether a state court rested on state or federal grounds when it held that a defendant's constitutional rights have been violated—the Court established the following conclusive presumption:

> When a state court decision fairly appears to rest primarily on federal law, or to be interwoven with federal law, and when the adequacy and independence of any possible state law ground is not clear from the face of the opinion, we will accept as the most reasonable explanation that the state

court decided the case the way it did because it believed that federal law required it to do so.

Michigan v. Long, 463 U.S. 1032, 1041–42 (1983).

In Harris v. Reed, 489 U.S. 255 (1989), the Court applied the *Long* presumption to determine whether a state court's decision rested on adequate and independent state grounds so as to preclude federal habeas review. The Court reasoned that because it was "faced with a common problem" as it found in *Long*, it would "adopt a common solution." Thus, *Harris* establishes a presumption that the state decision does not rest on an independent state ground. The state court must explicitly rely on a state ground to overcome this presumption—this is known as the "plain statement" rule.

Adequate State Ground Without an Explicit Statement: Coleman v. Thompson

The question in Coleman v. Thompson, 501 U.S. 722 (1991), was whether an adequate and independent state ground could be found in a state appellate court's summary order of dismissal. Coleman brought a state habeas proceeding alleging various federal constitutional errors. The trial court denied relief. Coleman's notice of appeal to the Virginia Supreme Court from the trial court's decision was untimely under Virginia law. The Commonwealth moved to dismiss the appeal on the sole ground that it was untimely. The Virginia Supreme Court delayed ruling on the motion to dismiss, and consequently briefs on both the motion and the merits were filed. Six months later, stating that it had considered all the briefs, the Virginia Supreme Court summarily granted the motion to dismiss the appeal and dismissed the petition for appeal. So the question was whether the Virginia court relied on the procedural bar to dismiss the action (in which case habeas relief would be denied), or relied instead on its interpretation of Coleman's constitutional claim.

Justice O'Connor, writing for the Court, found that the summary order rested on the adequate and independent state ground, i.e., the state law allowing dismissal of an appeal that was untimely filed. She rejected, for two reasons, Coleman's argument that the state court should be required to state explicitly that it is relying on an independent state ground in order to preclude federal habeas review. First, she asserted that an absolute requirement of an explicit statement misreads *Long*, which requires an explicit statement only upon a predicate finding that the state decision "must fairly appear to rest primarily on federal law or to be interwoven with federal law." Second, the proposal for a per se plain statement rule would "greatly and unacceptably expand the risk" that federal habeas courts would review state decisions that were in fact based on adequate and independent state grounds.

Justice O'Connor explained that where it does not fairly appear that the state court decision is based primarily on federal grounds, "it is simply not true that the most reasonable explanation is that the state judgment rested on federal grounds," and that a conclusive presumption to that effect "is simply not worth the cost in the loss of respect for the State that such a rule would entail." She concluded that "we will not impose on state courts the responsibility for using particular language in every case in which a state prisoner presents a federal claim * * * in order that federal courts might not be bothered with reviewing state law and the record in the case." Rather, federal courts on habeas must consider the nature of the disposition and the surrounding circumstances of the order to determine whether the state court relied on an adequate state ground.

On the facts, the Court found that the Virginia Supreme Court's summary order did not "fairly appear" to rest on or to be interwoven with federal law. Justice O'Connor noted that the summary order granted the Commonwealth's motion to dismiss, which was based solely upon Coleman's failure to meet the time requirements for a notice of appeal. Federal law was not mentioned in the order. She recognized that the Virginia Supreme Court's explicit consideration of briefs discussing the merits "adds some ambiguity," but concluded that this did not override the "explicit grant of a dismissal motion based solely on procedural grounds." Compare Brown v. Collins, 937 F.2d 175 (5th Cir.1991)(state court addressed federal constitutional claims where the government claimed a procedural bar, and the state court specifically noted that it "considered the petition" of the defendant alleging constitutional error; therefore there was no independent state ground precluding habeas review).

Justice White wrote a concurring opinion in *Coleman*, emphasizing that he was not convinced that the Virginia Supreme Court followed a practice of waiving a procedural bar when constitutional issues are at stake.

Justice Blackmun, joined by Justices Marshall and Stevens, filed a lengthy dissent, criticizing the Court's "crusade to erect petty procedural barriers in the path of any state prisoner seeking review of his federal constitutional claims." He argued that the Court "is creating a Byzantine morass of arbitrary, unnecessary and unjustifiable impediments to the vindication of federal rights" and "subordinates fundamental constitutional rights to mere utilitarian interests."

Justice Blackmun argued that states should be required to make a plain statement of reliance on state law in order to establish an independent state ground precluding habeas review. He asserted that "the plain-statement rule provides a simple mechanism by which a state court may invoke the discretionary deference of the federal court and virtually insulate its judgment from federal review." He contended that the majority's approach of looking to the nature of the disposition and the circumstances surrounding a summary order was "inherently indeterminate" and that the plain statement rule "effectively and equitably eliminates this unacceptable uncertainty."

Note that on the habeas corpus flow chart, the Court's finding that Virginia relied on a state rule to dismiss the appeal does not end the case. Rather, it means that the state applied a procedural bar. Coleman could still have his habeas petition heard—but only if he could establish cause and prejudice or actual innocence. As discussed above, Coleman could not do so. If the state procedural bar had not been applied, then Virginia would have ruled on the constitutional claims, there would have been no procedural defaults, and Coleman's habeas petition would have been heard.

Coleman and the Plain Statement Rule

After *Coleman,* is there anything left of the Harris v. Reed "plain statement" rule? Consider the views of Judge Williams, concurring in Young v. Herring, 938 F.2d 543 (5th Cir.1991)(en banc).

> [The plain statement] requirement is to be applied narrowly—only in those cases where the state court considers both the procedural bar and explicitly the federal constitutional issue on the merits. The fact that the [state] court is fully aware of the presence of the federal constitutional issue is not enough even though the court does not clearly and expressly rely upon the procedural bar.

See also Hunter v. Aispuro, 958 F.2d 955 (9th Cir.1992)("*Coleman* reexamined *Harris* and explained that a predicate to the application of the *Harris* presumption is that the decision of the last state court must fairly appear to rest primarily on federal law or to be interwoven with federal law"; plain statement rule is not applicable where the state court ruling made "no reference to federal law and give no indication that federal law was consulted in reaching a decision").

"Looking Through" to a Prior State Decision: Ylst v. Nunnemaker

In Ylst v. Nunnemaker, 501 U.S. 797 (1991), the California Supreme Court denied without explanation Nunnemaker's state petition for habeas corpus. Twelve years earlier, the California Court of Appeal had affirmed Nunnemaker's conviction, rejecting his constitutional claims solely and explicitly on the ground of failure to object at trial (i.e., a state procedural bar). Nunnemaker's petition for state habeas to the California Supreme Court specifically addressed both procedural and constitutional issues. Justice Scalia, writing for a six-person majority, held that the California Supreme Court's unexplained denial of Nunnemaker's habeas petition was based on the independent and adequate state ground of procedural default. Justice Scalia noted that "procedural bars are not immortal" and that "if the last state court to be presented with a particular federal claim reaches the merits, it removes any bar to federal court review that might otherwise have been available." He recognized that it is often difficult to determine whether the later court lifted the procedural bar or instead rested on the independent state ground. Justice Scalia stated that the process used in *Coleman* of determining the nature of the disposition and the circumstances surrounding the unexplained order could not be used in every case, because "such clues will not always, or even ordinarily, be available." He noted that "many formulary orders are not meant to convey anything as to the reason for the decision" and that attributing a reason in these circumstances was "difficult and artificial." He stated the rule to guide such circumstances as follows:

> We think that the attribution necessary for federal habeas purposes can be facilitated, and sound results more often assured, by applying the following presumption: where there has been one reasoned state judgment rejecting a federal claim, later unexplained orders upholding that judgment or rejecting the same claim rest upon the same ground. * * * The maxim is that silence implies consent, not the opposite. * * * The essence of unexplained orders is that they say nothing. We think that a presumption which gives them no effect—which simply "looks through" them to the last reasoned decision—most nearly reflects the role that they are ordinarily intended to play.

Justice Scalia emphasized that the presumption of reliance on a state ground derived from "looking through" silent orders was rebuttable. He gave as an example a situation where the last reasoned state court decision relied on a procedural default, but a retroactive change in law eliminated that ground as a basis for decision, and the reviewing court directed briefing on the merits of the constitutional claim.

Applying the "looking through" analysis to the facts of *Nunnemaker,* the Court looked through the California Supreme Court's unexplained denial of state habeas to the last reasoned state court decision, that of the California Court of Appeal twelve years earlier. Because that prior decision had expressly and unequivocally relied on the independent state ground of procedural default, the California Supreme Court's unexplained order was deemed to have done so as well.

Justice Blackmun, joined by Justices Stevens and Marshall, dissented. Justice Blackmun argued that the process of "looking through" silent orders would complicate the efforts of state courts to understand and accommodate the Court's habeas jurisprudence. He pointed out that "a state court that does not intend to rely on a procedural default but wishes to deny a meritless petition in a summary order must now remember that its unexplained order will be ignored by the federal habeas court. Thus, the state court must review the procedural history of the petitioner's claim and determine which state court judgment a federal habeas court is likely to recognize" as the last reasoned decision. Justice Blackmun concluded that he saw "no benefit in abandoning a clear rule to create chaos."

Coleman and *Nunnemaker* were decided on the same day. After these cases, how does a habeas court, in evaluating a summary order of a state court, determine whether to consider the nature of the disposition and the surrounding circumstances, as set forth in *Coleman,* or whether to use the "looking through" process of *Nunnemaker?*

State Ground That Is Not Adequate

A state procedural bar will be deemed "adequate" to preclude habeas review only if it is regularly followed and firmly established in practice. See James v. Kentucky, 466 U.S. 341 (1984), where the defendant asked the judge to admonish the jury not to draw an inference from his failure to testify. The judge refused the request, and James appealed the refusal. The state supreme court held that a request for an admonition was not adequate to preserve a claim on appeal for a failure to give an instruction. But the U.S. Supreme Court stated that "for federal constitutional purposes, James adequately invoked his substantive right to jury guidance." The Court held that "Kentucky's distinction between admonitions and instructions is not the sort of firmly established and regularly followed state practice that can prevent implementation of federal constitutional rights."

In Ford v. Georgia, 498 U.S. 411 (1991), a unanimous Supreme Court held that a state procedural rule could not be applied retroactively to prevent federal review of a constitutional claim. Justice Souter's opinion for the Court concluded that a rule unannounced at the time of petitioner's trial could not have been firmly established at that time, and was thus "inadequate to serve as an independent state ground within the meaning of *James.*" See also Johnson v. Mississippi, 486 U.S. 578 (1988)(no adequate state ground where Mississippi law did not consistently require a claim such as the defendant's to be asserted on direct appeal).

"Exorbitant" Application of an Adequate State Ground: Lee v. Kemna

In Lee v. Kemna, 534 U.S. 362 (2002), the Court found an exception to procedural default on an adequate state ground, for "exceptional cases in which exorbitant application of a generally sound rule renders the state ground inadequate to stop consideration of a federal question" on habeas review. Lee was being tried for murder in Missouri, and had produced alibi witnesses from California, who would have testified that Lee was with them in California on the day of the murder. When it came time to present the witnesses, however, on the third day of trial, they were not in court and Lee's counsel did not know where they were. He asked for a day's continuance so that he could locate the witnesses, and assured the court that the witnesses had not left the jurisdiction because they had business to attend to locally. The trial judge refused to continue the trial, because he wanted to be with his daughter, who was having surgery, the next day, and had other trials to attend to after that. Lee presented no witnesses and was convicted. He brought a habeas action, arguing that the refusal to grant a continuance violated his due process rights, and presented affidavits from the alibi witnesses who stated that they were not in the courtroom on the third day of trial because they had been informed by court personnel that they would not be testifying that day.

The state appellate court refused to consider the merits of Lee's due process argument, relying on a procedural bar: Missouri rules of procedure (Court Rules 24.09 and 24.10) that require a motion for continuance to be submitted in writing with a supporting affidavit. The question for the Supreme Court was whether this procedural bar prohibited a habeas action in the absence of a showing of cause and prejudice or actual innocence.

Justice Ginsburg, writing for six Justices, declared that this case fit into the "limited category" of exceptional cases in which a generally sound state rule of procedure must be found inadequate. She summarized as follows:

> Three considerations, in combination, lead us to conclude that this case falls within the small category of cases in which asserted state grounds are inadequate to block adjudication of a federal claim. First, when the trial judge denied Lee's motion, he stated a reason that could not have been countered by a perfect motion for continuance. The judge said he could not carry the trial over until the next day because he had to be with his daughter in the hospital; the judge further informed counsel that another scheduled trial prevented him from concluding Lee's case on the following business day. Although the judge hypothesized that the witnesses had "abandoned" Lee, he had not a scintilla of evidence or a shred of information on which to base this supposition.

> Second, no published Missouri decision directs flawless compliance with Rules 24.09 and 24.10 in the unique circumstances this case presents—the sudden, unanticipated, and at the time unexplained disappearance of critical, subpoenaed witnesses on what became the trial's last day. Lee's predica-

ment, from all that appears, was one Missouri courts had not confronted before. * * *

Third and most important, given the realities of trial, Lee substantially complied with Missouri's key Rule. As to the "written motion" requirement * * * Missouri does not rule out oral continuance motions; they are expressly authorized, upon consent of the adverse party, by Rule 24.09. And the written transcript of the brief trial court proceedings enabled an appellate court to comprehend the situation quickly. In sum, we are drawn to the conclusion reached by the Eighth Circuit dissenter: "[A]ny seasoned trial lawyer would agree" that insistence on a written continuance application, supported by an affidavit, "in the midst of trial upon the discovery that subpoenaed witnesses are suddenly absent, would be so bizarre as to inject an Alice-in-Wonderland quality into the proceedings."

Justice Ginsburg concluded as follows:

We hold that the Missouri Rules, as injected into this case by the state appellate court, did not constitute a state ground adequate to bar federal habeas review. Caught in the midst of a murder trial and unalerted to any procedural defect in his presentation, defense counsel could hardly be expected to divert his attention from the proceedings rapidly unfolding in the courtroom and train, instead, on preparation of a written motion and affidavit. Furthermore, the trial court, at the time Lee moved for a continuance, had in clear view the information needed to rule intelligently on the merits of the motion. Beyond doubt, Rule 24.10 serves the State's important interest in regulating motions for a continuance—motions readily susceptible to use as a delaying tactic. But under the circumstances of this case, we hold that petitioner Lee, having substantially, if imperfectly, made the basic showings Rule 24.10 prescribes, qualifies for adjudication of his federal, due process claim.

Justice Kennedy, joined by Justices Scalia and Thomas, dissented. Justice Kennedy argued that a regularly followed state rule had previously been found inadequate "only when the state had no legitimate interest in the rule's enforcement." The need to provide regulations on possibly spurious motions for continuance meant that the Missouri rules were "adequate" within the meaning of Supreme Court jurisprudence. Justice Kennedy concluded that the Court's new exception "does not bode well for the adequacy doctrine or federalism."

5. *Abuse of the Writ*

Successive habeas petitions (i.e., multiple collateral attacks on the same judgment) ordinarily constitute "abuse of the writ," which generally precludes review regardless of the merits of the subsequent petition. In McCleskey v. Zant, 499 U.S. 467 (1991), the Court held that a petitioner is generally not permitted to bring a successive habeas petition, but must ordinarily bring all claims in a single petition. Justice Kennedy wrote the opinion for six members of the Court. The majority held that it was not necessary for the state to show that the petitioner had deliberately abandoned a claim in a prior habeas petition; a petitioner may also abuse the writ by failing to raise a claim through neglect.

Justice Kennedy accepted McCleskey's argument that the comity notions behind the procedural default doctrine were not applicable to successive federal habeas petitions. He responded as follows:

Nonetheless, the doctrines of procedural default and abuse of the writ are both designed to lessen the injury to a State that results through reexamination of a state conviction on a ground that the State did not have the opportunity to address at a prior, appropriate time; and both doctrines seek to vindicate the State's interest in the finality of its criminal judgments.

The analogy of abuse of the writ and procedural default led the Court in *McCleskey* to hold that a successive habeas petition could be entertained only if the petitioner could show cause and prejudice for failing to bring all claims together in a single petition, or if he could show that the successive petition established his actual innocence. As discussed above, these standards have been established by the Court to permit a habeas court to excuse procedural defaults in truly exceptional cases. *McCleskey* held that satisfaction of these standards would cure abuse of the writ as well.

Effect of the AEDPA

The AEDPA, however, tightens up the use of successive petitions even further than the Court had done in *McCleskey*. The *McCleskey* Court held that a showing of cause and prejudice, or actual innocence, would permit a successive petition. The AEDPA, in contrast, provides for absolute dismissal of claims identical to those previously brought (no exceptions), and dismissal of new claims with two minor exceptions: 1) if they are based on a new rule made retroactive to habeas cases by the Supreme Court (which essentially can never happen), or 2) if the claims were not included in the initial petition due to an unavailable factual predicate (as with the suppression of information that occurred in Amadeo v. Zant, supra). These two extremely limited grounds are the only permissible grounds for establishing cause. Moreover, assuming that one of these causes are shown, the petitioner then has to show by clear and convincing evidence that no reasonable factfinder could have convicted him. Thus, there is no actual innocence exception to excuse the cause requirement— the petitioner must establish not only cause, but also a standard of prejudice more rigorous than the actual innocence exception to the cause and prejudice requirement had been, i.e., clear and convincing evidence that but for the constitutional violation, no reasonable factfinder could have convicted the petitioner. Finally, the petitioner must obtain clearance from a three-member panel of the court of appeals (which must be satisfied of a prima facie case) before a successive petition can even be brought.

In Felker v. Turpin, 518 U.S. 651 (1996), the petitioner argued that the above provisions operate as a "suspension" of the writ of habeas corpus, in violation of Article I, section 9 of the Constitution. That clause provides that "the Privilege of the Writ of Habeas Corpus shall not be suspended, unless when in Cases of Rebellion or Invasion the public Safety may require it." But the Suspension Clause argument was unanimously rejected in an opinion by Chief Justice Rehnquist. The Chief Justice reasoned as follows:

> The new restrictions on successive petitions constitute a modified res judicata rule, a restraint on what is called in habeas corpus practice "abuse of the writ." In McCleskey v. Zant, we said that "the doctrine of abuse of the writ refers to a complex and evolving body of equitable principles informed and controlled by historical usage, statutory developments, and

judicial decisions." The added restrictions which the Act places on second habeas petitions are well within the compass of this evolutionary process, and we hold that they do not amount to a "suspension" of the writ contrary to Article I, § 9.

Premature Claims and Successive Petitions:
Stewart v. Martinez–Villareal

In Stewart v. Martinez–Villareal, 523 U.S. 637 (1998), Martinez brought a habeas petition challenging his capital conviction. The petition contained a number of claims; one claim was that Martinez was incompetent and therefore could not be executed. Such a claim is called a *"Ford"* claim, after Ford v. Wainright, 477 U.S. 399 (1986) (holding that the Eight Amendment prohibits the execution of an incompetent person). The lower courts held that the *Ford* claim was procedurally premature, and the remaining claims were eventually dismissed on the merits. When the state proceeded to set a date certain for the execution, Martinez sought to reopen his *Ford* claim. The state argued that this was a successive petition, barred by the terms of the AEDPA. But the Supreme Court, in an opinion by Chief Justice Rehnquist, held that the incompetence claim could not be treated as a successive petition; therefore the petitioner had the right to have it considered on the merits. The Chief Justice's analysis proceeded as follows:

> The State contends that because respondent has already had one "fully-litigated habeas petition, the plain meaning of [the AEDPA] requires his new petition to be treated as successive." Under that reading of the statute, respondent is entitled to only one merits judgment on his federal habeas claims. * * *

> This may have been the second time that respondent had asked the federal courts to provide relief on his *Ford* claim, but this does not mean that there were two separate applications, the second of which was necessarily subject to [the AEDPA]. There was only one application for habeas relief, and the District Court ruled (or should have ruled) on each claim at the time it became ripe. Respondent was entitled to an adjudication of all of the claims presented in his earlier, undoubtedly reviewable, application for federal habeas relief. The Court of Appeals was therefore correct in holding that respondent was not required to get authorization to file a "second or successive" application before his *Ford* claim could be heard.

> If the State's interpretation of "second or successive" were correct, the implications for habeas practice would be far-reaching and seemingly perverse. * * * [It] would mean that a dismissal of a first habeas petition for technical procedural reasons would bar the prisoner from ever obtaining federal habeas review.

Justices Scalia and Thomas dissented; each wrote separate opinions joined by the other. Both opinions made the point that however "perverse" the result, the plain meaning of the AEDPA was that the revival of a petition dismissed or deferred on procedural grounds constitutes a successive petition, and is therefore prohibited, subject to the two very limited exceptions not at issue in this case.

Note that the *Martinez* rule would also apply in situations where a habeas claim is dismissed because the petitioner has not exhausted state remedies. If the petitioner then goes to state court and exhausts his remedies, but gets no relief, he can then refile his habeas petition. Such a petition is not "successive" within the meaning of the AEDPA, because, like Martinez, the petitioner never had his claims considered on the merits by the federal court.

6. *Newly Discovered Evidence*

Chief Justice Rehnquist wrote for the Court in Herrera v. Collins, 506 U.S. 390 (1993), as it rejected a habeas corpus challenge to a death penalty conviction based upon a claim of newly discovered evidence purporting to demonstrate innocence. Herrera was convicted of killing two police officers. He was identified by an eyewitness and in a dying declaration made by one of the officers. A note written by Herrera, implicating him in one of the murders, was found on his person when he was arrested. Forensic evidence also connected him to the crimes. Herrera filed a habeas corpus petition in state court. He did not contend that an error had been made at his trial. Rather, he contended that he had discovered new evidence proving that his brother Raul had actually killed the officers. He supported the petition with affidavits of Raul's lawyer and former cellmate, both relating inculpatory statements made by Raul, as well as an affidavit from Raul's son who purported to be an eyewitness to his father's murder of the officers. These affidavits were inconsistent with some details about the murders. Herrera's petition was filed 10 years after his conviction, and eight years after Raul's death.

Herrera's state habeas petition was dismissed as untimely by the Texas courts. He then filed a federal habeas petition asserting "that the Eighth and Fourteenth Amendments to the United States Constitution prohibit the execution of a person who is innocent of the crime for which he was convicted." In rejecting the assertion, the Chief Justice reasoned that innocence "must be determined in some sort of a judicial proceeding" and that when a defendant has been afforded a fair trial "and convicted of the offense for which he was charged, the presumption of innocence disappears." He stated that the writ of habeas corpus was not an appropriate vehicle for assessing factual innocence, in the absence of a claim that the trial itself was unfair—and Herrera made no such claim:

> Claims of actual innocence based on newly discovered evidence have never been held to state a ground for federal habeas relief absent an independent constitutional violation occurring in the underlying state criminal proceeding. * * * This rule is grounded in the principle that federal habeas courts sit to ensure that individuals are not imprisoned in violation of the Constitution—not to correct errors of fact.

Herrera relied on Sawyer v. Whitley, supra, where the Court held that a habeas petitioner who procedurally defaulted his claim may still have his federal constitutional claims heard if he makes a proper showing of actual innocence. But the Chief Justice distinguished *Sawyer* on the ground that it "makes clear that a claim of actual innocence is not itself a constitutional claim, but instead a gateway through which a habeas petitioner must pass to have his otherwise barred constitutional claim considered on the merits." In contrast, Herrera made no argument that his trial was tainted by constitutional error. The Chief Justice concluded that the "actual innocence" exception set forth in *Sawyer* did not extend to "freestanding claims of actual innocence." Compare Schlup v.

Delo, 513 U.S. 298 (1995) (petitioner can rely on newly discovered evidence to establish actual innocence, where he claims that there was a constitutional error at his trial).

In denying habeas relief, the Court relied on the fact that Herrera was not "left without a forum to raise his actual innocence claim." The Court noted that under Texas law, Herrera could seek executive clemency, and stated that clemency "is deeply rooted in our Anglo–American tradition of law, and is the historic remedy for preventing miscarriage of justice where judicial process has been exhausted."

Ultimately, the Court found it unnecessary to reach the question whether federal habeas relief would *ever* be available to prevent the execution of an innocent person when there is no possible state relief. The Chief Justice assumed *arguendo* that the Constitution prohibited such an execution; but he stated that, even if that were so, a defendant who claimed actual innocence after an error-free trial would have to make an "extraordinarily high" showing that the newly discovered evidence proved his innocence. This high threshold was required due to the "very disruptive effect that entertaining claims of actual innocence would have on the need for finality in capital cases, and the enormous burden that having to retry cases based on often stale evidence would place on the States."

The Court found that Herrera had not come close to satisfying an "extraordinarily high" threshold of proof of actual innocence. The Chief Justice stated that the evidence presented against Herrera at trial was strong, and that his purported evidence of innocence consisted of inconsistent and suspiciously-timed affidavits implicating a person who was now dead. He concluded that "coming 10 years after petitioner's trial, this showing of innocence falls far short of that which would have to be made in order to trigger the sort of constitutional claim which we have assumed, *arguendo,* to exist."

Justice O'Connor, joined by Justice Kennedy, wrote a concurring opinion and stated that she could "not disagree with the fundamental legal principle that executing the innocent is inconsistent with the Constitution." However, she found that Herrera was not "an innocent man on the verge of execution. He is instead a legally guilty one who, refusing to accept the jury's verdict, demands a hearing in which to have his culpability determined once again."

Justice Scalia, joined by Justice Thomas, concurred and argued that "[t]here is no basis in text, tradition, or even in contemporary practice (if that were enough) for finding in the Constitution a right to demand judicial consideration of newly discovered evidence of innocence brought forward after conviction."

Justice White concurred in the judgment. He assumed that a persuasive showing of actual innocence would bar execution, but found that Herrera had not made a sufficient showing of his innocence.

Justice Blackmun, joined by Justices Stevens and in large part by Justice Souter, dissented. He argued that the Eighth Amendment and the Due Process Clause forbid the execution of a person who can prove his innocence with newly discovered evidence. Justice Blackmun contended that the remedy of executive clemency is not adequate to satisfy the Constitution, because that remedy is too idiosyncratic and politicized to protect against the execution of an innocent person. He therefore concluded that the courts must review a claim of innocence based upon newly discovered evidence. He would "hold that, to obtain relief on a claim of actual innocence, the petitioner must show that he probably is innocent."

7. *Limitations on Obtaining a Hearing*

What happens if a habeas petitioner claims that constitutional error occurred at his state trial, but the argument of error is dependent on a factual predicate that remains undeveloped? For example, if the defendant argues that the prosecutor exercised peremptory challenges in a discriminatory manner, certain factual issues will be important, e.g., how many were struck, who were they, what was said on voir dire, what rationale did the prosecutor give for striking the juror, etc. If these facts were not developed in the state court, the petitioner will need to move for an evidentiary hearing to develop his claims. However, if the petitioner should have developed the facts in the state system, and failed to do so, a question similar to that discussed in Wainwright v. Sykes, supra, arises—why should the petitioner be permitted an evidentiary hearing if he failed to develop the necessary facts in the state proceeding? Such a petitioner would seem to have run aground on a state procedural bar.

In Keeney v. Tamayo–Reyes, 504 U.S. 1 (1992), the Court relied on its procedural default cases such as Wainwright v. Sykes to hold that a petitioner who failed to develop facts in the state proceeding could be denied an evidentiary hearing in federal court (and thus, as a practical matter, denied habeas relief on the merits) unless he could establish "cause and prejudice" for the failure to develop the facts below. Tamayo–Reyes had pleaded nolo contendere to a charge of first-degree manslaughter. In his habeas action, he argued that his plea was not knowing and intelligent because his translator had not translated accurately and completely for him the *mens rea* element of the crime. He also contended that he did not understand the purposes of the plea form and the plea hearing, and that he thought he was agreeing to be tried for manslaughter rather than agreeing to plead guilty. The merits of his claim were obviously fact-dependent, but his counsel had failed to develop the necessary facts in state collateral proceedings. Justice White, writing for the Court, declared that "encouraging the full factual development in state court of a claim that state courts committed constitutional error advances comity by allowing a coordinate jurisdiction to correct its own errors in the first instance." He concluded that the state court "is the appropriate forum for resolution of factual issues in the first instance, and creating incentives for the deferral of factfinding to later federal-court proceedings can only degrade the accuracy and efficiency of judicial proceedings. This is fully consistent with and gives meaning to the requirement of exhaustion."

The AEDPA

After the 1996 Antiterrorism and Effective Death Penalty Act (AEDPA), there are only a few reasons for which a habeas court can hold a factfinding hearing; the standards set forth in *Tamayo-Reyes* are restricted even further. The Court construed the AEDPA provisions concerning hearings in Williams v. Taylor, 529 U.S. 420 (2000). As amended by the AEDPA, 28 U.S.C. § 2254(e)(2)—the provision that controls whether a habeas petitioner may receive an evidentiary hearing in federal district court on claims that were not developed in the state court—provides as follows:

If the applicant has failed to develop the factual basis of a claim in State court proceedings, the court shall not hold an evidentiary hearing on the claim unless the applicant shows that—

(A) the claim relies on—

(i) a new rule of constitutional law, made retroactive to cases on collateral review by the Supreme Court, that was previously unavailable; or

(ii) a factual predicate that could not have been previously discovered through the exercise of due diligence; and

(B) the facts underlying the claim would be sufficient to establish by clear and convincing evidence that but for constitutional error, no reasonable factfinder would have found the applicant guilty of the underlying offense.

In his habeas petition, Williams sought an evidentiary hearing to develop three claims: 1) a claim under *Brady* that the prosecution failed to disclose a psychological report on the prosecution's star witness; 2) a claim that a juror had lied on voir dire by failing to disclose a source of bias; and 3) a related claim that the prosecutor committed misconduct because he knew that the juror was biased and failed to disclose that fact. In the Supreme Court, Williams conceded that he could not satisfy the stringent standards for relief set forth in subdivision (B) of the statute (i.e., actual innocence). Resolution of the right to an evidentiary hearing therefore depended on whether Williams had "failed to develop" the basis of the factual claim in state court. The parties agreed that the facts necessary to support Williams' habeas claims had *not* been developed in the state court. Williams argued, however, that he had not *failed* to develop the claims, because he was *unable* to pursue the claims during the state court proceeding, i.e., he was not at fault. The government argued for a no-fault interpretation of the statutory term "failed", i.e., if the claims were not developed in the state court—no matter the reason—then there is no right to an evidentiary hearing to develop the claims in the federal district court.

The Supreme Court, in a unanimous opinion by Justice Kennedy, rejected the government's no-fault construction of the AEDPA term "failed", and held that the term "failed to develop" requires some "lack of diligence" on the petitioner's part. Justice Kennedy explained this ruling in the following passage:

Under [the government's] no-fault reading of the statute, if there is no factual development in the state court, the federal habeas court may not inquire into the reasons for the default when determining whether the opening clause of § 2254(e)(2) applies. We do not agree with the Commonwealth's interpretation of the word "failed."

* * *

We give the words of a statute their ordinary, contemporary, common meaning, absent an indication Congress intended them to bear some different import. In its customary and preferred sense, "fail" connotes some omission, fault, or negligence on the part of the person who has failed to do something. To say a person has failed in a duty implies he did not take the necessary steps to fulfill it. He is, as a consequence, at fault and bears responsibility for the failure. In this sense, a person is not at fault when his diligent efforts to perform an act are thwarted, for example, by the conduct of another or by happenstance. Fault lies, in those circumstances, either with the person who interfered with the accomplishment of the act or with no one at all. We conclude Congress used the word "failed" in the sense just described. * * *

Under the opening clause of § 2254(e)(2), a failure to develop the factual basis of a claim is not established unless there is lack of diligence, or some greater fault, attributable to the prisoner or the prisoner's counsel. * * *

* * *

Justice Kennedy explained that the statute required the defendant and counsel to pursue factfinding with "diligence" in the state court:

> Federal habeas corpus principles must inform and shape the historic and still vital relation of mutual respect and common purpose existing between the States and the federal courts. In keeping this delicate balance we have been careful to limit the scope of federal intrusion into state criminal adjudications and to safeguard the States' interest in the integrity of their criminal and collateral proceedings.
>
> It is consistent with these principles to give effect to Congress' intent to avoid unneeded evidentiary hearings in federal habeas corpus, while recognizing the statute does not equate prisoners who exercise diligence in pursuing their claims with those who do not. Principles of exhaustion are premised upon recognition by Congress and the Court that state judiciaries have the duty and competence to vindicate rights secured by the Constitution in state criminal proceedings. Diligence will require in the usual case that the prisoner, at a minimum, seek an evidentiary hearing in state court in the manner prescribed by state law. * * * For state courts to have their rightful opportunity to adjudicate federal rights, the prisoner must be diligent in developing the record and presenting, if possible, all claims of constitutional error. If the prisoner fails to do so, himself or herself contributing to the absence of a full and fair adjudication in state court, § 2254(e)(2) prohibits an evidentiary hearing to develop the relevant claims in federal court, unless the statute's other stringent requirements are met. Federal courts sitting in habeas are not an alternative forum for trying facts and issues which a prisoner made insufficient effort to pursue in state proceedings. Yet comity is not served by saying a prisoner "has failed to develop the factual basis of a claim" where he was unable to develop his claim in state court despite diligent effort. In that circumstance, an evidentiary hearing is not barred by § 2254(e)(2).

Justice Kennedy then applied the "diligence" test to the facts of the case. He found that Williams had not been diligent in pursuing his *Brady* claim, because the witness' psychological history had been disclosed at that witness' sentencing proceeding, well in time for Williams to use it in his state proceedings. Williams and his counsel were thus aware of the report and yet took no steps to have it produced. In contrast, Williams was not at fault for the failure to develop the claim of juror bias and the related claim of prosecutorial misconduct for failure to disclose the juror bias. The juror had misrepresented her background in answering a question on voir dire. There was no reason for Williams or his counsel to believe that the juror and the prosecutor were hiding anything. The Court noted that it would be "surprised, to say the least, if a district court familiar with the standards of trial practice were to hold that in all cases diligent counsel must check public records containing personal information pertaining to each and every juror."

8. *Harmless Error In Habeas Corpus Cases*

A Less Onerous Standard of Harmlessness:
Brecht v. Abrahamson

In Brecht v. Abrahamson, 507 U.S. 619 (1993), the Court considered the standard that should be applied by a federal habeas court in assessing whether a constitutional error in a state court was harmless. The state urged as a standard that an error should be presumed harmless unless it had a "substantial and injurious effect on the verdict." This standard, which is employed by the Court for review of non-constitutional error on direct review, is referred to as the *"Kotteakos"* standard. See Kotteakos v. United States, 328 U.S. 750 (1946). The *Kotteakos* standard is less onerous for the state to meet (i.e., the error is less likely to create a reversal) than is the "harmless beyond a reasonable doubt" standard applied by the Court to constitutional errors on direct review; this more stringent test of harmlessness—understandably advocated by the petitioner in *Brecht*—is known as the *"Chapman"* standard. See Chapman v. California, discussed earlier in this Chapter in the section on harmless error on direct review.

The 5–4 majority in *Brecht* held that the *Chapman* standard was too stringent to be applied in a collateral attack of a state court conviction. Instead the more permissive *Kotteakos* test applied. The Court concluded that the *"Kotteakos* harmless-error standard is better tailored to the nature and purpose of collateral review than the *Chapman* standard, and application of a less onerous harmless-error standard on habeas promotes the considerations underlying our habeas jurisprudence."

Writing for the majority, Chief Justice Rehnquist emphasized the difference between collateral review and direct appeal:

> The reason most frequently advanced in our cases for distinguishing between direct and collateral review is the State's interest in the finality of convictions that have survived direct review within the state court system. We have also spoken of comity and federalism. * * * Finally, we have recognized that liberal allowance of the writ degrades the prominence of the trial itself, and at the same time encourages habeas petitioners to relitigate their claims on collateral review.

> * * * State courts are fully qualified to identify constitutional error and evaluate its prejudicial effect on the trial process under *Chapman,* and state courts often occupy a superior vantage point from which to evaluate the effect of trial error. For these reasons, it scarcely seems logical to require federal habeas courts to engage in the identical approach to harmless-error review that *Chapman* requires state courts to engage in on direct review.

The Chief Justice emphasized the following costs of "overturning final and presumptively correct convictions on collateral review because the State cannot prove that an error is harmless under *Chapman*": 1) the State's interest in finality and in sovereignty over criminal matters is undermined; 2) granting habeas relief "merely because there is a reasonable possibility that trial error contributed to the verdict is at odds with the historic meaning of habeas corpus—to afford relief to those whom society has grievously wronged"; and 3) the State suffers "social costs" due to the necessity to retry a case after a significant passage of time. The Chief Justice concluded as follows:

> The imbalance of the costs and benefits of applying the *Chapman* harmless-error standard on collateral review counsels in favor of applying a less onerous standard on habeas review of constitutional error. The *Kotteakos* standard, we believe, fills the bill. The test under *Kotteakos* is whether the error "had substantial and injurious effect or influence in determining the jury's verdict." Under this standard, habeas petitioners may obtain plenary review of their constitutional claims, but they are not entitled to habeas relief based on trial error unless they can establish that it resulted in "actual prejudice."

In a footnote, the Court left open the possibility that "in an unusual case, a deliberate and especially egregious error of the trial type, or one that is combined with a pattern of prosecutorial misconduct, might so infect the integrity of the proceeding as to warrant the grant of habeas relief, even if it did not substantially influence the jury's verdict." The Chief Justice was also careful to note that the *Kotteakos* standard would be applied only to constitutional errors of the "trial type." If the constitutional error is "structural" in the sense that it tainted the entirety of the trial, then per se reversal is required whether the error is discovered on direct or habeas review. See the discussion earlier in this Chapter about errors that cannot be harmless.

Justice Stevens filed a concurring opinion in which he emphasized that, even under *Kotteakos,* the reviewing court must make a *de novo* examination of the trial record. He also emphasized that the reviewing court must focus on the effect of the error, not on whether it thinks that a defendant would have been convicted absent the error. He concluded that "the way we phrase the governing standard is far less important than the quality of the judgment with which it is applied."

Justice White dissented, joined by Justice Blackmun and in substantial part by Justice Souter. He argued that the *Chapman* standard was essential to the safeguard of constitutional rights.

Justice O'Connor dissented in a separate opinion in which she argued that "[i]f there is a unifying theme to this Court's habeas jurisprudence, it is that the ultimate equity on the prisoner's side—the possibility that an error may have caused the conviction of an actually innocent person—is sufficient by itself to permit plenary review of the prisoner's federal claim." Justice O'Connor concluded that "the harmless-error standard often will be inextricably intertwined with the interest of reliability," and that when constitutional errors—such as, for example, a denial of confrontation or the introduction of an involuntary confession—are detected, "the harmless-error standard is crucial to our faith in the accuracy of the outcome."

Burden of Proof as to Harmlessness: O'Neal v. McAninch

Who bears the burden on the harmlessness question in habeas cases? Must the defendant show that the error was harmful, or must the state show that the error was harmless? In O'Neal v. McAninch, 513 U.S. 432 (1995), the Court held that where a judge has "grave doubt" as to whether an error was harmless or not under the *Kotteakos* standard, the petitioner is entitled to habeas relief. Justice Breyer, writing for six Justices, defined "grave doubt" as arising when, "in the judge's mind, the matter is so evenly balanced that he feels himself in virtual equipoise as to the harmlessness of the error." Where "grave doubt" as to harmlessness exists, "the uncertain judge should treat the error, not as if it were harmless, but as if it affected the verdict."

Justice Breyer reasoned that allowing the petitioner to win in cases of "grave doubt" as to harmlessness was a result that was consistent with other harmless-error cases such as *Kotteakos* and *Chapman,* where the Court imposed the burden of showing harmlessness on the government. He contended that a rule "denying the writ in cases of grave uncertainty, would virtually guarantee that many, in fact, will be held in unlawful custody—contrary to the writ's most basic traditions and purposes." Justice Breyer recognized the state's interest in finality but declared that "this interest is somewhat diminished by the legal circumstance that the State normally bears responsibility for the error that infected the initial trial."

Justice Thomas, joined by Chief Justice Rehnquist and Justice Scalia, dissented. He argued that the burden should be placed on the petitioner, as it was the petitioner who was bringing the action. He elaborated as follows:

> The habeas petitioner comes to federal court as a plaintiff. Because the plaintiff seeks to change the present state of affairs, he naturally should be expected to bear the risk of failure of proof or persuasion. Part of that burden is the requirement that the plaintiff show that the defendant's actions caused harm. In other areas of the law, the plaintiff almost invariably bears the burden of persuasion with respect to whether the defendant's actions caused harm. * * * Under the majority's rationale, however, the habeas petitioner need not prove causation at all; once a prisoner establishes error, the government must affirmatively persuade the court of the harmlessness of that error. Without explaining why it favors habeas plaintiffs over other plaintiffs, the Court thus treats the question of causation as an affirmative defense.

Justice Thomas also noted the limited impact that the majority's decision would have, because "cases in which habeas courts are in equipoise on the issue of harmlessness are astonishingly rare."

Index

References are to Pages Where Topic Begins

1703

†